Pocket Kenkyusha Japanese Dictionary

To my dear friend Elliott,

may your foreign language studies lead you to discover not only new places in the world, but also within yourself.

Dylan

Pocket Kenkyusha Japanese Dictionary

Editor in chief

Shigeru Takebayashi

OXFORD
UNIVERSITY PRESS

Great Clarendon Street, Oxford OX2 6DP

Oxford University Press is a department of the University of Oxford. It furthers the University's objective of excellence in research, scholarship, and education by publishing worldwide in

Oxford New York

Auckland Cape Town Dar es Salaam Hong Kong Karachi Kuala Lumpur Madrid Melbourne Mexico City Nairobi New Delhi Shanghai Taipei Toronto

With offices in

Argentina Austria Brazil Chile Czech Republic France Greece Guatemala Hungary Italy Japan South Korea Poland Portugal Singapore Switzerland Thailand Turkey Ukraine Vietnam

First published as *The Kenkyusha English-Japanese Japanese-English Learner's Pocket Dictionary* 1996

Published as the *Pocket Kenkyusha Japanese Dictionary* 2003

British Library Cataloguing in Publication Data
Data available

Library of Congress Cataloging in Publication Data
Data available

ISBN-13: 978-0-19-860748-9

9

Printed in Great Britain by
Clays Ltd, St Ives plc

Contents

Editors and Contributors

Editor in Chief
Shigeru Takebayashi
Professor Emeritus at Tokyo University of Foreign Studies

Managing Editor
Kazuhiko Nagai

Senior Editors
Christopher Barnard
Hiroko Endo
Atsuko S. Kondoh

Lexicographers
Fumihiro Aoyama
Toru Bizen
Valerie Durham
Yasutoshi Hanada
Kenneth Jones
Yo Kitamura
Yukie Masuko
Michiyo Moriya
Yoko Nishino
Hiroko Saito
Chieko Shimazu
Shigeko Tanaka
Koichi Tonegawa
Shigeru Yamada

Publishing Administration
Josuke Okada
Hiroshi Hiruma
Osamu Hijikata
Koicki Kurosawa
Shigeki Sasaki

Printing Administration
Eiichiro Kosakai
Takashi Suzuki

Keyboarders
Susumu Enomoto
Ichiro Hashimoto
Noriko Shimada

Editorial Assistance
Kikue Suzuki

Preface

This easy-to-use pocket dictionary is the ideal reference tool for any English-speaker learning Japanese, whether you're studying the language at school or university, or learning it on your own. Its compact format and ultra-clear layout give quick access to all the vocabulary learners need. It combines extensive language resources with the lexicographic expertise of Kenkyusha, one of Japan's leading language publishers.

The dictionary provides comprehensive coverage of Japanese vocabulary across a broad spectrum of contemporary written and spoken language, incorporating many idiomatic phrases and expressions. Headwords and examples are given in both romanized and script form, and thousands of examples lead you to the translation you need quickly and easily. The dictionary also offers extensive guidance on Japanese pronunciation and grammar, and includes useful appendices covering cultural topics such as government ministries, political parties, and historical periods. A full table of Japanese sounds is included at the back of the book for quick reference.

Designed to meet the needs of a wide range of users, from the student to the traveller or business professional, the *Pocket Kenkyusha Japanese Dictionary* is the most comprehensive, accessible, and user-friendly Japanese-English English-Japanese dictionary for English-speaking learners available.

Guide to the Use of the Dictionary

1. Romanization

The romanization used in this dictionary is based on the standard Hepburn system with the following modifications:

1. 1 Long vowels are indicated by doubled vowel letters, '*aa*, *ii*, *uu*, *ee*, *oo*,' instead of the conventional transcription which, depending on the particular vowel, either uses macrons or doubles the vowel letter.

> **to˥oki** とうき (earthenware)
> **shu⌈uchuu** しゅうちゅう (concentration)
> **pa˥atii** パーティー (party)

1. 2 When the vowel sequence '*ei*' is pronounced as a long '*e*,' it is written as '*ee*.'

> **se˥eto** せいと (pupil)
> **se⌈tsumee** せつめい (explanation)

But a word like けいと (knitting wool) is written as *keito* in order to show that it is composed of two separate word elements, *ke* (wool) and *ito* (thread).

1. 3 When there is a sequence of three or more identical vowel letters, a hyphen is used to clarify the word elements.

> **ke⌈e-ee** けいえい (management)
> **so⌈o-oñ** そうおん (noise)

1. 4 '*ñ*' is used to transcribe the syllabic '*n*' (ん/ン).

> **shi⌈ñbuñ** しんぶん (newspaper)
> **ke⌈ñkoo** けんこう (health)

1. 5 When the small 'っ/ッ' precedes a consonant, the sequence is transcribed as a double consonant, except in the case of '*ch*,' which is written '*tch*.'

> **a⌈ppaku** あっぱく (pressure)
> **hi˥tto** ヒット (hit)
> **shu⌈tchoo** しゅっちょう (business trip)

1. 6 The small 'っ / ッ' in interjections such as 'あっ' and 'えっ' is transcribed with an apostrophe. This sign represents a glottal stop (an abrupt tightening of the vocal cords) after the preceding vowel.

a' あっ (Oh!) **e'** えっ (Eh!)

2. Headwords

2. 1 Headwords are arranged in alphabetical order with accent marks. The accent of a prefix or suffix is not given unless the accent of the derived compound is invariant.

2. 2 Headwords are written in roman letters followed by the standard writing in *hiragana* or *katakana* (the two Japanese syllabaries), and, where appropriate, *kanji* (Chinese characters). This is followed by an abbreviation indicating the part of speech.

a⌈tama⌉ あたま (頭) ***n.*** head
bo⌈oeki ぼうえき (貿易) ***n.*** trade

2. 3 Numbered superscripts are used to distinguish different words with the same romanization.

ha⌈shi[1] はし (橋) ***n.*** bridge
ha⌉shi[2] はし (箸) ***n.*** chopsticks

2. 4 Prefixes are followed, and suffixes preceded, by a hyphen, thus indicating position at either the beginning or end of a word.

da⌈i- だい (big; large) > **dai-toshi** (a *large* city)
-dañ だん (group) > **ooeñ-dañ** (a *group* of cheerleaders)

As a general principle, a word which can stand alone as a single unit is left as one word without a hyphen. However, in the case of examples which are listed under suffixes and prefixes which themselves constitute headwords, the hyphen is used to clarify the word elements.

oo-goe (大声) (under headword, **oo-**)
o⌈ogo⌉e (大声) (headword) a *loud* voice
jidoo-*sha* (自動車) (under headword, **-sha**)
ji⌈do⌉osha (自動車) (headword) a motor *vehicle*

2. 5 The swung dash, ~, is used to avoid repetition of the Japanese headword.

u⌈ñdoo うんどう (exercise)
uñdoo (**o**) **suru** (〜(を)する) (take exercise)

2. 6 Set phrases are shown in boldfaced type.

atama ga kireru (〜が切れる) have a sharp mind
me ga mawaru (〜が回る) feel giddy

2. 7 The raised dot in a headword distinguishes the stem of verbs and adjectives from the part to be inflected.

ka⌉k·u かく (書く), **a⌈buna·i** あぶない (危ない)

2. 8 When a headword comprises more than one part of speech, each part is dealt with separately under a different subheading.

ma⌉ñzoku まんぞく (満足) *n.* satisfaction; contentment.
— *a.n.* (〜 na, ni) satisfactory; contented.

The parts of speech of some words differ according to the context. In that case, they are given together.

3. Meaning and usage

3. 1 Different senses of a headword which are subsumed under one meaning are separated by semicolons.

na⌈yami⌉ なやみ (悩み) *n.* worry; trouble; sufferings; anguish.

3. 2 When a headword has more than one meaning, each meaning is listed in a numbered sequence, with the most common and important meaning shown first.

ho⌈okoo ほうこう (方向) *n.*
1 direction; way; course.
2 aim; object; course.

3. 3 Special notes on both the grammatical and social usage of words, and relevant cultural information are introduced by a ★.

4. Illustrative examples

4. 1 Example phrases and sentences are presented in the following order: romanized Japanese, normal Japanese orthography, the corresponding English translation.

Watashi wa maiasa hachi-ji ni ie o demasu. (私は毎朝8時に家を出ます) I *leave* the house at eight every morning.

4.2 Romanized Japanese is printed in italics with the headword of that particular entry set in upright style. In the illustrative phrase or sentence, the English translation of the headword is given in italics. The user should note that the parts of speech of the Japanese headword and its English translation equivalent will often be different, and also that it is sometimes difficult to define precisely the exact English word or words that correspond to the Japanese headword.

4.3 In example sentences featuring dialogue, Japanese style quotation marks, 「 」, are used in the Japanese text, and conventional English quotation marks in the romanization and translation.

> "*O-geñki desu ka?*" "Okagesama de." (「お元気ですか」「おかげさまで」) "How are you?" "*I'm fine, thank you.*"

4.4 Many of the Japanese sentences are subject to several interpretations depending on context, which of course cannot be given in any detail in a dictionary such as this. It should be borne in mind that in Japanese the grammatical subject is often not expressed, and the distinction between singular and plural, or between definite (e.g. 'the pen') and indefinite (e.g. 'a pen'), is not as clearcut as in English.

5. Orthography

5.1 The orthography of headwords and entries reflects current educated usage, while at the same time taking into account the recommendations of the Government Committee on 'Chinese Characters for Daily Use' (1981). The general principles that have been followed are:

5.2 When there is a *kanji* listed after the *hiragana* immediately following the headword and all example phrases and sentences use that *kanji*, you may assume that the word is normally written in *kanji*, rather than *hiragana*.

> **na[game]ru** ながめる (眺める) *vt.* look at; watch; view: *mado kara soto o* nagameru (窓から外を眺める) *look* out of the window.

5.3 When there is a *kanji* listed after the *hiragana*, but no example phrases or sentences with that *kanji*, you may assume that whilst the *kanji* for that particular word does exist, it is common and perfectly acceptable not to use it in everyday written Japanese.

> **ma⌉ku** まく(蒔く) *vt.* plant; sow:
> *hana no tane o* maku (花の種をまく) *plant* flower seeds.

5. 4 You will also find illustrative examples in which example sentences using the headword is sometimes in *kana*, and sometimes in *kanji*. In such cases you may assume that both usages are perfectly acceptable, although some senses of the word may more commonly be written in *kana*, and other senses in *kanji*. (For example, see the entries under '**a⌈taru**.')

6. Conjugations of verbs

6. 1 Consonant-stem verbs

Consonant-stem verbs are marked [C] in this dictionary and the two basic forms, to which '*-masu*' and '*-nai*' are attached, and the *te*-form are given in this order.

> **ka⌉k·u** かく(書く) *vt.* (kak·i-; kak·a-; ka·i-te [C])
> **no⌉m·u** のむ(飲む) *vt.* (nom·i-; nom·a-; noñ-de [C])

6. 2 Vowel-stem verbs

Vowel-stem verbs are marked [V] in this dictionary, and only the *te*-form is given, since the '*-masu*' and '*-nai*' are attached to the stem without any changes.

> **ta⌈be⌉·ru** たべる(食べる) *vt.* (tabe-te [V])

6. 3 Irregular verbs

Irregular verbs are marked [I] in this dictionary, and the two basic forms, to which '*-masu*' and '*-nai*' are attached, and the *te*-form are given.

> **s·u⌈ru** する *vt.* (sh·i-; sh·i-; sh·i-te [I])
> **me⌈ñs·u⌉ru** めんする(面する) *vi.* (meñsh·i-; meñsh·i-; meñsh·i-te [I])
> **k·u⌉ru** くる(来る) *vi.* (k·i-; k·o-; k·i-te [I])

6. 4 With longer verbs, the conjugational information is given in abbreviated form in the interests of both clarity and economy of space.

> **chi⌈rakas·u** ちらかす(散らかす) *vt.* (-kash·i-; -kas·a-; -kash·i-te [C]) scatter; litter.

7. Conjugation of adjectives

7.1 Only the *ku*-form is given.

> **ta⌈ka⌉·i** たかい(高い) *a.* (-ku) high; tall; lofty.

7.2 Most adjectives are used attributively and predicatively. But in those cases in which adjectives are restricted in their usage, those that are used only attributively are marked '*attrib.*' (attributive), and those used only predicatively are marked '*pred.*' (predicative).

> **shi⌈katana⌉·i** しかたない(仕方ない) *a.* (-ku) (*pred.*) cannot help doing; be no use doing.

8. Adjectival nouns

The entry that follows an adjectival noun is as follows:

> **shi⌉zuka** しずか(静か) *a.n.* (~ na, ni) quiet

The word '*na*' is used to link the adjectival noun to a following noun or another adjectival noun which it modifies.

> shizuka *na ashioto* (*quiet* footsteps)

The '*ni*' indicates that the adjectival noun can be adverbialized.

> shizuka *ni aruku* (walk *quietly*)

9. Adverbs

Inflected forms of some verbs or adjectives are used as adverbs, and when such a form is common, it is listed as a headword.

> **a⌈a-shite** ああして *adv.* like that

When adverbs are commonly followed by '*to*,' or '*suru*,' this information is given in round brackets immediately following.

> **do⌈shi⌉ñ** どしん *adv.* (~ to) with a thud
> **fu⌉rafura** ふらふら *adv.* (~ suru) feel dizzy

When '*to*' is optional, an attempt is made to show this in the illustrative examples.

10. Levels of usage

Levels of usage or register are indicated as follows:

formal	=	a word used in formal or official situations
informal	=	a word used in relaxed and friendly situations

colloquial	=	an informal word used in conversation
polite	=	a polite word
honorific	=	a word indicating respect for others
humble	=	a word indicating humility
brusque	=	a potentially rough or abrupt word
rude	=	a potentially impolite or offensive word
literary	=	a word used in the written language

The above is to be taken only as a guide. There will be great variations in usage amongst native speakers of Japanese.

11. Cross-references

Reference to another word with a related meaning is indicated by ⟪⇨⟫.
Reference to a word with a contrasting meaning is indicated by ⟪↔⟫.

12. Brackets in illustrative examples

Round brackets (   ) indicate that omission is possible.
Square brackets [   ] indicate alternative possibilities.

13. Abbreviations

a.	adjective	*infl. end.*	inflected ending
a.n.	adjectival noun	*int.*	interjection
adv.	adverb	*n.*	noun
app.	appendix	*neg.*	negative
attrib.	attributive	*p.*	particle
colloq.	colloquial	*pred.*	predicative
conj.	conjunction	*pref.*	prefix
derog.	derogatory	*suf.*	suffix
fig.	figurative	*vi.*	intransitive verb
illus.	illustration	*vt.*	transitive verb

A

a'˥ あっ *int.* oh; ah: ★ Used to express admiration, wonder, danger, etc. A', *wakatta.* (あっ, わかった) *Oh,* I see.

a⌈a[1] ああ *adv.* such; that; to such a degree; to such an extent: *Niku ga* aa *takakute wa totemo kaemaseñ.* (肉がああ高くてはとても買えません) If meat costs *that much,* I just cannot afford to buy it. ⟪⇨ doo[1]; koo; soo[1]⟫

a˥a[2] ああ *int.* oh; ah; well; yes: ★ Used to express admiration, wonder, sorrow, etc. Aa, *kiree da.* (ああ, きれいだ) *Oh,* that's beautiful. ⟪⇨ oo[2]⟫

a⌈a-iu ああいう *attrib.* that; like that; that kind of; such: *Watashi wa* aa-iu *zasshi ni wa kyoomi ga arimaseñ.* (私はああいう雑誌には興味がありません) I am not interested in *that kind* of magazine. ⟪⇨ doo-iu; koo-iu; soo-iu⟫

a⌈a-shite ああして *adv.* like that; in that way: *Kanojo wa* aa-shite *itsu-mo hito ni damasareru.* (彼女はああしていつも人にだまされる) She is always deceived *like that* by people. ⟪⇨ doo-shite; koo-shite; soo-shite⟫

a⌈ba˥k·u あばく (暴く) *vt.* (abak·i-; abak·a-; aba·i-te Ⓒ) expose; disclose; reveal: *himitsu o* abaku (秘密を暴く) *expose* a confidence.

a⌈bare·ru あばれる (暴れる) *vi.* (abare-te Ⓥ) act violently; rage; struggle: *Kodomo wa chuusha o iyagatte* abareta. (子どもは注射をいやがって暴れた) The child *struggled* to get away from the injection.

a⌈bekobe あべこべ *n.* (*informal*) opposite; upside down; reverse.

a⌈bi·ru あびる (浴びる) *vt.* (abi-te Ⓥ) **1** bathe: *shawaa o* abiru (シャワーを浴びる) *take* a shower.
2 get covered with: *hokori o* abiru (ほこりを浴びる) *get covered* with dust.
3 bask: *nikkoo o* abiru (日光を浴びる) *bask* in the sun.
4 be an object of praise [attack; criticism]: *zessañ o* abiru (絶賛を浴びる) *receive* great praise. ⟪⇨ abiseru⟫

a⌈bise·ru あびせる (浴びせる) *vt.* (abise-te Ⓥ) **1** throw; pour (water): *hito ni mizu o* abiseru (人に水を浴びせる) *throw* water on a person.
2 (*fig.*) shower (with questions); heap (abuse on).

a⌈buna·i あぶない (危ない) *a.* (-ku) **1** dangerous; risky: *Dooro de asobu no wa* abunai. (道路で遊ぶのは危ない) It is *dangerous* to play in the road.
2 critical: *Kaneko-sañ wa inochi ga* abunai. (金子さんは命が危ない) Mr. Kaneko is in *critical* condition.

a⌈bura[1] あぶら (油) *n.* oil.

a⌈bura[2] あぶら (脂) *n.* fat; grease. ⟪⇨ shiboo[3]⟫

a⌈bura˥e あぶらえ (油絵) *n.* an oil painting.

a⌈chi˥-kochi あちこち *n.* =achira-kochira.

a⌈chira あちら *n.* **1** that place; that way; over there: ★ More polite than '*asoko*' and '*atchi*.' Achira *ni irassharu no wa donata desu ka?* (あちらにいらっしゃるのはどなたですか) Who is that person *over there*? (*polite*).
2 that thing; that person: ★ More polite than '*are*[1].' Achira *ga yuumee na Nakamura señsee desu.* (あちらが有名な中村先

生です) *That person over there* is the famous Prof. Nakamura. ⟪⇨ dochira; kochira; sochira⟫

a⌈chira-ko⌉chira あちらこちら *n.* here and there: ★ Abbreviated to '*achi-kochi*.'
Achira-kochira *de sakura ga saki-hajimeta.* (あちらこちらで桜が咲き始めた) The cherry trees started to bloom *here and there.*

a⌈e⌉g·u あえぐ (喘ぐ) *vi.* (aeg·i-; aeg·a-; ae·i-de Ⓒ) **1** pant; gasp:
aegi aegi *yama o noboru* (あえぎあえぎ山を登る) climb a mountain, *gasping for* breath.
2 suffer:
fukyoo ni aegu (不況にあえぐ) *suffer* an economic depression.

a⌈fure⌉·ru あふれる (溢れる) *vi.* (afure-te Ⓥ) **1** overflow; flood:
Ooame de kawa ga afureta. (大雨で川があふれた) The river *overflowed* because of the heavy rain.
2 be crowded with:
Shiñjuku wa hito de afurete iru. (新宿は人であふれている) Shinjuku *is crowded* with people.
3 be full of:
Kare wa kiboo ni afurete iru. (彼は希望にあふれている) He *is full* of hope.

a⌈gar·u あがる (上がる) *vi.* (agar·i-; agar·a-; agat-te Ⓒ) **1** go up; rise; come up:
Kare wa go-kai made aruite agatta. (彼は5階まで歩いて上がった) He *walked up* to the fifth floor.
2 (of degree, quantity, prices, etc.) rise, be raised; be promoted:
oñdo ga agaru (温度が上がる) the temperature *rises.* ⟪⇨ ageru[1]⟫ ⟪↔ sagaru⟫
3 improve; make progress:
seeseki ga agaru (成績が上がる) one's (school) grades *improve.* ⟪↔ ochiru; sagaru⟫
4 (of a child) enter (school):
Kare no kodomo wa kotoshi shoogakkoo ni agarimashita. (彼の子どもは今年小学校に上がりました) His child *started* elementary school this year.
5 (of rain) stop; clear up:
Ame ga agarimashita. (雨が上がりました) The rain *has stopped.*
6 (of a person) get nervous; get stage fright.
7 (*polite*) eat; drink:
Doozo o-agari *kudasai.* (どうぞお上がりください) Please *help yourself.* ⟪⇨ nomu; taberu⟫

a⌈ge·ru[1] あげる (上げる) *vt.* (age-te Ⓥ) **1** raise; lift:
Shitsumoñ ga areba te o age nasai. (質問があれば手を上げなさい) If you have any questions, please *raise* your hands. ⟪⇨ agaru⟫
2 give: ★ Not used toward one's superiors.
Anata ni kono hoñ o agemasu. (あなたにこの本をあげます) I will *give* you this book. ⟪↔ kureru[1]⟫ ⟪⇨ yaru[2]⟫
3 raise:
oñdo [*nedañ*] *o* ageru (温度[値段]を上げる) *raise* the temperature [price]. ⟪↔ sageru⟫ ⟪⇨ agaru⟫
4 improve; increase:
nooritsu o ageru (能率を上げる) *improve* the efficiency. ⟪⇨ agaru⟫
-te ageru (て〜) (used when doing a favor for someone else):
Watashi wa kare ni kasa o kashite ageta. (私は彼に傘を貸してあげた) I *lent* him an umbrella.

a⌈ge·ru[2] あげる (揚げる) *vt.* (age-te Ⓥ) deep-fry: *sakana o* ageru (魚を揚げる) *deep-fry* fish. ⟪⇨ itameru⟫

a⌈go⌉ あご (顎) *n.* jaw; chin.

a⌈go⌉hige あごひげ (顎髭) *n.* beard. ⟪⇨ hige⟫

a⌈gura あぐら *n.* (way of sitting with one's legs crossed).
agura o kaku (〜をかく) sit cross-legged.

a⌈hiru あひる (家鴨) *n.* domestic duck. ⟪⇨ kamo⟫

a⌉i あい (愛) *n.* love. ⟪⇨ aisuru; koi[2]⟫

a⌉ida あいだ (間) *n.* **1** (of place)

between; among:
Gyoo to gyoo no aida *o sukoshi ake nasai.* (行と行の間を少しあけなさい) Leave a little space *between* the lines.
2 (of time) for; while; during:
Watashi wa nagai aida *matasareta.* (私は長い間待たされた) I was kept waiting *for* a long time.
3 (of relations) between; among:
Kanojo wa daigakusee no aida *de niñki ga aru.* (彼女は大学生の間で人気がある) She is popular *among* college students.

a⌈idagara あいだがら (間柄) *n.* relation; terms:
Takahashi to wa shitashii aidagara *desu.* (高橋とは親しい間がらです) I'm on friendly *terms* with Takahashi.

a⌈ijiñ あいじん (愛人) *n.* lover; love; mistress. (⇨ koibito)

a⌈ijoo あいじょう (愛情) *n.* love; affection; attachment.

a⌈ikagi あいかぎ (合鍵) *n.* duplicate key. (⇨ kagi)

a⌈ikawarazu あいかわらず (相変わらず) *adv.* still; as...as ever; as usual:
Kanojo wa aikawarazu *yoku hataraku.* (彼女は相変わらずよく働く) She works *as* hard *as ever*.

a⌈ikyo⌉o あいきょう (愛敬) *n.* charm; amiability. (⇨ aiso)

a⌈ima あいま (合間) *n.* interval; recess:
shigoto no aima *ni sukoshi uñdoo o suru* (仕事の合間に少し運動をする) do some exercise *during* one's work breaks.

a⌈imai あいまい (曖昧) *a.n.* (~ na, ni) vague; ambiguous:
aimai *na heñji o suru* (あいまいな返事をする) give a *vague* answer.

a⌈iniku あいにく (生憎) *adv.* unfortunately; unluckily:
Ainiku *kare wa fuzai datta.* (あいにく彼は不在だった) *Unfortunately*, he was not at home.
— *a.n.* (~ na/no) unfortunate; unexpected:
Ainiku *no ame de eñsoku wa eñki sareta.* (あいにくの雨で遠足は延期された) The excursion was postponed on account of the *unexpected* rain.

a⌉isatsu あいさつ (挨拶) *n.*
1 greeting; salutation:
aisatsu *o kawasu* (あいさつを交わす) exchange *greetings*.
2 speech; address:
kaikai no aisatsu *o suru* (開会のあいさつをする) give an opening *address*.
3 call; visit:
shiñneñ no aisatsu *ni mawaru* (新年のあいさつに回る) make New Year's *calls*.
aisatsu (o) suru (~(を)する) *vi.* greet; salute.

a⌈iso⌉ あいそ (愛想) *n.* amiability; sociability; civility.
aiso ga ii (~がいい) get along well.
aiso ga tsukiru (~がつきる) be disgusted with.
aiso ga warui (~が悪い) be rather brusque.
... ni aiso o tsukasu (...に~をつかす) be out of patience with....
(↔ buaisoo) (⇨ aikyoo)

a⌈is·u⌉ru あいする (愛する) *vt.* (aish·i-; ais·a-; aish·i-te Ⓒ) love:
Kare wa miñna ni aisarete iru. (彼はみんなに愛されている) He *is loved* by all. (⇨ ai; koi²)

a⌈ite⌉ あいて (相手) *n.* mate; partner; opponent; companion.

a⌉itsu あいつ *n.* that fellow [woman]; that one [thing]. (⇨ kanojo; kare)

a⌉izu あいず (合図) *n.* signal; sign; alarm.
... ni aizu (o) suru (...に~(を)する) *vi.* signal; make a sign: *Keekañ wa kuruma ni tomare to* aizu shita. (警官は車に止まれと合図した) The policeman *signaled* the car to stop.

a⌉ji¹ あじ (味) *n.* taste; savor; flavor. (⇨ ajiwau)

a⌉ji² あじ (鯵) *n.* horse mackerel.

a⌈jiwa⌉·u あじわう(味わう) *vt.* (aji-wa·i-; ajiwaw·a-; ajiwat-te Ⓒ)
1 taste; relish:
hoñba no Chuugoku-ryoori o aji-wau (本場の中国料理を味わう) *relish* real Chinese cooking.
2 enjoy; appreciate:
Tanoshii tabi o ajiwatta. (楽しい旅を味わった) I *enjoyed* a pleasant journey.
3 experience; go through:
kanashimi o ajiwau (悲しみを味わう) *experience* sorrow.

a⌉ka[1] あか(赤) *n.* red. ⟪⇨ akai⟫

a⌈ka⌉[2] あか(垢) *n.* dirt; grime.

a⌉kachañ あかちゃん(赤ちゃん) *n.* baby. ★ Usually refers to someone else's baby. ⟪⇨ akañboo⟫

a⌈ka·i あかい(赤い) *a.* (-ku) red; crimson; scarlet. ⟪⇨ aka[1]⟫

a⌈kaji あかじ(赤字) *n.* the red; red figures; deficit. ⟪↔ kuroji⟫

a⌈kañboo あかんぼう(赤ん坊) *n.* baby. ⟪⇨ akachañ⟫

a⌈kari あかり(明り) *n.* light; lamp: akari *o tsukeru* [*kesu*] (明りをつける[消す]) turn on [off] the *light*.

a⌈karu·i あかるい(明るい) *a.* (-ku)
1 bright; light: akarui *iro* (明るい色) *bright* colors. ⟪↔ kurai[1]⟫
2 cheerful; happy: akarui *kibuñ* (明るい気分) a *happy* feeling. ⟪↔ kurai[1]⟫
3 (of prospects, etc.) bright: akarui *mirai* (明るい未来) a *bright* future. ⟪↔ kurai[1]⟫
4 be familiar with; be well informed:
Kare wa hooritsu ni akarui. (彼は法律に明るい) He *is well versed in* the law. ⟪↔ kurai[1]⟫ ⟪⇨ kuwashii⟫

a⌈kashi⌉ñgoo あかしんごう(赤信号) *n.* red light; stoplight. ⟪⇨ aoshiñgoo⟫

a⌈kas·u あかす(明かす) *vt.* (aka-sh·i-; akas·a-; akash·i-te Ⓒ)
1 spend; pass (a night):
koya de ichi-ya o akasu (小屋で一夜を明かす) *spend* a night in a hut.
2 reveal; disclose (a secret, etc.):
shiñjitsu o akasu (真実を明かす) *tell* the truth.

a⌈kegata あけがた(明け方) *n.* dawn; daybreak.

a⌈ke·ru[1] あける(開ける) *vt.* (ake-te Ⓥ) open; unpack; unlock:
doa [*hikidashi; kañzume*] *o* akeru (ドア[引き出し;缶詰]を開ける) *open* a door [drawer; can]. ⟪↔ shimeru[1]⟫ ⟪⇨ aku[1]⟫

a⌈ke·ru[2] あける(明ける) *vi.* (ake-te Ⓥ) **1** (of day) break; dawn:
Moo sugu yo ga akeru. (もうすぐ夜が明ける) The day will *break* soon.
2 (of a new year) begin:
toshi ga akeru (年が明ける) a new year *begins*.
3 end; be over:
Yatto tsuyu ga aketa. (やっと梅雨が明けた) At last the rainy season *is over*. ⟪⇨ owaru⟫

a⌈ke·ru[3] あける(空ける) *vt.* (ake-te Ⓥ) **1** empty; vacate.
2 make room for.
3 make an opening:
kabe ni ana o akeru (壁に穴をあける) *make* a hole in the wall. ⟪⇨ aku[2]⟫
4 make time:
Chotto o-jikañ o akete *itadakemasu ka?* (ちょっとお時間をあけていただけますか) Can you *spare* me a little time? ⟪⇨ aki[2]; aku[2]⟫

a⌉ki[1] あき(秋) *n.* autumn; fall.

a⌈ki[2] あき(空き) *n.* **1** vacancy. ⟪⇨ aku[2]⟫
2 space; room:
gyoo to gyoo no aida ni motto aki *o toru* (行と行の間にもっと空きをとる) leave more *space* between lines. ⟪⇨ akeru[3]⟫
3 spare time. ⟪⇨ akeru[3]⟫

a⌈kichi あきち(空き地) *n.* vacant land; empty lot. ⟪⇨ tochi⟫

a⌈kikañ あきかん(空き缶) *n.* empty can.

a⌈ki⌉raka あきらか(明らか) *a.n.* (~ na, ni) evident; obvious; clear:
Sono koto wa dare no me ni mo akiraka *desu.* (そのことはだれの目にも

明らかです) That is *evident* to everybody.

a⌈**kirame** あきらめ (諦め) *n.* resignation; abandonment:
Akirame ga kañjiñ desu. (あきらめが肝心です) We should know when to *give up*. (⇨ akirameru)

a⌈**kirame⌉·ru** あきらめる (諦める) *vt.* (akirame-te [V]) give up; abandon (a plan). (⇨ akirame; yameru[1])

a⌈**kire·ru** あきれる (呆れる) *vi.* (akire-te [V]) be astonished; be dumbfounded:
Kare no jooshiki no nasa ni wa akireta. (彼の常識のなさにはあきれた) I *was shocked* by his lack of common sense.

a⌈**ki⌉·ru** あきる (飽きる) *vi.* (aki-te [V]) get [be] tired of:
Tokai no seekatsu ni wa akita. (都会の生活には飽きた) I *have become weary* of city life. (⇨ kikiakiru)

a⌈**kiya** あきや (空き家) *n.* vacant [empty] house.

a⌈**kka** あっか (悪化) *n.* worsening; deterioration; aggravation.
akka suru (〜する) *vi.* become worse; deteriorate.

a⌈**kkena·i** あっけない (呆気ない) *a.* (-ku) disappointingly short [brief; quick]:
Is-shuukañ ga akkenaku *sugita.* (一週間があっけなく過ぎた) A week has passed *too quickly*.

a⌈**kogare** あこがれ (憧れ) *n.* yearning; longing. (⇨ akogareru)

a⌈**kogare·ru** あこがれる (憧れる) *vt.* (akogare-te [V]) **1** long for; yearn for:
Kanojo wa fasshoñ-moderu ni akogarete iru. (彼女はファッションモデルに憧れている) She *longs* to become a fashion model. (⇨ akogare)
2 admire:
sutaa ni akogareru (スターに憧れる) *admire* a star. (⇨ akogare)

a⌈**k·u**[1] あく (開く) *vi.* (ak·i-; ak·a-; a·i-te [C]) open:
Kono doa wa sayuu ni akimasu. (このドアは左右にあきます) This door *opens* sideways. (↔ shimaru[1]) (⇨ akeru[1]; hiraku)

a⌈**k·u**[2] あく (空く) *vi.* (ak·i-; ak·a-; a·i-te [C]) **1** get [be] empty [vacant]:
Sumimaseñ ga, sono seki wa aite imasu *ka?* (すみませんが, その席はあいていますか) Excuse me, but *is* that seat *occupied*? (⇨ akeru[3]; aki[2])
2 have a gap. (⇨ akeru[3])
3 (of a hole) have an opening. (⇨ akeru[3])
4 be free. (⇨ akeru[3])
5 finish with something:
Te ga aitara, *kono shigoto o tetsudatte kudasai.* (手があいたら, この仕事を手伝ってください) When you'*re finished*, please help me with this job.

a⌉**ku**[3] あく (悪) *n.* vice; evil. (↔ zeñ[1]) (⇨ zeñaku)

a⌈**kubi** あくび (欠伸) *n.* yawn:
akubi *o suru* (あくびをする) give a *yawn*.

a⌉**kui** あくい (悪意) *n.* ill will; malice; spite: akui *o idaku* (悪意を抱く) bear *ill will*.

a⌉**kuji** あくじ (悪事) *n.* evil [wicked] deed; crime: akuji *o hataraku* (悪事を働く) do *evil*.

a⌉**kuma** あくま (悪魔) *n.* devil; demon.

a⌈**ku⌉made (mo)** あくまで(も) (飽く迄(も)) *adv.* to the last; persistently.

a⌈**kuniñ** あくにん (悪人) *n.* bad [wicked] person; villain.

a⌉**kuseñto** アクセント *n.* **1** (pitch or stress) accent. ★ Not used in the sense of 'a (foreign) accent.'
2 emphasis; stress; accent:
Ooki-na riboñ ga kanojo no fuku no akuseñto ni natte ita. (大きなリボンが彼女の服のアクセントになっていた) A large ribbon *set off* her dress.

a⌉**kushu** あくしゅ (握手) *n.* handshake; handclasp.
akushu (o) suru (〜(を)する) *vi.* shake hands.

a
a⌈ma⌉do あまど(雨戸) *n.* sliding storm door made of thin boards; shutter.

a⌈mae·ru あまえる(甘える) *vi.* (amae-te [V]) **1** behave like a spoiled child; have a coquettish way:
Sono ko wa haha-oya ni amaeta. (その子は母親に甘えた) The child *behaved like a baby* with his mother.
2 depend on; take advantage of:
hito no kooi [shiñsetsu] ni amaeru (人の好意[親切]に甘える) *depend* on a person's goodwill [kindness].

a⌈ma⌉gu あまぐ(雨具) *n.* rainwear; umbrella; raincoat.

a⌈ma·i あまい(甘い) *a.* (-ku)
1 (of taste) sweet; sugary.
2 (of voice, melody, etc.) sweet; attractive.
3 not salty:
Kyoo no misoshiru wa chotto amai. (きょうのみそ汁はちょっと甘い) Today's miso soup is *not salty* enough. ⟪↔ karai⟫
4 lenient; not severe in discipline:
Shujiñ wa kodomo ni amai. (主人は子どもに甘い) My husband is *too easy* on the children. ⟪↔ karai⟫
5 optimistic; easygoing; underestimating the results.

a⌈ma⌉mizu あまみず(雨水) *n.* rainwater.

a⌈mari⌉[1] あまり(余り) *n.* the rest; the balance; remains. ⟪⇨ amaru⟫

a⌈mari[2] あまり(余り) *adv.* **1** too; very:
Kono ryoori wa amari *karakute, taberarenai.* (この料理はあまり辛くて, 食べられない) This dish is *too* peppery for me to eat.
2 (with a negative) not...much; not very; seldom; rarely:
Yasai wa amari *suki de wa arimaseñ.* (野菜はあまり好きではありません) I don't like vegetables *very much.*

-a⌉mari あまり(余り) *suf.* over...; more than...:
*Nihoñ ni kite sañ-neñ-*amari *ni narimasu.* (日本に来て3年あまりになります) I have been in Japan *over* three years now.

a⌈ma⌉r·u あまる(余る) *vt.* (amar·i-; amar·a-; amat-te [C])
1 be left (over):
Baageñ de yasuku kaeta no de, sañzeñ-eñ o-kane ga amatta. (バーゲンで安く買えたので, 3,000円お金が余った) As I could buy it at a bargain, I *saved* 3,000 yen. ⟪⇨ amari[1]⟫
2 be in excess; be more than enough.

a⌈ma⌉s·u あます(余す) *vt.* (amash·i-; amas·a-; amash·i-te [C])
1 leave:
Amasanai *de, miñna tabe nasai.* (余さないで, みんな食べなさい) *Don't leave* anything. Eat it all. ⟪⇨ nokosu⟫
2 be left; remain. ⟪⇨ nokosu⟫
amasu tokoro naku (～ところなく) completely; fully.

a⌈maya⌉dori あまやどり(雨宿り) *n.* taking shelter from the rain.

a⌈mayaka⌉s·u あまやかす(甘やかす) *vt.* (-kash·i-; -kas·a-; -kash·i-te [C]) spoil; pamper.

a⌉me[1] あめ(雨) *n.* rain. ⟪⇨ amefuri; hare; kumori⟫

a⌈me[2] あめ(飴) *n.* candy; sweet; lollipop:
ame *o shaburu* (あめをしゃぶる) suck a piece of *candy.*

a⌈me⌉furi あめふり(雨降り) *n.* rain; rainy weather. ⟪⇨ ame[1]⟫

a⌈mi⌉ あみ(網) *n.* net:
ami *o haru* (網を張る) lay a net / ami *o utsu* (網を打つ) cast a net.

a⌈mi⌉mono あみもの(編み物) *n.* knitting; crochet.

a⌉m·u あむ(編む) *vt.* (am·i-; am·a-; añ-de [C]) knit; crochet; braid; weave:
keito no seetaa o amu (毛糸のセーターを編む) *knit* a woolen sweater.

a⌉ñ あん(案) *n.* plan; idea; proposal; draft.

a⌈na⌉ あな (穴) *n.* **1** hole; opening; perforation.
2 defect; deficit; loophole:
Kimi no keekaku ni wa ana *ga aru.* (君の計画には穴がある) There is a *defect* in your plan.
3 gap:
Sekiya-sañ no yasuñda ana *o umenakereba naranai.* (関谷さんの休んだ穴を埋めなければならない) We have to fill the *gap* left by Mr. Sekiya's absence.

a⌈nado⌉r·u あなどる (侮る) *vt.* (anador·i-; anador·a-; anadot-te Ⓒ)
1 despise; look down on:
Wakai kara to itte kare o anadotte *wa ikenai.* (若いからといって彼を侮ってはいけない) You shouldn't *look down* on him just because he is young.
2 make light of.

a⌈na⌉ta あなた *n.* you: ★ Plural forms are '*anata-tachi*,' '*anata-gata*' (*polite*) and '*anata-ra*' (*slightly derog.*). Not used when addressing one's superiors.
Kore wa anata no *desu ka*? (これはあなたのですか) Is this *yours*?
《⇨ kimi[1]》

a⌈nau⌉ñsu アナウンス *n.* announcement.

a⌈ñba⌉rañsu アンバランス *a.n.* (~ na/ni) imbalance.

a⌈ñdo あんど (安堵) *n.* (*formal*) relief; reassurance. 《⇨ añshiñ》
... ni añdo suru (...に~する) *vi.* be [feel] relieved.

a⌈ne あね (姉) *n.* one's older [elder; big] sister. 《⇨ imooto》

a⌈ñgai あんがい (案外) *adv.* unexpectedly; against expectations.
— *a.n.* (~ na, ni) unexpected; surprising.

a⌈ñgoo あんごう (暗号) *n.* code; cipher; cryptogram.

a⌈ni あに (兄) *n.* one's older [elder; big] brother. 《↔ otooto》

a⌈ñi あんい (安易) *a.n.* (~ na, ni) (*formal*) easy; easygoing; happy-go-lucky.

a⌈ñji あんじ (暗示) *n.* hint; suggestion; intimation.
añji suru (~する) *vt.* hint; suggest; imply.

a⌈ñji⌉·ru あんじる (案じる) *vt.* (añjite Ⓥ) worry; be anxious:
Kare wa chichi-oya no keñkoo o añjite iru. (彼は父親の健康を案じている) He *is worried* about his father's health.

a⌈ñki あんき (暗記) *n.* memorization; memorizing.
añki suru (~する) *vt.* memorize; learn by heart.

a⌈ñma あんま (按摩) *n.* Japanese massage; masseur; masseuse.

a⌈ñmari あんまり *a.n.* (~ na/no, ni) beyond the ordinary degree; extreme:
Sore wa añmari *da.* (それはあんまりだ) That's going *too far*.
— *adv.* (*colloq.*) = amari[2].

a⌈ñmiñ あんみん (安眠) *n.* sound [good] sleep.

a⌈ñmoku あんもく (暗黙) *n.* implicitness; tacitness:
añmoku *no ryookai* (暗黙の了解) an *implicit* understanding.

a⌈ñna あんな *attrib.* such; like that:
Añna *tokoro de asoñde wa abunai na.* (あんな所で遊んでは危ないな) It is dangerous to play in *such* a place.
《⇨ doñna; koñna; soñna》

a⌈ñna⌉i あんない (案内) *n.* **1** guidance; guide.
2 notice; invitation:
añnai-joo (案内状) an *invitation* letter [card].
añnai suru (~する) *vt.* guide; show.

a⌈ñna ni あんなに *adv.* such ; so:
Añna ni *okoranakute mo* yokkatta no ni. (あんなに怒らなくてもよかったのに) It was unnecessary for you to get so angry. 《⇨ doñna ni; koñna ni; soñna ni》

a⌈no あの *attrib.* **1** that; the:
Asoko ni suwatte iru ano *hito wa dare desu ka?* (あそこに座っているあの

人はだれですか) Who is *that* person sitting over there?
2 that; the: ★ Refers to a person or thing that is, in time or space, distant from both the speaker and the listener.
*"Kinoo Akihabara e itte kimashita." "*Ano *atari mo nigiyaka ni narimashita ne."* (「きのう秋葉原へ行って来ました」「あの辺りもにぎやかになりましたね」) "I went to Akihabara yesterday." "*That* area has become a lively place, hasn't it?"
3 that: ★ Refers to a person or thing known to both the speaker and the listener.
"Mada ano *koto o ki ni shite iru ñ desu ka?" "*Ano *koto tte, nañ desu ka?"* (「まだあの事を気にしているんですか」「あの事って, 何ですか」) "Are you still worried about *that* matter?" "What do you mean by *that* matter?" ⟪⇨ dono; kono; sono⟫

a⌈noo あのう *int.* excuse me; say; well:
Anoo, *Tookyoo-daigaku wa doo ittara ii deshoo ka?* (あのう, 東京大学はどう行ったらいいでしょうか) *Excuse me*, but how can I get to Tokyo University?

a⌈ñpi あんぴ (安否) *n.* safety:
Kare no añpi *ga shiñpai desu.* (彼の安否が心配です) I am worried about his *safety*.

a⌈ñsatsu あんさつ (暗殺) *n.* assassination.

a⌈ñsee あんせい (安静) *n.* rest; quiet; repose.
añsee ni suru (～にする) lie quietly in bed; take bed rest.

a⌈ñshiñ あんしん (安心) *n.* peace of mind; relief.
añshiñ suru (～する) *vi.* feel relieved [assured].
— *a.n.* (～ na) safe; reassuring; secure.

a⌈ñshoo あんしょう (暗礁) *n.*
1 reef.
2 (*fig.*) deadlock:
Kare-ra no hanashiai wa añshoo *ni noriageta.* (彼らの話し合いは暗礁に乗り上げた) Their talks came to a *deadlock*.

a⌈ñshoo-ba⌉ñgoo あんしょうばんごう (暗証番号) *n.* code number:
añshoo-bañgoo *o osu* (暗証番号を押す) enter one's *code number*.

a⌈ñta あんた *n.* (*informal*) = anata.

a⌈ñtee あんてい (安定) *n.* stability; balance; steadiness.
añtee suru (～する) *vi.* become stable; be stabilized.

a⌈ñzañ あんざん (暗算) *n.* mental arithmetic [calculation].
añzañ suru (～する) *vt.* do sums in one's head.

a⌈ñzeñ あんぜん (安全) *n.* safety; security.
— *a.n.* (～ na, ni) safe; secure.

a⌈ñzu あんず (杏) *n.* apricot.

a⌉o あお (青) *n.* **1** blue.
2 (of a traffic light, plants, vegetables, etc.) green:
ao-*yasai* (青野菜) *green* vegetables / ao-*riñgo* (青りんご) *a* green *apple*. ⟪⇨ aoi; aojiroi; midori⟫

a⌈oa⌉o to あおあおと (青々と) *adv.* (～ suru) (of trees, leaves, etc.) fresh and green; verdant.

a⌈o⌉g·u[1] あおぐ (仰ぐ) *vt.* (aog·i-; aog·a-; ao·i-de Ⓒ) **1** look up at: *sora no hoshi o* aogu (空の星を仰ぐ) *look up* at the stars in the sky.
2 respect; look up to.

a⌈o⌉g·u[2] あおぐ (扇ぐ) *vt.* (aog·i-; aog·a-; ao·i-de Ⓒ) fan:
uchiwa de jibuñ o aogu (うちわで自分をあおぐ) *fan* oneself with a round fan.

a⌈o⌉·i あおい (青い) *a.* (-ku) **1** blue.
2 green; unripe. ⟪⇨ ao; midori⟫
3 (of a person's face, look) pale. ⟪⇨ aojiroi⟫

a⌈ojiro⌉·i あおじろい (青白い) *a.* (-ku) **1** bluish white.
2 pale; pallid:
Kare wa aojiroi *kao o shite iru.* (彼は青白い顔をしている) He looks

pale. ⟪⇨ aoi⟫

a⌈o⌉r·u あおる (煽る) *vt.* (aor·i-; aor·a-; aot-te Ⓒ) **1** fan; flap: *Kaateñ ga kaze ni* aorarete iru. (カーテンが風にあおられている) The curtains *are flapping* in the wind.
2 stir up; incite: *kyoosooshiñ o* aoru (競争心をあおる) *arouse* a sense of rivalry.

a⌈oshi⌉ñgoo あおしんごう (青信号) *n.* green light. ⟪⇨ akashiñgoo⟫

a⌈ozame⌉·ru あおざめる (青ざめる) *vi.* (aozame-te Ⓥ) turn pale. ⟪⇨ aoi⟫

a⌈ozo⌉ra あおぞら (青空) *n.* the blue (azure) sky.

a⌈pa⌉ato アパート *n.* an apartment; an apartment house. ⟪⇨ mañshoñ⟫

a⌈ppaku あっぱく (圧迫) *n.* pressure; oppression.
appaku suru (〜する) *vt.* oppress; suppress; strain.

a⌉ra あら *int.* my goodness; why. ★ Used by women to express wonder, surprise, etc. Men use '*are*[2].' ⟪⇨ maa[2]⟫

a⌈ra·i[1] あらい (荒い) *a.* (-ku) rough; rude; violent: *Kyoo wa nami ga* arai. (きょうは波が荒い) The sea is *rough* today. ⟪↔ shizuka⟫

a⌈ra·i[2] あらい (粗い) *a.* (-ku) coarse; rough: arai *suna* (粗い砂) *coarse* sand. ⟪↔ komakai⟫

a⌈rakajime あらかじめ *adv.* beforehand; in advance: *Kare wa jikeñ no naiyoo o* arakajime *shitte ita.* (彼は事件の内容をあらかじめ知っていた) He knew the details of the affair *in advance.*

a⌈rappo⌉·i あらっぽい (荒っぽい) *a.* (-ku) rough; rude: arappoi *uñteñ* (荒っぽい運転) *unruly* driving.

a⌈rare あられ *n.* hail; hailstone.

a⌈rasa⌉gashi あらさがし (粗探し) *n.* faultfinding; picking flaws: *hito no* arasagashi o suru (人のあらさがしをする) *find fault* with others.

a⌉rashi あらし (嵐) *n.* storm; tempest. ⟪⇨ taifuu⟫

a⌈raso⌉i あらそい (争い) *n.* dispute; quarrel; trouble. ⟪⇨ arasou⟫

a⌈raso⌉·u あらそう (争う) *vi.* (araso·i-; arasow·a-; arasot-te Ⓒ)
1 quarrel; dispute: *tochi no shoyuukeñ o* arasou (土地の所有権を争う) *dispute* the ownership of land. ⟪⇨ arasoi⟫
2 compete: *Jookyaku wa saki o* arasotte, *deñsha ni noroo to shita.* (乗客は先を争って, 電車に乗ろうとした) The passengers *pushed* in front of one another to get on the train.

a⌈ras·u あらす (荒らす) *vt.* (arash·i-; aras·a-; arash·i-te Ⓒ)
1 damage. ⟪⇨ areru⟫
2 ransack; break in: *Doroboo ni heya o* arasareta. (泥棒に部屋を荒らされた) My room was *ransacked* by a thief.

a⌈rasuji あらすじ (粗筋) *n.* outline; synopsis; plot.

a⌉rata あらた (新た) *a.n.* (〜 na, ni) (*formal*) new; fresh. ⟪⇨ atarashii⟫

a⌈ratama⌉r·u あらたまる (改まる) *vi.* (-mar·i-; -mar·a-; -mat-te Ⓒ)
1 be improved. ⟪⇨ aratameru⟫
2 (of a year, semester, etc.) begin; come around: *Toshi ga* aratamatta. (年が改まった) The new year *has come around.*
aratamatta (改まった) *attrib.* formal; ceremonious.
aratamatte (改まって) *adv.* in a formal way.

a⌈ratame⌉·ru あらためる (改める) *vt.* (-me-te Ⓥ) **1** change; renew: *fukusoo o* aratameru (服装を改める) *change* one's clothes. ⟪⇨ aratamaru⟫
2 correct; reform: *zeesee o* aratameru (税制を改める) *reform* the tax system. ⟪⇨ aratamaru⟫
3 examine; check:

Keekañ wa kabañ no nakami o aratameta. (警官はかばんの中身を改めた) The policeman *checked* the contents of the bag.

a⌈rata⌉mete あらためて (改めて) *adv.* another time; again.

a⌈ra·u あらう (洗う) *vt.* (ara·i-; araw·a-; arat-te Ⓒ) **1** wash; clean: *sara o* arau (皿を洗う) *wash* the dishes.

2 wash; flow against [over]: *Nami ga kishi o* aratte iru. (波が岸を洗っている) Waves *are washing* the beach.

a⌈rau⌉mi あらうみ (荒海) *n.* rough [stormy] sea. (⇨ umi[1])

a⌈raware⌉·ru あらわれる (現れる) *vi.* (-ware-te Ⓥ) **1** appear; come out: *Kumo no aida kara tsuki ga* arawareta. (雲の間から月が現れた) The moon *appeared* from behind the clouds. (⇨ arawasu[2])

2 arrive; show up: *Sañjup-puñ matte, kare ga* arawarenakereba, *saki ni ikimashoo.* (30 分待って, 彼が現れなければ, 先に行きましょう) We'll wait for thirty minutes and if he *doesn't show up*, let's go on ahead. (⇨ arawasu[2])

3 (of hidden nature, facts, etc.) be discovered; be revealed.

a⌈rawa⌉s·u[1] あらわす (表す) *vt.* (-wash·i-; -was·a-; -wash·i-te Ⓒ) **1** show; reveal; express.

2 signify; stand for; symbolize: *Kono kigoo wa nani o* arawashite *imasu ka?* (この記号は何を表していますか) What does this symbol *stand for*?

a⌈rawa⌉s·u[2] あらわす (現す) *vt.* (-wash·i-; -was·a-; -wash·i-te Ⓒ) **1** show up; appear; reveal: *Hisashiburi ni kare wa paatii ni sugata o* arawashita. (久しぶりに彼はパーティーに姿を現した) He *showed up* at the party—the first time in quite a while. (⇨ arawareru)

2 take effect: *Kono kusuri wa sugu ni kooka o* arawashimasu. (この薬はすぐに効果を現します) This medicine will soon *take effect*.

a⌈rawa⌉s·u[3] あらわす (著す) *vt.* (-wash·i-; -was·a-; -wash·i-te Ⓒ) (*formal*) write; publish: *hoñ o* arawasu (本を著す) *write* a book.

a⌈rayu⌉ru あらゆる *attrib.* all; every: arayuru *kikai o riyoo suru* (あらゆる機会を利用する) make use of *every* opportunity.

a⌈re[1] あれ *n.* **1** that over there: ★ Refers to something located at some distance from both the speaker and the listener. Are *wa Tookyoo-tawaa desu.* (あれは東京タワーです) *That* is the Tokyo Tower. (⇨ dore[1]; kore; sore[1])

2 that, it: ★ Refers to something, which is, in time or space, distant from both the speaker and the listener. Are *wa nañ-neñ-mae deshita kke, Izu ni jishiñ ga atta no wa?* (あれは何年前でしたっけ, 伊豆に地震があったのは) How many years ago was *it* when there was the earthquake in Izu?

3 that, it: ★ Refers to something known to both the speaker and the listener. *"Nee, are kaita?" "Are tte geñgogaku no repooto no koto?"* (「ねえ, あれ書いた」「あれって, 言語学のレポートのこと」) "Say, have you written *that*?" "By 'that,' do you mean the linguistics paper?"

4 she; he: ★ Refers to one's wife or one's subordinate. *Kanai desu ka? Are wa ima jikka e itte imasu.* (家内ですか. あれは今実家へ行っています) My wife? *She* is visiting her parents' house.

are irai (～以来) since then.

a⌈re[2] あれ *int.* oh; look; really. ★ Used by men to express surprise, doubt, etc. Women use '*ara*.'

a|re de あれで *adv.* **1** with that: Are de *kare wa jishiñ o torimodoshita.* (あれで彼は自信を取り戻した) *With that*, he regained his self-confidence.
2 in one's own way: *Kare wa* are de *nakanaka omoiyari ga aru.* (彼はあれでなかなか思いやりがある) He is very considerate *in his own way.*

a|re-(k)kiri あれ(っ)きり *adv.* (with a negative) since then: Are-(k)kiri *kare ni atte imaseñ.* (あれっきり彼に会っていません) I haven't met him *since then.* ⟪⇨ kore-(k)kiri; sore-(k)kiri⟫

a|re|-kore あれこれ *adv.* this and that; one thing and another; in various ways: Are-kore *yatte iru uchi ni, yoi hoohoo ga mitsukatta.* (あれこれやっているうちに, 良い方法が見つかった) While trying out *various ways*, I discovered a good method. ⟪⇨ iroiro²⟫

a|re·ru あれる (荒れる) *vi.* (are-te Ⓥ) **1** be stormy; be rough.
2 lie waste; be dilapidated. ⟪⇨ arasu⟫
3 (of lips and skin) become rough: *Fuyu ni naru to te ga* areru. (冬になると手が荒れる) In winter, my hands *become chapped.*
4 be in a bad mood.

a|re|rugii アレルギー *n.* allergy.

a|ri あり (蟻) *n.* ant.

a|rifureta ありふれた (有り触れた) *attrib.* common; everyday; commonplace: arifureta *hanashi* (ありふれた話) just *another* story.

a|rigata|·i ありがたい (有り難い) *a.* (-ku) **1** thankful; grateful; pleasant: *Tetsudatte itadaketara,* arigatai *desu.* (手伝っていただけたら, ありがたいです) I would be *grateful* if you helped me.
2 edifying and merciful: *Kyoo wa boosañ kara* arigatai *hanashi o kiita.* (きょうは坊さんからありがたい話を聞いた) I listened to the *edifying* teachings of the Buddhist priest today.

a|ri|gatoo ありがとう (有り難う) thank you; thanks: Arigatoo *gozaimasu.* (ありがとうございます) *Thank you* very much.

a|ri|sama ありさま (有様) *n.* state; circumstances; scenes.
★ Often refers to a bad state.

a|ru[1] ある (或る) *attrib.* a certain; some: Aru *hi kare ga totsuzeñ tazunete kita.* (ある日彼が突然訪ねて来た) *One* day he suddenly called on me.

a|r·u[2] ある (有る・在る) *vi.* (ar·i-; at-te Ⓒ) **1** be; exist; there is [are]: *Kagi wa tsukue no ue ni* arimasu. (鍵は机の上にあります) The key *is* on the desk. ⟪↔ nai⟫ ⟪⇨ da; desu; iru¹⟫
2 be located: *Sono shiro wa yama no naka ni* arimasu. (その城は山の中にあります) The castle *is located* in the mountains. ⟪↔ nai⟫
3 have: *Kanojo wa e no sainoo ga* aru. (彼女は絵の才能がある) She *has* a talent for painting. ⟪↔ nai⟫
4 (of quantity, height, width, etc.) be: *Taijuu wa dono kurai* arimasu *ka?* (体重はどのくらいありますか) How much *do* you *weigh*?
5 be found: *Kono ki wa Nihoñ-juu doko ni mo* arimasu. (この木は日本中どこにもあります) This tree *is found* throughout Japan. ⟪↔ nai⟫
6 have the experience of: *Kare ni* wa atta koto ga arimasu *ka?* (彼には会ったことがありますか) / *Have* you *ever met* him? ⟪⇨ koto¹⟫
7 happen: *Yuube kiñjo de kaji ga* arimashita. (ゆうべ近所で火事がありました) A fire *broke out* in the neighborhood

last night.
8 take place; be held:
Sakuneñ kono keñ de kokutai ga arimashita. (昨年この県で国体がありました) The National Athletic Meet *was held* in this prefecture last year.

a⌈ruba⌉ito アルバイト *n.* part-time job; job on the side; part-timer.

a⌈ru⌉iwa[1] あるいは (或は) *conj.* (*formal*) or; either...or:
Anata ka aruiwa *watashi ga ikanakereba narimaseñ.* (あなたかあるいは私が行かなければなりません) *Either* you *or* I have to go. ⟪⇨ mata-wa⟫

a⌈ru⌉iwa[2] あるいは (或は) *adv.* perhaps; probably: ★ Usually followed by '*ka mo shirenai.*'
Sono keekaku wa aruiwa *chuushi ni naru ka mo shirenai.* (その計画はあるいは中止になるかもしれない) The project will *probably* be halted.

a⌈rukari アルカリ *n.* alkali. ⟪↔ sañ[2]⟫

a⌈rukooru アルコール *n.* **1** alcohol. **2** alcoholic beverage.

a⌈ru⌉k·u あるく (歩く) *vi.* (aruk·i-; aruk·a-; aru·i-te Ⓒ) walk:
Eki made aruite *go-fuñ desu.* (駅まで歩いて5分です) It takes five minutes to *walk* to the station.

a⌈rumi アルミ *n.* aluminum:
arumi *sasshi* (アルミサッシ) an *aluminum* window sash.

a⌉sa[1] あさ (朝) *n.* morning. ⟪↔ bañ[1]; yoru[1]⟫

a⌈sa⌉[2] あさ (麻) *n.* hemp; hemp plant [cloth].

a⌉sabañ あさばん (朝晩) *n.* morning and evening. ⟪⇨ asayuu⟫
— *adv.* always; from morning till night.

a⌈sa⌉gao あさがお (朝顔) *n.* morning glory plant.

a⌈sago⌉hañ あさごはん (朝ご飯) *n.* breakfast. ★ More polite than '*asameshi.*' ⟪↔ bañgohañ⟫ ⟪⇨ chooshoku; gohañ; hirugohañ⟫

a⌉sahi あさひ (朝日) *n.* morning [rising] sun. ⟪↔ yuuhi⟫

a⌈sa·i あさい (浅い) *a.* (-ku) **1** shallow:
asai *nabe* (浅い鍋) a *shallow* pan / *isu ni* asaku *koshikakeru* (いすに浅く腰掛ける) sit *on the edge* of a chair. ⟪↔ fukai⟫
2 (of time, etc.) short:
Kono kaisha wa dekite kara, hi ga asai. (この会社はできてから, 日が浅い) This company was established *not so long ago.*
3 (of experience, knowledge) lacking; green; superficial:
Kare wa mada keekeñ ga asai. (彼はまだ経験が浅い) He *doesn't have much* experience.
4 light; slight:
asai *kizu* (浅い傷) a *slight* cut. ⟪↔ fukai⟫

a⌈sameshi あさめし (朝飯) *n.* (*slightly rude*) breakfast. ⟪⇨ asagohañ; chooshoku⟫
asameshi mae (～前) **1** before breakfast. **2** very easy.

a⌈sa⌉ne あさね (朝寝) *n.* late rising.
asane (o) suru (～(を)する) *vi.* get up late. ⟪⇨ hirune⟫

a⌈sa-ne⌉boo あさねぼう (朝寝坊) *n.* late riser. ⟪⇨ yofukashi⟫
asa-neboo (o) suru (～(を)する) *vi.* get up late in the morning.

a⌈sa⌉tte あさって (明後日) *n.* the day after tomorrow. ⟪⇨ kyoo; myoogonichi⟫

a⌈sayake あさやけ (朝焼け) *n.* morning glow in the sky. ⟪↔ yuuyake⟫

a⌉sayuu あさゆう (朝夕) *n.* morning and evening. ⟪⇨ asabañ⟫

a⌉se あせ (汗) *n.* sweat; perspiration.

a⌈se⌉r·u[1] あせる (焦る) *vi.* (aser·i-; aser·a-; aset-te Ⓒ) hurry; be impatient.

a⌈se⌉r·u[2] あせる (褪せる) *vi.* (aser·i-; aser·a-; aset-te Ⓒ) fade; be discolored:
Kaateñ no iro ga asete kita. (カーテンの色があせてきた) The curtains

have faded.

a⌈shi⌉ あし(足・脚) *n.* **1** foot; leg; paw. ★'脚' usually refers to some sort of support.
2 step; pace:
ashi *ga hayai* [*osoi*] (足が速い[遅い]) be quick [slow] of *foot.*
3 means of transport:
Kootsuu suto ga shimiñ no ashi *o ubatta.* (交通ストが市民の足を奪った) The transport strike deprived the citizens of *transportation.*
ashi ga deru (〜が出る) exceed the budget.
... kara ashi o arau (...から〜を洗う) wash one's hands of (crime).
... ni ashi o hakobu (...に〜を運ぶ) visit; make a call on.
... no ashi o hipparu (...の〜を引っ張る) get in a person's way; hold back (from success, etc.)

a⌈shia⌉to あしあと(足跡) *n.* footprint; track.

a⌈shibu⌉mi あしぶみ(足踏み) *n.*
1 stepping; stamping.
2 standstill:
ashibumi-*jootai ni aru* (足踏み状態にある) be at a *standstill.*
ashibumi (o) suru (〜(を)する) *vi.* mark time.

a⌈shidori あしどり(足取り) *n.*
1 step; gate; pace:
Kare wa omoi [*karui*] ashidori *de ie e kaetta.* (彼は重い[軽い]足どりで家へ帰った) He returned home with heavy [light] *steps.*
2 trace; track:
Keesatsu wa hañniñ no ashidori *o otta.* (警察は犯人の足どりを追った) The police followed the *tracks* of the criminal.

a⌈shiga⌉kari あしがかり(足掛かり) *n.* footing; foothold.

a⌈shi⌉kubi あしくび(足首) *n.* ankle.

a⌈shimoto⌉ あしもと(足元) *n.* at (near) one's foot:
Ashimoto *ni ki o tsuke nasai.* (足元に気をつけなさい) Watch your *step!*

a⌈shinami あしなみ(足並み) *n.* (of two or more people) pace; step:
Kooshiñ-chuu ni miñna no ashinami *ga midareta.* (行進中にみんなの足並みが乱れた) They got out of *step* during the procession.

a⌈shioto⌉ あしおと(足音) *n.* sound of footsteps.

a⌈shita⌉ あした(明日) *n.* tomorrow. ⟪⇨ kinoo[1]; kyoo⟫

a⌈sobi あそび(遊び) *n.* play; game; fun; amusement.
asobi ni iku (〜に行く) visit; call on; make a trip for pleasure. ⟪⇨ asobu⟫

a⌈sob·u あそぶ(遊ぶ) *vi.* (asob·i-; asob·a-; asoñ-de [C]) **1** play; amuse oneself:
kooeñ de asobu (公園で遊ぶ) *play* in the park. ⟪⇨ asobi⟫
2 be idle; idle away.
3 (of a place, a room, an instrument, etc.) be not in use:
asoñde iru *heya* (遊んでいる部屋) a room *not in use.*

a⌈soko あそこ *n.* **1** that place; over there: ★ Refers to a place which is some distance away from both the speaker and the listener.
Asoko *ni takai too ga mieru deshoo.* (あそこに高い塔が見えるでしょう) You should be able to see a tall tower *over there.*
2 that place: ★ Refers to a place which is removed from both the speaker and the listener, but is known to them.
Izu mo ii kedo, watashi wa asoko *yori Shiñshuu no hoo ga suki desu.* (伊豆もいいけど, 私はあそこより信州の方が好きです) Izu is a nice place to visit, but I like Shinshu better. ⟪⇨ soko[1]⟫
3 that place: ★ Refers to a place which the speaker expects the listener to know about.
"Koñbañ asoko *e nomi ni ikanai?" "Ii ne. Ikimashoo."* (「今晩あ

そこへ飲みに行かない」「いいね. 行きましょう」) "How about going for a drink at *that place* this evening?" "Yes. Let's go."
2 that: ★ Used to emphasize a degree.
Kare ga asoko *made gañbaru to wa omoimaseñ deshita.* (彼があそこまでがんばるとは思いませんでした) I never thought that he would try *that* hard. ⟪⇨ doko; koko[1]; soko[1]⟫

a⌈ssa⌉ri あっさり *adv.* (~ to) easily; readily.
assari (to) suru (~(と)する) (of dish, appetite, desire, etc.) plain; simple; light: *Niku-ryoori no ato wa* assari (to) shita *mono ga tabetaku naru.* (肉料理の後はあっさり(と)したものが食べたくなる) After a meat dish, I feel like eating something *plain and simple.*

a⌈sseñ あっせん(斡旋) *n.* good offices; mediation; help.
asseñ suru (~する) *vt.* use one's good offices; mediate.

a⌈su⌉ あす(明日) *n.* = ashita.

a⌈tae·ru あたえる(与える) *vt.* (ataete [V]) **1** give; award.
2 give; cause (shock, damage, pain, etc.).
3 afford (pleasure, etc.).
4 assign; provide (a job, a question, etc.):
Hayashi-sañ wa ataerareta *shigoto o isshoo-keñmee yatte imasu.* (林さんは与えられた仕事を一生懸命やっています) Ms. Hayashi is putting her all into the work that *was assigned* to her.

a⌈takushi あたくし *n.* (*informal*) = watakushi. ★ Used mainly by women.

a⌈tama⌉ あたま(頭) *n.* **1** head:
★ Usually indicates the portion from the eyebrows up, or the top part covered with hair.
Atama ga itai. (頭が痛い) *I have a headache.*
2 brain: atama ga ii (頭がいい) *be smart* / atama *o tsukau* (頭を使う) use one's *brains.* ⟪⇨ chie⟫
3 hair: atama *o arau* (頭を洗う) shampoo one's *hair.*
⟪⇨ kami-no-ke⟫
atama ga agaranai (~が上がらない) cannot compete with; be indebted to.
atama ga kireru (~が切れる) have a sharp mind.
atama ni kuru (~にくる) get angry.
atama o hineru (~をひねる) rack one's brains.
atama o itameru (~を痛める) be worried.

a⌈tamaka⌉zu あたまかず(頭数) *n.* the number of persons.
⟪⇨ niñzuu⟫

a⌈tamakiñ あたまきん(頭金) *n.* down payment.

a⌈tarashi⌉·i あたらしい(新しい) *a.* (-ku) **1** new; latest. ⟪↔ furui⟫
2 fresh. ⟪↔ furui⟫ ⟪⇨ arata⟫

a⌉tari あたり(辺り) *n.* **1** neighborhood; vicinity. ⟪⇨ heñ[2]⟫
2 about; around:
atari *o mimawasu* (辺りを見回す) look *around.*

a⌈tarimae あたりまえ(当たり前) *a.n.* (~ na/no, ni) **1** natural; reasonable. ⟪⇨ toozeñ⟫
2 ordinary.

a⌈tar·u あたる(当たる) *vi.* (atar·i-; atar·a-; atat-te [C]) **1** hit; strike:
Booru ga kare no atama ni atatta. (ボールが彼の頭に当たった) A ball *hit* him on the head. ⟪⇨ ateru⟫
2 (of a prediction, a forecast) be right:
Kyoo no teñki-yohoo wa atatta. (きょうの天気予報は当たった) Today's weather forecast *was right.*
3 win:
Kono kuji ga it-too ni atarimashita. (このくじが一等に当たりました) This lottery ticket *won* first prize.
⟪⇨ ateru⟫
4 make a hit; succeed:
Shiñ-seehiñ ga atatta. (新製品が当たった) The new product *was a hit.*

a

5 (of a date) fall on:
Kotoshi wa Kurisumasu ga nichiyoo ni ataru. (ことしはクリスマスが日曜に当たる) This year Christmas *falls on* Sunday.
6 correspond; be equivalent to:
Ich-mairu wa it-teñ-rok-kiro ni ataru. (1 マイルは 1.6 キロに当たる) One mile *is equivalent* to 1.6 kilometers.
7 lie; be located:
Sono machi wa Tookyoo no kita ni ataru. (その町は東京の北に当たる) That town *lies* to the north of Tokyo.
8 be assigned; be allotted; be called on:
Koñdo no geki de kanojo wa ii yaku ni atatta. (今度の劇で彼女はいい役に当たった) In the recent play, she *was given* a good part.
《⇨ ateru》
9 (of light, rays, etc.) shine; get sunshine. 《⇨ ateru》
10 (of a person) be poisoned; get food poisoning:
fugu ni ataru (ふぐにあたる) *be poisoned* by globefish.
11 consult; look up; check (a source of information):
Jisho ni atatte, *kañji no imi o shirabeta.* (辞書にあたって, 漢字の意味を調べた) I *looked* in the dictionary for the meaning of the Chinese character.
12 be hard on (a person):
Kimura-sañ wa itsu-mo watashi ni tsuraku ataru. (木村さんはいつも私につらく当たる) Mr. Kimura *is* always *hard* on me.
13 undertake; be in charge of.
《⇨ ateru》
14 expose oneself to heat [wind, etc.]:
sutoobu ni ataru (ストーブにあたる) *warm oneself* at the heater.
... (suru) ni wa ataranai (...(する)にはあたらない) be not worth (doing).
... ni atari [atatte] (...するにあたり[あたって]) (*formal*) on the occasion of. 《⇨ saishite》

a⌈tashi あたし *n.* (*informal*) = watakushi. ★ Used mainly by women.

a⌈tata⌉ka あたたか (暖か) *a.n.* (~ na, ni) warm; mild. 《⇨ atatakai》

a⌈tataka⌉·i あたたかい (暖かい・温かい) *a.* (-ku) (*informal* =attaka)
1 warm; mild:
Dañdañ atatakaku *natte kita.* (だんだん暖かくなってきた) It has become *warmer and warmer.* 《↔ samui》
《⇨ atataka》
2 warm-hearted; cordial:
Miñna wa kare o atatakaku *mukaeta.* (みんなは彼を温かく迎えた) They gave him a *cordial* welcome. 《↔ tsumetai》

a⌈tatama⌉r·u あたたまる (暖まる・温まる) *vi.* (-mar·i-; -mar·a-; -mat-te Ⓒ) get warm; warm up; be heated. 《⇨ atatameru》

a⌈tatame⌉·ru あたためる (暖める・温める) *vt.* (-me-te Ⓥ) **1** warm (up); heat. 《⇨ atatamaru》
2 nurse (a thought); have (a plan) in mind.

a⌈tchi⌉ あっち *n.* (*colloq.*) =achira.

a⌈te あて (当て) *n.* **1** object; aim; goal. 《⇨ mokuteki》
2 expectation; hope.
3 dependence; reliance:
Watashi-tachi wa anata o ate ni shite imasu. (私たちはあなたを当てにしています) We *depend* on you.

-ate あて (宛) *suf.* addressed to:
Suzuki-sañ-ate *no kozutsumi* (鈴木さんあての小包) a parcel *addressed to* Miss Suzuki.

a⌈tehama⌉r·u あてはまる (当てはまる) *vi.* (-hamar·i-; -hamar·a-; -hamat-te Ⓒ) **1** hold true; fit:
Kono kotowaza wa geñdai ni mo atehamaru. (このことわざは現代にも当てはまる) This proverb *holds true* even in our time. 《⇨ atehameru》
2 fulfill:
Koo-iu jookeñ ni atehamaru *hito wa nakanaka mitsukaranai.* (こうい

う条件に当てはまる人はなかなか見つからない) It is hard to find a person who *fulfills* these conditions. 《⇨ atehameru》

a⌈tehame⌉·ru あてはめる(当てはめる) *vt.* (-hame-te Ⅴ) apply; adapt:
Gaikoku no shuukañ o subete Nihoñ ni atehameru *wake ni wa ikanai.* (外国の習慣をすべて日本に当てはめるわけにはいかない) You cannot expect us to *adapt* all foreign customs to Japan. 《⇨ atehamaru》

a⌈tena あてな(宛名) *n.* address.

a⌈te·ru あてる(当てる) *vt.* (ate-te Ⅴ) **1** hit; strike:
Kare wa ya o mato ni ateta. (彼は矢を的に当てた) He *shot* the arrow into the target. 《⇨ ataru》
2 put:
Kanojo wa kodomo no hitai ni te o ateta. (彼女は子どもの額に手を当てた) She *put* her hand to her child's forehead.
3 guess; give a right answer:
Kare ga seekai o ateta. (彼が正解を当てた) He *guessed* the right answer. 《⇨ ataru》
4 expose:
Nureta fuku o hi ni atete *kawakashita.* (ぬれた服を日に当てて乾かした) I *put* the wet clothes out in the sun to dry them. 《⇨ ataru》
5 (of a lottery) win. 《⇨ ataru》
6 use; spend (money, time, etc.):
Kanojo wa ichi-nichi ichi-jikañ o Nihoñgo no beñkyoo ni atete iru. (彼女は1日1時間を日本語の勉強に当てている) She *devotes* an hour a day to studying Japanese.
7 call on (somebody):
Kyoo watashi wa señsee ni aterareta. (きょう私は先生に当てられた) Today the teacher *called on* me in class. 《⇨ ataru》

a⌈tesaki あてさき(宛て先) *n.* address; destination.

a⌉to[1] あと(後) *n.* **1** back; rear:
ato o ou (後を追う) *pursue* / ato ni tsuzuku (後に続く) *follow.* 《↔ mae》
2 after; later: ★ Usually in the pattern '(...*no*/-*ta*) ato *de*.'
Ato *de deñwa shimasu.* (後で電話します) I'll call you *later.* 《↔ mae》
3 rest; remainder.

a⌉to[2] あと(跡) *n.* mark; trace; track; ruins; remains:
kutsu no ato (靴の跡) the *marks* of shoes.

a⌈to⌉ashi あとあし(後足) *n.* (of an animal) hind leg. 《↔ maeashi》

a⌈toka⌉tazuke あとかたづけ(後片付け) *n.* clearing away; put back in order:
shokuji no atokatazuke o suru (食事の後片付けをする) *clear* the table after a meal.

a⌉tosaki あとさき(後先) *n.* **1** before and behind; both ends.
2 consequences:
Kare wa atosaki *no kañgae mo naku, keeyakusho ni saiñ shita.* (彼は後先の考えもなく,契約書にサインした) He signed the contract without any consideration of the *consequences.*

a⌈toshi⌉matsu あとしまつ(後始末) *n.* **1** putting things in order:
hi no atoshimatsu o suru (火の後始末をする) *put out* a fire *completely.*
2 settlement:
Chichi ga watashi no shakkiñ no atoshimatsu o shite kureta. (父が私の借金の後始末をしてくれた) My father *settled* my debts for me.

a⌈tsugami あつがみ(厚紙) *n.* thick paper; cardboard; pasteboard.

a⌈tsugi あつぎ(厚着) *n.* heavy [thick] clothes [clothing]. 《↔ usugi》

a⌈tsu⌉·i[1] あつい(熱い) *a.* (-ku)
1 (of temperature) hot; heated. 《↔ tsumetai; nurui》《⇨ atsusa[2]》
2 emotionally excited.

a⌈tsu⌉·i[2] あつい(暑い) *a.* (-ku) hot; very warm. 《↔ samui》《⇨ atsusa[1]》

a⌈tsu·i[3] あつい(厚い) *a.* (-ku)
1 thick; heavy:

Kono oreñji wa kawa ga atsui. (このオレンジは皮が厚い) This orange has a *thick* skin. 《↔ usui》 《⇨ atsusa[3]; buatsui》
2 warm; hearty:
atsui *motenashi* (厚いもてなし) a *warm and friendly* welcome.

a⌈tsukai あつかい (扱い) *n.* handling; dealing; treatment:
Gasoriñ no atsukai *ni wa ki o tsukete kudasai.* (ガソリンの扱いには気をつけてください) Please be careful when *handling* gasoline. 《⇨ atsukau》

a⌈tsukamashi⌉·i あつかましい (厚かましい) *a.* (-ku) impudent; shameless; presumptuous. 《⇨ zuuzuushii》

a⌈tsuka·u あつかう (扱う) *vt.* (-ka·i-; -kaw·a-; -kat-te Ⓒ)
1 handle; operate.
2 treat; take care of; deal with:
Koko no teñiñ wa o-kyaku o taisetsu ni atsukaimasu. (ここの店員はお客を大切に扱います) The clerks in this shop *treat* customers with courtesy.
3 accept; deal in.
4 write up in a newspaper or a magazine. 《⇨ atsukai》

a⌈tsukurushi⌉·i あつくるしい (暑苦しい) *a.* (-ku) sultry; humid and uncomfortable.

a⌈tsumari⌉ あつまり (集まり) *n.*
1 meeting; gathering.
2 attendance; collection:
Atsumari *ga yoi* [*warui*]. (集まりがよい[悪い]) There is a large [small] *attendance.*

a⌈tsuma⌉r·u あつまる (集まる) *vi.* (-mar·i-; -mar·a-; -mat-te Ⓒ)
1 gather; assemble. 《⇨ atsumari; atsumeru》
2 be collected. 《⇨ atsumeru》
3 be concentrated; be centered:
Hitobito no doojoo ga kanojo ni atsumatta. (人々の同情が彼女に集まった) Their sympathy *was centered* on her.

a⌈tsume⌉·ru あつめる (集める) *vt.* (-me-te Ⓥ) **1** gather; assemble:
gakusee o uñdoojoo ni atsumeru (学生を運動場に集める) *assemble* the students on the sports field. 《⇨ atsumaru》
2 collect:
mezurashii kitte o takusañ atsumeru (珍しい切手をたくさん集める) *collect* many rare stamps. 《⇨ atsumaru; shuushuu》
3 attract:
Sono nyuusu wa hitobito no kañshiñ o atsumeta. (そのニュースは人々の関心を集めた) The news *attracted* people's interest.

a⌈tsurae⌉·ru あつらえる (誂える) *vt.* (-rae-te Ⓥ) order (goods):
Yuumee na mise de suutsu o atsuraeta. (有名な店でスーツをあつらえた) I *ordered* a suit at a famous store.

a⌈tsu⌉ryoku あつりょく (圧力) *n.* pressure; stress.

a⌉tsusa[1] あつさ (暑さ) *n.* heat; hot weather; hotness. 《↔ samusa》 《⇨ atsui[2]》

a⌉tsusa[2] あつさ (熱さ) *n.* hotness; heat; warmth:
furo no atsusa *o miru* (風呂の熱さをみる) check the *temperature* of a bath. 《⇨ atsui[1]》

a⌈tsusa[3] あつさ (厚さ) *n.* thickness. 《⇨ atsui[3]》

a⌈tta⌉ka あったか (暖か) *a.n.* (*colloq.*) = atataka.

a⌈ttoo あっとう (圧倒) *n.* being overwhelming.
attoo suru (〜する) *vt.* overwhelm; overpower: *Wareware wa kazu no ue de teki o* attoo shita. (われわれは数の上で敵を圧倒した) We *overwhelmed* the enemy numerically.

a⌈ttoo-teki あっとうてき (圧倒的) *a.n.* (〜 na, ni) overwhelming:
attoo-teki *tasuu* (圧倒的多数) an *overwhelming* majority.

a⌉·u[1] あう (会う·逢う·遇う) *vi.* (a·i-; aw·a-; at-te Ⓒ) meet; see; come across: ★ Used with '*ni* [*to*].' A

more polite expression is '*o-me-ni-kakaru*.'
Watashi wa Giñza de kare ni battari atta. (私は銀座で彼にばったり会った) I *came across* him in Ginza.

a˥·u[2] あう (合う) *vi.* (a·i-; aw·a-; at-te [C]) **1** fit; suit:
Kono fuku wa watashi ni pittari aimasu. (この服は私にぴったり合います) This dress *fits* me perfectly. ⟪⇨ awaseru⟫
2 agree with; correspond. ⟪⇨ awaseru⟫
3 (in the form of '*atte iru*') be correct; be right:
Kono tokee wa atte imasu. (この時計は合っています) This clock *has the right time.*
4 (with a negative) pay:
Kore ijoo yasuku shite wa (*wari ni*) awanai. (これ以上安くしては(割に)合わない) It *does not pay* if I sell at a lower price. ⟪⇨ wari⟫

a˥·u[3] あう (遭う) *vi* (a·i-; aw·a-; at-te [C]) meet with; have an unfavorable experience:
jiko ni au (事故にあう) *meet with* an accident / *hidoi me ni* au (ひどい目にあう) *have* a bad experience.

a⌈wa˥ あわ (泡) *n.* bubble; foam; lather: awa *ga tatsu* (泡が立つ) *bubbles* form.
awa o kuu (～を食う) be confused. ⟪⇨ awateru⟫

a⌈wa˥·i あわい (淡い) *a.* (-ku) (*literary*) **1** pale; light: awai *aoiro* (淡い青色) *pale* blue.
2 faint: awai *nozomi* (淡い望み) a *faint* hope.
3 transitory; fleeting: awai *koi* (淡い恋) a *fleeting* love.

a˥ware あわれ (哀れ) *n.* pity:
aware *o sasou* (哀れを誘う) arouse one's *pity*.
— *a.n.* (～ na, ni) pitiful; miserable; pathetic:
Hitori-gurashi no roojiñ o aware ni omou. (一人暮らしの老人を哀れに思う) I *pity* the old man living alone.

a⌈wase˥·ru あわせる (合わせる) *vt.* (awase-te [V]) **1** put [join] together:
chikara o awaseru (力を合わせる) *unite* efforts. ⟪⇨ au[2]⟫
2 add (up):
Zeñbu awasete *ikura desu ka?* (全部合わせていくらですか) How much does it come to *altogether*?
3 fit:
Karada ni awasete *doresu o tsukutta.* (体に合わせてドレスを作った) I had a dress made to *fit* me. ⟪⇨ au[2]⟫
4 adjust; set:
kamera no piñto o awaseru (カメラのピントを合わせる) *adjust* the focus of a camera. ⟪⇨ au[2]⟫
5 accompany:
piano no bañsoo ni awasete *utau* (ピアノの伴奏に合わせて歌う) sing *to the accompaniment* of the piano.
6 adapt:
Watashi wa kare no yarikata ni awaseta. (私は彼のやり方に合わせた) I *adapted myself* to his way of working. ⟪⇨ au[2]⟫
7 mix:
kechappu to mayoneezu o awaseru (ケチャップとマヨネーズを合わせる) *mix* ketchup and mayonnaise.

a⌈watadashi˥·i あわただしい (慌ただしい) *a.* (-ku) hasty; hurried; quick; busy.

a⌈watemono あわてもの (慌て者) *n.* rash person.

a⌈wate·ru あわてる (慌てる) *vi.* (awate-te [V]) **1** hurry; panic.
2 get flustered; be confused. ⟪⇨ magotsuku⟫

a⌈yafuya あやふや *a.n.* (～ na, ni) vague; uncertain:
ayafuya *na heñji* (あやふやな返事) a *vague* answer.

a⌈yamachi˥ あやまち (過ち) *n.* mistake; error; fault; sin:
ayamachi *o okasu* (過ちを犯す) make a *mistake*.

a⌈yamari˥ あやまり (誤り) *n.* error; mistake; slip: ★ Interchangeable

with '*machigai*,' but more formal.
Ayamari *ga attara, naoshi nasai.* (誤りがあったら, 直しなさい) Correct *errors*, if any. ((⇨ ayamaru²))

a⌈yama⌉r·u¹ あやまる (謝る) *vt.* (-mar·i-; -mar·a-; -mat-te Ⓒ) apologize; beg a person's pardon.

a⌈yama⌉r·u² あやまる (誤る) *vi.*, *vt.* (-mar·i-; -mar·a-; -mat-te Ⓒ) make a mistake:
hoogaku o ayamaru (方角を誤る) *take the wrong* direction. ((⇨ ayamari))

a⌈yame あやめ (菖蒲) *n.* sweet flag; iris.

a⌈yashi·i あやしい (怪しい) *a.* (-ku)
1 suspicious; strange.
2 doubtful; dubious; uncertain.
3 clumsy; poor:
Kare wa ashimoto ga ayashikatta. (彼は足元が怪しかった) He walked *unsteadily*.

a⌈ya⌉s·u あやす *vi.* (ayash·i-; aya-s·a-; ayash·i-te Ⓒ) fondle; lull; dandle; soothe:
akañboo o ayasu (赤ん坊をあやす) *cuddle* a baby.

a⌈yatsu⌉r·u あやつる (操る) *vt.* (ayatsur·i-; ayatsur·a-; ayatsut-te Ⓒ) manipulate; handle; manage:
niñgyoo o ayatsuru (人形を操る) *manipulate* a puppet / *fune o* ayatsuru (船を操る) *steer* a boat.

a⌈za⌉yaka あざやか (鮮やか) *a.n.* (~ na, ni) 1 bright; vivid; fresh:
Ame no ato de, ki no midori ga azayaka *datta.* (雨のあとで, 木の緑が鮮やかだった) After the rain, the green of the trees was *fresh*.
2 splendid, skillful:
azayaka *na eñgi* (鮮やかな演技) a *splendid* performance.

a⌈zuka⌉r·u あずかる (預かる) *vt.* (-kar·i-; -kar·a-; -kat-te Ⓒ)
1 keep:
Yamada-sañ ga anata no nimotsu o azukatte imasu. (山田さんがあなたの荷物を預かっています) Mr. Yamada *has* your baggage. ((⇨ azukeru))
2 look after; take charge of:
Hoikueñ wa kodomo o go-ji made azukatte *kureru.* (保育園は子どもを5時まで預かってくれる) At the nursery, they *look after* the children until five o'clock. ((⇨ azukeru))
3 withhold:
Kimi no jihyoo wa toriaezu azukatte *okoo.* (君の辞表はとりあえず預かっておこう) I will *sit on* your resignation for the time being. ((⇨ azukeru))

a⌈zuke⌉·ru あずける(預ける) *vt.* (-ke-te Ⓥ) 1 leave:
Kurooku ni mochimono o azuketa. (クロークに持ち物を預けた) I *left* my things in the cloakroom. ((⇨ azukaru))
2 deposit:
Giñkoo ni gomañ-eñ azuketa. (銀行に5万円預けた) I *deposited* 50,000 yen in the bank. ((⇨ azukaru))
3 entrust:
Kodomo wa haha ni azukete, *shigoto ni ikimasu.* (子どもは母に預けて, 仕事に行きます) I *entrust* my child to my mother's care and go to work. ((⇨ azukaru))

a⌈zuki⌉ あずき (小豆) *n.* adzuki bean.

b

B

ba ば(場) *n.* **1** place; spot:
ba *o hazusu* (場を外す) leave the *room* / ba *o fusagu* (場をふさぐ) take up much *space*. ⟪⇨ basho⟫
2 occasion; case:
sono ba *ni fusawashii fuku o kiru* (その場にふさわしい服を着る) wear clothes suitable for the *occasion*.
3 (of a drama) scene:
ni-maku sañ-ba (2幕3場) Act 2, *Scene* 3.

-ba[1] ば *infl. end.* [attached to the conditional base of a verb, adjective or the copula] ★ The *ba*-form of a verb is made by replacing the final '*-u*' with '*e*' and adding '*-ba*,' and the *ba*-form of an adjective by dropping the final '*-i*' and adding '*-kereba*.' The *ba*-form of the copula '*da*' is '*naraba*.' ⟪⇨ APP. 2⟫
1 if; provided; when:
a (the *ba*-form clause indicates a condition and the following clause the consequent result):
Ame ga fureba *eñsoku wa chuushi desu.* (雨が降れば遠足は中止です) *If it rains*, our outing will be canceled. ⟪⇨ -tara⟫
b (the *ba*-form clause indicates an assumed or possible situation and the following clause the speaker's intention, request, advice, etc.):
Jikañ ga areba *Kyooto e mo ikitai.* (時間があれば京都へも行きたい) *Provided there is time*, I would like to go to Kyoto as well.
c (the *ba*-form clause indicates an unfulfilled or unreal condition and the following clause the speaker's judgment, wish, reaction, etc.):
Moo sukoshi gañbareba *dekita to omoimasu.* (もう少しがんばればできたと思います) I feel I could have succeeded *if I had tried a bit harder*. ⟪⇨ -tara⟫
2 when; whenever: ★ The *ba*-form clause indicates a habitual action in the past and the following clause the consequence of that action.
Chichi wa nomeba *kanarazu utatta mono da.* (父は飲めば必ず歌ったものだ) My father always used to sing *when he drank*.
3 and; both...and; neither...nor: ★ Used to link similar items in a parallel relationship.
Ano hito wa tabako mo sueba *sake mo nomu.* (あの人はたばこも吸えば酒も飲む) He smokes *and* drinks.

-ba[2] ば(羽) *suf.* counter for birds and rabbits. ⟪⇨ APP. 4⟫

ba⌈a ばあ *int.* boo; bo. ★ Used when playing with babies.

ba⌈ai ばあい(場合) *n.* **1** case; occasion; circumstance:
Sono kisoku wa kono baai *atehamaranai.* (その規則はこの場合あてはまらない) That rule does not apply in this *case*.
2 in case of; if; when:
Kaji no baai *wa beru ga narimasu.* (火事の場合はベルが鳴ります) *In the event of* fire, the bell will ring. ⟪⇨ toki⟫

ba⌉asañ ばあさん(婆さん) *n.* (*informal*) **1** one's grandmother.
2 old woman. ⟪↔ jiisañ⟫ ⟪⇨ o-baasañ⟫

ba⌈chi⌉ ばち(罰) *n.* punishment inflicted by gods or Buddha:
bachi ga ataru (罰が当たる) *be punished; get it.*

ba⌈i ばい(倍) *n.* double; twice:
Go-neñ de shuunyuu ga bai ni natta. (5年で収入が倍になった) My income *doubled* in five years.

-bai[1] ばい(倍) *suf.* times; -fold: *Bukka ga* sañ-bai *ni natta.* (物価が3倍になった) Prices *tripled*.

-bai[2] ばい(杯) *suf.* =-hai. ⟪⇨ APP. 4⟫

ba⌉ibai ばいばい(売買) *n.* buying and selling; trade.
baibai suru (〜する) *vt.* deal in; trade.

ba⌈ieñ ばいえん(煤煙) *n.* soot; smoke.

ba⌈ikai ばいかい(媒介) *n.* mediation; medium.
baikai suru (〜する) *vt.* mediate: *Mararia wa ka ni yotte* baikai sareru. (マラリアは蚊によって媒介される) Malaria *is carried* by mosquitoes.

ba⌈ikiñ ばいきん(ばい菌) *n.* germ; bacteria. ★ Informal equivalent for '*saikiñ*,' emphasizing filthiness. ⟪⇨ saikiñ[2]⟫

ba⌈imee ばいめい(売名) *n.* self-advertisement; publicity:
baimee *o hakaru* (売名を図る) seek *publicity*.

ba⌈ioriñ バイオリン *n.* violin.
baioriñ *o hiku* (バイオリンを弾く) play the *violin*.

ba⌈iritsu ばいりつ(倍率) *n.*
1 magnification; power.
2 competition:
Kono gakkoo wa bairitsu *ga takai.* (この学校は倍率が高い) There is keen *competition* to enter this school.

ba⌈ishoo ばいしょう(賠償) *n.* reparation; compensation:
baishoo *o yookyuu suru* (賠償を要求する) demand *reparations*.

ba⌈ishuñ ばいしゅん(売春) *n.* prostitution:
baishuñ-fu (売春婦) a *prostitute*.

ba⌈ishuu ばいしゅう(買収) *n.*
1 buying up; purchase.
2 bribery; corruption.
baishuu (o) suru (〜(を)する) *vt.*
1 buy up; purchase (a building, land, etc.).
2 bribe; corrupt: *shooniñ o* baishuu suru (証人を買収する) *corrupt* a witness.

ba⌈iteñ ばいてん(売店) *n.* stand; stall; kiosk; store.

ba⌉iu ばいう(梅雨) *n.* the rainy season. ⟪⇨ tsuyu[2]; uki[1]⟫

ba⌈iyaku ばいやく(売約) *n.* sales contract.

ba⌉jji バッジ *n.* badge; pin.
★ Usually refers to the badge that businessemen wear on their lapels to identify their companies.

ba⌉ka ばか(馬鹿) *n.* fool; stupid [silly] person:
Soñna koto o suru to wa kare mo baka *da.* (そんなことをするとは彼もばかだ) He is a *fool* to do such a thing.
baka ni naranai (〜にならない) be not negligible.
baka ni suru (〜にする) make a fool of.
baka o miru (〜を見る) feel like a fool.
— *a.n.* (〜 na) foolish; stupid; ridiculous; unreasonable.

ba⌈ka- ばか(馬鹿) *pref.* too...; extremely; excessively:
baka-*shoojiki* (ばか正直) *too* honest *for one's own good* / baka-*teenee* (ばかていねい) *excessive* politeness.

ba⌈kabakashi⌉·i ばかばかしい(馬鹿馬鹿しい) *a.* (-ku) foolish; silly; absurd. ⟪⇨ bakarashii⟫

ba⌉ka ni ばかに(馬鹿に) *adv.* awfully; terribly; very:
Kyoo wa baka ni *isogashii.* (きょうはばかに忙しい) I'm *terribly* busy today.

ba⌉kañsu バカンス *n.* vacation; holidays.

ba⌈karashi⌉·i ばからしい(馬鹿らしい) *a.* (-ku) foolish; silly; absurd; ridiculous. ⟪⇨ bakabakashii⟫

ba⌉kari ばかり *p.* ★ Follows a noun, adjective or the dictionary form of a verb, or the *te*-form of a verb in the pattern '*-te bakari iru.*'
1 only; no other than...; nothing but:

Señsee wa watashi bakari *ni shitsumoñ suru.* (先生は私ばかりに質問する) The teacher asks questions to *no one but* me. 《⇨ dake; nomi[2]》
2 just:
Nihoñ ni tsuita bakari *de mada nani mo mite imaseñ.* (日本に着いたばかりでまだ何も見ていません) I've *just* arrived in Japan, so I haven't yet seen anything.
3 about; approximately; thereabouts:
Juugo-fuñ bakari *matte kudasai.* (15分ばかり待ってください) Please wait for *about* fifteen minutes. 《⇨ kurai[2]; hodo》
4 be about [ready] to do:
Itsu de mo shuppatsu dekiru bakari *ni yooi wa dekite imasu.* (いつでも出発できるばかりに用意はできています) We *are ready to* set off at any time.
5 just [simply] because:
Koñpyuutaa ga tsukaenai bakari *ni, ii shigoto ni tsukenakatta.* (コンピューターが使えないばかりに, いい仕事につけなかった) *Just because* I can't use a computer, I couldn't get a decent job.
6 (used for emphasis): ★ Emphatic form is '*bakkari.*'
Koñdo bakari *wa gamañ ga dekinai.* (今度ばかりはがまんができない) *This time* I am not going to put up with it.

ba[ka]s·u ばかす (化かす) *vt.* (bakash·i-; bakas·a-; bakash·i-te [C]) bewitch; play a trick on:
Nihoñ de wa, kitsune ga hito o bakasu *to iwareru.* (日本では, 狐が人を化かすといわれる) In Japan, it is said that foxes *play tricks* on people.

ba[kemono] ばけもの (化け物) *n.* monster; ghost; specter.

ba[ke]·ru ばける (化ける) *vi.* (bake-te [V]) **1** take the form of:
Mahootsukai ga raioñ ni baketa. (魔法使いがライオンに化けた) The witch *took the form of* a lion.
2 disguise oneself as:
Gootoo wa keekañ ni bakete ita. (強盗は警官に化けていた) The robber *disguised himself* as a policeman.

ba[ketsu バケツ *n.* bucket; pail.

ba[kka]ri ばっかり *p.* = bakari.

ba[kkiñ ばっきん (罰金) *n.* fine; penalty.

ba]kku バック *n.* back; background. 《⇨ haikee[2]》
bakku suru (〜する) *vi.* reverse (a car).

ba[kuchi ばくち (博打) *n.* gambling; speculation. 《⇨ kakegoto》

ba[kudai ばくだい (莫大) *a.n.* (〜 na) huge; enormous; vast:
bakudai *na kiñgaku* (莫大な金額) a *huge* sum of money.

ba[kudañ ばくだん (爆弾) *n.* bomb.

ba]kufu ばくふ (幕府) *n.* shogunate.

ba[kugeki ばくげき (爆撃) *n.* bombing.
bakugeki suru (〜する) *vt.* bomb.

ba[kuhatsu ばくはつ (爆発) *n.* explosion; eruption; burst.
bakuhatsu suru (〜する) *vi.* explode; blow up; burst.

ba]kuro ばくろ (暴露) *n.* exposure; disclosure.
bakuro suru (〜する) *vt.* expose; disclose: *himitsu o* bakuro suru (秘密を暴露する) *disclose* a secret.

ba[kuzeñ ばくぜん (漠然) *adv.* (〜 to) vaguely; aimlessly:
Kodomo no koro no koto wa bakuzeñ *to oboete imasu.* (子どものころのことは漠然と覚えています) I remember my childhood *vaguely.*

ba]meñ ばめん (場面) *n.* scene; sight; spectacle.

ba[ñ[1] ばん (晩) *n.* evening; night. 《↔ asa[1]》 《⇨ yoru[1]; yuube[1]; yuugata》

ba]ñ[2] ばん (番) *n.* one's turn; order:
Saa kimi ga utau bañ *da.* (さあ君が歌う番だ) Now it's your *turn* to

sing. (⇨ juñbañ)

ba˥ñ[3] ばん(番) *n.* watch; guard: *nimotsu no* bañ *o suru* (荷物の番をする) keep *watch* over the baggage.

ba˥ñ[4] ばん(盤) *n.* board; disk.

-bañ ばん(番) *suf.* **1** order in a series:
Kare wa ni-bañ *ni toochaku shita.* (彼は2番に到着した) He was the *second* to arrive.
2 number:
Nañ-bañ *ni o-kake desu ka?* (何番におかけですか) What *number* are you phoning? (⇨ bañgoo)

ba˹ñcha ばんちゃ(番茶) *n.* coarse green tea. (⇨ o-cha; señcha)

ba˹ñchi ばんち(番地) *n.* house [street] number; address.

ba˹ñdo バンド *n.* **1** strap; band: tokee no bañdo (時計のバンド) a *watchband.*
2 belt: *kawa no* bañdo (皮のバンド) a leather *belt.*
3 musical band: *burasu*-bañdo (ブラスバンド) a brass *band.*

ba˥ne ばね *n.* spring.

ba˹ñgo˥hañ ばんごはん(晩ご飯) *n.* dinner; supper. ★ More polite than '*bañmeshi*.'
(⇨ gohañ; hirugohañ; yuushoku)
(↔ asagohañ)

ba˹ñgo˥o ばんごう(番号) *n.* number. ★ When asking the number, say '*nañ-bañ*,' not '*nañ bañgoo*.' (⇨ -bañ)

ba˹ñgumi ばんぐみ(番組) *n.* program:
rajio [*terebi*] (*no*) bañgumi (ラジオ[テレビ](の)番組) a radio [television] *program.*

ba˥ñji ばんじ(万事) *n.* everything; all:
Bañji *umaku ikimashita.* (万事うまく行きました) *Everything* went well.

ba˹ñkeñ ばんけん(番犬) *n.* watchdog. (⇨ inu)

ba˹ñku˥ruwase ばんくるわせ(番狂わせ) *n.* unexpected result; surprise; upset.

-bañme˥ ばんめ(番目) *suf.* (designates the place in a sequence):
mae kara sañ-bañme (前から3番目) *third* from the front.

ba˹ñmeshi ばんめし(晩飯) *n.* (*informal*) supper. (⇨ bañgohañ; yuushoku)

ba˹ñneñ ばんねん(晩年) *n.* one's later years.

ba˹ñni˥ñ ばんにん(番人) *n.* watchman; watch; guard.

ba˹ñnoo ばんのう(万能) *n.* omnipotence:
bañnoo-*señshu* (万能選手) an *all-around* player.

ba˹ñsañ ばんさん(晩餐) *n.* (*formal*) dinner; banquet. (⇨ yuushoku)

-bañseñ ばんせん(番線) *suf.* platform; track:
Señdai-yuki no ressha wa go-bañseñ *kara demasu.* (仙台行きの列車は5番線から出ます) The train for Sendai leaves from *track 5.*

ba˹ñsoo ばんそう(伴奏) *n.* accompaniment.
bañsoo (o) suru (～(を)する) *vi.* accompany (a song on the piano).

ba˹ñsookoo ばんそうこう(絆創膏) *n.* sticking plaster; adhesive tape.

ba˹ñza˥i ばんざい(万歳) *n.* cheers:
bañzai *o sañshoo suru* (万歳を三唱する) give three *cheers.*

ba˹ñzeñ ばんぜん(万全) *n.* absolute sureness:
Taifuu ni taisuru sonae wa bañzeñ desu. (台風に対する備えは万全です) We *are well prepared* against typhoons.

ba˹ra ばら(薔薇) *n.* rose.

ba˹rabara[1] ばらばら *a.n.* (～ na/no, ni) apart; in [to] pieces:
Kaze de shorui ga barabara *ni natte shimatta.* (風で書類がばらばらになってしまった) The papers were *scattered* by the wind.

ba˥rabara[2] ばらばら *adv.* (～ to) (the sound of large drops of rain or lots of small rocks pelting down):
Barabara (*to*) *yuudachi ga futte*

kita. (ばらばら(と)夕立が降ってきた) The evening rain came *pelting down.*

ba⌈rama⌉k·u ばらまく (ばら蒔く) *vt.* (-mak·i-; -mak·a-; -ma·i-te [C])
1 scatter; spread:
uwasa o baramaku (うわさをばらまく) *spread* the rumor.
2 hand out indiscriminately; throw around:
meeshi o baramaku (名刺をばらまく) *hand out* name cards indiscriminately.

ba⌈rañsu バランス *n.* balance:
barañsu no toreta *shokuji* (バランスのとれた食事) a *well-balanced* diet. 《↔ añbarañsu》

ba⌈ree-bo⌉oru バレーボール *n.* volleyball. ★ Often abbreviated to simply '*baree*.'

ba⌈sho ばしょ (場所) *n.* **1** place; spot; location. 《⇨ ba; kasho》
2 space; room:
Piano wa basho *o toru.* (ピアノは場所をとる) The piano takes up a lot of *space.*
3 (of sumo wrestling) tournament:
haru-basho (春場所) the spring *sumo tournament.*

ba⌈ssui ばっすい (抜粋) *n.* extract; excerpt.
bassui suru (～する) *vt.* extract; excerpt.

ba⌈ss·uru ばっする (罰する) *vt.* (bassh·i-; bassh·i-; bassh·i-te [I]) punish; inflict punishment for (a crime). 《⇨ batsu》

ba⌉su バス *n.* bus; coach. 《⇨ shibasu; tobasu[2]》

ba⌈suketto-bo⌉oru バスケットボール *n.* basketball. ★ Often abbreviated to simply '*basuketto.*'

ba⌈sutee バスてい (バス停) *n.* bus stop. 《⇨ teeryuujo》

ba⌉tabata ばたばた *adv.* (～ to)
1 (the sound of flapping, rattling or clattering):
Kaateñ ga kaze de batabata (*to*) *oto o tatete iru.* (カーテンが風でばたばた(と)音をたてている) The curtains are *flapping* in the wind.
2 in a flurry:
batabata (*to*) *beñkyoo o hajimeru* (ばたばた(と)勉強を始める) begin to study *in a fluster.*
3 one after another:
kaisha ga batabata (*to*) *toosañ suru* (会社がばたばた(と)倒産する) firms go bankrupt *one after another.*

ba⌉tsu ばつ (罰) *n.* punishment; penalty. 《⇨ bassuru》

ba⌈tsuguñ ばつぐん (抜群) *a.n.* (～ no, ni) outstanding; unrivaled:
Kanojo wa uta ga batsuguñ *ni umai.* (彼女は歌が抜群にうまい) Her singing *is unrivaled* in excellence.

ba⌈tta⌉ri ばったり *adv.* (～ to)
1 with a thud:
battari (*to*) *taoreru.* (ばったり(と)倒れる) fall down *with a thud.*
2 unexpectedly; by chance:
Sakki Tanaka-sañ to battari *aimashita.* (さっき田中さんとばったり会いました) I met Ms. Tanaka *by chance* a little while ago.
3 suddenly:
Kare kara no tegami ga battari *konaku natta.* (彼からの手紙がばったり来なくなった) His letters *suddenly* stopped coming.

ba⌉tterii バッテリー *n.* car battery. 《⇨ deñchi》

-be べ (辺) *suf.* around; nearby; neighborhood:
kishi-be (岸辺) a *shore* / *mado*-be (窓辺) *by* the window.

Be⌈ekoku べいこく (米国) *n.* America; the United States (of America).

be⌉esu ベース *n.* **1** base; basis:
chiñgiñ-beesu (賃金ベース) the wage *base.*
2 (of baseball) base.

be⌈esu-a⌉ppu ベースアップ *n.* pay raise [hike].

be⌉ki べき *n.* [follows the dictionary form of a verb, except

that '*suru beki*' is usually '*su beki*.']
1 should; ought to:
Miñna ga kono teñ o kañgaeru beki *desu*. (みんながこの点を考えるべきです) Everyone *should* consider this point.
2 worthy of; deserve to be:
odoroku beki *dekigoto* (驚くべき出来事) a *remarkable* [*surprising*] incident / kanashimu beki *koto* (悲しむべきこと) a matter of *regret*.

be⌈kkyo べっきょ (別居) *n.* living apart; separation.
bekkyo suru (～する) *vi.* live apart; separate. ⟪⇨ rikoñ⟫

be⌉ñ べん (便) *n.* **1** convenience; facilities; service:
Kare no uchi wa kootsuu no beñ ga yoi. (彼の家は交通の便が良い) His house *is easy of access*.
2 feces; stool.

-beñ べん (遍) *suf.* (the number of) times. ⟪⇨ APP. 4⟫

be⌉ñgo べんご (弁護) *n.* (legal) defense; justification.
beñgo (o) suru (～(を)する) *vt.* defend; justify.

be⌈ñgoniñ べんごにん (弁護人) *n.* defense lawyer; counsel.

be⌈ñgo⌉shi べんごし (弁護士) *n.* lawyer; attorney.

be⌈ñjo⌉ べんじょ (便所) *n.* toilet; lavatory. ★ Avoid in polite conversation. Use '*tearai*' (*literally* 'hand-washing place') or '*o-tearai*' (*polite*) instead.
⟪⇨ kooshuu-beñjo; toire⟫

be⌉ñkai べんかい (弁解) *n.* excuse; explanation.
beñkai suru (～する) *vt.* make excuses; explain.

be⌈ñkyoo べんきょう (勉強) *n.*
1 study:
beñkyooo *o namakeru* (勉強を怠ける) neglect one's *studies*.
2 experience; lesson:
Shippai ga ii beñkyoo ni natta. (失敗がいい勉強になった) I *learned* much from my failure.
⟪⇨ taikeñ⟫
beñkyoo (o) suru (～(を)する) *vi.*, *vt.* **1** study; work.
2 make a discount; reduce the price. ⟪⇨ makeru⟫

be⌈ñpi べんぴ (便秘) *n.* constipation.
beñpi suru (～する) *vi.* be constipated.

be⌈ñri べんり (便利) *a.n.* (～ na, ni) convenient; useful; handy.
⟪↔ fubeñ⟫ ⟪⇨ choohoo⟫

be⌈ñshoo べんしょう (弁償) *n.* compensation; indemnification.
beñshoo (o) suru (～(を)する) *vt.* compensate; indemnify; pay.

be⌈ñto⌉o べんとう (弁当) *n.* packed [box] lunch; lunch box.

be⌉rabera べらべら *adv.* (～ to) glibly:
himitsu o berabera (to) hanasu (秘密をべらべら(と)話す) *babble out* a secret. ⟪⇨ perapera[1]⟫

be⌈rañda ベランダ *n.* veranda; porch.

be⌈sso⌉o べっそう (別荘) *n.* country [summer] house; villa; cottage.

be⌉suto ベスト *n.* best:
besuto *o tsukusu* (ベストをつくす) do one's *best*.

be⌈terañ ベテラン *n.* expert; experienced person:
beterañ *no kañgofu* (ベテランの看護婦) an *experienced* nurse.

be⌈tsu[1] べつ (別) *n.* distinction; exception.
betsu to shite (～として) except:
Ookisa wa betsu to shite, *iro ga ki ni iranakatta*. (大きさは別として, 色が気に入らなかった) *Regardless of* the size, I didn't like the color.

be⌈tsu[2] べつ (別) *a.n.* (～ na/no, ni) another; different.

-betsu べつ (別) *suf.* classified by...; according to...:
shokugyoo-betsu *deñwachoo* (職業別電話帳) a *classified* telephon[e] directory.

be⌈tsubetsu べつべつ (別々

b

(～ na/no, ni) different(ly); separate(ly); respective(ly): *Futari wa* betsubetsu *no michi o itta.* (二人は別々の道を行った) The two of them went their *respective* ways.

be⌈tsujoo べつじょう (別状) *n.* (with a negative) something wrong; something unusual: *Kare wa atama ni kega o shita ga, inochi ni wa* betsujoo wa nakatta. (彼は頭にけがをしたが, 命には別状なかった) He got hurt on the head, but his life *was not in danger*.

be⌈tsu ni べつに (別に) *adv.* (with a negative) particularly; in particular: *Ima no tokoro* betsu ni *suru koto wa arimaseñ.* (今のところ別にすることはありません) I have nothing *particular* to do at the moment.

-bi び (日) *suf.* day: *kineñ*-bi (記念日) a memorial *day*. ⟪⇨ APP. 5⟫.

bi⌉deo ビデオ *n.* video (tape); videocassette recorder.

bi⌉jiñ びじん (美人) *n.* good-looking [beautiful] woman; beauty.

bi⌉jutsu びじゅつ (美術) *n.* art; fine arts.

bi⌈jutsu⌉kañ びじゅつかん (美術館) *n.* art museum.

-biki びき (匹) *suf.* counter for small animals, fish and insects. ⟪⇨ APP. 4⟫

bi⌈kku⌉ri s·uru びっくりする *vi.* (sh·i-; sh·i-; sh·i-te [1]) be surprised; be astonished; be amazed. ⟪⇨ odoroku⟫

bi⌉kubiku s·uru びくびくする *vi.* (sh·i-; sh·i-; sh·i-te [1]) be timid [nervous; afraid]: *machigai o* bikubiku suru (間違いをびくびくする) *be afraid* of mistakes. ⟪⇨ osoreru⟫

bi⌈myoo びみょう (微妙) *a.n.* (～ na, ni) delicate; subtle; nice; fine: bimyoo *na moñdai* (微妙な問題) a *delicate* matter.

bi⌉ñ[1] びん (瓶) *n.* bottle; jar.

bi⌉ñ[2] びん (便) *n.* flight; service: *Sono* biñ *wa shoogo ni demasu.* (その便は正午に出ます) The *flight* leaves at noon.

bi⌉ñboo びんぼう (貧乏) *n.* poverty; destitution.

biñboo suru (～する) *vi.* be poor; be badly off.

— *a.n.* (～ na, ni) poor; needy. ⟪⇨ mazushii⟫

bi⌈ñbooniñ びんぼうにん (貧乏人) *n.* poor person. ⟪↔ kanemochi⟫

bi⌈ni⌉iru ビニール *n.* plastic; vinyl. ⟪⇨ purasuchikku⟫

bi⌈ñjoo びんじょう (便乗) *n.* free ride in a car.

biñjoo suru (～する) *vi.* **1** get a lift.

2 take advantage of: *Kare-ra wa uñchiñ no neage ni* biñjoo shite, *nedañ o ageta.* (彼らは運賃の値上げに便乗して, 値段を上げた) They *took advantage of* the rise in transport costs to increase their prices.

bi⌈ñkañ びんかん (敏感) *a.n.* (～ na, ni) sensitive; susceptible: *Wakamono wa ryuukoo ni* biñkañ *da.* (若者は流行に敏感だ) Young people are *very aware* of changes in fashion. ⟪↔ doñkañ⟫

bi⌈ñseñ びんせん (便箋) *n.* letter paper; letterhead; writing pad.

bi⌈ñshoo びんしょう (敏捷) *a.n.* (～ na, ni) agile; nimble; quick; prompt: biñshoo *ni koodoo suru* (敏しょうに行動する) act *promptly*. ⟪⇨ subayai⟫

bi⌈ñwañ びんわん (敏腕) *n.* (great) ability: biñwañ *o furuu* (敏腕をふるう) show one's *ability*.

— *a.n.* (～ na) able; capable: biñwañ *na keeji* (敏腕な刑事) a *shrewd* detective.

bi⌈ñzume びんづめ (瓶詰) *n.* bottling; bottled food [beverage]. ⟪⇨ kañzume⟫

bi⌉ribiri びりびり *adv.* (～ to) (the sound of trembling or ripping):

Kare wa sono tegami o biribiri (to) yabuita. (彼はその手紙をびりびり(と)やぶいた) He *tore* the letter into pieces.

bi⌈roodo ビロード *n.* velvet.

bi⌉ru ビル *n.* building. ★ Shortened form of '*birudiñgu*' (building).

bi⌉rudiñgu ビルディング *n.* building. ★ Refers mainly to western-style structures three stories and over.

bi⌈shobisho びしょびしょ *a.n.* (~ na/no, ni) wet through; soaked:
bishobisho ni naru (びしょびしょになる) *get wet to the skin.*

bi⌈shoo びしょう(微笑) *n.* smile.
bishoo suru (~する) *vi.* make a smile. (⇨ hohoemu)

bi⌈suke⌉tto ビスケット *n.* cracker; cookie.

bi⌈yoo びよう(美容) *n.* personal beauty; beauty culture:
Earobikusu wa biyoo *ni yoi.* (エアロビクスは美容によい) Aerobics is good for *keeping your figure.*

bi⌈yo⌉oiñ びよういん(美容院) *n.* beauty shop [salon].

bo⌉chi ぼち(墓地) *n.* graveyard; cemetery.

bo⌈iñ ぼいん(母音) *n.* vowel:
tañ[*choo*]-boiñ (短[長]母音) a short [long] *vowel.* (⇨ APP. 1)

bo⌈ke⌉-ru ぼける(惚ける) *vi.* (bo-ke-te [V]) grow senile:
Kare mo dañdañ bokete kita. (彼もだんだんぼけてきた) He too *became* increasingly *affected by senility.*

bo⌉ki ぼき(簿記) *n.* bookkeeping:
boki *o tsukeru* (簿記をつける) keep *books.*

bo⌈kiñ ぼきん(募金) *n.* fund-raising; collection of contributions.
bokiñ suru (~する) *vi.* raise funds; collect money.

bo⌉koku ぼこく(母国) *n.* one's mother country; one's homeland. (⇨ kuni)

bo⌈kokugo ぼこくご(母国語) *n.* one's mother tongue.

bo⌉koo ぼこう(母校) *n.* one's alma mater.

bo⌉ku ぼく(僕) *n.* I. ★ 'boku no' = my, 'boku ni/o' = me. Plural forms are '*boku-tachi*' or '*boku-ra*' (*humble*). (⇨ kimi[1]; kare; kanojo)

bo⌈kuchiku ぼくちく(牧畜) *n.* stock farming; cattle breeding.

bo⌈kujoo ぼくじょう(牧場) *n.* stock farm; pasture; ranch.

bo⌉kushi ぼくし(牧師) *n.* clergyman; minister. (⇨ shiñpu[1])

bo⌈ñ[1] ぼん(盆) *n.* tray; server. ★ Usually with '*o*-.'

bo⌉ñ[2] ぼん(盆) *n.* Bon Festival. ★ '*Boñ*' is a Buddhist observance celebrated on July 15 or August 15, depending on the district.

-boñ ぼん(本) *suf.* counter for long cylindrical objects. (⇨ APP. 4)

bo⌈ñchi ぼんち(盆地) *n.* basin; valley: *Koofu* Boñchi (甲府盆地) the Kofu *Basin.*

bo⌈ñ-o⌉dori ぼんおどり(盆踊り) *n.* Bon dances. (⇨ boñ[2])

bo⌈ñya⌉ri ぼんやり *adv.* (~ to; ~ suru) **1** absent-mindedly; vacantly; carelessly:
Boñyari *shite ite, oriru eki o machigaete shimatta.* (ぼんやりしていて, 降りる駅を間違えてしまった) I *carelessly* went and got off at the wrong station. (⇨ boyaboya suru)
2 idly:
Boñyari (*to*) *tatte inai de, tetsudai nasai.* (ぼんやり(と)立っていないで, 手伝いなさい) Don't stand there *doing nothing.* Give me a hand.
3 (of memory, sight, etc.) vaguely; unclearly; obscurely:
Kare no koto wa boñyari (*to*) *shika oboete imaseñ.* (彼のことはぼんやり(と)しか覚えていません) I only *vaguely* remember him. (⇨ bakuzeñ)
4 drowsy:

Nebusoku de atama ga boñyari (*to*) *shite iru.* (寝不足で頭がぼんやり(と)している) I feel *drowsy* because of lack of sleep.

bo^ro ぼう(棒) *n.* stick; pole; rod.

bo⌈ochoo ぼうちょう(膨張) *n.* expansion; swelling.
boochoo suru (〜する) *vi.* expand; swell.

bo⌈odoo ぼうどう(暴動) *n.* riot: boodoo *o okosu* [*shizumeru*] (暴動を起こす[しずめる]) start [suppress] a *riot.*

bo⌈oee ぼうえい(防衛) *n.* defense.
booee suru (〜する) *vt.* defend. ⟪⇨ mamoru⟫

bo⌈oeki ぼうえき(貿易) *n.* trade; commerce.
... to booeki (o) suru (...と〜(を)する) *vi.* carry on trade.

bo⌈oeñkyoo ぼうえんきょう(望遠鏡) *n.* telescope.

bo⌈ofu⌉u ぼうふう(暴風) *n.* storm; windstorm.

bo⌈ogai ぼうがい(妨害) *n.* disturbance; obstruction; interference.
boogai suru (〜する) *vt.* disturb; obstruct; interfere.

bo⌉ogyo ぼうぎょ(防御) *n.* defense; safeguard. ⟪↔ koogeki⟫
boogyo suru (〜する) *vt.* defend. ⟪⇨ mamoru⟫

bo⌈oi ボーイ *n.* waiter; bellboy; porter.

bo⌈oka ぼうか(防火) *n.* fire prevention.

bo⌈okeñ ぼうけん(冒険) *n.* adventure; venture; risk.
bookeñ (o) suru (〜(を)する) *vi.* make a venture; run a risk.

bo⌈okoo ぼうこう(暴行) *n.* violence; assault; rape.
bookoo suru (〜する) *vt.* use violence; make an assault; rape.

bo⌈omee ぼうめい(亡命) *n.* defection; asylum.
boomee suru (〜する) *vi.* defect; take [seek] asylum.

bo⌉onasu ボーナス *n.* bonus.
★ Japanese 'permanent' workers usually receive extra remuneration, called '*boonasu*' twice a year in June and December.

bo⌈one⌉ñkai ぼうねんかい(忘年会) *n.* year-end party.

bo⌈orubako ボールばこ(ボール箱) *n.* cardboard box; carton.

bo⌈orugami ボールがみ(ボール紙) *n.* cardboard.

bo⌈oru-peñ ボールペン *n.* ball-point pen.

bo⌉oryoku ぼうりょく(暴力) *n.* violence; force.

bo⌈oryoku⌉dañ ぼうりょくだん(暴力団) *n.* gang; crime syndicate: booryokudañ-*in* (暴力団員) a *gang* member.

bo⌈osañ ぼうさん(坊さん) *n.* Buddhist priest; bonze.

bo⌈oshi[1] ぼうし(帽子) *n.* hat; cap.

bo⌈oshi[2] ぼうし(防止) *n.* prevention; check.
booshi suru (〜する) *vt.* prevent; check. ⟪⇨ fusegu⟫

bo⌈osui ぼうすい(防水) *n.* waterproofing.

bo⌉oto ボート *n.* rowboat: booto *o kogu* (ボートをこぐ) row a *boat.*

bo⌉ribori ぼりぼり *adv.* (〜 to) (the sound of scratching, crunching, etc.):
ka ni sasareta tokoro o boribori (to) kaku (蚊に刺された所をぼりぼり(と)かく) *scratch away* at the place a mosquito has bitten one.

bo⌈roboro[1] ぼろぼろ *a.n.* (〜 na/no, ni) (the state of being worn or torn):
Watashi no kutsu wa moo boroboro *desu.* (私の靴はもうぼろぼろです) My shoes are completely *worn out.*

bo⌉roboro[2] ぼろぼろ *adv.* (〜 to) (the state of grains, drops, etc., falling down):
Furui kabe ga boroboro (*to*) *kuzure-ochita.* (古い壁がぼろぼろ(と)くずれ落ちた) The old wall *fell down.*

bo⌈shuu ぼしゅう(募集) *n.* re-

cruitment; collection.
boshuu suru (～する) *vt.* recruit; collect.

bo⌈sshuu ぼっしゅう (没収) *n.* confiscation; forfeit.
bosshuu suru (～する) *vt.* confiscate; impound. ⟪⇨ toriageru⟫

bo⌈tañ[1] ボタン *n.* button; push button.

bo⌉tañ[2] ぼたん (牡丹) *n.* tree peony; *Paeonia suffruticosa.*

bo⌉tchañ ぼっちゃん (坊ちゃん) *n.*
1 (*polite*) your son. ⟪↔ o-joosañ⟫
2 (*derog.*) naive person:
Kare wa sekeñ shirazu no botchañ *da.* (彼は世間知らずの坊ちゃんだ) He is an *unsophisticated fellow* who knows nothing of the world.

bo⌈ttoo ぼっとう (没頭) *n.* absorption; devotion.
bottoo suru (～する) *vi.* be absorbed; be devoted.

bo⌉ya ぼや *n.* small fire.

bo⌉yaboya s·uru ぼやぼやする *vi.* (sh·i-; sh·i-; sh·i-te [1]) be careless; be absent-minded:
Boyaboya shite iru *to kuruma ni hikaremasu yo.* (ぼやぼやしていると車にひかれますよ) If *you are not on your toes*, you will be hit by a car. ⟪⇨ boñyari⟫

bu[1] ぶ (分) *n.* advantage.
bu ga aru (～がある) have an advantage.

bu[2] ぶ (分) *n.* (a unit of rate) one percent: ★ One tenth of '*wari*.'
hachi bu *no rishi* (8 分の利子) eight *percent* interest. ⟪⇨ wari⟫
...bu-doori (...～どおり) ten percent: *Geñkoo wa* hachi-bu-doori *kañsee shimashita.* (原稿は八分どおり完成しました) I have finished eighty *percent* of the manuscript.

bu[3] ぶ (部) *n.* **1** department:
hañbai-bu (販売部) the sales *department.*
2 club; society:
tenisu-bu (テニス部) a tennis *club* / *eñgeki*-bu (演劇部) a theatrical *society.*

-bu ぶ (部) *suf.* **1** part:
*Kono shoosetsu wa sañ-*bu *kara naru.* (この小説は 3 部からなる) This novel consists of three *parts.*
2 (of a book) copy. ⟪⇨ -satsu⟫

bu⌈a⌉isoo ぶあいそう (無愛想) *a.n.* (～ na, ni) unsociable; blunt:
Ano mise no teñiñ wa buaisoo *da.* (あの店の店員は無愛想だ) The clerks at that shop are *not courteous.* ⟪↔ aiso⟫

bu⌈atsu·i ぶあつい (分厚い) *a.* (-ku) thick: buatsui *hoñ* (分厚い本) a *thick* book. ⟪⇨ atsui[3]⟫

bu⌉buñ ぶぶん (部分) *n.* part; portion.

bu⌈buñ-teki ぶぶんてき (部分的) *a.n.* (～ na, ni) partial; partly:
Kanojo no iu koto wa bubuñ-teki *ni wa tadashii.* (彼女の言うことは部分的には正しい) What she says is *partly* right.

bu⌈choo ぶちょう (部長) *n.* manager; the head [chief] of a department.

bu⌈doo ぶどう (葡萄) *n.* grape; grapevine.

bu⌈do⌉oshu ぶどうしゅ (葡萄酒) *n.* wine.

bu⌈e⌉ñryo ぶえんりょ (無遠慮) *a.n.* (～ na, ni) rude; impolite; forwardness. ⟪↔ eñryo⟫

bu⌈hiñ ぶひん (部品) *n.* parts:
jidoosha no buhiñ (自動車の部品) automobile *parts.*

bu⌈ji ぶじ (無事) *n.* safety; peace.
— *a.n.* (～ na, ni) safe; peaceful; all right:
Sono ko wa buji *ni kyuushutsu sareta.* (その子は無事に救出された) The child was rescued *safely.* ⟪⇨ añzeñ⟫

bu⌈joku ぶじょく (侮辱) *n.* insult; contempt; affront.
bujoku suru (～する) *vt.* insult.

bu⌉ka ぶか (部下) *n.* subordinate (at a workplace).

bu⌈ka⌉kkoo ぶかっこう (不格好) *a.n.* (～ na, ni) unshapely; awkward; clumsy:

bukakko *na booshi* (不格好な帽子) an *unshapely* hat. 《⇨ kakkoo[1]》

bu˥ki ぶき (武器) *n.* arms; weapon; ordnance.

bu˥kimi ぶきみ (無気味) *a.n.* (~ na, ni) weird; uncanny: bukimi *na oto* (無気味な音) a *weird* noise.

bu˥ki˥yoo ぶきよう (不器用) *n.* clumsiness; awkwardness.

— *a.n.* **1** (~ na, ni) clumsy; unskilled; awkward:
Watashi wa totemo bukiyoo *da.* (私はとても不器用だ) I'm *all thumbs.* 《↔ kiyoo》
2 unable to deal with a situation with finesse:
Watashi wa doomo bukiyoo *de oseji mo ienai.* (私はどうも不器用でお世辞も言えない) I am a *poor hand* at paying compliments.

bu˥kka ぶっか (物価) *n.* (commodity) prices. ★ Means general prices of commodities. The price of a specific article is '*nedañ.*' 《⇨ kakaku》

Bu˥kkyoo ぶっきょう (仏教) *n.* Buddhism.

bu˥kubuku ぶくぶく *adv.* **1** (~ to, ni) (the state of being fat or baggy):
Kare wa saikiñ bukubuku (*to* [*ni*]) *futotte kita.* (彼は最近ぶくぶく(と[に])太ってきた) He is getting *fatter* these days.
2 (~ to) (the state of bubbling):
Fune wa bukubuku (*to*) *shizuñde shimatta.* (船はぶくぶく(と) 沈んでしまった) The ship sank, *leaving a trail of bubbles.*

bu˥ñ[1] ぶん (文) *n.* sentence; composition.

bu˥ñ[2] ぶん (分) *n.* **1** share; part; portion:
Kore wa kimi no buñ *da.* (これは君の分だ) This is your *share.*
2 place; station:
jibuñ no buñ *o shiru* (自分の分を知る) know one's *place.*
3 condition:
Kono buñ *nara, bañji umaku iku daroo.* (この分なら, 万事うまく行くだろう) Under the present *conditions,* everything should go well. 《⇨ chooshi》

-buñ ぶん (分) *suf.* (the amount or percentage contained in materials): *too*-buñ (糖分) the *amount* [*percentage*] of sugar / *eñ*-buñ (塩分) salt *content.*

bu˥nañ ぶなん (無難) *n.* safety; security.

— *a.n.* (~ na, ni) safe; passable:
Sono koto ni tsuite wa damatte iru hoo ga bunañ *da.* (そのことについてはだまっているほうが無難だ) Regarding that matter, it would be *safer* to keep silent.

bu˥ñbo ぶんぼ (分母) *n.* denominator. 《⇨ buñsuu》

bu˥ñbo˥ogu ぶんぼうぐ (文房具) *n.* stationery; writing materials.

bu˥ñboogu˥teñ ぶんぼうぐてん (文房具店) *n.* stationer's; stationery store.

bu˥ñbuñ ぶんぶん *adv.* (~ to) (the buzzing noise made when bees or flies are flying; the droning noise made by the rotation of motors):
katana [*boo*] *o* buñbuñ (*to*) *furimawasu* (刀[棒]をぶんぶん(と)振り回す) wave a sword [club] about *vigorously.*

bu˥ñgaku ぶんがく (文学) *n.* literature.

bu˥ñga˥kusha ぶんがくしゃ (文学者) *n.* literary man; man of letters; writer.

bu˥ñgo ぶんご (文語) *n.* written [literary] language. 《↔ koogo》

bu˥ñjoo-ju˥utaku ぶんじょうじゅうたく (分譲住宅) *n.* condominium; house in a development project. 《⇨ chiñtai-juutaku》

bu˥ñka[1] ぶんか (文化) *n.* culture: buñka *no kooryuu* (文化の交流) *cultural* exchange.

bu˥ñka[2] ぶんか (文科) *n.* the department of liberal arts; the humanities. 《⇨ rika》

bu⌈ñkai ぶんかい (分解) *n.* resolution; taking to pieces.
buñkai suru (〜する) *vi., vt.* resolve; take to pieces.

bu⌈ñka⌉jiñ ぶんかじん (文化人) *n.* person following an academic or artistic career; cultured person.

Bu⌈ñka-ku⌉ñshoo ぶんかくんしょう (文化勲章) *n.* Order of Culture.

bu⌈ñka-teki ぶんかてき (文化的) *a.n.* (〜 na, ni) cultural; civilized:
buñka-teki *na seekatsu o suru* [*okuru*] (文化的な生活をする[送る]) lead a *civilized* life.

bu⌈ñka⌉zai ぶんかざい (文化財) *n.* cultural property [assets]:
juuyoo-buñkazai (重要文化財) an Important *Cultural Property*.

bu⌈ñkeñ ぶんけん (文献) *n.* books or documents on a particular subject; literature.

bu⌈ñmee ぶんめい (文明) *n.* civilization.

bu⌈ñmyaku ぶんみゃく (文脈) *n.* context.

bu⌈ñpai ぶんぱい (分配) *n.* distribution; division.
buñpai suru (〜する) *vt.* distribute; divide. 《⇨ yamawake》

bu⌈ñpoo ぶんぽう (文法) *n.* grammar.

bu⌈ñpu ぶんぷ (分布) *n.* distribution; spread.
buñpu suru (〜する) *vi.* be distributed; range.

bu⌉ñraku ぶんらく (文楽) *n.* traditional Japanese puppet theater.

bu⌈ñretsu ぶんれつ (分裂) *n.* split; division.
buñretsu suru (〜する) *vi.* split; divide. 《⇨ wakareru[1]》

bu⌈ñri ぶんり (分離) *n.* separation; disunion.
buñri suru (〜する) *vi., vt.* separate: *gyuunyuu kara kuriimu o* buñri suru (牛乳からクリームを分離する) *separate* cream from milk.

bu⌈ñrui ぶんるい (分類) *n.* classification; grouping.
buñrui suru (〜する) *vt.* classify; group.

bu⌈ñryo⌉o ぶんりょう (分量) *n.* quantity or amount that can be measured. 《⇨ ryoo[1]》

bu⌈ñsañ ぶんさん (分散) *n.* dispersion; decentralization.
buñsañ suru (〜する) *vi., vt.* disperse; decentralize. 《↔ shuuchuu》

bu⌈ñseki ぶんせき (分析) *n.* analysis.
buñseki suru (〜する) *vt.* make an analysis; analyze.

bu⌉ñshi ぶんし (分子) *n.* **1** numerator. 《⇨ buñsuu》
2 molecule; element.

bu⌉ñsho ぶんしょ (文書) *n.* document; writing.

bu⌉ñshoo ぶんしょう (文章) *n.* sentences; writing.

bu⌈ñsu⌉u ぶんすう (分数) *n.* fraction. ★ The numerator is called '*buñshi*' (分子), and the denominator '*buñbo*' (分母). Y/X is read as '*X buñ no Y*.'

bu⌈ñtai ぶんたい (文体) *n.* style of writing.

bu⌈ñtañ ぶんたん (分担) *n.* partial charge; allotment; share.
buñtañ suru (〜する) *vt.* share. 《⇨ wakeru》

bu⌈ñtsuu ぶんつう (文通) *n.* correspondence.
buñtsuu suru (〜する) *vi.* correspond with; exchange letters. 《⇨ tegami》

bu⌉ñya ぶんや (分野) *n.* field; sphere; branch:
Kare wa kono buñya *de yuumee desu.* (彼はこの分野で有名です) He is famous in this *field*.

bu⌉rabura ぶらぶら *adv.* (〜 to; 〜 suru) **1** (the state of legs or arms hanging loosely, or of a pendulum swinging):
burabura *yureru* (ぶらぶら揺れる) sway *back and forth*.
2 (the state of moving aimlessly about):

Kooeň o bura-bura *saňpo shita.* (公園をぶらぶら散歩した) I went out for a *stroll* around the park.
3 (the state of idling about): *Sotsugyoo shite kara, ano hito wa mainichi* burabura *shite iru.* (卒業してから, あの人は毎日ぶらぶらしている) Since he graduated from school, he has been *lazing about* every day.

bu'raňko ぶらんこ *n.* swing.

bu'rasagar·u ぶらさがる (ぶら下がる) *vi.* (-sagar·i-; -sagar·a-; -sagat-te [C]) hang:
tetsuboo ni burasagaru (鉄棒にぶら下がる) *hang* from a horizontal bar. ⟪⇨ burasageru⟫

bu'rasage·ru ぶらさげる (ぶら下げる) *vt.* (-sage-te [V]) hang:
kata kara baggu o burasageru (肩からバッグをぶら下げる) *sling* a bag on one's shoulder. ⟪⇨ burasagaru⟫

bu'rashi ブラシ *n.* brush.
⟪⇨ fude; hake⟫

bu'ree ぶれい (無礼) *n.* impolite behavior; rudeness: buree o hataraku (無礼をはたらく) *be rude.*
— *a.n.* (~ na) rude; impolite.
⟪⇨ shitsuree⟫

-buri ぶり (振り) *suf.* **1** [with a noun or the continuative base of a verb] manner; way:
hanashi-buri (話しぶり) someone's *way* of talking.
2 after: ★ Used after words denoting duration and indicates that something occurred again after the interval of time stated.
Goneň-buri *ni furusato e kaetta.* (五年ぶりにふるさとへ帰った) I went back to my hometown *for the first time in five years.*
⟪⇨ hisashiburi⟫

-bu'r·u ぶる *suf.* (*vi.*) (-bur·i-; -bur·a-; -but-te [C]) pose as...; behave like...: ★ Used to form a verb from a noun, adjective, or adjectival noun. It conveys a derogatory meaning.
1 [after a noun] *Kare wa geejutsuka*-butte iru. (彼は芸術家ぶっている) He *poses as* an artist.
2 [after the stem of an adjective] *era*-buru (偉ぶる) *act* big.
3 [after an adjectival noun] *joohiň*-buru (上品ぶる) *put on* airs; *pretend* to be refined.

bu'ruburu ぶるぶる *adv.* (~ to) (the state of the body or limbs shaking or quivering from cold, fear, etc.):
Watashi wa osoroshikute, buruburu (to) *furueta.* (私は恐ろしくて, ぶるぶる(と)震えた) I *trembled* with fear.

bu'sa'hoo ぶさほう (無作法) *n.* bad manners; breach of etiquette.
— *a.n.* (~ na, ni) ill-mannered; impolite. ⟪⇨ shitsuree⟫

bu'shi ぶし (武士) *n.* warrior; samurai. ★ A man of arms in the service of a feudal lord in Japan.

bu'sho'o ぶしょう (不精·無精) *n.* laziness; indolence:
bushoo-*mono* (不精者) a *lazy* fellow / bushoo-hige (不精ひげ) a *stubbly beard.*
— *a.n.* (~ na, ni) lazy; indolent.
bushoo suru (~する) *vi.* be lazy; be remiss.

bu'shu ぶしゅ (部首) *n.* the radical of a Chinese character.
★ Used as a classificatory element in *kaňji.* ⟪⇨ heň[3]; tsukuri⟫

-bu'soku ぶそく (不足) *suf.* insufficient; short; lacking:
suimiň-busoku (睡眠不足) *insufficient* sleep / *uňdoo*-busoku (運動不足) *lack* of exercise. ⟪⇨ fusoku⟫

bu'soo ぶそう (武装) *n.* armaments; military equipment.
busoo suru (~する) *vi.* take up arms. ⟪↔ hibusoo⟫

bu'sshi ぶっし (物資) *n.* goods; necessities; supplies:
kyuueň-busshi (救援物資) relief *supplies.*

bu'sshiki ぶっしき (仏式) *n.* Buddhist rites. ⟪⇨ shiňshiki⟫

buˈsshitsu ぶっしつ(物質) *n.* matter; substance.

buˈsshitsu-teki ぶっしつてき(物質的) *a.n.* (~ na, ni) material; physical:
Kanojo wa busshitsu-teki ni megumarete iru. (彼女は物質的に恵まれている) She *is well off*.

buˈssoˈo ぶっそう(物騒) *n.* lack of safety; danger.
— *a.n.* (~ na, ni) unsafe; dangerous. 《⇨ kikeñ[1]》

buˈta ぶた(豚) *n.* pig; hog.

buˈtai ぶたい(舞台) *n.* **1** stage:
butai *ni tatsu* (舞台に立つ) appear on the *stage*.
2 setting; scene.
butai-ura (~裏) backstage; behind the scenes.

buˈtaniku ぶたにく(豚肉) *n.* pork.

buˈtoo ぶとう(舞踏) *n.* (*formal*) dance: butoo-kai (舞踏会) a *ball*. 《⇨ odori》

-butsu ぶつ(物) *suf.* thing; object; matter:
iñsatsu-butsu (印刷物) printed *matter* / yuubiñ-butsu (郵便物) *mail*.

buˈtsubutsu[1] ぶつぶつ *adv.*
1 (the state of many small swellings appearing):
kao ni nikibi ga butsubutsu *dekiru* (顔ににきびがぶつぶつできる) have one's face come out in *pimples*.
2 (the state of talking to oneself in a low voice or mumbling complaints to someone):
Kare wa ki ni iranai to sugu butsubutsu iu. (彼は気に入らないとすぐぶつぶつ言う) When there is something he doesn't like, he soon *grumbles*. 《⇨ fuhee》

buˈtsubutsu[2] ぶつぶつ *n.* rash; pimple.

buˈtsudañ ぶつだん(仏壇) *n.* Buddhist altar for enshrining the spirits of a family.

buˈtsukar·u ぶつかる *vt.* (-kar·i-; -kar·a-; -kat-te Ⓒ) **1** bump into; crash against; collide:
Kuruma ga kabe ni butsukatta. (車が壁にぶつかった) A car *crashed into* the wall. 《⇨ butsukeru》
2 encounter; run into; meet (difficulties, hardship, a problem, etc.).
3 wrangle; have a run-in with:
shigoto no koto de jooshi to butsukaru (仕事のことで上司とぶつかる) *have a disagreement* with one's boss about the job. 《⇨ shoototsu》

buˈtsuke·ru ぶつける *vt.* (-ke-te Ⓥ) **1** bump; knock:
kuruma o deñchuu ni butsukeru (車を電柱にぶつける) *drive* one's car into a utility pole. 《⇨ ataru; butsukaru》
2 throw:
Neko ni ishi o butsukete *wa ikemaseñ.* (猫に石をぶつけてはいけません) Don't *throw* stones at the cat.
3 give vent to:
fumañ o hito ni butsukeru (不満を人にぶつける) *give vent* to one's discontent on somebody.

buˈtsuri ぶつり(物理) *n.* physics.
★ Shortened form of '*butsurigaku*.'

buˈtsuriˈgaku ぶつりがく(物理学) *n.* physics.

buˈttai ぶったい(物体) *n.* object; thing; substance.

buˈyoˈojiñ ぶようじん(不用心) *a.n.* (~ na, ni) unsafe; insecure; careless. 《↔ yoojiñ》

byoˈo[1] びょう(秒) *n.* second:
Kono tokee wa go-byoo *okurete iru.* (この時計は5秒遅れている) This watch is five *seconds* slow. 《⇨ fuñ[1]; byooshiñ》

byoˈo[2] びょう(鋲) *n.* tack; thumbtack; drawing pin. 《⇨ gabyoo》

-byoo びょう(病) *suf.* disease:
shiñzoo-byoo (心臓病) heart *disease*.

byoˈobu びょうぶ(屏風) *n.* folding screen.

byoˈodoo びょうどう(平等) *n.* equality; impartiality.

— *a.n.* (~ na, ni) equal; impartial; even. ⟪⇨ taitoo⟫

byoˈoiñ びょういん (病院) *n.* hospital. ⟪⇨ nyuuiñ; taiiñ⟫

byoˈoki びょうき (病気) *n.* illness; sickness; disease:
byooki *ni naru* (病気になる) become *ill* | *Kare wa* byooki *da.* (彼は病気だ) He is *ill.* ⟪⇨ hatsubyoo⟫

byoˈoniñ びょうにん (病人) *n.* patient; sick person.

byoˈosha びょうしゃ (描写) *n.* description; portrait.
byoosha suru (~する) *vt.* describe; portray.

byoˈoshi びょうし (病死) *n.* death from a disease.
byooshi suru (~する) *vi.* die from an illness.

byoˈoshiñ びょうしん (秒針) *n.* (of a clock) second hand.
⟪⇨ byoo[1]; fuñshiñ⟫

byoˈoshitsu びょうしつ (病室) *n.* sickroom; ward.

byoˈotoo びょうとう (病棟) *n.* ward (in a hospital).

C

cha ちゃ (茶) *n.* **1** tea; green tea. ★ When referring to the beverage, it is usually called '*o-cha.*'
2 tea plant.
3 brown. ⟪⇨ chairo⟫

chaˈiro ちゃいろ (茶色) *n.* brown.

chaˈkkaˈri ちゃっかり *adv.* (~ to; ~ suru) shrewdly; smartly; cleverly:
Ano ko wa chakkari shite iru. (あの子はちゃっかりしている) That boy *is shrewd.*

-chaku[1] ちゃく (着) *suf.* (after a numeral) the order of arrival; place:
Marasoñ de it-chaku *ni natta.* (マラソンで1着になった) I came in *first* in the marathon. ⟪⇨ -i[1]⟫

-chaku[2] ちゃく (着) *suf.* [after a place name] arrival:
gogo ni-ji Narita-chaku *no biñ* (午後2時成田着の便) the plane *arriving* at Narita at two P.M.

-chaku[3] ちゃく (着) *suf.* counter for dresses, suits, etc.

chaˈkuchaku ちゃくちゃく (着々) *adv.* (~ to) steadily; according to plan; step by step:
Kooji wa chakuchaku *to susuñde imasu.* (工事は着々と進んでいます) The construction work is proceeding *according to plan.*

chaˈkujitsu ちゃくじつ (着実) *a.n.* (~ na, ni) steady; sound; solid:
Keekaku wa chakujitsu *ni susuñde imasu.* (計画は着実に進んでいます) The plan is making *steady* progress.

chaˈkuriku ちゃくりく (着陸) *n.* landing.
chakuriku suru (~する) *vi.* make a landing; land. ⟪↔ ririku⟫

chaˈkuseki ちゃくせき (着席) *n.* taking a seat; sitting.
chakuseki suru (~する) *vi.* sit down; have a seat.

chaˈkushoku ちゃくしょく (着色) *n.* coloration; coloring.
chakushoku suru (~する) *vt.* color; paint.

chaˈkushu ちゃくしゅ (着手) *n.* start; commencement.
chakushu suru (~する) *vi.* start; begin; set about. ⟪⇨ hajimeru⟫

chaˈkusoo ちゃくそう (着想) *n.* idea; conception.

-chañ ちゃん *suf.* **1** (used after a given name to address children affectionately): ★ The first name is often shortened. *Sachiko* >*Sat*-chañ, *Hiroshi*>*Hiro*-chañ.
2 (used after a kinship word by a small child):
o-nee-chañ (おねえちゃん) one's

older sister / o-jii-chañ (おじいちゃん) one's *grandfather*.

cha-ˈno-ma ちゃのま (茶の間) *n.* living [sitting] room. ⟪⇨ ima²⟫

cha-ˈno-yu ちゃのゆ (茶の湯) *n.* tea ceremony. ⟪⇨ sadoo⟫

chaˈñsu チャンス *n.* good chance; opportunity. ★ Used only with reference to a favorable occasion.

chaˈñto ちゃんと *adv.* (～ suru) (of an action) properly done; without fail; exactly:
Kaze ga hairanai yoo ni doa o chañto *shime nasai.* (風が入らないようにドアをちゃんと閉めなさい) Please shut the door *properly* to keep the wind out. ⟪⇨ kichiñto⟫

chaˈwañ ちゃわん (茶碗) *n.* teacup; rice bowl. ⟪⇨ yunomi⟫

chi¹ ち (血) *n.* **1** blood:
chi *o tomeru* (血を止める) stop the *bleeding*.
2 family relation:
Kare-ra wa chi *no tsunagari ga aru.* (彼らは血のつながりがある) They are related by *blood*.

chiˈ² ち (地) *n.* the earth; the ground; district.

chiˈchiˈ¹ ちち (父) *n.* **1** father. ⟪↔ haha⟫ ⟪⇨ chichi-oya; o-too-sañ⟫
2 originator:
Kare wa Nihoñ no kiñdai-kagaku no chichi *desu.* (彼は日本の近代科学の父です) He is the *father* of modern science in Japan.

chiˈchiˈ² ちち (乳) *n.* **1** milk:
akañboo ni chichi o nomaseru (赤ん坊に乳を飲ませる) *breast-feed* a baby.
2 (mother's) breast.

chiˈchi-oya ちちおや (父親) *n.* male parent; father. ⟪↔ haha-oya⟫ ⟪⇨ chichi¹⟫

chiˈe ちえ (知恵) *n.* wisdom; sense; brains.
chie o shiboru (～をしぼる) think hard: *Watashi-tachi wa miñna de* chie o shibotta. (私たちはみんなで知恵をしぼった) We all *racked our brains*. ⟪⇨ atama⟫

chiˈgai ちがい (違い) *n.* difference; distinction; disparity. ⟪⇨ sa¹⟫

-chigai ちがい (違い) *suf.* **1** mis-; error; mistake: ★ Attached to a noun or the continuative base of a verb.
kañ-chigai (勘違い) a *mistaken* idea / *kiki*-chigai (聞き違い) a *mis*-hearing. ⟪⇨ hitochigai⟫
2 (with a numeral) difference: ★ Often the difference in age between siblings.
Watashi to ani wa mittsu-chigai *desu.* (私と兄は三つ違いです) My brother is three years *older* than me.

chiˈgainaˈi ちがいない (違いない) must; be certain; be sure: ★ Polite equivalent is '*chigai arimaseñ*.'
Kare ga itte iru koto wa hoñtoo ni chigainai. (彼が言っていることは本当に違いない) What he says *must be* true. ⟪⇨ tashika⟫

chiˈga·u ちがう (違う) *vi.* (chiga-i-; chigaw·a-; chigat-te Ⓒ)
1 be different; differ:
Kuni ni yotte kotoba ya shuukañ ga chigaimasu. (国によって言葉や習慣が違います) Language and customs *differ* from country to country. ⟪⇨ sooi¹⟫
2 wrong; incorrect:
Kotae ga chigatte iru. (答えが違っている) The answer to the question *is wrong*.

chiˈgiˈr·u¹ ちぎる (千切る) *vt.* (chi-gir·i-; chigir·a-; chigit·te Ⓒ) tear off; tear to pieces:
Pañ o komakaku chigitte, *tori ni yatta.* (パンを細かくちぎって, 鳥にやった) I *broke* the bread *into pieces* and gave it to the birds.

chiˈgiˈr·u² ちぎる (契る) *vt.* (chi-gir·i-; chigir·a-; chigit-te Ⓒ)
1 pledge; vow; promise:
Futari wa ee-eñ no ai o chigitta. (二人は永遠の愛を契った) The two

pledged their eternal love.
2 share a bed.

chiʳheeseñ ちへいせん (地平線) *n.* horizon. ★ The line where the sky and the land seem to meet. ⟪⇨ suiheeseñ⟫

chiʳhoˀo ちほう (地方) *n.* **1** district; region; area: ★ Refers to a particular region of a country.
Kañtoo-chihoo (関東地方) the Kanto *district*. ⟪⇨ chiiki⟫
2 the country; the provinces. ⟪⇨ inaka⟫

chiˀi ちい (地位) *n.* position; status; standing.

chiˀiki ちいき (地域) *n.* area; region; zone: ★ '*Chiiki*' implies a more limited area than '*chihoo*.'
Hiroi chiiki *ni watatte sakumotsu ga higai o uketa.* (広い地域にわたって作物が被害を受けた) The crops were badly damaged over a large *area*. ⟪⇨ chiku; chitai⟫

chiʳisaˀ·i ちいさい (小さい) *a.* (-ku)
1 small; little:
chiisai *kuruma* (小さい車) a *small* car. ⟪↔ ookii⟫
2 trivial; petty:
Chiisai *koto ni kuyokuyo suru no wa yame nasai.* (小さいことにくよくよするのはやめなさい) Don't worry about *trivial* matters. ⟪↔ ookii⟫ ⟪⇨ komakai⟫

chiˀisa-na ちいさな (小さな) *attrib.* small; little; trivial:
Kare wa chiisa-na *mondai ni wa kodawaranai.* (彼は小さな問題にはこだわらない) He does not care about *trivial* matters. ⟪↔ ooki-na⟫ ⟪⇨ chiisai⟫

chiˀji ちじ (知事) *n.* (prefectural) governor:
keñ[*fu*]-chiji (県[府]知事) the *governor* of a prefecture.

chiʳjimar·u ちぢまる (縮まる) *vi.* (-mar·i-; -mar·a-; -mat·te [C]) get shorter or smaller:
Kondo no taikai de kiroku ga ni-byoo chijimatta. (今度の大会で記録が2秒縮まった) In this meet, two seconds *were clipped off* the record. ⟪⇨ chijimeru⟫

chiʳjime·ru ちぢめる (縮める) *vt.* (-me-te [V]) shorten; reduce:
sukaato no take o chijimeru (スカートの丈を縮める) *shorten* the length of a skirt. ⟪⇨ chijimaru⟫

chiʳjim·u ちぢむ (縮む) *vi.* (chiji-m·i-; chijim·a-; chijiñ-de [C]) shrink; contract:
Kono shatsu wa aratte mo chijimanai. (このシャツは洗っても縮まない) This shirt *doesn't shrink* in the wash.

chiʳjiñ ちじん (知人) *n.* acquaintance; friend.

chiʳjire·ru ちぢれる (縮れる) *vi.* (chijire-te [V]) (of hair) wave; curl; frizz.

chiʳjoo ちじょう (地上) *n.* the ground; the land surface:
chijoo *juuni-kai no biru* (地上12階のビル) a building with twelve stories above *the ground*. ⟪↔ chika⟫

chiʳkaˀ ちか (地下) *n.* underground:
Chuushajoo wa chika *ni arimasu.* (駐車場は地下にあります) The parking space is down in the *basement*. ⟪↔ chijoo⟫

chiʳkaˀdoo ちかどう (地下道) *n.* underground passage.

chiʳkaˀgoro ちかごろ (近頃) *adv.* (~ no) lately; recently; nowadays:
Chikagoro *no wakai hito wa yoku kaigai e iku.* (近ごろの若い人はよく海外へ行く) *Today's* youngsters frequently go abroad. ⟪⇨ kono-goro⟫

chiʳkaˀ·i[1] ちかい (近い) *a.* (-ku)
1 near; close:
Tookyoo-eki wa koko kara chikai. (東京駅はここから近い) Tokyo Station is *near* here. ⟪↔ tooi⟫
2 almost; nearly:
Natsu mo owari ni chikai. (夏も終わりに近い) Summer is *almost* over.

chiʳkai[2] ちかい (誓い) *n.* oath; vow; pledge:

chikai *o tateru* (誓いをたてる) swear an *oath*. ⟪⇨ chikau⟫

chi⌈ka⌉ku ちかく (近く) *n.* neighborhood:
Kono chikaku *ni wa suupaa ga takusañ arimasu.* (この近くにはスーパーがたくさんあります) There are a lot of supermarkets *around here*. ⟪↔ tooku⟫ ⟪⇨ chikai[1]⟫
— *adv.* **1** almost; nearly:
★ Often with a numeral.
Kare wa moo ik-kagetsu chikaku *yasuñde iru.* (彼はもう1か月近く休んでいる) He has been absent *nearly* a month now.
2 (of time) soon; before long:
Ano futari wa chikaku *kekkoñ suru soo desu.* (あの二人は近く結婚するそうです) I hear that those two are going to get married *soon*.

chi⌈ka⌉michi ちかみち (近道) *n.* shortcut; the shortest way. ⟪↔ toomawari⟫

chi⌈kara⌉ ちから (力) *n.* **1** power; ability:
Watashi no chikara *de dekiru koto wa nañ de mo yarimasu.* (私の力でできることは何でもやります) I will do everything in my *power*.
2 strength; force; might.
chikara-ippai (〜いっぱい) with all one's might.
chikara o ireru (〜を入れる) make efforts.

chi⌈karazuyo⌉·i ちからづよい (力強い) *a.* (-ku) powerful; strong; reassuring:
Kare kara chikarazuyoi *hagemashi o uketa.* (彼から力強い励ましを受けた) I received *reassuring* encouragement from him.

chi⌈katetsu ちかてつ (地下鉄) *n.* subway; underground railway.

chi⌈ka⌉·u ちかう (誓う) *vt.* (chikai-; chikaw·a-; chikat-te Ⓒ) swear; pledge; vow:
Shooniñ wa shiñjitsu o noberu to chikatta. (証人は真実を述べると誓った) The witness *swore* to tell the truth. ⟪⇨ chikai[2]⟫

chi⌈kayo⌉r·u ちかよる (近寄る) *vi.* (-yor·i-; -yor·a-; -yot-te Ⓒ) approach; get near:
Abunai tokoro ni wa chikayoranai *hoo ga ii.* (危ないところには近寄らないほうがいい) You'd better *keep away* from dangerous places.

chi⌈kazuke⌉·ru ちかづける (近付ける) *vt.* (-zuke-te Ⓥ) bring close; move nearer. ⟪⇨ chikazuku⟫

chi⌈kazu⌉k·u ちかづく (近付く) *vi.* (-zuk·i-; -zuk·a-; -zu·i-te Ⓒ) **1** approach; come [draw] near:
Taifuu ga Nihoñ ni chikazuite iru. (台風が日本に近づいている) A typhoon *is approaching* Japan.
2 become acquainted; approach:
Añna otoko ni wa chikazukanai *hoo ga ii.* (あんな男には近づかないほうがいい) You had better *keep away from* such a fellow. ⟪⇨ chikazukeru⟫

chi⌈kee ちけい (地形) *n.* the lay of the land; geographical features.

chi⌈koku ちこく (遅刻) *n.* late coming; being late.
chikoku suru (〜する) *vi.* be [come] late. ⟪⇨ okureru⟫

chi⌉ku ちく (地区) *n.* district; zone; area: ★ Refers to a section or an area with some distinctive feature.
Kare wa kono chiku *no daihyoo desu.* (彼はこの地区の代表です) He is the representative of this *district*. ⟪⇨ chiiki⟫

chi⌈ku⌉bi ちくび (乳首) *n.* nipple; teat.

chi⌈kuseki ちくせき (蓄積) *n.* accumulation.
chikuseki suru (〜する) *vt.* accumulate; store up: *tomi o* chikuseki suru (富を蓄積する) *accumulate* a fortune.

chi⌈kyuu ちきゅう (地球) *n.* the earth; the globe.

chi⌈mamire ちまみれ (血塗れ) *n.* being bloody:
chimamire *no taoru* (血まみれのタオル) a *bloodstained* towel.

chi⌈mee ちめい(地名) *n.* place-name.

chi⌈me⌉eshoo ちめいしょう(致命傷) *n.* fatal wound [injury]; deathblow.

-chiñ ちん(賃) *suf.* pay; fare; rate; charge:
deñsha-chiñ (電車賃) a train *fare* / kari-chiñ (借り賃) a *rent*; *hire*.
(⇨ -ryoo; -dai²)

chi⌈ñbotsu ちんぼつ(沈没) *n.* sinking (of a ship).
chiñbotsu suru (〜する) *vi.* sink; go down. (⇨ shizumu)

chi⌉ñchiñ ちんちん *adv.* (the sound of whistling):
Yakañ ga chiñchiñ *natte iru.* (やかんがちんちんなっている) The kettle is *singing*.

chi⌈ñgiñ ちんぎん(賃金) *n.* wages; pay. (⇨ gekkyuu; kyuuryoo)

chi⌈ñmoku ちんもく(沈黙) *n.* silence; reticence.
chiñmoku suru (〜する) *vi.* hold one's tongue; be silent. (⇨ damaru)

chi⌉noo ちのう(知能) *n.* intelligence; mental ability:
chinoo-*shisuu* (知能指数) an *intelligence* quotient. (⇨ chisee)

chi⌈ñretsu ちんれつ(陳列) *n.* exhibition; display.
chiñretsu suru (〜する) *vt.* exhibit; display.

chi⌈ñtai-ju⌉utaku ちんたいじゅうたく(賃貸住宅) *n.* rental house [apartment]. (⇨ buñjoo-juutaku)

chi⌈rabar·u ちらばる(散らばる) *vi.* (-bar·i-; -bar·a-; -bat-te Ⓒ) scatter; be strewn:
Akikañ ga hiroba ni takusañ chirabatte iru. (空き缶が広場にたくさん散らばっている) Many empty cans *are strewn* over the square. (⇨ chiru)

chi⌉rachira ちらちら *adv.* (〜 to; 〜 suru) **1** (the state of something small and light falling slowly):
Yuki ga chirachira *(to) furi-hajimeta.* (雪がちらちら(と)降り始めた) Snow has started to fall *lightly*.
2 (the state of small lights twinkling):
Terebi no gameñ ga chirachira *shite iru.* (テレビの画面がちらちらしている) There is a *flutter* on the TV screen.
3 (the state of seeing or hearing on and off):
Kare wa chirachira *(to) kochira o mita.* (彼はちらちら(と)こちらを見た) He kept *glancing* in my direction.

chi⌈rakar·u ちらかる(散らかる) *vi.* (-kar·i-; -kar·a-; -kat-te Ⓒ) be scattered; be littered; be untidy:
Kare no heya wa chirakatte ita. (彼の部屋は散らかっていた) His room *was a mess*. (⇨ chirakasu)

chi⌈rakas·u ちらかす(散らかす) *vt.* (-kash·i-; -kas·a-; -kash·i-te Ⓒ) scatter; litter:
Gomi o chirakasanai de *kudasai*. (ごみを散らかさないでください) *Don't litter*, please. (⇨ chirakaru)

chi⌈ras·u ちらす(散らす) *vt.* (chirash·i-; chiras·a-; chirash·i-te Ⓒ) (*literary*) scatter:
Kaze ga niwa ichimeñ ni ko no ha o chirashita. (風が庭一面に木の葉を散らした) The wind *scattered* leaves all over the garden.
(⇨ chiru)

chi⌈ri¹ ちり(塵) *n.* dust; dirt.
(⇨ gomi; hokori²)

chi⌉ri² ちり(地理) *n.* geography; geography of a neighborhood.

chi⌈rigami ちりがみ(ちり紙) *n.* tissue; toilet paper (in separate sheets).

chi⌈rigami-ko⌉okañ ちりがみこうかん(ちり紙交換) *n.* an exchange of old newspapers and magazines for tissue or toilet rolls.

chi⌈r·u ちる(散る) *vi.* (chir·i-; chir·a-; chit-te Ⓒ) **1** fall:
Ame de sakura no hana ga sukkari chitte *shimatta.* (雨で桜の花がすっかり散ってしまった) The cherry blossoms have all *fallen* in the rain.
(⇨ chirasu)

2 scatter; disperse:
Kooeñ ni kamikuzu ga chitte iru. (公園に紙くずが散っている) *There is* paper *all over* the park.
《⇨ chirasu》

chi⌈ryoo ちりょう(治療) *n.* medical treatment.
chiryoo suru (〜する) *vt.* treat; cure: *Watashi wa me o* chiryoo shite moratta. (私は眼を治療してもらった) I *had* my eyes *treated.*

chi⌉see ちせい(知性) *n.* intellect; intelligence. 《⇨ chiteki》

chi⌉shiki ちしき(知識) *n.* knowledge; information; learning.

chi⌉sso ちっそ(窒素) *n.* nitrogen: chisso-*sañkabutsu* (窒素酸化物) *nitrogen* oxide.

chi⌈ssoku ちっそく(窒息) *n.* suffocation; choking.
chissoku suru (〜する) *vi.* be suffocated; be choked.

chi⌉tai ちたい(地帯) *n.* zone; area; region; belt:
añzeñ-chitai (安全地帯) a safety *zone.* 《⇨ chiiki; chiku》

chi⌈teki ちてき(知的) *a.n.* (〜 na, ni) intellectual; intelligent.
《⇨ chisee; chinoo》

chi⌈tsu⌉jo ちつじょ(秩序) *n.* order; system:
shakai no chitsujo *o tamotsu* [*midasu*] (社会の秩序を保つ[乱す]) maintain [disturb] social *order.*

chi⌈tto⌉-mo ちっとも *adv.* (with a negative) (not) a bit; (not) at all:
Kono bañgumi wa chitto-mo *omoshirokunai.* (この番組はちっともおもしろくない) This program is *not at all* interesting. 《⇨ sukoshi mo》

chi⌉zu ちず(地図) *n.* map; atlas; chart.

-cho ちょ(著) *suf.* written by:
Kawabata Yasunari-cho *"Yukiguni"* (川端康成著『雪国』) "Snow Country" *written by* Yasunari Kawabata.

cho⌈chiku ちょちく(貯蓄) *n.* savings.
chochiku suru (〜する) *vi.* save up: *roogo ni sonaete* chochiku suru (老後に備えて貯蓄する) *save up* for one's old age. 《⇨ chokiñ; yokiñ》

cho⌈kiñ ちょきん(貯金) *n.* savings; deposit.
chokiñ suru (〜する) *vi., vt.* save; deposit: *Watashi wa maitsuki sañmañ-eñ* chokiñ shite imasu. (私は毎月 3 万円貯金しています) I *save* 30,000 yen every month.
《⇨ yokiñ; chochiku》

cho⌈kkaku ちょっかく(直角) *n.* right angle.

cho⌈kkee ちょっけい(直径) *n.* diameter.

cho⌈kki チョッキ *n.* vest; waistcoat.

cho⌈kkoo ちょっこう(直行) *n.* going straight [direct].
chokkoo suru (〜する) *vi.* go straight [direct].

cho⌈kumeñ ちょくめん(直面) *n.* confrontation; facing.
chokumeñ suru (〜する) *vi.* be faced; be confronted.
《⇨ butsukaru》

cho⌈kuseñ ちょくせん(直線) *n.* straight line. 《↔ kyokuseñ》

cho⌈kusetsu ちょくせつ(直接) *adv.* (〜 no) directly; immediately:
Kare to chokusetsu *kooshoo shite mimasu.* (彼と直接交渉してみます) I will try to negotiate *directly* with him. 《↔ kañsetsu[1]》 《⇨ jika ni》

cho⌈kusetsu-teki ちょくせつてき(直接的) *a.n.* (〜 na, ni) direct; immediate: 《↔ kañsetsu-teki》
chokusetsu-teki *na geñiñ* (直接的な原因) the *immediate* cause.

cho⌉o[1] ちょう(腸) *n.* intestines; bowels.

cho⌉o[2] ちょう(兆) *n.* one trillion (U.S.); one billion (Brit.).
《⇨ APP. 3》

cho⌉o[3] ちょう(蝶) *n.* butterfly.

cho⌉o[4] ちょう(庁) *n.* agency; government office. 《⇨ APP. 7》

cho⌉o- ちょう(超) *pref.* super-; ultra-: choo-*tokkyuu* (超特急) *super*express / choo-koosoobiru (超高層ビル) a *skyscraper*.

-choo[1] ちょう(町) *suf.* town; block; street. ★ An administrative division of a city or metropolitan area. ⟪⇨ -machi; juusho⟫

-choo[2] ちょう(長) *suf.* head; boss; chief; leader: *bu*-choo (部長) the *head* of a division / eki-choo (駅長) a *stationmaster* / iiñ-choo (委員長) a *chairman*.

cho⌈obo ちょうぼ(帳簿) *n.* account book: choobo *o tsukeru* [*shimeru*] (帳簿をつける[締める]) keep [close] the *accounts*. ⟪⇨ choomeñ⟫

cho⌈ochi⌉ñ ちょうちん(提灯) *n.* (paper) lantern.

cho⌉ocho(o) ちょうちょ(う)(蝶々) *n.* = choo[3].

cho⌈oda⌉i ちょうだい(頂戴) please; please do [give] ...: ★ Used at the end of a sentence and follows a noun or the *te*-form of a verb. Informal equivalent of '*kudasai*.' Used mainly by children and women, and by men to their inferiors.
Kore o choodai. (これをちょうだい) *Please give* this to me. / *Kono tegami o kare ni* watashite choodai. (この手紙を彼に渡してちょうだい) *Please hand over* this letter to him.

cho⌈odai s·uru ちょうだいする(頂戴する) *vt.* (sh·i-; sh·i-; sh·i-te ⓘ)
1 (*humble*) receive; get:
Koko ni iñkañ o choodai shitai *no desu ga.* (ここに印鑑をちょうだいしたいのですが) May I *have* your seal impression here?
2 (*humble*) eat; drink:
Moo juubuñ choodai shimashita. (もう十分ちょうだいしました) I *have had* enough, thank you. ⟪⇨ itadaku⟫

cho⌈odo ちょうど(丁度) *adv.* just; exactly:
Ima choodo *shichi-ji desu.* (今ちょうど7時です) It is *exactly* seven o'clock.

cho⌈ofuku ちょうふく(重複) *n.* overlap; duplication: repetition.
choofuku suru (～する) *vi.* repeat; overlap.

cho⌉ohoo ちょうほう(重宝) *a.n.* (～ na) useful; handy; helpful. ⟪⇨ beñri⟫
choohoo suru (～する) *vt.* find something handy [useful].

cho⌈ohookee ちょうほうけい(長方形) *n.* rectangle.

cho⌈oiñ ちょういん(調印) *n.* signing; signature.
... ni chooiñ suru (...に～する) *vi.* sign (a treaty, contract, etc.). ⟪⇨ saiñ⟫

cho⌉ojo ちょうじょ(長女) *n.* eldest [oldest] daughter. ⟪↔ choonañ⟫

cho⌈ojo⌉o ちょうじょう(頂上) *n.* top; summit; peak.

cho⌈oka ちょうか(超過) *n.* excess; surplus.
chooka suru (～する) *vt.* exceed; be more than. ⟪⇨ koeru[2]⟫

cho⌈okañ[1] ちょうかん(朝刊) *n.* morning paper; the morning edition of a paper. ⟪↔ yuukañ[2]⟫ ⟪⇨ shiñbuñ⟫

cho⌈okañ[2] ちょうかん(長官) *n.* the director [head] of a (government) office.

cho⌉oki ちょうき(長期) *n.* a long (period of) time. ⟪↔ tañki[1]⟫

cho⌈okoku ちょうこく(彫刻) *n.* sculpture; carving.
chookoku suru (～する) *vt.* sculpt; carve.

cho⌈ome ちょうめ(丁目) *n.* chome: ★ A section of a city, larger than '*bañchi*.'
Giñza yoñ-choome (銀座4丁目) Ginza 4-chome. ⟪⇨ bañchi; juusho⟫

cho⌈ome⌉ñ ちょうめん(帳面) *n.* notebook; account book:
choomeñ *o tsukeru* (帳面をつける) keep an *account book*. ⟪⇨ choobo; nooto⟫

cho[oomi]ryoo ちょうみりょう (調味料) *n.* seasoning; flavoring.

cho[oona]ñ ちょうなん (長男) *n.* eldest [oldest] son. ⟪↔ choojo⟫

cho[oori]shi ちょうりし (調理師) *n.* qualified cook.

cho]osa ちょうさ (調査) *n.* investigation; survey; research.
choosa suru (〜する) *vt.* investigate; make a survey.

cho[oosa]dañ ちょうさだん (調査団) *n.* survey group; investigating commission.

cho[oosee ちょうせい (調整) *n.* adjustment; regulation.
choosee suru (〜する) *vt.* adjust; regulate.

cho[oosen ちょうせん (挑戦) *n.* challenge; attempt.
chooseñ suru (〜する) *vi.* challenge; attempt; try. ⟪⇨ idomu⟫

cho[oosetsu ちょうせつ (調節) *n.* control; adjustment; regulation.
choosetsu suru (〜する) *vt.* control; adjust; regulate.

cho[ooshi ちょうし (調子) *n.*
1 condition:
Kono kuruma wa chooshi *ga yoi.* (この車は調子が良い) This car is in good *condition.*
2 way; manner:
Sono chooshi *de yari nasai.* (その調子でやりなさい) Keep trying in that *way.*
3 tune; tone:
Kono gitaa wa chooshi *ga atte* [*hazurete*] *iru.* (このギターは調子が合って[はずれて]いる) This guitar is in [out of] *tune.*
chooshi o awaseru (〜を合わせる) adapt oneself; humor.

cho]osho ちょうしょ (長所) *n.* strong [good] point; merit; advantage. ⟪↔ tañsho; ketteñ⟫

cho[ooshoku ちょうしょく (朝食) *n.* breakfast. ⟪⇨ asagohañ; asameshi⟫ ⟪↔ bañgohañ⟫

cho[ooshuu ちょうしゅう (聴衆) *n.* audience; attendance.

cho]oteñ ちょうてん (頂点) *n.* peak; top; climax:
chooteñ *ni tassuru* (頂点に達する) reach the *peak.*

cho[oowa ちょうわ (調和) *n.* harmony.
choowa suru (〜する) *vi.* harmonize; match.

cho]sha ちょしゃ (著者) *n.* writer of a book; author.

cho]sho ちょしょ (著書) *n.* book written by the author; work.

cho[su]ichi ちょすいち (貯水池) *n.* reservoir.

cho]tto ちょっと *adv.* **1** (of degree, quality, quantity, etc.) just a little; slightly:
Satoo o moo chotto *irete kudasai.* (砂糖をもうちょっと入れてください) Please add *a little more* sugar.
2 (of time) just a minute; for a moment:
Chotto *o-machi kudasai.* (ちょっとお待ちください) Please wait *a moment.*
3 rather; pretty:
Sore wa chotto *omoshiro-soo desu ne.* (それはちょっとおもしろそうですね) That sounds *rather* interesting.
4 (with a negative) just; easily:
Kare ni doko de atta ka chotto *omoidasenai.* (彼にどこで会ったかちょっと思い出せない) I *just* cannot remember where I met him.

cho[zoo ちょぞう (貯蔵) *n.* storage; preservation; stock.
chozoo suru (〜する) *vt.* store; preserve.

chu]u[1] ちゅう (中) *n.* middle; medium; average:
Kare no seeseki wa chuu *no joo desu.* (彼の成績は中の上です) His school record is slightly above *average.*

chu[u[2] ちゅう (注) *n.* note; annotation:
chuu o tsukeru (注をつける) *annotate.*

-chuu ちゅう (中) *suf.* **1** (used to express time) in; during; within; through; throughout:
Koñshuu-chuu *ni reñraku itashimasu.* (今週中に連絡いたします) I

will get in touch with you *during* the week. 《⇨ -juu[1]》
2 (used to express a continuing state, condition or situation) under; in; during:
Sono dooro wa ima kooji-chuu *desu.* (その道路は今工事中です) The road is now *under* construction.
3 out of (the stated number):
Juuniñ-chuu *hachi-niñ ga sono añ ni sañsee shita.* (10人中8人がその案に賛成した) Eight *out of* ten were in favor of the proposal.

chu^r^uburu ちゅうぶる (中古) *n.* used [secondhand] article. 《⇨ chuuko》

chu^1^ucho ちゅうちょ (躊躇) *n.* hesitation; indecision.
chuucho suru (～する) *vi.* hesitate; waver. 《⇨ tamerau》

chu^r^udañ ちゅうだん (中断) *n.* discontinuance; interruption.
chuudañ suru (～する) *vi.*, *vt.* stop; discontinue; interrupt.

chu^1^udoku ちゅうどく (中毒) *n.* poisoning:
shoku[*gasu*]-chuudoku (食[ガス]中毒) food [gas] *poisoning.*
chuudoku suru (～する) *vi.* be poisoned.

chu^r^uga^1^eri ちゅうがえり (宙返り) *n.* somersault; looping.

chu^r^uga^1^kkoo ちゅうがっこう (中学校) *n.* junior high school; lower secondary school. 《⇨ gakkoo》

chu^1^ugaku ちゅうがく (中学) *n.* Shortened form of '*chuugakkoo*' (junior high school).

chu^r^uga^1^kusee ちゅうがくせい (中学生) *n.* junior high school pupil.

chu^r^ugata ちゅうがた (中型) *n.* medium size:
chuugata *no kuruma* (中型の車) a *medium-sized* car. 《⇨ oogata; kogata》

chu^r^ugeñ ちゅうげん (中元) *n.* midyear gift. ★ Usually used with an honorific '*o*-.' In appreciation of special favors received, it is sent between July and August. 《⇨ (o)seebo》

chu^1^ui ちゅうい (注意) *n.* **1** attention:
Dare mo kare no itta koto ni chuui *o harawanakatta.* (だれも彼の言ったことに注意を払わなかった) Nobody paid *attention* to what he said.
2 care; caution:
Kono shigoto wa tokubetsu no chuui *ga iru.* (この仕事は特別の注意がいる) This work needs special *care.*
3 warning:
Kanojo wa watashi no chuui *o mushi shita.* (彼女は私の注意を無視した) She disregarded my *warning.*
chuui suru (～する) *vi.* take care; caution; advise; warn: *Korobanai yoo ni* chuui shi nasai. (転ばないように注意しなさい) *Take care* that you don't fall.

chu^r^uibuka^1^·i ちゅういぶかい (注意深い) *a.* (-ku) careful; cautious; watchful. 《⇨ shiñchoo[2]; yoojiñbukai》

chu^r^ujitsu ちゅうじつ (忠実) *a.n.* (～ na, ni) **1** loyal; faithful:
Kare ni wa chuujitsu *na buka ga oozee iru.* (彼には忠実な部下がおおぜいいる) He has many *loyal* people working under him.
2 true to fact:
Kore wa geñbuñ ni chuujitsu *na yaku da.* (これは原文に忠実な訳だ) This is a translation *true* to the original.

chu^r^ujuñ ちゅうじゅん (中旬) *n.* the middle ten days of a month. 《⇨ joojuñ; gejuñ》

chu^r^ukai ちゅうかい (仲介) *n.* intermediation; mediation:
ryoosha no chuukai o suru (両者の仲介をする) *mediate* between two parties.

chu^r^ukañ ちゅうかん (中間) *n.* interim; middle:
Eki wa sono futatsu no machi no chuukañ *ni dekimasu.* (駅はその二つの町の中間にできます) The train station will be built *in between* the

two towns.

chu⌈uka-ryo⌉ori ちゅうかりょうり (中華料理) *n.* Chinese dishes [food]; Chinese cooking [cuisine].

chu⌈uka-so⌉ba ちゅうかそば (中華そば) *n.* Chinese noodles. (⇨ raameñ)

chu⌈ukee ちゅうけい (中継) *n.* relay; hookup; transmission.
chuukee suru (〜する) *vt.* relay.

chu⌈uko ちゅうこ (中古) *n.* used [secondhand] article:
chuuko-*sha* (中古車) a *secondhand* car. (⇨ chuuburu)

chu⌈ukoku ちゅうこく (忠告) *n.* advice; counsel.
chuukoku suru (〜する) *vt.* advise; counsel.

chu⌈uko⌉oneñ ちゅうこうねん (中高年) *n.* (people of) middle and advanced age; senior citizen. (⇨ chuuneñ)

chu⌈ukyuu ちゅうきゅう (中級) *n.* medium level. (⇨ shokyuu; jookyuu)

chu⌈umoku ちゅうもく (注目) *n.* attention; notice.
chuumoku suru (〜する) *vi.*, *vt.* pay attention; watch.

chu⌈umoñ ちゅうもん (注文) *n.*
1 order (of goods):
Chuumoñ *o sabaku no ni isogashii.* (注文をさばくのに忙しい) We are busy filling *orders*.
2 request; demand:
Soñna chuumoñ *ni wa oojirarenai.* (そんな注文には応じられない) I cannot comply with such a *demand*.
chuumoñ suru (〜する) *vt.* give an order; order.

chu⌈uneñ ちゅうねん (中年) *n.* middle age:
chuuneñ *no fuufu* (中年の夫婦) a *middle-aged* couple.

chu⌈uo⌉o ちゅうおう (中央) *n.* center; middle. (⇨ mañnaka)

chu⌈uritsu ちゅうりつ (中立) *n.* neutrality:
chuuritsu *o mamoru* (中立を守る) observe *neutrality*.

chu⌈uryuu ちゅうりゅう (中流) *n.*
1 middle class:
chuuryuu *no katee* (中流の家庭) a *middle-class* family. (⇨ jooryuu; kasoo)
2 the middle of a river.

chu⌈usai ちゅうさい (仲裁) *n.* arbitration; mediation.
chuusai (o) suru (〜(を)する) *vt.* arbitrate; mediate.

chu⌉usee ちゅうせい (中世) *n.* the Middle Ages; medieval times.
★ The Japanese Middle Ages comprise the Kamakura period (12th century) to the Azuchi-Momoyama period (late 16th–early 17th centuries). (⇨ APP. 9)

chu⌈useñ ちゅうせん (抽選) *n.* drawing; lot: chuuseñ *de kimeru* (抽選で決める) decide by *lot*.

chu⌈usha[1] ちゅうしゃ (駐車) *n.* parking:
Koko wa chuusha-*kiñshi desu.* (ここは駐車禁止です) *Parking* is prohibited here.
chuusha suru (〜する) *vi.* park. (⇨ chuushajoo)

chu⌈usha[2] ちゅうしゃ (注射) *n.* injection; shot.
chuusha suru (〜する) *vt.* inject.

chu⌈ushajoo ちゅうしゃじょう (駐車場) *n.* parking lot; car park. (⇨ chuusha[1])

chu⌈ushi ちゅうし (中止) *n.* stoppage; discontinuance; suspension.
chuushi suru (〜する) *vt.* stop; call off; discontinue; suspend.

chu⌈ushiñ ちゅうしん (中心) *n.*
1 center:
Sono biru wa shi no chuushiñ *ni aru.* (そのビルは市の中心にある) That building is in the *center* of the city.
2 focus; core:
Kuruma no yushutsu ga wadai no chuushiñ *datta.* (車の輸出が話題の中心だった) Car exports were the *focus* of our discussions.

chu⌈ushoku ちゅうしょく (昼食) *n.*

(*formal*) lunch. ⟪⇨ hirumeshi; hirugohañ⟫

chu⌈ushoo ちゅうしょう (中傷) *n.* slander.
chuushoo suru (〜する) *vt.* slander; speak ill of.

chu⌈ushoo-ki⌉gyoo ちゅうしょうきぎょう (中小企業) *n.* small and medium-sized enterprises.

chu⌈ushoo-teki ちゅうしょうてき (抽象的) *a.n.* (〜 na, ni) abstract:
chuushoo-teki *na giroñ* (抽象的な議論) *abstract* discussion. ⟪↔ gutaiteki⟫

chu⌈utai ちゅうたい (中退) *n.* leaving school in mid-course.
chuutai suru (〜する) *vi.* drop out; quit (school, university, etc.). ⟪⇨ taigaku⟫

chu⌈uto ちゅうと (中途) *n.* middle; the midway point:
Teñki ga warui no de chuuto *de hikikaeshita.* (天気が悪いので中途で引き返した) We turned back *halfway* because the weather was bad. ⟪⇨ tochuu⟫

D

da だ *copula.* (*informal*) ★ The corresponding formal equivalent in the written language is '*de aru*,' and the polite colloquial equivalent is '*desu*.' ⟪⇨ APP. 2⟫
1 be [am/is/are]: ★ Indicates that the subject equals the complement.
Kare wa haisha da. (彼は歯医者だ) He *is* a dentist.
2 be located in a certain place:
Boku no kuruma wa doko da? (僕の車はどこだ) Where *is* my car?
3 (indicates a situation or condition):
Kyoo wa ichi-nichi ame datta. (きょうは一日雨だった) It *rained* all day today.
4 (used as a verb substitute):
"Nomimono wa nani ni shimasu ka?" "Boku wa koohii da." (「飲物は何にしますか」「僕はコーヒーだ」) "What would you like to drink?" "I'll *drink* coffee."

da⌉asu ダース *n.* dozen.

da⌈budabu だぶだぶ *a.n.* (〜 na, ni) too large; baggy; loose.

da⌉ ga だが *conj.* but; however:
Kare wa byooiñ e katsugi-komareta. Da ga *osokatta.* (彼は病院へかつぎ込まれた. だが遅かった) He was carried into the hospital. *But* it was too late.

da⌈geki だげき (打撃) *n.* **1** hard hit; blow.
2 damage:
kañbatsu de hidoi dageki *o ukeru* (かんばつでひどい打撃を受ける) suffer serious *damage* because of the drought.
3 emotional disturbance; shock.
4 (of baseball) batting.

da⌉i[1] だい (大) *n.* bigness; large size:
Dai *wa shoo o kaneru.* (*saying*) (大は小をかねる) '*Big*' always includes 'small.'

da⌉i[2] だい (代) *n.* generation; time:
Sono mise wa kare no dai *ni sakaeta.* (その店は彼の代に栄えた) The shop flourished in his *time*.

da⌉i[3] だい (題) *n.* subject; theme.

da⌈i-[1] だい (大) *pref.* **1** big; large:
dai-*toshi* (大都市) a *large* city. ⟪↔ shoo-⟫
2 great: dai-*seekoo* (大成功) a *great* success.
3 serious; grave: dai-*moñdai* (大問題) a *serious* issue.

da⌉i-[2] だい (第) *pref.* (indicates an ordinal number):
dai-niji *sekai-taiseñ* (第二次世界大戦) *the Second* World War.

-dai[1] だい (台) *suf.* **1** (counter for relatively large vehicles or machines):
Uchi ni wa terebi ga ni-dai *aru.* (うちにはテレビが2台ある) We have *two* TVs at home.
2 mark:
*Kabuka ga niseñ-eñ-*dai *ni tasshita.* (株価が2,000円台に達した) The price of the stock reached the 2,000-yen *mark.*
3 between...and...:
asa shichi-ji-dai *no deñsha* (朝7時台の電車) the trains *between seven and eight* in the morning.

-dai[2] だい (代) *suf.* fare; rate; charge:
takushii-dai (タクシー代) a taxi *fare* / *heya*-dai (部屋代) room *rent.* ((⇨ -chiñ; -ryoo))

-dai[3] だい (代) *suf.* age; period:
Kare wa mada sañjuu-dai *desu.* (彼はまだ30代です) He is still in his *thirties.*

da⌈ibe⌉ñ だいべん (大便) *n.* feces; stool; excrement. ((⇨ fuñ[2]; kuso))

da⌈ibu だいぶ (大分) *adv.* considerably; quite; very:
Daibu *suzushiku natte kita.* (だいぶ涼しくなってきた) It has become *considerably* cool. ((⇨ kanari))

da⌈ibu⌉buñ だいぶぶん (大部分) *n.* the greater part; most:
Daibubuñ *no hito wa sono hooañ ni hañtai desu.* (大部分の人はその法案に反対です) *Most* of the people are against the bill.
— *adv.* mostly. ((⇨ hotoñdo))

da⌈ibutsu だいぶつ (大仏) *n.* huge statue of Buddha.

da⌉ichoo だいちょう (大腸) *n.* the large intestine.

da⌉idai だいだい (代々) *n.* from generation to generation; generation after generation.

da⌈idoko(ro) だいどこ(ろ) (台所) *n.* kitchen. ((⇨ katte[1]))

da⌈igaku だいがく (大学) *n.* university; college.

da⌈igaku⌉iñ だいがくいん (大学院) *n.* graduate school.

da⌈iga⌉kusee だいがくせい (大学生) *n.* university [college] student; undergraduate.

da⌈igi⌉shi だいぎし (代議士) *n.* Diet member. ★ Usually refers to a member of the House of Representatives (*Shuugiiñ*).

da⌈ihyoo だいひょう (代表) *n.* representative; delegate.
daihyoo suru (〜する) *vt.* represent.

da⌈ihyoo-teki だいひょうてき (代表的) *a.n.* (〜 na) typical; representative.

da⌉i-ichi だいいち (第一) *n.* the first; the most important thing:
Keñkoo ga dai-ichi *da.* (健康が第一だ) Health is *everything.*
— *adv.* first; to begin with:
Dai-ichi *sore wa taka-sugimasu.* (第一それは高すぎます) *To begin with,* it is too expensive.

da⌈iji[1] だいじ (大事) *a.n.* (〜 na, ni) important; valuable; precious. ((⇨ o-daiji ni; juuyoo; taisetsu))

da⌈iji[2] だいじ (大事) *n.* serious matter; crisis; emergency:
Kaji wa daiji *ni itaranakatta.* (火事は大事に至らなかった) The fire did not get *serious.* ((⇨ ichidaiji))

da⌉ijiñ だいじん (大臣) *n.* minister; secretary; cabinet member.

da⌈ijo⌉obu だいじょうぶ (大丈夫) *a.n.* (〜 na) all right; sure:
Watashi wa hitori de daijoobu *desu.* (私は一人でだいじょうぶです) I can *manage* it by myself.

da⌈iki⌉bo だいきぼ (大規模) *a.n.* (〜 na, ni) large-scale. ((⇨ oogakari))

da⌉ikiñ だいきん (代金) *n.* price; charge; bill. ((⇨ ryookiñ))

da⌉ikirai だいきらい (大嫌い) *a.n.* (〜 na) have a strong dislike; hate. ((⇨ kirai)) ((↔ daisuki))

da⌉ikoñ だいこん (大根) *n.* Japanese white radish. ((⇨ hatsukadaikoñ))

da⌉iku だいく (大工) *n.* carpenter.

《⇨ nichiyoo daiku》

-daime だいめ (代目) *suf.* the order of generations:
go-daime *no shachoo* (5 代目の社長) the *fifth* president of the company.

da⌈imee だいめい (題名) *n.* title.

da⌈ime⌉eshi だいめいし (代名詞) *n.* pronoun; synonym; epithet.

da⌈imyo⌉o だいみょう (大名) *n.* daimyo. ★ Japanese feudal lord.

da⌈inashi だいなし (台無し) *a.n.* (~ ni) ruining; spoiling:
Ame de ryokoo ga dainashi ni natta. (雨で旅行が台なしになった) Our trip *was spoiled* by the rain.

da⌈iri だいり (代理) *n.* representative; proxy:
kachoo no dairi o tsutomeru (課長の代理を務める) *act* for the section chief.

da⌉ishoo だいしょう (大小) *n.* size; measure. 《⇨ ookisa》

da⌉isuki だいすき (大好き) *a.n.* (~ na) favorite:
daisuki *na tabemono* (大好きな食べ物) one's *favorite* food. 《⇨ suki[1]》

da⌈itai だいたい (大体) *n.* outline; summary; sketch.
— *adv.* about; almost; generally:
Kare no toshi wa daitai *watashi to onaji-gurai desu.* (彼の年は大体私と同じぐらいです) He is *almost* as old as I am.

da⌈ita⌉ñ だいたん (大胆) *a.n.* (~ na, ni) daring; bold; audacious.

da⌈ito⌉oryoo だいとうりょう (大統領) *n.* president (of a country).

da⌉iya[1] ダイヤ *n.* train [bus] schedule; timetable. 《⇨ jikokuhyoo》

da⌉iya[2] ダイヤ *n.* diamond.

da⌈iyaru ダイヤル *n.* dial.
daiyaru suru (~する) *vi.* call on the phone; dial.

da⌈iyoo だいよう (代用) *n.* substitution. 《⇨ kawari》

da⌈izu だいず (大豆) *n.* soybean.

da⌉ kara だから *conj.* so; therefore; because:
Kinoo wa netsu ga atta. Da kara *gakkoo o yasuñda.* (きのうは熱があった. だから学校を休んだ) I had a temperature yesterday. *That's why* I took the day off from school.

da⌈ke だけ (丈) *p.* [follows a noun, the dictionary form and *ta*-form of a verb or adjective, an adjectival noun with '*na*' or particles]
1 only; just; no more: ★ Used to indicate a limit.
Sore o shitte iru no wa watashi dake *desu.* (それを知っているのは私だけです) I am the *only* person who knows that.
2 as...as; enough to do: ★ Used for emphasis or to indicate a limit.
Doozo suki na dake *meshiagatte kudasai.* (どうぞ好きなだけ召し上がってください) Please go ahead and eat *as much as* you wish. 《⇨ nomi[2]; shika[3]》

da⌉ kedo だけど *conj.* (*informal*) = da keredo (mo).

da⌉ keredo (mo) だけれど(も) *conj.* but; however; yet:
Ano hito wa uñdoo wa nañ de mo tokui desu. Da keredo (mo) *oyogemaseñ.* (あの人は運動は何でも得意です. だけれど(も)泳げません) He excels at all sorts of sports. *However*, he cannot swim.

da⌈ketsu だけつ (妥結) *n.* agreement; compromise settlement.
daketsu suru (~する) *vi.* come to an agreement [a settlement].

da⌈kia⌉·u だきあう (抱き合う) *vi.* (-a·i-; -a·wa-; -at-te Ⓒ) embrace [hug] each other.

da⌉kko だっこ *n.* carrying [holding] (a baby) in one's arms.
dakko suru (~する) *vt.* carry [hold] (a baby) in one's arms. 《⇨ daku》

da⌈k·u だく (抱く) *vt.* (dak·i-; dak·a-; da·i-te Ⓒ) **1** hold (a thing; a person) in one's arms; hug; embrace. 《⇨ dakko》

2 (of a bird) sit on (an egg).

da⌈kuoñ だくおん(濁音) *n.* syllables in Japanese that have a voiced consonant. ★ Indicated in writing with '゛' on the upper right-hand side of the *kana* letters. ガ (*ga*), ザ (*za*), ダ (*da*), バ (*ba*). ⟪⇨ hañ-dakuoñ; seeoñ; APP. 1⟫

da⌈kyoo だきょう(妥協) *n.* compromise; agreement.
dakyoo suru (～する) *vi.* compromise.

da⌈ma⌉r·u だまる(黙る) *vi.* (damar·i-; damar·a-; damat-te Ⓒ) stop talking [crying]; keep silent.

da⌈ma⌉s·u だます(騙す) *vt.* (damash·i-; damas·a-; damash·i-te Ⓒ) **1** cheat; trick; deceive.
2 coax (a child); use every trick to coax. ⟪⇨ gomakasu; sagi[1]⟫

da⌈ma⌉tte だまって(黙って) *adv.* without telling a person; without permission [notice]; without complaints.

da⌈me[1] だめ(駄目) *a.n.* (～ na, ni)
1 no good; useless:
Kono kamisori wa zeñzeñ dame *da.* (このかみそりは全然だめだ) This razor is completely *useless.*
2 vain; of no use:
Doryoku shita ga dame *datta.* (努力したがだめだった) I made every effort, but *in vain.* ⟪⇨ muda⟫
3 fail:
Shikeñ wa dame *datta.* (試験はだめだった) I *failed* in the examination.
4 cannot do; be poor at:
Ryoori wa dame *na ñ desu.* (料理はだめなんです) I am *not good* at cooking.
5 must not do; should not do:
O-sake o noñde wa dame *desu.* (お酒を飲んではだめです) You *shouldn't* drink. ⟪⇨ ikemaseñ; ikenai⟫
dame ni naru (～になる) *vi.* be spoiled; be ruined; go bad.
dame ni suru (～にする) *vt.* spoil; ruin.

da⌉ñ[1] だん(段) *n.* **1** step; stair; rung (of a ladder).
2 column:
*shiñbuñ no go-*dañ *kookoku* (新聞の5段広告) a five-*column* newspaper advertisement.
3 (in judo, kendo, karate, go, shogi, etc.) a degree of proficiency. ⟪⇨ kyuu[2]⟫
4 the holder of *dan.*

da⌉ñ[2] だん(壇) *n.* platform; podium.

-dañ だん(団) *suf.* group; troupe; party: *ooeñ-*dañ (応援団) a *group* of cheerleaders.

da⌈ñatsu だんあつ(弾圧) *n.* oppression; suppression; pressure.
dañatsu suru (～する) *vt.* oppress; suppress.

da⌈ñboo だんぼう(暖房) *n.* heating of a room, building, etc.
dañboo suru (～する) *vt.* heat.
⟪↔ reeboo⟫

da⌈ñbo⌉oru だんボール(段ボール) *n.* corrugated cardboard.

da⌈ñchi だんち(団地) *n.* public apartment [housing] complex.

da⌈ñdañ だんだん(段々) *adv.* (～ to, ni) gradually; little by little; one after another.
⟪⇨ sukoshi-zutsu⟫

da⌉ñjo だんじょ(男女) *n.* man and woman; both sexes.

da⌉ñjo kyo⌈ogaku だんじょきょうがく(男女共学) *n.* coeducation.
★ Sometimes abbreviated to '*kyoogaku.*'

da⌈ñkai だんかい(段階) *n.* **1** step; stage; phase:
Ima no dañkai *de wa happyoo dekimaseñ.* (今の段階では発表できません) We cannot make an announcement at this *stage.*
2 grade; rank; level.

da⌈ñketsu だんけつ(団結) *n.* union; solidarity.
dañketsu suru (～する) *vi.* unite; join together.

da⌉no だの *p.* and; or; and the like; and so forth; and what not:
Watashi wa jisho dano *sañkoosho* dano *o tsukatte shirabemashita.*

(私は辞書だの参考書だのを使って調べました) I checked it using dictionaries, reference books *and so forth*. 《⇨ ya[1]; to ka》

da⌈ñsee だんせい (男性) *n.* adult man; male. 《↔ josee》《⇨ dañshi; otoko》

da⌈ñsee-teki だんせいてき (男性的) *a.n.* (~ na, ni) (of men, women and things) manly; masculine; mannish. 《⇨ josee-teki; otokorashii》

da⌉ñshi だんし (男子) *n.* **1** boy. **2** man; male:
dañshi-*yoo toire* (男子用トイレ) the *men's* toilet. 《↔ joshi[1]》《⇨ dañsee》

da⌈ñtai だんたい (団体) *n.* party; group; body.

da⌈ñtee だんてい (断定) *n.* conclusion; decision.
dañtee suru (~する) *vt.* conclude; decide.

da⌉ñtoo だんとう (暖冬) *n.* mild winter.

-dara だら *infl. end.* ⇨ -tara.

-da⌉rake だらけ *suf.* (*n.*) [attached to a noun] be full of; be covered with: ★ Used in an unfavorable situation.
machigai-darake (間違いだらけ) *be full of* mistakes.

da⌈rashina⌉·i だらしない *a.* (-ku) **1** slovenly; sloppy; untidy. **2** weak-willed; spineless.

da⌉re だれ (誰) *n.* who; whose; whom:
Kore wa dare no *kutsu desu ka?* (これはだれの靴ですか) *Whose* shoes are these? 《⇨ donata》

da⌉re-ka だれか (誰か) *n.* someone; anyone:
Dare-ka *kanojo no juusho o shirimaseñ ka?* (だれか彼女の住所を知りませんか) Doesn't *anyone* know her address? 《⇨ donata-ka》

da⌈re⌉·ru だれる *vi.* (dare-te ⓥ) become dull; become tedious; become listless.

-dari だり *infl. end.* ⇨ -tari.

da⌈ro⌉o だろう [follows a verb, noun, adjectival noun, or adjective] (*polite*=deshoo) I think; I suppose; I wonder:
Ame wa furanai daroo. (雨は降らないだろう) *I* don't *think* it will rain. 《⇨ da; deshoo》

da⌈ru⌉·i だるい *a.* (-ku) listless; feel languid [tired].

da⌈sseñ だっせん (脱線) *n.* derailment; digression.
dasseñ suru (~する) *vi.* be derailed; digress.

da⌉s·u だす (出す) *vt.* (dash·i-; das·a-; dash·i-te ⓒ) **1** hold out; stick out:
mado kara kubi o dasu (窓から首を出す) *lean* out of the window.
2 take out:
kimerareta basho ni gomi o dasu (決められた場所にごみを出す) *take* the garbage *out* to the designated place.
3 issue; publish:
hoñ o dasu (本を出す) *publish* a book. 《⇨ hakkoo; shuppañ[1]》
4 give; hand in:
jihyoo o dasu (辞表を出す) *hand in* one's resignation.
5 send:
tegami o sokutatsu de dasu (手紙を速達で出す) *send* a letter by special delivery. 《⇨ okuru[1]》
6 serve (a dish); pay (expenses):
o-kyaku ni koohii o dasu (お客にコーヒーを出す) *serve* coffee to a visitor.
7 give out; break out:
Kaze o hiite, netsu o dashita. (かぜを引いて, 熱を出した) I caught a cold and *ran* a fever.
8 show; display:
paatii ni kao o dasu (パーティーに顔を出す) *make an appearance* at a party.
9 put forth; stir (power, energy, etc.):
supiido o dasu (スピードを出す) *gather* speed / Geñki o dashi nasai. (元気を出しなさい) *Cheer up!*
10 start; result in; cause (a fire,

casualties, etc.):
Kon̄kai no jiko wa ooku no shishoosha o dashita. (今回の事故は多くの死傷者を出した) The accident *resulted in* many dead and injured.
11 draw; work out (a conclusion, an answer, etc.):
ketsuron̄ o dasu (結論を出す) *draw* a conclusion.
12 open (a shop):
Amerika ni shiten̄ o dasu (アメリカに支店を出す) *open* a branch office in America.

-da¹s·u だす (出す) (-dash·i-; -da-s·a-; -dash·i-te Ⓒ) ★ Occurs as the second element of compound verbs. Added to the continuative base of a verb.
1 [with a transitive verb] take out; put out; bring out:
mochi-dasu (持ち出す) carry *out* / *oi*-dasu (追い出す) drive *away*.
2 [with an intransitive verb] go out; come out:
nige-dasu (逃げ出す) run *away* / *nuke*-dasu (抜け出す) sneak *out*.
3 [with a transitive or intransitive verb] start; begin:
aruki-dasu (歩き出す) *start* walking / *furi*-dasu (降り出す) *begin* to rain [snow]. ⟪⇨ -hajimeru⟫

daᶠtoo だとう (妥当) *a.n.* (~ na) appropriate; proper; reasonable.

daᶠttai だったい (脱退) *n.* withdrawal; secession.
dattai suru (~する) *vt.* withdraw; secede. ⟪↔ kanyuu⟫ ⟪⇨ nukeru (5)⟫

da¹tte¹ だって *p.* [an informal variant of '*de mo*' and follows a noun] **1** even:
a (used to give an extreme example):
Kon̄na kan̄tan̄ na koto, kodomo datte *shitte iru yo.* (こんな簡単なこと，子どもだって知っているよ) *Even* a child knows something as simple as this. ⟪⇨ de mo¹⟫
b (with a number or quantity expression, indicates an emphatic negative):
Ano hito ni wa ichi-en̄ datte *kashitaku arimasen̄.* (あの人には１円だって貸したくありません) I wouldn't lend him *even* one *single* yen.
2 always; everyone; everywhere: ★ Used with interrogatives such as '*itsu*,' '*dare*,' and '*doko*.'
Ano hito wa itsu datte *hima-soo da.* (あの人はいつだって暇そうだ) She *always* seems to have time on her hands. ⟪⇨ de mo¹⟫

da¹tte² だって *conj.* (*informal*) because; but: ★ Used at the beginning of a sentence.
*"Doo-shite okureta no?" "*Datte *basu ga okureta n̄ da mono."* (「どうして遅れたの」「だってバスが遅れたんだもの」) "Why are you late?" "Well, *because* the bus was late." ⟪⇨ de mo²⟫

de¹ で *p.* [follows a noun]
1 (indicates the location of an action) at; in; on:
dooro de *asobu* (道路で遊ぶ) play *on* the street.
2 (indicates a means or method) by; with; in:
takushii de *iku* (タクシーで行く) go *by* taxi.
3 (indicates a substance or material) of; with:
Kono nin̄gyoo wa kami de *dekite imasu.* (この人形は紙でできています) This doll is made *of* paper.
4 (sets the limits of a time or space) in:
Nihon̄ de *ichi-ban̄ takai yama* (日本で一番高い山) the highest mountain *in* Japan.
5 (indicates cause or reason) because of; by; owing to:
Byooki de *kaisha o yasumimashita.* (病気で会社を休みました) I was absent from the company *due to* illness.
6 (delimits the time in which an action or event occurs) in:

Is-shuukañ de *sañ-satsu hoñ o yomimashita.* (一週間で 3 冊本を読みました) I read three books *in* a week.

7 (sets the limits of a price or quantity) for; by:

Riñgo wa sañ-ko de *hyaku-eñ desu.* (りんごは 3 個で 100 円です) Apples are 100 yen *for* three.

de[2] て *copula* [the *te*-form of '*da*'] be:

Chichi wa isha de, *ani wa kyooshi desu.* (父は医者で, 兄は教師です) My father *is* a doctor and my older brother is a teacher.

-de て *infl. end.* ⇨ -te.

de⌈a·u であう (出会う) *vi.* (dea·i-; deaw·a-; deat-te Ⓒ) **1** come across; run into; meet.

2 encounter (difficulties, hardship, etc.).

de⌈fure デフレ *n.* deflation. ⟪↔ iñfure⟫

de⌉guchi でぐち (出口) *n.* exit; way out. ⟪↔ iriguchi⟫

de⌈iri でいり (出入り) *n.* going in and out.

deiri suru (～する) *vi.* go in and out; come and go.

de⌈iri⌉guchi でいりぐち (出入り口) *n.* entrance; doorway; gateway.

de⌈kake·ru でかける (出掛ける) *vi.* (dekake-te Ⓥ) go out; leave the house. ⟪⇨ gaishutsu⟫

de⌈ki でき (出来) *n.* **1** workmanship; craftsmanship; make.

2 crop; harvest.

3 result:

Shikeñ no deki *wa maamaa datta.* (試験の出来はまあまあだった) The *result* of the examination was not so bad.

de⌈kiagari できあがり (出来上がり) *n.* completion; workmanship. ⟪⇨ deki⟫

de⌈kiagar·u できあがる (出来上がる) *vi.* (-agar·i-; -agar·a-; -agat-te Ⓒ) be completed; be finished.

de⌈ki⌉goto できごと (出来事) *n.* occurrence; happening; event; accident.

de⌈kimo⌉no できもの (出来物) *n.* boil; tumor; eruption.

de⌈ki⌉·ru できる (出来る) *vi.* (deki-te Ⓥ) **1** be able to do; can do:

Watashi wa kuruma no uñteñ ga dekimasu. (私は車の運転ができます) I *can* drive a car.

2 be competent; be capable:

Kanojo wa suugaku ga dekiru. (彼女は数学ができる) She *is good* at mathematics.

3 be completed; be organized:

Sono biru wa ku-gatsu ni dekimasu. (そのビルは 9 月にできます) The building will *be completed* in September.

4 be ready:

Yuushoku no yooi ga dekimashita. (夕食の用意ができました) Dinner *is ready.*

5 be made:

Kono kutsu wa gañjoo ni dekite iru. (この靴はがんじょうにできている) These shoes *are made* strong.

6 form:

Kao ni nikibi ga dekita. (顔ににきびができた) Pimples have *come out* on my face.

7 grow; yield:

Kono chihoo de wa riñgo ga dekimasu. (この地方ではりんごができます) Apples *are grown* in this district.

de⌈kiru dake できるだけ (出来る丈) *adv.* as...as possible; to the best of one's ability:

Dekiru dake *hayaku kite kudasai.* (できるだけ早く来てください) Please come *as* early *as possible.*

de⌈koboko でこぼこ (凸凹) *a.n.* (～ na, ni) uneven; rough.

de⌉ mo[1] でも *p.* [the *te*-form of '*da*' plus the particle '*mo*']

1 even:

a (used to give an extreme example):

Ame de mo *uñdookai wa okonaimasu.* (雨でも運動会は行います) *Even* if it rains, we will hold sports day. ⟪⇨ datte[1]⟫

b (used to emphasize the preceding noun):
Ichi-eñ de mo *yasuku kaitai mono desu.* (1円でも安く買いたいものです) It is natural that we want to buy things *even* one yen more cheaply. (⇨ datte[1])
2 any: ★ Used with interrogatives such as '*itsu*,' '*dare*,' and '*doko*.'
Sono shina wa doko de mo *te ni hairimasu.* (その品はどこでも手に入ります) The goods are available *anywhere*. (⇨ datte[1])
3 or something:
Sono heñ de koohii de mo *ikaga desu ka?* (その辺でコーヒーでもいかがですか) What about having a coffee *or something* over there?

de˥ mo[2] でも *conj.* (*informal*) but; and yet: ★ Used only at the beginning of a sentence.
De mo *watashi wa hañtai desu.* (でも私は反対です) *But* I am against it. (⇨ datte[2])

de˥mukae でむかえ (出迎え) *n.* meeting; reception:
Eki made demukae *ni kite kudasai.* (駅まで出迎えに来てください) Please come to the station to *meet* me. (↔ miokuri) (⇨ demukaeru)

de˥mukae·ru でむかえる (出迎える) *vt.* (-kae-te [V]) meet; greet; receive:
kuukoo de kare o demukaeru (空港で彼を出迎える) *meet* him at the airport. (↔ miokuru) (⇨ demukae)

de˥ñatsu でんあつ (電圧) *n.* voltage.

de˥ñchi でんち (電池) *n.* battery; (electric) cell. (⇨ batterii)

de˥ñchuu でんちゅう (電柱) *n.* utility pole; electric light [telephone] pole.

de˥ñeñ でんえん (田園) *n.* the country; rural districts.

de˥ñgeñ でんげん (電源) *n.* power supply; switch; outlet:
deñgeñ o ireru [kiru] (電源を入れる [切る]) *turn the switch on* [*off*].

de˥ñki でんき (電気) *n.* **1** electricity:
deñki-*ryookiñ* (電気料金) *electric* charges / deñki-*kigu* (電気器具) *electric* appliances.
2 electric light:
deñki *o tsukeru* [*kesu*] (電気をつける [消す]) turn on [off] the *light*.

de˥ñki-go˥tatsu でんきごたつ (電気炬燵) *n.* electric foot warmer. (⇨ kotatsu)

de˥ñki-sooji˥ki でんきそうじき (電気掃除機) *n.* vacuum cleaner.

de˥ñki-suta˥ñdo でんきスタンド (電気スタンド) *n.* desk lamp; floor lamp.

de˥ñkyuu でんきゅう (電球) *n.* electric light bulb. (⇨ tama[1])

de˥ñpa でんぱ (電波) *n.* electric wave; radio wave.

de˥ñpoo でんぽう (電報) *n.* telegram; wire; telegraph.

de˥ñryoku でんりょく (電力) *n.* electric power; electricity.

de˥ñryuu でんりゅう (電流) *n.* electric current.

de˥ñseñ[1] でんせん (電線) *n.* electric wire; telephone line.

de˥ñseñ[2] でんせん (伝染) *n.* contagion; infection:
deñseñ-byoo (伝染病) an infectious *disease*.
deñseñ suru (～する) *vi.* be contagious; be infectious.

de˥ñsetsu でんせつ (伝説) *n.* legend; tradition.

de˥ñsha でんしゃ (電車) *n.* (electric) train; streetcar; tram (car). (⇨ ressha; kisha[2])

de˥ñshi-re˥ñji でんしレンジ (電子レンジ) *n.* microwave oven.

de˥ñtaku でんたく (電卓) *n.* desk [pocket] calculator.

de˥ñtoo[1] でんとう (電灯) *n.* electric light.

de˥ñtoo[2] でんとう (伝統) *n.* tradition; heritage.

de˥ñtoo-teki でんとうてき (伝統的) *a.n.* (～ na, ni) traditional.

de⸢ñwa でんわ(電話) *n.* telephone; (tele)phone call:
deñwa o kakeru [kiru] (電話をかける[切る]) *dial* [*hang up*].
deñwa (o) suru (~(を)する) *vt.* call up; telephone. ⟪⇨ kooshuudeñwa⟫

d

de⸢ñwa-ba⸣ñgoo でんわばんごう (電話番号) *n.* telephone number.

de⸢ñwachoo でんわちょう(電話帳) *n.* telephone book [directory].

de⸢pa⸣ato デパート *n.* department store.

de⸣·ru でる(出る) *vi.* (de-te [V])
1 go out; leave; depart:
Watashi wa maiasa hachi-ji ni ie o demasu. (私は毎朝 8 時に家を出ます) I *leave* the house at eight every morning. ⟪⇨ shuppatsu⟫
2 go to; get to:
Kono michi o massugu ni iku to eki ni demasu. (この道をまっすぐに行くと駅に出ます) Go straight along this road, and you'll *get to* the station.
3 attend; take part in:
jugyoo [*kaigi*] *ni* deru (授業[会議]に出る) *attend* class [a meeting]. ⟪⇨ shusseki⟫
4 appear; come out:
Nishi no sora ni tsuki ga deta. (西の空に月が出た) The moon *appeared* in the western sky.
5 graduate:
Daigaku o deta *no wa go-neñ mae desu.* (大学を出たのは 5 年前です) It is five years since I *graduated* from university. ⟪⇨ sotsugyoo⟫
6 produce; yield:
Kono chihoo de wa oñseñ ga deru. (この地方では温泉が出る) There *are* hot springs in this area.
7 (of physiological phenomena) have:
Yoñjuu-do chikai netsu ga deta. (40度近い熱が出た) I *had* a fever of almost forty degrees.
8 (of liquid) run; flow; come out:
Kemuri ga shimite, namida ga deta. (煙がしみて, 涙が出た) The smoke stung and made my eyes *water*.
9 (of emotions and spirits) show; raise:
Kore o nomeba geñki ga demasu. (これを飲めば元気が出ます) Drinking this will *raise* your spirits.
10 stick out:
Koñna tokoro ni kugi ga dete iru. (こんなところにくぎが出ている) There's a nail *sticking out* here.
11 be published; be printed:
Kono hoñ wa deta *bakari desu.* (この本は出たばかりです) This book *has* just *been published*. ⟪⇨ shuppañ[1]⟫
12 be given:
Señsee kara shukudai ga deta. (先生から宿題が出た) Our teacher *gave* us homework.
13 be reached; come up with:
Yatto ketsuroñ ga deta. (やっと結論が出た) At last a conclusion *was reached*.
14 be found; turn up:
Ikura sagashite mo ano tegami ga dete konai. (いくら探してもあの手紙が出てこない) Although I've looked everywhere, the letter *has not been found*.
15 exceed; be over:
Kanojo wa sañjuu o sukoshi dete iru. (彼女は 30 を少し出ている) She *is* a little *over* thirty.
16 sell:
Kono hoñ wa saikiñ yoku demasu. (この本は最近良く出ます) This book *has been selling* very well recently. ⟪⇨ ureru[1]⟫
17 take an attitude:
Aite ga doo deru *ka ga moñdai desu.* (相手がどう出るかが問題です) It is a question of what move the other party *makes*.

-de⸣·ru でる(出る) (-de-te [V])
★ Occurs as the second element of compound verbs. Added to the continuative base of a verb.
1 [with an intransitive verb] appear; come out:

tsuki-deru (突き出る) stick *out* / *shimi*-deru (しみ出る) ooze *out*.
2 [with a transitive verb] apply; announce:
mooshi-deru (申し出る) *offer* / todoke-deru (届け出る) *report*.

de⌈shi⌉ でし (弟子) *n.* pupil; apprentice; disciple.

deshoo でしょう I suppose [wonder]: ★ Polite equivalent of '*daroo*.'
Chichi wa osoraku uchi ni iru deshoo. (父はおそらく家にいるでしょう) *I think* my father will probably be at home. ⟪⇨ da; daroo⟫

desu です *copula.* (*polite*) (*informal*=da) **1** be [am/is/are]:
★ Indicates that the subject equals the complement.
"*Anata wa gakusee* desu *ka?*" "*Hai, soo* desu. [*Iie, soo* de wa arimaseñ.]" (「あなたは学生ですか」「はい, そうです[いいえ, そうではありません]」 "*Are* you a student?" "Yes, I *am*. [No, I *am not*.]" ⟪⇨ APP. 2⟫
2 be located in a certain place:
Omocha-uriba wa sañ-gai desu. (おもちゃ売り場は3階です) The toy section *is* on the third floor. ⟪⇨ aru²⟫
3 (indicates a situation or condition):
Kanojo wa byooki desu. (彼女は病気です) She *is* sick.
4 (used as a verb substitute):
"*Anata wa nani o chuumoñ shimashita ka?*" "*Watashi wa o-sushi* desu." (「あなたは何を注文しましたか」「私はおすしです」) "What did you order?" "I *ordered* sushi."
5 (after an adjective, makes the expression polite):
Kono riñgo wa totemo oishii desu. (このりんごはとてもおいしいです) This apple *is* very *delicious*.

de⌈tarame でたらめ (出鱈目) *n.* nonsense; irresponsible remark; lie. ⟪⇨ uso⟫
— *a.n.* (~ na, ni) random; haphazard; irresponsible.

de⌉ wa¹ では [used in conditional sentences] with: ★ The '*de wa*' clause indicates the condition and the second clause the natural or obvious result.
Kono chooshi de wa *kotoshi no keeki wa kitai dekimaseñ.* (この調子ではことしの景気は期待できません) *If* things are like this, we cannot expect good business this year.

de⌉ wa² では *conj.* then; well; if so: ★ '*De wa*' becomes '*jaa*' in informal speech. ⟪⇨ sore ja(a)⟫
De wa *kore kara kaigi o hajimemasu.* (ではこれから会議を始めます) *Well then*, we will now start the meeting / De wa mata *ashita.* (ではまたあした) *So long*, see you again tomorrow.

-de wa では [*te*-form of '*da*' plus the paticle '*wa*'] ⇨ -te wa.

do ど (度) *n.* **1** (of myopia, glasses) degree:
do no tsuyoi [yowai] *megane* (度の強い[弱い]眼鏡) *strong* [*weak*] glasses.
2 extent; amount; limit.
do ga sugiru (~が過ぎる) carry things too far.

-do ど (度) *suf.* **1** (a unit of measure) degree: *sesshi nijuu*-do (摂氏20度) twenty *degrees* centigrade.
2 time: ichi-do (一度) *once* / nido (二度) *twice* / *sañ*-do (三度) three *times*. ⟪⇨ -kai¹⟫

do⌈bu⌉ñ どぶん *adv.* (~ to) with a plop; with a splash: ★The sound of an object falling into water.
puuru e dobuñ to *tobikomu* (プールへどぶんと飛び込む) dive into a pool *with a splash*.

do⌉chira どちら *n.* **1** where:
★ More polite than '*doko*.'
Deguchi wa dochira *desu ka?* (出口はどちらですか) *Where* is the exit?
2 which: ★ More polite than '*dotchi*.'
Koohii to koocha to dochira *ga suki desu ka?* (コーヒーと紅茶とどちら

が好きですか) *Which* do you like better, coffee or tea?

3 who:
Dochira-*sama deshoo ka?* (どちら様でしょうか) May I have your name? (*literally*, *Who* would you be?)
《⇨ achira; kochira; sochira》

d

do¹chira mo どちらも both; either:
Ryooshiñ wa dochira mo *señsee desu.* (両親はどちらも先生です) *Both* of my parents are teachers.

do⌐ke·ru どける(退ける) *vt.* (dokete Ⓥ) remove; take away.
《⇨ doku[1]》

do¹kidoki どきどき *adv.* (～ to; ～ suru) (the state of one's heart beating faster):
Mune ga dokidoki shita. (胸がどきどきした) *There was a pounding* in my chest.

do¹ko どこ(何処) *n.* where; wherever:
Koobañ wa doko *desu ka?* (交番はどこですか) *Where* is the police box? / Doko de mo *suki na tokoro e iki nasai.* (どこでも好きな所へ行きなさい) You may go *wherever* you like. 《⇨ asoko; dochira; koko[1]; soko[1]》

do¹ko-ka どこか(何処か) somewhere; someplace:
Doko-ka *shizuka na tokoro e ryokoo shite mitai.* (どこか静かな所へ旅行してみたい) I want to take a trip to *someplace* quiet.
— *adv.* somewhat; something.

do¹ko made mo どこまでも(何処迄も) *adv.* to the last; endlessly:
Kare wa doko made mo *jibuñ no ikeñ o shuchoo shita.* (彼はどこまでも自分の意見を主張した) He *persistently* held to his opinion.

do¹ko mo どこも(何処も) *adv.* everywhere; (*neg.*) nowhere:
Natsu-yasumi ni naru to kaisuiyokujoo wa doko mo *hito de ippai ni naru.* (夏休みになると海水浴場はどこも人でいっぱいになる) With summer break starting, beaches *everywhere* become crowded.

do¹koro ka どころか *p.* [precedes a contradictory or qualifying statement]
1 far from; on the contrary:
Kare wa byooki dokoro ka, *totemo geñki desu.* (彼は病気どころか, とても元気です) *Far from* being ill, he is in excellent health.
2 not to mention; to say nothing of:
Uchi de wa jidoosha dokoro ka, *jiteñsha mo arimaseñ.* (うちでは自動車どころか, 自転車もありません) We do not have a bicycle, *not to mention* a car.

do⌐k·u[1] どく(退く) *vi.* (dok·i-; dok·a-; do·i-te Ⓒ) move; make room; step aside. 《⇨ dokeru》

do⌐ku[2] どく(毒) *n.* poison; harm:
Tabako wa karada ni doku *da.* (たばこは体に毒だ) Smoking is *bad* for your health.

do¹kuji どくじ(独自) *a.n.* (～ na/no, ni) one's own; unique; original; personal.

do⌐kuritsu どくりつ(独立) *n.* independence.
dokuritsu suru (～する) *vi.* become independent. 《⇨ hitoridachi》

do⌐kusai どくさい(独裁) *n.* dictatorship; despotism.

do⌐kuseñ どくせん(独占) *n.* monopoly; exclusive possession.
dokuseñ suru (～する) *vt.* monopolize.

do¹kusha どくしゃ(読者) *n.* subscriber; reader.

do⌐kushiñ どくしん(独身) *n.* bachelorhood; spinsterhood.

do¹kusho どくしょ(読書) *n.* reading (a book).
dokusho (o) suru (～(を)する) *vi.* read (a book).

do⌐kutoku どくとく(独特) *a.n.* (～ na/no, ni) characteristic; peculiar; unique. 《⇨ tokuyuu》

do⌐kuyaku どくやく(毒薬) *n.* poison. ⟪⇨ gekiyaku⟫

-do¹mo ども(共) *suf.* (used to form the plural of a noun).
1 (expresses humility): ★ Attached to a noun indicating the speaker. ⟪⇨ -tachi⟫
Watashi-domo *ni o-makase kudasai.* (私どもにおまかせください) Please leave it to *us*.
2 (implies a contemptuous or belittling attitude): ★ Attached to a noun indicating others.
Wakamono-domo *wa mattaku reegi o shiranai.* (若者どもはまったく礼儀を知らない) *Young people* have no manners at all.

do⌐na¹r·u どなる(怒鳴る) *vi.* (donar·i-; donar·a-; donat-te Ⓒ) shout; cry; yell:
tasukete kure to donaru (助けてくれとどなる) *cry* for help. ⟪⇨ sakebu⟫

do¹nata どなた(何方) *n.* (*polite*) = dare. who; whose; whom:
Kore wa donata no *kasa desu ka?* (これはどなたの傘ですか) *Whose* umbrella is this?

do¹nata-ka どなたか(何方か) *n.* (*polite*) =dare-ka. anyone:
Donata-ka *tetsudatte kureru hito wa imaseñ ka?* (どなたか手伝ってくれる人はいませんか) Isn't there *anyone* who can help me?

do⌐ñbu¹ri どんぶり(丼) *n.* porcelain bowl; large rice bowl:
oyako-doñburi (親子どんぶり) a *bowl* of rice topped with chicken and eggs.

do¹ñdoñ¹ どんどん *adv.* (~ to) rapidly; steadily:
Yama-kaji ga doñdoñ (*to*) *moe-hirogatta.* (山火事がどんどん(と)燃え広がった) The forest fire spread *rapidly*.

do¹ñdoñ² どんどん *adv.* (~ to) (the sound made when knocking strongly on a door or beating a drum):
to o doñdoñ (*to*) *tataku* (戸をどんどん(と)たたく) *bang* at a door.

do⌐ñkañ どんかん(鈍感) *a.n.* (~ na, ni) insensible; insensitive; dull. ⟪↔ biñkañ⟫

do⌐ñkoo どんこう(鈍行) *n.* (*informal*) local [slow] train. ⟪⇨ futsuu²⟫

do¹ñna どんな *attrib.* **1** what; what kind of:
Saikiñ doñna *mono o yomimashita ka?* (最近どんなものを読みましたか) *What* have you read recently?
2 however; no matter how:
Doñna *chiisa-na koto de mo kiroku shite kudasai.* (どんな小さなことでも記録してください) *However* minor it is, please make a record of it.
3 any; every:
Soñna koto wa doñna hito *de mo shitte iru.* (そんなことはどんな人でも知っている) *Everyone* is aware of such a thing. ⟪⇨ añna; koñna; soñna⟫

do¹ñna ni どんなに *adv.* **1** how; how much; to what extent:
Sore ga doñna ni *juuyoo ka wakatte imasu.* (それがどんなに重要かわかっています) I know *how* important it is. ⟪⇨ ika ni⟫
2 (with a negative) no matter how; whatever; however:
Doñna ni *ooki-na jishiñ de mo kono biru wa taoremaseñ.* (どんなに大きな地震でもこのビルは倒れません) *However* great the earthquake may be, this building will not collapse.
⟪⇨ añna ni; koñna ni; soñna ni⟫

do¹no どの *attrib.* **1** which; what; who:
Dono *kisetsu ga ichibañ suki desu ka?* (どの季節が一番好きですか) *Which* season do you like best?
2 any; every:
Koñshuu wa dono *hi mo isogashii.* (今週はどの日も忙しい) I am busy *every* day this week. ⟪⇨ ano; kono; sono⟫

-do¹no どの(殿) *suf.* (one of the titles used after the addressee's name in a formal letter):
★ Used by public offices while '*-sama*' is used by private individuals.

Yamada Taroo-dono (山田太郎殿) *Mr.* Taro Yamada.

do[no-kurai どのくらい (どの位) *adv.* (~ no) how much [many; long; far, etc.]: ★ Also '*dono-gurai*.'
Kono suutsukeesu no omosa wa dono-kurai *desu ka?* (このスーツケースの重さはどのくらいですか) *How much* does this suitcase weigh?

d

do]o[1] どう *adv.* **1** how:
Kibuñ wa doo *desu ka?* (気分はどうですか) *How* are you feeling?
2 what:
Moshi shippai shitara, doo *shimasu ka?* (もし失敗したら, どうしますか) *What* if you should fail?
⟪⇨ aa[1]; koo; soo[1]⟫

do]o[2] どう (胴) *n.* the trunk of the body. ★ The body not including the head and limbs. ⟪⇨ dootai⟫

do]o[3] どう (銅) *n.* copper; bronze.

doo- どう (同) *pref.* **1** the same:
doo-sedai *no wakamono* (同世代の若者) the youth of *one's generation.*
2 (used in documents, newspaper articles, etc. to avoid repetition of the same word):
Higaisha wa chikaku no byooiñ ni hakobare, doo-*byooiñ de teate o uketa.* (被害者は近くの病院に運ばれ, 同病院で手当を受けた) The injured were taken to a nearby hospital and treated in *that* hospital.

do[obutsu どうぶつ (動物) *n.*
1 animal. ★ Any living thing that is not a plant.
2 any animal other than man:
doobutsu *o hogo* [*gyakutai*] *suru* (動物を保護[虐待]する) protect [be cruel to] *animals.*

do[obutsu]eñ どうぶつえん (動物園) *n.* zoo. ⟪⇨ shokubutsueñ⟫

do[odoo どうどう (堂々) *adv.* (~ to) **1** in a dignified manner; magnificently.
2 (of competition, play, etc.) fairly: doodoo to *tatakau* (堂々と戦う) play *fair.*

do[ofuu どうふう (同封) *n.* enclosing.
doofuu suru (~する) *vt.* enclose.

do[ogu] どうぐ (道具) *n.* tool; utensil; instrument.

do[ohañ どうはん (同伴) *n.* company; accompanying.
doohañ suru (~する) *vt.* go with; accompany; escort.

do[oi どうい (同意) *n.* agreement; consent; assent.
... ni dooi suru (...に~する) *vt.* agree with; consent to.

do[oigo どういご (同意語) *n.* synonym. ⟪↔ hañigo⟫

do]o i[tashima]shite どういたしまして (どう致しまして) you're welcome; don't mention it; not at all; it's my pleasure.

do[oitsu どういつ (同一) *a.n.* (~ na/no, ni) identical; the same. ⟪⇨ onaji⟫

do]o-iu どういう (どう言う) *attrib.* how; why; what:
Sore wa doo-iu *koto desu ka?* (それはどういうことですか) *What* do you mean by that? ⟪⇨ aa-iu; koo-iu; soo-iu⟫

do]oji どうじ (同時) *n.* simultaneity; occurrence at the same time. ⟪⇨ dooji ni⟫

do[oji ni どうじに (同時に) *adv.*
1 at the same time; simultaneously.
2 soon; immediately:
Yo ga akeru to dooji ni *ame ga furi-dashita.* (夜が明けると同時に雨が降りだした) *At* the break of day, it started to rain.
3 as well as; while:
Watashi-tachi wa kare-ra ni taberu mono to dooji ni *kiru mono mo ataeta.* (私たちは彼らに食べる物と同時に着る物も与えた) We gave them clothes *as well as* food.

do[oji-tsu]uyaku どうじつうやく (同時通訳) *n.* simultaneous interpretation; simultaneous interpreter. ⟪⇨ tsuuyaku⟫

do⌐ojoo どうじょう (同情) *n.* sympathy; compassion.
... ni doojoo suru (...に〜する) *vt.* sympathize.

do⌝o ka どうか *adv.* **1** please:
Doo ka *o-kane o kashite kudasai.* (どうかお金を貸してください) *Please* lend me some money.
2 if; whether:
Sore ga hoñtoo ka doo ka *shirimaseñ.* (それが本当かどうか知りません) I don't know *whether* that is true or not.
doo ka shite iru (〜している) be strange; be wrong.

do⌐okañ どうかん (同感) *n.* agreement; feeling the same way.
... ni dookañ suru (...に〜する) *vi.* agree; sympathize; feel the same way.

do⌐oki どうき (動機) *n.* motive; motivation; reason.

do⌐omee[1] どうめい (同盟) *n.* alliance; league; union.
... to doomee suru (...と〜する) *vi.* make an alliance with; ally.

do⌐omee[2] どうめい (同名) *n.* the same name.

do⌝omo どうも *adv.* **1** very:
Doomo *arigatoo gozaimasu.* (どうもありがとうございます) Thank you *very* much. ★ '*Doomo*' is often used as an abbreviation of either '*doomo arigatoo*' or '*doomo sumimaseñ.*' In that sense, '*doomo*' is more like 'thank you' or 'I'm sorry.' 《⇨ señjitsu》
2 it seems...: ★ Used when making unfavorable judgments or predictions. In this usage '*yoo da*' or '*rashii*' often come at the end of the sentence.
Doomo *ano hanashi wa uso no yoo da.* (どうもあの話はうそのようだ) The story *seems* like a lie.
3 (with a negative) just cannot; there is no way:
Urusai oñgaku wa doomo *suki ni naremaseñ.* (うるさい音楽はどうも好きになれません) I *just don't seem* able to enjoy loud music.
4 somehow:
Doomo *watashi-tachi wa itsu-mo keñka ni natte shimau.* (どうも私たちはいつもけんかになってしまう) *Somehow* we always end up arguing.

do⌝o ni ka どうにか *adv.* = nañ to ka.

-do⌝ori どおり *suf.* = -toori.

do⌝oro どうろ (道路) *n.* road; way; street. 《⇨ koosoku-dooro》

do⌝osa どうさ (動作) *n.* movement; manners; action.

do⌐ose どうせ *adv.* **1** after all:
★ Used when past experience suggests an unfavorable result.
Soñna hanashi wa doose *uso ni kimatte iru.* (そんな話はどうせうそに決まっている) *After all*, such a story must be a lie.
2 as a matter of course; anyhow: ★ Used when a certain limit is known and the speaker is pessimistic.
Doose *watashi no inochi wa nagaku nai no da.* (どうせ私の命は長くないのだ) *Anyhow*, I know that I cannot live long.

do⌐osee[1] どうせい (同性) *n.* **1** the same sex: doosee-*ai* (同性愛) *homosexual* love.
2 person of the same sex.

do⌐osee[2] どうせい (同姓) *n.* the same family name:
doosee *doomee* (同姓同名) *the same family* and given *names.*

do⌐osee[3] どうせい (同棲) *n.* cohabitation; living together.
doosee suru (同せいする) cohabit; live together.

do⌐oshi どうし (動詞) *n.* verb. 《⇨ APP. 2》

-do⌝oshi[1] どうし (同士) *suf.*
1 persons who belong to the same group or class:
Kodomo-dooshi *de keñka o hajimeta.* (子どもどうしでけんかを始めた) The children began to quarrel *among themselves.*
2 persons who stand in the same

relationship to each other:
Futari wa koibito-dooshi *da.* (二人は恋人どうしだ) They are *lovers.*

-dooshi[2] どおし (通し) *suf.* keep doing: ★ Added to the continuative base of a verb.
Asa kara tachi-dooshi *de tsukareta.* (朝から立ち通しで疲れた) As I *have been standing* since morning, I am tired.

do͞o-shite どうして *adv.* **1** why:
Doo-shite *koñna koto ni natta no ka, setsumee shite kudasai.* (どうしてこんなことになったのか, 説明してください) Please explain *why* this happened.
2 how:
Kono moñdai wa doo-shite *toku ñ desu ka?* (この問題はどうして解くんですか) *In what way* can we solve this problem?
《⇨ aa-shite; koo-shite; soo-shite》

do͞o-shite mo どうしても *adv.*
1 by all means; at any cost.
2 (with a negative) just cannot:
Kare no iu koto wa doo-shite mo *shiñjirarenai.* (彼の言うことはどうしても信じられない) I *just cannot* believe what he says.

do⌈oso⌉okai どうそうかい (同窓会) *n.* alumni association [reunion].

do͞otai どうたい (胴体) *n.* trunk; body; torso. 《⇨ doo[2]》

do⌈otoku どうとく (道徳) *n.* morality; morals.

do⌈otoku-teki どうとくてき (道徳的) *a.n.* (~ na, ni) moral; morally.

do⌈owa どうわ (童話) *n.* fairy [nursery] tale; children's story.

do͞o-yara どうやら *adv.* **1** probably; apparently: ★ Usually occurs with '*rashii*,' '*yoo da*,' etc.
Ashita wa doo-yara *ame no yoo desu.* (あしたはどうやら雨のようです) It *certainly* looks like rain tomorrow.
2 somehow:
Doo-yara *shujutsu wa seekoo shita.* (どうやら手術は成功した) The operation was *somehow* a success.

do⌈oyoo[1] どうよう (同様) *a.n.* (~ na, ni) the same; similar:
Dooyoo *na ikeñ wa hoka kara mo deta.* (同様な意見はほかからも出た) *Similar* opinions were given by other people. 《⇨ onaji》
— *adv.* in the same way; likewise.

do⌈oyoo[2] どうよう (動揺) *n.* shakiness; disturbance; agitation.
... ni dooyoo suru (...に～する) *vi.* be shaken by; be disturbed by.

do⌈oyoo[3] どうよう (童謡) *n.* children's song; nursery rhyme.

do͞ozo どうぞ (何卒) *adv.*
1 please:
Doozo *o-kake kudasai.* (どうぞお掛けください) *Please* have a seat.
2 certainly; sure; of course:
"Deñwa o o-kari dekimasu ka?" "Ee, doozo." (「電話をお借りできますか」「ええ, どうぞ」) "May I use your telephone?" "*Certainly.*"

do͞re[1] どれ (何れ) *n.* **1** which:
Dore *ga anata no nimotsu desu ka?* (どれがあなたの荷物ですか) *Which* one is your baggage?
2 whichever:
Dore de mo *ichibañ suki na mono o tori nasai.* (どれでも一番好きなものをとりなさい) Take *whichever* one you like best.
3 all:
Karita hoñ wa dore *mo omoshiroku nakatta.* (借りた本はどれもおもしろくなかった) *All* the books I borrowed were boring.
《⇨ are[1]; kore; sore[1]》

do͞re[2] どれ *int.* now; well; let me see. 《⇨ saa》

do⌈ro⌉ どろ (泥) *n.* mud.

do⌈roboo どろぼう (泥棒) *n.* thief; robber; burglar.

do͞ru ドル (弗) *n.* dollar. 《⇨ dorudaka; doruyasu》

do⌈rubako ドルばこ (弗箱) *n.* money-maker; gold mine.

do⌈rudaka ドルだか (弗高) *n.* strong dollar; appreciation of the dollar. ⟪↔ doruyasu⟫

do⌈ruyasu ドルやす (弗安) *n.* weak dollar; depreciation of the dollar. ⟪↔ dorudaka⟫

do⌉ryoku どりょく (努力) *n.* effort; endeavor.
doryoku suru (～する) *vi.* make efforts; endeavor.

do⌈shi⌉ñ どしん *adv.* (～ to) with a thud [thump]; plump:
Kuruma ga hee ni doshiñ *to butsukatta.* (車が塀にどしんとぶつかった) The car *thudded* into the wall.

do⌈soku どそく (土足) *n.* with one's shoes on:
Kare wa dosoku *no mama uchi ni agatta.* (彼は土足のまま家にあがった) He entered the house *without removing his shoes.*

do⌉tchi どっち *n.* (*colloq.*) = dochira. **1** which:
Waiñ wa aka to shiro, dotchi *ni shimasu ka?* (ワインは赤と白, どっちにしますか) *Which* will you have, red or white wine?
2 both; either:
Watashi-tachi wa dotchi *mo sarariimañ desu.* (私たちはどっちもサラリーマンです) We are *both* office workers. ⟪⇨ atchi; kotchi; sotchi⟫

do⌈tchimichi どっちみち *adv.* anyway; in either case; sooner or later.

do⌈te どて (土手) *n.* bank; embankment.

do⌈tto どっと *adv.* **1** (the state of giving a roar of laughter):
Kañkyaku wa dotto *waratta.* (観客はどっと笑った) The audience *burst* into laughter.
2 in a rush; all of a sudden:
Deñsha kara hito ga dotto *orita.* (電車から人がどっと降りた) People *rushed* off the train.

do⌉yadoya どやどや *adv.* (～ to) (the state of many people moving together in a crowd):
Siñbuñ-kisha ga kaijoo ni doyadoya (*to*) *haitte kita.* (新聞記者が会場にどやどや(と)入って来た) The reporters rushed *noisily* into the meeting room.

do⌈yo⌉o(bi) どよう(び) (土曜(日)) *n.* Saturday. ⟪⇨ APP. 5⟫

E

e⌉[1] え (絵) *n.* picture; drawing; painting. ⟪⇨ egaku; kaiga⟫

e[2] え (柄) *n.* handle (of a tool, etc.).

e[3] へ *p.* [follows a noun and indicates a direction or goal]
1 to; for:
Giñza e *itte, eega o mimashoo.* (銀座へ行って, 映画を見ましょう) Let's go *to* Ginza and see a film.
2 on; onto:
Kono hako o tana no ue e *oite kudasai.* (この箱を棚の上へ置いてください) Please put this box *on* the shelf.
3 in; into:
Shorui wa hikidashi e *iremashita.* (書類は引き出しへ入れました) I put the papers *in* the drawer.
★ In the above examples '*ni*' can be used instead of '*e*.' ⟪⇨ ni[2]⟫

e' えっ *int.* oh; hah; eh: ★ Used when one fails to hear what is said, or to indicate surprise.
E', *nañ desu ka?* (えっ, 何ですか) *What?* What did you say?

e⌈akoñ エアコン *n.* air conditioner; air conditioning. ⟪⇨ kuuraa⟫

e⌈bi えび (海老) *n.* lobster; prawn; shrimp.

e⌈da えだ (枝) *n.* branch; bough; twig; sprig.

e⌉e ええ *int.* yes; no: ★ '*Ee*' literally means 'That's right' and is used to confirm a statement, whether affirmative or negative.
"Anata wa Nihoñjiñ desu ka?"

"Ee, *soo desu.*" (「あなたは日本人ですか」「ええ, そうです」) "Are you Japanese?" "*Yes*, I am." / "*Kore wa anata no kasa de wa arimaseñ ne?*" "Ee, *chigaimasu.*" (「これはあなたの傘ではありませんね」「ええ, 違います」) "Isn't this your umbrella?" "*No*, it isn't." ⟪⇨ hai[1]; iie⟫

e

e⌈ebuñ えいぶん(英文) *n.* English; English sentence.

e⌈ebu⌉ñgaku えいぶんがく(英文学) *n.* English literature.

e⌈e-eñ えいえん(永遠) *a.n.* (~ ni / no) eternity; permanence. ⟪⇨ eekyuu⟫

e⌉ega えいが(映画) *n.* movie; the movies; film.

e⌈ega⌉kañ えいがかん(映画館) *n.* movie theater; cinema.

E⌈ego えいご(英語) *n.* English; the English language.

e⌈egyoo えいぎょう(営業) *n.* sales; business; trade:
Eegyoo-chuu. (*sign*) (営業中) *Open* (for business).
eegyoo suru (~する) *vi.* do business.

E⌈ekoku えいこく(英国) *n.* Great Britain; England; the United Kingdom.

e⌈ekyoo えいきょう(影響) *n.* influence; effect; impact.
... ni eekyoo suru (...に~する) *vi.* influence; affect.

e⌈ekyuu えいきゅう(永久) *a.n.* (~ ni / no) permanence; eternity:
eekyuu *no heewa o negau* (永久の平和を願う) wish for *eternal* peace. ⟪⇨ ee-eñ⟫

e⌈enichi-ji⌉teñ えいにちじてん(英日辞典) *n.* English-Japanese dictionary for English speaking people. ⟪⇨ eewa-jiteñ; nichiee-jiteñ; waee-jiteñ⟫

e⌈esee[1] えいせい(衛生) *n.* hygiene; sanitation; health.

e⌈esee[2] えいせい(衛星) *n.* satellite: ⟪⇨ jiñkoo-eesee⟫
eesee-*hoosoo* (衛星放送) *satellite* broadcasting.

e⌈esee-teki えいせいてき(衛生的) *a.n.* (~ na, ni) sanitary:
Shokudoo no eesee-teki *na kañri ga hitsuyoo desu.* (食堂の衛生的な管理が必要です) Conditions in restaurants must be kept *sanitary*.

e⌈ewa-ji⌉teñ えいわじてん(英和辞典) *n.* English-Japanese dictionary for Japanese people. ⟪⇨ eenichi-jiteñ; nichiee-jiteñ; waee-jiteñ⟫

e⌈eyoo えいよう(栄養) *n.* nutrition; nourishment. ⟪⇨ jiyoo⟫

e⌈eyuu えいゆう(英雄) *n.* hero.

e⌈ga⌉k·u えがく(描く) *vt.* (egak·i-; egak·a-; ega·i-te [C]) **1** paint; draw:
e o egaku (絵を描く) *draw* a picture. ⟪⇨ kaku[2]⟫
2 take form; describe:
Booru wa aozora ni ko o egaite *toñde itta.* (ボールは青空に弧を描いて飛んで行った) The ball went flying, *describing* an arc against the sky.
3 form a picture in the mind; imagine.

e⌉gao えがお(笑顔) *n.* smile; smiling [beaming] face.

e-⌈ha⌉gaki えはがき(絵葉書) *n.* picture postcard. ⟪⇨ hagaki⟫

e⌈ho⌉ñ えほん(絵本) *n.* picture [illustrated] book.

e⌉ki えき(駅) *n.* (railroad) station.

e⌈kibeñ えきべん(駅弁) *n.* box lunch sold at a railroad station.

e⌈kichoo えきちょう(駅長) *n.* stationmaster.

e⌈ki⌉iñ えきいん(駅員) *n.* station employee; station staff.

e⌈kimae えきまえ(駅前) *n.* the place [street] in front of [near] a (railroad) station.

e⌈kitai えきたい(液体) *n.* liquid; fluid. ⟪⇨ kitai[2]; kotai⟫

e⌈mono えもの(獲物) *n.* game; catch; take:
Emono *ga wana ni kakatta.* (獲物がわなにかかった) There was an *animal* caught in the trap.

e⌉ñ[1] えん(円) *n.* yen. ★ The

monetary unit of Japan. ⟪⇨ eñdaka; eñyasu; kooka[3]; shihee⟫

e˥ñ[2] えん (円) *n.* circle.

e˥ñ[3] えん (縁) *n.* relation; connection; affinity:
Ano hito to wa eñ *o kirimashita.* (あの人とは縁を切りました) I broke off *relations* with him.

e˥ñchoo えんちょう (延長) *n.* extension; prolongation.
eñchoo suru (～する) *vt.* extend; lengthen; prolong. ⟪↔ tañshuku⟫

e˥ñdaka えんだか (円高) *n.* strong yen; appreciation of the yen. ⟪↔ eñyasu⟫

e˥ñdañ えんだん (縁談) *n.* an offer of marriage; marriage arrangements.

e˥ñdoo えんどう (沿道) *n.* route; roadside:
Eñdoo *wa keñbutsuniñ de ippai datta.* (沿道は見物人でいっぱいだった) *Both sides of the street* were crowded with spectators.

e˥ñgañ えんがん (沿岸) *n.* coast; shore.

e˥ñgawa えんがわ (縁側) *n.* corridor-like veranda. ★ A long, narrow wooden floor laid outside the rooms of a Japanese house.

e˥ñgee えんげい (園芸) *n.* gardening; horticulture.

e˥ñgeki えんげき (演劇) *n.* play; theatrical performance. ★ Usually refers to dramatic performances as a branch of art.

e˥ñgi[1] えんぎ (演技) *n.* performance; acting.

e˥ñgi[2] えんぎ (縁起) *n.* omen; luck; portent:
Kore wa eñgi *ga yoi* [*warui*]. (これは縁起がよい[悪い]) This is a sign of good [bad] *luck.*
eñgi o katsugu (～をかつぐ) be superstitious.

e˥ñji·ru えんじる (演じる) *vt.* (eñjite Ⓥ) perform; play; act:
Kooshoo ni atari, kare wa juuyoo na yakuwari o eñjita. (交渉にあたり，彼は重要な役割を演じた) He *played* an important role in the negotiation.

e˥ñjo えんじょ (援助) *n.* help; aid; assistance; support.
eñjo suru (～する) *vt.* help; aid; assist; support.

e˥ñka えんか (演歌) *n.* traditional Japanese popular songs. ★ Typically with sad lyrics and melancholy melodies.

e˥ñkai えんかい (宴会) *n.* party; dinner (party); banquet.

e˥ñkatsu えんかつ (円滑) *a.n.* (～ na, ni) smooth; without a hitch:
Hanashiai wa eñkatsu *ni susuñda.* (話し合いは円滑に進んだ) The talks went off *smoothly.*

e˥ñki えんき (延期) *n.* postponement; adjournment.
eñki suru (～する) *vt.* postpone; put off; adjourn. ⟪⇨ nobasu[2]⟫

e˥nogu えのぐ (絵の具) *n.* paints; colors.

e˥ñpitsu えんぴつ (鉛筆) *n.* pencil.

e˥ñryo えんりょ (遠慮) *n.* reserve; restraint; modesty.
eñryo suru (～する) *vi., vt.* **1** reserve: *Watashi no hihañ wa* eñryo shite okimasu. (私の批判は遠慮しておきます) I will *reserve* my criticism.
2 refrain: *Tabako wa* eñryo shite *kudasai.* (たばこは遠慮してください) Please *refrain* from smoking.

e˥ñshi えんし (遠視) *n.* farsightedness; longsightedness. ⟪↔ kiñshi[2]⟫

e˥ñshutsu えんしゅつ (演出) *n.* production; direction.
eñshutsu suru (～する) *vt.* produce; direct (a play).

e˥ñshuu えんしゅう (演習) *n.* **1** maneuvers.
2 seminar:
Nihoñ-buñgaku no eñshuu (日本文学の演習) a *seminar* in Japanese literature.

e˥ñsoku えんそく (遠足) *n.* outing; excursion; hike.

e⌈ñsoo えんそう(演奏) *n.* (musical) performance; recital.
eñsoo suru (～する) *vt.* play; perform.

e⌈ñtotsu えんとつ(煙突) *n.* chimney; stovepipe; funnel.

e⌈ñyasu えんやす(円安) *n.* weak yen; depreciation of the yen. 《↔ eñdaka》

e⌈ñzetsu えんぜつ(演説) *n.* address; speech; oration:
Kare wa mijikai enzetsu o shita. (彼は短い演説をした) He *made* a short *speech*. 《⇨ kooeñ[2]》

e⌈ra えら(鰓) *n.* gills.

e⌈ra⌉b·u えらぶ(選ぶ) *vt.* (erab·i-; erab·a-; erañ-de Ⓒ) **1** choose; select: *okurimono o* erabu (贈り物を選ぶ) *choose* a present.
2 elect (a chairman).

e⌈ra⌉·i[1] えらい(偉い) *a.* (-ku) **1** distinguished; high:
erai *hito to au* (偉い人) meet a *distinguished* person.
2 great; admirable:
Jibuñ de hataraite, daigaku o deta nañte erai *desu ne.* (自分で働いて, 大学を出たなんて偉いですね) It is *admirable* that you worked your way through college. 《⇨ rippa》

e⌈ra⌉·i[2] えらい *a.* (-ku) serious; awful:
Erai *koto ni natta zo.* (えらいことになったぞ) Now we are *in a fix.* 《⇨ taiheñ》

e⌈ri⌉ えり(襟) *n.* collar; neck; neckband; lapel.

e⌉·ru える(得る) *vt.* (e-te Ⓥ) gain; obtain; get:
Kanojo wa señsee no shikaku o eru *tame ni beñkyoo shite imasu.* (彼女は先生の資格を得るために勉強しています) She is studying to *obtain* a teaching certificate. 《⇨ toru[1]》
-zaru o enai (ざるを得ない) can do nothing but...: ★ Attached to the negative base of a verb; '*suru*' is irregular: '*sezaru o enai*.'
Sono keekaku wa akiramezaru o enai. (その計画はあきらめざるを得ない) We *can do nothing but give up* the plan.

e⌈sa⌉ えさ(餌) *n.* bait; food; feed.

F

fa⌉ito ファイト *n.* fight; fighting spirit:
faito *o moyasu* (ファイトを燃やす) be full of *fight*.
— *int.* a shout given when encouraging other people:
Faito! (ファイト) *Stick to it* [*Come on*]*!*

fa⌉sunaa ファスナー *n.* zipper; zip fastener.

fu ふ(府) *n.* prefecture: ★ An administrative division of Japan, but only used with reference to Osaka (大阪) and Kyoto (京都).
Oosaka-fu (大阪府) Osaka *Prefecture*. 《⇨ ken[1]》

fu- ふ(不) *pref.* not; un-; in-: ★ Gives a negative or contrary meaning to a word.
fu-*goori na* (不合理な) *ir*rational / fu-*hitsuyoo na* (不必要な) *un*necessary / fu-*jiyuu* (不自由) *in*convenience.

fu⌈añ ふあん(不安) *n.* worry; uneasiness; anxiety:
fuañ *o kañjiru* (不安を感じる) feel *anxiety*.
— *a.n.* (～ na, ni) afraid; uneasy; anxious; worried. 《⇨ shiñpai》

fu⌉beñ ふべん(不便) *n.* inconvenience; unhandiness:
Teedeñ de zuibuñ fubeñ o shita. (停電でずいぶん不便をした) We *were put to great inconvenience* because of the power failure.

— *a.n.* (~ na, ni) inconvenient; not handy. ⟪↔ beñri⟫ ⟪⇨ fujiyuu⟫

fu⌈be⌉ñkyoo ふべんきょう (不勉強) *n.* laziness (in one's studies).
— *a.n.* (~ na) idle; lazy.
★ Not trying hard enough to acquire knowledge.

fu⌉bo ふぼ (父母) *n.* parents; one's father and mother. ⟪⇨ fukee⟫

fu⌉buki ふぶき (吹雪) *n.* snowstorm; blizzard. ⟪⇨ kamifubuki⟫

fu⌈chi⌉ ふち (縁) *n.* brim; rim; edge; brink.

fu⌈choo ふちょう (不調) *n.* failure; bad condition:
fuchoo *ni owaru* (不調に終わる) end in *failure* / fuchoo *de aru* (不調である) be in *bad condition*.
⟪↔ koochoo[1]⟫

fu⌈chu⌉ui ふちゅうい (不注意) *n.* carelessness; negligence.
— *a.n.* (~ na) careless; thoughtless; negligent:
fuchuui *na ayamari* (不注意な誤り) *careless* mistakes.

fu⌈da ふだ (札) *n.* check; tag; card.

fu⌉dañ ふだん (普段) *n., adv.* usual(ly); ordinary; ordinarily; always:
fudañ *to kawaranai fukusoo o suru* (普段と変わらない服装をする) wear the same clothes as *always*.

fu⌈dañgi⌉ ふだんぎ (普段着) *n.* everyday clothes; casual wear.

fu⌈de ふで (筆) *n.* writing brush (for Japanese calligraphy); brush for painting a picture.

fu⌈doosañ ふどうさん (不動産) *n.* real estate [property]; immovables: fudoosañ*-ya* (不動産屋) a *real estate* agent.

fu⌈e ふえ (笛) *n.* flute; whistle.

fu⌈e⌉·ru ふえる (増える・殖える) *vi.* (fue-te [V]) **1** increase:
Taijuu ga ichi-kiro fueta. (体重が1キロ増えた) I *have gained* a kilo in weight. ⟪↔ heru⟫
2 breed; propagate:
Neko ga fuete, *komatte iru.* (猫が殖えて, 困っている) We don't know what to do about the cats *breeding*.

fu⌈goo ふごう (符号) *n.* sign; mark; symbol. ⟪⇨ kigoo⟫

fu⌈hee ふへい (不平) *n.* dissatisfaction; discontent; complaint.

fu⌈hitsu⌉yoo ふひつよう (不必要) *a.n.* (~ na, ni) unnecessary; needless. ⟪↔ hitsuyoo⟫

fu⌈i ふい (不意) *n.* unexpectedness; suddenness; surprise.
fui o tsuku (~をつく) catch a person off guard.
— *a.n.* (~ na/no, ni) unexpected; sudden; all of a sudden:
Mukashi no tomodachi ga fui *ni yatte kita.* (昔の友だちが不意にやって来た) An old friend *unexpectedly* dropped by.

fu⌈jiñ[1] ふじん (夫人) *n.* **1** wife:
Saitoo-sañ wa fujiñ *doohañ de ryokoo shita.* (斎藤さんは夫人同伴で旅行した) Mr. Saito went on a trip with his *wife*.
2 Mrs.:
Hiroma de Satoo fujiñ *ni shookai sareta.* (広間で佐藤夫人に紹介された) I was introduced to *Mrs.* Sato in the hall.

fu⌈jiñ[2] ふじん (婦人) *n.* lady; female; adult woman. ⟪⇨ josee; joshi[1]; oñna⟫

fu⌈jiñka ふじんか (婦人科) *n.* gynecology. ⟪⇨ sañfujiñka⟫

fu⌈jiñka⌉-i ふじんかい (婦人科医) *n.* gynecologist.

fu⌈jiñke⌉ekañ ふじんけいかん (婦人警官) *n.* policewoman. ⟪⇨ omawari-sañ⟫

fu⌉jiyuu ふじゆう (不自由) *a.n.* (~ na) **1** (of one's lifestyle) inconvenient; needy:
Deñwa ga nai to nani-ka to fujiyuu *desu.* (電話がないと何かと不自由です) It is somewhat *inconvenient* to be without a telephone. ⟪↔ beñri⟫ ⟪⇨ fubeñ⟫
2 physically handicapped; dis-

abled:
me no fujiyuu *na hito* (目の不自由な人) a person with *weak* eyes; a *blind* person.
fujiyuu suru (～する) *vi.* be inconvenient; be needy; be short of.

fu⌈ju⌉ubuñ ふじゅうぶん (不十分) *a.n.* (～ na) not enough; unsatisfactory; imperfect:
Setsumee ga fujuubuñ *da.* (説明が不十分だ) The explanation is *insufficient.* ⟪↔ juubuñ⟫

fu⌈ka⌉ ふか (不可) *n.* (of a grade rating) failure; F in schoolwork. ⟪↔ ka²⟫

fu⌈ka⌉·i ふかい (深い) *a.* (-ku)
1 deep:
fukai *kawa* (深い川) a *deep* river / fukai *kizu* (深い傷) a *deep* wound. ⟪↔ asai⟫ ⟪⇨ fukasa⟫
2 profound; deep:
fukai *kanashimi* (深い悲しみ) *deep* sorrow.
3 dense; thick:
fukai *kiri* (深い霧) a *dense* fog.

fu⌈kama⌉r·u ふかまる (深まる) *vi.* (-mar·i-; -mar·a-; -mat-te Ⓒ) deepen; become deeper:
Nihoñgo e no kyoomi ga fukamatta. (日本語への興味が深まった) My interest in the Japanese language *has deepened.* ⟪⇨ fukameru⟫

fu⌈kame⌉·ru ふかめる (深める) *vt.* (-me-te Ⓥ) deepen; enrich:
chishiki o fukameru (知識を深める) *deepen* one's knowledge. ⟪⇨ fukamaru⟫

fu⌈ka⌉noo ふかのう (不可能) *n.* impossibility; impracticability.
— *a.n.* (～ na, ni) impossible; impracticable. ⟪↔ kanoo⟫

fu⌈ka⌉ñzeñ ふかんぜん (不完全) *a.n.* (～ na) incomplete; imperfect. ⟪↔ kañzeñ⟫

fu⌈ka⌉sa ふかさ (深さ) *n.* depth:
Kono kawa wa fukasa *ga go-meetoru aru.* (この川は深さが５メートルある) This river is five meters *deep.* ⟪⇨ fukai⟫

fu⌈ka⌉s·u¹ ふかす (吹かす) *vt.* (fukash·i-; fukas·a-; fukash·i-te Ⓒ)
1 puff:
tabako o fukasu (たばこを吹かす) *puff on* a cigarette.
2 race (an engine).

fu⌈ka⌉s·u² ふかす (蒸かす) *vt.* (fukash·i-; fukas·a-; fukash·i-te Ⓒ) steam:
jagaimo [gohañ] o fukasu (じゃがいも[ご飯]をふかす) *steam* potatoes [rice]. ⟪⇨ musu⟫

fu⌈ke⌉e ふけい (父兄) *n.* parents of schoolchildren. ⟪⇨ fubo⟫

fu⌈ke⌉eki ふけいき (不景気) *n.* economic depression; hard times; recession; slump. ⟪↔ keeki²⟫
— *a.n.* (～ na) **1** dull; slack; depressed:
Doko mo fukeeki *da.* (どこも不景気だ) Business is *slack* everywhere. ⟪⇨ fukyoo⟫
2 (*informal*) cheerless; gloomy:
Kare wa fukeeki *na kao o shite ita.* (彼は不景気な顔をしていた) He looked *gloomy.*

fu⌈ke⌉·ru¹ ふける (老ける) *vi.* (fukete Ⓥ) grow old; look old for one's age.

fu⌈ke⌉·ru² ふける (更ける) *vi.* (fukete Ⓥ) grow late:
Yoru mo daibu fukete kimashita *kara sorosoro o-itoma itashimasu.* (夜もだいぶ更けてきましたからそろそろおいとま致します) As *it is getting* quite late, I must be leaving now.

fu⌈ketsu ふけつ (不潔) *a.n.* (～ na) unclean; dirty; filthy; unsanitary. ⟪↔ seeketsu⟫

fu⌈ki⌉ñ¹ ふきん (付近) *n.* neighborhood; vicinity.

fu⌈ki⌉ñ² ふきん (布巾) *n.* dish [tea] towel; dishcloth.

fu⌈ki⌉soku ふきそく (不規則) *a.n.* (～ na, ni) irregular:
fukisoku *na seekatsu o suru* (不規則な生活をする) lead an *irregular* life.

fu⌈kitobas·u ふきとばす (吹き飛ばす) *vt.* (-tobash·i-; -tobas·a-;

-tobash·i-te [C]) blow off:
Kaze de booshi o fukitobasareta. (風で帽子を吹き飛ばされた) My hat *was blown off* by the wind. 《⇨ fukitobu》

fuˈkitob·u ふきとぶ (吹き飛ぶ) *vi.* (-tob·i-; -tob·a-; -toñ-de [C]) blow off:
Shorui ga kaze de fukitoñda. (書類が風で吹き飛んだ) The papers *flew away* in the wind. 《⇨ fukitobasu; tobu[1]》

fuˈkitsu ふきつ (不吉) *a.n.* (~ na) ominous; unlucky:
Fukitsu *na yokañ ga suru.* (不吉な予感がする) I have an *ominous* presentiment.

fuˈkitsukeˈ·ru ふきつける (吹き付ける) (-tsuke-te [V]) **1** *vi.* blow against:
Kaze ga shoomeñ kara hageshiku fukitsuketa. (風が正面から激しく吹き付けた) The wind *blew* violently from in front.
2 *vt.* spray:
kabe ni peñki o fukitsukeru (壁にペンキを吹き付ける) *spray* paint on the wall.

fuˈkkatsu ふっかつ (復活) *n.* revival; restoration; resurgence.
fukkatsu suru [saseru] (~する[させる]) *vi., vt.* come [bring] back; revive; restore.

Fuˈkkatsuˈsai ふっかつさい (復活祭) *n.* Easter; Easter Day [Sunday].

fuˈkoˈo ふこう (不幸) *n.* **1** unhappiness; misfortune.
2 death:
Kanojo no uchi de fukoo *ga atta rashii.* (彼女の家で不幸があったらしい) She seems to have had a *death* in the family.
— *a.n.* (~ na, ni) unhappy; unlucky; unfortunate. 《⇨ fushiawase》
fukoo chuu no saiwai (~中の幸い) a stroke of good luck in the midst of ill fortune.

fuˈkoˈohee ふこうへい (不公平) *n.* unfairness; partiality; injustice.
— *a.n.* (~ na, ni) unfair; partial; unjust. 《↔ koohee》

fuˈk·u[1] ふく (吹く) (fuk·i-; fuk·a-; fu·i-te [C]) *vi.* blow:
Kaze ga fuite iru. (風が吹いている) The wind *is blowing.*
— *vt.* **1** play a musical instrument:
fue [torañpetto] o fuku (笛[トランペット]を吹く) *play* the flute [trumpet].
2 send forth air; blow:
Kare wa roosoku no hi o fuite, *keshita.* (彼はろうそくの火を吹いて, 消した) He *blew* out the candle.
3 put forth a bud:
Sakura no ki ga me o fuita. (桜の木が芽をふいた) The cherry trees *have put forth* buds.

fuˈku[2] ふく (服) *n.* clothes; dress; suit. 《⇨ ifuku; yoofuku; wafuku》

fuˈk·u[3] ふく (拭く) *vt.* (fuk·i-; fuk·a-; fu·i-te [C]) **1** wipe (off); clean:
mado o fuite, *kiree ni suru* (窓をふいて, きれいにする) *wipe* the windows clean.
2 dry:
hañkachi de namida [ase] o fuku (ハンカチで涙[汗]をふく) *dry* one's tears [perspiration] with one's handkerchief.

fuˈku[4] ふく (福) *n.* good luck [fortune]; happiness.

fuˈku- ふく (副) *pref.* vice; deputy; assistant:
fuku-*chiji* (副知事) a *deputy* governor / fuku-*gichoo* (副議長) a *vice*-chairman.

fuˈkumeˈ·ru ふくめる (含める) *vt.* (fukume-te [V]) include:
Riñgo wa sooryoo o fukumete, *rokuseñ-eñ desu.* (りんごは送料を含めて, 6千円です) The apples will be 6,000 yen, *including* delivery charges. 《⇨ fukumu》

fuˈkuˈm·u ふくむ (含む) *vt.* (fukum·i-; fukum·a-; fukuñ-de [C]) **1** contain; include:
Hooreñsoo wa bitamiñ o takusañ

fukuñde iru. (ほうれん草はビタミンをたくさん含んでいる) Spinach *contains* plenty of vitamins.
2 hold a thing in one's mouth: *mizu o kuchi ni* fukuñde, *ugai suru* (水を口に含んで, うがいする) *hold* water in one's mouth and gargle. ((⇨ fukumeru))
3 imply: *Kare no kotoba wa hiniku o* fukuñde ita. (彼の言葉は皮肉を含んでいた) *There was* sarcasm in his words.
4 bear in mind: *Doo ka kono teñ o o*-fukumi *oki kudasai.* (どうかこの点をお含みおきください) Please *bear* this point *in mind.*

fu⌈kurahagi ふくらはぎ (張ら脛) *n.* calf of the leg.

fu⌈kuramas·u ふくらます (膨らます) *vt.* (-mash·i-; -mas·a-; -mash·i-te [C]) **1** inflate; swell; blow up: *kuchi de fuuseñ o* fukuramasu (口で風船をふくらます) *blow up* a balloon. ((⇨ fukuramu))
2 puff out; expand: *Kare wa fumañ-soo ni hoo o* fukuramashita. (彼は不満そうにほおをふくらました) He *puffed out* his cheeks with apparent dissatisfaction. ((⇨ fukureru))

fu⌈kuram·u ふくらむ (膨らむ) *vi.* (-ram·i-; -ram·a-; -rañ-de [C])
1 swell; expand: *Hana no tsubomi ga* fukuramihajimeta. (花のつぼみがふくらみ始めた) The flower buds *have begun to swell.* ((⇨ fukureru))
2 bulge: *Kabañ wa nimotsu de* fukurañde ita. (かばんは荷物でふくらんでいた) The bag *was bulgy* with its contents.

fu⌈kure·ru ふくれる (膨れる) *vi.* (fukure-te [V]) **1** swell: *Mochi wa yaku to* fukureru. (もちは焼くとふくれる) Rice cakes *swell* when grilled.
2 sulk; become sulky: *Kare wa shikarareru to sugu ni* fukureru. (彼はしかられるとすぐにふくれる) He soon *sulks* when he is scolded.

fu⌈kuro⌉ ふくろ (袋) *n.* bag; sack; pouch.

fu⌈kusa⌉yoo ふくさよう (副作用) *n.* side effect.

fu⌈kuseñ ふくせん (複線) *n.* two-track line; double track. ((↔ tañseñ))

fu⌈ku-sha⌉choo ふくしゃちょう (副社長) *n.* executive vice president.

fu⌈ku⌉shi[1] ふくし (福祉) *n.* welfare; well-being: *shakai*-fukushi (社会福祉) social *welfare.*

fu⌈kushi[2] ふくし (副詞) *n.* adverb. ((⇨ APP. 1))

fu⌈kushuu ふくしゅう (復習) *n.* review; revision.
fukushuu suru (～する) *vt.* review [go over] one's lessons. ((↔ yoshuu))

fu⌈kusoo ふくそう (服装) *n.* dress; costume; clothes: *Uchi no musuko wa* fukusoo *o amari kamawanai.* (うちの息子は服装をあまり構わない) My son doesn't care much about his *clothes.* ((⇨ minari))

fu⌈kuzatsu ふくざつ (複雑) *a.n.* (～ na, ni) complicated; complex; intricate: fukuzatsu *na koozoo* (複雑な構造) a *complex* structure. ((↔ kañtañ))

fu⌈kyoo ふきょう (不況) *n.* recession; depression; slump. ((↔ kookyoo[2])) ((⇨ fukeeki))

fu⌈kyuu ふきゅう (普及) *n.* popularization; spread; diffusion:
fukyuu suru (～する) *vi.* spread; diffuse; popularize. ((⇨ hiromaru))

fu⌈ma⌉jime ふまじめ (不真面目) *a.n.* (～ na, ni) not serious; frivolous; insincere. ((↔ majime))

fu⌈mañ ふまん (不満) *n.* dissatisfaction; discontent.
— *a.n.* (～ na, ni) unsatisfactory; unsatisfied; dissatisfied: *Ima no kyuuryoo ni wa* fumañ

desu. (今の給料には不満です) I am *dissatisfied* with my present salary. 《↔ mañzoku》

fu⌈mee ふめい (不明) *a.n.* (~ na/no) unclear; obscure; unknown: *kokuseki* fumee *no hikooki* (国籍不明の飛行機) an aircraft of *unidentified* nationality.

fu⌈me⌉eyo ふめいよ (不名誉) *a.n.* (~ na) disgraceful; shameful; discreditable:
Booryoku o furuu no wa fumeeyo *na koto da.* (暴力をふるうのは不名誉なことだ) It is a *disgraceful* act to use violence. 《↔ meeyo》

fu⌈mikiri ふみきり (踏切) *n.* railroad crossing; level crossing.

fu⌈mitsuke⌉·ru ふみつける (踏み付ける) *vt.* (-tsuke-te [V]) trample; stamp:
Dare-ka ga kadañ o fumitsuketa. (だれかが花壇を踏みつけた) Someone *trampled down* the flower bed.

fu⌈moto⌉ ふもと (麓) *n.* lowest part of a mountain; foot of a hill.

fu⌈m·u ふむ (踏む) *vt.* (fum·i-; fum·a-; fuñ-de [C]) **1** trample; step:
bureeki o fumu (ブレーキを踏む) *step* on the brakes.
2 set foot on:
hajimete Amerika no chi o fumu (初めてアメリカの地を踏む) *set foot* on American soil for the first time.
3 go through; follow (a procedure):
seeki no tetsuzuki o fumu (正規の手続きを踏む) *go through* the due formalities.

fu⌉ñ[1] ふん (分) *n.* minute:
*Sañ-ji go-*fuñ *mae* [*sugi*] *desu.* (3時5分前[過ぎ]です) It is five *minutes* to [past] three. 《⇨ APP. 4》

fu⌉ñ[2] ふん (糞) *n.* excrement; feces; dung. 《⇨ daibeñ; kuso》

fu⌈nabiñ ふなびん (船便) *n.* sea [surface] mail.

fu⌈ñba⌉r·u ふんばる (踏ん張る) *vi.* (-bar·i-; -bar·a-; -bat-te [C]) **1** stand firm; brace one's legs.
2 hold out:
Akirameru na. Ima koso fuñbaru *toki da.* (あきらめるな. 今こそ踏ん張るときだ) Don't give up. Now is the time to *hang on.* 《⇨ gañbaru》

fu⌉ne ふね (舟·船) *n.* boat; ship; vessel. ★ '舟' usually refers to a small vessel like a rowboat, and '船' to a large vessel like a steamship. 《⇨ watashibune》

fu⌈neñ ふねん (不燃) *n.* nonflammability; incombustibility:
funeñ-butsu (不燃物) *incombustibles.*

fu⌈ñeñ ふんえん (噴煙) *n.* smoke of a volcano.

fu⌈ñgai ふんがい (憤慨) *n.* indignation; resentment.
fuñgai suru (~する) *vi.* resent; be indignant.

fu⌈ñi⌉ki ふんいき (雰囲気) *n.* mood; atmosphere; ambience.

fu⌈ñka ふんか (噴火) *n.* eruption; volcanic activity.
fuñka suru (~する) *vi.* erupt.

fu⌈ñka⌉koo ふんかこう (噴火口) *n.* volcanic crater.

fu⌈ñshiñ ふんしん (分針) *n.* (of a clock) minute hand. 《⇨ byooshiñ》

fu⌈ñshitsu ふんしつ (紛失) *n.* loss.
fuñshitsu suru (~する) *vt.* (*formal*) lose; miss. 《⇨ nakusu[1]》

fu⌈ñwa⌉ri ふんわり *adv.* (~ to) softly; lightly; gently:
Akañboo ni moofu o fuñwari (*to*) *kaketa.* (赤ん坊に毛布をふんわり(と)掛けた) I put a blanket *gently* over the baby. 《⇨ fuwari》

fu⌈ñzuke⌉·ru ふんづける (踏ん付ける) *vt.* (-zuke-te [V]) (*informal*) = fumitsukeru.

fu⌈rafura[1] ふらふら *a.n.* (~ na, ni) unsteady; staggering; groggy:
Kare wa furafura *to tachiagatta.* (彼はふらふらと立ち上がった) He *unsteadily* got to his feet.

fu⌉rafura[2] ふらふら *adv.* (~ to; ~ suru) **1** impulsively; uncon-

sciously:
Kanojo wa furafura *to kare no sasoi ni notte shimatta.* (彼女はふらふらと彼の誘いに乗ってしまった) She yielded to his temptation *in spite of herself*.
2 feel dizzy; be faint; waver:
Onaka ga suite furafura *suru.* (おなかがすいてふらふらする) I am *faint* with hunger.

fu'rai フライ *n.* fried food.

fu'raipañ フライパン *n.* frying pan; skillet.

fu're·ru ふれる (触れる) *vi.* (fure-te Ⓥ) **1** touch; feel:
E ni te o furenai *de kudasai.* (絵に手を触れないでください) *Don't touch* the paintings.
2 mention; refer to:
Kare wa jibuñ no misu ni tsuite hitokoto mo furenakatta. (彼は自分のミスについて一言も触れなかった) He *did not mention* even one word about his blunder.
3 affect the emotions or feelings of (a person):
Shachoo no ikari ni furete, *kare wa kubi ni natta.* (社長の怒りに触れて, 彼は首になった) Having *incurred* the president's anger, he was fired.
4 perceive; experience:
Me ni fureru *mono subete ga watashi ni wa mezurashii.* (目に触れるものすべてが私には珍しい) Everything that I *see* is new to me.
5 infringe (a law, a regulation, a rule, etc.).

fu'ri[1] ふり (不利) *n.* disadvantage; handicap.
— *a.n.* (~ na, ni) disadvantageous; unfavorable:
Kare ni totte furi *na shooko ga mitsukatta.* (彼にとって不利な証拠が見つかった) A piece of evidence *against* him has been found. ⟪↔ yuuri⟫

fu'ri[2] ふり (振り) *n.* personal appearance.
... furi o suru (~をする) pretend; affect; feign: *neta* furi o suru (寝たふりをする) *pretend* to be asleep.

fu'rigana ふりがな (振り仮名) *n.* 'kana' written next to or above Chinese characters to show the pronunciation. ⟪⇨ kana⟫

fu'rika'er·u ふりかえる (振り返る) *vi.* (-kaer·i-; -kaer·a-; -kaet-te Ⓒ) **1** turn around; look back.
2 recollect; look back:
kako [gakusee jidai] o furikaeru (過去[学生時代]を振り返る) *look back* on the past [one's college days].

fu'rimu'k·u ふりむく (振り向く) *vi.* (-muk·i-; -muk·a-; -mu·i-te Ⓒ)
1 turn one's face; turn around. ⟪⇨ muku[1]⟫
2 (with a negative) pay attention to; care for:
Kanojo wa kanemochi igai no otoko ni wa furimuki mo shinai. (彼女は金持ち以外の男には振り向きもしない) She *doesn't care for* men unless they are rich.

fu'ro' ふろ (風呂) *n.* **1** bath; bathtub: ★ Often with '*o*-.'
furo *ni hairu* (ふろに入る) take a *bath*. ⟪⇨ nyuuyoku⟫
2 public bath:
furo *ni iku* (ふろに行く) go to the *public bath*. ★ The public bath is called '*furoya*' or '*señtoo*.'

fu'roba' ふろば (風呂場) *n.* a room with a bathtub; bathroom.

fu'roku ふろく (付録) *n.* supplement; appendix.

fu'roñto フロント *n.* (of a hotel) front desk; reception desk.

fu'roñto-ga'rasu フロントガラス *n.* windshield; windscreen.

fu'roshiki ふろしき (風呂敷) *n.* wrapping cloth. ★ A square scarf-like cloth used for wrapping and carrying things.

fu'ro'ya ふろや (風呂屋) *n.* public bath. ⟪⇨ señtoo[3]⟫

fu'r·u[1] ふる (降る) *vi.* (fur·i-; fur·a-; fut-te Ⓒ) **1** (of rain, snow, hail) fall:
Ame ga hageshiku futte iru. (雨が激しく降っている) *It is raining* hard.

2 (of ash, dust, etc.) fall; come down.

fu⌈r·u[2] ふる(振る) *vt.* (fur·i-; fur·a-; fut-te Ⓒ) **1** shake; move: *Keekañ wa te o* futte, *tomare to aizu shita.* (警官は手を振って, 止まれと合図した) The policeman *waved* his hand to signal me to halt.
2 sprinkle:
niku ni shio to koshoo o furu (肉に塩とこしょうを振る) *sprinkle* the meat with salt and pepper.
3 assign; add (a letter, a number, etc.):
kañji ni furigana o furu (漢字にふりがなを振る) *put* the corresponding 'furigana' next to the Chinese characters.
4 (often in the passive) refuse; abandon:
Kare wa koibito ni furareta. (彼は恋人に振られた) He *was jilted* by his girlfriend.

fu⌈rue·ru ふるえる(震える) *vi.* (furue-te Ⓥ) tremble; shake; shiver; shudder. (⇨ furuwaseru)

fu⌈ru⌉·i ふるい(古い) *a.* (-ku) old; stale; old-fashioned; out-of-date. (↔ atarashii)

fu⌈ruma⌉·u ふるまう(振る舞う) *vi.* (-ma·i-; -maw·a-; -mat-te Ⓒ)
1 behave; act:
Kare wa shachoo rashiku furumatta. (彼は社長らしく振る舞った) He *behaved* just as the president of a company should.
2 treat; entertain.

fu⌈ru⌉sato ふるさと(故郷) *n.* one's home; one's hometown.

fu⌈rushi⌉ñbuñ ふるしんぶん(古新聞) *n.* old newspaper. (⇨ chiri-gami-kookañ)

fu⌈ruwase·ru ふるわせる(震わせる) *vt.* (furuwase-te Ⓥ) cause to tremble:
Shoojo wa samu-soo ni karada o furuwasete ita. (少女は寒そうに体を震わせていた) The girl *was shaking* all over as if she were cold.
(⇨ furueru)

fu⌈ryoo ふりょう(不良) *a.n.* (~ na/no) bad; poor; defective:
Kotoshi wa ine no sakugara ga furyoo *da.* (今年は稲の作柄が不良だ) We had a *poor* rice crop this year.
(⇨ yoi[1])

fu⌈sa⌉ ふさ(房) *n.* tuft; fringe; tassel; bunch.

fu⌈sagar·u ふさがる(塞がる) *vi.* (fusagar·i-; fusagar·a-; fusagat-te Ⓒ) **1** close; be closed:
Kizuguchi ga yatto fusagatta. (傷口がやっとふさがった) The wound has *closed up* at last. (⇨ fusagu)
2 be blocked; be packed:
Jiko de dooro ga fusagatte, *ugokenakatta.* (事故で道路がふさがって, 動けなかった) The road *was blocked* by the accident and we were stuck. (⇨ fusagu)
3 be occupied; be used:
Zaseki wa miñna fusagatte imasu. (座席はみんなふさがっています) The seats *are* all *occupied.*

fu⌈sag·u ふさぐ(塞ぐ) *vt.* (fusag·i-; fusag·a-; fusa·i-de Ⓒ)
1 stop; cover:
Ana o ishi de fusaida. (穴を石でふさいだ) I *stopped up* the hole with a stone. (⇨ fusagaru)
2 block; occupy:
Ooki-na torakku ga michi o fusaide ita. (大きなトラックが道をふさいでいた) A large truck *was blocking* the road. (⇨ fusagaru)

fu⌈sa⌉i ふさい(夫妻) *n.* husband and wife.

fu⌈sawashi⌉·i ふさわしい *a.* (-ku) suitable; proper; appropriate:
sono ba ni fusawashii *fuku* (その場にふさわしい服) clothes *suitable* for the occasion. (⇨ tekisetsu)

fu⌈se⌉ekaku ふせいかく(不正確) *n., a.n.* (~ na, ni) incorrect; inaccurate; inexact; uncertain.
(↔ seekaku[2])

fu⌈se⌉g·u ふせぐ(防ぐ) *vt.* (fuseg·i-; fuseg·a-; fuse·i-de Ⓒ)
1 protect; defend:
Samusa o fusegu *tame ni, jañpaa*

o kita. (寒さを防ぐために, ジャンパーを着た) I wore a windbreaker to *protect* myself from the cold.
2 guard; prevent:
jiko o fusegu (事故を防ぐ) *prevent* an accident. ⟪⇨ booshi²⟫

fu⌈se⌉·ru ふせる (伏せる) *vt.* (fusete Ⓥ) **1** put a thing upside down; put a thing face down.
2 look downward; lower one's eyes:
Kanojo wa hazukashi-soo ni me o fuseta. (彼女は恥ずかしそうに目を伏せた) She *lowered* her eyes bashfully.
3 keep a thing secret.

fu⌈shi⌉¹ ふし (節) *n.* **1** knot:
Kono ita wa fushi *ga ooi.* (この板は節が多い) This plank is full of *knots.*
2 joint:
take no fushi (竹の節) a *joint* in a piece of bamboo.

fu⌈shi⌉² ふし (節) *n.* melody; tune; strain.

fu⌈shia⌉wase ふしあわせ (不幸せ) *n.* unhappiness; misfortune.
— *a.n.* (~ na, ni) unhappy; unfortunate. ⟪↔ shiawase⟫ ⟪⇨ fukoo⟫

fu⌈shigi ふしぎ (不思議) *n.* wonder; mystery; miracle.
— *a.n.* (~ na, ni) difficult to explain the reason or cause; mysterious; strange.

fu⌈shi⌉matsu ふしまつ (不始末) *n.* carelessness; misconduct:
Kaji no geñiñ wa tabako no hi no fushimatsu *datta.* (火事の原因はたばこの火の不始末だった) The cause of the fire was *careless handling* of cigarette butts.

fu⌈shi⌉ñsetsu ふしんせつ (不親切) *a.n.* (~ na, ni) unkind; insufficient inconsiderate. ⟪↔ shiñsetsu⟫

fu⌈shi⌉zeñ ふしぜん (不自然) *a.n.* (~ na, ni) unnatural; artificial; forced. ⟪↔ shizeñ⟫

fu⌈shoo ふしょう (負傷) *n.* injury; wound; cut; bruise. ⟪⇨ kega⟫
fushoo suru (~する) *vi.* be injured; be wounded.

fu⌈soku ふそく (不足) *n.* shortage; lack; want; insufficiency.
fusoku suru (~する) *vi.* be short; be lacking. ⟪⇨ -busoku⟫

fu⌈suma ふすま (襖) *n.* Japanese sliding door. ★ Both sides are covered with thick paper.

fu⌈ta ふた (蓋) *n.* lid; cap; cover:
nabe ni futa *o suru* (なべにふたをする) put the *lid* on a pot.

fu⌈ta- ふた (二) *pref.* double; two:
futa-*keta* (二桁) *double* digits / futa-*kumi* (二組) *two* pairs.

fu⌈tañ ふたん (負担) *n.* burden; load; charge; obligation.
futañ suru (~する) *vt.* bear; share; cover: *Sooryoo wa kochira de* futañ shimasu. (送料はこちらで負担します) We *will cover* the postage.

fu⌈tari⌉ ふたり (二人) *n.* two persons; couple.

fu⌈ta⌉shika ふたしか (不確か) *a.n.* (~ na, ni) uncertain; unreliable. ⟪↔ tashika⟫

fu⌈tatabi ふたたび (再び) *adv.* again; once more; for the second time: ★ Similar in meaning to '*mata*' but slightly formal.
Kooshoo ga futatabi *hajimatta.* (交渉が再び始まった) The negotiations have started *once more.*

fu⌈tatsu⌉ ふたつ (二つ) *n.* couple; two. ★ Used when counting. ⟪⇨ ni¹; APP. 3⟫

fu⌈te⌉kitoo ふてきとう (不適当) *a.n.* (~ na, ni) unsuitable; unfit. ⟪↔ tekitoo⟫

fu⌈to ふと *adv.* suddenly; by chance; unexpectedly:
Futo *ii aidea ga ukañda.* (ふといいアイデアが浮かんだ) *Suddenly* a good idea came to me.

fu⌈to⌉·i ふとい (太い) *a.* (-ku)
1 (of round objects such as sticks or string) thick; bold:

futoi *keito* (太い毛糸) *thick* wool / futoi *señ* (太い線) a *bold* line. ⟪↔ hosoi⟫
2 (of a voice) deep. ⟪↔ hosoi⟫

fu⌈tokoro ふところ(懐) *n.* breast; bosom; breast pocket.

fu⌈tomomo ふともも(太股) *n.* thigh. ⟪⇨ momo[1]⟫

fu⌈toñ ふとん(布団) *n.* padded floor mattress used as a bed; bedding; quilt.

fu⌈too ふとう(不当) *a.n.* (~ na, ni) unfair; unjust; unreasonable. ⟪↔ seetoo[1]⟫

fu⌈to⌉r·u ふとる(太る) *vi.* (futor·i-; futor·a-; futot-te Ⓒ) **1** grow fat; gain weight.
2 be fat; be plump: ★ '*Futotte iru*' is the pattern used in this sense.
Futotte iru *hito wa tsukare-yasui.* (太っている人は疲れやすい) *Fat* people get tired easily.

fu⌈tsuka ふつか(二日) *n.* two days; the second day. ⟪⇨ APP. 5⟫

fu⌈tsukayoi ふつかよい(二日酔い) *n.* hangover (from alcohol).

fu⌈tsuu[1] ふつう(普通) *a.n.* (~ na/no, ni) common; ordinary; normal; usual; average:
Nihoñ de wa busshiki no sooshiki ga futsuu *desu.* (日本では仏式の葬式が普通です) In Japan Buddhist funerals are the *norm.*
— *adv.* usually; commonly; ordinarily; normally. ⟪⇨ heejoo; nami[1]⟫

fu⌈tsuu[2] ふつう(普通) *n.* local train; one that stops at every station along the line. ⟪⇨ doñkoo⟫

fu⌈tsuu[3] ふつう(不通) *n.* interruption; suspension:
Yamanote-señ wa ima futsuu *desu.* (山の手線はいま不通です) The Yamanote Line *is not in service* now.

fu⌈ttoo ふっとう(沸騰) *n.* boiling; seething.
futtoo suru (~する) *vi.* **1** boil; come to the boil.
2 be heated:
Giroñ ga futtoo shita. (議論がふっとうした) The discussion *became heated.*

fu⌉u[1] ふう(風) *n.* **1** look; appearance; air:
Kare wa nanigenai fuu o shite ita. (彼は何気ない風をしていた) He *pretended* nonchalance.
2 way; manner:
Sore wa koñna fuu ni *yatte gorañ nasai.* (それはこんな風にやってごらんなさい) Try to do it *in this manner.* ⟪⇨ guai⟫

fu⌉u[2] ふう(封) *n.* seal:
tegami no fuu o suru [kiru] (手紙の封をする[切る]) *seal* [*open*] a letter.

-fuu ふう(風) *suf.* style; type:
Nihoñ-fuu *no furo* (日本風のふろ) a Japanese *style* bath.

fu⌉ufu ふうふ(夫婦) *n.* man [husband] and wife; married couple.

fu⌉ufuu ふうふう *adv.* (~ to) (used when blowing on something hot to cool it):
Miñna fuufuu *ii-nagara sukiyaki o tabeta.* (みんなふうふう言いながらすき焼きを食べた) Everyone was *blowing* on the sukiyaki as they ate it.
fuufuu iu (~言う) pant; breathe hard. ⟪⇨ aegu⟫

fu⌉ukee ふうけい(風景) *n.* landscape; scene; scenery.

fu⌉uki ふうき(風紀) *n.* social morality; discipline:
fuuki *o midasu* (風紀を乱す) corrupt *public morals.*

fu⌈uñ[1] ふうん *int.* hum; oh.
★ Used to express a half-hearted reply. It is rude to use this expression in reply to one's superiors.

fu⌉uñ[2] ふうん(不運) *n.* bad luck; misfortune.
— *a.n.* (~ na, ni) unlucky; unfortunate:
fuuñ *na jiko* (不運な事故) an *unfortunate* accident. ⟪↔ koouñ⟫

fu⌈useñ ふうせん(風船) *n.* balloon.

fu⌈ushuu ふうしゅう(風習) *n.* custom; manners; practices.

fu⌉utoo ふうとう(封筒) *n.* envelope.

fu⌉u-u ふうう(風雨) *n.* wind and rain; storm.

fu⌉uzoku ふうぞく(風俗) *n.* manners; public morals.

fu⌈uzoku-e⌉egyoo ふうぞくえいぎょう(風俗営業) *n.* entertainment and amusement trades. ★ Usually used as a euphemism for prostitution.

fu⌈wafuwa[1] ふわふわ *a.n.* (~ no, ni) gentle; soft: ★ Used for objects which are light and fluffy.
fuwafuwa *no kusshoñ* (ふわふわのクッション) a *soft* cushion.

fu⌉wafuwa[2] ふわふわ *adv.* (~ to, ~ suru) **1** lightly; buoyantly:
Sono fuuseñ wa doko-ka e fuwafuwa (*to*) *tonde itta.* (その風船はどこかへふわふわ(と)飛んで行った) The balloon *gently* floated away somewhere.
2 restless; unsettled. ★ Used about people who cannot settle down or pay attention to what they should be doing.

fu⌈wa⌉ri ふわり *adv.* (~ to) gently; softly; lightly. ★ Used for objects moving slowly in the air. '*Fuñwari*' is also used when referring to something softer or lighter. ⟪⇨ fuñwari⟫

fu⌈ya⌉s·u ふやす(増やす) *vt.* (fuyash·i-; fuyas·a-; fuyash·i-te Ⓒ) increase; add to:
hito o fuyasu (人を増やす) *increase* the staff / *zaisañ o* fuyasu (財産を増やす) *add to* one's fortune.

fu⌈yu⌉ ふゆ(冬) *n.* winter.

fu⌈yu⌉kai ふゆかい(不愉快) *a.n.* (~ na, ni) unpleasant; disagreeable. ⟪↔ yukai⟫

fu⌈yu-ya⌉sumi ふゆやすみ(冬休み) *n.* winter vacation.

fu⌈zai ふざい(不在) *n.* absence:
Anata no fuzai*-chuu ni raikyaku ga arimashita.* (あなたの不在中に来客がありました) A visitor came to see you during your *absence.*

fu⌈zake⌉-ru ふざける *vi.* (fuzakete Ⓥ) **1** joke; jest; talk nonsense:
Kare ga fuzakete *itta koto nado, ki ni suru na.* (彼がふざけて言ったことなど, 気にするな) Don't worry about something he said *in jest.*
2 frisk; frolic.

fu⌈zoku ふぞく(付属) *n.* attachment; accessory.
fuzoku suru (~する) *vi.* be attached; be affiliated.

G

ga[1] が *p.* **1** (used to mark the topic of a sentence):
Kyooto ni wa furui tatemono ga *takusañ arimasu.* (京都には古い建物がたくさんあります) There are a lot of old *buildings* in Kyoto. ★ Generally speaking, '*ga*' is used to stress the subject and '*wa*' is used to emphasize the predicate. When a noun is first mentioned, it is usually followed by '*ga*,' but on later mentions, by '*wa*.' ⟪⇨ wa[3]⟫
2 [follows a nominalized verb which is the subject of its clause]:
Oñgaku o kiku no ga *nani yori no tanoshimi desu.* (音楽を聞くのがなによりの楽しみです) Nothing is more enjoyable than *listening to music.*
3 (used with certain expressions indicating likes, dislikes, desires and wishes):
Watashi wa yasai ga *kirai desu.* (私は野菜がきらいです) I dislike *vegetables.*
4 (used with certain expressions indicating ability or skill):

Yamada-sañ wa sukii ga *joozu desu.* (山田さんはスキーがじょうずです) Mrs. Yamada is good at *skiing.*

ga[2] が *p.* **1** but; although:

a (used to link two clauses, the second of which is an unexpected outcome or result of the first):

Yuujiñ ni ai ni ikimashita ga, *ainiku rusu deshita.* (友人に会いに行きましたが, あいにく留守でした) I went to see my friend, *but* unfortunately she was not at home.

《⇨ kakawarazu; keredo (mo); no ni》

b (used to link two clauses that are in direct contrast):

Peñ wa arimasu ga, *kami ga arimaseñ.* (ペンはありますが, 紙がありません) I have a pen, *but* no paper.

《⇨ kakawarazu; keredo (mo); no ni》

2 (used in a non-contrastive way to link two clauses, the first of which is a preliminary to the second):

Sumimaseñ ga, *eki e wa doo ikeba ii ñ deshoo ka?* (すみませんが, 駅へはどう行けばいいんでしょうか) *Excuse me, but* what would be the best way of going to the station?

3 and also: ★ Used to link two clauses, the second of which supplements the first.

Kanojo wa kiryoo mo ii ga, *atama mo ii.* (彼女は器量もいいが, 頭もいい) She is good-looking, *and* what is more, clever.

4 (used at the end of an unfinished sentence to politely express modesty or reserve, or to avoid making an overly direct statement):

Anoo, sore watashi no na ñ desu ga ... (あのう, それ私のなんですが...) Excuse me, but *I think* that is mine.

ga⌉bugabu がぶがぶ *adv.* (~ to) (the sound of noisily drinking a liquid):

Kare wa mizu o nañbai mo gabugabu (*to*) *noñda.* (彼は水を何杯もがぶがぶ(と)飲んだ) He *noisily* drank several cups of water.

《⇨ gatsugatsu》

ga⌈byoo がびょう(画鋲) *n.* thumbtack; drawing pin. 《⇨ byoo[2]》

-gachi がち(勝ち) *suf.* tend to do; be apt [liable] to do:

★ Added to a noun or the continuative base of a verb. Often used when the tendency is unfavorable.

Kare wa karada ga yowai no de gakkoo o yasumi-gachi *desu.* (彼は体が弱いので学校を休みがちです) Since he is physically delicate, he *is often absent* from school.

ga⌉i がい(害) *n.* harm; damage:

Tabako wa keñkoo ni gai ga aru. (たばこは健康に害がある) Smoking *is harmful* to your health.

-gai がい(外) *suf.* outside:

moñdai-gai (問題外) *out of* the question / jikañ-gai *roodoo* (時間外労働) *overtime* work.

ga⌈iatsu がいあつ(外圧) *n.* external pressure:

gaiatsu *ni makeru* (外圧に負ける) yield to *external pressure.*

ga⌉ibu がいぶ(外部) *n.* **1** outside; exterior:

tatemono no gaibu (建物の外部) the *exterior* of a building.

《↔ naibu》

2 outside (one's circle); external (to one's interests):

Himitsu ga gaibu *ni moreta.* (秘密が外部に漏れた) The secret leaked to *outsiders.* 《↔ naibu》

ga⌈ido-bu⌉kku ガイドブック *n.*

1 guidebook for travelers or tourists.

2 manual; handbook.

ga⌈ijiñ がいじん(外人) *n.* foreigner. ★ Abbreviation of '*gaikokujiñ.*'

ga⌉ika がいか(外貨) *n.* foreign currency [money].

ga⌈ikañ がいかん(外観) *n.* appearance; exterior view.

ga⌈ikoku がいこく(外国) *n.* foreign country [land].

ga⌈ikokugo がいこくご(外国語) *n.* foreign language.

ga⌈ikoku⌉jiñ がいこくじん(外国人) *n.* foreigner; alien.

ga⌈ikoo がいこう(外交) *n.* **1** diplomacy; foreign affairs.
2 door-to-door sales:
Kanojo wa hokeñ no gaikoo o shite iru. (彼女は保険の外交をしている) She *goes from house to house* selling insurance.

g

ga⌈iko⌉oiñ がいこういん(外交員) *n.* salesman; saleswoman.

ga⌈iko⌉okañ がいこうかん(外交官) *n.* diplomat.

ga⌉ineñ がいねん(概念) *n.* notion; general idea; concept.

ga⌈iraigo がいらいご(外来語) *n.* loanword; Japanized foreign word. ★ Usually written in 'katakana.'

ga⌉ishite がいして(概して) *adv.* (*formal*) generally; in general; on the whole:
Nihoñ no dooro wa gaishite *semai.* (日本の道路は概して狭い) Roads in Japan are *generally* narrow.

ga⌈ishoku がいしょく(外食) *n.* eating out.

ga⌈ishutsu がいしゅつ(外出) *n.* going out.
gaishutsu suru (～する) *vi.* go out. ⟪⇨ dekakeru⟫

ga⌈isoo がいそう(外装) *n.* the exterior (of a building, car, etc.); external ornament. ⟪↔ naisoo⟫

ga⌉is·u がいす(害す) *vt.* (gaish·ite V) injure; hurt:
Kare wa kañjoo o gaishita *rashii.* (彼は感情を害したらしい) He seems to *be offended*.

ga⌈itoo[1] がいとう(該当) *n.* application; correspondence.
gaitoo suru (～する) *vi.* come [fall] under; apply; correspond. ⟪⇨ atehamaru⟫

ga⌈itoo[2] がいとう(街頭) *n.* street.

ga⌈itoo[3] がいとう(街灯) *n.* street lamp.

ga⌈ito⌉osha がいとうしゃ(該当者) *n.* applicable person:
Sono shoo no gaitoosha *wa inakatta.* (その賞の該当者はいなかった) There was nobody *deserving* of the prize.

ga⌈iyoo がいよう(概要) *n.* outline; summary. ⟪↔ shoosai⟫

ga⌈ka がか(画家) *n.* painter; artist.

-ga⌉kari[1] がかり(係) *suf.* **1** clerk:
añnai-gakari (案内係) a *receptionist*; an *usher*.
2 section (of a company, organization, etc.). ⟪⇨ kakari⟫

-ga⌉kari[2] がかり(掛かり) *suf.* take; require:
Sañ-niñ-gakari *de piano o ugokashita.* (三人がかりでピアノを動かした) It *took* three people to move the piano.

ga⌈ke がけ(崖) *n.* cliff; precipice; bluff.

ga⌈keku⌉zure がけくずれ(崖崩れ) *n.* landslide.

ga⌈kka がっか(学科) *n.* **1** department (of a university).
2 subject; a course of study.

ga⌈kkai がっかい(学会) *n.* learned society; academic conference.

ga⌈kka⌉ri がっかり *adv.* (～ suru) be disappointed; lose heart:
Shiai ga ame de chuushi ni nari, gakkari *shita.* (試合が雨で中止になり,がっかりした) I *was* very *disappointed*, because the game was rained out. ⟪⇨ shitsuboo⟫

ga⌈kki[1] がっき(学期) *n.* term; semester. ★ Japanese elementary schools and junior and senior high schools have three terms. Universites and colleges have two terms. ⟪⇨ shiñgakki⟫

ga⌈kki[2] がっき(楽器) *n.* (musical) instrument.

ga⌈kkoo がっこう(学校) *n.* school.

ga⌉ku[1] がく(額) *n.* sum; amount.

ga⌈ku[2] がく(額) *n.* framed picture; frame.

ga⌝ku³ がく(学) *n.* learning; knowledge; education:
Ano hito wa gaku ga aru. (あの人は学がある) He *is well-educated.*

-gaku がく(学) *suf.* science; study:
butsuri-gaku (物理学) *physics* / geñgo-gaku (言語学) *linguistics.*

ga⌝kubu がくぶ(学部) *n.* college; faculty; department; school:
koo-gakubu (工学部) the *college* of engineering / *hoo*-gakubu (法学部) the *faculty* of law. ⟪⇨ bu³⟫

ga⌈kuchoo がくちょう(学長) *n.* the president of a university; chancellor.

ga⌈kufu がくふ(楽譜) *n.* (sheet) music; score.

ga⌈kuhi がくひ(学費) *n.* school expenses; tuition.

ga⌈ku⌝moñ がくもん(学問) *n.* learning; study; education.

ga⌈kuneñ がくねん(学年) *n.* school [academic] year; grade.

ga⌈kureki がくれき(学歴) *n.* educational background; schooling.

ga⌈kuryoku がくりょく(学力) *n.* academic ability; scholarship.

ga⌈kusee がくせい(学生) *n.* student. ★ Refers to older students, especially college students. ⟪⇨ seeto⟫

ga⌈kusetsu がくせつ(学説) *n.* theory.

ga⌈kusha がくしゃ(学者) *n.* scholar; learned man.

ga⌈kushuu がくしゅう(学習) *n.* learning; study. ★ Usually refers to the process of studying.
gakushuu suru (～する) *vt.* learn; study.

ga⌈kushu⌝usha がくしゅうしゃ(学習者) *n.* learner.

ga⌝mañ がまん(我慢) *n.* endurance; patience; perseverance.
gamañ ga naranai (～がならない) cannot stand.
gamañ suru (～する) *vt.* **1** endure; stand; put up with. ⟪⇨ shiñboo⟫
2 manage; make do with: *Kono fuyu wa furui oobaa de* gamañ shita. (この冬は古いオーバーで我慢した) I *made do with* my old overcoat this winter.
gamañ-zuyoi (～強い) be very patient.

-gamashi⌝i がましい *suf.* (*a.*) (-ku) sound like; smack of:
Kare no setsumee wa iiwake-gamashikatta. (彼の説明は言い訳がましかった) His explanation *sounded like* an excuse.

ga⌝migami がみがみ *adv.* (～ to) (the manner of insisting or needlessly saying something):
Uchi no kachoo wa itsu-mo gamigami (to) urusai. (うちの課長はいつもがみがみ(と)うるさい) Our section chief *is* always *nagging* us.

ga⌝ñ がん(癌) *n.* cancer.

ga⌈ñba⌝r·u がんばる(頑張る) *vi.* (-bar·i-; -bar·a-; -bat-te Ⓒ)
1 work hard; persevere:
Atarashii shokuba de gañbarimasu. (新しい職場で頑張ります) I will *do my utmost* in my new place of work.
2 insist:
Kare wa jibuñ ga tadashii to gañbatta. (彼は自分が正しいと頑張った) He *insisted* that he was right.
Gañbatte (ne). (頑張って(ね)) Good luck. ★ Used in giving encouragement.

ga⌈ñjoo がんじょう(頑丈) *a.n.* (～ na, ni) strong; firm; sturdy:
Kono hoñbako wa gañjoo *ni dekite iru.* (この本箱はがんじょうにできている) This bookcase is *well put together.*

ga⌈ñka がんか(眼科) *n.* ophthalmology: gañka-i (眼科医) an *eye doctor.* ⟪⇨ meisha⟫

ga⌝ñkiñ がんきん(元金) *n.* monetary principal. ⟪↔ rishi⟫

ga⌝ñko がんこ(頑固) *a.n.* (～ na, ni) **1** (of a person) stubborn; obstinate.
2 (of a disease, stains, etc.)

incurable; stubborn.

ga⌈ñpeki がんぺき (岸壁) *n.* quay; wharf.

ga⌉ñrai がんらい (元来) *adv.* originally; by nature. ⟪⇨ hoñrai (wa)⟫

ga⌉ñsho がんしょ (願書) *n.* (written) application; written request.

ga⌈ppee がっぺい (合併) *n.* merger; combination; amalgamation.
gappee suru (～する) *vi., vt.* merge; combine.

g

ga⌈ra がら (柄) *n.* **1** pattern; design.
2 build:
Kare wa gara ga ookii. (彼は柄が大きい) He *has a large build.*

-gara がら (柄) *suf.* **1** pattern:
*hana-*gara *no sukaato* (花柄のスカート) a skirt with a flower *pattern.*
2 pertinent to the situation:
Shigoto-gara *sake o nomu kikai ga ooi.* (仕事柄酒を飲む機会が多い) *My job being what it is,* I often have occasion to drink.

ga⌈ragara[1] がらがら *a.n.* (～ na/no, ni) empty. ⟪⇨ kara[1]⟫

ga⌉ragara[2] ガラガラ *adv* (the sound of things crashing or collapsing):
Jishiñ de tatemono ga garagara (to) kuzureta. (地震で建物がガラガラ(と)崩れた) The earthquake caused the building to *come crashing down.*

ga⌈rakuta がらくた *n.* useless articles; junk; rubbish. ⟪⇨ kuzu⟫

ga⌈ra⌉ri to ガラリと *adv.* **1** with a clatter [noise]:
to o garari to *akeru* (戸をガラリと開ける) slide open a door *with a noise.* ★ Used only for sliding doors.
2 (of attitude, situation, etc.) completely; suddenly:
Machi no yoosu ga garari to *kawatta.* (町のようすががらりと変わった) The look of the town has changed *completely.*

ga⌈rasu ガラス *n.* glass; pane

ga⌉reeji ガレージ *n.* garage.
★ '*Gareeji*' does not refer to a place where cars are repaired and gasoline sold. ⟪⇨ shako⟫

-gari がり *suf.* (*n.*) (refers to a person sensitive to the quality suggested by the adjective): ★ Attached to the stem of an adjective to form a noun. It is often followed by '*-ya* (*-sañ*),' which implies familiarity.
samu-gari *no hito* (寒がりの人) a person *sensitive to the cold* / sabishigari-ya (寂しがり屋) a person *who always feels lonely and longs for company.*

ga⌈roo がろう (画廊) *n.* gallery.
★ Refers to a store that sells art work, usually Western art.

-ga⌉r·u がる *suf.* (*vi.*) (-gar·i-; -gar·a-; -gat-te Ⓒ) [attached to the stem of an adjective or adjectival noun] ★ Not used when asking others about their feelings, emotions, etc.
1 (expresses the feelings or emotions of someone other than the speaker):
Kodomo-tachi wa miñna samugatte *iru.* (子どもたちはみんな寒がっている) The children are all *complaining that they are cold.*
2 pretend:
Kare wa tsuyo-gatte *iru dake da.* (彼は強がっているだけだ) He is only *pretending to be* strong.

ga⌈soriñ ガソリン *n.* gasoline; petrol.

ga⌈soriñ-suta⌉ñdo ガソリンスタンド *n.* gas [filling] station.

ga⌈sshoo がっしょう (合唱) *n.* chorus; concerted singing.

ga⌈sshuku がっしゅく (合宿) *n.* lodging together for training.

ga⌉su ガス *n.* gas; dense fog.

-gata がた (方) *suf.* toward:
*ake-*gata (明け方) daybreak / *yuu-*gata (夕方) evening.

ga⌉tagata[1] がたがた *adv.* (～ to; suru) **1** rattle; clatter:
Tsuyoi kaze de mado ga gatagata

(to) natta. (強い風で窓ががたがた(と)鳴った) The windows *rattled* in the strong wind.
2 shiver; tremble:
Samukute, karada ga gatagata (to) furueta. (寒くて, 体ががたがた(と)震えた) My body *trembled* with cold.

gaˈtagata[2] がたがた *a.n.* (~ na/no, ni) shaky; rickety:
gatagata *no teeburu* (がたがたのテーブル) a *rickety* table.

-gataˈ·i がたい (難い) *suf.* (*a.*) (-ku) (*formal*) difficult; impossible:
★ Added to the continuative base of a verb.
Kare no koodoo wa rikai shi-gatai. (彼の行動は理解しがたい) His behavior *is difficult* to understand.
《↔ -yasui》《⇨ -nikui; -zurai》

-gaˈtera (ni) がてら(に) *suf.* while; at the same time; by way of: ★ Attached to the continuative base of volitional verbs or nouns that denote action. Note that the last verb phrase indicates the main action.
Sañpo-gatera (ni), *chotto yotte mita dake desu.* (散歩がてら(に), ちょっと寄ってみただけです) I just dropped by *while taking a walk.*

gaˈtsugatsu がつがつ *adv.* (~ to; ~ suru) hungrily; greedily:
gatsugatsu (*to*) *taberu* (がつがつ(と)食べる) eat *greedily.* 《⇨ gabugabu》

gaˈwa がわ (側) *n.* side:
migi [*hidari*]-gawa (右[左]側) the right [left] *side* / *ryoo*-gawa (両側) both *sides.*

gaˈyagaya がやがや *adv.* (~ to) (the noise made by many people talking and laughing):
gayagaya (*to*) *sawagu* (がやがや(と)騒ぐ) make *a lot of noise.* 《⇨ zawazawa》

geˈ げ (下) *n.* lowest grade [class]; inferiority. 《⇨ chuu[1]; joo[2]》

-ge げ (気) *suf.* (*a.n.*) (~ na, ni) (indicates the feeling or appearance of others): ★ Attached to the stem of an adjective.
tanoshi-ge *na waraigoe* (楽しげな笑い声) *happy* laughter.

geˈe げい (芸) *n.* **1** art; skill.
2 trick:
Inu ni gee *o shikoñda.* (犬に芸を仕込んだ) I taught my dog *tricks.*

geˈejutsu げいじゅつ (芸術) *n.* art; fine arts.

geˈejutsuka げいじゅつか (芸術家) *n.* artist.

geˈenoo げいのう (芸能) *n.* public entertainment; performing arts:
geenoo-jiñ (芸能人) *public entertainer; show business personality.*

geˈeto-boˈoru ゲートボール *n.* 'gate ball.' ★ A variant of croquet created in Japan.

geˈhiˈñ げひん (下品) *a.n.* (~ na, ni) vulgar; coarse; unrefined:
gehiñ *na kotoba o tsukau* (下品な言葉を使う) use *coarse* language.
《↔ joohiñ》

geˈjuñ げじゅん (下旬) *n.* the last ten days of a month. 《⇨ chuujuñ; joojuñ》

geˈka げか (外科) *n.* surgery:
geka-i (外科医) a *surgeon.*
《⇨ naika》

geˈki げき (劇) *n.* drama; play.

geˈkijoo げきじょう (劇場) *n.* theater; playhouse.

geˈkiree げきれい (激励) *n.* encouragement; urging.
gekiree suru (~する) *vt.* encourage; cheer up.

geˈkiyaku げきやく (劇薬) *n.* powerful drug; poison. 《⇨ dokuyaku》

geˈkkañ げっかん (月間) *n.* by the month; monthly:
gekkañ *no uriage* (月間の売り上げ) *monthly* sales. 《⇨ neñkañ》

geˈkkyuu げっきゅう (月給) *n.* monthly pay [salary]. 《⇨ chiñgiñ》

geˈkoo げこう (下校) *n.* leaving school.
gekoo suru (~する) *vi.* leave school. 《↔ tookoo》

geˈñba げんば (現場) *n.* the scene;

the spot:
Koko ga jiko-geñba *desu.* (ここが事故現場です) This is the *spot* where the accident occurred.

ge⌈ñbaku げんばく(原爆) *n.* = geñshi-bakudañ.

ge⌉ñchi げんち(現地) *n.* the spot; the place:
Geñchi *kara no hookoku wa mada kite imaseñ.* (現地からの報告はまだ来ていません) Reports from *the scene* have not yet come in.

g

ge⌉ñdai げんだい(現代) *n.* the present age [day]; today. ⟪⇨ kindai⟫

ge⌈ñdai-teki げんだいてき(現代的) *a.n.* (~ na, ni) modern:
geñdai-teki *na keñchiku* (現代的な建築) *modern* architecture.

ge⌉ñdo げんど(限度) *n.* limit; limitations; bounds.

ge⌉ñgo げんご(言語) *n.* language; speech; words. ⟪⇨ kokugo⟫

ge⌈ñgo⌉gaku げんごがく(言語学) *n.* linguistics.

ge⌈ñgo⌉o げんごう(元号) *n.* an era name. ⟪⇨ APP. 9⟫

ge⌈ñiñ げんいん(原因) *n.* cause; factor; origin:
kaji no geñiñ *o shiraberu* (火事の原因を調べる) try to find the *cause* of the fire. ⟪↔ kekka⟫

ge⌈ñjitsu げんじつ(現実) *n.* actuality; reality:
Yume ga geñjitsu *to natta.* (夢が現実となった) The dream came *true.*

ge⌈ñjitsu-teki げんじつてき(現実的) *a.n.* (~ na, ni) realistic; down-to-earth.

ge⌈ñjoo げんじょう(現状) *n.* the present condition.

ge⌈ñjuu げんじゅう(厳重) *a.n.* (~ na, ni) strict; severe; strong:
Kyootee-ihañ ni taishite, geñjuu *ni koogi shita.* (協定違反に対して, 厳重に抗議した) We made a *strong* protest against their breach of the agreement.

ge⌈ñju⌉usho げんじゅうしょ(現住所) *n.* one's present address. ⟪⇨ juusho; sumai⟫

ge⌉ñkai げんかい(限界) *n.* boundary; limit; limitations.

ge⌉ñkañ げんかん(玄関) *n.* front door; entrance; porch.

ge⌉ñki げんき(元気) *n.* spirits; vigor; energy.
geñki-zukeru (~づける) *vt.* encourage.
— *a.n.* (~ na, ni) **1** well; fine; healthy: ★ The honorific '*o*' ('*o-geñki*') is often used when enquiring about someone's health, but never used when referring to oneself, one's family members, etc.
"O-geñki desu ka?" "Hai, geñki *desu."* (「お元気ですか」「はい, 元気です」) "How are you?" "*Fine,* thank you."
2 lively; high-spirited; energetic; vigorous; active.

ge⌈ñki⌉ñ[1] げんきん(現金) *n.* cash:
geñkiñ *de harau* (現金で払う) pay in *cash.*

ge⌈ñki⌉ñ[2] げんきん(現金) *a.n.* (~ na, ni) calculating; mercenary:
Kare wa geñkiñ *na otoko da.* (彼は現金な男だ) He is a *calculating* fellow.

ge⌈ñki⌉ñ[3] げんきん(厳禁) *n.* strict prohibition:
Chuusha geñkiñ. (*sign*) (駐車厳禁) *No* Parking.
geñkiñ suru (~する) *vt.* strictly prohibit [forbid].

ge⌉ñkoo げんこう(原稿) *n.* manuscript; copy.

ge⌈ñkoo-yo⌉oshi げんこうようし(原稿用紙) *n.* manuscript [writing] paper:
yoñhyaku-ji-zume geñkoo-yooshi (四百字詰め原稿用紙) *manuscript paper* with four hundred squares for characters.

ge⌉ñ ni げんに(現に) *adv.* actually; really:
Watashi wa geñ ni *sore o kono me de mimashita.* (私は現にそれをこ

の目で見ました) I *actually* saw it with my own eyes.

ge⌈ñpatsu げんぱつ (原発) *n.* nuclear power plant. ★ Abbreviation of '*geñshiryoku hatsudeñsho.*' ⟪⇨ geñshiryoku⟫

ge⌉ñri げんり (原理) *n.* principle; theory.

ge⌈ñroñ げんろん (言論) *n.* speech; writing:
geñroñ *no jiyuu* (言論の自由) freedom of *speech.*

ge⌈ñryo⌉o げんりょう (原料) *n.* raw materials; ingredient.

ge⌈ñsaku げんさく (原作) *n.* the original (work).

ge⌉ñshi げんし (原子) *n.* atom.

ge⌈ñshi-ba⌉kudañ げんしばくだん (原子爆弾) *n.* atomic bomb. ⟪⇨ geñbaku⟫

ge⌈ñshi⌉kaku げんしかく (原子核) *n.* atomic nucleus.

ge⌈ñshi⌉ro げんしろ (原子炉) *n.* nuclear reactor.

ge⌈ñshi⌉ryoku げんしりょく (原子力) *n.* atomic energy; nuclear power. ⟪⇨ geñpatsu⟫

ge⌈ñsho げんしょ (原書) *n.* the original (book) written in a foreign language.

ge⌈ñshoo[1] げんしょう (減少) *n.* decrease; diminution.
geñshoo suru (～する) *vi.* decrease; diminish; lessen. ⟪↔ zoodai; zooka⟫

ge⌈ñshoo[2] げんしょう (現象) *n.* phenomenon.

ge⌉ñshu げんしゅ (厳守) *n.* strict observance; rigid adherence.
geñshu suru (～する) *vt.* observe strictly.

ge⌈ñshuu げんしゅう (減収) *n.* decrease in income [revenue]. ⟪↔ zooshuu⟫

ge⌉ñso げんそ (元素) *n.* chemical element.

ge⌈ñsoku げんそく (原則) *n.* principle; general rule.
geñsoku to shite (～として) in principle.

ge⌉ñzai げんざい (現在) *n.* the present time; now. ⟪⇨ ima[1]⟫
... geñzai (...～) as of...: *Hachigatsu tooka* geñzai, *oobosha wa gojuu-niñ desu.* (8月10日現在, 応募者は50人です) The number of applicants is fifty *as of* August 10.

ge⌉ñzoo げんぞう (現像) *n.* (of photography) development.
geñzoo suru (～する) *vt.* develop (a film).

ge⌈ppu げっぷ (月賦) *n.* monthly installment [payment].

ge⌉ragera げらげら *adv.* (～ to) (the act of laughing loudly):
geragera (to) warau (げらげら(と)笑う) *guffaw.*

ge⌈ri げり (下痢) *n.* diarrhea. ⟪⇨ kudaru⟫

ge⌉sha げしゃ (下車) *n.* getting off (a train). ⟪↔ joosha⟫
gesha suru (～する) *vi.* get off (a train). ⟪⇨ tochuu-gesha; oriru⟫

ge⌈shi げし (夏至) *n.* summer solstice (about June 21). ⟪⇨ tooji[2]⟫

ge⌈shuku げしゅく (下宿) *n.*
1 boardinghouse; rooming house.
2 boarding; lodging.
geshuku suru (～する) *vi.* board; live in a rooming house.

ge⌈ssha げっしゃ (月謝) *n.* monthly tuition; tuition fee.

ge⌈sshoku げっしょく (月食) *n.* lunar eclipse. ⟪⇨ nisshoku⟫

ge⌈ta げた (下駄) *n.* Japanese wooden sandals.

ge⌈tsumatsu げつまつ (月末) *n.* the end of the month. ⟪⇨ shuumatsu; neñmatsu⟫

ge⌈tsuyo⌉o(bi) げつよう(び) (月曜(日)) *n.* Monday. ⟪⇨ APP. 5⟫

gi⌉choo ぎちょう (議長) *n.* chairperson; the speaker.

gi⌈dai ぎだい (議題) *n.* topic [subject] for discussion; agenda.

gi⌉iñ ぎいん (議員) *n.* Diet member; member of an assembly. ⟪⇨ Shuugiiñ; Sañgiiñ⟫

gi⌉jutsu ぎじゅつ (技術) *n.* technique; technology; art; skill.

gi˥kai ぎかい (議会) *n.* assembly; the Diet; Congress; Parliament. ⟪⇨ kokkai⟫

gi˹kyoku ぎきょく (戯曲) *n.* play; drama.

-gimi ぎみ (気味) *suf.* touch; shade:
Watashi wa kaze-gimi *desu.* (私はかぜぎみです) I have a *bit* of a cold.

gi˹moñ ぎもん (疑問) *n.* question; doubt; problem. ⟪⇨ utagai⟫

g

gi˥mu ぎむ (義務) *n.* duty; obligation:
gimu *o hatasu* [*okotaru*] (義務を果たす[怠る]) perform [neglect] one's *duty.* ⟪↔ keñri⟫

gi˥ñ ぎん (銀) *n.* silver.

gi˹ñkoo ぎんこう (銀行) *n.* bank:
giñkoo *ni yokiñ suru* (銀行に預金する) deposit money in a *bank.*

gi˹ñko˥oiñ ぎんこういん (銀行員) *n.* bank clerk.

gi˥ragira ぎらぎら *adv.* (～ to) (the state of shining with unpleasant brightness):
Taiyoo ga giragira (to) teritsukete ita. (太陽がぎらぎら(と)照りつけていた) The sun *was glaring down.* ⟪⇨ kirakira⟫

gi˹ri˥ ぎり (義理) *n.* duty; obligation; debt of gratitude:
Watashi wa kare ni giri *ga aru.* (私は彼に義理がある) I am under an *obligation* to him.
giri no ... (～の...) ...-in-law: giri no *chichi* [*imooto*] (義理の父[妹]) a father[sister]*-in-law.*

gi˥roñ ぎろん (議論) *n.* argument; discussion; dispute.
giroñ (o) suru (～(を)する) *vt.* argue; discuss; dispute.

gi˹see ぎせい (犠牲) *n.* **1** sacrifice: gisee *o harau* (犠牲を払う) make *sacrifices.*
2 victim:
Chichi wa señsoo no gisee *to natte shiñda.* (父は戦争の犠牲となって死んだ) My father died, a *victim* of war.

gi˥shi ぎし (技師) *n.* engineer.

gi˹sshi˥ri ぎっしり *adv.* (～ to) closely; tightly; to the full:
Hoñbako ni hoñ ga gisshiri (*to*) *tsumatte iru.* (本箱に本がぎっしり(と)詰まっている) The bookcase is *tightly* packed with books. ⟪⇨ ippai[2]; mañiñ⟫

go[1] ご (語) *n.* **1** language:
gaikoku-go (外国語) a foreign *language.*
2 word:
Kono go *no imi wa nañ desu ka?* (この語の意味は何ですか) What does this *word* mean?
3 term: *señmoñ*-go (専門語) a technical *term.*

go˥[2] ご (碁) *n.* (the game of) go.

go˥[3] ご (五) *n.* five. ⟪⇨ itsutsu; APP. 3⟫

go- ご (御) *pref.* [added to a noun, usually of Chinese origin]
1 (indicates respect toward the listener):
Go-kekkoñ *wa itsu desu ka?* (ご結婚はいつですか) When is *your marriage*?
2 (indicates humility on the part of the speaker):
Watashi ga go-añnai itashimasu. (私がご案内いたします) I'll *show* you *around.*

-go ご (後) *suf.* after; in:
Kare no shujutsu-go *no keeka wa ryookoo desu.* (彼の手術後の経過は良好です) He is doing well *after* the operation. ⟪⇨ -mae[1]⟫

go-˹busata ごぶさた (御無沙汰) *n.* long silence (not having been in touch). ★ Humble form of '*busata.*' This word is only used with reference to oneself.
go-busata suru (～する) *vi.* do not see [write] for a long time:
Go-busata shite imasu [shimashita]. (ご無沙汰しています[しました]) I *haven't seen* [*written to*] *you for a long time.*

go˹chisoo ごちそう (御馳走) *n.* treat; feast; entertainment:

Kare wa watashi ni teñpura o gochisoo shite kureta. (彼は私にてんぷらをごちそうしてくれた) He *treated* me to tempura.

go⌈chisoosama ごちそうさま (御馳走さま) **1** (used to express thanks after a meal):
Gochisoosama (*deshita*). (ごちそうさま(でした)) *Thank you. I* really *enjoyed the meal.* (⇨ itadakimasu)
2 (used to express thanks for hospitality):
Kyoo wa hoñtoo ni gochisoosama *deshita.* (きょうは本当にごちそうさまでした) *Thank you very much for your hospitality* today.

go⌉gaku ごがく (語学) *n.* language study; linguistics.

go⌉-gatsu ごがつ (五月) *n.* May. (⇨ APP. 5)

go⌈geñ ごげん (語源) *n.* origin of a word; etymology.

go⌉go ごご (午後) *n.* afternoon; P.M. (↔ gozeñ)

go⌉hañ ごはん (ご飯) *n.*
1 (cooked [boiled]) rice:
Gohañ *o ni-hai tabeta.* (ご飯を2杯食べた) I ate two bowls of *rice.*
2 meal; food:
Ohiru da kara gohañ *ni shiyoo.* (お昼だからご飯にしよう) Since it is noon, let's have *lunch.* (⇨ asagohañ; bañgohañ; hirugohañ)

go⌉i ごい (語彙) *n.* vocabulary.

go⌈ju⌉u ごじゅう (五十) *n.* fifty.

go⌈juu-no⌉-too ごじゅうのとう (五重の塔) *n.* five-storied pagoda.

go⌈ju⌉uoñ ごじゅうおん (五十音) *n.* the Japanese syllabary. (⇨Table of Japanese symbols)

go⌈kai ごかい (誤解) *n.* misunderstanding; misapprehension.
gokai (o) suru (~(を)する) *vt.* misunderstand; mistake.

go⌈ka⌉ku-kee ごかくけい (五角形) *n.* pentagon.

go⌈kiburi ごきぶり *n.* cockroach.

-go⌉kko ごっこ *suf.* play...:
o-isha-sañ-gokko *o suru* (お医者さんごっこをする) play *doctor.*

-gokochi ごこち (心地) *suf.* feeling:
sumi-gokochi *ga ii* (住み心地がいい) be comfortable to *live in.*

go⌉ku ごく (極) *adv.* very; extremely: (⇨ kiwamete)
Sore wa goku *saikiñ no dekigoto desu.* (それはごく最近のでき事です) That is a *very* recent occurrence.

go⌈ku⌉roo ごくろう (ご苦労) *n.* trouble:
Gokuroo *o kakete, mooshiwake arimaseñ.* (ご苦労をかけて, 申し訳ありません) I am very sorry for causing so much *trouble.*
— *a.n.* (~ na/no) painful; hard: ★ Sometimes used sarcastically.
Kono samui no ni suiee to wa gokuroo *na koto da.* (この寒いのに水泳とはご苦労なことだ) It is an *ordeal* to go swimming when it is cold like this. (⇨ gokuroosama)

go⌈ku⌉roosama ごくろうさま (御苦労様) thank you for your trouble; thank you very much. ★ Used to express thanks for a task well done or trouble expended. Not used to superiors.

go⌈maka⌉s·u ごまかす (誤魔化す) *vt.* (-kash·i-; -kas·a-; -kash·i-te Ⓒ) **1** cheat; deceive; take in. (⇨ damasu)
2 tell a lie:
neñree o gomakasu (年齢をごまかす) *lie* about one's age.
3 gloss over:
Kare wa shippai o waratte gomakashita. (彼は失敗を笑ってごまかした) He *laughed off* his blunder.
4 embezzle; (of accounts) cook.

go⌈meñ[1] ごめん (御免) excuse me; pardon me; I'm sorry. ★ '*Gomeñ nasai*' is more polite. (⇨ gomeñ kudasai)

go⌈meñ[2] ごめん (御免) *n.* (used to express refusal):
Soñna shigoto wa gomeñ *da.* (そんな仕事はごめんだ) That kind of job *is not for me.*

go⌈meñ kudasa⌉i ごめんください

g

(御免下さい) **1** excuse me: ★ Used when arriving or taking one's leave.
Kore de shitsuree shimasu. Gomeñ kudasai. (これで失礼します. ごめんください) I will now say goodbye here. *Please excuse me.*
2 I am sorry; pardon [forgive] me. ((⇨ gomeñ[1]))

go[meñ nasa]i ごめんなさい (御免なさい) I am sorry; excuse me; forgive me:
Okurete gomeñ nasai. (遅れてごめんなさい) *I'm sorry* to be late.

g

go[mi] ごみ (塵·芥) *n.* trash; rubbish; litter; garbage. ((⇨ chiri[1]))

go[mi]bako ごみばこ (ごみ箱) *n.* trash [garbage] can; dustbin.

go]mu ゴム *n.* rubber.

-goo ごう (号) *suf.* **1** number: *taifuu juusañ*-goo (台風 13 号) Typhoon *No.* 13.
2 issue (of a magazine).
3 building number. ((⇨ juusho))

go[oiñ ごういん (強引) *a.n.* (~ na, ni) forcible; high-handed:
gooiñ *na seerusumañ* (強引なセールスマン) a *high-handed* salesman.

go]oka ごうか (豪華) *a.n.* (~ na, ni) luxurious; magnificent:
gooka *na kekkoñ-shiki* (豪華な結婚式) a *splendid* wedding ceremony.

go[okaku ごうかく (合格) *n.* passing (an examination); success.
gookaku suru (~する) *vi.* pass; succeed: *keñsa ni* gookaku suru (検査に合格する) *pass* an inspection.

go[okee ごうけい (合計) *n.* total; sum; the sum total.
gookee suru (~する) *vt.* sum up; total. ((⇨ sashihiki))

go[orika ごうりか (合理化) *n.* rationalization.
goorika suru (~する) *vt.* rationalize.

go[ori-teki ごうりてき (合理的) *a.n.* (~ na, ni) rational; reasonable; practical:
kaji o goori-teki ni suru (家事を合理的にする) *streamline* housework.

go[orudeñ-ui]iku ゴールデンウイーク *n.* 'Golden Week.' ★ Refers to the period from April 29 to May 5, which is full of national holidays. ((⇨ APP. 6))

go[oru]-iñ ゴールイン *n.* finish; breasting the tape.
gooru-iñ suru (~する) **1** reach the finish line.
2 get married: *Futari wa yatto* gooru-iñ shita. (二人はやっとゴールインした) The two of them finally *got married.*

go[osee ごうせい (合成) *n.* synthesis; composition:
goosee-*señi* (合成繊維) *synthetic* fiber.

go[otoo ごうとう (強盗) *n.* **1** burglar; robber. ((⇨ doroboo))
2 robbery:
gootoo *o hataraku* (強盗をはたらく) commit a *robbery.*

go[raku ごらく (娯楽) *n.* amusement; recreation; entertainment.

go[rañ ごらん (ご覧) *n.* (*honorific*)
1 see; look at:
Kore o gorañ *kudasai.* (これをご覧ください) Please *look at* this.
2 try:
Moo ichi-do yatte gorañ nasai (もう一度やってご覧なさい) *Try* it again.

-go]ro ごろ (頃) *suf.* about; around:
Juuji-goro *uchi ni kite kudasai.* (10 時ごろうちに来てください) I would like you to come to my house at *about* ten o'clock. ((⇨ koro))

go]rogoro ごろごろ *adv.* (~ to)
1 (the sound of rolling, rumbling and purring):
Kaminari ga gorogoro (to) natte iru. (雷がゴロゴロ(と)鳴っている) The thunder *is rolling.*
2 (the state of something rolling):
Ooki-na iwa ga yama no shameñ o gorogoro (to) ochite itta. (大きな岩が山の斜面をゴロゴロ(と)落ちて行った) A large rock *rolled down* the

mountainside.
3 (the state of being plentiful):
Suisu de wa ni-ka-koku-go o hanaseru hito ga gorogoro iru. (スイスでは2か国語を話せる人がごろごろいる) In Switzerland *there are many* who can speak two languages.
4 (the state of being lazy):
Kare wa yasumi-juu ie de gorogoro (to) shite ita. (彼は休み中家でごろごろ(と)していた) He *lolled around* the house all through the holidays.

go⌈ro⌉ri ごろり *adv.* (~ to) (used to express the action of lying down):
Kare wa gorori *to tatami no ue ni* yoko ni natta. (彼はごろりと畳の上に横になった) He *plopped himself down* full length on the tatami.

-goshi ごし(越し) *suf.* **1** through; over:
*Kare wa megane-*goshi *ni watashi o niramitsuketa.* (彼は眼鏡越しに私をにらみつけた) He glared at me *over* his glasses.
2 [after a noun denoting a long period of time] for; over:
Go-neñ-goshi *no koi ga minotte, futari wa kekkoñ shita.* (五年越しの恋が実って, 二人は結婚した) Their love of *five years* matured and they got married.

-goto ごと *suf.* and all; together with:
*riñgo o kawa-*goto *taberu* (りんごを皮ごと食べる) eat an apple, peel *and all.*

-go⌉to ni ごとに *suf.* **1** every; each:
*Sooji toobañ wa ik-kagetsu-*goto ni *kawarimasu.* (掃除当番は1か月ごとに替わります) Cleaning duty changes *every* month.
2 every time; whenever; whoever:
*Kare wa au hito-*goto ni *sono hanashi o shite iru.* (彼は会う人ごとにその話をしている) He tells that story to *whoever* he meets.

go⌈zaima⌉su ございます(御座居ます) be; have; there is [are]:
★ Polite equivalent of '*arimasu*.' The polite equivalent of '*desu*' is '*de gozaimasu*.'
Nani-ka go-yoo ga gozaimashitara, *o-shirase kudasai.* (何かご用がございましたら, お知らせください) If *there is* anything I can do for you, please let me know.
Arigatoo gozaimasu. (ありがとうございます) Thank you very much.
Ohayoo gozaimasu. (お早うございます) Good morning.

go⌉zeñ ごぜん(午前) *n.* forenoon; morning; A.M. 《↔ gogo》《⇨ asa[1]》

go⌈zeñ-chuu ごぜんちゅう(午前中) *n., adv.* in the morning; any time from sunrise to noon.

go⌈zo⌉ñji ごそんじ(ご存じ) (*honorific*) know; be aware:
Kare no atarashii juusho o gozoñji *desu ka?* (彼の新しい住所をご存じですか) *Do* you *know* his new address? 《⇨ zoñjiru》

gu⌈ai ぐあい(具合) *n.* **1** condition:
Onaka no guai ga okashii. (おなかのぐあいがおかしい) I *am sick* to my stomach.
2 convenience:
Kare wa guai no warui *toki ni yatte kita.* (彼はぐあいの悪いときにやって来た) He showed up at an *inconvenient* time.
3 manner; way:
Koñna guai *ni yareba, umaku ikimasu.* (こんなぐあいにやれば, うまく行きます) If you do it *this way*, you will succeed.

gu⌉ñ[1] ぐん(群) *n.* group; crowd.
guñ o nuku (~を抜く) excel [surpass] all.

gu⌉ñ[2] ぐん(軍) *n.* force; army; troops. 《⇨ Jieetai》

gu⌉ñ[3] ぐん(郡) *n.* county; district.

gu⌉ñbi ぐんび(軍備) *n.* armaments; military preparations.

gu⌉ñguñ ぐんぐん *adv.* (~ to) quickly; rapidly; steadily:

g

shiñchoo ga guñguñ (to) nobiru (身長がぐんぐん(と)伸びる) *shoot up* in height.

guʻñji-eˈñjo ぐんじえんじょ (軍事援助) *n.* military aid.

guʻñjiñ ぐんじん (軍人) *n.* military man; soldier; sailor; airman.

guʻñkañ ぐんかん (軍艦) *n.* warship; man-of-war.

guʻñshuu ぐんしゅう (群衆・群集) *n.* crowd; throng; mob.

guˈñtai ぐんたい (軍隊) *n.* armed forces; troops.

g

guʻñtoo ぐんとう (群島) *n.* a group of islands; archipelago. ⟪⇨ rettoo[1]⟫

guˈragura ぐらぐら *adv.* (~ to)
1 (unstable shaking or moving): *Jishiñ de ie ga* guragura (*to*) *yureta.* (地震で家がぐらぐら(と)揺れた) The house shook *unsteadily* in the earthquake.
2 (the state of water boiling): *Yakañ no yu ga* guragura (*to*) *nitatte iru.* (やかんの湯がぐらぐら(と)煮立っている) The water in the kettle is boiling *vigorously*.

guˈrai ぐらい (位) *p.* = kurai[2].

guˈramu グラム *n.* gram.

guʻrañdo グランド *n.* playground; sports ground; stadium.

guʻriiñsha グリーンしゃ (グリーン車) *n.* 'green car'; first-class railway carriage.

guʻroˈobu グローブ *n.* glove.

guˈruguru ぐるぐる *adv.* (~ to) (the state of something moving around or rotating continuously): *Kare wa te o* guruguru (*to*) *mawashite aizu shita.* (彼は手をぐるぐる(と)回して合図した) He signaled by *waving* his hand *around*.

guʻruˈri ぐるり *adv.* = gurutto.

guʻruˈtto ぐるっと *adv.* (the action of looking around or the feeling of being completely surrounded): *koosoo-biru ni* gurutto *torikakomareta kooeñ* (高層ビルにぐるっと取り囲まれた公園) a park *completely* surrounded by high-rise buildings.

guʻssuˈri ぐっすり *adv.* (~ to) (the state of sleeping soundly): *Yuube wa* gussuri (*to*) *nemureta.* (ゆうべはぐっすり(と)眠れた) I was able to sleep *soundly* last night.

guʻtai-teki ぐたいてき (具体的) *a.n.* (~ na, ni) concrete; definite; physical: gutai-teki *na ree o ageru* (具体的な例をあげる) give *concrete* examples. ⟪↔ chuushoo-teki⟫

guʻtto ぐっと *adv.* **1** suddenly; firmly; fast; hard: gutto *tsukamu* (ぐっとつかむ) grasp *firmly* / gutto *hipparu* (ぐっと引っ張る) pull *with a jerk*.
2 much; by far: *Kotchi no hoo ga* gutto *hikitatsu.* (こっちのほうがぐっと引き立つ) This one looks *much* better.

guˈuguu ぐうぐう *adv.* (~ to) (the sound of snoring or of an empty stomach): *Kare wa* guuguu (*to*) *ooki-na ibiki o kaite ita.* (彼はグウグウ(と)大きないびきをかいていた) He was snoring *loudly*.

guʻusuˈu ぐうすう (偶数) *n.* even number(s). ⟪↔ kisuu⟫

guʻuzeñ ぐうぜん (偶然) *a.n.* (~ na/no, ni) chance; accident: guuzeñ *no dekigoto* (偶然の出来事) a *chance* occurrence.
— *adv.* by chance: *Watashi wa* guuzeñ, *sono jiko geñba ni* ita. (私は偶然, その事故現場にいた) I just *happened to be* at the scene of the accident. ⟪⇨ tamatama⟫

guˈzuguzu ぐずぐず *adv.* (~ to; ~ suru) slowly; lazily: Guzuguzu shite iru *to, okuremasu yo.* (ぐずぐずしていると, 遅れますよ) If you *dawdle along*, you will be late.
guzuguzu iu (~言う) grumble; complain. ⟪⇨ fuhee⟫

gyaʻku ぎゃく (逆) *n.* reverse; contrary; opposite.

— *a.n.* (～ na/no, ni) reverse; contrary; opposite:
gyaku *no hookoo* (逆の方向) the *opposite* direction.

gyo⌝gyoo ぎょぎょう (漁業) *n.* fishery; fishing industry.
《⇨ noogyoo》

gyo⌝kuro ぎょくろ (玉露) *n.* green tea of the highest quality.
《⇨ bañcha; señcha》

gyo⌝o ぎょう (行) *n.* **1** row of words; line:
ichi gyoo *oki ni kaku* (一行おきに書く) write on every other *line.*
2 (of the Japanese syllabary) series:
gojuuoñ-zu no ka gyoo (五十音図のカ行) the 'k' *series* in the list of the Japanese syllabary. 《⇨ inside front cover》

gyo⌜ogi ぎょうぎ (行儀) *n.* manners; behavior.

gyo⌝oji ぎょうじ (行事) *n.* event; function.

gyo⌜oretsu ぎょうれつ (行列) *n.*
1 line; queue.
2 procession; parade:
soogi no gyooretsu (葬儀の行列) a funeral *procession.*
gyooretsu suru (～する) *vi.* stand in line; queue up.

gyo⌜osee ぎょうせい (行政) *n.* administration:
gyoosee-*kaikaku* (行政改革) *administrative* reform. 《⇨ sañkeñ-buñritsu》

gyo⌜oseki ぎょうせき (業績) *n.* achievements; results; work:
Kaisha no gyooseki *wa amari yoku arimaseñ.* (会社の業績はあまり良くありません) Company *business* is not so good.

gyo⌝osha ぎょうしゃ (業者) *n.* dealer; trader; manufacturer.

gyo⌜oza ぎょうざ *n.* Chinese dumplings.

gyo⌜señ ぎょせん (漁船) *n.* fishing boat [vessel].

gyo⌜soñ ぎょそん (漁村) *n.* fishing village.

gyo⌜tto s·uru ぎょっとする *vi.* (sh·i-; sh·i-; sh·i-te [I]) be startled; be frightened.

gyu⌝ugyuu ぎゅうぎゅう *adv.* (～ to, ni) (the state of squeezing something, or of it being tightly packed):
Watashi wa kabañ ni irui o gyuugyuu (*to* [*ni*]) tsumeta. (私はかばんに衣類をぎゅうぎゅう(と[に])詰めた) I *squeezed* my clothes into the bag.

gyu⌜uniku ぎゅうにく (牛肉) *n.* beef. 《⇨ niku》

gyu⌜unyuu ぎゅうにゅう (牛乳) *n.* cow's milk.

H

ha⌝[1] は (歯) *n.* tooth:
ha *o migaku* (歯を磨く) brush one's *teeth.*
ha ga tatanai (～がたたない) be beyond one's power.

ha⌝[2] は (刃) *n.* edge; blade.

ha[3] は (葉) *n.* leaf; foliage.

ha⌝a[1] はあ *int.* yes; indeed; well:
"Issho ni ikimasu ka?" "Haa, *ikimasu."* (「一緒に行きますか」「はあ, 行きます」) "Are you coming with me?" "*Yes,* I am." 《⇨ hai[1]》

ha⌜a[2] はあ *int.* what: ★ With a rising tone.
"Raishuu Chuugoku e ikimasu." "Haa?" (「来週中国へ行きます」「はあ」) "I am going to China next week." "*What did you say?*"

ha⌜aku はあく (把握) *n.* grasp; hold; grip. ★ Usually used figuratively.
haaku suru (～する) *vt.* grasp; hold; seize: *jitai o* haaku suru (事態を把握する) *grasp* the situation.

《⇨ rikai; tsukamu》

ha⌈ba はば (幅) *n.* width; range; breadth. 《⇨ nagasa; takasa》

ha⌈ba⌉m·u はばむ (阻む) *vt.* (ha-bam·i-; habam·a-; habañ-de Ⓒ) prevent; block; check. 《⇨ jama》

ha⌈bu⌉k·u はぶく (省く) *vt.* (ha-buk·i-; habuk·a-; habu·i-te Ⓒ) cut down; save; omit:
tema o habuku (手間を省く) *save* a labor.

ha⌈bu⌉rashi はブラシ (歯ブラシ) *n.* toothbrush.

ha⌈chi[1] はち (八) *n.* eight. 《⇨ yattsu; APP. 3》

ha⌈chi[2] はち (鉢) *n.* flower pot; container; bowl; basin. 《⇨ chawañ; doñburi》

ha⌈chi[3] はち (蜂) *n.* bee; wasp.

ha⌈chi-gatsu⌉ はちがつ (八月) *n.* August. 《⇨ APP. 5》

ha⌈chi⌉maki はちまき (鉢巻き) *n.* headband.

ha⌉da はだ (肌) *n.* **1** skin:
Kanojo wa hada *ga shiroi.* (彼女は肌が白い) She has fair *skin.*
2 temperament:
*Kare wa geejutsuka-*hada *da.* (彼は芸術家肌だ) He has an artistic *temperament.*

ha⌈dagi⌉ はだぎ (肌着) *n.* underwear; underclothes.

ha⌈daka はだか (裸) *n.* naked body; nakedness; nudity.

ha⌈dashi はだし (裸足) *n.* bare foot.

ha⌈de⌉ はで (派手) *a.n.* (～ na, ni)
1 showy; bright; gaudy:
Kono fuku wa sukoshi hade-*sugiru.* (この服は少し派手すぎる) This garment is a bit too *gaudy.* 《↔ jimi》
2 spectacular; conspicuous:
Futari wa hade *na keñka o shita.* (二人は派手なけんかをした) The two of them had a *spectacular* fight.
3 lavish:
hade *ni kane o tsukau* (派手に金を使う) spend money *lavishly.*

ha⌈e はえ (蝿) *n.* fly.

ha⌈e⌉·ru[1] はえる (生える) *vi.* (hae-te Ⓥ) **1** (of a plant) come out; grow:
Kono ki wa nettai dake ni haete iru. (この木は熱帯だけに生えている) This tree *grows* only in tropical regions.
2 (of tooth, hair, etc.) grow:
Akañboo ni ha ga haeta. (赤ん坊に歯が生えた) The baby *cut* a tooth. 《⇨ hayasu》

ha⌈e⌉·ru[2] はえる (映える) *vi.* (hae-te Ⓥ) **1** shine:
Fuji-sañ ga asahi ni haete, *utsukushii.* (富士山が朝日に映えて, 美しい) Mt. Fuji is beautiful—*shining* in the morning sun.
2 look beautiful:
Kanojo ni wa shiroi doresu ga yoku haeru. (彼女には白いドレスがよく映える) White dresses *look very nice* on her.

ha⌈gaki はがき (葉書) *n.* postcard. 《⇨ e-hagaki; oofuku-hagaki》

ha⌈gare⌉·ru はがれる (剝がれる) *vi.* (hagare-te Ⓥ) peel [come] off:
Posutaa ga kaze de hagarete shimatta. (ポスターが風ではがれてしまった) The poster *came off* in the wind. 《⇨ hagasu》

ha⌈ga⌉s·u はがす (剝がす) *vt.* (ha-gash·i-; hagas·a-; hagash·i-te Ⓒ) peel off:
Fuutoo kara kitte o hagashita. (封筒から切手をはがした) I *peeled* the stamp off the envelope. 《⇨ hagu; hagareru》

ha⌈gema⌉s·u はげます (励ます) *vt.* (-mash·i-; -mas·a-; -mash·i-te Ⓒ) encourage; cheer up.

ha⌈ge⌉m·u はげむ (励む) *vi.* (ha-gem·i-; hagem·a-; hageñ-de Ⓒ) work hard; apply oneself to.

ha⌈ge⌉·ru[1] はげる (剝げる) *vi.* (ha-ge-te Ⓥ) **1** come off; wear off:
Tokorodokoro peñki ga hagete iru. (ところどころペンキがはげている) The paint *has come off* in places. 《⇨ hagasu》
2 (of color) fade. 《⇨ aseru[2]》

ha[ge·]ru[2] はげる(禿る) *vi.* (hagete [V]) become bald:
Kare wa sukoshi hagete iru. (彼は少しはげている) He *is* slightly *bald*.

ha[geshi]·i はげしい(激しい) *a.* (-ku) intense; violent; severe:
hageshii *atsusa* (激しい暑さ) *intense* heat / hageshii *itami* (激しい痛み) an *acute* pain.

ha]g·u はぐ(剝ぐ) *vt.* (hag·i-; hag·a-; ha·i-de [C]) tear off; strip off; remove the skin.
《⇨ hagasu》

ha[gu]ruma はぐるま(歯車) *n.* cogwheel; gear.

ha]ha はは(母) *n.* mother. 《↔ chichi[1]》《⇨ haha-oya》

ha[haa ははあ *int.* well; I see; oh; now:
Hahaa, *sore de wakarimashita.* (ははあ, それでわかりました) *I see.* I understand now.

ha[ha-oya ははおや(母親) *n.* female parent; mother. 《↔ chichi-oya》《⇨ haha》

ha]i[1] はい *int.* **1** yes; no: ★ '*Hai*' literally means 'That's right' and is used to confirm a statement, whether affirmative or negative.
"Kore wa kawa desu ka?" "Hai, *soo desu."* (「これは革ですか」「はい, そうです」) "Is this leather?" "*Yes*, it is." / *"Anata wa Nihoñ no kata de wa arimaseñ ne?"* "Hai, *Chuugokujiñ desu."* (「あなたは日本の方ではありませんね」「はい, 中国人です」) "You aren't Japanese, are you?" "*No*, I'm Chinese." 《↔ iie》
2 (when the roll is called) yes; here; present:
"Suzuki(-kuñ)." "Hai." (「鈴木(君)」「はい」) "Suzuki." "*Here.*"
3 certainly; of course:
"Deñwa o o-kari shite yoroshii desu ka?" "Hai, *doozo."* (「電話をお借りしてよろしいですか」「はい, どうぞ」) "May I use your phone?" "*Certainly.* Please go ahead."

ha[i[2] はい(灰) *n.* ash.

ha[i[3] はい(肺) *n.* lungs.

-hai はい(杯) *suf.* cup; glass; bowl. ★ Liquid measure counter used to count glassfuls or cupfuls. 《⇨ APP. 4》

ha[iaga]r·u はいあがる(這い上がる) *vt.* (-agar·i-; -agar·a-; -agat-te [C]) creep up; crawl up:
Kono gake o haiagaru *no wa muzukashii.* (このがけをはい上がるのは難しい) It is difficult to *climb up* this cliff.

ha[iboku はいぼく(敗北) *n.* defeat.
haiboku suru (～する) *vi.* be defeated be beaten. 《↔ shoori》《⇨ makeru》

ha[ibo]oru ハイボール *n.* highball. ★ In Japan, refers to whisky and soda. 《⇨ mizuwari》

ha[ichi はいち(配置) *n.* arrangement; stationing.
haichi suru (～する) *vt.* arrange; station; post.

ha[igañ はいがん(肺癌) *n.* lung cancer. 《⇨ gañ》

ha[igu]usha はいぐうしゃ(配偶者) *n.* (*legal*) spouse; one's husband; one's wife.

ha[i-iro はいいろ(灰色) *n.* gray.

ha[ikee[1] はいけい(拝啓) *n.* Dear...; Gentlemen; Dear Sir or Madam. ★ Used in the salutation of a formal letter. 《⇨ keegu; zeñryaku》

ha[ikee[2] はいけい(背景) *n.* **1** background.
2 scenery; setting; scene:
Sono monogatari no haikee *wa Yokohama desu.* (その物語の背景は横浜です) The *setting* of the story is Yokohama.

ha[ikeñ はいけん(拝見) *n.* (humble equivalent of 'see' or 'read'):
"Doozo." "De wa chotto haikeñ." (「どうぞ」「ではちょっと拝見」) "Please go ahead." "Then let me *have a look* at it."
haikeñ suru (～する) *vt.* (*humble*) see; look at; watch; read: *O-tegami o* haikeñ shimashita. (お手紙を拝見しました) I *have read* your letter.

h

ha¹ikiñgu ハイキング *n.* hike; hiking.

ha⌈iku はいく(俳句) *n.* haiku. ★ A poem with lines of five, seven, and five syllables.

ha⌈iretsu はいれつ(配列) *n.* arrangement; placement in order.
hairetsu suru (～する) *vt.* arrange; place in order.

ha¹ir·u はいる(入る) *vi.* (hair·i-; hair·a-; hait-te Ⓒ) ★ '*haitte iru*' =be in [inside]. **1** enter; come [go] in:
Deñsha ga hoomu ni haitte kita. (電車がホームに入ってきた) The train *pulled in* to the platform.
2 be admitted; enter; join:
daigaku ni hairu (大学に入る) *matriculate* at a university.
3 contain; include:
Kono biiru ni wa amari arukooru ga haitte imaseñ. (このビールにはあまりアルコールが入っていません) This beer *does not contain* much alcohol.
4 hold; seat:
Kono gekijoo wa gohyaku-niñ hairu. (この劇場は500人入る) This theater *accommodates* 500 people.
5 (of a season, a vacation, etc.) begin; set in:
Moo tsuyu ni hairimashita. (もう梅雨に入りました) We have already *entered* the rainy season.
6 get; obtain; have:
Dai-nyuusu ga haitta. (大ニュースが入った) We *have had* some big news.
7 be installed:
Kaku heya ni deñwa ga haitta. (各部屋に電話が入った) Telephones *have been installed* in each room. ⟨⇨ setchi⟩

ha⌈iseki はいせき(排斥) *n.* exclusion; boycott; shut-out.
haiseki suru (～する) *vt.* expel; boycott; shut out.

ha⌈iseñ はいせん(敗戦) *n.* loss of a battle [game]; defeat.

ha¹isha[1] はいしゃ(歯医者) *n.* dentist. ⟨⇨ isha⟩

ha¹isha[2] はいしゃ(敗者) *n.* loser; defeated peson. ⟨↔ shoosha[2]⟩

ha⌈ishi はいし(廃止) *n.* abolition; discontinuance; repeal.
haishi suru (～する) *vt.* abolish; discontinue; repeal.

ha⌈isui はいすい(排水) *n.* draining; drainage.
haisui suru (～する) *vt.* drain; pump water out.

ha⌈itatsu はいたつ(配達) *n.* delivery.
haitatsu suru (～する) *vt.* deliver (newspapers, letters, etc.).

ha¹iyaa ハイヤー *n.* chauffeur-driven limousine. ★ From 'hire.' ⟨⇨ takushii⟩

ha⌈iyuu はいゆう(俳優) *n.* actor; actress. ⟨⇨ yakusha⟩

ha⌈izara はいざら(灰皿) *n.* ashtray.

ha⌈ji¹ はじ(恥) *n.* shame; disgrace; humiliation:
Watashi wa miñna no mae de haji *o kaita.* (私はみんなの前で恥をかいた) I was put to *shame* in public.

ha⌈jike¹·ru はじける(弾ける) *vi.* (hajike-te Ⓥ) burst [crack] open; pop:
Kuri ga hi no naka de hajiketa. (栗が火の中ではじけた) The chestnut *burst open* in the fire. ⟨⇨ hajiku⟩

ha⌈ji¹k·u はじく(弾く) *vt.* (hajik·i-; hajik·a-; haji·i-te Ⓒ) flip; fillip; repel:
Kono reeñkooto wa ame o yoku hajikimasu. (このレインコートは雨をよくはじきます) This raincoat *repels* rain well. ⟨⇨ hajikeru⟩

ha⌈jimar·u はじまる(始まる) *vi.* (hajimar·i-; hajimar·a-; hajimat-te Ⓒ) begin; start. ⟨⇨ hajimeru⟩

ha⌈jime はじめ(初め) *n.* beginning; start:
Watashi wa kotoshi no hajime *ni Nihoñ e kimashita.* (私は今年の初めに日本へ来ました) I came to Japan at the *beginning* of this year.

ha⌈jimema¹shite はじめまして(始

めまして) How do you do?; I'm glad to meet you.

ha⌈jime·ru はじめる(始める) *vt.* (hajime-te [V]) begin; start:
Sore de wa jugyoo o hajimemasu. (それでは授業を始めます) Now we'll *begin* the lesson. ⟪⇨ hajimaru⟫

-hajime·ru はじめる(始める) (-hajime-te [V]) start (doing): ★ Occurs as the second element of compound verbs. Added to the continuative base of a verb.
yomi-hajimeru (読み始める) *start* reading / *tabe*-hajimeru (食べ始める) *begin* eating. ⟪⇨ -dasu (3)⟫

ha⌈ji⌉mete はじめて(初めて) *adv.* first; for the first time:
Fuji-sañ o mita no wa kore ga hajimete *desu.* (富士山を見たのはこれが初めてです) This is *the first time* that I have seen Mt. Fuji.

ha⌈ji⌉·ru はじる(恥じる) *vi.* (haji-te [V]) feel ashamed:
Watashi wa jibuñ no chikara-busoku o hajite iru. (私は自分の力不足を恥じている) I *am ashamed* of my lack of ability.

ha⌈ka⌉ はか(墓) *n.* grave; tomb.

ha⌈kai はかい(破壊) *n.* destruction; demolition.
hakai suru (～する) *vt.* destroy; demolish.

ha⌈kai-teki はかいてき(破壊的) *a.n.* (～ na, ni) destructive.

ha⌈kama⌉ はかま(袴) *n.* Long pleated trousers chiefly worn by men over a kimono.

ha⌈kama⌉iri はかまいり(墓参り) *n.* visit to a grave. ⟪⇨ higañ⟫

ha⌈kari⌉ はかり(秤) *n.* balance; scales.

ha⌈ka⌉r·u[1] はかる(計る) *vt.* (haka-r·i-; hakar·a-; hakat-te [C])
1 record the time; time:
kuruma no sokudo o hakaru (車の速度を計る) *time* the speed of a car.
2 measure (blood pressure or temperature); take.

ha⌈ka⌉r·u[2] はかる(量る) *vt.* (haka-r·i-; hakar·a-; hakat-te [C]) weigh; measure:
taijuukee de taijuu o hakaru (体重計で体重を量る) *weigh* oneself on scales / *komugiko no ryoo o kappu de* hakaru (小麦粉の量をカップで量る) *measure* the amount of flour with a measuring cup.

ha⌈ka⌉r·u[3] はかる(測る) *vt.* (haka-r·i-; hakar·a-; hakat-te [C])
1 take the measurement; fathom:
kawa no fukasa o hakaru (川の深さを測る) *measure* the depth of a river.
2 = hakaru[2].

ha⌈ka⌉r·u[4] はかる(図る) *vt.* (haka-r·i-; hakar·a-; hakat-te [C])
1 strive; make an effort:
imeeji-appu o hakaru (イメージアップを図る) *strive* to improve one's image.
2 plan; attempt: *jisatsu o* hakaru (自殺を図る) *attempt* suicide.

ha⌈ka⌉r·u[5] はかる(謀る) *vt.* (haka-r·i-; hakar·a-; hakat-te [C]) plot; attempt:
shushoo no añsatsu o hakaru (首相の暗殺を謀る) *plot* the assassination of the prime minister.

ha⌉kase はかせ(博士) *n.* doctor. ⟪⇨ hakushi[1]⟫

ha⌈ke⌉ はけ(刷毛) *n.* flat brush. ⟪⇨ burashi⟫

ha⌈keñ はけん(派遣) *n.* dispatch.
hakeñ suru (～する) *vt.* dispatch; send.

ha⌉kihaki はきはき *adv.* (～ to) crisply; briskly; smartly:
Kanojo wa shitsumoñ ni hakihaki (*to*) *kotaeta.* (彼女は質問にはきはき(と)答えた) She *briskly* replied to the questions.

ha⌈kimono はきもの(履物) *n.* footwear; shoes.

ha⌈kkeñ はっけん(発見) *n.* discovery; detection.
hakkeñ suru (～する) *vt.* discover; find; detect. ⟪⇨ mitsukeru⟫

ha⌈kki はっき(発揮) *n.* demonstration; display.

hakki suru (～する) *vt.* demonstrate; display; show: *jitsuryoku o* hakki suru (実力を発揮する) *show* one's ability.

ha⌈kki⌉ri はっきり *adv.* (～ to; ～ suru) clearly; distinctly; definitely:
Sono koto wa asu ni nareba, hakkiri *shimasu.* (そのことは明日になれば, はっきりします) The matter will become *clear* tomorrow.
《⇨ akiraka》

ha⌈kkoo はっこう (発行) *n.* publication; issue.
hakkoo suru (～する) *vt.* publish; issue (a magazine). 《⇨ dasu (3)》

h

ha⌈kkutsu はっくつ (発掘) *n.* digging; excavation.
hakkutsu suru (～する) *vt.* dig out; unearth; excavate.

ha⌈ko はこ (箱) *n.* box; case.

ha⌈kob·u はこぶ (運ぶ) (hakob·i-; hakob·a-; hakoñ-de Ⓒ)
1 *vt.* carry; transport:
Keganiñ wa kyuukyuusha de byooiñ ni hakobareta. (けが人は救急車で病院に運ばれた) The injured *were taken* to the hospital by ambulance.
2 *vt.* move forward; carry out:
umaku koto o hakobu (うまくことを運ぶ) *carry out* a plan smoothly.
3 *vi.* make progress; go:
Shigoto wa umaku hakoñde imasu. (仕事はうまく運んでいます) The work *is going* forward nicely.

ha⌈k·u[1] はく (履く) *vt.* (hak·i-; hak·a-; ha·i-te Ⓒ) put on (footwear, trousers, skirts, etc.):
★ '*haite iru*'= wear. 《↔ nugu》
Kono jiiñzu o haite mite *mo ii desu ka?* (このジーンズをはいてみてもいいですか) May I *try* on these jeans?

ha⌉k·u[2] はく (掃く) *vt.* (hak·i-; hak·a-; ha·i-te Ⓒ) sweep:
niwa o haku (庭を掃く) *sweep* the garden.

ha⌉k·u[3] はく (吐く) *vt.* (hak·i-; hak·a-; ha·i-te Ⓒ) **1** vomit; spit:
Michi ni tsuba o haite *wa ikemaseñ.* (道につばを吐いてはいけません) You must not *spit* on the street.
2 send out; emit; belch:
Yukkuri iki o haite *kudasai.* (ゆっくり息を吐いてください) Please *breathe out* slowly.

-haku はく (泊) *suf.* counter for overnight stays.
《⇨ tomaru[2]; APP. 4》

ha⌈kubutsu⌉kañ はくぶつかん (博物館) *n.* museum.

ha⌈kusa⌉i はくさい (白菜) *n.* Chinese cabbage.

ha⌈kuseñ はくせん (白線) *n.* white line:
Hakuseñ *no uchigawa ni o-sagari kudasai.* (*station announcement*) (白線の内側にお下がりください) Please keep behind the *warning line.*

ha⌉kushi[1] はくし (博士) *n.* doctor:
buñgaku-hakushi (文学博士) a *Doctor* of Literature. 《⇨ hakase》

ha⌈kushi[2] はくし (白紙) *n.* white paper; blank paper.
hakushi ni modosu (～に戻す) make a fresh start.

ha⌉kushu はくしゅ (拍手) *n.* applause; hand clapping.
hakushu suru (～する) *vi.* clap one's hands.

ha⌈me·ru はめる (嵌める) *vt.* (hame-te Ⓥ) **1** put on (gloves, rings, etc.): ★ '*hamete iru*'= have on; wear.
Kare wa kawa no tebukuro o hamete ita. (彼は革の手袋をはめていた) He *was wearing* leather gloves.
2 fit; put:
Watashi wa sono e o gaku ni hameta. (私はその絵を額にはめた) I *set* the picture into the frame.
3 take in; entrap:
hito o wana ni hameru (人をわなにはめる) *entrap* a person.

ha⌈mi⌉gaki はみがき (歯磨き) *n.* toothpaste; dental cream.

ha⌉ñ[1] はん (班) *n.* group; squad.

ha⌉ñ[2] はん (判) *n.* seal; stamp.
★ A seal is used in Japan instead

of a signature. ⟪⇨ iñkañ⟫

ha˥ñ³ はん (版) *n.* edition; printing:
*Kono jisho wa go-*hañ *o kasaneta.* (この辞書は 5 版を重ねた) This dictionary has gone through five *printings.*

hañ- はん (反) *pref.* **1** anti-:
hañ-*kaku uñdoo* (反核運動) an *anti*-nuclear campaign.
2 re-:
hañ-sayoo (反作用) a *reaction.*

-ha˥ñ はん (半) *suf.* half:
*Kesa wa go-ji-*hañ *ni okimashita.* (今朝は 5 時半に起きました) I got up at five-*thirty* this morning.

ha⌈na¹ はな (鼻) *n.* **1** (of a human being) nose.
2 (of an animal) muzzle; snout; trunk.
3 nasal mucus:
Hana *o kami nasai.* (はなをかみなさい) Blow your *nose.*
4 the sense of smell:
Kare wa hana *ga kiku.* (彼は鼻がきく) He has a good *nose.*

ha⌈na˥² はな (花) *n.* flower; blossom. ⟪⇨ o-hana⟫

ha⌈nabanashi˥·i はなばなしい (華々しい) *a.* (-ku) brilliant; splendid; active:
hanabanashii *katsuyaku o suru* (はなばなしい活躍をする) lead an *active* career.

ha˥nabi はなび (花火) *n.* fireworks; sparkler.

ha⌈nabi˥ra はなびら (花びら) *n.* petal.

ha⌈nahada はなはだ (甚だ) *adv.* (*formal*) very; greatly; extremely:
Sono soo-oñ wa hanahada *meewaku da.* (その騒音ははなはだ迷惑だ) The noise is *terribly* annoying.

ha⌈nahadashi˥·i はなはだしい (甚だしい) *a.* (-ku) serious; gross; excessive:
Mattaku gokai mo hanahadashii. (全く誤解もはなはだしい) It is a *gross* misunderstanding.

ha⌈nami˥ はなみ (花見) *n.* cherry blossom viewing. ★ Often with '*o-*.'

ha⌈namu˥ko はなむこ (花婿) *n.* bridegroom. ⟪↔ hanayome⟫

ha⌈nare-ba˥nare はなればなれ (離れ離れ) *n.* being separated; being split up:
hanare-banare *ni kurasu* (離ればなれに暮らす) live *separately.*

ha⌈nare˥·ru¹ はなれる (離れる) *vi.* (hanare-te [V]) **1** separate; be separated:
Kare wa kazoku to hanarete, *kurashite iru.* (彼は家族と離れて, 暮らしている) He is living *apart* from his family. ⟪⇨ hanasu²⟫
2 leave:
kokyoo o hanareru (故郷を離れる) *leave* one's hometown.
3 be away from; be apart from:
Watashi no ie wa eki kara ni-kiro hanarete imasu. (私の家は駅から 2 キロ離れています) My house *is* two-kilometers *away* from the station.

ha⌈nare˥·ru² はなれる (放れる) *vi.* (hanare-te [V]) get free:
Tora ga ori o hanarete *nigeta.* (虎がおりを放れて逃げた) The tiger *got free* from its cage and escaped.

ha⌈nase˥·ru はなせる (話せる) *vi.* (hanase-te [V]) ★ Potential form of '*hanasu*¹.'
1 be able to speak:
Kono tori wa kotoba ga hanaseru. (この鳥は言葉が話せる) This bird *can talk.*
2 talk sense; be understanding:
Kare wa hanaseru *otoko da.* (彼は話せる男だ) He is an *understanding* person.

ha⌈nashi˥ はなし (話) *n.* **1** talk; chat; conversation:
Kare to hanashi *o shita.* (彼と話をした) I had a *talk* with him.
2 speech; address.
3 topic; subject:
Hanashi *o kaemashoo.* (話をかえましょう) Let's change the *subject.*
4 story; tale:

Kodomo ga neru mae ni hanashi *o shite yatta.* (子どもが寝る前に話をしてやった) I told my child a *story* before he went to sleep.

5 rumor:

Kare wa byooki da to iu hanashi *desu.* (彼は病気だという話です) There is a *rumor* that he is ill.

ha⌈nashiai はなしあい (話し合い) *n.* talks; consultation; negotiations.

ha⌈nashia⌉·u はなしあう (話し合う) *vi.* (-a·i-; -aw·a-; -at-te [C]) talk with; consult with; discuss:

Keekaku wa miñna to hanashiatte *kara kimemasu.* (計画はみんなと話し合ってから決めます) I will decide on a plan after *discussing* it with the others.

ha⌈nashigo⌉e はなしごえ (話し声) *n.* voice; the sound of voices.

ha⌈nashikake⌉·ru はなしかける (話し掛ける) *vt.* (-kake-te [V]) speak to; address; begin to speak [talk]:

Watashi wa kare ni Nihoñgo de hanashikaketa. (私は彼に日本語で話しかけた) I *spoke* to him in Japanese.

ha⌈nashi-ko⌉toba はなしことば (話し言葉) *n.* spoken language; speech. ⟪↔ kaki-kotoba⟫

ha⌈nashite はなして (話し手) *n.* speaker; the person (in a conversation) who is talking. ⟪↔ kikite⟫

ha⌈na⌉s·u[1] はなす (話す) *vi.* (hanash·i-; hanas·a-; hanash·i-te [C]) talk; speak; tell:

Motto yukkuri hanashite *kudasai.* (もっとゆっくり話してください) Will you please *speak* a little more slowly? ⟪⇨ hanaseru; kataru⟫

ha⌈na⌉s·u[2] はなす (離す) *vt.* (hanash·i-; hanas·a-; hanash·i-te [C]) **1** separate; part; keep apart; isolate. ⟪⇨ hikihanasu⟫

2 (with a negative) do without:

Kono jiteñ wa hanasu *koto ga dekinai.* (この辞典は離すことができない) I *cannot do without* this dictionary.

ha⌈na⌉s·u[3] はなす (放す) *vt.* (hanash·i-; hanas·a-; hanash·i-te [C]) **1** let go; take one's hand off:

Kare wa roopu kara te o hanashita. (彼はロープから手を放した) He *let go* of the rope.

2 let loose; set free (an animal):

Sakana o kawa e hanashite yatta. (魚を川へ放してやった) I *put* the fish *back* into the river.

ha⌈nawa はなわ (花輪) *n.* floral wreath.

ha⌈na⌉yaka はなやか (華やか) *a.n.* (~ na, ni) bright; flowery; gorgeous; luxurious:

hanayaka *na doresu* (華やかなドレス) a *gorgeous* dress.

ha⌈na⌉yome はなよめ (花嫁) *n.* bride. ⟪↔ hanamuko⟫

ha⌈ñbai はんばい (販売) *n.* sale; selling; marketing.

hañbai suru (~する) *vt.* sell; deal. ⟪⇨ uru[1]⟫

ha⌈ñ-Bee はんべい (反米) *n.* anti-American. ⟪↔ shiñ-Bee⟫

ha⌈ñbu⌉ñ はんぶん (半分) *n.* half.

— *adv.* half:

Shigoto wa hañbuñ *owarimashita.* (仕事は半分終わりました) The work is now *half* finished. ⟪⇨ nakaba⟫

ha⌈ñ-da⌉kuoñ はんだくおん (半濁音) *n.* *kana* letters with '°' attached. These change the original consonant pronunciation to '*p*': パ (*pa*), ピ (*pi*), プ (*pu*), ペ (*pe*) and ポ (*po*). ⟪⇨ dakuoñ; seeoñ; APP. 1⟫

ha⌈ñdañ はんだん (判断) *n.* judgment; decision:

Dochira ga hoñmono ka hañdañ ga tsukanai. (どちらが本物か判断がつかない) I *cannot tell* which is genuine.

hañdañ suru (~する) *vt.* judge; decide.

ha⌈ñdo-ba⌉ggu ハンドバッグ *n.* handbag; purse.

ha⌈ñdoru ハンドル *n.* **1** steering wheel.

2 (of a bicycle) handlebars.

ha⌈ne はね (羽) *n.* feather; wing; plume.

ha⌈ñee[1] はんえい (繁栄) *n.* prosperity.
hañee suru (～する) *vi.* prosper; thrive; flourish.

ha⌈ñee[2] はんえい (反映) *n.* reflection.
hañee suru (～する) *vt.* reflect.

ha⌈nekaes·u はねかえす (跳ね返す) *vt.* (-kaesh·i-; -kaes·a-; -kaesh·i-te Ⓒ) repel; reject:
Teki no koogeki o hanekaeshita. (敵の攻撃を跳ね返した) We *repelled* the attack of the enemy.

ha⌈ne⌉·ru はねる (跳ねる) *vi.* (hanete Ⓥ) **1** jump; leap; spring; bound:
Koi ga ike de haneta. (こいが池で跳ねた) A carp *jumped* in the pond.
2 (of mud, water, etc.) splash.
3 (of a performance) close; be over.

ha⌈ñga はんが (版画) *n.* woodblock print; woodcut.

ha⌈ñgaku はんがく (半額) *n.* half the price.

ha⌈ñgeki はんげき (反撃) *n.* counterattack.
hañgeki suru (～する) *vi.* counterattack; fight back.

ha⌉ñhañ はんはん (半々) *n.* half-and-half; fifty-fifty:
rieki o hañhañ *ni wakeru* (利益を半々にわける) divide the profit *equally*.

ha⌉ñi はんい (範囲) *n.* scope; sphere; range:
Kare no kyoomi wa hiroi hañi *ni wataru.* (彼の興味は広い範囲にわたる) His interests are wide *ranging*.

ha⌈ñi⌉go はんいご (反意語) *n.* antonym. ⟪↔ dooigo⟫

ha⌉ñji はんじ (判事) *n.* judge.

ha⌉ñjoo はんじょう (繁盛) *n.* (of business) prosperity.
hañjoo suru (～する) *vi.* (of business) prosper; thrive, flourish.

ha⌈ñjuku はんじゅく (半熟) *n.* half-boiled egg. ⟪⇨ tamago⟫

ha⌈ñkachi ハンカチ *n.* handkerchief.

ha⌈ñkañ はんかん (反感) *n.* antipathy; ill feeling.

ha⌉ñkee はんけい (半径) *n.* radius.

ha⌈ñko⌉ はんこ (判子) *n.* seal; stamp. ⟪⇨ hañ[2]⟫

ha⌈ñkyoo はんきょう (反響) *n.* echo; sensation; repercussion:
Sono eega wa ooki-na hañkyoo *o* yoñda. (その映画は大きな反響を呼んだ) The movie created a great *sensation*.
hañkyoo suru (～する) *vi.* echo; reverberate.

ha⌈ñnichi はんにち (半日) *n.* half a day; a half day.

ha⌉ñniñ はんにん (犯人) *n.* criminal; culprit; offender.

ha⌈ñnoo はんのう (反応) *n.* reaction; response; effect.
hañnoo suru (～する) *vi.* react: respond. ⟪⇨ eekyoo⟫

ha⌈ñrañ はんらん (反乱) *n.* rebellion; revolt; insurrection:
hañrañ *o okosu* (反乱を起こす) rise in *rebellion*.

ha⌈ñsee はんせい (反省) *n.* reflection; reconsideration; introspection.
hañsee suru (～する) *vt.* reflect; feel sorry.

ha⌈ñsha はんしゃ (反射) *n.* reflection; reflex.
hañsha suru (～する) *vt.* reflect.

ha⌉ñshite はんして (反して) be contrary to: ★ Used in the pattern '*... ni hañshite.*'
Kare wa oya no kiboo ni hañshite, *isha ni naranakatta.* (彼は親の希望に反して, 医者にならなかった) *Contrary to* his parents' wishes, he did not become a doctor. ⟪⇨ hañsuru⟫

ha⌈ñshoku はんしょく (繁殖) *n.* breeding; propagation.
hañshoku suru (～する) *vi.* breed; propagate.

ha⌈ñs·u⌉ru はんする (反する) *vi.* (hañsh·i-; hañsh·i-; hañsh·i-te

[I]) be against; breach (a regulation, rule, contract, etc.):
Sore wa keeyaku ni hañsuru. (それは契約に反する) That *breaches* the contract. 《⇨ hañshite; ihañ》

ha⌈ñtai はんたい (反対) *n.* **1** opposite; contrary:
Kono e wa jooge hañtai *da.* (この絵は上下反対だ) This picture is *upside-down.*
2 opposition; objection:
Watashi wa sono ikeñ ni hañtai *desu.* (私はその意見に反対です) I am *against* that opinion. 《↔ sañsee[1]》
hañtai suru (～する) *vi.* oppose.

ha⌈ñ-ta⌉isee はんたいせい (反体制) *n.* anti-establishment. 《↔ taisee》

ha⌈ñtee はんてい (判定) *n.* judgment; decision.
hañtee suru (～する) *vt.* judge; decide.

ha⌈ñtoo はんとう (半島) *n.* peninsula.

ha⌈ñtoshi はんとし (半年) *n.* six months; half a year.

ha⌈ñtsuki⌉ はんつき (半月) *n.* fortnight; two weeks; half a month.

ha⌈ñzai はんざい (犯罪) *n.* crime; offense; delinquency.

ha⌈ori はおり (羽織) *n.* short overgarment. ★ Usually worn over a kimono.

ha⌈ppi はっぴ (法被) *n.* happi coat.

ha⌈ppyoo はっぴょう (発表) *n.* announcement; publication; release.
happyoo suru (～する) *vt.* announce; publish; release.
《⇨ dasu (3)》

ha⌈ra⌉[1] はら (腹) *n.* **1** belly; bowels; stomach: ★ Informal expression used by men. '*Onaka*' is more polite.
Hara ga itai. (腹が痛い) I *have a stomachache.*
2 mind; heart:
Hara *no naka de kanojo wa kare o keebetsu shite ita.* (腹の中で彼女は彼を軽蔑していた) She despised him in her *heart.*
hara ga tatsu (～が立つ) be [get] angry.
hara o kimeru (～を決める) make up one's mind.
hara o tateru (～を立てる) lose one's temper.

ha⌉ra[2] はら (原) *n.* field; plain. 《⇨ nohara》

ha⌉ra⌉gee はらげい (腹芸) *n.* implicit mutual understanding.

ha⌉rahara はらはら *adv.* (～ suru) (the state of being nervous or uneasy):
Kare ga nani o ii-dasu ka wakaranai no de harahara *shita.* (彼が何を言い出すかわからないのではらはらした) I didn't know what he was going to say, so I felt *uneasy.*
《⇨ fuañ; shiñpai》

ha⌉rappa はらっぱ (原っぱ) *n.* field; plain. 《⇨ nohara》

ha⌈ra⌉·u はらう (払う) *vt.* (hara·i-; haraw·a-; harat-te [C]) **1** pay; pay back: *Kuruma ni ni-hyakumañ-eñ* haratta. (車に200万円払った) I *paid* two million yen for the car.
2 dust; brush; clear:
hoñ no hokori o harau (本のほこりを払う) *dust* the books.
3 pay; show (attention):
hokoosha no añzeñ ni chuui o harau (歩行者の安全に注意を払う) *pay* attention to the safety of pedestrians.

ha⌈re⌉ はれ (晴れ) *n.* fine [clear] weather:
Asu wa hare *deshoo.* (あすは晴れでしょう) It is likely to be *fine* tomorrow. 《⇨ hareru[1]; ame[1]; kumori》
hare no (～の) **1** fine; fair:
hare no *hi* (晴れの日) a *clear* day.
2 auspicious; grand: hare no *butai* (晴れの舞台) a *grand* occasion.

ha⌈re⌉·ru[1] はれる (晴れる) *vi.* (harete [V]) **1** (of weather, sky) clear up; become clear. 《⇨ hare》
2 be cheered up; be refreshed:
Sañpo de mo sureba ki ga hare-

masu *yo.* (散歩でもすれば気が晴れますよ) If you were to, say, go for a stroll, you'd *feel much better.*
3 be cleared; be dispelled:
Kare ni taisuru utagai ga hareta. (彼に対する疑いが晴れた) The suspicion against him *has been dispelled.*

ha⌈re·ru[2] はれる (腫れる) *vi.* (harete [V]) swell up; become swollen.

ha⌉ri[1] はり (針) *n.* **1** needle.
2 the hands of a clock.
3 fishhook. ⟪⇨ tsuri[1]⟫

ha⌉ri[2] はり (鍼) *n.* acupuncture.

ha⌈rigane はりがね (針金) *n.* wire.

ha⌈riki⌉r·u はりきる (張り切る) *vi.* (-kir·i-; -kir·a-; -kit-te [C]) be in high spirits; be full of vitality; be fired up:
Kanojo wa atarashii shigoto ni harikitte imasu. (彼女は新しい仕事に張り切っています) She *is very enthusiastic* about her new job.

ha⌉ru[1] はる (春) *n.* spring:
Moo sugu haru *ga kuru.* (もうすぐ春が来る) *Spring* will come soon.

ha⌈r·u[2] はる (貼る) *vt.* (har·i-; har·a-; hat-te [C]) put; stick:
kabe ni posutaa o haru (壁にポスターをはる) *stick* a poster on the wall.

ha⌈r·u[3] はる (張る) *vi., vt.* (har·i-; har·a-; hat-te [C]) **1** set up; put up; spread:
teñto o haru (テントを張る) *pitch* a tent / *ho o* haru (帆を張る) *set* a sail.
2 stretch; strain:
Geñba ni wa tsuna ga hatte atte, dare mo hairemaseñ. (現場には綱が張ってあって, だれも入れません) A rope *is stretched* around the spot and no one can get in.
3 cover; freeze; tile:
Ike ni koori ga hatta. (池に氷が張った) Ice *covered* the pond.

ha⌈ruba⌉ru はるばる (遥々) *adv.* (~ to) all the way; from afar:
Kinoo haha ga kyoori kara harubaru (*to*) *dete kimashita.* (きのう母が郷里からはるばる(と)出てきました) Yesterday my mother came up *all the way* from our hometown.

ha⌉ruka はるか (遥か) *adv.* **1** (of distance) far away:
Haruka *mukoo ni Fuji-sañ ga mieta.* (はるか向こうに富士山が見えた) I could see Mt. Fuji *far away* over there.
2 (of time) far back:
Haruka *mukashi no koto na no de yoku oboete imaseñ.* (はるか昔のことなのでよく覚えていません) It is something that happened *a very long time ago*, so I don't remember clearly.

ha⌉ruka ni はるかに (遥かに) *adv.* much; by far:
Kono kuruma no hoo ga haruka ni *seenoo ga ii.* (この車のほうがはるかに性能がいい) This car's performance is *far* better. ⟪⇨ zutto⟫

ha⌈ru-ya⌉sumi はるやすみ (春休み) *n.* spring vacation. ★ Schools are on vacation from the middle of March until the beginning of April. ⟪⇨ yasumi⟫

ha⌈sami⌉ はさみ (鋏) *n.* scissors; shears.

ha⌈sa⌉m·u はさむ (挟む) *vt.* (hasam·i-; hasam·a-; hasañ-de [C]) put in; insert; catch in:
doa ni yubi o hasamu (ドアに指を挟む) *get* one's fingers *caught* in the door.

ha⌉sañ はさん (破産) *n.* bankruptcy; insolvency.
hasañ suru (~する) *vi.* go bankrupt.

ha⌈shi⌉[1] はし (橋) *n.* bridge.

ha⌉shi[2] はし (箸) *n.* chopsticks.

ha⌈shi[3] はし (端) *n.* end; edge.

ha⌈shigo はしご (梯子) *n.* ladder; stairs.

ha⌈shira はしら (柱) *n.* pillar; post; column.

ha⌈shi⌉r·u はしる (走る) *vi.* (hashir·i-; hashir·a-; hashit-te [C])
1 (of people and animals) run; dash; rush; jog. ⟪⇨ kakeru[7]⟫
2 (of vehicles) run; travel:
Kono dooro wa basu ga hashitte

imasu. (この道路はバスが走っています) Buses *run* along this street.
3 (of a railroad, a road, etc.) run:
Kono michi wa toozai ni hashitte imasu. (この道は東西に走っています) This road *runs* east-west.

ha⌈soñ はそん (破損) *n.* damage; breakage.
hasoñ suru (～する) *vi.* be damaged; be broken.

ha⌈ssee はっせい (発生) *n.* occurrence; outbreak.
hassee suru (～する) *vi.* occur; break out: *Jiko ga* hassee shita. (事故が発生した) An accident has *occurred.*

ha⌈ssha はっしゃ (発車) *n.* (of a train, bus, etc.) departure.
hassha suru (～する) *vi.* start; leave; depart. ⟪↔ teesha⟫

ha⌈sumu⌉kai はすむかい (斜向かい) *n.* the diagonally opposite side:
hasumukai *no ie* (はす向かいの家) a house standing *diagonally opposite.*

ha⌈ta⌉ はた (旗) *n.* flag; banner.

ha⌉tachi はたち (二十歳) *n.* twenty years of age.

ha⌈take はたけ (畑) *n.* field; farm.
hatake chigai (～違い) outside one's field: *Kagaku wa* hatake chigai *desu.* (化学は畑違いです) Chemistry is *outside my field.*

ha⌈taki⌉ はたき (叩き) *n.* duster.
★ Made of strips of cloth tied at the end of a long stick.

ha⌈tame⌉k·u はためく *vi.* (-mek·i-; -mek·a-; -me·i-te Ⓒ) (of a flag) flutter; wave.

ha⌈tañ はたん (破綻) *n.* failure; breakdown; rupture.
hatañ suru (～する) *vi.* fail; break down; rupture.

ha⌈taraki はたらき (働き) *n.*
1 work; service:
hataraki *ni deru* (働きに出る) go to *work.*
2 function; operation:
i no hataraki (胃の働き) the *function* of the stomach.
hataraki o suru (～をする) *vi.* do work; make a contribution:
★ Preceded by a modifier.
Kare wa mezamashii hataraki o shita. (彼は目覚ましい働きをした) He *has done* remarkable *work.*

ha⌈tarak·u はたらく (働く) *vi., vt.* (hatarak·i-; hatarak·a-; hatara·ite Ⓒ) **1** work; labor; serve:
giñkoo de hataraku (銀行で働く) *work* at a bank.
2 function; work:
Kyoo wa atama ga hatarakanai. (きょうは頭が働かない) My brain *is not working* today.
3 commit (violence, a crime, etc.):
nusumi o hataraku (盗みを働く) *commit* theft.

ha⌈ta⌉shite はたして (果たして) *adv.* (often in questions) really; as was expected; sure enough:
Hatashite *hoñtoo daroo ka?* (はたして本当だろうか) Is it *really* true?

ha⌉to はと (鳩) *n.* pigeon; dove.

ha⌈tsu- はつ (初) *pref.* first:
hatsu-*koi* (初恋) one's *first* love / hatsu-*yuki* (初雪) the *first* snow of the winter.

-hatsu[1] はつ (発) *suf.* **1** (of a train, bus, etc.) leaving:
Ueno-hatsu *no shiñdaisha* (上野発の寝台車) the sleeper *leaving* Ueno.
2 (of a news source) from; datelined:
Pekiñ-hatsu *no nyuusu* (北京発のニュース) news *datelined* Beijing.

-hatsu[2] はつ (発) *suf.* counter for bullets, shells and large fireworks. ⟪⇨ APP. 4⟫

ha⌈tsubai はつばい (発売) *n.* sale.
hatsubai suru (～する) *vt.* sell; put on sale. ⟪⇨ uru[1]⟫

ha⌈tsubyoo はつびょう (発病) *n.* onset of a disease; attack.
hatsubyoo suru (～する) *vi.* become sick; be taken ill. ⟪⇨ byooki⟫

ha⌈tsugeñ はつげん (発言) *n.*

speech; remark.
hatsugeñ suru (〜する) *vi.* speak; utter; say a word.

ha⌈tsu-hi⌉node はつひので (初日の出) *n.* the sunrise on New Year's Day.

ha⌈tsuiku はついく (発育) *n.* development; growth.
hatsuiku suru (〜する) *vi.* grow; develop.

ha⌈tsuka はつか (二十日) *n.* twenty days; the twentieth. 《⇨ APP. 5》

ha⌈tsuka-da⌉ikoñ はつかだいこん (二十日大根) *n.* radish. 《⇨ daikoñ》

ha⌈tsumee はつめい (発明) *n.* invention.
hatsumee suru (〜する) *vt.* invent.

ha⌈tsumo⌉ode はつもうで (初詣) *n.* the first New Year's visit to a shrine or a temple.

ha⌈tsuoñ[1] はつおん (発音) *n.* pronunciation.
hatsuoñ suru (〜する) *vt.* pronounce. 《⇨ APP. 1》

ha⌈tsu⌉oñ[2] はつおん (撥音) *n.* the Japanese syllabic nasal, written '*ñ*' in this dictionary:
hatsuoñ-*biñ* (はつ音便) the *nasal sound* change. 《⇨ sokuoñ; yooñ; APP. 1》

ha⌈ttatsu はったつ (発達) *n.* development; growth.
hattatsu suru (〜する) *vi.* grow; develop: *Taifuu ga minami no kaijoo de* hattatsu shite iru. (台風が南の海上で発達している) A typhoon *is developing* over the ocean in the south. 《⇨ hatteñ》

ha⌈tteñ はってん (発展) *n.* expansion; development; progress.
hatteñ suru (〜する) *vi.* develop; grow; expand. 《⇨ hattatsu》

ha⌈tteñ-tojo⌉o-koku はってんとじょうこく (発展途上国) *n.* developing country.

ha⌈tto はっと *adv.* (〜 suru) (the state of being startled):
Watashi wa ushiro kara yobikakerarete, hatto *shita.* (私は後ろから呼びかけられて, はっとした) I was *startled* when called to from behind.

ha⌉·u はう (這う) *vi.* (ha·i-; ha-w·a-; hat-te [C]) creep; crawl.

ha⌉usu ハウス *n.* hothouse; (plastic) greenhouse.

ha⌈ya⌉·i[1] はやい (早い) *a.* (-ku) (of time) early; soon:
Akirameru no wa mada hayai. (あきらめるのはまだ早い) It is still too *early* to give up. 《↔ osoi》

ha⌈ya⌉·i[2] はやい (速い) *a.* (-ku) (of motion) fast; quick; rapid; speedy:
Kono kawa wa nagare ga hayai. (この川は流れが速い) The current in this river is very *fast.* 《↔ osoi》

ha⌈ya⌉kuchi はやくち (早口) *n.* fast talking:
Kanojo wa hayakuchi *da.* (彼女は早口だ) She *talks fast.*

ha⌈yama⌉r·u はやまる (早まる) *vi.* (-mar·i-; -mar·a-; -mat-te [C]) (of time) be made earlier; be brought forward:
Dañtoo de sakura no kaika ga hayamatta. (暖冬で桜の開花が早まった) Because of the warm winter, the opening of the cherry blossoms *occurred early.* 《⇨ hayameru[1]》

ha⌈yame⌉·ru[1] はやめる (早める) *vt.* (-me-te [V]) **1** hasten; speed up:
Karoo ga kare no shi o hayameta. (過労が彼の死を早めた) Overwork *hastened* his death. 《⇨ hayamaru》
2 advance; bring forward:
Kare-ra wa kekkoñ-shiki o ni-shuukañ hayameta. (彼らは結婚式を2週間早めた) They *advanced* their wedding by two weeks. 《⇨ hayamaru》

ha⌈yame⌉·ru[2] はやめる (速める) *vt.* (-me-te [V]) quicken; hasten:
Kuruma wa supiido o hayameta. (車はスピードを速めた) The car *speeded up.*

ha⌈ya⌉ne はやね (早寝) *n.* going to bed early.

h

hayane (o) suru (～(を)する) *vi.* go to bed early.

ha⌈ya⌉oki はやおき (早起き) *n.* early rising.
hayaoki (o) suru (～(を)する) *vi.* get up early; rise early.

ha⌈ya⌉r·u はやる (流行る) *vi.* (hayar·i-; hayar·a-; hayat-te [C])
1 be popular; be in fashion:
Ima sono uta ga hayatte imasu. (今その歌がはやっています) That song *is* now *popular*. ⟪⇨ ryuukoo⟫
2 (of a shop, an enterprise, etc.) prosper; do good business:
Ano mise wa hayatte iru. (あの店ははやっている) That shop *is doing well*.
3 (of disease) be raging; be prevalent:
Ryuukañ ga Nihoñ-juu de hayatte imasu. (流感が日本中ではやっています) Influenza *is prevalent* throughout Japan.

ha⌉yasa はやさ (速さ) *n.* speed; quickness; rapidity. ⟪⇨ sokudo; supiido⟫

ha⌈yashi はやし (林) *n.* grove; woods. ★ A large area of land more thickly covered with trees than '*hayashi*' is called '*mori*' (森).

ha⌈ya⌉s·u はやす (生やす) *vt.* (hayash·i-; hayas·a-; hayash·i-te [C]) grow (a beard, etc.): ★ '*hayashite iru*' = wear.
Kare wa hige o hayashite iru. (彼はひげを生やしている) He *wears* a beard. ⟪⇨ haeru¹⟫

ha⌈zu はず (筈) *n.* supposed; expected:
Tanaka-sañ wa jimusho ni iru hazu *desu*. (田中さんは事務所にいるはずです) Miss Tanaka is *supposed* to be in the office. ⟪⇨ hazu wa nai⟫

ha⌈zukashi⌉·i はずかしい (恥ずかしい) *a.* (-ku) ashamed; shameful:
Koñna kañtañ na koto ga dekinakute, hazukashii. (こんな簡単なことができなくて, 恥ずかしい) I feel *ashamed* that I cannot do such a simple thing. ⟪⇨ kimari ga warui⟫

ha⌈zumi はずみ (弾み) *n.* momentum; impulse:
hazumi *ga tsuku* (はずみがつく) gain *momentum*. ⟪⇨ hazumu⟫

ha⌈zum·u はずむ (弾む) *vi.* (hazum·i-; hazum·a-; hazuñ-de [C])
1 bounce; bound:
Kono booru wa yoku hazumu. (このボールはよく弾む) This ball *bounces* well. ⟪⇨ hazumi⟫
2 become lively; bound:
Watashi-tachi no hanashi wa hazuñda. (私たちの話は弾んだ) Our conversation *became lively*.

ha⌈zure·ru はずれる (外れる) *vi.* (hazure-te [V]) **1** come off; be undone; be out of joint:
Juwaki ga hazurete imasu. (受話器がはずれています) The receiver *is off the hook*. ⟪⇨ hazusu⟫
2 miss (a target); fail; (of a prediction, a forecast, a guess, etc.) prove wrong.
3 be out of the way; be contrary:
chuushiñ kara hazureru (中心からはずれる) *be off* center.

ha⌈zus·u はずす (外す) *vt.* (hazush·i-; hazus·a-; hazush·i-te [C])
1 take off; remove:
megane [*tokee*] *o* hazusu (眼鏡[時計]を外す) *take off* one's glasses [watch] / *botañ o* hazusu (ボタンをはずす) *undo* a button. ⟪⇨ hazureru⟫
2 leave (one's seat); slip away from:
Kare wa kaigi-chuu, seki o hazushita. (彼は会議中, 席をはずした) He *left* his seat in the middle of the meeting.

ha⌈zu wa na⌉i はずはない (筈は無い) (*formal* = '*hazu wa arimaseñ*') be hardly possible; cannot expect:
Soñna hazu wa nai. (そんなはずはない) That's *impossible*.
★ Note the use of a double negative, '*nai hazu wa nai*': *Kimi ga sore o* shiranai hazu wa nai. (君が

それを知らないはずはない) *There is no reason* for you *not to know* that.

he⁽bi へび(蛇) *n.* snake; serpent.

he⁽e へい(塀) *n.* wall; fence.

he⁽ebon̄ へいぼん(平凡) *a.n.* (~ na, ni) ordinary; common; uneventful:
Heebon̄ *da keredo, shiawase na mainichi o okutte imasu.* (平凡だけれど, 幸せな毎日を送っています) I lead an *uneventful*, but happy life. ⟪⇨ futsuu[1]⟫

he⁽ehoo へいほう(平方) *n.* square: *ni-meetoru* heehoo (2メートル平方) 2 meters *square* / *ni*-heehoo *meetoru* (2平方メートル) two *square* meters.
heehoo suru (~する) *vt.* square. ⟪↔ rippoo[1]⟫

he⁽ejitsu へいじつ(平日) *n.* weekday; workday. ⟪⇨ kyuujitsu; shukujitsu; shuumatsu⟫

he⁽ejoo へいじょう(平常) *n.* normal; usual:
Shiñkañseñ no daiya wa heejoo *ni modotta.* (新幹線のダイヤは平常に戻った) The schedule of the Shinkansen has returned to *normal*. ⟪⇨ futsuu[1]⟫

he⁽ekai へいかい(閉会) *n.* closing of a meeting [session].
heekai suru (~する) *vi.* close [adjourn] a meeting. ⟪↔ kaikai⟫

he⁽eki[1] へいき(平気) *n.* indifference; calmness:
Kanojo wa heeki *o yosootta.* (彼女は平気を装った) She assumed an air of *indifference*.
— *a.n.* (~ na, ni) calm; cool; indifferent; unconcerned:
Nani o iwarete mo watashi wa heeki *desu.* (何を言われても私は平気です) I *do not care* what is said to me.

he⁽eki[2] へいき(兵器) *n.* weapon; arms.

he⁽ekin̄[1] へいきん(平均) *n.* average; mean: heekin̄ *o dasu* (平均を出す) find the *average*.
heekin̄ suru (~する) *vi.* calculate the average: Heekin̄ shite, *futari ni hitori ga megane o kakete imasu.* (平均して, 二人に一人が眼鏡をかけています) *On the average*, every second person wears glasses.

he⁽ekin̄[2] へいきん(平均) *n.* balance:
heekin̄ *o tamotsu* [*ushinau*] (平均を保つ[失う]) keep [lose] one's *balance*.

he⁽ekoo[1] へいこう(平行) *n.* parallel.

he⁽ekoo[2] へいこう(並行) *n.* going side by side.

he⁽ekoo[3] へいこう(閉口) *n.* being annoyed; being bothered.
heekoo suru (~する) *vi.* be annoyed; be bothered: *Shichoo no nagai eñzetsu ni wa* heekoo shita. (市長の長い演説には閉口した) We *got fed up* with the mayor's long speech.

he⁽emen̄ へいめん(平面) *n.* level; plane.

he⁽eme⁾n̄zu へいめんず(平面図) *n.* floor [ground] plan.

he⁽etai へいたい(兵隊) *n.*
1 a group of soldiers; troops.
2 soldier; sailor. ★ Especially those lower in rank. Often figuratively refers to a common company employee. ⟪⇨ gun̄jin̄⟫

he⁽ewa へいわ(平和) *n.* peace.
— *a.n.* (~ na, ni) peaceful: heewa *ni kurasu* (平和に暮らす) live in *peace*. ⟪↔ señsoo⟫

he⁽eya へいや(平野) *n.* plain; open field.

he⁾n̄[1] へん(変) *a.n.* (~ na, ni) strange; odd; queer; peculiar:
Kono kuruma wa tokidoki heñ *na oto ga suru.* (この車はときどき変な音がする) This car sometimes makes a *strange* noise.

he⁽n̄[2] へん(辺) *n.* **1** part; region; neighborhood:
Kare no ie wa kono heñ *ni aru hazu desu.* (彼の家はこの辺にあるはずです) His house should be *around* here. ⟪⇨ atari⟫

2 degree; range; limit:
Kyoo wa kono heñ *de owari ni shiyoo.* (きょうはこの辺で終わりにしよう) Let's finish up *here* today.

he⌈ñ³ へん (偏) *n.* the left-hand radical of a Chinese character. ((⇨ bushu; tsukuri))

-heñ へん (遍) *suf.* counter for the number of times. ((⇨ -kai¹; APP. 4))

he⌉ñi へんい (変異) *n.* variation: totsuzeñ-heñi (突然変異) *mutation.*

he⌈ñji⌉ へんじ (返事) *n.* answer; reply:
Yobaretara, sugu heñji o shi nasai. (呼ばれたら, すぐ返事をしなさい) *Answer* immediately when your name is called. ((⇨ kotaeru))

he⌉ñka へんか (変化) *n.*
1 change; variation; alteration:
Kono atari no keshiki wa heñka *ni toñde iru.* (この辺りの景色は変化に富んでいる) The landscapes around here are full of *variety.*
2 inflection; conjugation:
dooshi no heñka (動詞の変化) *conjugation* of verbs.
heñka suru (～する) *vi.* **1** change; vary; alter.
2 inflect; conjugate.

he⌈ñkeñ へんけん (偏見) *n.* prejudice; bias.

he⌈ñkoo へんこう (変更) *n.*
change; alteration; modification.
heñkoo suru (～する) *vt.* change; alter; modify: *yotee o* heñkoo suru (予定を変更する) *change* one's schedule.

he⌈ñsai へんさい (返済) *n.* repayment; refund.
heñsai suru (～する) *vt.* pay back; repay; refund.

he⌈ñshuu へんしゅう (編集) *n.*
editing; compilation.
heñshuu suru (～する) *vi.* edit; compile: *bideo o* heñshuu suru (ビデオを編集する) *edit* video tapes.

he⌈ñshu⌉uchoo へんしゅうちょう (編集長) *n.* editor-in-chief; chief editor.

he⌈ras·u へらす (減らす) *vt.* (herash·i-; heras·a-; herash·i-te Ⓒ) reduce; decrease; cut down; diminish:
Anata wa taijuu o herashita *hoo ga yoi.* (あなたは体重を減らしたほうがよい) You should *lose* weight. ((⇨ heru))

he⌈r·u へる (減る) *vi.* (her·i-; her·a-; het-te Ⓒ) **1** become less [fewer]; decrease:
Kuruma no gasoriñ ga hette kita. (車のガソリンが減ってきた) The car *has run low* on gas. ((↔ fueru)) ((⇨ herasu))
2 (of shoes, tires) wear out.
3 get hungry:
Onaka ga hette kita. (おなかが減ってきた) I'*ve gotten hungry.* ★ '*Onaka ga suite kimashita.*' is more polite. ((⇨ suku¹))

he⌈so へそ (臍) *n.* navel. ★ Often '*o-heso.*'

he⌈ta⌉ へた (下手) *a.n.* (～ na, ni) poor; bad:
Watashi wa uñteñ ga heta *desu.* (私は運転がへたです) I am *not* very *good* at driving. ((↔ joozu))
heta o suru to (～をすると) if one is not careful; if not properly handled.

he⌉te へて (経て) via; by way of:
Kare wa Hawai o hete *Tookyoo ni tsukimashita.* (彼はハワイを経て東京に着きました) He arrived in Tokyo *via* Hawaii. ((⇨ keeyu¹))

he⌈ya⌉ へや (部屋) *n.* room; chamber; apartment.

hi¹ ひ (日) *n.* **1** day (24 hours); time:
Doñdoñ hi *ga tatte yuku.* (どんどん日がたってゆく) The *days* go by so quickly.
2 date:
Shuppatsu no hi *wa mitee desu.* (出発の日は未定です) The *date* of departure is not fixed yet.

hi² ひ (日) *n.* **1** the sun.
2 sun (＝sunbeam):
Kono heya ni wa hi *ga sasanai.* (こ

の部屋には日がささない) The *sun* does not shine into this room.

3 period of light; day (as opposed to night):
Hi *ga nagaku [mijikaku] natta.* (日が長く[短く]なった) The *days* are getting longer [shorter].

hiˀ[3] ひ (火) *n.* fire:
tabako ni hi o tsukeru (たばこに火をつける) *light* a cigarette.

hiˀ[4] ひ (灯) *n.* light:
hi *o tomosu [kesu]* (灯をともす[消す]) turn on [off] a *light*.

hiˀ[5] ひ (比) *n.* ratio. ⟪⇨ hiritsu⟫

hi[6] ひ (碑) *n.* monument.

hiˀ**-** ひ (非) *pref.* un-; non-:
hi-*kyooryoku-teki na taido* (非協力的な態度) an *un*cooperative attitude.

-hi ひ (費) *suf.* expenses:
kootsuu-hi (交通費) traveling *expenses* / *seekatsu*-hi (生活費) living *expenses*.

hiˁ**atari** ひあたり (日当たり) *n.* exposure to the sun; sunshine:
hiatari no yoi *heya* (日当たりのよい部屋) a *sunny* room. ⟪⇨ hikage; hinata⟫

hiˀ**bachi** ひばち (火鉢) *n.* brazier.
★ The hibachi has no grill. It is used basically for heating, not cooking.

hiˀ**bana** ひばな (火花) *n.* sparks.

hiˁ**bari** ひばり (雲雀) *n.* skylark; lark.

hiˀ**bashi** ひばし (火箸) *n.* chopsticks made of metal. ★ Used like tongs and fire irons to tend heated charcoal, etc.

hiˁ**bi**ˀ ひび *n.* **1** crack:
Kono koppu ni wa hibi *ga haitte iru.* (このコップにはひびが入っている) There is a *crack* in this glass.
2 split:
Sono koto de futari no kañkee ni hibi *ga haitta.* (そのことで二人の関係にひびが入った) The incident caused a *split* in their relationship.

hiˁ**biki**ˀ ひびき (響き) *n.* sound; peal; echo. ⟪⇨ hibiku⟫

hiˁ**bi**ˀ**k·u** ひびく (響く) *vi.* (hibik·i-; hibik·a-; hibi·i-te Ⓒ) **1** sound; ring; resound; echo:
Tera no kane ga mura-juu ni hibiita. (寺の鐘が村中に響いた) The bell of a temple *resounded* throughout the village. ⟪⇨ hibiki⟫
2 affect; have an unfavorable influence on:
Naga-ame ga sakumotsu no shuukaku ni hibiita. (長雨が作物の収穫に響いた) The long rains *had an adverse effect* on the harvest.

hiˁ**bu**ˀ**soo** ひぶそう (非武装) *n.* demilitarization. ⟪↔ busoo⟫

hiˁ**dari** ひだり (左) *n.* left. ⟪↔ migi⟫

hiˁ**darigawa** ひだりがわ (左側) *n.* left side. ⟪↔ migigawa⟫

hiˁ**darikiki** ひだりきき (左利き) *n.* left-handed person. ⟪↔ migikiki⟫

hiˁ**darite** ひだりて (左手) *n.*
1 left hand. ⟪↔ migite⟫
2 left direction:
Hidarite *ni kawa ga mieru.* (左手に川が見える) I can see a river on the *left*. ⟪↔ migite⟫

hiˁ**do**ˀ**·i** ひどい (酷い) *a.* (-ku) **1** serious; hard; violent:
Ame ga hidoku *natte kita.* (雨がひどくなってきた) It has started to rain *hard*.
2 cruel; terrible:
Ano otoko wa hidoi *yatsu da.* (あの男はひどいやつだ) He is a *cruel* man.

hiˁ**e**ˀ**·ru** ひえる (冷える) *vi.* (hie-te Ⓥ) get cold [chilly; cool]:
Yoru ni natte, dañdañ hiete kita. (夜になって, だんだん冷えてきた) It *is* gradually *getting cold* as night comes on. ⟪⇨ hiyasu⟫

hiˀ**fu** ひふ (皮膚) *n.* skin. ⟪⇨ hada⟫

hiˁ**fuka** ひふか (皮膚科) *n.* dermatology.

hiˁ**gaeri**ˀ ひがえり (日帰り) *n.* day-trip; one day trip.

hiˀ**gai** ひがい (被害) *n.* **1** damage.
2 loss:
Sono kaisha no uketa higai *wa wazuka datta.* (その会社の受けた被害

はわずかだった) The *loss* the company sustained was slight.

hi⌈ga⌉isha ひがいしゃ (被害者) *n.* victim; sufferer.

hi⌈ga⌉ñ ひがん (彼岸) *n.* the equinoctial week. ★ Politely '*o-higañ*.' It is a Japanese custom to visit one's family grave during the spring and autumn equinoctial weeks. ⟪⇨ hakamairi⟫

hi⌈gashi⌉ ひがし (東) *n.* east; (~ ni/e) eastward. ⟪↔ nishi⟫

hi⌈ge ひげ (髭) *n.* general term for facial hair:
hige *o hayasu* (ひげを生やす) grow a *beard.* ⟪⇨ kuchihige⟫

hi⌉geki ひげき (悲劇) *n.* tragedy. ⟪↔ kigeki⟫

hi⌈goro ひごろ (日頃) *n.* everyday; always; usually:
Higoro *no doryoku ga taisetsu desu.* (日ごろの努力が大切です) One's *daily* efforts are important.

hi⌈hañ ひはん (批判) *n.* criticism.
hihañ suru (~する) *vt.* criticize.

hi⌈hyoo ひひょう (批評) *n.* comment; criticism; review.
hihyoo suru (~する) *vt.* criticize; review; comment.

hi⌈ji⌉ ひじ (肘) *n.* elbow.

hi⌈joo ひじょう (非常) *n.* emergency; contingency:
Hijoo *no baai wa koko kara deraremasu.* (非常の場合はここから出られます) You can go out this way in an *emergency.*
— *a.n.* (~ na, ni) great; extreme; very:
Kare wa hijoo ni *yorokoñde imashita.* (彼は非常に喜んでいました) He was *absolutely* delighted.
⟪⇨ taiheñ; taisoo[2]⟫

hi⌈jo⌉oguchi ひじょうぐち (非常口) *n.* emergency exit.

hi⌈joo ni ひじょうに (非常に) *adv.* ⇨ hijoo.

hi⌈jooseñ ひじょうせん (非常線) *n.* police cordon.

hi⌈jo⌉oshiki ひじょうしき (非常識) *a.n.* (~ na, ni) lacking in common sense; unreasonable.

hi⌈kae⌉shitsu ひかえしつ (控室) *n.* anteroom; waiting room.

hi⌈kage ひかげ (日陰) *n.* shade. ⟪↔ hinata⟫

hi⌈kaku ひかく (比較) *n.* comparison; parallel. ⟪⇨ kuraberu⟫
hikaku suru (~する) *vt.* compare.

hi⌈kaku-teki ひかくてき (比較的) *adv.* comparatively; relatively:
★ Note that this word is an adverb, not an adjectival noun.
Mondai wa hikaku-teki *yasashikatta.* (問題は比較的やさしかった) I found the problems *comparatively* easy.

hi⌈kari⌉ ひかり (光) *n.* light; ray.

hi⌈ka⌉r·u ひかる (光る) *vi.* (hikar·i-; hikar·a-; hikat-te [C])
1 shine; twinkle; gleam; glitter:
Tooku de nani-ka ga hikatta. (遠くで何かが光った) Something *glinted* in the distance.
2 stand out; be prominent:
Kono zasshi de wa kare no shoosetsu ga hikatte iru. (この雑誌では彼の小説が光っている) His novel *figures prominently* in this magazine.

-hiki ひき (匹) *suf.* counter for small animals, fish and insects. ⟪⇨ APP. 4⟫

hi⌈kiage⌉·ru ひきあげる (引き上げる・引き揚げる) *vt.* (-age-te [V])
1 pull up; salvage:
Chiñbotsu shita fune o hikiageta. (沈没した船を引き揚げた) We *salvaged* the sunken ship.
2 raise:
chiñgiñ o hikiageru (賃金を引き上げる) *raise* wages. ⟪↔ hikisageru⟫
3 withdraw (an army):
guñtai o hikiageru (軍隊を引き揚げる) *withdraw* troops.

hi⌈kidashi ひきだし (引き出し) *n.* drawer.

hi⌈kida⌉s·u ひきだす (引き出す) *vt.* (-dash·i-; -das·a-; -dash·i-te [C])
1 draw (a conclusion, etc.).
2 draw (money from a deposit):
giñkoo kara hyakumañ-eñ hiki-

dasu (銀行から100万円引き出す) *withdraw* one million yen from the bank.

hi⌈kihana⌉s·u ひきはなす (引き離す) *vt.* (-hanash·i-; -hanas·a-; -hanash·i-te Ⓒ) **1** outdistance; outrun:
aite o hikihanasu (相手を引き離す) *run ahad of* one's competitors.
2 separate:
hahaoya kara kodomo o hikihanasu (母親から子どもを引き離す) *separate* a mother from her child. 《⇨ hanasu[2]》

hi⌈kika⌉es·u ひきかえす (引き返す) *vi.* (-kaesh·i-; -kaes·a-; -kaesh·i-te Ⓒ) come [go] back; return:
Hikooki wa eñjiñ no koshoo de tochuu kara hikikaeshita. (飛行機はエンジンの故障で途中から引き返した) The plane *turned back* half way because of engine trouble.

hi⌈kiniku ひきにく (挽き肉) *n.* ground meat; minced meat.

hi⌈kinobashi[1] ひきのばし (引き延ばし) *n.* delaying; postponement. 《⇨ hikinobasu[1]》

hi⌈kinobashi[2] ひきのばし (引き伸ばし) *n.* enlargement. 《⇨ hikinobasu[2]》

hi⌈kinoba⌉s·u[1] ひきのばす (引き延ばす) *vt.* (-nobash·i-; -nobas·a-; -nobash·i-te Ⓒ) extend; prolong; put off:
Shiharai kigeñ o hikinobashite moratta. (支払い期限を引き延ばしてもらった) The payment deadline *was extended* for me. 《⇨ hikinobashi[1]》

hi⌈kinoba⌉s·u[2] ひきのばす (引き伸ばす) *vt.* (-nobash·i-; -nobas·a-; -nobash·i-te Ⓒ) enlarge:
Shashiñ o hikinobashite moratta. (写真を引き伸ばしてもらった) I *had* the photograph *enlarged*. 《⇨ hikinobashi[2]》

hi⌈kinu⌉k·u ひきぬく (引き抜く) *vt.* (-nuk·i-; -nuk·a-; -nu·i-te Ⓒ)
1 pull out; draw; extract:
kugi o hikinuku (くぎを引き抜く) *pull out* a nail. 《⇨ nuku》
2 hire away; transfer:
Uchi no kaisha de wa shaiñ o sañniñ hikinukareta. (うちの会社では社員を3人引き抜かれた) Three people *were hired away* from our company.

hi⌈kisaga⌉r·u ひきさがる (引き下がる) *vi.* (-sagar·i-; -sagar·a-; -sagat-te Ⓒ) withdraw; leave:
Kumiaiiñ-tachi wa sunao ni hikisagaranakatta. (組合員たちは素直に引き下がらなかった) The union members *did not withdraw* obediently. 《⇨ hiku[1]》

hi⌈kisage⌉·ru ひきさげる (引き下げる) *vt.* (-sage-te Ⓥ) lower; reduce; cut [bring] down:
nedañ o hikisageru (値段を引き下げる) *lower* the price. 《⇨ hikiageru》

hi⌈kitate⌉·ru ひきたてる (引き立てる) *vt.* (-tate-te Ⓥ) **1** favor; patronize; support:
Kachoo wa itsu-mo kare o hikitatete iru. (課長はいつも彼を引き立てている) Our boss *is* always *favoring* him.
2 set off:
Bakku no aozora ga kanojo no fukusoo o hikitatete iru. (バックの青空が彼女の服装を引き立てている) The blue sky in the background *sets off* her clothes. 《⇨ hikitatsu》

hi⌈kita⌉ts·u ひきたつ (引き立つ) *vi.* (-tach·i-; -tat·a-; -tat-te Ⓒ) look nice; be set off:
Soko ni hana o ikeru to issoo hikitachimasu. (そこに花を生けるといっそう引き立ちます) If you put a flower arrangement there, the place will *look much better*. 《⇨ hikitateru》

hi⌈kitome⌉·ru ひきとめる (引き止める・引き留める) *vt.* (-tome-te Ⓥ) keep; prevent:
Kare o hikitomeru *koto wa dekinakatta.* (彼を引き止めることはできなかった) We could not *prevent* him *from leaving*.

hi⌈kito⌉r·u ひきとる (引き取る) *vt.* (-tor·i-; -tor·a-; -tot-te Ⓒ)

1 take [buy] back:
Urenokotta shinamono wa hikitorimasu. (売れ残った品物は引き取ります) We will *take back* unsold goods.
2 take care of; take in (a child, an old person, etc.).

hi⌈kitsuke⌉·ru ひきつける (引き付ける) *vt.* (-tsuke-te [V]) **1** attract; charm; magnetize:
Kare no eñzetsu wa chooshuu o hikitsuketa. (彼の演説は聴衆を引きつけた) His speech *charmed* the audience.
2 (of a magnet) attract.

hi⌈kiuke⌉·ru ひきうける (引き受ける) *vt.* (-uke-te [V]) take; undertake:
Sono yakume wa watashi ga hikiukemasu. (その役目は私が引き受けます) I will *undertake* that duty.

hi⌈kiwake ひきわけ (引き分け) *n.* drawn game; draw; tie. 《⇨ hikiwakeru》

hi⌈kiwake⌉·ru ひきわける (引き分ける) *vi.*, *vt.* (-wake-te [V]) draw; tie:
Jaiañtsu wa Taigaasu to no shiai o hikiwaketa. (ジャイアンツはタイガースとの試合を引き分けた) The Giants *drew* in the game with the Tigers. 《⇨ hikiwake》

hi⌈kiwata⌉s·u ひきわたす (引き渡す) *vt.* (-watash·i-; -watas·a-; -watash·i-te [C]) hand over; deliver:
Kare-ra wa doroboo o keesatsu ni hikiwatashita. (彼らは泥棒を警察に引き渡した) They *handed* the thief *over* to the police. 《⇨ watasu》

hi⌈ki⌉zañ ひきざん (引き算) *n.* (of arithmetic) subtraction. 《↔ tashizañ》

hi⌈kizur·u ひきずる (引きずる) *vt.* (-zur·i-; -zur·a-; -zut-te [C]) drag; trail: *ashi o* hikizuru (足を引きずる) *drag* one's feet / *kimono no suso o* hikizuru (着物のすそを引きずる) *trail* the hem of one's kimono.

hi⌈kkaka⌉r·u ひっかかる (引っ掛かる) *vi.* (-kakar·i-; -kakar·a-; -kakatte [C]) **1** get caught:
Zuboñ ga kugi ni hikkakatta. (ズボンがくぎに引っ掛かった) My trousers *got caught* on a nail. 《⇨ hikkakeru》
2 fall for; be deceived:
Kanojo wa sagi ni hikkakatta. (彼女は詐欺に引っ掛かった) She *fell for* a confidence trick. 《⇨ hikkakeru》

hi⌈kkake⌉·ru ひっかける (引っ掛ける) *vt.* (-kake-te [V]) **1** catch:
Kare wa shatsu o kugi ni hikkaketa. (彼はシャツをくぎに引っ掛けた) He *caught* his shirt on a nail. 《⇨ hikkakaru》
2 (of clothes) throw on:
Kare wa uwagi o hikkakete, *soto ni deta.* (彼は上着を引っ掛けて, 外に出た) He *threw on* his jacket and went out.
3 splash:
Kodomo-tachi wa otagai ni mizu o hikkakete, *asoñda.* (子どもたちはお互いに水を引っ掛けて, 遊んだ) The children played, *splashing* water at each other. 《⇨ hikkakaru》
4 deceive; trap; seduce:
Kare o hikkakeyoo *to shite mo, muda desu.* (彼を引っ掛けようとしても, 無駄です) It is no use trying to *deceive* him. 《⇨ hikkakaru》

hi⌈kki ひっき (筆記) *n.* notetaking; writing.
hikki suru (～する) *vt.* take notes.

hi⌈kko⌉m·u ひっこむ (引っ込む) *vi.* (-kom·i-; -kom·a-; -koñ-de [C])
1 retire; withdraw:
Kare wa kokyoo ni hikkoñda. (彼は故郷に引っ込んだ) He *retired* to his hometown.
2 stand back:
Kare no ie wa dooro kara yaku gojuu-meetoru hikkoñde iru. (彼の家は道路から約 50 メートル引っ込んでいる) His house *stands back* about fifty meters from the road.

hi⌈kkoshi ひっこし (引っ越し) *n.* move; removal. 《⇨ hikkosu》

hi⌈kko⌉s·u ひっこす (引っ越す) *vi.* (-kosh·i-; -kos·a-; -kosh·i-te [C]) move:
Ikka wa Nagoya kara Oosaka e

hikkoshita. (一家は名古屋から大阪へ引っ越した) The family *moved* from Nagoya to Osaka. ⟪⇨ hikkoshi⟫

hi⌈kkurika⌉er·u ひっくりかえる (ひっくり返る) *vi.* (-kaer·a-; -kaer·i-; -kaet-te Ⓒ) overturn; upset:
Tsuri-bune ga hikkurikaetta. (釣り舟がひっくり返った) The fishing boat *overturned*. ⟪⇨ hikkurikaesu⟫

hi⌈kkurika⌉es·u ひっくりかえす (ひっくり返す) *vt.* (-kaesh·i-; -kaes·a-; -kaesh·i-te Ⓒ) turn over; upset:
Kare wa koppu o hikkurikaeshita. (彼はコップをひっくり返した) He *upset* the glass. ⟪⇨ hikkurikaeru⟫

hi⌈koo ひこう (飛行) *n.* flight; flying.
hikoo suru (～する) *vi.* fly; make a flight.

hi⌈koojoo ひこうじょう (飛行場) *n.* airfield; airport. ⟪⇨ kuukoo⟫

hi⌈ko⌉oki ひこうき (飛行機) *n.* airplane; plane.

hi⌈koosen̄ ひこうせん (飛行船) *n.* airship; dirigible; blimp.

hi⌈k·u[1] ひく (引く) *vt.* (hik·i-; hik·a-; hi·i-te Ⓒ) **1** pull; draw; tow; tug:
Himo o hiite, *den̄ki o tsuketa.* (ひもを引いて, 電気をつけた) I switched on the light by *pulling* the cord.
2 lead by the hand:
Kanojo wa kodomo no te o hiite, *aruita.* (彼女は子どもの手を引いて, 歩いた) She walked along, *leading* her child *by the hand.*
3 catch; attract:
chuui o hiku (注意を引く) *attract* someone's attention.
4 consult (a dictionary); look up:
Jisho o hiite, *sono imi o shirabeta.* (辞書を引いて, その意味を調べた) I *consulted* a dictionary and checked the meaning.
5 lay; install:
suidoo o hiku (水道を引く) *lay* a water pipe / *den̄wa o* hiku (電話を引く) *install* a telephone.
6 draw (a line):
sen̄ o hiku (線を引く) *draw* a line.
7 subtract; take:
Juu kara san̄ o hiku *to nana nokoru.* (10 から 3 を引くと 7 残る) *Take* 3 from 10 and it leaves 7. ⟪↔ tasu⟫
8 catch (a cold).
9 *vi.* go down; subside:
Netsu wa hikimashita *ka?* (熱は引きましたか) *Has* the fever *subsided?*
10 *vi.* yield; pull out:
Kare wa ip-po mo ato e hikanakatta. (彼は一歩も後へ引かなかった) He *did not yield* a single step.
11 (of the tide) ebb. ⟪↔ michiru⟫

hi⌈k·u[2] ひく (弾く) *vt.* (hik·i-; hik·a-; hi·i-te Ⓒ) play (a musical instrument):
Kanojo wa joozu ni piano o hiku. (彼女は上手にピアノを弾く) She *plays* the piano well.

hi⌈k·u[3] ひく (轢く) *vt.* (hik·i-; hik·a-; hi·i-te Ⓒ) hit; run over [down]:
Kare no kuruma wa neko o hiita. (彼の車は猫をひいた) His car *ran over* a cat.

hi⌈ku⌉·i ひくい (低い) *a.* (-ku)
1 (of height) low; short:
Chichi wa watashi yori se ga hikui. (父は私より背が低い) My father is *shorter* than me. ⟪↔ takai⟫
2 (of a position, degree, level) low:
Kyoo wa kinoo yori on̄do ga hikui. (きょうはきのうより温度が低い) Today the temperature is *lower* than yesterday. ⟪↔ takai⟫
3 (of sound, voice) not loud; low:
hikui *koe de hanasu* (低い声で話す) speak in a *low* voice. ⟪↔ takai⟫

hi⌈kyo⌉o ひきょう (卑怯) *a.n.* (～ na, ni) foul; unfair; cowardly; mean:
Imasara te o hiku nan̄te hikyoo *da.* (いまさら手を引くなんてひきょうだ) It is *cowardly* of you to back out now.

hi⌈ma ひま (暇) *n.* time; free time; leisure.

— *a.n.* (~ na) free; not busy: *Kyoo wa kyaku ga sukunakute,* hima *desu.* (きょうは客が少なくて，暇です) There are only a few customers today, so we are *not busy.* ⟪↔ isogashii⟫

hima o dasu (~を出す) dismiss; fire. ⟪⇨ kubi⟫

hi⌈mee ひめい (悲鳴) *n.* shriek; scream: himee *o ageru* (悲鳴を上げる) give a *scream.*

hi⌈mitsu ひみつ (秘密) *n.* secret.

hi⌈mo ひも (紐) *n.* string; cord; band.

h

hi⌈ñ ひん (品) *n.* elegance; grace; refinement: hiñ no yoi *fujiñ* (品の良い婦人) an *elegant* lady. ⟪⇨ hiñi⟫

hi⌉na ひな (雛) *n.* chick; young bird.

hi⌈nama⌉tsuri ひなまつり (雛祭り) *n.* the Doll Festival celebrated on March 3. ★ Also known as the Girls' Festival.

hi⌉nañ[1] ひなん (非難) *n.* blame; criticism; attack.

hinañ suru (~する) *vt.* criticize; blame; attack.

hi⌉nañ[2] ひなん (避難) *n.* shelter; refuge; evacuation.

hinañ suru (~する) *vi.* take shelter [refuge]; evacuate.

hi⌈nani⌉ñgyoo ひなにんぎょう (雛人形) *n.* a doll made of paper or clay, usually colorfully clad. ⟪⇨ hinamatsuri⟫

hi⌈nata ひなた (日向) *n.* sunny place. ⟪↔ hikage⟫ ⟪⇨ hiatari⟫

hinata-bokko (~ぼっこ) sunbath: hinata-bokko o suru (日なたぼっこをする) *bask in the sun.*

hi⌈ne⌉r·u ひねる (捻る) *vt.* (hiner·i-; hiner·a-; hinet-te Ⓒ) turn (a faucet, tap, knob); twist: *Kare wa sukeeto de ashi o* hinetta. (彼はスケートで足をひねった) He *twisted* his foot ice-skating.

hi⌉ñi ひんい (品位) *n.* dignity; grace; elegance. ⟪⇨ hiñ⟫

hi⌈niku ひにく (皮肉) *n.* irony; sarcasm; cynicism.

— *a.n.* (~ na, ni) ironic: *Gyaku no kekka ni naru to wa* hiniku *da.* (逆の結果になるとは皮肉だ) It's *ironic* that things turned out exactly opposite.

hi⌈ñjaku ひんじゃく (貧弱) *a.n.* (~ na, ni) poor; feeble: hiñjaku *na karadatsuki* (貧弱な体つき) a *feeble* body.

hi⌈node ひので (日の出) *n.* sunrise.

hi⌈noiri ひのいり (日の入り) *n.* sunset. ⟪↔ hinode⟫

hi⌈ñshi ひんし (品詞) *n.* part of speech. ⟪⇨ APP. 2⟫

hi⌈ñshitsu ひんしつ (品質) *n.* quality: hiñshitsu *ga yoi* [*warui*] (品質が良い[悪い]) be good [bad] in *quality.*

hi⌈nyookika ひにょうきか (泌尿器科) *n.* urology department.

hi⌈ppa⌉r·u ひっぱる (引っ張る) *vt.* (-par·i-; -par·a-; -pat-te Ⓒ)

1 pull; tug; jerk: *Dare-ka ga watashi no sode o* hippatta. (だれかが私のそでを引っ張った) Someone *tugged* at my sleeve.

2 bring; take (a person): *Kare wa keesatsu e* hipparareta. (彼は警察へ引っ張られた) He *was taken along* to the police.

3 lead: *Kare wa chiimu no hoka no mono o yoku* hippatte iru. (彼はチームの他の者をよく引っ張っている) He *leads* the others in the team well.

hi⌈raga⌉na ひらがな (平仮名) *n.* the Japanese cursive syllabary. ⟪⇨ inside front cover⟫

hi⌉rahira ひらひら *adv.* (~ to) (the motion of light, thin or soft things, fluttering, swaying, or falling): *Choochoo ga* hirahira (*to*) *toñde iru.* (蝶々がひらひら(と)飛んでいる) The butterflies are *fluttering* around.

hi⌈rake⌉·ru ひらける (開ける) *vi.* (hirake-te Ⓥ) **1** (of a place) become modernized [civilized]; develop:

Kono machi wa saikiñ hirakemashita. (この町は最近開けました) This town *has* recently *developed*.
2 (of scenery) open; spread out: *Me no mae ni utsukushii keshiki ga* hiraketa. (目の前に美しい景色が開けた) A beautiful view *opened* in front of our eyes.

hiˈrakiˀ ひらき (開き) *n.*
1 opening:
Kono tobira wa hiraki ga warui. (このとびらは開きが悪い) This door *won't open easily*. ⟪⇨ hiraku⟫
2 difference:
Futari no ikeñ ni wa ooki-na hiraki *ga aru*. (二人の意見には大きな開きがある) There is a great *difference* of opinion between them.
3 fish cut open, flattened and dried:
aji no hiraki (あじの開き) a horse mackerel *cut open and dried*.

hiˈraˀk·u ひらく (開く) (hirak·i-; hirak·a-; hira·i-te Ⓒ)
1 *vt.* open; undo; unpack; unseal:
Kare wa doa o hiraite, *heya ni haitta*. (彼はドアを開いて, 部屋に入った) He *opened* the door and went into the room. ⟪⇨ akeru[1]⟫
2 *vi.* (of an office, shop, etc.) start; begin; establish; found:
Yuubiñkyoku wa ku-ji ni hirakimasu. (郵便局は9時に開きます) The post office *opens* at nine. ⟪⇨ aku[1]⟫
3 *vt.* hold (a meeting); give (a party).
4 *vi.* (of flowers) come out:
Sakura ga hiraki-*hajimemashita*. (桜が開き始めました) The cherry blossoms have started to *open*.

hiˈrata·i ひらたい (平たい) *a.* (-ku) flat; even:
hiratai *sara* (平たい皿) a *flat* plate / *hyoomeñ o* hirataku *suru* (表面を平たくする) make a surface *even*.
⟪⇨ taira⟫

hiˈritsu ひりつ (比率) *n.* ratio; percentage. ⟪⇨ hi[5]⟫

hiˈroba ひろば (広場) *n.* open space; square; plaza.

hiˈrogar·u ひろがる (広がる) *vi.* (hirogar·i-; hirogar·a-; hirogat-te Ⓒ) **1** extend; expand; widen:
Eki no mae no michi ga hirogatta. (駅の前の道が広がった) The road in front of the station *widened*.
⟪⇨ hirogeru⟫
2 (of a rumor) spread.
⟪⇨ hiromaru⟫

hiˈroge·ru ひろげる (広げる) *vt.* (hiroge-te Ⓥ) **1** spread; unfold; unroll:
Sono tori wa tsubasa o hirogeta. (その鳥は翼を広げた) The bird *spread* its wings. ⟪⇨ hirogaru⟫
2 widen (a field of activity); enlarge; extend:
shoobai o hirogeru (商売を広げる) *expand* one's business. ⟪⇨ hirogaru⟫

hiˈroˀ·i ひろい (広い) *a.* (-ku) large; big; wide; broad:
hiroi *ie* (広い家) a *roomy* house / hiroi *chishiki* (広い知識) *broad* knowledge. ⟪↔ semai⟫

hiˈromar·u ひろまる (広まる) *vi.* (hiromar·i-; hiromar·a-; hiromat-te Ⓒ) spread; come into fashion; be circulated:
Sono uwasa wa machi-juu ni hiromatta. (そのうわさは町中に広まった) The rumor *spread* throughout the town. ⟪⇨ hiromeru⟫

hiˈrome·ru ひろめる (広める) *vt.* (hirome-te Ⓥ) spread; popularize:
kañkyoo-hakai ni kañsuru chishiki o hiromeru (環境破壊に関する知識を広める) *spread* knowledge about environmental destruction.
⟪⇨ hiromaru⟫

hiˈroo[1] ひろう (疲労) *n.* fatigue; tiredness; exhaustion.
hiroo suru (～する) *vi.* be tired; be fatigued; be exhausted.
⟪⇨ kutabireru; tsukareru⟫

hiˈroo[2] ひろう (披露) *n.* introduction; announcement.
hiroo suru (～する) *vt.* introduce;

h

announce; show: *Kare wa watashi-tachi ni atarashii sakuhiñ o* hiroo shita. (彼は私たちに新しい作品を披露した) He *showed* us his new work.

hi⌉rosa ひろさ (広さ) *n.* area; extent; size; width:
Sono heya no hirosa *wa dono kurai desu ka?* (その部屋の広さはどのくらいですか) What is the *size* of that room?

hi⌈ro·u ひろう (拾う) *vt.* (hiro·i-; hirow·a-; hirot-te Ⓒ) **1** pick up; find:
Saifu o hirotte, *keesatsu ni todoketa.* (財布を拾って, 警察に届けた) I *picked up* a wallet and turned it in to the police.
2 get; pick up (a taxi).

hi⌈ru⌉ ひる (昼) *n.* noon; day; daytime. (⇨ asa¹)

hi⌈rugo⌉hañ ひるごはん (昼ご飯) *n.* lunch. ★ More polite than '*hirumeshi*.' (⇨ asagohañ; bañgohañ; chuushoku; gohañ)

hi⌈ruma⌉ ひるま (昼間) *n.* daytime.

hi⌈rumeshi ひるめし (昼飯) *n.* (*informal*) lunch. (⇨ hirugohañ; chuushoku)

hi⌈ru⌉m·u ひるむ (怯む) *vi.* (hirum·i-; hirum·a-; hiruñ-de Ⓒ) flinch (from); shrink (from):
Kare wa kikeñ ni mo hirumanakatta. (彼は危険にもひるまなかった) He *did not shrink* from danger.

hi⌈rune ひるね (昼寝) *n.* nap.

hi⌈ruya⌉sumi ひるやすみ (昼休み) *n.* lunch break; noon recess.

hi⌉ryoo ひりょう (肥料) *n.* manure; fertilizer.

hi⌈sa⌉isha ひさいしゃ (被災者) *n.* victim (of a disaster); sufferer.

hi⌈sañ ひさん (悲惨) *a.n.* (~ na, ni) wretched; miserable; terrible; tragic:
hisañ *na jiko* (悲惨な事故) a *tragic* accident.

hi⌈sashi ひさし (庇) *n.* **1** eaves.
2 visor (to a cap).

hi⌈sashiburi ひさしぶり (久し振り) *a.n.* (~ na/no, ni) after a long time [silence; separation]:
Hisashiburi *desu ne.* (久しぶりですね) It's *a long time* since I saw you last. ★ In greetings, '*o-hisashiburi desu ne*' is more polite.

hi⌈sa⌉shiku ひさしく (久しく) *adv.* (*formal*) for a long time:
Suzuki-sañ to wa hisashiku *atte imaseñ.* (鈴木さんとは久しく会っていません) I haven't met Mrs. Suzuki *for a long time.*

hi⌈sho⌉¹ ひしょ (秘書) *n.* secretary.

hi⌈sho² ひしょ (避暑) *n.* summering; going somewhere cool during the hot months.

hi⌈so⌉ka ひそか (密か) *a.n.* (~ na, ni) in secret; in private:
Kagekiha wa hisoka *ni bakudañ o tsukutte ita.* (過激派はひそかに爆弾を作っていた) The radicals were *secretly* making bombs.

hi⌉ssha ひっしゃ (筆者) *n.* writer; author.

hi⌉sshi ひっし (必死) *a.n.* (~ na/no, ni) desperate; frantic:
Kare wa hisshi *ni nigeta.* (彼は必死に逃げた) He ran away *desperately.*

hi⌈sso⌉ri ひっそり *adv.* (~ to; ~ suru) (the state of being quiet, still or deserted):
Mori no naka wa hissori (*to*) *shite ita.* (森の中はひっそり(と)していた) All was *hushed* in the forest.

hi⌈tai ひたい (額) *n.* forehead; brow.

hi⌈tar·u ひたる (浸る) *vi.* (hitar·i-; hitar·a-; hitat-te Ⓒ) **1** be flooded; be under water:
Koozui de hatake ga mizu ni hitatta. (洪水で畑が水に浸った) The fields *were inundated* because of flooding. (⇨ hitasu)
2 be immersed in; be given to:
Kare wa sono ba no tanoshii fuñiki ni hitatta. (彼はその場の楽しい雰囲気に浸った) He *steeped himself* in the merry atmosphere of the place.

hi⌈tas·u ひたす (浸す) *vt.* (hita-

sh·i-; hitas·a-; hitash·i-te Ⓒ)
dip; soak:
mame o mizu ni hitasu (豆を水に浸す) *soak* beans in water.
《⇨ hitaru》

hi⌈tee ひてい (否定) *n.* denial; negation.
hitee suru (～する) *vt.* deny; make a denial. 《↔ kootee[1]》

hi⌈to ひと (人) *n.* **1** person; man; woman: ★ In polite speech, '*kata*' is used.
Ano hito *wa dare desu ka?* (あの人はだれですか) Who is that *man* [*woman*]? 《⇨ kata[3]》
2 (other) people:
Wakai hito *ga urayamashii.* (若い人がうらやましい) I envy young *people.*
3 human being; man:
Hito *wa dare de mo shinu.* (人はだれでも死ぬ) *Man* is mortal.
4 worker; hand:
Hito *ga tarinai.* (人が足りない) We are short of *workers.* 《⇨ hitode》

hi⌈to-[1] ひと (一) *pref.* one:
Watashi wa ichi-nichi ni tabako o hito-*hako suimasu.* (私は一日にたばこを一箱吸います) I smoke *a* pack of cigarettes a day.

hi⌈to-[2] ひと (一) *pref.* a [an]:
★ Precedes a noun and indicates one (short) action.
hito-*shigoto suru* (一仕事する) do *a* job of work / hito-*nemuri suru* (一眠りする) have *a* nap.

hi⌈to⌉bito ひとびと (人々) *n.* (many) people.

hi⌈tochi⌉gai ひとちがい (人違い) *n.* mistaking a person for somebody else:
Gomeñ nasai. Hitochigai deshita. (ごめんなさい. 人違いでした) I'm sorry. I *took you for someone I know.*
《⇨ -chigai》

hi⌈tode ひとで (人手) *n.*
1 worker; hand:
Hitode *ga tarinai.* (人手が足りない) We are short of *hands.* 《⇨ hito》
2 another's help:
Kono shigoto wa hitode *o karizu ni, yarimashita.* (この仕事は人手を借りずに, やりました) I have done this work without *anyone else's help.*
3 another's possession:
Sono uchi wa tsui-ni hitode *ni watatta.* (その家はついに人手に渡った) The house finally passed into *another's possession.*

hi⌈todoori ひとどおり (人通り) *n.* pedestrian traffic.

hi⌈togara ひとがら (人柄) *n.* personality; personal character.

hi⌈togomi ひとごみ (人込み) *n.* crowd:
Depaato wa taiheñ na hitogomi *datta.* (デパートは大変な人込みだった) The department store was very *crowded.*

hi⌈togoto ひとごと (人事) *n.* other people's affairs: ★ Often used with a negative.
Sono jiko wa hitogoto de wa nai. (その事故はひと事ではない) *Everyone has the possibility* of encountering such an accident.

hi⌈tokage ひとかげ (人影) *n.* shadow of a person; human figure.

hi⌈to⌉koto ひとこと (一言) *n.* single word:
Kare wa kaigi-chuu, hitokoto mo shaberanakatta. (彼は会議中, ひと言もしゃべらなかった) He *remained silent* during the meeting.

hi⌈toma⌉kase ひとまかせ (人任せ) *n.* leaving a matter to others:
Kare wa nañ de mo hitomakase *da.* (彼は何でも人まかせだ) He *leaves everything to others.*

hi⌈tomane ひとまね (人真似) *n.* (of people) mimicry; imitation:
Oomu wa hitomane *ga umai.* (おうむは人まねがうまい) Parrots are good at *copying what people say.*

hi⌈to⌉mazu ひとまず *adv.* first (of all); for a while; for the time being:
Hitomazu, *yasumi o torimashoo.* (ひとまず, 休みをとりましょう) Let's

h

take a break *for a while.*

hi⌈to⌉me[1] ひとめ (一目) *n.* look; sight; glance:
Kare wa hitome *de kanojo ga suki ni natta.* (彼はひと目で彼女が好きになった) With *one glance*, he took a fancy to her.

hi⌈tome[2] ひとめ (人目) *n.* public attention; notice:
Sono atarashii biru wa hitome *o hiita.* (その新しいビルは人目を引いた) The new building attracted *public attention.*

hi⌈to⌉mi ひとみ (瞳) *n.* pupil of the eye.

hi⌈to⌉ri ひとり (一人・独り) *n.* one (person); each; by oneself:
Kanojo wa hitori de *kurashite imasu.* (彼女は一人で暮らしています) She lives *by herself.*

hi⌈toridachi ひとりだち (独り立ち) *n.* independence.
hitoridachi suru (～する) *vi.* become independent; stand on one's own feet. ⟪⇨ dokuritsu⟫

hi⌈toride ni ひとりでに (独りでに) *adv.* by itself; automatically:
Kono deñtoo wa kuraku naru to hitoride ni *tsukimasu.* (この電灯は暗くなるとひとりでにつきます) When it gets dark, this light comes on *automatically.* ⟪⇨ shizeñ ni⟫

hi⌈torigoto ひとりごと (独り言) *n.* soliloquy; talking to oneself.

hi⌈tori-hito⌉ri ひとりひとり (一人一人) *n.* every one; one by one; one after another.

hi⌈tosashi⌉yubi ひとさしゆび (人差し指) *n.* forefinger; index finger. ⟪⇨ yubi⟫

hi⌈toshi⌉·i ひとしい (等しい) *a.* (-ku)
1 equal; the same:
Kono futatsu no kozutsumi wa mekata ga hitoshii. (この二つの小包は目方が等しい) These two parcels are *equal* in weight.
2 almost; practically:
Rieki ga tatta señ-eñ de wa nai ni hitoshii. (利益がたった千円ではないに等しい) The profit was only one thousand yen, which is *almost* nothing.

hi⌈to⌉tobi ひととび (一飛び) *n.* jump; hop:
Hikooki nara, Tookyoo to Fukuoka wa hitotobi *desu.* (飛行機なら, 東京と福岡はひととびです) It is just a *hop* between Tokyo and Fukuoka if you go by airplane.

hi⌈totoori ひととおり (一通り) *n.* all; generality; ordinariness:
hitotoori *no setsumee* (一通りの説明) a *general* explanation.
— *adv.* briefly; hurriedly; roughly:
maiasa hitotoori *shiñbuñ ni me o toosu* (毎朝一通り新聞に目を通す) glance *through* newspapers every morning. ⟪⇨ zatto⟫

hi⌈to⌉tsu[1] ひとつ (一つ) *n.* **1** one; single: ★ Used when counting.
Kore o hitotsu *kudasai.* (*at a store*) (これを一つ下さい) Give me *one* of these, please. ⟪⇨ APP. 3⟫
2 one-year old:
Kono ko wa hitotsu *hañ desu.* (この子は一つ半です) This child is *one* and a half years old.

hi⌈to⌉tsu[2] ひとつ *adv.* just; anyway; at any rate:
Mono wa tameshi da. Hitotsu *yatte miyoo.* (ものは試しだ. ひとつやってみよう) You will never know if you don't try. Let's have *a go.*

hi⌈to⌉tsuki ひとつき (一月) *n.* one month.

hi⌈to⌉yasumi ひとやすみ (一休み) *n.* a short rest; break.
hitoyasumi suru (～する) *vi.* take a short rest. ⟪⇨ kyuukee⟫

hi⌈tsuji ひつじ (羊) *n.* sheep.

hi⌈tsuyoo ひつよう (必要) *n.* necessity; need.
— *a.n.* (～ na, ni) necessary; essential; indispensable:
Hitsuyoo *na mono ga attara, osshatte kudasai.* (必要なものがあったら, おっしゃってください) If there is anything you *need*, please let me know. ⟪↔ fuhitsuyoo⟫

hi⌈tsuzeñ-teki ひつぜんてき(必然的) *a.n.* (~ na, ni) necessary; natural; inevitable:
hitsuzeñ-teki *na kekka* (必然的な結果) an *inevitable* result.

hi⌉tto ヒット *n.* **1** (of baseball) hit; single.
2 great success; hit.
hitto suru (~する) *vi.* make a hit.

hi⌈ya-a⌉se ひやあせ(冷や汗) *n.* cold sweat:
hiya-ase *o kaku* (冷や汗をかく) break into a *cold sweat.*

hi⌈yaka⌉s·u ひやかす(冷やかす) *vt.* (hiyakash·i-; hiyakas·a-; hiyakash·i-te Ⓒ) **1** make fun of; tease:
Futari ga aruite iru no o mite, hiyakashite *yatta.* (二人が歩いているのを見て, 冷やかしてやった) We saw the couple strolling and *made fun of* them.
2 window-shop:
Mise o hiyakashite *jikañ o tsubushita.* (店を冷やかして時間をつぶした) I idled away the time *window-shopping.*

hi⌈yake ひやけ(日焼け) *n.* sunburn; suntan.
hiyake suru (~する) *vi.* get sunburned; get a suntan.

hi⌈ya⌉s·u ひやす(冷やす) *vt.* (hiyash·i-; hiyas·a-; hiyash·i-te Ⓒ) cool; ice; refrigerate:
reezooko de biiru o hiyasu (冷蔵庫でビールを冷やす) *cool* beer in the fridge. ⟪⇨ hieru⟫

hi⌈ya⌉yaka ひややか(冷ややか) *a.n.* (~ na, ni) cold; coldhearted; cool; icy:
Kare wa hiyayaka *na me de watashi o mita.* (彼は冷ややかな目で私を見た) He gave me a *cold* look.

hi⌈yoko ひよこ *n.* chick; chicken.

hi⌉yoo ひよう(費用) *n.* expense; expenditure; cost.

hi⌈za ひざ(膝) *n.* knee; lap.

hi⌈zashi ひざし(日差し) *n.* sunlight; sun.

hi⌈zuke ひづけ(日付) *n.* date.

hi⌈zumi ひずみ(歪み) *n.* warp; distortion:
keezai no hizumi (経済のひずみ) *distortions* in the economy.

ho[1] ほ(穂) *n.* (of a plant) ear.

ho[2] ほ(帆) *n.* sail:
ho *o ageru [orosu]* (帆を揚げる[下ろす]) hoist [lower] a *sail.*

-ho ほ(歩) *suf.* counter for steps. ⟪⇨ APP. 4⟫

ho⌉bo ほぼ *adv.* almost; nearly; about:
Biru wa hobo *dekiagarimashita.* (ビルはほぼでき上がりました) The building is *almost* completed.

hodo ほど(程) *p.* **1** about; some:
Ato juugo-fuñ hodo *de Narita ni tsukimasu.* (あと15分ほどで成田に着きます) We will be arriving at Narita in *about* fifteen minutes. ⟪⇨ kurai[2]⟫
2 not as [so]...as: ★ Follows a noun and used with a negative.
Kotoshi no natsu wa kyoneñ hodo *atsuku nai.* (今年の夏は去年ほど暑くない) This summer is *not as* hot *as* last year's.
3 the more...the more:
Reñshuu sureba suru hodo *umaku narimasu.* (練習すればするほどうまくなります) *The more* you practice, *the better* you become.
4 so...that:
Tsukarete, moo ip-po mo arukenai hodo *datta.* (疲れて, もう一歩も歩けないほどだった) I was *so* exhausted *that* I was unable to take even one step more.
5 almost:
Sono shirase o kiite tobiagaru hodo *bikkuri shita.* (その知らせを聞いて飛び上がるほどびっくりした) On hearing the news, I *almost* jumped up in surprise.

ho⌈do⌉k·u ほどく(解く) *vt.* (hodok·i-; hodok·a-; hodo·i-te Ⓒ) undo; untie; unpack; unfasten:
kutsu no himo o hodoku (靴のひもをほどく) *untie* one's shoelaces / *seetaa o* hodoku (セーターをほどく) *un-*

ravel a sweater.

ho⌈doo ほどう(歩道) *n.* sidewalk; pavement. 《↔ shadoo》

ho⌈dookyoo ほどうきょう(歩道橋) *n.* pedestrian overpass.

ho⌈e⌉·ru ほえる(吠える) *vi.* (hoe-te [V]) bark; howl; roar:
Sono inu wa watashi ni mukatte hoeta. (その犬は私に向かってほえた) The dog *barked* at me.

ho⌈ga⌉raka ほがらか(朗らか) *a.n.* (~ na, ni) cheerful; bright:
hogaraka *na seekaku* (朗らかな性格) a *cheerful* disposition.

h

ho⌉go ほご(保護) *n.* protection; guardianship; preservation.
hogo suru (~する) *vt.* **1** protect; take care of; preserve.
2 take into protective custody; shelter.

ho⌉ho ほほ(頬) *n.* cheek. 《⇨ hoo[3]》

ho⌈hoe⌉m·u ほほえむ(微笑む) *vi.* (-em·i-; -em·a-; -eñ-de [C]) smile. 《⇨ bishoo》

ho⌈ka ほか(外・他) *n.* other; another; else:
Kono kutsu wa sukoshi ooki-sugi-masu. Hoka *no o misete kudasai.* (この靴は少し大き過ぎます. ほかのを見せてください) These shoes are a bit too big. Can you show me some *others*? 《⇨ sono-hoka; ta no》

ho⌉kahoka ほかほか *a.n.* (~ no) nice and warm; steaming hot:
hokahoka *no satsumaimo* (ほかほかのさつまいも) *steaming* hot sweet potatoes.
— *adv.* (~ suru) warm: *Furo ni hairu to karada ga* hokahoka *suru.* (ふろに入ると体がほかほかする) You will feel *warm* after taking a bath.

ho⌈kañ ほかん(保管) *n.* safekeeping; custody; storage.
hokañ suru (~する) *vt.* keep; have a thing in one's custody.

ho⌈ka ni ほかに(他に) *adv.* **1** besides; else; as well as:
Hoka ni *nani-ka suru koto wa ari-masu ka?* (ほかに何かすることはありますか) Is there anything *else* left to do? 《⇨ sono-hoka》
2 except (for):
Kare no hoka ni *sore ga dekiru mono wa imaseñ.* (彼のほかにそれができる者はいません) *Except for* him, there is no one who can do that.

ho⌈keñ[1] ほけん(保険) *n.* insurance; assurance:
Kuruma ni hokeñ *o kaketa.* (車に保険をかけた) I've taken out *insurance* on my car.

ho⌈keñ[2] ほけん(保健) *n.* preservation of health; health.

ho⌈keñjo ほけんじょ(保健所) *n.* health center.

ho⌈ke⌉ñshoo ほけんしょう(保険証) *n.* = keñkoo-hokeñshoo.

ho⌈keñ-ta⌉iiku ほけんたいいく(保健体育) *n.* health and physical education.

Ho⌈kkyoku ほっきょく(北極) *n.* North Pole. 《↔ Nañkyoku》

ho⌈kori[1] ほこり(誇り) *n.* pride:
Kare wa musuko o hokori *ni omotte iru.* (彼は息子を誇りに思っている) He takes *pride* in his son. 《⇨ hokoru》

ho⌈kori[2] ほこり(埃) *n.* dust. 《⇨ chiri[1]; gomi》

ho⌈korobi⌉·ru ほころびる(綻びる) *vi.* (hokorobi-te [V]) **1** be torn; come apart:
nuime ga hokorobiru (縫い目がほころびる) *come apart* at the seams.
2 (of a flower bud) begin to bloom.

ho⌈kor·u ほこる(誇る) *vt.* (hoko-r·i-; hokor·a-; hokot-te [C]) be proud; boast; brag:
Kare wa umare no yoi no o ho-kotte iru. (彼は生まれの良いのを誇っている) He *is proud* of being well-born. 《⇨ hokori[1]》

ho⌈me⌉·ru ほめる(褒める) *vt.* (home-te [V]) praise; speak well of; compliment:
Señsee wa kare no Nihoñgo no hatsuoñ o hometa. (先生は彼の日本語の発音をほめた) The teacher *praised* his Japanese pronuncia-

tion. ⟪↔ kenasu⟫

ho˥ñ ほん(本) *n.* book; volume.

hoñ- ほん(本) *pref.* **1** real; genuine; regular:
hoñ-*shiñju* (本真珠) a *genuine* pearl / hoñ-*shikeñ* (本試験) the *final* examination.
2 (*formal*) this; current:
hoñ-*añ* (本案) *this* plan.

-hoñ ほん(本) *suf.* counter for long objects. ⟪⇨ APP. 4⟫

ho˥ñba ほんば(本場) *n.* center of production; home:
Riñgo no hoñba *wa Aomori desu.* (りんごの本場は青森です) The *home of* Japanese apple *production* is Aomori.

ho˥ñbako ほんばこ(本箱) *n.* bookcase. ⟪⇨ hoñdana⟫

ho˥ñbuñ ほんぶん(本文) *n.* text; body:
keeyakusho no hoñbuñ (契約書の本文) the *text* of a contract.

ho˥ñdana ほんだな(本棚) *n.* bookshelf. ⟪⇨ hoñbako⟫

ho˥ne˥ ほね(骨) *n.* **1** bone:
Kono sakana wa hone *ga ooi.* (この魚は骨が多い) This fish has a lot of *bones.*
2 rib; frame:
Kasa no hone *ga ip-poñ orete shimatta.* (傘の骨が一本折れてしまった) A *rib* of my umbrella broke.
3 hardness; difficulty:
Sono yama ni noboru no wa hone da. (その山に登るのは骨だ) It *is hard* to climb that mountain.
4 backbone; pluck:
Kare wa hone *no aru otoko da.* (彼は骨のある男だ) He is a man with *backbone.*
hone o oru (～を折る) take great pains.

ho˥ñgoku ほんごく(本国) *n.* one's own country; one's home country. ⟪⇨ bokoku⟫

ho˥ñjitsu ほんじつ(本日) *n.* today; this day. ★ Formal equivalent of '*kyoo.*'

ho˥ñkaku-teki ほんかくてき(本格的) *a.n.* (～ na, ni) full; full-scale; real:
hoñkaku-teki *na Furañsu ryoori* (本格的なフランス料理) *real* French cooking.

ho˥ñkañ ほんかん(本館) *n.* the main building; this building.

ho˥ñki ほんき(本気) *n.* earnestness; seriousness:
Tanaka-sañ wa joodañ o hoñki ni shita. (田中さんは冗談を本気にした) Ms. Tanaka *took* the joke *seriously.* ⟪⇨ majime⟫
— *a.n.* (～ na, ni) earnest; serious:
Kare-ra wa hoñki *ni natte, choosa o hajimeta.* (彼らは本気になって，調査を始めた) They have become *serious* and started the investigation.

ho˥ñmono ほんもの(本物) *n.* genuine article; the real thing.

ho˥ñmyoo ほんみょう(本名) *n.* one's real name. ⟪⇨ namae⟫

ho˥ñne ほんね(本音) *n.* real intention [feeling]:
Ano hito wa nakanaka hoñne *o iwanai.* (あの人はなかなか本音を言わない) He doesn't readily disclose his *real intentions* [*feelings*]. ⟪⇨ tatemae⟫

ho˥ñneñ ほんねん(本年) *n.* the current year; this year. ★ More formal than '*kotoshi.*'

ho˥ñniñ ほんにん(本人) *n.* the person in question:
Hoñniñ *wa sono jijitsu o hitee shite imasu.* (本人はその事実を否定しています) *The man himself* denies the fact. ⟪⇨ tooniñ⟫

ho˥ñno ほんの(本の) *attrib.* only; mere; just: ⟪⇨ wazuka⟫
Shio o hoñno *sukoshi irete kudasai.* (塩をほんの少し入れてください) Please add *just* a little salt.

ho˥ñnoo ほんのう(本能) *n.* instinct.

ho˥ñnoo-teki ほんのうてき(本能的) *a.n.* (～ na, ni) instinctive:
Doobutsu wa hoñnoo-teki *ni ki-*

keñ o kañjiru. (動物は本能的に危険を感じる) Animals sense danger *instinctively*.

ho˥noo ほのお (炎) *n.* flame; blaze.

ho˥ñrai (wa) ほんらい(は) (本来(は)) *adv.* **1** originally; by nature:
Sushi wa hoñrai (wa) hozoñshoku de atta. (すしは本来(は)保存食であった) Sushi was *originally* a preserved food.
2 essentially:
Kore to sore wa hoñrai *(wa) betsu no mono da.* (これとそれは本来(は)別のものだ) This and that are *essentially* different matters. 《⇨ gañrai; motomoto》

ho˥ñryoo ほんりょう (本領) *n.* one's real ability; one's specialty:
Kare wa hañbaibu de hoñryoo *o hakki shita.* (彼は販売部で本領を発揮した) He showed *what he could do* in the sales department.

ho˥ñshitsu ほんしつ (本質) *n.* essence; substance; real nature:
Kare-ra no ikeñ wa hoñshitsu *ni oite onaji desu.* (彼らの意見は本質において同じです) Their opinions are the same in *essence*.

ho˥ñshitsu-teki ほんしつてき (本質的) *a.n.* (~ na, ni) essential; intrinsic:
Ryoosha no aida ni hoñshitsu-teki *na chigai wa nai.* (両者の間に本質的な違いはない) There is not an *essential* difference between the two of them.

ho˥ñteñ ほんてん (本店) *n.* head office; main store.

ho˥ñto ほんと *n.*, *a.n.* (*informal*) = hoñtoo.

ho˥ñtoo ほんとう (本当) *n.* truth; fact; reality:
Hoñtoo *no koto o itte kudasai.* (本当のことを言ってください) Please tell me the *truth*.
— *a.n.* (~ na, ni) true; actual; real:
Sono hanashi wa hoñtoo *desu.* (その話は本当です) The story is *true*.

ho˥ñya ほんや (本屋) *n.* book-store; bookshop.

ho˥ñyaku ほんやく (翻訳) *n.* translation.
hoñyaku suru (~する) *vt.* translate. 《⇨ yaku[4]》

ho˥o[1] ほう (法) *n.* **1** law:
Kimi no kooi wa hoo *ni hañsuru.* (君の行為は法に反する) Your conduct is against the *law*.
2 method; way:
*Watashi wa ii keñkoo-*hoo *o shitte imasu.* (私はいい健康法を知っています) I know a very effective *way* of keeping one's health. 《⇨ hoohoo》

ho˥o[2] ほう (方) *n.* **1** direction:
Kare wa dotchi no hoo *e ikimashita ka?* (彼はどっちの方へ行きましたか) In which *direction* did he go?
2 (as far as) something [someone] (is concerned): ★ Used in comparison or contrast.
Boku no hoo *ga kare yori mo se ga takai.* (ぼくのほうが彼よりも背が高い) *I* am taller than him.

ho˥o[3] ほお (頰) *n.* cheek. 《⇨ hoho》

ho˥oañ ほうあん (法案) *n.* bill:
Sono hooañ *wa gikai o tsuuka shita.* (その法案は議会を通過した) The *bill* passed the Diet.

ho˥obi ほうび (褒美) *n.* reward; prize:
Watashi wa hoobi *ni mañneñhitsu o moratta.* (私はほうびに万年筆をもらった) I got a fountain pen as a *prize*.

ho˥oboo ほうぼう (方々) *n.* every direction; everywhere; here and there:
Kagi o hooboo *sagashita ga, mitsukaranakatta.* (鍵をほうぼう捜したが, 見つからなかった) I searched for the key *high and low*, but it did not turn up.

ho˥ochi ほうち (放置) *n.* leaving (a thing).
hoochi suru (~する) *vt.* leave; let alone: *Jiteñsha o koko ni* hoochi shinai *de kudasai.* (自転車をここに放置しないでください) Please *don't leave* your bicycle here.

ho⌈ochoo ほうちょう(包丁) ***n.*** kitchen knife.

ho⌈odoo ほうどう(報道) ***n.*** news; report; information.
hoodoo suru (～する) *vt.* report; inform.

ho⌈odo⌉ojiñ ほうどうじん(報道陣) ***n.*** a group of reporters; the press.

ho⌈ofu ほうふ(豊富) ***a.n.*** (～ na, ni) plentiful; ample; rich:
Ano kañgofu-sañ wa keekeñ ga hoofu *desu.* (あの看護婦さんは経験が豊富です) That nurse has *a lot of* experience.

ho⌉o ga ⌈i⌉i ほうがいい(方が良い)
★ Used in the patterns, '*n.*+*no hoo ga ii*; *a.n.*+*na hoo ga ii*; *v.* [*a.*; *attrib.*]+*hoo ga ii*.'
1 be better:
Chiisai no yori ookii hoo ga ii. (小さいのより大きいほうがいい) The big one *is better* than the small one.
2 I suggest...; be better; had better (do); should (do): ★ Used in making recommendations.
Hokkaidoo nara, hikooki de itta hoo ga ii *ka mo shiremaseñ.* (北海道なら, 飛行機で行ったほうがいいかもしれません) If you are going to Hokkaido, *it might be better* to go by plane.

ho⌈ogaku ほうがく(方角) ***n.*** direction; bearings.

ho⌈oge⌉ñ ほうげん(方言) ***n.*** dialect.

ho⌉ohige ほおひげ(頰髭) ***n.*** whiskers. ⟪⇨ hige⟫

ho⌈ohoo ほうほう(方法) ***n.*** method; way; measure. ⟪⇨ hoo[1]⟫

ho⌈oji·ru ほうじる(報じる) ***vt.*** (hooji-te [V]) report; inform; broadcast; televise:
Dono shiñbuñ mo sono kuni no jishiñ no koto o hoojita. (どの新聞もその国の地震のことを報じた) All the newspapers *reported* the earthquake in that country.

ho⌈okai ほうかい(崩壊) ***n.*** (*formal*) collapse; breakdown; disintegration.
hookai suru (～する) *vi.* collapse; disintegrate; decay. ⟪⇨ kowareru; kuzureru⟫

ho⌈okeñ-shu⌉gi ほうけんしゅぎ(封建主義) ***n.*** feudalism.

ho⌈okeñ-teki ほうけんてき(封建的) ***a.n.*** (～ na, ni) feudal; feudalistic:
hookeñ-teki *na kañgaekata* (封建的な考え方) a *feudalistic* way of thinking.

ho⌉oki[1] ほうき(放棄) ***n.*** abandonment; renunciation.
hooki suru (～する) *vt.* give up; abandon; renounce.

ho⌉oki[2] ほうき(箒) ***n.*** broom.

ho⌈okoku ほうこく(報告) ***n.*** report.
hookoku suru (～する) *vt.* report; inform; give an account.

ho⌈okoo ほうこう(方向) ***n.***
1 direction; way; course.
2 aim; object; course:
jibuñ no shoorai no hookoo *o kimeru* (自分の将来の方向を決める) make a decision about the future *course* of one's life.

ho⌈ome⌉ñ ほうめん(方面) ***n.***
1 district:
Taifuu wa Shikoku hoomeñ *o osotta.* (台風は四国方面を襲った) The typhoon hit the Shikoku *district.*
2 direction:
Kare wa Ueno hoomeñ *e ikimashita.* (彼は上野方面へ行きました) He went in the *direction* of Ueno.
3 field:
Yamada-hakase wa kono hoomeñ *no keñi desu.* (山田博士はこの方面の権威です) Dr. Yamada is an authority in this *field.*

ho⌈omoñ ほうもん(訪問) ***n.*** visit; call.
hoomoñ suru (～する) *vt.* call at [on]; visit.

ho⌉omu[1] ホーム ***n.*** platform.

ho⌉omu[2] ホーム ***n.*** home; asylum: *roojiñ*-hoomu (老人ホーム) an old people's *home.*

ho˥omu[3] ホーム *n.* (of baseball) home plate.

ho˩omu˥r·u ほうむる (葬る) *vt.* (hoomur·i-; hoomur·a-; hoomut-te [C]) **1** bury (a dead body): *Kare wa kono bochi ni* hoomura-rete imasu. (彼はこの墓地に葬られています) He *is buried* in this graveyard.
2 shelve (a plan); hush up (an incident):
Sono oshoku-jikeñ wa yami ni hoomurareta. (その汚職事件は闇に葬られた) The corruption case *was swept under the carpet.*

ho˩ore˥ñsoo ほうれんそう (菠薐草) *n.* spinach.

ho˩oritsu ほうりつ (法律) *n.* law.

ho˩or·u[1] ほうる (放る) *vt.* (hoor·i-; hoor·a-; hoot-te [C]) throw; toss; pitch:
Sono booru o hootte *kudasai.* (そのボールを放ってください) Please *throw* the ball to me. ⟪⇨ nageru⟫

ho˥oru[2] ホール *n.* hall. ★ Used for public events.

ho˩osaku[1] ほうさく (豊作) *n.* good crop; rich harvest.

ho˩osaku[2] ほうさく (方策) *n.* measures; plan; means:
hoosaku ga tsukiru (方策が尽きる) *be at one's wits' end.* ⟪⇨ shudañ⟫

ho˩oseki ほうせき (宝石) *n.* jewel; gem; jewelry.

ho˥oshi ほうし (奉仕) *n.* service.
... ni hooshi suru (...に～する) *vt.* serve: *shakai ni* hooshi suru (社会に奉仕する) *serve* the community. ⟪⇨ tsukusu⟫

ho˩oshiñ ほうしん (方針) *n.* policy; course; principle:
atarashii hooshiñ *o tateru* (新しい方針を立てる) make a new *policy.*

ho˩oshuu ほうしゅう (報酬) *n.* remuneration; reward; fee.

ho˩osoku ほうそく (法則) *n.* law; rule:
juyoo to kyookyuu no hoosoku (需要と供給の法則) the *law* of supply and demand.

ho˩osoo[1] ほうそう (放送) *n.* broadcasting; broadcast.
hoosoo suru (～する) *vt.* broadcast; televise; put on the air.

ho˩osoo[2] ほうそう (包装) *n.* packing; wrapping.
hoosoo suru (～する) *vt.* pack; wrap. ⟪⇨ tsutsumu⟫

ho˩oso˥ogeki ほうそうげき (放送劇) *n.* radio [TV] drama.

ho˩oso˥okyoku ほうそうきょく (放送局) *n.* broadcasting station; radio [TV] station.

ho˩otai ほうたい (包帯) *n.* bandage; dressing:
kizuguchi ni hootai *o suru* (傷口に包帯をする) put a *bandage* on the wound.

ho˥ra ほら *int.* look; look here; listen:
Hora, *mukoo ni shima ga mieru yo.* (ほら, 向こうに島が見えるよ) *Look!* You can see an island over there.

ho˩ra-ana ほらあな (洞穴) *n.* cave; cavern.

ho˩ri˥ ほり (堀) *n.* moat; canal.

ho˩robi˥·ru ほろびる (滅びる) *vi.* (horobi-te [V]) fall; die out; be ruined; perish:
Sono kuni wa sañzeñ-neñ mae ni horobimashita. (その国は 3 千年前に滅びました) That country *perished* 3,000 years ago. ⟪⇨ horobosu⟫

ho˩robo˥s·u ほろぼす (滅ぼす) *vt.* (horobosh·i-; horobos·a-; horobosh·i-te [C]) destroy; ruin:
Kaku-señsoo wa jiñrui o horoboshimasu. (核戦争は人類を滅ぼします) Nuclear war will *destroy* humanity. ⟪⇨ horobiru⟫

ho˥r·u[1] ほる (掘る) *vt.* (hor·i-; hor·a-; hot-te [C]) dig; excavate:
ana o horu (穴を掘る) *dig* a hole.

ho˥r·u[2] ほる (彫る) *vt.* (hor·i-; hor·a-; hot-te [C]) carve; engrave; chisel; inscribe:
Kare wa ki o hotte *niñgyoo o tsukutta.* (彼は木を彫って人形を作った) He made a doll by *carving* the wood.

ho⌉ryo ほりょ(捕虜) *n.* prisoner (of war); captive.

ho⌈shi ほし(星) *n.* star.

ho⌈shi⌉·i ほしい(欲しい) *a.* (-ku) want; would like; wish; hope: *Motto jikañ ga* hoshii. (もっと時間が欲しい) I *want* more time.

ho⌈shi⌉mono ほしもの(干し物) *n.* washing; clothes for drying. ⟨⇨ señtaku[1]; señtakumono⟩

ho⌈shoo[1] ほしょう(保証) *n.* guarantee; warranty; assurance.
hoshoo suru (〜する) *vt.* guarantee; warrant; assure.

ho⌈shoo[2] ほしょう(保障) *n.* security: *shakai*-hoshoo (社会保障) social *security*.
hoshoo suru (〜する) *vt.* secure; guarantee.

ho⌈shoo[3] ほしょう(補償) *n.* compensation; indemnity.
hoshoo suru (〜する) *vt.* compensate; indemnify.

ho⌈shooniñ ほしょうにん(保証人) *n.* guarantor.

ho⌉shu ほしゅ(保守) *n.* conservatism: hoshu-*too* (保守党) a conservative party. ⟨↔ kakushiñ[2]⟩

ho⌈shu-teki ほしゅてき(保守的) *a.n.* (〜 na, ni) conservative. ⟨↔ shiñpo-teki⟩

ho⌈so⌉·i ほそい(細い) *a.* (-ku)
1 (of round objects such as sticks or string) thin; small; fine: hosoi *hari* (細い針) a *thin* needle / hosoi *señ* (細い線) a *fine* line. ⟨↔ futoi⟩
2 (of a voice) thin. ⟨↔ futoi⟩

ho⌈sonaga⌉·i ほそながい(細長い) *a.* (-ku) long and narrow; slender: *Kono heya wa* hosonagakute *tsukainikui.* (この部屋は細長くて使いにくい) This room is *long and narrow*, and awkward to use. ⟨⇨ hosoi; nagai⟩

ho⌈ssoku ほっそく(発足) *n.* start; inauguration.
hossoku suru (〜する) *vi.* make a start; be inaugurated.

ho⌉s·u ほす(干す) *vt.* (hosh·i-; hos·a-; hosh·i-te Ⓒ) **1** dry: *Kanojo wa nureta taoru o hinata ni* hoshita. (彼女はぬれたタオルを日なたに干した) She *dried* the wet towel in the sun.
2 drink up; empty: *Kare wa koppu no biiru o* hoshita. (彼はコップのビールを干した) He *drained* the beer in the glass.

ho⌉taru ほたる(蛍) *n.* firefly.

ho⌉tchikisu ホッチキス *n.* stapler.

ho⌈toke⌉ ほとけ(仏) *n.* **1** the Buddha.
2 the deceased: hotoke *ni hana o sonaeru* (仏に花を供える) offer flowers before *the deceased*.

ho⌈to⌉ñdo ほとんど(殆ど) *n., adv.*
1 almost; nearly: *Sono ie wa* hotoñdo *dekiagarimashita.* (その家はほとんどでき上がりました) The house is *nearly* completed.
2 (with a negative) hardly; few; little: *Watashi wa sore ni tsuite wa* hotoñdo *shirimaseñ.* (私はそれについてはほとんど知りません) I *hardly* know anything about that.

ho⌈tto ほっと *adv.* (〜 suru) (the state of being relieved): *Shikeñ ga owatte,* hotto shita. (試験が終わって, ほっとした) I *was relieved* when the exam was over.

ho⌈yahoya ほやほや *n.* (the state of being new or fresh): *Kare-ra wa shiñkoñ* hoyahoya *desu.* (彼らは新婚ほやほやです) They have *just* married.

ho⌈zoñ ほぞん(保存) *n.* preservation; conservation.
hozoñ suru (〜する) *vt.* preserve; keep.

ho⌈zo⌉ñshoku ほぞんしょく(保存食) *n.* preserved food; emergency provisions.

hya⌈kkaji⌉teñ ひゃっかじてん(百科事典) *n.* encyclopedia.

hya⌈ku⌉ ひゃく(百) *n.* one hundred. ⟨⇨ APP. 3⟩

hyo⌈ito ひょいと *adv.* unexpectedly; suddenly; casually; lightly: *Michi no kado kara* hyoito *jiteñsha ga dete kite, bikkuri shita.* (道の角からひょいと自転車が出て来て，びっくりした) I was surprised when a bicycle *suddenly* came around the corner.

hyo⌈o ひょう (表) *n.* table; list.

hyo⌈obañ ひょうばん (評判) *n.* reputation; popularity; rumor.

hyo⌈oge⌉ñ ひょうげん (表現) *n.* verbal expression; representation.
hyoogeñ suru (～する) *vt.* express; represent.

hyo⌈ojo⌉o ひょうじょう (表情) *n.* facial expression; look.

hyo⌈ojuñ ひょうじゅん (標準) *n.* standard; normal; average.

hyo⌈ojuñgo ひょうじゅんご (標準語) *n.* the standard language. ★ Often called '*kyootsuugo.*'

hyo⌈ojuñ-teki ひょうじゅんてき (標準的) *a.n.* (～ na, ni) standard; average; typical.

hyo⌉oka ひょうか (評価) *n.* valuation; appraisal; rating; assessment.
hyooka suru (～する) *vt.* value; appraise; estimate.

hyo⌈ome⌉ñ ひょうめん (表面) *n.*
1 surface:
Teeburu no hyoomeñ *wa pikapika shite ita.* (テーブルの表面はぴかぴかしていた) The *surface* of the table was shiny.
2 outside:
Tatemono no hyoomeñ *wa rippa datta.* (建物の表面はりっぱだった) The *outside* of the building was gorgeous.
3 appearance:
Kare wa hyoomeñ *wa otonashisoo ni mieru.* (彼は表面はおとなしそうに見える) In *appearance*, he seems easy to deal with.

hyo⌈oroñ ひょうろん (評論) *n.* criticism; review; critical essay.

hyo⌈oryuu ひょうりゅう (漂流) *n.* drifting.
hyooryuu suru (～する) *vt.* drift; go adrift.

hyo⌈oshi⌉ ひょうし (表紙) *n.* the cover of a book or a magazine. ★ Often refers to the jacket of a book. ⟪⇨ kabaa⟫

hyo⌉rohyoro[1] ひょろひょろ *adv.* (～ to; ～ suru) **1** tall and thin: hyorohyoro (*to*) *nobita kusa* (ひょろひょろ(と)伸びた草) grass which has grown *tall and thin.*
2 staggeringly; totteringly: *Kare wa sake ni yotte* hyorohyoro (to) aruita. (彼は酒に酔ってひょろひょろ(と)歩いた) He *staggered* along drunk. ⟪⇨ yoroyoro⟫

hyo⌈rohyoro[2] ひょろひょろ *a.n.* (～ na, ni) lanky; slender; frail; feeble:
Kare wa karada ga hyorohyoro *de tayorinai.* (彼は体がひょろひょろで頼りない) He is *tall and slim* and looks unreliable.

I

i い (胃) *n.* stomach.

-i[1] い *suf.* place; rank:
hyaku-meetoru kyoosoo de ni-i *ni naru* (百メートル競走で2位になる) come in *second* in the 100-meter race.

-i[2] い (医) *suf.* medical doctor; general practitioner:
gañka-i (眼科医) an eye *doctor* / geka-i (外科医) a *surgeon* / naika-i (内科医) a *physician.* ⟪⇨ isha⟫

i⌈ba⌉r·u いばる (威張る) *vi.* (ibar·i-; ibar·a-; ibat-te Ⓒ) put on airs; boast; be haughty. ⟪⇨ karaibari⟫

i⌈basho いばしょ (居場所) *n.* whereabouts.

i⌈biki⌉ いびき (鼾) *n.* snore.

i⌈chi⌉[1] いち (一·壱) *n.* one; the first; No. 1:
Nihoñ-ichi (日本一) *No. 1* in Japan. (⇨ hitotsu[1]; APP. 3)

i⌉chi[2] いち (位置) *n.* position; location; situation.
ichi suru (〜する) *vi.* lie; be located.

i⌉chiba いちば (市場) *n.* market.
★ Never used to mean 'supermarket' or 'store.'

i⌈chi⌉bañ[1] いちばん (一番) *n.* first.

i⌈chibañ[2] いちばん (一番) *adv.* most; best:
Dono kisetsu ga ichibañ *suki desu ka?* (どの季節がいちばん好きですか) Which season do you like *best*?

i⌈chi⌉bu いちぶ (一部) *n.* (a) part; portion; section.
— *adv.* partially; in part:
sekkee o ichibu *shuusee suru* (設計を一部修正する) correct the design *in part*.

i⌈chibu⌉buñ いちぶぶん (一部分) *n.* (a) part; section. (⇨ ichibu)

i⌈chida⌉iji いちだいじ (一大事) *n.* serious [grave] matter. (⇨ daiji[2])

i⌈chidañ いちだん (一団) *n.* group: party; body:
Kare-ra wa ichidañ to natte *heya kara dete itta.* (彼らは一団となって部屋から出て行った) They walked out of the room *in a body*. (⇨ -dañ)

i⌈chido いちど (一度) *n.* once; one time.

i⌈chido⌉ ni いちどに (一度に) *adv.* all at once; at a time; at the same time.

i⌈chido⌉o いちどう (一同) *n.* everyone; all present:
ichidoo *o daihyoo shite, aisatsu suru* (一同を代表して, 挨拶する) make an address as the representative of *all those present*.

i⌈chi⌉gai ni いちがいに (一概に) *adv.* (〜 wa) (with a negative) generally; necessarily; indiscriminately:
Kare ga machigatte iru to wa ichigai ni (*wa*) *kimeraremaseñ.* (彼が間違っているとは一概に(は)決められません) We cannot *necessarily* conclude that he is wrong.

i⌈chi-gatsu⌉ いちがつ (一月) *n.* January. (⇨ APP. 5)

i⌈chigo いちご (苺) *n.* strawberry.

i⌈chiguñ いちぐん (一軍) *n.* (of baseball) the first team; major league. (⇨ niguñ)

i⌈chiha⌉yaku いちはやく (逸早く) *adv.* quickly; without delay.

i⌈chi⌉ichi いちいち (一々) *adv.* in detail; one by one:
Chichi wa watashi no suru koto ni ichiichi *kuchi o dasu.* (父は私のすることにいちいち口を出す) My father meddles in *everything* I do.

i⌈chi⌉ji いちじ (一時) *adv.* **1** once; at one time:
Sono uta wa ichiji *hayatta koto ga arimasu.* (その歌は一時はやったことがあります) That song was *at one time* popular.
2 for a while; for the time being:
Watashi wa sañ-neñ hodo mae ni ichiji *koko ni suñde ita koto ga arimasu.* (私は三年ほど前に一時ここに住んでいたことがあります) Three years ago I used to live here *for a while*.

i⌈chijirushi⌉·i いちじるしい (著しい) *a.* (-ku) remarkable; marked; noticeable.

i⌈chimeñ いちめん (一面) *n.* **1** one side; one aspect:
Anata wa yo-no-naka no ichimeñ *shika mite inai.* (あなたは世の中の一面しか見ていない) You have only seen *one side* of life.
2 the front page of a newspaper.
— *adv.* **1** on the other hand:
Kanojo wa yasashii ga ichimeñ *kibishii tokoro mo aru.* (彼女は優しいが一面厳しい所もある) She is tenderhearted, but *on the other hand* she has a strict side.
2 all over; the whole place:
Mizuumi wa ichimeñ *koori de oowarete ita.* (湖は一面氷でおおわれて

いた) *The whole surface* of the lake was covered with ice.

i⌈chinichi-juu いちにちじゅう(一日中) *adv.* all day (long).

i⌈chioo いちおう(一応) *adv.* anyway; just in case; for the time being:
Kare ga iru ka doo ka wakaranai ga, ichioo *reñraku shite mimashoo.* (彼がいるかどうかわからないが, 一応連絡してみましょう) I don't know if he is there or not, but *anyway* let's try to get in touch with him. 《⇨ toriaezu》

i⌈chiritsu いちりつ(市立) *n.* = shiritsu[2].

i⌈chiryuu いちりゅう(一流) *n.* first-class; first-rate:
ichiryuu *no hoteru* (一流のホテル) a *first-rate* hotel. 《⇨ ikkyuu; sañryuu》

i⌈chi⌉ya いちや(一夜) *n.* a [one] night:
Watashi wa sono koya de ichiya o *sugoshita.* (私はその小屋で一夜を過ごした) I spent *a night* in the hut.

i⌈dai いだい(偉大) *a.n.* (~ na, ni) great; grand: idai *na sakka* (偉大な作家) a *great* novelist.

i⌉do いど(井戸) *n.* well.

i⌈do⌉m·u いどむ(挑む) *vt.* (idom·i-; idom·a-; idoñ-de Ⓒ) try; challenge; defy: *shiñ-kiroku ni* idomu (新記録に挑む) *try to set* a new record. 《⇨ chooseñ》

i⌈doo[1] いどう(移動) *n.* **1** movement; transfer.
2 removal; migration:
miñzoku no idoo (民族の移動) a racial *migration.*
idoo suru (~する) *vi., vt.* move; travel; migrate.

i⌈doo[2] いどう(異動) *n.* personnel change; reshuffle.

i⌈e⌉[1] いえ(家) *n.* home; house.
★ A little more formal than '*uchi*[1].'

i⌈e⌉[2] いえ *int.* no. ★ Less formal than '*iie.*'

i⌈ede いえで(家出) *n.* running away from home.

i⌈emoto⌉ いえもと(家元) *n.* master [leader] of a school (of flower arrangement, tea ceremony, etc.).

i⌉fuku いふく(衣服) *n.* clothes; clothing. 《⇨ fuku[2]》

i⌈gai いがい(意外) *a.n.* (~ na, ni) unexpected; surprising:
igai *na dekigoto* (意外な出来事) an *unexpected* occurrence.

-i⌉gai いがい(以外) *suf.* **1** except; but; other than:
*Mokuyoo-*igai *nara, itsu de mo kekkoo desu.* (木曜以外なら, いつでもけっこうです) As long as it is a day *other than* Thursday, anytime is fine.
2 in addition to; besides:
*Kare wa hyooroñ-*igai *ni shoosetsu mo kakimasu.* (彼は評論以外に小説も書きます) *In addition to* reviews, he also writes novels.

i⌉gaku いがく(医学) *n.* medical science; medicine.

i⌈gañ いがん(胃癌) *n.* stomach [gastric] cancer. 《⇨ gañ》

i⌈geñ いげん(威厳) *n.* dignity; majesty: igeñ *o tamotsu* [*sokonau*] (威厳を保つ[損なう]) maintain [impair] one's *dignity.*

i⌉gi[1] いぎ(意義) *n.* meaning; significance:
Oriñpikku wa sañka suru koto ni igi *ga aru.* (オリンピックは参加することに意義がある) In the Olympics, the *importance* lies in participating.

i⌉gi[2] いぎ(異議) *n.* objection; dissent; protest: igi *o tonaeru* (異議を唱える) raise an *objection.*

i⌉go[1] いご(以後) *n.* after this; from that time on; ever since:
Sono kaisha wa sekiyu shokku igo, *sugu ni tachinaotta.* (その会社は石油ショック以後, すぐに立ち直った) The company recovered soon *after* the oil crisis. 《↔ izeñ[1]》

i⌉go[2] いご(囲碁) *n.* the game of go.

i⌈hañ いはん(違反) *n.* violation; breach.
... ni ihañ suru (...に~する) *vt.* vio-

late; break. 《⇨ hañsuru》

i'i いい(良い) *a.* good; nice; fine: ★ Used only in this form. More informal than '*yoi*[1]' and often used ironically.
Kanojo wa fukusoo no señsu ga ii. (彼女は服装のセンスがいい) She has *good* taste in clothes.

i'iarawa's·u いいあらわす(言い表す) *vt.* (-arawash·i-; -arawas·a-; -arawash·i-te [C]) say; express; describe.

i'ia'·u いいあう(言い合う) *vt.* (-a·i-; -aw·a-; -at-te [C]) quarrel; dispute. 《⇨ arasou》

i'ida's·u いいだす(言い出す) *vt.* (-dash·i-; -das·a-; -dash·i-te [C]) start speaking; propose; suggest.

i'ie' いいえ *int.* no; yes: ★ '*Iie*' literally means 'That's wrong,' and is used to confirm a statement, whether affirmative or negative.
"Ima isogashii desu ka?" "Iie, isogashiku arimaseñ." (「今忙しいですか」「いいえ, 忙しくありません」) "Are you busy now?" "*No*, I am not." / *"Moo sukoshi o-nomi ni narimaseñ ka?" "Iie, moo kekkoo desu."* (「もう少しお飲みになりませんか」「いいえ, もう結構です」) "Won't you have a bit more to drink?" "*No*, thank you. 《↔ hai[1]》 《⇨ iya[2]》

i'ika'es·u いいかえす(言い返す) *vi.* (-kaesh·i-; -kaes·a-; -kaesh·i-te [C]) talk back; retort.

i'ikageñ いいかげん(いい加減) *a.n.* (~ na, ni) irresponsible; noncommittal; vague:
Kare wa suru koto ga iikageñ *da.* (彼はすることがいいかげんだ) He *never takes responsibility* for what he does.
— *adv.* rather; pretty:
Tañjuñ na shigoto na no de iikageñ *iya ni natta.* (単純な仕事なのでいいかげんいやになった) Since it is a monotonous job, I am *rather* bored with it.
Iikageñ ni shinai ka. (~にしないか) That's enough! Come off it!

i'ikata いいかた(言い方) *n.* expression; way of speaking:
Kanojo wa mono no iikata *ga teenee da.* (彼女は物の言い方が丁寧だ) Her *manner of speaking* is polite.

i'ikikase'·ru いいきかせる(言い聞かせる) *vi.* (-kikase-te [V]) tell a person to (do); persuade; admonish.

i'iñ いいん(委員) *n.* member of a committee.

i'i'ñchoo いいんちょう(委員長) *n.* chairman; chairperson.

i'i'ñkai いいんかい(委員会) *n.* committee; committee meeting.

i'itsuke'·ru いいつける(言い付ける) *vi., vt.* (-tsuke-te [V]) **1** tell a person to (do):
Kare wa musuko ni shigoto o tetsudau yoo iitsuketa. (彼は息子に仕事を手伝うよう言いつけた) He *told* his son to help him with his work.
2 tell on:
Soñna koto o shitara, señsee ni iitsukemasu *yo.* (そんなことをしたら, 先生に言いつけますよ) If you do such a thing, I will *tell* the teacher *on* you.

i'itsutae いいつたえ(言い伝え) *n.* tradition; legend.

i'iwake いいわけ(言い訳) *n.* excuse; explanation; justification:
kurushii iiwake o suru (苦しい言い訳をする) *make* a poor *excuse*.

i'ji[1] いじ(意地) *n.* **1** pride:
Watashi ni mo iji *ga aru.* (私にも意地がある) I, too, have my *pride*.
2 nature; disposition:
Ano hito wa iji ga warui. (あの人は意地が悪い) She is *ill-natured*.
iji o haru (~を張る) do not give in.

i'ji[2] いじ(維持) *n.* maintenance; upkeep.
iji suru (~する) *vt.* maintain; keep up: *keñkoo o* iji suru (健康を維持する) *keep* oneself in good health.

i'jime·ru いじめる(苛める) *vt.* (ijime-te [V]) tease; annoy; bully.

i⌈jiwa⌉ru いじわる(意地悪) *n.* nastiness; maliciousness.
— *a.n.* (~ na, ni) nasty; ill-natured; malicious.

i⌉joo[1] いじょう(以上) *n.* **1** the above; the foregoing:
Ijoo *ga watashi no kiita koto no subete desu.* (以上が私の聞いたことのすべてです) *The foregoing* is everything I heard. 《↔ ika[1]》
2 that's all; concluded:
Ijoo, *watashi no kañgae o nobesasete itadakimashita.* (以上, 私の考えを述べさせていただきました) *That is* what I wanted to say.

i⌉joo[2] いじょう(以上) *conj.* since; once; as long as:
Yakusoku shita ijoo, *watashi wa kanarazu jikkoo shimasu.* (約束した以上, 私は必ず実行します) *Once* I have made a promise, I will certainly carry it out.

i⌈joo[3] いじょう(異常) *a.n.* (~ na, ni) abnormal; unusual; extraordinary. 《↔ seejoo》

-i⌉joo いじょう(以上) *suf.* **1** above; over; not less than:
*Juuhas-sai-*ijoo *nara dare de mo meñkyo ga toremasu.* (18 歳以上ならだれでも免許が取れます) Anybody who is eighteen *and over* can get a driver's license. 《↔ -ika》
★ '*-ijoo*' includes the preceding number, so, strictly speaking, '18-*ijoo*' means 'more than 17.'
2 more than:
*Kono mae kanojo ni atte kara ichi-neñ-*ijoo *ni narimasu.* (この前彼女に会ってから一年以上になります) It is now *more than* a year since I last met her.

i⌈juu いじゅう(移住) *n.* migration; emigration; immigration.
ijuu suru (~する) *vi.* migrate; emigrate; immigrate.

i⌉ka[1] いか(以下) *n.* the following; as follows:
Kare kara kiita hanashi wa ika *no toori desu.* (彼から聞いた話は以下の通りです) What I heard from him is *as follows*: 《↔ ijoo[1]》

i⌈ka[2] いか(烏賊) *n.* cuttlefish; squid. 《⇨ surume》

-i⌉ka いか(以下) *suf.* **1** less than:
Kono kuruma wa juumañ-eñ ika *no kachi shika nai.* (この車は 10 万円以下の価値しかない) This car only has a value of *less than* 100,000 yen. ★ '*-ika*' includes the preceding number, so, strictly speaking, '19 *ika*' means 'less than 20.' 《↔ -ijoo》 《⇨ -mimañ》
2 below; under:
*Koñdo no watashi no seeseki wa heekiñ-*ika *datta.* (今度の私の成績は平均以下だった) My grades this time were *below* average.

i⌈kada いかだ(筏) *n.* raft.

i⌈ka⌉ga いかが(如何) *adv.*
1 how:
O-karada wa ikaga *desu ka?* (お体はいかがですか) *How* is your health?
2 Would you like...?: ★ Used when offering food, etc.
Biiru wa ikaga *desu ka?* (ビールはいかがですか) *Would you like* some beer?
3 How [What] about...?:
Kare o sasottara ikaga *desu ka?* (彼を誘ったらいかがですか) *What about* inviting him?
4 what:
Anata no go-ikeñ wa ikaga *desu ka?* (あなたのご意見はいかがですか) *What* is your opinion?

i⌈ka⌉iyoo いかいよう(胃潰瘍) *n.* an ulcer of the stomach.

i⌈ka⌉ ni いかに(如何に) *adv.* **1** (of degree) how:
Itte minai to sono taki ga ika ni *ookii ka wakarimaseñ.* (行って見ないとその滝がいかに大きいかわかりません) You will not appreciate *how* large the waterfall is unless you go and see for yourself.
2 (of manner) how:
Ika ni *shite uriage o nobasu ka ga moñdai desu.* (いかにして売上を伸ばすかが問題です) The question is *how* to increase sales.

3 (*formal*) however:
Ika ni *kurushikute mo kono shigoto o tsuzukeru tsumori desu.* (いかに苦しくてもこの仕事を続けるつもりです) *However* painful it is, I intend to continue this work.

i⸢ka⸣ ni mo いかにも (如何にも) *adv.* really; truly; typically:
Sono hanashi wa ika ni mo *hoñtoo ni kikoeru.* (その話はいかにも本当に聞こえる) That story sounds as if it were *really* true.

i⸢kari いかり (怒り) *n.* anger; rage; wrath. ⟪⇨ okoru[2]⟫

i⸢ka⸣s·u いかす (生かす) *vt.* (ika-sh·i-; ikas·a-; ikash·i-te Ⓒ) make the most of:
jibuñ no chishiki [*sainoo; keekeñ*] *o* ikasu (自分の知識[才能; 経験]を生かす) *make good use of* one's knowledge [talent; experience].

i⸢ke⸣ いけ (池) *n.* pond. ⟪⇨ numa⟫

i⸢ke⸣bana いけばな (生け花) *n.* flower arrangement. ⟪⇨ ikeru⟫

i⸢kemase⸣ñ いけません ★ Polite equivalent of '*ikenai.*'
1 must not (do); will not (do); be no good:
Uchi no inu o ijimete wa ikemaseñ. (うちの犬をいじめてはいけません) You *must not* tease our dog. ⟪⇨ dame⟫
2 (with a negative verb) must (do); have to (do):
Anata wa kanojo ni ayamaranakute wa ikemaseñ. (あなたは彼女に謝らなくてはいけません) You *must* apologize to her. ⟪⇨ beki; dame⟫

i⸣keñ いけん (意見) *n.* **1** opinion; view; idea:
jibuñ no ikeñ *o noberu* (自分の意見を述べる) express one's *opinion.*
2 advice:
isha no ikeñ *ni shitagau* (医者の意見に従う) follow one's doctor's *advice.*

i⸢kena·i いけない *a.* (-ku) bad; wrong:
Doko-ka ikenai *tokoro ga arimasu ka?* (どこかいけないところがありますか) Is there anything *wrong* with it?
-te wa ikenai (ては〜) **1** must not (do); should not (do): *Soñna koto o* shite wa ikenai. (そんなことをしてはいけない) You *should not do* such a thing. ⟪⇨ dame⟫
2 (with a negative verb) must (do); should (do): *Sugu ikanakereba* ikenai. (すぐ行かなければいけない) I *must* go at once.
... to ikenai kara [no de] (...と〜から[ので]) in case: *Ame ga furu* to ikenai kara, *kasa o motte iki nasai.* (雨が降るといけないから, 傘を持って行きなさい) Take an umbrella with you *in case* it rains.
★ Polite forms are '*ikenai desu, ikemaseñ.*'

i⸢ke⸣·ru いける (生ける) *vt.* (ike-te Ⓥ) arrange (flowers). ⟪⇨ ikebana⟫

i⸣ki[1] いき (息) *n.* breath; breathing.
iki ga kireru (〜が切れる) be out of breath.
iki o hikitoru (〜を引き取る) breathe one's last.
iki o korosu (〜を殺す) hold one's breath.
iki o tsuku (〜をつく) take a rest.

i⸢ki[2] いき (行き) *n.* (＝yuki[2]) going (to the destination):
Iki *wa takushii, kaeri wa basu deshita.* (行きはタクシー, 帰りはバスでした) The *trip there* was by taxi, and the return by bus. ⟪↔ kaeri⟫

i⸢ki[3] いき (粋) *a.n.* (〜 na, ni) chic; stylish; smart.

i⸢kichigai いきちがい (行き違い) *n.* crossing each other. ⟪⇨ yukichigai⟫

i⸢kidomari いきどまり (行き止まり) *n.* dead end. ⟪⇨ yukidomari⟫

i⸢kigire いきぎれ (息切れ) *n.* being short of breath. ⟪⇨ iki[1]⟫

i⸢ki-i⸣ki いきいき (生き生き) *adv.* (〜 to) vividly:
Mizu o yattara, nae ga iki-iki *to shite kita.* (水をやったら, 苗が生き生きとしてきた) When I watered the young plants, they *freshened up.*

i⌈kikaer·u いきかえる(生き返る) *vi.* (-kaer·i-; -kaer·a-; -kaet-te Ⓒ)
1 revive; come to life.
2 feel refreshed:
Tsumetai shawaa o abitara, iki-kaetta *yoo na kokochi ga shita.* (冷たいシャワーを浴びたら，生き返ったような心地がした) I *felt refreshed* after taking a cold shower.

i⌈ki⌉mono いきもの(生き物) *n.* living thing; creature; animal. 《⇨ seebutsu》

i⌈kinari いきなり *adv.* all of a sudden; abruptly; without notice.

i⌈kinoko⌉r·u いきのこる(生き残る) *vi.* (-nokor·i-; -nokor·a-; -nokot-te Ⓒ) survive.

i⌈kio⌉i[1] いきおい(勢い) *n.* force; might; vigor; energy; influence:
Miñna de booto o ikioi yoku *koida.* (みんなでボートを勢いよくこいだ) We all rowed the boat *powerfully.*

i⌈kio⌉i[2] いきおい(勢い) *adv.* in the course of; consequently; naturally; necessarily:
Ikioi, *sono yaku o hikiukeru koto ni natte shimatta.* (勢い，その役を引き受けることになってしまった) *By force of circumstances,* I ended up accepting the role.

i⌈ki⌉·ru いきる(生きる) *vi.* (iki-te Ⓥ) 1 live: ★ '*ikite iru*'=be alive. 《↔ shinu》
Sono inu wa mada ikite *imasu.* (その犬はまだ生きています) The dog *is* still *alive.*
2 (of a rule, convention, etc.) be valid; be good; live. ★ Usually used in '*ikite iru.*'

i⌈kisatsu いきさつ(経緯) *n.* circumstances; story; reason:
Kanojo to shiriatta ikisatsu *o kare ni hanashita.* (彼女と知り合ったいきさつを彼に話した) I told him the *story* of how I had come to know her.

i⌈kka いっか(一家) *n.* family:
Yamada-sañ ikka *wa Yokohama e hikkoshimashita.* (山田さん一家は横浜へ引っ越しました) *The Yamadas* moved to Yokohama.

i⌈kkoo[1] いっこう(一行) *n.* party; group; company.

i⌈kkoo[2] いっこう(一向) *adv.* (~ ni) (with a negative) at all; in the least:
Kare no gorufu wa ikkoo *ni joota-tsu shinai.* (彼のゴルフは一向に上達しない) His golf does not improve *at all.* 《⇨ sappari[2]》

i⌈kkyuu いっきゅう(一級) *n.* first class [rate]; top grade. 《⇨ ichi-ryuu; saikoo》

-i⌉koo いこう(以降) *suf.* after; on or after:
Yoru hachi-ji-ikoo *ni o-deñwa o kudasai.* (夜8時以降にお電話を下さい) Please phone me *after* eight in the evening. ★ '*-ikoo*' includes the preceding number, so, strictly speaking, '*sañ-ji-ikoo*' means 'at and after three o'clock.'

i⌈k·u いく(行く) *vi.* (ik·i-; ik·a-; it-te Ⓒ) ★ Also pronounced '*yuku,*' an alternate form of '*iku,*' which is somewhat formal and old-fashioned but is used in forming compounds.
1 go away; leave:
Kare wa moo ikimashita. (彼はもう行きました) He *has* already *left.* 《↔ kuru》
2 go; come:
Kanojo wa kotoshi Oosutoraria ni ikimasu. (彼女は今年オーストラリアに行きます) She *is going* to Australia this year. 《↔ kaeru[1]》
3 go doing: ★ Used with a noun in '... *ni iku.*'
Kanojo wa suupaa e kaimono ni ikimashita. (彼女はスーパーへ買い物に行きました) She *has gone* shopping at the supermarket.
4 go in order to do: ★ Used with a verb in '... *ni iku.*'
Kinoo wa eega o mi ni ikimashita. (きのうは映画を見に行きました) I *went* to see a movie yesterday.
5 proceed; go:
Subete ga umaku ikimashita. (すべてがうまくいきました) Everything

went smoothly. ★ Note that '*iku*' is equivalent to 'come' in the following kind of situation. "*Hayaku, kochira ni kite kudasai.*" "*Hai, ima* ikimasu." (「早く, こちらに来てください」「はい, いま行きます」) "Please come here quickly." "All right, I'*m coming* (*literally* 'going') now."

i˥ku- いく (幾) *pref.* (*formal*)
1 how many:
Fune de iku-*nichi kakarimashita ka?* (船で幾日かかりましたか) *How many* days did it take by ship? 《⇨ nañ》
2 some; several:
Sono jiko de iku-*niñ mo keganiñ ga deta.* (その事故で幾人もけが人がでた) *Several* people were injured in that accident. 《⇨ nañ》

i˥kubuñ いくぶん (幾分) *adv.* (~ ka) a little; somewhat; more or less. 《⇨ ikura ka》

i˥ku-do いくど (幾度) *adv.* how often: 《⇨ nañ-do》
Iku-do *ittara wakaru ñ da.* (いくど言ったらわかるんだ) *How many times* do I have to tell you before you understand?
iku-do mo (~も) very often; again and again.

i˥kuji ga nai いくじがない (意気地がない) chickenhearted; cowardly:
Kare wa ikuji ga nai. (彼は意気地がない) He *has no guts.*

i˥kura いくら (幾ら) *adv.* (of a price) how much.
ikura mo (~も) (with a negative) not many [much]: *Kono biñ ni wa uisukii ga* ikura mo *nokotte inai.* (このびんにはウイスキーがいくらも残っていない) There is *not much* whisky left in this bottle.
ikura ... -te [-de] mo (~...て[で]も) (with a negative) no matter how; however:
Ikura *hayaku* aruite mo, *kare ni oitsukenakatta.* (いくら速く歩いても, 彼に追いつけなかった) *No matter how* fast I *walked*, I could not catch up with him.

i˥kura ka いくらか (幾らか) *adv.* a little; somewhat; more or less:
Kanojo wa ikura ka *Nihoñ-go ga hanasemasu.* (彼女はいくらか日本語が話せます) She can speak Japanese *after a fashion.* 《⇨ ikubuñ》

i˥kusaki いくさき (行く先) *n.* destination. 《⇨ yukusaki》

i˥kutsu いくつ (幾つ) *adv.* (of a number, age) how many; how old. 《⇨ APP. 3》
ikutsu ka (~か) some; several:
Kono hoñyaku ni wa ikutsu ka *machigai ga aru.* (この翻訳にはいくつか間違いがある) There are *some* mistakes in this translation.
ikutsu mo (~も) many; a large number of; a lot of. 《⇨ takusañ》

i˥ma[1] いま (今) *n.* now; at present; at the moment.
— *adv.* **1** at once; right [just] now: Ima (*sugu*) *ikimasu.* (今(すぐ)行きます) I am coming (right) *now.*
2 more: Ima *shibaraku matte kudasai.* (今しばらく待ってください) Please wait a little *longer.*

i˥ma[2] いま (居間) *n.* living room; sitting room. 《⇨ cha-no-ma》

i˥magoro いまごろ (今頃) *n.* now; (about) this time:
Kanojo wa imagoro *ni natte, ikanai to ii-dashita.* (彼女は今ごろになって, 行かないと言い出した) *At this stage* she has announced that she is not going.

i˥ma ma˥de いままで (今迄) *adv.* (~ no) until now; so far:
Ima made, *doko e itte ita ñ desu ka?* (今まで, どこへ行っていたんですか) Where have you been *until now*?

i˥ma ni いまに (今に) *adv.* soon; before long:
Ima ni *anata mo Nihoñgo ga hanaseru yoo ni narimasu yo.* (今にあなたも日本語が話せるようになりますよ) *Before long* you too will be able to speak Japanese.

i˥ma ni mo いまにも (今にも) *adv.*

at any moment; be ready to:
Ima ni mo *ame ga furi-soo da.* (今にも雨が降りそうだ) It looks as if it will rain *at any moment*.

i⌈masara いまさら(今更) *adv.*
1 (with a negative) now; after so long; at this late stage:
Imasara, *iya to wa ienai.* (いまさら, いやとは言えない) I can't say no *at this stage*.
2 (with a negative) again:
Imasara *iu made mo nai ga, ashita wa chikoku shinai yoo ni.* (いまさら言うまでもないが, あしたは遅刻しないように) It is hardly necessary to tell you *again*, but make sure that tomorrow you are not late.

i⌉meeji イメージ *n.* image; picture; impression.

i⌈meeji-a⌉ppu イメージアップ *n.* improving one's image.
⟪↔ imeeji-dauñ⟫

i⌈meeji-che⌉ñji イメージチェンジ *n.* changing one's image.

i⌈meeji-da⌉uñ イメージダウン *n.* damaging one's image.
⟪⇨ imeeji-appu⟫

i⌉mi いみ(意味) *n.* **1** meaning; sense; implication:
Kono go ni warui imi *wa arimaseñ.* (この語に悪い意味はありません) This word has no bad *implications*.
3 significance:
Kare no shite iru koto wa imi *ga arimasu.* (彼のしていることは意味があります) What he is doing has *significance*.

i⌈miñ いみん(移民) *n.* **1** emigration; immigration.
2 emigrant; immigrant.
imiñ suru (〜する) *vi.* emigrate; immigrate.

i⌈mo⌉ いも(芋) *n.* potato; sweet potato; taro.

i⌈mooto いもうと(妹) *n.* one's younger sister. ★ When referring to someone else's sister, '*imooto-sañ*' is usually used.
⟪↔ ane⟫

-iñ いん(員) *suf.* person in charge; member: *eki*-iñ (駅員) a station *employee* | *kaisha*-iñ (会社員) a company *worker*.

i⌉na いな(否) *n.* (*formal*) no; nay.
⟪↔ ka[2]⟫
... ya ina ya (...や〜や) as soon as; hardly...when: *Kodomo-tachi wa watashi o miru* ya ina ya *nigedashita.* (子どもたちは私を見るやいなや逃げ出した) *The moment* the children saw me, they ran away.

-i⌉nai いない(以内) *suf.* within; in:
Hoñ wa ni-shuukañ-inai *ni kaeshite kudasai.* (本は2週間以内に返してください) Please return the book *in* two weeks. ★ '*-inai*' includes the preceding number, so, strictly speaking, '*hyaku-eñ-inai*' means '100 yen or less than 100 yen.'

i⌈naka いなか(田舎) *n.* **1** the country; the countryside.
2 one's home; one's hometown.

i⌈nazuma いなずま(稲妻) *n.* lightning.

i⌈ñboo いんぼう(陰謀) *n.* plot; intrigue; conspiracy.

i⌉ñchiki いんちき *n.* (*colloq.*) fake; fraud; forgery:
Iñchiki o suru *na yo.* (いんちきをするなよ) Don't *cheat*.
— *a.n.* (〜 na, ni) (*colloq.*) fake; fraudulent; bogus:
Kono shorui wa iñchiki *da.* (この書類はいんちきだ) These documents are *forgeries*.

i⌉ne いね(稲) *n.* rice plant.
⟪⇨ kome⟫

i⌈ñfure インフレ *n.* inflation.
⟪↔ defure⟫

i⌈ñkañ いんかん(印鑑) *n.* personal seal; stamp. ⟪⇨ hañ[2]⟫

i⌈ñmetsu いんめつ(隠滅) *n.* destruction; disappearance.
iñmetsu suru (〜する) *vt.* destroy: *shooko o* iñmetsu suru (証拠を隠滅する) *destroy* evidence.

i⌉nochi いのち(命) *n.* life:

Sono jiko de shichi-niñ ga inochi *o ushinatta.* (その事故で7人が命を失った) Seven people lost their *lives* in that accident.
inochi-gake de (～がけで) at the risk of one's life.

i⌈noko⌉r·u いのこる (居残る) *vi.* (inokor·i-; inokor·a-; inokot-te Ⓒ) stay; remain; work overtime. (⇨ nokoru)

i⌈nori⌉ いのり (祈り) *n.* prayer; grace. (⇨ inoru)

i⌈no⌉r·u いのる (祈る) *vi., vt.* (ino-r·i-; inor·a-; inot-te Ⓒ) pray; wish:
Koouñ [Seekoo] o inorimasu. (幸運[成功]を祈ります) I *wish* you good luck [success]. (⇨ inori)

i⌉ñryoku いんりょく (引力) *n.* gravitation.

i⌈ñryo⌉osui いんりょうすい (飲料水) *n.* drinking water.

i⌈ñsatsu いんさつ (印刷) *n.* printing; print; press.
iñsatsu suru (～する) *vt.* print; put into print.

i⌈ñsatsu⌉butsu いんさつぶつ (印刷物) *n.* printed matter.

i⌈ñshi いんし (印紙) *n.* = shuu-nyuu-iñshi.

i⌈ñshoo いんしょう (印象) *n.* impression:
Kare wa miñna ni yoi iñshoo *o ataeta.* (彼はみんなに良い印象を与えた) He made a good *impression* on everybody.

i⌈ñshoo-teki いんしょうてき (印象的) *a.n.* (～ na, ni) impressive.

in⌈sutañto ra⌉ameñ インスタントラーメン *n.* instant Chinese noodles. (⇨ raameñ)

i⌈ñteri インテリ *n.* intellectual; the intelligentsia.

i⌈nu⌉ いぬ (犬) *n.* dog. (⇨ bañkeñ)

i⌈nugoya いぬごや (犬小屋) *n.* doghouse; kennel.

i⌈ñyoo いんよう (引用) *n.* quotation; citation.
iñyoo suru (～する) *vt.* quote; cite.

i⌉ppai[1] いっぱい (一杯) *n.* **1** a cup [glass; bowl]:
koohii ippai (コーヒー一杯) *a cup* of coffee. (⇨ -hai; APP. 4)
2 (having) a drink:
Kaeri ni ippai *yarimaseñ ka?* (帰りに一杯やりませんか) Won't you have *a drink* on the way back?
ippai kuwasu (～食わす) deceive; cheat. (⇨ damasu)

i⌈ppai[2] いっぱい *a.n.* (～ na/no, ni) be full; be filled; be crowded:
Depaato wa hito de ippai *datta.* (デパートは人でいっぱいだった) The department store was *crowded* with people.

i⌉ppai[3] いっぱい *adv.* until (the end of):
Kono shigoto wa koñgetsu ippai *kakarimasu.* (この仕事は今月いっぱいかかります) This job will take *until the end of* this month.

i⌈ppañ ni いっぱんに (一般に) *adv.* generally; in general.

i⌈ppo⌉o[1] いっぽう (一方) *n.* **1** one end [side]; the other end [side].
2 one-way: ippoo-*tsuukoo* (一方通行) *one-way* traffic.
3 continuation:
Tochi no nedañ wa agaru ippoo *desu.* (土地の値段は上がる一方です) Land prices *continue* to rise.

i⌈ppo⌉o[2] いっぽう (一方) *conj.* on the other hand; while:
Shuunyuu wa fueta ga, ippoo, *isogashiku natta.* (収入は増えたが，一方，忙しくなった) My income has gone up, but, *on the other hand*, I have become busier.

i⌈rai いらい (依頼) *n.* **1** request:
hito no irai *o kotowaru* (人の依頼を断る) decline a person's *request*.
2 dependence; reliance:
Kanojo wa irai-shiñ ga tsuyoi. (彼女は依頼心が強い) She *relies too much* on other people.
irai suru (～する) *vt.* ask; request.

-i⌉rai いらい (以来) *suf.* since; after:
Sotsugyoo-irai *kare to wa atte*

imaseñ. (卒業以来彼とは会っていません) I have not seen him *since* graduation.

iˡrainiñ いらいにん (依頼人) *n.* client. ⟪⇨ kyaku⟫

iˡraira いらいら *adv.* (~ suru) (the state of being impatient [nervous]):
Kare o matte mo konai no de iraira *shite kita.* (彼を待っても来ないのでいらいらしてきた) I waited for him but he did not come, so I got *impatient.*

iˡrassha˥i いらっしゃい = irasshaimase.

iˡrasshaima˥se いらっしゃいませ
1 (to a visitor) welcome:
Irasshaimase. *Doozo o-hairi kudasai.* (いらっしゃいませ. どうぞお入りください) *Welcome.* Please come in.
2 (to a customer at a store) welcome.

iˡrassha˥r·u いらっしゃる *vi.* (irassha·i-; irasshar·a-; irasshat-te Ⓒ) ★ Honorific form of '*kuru, iku, iru.*' The *te*-form is often pronounced '*irashite.*'
1 come:
Yoku irasshaimashita. (よくいらっしゃいました) I am glad you *have come.*
2 go:
Kyooto e wa itsu irasshaimasu *ka?* (京都へはいついらっしゃいますか) When *are* you *going* to Kyoto?
3 be; be present:
Señsee wa ima irasshaimasu *ka?* (先生は今いらっしゃいますか) *Is* the teacher *in* now?

iˡrechigai ni いれちがいに (入れ違いに) *adv.* passing [crossing] each other:
Anata to irechigai ni Tanaka-sañ ga miemashita. (あなたと入れ違いに田中さんが見えました) *Just as you went out,* Miss Tanaka came to see you.

iˡre˥esai いれいさい (慰霊祭) *n.* memorial service.

iˡrekae˥·ru いれかえる (入れ替える) *vt.* (-kae-te Ⓥ) replace; substitute; change.
2 refresh:
kuuki o irekaeru (空気を入れ替える) *change* the air (of a room). ⟪⇨ irekawaru⟫

iˡrekawa˥r·u いれかわる (入れ代わる) *vi.* (-kawar·i-; -kawar·a-; -kawat-te Ⓒ) be replaced; change:
Kaichoo ga irekawatta. (会長が入れ代わった) The company chairman *was replaced.* ⟪⇨ irekaeru⟫

iˡremono いれもの (入れ物) *n.* container; vessel.

iˡre·ru いれる (入れる) *vt.* (ire-te Ⓥ) **1** put in [into]; pour; fill:
koohii ni satoo o ireru (コーヒーに砂糖を入れる) *put* sugar into coffee.
2 insert; enclose:
Tegami ni shashiñ o ireta. (手紙に写真を入れた) I *enclosed* some photos with the letter.
3 let in:
Mado o akete shiñseñ na kuuki o ireta. (窓を開けて新鮮な空気を入れた) I opened the windows and *let in* some fresh air.
4 send (a person to school, an organization, etc.):
Kare wa musuko o gaikoku no daigaku ni ireta. (彼は息子を外国の大学に入れた) He *sent* his son to a university overseas.
5 include:
Tesuuryoo o irete, *goseñ-eñ ni narimasu.* (手数料を入れて, 5千円になります) It comes to 5,000 yen, *including* commission.
6 admit:
Sono kai no meñbaa ni irete moratta. (その会のメンバーに入れてもらった) I *was admitted* as a member of the society.
7 accept (a demand, request, etc.):
Kaisha-gawa wa kumiai no yookyuu o ireta. (会社側は組合の要求を入れた) The management *accepted* the union's demands.
8 switch on:

terebi no suitchi o ireru (テレビのスイッチを入れる) *switch on* the television.

i⌈riguchi いりぐち (入り口) *n.* entrance; way in; doorway. 《↔ deguchi》

i⌈rita⌉mago いりたまご (煎り卵) *n.* scrambled eggs.

i⌈ro⌉ いろ (色) *n.* color; tint; complexion:
Kanojo wa iro *ga shiroi.* (彼女は色が白い) She has a fair *complexion.*
iro o tsukeru (~をつける) add a little something extra.

i⌈roiro[1] いろいろ (色々) *n.* variety:
choo no iroiro (蝶のいろいろ) a *variety* of butterflies.
— *a.n.* (~ na, ni) various; all kinds of. 《⇨ samazama》

i⌈roiro[2] いろいろ (色々) *adv.* (~ to) variously; differently; all kinds of:
iroiro *yatte miru* (いろいろやってみる) try *all sorts of things.*

i⌈rojiro いろじろ (色白) *a.n.* (~ na/no) fair-complexioned:
irojiro *no bijiñ* (色白の美人) a *fair-skinned* beauty.

i⌈roñna いろんな *attrib.* (*informal*) various; all kinds of. 《⇨ iroiro[1]》

i·⌈ru[1] いる (居る) *vi.* (i-te [V])
1 (of a person, animal) be; there is [are]; exist: ★ When the subject is animate (a person or animal), '*iru*' is used, while '*aru*' is used to indicate the existence of something inanimate (a thing or plant).
Kare wa niwa ni imasu. (彼は庭にいます) He *is* in the garden.
2 have:
Watashi ni wa ani ga hitori imasu. (私には兄が一人います) I *have* one older brother.
3 live:
Ryooshiñ wa Hokkaidoo ni imasu. (両親は北海道にいます) My parents *live* in Hokkaido.
4 be present:
Anata ga ite *kuretara, tasukarimasu.* (あなたがいてくれたら, 助かります) If you *are present,* it will be of great help to us.
-te [-de] iru (て[で]~) ★ Attached to the *te*-form of a verb, it indicates a continuing action, the state of being engaged in something, or a resulting state.
Kanojo wa gakkoo de Nihoñgo o oshiete imasu. (彼女は学校で日本語を教えています) She *teaches* Japanese at a school.

i⌈r·u[2] いる (要る) *vi.* (ir·i-; ir·a-; itte [C]) need; want; be necessary:
Kono hoñ wa moo irimaseñ. (この本はもう要りません) I *no longer need* this book.

i⌉r·u[3] いる (炒る) *vt.* (ir·i-; ir·a-; itte [C]) roast (beans); parch.

i⌉·ru[4] いる (射る) *vt.* (i-te [V]) shoot (an arrow); hit.

i⌉rui いるい (衣類) *n.* clothing; clothes; garments.

i⌈ryoo[1] いりょう (医療) *n.* medical treatment.

i⌉ryoo[2] いりょう (衣料) *n.* clothing; clothes.

i⌈ryoohiñ いりょうひん (衣料品) *n.* articles of clothing.

i⌈samashi⌉·i いさましい (勇ましい) *a.* (-ku) brave; courageous:
isamashiku *tatakau* (勇ましく戦う) fight *bravely.*

i⌈see[1] いせい (異性) *n.* the opposite [other] sex.

i⌈see[2] いせい (威勢) *n.* spirits:
Kare-ra wa isee yoku, *shuppatsu shita.* (彼らは威勢よく, 出発した) They set out *in high spirits.*

i⌈sha いしゃ (医者) *n.* doctor; physician:
isha *ni mite morau* (医者に診てもらう) consult a *doctor.* 《⇨ -i[2]》

i⌈shi[1] いし (石) *n.* stone; rock; pebble.

i⌉shi[2] いし (意志) *n.* will:
Kare wa ishi *ga tsuyoi [yowai].* (彼は意志が強い[弱い]) He is a man of strong [weak] *will.*

i⌉shi[3] いし (意思) *n.* intention.

iˡshi[4] いし (医師) *n.* doctor. ((⇨ isha))

iˡshiki いしき (意識) *n.* consciousness; one's senses.
ishiki suru (～する) *vt.* be conscious [aware] of.

iˈshoku いしょく (移植) *n.* transplantation; grafting.
ishoku suru (～する) *vt.* transplant; graft.

i-ˈshokuˡ-juu いしょくじゅう (衣食住) *n.* food, clothing and shelter.

iˡshoo いしょう (衣装) *n.* clothes; dress; costume.

iˈsogashiˡ·i いそがしい (忙しい) *a.* (-ku) busy:
shigoto de isogashii (仕事で忙しい) *be busy* with one's work.
((↔ hima)) ((⇨ taboo))

iˈsogaˡs·u いそがす (急がす) *vt.* (isogash·i-; isogas·a-; isogash·i-te [C]) hurry; hasten.
((⇨ isogu))

iˈsoˡg·u いそぐ (急ぐ) *vi.* (isog·i-; isog·a-; iso·i-de [C]) hurry; make haste; hasten. ((⇨ isogasu))

iˡssai いっさい (一切) *n.* all; everything.
— *adv.* (with a negative) not at all:
Watashi wa sono moñdai to issai *kañkee arimaseñ.* (私はその問題と一切関係ありません) I am *not in any way* connected with that matter.

iˈssakuˡjitsu いっさくじつ (一昨日) *n.* (*formal*) = ototoi.

iˈssakuneñ いっさくねん (一昨年) *n.* (*formal*) = ototoshi.

iˈssee[1] いっせい (一斉) *adv.* (～ ni) at the same time; all together; simultaneously.

iˡssee[2] いっせい (一世) *n.* Issei; Japanese immigrant, usually to North and South American countries. ((⇨ nisee; sañsee[2]))

iˈsshiˡñ ni いっしんに (一心に) *adv.* earnestly; fervently:
kami ni isshiñ ni *inoru* (神に一心に祈る) pray to God *intently.*

iˈssho いっしょ (一緒) *n.* the same:
Watashi wa Yamada to kurasu ga issho *datta.* (私は山田とクラスがいっしょだった) I was in *the same* class as Yamada. ((⇨ onaji))

iˈssho ni いっしょに (一緒に) *adv.* (all) together; at the same time.
issho ni naru (～なる) meet; get married.
issho ni suru (～する) put together; mix up.

iˈsshoo いっしょう (一生) *n.* lifetime; life:
Kare wa isshoo *dokushiñ de sugoshita.* (彼は一生独身で過ごした) He was a bachelor *all his life.*

iˈsshoo-keˡñmee いっしょうけんめい (一生懸命) *a.n.* (～ na, ni) very hard; with all one's might:
isshoo-keñmee (*ni*) *hataraku* (一生懸命(に)働く) work *as hard as one could.* ((⇨ keñmee[2]))

iˡsshu いっしゅ (一種) *n.* kind; sort; variety:
Kono ki wa sakura no isshu *desu.* (この木は桜の一種です) This tree is *a variety* of cherry.

iˈsshuñ いっしゅん (一瞬) *n.* an instant; a moment.
— *adv.* for a moment:
Kare wa isshuñ *ishiki o ushinatta.* (彼は一瞬意識を失った) He lost consciousness *for just a moment.*

iˈsshuu いっしゅう (一周) *n.* one round.
isshuu suru (～する) *vi.* go around: *sekai o* isshuu suru (世界を一周する) *travel around* the world.

iˈsso いっそ *adv.* rather; preferably; once and for all.
isso no koto (～の事) rather; preferably: Isso no koto *saisho kara yarinaoshita hoo ga ii.* (いっその事最初からやり直したほうがいい) We *had better* do it all over again from the beginning.

iˈssoo いっそう (一層) *adv.* (～ no) all the more; further; still:
issoo *doryoku suru* (いっそう努力す

る) make *even* greater efforts.

iˈsu いす(椅子) *n.* **1** chair; stool. **2** post; position: *shachoo no* isu *o nerau* (社長のいすをねらう) aim for the *post* of president.

iˈta いた(板) *n.* board; plank.

iˈtabaˈsami いたばさみ(板挟み) *n.* dilemma; fix: *giri to niñjoo no* itabasami ni naru (義理と人情の板挟みになる) *be torn between* duty and sentiment. 《⇨ nayamu》

iˈtadakimaˈsu いただきます(頂きます・戴きます) ★ This is what the Japanese say before they start eating. Literally it means, "We are going to eat [partake]." 《⇨ itadaku; gochisoosama》

iˈtadak·u いただく(頂く・戴く) *vt.* (itadak·i-; itadak·a-; itada·i-te Ⓒ) **1** (*humble*) have; get; take; receive: *Kinoo, o-tayori o* itadakimashita. (きのう, お便りをいただきました) I *received* your letter yesterday. 《⇨ morau》
2 (*humble*) eat; drink: *Moo juubuñ* itadakimashita. (もう十分いただきました) I *have had* plenty, thanks. 《⇨ choodai suru; itadakimasu; taberu; nomu》
3 (*literary*) be capped: *yuki o* itadaita *yama* (雪をいただいた山) a mountain *capped* with snow. 《⇨ oou》
-te itadaku [itadakeru] (ていただく[いただける] (*humble*) have something done for one; be allowed to do something: ★ Used when asking a favor of a person, who is higher in status. When the person is equal or lower in status, '*-te morau*' is used.
Eki e iku michi o oshiete itadakemasu *ka?* (駅へ行く道を教えていただけますか) *Would you be kind enough to tell me* the way to the station?

iˈtaˈ·i いたい(痛い) *a.* (-ku) painful; sore: Ha ga itai. (歯が痛い) I *have a toothache.*

iˈtameˈ·ru いためる(炒める) *vt.* (itame-te Ⓥ) fry; panfry; sauté: *niku o abura de* itameru (肉を油でいためる) *fry* meat in oil. 《⇨ ageru[2]》

iˈtamiˈ いたみ(痛み) *n.* pain; ache: *Senaka ni* itami *o kañjiru.* (背中に痛みを感じる) I can feel a *pain* in my back. 《⇨ itamu; itai》

iˈtaˈm·u いたむ(痛む) *vi.* (itam·i-; itam·a-; itañ-de Ⓒ) **1** hurt; ache; have a pain: *Ha ga mada* itamu. (歯がまだ痛む) My tooth still *hurts.* 《⇨ itami》
2 (of one's heart) ache: *Sono ko no koto o omou to kanojo wa kokoro ga* itañda. (その子のことを思うと彼女は心が痛んだ) When she thought of the child, her heart *ached.* 《⇨ itami》

iˈtashimaˈsu いたします(致します) *vt.* = itasu.

iˈtas·u いたす(致す) *vt.* (itash·i-; itas·a-; itash·i-te Ⓒ) do: ★ The humble form of '*suru.*' Usually used in the *masu*-form.
Asu o-ukagai itashimasu. (あすお伺いいたします) I *will* call on you tomorrow.

iˈtawaˈr·u いたわる(労る) *vt.* (itawar·i-; itawar·a-; itawat-te Ⓒ) treat kindly; be kind; take care of: *roojiñ o* itawaru (老人をいたわる) *be kind* to old people.

iˈtazura いたずら(悪戯) *n.* mischief; prank: itazura *o suru* (いたずらをする) play a *trick.*
— *a.n.* (~ na) naughty; mischievous.

iˈtchi いっち(一致) *n.* agreement; accord; coincidence.
itchi suru (~する) *vi.* match; agree; accord; coincide.

iˈto[1] いと(糸) *n.* thread; yarn; string.

iˈto[2] いと(意図) *n.* intention; purpose.

ito suru (～する) *vt.* intend; aim at. ⟪⇨ mokuromu⟫

i⌈to⌉guchi いとぐち (糸口) *n.*
1 the end of a thread.
2 beginning; clue; lead:
hanashi no itoguchi *o mitsukeru* (話の糸口を見つける) try to *break the ice in a conversation.*

i⌈to⌉ko いとこ (従兄弟・従姉妹) *n.* cousin. ★ '従兄弟' is used to refer to male cousins or a mixed group of male and female cousins. '従姉妹' refers to female cousins.

i⌈toma いとま (暇) *n.* (*formal*)
1 spare time. ⟪⇨ hima⟫
2 taking one's leave: ★ Often with '*o-*.'
Moo o-itoma *shinakereba narimaseñ.* (もうおいとましなければなりません) I must *be leaving* now.

i⌈tona⌉m·u いとなむ (営む) *vt.* (itonam·i-; itonam·a-; itonañ-de Ⓒ) run; be engaged in; lead:
Kare wa ryokañ o itonañde iru. (彼は旅館を営んでいる) He *runs* a Japanese inn. ⟪⇨ kee-ee⟫

i⌉tsu いつ (何時) *adv.* when; what time:
Kono koinu wa itsu *umaremashita?* (この小犬はいつ生まれました) *When* was this puppy born? / *Anata wa* itsu *made Hokkaidoo ni iru yotee desu ka?* (あなたはいつまで北海道にいる予定ですか) *How long* do you plan to stay in Hokkaido?

i⌉tsu de mo いつでも (何時でも) *adv.* 1 always; all the time.
2 at any time; whenever:
Kaesu no wa itsu de mo *kekkoo desu.* (返すのはいつでもけっこうです) You can return it *anytime.*

i⌈tsuka いつか (五日) *n.* five days; the fifth day of the month. ⟪⇨ APP. 5⟫

i⌉tsu-ka いつか (何時か) *adv.*
1 (of future) someday; sometime:
Sono shiñsoo wa itsu-ka *wakaru deshoo.* (その真相はいつかわかるでしょう) The truth will come out *someday.*
2 (of the past) once; before:
Kanojo ni wa itsu-ka *doko-ka de atta oboe ga arimasu.* (彼女にはいつかどこかで会った覚えがあります) I have a recollection of meeting her somewhere *sometime before.*

i⌉tsu made mo いつまでも (何時迄も) *adv.* forever; endlessly; as long as (one likes).

i⌉tsu-mo いつも (何時も) *adv.* (～ no) always; usually:
Itsu-mo *neru mae ni shawaa o abimasu.* (いつも寝る前にシャワーを浴びます) I *usually* take a shower before going to bed. ⟪⇨ maido; shotchuu⟫

i⌈tsu-no-ma-ni⌉-ka いつのまにか (何時の間にか) *adv.* before one knows it; too soon.

i⌈tsu⌉tsu いつつ (五つ) *n.* five.
★ Used when counting.
⟪⇨ go[3]; APP. 3⟫

i⌈ttai[1] いったい (一体) *n.* one; one body:
Futatsu no kaisha ga gappee shite, ittai to natta. (二つの会社が合併して, 一体となった) The two companies merged and became *one.*

i⌈ttai[2] いったい (一体) *adv.* (with an interrogative) on earth; in the world; even:
Ittai *nani ga okotta no desu ka?* (いったい何が起こったのですか) What *on earth* has happened?

i⌈ttañ いったん (一旦) *adv.* 1 once:
Ittañ *hajimeta koto wa saigo made yari nasai.* (いったん始めたことは最後までやりなさい) *Once* you have started something, continue until you have finished it.
2 temporarily; for a while:
Watashi wa raishuu ittañ *kuni ni kaerimasu.* (私は来週いったん国に帰ります) I am going home *for just a short while* next week.

i⌉tte いって (一手) *n.* 1 monopoly; exclusiveness:
Kono shina wa kare no kaisha ga

itte *ni hañbai shite iru.* (この品は彼の会社が一手に販売している) This article is sold *exclusively* by his company.
2 (of chess, shoogi, go, etc.) move.

i⌈ttee いってい (一定) *n.* fixed (condition); definite (condition); uniform (circumstances).
ittee no (〜の) fixed; regular:
Watashi wa ittee *no sokudo de uñteñ shita.* (私は一定の速度で運転した) I drove at a *steady* speed.
ittee suru (〜する) *vi.* fix; set; standardize: *Okiru jikañ wa* ittee shite imaseñ. (起きる時間は一定していません) The time I get up *is irregular*.

i⌈tte-kimasu いってきます (行って来ます) I'll go and come back. ★ A set expression used when leaving home. A more polite form is '*itte-mairimasu*.' (⇨ itte-(i)rasshai)

i⌈tte-(i)rasshai いって(い)らっしゃい (行って(い)らっしゃい) Please go and come back. ★ A set expression used when someone is going out. (⇨ itte-kimasu)

i⌈ttoo いっとう (一等) *n.* first class; first prize; first place. (⇨ nitoo)

i·⌈u いう (言う) *vt.* (i·i-; iw·a-; it-te Ⓒ) ★ '言う' (*iu*) is often pronounced '*yuu*.' In the *te*-form and the past '*yutte*' and '*yutta*' are common, but slightly more informal than the equivalent standard form, '*itte*' and '*itta*.'
1 say; tell; talk; speak:
Kare wa watashi ni "Isoge" to itta. (彼は私に「急げ」と言った) He *said* "Hurry up" to me.
2 mention; refer to:
Shachoo wa atarashii keekaku ni tsuite nani mo iwanakatta. (社長は新しい計画について何も言わなかった) The president *did not refer* to the new project.
3 express; call:
Anata no kañgae o itte *kudasai.* (あなたの考えを言ってください) Please *express* your thoughts.
4 tell; order:
Kare-ra ni sugu dete iku yoo ni itta. (彼らにすぐ出て行くように言った) I *told* them to get out at once.
... to iu (…と〜) **1** people say:
Kare wa kaisha o yameru to iu *uwasa ga aru.* (彼は会社を辞めるといううわさがある) Rumor has it *that* he will quit his company.
2 (used for emphasis or explanation): *Watashi wa mada tako* to iu *mono o tabeta koto ga nai.* (私はまだたこというものを食べたことがない) I have not yet eaten *octopus*.

i⌈wa⌉ いわ (岩) *n.* rock; crag. (⇨ ishi[1])

i⌈waba いわば (言わば) *adv.* so to speak; as it were, in a sense; practically.

i⌈wa⌉i いわい (祝い) *n.* **1** celebration; congratulation.
★ Usually with '*o-*.' (⇨ iwau)
2 present:
kekkoñ no o-iwai (結婚のお祝い) a wedding *present*.

i⌈washi いわし (鰯) *n.* sardine.

i⌈wa⌉·u いわう (祝う) *vt.* (iwa·i-; iwaw·a-; iwat-te Ⓒ) celebrate; congratulate:
tañjoobi o iwau (誕生日を祝う) *celebrate* a birthday. (⇨ iwai; shukusu)

i⌈wa⌉yuru いわゆる (所謂) *attrib.* what is called; so-called.

i⌈ya[1] いや (嫌) *a.n.* (〜 na, ni) disagreeable; disgusting; horrible:
Beñkyoo ga iya ni natta. (勉強がいやになった) I *am fed up* with my studies.

i⌈ya[2] いや *int.* no; yes: ★ '*Iya*' literally means 'That's wrong,' and is used to confirm a statement, whether affirmative or negative.
"Kare wa kimasu ka?" "Iya, konai to omoimasu." (「彼は来ますか」「いや, 来ないと思います」) "Is he

coming?" "*No*, I do not think so." / *"Mada ame wa yamimaseñ ka?" "*Iya, *yamimashita."* (「まだ雨はやみませんか」「いや, やみました」) "Hasn't the rain stopped yet?" "*Yes*, it has." ((⇨ iie))

iya to iu (～と言う) say no.

i⌈yagarase いやがらせ (嫌がらせ) *n.* harassment:
iyagarase *no deñwa* (嫌がらせの電話) a *harassing* phone call. ((⇨ sekuhara))

i⌈yaga⌉r·u いやがる (嫌がる) *vt.* (iyagar·i-; iyagar·a-; iyagat-te Ⓒ) dislike; hate; be unwilling; be reluctant.

i⌈yaiya いやいや *adv.* unwillingly; reluctantly; against one's will.

i⌈yarashi⌉·i いやらしい *a.* (-ku) disgusting; offensive; nasty:
iyarashii *yatsu* (いやらしいやつ) a *nasty* fellow.

i⌈yashi·i いやしい (卑しい) *a.* (-ku)
1 vulgar; coarse.
2 greedy; gluttonous:
Kare wa kane ni iyashii. (彼は金に卑しい) He is *mean* with money.

i⌈yo⌉iyo いよいよ *adv.* **1** more and more; all the more. ((⇨ masumasu))
2 at last; finally:
Iyoiyo *ashita wa nyuugaku-shikeñ da.* (いよいよあしたは入学試験だ) Tomorrow is the entrance exam *at long last*.

i⌉yoku いよく (意欲) *n.* will; eagerness; desire; volition:
Kanojo ni wa beñkyoo shitai to iu iyoku ga aru. (彼女には勉強したいという意欲がある) She *is eager* to study.

i⌈yoku-teki いよくてき (意欲的) *a.n.* (～ na, ni) eager; active; positive enthusiastic.

i⌉zeñ[1] いぜん (以前) *n.* **1** before a certain time:
Kyoo wa shichi-ji izeñ *ni kaerimasu.* (きょうは7時以前に帰ります) Today I'll return *before* seven. ((↔ igo[1]))
2 ago; once; formerly:
Kare ni atta no wa zutto izeñ *desu.* (彼に会ったのはずっと以前です) It was a long time *ago* that I met him.

i⌈zeñ[2] いぜん (依然) *adv.* (～ to shite) still; as ever; as before:
Eñ wa izeñ (*to shite*) *agari tsuzukete iru.* (円は依然(として)上がり続けている) The Japanese yen *still* shows a tendency to go up.

i⌈zumi いずみ (泉) *n.* spring; fountain.

i⌈zure いずれ (何れ) *adv.* (～ no) some day; one day; before long.
izure ni shite mo [seyo] (～にしても[せよ]) in any event; at any rate.

i⌈zure mo いずれも (何れも) *adv.* both; either; any; all:
Sono ni-satsu no shoosetsu wa izure mo *yomimashita.* (その2冊の小説はいずれも読みました) I have read *both* those novels.

J

ja じゃ *conj.* = jaa.

ja⌉a じゃあ *conj.* (*formal* = de wa) well; then:
Jaa, *mata ashita.* (じゃあ, またあした) *Well*, I'll see you tomorrow.

ja⌉bujabu じゃぶじゃぶ *adv.* (～ to) (the sound or action of water splashing around):
kawa o jabujabu (*to*) *wataru* (川をじゃぶじゃぶ(と)渡る) *splash* one's way across a river.

ja⌈gaimo じゃがいも (じゃが芋) *n.* potato.

ja⌈guchi じゃぐち (蛇口) *n.* tap; faucet.

ja⌈ma じゃま (邪魔) *n.* disturbance; hindrance; interference.
jama (o) suru (～(を)する) *vt.*

1 disturb; hinder; interfere.
2 visit: ★ Usually with '*o-*.'
Asu o-jama shimasu. (あすおじゃまします) I'll *visit* you tomorrow.
— *a.n.* (~ na, ni) obstructive; hampering; burdensome:
Soko ni iru to jama *desu.* (そこにいるとじゃまです) You are *in the way.*

ja⌈ñkeñ じゃんけん *n.* the game of 'paper, scissors, stone.'

ja⌈re⌉·ru じゃれる *vi.* (jare-te [V]) play with:
Neko ga mari to jarete iru. (猫がまりとじゃれている) The cat *is playing* with a ball.

-jau じゃう *suf.* ⇨ shimau[2].

je⌈tto⌉ki ジェットき (ジェット機) *n.* jet (plane).

ji⌉ じ (字) *n.* **1** letter; character. 《⇨ moji》
2 handwriting:
Kare no ji *wa yomi-nikui.* (彼の字は読みにくい) His *handwriting* is hard to read.

-ji[1] じ (時) *suf.* o'clock:
gozeñ roku-ji (午前6時) *six* in the morning. 《⇨ jikañ》

-ji[2] じ (寺) *suf.* temple:
Hooryuu-ji (法隆寺) Horyuji *Temple.* 《⇨ tera》

-ji[3] じ (次) *suf.* the number in a series; order:
ichi-ji (一次) the *first* / ni-ji (二次) the *second* / *seki*-ji (席次) seating *order.*

ji⌈bi-iñkooka じびいんこうか (耳鼻咽喉科) *n.* otolaryngology; ear, nose and throat department.

ji⌈bika じびか (耳鼻科) *n.* = jibi-iñkooka.

ji⌈biki じびき (字引) *n.* dictionary. ★ Not as common as '*jisho*' anymore. 《⇨ jisho[2]; jiteñ》

ji⌈buñ じぶん (自分) *n.* oneself:
Jibuñ *no koto wa* jibuñ *de shi nasai.* (自分のことは自分でしなさい) *You yourself* do *your own* business.

ji⌉chi じち (自治) *n.* self-government; autonomy.

ji⌉choo じちょう (次長) *n.* deputy chief; vice-director.

ji⌈dai じだい (時代) *n.* **1** era; period; age. 《⇨ APP. 9》
2 days: *gakusee* jidai (学生時代) one's student *days.*
3 times:
Kimi no kañgae wa jidai*-okure da.* (君の考えは時代遅れだ) You ideas are behind the *times.*

ji⌈dai-sa⌉kugo じだいさくご (時代錯誤) *n.* anachronism.

ji⌈doo[1] じどう (自動) *n.* automatic:
jidoo*-shooteñ no kamera* (自動焦点のカメラ) an *automatic* focusing camera

ji⌉doo[2] じどう (児童) *n.* child; juvenile. 《⇨ kodomo》

ji⌈do⌉osha じどうしゃ (自動車) *n.* car; automobile; motor vehicle. 《⇨ kuruma》

ji⌈do⌉oshi じどうし (自動詞) *n.* intransitive verb. 《↔ tadooshi》 《⇨ APP. 2》

ji⌈ee じえい (自衛) *n.* self-defense.
jiee suru (~する) *vi.* defend oneself.

Ji⌈eetai じえいたい (自衛隊) *n.* the Self-Defense Forces:
Rikujoo [*Kaijoo; Kookuu*] Jieetai (陸上[海上; 航空]自衛隊) the Ground [Maritime; Air] *Self-Defense Force.* 《⇨ guñ[2]》

ji⌈goku⌉ じごく (地獄) *n.* hell.

ji⌉gyoo じぎょう (事業) *n.* business; enterprise:
jigyoo *ni seekoo* [*shippai*] *suru* (事業に成功[失敗]する) succeed [fail] in *business.*

ji⌈hi⌉biki じひびき (地響き) *n.* rumbling of the ground:
Sono ki wa jihibiki o tatete, *taoreta.* (その木は地響きを立てて, 倒れた) The tree fell *with a thud.*

ji⌈hyoo じひょう (辞表) *n.* resignation:
jihyoo *o dasu* (辞表を出す) hand in one's *resignation.*

ji⌉isañ じいさん (爺さん) *n.* (*informal*) **1** one's grandfather.

2 old man. 《↔ baasañ》《⇨ o-jiisañ》

ji¹jitsu[1] じじつ(事実) *n.* fact; truth; reality:
Kono shoosetsu wa jijitsu *ni motozuite imasu.* (この小説は事実に基づいています) This novel is based on *fact.*
jijitsu joo (no) (〜上(の)) actual:
Kare wa jijitsu joo (no) *shachoo no yoo ni furumatte iru.* (彼は事実上(の)社長のように振る舞っている) He carries on as if he were the *actual* president.

ji¹jitsu[2] じじつ(事実) *adv.* as a matter of fact; actually:
Jijitsu *kare wa soo iimashita.* (事実彼はそう言いました) *As a matter of fact*, he said so.

ji¹jo じじょ(次女・二女) *n.* one's second daughter.

ji⌈joo じじょう(事情) *n.* **1** circumstances; conditions:
Jijoo *ga yuruseba sono kai ni shusseki shimasu.* (事情が許せばその会に出席します) I'll attend the party if *circumstances* permit.
2 reasons:
Kanojo wa katee no jijoo *de kaisha o yamemashita.* (彼女は家庭の事情で会社を辞めました) She left the company for family *reasons.*
3 affairs:
Kare wa Nihoñ no jijoo *o yoku shitte iru.* (彼は日本の事情をよく知っている) He is familiar with Japanese *affairs.*

ji¹kai じかい(次回) *n.* next; next time:
jikai *no kaigi* (次回の会議) the *next* meeting. 《⇨ tsugi》

ji⌈kaku じかく(自覚) *n.* consciousness; awareness.
jikaku suru (〜する) *vt.* realize; awaken; be aware of: *Watashi wa chiimu no kyaputeñ to shite* jikaku shite imasu. (私はチームのキャプテンとして自覚しています) I *am well aware* that I am captain of this team.

ji⌈kañ じかん(時間) *n.* **1** time; period:
Jikañ *wa juubuñ ni arimasu.* (時間は十分にあります) We have plenty of *time.*
2 time; hour:
Shuppatsu no jikañ *ga heñkoo ni natta.* (出発の時間が変更になった) The *hour* of departure has been changed.
3 lesson; class:
Tsugi no jikañ *wa suugaku desu.* (次の時間は数学です) The next *lesson* is mathematics.

-ji¹kañ じかん(時間) *suf.* hour:
*Hakone made kuruma de sañ-*jikañ *kakatta.* (箱根まで車で3時間かかった) It took three *hours* to Hakone by car.

ji¹ka ni じかに(直に) *adv.* directly; at first hand; in person:
Sono hanashi wa kare kara jika ni *kikimashita.* (その話は彼からじかに聞きました) I heard the news *directly* from him. 《⇨ chokusetsu》

ji⌈kañwari じかんわり(時間割) *n.* class schedule.

ji¹keñ じけん(事件) *n.* **1** event; affair:
Kare wa sono jikeñ *ni makikomareta.* (彼はその事件に巻き込まれた) He was involved in that *affair.*
2 incident; case.

ji¹ki[1] じき(時期) *n.* **1** time:
Ima ga ichineñ-juu de ichibañ isogashii jiki *desu.* (今が一年中で一番忙しい時期です) This is the busiest *time* of the whole year. 《⇨ toki》
2 season:
Aki wa ryokoo o suru no ni ichibañ ii jiki *desu.* (秋は旅行をするのに一番いい時期です) Autumn is the best *season* for traveling.

ji¹ki[2] じき(時機) *n.* opportunity; chance.

ji¹ki[3] じき(磁器) *n.* porcelain; china. 《⇨ tooki[1]》

ji⌈ki ni じきに(直に) *adv.* **1** soon; in a moment:
Shujiñ wa jiki ni *modotte kimasu.*

(主人はじきに戻ってきます) My husband will *soon* be back.
2 easily; readily:
Yasui shinamono wa jiki ni *kowareru.* (安い品物はじきに壊れる) Cheap goods *easily* break.

ji⌈kkañ じっかん (実感) *n.* actual feeling; realization.
jikkañ suru (~する) *vt.* fully realize.

ji⌈kkeñ じっけん (実験) *n.* experiment; test.
jikkeñ (o) suru (~(を)する) *vt.* make an experiment.

ji⌈kkeñdai じっけんだい (実験台) *n.*
1 laboratory table.
2 the subject of an experiment:
jikkeñdai *ni sareru* (実験台にされる) be used as a *guinea pig*.

ji⌈kke⌉ñshitsu じっけんしつ (実験室) *n.* laboratory.

ji⌈kkoo じっこう (実行) *n.* practice; action; execution.
jikkoo suru (~する) *vt.* carry out; execute: *yakusoku o* jikkoo suru (約束を実行する) *fulfill* a promise.

ji⌈kku⌉ri じっくり *adv.* (~ to) closely; carefully; thoroughly:
Watashi wa kanojo to sono koto ni tsuite jikkuri (*to*) *hanashiatta.* (私は彼女とそのことについてじっくり(と)話し合った) I discussed the matter *thoroughly* with her.

ji⌉ko[1] じこ (事故) *n.* accident:
jiko *o okosu* (事故を起こす) cause an *accident*.

ji⌉ko[2] じこ (自己) *n.* self; oneself:
jiko-*mañzoku* (自己満足) *self*-satisfaction.

ji⌉koku じこく (時刻) *n.* time:
Tokee o tadashii jikoku *ni awaseta.* (時計を正しい時刻に合わせた) I set my watch to the right *time*.

ji⌈kokuhyoo じこくひょう (時刻表) *n.* (train) schedule; timetable. ⟪⇨ daiya[1]⟫

ji⌈ko-sho⌉okai じこしょうかい (自己紹介) *n.* self-introduction.
jiko-shookai (o) suru (~(を)する) *vi.* introduce oneself.

ji⌈ku⌉ じく (軸) *n.* axis; axle; shaft.

ji⌈mañ じまん (自慢) *n.* pride; boast:
Kare wa haha-oya no jimañ no *tane da.* (彼は母親の自慢の種だ) He is his mother's *pride*.
jimañ (o) suru (~(を)する) *vt.* be proud of; boast; brag.

ji⌉meñ じめん (地面) *n.* surface of the earth; ground.

ji⌈mi⌉ じみ (地味) *a.n.* (~ na, ni) plain; quiet; modest:
jimi *na nekutai* (地味なネクタイ) a *quiet* tie. ⟪↔ hade⟫

Ji⌈miñtoo じみんとう (自民党) *n.* = Jiyuu Miñshutoo ⟪⇨ APP. 8⟫

ji⌉mu じむ (事務) *n.* office [clerical] work; business.

ji⌈mu⌉iñ じむいん (事務員) *n.* office worker; clerk; secretary.

ji⌈mu⌉shitsu じむしつ (事務室) *n.* office room.

ji⌈mu⌉sho じむしょ (事務所) *n.* office.

-jiñ じん (人) *suf.* person:
geenoo-jiñ (芸能人) a show business [TV] *personality*.

ji⌉nañ じなん (次男·二男) *n.* one's second son.

ji⌈ñbuñka⌉gaku じんぶんかがく (人文科学) *n.* the humanities.

ji⌉ñbutsu じんぶつ (人物) *n.*
1 character:
Kare no jiñbutsu *wa hoshoo shimasu.* (彼の人物は保証します) I vouch for his *character*.
2 person; figure.

ji⌉ñja じんじゃ (神社) *n.* Shinto shrine. ⟪⇨ tera⟫

ji⌉ñji じんじ (人事) *n.* personnel affairs:
Atarashii jiñji *ga happyoo ni natta.* (新しい人事が発表になった) The new *personnel appointments* were announced.

ji⌈ñkaku じんかく (人格) *n.* character; personality.

ji⌈ñkoo じんこう (人口) *n.* population.

ji⌈ñkoo-e⌉esee じんこうえいせい

(人工衛星) *n.* artificial satellite. ⟪⇨ eesee²⟫

ji[ñkoo-ko]kyuu じんこうこきゅう (人工呼吸) *n.* artificial respiration.

ji[ñkoo-teki じんこうてき (人工的) *a.n.* (~ na, ni) artificial: jiñkoo-teki *ni ame o furaseru* (人工的に雨を降らせる) make rain fall *artificially*.

ji[ñmee じんめい (人命) *n.* human life.

ji[ñmi]ñ じんみん (人民) *n.* the people; the members of a nation-state.

ji]ñrui じんるい (人類) *n.* humankind; the human race. ⟪⇨ niñgeñ⟫

ji]ñsee じんせい (人生) *n.* human life; life: *Kanojo wa shiawase na* jiñsee *o okutta.* (彼女は幸せな人生を送った) She lived a happy *life*.

ji[ñshu じんしゅ (人種) *n.* race; ethnic group: jiñshu-*sabetsu* (人種差別) *racial* discrimination.

ji]ñtai じんたい (人体) *n.* human body. ⟪⇨ karada⟫

ji[nushi じぬし (地主) *n.* landowner; landlord. ⟪⇨ ooya⟫

ji[ñzoo じんぞう (腎臓) *n.* kidney.

ji]rojiro じろじろ *adv.* (~ to) **jirojiro (to) miru** (~(と)見る) stare at.

ji[satsu じさつ (自殺) *n.* suicide. **jisatsu suru** (~する) *vi.* commit suicide; kill oneself.

ji[shiñ¹ じしん (自信) *n.* confidence; assurance: *Watashi wa shikeñ ni ukaru* jishiñ *ga aru.* (私は試験に受かる自信がある) I *am confident* of passing the examination.

ji[shiñ² じしん (地震) *n.* earthquake; earth tremor.

ji]shiñ³ じしん (自身) *n.* oneself; itself: *Kare* jishiñ *ga soo iimashita.* (彼自身がそう言いました) He told me so *himself*.

ji]sho¹ じしょ (地所) *n.* land; ground; lot.

ji]sho² じしょ (辞書) *n.* dictionary. ★ More formal than '*jibiki*.' ⟪⇨ jibiki; jiteñ⟫

ji[shuu じしゅう (自習・自修) *n.* studying for [by] oneself. **jishuu suru** (~する) *vi.* study for [by] oneself.

ji[ssai じっさい (実際) *n.* fact; truth; practice: *Sono hanashi wa* jissai *to chigaimasu.* (その話は実際と違います) Your story differs from the *facts*. **jissai wa** (~は) as a matter of fact: *Kare wa reetañ ni mieru ga* jissai wa *shiñsetsu na hito desu.* (彼は冷淡に見えるが実際は親切な人です) He appears coldhearted, but he is *really* a kind man.
— *adv.* (~ no, ni) actually; really.

ji[ssai-teki じっさいてき (実際的) *a.n.* (~ na, ni) practical; matter-of-fact: jissai-teki *na chishiki* (実際的な知識) *practical* knowledge.

ji[sseki じっせき (実績) *n.* actual results; one's achievements.

ji[sseñ じっせん (実践) *n.* practice. **jisseñ suru** (~する) *vt., vi.* practice: *Jibuñ ga shiñjiru yoo ni* jisseñ shi nasai. (自分が信じるように実践しなさい) *Act* in accordance with your beliefs.

ji[sshi じっし (実施) *n.* enforcement; operation. **jisshi suru** (~する) *vt.* enforce; carry out; put into force.

ji[sshitsu-teki じっしつてき (実質的) *a.n.* (~ na, ni) substantial; essential; material.

ji[sshuu じっしゅう (実習) *n.* practice; practical training: *ryoori no* jisshuu o suru (料理の実習をする) *practice* cooking.

ji]tai じたい (事態) *n.* situation: Saiaku no jitai *wa sakerareta.* (最悪の事態は避けられた) We were able to avert *the worst*.

ji⌈taku じたく(自宅) *n.* one's own house; one's home.

ji⌈teñ じてん(辞典) *n.* dictionary. ★ More formal than '*jisho.*' Usually used in the title of a dictionary. 《⇨ jisho[2]; jibiki》

ji⌈te⌉ñsha じてんしゃ(自転車) *n.* bicycle: jiteñsha *ni noru* (自転車に乗る) ride a *bicycle.*

ji⌈tsubutsu じつぶつ(実物) *n.* real thing; original:
Kono e wa jitsubutsu *sokkuri da.* (この絵は実物そっくりだ) This picture looks just like the *real thing.*

ji⌈tsugeñ じつげん(実現) *n.* realization; materialization.
jitsugeñ suru (～する) *vi., vt.* come true; realize.

ji⌈tsujoo じつじょう(実情) *n.* actual circumstances; the real state of affairs.

ji⌈tsu⌉ ni じつに(実に) *adv.* very; terribly; really; extremely:
Koko kara miru Fuji-sañ wa jitsu ni *utsukushii.* (ここから見る富士山は実に美しい) Mt. Fuji seen from here is *very* beautiful.

ji⌈tsuree じつれい(実例) *n.* example; instance:
Kare wa jitsuree *o agete, setsumee shita.* (彼は実例をあげて, 説明した) He explained by giving *examples.*

ji⌈tsuryoku じつりょく(実力) *n.*
1 real ability; merit:
jitsuryoku *o hakki suru* (実力を発揮する) demonstrate one's *ability.*
2 force:
jitsuryoku *o kooshi suru* (実力を行使する) use *force.*

ji⌈tsu⌉-wa じつは(実は) *adv.* to tell the truth; actually; as a matter of fact.

ji⌈tsuyoo じつよう(実用) *n.* practical use; utility:
Kono doogu wa jitsuyoo *ni wa yakudatanai.* (この道具は実用には役立たない) This tool is of little *practical use.*

ji⌈tsuyooka じつようか(実用化) *n.* practical use.
jitsuyooka suru (～する) *vt., vi.* put [turn] (a thing) to practical use.

ji⌈tsuyoo-teki じつようてき(実用的) *a.n.* (～ na, ni) practical.

ji⌈ttai じったい(実態) *n.* actual condition:
Roodoosha no jittai *o shirabeta.* (労働者の実態を調べた) We researched the *actual conditions* of the workers.

ji⌈tto じっと *adv.* **1** still; quietly; motionlessly:
Shashiñ o torimasu kara jitto *shite ite kudasai.* (写真を撮りますからじっとしていてください) I am going to take a photo, so please keep *still.*
2 fixedly; steadily; intently; attentively: jitto *mitsumeru* (じっと見つめる) stare *intently.*
3 patiently:
Watashi wa sono itami o jitto *gamañ shita.* (私はその痛みをじっと我慢した) I *patiently* endured the pain.

ji⌈yoo じよう(滋養) *n.* nourishment; nutrition. 《⇨ eeyoo》

ji⌈yu⌉u じゆう(自由) *n.* freedom; liberty:
Iku ikanai wa kimi no jiyuu *da.* (行く行かないは君の自由だ) It is *up to* you whether you go or not.
— *a.n.* (～ na, ni) free; easy.

ji⌈yuushu⌉gi じゆうしゅぎ(自由主義) *n.* liberalism.

ji⌈zeñ じぜん(慈善) *n.* charity.

ji⌈zoo じぞう(地蔵) *n.* guardian deity of children and travelers.

-jo じょ(所) *suf.* office; institute; works:
iñsatsu-jo (印刷所) printing *plant* / *keñkyuu*-jo (研究所) a research *institute* / seesaku-jo (製作所) a *factory.* 《⇨ -sho[1]》

jo⌈do⌉oshi じょどうし(助動詞) *n.* auxiliary verb.

jo⌈gai じょがい(除外) *n.* exclusion; exception.

jogai suru (〜する) *vt.* exclude; except.

jo⌈koo じょこう(徐行) *n.* going slow.

jokoo suru (〜する) *vi.* go slow; slow down.

jo⌈kyo⌉oju じょきょうじゅ(助教授) *n.* assistant professor.

jo⌈o[1] じょう(情) *n.* **1** affection; love:

oyako no joo (親子の情) the *affection* between parent and child.

2 feeling; sentiment:

Kare wa joo ni moroi. (彼は情にもろい) He *is easily moved emotionally.*

joo ga utsuru (〜が移る) become attached.

jo⌉o[2] じょう(上) *n.* the best; the top:

Kono shina wa joo *no bu desu.* (この品は上の部です) This article is one of the *best.*

-joo[1] じょう(場) *suf.* ground; links; track:

uñdoo-joo (運動場) a *playground* / *yakyuu*-joo (野球場) a baseball *ground* / *gorufu*-joo (ゴルフ場) golf *links* / *keeba*-joo (競馬場) a race *track.*

-joo[2] じょう(状) *suf.* letter:

shootai-joo (招待状) an *invitation* / *suiseñ*-joo (推薦状) a *letter* of recommendation. 《⇨ tegami》

-joo[3] じょう(状) *suf.* -like; -shaped; form:

kyuu-joo no (球状の) *globular* / kuriimu-joo no (クリーム状の) *creamy.* 《⇨ jootai》

-joo[4] じょう(上) *suf.* concerning; from the viewpoint of:

kyooiku-joo *konomashiku nai* (教育上好ましくない) be unsuitable *from the educational point of view.*

-joo[5] じょう(畳) *suf.* counter for tatami mats:

roku-joo *ma* (6畳間) a six-*mat* room / *hachi*-joo *no heya* (8畳の部屋) a room with eight *mats.* 《⇨ tatami》

jo⌈obu じょうぶ(丈夫) *a.n.* (〜 na, ni) **1** (of a person) healthy.

2 (of substance) strong; durable; firm; tough.

jo⌉ocho じょうちょ(情緒) *n.* **1** atmosphere: *ikoku*-joocho (異国情緒) an exotic *atmosphere.*

2 emotion:

Kare wa joocho *ga fuañtee da.* (彼は情緒が不安定だ) He is *emotionally* unstable.

jo⌈oda⌉ñ じょうだん(冗談) *n.* joke; humor; fun:

Joodañ *hañbuñ ni itta dake desu.* (冗談半分に言っただけです) I just said it in *fun.*

joodañ deshoo (〜でしょう) you're kidding.

joodañ ja nai (〜じゃない) you can't be serious.

joodañ wa sate oki (〜はさておき) joking apart.

jo⌈oee じょうえい(上映) *n.* showing of a movie.

jooee suru (〜する) *vt.* show; present.

jo⌈oeñ じょうえん(上演) *n.* (of a play) presentation; performance.

jooeñ suru (〜する) *vt.* present; perform; put on the stage.

jo⌉oge じょうげ(上下) *n.* **1** upper and lower parts:

sebiro no jooge (背広の上下) the *jacket and trousers* of a suit.

2 social standing:

jooge kañkee (上下関係) the *pecking order.*

3 up and down:

hata o jooge *ni furu* (旗を上下に振る) wave a flag *up and down.*

jooge suru (〜する) *vi.* rise and fall; fluctuate. 《↔ sayuu》 《⇨ ueshita》

jo⌈ohatsu じょうはつ(蒸発) *n.*

1 evaporation; vaporization.

2 (of a person) disappearance.

joohatsu suru (〜する) *vi.* **1** evaporate; vaporize.

2 (of a person) disappear; run away.

jo⌈ohi⌉ñ じょうひん(上品) *a.n.* (~ na, ni) graceful; elegant; refined. ⟪↔ gehiñ⟫

jo⌈ohoo じょうほう(情報) *n.* information; intelligence.

jo⌈ojuñ じょうじゅん(上旬) *n.* the first ten days of a month. ⟪⇨ chuujuñ; gejuñ⟫

jo⌈oke⌉ñ じょうけん(条件) *n.* condition; terms:
jookeñ *o tsukeru* (条件をつける) impose *conditions.*

jo⌉oki じょうき(蒸気) *n.* steam; vapor.

jo⌈oki⌉geñ じょうきげん(上機嫌) *n.* good humor; high spirits.

jo⌈oko⌉okyaku じょうこうきゃく(乗降客) *n.* passengers getting on and off.

jo⌈okuu じょうくう(上空) *n.* the sky:
Hikooki wa Tookyoo-wañ jookuu *o señkai shita.* (飛行機は東京湾上空を旋回した) The airplane circled *over* Tokyo Bay.

jo⌈okyaku じょうきゃく(乗客) *n.* passenger.

jo⌈okyoo[1] じょうきょう(状況) *n.* situation; circumstances; conditions.

jo⌈okyoo[2] じょうきょう(上京) *n.* going [coming] up to Tokyo.
jookyoo suru (~する) *vi.* go [come] up to Tokyo.

jo⌈okyuu じょうきゅう(上級) *n.* advanced course. ⟪⇨ chuukyuu; shokyuu⟫

jo⌈omae じょうまえ(錠前) *n.* lock:
to ni joomae *o kakeru* (戸に錠前を掛ける) *lock* a door. ⟪⇨ kagi⟫

jo⌉omu (to⌈rishimari⌉yaku) じょうむ(とりしまりやく)(常務(取締役)) *n.* managing director.

jo⌈onetsu じょうねつ(情熱) *n.* passion; enthusiasm:
Kare wa joonetsu *o komete katatta.* (彼は情熱を込めて語った) He spoke with *passion.*

jo⌈onetsu-teki じょうねつてき(情熱的) *a.n.* (~ na, ni) passionate; enthusiastic; ardent:
joonetsu-teki *na odori* (情熱的な踊り) a *passionate* dance.

jo-⌈o⌉o じょおう(女王) *n.* queen. ⟪↔ oo[1]⟫

jo⌈o-oñ じょうおん(常温) *n.* normal [room] temperature; fixed temperature.

jo⌈oriku じょうりく(上陸) *n.* landing; disembarkation.
jooriku suru (~する) *vi.* land; disembark: *Taifuu ga Kyuushuu ni* jooriku *shita.* (台風が九州に上陸した) The typhoon *came ashore* in Kyushu.

jo⌈oruri じょうるり(浄瑠璃) *n.* narrative ballad sung for traditional puppet theater.

jo⌈oryuu じょうりゅう(上流) *n.*
1 the upper course [reaches] of a river. ⟪↔ karyuu⟫
2 the upper class. ⟪⇨ chuuryuu; kasoo⟫

jo⌈osee じょうせい(情勢) *n.* the state of affairs; situation; conditions.

jo⌈osha じょうしゃ(乗車) *n.* boarding a train [bus]; taking a taxi.
joosha suru (~する) *vt.* get on a train [bus, etc.]. ⟪↔ gesha⟫ ⟪⇨ noru[1]⟫

jo⌈osha⌉keñ じょうしゃけん(乗車券) *n.* train [bus] ticket.

jo⌉oshi じょうし(上司) *n.* one's superior; boss.

jo⌈oshiki じょうしき(常識) *n.* common knowledge; common sense.
jooshiki hazure (~はずれ) eccentric; absurd: jooshiki hazure *no furumai* (常識はずれの振る舞い) *senseless* behavior.

jo⌈oshiki-teki じょうしきてき(常識的) *a.n.* (~ na, ni) commonsense; practical; ordinary; commonplace:
Sono nedañ wa jooshiki-teki *da to omou.* (その値段は常識的だと思う) I think that price is *reasonable.*

jo⌈oshoo じょうしょう(上昇) *n.*

rise; ascent.
jooshoo suru (～する) *vi.* rise; go up. ⟪↔ kakoo[2]; teeka[1]⟫

jo⌈otai じょうたい (状態) *n.* state; condition:
Kono ie wa hidoi jootai *da.* (この家はひどい状態だ) This house is in a bad *state.*

jo⌈otoo じょうとう (上等) *a.n.* (～ na, ni) of good quality; excellent.

jo⌈owañ じょうわん (上腕) *n.* upper arm. ⟪⇨ ude⟫

jo⌈oyaku じょうやく (条約) *n.* treaty:
jooyaku *ni chooiñ suru* (条約に調印する) sign a *treaty.*

jo⌈oyoo-ka⌉ñji じょうようかんじ (常用漢字) *n.* Chinese characters in common use. ★ The 1945 characters designated by the Cabinet in 1981 for everyday use. ⟪⇨ kañji[2]⟫

jo⌈ozu⌉ じょうず (上手) *a.n.* (～ na, ni) good; well:
Nakanaka joozu *ni utaenai.* (なかなかじょうずに歌えない) I can't sing at all *well.* ⟪↔ heta⟫ ⟪⇨ umai⟫

jo⌈see じょせい (女性) *n.* adult woman; lady; female. ★ A more refined word than '*oñna*,' which often sounds rude. ⟪↔ dañsee⟫ ⟪⇨ fujiñ[2]; joshi[1]; oñna⟫

jo⌈see-teki じょせいてき (女性的) *a.n.* (～ na, ni) (of women, men and things) womanly, feminine; womanish. ⟪↔ dañsee-teki⟫ ⟪⇨ oñnarashii⟫

jo⌉shi[1] じょし (女子) *n.* **1** girl.
2 woman; lady; female. ⟪↔ dañshi⟫ ⟪⇨ fujiñ[2]; josee; oñna⟫

jo⌈shi[2] じょし (助詞) *n.* (postpositional) particle. ⟪⇨ APP. 2⟫

jo⌈shidai じょしだい (女子大) *n.* women's university. ★ Shortened form of '*joshi-daigaku.*'

jo⌈shi-da⌉igaku じょしだいがく (女子大学) *n.* women's university. ⟪⇨ daigaku; joshidai⟫

jo⌈shu じょしゅ (助手) *n.* assistant; helper; tutor.

jo⌈yuu じょゆう (女優) *n.* actress. ⟪⇨ haiyuu⟫

ju⌉gyoo じゅぎょう (授業) *n.* lesson; class; school:
Señsee wa Nihoñgo de jugyoo (*o*) *shita.* (先生は日本語で授業(を)した) The teacher conducted her *class* in Japanese.

ju⌈keñ じゅけん (受験) *n.* taking an (entrance) examination.
jukeñ suru (～する) *vt.* take an (entrance) examination.

ju⌈kugo じゅくご (熟語) *n.* **1** compound word consisting of two or more Chinese characters. *e.g.* 手荷物 (*tenimotsu*), 登山 (*tozañ*).
2 idiom; set phrase.

ju⌈ku⌉s·u じゅくす (熟す) *vi.* (jukush·i-; jukus·a-; jukush·i-te Ⓒ)
1 ripen:
Kono kaki wa jukushite iru. (この柿は熟している) This persimmon *is ripe.*
2 (of opportunity, etc.) be ripe:
Ki no jukusu *no o matoo.* (機の熟すのを待とう) Let's wait until the time *is ripe.*

ju⌈myoo じゅみょう (寿命) *n.* life span; life:
jumyoo ga nagai [mijikai] (寿命が長い[短い]) be *long-lived* [*short-lived*].
jumyoo ga chijimaru (～が縮まる) one's life is shortened: *Sono jiko de* jumyoo ga chijimatta. (その事故で寿命が縮まった) The accident *took years off my life.*

ju⌈ñ[1] じゅん (順) *n.* order; turn:
Se no takai juñ *ni narabi nasai.* (背の高い順に並びなさい) Line up in *order* of height. ⟪⇨ juñbañ; juñjo⟫
juñ o otte (～を追って) in the proper order.

ju⌉ñ[2] じゅん (純) *a.n.* (～ na) pure; innocent; simplehearted:
Juñ *na hito hodo damasare-yasui.* (純な人ほどだまされやすい) Those who are *unsophisticated* are apt to be taken in easily.

juñ-[1] じゅん (準) *pref.* quasi-;

semi-; associate:
juñ-*kyuu* (*ressha*) (準急(列車)) a *semi*-express train / juñ-*kesshoo* (準決勝) a *semi*-final match [game].

ju⌈ñ-[2] じゅん (純) *pref.* pure; all: juñ-*kiñ* (純金) *pure* gold / juñ-*moo* (純毛) *all* wool.

ju⌈ñbañ じゅんばん (順番) *n.* one's turn:
narañde, juñbañ *o matsu* (並んで, 順番を待つ) line up and wait for one's *turn.*

ju⌉ñbi じゅんび (準備) *n.* preparation; arrangements.

ju⌈ñchoo じゅんちょう (順調) *a.n.* (~ na, ni) smooth; favorable; all right:
Shujutsu-go no keeka wa juñchoo *desu.* (手術後の経過は順調です) Post-operative progress has been *satisfactory.*

ju⌈ñeñ じゅんえん (順延) *n.* postponement of something scheduled.
juñeñ suru (~する) *vt.* postpone; put off. ⟪⇨ nobasu[2]⟫

ju⌉ñjo じゅんじょ (順序) *n.* order:
Juñjo *ga gyaku desu.* (順序が逆です) The *order* is reversed. ⟪⇨ jun[1]⟫

ju⌈ñjoo じゅんじょう (純情) *a.n.* (~ na) unsophisticated; naive; pure.

ju⌈ñju⌉ñ ni じゅんじゅんに (順々に) *adv.* one by one.

ju⌈ñkañ じゅんかん (循環) *n.* circulation; rotation.
juñkañ suru (~する) *vi.* circulate; cycle. ⟪⇨ mawaru⟫

ju⌈ñkyuu じゅんきゅう (準急) *n.* semi-express train. ⟪⇨ kyuukoo[1]⟫

ju⌉ñsa じゅんさ (巡査) *n.* policeman (the lowest rank in the police).

ju⌈ñsui じゅんすい (純粋) *a.n.* (~ na, ni) pure; genuine:
juñsui *na Akita-keñ* (純粋な秋田犬) a *pure-blooded* Akita dog.

ju⌈tsugo じゅつご (術語) *n.* technical term.

ju⌉u[1] じゅう (十) *n.* ten.
jut-chuu hakku (~中八九) highly likely to occur.
⟪⇨ too[1]; APP. 3⟫

ju⌉u[2] じゅう (銃) *n.* gun; rifle.

-juu[1] じゅう (中) *suf.* **1** through; throughout:
*Ichinichi-*juu *ame ga futta.* (一日中雨が降った) It rained *all* day *long.* ⟪⇨ -chuu⟫
2 all over:
*Kare wa sekai-*juu *o ryokoo shita.* (彼は世界中を旅行した) He has traveled *all over* the world.

-juu[2] じゅう (重) *suf.* -fold:
ni-juu no (二重の) *twofold* / sañ-juu no (三重の) *threefold* / go-juu-no-*too* (五重の塔) a *five-storied* pagoda.

ju⌈ubu⌉ñ じゅうぶん (十分) *a.n.* (~ na, ni) enough; sufficient; ample:
Jikañ wa juubuñ *ni arimasu.* (時間は十分にあります) We have *plenty of* time. ⟪↔ fujuubuñ⟫
— *adv.* enough; to the full; thoroughly:
Añzeñ ni juubuñ *go-chuui kudasai.* (安全に十分ご注意ください) Please pay *close* attention to safety.

ju⌈udai じゅうだい (重大) *a.n.* (~ na) serious; important; grave:
Kare no sekiniñ wa juudai *desu.* (彼の責任は重大です) His responsibility is *great.*

ju⌈udeñ じゅうでん (充電) *n.* charge of electricity.
juudeñ suru (~する) *vt.* charge.

ju⌉udoo じゅうどう (柔道) *n.* judo.

ju⌈ufuku じゅうふく (重複) *n.* = choofuku.

ju⌈u-gatsu⌉ じゅうがつ (十月) *n.* October. ⟪⇨ APP. 5⟫

ju⌈ugoya じゅうごや (十五夜) *n.* a full moon night.

ju⌈ugyo⌉oiñ じゅうぎょういん (従業員) *n.* employee; worker.
⟪⇨ shaiñ⟫

ju⌈uichi-gatsu⌉ じゅういちがつ (十

一月) *n.* November. ⟪⇨ APP. 5⟫

ju⌈uji⌉ro じゅうじろ(十字路) *n.* crossroads. ⟪⇨ **koosateñ**⟫

ju⌈ujitsu じゅうじつ(充実) *n.* fullness; substantiality.
juujitsu suru (〜する) *vi.* be rich in content: *Kono gakkoo wa uñdoo shisetsu ga* juujitsu shite iru. (この学校は運動施設が充実している) This school has a *full range* of sports facilities.

ju⌉ukyo じゅうきょ(住居) *n.* dwelling; residence. ⟪⇨ **sumai**⟫

ju⌈umiñ じゅうみん(住民) *n.* inhabitant; dweller; resident.

ju⌈uni-gatsu⌉ じゅうにがつ(十二月) *n.* December. ⟪⇨ APP. 5⟫

ju⌈uni⌉shi じゅうにし(十二支) *n.* the twelve Chinese year signs.

ju⌉usho じゅうしょ(住所) *n.* one's address; one's dwelling place.

ju⌉usu ジュース *n.* soft drink; juice. ★ Usually refers to sweetened and flavored carbonated drinks. Fruit and vegetable juice is called '*nama* (*no*) *juusu*' (fresh juice).

ju⌈utaku じゅうたく(住宅) *n.* house; housing.

ju⌉utañ じゅうたん(絨毯) *n.* carpet; rug.

ju⌈uteñ じゅうてん(重点) *n.* stress; importance; priority:
Kono gakkoo de wa supootsu ni juuteñ *o oite iru.* (この学校ではスポーツに重点を置いている) This school lays *stress* on sports.

ju⌈uteñ-teki じゅうてんてき(重点的) *a.n.* (〜 **na, ni**) intensive; preponderant:
juuteñ-teki *ni soosaku suru* (重点的に捜索する) make an *intensive* search.

ju⌈uyaku じゅうやく(重役) *n.* corporate executive; company director.

ju⌈uyoo じゅうよう(重要) *a.n.* (〜 **na**) important; major; essential.

ju⌈uyu じゅうゆ(重油) *n.* heavy oil. ⟪↔ **keeyu**[2]⟫

ju⌈wa⌉ki じゅわき(受話器) *n.* (telephone) receiver.

ju⌈yoo じゅよう(需要) *n.* demand; request:
Kyookyuu ga juyoo *ni oitsukanai.* (供給が需要に追いつかない) The supply does not meet the *demand.* ⟪↔ **kyookyuu**⟫

ju⌈yo⌉osha じゅようしゃ(需要者) *n.* consumer; user; customer.

K

ka[1] か(蚊) *n.* mosquito.

ka⌉[2] か(可) *n.* **1** (of a grade rating) being passable; C or D in schoolwork. ⟪⇨ **fuka**; **ryoo**[3]; **yuu**[2]⟫
2 (*formal*) approval. ⟪↔ **ina**⟫

ka[3] か *p.* **1** (used to make questions): ★ Changes an ordinary declarative sentence to an interrogative sentence.
Anata wa Tanaka-sañ desu ka*?* (あなたは田中さんですか) *Are you* Mrs. Tanaka?
2 won't you...; what about...; shall I [we]...: ★ Used in invitations, requests or proposals.
Koohii de mo nomimaseñ ka*?* (コーヒーでも飲みませんか) *Won't you have* a coffee, or something?
3 I wonder: ★ Used with the tentative of the copula.
Ashita wa teñki ni naru daroo ka*?* (あしたは天気になるだろうか) *I wonder* if it will be fine tomorrow.
4 (used rhetorically when confirming a fact to oneself):
Are, moo koñna jikañ ka. (あれ, もうこんな時間か) What! *Is it* already *so late*?
5 (used rhetorically when encouraging oneself to do some-

thing):
Sorosoro kaeru ka. (そろそろ帰るか) I *must be off on my way* now.
6 (used when questioning or refuting someone's opinion):
Soñna kodomo ni nani ga dekiru ka. (そんな子どもに何ができるか) *What can* a child like that *do*?

ka[4] か *p.* **1** (used after interrogatives to form indefinites):
Nani-ka *tsumetai mono o kudasai.* (何か冷たいものを下さい) Please give me *something* cold to drink.
2 perhaps [probably] because: ★ Used to indicate a possible reason or cause.
Tsukarete iru see ka *shokuyoku ga arimaseñ.* (疲れているせいか食欲がありません) *Perhaps* it is *because* I am tired, but I have no appetite.
3 or: ★ Used when listing examples from among two or more alternatives.
Kyooto ka *Nara e ikitai.* (京都か奈良へ行きたい) I want to go to *either* Kyoto *or* Nara.
4 (used with embedded questions):
Tsugi no deñsha wa nañ-ji ni deru ka *shitte imasu ka?* (次の電車は何時に出るか知っていますか) Do you know *what time the next train leaves*?
5 whether or...; whether or not: ★ Used with embedded alternate questions.
Kare ni heñji o dashita ka, *doo* ka *oboete imaseñ.* (彼に返事を出したか, どうか覚えていません) I can't remember *whether* I sent him the answer *or not*. ★ Note that '*ka*' can be followed by other particles, particularly '*wa*,' '*ga*' and '*o*.' *e.g.* Doko e iku ka wa, *mada kimete imaseñ.* (どこへ行くかは, まだ決めていません) I have not yet decided *where to go.* / Doo kaiketsu suru ka ga, *moñdai desu.* (どう解決するかが, 問題です) The problem is *how we are going to solve it.*

-ka[1] か(日) *suf.* day:
futsu-ka (二日) the 2nd (*day*); two *days* / *too*-ka (十日) the 10th (*day*); ten *days.* 《⇨ APP. 5》

-ka[2] か(下) *suf.* under; below:
... *no shihai*-ka (...の支配下) *under* the rule of... / *ree-ka* (零下) *below* zero (degrees).

-ka[3] か(化) *suf.* -ization: ★ A change into the stated condition.
eega-ka (映画化) *making* into a movie / goori-ka (合理化) *rationalization.*
-ka suru (~する) *vt., vi.* -ize:
kikai-ka suru (機械化する) *mechanize.*

-ka[4] か(科) *suf.* course; department; studies:
Nihoñgo gak-ka (日本語学科) a Japanese language *course* / *nai*-ka (内科) the *department* of internal medicine.

-ka[5] か(課) *suf.* **1** lesson; work:
dai ik-ka (第一課) *Lesson* 1 / *nik*-ka (日課) daily *work.*
2 section (of a company): *jiñji*-ka (人事課) the personnel *section.*

-ka[6] か(家) *suf.* **1** (signifies a possessor):
shihoñ-ka (資本家) a *capitalist.*
2 a person of the stated quality or tendency:
kuusoo-ka (空想家) a *dreamer.*
3 specialist:
oñgaku-ka (音楽家) a *musician.*

-ka[7] か(箇) *suf.* counter used with numerals: ★ Sometimes 'ケ' is used instead of 'か.'
ni-ka-*getsu* (二か月) *two* months / go-ka-*koku* (五か国) *five* countries.

ka]asañ かあさん(母さん) *n.* (*informal*) momma; mother.
★ Usually with '*o*-.' 《↔ toosañ》 《⇨ haha; haha-oya; o-kaasañ》

ka]baa カバー *n.* **1** cover; covering:
sofaa ni kabaa *o kakeru* (ソファーにカバーをかける) put a *cover* on the sofa.
2 dust jacket; wrapper.

k

《⇨ hyooshi》

kabaa suru (〜する) *vt.* **1** cover; make up: *akaji o* kabaa suru (赤字をカバーする) *make up* the deficit.
2 (of baseball) cover; back up.

ka⌈bañ かばん (鞄) *n.* bag; satchel; briefcase.

ka⌈ba⌉·u かばう (庇う) *vt.* (kaba·i-; kabaw·a-; kabat-te Ⓒ) protect; defend:
Dare mo kanojo o kabawanakatta. (だれも彼女をかばわなかった) *Nobody pleaded* for her.

ka⌈bayaki かばやき (蒲焼き) *n.* broiled eels. ★ Eels are split and barbecued over a charcoal fire. 《⇨ unagi》

ka⌈be かべ (壁) *n.* **1** wall.
2 obstacle; deadlock:
Jiñshu-moñdai ga kabe *ni natte iru.* (人種問題が壁になっている) The racial problem constitutes an *obstacle.*

ka⌈bi かび (黴) *n.* mold.

ka⌈biñ かびん (花瓶) *n.* flower vase.

ka⌈bocha かぼちゃ *n.* pumpkin; squash.

ka⌈bu[1] かぶ (株) *n.* **1** stock; share. 《⇨ kabukeñ; kabunushi》
2 roots; stump:
*Pañjii no nae o sañ-*kabu *katta.* (パンジーの苗を3株買った) I bought three pansy *seedlings.*

ka⌈bu[2] かぶ (蕪) *n.* turnip.

ka⌈bukeñ かぶけん (株券) *n.* stock [share] certificate.

ka⌈buki かぶき (歌舞伎) *n.* Japanese traditional drama.

ka⌈bu⌉nushi かぶぬし (株主) *n.* stockholder; shareholder. 《⇨ kabu[1]》

ka⌈bu⌉r·u かぶる (被る) *vt.* (kabur·i-; kabur·a-; kabut-te Ⓒ)
1 put on (headwear): ★ '*kabutte iru*'=wear.
Giñkoo-gootoo wa fukumeñ o kabutte ita. (銀行強盗は覆面をかぶっていた) The bank robber *wore* a mask. 《⇨ kabuseru》
2 be covered:
hokori o kaburu (ほこりをかぶる) *be covered* with dust. 《⇨ kabuseru》
3 take on (responsibility):
Kare wa hitori de sono jikeñ no sekiniñ o kabutta. (彼は一人でその事件の責任をかぶった) He alone *took* responsibility for the affair.

ka⌈buse⌉·ru かぶせる (被せる) *vt.* (kabuse-te Ⓥ) put...on; cover...with:
kodomo ni booshi o kabuseru (子どもに帽子をかぶせる) *put* a cap on a child's head. 《⇨ kaburu》

ka⌈bushikiga⌉isha かぶしきがいしゃ (株式会社) *n.* incorporated company; joint-stock company. 《⇨ kaisha》

ka⌉chi[1] かち (価値) *n.* worth; value; merit. 《⇨ neuchi》

ka⌈chi⌉[2] かち (勝ち) *n.* victory. 《↔ make》

ka⌈chikachi[1] かちかち *a.n.* (〜 no, ni) **1** be frozen hard:
Ike (*no mizu*) *ga* kachikachi *ni kootte iru.* (池(の水)がかちかちに凍っている) The (water in the) pond is frozen *hard.*
2 tense:
Sono oñna-no-ko wa kiñchoo shite, kachikachi *ni natte ita.* (その女の子は緊張して，かちかちになっていた) The girl was *rigid* with tension.

ka⌉chikachi[2] カチカチ *adv.* (〜 to) (tick of a clock):
Kono tokee wa amari kachikachi (*to*) *iwanai.* (この時計はあまりカチカチ(と)いわない) This clock hardly makes any *ticking sound.*

ka⌈chiku かちく (家畜) *n.* livestock; domestic animal.

ka⌈choo かちょう (課長) *n.* section chief; manager.

ka⌈dai かだい (課題) *n.* **1** problem; question.
2 assignment:
natsu-yasumi no kadai (夏休みの課題) *assignments* for the summer vacation.

ka⌉do[1] かど (角) *n.* corner.

ka˥do[2] かど (過度) *a.n.* (~ no, ni) excessive; too much:
Kado *no kitai wa kiñmotsu desu.* (過度の期待は禁物です) You should not expect *too much.*

ka˥do˥matsu かどまつ (門松) *n.* New Year's pine decorations.

ka˥eri˥ かえり (帰り) *n.* return:
Koñya wa kaeri *ga osoku narimasu.* (今夜は帰りが遅くなります) I will *be coming home* late this evening. ⟪↔ iki[2]; yuki[2]⟫

ka˥erimi˥·ru かえりみる (顧みる) *vt.* (kaerimi-te [V]) **1** look back on:
jibuñ no kako o kaerimiru (自分の過去を顧みる) *look back on* one's past.
2 think of; pay attention:
Isogashikute, kazoku o kaerimiru *hima mo nakatta.* (忙しくて, 家族を顧みるひまもなかった) I was so busy that I did not even have time to *consider* my family.

ka˥er·u[1] かえる (帰る) *vi.* (kaer·i-; kaer·a-; kaet-te [C]) (of a person) come back; return:
Moo kaeranakereba *narimaseñ.* (もう帰らなければなりません) I *must be going* now. ⟪↔ iku⟫ ⟪⇨ modoru⟫

ka˥er·u[2] かえる (返る) *vi.* (kaer·i-; kaer·a-; kaet-te [C]) (of an object) return; get back:
Nusumareta e wa buji ni mochinushi no tokoro e kaetta. (盗まれた絵は無事に持ち主の所へ返った) The stolen picture *was* safely *returned* to its owner. ⟪⇨ modoru⟫

ka˥e·ru[3] かえる (変える) *vt.* (kae-te [V]) change; alter:
Taifuu wa shiñro o kaeta. (台風は進路を変えた) The typhoon *altered* its course. ⟪⇨ kawaru[1]⟫

ka˥e·ru[4] かえる (代える·替える·換える) *vt.* (kae-te [V]) change:
ichimañ-eñ satsu o señ-eñ satsu ni kaeru (一万円札を千円札にかえる) *change* a 10,000-yen bill into 1,000-yen bills. ⟪⇨ kawaru[2]⟫

ka˥er·u[5] かえる (孵る) *vi.* (kaer·i-; kaer·a-; kaet-te [C]) hatch; be hatched.

ka˥eru[6] かえる (蛙) *n.* frog; toad.

ka˥es·u かえす (返す) *vt.* (kaesh·i-; kaes·a-; kaesh·i-te [C]) return; give back. ⟪⇨ modosu⟫

ka˥ette かえって (却って) *adv.* on the contrary; after all; rather:
Kuruma yori aruita hoo ga, kaette *hayai koto ga arimasu.* (車より歩いたほうが, かえって早いことがあります) Walking, *rather* than going by car, is sometimes quicker.

ka˥fuñshoo かふんしょう (花粉症) *n.* hay fever; pollen allergy.

ka˥gaku[1] かがく (科学) *n.* science.

ka˥gaku[2] かがく (化学) *n.* chemistry. ★ Sometimes called '*bakegaku*' to distinguish it from '*kagaku*[1].'

ka˥ga˥kusha[1] かがくしゃ (科学者) *n.* scientist.

ka˥ga˥kusha[2] かがくしゃ (化学者) *n.* chemist.

ka˥gaku-teki かがくてき (科学的) *a.n.* (~ na, ni) scientific:
kagaku-teki *ni setsumee suru* (科学的に説明する) explain something *scientifically.*

ka˥game·ru かがめる (屈める) *vt.* (kagame-te [V]) bend; stoop:
mi o kagameru (身をかがめる) *bend down.* ⟪⇨ kagamu⟫

ka˥gami˥ かがみ (鏡) *n.* mirror; looking glass.

ka˥gami˥-mochi かがみもち (鏡餅) *n.* round rice cake offered to gods at New Year's time. ⟪⇨ mochi⟫

ka˥gam·u かがむ (屈む) *vi.* (kagam·i-; kagam·a-; kagañ-de [C]) bend; stoop; crouch:
kagañde *kusa o toru* (かがんで草を取る) *bend down* and pull up the weeds. ⟪⇨ kagameru⟫

ka˥gayaki˥ かがやき (輝き) *n.* brightness; brilliance; radiance. ⟪⇨ kagayaku⟫

ka˥gaya˥k·u かがやく (輝く) *vi.* (-yak·i-; -yak·a-; -ya·i-te [C]) **1** shine; flash; glitter; twinkle.

2 be radiant; sparkle:
Shoojo no kao wa yorokobi de kagayaite ita. (少女の顔は喜びで輝いていた) The girl's face *was radiant* with joy.

ka⌉ge[1] かげ (影) *n.* **1** shadow.
2 silhouette:
Shooji ni hito no kage *ga utsutta.* (障子に人の影が映った) *The outline of a figure* was cast onto the paper sliding door.
3 reflection:
Mizuumi ni yama no kage *ga utsutte iru.* (湖に山の影が映っている) The *image* of the mountain is reflected in the lake.

ka⌉ge[2] かげ (陰) *n.* **1** shade.
2 back; rear:
Otoko wa kaateñ no kage *ni kakureta.* (男はカーテンの陰に隠れた) The man hid *behind* the curtain.
3 behind one's back; behind the scenes.

ka⌈geki かげき (過激) *a.n.* (~ na, ni) extreme; radical:
kageki *na shisoo* (過激な思想) *radical* ideology.

ka⌈geñ かげん (加減) *n.* **1** addition and subtraction.
2 state; condition:
Kyoo no kañja no kageñ wa yosa [waru]-soo da. (きょうの患者のかげんは良さ[悪]そうだ) The *condition* of the patient today seems to be good [bad].
kageñ suru (~する) *vt.* regulate; adjust (something physical):
heya no oñdo o kageñ suru (部屋の温度を加減する) *regulate* the temperature of the room.

ka⌈gi⌉ かぎ (鍵) *n.* key. ★ Can also refer to a lock. ⟪⇨ aikagi⟫

ka⌈giri⌉ かぎり (限り) *n.* **1** limit:
Niñgeñ no yokuboo ni wa kagiri *ga nai.* (人間の欲望には限りがない) There are no *bounds* to human greed. ⟪⇨ kagiru⟫
2 end:
Kono teñrañkai wa koñgetsu-kagiri *de owari desu.* (この展覧会は今月限りで終わりです) This exhibition finishes at the *end* of this month.
... kagiri (...~) as long as; as far as: *Miwatasu* kagiri, *umi ga hirogatte ita.* (見渡す限り, 海が広がっていた) The sea extended *as far as* the eye could see.

ka⌈gi⌉r·u かぎる (限る) *vt.* (kagir·i-; kagir·a-; kagit-te Ⓒ)
1 limit; restrict:
Kono shoohiñ wa kazu ga kagirarete imasu. (この商品は数が限られています) These goods *are limited* in quantity. ⟪⇨ kagiri⟫
2 be (the) best; be (the) most suitable:
Natsu wa biiru ni kagirimasu. (夏はビールに限ります) In summer *there is nothing like* beer.
... ni kagiri (...に限り) just: Koñdo ni kagiri, *muryoo to shimasu.* (今度に限り, 無料とします) *Just this once*, we will make it free.
... ni kagitte (...に限って) be the last person: Kare ni kagitte, *soñna koto wa shimaseñ.* (彼に限って, そんなことはしません) *He is the last person* to do a thing like that.

ka⌈go かご (籠) *n.* basket; cage.

ka⌈goo かごう (化合) *n.* chemical combination.
kagoo suru (~する) *vi.* combine with.

ka⌉gu[1] かぐ (家具) *n.* furniture.

ka⌈g·u[2] かぐ (嗅ぐ) *vt.* (kag·i-; kag·a-; ka·i-de Ⓒ) smell; scent; sniff:
Kanojo wa bara no hana no nioi o kaida. (彼女はばらの花のにおいをかいだ) She *smelled* the roses.

ka⌈ha⌉ñsuu かはんすう (過半数) *n.* majority; the greater number.

ka⌉hee かへい (貨幣) *n.* money; currency. ⟪⇨ kane[1]⟫

ka⌉i[1] かい (会) *n.* **1** meeting; party; assembly; gathering.
2 society; club:
Yamada-shi o ooeñ suru kai *o tsukutta.* (山田氏を応援する会をつくった)

We organized a *society* in support of Mr. Yamada.

kaʹi² かい (貝) *n.* shellfish; shell.

-kai¹ かい (回) *n.* **1** time:
Watashi wa ik-kagetsu ni ni-kai *Oosaka e ikimasu.* (私は1か月に2回大阪へ行きます) I go to Osaka *twice* a month. (⇨ -do)
2 (of baseball) inning.

-kai² かい (界) *suf.* community; world; circle; kingdom:
buñgaku-kai (文学界) the literary *world* / *keezai*-kai (経済界) financial *circles.*

-kai³ かい (階) *n.* **1** (used for counting floors):
ik-kai (1階) the first *floor* / *ni*-kai (2階) the second *floor.* ★ The floors of a house or a building are counted in the same way as in the U.S.A., the ground floor being the first floor.
2 (used for naming floors):
Omocha wa go-kai *de utte imasu.* (おもちゃは5階で売っています) Toys are sold on the fifth *floor.*
(⇨ APP. 4)

-kai⁴ かい (会) *suf.* party; gathering:
kañgee-kai (歓迎会) a welcome *party* / *soobetsu*-kai (送別会) a farewell *party.*

-kai⁵ かい (海) *suf.* sea:
Nihoñ-kai (日本海) the *Sea* of Japan / *Kasupi*-kai (カスピ海) the Caspian *Sea.*

kaʹiageʹ·ru かいあげる (買い上げる) *vt.* (-age-te [V]) (of a government) buy; purchase:
Seefu wa kome o nooka kara kaiagete iru. (政府は米を農家から買い上げている) The government *purchases* rice from farmers. (⇨ kau¹)

kaʹichoo かいちょう (会長) *n.* the president (of a company); the chairman (of a corporation).

kaʹichuudeʹñtoo かいちゅうでんとう (懐中電灯) *n.* flashlight; electric torch.

kaʹichuudoʹkee かいちゅうどけい (懐中時計) *n.* pocket watch.

kaʹidañ¹ かいだん (階段) *n.* stairs; steps; staircase.

kaʹidañ² かいだん (会談) *n.* talks; conference.
... to kaidañ suru (...と～する) *vi.* talk together with; confer with.

kaʹifuku かいふく (回復) *n.* **1** recovery:
Kare no kaifuku *wa hayakatta.* (彼の回復は早かった) He made a quick *recovery.*
2 restoration:
shiñyoo no kaifuku *o hakaru* (信用の回復を図る) seek to *restore* one's reputation.
kaifuku suru (～する) *vt., vi.* restore; improve; recover.

kaʹiga かいが (絵画) *n.* picture; painting. (⇨ e¹; egaku)

kaʹigai かいがい (海外) *n.* lands beyond the sea; overseas countries:
kaigai-*ryokoo* (海外旅行) an *overseas* trip. (↔ kokunai) (⇨ kokugai)

kaʹigañ かいがん (海岸) *n.* seashore; coast; beach.

kaʹigara かいがら (貝殻) *n.* seashell.

kaʹigi かいぎ (会議) *n.* conference; meeting; council:
Kare wa kaigi-*chuu desu.* (彼は会議中です) He is in *conference.*

kaʹigo かいご (介護) *n.* nursing; care.
kaigo suru (～する) *vt.* nurse; look after; care for.

kaʹigoo かいごう (会合) *n.* meeting; gathering; assembly.

kaʹiguñ かいぐん (海軍) *n.* navy; naval forces. (⇨ Jieetai; kuuguñ; rikuguñ)

kaʹihatsu かいはつ (開発) *n.* development; exploitation.
kaihatsu suru (～する) *vt.* develop; exploit.

kaʹihoo¹ かいほう (解放) *n.* release; liberation.
kaihoo suru (～する) *vt.* release;

k

free; liberate: *hitojichi o* kaihoo suru (人質を解放する) *free* hostages.

ka⌈ihoo[2] かいほう (開放) *n.* opening.
kaihoo suru (～する) *vt.* be open (to the public); leave open.

ka⌈ihyoo かいひょう (開票) *n.* ballot [vote] counting.
kaihyoo suru (～する) *vi.* count the ballots [votes].

ka⌈iiñ かいいん (会員) *n.* member; membership.

ka⌈ijoo[1] かいじょう (会場) *n.* meeting place; site.

ka⌈ijoo[2] かいじょう (海上) *n.* the sea:
Sono booto wa kaijoo *o hyooryuu shita.* (そのボートは海上を漂流した) The boat was adrift on *the sea.*
《⇨ kuuchuu; rikujoo》

k

ka⌈ikai かいかい (開会) *n.* the opening of a meeting [session].
kaikai suru (～する) *vi.*, *vt.* open a meeting. 《↔ heekai》

ka⌈ikaku かいかく (改革) *n.* reform; revision.
kaikaku suru (～する) *vt.* reform; revise: *zeesee o* kaikaku suru (税制を改革する) *make reforms* in the taxation system.

ka⌈ikee かいけい (会計) *n.* **1** accounts; accounting.
2 payment; check; bill:
Kaikee *wa sumasemashita.* (会計は済ませました) I paid the *bill.*
《⇨ shiharai》

ka⌈ikeñ かいけん (会見) *n.* interview.
kaikeñ suru (～する) *vi.* have an interview.

ka⌈iketsu かいけつ (解決) *n.* solution; settlement.
kaiketsu suru (～する) *vi.*, *vt.* solve; settle; clear up.

ka⌉iko かいこ (解雇) *n.* dismissal; discharge; layoff.
kaiko suru (～する) *vt.* dismiss; lay off. 《⇨ kubi》

ka⌈ikyoo かいきょう (海峡) *n.* strait; channel:
Tsugaru-kaikyoo (津軽海峡) the Tsugaru *Straits.*

Ka⌉ikyoo かいきょう (回教) *n.* Islam.

ka⌈ikyuu かいきゅう (階級) *n.*
1 class:
jooryuu [chuuryuu; kasoo] kaikyuu (上流[中流; 下層]階級) the upper [middle; lower] *class.*
2 rank.

ka⌈imono かいもの (買い物) *n.* shopping; purchase:
yasui [takai] kaimono *o suru* (安い[高い]買い物をする) make a good [bad] *purchase.*

ka⌈inañ かいなん (海難) *n.* shipwreck; sea disaster; marine accident.

ka⌈iryoo かいりょう (改良) *n.* improvement; reform.
kairyoo suru (～する) *vt.* improve; reform. 《⇨ kaizeñ》

ka⌈iryuu かいりゅう (海流) *n.* ocean current:
Nihoñ-kairyuu (日本海流) the Japan *Current.*

ka⌈isai かいさい (開催) *n.* holding (of a conference, exhibition, etc.).
kaisai suru (～する) *vt.* hold; open. 《⇨ hiraku》

ka⌈isañ かいさん (解散) *n.* breakup; dissolution.
kaisañ suru (～する) *vi.*, *vt.* break up (a meeting); dissolve.

ka⌈isatsu かいさつ (改札) *n.* examination of tickets.
kaisatsu suru (～する) *vt.* punch [inspect] tickets.

ka⌈isee[1] かいせい (改正) *n.* revision; amendment.
kaisee suru (～する) *vt.* revise; amend: *keñpoo o* kaisee suru (憲法を改正する) *amend* the constitution.

ka⌈isee[2] かいせい (快晴) *n.* fine weather. 《⇨ teñki》

ka⌈isetsu[1] かいせつ (解説) *n.* explanation; commentary (by an expert).
kaisetsu suru (～する) *vt.* explain,

comment: *jiji-mondai o* kaisetsu suru (時事問題を解説する) *comment* on current events.

ka⌈isetsu[2] かいせつ (開設) *n.* establishment; foundation; inauguration.

kaisetsu suru (〜する) *vt.* establish; set up: *jibuñ no jimusho o* kaisetsu suru (自分の事務所を開設する) *set up* one's own office.

ka⌈isha かいしゃ (会社) *n.* **1** company; corporation; firm.

2 office:

Kaisha *o deru no wa roku-ji-goro desu.* (会社を出るのは6時ごろです) It is at about six o'clock that I leave the *office.*

ka⌈isha⌉iñ かいしゃいん (会社員) *n.* company employee; office worker. ★ Considered an occupational category.

ka⌉ishaku かいしゃく (解釈) *n.* interpretation; explanation.

kaishaku suru (〜する) *vt.* interpret; construe.

ka⌈ishi かいし (開始) *n.* beginning; start; opening.

kaishi suru (〜する) *vt.* begin; start; open. ⟪↔ shuuryoo⟫ ⟪⇨ hajimeru⟫

ka⌈ishoo かいしょう (解消) *n.* cancellation; annulment.

kaishoo suru (〜する) *vt.* cancel (a contract); annul; break off.

ka⌈isu⌉iyoku かいすいよく (海水浴) *n.* sea bathing.

ka⌈isu⌉u かいすう (回数) *n.* the number of times; frequency: *Basu no deru* kaisuu *wa ichi-jikañ ni ni-hoñ desu.* (バスの出る回数は1時間に2本です) The bus runs twice each hour.

ka⌈isu⌉ukeñ かいすうけん (回数券) *n.* coupon; ticket: *juu-mai tsuzuri no* kaisuukeñ (十枚つづりの回数券) a book of 10 *bus* [*train*] *tickets.*

ka⌈itaku かいたく (開拓) *n.* **1** reclamation; cultivation.

2 opening up.

kaitaku suru (〜する) *vt.* **1** reclaim; cultivate: *arechi o* kaitaku suru (荒れ地を開拓する) *cultivate* waste land.

2 open up a new field [market, etc.]: *atarashii shijoo o* kaitaku suru (新しい市場を開拓する) *develop* a new market.

ka⌈iteñ[1] かいてん (回転) *n.* **1** revolution; rotation; spin: kaiteñ-*doa* (回転ドア) a *revolving* door.

2 turnover; circulation: *Ano mise wa kyaku no* kaiteñ *ga ii.* (あの店は客の回転がいい) That store has a *constant flow* of customers.

kaiteñ suru (〜する) *vi.* **1** revolve; rotate; spin.

2 circulate; turn over.

ka⌈iteñ[2] かいてん (開店) *n.* opening of a store.

kaiteñ suru (〜する) *vt., vi.* open [set up] a store.

ka⌈itoo[1] かいとう (回答) *n.* reply; answer.

kaitoo suru (〜する) *vt.* reply; answer: *buñsho de* kaitoo suru (文書で回答する) *reply* in writing.

ka⌈itoo[2] かいとう (解答) *n.* solution; answer.

kaitoo (o) suru (〜(を)する) *vt.* answer; solve. ⟪⇨ toku[1]⟫.

ka⌈itoo[3] かいとう (解凍) *n.* thawing; defrosting.

kaitoo suru (〜する) *vt.* thaw; defrost: *reetoo-shokuhiñ o* kaitoo suru (冷凍食品を解凍する) *thaw out* frozen food.

ka⌈iwa かいわ (会話) *n.* conversation; talk; dialogue.

ka⌈iyoo かいよう (潰瘍) *n.* ulcer. ⟪⇨ ikaiyoo⟫

ka⌈izeñ かいぜん (改善) *n.* improvement; betterment.

kaizeñ suru (〜する) *vt.* improve; better: *roodoo-jookeñ o* kaizeñ suru (労働条件を改善する) *improve* labor conditions. ⟪⇨ kairyoo⟫

ka⌉ji[1] かじ (家事) *n.* housework;

household chores; housekeeping.
kaji no tsugoo (～の都合) family reasons.

ka⌉ji[2] かじ (火事) *n.* fire:
Sakuya kiñjo de kaji *ga atta.* (昨夜近所で火事があった) There was a *fire* in the neighborhood last night.

ka⌉ji[3] かじ (舵) *n.* tiller; rudder; helm.

ka⌈jiritsu⌉k·u かじりつく (齧り付く) *vt.* (-tsuk·i-; -tsuk·a-; -tsu·i-te Ⓒ) **1** bite at [into]:
Kare wa ooki-na riñgo ni kajiritsuita. (彼は大きなりんごにかじりついた) He *bit* into a large apple.
2 hold on to; cling to:
Kanojo wa sutoobu ni kajiritsuite ita. (彼女はストーブにかじりついていた) She *stayed close up to* the heater.

ka⌈ji⌉r·u かじる (齧る) *vt.* (kajir·i-; kajir·a-; kajit-te Ⓒ) **1** gnaw; bite:
Sono kaki o kajittara, *shibukatta.* (その柿をかじったら, 渋かった) When I *took a bite* of the persimmon, it was bitter.
2 know a little of (learning):
Watashi wa Rateñgo o sukoshi kajirimashita. (私はラテン語を少しかじりました) I *have learned* a bit of Latin.

ka⌈kae·ru かかえる (抱える) *vt.* (kakae-te Ⓥ) **1** have [hold] (a parcel, bag, baggage, etc.) in [under] one's arms.
2 have (a problem, difficulty, etc.):
Kare wa dai-kazoku o kakaete iru. (彼は大家族を抱えている) He *has* a large family to support.

ka⌈kage·ru かかげる (掲げる) *vt.* (kakage-te Ⓥ) fly; put up; hang up (a flag, sign, etc.):
kañbañ o kakageru (看板を掲げる) *put up* a signboard.

ka⌈kaku かかく (価格) *n.* price; cost; value:
kakaku *o ageru* [*sageru*] (価格を上げる[下げる]) raise [lower] the *price.*

ka⌉kari かかり (係り) *n.* charge; duty; a person in charge:
Kare wa eñkai no kakari *desu.* (彼は宴会の係りです) He is in *charge* of the banquet. 《⇨ -gakari[1]》

ka⌈kari⌉choo かかりちょう (係長) *n.* group chief; chief clerk.

ka⌈ka⌉r·u[1] かかる (掛かる) *vi.* (kakar·i-; kakar·a-; kakat-te Ⓒ)
1 (of time) take:
Koko kara eki made aruite, dono kurai kakarimasu *ka?* (ここから駅まで歩いて, どのくらいかかりますか) How long does it *take* to walk from here to the station? 《⇨ kakeru[2]》
2 (of money) cost:
Terebi no shuuri ni goseñ-eñ kakatta. (テレビの修理に 5 千円かかった) The television repair *cost* me five thousand yen. 《⇨ kakeru[2]》
3 hang:
Kabe ni hana no e ga kakatte *imasu.* (壁に花の絵が掛かっています) There is a picture of flowers *hanging* on the wall. 《⇨ kakeru[1]》
4 be locked; button:
Kono kuruma wa kagi ga kakatte inai. (この車は鍵がかかっていない) This car *is not locked.* 《⇨ kakeru[1]》
5 be caught:
Kare wa wana ni kakatta. (彼はわなにかかった) He *was caught* in a trap.
6 splash:
Mizu ga zuboñ ni kakatta. (水がズボンにかかった) Water *splashed* on my trousers. 《⇨ kakeru[1]》
7 (of suspicion) rest:
Kare ni utagai ga kakatta. (彼に疑いがかかった) Suspicion *has rested* on him.
8 (of tax) be imposed:
Gasoriñ ni wa zeekiñ ga kakatte imasu. (ガソリンには税金がかかっています) *There is* a tax on gasoline.
9 consult (a doctor):
Hayaku isha ni kakari nasai. (早く医者にかかりなさい) You should *consult* a doctor immediately.
10 be telephoned:
Kanojo kara deñwa ga kakatta. (彼女から電話がかかった) *There was* a

phone call from her. ⟪⇨ kakeru[1]⟫
11 work:
Kuruma no eñjiñ wa sugu ni kakatta. (車のエンジンはすぐにかかった) The car engine soon *started*. ⟪⇨ kakeru[1]⟫
12 be covered:
Sora ni kumo ga kakatte kita. (空に雲がかかってきた) The sky *became cloudy*.
13 begin start; set about:
shigoto ni kakaru (仕事にかかる) *start* a job.

ka⌈ka⌉r·u[2] かかる (架かる) *vi.* (kakar·i-; kakar·a-; kakat-te Ⓒ)
span:
Kono kawa ni chikai uchi ni hashi ga kakarimasu. (この川に近いうちに橋がかかります) A bridge will *span* this river in the near future. ⟪⇨ kakeru[5]⟫

ka⌈ka⌉r·u[3] かかる (罹る) *vi.* (kakar·i-; kakar·a-; kakat-te Ⓒ)
become [fall] sick [ill]; catch (a disease):
Kono ko wa kaze ni kakari-yasui. (この子はかぜにかかりやすい) This child *catches* colds *easily*.

ka⌈ka⌉r·u[4] かかる (懸かる) *vi.* (kakar·i-; kakar·a-; kakat-te Ⓒ)
appear; form:
Sora ni niji ga kakatta. (空に虹がかかった) A rainbow *formed* in the sky.

ka⌈kato かかと *n.* heel.

ka⌈kawa⌉razu かかわらず (拘らず)
irrespective of; regardless of:
★ Used in the pattern, '... *ni kakawarazu*.'
Neñree ni kakawarazu, *dare de mo sañka dekimasu*. (年齢にかかわらず, だれでも参加できます) Anyone can take part, *irrespective of* age.
... ni mo kakawarazu (...にも～) although; in spite of: *Nañ-do mo chuui shita* ni mo kakawarazu, *kare wa aikawarazu kuru no ga osoi*. (何度も注意したにもかかわらず, 彼は相変わらず来るのが遅い) *Although* I have repeatedly warned him, he still continues to arrive late.
⟪⇨ ga[2]; keredo (mo); no ni⟫

ka⌈kawa⌉r·u かかわる (関わる) *vi.* (kakawar·i-; kakawar·a-; kakawat-te Ⓒ) **1** have to do with; concern; affect:
hito no inochi ni kakawaru *moñdai* (人の命にかかわる問題) a problem *affecting* people's lives.
⟪⇨ kañkee⟫
2 get involved; involve oneself with:
Yopparai ni wa kakawaranai *hoo ga yoi*. (酔っ払いにはかかわらないほうがよい) You had better *not get involved* with drunks.

ka⌈ke⌉ かけ (賭け) *n.* bet; stake; gamble: kake *o suru* (賭けをする) make a *bet*. ⟪⇨ kakeru[4]⟫

ka⌈ke⌉ashi かけあし (駆け足) *n.*
run; gallop.
kakeashi de (～で) hurriedly:
Watashi wa Amerika o kakeashi de *ryokoo shita*. (私はアメリカを駆け足で旅行した) I made a *quick* tour of the United States.

ka⌈kebu⌉toñ かけぶとん (掛け布団)
n. covers; quilt; eiderdown.

ka⌈kedas·u かけだす (駆け出す) *vi.* (-dash·i-; -das·a-; -dash·i-te Ⓒ)
run out; start running.

ka⌈kedo⌉kee かけどけい (掛け時計)
n. wall clock.

ka⌈kee かけい (家計) *n.* family budget; housekeeping expenses.

ka⌈kego⌉e かけごえ (掛け声) *n.*
shout; cheer: kakegoe o kakeru (掛け声をかける) *call out*.

ka⌈ke⌉goto かけごと (賭事) *n.*
gambling. ⟪⇨ bakuchi; kake⟫

ka⌈ke⌉jiku かけじく (掛け軸) *n.*
hanging scroll. ★ Traditionally hung in the '*tokonoma*.'

ka⌈kekomi かけこみ (駆け込み) *n.*
running into:
Kakekomi-joosha *wa kikeñ desu*. (駆け込み乗車は危険です) It is dangerous to try to *dash onto a train* just before it leaves.
⟪⇨ kakekomu⟫

k

ka'kekomu かけこむ(駆け込む) *vi.* (-kom·i-; -kom·a-; -koñ-de [C]) run into; seek refuge:
Kanojo wa tasuke o motomete koobañ ni kakekoñda. (彼女は助けを求めて交番に駆け込んだ) Seeking help, she *took refuge* in a police box. (⇨ kakekomi)

ka'kemawar·u かけまわる(駆け回る) *vi.* (-mawar·i-; -mawar·a-; -mawat-te [C]) **1** run about. (⇨ kakeru[7])
2 busy oneself (doing):
Kare-ra wa kifu-atsume ni kakemawatte iru. (彼らは寄付集めに駆け回っている) They *are busying themselves* collecting contributions.

ka'kera かけら(欠片) *n.* fragment; broken piece. (⇨ kakeru[6])

ka'ke'·ru[1] かける(掛ける・懸ける) *vt.* (kake-te [V]) **1** hang:
kabe ni e o kakeru (壁に絵をかける) *hang* a picture on the wall. (⇨ kakaru[1])
2 set up:
yane ni hashigo o kakeru (屋根にはしごをかける) *set up* a ladder against the roof. (⇨ kakaru[2])
3 place; put:
hi ni nabe o kakeru (火になべをかける) *put* a pot on the fire.
4 put on: ★'*kakete iru*' = wear.
Kanojo wa hoñ o yomu toki, itsumo megane o kakete iru. (彼女は本を読むとき, いつも眼鏡をかけている) She always *wears* glasses for reading.
5 cover; lay; put:
Samui no de hiza ni moofu o kaketa. (寒いのでひざに毛布をかけた) It was cold, so I *covered* my knees with a blanket.
6 lock:
mado ni kagi o kakeru (窓に鍵をかける) *lock* the window. (⇨ kakaru[1])
7 telephone; make a phone call:
Ato de deñwa o kakete *kudasai*. (あとで電話をかけてください) Please *phone* me later. (⇨ kakaru[1])
8 play; start; switch on:
rekoodo o kakeru (レコードをかける) *put* a record *on* / *rajio o* kakeru (ラジオをかける) *turn on* the radio. (⇨ kakaru[1])
9 sit down; take a seat:
beñchi ni koshi o kakeru (ベンチに腰をかける) *sit down* on a bench.
10 fasten; tie; bind:
furu-shiñbuñ no taba ni himo o kakeru (古新聞の束にひもをかける) *bind up* a sheaf of old newspapers with a cord.
11 pour; sprinkle; splash; water:
Sono kuruma wa watashi no fuku ni doromizu o kaketa. (その車は私の服に泥水をかけた) The car *splashed* muddy water on my clothes. (⇨ kakaru[1])

ka'ke'·ru[2] かける(掛ける) *vt.* (kake-te [V]) spend; take:
Kare wa sono sakuhiñ no kañsee ni go-neñ kaketa. (彼はその作品の完成に5年かけた) He *took* five years to complete the work. (⇨ kakaru[1])

ka'ke'·ru[3] かける(掛ける) *vt.* (kake-te [V]) multiply:
Sañ kakeru *ni wa roku desu*. (3掛ける2は6です) Three *times* two is six. (↔ waru)

ka'ke'·ru[4] かける(賭ける) *vt.* (kake-te [V]) **1** bet; stake; gamble:
Kare wa sono reesu ni gomañ-eñ kaketa. (彼はそのレースに5万円賭けた) He *bet* 50,000 yen on the race. (⇨ kake)
2 risk: *inochi o* kakeru (命を賭ける) *risk* one's life.

ka'ke'·ru[5] かける(架ける) *vt.* (kake-te [V]) build; span:
kawa ni tsuribashi o kakeru (川につり橋をかける) *build* a suspension bridge across a river. (⇨ kakaru[2])

ka'ke·ru[6] かける(欠ける) *vi.* (kake-te [V]) **1** chip; break:
Kono chawañ wa fuchi ga kakete iru. (この茶碗は縁が欠けている) The rim of this rice bowl *is chipped*.

2 lack; want; missing:
Kono hoñ wa ni-peeji kakete imasu. (この本は2ページ欠けています) This book *is missing* two pages.

ka⌈ke⌉·ru[7] かける(駆ける) *vi.* (kake-te [V]) run. ⟪⇨ hashiru⟫

ka⌈ketsuke·ru かけつける(駆け付ける) *vi.* (-tsuke-te [V]) run [rush] to; come running:
Keekañ ga sugu sono geñba ni kaketsuketa. (警官がすぐその現場に駆けつけた) A policeman *rushed* to the scene immediately. ⟪⇨ isogu⟫

ka⌈keyor·u かけよる(駆け寄る) *vi.* (-yor·i-; -yor·a-; -yot-te [C]) run up (to a child).

ka⌈ke⌉zañ かけざん(掛け算) *n.* (of arithmetic) multiplication. ⟪⇨ kakeru[3]⟫ ⟪↔ warizañ⟫

ka⌈ki[1] かき(柿) *n.* persimmon.

ka⌉ki[2] かき(牡蠣) *n.* oyster.

ka⌉ki[3] かき(夏期) *n.* summer; summertime:
kaki-*kyuuka* (夏期休暇) *summer* vacation [holidays]. ⟪⇨ tooki[4]; shuñki; shuuki[2]⟫

ka⌈kiarawa⌉s·u かきあらわす(書き表す) *vt.* (-arawash·i-; -arawas·a-; -arawash·i-te [C]) describe in writing:
Sono kimochi wa kotoba de wa kakiarawasemaseñ. (その気持ちは言葉では書き表せません) I *cannot express* that feeling in writing.

ka⌈kidas·u かきだす(書き出す) *vt.* (-dash·i-; -das·a-; -dash·i-te [C]) make a list of:
kau mono o kakidasu (買う物を書き出す) *make a* shopping *list*.

ka⌈kiire·ru かきいれる(書き入れる) *vt.* (-ire-te [V]) write [put] in; enter. ⟪⇨ kakikomu⟫

ka⌈kikae·ru かきかえる(書き換える) *vt.* (-kae-te [V]) **1** rewrite; retell; paraphrase. ⟪⇨ kakinaosu⟫
2 renew (a license, certificate, etc.).

ka⌈kika⌉ta かきかた(書き方) *n.* manner of writing; how to write; how to fill in [out].

ka⌈kikom·u かきこむ(書き込む) *vt.* (-kom·i-; -kom·a-; -koñ-de [C]) write; jot down; fill in [out]:
yooshi ni kakikomu (用紙に書き込む) *fill out* a form.

ka⌈ki-ko⌉toba かきことば(書き言葉) *n.* written language; literary expression. ⟪↔ hanashi-kotoba⟫

ka⌈kimawas·u かきまわす(掻き回す) *vt.* (-mawash·i-; -mawas·a-; -mawash·i-te [C]) **1** stir; rummage:
Hikidashi o kakimawashite *hañko o sagashita.* (引き出しをかき回してはんこを捜した) I *rummaged around* in the drawer looking for my seal.
2 ruin; throw into confusion:
Iiñkai wa kare hitori ni kakimawasarete iru. (委員会は彼一人にかき回されている) The committee *has been thrown into confusion* just by him.

ka⌈kinaos·u かきなおす(書き直す) *vt.* (-naosh·i-; -naos·a-; -naosh·i-te [C]) rewrite; write again. ⟪⇨ kakikaeru⟫

ka⌈kine かきね(垣根) *n.* fence; hedge.

ka⌈kitate·ru かきたてる(書き立てる) *vt.* (-tate-te [V]) write up:
Shiñbuñ wa issee ni sono jikeñ o kakitateta. (新聞は一斉にその事件を書き立てた) All the newspapers *played up* that affair.

ka⌈kitome かきとめ(書留) *n.* registered mail.

ka⌈kitome·ru かきとめる(書き留める) *vt.* (-tome-te [V]) write [jot] down:
deñwa-bañgoo o kakitomeru (電話番号を書き留める) *write down* a telephone number.

ka⌈kitori かきとり(書き取り) *n.* dictation. ⟪⇨ kakitoru⟫

ka⌈kitor·u かきとる(書き取る) *vt.* (-tor·i-; -tor·a-; -tot-te [C]) write down; dictate; copy. ⟪⇨ kakitori⟫

ka⌈kitsuke·ru かきつける(書き付ける) *vt.* (-tsuke-te [V]) note [jot] down. ⟪⇨ kakitomeru⟫

ka⌈kizome かきぞめ(書き初め) *n.* the New Year's writing.

ka⌉kko かっこ(括弧) *n.* parentheses; brackets; braces.

ka⌈kkoi⌉·i かっこいい *a.* (kakkoyoku) (*informal*) good-looking; handsome; stylish: ★ Abbreviation of '*kakkoo ga ii.*'
Kare wa kakkoii *kuruma o motte iru.* (彼はかっこいい車を持っている) He has a *stylish* car.

ka⌉kkoku かっこく(各国) *n.* every country; each nation; various countries.

ka⌈kkoo[1] かっこう(格好) *n.* appearance; shape; style:
kakkoo *ga onaji* (格好が同じ) be similar in *shape* / kakkoo ga ii (格好がいい) *look nice* / kakkoo no warui (格好の悪い) *unattractive.*
⟪↔ bukakko⟫ ⟪⇨ teesai⟫
— *a.n.* (~ na/no) suitable; fit; ideal: kakkoo *na nedañ* (格好な値段) a *reasonable* price.

ka⌉kkoo[2] かっこう(郭公) *n.* Japanese cuckoo.

ka⌉ko かこ(過去) *n.* the past:
Kako *no koto wa wasuremashoo.* (過去のことは忘れましょう) Let's forget *the past.*

ka⌈koi かこい(囲い) *n.* enclosure; fence; railing. ⟪⇨ kakou⟫

ka⌈kom·u かこむ(囲む) *vt.* (kakom·i-; kakom·a-; kakoñ-de Ⓒ)
1 enclose; surround:
Sono mura wa yama ni kakomarete iru. (その村は山に囲まれている) The village *is surrounded* by mountains.
2 circle:
Tadashii kotae o maru de kakomi nasai. (正しい答えを丸で囲みなさい) *Circle* the correct answers.

ka⌈koo[1] かこう(加工) *n.* processing; manufacturing.
kakoo suru (~する) *vt.* process; manufacture; work: *geñryoo o* kakoo suru (原料を加工する) *process* raw materials.

ka⌈koo[2] かこう(下降) *n.* descent; fall; downturn.
kakoo suru (~する) *vi.* go down; descend; decline. ⟪↔ jooshoo⟫

ka⌈ko·u かこう(囲う) *vt.* (kako·i-; kakow·a-; kakot-te Ⓒ) enclose; fence:
Shikichi o saku de kakotta. (敷地を柵で囲った) I *enclosed* the site with a fence. ⟪⇨ kakoi⟫

ka⌉k·u[1] かく(書く) *vt.* (kak·i-; kak·a-; ka·i-te Ⓒ) write:
tegami [*shi*] *o* kaku (手紙[詩]を書く) *write* a letter [poem].
kaite aru (書いてある) be written; say: *Shiñbuñ ni wa nañ to* kaite arimasu *ka?* (新聞には何と書いてありますか) What does it *say* in the paper?

ka⌉k·u[2] かく(描く) *vt.* (kak·i-; kak·a-; ka·i-te Ⓒ) draw; paint:
kabe ni e o kaku (壁に絵をかく) *draw* a picture on the wall.
⟪⇨ egaku⟫

ka⌉k·u[3] かく(掻く) *vt.* (kak·i-; kak·a-; ka·i-te Ⓒ) **1** scratch:
kayui tokoro o kaku (かゆい所をかく) *scratch* where it itches.
2 shovel: *yuki o* kaku (雪をかく) *shovel* snow away.

ka⌈ku[4] かく(格) *n.* status; rank; class; grade.
kaku ga chigau (~が違う) be not comparable: *Kare to watashi de wa* kaku ga chigau. (彼と私では格が違う) I *am just not in his class.*

ka⌉ku[5] かく(核) *n.* **1** nucleus:
kaku-*jikkeñ* (核実験) a *nuclear* test.
2 core; kernel.

ka⌈ku[6] かく(角) *n.* angle.
⟪⇨ kakudo; shikaku[2]⟫

ka⌉ku- かく(各) *pref.* each:
kaku-*katee* (各家庭) *each* family.

-ka⌉ku かく(画) *suf.* **1** (of rooms) partition:
ik-kaku (一画) a *partition.*
2 (of Chinese characters) stroke:
rok-kaku *no kañji* (6画の漢字) a Chinese character of six *strokes.*

ka˥kuchi かくち(各地) *n.* various parts of the country.

ka┌kudai かくだい(拡大) *n.* expansion; magnification.
kakudai suru (～する) *vi., vt.* expand; magnify; enlarge: *kaigai-eñjo no waku o* kakudai suru (海外援助の枠を拡大する) *increase* the range of overseas aid. ⟪↔ shukushoo⟫

ka˥kudo かくど(角度) *n.* **1** angle.
2 viewpoint:
Sono moñdai o chigau kakudo *kara keñtoo shite mimashoo.* (その問題を違う角度から検討してみましょう) Let's examine the problem from a different *viewpoint.*

ka˥kugo かくご(覚悟) *n.* **1** preparedness; readiness:
Hinañ wa kakugo no ue desu. (非難は覚悟のうえです) I *am prepared* for criticism.
2 resolution; determination:
Watashi wa jihyoo o dasu kakugo desu. (私は辞表を出す覚悟です) I *am determined* to hand in my resignation.
kakugo suru (～する) *vt.* **1** be prepared; be ready.
2 be determined; be resigned:
shi o kakugo suru (死を覚悟する) *be resigned* to death.

ka˥kuho かくほ(確保) *n.* securing; ensuring; guarantee.
kakuho suru (～する) *vt.* secure; ensure: *zaseki o* kakuho suru (座席を確保する) *secure* a seat.

ka˥kuji かくじ(各自) *n.* (*formal*) each person. ⟪⇨ meemee; onoono⟫

ka┌kujitsu かくじつ(確実) *a.n.* (～ na, ni) certain; sure:
Tanaka-shi no tooseñ wa hobo kakujitsu *desu.* (田中氏の当選はほぼ確実です) Mr. Tanaka's victory in the election is almost *certain.*

ka┌kumee かくめい(革命) *n.* revolution.

ka┌kumee-teki かくめいてき(革命的) *a.n.* (～ na, ni) revolutionary.

ka┌kuneñ かくねん(隔年) *n.* every other [second] year.

ka┌kuniñ かくにん(確認) *n.* confirmation; verification.
kakuniñ suru (～する) *vt.* confirm; make sure: *hoteru no yoyaku o* kakuniñ suru (ホテルの予約を確認する) *confirm* the hotel reservation.

ka┌kure˥ñbo(o) かくれんぼ(う)(隠れん坊) *n.* hide-and-seek.

ka┌kure˥·ru かくれる(隠れる) *vi.* (kakure-te [V]) hide; hide oneself. ⟪⇨ kakusu⟫

ka┌kuritsu[1] かくりつ(確立) *n.* establishment.
kakuritsu suru (～する) *vi., vt.* establish; build up: *yuukoo-kañkee o* kakuritsu suru (友好関係を確立する) *build up* friendly relations.

ka┌kuritsu[2] かくりつ(確率) *n.* probability; likelihood:
Kare ga seekoo suru kakuritsu *wa takai* [*hikui*]. (彼が成功する確率は高い[低い]) There is a good [small] *chance* of his success.

ka┌kushiñ[1] かくしん(確信) *n.* conviction; confidence.
kakushiñ suru (～する) *vt.* be convinced; strongly believe.

ka┌kushiñ[2] かくしん(革新) *n.*
1 reform; innovation:
gijutsu no kakushiñ (技術の革新) technological *innovation.*
2 reformist; progressive; reformist [progressive] party. ⟪↔ hoshu⟫
kakushiñ suru (～する) *vt.* reform; innovate. ⟪⇨ kaikaku⟫

ka˥kushu かくしゅ(各種) *n.* various kinds; all kinds:
kakushu *no mihoñ* (各種の見本) *all kinds* of samples.

ka┌kushuu かくしゅう(隔週) *n.* every other [second] week.

ka┌ku˥s·u かくす(隠す) *vt.* (kakush·i-; kakus·a-; kakush·i-te [C])
1 hide; put out of sight. ⟪⇨ kakureru⟫

2 keep secret from; conceal; cover up:
Nani mo kakusazu *ni hanashi nasai.* (何も隠さずに話しなさい) Speak out *without concealing* anything.

ka⌈kutee かくてい (確定) *n.* decision; settlement.
kakutee suru (〜する) *vi., vt.* decide; settle; fix: *Hikoku no yuuzai ga* kakutee shita. (被告の有罪が確定した) The defendant's guilt *was decided.*

ka⌈kutoku かくとく (獲得) *n.* acquisition; acquirement.
kakutoku suru (〜する) *vt.* acquire; win; obtain.

ka⌈ma[1] かま (釜) *n.* iron pot; kettle.

ka⌉ma[2] かま (鎌) *n.* sickle; scythe.

ka⌈mae⌉·ru かまえる (構える) *vt.* (kamae-te Ⓥ) **1** take a posture; prepare oneself:
pisutoru o kamaeru (ピストルを構える) *have* a pistol *ready.*
2 set up; build:
mise o kamaeru (店を構える) *set up* a shop.

ka⌈ma⌉·u かまう (構う) *vi., vt.* (kama·i-; kamaw·a-; kamat-te Ⓒ)
1 (in the negative) (not) mind:
"Tabako o sutte mo kamaimaseñ *ka?" "Ee,* kamaimaseñ." (「たばこを吸ってもかまいませんか」「ええ, かまいません」) "Do you *mind* if I smoke?" "No, I *don't.*"
2 (in the negative) (not) meddle; (not) interfere:
Hito [Watashi] ni kamau *na.* (ひと[私]にかまうな) *Leave* me *alone.*
3 (in the negative) (not) look after; (not) care for; (not) pay attention to.

ka⌉me かめ (亀) *n.* tortoise; turtle. ⟪⇨ tsuru[3]⟫

ka⌈mera⌉mañ カメラマン *n.* photographer; cameraman.

ka⌈mi[1] かみ (紙) *n.* paper.

ka⌈mi[2] かみ (髪) *n.* hair.

ka⌉mi[3] かみ (神) *n.* deity; god; God. ★ Often called '*kamisama.*'

ka⌈mi- かみ (上) *pref.* **1** upper:
kami-*te* (上手) the *upper* part; the right of the stage / kami-*za* (上座) the seat of *honor.* ⟪↔ shimo-⟫
2 the first:
kami-*hañki* (上半期) the *first* half of the year. ⟪↔ shimo-⟫

ka⌈mia⌉·u かみあう (嚙み合う) *vi.* (-a·i-; -aw·a-; -at-te Ⓒ) **1** (of gears) mesh; engage.
2 (of an opinion, view, etc.) agree: ★ Used usually in the negative.
Futari no ikeñ wa kamiawanakatta. (二人の意見はかみ合わなかった) They *argued on different planes.*

ka⌈mifu⌉buki かみふぶき (紙吹雪) *n.* confetti. ⟪⇨ fubuki⟫

ka⌈mikuda⌉k·u かみくだく (嚙み砕く) *vt.* (-kudak·i-; -kudak·a-; -kuda·i-te Ⓒ) **1** crush with one's teeth. ⟪⇨ kamu⟫
2 explain in easy words.

ka⌈miku⌉zu かみくず (紙屑) *n.* wastepaper.

ka⌈mina⌉ri かみなり (雷) *n.* thunder; lightning.

ka⌈mi-no⌉-ke かみのけ (髪の毛) *n.* hair of the head. ⟪⇨ kami[2]; ke[1]⟫

ka⌉misama かみさま (神様) *n.* deity; god; God. ⟪⇨ kami[3]⟫

ka⌈misori⌉ かみそり (剃刀) *n.* razor.

ka⌉mo かも (鴨) *n.* wild duck. ⟪⇨ ahiru⟫

ka⌈moku かもく (科目) *n.* subject; course of study.

ka⌉ mo shirenai かもしれない (かも知れない) (*polite*='*ka mo shiremaseñ*' or '*ka mo shirenai desu*')
1 it may be; perhaps:
Sore wa hoñtoo ka mo shirenai. (それは本当かもしれない) It *might be* true.
2 there is no way to tell...:
Itsu ame ga furi-hajimeru ka mo shirenai. (いつ雨が降り始めるかもしれない) *There is no telling* when it might start raining.

ka⌉motsu かもつ (貨物) *n.*

freight; goods; cargo.

ka|m·u かむ(噛む) *vt.* (kam·i-; kam·a-; kañ-de Ⓒ) bite; chew; gnaw:
Inu ni te o kamareta. (犬に手をかまれた) My hand *was bitten* by a dog.

ka|ñ[1] かん(缶) *n.* can; tin:
kañ-*kiri* (缶切り) a *can* opener.

ka|ñ[2] かん(管) *n.* pipe; tube.
⟪⇨ shikeñkañ; shiñkuukañ; suidookañ⟫

ka|ñ[3] かん(勘) *n.* intuition; perception:
Watashi wa kañ *de wakatta.* (私は勘でわかった) I felt it *intuitively.*

-kañ[1] かん(間) *suf.* **1** (of places, persons, etc.) between; among:
Tookyoo Oosaka-kañ (東京・大阪間) *between* Tokyo and Osaka.
2 (of time, period) in; for; during:
Is-shuu-kañ *Señdai ni taizai shita.* (一週間仙台に滞在した) I stayed in Sendai *for* a week.

-ka|ñ[2] かん(巻) *suf.* volume; reel.
★ Counter for books, dictionaries, and reels of film.

ka|na かな(仮名) *n.* Japanese syllabary. ★ There are two systems, '*hiragana*' and '*katakana*.' ⟪⇨ furigana; inside front cover⟫

ka|na かな *p.* **1** I wonder (if):
★ Usually used in addressing oneself. Most often used by men; women use '*ka shira*.' '*Ka naa*' is a variant.
Ashita wa teñki ka na? (あしたは天気かな) Will the weather be fine tomorrow, *I wonder*?
2 I don't know (whether or not):
Kimi ni kore wakaru ka na? (君にこれわかるかな) *I don't know whether or not* you can understand this.

ka|naa かなあ *p.* = ka na.

ka|nai かない(家内) *n.* one's own wife. ⟪↔ otto; shujiñ⟫ ⟪⇨ tsuma⟫

ka|namonoya かなものや(金物屋) *n.* hardware dealer; hardware store; ironmonger.

ka|narazu かならず(必ず) *adv.* certainly; surely; without fail; by all means.

ka|narazu| shimo かならずしも(必ずしも) *adv.* (with a negative) always; necessarily:
Kanemochi ga kanarazu shimo *shiawase to wa kagiranai.* (金持ちが必ずしも幸せとは限らない) The rich are not *always* happy.

ka|nari かなり(可成) *adv.* pretty; fairly; considerably:
Yasuñdara, kanari *geñki ni narimashita.* (休んだら, かなり元気になりました) I took a day off, so I feel *pretty* good now. ⟪⇨ daibu⟫

ka|nashi·i かなしい(悲しい) *a.* (-ku) sad; sorrowful:
kanashii *monogatari* (悲しい物語) a *sad* tale. ⟪↔ ureshii⟫ ⟪⇨ kanashimi; kanashimu⟫

ka|nashimi かなしみ(悲しみ) *n.* sadness; sorrow; grief:
kanashimi *ni shizumu* (悲しみに沈む) be deep in *grief.* ⟪↔ yorokobi⟫ ⟪⇨ kanashimu; kanashii⟫

ka|nashi|m·u かなしむ(悲しむ) *vt.* (kanashim·i-; kanashim·a-; kanashiñ-de Ⓒ) feel sad; grieve; mourn; lament. ⟪↔ yorokobu⟫ ⟪⇨ kanashimi; kanashii⟫

ka|na|·u かなう(適う) *vi.* (kana·i-; kanaw·a-; kanat-te Ⓒ) suit; meet; serve:
Sore wa rikutsu ni kanatte iru. (それは理屈にかなっている) That *is in conformity* with logic.

ka|nawa|nai かなわない(適わない) cannot bear [compete]: ★ The *nai*-form of the verb '*kanau*.'
Mushiatsukute kanawanai. (蒸し暑くてかなわない) I *cannot stand* this sultry weather. ★ '*Kanaimaseñ*' and '*kanawanai desu*' are polite forms.

ka|nazu|chi かなづち(金槌) *n.* **1** hammer:
kanazuchi *de kugi o utsu* (金づちで釘を打つ) drive a nail in with a

hammer.
2 (*colloq.*) a person who can not swim at all.

ka[nazu]kai かなづかい (仮名遣い) *n*. rules for the use of *kana*.

ka[ñbañ かんばん (看板) *n*. signboard; sign.

ka[ñbatsu かんばつ (干魃) *n*. drought; dry weather.

ka]ñbeñ かんべん (勘弁) *n*. pardon; excuse; tolerance.
kañbeñ suru (〜する) *vt*. pardon; forgive; excuse. ⟪⇨ yurusu⟫

ka]ñbu かんぶ (幹部) *n*. management; executives; leaders.

ka]ñbyoo かんびょう (看病) *n*. nursing; attendance.
kañbyoo (o) suru (〜(を)する) *vt*. nurse; attend (a patient).

ka]ñchoo かんちょう (官庁) *n*. government office. ⟪⇨ APP. 7⟫

ka[ñdañkee かんだんけい (寒暖計) *n*. thermometer. ⟪⇨ oñdokee⟫

ka[ñdoo かんどう (感動) *n*. deep emotion; strong impression.
kañdoo suru (〜する) *vi*. be impressed; be moved; be touched.

ka[ñdo]oshi かんどうし (感動詞) *n*. (of grammar) interjection. ⟪⇨ APP. 2⟫

ka[ne[1] かね (金) *n*. money.
★ Often used with '*o*-.'
⟪⇨ kahee; kiñseñ; kooka[3]; shihee⟫

ka[ne[2] かね (鐘) *n*. bell; gong; chime.

ka[nemo]chi かねもち (金持ち) *n*. rich person; wealthy person; the rich. ⟪↔ biñbooniñ⟫

ka[ne]·ru かねる (兼ねる) *vt*. (kane-te [V]) serve both as; double as:
Kono heya wa shosai to oosetsuma o kanete imasu. (この部屋は書斎と応接間を兼ねています) This room *serves both as* a study and a reception room.

-kane]·ru かねる (-kane-te [V]) cannot; be unable to; be not allowed to: ★ Occurs as the second element of compound verbs. Added to the continuative base of a verb.
Ano hito nara sore o yari-kanenai. (あの人ならそれをやりかねない) He *is likely* to do that.

ka]nete かねて (予て) *adv*. before; beforehand; previously:
kanete *yotee sarete ita yoo ni* (かねて予定されていたように) as *previously* scheduled.

ka[netsu[1] かねつ (加熱) *n*. heating.
kanetsu suru (〜する) *vt*. heat; cook. ⟪↔ reekyaku⟫ ⟪⇨ nessuru⟫

ka[netsu[2] かねつ (過熱) *n*. overheating.
kanetsu suru (〜する) *vi*. overheat; (*fig*.) go to excess.

ka[ñga]e かんがえ (考え) *n*.
1 thought:
kañgae *o matomeru* (考えをまとめる) collect one's *thoughts*. ⟪⇨ kañgaeru⟫
2 idea:
Sore wa yoi kañgae *da*. (それはよい考えだ) That is a good *idea*.
3 opinion; view:
Watashi no kañgae *de wa, anata no* kañgae *wa machigatte imasu*. (私の考えでは, あなたの考えは間違っています) In my *opinion*, your *view* is wrong.
4 intention:
Ima no shigoto wa yameru kañgae desu. (今の仕事はやめる考えです) I *intend* to quit my present job.

ka[ñgaeko]m·u かんがえこむ (考え込む) *vi*. (-kom·i-; -kom·a-; -koñde [C]) think hard; brood over; be lost in thought.

ka[ñgaenao]s·u かんがえなおす (考え直す) *vt*. (-naosh·i-; -naos·a-; -naosh·i-te [C]) reconsider; rethink; give up.

ka[ñgae]·ru かんがえる (考える) *vt*. (kañgae-te [V]) 1 think; consider:
Yoku kañgaete *kara kimetai to omoimasu*. (よく考えてから決めたいと思います) I would like to decide

after I *have considered* carefully. ⟪⇨ kañgae⟫

2 expect; imagine:
Sono shigoto wa kañgaete *ita yori mo kañtañ datta.* (その仕事は考えていたよりも簡単だった) The job was easier than I *had expected.* ⟪⇨ omou⟫

3 regard; take; believe:
Watashi wa ima made ano hito o shiñshi da to kañgaete imashita. (私は今まであの人を紳士だと考えていました) Up to now I *had believed* that he was a gentleman.

4 devise:
Kore wa watashi ga kañgaeta *omocha desu.* (これは私が考えたおもちゃです) This is a toy which I *thought up.*

ka⌈ñgaetsu⌉k·u かんがえつく (考え付く) *vt.* (-tsuk·i-; -tsuk·a-; -tsu-i-te Ⓒ) think of; hit upon; call to mind; recollect.

ka⌈ñgai[1] かんがい (感慨) *n.* deep emotion; strong feelings:
kañgai *ni fukeru* (感慨にふける) be overcome by *deep emotion.*

ka⌈ñgai[2] かんがい (灌漑) *n.* irrigation.
kañgai suru (～する) *vt.* irrigate; water: *tochi o* kañgai suru (土地をかんがいする) *irrigate* land.

ka⌈ñgee かんげい (歓迎) *n.* welcome; reception.
kañgee suru (～する) *vt.* welcome.

ka⌈ñgeki かんげき (感激) *n.* deep emotion; strong impression.
kañgeki suru (～する) *vi.* be deeply moved; be impressed.

ka⌉ñgo かんご (看護) *n.* nursing.
kañgo suru (～する) *vt.* nurse; look after: *byooniñ o* kañgo suru (病人を看護する) *care for* a sick person.

ka⌈ñgo⌉fu かんごふ (看護婦) *n.* female nurse. ⟪⇨ kañgo⟫

ka⌈ni かに (蟹) *n.* crab.

ka⌈ñja かんじゃ (患者) *n.* patient; sufferer; case.

ka⌈ñji[1] かんじ (感じ) *n.* **1** impression; effect:
Kare wa kañji *ga yoi* [*warui*]. (彼は感じが良い[悪い]) He makes a good [bad] *impression.*

2 feeling; feel:
Watashi no kañji *de wa kare wa konai to omou.* (私の感じでは彼は来ないと思う) I have a *feeling* that he will not come.

ka⌈ñji[2] かんじ (漢字) *n.* Chinese character; 'kanji.' ⟪⇨ jooyoo-kañji⟫

ka⌉ñji[3] かんじ (幹事) *n.* secretary; manager; steward:
booneñ-kai no kañji (忘年会の幹事) the *organizer* of a year-end party.

ka⌈ñjiñ かんじん (肝心) *a.n.* (～ na, no) essential; important:
Nañ de mo hajime ga kañjiñ *desu.* (何でも初めが肝心です) In all things the first step is the most *important.* ⟪⇨ juuyoo; taisetsu⟫

ka⌈ñji·ru かんじる (感じる) *vt.* (ka-ñji-te Ⓥ) feel; sense; be impressed:
nani-ka kikeñ o kañjiru (何か危険を感じる) *sense* some danger.

ka⌈ñjo⌉o[1] かんじょう (勘定) *n.*

1 calculation; count:
Gookee no kañjoo *ga awanai.* (合計の勘定が合わない) The *figures* for the total do not come out right.

2 account; payment; bill:
Kañjoo *wa watashi ga haraimasu.* (勘定は私が払います) I'll pay the *bill.*

3 consideration; account:
Kare no koto wa kañjoo *ni irete nakatta.* (彼のことは勘定に入れてなかった) I did not take him into *consideration.*
kañjoo suru (～する) *vt.* count; calculate. ⟪⇨ kazoeru⟫

ka⌈ñjoo[2] かんじょう (感情) *n.* feeling(s); emotion; sentiment:
Kare no kotoba wa kanojo no kañjoo *o gaishita.* (彼の言葉は彼女の感情を害した) His words hurt her *feelings.*

ka⌈ñjoo-teki かんじょうてき (感情的) *a.n.* (～ na, ni) emotional;

k

sentimental:
Kare wa sugu kañjoo-teki ni naru. (彼はすぐ感情的になる) He soon *gives way to his feelings.*

ka⌈ñkaku[1] かんかく (間隔) *n.* interval; space:
juugo-fuñ kañkaku *de* (15分間隔で) at fifteen-minute *intervals* / kañkaku *o akeru* (間隔をあける) leave a *space.*

ka⌈ñkaku[2] かんかく (感覚) *n.* sense; sensation:
*Kanojo wa shikisai-*kañkaku *ga sugurete iru.* (彼女は色彩感覚がすぐれている) She has an excellent *sense* of color.

ka⌈ñkaku-teki かんかくてき (感覚的) *a.n.* (~ na, ni) sensuous; related to the senses.

ka⌉ñkañ[1] かんかん *adv.* (~ to)
1 (used to describe the heat and brightness of the sun):
Hi ga kañkañ (to) tette iru. (日がかんかん(と)照っている) The sun *is blazing hot.*
2 clang; loud ringing sound.

ka⌈ñkañ[2] かんかん *a.n.* (~ ni) furious:
Chichi wa kañkañ ni natte okotta. (父はかんかんになって怒った) My father *flew into a rage.*

ka⌈ñkee かんけい (関係) *n.*
1 connection:
Kare wa shigoto no kañkee de *Oosaka e ikimashita.* (彼は仕事の関係で大阪へ行きました) He went to Osaka *in connection with* his business.
2 relation; relationship:
Kanojo wa watashi no uchi to nañ no kañkee *mo arimaseñ.* (彼女は私の家と何の関係もありません) She is of no *relation* to my family.
3 concern; involvement:
Anata ni wa kañkee no nai koto *desu.* (あなたには関係のないことです) It is *none of your business.*
4 influence:
Teñkoo wa shuukaku ni juuyoo na kañkee *ga arimasu.* (天候は収穫に重要な関係があります) The weather has an important *influence* on the harvest.
5 sexual relations.
kañkee suru (~する) *vi.* be concerned; be involved; be related; be affected. ⟪↔ mukañkee⟫

ka⌈ñke⌉esha かんけいしゃ (関係者) *n.* person concerned.

ka⌉ñki[1] かんき (喚起) *n.* arousing; stirring up.
kañki suru (~する) *vt.* arouse; stir up: *hitobito no chuui o* kañki suru (人々の注意を喚起する) *arouse* the attention of people.

ka⌉ñki[2] かんき (乾期) *n.* dry season. ⟪↔ uki[1]⟫

ka⌈ñkoo かんこう (観光) *n.* sightseeing; tourism.
kañkoo suru (~する) *vt.* see the sights.

ka⌈ñkyaku かんきゃく (観客) *n.* audience; spectator. ⟪⇨ keñbutsuniñ⟫

ka⌈ñkyoo かんきょう (環境) *n.* (natural) environment; surroundings.

ka⌈ñkyoo-e⌉esee かんきょうえいせい (環境衛生) *n.* environmental hygiene [sanitation].

ka⌈ñkyoo-ha⌉kai かんきょうはかい (環境破壊) *n.* environmental destruction.

ka⌈ñmuri かんむり (冠) *n.* crown.

ka⌉ñneñ かんねん (観念) *n.*
1 sense:
Kare wa jikañ no kañneñ *ga nai.* (彼は時間の観念がない) He has no *sense* of time.
2 idea: *kotee-*kañneñ (固定観念) fixed *ideas.*
kañneñ suru (~する) *vi.* give up; resign oneself to.

ka⌉ñnushi かんぬし (神主) *n.* Shinto priest.

ka⌉nojo かのじょ (彼女) *n.* **1** she.
★ 'kanojo no'=her; 'kanojo o'=her. ⟪↔ kare⟫
2 girlfriend.

ka⌈noo かのう (可能) *a.n.* (~ na,

k

ni) possible; practicable. 《↔ fukanoo》

ka⌈noosee かのうせい (可能性) ***n.*** possibility; potentiality.

ka⌉ñpa カンパ ***n.*** fund-raising campaign; contribution.
kañpa suru (～する) *vt.* make a contribution.

ka⌈ñpai かんぱい (乾杯) ***n.*** toast.
kañpai suru (～する) *vi.* drink a toast.

ka⌈ñreñ かんれん (関連) ***n.*** relation; connection; association.
kañreñ suru (～する) *vi.* be related; be connected.

ka⌉ñri かんり (管理) ***n.*** administration; management; control: kañri-niñ (管理人) a *janitor*; a *concierge.*
kañri suru (～する) *vt.* administer; manage; take care of.

ka⌈ñroku かんろく (貫録) ***n.*** presence; dignity:
Kare wa kañroku *ga aru.* (彼は貫録がある) He is a man of *presence.*

ka⌈ñryoo[1] かんりょう (完了) ***n.*** completion.
kañryoo suru (～する) *vi., vt.* complete; finish. 《⇨ owaru》

ka⌈ñryoo[2] かんりょう (官僚) ***n.*** bureaucrat; bureaucracy.

ka⌈ñryoo-teki かんりょうてき (官僚的) ***a.n.*** (～ na, ni) bureaucratic.

ka⌈ñsañ かんさん (換算) ***n.*** (of numerical units) conversion; change.
kañsañ suru (～する) *vt.* convert; change: *eñ o doru ni* kañsañ suru (円をドルに換算する) *convert* yen into dollars.

ka⌈ñsatsu かんさつ (観察) ***n.*** observation.
kañsatsu suru (～する) *vt.* observe; watch: *hoshi no ugoki o* kañsatsu suru (星の動きを観察する) *observe* the movement of the stars.

ka⌈ñsee かんせい (完成) ***n.*** completion; perfection.
kañsee suru (～する) *vt., vi.* complete; finish. 《↔ mikañsee》

ka⌈ñseñ かんせん (感染) ***n.*** infection; contagion; transmission.
kañseñ suru (～する) *vi.* catch; contract. 《⇨ utsuru[1]》

ka⌈ñsetsu[1] かんせつ (間接) ***n.*** indirectness; being secondhand:
Sono koto wa kañsetsu *ni kikimashita.* (そのことは間接に聞きました) I heard it *indirectly.* 《↔ chokusetsu》

ka⌈ñsetsu[2] かんせつ (関節) ***n.*** (of a body) joint.

ka⌈ñsetsu-teki かんせつてき (間接的) ***a.n.*** (～ na, ni) indirect; secondhand. 《↔ chokusetsu-teki》

ka⌉ñsha かんしゃ (感謝) ***n.*** thanks; gratitude.
kañsha suru (～する) *vt., vi.* thank; be grateful; be thankful.

ka⌈ñshi かんし (監視) ***n.*** watch; surveillance.
kañshi suru (～する) *vt.* watch; observe.

ka⌈ñshiñ[1] かんしん (感心) ***n.*** admiration.
kañshiñ suru (～する) *vi.* be impressed; admire.
— *a.n.* (～ na) admirable; good; praiseworthy.

ka⌈ñshiñ[2] かんしん (関心) ***n.*** interest; concern:
seeji ni kañshiñ ga aru (政治に関心がある) *be interested* in politics.

ka⌈ñshoo[1] かんしょう (鑑賞) ***n.*** (usually of works of art, etc.) appreciation.
kañshoo suru (～する) *vt.* appreciate; enjoy: *oñgaku o* kañshoo suru (音楽を鑑賞する) *listen to and enjoy* music.

ka⌈ñshoo[2] かんしょう (干渉) ***n.*** interference; intervention.
kañshoo suru (～する) *vi.* interfere; meddle.

ka⌈ñshuu[1] かんしゅう (慣習) ***n.*** custom; convention.

ka⌈ñshuu[2] かんしゅう (観衆) ***n.*** audience; spectators.

ka⌈ñsoku かんそく (観測) ***n.*** obser-

vation; survey:
kishoo no kañsoku (気象の観測) meteorological *observation*.
kañsoku suru (～する) *vt.* observe; survey.

ka⌈ñsoo[1] かんそう (乾燥) *n.* dryness:
kañsoo-zai (乾燥剤) a *desiccant*.
kañsoo suru (～する) *vt., vi.* dry; desiccate.

ka⌈ñsoo[2] かんそう (感想) *n.* impression; thoughts; comment:
kañsoo *o noberu* (感想を述べる) give one's *impressions*.

ka⌈ñs·u⌉ru かんする (関する) *vi.* (kañsh·i-; kañsh·i-; kañsh·i-te [I]) concern.
... ni kañshite (...に関して) concerning; about: *Sono koto* ni kañshite, *shitte iru koto o o-hanashi shimasu.* (そのことに関して, 知っていることをお話しします) I will tell you what I know *concerning* that matter.
... ni kañsuru (...に～) concerning; about: *Nihoñ* ni kañsuru *hoñ* (日本に関する本) a book *about* Japan.

ka⌈ñtai かんたい (寒帯) *n.* frigid zone. ⟪↔ nettai; oñtai⟫

ka⌈ñtañ かんたん (簡単) *a.n.* (～ na, ni) **1** easy; simple: *Soñna moñdai wa* kañtañ *ni tokeru.* (そんな問題は簡単に解ける) I can *easily* solve a problem like that.
2 brief: kañtañ *ni ieba* (簡単に言えば) *briefly* speaking.

ka⌈ñtoku かんとく (監督) *n.*
1 supervision:
Watashi-tachi wa kare no kañtoku *no moto ni hataraita.* (私たちは彼の監督のもとに働いた) We worked under his *supervision*.
2 supervisor; foreman; manager; director.
kañtoku suru (～する) *vt.* supervise.

ka⌈ñtsuu かんつう (貫通) *n.* penetration.
kañtsuu suru (～する) *vi.* penetrate; go through.

ka⌈ñwa かんわ (緩和) *n.* relaxation; mitigation.
kañwa suru (～する) *vt., vi.* relax; ease: *seegeñ o* kañwa *suru* (制限を緩和する) *relax* restrictions. ⟪⇨ yurumeru⟫

ka⌈ñwa-ji⌉teñ かんわじてん (漢和辞典) *n.* dictionary of Chinese explained in Japanese.

ka⌈nyuu かにゅう (加入) *n.* joining; entry; admission.
... ni kanyuu suru (...に～する) *vi.* join; enter. ⟪↔ dattai⟫

ka⌈nyu⌉usha かにゅうしゃ (加入者) *n.* member; subscriber:
hokeñ kanyuusha (保険加入者) a *holder* of an insurance policy.

ka⌈ñzee かんぜい (関税) *n.* customs; customs duties; tariff.

ka⌈ñzeñ かんぜん (完全) *n.* perfection; completeness:
kañzeñ-*hañzai* (完全犯罪) a *perfect* crime.
— *a.n.* (～ na, ni) perfect; complete; fully. ⟪↔ fukañzeñ⟫

ka⌈ñzoo かんぞう (肝臓) *n.* liver.

ka⌈ñzume⌉ かんづめ (缶詰) *n.* canned [tinned] food.

ka⌈o かお (顔) *n.* **1** face; features.
2 look; expression:
Kanojo wa kanashi-soo na kao o shite ita. (彼女は悲しそうな顔をしていた) She *looked* sad.
3 head: ★ The part of the head where hair grows is called '*atama*.'
mado kara kao *o dasu* (窓から顔を出す) put one's *head* out of the window.
4 honor; influence:
Kare wa oji no kao *de kono kaisha ni haitta.* (彼は叔父の顔でこの会社に入った) He got into this company through the *influence* of his uncle.
kao ga hiroi (～が広い) know a lot of people.
kao ga kiku (～がきく) have influence.

kao o dasu (～を出す) make an appearance.
kao o tateru (～を立てる) save a person's face.

ka⌈odachi かおだち (顔立ち) *n.* features; looks:
Kanojo no kaodachi *wa haha-oya ni nite iru.* (彼女の顔立ちは母親に似ている) Her *features* resemble her mother's.

ka⌈oiro かおいろ (顔色) *n.* complexion; look; expression.
kaoiro o kaeru (～を変える) change color: *Kare wa* kaoiro o kaete *okotta.* (彼は顔色を変えて怒った) He *turned red* with anger.

ka⌉oku かおく (家屋) *n.* (*literary*) house; building. 《⇨ ie[1]; uchi[1]》

ka⌈ori かおり (香り) *n.* smell; fragrance; aroma:
Kono bara wa yoi kaori *ga suru.* (このバラはよい香りがする) This rose *smells* sweet. 《⇨ nioi》

ka⌈otsuki かおつき (顔付き) *n.* looks; countenance:
kiñchoo shita kaotsuki (緊張した顔つき) a strained *look.*

ka⌈ppa かっぱ (河童) *n.* imaginary Japanese river-sprite.

ka⌈ppatsu かっぱつ (活発) *a.n.* (～ na, ni) lively; active:
Giroñ ga kappatsu *ni natte kita.* (議論が活発になってきた) The discussion has become *heated.*

ka⌈ra[1][1] から (空) *n.* emptiness:
Sono hako wa kara *desu.* (その箱は空です) The box is *empty.*

ka⌈ra[1][2] から (殻) *n.* shell; husk; hull.

kara[3] から *p.* [follows a noun]
1 (indicates a point of origin in time or space) from:
Soko wa eki kara *aruite, dono kurai kakarimasu ka?* (そこは駅から歩いて, どのくらいかかりますか) How long does it take to go there on foot *from* the station? 《↔ made》
2 (indicates a source) from:
Tomodachi kara *purezeñto o moraimashita.* (友達からプレゼントをもらいました) I received a present *from* a friend.
3 (indicates origin or provenance) from:
Wain wa budoo kara *tsukuraremasu.* (ワインはぶどうから作られます) Wine is made *from* grapes.
4 (indicates movement or action from or through a place) from; through:
Watashi no ie kara *Fuji-sañ ga miemasu.* (私の家から富士山が見えます) Mt. Fuji is visible *from* my house.
5 (indicates the first item in a series) from; with:
Chiisai hito kara *juñ ni narañde kudasai.* (小さい人から順に並んでください) Please line up in order, starting *with* the smaller children.
6 (indicates cause or reason) from:
Chotto shita kooroñ kara *oogeñka ni natta.* (ちょっとした口論から大げんかになった) A big fight developed *from* a minor argument.

kara[4] から *p.* so; therefore; because: ★ Follows a verb, adjective or the copula and indicates cause or reason.
Sukoshi samui kara *sutoobu o tsukemashoo ka?* (少し寒いからストーブをつけましょうか) *As* it's a bit chilly, shall I put on the heater? 《⇨ da kara; no de》
... kara da (...～だ) because: *Nihoñgo o narai-hajimeta no wa Nihoñ de beñkyoo shitakatta* kara desu. (日本語を習い始めたのは日本で勉強したかったからです) It is *because* I wanted to study in Japan that I started studying Japanese.

ka⌈rada からだ (体) *n.* **1** body; physique; build; constitution.
2 health:
Kare wa karoo de karada *o kowashita.* (彼は過労で体をこわした) He injured his *health* by overwork.

ka⌈radatsuki からだつき (体つき) *n.* one's figure; build.

ka⌈ra⌉·i からい (辛い) *a.* (-ku)
1 salty; hot; peppery; spicy.
2 severe; strict:
Ano señsee wa saiteñ ga karai. (あの先生は採点が辛い) That teacher is *strict* in grading. ⟪↔ amai⟫

ka⌈rai⌉bari からいばり (空威張り) *n.* bravado; bluff.
karaibari suru (～する) *vi.* bluster; bluff. ⟪⇨ ibaru⟫

ka⌈rakara からから *a.n.* (～ na/no, ni) dry; thirsty:
karakara *no teñki* (からからの天気) *dry* weather.

ka⌈raka⌉·u からかう *vt.* (karaka-i-; karakaw·a-; karakat-te Ⓒ) tease; play a trick; make fun of.

ka⌈raoke カラオケ *n.* karaoke; recorded musical backing for vocal accompaniment.

k

ka⌈rappo からっぽ *a.n.* (～ na/no, ni) empty. ⟪⇨ kara[1]⟫

ka⌈rashi からし (芥子) *n.* mustard.

ka⌉rasu[1] からす (烏) *n.* crow; raven.

ka⌈ras·u[2] からす (枯らす) *vt.* (karash·i-; karas·a-; karash·i-te Ⓒ) wither; kill (a plant). ⟪⇨ kareru⟫

ka⌈rasumu⌉gi からすむぎ (烏麦) *n.* oats.

ka⌈rate[1] からて (空手) *n.* state of being empty-handed:
Kanojo wa karate *de kaette kita.* (彼女は空手で帰って来た) She came back *empty-handed*.

ka⌈rate[2] からて (空手) *n.* karate.

ka⌉re かれ (彼) *n.* **1** he. ★ 'kare no'＝his, 'kare o'＝him.
2 boyfriend. ⟪↔ kanojo⟫

ka⌈re·ru かれる (枯れる) *vi.* (kare-te Ⓥ) (of a plant) die; wither. ⟪⇨ karasu[2]⟫

ka⌉ri かり (借り) *n.* debt:
Kare ni wa ooki-na kari *ga aru.* (彼には大きな借りがある) I am greatly in *debt* to him. ⟪↔ kashi[2]⟫ ⟪⇨ kariru⟫

ka⌈ri ni かりに (仮に) *adv.* **1** if; even if; supposing:
Kari ni *ame dattara doo shimasu ka?* (かりに雨だったらどうしますか) *Supposing* it rains, what shall we do? ⟪⇨ moshi (mo)⟫
2 for the time being; temporarily:
Kono heya wa kari ni *kyooshitsu ni shiyoo shite imasu.* (この部屋はかりに教室に使用しています) We are using this room as a classroom *for the time being.*

ka⌈ri·ru かりる (借りる) *vt.* (kari-te Ⓥ) **1** borrow; rent; lease. ⟪↔ kasu⟫
2 use (equipment, facilities, etc.):
Deñwa o o-kari *dekimasu ka?* (電話をお借りできますか) Can I *use* your phone? ⟪↔ kasu⟫
3 receive; need:
hito no chikara o kariru (人の力を借りる) *receive* someone's help.

ka⌈roñji·ru かろんじる (軽んじる) *vt.* (karoñji-te Ⓥ) neglect; make little [light] of. ⟪↔ omoñjiru⟫

ka⌈roo かろう (過労) *n.* overwork; strain. ⟪⇨ karooshi⟫

ka⌈ro⌉ojite かろうじて (辛うじて) *adv.* barely; narrowly:
karoojite *shikeñ ni ukaru* (かろうじて試験に受かる) *barely* pass the examination.

ka⌈ro⌉oshi かろうし (過労死) *n.* death from overwork. ⟪⇨ karoo⟫

ka⌈r·u かる (刈る) *vt.* (kar·i-; kar·a-; kat-te Ⓒ) cut; reap; crop; mow:
Kami o mijikame ni katte *kudasai.* (髪を短めに刈ってください) Please *cut* my hair a bit short.

ka⌈ru·i かるい (軽い) *a.* (-ku) **1** (of weight) light. ⟪↔ omoi[1]⟫
2 easy:
Watashi wa karui *kimochi de demo ni sañka shita.* (私は軽い気持ちでデモに参加した) I *casually* participated in the demonstration.
3 (of crime, disease, etc.) slight; minor:
Karui *kaze o hiita.* (軽いかぜをひいた) I have caught a *slight* cold. ⟪↔ omoi[1]⟫

4 relieved; relaxed:
Ima wa kibuñ mo karui. (今は気分も軽い) I feel *relieved* now.
《↔ omoi[1]》

ka⌉ruta カルタ *n.* traditional Japanese playing cards; card game.

ka⌈ryoku かりょく (火力) *n.* heat; heating power:
karyoku-*hatsudeñsho* (火力発電所) a *thermal* power plant. 《↔ sui-ryoku》

ka⌈ryuu かりゅう (下流) *n.* lower course [reaches] of a river.
《↔ jooryuu》

ka⌉sa かさ (傘) *n.* umbrella; parasol. 《⇨ amagu》

ka⌈sai かさい (火災) *n.* fire:
★ More formal than '*kaji*.'
Shiñriñ ni kasai *ga hassee shita.* (森林に火災が発生した) A *fire* broke out in the forest.

ka⌉sakasa[1] カサカサ *adv.* (～ to) (the sound of a thin, light object moving):
kasakasa *to iu oto* (カサカサという音) a *rustling* sound.

ka⌈sakasa[2] かさかさ *a.n.* (～ no, ni) (the state of being dry):
Fuyu ni naru to te ga kasakasa *ni naru.* (冬になると手がかさかさになる) Whenever winter comes, my hands get *dry*.

ka⌈sanar·u かさなる (重なる) *vi.* (kasanar·i-; kasanar·a-; kasanat-te [C]) **1** happen at the same time; occur one after another:
Kyuujitsu ga nichiyoo to kasanaru. (休日が日曜と重なる) The public holiday *falls* on Sunday.
2 pile up:
Tsukue no ue ni shorui ga kasanatte iru. (机の上に書類が重なっている) There *are* papers *piled up* on the desk. 《⇨ kasaneru》

ka⌈sane·ru かさねる (重ねる) *vt.* (kasane-te [V]) **1** pile up; put on top:
tsukue no ue ni hoñ o kasaneru (机の上に本を重ねる) *pile* books *up* on the desk. 《⇨ kasanaru; tsumu[1]》
2 repeat:
Kare no kasaneta *kuroo ga mi o musuñda.* (彼の重ねた苦労が実を結んだ) His *repeated* toil produced favorable results.

ka⌉segi かせぎ (稼ぎ) *n.* income; earnings:
Kare wa kasegi *ga ii.* (彼は稼ぎがいい) He *earns* a good income.
《⇨ kasegu; shuunyuu》

ka⌈se⌉g·u かせぐ (稼ぐ) *vt.* (kaseg·i-; kaseg·a-; kase·i-de [C]) earn; make money; work.
《⇨ kasegi》

ka⌈seki かせき (化石) *n.* fossil.

ka⌉shi[1] かし (菓子) *n.* confectionery; cake; candy; sweets.
★ Often '*o-kashi*.' 《⇨ keeki[1]》

ka⌈shi[2] かし (貸し) *n.* loan:
★ Used both literally and figuratively.
Kare ni wa takusañ kashi ga aru. (彼にはたくさん貸しがある) He *owes me* a lot. 《↔ kari》

ka⌈shidashi かしだし (貸し出し) *n.* loan; lending service:
Sono hoñ wa kashidashi-*chuu desu.* (その本は貸し出し中です) That book is out on *loan*. 《⇨ kashidasu》

ka⌈shida⌉s·u かしだす (貸し出す) *vt.* (-dash·i-; -das·a-; -dash·i-te [C]) lend [loan] out; rent. 《⇨ kashidashi; kasu》

ka⌉shiko かしこ *n.* Yours sincerely. ★ Used at the end of a woman's letter. 《⇨ keegu; tegami》

ka⌈shiko⌉·i かしこい (賢い) *a.* (-ku) wise; clever; smart:
kashikoi *ko* (賢い子) a *bright* child.
《⇨ rikoo》

ka⌈shikomarima⌉shita かしこまりました (畏まりました) certainly:
★ Indicates that the speaker will carry out an order or request given by a superior. Often used by service personnel to customers.

"Kono hañkachi o kudasai." "Kashikomarimashita." (「このハンカチをください」「かしこまりました」) "Please let me have this handkerchief." "*Certainly.*"

ka⸢shima かしま(貸間) *n.* = kashishitsu.

ka shira かしら *p.* (*informal*)
1 I wonder: ★ Used, often rhetorically, to indicate a question or express doubt. Used mainly by women. Men use '*ka na*.'
Ano hito wa ima-goro nani o shite iru ka shira. (あの人は今ごろ何をしているかしら) *I wonder* what he is doing at the moment.
2 (used to pose a question):
Anata wa ashita o-taku ni irassharu ka shira. (あなたはあしたお宅にいらっしゃるかしら) *Are* you *going to be* home tomorrow?
-nai ka shira (ない〜) I hope; I would like: *Hayaku yasumi ni* naranai ka shira. (早く休みにならないかしら) *I hope* the vacation begins soon.

ka⸢shishitsu かししつ(貸し室) *n.* room for rent; room to let.

ka⸢shiya[1] かしや(貸家) *n.* house for rent; house to let.

ka⸢shi⸣ya[2] かしや(菓子屋) *n.* confectioner; confectionery.

ka⸣sho かしょ(箇所) *n.* place; spot; point:
Kono shirushi wa kikeñ na kasho *o shimeshimasu.* (この印は危険な箇所を示します) These marks show the dangerous *places.* ⟪⇨ basho⟫

-ka⸣sho かしょ(箇所) *suf.* part; place; passage:
Shikeñ de ni-kasho *machigaeta.* (試験で2か所間違えた) I made *two* mistakes in the examination.

ka⸣shu かしゅ(歌手) *n.* singer; vocalist.

ka⸢soo かそう(下層) *n.* **1** lower layer [stratum].
2 the lower class. ⟪⇨ chuuryuu; jooryuu⟫

ka⸢s·u かす(貸す) *vt.* (kash·i-; kas·a-; kash·i-te Ⓒ) **1** lend; loan; rent; lease:
tochi o kare ni kasu (土地を彼に貸す) *lease* the land to him.
⟪↔ kariru⟫ ⟪⇨ kashi[2]⟫
2 let use (equipment, facilities, etc.). ⟪↔ kariru⟫
3 give:
hito ni chikara o kasu (人に力を貸す) *give* a person assistance.
⟪↔ kariru⟫

ka⸣suka かすか(微か) *a.n.* (〜 na, ni) faint; vague; dim:
Tooku ni akari ga kasuka *ni mieta.* (遠くに明りがかすかに見えた) I could see a light shining *dimly* in the distance.

ka⸢sumi かすみ(霞) *n.* haze; mist.

ka⸢sum·u かすむ(霞む) *vi.* (kasum·i-; kasum·a-; kasuñ-de Ⓒ)
1 (of a view, sky, etc.) be hazy.
2 (of vision) be blurred.

ka⸣ta[1] かた(肩) *n.* shoulder.
kata no ni ga oriru (〜の荷がおりる) a load off one's mind.
kata o motsu (〜をもつ) take sides.

ka⸢ta[2] かた(型) *n.* **1** pattern:
doresu no kata *o toru* (ドレスの型をとる) make a *pattern* of a dress.
2 type; style; model:
ichibañ atarashii kata (一番新しい型) the latest *model.*
3 mold:
zerii o kata *ni nagashikomu* (ゼリーを型に流し込む) pour jelly into a *mold.*

ka⸢ta[3] かた(方) *n.* (*polite*) person; lady; gentleman:
Kono kata *ga Suzuki-sañ desu.* (この方が鈴木さんです) This *lady* is Miss Suzuki. ⟪⇨ hito⟫

-kata[1] かた(方) *suf.* care of:
*Itoo-sama-*kata *Suzuki-sama* (伊藤様方鈴木様) Mr. Suzuki *c/o* Mr. Ito.

-kata[2] かた(方) *suf.* way; manner: ★ Added to the continuative base of a verb.
*Kono kudamono no tabe-*kata *ga wakarimaseñ.* (この果物の食べ方がわ

かりません) I don't know *how to* eat this fruit.

ka[tachi かたち(形) *n.* shape; form; figure; appearance:
marui katachi *no tatemono* (丸い形の建物) a building with a round *shape* | *Shiki to itte mo,* katachi *dake no mono datta.* (式と言っても, 形だけのものだった) Although it was a ceremony, it was only a matter of *form.*

ka[tagaki かたがき(肩書) *n.* title; degree:
Nihoñ de wa katagaki *ga mono o iu.* (日本では肩書がものをいう) In Japan *titles* have weight.

ka[ta]gata かたがた(方々) *n.* (*polite*) the people (concerned).

ka[tagawa かたがわ(片側) *n.* one side:
michi no katagawa *o tooru* (道の片側を通る) pass on *one side* of the road. ⟪⇨ ryoogawa⟫

ka[tagu]ruma かたぐるま(肩車) *n.* riding on someone's shoulders.
kataguruma suru (～する) *vt.* give someone a piggyback.

ka[tahashi かたはし(片端) *n.* one end; one side:
tsuna no katahashi *o hipparu* (綱の片端を引っ張る) pull *one end* of the rope. ⟪↔ ryoohashi⟫

ka[ta]hoo かたほう(片方) *n.* one side; one of a pair; the other:
Tebukuro no katahoo *o nakushite shimatta.* (手袋の片方をなくしてしまった) I have lost *one of* my gloves. ⟪⇨ ryoohoo⟫

ka[ta·i かたい(堅い·固い·硬い) *a.* (-ku) **1** hard; solid; stiff; firm; tough:
Daiyamoñdo wa katai. (ダイヤモンドは硬い) Diamonds are *hard.* ⟪↔ yawaraka; yawarakai⟫
2 stiff:
Kare wa katai *buñshoo o kaku.* (彼は硬い文章を書く) He writes in a *stiff* style.
3 firm; tight:
Kono musubime wa katakute, *hodokenai.* (この結び目は固くて, ほどけない) This knot is so *tight* I cannot undo it.
4 sure:
Ano señshu no nyuushoo wa katai. (あの選手の入賞は堅い) That player's winning the prize is a *sure* thing.
5 steady; sound; serious:
Katai *hanashi wa kore-gurai ni shimashoo.* (堅い話はこれぐらいにしましょう) Let's talk no more of *serious* matters.
6 obstinate; stubborn:
Uchi no kachoo wa atama ga katai. (うちの課長は頭が固い) Our section chief is *obstinate* in his way of thinking.

ka[taka]na かたかな(片仮名) *n.* one of the Japanese syllabaries. ⟪⇨ inside front cover⟫

ka[taki] かたき(敵) *n.* enemy; foe; rival:
shoobai-gataki (商売がたき) a *rival* in business. ★ The initial /k/ changes to /g/ in compounds.
kataki o utsu (～を討つ) revenge oneself.

ka[tamari かたまり(塊) *n.* lump; mass; clod; chunk:
koori no katamari (氷の塊) a *lump* of ice.

ka[tamar·u かたまる(固まる) *vi.* (-mar·i-; -mar·a-; -mat-te [C]) become hard; harden; set:
Kono semeñto wa mada katamatte *imaseñ.* (このセメントはまだ固まっていません) This cement *has* not *set* yet. ⟪⇨ katameru⟫

ka[tame·ru かためる(固める) *vt.* (-me-te [V]) **1** harden:
yuki o fuñde katameru (雪を踏んで固める) *tread down* the snow. ⟪⇨ katamaru⟫
2 strengthen; tighten; fortify:
ketsui o katameru (決意を固める) *make a firm* resolution. ⟪⇨ katamaru⟫

ka[tamichi かたみち(片道) *n.* one-way (ticket). ⟪↔ oofuku⟫

k

ka⌈tamuke⌉·ru かたむける (傾ける) *vt.* (-muke-te [V]) **1** incline; lean; slant; tilt. ⟪⇨ katamuku⟫
2 devote (one's energy).

ka⌈tamuki⌉ かたむき (傾き) *n.*
1 slant; slope; tilt. ⟪⇨ katamuku⟫
2 tendency; trend:
Kare wa monogoto o karuku miru katamuki *ga aru.* (彼は物事を軽く見る傾きがある) He has a *tendency* to take things lightly. ⟪⇨ keekoo⟫

ka⌈tamu⌉k·u かたむく (傾く) *vi.* (-muk·i-; -muk·a-; -mu·i-te [C])
1 lean; slope; slant; tilt:
Kono to wa sukoshi katamuite iru. (この戸は少し傾いている) This door *leans* slightly to one side. ⟪⇨ katamukeru; katamuki⟫
2 be inclined; lean:
Kare wa tasuu-ha ni katamuite iru. (彼は多数派に傾いている) He *is inclining* toward the majority faction.
3 (of the sun or the moon) go down; sink; set.

ka⌈tana⌉ かたな (刀) *n.* sword:
katana *o nuku* (刀を抜く) draw a *sword.*

ka⌈tar·u かたる (語る) *vt.* (katar·i-; katar·a-; katat-te [C]) (*slightly formal*) talk; tell; relate.
shiñsoo o kataru (真相を語る) *tell* the truth. ⟪⇨ hanasu[1]; shaberu⟫

ka⌈tasa かたさ (堅さ・固さ・硬さ) *n.*
1 hardness; solidity; firmness; stiffness. ⟪⇨ katai⟫
2 stubbornness. ⟪⇨ katai⟫

ka⌈tate かたて (片手) *n.* one hand. ⟪⇨ ryoote⟫

ka⌈tayo⌉r·u かたよる (偏る) *vi.* (-yor·i-; -yor·a-; -yot-te [C]) be partial; be prejudiced; be slanted.

ka⌈tazuke⌉·ru かたづける (片付ける) *vt.* (-zuke-te [V]) **1** put in order; tidy up; put away.
2 settle (a dispute); solve (a problem); finish (a job).

ka⌈tee[1] かてい (家庭) *n.* home; family; household.

ka⌈tee[2] かてい (仮定) *n.* assumption; supposition; hypothesis.
katee suru (～する) *vi., vt.* assume; suppose; postulate.

ka⌈tee[3] かてい (過程) *n.* process; course:
*seezoo-*katee (製造過程) the *course* of production.

ka⌈tee-teki かていてき (家庭的) *a.n.* (～ na, ni) homely; homelike; domestic:
katee-teki *na josee* (家庭的な女性) a *domestic* woman.

ka⌉ts·u[1] かつ (勝つ) *vi.* (kach·i-; kat·a-; kat-te [C]) **1** win; beat; defeat:
tatakai ni katsu (戦いに勝つ) *win* a battle. ⟪↔ makeru⟫
2 overcome (temptation, difficulties, etc.). ⟪↔ makeru⟫

ka⌉tsu[2] かつ (且つ) *conj.* (*formal*) and; moreover; also:
hitsuyoo katsu *juubuñ na jookeñ* (必要かつ十分な条件) a necessary *and* sufficient condition.

ka⌈tsudoo かつどう (活動) *n.* activity; action; operation.
katsudoo suru (～する) *vi.* be active; work.

ka⌈tsudoo-teki かつどうてき (活動的) *a.n.* (～ na, ni) active; energetic.

ka⌈tsu⌉g·u かつぐ (担ぐ) *vt.* (katsug·i-; katsug·a-; katsu·i-de [C])
1 carry (a burden) on one's shoulder.
2 play a trick on; make a fool of; take in. ⟪⇨ damasu⟫

ka⌈tsuji かつじ (活字) *n.* printing type.

ka⌉tsute かつて (曾て) *adv.* (～ no) **1** once; at one time; formerly:
Katsute *kanojo wa niñki-kashu datta.* (かつて彼女は人気歌手だった) She was a popular singer *at one time.*
2 ever; never:
Koñna keekeñ wa imada katsute *shita koto ga arimaseñ.* (こんな経験はいまだかつてしたことがありません) So

far I have *never* had this kind of experience.

ka⌈tsuyaku かつやく (活躍) *n.* remarkable activity.

katsuyaku suru (～する) *vi.* take an active part; participate actively: *terebi de* katsuyaku suru (テレビで活躍する) *be active* in TV.

ka⌈tsuyoo かつよう (活用) *n.*

1 practical use; utilization.

2 (of grammar) inflection; conjugation.

katsuyoo suru (～する) **1** *vt.* make use of; utilize; make the most of.

2 *vi.* inflect; conjugate.

ka⌈tte[1] かって (勝手) *n.* **1** kitchen. ★ Usually with '*o-*.' ⟪⇨ daidokoro⟫

2 way; convenience:

Kono apaato wa katte ga warui. (このアパートは勝手が悪い) This apartment *is inconvenient*.

ka⌈tte[2] かって (勝手) *n.* selfishness; willfulness:

Soñna katte *wa yurusenai.* (そんな勝手は許せない) I won't stand for that sort of *selfish behavior*.

— *a.n.* (～ na, ni) selfish:

katte *na hito* (勝手な人) a *selfish* person. ⟪⇨ wagamama⟫

ka·⌈u[1] かう (買う) *vt.* (ka·i-; ka-w·a-; kat-te Ⓒ) **1** buy; purchase; get. ⟪↔ uru[1]⟫ ⟪⇨ koonyuu⟫

2 incur; take up (an ill feeling, quarrel, etc.):

hito no urami o kau (人の恨みを買う) *incur* a person's ill will.

3 recognize; think much of (a person's ability).

ka⌉·u[2] かう (飼う) *vt.* (ka·i-; ka-w·a-; kat-te Ⓒ) keep (an animal); have; raise; rear.

ka⌈wa⌉[1] かわ (川) *n.* river; stream; brook.

ka⌈wa⌉[2] かわ (皮) *n.* skin; hide; peel; rind; bark.

ka⌈wa⌉[3] かわ (革) *n.* leather.

ka⌈wa[4] かわ (側) *n.* = gawa.

ka⌈waiga⌉r·u かわいがる (可愛がる) *vt.* (-gar·i-; -gar·a-; -gat-te Ⓒ) love; pet; caress.

ka⌈wai⌉·i かわいい (可愛い) *a.* (-ku)

1 cute; pretty; lovely.

2 dear:

Seeto wa miñna kawaii. (生徒はみんなかわいい) My pupils are all *dear* to me.

3 (of a vehicle, instrument, etc.) little; tiny.

ka⌈wairashi⌉·i かわいらしい (可愛らしい) *a.* (-ku) = kawaii.

ka⌈waiso⌉o かわいそう (可哀相) *a.n.* (～ na, ni) poor; pitiful; miserable; sad:

Sono hanashi o kiite, roojiñ ga kawaisoo *ni natta.* (その話を聞いて、老人がかわいそうになった) I felt *sorry* for the old man when I heard the story.

ka⌈waka⌉s·u かわかす (乾かす) *vt.* (-kash·i-; -kas·a-; -kash·i-te Ⓒ) dry (wet things). ⟪⇨ kawaku⟫

ka⌈wa⌉k·u かわく (乾く) *vi.* (kawa-k·i-; kawak·a-; kawa·i-te Ⓒ) dry. ⟪⇨ kawakasu⟫

ka⌈wara かわら (瓦) *n.* roof tile.

ka⌈wari かわり (代わり) *n.* substitute; replacement:

Dare ga kare no kawari *o tsutomemashita ka?* (だれが彼の代わりをつとめましたか) Who acted as his *substitute*?

ka⌈wari ni かわりに (代わりに) *adv.*

1 instead (of):

Kare ga ikenakereba, watashi ga kawari ni *ikimasu.* (彼が行けなければ、私が代わりに行きます) If he cannot go, I will go *instead*.

2 in return; in exchange.

ka⌈war·u[1] かわる (変わる) *vi.* (ka-war·i-; kawar·a-; kawat-te Ⓒ)

1 change; turn:

Shiñgoo ga aka kara ao ni kawatta. (信号が赤から青に変わった) The traffic light *changed* from red to green. ⟪⇨ kaeru[3]⟫

2 differ; vary:

Kuni ni yotte fuuzoku shuukañ wa kawaru. (国によって風俗習慣は

変わる) Manners and customs *differ* from country to country. 《⇨ kaeru[3]》

ka⌈war·u[2] かわる(代わる·替わる) *vi.* (kawar·i-; kawar·a-; kawat-te Ⓒ) replace; displace; substitute: *Kaeri wa watashi ga kuruma no uñteñ o kare to* kawatta. (帰りは私が車の運転を彼と代わった) On the way back I did the driving *instead of* him. 《⇨ kaeru[4]》

ka⌈waru-ga⌉waru かわるがわる(代わる代わる) *adv.* (~ ni) by turns; in turn. 《⇨ kootai》

ka⌈wase かわせ(為替) *n.*
1 money order.
2 monetary exchange:
kawase-*sooba* (為替相場) the *exchange* rate.

ka⌈yo⌉o(bi) かよう(び)(火曜(日)) *n.* Tuesday. 《⇨ APP. 5》

ka⌈yo⌉okyoku かようきょく(歌謡曲) *n.* popular song.

ka⌈yo·u かよう(通う) *vi.* (kayo·i-; kayow·a-; kayot-te Ⓒ) **1** go; commute:
Kare wa kuruma de kaisha e kayotte imasu. (彼は車で会社へ通っています) He *commutes* to his office by car.
2 (of a vehicle) run:
Sono machi made basu ga kayotte *imasu.* (その町までバスが通っています) There are buses *running* as far as that town.

ka⌈yowa⌉·i かよわい(か弱い) *a.* (-ku) weak; frail; helpless:
kayowai *josee* (か弱い女性) a *frail* woman.

ka⌈yu⌉·i かゆい(痒い) *a.* (-ku) itchy; itching:
Senaka ga kayui. (背中がかゆい) My back is *itching.*

ka⌉zañ かざん(火山) *n.* volcano.

ka⌈zari かざり(飾り) *n.* decoration; ornament. 《⇨ kazaru》

ka⌈zar·u かざる(飾る) *vt.* (kazar·i-; kazar·a-; kazat-te Ⓒ)
1 decorate; ornament:
heya o hana de kazaru (部屋を花で飾る) *decorate* a room with flowers. 《⇨ kazari》
2 display:
heya ni Nihoñ-niñgyoo o kazaru (部屋に日本人形を飾る) *display* a Japanese doll in a room.

ka⌈ze[1] かぜ(風) *n.* wind; draft; breeze:
Kaze *ga yañda.* (風がやんだ) The *wind* has died down.

ka⌈ze[2] かぜ(風邪) *n.* cold; influenza: kaze *o hiku* (かぜをひく) catch a *cold.*

ka⌈zoe⌉doshi かぞえどし(数え年) *n.* a person's age counted on the basis of the calendar year. 《⇨ toshi[1]》

ka⌈zoe⌉·ru かぞえる(数える) *vt.* (kazoe-te Ⓥ) count:
ichi kara juu made kazoeru (1から10まで数える) *count* from one to ten. 《⇨ kañjoo[1]》

ka⌉zoku かぞく(家族) *n.* family:
Uchi wa roku-niñ kazoku *desu.* (うちは6人家族です) We have six *family members.*

ka⌉zu かず(数) *n.* number. 《⇨ APP. 3》

ke[1] け(毛) *n.* **1** (body) hair:
Kare wa ke *ga koi [usui].* (彼は毛が濃い[薄い]) He has thick [thin] *hair.* 《⇨ kami-no-ke》
2 fur; feather; wool: ke *no kooto* (毛のコート) a *woolen* coat.

ke[2] け(気) *n.* sign; touch; taste:
Doko ni mo hi no ke *wa nakatta.* (どこにも火の気はなかった) There was no *sign* of fire.

-ke け(家) *suf.* family:
Yamada-ke (山田家) the Yamada *family* / Maeda-ke (前田家) *the Maedas.*

ke⌉chi けち *n.* stinginess; stingy person; miser.
— *a.n.* (~ na, ni) **1** stingy; mean; miserly.
2 narrow-minded:
kechi *na kañgae* (けちな考え) a *narrow-minded* idea.

ke⌈damono けだもの(獣) *n.*

beast; brute. ★ More emphatic than '*kemono*' and often has a derogatory connotation. ⟪⇨ kemono⟫

ke⌉e[1] けい (刑) *n.* punishment; penalty; sentence: kee *ni fukusuru* (刑に服する) serve a *sentence.*

ke⌉e[2] けい (計) *n.* **1** total; sum: kee *o dasu* (計を出す) figure out a *sum.* ⟪⇨ gookee⟫

2 plan; plot:
Ichi-neñ no kee *wa gañtañ ni ari.* (一年の計は元旦にあり) New Year's Day is the day to make your *plans* for the year. ⟪⇨ keekaku⟫

-kee けい (形) *suf.* shape; form; type:
kyuu-kee (球形) a round *shape* / *chi*-kee (地形) the *lay* of the land.

ke⌈eba けいば (競馬) *n.* horse racing.

ke⌈ebetsu けいべつ (軽蔑) *n.* contempt; scorn; disdain.
keebetsu suru (〜する) *vt.* look down on; despise; disdain.

ke⌈e-ee けいえい (経営) *n.* management; administration.
kee-ee suru (〜する) *vt.* manage; operate; run (a shop). ⟪⇨ uñee; itonamu⟫

ke⌈e-e⌉esha けいえいしゃ (経営者) *n.* manager; the management; proprietor.

ke⌈ego けいご (敬語) *n.* honorific; polite expression. ★ Comprising the three categories of honorific, polite and humble expressions.

ke⌉egu けいぐ (敬具) *n.* Yours truly; Sincerely yours. ★ Used in the complimentary close of a letter. ⟪⇨ haikee[1]; kashiko⟫

ke⌉ehi けいひ (経費) *n.* expense; cost; upkeep:
keehi *o kiritsumeru* (経費を切り詰める) cut down on *expenses.*

ke⌉eji けいじ (刑事) *n.* **1** (police) detective.

2 criminal affairs:
keeji-*jikeñ* (刑事事件) a *criminal* case. ⟪⇨ miñji⟫

ke⌈eka けいか (経過) *n.* [...]ress; development; cou[...]
jikeñ no keeka (事件の経[...]) [...] *development* of an affair.

2 lapse; passage:
Ip-puñ keeka. (1 分経過) Or[...]ute *has passed.*
keeka suru (〜する) *vi.* pass: ★ More formal than '*tatsu*⁴.'
Sutaato shite kara sañjup-puñ keeka shimashita. (スタートしてから30 分経過しました) Thirty minutes *have passed* since they started.

ke⌈ekai[1] けいかい (警戒) *n.* caution; precaution; watch; guard.
keekai suru (〜する) *vt.* be cautious of; look [watch] out for; guard against.

ke⌈ekai[2] けいかい (軽快) *a.n.* (〜 na, ni) light; nimble:
keekai *na ashidori de aruku* (軽快な足どりで歩く) walk with *light steps.*

ke⌈ekaku けいかく (計画) *n.* plan; design; project; scheme:
keekaku *o tateru* (計画を立てる) work out a *plan.*
keekaku suru (〜する) *vt.* plan; project; scheme.

ke⌈ekañ けいかん (警官) *n.* policeman; police officer. ★ More formal than '*omawari-sañ.*' ⟪⇨ fujiñkeekañ; keesatsu⟫

ke⌈ekeñ けいけん (経験) *n.* experience:
keekeñ *o tsumu* (経験を積む) gain *experience.* ⟪⇨ taikeñ⟫
keekeñ suru (〜する) *vt.* experience; go through; undergo.

ke⌉eki[1] ケーキ *n.* cake. ★ Japanese confectionery is called '*kashi.*' ⟪⇨ kashi[1]⟫

ke⌈eki[2] けいき (景気) *n.* business; economy; economic conditions:
Keeki *ga yoi* [*warui*]. (景気が良い[悪い]) *Business* is brisk [slow].

ke⌉eko けいこ (稽古) *n.* practice; exercise; lesson; rehearsal:
señsee ni tsuite ikebana no keeko *o suru* (先生について生け花の稽古をす

take *lessons* in ikebana from a teacher.

ke⌈ekoku けいこく(警告) *n.* warning; caution.
keekoku suru (～する) *vt.* warn; caution. 《⇨ chuui》

ke⌈ekoo けいこう(傾向) *n.* tendency; trend; inclination:
Kare wa chikagoro monowasure o suru keekoo ga aru. (彼は近ごろ物忘れをする傾向がある) He *is inclined* to be forgetful these days.

ke⌈ekootoo けいこうとう(蛍光灯) *n.* fluorescent lamp.

ke⌈ekoo-to⌉ryoo けいこうとりょう(蛍光塗料) *n.* fluorescent [luminous] paint.

ke⌈ereki けいれき(経歴) *n.* career; background; one's personal history. 《⇨ rireki》

ke⌈esai けいさい(掲載) *n.* publication; insertion.
keesai suru (～する) *vt.* publish; insert; print: *Sono kookoku wa shiñbuñ ni* keesai sareta. (その広告は新聞に掲載された) That advertisement *appeared* in a newspaper. 《⇨ noseru[2]》

ke⌈esañ けいさん(計算) *n.* calculation; sums; figures.
keesañ ni ireru (～に入れる) take account of.
keesañ suru (～する) *vt.* calculate; count; reckon; figure.

ke⌈esa⌉ñki けいさんき(計算機) *n.* calculator.

ke⌈esatsu けいさつ(警察) *n.* the police; police station. 《⇨ keekañ》

ke⌈esatsusho けいさつしょ(警察署) *n.* police station.

ke⌈esee-ge⌉ka けいせいげか(形成外科) *n.* plastic surgery.

ke⌈esha けいしゃ(傾斜) *n.* slant; slope; inclination:
yane no keesha (屋根の傾斜) the *slope* of a roof.
keesha suru (～する) *vi.* incline; slant; slope; descend. 《⇨ katamuku》

Ke⌈eshi⌉-choo けいしちょう(警視庁) *n.* Metropolitan Police Department.

ke⌈eshiki けいしき(形式) *n.* form; formality:
keeshiki *ni kodawaru* (形式にこだわる) stick to *formalities.* 《↔ naiyoo》

ke⌈eshiki-teki けいしきてき(形式的) *a.n.* (～ na, ni) formal; perfunctory:
keeshiki-teki *na aisatsu* (形式的なあいさつ) a *perfunctory* greeting.

ke⌈esotsu けいそつ(軽率) *a.n.* (～ na, ni) careless; rash; hasty:
keesotsu *na koto o suru* (軽率なことをする) do something *rash.* 《↔ shiñchoo[2]》

ke⌈etai けいたい(携帯) *n.* carrying: keetai-hiñ (携帯品) one's *personal effects.*
keetai suru (～する) *vt.* carry a thing with one.

ke⌈eto けいと(毛糸) *n.* = keito.

ke⌈etoo けいとう(系統) *n.*
1 system:
Meeree-keetoo *ga barabara da.* (命令系統がばらばらだ) The *system* of command is in disorder.
2 lineage; descent:
Ano hito wa Geñji no keetoo o *hiite iru.* (あの人は源氏の系統を引いている) He *is descended* from the Genji family.

ke⌈etoo-teki けいとうてき(系統的) *a.n.* (～ na, ni) systematic.

ke⌈eyaku けいやく(契約) *n.* contract; agreement.
keeyaku suru (～する) *vi.* make a contract.

ke⌈eyakusho けいやくしょ(契約書) *n.* (written) contract:
keeyakusho *o torikawasu* (契約書を取り交わす) exchange *written contracts.*

ke⌈eyoo けいよう(掲揚) *n.* (of a flag) hoist; fly.
keeyoo suru (～する) *vt.* hoist; raise.

ke⌈eyu[1] けいゆ(経由) *n.* by way of; via:

Roñdoñ keeyu *de Pari e iku* (ロンドン経由でパリへ行く) go to Paris *via* London. 《⇨ hete》

ke⌈eyu[2] けいゆ (軽油) *n.* light oil. 《↔ juuyu》

ke⌉ezai けいざい (経済) *n.* economy; finance:
keezai *seechoo-ritsu* (経済成長率) *economic* growth rate.

ke⌈ezai-teki けいざいてき (経済的) *a.n.* (~ na, ni) **1** economic; financial:
Kare wa keezai-teki *ni moñdai ga aru yoo da.* (彼は経済的に問題があるようだ) He seems to have *financial* problems.
2 economical:
Chiisai kuruma no hoo ga keezai-teki *da.* (小さい車のほうが経済的だ) Small cars are more *economical*.

ke⌈ezoku けいぞく (継続) *n.* continuation; renewal.
keezoku suru (~する) *vi., vt.* continue; go on. ★ More formal than '*tsuzuku*.'

ke⌈ga⌉ けが (怪我) *n.* injury; hurt; wound.
kega (o) suru (~(を)する) *vt.* injure; wound; hurt: *te ni* kega o suru (手にけがをする) *hurt* one's hand.

ke⌉hai けはい (気配) *n.* sign; indication:
Heya ni wa hito no kehai *wa nakatta.* (部屋には人の気配はなかった) There were no *signs* of life in the room.

ke⌈ito けいと (毛糸) *n.* woolen yarn; knitting wool.

ke⌈kka けっか (結果) *n.* result; effect; consequence; outcome:
geñiñ to kekka (原因と結果) cause and *effect*. 《↔ geñiñ》

ke⌈kkaku けっかく (結核) *n.* tuberculosis.

ke⌈kkañ[1] けっかん (欠陥) *n.* flaw; defect; shortcomings:
kekkañ *shoohiñ* (欠陥商品) *defective* merchandise. 《⇨ ketteñ》

ke⌈kkañ[2] けっかん (血管) *n.* blood vessel; vein; artery.

ke⌈kkoñ けっこん (結婚) *n.* marriage; matrimony.
kekkoñ suru (~する) *vi.* marry; get married.

ke⌈kko⌉ñshiki けっこんしき (結婚式) *n.* wedding ceremony:
kekkoñshiki *o ageru* (結婚式を挙げる) hold a *wedding ceremony*.

ke⌉kkoo[1] けっこう (結構) *a.n.* (~ na, ni) good; nice; excellent; splendid:
kekkoo *na okurimono* (結構な贈り物) a *nice* present.
kekkoo desu (~です) **1** fine:
Nani-ka kakumono o kashite kudasai. Nañ de mo kekkoo desu. (何か書くものを貸してください. 何でも結構です) Please lend me something to write with. Anything is *fine*.
2 (refusal) no, thank you: *"Moo ip-pai biiru o ikaga desu ka?" "Moo* kekkoo desu." (「もう一杯ビールをいかがですか」「もう結構です」) "What about another glass of beer?" "*No, thank you.*" 《⇨ takusañ》

ke⌉kkoo[2] けっこう (結構) *adv.* fairly; quite; rather:
Sono gekijoo wa heejitsu de mo kekkoo *koñde imasu.* (その劇場は平日でもけっこう込んでいます) The theater is *quite* crowded even on weekdays.

ke⌈kkoo[3] けっこう (決行) *n.* carrying out as scheduled.
kekkoo suru (~する) *vt.* carry out as scheduled.

ke⌈kkoo[4] けっこう (欠航) *n.* cancellation (of a flight, voyage).
kekkoo suru (~する) *vi.* do not fly [sail].

ke⌈kkyoku けっきょく (結局) *adv.* after all; in the end; in the long run.

ke⌈mono けもの (獣) *n.* beast; wild animal. 《⇨ kedamono》

ke⌈mu·i けむい (煙い) *a.* (-ku) smoky:
Takibi ga kemui. (たき火が煙い)

The bonfire is *smoky*. ⟪⇨ kemutai⟫

ke⌈muri けむり(煙り) *n.* smoke; fumes. ⟪⇨ kemuru⟫

ke⌈mur·u けむる(煙る) *vi.* (kemur·i-; kemur·a-; kemut-te Ⓒ)
1 smoke; smolder:
Kono dañro wa hidoku kemuru. (この暖炉はひどく煙る) This fireplace *smokes* badly. ⟪⇨ kemuri⟫
2 look dim; be obscured:
Shima wa kiri ni kemutte ita. (島は霧に煙っていた) The island *was shrouded* in fog.

ke⌈muta·i けむたい(煙たい) *a.* (-ku)
1 smoky:
Heya ga kemutai. (部屋が煙たい) The room is *smoky*. ⟪⇨ kemui⟫
2 unapproachable; uncomfortable:
Kono-goro chichi ga kemutaku *natte kita.* (このごろ父が煙たくなってきた) These days I have begun to feel *awkward* in my father's presence.

ke⌉ñ[1] けん(県) *n.* prefecture.
★ A basic administrative unit in Japan. ⟪⇨ inside back cover⟫

ke⌉ñ[2] けん(券) *n.* ticket; coupon.

-keñ[1] けん(軒) *suf.* counter for a house [door]. ⟪⇨ APP. 4⟫

-keñ[2] けん(権) *suf.* right:
señkyo-keñ (選挙権) the *right* to vote / *jiñ*-keñ (人権) human *rights*.

ke⌈nas·u けなす(貶す) *vt.* (kenash·i-; kenas·a-; kenash·i-te Ⓒ) speak ill of; run down; criticize.

ke⌈ñbeñ けんべん(検便) *n.* stool test.
keñbeñ (o) suru (〜(を)する) *vi.* examine a person's stool.

ke⌈ñbutsu けんぶつ(見物) *n.* sightseeing; visit; sightseer; spectator.
keñbutsu suru (〜する) *vt.* see; see the sights of; watch.

ke⌈ñbutsuniñ けんぶつにん(見物人) *n.* spectator; onlooker.

ke⌉ñchi けんち(見地) *n.* viewpoint; standpoint:
kotonatta keñchi *kara ikeñ o noberu* (異なった見地から意見を述べる) express one's opinion from a different *viewpoint*.

ke⌈ñ-chi⌉ji けんちじ(県知事) *n.* (prefectural) governor. ⟪⇨ chiji⟫

ke⌈ñchiku けんちく(建築) *n.* building; construction; architecture. ⟪⇨ tatemono⟫
keñchiku suru (〜する) *vt.* build; put up: ★ More formal than '*tateru*[2].'

ke⌉ñchoo けんちょう(県庁) *n.* prefectural office.

ke⌉ñdoo けんどう(剣道) *n.* Japanese swordsmanship [fencing]; kendo.

ke⌈ñgaku けんがく(見学) *n.* study by observation; study visit.
keñgaku suru (〜する) *vt.* visit for study; inspect; observe:
Ashi o kega shita no de, taiiku wa keñgaku shita. (足をけがしたので, 体育は見学した) As I had injured my leg, I only *observed* the physical education class.

ke⌉ñi けんい(権威) *n.* authority; expert.

ke⌉ñji けんじ(検事) *n.* public prosecutor.

ke⌈ñka けんか(喧嘩) *n.* quarrel; fight; brawl.
keñka (o) suru (〜(を)する) *vi.* quarrel; have a fight.
keñka o uru (〜を売る) pick a fight.

ke⌈ñkai けんかい(見解) *n.* opinion; view; outlook.

ke⌈ñketsu けんけつ(献血) *n.* blood donation.
keñketsu suru (〜する) *vi.* donate [give] blood.

ke⌈ñkoo けんこう(健康) *n.* health:
keñkoo-*shiñdañ* (健康診断) a *medical* checkup / keñkoo-*hokeñ* (健康保険) *health* insurance.
— *a.n.* (〜 na, ni) healthy; healthful.

ke⌈ñkoo-hoke⌉ñshoo けんこうほ

けんしょう (健康保険証) *n.* health insurance card.

ke⌈ñkyuu けんきゅう (研究) *n.* study; research; investigation.
keñkyuu suru (〜する) *vt., vi.* make a study; do research.

ke⌈ñmee[1] けんめい (賢明) *a.n.* (〜 na, ni) wise; sensible; judicious.

ke⌈ñmee[2] けんめい (懸命) *a.n.* (〜 na/no, ni) eager; hard; strenuous:
Keñmee *na soosa ga tsuzukerareta.* (懸命な捜査が続けられた) A *diligent* investigation was carried out. ⟪⇨ isshoo-keñmee⟫

ke⌉ñpoo けんぽう (憲法) *n.* constitution:
keñpoo-*ihañ* (憲法違反) a breach of the *constitution.*

ke⌉ñri けんり (権利) *n.* right; claim; privilege:
keñri *o yookyuu suru* (権利を要求する) claim a *right.* ⟪↔ gimu⟫

ke⌈ñrikiñ けんりきん (権利金) *n.* key money; premium. ★ Money additional to the rent requested when renting an apartment or house. ⟪⇨ reekiñ; shikikiñ; yachiñ⟫

ke⌉ñryoku けんりょく (権力) *n.* power; authority; influence:
Kare wa kono kaisha de keñryoku ga aru. (彼はこの会社で権力がある) He is an *influential man* in this company.

ke⌉ñsa けんさ (検査) *n.* inspection; examination; test:
hiñshitsu no keñsa *o suru* (品質の検査をする) carry out quality *inspections.*

ke⌈ñsaku けんさく (検索) *n.* reference; access; retrieval.
keñsaku suru (〜する) *vt.* refer to; look up; search.

ke⌈ñsatsu[1] けんさつ (検札) *n.* inspection of tickets.

ke⌈ñsatsu[2] けんさつ (検察) *n.* prosecution.

ke⌈ñsetsu けんせつ (建設) *n.* construction; establishment.
keñsetsu suru (〜する) *vt.* build; construct; establish.

ke⌈ñshoo けんしょう (懸賞) *n.* prize; prize contest; reward.

ke⌈ñshu⌉usee けんしゅうせい (研修生) *n.* trainee.

ke⌈ñsoñ けんそん (謙遜) *n.* modesty; humility.
keñsoñ suru (〜する) *vi.* be modest; be humble.

ke⌈ñto⌉o[1] けんとう (見当) *n.*
1 guess; estimate; idea:
keñtoo *o tsukeru* (見当をつける) make a *guess.*
2 direction:
Byooiñ wa daitai kono keñtoo *ni arimasu.* (病院は大体この見当にあります) The hospital is roughly in this *direction.*
keñtoo-chigai[-hazure] (〜違い[はずれ]) be wrong; be off the point.

ke⌈ñtoo[2] けんとう (検討) *n.* examination; study; investigation.
keñtoo suru (〜する) *vt.* examine; study; investigate.

ke⌈ñtoo[3] けんとう (健闘) *n.* good fight; strenuous efforts.
keñtoo suru (〜する) *vi.* put up a good fight; make strenuous efforts.

ke⌈ñyaku けんやく (倹約) *n.* thrift; economy.
keñyaku suru (〜する) *vt.* save; economize: *shokuhi o* keñyaku suru (食費を倹約する) *economize* on food expenses. ⟪↔ roohi⟫

ke⌈ñzeñ けんぜん (健全) *a.n.* (〜 na, ni) healthy; wholesome; sound:
keñzeñ *na yomimono* (健全な読み物) *wholesome* reading.

ke⌈ppaku けっぱく (潔白) *n.* innocence; guiltlessness:
mi no keppaku *o shoomee suru* (身の潔白を証明する) prove one's *innocence.*

ke⌉redo (mo) けれど(も) *conj.* but; however:

k

Kanojo wa kai ni shootai sareta. Keredo mo *shusseki shinakatta.* (彼女は会に招待された．けれども出席しなかった) *Though* she was invited, she did not attend the party.
《⇨ ga[2]; kakawarazu; no ni》

keˈr·u ける(蹴る) *vt.* (ker·i-; ke-r·a-; ket-te Ⓒ) **1** kick.
2 reject; refuse (a request, demand, etc.):
Kare wa watashi-tachi no yoo-kyuu o ketta. (彼は私たちの要求をけった) He *rejected* our demands.

keˈsa けさ(今朝) *n.* this morning.
《↔ myoochoo; yokuasa》

keˈshigomu けしごむ(消しゴム) *n.* eraser; rubber.

keˈshiki けしき(景色) *n.* scenery; scene; landscape; view.

keˈshoˈo けしょう(化粧) *n.* makeup: keshoo-shitsu (化粧室) a *toilet*; a *restroom.*
keshoo (o) suru (〜(を)する) *vi.* make oneself up; paint.

keˈssaku けっさく(傑作) *n.* masterpiece.

keˈssañ けっさん(決算) *n.* closing accounts; settlement of accounts.
kessañ (o) suru (〜(を)する) *vt.* settle [balance] accounts.

keˈssee けっせい(結成) *n.* organization; formation.
kessee suru (〜する) *vt.* organize; form: *atarashii too o* kessee suru (新しい党を結成する) *form* a new political party.

keˈsseki けっせき(欠席) *n.* absence.
kesseki suru (〜する) *vt.* stay away; absent oneself: *gakkoo o* kesseki suru (学校を欠席する) *be absent* from school.
《↔ shusseki》

keˈsshiñ けっしん(決心) *n.* decision; determination; resolution.
kesshiñ suru (〜する) *vi., vt.* make up one's mind; decide; determine; resolve.

keˈsshite けっして(決して) *adv.* (with a negative) never; by no means; not at all:
Kanojo wa kesshite *yakusoku o yaburanai.* (彼女は決して約束を破らない) She *never* breaks a promise.

keˈsshoo[1] けっしょう(決勝) *n.* final game [match]; finals.

keˈsshoo[2] けっしょう(結晶) *n.*
1 crystal; crystallization.
2 (*fig.*) result; fruit:
ase no kesshoo (汗の結晶) the *result* of much effort.

keˈssoñ けっそん(欠損) *n.* deficit; loss:
hyakumañ-eñ no kessoñ *o dasu* (100万円の欠損を出す) have a *deficit* of a million yen. 《↔ rieki》

keˈs·u けす(消す) *vt.* (kesh·i-; ke-s·a-; kesh·i-te Ⓒ) **1** extinguish; put out; blow out:
kaji o kesu (火事を消す) *extinguish* a fire / *akari o* kesu (明かりを消す) *put out* a light. 《⇨ kieru》
2 switch off; turn off:
Rajio o keshite *kudasai.* (ラジオを消してください) Please *turn off* the radio.
3 erase; rub [wipe] off; cross out:
Kare wa kanojo no namae o meebo kara keshita. (彼は彼女の名前を名簿から消した) He *crossed* her name *off* the list. 《⇨ kezuru》
4 remove; deaden; absorb:
iya na nioi o kesu (いやなにおいを消す) *get rid of* a bad smell.
《⇨ kieru》

keˈtobas·u けとばす(蹴飛ばす) *vt.* (-tobash·i-; -tobas·a-; -tobash·i-te Ⓒ) kick (away). 《⇨ keru》

keˈtsuatsu けつあつ(血圧) *n.* blood pressure:
ketsuatsu *ga takai* [*hikui*] (血圧が高い[低い]) have a high [low] *blood pressure.*

keˈtsudañ けつだん(決断) *n.* decision; determination; resolution.
ketsudañ suru (〜する) *vi.* decide; determine; resolve.

keˈtsuˈeki けつえき(血液) *n.* blood: ketsueki-*gata* (血液型) a

blood type.

ke˥tsui けつい(決意) *n.* determination; resolution.
ketsui suru (〜する) *vt.* determine; resolve: *jiniñ o* ketsui suru (辞任を決意する) *decide* to resign one's post.

ke˹tsuroñ けつろん(結論) *n.* conclusion:
ketsuroñ *o dasu* (結論を出す) form a *conclusion*.

ke˹ttee けってい(決定) *n.* decision; determination; conclusion; settlement.
kettee suru (〜する) *vi.*, *vt.* decide; determine; conclude; settle: *nani o suru ka o* kettee suru (何をするかを決定する) *decide* what to do. ⟪⇨ kimeru; kimaru⟫

ke˹tte˥ñ けってん(欠点) *n.* fault; drawback; weak point:
jibuñ no ketteñ *o naosu* (自分の欠点を直す) correct one's *weak points.* ⟪↔ choosho⟫ ⟪⇨ tañsho⟫

ke˹washi˥·i けわしい(険しい) *a.* (-ku) **1** steep:
kewashii *yama-michi* (険しい山道) a *steep* mountain path.
2 grim; severe; critical:
Joosee ga kewashiku *natte kita.* (情勢が険しくなってきた) The situation has become *grave.*

ke˹zur·u けずる(削る) *vt.* (kezur·i-; kezur·a-; kezut-te Ⓒ)
1 shave; plane; sharpen:
ita o taira ni kezuru (板を平らに削る) *plane* a board smooth / *eñpitsu o* kezuru (鉛筆を削る) *sharpen* a pencil.
2 delete; cross out. ⟪⇨ kesu⟫
3 reduce; curtail; cut:
koosaihi o kezuru (交際費を削る) *cut down on* entertainment expenses.

ki[1]˥ き(木) *n.* **1** tree; shrub.
2 wood; lumber; timber.

ki[2] き(気) *n.* **1** mind; mood; feeling:
Kare wa shippai suru yoo na ki *ga suru.* (彼は失敗するような気がする) I have a *feeling* that he will fail.
2 nature; disposition; temper:
Kare no musume wa ki ga tsuyoi *ga, musuko wa* ki ga yowai. (彼の娘は気が強いが, 息子は気が弱い) His daughter is *unyielding*, but his son is *timid.*
3 intention; will:
Ano hito to kekkoñ suru ki *wa arimaseñ.* (あの人と結婚する気はありません) I have no *intention* of marrying him.
ki ga au (〜が合う) get along well.
ki ga chiisai (〜が小さい) be timid.
ki ga chiru (〜が散る) be distracted.
ki ga kiku (〜が利く) be considerate; be attentive; be thoughtful.
ki ga omoi (〜が重い) be heavy-hearted.
ki ga sumu (〜が済む) be satisfied.
ki ga tsuku (〜がつく) notice; come to one's senses.
ki ni iru (〜に入る) like; be pleased.
ki ni kuwanai (〜に食わない) be disagreeable.
ki ni naru (〜になる) bother; get on one's nerves.
ki ni suru (〜にする) worry; mind; care.
ki o kubaru (〜を配る) be attentive to.
ki o tsukeru (〜をつける) be careful; take care.

-ki[1] き(器) *suf.* **1** -ware; utensil; apparatus:
too-ki (陶器) ceramic *ware* / *gak*-ki (楽器) a musical *instrument* / *juwa*-ki (受話器) a telephone *receiver.*
2 organ: *shooka*-ki (消化器) the digestive *organs.*

-ki[2] き(機) *suf.* **1** plane:
hikoo-ki (飛行機) an *airplane* / *jetto-ki* (ジェット機) a jet *plane.*
2 machine:
señtaku-ki [*sentak*-ki] (洗濯機) a washing *machine* / *señpuu*-ki (扇風機) an electric *fan.*

ki˹atsu きあつ(気圧) *n.* atmospheric pressure.

ki⌈bishi⌉·i きびしい (厳しい) *a.* (-ku) severe; stern; strict:
Kanojo wa kodomo ni kibishii. (彼女は子どもに厳しい) She is *strict* with her children.

ki⌉bo きぼ (規模) *n.* scale; size:
Sono taikai wa kokusai-teki na kibo *de hirakareta.* (その大会は国際的な規模で開かれた) The convention was held on an international *scale.*

ki⌈boo きぼう (希望) *n.* hope; wish; request; expectation:
kiboo *o idaku* (希望を抱く) cherish a *hope* / kiboo *o ushinau* (希望を失う) lose *hope.*
kiboo suru (～する) *vt.* hope; wish. ⟪⇨ nozomu'⟫

ki⌉buñ きぶん (気分) *n.* feeling; mood; sentiment:
Kyoo wa kibuñ ga yoi [warui]. (きょうは気分が良い[悪い]) I feel [*don't feel*] *well* today.

ki⌉chi きち (基地) *n.* base: *guñji-*kichi (軍事基地) a military *base.*

ki⌈chi⌉ñto きちんと *adv.* neatly; exactly; properly; in good order:
hikidashi o kichiñto *seeri shite oku* (引き出しをきちんと整理しておく) keep the drawers *tidy.* ⟪⇨ chañto⟫

ki⌈choo きちょう (貴重) *a.n.* (～ na) precious; valuable:
kichoo *na taikeñ* (貴重な体験) a *precious* experience.

ki⌈choohiñ きちょうひん (貴重品) *n.* (one's) valuables.

ki⌈dootai きどうたい (機動隊) *n.* riot police [squad].

ki⌈dor·u きどる (気取る) *vi., vt.* (kidor·i-; kidor·a-; kidot-te Ⓒ)
1 put on airs; give oneself airs.
2 pose as:
Kare wa gakusha o kidotte iru. (彼は学者を気取っている) He *affects* to be a scholar.

ki⌈e·ru きえる (消える) *vi.* (kie-te Ⓥ) **1** (of a fire, light, etc.) go out; die out. ⟪⇨ kesu⟫
2 disappear; vanish; go out of sight. ⟪⇨ kesu⟫
3 (of snow) melt away.
4 go away; die out:
Itami ga kieta. (痛みが消えた) The pain *has gone away.*

ki⌉fu きふ (寄付) *n.* contribution; donation:
kifu *o atsumeru* (寄付を集める) collect *contributions.*
kifu suru (～する) *vt.* contribute; donate.

ki⌈gae きがえ (着替え) *n.* change of clothes:
kigae o suru (着替えをする) *change one's clothes.* ⟪⇨ kigaeru⟫

ki⌈gae⌉·ru きがえる (着替える) *vt.* (kigae-te Ⓥ) change one's clothes. ⟪⇨ kigae⟫

ki⌉gai きがい (機外) *n.* outside an airplane. ⟪↔ kinai⟫

ki⌈ga⌉kari きがかり (気掛り) *a.n.* (～ na, ni) worry; anxiety; concern:
Musuko no shoorai ga kigakari *desu.* (息子の将来が気がかりです) We *are worried* about our son's future. ⟪⇨ shiñpai⟫

ki⌈gane きがね (気兼ね) *n.* constraint.
kigane suru (～する) *vi.* feel constrained; worry about giving trouble: *Shuuto ni wa* kigane shite imasu. (しゅうとには気兼ねしています) I *feel ill at ease* with my mother-in-law.

ki⌈garu きがる (気軽) *a.n.* (～ na, ni) lighthearted; cheerful; buoyant:
Kigaru *ni asobi ni kite kudasai.* (気軽に遊びに来てください) Please feel *free* to come and visit us. ⟪⇨ kiraku⟫

ki⌉geki きげき (喜劇) *n.* comedy. ⟪↔ higeki⟫

ki⌉geñ¹ きげん (期限) *n.* time limit; deadline:
Koñgetsu de keeyaku no kigeñ ga kireru. (今月で契約の期限が切れる) The agreement *expires* this month.

ki⌈geñ[2] きげん(機嫌) *n.* humor; temper; mood:
kigeñ *ga ii* [*warui*] (きげんがいい[悪い]) be in good [bad] *humor* today.
kigeñ o toru (～を取る) play up to: *Kare wa uwayaku no go*kigeñ *o totta.* (彼は上役のごきげんを取った) He *got on the right side of* his boss.

ki⌉geñ[3] きげん(起源) *n.* origin; beginning:
seemee no kigeñ (生命の起源) the *origin* of life.

ki⌈goo きごう(記号) *n.* mark; sign; symbol. 《⇨ fugoo》

ki⌉gu きぐ(器具) *n.* appliance; utensil; instrument.

ki⌉gyoo きぎょう(企業) *n.* company; business; enterprise.

ki⌈hoñ きほん(基本) *n.* fundamentals; basics; basis; standard:
Kihoñ *o wasureru na.* (基本を忘れるな) Never forget *basics*. 《⇨ kiso》

ki⌈hoñ-teki きほんてき(基本的) *a.n.* (～ na, ni) fundamental; basic.

ki⌈iro きいろ(黄色) *n.* yellow. 《⇨ kiiroi》

ki⌈iro·i きいろい(黄色い) *a.* (-ku) yellow. 《⇨ kiiro》

ki⌉ji[1] きじ(記事) *n.* news; article:
Sono kiji *wa kesa no shiñbuñ de yomimashita.* (その記事は今朝の新聞で読みました) I read the *news* in this morning's paper.

ki⌉ji[2] きじ(生地) *n.* cloth; material; texture.

ki⌈ji[3] きじ(雉) *n.* pheasant.

ki⌉jitsu きじつ(期日) *n.* fixed date; deadline; appointed day:
Kare wa itsu-mo kijitsu *o mamoranai.* (彼はいつも期日を守らない) He always fails to meet the *deadline*.

ki⌈juñ[1] きじゅん(基準) *n.* standard; criterion; basis:
Yosañ wa sakuneñ-do no jisseki o kijuñ *ni shite iru.* (予算は昨年度の実績を基準にしている) The budget was made on the *basis* of last year's actual results.

ki⌈juñ[2] きじゅん(規準) *n.* norm; standard.

ki⌈ka⌉i[1] きかい(機械) *n.* machine; machinery.

ki⌈ka⌉i[2] きかい(機会) *n.* opportunity; chance; occasion:
ii kikai *o nogasu* (いい機会を逃す) miss a good *opportunity*.

ki⌈kaika きかいか(機械化) *n.* mechanization.
kikaika suru (～する) *vt.* mechanize: *noogyoo o* kikaika suru (農業を機械化する) *mechanize* farming.

ki⌈kaku[1] きかく(企画) *n.* plan; project; planning: kikaku *o tateru* (企画を立てる) make a *plan*.
kikaku suru (～する) *vt.* plan; arrange.

ki⌈kaku[2] きかく(規格) *n.* standard; requirements.

ki⌈ka⌉ñ きかん(期間) *n.* term; period:
Keeyaku no kikañ *wa go-neñ desu.* (契約の期間は5年です) The *term* of the contract is five years.

-ki⌉kañ きかん(機関) *suf.* **1** engine: *jooki*-kikañ (蒸気機関) a steam *engine*.
2 institution; system; means: *kyooiku*-kikañ (教育機関) an educational *institution* / *kootsuu*-kikañ (交通機関) a *means* of transport.

ki⌈ka⌉ñsha きかんしゃ(機関車) *n.* locomotive.

ki⌈kas·u きかす(聞かす) *vt.* (kikash·i-; kikas·a-; kikash·i-te Ⓒ) tell; let hear:
Sono hanashi wa nañ-do mo kikasareta. (その話は何度も聞かされた) I *was told* the story many times. 《⇨ kiku[1]》

ki⌈keñ[1] きけん(危険) *n.* danger; peril; risk; hazard:
kikeñ *o kañjiru* (危険を感じる) sense *danger*.
— *a.n.* (～ na) dangerous; perilous; risky; hazardous; unsafe.

ki⌈keñ[2] きけん(棄権) *n.* abstention; withdrawal.

kikeñ suru (～する) *vt.* abstain; withdraw; default: *toohyoo o* kikeñ suru (投票を棄権する) *abstain* from voting.

ki⌉ki きき (危機) *n.* crisis; emergency.

kiki-ippatsu (～一髪) a hair's breadth: *Kare wa* kiki-ippatsu de *shi o manugareta.* (彼は危機一髪で死を免れた) He escaped death *by the skin of his teeth.*

ki⌈kiaki⌉·ru ききあきる (聞き飽きる) *vi.* (-aki-te [V]) be tired of hearing. ((⇨ akiru))

ki⌈kichigae⌉·ru ききちがえる (聞き違える) *vt.* (-chigae-te [V]) mishear; hear a thing wrong. ((⇨ kikichigai))

ki⌈kichigai ききちがい (聞き違い) *n.* hearing wrongly:
Sore wa anata no kikichigai *desu.* (それはあなたの聞き違いです) You *didn't hear* me *correctly.* ((⇨ kikichigaeru))

ki⌈kida⌉s·u ききだす (聞き出す) *vt.* (-dash·i-; -das·a-; -dash·i-te [C]) get (information); find out:
Kare kara nani mo kikidasu *koto ga dekinakatta.* (彼から何も聞き出すことができなかった) We could not *find out* anything from him.

ki⌈kigurushi⌉·i ききぐるしい (聞き苦しい) *a.* (-ku) disagreeable to hear; harsh to the ear:
Kare no iiwake wa kikigurushikatta. (彼の言い訳は聞き苦しかった) I *could not bear* to listen to his excuses.

ki⌈kika⌉es·u ききかえす (聞き返す) *vt.* (-kaesh·i-; -kaes·a-; -kaesh·i-te [C]) repeat a question; ask again. ((⇨ kikinaosu))

ki⌈kime ききめ (効き目) *n.* effect; efficacy; virtue:
Kare ni chuukoku shite mo, kikime *wa nakatta.* (彼に忠告しても, 効き目はなかった) Although I warned him, it had no *effect.* ((⇨ kiku[2]; kooka[1]))

ki⌈kinao⌉s·u ききなおす (聞き直す) *vt.* (-naosh·i-; -naos·a-; -naosh·i-te [C]) ask again. ((⇨ kikikaesu))

ki⌈kinoga⌉s·u ききのがす (聞き逃す) *vt.* (-nogash·i-; -nogas·a-; -nogash·i-te [C]) fail to hear:
Sono nyuusu wa kikinogashimashita. (そのニュースは聞き逃しました) I *failed to hear* the news.

ki⌈kisokona⌉·u ききそこなう (聞き損なう) *vt.* (-sokona·i-; -sokonaw·a-; -sokonat-te [C]) hear amiss; fail to catch:
Kare ga itta koto o kikisokonaimashita. (彼が言ったことを聞き損ないました) I *could not catch* what he said. ((⇨ -sokonau))

ki⌈kite ききて (聞き手) *n.* hearer; listener; interviewer; audience. ((↔ hanashite))

ki⌈kito⌉r·u ききとる (聞き取る) *vt.* (-tor·i-; -tor·a-; -tot-te [C]) hear; catch:
Watashi no iu koto ga kikitoremasu *ka?* (私の言うことが聞き取れますか) *Can* you *hear* what I am saying?

ki⌈koe·ru きこえる (聞こえる) *vi.* (kikoe-te [V]) **1** hear; be audible:
Deñwa ga tookute, yoku kikoemaseñ. (電話が遠くて, よく聞こえません) I *cannot hear* you properly because of the bad phone connection.
2 sound (like...):
Anata no kotoba wa iiwake ni kikoeru. (あなたの言葉は言い訳に聞こえる) What you say *sounds* like an excuse.

ki⌈koku きこく (帰国) *n.* return to one's country [homeland].

ki⌈koku-shi⌉jo きこくしじょ (帰国子女) *n.* Japanese children [students] who have recently returned home from living abroad.

ki⌈koo きこう (気候) *n.* climate; weather.

ki⌈k·u[1] きく (聞く・聴く・訊く) *vt.* (kik·i-; kik·a-; ki·i-te [C])
1 listen to:

Maiasa shichi-ji no nyuusu o kikimasu. (毎朝7時のニュースをききます) Every morning I *listen to* the seven o'clock news.

2 hear of [about]:
Soñna koto wa kiita *koto ga arimaseñ.* (そんなことは聞いたことがありません) I *have* never *heard of* such a thing.

3 ask; inquire:
Keesatsukañ ni eki e iku michi o kiita. (警察官に駅へ行く道を聞いた) I *asked* a policeman the way to the station.

4 obey; follow:
Sono ko wa oya no iu koto o yoku kiku. (その子は親の言うことをよく聞く) That boy faithfully *obeys* what his parents tell him.
《⇨ shitagau》

ki⌈k·u[2] きく(効く・利く) *vi.* (kik·i-; kik·a-; ki·i-te Ⓒ) **1** (of medicine, remedy, etc.) have an effect; work.

2 (of apparatus) act; work:
Kono jiteñsha wa bureeki ga kikanai. (この自転車はブレーキが利かない) The brakes on this bicycle *do not work.*

... ga kiku (...が〜) can be done: señtaku ga kiku (洗濯がきく) *be washable* / shuuri ga kiku (修理がきく) *be repairable.* 《⇨ dekiru》

ki⌈ku⌉[3] きく(菊) *n.* chrysanthemum.

ki⌈ku⌉bari きくばり(気配り) *n.* attention; care; consideration.

ki⌈kyoo ききょう(帰郷) *n.* homecoming.
kikyoo suru (〜する) *vi.* return to one's hometown.

ki⌈mae ga i⌉i きまえがいい(気前がいい) generous; liberal; openhanded:
Ano hito wa itsu-mo kimae ga ii. (あの人はいつも気前がいい) He *is* always *generous* with his money.

ki⌈magure きまぐれ(気紛れ) *n.* caprice; whim; fancy.
— *a.n.* (〜 na, ni) capricious; whimsical:
Kimagure *ni itta koto ga hoñtoo ni natta.* (気まぐれに言ったことが本当になった) What I had said *frivolously* came true.

ki⌈mama きまま(気まま) *a.n.* (〜 na, ni) easy; carefree:
kimama *ni kurasu* (気ままに暮らす) live an *easy* life.

ki⌈mari きまり(決まり) *n.* **1** rule; regulation:
kimari *o mamoru* [*yaburu*] (決まりを守る[破る]) obey [break] a *rule.*

2 settlement; conclusion:
Hayaku kono shigoto ni kimari o tsuketai. (早くこの仕事に決まりをつけたい) I *want to finish up* this job as soon as possible.

3 habit; custom:
Yuuhañ mae ni biiru o nomu no ga kare no kimari *desu.* (夕飯前にビールを飲むのが彼の決まりです) It is his *custom* to have a beer before dinner.

ki⌈mari ga waru⌉i きまりがわるい(きまりが悪い) feel embarrassed.
《⇨ hazukashii》

ki⌈mar·u きまる(決まる) *vi.* (kimar·i-; kimar·a-; kimat-te Ⓒ) be decided; be settled; be fixed:
Sono hanashi wa sugu ni kimatta. (その話はすぐに決まった) The negotiations *were* soon *concluded.*
《⇨ kettee; kimeru》
kimatta (決まった) regular: *Kare ni wa* kimatta *shoku ga nai.* (彼には決まった職がない) He has no *regular* job.
kimatte (決まって) always: *Kaigi ni kare wa* kimatte *okureru.* (会議に彼は決まって遅れる) He is *always* late for meetings.

ki⌈me·ru きめる(決める) *vt.* (kimete Ⓥ) **1** decide; determine:
Doko e iku ka mada kimete *imaseñ.* (どこへ行くかまだ決めていません) I have not yet *made up my mind* where to go. 《⇨ kimaru》

2 arrange (a time, a place, etc.); fix; settle. 《⇨ kimaru》

k

ki⌈mi[1] きみ(君) *n.* you. ★ The plural forms are '*kimi-tachi*' and '*kimi-ra*' (*slightly derog.*).
★ Used by men when talking to close friends, subordinates, or juniors. ⟪⇨ anata⟫

ki⌈mi⌉[2] きみ(気味) *n.* **1** feeling; sensation:
Ii kimi da. (いい気味だ) *It serves you right.*
2 tendency.
kimi ga ii (～がいい) feel satisfied.
kimi ga warui (～が悪い) weird; creepy; uncanny.

ki⌈mitsu きみつ(機密) *n.* secret [classified] information:
kimitsu-*buñsho* (機密文書) a *secret* [*confidential*] document.

ki⌈mochi きもち(気持ち) *n.* feeling; mood:
Kare no kimochi *wa wakaru.* (彼の気持ちはわかる) I know *how he feels.*
kimochi ga yoi [warui] (～が良い[悪い]) feel good [sick].

ki⌈mono きもの(着物) *n.* **1** kimono; traditional Japanese costume.
2 clothes; clothing.

ki⌈muzukashi⌉·i きむずかしい(気難しい) *n.* (-ku) hard to please; grouchy:
Kaneko-sañ wa kimuzukashii. (金子さんは気難しい) Mr. Kaneko is *hard to please.*

ki⌉myoo きみょう(奇妙) *a.n.* (～ na, ni) strange; odd; queer:
Kimi ga sono koto o shiranai nañte kimyoo *da.* (きみがそのことを知らないなんて奇妙だ) It is rather *odd* that you know nothing about that.

ki⌉ñ[1] きん(金) *n.* gold.

ki⌉ñ[2] きん(菌) *n.* germ; bacterium; fungus.

ki⌉nai きない(機内) *n.* inside an airplane:
kinai *ni ooki-na nimotsu o mochikomu* (機内に大きな荷物を持ち込む) take large items of luggage *onto the plane.* ⟪↔ kigai⟫

ki⌈ñbeñ きんべん(勤勉) *n.* diligence; industry. ⟪↔ namakeru⟫
— *a.n.* (～ na, ni) hardworking; diligent:
Ano hito wa kiñbeñ *da.* (あの人は勤勉だ) He is *industrious.*

ki⌈ñchoo きんちょう(緊張) *n.* strain; tension.
kiñchoo suru (～する) *vi.* feel nervous; tense up.

ki⌉ñdai きんだい(近代) *n.* modern ages [times]:
kiñdai-*kokka* (近代国家) a *modern* nation. ⟪⇨ geñdai⟫

ki⌈ñdaika きんだいか(近代化) *n.* modernization.
kiñdaika suru (～する) *vt.* modernize: *mura o* kiñdaika suru (村を近代化する) *modernize* a village.

ki⌈neñ きねん(記念) *n.* souvenir; commemoration.
kineñ suru (～する) *vt.* commemorate. ⟪⇨ kineñbi⟫

ki⌈ñeñ きんえん(禁煙) *n.* prohibition of smoking: kiñeñ-*sha* (禁煙車) a *no-smoking* (railroad) car.
kiñeñ suru (～する) *vi.* give up smoking.

ki⌈ne⌉ñbi きねんび(記念日) *n.* memorial [commemoration] day; anniversary.

ki⌈ñgaku きんがく(金額) *n.* amount [sum] of money.

ki⌈ñgañ きんがん(近眼) *n.* nearsightedness; shortsightedness.

ki⌉ñgyo きんぎょ(金魚) *n.* goldfish.

ki⌈ñiro きんいろ(金色) *n.* color of gold; gold.

ki⌈ñji·ru きんじる(禁じる) *vt.* (kiñjite [V]) forbid; prohibit; ban:
Koko de wa kitsueñ ga kiñjirarete imasu. (ここでは喫煙が禁じられています) Smoking *is prohibited* here.

ki⌉ñjo きんじょ(近所) *n.* neighborhood; vicinity.

ki⌈ñjo-me⌉ewaku きんじょめいわく(近所迷惑) *n.* a nuisance to the neighbors.

ki⌉ñko きんこ(金庫) *n.* safe:
o-kane o kiñko *ni shimau* (お金を金

庫にしまう) put money in a *safe*.

ki͡ñkoo きんこう (均衡) *n.* balance; equilibrium:
chikara no kiñkoo *o tamotsu* [*yaburu*] (力の均衡を保つ[破る]) maintain [upset] the *balance* of power.

ki͡ñkyuu きんきゅう (緊急) *n.* emergency; urgency.
— *a.n.* (~ na, ni) urgent; pressing; immediate:
Kiñkyuu *na yooji ga dekimashita.* (緊急な用事ができました) Some *pressing* business has come up.

ki͡ñmotsu きんもつ (禁物) *n.* prohibited thing; taboo:
Yudañ wa kiñmotsu *desu.* (油断は禁物です) Carelessness is *not tolerated.*

ki͝ñmu きんむ (勤務) *n.* service; duty; work:
kiñmu-*jikañ* (勤務時間) *office* hours / kiñmu-*saki* (勤務先) one's place of *employment*.
kiñmu suru (~する) *vi.* be on duty; be at work. ⟪⇨ tsutomeru[1]⟫

ki͝ñniku きんにく (筋肉) *n.* muscle; brawn:
Kare wa kiñniku takumashii *ude o shite iru.* (彼は筋肉たくましい腕をしている) He has *brawny* arms.

ki͡nodoku͝ きのどく (気の毒) *a.n.* (~ na, ni) pitiable; pitiful; unfortunate; regrettable; sorry:
*Sore wa o-*kinodoku *desu.* (それはお気の毒です) I'm *sorry* to hear that.

ki͝noko きのこ *n.* mushroom.

ki͡no͝o[1] きのう (昨日) *n.* yesterday. ⟪⇨ ashita; kyoo; myoogonichi⟫

ki͝noo[2] きのう (機能) *n.* function:
kinoo-*shoogai* (機能障害) a *functional* disorder (of the body).
kinoo suru (~する) *vi.* function; work. ⟪⇨ ugoku⟫

ki͡ñpatsu きんぱつ (金髪) *n.* blond [golden] hair.

ki͝ñseñ きんせん (金銭) *n.* money; cash. ⟪⇨ kane[1]⟫

ki͡ñshi[1] きんし (禁止) *n.* prohibition; ban:
Koko wa chuusha kiñshi desu. (ここは駐車禁止です) Parking *is prohibited* here.
kiñshi suru (~する) *vt.* prohibit; forbid; ban. ⟪↔ kyoka⟫

ki͡ñshi[2] きんし (近視) *n.* nearsightedness; shortsightedness. ⟪↔ eñshi⟫ ⟪⇨ kiñgañ⟫

ki͝nu きぬ (絹) *n.* silk.

ki͡ñyo͝o(bi) きんよう(び) (金曜(日)) *n.* Friday. ⟪⇨ APP. 5⟫

ki͡nyuu きにゅう (記入) *n.* entry.
kinyuu (o) suru (~(を)する) *vt.* make an entry; write; fill out.

ki͝ñzoku きんぞく (金属) *n.* metal.

ki͡oku きおく (記憶) *n.* memory; recollection; remembrance:
kioku *o ushinau* (記憶を失う) lose one's *memory*.
kioku suru (~する) *vt.* remember; memorize. ⟪⇨ mono-oboe; oboe⟫

ki͡oñ きおん (気温) *n.* (atmospheric) temperature.

ki͡ppa͝ri きっぱり *adv.* (~ to) flatly; definitely; for good:
kippari (*to*) *sake o yameru* (きっぱり(と)酒をやめる) give up drinking *for good*.

ki͡ppu きっぷ (切符) *n.* ticket:
*oofuku-*kippu (往復切符) a roundtrip *ticket*. ⟪⇨ keñ[2]⟫

ki͡rai きらい (嫌い) *a.n.* (~ na) dislike; hate:
Toku ni kirai *na tabemono wa arimaseñ.* (特に嫌いな食べ物はありません) There isn't any food I *dislike* in particular. ⟪↔ suki[1]⟫ ⟪⇨ kirau⟫

ki͝rakira きらきら *adv.* (~ to) (the state of things that shine brightly):
kirakira (to) hikaru (きらきら(と)光る) *glitter*; *glisten*. ⟪⇨ giragira⟫

ki͡raku きらく (気楽) *a.n.* (~ na, ni) carefree; easy; comfortable:
Doozo, kiraku *ni shite kudasai.* (どうぞ, 気楽にしてください) Please make yourself *comfortable*. ⟪⇨ noñbiri; noñki⟫

ki⌈ra⌉ri きらり *adv.* (~ to) shine or glitter briefly:
Kanojo no me ni namida ga kirari *to hikatta.* (彼女の目に涙がきらりと光った) The tears *glistened* in her eyes.

ki⌈ra·u きらう (嫌う) *vt.* (kira·i-; kiraw·a-; kirat-te Ⓒ) dislike; hate:
hito ni kirawareru (人に嫌われる) *be disliked* by everyone. 《⇨ kirai》

ki⌈re⌉ きれ (切れ) *n.* cloth; rag. 《⇨ nuno》

-kire きれ (切れ) *suf.* piece; slice; strip:
*niku go-*kire (肉 5 切れ) five *pieces* of meat / *pañ hito-*kire (パン 1 切れ) a *slice* of bread.

ki⌉ree きれい (綺麗) *a.n.* (~ na, ni) **1** beautiful; pretty; lovely:
kiree *na josee* [*keshiki*] (きれいな女性[景色]) a *beautiful* woman [view] 《⇨ utsukushii》
2 clean; clear; tidy; neat:
Heya o kiree ni sooji shita. (部屋をきれいに掃除した) I *cleaned* the room thoroughly. 《↔ kitanai》
3 (~ ni) completely; wholly; entirely:
Sono koto wa kiree *ni wasurete ita.* (そのことはきれいに忘れていた) I had *completely* forgotten that. 《⇨ sukkari》
4 (~ na) (of politics) fair; clean:
kiree *na señkyo* (きれいな選挙) a *clean and fair* election.

ki⌈re⌉·ru きれる (切れる) *vi.* (kire-te Ⓥ) **1** (of a blade, knife, sword, etc.) cut; be sharp:
Kono naifu wa (*yoku*) kireru. (このナイフは(よく)切れる) This knife *cuts* well.
2 (of a thread, rope, etc.) break; be broken; snap:
Ito [*Tsuna*] *ga* kireta. (糸[綱]が切れた) The thread [rope] *broke*. 《⇨ kiru[1]》
3 (of a telephone, communication, relations, etc.) cut off:
Deñwa ga tochuu de kireta. (電話が途中で切れた) I *was cut off* in the middle of my phone call. 《⇨ kiru[1]》
4 (of a bank, dam) collapse; burst:
Totsuzeñ damu ga kireta. (突然ダムが切れた) The dam suddenly *burst*.
5 (of food, goods) run out; be out of stock:
Bataa ga kirete shimatta. (バターが切れてしまった) The butter *has run out*.
6 (of a contract, deadline, etc.) expire:
Kono keeyaku wa kotoshi de kiremasu. (この契約は今年で切れます) This contract *expires* this year.
7 (of a person) able; competent:
Kanojo wa kireru. (彼女は切れる) She is *very able*.

ki⌈ri[1] きり (霧) *n.* fog; mist.

ki⌉ri[2] きり (錐) *n.* drill; gimlet; awl.

-kiri きり (切り) *suf.* **1** only:
★ The emphatic form is '*-kkiri*.'
*Josee wa watashi hitori-*kiri *datta.* (女性は私一人きりだった) I was the *only* woman there.
2 since:
*Kare wa itta-*kiri *kaette konakatta.* (彼は行ったきり帰って来なかった) He has never returned *since* he left.

ki⌈riage·ru きりあげる (切り上げる) *vt.* (-age-te Ⓥ) **1** knock off; leave off; finish:
go-ji ni shigoto o kiriageru (5 時に仕事を切り上げる) *knock off* work at five.
2 raise; round up:
shoosuu-teñ ika o kiriageru (小数点以下を切り上げる) *raise* the decimals to the nearest whole number. 《⇨ kirisuteru; shisha-gonyuu》
3 revalue:
tsuuka o juugo-paaseñto kiriageru (通貨を 15% 切り上げる) *revalue* the currency by fifteen percent.

ki⌈ridas·u きりだす (切り出す) *vi.*, *vt.* (-dash·i-; -das·a-; -dash·i-te

[C]) **1** begin to talk:
Kare wa yooyaku sono moñdai o kiridashita. (彼はようやくその問題を切り出した) He finally *broached* the matter.
2 cut down; log; quarry:
ki o kiridasu (木を切り出す) *cut down* a tree.

ki⌈rihana⌉s·u きりはなす (切り離す) *vt.* (-hanash·i-; -hanas·a-; -hanash·i-te [C]) cut off; separate.

ki⌈rikae·ru きりかえる (切り替える) *vt.* (-kae-te [V]) change; renew; switch:
chañneru o kirikaeru (チャンネルを切り替える) *change* the (TV) channel.

ki⌈rinuk·u きりぬく (切り抜く) *vt.* (-nuk·i-; -nuk·a-; -nu·i-te [C]) clip; cut out:
Sono kiji o shiñbuñ kara kirinuita. (その記事を新聞から切り抜いた) I *clipped* the article out of the newspaper.

ki⌈risage·ru きりさげる (切り下げる) *vt.* (-sage-te [V]) **1** cut; reduce:
nedañ o subete go-paaseñto kirisageru (値段をすべて 5% 切り下げる) *reduce* all prices by five percent.
2 devalue:
tsuuka o juugo-paaseñto kirisageru (通貨を 15% 切り下げる) *devalue* the currency by fifteen percent.

ki⌈risute·ru きりすてる (切り捨てる) *vt.* (-sute-te [V]) round down; cut off; omit:
hasuu o kirisuteru (端数を切り捨てる) *cut off* fractions. ((⇨ kiriageru; shisha-gonyuu))

Ki⌈risuto キリスト *n.* Christ.

Ki⌈risuto-kyoo キリストきょう (基督教) *n.* Christianity:
Kirisuto-kyooto (キリスト教徒) a *Christian.*

ki⌈ritor·u きりとる (切り取る) *vt.* (-tor·i-; -tor·a-; -tot-te [C]) cut away [off]; clip:
ki no eda o kiritoru (木の枝を切り取る) *cut away* the branches of a tree.

ki⌈ritsu きりつ (規律) *n.* **1** rules; regulations:
kiritsu *o mamoru* [*yaburu*] (規律を守る[破る]) observe [break] the *rules.*
2 order; discipline.

ki⌈ritsume⌉·ru きりつめる (切り詰める) *vt.* (-tsume-te [V]) cut down; reduce; shorten:
keehi o kiritsumeru (経費を切り詰める) *cut down* on expenses.

ki⌉ro キロ *n.* ★ Shortened form of '*kiromeetoru*' and '*kiroguramu.*'

ki⌈rogu⌉ramu キログラム *n.* kilogram. ((⇨ kiro))

ki⌈roku きろく (記録) *n.* record; minutes.
kiroku suru (〜する) *vt.* record; write down: *kaigi no naiyoo o* kiroku suru (会議の内容を記録する) *record* the content of a meeting.

ki⌈rome⌉etoru キロメートル *n.* kilometer. ((⇨ kiro))

ki⌈r·u[1] きる (切る) *vt.* (kir·i-; kir·a-; kit-te [C]) **1** cut; chop; slice; saw; shear:
Kanojo wa hoochoo de yubi o kitta. (彼女は包丁で指を切った) She *cut* her finger with a kitchen knife.
2 sever (relations):
Kare wa sono kai to eñ o kitta. (彼はその会と縁を切った) He *severed* his connection with the society. ((⇨ kireru))
3 hang up (a telephone):
Deñwa o kiranai *de kudasai.* (電話を切らないでください) Please *do not hang up.* ((⇨ kireru))
4 switch off:
deñki (*no suitchi*) *o* kiru (電気(のスイッチ)を切る) *switch off* the electricity.
5 punch (a ticket):
kippu o kitte morau (切符を切ってもらう) *get* one's ticket *punched.*
6 drain:
hooreñsoo no mizu o kiru (ほうれん草の水を切る) *drain* water from

spinach.
7 be less than...:
Kare wa hyaku-meetoru de juu-ichi-byoo o kitta. (彼は100メートルで11秒を切った) He *did* 100 meters *in less than* eleven seconds.
8 shuffle:
torañpu o kiru (トランプを切る) *shuffle* playing cards.

ki·ʳru² きる(着る) *vt.* (ki-te Ⓥ)
1 put on:
Kare wa oobaa o kinai de *soto e deta.* (彼はオーバーを着ないで外へ出た) He went out *without putting on* his overcoat. ⟪⇨ kiseru⟫
2 wear; have on: ★ Used in '*kite iru*.'
Yamada-sañ wa wafuku o kite ita. (山田さんは和服を着ていた) Miss Yamada *was wearing* Japanese clothes.

kiʳseñ きせん(汽船) *n.* steamer; steamship; steamboat.

kiʳse·ru きせる(着せる) *vt.* (kise-te Ⓥ) dress; clothe:
kodomo ni wafuku o kiseru (子どもに和服を着せる) *dress* a child in Japanese style clothes. ⟪⇨ kiru²⟫

kiʳseˀtsu きせつ(季節) *n.* season; time of the year.

kiʳshaˀ¹ きしゃ(記者) *n.* reporter; journalist.

kiʳshaˀ² きしゃ(汽車) *n.* train. ⟪⇨ ressha; deñsha⟫

kiʳsha-kaˀikeñ きしゃかいけん(記者会見) *n.* press conference.

kiʳshiˀ きし(岸) *n.* bank; shore; coast.

kiʳshitsu きしつ(気質) *n.* disposition; temper; nature:
kimuzukashii [yasashii] kishitsu *no otoko* (気難しい[優しい]気質の男) a man of grumpy [affectionate] *disposition.*

kiʳshoo¹ きしょう(気性) *n.* temper; disposition; nature:
Kare wa kishoo *ga hageshii.* (彼は気性が激しい) He has a fiery *temper.* ⟪⇨ kishitsu⟫

kiʳshoo² きしょう(気象) *n.* weather conditions.

kiʳshoo³ きしょう(起床) *n.* getting up; rising.
kishoo suru (〜する) *vi.* rise from one's bed. ⟪⇨ okiru⟫

kiʳsoˀ きそ(基礎) *n.* foundation; basis; base; basics. ⟪⇨ kihoñ⟫

kiʳsoˀku きそく(規則) *n.* rule; regulations.

kiʳsoku-teki きそくてき(規則的) *a.n.* (〜 na, ni) regular; systematic:
kisoku-teki *na seekatsu o suru* (規則的な生活をする) lead a *well-regulated* life.

kiʳso-teki きそてき(基礎的) *a.n.* (〜 na, ni) fundamental; basic; elementary:
kiso-teki *na buñpoo* (基礎的な文法) *elementary* grammar.

kiʳssaˀteñ きっさてん(喫茶店) *n.* coffeehouse; coffee shop; tearoom.

kiʳsuˀu きすう(奇数) *n.* odd number(s). ⟪↔ guusuu⟫

kiʳta きた(北) *n.* north; (〜 ni/e) northward. ⟪↔ minami⟫

kiʳtaeˀ·ru きたえる(鍛える) *vt.* (kitae-te Ⓥ) train; build up; strengthen:
wakai uchi ni karada o kitaeru (若いうちに体を鍛える) *harden* one's body while young.

kiʳtai¹ きたい(期待) *n.* expectation; anticipation; hope:
kitai-hazure (期待外れ) a *disappointment.*
kitai suru (〜する) *vt.* count on; expect; anticipate; hope for.

kiʳtai² きたい(気体) *n.* gas. ⟪⇨ ekitai; kotai⟫

kiʳtaku きたく(帰宅) *n.* returning home.
kitaku suru (〜する) *vi.* return home. ⟪⇨ kaeru¹⟫

kiʳtanaˀ·i きたない(汚い) *a.* (-ku)
1 dirty; filthy; foul. ⟪↔ kiree⟫
2 mean; low; dirty:
Ano hito wa o-kane ni kitanai. (あの人はお金に汚い) He is *mean* with

his money.
3 indecent; filthy; nasty:
kitanai *kotoba* (汚い言葉) *indecent* language.

ki⌈tee きてい (規定) *n.* rule; regulation; stipulation.
kitee suru (~する) *vt.* prescribe; provide. ⟪⇨ sadameru⟫

ki⌈teñ きてん (起点) *n.* starting point. ⟪⇨ shuuteñ⟫

ki⌈tsueñ きつえん (喫煙) *n.* smoking. ⟪⇨ tabako⟫
kitsueñ suru (~する) *vi.* have a smoke.

ki⌈tsu·i きつい *a.* (-ku) **1** tight:
Kono sukaato wa sukoshi kitsui. (このスカートは少しきつい) This skirt is a bit *tight.* ⟪↔ yurui; yuruyaka⟫
2 hard; severe:
Kono-goro no samusa wa kitsui. (この頃の寒さはきつい) The recent cold weather has been *severe.*
3 stern; strong-minded:
kitsui *seekaku* (きつい性格) a *stern* and *strong-minded* personality.

ki⌈tsune きつね (狐) *n.* fox.

ki⌈tte きって (切手) *n.* postage stamp.

ki⌈tto きっと *adv.* surely; without fail; undoubtedly:
Kare wa kitto *kimasu.* (彼はきっと来ます) He will *certainly* come. ⟪⇨ kanarazu⟫

ki⌈wa⌉mete きわめて (極めて) *adv.* (*formal*) extremely; exceedingly.

ki⌈yo⌉·i きよい (清い) *a.* (-ku) (*literary*) clean; pure:
kiyoku *suñda nagare* (清く澄んだ流れ) a *crystal clear* stream. ⟪⇨ kiyoraka⟫

ki⌉yoo きよう (器用) *a.n.* (~ na, ni) **1** skillful; handy; deft:
Kanojo wa tesaki ga kiyoo *da.* (彼女は手先が器用だ) She is *good* with her hands. ⟪↔ bukiyoo⟫
2 clever: kiyoo *na hito* (器用な人) a *clever* person.

ki⌈yo⌉raka きよらか (清らか) *a.n.* (~ na, ni) (*literary*) pure; clear; noble:
kiyoraka *na hitomi* (清らかなひとみ) *bright, clear* eyes. ⟪⇨ kiyoi⟫

ki⌈zam·u きざむ (刻む) *vt.* (kizam·i-; kizam·a-; kizañ-de Ⓒ)
1 mince; chop up:
tamanegi o kizamu (たまねぎを刻む) *chop up* an onion.
2 carve; engrave.

ki⌈zetsu きぜつ (気絶) *n.* fainting; faint; swoon.
kizetsu suru (~する) *vi.* faint:
Kanojo wa kizetsu shite *taoreta.* (彼女は気絶して倒れた) She fell *in a faint.*

ki⌉zoku きぞく (貴族) *n.* aristocracy; noble; nobleman; peer; peeress.

ki⌈zu[1] きず (傷) *n.* injury; wound; hurt; cut.

ki⌈zu[2] きず (疵) *n.* crack; flaw; bruise; defect.
kizu o tsukeru (~をつける) damage; ruin; spoil.

ki⌈zu⌉kai きづかい (気遣い) *n.* worry; fear:
Kare ga shippai suru kizukai *wa arimaseñ.* (彼が失敗する気遣いはありません) There is no *fear* of his failing. ⟪⇨ kizukau⟫

ki⌈zuka⌉·u きづかう (気遣う) *vt.* (kizuka·i-; kizukaw·a-; kizukat-te Ⓒ) be anxious about; worry about:
hito no añpi o kizukau (人の安否を気づかう) *be anxious* about a person's safety. ⟪⇨ kizukai⟫

ki⌈zu⌉k·u[1] きづく (気付く) *vi.* (kizuk·i-; kizuk·a-; kizu·i-te Ⓒ) become aware; notice; find out:
buñshoo no ayamari ni kizuku (文章の誤りに気づく) *notice* a mistake in a sentence.

ki⌈zu⌉k·u[2] きずく (築く) *vt.* (kizuk·i-; kizuk·a-; kizu·i-te Ⓒ) build; construct; erect:
ooki-na zaisañ o kizuku (大きな財産を築く) *build up* a large fortune.

ki⌉zuna きずな (絆) *n.* bond; ties:
Futari wa tsuyoi yuujoo no kizuna *de musubarete ita.* (二人は強い友情

のきずなで結ばれていた) The two of them were bound together by firm *ties* of friendship.

ki⌈zutsuke⌉·ru きずつける (傷付ける) *vt.* (-tsuke-te [V]) wound; injure; hurt (physically or mentally). 《⇨ kizutsuku》

ki⌈zutsu⌉k·u きずつく (傷付く) *vi.* (-tsuk·i-; -tsuk·a-; -tsu·i-te [C]) be [get] injured; be [get] hurt (usually mentally):
Sono uwasa de kanojo no kokoro wa kizutsuita. (そのうわさで彼女の心は傷ついた) She *was deeply hurt* by the rumor. 《⇨ kizutsukeru》

ko こ (子) *n.* **1** child; son; daughter: ★ Usually used with a modifier.
otoko-no-ko (男の子) a *boy* / oñna-no-ko (女の子) a *girl*. 《⇨ kodomo》
2 (of animals) the young:
inu no ko (犬の子) a *puppy* / neko no ko (猫の子) a *kitten*. 《↔ oya》

ko-[1] こ (小) *pref.* small; little:
ko-*tori* (小鳥) a *little* bird / ko-*zeni* (小銭) *small* change / ko-*same* (小雨) *light* rain.

ko⌉-[2] こ (故) *pref.* the late; the deceased:
ko-*Yamada-shi* (故山田氏) *the late* Mr. Yamada.

-ko[1] こ (個) *suf.* piece; item:
★ Counter for small objects.
tamago sañ-ko (卵 3 個) *three* eggs / *sekkeñ go*-ko (石けん 5 個) five *cakes* of soap.

-ko[2] こ (戸) *suf.* house: *nijuk*-ko *no ie* (20 戸の家) twenty *houses*.

-ko[3] こ (粉) *suf.* powder; flour:
karee-ko (カレー粉) curry *powder* / *komugi*-ko (小麦粉) wheat *flour*.

-ko[4] こ (湖) *suf.* lake:
Kawaguchi-ko (河口湖) *Lake* Kawaguchi.

ko⌈ba⌉m·u こばむ (拒む) *vt.* (ko-bam·i-; kobam·a-; kobañ-de [C]) refuse (a demand, request); decline. 《⇨ kotowaru》

ko⌈bore⌉·ru こぼれる (零れる) *vi.* (kobore-te [V]) (of fluid, grains, etc.) fall; slop; spill:
Kanojo no me kara namida ga koboreta. (彼女の目から涙がこぼれた) Tears *fell* from her eyes.
《⇨ kobosu》

ko⌈bo⌉s·u こぼす (零す) *vt.* (kobo-sh·i-; kobos·a-; kobosh·i-te [C])
1 spill (fluid, grains, etc.); shed; drop. 《⇨ koboreru》
2 complain; grumble:
Kanojo wa itsu-mo kodomo no koto o koboshite iru. (彼女はいつも子どものことをこぼしている) She *is* always *grumbling* about her children.

ko⌈chira こちら *n.* **1** this place; this way; here: ★ Refers to a direction or a place close to the speaker. More polite than '*koko*' and '*kotchi*.'
Kochira *ga o-tearai desu*. (こちらがお手洗いです) *This* is the bathroom.
《⇨ mukoo[1]》
2 this thing; this person:
★ More polite than '*kore*.'
Kochira *wa hoñjitsu no tokubetsu ryoori desu*. (こちらは本日の特別料理です) *This* is today's special dish.
3 I; we:
Ato de kochira *kara moo ichido o-deñwa itashimasu*. (あとでこちらからもう一度お電話いたします) *I* will call you back again later. 《⇨ achira; dochira; sochira》

ko⌈choo こちょう (誇張) *n.* exaggeration; overstatement.
kochoo suru (～する) *vt.* exaggerate; overstate.

ko⌉dai こだい (古代) *n.* ancient times; remote ages.

ko⌈doku こどく (孤独) *n.* loneliness; solitude.
— *a.n.* (～ na, ni) lonely; solitary:
kodoku *na seekatsu o suru* (孤独な生活をする) lead a *solitary* life.

ko⌈domo こども (子供) *n.* child; boy; girl. 《↔ otona》《⇨ ko》

ko⌉e こえ (声) *n.* **1** human voice; cry:

koe o dashite, *hoñ o yomu* (声を出して, 本を読む) read a book *aloud.*
2 sound; note; song: *mushi no* koe *o kiku* (虫の声を聞く) listen to the *singing* of insects.
3 opinion; view: *kokumiñ no* koe (国民の声) the *opinions* of the people.

ko⌈e·ru[1] こえる (越える) *vi.* (koe-te Ⓥ) go beyond; go over: *yama o* koeru (山を越える) *go over* a mountain / *kawa o* koeru (川を越える) *cross* a river.

ko⌈e·ru[2] こえる (超える) *vi.* (koe-te Ⓥ) exceed; be more than: *Kanojo wa sañjuu o* koete iru. (彼女は30を超えている) She *is more than* thirty. ⟪⇨ kosu[2]⟫

ko⌈e⌉·ru[3] こえる (肥える) *vi.* (koe-te Ⓥ) **1** be fertile: *Kono tochi wa* koete iru. (この土地は肥えている) This soil *is fertile.*
2 grow fat; put on flesh.
... ga koete iru (...が肥えている) have a delicate...: me ga koete iru (目が肥えている) *have an eye for* (beauty).

ko⌈fuñ こふん (古墳) *n.* ancient tomb; old mound. ⟪⇨ APP. 9⟫

ko⌈ga⌉s·u こがす (焦がす) *vt.* (kogash·i-; kogas·a-; kogash·i-te Ⓒ) burn; singe; scorch: *airoñ de shatsu o* kogasu (アイロンでシャツを焦がす) *scorch* one's shirt with an iron. ⟪⇨ kogeru⟫

ko⌈gata こがた (小型) *n.* small size; pocket size: kogata *no kuruma* (小型の車) a *small* car / kogata *no kamera* (小型のカメラ) a *pocket* camera. ⟪⇨ oogata; chuugata⟫

ko⌈ge⌉·ru こげる (焦げる) *vi.* (koge-te Ⓥ) burn; scorch: *Mochi ga makkuro ni* kogete shimatta. (餅が真っ黒に焦げてしまった) The rice cake *has been burned* black. ⟪⇨ kogasu⟫

ko⌈gi⌉tte こぎって (小切手) *n.* check; cheque: kogitte *de harau* (小切手で払う) pay by *check.*

ko⌈goe こごえ (小声) *n.* low voice; whisper. ⟪↔ oogoe⟫

ko⌈goe·ru こごえる (凍える) *vi.* (kogoe-te Ⓥ) freeze; be frozen: *Samukute, te ga* kogoeta. (寒くて, 手が凍えた) My hands *were numb* with the cold.

ko⌉g·u こぐ (漕ぐ) *vt.* (kog·i-; kog·a-; ko·i-de Ⓒ) **1** row; paddle: *booto o* kogu (ボートをこぐ) *row* a boat.
2 pedal; swing: *jiteñsha o* kogu (自転車をこぐ) *pedal* a bicycle.

ko⌉·i[1] こい (濃い) *a.* (-ku) **1** (of color) dark; deep: koi *iro* (濃い色) a *dark* color / koi *aka* (濃い赤) *deep* red. ⟪↔ usui⟫
2 (of taste, density, etc.) thick; strong; dense: *Ani wa hige ga* koi. (兄はひげが濃い) My brother has a *thick* beard. ⟪↔ usui⟫
3 (of degree) strong: *Kare ga sore o shita utagai ga* koi. (彼がそれをした疑いが濃い) The suspicion he did that is *strong.*

ko⌉i[2] こい (恋) *n.* love: koi *ni ochiru* (恋に落ちる) fall in *love.* ⟪⇨ ai; aisuru⟫

ko⌉i[3] こい (故意) *n.* intention; deliberation; purpose: *Watashi wa* koi ni *okureta wake de wa arimaseñ.* (私は故意に遅れたわけではありません) I did not come late *intentionally.* ⟪⇨ waza-to⟫

ko⌉i[4] こい (鯉) *n.* carp. ⟪⇨ koinobori⟫

ko⌈ibito こいびと (恋人) *n.* boyfriend; girlfriend; love. ★ Refers to a steady male or female companion. ⟪⇨ aijiñ⟫

ko⌈ino⌉bori こいのぼり (鯉のぼり) *n.* carp streamer. ★ Carp-shaped streamers traditionally flown on Children's Day (May 5).

ko⌈ishi こいし (小石) *n.* small stone [rock]. ⟪⇨ ishi[1]⟫

ko⌈ishi⌉·i こいしい (恋しい) *a.* (-ku) miss; long for; beloved: *Kokyoo ga* koishiku *natte kita.* (故

k

郷が恋しくなってきた) I have come to *long for* my hometown.

ko⌈is·u⌉ru こいする(恋する) *vt.* (koish·i-; koish·i-; koish·i-te ①) love; fall in love. ⟪⇨ koi[2]⟫

ko⌉ji こじ(孤児) *n.* orphan.

ko⌉jiñ[1] こじん(個人) *n.* **1** individual:
kojiñ *no jiyuu [keñri]* (個人の自由[権利]) the freedom [rights] of the *individual*.
2 each person:
Mochimono wa kojiñ kojiñ *de chuui shite kudasai.* (持ち物は個人個人で注意してください) *Each person* please take care of his or her possessions.

ko⌉jiñ[2] こじん(故人) *n.* the deceased. ⟪⇨ ko-[2]⟫

ko⌈jiñ-teki こじんてき(個人的) *a.n.* (~ na, ni) personal; private:
Kare wa kojiñ-teki *na riyuu de tsutome o yamemashita.* (彼は個人的な理由で勤めをやめました) He quit his job for *private* reasons.

ko⌈ke⌉ こけ(苔) *n.* moss.

ko⌉kka[1] こっか(国家) *n.* nation; state; country.

ko⌉kka[2] こっか(国歌) *n.* national anthem.

ko⌉kka[3] こっか(国花) *n.* national flower.

ko⌈kkai こっかい(国会) *n.* national assembly; legislature of a nation; the Diet. ★ The Japanese Diet is made up of the House of Representatives (*Shuugiiñ*) and the House of Councilors (*Sañgiiñ*). ⟪⇨ Shuugiiñ; Sañgiiñ⟫

ko⌈kkee こっけい(滑稽) *a.n.* (~ na, ni) funny; humorous; comical; ridiculous:
kokkee *na koto o iu* (滑稽なことを言う) say something *foolishly comical*.

ko⌈kki こっき(国旗) *n.* national flag.

ko⌈kkoo こっこう(国交) *n.* diplomatic relations; national friendship:
kokkoo *o musubu* (国交を結ぶ) establish *diplomatic relations*.

ko⌈kkyoo こっきょう(国境) *n.* national border; frontier of a country.

ko⌈ko[1] ここ(此処) *n.* **1** here; this place: ★ Refers to a place close to the speaker.
Koko *kara eki made dono kurai arimasu ka?* (ここから駅までどのくらいありますか) How far is it from *here* to the station?
2 here; this place: ★ Used when the speaker indicates a location by way of explanation, etc.
Kono chizu no koko *ga watashitachi no machi desu.* (この地図のここが私たちの町です) *This part* of the map is our town.
3 this: ★ Refers to something the speaker has just mentioned or intends to mention.
Kyoo no koogi wa koko *made desu.* (きょうの講義はここまでです) *This* concludes my lecture for today.
4 next; past: ★ Refers to a period of time.
Kare wa koko *shibaraku byooki deshita.* (彼はここしばらく病気でした) He had been sick for some time *past*.
5 so far: ★ Refers to a time in the present.
Koko made *wa subete umaku ikimashita.* (ここまではすべてうまくいきました) *So far* everything has gone well. ⟪⇨ asoko; doko; soko[1]⟫

ko⌉ko[2] ここ(個々) *n.* (*formal*) individual; each:
Sore wa koko *no hito no sekiniñ desu.* (それは個々の人の責任です) *Each individual* person is responsible for it.

ko⌈kochi ここち(心地) *n.* feeling; sensation:
Kono isu wa kokochi ga yoi. (このいすは心地がよい) This chair *is comfortable*.

ko⌉koku ここく(故国) *n.* homeland [country].

ko⌈konoka⌉ ここのか (九日) *n.* nine days; the ninth day of the month. (⇨ APP. 5)

ko⌈ko⌉notsu ここのつ (九つ) *n.* nine. ★ Used when counting. (⇨ ku[1]; kyuu[5]; APP. 3)

ko⌈ko⌉ro こころ (心) *n.* heart; mind; spirit:
kokoro *o kimeru* (心を決める) make up one's *mind*. (⇨ shiñ[2])
kokoro kara (〜から) from the bottom of one's heart.
kokoro o utsu (〜を打つ) strike home.

ko⌈koroa⌉tari こころあたり (心当たり) *n.* idea; clue:
Kare ga doko ni iru ka kokoroatari *wa arimasu ka?* (彼がどこにいるか心当たりはありますか) Do you have any *idea* where he is?

ko⌈koroboso⌉·i こころぼそい (心細い) *a.* (-ku) lonely; helpless; uncertain:
kokorobosoku *omou* (心細く思う) feel *helpless*.

ko⌈koro⌉e こころえ (心得) *n.* knowledge; skill:
Kanojo wa ikebana no kokoroe *ga arimasu.* (彼女は生け花の心得があります) She has a good *knowledge* of flower arrangement.

ko⌈koroe⌉·ru こころえる (心得る) *vt.* (kokoroe-te [V]) know; be aware:
Sono heñ no jijoo wa yoku kokoroete imasu. (その辺の事情はよく心得ています) I *am well aware* of that situation.

ko⌈korogake こころがけ (心掛け) *n.* care; prudence; intention:
Kare wa itsu-mo kokorogake ga yoi. (彼はいつも心がけがよい) He *is* always *prudent*. (⇨ kokorogakeru)

ko⌈korogake⌉·ru こころがける (心掛ける) *vt.* (-gake-te [V]) try; keep in mind; do one's best. (⇨ kokorogake)

ko⌈korogurushi⌉·i こころぐるしい (心苦しい) *a.* (-ku) feel sorry; painful. (⇨ sumanai)

ko⌈koromi⌉ こころみ (試み) *n.* trial; attempt; test:
kokoromi *ni sore o yatte miru* (試みにそれをやってみる) give it a *try*. (⇨ kokoromiru)

ko⌈koromi⌉·ru こころみる (試みる) *vt.* (-mi-te [V]) try; attempt; experiment. (⇨ kokoromi; kuwadateru)

ko⌈koromochi こころもち (心持ち) *adv.* a little; a bit; slightly:
Kyoo wa kokoromochi *atatakai.* (きょうは心持ち暖かい) It is *a bit* warm today.

ko⌈koroyo⌉·i こころよい (快い) *a.* (-ku) pleasant; agreeable; delightful.

ko⌈korozashi こころざし (志) *n.* one's will; resolution; ambition:
kokorozashi *o tateru* (志を立てる) make up one's *mind*. (⇨ kokorozasu)

ko⌈koroza⌉s·u こころざす (志す) *vt.* (-zash·i-; -zas·a-; -zash·i-te [C]) intend; aim; plan:
Kare wa sakka o kokorozashite iru. (彼は作家を志している) He *has set his heart* on becoming a writer. (⇨ kokorozashi)

ko⌈korozu⌉kai こころづかい (心遣い) *n.* thoughtfulness; consideration.

ko⌈korozuyo⌉·i こころづよい (心強い) *a.* (-ku) reassuring:
Anata ga ite kureru to kokorozuyoi. (あなたがいてくれると心強い) Your presence *reassures* me.

ko⌈kubañ こくばん (黒板) *n.* blackboard.

ko⌈kuboo こくぼう (国防) *n.* national defense.

ko⌉kudo こくど (国土) *n.* country; territory; land area.

ko⌈ku⌉gai こくがい (国外) *n.* outside the country; abroad; overseas. (↔ kokunai) (⇨ kaigai)

ko⌈kugo こくご (国語) *n.* **1** Japanese language (as an academic

k

subject in Japan). 《⇨ Nihoñgo》
2 language; one's mother tongue. 《⇨ geñgo》

ko⌈kuhaku こくはく(告白) *n.* confession; declaration.
kokuhaku suru (〜する) *vt.* confess; declare.

ko⌈kuhoo こくほう(国宝) *n.* National Treasure.

ko⌈kumee こくめい(国名) *n.* name of a country.

ko⌈kumiñ こくみん(国民) *n.* nation; people; citizen:
kokumiñ *no shukujitsu* (国民の祝日) a *national* holiday. 《⇨ APP. 6》

ko⌈kumu-da⌉ijiñ こくむだいじん(国務大臣) *n.* minister of state.

ko⌈ku⌉nai こくない(国内) *n.* inside the country; domestic; home:
Kare wa Nihoñ kokunai *o jiteñsha de ryokoo shita.* (彼は日本国内を自転車で旅行した) He has traveled *around Japan* by bicycle.
《↔ kokugai; kaigai》

ko⌈kuritsu こくりつ(国立) *n.* national; state:
kokuritsu-*daigaku* (国立大学) a *national* university / kokuritsu-*kooeñ* (国立公園) a *national* park.

ko⌈kusai- こくさい(国際) *pref.* international: kokusai-*kaigi* (国際会議) an *international* conference.

ko⌈kusaika こくさいか(国際化) *n.* internationalization.
kokusaika suru (〜する) *vi.* internationalize: *Kono moñdai wa* kokusaika shi-soo *da.* (この問題は国際化しそうだ) This problem will *become a matter of international concern.*

ko⌈kusai-teki こくさいてき(国際的) *a.n.* (〜 na, ni) international:
kokusai-teki *ni katsuyaku shite iru pianisuto* (国際的に活躍しているピアニスト) a pianist who is active *on the world stage.*

ko⌈kusañ こくさん(国産) *n.* domestic production; home-produced:
kokusañ-*sha* (国産車) a *domestically produced* car.

ko⌈kuseki こくせき(国籍) *n.* (country of) nationality; citizenship:
Kare no kokuseki *wa Nihoñ desu.* (彼の国籍は日本です) His *country of nationality* is Japan.

ko⌈kuyuu こくゆう(国有) *n.* national; state:
kokuyuu-*chi* (国有地) *state-owned* land / kokuyuu-*riñ* (国有林) a *state* forest.

ko⌉kyoo こきょう(故郷) *n.* one's home; one's birthplace; hometown:
Watashi no kokyoo *wa Hokkaidoo* desu. (私の故郷は北海道です) I *come from* Hokkaido.

ko⌈kyuu こきゅう(呼吸) *n.*
1 breathing; respiration:
Byooniñ wa kokyuu *ga arakatta.* (病人は呼吸が荒かった) The patient was *breathing* hard. 《⇨ iki[1]》
2 knack; trick; craft:
Watashi wa yatto sono shigoto no kokyuu *ga nomikometa.* (私はやっとその仕事の呼吸が飲み込めた) Finally I got the *hang* of how to do the work.
3 harmony:
Shikisha to eñsoosha no kokyuu *wa pittari atte ita.* (指揮者と演奏者の呼吸はぴったり合っていた) The conductor and musicians were in perfect *harmony.*
kokyuu suru (〜する) *vi., vt.* breathe; respire.

ko⌈ma⌉ka こまか(細か) *a.n.* (〜na, ni) fine; attentive; detailed:
komaka *na chuui* (細かな注意) *meticulous* care / komaka *ni shiraberu* (細かに調べる) examine *minutely.* 《⇨ komakai》

ko⌈maka⌉·i こまかい(細かい) *a.* (-ku) **1** (of grains, particles, etc.) very small; fine. 《↔ arai[2]》 《⇨ komaka》
2 (of money) small:

señ-eñ satsu o komakaku *suru* (千円札を細かくする) *change* a 1000-yen bill.
3 detailed; careful:
Komakai koto *wa ato de setsumee shimasu.* (細かいことはあとで説明します) I will explain the *details* later.
4 minor; trifling:
komakai *koto de kuyokuyo suru* (細かいことでくよくよする) worry about *trifling* matters.
5 thrifty; stingy:
Kare wa kane ni komakai. (彼は金に細かい) He is *tight* with money.

ko⌈ma⌉r·u こまる(困る) *vi.* (komar·i-; komar·a-; komat-te [C])
1 be in an awkward position; be in a fix; have a hard time.
2 be in financial difficulties; be hard up.

ko⌈me⌉ こめ(米) *n.* rice.
★ With '*o-*' in polite speech.

ko⌈me⌉·ru こめる(込める) *vt.* (kome-te [V]) load:
juu ni tama o komeru (銃に弾を込める) *load* a gun.

ko⌈mori⌉uta こもりうた(子守歌) *n.* lullaby.

ko⌉m·u こむ(込む・混む) *vi., vt.* (kom·i-; kom·a-; koñ-de [C]) be crowded; be packed; be full; be jammed. 《⇨ koñzatsu》

ko⌈mu⌉gi こむぎ(小麦) *n.* wheat.

ko⌈mugiko こむぎこ(小麦粉) *n.* wheat flour.

ko⌉ñ こん(紺) *n.* dark blue; navy blue.

ko⌈ñ- こん(今) *pref.* this; the present; the coming:
koñ-*neñdo* (今年度) *this* year / koñ-*seeki* (今世紀) *the present* century.

ko⌈na⌉ こな(粉) *n.* powder; flour; meal.

ko⌈naida こないだ *n.* (*informal*) recently; the other day:
Sore wa tsui konaida *no dekigoto da.* (それはついこないだの出来事だ) That is a very *recent* event. 《⇨ kono-aida》

ko⌉ñbañ こんばん(今晩) *n.* this evening; tonight. 《⇨ koñya》

ko⌈ñbañ wa⌉ こんばんは(今晩は) Good evening.

ko⌉ñbu こんぶ(昆布) *n.* sea tangle; kelp. ★ Also called '*kobu*.'

ko⌈ñchuu こんちゅう(昆虫) *n.* insect; bug. 《⇨ mushi[1]》

ko⌈ñdate こんだて(献立) *n.* menu: *kyoo no* koñdate (きょうの献立) today's *menu.*

ko⌉ñdo こんど(今度) *n.* **1** this time; now:
Koñdo *wa kimi no bañ desu.* (今度は君の番です) *Now,* it's your turn.
2 next time:
Koñdo *wa itsu kimasu ka?* (今度はいつ来ますか) When are you coming *next time*?
3 recently:
Kare wa koñdo *hoñ o dashita.* (彼は今度本を出した) He has *recently* published a book. 《⇨ kono-tabi》

ko⌈ñgetsu こんげつ(今月) *n.* this month. 《⇨ señgetsu; raigetsu》

ko⌉ñgo こんご(今後) *n., adv.* after this; from now on; in the future.
koñgo tomo (〜とも) continually:
Koñgo tomo *yoroshiku o-negai itashimasu.* (今後ともよろしくお願いいたします) I'm looking forward to enjoying good relations with you.
★ Set phrase used upon meeting someone for the first time.

ko⌈ñgoo こんごう(混合) *n.* mixing; mixture.
koñgoo suru (〜する) *vi., vt.* mix; mingle; blend. 《⇨ majiru; mazeru》

ko⌉ñjoo こんじょう(根性) *n.* spirit; guts: koñjoo *no aru otoko* (根性のある男) a man of *spirit.*

ko⌉ñkai こんかい(今回) *n.* this time:
Koñkai *wa nyuushoo shita hito ga inakatta.* (今回は入賞した人がいなかった) There was nobody who won the prize *this time.*

ko⌈ñku⌉uru コンクール *n.* contest; competition.

ko⌉ñkyo こんきょ(根拠) *n.*
1 basis; foundation; ground:
Sono uwasa wa mattaku koñkyo *ga arimaseñ.* (そのうわさは全く根拠がありません) The rumor is completely without *foundation.*
2 reason:
Kare ga soo iu no ni wa koñkyo *ga aru.* (彼がそう言うのには根拠がある) He has his *reasons* for saying so.

ko⌈ñmo⌉ri こんもり *adv.* (~ to; ~ suru) thick; dense:
koñmori to shita *mori* (こんもりとした森) *thick* woods.

ko⌈ñna こんな *attrib.* this; like this: ★ Refers to something close to the speaker.
Koñna *sakana wa mita koto ga arimaseñ.* (こんな魚は見たことがありせん) I have never seen a fish *like this.* ⟪⇨ añna; doñna; soñna⟫

ko⌉ñnañ こんなん(困難) *n.* difficulty; hardship; trouble:
koñnañ *ni taeru* (困難に耐える) endure *hardships.*
— *a.n.* (~ na, ni) difficult; hard; troublesome:
Kono moñdai wa kaiketsu ga koñnañ *desu.* (この問題は解決が困難です) It is *difficult* to solve this problem.

ko⌈ñna ni こんなに *adv.* this; like this; so:
Koñna ni *osoku made doko ni ita no?* (こんなに遅くまでどこにいたの) Where have you been until *so* late? ⟪⇨ añna ni; doñna ni; soñna ni⟫

ko⌉ñnichi こんにち(今日) *n.* today; the present day:
koñnichi *no sekai* (今日の世界) the world of *today.* ⟪⇨ hoñjitsu; kyoo⟫

ko⌈ñnichi wa⌉ こんにちは(今日は) Good day; Good morning; Good afternoon; Hello.

ko⌈ñnyaku⌉ こんにゃく *n.* devil's tongue. ★ Jelly-like food made from the starch of devil's tongue root.

ko⌈no この(此の) *attrib.* 1 this: ★ Refers to a person or thing that is close to the speaker.
Kono *fairu o tana ni modoshite kudasai.* (このファイルを棚に戻してください) Please put *this* file back on the shelf.
2 this: ★ Refers to a time in the immediate future.
Kono *natsu-yasumi wa doko-ka e ikimasu ka?* (この夏休みはどこかへ行きますか) Are you going anywhere *this* summer vacation?
3 this: ★ Introduces something as a subject of conversation.
Kono *koto wa dare ni mo iwanai de kudasai.* (このことはだれにも言わないでください) Please don't tell anybody about *this.* ⟪⇨ ano; dono; sono⟫

ko⌈no-aida⌉ このあいだ(此の間) *n.* the other day; some time ago; recently: ★ *informal* = konaida.
Kono-aida *wa o-sewa ni narimashita.* (この間はお世話になりました) Thank you for the kindness I received *the other day.* ⟪⇨ kono-mae⟫

ko⌈no-goro このごろ(此の頃) *adv.* (~ no) now; these days; recently. ⟪⇨ chikagoro; saikiñ[1]⟫

ko⌈no-ma⌉e このまえ(此の前) *n.* the other day; last; the last time:
Kono-mae *no kaigi ni wa demaseñ deshita.* (この前の会議には出ませんでした) I did not attend the *last* meeting. ⟪⇨ kono-aida⟫

ko⌈no-mama このまま(此の儘) *n.* the present state; as it is; as they are:
Kono shorui wa kono-mama *koko ni oite oite kudasai.* (この書類はこのままここに置いておいてください) Please leave these papers here *just as they are.* ⟪⇨ mama[1]⟫

ko⌈nomashi⌉i このましい(好ましい) *a.* (-ku) good; desirable; favorable: ⟪⇨ nozomashii⟫
Kitsueñ wa keñkoo-joo konomashiku *nai.* (喫煙は健康上好ましくない)

Smoking is not *good* for the health.

ko⌈nomi⌉ このみ(好み) *n.* liking; taste; fancy:
Kono nekutai wa watashi no konomi *ni atte iru.* (このネクタイは私の好みに合っている) This tie is to my *taste.* ((⇨ konomu))

ko⌈no⌉m·u このむ(好む) *vt.* (konom·i-; konom·a-; konoñ-de [C]) like; prefer. ★ '*suki da* [*desu*]' is more common. ((⇨ konomi))

ko⌈no⌉-tabi このたび(此の度) *n.* (*formal*) this (present; previous) time [occasion]:
Watashi wa kono-tabi *Shiñgapooru ni teñkiñ to narimashita.* (私はこの度シンガポールに転勤となりました) I have been transferred to Singapore *this time.* ((⇨ koñdo))

ko⌈no-tsugi⌉ このつぎ(此の次) *n.* next:
Kono-tsugi *no deñsha ni noroo.* (この次の電車に乗ろう) Let's take the *next* train.

ko⌈no-ue このうえ(此の上) *n.* more; further; in addition to this.
kono-ue (mo) nai (~(も)ない) most; greatest: kono-ue mo nai *kooee* (この上もない光栄) the *greatest* honor.

ko⌈ñpoñ こんぽん(根本) *n.* foundation; basis; root.

ko⌈ñpoñ-teki こんぽんてき(根本的) *a.n.* (~ na, ni) fundamental; basic.

ko⌈ñrañ こんらん(混乱) *n.* confusion; disorder; chaos.
koñrañ suru (~する) *vi.* be confused; be mixed up: *Jishiñ no tame ressha no daiya ga* koñrañ shita. (地震のため列車のダイヤが混乱した) The train schedule *was disrupted* because of the earthquake. ((⇨ midareru))

ko⌉ñseñto コンセント *n.* electrical outlet; wall socket.

ko⌉ñshuu こんしゅう(今週) *n.* this week. ((⇨ señshuu))

ko⌉ñya こんや(今夜) *n.* this evening; tonight. ((⇨ koñbañ))

ko⌉ñyaku こんやく(婚約) *n.* marriage engagement.
koñyaku suru (~する) *vi.* get engaged.

ko⌉ñzatsu こんざつ(混雑) *n.* congestion; jam.
koñzatsu suru (~する) *vi.* be crowded; be jammed. ((⇨ komu))

ko⌈o こう(斯う) *adv.* **1** this; like this: ★ Refers to something close to the speaker.
Koo *atsukute wa gaishutsu shitaku nai.* (こう暑くては外出したくない) I don't want to go out in *such* heat.
2 this: ★ Refers to something just mentioned or about to be mentioned.
Kono hoñ ni wa koo *kaite arimasu.* (この本にはこう書いてあります) This book says *as follows*: ((⇨ aa[1]; doo[1]; soo[1]))

-koo こう(港) *suf.* port; harbor:
Yokohama-koo (横浜港) Yokohama *Harbor* / *Niigata*-koo (新潟港) the *port* of Niigata.

ko⌈oba⌉ こうば(工場) *n.* factory; workshop. ★ Refers to a small factory, often under private management. ((⇨ koojoo[1]))

ko⌈obai こうばい(勾配) *n.* slope; grade; slant:
kyuu na koobai *no yama-michi* (急な勾配の山道) a mountain path with a steep *slope.*

ko⌈obañ こうばん(交番) *n.* police box. ((⇨ keesatsu))

ko⌉obutsu[1] こうぶつ(好物) *n.* one's favorite food.

ko⌉obutsu[2] こうぶつ(鉱物) *n.* mineral.

ko⌈ocha こうちゃ(紅茶) *n.* black tea. ((⇨ o-cha))

ko⌉ochi[1] コーチ *n.* coach.
koochi suru (~する) *vt.* coach (a team).

ko⌉ochi[2] こうち(耕地) *n.* cultivated land; arable land.

k

ko⌉ochi[3] こうち (高地) *n.* highlands; upland. ⟪↔ teechi⟫

ko⌈ochoo[1] こうちょう (好調) *a.n.* (~ na, ni) in good shape [condition]; favorable; satisfactory. ⟪↔ fuchoo⟫

ko⌈ochoo[2] こうちょう (校長) *n.* principal; headmaster; headmistress.

ko⌈odai こうだい (広大) *a.n.* (~ na) extensive; vast: koodai *na sabaku* (広大な砂漠) an *extensive* desert.

ko⌈odeñ こうでん (香典) *n.* monetary offering to a departed soul.

ko⌉odo[1] コード *n.* electrical cord; flex.

ko⌉odo[2] こうど (高度) *n.* height; altitude: koodo *goseñ-meetoru* (高度5千メートル) a *height* of 5,000 meters.

ko⌉odo[3] こうど (高度) *a.n.* (~ na/no, ni) advanced; highly developed: koodo *ni hattatsu shita kagaku-gijutsu* (高度に発達した科学技術) scientific technology which has developed to a *high level*.

ko⌉odo[4] こうど (硬度) *n.* hardness.

ko⌈odoo[1] こうどう (行動) *n.* act; action; behavior; conduct.
koodoo suru (~する) *vi.* act; behave; conduct oneself.

ko⌈odoo[2] こうどう (講堂) *n.* lecture hall; auditorium; assembly hall.

ko⌈oeñ[1] こうえん (公園) *n.* park; public playground.

ko⌈oeñ[2] こうえん (講演) *n.* lecture; speech; talk.
kooeñ (o) suru (~(を)する) *vi.* give a lecture; make a speech. ⟪⇨ eñzetsu⟫

ko⌈oeñ[3] こうえん (公演) *n.* public performance.
kooeñ suru (~する) *vt.* perform; present (a play). ⟪⇨ jooeñ⟫

ko⌈oeñ[4] こうえん (後援) *n.* support; sponsorship: kooeñ-*kai* (後援会) a *supporters'* association; a *fan* club.
kooeñ suru (~する) *vt.* support; sponsor.

ko⌉ofu こうふ (交付) *n.* issue; grant.
koofu suru (~する) *vt.* issue (a passport); grant.

ko⌈ofuku こうふく (幸福) *n.* happiness; fortune.
— *a.n.* (~ na, ni) happy; fortunate. ⟪⇨ shiawase⟫

ko⌈ofuñ こうふん (興奮) *n.* excitement; stimulation.
koofuñ suru (~する) *vi.* be [get] excited.

ko⌉ogai[1] こうがい (郊外) *n.* suburbs; outskirts: *Kare wa* koogai *no ie ni hikkoshita.* (彼は郊外の家に引っ越した) He moved to a house on the *outskirts of town.* ⟪⇨ shigai[2]⟫

ko⌈ogai[2] こうがい (公害) *n.* pollution; public nuisance.

ko⌈ogaku こうがく (高額) *n.* large sum of money: *Kare wa* koogaku *no kifu o shita.* (彼は高額の寄付をした) He made a *large* contribution. ⟪↔ teegaku[2]⟫

ko⌈ogeehiñ こうげいひん (工芸品) *n.* craftwork.

ko⌈ogeki こうげき (攻撃) *n.* attack; criticism; offensive.
koogeki suru (~する) *vt.* attack; criticize. ⟪↔ boogyo; shubi⟫

ko⌈ogeñ こうげん (高原) *n.* plateau; tableland; highlands.

ko⌉ogi[1] こうぎ (抗議) *n.* protest; objection.
koogi suru (~する) *vi.* protest; object.

ko⌉ogi[2] こうぎ (講義) *n.* lecture.
koogi (o) suru (~(を)する) *vt.* give a lecture; lecture.

ko⌉ogo こうご (口語) *n.* spoken [colloquial] language: koogo-*tai* (口語体) *colloquial* style. ⟪↔ buñgo⟫

ko⌉ogo ni こうごに (交互に) *adv.* by [in] turns; alternately: *Futari wa* koogo ni *keebi ni tsuite* *ita.* (二人は交互に警備についていた) The two persons were on guard *in turns.*

ko⌈ogo⌉o こうごう (皇后) *n.* empress:
Koogoo *Heeka* (皇后陛下) Her Majesty the *Empress.* ⟪⇨ teñnoo⟫

ko⌉ogu こうぐ (工具) *n.* tool; implement.

ko⌉ogyoo[1] こうぎょう (工業) *n.* industry: koogyoo-chitai (工業地帯) an *industrial* district.

ko⌉ogyoo[2] こうぎょう (鉱業) *n.* mining (industry).

ko⌈ohai こうはい (後輩) *n.* one's junior; underclassman:
Watashi wa kare no ichi-neñ koohai *desu.* (私は彼の一年後輩です) I am his *junior* by a year. ⟪↔ señpai⟫

ko⌉ohaku こうはく (紅白) *n.* red and white.

ko⌈ohañ こうはん (後半) *n.* second [latter] half. ⟪↔ zeñhañ⟫

ko⌈ohee こうへい (公平) *n.* fairness; impartiality.
— *a.n.* (~ na, ni) fair, just; impartial: koohee *na saibañ* (公平な裁判) a *fair* trial.
⟪↔ fukoohee⟫

ko⌈ohi⌉i コーヒー (咖啡) *n.* coffee: koohii *o ireru* [*nomu*] (コーヒーを入れる[飲む]) make [drink] *coffee.*

ko⌉oho こうほ (候補) *n.* **1** candidacy; candidature; candidate: kooho ni tatsu (候補に立つ) *run* [*stand*] *for election.*
2 favorite:
Kare no chiimu wa yuushoo kooho *da.* (彼のチームは優勝候補だ) His team is the top *favorite.*

ko⌈ohoo[1] こうほう (広報) *n.* public information; public relations.

ko⌈ohoo[2] こうほう (公報) *n.* official bulletin.

ko⌉oi[1] こうい (行為) *n.* act; action; deed; behavior; conduct.

ko⌉oi[2] こうい (好意) *n.* goodwill; kindness; favor:
Kanojo wa kimi ni kooi o motte iru *yoo da.* (彼女は君に好意を持っているようだ) She seems to *be fond of* you. ⟪↔ tekii⟫

ko⌈oiñ こういん (工員) *n.* factory worker.

ko⌈oi-teki こういてき (好意的) *a.n.* (~ na, ni) friendly; kind; favorable: kooi-teki *na heñji* (好意的な返事) a *favorable* reply.

ko⌈o-iu こういう (斯ういう) *attrib.* like this; thus: ★ Refers to something close to the speaker.
koo-iu *koto* (こういうこと) *this sort of* thing. ⟪⇨ aa-iu; doo-iu; soo-iu⟫

ko⌉oji こうじ (工事) *n.* construction work:
Kooji-*chuu.* (*sign*) (工事中) Under *Construction.* / kooji-*geñba* (工事現場) a *construction* site.
kooji suru (~する) *vi.* construct; work on.

ko⌈ojo⌉o[1] こうじょう (工場) *n.* factory; mill; plant; workshop.
★ Refers to a larger, well-equipped factory. More formal than '*kooba.*'

ko⌈ojoo[2] こうじょう (向上) *n.* rise; improvement; progress:
gijutsu no koojoo (技術の向上) an *improvement* in techniques.
koojoo suru (~する) *vi.* rise; improve; progress.

ko⌉oka[1] こうか (効果) *n.* effect; efficacy; efficiency:
Kono kusuri wa zutsuu ni kooka ga arimasu. (この薬は頭痛に効果があります) This medicine *is effective* for headaches.

ko⌉oka[2] こうか (高価) *a.n.* (~ na, ni) expensive; high-priced; costly:
kooka *na shinamono* (高価な品物) *high-priced* goods. ⟪↔ yasui⟫ ⟪⇨ takai⟫

ko⌉oka[3] こうか (硬貨) *n.* coin.
⟪↔ satsu; shihee⟫

ko⌈okai[1] こうかい (公開) *n.* open to the public.
kookai suru (~する) *vt.* make public; exhibit; release.

k

ko¹okai² こうかい(航海) *n.* voyage; navigation; cruise; sailing.
kookai suru (~する) *vi.* go by sea; sail; cruise.

ko¹okai³ こうかい(後悔) *n.* regret; repentance.
kookai suru (~する) *vi., vt.* regret; repent; feel remorse.

ko⌈okai⁴ こうかい(公海) *n.* the high seas.

ko⌈okañ こうかん(交換) *n.* exchange; replacement; barter.
kookañ suru (~する) *vt.* change; exchange; replace; barter.
《⇨ torikaeru》

ko⌈oka-teki こうかてき(効果的) *a.n.* (~ na, ni) effective; successful: kooka-teki *na taisaku* (効果的な対策) *effective* measures.

ko⌈okee こうけい(光景) *n.* scene; sight; view:
Sono tani no kookee *wa ima de mo oboete imasu.* (その谷の光景は今でも覚えています) I still remember the *view* of that valley.

ko¹oki こうき(後期) *n.* latter half of the year; second term [semester]. 《↔ zeñki》

ko⌈oki¹shiñ こうきしん(好奇心) *n.* curiosity; inquisitiveness:
Kare wa kookishiñ ga tsuyoi. (彼は好奇心が強い) He *is very inquisitive.* 《⇨ kyoomi; yajiuma》

ko⌈okoku こうこく(広告) *n.* advertisement:
shiñbuñ ni kookoku *o dasu* [*noseru*] (新聞に広告を出す[載せる]) put an *advertisement* in a newspaper.
kookoku suru (~する) *vt.* advertise. 《⇨ señden》

ko⌈okoo¹ こうこう(高校) *n.* (senior) high school. ★ Shortened form of '*kootoo-gakkoo.*'

ko¹okoo² こうこう(孝行) *n.* being obedient (to one's parents).
— *a.n.* (~ na) good; obedient; dutiful: kookoo *na musuko* (孝行な息子) a *dutiful* son.

ko⌈oko¹osee こうこうせい(高校生) *n.* (senior) high school student.

ko⌈oku¹ubiñ こうくうびん(航空便) *n.* airmail:
tegami o kookuubiñ *de okuru* [*dasu*] (手紙を航空便で送る[出す]) send a letter by *airmail.*

ko⌈oku¹ukeñ こうくうけん(航空券) *n.* airline ticket.

ko⌈oku¹uki こうくうき(航空機) *n.* airplane; aircraft.

Ko¹okyo こうきょ(皇居) *n.* the Imperial Palace.

ko⌈okyoo¹ こうきょう(公共) *n.* the community; public:
kookyoo *no fukushi* (公共の福祉) *public* welfare.

ko⌈okyoo² こうきょう(好況) *n.* brisk market; prosperous conditions. 《↔ fukyoo》

ko⌈okyuu こうきゅう(高級) *a.n.* (~ na, ni) high-class; high-grade; exclusive:
kookyuu (*na*) *hoteru* (高級(な)ホテル) an *exclusive* hotel / kookyuu-*sha* (高級車) a *high-class* car.

ko⌈omi¹ñkañ こうみんかん(公民館) *n.* public hall; community center.

ko⌈omiñ¹keñ こうみんけん(公民権) *n.* civil rights.

ko⌈omoku こうもく(項目) *n.* item; heading; clause.

ko⌈omu¹iñ こうむいん(公務員) *n.* public worker; government employee; civil servant.

ko⌈omu¹r·u こうむる(被る) *vt.* (-mur·i-; -mur·a-; -mut-te Ⓒ) receive; sustain; suffer:
taifuu de ooki-na higai o koomuru (台風で大きな被害を被る) *suffer* heavy damage from the typhoon.
《⇨ ukeru》

ko⌈omyoo こうみょう(巧妙) *a.n.* (~ na, ni) clever; cunning; smart; crafty:
koomyoo *na yarikata* (巧妙なやり方) a *clever* trick.

ko⌈onyuu こうにゅう(購入) *n.* purchase; buying.
koonyuu suru (~する) *vt.* buy; purchase. 《⇨ kau¹》

k

ko⌈o-oñ こうおん (高温) *n.* high temperature. 《↔ teeoñ》

ko⌈ori こおり (氷) *n.* ice.

ko⌈oritsu[1] こうりつ (公立) *n.* public; prefectural; municipal: kooritsu *no toshokañ* (公立の図書館) a *public* library. 《↔ shiritsu[1]》

ko⌈oritsu[2] こうりつ (効率) *n.* efficiency: kooritsu *o takameru* (効率を高める) increase the *efficiency*.

ko⌈oritsu-teki こうりつてき (効率的) *a.n.* (~ na, ni) efficient: kooritsu-teki *na kikai* (効率的な機械) an *efficient* machine.

ko⌈or·u こおる (凍る) *vi.* (koor·i-; koor·a-; koot-te Ⓒ) freeze: *Kesa niwa no ike ga* kootta. (けさ庭の池が凍った) This morning the pond in the garden *was frozen*.

ko⌉oryo こうりょ (考慮) *n.* (*formal*) consideration: *Sono kikaku wa* kooryo-*chuu desu*. (その企画は考慮中です) The project is now under *consideration*.
kooryo suru (~する) *vt.* consider; take into account.

ko⌉oryoku こうりょく (効力) *n.* effect; force; validity: *Sono hooritsu wa mada* kooryoku *ga arimasu*. (その法律はまだ効力があります) That law is still in *force*.

ko⌈osa こうさ (交差) *n.* crossing; intersection.
koosa suru (~する) *vi.* cross; intersect. 《⇨ majiwaru》

ko⌈osai こうさい (交際) *n.* company; association; friendship; acquaintance: koosai-*hi* (交際費) an *expense* account; *entertainment* [*social*] expenses.
koosai suru (~する) *vi.* keep company; associate.

ko⌈osaku[1] こうさく (工作) *n.*
1 handicraft; woodwork: koosaku *de take no fue o tsukuru* (工作で竹の笛を作る) make a bamboo flute in *handicraft class*.
2 maneuvering; move: *Kare wa kooshoo no ura de* koosaku *o shita*. (彼は交渉の裏で工作をした) He *maneuvered* behind the scenes at the negotiations.

ko⌈osaku[2] こうさく (耕作) *n.* cultivation: koosaku-*chi* (耕作地) *cultivated* land.
koosaku suru (~する) *vt.* cultivate. 《⇨ tagayasu》

ko⌈osa⌉teñ こうさてん (交差点) *n.* crossing; intersection. 《⇨ juujiro》

ko⌈osee[1] こうせい (構成) *n.* makeup; organization; composition; structure.
koosee suru (~する) *vt.* make up; organize; compose: *Iiñkai wa shichi-niñ de* koosee sarete imasu. (委員会は7人で構成されています) The committee *is made up* of seven members.

ko⌈osee[2] こうせい (校正) *n.* proofreading: *zasshi o* koosee suru (雑誌を校正する) *read proofs* of a magazine.

ko⌈oseñ こうせん (光線) *n.* light; beam; ray: *taiyoo no* kooseñ (太陽の光線) the *rays* of the sun.

ko⌉osha[1] こうしゃ (校舎) *n.* school building; schoolhouse. 《⇨ gakkoo》

ko⌉osha[2] こうしゃ (後者) *n.* (*formal*) the latter: *Washitsu to yooshitsu de wa,* koosha *no hoo ga suki desu*. (和室と洋室では, 後者のほうが好きです) Between a Japanese-style room and a western-style room, I prefer *the latter*. 《↔ zeñsha》

ko⌉oshi[1] こうし (講師) *n.* lecturer; instructor.

ko⌉oshi[2] こうし (公使) *n.* minister (in the diplomatic service): *chuu-Nichi Furansu* kooshi (駐日フランス公使) the French *minister* to Japan.

ko⌈oshi⌉kañ こうしかん (公使館) *n.* legation.

ko⌈oshiki[1] こうしき (公式) *n.* offi-

k

cial; formal: kooshiki *hoomoñ* (公式訪問) a *formal* visit. ⟪⇨ seeshiki⟫

ko⌈oshiki[2] こうしき (公式) *n.* formula: *suugaku no* kooshiki (数学の公式) a mathematical *formula.*

ko⌈oshiñ こうしん (行進) *n.* march; parade: kooshiñ-*kyoku* (行進曲) a musical *march.*
kooshiñ suru (〜する) *vi.* march; parade.

ko⌈oshi⌉see こうしせい (高姿勢) *n.* aggressive [high-handed] attitude. ⟪↔ teeshisee⟫

ko⌈o-shite こうして *adv.* in this way:
Isogashikute, koo-shite *jitto suwatte wa irarenai.* (忙しくて, こうしてじっとすわってはいられない) I am too busy to sit around *in this way* doing nothing. ⟪⇨ aa-shite; soo-shite⟫

ko⌈oshoo こうしょう (交渉) *n.*
1 negotiations; talks:
Sono kooshoo *wa matomarimashita.* (その交渉はまとまりました) The *negotiations* were concluded.
2 connection; relations:
Watashi wa seejika to wa nañ no kooshoo *mo arimaseñ.* (私は政治家とは何の交渉もありません) I have no *connections* with politicians.
kooshoo suru (〜する) *vt.* negotiate.

ko⌈oshuu こうしゅう (公衆) *n.* the general public:
Kooshuu *no meñzeñ de haji o kakasareta.* (公衆の面前で恥をかかされた) I was put to shame in *public.*

ko⌈oshuu-be⌉ñjo こうしゅうべんじょ (公衆便所) *n.* public lavatory [toilet]. ⟪⇨ beñjo⟫

ko⌈oshuu-de⌉ñwa こうしゅうでんわ (公衆電話) *n.* public telephone; pay phone. ⟪⇨ deñwa⟫

ko⌈oshuu-do⌉otoku こうしゅうどうとく (公衆道徳) *n.* public morals. ⟪⇨ dootoku⟫

ko⌈osoku-do⌉oro こうそくどうろ (高速道路) *n.* expressway; freeway; motorway. ⟪⇨ dooro⟫

ko⌈osoo こうそう (構想) *n.* plan; idea; design; plot:
koosoo *o tateru* [*neru*] (構想を立てる[練る]) map out [refine] a *plan.*
koosoo suru (〜する) *vt.* plan; design; plot.

ko⌉osu コース *n.* **1** (of lessons) course:
Nihoñgo no shokyuu koosu (日本語の初級コース) the beginners' Japanese *course.*
2 (of a race) course; lane:
dai-sañ koosu *o hashiru* (第3コースを走る) run in *Lane* No. 3.
3 (of a meal) course:
*furu-*koosu *no shokuji* (フルコースの食事) a meal with all the *courses.*

ko⌈osui こうすい (香水) *n.* perfume; scent.

ko⌈otai こうたい (交替) *n.* shift; change:
Watashi-tachi wa kootai *de uñteñ o shita.* (私たちは交替で運転をした) We took *turns* doing the driving.
kootai suru (〜する) *vi.* take turns; change.

ko⌈otee[1] こうてい (肯定) *n.* affirmation; affirmative.
kootee suru (〜する) *vt.* affirm; acknowledge; confirm. ⟪↔ hitee⟫

ko⌈otee[2] こうてい (皇帝) *n.* emperor. ★ The Japanese emperor is known as '*teñnoo.*'

ko⌈oteñ-teki こうてんてき (後天的) *a.n.* (〜 na, ni) acquired; a posteriori:
kooteñ-teki *na seekaku* (後天的な性格) a personality *acquired because of one's upbringing and environment.* ⟪↔ señteñ-teki⟫

ko⌉oto[1] コート *n.* coat; overcoat; raincoat; trenchcoat.

ko⌉oto[2] コート *n.* court: *tenisu* kooto (テニスコート) a tennis *court.*

ko⌈otoo こうとう (高等) *a.n.* (〜 na) high; higher; advanced:
kootoo-*kyooiku* (高等教育) *higher* education.

ko⌈otoo-ga⌉kkoo こうとうがっこう

k

(高等学校) *n.* senior high school; upper secondary school. ⟪⇨ koo-koo¹⟫

ko⌈otsuu こうつう (交通) *n.* traffic; transportation; communication.

ko⌈otsuu-do⌉otoku こうつうどうとく (交通道徳) *n.* good driving manners; consideration for others when driving. ⟪⇨ doo-toku⟫

ko⌈otsu⌉uhi こうつうひ (交通費) *n.* traveling expenses; carfare.

ko⌈otsuu-ji⌉ko こうつうじこ (交通事故) *n.* traffic accident.

ko⌈oun̄ こううん (幸運) *n.* good luck [fortune].
— *a.n.* (~ na, ni) lucky; fortunate. ⟪↔ fuun̄²⟫

ko⌈oyoo こうよう (紅葉) *n.* red leaves; autumn colors [tints].
kooyoo suru (~する) *vi.* turn red [yellow]. ⟪⇨ momiji⟫

ko⌉ozan̄¹ こうざん (鉱山) *n.* mine.

ko⌉ozan̄² こうざん (高山) *n.* high mountain.

ko⌈ozen̄ こうぜん (公然) *a.n.* (~ no / to; ~ taru) open; public: *Sore wa* koozen̄ no himitsu *desu.* (それは公然の秘密です) It is an *open secret.*

ko⌈ozoo こうぞう (構造) *n.* structure; construction:
bun̄ [*shakai*] *no* koozoo (文[社会]の構造) the *structure* of a sentence [society].

ko⌈ozui こうずい (洪水) *n.* flood; inundation.

ko⌉pii コピー *n.* copy; photocopy.
kopii suru (~する) *vt.* copy; photocopy.

ko⌈ppu コップ *n.* glass; tumbler.

ko⌉ra こら *int.* (*rude*) hey (you)!; hi!; there! ★ Used by men when reprimanding someone.

ko⌈rae⌉·ru こらえる (堪える) *vt.* (korae-te [V]) **1** bear; stand; endure: *itami o* koraeru (痛みをこらえる) *endure* pain. ⟪⇨ gaman̄⟫
2 control; subdue; suppress: *namida o* koraeru (涙をこらえる) *keep back* one's tears.

ko⌈re これ (此れ) *n.* **1** this: ★ Refers to something or someone that is close to the speaker.
Kore *wa dare no hon̄ desu ka?* (これはだれの本ですか) Whose book is *this*?
2 this: ★ Introduces or refers to one's own wife or child.
Kore *ga uchi no kanai* [*musuko*] *desu.* (これがうちの家内[息子]です) *This* is my wife [son].
3 this; it: ★ Refers to something or someone that was previously mentioned or that is about to be mentioned.
Zairyoo o yoku maze, kore *ni tamago o kuwaemasu.* (材料をよく混ぜ, これに卵を加えます) Mix the ingredients well, and then add the egg to *it*.
4 this; that: ★ Refers to a continuing state or action.
Kore *de yoshi.* (これでよし) *This* will do.
5 this; that: ★ Used for emphasis.
Kore *wa hidoi netsu da.* (これはひどい熱だ) What a fever *this* is!
⟪⇨ are¹; dore¹; sore¹⟫

ko⌈re de これで (此れで) *adv.* now; under the circumstances; with this:
Kore de *an̄shin̄ shita.* (これで安心した) I *now* feel relieved.

ko⌈re kara⌉ これから (此れから)
1 now:
Kore kara *shusseki o torimasu.* (これから出席をとります) I am *now* going to take attendance.
2 from now on; after this; in the future. ⟪⇨ are¹ irai; sore kara⟫

ko⌈re-(k)kiri これっきり (此れっきり) *adv.* (with a negative) **1** (of future) never:
Kore-kkiri *kanojo to wa aenai ka mo shirenai.* (これっきり彼女とは会えないかもしれない) I'm afraid I will

k

never be able to see her again.
2 (of a thing) only:
O-kane wa kore-kkiri *shika motte imaseñ.* (お金はこれっきりしか持っていません) This is the *only* money I have. 《⇨ are-(k)kiri; sore-(k)kiri》

ko⌈re ma⌉de これまで (此れ迄)
1 so far; until now:
Kare wa kore made *gakkoo o yasuñda koto ga arimaseñ.* (彼はこれまで学校を休んだことがありません) *So far* he has not missed a day from school.
2 here:
Kyoo wa kore made. (きょうはこれまで) Let us finish *here* today.

ko⌈ri⌉·ru こりる (懲りる) *vi.* (kori-te [V]) **1** learn a lesson:
Kare wa mada sono shippai ni korinai *yoo da.* (彼はまだその失敗に懲りないようだ) It seems he *has not learned a lesson* from his failure.
2 have enough (on); be soured:
Kekkoñ ni wa korite imasu. (結婚には懲りています) I'*ve had a bitter experience* with marriage.

k

ko⌉ro ころ (頃) *n.* the time:
Sakura wa ima ga ichibañ ii koro *desu.* (桜は今がいちばんいいころです) Now is the best *time* for cherry blossoms. 《⇨ -goro》

ko⌈rob·u ころぶ (転ぶ) *vi.* (korob·i-; korob·a-; koroñ-de [C]) fall; tumble:
Kare wa ne ni tsumazuite koroñda. (彼は根につまずいて転んだ) He tripped on a root and *fell.* 《⇨ taoreru》

ko⌈rogar·u ころがる (転がる) *vi.* (-gar·i-; -gar·a-; -gat-te [C])
1 roll; fall; tumble:
Booru ga saka o korogatte itta. (ボールが坂を転がっていった) The ball *rolled down* away the slope. 《⇨ korogasu》
2 lie down:
shibafu ni korogaru (芝生に転がる) *lie down* on the lawn.

ko⌈rogas·u ころがす (転がす) *vt.* (-gash·i-; -gas·a-; -gash·i-te [C]) roll; tumble over:
Sono ooki-na ishi o korogashite *ugokashita.* (その大きな石を転がして動かした) We moved that large stone by *rolling* it along. 《⇨ korogaru》

ko⌉rokoro ころころ *adv.* (~ to) (the sound or manner of a small, round object rolling):
Booru ga korokoro (*to*) *korogatte kita.* (ボールがころころ(と)転がって来た) A ball came *rolling up* to me.

ko⌈ro⌉ri ころり *adv.* (~ to) **1** easily; suddenly:
Kanojo wa kare ni korori *to damasareta.* (彼女は彼にころりとだまされた) She was *easily* taken in by him.
2 quite; entirely:
Sono yakusoku o korori *to wasurete ita.* (その約束をころりと忘れていた) I *quite* forgot the appointment.

ko⌈ros·u ころす (殺す) *vt.* (korosh·i-; koros·a-; korosh·i-te [C])
1 kill; murder.
2 suppress (breathing, a yawn, etc.); restrain.

ko⌉r·u[1] こる (凝る) *vi.* (kor·i-; kor·a-; kot-te [C]) be crazy; be devoted:
Kare wa gorufu ni kotte iru. (彼はゴルフに凝っている) He *is crazy* about golf.

ko⌉r·u[2] こる (凝る) *vi.* (kor·i-; kor·a-; kot-te [C]) (of shoulders) be stiff.

ko⌈same こさめ (小雨) *n.* light rain; drizzle. 《↔ ooame》

ko⌈see こせい (個性) *n.* individuality; personality:
kosee *o nobasu* (個性を伸ばす) develop one's *individuality.*

ko⌈see-teki こせいてき (個性的) *a.n.* (~ na, ni) distinctive:
Ano haiyuu wa kosee-teki *na kao o shite iru.* (あの俳優は個性的な顔をしている) The actor has a *distinctive* face.

ko⌈seki こせき (戸籍) *n.* family register.

ko⌈shi こし (腰) *n.* waist; hip:
isu ni koshi o orosu (椅子に腰を下

ろす) *sit* on a chair. 《⇨ shiri》

ko⌈shikake⌉ こしかけ (腰掛け) *n.*
1 chair; stool:
koshikake *ni suwaru* (腰掛けに座る) sit on a *chair*. 《⇨ isu; koshikakeru》
2 temporary work; makeshift job:
Kanojo no shigoto wa kekkoñ made no koshikake *da.* (彼女の仕事は結婚までの腰掛けだ) Her job is a *temporary one* until marriage. 《⇨ riñji》

ko⌈shikake⌉·ru こしかける (腰掛ける) *vi.* (-kake-te Ⓥ) sit down; take a seat. 《⇨ koshikake》

ko⌈shirae·ru こしらえる (拵える) *vt.* (-rae-te Ⓥ) make; build:
inugoya o koshiraeru (犬小屋をこしらえる) *make* a doghouse. 《⇨ tsukuru[1]》

ko⌈shoo[1] こしょう (故障) *n.* breakdown; trouble.
koshoo suru (〜する) *vi.* go out of order; break down; be in trouble. 《⇨ kowareru》

ko⌈sho⌉o[2] こしょう (胡椒) *n.* pepper.

koso こそ *p.* indeed; just:
★ Used to emphasize the preceding word.
Koñdo koso *seekoo shite miseru.* (今度こそ成功して見せる) *This one time* I will show you I can succeed.

ko⌈sso⌉ri こっそり *adv.* (〜 to) secretly; stealthily; in private:
Kare wa kanojo ni kossori (*to*) *atte ita.* (彼は彼女にこっそり(と)会っていた) He was meeting with her *secretly.*

ko⌈s·u[1] こす (越す) *vt.* (kosh·i-; kos·a-; kosh·i-te Ⓒ) **1** go over; cross:
Kare no utta booru wa feñsu o koshita. (彼の打ったボールはフェンスを越した) The ball he hit *went over* the fence.
2 move (to a new house). 《⇨ hikkoshi》
3 spend (time):
Kare wa Hokkaidoo de sukii o shite, fuyu o koshita. (彼は北海道でスキーをして, 冬を越した) He *spent* winter skiing in Hokkaido. 《⇨ sugosu》

ko⌈s·u[2] こす (超す) *vt.* (kosh·i-; kos·a-; kosh·i-te Ⓒ) be over; be more than:
Shachoo wa nanajuu o koshite iru. (社長は70を超している) Our president *is more than* seventy. 《⇨ koeru[2]》

ko⌈su⌉r·u こする (擦る) *vt.* (kosur·i-; kosur·a-; kosut-te Ⓒ) rub; scrub: 《⇨ masatsu》
Kare wa nemui me o kosutta. (彼は眠い目をこすった) He *rubbed* his sleepy eyes.

ko⌈ta⌉e こたえ (答え) *n.* answer; reply; response. 《⇨ kotaeru》

ko⌈tae⌉·ru こたえる (答える) *vi.* (kotae-te Ⓥ) answer; reply:
Sono ko wa nani o kiite mo kotaenakatta. (その子は何を聞いても答えなかった) Whatever I asked the child, he *did not reply.* 《⇨ kotae》

ko⌈tai こたい (固体) *n.* solid. 《⇨ ekitai; kitai[2]》

ko⌈tatsu こたつ (炬燵) *n.* Japanese foot warmer. 《⇨ deñkigotatsu》

ko⌈tchi⌉ こっち *n.* (*colloq.*) = kochira.
1 this; here:
Kare wa ma-mo-naku kotchi *e kimasu.* (彼は間もなくこっちへ来ます) He will be *here* very soon.
2 we; I:
Kotchi *ni wa sekiniñ wa arimaseñ.* (こっちには責任はありません) *We* are not to blame. 《⇨ atchi; dotchi; sotchi》

ko⌈tee こてい (固定) *n.* fixation.
kotee-*shisañ zee* (固定資産税) a *fixed* property tax.
kotee suru (〜する) *vt.* fix; settle.

ko⌈teñ こてん (古典) *n.* classics.

ko⌈to[1] こと (事) *n.* **1** thing; matter; affair; fact: ★ The meaning

k

is defined by the preceding noun or modifier.
Kyoo wa suru koto *ga takusañ aru.* (きょうはすることがたくさんある) I have a lot of *things to do* today.
2 incident; problem; plan:
Koto *wa juñchoo ni susuñde imasu.* (ことは順調に進んでいます) The *plan* is well under way.
3 (used in giving impersonal orders or instructions):
Shimee oyobi juusho o kinyuu no koto. (氏名および住所を記入のこと) *Enter* both full name and address.
... koto ga aru (...～がある) have experienced: ★ Preceded by the past form of a verb and refers to experiences in the past. *Kare wa chuugaku de oshieta* koto ga arimasu. (彼は中学で教えたことがあります) He *has experience* of teaching at a junior high school.
... koto ga dekiru (...～ができる) be able to do: ★ Preceded by the dictionary form of a verb. *Sono ooki-na iwa wa ugokasu* koto ga dekinakatta. (その大きな岩は動かすことができなかった) We *were unable to* move that large rock.
... koto ni natte iru (...～になっている) be supposed [scheduled] to do: ★ Preceded by the dictionary form of a verb. *Kare to wa go-ji ni au* koto ni natte imasu. (彼とは 5 時に会うことになっています) I *am set to* meet him at five.
... koto ni shite iru (...～にしている) make it a rule to do: ★ Preceded by the dictionary form of a verb. *Asa wa hayaku okiru* koto ni shite imasu. (朝は早く起きることにしています) I *make it a rule to* get up early in the morning.
... koto ni suru (...～にする) decide to do: ★ Preceded by the dictionary form of a verb. *Kuuraa o kau* koto ni shimashita. (クーラーを買うことにしました) I *decided to* buy an air conditioner.

ko⌉to[2] こと(琴) *n.* koto; traditional Japanese harp.

ko⌉to[3] こと(古都) *n.* ancient city [capital]. ★ Often refers to Kyoto or sometimes to Nara.

ko⌈toba⌉ ことば(言葉) *n.* language; word; speech.

ko⌈tobazu⌉kai ことばづかい(言葉遣い) *n.* wording; language; one's way of speaking.

ko⌈togara⌉ ことがら(事柄) *n.* thing; matter; subject:
Kore wa hijoo ni juuyoo na kotogara desu. (これは非常に重要な事柄です) This is a very important *matter.* ⟪⇨ koto[1]⟫

ko⌈togo⌉toku ことごとく(悉く) *adv.* (*formal*) entirely; utterly:
Yatoo wa yotoo no teeañ ni, kotogotoku *hañtai shite iru.* (野党は与党の提案に, ことごとく反対している) The opposition is *utterly* against the ruling party's proposal.

ko⌈tona⌉r·u ことなる(異なる) *vi.* (-nar·i-; -nar·a-; -nat-te Ⓒ) differ; vary; be different: ★ More formal than '*chigau.*'
Watashi-tachi no kañgae-kata wa kotonatte iru. (私たちの考え方は異なっている) Our ways of thinking *are different.*

ko⌉to ni ことに(殊に) *adv.* (*formal*) especially; particularly. ⟪⇨ toku ni⟫

ko⌈to ni yoru to ことによると(事に依ると) *adv.* probably; possibly:
Koto ni yoru to *gogo wa ame ga furu ka mo shirenai.* (ことによると午後は雨が降るかもしれない) There will *probably* be rain in the afternoon.

ko⌈tori ことり(小鳥) *n.* little bird.

ko⌈toshi ことし(今年) *n.* this year. ⟪⇨ kyoneñ; raineñ⟫

ko⌈towa⌉r·u ことわる(断る) *vt.* (-war·i-; -war·a-; -wat-te Ⓒ)
1 refuse (a demand, request, admission, etc.); decline; reject; turn down. ⟪⇨ o-kotowari⟫
2 get permission:
Kuruma o tsukau toki wa watashi

ni kotowatte *kudasai*. (車を使うときは私に断ってください) When you are going to use the car, please *get permission* from me.
3 give notice:
Kare wa arakajime kotowaranai de *kaisha o yamete shimatta*. (彼はあらかじめ断らないで会社を辞めてしまった) *Without giving notice* beforehand, he just went and quit the company.

ko⌈towaza ことわざ (諺) *n*. proverb; saying.

ko⌈tozuke⌉·ru ことづける (言付ける) *vt*. (-zuke-te [V]) leave a message; ask a person to do. ((⇨ tanomu))

ko⌈tsu こつ (骨) *n*. knack; secret:
Kare wa tsuri no kotsu *o shitte iru*. (彼は釣りのこつを知っている) He has the *knack* of fishing.

ko⌉tsukotsu こつこつ *adv*. (～ to) **1** (the sound of a step; tap):
Kotsukotsu *to dare-ka no kutsu no oto ga kikoeru*. (こつこつとだれかの靴の音が聞こえる) I hear the *clicking* sound of someone's heels.
2 steadily; patiently; little by little:
kotsukotsu (*to*) *kane o tameru* (こつこつ(と)金をためる) save money *little by little*.

ko⌈uri こうり (小売り) *n*. retail:
Kore wa kouri *de gohyaku-eñ desu*. (これは小売りで 500 円です) This is 500 yen *retail*. ((⇨ oroshi))

ko⌈waga⌉r·u こわがる (怖がる) *vi*. (-gar·i-; -gar·a-; -gat-te [C]) be afraid; be frightened; be scared:
takai tokoro o kowagaru (高い所を怖がる) *be afraid* of heights. ((⇨ kowai))

ko⌈wa⌉·i こわい (怖い) *a*. (-ku)
1 dreadful; horrible; frightening:
kowai *omoi o suru* (怖い思いをする) have a *frightening* experience. ((⇨ kowagaru; osoroshii))
2 strict:
Yamada señsee wa kowai. (山田先生は怖い) Our teacher, Mr. Yamada, is very *strict*.

ko⌈ware⌉·ru こわれる (壊れる) *vi*. (koware-te [V]) **1** break; be broken; be damaged:
Kabiñ ga yuka ni ochite kowareta. (花びんが床に落ちてこわれた) The vase fell on the floor and *broke*. ((⇨ kowasu))
2 get out of order:
Kono terebi wa kowarete imasu. (このテレビはこわれています) This television *is out of order*. ((⇨ koshoo[1]))
3 (of a hope, dream, etc.) be destroyed; be broken off. ((⇨ kowasu))

ko⌈wa⌉s·u こわす (壊す) *vt*. (kowash·i-; kowas·a-; kowash·i-te [C]) **1** break; pull down:
Dare-ka ga doa o kowashita. (だれかがドアをこわした) Someone *broke* the door. ((⇨ kowareru))
2 wreck; destroy; ruin; spoil (a hope, dream, etc.):
shizeñ o kowasu (自然をこわす) *destroy* nature / *yume o* kowasu (夢をこわす) *ruin* one's dreams. ((⇨ kowareru))
3 injure (health); upset:
Kare wa muri o shite karada o kowashita. (彼は無理をして体をこわした) He *injured* his health by overworking.

ko⌈ya こや (小屋) *n*. hut; shack; shed.

ko⌈yomi⌉ こよみ (暦) *n*. calendar; almanac.

ko⌈yubi こゆび (小指) *n*. little finger; little toe.

ko⌈yuki こゆき (小雪) *n*. light snow. ((⇨ ooyuki; yuki[1]))

ko⌈yuu こゆう (固有) *a.n*. (～ na/no, ni) peculiar; characteristic; inherent:
Shiñtoo wa Nihoñ koyuu *no shuukyoo desu*. (神道は日本固有の宗教です) Shinto is a religion *peculiar* to Japan.

ko⌉zukai こづかい (小遣い) *n*. allowance; pocket money.

k

ko⌈zu⌉tsumi こづつみ(小包) *n.* parcel; package; parcel post.

ku⌉¹ く(九) *n.* nine: ★「九」is sometimes pronounced '*kyuu*.' For counting days, the ninth day is pronounced '*kokonoka*.' 《⇨ kokonotsu; APP. 3》

ku² く(区) *n.* **1** ward. ★ The basic administrative unit in metropolitan areas. 《⇨ kuyakusho》
2 district; zone:
Basu wa ik-ku *hyakuhachijuu-eñ desu.* (バスは1区180円です) The bus fare is 180 yen per *zone*.

ku⌉³ く(句) *n.* phrase.

ku⌈ba⌉r·u くばる(配る) *vt.* (kubar·i-; kubar·a-; kubat-te Ⓒ) distribute; deliver; pass out:
bira o kubaru (ビラを配る) *distribute* handbills / *shiñbuñ o* kubaru (新聞を配る) *deliver* newspapers. 《⇨ haitatsu》

ku⌉betsu くべつ(区別) *n.* distinction; difference.
kubetsu suru (〜する) *vt.* tell... from; distinguish; discriminate.

ku⌈bi くび(首) *n.* neck; head:
Mado kara kubi *o dasu to kikeñ desu.* (窓から首を出すと危険です) It is dangerous to stick your *head* out of the window. 《⇨ atama》
kubi ni naru (〜になる) be dismissed [fired]. 《⇨ kaiko》
kubi o tsukkomu (〜を突っ込む) consciously involve oneself; stick one's nose into.

ku⌈cha⌉kucha くちゃくちゃ *adv.* (〜 to) (the sound of chewing things):
mono o taberu toki, kuchakucha (*to*) *oto o saseru* (物を食べるとき, くちゃくちゃ(と)音をさせる) make a *smacking* noise while eating food.

ku⌈chi¹ くち(口) *n.* **1** mouth.
2 (of a container) mouth:
biñ no kuchi (びんの口) the *mouth* of a bottle.
kuchi ga karui (〜が軽い) indiscreet; talkative.
kuchi ga omoi (〜が重い) be close-mouthed. 《⇨ mukuchi》
kuchi ga suberu (〜が滑る) let slip.
kuchi ga umai (〜がうまい) be a smooth talker.
kuchi ga warui (〜が悪い) have a sharp tongue.
kuchi ni au (〜に合う) suit one's taste.

ku⌈chi² くち(口) *n.* job; position; opening:
taipisuto no kuchi (タイピストの口) a *job* as a typist.

ku⌈chibeni くちべに(口紅) *n.* rouge; lipstick.

ku⌈chibiru くちびる(唇) *n.* lip.

ku⌈chi⌉guchi ni くちぐちに(口々に) *adv.* unanimously; in unison; at once:
Miñna wa kuchiguchi ni *kanojo no e o hometa.* (みんなは口々に彼女の絵をほめた) They were *all* in agreement in praising her painting.

ku⌈chihige くちひげ(口髭) *n.* mustache. 《⇨ hige》

ku⌉da くだ(管) *n.* pipe; tube.

ku⌈dake⌉·ru くだける(砕ける) *vi.* (kudake-te Ⓥ) break; go to pieces:
Ishi ga atatte, kagami ga kudaketa. (石が当たって, 鏡が砕けた) A stone hit the mirror and it *smashed*. 《⇨ kudaku》

ku⌈da⌉keta くだけた **1** (of language) colloquial; informal:
kudaketa *iikata* (くだけた言いかた) a *colloquial* expression.
2 (of a person) affable:
kudaketa *hito* (くだけた人) an *affable* person.

ku⌈da⌉k·u くだく(砕く) *vt.* (kudak·i-; kudak·a-; kuda·i-te Ⓒ)
1 break; smash; shatter; crush.
2 destroy; ruin (a hope, dream, etc.). 《⇨ kudakeru》

ku⌈da⌉mono くだもの(果物) *n.* fruit.

ku⌈darana·i くだらない *a.* (-ku)
1 worthless; trivial:

kudaranai *mondai* (くだらない問題) a *trivial* matter. ⟪⇨ tsumaranai⟫
2 absurd; nonsense:
Kudaranai koto *o iu na.* (くだらないことを言うな) Don't talk *nonsense.*

ku꜔dari くだり (下り) *n.* **1** descent; downhill slope. ⟪↔ nobori⟫ ⟪⇨ kudaru⟫
2 down train. ★ The train going away from Tokyo or a major city. ⟪↔ nobori⟫

ku꜔dar·u くだる (下る) *vi.* (kudar·i-; kudar·a-; kudat-te Ⓒ)
1 descend; go down; come down:
yama o kudaru (山を下る) *go down* a mountain. ⟪↔ noboru[3]⟫
2 (of an order) be passed; be issued:
Kare-ra ni shuppatsu no meeree ga kudatta. (彼らに出発の命令が下った) The order for departure *was issued* to them.
3 have loose bowels:
Watashi wa o-naka ga kudatte iru. (私はおなかが下っている) My bowels *are loose.* ⟪⇨ geri⟫

ku꜔dasa꜔i ください (下さい) [the imperative of '*kudasaru*']
1 (*polite*) please give me; let me have: *O-cha o ip-pai* kudasai. (お茶を一杯下さい) *Please give me* a cup of tea.
2 (*polite*) please do (for me): ★ Preceded by the *te*-form of a verb. *Moo sukoshi yukkuri* hanashite kudasai. (もう少しゆっくり話してください) *Speak* more slowly, *please.*
3 (*honorific*) please do: ★ Preceded by '*o*-'+the continuative base of a verb. Doozo o-kake kudasai. (どうぞお掛けください) *Please have a seat.*
-nai de kudasai (ないで〜) (*polite*) please do not: *Doo-ka* ikanai de kudasai. (どうか行かないでください) Please *don't go away.*

ku꜔dasa꜔r·u くださる (下さる) *vt.* (-sa·i-; -sar·a-; -sat-te Ⓒ) give me [us] (something): ★ Honorific alternative of '*kureru*[1].'
Sensee wa watashi ni nooto o kudasatta. (先生は私にノートを下さった) The teacher *gave me* a notebook.
-te kudasaru (て〜) (used when a person's superior does something for that person): *Kore wa ano yuumee na gaka ga* kaite kudasatta *e desu.* (これはあの有名な画家がかいてくださった絵です) This is the picture which that famous painter *drew* for me.

ku꜔fuu くふう (工夫) *n.* idea; device; contrivance.
kufuu suru (〜する) *vt.* devise; contrive; think out.

ku꜔-gatsu くがつ (九月) *n.* September. ⟪⇨ APP. 5⟫

ku꜔gi くぎ (釘) *n.* nail:
kugi *o utsu* [*nuku*] (釘を打つ[抜く]) drive [pull out] a *nail.*

ku꜔gi꜔r·u くぎる (区切る) *vt.* (kugir·i-; kugir·a-; kugit-te Ⓒ) divide; partition; space; punctuate:
heya o futatsu ni kugiru (部屋を2つに区切る) *divide* a room into two.

ku꜔i くい (杭) *n.* stake; pile; post:
kui *o utsu* (杭を打つ) drive in a *pile.*

ku꜔izu クイズ *n.* quiz: ★ Not used in the sense of a short exam.
kuizu *bangumi* (クイズ番組) a *quiz* show.

ku꜔ji くじ (籤) *n.* lot; lottery. ⟪⇨ takarakuji⟫

ku꜔ji꜔k·u くじく (挫く) *vt.* (kujik·i-; kujik·a-; kuji·i-te Ⓒ) **1** sprain; wrench:
ashikubi o kujiku (足首をくじく) *sprain* one's ankle.
2 frustrate; baffle; crush:
yowaki o tasuke, tsuyoki o kujiku (弱きを助け,強きをくじく) help the weak and *crush* the strong.

ku꜔ki꜔ くき (茎) *n.* stalk; stem.

ku꜔kyoo くきょう (苦境) *n.* difficult situation; adversity.

ku꜔ma꜔ くま (熊) *n.* bear.

ku⌈mi⌉ くみ(組) *n.* **1** class:
Watashi-tachi wa onaji kumi *desu.* (私たちは同じ組です) We are in the same *class.* ((⇨ kurasu²))
2 group; party; team:
*Go-niñ-zutsu, sañ-*kumi *ni wakareta.* (五人ずつ, 3組に分かれた) We were divided into three *groups* of five.
3 set; pair:
*Kono sara wa go-ko de, hito-*kumi *desu.* (この皿は5個で, ひと組です) These plates come five to a *set.*

ku⌈miai くみあい(組合) *n.* union; association. ((⇨ roodoo-kumiai))

ku⌈miawase くみあわせ(組み合わせ) *n.* combination; pairing:
shiai no kumiawase (試合の組み合わせ) the *pairings* for a tournament. ((⇨ kumiawaseru))

ku⌈miawase·ru くみあわせる(組み合わせる) *vt.* (-awase-te [V]) put together; combine; match. ((⇨ kumiawase))

ku⌈mitate くみたて(組み立て) *n.* assembly; structure; construction; composition:
buhiñ no kumitate (部品の組み立て) the *assembly* of parts. ((⇨ kumitateru))

ku⌈mitate⌉·ru くみたてる(組み立てる) *vt.* (-tate-te [V]) put together; assemble; construct; compose:
mokee hikooki o kumitateru (模型飛行機を組み立てる) *build* a model airplane. ((⇨ kumitate))

ku⌉mo¹ くも(雲) *n.* cloud.

ku⌉mo² くも(蜘蛛) *n.* spider.

ku⌈mori⌉ くもり(曇り) *n.* cloudiness; cloudy weather. ((⇨ ame¹; hare; kumoru))

ku⌈mori-ga⌉rasu くもりガラス(曇りガラス) *n.* frosted glass; ground glass. ((⇨ garasu))

ku⌈mo⌉r·u くもる(曇る) *vi.* (kumor·i-; kumor·a-; kumot-te [C])
1 become cloudy; cloud over; become overcast. ((↔ hareru¹)) ((⇨ kumori))
2 fog up; collect moisture:
Yuge de megane ga kumotta. (湯気で眼鏡が曇った) My glasses *misted up* with the steam.
3 (of a facial expression) grow cloudy.

ku⌉m·u¹ くむ(組む) *vt.* (kum·i-; kum·a-; kuñ-de [C]) **1** cross; fold:
ude o kuñde *aruku* (腕を組んで歩く) walk *arm in arm.*
2 cooperate; pair with:
Watashi wa tenisu de Yamada-sañ to kuñda. (私はテニスで山田さんと組んだ) I *paired up* with Mr. Yamada for tennis.
3 put together; assemble:
retsu o kumu (列を組む) *form* a line.

ku⌈m·u² くむ(汲む) *vt.* (kum·i-; kum·a-; kuñ-de [C]) **1** draw; ladle; scoop up; pump:
baketsu ni mizu o kumu (バケツに水をくむ) *ladle* water into a bucket.
2 understand (a person's feeling); take into consideration:
Kare wa watashi no kimochi o kuñde kureta. (彼は私の気持ちをくんでくれた) He *took* my feelings *into consideration.*

ku⌈ñ くん(訓) *n.* the Japanese reading of a Chinese character.
★ A single Chinese character with different meanings may have more than one '*kuñ*' reading. ((⇨ oñ²))

-kuñ くん(君) *suf.* Mr.:
★ Added to either the given or family name of male friends or someone of lower status. ((⇨ -sañ¹))
*Suzuki-*kuñ (鈴木君) (*Mr.*) Suzuki.

ku⌈ni くに(国) *n.* country; nation; home; hometown. ((⇨ furusato; kokyoo))

ku⌉ñreñ くんれん(訓練) *n.* training; drill; practice.
kuñreñ (o) suru (～(を)する) *vt.* train; drill.

ku⌈rabe·ru くらべる(比べる) *vt.* (kurabe-te [V]) compare:
hoñyaku to geñsho o kuraberu (翻

訳と原書を比べる) *compare* the translation with the original. ⟪⇒ hikaku; terashiawaseru⟫

ku⌈ra·i[1] くらい(暗い) *a.* (-ku)

1 dim; dark:
Soto ga kuraku *natte kita.* (外が暗くなってきた) It is getting *dark* outside. ⟪↔ akarui⟫

2 (of character, mood, etc.) gloomy; shadowy:
Suzuki-sañ wa itsu-mo kurai kao o shite iru. (鈴木さんはいつも暗い顔をしている) Miss Suzuki always *has a long face.* ⟪↔ akarui⟫

3 (of prospects, etc.) gloomy; dark:
Keezai no mitooshi wa kurai. (経済の見通しは暗い) The economic outlook is *gloomy.* ⟪↔ akarui⟫

4 (of knowledge) be unfamiliar with:
Watashi wa hooritsu ni kurai. (私は法律に暗い) I am *unfamiliar* with the law. ⟪↔ akarui⟫

ku⌉rai[2]**/gu⌉rai** くらい/ぐらい(位) *p.*
★ In the following examples, '*kurai*' can be replaced by '*gurai*.' ⟪⇒ bakari; hodo⟫

1 (of time and quantity) about; approximately:
Go-fuñ kurai *de modorimasu.* (5分くらいで戻ります) I will be back in *approximately* five minutes.

2 like; such that:
Koñna koto kurai *kodomo datte dekiru.* (こんなことくらい子どもだってできる) Even a child can do something *like* this.

3 too...to:
Watashi wa ip-po mo arukenai kurai *tsukareta.* (私は一歩も歩けないくらい疲れた) I was *too* tired *to* take another step forward.

4 not as [so]...as: ★ Follows nouns and occurs with a negative.
Anata kurai *isogashii hito wa hoká ni* imaseñ. (あなたくらい忙しい人はほかにいません) There is *no one* who is *as* busy *as* you.

5 only; at least:
Soñna baka na koto o kañgaeru no wa kimi kurai *no mono da.* (そんなばかなことを考えるのは君くらいのものだ) You are the *only* person that would think of something idiotic like that.

... kurai nara (...〜なら) if:
Tochuu de nagedasu kurai nara, *hajime kara yaranai hoo ga ii.* (途中で投げ出すくらいなら, 初めからやらないほうがいい) *If* you are going to give up halfway through, you had better not start at all.

ku⌈rashi くらし(暮らし) *n.* life; living; livelihood. ⟪⇒ kurasu[1]⟫

ku⌈rashi⌉kku (o⌉ñgaku) クラシックおんがく(クラシック音楽) *n.* classical music.

ku⌈ras·u[1] くらす(暮らす) *vi., vt.* (kurash·i-; kuras·a-; kurash·i-te Ⓒ) live; make a living; get along; stay:
Sono sakka wa ik-ka-getsu hoteru de kurashita. (その作家は一か月ホテルで暮らした) The author *stayed* at a hotel for a month.

ku⌉rasu[2] クラス *n.* class.

ku⌈re くれ(暮れ) *n.* end of the year. ⟪⇒ kureru[2]⟫

ku⌈regu⌉re mo くれぐれも(呉々も) *adv.* please: ★ Used as an intensifier in expressions indicating one's sincere desire.
Kuregure mo *keñkoo ni go-chuui* kudasai. (くれぐれも健康にご注意ください) *Please* take good care of yourself.

ku⌈re·ru[1] くれる(呉れる) *vt.* (kurete Ⓥ) give: ★ '*Kudasaru*' is the honorific alternative.
Kare wa watashi ni jisho o kureta. (彼は私に辞書をくれた) He *gave* me a dictionary.

-te kureru (て〜) (used when a person's equal or subordinate does something for that person):
Yamada-sañ wa shiñsetsu ni mo watashi o eki made okutte kureta. (山田さんは親切にも私を駅まで送ってくれた) Mr. Yamada was kind

enough to *take* me to the station. ⟪↔ ageru[1]⟫

ku⌈re·ru[2] くれる(暮れる) *vi.* (kurete [V]) **1** (of a day) get dark.
2 (of a year) draw to an end:
Kotoshi mo kurete kita. (今年も暮れてきた) The year *is drawing to an end.* ⟪⇨ kure⟫
... ni kureru (...に暮れる) be lost (in thought): *Doo shite yoi ka* tohoo ni kureta. (どうしてよいか途方に暮れた) I *was at a loss* what to do.

ku⌈ri⌉iniñgu クリーニング *n.* cleaning; laundry:
Zuboñ o kuriiniñgu *ni dashita.* (ズボンをクリーニングに出した) I sent my trousers to the *cleaner's.*

ku⌈rika⌉es·u くりかえす(繰り返す) *vt.* (-kaesh·i-; -kaes·a-; -kaesh·i-te [C]) repeat; do over again:
onaji machigai o kurikaesu (同じ間違いを繰り返す) *repeat* the same mistake.

Ku⌈risu⌉masu クリスマス *n.* Christmas.

ku⌉ro くろ(黒) *n.* **1** black; brown:
kuro *no kutsu* (黒の靴) *black* shoes.
2 guilty:
Kare wa kuro *da to omou.* (彼は黒だと思う) I think he is *guilty.*
⟪↔ shiro[1]⟫

ku⌈ro⌉·i くろい(黒い) *a.* (-ku)
1 black; dark; tanned. ⟪⇨ kuro⟫
2 (of rumors, etc.) dark:
Ano kaisha wa saikiñ kuroi *uwasa ga aru.* (あの会社は最近黒いうわさがある) Recently there have been *dark* rumors concerning that company.

ku⌈roji くろじ(黒字) *n.* black-ink balance; surplus:
Kaisha wa kuroji *desu.* (会社は黒字です) Our company is in the *black.*
⟪↔ akaji⟫

ku⌉roo くろう(苦労) *n.* trouble; difficulty; hardship; pains.
kuroo suru (〜する) *vi.* have trouble [difficulty]; have a hard time.
⟪⇨ gokuroosama⟫

ku⌉rooto くろうと(玄人) *n.* expert; professional; specialist.
⟪↔ shirooto⟫

k·u⌉ru くる(来る) *vi.* (k·i-; k·o-; k·i-te [I]) **1** come; arrive:
Koko ni kite *kudasai.* (ここに来てください) Please *come* here. ⟪↔ iku⟫
2 come from; be caused:
Kare no byooki wa karoo kara kita. (彼の病気は過労からきた) His illness *was caused* by overwork.
-te kuru (て〜) become [come to ...]: *Dañdañ samuku* natte kita. (だんだん寒くなってきた) It *has become* colder and colder.

ku⌉rukuru くるくる *adv.* (〜 to)
1 (used to express an object rotating):
Fuusha ga kurukuru *to mawatte ita.* (風車がくるくると回っていた) The sails of the windmill were turning *round and round.*
2 (used to express the state of being unstable):
Kare wa kañgae ga kurukuru *(to) kawaru.* (彼は考えがくるくる(と)変わる) His ideas are *always* changing.

ku⌈ruma くるま(車) *n.* **1** vehicle; car; automobile.
2 taxi:
Kuruma *o yoñde kudasai.* (車を呼んでください) Please call me a *taxi.*
3 wheel; caster.

ku⌈ru⌉m·u くるむ *vt.* (kurum·i-; kurum·a-; kuruñ-de [C]) wrap:
Kanojo wa akañboo o moofu de kuruñda. (彼女は赤ん坊を毛布でくるんだ) She *wrapped* her baby in a blanket.

ku⌈ru⌉ri to くるりと *adv.* **1** (used to express the action of turning around):
Kare wa kururi to *ushiro o furimuita.* (彼はくるりと後ろを振り向いた) He *spun around* and looked back.
2 suddenly; abruptly:
Kare wa kururi to *keekaku o kaeta.* (彼はくるりと計画を変えた) He *suddenly* changed his plan.

ku⌈rushi⌉·i くるしい(苦しい) *a.*

(-ku) **1** painful; hard:
Sono tozañ wa kurushikatta. (その登山は苦しかった) The mountain climb was *very hard*. 《⇨ kurushimu》
2 needy:
Koñgetsu wa kakee ga kurushii. (今月は家計が苦しい) This month we are in financially *straitened circumstances* at home.
3 awkward:
Watashi no tachiba ga kurushiku *natte kita*. (私の立場が苦しくなってきた) My position has become *awkward*.

ku⌈rushime⌉·ru くるしめる (苦しめる) *vt.* (-shime-te Ⓥ) distress; annoy; torment:
Shakkiñ ga kare o kurushimete iru. (借金が彼を苦しめている) The loan *is causing* him *distress*. 《⇨ kurushimu》

ku⌈rushimi⌉ くるしみ (苦しみ) *n.* pain; hardship; agony:
kurushimi *ni taeru* (苦しみに耐える) bear *hardship*. 《⇨ kurushimu》

ku⌈rushi⌉m·u くるしむ (苦しむ) *vi.* (-shim·i-; -shim·a-; -shiñ-de Ⓒ)
1 suffer from; feel pain; be afflicted:
ue ni kurushimu (飢えに苦しむ) *suffer* from hunger. 《⇨ kurushimeru; kurushimi》
2 be troubled; be worried; be at a loss:
Kare wa iiwake ni kurushiñda. (彼は言い訳に苦しんだ) He *was at a loss* for an excuse.
3 have difficulty:
Kare no koodoo wa rikai ni kurushimu. (彼の行動は理解に苦しむ) I *have difficulty* in understanding his behavior.

ku⌈sa⌉ くさ (草) *n.* grass; weed. 《⇨ zassoo; shiba; shibafu》

ku⌈sa⌉bana くさばな (草花) *n.* flowering plant.

kusa⌉·i くさい (臭い) *a.* (-ku)
1 smelly; stinking:
Kono kutsushita wa kusai. (この靴下は臭い) These socks are *smelly*.
2 suspicious; dubious; fishy:
Sono hanashi wa kusai. (その話は臭い) That story is *dubious*.

-ku⌈sa⌉i くさい (臭い) *suf.*
1 smelly; stinking:
koge-kusai (焦げ臭い) have a burnt *smell* / *sake*-kusai (酒臭い) *reek* of alcohol.
2 seem; look; sound:
iñchiki-kusai (インチキくさい) be phony *sounding* / *uso*-kusai (うそくさい) *seem like* a lie.
3 (used as an intensifier):
baka-kusai (ばかくさい) *completely* foolish / *meñdoo*-kusai (面倒くさい) *very* troublesome.

ku⌈sa⌉ki くさき (草木) *n.* grass and trees; plants.

ku⌈sari くさり (鎖) *n.* chain.

ku⌈sa⌉r·u くさる (腐る) *vi.* (kusa-r·i-; kusar·a-; kusat-te Ⓒ) **1** go bad; decay; rot.
2 be discouraged:
Koto ga umaku ikanakute, kare wa kusatte iru. (ことがうまくいかなくて, 彼はくさっている) Things have gone wrong for him, so he *is discouraged*.

ku⌈se⌉ くせ (癖) *n.* **1** habit:
tsume o kamu kuse (つめをかむ癖) a *habit* of biting one's nails.
2 peculiarity:
Kare wa kuse no aru *ji o kaku*. (彼は癖のある字を書く) He writes in a *characteristic* way.

ku⌈se⌉ ni くせに (癖に) although; when; in spite of: ★ Usually belittling or disparaging.
Kare wa nani mo shiranai kuse ni, *nañ de mo shitte iru yoo ni hanasu*. (彼は何も知らないくせに, 何でも知っているように話す) *Although* he knows nothing, he talks as if he knew everything.

ku⌈shakusha くしゃくしゃ *adv.* (~ no, ni) (used to express something that is wrinkled, creased or crumpled):
Kami no ke ga kushakusha *da*. (髪

k

の毛がくしゃくしゃだ) My hair is all *messed up*.

ku⌈sha⌉mi くしゃみ *n.* sneeze: *Kare wa nañ-do mo* kushami (o) shita. (彼は何度もくしゃみ(を)した) He *sneezed* many times.

ku⌈shi⌉ くし(櫛) *n.* comb.

ku⌈shi⌉ñ くしん(苦心) *n.* pains; hard work; effort.
kushiñ suru (～する) *vi.* take pains; work hard; make great efforts.

ku⌈so⌉ くそ(糞) *n.* shit. ★ Often used as an exclamation of disgust, anger, etc. ⟪⇨ daibeñ; fuñ[2]⟫

ku⌈sudama くすだま(薬玉) *n.*
1 decorative paper ball. ★ It is usually hung on festive occasions.
2 ornamental scent bag.

k

ku⌈sugur·u くすぐる(擽る) *vt.* (-gur·i-; -gur·a-; -gut-te [C]) tickle (a person).

ku⌈sugutta⌉·i くすぐったい *a.* (-ku) tickling; ticklish: *Senaka ga* kusuguttai. (背中がくすぐったい) My back is *ticklish*.

ku⌈su⌉kusu くすくす *adv.* (～ to) (used to express the manner of giggling [tittering; chuckling]): *hitori de* kusukusu (to) warau (ひとりでくすくす(と)笑う) *chuckle* to oneself.

ku⌈suri くすり(薬) *n.* medicine; drug: kusuri *o nomu* (薬を飲む) take *medicine*. ⟪⇨ naifukuyaku⟫

ku⌈suriya くすりや(薬屋) *n.* pharmacy; drugstore. ⟪⇨ yakkyoku⟫

ku⌈suri⌉yubi くすりゆび(薬指) *n.* ring finger.

ku⌈tabire⌉·ru くたびれる *vi.* (-bire-te [V]) **1** be tired; get tired; get exhausted: *Kanojo wa sugu ni* kutabireru. (彼女はすぐにくたびれる) She soon *gets tired out*.
2 (of clothes) be worn out: *Kare wa* kutabireta *kutsu o haite ita*. (彼はくたびれた靴をはいていた) He was wearing *worn-out* shoes.

ku⌈takuta くたくた *adv.* (～ ni) dead tired; exhausted: *Kare wa tsukarete* kutakuta *datta*. (彼は疲れてくたくただった) He was *utterly exhausted*.

ku⌈teñ くてん(句点) *n.* period. ★ The Japanese period is '。'. ⟪⇨ tooteñ⟫

ku⌈to⌉oteñ くとうてん(句読点) *n.* punctuation marks. ⟪⇨ kuteñ; tooteñ⟫

ku⌈tsu⌉ くつ(靴) *n.* shoes; boots.

ku⌈tsu⌉shita くつした(靴下) *n.* socks; stockings: kutsushita *o haku* [*nugu*] (靴下をはく[脱ぐ]) put on [take off] one's *socks*. ⟪⇨ tebukuro⟫

ku⌈tsuu くつう(苦痛) *n.* pain; pang; agony: kutsuu *o kañjiru* (苦痛を感じる) feel *pain*.

ku⌉·u くう(食う) *vt.* (ku·i-; ku-w·a-; kut-te [C]) **1** (*rude*) eat: ★ '*Taberu*' is more polite and usual.
Kyoo wa mada nani mo kutte inai. (きょうはまだ何も食っていない) I *have not eaten* anything yet today.
2 (*rude*) live; earn a living: ★ '*Taberu*' is more polite.
Kare wa arubaito o shite, kutte iru. (彼はアルバイトをして, 食っている) He *gets by* doing a part-time job.
3 (of an insect) eat; bite: *Kono moofu wa mushi ga* kutte iru. (この毛布は虫が食っている) The moths *have eaten* this blanket.
4 (of time, fuel, etc.) consume; waste: *Ookii kuruma wa gasoriñ o* kuu. (大きい車はガソリンを食う) Large cars *consume* lots of gasoline.
5 be taken in: *Sono te wa* kuwanai *zo*. (その手は食わないぞ) I *will not fall* for that trick.

ku⌈uchuu くうちゅう(空中) *n.* the air; the sky: kuuchuu *ni tadayou* (空中に漂う) float in *the air*. ⟪⇨ kaijoo[2]; rikujoo⟫

ku⌈ufuku くうふく(空腹) *n.* hunger; empty stomach.

ku⌈uguñ くうぐん(空軍) *n.* air force. ⟪⇨ Jieetai; kaiguñ; rikuguñ⟫

ku⌈ukañ くうかん(空間) *n.* space; room: kuukañ *o akeru* (空間をあける) make *room.*

ku⌉uki くうき(空気) *n.* air: *heya no* kuuki o irekaeru (部屋の空気を入れ替える) *air* a room.

ku⌈ukoo くうこう(空港) *n.* airport. ⟪⇨ hikoojoo⟫

ku⌈upoñ⌉keñ クーポンけん(クーポン券) *n.* coupon ticket.

ku⌉uraa クーラー *n.* air conditioner. ⟪⇨ eakoñ⟫

ku⌈urañ くうらん(空欄) *n.* blank column [space].

ku⌈usoo くうそう(空想) *n.* fancy; imagination; daydream.
kuusoo suru (~する) *vt.* fancy; imagine; daydream.

ku⌈wadate⌉·ru くわだてる(企てる) *vt.* (-date-te Ⓥ) **1** attempt; try: *jisatsu o* kuwadateru (自殺を企てる) *attempt* suicide.
2 plan:
Sono kaisha wa atarashii koojoo no keñsetsu o kuwadatete iru. (その会社は新しい工場の建設を企てている) The company *is planning* the construction of a new factory.

ku⌈wae·ru くわえる(加える) *vt.* (-e-te Ⓥ) **1** add; sum up; include; join: ⟪⇨ tsukekuwaeru⟫
Satoo o moo sukoshi kuwaete *kudasai.* (砂糖をもう少し加えてください) Please *add* a little more sugar.
2 increase; gather; pick up:
Kuruma wa shidai ni sokudo o kuwaeta. (車は次第に速度を加えた) The car gradually *picked up* speed. ⟪⇨ kuwawaru⟫
3 give; put; deal:
hito ni atsuryoku o kuwaeru (人に圧力を加える) *put* pressure on a person.

ku⌈washi⌉·i くわしい(詳しい) *a.* (-ku) **1** full; detailed; minute:
Kuwashii *koto wa shirimaseñ.* (詳しいことは知りません) I do not know the *full details.*
2 (of knowledge) well versed; familiar.

ku⌈wawa⌉r·u くわわる(加わる) *vi.* (-war·i-; -war·a-; -wat-te Ⓒ)
1 join; take part in:
Kanojo mo sono asobi ni kuwawatta. (彼女もその遊びに加わった) She too *joined* in the game. ⟪⇨ kuwaeru⟫
2 increase; gain:
Higoto ni samusa ga kuwawatte imasu. (日ごとに寒さが加わっています) It *is getting* colder day by day.

ku⌈ya⌉kusho くやくしょ(区役所) *n.* ward office. ★ The equivalent of city hall in metropolitan areas. ⟪⇨ ku[2]; shiyakusho⟫

ku⌈yashi⌉·i くやしい(悔しい) *a.* (-ku) mortifying; regrettable:
Makete kuyashii. (負けて悔しい) How *mortifying* it is to be defeated.

ku⌉zu くず(屑) *n.* **1** waste; rubbish; trash. ⟪⇨ garakuta⟫
2 (*informal*) worthless [useless] person:
Aitsu wa niñgeñ no kuzu *da.* (あいつは人間のくずだ) He is a *good-for-nothing.*

ku⌈zure⌉·ru くずれる(崩れる) *vi.* (-re-te Ⓥ) **1** collapse; break; be destroyed; give way:
Toñneru ga kuzureta. (トンネルがくずれた) The tunnel *caved in.* ⟪⇨ kuzusu⟫
2 lose shape:
Sono fuku wa katachi ga kuzurete iru. (その服は形がくずれている) Those clothes *have lost* their shape.
3 (of weather) change; deteriorate:
Teñki ga kuzure-*soo da.* (天気がくずれそうだ) The weather is likely to *deteriorate.*
4 (of money) be changed:
Ichimañ-eñ satsu kuzuremasu ka? (一万円札くずれますか) Can you

change a ¥10,000 note?
《⇨ kuzusu》

ku⌈zu⌉s·u くずす(崩す) *vt.* (-sh·i-; -s·a-; -sh·i-te Ⓒ) **1** break down; pull down:
furui biru o kuzusu (古いビルをくずす) *knock down* an old building.
《⇨ kuzureru》
2 change (money); break:
Ichimañ-eñ o kuzushite, *señ-eñ satsu ni shita.* (一万円をくずして, 千円札にした) I *have changed* ¥10,000 into thousand yen notes.
《⇨ kuzureru》
3 write (letters, characters) in a cursive style.

kya⌉betsu キャベツ *n.* cabbage.

kya⌈kkañ-teki きゃっかんてき(客観的) *a.n.* (~ na, ni) objective:
kyakkañ-teki *na mikata* (客観的な見方) an *objective* point of view.
《↔ shukañ-teki》

kya⌈ku きゃく(客) *n.* **1** caller; visitor; guest. ★ Polite form is '*o-kyaku(-sañ).*'
2 customer; client; audience; spectator; passenger.

kya⌈kuhoñ きゃくほん(脚本) *n.* play; drama; scenario; screenplay.

kya⌈kuma きゃくま(客間) *n.* drawing room; guest room.

kya⌈kuseñ きゃくせん(客船) *n.* passenger boat [ship].

kya⌈kushoku きゃくしょく(脚色) *n.* dramatization; adaptation.
kyakushoku suru (~する) *vt.* dramatize; adapt.

kya⌈sshu-ka⌉ado キャッシュカード *n.* debit card; bank card.

kyo⌈dai きょだい(巨大) *a.n.* (~ na, ni) huge; gigantic:
kyodai *na tatemono* (巨大な建物) a *huge* building. 《⇨ ookii》

kyo⌉hi きょひ(拒否) *n.* refusal; rejection; denial; veto.
kyohi suru (~する) *vt.* refuse; reject; deny; turn down; veto.
《⇨ kotowaru》

kyo⌉ka きょか(許可) *n.* permission; license; approval; leave:
gaishutsu no kyoka *o morau* (外出の許可をもらう) get *permission* to go out. 《⇨ shooniñ[1]; yurushi》
kyoka suru (~する) *vt.* permit; allow; license; approve. 《↔ kiñshi[1]》《⇨ yurusu》

kyo⌉ku きょく(曲) *n.* music; tune.

-kyoku きょく(局) *suf.* **1** bureau; department:
Seesoo-kyoku (清掃局) Public Sanitation *Department.* 《⇨ -ka[5]》
2 office; station:
yuubiñ-kyoku (郵便局) a post *office* / *heñshuu*-kyoku (編集局) an editorial *office* / *hoosoo*-kyoku (放送局) a broadcasting *station.*

kyo⌈kuseñ きょくせん(曲線) *n.* curve; curved line. 《↔ chokuseñ》

kyo⌈kuta⌉ñ きょくたん(極端) *n.* extreme: kyokutañ *ni hashiru* (極端に走る) go to *extremes.*
— *a.n.* (~ na, ni) extreme; radical: kyokutañ *na ikeñ* (極端な意見) an *extreme* opinion.

kyo⌉neñ きょねん(去年) *n.* last year. 《⇨ kotoshi; raineñ》

kyo⌉o きょう(今日) *n.* today; this day. 《⇨ ashita; koñnichi; kinoo[1]》

-kyoo きょう(鏡) *suf.* -scope:
booeñ-kyoo (望遠鏡) a *telescope* / keñbi-kyoo (顕微鏡) a *microscope.*

kyo⌈ochoo きょうちょう(強調) *n.* emphasis; stress.
kyoochoo suru (~する) *vt.* emphasize; stress.

kyo⌉odai きょうだい(兄弟) *n.* sibling; brother; sister.

kyo⌈odoo きょうどう(共同) *n.* collaboration; partnership:
kyoodoo *jigyoo* (共同事業) a *joint* venture / kyoodoo *seemee* (共同声明) a *joint* statement.
kyoodoo suru (~する) *vt.* share; combine one's efforts.

kyo⌉ofu きょうふ(恐怖) *n.* fear; terror; horror:
kyoofu *ni osowareru* (恐怖に襲われる) be seized with *fear.*

kyo⌈oge⌉ñ きょうげん(狂言) *n.*

1 traditional comic drama.
★ Performed as supplementary entertainment to fill the intervals between Noh plays.
2 sham; make-believe:
Kare no shita koto wa kyoogeñ *datta.* (彼のしたことは狂言だった) What he did was a *sham.*
《⇨ shibai》

kyo⌉ogi[1] きょうぎ (競技) *n.* contest; competition; match; game; event:
kyoogi-joo (競技場) a *sports ground*; a *stadium.*
kyoogi suru (～する) *vt.* play a game; have a contest; compete.

kyo⌉ogi[2] きょうぎ (協議) *n.* conference; discussion; deliberation.
kyoogi suru (～する) *vt.* discuss; talk; consult. 《⇨ soodañ》

kyo⌈oguu きょうぐう (境遇) *n.* surroundings; circumstances:
Kanojo wa megumareta kyooguu *ni sodatta.* (彼女は恵まれた境遇に育った) She grew up in favorable *surroundings.*

kyo⌈ohaku きょうはく (脅迫) *n.* threat; intimidation; menace:
kyoohaku-*joo* (脅迫状) a *threatening* [*blackmail*] letter.
kyoohaku suru (～する) *vt.* threaten; intimidate; menace.

kyo⌈oiku きょういく (教育) *n.* education; teaching; training.
kyooiku suru (～する) *vt.* educate; train.

kyo⌈oiñ きょういん (教員) *n.* teacher. 《⇨ señsee》

kyo⌈oju きょうじゅ (教授) *n.* (full) professor. 《⇨ jokyooju; kooshi[1]》

kyo⌉oka きょうか (強化) *n.* strengthening; reinforcement; buildup: kyooka-*garasu* (強化ガラス) *reinforced* glass.
kyooka suru (～する) *vt.* strengthen; reinforce; build up: *keebi o* kyooka suru (警備を強化する) *strengthen* the guard.

kyo⌈okai[1] きょうかい (境界) *n.* boundary; border. 《⇨ sakai》

kyo⌈okai[2] きょうかい (教会) *n.* church.

kyo⌈oka⌉sho きょうかしょ (教科書) *n.* textbook; schoolbook.

kyo⌈okuñ きょうくん (教訓) *n.* lesson; moral:
Sono shippai wa yoi kyookuñ *ni natta.* (その失敗は良い教訓になった) The failure was a good *lesson* to me.

kyo⌈okyuu きょうきゅう (供給) *n.* supply; service:
deñryoku no kyookyuu (電力の供給) the *supply* of electric power.
《↔ juyoo》
kyookyuu suru (～する) *vt.* supply; provide.

kyo⌉omi きょうみ (興味) *n.* interest:
Watashi wa seeji ni wa kyoomi *ga nai.* (私は政治には興味がない) I have no *interest* in politics.
《⇨ kañshiñ[2]》

kyo⌈oretsu きょうれつ (強烈) *a.n.* (～ na, ni) strong; intense:
Sono jishiñ wa kyooretsu *datta.* (その地震は強烈だった) The earthquake was very *strong.*

kyo⌉ori きょうり (郷里) *n.* one's hometown; one's home

kyo⌈oryoku[1] きょうりょく (協力) *n.* cooperation; collaboration; working together.
kyooryoku suru (～する) *vi.* cooperate; collaborate; work together.
《⇨ kyoodoo》

kyo⌈oryoku[2] きょうりょく (強力) *a.n.* (～ na, ni) strong; powerful.
《⇨ chikarazuyoi》

kyo⌈osañshu⌉gi きょうさんしゅぎ (共産主義) *n.* communism.

Kyo⌈osañtoo きょうさんとう (共産党) *n.* = Nihoñ Kyoosañtoo.
《⇨ APP. 8》

kyo⌈osee きょうせい (強制) *n.* compulsion; coercion.
kyoosee suru (～する) *vt.* force; compel; coerce.

kyo⌈osee-teki きょうせいてき (強制的) *a.n.* (～ na, ni) compulsory;

k

obligatory:
Watashi-tachi wa kyoosee-teki *ni sore o yarasareta.* (私たちは強制的にそれをやらされた) We were made to do it *by force.*

kyoˈoshi きょうし (教師) *n.* teacher; instructor. 《⇨ señsee》

kyoˊoshiˈñshoo きょうしんしょう (狭心症) *n.* angina (pectoris).

kyoˊoshitsu きょうしつ (教室) *n.* classroom; schoolroom.

kyoˊoshuku きょうしゅく (恐縮) *n.* being obliged; feeling sorry:
Wazawaza oide itadaite, kyooshuku *desu.* (わざわざお出でいただいて, 恐縮です) I *am much obliged* to you for taking the trouble to come.
kyooshuku suru (〜する) *vi.* be obliged; feel sorry.

kyoˊosoñ きょうそん (共存) *n.* coexistence.
kyoosoñ suru (〜する) *vi.* coexist; live together.

kyoˊosoo きょうそう (競争) *n.* competition; contest:
kyoosoo *ni katsu* [*makeru*] (競争に勝つ[負ける]) win [lose] in a *competition.*
kyoosoo suru (〜する) *vt.* compete; contest.

kyoˊotsuu きょうつう (共通) *a.n.* (〜 na/no, ni) common; mutual:
wareware kyootsuu *no rieki* (われわれ共通の利益) our *mutual* advantage.
kyootsuu suru (〜する) *vi.* have in common.

kyoˊotsuugo きょうつうご (共通語) *n.* common language.
《⇨ kokugo》

kyoˊowaˈkoku きょうわこく (共和国) *n.* republic.

kyoˊoyoo きょうよう (教養) *n.* culture; education:
kyooyoo *o mi ni tsukeru* (教養を身につける) acquire *education and culture.*

kyoˈri きょり (距離) *n.* distance; interval:
kyori *o hakaru* (距離を測る) measure the *distance.*

kyoˈrokyoro きょろきょろ *adv.* (〜 to; 〜 suru) (used to express the action of looking around nervously or restlessly):
kyorokyoro *suru* (きょろきょろする) *look around restlessly.*

kyuˊu[1] きゅう (急) *n.* emergency; urgency:
Kono keñ wa kyuu *o yoo shimasu.* (この件は急を要します) This matter demands *immediate attention.*
— *a.n.* (〜 na, ni) **1** urgent; pressing:
Kare wa kyuu *na yooji de Oosaka e ikimashita.* (彼は急な用事で大阪へ行きました) He went to Osaka on *urgent* business.
2 sudden; unexpected:
Kare no shi wa amari ni mo kyuu *datta.* (彼の死はあまりにも急だった) His death was very *sudden.*
3 steep; sharp:
Kono saka wa kyuu *da.* (この坂は急だ) This slope is *steep.*
4 swift; rapid:
Koko wa nagare ga kyuu *da.* (ここは流れが急だ) The flow of the river is *swift* hereabouts.

kyuˈu[2] きゅう (級) *n.* **1** class; grade; rank:
daijiñ kyuu *no jiñbutsu* (大臣級の人物) a person of ministerial *rank.*
2 (in judo, kendo, karate, go, shogi, etc.) the name for the degree given to the less proficient:
karate no ni-kyuu (空手の2級) a second *grade* in karate.
3 the holder of *kyuu.* 《⇨ dañ[1]》

kyuˈu[3] きゅう (旧) *n.* old; former:
kyuu *shoogatsu* (旧正月) New Year's Day according to the *old* [*lunar*] *calendar.*
— *pref.* ex-: kyuu-*shichoo* (旧市長) an *ex*-mayor. 《⇨ moto[2]》

kyuˈu[4] きゅう (球) *n.* globe; sphere; ball; bulb.

kyuˈu[5] きゅう (九) *n.* nine.

★ Also pronounced '*ku*.' ⟪⇨ kokonotsu; APP. 3⟫

kyu⌈ubyoo きゅうびょう (急病) *n.* sudden illness; acute disease.

kyu⌈ugaku きゅうがく (休学) *n.* temporary absence from school.
kyuugaku suru (～する) *vi.* withdraw from school temporarily.

kyu⌈ugeki きゅうげき (急激) *a.n.* (～ na, ni) sudden; abrupt; rapid:
Saikiñ no yo-no-naka wa heñka ga kyuugeki *desu.* (最近の世の中は変化が急激です) The changes in recent society are very *rapid*.

kyu⌈ugyoo きゅうぎょう (休業) *n.* suspension of business; shutdown.
kyuugyoo suru (～する) *vi.* suspend business; be closed; take a holiday. ⟪⇨ yasumu⟫

kyu⌈ujiñ きゅうじん (求人) *n.* offer of a situation [job]:
kyuujiñ-*kookoku ni oobo suru* (求人広告に応募する) apply for a job in the *wanted* ads.

kyu⌈ujitsu きゅうじつ (休日) *n.* holiday. ⟪⇨ APP. 6⟫

kyu⌈uka きゅうか (休暇) *n.* vacation; holiday:
Isogashikute, kyuuka *ga torenai.* (忙しくて, 休暇がとれない) I am too busy to *take time off*. ⟪⇨ yasumi⟫

kyu⌈ukee きゅうけい (休憩) *n.* break; rest; intermission:
kyuukee-jikañ (休憩時間) a *recess*; an *intermission*. ⟪⇨ kyuusoku; yasumi⟫
kyuukee suru (～する) *vt.* take [have] a break [rest]. ⟪⇨ hito-yasumi⟫

kyu⌈ukoo[1] きゅうこう (急行) *n.* express train. ⟪⇨ futsuu[2]; tokkyuu⟫

kyu⌈ukoo[2] きゅうこう (休講) *n.* no lecture.
kyuukoo suru (～する) *vt.* cancel a class [lecture].

kyu⌉ukutsu きゅうくつ (窮屈) *a.n.* (～ na, ni) **1** small; close; tight:
Kono kuruma wa roku-niñ noru to, kyuukutsu *desu.* (この車は6人乗ると, 窮屈です) If six people get in this car, it will *be cramped*.
2 (of regulations, etc.) strict; rigid:
Kono gakkoo no kisoku wa kyuukutsu *da.* (この学校の規則は窮屈だ) The rules at this school are *strict*.
3 stiff; formal; serious; uncomfortable:
Soñna ni kyuukutsu *ni kañgaenai de kudasai.* (そんなに窮屈に考えないでください) Don't take it so *seriously*.

kyu⌈ukyuu きゅうきゅう (救急) *n.* emergency:
kyuukyuu-*bako* (救急箱) a *first-aid* kit / kyuukyuu-*byooiñ* (救急病院) an *emergency* hospital / kyuukyuu-sha (救急車) an *ambulance*.

kyu⌉uri きゅうり (胡瓜) *n.* cucumber.

kyu⌉uryoo きゅうりょう (給料) *n.* pay; wages; salary:
kyuuryoo *o morau* (給料をもらう) get one's *salary*. ⟪⇨ chiñgiñ⟫

kyu⌈ushoku[1] きゅうしょく (求職) *n.* job hunting:
kyuushoku *no mooshikomi o suru* (求職の申し込をする) ask for *employment* [*a position*].

kyu⌈ushoku[2] きゅうしょく (給食) *n.* provision of meals; school meal [lunch].
kyuushoku suru (～する) *vt.* provide lunches [meals] (for schoolchildren, employees, etc.).

kyu⌈ushuu きゅうしゅう (吸収) *n.* absorption; suction.
kyuushuu suru (～する) *vt.* absorb; suck in. ⟪⇨ suu[1]⟫

kyu⌈usoku きゅうそく (休息) *n.* rest; repose.
kyuusoku suru (～する) *vi.* take [have] a rest. ⟪⇨ kyuukee⟫

kyu⌈uyoo きゅうよう (急用) *n.* urgent business.

M

ma ま(間) *n.* **1** time; interval: *Isogashikute, yasumu* ma *mo nai.* (忙しくて, 休む間もない) I am so busy I do not even have *time* to rest.
2 interval; space: *ie to dooro no aida ni ittee no* ma *o toru* (家と道路の間に一定の間を取る) leave a certain *space* between a house and a road.
3 room. ⟪⇨ heya; -ma⟫
ma ga [no] warui (〜が[の]悪い) unlucky; unfortunate; be embarrassed; feel awkward.

-ma ま(間) *suf.* room: ★ Also used as counter for rooms. *Nihoñ*-ma (日本間) a Japanese-style *room* / *roku-joo*-ma (六畳間) a six-tatami-mat *room.* ⟪⇨ heya; ma⟫

m

ma¹a[1] まあ *adv.* (*informal*) **1** just: Maa *chotto yatte mimashoo.* (まあちょっとやってみましょう) I will *just* have a quick try.
2 well; say; probably; now: ★ Used to soften a statement or opinion. Maa *kañgaete okimasu.* (まあ考えておきます) *Well*, I will give it some thought.
3 about; by and large: *Kanojo wa* maa *sañ-juu* gurai *desu.* (彼女はまあ30ぐらいです) She would be, *about*, thirty.

ma¹a[2] まあ *int.* oh; well; good heavens; goodness: ★ Used by women to express surprise, embarrassment or admiration. Maa, *odoroita.* (まあ, 驚いた) *Well!* I am surprised! ⟪⇨ ara⟫

ma¹aku マーク *n.* mark; sign; insignia; design.
maaku suru (〜する) *vt.* **1** make a mark.
2 keep an eye on: *Keesatsu de wa kare o* maaku shite iru. (警察では彼をマークしている) The police *are keeping a close eye* on him.

ma¹amaa まあまあ *adv.* so-so; not so bad; all right.
— *int.* come now; well: Maamaa, *sonna ni koofuñ shinai de.* (まあまあ, そんなに興奮しないで) *Come now*, do not get so excited.

ma⌈bushi¹·i まぶしい(眩しい) *a.* (-ku) glaring; dazzling.

ma¹buta まぶた(瞼) *n.* eyelid.

ma⌈chi¹ まち(町·街) *n.* town; city; street. ⟪⇨ mura⟫

-machi まち(町) *suf.* town; block; street. ★ An administrative division of a town. ⟪⇨ -choo[1]⟫

ma⌈chia¹ishitsu まちあいしつ(待合室) *n.* waiting room.

ma⌈chiawase まちあわせ(待ち合わせ) *n.* meeting by appointment. ⟪⇨ machiawaseru⟫

ma⌈chiawase·ru まちあわせる(待ち合わせる) *vt.* (-awase-te V) meet a person by appointment. ⟪⇨ machiawase⟫

ma⌈chidooshi¹·i まちどおしい(待ち遠しい) *a.* (-ku) look forward to; wait anxiously for; long for. ⟪⇨ machinozomu⟫

ma⌈chigae¹·ru まちがえる(間違える) *vt.* (-gae-te V) make a mistake; make an error; confuse: *Dare-ka ga* machigaete, *watashi no kutsu o haite itta.* (だれかが間違えて, 私の靴をはいて行った) Someone *mistakenly* put on my shoes and went off. ⟪⇨ machigai⟫

ma⌈chiga¹i まちがい(間違い) *n.*
1 mistake; error; blunder; fault: machigai *o suru* (間違いをする) make a *mistake.* ⟪⇨ machigau⟫
2 accident; trouble: machigai *o okosu* (間違いを起こす) get into *trouble.* ⟪⇨ jiko[1]; misu[1]⟫

ma⌈chiga⌉·u まちがう (間違う) *vi.*, *vt.* (-ga·i-; -gaw·a-; -gat-te Ⓒ) be wrong: ★ Usually in the phrase '*machigatte iru*.'
Kono deñwa bañgoo wa machigatte iru. (この電話番号は間違っている) This telephone number *is wrong*. ((⇨ machigaeru; machigai))

ma⌈chi⌉machi まちまち *a.n.* (~ na/no, ni) different; various; divided:
Ikeñ ga machimachi *ni wakareta.* (意見がまちまちに分かれた) Opinion was divided *in many ways*.

ma⌈chinozom·u まちのぞむ (待ち望む) *vt.* (-nozom·i-; -nozom·a-; -nozoñ-de Ⓒ) wait for; look forward to. ((⇨ machidooshii))

ma⌉da まだ (未だ) *adv.* **1** (with a negative) yet:
Kanojo wa mada *kite imaseñ.* (彼女はまだ来ていません) She has not come *yet*.
2 still:
Kare wa mada *miseeneñ desu.* (彼はまだ未成年です) He is *still* under age.
3 more:
Taifuu wa mada *yatte kuru deshoo.* (台風はまだやって来るでしょう) Some *more* typhoons will be coming our way.
4 only:
Nihoñ ni kite, mada *hañtoshi desu.* (日本に来て，まだ半年です) It is *only* six months since I came to Japan.

ma⌉damada まだまだ (未だ未だ) *adv.* still; (not) yet:
Kono shoobai wa madamada *kore kara nobimasu.* (この商売はまだまだこれから伸びます) This business will expand *still* more from now.

ma⌉de まで (迄) *p.* **1** to; till; as far as: ★ Indicates the forward limits of an action or state in time or space. Often used with '*kara*[3].'
Mainichi asa ku-ji kara gogo go-ji made *hatarakimasu.* (毎日朝9時から午後5時まで働きます) I work from nine in the morning *till* five in the afternoon every day. ((↔ kara[3]))
2 till: ★ Follows the dictionary form of a verb and indicates the time limit of an action or state.
Shiñbuñ o yomu made *sono jikeñ no koto wa shiranakatta.* (新聞を読むまでその事件のことは知らなかった) I didn't know about the incident *till* I read the paper. ((⇨ made ni))
3 also; even: ★ Emphasizes an extreme limit.
Kodomo ni made *baka ni sareta.* (子どもにまでばかにされた) I was made a fool of *even* by the children.

ma⌉de ni までに (迄に) **1** by; before; not later than: ★ Follows time expressions. ((⇨ made))
Kono shigoto wa getsumatsu made ni *shiagete kudasai.* (この仕事は月末までに仕上げてください) Please finish up this work *by* the end of this month.
2 by the time: ★ Follows the dictionary form of a verb.
Kodomo-tachi ga kaette kuru made ni *yuuhañ no shitaku o shita.* (子どもたちが帰って来るまでに夕飯の支度をした) I had prepared dinner *by the time* the children got back.

ma⌉do まど (窓) *n.* window:
mado *o akeru* [*shimeru*] (窓を開ける[閉める]) open [shut] the *window*.

ma⌈do⌉guchi まどぐち (窓口) *n.* window; wicket; clerk at the window.

ma⌉e まえ (前) *n.* **1** front:
★ '*Mae*' covers the meanings 'front' and 'in front (of).' *e.g.* *biru no mae* = the front of the building; in front of the building. ((↔ ura; ushiro)) ((⇨ shoomeñ))
2 the first part:
Sono monogatari no mae *no bubuñ wa taikutsu desu.* (その物語の前の部分は退屈です) The *first part* of the story is tedious. ((↔ ato[1]))
3 the previous [former] time; ago; before:

Mae *wa koko ni eki ga arimashita.* (前はここに駅がありました) In *former times* there was a station here. 《⇨ izen[1]》

-mae[1] まえ(前) *suf.* **1** in front of:
Kono basu wa shiyakusho-mae *ni tomarimasu.* (このバスは市役所前に止まります) This bus stops *in front of* the city hall.
2 ago; before:
Kanojo wa hito-tsuki-mae *ni Nihoñ e kimashita.* (彼女は一月前に日本へ来ました) She came to Japan one month *ago.* 《⇨ -go; -sugi》

-mae[2] まえ(前) *suf.* for (the stated number of people):
shokuji o go-niñ-mae *tanomu* (食事を5人前頼む) order food *for five.*

ma˥eashi まえあし(前足) *n.* (of an animal) forefoot; foreleg. 《↔ atoashi》

ma˥egaki まえがき(前書き) *n.* preface; foreword.

ma˥emuki まえむき(前向き) *n.*
1 facing front.
2 positive attitude:
moñdai ni motto maemuki *ni torikumu* (問題にもっと前向きに取り組む) take a more *positive attitude* to the problem. 《⇨ sekkyoku-teki》

ma˥garikado まがりかど(曲がり角) *n.* **1** street corner; bend; turn.
2 turning point:
Gakkoo kyooiku wa magarikado *ni kite iru.* (学校教育は曲がり角に来ている) School education is now at a *turning point.*

ma˥gar·u まがる(曲がる) *vi.* (magar·i-; magar·a-; magat-te Ⓒ)
1 bend; curve:
koshi ga magaru (腰が曲がる) *be bent over* at the waist. 《⇨ mageru》
2 turn; wind:
Tsugi no shiñgoo o hidari ni magari nasai. (次の信号を左に曲がりなさい) *Turn* left at the next traffic light.

ma˥ge·ru まげる(曲げる) *vt.* (mage-te Ⓥ) **1** bend:
harigane o mageru (針金を曲げる) *bend* a wire. 《⇨ magaru》
2 depart from (one's principles); deviate from:
Watashi no kotoba o magete *toranai de kudasai.* (私の言葉を曲げて取らないでください) Please do not *wrongly* interpret my words.

ma˥gira˥s·u まぎらす(紛らす) *vt.* (-rash·i-; -ras·a-; -rash·i-te Ⓒ) divert; beguile:
oñgaku o kiite ki o magirasu (音楽を聞いて気を紛らす) *divert oneself* by listening to music. 《⇨ magireru》

ma˥gire˥·ru まぎれる(紛れる) *vi.* (-re-te Ⓥ) **1** get mixed up:
yami ni magirete *nigeru* (闇に紛れて逃げる) run away *under cover of* darkness.
2 be diverted:
Tabi ni dereba ki ga magireru *deshoo.* (旅に出れば気が紛れるでしょう) If you go on a trip, you will *be diverted from worry.* 《⇨ magirasu》

ma˥go˥ まご(孫) *n.* grandchild; grandson; granddaughter.

ma˥gomago まごまご *adv.* (~ suru) **1** get confused; lose one's presence of mind.
2 loiter; hang around:
Magomago shite iru *to deñsha ni maniaimaseñ yo.* (まごまごしていると電車に間に合いませんよ) If you *waste time*, we will not be in time for the train.

ma˥gotsuk·u まごつく *vi.* (-tsuk·i-; -tsuk·a-; -tsu·i-te Ⓒ) get confused; be embarrassed; be at a loss.

ma˥guro まぐろ(鮪) *n.* tuna.

ma˥hi まひ(麻痺) *n.* paralysis; numbness.
mahi suru (~する) *vi.* be paralyzed; be numbed.

ma˥hoo まほう(魔法) *n.* magic; witchcraft.

mai- まい(毎) *pref.* every; each:

m

mai-*nichi* (毎日) *every* day / mai-*shuu* (毎週) *every* week.

-mai[1] まい *infl. end.* [attached to the dictionary form of a consonant-stem verb or the continuative base of a vowel-stem verb] **1** think not; probably not: *Osoraku kare wa* ikumai. (おそらく彼は行くまい) Probably he *will not go.* / *Koñna mono wa inu de mo* tabemai. (こんなものは, 犬でも食べまい) Even a dog *wouldn't eat* stuff like this. ⟪⇨ daroo⟫
2 do not want to: ★ Often in the pattern '*ni-do to ...-mai to omou.*'
Kare ni wa ni-do to aumai *to omotte imasu.* (彼には二度と会うまいと思っています) I am determined *never to meet* him again.

-mai[2] まい (枚) *suf.* sheet; piece; leaf; slice: ★ Counter for flat objects.
*kami yoñ-*mai (紙 4 枚) four *sheets* of paper / *garasu ni-*mai (ガラス 2 枚) two *panes* of glass.

ma˥iasa まいあさ (毎朝) *n.* every morning.

ma˥ibañ まいばん (毎晩) *n.* every evening; every night.

ma˥ido まいど (毎度) *n.* every [each] time; always:
Kare ga moñku o iu no wa maido no koto *da.* (彼が文句を言うのは毎度のことだ) His complaining is an *everyday affair.*
— *adv.* often; frequently. ⟪⇨ itsu-mo⟫
maido arigatoo (〜ありがとう) thank you: Maido arigatoo *gozaimasu.* (毎度ありがとうございます) *Thank you* very much. ★ A set phrase used by service personnel.

ma˥igo まいご (迷子) *n.* lost [stray; missing] child:
maigo ni naru (迷子になる) *lose one's way.*

ma˥i-ho˥omu マイホーム *n.* one's own home.

ma˥i-ka˥a マイカー *n.* one's own car; private [family] car.

ma˥ikai まいかい (毎回) *adv.* every [each] time; every inning [round].

ma˥iku マイク *n.* microphone.

ma˥inasu マイナス *n.* **1** minus: mainasu *go-do* (マイナス 5 度) five degrees *below zero.*
2 disadvantage; handicap: *Sono koto wa wareware ni totte* mainasu *da.* (そのことはわれわれにとってマイナスだ) That is a *disadvantage* to us. ⟪↔ purasu⟫
mainasu suru (〜する) *vt.* subtract.

ma˥inichi まいにち (毎日) *n.* every day.

ma˥ir·u[1] まいる (参る) *vi.* (mair·i-; mair·a-; mait-te Ⓒ) **1** (*humble*) go; come:
Sugu mairimasu. (すぐ参ります) I *am coming* right away. / *Itte* mairimasu. (行って参ります) I *am going out* (*and will be back soon*).
2 visit a shrine [temple]; go to worship. ⟪⇨ omairi⟫

ma˥ir·u[2] まいる (参る) *vi.* (mair·i-; mair·a-; mait-te Ⓒ) **1** cannot stand; give up:
Kono atsusa ni wa maitta. (この暑さには参った) I *cannot stand* this heat.
2 be defeated:
Kare wa maitta *to itta.* (彼は参ったと言った) He admitted his *defeat.*
3 be at a loss; be embarrassed:
Doo shite yoi ka wakarazu, maitta. (どうしてよいかわからず, 参った) I *was at a loss* what to do.

ma˥ishuu まいしゅう (毎週) *n.* every week.

ma˥itoshi まいとし (毎年) *n.* every [each] year.

ma˥itsuki まいつき (毎月) *n.* every [each] month.

ma˥jime まじめ (真面目) *a.n.* (~ na, ni) serious; honest; sober; earnest. ⟪↔ fumajime⟫ ⟪⇨ hoñki⟫

ma˥ji˥r·u まじる (混じる) *vi.* (maji-

m

r·i-; majir·a-; majit-te [C]) be mixed; be mingled. ⟪⇨ koñgoo; mazeru⟫

ma[ji wa]r·u まじわる（交わる） *vi.* (-war·i-; -war·a-; -wat-te [C])
1 cross; intersect:
Sono futatsu no dooro wa yaku ichi-kiro saki de majiwatte imasu. (その二つの道路は約1キロ先で交わっています) The two roads *cross each other* about one kilometer ahead. ⟪⇨ koosa⟫
2 associate (with a person); get along with.

ma[kase]·ru まかせる（任せる） *vt.* (makase-te [V]) leave; trust:
Sono shigoto wa watashi ni makase *nasai.* (その仕事は私に任せなさい) Please *leave* that job to me.

ma[kas·u まかす（負かす） *vt.* (makash·i-; makas·a-; makash·i-te [C]) beat; defeat. ⟪⇨ makeru⟫

ma[ke まけ（負け） *n.* defeat; loss; lost game. ⟪↔ kachi[2]⟫ ⟪⇨ makeru⟫

ma[keoshimi まけおしみ（負け惜しみ） *n.* sour grapes: *Kare wa* makeoshimi ga tsuyoi. (彼は負け惜しみが強い) He is a *bad loser*.

ma[ke·ru まける（負ける） *vi.* (make-te [V]) **1** be beaten [defeated]; lose. ⟪↔ katsu[1]⟫ ⟪⇨ makasu; make⟫
2 discount; reduce; cut:
Sukoshi makete *kuremaseñ ka?* (少しまけてくれませんか) Can't you *reduce* the price slightly?
3 give in (to temptation); yield. ⟪↔ katsu[1]⟫

ma[kiko]m·u まきこむ（巻き込む） *vt.* (-kom·i-; -kom·a-; -koñ-de [C]) involve:
Watashi wa sono keñka ni makikomarete shimatta. (私はそのけんかに巻き込まれてしまった) I *got involved* in the fight.

ma[kka] まっか（真っ赤） *a.n.* (～ na, ni) (deep) red; crimson; scarlet: makka *ni natte okoru* (まっかになって怒る) become *red* with anger. ⟪↔ massao⟫

ma[kko]o kara まっこうから（真っ向から） *adv.* head-on; squarely:
Kare wa sono keekaku ni makkoo kara *hañtai shita.* (彼はその計画にまっこうから反対した) He opposed that plan *head-on*.

ma[kku]ra まっくら（真っ暗） *a.n.* (～ na, ni) pitch-dark.

ma[kku]ro まっくろ（真っ黒） *a.n.* (～ na, ni) coal-black; tanned all over. ⟪↔ masshiro⟫

ma[koto ni まことに（誠に） *adv.* (*formal*) very; very much; truly:
Makoto ni *mooshiwake arimaseñ.* (まことに申しわけありません) I am *sincerely* sorry.

ma[k·u[1] まく（巻く） *vt.* (mak·i-; mak·a-; ma·i-te [C]) **1** wind; wrap:
ude ni hootai o maku (腕に包帯を巻く) *wind* a bandage around one's arm.
2 roll up; coil up:
roopu o guruguru maku (ロープをぐるぐる巻く) *coil* a rope *up*.

ma[ku][2] まく（幕） *n.* **1** curtain (in a theater).
2 act:
sañ-maku *no kigeki* (3幕の喜劇) a comedy in three *acts*.

ma]k·u[3] まく（蒔く） *vt.* (mak·i-; mak·a-; ma·i-te [C]) plant; sow:
hana no tane o maku (花の種をまく) *plant* flower seeds.

ma[ku][4] まく（膜） *n.* membrane; film.

ma[ku-no]-uchi(-be]ñtoo) まくのうち(べんとう)（幕の内(弁当)） *n.* Japanese-style variety box lunch.

ma]kura まくら（枕） *n.* pillow.

ma[ma][1] まま（儘） *n.* **1** remaining in the same state [condition]:
Deñsha wa mañiñ de, zutto tatta mama *datta.* (電車は満員で，ずっと立ったままだった) The train was full, and I *remained standing* all the way. ⟪⇨ kono-mama; sono-mama⟫
2 with; having:
Kanojo wa booshi o kabutta ma-

ma, *heya ni haitta.* (彼女は帽子をかぶったまま, 部屋に入った) She entered the room *with* her hat on.

3 as it is:
Watashi wa mita mama (no koto) *o keesatsu ni hanashita.* (私は見たまま(のこと)を警察に話した) I reported it to the police just *as I saw it happen*.

4 in accordance with; as:
Watashi wa iwareru (ga) mama *ni soko e itta.* (私は言われる(が)ままにそこへ行った) I went there *as I was told to.*

ma^l^ma[2] ママ *n.* mom; mum; mommy; mammy; mother. ⟪⇨ papa⟫

ma^r^mahaha ままはは (継母) *n.* stepmother.

ma^r^me^l^[1] まめ (豆) *n.* bean; pea.

ma^r^me^l^[2] まめ *n.* blister; corn.

ma^r^me[3] まめ *a.n.* (~ na, ni) faithful; hardworking:
mame *ni hataraku* (まめに働く) *work like a beaver.*

ma^r^metsu まめつ (摩滅) *n.* wear and tear.
mametsu suru (~する) *vi.* be worn down [out]. ⟪⇨ heru⟫

-mamire まみれ (塗れ) *suf.* (*n.*) [after a noun] be covered:
★ Used in an unfavorable situation.
*ase-*mamire (汗まみれ) *covered* in sweat / *chi-*mamire (血まみれ) *all bloody.*

ma^r^mire^l^·ru まみれる (塗れる) *vi.* (mamire-te Ⓥ) be covered; be smeared:
Kare no zuboñ wa doro ni mamirete ita. (彼のズボンは泥にまみれていた) His trousers *were covered* in mud.

ma-^r^mo^l^-naku まもなく (間も無く) *adv.* soon; shortly; before long.

ma^r^mo^l^r·u まもる (守る) *vt.* (mamor·i-; mamor·a-; mamot-te Ⓒ)
1 defend:
kuni o mamoru (国を守る) *defend* one's country. ⟪↔ semeru[1]⟫
2 protect; guard:
kodomo-tachi o kootsuu-jiko kara mamoru (子どもたちを交通事故から守る) *protect* children from traffic accidents.
3 keep (a promise); observe (a rule, etc.).

ma^l^ñ まん (万) *n.* ten thousand. ⟪⇨ APP. 3⟫

ma^l^naa マナー *n.* manners:
manaa *ga yoku nai* (マナーがよくない) have no *manners.*

ma^r^nab·u まなぶ (学ぶ) *vt.* (manab·i-; manab·a-; manañ-de Ⓒ) learn; study; take lessons. ⟪⇨ narau⟫

ma^r^ne まね (真似) *n.* imitation; mimicry:
señsee no mane *o suru* (先生のまねをする) *mimic* a teacher. ⟪⇨ maneru⟫

ma^r^neki^l^ まねき (招き) *n.* invitation. ⟪⇨ maneku; shootai[1]⟫

ma^r^ne^l^k·u まねく (招く) *vt.* (manek·i-; manek·a-; mane·i-te Ⓒ)
1 invite; call:
Kanojo wa watashi o paatii ni maneite kureta. (彼女は私をパーティーに招いてくれた) She *invited* me to the party. ⟪⇨ maneki⟫
2 beckon; gesture:
Watashi wa sono ko o te de maneita. (私はその子を手で招いた) I *beckoned* the child over.
3 cause (an accident, trouble, etc.); result in; bring about.

ma^r^ne·ru まねる (真似る) *vt.* (mane-te Ⓥ) imitate; copy; mimic:
dezaiñ o maneru (デザインをまねる) *copy* a design.

ma^r^ñga まんが (漫画) *n.* cartoon; comics; caricature.

ma^l^ñgetsu まんげつ (満月) *n.* full moon. ⟪⇨ tsuki[2]⟫

ma^r^nia^l^·u まにあう (間に合う) *vi.* (-a·i-; -aw·a-; -at-te Ⓒ)
1 be in time:
shuudeñ ni maniau (終電に間に合う) *be in time* for the last train.
2 be useful; be enough; do:
Kono jisho de maniaimasu. (この辞書で間に合います) I can make *do*

with this dictionary.

ma⌉ñichi まんいち (万一) *n.* emergency; the worst: ★ Literally 'one out of ten thousand.'
Mañichi *no baai wa koko ni reñraku shite kudasai.* (万一の場合はここに連絡してください) In the event of an *unforseen occurrence*, please contact this place.
— *adv.* in case; by some chance.

ma⌈ñiñ まんいん (満員) *n.* being full; no vacancy; full house.

ma⌈ñjoo-itchi まんじょういっち (満場一致) *n.* unanimity:
Sono keekaku wa mañjoo-itchi *de kimatta.* (その計画は満場一致で決まった) The plan was *unanimously* adopted. ⟪⇨ itchi⟫

ma⌈ñnaka まんなか (真ん中) *n.* the middle; center:
machi no mañnaka (町の真ん中) the *heart* of town. ⟪⇨ chuuoo⟫

ma⌈ñne⌉ñhitsu まんねんひつ (万年筆) *n.* fountain pen.

ma⌈ñseki まんせき (満席) *n.* full house; the seats being filled.

ma⌉ñshoñ マンション *n.* **1** condominium; apartment complex.
2 individual unit of same.

ma⌈ñte⌉ñ まんてん (満点) *n.* full marks; perfect score:
mañteñ *o toru* (満点を取る) get *full marks.*

ma⌈ñza⌉i まんざい (漫才) *n.* comic dialogue on stage. ★ A vaudeville act performed by a pair of comedians.

ma⌉ñzoku まんぞく (満足) *n.* satisfaction; contentment.
mañzoku suru (～する) *vi.* be satisfied; be contented.
— *a.n.* (～ na, ni) **1** satisfactory; contented. ⟪↔ fumañ⟫
2 enough; complete; proper:
Isogashikute, kono mikka-kañ mañzoku *na shokuji o shite imaseñ.* (忙しくて，この 3 日間満足な食事をしていません) I have not had a *proper* meal these three days as I have been so busy.

ma⌈ppu⌉tatsu まっぷたつ (真っ二つ) *n.* right in half [two].

ma⌈re まれ (希) *a.n.* (～ na, ni) rare; uncommon; unusual. ⟪⇨ mezurashii⟫

ma⌈ri⌉ まり (鞠) *n.* ball.

ma⌈ru まる (丸) *n.* circle. ⟪⇨ marui⟫

ma⌈ru- まる (丸) *pref.* full; whole:
Kañsee made ni wa maru-*ik-kagetsu kakarimasu.* (完成までには丸 1 か月かかります) It will take a *whole* month before completion.

-maru まる (丸) *suf.* (attached to the name of a Japanese civilian vessel).

ma⌈rude まるで (丸で) *adv.*
1 (with a negative) absolutely; entirely; quite; altogether:
Watashi no Nihoñgo wa marude *dame desu.* (私の日本語はまるでだめです) My Japanese is *absolutely* useless.
2 just (like; as if): ★ Used with '*yoo da.*'
Sono oñna-no-ko wa marude *otona no* yoo *na kuchi o kiku.* (その女の子はまるで大人のような口をきく) The girl talks *just as if* she were an adult.

ma⌈ru·i まるい (丸い) *a.* (-ku)
1 round; spherical; circular. ⟪⇨ maru; shikakui⟫
2 plump; chubby:
akañboo no marui *hoo* (赤ん坊の丸いほお) the *chubby* cheeks of a baby.
3 bent; stooped:
Kare wa toshi o totte, senaka ga maruku *natte kita.* (彼は年をとって，背中が丸くなってきた) As he grew older, he became *stooped.*

ma⌈rume·ru まるめる (丸める) *vt.* (marume-te [V]) form into a ball; roll (up): *kami o* marumeru (紙を丸める) *roll up* a piece of paper.

ma⌉saka まさか *adv.* surely (not); cannot be: ★ Used to express unlikelihood or unwillingness to believe.

Sore wa masaka *hoñtoo no hanashi ja nai deshoo ne?* (それはまさか本当の話じゃないでしょうね) That is not *really* a true story, is it?
masaka no toki (〜のとき) (*formal*) in case of emergency [need].

ma'sa ni まさに (正に) *adv.*
1 just; exactly; really; surely:
Masa ni *anata no ossharu toori desu.* (まさにあなたのおっしゃるとおりです) It is *just* as you say.
2 be about to (do); be just going to (do):
Eki ni tsuitara, deñsha ga masa ni *deyoo to shite ita.* (駅に着いたら，電車がまさに出ようとしていた) When I arrived at the station, the train was *just about to* pull out.

ma'sa'r·u まさる (勝る) *vi.* (masar·i-; masar·a-; masat-te Ⓒ) surpass; excel; exceed.

ma'satsu まさつ (摩擦) *n.* rubbing; friction; discord:
booeki-masatsu *o okosu* (貿易摩擦を起こす) give rise to trade *friction.*
masatsu suru (〜する) *vt., vi.* rub. ⟪⇨ kosuru⟫

ma'shite まして *adv.* **1** (with a negative) much [still] less; let alone:
Chuugokugo wa hanasemaseñ shi, mashite *kaku koto wa dekimaseñ.* (中国語は話せませんし，まして書くことはできません) I cannot speak Chinese, *much less* write it.
2 (with an affirmative) much [still] more; even more.

ma'ssa'ichuu まっさいちゅう (真っ最中) *n.* right in the middle (of); (at) the height (of). ⟪⇨ saichuu⟫

ma'ssa'ki まっさき (真っ先) *n.* the very first; (at) the head (of).

ma'ssa'o まっさお (真っ青) *a.n.* (〜 na, ni) **1** (deep) blue; azure.
2 pale; white:
Kare wa kyoofu de massao *ni natta.* (彼は恐怖で真っ青になった) He grew *pale* with terror. ⟪↔ makka⟫

ma'sshi'ro まっしろ (真っ白) *a.n.* (〜 na, ni) pure-white; white as snow. ⟪↔ makkuro⟫

ma'sshiro'·i まっしろい (真っ白い) *a.* (-ku) pure-white; white as snow.

ma'ssu'gu まっすぐ (真っ直ぐ) *a.n.* (〜 na, ni) **1** straight; direct.
massugu *na michi* (真っすぐな道) a *straight* road.
2 upright; honest:
Kare wa massugu *na seekaku o shite iru.* (彼は真っすぐな性格をしている) He has an *honest and upright* personality.

ma's·u[1] ます (増す) *vi.* (mash·i-; mas·a-; mash·i-te Ⓒ) increase; gain; add. ★ Slightly more formal than '*fueru.*'

ma'su[2] ます (鱒) *n.* trout.

ma'su[3] ます (升) *n.* small square measuring box.

-masu ます *infl. end.* [attached to the continuative base of a verb] ★ Used to make the style of speech polite without adding any concrete meaning. ⟪⇨ APP. 2⟫
Watashi wa maiasa shiñbuñ o yomimasu. (私は毎朝新聞を読みます) I *read* the newspaper every morning. / *Watashi wa tabako o* suimaseñ. (私はたばこを吸いません) I *don't smoke.*

ma'sukomi マスコミ *n.* mass media; journalism.

ma'suku マスク *n.* (face) mask; features.

ma'su'masu ますます (益々) *adv.* more and more; less and less; increasingly. ⟪⇨ iyoiyo⟫

ma'sutaa[1] マスター *n.* mastery.
masutaa suru (〜する) *vt.* master: *Nihoñgo o* masutaa suru (日本語をマスターする) *master* the Japanese language.

ma'sutaa[2] マスター *n.* owner (of a bar, club, etc.); proprietor. ⟪⇨ shujiñ⟫

ma'ta[1] また (股) *n.* crotch; thigh.

ma'ta[2] また (又) *adv.* **1** again:
Mata, *kare wa chikoku da.* (また，彼は遅刻だ) He is late *again.*

m

2 also; too:
Kare wa isha de ari, mata *sakka de mo aru.* (彼は医者であり，また作家でもある) He is a doctor and *also* a writer.

ma|ta[3] また (又) *conj.* moreover; besides; what is more. ⟪⇨ sara ni⟫

ma|taga|r·u またがる (跨る) *vi.* (matagar·i-; matagar·a-; matagat-te Ⓒ) **1** straddle; sit astride (a horse).
2 extend; span:
Fuji-sañ wa futatsu no keñ ni matagatte imasu. (富士山は２つの県にまたがっています) Mt. Fuji *sits on* two prefectures.

ma|ta|g·u またぐ (跨ぐ) *vt.* (matag·i-; matag·a-; mata·i-de Ⓒ) step over; cross:
Kare wa mizutamari o mataida. (彼は水たまりをまたいだ) He *stepped over* the puddle.

ma|ta|-wa または (又は) *conj.* or:
kuro mata-wa *ao no boorupeñ* (黒または青のボールペン) a black *or* a blue ballpoint pen. ⟪⇨ aruiwa[1]; moshikuwa⟫

ma|to まと (的) *n.* mark; target; object; focus:
chuumoku no mato (注目の的) the *focus* of public attention.
mato-hazure (～外れ) off the point.

ma|tomari まとまり (纏り) *n.*
1 unity; organization; solidarity. ⟪⇨ matomaru⟫
2 coherence; order:
Kare no hanashi wa matomari *ga nai.* (彼の話はまとまりがない) His talk lacks *coherence.*

ma|tomar·u まとまる (纏まる) *vi.* (matomar·i-; matomar·a-; matomat-te Ⓒ) **1** be collected; be brought together. ⟪⇨ matomeru⟫
2 be united; be organized:
Kañgae wa mada matomatte imaseñ. (考えはまだまとまっていません) My thoughts *are not organized* yet. ⟪⇨ matomeru; matomari⟫
3 (of a negotiation, contract, etc.) be settled; be concluded; come to an agreement. ⟪⇨ matomeru⟫

ma|tome まとめ (纏め) *n.* summary; conclusion. ⟪⇨ matomeru⟫

ma|tome·ru まとめる (纏める) *vt.* (matome-te Ⓥ) **1** collect; gather together:
Kamikuzu o matomete *moyashita.* (紙くずをまとめて燃やした) I *collected* the wastepaper and burned it.
2 arrange; put into shape:
Kare wa sono eñdañ o matometa. (彼はその縁談をまとめた) He *arranged* the marriage. ⟪⇨ matomaru⟫
3 settle (a negotiation, contract, etc.); mediate. ⟪⇨ matomaru⟫

ma|ts·u[1] まつ (待つ) *vt.* (mach·i-; mat·a-; mat-te Ⓒ) wait; look forward to:
Dare o matte iru *ñ desu ka?* (だれを待っているんですか) Who *are* you *waiting* for?

ma|tsu[2] まつ (松) *n.* pine (tree):
matsu-*kazari* (松飾り) the New Year's pine decorations. ⟪⇨ kadomatsu; shoo-chiku-bai⟫

-matsu まつ (末) *suf.* the end:
shuu-matsu (週末) the week-*end* / *getsu*-matsu (月末) the *end* of the month. ⟪⇨ sue⟫

ma|tsuri まつり (祭り) *n.* festival; fete.

ma|tsur·u まつる (祭る) *vt.* (matsur·i-; matsur·a-; matsut-te Ⓒ) deify; enshrine.

ma|tsutake まつたけ (松茸) *n.* matsutake. ★ A large brown edible mushroom. ⟪⇨ kinoko⟫

ma|ttaku まったく (全く) *adv.*
1 completely; utterly:
Sore wa mattaku *bakageta hanashi da.* (それはまったくばかげた話だ) That is an *utterly* ridiculous story.
2 (with a negative) (not) at all:
Watashi wa mattaku *oyogemaseñ.* (私はまったく泳げません) I cannot swim *at all.* ⟪⇨ zeñzeñ⟫
3 really; indeed:

"Kyoo wa ii teñki desu ne." "Mattaku desu." (「きょうはいい天気ですね」「まったくです」) "It is nice weather today." "It *certainly* is."

ma·⌈u まう (舞う) *vi.* (ma·i-; ma-w·a-; mat-te Ⓒ) dance; flutter; whirl.

ma⌈wari まわり (回り・周り) *n.*
1 circumference; edge:
ike no mawari *o aruku* (池の周りを歩く) walk around the *edge* of a pond.
2 neighborhood; environment:
Watashi no ie no mawari *ni takusañ ie ga tachimashita.* (私の家の周りにたくさん家が建ちました) Many houses were built in my *neighborhood.*

ma⌈wari⌉michi まわりみち (回り道) *n.* detour; roundabout course: mawarimichi *o suru* (回り道をする) make a *detour.*

ma⌈war·u まわる (回る) *vi.* (ma-war·i-; mawar·a-; mawat-te Ⓒ)
1 turn; rotate; revolve; spin:
Kono koma wa yoku mawaru. (このこまはよく回る) This top *spins* well. ⟪⇨ mawasu⟫
2 make the rounds; look around:
Keekañ ga kono heñ o mawatte *iru no o mimashita.* (警官がこの辺を回っているのを見ました) I saw a policeman *making the rounds* in this area.
3 come around; go around:
Uraguchi e mawatte *kudasai.* (裏口へ回ってください) Please *come around* to the back door.

-mawar·u まわる (回る) (-mawa-r·i-; -mawar·a-; -mawat-te Ⓒ)
★ Occurs as the second element of compound verbs. Added to the continuative base of a verb. go about; move around:
aruki-mawaru (歩き回る) walk *about* / *kake*-mawaru (駆け回る) run *around.*

ma⌈was·u まわす (回す) *vt.* (ma-wash·i-; mawas·a-; mawash·i-te Ⓒ) **1** turn; rotate; spin:
daiyaru o mawasu (ダイヤルを回す) *dial* a number / *totte o* mawasu (取っ手を回す) *rotate* a handle. ⟪⇨ mawaru⟫
2 send around; pass; forward:
Sono shio o mawashite *kudasai.* (その塩を回してください) *Pass* me the salt, please.
3 (of a phone call) transfer.

ma⌈yo⌉naka まよなか (真夜中) *n.* midnight; the middle of the night.

ma⌈yone⌉ezu マヨネーズ *n.* mayonnaise.

ma⌈yo⌉·u まよう (迷う) *vi.* (mayo-i-; mayow·a-; mayot-te Ⓒ)
1 get lost; lose one's way.
2 be puzzled; be at a loss:
Watashi wa nañ to itte yoi ka mayotta. (私は何と言ってよいか迷った) I *was at a loss* what to say.
3 hesitate; be undecided:
Kare wa dare ni toohyoo suru ka mada mayotte iru. (彼はだれに投票するかまだ迷っている) He *is* still *undecided* who to vote for.

ma⌉yu まゆ (眉) *n.* eyebrow:
mayu *o hisomeru* (眉をひそめる) knit one's *eyebrows.*

ma⌉yuge まゆげ (眉毛) *n.* eyebrow.

ma⌈za⌉r·u まざる (混ざる) *vi.* (ma-zar·i-; mazar·a-; mazat-te Ⓒ) = majiru. ⟪⇨ mazeru⟫

ma⌈ze⌉·ru まぜる (混ぜる) *vt.* (ma-ze-te Ⓥ) mix; combine; mingle; blend. ⟪⇨ majiru⟫

ma⌉zu まず (先ず) *adv.* **1** first of all; to begin with.
2 probably; almost certainly:
Gogo wa mazu *ame deshoo.* (午後はまず雨でしょう) It will *probably* rain this afternoon.

ma⌈zu⌉·i[1] まずい (不味い) *a.* (-ku)
1 (of taste) not good; bad. ⟪↔ oishii⟫
2 awkward; unfavorable:
Kanojo wa mazui *toki ni kita.* (彼女はまずいときに来た) She showed up at an *awkward* moment.

m

ma⌈zu⌉·i[2] まずい (拙い) *a.* (-ku) (of skill) clumsy; poor:
mazui *hoñyaku* (まずい翻訳) a *poor* translation. ⟪⇨ heta⟫

ma⌈zushi⌉·i まずしい (貧しい) *a.* (-ku) poor; needy. ⟪↔ yutaka⟫ ⟪⇨ biñboo⟫

me⌉[1] め (目) *n.* **1** eye:
Haha wa hidari no me *ga mienai.* (母は左の目が見えない) My mother is blind in the left *eye.*
2 eyesight; sight:
Me *ga waruku natte kita.* (目が悪くなってきた) My *sight* began to fail.
3 viewpoint:
Oya no me *kara mireba, dono ko mo kawaii.* (親の目から見れば, どの子もかわいい) In the *eyes* of the parents, all children are sweet and dear.
4 bad experience:
Ikka wa hidoi me *ni atta.* (一家はひどい目にあった) The whole family had a very bad *experience.*
5 eye-like object:
hari no me (針の目) the *eye* of a needle / *taifuu no* me (台風の目) the *eye* of a typhoon.
me ga mawaru (〜が回る) feel giddy.
me o hikaraseru (〜を光らせる) keep a sharp eye out.
me o hiku (〜を引く) attract a person's attention.
me o mawasu (〜を回す) faint; be astonished.
me o toosu (〜を通す) run one's eye over.
me o tsukeru (〜をつける) have one's eye (on something). ⟪⇨ ome-ni-kakaru⟫

me⌉[2] め (芽) *n.* shoot; sprout; bud.

-me[1] め (目) *suf.* (the position of something in an ordered group or arrangement):
hidari kara ni-keñ-me *no uchi* (左から2軒目の家) the *second* house from the left.

-me[2] め *suf.* (degree or tendency): ★ Added to the stem of an adjective.
haya-me *ni shuppatsu suru* (早めに出発する) start *a bit early* / ooki-me *no kutsu* (大きめの靴) a pair of shoes *on the large side.*

me⌈atarashi⌉·i めあたらしい (目新しい) *a.* (-ku) new; fresh; novel; original. ⟪⇨ atarashii⟫

me⌉ate めあて (目当て) *n.* **1** aim; object:
o-kane meate *ni hataraku* (お金目当てに働く) work *for* money.
2 guide; landmark:
Ano takai biru o meate *ni aruite iki nasai.* (あの高いビルを目当てに歩いて行きなさい) Continue walking, *keeping an eye on* that tall building.

me⌈chakucha めちゃくちゃ *a.n.* (〜 na, ni) messy; unreasonable; reckless:
Kare no yookyuu wa mechakucha *da.* (彼の要求はめちゃくちゃだ) His demands are *unreasonable.*

me⌈chamecha めちゃめちゃ *a.n.* (〜 na, ni) (*informal*) smashed up; ruined; messed up.

me⌈da⌉ts·u めだつ (目立つ) *vi.* (medach·i-; medat·a-; medat-te Ⓒ) stand out; be conspicuous; be prominent.

me⌈deta⌉·i めでたい (目出度い) *a.* (-ku) happy; joyful:
Musuko wa medetaku *daigaku ni gookaku shimashita.* (息子はめでたく大学に合格しました) *Happily* my son was able to pass the exam to university. ⟪⇨ omedetai⟫

me⌉e めい (姪) *n.* niece.
★ When another family's niece is referred to, '*meego-sañ*' is used. ⟪↔ oi[1]⟫

me⌈e- めい (名) *pref.* famous; great; excellent:
mee-*bameñ* (名場面) a *famous* scene / mee-*señshu* (名選手) a *star* player.

-mee めい (名) *suf.* number of people:

nijuu-mee (20 名) twenty *people.*

me⌈ean[1] めいあん (名案) *n.* good idea; splendid plan.

me⌈ean[2] めいあん (明暗) *n.* light and shade; bright and dark sides.
meeañ o wakeru (～を分ける) decide: *Sono dekigoto ga kare no jiñsee no* meeañ o waketa. (その出来事が彼の人生の明暗を分けた) The incident *decided* his fate.

me⌈ebo めいぼ (名簿) *n.* name list; directory; roll.

me⌉ebutsu めいぶつ (名物) *n.* special [noted] product; specialty.

me⌈echuu めいちゅう (命中) *n.* hit.
meechuu suru (～する) *vt.* hit the target. ⟪⇨ ataru⟫

me⌈ehaku めいはく (明白) *a.n.* (～ na, ni) clear; obvious; plain; evident. ⟪⇨ meeryoo⟫

me⌈eji⌉ñ めいじん (名人) *n.* expert; master: *tsuri no* meejiñ (つりの名人) an *expert* at fishing.

me⌈eji·ru めいじる (命じる) *vt.* (meeji-te [V]) **1** tell; order; command. ⟪⇨ meeree⟫
2 appoint; place:
Kare wa koochoo ni meejirareta. (彼は校長に命じられた) He *was appointed* school principal.

me⌈ekaku めいかく (明確) *a.n.* (～ na, ni) clear and accurate; distinct; definite.

me⌈eme⌉e めいめい (銘々) *n.* (～ ni) each; individually. ⟪⇨ kakuji; ono-ono⟫

me⌈eree めいれい (命令) *n.* order; command; instructions.
meeree suru (～する) *vt.* order; command; instruct.

me⌈eroo めいろう (明朗) *a.n.* (～ na, ni) **1** cheerful; openhearted:
meeroo *na hito* (明朗な人) an *openhearted* person. ⟪⇨ hogaraka⟫
2 (of accounts, bills, etc.) clean; aboveboard.

me⌈eryoo めいりょう (明瞭) *a.n.* (～ na, ni) clear; evident; articulate:
Sono jijitsu wa dare ni mo meeryoo *desu.* (その事実はだれにも明瞭です) That fact is *evident* to everyone. ⟪⇨ meehaku⟫

me⌈esaku めいさく (名作) *n.* fine work; masterpiece.

me⌈eshi[1] めいし (名刺) *n.* calling [visiting] card; business card.

me⌈eshi[2] めいし (名詞) *n.* noun; substantive. ⟪⇨ APP. 2⟫

me⌈eshiñ めいしん (迷信) *n.* superstition.

me⌈esho めいしょ (名所) *n.* noted place; place of interest; sights to see.

me⌈eshoo めいしょう (名称) *n.* name; title:
shiñ-seehiñ ni meeshoo *o tsukeru* (新製品に名称をつける) give a *name* to a new product.

me⌈etaa メーター *n.* meter:
gasu [*suidoo; deñki*] *no* meetaa (ガス[水道; 電気]のメーター) a gas [water; electricity] *meter.*

me⌈etoru メートル (米) *n.* meter.

me⌉ewaku めいわく (迷惑) *n.* trouble; annoyance; nuisance:
hito ni meewaku *o kakeru* (人に迷惑をかける) cause a person *trouble.* ⟪⇨ meñdoo⟫
meewaku suru (～する) *vi.* be annoyed; be bothered.
— *a.n.* (～ na) annoying; bothering; troublesome; inconvenient.

me⌉eyo めいよ (名誉) *n.* honor; glory:
Subarashii shoo o itadaite meeyo *ni omoimasu.* (素晴らしい賞をいただいて名誉に思います) I *am honored* to have received such a wonderful prize.
— *a.n.* (～ na) honorable. ⟪↔ fumeeyo⟫

me⌈eyoki⌉soñ めいよきそん (名誉棄損) *n.* defamation; libel; slander.

me⌉gane めがね (眼鏡) *n.* glasses; spectacles:
megane *o kakeru* [*hazusu*] (眼鏡を

かける[はずす]) put on [take off] one's *glasses*.

me⌈gumare·ru めぐまれる(恵まれる) *vi*. (megumare-te [V]) **1** be blessed; be gifted:
keñkoo ni megumareru (健康に恵まれる) *be blessed* with good health.
2 be rich:
Sono kuni wa teñneñ shigeñ ni megumarete iru. (その国は天然資源に恵まれている) That country *is rich* in natural resources.

me⌈gum·u めぐむ(恵む) *vt*. (megum·i-; megum·a-; meguñ-de [C]) give in charity; do a person a kindness.

me⌈gur·u めぐる(巡る) *vt*. (megur·i-; megur·a-; megut-te [C])
1 come around; make a tour. (⇨ mawaru)
2 concern; relate:
Isañ o megutte, *kyoodai ga arasotte iru*. (遺産を巡って兄弟が争っている) The brothers are fighting *over* the legacy.

me⌈gu⌉suri めぐすり(目薬) *n*. eyewash; eye lotion.

me⌉isha めいしゃ(目医者) *n*. eye doctor; oculist. (⇨ gañka)

me⌈kata めかた(目方) *n*. weight:
tsutsumi no mekata o hakaru (包みの目方を計る) *weigh* a parcel. (⇨ omosa)

me⌈kki めっき(鍍金) *n*. plating; gilding.
mekki suru (～する) *vt*. plate; gild.

me⌈kur·u めくる(捲る) *vt*. (mekur·i-; mekur·a-; mekut-te [C]) turn over [up]:
peeji o mekuru (ページをめくる) *turn over* a page.

me⌈ma⌉i めまい(眩暈) *n*. giddiness; dizziness: memai ga suru (めまいがする) *feel dizzy*.

me⌉mo メモ *n*. memo; note.
memo suru (～する) *vt*. put down; make a note of.

me⌈mori⌉ めもり(目盛り) *n*. scale; graduation (on a thermometer).

me⌈ñ[1] めん(面) *n*. **1** mask; face guard.
2 plane; surface: *suihee*-meñ (水平面) a horizontal *plane*.
3 aspect; side:
monogoto no akarui meñ *o miru* (物事の明るい面を見る) look on the bright *side* of things.
4 (of a newspaper) page:
shiñbuñ no dai ichi-meñ (新聞の第一面) the front *page* of a newspaper.

me⌉ñ[2] めん(綿) *n*. cotton:
meñ *no kutsushita* (綿の靴下) *cotton* socks. (⇨ momeñ; wata)

me⌈ñboku めんぼく(面目) *n*. honor; face; prestige:
Añna machigai o shite, meñboku nai. (あんな間違いをして, 面目ない) I *am ashamed* of having made such a mistake.

me⌈ñdo⌉o めんどう(面倒) *n*.
1 trouble; inconvenience:
Hito ni meñdoo *wa kaketaku arimaseñ*. (人に面倒はかけたくありません) I don't want to cause any *trouble* to others. (⇨ meewaku)
2 care:
Ane ga byooki no haha no meñdoo *o mite imasu*. (姉が病気の母の面倒を見ています) My sister takes *care* of our sick mother.
— *a.n.* (～ na, ni) troublesome; difficult; complicated. (⇨ yakkai)

me⌈ñdookusa⌉·i めんどうくさい(面倒臭い) *a*. (-ku) troublesome; wearisome; reluctant:
Ame ga futte iru no de gaishutsu suru no wa meñdookusai. (雨が降っているので外出するのは面倒くさい) It is raining, so I am *reluctant* to go out.

me⌈ñji·ru めんじる(免じる) *vt*. (meñji-te [V]) (*formal*) exempt; excuse:
shikeñ o meñjiru (試験を免じる) *exempt* a person from an examination. (⇨ meñjo)
... ni meñjite (...に免じて) in consideration of: *Watashi* ni meñjite

m

kare o yurushite yatte kudasai. (私に免じて彼を許してやってください) Please forgive him *for my sake.*

me˥ñjo めんじょ (免除) *n.* exemption; remission.
meñjo suru (～する) *vt.* exempt; remit: *zeekiñ ga* meñjo sareru (税金が免除される) *be exempted* from taxation.

me˥ñkai めんかい (面会) *n.* interview; meeting.
meñkai suru (～する) *vt.* see; meet; visit; interview.

me˥ñkyo めんきょ (免許) *n.* license; certificate.

me┌ñkyo˥joo めんきょじょう (免許状) *n.* license; certificate.

me┌ñkyo˥shoo めんきょしょう (免許証) *n.* license; driver's license.

me┌ñmoku めんもく (面目) *n.* honor. (⇨ meñboku)

me˥ñseki めんせき (面積) *n.* area; size; floor space. (⇨ taiseki)

me┌ñs·u˥ru めんする (面する) *vi.* (meñsh·i-; meñsh·i-; meñsh·i-te [I]) face; look out:
Sono heya wa minami [*umi*] *ni* meñshite iru. (その部屋は南[海]に面している) The room *faces* south [the sea].

me˥nyuu メニュー *n.* menu; bill of fare.

me┌ñzee めんぜい (免税) *n.* tax exemption: meñzee-*hiñ* (免税品) a *duty-free* article.

me˥rodii メロディー *n.* melody; tune.

-me˥·ru める *suf.* (*v.*) (-me-te [V]) make; -en: ★ Added to the stem of an adjective describing quality.
haya-meru (早める) *hasten*; *quicken* / *usu*-meru (薄める) *make* thinner.

me┌shi˥ めし (飯) *n.* ★ Used by men. **1** (*informal*) (cooked [boiled]) rice:
meshi *o taku* (飯を炊く) cook [boil] *rice.* (⇨ gohañ)
2 (*informal*) meal; food:
Saa meshi *no jikañ da.* (さあ飯の時間だ) Well, now it's time *to eat.* (⇨ asameshi; bañmeshi; hirumeshi)
3 (*informal*) living; livelihood:
Kono kyuuryoo de wa meshi wa kuenai. (この給料では飯は食えない) I *cannot make a living* on this salary.

me┌shiagar·u めしあがる (召し上がる) *vt.* (-agar·i-; -agar·a-; -agat-te [C]) ★ Honorific equivalent of '*taberu*' and '*nomu*.'
eat; drink; have:
Nani o meshiagarimasu *ka?* (何を召し上がりますか) What would you like to *have*?

me┌shita˥ めした (目下) *n.* one's inferior; subordinate. (↔ meue)

me┌su˥ めす (雌) *n.* female; she:
mesu no niwatori (めすの鶏) a *hen* / mesu *inu* (めす犬) a *female* dog. (↔ osu[2])

me┌tsuboo めつぼう (滅亡) *n.* fall; downfall.
metsuboo suru (～する) *vi.* fall; perish; collapse. (⇨ horobiru)

me˥tsuki めつき (目付き) *n.* look; eyes: *surudoi* metsuki (鋭い目つき) a piercing *look.*

me˥tta めった (滅多) *a.n.* (～ na) rash; thoughtless; reckless:
Metta na koto wa iwanai *hoo ga ii.* (めったなことは言わないほうがいい) You had better *be careful about what you say.*

me˥tta ni めったに (滅多に) *adv.* (with a negative) rarely; seldom; hardly ever:
Koñna ii chañsu wa metta ni nai. (こんないいチャンスはめったにない) One *seldom has* a chance as good as this.

me┌ue めうえ (目上) *n.* one's superior. (↔ meshita)

me┌zamashi˥·i めざましい (目覚ましい) *a.* (-ku) remarkable; startling; wonderful.

me┌za˥s·u めざす (目指す) *vt.* (mezash·i-; mezas·a-; mezash·i-te [C]) aim:

m

Fune wa Ooshima o mezashite *shukkoo shita.* (船は大島を目指して出港した) The ship left port, *heading for* Oshima.

me⌈zurashi⌉·i めずらしい (珍しい) *a.* (-ku) rare; unusual; uncommon.

mi[1] み (身) *n.* **1** one's body; person; oneself:
doa no ushiro ni mi *o kakusu* (ドアの後ろに身を隠す) hide *oneself* behind the door.
2 position; place:
Watashi no mi *ni mo natte kudasai.* (私の身にもなってください) Please put yourself in my *place.*
mi ni shimiru (~にしみる) touch one's heart.
mi ni tsukeru (~につける) put on; acquire.

mi[2] み (実) *n.* fruit; nut; berry.
mi o musubu (~を結ぶ) yield fruit; (*fig.*) bear fruit.

mi- み (未) *pref.* un-:
mi-*tee* (未定) *un*decided / mi-*kañsee* (未完成) *un*finished.

-mi み (味) *suf.* taste:
ama-mi (甘味) *sweetness* / *kara*-mi (辛味) a hot *taste.*

mi⌈age·ru みあげる (見上げる) *vt.* (-age-te [V]) look up at; raise one's eyes toward. ⟪↔ miorosu⟫

mi⌈ai みあい (見合い) *n.* an arranged meeting with a view to marriage. ★ Often with '*o*-.'
miai (o) suru (~(を)する) *vi.* see each other with a view to marriage. ⟪⇨ nakoodo⟫

mi⌈awase·ru みあわせる (見合わせる) *vt.* (-awase-te [V]) **1** look at each other.
2 put off; postpone.

mi⌉buñ みぶん (身分) *n.* social status [standing]; position.

mi⌈buñ-shoomeesho みぶんしょうめいしょ (身分証明書) *n.* identification card; ID (card).

mi⌉buri みぶり (身振り) *n.* gesture; motion; way of acting.

mi⌈chi[1] みち (道) *n.* **1** road; way; street; path.
2 course; means:
Kore ga nokosareta tada hitotsu no michi *desu.* (これが残されたただ一つの道です) This is the only *course* left open to us.
3 field:
Yamada-shi wa kono michi *no keñi desu.* (山田氏はこの道の権威です) Mr. Yamada is an authority in this *field.*
4 public morals; the path of righteousness.

mi⌉chi[2] みち (未知) *n.* unknown:
michi *no sekai* (未知の世界) the *unknown* world.

mi⌈chibi⌉k·u みちびく (導く) *vt.* (-bik·i-; -bik·a-; -bi·i-te [C]) guide; lead:
Kakegoto ga kare o hametsu e michibiita. (賭け事が彼を破滅へ導いた) Gambling *led* him to his ruin.

mi⌈chigae·ru みちがえる (見違える) *vt.* (-gae-te [V]) mistake for:
Kare to kare no niisañ o michigaete shimatta. (彼と彼の兄さんを見違えてしまった) I *mistook* his older brother for him.

mi⌈chijuñ みちじゅん (道順) *n.* route; way; course:
Kare ni yuubiñkyoku made no michijuñ *o oshiete yatta.* (彼に郵便局までの道順を教えてやった) I told him the *way* to the post office. ⟪⇨ michi[1]⟫

mi⌈chi⌉·ru みちる (満ちる) *vi.* (michi-te [V]) **1** be filled; be full:
Sono machi wa kakki ni michite ita. (その町は活気に満ちていた) The town *was full* of activity.
2 (of the tide) rise; come in. ⟪↔ hiku[1]⟫

mi⌈dare⌉·ru みだれる (乱れる) *vi.* (midare-te [V]) be in disorder; be in a mess; be confused; be disrupted. ⟪⇨ midasu⟫

mi⌈da⌉s·u みだす (乱す) *vt.* (midash·i-; midas·a-; midash·i-te [C]) put into disorder; disturb; confuse; disrupt:
Retsu o midasanai *de kudasai.* (列

を乱さないでください) Please *do not fall out of* line. ⟪⇨ midareru⟫

mi˥dori みどり(緑) *n.* green; greenery; verdure. ⟪⇨ ao; aoi; midori-iro⟫

mi˹dori-iro みどりいろ(緑色) *n.* green color. ⟪⇨ ao; midori⟫

mi˹e˥·ru みえる(見える) *vi.* (mie-te Ⓥ) **1** be seen; be visible; be in sight:
Kiri de nani mo mienakatta. (霧で何も見えなかった) We *could see nothing* because of the fog. ⟪⇨ miru⟫
2 look; seem:
Kanojo wa toshi yori mo wakaku mieru. (彼女は年よりも若く見える) She *looks* young for her age.
3 (*honorific*) come; appear:
Shachoo wa mada miemaseñ. (社長はまだ見えません) The president *has not appeared* yet.

mi˹gak·u みがく(磨く) *vt.* (miga-k·i-; migak·a-; miga·i-te Ⓒ)
1 polish; shine; brush:
kutsu o migaku (靴を磨く) *shine* one's shoes.
2 improve (one's skill); cultivate (one's character).

mi˹gi みぎ(右) *n.* right:
tsumami o migi *e mawasu* (つまみを右へ回す) turn a handle to the *right*. ⟪↔ hidari⟫

mi˹gigawa みぎがわ(右側) *n.* right side. ⟪↔ hidarigawa⟫

mi˹gikiki みぎきき(右利き) *n.* right-handed person. ⟪↔ hidari-kiki⟫

mi˹gite みぎて(右手) *n.* **1** right hand. ⟪↔ hidarite⟫
2 right direction:
Migite *ni Fuji-sañ ga mieta.* (右手に富士山が見えた) We saw Mt. Fuji on our *right*. ⟪↔ hidarite⟫

mi˥goto みごと(見事) *a.n.* (~ na, ni) splendid; wonderful; excellent; beautiful. ⟪⇨ subarashii⟫

mi˹gurushi˥·i みぐるしい(見苦しい) *a.* (-ku) unsightly; indecent; disgraceful.

mi˹harashi みはらし(見晴らし) *n.* view:
miharashi *no yoi heya* (見晴らしのよい部屋) a room with a good *view*.

mi˹hari みはり(見張り) *n.* watch; guard. ⟪⇨ miharu⟫

mi˹har·u みはる(見張る) *vt.* (-ha-r·i-; -har·a-; -hat-te Ⓒ) keep watch; keep a lookout:
teki o miharu (敵を見張る) *keep a lookout* for the enemy.

mi˹hoñ みほん(見本) *n.* sample; specimen.

mi˹idas·u みいだす(見い出す) *vt.* (-dash·i-; -das·a-; -dash·i-te Ⓒ) find; discover:
Watashi-tachi wa nañ to ka kaiketsu-saku o miidashita. (私達はなんとか解決策を見いだした) We managed somehow to *find* the solution.

mi˹jika みぢか(身近) *a.n.* (~ na, ni) familiar; close; near oneself:
Watashi wa sono chosha o mijika *ni kañjita.* (私はその著者を身近に感じた) I felt myself *close* to the author.

mi˹jika˥·i みじかい(短い) *a.* (-ku)
1 (of length, distance) short:
Kanojo wa kami o mijikaku *shite iru.* (彼女は髪を短くしている) She wears her hair *short*. ⟪↔ nagai⟫
2 (of time) short; brief:
Kare no supiichi wa mijikakatta. (彼のスピーチは短かった) His speech *was short*. ⟪↔ nagai⟫

mi˥jime みじめ(惨め) *a.n.* (~ na, ni) miserable; wretched; pitiful:
mijime *na seekatsu o okuru* (惨めな生活を送る) lead a *miserable* life.

mi˹ka˥iketsu みかいけつ(未解決) *n.*, *a.n.* (~ na/no, ni) unsolved; unsettled. ⟪↔ kaiketsu⟫

mi˹kake みかけ(見掛け) *n.* appearance; look; show:
Hito wa mikake *ni yoranai.* (人は見かけによらない) People's *appearances* are deceptive.

mi˹kake·ru みかける(見掛ける) *vt.* (-kake-te Ⓥ) happen to see; come across; catch sight of.

m

mi¹kañ みかん(蜜柑) *n.* mandarin orange.

mi⌈ka¹ñsee みかんせい(未完成) *a.n.* (~ na/no, ni) unfinished; incomplete. ⟨↔ kañsee⟩

mi⌈kata¹¹ みかた(見方) *n.* point of view; standpoint; attitude.

mi⌈kata² みかた(味方) *n.* friend; side; ally; supporter:
Ano hito wa watashi-tachi no mikata *desu.* (あの人は私たちのみかたです) He is *on our side.* ⟨↔ teki⟩

mi⌈kazuki みかづき(三日月) *n.* crescent; new moon. ⟨⇨ tsuki²⟩

mi¹ki みき(幹) *n.* main stem of a tree; trunk.

mi⌈kka みっか(三日) *n.* three days; the third day of the month. ⟨⇨ APP. 5⟩

mi⌈komi みこみ(見込み) *n.*
1 hope; chance; possibility:
Seekoo no mikomi *wa gobu-gobu desu.* (成功の見込みは五分五分です) There is a fifty-fifty *chance* of success. ⟨⇨ chañsu⟩
2 expectation; prospect:
Watashi-tachi no mikomi *wa atatta [hazureta].* (私たちの見込みは当たった[はずれた]) Our *expectations* proved right [wrong].
mikomi no aru (~のある) promising.

mi⌈koñ みこん(未婚) *n.* unmarried; single:
mikoñ *no haha* (未婚の母) an *unmarried* mother.

mi⌈kudas·u みくだす(見下す) *vt.* (-kudash·i-; -kudas·a-; -kudash·i-te Ⓒ) look down on; despise.

mi⌈kurabe·ru みくらべる(見比べる) *vt.* (-kurabe-te Ⓥ) compare. ⟨⇨ hikaku; kuraberu⟩

mi⌈mai みまい(見舞い) *n.* **1** visit (to a hospital or a sick person); call; inquiry. ★ Often with '*o*-.' ⟨⇨ mimau⟩
2 expression of one's sympathy [concern]:
Shichoo wa higaisha ni mimai *no kotoba o nobeta.* (市長は被害者に見舞いの言葉を述べた) The mayor expressed his *sympathy* for the victims.

-mi¹mañ みまん(未満) *suf.* under; below; less than:
Juuhas-sai-mimañ *wa nyuujoo dekimaseñ.* (18歳未満は入場できません) Those *under* eighteen years of age are not permitted to enter.
★ '*-mimañ*' does not include the preceding number, so, strictly speaking, '*jus-sai-mimañ*' is 'under nine years of age.' ⟨⇨ -ika⟩

mi⌈ma·u みまう(見舞う) *vt.* (mima·i-; mimaw·a-; mimat-te Ⓒ)
1 visit; inquire after:
Kinoo nyuuiñ-chuu no itoko o mimatta. (きのう入院中のいとこを見舞った) Yesterday I *visited* my cousin who is in the hospital. ⟨⇨ mimai⟩
2 (of disaster) hit; strike.

mi⌈mawari みまわり(見回り) *n.* patrol; inspection:
koojoo no mimawari *o suru* (工場の見回りをする) make an *inspection* visit to a factory. ⟨⇨ mimawaru⟩

mi⌈mawar·u みまわる(見回る) *vt.* (-mawar·i-; -mawar·a-; -mawat-te Ⓒ) patrol; make one's rounds; inspect. ⟨⇨ mimawari⟩

mi⌈mawas·u みまわす(見回す) *vt.* (-mawash·i-; -mawas·a-; -mawash·i-te Ⓒ) look around [about].

mi⌈mi¹ みみ(耳) *n.* **1** ear.
2 hearing:
Kare wa mimi *ga tooi.* (彼は耳が遠い) He is hard of *hearing.*
mimi o sumasu (~を澄ます) strain one's ears; listen carefully.

mi⌈na¹ みな(皆) *n., adv.* all; everyone; everything. ⟨⇨ miñna⟩

mi⌈nami みなみ(南) *n.* south; (~ ni/e) southward. ⟨↔ kita⟩

mi⌈nara·u みならう(見習う) *vt.* (-nara·i-; -naraw·a-; -narat-te Ⓒ) follow a person's example;

imitate; learn:
shigoto o minarau (仕事を見習う) *learn* a job.

mi⌉nari みなり (身なり) *n.* appearance; dress; clothes:
Kare wa minari *o kamawanai.* (彼は身なりを構わない) He is indifferent about his *appearance.*
《⇨ fukusoo》

mi⌈na⌉-sama みなさま (皆様) *n.* (*honorific*) = mina-sañ.

mi⌈na⌉-sañ みなさん (皆さん) *n.*
1 everybody; everyone; all:
Mina-sañ, *ohayoo gozaimasu.* (皆さん, お早うございます) Good morning, *everybody.*
2 ladies and gentlemen:
Mina-sañ, *kore o gorañ kudasai.* (皆さん, これをご覧ください) *Ladies and gentlemen*, please look at this.

mi⌈nas·u みなす (見なす) *vt.* (minash·i-; minas·a-; minash·i-te Ⓒ)
regard; consider:
Sañjup-puñ ijoo tatte mo konai hito wa kesseki to minashimasu. (30 分以上たっても来ない人は欠席とみなします) Those who are over thirty minutes late will *be considered* absent.

mi⌈nato みなと (港) *n.* port; harbor.

mi⌈ne みね (峰) *n.* mountain peak; ridge.

mi⌈niku⌉·i[1] みにくい (見難い) *a.* (-ku) hard [difficult] to see.

mi⌈niku⌉·i[2] みにくい (醜い) *a.* (-ku)
1 ugly:
minikui *kizu* (醜いきず) an *ugly* scar.
2 (of conduct, trouble, etc.) scandalous; ignoble:
minikui *arasoi* (醜い争い) a *scandalous* dispute.

mi⌉ñji みんじ (民事) *n.* (of law) civil affairs: miñji-*soshoo* (民事訴訟) a *civil* action. 《⇨ keeji》

mi⌈ñkañ みんかん (民間) *n.* private; civilian:
miñkañ-*kigyoo* (民間企業) a *private* enterprise.

mi⌈ñna⌉ みんな (皆) *n., adv.* all; everyone; everything:
miñna *no ikeñ o kiku* (みんなの意見を聞く) listen to *everyone*'s opinion.
《⇨ mina》

mi⌈no⌉r·u みのる (実る) *vi.* (minor·i-; minor·a-; minot-te Ⓒ)
1 bear fruit.
2 (of an effort, etc.) have results:
Kare no doryoku wa amari minoranakatta. (彼の努力はあまり実らなかった) His efforts *hardly produced anything.*

mi⌈noshirokiñ みのしろきん (身代金) *n.* ransom.

mi⌈noue みのうえ (身の上) *n.*
one's personal affairs; one's personal history.

mi⌈ñshuku みんしゅく (民宿) *n.*
private home which takes in paying guests.

mi⌈ñshu-shu⌉gi みんしゅしゅぎ (民主主義) *n.* democracy.

mi⌈nu⌉k·u みぬく (見抜く) *vt.*
(-nuk·i-; -nuk·a-; -nu·i-te Ⓒ) see through; figure out; perceive:
hito no kokoro o minuku (人の心を見抜く) *see into* a person's mind.

mi⌈ñyoo みんよう (民謡) *n.* folk song; popular ballad.

mi⌉ñzoku みんぞく (民族) *n.* race; people; nation:
miñzoku *no dai-idoo* (民族の大移動) a *racial* migration.

mi⌈oboe みおぼえ (見覚え) *n.* recognition; remembrance:
Ano otoko ni wa mioboe *ga aru.* (あの男には見覚えがある) I *remember* having seen that man.

mi⌈okuri みおくり (見送り) *n.*
send-off; seeing a person off.
《↔ demukae》《⇨ miokuru》

mi⌈okur·u みおくる (見送る) *vt.*
(-okur·i-; -okur·a-; -okut-te Ⓒ)
1 see off:
Tookyoo-eki de kare o miokutta. (東京駅で彼を見送った) We *saw* him *off* at Tokyo Station. 《↔ demukaeru》《⇨ miokuri》
2 pass up (one's turn, opportunity, etc.).

m

mi⌈oros·u みおろす(見下ろす) *vt.* (-orosh·i-; -oros·a-; -orosh·i-te Ⓒ) look down; overlook; command. ⟪↔ miageru⟫

mi⌈otoshi みおとし(見落とし) *n.* oversight; careless mistake. ⟪⇨ miotosu⟫

mi⌈otos·u みおとす(見落とす) *vt.* (-otosh·i-; -otos·a-; -otosh·i-te Ⓒ) overlook; miss: *Watashi wa sono machigai o* miotoshite ita. (私はその間違いを見落としていた) I *missed* the mistake. ⟪⇨ miotoshi⟫

mi⌉rai みらい(未来) *n.* future.

mi⌉ri ミリ *n.* millimeter; milligram. ★ Shortened form of '*miri-meetoru*' and '*miri-guramu*.'

mi⌈ri-gu⌉ramu ミリグラム(瓱) *n.* milligram. ★ Shortened form, '*miri*' is more common. ⟪⇨ miri⟫

mi⌈ri-me⌉etoru ミリメートル(粍) *n.* millimeter. ★ Shortened form, '*miri*' is more common. ⟪⇨ miri⟫

mi⌈ri-ri⌉ttoru ミリリットル(竓) *n.* milliliter.

mi⌉·ru みる(見る・診る) *vt.* (mi-te Ⓥ) **1** see; look at; watch.
2 read; look through: *Kyoo no shiñbuñ o* mimashita *ka?* (きょうの新聞を見ましたか) *Have* you *read* today's paper?
3 inspect; check; consult: *Haisha de ha o* mite moratta. (歯医者で歯を診てもらった) I *had* my teeth *looked at* by the dentist.
4 look after; help: *Kono kabañ o* mite ite *kudasai*. (このかばんを見ていてください) Will you please *keep an eye* on this bag?
-te miru (て〜) try doing: *Atarashii waapuro wa* tsukatte mimashita *ka?* (新しいワープロは使ってみましたか) *Have* you *tried using* your new word processor?

mi⌉ruku ミルク *n.* milk. ★ Often refers to processed milk and creamers. Cows' milk is called '*gyuunyuu*.'

mi⌈ryoku みりょく(魅力) *n.* charm; attraction; appeal; fascination.

mi⌈sage·ru みさげる(見下げる) *vt.* (misage-te Ⓥ) = mikudasu.

mi⌈saki みさき(岬) *n.* cape; promontory.

mi⌈se⌉ みせ(店) *n.* store; shop.

mi⌈sebiraka⌉s·u みせびらかす(見せびらかす) *vt.* (-kash·i-; -kas·a-; -kash·i-te Ⓒ) show off.

mi⌈semono⌉ みせもの(見せ物) *n.* show; exhibition.

mi⌈se⌉·ru みせる(見せる) *vt.* (mi-se-te Ⓥ) **1** show; display; let a person see.
2 show on purpose; pretend: *Heya o hiroku* miseru *tame ni teeburu o ugokashita.* (部屋を広く見せるためにテーブルを動かした) I moved the table so that the room *would look* larger.
-te miseru (て〜) **1** show how to do: oyoide miseru (泳いで見せる) *show* someone *how to swim.*
2 (show a firm decision): *Kon̄do koso kare o* makashite miseru. (今度こそ彼を負かして見せる) You just *watch* me *beat* him this time.

mi⌉shiñ ミシン *n.* sewing machine.

mi⌉so みそ(味噌) *n.* soybean paste; miso.

mi⌈soshi⌉ru みそしる(味噌汁) *n.* miso soup.

mi⌈ssetsu みっせつ(密接) *a.n.* (〜 na, ni) close; closely related: missetsu *na kañkee ga aru* (密接な関係がある) have a *close* relation.

mi⌉su[1] ミス *n.* mistake; error.
misu (o) suru (〜(を)する) *vi.* make a mistake. ⟪⇨ machigai⟫

mi⌉su[2] ミス *n.* Miss; being single.

mi⌈suborashi⌉·i みすぼらしい *a.* (-ku) humble; scruffy; shabby; wretched.

mi⌈sui みすい(未遂) *n.* attempt: *satsujiñ*-misui (殺人未遂) an *attempted* murder.

mi⌈sumisu みすみす *adv.* before

one's eyes; helplessly:
Kare wa misumisu *sono kikai o nogashite shimatta.* (彼はみすみすその機会を逃してしまった) He *helplessly* let the chance slip by.

mi⌈sute·ru みすてる (見捨てる) *vt.* (-sute-te [V]) forsake; desert; leave.

mitai みたい *a.n.* (~ na, ni) [immediately follows a preceding noun or adjectival noun] **1** similar to; like:
yume mitai *na hanashi* (夢みたいな話) a story *like* a dream.
2 such as; like: ★ Refers to something by way of example.
Kare mitai *ni atama no yoi hito ni wa atta koto ga nai.* (彼みたいに頭のよい人には会ったことがない) I have never met a smart person *like* him.
3 seem; appear:
Kanojo wa kanemochi mitai *da.* (彼女は金持ちみたいだ) She *appears* to be rich. ⇨ rashii; soo[2]; yoo[2]

mi⌈ta⌉s·u みたす (満たす) *vt.* (mi-tash·i-; mitas·a-; mitash·i-te [C]) **1** fill up:
koppu ni biiru o mitasu (コップにビールを満たす) *fill* a glass with beer.
2 satisfy (desire); meet (a condition, etc.).

mi⌈tee みてい (未定) *n.* undecided; uncertain.

mi⌈tome·ru みとめる (認める) *vt.* (mitome-te [V]) **1** recognize; admit; concede:
Kare wa jibuñ no machigai o mitometa. (彼は自分の間違いを認めた) He *admitted* his mistake.
2 allow; approve:
Chichi wa watashi no gaihaku o mitomete kuremaseñ. (父は私の外泊を認めてくれません) My father *does not allow* me to sleep out.
3 see; find; notice (an unusual thing, change, etc.).

mi⌈tooshi みとおし (見通し) *n.* **1** visibility:
Kono atari wa mitooshi *ga ii* [*warui*]. (このあたりは見通しがいい[悪い]) *Visibility* is good [poor] around here.
2 prospects; outlook:
Shoobai no mitooshi *wa akarui.* (商売の見通しは明るい) Business *prospects* are bright.

mi⌉tsu みつ (蜜) *n.* honey; molasses; treacle.

mi⌈tsu⌉bachi みつばち (蜜蜂) *n.* honeybee.

mi⌉tsudo みつど (密度) *n.* density:
jiñkoo mitsudo (人口密度) population *density*.

mi⌈tsukar·u みつかる (見付かる) *vi.* (-kar·i-; -kar·a-; -kat-te [C]) be found; be discovered; be caught. ⇨ mitsukeru

mi⌈tsuke·ru みつける (見付ける) *vt.* (-tsuke-te [V]) find; discover; catch:
Kinoo yasui mise o mitsuketa. (きのう安い店を見つけた) Yesterday I *found* a shop with good prices. ⇨ mitsukaru; sagasu

mi⌈tsume·ru みつめる (見詰める) *vt.* (-tsume-te [V]) gaze; stare; study.

mi⌈tsumori みつもり (見積もり) *n.* estimate; quotation:
shuuri no mitsumori *o dasu* [*suru*] (修理の見積もりを出す[する]) make an *estimate* for the repairs. ⇨ mitsumoru

mi⌈tsumor·u みつもる (見積もる) *vt.* (-tsumor·i-; -tsumor·a-; -tsumot-te [C]) estimate; make an estimate. ⇨ mitsumori

mi⌈ttomona⌉·i みっともない *a.* (-ku) shabby; clumsy-looking; shameful; disgraceful.

mi⌈ttsu⌉ みっつ (三つ) *n.* three. ★ Used when counting. ⇨ sañ[1]; APP. 3

mi⌈ushina·u みうしなう (見失う) *vt.* (-ushina·i-; -ushinaw·a-; -ushi-nat-te [C]) lose sight [track] of.

mi⌈wake·ru みわける (見分ける) *vt.* (-wake-te [V]) distinguish; tell from. ⟪⇨ kubetsu⟫

mi⌈watas·u みわたす (見渡す) *vt.* (-watash·i-; -watas·a-; -watash·i-te Ⓒ) look around; survey.

mi⌈yage みやげ (土産) *n.* present; souvenir. ★ Something you buy as a present when returning from a trip or visiting someone. ⟪⇨ o-miyage; purezeñto⟫

mi⌈yako みやこ (都) *n.* capital; metropolis; city.

mi⌈zo みぞ (溝) *n.* ditch; gutter; groove.
2 gap; gulf:
Futari no aida ni mizo *ga dekita.* (二人の間に溝ができた) A *gulf* has developed between the couple.

mi⌈zu みず (水) *n.* water; cold water.
mizu ni nagasu (～に流す) forgive and forget.

mi⌈zugi みずぎ (水着) *n.* swimsuit; bathing suit.

mi⌈zuiro みずいろ (水色) *n.* pale [light] blue.

mi⌉zukara みずから (自ら) *adv.* personally; in person:
Shachoo mizukara *sono kooshoo ni atatta.* (社長自らその交渉にあたった) The president *personally* carried on the negotiations.

mi⌈zumushi みずむし (水虫) *n.* athlete's foot.

mi⌈zusashi⌉ みずさし (水差し) *n.* pitcher; water jug.

mi⌈zuu⌉mi みずうみ (湖) *n.* lake. ⟪⇨ ike⟫

mi⌈zuwari みずわり (水割り) *n.* whisky and water. ⟪⇨ haibooru⟫

mo[1] も (藻) *n.* waterweed; seaweed.

mo[2] も *p.* **1** also; too; besides:
Watashi mo *ikitai.* (私も行きたい) I want to go, *too.*
2 both...and; either...or; neither...nor: ★ Usually occurs as a pair.
Kare wa sukii mo *sukeeto* mo *dekimasu.* (彼はスキーもスケートもできます) He can *both* ski *and* skate.
Watashi wa hima mo *okane* mo *arimaseñ.* (私は暇もお金もありません) I have *neither* time *nor* money.
3 even: ★ Used to emphasize a situation by giving one extreme negative example.
Isogashikute, deñwa mo *kakerarenai.* (忙しくて, 電話もかけられない) I'm so busy that I can't *even* make a phone call. ⟪⇨ sae; sura⟫
4 (used with interrogatives to emphasize a negative):
Kinoo wa doko e mo *ikanakatta.* (きのうはどこへも行かなかった) I did not go *anywhere* yesterday.
5 as many as; as much as:
★ Used with a number or quantity expression to emphasize that the number or quantity is unexpectedly either large or small.
Kekkoñ-shiki ni hyaku-niñ mo *kite kureta.* (結婚式に100人も来てくれた) A *full* hundred people came to our wedding.
6 within, as little as: ★ Used with number or quantity expressions to indicate a limit.
Ichi-neñ mo *sureba, shigoto ni nareru deshoo.* (一年もすれば, 仕事に慣れるでしょう) I am sure you will get used to the job *in* a year.
7 not one; not any; not a single: ★ Follows counters and used with a negative for emphasis.
Gaikoku e wa ichi-do mo *itta koto ga arimaseñ.* (外国へは一度も行ったことがありません) I have not been abroad *even once.*
8 (used in sentences expressing emotion, especially nostalgia):
Natsu-yasumi mo *moo owari da.* (夏休みももう終わりだ) *Ah! The summer vacation* is now over.

mo⌈chi もち (餅) *n.* rice cake. ⟪⇨ mochitsuki; yakimochi⟫

mo⌈chiage·ru もちあげる (持ち上げる) *vt.* (-age-te Ⓥ) **1** lift; heave.
2 flatter; cajole:
Kare wa mochiagerarete *jookigeñ datta.* (彼は持ち上げられて上機嫌だっ

た) He *was flattered* into good spirits.

mo⌈chidas·u もちだす(持ち出す) *vt.* (-dash·i-; -das·a-; -dash·i-te Ⓒ) **1** take out:
Kono hoñ wa damatte, mochidasanai de *kudasai.* (この本は黙って, 持ち出さないでください) Please *do not take out* this book without asking.
2 bring up; propose (a plan, suggestion, etc.).

mo⌈chii⌉·ru もちいる(用いる) *vt.* (mochii-te Ⓥ) use; make use of; employ. (⇨ tsukau)

mo⌈chikomi もちこみ(持ち込み) *n.* bringing in:
Kikeñbutsu no mochikomi kiñshi. (*sign*) (危険物の持ち込み禁止) Dangerous Articles *Prohibited.* (⇨ mochikomu)

mo⌈chikom·u もちこむ(持ち込む) *vt.* (-kom·i-; -kom·a-; -koñ-de Ⓒ) carry into; lodge:
kujoo o mochikomu (苦情を持ち込む) *lodge* a complaint. (⇨ mochikomi)

mo⌈chi⌉mono もちもの(持ち物) *n.* one's belongings; one's property; one's personal effects.

mo⌈chi⌉nushi もちぬし(持ち主) *n.* owner; possessor; proprietor.

mo⌈chi⌉roñ もちろん(勿論) *adv.*
1 of course; certainly; sure.
2 (~ no koto) not to mention; to say nothing of:
Kanojo wa Nihoñ no geñdai-buñ wa mochiroñ *(no koto), koteñ mo yomemasu.* (彼女は日本の現代文はもちろん(のこと), 古典も読めます) She can read the Japanese classics, *to say nothing of* contemporary writing.

mo⌈chitsuki⌉ もちつき(餅つき) *n.* making of rice cake. (⇨ mochi)

mo⌈do⌉r·u もどる(戻る) *vi.* (modor·i-; modor·a-; modot-te Ⓒ)
1 go [come] back; return. (⇨ kaeru[1]; kaeru[2])
2 be restored; regain:
Shiñkañseñ no daiya wa heejoo ni modorimashita. (新幹線のダイヤは平常に戻りました) The Shinkansen schedule *has been restored* to normal. (⇨ modosu)

mo⌈do⌉s·u もどす(戻す) *vt.* (modosh·i-; modos·a-; modosh·i-te Ⓒ) **1** put back; return; restore. (⇨ kaesu; modoru)
2 throw up; vomit.

mo⌈e·ru もえる(燃える) *vi.* (moete Ⓥ) **1** burn; blaze.
2 glow (with hope, ambition, etc.); burn:
Kanojo wa kiboo ni moete ita. (彼女は希望に燃えていた) She *was burning* with hope. (⇨ moyasu)

mo⌈ga⌉k·u もがく *vi.* (mogak·i-; mogak·a-; moga·i-te Ⓒ) struggle; writhe:
Inu wa ana kara deyoo to mogaite ita. (犬は穴から出ようともがいていた) The dog *was struggling* to get out of the hole.

mo⌉g·u もぐ *vt.* (mog·i-; mog·a-; mo·i-de Ⓒ) pick (fruit); pluck.

mo⌉gumogu もぐもぐ *adv.* (~ to) mumblingly:
nani-ka mogumogu (to) iu (何かもぐもぐ(と)言う) *mumble* something.

mo⌈gu⌉r·u もぐる(潜る) *vi.* (mogur·i-; mogur·a-; mogut-te Ⓒ)
1 dive; go [stay] underwater.
2 get into (a hole, the ground, etc.); creep into; hide.

mo⌈hañ もはん(模範) *n.* model; example; pattern.

mo⌉haya もはや(最早) *adv.* now; by now; already:
Mohaya *ososugimasu.* (もはや遅すぎます) It is too late *now.*

mo⌉ji もじ(文字) *n.* letter; character. (⇨ ji)

mo⌉jimoji もじもじ *adv.* (~ to; ~ suru) hesitatingly; timidly; reservedly:
Kanojo wa meñsetsu no toki mojimoji *(to) shite ita.* (彼女は面接のときもじもじ(と)していた) She acted *nervously* at the interview.

mo⌈kee もけい(模型) *n.* model;

m

miniature: mokee *hikooki* (模型飛行機) a *model* plane.

mo⌉kka もっか (目下) *n.*, *adv.* (*formal*) now; currently; at present. ⟨⇨ geñzai⟩

mo⌈kuhi⌉keñ もくひけん (黙秘権) *n.* the right of silence.

mo⌈kuhyoo もくひょう (目標) *n.* goal; target; object; mark.

mo⌈kuji もくじ (目次) *n.* table of contents.

mo⌈kumoku もくもく (黙々) *adv.* (~ to) in silence; without saying anything:
mokumoku *to hataraku* (黙々と働く) work *without saying anything.*

mo⌈kuroku もくろく (目録) *n.* catalog; list.

mo⌈kuromi⌉ もくろみ (目論見) *n.* plan; scheme; intention:
Watashi no mokuromi *wa hazureta.* (私のもくろみははずれた) My *plan* fell through. ⟨⇨ mokuromu⟩

m

mo⌈kuro⌉m·u もくろむ (目論む) *vt.* (-rom·i-; -rom·a-; -roñ-de [C]) plan; scheme; intend:
Kare wa nani-ka mokuroñde iru. (彼は何かもくろんでいる) He *is up to* something. ⟨⇨ mokuromi⟩

mo⌈kuteki もくてき (目的) *n.* purpose; aim; objective.

mo⌈kuteki⌉chi もくてきち (目的地) *n.* one's destination; one's; goal.

mo⌈kuyo⌉o(bi) もくよう(び) (木曜(日)) *n.* Thursday. ⟨⇨ APP. 5⟩

mo⌈ku⌉zai もくざい (木材) *n.* wood; lumber; timber.

mo⌈kuzoo もくぞう (木造) *n.* made of wood; wooden:
Kono jiñja wa mokuzoo *desu.* (この神社は木造です) This shrine is *built of wood.*

mo⌈meñ もめん (木綿) *n.* cotton; cotton thread. ⟨⇨ meñ[2]; wata⟩

mo⌈me·ru もめる (揉める) *vi.* (mo-me-te [V]) have trouble; have an argument.

mo⌉miji もみじ (紅葉) *n.* maple; autumn [red] leaves. ⟨⇨ kooyoo⟩

mo⌉mo[1] もも (股) *n.* thigh.

mo⌈mo[2] もも (桃) *n.* peach; peach tree.

mo⌈moiro ももいろ (桃色) *n.* pink. ★ Has a pornographic implication like English 'blue.' ⟨⇨ piñku⟩

mo⌈m·u もむ (揉む) *vt.* (mom·i-; mom·a-; moñ-de [C]) massage; rub.

mo⌉ñ もん (門) *n.* gate.

mo⌉naka もなか (最中) *n.* Japanese wafer cake. ⟨⇨ wagashi⟩

mo⌈ñdai もんだい (問題) *n.*
1 question; issue; problem:
moñdai *o kaiketsu suru* (問題を解決する) settle a *question.*
2 problem (to be answered):
moñdai *o toku* (問題を解く) solve a *problem.* ⟨↔ tooañ⟩ ⟨⇨ kotae⟩
3 matter:
Sore wa betsu moñdai *desu.* (それは別問題です) That is another *matter.*
4 trouble:
Kare wa mata moñdai *o okoshita.* (彼はまた問題を起こした) He has once more caused *trouble.*

mo⌈ñdo⌉o もんどう (問答) *n.* argument; questions and answers.
moñdoo suru (~する) *vi.* have an argument. ⟨⇨ tooroñ⟩

mo⌉ñku もんく (文句) *n.* **1** words; phrase: *kimari-*moñku (決まり文句) a set *phrase.*
2 complaint; objection.

mo⌈no[1]⌉ もの (物) *n.* **1** thing; material; article:
Nani-ka taberu mono *wa arimasu ka?* (何か食べる物はありますか) Is there any*thing* to eat?
2 one's possessions:
Kore wa watashi no mono *da.* (これは私のものだ) This is *mine.*
3 quality:
Kono shina wa mono *ga ii.* (この品は物がいい) This article is of good *quality.*
4 word:
Tsukarete, mono *mo ienai.* (疲れて、物も言えない) I am too tired to

even say a *word*.

mono ni naru (～になる) make good: *Sono keekaku wa* mono ni naranakatta. (その計画はものにならなかった) The plan *did not materialize*.

mono ni suru (～にする) master.

mo⌈no⌉² もの (者) *n.* person; fellow; one:

Kare wa kono kaisha no mono *de wa arimaseñ.* (彼はこの会社の者ではありません) He is not an *employee* of this company. 《⇨ hito; kata³》

-mono もの (物) *suf.* thing; article; clothes: *uri*-mono (売り物) an *article* for sale / *fuyu*-mono (冬物) winter *clothes*.

mo⌈no⌉ da ものだ **1** be natural:

★ Polite form is '*mono desu*.' Denotes that a certain result or consequence is natural under given circumstances.

Ryokoo ni deru to hoñ ga yomitaku naru mono da. (旅行に出ると本が読みたくなるものだ) When one goes on a trip, one *usually* feels like reading a book.

2 used to (do): ★ Refers to past habits and states.

Mukashi wa kono atari ni norainu ga takusañ ita mono desu. (昔はこのあたりに野良犬がたくさんいたものです) There *used to* be many stray dogs around this place a while back.

3 should (do): ★ Denotes obligation or duty.

Hito ni mono o morattara, oree o iu mono da. (人に物をもらったら, お礼をいうものだ) When you receive something from someone, you *should* say 'thank you.'

4 how...! ★ Denotes the speaker's sentiment.

Hito no isshoo wa mijikai mono da. (人の一生は短いものだ) *How* short life is!

5 how could...? ★ Denotes the speaker's criticism or judgment.

Baka na koto o shita mono da. (ばかなことをしたものだ) *It was* very foolish of me.

mo⌈noga⌉tari ものがたり (物語) *n.* story; tale; narrative.

mo⌈nogata⌉r·u ものがたる (物語る) *vt.* (-gatar·i-; -gatar·a-; -gatatte Ⓒ) tell of; show; describe.

mo⌈no⌉goto ものごと (物事) *n.* things; everything:

Anata wa monogoto *o majime ni kañgae-sugiru.* (あなたは物事をまじめに考え過ぎる) You take *things* too seriously.

mo⌈no⌉ ka ものか (*informal*) never:

★ Placed at the end of a sentence to express strong negation.

Añna yatsu to moo kuchi o kiku mono ka. (あんなやつともう口をきくものか) *Do you expect* me to talk to a fellow like him again?

mo⌈no-o⌉boe ものおぼえ (物覚え) *n.* memory:

Kare wa mono-oboe *ga ii.* (彼は物覚えがいい) He has a good *memory*. 《⇨ kioku》

mo⌈nooki⌉ ものおき (物置) *n.* storeroom; shed; closet.

mo⌈nooto⌉ ものおと (物音) *n.* (strange) sound; noise:

Monooto *hitotsu shinai*. (物音一つしない) There is no *sound*.

mo⌈nosa⌉shi ものさし (物差し) *n.* ruler; measure.

mo⌈nosugo⌉·i ものすごい (物凄い) *a.* (-ku) (*informal*) terrible; terrific:

Kare wa kimi no koto o monosugoku *okotte iru zo.* (彼は君のことをものすごく怒っているぞ) He is *hopping* mad at you.

mo⌈no⌉zuki ものずき (物好き) *n.* strange [eccentric] person.

— *a.n.* (～ na, ni) curious; weird; eccentric.

mo⌉o もう *adv.* **1** already; yet; now:

Depaato wa moo *hiraite imasu ka?* (デパートはもう開いていますか) Are the department stores open *yet*?

2 more; further; again:

Moo *ichi-do sono eega o mitai.* (もう一度その映画を見たい) I would like to see that film once *more.*
3 soon; before long:
Moo *sorosoro kanojo wa kuru to omoimasu.* (もうそろそろ彼女は来ると思います) I think she will be coming *soon.* ⟪⇨ moo sugu⟫

mo⌈o- もう(猛) *pref.* hard; heavy; intensive:
moo-*beñkyoo* (猛勉強) *hard* study / moo-*reñshuu* (猛練習) *intensive* training.

mo⌉ochoo もうちょう(盲腸) *n.* appendix:
moochoo-eñ (盲腸炎) *appendicitis.*
★ '*Chuusuieñ*' (虫垂炎) is the technical term.

mo⌉ofu もうふ(毛布) *n.* blanket.

mo⌈o jiki もうじき *adv.* soon; shortly. ⟪⇨ moo sugu⟫

mo⌈oka⌉r·u もうかる(儲かる) *vi.* (-kar·i-; -kar·a-; -kat-te Ⓒ) make money; make a profit; be profitable. ⟪⇨ mookeru[1]; mooke⟫

mo⌈oke もうけ(儲け) *n.* profit; gains; earnings. ⟪↔ soñ⟫ ⟪⇨ mookeru[1]; mookaru; rieki⟫

mo⌈oke⌉·ru[1] もうける(儲ける) *vt.* (-ke-te Ⓥ) make money; make a profit:
Kare wa kabu de ni-hyakumañ-eñ mooketa. (彼は株で200万円もうけた) He *made* two million yen on stocks. ⟪⇨ mookaru; mooke⟫

mo⌈oke⌉·ru[2] もうける(設ける) *vt.* (-ke-te Ⓥ) set up (an organization, rule, etc.); lay down:
shiteñ o mookeru (支店を設ける) *set up* a branch office.

mo⌈oretsu もうれつ(猛烈) *a.n.* (~ na, ni) violent; fierce; terrible:
mooretsu *na taifuu* (猛烈な台風) a *violent* typhoon.

mo⌈oshiage·ru もうしあげる(申し上げる) *vt.* (-age-te Ⓥ) express; say: ★ Humble equivalent of '*iu.*' More humble than '*moosu.*'
Hoñ-neñ mo yoroshiku onegai mooshiagemasu. (*on a New Year's card*) (本年もよろしくお願い申し上げます) I *would appreciate* your further kindness this year.
o[go]-... mooshiagemasu (お[ご]...申し上げます) (*humble*) will do:
O-seki e go-añnai mooshiagemasu. (お席へご案内申し上げます) I *will show* you to your seat.

mo⌈oshide·ru もうしでる(申し出る) *vt.* (-de-te Ⓥ) propose; offer; request; apply for.

mo⌈oshikomi もうしこみ(申し込み) *n.* application; offer; proposal; request. ⟪⇨ mooshikomu⟫

mo⌈oshikom·u もうしこむ(申し込む) *vt.* (-kom·i-; -kom·a-; -koñ-de Ⓒ) apply for; propose:
Kare wa kanojo ni kekkoñ o mooshikoñda. (彼は彼女に結婚を申し込んだ) He *proposed* marriage to her. ⟪⇨ mooshikomi⟫

mo⌈oshiwake もうしわけ(申し訳) *n.* apology; excuse.
mooshiwake arimaseñ (~ありません) I am sorry; excuse me. ⟪⇨ mooshiwake nai⟫

mo⌈oshiwake na⌉·i もうしわけない(申し訳ない) (-ku) be sorry:
Go-meewaku o o-kakeshite, mooshiwake naku *omotte orimasu.* (ご迷惑をおかけして, 申し訳なく思っております) *I feel very sorry* for causing you so much trouble.

mo⌉os·u もうす(申す) *vt.* (moosh·i-; moos·a-; moosh·i-te Ⓒ) (*humble*) say; tell; call:
Chichi wa sugu ni mairu to mooshite orimasu. (父はすぐに参ると申しております) My father *says* that he will soon come.
o-... mooshimasu (お...申します) (*humble*) will do: *Nochi-hodo* o-ukagai mooshimasu. (後ほどお伺い申します) I *will call on* you later. ⟪⇨ mooshiageru⟫

mo⌈o su⌉gu もうすぐ *adv.* soon; shortly; before long.

mo⌉ppara もっぱら(専ら) *adv.* exclusively; wholly; mostly.

mo⌈ra⌉s·u もらす(漏らす) *vt.* (mo-rash·i-; moras·a-; morash·i-te [C]) **1** let leak (water, oil, etc.); let out (a secret, complaint, etc.). ⟪⇨ moreru⟫
2 fail to do: ★ Attached to the continuative base of a verb.
kiki-morasu (聞き漏らす) *fail to* hear / *kaki*-morasu (書き漏らす) *fail to* write down.

mo⌈ra·u もらう(貰う) *vt.* (mora·i-; moraw·a-; morat-te [C]) get; receive (a present).
-te morau (て~) ★ Used when asking someone to do something, or when receiving benefit from someone.
Kanojo ni tegami o taipu shite moratta. (彼女に手紙をタイプしてもらった) I *had* her *type* the letter *for me.* ⟪⇨ itadaku⟫

mo⌈re⌉·ru もれる(漏れる) *vi.* (more-te [V]) **1** (of water) leak; escape; (of a secret) leak out. ⟪⇨ morasu; moru[1]⟫
2 be left out (of a list, selection, etc.); be omitted.

mo⌈ri もり(森) *n.* woods; forest. ⟪⇨ hayashi; shiñriñ⟫

mo⌈ribachi もりばち(盛り鉢) *n.* bowl. ⟪⇨ wañ[1]⟫

mo⌈ro⌉·i もろい(脆い) *a.* (-ku)
1 fragile; weak.
2 (of feeling, emotion, etc.) be moved easily:
Haha wa joo ni moroi. (母は情にもろい) My mother *is easily moved* emotionally.

mo⌉r·u[1] もる(漏る) *vi.* (mor·i-; mor·a-; mot-te [C]) leak:
Kono heya wa ame ga moru. (この部屋は雨が漏る) Rain *leaks* into this room. ⟪⇨ moreru⟫

mo⌉r·u[2] もる(盛る) *vt.* (mor·i-; mor·a-; mot-te [C]) pile up; heap up. ⟪⇨ tsumu[1]⟫

mo⌉shi (mo) もし(も)(若し(も)) *adv.* if; in case:
Moshi mo *ashita yoi teñki nara, pikunikku ni ikimasu.* (もしもあした良い天気なら, ピクニックに行きます) We are going on a picnic *if* it is fine tomorrow. ⟪⇨ kari ni⟫

mo⌉shi-ka shitara もしかしたら(若しかしたら) *adv.* perhaps; maybe; possibly.

mo⌉shi-ka suru to もしかすると(若しかすると) *adv.* = moshi-ka shitara.

mo⌉shikuwa もしくは(若しくは) *conj.* (*formal*) or:
hoñniñ moshikuwa *dairiniñ* (本人もしくは代理人) *either* the person in question *or* his or her representative. ⟪⇨ aruiwa[1]; mata-wa⟫

mo⌉shimoshi もしもし *int.*
1 hello: ★ Used when answering a telephone call.
Moshimoshi, *Yamada-sañ desu ka?* (もしもし, 山田さんですか) *Hello.* Is that Mrs. Yamada?
2 excuse me: ★ Used when addressing a stranger.
Moshimoshi, *kippu o otoshimashita yo.* (もしもし, 切符を落としましたよ) *Excuse me.* You have dropped your ticket.

mo⌈tara⌉s·u もたらす *vt.* (-rash·i-; -ras·a-; -rash·i-te [C]) bring (about); lead to:
yoi kekka o motarasu (良い結果をもたらす) *produce* good results. ⟪⇨ shoojiru⟫

mo⌈tare⌉·ru もたれる(凭れる) *vi.* (-re-te [V]) **1** lean:
kabe ni motareru (壁にもたれる) *lean* against a wall.
2 (of food) sit heavy on one's stomach; be hard to digest.

mo⌈tenas·u もてなす(持て成す) *vt.* (-nash·i-; -nas·a-; -nash·i-te [C]) entertain; treat:
kyaku o atsuku motenasu (客を厚くもてなす) *give* a guest *warm welcome.*

mo⌈te⌉·ru もてる(持てる) *vi.* (mote-te [V]) be popular; be a favorite:
Kare wa oñna-no-ko ni yoku moteru. (彼は女の子によくもてる) He *is*

m

very popular with the girls.

mo⌈to[1] もと(元・基・本・素) *n.*

1 cause; beginning; origin: *keñka no* moto (けんかの元) the *cause* of a quarrel.

2 basis; foundation: *Kono deeta wa nani o* moto *ni shite imasu ka?* (このデータは何を基にしていますか) What is the *basis* for these data?

3 material; basic ingredient: *Miso no* moto *wa daizu desu.* (みその素は大豆です) The *basic material* for miso is soybeans.

4 capital; funds. 《⇨ motode》

mo⌉to[2] もと(元・旧) *n.* original [former] state: *teeburu o* moto no toori *naraberu* (テーブルをもとの通り並べる) put the tables *as they were.* 《⇨ kyuu[3]; zeñ-[2]》

mo⌈tode もとで(元手) *n.* capital; funds. 《⇨ shihoñ; shikiñ》

mo⌈tome⌉·ru もとめる(求める) *vt.* (-me-te [V]) **1** request; demand.

2 seek; look for: *shoku o* motomeru (職を求める) *look for* employment.

3 buy; purchase.

mo⌈tomoto もともと(元々) *adv.* from the first [beginning]; by nature.

motomoto da (～だ) remain unchanged: *Soñ shite* motomoto da. (損してもともとだ) Even if I lose money, I will be *none the worse* for it.

mo⌈tozu⌉k·u もとづく(基づく) *vi.* (-zuk·i-; -zuk·a-; -zu·i-te [C]) be based on; be founded on.

mo⌉ts·u もつ(持つ) *vt.* (moch·i-; mot·a-; mot-te [C]) **1** take; hold; carry: *Sono nimotsu wa watashi ga* mochimashoo. (その荷物は私が持ちましょう) I'll *take* that luggage.

2 possess; own: ★ Usually used in the form '*motte iru.*' *Kare wa supootsukaa o* motte iru. (彼はスポーツカーを持っている) He *has* a sports car. 《⇨ shoyuu》

3 cherish (a feeling); harbor (a desire): *Watashi wa Nihoñ no rekishi ni kyoomi o* motte imasu. (私は日本の歴史に興味を持っています) I *have* an interest in Japanese history.

4 last; hold; keep; wear: *Kono fuku wa ato go-neñ* mochimasu. (この服はあと5年もちます) These clothes *will last* five more years.

5 bear; cover; pay: *Kañjoo wa kare ga* motta. (勘定は彼が持った) He *paid* the bill. 《⇨ harau》

mo⌈ttaina⌉·i もったいない(勿体無い) *a.* (-ku) **1** wasteful: *Jikañ ga* mottainai. (時間がもったいない) It is a *waste* of time.

2 too good: *Watashi ni wa* mottainai *heya desu.* (私にはもったいない部屋です) This is a room that is *too good* for me. 《⇨ oshii》

mo⌈tte ik·u もっていく(持って行く) *vt.* (ik·i-; ik·a-; it-te [C]) take (a thing with one); carry: *pikunikku ni iroiro na tabemono o* motte iku (ピクニックにいろいろな食べ物を持って行く) *take* various foods to a picnic. 《↔ motte kuru》

mo⌈tte k·u⌉ru もってくる(持って来る) *vt.* (k·i-; k·o-; k·i-te [I]) bring; get: *Kasa o* motte kuru *no o wasurete shimatta.* (かさを持って来るのを忘れてしまった) I forgot to *bring* my umbrella. 《↔ motte iku》

mo⌉tto もっと *adv.* more: Motto *motte kite kudasai.* (もっと持って来てください) Please bring some *more.*

mo⌈tto⌉mo[1] もっとも(最も) *adv.* most: *Nihoñ de* mottomo *takai yama* (日本で最も高い山) the *highest* mountain in Japan. 《⇨ ichibañ[2]》

mo⌈tto⌉mo[2] もっとも(尤も) *a.n.* (～ na, ni) reasonable; natural;

right. ⟪⇨ toozeñ⟫

mo˥ttomo[3] もっとも（尤も）*conj.* however; but; though:
Kanojo wa keesañ ga hayai. Mottomo *tokidoki machigaeru.*（彼女は計算が速い. もっともときどき間違える）She is quick at figures. *But* she sometimes makes mistakes.
⟪⇨ tadashi⟫

mo┌yas·u もやす（燃やす）*vt.* (moyash·i-; moyas·a-; moyash·i-te Ⓒ) burn (wastepaper).
⟪⇨ moeru⟫

mo┌yoo もよう（模様）*n.* **1** pattern; design:
hana no moyoo *no kabegami*（花の模様の壁紙）wallpaper with a floral *pattern.*
2 look; appearance:
Kaigi wa eñki ni naru moyoo da.（会議は延期になるもようだ）It *looks like* the meeting is going to be postponed.
3 development; circumstances:
Kare wa sono kuni no saikiñ no moyoo *o hanashite kureta.*（彼はその国の最近のもようを話してくれた）He told us about the latest *developments* in the country.
⟪⇨ yoosu⟫

mo┌yooshi もよおし（催し）*n.* meeting; party; function.
⟪⇨ moyoosu⟫

mo┌yoos·u もよおす（催す）*vt.* (moyoosh·i-; moyoos·a-; moyoosh·i-te Ⓒ) **1** hold; have; give (a party). ⟪⇨ hiraku; moyooshi⟫
2 feel:
nemuke o moyoosu（眠気を催す）*feel* sleepy / *samuke o* moyoosu（寒気を催す）*feel* a chill.

mu˥ む（無）*n.* nothing; naught; nil:
Watashi-tachi no doryoku wa subete mu *ni natta.*（私たちの努力はすべて無になった）All our efforts have come to *nothing.*

mu- む（無）*pref.* un-; -less; free:
mu-*yoku*（無欲）*un*selfish / mu-zai（無罪）*innocent.*

mu˥cha むちゃ（無茶）*n.* being unreasonable; being absurd:
mucha *o suru*（無茶をする）do *reckless things.*
— *a.n.* (～ na, ni) unreasonable; absurd; reckless.

mu┌chakucha むちゃくちゃ（無茶苦茶）*a.n.* (～ na, ni) (*informal*) absurd; reckless; awful.
⟪⇨ mucha; mechamecha⟫

mu˥chi[1] むち（無知）*n.* ignorance; innocence.
— *a.n.* (～ na) ignorant.

mu˥chi[2] むち（鞭）*n.* whip; lash.

mu┌chuu むちゅう（夢中）*a.n.* (～ na, ni) absorbed; crazy:
terebi-geemu ni muchuu ni naru（テレビゲームに夢中になる）*be absorbed* in a video game.
muchuu de（～で）for one's life:
Watashi wa muchuu de *nigeta.*（私は夢中で逃げた）I ran *for my life.*

mu┌da むだ（無駄）*n.* waste; uselessness:
muda *o habuku*（無駄を省く）cut down on *waste.*
— *a.n.* (～ na, ni) wasteful; useless. ⟪⇨ dame⟫

mu┌dañ むだん（無断）*n.* without permission [leave; notice]:
mudañ *de gakkoo o yasumu*（無断で学校を休む）be absent from school *without notice.*

mu┌dazu˥kai むだづかい（無駄遣い）*n.* waste; wasting:
zeekiñ no mudazukai（税金のむだづかい）a *waste* of tax money.
mudazukai suru（～する）*vt.* waste.

mu˥eki むえき（無益）*a.n.* (～ na, ni) useless; futile:
mueki *na arasoi*（無益な争い）a *useless* controversy. ⟪↔ yuueki⟫

mu˥gai むがい（無害）*a.n.* (～ na, ni) harmless; innocuous.
⟪↔ yuugai⟫

mu┌geñ むげん（無限）*n.* boundless; limitless:
mugeñ *no yorokobi*（無限の喜び）*boundless* joy.

m

— *a.n.* (~ na, ni) infinite; boundless; limitless.

mu⌉gi むぎ (麦) *n.* wheat; barley; oats.

mu⌈goñ むごん (無言) *n.* silence; muteness:
Kare wa mugoñ *de heya kara dete itta.* (彼は無言で部屋から出て行った) He went out of the room *without a word.* ⟪⇨ damatte⟫

mu⌉hoñ むほん (謀反) *n.* rebellion:
muhoñ *o okosu* (謀反を起こす) *rebel.*

mu⌈ika むいか (六日) *n.* six days; the sixth day of the month. ⟪⇨ APP. 5⟫

mu⌈i⌉mi むいみ (無意味) *a.n.* (~ na, ni) meaningless; senseless: muimi *na giroñ* (無意味な議論) *meaningless* arguments.

mu⌉jaki むじゃき (無邪気) *a.n.* (~ na, ni) innocent; childlike:
Kodomo wa mujaki *da.* (子どもは無邪気だ) Children are *without guile.*

mu⌉ji むじ (無地) *n.* plain; having no pattern or design.

mu⌈jiñ むじん (無人) *n.* vacant; uninhabited:
mujiñ-*fumikiri* (無人踏切) an *unattended* railroad crossing.

mu⌈juñ むじゅん (矛盾) *n.* contradiction; inconsistency; incompatibility.
mujuñ suru (~する) *vi.* contradict; be inconsistent; be incompatible.

mu⌈kae·ru むかえる (迎える) *vt.* (mukae-te [V]) **1** meet; come to meet; welcome; receive:
Watashi-tachi wa kare o eki de mukaemashita. (私たちは彼を駅で迎えました) We *met* him at the station.
2 invite:
kyaku o yuushoku ni mukaeru (客を夕食に迎える) *invite* a guest to dinner.
3 greet (a new year); see (one's birthday); attain.

mu⌈kai むかい (向かい) *n.* opposite side [place]:
Gakkoo no mukai *ni hoñya ga arimasu.* (学校の向かいに本屋があります) There is a bookstore *across* from the school. ⟪⇨ mukau⟫

mu⌈ka⌉ñkee むかんけい (無関係) *a.n.* (~ na, ni) unrelated; irrelevant:
Watashi wa koñdo no jikeñ to wa mukañkee desu. (私は今度の事件とは無関係です) I *have nothing to do* with this affair. ⟪↔ kañkee⟫

mu⌈kashi むかし (昔) *n.* the past; old days; ancient times. ⟪↔ ima[1]⟫

mu⌈kashi-ba⌉nashi むかしばなし (昔話) *n.* old tale [story].

mu⌈kashi-mukashi むかしむかし (昔々) *n.* once upon a time.

mu⌈ka·u むかう (向かう) *vi.* (muka-i-; mukaw·a-; mukat-te [C])
1 face; front:
Mukatte *migi ni mieru no ga shiyakusho desu.* (向かって右に見えるのが市役所です) The building *you can see* on the right is the town hall. ⟪⇨ mukai⟫
2 head; leave for...:
Hikooki wa Tookyoo kara Oosaka e mukatta. (飛行機は東京から大阪へ向かった) The airplane *set course* from Tokyo for Osaka.
3 against; to:
Señsee ni mukatte, *soñna koto o itte wa ikemaseñ.* (先生に向かって，そんなことを言ってはいけません) You must not say that kind of thing directly *to* your teacher.

-muke むけ (向け) *suf.* for:
*kodomo-*muke *no bañgumi* (子ども向けの番組) a program *for* children. ⟪⇨ muki⟫

mu⌈ke·ru むける (向ける) *vt.* (muke-te [V]) **1** turn; direct:
Kare wa kanojo no hoo ni me o muketa. (彼は彼女のほうに目を向けた) He *turned* his eyes toward her. ⟪⇨ muku[1]⟫
2 aim; point:

Gootoo wa keekañ ni juu o muketa. (強盗は警官に銃を向けた) The robber *aimed* his pistol at the policeman.

muˈki むき (向き) *n.* **1** way; direction:
Kaze no muki *ga kawatta.* (風の向きが変わった) The *direction* of the wind has changed. 《⇨ muku[1]》
2 suitable; suited:
Kono fuku wa wakai hito muki *desu.* (この服は若い人向きです) These clothes are *suitable* for young people. 《⇨ muku[1]》

muˈko むこ (婿) *n.* **1** bridegroom.
2 son-in-law. 《↔ yome》

muˈkoo[1] むこう (向こう) *n.* **1** the other [opposite] side; over there. 《⇨ kochira》
2 (used to refer to the third person) the other party; he; she; they:
Warui no wa mukoo *da.* (悪いのは向こうだ) It is *they* who are in the wrong. 《⇨ kochira》
3 destination:
Mukoo *ni tsuitara, o-shirase shimasu.* (向こうに着いたら, お知らせします) I will let you know when I reach my *destination.*
4 the near future; the coming period of time:
Mukoo *is-shuukañ kyuugyoo shimasu.* (向こう一週間休業します) We will be closed for business for the *next* week.

muˈkoo[2] むこう (無効) *a.n.* (～ na) invalid; no good; void. 《↔ yuukoo[2]》

muˈkoozune むこうずね (向こう脛) *n.* shin.

muˈk·u[1] むく (向く) *vi.* (muk·i-; muk·a-; mu·i-te Ⓒ) **1** turn; look: *ushiro o* muku (後ろを向く) *look* back. 《⇨ mukeru》
2 face:
Watashi no heya wa nishi ni muite imasu. (私の部屋は西に向いています) My room *faces* west. 《⇨ mukeru; muki》
3 be fit; be suitable; suit:
Kono shigoto wa kanojo ni muite iru. (この仕事は彼女に向いている) This work *suits* her.
《⇨ fusawashii》

muˈk·u[2] むく (剝く) *vt.* (muk·i-; muk·a-; mu·i-te Ⓒ) peel; pare.

muˈkuchi むくち (無口) *a.n.* (～ na) taciturn; reticent:
Kare wa mukuchi desu. (彼は無口です) He *does not talk much.*
《⇨ kuchi[1]》

muˈmee むめい (無名) *n.* nameless; unknown:
mumee no *sakka* (無名の作家) an *obscure* writer. 《↔ yuumee》

muˈnashiˈ·i むなしい (空しい) *a.* (-ku) fruitless; futile; empty:
munashii *doryoku* (むなしい努力) *fruitless* efforts. 《⇨ muda》

muˈneˈ むね (胸) *n.* **1** chest; breast; bust.
2 heart:
Mada mune *ga dokidoki shite iru.* (まだ胸がどきどきしている) My *heart* is still pounding.
mune ga ippai ni naru (～がいっぱいになる) one's heart is full of (emotion).
mune ga itamu (～が痛む) pain one's heart.

muˈnoo むのう (無能) *a.n.* (～ na) incompetent; incapable.
《↔ yuunoo》

muˈraˈ むら (村) *n.* village:
mura-*yakuba* (村役場) a *village* office. 《⇨ machi》

-mura むら (村) *suf.* village:
Ogawa-mura (小川村) Ogawa *Village.*

muˈraˈsaki むらさき (紫) *n.* purple; violet.

muˈreˈ むれ (群れ) *n.* group; crowd:
hitsuji no mure (羊の群れ) a *flock* of sheep / *ushi no* mure (牛の群れ) a *herd* of cattle.

muˈri むり (無理) *n.* unreasonable; unjust:
Amari muri *o iwanai de kudasai.*

m

(あまり無理を言わないでください) Do not be so *unreasonable.*
muri (o) suru (～(を)する) *vi.* overwork; strain oneself.
— *a.n.* (～ na, ni) impossible; unreasonable; unjust.

mu⌈ri⌉kai むりかい (無理解) *n., a.n.* (～ na) lack of understanding [sympathy]; inconsiderate. 《↔ rikai》

mu⌈ri-shi⌉ñjuu むりしんじゅう (無理心中) *n.* forced double suicide. 《⇨ shiñjuu》

mu⌈roñ むろん (無論) *adv.* = mochiroñ.

mu⌉ryoku むりょく (無力) *a.n.* (～ na/no) powerless; helpless; incompetent. 《↔ yuuryoku》

mu⌉ryoo むりょう (無料) *n.* no charge; free:
Sooryoo wa muryoo *desu.* (送料は無料です) The postage is *free.* 《↔ yuuryoo》

mu⌈señ むせん (無線) *n.* radio; wireless.

mu⌈shi[1] むし (虫) *n.* insect; bug; worm; vermin.
mushi ga [no] yoi (～が[の]よい) be selfish. 《⇨ wagamama》

mu⌉shi[2] むし (無視) *n.* disregard; neglect.
mushi suru (～する) *vt.* ignore; disregard.

mu⌈shiatsu⌉·i むしあつい (蒸し暑い) *a.* (-ku) sultry; hot and humid. 《⇨ musu》

mu⌈shiba むしば (虫歯) *n.* decayed [bad] tooth; cavity; caries.

mu⌉shiro むしろ (寧ろ) *adv.* rather (than):
Kare wa shoosetsuka to iu yori, mushiro *shijiñ desu.* (彼は小説家というより, むしろ詩人です) He is *more* of a poet than a novelist.

mu⌈shir·u むしる *vt.* (mushir·i-; mushir·a-; mushit-te [C]) pull up (weeds); pluck (feathers).

mu⌉s·u むす (蒸す) (mush·i-; mus·a-; mush·i-te [C]) **1** *vt.* steam:
jagaimo o musu (じゃがいもを蒸す) *steam* potatoes. 《⇨ fukasu[2]》
2 *vi.* (of weather, place, etc.) be sultry; be stuffy.

mu⌈subi むすび (結び) *n.* **1** end; finish; conclusion:
Kare ni musubi *no kotoba o tanoñda.* (彼に結びの言葉を頼んだ) We asked him to make some *closing* remarks. 《⇨ musubu》
2 rice ball. 《⇨ omusubi》

mu⌈subitsuke⌉·ru むすびつける (結び付ける) *vt.* (-tsuke-te [V])
1 tie; fasten:
inu no kusari o ki ni musubitsukeru (犬の鎖を木に結び付ける) fasten the dog's chain to a tree.
2 link; relate:
Sono futatsu no hañzai o musubitsukeru *shooko wa nani mo nai.* (その二つの犯罪を結び付ける証拠は何もない) There is no evidence at all that *links* the two crimes.

mu⌈sub·u むすぶ (結ぶ) *vt.* (musub·i-; musub·a-; musuñ-de [C])
1 tie (a ribbon); knot (a rope). 《⇨ musubi》
2 link; connect:
Hoñshuu to Shikoku o musubu *hashi ga kañsee shita.* (本州と四国を結ぶ橋が完成した) The bridges which *link* Honshu and Shikoku have been completed. 《⇨ musubitsukeru》
3 (*fig.*) bind:
Kare-ra wa yuujoo de musubarete ita. (彼らは友情で結ばれていた) They *were bound* together by their friendship.
4 conclude (a treaty, contract); form (an alliance).

mu⌈suko むすこ (息子) *n.* son.
★ Another person's son is called '*musuko-sañ.*' 《↔ musume》

mu⌈sume⌉ むすめ (娘) *n.*
1 daughter. ★ Another person's daughter is called '*musume-sañ.*' 《↔ musuko》
2 unmarried young woman; girl.

musu⌉u むすう (無数) *a.n.* (～ ni) countless; numberless.

mu⌈ttsu⌉ むっつ(六つ) *n.* six.
★ Used when counting.
《⇨ roku; APP. 3》

mu⌉udo ムード *n.* atmosphere.

mu⌉yami むやみ(無闇) *a.n.* (~ na, ni) **1** reckless; excessive:
Muyami *ni uñdoo suru no wa karada ni yoku nai.* (むやみに運動するのは体によくない) Exercising *excessively* is not good for you.
2 indiscriminate:
Muyami *ni kodomo o shikaranai hoo ga yoi.* (むやみに子どもをしからないほうがよい) You should not *indiscriminately* scold children.

mu⌉yoku むよく(無欲) *a.n.* (~ na, ni) disinterested; unselfish.
《↔ yokubari》

mu⌈yoo むよう(無用) *a.n.* (~ na, ni) unnecessary; useless:
Shiñpai wa muyoo *desu.* (心配は無用です) There is *no need* to worry.

mu⌈zukashi·i むずかしい(難しい) *a.* (-ku) **1** hard; difficult:
Kyoo no tesuto wa muzukashikatta. (きょうのテストは難しかった) Today's test *was difficult.*
《↔ yasashii[1]》
2 (of a procedure, a situation, etc.) troublesome; complicated.
★ Often used as a euphemism for the impossible.
3 (of character, personality, etc.) difficult to please; particular.

mya⌈ku⌉ みゃく(脈) *n.* pulse.

myo⌉o みょう(妙) *a.n.* (~ na, ni) strange; queer; funny; odd.

myo⌉obañ みょうばん(明晩) *n.* (*formal*) tomorrow evening; tomorrow night. 《↔ koñbañ》

myo⌈ochoo みょうちょう(明朝) *n.*, *adv.* (*formal*) tomorrow morning.
《↔ kesa》

myo⌈ogo⌉nichi みょうごにち(明後日) *n.* the day after tomorrow.
★ Formal equivalent of '*asatte*.'

myo⌉oji みょうじ(名字) *n.* family name; surname. 《⇨ namae》

myo⌉onichi みょうにち(明日) *n.* (*formal*) tomorrow. 《⇨ ashita》

N

ñ ん [the contracted form of either the noun or particle '*no*']
★ In speech, '*no da* [*desu*]' is often contracted to '*ñ da* [*desu*].'
Kono kasa wa watashi ñ [no] *desu.* (この傘は私ん[の]です) This umbrella is *mine.* / *Doo sureba ii* ñ [no] *deshoo ka?* (どうすればいいん[の]でしょうか) What shall I do?
《⇨ no[1], no[2] (3)》

na[1] な(名) *n.* **1** name; title.
《⇨ namae》
2 fame; reputation:
Kare wa Nihoñ de wa na ga shirarete iru. (彼は日本では名が知られている) He is *well-known* in Japan.
na mo nai (~もない) nameless; obscure.

na[2] な *p.* (*rude*) do not (do):
★ Used to indicate prohibition or to give a negative order. Used usually by men.
Shibafu ni hairu na. (芝生に入るな) *Do not walk* on the grass.

na[3] な *p.* (*rude*) (used to give an order): ★ An abbreviation of '*nasai*.'
Motto hayaku aruki na. (もっと速く歩きな) *Walk* faster.

na(a) な(あ) *p.* **1** (used to indicate emotion):
Ii teñki da na. (いい天気だな) *What* nice weather it is!
2 (used when seeking agreement): ★ Used mainly by men.
Ashita wa atsui deshoo na. (あしたは暑いでしょうな) It will be hot tomorrow, *won't it*?

na⌉be なべ(鍋) *n.* pan; pot.

na⌈bi⌉k·u なびく(靡く) *vi.* (nabik·i-; nabik·a-; nabi·i-te [C]) (of a flag) flutter; wave; stream.

na⌈daka⌉·i なだかい (名高い) *a.* (-ku) famous; well-known; noted. ⟪⇨ yuumee⟫

na⌈dare⌉ なだれ (雪崩) *n.* snow-slide; avalanche.

na⌈de⌉·ru なでる (撫でる) *vt.* (na-de-te [V]) stroke; pat; pet: *kodomo no atama o* naderu (子どもの頭をなでる) *stroke* a child's head.

na⌉do など (等) *p.* **1** such as; and the like: ★ Used to give examples. Follows nouns, usually in the pattern '*ya* ... (*ya*) ... *nado*.'
Kono machi ni wa jiñja ya tera nado *furui tatemono ga takusañ arimasu.* (この町には神社や寺など古い建物がたくさんあります) In this town there are lots of old buildings, *such as* temples and shrines.
2 or whatever: ★ Used when giving one representative example.
Sono heñ de biiru nado *ip-pai ikaga desu ka?* (その辺でビールなど一杯いかがですか) What about a beer, *or whatever*, over there?
3 (used to express humility when referring to oneself, one's relatives, or one's possessions):
Watashi no koto nado *doozo o-kamai naku.* (私のことなどどうぞおかまいなく) Please don't worry yourself *about me*.
4 (used in expressions of negation, disavowal, or scorn):
Koñna tsumaranai koto de keñka nado *yoshi nasai.* (こんなつまらないことでけんかなどよしなさい) Don't argue about *something* that is as unimportant as this. ⟪⇨ nañte[2]⟫
5 (used to add emphasis):
Kare wa uso nado *tsuku yoo na hito de wa arimaseñ.* (彼はうそなどつくような人ではありません) He is not the kind of person that would do *something like* tell a lie.

na⌉e なえ (苗) *n.* seedling; young plant.

na⌈fuda なふだ (名札) *n.* name card; tag; nameplate.

na⌈ga- なが (長) *pref.* long: naga-*ame* (長雨) a *long* rain / naga-*banashi* (長話) a *long* talk.

na⌈gabi⌉k·u ながびく (長引く) *vi.* (-bik·i-; -bik·a-; -bi·i-te [C]) be prolonged; drag on.

na⌈gagutsu ながぐつ (長靴) *n.* boots; rubber boots; Wellington boots.

na⌈ga⌉·i ながい (長い) *a.* (-ku)
1 (of length, distance) long:
Nihoñ de ichibañ nagai *kawa* (日本で一番長い川) the *longest* river in Japan. ⟪↔ mijikai⟫ ⟪⇨ nagasa⟫
2 (of time) long:
Koochoo señsee no hanashi wa totemo nagakatta. (校長先生の話はとても長かった) The headmaster's speech was very *long*.
⟪↔ mijikai⟫

na⌈gaiki⌉ ながいき (長生き) *n.* long life; longevity.
nagaiki (o) suru (〜(を)する) *vi.* live long; outlive.

na⌈game⌉ ながめ (眺め) *n.* view; scene; prospect. ⟪⇨ nagameru⟫

na⌈game⌉·ru ながめる (眺める) *vt.* (nagame-te [V]) look at; watch; view:
mado kara soto o nagameru (窓から外を眺める) *look* out of the window. ⟪⇨ nagame⟫

na⌈ganeñ ながねん (長年) *n.* many years; a long time.

-nagara ながら (乍ら) *suf.* [attached to the continuative base of a verb, an adjectival noun or the dictionary form of an adjective]
1 while; as: ★ Used to show that two actions are simultaneous.
Watashi wa sutereo o kiki-nagara, *beñkyoo shimasu.* (私はステレオを聞きながら, 勉強します) I study *while* listening to the stereo.
2 though; yet: ★ Used to indicate a contrast or an unexpected

result or situation.
Karada ni warui to shiri-nagara, *tabako wa yameraremaseñ.* (体に悪いと知りながら, たばこはやめられません) *Though* I know cigarettes are bad for me, I cannot give them up.
3 (used in fixed, introductory expressions):
Zañneñ-nagara, *kono jiko de ooku no kata ga nakunarimashita.* (残念ながら, この事故で多くの方が亡くなりました) *To my deep regret*, a great many people died in this accident.

na⌈gare⌉ ながれ (流れ) *n.* **1** flow; stream:
Kono kawa wa nagare ga hayai. (この川は流れが速い) This river *flows fast.* 《⇨ nagareru》
2 current; momentum:
Kare wa toki no nagare *ni umaku notta.* (彼は時の流れにうまくのった) He skillfully took advantage of the *current* of the times.

na⌈gare⌉·ru ながれる (流れる) *vi.* (nagare-te Ⓥ) **1** flow; run; stream. 《⇨ nagare》
2 (of a bridge, building, etc.) be washed away. 《⇨ nagasu》
3 pass:
Are kara juu-neñ no saigetsu ga nagareta. (あれから10年の歳月が流れた) Ten years *have passed* since then. 《⇨ nagare》
4 (of a game, meeting, etc.) be rained out. 《⇨ chuushi》

na⌉gasa ながさ (長さ) *n.* length. 《⇨ haba; nagai》

na⌈gashi⌉[1] ながし (流し) *n.* sink.

na⌉gashi[2] ながし (流し) *n.* cruising (taxi): nagashi *no takushii* (流しのタクシー) a *cruising* taxi.

na⌈ga⌉s·u ながす (流す) *vt.* (nagash·i-; nagas·a-; nagash·i-te Ⓒ) **1** pour; let flow; shed:
furo no mizu o nagasu (ふろの水を流す) *let* the bath water *out.* 《⇨ nagareru》
2 wash away (a bridge, etc.):
Taifuu de hashi ga nagasareta. (台風で橋が流された) A bridge *was washed away* in the typhoon. 《⇨ nagareru》
3 wash down:
Señtoo de kare no senaka o nagashite yatta. (銭湯で彼の背中を流してやった) I *washed down* his back in the public bath.

na⌈ge⌉k·u なげく (嘆く) *vi.* (nagek·i-; nagek·a-; nage·i-te Ⓒ) grieve; deplore; regret. 《⇨ kanashimu》

na⌈ge⌉·ru なげる (投げる) *vt.* (nage-te Ⓥ) **1** throw; hurl; fling; pitch; toss: *inu ni ishi o* nageru (犬に石を投げる) *throw* a stone at a dog. 《⇨ hooru[1]》
2 abandon (a plan, attempt, etc.); give up.

na⌈gori⌉ なごり (名残) *n.* **1** parting; farewell:
Futari wa nagori o oshiñda. (二人は名残を惜しんだ) The couple were *reluctant to part.*
2 trace; remains:
Sono mura ni wa mada señsoo no nagori *ga atta.* (その村にはまだ戦争の名残があった) There were still *traces* of the war in the village.

na⌈go⌉yaka なごやか (和やか) *a.n.* (~ na, ni) peaceful; friendly.

na⌈gu⌉r·u なぐる (殴る) *vt.* (nagur·i-; nagur·a-; nagut-te Ⓒ) strike; hit; knock; beat.

na⌈gusame⌉·ru なぐさめる (慰める) *vt.* (nagusame-te Ⓥ) comfort; console; cheer up.

na⌉·i ない (無い) *a.* (-ku) ★ Not used attributively. Polite forms are '*arimaseñ*' and '*nai desu.*'
1 no; do not exist:
Kono buñ ni machigai wa nai. (この文に間違いはない) There are *no* mistakes in this sentence. 《↔ aru[2]》
2 no; do not have:
Hoñ o yomu hima ga nai. (本を読む暇がない) I *have no* time to read. 《↔ aru[2]》

3 be free (from):
Kare no seekatsu wa mattaku kuroo ga nai. (彼の生活はまったく苦労がない) His life *is* quite *free* from care. ⟪↔ aru²⟫
4 (of a thing, an article, etc.) be missing: ⟪↔ aru²⟫
★ Follows the *ku*-form of other adjectives to make the negative form. *Kyoo wa isogashiku* nai. (きょうは忙しくない) I am *not* busy today.

-na·i¹ ない *infl. end.* (-ku) [attached to the negative base of a verb, and inflected like an adjective] do not; will not; cannot:
Kono mado wa dooshite mo akanai. (この窓はどうしても開かない) This window *won't open.*

-na˥·i² ない (無い) *suf.* (*a.*) (-ku) [added to a limited number of nouns to make a negative adjective]
nasake-nai (情けない) *shameful* / shikata-nai (仕方ない) *unavoidable.*

-nai³ ない (内) *suf.* in; inside; within:
Sha-nai *no o-tabako wa go-eñryo kudasai.* (車内のおたばこはご遠慮ください) Please refrain from smoking *in* the vehicle.

na˥ibu ないぶ (内部) *n.* **1** inside; interior:
kyookai no naibu (教会の内部) the *interior* of a church. ⟪↔ gaibu⟫
2 internal affairs. ⟪↔ gaibu⟫

na˥ifu ナイフ *n.* knife. ★ 'Kitchen knife' is called '*hoochoo.*'

na⌈ifuku˥yaku ないふくやく (内服薬) *n.* medicine to be taken internally. ⟪⇨ kusuri⟫

na⌈ika ないか (内科) *n.* internal medicine: naika-i (内科医) a *physician.* ⟪⇨ geka⟫

na˥ikaku ないかく (内閣) *n.* cabinet:
naikaku *o soshiki* [*kaizoo*] *suru* (内閣を組織[改造]する) form [reshuffle] a *cabinet.*

Na˥ikaku-so⌈orida˥ijiñ ないかくそうりだいじん (内閣総理大臣) *n.* the Prime Minister.

na˥ishi ないし (乃至) *conj.* (*formal*)
1 from...to...; between...and...:
Kono shigoto wa kañsee made ni, tooka naishi *ni-shuukañ kakarimasu.* (この仕事は完成までに, 10 日ないし 2 週間かかります) It will take *between* ten days *and* two weeks before this job is finished.
⟪⇨ mata-wa⟫
2 or:
Dairiniñ wa haiguusha naishi *oyako ni kagirimasu.* (代理人は配偶者ないし親子に限ります) The proxy must be a spouse, *or* parent or child.

na⌈ishiñ ないしん (内心) *n.*, *adv.* one's inmost heart; at heart; inwardly:
Kare wa naishiñ *bikubiku shite ita.* (彼は内心びくびくしていた) He was *inwardly* nervous. ⟪⇨ kokoro⟫

na⌈isho˥ ないしょ (内緒·内証) *n.* secrecy; secret:
Kono keekaku wa kare ni wa naisho *ni shite kudasai.* (この計画は彼にはないしょにしてください) Please keep this plan a *secret* from him.

na⌈isoo ないそう (内装) *n.* interior decoration [furnishings]; upholstery. ⟪↔ gaisoo⟫

na⌈iyoo ないよう (内容) *n.* contents; substance. ⟪↔ keeshiki⟫

na⌈iyoo-mi˥hoñ ないようみほん (内容見本) *n.* sample pages; prospectus.

na⌈izoo ないぞう (内臓) *n.* internal organs.

na˥ka¹ なか (中) *n.* **1** inside; interior:
Kono koppu wa naka *ga yogorete iru.* (このコップは中が汚れている) This glass is dirty on the *inside.*
⟪↔ soto⟫ ⟪⇨ uchi²⟫
2 in; into:
Uchi no naka *e hairi nasai.* (家の中へ入りなさい) Please come *into* the house. ⟪↔ soto⟫
3 middle:

Kare-ra wa fubuki no naka *o deka-keta.* (彼らは吹雪の中を出かけた) They went out in the *middle* of the blizzard.

4 of; among:

Sono shinamono no naka *ni wa furyoohiñ ga atta.* (その品物の中には不良品があった) There were some defective items *among* the goods.

na⌉ka[2] なか (仲) *n.* relation; terms: naka *ga ii* [*warui*] (仲がいい[悪い]) be on good [bad] *terms.*

na⌈kaba⌉ なかば (半ば) *n.* middle; halfway:

sañ-gatsu nakaba (三月半ば) *mid-*March.

— *adv.* half; partly:

Ima no wa nakaba *joodañ desu.* (今のは半ば冗談です) I was *half* joking. ⟪⇨ hañbuñ⟫

na⌈kama⌉ なかま (仲間) *n.* friend; fellow; comrade:

Watashi wa sono nakama *ni haitta.* (私はその仲間に入った) I joined in the *group.*

na⌈ka⌉mi なかみ (中身) *n.* contents; substance. ⟪⇨ naiyoo⟫

na⌈kanaka なかなか (中々) *adv.*

1 very; quite:

Kanojo no Nihoñgo wa nakanaka *umai.* (彼女の日本語はなかなかうまい) Her Japanese is *pretty* good.

2 (with a negative) easily; readily:

Kono futa wa nakanaka *torenai.* (このふたはなかなか取れない) This lid will not come off *easily.*

na⌈kana⌉ori なかなおり (仲直り) *n.* reconciliation.

nakanaori suru (～する) *vi.* be reconciled; make up.

na⌈kase·ru なかせる (泣かせる) *vt.* (nakase-te [V]) **1** make a person cry; move a person to tears. ⟪⇨ naku[1]⟫

2 (*fig.*) cause trouble [a problem].

na⌈kas·u なかす (泣かす) *vt.* (na-kash·i-; nakas·a-; nakash·i-te [C]) = nakaseru.

na⌉kayoku s·uru なかよくする (仲良くする) *vi.* (sh·i-; sh·i-; sh·i-te [I]) make friends with; get on well.

na⌈ka⌉yubi なかゆび (中指) *n.* middle finger.

-na⌉kereba i⌈kenai なければいけない (*polite*＝'*-nakereba ikemaseñ*') must do (something): ★ Literally 'Unless someone does..., it cannot go.'

Isha ni kono kusuri o nomanakereba ikenai *to iwareta.* (医者にこの薬を飲まなければいけないと言われた) I was told by the doctor that I *had to take* this medicine.

-na⌉kereba na⌈ra⌉nai なければならない (*polite*＝'*-nakereba narimaseñ*') must do (something): ★ Literally, 'Unless someone does..., it will not do.'

Koñshuu-chuu ni kore o shinakereba naranai. (今週中にこれをしなければならない) I *must finish* this within this week.

na⌈kigo⌉e[1] なきごえ (泣き声) *n.* cry; sob; whine. ⟪↔ waraigoe⟫

na⌈kigo⌉e[2] なきごえ (鳴き声) *n.* song; note; bark:

kotori no nakigoe (小鳥の鳴き声) a little bird's *song.* ⟪⇨ naku[2]⟫

na⌈ko⌉odo なこうど (仲人) *n.* matchmaker; go-between:

nakoodo *o suru* (仲人をする) act as *go-between.* ⟪⇨ miai⟫

na⌈k·u[1] なく (泣く) *vi.* (nak·i-; nak·a-; na·i-te [C]) cry; weep; sob; shed tears. ⟪⇨ nakaseru⟫

na⌈k·u[2] なく (鳴く) *vi.* (nak·i-; nak·a-; na·i-te [C]) **1** (of insects, birds) sing; cry.

2 (of animals) bark; roar; bleat.

na⌈kunar·u[1] なくなる (無くなる) *vi.* (-nar·i-; -nar·a-; -nat-te [C])

1 run out:

Kozukai ga nakunatte shimatta. (小遣いがなくなってしまった) I *have used up* all my pocket money. ⟪⇨ nakusu[1]⟫

2 be missing:

Kono hoñ wa ni-peeji nakunatte

iru. (この本は2ページなくなっている) This book *is missing* two pages.

3 be gone; disappear:
Ha no itami ga nakunatta. (歯の痛みがなくなった) The pain in my tooth *has gone*.

na'kunar·u² なくなる (亡くなる) *vi.* (-nar·i-; -nar·a-; -nat-te Ⓒ) pass away; die. ★ Euphemistic equivalent of '*shinu*.' ⟪⇨ nakusu²⟫

na'kus·u¹ なくす (無くす) *vt.* (nakush·i-; nakus·a-; nakush·i-te Ⓒ) **1** lose:
Watashi wa kurejitto kaado o nakushite shimatta. (私はクレジットカードをなくしてしまった) I *have lost* my credit card. ⟪⇨ nakunaru¹⟫

2 get rid of; abolish:
Koñna warui shuukañ wa nakusu *beki da*. (こんな悪い習慣はなくすべきだ) This kind of evil custom should *be abolished*.

na'kus·u² なくす (亡くす) *vt.* (nakush·i-; nakus·a-; nakush·i-te Ⓒ) lose (a close relative); be bereft of:
Kare wa tsuma o gañ de nakushita. (彼は妻をがんで亡くした) He *lost* his wife to cancer. ⟪⇨ nakunaru²⟫

n

na'ma なま (生) *n.* **1** raw; uncooked:
Kono sakana wa nama *de taberaremasu*. (この魚は生で食べられます) You can eat this fish *raw*.

2 live; direct: nama *no oñgaku* (生の音楽) *live* music.

na'ma- なま (生) *pref.* **1** raw; fresh: nama-*yasai* (生野菜) *raw* vegetables.

2 live: nama-*hoosoo* (生放送) a *live* broadcast.

na'ma-bi'iru なまビール (生ビール) draft beer. ★ Beer not sterilized by heating.

na'mae なまえ (名前) *n.* **1** name.

2 given name. ⟪⇨ myooji; na¹⟫

na'magusa'·i なまぐさい (生臭い) *a.* (-ku) (of smell) fishy:
namagusai *nioi* (生臭いにおい) a *fishy* smell.

na'maiki なまいき (生意気) *a.n.* (~ na, ni) cheeky; saucy; impudent; impertinent.

na'make'·ru なまける (怠ける) *vi.* (namake-te Ⓥ) be lazy; idle away; neglect. ⟪↔ kiñbeñ⟫

na'manuru'·i なまぬるい (生温い) *adj.* (-ku) **1** (of liquid) lukewarm; tepid.

2 (of a method) mild; soft; wishy-washy.

na'mari¹ なまり (訛) *n.* dialect; accent.

na'mari'² なまり (鉛) *n.* lead.

na'ma-ta'mago なまたまご (生卵) *n.* raw egg.

na'me'raka なめらか (滑らか) *a.n.* (~ na, ni) smooth.

na'me'·ru なめる (嘗める) *vt.* (name-te Ⓥ) **1** lick; lap.

2 suck (candy); eat:
ame o nameru (あめをなめる) *suck* a candy.

3 make light of:
aite o nameru (相手をなめる) *underestimate* one's rival.

na'mi¹ なみ (並) *n.* average; medium; ordinary; common. ⟪⇨ futsuu¹⟫

na'mi'² なみ (波) *n.* wave; surf.

-nami なみ (並み) *suf.* ordinary; the same level:
Kare wa kazoku-nami *ni atsukawareta*. (彼は家族並みに扱われた) He was treated *like* a member of the family.

na'mida なみだ (涙) *n.* tear:
namida *o nagasu* (涙を流す) shed *tears*.

na'miki なみき (並木) *n.* row of trees.

na'ñ なん (何) *n.* ★ Variant of '*nani*.' ⟪⇨ nani⟫

1 what:
Are wa nañ *desu ka?* (あれは何ですか) *What* is that?

2 how:
Anata wa kono kaisha ni nañ-*neñ tsutomemashita ka?* (あなたはこの会

社に何年勤めましたか) *How* many years have you worked for this company? ⟪⇨ iku-⟫

3 many:

Kono shigoto o oeru no ni nañ-neñ *mo kakarimashita.* (この仕事を終えるのに何年もかかりました) It took *many* years to finish this work.

na⌉na なな(七) *n.* seven. ★ Usually used in compounds. ⟪⇨ nanatsu; shichi; APP. 3⟫

na⌈na⌉me ななめ(斜め) *a.n.* (~ no, ni) **1** oblique; slant:

michi o naname *ni oodañ suru* (道を斜めに横断する) cross a road *diagonally.*

2 in a bad humor:

Kanojo wa ima go-kigeñ naname *da.* (彼女は今ご機嫌斜めだ) She is now *in a bad mood.*

na⌈na⌉tsu ななつ(七つ) *n.* seven; the seventh. ★ Used when counting. ⟪⇨ nana; shichi; APP. 3⟫

na⌉ñboku なんぼく(南北) *n.* north and south. ⟪⇨ toozai⟫

na⌉ñ da ka なんだか(何だか) *adv.* somehow; somewhat:

Kyoo wa nañ da ka *kibuñ ga warui.* (きょうは何だか気分が悪い) Today I feel *somewhat* out of sorts.

na⌉ñ de なんで(何で) *adv.* why:

Kare wa nañ de *okotta ñ desu ka?* (彼は何で怒ったんですか) *Why* is it that he got angry? ⟪⇨ naze⟫

na⌉ñ de mo なんでも(何でも) *adv.*

1 anything; everything; whatever:

Nañ de mo *hoshii mono ga attara, ii nasai.* (何でも欲しいものがあったら, 言いなさい) If there is *anything* you want, please mention it.

2 I hear; they say: ★ Used to avoid direct agreement, judgment, or opinion.

Nañ de mo *kare no byooki wa omoi rashii.* (何でも彼の病気は重いらしい) *They say* that his illness seems grave.

3 (with a negative) nothing:

Koñna shigoto wa nañ de mo *nai.* (こんな仕事は何でもない) There is *nothing* to this kind of job.

na⌉ñ-do なんど(何度) *adv.*

1 how many times; how often:

Kyooto ni wa nañ-do *ikimashita ka?* (京都には何度行きましたか) *How often* have you been to Kyoto?

2 how many degrees:

Netsu wa nañ-do *arimasu ka?* (熱は何度ありますか) *How much* is your temperature?

nañ-do mo (~も) many times.

na⌉ni なに(何) *n.* what:

Nani *ga atta ñ desu ka?* (何があったんですか) *What* happened? ⟪⇨ nani-ka⟫

— *int.* what; why:

Nani, *kare ga jiko o okoshita tte.* (なに, 彼が事故を起こしたって) *What!* You mean he has caused an accident!

na⌉ni-ka なにか(何か) *n., adv.* something; anything:

Nani-ka *nomimono o kudasai.* (何か飲み物を下さい) Please give me *something* to drink.

na⌈ni mo なにも(何も) *adv.* (with a negative) nothing:

Watashi wa kare to nani mo *kañkee arimaseñ.* (私は彼と何も関係ありません) I have *nothing* to do with him.

na⌉ni-shiro なにしろ(何しろ) *adv.* at any rate; anyway:

Nani-shiro *yatte miru koto desu.* (何しろやってみることです) *At any rate,* the important thing is to try.

na⌉ni-yara なにやら(何やら) *adv.* some; something:

Inaka kara nani-yara *okutte kita.* (田舎から何やら送ってきた) I have received *something* sent from the country.

na⌉ni-yori なにより(何より) *adv.* (~ no) better [more] than anything else:

Keñkoo ga nani-yori *desu.* (健康が何よりです) Health is the *most important* thing.

n

na]ñ-ka なんか（何か）*n., adv.* (*informal*) = nani-ka.

na[ñkyoku なんきょく（難局）*n.* difficult situation; difficulty.

Na[ñkyoku なんきょく（南極）*n.* South Pole:
Nañkyoku-*tairiku*（南極大陸）the *Antarctic* Continent. ⟪↔ Hokkyoku⟫

na[noka] なのか（七日）*n.* seven days; the seventh day of the month. ★ Also pronounced '*nanuka*.' ⟪⇨ APP. 5⟫

na]ñra-ka なんらか（何らか）*n.* some; any:
Fukeeki ni taishite nañra-ka *no taisaku o tateru hitsuyoo ga aru.*（不景気に対してなんらかの対策を立てる必要がある）We have to take *some* measures against the business depression.

na]ñte[1] なんて（何て）*adv.* how; what:
Kesa wa nañte *samui ñ daroo.*（今朝は何て寒いんだろう）*How* cold it is this morning!

nañte[2] なんて *p.* such; like:
★ Follows a noun or the dictionary form of a verb and implies a degree of criticism.
Ano hito ga nusumi o suru nañte *shiñjirarenai.*（あの人が盗みをするなんて信じられない）I cannot believe that he would do *such* a thing *as* steal.

na]ñ to なんと（何と）*adv.*
1 what: ★ Used in a question.
Kare wa ima nañ to *iimashita ka?*（彼はいま何と言いましたか）*What* did he say just now?
2 how; in what way:
Nañ to *o-wabi shite yoi ka wakarimaseñ.*（何とおわびしてよいかわかりません）I do not kow *how* I can apologize.
3 what; how: ★ Used in an exclamation of surprise.
Nañ to *kare wa kyuujus-sai datta.*（何と彼は90歳だった）*To my surprise*, he was ninety.

na]ñ to ka なんとか（何とか）*adv.* one way or another; anyhow; somehow:
Nañ to ka *shikeñ ni gookaku shimashita.*（何とか試験に合格しました）I *barely* passed the exam.
nañ to ka suru（～する）manage to do: *Kono keñ wa getsumatsu made ni* nañ to ka shimasu.（この件は月末までに何とかします）I will *manage to do* it by the end of this month.

na[ñ-to-na]ku なんとなく（何と無く）*adv.* somehow; vaguely; for some reason or other:
Kyoo wa nañ-to-naku, *sore o yaru ki ga shinai.*（きょうは何となく，それをやる気がしない）*Somehow* I have no mind to do it today.

na[nuka なぬか（七日）*n.* = nanoka. ⟪⇨ APP. 5⟫

na]o[1] なお（尚）*adv.* still; even:
Daibu yoku natte kimashita ga nao *chuui ga hitsuyoo desu.*（だいぶよくなってきましたがなお注意が必要です）You have gotten much better, but care is *still* necessary.

na]o[2] なお（尚）*conj.* furthermore:
Nao, *shoosai wa nochi-hodo o-shirase itashimasu.*（なお，詳細は後ほどお知らせいたします）*Furthermore*, we will inform you of the details later.

na[o]r·u[1] なおる（直る）*vi.* (naor·i-; naor·a-; naot-te Ⓒ) **1** be fixed; be mended; be repaired. ⟪⇨ naosu[1]⟫
2 (of a mistake) be corrected. ⟪⇨ naosu[1]⟫
3 (of a mood, temper) be restored:
Kanojo no kigeñ ga naotta.（彼女の機嫌が直った）Her good mood *has been restored*. ⟪⇨ naosu[1]⟫

na[o]r·u[2] なおる（治る）*vi.* (naor·i-; naor·a-; naot-te Ⓒ) (of a person, injury, illness, etc.) recover; get well; be cured; be healed. ⟪⇨ naosu[2]⟫

na[o-sara なおさら（尚更）*adv.* all

the more; still more.

na[o]s·u[1] なおす (直す) *vt.* (nao-sh·i-; naos·a-; naosh·i-te C)
1 mend; repair; fix. ⟪⇨ naoru[1]⟫
2 correct (a mistake); remedy.
3 adjust:
tokee no hari o naosu (時計の針を直す) *adjust* a watch.
4 translate; convert; turn:
Nihoñgo o Eego ni naosu (日本語を英語に直す) *translate* Japanese into English. ⟪⇨ yakusu⟫

na[o]s·u[2] なおす (治す) *vt.* (nao-sh·i-; naos·a-; naosh·i-te C)
cure (a disease); heal. ⟪⇨ naoru[2]⟫

nara なら [provisional form of '*da*'] ★ The more literary variant '*naraba*' can be used to emphasize the idea of condition.
1 when it comes to...; as far as... is concerned; if:
Deñsha nara, *nijip-puñ mo kakarimaseñ.* (電車なら, 20 分もかかりません) *If* you go by train, it won't even take twenty minutes.
2 provided that; if:
Tanaka-sañ ga ikanai no nara, *boku mo ikimaseñ.* (田中さんが行かないのなら, ぼくも行きません) *If* Miss Tanaka does not go, I will not go, either.
3 the more...the more:
Fukuzatsu nara *fukuzatsu na hodo tsukai nikui.* (複雑なら複雑なほど使いにくい) *The more* complicated it is, *the harder* it is to use.
⟪⇨ -ba[1]; to[1]; -tara⟫

na[rabe·ru ならべる (並べる) *vt.* (narabe-te V) **1** arrange; line up:
tsukue o ichi-retsu ni naraberu (机を一列に並べる) *arrange* the desks in one row. ⟪⇨ narabu⟫
2 display; spread (dishes).
⟪⇨ narabu⟫

na[rabi ni ならびに (並びに) *conj.* (*formal*) and; as well as:
Nihoñ narabi ni *Kañkoku* (日本ならびに韓国) Japan *and* Korea.
⟪⇨ soshite; to[2]⟫

na[rab·u ならぶ (並ぶ) *vi.* (nara-b·i-; narab·a-; narañ-de C)
1 stand in a row; form a line [queue]. ⟪⇨ naraberu⟫
2 rank; be equal:
Watashi-tachi no aida de wa go-rufu de kare ni narabu *mono wa imaseñ.* (私たちの間ではゴルフで彼に並ぶものはいません) In our group, there is no one *equal* to him in golf.

na[ra]nai ならない (*polite* = *nari-maseñ*) **1** must not; should not:
★ Used in the pattern '*-te wa naranai*' to indicate prohibition.
Kono koto o kare ni itte wa naranai. (このことを彼に言ってはならない) You *should not* tell him about this matter.
2 must; have to; need to:
★ Used in the pattern '*-nakereba [-nakute wa] naranai*' to indicate necessity.
Moo ikanakereba naranai. (もう行かなければならない) I *must* be going now.
3 cannot help: ★ Used with a *te*-form of a verb, adjective or the copula to indicate that one cannot prevent oneself from doing something.
Kare wa uso o tsuite iru yoo ni omoete naranai. (彼はうそをついているように思えてならない) I *cannot help* thinking that he is telling a lie.
4 cannot:
Moo gamañ ga naranai. (もうがまんがならない) I *cannot* stand any more.

na[ras·u[1] ならす (鳴らす) *vt.* (na-rash·i-; naras·a-; narash·i-te C)
1 ring (a bell); sound (a siren); blow (a horn). ⟪⇨ naru[2]⟫
2 (of a person) be popular.

na[ra]s·u[2] ならす (慣らす) *vt.* (na-rash·i-; naras·a-; narash·i-te C)
accustom; train:
Nihoñgo no hatsuoñ ni mimi o narasu (日本語の発音に耳を慣らす) *accustom* one's ears to the pronunciation of Japanese.
⟪⇨ nareru⟫

na⌈ra⌉·u ならう(習う) *vt.* (nara·i-; naraw·a-; narat-te Ⓒ) learn; study; practice; take lessons: *piano o* narau (ピアノを習う) *take* piano lessons. ⟪⇨ manabu⟫

na⌈renareshi⌉·i なれなれしい(馴れ馴れしい) *a.* (-ku) overfamiliar; too friendly.

na⌈re⌉·ru なれる(慣れる) *vi.* (nare-te Ⓥ) become accustomed: *Nihoñ no seekatsu ni* nareru (日本の生活に慣れる) *become accustomed* to life in Japan. ⟪⇨ narasu[2]⟫

nari[1] なり *p.* or: ★ Follows a noun or the dictionary form of a verb and implies a choice among two or more alternatives.
Wakaranai toki wa señsee ni kiku nari *jisho de shiraberu* nari *shi nasai.* (わからないときは先生に聞くなり辞書で調べるなりしなさい) When you do not understand, ask the teacher, look it up in your dictionary, *or* do something. ⟪⇨ aruiwa[1]; mata-wa⟫

nari[2] なり *p.* as soon as: ★ Follows the dictionary form of a verb.
Kare wa kaette kuru nari, *nete shimatta.* (彼は帰ってくるなり，寝てしまった) He went straight to sleep *as soon as* he returned.

na⌈ritats·u なりたつ(成り立つ) *vi.* (-tach·i-; -tat·a-; -tat-te Ⓒ)
1 be made up; consist.
2 materialize; be realized:
Shikiñ ga areba kono kikaku wa naritachimasu. (資金があればこの企画は成り立ちます) Provided we have the funds, this project will *be realized.* ⟪⇨ seeritsu⟫

na⌉r·u[1] なる(成る) *vi.* (nar·i-; nar·a-; nat-te Ⓒ) **1** (of a person) become; grow:
Kare wa isha ni natta. (彼は医者になった) He *became* a doctor.
2 (of time, season, etc.) come; grow; set in:
Yatto haru ni natta. (やっと春になった) At last spring *has come.*
3 come to do; begin to do:
Watashi wa kare ga suki ni natta. (私は彼が好きになった) I *have come* to like him.
4 change; turn:
Shiñgoo ga ao ni natta. (信号が青になった) The traffic light *turned* green.
5 become of:
Sono go kare ga doo natta *ka shirimaseñ.* (その後彼がどうなったか知りません) I do not know what *became of* him after that.
6 (of a number, quantity, etc.) amount; total:
Zeñbu de ikura ni narimasu *ka?* (全部でいくらになりますか) How much does it *come* to altogether?
7 (of age) reach:
Kanojo wa raineñ hatachi ni narimasu. (彼女は来年二十歳になります) She will *be* twenty next year.
8 (*formal*) (of time) pass:
Nihoñ ni kite, ni-neñ ni narimasu. (日本に来て，2年になります) Two years *have passed* since I came to Japan.
9 act; serve:
Kare wa sono kaigi de gichoo to natta. (彼はその会議で議長となった) He *was elected* chairman at the meeting.
10 be made up; consist:
Kono kurasu wa yoñjuugo-niñ kara natte imasu. (このクラスは45人からなっています) This class *is made up* of forty-five people.
★ Honorific expressions are formed with '*o-*' plus the continuative base of a verb plus '*ni naru.*' *e.g. Kono hoñ o* o-yomi ni narimasu *ka?* (この本をお読みになりますか) Would you like to *read* this book?

na⌈r·u[2] なる(鳴る) *vi.* (nar·i-; nar·a-; nat-te Ⓒ) ring; sound; chime; toll. ⟪⇨ narasu[1]⟫

na⌉r·u[3] なる(生る) *vi.* (nar·i-; nar·a-; nat-te Ⓒ) (of a plant) bear fruit; (of fruit) grow.

na⌈rubeku なるべく(成る可く) *adv.*
1 as...as possible; to the best of one's ability:
Narubeku *ooki-na koe de hanashite kudasai.* (なるべく大きな声で話してください) Please speak *as* loudly *as possible.*
2 if possible:
Narubeku (*nara*) *ashita made ni kono shigoto o shiagete kudasai.* (なるべく(なら)あしたまでにこの仕事を仕上げてください) I want you to finish this work by tomorrow, *if possible.*

na⌈ruhodo なるほど(成る程) *adv.*
1 I see; I admit:
Naruhodo, *watashi no machigai deshita.* (なるほど, 私の間違いでした) *I admit* it was my mistake.
2 indeed; to be sure.

na⌈sa⌉i なさい (used to express an imperative): ★ The imperative form of '*nasaru*.' Follows the continuative base of a verb.
Tsugi no moñdai o toki nasai. (次の問題を解きなさい) *Solve* the following problems.

na⌉sake なさけ(情け) *n.* sympathy; mercy; charity; kindness:
hito ni nasake *o kakeru* (人に情けをかける) show *sympathy* to a person.

na⌈sakebuka⌉·i なさけぶかい(情け深い) *a.* (-ku) kindhearted; warmhearted; merciful.

na⌈sakena⌉·i なさけない(情けない) *a.* (-ku) shameful; deplorable; miserable.

na⌈sa⌉r·u なさる(為さる) *vt.* (nasai-; nasar·a-; nasat-te Ⓒ) do:
★ Honorific equivalent of '*suru*.'
Ashita wa doo nasaimasu *ka?* (あしたはどうなさいますか) What are you going to *do* tomorrow?
《⇨ nasai》

na⌉shi[1] なし(無し) *n.* nothing:
Ijoo nashi. (異常なし) There is *nothing* abnormal. 《⇨ nai》

na⌈shi⌉[2] なし(梨) *n.* pear; pear tree.

na⌉su[1] なす(茄子) *n.* eggplant.

na⌉s·u[2] なす(為す) *vt.* (nash·i-; nas·a-; nash·i-te Ⓒ) (*formal*) do:
Kare ni wa kare no nasu *beki koto ga aru.* (彼には彼のなすべきことがある) He has to do what he has to *do.*

na⌈tsu⌉ なつ(夏) *n.* summer.
《⇨ shiki[1]》

na⌈tsukashi⌉·i なつかしい(懐かしい) *a.* (-ku) dear; good old; longed-for:
Furusato ga natsukashii. (ふるさとが懐かしい) I *long for* my hometown.

na⌈tsumi⌉kañ なつみかん(夏蜜柑) *n.* Chinese citron.

na⌈tsu-ya⌉sumi なつやすみ(夏休み) *n.* summer vacation. 《⇨ yasumi》

na⌈ttoku なっとく(納得) *n.* understanding; satisfaction.
nattoku saseru (〜させる) *vt.* convince; persuade.
nattoku suru (〜する) *vi.* understand; be satisfied.

na⌈tto⌉o なっとう(納豆) *n.* fermented soybeans.

na⌈wa⌉ なわ(縄) *n.* rope; cord.

na⌈yamashi⌉·i なやましい(悩ましい) *a.* (-ku) sexy; amorous; voluptuous.

na⌈yami⌉ なやみ(悩み) *n.* worry; trouble; sufferings; anguish.
《⇨ nayamu》

na⌈ya⌉m·u なやむ(悩む) *vi.* (nayam·i-; nayam·a-; nayañ-de Ⓒ) worry; suffer:
Kare wa doo shitara yoi ka nayañde imasu. (彼はどうしたらよいか悩んでいます) He *is worrying* about what to do. 《⇨ nayami》

na⌉ze なぜ(何故) *adv.* why; what for:
Naze *paatii ni konakatta ñ desu ka?* (なぜパーティーに来なかったんですか) *Why* didn't you come to our party? 《⇨ nañde》

na⌉ze nara(ba) なぜなら(ば)(何故なら(ば)) *conj.* the reason is; that is so because. ★ Used at the beginning of a sentence.

na⌈zo なぞ(謎) *n.* mystery; enig-

n

ma; riddle; puzzle:
nazo *o toku* (謎を解く) solve a *mystery* [*riddle*].

na[zonazo なぞなぞ (謎々) *n.* riddle. ⟪⇨ nazo⟫

na[zuke]·ru なづける (名付ける) *vt.* (nazuke-te [V]) name; call:
Ryooshiñ wa kodomo o Akemi to nazuketa. (両親は子どもを明美と名づけた) The parents *named* their child Akemi. ⟪⇨ namae⟫

ne[1] ね (根) *n.* **1** root:
Sono ki wa sugu ni ne *ga tsuita.* (その木はすぐに根がついた) The tree soon took *root.*
2 (*fig.*) root:
aku no ne *o tatsu* (悪の根を断つ) eradicate the *root* of evil.

ne[2] ね (値) *n.* price; cost. ⟪⇨ nedañ⟫

ne[3] ね *p.* **1** (used when seeking agreement from someone):
Ashita kimasu ne. (あした来ますね) You are coming tomorrow, *aren't you*?
2 (used after a phrase to obtain confirmation from the listener):
★ Overuse sounds too familiar.
Ano ne, *kinoo* ne, *Giñza de* ne, *shokuji shite* ne ... (あのね, きのうね, 銀座でね, 食事してね...) *Look*...yesterday, *okay*? In Ginza, *understand*? We had a meal, *right*?
3 (used as an exclamation, or to indicate surprise):
Zuibuñ muzukashii desu ne. (ずいぶん難しいですね) Well, it is very difficult, *isn't it*?
4 (used to slightly emphasize one's opinion):
Hayaku kaetta hoo ga ii to omoimasu ne. (早く帰ったほうがいいと思いますね) *I think* you had better go back soon.

ne[4] ね *int.* look; listen; say:
★ Used to get attention.
Ne, *kore kiree deshoo.* (ね, これきれいでしょう) *Look*, isn't this lovely?

ne[agari ねあがり (値上がり) *n.* increase in price; appreciation.
neagari suru (～する) *vi.* (of a price) rise; go up. ⟪↔ nesagari⟫

ne[age ねあげ (値上げ) *n.* price rise; increase; raise.
neage suru (～する) *vt.* raise the price. ⟪↔ nesage⟫

ne[bari] ねばり (粘り) *n.* **1** stickiness; adhesiveness. ⟪⇨ nebaru⟫
2 tenacity; perseverance:
Kimi wa nebari *ga tarinai.* (きみは粘りが足りない) You lack *tenacity.* ⟪⇨ nebaru⟫

ne[ba]r·u ねばる (粘る) *vi.* (nebar·i-; nebar·a-; nebat-te [C])
1 be sticky; be glutinous. ⟪⇨ nebari⟫
2 (of a person) stick; persist. ⟪⇨ nebari⟫

ne[biki ねびき (値引き) *n.* discount; reduction in price. ⟪⇨ waribiki⟫
nebiki suru (～する) *vt.* discount; reduce a price.

ne[boke]·ru ねぼける (寝惚ける) *vi.* (-boke-te [V]) be half asleep; be not fully awake.

ne[boo ねぼう (寝坊) *n.* late riser; sleepyhead; oversleeping.
neboo suru (～する) *vi.* oversleep; get up late.

ne[dañ ねだん (値段) *n.* price; cost. ⟪⇨ ne[2]⟫

ne[da]r·u ねだる *vt.* (nedar·i-; nedar·a-; nedat-te [C]) ask; beg; press; plead.

ne[doko ねどこ (寝床) *n.* bed:
nedoko *ni hairu* (寝床に入る) go to *bed.* ⟪⇨ neru[1]⟫

ne[esañ ねえさん (姉さん) *n.* one's own older sister. ⟪⇨ ane; niisañ⟫

ne[fuda ねふだ (値札) *n.* price tag [label].

ne[ga]i ねがい (願い) *n.* wish; desire; request: *heewa e no* negai (平和への願い) *desire* for peace. ⟪⇨ o-negai; negau⟫

ne[ga]·u ねがう (願う) *vt.* (nega·i-; negaw·a-; negat-te [C]) wish; desire; hope:
Mata o-me ni kakareru koto o

negatte imasu. (またお目にかかれることを願っています) I *hope* to see you again. ⟪⇨ negai⟫

ne|gi ねぎ (葱) *n.* Welsh onion; scallion. ⟪⇨ tamanegi⟫

ne|ji ねじ *n.* **1** screw:
neji *o shimeru* [*yurumeru*] (ねじを締める[ゆるめる]) turn [loosen] a *screw.*
2 the spring of a watch.

ne|jire|·ru ねじれる (捩れる) *vi.* (nejire-te Ⓥ) be twisted. ⟪⇨ nejiru⟫

ne|ji|r·u ねじる (捩る) *vt.* (nejir·i-; nejir·a-; nejit-te Ⓒ) twist; screw; wring:
futa o nejitte *shimeru* [*akeru*] (ふたをねじって閉める[開ける]) *screw* a cap on [off]. ⟪⇨ nejireru⟫

ne|kase·ru ねかせる (寝かせる) *vt.* (nekase-te Ⓥ) put to bed; let sleep. ⟪⇨ nekasu⟫

ne|kas·u ねかす (寝かす) *vt.* (nekash·i-; nekas·a-; nekash·i-te Ⓒ) put to bed; let sleep. ⟪⇨ neru[1]⟫

ne|ko ねこ (猫) *n.* cat.

ne|koro|b·u ねころぶ (寝転ぶ) *vi.* (-korob·i-; -korob·a-; -koroñ-de Ⓒ) lie down; throw oneself down. ⟪⇨ neru[1]⟫

ne|maki ねまき (寝巻) *n.* nightclothes; nightgown; pajamas.

ne|mu·i ねむい (眠い) *a.* (-ku) sleepy; drowsy:
Kaigi no toki, totemo nemukatta. (会議のとき, とても眠かった) I *felt* very *drowsy* during the meeting.

ne|mure·ru ねむれる (眠れる) *vi.* (nemure-te Ⓥ) be able to sleep. ⟪⇨ nemuru⟫

ne|mur·u ねむる (眠る) *vi.* (nemur·i-; nemur·a-; nemut-te Ⓒ) sleep; fall asleep:
Akañboo wa gussuri nemutte imasu. (赤ん坊はぐっすり眠っています) The baby *is sleeping* soundly. ⟪⇨ nemureru; neru[1]⟫

ne|muta·i ねむたい (眠たい) *a.* (-ku) = nemui.

ne|ñ[1] ねん (年) *n.* **1** year:
Kare wa neñ *ni ichi-do gaikoku e iku.* (彼は年に一度外国へ行く) He goes abroad once a *year.*
2 grade:
*Musuko wa kookoo ichi-*neñ *desu.* (息子は高校 1 年です) My son is in the first *year* of high school. ⟪⇨ gakuneñ⟫

ne|ñ[2] ねん (念) *n.* sense; feeling:
Kimi wa kañsha no neñ *ga tarinai.* (きみは感謝の念が足りない) You lack a *sense* of gratitude.
neñ no tame (〜のため) just in case.
neñ o ireru (〜を入れる) do with great care.

ne|ñbutsu ねんぶつ (念仏) *n.* Buddhist invocation.

ne|ñchoo ねんちょう (年長) *n.* seniority:
Kare wa watashi yori mittsu neñ*choo desu.* (彼は私より 3 つ年長です) He is *older* than me by three years. ⟪⇨ toshi-ue⟫

ne|ñdai ねんだい (年代) *n.* generation; date; age; period. ⟪⇨ jidai; APP. 9⟫

ne|ñdo[1] ねんど (年度) *n.* year; fiscal [financial] year:
*rai-*neñdo *no yosañ* (来年度の予算) the budget for the next *year.*

ne|ñdo[2] ねんど (粘土) *n.* clay.

ne|ñga ねんが (年賀) *n.* New Year's greetings.

ne|ñga-ha|gaki ねんがはがき (年賀葉書) *n.* New Year's greeting postcard. ⟪⇨ neñgajoo⟫

ne|ñgajoo ねんがじょう (年賀状) *n.* New Year's card. ⟪⇨ neñgahagaki⟫

ne|ñga|ppi ねんがっぴ (年月日) *n.* date. ★ A particular day, month and year.

ne|ñgetsu ねんげつ (年月) *n.* time; years:
Sono toñneru o kañsee suru no ni nagai neñgetsu *ga kakatta.* (そのトンネルを完成するのに長い年月がかかった) It took many *years* to build the tunnel. ⟪⇨ toshitsuki; tsukihi⟫

ne|ñgo|o ねんごう (年号) *n.* the

name of an era; the posthumous name of a Japanese emperor and of his reign. ⟪⇨ APP. 9⟫

ne⌈ñjuu ねんじゅう(年中) *n.*, *adv.* all the year round; throughout the year; always.

ne⌈ñkañ ねんかん(年間) *n.* year:
Watashi wa juugo-neñkañ *mujiko desu.* (私は15年間無事故です) I've had a clean driving record *for fifteen years.* ⟪⇨ gekkañ⟫

ne⌈ñmatsu ねんまつ(年末) *n.* the end of the year. ⟪↔ neñtoo⟫

ne⌈ñree ねんれい(年齢) *n.* age. ⟪⇨ toshi[1]⟫

ne⌈ñryo⌉o ねんりょう(燃料) *n.* fuel.

-ne⌉ñsee ねんせい(年生) *suf.* a student of the stated academic year:
shoogaku roku-neñsee (小学6年生) a sixth *year* elementary school pupil.

ne⌈ñtoo ねんとう(年頭) *n.* the beginning of a year. ⟪↔ neñmatsu⟫

ne⌈rai ねらい(狙い) *n.* aim; mark; target; purpose:
mato ni nerai *o sadameru* (的にねらいを定める) take *aim* at a target. ⟪⇨ nerau⟫

ne⌈ra·u ねらう(狙う) *vt.* (nera·i-; neraw·a-; nerat-te [C]) **1** take aim; set one's sights. ⟪⇨ nerai⟫
2 aim (a goal, victory, success, etc.). ⟪⇨ nerai⟫

ne·⌈ru[1] ねる(寝る) *vi.* (ne-te [V])
1 go to bed; sleep. ⟪⇨ nekasu⟫
2 be sick in bed: ⟪⇨ yasumu⟫
Kinoo wa kaze de nete imashita. (きのうはかぜで寝ていました) I *was sick in bed* with a cold yesterday.
3 lie down. ⟪⇨ nesoberu⟫

ne⌉r·u[2] ねる(練る) *vi.* (ner·i-; ner·a-; net-te [C]) **1** knead:
komugi-ko no kiji o neru (小麦粉の生地を練る) *knead* dough.
2 work out (a plan, etc.) carefully; elaborate.

ne⌈sagari ねさがり(値下がり) *n.* fall in price; depreciation. ⟪↔ neagari⟫

nesagari suru (〜する) *vi.* fall; go down; become cheaper.

ne⌈sage ねさげ(値下げ) *n.* reduction in price; price cut. ⟪↔ neage⟫

nesage suru (〜する) *vt.* reduce; cut the price; mark down.

ne⌈sobe⌉r·u ねそべる(寝そべる) *vi.* (nesober·i-; nesober·a-; nesobet-te [C]) lie down; sprawl; stretch.

ne⌉sshiñ ねっしん(熱心) *a.n.* (〜 na, ni) eager; hardworking; devoted.

ne⌈ss·u⌉ru ねっする(熱する) *vi.*, *vt.* (nessh·i-; nessh·i-; nessh·i-te [I]) heat; become hot. ⟪⇨ kanetsu[1]; netsu⟫

ne⌈takiri ねたきり(寝たきり) *n.* bedridden:
Chichi wa netakiri *desu.* (父は寝たきりです) My father is *bedridden.*

ne⌈tsu[1] ねつ(熱) *n.* **1** heat:
taiyoo no netsu (太陽の熱) the *heat* of the sun.
2 fever; temperature:
Kono ko wa netsu *ga aru.* (この子は熱がある) This child has a *fever.*
3 enthusiasm; craze.

ne⌉ttai ねったい(熱帯) *n.* torrid zone; tropics. ⟪↔ kañtai; oñtai⟫

ne⌉ttoo ねっとう(熱湯) *n.* boiling water. ⟪⇨ o-yu⟫

ne⌈uchi ねうち(値打ち) *n.* value; worth; price. ⟪⇨ kachi[1]⟫

ne⌈zumi ねずみ(鼠) *n.* mouse; rat.

ni[1][1] に(二) *n.* two. ⟪⇨ APP. 3⟫

ni[2] に *p.* **1** (indicates a place):
a at; in: ★ Indicates existence at a location.
Ashita wa watashi wa uchi ni *imasu.* (あしたは私は家にいます) I will be *at* home tomorrow.
b on; onto: ★ Indicates the final location of an object that is moved.
Hoñ wa tsukue no ue ni *oite kudasai.* (本は机の上に置いてください) Put the book *on* the desk, please.

c to; toward: ★ Indicates direction or final destination. Used with verbs of movement.
Watashi wa mainichi gakkoo ni *ikimasu.* (私は毎日学校に行きます) I go *to* school every day. ★ Direction can also be indicated by '*e*.' ((⇨ e[3]))
2 to; from; by: ★ Indicates the direction of giving or receiving.
Nokorimono o inu ni *yatta.* (残り物を犬にやった) I gave the leftovers *to* the dog. ((⇨ kara[3]))
3 at; in: ★ Indicates the time of an action or event.
Watashi wa maiasa roku-ji ni *okimasu.* (私は毎朝6時に起きます) I get up *at* six every morning.
4 in; to: ★ Used in expressions of frequency or proportion.
Kare wa ichi-nichi ni *tabako o futa-hako suimasu.* (彼は1日にたばこを2箱吸います) He smokes two packs of cigarettes *in* a day.
5 to; into: ★ Indicates a change or resulting condition.
Shiñgoo ga aka kara ao ni *kawatta.* (信号が赤から青にかわった) The traffic lights changed from red *to* green.
6 (used with verbs of decision):
Kaisha o yameru koto ni *kimeta.* (会社をやめることに決めた) I have decided *to quit* the company.
7 to: ★ Indicates a recipient.
Gaikoku no tomodachi ni *tegami o kaita.* (外国の友だちに手紙を書いた) I wrote a letter *to* a friend abroad.
8 by: ★ Indicates the agent of a passive sentence.
Kyoo wa señsee ni *homerareta.* (きょうは先生にほめられた) I was praised *by* my teacher today. ★ '*Kara*' can also be used. ((⇨ kara[3]))
9 (indicates the person who is made or allowed to do an action): ★ Used with a causative verb.
Sono shigoto o watashi ni *sasete kudasai.* (その仕事を私にさせてください) I beg you to let *me* do the job.
10 for: ★ Used when comparing, differentiating, estimating, etc.
Kono doresu wa watashi ni *choodo ii.* (このドレスは私にちょうどいい) This dress is just right *for* me.
11 in order to; for the purpose of: ★ Indicates purpose or reason. Used with verbs of movement, especially '*iku*' and '*kuru.*'
Sañpo ni *ikimashoo.* (散歩に行きましょう) Let's go *for* a walk.
12 for; as: ★ Indicates purpose or means.
Kono sakana wa shokuyoo ni *naranai.* (この魚は食用にならない) This fish is not fit *for* food.
13 from; by: ★ Indicates the cause or reason for a state or situation.
Shigoto ni *tsukaremashita.* (仕事に疲れました) I am tired *from* work.
14 at; in: ★ Used in expressions indicating ability, skill or knowledge.
Kare wa suugaku ni *tsuyoi.* (彼は数学に強い) He is good *at* math.
15 in (a stated way): ★ Used in expressions indicating manner.
Kare wa sono buñshoo o machigawazu ni *yoñda.* (彼はその文章を間違わずに読んだ) He read the sentence *faultlessly.*

ni[3] に *p.* and: ★ Used in listing, recalling or restating items.
Kyoo kau mono wa tamago ni *miruku desu.* (きょう買うものは卵にミルクです) Today I have to buy eggs *and* milk. ((⇨ to[2]; ya[1]; yara))

ni˥[4] に (荷) *n.* load; freight; cargo: *kuruma ni* ni o tsumu (車に荷を積む) *load up* a car. ((⇨ kamotsu; nimotsu))

ni⌈a˥·u にあう (似合う) *vi.* (nia·i-; niaw·a-; niat-te Ⓒ) suit; become. ((⇨ au[2]))

ni⌈bu˥·i にぶい (鈍い) *a.* (-ku) dull; blunt; slow:
Mada ki ga tsukanai nañte kare

mo nibui *desu ne.* (まだ気がつかないなんて彼も鈍いですね) He still does not understand. He is a bit *slow,* isn't he? ⟪↔ surudoi⟫

-nichi にち (日) *suf.* day:
*Ni, sañ-*nichi *koko ni taizai shimasu.* (2, 3 日ここに滞在します) I will stay here for a few *days.*

ni⌈chiee-ji⌉teñ にちえいじてん (日英辞典) *n.* a Japanese-English dictionary for English-speaking people. ★ A Japanese-English dictionary for Japanese is called '*waee-jiteñ*' (和英辞典). ⟪⇨ jiteñ⟫

ni⌉chiji にちじ (日時) *n.* time and date.

ni⌈chijoo-ka⌉iwa にちじょうかいわ (日常会話) *n.* everyday conversation.

ni⌈chijoo-se⌉ekatsu にちじょうせいかつ (日常生活) *n.* daily life.

ni⌈chiyoo da⌉iku にちようだいく (日曜大工) *n.* Sunday [weekend] carpenter. ⟪⇨ daiku⟫

ni⌈chiyo⌉o(bi) にちよう (び) (日曜 (日)) *n.* Sunday. ⟪⇨ APP. 5⟫

ni⌈chiyoohiñ にちようひん (日用品) *n.* daily necessities.

ni⌈e·ru にえる (煮える) *vi.* (nie-te [V]) cook; be cooked. ⟪⇨ niru¹⟫

ni⌈ga⌉·i にがい (苦い) *a.* (-ku)
1 (of taste) bitter. ⟪↔ amai⟫
2 (of experience) hard; bitter: nigai *keekeñ o suru* (苦い経験をする) have a *bitter* experience.
3 (of a countenance) sour; unpleasant: nigai *kao o suru* (苦い顔をする) make a *wry* face.

ni⌈ga⌉s·u にがす (逃がす) *vt.* (nigash·i-; nigas·a-; nigash·i-te [C]) set free; let go; let escape. ⟪⇨ nigeru; torinigasu⟫

ni⌈gate⌉ にがて (苦手) *a.n.* (~ na)
1 one's weak point. ⟪↔ tokui⟫
2 person who is hard to deal with; tough customer.

ni-⌈gatsu⌉ にがつ (二月) *n.* February. ⟪⇨ APP. 5⟫

ni⌈gedas·u にげだす (逃げ出す) *vi.* (-dash·i-; -das·a-; -dash·i-te [C]) run away; take to one's heels.

ni⌈ge⌉·ru にげる (逃げる) *vi.* (nige-te [V]) run away; escape; flee. ⟪⇨ nigasu; nogareru⟫

ni⌈giri にぎり (握り) *n.* **1** grip; handle. ⟪⇨ nigiru⟫
2 = nigirizushi.

ni⌈giri⌉zushi にぎりずし (握り鮨) *n.* hard-rolled sushi. ⟪⇨ sushi⟫

ni⌈gir·u にぎる (握る) *vt.* (nigir·i-; nigir·a-; nigit-te [C]) **1** grasp; grip; hold.
2 dominate (an organization); rule; control:
Kare ga kaisha no subete o nigitte iru. (彼が会社のすべてを握っている) He *controls* everything in the company.

ni⌈giwa⌉·u にぎわう (賑わう) *vi.* (-wa·i-; -waw·a-; -wat-te [C]) be crowded; be alive; be prosperous. ⟪⇨ nigiyaka⟫

ni⌈gi⌉yaka にぎやか (賑やか) *a.n.* (~ na, ni) **1** (of place) busy; crowded. ⟪⇨ nigiwau⟫
2 (of people, crowds, etc.) merry; lively; cheerful; noisy. ⟪↔ sabishii⟫

ni⌈gori⌉ にごり (濁り) *n.* **1** muddiness; unclearness:
Kono mizu wa nigori *ga aru.* (この水は濁りがある) This water is *not clear.* ⟪⇨ nigoru⟫
2 voiced consonant. ⟪⇨ dakuoñ; nigoru⟫

ni⌈go⌉r·u にごる (濁る) *vi.* (nigor·i-; nigor·a-; nigot-te [C])
1 become muddy; become cloudy. ⟪⇨ nigori⟫
2 (of some *kana* letters) be voiced:
'Ta' ga nigoru *to 'da' ni narimasu.* (「た」が濁ると「だ」になります) 'Da' is the *voiced* equivalent of 'ta.' ⟪⇨ nigori⟫

ni⌈guñ にぐん (二軍) *n.* (of baseball) farm team [club]; the minors. ⟪⇨ ichiguñ⟫

Ni⌈ho⌉ñ にほん (日本) *n.* Japan. ★ Also '*Nippoñ.*' ⟪⇨ Nippoñ⟫

Ni⌈hoñgo にほんご (日本語) *n.* Japanese language; Japanese. ((⇨ kokugo))

Ni⌈hoñji⌉ñ にほんじん (日本人) *n.* Japanese people; Japanese.

ni⌉isañ にいさん (兄さん) *n.* one's own older brother. ((⇨ ani; nee-sañ))

ni⌈ji にじ (虹) *n.* rainbow.

ni⌈ji⌉m·u にじむ (滲む) *vi.* (nijim·i-; nijim·a-; nijiñ-de Ⓒ) (of ink) run; blot; get blurred.

ni⌈kai にかい (二階) *n.* the second (American) floor; the first (British) floor.

ni⌈kka にっか (日課) *n.* one's daily work [task]:
Maiasa jogiñgu o suru no ga nikka *desu.* (毎朝ジョギングをするのが日課です) I make a *practice* of jogging every morning.

ni⌈kki にっき (日記) *n.* diary.

ni⌉kkoo にっこう (日光) *n.* sunlight; sunshine; sun.

ni⌈kko⌉ri にっこり *adv.* (~ to; ~ suru) with a smile:
Sono oñna-no-ko wa watashi ni mukatte nikkori (*to*) *waratta.* (その女の子は私に向かってにっこり(と)笑った) The girl gave me a *smile.*

ni⌉koniko にこにこ *adv.* (~ to; ~ suru) with a smile:
Kanojo wa itsu-mo nikoniko *shite iru.* (彼女はいつもにこにこしている) She is always *smiling cheerfully.*

ni⌈ku⌉ にく (肉) *n.* meat; flesh.

ni⌈ku⌉·i にくい (憎い) *a.* (-ku)
1 hateful. ((⇨ nikumu))
2 (*ironic*) smart; clever:
Kimi mo nakanaka nikui *koto o iu ne.* (君もなかなか憎いことを言うね) *Well* said.

-niku⌉·i にくい (難い) *suf.* (*a.*) (-ku) hard; difficult: ★ Added to the stem of a volitional verb.
Kono doogu wa tsukai-nikui. (この道具は使いにくい) This tool is *difficult* to handle. ((↔ -yasui)) ((⇨ -gatai))

ni⌈ku⌉m·u にくむ (憎む) *vt.* (nikum·i-; nikum·a-; nikuñ-de Ⓒ) hate; abhor; despise. ((⇨ nikushimi))

ni⌈kurashi⌉·i にくらしい (憎らしい) *a.* (-ku) hateful; spiteful:
Dañdañ kare ga nikurashiku *natte kita.* (だんだん彼が憎らしくなってきた) He has gradually become *detestable* to me.

ni⌈kushimi にくしみ (憎しみ) *n.* hatred; hate; enmity. ((⇨ nikumu; nikui))

ni⌈kutai にくたい (肉体) *n.* body; the flesh. ((⇨ karada))

ni⌈ku⌉ya にくや (肉屋) *n.* butcher; meat shop.

ni⌈kyuu にきゅう (二級) *n.* second class; second rate. ((⇨ ikkyuu))

ni⌉motsu にもつ (荷物) *n.* load; baggage; luggage.

-niñ にん (人) *suf.* counter for people: *Kodomo wa* sañ-niñ *desu.* (子どもは 3 人です) I have *three* children. ★ Exceptions are '*hitori*' (one person) and '*futari*' (two persons).

ni⌈na⌉·u になう (担う) *vt.* (nina·i-; ninaw·a-; ninat-te Ⓒ) (*formal*) bear (a burden); take (responsibility).

ni⌈ñgeñ にんげん (人間) *n.* human being; man. ((⇨ hito; jiñrui))

ni⌈ñgyoo にんぎょう (人形) *n.* doll; puppet.

ni⌈ñjiñ にんじん (人参) *n.* carrot.

ni⌉ñjoo にんじょう (人情) *n.* human nature; humanity; kindness:
niñjoo no atsui [usui] *hito* (人情の厚い[薄い]人) a *warmhearted* [*coldhearted*] man.

ni⌈ñki にんき (人気) *n.* popularity; public interest.

ni⌉ñmu にんむ (任務) *n.* duty; task; office:
niñmu *o hatasu* [*okotaru*] (任務を果たす[怠る]) fulfill [neglect] one's *duty.*

ni⌈ñshiki にんしき (認識) *n.* understanding; recognition:

n

niñshiki *ga tarinai* (認識が足りない) have little *understanding.*
niñshiki suru (～する) *vt.* understand; recognize; be aware of. 《⇨ rikai》

ni⌈ñshiñ にんしん (妊娠) *n.* pregnancy.
niñshiñ suru (～する) *vi.* become pregnant.

ni⌉ñzuu にんずう (人数) *n.* the number of people. 《⇨ atamakazu》

ni⌈o⌉i におい (匂い・臭い) *n.* smell; odor; fragrance. 《⇨ kaori; niou》

ni⌈o⌉·u におう (匂う・臭う) *vi.* (nioi-; niow·a-; niot-te Ⓒ) smell; be fragrant; stink. 《⇨ nioi》

Ni⌈ppo⌉ñ にっぽん (日本) *n.* Japan. ★ Both '*Nippoñ*' and '*Nihoñ*' are often used in isolation interchangeably. Generally, however, '*Nihoñ*' is preferred when forming compounds. 《⇨ Nihoñ》

ni⌈ra⌉m·u にらむ (睨む) *vt.* (niram·i-; niram·a-; nirañ-de Ⓒ)
1 glare; stare.
2 (in the passive) be in disfavor: *Kare wa buchoo ni* niramarete iru. (彼は部長ににらまれている) He *is in disfavor* with the general manager.
3 suspect; spot.

ni·⌈ru[1] にる (煮る) *vt.* (ni-te Ⓥ) boil; simmer; cook. 《⇨ nieru》

ni·⌈ru[2] にる (似る) *vi.* (ni-te Ⓥ) resemble; be like; be similar.

ni⌈ryuu にりゅう (二流) *n.* second-class; second-rate. 《⇨ ichiryuu; sañryuu》

ni⌈se にせ (偽) *n.* sham; counterfeit; imitation: nise *no daiya* (偽のダイヤ) a *fake* diamond.

ni⌉see にせい (二世) *n.* Nisei; the second-generation of Japanese immigrants; a member of this generation. 《⇨ issee[2]; sañsee[2]》

ni⌈semono にせもの (偽物) *n.* forgery; counterfeit; imitation.

ni⌈shi にし (西) *n.* west; (～ ni/e) westward. 《↔ higashi》

ni shiro にしろ ★ The particle '*ni*' plus the imperative of '*suru*.'
1 even if: ★ Used to form a weak conditional.
Oseji ni shiro, *homerarereba dare de mo warui ki wa shinai.* (お世辞にしろ, ほめられればだれでも悪い気はしない) *Even if* it is flattery, no one feels displeased when he is praised.
2 and; or: ★ Used to give illustrative examples or possibilities.
Beñkyoo ni shiro *uñdoo* ni shiro, *mainichi no doryoku ga taisetsu desu.* (勉強にしろ運動にしろ, 毎日の努力が大切です) In *both* studies *and* physical training, continued daily effort is important.

ni shi⌈te⌉ mo にしても even if: *Joodañ* ni shite mo, *do ga sugiru.* (冗談にしても, 度が過ぎる) *Even if* you did it in jest, you've carried things too far. 《⇨ ni shiro》

ni shi⌈te⌉ wa にしては **1** even if; for: ★ Used when the speaker accepts the situation or explanation in the first clause, but finds that the consequent result, as specified in the second clause, is contrary to normal expectation.
Kare wa daigaku o deta ni shite wa, *jooshiki ni kakete iru.* (彼は大学を出たにしては, 常識に欠けている) *For* someone who graduated from college, he lacks common sense.
2 considering; for: ★ Follows a noun and indicates that, considering the characteristics normally associated with that noun, the judgment the speaker makes is contrary to expectation.
Ano hito wa gaikoku-jiñ ni shite wa, *Nihoñgo ga umai.* (あの人は外国人にしては, 日本語がうまい) *For* a foreigner, his Japanese is good.

ni⌈sshoku にっしょく (日食) *n.* solar eclipse. 《⇨ gesshoku》

ni⌈ssu⌉u にっすう (日数) *n.* the

number of days; time.

ni[ta]ts·u にたつ(煮立つ) *vi.* (-tach·i-; -tat·a-; -tat·te Ⓒ) (of water, vessel) boil; come to a boil.

ni[tchuu にっちゅう(日中) *n.* the daytime. ⟪↔ yakañ[1]⟫

ni[too にとう(二等) *n.* second class; second prize; second place. ⟪⇨ ittoo⟫

ni[ttee にってい(日程) *n.* one's day's schedule; itinerary.

ni[wa にわ(庭) *n.* garden; yard; court.

ni] wa には *p.* for; to; in:
Kore wa watashi ni wa *taisetsu na shashiñ desu.* (これは私には大切な写真です) This is a photo which is important *for* me. ⟪⇨ ni[2]; wa[3]⟫

ni]waka にわか(俄か) *a.n.* (～ na, ni) sudden; immediate; unexpected:
Niwaka *ni ame ga furi-dashita.* (にわかに雨が降りだした) It *suddenly* started raining.

ni[waka-a]me にわかあめ(俄か雨) *n.* rain shower.

ni[watori にわとり(鶏) *n.* chicken; rooster; hen. ⟪⇨ hiyoko⟫

ni]yaniya にやにや *adv.* (～ to; ～ suru) (the manner of grinning [smirking]):
niyaniya (to) warau (にやにや(と)笑う) *grin broadly.*

ni[zu]kuri にづくり(荷造り) *n.* packing:
hikkoshi no nizukuri o suru (引っ越しの荷造りをする) do the *packing* for moving.

no[1] の *p.* **1** of; at; in; on:
★ Used to link two nouns. The first noun describes the latter in some way.
kinu no *hañkachi* (絹のハンカチ) a *silk* handkerchief / *watashi* no *hoñ* (私の本) a book *of* mine / *machi* no *yuubiñkyoku* (町の郵便局) a post office *in* town.
★ Also note the pattern: noun＋particle＋'*no*'＋noun. *e.g. tomodachi* kara no *deñwa* (友だちからの電話) a phone call *from* a friend / *haha* e no *tegami* (母への手紙) a letter *to* my mother.
2 (used as the subject marker in a clause modifying a noun):
Watashi no *yomitai hoñ wa kore desu.* (私の読みたい本はこれです) The book *I* want to read is this one.
3 (used to link two nouns, which are in apposition):
beñgoshi no *Tanaka-sañ* (弁護士の田中さん) Mr. Tanaka, *who is* a lawyer.
★ Note the ambiguity: '*isha* no *tomodachi*' (医者の友だち) has two meanings, 'the doctor's friend' (as in **1**) and 'my friend, who is a doctor' (as in **3**).
4 (used to link quantity expressions to a following noun):
sañ-biki no *kobuta* (三匹のこぶた) *three* little pigs.

no[2] の *n.* **1** one: ★ Used to substitute for another noun and often modified by a verb or adjective.
Motto yasui no *wa arimaseñ ka?* (もっと安いのはありませんか) Isn't there a cheaper *one*?
2 the fact; that: ★ Used to nominalize the previous clause.
Kanojo ga nyuuiñ shita no *o shitte imasu ka?* (彼女が入院したのを知っていますか) Do you know *that* she was hospitalized?
3 (used in giving explanations, or in eliciting or confirming information): ★ Added to the end of a clause as '*no da*' or '*no desu.*' In speech, usually '*ñ da*' or '*ñ desu.*'
Nani-ka atta ñ desu *ka?* (何かあったんですか) *Has* something *happened*?

no[3] の *p.* (*colloq.*) [added to the end of a sentence]
1 (signifies a question): ★ With rising intonation. Equivalent to '*no desu ka.*'

Doko e iku no? (どこへ行くの) Where *are* you *off* to?

2 (suggests an explanation): ★ With falling intonation. Used mainly by women and children. Equivalent to '*no desu*.'

"Doo shita?" "Atama ga itai no." (「どうした」「頭が痛いの」) "What's the matter?" "I have a headache."

no[14] の (野) *n.* field. ⟪⇨ nohara⟫

no⌈ba⌉s·u[1] のばす (伸ばす) *vt.* (nobash·i-; nobas·a-; nobash·i-te Ⓒ) **1** lengthen; make longer.

2 straighten; stretch; reach: *Kanojo wa te o* nobashite *posutaa o hagashita.* (彼女は手を伸ばしてポスターをはがした) She *reached out* and pulled down the poster.

3 smooth out (a wrinkle, surface, etc.); iron out. ⟪⇨ nobiru[1]⟫

4 let grow (a beard, hair). ⟪⇨ nobiru[1]⟫

5 develop; improve; better: *Kare wa mata kiroku o* nobashita. (彼はまた記録を伸ばした) He *bettered* his record once more. ⟪⇨ nobiru[1]⟫

no⌈ba⌉s·u[2] のばす (延ばす) *vt.* (nobash·i-; nobas·a-; nobash·i-te Ⓒ) **1** extend; prolong: *taizai kikañ o* nobasu (滞在期間を延ばす) *extend* one's length of stay. ⟪⇨ nobiru[2]⟫

2 postpone; put off: *shuppatsu o* nobasu (出発を延ばす) *postpone* one's departure. ⟪⇨ eñki⟫

no⌉be- のべ (延べ) *pref.* aggregate; total number: *Nyuujoosha wa* nobe-*hasseñ-niñ ni tasshita.* (入場者は延べ 8,000 人に達した) *The total number* of visitors reached 8,000.

no⌈be⌉·ru のべる (述べる) *vt.* (nobe-te Ⓥ) state (an opinion); express (one's ideas); mention.

no⌈bi⌉·ru[1] のびる (伸びる) *vi.* (nobi-te Ⓥ) **1** (of a plant, hair, etc.) grow. ⟪⇨ nobasu[1]⟫

2 lengthen, extend: *Kare wa saikiñ shiñchoo ga kyuu ni* nobita. (彼は最近身長が急に伸びた) He *has* recently *shot up* in height.

3 improve; develop; increase: *Yushutsu wa* nobiru *keekoo ni arimasu.* (輸出は伸びる傾向にあります) Exports show a tendency to *increase.* ⟪⇨ nobasu[1]⟫

4 (*colloq.*) be tired out; pass out.

no⌈bi⌉·ru[2] のびる (延びる) *vi.* (nobite Ⓥ) **1** lengthen; be extended: *Hi ga* nobimashita *ne.* (日が延びましたね) The days *have gotten longer*, haven't they?

2 be postponed; be delayed. ⟪⇨ nobasu[2]⟫

no⌈bori のぼり (上り) *n.* **1** ascent. ⟪↔ kudari⟫

2 up train. ★ '*Nobori*' is a train going in the direction of a major city, especially Tokyo, and '*kudari*' is a train going out of a major city. ⟪↔ kudari⟫

no⌈bor·u[1] のぼる (上る) *vi.* (nobor·i-; nobor·a-; nobot-te Ⓒ)

1 go up; ascend: *kaidañ* [*saka*] *o* noboru (階段[坂]を上る) *go up* stairs [a slope]. ⟪↔ oriru⟫

2 amount to; reach: *Sono jiko ni yoru shishoosha wa gojuu-niñ ijoo ni* nobotta. (その事故による死傷者は 50 人以上に上った) The dead and injured in the accident *reached* more than fifty.

3 rise: *shachoo no chii ni* noboru (社長の地位に上る) *rise* to the position of president.

no⌈bor·u[2] のぼる (昇る) *vi.* (nobor·i-; nobor·a-; nobot-te Ⓒ) go up; rise. ⟪⇨ agaru⟫

no⌈bor·u[3] のぼる (登る) *vi.* (nobor·i-; nobor·a-; nobot-te Ⓒ) climb (a mountain).

no⌈chi⌉ のち (後) *n.* later; after. ⟪⇨ ato[1]⟫

no⌈chi-hodo のちほど (後程) *adv.* later (on):

Nochi-hodo *go-reñraku itashimasu.* (後ほどご連絡いたします) I will get in touch with you *later on.*

no de ので because; so; owing to; therefore:
Sakuya wa osoku made shigoto o shita no de, *nemui.* (昨夜は遅くまで仕事をしたので, 眠い) I worked late last night and I am *therefore* sleepy. 《⇨ kara[4]》

no⌉do のど (喉) *n.* throat:
Nodo ga kawaita. (のどが渇いた) I *am thirsty.*

no⌉doka のどか (長閑) *a.n.* (～ na, ni) calm; peaceful:
nodoka *na haru no hi* (のどかな春の日) a *calm* spring day.

no⌈gare⌉·ru のがれる (逃れる) *vi.* (nogare-te [V]) escape; run away; avoid. 《⇨ nigeru; nogasu》

no⌈ga⌉s·u のがす (逃す) *vt.* (nogash·i-; nogas·a-; nogash·i-te [C]) miss (a chance, an opportunity, etc.); lose; let slip. 《⇨ nigasu; nogareru》

no⌉hara のはら (野原) *n.* field; plain. 《⇨ hara[2]; harappa; no[4]》

no⌈iro⌉oze ノイローゼ *n.* neurosis; nervous breakdown.

no⌈ki のき (軒) *n.* eaves.

no⌉kku ノック *n.* **1** knock.
2 (of baseball) hitting grounders and flies for practice.
nokku suru (～する) *vt.* rap on a door; knock.

no⌈kogiri⌉ のこぎり (鋸) *n.* saw.

no⌈ko⌉razu のこらず (残らず) *adv.* all; entirely; without exception. 《⇨ subete; zeñbu》

no⌈kori⌉ のこり (残り) *n.* the remainder; the rest; leftovers.

no⌈ko⌉r·u のこる (残る) *vi.* (nokor·i-; nokor·a-; nokot-te [C]) remain; be left:
Watashi wa shibaraku sono ba ni nokotta. (私はしばらくその場に残った) I *remained* there for a short while. 《⇨ inokoru; nokosu》

no⌈ko⌉s·u のこす (残す) *vt.* (nokosh·i-; nokos·a-; nokosh·i-te [C]) leave (behind); set aside; reserve. 《⇨ amasu; nokoru》

no⌉mi[1] のみ (鑿) *n.* chisel.

no⌉mi[2] のみ *p.* (*formal*) only; alone: ★ Used after a noun or verb to express a limit.
Watashi wa jibuñ ga shitte iru koto nomi *hanashita.* (私は自分が知っていることのみ話した) I told *only* what I knew. 《⇨ bakari; dake; shika[3]》
... nomi narazu ... mo (...～ならず...も) not only...but also: *Kono hoñ wa kodomo* nomi narazu *otona ni* mo *omoshiroi.* (この本は子どものみならず大人にもおもしろい) This book is interesting, *not only* for children, *but also* for adults.

no⌈mikom·u のみこむ (飲み込む) *vt.* (-kom·i-; -kom·a-; -koñ-de [C])
1 swallow; gulp; choke down.
2 understand; learn; grasp:
Kanojo wa watashi no setsumee o sugu nomikoñda. (彼女は私の説明をすぐ飲み込んだ) She *grasped* my explanation right away.

no⌈mi⌉mizu のみみず (飲み水) *n.* drinking water.

no⌈mi⌉mono のみもの (飲み物) *n.* drink; beverage.

no⌉m·u のむ (飲む) *vt.* (nom·i-; nom·a-; noñ-de [C]) **1** drink (coffee, milk, etc.); take alcohol; take (medicine).
2 accept (a demand, request, etc.); agree.

no⌈ñbi⌉ri のんびり *adv.* (～ to; ～ suru) leisurely; quietly; peacefully.

no ni のに although; but; in spite of:
Isshoo-keñmee hataraite iru no ni *seekatsu wa raku ni naranai.* (一生懸命働いているのに生活は楽にならない) *In spite of* my working hard, life has not become any easier. 《⇨ ga[2]; kakawarazu; keredo (mo)》

no⌉ñki のんき (呑気) *a.n.* (～ na, ni) easygoing; happy-go-lucky; carefree; optimistic.

no˥o[1] のう(脳) *n.* brain; brains.

no˥o[2] のう(能) *n.* Noh play.

no˥ochi のうち(農地) *n.* farmland; agricultural land.

no˥oeñ のうえん(農園) *n.* farm; plantation. ⟨⇨ noojoo⟩

no˥ogyoo のうぎょう(農業) *n.* agriculture; farming.

no˥oi˥kketsu のういっけつ(脳溢血) *n.* cerebral hemorrhage.

no˥ojoo のうじょう(農場) *n.* farm; ranch.

no˥oka のうか(農家) *n.* farmhouse; farmer.

no˥oke˥sseñ のうけっせん(脳血栓) *n.* cerebral thrombosis.

no˥oko˥osoku のうこうそく(脳梗塞) *n.* cerebral infarction.

no˥omiñ のうみん(農民) *n.* landed farmer; peasant.

no˥oritsu のうりつ(能率) *n.* efficiency:
shigoto no nooritsu *o ageru* (仕事の能率を上げる) improve the *efficiency* of the work.

no˥oritsu-teki のうりつてき(能率的) *a.n.* (～ na, ni) efficient.

no˥oryoku のうりょく(能力) *n.* ability; capacity; faculty.

no˥oshi のうし(脳死) *n.* brain death.

no˥osoñ のうそん(農村) *n.* farm village; farming district.

no˥oto ノート *n.* notebook. ⟨⇨ choomeñ⟩
nooto suru (～する) *vt.* write down; take notes.

no˥oyaku のうやく(農薬) *n.* artificially synthesized fertilizers and pesticides.

no˥rainu のらいぬ(野良犬) *n.* homeless dog; stray dog.

no˥reñ のれん(暖簾) *n.* short split curtain. ★ Hung outside the entrance of a Japanese-style shop, restaurant, bar, etc.

no˥ri˥[1] のり(糊) *n.* glue; paste; starch. ⟨⇨ norizuke⟩

no˥ri˥[2] のり(海苔) *n.* laver; seaweed. ⟨⇨ norimaki⟩

no˥riage˥·ru のりあげる(乗り上げる) *vi.* (-age-te Ⓥ) run onto; run aground.

no˥riba のりば(乗り場) *n.* stop; stand; platform:
Chikatetsu no noriba *wa doko desu ka?* (地下鉄の乗り場はどこですか) *Where* can I take the subway?

no˥rida˥s·u のりだす(乗り出す) *vi.* (-dash·i-; -das·a-; -dash·i-te Ⓒ)
1 sail out:
araumi ni noridasu (荒海に乗り出す) *sail out* on the rough sea.
2 set about; embark; start (an enterprise):
atarashii jigyoo ni noridasu (新しい事業に乗り出す) *embark* on a new business.
3 lean forward:
mado kara noridasu (窓から乗り出す) *lean* out of a window.

no˥riire のりいれ(乗り入れ) *n.*
1 driving (a car) into:
Kuruma no noriire *kiñshi.* (*sign*) (車の乗り入れ禁止) No *Entry* for Motor Vehicles. ⟨⇨ noriireru⟩
2 the extension of (a railroad line) into (another line). ⟨⇨ noriireru⟩

no˥riire˥·ru のりいれる(乗り入れる) *vi.* (-ire-te Ⓥ) **1** drive [ride] into (a place). ⟨⇨ noriire⟩
2 extend into:
Raineñ wa chikatetsu ga kono eki made noriiremasu. (来年は地下鉄がこの駅まで乗り入れます) The subway will *be extended* to this station next year. ⟨⇨ noriire⟩

no˥rikae のりかえ(乗り換え) *n.* change; transfer. ⟨⇨ norikaeru⟩

no˥rikae˥·ru のりかえる(乗り換える) *vi.* (-kae-te Ⓥ) change; transfer:
Ueno de Giñza-señ ni norikaeru (上野で銀座線に乗り換える) *change* at Ueno for the Ginza Line. ⟨⇨ norikae⟩

no˥rikoe˥·ru のりこえる(乗り越える) *vi.* (-koe-te Ⓥ) get over; climb over; overcome.

no˥riko˥m·u のりこむ(乗り込む) *vi.*

(-kom·i-; -kom·a-; -koñ-de [C])
1 get on [in] (a vehicle); board: *takushii ni* norikomu (タクシーに乗り込む) *get in* a taxi.
2 march [ride] into (a place).

no⌈rikoshi のりこし (乗り越し) *n.* riding beyond one's station. ((⇨ norikosu))

no⌈riko⌉s·u のりこす (乗り越す) *vt.* (-kosh·i-; -kos·a-; -kosh·i-te [C]) ride past one's station. ((⇨ norikoshi))

no⌈ri⌉maki のりまき (海苔巻き) *n.* vinegared rice rolled in dried laver. ((⇨ nori[2]))

no⌈rimono のりもの (乗り物) *n.* vehicle; (a means of) transport.

no⌈riokure⌉·ru のりおくれる (乗り遅れる) *vi.* (-okure-te [V]) fail to catch (a train, bus, etc.); miss.

no⌈ri⌉ori のりおり (乗り降り) *n.* getting on and off trains.
noriori suru (～する) *vi.* get on and off.

no⌈risokona⌉·u のりそこなう (乗り損なう) *vt.* (-sokona·i-; -sokonaw·a-; -sokonat-te [C]) fail to catch (a train, bus, etc.); miss.

no⌈rizuke のりづけ (糊付け) *n.* pasting; gluing. ((⇨ nori[1]))

no⌈ro⌉·i のろい (鈍い) *a.* (-ku) (*colloq.*) (of motion, work, etc.) slow; dull.

no⌉ronoro のろのろ *adv.* (～ to; ～ suru) slowly; sluggishly.

no⌈r·u[1] のる (乗る) *vi.* (nor·i-; nor·a-; not-te [C]) **1** take (a bus, train, etc.); ride (a horse); get on. ((↔ oriru)) ((⇨ noseru[1]))
2 step on; get on:
Kanojo wa isu ni notte, *sono hoñ o totta.* (彼女はいすに乗って, その本を取った) She *got on* a chair and got the book.
3 give advice; take an interest:
Kare wa watashi no soodañ ni notte kureta. (彼は私の相談に乗ってくれた) He was kind enough to *give* me *advice*.

no⌈r·u[2] のる (載る) *vi.* (nor·i-; nor·a-; not-te [C]) **1** lie on; rest:
Shiryoo wa anata no tsukue no ue ni notte imasu. (資料はあなたの机の上にのっています) The data *are on* your desk.
2 (of an article, advertisement, etc.) appear (in a magazine, newspaper, etc.); (of a name, etc.) be listed. ((⇨ noseru[2]))

no⌈se·ru[1] のせる (乗せる) *vt.* (nosete [V]) give a ride; load; pick up. ((↔ orosu[1])) ((⇨ noru[1]))

no⌈se·ru[2] のせる (載せる) *vt.* (nosete [V]) **1** put on; load:
Watashi wa sono tsutsumi o tana no ue ni noseta. (私はその包みを棚の上に載せた) I *put* the parcel on the shelf.
2 publish:
Kono kiji wa sañ-gatsu-goo ni nosemasu. (この記事は3月号に載せます) We are going to *publish* this article in the March issue. ((⇨ noru[2]))

no⌈shi⌉ のし (熨斗) *n.* decoration for gifts. ★ Thin strip of dried abalone wrapped in red and white paper. These days the abalone is usually omitted.

no⌈zok·u[1] のぞく (除く) *vt.* (nozok·i-; nozok·a-; nozo·i-te [C]) remove; exclude; get rid of. ((⇨ torinozoku))

no⌈zok·u[2] のぞく (覗く) *vt.* (nozok·i-; nozok·a-; nozo·i-te [C]) peep; look in.

no⌈zomashi⌉·i のぞましい (望ましい) *a.* (-ku) desirable; preferable. ((⇨ konomashii))

no⌈zomi のぞみ (望み) *n.* **1** wish; desire; hope. ((⇨ nozomu[1]))
2 chance; prospect; likelihood:
Shoori no nozomi *wa mada juubuñ ni arimasu.* (勝利の望みはまだ十分にあります) We still have a good *chance* of victory.

no⌈zom·u[1] のぞむ (望む) *vt.* (nozom·i-; nozom·a-; nozoñ-de [C])
1 want; wish; hope for. ((⇨ nozomi))

n

2 like; prefer:
Inaka no seekatsu o nozomu *hito ga ooi.* (田舎の生活を望む人が多い) There are many people who *prefer* life in the country. 《⇨ nozomi》

no⌈zom·u[2] のぞむ (臨む) *vi.* (nozom·i-; nozom·a-; nozoñ-de C)
1 face (a place); overlook.
2 attend (a ceremony).
3 face (danger, crisis, etc.).

nu⌉g·u ぬぐ (脱ぐ) *vt.* (nug·i-; nug·a-; nu·i-de C) take off; get undressed. 《↔ haku[1]; kiru[2]》

nu⌈karumi ぬかるみ (泥濘) *n.* mud; muddy place.

nu⌈keda⌉s·u ぬけだす (抜け出す) *vi.* (-dash·i-; -das·a-; -dash·i-te C) get away; slip away; get out of:
heya kara nukedasu (部屋から抜け出す) *slip* out of a room.

nu⌈ke·ru ぬける (抜ける) *vi.* (nukete V) **1** come out; fall (out):
Kugi ga nakanaka nukenai. (くぎがなかなか抜けない) The nail *won't come out* easily. 《⇨ nuku》
2 come off; go off; wear off:
Baketsu no soko ga nukete shimatta. (バケツの底が抜けてしまった) The bottom of the bucket *came out.* 《⇨ nuku》
3 be missing; be left out:
Kono geñkoo wa sañ-mai nukete imasu. (この原稿は3枚抜けています) This manuscript *is missing* three pages. 《⇨ nuku》
4 go through:
Deñsha wa toñneru o nuketa. (電車はトンネルを抜けた) The train *went* through the tunnel.
5 leave (a group, organization, etc.); quit. 《⇨ dattai; nuku》

nu⌈kito⌉r·u ぬきとる (抜き取る) *vt.* (-tor·i-; -tor·a-; -tot-te C) pull out; extract; take out. 《⇨ nuku》

nu⌈k·u ぬく (抜く) *vi., vt.* (nuk·i-; nuk·a-; nu·i-te C) **1** pull out; extract:
biiru no señ o nuku (ビールの栓を抜く) *open* the bottle of beer. 《⇨ hikinuku; nukeru》
2 take out; remove (a stain). 《⇨ nukeru》
3 beat; outrun; outstrip:
mae o hashitte iru kuruma o nuku (前を走っている車を抜く) *overtake* the car traveling in front.

nu⌈ma⌉ ぬま (沼) *n.* swamp; marsh. 《⇨ ike》

nu⌈no ぬの (布) *n.* cloth. 《⇨ kire》

nu⌈ras·u ぬらす (濡らす) *vt.* (nurash·i-; nuras·a-; nurash·i-te C) wet; moisten; dampen. 《⇨ nureru》

nu⌈re·ru ぬれる (濡れる) *vi.* (nurete V) get wet; be moistened. 《⇨ nurasu》

nu⌈r·u ぬる (塗る) *vt.* (nur·i-; nur·a-; nut-te C) paint; spread; plaster; apply.

nu⌈ru⌉·i ぬるい (温い) *a.* (-ku) lukewarm; tepid. 《⇨ atsui[1]》

nu⌉shi ぬし (主) *n.* the person:
Ano hito ga uwasa no nushi *desu.* (あの人がうわさの主です) He is *the person* we have been talking about. 《⇨ hoñniñ》

nu⌈sumi⌉ ぬすみ (盗み) *n.* theft; pilferage; stealing:
nusumi *o hataraku* (盗みを働く) commit *theft.* 《⇨ nusumu》

nu⌈su⌉m·u ぬすむ (盗む) *vt.* (nusum·i-; nusum·a-; nusuñ-de C) steal; rob; pilfer. 《⇨ nusumi; toru[1]》

nu⌉·u ぬう (縫う) *vt.* (nu·i-; nuw·a-; nut-te C) sew; stitch:

nyo⌉o にょう (尿) *n.* urine.

nyu⌈u- にゅう (入) *pref.* entry; entrance:
nyuu-*koku* (入国) *entry* into a country / nyuu-*koo* (入港) *arrival* of a ship in port.

nyu⌈ugaku にゅうがく (入学) *n.* entrance into a school; admission to a school.
nyuugaku suru (～する) *vi.* start to go to school; be admitted to a school. 《↔ sotsugyoo》

nyu⌉ugañ にゅうがん (乳癌) *n.*

breast cancer. 《⇨ gañ》

nyu⌈uiñ にゅういん(入院) *n.* admission to a hospital; hospitalization.
nyuuiñ suru (〜する) *vi.* be hospitalized; enter the hospital.
《↔ taiiñ》《⇨ byooiñ》

nyu⌈ujoo にゅうじょう(入場) *n.* entrance; admission:
Kodomo wa nyuujoo *o-kotowari.* (*sign*) (子どもは入場お断わり) No *Admission* to Children.
nyuujoo suru (〜する) *vi.* enter; be admitted. 《↔ taijoo》《⇨ hairu》

nyu⌈ujo⌉okeñ にゅうじょうけん(入場券) *n.* admission ticket.

nyu⌈ukoku にゅうこく(入国) *n.* entry into a country:
nyuukoku-*tetsuzuki* (入国手続き) *immigration* formalities.
nyuukoku suru (〜する) *vi.* enter a country. 《↔ shukkoku》

nyu⌈usha にゅうしゃ(入社) *n.* joining a company.
nyuusha suru (〜する) *vi.* join a company. 《↔ taisha》

nyu⌈ushoo にゅうしょう(入賞) *n.* winning a prize.
nyuushoo suru (〜する) *vi.* win a prize.

nyu⌉usu ニュース *n.* news:
Nani-ka ii nyuusu *wa arimasu ka?* (何かいいニュースはありますか) Do you have any good *news*?

nyu⌈uyoku にゅうよく(入浴) *n.* bath; bathing. 《⇨ furo》
nyuuyoku suru (〜する) *vi.* take a bath.

O

o[1] お(尾) *n.* **1** tail. 《⇨ shippo》
2 (of a comet) trail.

o[2] を *p.* [follows a noun]
1 (indicates the direct object):
Maiasa shiñbuñ o *yomimasu.* (毎朝新聞を読みます) I read the *newspaper* every morning.
2 (indicates location or movement):
Tsugi no kado o *hidari e magari nasai.* (次の角を左へ曲がりなさい) Turn left *at* the next corner.
3 (indicates movement away from a place, institution, etc.):
Kyoneñ koko no daigaku o *demashita.* (去年ここの大学を出ました) I graduated *from* a university here last year.

o- お *pref.* [added to a noun, verb or adjective to indicate respect, humility or politeness]
1 (respect toward the listener):
O-tegami *arigatoo gozaimashita.* (お手紙ありがとうございました) Thank you for *your letter*. ★ Verbs are used in the following pattern: '*o-* + *v.* (continuative base) + *ni naru.*' 《⇨ naru[1]》
2 (humility on the part of the speaker):
Ato de o-deñwa *itashimasu.* (あとでお電話いたします) I'll give you a *call* later. ★ Verbs are used in the following pattern: '*o-* + *v.* (continutative base) + *suru* [*itasu*].' 《⇨ suru[1]》
3 (politeness):
o-kashi (お菓子) *sweets* / o-kane (お金) *money* / o-kome (お米) *rice*.

o⌈ba おば(伯母・叔母) *n.* one's aunt. ★ Older sisters of one's father or mother are '伯母,' and younger sisters are '叔母.' 《⇨ obasañ》

o-⌈ba⌉asañ おばあさん(お祖母さん・お婆さん) *n.* ★ '祖母' is used for 1, while '婆' is used for 2.
1 one's grandmother. 《⇨ sobo》
2 old woman. 《⇨ baasañ》

o⌈basañ おばさん(伯母さん・叔母さん・小母さん) *n.* ★ '伯母, 叔母' are used for 1, while '小母' is used for 2. 《⇨ oba》

n o

1 one's aunt.
2 middle-aged woman.

o⌉bi おび (帯) *n.* obi; belt for a kimono; broad sash.

o⌈biyaka⌉s·u おびやかす (脅かす) *vt.* (-kash·i-; -kas·a-; -kash·i-te Ⓒ) threaten; menace; frighten.

o⌈bo⌉e おぼえ (覚え) *n.* memory; remembrance; recollection:
Kanojo ni wa mae ni doko-ka de atta oboe ga aru. (彼女には前にどこかで会った覚えがある) I *remember* seeing her somewhere before. ⟪⇨ kioku⟫

o⌈boe⌉·ru おぼえる (覚える) *vt.* (oboe-te Ⓥ) 1 remember; memorize. ⟪⇨ omoidasu⟫
2 learn:
Suiee wa doko de oboemashita *ka?* (水泳はどこで覚えましたか) Where *did* you *learn* swimming?

o⌈bore·ru おぼれる (溺れる) *vi.* (obore-te Ⓥ) 1 (almost) drown; be (almost) drowned.
2 indulge in (excessibly):
sake ni oboreru (酒におぼれる) *abandon oneself* to drink.

o⌈busa⌉r·u おぶさる (負ぶさる) *vi.* (obusar·i-; obusar·a-; obusat-te Ⓒ) ride on a person's back; rely on. ⟪⇨ oñbu⟫

o-⌈cha おちゃ (お茶) *n.* 1 tea; green tea:
O-cha *o nomimaseñ ka?* (お茶を飲みませんか) How about a cup of *tea*? ★ This expression often implies "Let's have a chat." ⟪⇨ cha⟫
2 tea break:
O-cha *ni shimashoo.* (お茶にしましょう) Let's have a *tea break.*
3 tea ceremony:
o-cha *o narau* (お茶を習う) learn the *tea ceremony.*

o⌉chiba おちば (落ち葉) *n.* fallen leaves.

o⌈chi⌉·ru おちる (落ちる) *vi.* (ochite Ⓥ) 1 come [go] down; fall; drop. ⟪⇨ otosu⟫
2 fall [drop] off:
Koñgetsu wa uriage ga ochita. (今月は売上が落ちた) This month's sales *have fallen off*. ⟪↔ agaru⟫
3 fail an examination. ⟪⇨ otosu⟫
4 (of stains) come out [off]. ⟪⇨ otosu⟫
5 (of a name, item, etc.) be missing. ⟪⇨ otosu⟫

o⌈chitsuk·u おちつく (落ち着く) *vi.* (-tsuk·i-; -tsuk·a-; -tsu·i-te Ⓒ)
1 calm down; cool down.
2 (of trouble, a quarrel, etc.) subside; die down.
3 settle down (in an apartment).

o-⌈chuugeñ おちゅうげん (お中元) *n.* = chuugeñ.

o-⌈dai おだい (お代) *n.* price; rate; charge; fare. ⟪⇨ -dai[2]⟫

o-⌈daiji ni おだいじに (お大事に) take care of yourself. ★ An idiomatic expression of sympathy to a sick person.

o⌈date·ru おだてる (煽てる) *vt.* (odate-te Ⓥ) flatter; incite.

o⌈da⌉yaka おだやか (穏やか) *a.n.* (~ na, ni) 1 calm; quiet; peaceful. ⟪⇨ shizuka⟫
2 (of personality, atmosphere, etc.) mild; gentle; amicable.

o⌈de⌉ki おでき *n.* = dekimono.

o⌈de⌉ñ おでん *n.* Japanese hotchpotch.

o⌈dokas·u おどかす (脅かす) *vt.* (odokash·i-; odokas·a-; odokash·i-te Ⓒ) threaten; frighten; startle. ⟪⇨ odosu⟫

o⌉do-odo おどおど *adv.* (~ to) timidly; shyly.
odo-odo suru (~する) *vi.* be timid. ⟪⇨ bikubiku suru⟫

o⌈dori おどり (踊り) *n.* dance; dancing. ⟪⇨ butoo; odoru⟫

o⌈doriba おどりば (踊り場) *n.* landing (of stairs).

o⌈doroka⌉s·u おどろかす (驚かす) *vt.* (-kash·i-; -kas·a-; -kash·i-te Ⓒ) surprise; astonish; startle. ⟪⇨ odoroku⟫

o⌈doroki⌉ おどろき (驚き) *n.* surprise; astonishment; shock. ⟪⇨ odoroku⟫

o⌈doro⌉k·u おどろく(驚く) *vi.* (o-dorok·i-; odorok·a-; odoro·i-te Ⓒ) **1** be surprised; be astonished; be shocked. ⟪⇨ odorokasu⟫
2 wonder; marvel:
Sono sakuhiñ no amari no dekibae ni odorokimashita. (その作品のあまりのできばえに驚きました) I *marveled* at that wonderful work.
⟪⇨ odoroki⟫

o⌈dor·u おどる(踊る) *vi.* (odor·i-; odor·a-; odot-te Ⓒ) dance:
warutsu o odoru (ワルツを踊る) *dance* a waltz. ⟪⇨ odori⟫

o⌈doshi おどし(脅し) *n.* threat; menace; bluff. ⟪⇨ odosu⟫

o⌈dos·u おどす(脅す) *vt.* (odosh·i-; odos·a-; odosh·i-te Ⓒ) threaten; menace. ⟪⇨ odoshi⟫

o⌈e·ru おえる(終える) *vt.* (oe-te Ⓥ) finish; end; complete. ⟪⇨ owaru⟫

o⌈ga⌉m·u おがむ(拝む) *vt.* (ogam·i-; ogam·a-; ogañ-de Ⓒ) pray; worship:
hotoke-sama o ogamu (仏様を拝む) *worship* the Buddha.

o⌈gawa おがわ(小川) *n.* brook; small stream.

o⌈gina⌉·u おぎなう(補う) *vt.* (oginai-; oginaw·a-; oginat-te Ⓒ) make up for; compensate; fill:
akaji o oginau (赤字を補う) *make up* the deficit.

o⌈gor·u[1] おごる(奢る) *vt.* (ogor·i-; ogor·a-; ogot-te Ⓒ) treat:
Kyoo no o-hiru wa watashi ga ogorimasu. (きょうのお昼は私がおごります) I'll *treat* you to lunch today.

o⌈gor·u[2] おごる(驕る) *vi.* (ogor·i-; ogor·a-; ogot-te Ⓒ) be proud; be haughty:
Saikiñ yuumee ni natte, kare wa sukoshi ogotte iru. (最近有名になって, 彼は少しおごっている) Recently he has become famous and *is* a little *proud and arrogant.*

o⌈go⌉soka おごそか(厳か) *a.n.* (~ na, ni) solemn; grave; dignified.

o⌈ha⌉gi おはぎ(お萩) *n.* glutinous rice ball coated with sweet red-bean paste or soybean powder.

o-⌈hana おはな(お花) *n.* flower arrangement; ikebana.
⟪⇨ hana[2]; ikebana⟫

o⌈hayoo おはよう(お早よう) good morning. ★ Expression used when people first see each other in the early morning. '*Ohayoo.*' is used between close friends or when addressing a person lower in status. The more polite expression is '*Ohayoo gozaimasu.*'

o-⌈hi⌉ru おひる(お昼) *n.* noon; lunch:
O-hiru *wa doko de tabemashita ka?* (お昼はどこで食べましたか) Where did you have *lunch?* ⟪⇨ shoogo⟫

o⌈i[1] おい(甥) *n.* nephew. ★ When another family's nephew is referred to, '*oigo-sañ*' is used.
⟪↔ mee⟫

o⌉i[2] おい *int.* (*rude*) hey; hi; say; hello; look: ★ Used by men.
Oi. *Doko e iku ñ da.* (おい. どこへ行くんだ) *Hey!* Where are you going?

o⌈ida⌉s·u おいだす(追い出す) *vi.* (-dash·i-; -das·a-; -dash·i-te Ⓒ) drive out; expel; oust.

o⌈ide おいで(お出で) *n.* ★ Both '*oide desu*' and '*oide ni naru*' are honorific equivalents of '*iru,*' '*kuru*' and '*iku.*'
1 presence:
O-kaasañ wa oide *desu ka?* (お母さんはおいでですか) *Is* your mother *in*?
⟪⇨ iru[1]⟫
2 coming:
Doozo oide *kudasai.* (どうぞおいでください) Please *come and visit* us.
⟪⇨ kuru⟫
3 going:
Dochira e oide *desu ka?* (どちらへおいでですか) Where *are* you *going*?
⟪⇨ iku⟫
4 be present; go; come: ★ Shortened form of '*oide nasai,*' which implies an order or request.
Koko ni shibaraku oide. (ここにしばら

くおいで) *Stay* here for a while.

o⌈ihara⌉·u おいはらう (追い払う) *vt.* (-hara·i-; -haraw·a-; -harat-te [C]) (*informal* = opparau) drive [turn] away; disperse.

o⌈ikake⌉·ru おいかける (追い掛ける) *vt.* (-kake-te [V]) run after; chase; pursue.

o⌈iko⌉s·u おいこす (追い越す) *vt.* (-kosh·i-; -kos·a-; -kosh·i-te [C]) pass; overtake; outstrip. ⟪⇨ oi-tsuku⟫

o⌈inu⌉k·u おいぬく (追い抜く) *vt.* (-nuk·i-; -nuk·a-; -nu·i-te [C]) overtake. ⟪⇨ oikosu⟫

o⌈ishi·i おいしい (美味しい) *a.* (-ku) delicious; tasty; good. ⟪↔ mazui[1]⟫ ⟪⇨ umai⟫

o⌉ite おいて (於いて) ★ Used in the pattern '... *ni oite*.' Compared to '*de*,' it is a written form. Before a noun '... *ni okeru*' or '... *ni oite no*.'

1 in: ★ Indicates location in place or time.

Shikeñ wa kaigishitsu ni oite *okonawareta.* (試験は会議室において行われた) The examination was given *in* the conference room.

2 as for; in the matter of:

Kono teñ ni oite *watashi wa kare to ikeñ ga kuichigatte imasu.* (この点において私は彼と意見が食い違っています) *As for* this point, my opinion differs from his.

o⌈itsu⌉k·u おいつく (追い付く) *vt.* (-tsuk·i-; -tsuk·a-; -tsu·i-te [C]) catch up with; overtake. ⟪⇨ oikosu⟫

o⌈ji おじ (伯父·叔父) *n.* one's uncle. ★ Older brothers of one's father or mother are '伯父,' and younger brothers are '叔父.' ⟪⇨ ojisañ⟫

o⌈jigi おじぎ (お辞儀) *n.* bow:

Sono ko wa watashi ni teenee ni ojigi o shita. (その子は私にていねいにおじぎをした) The child *bowed* politely to me.

o-⌈ji⌉isañ おじいさん (お祖父さん·お爺さん) *n.* ★ '祖父' is used for 1, while '爺' is used for 2.

1 one's grandfather. ⟪⇨ sofu⟫

2 old man. ⟪⇨ jiisañ⟫

o⌈jisañ おじさん (伯父さん·叔父さん·小父さん) *n.* ★ '伯父, 叔父' is used for 1, while '小父' is used for 2.

1 one's uncle. ⟪⇨ oji⟫

2 middle-aged man.

o-⌈jo⌉osañ おじょうさん (お嬢さん) *n.*

1 your [his; her] daughter.

2 young lady; girl. ⟪↔ botchañ⟫

o⌈ka おか (丘) *n.* hill; heights. ⟪⇨ yama⟫

o-⌈ka⌉achañ おかあちゃん (お母ちゃん) *n.* mother; mom. ★ Used chiefly by small children. ⟪↔ o-toochañ⟫

o-⌈ka⌉asañ おかあさん (お母さん) *n.* mother; mom. ⟪↔ o-toosañ⟫ ⟪⇨ haha⟫

o⌈kaeri nasa⌉i おかえりなさい (お帰りなさい) welcome home; I'm glad you're home again. ★ Literally 'You've come home.' A set phrase used in response to '*Tadaima*.' (I'm home.) ⟪⇨ tadaima[2]⟫

o⌈kage おかげ (お陰) *n.* thanks to; owing to:

Anata ga tetsudatte kureta okage *de, mikka de shigoto ga owarimashita.* (あなたが手伝ってくれたおかげで, 3日で仕事が終わりました) *Thanks to* your help, I was able to finish the work in three days. ⟪⇨ see[5]⟫

o⌈kagesama de おかげさまで (お陰さまで) ★ An idiomatic expression used in response to a greeting.

"O-geñki desu ka?" "Okagesama de." (「お元気ですか」「おかげさまで」) "How are you?" "*I'm fine, thank you.*"

o-⌈kane おかね (お金) *n.* = kane[1].

o-⌈ka⌉shi おかし (お菓子) *n.* confectionery; cake; sweets; candy. ⟪⇨ kashi[1]⟫

o⌈kashi⌉·i おかしい (可笑しい) *a.* (-ku) **1** amusing; funny; ridiculous. ⟪⇨ okashi-na; omoshiroi⟫

2 strange; odd:

Kare ga mada konai no wa okashii. (彼がまだ来ないのはおかしい) His not

arriving yet is *strange*.

3 queer; unusual:
I no guai ga chotto okashii. (胃の具合がちょっとおかしい) My stomach feels a bit *queer*.

o⌈ka⌉shi-na おかしな (可笑しな) *attrib.* **1** amusing; funny; ridiculous. (⇒ okashii)
2 strange; queer; odd. (⇒ okashii)

o⌈ka⌉s·u[1] おかす (犯す) *vt.* (okash·i-; okas·a-; okash·i-te Ⓒ) commit (a crime); violate (a law); break.

o⌈ka⌉s·u[2] おかす (侵す) *vt.* (okash·i-; okas·a-; okash·i-te Ⓒ) invade; infringe; violate:
hoka no hito no puraibashii o okasu (ほかの人のプライバシーを侵す) *invade* another person's privacy.

o⌈kazu おかず (お数) *n.* side dish.

o⌈ke おけ (桶) *n.* tub; pail; wooden bucket.

o⌈ke⌉ru おける (於ける) at; in:
★ Used in the pattern '*... ni okeru*.'
Igaku ni okeru *shiñpo wa subarashii.* (医学における進歩はすばらしい) The progress *in* medical science is remarkable. (⇒ oite)

o⌈ki おき (沖) *n.* offing; open sea.

-o⌈ki おき (置き) *suf.* every; at intervals of:
ichi-meetoru-oki *ni kui o utsu* (1メートルおきにくいを打つ) drive in the stakes *at intervals of* one meter.

o⌈kiba おきば (置き場) *n.* place (for leaving something); space; room.

o⌈kido⌉kee おきどけい (置き時計) *n.* table [desk; mantel] clock. (⇒ tokee)

o⌈kimono おきもの (置物) *n.* ornament. ★ China, carving, figurines, etc., that are displayed in one's home.

o⌈ki⌉·ru おきる (起きる) *vi.* (oki-te Ⓥ) **1** get up; rise. (⇒ okosu)
2 wake up; stay awake. (⇒ okosu)
3 happen; occur. (⇒ okoru[1])

o⌈kiwasure⌉·ru おきわすれる (置き忘れる) *vt.* (-wasure-te Ⓥ) leave; forget; put down and forget:
deñsha ni kasa o okiwasureru (電車に傘を置き忘れる) *leave* one's umbrella in a train. (⇒ wasureru; wasuremono)

o⌈kona·u おこなう (行う) *vt.* (okona·i-; okonaw·a-; okonat-te Ⓒ) hold; give; practice:
shikeñ o okonau (試験を行う) *give* an examination.

o⌈kori⌉ おこり (起こり) *n.* **1** cause:
Koto no okori *wa nañ desu ka?* (事の起こりは何ですか) What is the *cause* of this?
2 origin; source:
buñmee no okori (文明の起こり) the *origin* of civilization.

o⌈ko⌉r·u[1] おこる (起こる) *vi.* (okor·i-; okor·a-; okot-te Ⓒ)
1 happen; occur; take place.
2 be caused; stem from:
Sono jiko wa fuchuui kara okotta. (その事故は不注意から起こった) The accident *stemmed* from carelessness. (⇒ okiru; okosu)

o⌈ko⌉r·u[2] おこる (怒る) (okor·i-; okor·a-; okot-te Ⓒ) **1** *vi.* get angry; lose one's temper.
2 *vt.* scold. (⇒ shikaru)

o⌈ko⌉r·u[3] おこる (興る) *vi.* (okor·i-; okor·a-; okot-te Ⓒ) spring up; come into existence.

o-⌈kosañ おこさん (お子さん) *n.* (*polite*) someone else's child.

o⌈ko⌉s·u おこす (起こす) *vt.* (okosh·i-; okos·a-; okosh·i-te Ⓒ)
1 wake up; awake:
Asu no asa roku-ji ni okoshite *kudasai.* (あすの朝6時に起こしてください) Please *wake* me *up* at six tomorrow morning. (⇒ okiru)
2 raise; set up:
Kare wa taoreta saku o okoshita. (彼は倒れたさくを起こした) He *raised* the fallen fence.
3 cause (an accident, trouble); bring about:
jiko [moñdai] o okosu (事故[問題]を起こす) *cause* an accident [trouble]. (⇒ okiru)

O

4 start (a movement):
shoohisha-uñdoo o okosu (消費者運動を起こす) *start* a consumer movement. ⟪⇨ okiru⟫
5 produce:
deñki o okosu (電気を起こす) *produce* electricity. ⟪⇨ okiru⟫

o-ʳkotowari おことわり (お断り) *n.* refusal; rejection; prohibition:
★ Used as a warning.
Meñkai wa o-kotowari *desu.* (面会はお断りです) We *cannot accept* visitors. ⟪⇨ kotowaru⟫

oʳk·u[1] おく (置く) *vt.* (ok·i-; ok·a-; o·i-te Ⓒ) **1** put; keep; place:
Kasa wa doko ni oitara *yoi deshoo ka?* (傘はどこに置いたらよいでしょうか) Where should I *put* my umbrella?
2 leave:
Kagi o doko e oita *ka wasurete shimatta.* (鍵をどこへ置いたか忘れてしまった) I have forgotten where I *left* the keys.
3 have for sale; deal in:
Kono mise wa iroiro na buñboogu o oite imasu. (この店はいろいろな文房具を置いています) At this shop they *handle* a variety of stationery goods.
4 take in; have:
Kare wa shiyooniñ o oite imasu. (彼は使用人を置いています) He *has* a servant.
-te[-de] oku (て[で]〜) leave a thing as it is; do something in advance: *Tomodachi ga sugu kuru kara doa o* akete oite *kudasai.* (友だちがすぐ来るからドアを開けておいてください) A friend is coming soon, so please *leave* the door *open*.

oˀku[2] おく (奥) *n.* inner part; interior; back.

oˀku[3] おく (億) *n.* one hundred million. ⟪⇨ APP. 3⟫

oʳkubyoˀo おくびょう (臆病) *a.n.* (〜 na, ni) cowardly; timid.

oʳkujoo おくじょう (屋上) *n.* roof; rooftop. ⟪↔ chika⟫

oʳkurase·ru おくらせる (遅らせる) *vt.* (okurase-te Ⓥ) delay; put off; turn back. ⟪⇨ okureru⟫

oʳkure おくれ (遅れ) *n.* delay:
Kootsuu juutai ga okure *no geñiñ datta.* (交通渋滞が遅れの原因だった) The traffic jam was the cause of the *delay*. ⟪⇨ okureru⟫

oʳkure·ru おくれる (遅れる) *vi.* (okure-te Ⓥ) **1** be late; be behind time:
Yakusoku no jikañ ni okurete shimatta. (約束の時間に遅れてしまった) I *was later* than the time agreed on. ⟪⇨ chikoku; okure⟫
2 (of a clock, watch) be slow; lose. ⟪↔ susumu⟫
3 fall behind; be behind.

oʳkurigana おくりがな (送り仮名) *n.* (inflectional) 'kana' ending.
★ The 'kana' added to a Chinese character to help show its Japanese grammatical ending.

oʳkurimono おくりもの (贈り物) *n.* present; gift. ⟪⇨ miyage; purezeñto⟫

oʳkur·u[1] おくる (送る) *vt.* (okur·i-; okur·a-; okut-te Ⓒ) **1** send:
Kare ni kookuubiñ de hoñ o okutta. (彼に航空便で本を送った) I *sent* him a book by airmail. ⟪⇨ dasu (5)⟫
2 see off; see home; take:
Kanojo o uchi made okutte *yari nasai.* (彼女を家まで送ってやりなさい) Please *see* her home.
3 pass; spend; lead:
Kare wa megumareta seekatsu o okutte imasu. (彼は恵まれた生活を送っています) He *leads* a privileged life.

oʳkur·u[2] おくる (贈る) *vt.* (okur·i-; okur·a-; okut-te Ⓒ) give; present:
Kanojo no kekkoñ iwai ni kabiñ o okutta. (彼女の結婚祝いに花瓶を贈った) I *gave* her a vase for a wedding present.

oˀkusama おくさま (奥様) *n.* (*polite*) someone else's wife; married woman. ⟪⇨ okusañ⟫

oˀkusañ おくさん (奥さん) *n.* someone else's wife; married woman.
★ Used when addressing some-

one else's wife or referring to her. A more polite word is '*okusama*.' The speaker's wife is referred to as '*kanai*.'

o-ˈkyaku-sañ おきゃくさん (お客さん) *n.* **1** (*polite*) caller; visitor; guest. **2** customer; client; audience; spectator; passenger. ⟪⇨ kyaku⟫

oˈmachidoosama おまちどうさま (お待ちどうさま) (*informal*) = omatase shimashita.

oˈmae おまえ (お前) *n.* (*rude*) you: ★ Used by men in addressing inferiors, particularly children. The plural forms are '*omae-tachi*' and (*derog.*) '*omae-ra*.'
Omae *mo kuru ka?* (おまえも来るか) *You* coming with me? ⟪⇨ ore⟫

oˈmairi おまいり (お参り) *n.* visit to a temple [shrine]; going to worship at a temple [shrine].
omairi suru (～する) *vi.* visit [go to] a temple [shrine]. ⟪⇨ sañpai⟫

oˈmamori おまもり (お守り) *n.* good luck talisman [charm].

oˈmatase shimaˈshita おまたせしました (お待たせしました) (*humble*= '*omatase itashimashita*') I am sorry to have kept you waiting.

oˈmaˈwari-sañ おまわりさん (お巡りさん) *n.* policeman; cop. ⟪⇨ keekañ⟫

oˈmedeta おめでた (御目出度) *n.* happy event. ★ Often used with reference to a forthcoming birth.

oˈmedeta·i おめでたい (御目出度い) *a.* (-ku) **1** = medetai. **2** (*derog.*) simple-minded.

oˈmedetoo おめでとう (御目出度う) congratulations: ★ '*Omedetoo gozaimasu*' is more polite.
Tañjoobi omedetoo. (誕生日おめでとう) *Many happy returns of the day.*

oˈmedetoo gozaimaˈsu おめでとうございます (御目出度う御座います) = omedetoo.

oˈme-ni-kakaˈr·u おめにかかる (お目に掛かる) *vt.* (-kakar·i-; -kakar·a-; -kakat-te Ⓒ) meet; see: ★ Humble equivalent of '*au*.'
Mata ome-ni-kakarete *ureshii desu.* (またお目にかかれてうれしいです) I'm glad to *see* you again.

oˈmikuji おみくじ (御神籤) *n.* sacred lot from a shrine; written oracle. ★ The fortune is written on a slip of paper.

o-ˈmiyage おみやげ *n.* present; gift; souvenir. ⟪⇨ miyage; okurimono⟫

oˈmoˈcha おもちゃ *n.* toy; plaything.
omocha ni suru (～にする) toy [play] with.

oˈmo·i[1] おもい (重い) *a.* (-ku) **1** heavy. ⟪↔ karui⟫ ⟪⇨ omosa⟫ **2** important; grave:
Watashi wa sono omoi *sekiniñ o hikiukeru koto ni shita.* (私はその重い責任を引き受けることにした) I've decided to assume that *grave* responsibility. ⟪↔ karui⟫
3 (of crime, disease, etc.) serious. ⟪↔ karui⟫

oˈmoˈi[2] おもい (思い) *n.* **1** thought; idea:
omoi *ni fukeru* (思いにふける) be lost in *thought*.
2 wish; expectation:
Subete wa omoi-doori *umaku ikimashita.* (すべては思い通りうまくいきました) Everything went off well, *as we had wished*.
3 attachment; affection:
Kare wa kanojo ni omoi *o yosete ita.* (彼は彼女に思いを寄せていた) He had an *attachment* for her.
4 feeling:
Kodomo ni wa kanashii omoi *o sasetaku nai.* (子どもには悲しい思いをさせたくない) I do not want to make my children *feel sad*.

oˈmoichigai おもいちがい (思い違い) *n.* misunderstanding; mistake.

oˈmoidaˈs·u おもいだす (思い出す) *vt.* (-dash·i-; -das·a-; -dash·i-te Ⓒ) remember; recall; remind:
mukashi o omoidasu (昔を思い出す) *think of* the good old days. ⟪⇨ oboeru⟫

o⌈moide おもいで（思い出） *n.* recollections; memory; reminiscence.

o⌈moigakena⌉·i おもいがけない（思いがけない） *a.* (-ku) unexpected:
Omoigakenaku, *tomodachi ga tazunete kita.* (思いがけなく，友だちが訪ねて来た) A friend *unexpectedly* visited me.

o⌈moikiri[1] おもいきり（思い切り） *n.* decisiveness; decision:
Kare wa omoikiri ga yoi [warui]. (彼は思い切りがよい[悪い]) He *is decisive* [*indecisive*]. ((⇨ omoikiru))

o⌈moikiri[2] おもいきり（思い切り） *adv.* thoroughly; to one's heart's content. ((⇨ omou-zoñbuñ))

o⌈moiki⌉r·u おもいきる（思い切る） *vt.* (-kir·i-; -kir·a-; -kit-te Ⓒ) give up; abandon; decide.
((⇨ omoikiri[1]; omoikitte))

o⌈mo⌉ikitte おもいきって（思い切って） *adv.* decisively; resolutely:
Kanojo wa omoikitte *señsee ni hoñtoo no koto o hanashita.* (彼女は思い切って先生にほんとうのことを話した) She *dared* to tell the truth to her teacher.
omoikitte ... suru (〜...する) make up one's mind to do.

o⌈moiko⌉m·u おもいこむ（思い込む） *vi.* (-kom·i-; -kom·a-; -koñ-de Ⓒ)
1 believe; be under the impression. ((⇨ shiñjiru))
2 take...for granted:
Miñna kare ga yuushoo suru mono to omoikoñde ita. (みんな彼が優勝するものと思い込んでいた) Everyone *took it for granted* that he would win the championship.

o⌈moi-no-hoka おもいのほか（思いの外） *adv.* unexpectedly; surprisingly. ((⇨ añgai))

o⌈moitodoma⌉r·u おもいとどまる（思い止まる） *vt.* (-todomar·i-; -todomar·a-; -todomat-te Ⓒ) change one's mind; hold oneself back. ((⇨ akirameru))

o⌈moitsuki おもいつき（思い付き） *n.* idea; thought:
Sore wa yoi omoitsuki *desu.* (それは良い思いつきです) That is a good *idea.*
((⇨ omoitsuku))

o⌈moitsu⌉k·u おもいつく（思い付く） *vt.* (-tsuk·i-; -tsuk·a-; -tsu·i-te Ⓒ) hit on; think of:
umai kañgae o omoitsuku (うまい考えを思いつく) *hit on* a good idea.
((⇨ omoitsuki))

o⌈moiyari おもいやり（思いやり） *n.* consideration; thoughtfulness; sympathy:
Kare wa hoka no hito ni taishite omoiyari ga aru. (彼はほかの人に対して思いやりがある) He *is considerate* to others.

o⌈mokurushi⌉·i おもくるしい（重苦しい） *a.* (-ku) heavy; gloomy; oppressive; stifling.

o⌈momuki おもむき（趣） *n.* **1** attractive atmosphere; charm:
Kono niwa wa omomuki *ga aru.* (この庭は趣がある) This garden has its *charm.*
2 look; appearance:
Kaateñ de heya no omomuki *ga kawatta.* (カーテンで部屋の趣が変わった) Because of the curtains the *appearance* of the room changed.

o⌉mo-na おもな（主な） *attrib.* chief; principal; main; leading:
Nihoñ no omo-na *toshi* (日本の主な都市) the *major* cities in Japan.

o⌈moni おもに（重荷） *n.* heavy load; burden:
Ryooshiñ no kitai ga kare no omoni *datta.* (両親の期待が彼の重荷だった) The expectations of his parents were a *burden* to him.

o⌉mo ni おもに（主に） *adv.* chiefly; mainly; mostly.

o⌈moñji⌉·ru おもんじる（重んじる） *vt.* (omoñji-te Ⓥ) respect; make much of; value. ((↔ karoñjiru))

o⌈mo-omoshi⌉·i おもおもしい（重々しい） *a.* (-ku) (of speech, attitude, etc.) grave; dignified; serious.

o⌈mosa おもさ（重さ） *n.* weight.
((⇨ omoi[1]; mekata))

o⌈moshiro⌉·i おもしろい（面白い） *a.* (-ku) interesting; amusing;

funny; exciting. ⟪↔ tsumaranai⟫

o⌈mota·i おもたい(重たい) *a.* (-ku) heavy. ⟪⇨ omoi[1]⟫

o⌈mote⌉ おもて(表) *n.* **1** front; the right side; surface. ⟪↔ ura⟫

2 front door:

Omote *kara haitte kudasai.* (表から入ってください) Please come in through the *front door.* ⟪↔ ura⟫

3 outside; the outdoors:

Omote *ni dare-ka tatte imasu.* (表にだれか立っています) There is someone standing *outside.*

4 (of baseball) the first half.

o⌈motemoñ おもてもん(表門) *n.* front gate. ⟪↔ uramoñ⟫

o⌈mo⌉·u おもう(思う) *vt.* (omo·i-; omow·a-; omot-te Ⓒ)

★ '*Omou*' refers to having thoughts and '*kañgaeru*' implies thinking about, pondering, considering, but there is some overlap in meaning.

1 think; believe:

Sore wa uso da to omou. (それはうそだと思う) I *think* that is a lie.

2 consider; regard:

Kare wa yuushuu na señshu da to omoimasu. (彼は優秀な選手だと思います) I *consider* him to be an excellent player.

3 expect:

Soko de kare ni au to wa omowanakatta. (そこで彼に会うとは思わなかった) I *never expected* I would meet him there.

4 want; wish; hope:

Yoroshikereba, sochira ni ukagaitai to omoimasu. (よろしければ, そちらにうかがいたいと思います) Provided it is convenient, I *would like* to pay you a visit. ★ In the pattern '*... tai to omou,*' '*omou*' is used to soften the force of '*tai*' and as such does not have a very specific meaning.

5 intend; be going to:

Kare wa isha ni naroo to omotte iru. (彼は医者になろうと思っている) He *intends* to become a doctor.

6 think of:

Kare wa itsu-mo byooki no haha no koto o omotte iru. (彼はいつも病気の母のことを思っている) He always *thinks of* his sick mother. ⟪⇨ kañgaeru⟫

o⌈mo⌉u-zoñbuñ おもうぞんぶん(思う存分) *adv.* (~ ni) to the full; to one's heart's content.

o⌈mowaku おもわく(思惑) *n.* expectation; calculation:

Watashi no omowaku *wa hazureta.* (私の思惑ははずれた) My *calculations* turned out to be wrong.

o⌈mo⌉wazu おもわず(思わず) *adv.* involuntarily; unconsciously; instinctively:

Sono shashiñ o mite, omowazu *waratte shimatta.* (その写真を見て, 思わず笑ってしまった) I *could not help* laughing when I saw the picture.

o⌈mu⌉subi おむすび(お結び) *n.* rice ball. ⟪⇨ onigiri⟫

o⌈mu⌉tsu おむつ *n.* diaper; nappy.

o⌉ñ[1] おん(恩) *n.* obligation; favor; kindness:

*Go-*oñ *wa wasuremaseñ.* (ご恩は忘れません) I will never forget your *kindness.*

o⌉ñ[2] おん(音) *n.* **1** (phonetics) speech sound.

2 the reading of a Chinese character taken from the original Chinese pronunciation. ⟪⇨ kuñ⟫

o⌉ñ- おん(御) *pref.* (used to indicate respect or politeness):

★ More formal than '*o-*,' but limited in use.

Oñ-ree *mooshi agemasu.* (御礼申し上げます) Please accept my *sincere thanks.*

o⌈naji おなじ(同じ) ★ '*Onaji*' is the form that precedes a noun. It is not followed by '*na*' or '*no.*'

1 same; similar; alike:

Watashi mo kore to onaji *jisho o motte imasu.* (私もこれと同じ辞書を持っています) I have the *same* dictionary as this. ⟪⇨ onajiku⟫

2 equivalent; equal:

Kono Nihoñgo to mattaku onaji

Eego wa arimaseñ. (この日本語とまったく同じ英語はありません) There is no English expression that is exactly *equivalent* to this Japanese. ⟪⇨ dooitsu; dooyoo[1]⟫

o⌈na⌉jiku おなじく(同じく) *adv.* similarly; in like manner:
Kare mo kimi to onajiku *gorufu ga suki da.* (彼も君と同じくゴルフが好きだ) He is fond of playing golf *like* you. ⟪⇨ onaji⟫

o⌈naka おなか(お腹) *n.* bowels; stomach: ★ More polite than '*hara.*'
Onaka ga suita. (おなかがすいた) I *am hungry.*
onaka ga ookii (〜が大きい) (*euphemistic*) be pregnant. ⟪⇨ hara[1]⟫

o⌉ñbiñ おんびん(音便) *n.* euphonic change in the pronunciation of a word. ⟪⇨ APP. 1⟫

o⌉ñbu おんぶ *n.* piggyback; pickaback. ⟪⇨ obusaru⟫
oñbu suru (〜する) *vt.* **1** carry a child piggyback.
2 rely on; depend upon.

o⌉ñchuu おんちゅう(御中) *n.* (*formal*) Messrs. ★ Used after the name of a firm or office on an envelope.

o⌈ñdañ おんだん(温暖) *a.n.* (〜 na, ni) (of climate) temperate; mild.

o⌉ñdo おんど(温度) *n.* temperature; heat. ⟪⇨ shitsuoñ⟫

o⌈ñdokee おんどけい(温度計) *n.* thermometer. ★ In Japan, the temperature is measured in Celsius. ⟪⇨ kañdañkee; sesshi⟫

o-⌈ne⌉esañ おねえさん(お姉さん) *n.*
1 someone else's older sister. ⟪↔ o-niisañ⟫
2 (as a term of address) my older sister. ★ When referring to one's own older sister, '*ane*' is used.

o-⌈negai おねがい(お願い) *n.* favor; request:
O-negai *ga aru ñ desu ga.* (お願いがあるんですが) I have a *favor* to ask of you.
o-negai suru (〜する) *vt.* request; ask: *Kore kara mo yoroshiku* o-negai shimasu. (これからもよろしくお願いします) I'*d appreciate* your support in the future. ⟪⇨ negai⟫

o⌉ñgaku おんがく(音楽) *n.* music; the musical art.

o⌈ñgakuka おんがくか(音楽家) *n.* musician.

o⌈ñgaku⌉kai おんがくかい(音楽会) *n.* concert.

o⌈ni⌉ おに(鬼) *n.* **1** demon; fiend; ogre.
2 (of the game of tag) "it."

o⌈ni⌉giri おにぎり(お握り) *n.* rice ball. ⟪⇨ omusubi⟫

o⌈ni-go⌉kko おにごっこ(鬼ごっこ) *n.* the game of tag.

o-⌈ni⌉isañ おにいさん(お兄さん) *n.*
1 someone else's older brother.
2 (as a term of address) my older brother. ★ When referring to one's own older brother, '*ani*' is used. ⟪⇨ o-neesañ⟫

o⌈ñna⌉ おんな(女) *n.* woman; female. ★ Often has a derogatory connotation; '*josee*' is preferable in many uses. ⟪↔ otoko⟫ ⟪⇨ fujiñ[2]; josee⟫

o⌈ñnade おんなで(女手) *n.* female breadwinner:
Kanojo wa oñnade *hitotsu de sañniñ no kodomo o sodateta.* (彼女は女手ひとつで3人の子どもを育てた) She brought up three children all by *herself.*

o⌈ñna⌉-no-ko おんなのこ(女の子) *n.* girl; daughter. ⟪↔ otoko-no-ko⟫ ⟪⇨ musume⟫

o⌈ñnarashi⌉i おんならしい(女らしい) *a.* (-ku) womanly; feminine; ladylike. ⟪↔ otokorashii⟫ ⟪⇨ joseeteki⟫

o⌈no⌉-ono おのおの(各々) *n.* (*slightly formal*) each:
Hito ni wa ono-ono *choosho to tañsho ga arimasu.* (人にはおのおの長所と短所があります) *Each* person has merits and shortcomings. ⟪⇨ kakuji; meemee⟫

o⌉ñsee おんせい(音声) *n.* voice;

vocal sound.

o⌈ñseñ おんせん (温泉) *n.* hot spring; spa.

o⌈ñsetsu おんせつ (音節) *n.* syllable.

o⌈ñshiñ-futsuu おんしんふつう (音信不通) *n.* no news; no correspondence.

o⌈ñshitsu おんしつ (温室) *n.* hothouse; greenhouse.

o⌈ñtai おんたい (温帯) *n.* temperate zone. ⟪⇨ kañtai; nettai⟫

o⌉o[1] おう (王) *n.* **1** king. ⟪↔ jo-oo⟫
2 king; magnate:
hyaku-juu no oo (百獣の王) the *king* of beasts / *sekiyu*-oo (石油王) an oil *magnate*.

o⌉o[2] おお *int.* oh; aah; well:
★ Used to express admiration, wonder, sorrow, etc.
Oo, *suteki da.* (おお, すてきだ) *Oh*, how fantastic. ⟪⇨ aa[2]⟫

oo- おお (大) *pref.* big; many; heavy; special:
oo-*doori* (大通り) a *main* street / oo-*goe* (大声) a *loud* voice.

-oo *infl. end.* [attached to the stem of a consonant-stem verb] ⟪⇨ -yoo⟫
1 intend; want:
Boku wa beñgoshi ni naroo to omotte imasu. (ぼくは弁護士になろうと思っています) I *intend to become* a lawyer.
2 be about to do:
Kare no uchi e ikoo to shitara, *kare ga tazunete kita.* (彼の家へ行こうとしたら, 彼が訪ねてきた) I *was on the point of going* to his house, when he came to see me.
3 let's:
Teñrañ-kai o mi ni ikoo. (展覧会を見に行こう) *Let's go* to see the exhibition.

o⌈oa⌉me おおあめ (大雨) *n.* heavy rain. ⟪↔ kosame⟫

o⌉obaa オーバー *a.n.* (~ na, ni) exaggerated. ⟪⇨ oogesa⟫
oobaa suru (~する) *vi.* exceed; go beyond. ⟪⇨ chooka⟫

o⌈obo おうぼ (応募) *n.* application; entry.
oobo suru (~する) *vi.* apply for; enter for. ⟪⇨ mooshikomu⟫

o⌈odañ[1] おうだん (横断) *n.* crossing; traversing:
oodañ-*hodoo* (横断歩道) a pedestrian *crossing*.
oodañ suru (~する) *vt.* go across; cross; traverse. ⟪⇨ wataru⟫

o⌈odañ[2] おうだん (黄疸) *n.* jaundice.

o⌈odo⌉ori おおどおり (大通り) *n.* main street; thoroughfare.

o⌈oeñ おうえん (応援) *n.* help; support; backing.
ooeñ suru (~する) *vt.* help; support; back up; cheer.

o⌈oe⌉ñdañ おうえんだん (応援団) *n.* cheering party; rooters.

o⌈o-e⌉ru オーエル *n.* female office worker. ★ Often written as 'OL,' an abbreviation of 'office lady.'

o⌈ofuku おうふく (往復) *n.* coming and going; going and returning. ⟪↔ katamichi⟫
oofuku suru (~する) *vi.* go and come back; make a round trip.

o⌈ofuku-ha⌉gaki おうふくはがき (往復葉書) *n.* reply-paid postcard. ⟪⇨ hagaki⟫

o⌈oga⌉kari おおがかり (大掛かり) *a.n.* (~ na, ni) great; large-scale:
oogakari *na kooji* (大がかりな工事) *large-scale* construction works. ⟪⇨ daikibo⟫

o⌈ogata おおがた (大型) *n.* large size:
oogata *no taifuu* (大型の台風) a *large* typhoon / oogata *no reezooko* (大型の冷蔵庫) a *large* refrigerator. ⟪⇨ chuugata; kogata⟫

o⌈ogesa おおげさ (大袈裟) *a.n.* (~ na, ni) exaggerated:
Kare no hanashi wa itsu-mo oogesa *da.* (彼の話はいつも大げさだ) His stories are always *exaggerated*.

o⌈ogo⌉e おおごえ (大声) *n.* loud voice:
oogoe o dasu (大声を出す) *raise one's voice*. ⟪↔ kogoe⟫

O

o⌈oguchi おおぐち (大口) *n.* **1** big [large] mouth:
ooguchi o akete *warau* (大口を開けて笑う) laugh *with one's mouth wide open.* 《⇨ kuchi[1]》
2 big:
ooguchi *no chuumoñ o morau* (大口の注文をもらう) receive a *big* order.

o⌈ohaba おおはば (大幅) *a.n.* (~ na, ni) large; big; drastic; substantial:
Jugyoo-ryoo ga oohaba *ni agatta.* (授業料が大幅に上がった) Tuition fees have gone up *substantially.*

o⌉o·i おおい (多い) *a.* (-ku) many; much; numerous:
Nihoñ wa jishiñ ga ooi. (日本は地震が多い) Earthquakes are *common* in Japan. 《↔ sukunai》

o⌉oi ni おおいに (大いに) *adv.* greatly; very (much):
ooi ni *yorokobu* (大いに喜ぶ) be *highly* pleased.

o⌈oi⌉sogi おおいそぎ (大急ぎ) *n.* being urgent; being pressed:
ooisogi *de eki e* iku (大急ぎで駅へ行く) *rush* to the station.

o⌈oji·ru おうじる (応じる) *vi.* (ooji-te [V]) **1** meet (a demand, order, etc.); accept; satisfy; respond.
2 be appropriate; be suitable (to one's ability):
nooryoku ni oojita *shoku o sagasu* (能力に応じた職を探す) look for employment that *is appropriate* to one's abilities.

o⌈okata[1] おおかた (大方) *adv.*
1 probably; perhaps:
Ookata *soñna koto daroo to omotte imashita.* (おおかたそんなことだろうと思っていました) I thought that was *perhaps* the case.
2 almost; nearly:
Sono atarashii ie wa ookata *dekiagarimashita.* (その新しい家はおおかたでき上がりました) The new house is *almost* finished. 《⇨ daitai》

o⌈okata[2] おおかた (大方) *n.* people in general:
Ookata no yosoo-doori, *Seebu ga yuushoo shimashita.* (おおかたの予想通り, 西武が優勝しました) *As generally expected,* the Seibu Lions won the pennant.

o⌈oke⌉sutora オーケストラ *n.* (symphony) orchestra; orchestral music.

o⌈oki⌉·i おおきい (大きい) *a.* (-ku)
1 big; large:
ookii *tsukue* (大きい机) a *large* desk. 《↔ chiisai》《⇨ ooki-na》
2 (of degree) great:
Fugookaku no shokku wa ookikatta. (不合格のショックは大きかった) Failure in the exam came as a *great* shock.
ookiku naru (大きくなる) grow up.

o⌉oki-na おおきな (大きな) *attrib.* big; large; great:
Yotee ni ooki-na *heñkoo wa nakatta.* (予定に大きな変更はなかった) There was no *great* change in the schedule. 《↔ chiisa-na》《⇨ ookii》

o⌈okisa おおきさ (大きさ) *n.* size; dimensions; volume:
ookisa *o hakaru* (大きさを測る) measure the *size.* 《⇨ daishoo; suñpoo》

o⌉oku おおく (多く) *n., adv.* many; much:
Kañkyaku no ooku *wa kodomotachi datta.* (観客の多くは子どもたちだった) *Most* of the audience were children.

o⌈okyuu おうきゅう (応急) *n.* emergency; temporary; makeshift:
★ Usually used in compounds.
ookyuu-teate (応急手当) *first aid.*

o⌈omi⌉zu おおみず (大水) *n.* flood:
oomizu ga deru (大水が出る) *be flooded.*

o⌈omu⌉gi おおむぎ (大麦) *n.* barley.

o⌈omu⌉kashi おおむかし (大昔) *n.* ancient times; antiquity.

o⌉opuñ[1] オープン *n.* opening.
oopuñ suru (~する) *vi.* open.

o⌉opuñ[2] オープン *a.n.* (~ na, ni) frank; open to the public.

o⌉orai オーライ *n.* all right; O.K.:
Hassha oorai. (*said by train conductors, etc.*) (発車オーライ) It is *all*

right to depart.

o⌈osee おうせい (旺盛) *a.n.* (~ na, ni) full of energy; eager:
Kodomo-tachi wa shokuyoku oosee *da.* (子どもたちは食欲おうせいだ) Children have a *good* appetite.

o⌈osetsu おうせつ (応接) *n.* reception (of a visitor).
oosetsu suru (~する) *vt.* receive (a guest).

o⌈osetsuma おうせつま (応接間) *n.* drawing room.

o⌈osetsu⌉shitsu おうせつしつ (応接室) *n.* reception room.

o⌈otai おうたい (応対) *n.* reception; meeting.
... ni ootai suru (...に~する) *vi.* receive (callers); deal with; wait on (customers).

o⌈oteñ おうてん (横転) *n.* turning sideways; overturning.
ooteñ suru (~する) *vi.* turn sideways; overturn.

o⌈oto⌉bai オートバイ *n.* motorcycle; motorbike.

o⌈o⌉·u おおう (覆う) *vt.* (oo·i-; oo-w·a-; oot-te Ⓒ) cover; veil; envelop. ⟪⇨ tsutsumu⟫

o⌉oya おおや (大家) *n.* owner of a house for rent; landlord; landlady. ⟪⇨ jinushi⟫

o⌈oyoo おうよう (応用) *n.* application; adaptation; practice.
ooyoo suru (~する) *vt.* apply; adapt; put to use.

o⌈oyo⌉rokobi おおよろこび (大喜び) *n.* delight; glee; joy:
Kare-ra wa shiai ni katte, ooyorokobi datta. (彼らは試合に勝って, 大喜びだった) They *were overjoyed* at winning the match.

o⌈oyoso おおよそ (大凡) *n.* outline:
Keekaku no ooyoso *o hanashite kudasai.* (計画のおおよそを話してください) Please tell us the *general outline* of your plan.
— *adv.* roughly; approximately; about. ⟪⇨ oyoso⟫

o⌈oyuki おおゆき (大雪) *n.* heavy fall of snow; heavy snowfall. ⟪↔ koyuki⟫ ⟪⇨ yuki[1]⟫

o⌈oza⌉ppa おおざっぱ (大雑把) *a.n.* (~ na, ni) rough; general:
Oozappa *ni mitsumotte, hyaku-mañ-eñ kakarimasu.* (おおざっぱに見積もって, 100 万円かかります) Estimating *roughly*, it will cost a million yen.

o⌈oze⌉e おおぜい (大勢) *n., adv.* crowd (of people).

o⌉ppai おっぱい *n.* = chichi[2].
★ Infant word for mother's milk or breast.

o⌈ppara⌉·u おっぱらう (追っ払う) *vt.* (-para·i-; -paraw·a-; -parat-te Ⓒ) = oiharau.

o⌈re おれ (俺) *n.* (*rude*) I.
★ Used by men. The plural form is '*ore-tachi*.' ⟪⇨ omae⟫

o-⌈ree おれい (お礼) *n.* ★ Polite form of '*ree*.' ⟪⇨ ree[2]⟫
1 thanks; gratitude:
Sono uchi o-ree *ni ukagaimasu.* (そのうちお礼に伺います) I will shortly pay you a visit *to thank you*.
2 reward; fee; remuneration.
o-ree (o) suru (~(を)する) *vt.* give a reward; pay a fee.

or⌈eñji-ka⌉ado オレンジカード *n.* a magnetic card with which one can buy Japan Railway tickets from vending machines.

o⌈re⌉·ru おれる (折れる) *vi.* (ore-te Ⓥ) **1** break; give way:
Yuki no omomi de ki no eda ga oreta. (雪の重みで木の枝が折れた) The branches *broke* under the weight of the snow. ⟪⇨ oru[1]⟫
2 give in; yield to.
3 turn:
Sono kuruma wa hidari ni oreta. (その車は左に折れた) The car *turned* left.

o⌈ri⌉ おり (折) *n.* occasion; time; chance:
Kono tsugi kare ni atta ori, *yoroshiku o-tsutae kudasai.* (この次彼に会った折, よろしくお伝えください) Please give him my best regards the next *time* you see him.
ori o mite (~をみて) at the first

opportunity.

o⌈ri⌉gami おりがみ（折り紙）*n.* origami; colored paper for paper folding.

o⌈rimono おりもの（織物）*n.* textile; fabric.

o⌈ri⌉·ru おりる（降りる・下りる）*vi.* (ori-te [V]) **1** get off (a vehicle); step off. 《↔ noru[1]》《⇨ gesha; orosu[1]》
2 come [go] down; step down:
kaidañ o oriru（階段を下りる）*go down* stairs.
3 (of frost and dew) fall:
Kesa wa hidoi shimo ga orita.（今朝はひどい霜が降りた）This morning the frost *was thick*.
4 quit (a position, etc.); resign.

o⌈ritatam·u おりたたむ（折り畳む）*vt.* (-tatam·i-; -tatam·a-; -tatañ-de [C]) fold; collapse (an umbrella). 《⇨ tatamu》

o⌉roka おろか（愚か）*a.n.* (~ na, ni) foolish; silly; stupid.

o⌈roshi⌉ おろし（卸し）*n.* wholesale. 《⇨ kouri; orosu[2]; toñya》

o⌈ro⌉soka おろそか（疎か）*a.n.* (~ na, ni) neglectful; negligent:
beñkyoo o orosoka *ni suru*（勉強をおろそかにする）*neglect* one's studies.

o⌈ro⌉s·u[1] おろす（降ろす・下ろす）*vt.* (orosh·i-; oros·a-; orosh·i-te [C])
1 drop; let off:
Tsugi no shiñgoo de oroshite *kudasai.*（次の信号で降ろしてください）Please *drop* me *off* at the next traffic light. 《↔ noseru[1]》《⇨ oriru》
2 unload; discharge; take down.
3 pull down; roll down; lower:
buraiñdo o orosu（ブラインドを下ろす）*lower* the blinds.
4 withdraw (a deposit).

o⌈ro⌉s·u[2] おろす（卸す）*vt.* (orosh·i-; oros·a-; orosh·i-te [C]) sell; wholesale:
Kono shoohiñ wa hitotsu señ-eñ de oroshite imasu.（この商品は一つ千円で卸しています）We *wholesale* these goods at 1,000 yen apiece.

o⌉r·u[1] おる（折る）*vt.* (or·i-; or·a-; ot-te [C]) **1** break; snap:
Kare wa hidari-ashi no hone o otta.（彼は左足の骨を折った）He *broke* a bone in his left leg.
2 fold:
Kanojo wa origami o otte, *tsuru o tsukutta.*（彼女は折り紙を折って，つるを作った）She *folded* a piece of paper into a crane.

o⌉r·u[2] おる（織る）*vt.* (or·i-; or·a-; ot-te [C]) weave.

o⌉r·u[3] おる（居る）*vi.* (or·i-; or·a-; ot-te [C]) be; exist:
1 [with an animate subject] (humble equivalent of '*iru*'):
Shujiñ wa ima ie ni orimasu.（主人は今家におります）My husband *is* at home now.
2 [with an inanimate subject] (polite equivalent of '(-*te*) *iru*'):
Kochira wa ima yuki ga futte orimasu.（こちらは今雪が降っております）It *is* now snowing here.

o⌈rugañ オルガン *n.* organ:
orugañ *o hiku*（オルガンをひく）play the *organ*.

o⌈sae⌉·ru おさえる（押さえる）*vt.* (osae-te [V]) **1** hold (down):
Kono roopu o shikkari osaete *kudasai.*（このロープをしっかり押さえてください）Please *hold* this rope tightly.
2 catch; arrest:
Doroboo wa geñkoohañ de osaerareta.（泥棒は現行犯で押さえられた）The thief *was caught* red-handed.

o⌈sama⌉r·u[1] おさまる（収まる）*vi.* (osamar·i-; osamar·a-; osamat-te [C]) **1** fit; be kept:
Sono tana ni kono hoñ ga zeñbu osamarimasu *ka?*（その棚にこの本が全部収まりますか）Will these books all *fit* onto that shelf? 《⇨ osameru[1]》
2 take office:
Kare wa kaichoo ni osamatta.（彼は会長に収まった）He *took* the post of chairman.

o⌈sama⌉r·u[2] おさまる（治まる）*vi.* (osamar·i-; osamar·a-; osamat-te [C]) **1** (of turmoil) settle

(down); be settled. ⟪⇨ osameru[2]⟫
2 (of the wind) calm down; die down.

o⌈sama⌉r·u[3] おさまる(納まる) *vi.* (osamar·i-; osamar·a-; osamatte Ⓒ) be paid:
Anata no zeekiñ ga mada osamatte *imaseñ.* (あなたの税金がまだ納まっていません) Your taxes *have* not *been paid* yet. ⟪⇨ osameru[3]⟫

o⌈same⌉·ru[1] おさめる(収める) *vt.* (osame-te Ⓥ) **1** put away (in); store; keep:
Tsukatta doogu wa moto no tokoro ni osamemashita. (使った道具は元の所に収めました) I *put* the tools *away* in their proper place. ⟪⇨ osamaru[1]⟫
2 get (a grade, mark); obtain; gain; attain:
Kare wa yuushuu na seeseki o osameta. (彼は優秀な成績を収めた) He *obtained* distinguished grades.

o⌈same⌉·ru[2] おさめる(治める) *vt.* (osame-te Ⓥ) **1** rule; govern; reign: *kuni o* osameru (国を治める) *govern* a country.
2 settle; put down:
sawagi o osameru (騒ぎを治める) *settle* a disturbance. ⟪⇨ osamaru[2]⟫

o⌈same⌉·ru[3] おさめる(納める) *vt.* (osame-te Ⓥ) **1** pay (a fee, charge, tax, etc.):
jugyoo-ryoo [*zeekiñ*] *o* osameru (授業料[税金]を納める) *pay* one's tuition [tax]. ⟪⇨ osamaru[3]⟫
2 supply; deliver:
Chuumoñ no shina wa getsumatsu made ni osamemasu. (注文の品は月末までに納めます) We will *deliver* the goods ordered by the end of the month.
3 accept:
Doo-ka kore o o-osame *kudasai.* (どうかこれをお納めください) Please *accept* this.

o⌈sana⌉·i おさない(幼い) *a.* (-ku)
1 very young.
2 childish; immature:
Ano hito wa toshi no wari ni osanai. (あの人は年の割に幼い) He is very *immature* for his age.

o-⌈satsu おさつ(お札) *n.* paper money; bill; note. ⟪⇨ satsu⟫

o⌈sechi-ryo⌉ori おせちりょうり(お節料理) *n.* special dishes served on the first three days of the New Year.

o-⌈seebo おせいぼ(お歳暮) *n.* = seebo.

o⌈seji おせじ(お世辞) *n.* compliment; flattery:
hito ni oseji o iu (人にお世辞を言う) *flatter* [*compliment*] a person.

o⌈sha⌉beri おしゃべり(お喋り) *n.* chat; chatter.
oshaberi (o) suru (〜(を)する) *vi.* chat away; chatter.
— *a.n.* (〜 na) talkative; gossipy.

o⌈sha⌉re おしゃれ(お洒落) *n.* dressing up; smart dresser.
oshare (o) suru (〜(を)する) *vi.* get dressed up.

o⌈shie おしえ(教え) *n.* teaching; instruction. ⟪⇨ oshieru⟫

o⌈shie·ru おしえる(教える) *vt.* (oshie-te Ⓥ) **1** teach (a lesson); instruct. ⟪↔ osowaru⟫ ⟪⇨ oshie⟫
2 tell (information); show (the way).

o⌈shi⌉·i おしい(惜しい) *a.* (-ku)
1 regrettable; unlucky:
Ii chañsu o nogashite, oshii *koto o shita.* (いいチャンスを逃して, 惜しいことをした) It was too *bad* that I let a great opportunity slip by.
2 precious; dear:
Dare de mo inochi ga oshii. (だれでも命が惜しい) Life is *dear* to everyone. ⟪⇨ oshimu⟫
3 too good:
Kono mañneñhitsu wa suteru no ga oshii. (この万年筆は捨てるのが惜しい) This fountain pen is *too good* to throw away. ⟪⇨ mottainai⟫

o⌈shiire おしいれ(押し入れ) *n.* closet; storage cupboard.

o⌈shi⌉kko おしっこ *n.* pee; piddle; urine. ★ Often used by

O

young children. ((⇨ shoobeñ))

o[shiko]m·u おしこむ (押し込む) *vi.* (-kom·i-; -kom·a-; -koñ-de [C]) push; thrust; stuff:
Kare wa kabañ ni hoñ o oshikoñda. (彼はかばんに本を押し込んだ) He *stuffed* the books into his bag.

o[shimai おしまい (お仕舞い) *n.* end; finish:
Kyoo wa kore de oshimai ni shiyoo. (きょうはこれでおしまいにしよう) *Let's finish off* here for today.
((⇨ shimai²))

o[shi]m·u おしむ (惜しむ) *vt.* (oshim·i-; oshim·a-; oshiñ-de [C])
1 grudge; spare:
Kare wa musume no tame ni hiyoo o oshimanakatta. (彼は娘のために費用を惜しまなかった) He *spared no* expense for his daughter.
2 regret:
Miñna ga kare no shi o oshiñda. (みんなが彼の死を惜しんだ) Everybody *regretted* his death.
((⇨ oshii))

o[shiroi おしろい (白粉) *n.* face powder.

o[shitsuke]·ru おしつける (押し付ける) *vt.* (-tsuke-te [V]) **1** push against; press against; thrust.
2 force (an unwelcome job) onto a person.

o[shiyose]·ru おしよせる (押し寄せる) *vi.* (-yose-te [V]) crowd; throng; surge:
Oozee no hito ga shiñ-kyuujoo ni oshiyoseta. (大勢の人が新球場に押し寄せた) Many people *crowded* into the new ballpark.

o[shoku おしょく (汚職) *n.* corruption; graft; bribery.

o-[shoosui おしょうすい (お小水) *n.* urine. ★ A common euphemism used in hospitals. ((⇨ shoobeñ))

o[so·i おそい (遅い) *a.* (-ku) **1** (of time) late:
Kotoshi wa haru ga osoi. (今年は春が遅い) Spring is *late* in coming this year. ((↔ hayai¹))
2 (of motion) slow. ((↔ hayai²))

o[sonae おそなえ (お供え) *n.* **1** offering. ((⇨ sonaeru²))
2 rice-cake offering.

o[so]raku おそらく (恐らく) *adv.* perhaps; probably; possibly; likely. ((⇨ tabuñ; tashika))

o[sore¹¹ おそれ (虞れ) *n.* **1** fear:
Kyoo wa ame no osore *wa arimaseñ.* (きょうは雨のおそれはありません) There is no *fear* of rain today.
2 possibility; likelihood:
Sono jikkeñ wa shippai suru osore ga arimasu. (その実験は失敗するおそれがあります) The experiment *is likely* to fail.

o[sore¹² おそれ (恐れ) *n.* terror; horror; dread. ((⇨ osoreru))

o[so]reirimasu おそれいります (恐れ入ります) (*humble*) thank you very much:
O-kokorozukai osoreirimasu. (お心づかい恐れ入ります) Your kind consideration *is much appreciated.*
osoreirimasu ga (〜が) excuse me, but: Osoreirimasu ga *mado o shimete itadakemasu ka?* (恐れ入りますが窓を閉めていただけますか) *Excuse me, but* would you mind closing the window?

o[sore]·ru おそれる (恐れる) *vi.* (osore-te [V]) fear; dread; be afraid; be frightened.
((⇨ osore²; osoroshii))

o[soroshi]·i おそろしい (恐ろしい) *a.* (-ku) fearful; terrible; horrible.
((⇨ osoreru; kowai))

o[soro]shiku おそろしく (恐ろしく) *adv.* very; awfully; terribly:
Kyoo wa osoroshiku *samui.* (きょうはおそろしく寒い) Today is a *terribly* cold day.

o[so]·u おそう (襲う) *vt.* (oso·i-; osow·a-; osot-te [C]) **1** attack; assault; raid.
2 (of disaster, tragedy, etc.) hit; strike:
Taifuu ga Kañtoo chihoo o osotta. (台風が関東地方を襲った) A typhoon *struck* the Kanto district.

o[sowar·u おそわる (教わる) *vi.*

(osowar·i-; osowar·a-; osowat-te [C]) be taught; learn:
Tanaka señsee kara Nihoñgo o osowaru (田中先生から日本語を教わる) *learn* Japanese from Miss Tanaka. ⟪↔ oshieru⟫

o⌈ssha⌉r·u おっしゃる (仰る) *vt.* (ossha·i-; osshar·a-; osshat-te [C]) say: ★ Honorific equivalent of '*iu.*'
Nañ to osshaimashita *ka?* (何とおっしゃいましたか) What was it you *said*?

o⌈s·u[1] おす (押す) *vt.* (osh·i-; o-s·a-; osh·i-te [C]) **1** push; press; shove; thrust.
2 stamp; seal:
hañ o osu (判を押す) *affix* a seal.

o⌈su⌉[2] おす (雄) *n.* male; he:
osu *no saru* (雄の猿) a *male* monkey / osu-neko (雄猫) a *tomcat.* ⟪↔ mesu⟫

o⌈tagaisama おたがいさま (お互い様) being in the same circumstances:
Kyuuryoo ga yasui no wa otagaisama *da.* (給料が安いのはお互いさまだ) *We are in the same boat* — having a low salary.

o-⌈taku おたく (お宅) *n.* **1** someone else's house: ★ Usually refers to the house of the listener.
Asu o-taku *ni ukagaimasu.* (あすお宅に伺います) I'll visit *your house* tomorrow.
2 you: ★ Polite equivalent of '*anata.*'
Kono kabañ wa o-taku no *desu ka?* (このかばんはお宅のですか) Is this bag *yours*?

o-⌈tazune[1] おたずね (お尋ね) *n.* (*polite*) question; inquiry.
o-tazune suru (〜する) *vt.* ask; inquire; question. ⟪⇨ tazuneru[1]⟫

o-⌈tazune[2] おたずね (お訪ね) *n.* (*polite*) visit.
o-tazune suru (〜する) *vt.* pay a visit. ⟪⇨ tazuneru[2]⟫

o-⌈tea⌉rai おてあらい (お手洗い) *n.* (*polite*) toilet; lavatory. ⟪⇨ tearai; beñjo; toire⟫

o-⌈te⌉tsudai-sañ おてつだいさん (お手伝いさん) *n.* home help; housemaid.

o⌈to⌉ おと (音) *n.* sound; noise.

o⌈togiba⌉nashi おとぎばなし (お伽話) *n.* fairy tale; nursery tale. ⟪⇨ doowa⟫

o⌈toko⌉ おとこ (男) *n.* man; male. ★ Has no derogatory connotation like '*oñna.*' ⟪⇨ dañsee⟫

o⌈toko⌉-no-ko おとこのこ (男の子) *n.* boy; son. ⟪↔ oñna-no-ko⟫ ⟪⇨ musuko⟫

o⌈tokorashi⌉·i おとこらしい (男らしい) *a.* (-ku) (*appreciative*) manly; masculine. ⟪↔ oñnarashii⟫ ⟪⇨ dañsee-teki⟫

o-⌈tokui(-sañ) おとくい(さん) (お得意(さん)) *n.* good customer.

o⌈tona おとな (大人) *n.* grown-up; adult. ⟪↔ kodomo⟫

o⌈tonashi⌉·i おとなしい (大人しい) *a.* (-ku) **1** (of a disposition) quiet; gentle; mild; meek; obedient.
2 (of a color, a pattern) quiet; soft; sober.

o-⌈to⌉ochañ おとうちゃん (お父ちゃん) *n.* father; dad. ★ Used chiefly by small children. ⟪↔ o-kaachañ⟫

o-⌈to⌉osañ おとうさん (お父さん) *n.* father; dad. ⟪↔ o-kaasañ⟫ ⟪⇨ chichi[1]⟫

o⌈tooto⌉ おとうと (弟) *n.* one's younger brother. ★ When referring to someone else's, '*ototosañ*' is usually used. ⟪↔ ani⟫

ot⌈oroe⌉ おとろえ (衰え) *n.* decline; weakening; failing:
kiokuryoku no otoroe (記憶力の衰え) the *failing* of one's memory. ⟪⇨ otoroeru⟫

o⌈toroe⌉·ru おとろえる (衰える) *vi.* (otoroe-te [V]) become weak; fail; decline:
Taifuu wa otoroete kita. (台風は衰えてきた) The typhoon *has lost its force.* ⟪⇨ otoroe⟫

o⌈tor·u おとる (劣る) *vi.* (otor·i-;

otor·a-; otot-te Ⓒ) be inferior; fall below.

o⌈toshimono おとしもの (落とし物) *n.* lost article [property]; something dropped by mistake. (⇨ otosu)

o⌈to⌉s·u おとす (落とす) *vt.* (otosh·i-; otos·a-; otosh·i-te Ⓒ)
1 drop:
Kare wa fooku o yuka ni otoshita. (彼はフォークを床に落とした) He *dropped* his fork on the floor. (⇨ ochiru)
2 lose:
Saifu o doko de otoshita *no ka wakarimaseñ.* (財布をどこで落としたのかわかりません) I do not know where I *lost* my purse.
3 reduce; lower:
supiido o otosu (スピードを落とす) *reduce* speed / *koe o* otosu (声を落とす) *lower* one's voice. (⇨ ochiru)
4 remove makeup; take out (stains, etc.). (⇨ ochiru)
5 fail (an examinee). (⇨ ochiru)

o⌈toto⌉i おととい (一昨日) *n.* the day before yesterday.

o⌈to⌉toshi おととし (一昨年) *n.* the year before last.

o⌈tozure⌉·ru おとずれる (訪れる) *vi.* (otozure-te Ⓥ) visit; call. (⇨ hoomoñ; tazuneru[2])

o⌈tsukaresama おつかれさま (お疲れ様) you must be tired; thank you for your hard work.
★ Used to express thanks to a person for doing something on one's behalf. '*Otsukaresama deshita.*' is used to superiors. (⇨ -sama)

o-⌈tsuri おつり (お釣り) *n.* change:
O-tsuri *wa totte oite kudasai.* (お釣りはとっておいてください) Please keep the *change*. (⇨ tsuri[2])

o⌈tto おっと (夫) *n.* husband.
★ '*Otto*' refers either to one's own husband, or is used as a generic term for husband. (↔ tsuma) (⇨ shujiñ)

o·⌈u[1] おう (追う) *vt.* (o·i-; ow·a-; ot-te Ⓒ) **1** chase; go after. (⇨ oikakeru)
2 drive away:
Kare wa sono chii o owareta. (彼はその地位を追われた) He *was driven* from his position.

o·⌈u[2] おう (負う) *vt.* (o·i-; ow·a-; ot-te Ⓒ) **1** carry (a load) on one's back. (⇨ seou)
2 assume (responsibility).
3 get wounded [injured]; suffer (an injury):
juushoo o ou (重傷を負う) *suffer* severe injury / *soñgai o* ou (損害を負う) *suffer* a loss.

o-⌈wabi おわび (お詫び) *n.* (*polite*) apology. (⇨ wabi; wabiru)

o-⌈wañ おわん (お椀) *n.* = wañ[1].

o⌈wari おわり (終わり) *n.* end; close. (↔ hajime) (⇨ owaru)

o⌈war·u おわる (終わる) *vi.* (owar·i-; owar·a-; owat-te Ⓒ) finish; end; be over. (⇨ oeru; owari; shuuryoo)

o⌈ya⌉ おや (親) *n.* parent(s). (↔ ko)

o⌈ya'⌉ おやっ *int.* oh; oh dear; dear me; good heavens:
Oya', *are wa nañ no oto da?* (おやっ, あれは何の音だ) *Oh!* What's that sound?

o⌉yako おやこ (親子) *n.* parent and child.

o⌉yaoya おやおや *int.* well; oh; oh dear; good heavens. ★ Intensive equivalent of '*oya'*.'

o⌈yasumi nasa⌉i おやすみなさい (お休みなさい) good night; sleep well.

o⌈ya⌉tsu おやつ (お八つ) *n.* **1** coffee [tea] break.
2 snack; refreshments.

o⌈yayubi おやゆび (親指) *n.* thumb. ★ In Japanese, the thumb is considered one of the fingers.

o⌈yobi および (及び) *conj.* (*formal*) and; both...and...:
Shimee oyobi *juusho o kinyuu no koto.* (氏名および住所を記入のこと)

Enter *both* name *and* address. 《⇨ soshite; to[2]》

o⌈yobos·u およぼす (及ぼす) *vt.* (oyobosh·i-; oyobos·a-; oyo-bosh·i-te Ⓒ) exert (influence); cause (harm). 《⇨ oyobu》

o⌈yob·u およぶ (及ぶ) *vi.* (oyob·i-; oyob·a-; oyoñ-de Ⓒ) **1** extend; spread; reach:
Kare no keñkyuu wa hiroi hañi ni oyobu. (彼の研究は広い範囲に及ぶ) His researches *extend* over a wide field. 《⇨ oyobosu》
2 (of time) last:
Kare no shukuji wa sañjup-puñ ni mo oyoñda. (彼の祝辞は 30 分にも及んだ) His congratulatory address *lasted* all of thirty minutes.
3 match:
Suugaku de wa kare ni oyobu *mono wa imaseñ.* (数学では彼に及ぶ者はいません) There is no one who can *match* him in math.
4 (in the negative) do not need:
Anata wa kuru ni wa oyobimaseñ. (あなたは来るには及びません) You *don't need* to come.

o⌈yo⌉g·u およぐ (泳ぐ) *vi.* (oyog·i-; oyog·a-; oyo·i-de Ⓒ) swim.

o-⌈yomesañ およめさん (お嫁さん) *n.* bride. 《⇨ yome》

o⌈yoso およそ (凡そ) *adv.*
1 about; nearly. 《⇨ yaku[3]》
2 (with a negative) quite; entirely:
Soñna koto o shite mo oyoso *imi ga arimaseñ.* (そんなことをしてもおよそ意味がありません) Even if you did that kind of thing, it would be *quite* meaningless.

o-⌈yu おゆ (お湯) *n.* hot water. 《⇨ yu》

P

-pa ぱ (羽) *suf.* counter for birds and rabbits. 《⇨ -wa; APP. 4》

pa⌉ama パーマ *n.* permanent wave; perm.

pa⌈ase⌉ñto パーセント *n.* percent; per cent. 《⇨ bu[2]; wari》

pa⌉atii パーティー *n.* **1** (of an occasion) party:
paatii *o hiraku* [*okonau*] (パーティーを開く[行う]) give a *party.*
2 (of a group) party. 《⇨ ikkoo[1]》

pa⌈chiñko パチンコ *n.* pinball (game); pachinko.

pa⌉chipachi ぱちぱち *adv.* (~ to) (the sound or action of crackling, clapping, etc.):
Kareki ga pachipachi (*to*) *moeta.* (枯れ木がぱちぱち(と)燃えた) The dry trees burned *with a crackling sound.*

-pai ぱい (杯) *suf.* counter for glassfuls or cupfuls. 《⇨ -hai; APP. 4》

pa⌈ipu パイプ *n.* pipe; tube; cigarette holder.

-paku ぱく (泊) *suf.* counter for overnight stays. 《⇨ APP. 4》

pa⌉ñ パン *n.* bread; toast; roll; bun.

pa⌈ñfure⌉tto パンフレット *n.* pamphlet; brochure; leaflet.

pa⌈ñku パンク *n.* flat tire; puncture.
pañku suru (~する) *vi.* have a flat tire; be punctured.

pa⌉ñtii-suto⌉kkiñgu パンティーストッキング *n.* panty hose.

pa⌉ñtsu パンツ *n.* underpants; briefs; shorts. ★ Not usually used for '*trousers.*'

pa⌉ñya パンや (パン屋) *n.* bakery; baker.

pa⌉pa パパ *n.* dad; daddy; papa; father. 《⇨ mama[2]》

pa⌉rapara[1] ぱらぱら *adv.* (~ to) (the sound or action of droplets or small objects falling or pages being turned):

o
p

Ame ga parapara (to) futte *kita.* (雨がぱらぱら(と)降って来た) The rain has started to *spatter down*.

pa⌈rapara[2] ぱらぱら *adv.* (the state of being sparse):
Dono sharyoo mo jookyaku wa parapara *datta.* (どの車両も乗客はぱらぱらだった) There were *just a few* passengers on every train.

pa⌉sapasa[1] ぱさぱさ *adv.* (~ to; ~ suru) (the state of being dry and bland):
Kono pañ wa pasapasa shite iru. (このパンはぱさぱさしている) This bread *is all dried up*.

pa⌈sapasa[2] ぱさぱさ *adv.* dry and brittle:
Kami ga pasapasa *da.* (髪がぱさぱさだ) My hair is *dry and brittle*.

pa⌈sokoñ パソコン *n.* personal computer.

pa⌈supo⌉oto パスポート *n.* passport. ⟪⇨ ryokeñ⟫

-patsu ぱつ(発) *suf.* counter used with bullets, shells and large fireworks. ⟪⇨ APP. 4⟫

pa⌉tto ぱっと *adv.* suddenly; all at once; quickly:
Ii kañgae ga patto *ukañda.* (いい考えがぱっと浮かんだ) A great idea *suddenly* occurred to me.
patto shinai (~しない) unattractive; inconspicuous; dull.

pe⌉chakucha ぺちゃくちゃ *adv.* (~ to) (used to express the manner of chattering or prattling):
pechakucha (to) shaberu (ぺちゃくちゃ(と)しゃべる) *chatter away*.

pe⌈epaa-te⌉suto ペーパーテスト *n.* written test.

pe⌈kopeko[1] ぺこぺこ *a.n.* (~ na, ni) (the state of being hungry):
Onaka ga pekopeko *da.* (おなかがぺこぺこだ) I am very *hungry*.

pe⌉kopeko[2] ぺこぺこ *adv.* (~ to; ~ suru) (bow) humbly.

-peñ ぺん(遍) *suf.* counter for the number of times. ⟪⇨ APP. 4⟫

pe⌉ñchi ペンチ *n.* cutting pliers.

pe⌈ñki ペンキ *n.* paint:
kabe ni peñki o nuru (壁にペンキを塗る) *paint* a wall. ⟪⇨ toryoo⟫

pe⌉rapera[1] ぺらぺら *a.n.* (~ na, ni) fluent; glib; voluble:
Kare wa Nihoñgo ga perapera *desu.* (彼は日本語がぺらぺらです) His Japanese is *fluent*.
— *adv.* (~ to) talkatively; noisily. ⟪⇨ berabera⟫

pe⌈rapera[2] ぺらぺら *a.n.* (~ na/no, ni) (of paper, board, etc.) thin; flimsy. ⟪⇨ usui⟫

pi⌉chipichi ぴちぴち *adv.* (~ to; ~ suru) (the state of being young, fresh and vigorous):
Sono shoojo wa pichipichi *(to) shite ita.* (その少女はぴちぴち(と)していた) The girl was *young and fresh*.

pi⌉imañ ピーマン *n.* green pepper; pimento.

pi⌉ipii ぴいぴい *adv.* (~ to; ~ suru) **1** (the song of birds):
Tori ga piipii (to) naite iru. (鳥がぴいぴい(と)鳴いている) Birds *are chirping*.
2 (of a financial condition) badly off; hard up:
Kare wa ima piipii shite iru. (彼は今ぴいぴいしている) He *is short of money* right now.

pi⌈kapika[1] ぴかぴか *a.n.* (~ na/no, ni) shining; glittering.

pi⌈ka⌉pika[2] ぴかぴか *adv.* (~ to) (the state of glittering, twinkling, etc.):
Inazuma ga pikapika to hikatta. (稲妻がピカピカと光った) *There was a flash* of lightning.

-piki ぴき(匹) *suf.* counter for small animals, fish and insects. ⟪⇨ APP. 4⟫

pi⌉kunikku ピクニック *n.* picnic.
★ Used for a pleasure trip which includes a picnic. Not used in the sense of a meal out of doors.

pi⌉kupiku ぴくぴく *adv.* (~ to; ~ suru) (the state of twitching):
Uki ga pikupiku shite iru. (浮きがぴくぴくしている) The float *is bobbing up and down*.

p

pi˥ñku ピンク *n.* pink. ★ Suggests something risqué, like 'blue' in English. *e.g.* piñku-*eega* (ピンク映画) a *pornographic* movie. ⟪⇨ momoiro⟫

pi˥ñto ピント *n.* focus: piñto *ga amai* [*zurete iru*] (ピントがあまい[ずれている]) be out of *focus*.
piñto-hazure (〜外れ) be wide of the mark. ⟪⇨ mato⟫

pi˥ta˥ri ぴたり *adv.* (〜 to)
1 closely; tightly.
2 suddenly; right away: *Sono kusuri o noñdara, itami ga* pitari (to) tomatta. (その薬を飲んだら, 痛みがぴたりと止まった) The pain *went right away* after I took the medicine.
3 exactly perfectly: *Yosoo ga* pitari (*to*) *atatta.* (予想がぴたり(と)当たった) My forecast hit the mark *exactly*.

pi˥tchi ピッチ *n.* pace; speed: *Koosoo-biru ga kyuu*-pitchi *de keñsetsu sarete iru.* (高層ビルが急ピッチで建設されている) High-rise buildings are being built at a fast *pace*.

pi˥tta˥ri ぴったり *adv.* (〜 no, to; 〜 suru) **1** = pitari.
2 right: *Kono fuku wa anata ni* pittari *desu.* (この服はあなたにぴったりです) These clothes are *just right* for you.

-po ぽ (歩) *suf.* counter for steps. ⟪⇨ APP. 4⟫

po˥kapoka ぽかぽか *adv.* (〜 to; 〜 suru) **1** (the state of being nice and warm): *Yooki ga* pokapoka *shite ite kimochi ga ii.* (陽気がぽかぽかしていて気持ちがいい) The weather is *nice and warm*.
2 (of beating) repeatedly.

po˥kka˥ri ぽっかり *adv.* (〜 to)
1 (the state of floating): *Shiroi kumo ga sora ni* pokkari (to) ukañde iru. (白い雲が空にぽっかり(と)浮かんでいる) There *is* a white cloud *suspended* in the sky.
2 (the state of being wide open): *Michi ni ana ga* pokkari aite ita. (道に穴がぽっかり開いていた) There *was* a hole *gaping wide open* in the road.

-poñ ぽん (本) *suf.* counter for long cylindrical objects. ⟪⇨ APP. 4⟫

po˥ñdo ポンド *n.* **1** pound sterling.
2 pound (unit of weight).

-ppo˥·i っぽい *suf.* (*a.*) (-ku) [attached to a noun, the continuative base of a verb, or the stem of an adjective] **1** something like; resembling; -ish: *Kare ni wa* kodomo-ppoi *tokoro ga aru.* (彼には子どもっぽいところがある) He has some *childish* points.
2 tending; looking: shime-ppoi (湿っぽい) *dampish* / yasu-ppoi *fuku* (安っぽい服) *cheap-looking* clothes.

po˥suto ポスト *n.* mailbox.

po˥tsupotsu ぽつぽつ *adv.* (〜 to) **1** (the state of small drops falling): *Ame ga* potsupostu futte *kita.* (雨がぽつぽつ降ってきた) The rain started *splattering down in drops*.
2 (the state of things occurring sporadically): *Joohoo ga* potsupostu haitte kita. (情報がぽつぽつ入ってきた) The reports *trickled in*.

po˥tto ポット *n.* thermos [vacuum] bottle; teapot; coffee pot.

-puñ ぷん (分) *suf.* counter for minutes. ⟪⇨ APP. 4⟫

pu˥ñpuñ ぷんぷん *adv.* (〜 to; 〜 suru) **1** a strong smell: *Kanojo wa koosui o* puñpuñ (to) sasete ita. (彼女は香水をぷんぷん(と)させていた) She *smelt strongly* of perfume.
2 (the state of being angry): *Kare wa* okotte puñpuñ shite iru. (彼は怒ってぷんぷんしている) He *is absolutely furious*.

p

pu¹ragu プラグ *n.* electric plug.
pu¹rasu プラス *n.* **1** plus. ⟪⇨ tasu⟫
2 advantage; gain; asset. ⟪↔ mainasu⟫
purasu suru (〜する) *vt.* add.
pu⌈rasuchi¹kku プラスチック *n.* plastic. ★ Refers only to rigid substances; vinyl is called '*biniiru*.'
pu⌈rattoho¹omu プラットホーム *n.* railroad station platform. ⟪⇨ hoomu[1]⟫
pu⌈re¹zeñto プレゼント *n.* present; gift.
purezeñto suru (〜する) *vt.* give a present. ⟪⇨ miyage; okurimono⟫
-puri ぷり(振り) *suf.* = -buri.
pu⌈riñto プリント *n.* **1** handout; copy; mimeographed copy.
2 (of a photograph) print.
puriñto suru (〜する) *vt.* make a handout [copy].
pu¹ripuri ぷりぷり *adv.* (〜 to; 〜 suru) (the state of being angry): puripuri suru (ぷりぷりする) *be very angry.*
pu¹ro[1] プロ *n.* professional; pro. ⟪⇨ señmoñka⟫
pu¹ro[2] プロ *n.* theatrical agency. ★ Originally from the shortened form of English 'production.'
pyu¹upyuu ぴゅうぴゅう *adv.* (〜 to) (used to express a shrill sound):
Soto wa tsumetai kaze ga pyuupyuu (to) fuite ita. (外は冷たい風がぴゅうぴゅう(と)吹いていた) The cold wind *was whistling* outside.

R

-ra ら(等) *suf.* **1** (used to form the plural of a noun referring to a person): ★ Used with reference to equals or subordinates. '*-tachi*' is more common.
boku-ra (ぼくら) *we; us* / kare-ra (彼ら) *they; them* / kodomo-ra (子どもら) *children.*
2 (used to form the plural of a pronoun referring to a thing):
kore-ra (これら) *these* / sore-ra (それら) *those.*
ra¹ameñ ラーメン *n.* Chinese noodles. ⟪⇨ chuuka-soba; iñsutañto raameñ⟫
ra¹igetsu らいげつ(来月) *n.* next month. ⟪⇨ koñgetsu; señgetsu⟫
ra⌈imu¹gi ライむぎ(ライ麦) *n.* rye.
ra⌈ineñ らいねん(来年) *n.* next year. ⟪⇨ kotoshi; kyoneñ⟫
ra⌈inichi らいにち(来日) *n.* visit to Japan.
rainichi suru (〜する) *vi.* visit [come to] Japan.
ra⌈ishuu らいしゅう(来週) *n.* next week. ⟪⇨ koñshuu; señshuu⟫
ra¹isu ライス *n.* cooked [boiled] rice. ★ Refers to cooked rice served on Western plates. When referring to rice served in Japanese-style bowls, use the word '*gohañ.*'
ra¹jio ラジオ *n.* radio:
rajio *o tsukeru* [*kesu*] (ラジオをつける[消す]) turn on [off] the *radio.*
ra⌈kkyoo らっきょう *n.* baker's garlic.
ra⌈ku¹ らく(楽) *n.* ease; comfort; relief.
— *a.n.* (〜 na, ni) **1** comfortable; easy:
Kusuri o noñdara, raku *ni narimashita.* (薬を飲んだら, 楽になりました) I felt more *comfortable* after taking the medicine.
2 simple; easy:
Kono nimotsu o hakobu no wa raku *desu.* (この荷物を運ぶのは楽です) It is quite *easy* to carry this baggage.

p
r

ra[kudai らくだい (落第) *n.* failure; flunking.
rakudai suru (〜する) *vi.* fail; flunk; repeat the same grade in school.

ra[kugo らくご (落語) *n.* comic story. ★ Told by a professional raconteur and with a witty ending.

ra[kunoo らくのう (酪農) *n.* dairy farming.

ra[kuseñ らくせん (落選) *n.* defeat in an election. ⟪↔ tooseñ⟫
rakuseñ suru (〜する) *vt.* **1** be defeated in an election.
2 be rejected: *Kanojo no e wa* rakuseñ shita. (彼女の絵は落選した) Her painting *was rejected.*

ra]ñ[1] らん (欄) *n.* column; space.

ra]ñ[2] らん (蘭) *n.* orchid.

ra[ñboo らんぼう (乱暴) *n.* violence; rudeness. ⟪⇨ booryoku⟫
rañboo suru (〜する) *vi.* **1** use violence; behave rudely.
2 violate; rape:
josee ni rañboo suru (女性に乱暴する) *rape* a woman.
— *a.n.* (〜 na, ni) violent; rude; rough; reckless:
Ano ko wa rañboo *da.* (あの子は乱暴だ) That child is *rude and rough.*

ra]ñpu[1] ランプ *n.* lamp.

ra]ñpu[2] ランプ *n.* exit [entrance] ramp of an expressway.

ra]ñshi らんし (卵子) *n.* ovum. ⟪⇨ seeshi[3]⟫

-rare·ru られる *infl. end.* (-rare-te [V]) [attached to the negative base of a vowel-stem verb and '*kuru*,' and itself inflected like a vowel-stem verb] ⟪⇨ -reru⟫
1 (indicates the passive) be...-ed:
Kanojo wa señsee ni homerareta. (彼女は先生にほめられた) She *was praised* by her teacher.
2 (indicates a sense of suffering, loss, etc.): ★ Usually used with reference to unfavorable occurrences.
Kitaku no tochuu de ame ni furareta. (帰宅の途中で雨に降られた) I *was caught* in the rain on my way home.
3 (indicates the potential) can:
Kono mi wa taberaremaseñ. (この実は食べられません) You *cannot eat* this fruit.
4 (indicates the natural potential): ★ Used when something naturally or involuntarily comes to mind.
Chichi no byooki no koto ga añjirareru. (父の病気のことが案じられる) I *cannot help worrying* about my father's illness.
5 (indicates the honorific):
Tanaka-sañ no kawari ni Yamada-sañ ga korareru *soo desu.* (田中さんの代わりに山田さんが来られるそうです) I hear that Mr. Yamada will *come* in place of Mr. Tanaka.

ra[shi]·i らしい *a.* (-ku) [follows a noun, adjective, adjectival noun, the dictionary form or the *ta*-form of a verb or the copula]
1 look like; seem:
Kono ike wa kanari fukai rashii. (この池はかなり深いらしい) This pond *seems* rather deep.
2 they say; I hear:
Kare wa kaisha o yameru rashii. (彼は会社を辞めるらしい) *They say* that he is leaving the company.

-rashi]·i らしい *suf.* (*a.*) (-ku) typical of; just like; befitting:
★ Added to a noun to make an adjective.
Soñna koto o suru nañte kimi-rashiku *nai.* (そんなことをするなんて君らしくない) It is not *like you* to do such a thing. / otoko-rashii *taido* (男らしい態度) a *manly* attitude.

re]e[1] れい (例) *n.* **1** example; instance: ree *o ageru* (例をあげる) give an *example.*
2 case:
mare na ree (まれな例) a rare *case.*
3 custom; habit; practice:
Soo suru no ga Nihoñ no ree *desu.*

(そうするのが日本の例です) It is a Japanese *custom* to do so.

re⌈e² れい(礼) *n.* **1** thanks; gratitude:
ree *o noberu* (礼を述べる) express one's *thanks.* ⦅⇨ o-ree⦆
2 reward; fee:
Watashi wa o-ree *ni ichimañ-eñ kare ni ageta.* (私はお礼に1万円彼にあげた) I gave him 10,000 yen as a *reward.*

re⌉e³ れい(礼) *n.* bow; salute:
Seeto-tachi wa señsee ni ree o shita. (生徒たちは先生に礼をした) The pupils *bowed* to the teacher. ⦅⇨ aisatsu⦆

re⌉e⁴ れい(零) *n.* zero; naught. ⦅⇨ zero⦆

re⌈eboo れいぼう(冷房) *n.* air conditioning.
reeboo suru (〜する) *vt.* air-condition. ⦅↔ dañboo⦆

re⌈ebuñ れいぶん(例文) *n.* example; illustrative sentence.

re⌈egai れいがい(例外) *n.* exception.

re⌈egi れいぎ(礼儀) *n.* manners; courtesy; politeness:
Ano hito wa reegi *o shiranai.* (あの人は礼儀を知らない) He does not understand the meaning of *manners.*

re⌉eka れいか(零下) *n.* below zero: reeka *juugo-do* (零下15度) fifteen degrees *below zero.*

re⌈ekiñ れいきん(礼金) *n.* reward; fee; thank-you money. ★ Money given to the landlord when renting an apartment or house. It is not refundable. ⦅⇨ shikikiñ; yachiñ⦆

re⌈ekoku れいこく(冷酷) *a.n.* (〜 na, ni) cruel; heartless; coldhearted.

re⌈ekyaku れいきゃく(冷却) *n.* cooling; refrigeration.
reekyaku suru (〜する) *vi., vt.* cool; chill; refrigerate. ⦅⇨ hiyasu⦆ ⦅↔ kanetsu¹⦆

re⌈esee れいせい(冷静) *a.n.* (〜 na, ni) calm; cool-headed:
Haha wa itsu-mo reesee *desu.* (母はいつも冷静です) My mother is always *calm and composed.*

re⌉esu¹ レース *n.* race:
reesu *ni katsu* [*makeru*] (レースに勝つ[負ける]) win [lose] a *race.*

re⌉esu² レース *n.* lace:
reesu *no kaateñ* (レースのカーテン) a *lace* curtain.

re⌈eta⌉ñ れいたん(冷淡) *a.n.* (〜 na, ni) cold; indifferent; coldhearted.

re⌈etoo れいとう(冷凍) *n.* freezing; refrigeration:
reetoo-*niku* (冷凍肉) *frozen* meat.
reetoo suru (〜する) *vt.* freeze; refrigerate. ⦅⇨ reezoo⦆

re⌈eto⌉oko れいとうこ(冷凍庫) *n.* freezer. ⦅⇨ reezooko⦆

re⌈ezoo れいぞう(冷蔵) *n.* cold storage; refrigeration.
reezoo suru (〜する) *vt.* refrigerate. ⦅⇨ reetoo⦆

re⌈ezo⌉oko れいぞうこ(冷蔵庫) *n.* refrigerator; icebox. ⦅⇨ reetooko⦆

-reki れき(歴) *suf.* career; experience; history:
gaku-reki (学歴) one's academic *career* / *shoku*-reki (職歴) one's working *experience.*

re⌈kishi れきし(歴史) *n.* history.
★ '*Nihoñ no rekishi*' is often shortened to '*Nihoñ-shi.*'

re⌈kishi-teki れきしてき(歴史的) *a.n.* (〜 na, ni) historic:
rekishi-teki *ni yuumee na tera* (歴史的に有名な寺) a *historically* famous temple. ⦅⇨ rekishi⦆

re⌈ko⌉odo レコード *n.* record; disk: rekoodo *o kakeru* (レコードをかける) play a *record.*

re⌉moñ レモン *n.* lemon. ★ In Japan the word suggests something fresh and pleasant.

re⌈ñai れんあい(恋愛) *n.* love:
Futari wa reñai-chuu *desu.* (二人は恋愛中です) Those two *are in love.*
reñai suru (〜する) *vi.* fall in love.

r

re¹ñga れんが(煉瓦) *n.* brick.

re⌈ñgoo れんごう(連合) *n.* coalition; alliance; union: reñgoo-*koku* (連合国) the *Allied* Powers.
reñgoo suru (～する) *vi., vt.* combine; ally; unite.

re⌈ñjitsu れんじつ(連日) *adv.* (～ no) every day; day after day. ⟨⇨ mainichi⟩

re⌈ñpoo れんぽう(連邦) *n.* federation; union: reñpoo-*seefu* (連邦政府) a *federal* government.

re⌈ñraku れんらく(連絡) *n.* connection; contact.
reñraku suru (～する) *vi., vt.* connect; contact; get in touch.

re⌈ñshuu れんしゅう(練習) *n.* practice; drill; exercise; training; rehearsal:
reñshuu-*moñdai* (練習問題) a *practice* exercise [drill].
reñshuu suru (～する) *vt.* practice; drill; train; rehearse.

re⌈ñsoo れんそう(連想) *n.* association of ideas.
reñsoo suru (～する) *vt.* remind; bring to mind; associate.

re⌈ñtai-hoshooniñ れんたいほしょうにん(連帯保証人) *n.* surety; person who accepts responsibility for another.

re⌈ñtogeñ レントゲン *n.* X-rays; Roentgen rays.

re⌈ñzoku れんぞく(連続) *n.* continuation; succession; series.
reñzoku suru (～する) *vi.* continue; go on; last. ⟨⇨ tsuzuku⟩

re¹ñzu レンズ *n.* lens:
totsu [*oo*] reñzu (凸[凹]レンズ) a convex [concave] *lens.*

re⌈po¹oto レポート *n.* **1** term paper; written report. ★ Students commonly call their term papers '*repooto.*' ⟨⇨ roñbuñ⟩
2 news report.
repooto suru (～する) *vt.* report (for a newspaper); cover.

-re·ru れる *infl. end.* (-re-te [V]) [attached to the negative base of a consonant-stem verb, and itself inflected like a vowel-stem verb. '*Suru*' becomes '*sareru.*'] ⟨⇨ -rareru; sareru⟩
1 (indicates the passive) be...-ed: *Watashi wa inu ni te o* kamareta. (私は犬に手をかまれた) I *was bitten* on the hand by a dog.
2 (indicates a sense of suffering, loss, etc.): ★ Usually used with reference to unfavorable occurrences.
Yuube wa akañboo ni nakarete, *yoku nemurenakatta.* (夕べは赤ん坊に泣かれて, よく眠れなかった) I could not sleep well last night because the baby *was crying.*
3 (indicates the potential) can: *Kono saki wa* ikaremaseñ. (この先は行かれません) You *cannot go* any further than this.
4 (indicates the natural potential): ★ Used when something naturally or involuntarily comes to mind.
Koñdo no shiai de wa kare no katsuyaku ga kitai sareru. (今度の試合では彼の活躍が期待される) A remarkable performance *is expected* of him in the coming match.
5 (indicates the honorific): *Shachoo wa moo* kitaku saremashita. (社長はもう帰宅されました) The president *has* already *left* for home.

re⌈ssee れっせい(劣勢) *n.* inferiority; inferior position.
— *a.n.* (～ na, ni) inferior.
⟨↔ yuusee⟩ ⟨⇨ otoru⟩

re⌈ssha れっしゃ(列車) *n.* railroad [railway] train. ★ Usually refers to a long-distance train.
⟨⇨ deñsha; kisha[2]⟩

re¹tsu れつ(列) *n.* row; line; queue. ⟨⇨ gyooretsu⟩

-retsu れつ(列) *suf.* counter for rows or columns:
zeñ-retsu (前列) the front *row* / *koo*-retsu (後列) the back *row* / *Yoko ni ichi*-retsu *ni narabi nasai.* (横に1列に並びなさい) Please get

into one *line* across.

re⌈tteru レッテル *n.* label:
'gekiyaku' no retteru (「劇薬」のレッテル) a *label* of 'poison' / *Kare wa kechi da to iu* retteru *o hararete iru.* (彼はけちだというレッテルをはられている) He *is labeled* as a stingy man.

re⌈ttoo[1] れっとう (列島) *n.* chain of islands; archipelago:
Nihoñ rettoo (日本列島) the Japanese *Archipelago.* (⇒ guñtoo)

re⌈ttoo[2] れっとう (劣等) *n.* inferiority; low grade:
rettoo-*kañ* (劣等感) an *inferiority* complex / rettoo-*see* (劣等生) a *poor* student.

ri⌉eki りえき (利益) *n.* **1** profit; gains:
juumañ-eñ no rieki *o eru* (10万円の利益を得る) make a *profit* of 100,000 yen. (↔ kessoñ) (⇒ mooke; saisañ)
2 benefit; good:
Kono torihiki ga otagai no rieki *ni naru koto o nozomimasu.* (この取引がお互いの利益になることを望みます) I hope this business will prove of mutual *benefit.*

ri⌈juñ りじゅん (利潤) *n.* profit:
rijuñ *o tsuikyuu suru* (利潤を追求する) pursue *profits.* (⇒ rieki)

ri⌉ka りか (理科) *n.* **1** science; natural science.
2 the department of science:
Kare wa rika-kee *ni susuñda.* (彼は理科系に進んだ) He took the *science course.* (⇒ buñka[2])

ri⌉kai りかい (理解) *n.* understanding; appreciation. (↔ murikai)
rikai suru (〜する) *vt.* understand; appreciate. (⇒ wakaru)

ri⌉kishi りきし (力士) *n.* sumo wrestler. (⇒ sumoo)

ri⌈koñ りこん (離婚) *n.* divorce.
rikoñ suru (〜する) *vi.* get divorced. (⇒ bekkyo)

ri⌈koo りこう (利口) *a.n.* (〜 na, ni) clever; wise; smart:
Kono inu wa totemo rikoo *desu.* (この犬はとても利口です) This dog is very *intelligent.* (⇒ kashikoi)

ri⌈ku りく (陸) *n.* land; shore. (↔ umi[1])

ri⌈ku⌉guñ りくぐん (陸軍) *n.* army. (⇒ Jieetai; kaiguñ; kuuguñ)

ri⌈kujoo りくじょう (陸上) *n.*
1 land; shore:
Rikujoo *o itta hoo ga añzeñ desu.* (陸上を行ったほうが安全です) It is safer to go by *land.* (⇒ kaijoo[2])
2 = rikujoo-kyoogi.

ri⌈kujoo-kyo⌉ogi りくじょうきょうぎ (陸上競技) *n.* track and field; track-and-field events:
rikujoo-kyoogi-joo (陸上競技場) an *athletic field.*

ri⌈kutsu りくつ (理屈) *n.* **1** reason; logic:
Kare no iu koto wa rikutsu ni atte *iru.* (彼の言うことは理屈に合っている) What he says is in conformity with *logic.*
2 argument:
Kare wa nañ ni de mo rikutsu *o iu.* (彼は何にでも理屈を言う) He puts forth an *argument* about everything.

ri⌈ñgo りんご (林檎) *n.* apple.

ri⌈ñji りんじ (臨時) *n.* **1** special; extraordinary:
riñji-*ressha* (臨時列車) a *special* train / riñji-*kyuugyoo* (臨時休業) an *unscheduled* holiday.
2 temporary; provisional:
riñji *no shigoto* (臨時の仕事) a *temporary* job. (⇒ riñji ni)

ri⌈ñjiñ りんじん (隣人) *n.* one's neighbor; people in the neighborhood.

ri⌈ñji ni りんじに (臨時に) *adv.* temporarily; specially; provisionally:
Kare o riñji ni *yatotta.* (彼を臨時に雇った) We employed him *temporarily.* (⇒ riñji)

ri⌈ppa りっぱ (立派) *a.n.* (〜 na, ni) **1** respectable; worthy; praiseworthy; honorable. (⇒ erai[1])
2 wonderful; magnificent; splen-

did; excellent.

ri⌈ppoo[1] りっぽう(立方) *n.* cube: *go*-rippoo-*meetoru* (5 立方メートル) five *cubic* meters. ⟪↔ heehoo⟫

ri⌈ppoo[2] りっぽう(立法) *n.* law making; legislation: Rippoo-*kikañ wa kokkai desu.* (立法機関は国会です) The *legislative* organ is the Diet. ⟪⇨ sañkeñ-buñritsu⟫

ri⌈reki りれき(履歴) *n.* one's personal history; one's career. ⟪⇨ keereki⟫

ri⌈re⌉kisho りれきしょ(履歴書) *n.* personal history; curriculum vitae.

ri⌈riku りりく(離陸) *n.* takeoff (of an airplane).
ririku suru (～する) *vi.* take off. ⟪↔ chakuriku⟫

ri⌉roñ りろん(理論) *n.* theory: riroñ *o jissai ni ooyoo suru* (理論を実際に応用する) apply *theory* to practice.

ri⌈see りせい(理性) *n.* reason: risee *o ushinau* (理性を失う) lose one's *reason.*

ri⌉shi りし(利子) *n.* interest: *Tooza-yokiñ ni wa* rishi *ga tsukanai.* (当座預金には利子がつかない) A checking account yields no *interest.* ⟪↔ gañkiñ⟫

ri⌈soku りそく(利息) *n.* = rishi.

ri⌈soo りそう(理想) *n.* ideal: *takai* risoo *o idaku* (高い理想を抱く) have lofty *ideals.*

ri⌈soo-teki りそうてき(理想的) *a.n.* (～ na, ni) ideal: *Kono basho wa teñtai-kañsoku ni* risoo-teki *da.* (この場所は天体観測に理想的だ) This spot is *ideal* for astronomical observations.

ri⌉sshiñ-shusse りっしんしゅっせ(立身出世) *n.* success in life.
risshiñ-shusse suru (～する) *vi.* succeed in life; get ahead in life. ⟪⇨ shusse⟫

-ritsu りつ(率) *suf.* rate; percentage; proportion: *shitsugyoo*-ritsu (失業率) the unemployment *rate* / *toohyoo*-ritsu (投票率) the voter *turnout.* ⟪⇨ wariai⟫

ri⌈ttaa リッター *n.* liter.
★ Often used when referring to gasoline. ⟪⇨ rittoru⟫

ri⌈ttai りったい(立体) *n.* three-dimensional object; solid.

ri⌈ttai-ko⌉osa りったいこうさ(立体交差) *n.* two-level crossing; overpass system.

ri⌈ttai-teki りったいてき(立体的) *a.n.* (～ na, ni) solid; three-dimensional.

ri⌈ttoru リットル(立) *n.* liter: *mizu ni*-rittoru (水 2 リットル) two *liters* of water. ⟪⇨ rittaa⟫

ri⌈yoo りよう(利用) *n.* use; utilization.
riyoo suru (～する) *vt.* use; utilize; make use of; take advantage of. ⟪⇨ tsukau⟫

ri⌈yuu りゆう(理由) *n.* reason; cause; grounds. ⟪⇨ wake⟫

ro⌈kka⌉kukee ろっかくけい(六角形) *n.* hexagon.

ro⌈kotsu ろこつ(露骨) *a.n.* (～ na, ni) candid; plain; open; outspoken: *Kare wa* rokotsu *ni fumañ o arawashita.* (彼は露骨に不満を表した) He expressed his dissatisfaction *openly.*

ro⌈ku⌉ ろく(六) *n.* six. ⟪⇨ muttsu; APP. 3⟫

ro⌈ku-gatsu⌉ ろくがつ(六月) *n.* June. ⟪⇨ APP. 5⟫

ro⌈kumaku ろくまく(肋膜) *n.* pleura.

ro⌈ku-na ろくな(碌な) *attrib.* (with a negative) (no) good: *Kotoshi wa* roku-na koto *ga nakatta.* (今年はろくなことがなかった) *Nothing good* has happened to me this year.

ro⌈ku ni ろくに(碌に) *adv.* (with a negative) (not) well; (not) properly; hardly: *Kyoo wa isogashikute,* roku ni *shokuji o shite imaseñ.* (きょうは忙しくて,

r

ろくに食事をしていません) I have been so busy today that I haven't eaten *properly*. 《⇨ rokuroku》

ro⌈kuoñ ろくおん(録音) *n.* recording; transcription.
rokuoñ suru (〜する) *vt.* record; tape.

ro⌈kuroku ろくろく *adv.* (with a negative) (not) well; hardly; scarcely:
Yuube wa rokuroku *nenakatta.* (ゆうべはろくろく寝なかった) I slept *badly* last night. 《⇨ roku ni》

-roñ ろん(論) *suf.* theory; essay; comment:
kyooiku-roñ (教育論) educational *theory* / *buñgaku*-roñ (文学論) an *essay* on literature.

ro⌈ñbuñ ろんぶん(論文) *n.* essay; thesis; paper:
hakase-roñbuñ (博士論文) a doctoral *dissertation*. 《⇨ repooto》

ro⌈ñji·ru ろんじる(論じる) *vt.* (roñji-te [V]) discuss; argue; treat.

ro⌉ñri ろんり(論理) *n.* logic:
Kimi no roñri *ni wa tsuite ikemaseñ.* (君の論理にはついていけません) I cannot follow your *logic*.

ro⌈ñri-teki ろんりてき(論理的) *a.n.* (〜 na, ni) logical:
Kare wa roñri-teki *na setsumee o shita.* (彼は論理的な説明をした) He gave a *logical* explanation.

ro⌉o ろう(労) *n.* labor; pains; trouble:
Kanojo wa kesshite roo *o oshimanai.* (彼女は決して労を惜しまない) She never spares *pains*.

ro⌈odoo ろうどう(労働) *n.* (manual) labor; work:
roodoo-*jikañ* [*jookeñ*] (労働時間[条件]) *working* hours [conditions].
roodoo suru (〜する) *vi.* labor; work. 《⇨ hataraku》

ro⌈odoo-ku⌉miai ろうどうくみあい(労働組合) *n.* labor union; trade union. 《⇨ kumiai》

ro⌈odo⌉osha ろうどうしゃ(労働者) *n.* laborer; worker.

ro⌈ogo ろうご(老後) *n.* one's old age.

ro⌈ohi ろうひ(浪費) *n.* waste; extravagance. 《⇨ muda》
roohi suru (〜する) *vt.* waste. 《↔ setsuyaku》

ro⌈ojiñ ろうじん(老人) *n.* old people; aged man [woman]; the aged. 《↔ wakamono》

ro⌈ojiñ-ho⌉omu ろうじんホーム(老人ホーム) *n.* home for old people; nursing home for the aged.

ro⌈oka ろうか(廊下) *n.* corridor; passage.

ro⌈oma⌉ji ローマじ(羅馬字) *n.* Roman letters; Roman alphabet. 《⇨ inside front cover》

ro⌉oryoku ろうりょく(労力) *n.* labor; effort; service.

ro⌈oso⌉ku ろうそく(蠟燭) *n.* candle; taper.

ro⌈shutsu ろしゅつ(露出) *n.*
1 outcropping:
iwa no roshutsu (岩の露出) an *outcropping* of rock.
2 exposure:
Kono shashiñ wa roshutsu ga fusoku *shite iru.* (この写真は露出が不足している) This picture is *underexposed*.
roshutsu suru (〜する) *vt.* expose; bare: *hada o* roshutsu suru (肌を露出する) *bare* one's body.

ru⌉i るい(類) *n.* kind; sort. 《⇨ shurui》

ru⌈iji るいじ(類似) *n.* similarity; likeness; resemblance.
ruiji suru (〜する) *vi.* be similar [alike]; resemble. 《⇨ niru[2]》

ru⌉su るす(留守) *n.* absence:
Chichi wa rusu desu. (父は留守です) My father *is not at home* now.

ru⌈subañ るすばん(留守番) *n.* looking after the house during a person's absence.

rya⌉ku りゃく(略) *n.* abbreviation; omission. 《⇨ shooryaku; tañshuku》

rya⌈kugo りゃくご(略語) *n.* abbreviated word; abbreviation.

r

rya⌈ku⌉s·u りゃくす (略す) *vt.* (rya-kush·i-; ryakus·a-; ryakush·i-te Ⓒ) abbreviate. 《⇨ shooryaku》

ryo⌈hi りょひ (旅費) *n.* traveling expenses.

ryo⌈kaku りょかく (旅客) *n.* passenger; traveler. ★ Also pronounced '*ryokyaku*.'

ryo⌈ka⌉kuki りょかくき (旅客機) *n.* passenger plane. ★ Also pronounced '*ryokakki*.'

ryo⌈kañ りょかん (旅館) *n.* Japanese inn. ★ The rooms have tatami floors, and the rate usually includes breakfast and dinner. 《⇨ yado; yadoya》

ryo⌈keñ りょけん (旅券) *n.* passport. 《⇨ pasupooto》

ryo⌈koo りょこう (旅行) *n.* trip; journey; tour; travel. 《⇨ tabi[1]》
ryokoo suru (〜する) *vi.* travel; make a trip.

-ryoku りょく (力) *suf.* power:
sui-ryoku (水力) hydraulic *power* / *seeji*-ryoku (政治力) political *power*.

ryo⌈kucha りょくちゃ (緑茶) *n.* green tea. 《⇨ o-cha》

ryo⌈kyaku りょきゃく (旅客) *n.* = ryokaku.

ryo⌉o[1] りょう (量) *n.* **1** quantity; amount. 《↔ shitsu》 《⇨ buñryoo》
2 volume:
Kootsuu no ryoo *ga sañ-neñ de ni-bai ni natta.* (交通の量が3年で2倍になった) The *volume* of traffic doubled in three years.

ryo⌉o[2] りょう (寮) *n.* dormitory.

ryo⌉o[3] りょう (良) *n.* (of a grade rating) being good or satisfactory; B or C in schoolwork. 《⇨ ka[2]; yuu[2]》

ryo⌉o[4] りょう (猟) *n.* shooting; hunting: ryoo *ni dekakeru* (猟に出かける) go *shooting* [*hunting*].

ryo⌉o[5] りょう (漁) *n.* **1** fishing; fishery: ryoo *ni iku* (漁に行く) go *fishing*.
2 catch:
Kyoo wa ryoo *ga sukunakatta.* (きょうは漁が少なかった) We had a poor *catch* today.

ryo⌉o- りょう (両) *pref.* both:
ryoo-*koku* (両国) *both* countries / ryoo-*niñ* (両人) *both* people.

-ryoo りょう (料) *suf.* charge; fee; rate:
deñwa-ryoo (電話料) a telephone *charge* / *jugyoo*-ryoo (授業料) a tuition *fee*. 《⇨ -chiñ; -dai[2]》

ryo⌈oashi りょうあし (両足) *n.* both feet [legs]. 《⇨ ryoote》

ryo⌉odo りょうど (領土) *n.* territory; possession; domain:
Kono shima wa Nihoñ no ryoodo *desu.* (この島は日本の領土です) This island is Japanese *territory*.

ryo⌈ogae りょうがえ (両替) *n.* money exchange.
ryoogae suru (〜する) *vt.* exchange (dollars into yen); change.

ryo⌈ogawa りょうがわ (両側) *n.* both sides. 《⇨ katagawa》

ryo⌈ohashi りょうはし (両端) *n.* both ends. 《⇨ katahashi》

ryo⌈oho⌉o りょうほう (両方) *n.* both; both parties [sides]:
Kare wa jookañ gekañ, ryoohoo *tomo yoñde shimatta.* (彼は上巻下巻, 両方とも読んでしまった) He read *both* Volume 1 and Volume 2. 《⇨ katahoo》

ryo⌉oji りょうじ (領事) *n.* consul.

ryo⌈oji⌉kañ りょうじかん (領事館) *n.* consulate.

ryo⌈okai[1] りょうかい (了解) *n.* understanding; agreement; consent:
ryookai *o eru* [*motomeru*] (了解を得る[求める]) obtain [ask for] a person's *consent*.
ryookai suru (〜する) *vt.* understand; consent.

ryo⌈okai[2] りょうかい (領海) *n.* territorial waters.

ryo⌉okiñ りょうきん (料金) *n.* rate; charge; fee; fare. 《⇨ daikiñ; uñchiñ》

ryo⌈okoo りょうこう (良好) *a.n.* (〜 na, ni) good; excellent; satisfactory:

r

Kotoshi no kome no shuukaku wa ryookoo *deshita.* (今年の米の収穫は良好でした) The rice harvest this year was *excellent*. 《⇨ yoi[1]》

ryo⌉ori りょうり (料理) *n.* cooking; cookery; cuisine; dish; food.
ryoori suru (〜する) *vt.* cook; prepare. 《⇨ suiji》

ryo⌈osañ りょうさん (量産) *n.* mass production.
ryoosañ suru (〜する) *vt.* mass-produce.

ryo⌉osha りょうしゃ (両者) *n.* both of the two people; each other:
Ryoosha *no setsumee ga kuichigatte ita.* (両者の説明が食い違っていた) Their accounts contradicted *each other*.

ryo⌉oshi りょうし (漁師) *n.* fisherman.

ryo⌉oshiñ[1] りょうしん (両親) *n.* one's parents.

ryo⌉oshiñ[2] りょうしん (良心) *n.* conscience:
Ryooshiñ *ni yamashii koto wa arimaseñ.* (良心にやましいことはありません) I have a clear *conscience*.

ryo⌉oshu りょうしゅ (領主) *n.* feudal lord.

ryo⌈oshuusho りょうしゅうしょ (領収書) *n.* receipt:
Ryooshuusho *o moraemasu ka?* (領収書をもらえますか) May I have a *receipt*, please? 《⇨ uketori》

ryo⌈oshuushoo りょうしゅうしょう (領収証) *n.* voucher; receipt.

ryo⌈ote りょうて (両手) *n.* both hands; both arms. 《⇨ katate; ryooashi》

ryu⌉u りゅう (龍) *n.* dragon.

-ryuu りゅう (流) *suf.* **1** style; type; way:
jiko-ryuu (自己流) one's own *way* (of doing things).
2 class; rate; grade:
ichi-ryuu (一流) first *class* / *ni*-ryuu (二流) second *rate* / *chuu*-ryuu (中流) middle *grade* / *joo*-ryuu (上流) upper *class*.
3 flow; stream; current:
deñ-ryuu (電流) electric *current* / shi-ryuu (支流) a *tributary*.

ryu⌈uchijoo りゅうちじょう (留置場) *n.* detention house; lockup.

ryu⌈udo⌉oshoku りゅうどうしょく (流動食) *n.* liquid food [diet].

ryu⌈ugaku りゅうがく (留学) *n.* studying abroad.
ryuugaku suru (〜する) *vi.* study abroad; go abroad for study.

ryu⌈uga⌉kusee りゅうがくせい (留学生) *n.* student studying abroad; foreign student.

ryu⌈uhyoo りゅうひょう (流氷) *n.* drift ice; ice floe.

ryu⌈ukañ りゅうかん (流感) *n.* influenza; flu:
ryuukañ *ni kakaru* (流感にかかる) catch *influenza*.

ryu⌈ukoo りゅうこう (流行) *n.* fashion; vogue; popularity:
ryuukoo-*ka* (流行歌) a *popular* song.
ryuukoo suru (〜する) *vi.* come into fashion; be in fashion; be popular.

ryu⌈uneñ りゅうねん (留年) *n.* remaining in the same class.
ryuuneñ suru (〜する) *vi.* repeat the same class for another year. 《⇨ rakudai》

ryu⌈uniñ りゅうにん (留任) *n.* remaining in office.
ryuuniñ suru (〜する) *vi.* remain in office.

r

S

sa[1] さ (差) *n.* difference; gap; margin:
sedai no sa (世代の差) a generation *gap.* ((⇨ chigai))

sa[2] さ *p.* **1** (used when casually emphasizing one's thoughts or opinions):
Kyoo dekinakereba, ashita suru sa. (きょうできなければ, あしたするさ) If I can't do it today, *well* then, I'll do it tomorrow.
2 (used to indicate a strong reaction):
Nani o baka na koto o itte iru no sa. (何をばかなことを言っているのさ) What nonsense you are talking!
3 (used after a phrase to hold the attention of the listener):
Kono aida karita hoñ sa, *moo yoñjatta.* (この間借りた本さ, もう読んじゃった) The book I borrowed from you the other day... *Well*, I've already read it.

-sa さ *suf.* (*n.*) [added to the stem of an adjective or to an adjectival noun to form a noun]
atsu-sa (暑さ) *heat* / seekaku-sa (正確さ) *exactness.*

sa˥a さあ *int.* now; here; well; come on:
Saa, *hajimeyoo.* (さあ, 始めよう) *Okay*, let's start. ((⇨ sate))

sa˥abisu サービス *n.* **1** service:
Kono ryokañ wa saabisu *ga yoi* [*warui*]. (この旅館はサービスが良い[悪い]) The *service* at this Japanese inn is good [poor].
2 discount; no charge; extra:
Kono eñpitsu o saabisu *ni agemasu.* (この鉛筆をサービスにあげます) I will throw in this pencil as an *extra.*
saabisu (o) suru (～(を)する) *vi., vt.* **1** give a service; attend to.
2 make a discount; give away for nothing.

sa˥abisu˥ryoo サービスりょう (サービス料) *n.* service charge.

sa˥akuru サークル *n.* club:
saakuru-*katsudoo* (サークル活動) *club* activities (at college).

sa˥baku さばく (砂漠) *n.* desert.

sa˥bi˥ さび (錆び) *n.* rust; tarnish.

sa˥bi˥·ru さびる (錆びる) *vi.* (sabi-te [V]) rust; get rusty. ((⇨ sabi))

sa˥bishi˥·i さびしい (寂しい・淋しい) *a.* (-ku) lonely; forlorn; deserted. ((↔ nigiyaka)) ((⇨ wabishii))

sa˥bo˥r·u サボる *vt.* (sabor·i-; sabor·a-; sabot-te [C]) (*colloq.*) play truant [hooky]; loaf on the job; cut classes.

sa˥boteñ サボテン (仙人掌) *n.* cactus. ★ Sometimes pronounced '*shaboteñ.*'

sa˥dama˥r·u さだまる (定まる) *vi.* (sadamar·i-; sadamar·a-; sadamat-te [C]) be decided; be fixed:
Kono natsu wa teñkoo ga sadamaranai. (この夏は天候が定まらない) This summer the weather *is* quite *changeable.* ((⇨ sadameru))

sa˥dame˥·ru さだめる (定める) *vt.* (sadame-te [V]) **1** provide; stipulate; lay down (a rule).
2 decide (an aim, goal, etc.); fix; set. ((⇨ sadamaru))

sa˥doo さどう (茶道) *n.* tea ceremony. ((⇨ cha-no-yu))

sa˥e さえ *p.* (not) even:
★ Used for extreme examples.
Ichi-nichi-juu tabemono wa mochiroñ, mizu sae *kuchi ni shinakatta.* (一日中食べ物はもちろん, 水さえ口にしなかった) No food of course, but not *even* water, passed my lips all day long.
sae ...-ba [-tara] (～…ば[たら]) (just) as long as; if only: ★ Used to indicate an emphatic condi-

tion. *O-kane* sae areba, *nañ de mo dekiru.* (お金さえあれば，何でもできる) *Just as long as you have* money, you can do anything.

sa⌈egi⌉r·u さえぎる (遮る) *vt.* (saegir·i-; saegir·a-; saegit-te Ⓒ) interrupt; obstruct; block: *kaateñ de hikari o* saegiru (カーテンで光をさえぎる) *block out* the light with a curtain.

sa⌈ezu⌉r·u さえずる (囀る) *vi.* (saezur·i-; saezur·a-; saezut-te Ⓒ) (of a bird) sing; twitter; chirp; warble. ⟪⇨ naku[2]⟫

sa⌈ga⌉r·u さがる (下がる) *vi.* (sagar·i-; sagar·a-; sagat-te Ⓒ)
1 go down; fall; lower; drop: *Kioñ ga kyuu ni* sagatta. (気温が急に下がった) The temperature *has* suddenly *gone down.* ⟪↔ agaru⟫ ⟪⇨ sageru⟫
2 step back; stand back.

sa⌈gas·u さがす (捜す·探す) *vt.* (sagash·i-; sagas·a-; sagash·i-te Ⓒ) look for; seek; search.

sa⌈ge⌉·ru さげる (下げる) *vt.* (sage-te Ⓥ) **1** lower; pull down: *nedañ o* sageru (値段を下げる) *lower* the price. ⟪↔ ageru[1]⟫ ⟪⇨ sagaru⟫
2 hang; wear (a pendant). ⟪⇨ sagaru⟫
3 move back; draw back: *teeburu o ushiro e* sageru (テーブルを後ろへ下げる) *move* a table *back.*
4 clear away (dishes); take away.

sa⌉gi[1] さぎ (詐欺) *n.* fraud; swindle; deception:
sagi *o hataraku* (詐欺を働く) practice a *deception.* ⟪⇨ damasu⟫

sa⌈gi[2] さぎ (鷺) *n.* heron.

sa⌈gur·u さぐる (探る) *vt.* (sagur·i-; sagur·a-; sagut-te Ⓒ)
1 grope for; fumble for; feel for:
poketto o saguru (ポケットを探る) *fumble* in one's pocket.
2 sound out (a person's intention); feel out.

sa⌉gyoo さぎょう (作業) *n.* (factory) work; operation.
sagyoo suru (〜する) *vi.* work.

sa⌉i さい (際) *n.* time; occasion: *Hijoo no* sai *wa kono botañ o oshite kudasai.* (非常の際はこのボタンを押してください) Press this button in *case* of emergency. ⟪⇨ toki⟫

sa⌈i-[1] さい (再) *pref.* re-; again: sai-*nyuukoku* (再入国) *re*-entry into a country / sai-*koñ* (再婚) *re*-marriage.

sa⌈i-[2] さい (最) *pref.* (often translated into English as most..., -est): sai-*dai* (最大) the larg*est* / sai-*shoo* (最小) the small*est* / sai-zeñ (最善) the *best* / sai-aku (最悪) the *worst.*

-sai[1] さい (歳) *suf.* age; years old: *Haha wa juuhas*-sai *de kekkoñ shimashita.* (母は18歳で結婚しました) My mother married at the *age* of eighteen.

-sai[2] さい (祭) *suf.* festival; anniversary:
gojuu-neñ-sai (50年祭) the fiftieth *anniversary* / *buñka*-sai (文化祭) a cultural *festival.*

sa⌈ibai さいばい (栽培) *n.* growing; cultivation.
saibai suru (〜する) *vt.* grow; raise; cultivate: *oñshitsu de bara o* saibai suru (温室でばらを栽培する) *grow* roses in a greenhouse.

sa⌉ibañ さいばん (裁判) *n.* trial; judgment; court. ⟪⇨ soshoo⟫

sa⌈iba⌉ñkañ さいばんかん (裁判官) *n.* judge.

sa⌈ibañsho さいばんしょ (裁判所) *n.* courthouse; a court of justice.

sa⌈iboo さいぼう (細胞) *n.* (of biology) cell.

sa⌉ichuu さいちゅう (最中) *n.* (in) the middle (of):
Eñkai no saichuu *ni kare wa seki o tatta.* (宴会の最中に彼は席を立った) He left his seat in the *middle* of the party. ⟪⇨ massaichuu⟫

sa⌉idaa サイダー *n.* soda pop.
★ From English 'cider,' but not made from apples and nonalcoholic.

S

sa⌈idai さいだい (最大) *n.* the largest [biggest]; the greatest; maximum. 《↔ saishoo[1]》

sa⌈ifu さいふ (財布) *n.* wallet; (coin) purse.

sa⌈igai さいがい (災害) *n.* disaster; calamity:
saigai *o koomuru* (災害を被る) suffer from a *disaster* / saigai-*chi* (災害地) a *disaster* area.

sa⌉igo[1] さいご (最後) *n.* **1** the last; the end:
Kore ga saigo *no chañsu desu.* (これが最後のチャンスです) This is the *last* chance. 《↔ saisho》
2 once: ★ Used like a conjunction.
Kare ni kane o kashitara saigo, *kaeshite moraemaseñ.* (彼に金を貸したら最後, 返してもらえません) *Once* you lend him money, you can never get it back.

sa⌉igo[2] さいご (最期) *n.* end of one's life:
hisañ na saigo *o togeru* (悲惨な最期を遂げる) *die* in misery.

sa⌈ihoo さいほう (裁縫) *n.* sewing; needlework.

sa⌈ijitsu さいじつ (祭日) *n.* national holiday; festival day. 《⇨ APP. 6》

sa⌈ijoo さいじょう (最上) *n.* the best: saijoo *no shina* (最上の品) the *highest* quality article. 《↔ saitee》 《⇨ saikoo》

sa⌈ikai さいかい (再開) *n.* reopening; resumption.
saikai suru (〜する) *vt.* reopen; resume: *Kaigi wa gogo ni-ji ni* saikai saremasu. (会議は午後2時に再開されます) The meeting will *be reconvened* at 2:00 P.M.

sa⌈ikeñ さいけん (再建) *n.* reconstruction; rebuilding.
saikeñ suru (〜する) *vt.* reconstruct; rebuild.

sa⌈ikiñ[1] さいきん (最近) *n.* recent date.
— *adv.* recently; lately:
Saikiñ *yatto Nihoñgo no shiñbuñ ga yomeru yoo ni narimashita.* (最近やっと日本語の新聞が読めるようになりました) Just *recently*, I have at last become able to read Japanese newspapers. 《⇨ kono-goro》

sa⌈ikiñ[2] さいきん (細菌) *n.* germ; bacteria. 《⇨ baikiñ》

sa⌈ikoo さいこう (最高) *n.* **1** the highest:
Kyoo wa kotoshi saikoo *no atsusa datta.* (きょうは今年最高の暑さだった) Today it was the *highest* temperature of the year. 《↔ saitee》
2 best; supreme; maximum:
saikoo *sokudo* (最高速度) the *maximum* speed.

Sa⌈iko⌉osai さいこうさい (最高裁) *n.* Supreme Court. ★ Shortened form of '*Saikoo-saibañsho.*'

Sa⌈ikoo-saibañsho さいこうさいばんしょ (最高裁判所) *n.* Supreme Court.

sa⌈iku さいく (細工) *n.* **1** work; workmanship:
Kono kagu no saiku *wa subarashii.* (この家具の細工はすばらしい) The *workmanship* of this furniture is excellent.
2 artifice; tactics:
Ano hito no saiku *wa te ga koñde iru.* (あの人の細工は手が込んでいる) He uses very skillful *tactics.*

sa⌉iñ サイン *n.* **1** signature; autograph. ★ Comes from English 'sign,' but used as a noun in Japanese. 《⇨ shomee》
2 sign; signal:
rañnaa ni toorui no saiñ *o dasu* (*in baseball*) (ランナーに盗塁のサインを出す) *signal* a runner to steal.
saiñ suru (〜する) *vi.* sign; autograph.

sa⌈ina⌉ñ さいなん (災難) *n.* misfortune; disaster; accident:
sainañ *ni au* (災難にあう) meet with a *misfortune.*

sa⌈inoo さいのう (才能) *n.* ability; talent; gift:
sainoo *o hakki suru* (才能を発揮する) give full play to one's *ability.*

sa⌈isañ さいさん(採算) *n.* profit; gain:
saisañ ga toreru [torenai] (採算がとれる[とれない]) *be profitable* [*unprofitable*]. ⟪⇨ rieki⟫

sa⌉iseñ さいせん(賽銭) *n.* offertory; money offering.

sa⌉ishi さいし(妻子) *n.* one's wife and children; a man's family.

sa⌉ishite さいして(際して) on the occasion of:
Shuppatsu ni saishite *señsee kara chuui ga atta.* (出発に際して先生から注意があった) The teacher gave us advice *when* we were going to depart.

sa⌈isho さいしょ(最初) *n.* **1** beginning; start:
hoñ o saisho *kara saigo made yomu* (本を最初から最後まで読む) read a book from *beginning* to end. ⟪↔ saigo[1]⟫
2 (the) first:
Saisho *ni hatsugeñ shita no wa Yamada-sañ desu.* (最初に発言したのは山田さんです) It was Mr. Yamada who spoke *first*.

sa⌈ishoku さいしょく(菜食) *n.* vegetable diet.
saishoku suru (~する) *vi.* live on vegetables.

sa⌈ishoo[1] さいしょう(最小) *n.* the smallest; minimum. ⟪↔ saidai⟫

sa⌈ishoo[2] さいしょう(最少) *n.* the least; the smallest. ⟪⇨ saitee⟫

sa⌈ishuu[1] さいしゅう(最終) *n.* the last; the final:
Kore ga saishuu *no kettee desu.* (これが最終の決定です) This is our *final* decision.

sa⌈ishuu[2] さいしゅう(採集) *n.* collection.
saishuu suru (~する) *vt.* collect; gather: *koñchuu o* saishuu suru (昆虫を採集する) *collect* insects.

sa⌉isoku さいそく(催促) *n.* demand; reminder.
saisoku suru (~する) *vt.* press; urge; ask: *Watashi wa kare ni kashita kane no heñsai o* saisoku shita. (私は彼に貸した金の返済を催促した) I *pressed* him to repay the money I loaned him.

sa⌉itee さいてい(最低) *n.* **1** the lowest:
Señgetsu wa uriage ga saitee *datta.* (先月は売上が最低だった) Last month sales were the *lowest*.
2 the worst; minimum:
Shikeñ wa saitee *no deki datta.* (試験は最低の出来だった) I got the *worst* mark in the examination. ⟪↔ saikoo⟫

sa⌉iteñ さいてん(採点) *n.* grading; marking; scoring.
saiteñ suru (~する) *vt.* grade; mark; score: *tooañ o* saiteñ suru (答案を採点する) *mark* test papers.

sa⌈iwai さいわい(幸い) *a.n.* (~ na, ni) happy; lucky; fortunate.
— *adv.* happily; luckily; fortunately: ★ Often used in the form '~ *ni mo*.'
Saiwai (*ni mo*) *o-teñki ni megumaremashita.* (幸い(にも)お天気に恵まれました) *Fortunately*, we were blessed with good weather. ⟪⇨ shiawase⟫

sa⌈iyoo さいよう(採用) *n.* adoption; acceptance; employment.
saiyoo suru (~する) *vt.* adopt; accept; employ: *Sono kaisha wa joshi o juu-mee* saiyoo shita. (その会社は女子を10名採用した) The company *took on* ten women.

sa⌈ji⌉ さじ(匙) *n.* spoon.

sa⌈ka⌉ さか(坂) *n.* slope; hill:
saka *o noboru* [*oriru*] (坂を上る[下りる]) go up [down] a *slope*.

sa⌈kae⌉-ru さかえる(栄える) *vi.* (sakae-te [V]) prosper; flourish; thrive.

sa⌈ka⌉i さかい(境) *n.* border; boundary. ⟪⇨ kyookai[1]⟫

sa⌈kañ さかん(盛ん) *a.n.* (~ na, ni) **1** prosperous; flourishing; thriving.
2 energetic; active; vigorous:
Kanojo wa ima sakañ *ni e o kaite iru.* (彼女は今盛んに絵をかいている)

S

She now *actively* paints pictures.
3 popular; enthusiastic:
Nihoñ wa yakyuu ga sakañ *desu.* (日本は野球が盛んです) Baseball is *popular* in Japan.

sa⌈kana[1] さかな (魚) *n.* fish. ((⇨ sakanaya; tsuru[1]))

sa⌈kana[2] さかな (肴) *n.* side dish. ★ Relishes eaten as an accompaniment to drinking. ((⇨ tsumami[2]))

sa⌈kanaya さかなや (魚屋) *n.* fish dealer; fishmonger; fish shop.

sa⌈kanobo⌉r·u さかのぼる (遡る) *vi.* (-nobor·i-; -nobor·a-; -nobot-te Ⓒ) **1** go [sail] upstream.
2 (of a practice, convention, custom, etc.) go back; date from.

sa⌈kari さかり (盛り) *n.* **1** the height:
Sakura no hana wa sakari *o sugimashita.* (桜の花は盛りを過ぎました) The cherry blossoms are now past their *best.*
2 prime; bloom; flower:
Kare wa hataraki-zakari *ni nakunatta.* (彼は働き盛りに亡くなった) He died in his *prime.* ★ '*Sakari*' usually changes to '*zakari*' in compounds.
3 (of animals) heat; rut.

sa⌈kariba さかりば (盛り場) *n.* the busiest quarters of a city; amusement quarters.

sa⌈kasa さかさ (逆さ) *n.* inversion; reverse:
sakasa ni suru (逆さにする) *turn upside down.*

sa⌈kaya さかや (酒屋) *n.* liquor store; sake shop; sake dealer.

sa⌈kazuki⌉ さかずき (杯) *n.* sake cup. ((⇨ tokkuri))

sa⌈ke[1] さけ (酒) *n.* **1** sake; fermented rice beverage.
2 alcoholic drink; liquor:
Kare wa sake *ni tsuyoi* [*yowai*]. (彼は酒に強い[弱い]) He can [can't] hold his *drink.*

sa⌉ke[2] さけ (鮭) *n.* salmon. ★ Sometimes pronounced '*shake.*'

sa⌈kebi(go⌉e) さけび(ごえ) (叫び(声)) *n.* cry; shout; yell; scream; shriek. ((⇨ sakebu))

sa⌈ke⌉b·u さけぶ (叫ぶ) *vi.* (sakeb·i-; sakeb·a-; sakeñ-de Ⓒ) shout; cry out; yell; scream. ((⇨ donaru))

sa⌈ke⌉·ru[1] さける (避ける) *vi.* (sake-te Ⓥ) avoid; avert; evade; shun:
Sono jiko o sakeru *no wa fukanoo datta.* (その事故を避けるのは不可能だった) It was impossible to *avert* the accident.

sa⌈ke⌉·ru[2] さける (裂ける) *vi.* (sake-te Ⓥ) tear; split; rip:
Shatsu ga kugi ni hikkakatte, sakete shimatta. (シャツがくぎに引っかかって, 裂けてしまった) My shirt got caught on a nail and *ripped.* ((⇨ saku[2]))

sa⌈ki さき (先) *n.* **1** point; tip; end; head:
yubi no saki (指の先) the *tip* of a finger.
2 future:
Saki *no koto wa wakarimaseñ.* (先のことはわかりません) I do not know what will happen in the *future.*
3 (~ ni) in advance; beforehand:
Saki *ni daikiñ o haratte kudasai.* (先に代金を払ってください) Please pay *in advance.* ((↔ ato[1]))
4 ahead;
Chichi wa saki *ni dekakemashita.* (父は先に出かけました) My father left *ahead* of us.
5 previous; former:
Watashi ga saki *ni nobeta-toori yatte gorañ nasai.* (私が先に述べた通りやってごらんなさい) Try to do it just as I told you *previously.*

sa⌈kihodo さきほど (先程) *n., adv.* (*formal*) a little while ago; some time ago. ★ A little more formal than '*sakki.*'

sa⌈kka さっか (作家) *n.* writer; author; novelist.

S

sa⌉kkaa サッカー *n.* soccer; association football.

sa⌈kkaku さっかく(錯覚) *n.* illusion; imagination.
sakkaku suru (〜する) *vi.* have an illusion. ⟪⇨ gokai⟫

sa⌉kki さっき *n., adv.* a little while ago; some time ago. ⟪⇨ sakihodo⟫

sa⌈kkyoku さっきょく(作曲) *n.* musical composition:
sakkyoku-ka (作曲家) a *composer.*
sakkyoku suru (〜する) *vi., vt.* compose; write music.

sa⌈k·u[1] さく(咲く) *vi.* (sak·i-; sak·a-; sa·i-te Ⓒ) (of a flower) blossom; come out; bloom. ⟪⇨ hiraku⟫

sa⌉k·u[2] さく(裂く) *vt.* (sak·i-; sak·a-; sa·i-te Ⓒ) **1** tear; split; rip; rend. ⟪⇨ sakeru[2]⟫
2 separate; break up (relation, friendship, etc.).

sa⌈ku[3] さく(柵) *n.* fence; railing.

sa⌉ku[4] さく(策) *n.* plan; scheme; measure; policy:
saku *o neru* (策を練る) carefully work out a *plan.*

sa⌉k·u[5] さく(割く) *vt.* (sak·i-; sak·a-; sa·i-te Ⓒ) spare (time); give:
Isogashikute zeñzeñ jikañ ga sakemaseñ. (忙しくて全然時間が割けません) I am too busy to *spare* any time.

sa⌈ku- さく(昨) *pref.* last:
saku-jitsu (昨日) *yesterday* / saku-*neñ* (昨年) *last* year. ⟪↔ yoku-⟫

sa⌈ku⌉bañ さくばん(昨晩) *n.* (*formal*) last night; yesterday evening. ⟪⇨ sakuya⟫

sa⌈kubuñ さくぶん(作文) *n.* essay; composition.

sa⌈kuhiñ さくひん(作品) *n.* work; production; creation.

sa⌈kuiñ さくいん(索引) *n.* index.

sa⌈ku⌉jitsu さくじつ(昨日) *n.* (*formal*) yesterday. ⟪⇨ kinoo[1]⟫

sa⌈ku⌉motsu さくもつ(作物) *n.* crops; farm products.

sa⌈kuneñ さくねん(昨年) *n.* (*formal*) last year. ⟪⇨ kyoneñ⟫

sa⌈kura さくら(桜) *n.* cherry tree; cherry blossoms. ★ The cherry blossom is Japan's national flower.

sa⌈kusee[1] さくせい(作成) *n.* drawing up; making out.
sakusee suru (〜する) *vt.* draw up; make out (a contract).

sa⌈kusee[2] さくせい(作製) *n.* = seesaku[1].

sa⌈kuseñ さくせん(作戦) *n.* strategy; tactics; operations.

sa⌉kusha さくしゃ(作者) *n.* author; writer; artist.

sa⌈kushi さくし(作詞) *n.* writing a lyric [song]:
sakushi-ka [-sha] (作詞家[者]) a *songwriter.*

sa⌈ku⌉ya さくや(昨夜) *n.* last night; yesterday evening. ⟪↔ koñya⟫

-sama さま(様) *suf.* ★ Polite equivalent of '*-sañ*[1].'
1 Mr.; Mrs.; Miss: ★ Used in formal situations but more of a written than conversational form.
Tanaka-sama (田中様) *Mr.* [*Mrs.*; *Miss*] Tanaka.
2 (used to express respect): ★ Added to a kinship word or a name signifying a post or position.
oji-sama (おじ様) *uncle* / shichoo-sama (市長様) *mayor.*
3 (used to express appreciation): ★ Added to a word meaning labor or hard work. Not used when speaking to one's superiors, but '*-sama deshita*' is often used to superiors. ⟪⇨ otsukaresama; gokuroosama⟫

sa⌈ma⌉s·u[1] さます(冷ます) *vt.* (samash·i-; samas·a-; samash·i-te Ⓒ) **1** cool:
o-yu o samasu (お湯を冷ます) *cool* hot water. ⟪⇨ sameru[1]⟫
2 spoil; dampen:
hito no netsu o samasu (人の熱を冷

ます) *dampen* a person's enthusiasm. ⟨⟨⇨ sameru[1]⟩⟩

sa⌈ma⌉s·u[2] さます(覚ます) *vt.* (samash·i-; samas·a-; samash·i-te [C]) **1** wake up; awake. ⟨⟨⇨ okiru; sameru[2]⟩⟩
2 awaken; sober up:
Yoi o samashite *kara, uñteñ shi nasai.* (酔いを覚ましてから, 運転しなさい) Please drive your car after you *have sobered up*. ⟨⟨⇨ sameru[2]⟩⟩

sa⌈matage⌉·ru さまたげる(妨げる) *vt.* (samatage-te [V]) disturb; obstruct; prevent.

sa⌈ma⌉zama さまざま(様々) *a.n.* (~ na, ni) various; different; all kinds of. ⟨⟨⇨ iroiro[1]⟩⟩

sa⌈me⌉·ru[1] さめる(冷める) *vi.* (same-te [V]) **1** cool; get cold. ⟨⟨⇨ samasu[1]⟩⟩
2 (of a feeling, enthusiasm, etc.) cool down.

sa⌈me⌉·ru[2] さめる(覚める) *vi.* (same-te [V]) **1** wake up; awake.
2 come to one's senses; sober up:
Kare no kotoba de mayoi ga sameta. (彼の言葉で迷いが覚めた) His words *brought* me *to my senses*. ⟨⟨⇨ samasu[2]⟩⟩

sa⌈me⌉·ru[3] さめる(褪める) *vi.* (same-te [V]) (of color) fade; go out: iro ga sameru (色がさめる) *be discolored*.

sa⌈mu⌉·i さむい(寒い) *a.* (-ku) cold; chilly; freezing. ⟨⟨↔ atatakai; atsui[2]⟩⟩ ⟨⟨⇨ samusa; suzushii⟩⟩

sa⌈muke⌉ さむけ(寒気) *n.* chill; cold fit: samuke *ga suru* (寒気がする) have a *chill*.

sa⌉musa さむさ(寒さ) *n.* cold; cold weather. ⟨⟨↔ atsusa[1]⟩⟩

sa⌈ñ[1] さん(三・参) *n.* three; third: *eñpitsu* sañ-*boñ* (鉛筆3本) *three* pencils / sañ-*neñ* (3年) *three* years. ⟨⟨⇨ APP. 3⟩⟩

sa⌉ñ[2] さん(酸) *n.* acid. ⟨⟨↔ arukari⟩⟩

-sañ[1] さん *suf.* **1** (used to express respect and friendliness):
★ Added to a family or given name. ⟨⟨⇨ -kuñ⟩⟩
Yamamoto-sañ (山本さん) *Mr.* [*Mrs.*; *Miss*] Yamamoto.
2 (used after a kinship word): oji-sañ (おじさん) *uncle* / oba-sañ (おばさん) *aunt*.
3 (used to express appreciation in certain set phrases): ★ Not used when speaking to one's superiors.
Otsukare-sañ. (お疲れさん) *You must be tired.* / Go-kuroo-sañ. (ご苦労さん) *Thank you for your help.* ⟨⟨⇨ -sama⟩⟩

-sañ[2] さん(山) *suf.* Mount; Mt.: ★ Added to the name of a mountain. *Fuji*-sañ (富士山) *Mt.* Fuji. ⟨⟨⇨ -yama⟩⟩

sa⌈ñbutsu さんぶつ(産物) *n.* product; produce.

sa⌉ñchi さんち(産地) *n.* producing district; production center.

sa⌈ñfujiñka さんふじんか(産婦人科) *n.* obstetrics and gynecology: sañfujiñka-i (産婦人科医) an *obstetrician and gynecologist*. ⟨⟨⇨ fujiñka⟩⟩

sa⌉ñ-gatsu さんがつ(三月) *n.* March. ⟨⟨⇨ APP. 5⟩⟩

Sa⌈ñgi⌉iñ さんぎいん(参議院) *n.* the House of Councilors: Sañgiiñ *giiñ* (参議院議員) a member of *the House of Councilors*. ⟨⟨⇨ Shuugiiñ; kokkai⟩⟩

sa⌉ñgo さんご(珊瑚) *n.* coral.

sa⌈ñgyoo さんぎょう(産業) *n.* industry.

sa⌈ñka[1] さんか(参加) *n.* participation; joining.
sañka suru (~する) *vi.* participate; take part in; join. ⟨⟨⇨ deru (3)⟩⟩

sa⌈ñka[2] さんか(酸化) *n.* oxidation.
sañka suru (~する) *vi.* oxidize.

sa⌉ñkaku さんかく(三角) *n.* triangle. ⟨⟨⇨ shikaku[2]⟩⟩

sa⌈ñka⌉kukee さんかくけい(三角形) *n.* triangle.

sa⌈ñkeñ-buñritsu さんけんぶんり

つ(三権分立) *n.* separation of the three powers of administration, legislation, and judicature. ⟪⇨ shihoo[2]; gyoosee; rippoo[2]⟫

saˈñketsu さんけつ(酸欠) *n.* oxygen shortage.

saˈñkoo さんこう(参考) *n.* reference; information; consultation:
Kono hoñ o sañkoo *ni shi nasai.* (この本を参考にしなさい) You *should refer* to this book.

saˈñkoosho さんこうしょ(参考書) *n.* study-aid book; student handbook; reference book.

saˈñma さんま(秋刀魚) *n.* Pacific saury.

saˈñmyaku さんみゃく(山脈) *n.* mountain range [chain].

saˈñpai さんぱい(参拝) *n.* visit to a shrine or temple for worship.
sañpai suru (～する) *vi.* go and worship. ⟪⇨ omairi⟫

saˈñpatsu さんぱつ(散髪) *n.* men's haircut; men's hairdressing. ⟪⇨ tokoya⟫
sañpatsu suru (～する) *vi.* have a haircut.

saˈñpo さんぽ(散歩) *n.* walk; stroll:
sañpo *ni iku* [*deru*] (散歩に行く[出る]) go for a *walk.*
sañpo suru (～する) *vi.* take a walk.

saˈñryuu さんりゅう(三流) *n.* third-class; third-rate. ⟪⇨ ichiryuu; niryuu⟫

saˈñsee[1] さんせい(賛成) *n.* agreement; approval; support; favor.
sañsee suru (～する) *vt.* agree; approve; be in favor. ⟪↔ hañtai⟫

saˈñsee[2] さんせい(三世) *n.* Sansei; the third generation of Japanese immigrants; a member of this generation. ⟪⇨ issee[2]; nisee⟫

saˈñshoo さんしょう(参照) *n.* reference.
sañshoo suru (～する) *vt.* see; refer to: *jiteñ o* sañshoo suru (辞典を参照する) *consult* a dictionary.

saˈñso さんそ(酸素) *n.* oxygen.

saˈñsuˈu さんすう(算数) *n.* arithmetic. ⟪⇨ suugaku⟫

saˈñtoo さんとう(三等) *n.* third class; third prize; third place. ⟪⇨ ittoo; nitoo⟫

saˈñzañ さんざん(散々) *a.n.* (～ na) severe; terrible:
Tozañ wa ame de sañzañ *datta.* (登山は雨でさんざんだった) Our mountain climbing was *ruined* by the rain.
— *adv.* severely; terribly:
Sono seeto wa señsee ni sañzañ *shikarareta.* (その生徒は先生にさんざんしかられた) The pupil was *severely* scolded by his teacher.

saˈoˈ さお(竿) *n.* pole; rod.

saˈppaˈri[1] さっぱり *adv.* (～ suru)
1 feel refreshed:
Furo ni haittara, sappari *shita.* (ふろに入ったら, さっぱりした) I felt *nice and fresh* after taking a bath.
2 (of clothes) neat:
Kanojo wa itsu-mo sappari *shita fukusoo o shite iru.* (彼女はいつもさっぱりした服装をしている) She is always dressed *neatly.*
3 (of personality) frank; openhearted.
4 (of a dish, taste, etc.) simple; plain; light.

saˈppaˈri[2] さっぱり *adv.* **1** no good:
Shikeñ no kekka wa sappari *datta.* (試験の結果はさっぱりだった) The exam result was *no good.*
2 (with a negative) not at all:
Roshiago wa sappari *wakarimaseñ.* (ロシア語はさっぱりわかりません) I do not understand Russian *at all.* ⟪⇨ sukoshi mo⟫

saˈra さら(皿) *n.* plate; dish; platter; saucer.

saˈraineñ さらいねん(再来年) *n.* the year after next. ⟪⇨ kotoshi; raineñ⟫

saˈraishuu さらいしゅう(再来週) *n.* the week after next. ⟪⇨ raishuu⟫

saˈra ni さらに(更に) *adv.* further; even [still] more:

S

Yoru ni naru to, ame wa sara ni *tsuyoku natta.* (夜になると, 雨はさらに強くなった) The rain became *even* heavier as night fell.

sa⌈rari⌉imañ サラリーマン *n.* office worker; white-collar worker; salaried worker. ★ Refers to male workers. Female workers are often called '*oo-eru*' (OL). ⟪⇒ oo-eru⟫

sa⌉rasara さらさら *adv.* (~ to) (the sound or state of moving or proceeding smoothly):
Kaze de ki no ha ga sarasara to natte iru. (風で木の葉がさらさらと鳴っている) The leaves are *rustling* in the wind.

sa⌈ra·u[1] さらう (攫う) *vt.* (sara·i-; saraw·a-; sarat-te Ⓒ) **1** sweep away:
Kodomo ga nami ni sarawareta. (子どもが波にさらわれた) A child *was swept away* by the waves.
2 kidnap:
Kare no hitori musume ga sarawareta. (彼の一人娘がさらわれた) His only daughter *was kidnapped.*
3 carry off (a victory); win (popularity, etc.).

sa⌈ra·u[2] さらう (浚う) *vt.* (sara·i-; saraw·a-; sarat-te Ⓒ) clean; dredge: *ike o* sarau (池をさらう) *dredge* a pond.

sare·ru される *vt.* (sare-te Ⓥ)
1 (honorific equivalent of '*suru*'):
Señsee mo shusseki sareru *soo desu.* (先生も出席されるそうです) I hear that the teacher will also *be present.*
2 be done: ★ The passive of '*suru.*'
Watashi wa kare ni ijiwaru sareta. (私は彼に意地悪された) I *was treated* meanly by him.

sa⌉r·u[1] さる (去る) *vi.* (sar·i-; sar·a-; sat-te Ⓒ) leave; pass; resign:
Taifuu wa sarimashita. (台風は去りました) The typhoon *has passed.*

sa⌉ru[2] さる (猿) *n.* monkey; ape.

sa⌉ru- さる (去る) *pref.* last:
Sono jikeñ wa saru *itsuka ni okotta.* (その事件は去る五日に起こった) The incident occurred on the fifth of *this* [*last*] month.

sa⌈sae·ru ささえる (支える) *vt.* (sasae-te Ⓥ) **1** prop up:
Tana o boo de sasaeta. (棚を棒で支えた) I *propped up* the shelf with a stick.
2 support (a family, group, organization, etc.).

sa⌈sa⌉r·u ささる (刺さる) *vi.* (sasar·i-; sasar·a-; sasat-te Ⓒ) stick; prick:
Hari ga yubi ni sasatta. (針が指に刺さった) A needle *pricked* my finger.

sa⌈sa⌉yaka ささやか *a.n.* (~ na, ni) small; humble; modest:
shomiñ no sasayaka *na negai* (庶民のささやかな願い) a *modest* request from common folk.

sa⌈serare·ru させられる *vt.* (-rare-te Ⓥ) be made to do:
Watashi wa toire no sooji o saserareta. (私はトイレの掃除をさせられた) I *was made* to clean the toilet.
⟪⇒ saseru; -rareru⟫

sa⌈se·ru させる *vt.* (sase-te Ⓥ)
1 make someone do; cause someone to do:
Koochi wa señshu ni mainichi reñshuu saseta. (コーチは選手に毎日練習させた) The coach *made* the players *practice* every day.
2 let someone do; allow someone do:
Watashi wa kare-ra ni yaritai-yoo ni saseta. (私は彼らにやりたいようにさせた) I *let* them *do* as they wished.

-sase·ru させる *infl. end.* (-sase-te Ⓥ) [attached to the negative base of a vowel-stem verb and '*kuru,*' and itself inflected like a vowel-stem verb]
1 make someone do; cause someone to do:
Kare no kañgae o kaesaseru *no*

S

wa muzukashii. (彼の考えを変えさせるのはむずかしい) It is difficult to *make* him *change* his mind. (⇨ -seru)

2 let someone do; allow someone to do:

Sono ko ni suki na dake tabesasete *yari nasai.* (その子に好きなだけ食べさせてやりなさい) *Let* the child *eat* as much as he likes. (⇨ -seru)

sa⌈shiage·ru さしあげる (差し上げる) *vt.* (-age-te [V]) (*honorific*) give; present. (⇨ ageru[1])

sa⌈shidas·u さしだす (差し出す) *vt.* (-dash·i-; -das·a-; -dash·i-te [C])

1 hold out (one's hand); reach out.

2 hand in; present; submit:

hookokusho o sashidasu (報告書を差し出す) *submit* a report. (⇨ teeshutsu)

sa⌈shi⌉hiki さしひき (差し引き) *n.* balance; total. (⇨ gookee)

sa⌈shimi⌉ さしみ (刺身) *n.* slices of raw fish for eating.

sa⌈shitsukae さしつかえ (差し支え) *n.* (with a negative) difficulty; obstruction; harm:

Sashitsukae nakereba, *ashita kite kudasai.* (差しつかえなければ, あした来てください) *If it is not inconvenient*, I would like you to come tomorrow. (⇨ sashitsukaeru)

sa⌈shitsukae·ru さしつかえる (差し支える) *vi.* (-tsukae-te [V]) interfere; affect; have difficulty. (⇨ sashitsukae)

sa⌉shizu さしず (指図) *n.* directions; instructions; orders.

sashizu suru (～する) *vt.* direct; instruct; order. (⇨ shiji[1])

sa⌈so·u さそう (誘う) *vt.* (saso·i-; sasow·a-; sasot-te [C]) **1** invite; ask; allure; tempt:

Watashi wa sukii ni ikoo to kanojo o sasotta. (私はスキーに行こうと彼女を誘った) I *asked* her to come skiing.

2 cause (tears, laughter, etc.).

sa⌉ssa to さっさと *adv.* quickly; promptly: sassa to *aruku* (さっさと歩く) walk *quickly.*

sa⌈sshi さっし (察し) *n.* understanding; guess; judgment:

Kare wa sasshi *ga ii* [*warui*]. (彼は察しがいい[悪い]) He is quick [slow] to *understand.* (⇨ sassuru)

sa⌈ssoku さっそく (早速) *adv.* immediately; promptly.

sa⌈ssoo to さっそうと *adv.* smartly; dashingly:

Kare wa atarashii fuku de sassoo to *arawareta.* (彼は新しい服でさっそうと現れた) He showed up *smartly* dressed in a new suit.

sa⌈ss·uru さっする (察する) *vt.* (sassh·i-; sassh·i-; sassh·i-te [I]) **1** guess; presume; suppose. (⇨ suisoku)

2 appreciate; understand:

*O-kimochi wa o-*sasshi *itashimasu.* (お気持ちはお察しいたします) I *appreciate* how you feel.

sa⌉s·u[1] さす (指す) *vt.* (sash·i-; sas·a-; sash·i-te [C]) **1** point; show; indicate:

Dore ga hoshii ka, yubi de sashi nasai. (どれが欲しいか, 指で指しなさい) *Point* to the one you want.

2 mean; refer to:

Anata no koto o sashite, *itta wake de wa arimaseñ.* (あなたのことを指して, 言った訳ではありません) I do not mean to imply that I *was referring to* you.

3 (in a classroom) call on.

sa⌉s·u[2] さす (刺す) *vt.* (sash·i-; sas·a-; sash·i-te [C]) **1** stab; pierce; thrust.

2 (of an insect) sting; bite:

Hachi ni te o sasareta. (蜂に手を刺された) I *was stung* on the hand by a bee.

3 (in baseball) throw out.

sa⌈suga さすが (流石) *adv.*

1 (～ ni) truly; indeed:

Sasuga *ni Fuji-sañ wa utsukushii.* (さすがに富士山は美しい) Mt. Fuji is *truly* beautiful.

2 (～ no) even:

Sasuga no *kare mo tsui ni maketa.* (さすがの彼もついに負けた) *Even* he finally suffered a defeat.
3 (~ ni/wa) just as one might expect:
Sasuga wa *taika da. Migoto na e da.* (さすがは大家だ. みごとな絵だ) *That's just what one would expect* of a master. It's a wonderful painting.

sa⌈tchuuzai さっちゅうざい (殺虫剤) *n.* insecticide.

sa⌉te さて *int.* now; well:
★ Used at the beginning of a sentence.
Sate, *tsugi no gidai ni utsurimasu.* (さて, 次の議題に移ります) *Now* we are going to move on to the next topic. ⟪⇨ saa⟫

sa⌈toimo さといも (里芋) *n.* taro.

sa⌈to⌉o さとう (砂糖) *n.* sugar.

sa⌈tor·u さとる (悟る) *vt.* (sator·i-; sator·a-; satot-te Ⓒ) **1** realize; find:
Koto no juudai-sa o satotta. (事の重大さを悟った) I *realized* the importance of the matter.
2 sense (danger):
Kikeñ o satotte, *kare wa sugu nigeta.* (危険を悟って, 彼はすぐ逃げた) *Sensing* danger, he quickly escaped.

sa⌈tsu さつ (札) *n.* paper money; bill; note. ★ '*O-satsu*' is more common when used independently. ⟪⇨ kahee; shihee⟫

-satsu さつ (冊) *suf.* volume; copy. ★ Counter for books and magazines.

sa⌈tsuee さつえい (撮影) *n.* photographing; shooting.
satsuee suru (~する) *vt.* take a picture; photograph; shoot. ⟪⇨ toru[4]⟫

sa⌈tsujiñ さつじん (殺人) *n.* homicide; murder:
satsujiñ-*jikeñ* (殺人事件) a *murder* case / satsujiñ-hañ (殺人犯) a *murderer.*

sa⌈tsumaimo さつまいも *n.* sweet potato.

sa⌈tsutaba さつたば (札束) *n.* roll [wad] of bills.

sa⌉tto さっと *adv.* quickly; suddenly:
Doa ga satto *hiraita.* (ドアがさっと開いた) The door opened *suddenly.*

sa⌈wagashi⌉·i さわがしい (騒がしい) *a.* (-ku) noisy; boisterous. ⟪⇨ sawagi; sawagu; soozooshii⟫

sa⌉wagi さわぎ (騒ぎ) *n.* noise; tumult; disturbance:
sawagi *o okosu* (騒ぎを起こす) cause a *disturbance.* ⟪⇨ sawagu; sawagashii⟫

sa⌈wa⌉g·u さわぐ (騒ぐ) *vi.* (sawag·i-; sawag·a-; sawa·i-de Ⓒ)
1 make a noise; clamor.
2 make merry:
Miñna de uta o utatte sawaida. (みんなで歌を歌って騒いだ) We all sang and *made merry.* ⟪⇨ sawagi⟫
3 make a fuss:
Ano kashu wa ima masukomi de sawagarete imasu. (あの歌手は今マスコミで騒がれています) *A great fuss is* now *made of* that singer by the media. ⟪⇨ sawagi⟫

sa⌈war·u[1] さわる (触る) *vi.* (sawar·i-; sawar·a-; sawat-te Ⓒ) touch; feel:
Teñjihiñ ni sawaranai de *kudasai.* (展示品に触らないでください) *Don't touch* the exhibits.

sa⌈war·u[2] さわる (障る) *vi.* (sawar·i-; sawar·a-; sawat-te Ⓒ)
1 hurt (a person's feelings); get on (a person's nerves); offend.
2 affect; be harmful (to health):
Nomi-sugi wa karada ni sawaru. (飲み過ぎは体にさわる) Drinking to excess *affects* the health.

sa⌈wa⌉yaka さわやか (爽やか) *a.n.* (~ na, ni) fresh; refreshing; crisp; pleasant:
sawayaka *na asa no kuuki* (さわやかな朝の空気) the *refreshing* morning air.

sa⌈yona⌉ra さよなら (*informal*) goodbye. ⟪⇨ sayoonara⟫

sa⌉yoo さよう(作用) *n.* action; operation; function:
sayoo *to hañ-sayoo* (作用と反作用) *action* and reaction.

sa⌈yoona⌉ra さようなら(左様なら) goodbye; so long.

sa⌉yuu さゆう(左右) *n.* right and left. ⟪↔ jooge⟫ ⟪⇨ ue-shita⟫
sayuu suru (〜する) decide; influence; control: *Sono mondai ga señkyo o ookiku* sayuu shita. (その問題が選挙を大きく左右した) That matter greatly *influenced* the election.

sa⌉zo さぞ *adv.* surely; I am sure:
Okaasañ wa sazo *yorokoñda deshoo.* (お母さんはさぞ喜んだでしょう) *I am sure* your mother was very pleased.

sa⌈zuka⌉r·u さずかる(授かる) *vi.* (sazukar·i-; sazukar·a-; sazukatte [C]) be given [awarded]; be blessed:
kodomo o sazukaru (子どもを授かる) *be blessed* with a child. ⟪⇨ sazukeru⟫

sa⌈zuke⌉·ru さずける(授ける) *vt.* (sazuke-te [V]) award (a prize); confer (a title); grant. ⟪⇨ sazukaru⟫

se せ(背) *n.* **1** back:
uma no se *ni noru* (馬の背に乗る) ride on a horse's *back* / se *o nobasu* (背を伸ばす) straighten one's *back.* ⟪⇨ senaka⟫
2 = see[1].

se⌈biro せびろ(背広) *n.* business suit; lounge suit.

se⌉dai せだい(世代) *n.* generation.

se⌉e[1] せい(背) *n.* height of a person; stature. ⟪⇨ se⟫

se⌉e[2] せい(性) *n.* sex. ★ The act of sex is called '*sekkusu.*'

se⌉e[3] せい(姓) *n.* family name; surname.

se⌉e[4] せい(精) *n.* energy; vigor.
see o dasu (〜を出す) work hard.

se⌉e[5] せい(所為) *n.* **1** blame; fault:
Sore wa watashi no see *de wa arimaseñ.* (それは私のせいではありません) It's not my *fault.*
2 because of; due to: ★ Indicates an unfavorable cause or reason.
Deñsha ga okureta no wa yuki no see *desu.* (電車が遅れたのは雪のせいです) The train was late *because of* the snow. ⟪⇨ okage⟫

-see せい(製) *suf.* made in [by; of]; -made:
garasu-see *no kabiñ* (ガラス製の花瓶) a vase *made* of glass.

se⌈ebetsu せいべつ(性別) *n.* distinction of sex.

se⌉ebi せいび(整備) *n.* maintenance; repair; improvement.
seebi suru (〜する) *vt.* maintain; service; improve.

se⌈ebo せいぼ(歳暮) *n.* year-end gift. ★ Usually with '*o-*.' Japanese people customarily send '*o-seebo*' to those to whom they feel indebted. ⟪⇨ chuugeñ⟫

se⌉ebuñ せいぶん(成分) *n.* ingredient; component.

se⌉ebutsu せいぶつ(生物) *n.* living thing; creature. ⟪⇨ ikimono⟫

se⌈ebyoo せいびょう(性病) *n.* venereal disease.

se⌈echoo せいちょう(成長・生長) *n.* growth. ★ '成長' is usually used for animals and '生長' for plants.
seechoo suru (〜する) *vi.* grow: seechoo shite *otona ni naru* (成長して大人になる) *grow* into a man [woman].

se⌉edo せいど(制度) *n.* system; institution:
atarashii seedo *o mookeru* (新しい制度を設ける) establish a new *system.*

se⌉e-eki せいえき(精液) *n.* semen; sperm.

se⌉efu せいふ(政府) *n.* government; administration.

se⌈efuku[1] せいふく(制服) *n.* uniform. 《⇨ fuku[2]; yoofuku》

se¹efuku² せいふく(正副) *n.* original and duplicate:
shorui o seefuku *ni-tsuu sakusee suru* (書類を正副2通作成する) make out documents in *duplicate* / seefuku gichoo (正副議長) the *chairman and vice-chairman.*

se⌈ege¹ñ せいげん(制限) *n.* restriction; limit: seegeñ *o kuwaeru* (制限を加える) impose *restrictions.*
seegeñ suru (～する) *vt.* restrict; limit. 《⇨ toosee》

se¹egi せいぎ(正義) *n.* justice; right.

se⌈ehiñ せいひん(製品) *n.* product; article; goods.

se⌈eho¹okee せいほうけい(正方形) *n.* square.

se⌈eiku せいいく(成育・生育) *n.* growth. ★'成育' is usually used for animals and '生育' for plants.
seeiku suru (～する) *vt., vi.* grow: *Ine wa juñchoo ni* seeiku shite imasu. (稲は順調に生育しています) The rice plants *are coming along* nicely. 《⇨ seechoo》

se⌈eji せいじ(政治) *n.* politics; government; administration.

se⌈ejika せいじか(政治家) *n.* statesman; politician.

se⌈ejiñ せいじん(成人) *n.* adult; grown-up.
seejiñ suru (～する) *vi.* become an adult; come of age. 《⇨ seeneñ[2]》

se⌈ejiñbyoo せいじんびょう(成人病) *n.* adult diseases; diseases which are often connected with aging.

se⌈ejitsu せいじつ(誠実) *a.n.* (～ na, ni) sincere; honest; faithful:
Kare wa yakusoku o seejitsu *ni jikkoo shita.* (彼は約束を誠実に実行した) He *faithfully* carried out his promise.

se⌈ejoo せいじょう(正常) *a.n.* (～ na, ni) normal; ordinary:
Taioñ wa seejoo *desu.* (体温は正常です) My temperature is *normal.* 《↔ ijoo[3]》

se⌈ejooka せいじょうか(正常化) *n.* normalization.
seejooka suru (～する) *vt.* normalize: *kokkoo o* seejooka suru (国交を正常化する) *normalize* diplomatic relations.

se⌈ejuku せいじゅく(成熟) *n.* ripeness; maturity.
seejuku suru (～する) *vt.* ripen; mature.

se⌈ekai せいかい(正解) *n.* correct answer.

se⌈ekaku¹ せいかく(性格) *n.* character; disposition; personality.

se⌈ekaku² せいかく(正確) *a.n.* (～ na, ni) correct; accurate; precise; exact. 《↔ fuseekaku》

se⌈ekatsu せいかつ(生活) *n.* life; living; livelihood:
seekatsu-*hi* (生活費) *living* expenses. 《⇨ seekee[1]》
seekatsu (o) suru (～(を)する) *vi.* live; make a living. 《⇨ kurasu[1]》

se⌈ekee¹ せいけい(生計) *n.* one's living; one's livelihood:
seekee *o tateru* (生計を立てる) earn a *living.*

se⌈ekee² せいけい(整形) *n.* orthopedic surgery; plastic surgery.
seekee suru (～する) *vt.* have plastic surgery.

se⌈ekee-ge¹ka せいけいげか(整形外科) *n.* orthopedics.

se⌈ekeñ せいけん(政権) *n.* political power:
Hoshutoo ga geñzai seekeñ *o nigitte iru.* (保守党が現在政権を握っている) The conservative party is now in *power.*

se⌈eketsu せいけつ(清潔) *a.n.* (～ na, ni) **1** clean; neat:
toire o seeketsu *ni shite oku* (トイレを清潔にしておく) keep the toilet *clean.* 《↔ fuketsu》
2 honest:
seeketsu *na seejika* (清潔な政治家) an *honest* politician.

se¹eki せいき(世紀) *n.* century.

se͡ekoo[1] せいこう(成功) *n.* success; prosperity; achievement.
seekoo suru (〜する) *vi.* succeed; be successful. 《↔ shippai》

se͡ekoo[2] せいこう(性交) *n.* sexual intercourse.
seekoo suru (〜する) *vi.* have sexual intercourse.

se͡eko͝oi せいこうい(性行為) *n.* sexual act.

se͡ekyuu せいきゅう(請求) *n.* demand; claim; request:
seekyuu-sho (請求書) a *bill*; a *request for payment*.
seekyuu suru (〜する) *vt.* demand; claim; request; charge.

se͝emee[1] せいめい(生命) *n.* life. 《⇨ inochi》

se͝emee[2] せいめい(姓名) *n.* one's full name. 《⇨ namae》

se͡emee[3] せいめい(声明) *n.* statement; declaration; announcement: seemee *o dasu* (声明を出す) make a *statement*.

se͡emitsu せいみつ(精密) *a.n.* (〜 na, ni) precise; detailed; minute:
seemitsu-*keñsa* (精密検査) a *detailed* (health) examination.

se͡emoñ せいもん(正門) *n.* front gate; main entrance.

se͡eneñ[1] せいねん(青年) *n.* youth; young man. 《⇨ shooneñ》

se͡eneñ[2] せいねん(成年) *n.* full age; majority:
seeneñ ni tassuru (成年に達する) *come of age*. 《⇨ seejiñ》

se͡eneñga͝ppi せいねんがっぴ(生年月日) *n.* date of one's birth.

se͡enoo せいのう(性能) *n.* efficiency; performance; power:
Kono kamera wa seenoo ga yoi. (このカメラは性能が良い) This camera *works well*.

se͝eoñ せいおん(清音) *n.* voiceless sound. ★ Japanese syllables with a consonant that is not voiced, *i.e.* か (*ka*), さ (*sa*), ち (*chi*), ほ (*ho*). 《⇨ dakuoñ; hañ-dakuoñ; inside front cover》

se͡ereki せいれき(西暦) *n.* Christian era; A.D.

se͝eri[1] せいり(整理) *n.* tidying up; putting things in order.
seeri suru (〜する) *vt.* **1** tidy up; put in order; arrange.
2 cut down; reduce:
juugyooiñ o seeri suru (従業員を整理する) *reduce* the number of employees.

se͝eri[2] せいり(生理) *n.* physiology; menses:
seeri *ni naru* (生理になる) have one's monthly *period*.

se͡eritsu せいりつ(成立) *n.* coming into existence; formation; conclusion.
seeritsu suru (〜する) *vi.* come into existence; be formed; be concluded: *Atarashii naikaku ga* seeritsu shita. (新しい内閣が成立した) A new cabinet *was formed*.

se͝eryoku せいりょく(勢力) *n.* influence; power; strength.

se͡e-sa͝betsu せいさべつ(性差別) *n.* sexism; sex discrimination.

se͡esaku[1] せいさく(製作) *n.* manufacture; production of machinery.
seesaku suru (〜する) *vt.* manufacture; produce. 《⇨ seezoo》

se͡esaku[2] せいさく(制作) *n.* production of works of art.
seesaku suru (〜する) *vt.* produce: *atarashii eega o* seesaku suru (新しい映画を制作する) *make* a new movie.

se͡esaku[3] せいさく(政策) *n.* policy:
gaikoo seesaku (外交政策) a foreign *policy*.

se͡esañ せいさん(生産) *n.* production; manufacture:
seesañ-daka (生産高) *output*.
seesañ suru (〜する) *vt.* produce; manufacture. 《↔ shoohi》

se͡esa͝ñsha せいさんしゃ(生産者) *n.* producer; maker; manufacturer. 《↔ shoohisha》

se͡eseki せいせき(成績) *n.*

S

school record; grade; result.

se͈eshi[1] せいし (生死) *n.* life and death:
Kare no seeshi *wa fumee desu.* (彼の生死は不明です) Nobody knows whether he is *alive or not.*

se͈eshi[2] せいし (制止) *n.* holding back; control.
seeshi suru (~する) *vt.* stop; hold back; restrain. ⟪⇨ tomeru[1]⟫

se͈eshi[3] せいし (精子) *n.* sperm. ⟪↔ rañshi⟫

se͈eshiki せいしき (正式) *a.n.* (~ na, ni) formal; official; regular:
seeshiki *kaiiñ* (正式会員) a *regular* member.

se͈eshiñ せいしん (精神) *n.*
1 mind; soul:
seeshiñ-*byoo* (精神病) a *mental* disease / seeshiñ-*ryoku* (精神力) *mental* power.
2 spirit:
keñpoo no seeshiñ (憲法の精神) the *spirit* of the constitution.

se͈eshiñ-teki せいしんてき (精神的) *a.n.* (~ na, ni) mental; spiritual:
Chichi-oya no shi wa kare ni totte ooki-na seeshiñ-teki *dageki datta.* (父親の死は彼にとって大きな精神的打撃だった) His father's death was a great *mental* blow to him.

se͈eshitsu せいしつ (性質) *n.*
1 nature; disposition; character.
2 property; quality:
abura ga mizu ni uku to iu seeshitsu *o riyoo suru* (油が水に浮くという性質を利用する) make use of oil's *property* of floating on water.

se͈esho[1] せいしょ (清書) *n.* fair copy; making a fair copy.
seesho suru (~する) *vt.* make a fair copy.

se͈esho[2] せいしょ (聖書) *n.* the Bible; Testament:
kyuuyaku seesho (旧約聖書) the Old *Testament* / *shiñyaku* seesho (新約聖書) the New *Testament.*

se͈eshuñ せいしゅん (青春) *n.* youth; the period of adolescence.

se͈esoo せいそう (清掃) *n.* cleaning: seesoo-sha (清掃車) a *garbage truck*; a *dustcart.*
seesoo suru (~する) *vt.* clean:
heya [*dooro*] *o* seesoo suru (部屋[道路]を清掃する) *clean* a room [street]. ⟪⇨ sooji⟫

se͈etaa セーター *n.* sweater.

se͈etee せいてい (制定) *n.* enactment; establishment.
seetee suru (~する) *vt.* enact; establish: *hooritsu o* seetee suru (法律を制定する) *enact* laws.

se͈e-teki せいてき (性的) *a.n.* (~ na, ni) sex; sexual; sexy:
see-teki *iyagarase* (性的いやがらせ) *sexual* harassment.

se͈eteñ せいてん (晴天) *n.* fair weather. ⟪↔ uteñ⟫

se͈etetsu せいてつ (製鉄) *n.* iron manufacture:
seetetsu-jo (製鉄所) an *ironworks.*

se͈eto せいと (生徒) *n.* pupil; student. ★ College students are called '*gakusee.*'

se͈etoñ せいとん (整頓) *n.* order.
seetoñ suru (~する) *vt.* put in order; tidy up. ⟪⇨ totonoeru⟫

se͈etoo[1] せいとう (正当) *a.n.* (~ na, ni) just; right; good; fair:
Kare ni wa seetoo *na riyuu ga arimasu.* (彼には正当な理由があります) He has a *good* reason. ⟪↔ futoo⟫

se͈etoo[2] せいとう (政党) *n.* political party. ⟪⇨ APP. 8⟫

se͈eyaku せいやく (制約) *n.* restriction; restraint; limitation:
yosañ no seeyaku (予算の制約) budgetary *limitations.*
seeyaku suru (~する) *vt.* limit; restrict; restrain.

Se͈eyoo せいよう (西洋) *n.* the West: seeyoo-*ryoori* (西洋料理) *Western* cooking. ⟪↔ Tooyoo⟫

Se͈eyo͈ojiñ せいようじん (西洋人) *n.* Westerner; European. ⟪↔ Tooyoojiñ⟫

se͈eza せいざ (正座) *n.* sitting in a formal posture. ★ To sit upright on the floor with one's shins fold-

S

ed under the haunches and the knees facing out.

se⌉ezee せいぜい (精々) *adv.*
1 as...as possible:
Seezee *o-yasuku shite okimasu.* (せいぜいお安くしておきます) We will give you *as* big a discount *as possible.*
2 (of cost, time, quantity, etc.) at (the) best [most]:
Soko made iku no ni kakatte mo, seezee *ichi-jikañ desu.* (そこまで行くのにかかっても, せいぜい1時間です) You can get there in an hour *at the most.*

se⌈ezoñ せいぞん (生存) *n.* existence; survival:
seezoñ-*sha* (生存者) a survivor.
seezoñ suru (～する) *vi.* exist; survive; live.

se⌈ezoo せいぞう (製造) *n.* manufacture; production.
seezoo suru (～する) *vt.* manufacture; produce; make. 《⇨ seesaku[1]; tsukuru[1]》

se⌉kai せかい (世界) *n.* **1** the world:
sekai *isshuu suru* (世界一周する) go around *the world.*
2 circle; sphere; realm:
seeji no sekai (政治の世界) political *circles.*

se⌉kaseka せかせか *adv.* (～ to; ～ suru) (the state of being restless or busy):
Kare wa itsu-mo sekaseka *shite iru.* (彼はいつもせかせかしている) He is always *restless.*

se⌈ka⌉s·u せかす (急かす) *vt.* (sekash·i-; sekas·a-; sekash·i-te Ⓒ) hurry; rush; press:
Sonna ni sekasanai de *kudasai.* (そんなにせかさないでください) Please *don't rush* me like that. 《⇨ seku》

se⌉keñ せけん (世間) *n.* the world; the public; society:
sekeñ *no chuumoku o atsumeru* (世間の注目を集める) attract *public* attention.

se⌉ki[1] せき (席) *n.* seat; one's place: 《⇨ zaseki》
seki *ni tsuku* (席に着く) take one's *seat* / seki *o tatsu* [*hanareru*] (席を立つ[離れる]) stand up from [leave] one's *seat.*

se⌈ki⌉[2] せき (咳) *n.* cough; coughing: seki o suru (せきをする) *cough.*

-seki せき (隻) *suf.* counter for large ships: *guñkañ* is-seki (軍艦一隻) *a* warship.

se⌈kiba⌉rai せきばらい (咳払い) *n.* cough.
sekibarai (o) suru (～(を)する) *vi.* clear one's throat.

se⌈kidoo せきどう (赤道) *n.* equator.

se⌈kigaiseñ せきがいせん (赤外線) *n.* infrared rays. 《↔ shigaiseñ》

se⌈kiju⌉uji せきじゅうじ (赤十字) *n.* the Red Cross:
Nihoñ Sekijuujisha (日本赤十字社) the Japanese *Red Cross Society.*

se⌈kiniñ せきにん (責任) *n.* responsibility; duty; obligation; liability:
sekiniñ ga aru (責任がある) *be responsible.*

se⌈kita⌉ñ せきたん (石炭) *n.* coal:
sekitañ *o horu* (石炭を掘る) mine *coal.*

se⌈kitate·ru せきたてる (急き立てる) *vt.* (-tate-te Ⓥ) urge; hurry; hasten; press:
Hayaku repooto o kaku yoo ni kare o sekitateta. (早くレポートを書くように彼をせきたてた) I *urged* him to write his school report soon. 《⇨ sekasu》

se⌈kiyu せきゆ (石油) *n.* petroleum; kerosene: sekiyu-*sutoobu* (石油ストーブ) a *kerosene* heater.

se⌉kkaku せっかく (折角) *adv.*
1 in spite of one's efforts:
Sekkaku *kita no ni doobutsu-eñ wa yasumi datta.* (せっかく来たのに動物園は休みだった) Although we *took the trouble* to come, the zoo was closed.
2 (～ no) kind:
Sekkaku no *o-maneki desu ga so-*

no hi wa tsugoo ga tsukimaseñ. (せっかくのお招きですがその日は都合がつきません) Thank you very much for your *kind* invitation, but I cannot make it on that day.

3 (~ no) precious; rare:

Sekkaku *no kikai o nogashita.* (せっかくの機会を逃した) I let a *rare* opportunity slip by.

se⌈kkee せっけい (設計) *n.* plan; design.

sekkee suru (~する) *vt.* plan; design (a house, car, etc.).

se⌈kkeñ せっけん (石鹸) *n.* soap.

se⌈kkiñ せっきん (接近) *n.* approach; access.

sekkiñ suru (~する) *vi.* approach; come [go] near.

se⌉kkusu セックス *n.* sexual intercourse; sex. ★ Japanese '*sekkusu*' is used only in this meaning.

se⌈kkyoku-teki せっきょくてき (積極的) *a.n.* (~ na, ni) positive; active; aggressive. (↔ shookyoku-teki) (⇨ maemuki)

se⌉k·u せく (急く) *vi.* (sek·i-; sek·a-; se·i-te [C]) hurry; be impatient. (⇨ isogu)

se⌈kuhara セクハラ *n.* sexual harassment. (⇨ iyagarase)

se⌈ma⌉·i せまい (狭い) *a.* (-ku) small; narrow:

Dooro ga semakute, *uñteñ shinikui.* (道路が狭くて, 運転しにくい) The road is so *narrow* that it is difficult to drive along it. (↔ hiroi)

se⌈ma⌉r·u せまる (迫る) *vi.* (semar·i-; semar·a-; semat-te [C])

1 draw near; approach; be at hand:

Shuppatsu no hi ga sematte kita. (出発の日が迫ってきた) The day of departure *is drawing near*.

2 force; press; urge:

Daijiñ wa sono jikeñ no sekiniñ o toware, jiniñ o semarareta. (大臣はその事件の責任を問われ, 辞任を迫られた) The minister *was urged* to take responsibility for the affair and resign. (⇨ shiiru)

se⌈me⌉·ru[1] せめる (攻める) *vt.* (seme-te [V]) attack; invade. (↔ mamoru) (⇨ osou)

se⌈me⌉·ru[2] せめる (責める) *vt.* (seme-te [V]) blame; accuse; criticize:

Señsee wa kare no fuchuui o semeta. (先生は彼の不注意を責めた) The teacher *criticized* him for his carelessness.

se⌉mete せめて *adv.* at least; just; only:

Semete *neñ ni ni-kai wa keñshiñ o uketa hoo ga yoi.* (せめて年に2回は検診を受けたほうがよい) You should undergo a medical examination twice a year *at least*.

se⌈mi せみ (蝉) *n.* cicada.

se⌉ñ[1] せん (線) *n.* line:

señ *o hiku* (線を引く) draw a *line*.

se⌉ñ[2] せん (千) *n.* one thousand. (⇨ APP. 3)

se⌉ñ[3] せん (栓) *n.* stopper; cork:

gasu [suidoo] no señ *o hiraku* [*shimeru*] (ガス[水道]の栓を開く[締める]) turn on [off] the *gas* [*water*].

se⌉ñ[4] せん (選) *n.* selection:

señ ni hairu [moreru] (選に入る[漏れる]) *be* [*not*] *selected*.

-señ せん (線) *suf.* transport system; line:

Chuuoo-señ *no deñsha* (中央線の電車) trains on the Chuo *Line*. (⇨ -bañseñ)

se⌈naka せなか (背中) *n.* one's back.

se⌈ñbazu⌉ru せんばづる (千羽鶴) *n.* a thousand folded paper cranes on a string. ★ Often used in praying for recovery from illness. (⇨ tsuru[3])

se⌉ñbee せんべい (煎餅) *n.* Japanese rice cracker.

se⌈ñcha せんちゃ (煎茶) *n.* green tea of middle grade. (⇨ o-cha)

se⌉ñchi センチ *n.* centimeter. ★ Shortened form of '*senchi-meetoru*.'

se⌈ñchi-me⌉etoru センチメートル

S

(糎) *n.* centimeter. ★ The shortened form '*señchi*' is more common. ⟪⇨ señchi⟫

se|ñchoo せんちょう(船長) *n.* captain (of a ship).

se|ñdeñ せんでん(宣伝) *n.* advertisement; publicity; propaganda.
señdeñ (o) suru (~(を)する) *vt.* advertise; propagandize. ⟪⇨ kookoku⟫

se|ñge|ñ せんげん(宣言) *n.* declaration; proclamation; announcement.
señgeñ (o) suru (~(を)する) *vt.* declare; proclaim; announce: *chuuritsu o* señgeñ suru (中立を宣言する) *declare* one's neutrality.

se|ñgetsu せんげつ(先月) *n.* last month. ⟪⇨ koñgetsu; raigetsu⟫

se|ñgo せんご(戦後) *n.* the postwar period; after the war. ⟪↔ señzeñ⟫

se|ñi せんい(繊維) *n.* fiber: *goosee*[*kagaku*]-señi (合成[化学]繊維) synthetic [chemical] *fiber*.

se|ñjitsu せんじつ(先日) *n.* the other day; a few days ago; some time ago:
Señjitsu *wa doomo.* (先日はどうも) Thank you very much for *the other day*.

se|ñkoo せんこう(専攻) *n.* academic specialty; special field; major.
señkoo suru (~する) *vt.* major in; specialize in.

se|ñkyo せんきょ(選挙) *n.* election:
señkyo-*keñ* (選挙権) the right *to vote* / señkyo-*uñdoo* (選挙運動) an *election* campaign.
señkyo suru (~する) *vt.* elect; vote for. ⟪⇨ toohyoo⟫

se|ñmeñ せんめん(洗面) *n.* washing one's face:
señmeñ-*doogu* (洗面道具) one's *washing* things.

se|ñmeñjo せんめんじょ(洗面所) *n.*
1 washroom; lavatory.
★ In an ordinary Japanese house, the bathtub and the toilet are installed in separate rooms.
2 washstand.

se|ñme|ñki せんめんき(洗面器) *n.* washbowl; washbasin.

se|ñmoñ せんもん(専門) *n.* specialty; special subject.

se|ñmoñka せんもんか(専門家) *n.* specialist; expert; professional.

se|ñmu (to|rishimari|yaku) せんむ(とりしまりやく)(専務(取締役)) *n.* senior [executive] managing director; senior vice president.

se|ñnuki| せんぬき(栓抜き) *n.* corkscrew; bottle opener.

se|nobi せのび(背伸び) *n.* standing on tiptoe.
senobi (o) suru (~(を)する) *vi.*
1 stand on tiptoe; stretch oneself.
2 (*fig.*) aim too high.

se|ñpai せんぱい(先輩) *n.* one's senior; elder:
Kare wa watashi no sañ-neñ señpai *desu.* (彼は私の3年先輩です) He is my *senior* by three years. ⟪↔ koohai⟫

se|ñpu|uki せんぷうき(扇風機) *n.* electric fan.

se|ñro せんろ(線路) *n.* railroad [railway] track; line.

se|ñryoo[1] せんりょう(占領) *n.* occupation; possession; capture.
señryoo suru (~する) *vt.* occupy; have all to oneself.

se|ñryo|o[2] せんりょう(染料) *n.* dye; dyestuffs.

se|ñse|e せんせい(先生) *n.* teacher; professor; doctor.

se|ñshi せんし(戦死) *n.* death in battle.
señshi suru (~する) *vi.* be killed in war.

se|ñshu せんしゅ(選手) *n.* player; athlete: *yakyuu no* señshu (野球の選手) a baseball *player*.

se|ñshuu せんしゅう(先週) *n.* last week. ⟪↔ koñshuu⟫

se|ñshu|uraku せんしゅうらく(千秋楽) *n.* the last day of a Grand

Sumo Tournament; the last day of a public performance.

se⌈ñsoo せんそう(戦争) *n.* war; battle; fight. ⟪↔ heewa⟫
señsoo (o) suru (〜(を)する) *vi.* make war; go to war.

se⌈ñsu せんす(扇子) *n.* folding fan. ⟪⇨ uchiwa[2]⟫

se⌈ñtaku[1] せんたく(洗濯) *n.* wash; washing; laundry.
señtaku suru (〜する) *vt.* wash; do the laundry. ⟪⇨ hoshimono; señtakumono⟫

se⌈ñtaku[2] せんたく(選択) *n.* choice; selection; option: señtaku *o ayamaru* (選択を誤る) make the wrong *choice.*
señtaku suru (〜する) *vt.* choose; select. ⟪⇨ erabu⟫

se⌈ñtaku⌉ki せんたくき(洗濯機) *n.* washing machine; washer.

se⌈ñtakumono せんたくもの(洗濯物) *n.* laundry; washing: señtakumono *o hosu* (洗濯物を干す) hang the *washing* out to dry. ⟪⇨ señtaku[1]⟫

se⌈ñteñ-teki せんてんてき(先天的) *a.n.* (〜 na, ni) native; innate; inborn: señteñ-teki *na sainoo* (先天的な才能) *innate* talent. ⟪↔ kooteñ-teki⟫

se⌈ñtoo[1] せんとう(先頭) *n.* the head; the lead: *ikkoo no* señtoo *ni tatte aruku* (一行の先頭に立って歩く) walk at the *head* of the group.

se⌈ñtoo[2] せんとう(戦闘) *n.* battle; combat; fight; action.

se⌉ñtoo[3] せんとう(銭湯) *n.* public bath. ⟪⇨ furo; furoya⟫

se⌈ñzai せんざい(洗剤) *n.* detergent: *chuusee*-señzai (中性洗剤) a neutral *detergent.*

se⌈ñzeñ せんぜん(戦前) *n.* the prewar period; before the war. ⟪↔ señgo⟫

se⌉ñzo せんぞ(先祖) *n.* ancestor; forefathers. ⟪↔ shisoñ⟫

se⌈o⌉·u せおう(背負う) *vt.* (seo·i-; seow·a-; seot-te Ⓒ) **1** carry (a load) on one's back.
2 shoulder (responsibility). ⟪⇨ ou[2]⟫

se⌈rifu せりふ(台詞) *n.* words; one's lines: serifu *o wasureru* (せりふを忘れる) forget one's *lines.*

se⌉roñ せろん(世論) *n.* public opinion. ⟪⇨ yoroñ⟫

-se·ru せる *infl. end.* (-se-te Ⓥ) [attached to the negative base of a consonant-stem verb and itself inflected like a vowel-stem verb]
1 make someone do; cause someone to do: *Kare ni sugu heñji o* kakasemasu. (彼にすぐ返事を書かせます) I'll *make* him *write* his answer immediately. ⟪⇨ -saseru⟫
2 let someone do; allow someone to do: *Watashi ni mo kono hoñ o* yomasete *kudasai.* (私にもこの本を読ませてください) Please *allow me* as well *to read* this book.

se⌉sse to せっせと *adv.* hard; busily: *Kanojo wa itsu-mo* sesse to *hataraite iru.* (彼女はいつもせっせと働いている) She always works *diligently.*

se⌉sshi せっし(摂氏) *n.* Celsius; centigrade. ★ The Fahrenheit scale is not used in Japan.

se⌈sshoku せっしょく(接触) *n.*
1 contact; touch; connection: *Kono puragu wa* sesshoku *ga warui.* (このプラグは接触が悪い) This plug gives a bad *connection.*
2 contact with a person.
sesshoku suru (〜する) *vi.*
1 contact; touch: *Kare no jiteñsha ga kuruma to* sesshoku shite, *kare wa taoreta.* (彼の自転車が車と接触して, 彼は倒れた) His bicycle *bumped* into a car and he fell over.
2 get in touch. ⟪⇨ sessuru⟫

se⌈ssui せっすい(節水) *n.* water saving.
sessui suru (〜する) *vi.* save water; use water sparingly.

S

se⌈ss·uru せっする(接する) *vi.* (sessh·i-; sessh·i-; sessh·i-te [1]) **1** touch:
Deñseñ ga noki ni sesshite *iru.* (電線が軒に接している) The electric wire *touches* the eaves.
2 come into contact with (a person); see.
3 attend to (a guest, customer, etc.); deal with.
4 border; abut:
Nihoñ wa dono gaikoku to mo sesshite *imaseñ.* (日本はどの外国とも接していません) Japan does not *border* any foreign countries.

se⌉tchi せっち(設置) *n.* formation; establishment; installation.
setchi suru (〜する) *vt.* form; establish; install.

se⌈tomono せともの(瀬戸物) *n.* china; porcelain; earthenware.

se⌉tsu[1] せつ(説) *n.* **1** theory:
atarashii setsu *o tateru* (新しい説を立てる) put forward a new *theory.*
2 opinion; view:
Kare wa jibuñ no setsu *o magenakatta.* (彼は自分の説を曲げなかった) He didn't change his own *views.*

se⌉tsu[2] せつ(節) *n.* **1** occasion; time; when:
Kochira e o-ide no setsu *wa zehi o-tachiyori kudasai.* (こちらへお出での節はぜひお立ち寄りください) By all means, please drop in *when* you happen to be in the neighborhood. ⟪⇨ toki⟫
2 (of grammar) clause.
3 section; paragraph; phrase.

se⌉tsubi せつび(設備) *n.* equipment; facilities; accommodations.
setsubi suru (〜する) *vt.* equip; accommodate. ⟪⇨ setchi⟫

se⌈tsubuñ せつぶん(節分) *n.* the day before the start of spring.
★ Usually falls on February 2 or 3. On the evening of this day, Japanese conduct the 'Bean-Throwing' ceremony and scatter roasted soybeans to drive away evil spirits.

se⌈tsudañ せつだん(切断) *n.* cutting; severance; amputation.
setsudañ suru (〜する) *vt.* cut off; sever; amputate. ⟪⇨ kiru[1]⟫

se⌈tsudeñ せつでん(節電) *n.* power saving.
setsudeñ suru (〜する) *vi.* save electricity.

se⌈tsujoku せつじょく(雪辱) *n.* vindication of one's honor; revenge.

se⌈tsumee せつめい(説明) *n.* explanation; illustration:
setsumee-*sho* (説明書) an *explanatory* leaflet; written *instructions.*
setsumee (o) suru (〜(を)する) *vt.* explain; illustrate; demonstrate.

se⌈tsuritsu せつりつ(設立) *n.* establishment; foundation.
setsuritsu suru (〜する) *vt.* set up; establish; found.

se⌈tsuyaku せつやく(節約) *n.* economy; saving; thrift.
setsuyaku suru (〜する) *vt.* economize; save; cut down. ⟪↔ roohi⟫ ⟪⇨ keñyaku⟫

se⌈tsuzoku せつぞく(接続) *n.* connection; joining; link.
setsuzoku suru (〜する) *vi., vt.* join; connect.

se⌈tsuzoku⌉shi せつぞくし(接続詞) *n.* (of grammar) conjunction.

se⌈wa⌉ せわ(世話) *n.* **1** care:
Oosaka ni itta toki, obasañ no sewa *ni narimashita.* (大阪に行ったときおばさんの世話になりました) When I went to Osaka, I *was looked after* by my aunt.
2 trouble:
hito ni sewa *o kakeru* (人に世話をかける) cause *trouble* to others.
3 help; kindness:
*Anata no o-toosañ ni wa taiheñ o-*sewa *ni natte imasu.* (あなたのお父さんには大変お世話になっています) I do appreciate the *help* I always receive from your father.
4 recommendation; introduction.

S

sewa (o) suru (～(を)する) *vt.*
1 take care of; look after; attend.
2 recommend; introduce: *Ueki-ya-sañ ga ii daiku-sañ o* sewa shite *kureta.* (植木屋さんがいい大工さんを世話してくれた) Our gardener was kind enough to *recommend* a good carpenter.

-sha しゃ (車) *suf.* car; vehicle: *jidoo*-sha (自動車) a motor *vehicle* / *res*-sha (列車) a long-distance *train.*

sha⌈be⌉r·u しゃべる (喋る) *vi.* (shaber·i-; shaber·a-; shabet-te Ⓒ) chat; chatter; talk. (⇨ hanasu[1]; kataru)

sha⌈bushabu しゃぶしゃぶ *n.* thin slices of beef and vegetables cooked portion by portion in boiling water on the table.

sha⌈choo しゃちょう (社長) *n.* president of a company; managing director.

sha⌈dañ しゃだん (遮断) *n.* cutting off; interruption: shadañ-ki (遮断機) a railroad *crossing gate.*
shadañ suru (～する) *vt.* cut off; interrupt; hold up. (⇨ tomeru[1])

sha⌈doo しゃどう (車道) *n.* roadway; carriageway. (↔ hodoo)

sha⌉gai しゃがい (車外) *n.* outside a vehicle [train]:
shagai no *fuukee* (車外の風景) the view *from a train.* (↔ shanai)

sha⌈gam·u しゃがむ *vi.* (shagam·i-; shagam·a-; shagañ-de Ⓒ) crouch; squat.

sha⌉iñ しゃいん (社員) *n.* company employee. (⇨ juugyooiñ; shokuiñ)

sha⌉kai しゃかい (社会) *n.* society; the world:
shakai *ni deru* (社会に出る) go out into the *world* / shakai-*hoshoo* (社会保障) *social* welfare guarantee / shakai-*kyooiku* (社会教育) *adult* education / shakai-shugi (社会主義) *socialism.*

sha⌈kki⌉ñ しゃっきん (借金) *n.* debt; loan:
Watashi wa yaku hyakumañ-eñ shakkiñ *ga aru.* (私は約 100 万円借金がある) I am in *debt* for about a million yen.
shakkiñ (o) suru (～(を)する) *vi.* borrow money.

sha⌉kkuri しゃっくり *n.* hiccup: shakkuri *ga deru* (しゃっくりが出る) have the *hiccups.*

sha⌉ko しゃこ (車庫) *n.* garage; carbarn. (⇨ gareeji)

sha⌉meñ しゃめん (斜面) *n.* slope; slant:
yama no shameñ *o noboru* (山の斜面を登る) go up the *slope* of a mountain.

sha⌉nai しゃない (車内) *n.* inside a vehicle [train]:
Shanai *wa kiñeñ desu.* (車内は禁煙です) Smoking is prohibited *in the train* [*bus*]. (↔ shagai)

sha⌈re しゃれ *n.* joke; witty remark; pun: share *o iu* [*tobasu*] (しゃれを言う[とばす]) crack a *joke.*

sha⌈riñ しゃりん (車輪) *n.* wheel: *jiteñsha no* shariñ (自転車の車輪) the *wheels* of a bicycle.

sha⌈ryoo しゃりょう (車両) *n.* vehicle; railway car.

sha⌈see しゃせい (写生) *n.* sketch; sketching.
shasee suru (～する) *vt.* make a sketch.

sha⌈setsu しゃせつ (社説) *n.* editorial; leading article.

sha⌈shiñ しゃしん (写真) *n.* photograph; picture: shashiñ *o toru* (写真を撮る) take a *photograph.*

sha⌈shi⌉ñki しゃしんき (写真機) *n.* camera.

sha⌈shoo しゃしょう (車掌) *n.* train [bus] conductor; guard.

sha⌉tai しゃたい (車体) *n.* body of a car; frame.

sha⌉tsu シャツ *n.* shirt; undershirt; underwear. ★ The type of shirt with which one wears a necktie is called '*waishatsu.*'

shi[1] し *p.* **1** and (also): ★ Used for emphatic listing.
Ano mise wa ryoori ga oishii shi,

S

fuñiki mo ii. (あの店は料理がおいしいし, 雰囲気もいい) The food in that restaurant is good, *and also* there is a pleasant atmosphere. ⟪⇨ to²; to ka⟫

2 (used at the end of an incomplete sentence in order to leave the rest to the imagination of the listener):
Asobi ni ikitai shi, *o-kane wa nai* shi ... (遊びに行きたいし, お金はないし…) I want to go off and enjoy myself, but I have no money, *and...*

shiˡ² し (市) *n.* city.

shi³ し (詩) *n.* poem; poetry; verse.

shiˡ⁴ し (四) *n.* four. ★ '四' is usually pronounced '*yoñ*,' as the pronunciation '*shi*' suggests 'death.' ⟪⇨ APP. 3⟫

shiˡ⁵ し (氏) *n.* **1** Mr:
Suzuki-shi *ga gichoo ni erabareta.* (鈴木氏が議長に選ばれた) *Mr.* Suzuki was elected chairman.
2 family:
Tokugawa-shi (徳川氏) the Tokugawa *family.*

shiˡ⁶ し (氏) *n.* he; him:
Shi *no keñkoo o shukushite, kañpai shiyoo.* (氏の健康を祝して, 乾杯しよう) Let's toast *his* health.

shiˡ⁷ し (死) *n.* death.

shiʳage しあげ (仕上げ) *n.* finish:
Kono teeburu wa shiage *ga suteki da.* (このテーブルは仕上げがすてきだ) This table has a nice *finish.* ⟪⇨ shiageru⟫

shiʳageˡ·ru しあげる (仕上げる) *vt.* (shiage-te [V]) finish; complete. ⟪⇨ shiage⟫

shiʳai しあい (試合) *n.* match; game; bout; competition.
shiai (o) suru (~(を)する) *vi.* play a game; have a match; compete.

shiʳasaˡtte しあさって *n.* three days from today. ⟪⇨ asatte⟫

shiʳawase しあわせ (幸せ) *n.* happiness; blessing; fortune. ⟪⇨ saiwai⟫
— *a.n.* (~ na, ni) happy; fortunate; lucky. ⟪↔ fukoo; fushiawase⟫ ⟪⇨ koofuku⟫

shiʳba しば (芝) *n.* turf; grass.

shiʳbafu しばふ (芝生) *n.* lawn; grass.

shiʳbai しばい (芝居) *n.* **1** play; drama; performance:
shibai *o mi ni iku* (芝居を見に行く) go to see a *play.*
2 put-on; acting: ⟪⇨ kyoogeñ⟫
Ani ga okotta no wa shibai *desu.* (兄が怒ったのは芝居です) My brother's anger is just a *put-on.*

shiʳbaˡraku しばらく (暫く) *adv.*
1 for a while [minute]:
Shibaraku, *o-machi kudasai.* (しばらく, お待ちください) Please wait *a little while.*
2 for the time being:
Shibaraku *kono hoteru ni taizai shimasu.* (しばらくこのホテルに滞在します) I will be staying in this hotel *for the time being.*
Shibaraku (buri) desu ne. (~(ぶり)ですね) I haven't seen you for a long time.

shiʳbaˡr·u しばる (縛る) *vt.* (shibar·i-; shibar·a-; shibat-te [C])
1 tie; bind:
Kanojo wa kizuguchi o hootai de shibatta. (彼女は傷口を包帯でしばった) She *bound up* the wound with a bandage.
2 (of time) restrict; bind:
jikañ ni shibarareru (時間に縛られる) *be restricted* by time.

shiˡbashiba しばしば (屢々) *adv.* many times; often; frequently. ⟪⇨ tabitabi⟫

shiʳbasu しバス (市バス) *n.* city bus. ★ This is a bus operated by a city. ⟪⇨ shideñ⟫

shiʳbireˡ·ru しびれる (痺れる) *vi.* (shibire-te [V]) be numbed; be paralyzed:
Ashi ga shibirete *tatenai.* (足がしびれて立てない) I cannot stand up because my feet *are asleep.*

shiʳboo¹ しぼう (志望) *n.* wish; desire; plan:

S

shiboo-sha (志望者) an *applicant*.
shiboo suru (～する) *vt.* want; desire; plan. ⟪⇨ nozomu[1]⟫

shi⌈boo[2] しぼう (死亡) *n.* death: shiboo-*jiko* (死亡事故) a *fatal* accident.
shiboo suru (～する) *vi.* die; be killed. ⟪⇨ shinu⟫

shi⌈boo[3] しぼう (脂肪) *n.* fat; grease:
Kono niku wa shiboo ga ooi. (この肉は脂肪が多い) This meat is *fatty*. ⟪⇨ abura[2]⟫

shi⌈bo⌉r·u しぼる (絞る) *vt.* (shibor·i-; shibor·a-; shibot-te Ⓒ)
1 squeeze; press: *remoñ o* shiboru (レモンを絞る) *squeeze* a lemon.
2 wring:
Nureta taoru o shibotte, *hoshita.* (濡れたタオルを絞って, 干した) I *wrung* the wet towel and put it out to dry.

sh⌈ibu⌉·i しぶい (渋い) *a.* (-ku)
1 (of taste) bitter; sharp and astringent.
2 (of color) sober; quiet; refined:
Kare wa itsu-mo shibui *fukusoo o shite iru.* (彼はいつも渋い服装をしている) He is always dressed in *quiet good taste.*
3 (of countenance) sullen: shibui *kao o suru* (渋い顔をする) make a *sour* face.
4 tight-fisted:
Ano hito wa kane ni shibui. (あの人は金に渋い) He is *stingy*.

shi⌈bu⌉r·u しぶる (渋る) *vi.* (shibur·i-; shibur·a-; shibut-te Ⓒ) hesitate; be reluctant:
Kare wa kanojo ni au no o shibutta. (彼は彼女に会うのを渋った) He *was reluctant* to meet her.

shi⌈chi⌉ しち (七) *n.* seven. ⟪⇨ nana; nanatsu; APP. 3⟫

shi⌈chi-gatsu⌉ しちがつ (七月) *n.* July. ⟪⇨ APP. 5⟫

shi⌈cho⌉o[1] しちょう (市長) *n.* mayor.

shi⌈cho⌉o[2] しちょう (支庁) *n.* the regional branch of a government agency.

shi⌈cho⌉o[3] しちょう (市庁) *n.* = shiyakusho.

shi⌈dai しだい (次第) *n.* **1** the instant; the moment: ★ Follows the continuative base of a verb.
Kekka ga wakari shidai *o-shirase shimasu.* (結果がわかり次第お知らせします) We will inform you *as soon as* we know the results.
2 being dependent:
Seekoo suru ka shinai ka wa anata no doryoku shidai *desu.* (成功するかしないかはあなたの努力次第です) Whether you succeed or not *depends* on your own efforts. ⟪⇨ yoru[3]⟫
3 circumstances:
Koo-iu shidai *de asu no kaigi ni wa shusseki dekimaseñ.* (こういう次第であすの会議には出席できません) Under these *circumstances*, I cannot attend tomorrow's meeting. ⟪⇨ wake⟫
4 order; program:
shiki-shidai (式次第) the *program* of a ceremony.

shi⌈dai ni しだいに (次第に) *adv.* gradually; by degrees; little by little.

shi⌈dareya⌉nagi しだれやなぎ (垂れ柳) *n.* weeping willow.

shi⌈deñ しでん (市電) *n.* streetcar; tram. ★ This is a streetcar operated by a city. ⟪⇨ shibasu⟫

shi⌈doo[1] しどう (指導) *n.* guidance; direction; leadership; instruction: shidoo-sha (指導者) a *leader*; a *guide*.
shidoo suru (～する) *vt.* guide; direct; coach; instruct; teach. ⟪⇨ oshieru⟫

shi⌈doo[2] しどう (私道) *n.* private road [path].

shi⌉gai[1] しがい (市街) *n.* the streets; city; town. ⟪⇨ machi⟫

shi⌉gai[2] しがい (市外) *n.* suburbs; outskirts:
shigai-*deñwa* (市外電話) an *out-*

of-town telephone call. ⟪↔ shinai⟫ ⟪⇨ koogai[1]⟫

shi⌈gaiseñ しがいせん (紫外線) *n.* ultraviolet rays. ⟪↔ sekigaiseñ⟫

shi⌈gamitsu⌉k·u しがみつく *vi.* (-tsuk·i-; -tsuk·a-; -tsu·i-te Ⓒ) cling to; hang [hold] on to.

shi-⌈gatsu⌉ しがつ (四月) *n.* April. ⟪⇨ APP. 5⟫

shi⌈geki しげき (刺激) *n.* stimulation; stimulus; incentive.
shigeki suru (～する) *vt.* stimulate; excite; provoke.

shi⌉geñ しげん (資源) *n.* resources: *teñneñ*-shigeñ *o kaihatsu suru* (天然資源を開発する) develop natural *resources.*

shi⌈ge⌉r·u しげる (茂る) *vi.* (shiger·i-; shiger·a-; shiget-te Ⓒ) (of plants) grow thickly; (of weeds) be overgrown.

shi⌈goto しごと (仕事) *n.*
1 work; job; business.
2 position; work; job; employment:
Kare wa ima shigoto *o sagashite iru tokoro desu.* (彼は今仕事を探しているところです) He is now seeking *employment.*

shi⌉hai しはい (支配) *n.* rule; government; control:
shihai-sha (支配者) a *ruler.*
shihai suru (～する) *vt.* rule; govern; control; dominate.

shi⌈ha⌉iniñ しはいにん (支配人) *n.* manager (of a store, restaurant, etc.).

shi⌈harai しはらい (支払い) *n.* payment:
Shiharai *wa getsumatsu ni narimasu.* (支払いは月末になります) *Payment* will be made at the end of the month. ⟪⇨ shiharau⟫

shi⌈hara⌉·u しはらう (支払う) *vt.* (-hara·i-; -haraw·a-; -harat-te Ⓒ) pay; defray:
Koñgetsu wa gasu-dai ni ichimañ-eñ shiharatta. (今月はガス代に1万円支払った) This month I *paid* 10,000 yen for gas. ⟪⇨ harau⟫

shi⌈hatsu しはつ (始発) *n.* **1** the first train; the first run. ⟪↔ shuudeñ(sha); shuusha⟫
2 starting:
Sono ressha wa Shiñjuku shihatsu *desu.* (その列車は新宿始発です) That train *starts* from Shinjuku.

shi⌉hee しへい (紙幣) *n.* paper money. ⟪⇨ satsu; kooka[3]⟫

shi⌈hoñ しほん (資本) *n.* capital; fund:
shihoñ-ka (資本家) a *capitalist* / shihoñ-shugi (資本主義) *capitalism.*

shi⌈ho⌉o[1] しほう (四方) *n.* all sides; all around:
Sono mura wa shihoo *o yama ni kakomarete iru.* (その村は四方を山に囲まれている) The village is surrounded *on all sides* by mountains.

shi⌉hoo[2] しほう (司法) *n.* jurisdiction:
shihoo-*keñ* (司法権) *judicial* power / shihoo-*shikeñ* (司法試験) a *bar* examination. ⟪⇨ sañkeñ-buñritsu⟫

shi⌈iñ しいん (子音) *n.* consonant. ⟪⇨ boiñ; APP. 1⟫

shi⌈ire しいれ (仕入れ) *n.* stocking; buying in:
shiire *kakaku* (仕入れ価格) the *buying* price ⟪⇨ shiireru⟫

shi⌈ire⌉·ru しいれる (仕入れる) *vt.* (shiire-te Ⓥ) **1** stock (goods); lay in stock. ⟪⇨ shiire⟫
2 get (information).

shi⌈i⌉·ru しいる (強いる) *vt.* (shii-te Ⓥ) force; compel; press:
Kare wa jishoku o shiirareta. (彼は辞職を強いられた) He *was forced* to resign.

shi⌉itsu シーツ *n.* bed sheet.

shi⌈izuñ-o⌉fu シーズンオフ *n.* off-season.

shi⌉ji[1] しじ (指示) *n.* directions; instructions.
shiji suru (～する) *vt.* direct; instruct; indicate.

shi⌉ji[2] しじ (支持) *n.* support; backing.

shiji suru (～する) *vt.* support; back up. ⟪⇨ kooeñ[4]⟫

shi⌈jiñ しじん (詩人) *n.* poet.

shi⌈joo しじょう (市場) *n.* market: shijoo-*choosa* (市場調査) a *market* survey.

shi⌉juu しじゅう (始終) *adv.* always; all the time; very often. ⟪⇨ itsu-mo⟫

shi⌈ka[1] しか (鹿) *n.* deer; stag; hind.

shi⌉ka[2] しか (歯科) *n.* dentistry: shika-i (歯科医) a *dentist.* ⟪⇨ haisha[1]⟫

shika[3] しか *p.* **1** only; except for: ★ Used after a noun or counter in negative sentences.
Kanojo wa kodomo ga hitori shika *inakatta.* (彼女は子どもが一人しかいなかった) She had *only* one child. ⟪⇨ dake; nomi[2]; bakari⟫
2 no other way: ★ Used after a verb in the dictionary form.
Koo nattara moo yaru shika *arimaseñ.* (こうなったらもうやるしかありません) If such is the case, there is *nothing* for us *but* to go ahead and do it.

shi⌈kaeshi しかえし (仕返し) *n.* revenge; retaliation.

shi⌈kai しかい (司会) *n.* master of ceremonies; chairperson.

shi⌈kake しかけ (仕掛け) *n.* device; mechanism; gadget.

shi⌈kake⌉·ru しかける (仕掛ける) *n.* (-kake-te Ⓥ) **1** start (a quarrel):
Kare wa watashi ni keñka o shikakete kita. (彼は私にけんかをしかけてきた) He *picked* a quarrel with me.
2 set (a trap); plant (a bomb).

shi⌈kaku[1] しかく (資格) *n.* **1** qualification; capacity:
shikaku no aru *kyooshi* (資格のある教師) a *qualified* teacher.
2 license; certificate:
isha no shikaku *o toru* (医者の資格を取る) get a doctor's *license.*

shi⌈kaku[⌉2] しかく (四角) *a.n.* (～ na, ni) square. ⟪⇨ shikakui⟫

shi⌈kaku[3] しかく (死角) *n.* dead angle; blind spot.

shi⌈kaku⌉·i しかくい (四角い) *a.* (-ku) square:
shikakui *teeburu* (四角いテーブル) a *square* table ⟪⇨ shikaku[2]; marui⟫

shi⌈ka⌉kukee しかくけい (四角形) *n.* quadrangle; tetragon.

shi⌈kame·ru しかめる *vt.* (shikame-te Ⓥ) frown; grimace:
Kanojo wa sono shirase o kiite, kao o shikameta. (彼女はその知らせを聞いて, 顔をしかめた) She *frowned* on hearing the news.

shi⌈ka⌉mo しかも (然も) *conj.*
1 moreover; besides:
Kanojo wa shigoto ga hayai. Shikamo *shiñchoo da.* (彼女は仕事が速い. しかも慎重だ) She does her work very quickly; *moreover*, she is careful.
2 yet; still; nevertheless:
Kare wa kikeñ ni chokumeñ shi, shikamo *heezeñ to shite ita.* (彼は危険に直面し, しかも平然としていた) He faced dangers, *and yet* he still remained calm.

shi⌈kar·u しかる (叱る) *vt.* (shikar·i-; shikar·a-; shikat-te Ⓒ) scold; reprove. ⟪⇨ okoru[2]⟫

shi⌈ka⌉shi しかし (然し) *conj.* but; however. ⟪⇨ da ga; keredo (mo); tokoro ga⟫

shi⌈kashi-na⌉gara しかしながら (然し乍ら) *conj.* however; but. ★ More formal than '*shikashi.*'

shi⌈kata しかた (仕方) *n.* way; method:
tadashii beñkyoo no shikata (正しい勉強のしかた) the right *way* of studying.

shi⌈katana⌉·i しかたない (仕方ない) *a.* (-ku) ★ Polite forms are '*shikatanai desu*' and '*shikata arimaseñ.*' '*Shikata ga nai*' is also used in the same meaning.
1 (*pred.*) cannot help doing; be no use doing:
Suñda koto wa shikatanai. (済んだことは仕方ない) What is done, *is done.* ⟪⇨ shiyoo ga nai⟫

S

2 (-ku) unwillingly; against one's will:
Watashi wa shikatanaku *sañsee shita.* (私は仕方なく賛成した) I approved it *reluctantly.*
-te shikatanai (て～) be dying to do: Ikitakute shikatanai. (行きたくて仕方ない) I'm *dying to go* there.

shi⌈ke⌉e しけい (死刑) *n.* death penalty.

shi⌈ke⌉ñ しけん (試験) *n.* examination; test: shikeñ *o ukeru* (試験を受ける) take an *examination.*
shikeñ (o) suru (～(を)する) *vt.* test; experiment. ⟪⇨ tesuto⟫

shi⌈keñkañ しけんかん (試験管) *n.* test tube. ⟪⇨ kañ[2]⟫

shi⌈ki⌉[1] しき (四季) *n.* the four seasons.

shi⌈ki⌉[2] しき (指揮) *n.* **1** command; direction: shiki *o toru* (指揮をとる) assume *command.*
2 conducting (an orchestra).
shiki suru (～する) *vt.* command (a ship); direct (a business); conduct (an orchestra).

shi⌈ki⌉[3] しき (式) *n.* **1** ceremony: shiki *o okonau* (式を行う) hold a *ceremony.* ⟪⇨ -shiki⟫
2 expression; formula: shiki de arawasu (式で表す) express something in a *formula.*

-shiki しき (式) *suf.* **1** ceremony: *sotsugyoo*-shiki (卒業式) a graduation *ceremony* / *kekkoñ*-shiki (結婚式) a wedding *ceremony.*
2 way; style; fashion:
Nihoñ-shiki *no toire* (日本式のトイレ) a Japanese-*style* toilet.

shi⌈kibu⌉toñ しきぶとん (敷き布団) *n.* mattress; sleeping pad.

shi⌈kichi しきち (敷地) *n.* site; lot; ground.

shi⌈ki⌉kiñ しききん (敷金) *n.* deposit. ★ Money paid to a landlord as a pledge for the rental contract. It is returnable.
⟪⇨ keñrikiñ; reekiñ; yachiñ⟫

shi⌈ki⌉ñ しきん (資金) *n.* fund; capital: shikiñ *o tsukuru* (資金をつくる) raise *funds.* ⟪⇨ motode⟫

shi⌈kiri しきり (仕切り) *n.* **1** partition; compartment:
heya no shikiri *o toru* (部屋の仕切りを取る) remove the *partitions* of a room. ⟪⇨ shikiru⟫
2 (of sumo wrestling) the warm-up process before a bout:
shikiri-*naoshi o suru* (仕切り直しをする) *toe the mark* again.

shi⌈kiri ni しきりに (頻りに) *adv.* very often; continually; eagerly.

shi⌈ki⌉r·u しきる (仕切る) *vt.* (shikir·i-; shikir·a-; shikit-te Ⓒ) divide; partition:
kaateñ de heya o futatsu ni shikiru (カーテンで部屋を2つに仕切る) *divide* the room into two with curtains.
⟪⇨ shikiri⟫

shi⌈kisai しきさい (色彩) *n.* color; coloration; coloring.

shi⌈kka⌉ri しっかり *adv.* (～ to; ～ suru) **1** firmly; tightly:
Kono tsuna ni shikkari *(to) tsukamari nasai.* (この綱にしっかり(と)つかまりなさい) Please take hold of this rope *firmly.*
2 hard; steadily; bravely:
Shikkari *(to) beñkyoo shi nasai.* (しっかり(と)勉強しなさい) Study *hard.* / Shikkari shi nasai. (しっかりしなさい) *Pull yourself together.*
shikkari shite iru [shita] (～している[した]) firm; reliable:
Kono tatemono wa kiso ga shikkari shite iru. (この建物は基礎がしっかりしている) The foundations of this building *are firm.*

shi⌈kke しっけ (湿気) *n.* moisture; humidity; damp.

shi⌈kki[1] しっき (漆器) *n.* lacquerware. ⟪⇨ urushi⟫

shi⌈kki[2] しっき (湿気) *n.* = shikke.

shi⌈k·u しく (敷く) *vt.* (shik·i-; shik·a-; shi·i-te Ⓒ) lay; spread; cover; stretch:
Doozo zabutoñ o shiite *kudasai.* (どうぞ座布団を敷いてください) Please *take* a cushion and sit down.

shi⌈kuji⌉r·u しくじる *vt.* (-jir·i-;

-jir·a-; -jit-te Ⓒ) fail; blunder; make a mistake. 《⇨ shippai》

shi⸢kumi しくみ (仕組み) *n.* structure; mechanism; setup:
koñpyuutaa no shikumi (コンピューターのしくみ) the *working* of a computer.

shi⸢ku⸣shiku しくしく *adv.*
shikushiku (to) itamu (～(と)痛む) have a dull pain.
shikushiku (to) naku (～(と)泣く) sob; weep.

shi⸢kyuu[1] しきゅう (至急) *n., adv.* urgently; immediately:
Shikyuu *go-heñji o kudasai.* (至急ご返事を下さい) Please let us have your reply *promptly.*

shi⸢kyuu[2] しきゅう (子宮) *n.* womb; uterus.

shi⸢ma[1] しま (島) *n.* island.

shi⸢ma[2] しま (縞) *n.* stripe:
aoi shima *no nekutai* (青い縞のネクタイ) a tie with blue *stripes.*

shi⸣mai[1] しまい (姉妹) *n.* sisters. 《⇨ kyoodai》

shi⸢mai[2] しまい (仕舞い) *n.* end:
Hajime kara shimai *made kare wa damatte ita.* (始めからしまいまで彼は黙っていた) He kept silent from beginning to *end.* 《⇨ oshimai》

shi⸢ma⸣r·u[1] しまる (閉まる) *vi.* (shimar·i-; shimar·a-; shimat-te Ⓒ)
1 close; be closed:
Kono doa wa jidoo-teki ni shimarimasu. (このドアは自動的に閉まります) This door *closes* automatically. 《⇨ shimeru[1]》
2 (of a shop) shut:
Sono mise wa hachi-ji ni shimarimasu. (その店は８時に閉まります) That shop *shuts* at eight. 《⇨ shimeru[1]》

shi⸢ma⸣r·u[2] しまる (締まる) *vi.* (shimar·i-; shimar·a-; shimat-te Ⓒ)
1 be tightened; become firm:
Neji wa shikkari shimatte imasu. (ねじはしっかり締まっています) The screws *are* good and *tight.* 《⇨ shimeru[2]》
2 become tense:
Kyoo no kare wa shimatte iru. (きょうの彼は締まっている) He *is tense* today.
3 be frugal:
Kanojo wa nakanaka shimatte iru. (彼女はなかなか締まっている) She *is* very *frugal* with money.

shi⸢ma⸣su します do: ★ Polite *masu*-form of '*suru.*'
Daigaku o detara nani o shimasu *ka?* (大学を出たら何をしますか) What will you *do* after college? 《⇨ suru[1]》

shi⸣matsu しまつ (始末) *n.* disposal; management; settlement:
Kono ko wa shimatsu ni oenai. (この子は始末に負えない) This child is *unmanageable.*
shimatsu ga warui (～が悪い) be impossible to handle.
shimatsu (o) suru (～(を)する) *vt.* dispose of; tidy up; put in order.

shi⸢matsusho しまつしょ (始末書) *n.* written apology. ★ Submitted to superiors by those who have caused an accident or made a blunder.

shi⸢ma⸣tta しまった *int.* gosh!; oh no!:
Shimatta! *Teeki o wasureta.* (しまった. 定期を忘れた) *Gosh!* I have forgotten my commuter pass.

shi⸢ma·u[1] しまう (仕舞う) *vi.* (shima·i-; shimaw·a-; shimat-te Ⓒ) stop (work); leave off:
Kyoo wa itsu-mo yori hayaku shigoto o shimatta. (きょうはいつもより早く仕事をしまった) Today I *left off* working earlier than usual.

shima·u[2] しまう (仕舞う) (shima·i-; shimaw·a-; shimat-te Ⓒ)
★ Follows the *te*-form of a verb. In conversation '*-te+shimau*' becomes '*-chau,*' and '*-de+shimau*' becomes '*-jau.*'
1 have done; (have) finished doing: ★ Used to emphasize the recent completion or occurrence of an action.
Shukudai wa moo yatte shimai-

mashita [yatchaimashita].（宿題はもうやってしまいました[やっちゃいました]）I *have* already *finished* my homework.

2 end up doing; go and do:
★ Used in reference to unfavorable consequences.
Kotori ga shiñde shimatta [shiñjatta].（小鳥が死んでしまった[死んじゃった]）The bird *went and died*.

shi⌈ma·u[3] しまう（仕舞う）*vi.* (shima·i-; shimaw·a-; shimat-te Ⓒ) put away; put back; keep. ⟪⇨ katazukeru⟫

shi⌈mauma しまうま（縞馬）*n.* zebra.

shi⌉mee[1] しめい（氏名）*n.* full name. ★ Literally 'family name'（氏）and 'personal name'（名）. ⟪⇨ namae⟫

shi⌉mee[2] しめい（使命）*n.* mission: shimee *o hatasu*（使命を果たす）carry out one's *mission*.

shi⌈mee[3] しめい（指名）*n.* nomination; designation; appointment:
shimee-*tehai*（指名手配）instituting a search for an *identified criminal*.
shimee suru（～する）*vt.* nominate; designate; name.

shi⌈mekiri しめきり（締め切り）*n.* deadline. ⟪⇨ shimekiru[2]⟫

shi⌈mekir·u[1] しめきる（閉め切る）*vt.* (-kir·i-; -kir·a-; -kit-te Ⓒ) close [shut] up:
Ame ga hidoi no de amado o shimekitte oita.（雨がひどいので雨戸をしめきっておいた）The rain was so heavy that I *kept* the shutters *closed*.

shi⌈mekir·u[2] しめきる（締め切る）*vt.* (-kir·i-; -kir·a-; -kit-te Ⓒ) close:
Boshuu wa koñgetsu ippai de shimekirimasu.（募集は今月いっぱいで締め切ります）Applications will *be closed* at the end of this month. ⟪⇨ shimekiri⟫

shi⌈menawa しめなわ（注連縄）*n.* sacred straw festoon. ★ A twisted rice-straw rope hung with strips of white paper.

shi⌈meppo⌉·i しめっぽい（湿っぽい）*a.* (-ku) **1** wet; damp; humid; moist:
Kono taoru wa shimeppoi.（このタオルはしめっぽい）This towel is *damp*.
2 gloomy:
Kyoo wa shimeppoi *hanashi wa yameyoo.*（きょうはしめっぽい話はやめよう）Let's put *gloomy* topics aside today.

shi⌈me⌉·ru[1] しめる（閉める）*vt.* (shime-te Ⓥ) close; shut:
Mado o shimete *kudasai.*（窓を閉めてください）Please *shut* the window. ⟪↔ akeru[1]⟫ ⟪⇨ shimaru[1]⟫

shi⌈me⌉·ru[2] しめる（締める）*vt.* (shime-te Ⓥ) **1** fasten:
shiito-beruto o shimeru（シートベルトを締める）*fasten* one's seatbelt.
2 put on (neckties, belts, etc.):
★ '*shimete iru*'＝wear.
3 lock:
doa no kagi o shimeru（ドアの鍵を締める）*lock* a door. ⟪⇨ shimaru[2]⟫
4 add up; total:
Shimete *ichimañ goseñ-eñ ni narimasu.*（締めて１万５千円になります）*Adding it up*, it comes to 15,000 yen.

shi⌈mer·u[3] しめる（湿る）*vi.* (shimer·i-; shimer·a-; shimet-te Ⓒ) get damp; get moist.

shi⌈me⌉·ru[4] しめる（占める）*vt.* (shime-te Ⓥ) occupy; hold:
Kare wa kaisha de juuyoo na chii o shimete iru.（彼は会社で重要な地位を占めている）He *occupies* an important position in the company. ⟪⇨ toru[1]⟫

shi⌈me⌉s·u しめす（示す）*vt.* (shimesh·i-; shimes·a-; shimesh·i-te Ⓒ) show; point out; indicate.

shi⌈mi しみ（染み）*n.* stain; spot; blot.

shi⌈miji⌉mi しみじみ *adv.* (～ to) deeply; really; keenly; quietly:
Byooki o shite, shimijimi (*to*) *keñkoo no taisetsu na koto ga wakat-*

ta. (病気をして，しみじみ(と)健康の大切なことがわかった) I *keenly* realized the importance of good health when I became ill.

shi|miñ しみん (市民) *n.* citizen: shimiñ-keñ (市民権) *citizenship.*

shi|mi·ru しみる (染みる) *vi.* (shimi-te [V]) **1** smart; sting; (of medicine) irritate:
Kono kusuri wa sukoshi shimimasu. (この薬は少ししみます) This medicine *stings* a little.
2 (of kindness, gentleness) touch:
Kare no shiñsetsu ga mi ni shimita. (彼の親切が身にしみた) His kindness *deeply touched* me.
3 (of cold) pierce:
Samusa ga mi ni shimita. (寒さが身にしみた) The cold *chilled* me to the bone.

shi|mo[1] しも (霜) *n.* frost.

shimo[2] しも *p.* (used with a negative) (not) always; (not) necessarily: ★ Used mainly with '*kanarazu.*'
Doryoku shite mo, kanarazu shimo *seekoo suru to wa kagiranai.* (努力しても，必ずしも成功するとは限らない) Even if you make every effort, it *doesn't always follow* that you will succeed.

shi|mo- しも (下) *pref.*
1 lower:
shimo-*te* (下手) the *lower* part; the left of the stage / shimo-*za* (下座) a *lower* seat. 《↔ kami-》
2 the second:
shimo-*hañki* (下半期) the *second* half of the year. 《↔ kami-》
3 last:
shimo-*futa-keta* (下2桁) the *last* two figures.

shi|moñ しもん (指紋) *n.* fingerprints.

shi|ñ[1] しん (芯) *n.* core; lead; wick:
eñpitsu no shiñ (鉛筆のしん) the *lead* of a pencil / *roosoku no* shiñ (ろうそくのしん) the *wick* in a candle.

shi|ñ[2] しん (心) *n.* heart; spirit:
Kare wa shiñ *wa yasashii hito da.* (彼は心はやさしい人だ) He is kind at *heart*. 《⇨ kokoro》

shi|ñ- しん (新) *pref.* new:
shiñ-*kiroku* (新記録) a *new* record / shiñ-*seehiñ* (新製品) a *new* product.

shi|na しな (品) *n.* **1** article; goods. 《⇨ shinamono》
2 quality; brand:
Kono kabañ wa shina *ga yoi* [*warui*]. (このかばんは品が良い[悪い]) This bag is of good [bad] *quality*.

shi|nabi·ru しなびる (萎びる) *vi.* (shinabi-te [V]) wither; shrivel. 《⇨ kareru》

shi|nai しない (市内) *n.* city; within the city. ★ This only applies to a city which is designated as '*shi.*' 《↔ shigai[2]》 《⇨ tonai》

shi|namono しなもの (品物) *n.* article; goods. 《⇨ shina》

shi|na|yaka しなやか *a.n.* (~ na, ni) soft and tender; flexible; supple: shinayaka *na eda* (しなやかな枝) a *supple* branch.

shi|ñ-Bee しんべい (親米) *n.* pro-American. 《↔ hañ-Bee》

shi|ñboo しんぼう (辛抱) *n.* patience; endurance; perseverance.
shiñboo suru (~する) *vi., vt.* be patient; endure; persevere. 《⇨ gamañ》

shi|ñboozuyo|·i しんぼうづよい (辛抱強い) *a.* (-ku) patient; persevering; tenacious.

shi|ñbuñ しんぶん (新聞) *n.* newspaper; paper. 《⇨ furushiñbuñ》

shi|ñchiku しんちく (新築) *n.* new building; new construction.
shiñchiku suru (~する) *vt.* build; construct. 《⇨ tateru[2]》

shi|ñchoo[1] しんちょう (身長) *n.* stature; height.

shi|ñchoo[2] しんちょう (慎重) *a.n.* (~ na, ni) careful; cautious; prudent. 《↔ keesotsu》

shi|ñchuu しんちゅう (真鍮) *n.* brass.

S

shi⌈ñdai しんだい (寝台) *n.* bed; berth: shiñdai-*sha* (寝台車) a *sleeping* car.

shi⌈ñdañ しんだん (診断) *n.* diagnosis: shiñdañ-*sho* (診断書) a *medical* certificate.
shiñdañ suru (～する) *vt.* diagnose.

shi⌉ñdo[1] しんど (震度) n. seismic intensity; intensity of a quake on the Japanese scale of eight.

shi⌉ñdo[2] しんど (進度) *n.* progress:
shiñdo *ga hayai* [*osoi*] (進度が速い[遅い]) make fast [slow] *progress.*

shi⌈ñdoo[1] しんどう (振動) *n.* vibration; swing; oscillation.
shiñdoo suru (～する) *vt.* vibrate; swing; oscillate.

shi⌈ñdoo[2] しんどう (震動) *n.* quake; tremor.
shiñdoo suru (～する) *vi.* shake; quake; tremble.

shi⌈ñfu⌉zeñ しんふぜん (心不全) *n.* heart failure.

shi⌈ñga⌉kki しんがっき (新学期) *n.* new school term. ⟪⇨ gakki[1]⟫

shi⌈ñgaku しんがく (進学) *n.* going on to a school of the next higher level.
shiñgaku suru (～する) *vi.* enter a school of a higher grade.

shi⌈ñgoo しんごう (信号) *n.* signal; traffic light:
shiñgoo *o mamoru* [*mushi suru*] (信号を守る[無視する]) observe [ignore] a *traffic signal.*

S

shi⌈nimonogu⌉rui しにものぐるい (死に物狂い) *n.* desperation:
shinimonogurui *ni* [*de*] *nigeru* (死に物狂いに[で]逃げる) run away *for dear life.*

shi⌈ñjiñ しんじん (新人) *n.* new star; new employee; rookie.

shi⌈ñji⌉·ru しんじる (信じる) *vt.* (shiñji-te [V]) **1** believe:
Anata no iu koto o shiñjimasu. (あなたの言うことを信じます) I *believe* what you say.
2 trust:
Watashi wa kare o shiñjite imasu. (私は彼を信じています) I *trust* him.
3 be sure; be confident:
Kanojo wa kitto seekoo suru to shiñjimasu. (彼女はきっと成功すると信じます) I *am confident* that she will succeed.
4 believe in (religions).
⟪⇨ shiñkoo[2]⟫

shi⌉ñjitsu しんじつ (真実) *n.* truth; reality; fact. ⟪⇨ shiñsoo⟫

shi⌈ñju しんじゅ (真珠) *n.* pearl.

shi⌈ñjuu しんじゅう (心中) *n.* double suicide; taking someone into death with one.
shiñjuu suru (～する) *vi.* commit a double suicide. ⟪⇨ muri-shiñjuu⟫

shi⌉ñkee しんけい (神経) *n.*
1 nerve:
Kare wa me no shiñkee *o yararete imasu.* (彼は目の神経をやられています) His visual *nerves* are damaged.
2 sensitivity:
shiñkee ga surudoi [nibui] (神経が鋭い[鈍い]) *be sensitive* [*insensitive*].

shi⌈ñkeeka しんけいか (神経科) *n.* neurology: shinkeeka-i (神経科医) a *neurologist.*

shi⌈ñke⌉eshitsu しんけいしつ (神経質) *a.n.* (～ na, ni) nervous:
shiñkeeshitsu *na hito* (神経質な人) a *nervous* person.

shi⌈ñkeñ しんけん (真剣) *a.n.* (～ na, ni) serious; earnest:
Watashi wa shiñkeñ *desu.* (私は真剣です) I am *serious.* ⟪⇨ majime⟫

shi⌈ñkiñ-ko⌉osoku しんきんこうそく (心筋梗塞) *n.* myocardial infarction.

shi⌈ñkoku しんこく (深刻) *a.n.* (～ na, ni) serious; grave:
Jitai wa shiñkoku *desu.* (事態は深刻です) The situation is *grave.*
⟪⇨ kibishii⟫

shi⌈ñkoñ しんこん (新婚) *n.* newly-married:
Ano futari wa shiñkoñ hoyahoya *desu.* (あの二人は新婚ほやほやです) They are *recently married.*

shi͡ñkoo[1] しんこう(進行) *n.* progress; advance.
shiñkoo suru (～する) *vi.* move; progress; advance. (⇨ susumu)

shi͡ñkoo[2] しんこう(信仰) *n.* faith; belief.
shiñkoo suru (～する) *vt.* believe in (Buddhism). (⇨ shiñjiru)

shi͡ñkuu しんくう(真空) *n.* vacuum.

shi͡ñkuukañ しんくうかん(真空管) *n.* vacuum tube; valve. (⇨ kañ[2])

shi͞ñneñ[1] しんねん(新年) *n.* new year; the New Year. (⇨ shoogatsu)

shi͞ñneñ[2] しんねん(信念) *n.* belief; faith; conviction:
shiñneñ *o tsuranuku* [*magenai*] (信念を貫く[曲げない]) stick to [do not deviate from] one's *faith*.

shi͡ñnyuu しんにゅう(侵入) *n.* invasion; intrusion; raid.
shiñnyuu suru (～する) *vi.* invade; intrude; break into.

shi͞-noo-koo-shoo しのうこうしょう(士農工商) *n.* the four classes in Japanese feudal society, from the highest to the lowest; warriors, farmers, artisans, and merchants.

shi͡ñpai しんぱい(心配) *n.* **1** anxiety; worry; concern; fear.
2 care; help:
Ojisañ ga shuushoku no shiñpai o shite kureta. (おじさんが就職の心配をしてくれた) My uncle *helped* me find employment.
shiñpai suru (～する) *vt.* worry; fear; care; be troubled.
— *a.n.* (～ na) worried; anxious; uneasy. (⇨ kigakari; fuañ)

shi͡ñpañ しんぱん(審判) *n.*
1 (of sports) umpire; referee.
2 judgment:
kainañ ni tsuite shiñpañ *o kudasu* (海難について審判を下す) pass *judgment* on a marine accident.

shi͞ñpi しんぴ(神秘) *n.* mystery.

shi͡ñpi-teki しんぴてき(神秘的) *a.n.* (～ na, ni) mysterious.

shi͞ñpo しんぽ(進歩) *n.* progress; advance; improvement.
shiñpo suru (～する) *vi.* progress; advance; improve.

shi͡ñpo-teki しんぽてき(進歩的) *a.n.* (～ na, ni) progressive; advanced:
Kare no kañgae wa shiñpo-teki *da.* (彼の考えは進歩的だ) His thinking is *forward-looking.* (↔ hoshuteki)

shi͞ñpu[1] しんぷ(神父) *n.* father.
★ A priest or clergyman in the Roman Catholic church.
(⇨ bokushi)

shi͞ñpu[2] しんぷ(新婦) *n.* bride.
★ Used only at a wedding ceremony or reception. (⇨ shiñroo)

shi͡ñrai しんらい(信頼) *n.* trust; confidence.
shiñrai suru (～する) *vt.* trust; rely on.

shi͞ñri[1] しんり(心理) *n.* state of mind; psychology:
shiñri-gaku (心理学) *psychology.*

shi͞ñri[2] しんり(真理) *n.* truth:
Kimi no iu koto ni wa ichimeñ no shiñri *ga aru.* (君の言うことには一面の真理がある) There is some *truth* in what you say.

shi͡ñriñ しんりん(森林) *n.* forest; woods. (⇨ mori; hayashi)

shi͡ñroo しんろう(新郎) *n.* bridegroom; groom. ★ Used only at a wedding ceremony or reception. (⇨ shiñpu[2])

shi͞ñrui しんるい(親類) *n.* relative; relation. (⇨ shiñseki)

shi͡ñryaku しんりゃく(侵略) *n.* invasion; aggression.
shiñryaku suru (～する) *vt.* invade.

shi͡ñryoo しんりょう(診療) *n.* medical treatment:
shiñryoo-jo (診療所) a *clinic*; a *dispensary.*
shiñryoo suru (～する) *vt.* treat (a patient). (⇨ chiryoo)

shi͡ñsatsu しんさつ(診察) *n.* medical examination.

shiñsatsu suru (〜する) *vt.* examine; see: *isha ni* shiñsatsu shite morau (医者に診察してもらう) *see* a doctor.

shi⌈ñsee[1] しんせい (申請) *n.* application; request:
shiñsee-*sho* (申請書) an *application* form; a written *application*.
shiñsee (o) suru (〜(を)する) *vt.* apply for. ⟪⇨ mooshikomu⟫

shi⌈ñsee[2] しんせい (神聖) *a.n.* (〜 na) sacred; holy; divine:
shiñsee *na basho* (神聖な場所) a *holy* place.

shi⌈ñseki しんせき (親戚) *n.* relative; relation. ⟪⇨ shiñrui⟫

shi⌈ñseñ しんせん (新鮮) *a.n.* (〜 na, ni) fresh; new; green:
shiñseñ *na yasai* (新鮮な野菜) *fresh* vegetables.

shi⌉ñsetsu しんせつ (親切) *n.* kindness; kindliness; tenderness. — *a.n.* (〜 na, ni) kind; kindly; friendly; hospitable:
Nihoñ de wa miñna ga shiñsetsu *ni shite kuremashita.* (日本ではみんなが親切にしてくれました) Everyone was *kind* to me in Japan. ⟪↔ fushiñsetsu⟫

shi⌉ñshi しんし (紳士) *n.* gentleman.

shi⌈ñshiki しんしき (神式) *n.* Shinto rites: shiñshiki no *kekkoñ* (神式の結婚) a *Shinto* wedding. ⟪⇨ busshiki⟫

shi⌈ñshiñ しんしん (深々) *adv.* (〜 to) (the state of increasing darkness or cold, or snow falling):
Yoru ga shiñshiñ to fukete iku. (夜がしんしんと更けていく) The night *is getting far advanced.*

shi⌈ñshitsu しんしつ (寝室) *n.* bedroom.

shi⌈ñshoku しんしょく (浸食) *n.* erosion.
shiñshoku suru (〜する) *vt.* erode; eat away.

shi⌈ñsho⌉osha しんしょうしゃ (身障者) *n.* abbreviation for '*shiñtai-shoogaisha*.' ⟪⇨ shiñtai-shoogaisha⟫

shi⌈ñshutsu しんしゅつ (進出) *n.* advance.
shiñshutsu suru (〜する) *vt.* advance; make one's way: *kesshoo-señ ni* shiñshutsu suru (決勝戦に進出する) *advance* to the finals.

shi⌈ñsoo しんそう (真相) *n.* the truth; fact:
Sono shiñsoo *wa dare mo shirimaseñ.* (その真相はだれも知りません) Nobody knows the *true facts.*

shi⌉ñtai しんたい (身体) *n.* body; constitution:
shiñtai-*keñsa* (身体検査) a *physical* examination. ⟪⇨ karada⟫

shi⌈ñtai-shooga⌉isha しんたいしょうがいしゃ (身体障害者) *n.* physically handicapped person; disabled person.

Shi⌉ñtoo しんとう (神道) *n.* Shintoism; Shinto.

shi⌈n·u しぬ (死ぬ) *vi.* (shin·i-; shin·a-; shiñ-de [C]) die; be killed: ★ A rather blunt expression. '*Nakunaru*' is more polite.
Chichi wa gañ de shinimashita. (父はがんで死にました) My father *died of* cancer. ⟪↔ ikiru⟫ ⟪⇨ shiboo[2]⟫

shi⌈ñya-ho⌉osoo しんやほうそう (深夜放送) *n.* late-night broadcasting.

shi⌈ñyoo しんよう (信用) *n.* confidence; trust; faith; reliance.
shiñyoo suru (〜する) *vt.* trust; put confidence in; rely on.

shi⌈ñyoo-ku⌉miai しんようくみあい (信用組合) *n.* credit union (association). ★ Operates as a bank for medium and small-sized enterprises.

shi⌈ñyuu しんゆう (親友) *n.* close friend; one's best friend.

shi⌈ñzeñ しんぜん (親善) *n.* friendship; goodwill:
shiñzeñ *o hakaru* (親善を図る) promote *friendly relations.*

S

shi⌈ñzeñ-ke⌉kkoñ しんぜんけっこん (神前結婚) *n.* wedding according to Shinto rites.

shi⌈ñzoo しんぞう (心臓) *n.* heart.
shiñzoo ga tsuyoi [yowai] (～が強い[弱い]) be bold [timid]: *Kare wa* shiñzoo ga tsuyoi. (彼は心臓が強い) He is *stout-hearted*.

shi⌈ñz·u⌉ru しんずる (信ずる) *vt.* (shiñj·i-; shiñj·i-; shiñj·i-te [I]) = shiñjiru.

shi⌈o[1] しお (塩) *n.* salt.

shi⌈o[2] しお (潮) *n.* tide:
shio *no michi-hi* (潮の満ち干) the ebb and flow of the *tide*.

shi⌈okara⌉·i しおからい (塩辛い) *a.* (-ku) salty. 《⇨ karai》

shi⌈oñ しおん (子音) *n.* = shiiñ.

shi⌈ore·ru しおれる (萎れる) *vi.* (shiore-te [V]) **1** (of a plant) wither; wilt; fade. 《⇨ kareru》
2 (of a person) be dejected.

shi⌈ppai しっぱい (失敗) *n.* failure; mistake.
shippai suru (～する) *vi.* fail. 《↔ seekoo[1]》 《⇨ shikujiru》

shi⌈ppitsu しっぴつ (執筆) *n.* writing: shippitsu-sha (執筆者) a *writer*; an *author*.
shippitsu suru (～する) *vt.* write: *hoñ* [*roñbuñ*] *o* shippitsu suru (本[論文]を執筆する) *write* a book [an essay].

shi⌈ppo⌉ しっぽ (尻尾) *n.* tail. 《⇨ o[1]》

shi⌈rabe[1] しらべ (調べ) *n.* examination; investigation; questioning:
shirabe o ukeru (調べを受ける) *be examined*. 《⇨ torishirabe》

shi⌈rabe[2] しらべ (調べ) *n.* melody; tune.

shi⌈rabemono しらべもの (調べ物) *n.* something to check up on.

shi⌈rabe⌉·ru しらべる (調べる) *vt.* (shirabe-te [V]) **1** examine; inspect; investigate:
kaji no geñiñ o shiraberu (火事の原因を調べる) *investigate* the cause of a fire. 《⇨ soosa[1]》
2 consult (a reference book); look up:
Sono go no imi o jisho de shirabeta. (その語の意味を辞書で調べた) I *consulted* the dictionary for the meaning of the word.

shi⌈rase しらせ (知らせ) *n.* news; information; report:
Kare kara nani-ka shirase *ga arimashita ka?* (彼から何か知らせがありましたか) Has there been any *news* from him? 《⇨ shiraseru》

shi⌈rase·ru しらせる (知らせる) *vt.* (shirase-te [V]) let know; inform; tell; report. 《⇨ shirase》

shi⌈razu-shi⌉razu しらずしらず (知らず知らず) *adv.* (～ ni) without knowing it; unconsciously:
Kodomo wa shirazu-shirazu (*ni*) *kotoba o oboeru.* (子どもは知らず知らず(に)言葉を覚える) Children learn language *unconsciously*.

shi⌈ri⌉ しり (尻) *n.* buttocks; bottom. ★ Often with '*o*-.'

shi⌈riai しりあい (知り合い) *n.* acquaintance:
Ano hito wa tañ-naru shiriai *desu.* (あの人は単なる知り合いです) He is just an *acquaintance*.

shi⌉riizu シリーズ *n.* series; serial.

shi⌉ritsu[1] しりつ (私立) *n.* private: ★ Sometimes '*watakushiritsu*' to distinguish it from '*shiritsu*[2]' (市立).
shiritsu-*daigaku* (私立大学) a *private* university [college]. 《↔ kooritsu[1]》

shi⌉ritsu[2] しりつ (市立) *n.* municipal: ★ Sometimes '*ichiritsu*' to distinguish it from '*shiritsu*[1]' (私立).
shiritsu *no toshokañ* (市立の図書館) a *municipal* library.

shi⌉ro[1] しろ (白) *n.* **1** white. 《⇨ shiroi》
2 innocence:
Kare wa zettai ni shiro *da to omou.* (彼は絶対に白だと思う) I am quite sure that he is *innocent*. 《↔ kuro》

S

shi⌈ro² しろ(城) *n.* castle.

shi⌈ro⌉·i しろい(白い) *a.* (-ku) white; (of skin) fair; (of hair) gray.

shi⌈ro-kuro しろくろ(白黒) *n.* black and white:
shiro-kuro *no fuirumu* (白黒のフイルム) *black-and-white* film.

shi⌉rooto しろうと(素人) *n.* amateur; layman. ⟪↔ kurooto⟫

shi⌈r·u¹ しる(知る) *vt.* (shir·i-; shir·a-; shit-te Ⓒ) **1** know; have knowledge of; be acquainted with: ★ The form '*shitte iru*' is used rather than '*shiru*.'
Kanojo no deñwa-bañgoo o shitte imasu *ka?* (彼女の電話番号を知っていますか) *Do* you *know* her phone number?
2 realize; notice; be aware:
Koñna ni osoi to wa shiranakatta. (こんなに遅いとは知らなかった) I *did not realize* it was this late.
3 discover; find:
Kare wa jibuñ ga machigatte iru koto o shitta. (彼は自分が間違っていることを知った) He *found* that he was wrong.

shi⌉ru² しる(汁) *n.* juice; soup.

shi⌈rubaa-shi⌉ito シルバーシート *n.* seat reserved for the elderly or handicapped on trains or buses. ★ Literally 'silver seat.'

shi⌈ruko⌉ しるこ(汁粉) *n.* sweet thick soup made from red beans with pieces of rice cake. ★ Often with '*o-*.'

shi⌈rushi しるし(印) *n.* **1** mark; check; sign:
kami ni shirushi *o tsukeru* (紙に印をつける) put a *mark* on paper.
2 token:
o-ree no shirushi *to shite* (お礼の印として) in *token* of one's gratitude.

shi⌈rus·u しるす(記す) *vt.* (shirush·i-; shirus·a-; shirush·i-te Ⓒ) (*formal*) write down. ⟪⇨ kaku¹⟫

shi⌉ryoo しりょう(資料) *n.* material; data:
roñbuñ no tame no shiryoo *o atsumeru* (論文のための資料を集める) collect *material* for an essay.

shi⌈satsu しさつ(視察) *n.* inspection; observation.
shisatsu suru (〜する) *vt.* inspect; observe.

shi⌈see しせい(姿勢) *n.* posture; carriage; position:
Kare wa shisee *ga ii* [*warui*]. (彼は姿勢がいい[悪い]) He has a fine [poor] *posture*.

shi⌈señ しせん(支線) *n.* branch line (of a railroad).

shi⌉setsu しせつ(施設) *n.* **1** facilities.
2 (*euphemistically*) institution; home; mental hospital.

shi⌉sha¹ ししゃ(死者) *n.* dead person; the dead.

shi⌉sha² ししゃ(支社) *n.* branch office. ⟪⇨ shiteñ⟫

shi⌉sha-gonyuu ししゃごにゅう(四捨五入) *n.* rounding off.
★ To round up to the nearest whole number when the figure is 5 and above, and round down when the figure is 4 and below. ⟪⇨ kiriageru; kirisuteru⟫

shi⌈sho⌉osha ししょうしゃ(死傷者) *n.* casualties:
Sono jiko de tasuu no shishoosha *ga deta.* (その事故で多数の死傷者が出た) There were many *dead and injured* in the accident.

shi⌈shutsu ししゅつ(支出) *n.* expenditure; outgoings; expense. ⟪↔ shuunyuu⟫ ⟪⇨ shuushi¹⟫
shishutsu suru (〜する) *vt.* pay; expend. ⟪⇨ shiharau⟫

shi⌈shuu ししゅう(刺繡) *n.* embroidery.
shishuu (o) suru (〜(を)する) *vt.* embroider.

shi⌉soku しそく(四則) *n.* the four basic operations of arithmetic. ⟪⇨ keesañ⟫

shi⌉soñ しそん(子孫) *n.* descendant; offspring. ⟪↔ señzo; soseñ⟫

shi⌈soo しそう(思想) *n.* thought;

idea: shisoo *no jiyuu* (思想の自由) freedom of *thought*.

shi˥sso しっそ(質素) *a.n.* (~ na, ni) simple; plain; homely:
Kare no seekatsu wa shisso *desu.* (彼の生活は質素です) His way of living is *plain and simple.*

shi˥su˥u しすう(指数) *n.* index number: *bukka*-shisuu (物価指数) a price *index.*

shi˥ta[1] した(下) *n.* **1** under; below:
Ki no shita *de inu ga nete iru.* (木の下で犬が寝ている) There is a dog asleep *under* the tree. ⟪↔ ue[1]⟫
2 down; downward:
Kono erebeetaa wa shita *e ikimasu.* (このエレベーターは下へ行きます) This elevator is going *down.* ⟪↔ ue[1]⟫
3 bottom. ⟪↔ ue[1]⟫
4 junior; younger:
Kanai wa mittsu shita *desu.* (家内は3つ下です) My wife is three years *younger* than me. ⟪↔ ue[1]⟫

shi˥ta˥[2] した(舌) *n.* tongue.

shi˥tagae˥·ru したがえる(従える) *vt.* (shitagae-te [V]) make (a person) follow; be accompanied by:
buka o shitagaeru (部下を従える) *be attended* by one's subordinates. ⟪⇨ shitagau⟫

shi˥tagaki したがき(下書き) *n.* draft:
supiichi no shitagaki o suru (スピーチの下書きをする) *make a draft* of one's speech.

shi˥tagatte[1] したがって(従って) ★ Used in the pattern '*... ni shitagatte.*' **1** in accordance with:
Subete, kare no sashizu ni shitagatte *okonatta.* (すべて, 彼の指図に従って行った) We have done everything *in accordance with* his instructions. ⟪⇨ shitagau⟫
2 as:
Taifuu no sekkiñ ni shitagatte, *fuu-u ga tsuyoku natta.* (台風の接近に従って, 風雨が強くなった) *As* the typhoon drew nearer, the wind got stronger and the rain heavier. ⟪⇨ tsurete⟫

shi˥tagatte[2] したがって(従って) *conj.* (*formal*) therefore; consequently; accordingly. ★ Used at the beginning of a sentence.

shi˥taga·u したがう(従う) *vi.* (shitaga·i-; shitagaw·a-; shitagat-te [C]) obey; follow; observe:
Iíñkai no kettee ni shitagaimasu. (委員会の決定に従います) We will *abide by* the decision of the committee. ⟪⇨ shitagaeru⟫

shi˥tagi したぎ(下着) *n.* underwear; underclothes.

shi˥tai したい(死体) *n.* dead body; corpse.

shi˥taku したく(支度) *n.* preparation; arrangements.
shitaku (o) suru (~(を)する) *vi.* prepare; get ready. ⟪⇨ yooi[1]⟫

shi˥tamachi したまち(下町) *n.*
1 the lower section of a city.
2 the old part of Tokyo.
★ Such as Asakusa and Kanda where family industries and commerce used to thrive.
⟪↔ yamanote⟫

shi˥tashi˥·i したしい(親しい) *a.* (-ku) friendly; familiar; intimate; close:
shitashii *tomodachi* (親しい友だち) a *good* friend / shitashii *kañkee* (親しい関係) *close* relations.

shi˥tashimi˥ したしみ(親しみ) *n.* friendly feeling; affection:
Watashi wa kanojo no hitogara ni shitashimi o kañjita. (私は彼女の人柄に親しみを感じた) I *felt myself drawn* to her because of her personality. ⟪⇨ shitashimu⟫

shi˥tashi˥m·u したしむ(親しむ) *vi.* (-shim·i-; -shim·a-; -shiñ-de [C])
1 be familiar [intimate]:
Sono otogibanashi wa kodomotachi ni shitashimarete imasu. (そのおとぎ話は子どもたちに親しまれています) That fairy tale *is familiar* to children.
2 enjoy; take an interest:

S

dokusho ni shitashimu (読書に親しむ) *enjoy* reading. ⟪⇨ shitashimi⟫

shi⌈tate⌉·ru したてる (仕立てる) *vt.* (shitate-te [V]) **1** tailor; make:
Kare wa atarashii suutsu o it-chaku shitateta. (彼は新しいスーツを一着仕立てた) He *had* a suit *made.*
2 raise; educate; train (a person).

shi⌈tauke したうけ (下請け) *n.* subcontract; subcontractor:
Kare wa sono shigoto o shitauke *ni dashita.* (彼はその仕事を下請けに出した) He gave the work to a *subcontractor.*

shi⌈tee してい (指定) *n.* appointment; designation:
shitee-*seki* [-*keñ*] (指定席[券]) a *reserved* seat [seat ticket].
shitee suru (～する) *vt.* appoint; designate; specify.

shi⌈teki してき (指摘) *n.* indication.
shiteki suru (～する) *vt.* point out; indicate.

shi⌈teñ してん (支店) *n.* branch office [store; shop]. ⟪⇨ shisha[2]⟫

shi⌈tetsu してつ (私鉄) *n.* private railroad [railway].

shi⌈to⌉shito しとしと *adv.* (～ to) (the state of fine rain falling):
Ame ga shitoshito (*to*) *futte iru.* (雨がしとしと(と)降っている) The rain is falling *softly.*

shi⌈to⌉yaka しとやか (淑やか) *a.n.* (～ na, ni) graceful; gentle:
shitoyaka *na josee* (しとやかな女性) a *graceful and modest* woman. ⟪⇨ joohiñ⟫

shi⌈tsu しつ (質) *n.* quality:
Ryoo yori mo shitsu *ga taisetsu desu.* (量よりも質が大切です) *Quality* matters more than quantity. ⟪↔ ryoo[1]⟫

-shitsu しつ (室) *suf.* room:
kyoo-shitsu (教室) a class*room* / *yoku*-shitsu (浴室) a bath*room.*

shi⌈tsuboo しつぼう (失望) *n.* disappointment; discouragement.
shitsuboo suru (～する) *vi.* be disappointed. ⟪⇨ gakkari⟫

shi⌈tsu⌉do しつど (湿度) *n.* humidity:
Kyoo wa shitsudo *ga takai* [*hikui*]. (きょうは湿度が高い[低い]) The *humidity* is high [low] today.

shi⌈tsu⌉gai しつがい (室外) *n.* outside a room; outdoors. ⟪↔ shitsunai⟫

shi⌈tsugyoo しつぎょう (失業) *n.* unemployment.
shitsugyoo suru (～する) *vt.* lose one's job; be out of work.

shi⌈tsuke しつけ (躾) *n.* training; discipline; manners:
Chichi wa shitsuke *ga kibishikatta.* (父はしつけが厳しかった) My father was very particular about our *upbringing.*

shi⌈tsuko⌉·i しつこい *a.* (-ku)
1 persistent; stubborn; importunate:
Onaji koto o shitsukoku *iwanai de kudasai.* (同じことをしつこく言わないでください) Please stop going *on and on* about the same thing.
2 (of food) heavy; cloying; greasy.

shi⌈tsumoñ しつもん (質問) *n.* question; inquiry.
shitsumoñ suru (～する) *vt., vi.* ask a question.

shi⌈tsu⌉nai しつない (室内) *n.* inside a room:
shitsunai-*sooshoku* (室内装飾) interior decoration. ⟪↔ shitsugai⟫

shi⌈tsuoñ しつおん (室温) *n.* room temperature. ⟪⇨ oñdo⟫

shi⌈tsu⌉ree しつれい (失礼) *n.* impoliteness.
shitsuree suru (～する) *vi.* **1** I'm sorry; Excuse me:
Kinoo wa rusu o shite, shitsuree shimashita. (きのうは留守をして, 失礼しました) I *am sorry* that I was not at home yesterday.
2 I must be going:
O-saki ni shitsuree shimasu. (お先に失礼します) Now *I must be going.*
— *a.n.* (～ na) impolite; discourteous; rude. ⟪⇨ busahoo⟫

S

shiˡtto しっと(嫉妬) *n.* jealousy; envy.
shitto suru (~する) *vt.* be jealous of; envy. ⟪⇨ yakimochi⟫

shiˡwa しわ(皺) *n.* **1** wrinkle:
Kare wa hitai ni shiwa *o yoseta.* (彼は額にしわを寄せた) He *wrinkled* his forehead.
2 crease:
airoñ de zuboñ no shiwa *o nobasu* (アイロンでズボンのしわを伸ばす) iron out the *creases* in the trousers.

shiˡwaza しわざ(仕業) *n.* one's doing; work:
Kore wa dare no shiwaza *desu ka?* (これはだれのしわざですか) Whose *doing* is this?

shiˡyaˡkusho しやくしょ(市役所) *n.* municipal [city] office; city hall. ⟪⇨ kuyakusho⟫

shiˡyoo[1] しよう(使用) *n.* use; employment.
shiyoo suru (~する) *vt.* use; employ. ⟪⇨ tsukau⟫

shiˡyoo[2] しよう(私用) *n.* private use; private business:
shiyoo *no deñwa* (私用の電話) a *private* telephone call.

shiˡyoo ga naˡ·i しようがない(仕様がない) *a.* (-ku) ★ Also pronounced '*shoo ga nai*.' Polite forms are '*shiyoo ga nai desu*' and '*shiyoo ga arimaseñ*.'
1 (*pred.*) be helpless; have no choice:
Dame nara, shiyoo ga nai. *Hoka no hito ni tanomimasu.* (だめなら, しようがない. ほかの人に頼みます) If your answer is 'No,' *there is no more to be said.* I will ask someone else. ⟪⇨ shikatanai⟫
2 (*attrib.*) good-for-nothing:
Aitsu wa shiyoo ga nai *yatsu da.* (あいつはしようがないやつだ) He is a *good-for-nothing.*

shiˡyuu しゆう(私有) *n.* private possession:
shiyuu-*zaisañ* (私有財産) *private property* / shiyuu-*chi* (私有地) *private land.*

shiˡzai しざい(資材) *n.* material; raw material.

shiˡzeñ しぜん(自然) *n.* nature:
Hokkaidoo ni wa mada shizeñ *ga nokotte iru.* (北海道にはまだ自然が残っている) The *natural environment* still survives in Hokkaido.
— *a.n.* (~ na, ni) natural:
shizeñ *ni furumau* (自然に振る舞う) behave *naturally.* ⟪↔ fushizeñ⟫
— *adv.* naturally; automatically.

shiˡzeñ ni しぜんに(自然に) *adv.* of oneself; automatically; spontaneously: ⟪⇨ hitoride ni⟫
Kaze wa shizeñ ni *naotta.* (かぜは自然に治った) My cold cured *itself.*

shiˡzuka しずか(静か) *a.n.* (~ na, ni) **1** quiet; still: shizuka *na ashioto* (静かな足音) *quiet* footsteps / shizuka *ni aruku* (静かに歩く) walk *quietly.* ⟪↔ urusai⟫
2 calm; soft:
Kyoo no umi wa shizuka *da.* (きょうの海は静かだ) The sea is *calm* today. ⟪⇨ arai[1]⟫

shiˡzukuˡ しずく(滴) *n.* drop:
Jaguchi kara mizu no shizuku ga ochite iru. (蛇口から水のしずくが落ちている) *Water is dripping* from the tap.

shiˡzumaˡr·u しずまる(静まる) *vi.* (shizumar·i-; shizumar·a-; shizumat-te Ⓒ) calm [quiet] down; subside:
Kaze ga shizumatta. (風が静まった) The wind *has died down.* ⟪⇨ shizumeru[2]⟫

shiˡzume·ru[1] しずめる(沈める) *vt.* (shizume-te Ⓥ) sink; submerge; put under water. ⟪⇨ shizumu⟫

shiˡzumeˡ·ru[2] しずめる(静める) *vt.* (shizume-te Ⓥ) calm; quiet; soothe; appease:
Kare wa koofuñ shita kañkyaku o shizumeta. (彼は興奮した観客を静めた) He *calmed* the excited spectators. ⟪⇨ shizumaru⟫

shiˡzum·u しずむ(沈む) *vi.* (shizum·i-; shizum·a-; shizuñ-de Ⓒ)
1 sink; go down:

Sono fune wa akkenaku shizuñde *shimatta.* (その船はあっけなく沈んでしまった) The ship *sank* quickly. 《⇨ chiñbotsu; shizumeru[1]》
2 be depressed:
Kare wa naze-ka shizuñde ita. (彼はなぜか沈んでいた) He *was depressed* for some reason or other.

sho- しょ (諸) *pref.* various:
sho-*koku* (諸国) *various* countries / sho-señsee (諸先生) *teachers.* 《⇨ kaku-》

-sho[1] しょ (所) *suf.* place; office; institute:
juu-sho (住所) an *address* / jimu-sho (事務所) an *office.* 《⇨ -jo》

-sho[2] しょ (書) *suf.* writing; letter; book: buñ-sho (文書) a *document* / doku-sho (読書) *reading.*

sho⌉batsu しょばつ (処罰) *n.* punishment; penalty:
shobatsu *o ukeru* (処罰を受ける) receive *punishment.*
shobatsu suru (~する) *vt.* punish.

sho⌉buñ しょぶん (処分) *n.* **1** disposal:
Gomi no shobuñ *ni komatte imasu.* (ごみの処分に困っています) I do not know what to do about *getting rid of* the rubbish.
2 punishment:
Kare wa uñteñmeñkyo-teeshi no shobuñ o uketa. (彼は運転免許停止の処分を受けた) He *was punished* by having his driving license suspended.
shobuñ suru (~する) *vt.* **1** dispose of; do away with; get rid of: *ie o* shobuñ suru (家を処分する) *sell off* one's house.
2 punish; discipline.

sho⌉chi しょち (処置) *n.* measure; treatment; disposal.
shochi suru (~する) *vt.* deal with; treat; dispose of: *moñdai o umaku* shochi suru (問題をうまく処置する) *deal with* a problem skillfully.

sho⌈chuu-mi⌉mai しょちゅうみまい (暑中見舞い) *n.* summer greeting card. ★ A postcard sent to inquire after a person's health in the hot season.

sho⌉ho しょほ (初歩) *n.* the first step; rudiments.

sho⌈kki しょっき (食器) *n.* tableware; the dishes.

sho⌉koku しょこく (諸国) *n.* various countries.

sho⌈kuba⌉ しょくば (職場) *n.* one's place of work; office; one's job.

sho⌈ku⌉butsu しょくぶつ (植物) *n.* plant; vegetation.

sho⌈kubutsu⌉eñ しょくぶつえん (植物園) *n.* botanical garden. 《⇨ doobutsueñ》

sho⌈kudoo[1] しょくどう (食堂) *n.* dining room; cafeteria; eating place; restaurant.

sho⌈kudoo[2] しょくどう (食道) *n.* gullet; esophagus.

sho⌈kudo⌉osha しょくどうしゃ (食堂車) *n.* dining car.

sho⌈ku⌉gyoo しょくぎょう (職業) *n.* occupation; profession; job; business.

sho⌈kuhi しょくひ (食費) *n.* food expenses; board.

sho⌈kuhiñ しょくひん (食品) *n.* food; foodstuffs: shokuhiñ-*teñkabutsu* (食品添加物) a *food* additive.

sho⌈ku⌉iñ しょくいん (職員) *n.* staff; staff member; personnel. 《⇨ juugyooiñ; shaiñ》

sho⌈kuji しょくじ (食事) *n.* meal; diet.
shokuji (o) suru (~(を)する) *vi.* have a meal.

sho⌈ku⌉motsu しょくもつ (食物) *n.* food. 《⇨ shokuryoo[1]》

sho⌈kuniñ しょくにん (職人) *n.* artisan; craftsman.

sho⌈ku⌉ryoo[1] しょくりょう (食料) *n.* foodstuffs. ★ Often refers to food other than staples. 《⇨ shokuryoo[2]》

sho⌈ku⌉ryoo[2] しょくりょう (食糧) *n.* food; provisions. ★ Often refers

S

to staple food. ⟪⇨ shokuryoo[1]⟫

sho⌈kutaku[1] しょくたく (食卓) *n.* dining table.

sho⌈kutaku[2] しょくたく (嘱託) *n.* part-time employee; nonregular employee.

sho⌈kuyoku しょくよく (食欲) *n.* appetite:
shokuyoku *ga aru* [*nai*] (食欲がある[ない]) have a good [poor] *appetite.*

sho⌈kyuu しょきゅう (初級) *n.* beginner's class:
shokyuu *Nihoñgo* (初級日本語) Japanese for *beginners.* ⟪⇨ chuukyuu; jookyuu⟫

sho⌈mee しょめい (署名) *n.* signature; autograph.
shomee suru (〜する) *vi.* sign; autograph: *keeyakusho ni* shomee suru (契約書に署名する) *sign* a contract. ⟪⇨ saiñ⟫

sho⌉miñ しょみん (庶民) *n.* ordinary citizen; common people; average person.

sho⌉motsu しょもつ (書物) *n.* (*formal*) book. ⟪⇨ hoñ⟫

sho⌉mu しょむ (庶務) *n.* general affairs:
shomu-*ka* (庶務課) the *general affairs* section (of a company).

sho⌉o[1] しょう (省) *n.* ministry:
Gaimu-shoo (外務省) the *Ministry* of Foreign Affairs. ⟪⇨ APP. 7⟫

sho⌉o[2] しょう (性) *n.* nature; disposition; temperament.
shoo ni au (〜に合う) be congenial to one: *Ima no shigoto wa kare no* shoo ni atte iru *yoo da.* (今の仕事は彼の性に合っているようだ) The present work seems to *be suited* to him.

sho⌉o[3] しょう (賞) *n.* prize; reward; award:
shoo *o toru* [*morau*] (賞を取る[もらう]) win a *prize.*

sho⌉o[4] しょう (章) *n.* **1** chapter: *dai is*-shoo (第1章) *Chapter* 1.
2 badge; emblem: *kaiiñ*-shoo (会員章) a membership *badge.*

sho⌉o[5] しょう (小) *n.* smallness: *Saizu wa dai to* shoo *ga arimasu.* (サイズは大と小があります) There are two sizes: large and *small.* ⟪⇨ dai[1]⟫

sho⌈o- しょう (小) *pref.* small; minor: shoo-*gekijoo* (小劇場) a *small* theater / shoo-*kibo* (小規模) *small* scale. ⟪↔ dai-[1]⟫

sho⌉obai しょうばい (商売) *n.* business; trade; occupation.
shoobai (o) suru (〜(を)する) *vi.* do business; engage in trade; deal in.

sho⌈obe⌉ñ しょうべん (小便) *n.* piss; urine. ★ Often pronounced '*shoñbeñ.*' ★ Considered vulgar and advisable not to use in public.
shoobeñ (o) suru (〜(を)する) *vi.* urinate: *tachi*-shoobeñ o suru (立ち小便をする) *urinate* in the street. ⟪↔ daibeñ; fuñ[2]; kuso⟫

sho⌈oboo しょうぼう (消防) *n.* fire fighting: shooboo-*sho* (消防署) a *fire* station / shooboo-*sha* (消防車) a *fire* engine.

sho⌉obu しょうぶ (勝負) *n.* game:
shoobu *ni katsu* [*makeru*] (勝負に勝つ[負ける]) win [lose] a *game.*
shoobu suru (〜する) *vi.* have a game; fight. ⟪⇨ tatakau⟫

sho⌈ochi しょうち (承知) *n.* knowing; being aware (of); consent:
Go-shoochi no yoo ni, *kare wa señgetsu taishoku shimashita.* (ご承知のように, 彼は先月退職しました) *As you know,* he retired last month.
shoochi suru (〜する) *vi.*
1 know; be aware (of); understand: *Sono koto wa* yoku shoochi shite imasu. (そのことはよく承知しています) I *am well aware* of that.
2 consent; agree; permit: *Chichi wa yatto watashi-no keekaku o* shoochi shite kureta. (父はやっと私の計画を承知してくれた) My father finally *agreed* to my plan.

sho⌈o-chiku⌉-bai しょうちくばい (松竹梅) *n.* pine, bamboo and

S

Japanese apricot. ★ These three plants are used together in making symbolic decorations on happy occasions. ⟪⇨ matsu[2]; take[1]; ume⟫

sho⌈ochoo[1] しょうちょう (象徴) *n.* symbol.
shoochoo suru (〜する) *vt.* symbolize.

sho˥ochoo[2] しょうちょう (小腸) *n.* the small intestine.

sho⌈odaku しょうだく (承諾) *n.* consent; agreement; permission; acceptance.
shoodaku suru (〜する) *vt.* consent; agree; permit; accept.

sho⌈odoku しょうどく (消毒) *n.* disinfection; sterilization.
shoodoku suru (〜する) *vt.* disinfect; sterilize: *kizuguchi o* shoodoku suru (傷口を消毒する) *disinfect* a wound.

sho⌈o-ene しょうエネ (省エネ) *n.* energy-saving.

sho⌈ogai[1] しょうがい (障害) *n.*
1 obstacle; obstruction; barrier: shoogai *ni butsukaru* (障害にぶつかる) encounter an *obstacle*.
2 defect; impediment: *Kare wa geñgo-*shoogai *ga aru.* (彼は言語障害がある) He has a speech *defect*.

sho˥ogai[2] しょうがい (生涯) *n.* one's whole life: *shiawase na* shoogai *o okuru* (幸せな生涯を送る) lead a happy *life*.

sho⌈oga˥kkoo しょうがっこう (小学校) *n.* elementary school. ⟪⇨ gakkoo⟫

sho⌈ogakukiñ しょうがくきん (奨学金) *n.* scholarship.

sho⌈oga˥kusee しょうがくせい (小学生) *n.* elementary school pupil; schoolchild. ⟪⇨ seeto⟫

sho⌈o ga na˥·i しょうがない *a.* (-ku) = shiyoo ga nai.

sho⌈ogatsu しょうがつ (正月) *n.* the New Year; January.

sho⌈ogi しょうぎ (将棋) *n.* Japanese chess.

sho˥ogo しょうご (正午) *n.* noon; midday. ⟪⇨ o-hiru⟫

sho⌈oguñ しょうぐん (将軍) *n.* general; shogun.

sho˥ogyoo しょうぎょう (商業) *n.* commerce; business: shoogyoo-*kookoo* (商業高校) a *commercial* high school.

sho⌈ohai しょうはい (勝敗) *n.* result of a game [battle]; victory or defeat.

sho⌈ohi しょうひ (消費) *n.* consumption; expenditure: shoohi-*zee* (消費税) a *consumption* tax.
shoohi suru (〜する) *vt.* consume; expend (time, energy, etc.). ⟪↔ seesañ⟫

sho˥ohiñ[1] しょうひん (商品) *n.* commodity; goods; merchandise. ⟪⇨ shinamono⟫

sho⌈ohiñ[2] しょうひん (賞品) *n.* prize; trophy.

sho⌈ohi˥sha しょうひしゃ (消費者) *n.* consumer. ⟪↔ seesañsha⟫

sho⌈oji しょうじ (障子) *n.* paper sliding door; shoji screen.

sho⌈oji˥ki しょうじき (正直) *n.* honesty; uprightness.
— *a.n.* (〜 na, ni) honest; frank; straightforward: *Hoñtoo no koto o* shoojiki *ni hanashite kudasai.* (本当のことを正直に話してください) Please speak the truth *frankly*.

sho⌈oji·ru しょうじる (生じる) *vi.* (shooji-te [V]) arise; happen; come about; result: *Gakusee no aida de fumañ ga* shoojita. (学生の間で不満が生じた) Discontent *arose* among the students.

sho˥ojo しょうじょ (少女) *n.* young [little] girl. ⟪↔ shooneñ⟫

sho⌈ojoo[1] しょうじょう (賞状) *n.* certificate of merit [commendation].

sho⌈ojo˥o[2] しょうじょう (症状) *n.* (disease) symptom; condition.

sho⌈oka[1] しょうか (消化) *n.* digestion.

S

shooka suru (～する) *vi., vt.* digest; assimilate.

sho⌈oka[2] しょうか (消火) *n.* fire extinguishing [fighting]:
shooka-ki (消火器) a *fire extinguisher* / shooka-señ (消火栓) a *fire hydrant.*
shooka suru (～する) *vt.* extinguish a fire; fight a fire.

sho⌈okai[1] しょうかい (紹介) *n.* introduction; presentation.
shookai suru (～する) *vt.* introduce; present.

sho⌉okai[2] しょうかい (商会) *n.* firm; company: *Sakamoto* shookai (坂本商会) Sakamoto & *Co.*

sho⌈oko しょうこ (証拠) *n.* proof; evidence:
shooko *o dasu* (証拠を出す) produce *evidence.*

sho⌈okyoku-teki しょうきょくてき (消極的) *a.n.* (～ na, ni) negative; passive. ⟪↔ sekkyoku-teki⟫

sho⌈omee[1] しょうめい (証明) *n.* proof; evidence; testimony:
shoomee-sho (証明書) a *certificate.*
shoomee suru (～する) *vt.* prove; testify; certify.

sho⌈omee[2] しょうめい (照明) *n.* lighting; illumination:
teñjihiñ ni shoomee *o ateru* (展示品に照明を当てる) direct a *light* onto an exhibit.
shoomee suru (～する) *vt.* light; illuminate.

sho⌈omeñ しょうめん (正面) *n.* the front; facade; the area in front. ⟪⇨ mae⟫

sho⌈omoo しょうもう (消耗) *n.* exhaustion; consumption.
shoomoo suru (～する) *vi., vt.* exhaust; consume.

sho⌈oneñ しょうねん (少年) *n.* (little) boy; lad. ⟪↔ shoojo⟫

sho⌈onika しょうにか (小児科) *n.* pediatrics:
shoonika-i (小児科医) a *pediatrician.*

sho⌈oniñ[1] しょうにん (承認) *n.* approval; recognition; permission:
shooniñ *o eru* [*morau*] (承認を得る[もらう]) get *permission.*
shooniñ suru (～する) *vt.* approve; recognize; permit. ⟪⇨ kyoka⟫

sho⌉oniñ[2] しょうにん (商人) *n.* merchant; tradesman; dealer; storekeeper; shopkeeper.

sho⌈oniñ[3] しょうにん (証人) *n.* witness.

sho⌈oniñ[4] しょうにん (昇任) *n.* promotion. ⟪⇨ shooshiñ⟫

sho⌉orai しょうらい (将来) *n.* future; the time [days] to come. ⟪⇨ mirai⟫

sho⌈oree しょうれい (奨励) *n.* encouragement.
shooree suru (～する) *vt.* encourage; recommend: *supootsu o* shooree suru (スポーツを奨励する) *encourages* sports.

sho⌉ori しょうり (勝利) *n.* victory: *attoo-teki na* shoori *o osameru* (圧倒的な勝利をおさめる) gain an overwhelming *victory.* ⟪↔ haiboku⟫

sho⌈oryaku しょうりゃく (省略) *n.* omission; abridgment; abbreviation. ⟪⇨ ryaku; ryakusu; tañshuku⟫
shooryaku suru (～する) *vt.* omit; abridge; abbreviate.

sho⌈oryo⌉o しょうりょう (少量) *n.* a small quantity [amount]. ⟪↔ tairyoo; taryoo⟫

sho⌈osai しょうさい (詳細) *n.* details; particulars:
Shoosai *wa ato de o-shirase shimasu.* (詳細は後でお知らせします) We will inform you of the *particulars* later on. ⟪↔ gaiyoo⟫
— *a.n.* (～ na, ni) detailed; particular; minute; full. ⟪⇨ kuwashii⟫

sho⌈osetsu しょうせつ (小説) *n.* novel; story; fiction:
shoosetsu-ka (小説家) a novelist.

sho⌉osha[1] しょうしゃ (商社) *n.* trading company; business firm.

sho⌉osha[2] しょうしゃ (勝者) *n.* winner; victor. ⟪↔ haisha[2]⟫

S

sho͞oshiñ しょうしん (昇進) *n.* promotion.
shooshiñ suru (～する) *vi.* be promoted.

sho͞oshoo しょうしょう (少々) *adv.* a little [few]; a moment [minute]:
Shooshoo *o-machi kudasai.* (少々お待ちください) Please wait *a moment.* ⟪⇨ sukoshi⟫

sho͞osu͞u[1] しょうすう (少数) *n.* a small number; minority. ⟪↔ tasuu⟫

sho͞osu͞u[2] しょうすう (小数) *n.* decimal: shoosuu-*teñ* (小数点) a *decimal* point.

sho͞otai[1] しょうたい (招待) *n.* invitation:
shootai *o ukeru* [*kotowaru*] (招待を受ける[断わる]) accept [decline] an *invitation.*
shootai suru (～する) *vt.* invite.

sho͞otai[2] しょうたい (正体) *n.* a person's true colors [character]; true nature.

sho͞oteñ[1] しょうてん (商店) *n.* store; shop. ⟪⇨ mise⟫

sho͞oteñ[2] しょうてん (焦点) *n.* focus:
shooteñ *ga atte iru* [*inai*] (焦点が合っている[いない]) be in [out of] *focus.*

sho͞otoo しょうとう (消灯) *n.* turning off the lights.
shootoo suru (～する) *vi.* turn off [put out] the lights.

sho͞ototsu しょうとつ (衝突) *n.*
1 collision; crash:
deñsha no shoototsu-*jiko* (電車の衝突事故) a *collision* between trains.
2 clash; conflict:
rigai no shoototsu (利害の衝突) a *clash* of interests.
shoototsu suru (～する) *vi.*
1 collide; run into; crash.
2 clash; conflict: *Guñshuu wa keekañ-tai to* shoototsu shita. (群衆は警官隊と衝突した) The crowd *clashed* with the police. ⟪⇨ butsukaru⟫

sho͞oyo しょうよ (賞与) *n.* bonus. ⟪⇨ boonasu⟫

sho͞oyu しょうゆ (醤油) *n.* soy sauce. ⟪⇨ miso⟫

sho͞ri しょり (処理) *n.* management; disposal; treatment.
shori suru (～する) *vt.* handle; deal with; manage.

sho͞rui しょるい (書類) *n.* document; papers.

sho͞sai しょさい (書斎) *n.* room for study.

sho͞tchuu しょっちゅう *adv.* (*informal*) always; very often. ⟪⇨ itsu-mo⟫

sho͞toku しょとく (所得) *n.* income; earnings:
shotoku-*zee* (所得税) an *income* tax.

sho͞yuu しょゆう (所有) *n.* possession; ownership:
shoyuu-butsu (所有物) one's *possessions* / shoyuu-sha (所有者) an *owner*.
shoyuu suru (～する) *vt.* possess; own. ⟪⇨ motsu⟫

sho͞zoku しょぞく (所属) *n.* one's position [post; place].
... ni shozoku suru (...に～する) *vi.* belong to; be attached to.

shu͞[1] しゅ (種) *n.* kind; sort; class; type:
Kono shu *no hoñ ga yoku urete imasu.* (この種の本がよく売れています) Books of this *kind* are selling well. ⟪⇨ shurui⟫

shu͞[2] しゅ (主) *n.* the chief [principal] thing:
Kono jigyoo wa kanemooke ga shu *de wa nai.* (この事業は金もうけが主ではない) It is not the *main purpose* of this enterprise to make money. ⟪⇨ shu to shite⟫

shu͞[3] しゅ (主) *n.* the Lord:
shu *Iesu Kirisuto* (主イエスキリスト) Jesus Christ, *Our Lord.*

-shu しゅ (酒) *suf.* alcoholic drink:
Nihoñ-shu (日本酒) Japanese *sake* / budoo-shu (ぶどう酒) *wine.*

shu͞bi しゅび (守備) *n.* defense; guard; fielding:
Ano señshu wa shubi *ga umai.* (あの

選手は守備がうまい) That player is good at *fielding*.
shubi suru (～する) *vi.* defend; guard. ⟪↔ koogeki⟫ ⟪⇨ mamoru⟫

shu⌈choo しゅちょう (主張) *n.* insistence; claim; assertion; opinion.
shuchoo suru (～する) *vt.* insist; maintain; claim: *jibuñ no keñri o* shuchoo suru (自分の権利を主張する) *assert* one's rights.

shu⌈dai しゅだい (主題) *n.* subject; theme:
shudai-*ka* (主題歌) a *theme* song.

shu⌉dañ しゅだん (手段) *n.* means; measures; step:
shudañ *o toru* (手段をとる) take a *step* [*measures*]. ⟪⇨ hoosaku[2]⟫

shu⌈ee しゅえい (守衛) *n.* guard; doorkeeper.

shu⌈eñ しゅえん (主演) *n.* having a leading role; the leading actor [actress].
shueñ suru (～する) *vi.* play the leading role; star.

shu⌉fu[1] しゅふ (主婦) *n.* housewife.

shu⌉fu[2] しゅふ (首府) *n.* capital; metropolis. ⟪⇨ shuto⟫

shu⌉gi しゅぎ (主義) *n.* principle; doctrine:
Kare wa jibuñ no shugi *o magenakatta.* (彼は自分の主義を曲げなかった) He did not deviate from his *principles*.

shu⌉go しゅご (主語) *n.* (of grammar) subject of a sentence.

shu⌉jiñ しゅじん (主人) *n.* **1** storekeeper; employer; owner.
2 husband. ★ *shujiñ*＝one's own husband; *go-shujiñ*＝someone else's husband. ⟪⇨ otto⟫

shu⌉ju しゅじゅ (種々) *n.* many kinds; various. ⟪⇨ iroiro[1]⟫

shu⌉jutsu しゅじゅつ (手術) *n.* operation. ★ Often pronounced '*shijitsu*.'
shujutsu (o) suru (～(を)する) *vt.* operate; be operated on.

shu⌈kañ しゅかん (主観) *n.* subjectivity.

shu⌈kañ-teki しゅかんてき (主観的) *a.n.* (～ na, ni) subjective:
Kare wa shukañ-teki *na ikeñ o nobeta.* (彼は主観的な意見を述べた) He gave his *subjective* opinion. ⟪↔ kyakkañ-teki⟫

shu⌈kketsu しゅっけつ (出血) *n.* bleeding; hemorrhage:
shukketsu *o tomeru* (出血を止める) stop the *bleeding*.
shukketsu suru (～する) *vt.* bleed.

shu⌈kkiñ しゅっきん (出勤) *n.* going to work; attendance.
shukkiñ suru (～する) *vt.* go to work; go [come] to the office.

shu⌈kkoku しゅっこく (出国) *n.* departure from a country:
shukkoku-*tetsuzuki* (出国手続き) *departure* formalities.
shukkoku suru (～する) *vt.* leave a country; get out of a country. ⟪↔ nyuukoku⟫

shu⌈kudai しゅくだい (宿題) *n.*
1 homework; assignment.
2 open [pending] question:
Kono moñdai wa tsugi no kai made shukudai ni shite okimashoo. (この問題は次の会まで宿題にしておきましょう) *Let's leave* this matter *as it is* until the next meeting.

shu⌈kujitsu しゅくじつ (祝日) *n.* national [legal; public] holiday. ⟪⇨ APP. 6⟫

shu⌈kusa⌉ijitsu しゅくさいじつ (祝祭日) *n.* national [public] holiday; red-letter day; festival.
★ Combination of '*shukujitsu*' (祝日) and '*saijitsu*' (祭日).

shu⌈kushoo しゅくしょう (縮小) *n.* reduction; curtailment.
shukushoo suru (～する) *vt.* reduce; curtail: *guñbi o* shukushoo suru (軍備を縮小する) *reduce* armaments. ⟪↔ kakudai⟫

shu⌈ku⌉s·u しゅくす (祝す) *n.* (shukush·i-; shukus·a-; shukush·i-te Ⓒ) (*formal*) congratulate; celebrate. ⟪⇨ iwau⟫

shu⌉mi しゅみ (趣味) *n.* **1** hobby; pastime; interest.
2 taste:

S

Kanojo wa kiru mono no shumi *ga ii [warui].* (彼女は着る物の趣味がいい[悪い]) She has fine [poor] *taste* in clothes.

shu⌈niñ しゅにん (主任) *n.* head; chief; boss: *kaikee*-shuniñ (会計主任) the *chief* accountant.

shu⌈ñkañ しゅんかん (瞬間) *n.* moment; instant:
Sore wa shuñkañ *no dekigoto datta.* (それは瞬間の出来事だった) It was something that happened in an *instant.*
...(shita) shuñkañ (...(した)〜) the moment (one has done...): *Hako no futa o aketa* shuñkañ *bakuhatsu shita.* (箱のふたを開けた瞬間爆発した) *The moment* I took off the lid, the box exploded.

shu⌉ñki しゅんき (春季) *n.* spring; springtime. ⇨ kaki[3]; shuuki[2]; tooki[4]

shu⌈ppañ[1] しゅっぱん (出版) *n.* publication; publishing:
shuppañ-*sha* (出版社) a *publishing* company; a *publisher.*
shuppañ suru (〜する) *vt.* publish; issue. ⇨ dasu (3); deru (11)

shu⌈ppañ[2] しゅっぱん (出帆) *n.* sailing; departure.
shuppañ suru (〜する) *vi.* set sail; leave; depart.

shu⌈ppatsu しゅっぱつ (出発) *n.* departure; start.
shuppatsu suru (〜する) *vi.* leave; start; depart; set out. ⟪↔ toochaku⟫ ⇨ deru (1)

shu⌈ppiñ しゅっぴん (出品) *n.* exhibition; display.
shuppiñ suru (〜する) *vt.* exhibit; display.

shu⌉rui しゅるい (種類) *n.* kind; sort; variety: ⇨ rui; shu[1]
Kore wa nañ to iu shurui *no inu desu ka?* (これは何という種類の犬ですか) What *kind* of dog is this?

shu⌈sai しゅさい (主催) *n.* sponsorship; promotion:
shusai-sha (主催者) a *sponsor*; a *promoter.*
shusai suru (〜する) *vt.* organize; sponsor; host.

shu⌉shi しゅし (趣旨) *n.* aim; object; point:
O-hanashi no shushi *wa yoku wakarimashita.* (お話しの趣旨はよくわかりました) I've understood the *point* of what you are saying.

shu⌈shoku しゅしょく (主食) *n.* staple food.

shu⌈shoo しゅしょう (首相) *n.* prime minister; premier. ⇨ Soori-daijiñ

shu⌈ssañ しゅっさん (出産) *n.* birth; childbirth; delivery.
shussañ suru (〜する) *vi., vt.* give birth. ⇨ umu[1]

shu⌈sse しゅっせ (出世) *n.* success in life; promotion.
shusse suru (〜する) *vi.* succeed in life; be promoted. ⇨ risshiñ-shusse

shu⌈ssee しゅっせい (出生) *n.* birth: ★ Also pronounced '*shusshoo.*'
shussee-chi (出生地) a *birthplace.*

shu⌈sseki しゅっせき (出席) *n.* presence; attendance.
shusseki suru (〜する) *vt.* attend; be present. ⟪↔ kesseki⟫ ⇨ deru (3)

shu⌈sshiñ しゅっしん (出身) *n.*
1 the place where one was born:
Kare wa Kyooto no shusshiñ *desu.* (彼は京都の出身です) He *comes from* Kyoto.
2 graduate:
Watashi wa kono daigaku no shusshiñ *desu.* (私はこの大学の出身です) I am a *graduate* of this university.

shu⌈sshoo しゅっしょう (出生) *n.* birth. ⇨ shussee

shu⌈tai しゅたい (主体) *n.* main constituent; core:
Sono chiimu wa wakai hito ga shutai ni natte imasu. (そのチームは若い人が主体になっています) The team *is made up mainly* of young players.

shu⌈tchoo しゅっちょう (出張) *n.* business [official] trip.

S

shutchoo suru (～する) *vi.* make a business [an official] trip.

shu'to しゅと (首都) *n.* capital; metropolis:
shuto-*keñ* (首都圏) *Tokyo* and the surrounding region / shuto-*koo-soku-dooro* (首都高速道路) the *Metropolitan* Expressway.

shu'toku しゅとく (取得) *n.* (*formal*) acquisition.
shutoku suru (～する) *vt.* acquire; obtain; get possession of.
《⇨ toru[1]》

shu' to shite しゅとして (主として) *adv.* mainly; chiefly; mostly:
Kaiiñ wa shu to shite *shufu desu.* (会員は主として主婦です) The members are *mostly* housewives.

shu'tsueñ しゅつえん (出演) *n.* appearance (on TV, the stage, etc.).
shutsueñ suru (～する) *vi.* appear; perform.

shu'tsujoo しゅつじょう (出場) *n.* participation; entry:
shutsujoo-sha (出場者) a *participant*; a *contestant*.
shutsujoo suru (～する) *vi.* take part in; participate in.

shu'u[1] しゅう (週) *n.* week.

shu'u[2] しゅう (州) *n.* state (of the U.S., Australia, etc.); county.

shu'uchaku しゅうちゃく (執着) *n.* attachment; adherance.
... ni shuuchaku suru (...に～する) *vi.* adhere to; be attached to:
jibuñ no añ ni saigo made shuuchaku suru (自分の案に最後まで執着する) *adhere* to one's own plan till the last.

shu'uchaku'-eki しゅうちゃくえき (終着駅) *n.* terminal station.

shu'uchuu しゅうちゅう (集中) *n.* concentration:
shuuchuu-*goou* (集中豪雨) a *localized* torrential downpour.
shuuchuu suru (～する) *vi., vt.* concentrate; focus; center.
《↔ buñsañ》

shu'udañ しゅうだん (集団) *n.* group; mass:
shuudañ *o tsukuru* (集団を作る) form a *group*.

shu'ude'ñ(sha) しゅうでん(しゃ) (終電(車)) *n.* the last train of the day. 《↔ shihatsu》

shu'ugeki しゅうげき (襲撃) *n.* attack; assault; raid.
shuugeki suru (～する) *vt.* raid; attack.

Shu'ugi'iñ しゅうぎいん (衆議院) *n.* the House of Representatives:
Shuugiiñ *giiñ* (衆議院議員) a member of the *House of Representatives.* 《⇨ Sañgiiñ; kokkai》

shu'ugoo しゅうごう (集合) *n.*
1 gathering; meeting; assembly:
shuugoo-*jikañ* [-*basho*] (集合時間[場所]) the *meeting* time [place].
2 (of mathematics) set:
shuugoo-*roñ* (集合論) *set* theory.
shuugoo suru (～する) *vi.* gather; meet; assemble. 《⇨ atsumaru》

shu'uheñ しゅうへん (周辺) *n.* vicinity; neighborhood; outskirts.
《⇨ mawari》

shu'ui しゅうい (周囲) *n.* **1** circumference. 《⇨ mawari》
2 surroundings; circumstances:
Shuui *ga urusakute, beñkyoo ga dekinakatta.* (周囲がうるさくて, 勉強ができなかった) I couldn't devote myself to my study because of the noisy *surroundings*.

shu'ukai しゅうかい (集会) *n.* meeting; assembly; gathering.

shu'ukaku しゅうかく (収穫) *n.* crop; harvest.
shuukaku suru (～する) *vt.* harvest; crop.

shu'ukañ[1] しゅうかん (習慣) *n.* habit; custom; practice:
Hayaku okiru no wa yoi shuukañ *desu.* (早く起きるのは良い習慣です) It is a good *habit* to get up early.

shu'ukañ[2] しゅうかん (週間) *n.* week:
Kootsuu Añzeñ Shuukañ (交通安全週間) Traffic Safety *Week*.

shu'uka'ñshi しゅうかんし (週刊誌) *n.* weekly magazine.

shu|uki[1] しゅうき (周期) *n.* cycle; period:
keeki no shuuki (景気の周期) a business [trade] *cycle.*

shu|uki[2] しゅうき (秋季) *n.* fall; autumn. ((⇨ kaki[3]; shuñki; tooki[4]))

-shu|uki しゅうき (周忌) *suf.* anniversary of a person's death:
*Kyoo wa haha no sañ-*shuuki *desu.* (きょうは母の 3 周忌です) Today is the third *anniversary* of our mother's death.

shu|ukiñ しゅうきん (集金) *n.* collection of money.
shuukiñ suru (〜する) *vt.* collect money.

shu|uki-teki しゅうきてき (周期的) *a.n.* (〜 na, ni) periodical:
Kono kazañ wa shuuki-teki *ni bakuhatsu shimasu.* (この火山は周期的に爆発します) This volcano erupts *periodically.*

shu|ukyoo しゅうきょう (宗教) *n.* religion: shuukyoo *o shiñjiru* (宗教を信じる) believe in *religion.*

shu|umatsu しゅうまつ (週末) *n.* weekend. ((⇨ heejitsu))

-shu|uneñ しゅうねん (周年) *suf.* anniversary: ★ Used for a happy event.
is-shuuneñ *kineñbi* (一周年記念日) the first *anniversary.*

shu|uniñ しゅうにん (就任) *n.* assumption of office; inauguration.
shuuniñ suru (〜する) *vi.* take office; assume.

shu|unyuu しゅうにゅう (収入) *n.* income; earnings; revenue. ((↔ shishutsu)) ((⇨ kasegi))

shu|unyuu-i|ñshi しゅうにゅういんし (収入印紙) *n.* revenue stamp. ★ Often called '*iñshi*,' and put on a bond, deed, etc.

shu|uri しゅうり (修理) *n.* repair; mending.
shuuri suru (〜する) *vt.* repair; mend; fix: *ie o* shuuri suru (家を修理する) *repair* a house.

shu|uryoo しゅうりょう (終了) *n.* end; close.
shuuryoo suru (〜する) *vi., vt.* end; close. ((↔ kaishi)) ((⇨ owaru))

shu|usee[1] しゅうせい (修正) *n.* amendment; revision; modification.
shuusee suru (〜する) *vt.* amend; revise; modify; correct.

shu|usee[2] しゅうせい (習性) *n.* habit; behavior:
saru no shuusee *o keñkyuu suru* (猿の習性を研究する) study the *behavior* of monkeys.

shu|usha しゅうしゃ (終車) *n.* the last train [bus]. ((↔ shihatsu))

shu|ushi[1] しゅうし (収支) *n.* incomings and outgoings; revenue and expenditure. ((⇨ shuunyuu; shishutsu))

shu|ushi[2] しゅうし (終始) *adv.* from beginning to end; throughout.
shuushi suru (〜する) *vi.* remain the same from beginning to end.

shu|ushoku しゅうしょく (就職) *n.* finding employment.
... ni shuushoku suru (...に〜する) *vi.* find work at; get a position at.

shu|ushokugo しゅうしょくご (修飾語) *n.* (of grammar) modifier; qualifier.

shu|ushuu しゅうしゅう (収集) *n.* collection.
shuushuu suru (〜する) *vt.* collect: *kitte o* shuushuu suru (切手を収集する) *collect* stamps. ((⇨ atsumeru))

shu|uteñ しゅうてん (終点) *n.* terminal station; terminus. ((↔ kiteñ))

shu|utoku|butsu しゅうとくぶつ (拾得物) *n.* article found; find. ((⇨ hirou))

shu|uyoo しゅうよう (収容) *n.* accommodation; seating.
shuuyoo suru (〜する) *vt.* accommodate; admit.

shu|uzeñ しゅうぜん (修繕) *n.* = shuuri.

shu|yaku しゅやく (主役) *n.* the leading part [role]; lead.

s

shu⌈yoo しゅよう(主要) *a.n.* (～ na) important; chief; principal; main:
shuyoo-*sañgyoo* (主要産業) *major* industries / shuyoo-*toshi* (主要都市) *chief* cities.

so⌉ba[1] そば(側) *n.* **1** side:
Sono ko wa haha-oya no soba *kara hanareyoo to shinakatta.* (その子は母親のそばから離れようとしなかった) The child wouldn't leave his mother's *side.*
2 (～ ni) next to; near; beside:
Chuushajoo wa eki no soba *ni arimasu.* (駐車場は駅のそばにあります) The parking lot is *next to* the station.

so⌉ba[2] そば(蕎麦) *n.* buckwheat (noodles).

so⌈bie⌉·ru そびえる(聳える) *vi.* (sobie-te [V]) rise; tower:
Me no mae ni sobiete iru *no ga Komagatake desu.* (目の前にそびえているのが駒ヶ岳です) That mountain *rising high* before us is Mt. Komagatake.

so⌉bo そぼ(祖母) *n.* one's grandmother. ⟪↔ sofu⟫ ⟪⇨ o-baasañ⟫

so⌈boku そぼく(素朴) *a.n.* (～ na, ni) simple; unsophisticated:
soboku *na hitogara* (素朴な人柄) an *unsophisticated* personality.

so⌈chira そちら *n.* ★ More polite than '*sotchi*.'
1 there; over there: ★ Refers to a direction or a place close to the listener.
Sochira *ga deguchi desu.* (そちらが出口です) *That way* is the exit.
2 that one; the other one: ★ Refers to something closer to the listener than the speaker.
Sochira *no o misete itadakemasu ka?* (そちらのを見せていただけますか) May I take a look at *that* one?
3 you; your side:
Sochira *no tsugoo no yoi toki ni itsu de mo oide kudasai.* (そちらの都合の良いときにいつでもおいでください) Please come any time when it is convenient to *you.* ⟪⇨ achira; kochira⟫

so⌈dachi⌉ そだち(育ち) *n.*
1 growth:
Kotoshi wa ine no sodachi *ga yoku nai.* (ことしは稲の育ちが良くない) This year the *growth* of rice is not good. ⟪⇨ sodatsu⟫
2 upbringing; breeding:
Watashi wa Tookyoo sodachi *desu.* (私は東京育ちです) I *grew up* in Tokyo. ⟪⇨ sodatsu⟫

so⌈date⌉·ru そだてる(育てる) *vt.* (sodate-te [V]) bring up; raise; cultivate; train:
Kare wa ooku no yuushuu na señshu o sodateta. (彼は多くの優秀な選手を育てた) He *has trained* many excellent players. ⟪⇨ sodatsu⟫

so⌈da⌉ts·u そだつ(育つ) *vi.* (sodach·i-; sodat·a-; sodat-te [C]) grow (up):
Riñgo wa koko de wa sodachimaseñ. (りんごはここでは育ちません) Apples *do not grow* here. ⟪⇨ sodateru; sodachi⟫

so⌈de そで(袖) *n.* sleeve.

so⌈e·ru そえる(添える) *vt.* (soe-te [V]) attach; add; garnish:
Okurimono ni tegami o soeta. (贈り物に手紙を添えた) I *attached* a letter to the gift.

so⌉fu そふ(祖父) *n.* one's grandfather.

so⌈futo-kuri⌉imu ソフトクリーム *n.* soft ice-cream (in a cone).

so⌈kku⌉ri そっくり *a.n.* (～ na/no, ni) similar; like:
Kanojo wa haha-oya ni sokkuri *desu.* (彼女は母親にそっくりです) She is *exactly like* her mother.
— *adv.* all; wholly; entirely:
Mochimono o sokkuri *nusumareta.* (持ち物をそっくり盗まれた) I had *all* my things stolen.

so⌈ko[1] そこ *n.* **1** that place; there: ★ Refers to a place near the listener and slightly distant from the speaker.
Suutsukeesu wa soko *ni oite kuda-*

sai. (スーツケースはそこに置いてください) Leave the suitcase *there*, please. ⟪⇨ asoko; doko; koko[1]⟫

2 there: ★ Refers to a place previously mentioned.
Saisho wa Oosaka e iki, soko *kara Okayama e ikimasu.* (最初は大阪へ行き, そこから岡山へ行きます) First I go to Osaka, and from *there* to Okayama.

3 that: ★ Refers to a subject mentioned by the listener.
Soko *no tokoro o moo ichido itte kudasai.* (そこの所をもう一度言ってください) Will you please repeat *what* you have just said?

4 then; when: ★ Refers to a particular time.
Dekakeyoo to shitara, soko *e deñwa ga kakatte kita.* (出かけようとしたら, そこへ電話がかかってきた) I was just going out, *when* the telephone rang.

so⌈ko² そこ (底) *n.* **1** bottom: *baketsu no* soko (バケツの底) the *bottom* of a bucket.

2 sole:
Kutsu ni atarashii soko *o tsukete moratta.* (靴に新しい底をつけてもらった) I had new *soles* put on my shoes.

so⌈ko de そこで *conj.* so; therefore. ★ Used at the beginning of a sentence.

so⌈kona⌉·u そこなう (損なう) *vt.* (sokona·i-; sokonaw·a-; sokonat-te Ⓒ) spoil; ruin; injure:
keñkoo o sokonau (健康を損なう) *ruin* one's health.

-sokona⌉·u そこなう (損なう) (-sokona·i-; -sokonaw·a-; -sokonat-te Ⓒ) miss; fail to (do): ★ Occurs as the second element of compound verbs. Added to the continuative base of a verb.
deñsha ni nori-sokonau (電車に乗りそこなう) *miss* a train.

so⌈ko⌉ra そこら *n.* **1** around there:
Megane nara, sokora *ni aru hazu desu.* (眼鏡なら, そこらにあるはずです) As for your glasses, they should be somewhere *around there.*

2 all over the place:
Karada ga sokora*-juu itai.* (体がそこらじゅう痛い) I have aches and pains *all over* my body.

3 approximately; or so:
Sono kamera nara, sañmañ-eñ ka sokora *de te ni hairimasu.* (そのカメラなら, 3万円かそこらで手に入ります) That camera is available at 30,000 yen *or so.*

-soku そく (足) *suf.* counter for footgear. ⟪⇨ APP. 4⟫

so⌈kubaku そくばく (束縛) *n.* restraint; restriction.
sokubaku suru (～する) *vt.* restrain; restrict: *geñroñ no jiyuu o* sokubaku suru (言論の自由を束縛する) *restrict* freedom of speech.

so⌈kudo そくど (速度) *n.* speed; velocity. ⟪⇨ sokuryoku; supiido⟫

so⌈kumeñ そくめん (側面) *n.* side; flank: sokumeñ *kara kare o eñjo suru* (側面から彼を援助する) help him *indirectly.*

so⌈kuoñ そくおん (促音) *n.* doubled consonant. ★ Represented in writing by a small '*tsu*' (っ). *e.g.* itta (行った). ⟪⇨ APP. 1⟫

so⌈ku⌉ryoku そくりょく (速力) *n.* speed:
*zeñ-*sokuryoku *de hashiru* (全速力で走る) run at full *speed.* ⟪⇨ sokudo; supiido⟫

so⌈kuryoo そくりょう (測量) *n.* survey; measurement.
sokuryoo suru (～する) *vt.* make a survey; measure.

so⌈kushiñ そくしん (促進) *n.* promotion; furtherance.
sokushiñ suru (～する) *vt.* promote; further; hasten: *booeki o* sokushiñ suru (貿易を促進する) *encourage* foreign trade.

so⌈kutatsu そくたつ (速達) *n.* special [express] delivery.

so⌈kutee そくてい (測定) *n.* measurement.
sokutee suru (～する) *vt.* mea-

sure; check: *kuruma no hayasa o* sokutee suru (車の速さを測定する) *measure* the speed of a car.

so⌈mar·u そまる(染まる) *vi.* (so-mar·i-; somar·a-; somat-te Ⓒ)
1 dye; be tinged:
Kono kiji wa yoku somaru. (この生地はよく染まる) This cloth *takes dye* well. ⟪⇨ someru⟫
2 be adversely influenced (by one's surroundings).

so⌉matsu そまつ(粗末) *a.n.* (～ na, ni) **1** poor; plain; humble:
somatsu *na shokuji o suru* (粗末な食事をする) have a *frugal* meal.
2 careless; rough; rude:
hoñ o somatsu *ni atsukau* (本を粗末に扱う) handle books *roughly*.

so⌈me·ru そめる(染める) *vt.* (some-te Ⓥ) dye; tinge:
Kanojo wa kami o chairo ni someta. (彼女は髪を茶色に染めた) She *dyed* her hair brown. ⟪⇨ somaru⟫

so⌈mu⌉k·u そむく(背く) *vi.* (so-muk·i-; somuk·a-; somu·i-te Ⓒ) disobey; disregard; violate:
Kare wa ryooshiñ no kitai ni somuite, *shikeñ ni shippai shita.* (彼は両親の期待に背いて, 試験に失敗した) *Contrary to* his parents' hopes, he failed the exam.

so⌉ñ そん(損) *n.* loss.
soñ (o) suru (～(を)する) *vt.* lose; suffer a loss.
— *a.n.* (～ na, ni) disadvantageous. ⟪↔ toku[2]⟫ ⟪⇨ soñshitsu⟫

so⌈nae⌉ そなえ(備え) *n.* preparations; provision; defense. ⟪⇨ sonaeru[1]⟫

so⌈nae⌉·ru[1] そなえる(備える) *vt.* (sonae-te Ⓥ) **1** prepare; provide:
Roogo ni sonaete *chokiñ shite imasu.* (老後に備えて貯金しています) I am saving up *for* my old age. ⟪⇨ sonae⟫
2 equip; furnish:
Kono kyooshitsu ni wa koñpyuutaa ga sonaete arimasu. (この教室にはコンピューターが備えてあります) Computers *are installed* in this classroom.

so⌈nae⌉·ru[2] そなえる(供える) *vt.* (sonae-te Ⓥ) offer:
Watashi wa kare no haka ni hana o sonaeta. (私は彼の墓に花を供えた) I *offered* flowers at his grave.

so⌈naetsuke そなえつけ(備え付け) *n.* equipment; fittings:
Doozo sonaetsuke *no shokki o o-tsukai kudasai.* (どうぞ備え付けの食器をお使いください) Please feel free to use the tableware *kept here*. ⟪⇨ sonaetsukeru⟫

so⌈naetsuke⌉·ru そなえつける(備え付ける) *vt.* (-tsuke-te Ⓥ) provide; furnish; equip; install:
Kono heya ni wa hitsuyoo na kagu ga subete sonaetsukete aru. (この部屋には必要な家具がすべて備え付けてある) This room *is* fully *equipped* with all the necessary furniture. ⟪⇨ sonaetsuke⟫

so⌈ñchoo[1] そんちょう(尊重) *n.* respect; high regard; esteem.
★ The grammatical object is usually inanimate.
soñchoo suru (～する) *vt.* respect; make much of. ⟪⇨ soñkee⟫

so⌉ñchoo[2] そんちょう(村長) *n.* village chief; the head of a village.

so⌈ñdai そんだい(尊大) *a.n.* (～ na, ni) arrogant; haughty; self-important:
Kare no soñdai *na taido ni hara ga tatta.* (彼の尊大な態度に腹がたった) I got angry at his *arrogant* attitude.

so⌈ñgai そんがい(損害) *n.* damage; loss:
Taifuu wa sono machi ni ooki-na soñgai *o ataeta.* (台風はその町に大きな損害を与えた) The typhoon caused great *damage* to the town.

so⌈ñkee そんけい(尊敬) *n.* respect; esteem; reverence. ★ The grammatical object is usually a person or the actions of a person.
soñkee suru (～する) *vt.* respect; esteem. ⟪⇨ soñchoo[1]⟫

so⌈ñna そんな *attrib.* **1** such; like that: ★ Refers to something men-

tioned or done by the listener.
Soñna *kanashi-soo na kao o shinai de kudasai.* (そんな悲しそうな顔をしないでください) Please don't put on *such* a sad look.
2 that; such: ★ Refers to something mentioned by the listener.
"Kare wa shutchoo-chuu desu." "Soñna *hazu wa arimaseñ."* (「彼は出張中です」「そんなはずはありません」) "He is on a business trip." "*That* cannot be true." ⟪⇨ añna; doñna; koñna⟫

so⌈ñna ni そんなに *adv.* that; like that; such; so:
Soñna ni *isogu hitsuyoo wa arimaseñ.* (そんなに急ぐ必要はありません) You needn't be in *such* a hurry.
⟪⇨ añna ni; doñna ni; koñna ni⟫

so⌈no その *attrib.* **1** the; that:
★ Refers to something which is located away from the speaker and close to the listener.
Sono *shio o totte kudasai.* (その塩をとってください) Could you pass me *the* salt, please.
2 the; that; it: ★ Refers to a person or thing just mentioned.
"Uchi wa eki no sugu soba desu." "Sono *eki wa kyuukoo mo tomarimasu ka?"* (「家は駅のすぐそばです」「その駅は急行も止まりますか」) "My house is near the station." "Do the expresses also stop at *that* station?" ⟪⇨ ano; dono; kono⟫

so⌈no-aida そのあいだ (その間) *adv.* during the time; in the meantime; all the while. ⟪⇨ aida⟫

so⌈no⌉-hoka そのほか (その他) *n.* the rest; the others:
Sono-hoka *no koto wa watashi ga yarimasu.* (そのほかのことは私がやります) I will do *the rest.*
— *adv.* (~ ni) else; besides:
Sono-hoka (*ni*) *nani-ka shitsumoñ wa arimasu ka?* (そのほか(に)何か質問はありますか) Are there *any other* questions? ⟪⇨ hoka⟫

so⌈no-mama そのまま (その儘) *n.*
1 the present state [situation]; as it is [stands]:
Kañja wa sono-mama *nekasete oite kudasai.* (患者はそのまま寝かせておいてください) Please leave the patient sleeping *as he is.* ⟪⇨ mama[1]⟫
2 immediately:
Kodomo wa gakkoo kara kaeru to sono-mama *asobi ni dekaketa.* (子どもは学校から帰るとそのまま遊びに出かけた) The child came home from school and *immediately* went out to play. ⟪⇨ mama[1]⟫

so⌈no-uchi そのうち (その内) *adv.* (~ ni) soon; before long; someday; sometime:
Sono-uchi *ame mo agaru deshoo.* (そのうち雨も上がるでしょう) The rain should let up *soon.*

so⌈no ue そのうえ (その上) *conj.* besides; moreover:
Kare wa yokubari de, sono ue *kechi datta.* (彼は欲張りで, その上けちだった) He was greedy, and *besides* he was stingy.

so⌈ñshitsu そんしつ (損失) *n.* loss: soñshitsu *o ataeru* [*koomuru*] (損失を与える[被る]) cause [suffer] a *loss.* ⟪⇨ soñ⟫

so⌈ñzai そんざい (存在) *n.* existence; presence; being.
soñzai suru (~する) *vi.* exist.

so⌉o[1] そう *adv.* **1** yes; no:
★ Used to express agreement with a question, regardless of whether it is affirmative or negative.
"Anata wa Doitsu no kata desu ka?" "Soo desu." (「あなたはドイツの方ですか」「そうです」) "Are you German?" "*That's right.*" / *"Anata wa o-sake o nomimaseñ ne?"* "Soo *desu. Zeñzeñ nomimaseñ."* (「あなたはお酒を飲みませんね」「そうです. 全然飲みません」) "You don't drink, do you?" "*That's right.* I don't drink at all."
2 so; like that; in that way:
Watashi wa soo *omoimasu.* (私はそう思います) I think *so.* ⟪⇨ aa[1]; doo[1]; koo⟫

so˥o[2] そう *n.* they say; I hear; I understand: ★ Preceded by a non-polite style predicate in either the present or past tense.
Yamada-sañ wa teñkiñ ni naru soo desu. (山田さんは転勤になるそうです) *I hear* that Mr. Yamada is to be transferred. ⟪⇨ mitai; rashii; yoo[2]⟫

so˥o[3] そう *int.* really; good:
*"Kuji ni atatta yo." "*Soo, *yokatta ne."* (「くじに当たったよ」「そう, よかったね」) "I won in the lottery." "*Really?* That's great!"

so˥o[4] そう(層) *n.* **1** layer; stratum: *gañseki no* soo (岩石の層) a rock *stratum.*
2 class; bracket:
chishiki-soo (知識層) the *intelligentsia* / *kooshotokusha*-soo (高所得者層) the high income *bracket.*

so˥o- そう(総) *pref.* all; general; total: soo-*señkyo* (総選挙) a *general* election / soo-*jiñkoo* (総人口) the *total* population.

-soo そう *suf.* (*a.n.*) (~ na, ni) look; seem; appear: ★ Attached to the continuative base of a verb, or the stem of an adjective, or to an adjectival noun. The adjectives '*yoi*' and '*nai*' take the form '*yosa-soo*' and '*nasa-soo.*'
Ame ga furi-soo da. (雨が降りそうだ) *It looks like rain.*

so˥oba そうば(相場) *n.* **1** market price; rate.
2 speculation:
Sooba *de soñ o shita.* (相場で損をした) I have lost money in *speculation.*

so˥ochi そうち(装置) *n.* device; equipment; apparatus:
Sono heya ni wa dañboo-soochi *ga nakatta.* (その部屋には暖房装置がなかった) There was no *kind of heating* in the room.

so˥odañ そうだん(相談) *n.* talks; consultation; conference.
soodañ suru (~する) *vi., vt.* talk; consult; confer. ⟪⇨ kyoogi[2]⟫

so˥odeñ そうでん(送電) *n.* transmission of electricity; power supply.
soodeñ suru (~する) *vt.* transmit [supply] electricity.

so˥odoo そうどう(騒動) *n.* disturbance; trouble; riot:
soodoo *o okosu* (騒動を起こす) make a *disturbance.*

so˥ogeñ そうげん(草原) *n.* grasslands; plain.

so˥ogo そうご(相互) *n.* mutual; reciprocal:
soogo *no rikai o fukameru* (相互の理解を深める) promote *mutual* understanding. ⟪⇨ tagai⟫

so˥ogo-no˥riire そうごのりいれ(相互乗り入れ) *n.* mutual use of each other's railroad tracks; mutual trackage agreement.

so˥ogoo そうごう(総合) *n.* synthesis; generalization.
soogoo suru (~する) *vt.* put together; synthesize.

so˥oi[1] そうい(相違) *n.* difference; divergence:
ikeñ no sooi (意見の相違) a *difference* of opinion.
sooi suru (~する) *vi.* differ; diverge. ⟪⇨ chigau; kotonaru⟫

so˥oi[2] そうい(総意) *n.* the general opinion [will]; the consensus.

so˥o-iu そういう *attrib.* **1** such; like that; that kind of: ★ Refers to something mentioned by the listener.
*"Kinoo Maruyama-sañ to iu kata ga tazunete kimashita." "*Soo-iu *hito wa shirimaseñ."* (「きのう丸山さんという方が訪ねて来ました」「そういう人は知りません」) "A Mrs. Maruyama came to see you yesterday." "I don't know *such* a person."
2 that: ★ Refers to what the speaker previously mentioned.
Soo-iu *wake de kyoo no kaigi ni wa shusseki dekimaseñ.* (そういう訳できょうの会議には出席できません) *That*'s why I am unable to attend today's meeting. ⟪⇨ aa-iu; doo-iu; koo-iu⟫

so⸢oji そうじ(掃除) *n.* cleaning.
sooji (o) suru (〜(を)する) *vt.* clean; sweep; dust. ⟪⇨ seesoo⟫

so⸢oji⸣ki そうじき(掃除機) *n.* (vacuum) cleaner.

so⸢ojuu そうじゅう(操縦) *n.* operation; maneuvering.
soojuu suru (〜する) *vt.* operate; pilot; fly; steer: *hikooki [fune] o* soojuu suru (飛行機[船]を操縦する) *pilot* a plane [ship].

so⸢okai そうかい(総会) *n.* general meeting:
kabunushi-sookai *o hiraku* (株主総会を開く) hold a *general meeting* of stockholders.

so⸢okiñ そうきん(送金) *n.* remittance of money.
sookiñ suru (〜する) *vi.* send money; remit.

so⸣oko そうこ(倉庫) *n.* warehouse; storehouse.

so⸢o-oñ そうおん(騒音) *n.* noise; din.

so⸣ori そうり(総理) *n.* abbreviation for '*Soori-daijiñ*.'
Soori-*fu* (総理府) the *Prime Minister*'s Office.

So⸢ori-da⸣ijiñ そうりだいじん(総理大臣) *n.* Prime Minister; Premier.

so⸢oritsu そうりつ(創立) *n.* establishment; foundation.
sooritsu suru (〜する) *vt.* establish; found.

so⸢oryo⸣oji そうりょうじ(総領事) *n.* consul general.

so⸢oryooji⸣kañ そうりょうじかん(総領事館) *n.* consulate general:
Nihoñ sooryoojikañ (日本総領事館) the Japanese *Consulate General*.

so⸣osa[1] そうさ(捜査) *n.* criminal investigation; search; manhunt.
soosa suru (〜する) *vt.* investigate. ⟪⇨ shiraberu⟫

so⸣osa[2] そうさ(操作) *n.* operation; handling; manipulation.
soosa suru (〜する) *vt.* operate (a machine); handle; manipulate.

so⸢osaku[1] そうさく(創作) *n.* creation; original work; novel.
soosaku suru (〜する) *vt.* create; originate; write.

so⸢osaku[2] そうさく(捜索) *n.* search; manhunt.
soosaku suru (〜する) *vt.* make a search.

so⸢oshiki そうしき(葬式) *n.* funeral (service): ★ Often '*o-sooshiki*.'
sooshiki *o suru [itonamu]* (葬式をする[営む]) perform a *funeral service*.

so⸢o shita⸣ra そうしたら *conj.*
1 after that; after all: ★ Used at the beginning of a sentence.
Ichi-jikañ mo matta. Soo shitara *yatto kare ga arawareta.* (1時間も待った. そうしたらやっと彼が現れた) I waited a full hour. *After that* he at last showed up.
2 then; if so; in that case:
Motto majime ni beñkyoo shi nasai. Soo shitara *baiku o katte agemasu.* (もっとまじめに勉強しなさい. そうしたらバイクを買ってあげます) Try to study more seriously. *If you do*, I will buy you a motorcycle. ⟪⇨ soo sureba⟫

so⸢o-shite そうして *conj.* and then:
Soo shite *kare wa shushoo ni niñmee sareta.* (そうして彼は首相に任命された) *And then* he was appointed prime minister. ⟪⇨ soshite⟫
— *adv.* that way; like that:
Soo shite *yaru no ga ichibañ da.* (そうしてやるのが一番だ) The best way to do it is *like that*.

so⸢oshoku そうしょく(装飾) *n.* decoration; ornament.
sooshoku suru (〜する) *vt.* decorate (an interior); ornament.

so⸣osoo[1] そうそう *int.* yes; oh; come to think of it; I remember:
Soosoo, *ano hito wa Yamada-sañ desu.* (そうそう, あの人は山田さんです) *Come to think of it*, he is Mr. Yamada.

so⸢osoo[2] そうそう(草々) *n.* Sincerely yours. ★ Polite way of ending a formal letter which begins with '*zeñryaku*.' (⇨ tegami)

so¹osu ソース *n.* sauce. ★ In Japan it often refers to a thick brown sauce.

so⌈o sure¹ba そうすれば *conj.* then; if so; in that case: ★ Used at the beginning of a sentence.
Kono kusuri o nomi nasai. Soo sureba, *sugu yoku narimasu.* (この薬を飲みなさい. そうすれば, すぐよくなります) Take this medicine. *If you do so,* you will soon get better.

so⌈otoo[1] そうとう (相当) *n.* worth:
Kare ni goseñ-eñ sootoo *no shina o okutta.* (彼に 5,000 円相当の品を贈った) I presented him with an article *worth* five thousand yen.
... ni sootoo suru (...に～する) *vi.* be equivalent to; correspond to.

so⌈otoo[2] そうとう (相当) *a.n.* (~ na/no, ni) considerable; quite; decent:
Kare no sukii no udemae wa sootoo *na mono desu.* (彼のスキーの腕前は相当なものです) His skill at skiing is *quite* something.
— *adv.* pretty; a lot:
Kyoo wa sootoo *atsuku nari-soo da.* (きょうは相当暑くなりそうだ) I think it is going to be *quite* hot today.

so⌈ozoo[1] そうぞう (想像) *n.* imagination; fancy; supposition:
soozoo *ga tsukanai* (想像がつかない) have no *idea.*
soozoo suru (～する) *vt.* imagine; fancy; guess.

so⌈ozoo[2] そうぞう (創造) *n.* creation.
soozoo suru (～する) *vt.* create.

so⌈ozooshi¹·i そうぞうしい (騒々しい) *a.* (-ku) noisy; boisterous. (⇨ sawagashii)

so¹ra[1] そら (空) *n.* the sky; the air.

so¹ra[2] そら *int.* look; there:
★ Not used to superiors.
Sora, *watashi no itta toori da.* (そら, 私の言ったとおりだ) *There,* I told you so. (⇨ sore[2])

so⌈re[1] それ *n.* **1** that; it: ★ Refers to something which is located away from the speaker and close to the listener.
Sore *wa dare no hoñ desu ka?* (それはだれの本ですか) Whose book is *that*?
2 that; it: ★ Refers to something mentioned by the listener.
"Jiko no koto shitte imasu ka?" "Sore *wa itsu no koto desu ka?"* (「事故のこと知っていますか」「それはいつのことですか」) "Do you know about the accident?" "When did *it* take place?"
3 it: ★ Refers to something previously mentioned.
Kinoo kasa o kaimashita ga, sore *o doko-ka e okiwasurete shimaimashita.* (きのう傘を買いましたが, それをどこかへ置き忘れてしまいました) I bought an umbrella yesterday, but I have left *it* somewhere. (⇨ are[1]; dore[1]; kore)

so¹re[2] それ *int.* there; now; look:
Sore, *isoge.* (それ, 急げ) *Look,* hurry up! (⇨ sora[2])

so⌈re da¹ kara それだから *conj.* so; that is why: ★ Used at the beginning of a sentence.
Kanojo wa seekaku ga yoi. Sore da kara *tomodachi ga takusañ iru.* (彼女は性格が良い. それだから友だちがたくさんいる) She has a nice personality. *That is why* she has got a lot of friends.

so⌈re de それで *conj.* **1** and; then:
Sore de *anata wa doo omoimasu ka?* (それであなたはどう思いますか) *And* what is your opinion?
2 therefore:
Netsu ga ari, sore de *gakkoo o yasumimashita.* (熱があり, それで学校を休みました) I had a fever, *therefore* I was absent from school.
— *adv.* now:
Sore de *jijoo ga wakarimashita.* (それで事情がわかりました) *Now* I have understood the circumstances.

s⌈ore de¹ mo それでも *conj.* but;

still; nevertheless; however: ★ Used at the beginning of a sentence.
Muzukashii ka mo shirenai. Sore de mo *yaru shika nai.* (難しいかもしれない. それでもやるしかない) It may be difficult. *Nevertheless*, there is nothing for it but to have a go.

so[re de] wa それでは *conj.* **1** if that is the case; if so; in that case: ★ Used at the beginning of a sentence.
"Watashi mo sono eega o mitai to omotte imasu." "Sore de wa, *issho ni ikimaseñ ka?"* (「私もその映画を見たいと思っています」「それでは, 一緒に行きませんか」) "I want to see that movie as well." "*In that case*, shall we go together?"
2 well; then: ★ Used at the beginning of a sentence.
Sore de wa, *kyoo wa kore de owarimasu.* (それでは, きょうはこれで終わります) *Well then*, we will finish here for today.

so[re do]koro ka それどころか on the contrary: ★ Used at the beginning of a sentence.
"Ima hima desu ka?" "Sore dokoro ka, *isogashii saichuu desu."* (「今暇ですか」「それどころか, 忙しい最中です」) "Are you free now?" "*Quite the opposite.* I am very busy right now."

so[re ja](a) それじゃ(あ) *int.* well (then): ⟪⇨ de wa²⟫
Sore jaa, *mata ashita.* (それじゃあ, またあした) *Well*, see you tomorrow.

so[re kara それから *conj.* and then; after that; afterward.

so[re-(k)kiri それ(っ)きり *adv.*
1 (with a negative) since:
Sore-(k)kiri *kanojo kara tayori wa arimaseñ.* (それ(っ)きり彼女から便りはありません) I haven't heard from her *since then.* ⟪⇨ are-(k)kiri⟫
2 all; no more than that:
Anata no chokiñ wa sore-(k)kiri *shika nai no desu ka?* (あなたの貯金はそれっきりしかないのですか) Are your savings *no more than* that? ⟪⇨ kore-(k)kiri⟫

so[re ma]de それまで(それ迄) up to that time; till then:
Kare no shoobai wa sore made *umaku itte ita.* (彼の商売はそれまでうまくいっていた) His business was successful *up to that time.*

so[re na]ra それなら *conj.* if so; in that case: ★ Used at the beginning of a sentence.
"Ogotte ageru yo." "Sore nara *issho ni itte mo ii."* (「おごってあげるよ」「それならいっしょに行ってもいい」) "I'll be glad to treat you." "*If so*, I'll come along with you."

so[re ni それに *conj.* and; besides; moreover: ★ Often used at the beginning of a sentence.
Koko wa yachiñ ga yasui shi, sore ni *eki ni mo chikai.* (ここは家賃が安いし, それに駅にも近い) The rent for this house is low, *and moreover* it is near the station.

so[re to]mo それとも *conj.* or:
Ocha ni shimasu ka, sore tomo *koohii ni shimasu ka?* (お茶にしますか, それともコーヒーにしますか) Do you wish green tea, *or* would you like coffee?

so[re wa so]o to それはそうと incidentally; by the way:
★ Used at the beginning of a sentence when changing the subject.
Sore wa soo to, *otoosañ no guai wa doo desu ka?* (それはそうと, お父さんの具合はどうですか) *By the way*, how is your father's health? ⟪⇨ tokoro de⟫

so[re]zore それぞれ *n., adv.* each; respectively:
Shussekisha wa sorezore *ikeñ o nobemashita.* (出席者はそれぞれ意見を述べました) The participants expressed their *respective* views.

so[robañ そろばん(算盤) *n.* abacus.

so[roe]·ru そろえる(揃える) *vt.* (soroe-te [V]) **1** arrange properly; put in order:
kaado o arufabetto juñ ni soroeru

(カードをアルファベット順にそろえる) *arrange* cards *in* alphabetical *order*. ⟪⇨ sorou⟫
2 get ready; collect:
Hitsuyoo na shorui wa zeñbu soroemashita. (必要な書類は全部そろえました) I *got* all the necessary documents *ready*. ⟪⇨ sorou⟫
3 make even:
ki o onaji takasa ni soroeru (木を同じ高さにそろえる) *make* the trees the same height. ⟪⇨ sorou⟫

so⌉rosoro そろそろ *adv.* **1** (of time) soon; before long; almost:
Sorosoro *shitsuree shimasu*. (そろそろ失礼します) *Now* I must be getting along. ⟪⇨ ma-mo-naku⟫
2 (～ to) (of movement) slowly; little by little.

so⌈ro⌉·u そろう (揃う) *vi.* (soro·i-; sorow·a-; sorot-te Ⓒ)
1 gather; meet; assemble:
Zeñiñ jikañ-doori ni sorotta. (全員時間通りにそろった) Everyone *assembled* at the appointed time.
2 be equal; be even; be uniform:
Kare-ra wa miñna fukusoo ga sorotte ita. (彼らはみんな服装がそろっていた) Their clothes *were* all *the same*. ⟪⇨ soroeru⟫
3 be [become] complete:
Koko ni wa Sheekusupia zeñshuu ga sorotte *imasu*. (ここにはシェークスピア全集がそろっています) We *have* a complete set of Shakespeare's works here. ⟪⇨ soroeru⟫

so⌉r·u[1] そる (剃る) *vi.* (sor·i-; sor·a-; sot-te Ⓒ) shave: *kao o* soru (顔をそる) *shave* one's face.

so⌉r·u[2] そる (反る) *vi.* (sor·i-; sor·a-; sot-te Ⓒ) warp; curve; bend.

so⌉señ そせん (祖先) *n.* ancestor; forefathers. ⟪↔ shisoñ⟫ ⟪⇨ señzo⟫

so⌉shiki そしき (組織) *n.* **1** organization; formation; system.
2 tissue.
soshiki suru (～する) *vt.* organize; form; compose: *roodoo-kumiai o* soshiki suru (労働組合を組織する) *organize* a labor union.

so⌈shite そして *conj.* and; and then: ★ A very common word for connecting words and clauses.
Furo ni hairi, soshite *sugu ni nemashita*. (風呂に入り, そしてすぐに寝ました) I took a bath, *and then* went to bed right away. ⟪⇨ soo-shite⟫

so⌈shitsu そしつ (素質) *n.* the makings; quality; aptitude:
Kare ni wa seerusumañ no soshitsu *wa nai*. (彼にはセールスマンの素質はない) He does not have the *makings* of a salesman.

so⌈shoo そしょう (訴訟) *n.* suit; lawsuit: soshoo *o okosu* (訴訟を起こす) file a *suit*. ⟪⇨ saibañ⟫

so⌈sog·u そそぐ (注ぐ) *vt.*, *vi.* (sosog·i-; sosog·a-; soso·i-de Ⓒ)
1 pour; water:
potto ni o-yu o sosogu (ポットにお湯を注ぐ) *pour* hot water into a thermos flask.
2 concentrate; devote oneself to; focus:
Kare wa jibuñ no keñkyuu ni zeñryoku o sosoida. (彼は自分の研究に全力を注いだ) He *put* everything into his studies.
3 flow:
Kono kawa wa Taiheeyoo ni sosogu. (この川は太平洋に注ぐ) This river *flows* into the Pacific Ocean.

so⌈sokkashi⌉·i そそっかしい *a.* (-ku) hasty; careless; thoughtless.

so⌈tchi⌉ そっち *n.* (*colloq.*) = sochira. **1** that; over there:
Sotchi *no o misete kudasai*. (そっちのを見せてください) Please show me *that* one.
2 (*colloq.*) you:
Kono moñdai ni tsuite sotchi no *kañgae wa doo desu ka?* (この問題についてそっちの考えはどうですか) What are *your* thoughts on this matter? ⟪⇨ atchi; dotchi; kotchi⟫

so⌈tchoku そっちょく (率直) *a.n.* (～ na, ni) frank; straightforward; candid. ⟪⇨ zakkubarañ⟫

so⌉to そと (外) *n.* outside; outdoors. ⟪↔ uchi[2]; naka[1]⟫

so⌈togawa そとがわ(外側) *n.* the outside; exterior:
Kono doa wa sotogawa *ni hiraki-masu.* (このドアは外側に開きます) This door opens *outward.* ⟪↔ uchi-gawa⟫

so⌈tsugyoo そつぎょう(卒業) *n.* graduation.
sotsugyoo suru (〜する) *vt.* graduate; finish. ⟪↔ nyuugaku⟫ ⟪⇨ deru (5)⟫

so⌈tto そっと *adv.* quietly; softly; lightly; gently:
Kare wa heya kara sotto *dete itta.* (彼は部屋からそっと出て行った) He went out of the room *quietly.*

so·⌈u[1] そう(沿う) *vi.* (so·i-; so-w·a-; sot-te Ⓒ) **1** go [run] along: ⟪⇨ -zoi⟫
Watashi-tachi wa kawa ni sotte *aruita.* (私たちは川に沿って歩いた) We walked *along* the riverbank.
2 be done according to:
Shigoto wa saisho no keekaku ni sotte *susumerareta.* (仕事は最初の計画に沿って進められた) The work was continued *according to* the original plan.

so·⌈u[2] そう(添う) *vt.* (so·i-; so-w·a-; sot-te Ⓒ) meet (expectations); answer; come up to:
Go-kitai ni sou *yoo, doryoku itashi-masu.* (ご期待に添うよう, 努力いたします) I will make every effort to *meet* your expectations.

su[1] す(巣) *n.* nest; web; comb.

su⌉[2] す(酢) *n.* vinegar.

su⌈barashi⌉·i すばらしい(素晴らしい) *a.* (-ku) wonderful; splendid; excellent:
subarashii *keshiki* (すばらしい景色) a *splendid* view. ⟪⇨ migoto⟫

su⌈bashiko⌉·i すばしこい *a.* (-ku) nimble; quick:
subashikoi *kodomo* (すばしこい子ども) a *nimble* child. ⟪⇨ subayai⟫

su⌈baya⌉·i すばやい(素早い) *a.* (-ku) quick; nimble:
Seefu wa sono jitai ni subayaku *taioo shita.* (政府はその事態にすばやく対応した) The government *promptly* dealt with the situation. ⟪⇨ subashikoi⟫

su⌈be⌉r·u すべる(滑る) *vi.* (sube-r·i-; suber·a-; subet-te Ⓒ)
1 slip; slide; glide: subette *korobu* (滑って転ぶ) *slip* and fall down.
2 fail (an examination).

su⌉bete すべて(全て) *n.*, *adv.* all; everything:
Subete *watashi no sekiniñ desu.* (すべて私の責任です) I am responsible for *everything.*

su⌈dare すだれ(簾) *n.* bamboo blind; reed screen.

su⌈de⌉ すで(素手) *n.* empty hand; bare hand:
Watashi wa sono sakana o sude *de tsukamaeta.* (私はその魚を素手で捕まえた) I caught that fish with my *bare hands.*

su⌉de ni すでに(既に) *adv.* already; previously; before; long ago:
Deñwa o shitara, kare wa sude ni *dekakete ita.* (電話をしたら, 彼はすでに出かけていた) When I telephoned, he had *already* left.

su⌈e すえ(末) *n.* **1** end:
Koñgetsu sue *ni kare wa Burajiru e ikimasu.* (今月末に彼はブラジルへ行きます) He is leaving for Brazil at the *end* of this month. ⟪⇨ -matsu⟫
2 after: ★ Follows the past of a verb.
Yoku kañgaeta sue *o-kotae itashi-masu.* (よく考えた末お答えいたします) I will give a reply *after* thinking it over carefully.
3 youngest child: sue *no musu-ko* (末の息子) the *youngest* son.

su⌈ekko すえっこ(末っ子) *n.* the youngest child.

su⌈e·ru すえる(据える) *vt.* (sue-te Ⓥ) **1** set; place; fix:
hoñbako o heya no sumi ni sueru (本箱を部屋の隅に据える) *place* a bookcase in a corner of the room.

S

2 appoint:
Shachoo wa jibuñ no musuko o kookeesha ni sueta. (社長は自分の息子を後継者に据えた) The president *appointed* his son as his successor.

su⌈gasugashi⌉·i すがすがしい (清々しい) *a.* (-ku) fresh; refreshing; bracing:
Yoku nemureta no de kesa wa sugasugashii. (よく眠れたのでけさはすがすがしい) I slept well, so I feel *refreshed* this morning.

su⌉gata すがた (姿) *n.* figure; shape:
Sono otoko no sugata *ni mioboe ga atta.* (その男の姿に見覚えがあった) I recognized the *figure* of that man.
sugata o arawasu (～を現す) appear; come into view.
sugata o kesu (～を消す) disappear.

su⌈gi すぎ (杉) *n.* Japanese cedar.

-sugi すぎ (過ぎ) *suf.* **1** (of times and dates) past; after:
Ima hachi-ji go-fuñ-sugi *desu.* (今8時5分過ぎです) It is now five *past* eight. ⟪↔ -mae⌉⟫
2 (of age) over; past:
Chichi wa nanajuu-sugi *desu.* (父は70過ぎです) My father is *over* seventy. ⟪↔ -mae⌉⟫
3 too much: ★ Added to the continuative base of a verb.
Tabe-sugi *wa keñkoo ni yoku arimaseñ.* (食べ過ぎは健康に良くありません) Eating *too much* is not good for the health. ⟪⇨ -sugiru⟫

su⌈gi⌉·ru すぎる (過ぎる) *vi.* (sugi-te [V]) **1** (of time) pass; be over:
Are kara ni-neñ (ga) sugimashita. (あれから2年(が)過ぎました) Since then two years *have passed.*
2 pass through:
Ressha wa moo Hiroshima o sugimashita. (列車はもう広島を過ぎました) The train *has* already *passed through* Hiroshima.
3 be past:
Kare wa go-juu o sugite iru *to omoimasu.* (彼は50を過ぎていると思います) I think he *is past* fifty.

-sugi·ru すぎる (過ぎる) (-sugi-te [V]) over-; too much: ★ Occurs as the second element of compound verbs. Added to the continuative base of a verb or the stem of an adjective.
hataraki-sugiru (働きすぎる) *overwork* / *omo*-sugiru (重すぎる) be *too* heavy.

su⌈go⌉·i すごい (凄い) *a.* (-ku)
1 (*informal*) great; superb; fantastic:
Shiñjuku wa sugoi *hito datta.* (新宿はすごい人だった) There was a *large* crowd in Shinjuku.
2 drastic; dreadful; horrible:
sugoi *jishiñ* (すごい地震) a *frightful* earthquake.
3 (-ku) awfully; terribly; extremely:
Kono hoñ wa sugoku *omoshiroi.* (この本はすごくおもしろい) This book is *terribly* interesting.

su⌈go⌉s·u すごす (過ごす) *vt.* (sugosh·i-; sugos·a-; sugosh·i-te [C]) pass; spend; idle away:
Watashi-tachi wa teñto de ichi-ya o sugoshita. (私たちはテントで一夜を過ごした) We *spent* the night in a tent.

su⌉gosugo すごすご *adv.* (～ to) dejectedly; with a heavy heart:
Shakkiñ o kotowararete kare wa sugosugo (*to*) *hikisagatta.* (借金を断られて彼はすごすご(と)引き下がった) Having been refused a loan, he *dejectedly* withdrew.

su⌉gu すぐ (直ぐ) *adv.* **1** (of time) at once; right away; soon.
2 (of distance) just; right:
Eki wa sugu *soko desu.* (駅はすぐそこです) The station is *just* over there.
3 easily; readily:
Kare wa sugu *okoru.* (彼はすぐ怒る) He gets angry *easily.*

su⌈gure⌉·ru すぐれる (優れる) *vi.* (sugure-te [V]) excel; surpass.

su⌈ibokuga すいぼくが (水墨画) *n.* a drawing in Indian ink. ⟪⇨ sumie⟫

su'ibuñ すいぶん(水分) *n.* water; moisture; juice:
suibuñ no ooi *kudamono* (水分の多い果物) *juicy* fruit.

su'ichoku すいちょく(垂直) *a.n.* (~ na, ni) perpendicular; vertical. ⟪↔ suihee⟫

su'ichuu すいちゅう(水中) *n.* underwater; in the water:
suichuu *ni tobikomu* (水中に飛び込む) jump *into the water.*

su'ideñ すいでん(水田) *n.* paddy; paddy field. ⟪⇨ ta[1]; tañbo⟫

su'idoo すいどう(水道) *n.* **1** water supply [service]:
Kono suidoo no mizu *wa nomemasu ka?* (この水道の水は飲めますか) Is this *tap water* good to drink?.
2 channel: *Buñgo*-suidoo (豊後水道) the Bungo *Channel.*

su'idookañ すいどうかん(水道管) *n.* water pipe; water main. ⟪⇨ kañ[2]⟫

su'iee すいえい(水泳) *n.* swimming; bathing. ⟪⇨ oyogu⟫

su'igara すいがら(吸い殻) *n.* cigarette butt [end]:
suigara-ire (吸い殻入れ) an *ashtray.*

su'igiñ すいぎん(水銀) *n.* mercury.

su'ihee すいへい(水平) *a.n.* (~ na, ni) horizontal; level. ⟪↔ suichoku⟫

su'iheeseñ すいへいせん(水平線) *n.* horizon. ★ The line where the sky and the sea meet. ⟪⇨ chiheeseñ⟫

su'iji すいじ(炊事) *n.* cooking; kitchen work. ⟪⇨ ryoori⟫
suiji (o) suru (~する) *vi.* cook.

su'ijuñ すいじゅん(水準) *n.* level; standard: *seekatsu*-suijuñ (生活水準) the *standard* of living.

su'ika すいか(西瓜) *n.* watermelon.

su'imase'ñ すいません (*colloq.*) = sumimaseñ.

su'imeñ すいめん(水面) *n.* the water surface.

su'imiñ すいみん(睡眠) *n.* sleep:
suimiñ *o toru* (睡眠をとる) have a *sleep.*

su'ioñ すいおん(水温) *n.* water temperature.

su'iri すいり(推理) *n.* reasoning; inference; guess.
suiri suru (~する) *vt.* reason; infer; deduce.

su'iryoku すいりょく(水力) *n.* waterpower:
suiryoku *hatsudeñsho* (水力発電所) a *hydroelectric power* plant. ⟪↔ karyoku⟫

su'iryoo すいりょう(推量) *n.* guess; surmise; inference.
suiryoo suru (~する) *vt.* guess; surmise; conjecture. ⟪⇨ suisoku⟫

su'isa'ñbutsu すいさんぶつ(水産物) *n.* marine products.

su'iseñ[1] すいせん(推薦) *n.* recommendation.
suiseñ suru (~する) *vt.* recommend. ⟪⇨ susumeru[2]⟫

su'iseñ[2] すいせん(水仙) *n.* narcissus; daffodil.

su'iseñ-be'ñjo すいせんべんじょ(水洗便所) *n.* flush toilet. ⟪⇨ beñjo⟫

su'ishiñ すいしん(推進) *n.* propulsion; drive.
suishiñ suru (~する) *vt.* propel; push on with. ⟪⇨ susumeru[1]⟫

su'ishitsu すいしつ(水質) *n.* quality of water.

su'ishoo すいしょう(水晶) *n.* crystal.

su'iso すいそ(水素) *n.* hydrogen.

su'isoku すいそく(推測) *n.* guess; conjecture.
suisoku suru (~する) *vt.* guess; conjecture; speculate.

su'isui すいすい *adv.* (~ to) lightly; easily:
Ike de koi ga suisui (to) oyoide iru. (池でこいがすいすい(と)泳いでいる) The carp *are gliding* through the pond.

su'itchi スイッチ *n.* switch:
hiitaa no suitch o ireru [kiru] (ヒーターのスイッチを入れる[切る]) *switch on* [*off*] a heater.

su'ito'r·u すいとる(吸い取る) *vt.* (-tor·i-; -tor·a-; -tot-te [C]) suck up; soak up; absorb (water).

su'iyo'o(bi) すいよう(び)(水曜(日)) *n.* Wednesday. ⟪⇨ APP. 5⟫

su⌈izoo すいぞう (膵臓) *n.* pancreas.

su⌉ji すじ (筋) *n.* **1** line; stripe: *akai* suji *no haitta tii-shatsu* (赤い筋の入った T シャツ) a T-shirt with red *stripes.*
2 muscle; tendon; sinew: *ashi no* suji *o itameru* (足の筋を痛める) hurt a *tendon* in one's leg.
3 string: *mame no* suji *o toru* (豆の筋を取る) remove the *strings* from beans.
4 story; plot: *Hanashi no* suji *wa heeboñ datta.* (話の筋は平凡だった) The *story* was commonplace.
5 sense; logic: *Kimi no iu koto wa* suji *ga tooranai.* (君の言うことは筋が通らない) There is no *sense* in what you say.

su⌈ke⌉eru スケール *n.* scale; caliber: sukeeru *no ooki-na jigyoo* (スケールの大きな事業) a large *scale* enterprise.

su⌈keeto スケート *n.* ice skating.

su⌈ke⌉juuru スケジュール *n.* schedule; program: sukejuuru *o tateru* (スケジュールを立てる) make out a *schedule.*

su⌈ki⌉[1] すき (好き) *a.n.* (~ na, ni) like; be fond of; love: *Tanaka-sañ wa e o kaku no ga* suki desu. (田中さんは絵をかくのが好きです) Ms. Tanaka *likes* to paint pictures. ⟪↔ kirai⟫ ⟪⇨ daisuki⟫
suki na yoo ni (~なように) as one likes [wishes].

su⌈ki[2] すき (隙) *n.* **1** unguarded moment; chance: Dare mo inai suki ni *tsumamigui o shita.* (だれもいないすきにつまみ食いをした) I took some snacks *while no one was around.*
2 fault; flaw: *Kare no toobeñ ni wa* suki *ga nakatta.* (彼の答弁にはすきがなかった) There were no *flaws* in his answer.
3 space; room: *Suutsukeesu wa ippai de sono hoñ o ireru* suki *wa arimaseñ.* (スーツケースはいっぱいでその本を入れるすきはありません) The suitcase is full and there is no *room* for the book.

su⌈ki[3] すき (鋤) *n.* plow; spade.

su⌈ki⌉i スキー *n.* ski; skiing: sukii *ni iku* (スキーに行く) go *skiing.*

su⌈kima すきま (隙間) *n.* **1** opening; gap; space: *kabe no* sukima (壁のすき間) an *opening* in the wall.
2 chink; crack: *mado-garasu no* sukima (窓ガラスのすき間) a *crack* between windowpanes.

su⌈kito⌉or·u すきとおる (透き通る) *vi.* (-toor·i-; -toor·a-; -toot-te [C]) be transparent; be seen through: sukitootta *garasu* (透き通ったガラス) *transparent* glass. ⟪⇨ toomee⟫

su⌈kiyaki すきやき (すき焼き) *n.* sukiyaki. ★ A dish of sliced beef and vegetables cooked in a shallow iron pan.

su⌈ki⌉zuki すきずき (好き好き) *n.* a matter of taste: *Hito ni wa sorezore* sukizuki *ga arimasu.* (人にはそれぞれ好き好きがあります) People have their *different tastes.* ⟪⇨ konomi⟫

su⌈kka⌉ri すっかり *adv.* completely; perfectly: *Sono koto o* sukkari *wasurete ita.* (そのことをすっかり忘れていた) I had *completely* forgotten about it.

su⌈kki⌉ri すっきり *adv.* (~ to; ~ suru) (the state of being refreshed, neat, clear-cut or simple): *Furo ni haittara, kibuñ ga* sukkiri *shita.* (ふろに入ったら, 気分がすっきりした) I felt *refreshed* after taking a bath.

su⌈ko⌉shi すこし (少し) *n., adv.*
1 a few [little]; some: *O-cha o moo* sukoshi *kudasai.* (お茶をもう少し下さい) Please give me a *little* more tea. ⟪↔ takusañ⟫ ⟪⇨ shooshoo⟫
2 a bit; somewhat: *Kono michi o* sukoshi *iku to hashi ni demasu.* (この道を少し行くと橋に出ます) Go along this road *a bit* and

you will come to a bridge.
3 a short time:
Kono heñ de sukoshi *yasumimashoo.* (この辺で少し休みましょう) Let's take *a short* rest somewhere around here.

su⌈ko⌉shi mo すこしも (少しも) *adv.* (with a negative) (not) at all; (not) in the least:
Sono eega wa sukoshi mo *omoshiroku nakatta.* (その映画は少しもおもしろくなかった) The film was *not in the least* interesting. ⟪⇨ chitto-mo⟫

su⌈koshi-zu⌉tsu すこしずつ (少しずつ) *adv.* little by little; gradually.

su⌈k·u[1] すく (空く) *vi.* (suk·i-; suk·a-; su·i-te Ⓒ) **1** become less crowded:
Deñsha wa suite ita. (電車はすいていた) The train *was* rather *empty.*
2 (of a stomach) become empty:
Onaka ga sukimashita. (おなかがすきました) I feel *hungry.*

su⌉k·u[2] すく (好く) *vt.* (suk·i-; suk·a-; su·i-te Ⓒ) like; love:
Kare wa miñna ni sukarete iru. (彼はみんなに好かれている) He *is liked* by everybody.

su⌈kui すくい (救い) *n.* **1** help; rescue:
sukui *o motomete sakebu* (救いを求めて叫ぶ) cry out for *help.*
⟪⇨ sukuu[1]⟫
2 relief; saving grace:
Sono jiko de shisha ga denakatta no ga sukui *datta.* (その事故で死者がでなかったのが救いだった) It was a great *relief* that there were no fatalities in the accident.

su⌈kuna⌉·i すくない (少ない) *a.* (-ku) few; little; small; scarce; short:
Koñgetsu wa ame ga sukunakatta. (今月は雨が少なかった) We have had *little* rain this month. ⟪↔ ooi⟫

su⌈ku⌉naku-tomo すくなくとも (少なくとも) *adv.* at least; not less than:
Kono kimono wa sukunaku-tomo *sañjuumañ-eñ wa shimasu.* (この着物は少なくとも30万円はします) This kimono costs *at least* 300,000 yen.

su⌈ku·u[1] すくう (救う) *vt.* (suku·i-; sukuw·a-; sukut-te Ⓒ) save; rescue; help:
Isha wa watashi no inochi o sukutte kureta. (医者は私の命を救ってくれた) The doctor *saved* my life.
⟪⇨ sukui⟫

su⌈ku·u[2] すくう (掬う) *vt.* (suku·i-; sukuw·a-; sukut-te Ⓒ) scoop (up); dip (up); ladle.

su⌈ma⌉ato スマート *a.n.* (~ na, ni) nice-looking; stylish; slender:
Kanojo wa itsu-mo fukusoo ga sumaato *da.* (彼女はいつも服装がスマートだ) Her clothes are always *chic.*
⟪⇨ iki[3]⟫

su⌉mai すまい (住まい) *n.* **1** address:
O-sumai *wa dochira desu ka?* (お住まいはどちらですか) May I ask *where you live*?
2 home; house; residence:
Koko wa kari no sumai *desu.* (ここは仮の住まいです) This is my temporary *residence.* ⟪⇨ juukyo⟫

su⌈ma⌉na·i すまない (済まない) *a.* (-ku) sorry; inexcusable:
Kimi ni wa hoñtoo ni sumanai *koto o shimashita.* (君には本当にすまないことをしました) I really did something *unpardonable* to you. ⟪⇨ kokoro-gurushii; sumimaseñ⟫

su⌈mase⌉·ru すませる (済ませる) *vt.* (sumase-te Ⓥ) finish; get through:
Moo chuushoku wa sumasemashita *ka?* (もう昼食は済ませましたか) *Have* you *finished* lunch yet?
⟪⇨ sumasu[1]⟫

su⌈ma⌉s·u[1] すます (済ます) *vt.* (sumash·i-; sumas·a-; sumash·i-te Ⓒ) **1** finish; settle:
Kare wa shiharai o sumasanai *de dete ikoo to shita.* (彼は支払いを済まさないで出て行こうとした) He tried to leave *without paying* the bill.
⟪⇨ sumaseru⟫
2 manage (with); make do:

S

Nihoñgo no beñkyoo ni jisho nashi de sumasu *koto wa dekimaseñ.* (日本語の勉強に辞書なしで済ますことはできません) In studying Japanese, one cannot *do* without a dictionary.

su[ma]s·u[2] すます (澄ます) *vi.* (sumash·i-; sumas·a-; sumash·i-te [C]) put on airs:
Kanojo wa sumashite ita. (彼女は澄ましていた) She *was prim and proper.*

su]mi[1] すみ (隅) *n.* corner.

su[mi][2] すみ (炭) *n.* charcoal.

su[mi][3] すみ (墨) *n.* India [Chinese] ink; ink stick.

su[mi]e すみえ (墨絵) *n.* India-ink painting. 《⇨ suibokuga》

su[mimase]ñ すみません **1** excuse [pardon] me; I'm sorry:
Go-meewaku o o-kakeshite, sumimaseñ. (ご迷惑をおかけして，すみません) *I am sorry* for causing you a lot of trouble.
2 thank you:
Tetsudatte itadaite, sumimaseñ. (手伝っていただいて，すみません) *Thank you* very much for helping me. 《⇨ arigatoo》

su[mire すみれ (菫) *n.* violet (flower).

su[moo すもう (相撲) *n.* sumo wrestling. 《⇨ rikishi》

su]m·u[1] すむ (住む) *vi.* (sum·i-; sum·a-; suñ-de [C]) live; reside: ★ Used in the '*-te iru*' form when referring to where a person currently lives.
Watashi wa apaato ni suñde imasu. (私はアパートに住んでいます) I *am living* in an apartment.

su]m·u[2] すむ (済む) *vi.* (sum·i-; sum·a-; suñ-de [C]) be finished; come to an end; get through:
Yatto shigoto ga suñda. (やっと仕事が済んだ) At last work *is finished.*

su]m·u[3] すむ (澄む) *vi.* (sum·i-; sum·a-; suñ-de [C]) become clear:
Koñya wa sora ga suñde iru. (今夜は空が澄んでいる) Tonight the sky *is clear.*

su[na すな (砂) *n.* sand; grain of sand.

su]nao すなお (素直) *a.n.* (~ na, ni) gentle; mild; obedient:
Sono ko wa watashi no iu koto o sunao *ni kiita.* (その子は私の言うことを素直に聞いた) The child listened *obediently* to what I said.

su[na]wachi すなわち (即ち) *conj.* (*formal*) that is (to say); namely.

su[ne] すね (脛) *n.* shank; shin.

su[ñpoo すんぽう (寸法) *n.* measure; measurements; size:
suñpoo *o toru* [*hakaru*] (寸法をとる[測る]) measure the *size.*
《⇨ ookisa》

su[ñzeñ すんぜん (寸前) *n.* just [right] before:
Sono kaisha wa toosañ sunzeñ *datta.* (その会社は倒産寸前だった) The company was *on the verge* of bankruptcy.

su[pa]supa すぱすぱ *adv.* (~ to) (with) quick puffs: ★ Used to express the action of smoking heavily.
tabako o supasupa (*to*) *suu* (たばこをすぱすぱ(と)吸う) *puff away* at a cigarette.

su[piido スピード *n.* speed:
supiido-*ihañ* (スピード違反) a *speeding* violation. 《⇨ hayasa; sokudo》

su[po]otsu スポーツ *n.* sport(s):
supootsu *o suru* (スポーツをする) go in for a *sport.*

su[ppa]·i すっぱい (酸っぱい) *a.* (-ku) acid; sour; vinegary.

su]ra すら *p.* even; if only:
★ Used for extreme examples.
Kodomo ni sura *dekiru no da kara anata ni dekinai wake ga nai.* (子どもにすらできるのだからあなたにできない訳がない) *Even* a child can do it, so there is no reason you can't.
《⇨ sae》

su]rasura すらすら *adv.* (~ to) smoothly; easily; fluently; readily.

su[rechiga·u すれちがう (すれ違う) *vi.* (-chiga·i-; -chigaw·a-; -chigat-te [C]) pass by:

S

Michi de señsee to surechigatta. (道で先生とすれ違った) I *passed* my teacher on the road.

su⌈ri すり(掏摸) *n.* pickpocket. ⟪⇨ suru[4]⟫

su⌈ri⌉ppa スリッパ *n.* scuffs; mules. ★ From English 'slippers.'

s·u⌈ru[1] する *vt.* (sh·i-; sh·i-; sh·i-te [I]) **1** do (something): *kaimono o* suru (買い物をする) *do* the shopping / *señtaku o* suru (洗濯をする) *do* the washing.
2 have (a wash, walk, etc.): *shokuji o* suru (食事をする) *have* a meal / *oshaberi o* suru (おしゃべりをする) *have* a chat / *keñka o* suru (けんかをする) *have* a fight.
3 take (a bath, break, etc.): *nyuuyoku* suru (入浴する) *take* a bath / *hirune o* suru (昼寝をする) *take* a nap.
4 make (a decision, discovery, etc.): *yakusoku o* suru (約束をする) *make* a promise / *iiwake o* suru (言い訳をする) *make* excuses.
5 play (baseball, chess, etc.): *yakyuu o* suru (野球をする) *play* baseball / *torañpu o* suru (トランプをする) *play* cards.
6 (of an article, goods, etc.) cost: *Kono yubiwa wa sañmañ-eñ* shimashita. (この指輪は3万円しました) This ring *cost* me 30,000 yen.
7 put on (a scarf, gloves, etc.): *tebukuro o* suru (手袋をする) *put on* gloves / *Kanojo wa kiiroi mafuraa* o shite *ita.* (彼女は黄色いマフラーをしていた) She *was wearing* a yellow muffler.
... ga suru (...が～) there is...: *Yoi kaori* ga suru. (良い香りがする) *There is* a nice smell.
... koto ni suru (...ことに～) decide: *Atarashii terebi o kau* koto ni shimashita. (新しいテレビを買うことにしました) I *have decided* to buy a new television.
... ni suru (...に～) **1** make into: *Tanaka-sañ o gichoo* ni shimashoo. (田中さんを議長にしましょう) *Let's make* Mr. Tanaka the chairman.
2 choose; decide: *"Kimi wa nani* ni suru?" *"Boku wa toñkatsu* ni suru." (「君は何にする」「ぼくはとんかつにする」) "What *would* you *like to eat*?" "I'll *have* a pork cutlet."
... o shite iru (...をしている) **1** be doing: *Haha wa señtaku o* shite imasu. (母は洗濯をしています) My mother *is doing the washing.*
2 work as; be engaged: *Ani wa isha* o shite imasu. (兄は医者をしています) My older brother *is* a doctor.
3 have (a shape, color, etc.): *Kanojo wa ooki-na me* o shite iru. (彼女は大きな目をしている) She *has* large eyes.
... to shitara (...としたら) as; when: *Dekakeyoo* to shitara, *deñwa ga kakatte kita.* (出かけようとしたら，電話がかかってきた) *As* I was about to go out, there was a phone call.

su⌉r·u[2] する(刷る) *vt.* (sur·i-; sur·a-; sut-te [C]) print: *Kono meeshi wa doko de* surimashita *ka?* (この名刺はどこで刷りましたか) Where *did* you *get* this name card *printed*?

su⌉r·u[3] する(擦る) *vt.* (sur·i-; sur·a-; sut-te [C]) **1** strike (a match); rub.
2 lose (at gambling).

su⌉r·u[4] する(掏る) *vt.* (sur·i-; sur·a-; sut-te [C]) pick; lift: *Watashi wa deñsha no naka de saifu o* surareta. (私は電車の中で財布をすられた) I *had* my wallet *lifted* in the train. ⟪⇨ suri⟫

su⌈rudo⌉·i するどい(鋭い) *a.* (-ku)
1 (of a blade, a claw, etc.) sharp; pointed.
2 (of a look, pain, etc.) sharp; acute: *senaka no* surudoi *itami* (背中の鋭い痛み) an *acute* pain in one's back.
3 (of a person etc.) sharp; keen: *kañsatsu ga* surudoi (観察が鋭い) have a *keen* eye.

su⌈rume するめ(鯣) *n.* dried squid. ⟪⇨ ika[2]⟫

S

su⌉rusuru するする *adv.* (～ to) easily; smoothly:
Saru wa surusuru (*to*) *ki ni nobotta.* (猿はするする(と)木に登った) The monkey climbed up the tree *with perfect ease.*

su⌉ru to すると *conj.* **1** and; then:
Kare wa neyoo to shite ita. Suru to *deñwa ga natta.* (彼は寝ようとしていた. すると電話が鳴った) He was going to sleep. *Just then* the telephone rang.
2 in that case:
"Ashita no yohoo wa ame desu." "Suru to *uñdookai wa chuushi desu ne."* (「あしたの予報は雨です」「すると運動会は中止ですね」) "Tomorrow the forecast is for rain." "*In that case*, we will have to cancel the athletic meet, won't we?"

su⌈shi⌉ すし (寿司·鮨) *n.* sushi.
★ Vinegared rice balls topped with slices of raw fish or egg.

su⌈so すそ (裾) *n.* **1** hem; bottom:
kimono no suso (着物のすそ) the *hem* of a kimono.
2 foot: *yama no* suso (山のすそ) the *foot* of a mountain.

su⌉su すす (煤) *n.* soot.

su⌈sume·ru[1] すすめる (進める) *vt.* (susume-te [V]) **1** proceed with (a procedure, project, etc.); carry forward: *kooshoo o* susumeru (交渉を進める) *proceed with* the negotiations. ⟪⇨ susumu⟫
2 promote; further:
sekai heewa o susumeru (世界平和を進める) *promote* world peace.
3 put forward (the hand of a clock [watch]). ⟪↔ okuraseru⟫ ⟪⇨ susumu⟫

su⌈sume·ru[2] すすめる (勧める) *vt.* (susume-te [V]) **1** advise; suggest; persuade:
Watashi wa kare ni tabako o yameru yoo susumeta. (私は彼にたばこをやめるよう勧めた) I *advised* him to give up smoking.
2 recommend:
Señsee wa sono jisho o seeto ni susumeta. (先生はその辞書を生徒に勧めた) The teacher *recommended* that dictionary to the pupils.
3 offer (a dish, drink, etc.).
4 tell; ask; invite:
Kare wa watashi ni kutsurogu yoo susumeta. (彼は私にくつろぐよう勧めた) He *told* me to make myself comfortable.

su⌈sum·u すすむ (進む) *vi.* (susum·i-; susum·a-; susuñ-de [C])
1 proceed; travel:
Watashi-tachi wa kita ni mukatte susuñda. (私たちは北に向かって進んだ) We *proceeded* northward.
2 (of a clock [watch]) gain; be fast. ⟪↔ okureru⟫ ⟪⇨ susumeru[1]⟫
3 (of a procedure, project, etc.) make progress; advance.
4 (of diseases) get worse.
5 (of appetite) be good:
Kyoo wa shoku ga susumanai. (きょうは食が進まない) I *do not have a good appetite* today.

su⌈sur·u すする (啜る) *vt.* (susur·i-; susur·a-; susut-te [C]) sip; slurp; suck:
o-cha o susuru (お茶をすする) *sip* tea / hana o susuru (鼻をすする) *sniffle.*

su⌈ta⌉a スター *n.* actor [actress, singer, player, etc.]; star.

su⌈ta⌉ato スタート *n.* start; getaway.
sutaato suru (～する) *vi.* start; begin. ⟪⇨ hajimaru⟫

su⌈tairi⌉suto スタイリスト *n.*
1 fashion-conscious person.
2 adviser on the hairstyle and clothes of models and actors.

su⌈ta⌉iru スタイル *n.* **1** figure:
Kanojo wa sutairu *ga ii.* (彼女はスタイルがいい) She has a good *figure.*
2 style:
Seekatsu no sutairu *ga kawatta.* (生活のスタイルが変わった) Life-*styles* have changed.

su⌈ta⌉jiamu スタジアム *n.* stadium.

su⌈ta⌉suta すたすた *adv.* (～ to) briskly; hurriedly: ★ Used to express a way of walking.

s

Kare wa sutasuta *to toori no hoo e aruite itta.* (彼はすたすたと通りの方へ歩いて行った) He walked ***briskly*** toward the street.

su⌈te⌉eki ステーキ *n.* steak; beefsteak.

su⌈teki すてき (素敵) *a.n.* (～ na) nice; splendid; marvelous; great: *Kimi no aidea wa* suteki *da.* (君のアイデアはすてきだ) That idea of yours is ***brilliant***.

su⌈te·ru すてる (捨てる) *vt.* (sute-te Ⓥ) **1** throw away; cast off; dump. **2** abandon; give up; forsake: *inochi o* suteru (命を捨てる) *throw away* one's life.

su⌈to⌉ スト *n.* strike. ((⇨ sutoraiki))

su⌈to⌉obu ストーブ *n.* heater. ★ Comes from English 'stove' but never refers to an apparatus for cooking food.

su⌈to⌉ppu ストップ *n.* stop; halt. **sutoppu suru** (～する) *vi.* stop. ((⇨ tomaru[1]))

su⌈tora⌉iki ストライキ *n.* strike: Sutoraiki *wa ma-mo-naku chuushi sareta.* (ストライキは間もなく中止された) The ***strike*** was soon called off. ((⇨ suto))

su⌈tto すっと *adv.* (～ suru) (feel) refreshed [relieved]: *Nayami o uchiakete* kimochi ga sutto shita. (悩みを打ち明けて気持ちがすっとした) ***A burden was removed from my mind*** after I disclosed my worries.

su·⌈u[1] すう (吸う) *vt.* (su·i-; su-w·a-; sut-te Ⓒ) **1** breathe (in): *asa no shiñseñ na kuuki o* suu (朝の新鮮な空気を吸う) ***breathe*** the fresh morning air. **2** sip; sup; suck; absorb: *Akañboo ga haha-oya no chichi o* sutte iru. (赤ん坊が母親の乳を吸っている) A baby ***is sucking*** at her mother's breast. **3** smoke: Tabako o sutte *mo ii desu ka?* (たばこを吸ってもいいですか) May I ***smoke***?

su⌉u[2] すう (数) *n.* number. ((⇨ APP. 3))

su⌈ugaku すうがく (数学) *n.* mathematics. ((⇨ sañsuu))

su⌈uhai すうはい (崇拝) *n.* worship; admiration; cult. **suuhai suru** (～する) *vt.* worship; admire; adore.

su⌈uji すうじ (数字) *n.* numeral; figure.

su⌉upaa(-ma⌉aketto) スーパー(マーケット) *n.* supermarket.

su⌉upu スープ *n.* soup; broth.

su⌈ushi すうし (数詞) *n.* (of grammar) numeral.

su⌈war·u すわる (座る) *vi.* (suwa-r·i-; suwar·a-; suwat-te Ⓒ) sit (down); take a seat. ((⇨ kakeru[1]))

su⌉yasuya すやすや *adv.* (～ to) calmly; quietly; peacefully: ★ Used to express the state of sleeping: *Akañboo wa* suyasuya (*to*) *nemutte imasu.* (赤ん坊はすやすや(と)眠っています) The baby is sleeping ***peacefully***.

su⌈zu[1] すず (鈴) *n.* bell.

su⌉zu[2] すず (錫) *n.* tin.

su⌈zume すずめ (雀) *n.* sparrow.

su⌈zuri⌉ すずり (硯) *n.* inkstone.

su⌈zushi⌉·i すずしい (涼しい) *a.* (-ku) cool; refreshing. ((↔ atatakai)) ((⇨ samui))

T

ta⌉[1] た (田) *n.* (rice) paddy. ((⇨ tañbo))

ta⌉[2] た (他) *n.* the rest; the other; the others. ((⇨ hoka))

-ta た *infl. end.* [attached to verbs, adjectives, and the copula] ★ The *ta*-form of a verb is made by dropping the final '*-te*' of the

te-form of a verb and adding '*-ta*.' When the *te*-form is '*-de*,' add '*-da*.' The *ta*-form of an adjective is made by dropping the final '*-i*,' and adding '*-katta*.' The *ta*-form of the copula is '*datta*.' 《⇨ APP. 2》
1 (indicates an action or a situation in the past):
Kesa wa go-ji ni okita. (今朝は5時に起きた) I *got up* at five this morning.
2 (indicates an action or a situation which is just finished or completed):
Kare wa ima dekaketa tokoro desu. (彼は今出かけたところです) He *has* just *gone out*.
3 (used to ask for confirmation or agreement):
Go-chuumoñ no shina wa kore deshita *ne*. (ご注文の品はこれでしたね) This *is* the article you ordered, isn't it?
4 (used to make a clause which modifies a noun):
Ano shiroi fuku o kita *hito wa dare desu ka?* (あの白い服を着た人はだれですか) Who is that person *wearing white?*

ta¹ba たば (束) *n.* bundle; bunch:
tegami no taba (手紙の束) a *bundle* of letters.

ta[bako たばこ (煙草) *n.* cigarette; cigar; tobacco:
tabako *o suu* [*nomu*] (たばこを吸う[のむ]) smoke a *cigarette*.

ta[bane¹·ru たばねる (束ねる) *vt.* (tabane-te [V]) bundle; tie up in a bundle.

ta[bemo¹no たべもの (食べ物) *n.* food; diet.

ta[be¹·ru たべる (食べる) *vt.* (tabe-te [V]) **1** eat (food); have; take. 《⇨ kuu; meshiagaru》
2 live on:
Hito-tsuki gomañ-eñ de wa tabete *ikemaseñ*. (ひと月5万円では食べていけません) One *cannot live* on fifty thousand yen a month.

ta[bi[1] たび (旅) *n.* trip; journey; tour; travel. 《⇨ ryokoo》

ta¹bi[2] たび (足袋) *n.* Japanese socks. ★ The front part is separated into two, the big toe and the other four toes.

ta[bi[3] たび (度) *n.* **1** every time:
Kono shashiñ o miru tabi *ni nakunatta chichi o omoidasu*. (この写真を見るたびに亡くなった父を思い出す) *Every time* I look at this photo I recall my dead father.
2 occasion:
Kono tabi *wa go-kekkoñ omedetoo gozaimasu*. (この度はご結婚おめでとうございます) Congratulations on this, the *occasion* of your wedding.

ta[bitabi たびたび (度々) *adv.* often; many times; repeatedly. 《⇨ shibashiba》

ta[boo たぼう (多忙) *a.n.* (~ na/no) busy. 《⇨ isogashii》

ta¹buñ たぶん (多分) *adv.* probably; perhaps; maybe:
Tabuñ *kanojo wa konai deshoo*. (たぶん彼女は来ないでしょう) *Maybe* she won't come. 《⇨ osoraku; tashika》

-tachi たち (達) *suf.* [attached to nouns indicating people and animals] (indicates the plural).
★ Note there are two uses: *señsee-tachi* = the teachers / the teacher(s) and others.

ta[chiagar·u たちあがる (立ち上がる) *vi.* (-agar·i-; -agar·a-; -agatte [C]) stand up; rise up:
Kokumiñ wa dokusai-seeji ni taishite tachiagatta. (国民は独裁政治に対して立ち上がった) The people *rose up* against the dictatorship.

ta[chiba¹ たちば (立場) *n.* **1** position; situation:
Kochira no tachiba *mo rikai shite kudasai*. (こちらの立場も理解してください) I hope you will understand our *position*.
2 standpoint:
Chigatta tachiba *kara arayuru kanoosee o kañgaemashita*. (違った

立場からあらゆる可能性を考えました) We considered all possibilities from a different *standpoint*.

ta⌈chidomar·u たちどまる(立ち止まる) *vi.* (-domar·i-; -domar·a-; -domat-te Ⓒ) stop; pause; stand still. ⟪⇨ tomaru[1]⟫

ta⌈chiiri たちいり(立ち入り) *n.* entrance; entry:
Koko wa tachiiri kiñshi *desu.* (ここは立ち入り禁止です) This area is *off-limits.* ⟪⇨ tachiiru⟫

ta⌈chii⌉r·u たちいる(立ち入る) *vi.* (-ir·i-; -ir·a-; -it-te Ⓒ) **1** trespass; enter:
tanin̄ no tochi ni tachiiru (他人の土地に立ち入る) *trespass* on other people's land. ⟪⇨ tachiiri⟫
2 meddle; pry into:
Kono mon̄dai ni wa tachiiritaku *arimasen̄.* (この問題には立ち入りたくありません) I don't wish to *meddle* in this problem.

ta⌈chimachi たちまち(忽ち) *adv.* in a moment; in no time:
Kinen̄-kitte wa tachimachi *uri-kireta.* (記念切手はたちまち売り切れた) The commemorative stamps were sold out *in no time.*

ta⌈chisar·u たちさる(立ち去る) *vi.* (-sar·i-; -sar·a-; -sat-te Ⓒ) leave; go away.

ta⌈chisuku⌉m·u たちすくむ(立ち竦む) *vi.* (-sukum·i-; -sukum·a-; -sukun̄-de Ⓒ) be [stand] petrified:
Osoroshii kookee o mite, watashi wa sono ba ni tachisukun̄de *shi-matta.* (恐ろしい光景を見て，私はその場に立ちすくんでしまった) I *stood rooted* to the spot at the horrible sight.

ta⌈chiyor·u たちよる(立ち寄る) *vi.* (-yor·i-; -yor·a-; -yot-te Ⓒ) drop in; stop by.

ta⌉da[1] ただ(唯) *adv.* only; simply; just:
Ima wa tada *kekka o matsu bakari desu.* (今はただ結果を待つばかりです) There is nothing to be done now but *simply* wait for the results. ⟪⇨ tan̄ ni⟫

ta⌉da[2] ただ(只) *n.* no charge; free:
Kono katarogu wa tada *desu.* (このカタログはただです) There is *no charge* for this catalog.

ta⌉dachi ni ただちに(直ちに) *adv.* at once; immediately; directly:
Ikkoo wa tadachi ni *shuppatsu shita.* (一行はただちに出発した) The party *immediately* set out. ⟪⇨ sugu⟫

ta⌈da⌉ima[1] ただいま(唯今) *n., adv.* now; (at) present; soon:
Tadaima *no jikoku wa ku-ji juu-go-fun̄ desu.* (ただいまの時刻は9時15分です) The time *now* is fifteen minutes past nine.

ta⌈daima[2] ただいま I'm home; I've just gotten back. ★ A greeting used by a person who has just come home. ⟪⇨ okaeri nasai⟫

ta⌉dashi ただし(但し) *conj.* (*formal*) but; however; provided. ⟪⇨ shikashi⟫

ta⌈dashi⌉·i ただしい(正しい) *a.* (-ku) correct; right; proper:
Kimi no han̄dan̄ wa tadashikatta. (きみの判断は正しかった) Your decision was *correct.*

ta⌈da⌉s·u ただす(正す) *vt.* (tadash·i-; tadas·a-; tadash·i-te Ⓒ)
1 correct; rectify:
ayamari o tadasu (誤りを正す) *correct* the errors.
2 reform; straighten:
shisee o tadasu (姿勢を正す) *straighten* one's posture.

ta⌈dayo⌉·u ただよう(漂う) *vi.* (tadayo·i-; tadayow·a-; tadayot-te Ⓒ) **1** drift; float:
Shiroi booto ga kaijoo o tadayotte *iru.* (白いボートが海上を漂っている) There *is* a white boat *afloat* on the sea.
2 be filled with:
Kaijoo ni wa nekki ga tadayotte *ita.* (会場には熱気が漂っていた) The hall *was alive* with excitement.

ta⌈do⌉oshi たどうし(他動詞) *n.*

t

transitive verb. ⟪↔ jidooshi⟫ ⟪⇨ APP. 2⟫

ta⌈doritsu⌉k·u たどりつく (辿り着く) *vi.* (-tsuk·i-; -tsuk·a-; -tsu·i-te Ⓒ) manage to arrive; work one's way.

ta⌈e⌉·ru[1] たえる (耐える) *vi.* (tae-te Ⓥ) bear; stand; endure: *kurushii seekatsu ni* taeru (苦しい生活に耐える) *endure* a hard life.

ta⌈e⌉·ru[2] たえる (絶える) *vi.* (tae-te Ⓥ) **1** become extinct; die out. **2** (of contact, relations, etc.) be cut off; come to an end: *Deñwa no koshoo de kare to no reñraku ga* taeta. (電話の故障で彼との連絡が絶えた) With the phone out of order, communication with him *was broken*.

ta⌉ezu たえず (絶えず) *adv.* always; continually; constantly.

ta⌈gai たがい (互い) *n.* each other; one another: ★ Often with '*o*-.' *Kare-ra wa* o-tagai *ni tasukeatta.* (彼らはお互いに助け合った) They helped *each other*. ⟪⇨ soogo⟫

-taga⌉r·u たがる *suf.* (*vi.*) (-taga-r·i-; -tagar·a-; -tagat-te Ⓒ) [attached to the continuative base of a verb] want (to do); be eager (to do): ★ Indicates the wishes and hopes of a person other than the speaker. ⟪⇨ -tai⟫ *Kare wa nañ de mo* shiritagaru. (彼は何でも知りたがる) He *is eager to know* everything.

ta⌈gaya⌉s·u たがやす (耕す) *vt.* (tagayash·i-; tagayas·a-; tagayash·i-te Ⓒ) cultivate (land); till; plow. ⟪⇨ koosaku[2]⟫

ta⌈gu⌉r·u たぐる (手繰る) *vt.* (ta-gur·i-; tagur·a-; tagut-te Ⓒ) haul in [up]; draw in: *tsuna o* taguru (綱をたぐる) *haul up* a rope.

ta⌉i[1] たい (対) *n.* versus; between: *sañ* tai *ni de katsu* (3 対 2 で勝つ) win by a score of three *to* one.

ta⌉i[2] たい (鯛) *n.* sea bream.

ta⌉i[3] たい (隊) *n.* party; company; band.

-ta·i たい *infl. end.* (*a.*) (-ku) [attached to the continuative base of a verb] want (to do); would like (to do): ★ Indicates the speaker's wishes or a desire to do something. ⟪⇨ -tagaru⟫ *Watashi wa nani-ka uñdoo ga* [*o*] shitai. (私は何か運動が[を]したい) I *want to do* some exercise. ⟪⇨ ga[1]⟫

ta⌈idañ たいだん (対談) *n.* talk between two people; interview.
taidañ suru (〜する) *vi.* have a talk.

ta⌉ido たいど (態度) *n.* attitude; manner; behavior.

ta⌈ifu⌉u たいふう (台風) *n.* typhoon.

ta⌈igai たいがい (大概) *n.* (〜 no) most; nearly all: taigai *no hito* (たいがいの人) *most* people.
— *adv.* usually; generally: *Nichiyoobi wa* taigai *ie ni imasu.* (日曜日はたいがい家にいます) On Sundays I am *generally* at home. ⟪⇨ taitee⟫

ta⌈igaku たいがく (退学) *n.* withdrawal from school; expulsion from school. ⟪⇨ teegaku[1]⟫
taigaku suru (〜する) *vi.* leave school.

ta⌈iguu たいぐう (待遇) *n.* **1** treatment; terms; pay: *Ano kaisha wa* taiguu ga yoi [warui]. (あの会社は待遇が良い[悪い]) That company *pays* its employees *well* [*badly*].
2 service: *Kono ryokañ wa* taiguu *ga yoi.* (この旅館は待遇が良い) The *service* at this inn is good.
taiguu suru (〜する) *vt.* treat; pay.

Ta⌈ihe⌉eyoo たいへいよう (太平洋) *n.* Pacific Ocean. ⟪⇨ Taiseeyoo⟫

ta⌈iheñ たいへん (大変) *a.n.* (〜 na) **1** very; awful; terrible: *Ryokoo de wa* taiheñ *na keekeñ o shimashita.* (旅行ではたいへんな経験をしました) I had an *awful* experience during the trip.

2 (of quantity) a lot of:
Sono shoobai ni wa taiheñ *na shikiñ ga iru.* (その商売にはたいへんな資金がいる) You need *a lot of* funds for that business.
3 hard; difficult:
Kare o settoku suru no wa taiheñ *desu.* (彼を説得するのはたいへんです) It is *hard* to persuade him.
4 serious; grave:
Taiheñ *na machigai o shite shimatta.* (たいへんな間違いをしてしまった) I have made a *serious* mistake.
— *adv.* (~ ni) very much; greatly; extremely.

ta⌉iho たいほ (逮捕) *n.* arrest.
taiho suru (~する) *vt.* arrest.

ta⌈ihoo たいほう (大砲) *n.* heavy gun; cannon.

ta⌉iiku たいいく (体育) *n.* physical education.

ta⌈iiñ たいいん (退院) *n.* leaving the hospital.
taiiñ suru (~する) *vi.* leave the hospital; be discharged from the hospital. ⟪↔ nyuuiñ⟫ ⟪⇨ byooiñ⟫

ta⌉iji たいじ (退治) *n.* getting rid of; extermination.
taiji suru (~する) *vt.* get rid of; exterminate: *gokiburi o* taiji suru (ごきぶりを退治する) *get rid of* cockroaches.

ta⌈ijoo たいじょう (退場) *n.* leaving; exit.
taijoo suru (~する) *vi.* leave; exit: *butai kara* taijoo suru (舞台から退場する) *leave* the stage. ⟪↔ nyuujoo; toojoo⟫

ta⌈ijuu たいじゅう (体重) *n.* one's body weight.

ta⌉ika たいか (大家) *n.* authority; expert; great master.

ta⌈ikai たいかい (大会) *n.* **1** convention; mass [general] meeting.
2 tournament; contest:
tenisu-taikai (テニス大会) a tennis *tournament.*

ta⌈ikaku たいかく (体格) *n.* physique; constitution; build.

ta⌈ikee たいけい (体系) *n.* system; organization.

ta⌈ikee-teki たいけいてき (体系的) *a.n.* (~ na, ni) systematic.

ta⌈ikeñ たいけん (体験) *n.* personal experience.
taikeñ suru (~する) *vt.* experience; undergo. ⟪⇨ keekeñ⟫

ta⌈ikiñ たいきん (大金) *n.* large sum of money.

ta⌈iko たいこ (太鼓) *n.* drum:
taiko *o tataku* (太鼓をたたく) beat a *drum.*

ta⌈ikoo たいこう (対抗) *n.* competition; rivalry.
taikoo suru (~する) *vi.* match; equal; compete. ⟪⇨ kyoosoo⟫

ta⌈ikutsu たいくつ (退屈) *a.n.* (~ na) tedious; boring; dull.
taikutsu suru (~する) *vi.* be bored; be weary. ⟪⇨ akiru⟫

ta⌉ioñ たいおん (体温) *n.* body temperature:
taioñ *o hakaru* (体温を測る) take a person's *temperature.*

ta⌈ioñkee たいおんけい (体温計) *n.* clinical thermometer.

ta⌉ipu[1] タイプ *n.* type; kind.

ta⌉ipu[2] タイプ *n.* typewriter; typing.
taipu suru (~する) *vt.* type.

ta⌈ira たいら (平ら) *a.n.* (~ na, ni) flat; even; level:
taira *na yane* (平な屋根) a *flat* roof.

ta⌈iriku たいりく (大陸) *n.* continent.

ta⌈iritsu たいりつ (対立) *n.* opposition; antagonism; confrontation.
tairitsu suru (~する) *vi.* be opposed; confront: *rigai ga* tairitsu suru (利害が対立する) interests *are in conflict.*

ta⌉iryoku たいりょく (体力) *n.* physical strength; powers.

ta⌈iryoo たいりょう (大量) *n.* a large quantity. ⟪↔ shooryoo⟫

ta⌈isaku たいさく (対策) *n.* measure; countermeasure:
taisaku *o neru* (対策を練る) work out *countermeasures.*

ta⌈isee たいせい (体制) *n.* system;

structure; establishment. ⟪↔ hañ-taisee⟫

Ta|ise|eyoo たいせいよう(大西洋) *n.* Atlantic Ocean. ⟪⇨ Taiheeyoo⟫

ta|iseki たいせき(体積) *n.* volume; capacity. ⟪⇨ meñseki⟫

ta|iseñ たいせん(大戦) *n.* great war:
dai ni-ji sekai taiseñ (第二次世界大戦) the Second World *War*.

ta|isetsu たいせつ(大切) *a.n.* (～ na, ni) important; valuable; precious. ⟪⇨ kañjiñ; daiji[1]⟫

ta|isha たいしゃ(退社) *n.* leaving one's office; resignation; retirement. ⟪↔ nyuusha⟫ ⟪⇨ taishoku⟫
taisha suru (～する) *vi.* leave one's office; resign; retire.

ta|ishi たいし(大使) *n.* ambassador.

ta|ishi|kañ たいしかん(大使館) *n.* embassy.

ta|ishita たいした(大した) *attrib.*
1 a lot of; great:
Kare no shageki no udemae wa taishita *mono da.* (彼の射撃の腕前はたいしたものだ) His skill in shooting is *quite* something.
2 (with a negative) not very; not much of:
Kare no kega wa taishita *koto wa nakatta.* (彼のけがはたいしたことはなかった) His injury was *nothing* serious.

ta|ishite[1] たいして(大して) *adv.* (with a negative) very (much):
Taishite *o-yaku ni tatezu, mooshiwake arimaseñ.* (たいしてお役に立てず, 申し訳ありません) I am sorry that I could not be of *much* assistance.

ta|ishite[2] たいして(対して)
★ Used in the pattern '*... ni taishite.*'
1 to; against; regarding:
Go-shitsumoñ ni taishite *o-kotae shimasu.* (ご質問に対してお答えします) I will reply *to* your question. ⟪⇨ taisuru⟫
2 in contrast to [with]:
Sono keekaku ni neñchoosha ga sañsee shita no ni taishite, *wakai hito-tachi wa hañtai shita.* (その計画に年長者が賛成したのに対して, 若い人たちは反対した) *In contrast to* the elderly people's support of the plan, the young were against it.

ta|ishoku たいしょく(退職) *n.* retirement; resignation.
taishoku suru (～する) *vi.* retire; resign; leave one's company. ⟪⇨ taisha⟫

ta|ishoo[1] たいしょう(対象) *n.* object; subject:
Kono shina wa kazee no taishoo ni narimasu. (この品は課税の対象になります) These goods *are subject* to taxation.

ta|ishoo[2] たいしょう(対照) *n.* contrast; comparison.
taishoo suru (～する) *vt.* contrast; compare. ⟪⇨ kuraberu⟫

ta|ishoo[3] たいしょう(対称) *n.* symmetry.

ta|ishoo[4] たいしょう(大将) *n.* general; admiral.

ta|ishuu たいしゅう(大衆) *n.* the general public; the people; the masses.

ta|isoo[1] たいそう(体操) *n.* gymnastics; physical exercise; calisthenics. ⟪⇨ uñdoo⟫

ta|isoo[2] たいそう(大層) *adv.* very (much); greatly:
Kanojo wa sono e ga taisoo *ki ni itte iru yoo datta.* (彼女はその絵がたいそう気に入っているようだった) She seemed to like the picture *very much*. ⟪⇨ hijoo⟫

ta|is·u|ru たいする(対する) *vi.* (taish·i-; tais·a-; taish·i-te Ⓒ)
... ni taisuru (...に～) to; against:
Sono moñdai ni taisuru *taisaku o tatenakereba naranai.* (その問題に対する対策を立てなければならない) We have to work out countermeasures *against* the problem. ⟪⇨ taishite[2]⟫

ta|itee たいてい(大抵) *n.* (～ no) most; just about:
Taitee *no kodomo wa chokoreeto*

t

ga suki desu. (たいていの子どもはチョコレートが好きです) *Most* children like chocolate.
— *adv.* usually; generally. ⟨⇨ taigai⟩

ta⌈itoo たいとう (対等) *a.n.* (～ na/no, ni) equal; even: *otagai ni* taitoo *no tachiba de hanashiau* (お互いに対等の立場で話し合う) talk with each other on an *equal* footing. ⟨⇨ byoodoo⟩

ta⌈iyaku たいやく (大役) *n.* important task [duty]: taiyaku *o hatasu* (大役を果たす) carry out an *important duty.*

ta⌉iyoo[1] たいよう (太陽) *n.* the sun.

ta⌈iyoo[2] たいよう (大洋) *n.* ocean: taiyoo-*koorosen̄* (大洋航路船) an *ocean* liner.

ta⌈iyoo-ne⌉n̄suu たいようねんすう (耐用年数) *n.* period of durability; life.

ta⌈izai たいざい (滞在) *n.* stay (at a place); visit.
taizai suru (～する) *vi.* make a stay. ⟨⇨ tomaru[2]⟩

ta⌈ka たか (鷹) *n.* hawk; falcon.

ta⌈ka⌉·i たかい (高い) *a.* (-ku)
1 high; tall; lofty. ⟨↔ hikui⟩ ⟨⇨ takasa⟩
2 expensive; high; dear: *Tookyoo wa bukka ga* takai. (東京は物価が高い) The price of goods in Tokyo is *high.* ⟨↔ yasui⟩
3 (of status, position, degree, etc.) high: *Kachoo wa Suzuki-san̄ o* takaku *hyooka shite iru.* (課長は鈴木さんを高く評価している) The manager thinks *highly* of Mr. Suzuki. ⟨↔ hikui⟩
4 (of sound, voice) loud; high-pitched. ⟨↔ hikui⟩

ta⌈kama⌉r·u たかまる (高まる) *vi.* (takamar·i-; takamar·a-; takamat-te [C]) rise; increase: *hyooban̄ ga* takamaru (評判が高まる) *rise* in popularity. ⟨⇨ takameru⟩

ta⌈kame⌉·ru たかめる (高める) *vt.* (takame-te [V]) raise; increase; improve: *kokumin̄ no seekatsu-suijun̄ o* takameru (国民の生活水準を高める) *increase* the people's standard of living. ⟨⇨ takamaru⟩

ta⌈kara⌉ たから (宝) *n.* treasure. ⟨⇨ takaramono⟩

ta⌈kara⌉kuji たからくじ (宝くじ) *n.* public lottery (ticket). ⟨⇨ kuji⟩

ta⌈karamono⌉ たからもの (宝物) *n.* treasure; heirloom. ⟨⇨ takara⟩

ta⌉kasa たかさ (高さ) *n.* **1** height; altitude: *biru no* takasa (ビルの高さ) the *height* of a building. ⟨⇨ haba; takai⟩
2 pitch; loudness: *oto no* takasa *o choosetsu suru* (音の高さを調節する) control the *pitch* [*loudness*] of a sound.

ta⌈ke[1] たけ (竹) *n.* bamboo. ⟨⇨ shoo-chiku-bai⟩

ta⌈ke⌉[2] たけ (丈) *n.* **1** length: *sukaato no* take o mijikaku suru (スカートの丈を短くする) *shorten* a skirt.
2 height: take ga nobiru (丈がのびる) *grow tall.*

ta⌈ki たき (滝) *n.* waterfall.

ta⌈kibi たきび (焚火) *n.* open-air fire; bonfire.

ta⌈kkyuu たっきゅう (卓球) *n.* table tennis; ping-pong.

ta⌈kkyuubin̄ たっきゅうびん (宅急便) *n.* (*trade name*) express home delivery.

ta⌉ko[1] たこ (蛸) *n.* octopus.

ta⌉ko[2] たこ (凧) *n.* kite.

ta⌉ko[3] たこ (胼胝) *n.* callus; corn.

ta⌈k·u[1] たく (炊く) *vt.* (tak·i-; tak·a-; ta·i-te [C]) cook (rice); boil. ⟨⇨ niru[1]⟩

ta⌈k·u[2] たく (焚く) *vt.* (tak·i-; tak·a-; ta·i-te [C]) burn (fuel): *sekitan̄* [*maki*] *o* taku (石炭[まき]をたく) *burn* coal [firewood]. ⟨⇨ moyasu⟩

ta⌈ku[3] たく (宅) *n.* ⇨ o-taku.

ta⌈kumashi⌉·i たくましい (逞しい) *a.* (-ku) **1** strong; robust: takumashii *karada* (たくましい体) a

t

robust physique.
2 powerful:
takumashii *soozooryoku* (たくましい想像力) a *powerful* imagination.

ta⌈kumi たくみ (巧み) *a.n.* (~ na, ni) skillful; clever:
hoochoo o takumi *ni tsukau* (包丁を巧みに使う) wield a kitchen knife with *skill.*

ta⌈kusa⌉ñ たくさん (沢山) *n., adv.*
1 many; much; a lot of:
Kare wa hoñ o takusañ *motte imasu.* (彼は本をたくさん持っています) He has *a lot of* books. ⟪↔ sukoshi; shooshoo⟫ ⟪⇨ ikutsu mo⟫
2 enough; sufficiently:
Kare no jimañ-banashi wa moo takusañ *da.* (彼の自慢話はもうたくさんだ) I have had *enough* of his boasting.

ta⌉kushii タクシー *n.* taxi:
takushii *o hirou* (タクシーを拾う) pick up a *taxi* / takushii-*noriba* (タクシー乗り場) a *taxi* stand. ⟪⇨ haiyaa⟫

ta⌈kuwae⌉·ru たくわえる (蓄える) *vt.* (takuwae-te [V]) save; put away; store:
roogo no seekatsu-shikiñ o takuwaeru (老後の生活資金を蓄える) *save* money to provide for one's old age.

ta⌈ma⌉[1] たま (球) *n.* **1** (of baseball, billiards, etc.) ball.
2 light bulb. ⟪⇨ deñkyuu⟫

ta⌈ma⌉[2] たま (玉) *n.* ball; bead.

ta⌈ma⌉[3] たま (弾) *n.* bullet.

ta⌈ma⌉go たまご (卵) *n.* egg:
tamago-yaki (卵焼き) an *omelet.* ⟪⇨ hañjuku; yude-tamago⟫

ta⌈mane⌉gi たまねぎ (玉葱) *n.* onion. ⟪⇨ negi⟫

ta⌈ma ni たまに *adv.* (~ wa) once in a while; occasionally; rarely:
Kare to wa tama ni *shika aimaseñ.* (彼とはたまにしか会いません) I meet him only *rarely.*

ta⌈marana·i たまらない (堪らない) *a.* (-ku) ★ Polite forms are '*tamaranai desu*' and '*tamarimaseñ.*' unbearable; intolerable.
-te tamaranai (て~) **1** so...that one cannot stand...: Sabishikute tamaranai. (寂しくてたまらない) I *am so lonely that* I *cannot stand* it.
2 be eager; be dying: *Jibuñ no kuruma ga* hoshikute tamaranai. (自分の車が欲しくてたまらない) I *cannot wait to have* my own car.

ta⌈mar·u[1] たまる (溜まる) *vi.* (tamar·i-; tamar·a-; tamat-te [C]) collect; pile up; accumulate; gather:
Tana no ue ni hokori ga tamatta. (棚の上にほこりがたまった) Dust *has collected* on the shelf. ⟪⇨ tameru[1]⟫

ta⌈mar·u[2] たまる (貯まる) *vi.* (tamar·i-; tamar·a-; tamat-te [C]) be saved:
Kare wa daibu o-kane ga tamatta *yoo da.* (彼はだいぶお金がたまったようだ) He seems to *have saved up* quite a bit of money. ⟪⇨ tameru[2]⟫

ta⌉mashii たましい (魂) *n.* soul; spirit.

ta⌈matama たまたま (偶々) *adv.* by chance. ⟪⇨ guuzeñ⟫

ta⌈me⌉ ため (為) *n.* **1** for the sake of; for the benefit of:
Watashi wa kimi no tame *ni, soo shita no desu.* (私は君のために, そうしたのです) I did so *for* your own *sake.*
2 for the purpose of; in order to:
Kanojo wa ryokoo e iku tame *ni, o-kane o tamete iru.* (彼女は旅行へ行くために, お金をためている) She is saving money *for the purpose of* going on a trip.
3 because of; owing to; as a result of:
Byooki no tame *ni, paatii ni derarenakatta.* (病気のために, パーティーに出られなかった) I could not attend the party *because of* my illness.

ta⌈mei⌉ki ためいき (溜息) *n.* sigh:
ooki-na tameiki *o tsuku* (大きなため息をつく) give a deep *sigh.*

ta⌈mera⌉·u ためらう(躊躇う) *vi.* (tamera·i-; tameraw·a-; tamerat-te Ⓒ) hesitate; waver; hang back. 《⇨ chuucho》

ta⌈me·ru[1] ためる(溜める) *vt.* (tame-te Ⓥ) store; cumulate: *amamizu o* tameru (雨水をためる) *collect and store* rainwater. 《⇨ tamaru[1]》

ta⌈me·ru[2] ためる(貯める) *vt.* (tame-te Ⓥ) save (money); amass. 《⇨ tamaru[2]》

ta⌈meshi⌉ ni ためしに(試しに) *adv.* tentatively; on trial.

ta⌈me⌉s·u ためす(試す) *vt.* (tamesh·i-; tames·a-; tamesh·i-te Ⓒ) try; test: *Kore wa kare no nooryoku o* tamesu *ii chañsu da.* (これは彼の能力を試すいいチャンスだ) This is a good chance to *test* his ability.

ta⌈mo⌉ts·u たもつ(保つ) *vi.* (tamoch·i-; tamot·a-; tamot-te Ⓒ) keep; hold; maintain; preserve; retain: *keñkoo* [*wakasa*] *o* tamotsu (健康[若さ]を保つ) *stay* healthy [young].

ta⌈na たな(棚) *n.* shelf; rack.

ta⌈nabata たなばた(七夕) *n.* the Star Festival celebrated on July 7.

ta⌈ñbo たんぼ(田圃) *n.* rice paddy. 《⇨ suideñ; ta[1]》

ta⌈ñchoo たんちょう(単調) *a.n.* (~ na, ni) monotonous; dull: Tañchoo *na seekatsu ni wa akimashita.* (単調な生活には飽きました) I am tired of my *dull* life.

ta⌉ne たね(種) *n.* **1** seed: tane *o maku* (種をまく) sow [plant] *seeds.*
2 cause; source: *Musume no koto ga itsu-mo shiñpai no* tane *desu.* (娘のことがいつも心配の種です) Our daughter is always a *cause* of anxiety.

ta⌈ñgo たんご(単語) *n.* word; vocabulary.

ta⌈ni⌉ たに(谷) *n.* valley; gorge.

ta⌉ñi たんい(単位) *n.* unit; (of a school) credit.

ta⌈niñ たにん(他人) *n.* others; unrelated person.

ta⌈ñjoo たんじょう(誕生) *n.* birth.
tañjoo suru (~する) *vi.* be born. 《⇨ umareru》

ta⌈ñjo⌉obi たんじょうび(誕生日) *n.* birthday.

ta⌈ñjuñ たんじゅん(単純) *a.n.* (~ na, ni) **1** simple: tañjuñ *na shigoto* (単純な仕事) a *simple* task.
2 (of people, ways of thinking, etc.) simple-minded.

ta⌉ñka[1] たんか(単価) *n.* unit price.

ta⌉ñka[2] たんか(担架) *n.* stretcher: tañka *de hito o hakobu* (担架で人を運ぶ) carry a person on *stretcher.*

ta⌉ñka[3] たんか(短歌) *n.* Japanese poem consisting of 31 syllables.
★ The syllables are arranged in five lines of 5, 7, 5, 7 and 7.

ta⌈ñkeñ たんけん(探検) *n.* exploration; expedition.
tañkeñ suru (~する) *vt.* explore.

ta⌉ñki[1] たんき(短期) *n.* a short (period of) time. 《↔ chooki》

ta⌉ñki[2] たんき(短気) *n., a.n.* (~ na) short temper; short-tempered.

ta⌈ñkoo たんこう(炭鉱) *n.* coal mine.

ta⌉ñ-naru たんなる(単なる) *attrib.* mere; simple; only: *Sore wa* tañ-naru *uwasa desu.* (それは単なるうわさです) That is a *mere* rumor.

ta⌉ñ ni たんに(単に) *adv.* only; merely; simply: *Watashi wa* tañ ni *shitte iru koto o hanashita dake desu.* (私は単に知っていることを話しただけです) I have just told them *only* what I know. 《⇨ tada[1]》

ta⌉ no たの(他の) *attrib.* other; another: ta no *hito* [*moñdai*] (他の人[問題]) *another* person [problem]. 《⇨ hoka》

ta⌉nomi たのみ(頼み) *n.* request; favor:

t

Anata ni tanomi *ga aru no desu ga.* (あなたに頼みがあるのですが) I have a *favor* to ask of you. 《⇨ tanomu》

ta⸢nomoshi⸣·i たのもしい (頼もしい) *a.* (-ku) reliable; promising; trustworthy.

ta⸢no⸣m·u たのむ (頼む) *vt.* (tanom·i-; tanom·a-; tanoñ-de Ⓒ)
1 ask (a favor); beg:
Watashi wa kare ni tasuke o tanoñda. (私は彼に助けを頼んだ) I *asked* him for assistance.
《⇨ tanomi》
2 order (goods); call (in); hire:
Hoñya ni hoñ o tanoñda *ga shinagire datta.* (本屋に本を頼んだが品切れだった) I *ordered* a book at the bookshop, but it was out of stock.

ta⸢noshi⸣·i たのしい (楽しい) *a.* (-ku) enjoyable; cheerful; happy. 《⇨ tanoshimi; tanoshimu》

ta⸢noshi⸣mi たのしみ (楽しみ) *n.*
1 pleasure; enjoyment; amusement; diversion. 《⇨ tanoshii; tanoshimu》
2 hope; expectation:
O-ai dekiru no o tanoshimi *ni shite imasu.* (お会いできるのを楽しみにしています) I *am looking forward to* seeing you.

ta⸢noshi⸣m·u たのしむ (楽しむ) *vt.*, *vi.* (-shim·i-; -shim·a-; -shiñ-de Ⓒ) enjoy; have a good time. 《⇨ tanoshii; tanoshimi》

ta⸢ñpaku⸣shitsu たんぱくしつ (蛋白質) *n.* protein.

ta⸢ñseñ たんせん (単線) *n.* single track (railroad). 《↔ fukuseñ》

ta⸢ñshiñ-fu⸣niñ たんしんふにん (単身赴任) *n.* taking up a new post and leaving one's family behind: tañshin-funiñsha (単身赴任者) a *business bachelor*.

ta⸣ñsho たんしょ (短所) *n.* shortcomings; weak point; fault. 《↔ choosho》

ta⸢ñshuku たんしゅく (短縮) *n.* shortening; curtailment; reduction.
tañshuku suru (〜する) *vt.* shorten; reduce: *eegyoo-jikañ o* tañshuku suru (営業時間を短縮する) *shorten* business hours. 《↔ eñchoo》

ta⸣ñso たんそ (炭素) *n.* carbon.

ta⸢ñsu たんす (箪笥) *n.* chest of drawers; wardrobe.

ta⸢ñtoo たんとう (担当) *n.* charge: tañtoo-*sha* (担当者) the person *in charge*.
tañtoo suru (〜する) *vt.* be in charge (of); take charge (of): *Kanojo wa kaikee o* tañtoo shite imasu. (彼女は会計を担当しています) She *is in charge of* accounting. 《⇨ ukemotsu》

ta⸣nuki たぬき (狸) *n.* raccoon dog.

ta⸢ore⸣·ru たおれる (倒れる) *vi.* (taore-te Ⓥ) **1** fall; topple:
Taifuu de taiboku ga taoreta. (台風で大木が倒れた) A big tree *fell down* in the typhoon. 《⇨ taosu》
2 become sick; (of a person) die; be killed:
karoo de taoreru (過労で倒れる) *collapse* from overwork.

ta⸣oru タオル *n.* towel.

ta⸢o⸣s·u たおす (倒す) *vt.* (taosh·i-; taos·a-; taosh·i-te Ⓒ) **1** throw [push] down; knock down; tip. 《⇨ taoreru》
2 beat; defeat; overthrow:
Kare wa yokozuna o taoshita. (彼は横綱を倒した) He *beat* the sumo grand champion. 《⇨ taoreru》

ta⸢ppu⸣ri たっぷり *adv.* (〜 to) fully; enough; in plenty:
Yosañ wa tappuri (*to*) *arimasu.* (予算はたっぷり(と)あります) We have *ample* funds.

-tara たら *infl. end.* [attached to verbs, adjectives, and the copula]
★ The *tara*-form is made by adding '*-ra*' to the *ta*-form. 《⇨ APP. 2》
1 if:
a (used in a conditional sentence):

Kirai dattara, *tabenakute mo ii desu yo.* (嫌いだったら, 食べなくてもいいですよ) *If* you do not like it, you don't have to eat it. ⟪⇨ ttara⟫
b (used in unreal or imaginary conditionals):
Byooki de nakattara, *ryokoo e ikeru ñ da ga.* (病気でなかったら, 旅行へ行けるんだが) If I *were not ill*, I would be able to go on a trip. ⟪⇨ -ba[1]⟫
c (used in fixed, introductory expressions):
Yoroshikattara, *kono heya o o-tsukai kudasai.* (よろしかったら, この部屋をお使いください) *If it is convenient for you*, please use this room.
2 when:
a (used to indicate a cause or reason): ★The second clause is often in the past.
Kanojo ni okurimono o shitara, *totemo yorokoñde kureta.* (彼女に贈物をしたら, とても喜んでくれた) *When* I gave her a present, she was very pleased.
b (used when an action occurs immediately after the *tara*-clause):
Kuukoo ni tsuitara, *o-deñwa shimasu.* (空港に着いたら, お電話します) I will phone you *on arriving* at the airport.
c (used when the action in the *tara*-clause leads to an unexpected occurrence): ★ The second clause is in the past.
Yamada no uchi e ittara, *rusu datta.* (山田の家へ行ったら, 留守だった) I went to Yamada's, but he was not at home.
-tara (**doo desu ka**) (～(どうですか)) what about; why don't you:
Koko de mattara, doo desu ka? (ここで待ったら, どうですか) *What about if* we wait here?

ta⌈ra⌉s·u たらす (垂らす) *vt.* (tara-sh·i-; taras·a-; tarash·i-te [C])
1 drop (liquid); drip:
Kare wa hitai kara ase o tarashite *ita.* (彼は額から汗を垂らしていた) He had sweat *dripping* from his brow. ⟪⇨ tareru⟫
2 hang down:
okujoo kara tsuna o tarasu (屋上から綱を垂らす) *hang down* a rope from the roof. ⟪⇨ tareru⟫

-ta⌉razu たらず (足らず) *suf.* less than; not more than:
hyaku-peeji-tarazu *no hoñ* (100 ページ足らずの本) a book of *less than* 100 pages.

ta⌈remaku たれまく (垂れ幕) *n.* banner hanging vertically; drop curtain.

ta⌈re⌉·ru たれる (垂れる) *vi.* (tare-te [V]) **1** drip; (of liquid) drop:
Jaguchi kara mizu ga tarete *imasu.* (蛇口から水が垂れています) Water *is dripping* from the faucet. ⟪⇨ tarasu⟫
2 hang; dangle:
Kanojo no kami wa kata made tarete ita. (彼女の髪は肩まで垂れていた) Her hair *hung down* to her shoulders. ⟪⇨ tarasu⟫

-tari たり *infl. end.* [attached to verbs, adjectives, and the copula] ★ The *tari*-form is made by adding '*-ri*' to the *ta*-form. ⟪⇨ APP. 2⟫
1 (indicates state(s) or action(s) occurring simultaneously or in succession): ★ Used usually in pairs, '*...-tari ...-tari*.'
Sono heya ni wa hito ga detari haittari shite ita. (その部屋には人が出たり入ったりしていた) Some people *were going into* the room, and others *were coming out*.
2 (indicates an example): ★ Often followed by '*nado*.'
Watashi wa donattari *nado shimaseñ.* (私はどなったりなどしません) I will not do such a thing as *shouting*.

ta⌈ri·ru たりる (足りる) *vi.* (tari-te [V]) be enough; be sufficient. ⟪⇨ juubuñ⟫

ta⌈ryoo たりょう (多量) *a.n.*

(~ na/no, ni) a large quantity [amount] (of):
Remoñ wa bitamiñ o taryoo ni fukuñde iru. (レモンはビタミンを多量に含んでいる) Lemons *are rich* in vitamins. ⟪↔ shooryoo⟫ ⟪⇨ tairyoo⟫

ta|shika たしか(確か) *a.n.* (~ na, ni) sure; certain; positive:
Kare ga kuru no wa tashika *desu.* (彼が来るのは確かです) It is *certain* that he will come. ⟪↔ futashika⟫
— *adv.* probably; perhaps; possibly:
Ano hito wa tashika *watashi yori wakai hazu desu.* (あの人は確か私より若いはずです) He is younger than me, *if I'm not mistaken.* ⟪⇨ chigainai; osoraku; tabuñ⟫.

ta|shikame|·ru たしかめる(確かめる) *vt.* (tashikame-te [V]) make sure; confirm; check.

ta|shi|zañ たしざん(足し算) *n.* (of arithmetic) addition. ⟪↔ hikizañ⟫

ta|shoo たしょう(多少) *n.* (a large or small) number; (a large or small) quantity.
— *adv.* some; a little; a few:
Nihoñ ni wa tashoo *shiriai ga imasu.* (日本には多少知り合いがいます) I have *a few* acquaintances in Japan.

ta|ssha たっしゃ(達者) *a.n.* (~ na, ni) **1** healthy; in good health. ⟪⇨ geñki⟫
2 proficient; expert; well:
Kanojo wa suiee ga tassha *desu.* (彼女は水泳が達者です) She is an *expert* swimmer.

ta|ss·uru たっする(達する) *vi., vt.* (tassh·i-; tassh·i-; tassh·i-te [I])
1 reach; arrive. ⟪⇨ tsuku[1]⟫
2 amount; reach:
Higai wa hyakumañ-eñ ni tasshita. (被害は100万円に達した) The damage *amounted* to one million yen.
3 attain; achieve:
Wareware wa mokuteki o tasshita. (われわれは目的を達した) We *attained* our purpose.

ta|s·u たす(足す) *vt.* (tash·i-; tas·a-; tash·i-te [C]) add; plus. ⟪↔ hiku[1]; herasu⟫

ta|sukaˈr·u たすかる(助かる) *vi.* (tasukar·i-; tasukar·a-; tasukatte [C]) **1** be saved; be rescued; survive. ⟪⇨ tasukeru⟫
2 (of aid, help, cooperation, etc.) be helpful:
Anata no go-kyooryoku ga areba, hijoo ni tasukarimasu. (あなたのご協力があれば，非常に助かります) If we have your cooperation it will *be a great help.* ⟪⇨ tasukeru⟫

ta|suke|·ru たすける(助ける) *vt.* (tasuke-te [V]) **1** help; assist; support:
Kanojo ga nimotsu o hakobu no o tasukete yatta. (彼女が荷物を運ぶのを助けてやった) I *helped* her carry the baggage. ⟪⇨ tasukaru⟫
2 save; rescue:
Kare wa oboreyoo to shite iru kodomo o tasuketa. (彼はおぼれようとしている子どもを助けた) He *saved* the child who was about to drown. ⟪⇨ tasukaru⟫

ta|su|u たすう(多数) *n.* a large [great] number; majority. ⟪↔ shoosuu[1]⟫

ta|takai たたかい(戦い) *n.* **1** war; battle. ⟪⇨ tatakau⟫
2 struggle:
hiñkoñ to no tatakai (貧困との戦い) the *struggle* against poverty. ⟪⇨ tatakau⟫

ta|taka·u たたかう(戦う) *vi.* (tataka·i-; tatakaw·a-; tatakat-te [C])
1 fight; struggle:
dokuritsu no tame ni tatakau (独立のために戦う) *fight* for independence. ⟪⇨ tatakai⟫
2 (of a game, match) play.

ta|ta|k·u たたく(叩く) *vt.* (tatak·i-; tatak·a-; tata·i-te [C])
1 beat; hit; knock; slap:
doa o tataku (ドアをたたく) *knock* on the door.
2 attack; criticize:

t

Yatoo wa seefu no seesaku o tataita. (野党は政府の政策をたたいた) The opposition *attacked* the government's policy.

ta[tami たたみ (畳) *n.* tatami (mat). (⇨ -joo[5])

ta[tam·u たたむ (畳む) *vt.* (tatam·i-; tatam·a-; tatañ-de C)
1 fold; double: *futoñ o* tatamu (ふとんをたたむ) *fold up* the bedding.
2 collapse (a desk, umbrella, etc.).
3 close down (a shop).

ta]te たて (縦) *n.* **1** length:
★ The vertical distance from end to end.
tate *no señ o hiku* (縦の線を引く) draw a *vertical* line. (↔ yoko)
2 (~ni) lengthwise; vertically.

ta[tegaki たてがき (縦書き) *n.* vertical writing. (↔ yokogaki)

ta[tekae·ru たてかえる (立て替える) *vt.* (-kae-te V) pay (for someone else); lend.

ta[temae たてまえ (建て前) *n.* principle; theory; opinion; official stance:
tatemae *to hoñne* (建て前と本音) the *principle* and the practice. (⇨ hoñne)

ta[te]mono たてもの (建物) *n.* building. (⇨ keñchiku)

ta[te]·ru[1] たてる (立てる) *vt.* (tate-te V) **1** set up; put up; stand:
tatefuda o tateru (立て札を立てる) *put up* a notice board. (⇨ tatsu[1])
2 raise (dust); make (a noise). (⇨ tatsu[1])

ta[te]·ru[2] たてる (建てる) *vt.* (tate-te V) build; erect:
tera o tateru (寺を建てる) *build* a temple. (⇨ keñchiku; tatsu[2])

ta[teuri-ju]utaku たてうりじゅうたく (建て売り住宅) *n.* ready-built house. ★ Often called '*tateuri*.'

ta[to]e[1] たとえ (譬え·例え) *n.* simile; metaphor; example.

ta[toe[2] たとえ (仮令) *adv.* even if; no matter what...:
Tatoe *anata ga hañtai shite mo watashi wa ikimasu.* (たとえあなたが反対しても私は行きます) *Even if* you are against it, I'm going.

ta[to]eba たとえば (例えば) *adv.* for example [instance]; such as.

ta[toe]·ru たとえる (譬える·例える) *vt.* (tatoe-te V) compare to; use a simile [metaphor].

ta]ts·u[1] たつ (立つ) *vi.* (tach·i-; tat·a-; tat-te C) **1** (of a person or an animal) stand; stand up:
seki o tatsu (席を立つ) *get up* from a seat.
2 (of a thing) stand.
3 (in an election) run; stand:
Koñdo no señkyo ni wa dare ga tachimasu *ka?* (今度の選挙にはだれが立ちますか) Who *is running* in the coming election?
4 (of steam, smoke, dust, etc.) rise. (⇨ tateru[1])

ta]ts·u[2] たつ (建つ) *vi.* (tach·i-; tat·a-; tat-te C) be built; be erected; be set up:
Kiñjo ni mañshoñ ga tatta. (近所にマンションが建った) A condominium *was built* in my neighborhood. (⇨ tateru[2])

ta]ts·u[3] たつ (絶つ) *vt.* (tach·i-; tat·a-; tat-te C) break off; sever; cut off:
gaikoo kañkee o tatsu (外交関係を絶つ) *break off* diplomatic relations.

ta]ts·u[4] たつ (経つ) *vi.* (tach·i-; tat·a-; tat-te C) (of time) pass by; go by:
Chichi-oya ga nakunatte kara sañ-neñ tatta. (父親が亡くなってから3年たった) Three years *have passed* since my father died. (⇨ keeka)

ta]ts·u[5] たつ (発つ) *vt.* (tach·i-; tat·a-; tat-te C) start; leave; depart. (⇨ shuppatsu)

ta]ts·u[6] たつ (断つ) *vt.* (tach·i-; tat·a-; tat-te C) quit; give up (smoking, alcohol, etc.).

ta[tta たった *adv.* only; just; no more than:
Eki made koko kara tatta *go-fuñ*

desu. (駅までここからたった5分です) It takes *no more than* five minutes from here to the station.

ta⌈ue⌉ たうえ(田植え) *n.* rice-planting; transplantation of rice seedlings.

ta⌈wara⌉ たわら(俵) *n.* straw bag.

ta⌈yasu⌉·i たやすい *a.* (-ku) easy; simple:
Koñna moñdai wa tayasuku *tokemasu.* (こんな問題はたやすく解けます) I can *easily* solve a problem like this. ⇨ yasashii[1]

ta⌉yori[1] たより(便り) *n.* letter; news. ⇨ tegami

ta⌉yori[2] たより(頼り) *n.* reliance; dependence; trust. ⇨ tayoru
tayori ni naru [naranai] (～になる[ならない]) reliable [unreliable].

ta⌈yo⌉r·u たよる(頼る) *vt.* (tayor·i-; tayor·a-; tayot-te Ⓒ) rely [count] on; depend on:
Kare wa mada oya ni tayotte iru. (彼はまだ親に頼っている) He still *depends* on his parents.

ta⌈zune⌉·ru[1] たずねる(尋ねる) *vt.* (tazune-te Ⓥ) **1** ask; inquire; question. ⇨ kiku[1]
2 look for; search for (a person): *nikushiñ o* tazuneru (肉親を尋ねる) *look for* one's relatives.

ta⌈zune⌉·ru[2] たずねる(訪ねる) *vt.* (tazune-te Ⓥ) visit; call on [at]; come [go round] to see.

te⌉ て(手) *n.* **1** hand.
2 means; way:
Keesatsu wa arayuru te *o tsukushite, sono ko o sagashita.* (警察はあらゆる手を尽くして，その子を捜した) The police tried every possible *means* to find the child.
3 kind; brand:
Kono te *no mono ga yoku uremasu.* (この手のものがよく売れます) Articles of this *kind* sell very well.
te ga denai (～が出ない) cannot possibly buy.
te ni ireru (～に入れる) get; obtain.
te o dasu (～を出す) start; dabble: *kabu ni* te o dasu (株に手を出す) *dabble* in stocks.
te o nuku (～を抜く) cut corners.
te o tsukeru (～をつける) start; set about.

-te て *infl. end.* [attached to the *ku*-form of an adjective. For the *te*-form of verbs, see APP. 2]
★ The *te*-form of the copula is '*de.*'
1 and: ★ Used to link similar items in a parallel relationship.
Terebi no nyuusu wa hayakute *seekaku da.* (テレビのニュースは速くて正確だ) The news on TV is *quick and* correct.
2 since; after: ★ Used to indicate a temporal sequence.
Kanojo wa daigaku o dete, *sugu kekkoñ shita.* (彼女は大学を出て，すぐ結婚した) She got married soon *after* graduating from college.
3 with: ★ Used when two actions occur almost simultaneously.
Kare wa udegumi o shite, *nani-ka kañgaete ita.* (彼は腕組みをして，何か考えていた) He was thinking about something *with* his arms folded.
4 because; since: ★ Used to indicate a cause or reason.
Kinoo no bañ wa atsukute, *nemurenakatta.* (きのうの晩は暑くて，眠れなかった) I could not sleep last night *for* the heat. ⇨ kara[4]; no de
5 by; on: ★ Used to indicate a means or method.
Kanojo wa jiteñsha ni notte, *kaimono ni ikimashita.* (彼女は自転車に乗って，買い物に行きました) She went shopping *by* bicycle.
6 but: ★ Used to indicate a contrast or opposition.
Koñna ni doryoku shite, *mada dekinai.* (こんなに努力して，まだできない) I have tried so hard, *but* I still cannot do it.
7 (used with other verbs such as '*iru,*' '*miru,*' '*oku,*' '*morau,*' '*age-*

ru,' 'kureru,' etc.):
Ima Nihoñgo o naratte imasu. (今日本語を習っています) I am now *studying* Japanese.

te⌈a⌉rai てあらい (手洗い) *n.* toilet; restroom; lavatory. ((⇨ beñjo))

te⌉-ashi てあし (手足) *n.* hand and foot; arms and legs; limbs.

te⌉ate てあて (手当て) *n.* **1** medical treatment [care]:
*ookyuu-*teate *o ukeru* (応急手当てを受ける) receive first *aid.*
2 allowance; bonus:
juutaku[*tsuukiñ*]-teate (住宅[通勤]手当て) a housing [commuting] *allowance.* ((⇨ boonasu; shooyo))
teate (o) suru (~(を)する) *vt.* treat (an illness).

te⌈bana⌉s·u てばなす (手放す) *vt.* (-banash·i-; -banas·a-; -banash·i-te Ⓒ) part with; sell; give up. ((⇨ uru[1]))

te⌈baya⌉·i てばやい (手早い) *a.* (-ku) quick:
Kare wa tebayaku *heya o katazuketa.* (彼は手早く部屋を片づけた) He *quickly* straightened up his room.

te⌉biki てびき (手引き) *n.* guide; guidebook; handbook.
tebiki (o) suru (~(を)する) *vt.* guide; lead; help.

te⌈bu⌉kuro てぶくろ (手袋) *n.* glove. ((⇨ kutsushita))

te⌉buri てぶり (手振り) *n.* gesture; signs. ((⇨ miburi))

te⌈chi⌉gai てちがい (手違い) *n.* mistake; fault; accident.

t

te⌈choo てちょう (手帳) *n.* small notebook; pocket diary.

te⌈da⌉suke てだすけ (手助け) *n.* help; assistance:
tedasuke ni naru (手助けになる) *be helpful.*
tedasuke (o) suru (~(を)する) *vt.* help; assist. ((⇨ tetsudau))

te⌈eañ ていあん (提案) *n.* proposal; suggestion; motion.
teeañ (o) suru (~(を)する) *vt.* propose (a plan); suggest; move.

te⌈eboo ていぼう (堤防) *n.* riverbank; embankment; levee. ((⇨ dote))

te⌈echi ていち (低地) *n.* lowlands; low ground. ((↔ koochi[3]))

te⌈edeñ ていでん (停電) *n.* blackout; power failure; power cut.
teedeñ suru (~する) *vi.* (of electric power) fail; be cut off.

te⌉edo ていど (程度) *n.* degree; extent; standard; level:
Sono uwasa wa aru teedo *made hoñtoo desu.* (そのうわさはある程度まで本当です) The rumor is true to some *extent.*

te⌈egaku[1] ていがく (停学) *n.* suspension from school (as punishment). ((⇨ taigaku))

te⌈egaku[2] ていがく (低額) *n.* small sum of money. ((⇨ koogaku))

te⌈eiñ ていいん (定員) *n.* (seating) capacity; the fixed number.

te⌈eka[1] ていか (低下) *n.* fall off; decline; deterioration.
teeka suru (~する) *vi.* fall; drop; lower. ((↔ jooshoo)) ((⇨ sagaru))

te⌈eka[2] ていか (定価) *n.* fixed [list] price.

te⌉eki ていき (定期) *n.* **1** fixed period:
kaigoo o teeki *ni hiraku* (会合を定期に開く) hold meetings at *regular intervals.*
2 commutation [season] ticket. ((⇨ teekikeñ))

te⌈eki⌉keñ ていきけん (定期券) *n.* commutation [season] ticket. ((⇨ kaisuukeñ))

te⌈ekoku ていこく (定刻) *n.* the scheduled [appointed] time.

te⌈ekoo ていこう (抵抗) *n.* **1** resistance; opposition.
2 reluctance:
Kare ni au no wa nañto-naku teekoo o kañjimasu. (彼に会うのは何となく抵抗を感じます) I *am* rather *reluctant* to meet him.
teekoo suru (~する) *vi.* resist; oppose.

te⌈ekyoo ていきょう (提供) *n.* offer; sponsorship.

teekyoo suru (～する) *vt.* offer; provide; donate. ⟪⇨ ataeru⟫

te⌈ekyu⌉ubi ていきゅうび (定休日) *n.* regular holiday.

te⌉ema テーマ *n.* theme; subject; topic.

te⌉enee ていねい (丁寧) *a.n.* (～ na, ni) **1** polite; courteous; kind: teenee *ni ojigi suru* (丁寧におじぎする) bow *politely.*
2 careful; close; thorough: *kañji o* teenee *ni kaku* (漢字を丁寧に書く) write Chinese characters *carefully.*

te⌈eneego ていねいご (丁寧語) *n.* polite word [expression].

te⌈eneñ ていねん (定年) *n.* retirement age; age limit.

te⌈eoñ ていおん (低温) *n.* low temperature. ⟪↔ koo-oñ⟫

te⌉epu テープ *n.* (of a cassette, video, etc.) tape; ticker tape; ribbon; adhesive tape.

te⌈eryuujo ていりゅうじょ (停留所) *n.* bus [streetcar] stop. ★ A train station is '*eki*.' ⟪⇨ basutee⟫

te⌈esai ていさい (体裁) *n.* appearance; show; style. ⟪⇨ kakkoo[1]⟫
teesai ga warui (～が悪い) feel awkward.

te⌈esee ていせい (訂正) *n.* correction; revision.
teesee suru (～する) *vt.* correct: *ayamari o* teesee suru (誤りを訂正する) *correct* a mistake. ⟪⇨ naosu[1]⟫

te⌈esha ていしゃ (停車) *n.* (of a train, bus, etc.) stop. ⟪↔ hassha⟫
teesha suru (～する) *vi.* stop.

te⌈eshi ていし (停止) *n.* **1** stop; halt. ⟪↔ zeñshiñ[1]⟫
2 suspension; cessation: *kaku-jikkeñ no* teeshi (核実験の停止) the *suspension* of nuclear tests.
teeshi suru (～する) *vi., vt.*
1 come to a stop; halt. ⟪⇨ tomaru[1]⟫
2 suspend (business, payment).

te⌈eshi⌉see ていしせい (低姿勢) *n.* modest attitude; low profile. ⟪↔ kooshisee⟫

te⌈eshoku ていしょく (定食) *n.* fixed meal; table d'hôte.

te⌈eshutsu ていしゅつ (提出) *n.* submission; presentation.
teeshutsu suru (～する) *vt.* submit; turn [send] in; present. ⟪⇨ dasu; sashidasu⟫

te⌈ga⌉kari てがかり (手掛かり) *n.* clue; key; track: *Hañniñ wa nani mo* tegakari *o nokosanakatta.* (犯人は何も手がかりを残さなかった) The culprit left no *traces* behind.

te⌈gami てがみ (手紙) *n.* letter: tegami *o dasu* [*uketoru*] (手紙を出す[受け取る]) send off [receive] a *letter.* ⟪⇨ buñtsuu; tayori[1]⟫

te⌈gara⌉ てがら (手柄) *n.* credit; meritorious deed: *Kono seekoo wa kimi no* tegara *da.* (この成功は君の手柄だ) *Credit* for this success goes to you.

te⌈garu てがる (手軽) *a.n.* (～ na, ni) handy; easy; light: tegaru *na jisho* (手軽な辞書) a *handy* dictionary.

te⌈giwa⌉ てぎわ (手際) *n.* skill; craftsmanship; efficiency: *Kare wa* tegiwa yoku *sono kooshoo o matometa.* (彼は手ぎわよくその交渉をまとめた) He concluded the negotiations *with skill.*

te⌉hai てはい (手配) *n.* arrangements; preparations.
tehai (o) suru (～(を)する) *vt.*
1 arrange; prepare; get ready.
2 search: *Sono jikeñ no yoogisha wa zeñkoku ni* tehai sarete imasu. (その事件の容疑者は全国に手配されています) The suspect in that case *is being searched for* nationwide.

te⌉hazu てはず (手筈) *n.* arrangements; plan; program: tehazu *o totonoeru* (手はずを整える) make *arrangements.*

te⌈ho⌉ñ てほん (手本) *n.* model; example; pattern.

te⌈ire⌉ ていれ (手入れ) *n.* **1** care: *Kono niwa wa* teire ga yukitodo-

t

ite iru. (この庭は手入れが行き届いている) This garden *is well cared for.*
2 raid; crackdown:
keesatsu no teire (警察の手入れ) a police *raid.*
teire (o) suru (～(を)する) *vt.*
1 take care of; care for; repair.
2 raid; crack down on.

te⌝jina てじな (手品) *n.* magic; conjuring trick.

te⌝juñ てじゅん (手順) *n.* plan; order; process; arrangement:
Subete wa tejuñ-*doori umaku itta.* (すべては手順どおりうまくいった) Everything went well according to *plan.*

te⌈ka⌝geñ てかげん (手加減) *n.* allowance; discretion; consideration.
tekageñ (o) suru (～(を)する) *vt.* make allowances; use discretion; take into consideration.

te⌝kazu てかず (手数) *n.* trouble. ⟪⇨ tesuu⟫

te⌈ki てき (敵) *n.* enemy; opponent; rival. ⟪↔ mikata[2]⟫

-teki てき (的) *suf.* (*a.n.*) (～ na, ni) concerning; having a certain character; resembling: ★ Added to a noun, usually of Chinese origin. '*-teki na* [*ni*]' is often equivalent to English '-al [-ally].'
roñri-teki *ni setsumee suru* (論理的に説明する) explain *logically* / ippañ-teki *na kañgae* (一般的な考え) a *common* notion.

te⌝kigi てきぎ (適宜) *a.n.* (～ na, ni), *adv.* appropriate; proper; suitable. ⟪⇨ tekitoo⟫

te⌝kii てきい (敵意) *n.* hostility; enmity. ⟪↔ kooi[2]⟫

te⌈kikaku てきかく (的確) *a.n.* (～ na, ni) accurate; exact; precise.

te⌈kisee てきせい (適性) *n.* aptitude: tekisee-*keñsa* (適性検査) an *aptitude* test.

te⌈kisetsu てきせつ (適切) *a.n.* (～ na, ni) suitable; appropriate; proper. ⟪⇨ fusawashii⟫

te⌈kis·u⌝ru てきする (適する) *vi.* (tekish·i-; tekis·a-; tekish·i-te [C]) be suitable; be good:
Kono shokubutsu wa shokuyoo ni tekishite imasu. (この植物は食用に適しています) This plant *is good* for food.

te⌝kisuto テキスト *n.* textbook.
★ Shortened form of '*tekisuto bukku*' (textbook). ⟪⇨ kyookasho⟫

te⌈kitoo てきとう (適当) *a.n.* (～ na, ni) **1** suitable; good:
tekitoo *na kikai ni* (適当な機会に) on a *suitable* occasion. ⟪↔ futekitoo⟫ ⟪⇨ tekisetsu⟫
2 (of work, method, etc.) irresponsible; taking things easy:
Muri shinai de, tekitoo ni yaroo. (無理しないで, 適当にやろう) *Let's take it easy* and not push ourselves too hard.

te⌈kiyoo てきよう (適用) *n.* application.
tekiyoo suru (～する) *vt.* apply (a rule).

te⌈kkiñ てっきん (鉄筋) *n.* steel rod [bar]: tekkiñ-koñkuriito (鉄筋コンクリート) *ferroconcrete.*

te⌈kkyoo てっきょう (鉄橋) *n.* iron bridge; railroad bridge.

te⌝ko てこ (梃子) *n.* lever.

te⌝kubi てくび (手首) *n.* wrist.

te⌈ma⌝ てま (手間) *n.* time; labor; trouble: tema *o habuku* (手間を省く) save *labor.*

te⌈mae てまえ (手前) *n.* **1** (～ ni, de) this side; before:
Koosateñ no temae de *tomatte kudasai.* (交差点の手前で止まってください) Please stop the car *before* you come to the intersection.
2 presence:
Ryooshiñ no temae *sono ko wa otonashiku shite ita.* (両親の手前その子はおとなしくしていた) The child remained quiet in the *presence* of her parents.

te⌈mane⌝ki てまねき (手招き) *n.* beckoning.

t

temaneki suru (〜する) *vt.* beckon. ⟪⇨ maneku⟫

-te mo ても [*te*-form of a verb or adjective plus the particle '*mo*']
1 (even) if; though:
Ame ga futte mo *shiai wa arimasu.* (雨が降っても試合はあります) *Even if* it rains, we will have the game. ⟪⇨ tatoe[2]⟫
2 however; whatever:
Doñna ni *sono shigoto ga* tsurakute mo *watashi wa yarimasu.* (どんなにその仕事がつらくても私はやります) I will carry out the task *however painful it is.*

te⌈moto⌉ てもと (手元) *n.* hand: *jisho o* temoto *ni oku* (辞書を手元に置く) keep a dictionary at *hand.*

te⌈ñ[1] てん (点) *n.* **1** dot; spot.
2 score; grade; mark. ⟪⇨ teñsuu⟫
3 point; respect:
Sono teñ *ni moñdai ga aru.* (その点に問題がある) There is a problem on that *point.*

te⌉ñ[2] てん (天) *n.* **1** the sky.
2 Heaven; Providence.

-teñ[1] てん (店) *suf.* store; shop; office:
sho-teñ (書店) a book*store* / *kissa*-teñ (喫茶店) a coffee *shop* / *shi*-teñ (支店) a branch *office.*

-teñ[2] てん (展) *suf.* exhibition: *ko*-teñ (個展) a one-man *show.*

te⌈na⌉oshi てなおし (手直し) *n.* readjustment; rectification; alteration; improvement.
tenaoshi suru (〜する) *vt.* readjust; rectify; alter; improve. ⟪⇨ naosu[1]⟫

te⌉ñchi てんち (天地) *n.* **1** heaven and earth; universe.
2 land; world: *jiyuu no* teñchi (自由の天地) a free *land.*
3 top and bottom:
Kono shashiñ wa teñchi ga gyaku *da.* (この写真は天地が逆だ) This photo is *upside down.*

te⌈ñdoñ てんどん (天丼) *n.* a bowl of rice topped with deep-fried shrimp and vegetables.

te⌉ñgoku てんごく (天国) *n.* heaven; Heaven; paradise. ⟪↔ jigoku⟫

te⌈ni⌉motsu てにもつ (手荷物) *n.* carry-on baggage; hand luggage: tenimotsu-azukarijo (手荷物預かり所) a *checkroom*; a *left-luggage office.*

te⌈ñiñ てんいん (店員) *n.* salesclerk; salesman; saleswoman.

te⌈ñjoo てんじょう (天井) *n.* ceiling; roof.

te⌈ñkai てんかい (展開) *n.* development.
teñkai suru (〜する) *vi., vt.* develop; unfold; spread out. ⟪⇨ hirogaru⟫

te⌈ñkee てんけい (典型) *n.* type; model; specimen.

te⌈ñkee-teki てんけいてき (典型的) *a.n.* (〜 na, ni) typical; model.

te⌈ñkeñ てんけん (点検) *n.* examination; check; inspection.
teñkeñ suru (〜する) *vt.* examine; check; inspect: *Gasoriñ-sutañdo de kuruma o* teñkeñ shite moratta. (ガソリンスタンドで車を点検してもらった) I *had* my car *checked* at a gas station. ⟪⇨ shiraberu⟫

te⌉ñki てんき (天気) *n.* weather; fine weather:
Kyoo wa teñki *da.* (きょうは天気だ) It's *fine* today. ⟪⇨ kaisee[2]; teñkoo⟫

te⌈ñkiñ てんきん (転勤) *n.* transfer.
teñkiñ suru (〜する) *vi.* be transferred.

te⌈ñki-yo⌉hoo てんきよほう (天気予報) *n.* weather forecast [report].

te⌈ñkoo てんこう (天候) *n.* weather conditions. ⟪⇨ teñki⟫

te⌈ñmo⌉ñgaku てんもんがく (天文学) *n.* astronomy.

te⌈ñneñ てんねん (天然) *n.* nature: teñneñ-*gasu* (天然ガス) *natural* gas / teñneñ-*kineñbutsu* (天然記念物) a *Natural* Monument.

te⌈ñno⌉o てんのう (天皇) *n.* emperor: ★ This only refers to the

t

Emperor of Japan.
Teñnoo-heeka (天皇陛下) *His Majesty the Emperor.* (⇨ Koogoo)

te-⌈no⌉-hira てのひら (手の平) *n.* the flat of the hand; palm.

te⌉ñpo テンポ *n.* tempo; pace; speed.

te⌈ñpura てんぷら (天ぷら) *n.* tempura. ★ A dish of seafood and vegetables, which are dipped in batter and deep-fried.

te⌈ñra⌉ñkai てんらんかい (展覧会) *n.* exhibition; show.

te⌈ñsai[1] てんさい (天災) *n.* natural disaster [calamity].

te⌈ñsai[2] てんさい (天才) *n.* genius.

te⌉ñshi てんし (天使) *n.* angel.

te⌈ñshoku てんしょく (転職) *n.* change of one's job.
teñshoku suru (〜する) *vi.* change one's occupation.

te⌈ñsu⌉u てんすう (点数) *n.* mark; point; score:
shikeñ de ii teñsuu *o toru* (試験でいい点数を取る) get a good *mark* on the test. (⇨ teñ[1])

te⌈ñteki てんてき (点滴) *n.* intravenous drip infusion.

te⌈ñtoo てんとう (点灯) *n.* lighting.
teñtoo suru (〜する) *vt., vi.* turn [switch] on a light; be turned on.

te⌈nugui てぬぐい (手拭) *n.* hand towel. ★ It is made of rough cotton cloth.

te⌈o⌉kure ておくれ (手遅れ) *n.* being too late; being beyond cure:
Ima to natte wa teokure *da.* (今となっては手遅れだ) It is *too late* now.

te⌈ppañ てっぱん (鉄板) *n.* iron [steel] plate:
teppañ-*yaki* (鉄板焼き) meat and vegetables cooked on an *iron plate.*

te⌈ppoo てっぽう (鉄砲) *n.* gun:
teppoo *o utsu* (鉄砲を撃つ) fire a *gun.*

te⌈ra⌉ てら (寺) *n.* (Buddhist) temple. ★ Also '*o-tera.*' (⇨ jiñja)

te⌈rashiawase⌉·ru てらしあわせる (照らし合わせる) *vt.* (-awase-te Ⓥ) compare with; check; test by comparison. (⇨ kuraberu)

te⌈ra⌉s·u てらす (照らす) *vt.* (terash·i-; teras·a-; terash·i-te Ⓒ) light; shine; illuminate. (⇨ teru)

te⌉rebi テレビ *n.* television (set); television (program); TV.

te⌈rehoñ-ka⌉ado テレホンカード *n.* telephone card. ★ A prepaid plastic card against which charges are debited when using a public phone.

te⌉r·u てる (照る) *vi.* (ter·i-; ter·a-; tet-te Ⓒ) shine; blaze:
Taiyoo ga kañkañ to tette iru. (太陽がかんかんと照っている) The sun *is shining* brightly. (⇨ terasu)

te⌈ruteru-bo⌉ozu てるてるぼうず (照る照る坊主) *n.* a simple, small doll, which children hang outside in the hope of it bringing good weather.

te⌈saki⌉ てさき (手先) *n.* **1** finger; hand:
Kare wa tesaki *ga kiyoo [bukiyoo] da.* (彼は手先が器用[不器用]だ) He is good [clumsy] with his *hands.*
2 tool; agent:
booryokudañ no tesaki (暴力団の手先) the *tool* of a criminal gang.

te⌈suri⌉ てすり (手摺り) *n.* rail; handrail.

te⌉suto テスト *n.* test; quiz. (⇨ shikeñ)
tesuto (o) suru (〜(を)する) *vt.* give a test: *kikai no seenoo o* tesuto suru (機械の性能をテストする) *test* the performance of a machine.

te⌈su⌉u てすう (手数) *n.* trouble:
Kare no okage de daibu tesuu *ga habuketa.* (彼のおかげでだいぶ手数が省けた) Thanks to him, we were able to save much *trouble.*

te⌈su⌉uryoo てすうりょう (手数料) *n.* commission; service charge.

te⌈tsu てつ (鉄) *n.* iron.

te⌈tsubiñ てつびん (鉄瓶) *n.* iron

kettle. ⟪⇨ yakañ[2]⟫

te⌈tsuboo てつぼう(鉄棒) *n.* horizontal bar; iron bar.

te⌈tsuda⌉i てつだい(手伝い) *n.*
1 help; assistance. ⟪⇨ tetsudau⟫
2 help(er); assistant:
Dare-ka tetsudai *o yokoshite kudasai.* (だれか手伝いをよこしてください) Please send *someone to help.*

te⌈tsuda⌉·u てつだう(手伝う) *vt.* (tetsuda·i-; tetsudaw·a-; tetsudat-te Ⓒ) help; assist:
Watashi wa kanojo no shigoto o tetsudatta. (私は彼女の仕事を手伝った) I *helped* her with her work. ⟪⇨ tetsudai⟫

te⌈tsudoo てつどう(鉄道) *n.* railroad; railway.

te⌈tsu⌉gaku てつがく(哲学) *n.* philosophy.

te⌈tsuya てつや(徹夜) *n.* staying up all night.
tetsuya suru (～する) *vi.* stay up all night.

te⌈tsu⌉zuki てつづき(手続き) *n.* procedure; formalities.

te⌈ttee てってい(徹底) *n.* thoroughness; completeness.
tettee suru (～する) *vi.* be thorough; be complete.

te⌈ttee-teki てっていてき(徹底的) *a.n.* (～ na, ni) thorough; exhaustive:
tettee-teki *ni choosa suru* (徹底的に調査する) make a *thorough* investigation.

-te wa ては [*te*-form of a verb or adjective plus the particle '*wa*']
1 (the '*-te wa*' clause indicates a condition and the following clause the natural or obvious result or conclusion):
Sonna ni tsukarete ite wa, *shigoto ni naranai.* (そんなに疲れていては，仕事にならない) *If* you are so tired, you will not be able to do your job properly.
2 (used to indicate an objection or prohibition):
Abunai tokoro e itte wa ikemaseñ. (危ない所へ行ってはいけません) You *must not go* to dangerous places.
★ Note: '*-te wa*' becomes '*-cha*' in informal speech, and '*de wa*' becomes '*ja.*' *e.g. Soko e* itcha *ikenai yo.* (そこへ行っちゃいけないよ) Don't *go* there.
-nakute wa naranai [dame da] (なくてはならない[だめだ]) must; should: ★ The form '*-nakereba*' is used similarly. ⟪⇨ -ba[1]⟫
Kodomo wa hayaku nenakute wa dame desu. (子どもは早く寝なくてはだめです) Children *should go to bed* early.

te⌈wake⌉ てわけ(手分け) *n.* division of labor.
tewake suru (～する) *vi.* divide; separate; share.

te⌈za⌉wari てざわり(手触り) *n.* feel; touch:
tezawari *ga yawarakai* (手触りが柔らかい) be soft to the *touch.*

ti⌈sshu-pe⌉epaa ティッシュペーパー *n.* tissue; Kleenex (*trade name*). ★ Also called simply '*tisshu.*' ⟪⇨ chirigami⟫

to[1] と *p.* **1** with; from: ★ Used after a noun.
Watashi wa kare to *yoku tenisu o shimasu.* (私は彼とよくテニスをします) I often play tennis *with* him.
2 to; into: ★ Used to indicate a resulting change.
Kaji de subete ga hai to *natta.* (火事ですべてが灰となった) Everything was reduced *to* ashes in the fire.
3 from; as; to: ★ Used in expressing difference, similarity, or comparison.
Kore to *onaji mono o kudasai.* (これと同じ物を下さい) Please give me the same one *as* this.
4 that: ★ Used as a quotative particle.
Ashita wa hareru to *omoimasu.* (あしたは晴れると思います) I think it will be fine tomorrow.
5 (used after adverbs, especially those signifying state, condition

or manner and after onomatopoeias):
Dokañ to *ooki-na oto ga shita.* (ドカンと大きな音がした) There was a loud *bang.*

to[2] と *p.* and: ★ Used to enumerate or list two or more nouns.
naifu to *fooku* (ナイフとフォーク) a knife *and* fork.

to[3] と (戸) *n.* door.

to[4] と (都) *n.* metropolis. ★ An administrative division of Japan, but only used with reference to Tokyo.

to⌈bas·u[1] とばす (飛ばす) *vt.* (tobash·i-; tobas·a-; tobash·i-te Ⓒ)
1 fly; let [make] fly:
mokee hikooki o tobasu (模型飛行機を飛ばす) *fly* a model airplane.
2 blow off:
Kaze de señtakumono ga tobasareta. (風で洗濯物が飛ばされた) The washing *was blown down* by the wind.
3 drive fast:
Kare wa moo-supiido de baiku o tobashita. (彼は猛スピードでバイクを飛ばした) He *drove* his motorbike at a furious speed.
4 skip; omit:
Watashi wa sono shoosetsu o tobasanai *de yoñda.* (私はその小説を飛ばさないで読んだ) I read the novel *without skipping.*
5 make (a joke); spread:
joodañ o tobasu (冗談を飛ばす) *crack* a joke / *dema o* tobasu (デマを飛ばす) *spread* a false rumor.
6 sputter; splash:
doromizu o tobasu (泥水を飛ばす) *splash* muddy water.

to⌈basu[2] とバス (都バス) *n.* a bus or the bus transportation system operated by the Tokyo Metropolitan Government. 《⇒ basu》

to⌈biaga⌉r·u とびあがる (飛び上がる) *vi.* (-agar·i-; -agar·a-; -agat-te Ⓒ) **1** jump; leap; spring to one's feet.
2 fly up:
Hibari ga mugibatake kara tobiagatta. (ひばりが麦畑から飛び上がった) A skylark *flew up* from the wheat field.

to⌈bida⌉s·u とびだす (飛び出す) *vi.* (-dash·i-; -das·a-; -dash·i-te Ⓒ) jump out; run out; rush out.

to⌈biko⌉m·u とびこむ (飛び込む) *vi.* (-kom·i-; -kom·a-; -koñ-de Ⓒ) jump [plunge] into; dive into:
puuru ni tobikomu (プールに飛び込む) *jump into* a pool.

to⌈bimawa⌉r·u とびまわる (飛び回る) *vt.* (-mawar·i-; -mawar·a-; -mawat-te Ⓒ) fly about; bustle about; romp about.

to⌈bino⌉k·u とびのく (飛び退く) *vi.* (-nok·i-; -nok·a-; -no·i-te Ⓒ) jump back [aside].

to⌈bino⌉r·u とびのる (飛び乗る) *vi.* (-nor·i-; -nor·a-; -not-te Ⓒ) jump on [into] (a vehicle). 《↔ tobioriru》

to⌈biori⌉·ru とびおりる (飛び下りる) *vi.* (-ori-te Ⓥ) jump down; leap down. 《↔ tobinoru》

to⌈bira とびら (扉) *n.* **1** door.
2 (of a book) title page.

to⌈bita⌉ts·u とびたつ (飛び立つ) *vi.* (-tach·i-; -tat·a-; -tat-te Ⓒ) fly away; (of an airplane) take off.

to⌈bitsu⌉k·u とびつく (飛び付く) *vi.* (-tsuk·i-; -tsuk·a-; -tsu·i-te Ⓒ) jump at; leap at.

to⌈boshi⌉·i とぼしい (乏しい) *a.* (-ku) scanty; scarce; poor:
Kimi wa mada keekeñ ga toboshii. (きみはまだ経験が乏しい) You are still *lacking* in experience.

to⌉botobo とぼとぼ *adv.* (～ to) (a weary or weak way of walking): tobotobo (to) aruku (とぼとぼ(と)歩く) *plod along.*

to⌈b·u[1] とぶ (飛ぶ) *vi.* (tob·i-; tob·a-; toñ-de Ⓒ) **1** (of a bird, aircraft) fly.
2 (of a person) fly; travel by plane:
Kare wa Sapporo made hikooki de toñda. (彼は札幌まで飛行機で飛ん

だ) He *flew* to Sapporo by plane.
3 rush; fly:
Kare wa jiko no geñba e toñda. (彼は事故の現場へ飛んだ) He *rushed* to the scene of the accident. (⇨ isogu)

to⌈b·u[2] とぶ(跳ぶ) *vi.* (tob·i-; to-b·a-; toñ-de [C]) jump; leap; hop. (⇨ haneru)

to⌈chi とち(土地) *n.* **1** land; lot; soil: tochi *o tagayasu* (土地を耕す) cultivate the *soil.* (⇨ akichi)
2 place:
Kono tochi *ni kita no wa hajimete desu.* (この土地に来たのは初めてです) This is the first time that I've visited this *place.*

to⌈chuu とちゅう(途中) *n.* on the way; halfway:
Yuubiñkyoku wa eki e iku tochuu *ni arimasu.* (郵便局は駅へ行く途中にあります) The post office is *on the way* to the station.

to⌈chuu-ge⌉sha とちゅうげしゃ(途中下車) *n.* (train) stopover.
tochuu-gesha suru (〜する) *vi.* stop over. (⇨ gesha; oriru)

to⌈dana とだな(戸棚) *n.* cupboard; closet.

to⌈den とでん(都電) *n.* a streetcar or the streetcar system operated by the Tokyo Metropolitan Government. (⇨ tobasu[2])

to⌈doke⌉·ru とどける(届ける) *vt.* (todoke-te [V]) **1** send; deliver; take; bring:
Kono kagu o jitaku made todokete *kudasai.* (この家具を自宅まで届けてください) Please *deliver* this furniture to my house. (⇨ todoku)
2 report; notify:
Toonañ o keesatsu ni todoketa. (盗難を警察に届けた) I *reported* the theft to the police.

to⌈do⌉k·u とどく(届く) *vi.* (todo-k·i-; todok·a-; todo·i-te [C])
1 arrive; get to:
Sokutatsu ga todokimashita. (速達が届きました) A special delivery *has arrived.* (⇨ todokeru)
2 reach:
Tana no ano hoñ ni te ga todoki-*masu ka?* (棚のあの本に手が届きますか) *Can* you *reach* that book on the shelf?

to-⌈doo-fu-ke⌉ñ とどうふけん(都道府県) *n.* all the major administrative divisions within Japan. (⇨ map (inside back cover))

to⌈ga⌉r·u とがる(尖る) *vi.* (toga-r·i-; togar·a-; togat-te [C]) taper off to a point; be sharp.
★ Often pronounced '*toñgaru.*'

to⌈ge⌉ とげ(刺) *n.* prick; splinter:
Toge *ga yubi ni sasatta.* (とげが指に刺さった) I got a *splinter* in my finger.

to⌈ge⌉·ru とげる(遂げる) *vt.* (toge-te [V]) accomplish; achieve; attain; realize:
mokuteki o togeru (目的を遂げる) *accomplish* one's purpose.

to⌈gire⌉·ru とぎれる(途切れる) *vi.* (togire-te [V]) break; be interrupted:
Deñwa ga natte, kaiwa ga togire-ta. (電話が鳴って, 会話が途切れた) The phone rang and our conversation *was interrupted.*

to⌉g·u とぐ(研ぐ) *vt.* (tog·i-; to-g·a-; to·i-de [C]) **1** sharpen (a knife); whet; grind.
2 wash (rice).

to⌉ho とほ(徒歩) *n.* walking:
Eki made toho *de jup-puñ desu.* (駅まで徒歩で10分です) It takes ten minutes to *walk* to the station. (⇨ aruku)

to⌈i とい(問い) *n.* question. (↔ kotae) (⇨ shitsumoñ)

to⌈iawase といあわせ(問い合わせ) *n.* inquiry. (⇨ toiawaseru)

to⌈iawase⌉·ru といあわせる(問い合わせる) *vt.* (-awase-te [V]) inquire; make inquiries:
Sono hoñ ga aru ka shoteñ ni toi-awaseta. (その本があるか書店に問い合わせた) I *inquired* at a bookstore whether the book was there. (⇨ toiawase)

t

to⌈ika⌉es·u といかえす(問い返す) *vi.* (-kaesh·i-; -kaes·a-; -kaesh·i-te Ⓒ) ask again; ask back; repeat one's question. (⇨ kiku[1])

to⌈ire トイレ *n.* toilet; lavatory. (⇨ beñjyo)

to⌈ishi といし(砥石) *n.* whetstone.

to⌈itada⌉s·u といただす(問い質す) *vt.* (-tadash·i-; -tadas·a-; -tadash·i-te Ⓒ) question closely; inquire. (⇨ kiku[1])

to⌈jikome⌉·ru とじこめる(閉じ込める) *vt.* (-kome-te Ⓥ) shut up; lock up; confine.

to⌈jikomi とじこみ(綴じ込み) *n.* file: *shiñbuñ no* tojikomi (新聞のとじ込み) a newspaper *file*. (⇨ tojikomu)

to⌈jiko⌉m·u とじこむ(綴じ込む) *vt.* (-kom·i-; -kom·a-; -koñ-de Ⓒ) file (papers); keep on file. (⇨ tojikomi; tojiru[2])

to⌈ji⌉mari とじまり(戸締まり) *n.* locking of doors.
tojimari (o) suru (〜(を)する) *vi.* lock up.

to⌈ji⌉·ru[1] とじる(閉じる) *vt.* (toji-te Ⓥ) close; shut:
me o tojiru (目を閉じる) *close* one's eyes / *hoñ o* tojiru (本を閉じる) *shut* a book / *mise o* tojiru (店を閉じる) *close* a store.

to⌈ji⌉·ru[2] とじる(綴じる) *vt.* (toji-te Ⓥ) bind; keep on file:
pañfuretto o hotchikisu de tojiru (パンフレットをホッチキスで綴じる) *staple* a pamphlet together.

to⌉ka とか(都下) *n.* **1** Tokyo Metropolitan area.
2 the cities, towns and villages of Metropolitan Tokyo, but excluding the 23 wards. (⇨ toshiñ)

to ka とか *p.* **1** and; or: ★ Used to link representative examples of a class.
Yasumi ni wa tenisu to ka *gorufu o shimasu.* (休みにはテニスとかゴルフをします) I go in for sports *like* tennis *and* golf on holidays. (⇨ ya[1])
2 or someone [something]: ★ Used when unable to recall something accurately.
Tanaka-sañ to ka *iu hito kara deñwa ga arimashita.* (田中さんとかいう人から電話がありました) There was a phone call from a Mr. Tanaka *or someone*.

to⌈kai とかい(都会) *n.* city; town.

to⌈kaku とかく(兎角) *adv.* having a tendency; being likely:
Wareware wa tokaku *jikañ o muda ni shi-gachi desu.* (われわれはとかく時間をむだにしがちです) We *are apt* to waste time.

to⌈ka⌉s·u とかす(溶かす) *vt.* (tokash·i-; tokas·a-; tokash·i-te Ⓒ) melt; dissolve; liquefy; fuse; thaw: *shio o mizu ni* tokasu (塩を水に溶かす) *dissolve* salt in water. (⇨ tokeru[1])

to⌈kee とけい(時計) *n.* clock; watch. ★ '*Tokee*' is a general word for watches and clocks.

to⌈kekom·u とけこむ(溶け込む) *vi.* (-kom·i-; -kom·a-; -koñ-de Ⓒ)
1 melt; dissolve:
shio ga tokekoñda *mizu* (塩が溶け込んだ水) water in which salt *is dissolved*.
2 adapt oneself (to the environment).

to⌈ke⌉·ru[1] とける(溶ける) *vi.* (toke-te Ⓥ) melt; dissolve. (⇨ tokasu)

to⌈ke⌉r·u[2] とける(解ける) *vi.* (toke-te Ⓥ) **1** (of a problem) be solved:
Kono moñdai wa nakanaka tokenai. (この問題はなかなか解けない) This problem *is not* easily *solved*. (⇨ toku[1])
2 (of a knot) come loose; come untied. (⇨ toku[1])
3 (of suspicion) be cleared; disappear. (⇨ toku[1])

to⌈ki⌉ とき(時) *n.* **1** time; hour:
Sono moñdai wa toki *ga kaiketsu shite kureru deshoo.* (その問題は時が解決してくれるでしょう) *Time* will take care of the problem.
2 when; while:

Shitsumoñ ga aru toki *wa te o age nasai.* (質問があるときは手を上げなさい) *When* you have a question, please raise your hand.

3 occasion; case:

Hijoo no toki *wa kono doa o akete kudasai.* (非常のときはこのドアを開けてください) Please open this door *in the event of* an emergency.

to⌈kidoki ときどき (時々) *adv.* from time to time; once in a while. ⟪⇨ shibashiba⟫

to⌈ki⌉ ni wa ときには (時には) *adv.* sometimes; at times; once in a while:

Toki ni wa *dare datte machigai o shimasu.* (時にはだれだって間違いをします) Everyone makes mistakes *at times.*

to⌈kkeñ とっけん (特権) *n.* privilege: tokkeñ-*kaikyuu* (特権階級) the *privileged* classes.

to⌈kku ni とっくに (疾っくに) *adv.* long ago; a long time ago:

Kare wa tokku ni *dekakemashita.* (彼はとっくに出かけました) He left *long ago.*

to⌈kkuri とっくり (徳利) *n.* sake flask. ⟪⇨ sakazuki⟫

to⌉kkyo とっきょ (特許) *n.* patent: tokkyo *o toru* (特許を取る) take out a *patent.*

to⌈kkyuu とっきゅう (特急) *n.* limited [special] express. ⟪⇨ kyuukoo⌉⟫

to⌈ko とこ (床) *n.* bed. ⟪⇨ futoñ⟫

toko ni tsuku (～につく) go to bed; (be sick) in bed.

to⌈konoma とこのま (床の間) *n.* tokonoma; alcove in a Japanese house.

to⌈koro⌉ de ところで *p.* [follows the past tense of a verb, adjective, or the copula]

even if: ★ The first clause introduces a condition and the second clause specifies a disagreeable or unfavorable consequence.

Kore kara isshoo-keñmee yatta tokoro de, *moo maniawanai daroo.* (これから一生懸命やったところで, もう間に合わないだろう) *Even if* you were to do your best from now on, it would be too late.

-ta [-da] tokoro de wa (た[だ]～は) as far as; according to:

★ The first clause puts a limit on the personal opinion or prediction in the second clause.

Watashi no kiita tokoro de wa, *mata kabu ga sagaru rashii.* (私の聞いたところでは, また株が下がるらしい) *As far as I have heard,* stocks will apparently continue to fall in value.

— *conj.* **1** well; now: ★ Used at the beginning of a sentence.

Tokoro de *koñdo wa nani o shimasu ka?* (ところで今度は何をしますか) *Well,* what shall we do this time?

2 by the way: ★ Used at the beginning of a sentence.

Tokoro de *okaasañ wa o-geñki desu ka?* (ところでお母さんはお元気ですか) *By the way,* is your mother in good health? ⟪⇨ sore wa soo to⟫

to⌈korodo⌉koro ところどころ (所所) *n., adv.* here and there; several places.

to⌈koro⌉ ga ところが *p.* when:

★ Follows the past tense of a verb, adjective or the copula. The second clause strongly suggests a realization or discovery occasioned by the action or state in the first clause. Similar to '*-tara.*' ⟪⇨ -tara⟫

Kare no uchi ni itta tokoro ga, *kare wa dekaketa ato datta.* (彼の家に行ったところが, 彼は出かけたあとだった) *When* I got to his house, he had already left.

— *conj.* but; while: ★ Used at the beginning of a sentence.

Chichi wa otooto ni wa yasashii. Tokoro ga *boku ni wa kibishii.* (父は弟には優しい. ところがぼくには厳しい) My father is very gentle with my younger brother, *but* he is really strict with me.

to⌈koya とこや (床屋) *n.* barbershop; barber. ⟪⇨ sañpatsu⟫

to⌉k·u[1] とく (解く) *vt.* (tok·i-; tok·a-; to·i-te Ⓒ) **1** untie; undo; unpack; loosen:
himo no musubime o toku (ひもの結び目を解く) *untie* the knot in a piece of string. ⟪⇨ tokeru[2]⟫
2 solve (a problem). ⟪⇨ kaitoo[2]⟫
3 dismiss; discharge; relieve:
Kare wa ma-mo-naku geñzai no niñmu o tokareru *deshoo.* (彼は間もなく現在の任務を解かれるでしょう) He will *be relieved* of his current duties very soon.

to⌈ku[2] とく (得) *n.* profit; benefit. — *a.n.* (~ na, ni) profitable; advantageous; economical. ⟪↔ soñ⟫ ⟪⇨ yuuri⟫

to⌉k·u[3] とく (説く) *vt.* (tok·i-; tok·a-; to·i-te Ⓒ) persuade; talk into; preach:
hotoke no michi o toku (仏の道を説く) *preach* the way of Buddha.

to⌈kubai とくばい (特売) *n.* sale; bargain sale.
tokubai (o) suru (~(を)する) *vt.* sell at a special price.

to⌈kubetsu とくべつ (特別) *a.n.* (~ na/no, ni), *adv.* special; extra; particular; exceptional:
tokubetsu *ni chuui o harau* (特別に注意を払う) take *special* care. ⟪⇨ toku ni⟫

to⌈kuchoo とくちょう (特徴) *n.* characteristic; feature. ⟪⇨ tokushoku⟫

to⌈ku⌉i とくい (得意) *a.n.* (~ na/no, ni) **1** good; favorite:
Kanojo wa ryoori ga tokui *desu.* (彼女は料理が得意です) She is *good* at cooking. ⟪↔ nigate⟫
2 proud; triumphant:
Kare wa jibuñ no keekeñ o tokui ni natte *hanashita.* (彼は自分の経験を得意になって話した) He talked about his experiences in a *proud manner.*

to⌈kuisaki とくいさき (得意先) *n.* custom; customer:
tokuisaki *o mawaru* (得意先を回る) make the rounds of the *customers.*

to⌉ku ni とくに (特に) *adv.* specially; especially; particularly:
Kotoshi no natsu wa toku ni *atsukatta.* (今年の夏は特に暑かった) This summer was *especially* hot. ⟪⇨ kotoni; tokubetsu⟫

to⌈kushoku とくしょく (特色) *n.* characteristic; feature. ⟪⇨ tokuchoo⟫

to⌈kushu とくしゅ (特殊) *a.n.* (~ na, ni) special; particular; unique; unusual:
tokushu *na jijoo* (特殊な事情) *special* circumstances.

to⌈kutee とくてい (特定) *n.* specification.
tokutee suru (~する) *vt.* specify:
Sono kaisha wa meekaa o tokutee shite kita. (その会社はメーカーを特定してきた) The company *specified* the manufacturer.

to⌈kuyuu とくゆう (特有) *a.n.* (~ na/no, ni) peculiar; characteristic; proper:
Kono o-matsuri wa Nihoñ tokuyuu *no mono desu.* (このお祭りは日本特有のものです) This festival is *peculiar* to Japan. ⟪⇨ dokutoku⟫

to⌈mar·u[1] とまる (止まる) *vi.* (tomar·i-; tomar·a-; tomat-te Ⓒ)
1 (of a moving thing) stop; pull up:
Kono deñsha wa kaku eki ni tomarimasu. (この電車は各駅に止まります) This train *stops* at every station. ⟪⇨ teeshi; tomeru[1]⟫
2 cease; stop:
Suidoo no mizumore ga tomatta. (水道の水漏れが止まった) The leak in the water pipe *has stopped.* ⟪⇨ tomeru[1]⟫
3 (of electricity [water, gas, etc.] supply) fail; be cut off:
Jiko de deñki ga tomatta. (事故で電気が止まった) The electricity *failed* because of an accident.

4 (of a bird) perch; alight; settle.

to⌈mar·u[2] とまる(泊まる) *vt.* (tomar·i-; tomar·a-; tomat-te Ⓒ)
1 (of a person) stay; lodge:
inaka no ryokañ ni tomaru (田舎の旅館に泊まる) *stay* at a country inn. 《⇨ -haku; taizai; tomeru[2]》
2 (of a ship) lie at anchor.

to⌈me·ru[1] とめる(止める) *vt.* (tome-te Ⓥ) **1** stop; bring to a halt; park:
Hoteru no mae de kuruma o tometa. (ホテルの前で車を止めた) I *stopped* the car in front of the hotel. 《⇨ tomaru[1]》
2 stop; forbid; prohibit:
Futari no keñka o tometa. (二人のけんかを止めた) I *stopped* their quarrel.

to⌈me·ru[2] とめる(泊める) *vt.* (tome-te Ⓥ) lodge; put up; accommodate:
Kare o sono bañ uchi ni tomete yatta. (彼をその晩家に泊めてやった) I *put* him *up* for the night. 《⇨ tomaru[2]》

to⌈me·ru[3] とめる(留める) *vt.* (tome-te Ⓥ) pin; tape; fasten:
posutaa o kabe ni byoo de tomeru (ポスターを壁にびょうで留める) *fix* a poster to a wall with tacks.

to⌉mi とみ(富) *n.* wealth; riches; fortune.

tomo[1] とも *p.* **1** all; both:
Watashi no kyoodai wa sañ-niñ tomo *isha desu.* (私の兄弟は３人とも医者です) *All* three of my brothers are doctors.
2 at the ...-est: ★ Indicates an approximate limit.
Sukunaku tomo *ichi-nichi ichi-jikañ wa uñdoo o shita hoo ga yoi.* (少なくとも１日１時間は運動をしたほうが良い) You should do *at least* one hour's exercise every day.

tomo[2] とも *p.* certainly; sure; of course: ★ Used when confidently expressing one's opinions or thoughts. Used mainly by men.
"Tetsudatte kurenai ka?" "Ii tomo." (「手伝ってくれないか」「いいとも」) "Won't you give me a hand?" "*Only too* pleased to."

to⌉mo[3] とも(友) *n.* friend. 《⇨ tomodachi; yuujiñ》

-tomo とも(共) *suf.* **1** both; all; (with a negative) neither; none:
Watashi no kodomo wa sañ-niñ-tomo *shoogakusee desu.* (私の子どもは３人とも小学生です) *All* three of my children are elementary school pupils.
2 including:
Kono yadoya no ryookiñ wa shokuhi-tomo *ip-paku ichimañ-eñ desu.* (この宿屋の料金は食費とも一泊１万円です) The charge for one night at this inn is 10,000 yen, *including* the cost of meals. 《⇨ fukumeru》

to⌈moba⌉taraki ともばたらき(共働き) *n.* husband and wife both working.

to⌈modachi ともだち(友達) *n.* friend; companion. 《⇨ tomo[3]; yuujiñ》

to⌉mokaku ともかく *adv.*
1 = tonikaku.
2 regardless of; apart from:
Hoka no hito wa tomokaku, *watashi wa hañtai desu.* (ほかの人はともかく，私は反対です) *Regardless of* the others, I am against it.

to⌈moka⌉segi ともかせぎ(共稼ぎ) *n.* = tomobataraki.

to⌈mona⌉·u ともなう(伴う) *vi.* (-na·i-; -naw·a-; -nat-te Ⓒ)
1 take; bring; be accompanied:
Kare wa kazoku o tomonatte *doraibu ni dekaketa.* (彼は家族を伴ってドライブに出かけた) He went for a drive *with* his family.
2 bring about (danger); go together; involve:
Kono shigoto wa kikeñ o tomonaimasu. (この仕事は危険を伴います) This work *involves* danger.

to⌈mo ni ともに(共に) *adv.* **1** together; with:

Señsee wa seeto to tomo ni *kyoo-shitsu no sooji o shita.* (先生は生徒とともに教室の掃除をした) The teacher cleaned the classroom *together* with the students.
2 both; as well as:
Watashi-tachi futari wa tomo ni *shikeñ ni ukarimashita.* (私たち二人はともに試験に受かりました) We *both* passed the examination. ⟪⇨ ryoohoo⟫
3 as:
Toshi o toru to tomo ni *kioku-ryoku wa otoroemasu.* (年をとるとともに記憶力は衰えます) *As* one grows older, one's memory becomes poor.

to⌈mor·u ともる (点る) *vt.* (tomo-r·i-; tomor·a-; tomot-te Ⓒ) be lit; burn:
Sono koya ni wa rañpu ga tomot-te ita. (その小屋にはランプがともっていた) A lamp *was burning* in the cabin. ⟪⇨ tsuku⁴⟫

to⌉m·u とむ (富む) *vi.* (tom·i-; to-m·a-; toñ-de Ⓒ) abound (in); be rich (in):
Kare no supiichi wa yuumoa ni toñde ita. (彼のスピーチはユーモアに富んでいた) His speech *was full* of humor.

to⌈nae⌉·ru となえる (唱える) *vt.* (tonae-te Ⓥ) **1** recite; chant; utter:
neñbutsu o tonaeru (念仏を唱える) *chant* (Buddhist) prayers / *bañzai o* tonaeru (万歳を唱える) *cry* 'ban-zai.'
2 advocate; advance:
Watashi no ikeñ ni igi o tonaeru *hito wa inakatta.* (私の意見に異議を唱える人はいなかった) There was nobody who *raised* objections to my opinion.

to⌉nai とない (都内) *n.* (within) the Tokyo Metropolitan area. ⟪⇨ shinai⟫

to⌈nari となり (隣) *n.* **1** next-door neighbor; the house next door.
2 next:
Tonari *no seki wa aite imasu ka?* (隣の席は空いていますか) Is that seat *next* to you free?

to⌈naria⌉wase となりあわせ (隣り合わせ) *n.* being side by side.

to⌈ñbo とんぼ *n.* dragonfly.

to⌈ñbo-ga⌉eri とんぼ返り *n.*
1 somersault.
2 quick round trip:
Toñbo-gaeri *de Nagano e itte kita.* (とんぼ返りで長野へ行ってきた) I made a *quick visit* to Nagano.

to⌈ñda とんだ *attrib.* terrible; unexpected; serious:
Sore wa toñda *sainañ deshita ne.* (それはとんだ災難でしたね) It was *quite* an unfortunate occurrence, wasn't it? ⟪⇨ toñde mo nai⟫

to⌈ñde mo na⌉·i とんでもない
1 absurd; outrageous; terrible; unexpected.
2 (used to express strong negation):
*"Watanabe-sañ wa rikoñ shita soo desu ne." "*Toñde mo nai.*"* (「渡辺さんは離婚したそうですね」「とんでもない」) "I hear Mrs. Watanabe got divorced." "*Goodness, no!*"

to⌈ñga⌉r·u とんがる *vi.* = togaru.

to⌉nikaku とにかく (兎に角) *adv.* anyway; in any case; at any rate. ⟪⇨ izure⟫

to⌈ñkatsu とんカツ (豚カツ) *n.* deep-fried breaded pork cutlet.

tono ko⌈to⌉ da [desu] とのことだ[です] I hear that...; they say that...:
Jee-aaru no uñchiñ heñkoo wa sugu ni jisshi sareru to no koto desu. (JRの運賃変更はすぐに実施されるとのことです) *They say that* the changes in JR fares will soon be put into effect.

to⌉ñtoñ¹ とんとん *adv.* (~ to) (the sound of a quick light strike):
toñtoñ *to doa o nokku suru oto* (とんとんとドアをノックする音) a *knock* on the door.

to⌈ñtoñ² とんとん *a.n.* (~ na, ni)

(*informal*) even; equal; the same:
Keehi o sashihiku to soñ-eki wa toñtoñ *desu.* (経費を差し引くと損益はとんとんです) If we deduct the expenses, gains and losses are *equal*.

to⌈ñya とんや (問屋) *n.* wholesale store; wholesaler. ⟪⇨ oroshi⟫

to⌉o[1] とう (十) *n.* ten. ★ Used when counting. ⟪⇨ juu[1]; APP. 3⟫

to⌉o[2] とう (党) *n.* (political) party. ⟪⇨ APP. 8⟫

to⌉o[3] とう (塔) *n.* tower; pagoda; steeple.

too- とう (当) *suf.* this; current: too-*chi* (当地) *this* city [town; country] / too-*teñ* (当店) *this* store.

-too[1] とう (等) *suf.* **1** class; grade: *it*-too (1 等) first *class* / *ni*-too (2 等) second *class*.
2 prize:
Kyoosoo de it-too *ni natta.* (競争で1 等になった) I won first *prize* in the race.

-too[2] とう (頭) *suf.* counter for large animals:
uma it-too (馬 1 頭) *one* horse / *ushi go*-too (牛 5 頭) five *head* of cattle. ⟪⇨ -hiki⟫

to⌈oañ とうあん (答案) *n.* examination answer sheet. ⟪↔ moñdai⟫ ⟪⇨ kotae⟫

to⌉obañ とうばん (当番) *n.* turn; duty:
Is-shuukañ ni ichi-do sooji toobañ *ni atarimasu.* (一週間に一度掃除当番にあたります) I take my *turn* to clean the room once a week.

to⌈obuñ とうぶん (当分) *adv.* for the time being; for some time.

to⌈ochaku とうちゃく (到着) *n.* arrival: toochaku-*jikoku* (到着時刻) the *arrival* time.
toochaku suru (〜する) *vi.* arrive (at one's destination). ⟪↔ shuppatsu⟫ ⟪⇨ tsuku[1]⟫

to⌈odai とうだい (灯台) *n.* lighthouse.

to⌈ofu とうふ (豆腐) *n.* soybean curd; tofu.

to⌈oga⌉rashi とうがらし (唐辛子) *n.* red pepper.

to⌈oge⌉ とうげ (峠) *n.* **1** the top of a mountain pass.
2 peak; height:
Atsusa wa ima ga tooge *da.* (暑さは今が峠だ) Now is *the hottest time* of the year.
tooge o kosu [koeru] (〜を越す[越える]) **1** cross over a peak.
2 get over the hump; overcome a difficulty.

to⌈ohyoo とうひょう (投票) *n.* vote; poll; ballot.
toohyoo (o) suru (〜(を)する) *vi.* vote; cast a vote. ⟪⇨ señkyo⟫

to⌈o·i とおい (遠い) *a.* (-ku) **1** far; distant; a long way. ⟪↔ chikai[1]⟫
2 (of time, relation, etc.) remote; distant:
Damu no kañsee wa mada tooi *hanashi da.* (ダムの完成はまだ遠い話だ) The completion of the dam is *a long way off*.

to⌈oitsu とういつ (統一) *n.* unity; unification; standardization.
tooitsu suru (〜する) *vt.* unify; standardize: *kakaku o* tooitsu *suru* (価格を統一する) *standardize* prices.

to⌉oji[1] とうじ (当時) *n.* at that time; then:
Tooji *wa shokuryoo ga fusoku shite ita.* (当時は食料が不足していた) *At that time* there was a shortage of food.

to⌈oji[2] とうじ (冬至) *n.* the winter solstice (about December 22). ⟪⇨ geshi⟫

to⌈ojitsu とうじつ (当日) *n.* that day; the very day:
Kare wa toojitsu *ni natte, kesseki no reñraku o shite kita.* (彼は当日になって, 欠席の連絡をしてきた) When *the day* came he reported that he would be absent.

to⌈ojoo とうじょう (登場) *n.* appearance; entrance. ⟪↔ taijoo⟫

toojoo suru (～する) *vi.* appear (on stage); enter.

to͡oka とおか(十日) *n.* ten days; the tenth day of the month. 《⇨ APP. 5》

to͡okee とうけい(統計) *n.* statistics: tookee *o toru* (統計をとる) collect *statistics.*

to͝oki[1] とうき(陶器) *n.* earthenware; pottery; ceramics. 《⇨ jiki[3]》

to͝oki[2] とうき(登記) *n.* registration (of a house or land).
tooki suru (～する) *vt.* register.

to͝oki[3] とうき(投機) *n.* speculation (in stocks); venture.

to͝oki[4] とうき(冬季) *n.* winter; wintertime. 《⇨ kaki[3]; shuñki; shuuki[2]》

to͡okoo とうこう(登校) *n.* school attendance: tookoo-*kyohi* (登校拒否) refusal to *attend school.*
tookoo suru (～する) *vi.* go to [attend] school. 《↔ gekoo》

to͡oku とおく(遠く) *n.* a long way (off):
Amari tooku *made asobi ni itte wa ikemaseñ.* (あまり遠くまで遊びに行ってはいけません) You must not go and play too *far off.* 《↔ chikaku》

to͝okyoku とうきょく(当局) *n.* the authorities:
*shi-*tookyoku *kara kyoka o morau* (市当局から許可をもらう) get permission from the ciy *authorities.*

to͡oma͝wari とおまわり(遠回り) *n.* roundabout way; detour:
Kono michi o iku to toomawari *ni narimasu.* (この道を行くと遠回りになります) If we go this way it will be *farther.*
toomawari (o) suru (～(を)する) *vi.* make a detour. 《↔ chikamichi》

to͡omee とうめい(透明) *a.n.* (～ na, ni) transparent; clear: toomee *na garasu* (透明なガラス) *transparent* glass. 《⇨ sukitooru》

to͝oniñ とうにん(当人) *n.* **1** the person concerned.
2 oneself:
Sono uwasa ni tooniñ *wa heeki datta.* (そのうわさに当人は平気だった) He *himself* was indifferent to the rumor. 《⇨ hoñniñ》

to͡ori[1] とおり(通り) *n.* street; road.

to͝ori[2] とおり(通り) *n.* as; like:
Kare wa itsu-mo no toori *ku-ji ni shussha shita.* (彼はいつものとおり9時に出社した) He came to the office at nine *as* usual.

-toori/doori とおり/どおり *suf.*
1 kind; sort:
*Jikkeñ wa iku-*toori *mo yatte mimashita.* (実験はいくとおりもやってみました) We carried out the experiment in many different *ways.*
2 about; approximately:
*Shigoto wa hachi-bu-*doori *owarimashita.* (仕事は8分どおり終わりました) *About* eighty percent of the work has been finished.

to͡orikakar·u とおりかかる(通り掛かる) *vi.* (-kakar·i-; -kakar·a-; -kakat-te Ⓒ) pass by casually; come along.

to͡orinuke とおりぬけ(通り抜け) *n.* passing through; through passage:
Toorinuke *kiñshi.* (*sign*) (通り抜け禁止) No *Thoroughfare.* 《⇨ toorinukeru》

to͡orinuke͝·ru とおりぬける(通り抜ける) *vi.* (-nuke-te Ⓥ) go [pass] through:
toñneru o toorinukeru (トンネルを通り抜ける) *pass through* a tunnel.

to͡orisugi·ru とおりすぎる(通り過ぎる) *vi.* (-sugi-te Ⓥ) pass; go by; go past. 《⇨ tooru》

to͡oroku とうろく(登録) *n.* registration; entry.
tooroku suru (～する) *vt.* register; enter: *shoohyoo o* tooroku suru (商標を登録する) *register* a trademark.

to͝oroñ とうろん(討論) *n.* discussion; debate; argument:
tooroñ-kai (討論会) a *debate*; a *panel discussion.*
tooroñ suru (～する) *vi.* discuss;

debate; argue.

to¹or·u とおる(通る) *vi.* (toor·i-; toor·a-; toot-te Ⓒ) **1** (of a vehicle, person, etc.) go; pass:
Kono dooro wa jidoosha ga yoku toorimasu. (この道路は自動車がよく通ります) Many cars *pass* along this road.
2 (of a bill, proposal, etc.) pass; be approved:
Kaisee-añ wa kinoo iiñkai o tootta. (改正案はきのう委員会を通った) The amended bill *passed* the committee yesterday. ⟪⇨ toosu⟫
3 (of a public vehicle) run:
Deñsha wa nijup-puñ goto ni tootte imasu. (電車は20分毎に通っています) The trains *come by* every twenty minutes.
4 (of a word, sentence, passage, etc.) make sense:
Kono buñshoo wa imi ga tooranai. (この文章は意味が通らない) This sentence *does not convey* any meaning.
5 (of a voice) carry.

to¹osañ とうさん(父さん) *n.* (*informal*) father; dad; daddy. ⟪↔ kaasañ⟫ ⟪⇨ chichi[1]; o-toosañ⟫

to⌈osee とうせい(統制) *n.* control; regulation.
toosee suru (〜する) *vt.* control; regulate. ⟪⇨ seegeñ⟫

to⌈oseñ とうせん(当選) *n.* **1** election; win in an election. ⟪↔ rakuseñ⟫
2 winning a prize:
tooseñ-sha (当選者) the *winner of a prize.*
tooseñ suru (〜する) *vi.* be elected; win a prize. ⟪⇨ ataru⟫

to⌈oshi とうし(投資) *n.* investment.
tooshi suru (〜する) *vi.* invest; put money in.

to⌈osho とうしょ(投書) *n.* letter; complaint [suggestion] by letter.
toosho suru (〜する) *vi., vt.* write in (to a newspaper).

to¹os·u とおす(通す) *vt.* (toosh·i-; toos·a-; toosh·i-te Ⓒ) **1** let (a person) pass:
Sumimaseñ ga chotto tooshite *kudasai.* (すみませんがちょっと通してください) Excuse me, but would you *let* me *pass*, please? ⟪⇨ tooru⟫
2 let in; admit:
Biniiru wa hikari wa toosu *ga mizu mo kuuki mo* toosanai. (ビニールは光は通すが水も空気も通さない) Plastic sheets *let in* light, but *let through* neither water nor air. ⟪⇨ tooru⟫
3 show in (a guest, etc.); usher in:
O-kyaku-sañ o heya ni tooshi nasai. (お客さんを部屋に通しなさい) Please *show* the guest into the room.
4 thread; pierce:
hari ni ito o toosu (針に糸を通す) *thread* a needle. ⟪⇨ tooru⟫
5 approve; pass (a bill). ⟪⇨ tooru⟫
6 stick to (one's opinion); persist:
Kare wa akumade jibuñ no shuchoo o toosoo *to shita.* (彼はあくまで自分の主張を通そうとした) He persistently *stuck* to his assertion.
7 continue; remain (in a certain state):
Kare wa isshoo dokushiñ de tooshita. (彼は一生独身で通した) He *remained* single all his life.

to⌈otatsu とうたつ(到達) *n.* arrival; attainment.
tootatsu suru (〜する) *vi.* reach; attain. ⟪⇨ tassuru⟫

to⌈otee とうてい(到底) *adv.* (with a negative) not possibly; by any means:
Soñna koto wa tootee *fukanoo desu.* (そんなことはとうてい不可能です) That kind of thing is *quite* impossible. ⟪⇨ totemo⟫

to¹oteñ とうてん(読点) *n.* Japanese-language comma (、). ★ An English-language comma (,) is called '*koñma.*' ⟪⇨ kuteñ⟫

to⌜oto⌝b·u とうとぶ(尊ぶ) *vt.* (-tob·i-; -tob·a-; -toñ-de [C]) value; respect: *inochi o* tootobu (命を尊ぶ) *value* life.

to⌜oto⌝·i とうとい(尊い・貴い) *a.* (-ku) precious; valuable; noble: tootoi *kyookuñ* (貴い教訓) an *invaluable* lesson / tootoi *gisee* (尊い犠牲) a *high* sacrifice.

to⌝otoo とうとう(到頭) *adv.*
★ More informal than '*tsui ni*'
1 at last; finally:
Kare wa tootoo *sono añ o akirameta.* (彼はとうとうその案をあきらめた) *At last* he gave up the plan.
2 after all:
Kanojo wa tootoo *sugata o misenakatta.* (彼女はとうとう姿を見せなかった) She did not show up *after all.*

To⌝oyoo とうよう(東洋) *n.* the Orient; the East:
Tooyoo *shokoku* (東洋諸国) *Oriental* [*Eastern*] countries.
⟪↔ Seeyoo⟫

To⌜oyo⌝ojiñ とうようじん(東洋人) *n.* an Oriental. ⟪↔ Seeyoojiñ⟫

to⌝ozai とうざい(東西) *n.* east and west. ⟪↔ nañboku⟫

to⌜ozaka⌝r·u とおざかる(遠ざかる) *vi.* (-zakar·i-; -zakar·a-; -zakatte [C]) **1** go away; fade away.
2 keep away:
Saikiñ gorufu kara toozakatte imasu. (最近ゴルフから遠ざかっています) I *haven't played* golf recently.
⟪⇨ toozakeru⟫

to⌜ozake⌝·ru とおざける(遠ざける) *vt.* (-zake-te [V]) keep away; avoid; ward off:
Kare wa yuujiñ o toozakete iru. (彼は友人を遠ざけている) He *keeps* his friends *at a distance.* ⟪⇨ toozakaru⟫

to⌜ozeñ とうぜん(当然) *a.n.* (~ na/no, ni) reasonable; natural; expected. ⟪⇨ atarimae⟫
— *adv.* naturally; of course:
Toozeñ, *kimi mo iku beki da.* (当然, きみも行くべきだ) *Of course,* you should go, too.

to⌝ppa とっぱ(突破) *n.* breakthrough; overcoming.
toppa suru (~する) *vt.* break through; overcome: *nañkañ o* toppa suru (難関を突破する) *overcome* a difficulty.

to⌜ra とら(虎) *n.* tiger.

to⌜rae⌝·ru とらえる(捕らえる) *vt.* (torae-te [V]) **1** catch; arrest:
Keesatsu wa sono doroboo o toraeta. (警察はその泥棒を捕らえた) The police *caught* the thief.
⟪⇨ tsukamaeru⟫
2 capture:
Kanojo no eñgi wa kañshuu no kokoro o toraeta. (彼女の演技は観衆の心を捕らえた) Her performance *captured* the hearts of the audience.

to⌜ra⌝kku トラック *n.* truck; lorry.

to⌜ra⌝ñpu トランプ *n.* playing cards. ★ Not used in the sense of 'trump(s),' as in bridge or whist.

to⌜re⌝·ru[1] とれる(取れる) *vi.* (torete [V]) **1** come off; be removed:
Shatsu no botañ ga toreta. (シャツのボタンがとれた) A button *has come off* my shirt. ⟪⇨ toru[1]⟫
2 (of pains) go away:
Kizu no itami ga toreta. (傷の痛みがとれた) The pain from the cut *has gone away.* ⟪⇨ toru[1]⟫
3 (of a word, sentence, passage, etc.) can be interpreted:
Kono buñ wa futatsu no imi ni toreru. (この文は二つの意味にとれる) This sentence *can be interpreted* in two ways. ⟪⇨ toru[1]⟫

to⌜re⌝·ru[2] とれる(捕れる) *vi.* (torete [V]) (of an animal) be caught.
⟪⇨ toru[2]⟫

to⌜re⌝·ru[3] とれる(採れる) *vi.* (torete [V]) (of a plant) be produced; be grown. ⟪⇨ toru[3]⟫

to⌜ri とり(鳥) *n.* **1** bird; fowl; poultry.
2 chicken. ⟪⇨ toriniku⟫

to⌜ria⌝ezu とりあえず(取り敢えず) *adv.* first of all; for the present:

t

Toriaezu *biiru o sañ-boñ kudasai.* (とりあえずビールを3本下さい) *To start with*, please give us three bottles of beer.

to⌈riage·ru とりあげる(取り上げる) *vt.* (-age-te [V]) **1** pick up: *juwaki o* toriageru (受話器を取り上げる) *pick up* the telephone receiver.
2 adopt (a proposal); accept (an opinion).
3 take up for discussion: *Sono moñdai wa tsugi ni* toriagemasu. (その問題は次に取り上げます) We will *take up* that problem next.
4 deprive (someone of a qualification, license, etc.); cancel.

to⌈riatsukai とりあつかい(取り扱い) *n.* treatment; handling. ⟪⇨ toriatsukau⟫

to⌈riatsuka·u とりあつかう(取り扱う) *vt.* (-atsuka·i-; -atsukaw·a-; -atsukat-te [C]) treat; handle; deal in [with]: *Kono shinamono wa chuui shite* toriatsukatte *kudasai.* (この品物は注意して取り扱ってください) Please *handle* these goods with care. ⟪⇨ toriatsukai⟫

to⌈ridas·u とりだす(取り出す) *vt.* (-dash·i-; -das·a-; -dash·i-te [C]) take out; pick out; produce: *Kanojo wa baggu kara techoo o* toridashita. (彼女はバッグから手帳を取り出した) She *took out* a small notebook from her bag.

to⌈rihazus·u とりはずす(取り外す) *vt.* (-hazush·i-; -hazus·a-; -hazush·i-te [C]) take away; remove.

to⌈ri⌉hiki とりひき(取り引き) *n.* business; dealings; transaction.
torihiki (o) suru (～(を)する) *vi.*, *vt.* do business; make a deal.

to⌈rii とりい(鳥居) *n.* torii.
★ The gateway at the entrance of a Shinto shrine.

to⌈riire⌉·ru とりいれる(取り入れる) *vt.* (-ire-te [V]) **1** take in: *señtakumono o* toriireru (洗濯物を取り入れる) *take in* the washing.
2 gather in (a crop); harvest.
3 adopt (an idea, opinion, etc.); introduce.

to⌈rikae とりかえ(取り替え) *n.* exchange; replacement. ⟪⇨ kookañ; torikaeru⟫

to⌈rikae·ru とりかえる(取り替える) *vt.* (-kae-te [V]) change; exchange; replace; renew: *Kanojo wa teeburu-kurosu o atarashii no to* torikaeta. (彼女はテーブルクロスを新しいのと取り替えた) She *changed* the tablecloth for a new one. ⟪⇨ torikae⟫

to⌈rikaes·u とりかえす(取り返す) *vt.* (-kaesh·i-; -kaes·a-; -kaesh·i-te [C]) get back; recover; regain.

to⌈rikakar·u とりかかる(取り掛かる) *vi.* (-kakar·i; -kakar·a-; -kakat-te [C]) begin; start; set about: *shigoto ni* torikakaru (仕事に取りかかる) *set to* work.

to⌈rikakom·u とりかこむ(取り囲む) *vt.* (-kakom·i-; -kakom·a-; -kakoñ-de [C]) surround; gather around. ⟪⇨ torimaku⟫

to⌈rikeshi とりけし(取り消し) *n.* cancellation; withdrawal. ⟪⇨ torikesu⟫

to⌈rikes·u とりけす(取り消す) *vt.* (-kesh·i-; -kes·a-; -kesh·i-te [C]) cancel; take back; withdraw: *yoyaku o* torikesu (予約を取り消す) *cancel* one's reservation. ⟪⇨ torikeshi⟫

to⌈rikumi とりくみ(取り組み) *n.* (of sumo wrestling) match; bout. ⟪⇨ torikumu⟫

to⌈rikum·u とりくむ(取り組む) *vi.* (-kum·i-; -kum·a-; -kuñ-de [C]) wrestle with; tackle; be engaged in: *Kare wa ima sono moñdai ni* torikuñde imasu. (彼は今その問題に取り組んでいます) He *is* now *tackling* the problem. ⟪⇨ torikumi⟫

to⌈rimak·u とりまく(取り巻く) *vt.* (-mak·i-; -mak·a-; -ma·i-te [C])

surround:
Señsee wa seeto-tachi ni torimakareta. (先生は生徒たちに取り巻かれた) The teacher *was surrounded* by her pupils.

to⌈rimodo⌉s·u とりもどす (取り戻す) *vt*. (-modosh·i-; -modos·a-; -modosh·i-te Ⓒ) get back; recover; regain:
keñkoo o torimodosu (健康を取り戻す) *regain* one's health.

to⌈rinigas·u とりにがす (取り逃がす) *vt*. (-nigash·i-; -nigas·a-; -nigash·i-te Ⓒ) fail to catch; miss. ((⇨ nigasu))

to⌈riniku とりにく (鶏肉) *n*. chicken meat; poultry.

to⌈rinozo⌉k·u とりのぞく (取り除く) *vt*. (-nozok·i-; -nozok·a-; -nozo-i-te Ⓒ) take away; remove. ((⇨ nozoku[1]))

to⌈rishimari とりしまり (取り締まり) *n*. control; regulation; crackdown. ((⇨ torishimaru))

to⌈rishimari⌉yaku とりしまりやく (取締役) *n*. director (of a company).

to⌈rishima⌉r·u とりしまる (取り締まる) *vt*. (-shimar·i-; -shimar·a-; -shimat-te Ⓒ) control; crack down:
Ima yopparai-uñteñ o torishimatte imasu. (今酔っ払い運転を取り締まっています) They *are* now *cracking down* on drunken driving. ((⇨ torishimari))

to⌈rishirabe とりしらべ (取り調べ) *n*. questioning; investigation; examination. ((⇨ torishiraberu))

to⌈rishirabe⌉·ru とりしらべる (取り調べる) *vt*. (-shirabe-te Ⓥ) examine (a suspect, etc.); investigate; inquire into:
Keesatsu wa yoogisha o torishirabete iru. (警察は容疑者を取り調べている) The police *are examining* the suspect. ((⇨ torishirabe))

to⌈ritsugi とりつぎ (取り次ぎ) *n*. agency; agent; wholesaler.

to⌈ritsu⌉g·u とりつぐ (取り次ぐ) *vt*. (-tsug·i-; -tsug·a-; -tsu·i-de Ⓒ)
1 act as an agent:
Go-chuumoñ wa watashi-domo ga toritsuide orimasu. (ご注文は私どもが取り次いでおります) We will *act as agent* for what you order. ((⇨ toritsugi))
2 convey (a message, telephone, etc.); answer.

to⌈ritsuke·ru とりつける (取り付ける) *vt*. (-tsuke-te Ⓥ) **1** install; furnish; equip; fit.
2 obtain (consent, permission, etc.):
Sono koto ni kañshite chichi no dooi o toritsuketa. (そのことに関して父の同意を取り付けた) I *obtained* my father's consent regarding that matter.

to⌈robi とろび (とろ火) *n*. very slow heat; low fire.

to⌉r·u[1] とる (取る) *vt*. (tor·i-; tor·a-; tot-te Ⓒ) **1** take; take hold of; seize:
Kare wa hoñdana kara jisho o totta. (彼は本棚から辞書を取った) He *took* a dictionary from the bookshelf.
2 get; take; receive; obtain; win:
Kyoo wa yasumi o torimashita. (きょうは休みをとりました) I *took* a day off today.
3 take off; remove:
Kare wa booshi o totte, *aisatsu shita*. (彼は帽子をとって, 挨拶した) He *took off* his hat and greeted me.
4 steal; rob:
Watashi wa jiteñsha o dare-ka ni torareta. (私は自転車をだれかにとられた) I *had* my bicycle *stolen* by someone. ((⇨ nusumu))
5 subscribe to (a newspaper, magazine); buy:
Watashi mo onaji shiñbuñ o totte *imasu*. (私も同じ新聞をとっています) I also *take* the same newspaper.
6 eat; have:
Moo chuushoku wa torimashita

ka? (もう昼食はとりましたか) *Have* you already *had* lunch?
7 take; make out; interpret; understand:
Watashi ga itta koto o waruku toranai de *kudasai.* (私が言ったことを悪くとらないでください) *Do not take* my words amiss.
8 take up; occupy (a place):
Kono tsukue wa basho o tori-*sugiru.* (この机は場所をとり過ぎる) This desk *takes up* too much space. ⟪⇨ shimeru[4]⟫
9 record; write down:
bañgumi o bideo ni toru (番組をビデオにとる) *record* a program on video / *kiroku o* toru (記録をとる) *keep* records.
10 charge (a fare, fee, etc.); demand:
Ano ryokañ wa ip-paku nimañ-eñ mo torimasu. (あの旅館は一泊２万円もとります) That inn *charges* all of 20,000 yen for one night.

to|r·u[2] とる (捕る) *vt.* (tor·i-; tor·a-; tot-te Ⓒ) catch (an animal, fish, etc.); get.

to|r·u[3] とる (採る) *vt.* (tor·i-; tor·a-; tot-te Ⓒ) **1** gather; pick (a plant).
2 adopt (a proposal, suggestion, etc.); choose; employ; engage.

to|r·u[4] とる (撮る) *vt.* (tor·i-; tor·a-; tot-te Ⓒ) take (a picture). ⟪⇨ satsuee⟫

to|ryoo とりょう (塗料) *n.* paint. ⟪⇨ peñki⟫

to|shi[1] とし (年) *n.* year; age.

to|shi[2] とし (都市) *n.* city; towns and cities.

to|shigoro としごろ (年頃) *n.*
1 marriageable age:
toshigoro *no musume* (年ごろの娘) a daughter of *marriageable age.*
2 about the same age:
Watashi ni mo añta to onaji toshigoro *no musuko ga imasu.* (私にもあんたと同じ年ごろの息子がいます) I also have a son *of your age.*

to|shiñ としん (都心) *n.* the heart [center] of Tokyo. ⟪⇨ toka⟫

to|shi-shita としした (年下) *n.* junior in age. ⟪↔ toshi-ue⟫

to shite として **1** as; for: ★ Indicates a role, position or qualification.
Yamamoto-shi wa taishi to shite *Chuugoku ni hakeñ sareta.* (山本氏は大使として中国に派遣された) Mr. Yamamoto was sent to China *as* ambassador.
2 not even a...: ★ Used after words such as '*hitori*,' '*ichi-nichi*,' '*ichi-do*,' etc., with a negative.
Dare hitori to shite *kare o tasukeyoo to shinakatta.* (だれ一人として彼を助けようとしなかった) *Not a single* person tried to help him.

to|shito|tta としとった (年とった) old; aged.

to|shi|tsuki としつき (年月) *n.* years. ⟪⇨ neñgetsu⟫

to|shi-ue としうえ (年上) *n.* senior in age. ⟪↔ toshi-shita⟫

to|shiyori| としより (年寄り) *n.* old person [people]. ⟪↔ wakamono⟫

to|sho としょ (図書) *n.* books. ⟪⇨ hoñ⟫

to|shokañ としょかん (図書館) *n.* (public) library. ⟪⇨ toshoshitsu⟫

to|sho|keñ としょけん (図書券) *n.* book token. ★ Often given as a gift.

to|sho|shitsu としょしつ (図書室) *n.* library; reading room.
★ Usually refers to a library in a school or an office. ⟪⇨ toshokañ⟫

to|ssa とっさ (咄嗟) *n.* (～ no) sudden; instant:
tossa *no dekigoto* (とっさの出来事) an *unexpected* occurrence.

to|ssa ni とっさに (咄嗟に) *adv.* immediately; instinctively.

to su|reba とすれば if; supposing; on the assumption that...:
★ The particle '*to*' plus the provisional of '*suru*.' The second clause indicates a judgment or inference based on the suppposi-

tion in the first clause.
Kimi ga dekinai to sureba, *tabuñ dare ni mo dekinai deshoo.* (君ができないとすれば, たぶんだれにもできないでしょう) *If* you are unable to do this, I doubt that anyone can.
(⇨ -tara; to[1])

to⌈tañ[1] とたん (途端) *n.* the moment; just as...:
Furo ni hairoo to shita totañ (*ni*) *deñwa ga naridashita.* (ふろに入ろうとしたとたん(に)電話が鳴りだした) *Just as* I was about to get into the bath, the phone started ringing.
(⇨ shuñkañ)

to⌈tañ[2] トタン *n.* galvanized iron.

tote とて *p.* even if: ★ Used when a fact is presented or an assumption made but the subsequent result or inference is contrary to expectation.
Shippai shita tote *gakkari suru na.* (失敗したとてがっかりするな) *Even if* you've failed, do not be discouraged.

to⌈temo とても *adv.* ★ Also '*tottemo.*' **1** very; really; awfully; extremely:
Kono hoñ wa totemo *omoshiroi.* (この本はとてもおもしろい) This book is *very* interesting.
2 (with a negative) not possibly; by any means:
Koñna muzukashii moñdai wa totemo *tokemaseñ.* (こんな難しい問題はとても解けません) I cannot *possibly* solve this sort of difficult problem. (⇨ tootee)

to⌈tonoe⌉·ru ととのえる (整える·調える) *vt.* (-noe-te [V]) **1** prepare; get ready:
yuushoku o totonoeru (夕食を整える) *get* dinner *ready.* (⇨ totonou)
2 make tidy; dress:
kami o totonoeru (髪を整える) *fix* one's hair.
3 settle; arrange (a marriage).
(⇨ totonou)

to⌈tono⌉·u ととのう (整う·調う) *vi.* (-no·i-; -now·a-; -not-te [C])
1 be ready; be prepared; be completed:
Juñbi ga sukkari totonotta. (準備がすっかり整った) The arrangements *are* fully *completed.* (⇨ totonoeru)
2 be settled; (of a marrige) be arranged. (⇨ totonoeru)

to⌈tsuzeñ とつぜん (突然) *a.n.* (~ na/no, ni) sudden; abrupt; unexpected.
— *adv.* suddenly; abruptly; unexpectedly: Totsuzeñ *deñwa ga natta.* (突然電話が鳴った) *Suddenly* the phone rang.

to⌉tte[1] とって to; for: ★ Used in making judgments or evaluations. Used in the pattern '*... ni totte.*'
Kaigai-ryokoo wa watashi ni totte *wasurerarenai omoide desu.* (海外旅行は私にとって忘れられない思い出です) The overseas trip is an unforgettable memory *to* me.

to⌈tte[2] とって (取っ手) *n.* handle; knob; pull; grip:
nabe no totte (なべの取っ手) the *handle* of a pan / *doa no* totte (ドアの取っ手) a door*knob.*

to⌈ttemo とっても *adv.* = totemo.

to⌉·u とう (問う) *vt.* (to·i-; tow·a-; to·u-te [C]) **1** ask; inquire:
hito no añpi o tou (人の安否を問う) *ask* about a person's safety.
(⇨ tazuneru[1])
2 (in the negative) care; mind:
Nedañ wa toimaseñ. (値段は問いません) I *don't care* about the price.

to wa ka⌈gira⌉nai とはかぎらない (とは限らない) not necessarily; not always: ★ This phrase is often preceded by '*kanarazu shimo.*' The polite equivalent is '*to wa kagirimaseñ.*'
Takai mono ga ii to wa kagiranai. (高いものがいいとは限らない) Expensive things are *not necessarily* good. (⇨ kagiru)

to⌈zañ とざん (登山) *n.* mountain climbing; going up a mountain.

tozañ (o) suru (〜(を)する) *vi.* climb a mountain.

tsu˥ba つば (唾) *n.* spit; saliva: *michi ni* tsuba o haku (道につばを吐く) spit *on the road.*

tsu┌baki˥[1] つばき (唾) *n.* = tsuba.

tsu˥baki[2] つばき (椿) *n.* camellia.

tsu┌bame つばめ (燕) *n.* swallow (bird).

tsu┌basa つばさ (翼) *n.* wing.

tsu┌bo[1] つぼ (壺) *n.* pot; jar; vase.

tsu┌bo[2] つぼ (坪) *n.* tsubo.
★ Unit of area. 1 tsubo = 3.3 square meters.

tsu┌bomi˥ つぼみ (蕾) *n.* flower bud.

tsu˥bu つぶ (粒) *n.* grain; drop: *kome*-tsubu (米粒) *grains* of rice / *oo*-tsubu *no ame* (大粒の雨) large *drops* of rain.

-tsu˥bu つぶ (粒) *suf.* counter for grain and small round objects: *kome hito*-tsubu (米 1 粒) *a grain* of rice / *mame* go-tsubu (豆 5 粒) *five* beans.

tsu┌bure·ru つぶれる (潰れる) *vi.* (tsubure-te [V]) **1** be crushed; be smashed; collapse. ⟪⇨ tsubusu⟫
2 (of a company) go bankrupt.

tsu┌bur·u つぶる (瞑る) *vt.* (tsubur·i-; tsubur·a-; tsubut-te [C]) close [shut] (one's eyes).

tsu┌bus·u つぶす (潰す) *vt.* (tsubush·i-; tsubus·a-; tsubush·i-te [C]) **1** crush; smash: *Kare wa hako o fuñzukete* tsubushita. (彼は箱を踏んづけてつぶした) He stepped on the box and *crushed* it. ⟪⇨ tsubureru⟫
2 thwart (a plan, project, etc.); ruin.
3 kill [pass] (time).

tsu┌buyaki つぶやき (呟き) *n.* mutter; murmur; grumble. ⟪⇨ tsubuyaku⟫

tsu┌buya˥k·u つぶやく (呟く) *vi.* (tsubuyak·i-; tsubuyak·a-; tsubuya·i-te [C]) murmur; mutter; grumble. ⟪⇨ tsubuyaki⟫

tsu┌chi˥ つち (土) *n.* **1** earth; soil; mud.
2 the ground: *bokoku no* tsuchi *o fumu* (母国の土を踏む) stand on the *ground* of one's homeland.

tsu˥e つえ (杖) *n.* stick; cane.

tsu┌geguchi つげぐち (告げ口) *n.* tattle; talebearing.
tsugeguchi (o) suru (〜(を)する) *vt.* tell on; let on.

tsu┌ge·ru つげる (告げる) *vt.* (tsuge-te [V]) (*formal*) tell; inform; report.

tsu┌gi˥ つぎ (次) *n.* next: Tsugi (*no eki*) *wa Ueno desu.* (次(の駅)は上野です) The *next* station is Ueno. ⟪⇨ koñdo; tsugitsugi⟫

tsu┌giko˥m·u つぎこむ (注ぎ込む) *vt.* (-kom·i-; -kom·a-; -koñ-de [C]) put into; invest: *Kare wa chokiñ o kabu ni* tsugikoñda. (彼は貯金を株につぎ込んだ) She *invested* her savings in stocks.

tsu┌gime つぎめ (継ぎ目) *n.* joint; seam: *Isu no* tsugime *ga yuruñde iru.* (いすの継ぎ目がゆるんでいる) The *joints* of the chair are loose.

tsu┌gi˥tsugi つぎつぎ (次々) *adv.* (〜 ni, to) one after another; in succession.

tsu┌goo つごう (都合) *n.* convenience; opportunity; circumstances.
tsugoo ga tsuku (〜がつく) suit one's convenience.
tsugoo o tsukeru (〜をつける) manage to do.

tsu┌g·u[1] つぐ (注ぐ) *vt.* (tsug·i-; tsug·a-; tsu·i-de [C]) pour; fill: *Kanojo wa o-cha o* tsuide kureta. (彼女はお茶をついでくれた) She *poured* me some tea.

tsu┌g·u[2] つぐ (次ぐ) *vi.* (tsug·i-; tsug·a-; tsu·i-de [C]) be [come] next to: ★ Used in the patterns '*... ni tsugu*' and '*... ni tsuide.*' *Oosaka wa Tookyoo ni* tsugu *daitokai desu.* (大阪は東京に次ぐ大都会

です) *Next* to Tokyo, Osaka is the biggest city.

tsu⌈g·u[3] つぐ(継ぐ) *vt.* (tsug·i-; tsug·a-; tsu·i-de Ⓒ) succeed; inherit; take over.

tsu⌈i[1] つい(対) *n.* pair:
Kono yunomi-jawañ wa tsui *ni natte imasu.* (この湯飲み茶わんは対になっています) These teacups make a *pair.*

tsu⌉i[2] つい *adv.* **1** (of time and distance) just; only:
Tsui *sakihodo koko ni tsuita tokoro desu.* (つい先ほどここに着いたところです) I got here *just* a little while ago.
2 carelessly; by mistake.

-tsui つい(対) *suf.* counter for a pair:
*it-*tsui *no yunomi-jawañ* (一対の湯飲み茶碗) a *pair* of teacups.

tsu⌈ide[1] ついで(序で) *n.* chance; opportunity; convenience:
Sono hoñ o o-kaeshi itadaku no wa tsuide *no toki de kekkoo desu.* (その本をお返しいただくのはついでのときで結構です) It will be perfectly all right if you return the book at your *convenience.*

tsu⌈ide[2] ついで(次いで) *adv.* next to; after:
Daitooryoo ni tsuide *shushoo ga eñzetsu shita.* (大統領に次いで首相が演説した) The prime minister gave his speech *after* that of the president.

tsu⌈ide ni ついでに(序でに) *adv.* while; on the way:
Hoñya e iku tsuide ni *kitte mo katte kimasu.* (本屋へ行くついでに切手も買って来ます) I will buy some stamps *on my way* to the bookstore.

tsu⌈ihoo ついほう(追放) *n.* exile; expulsion; purge.
tsuihoo suru (～する) *vt.* exile; banish; deport; oust.

tsu⌈ika ついか(追加) *n.* addition; supplement.
tsuika suru (～する) *vt.* add; supplement: *Biiru o* ato ni-hoñ tsuika shite *kudasai.* (ビールをあと2本追加してください) Please *bring us two more bottles* of beer.

tsu⌉i ni ついに(遂に) *adv.* **1** at last; finally. ⟪⇨ tootoo⟫
2 (with a negative) after all:
Kanojo ni nañ-do mo tegami o dashita ga, tsui ni *heñji ga konakatta.* (彼女に何度も手紙を出したが, ついに返事がこなかった) I wrote her many times, but *ended up* getting no answer.

tsu⌈iraku ついらく(墜落) *n.* (of an airplane) fall; crash.
tsuiraku suru (～する) *vi.* fall; crash. ⟪⇨ ochiru⟫

tsu⌈itachi⌉ ついたち(一日) *n.* the first day of the month.
⟪⇨ APP. 5⟫

tsu⌉ite ついて(就いて) ★ Used in the pattern '*... ni tsuite.*'
1 about; on; concerning: ★ Indicates the topic under discussion.
Atarashii seefu ni tsuite *doo omoimasu ka?* (新しい政府についてどう思いますか) What do you think *about* the new government?
2 per; for: ★ Indicates proportions or ratios. Also in the pattern '*... ni tsuki.*'
Chuusha-ryookiñ wa ichi-jikañ ni tsuki *sañbyaku-eñ desu.* (駐車料金は1時間につき300円です) The parking fee is 300 yen *per* hour.

tsu⌈iya⌉s·u ついやす(費やす) *vt.* (tsuiyash·i-; tsuiyas·a-; tsuiyash·i-te Ⓒ) spend (time, money); waste; consume.

tsu⌈kae⌉·ru[1] つかえる(支える) *vi.* (tsukae-te Ⓥ) **1** be choked; be stopped; be blocked:
Gesuikañ ni nani-ka ga tsukaete *iru.* (下水管に何かがつかえている) There is something *blocking* the drain.
2 be too big to go into:
Piano wa doa ni tsukaete *naka ni hairanakatta.* (ピアノはドアにつかえて中

に入らなかった) The piano *was too big* for the door and could not go into the room.

tsu⌈kae·ru[2] つかえる (仕える) *vi.* (tsukae-te [V]) serve; wait on.

tsu⌈kai つかい (使い) *n.* **1** errand: *kodomo o* tsukai *ni yaru* (子どもを使いにやる) send a child on an *errand.*
2 messenger; bearer.

tsu⌈kaihata⌉s·u つかいはたす (使い果たす) *vt.* (-hatash·i-; -hatas·a-; -hatash·i-te [C]) use up; exhaust: *kozukai o* tsukaihatasu (小遣いを使い果たす) *use up* all one's pocket money.

tsu⌈kaikomi つかいこみ (使い込み) *n.* embezzlement; misappropriation. ((⇨ tsukaikomu))

tsu⌈kaiko⌉m·u つかいこむ (使い込む) *vt.* (-kom·i-; -kom·a-; -koñ-de [C]) embezzle (company money). ((⇨ tsukaikomi))

tsu⌈kaikona⌉s·u つかいこなす (使いこなす) *vt.* (-konash·i-; -konas·a-; -konash·i-te [C]) make good use of; have a good command of.

tsu⌈kainare⌉·ru つかいなれる (使い慣れる) *vi.* (-nare-te [V]) be accustomed to using:
Kono waapuro wa tsukainarete imasu. (このワープロは使い慣れています) I *am accustomed to using* this word processor.

tsu⌈kaisute つかいすて (使い捨て) *n.* throwaway; disposable: tsukaisute *kamera* (使い捨てカメラ) a *throwaway* camera / tsukaisute *raitaa* (使い捨てライター) a *disposable* lighter.

tsu⌈kamae·ru つかまえる (捕まえる) *vt.* (tsukamae-te [V]) catch; arrest (a thief). ((⇨ taiho))

tsu⌈kamar·u つかまる (捕まる) *vi.* (tsukamar·i-; tsukamar·a-; tsukamat-te [C]) be caught; be arrested:
Sono seeto wa kañniñgu o shite iru tokoro o tsukamatta. (その生徒はカンニングをしているところを捕まった) The pupil *was caught* in the act of cheating. ((⇨ tsukamaeru))

tsu⌈ka⌉m·u つかむ (摑む) *vt.* (tsukam·i-; tsukam·a-; tsukañ-de [C])
1 catch; hold:
Kare wa ikinari watashi no ude o tsukañda. (彼はいきなり私の腕をつかんだ) He suddenly *caught* me by the arm.
2 get (money); grasp (a meaning, intention, etc.); seize (an opportunity).

tsu⌈kare⌉ つかれ (疲れ) *n.* fatigue; tiredness; exhaustion. ((⇨ tsukareru))

tsu⌈kare⌉·ru つかれる (疲れる) *vi.* (tsukare-te [V]) get tired; be tired out; be exhausted:
Kyoo wa zañgyoo de tsukaremashita. (きょうは残業で疲れました) Today I *am tired* from overtime work. ((⇨ tsukare))

tsu⌈ka·u つかう (使う) *vt.* (tsukai-; tsukaw·a-; tsukat-te [C])
1 use; handle; operate:
kikai o tsukau (機械を使う) *handle* a machine. ((⇨ shiyoo[1])).
2 spend (money, time); use.
3 employ; handle; manage:
arubaito o tsukau (アルバイトを使う) *employ* a part-timer.
4 speak (a language); write:
Eego o tsukatte *mo ii desu ka?* (英語を使ってもいいですか) Is it all right if I *speak* English?
5 use (a nonmaterial thing):
atama o tsukau (頭を使う) *use* one's head / ki o tsukau (気を使う) *worry* / *shiñkee o* tsukau (神経を使う) *pay* careful attention to.

tsu⌈kekuwae⌉·ru つけくわえる (付け加える) *vt.* (-kuwae-te [V]) add; append. ((⇨ kuwaeru))

tsu⌈kemono つけもの (漬け物) *n.* pickles. ★ Vegetables pickled in salt and rice bran. ((⇨ tsukeru[4]))

tsu⌈ke⌉·ru[1] つける (付ける) *vt.* (tsuke-te [V]) **1** attach (medicine); apply; spread (butter, jam):

t

suutsukeesu ni nafuda o tsukeru (スーツケースに名札をつける) *attach* a name tag to one's suitcase.
2 fix (equipment); install:
Kuruma ni eakoñ o tsukete moratta. (車にエアコンをつけてもらった) I *had* an air conditioner *installed* in my car.
3 write (a memo, diary, etc.):
nikki o tsukeru (日記をつける) *write* a diary.
4 give (a mark); grade:
Señsee wa kare no tooañ ni ii teñ o tsuketa. (先生は彼の答案にいい点をつけた) The teacher *gave* his answer a high mark.
5 tail; follow:
Kanojo wa dare-ka ni tsukerarete ita. (彼女はだれかにつけられていた) She *was being followed* by someone.

tsu⌈ke⌉·ru[2] つける (着ける) *vt.* (tsuke-te [V]) **1** put on (a dress, ring, etc.): ★ '*tsukete iru*'=wear.
atarashii doresu o mi ni tsukeru (新しいドレスを身に着ける) *put on* a new dress.
2 drive (a car) up to; draw (a ship) alongside:
geñkañ ni kuruma o tsukeru (玄関に車を着ける) *drive* a car up to the entrance.

tsu⌈ke⌉·ru[3] つける (点ける) *vt.* (tsuke-te [V]) switch on: light; set fire:
deñki o tsukeru (電気をつける) *switch on* the electricity / *tabako ni hi o* tsukeru (たばこに火をつける) *light* a cigarette. 《⇨ tsuku[4]》

tsu⌈ke·ru[4] つける (漬ける) *vt.* (tsuke-te [V]) pickle; preserve:
Niku o shio ni tsukete *hozoñ shita.* (肉を塩に漬けて保存した) I *salted* the meat to preserve it. 《⇨ tsukemono》

tsu⌈ki⌉[1] つき (月) *n.* month. 《⇨ APP. 5》

tsu⌈ki⌉[2] つき (月) *n.* the moon.

tsu⌈ki⌉[3] つき (付き) *n.* **1** adherence; stickiness:
Kono nori wa tsuki ga yoi [warui]. (この糊は付きが良い[悪い]) This glue *sticks well* [*badly*].
2 combustion:
Kono raitaa wa tsuki ga warui. (このライターは付きが悪い) This lighter *does not light easily*.

-tsuki つき (付き) *suf.* with:
Kono rajio wa ichi-neñ-kañ no hoshoo-tsuki *desu.* (このラジオは1年間の保証付きです) This radio comes *with* a one-year guarantee.

tsu⌈kiai つきあい (付き合い) *n.* association; friendship; acquaintance:
Kare to wa nagai tsukiai desu. (彼とは長いつきあいです) I *have known him* for a long time. 《⇨ tsukiau》

tsu⌈kiatari つきあたり (突き当たり) *n.* the end of a street.

tsu⌈kiata⌉r·u つきあたる (突き当たる) *vi.* (-atar·i-; -atar·a-; -atat-te [C]) **1** run into; collide; run against:
Torakku ga deñchuu ni tsukiatatta. (トラックが電柱に突き当たった) The truck *ran into* a utility pole.
2 face (a problem, difficulties, etc.):
muzukashii moñdai ni tsukiataru (むずかしい問題に突き当たる) *come up against* a tough problem.

tsu⌈kia⌉·u つきあう (付き合う) *vi.* (-a·i-; -aw·a-; -at-te [C]) associate with; keep company with. 《⇨ tsukiai》

tsu⌈kigime つきぎめ (月極め) *n.* (of payment) monthly:
Watashi wa chuushajoo o tsukigime *de karite iru.* (私は駐車場を月ぎめでかりている) I rent a parking space *by the month*.

tsu⌈ki⌉hi つきひ (月日) *n.* time; years. 《⇨ neñgetsu》

tsu⌈kioto⌉s·u つきおとす (突き落とす) *vt.* (-otosh·i-; -otos·a-; -otosh·i-te [C]) push over; thrust down:
gake kara hito o tsukiotosu (がけから人を突き落とす) *push* a person *off* a cliff.

t

tsu⌈ki⌉·ru つきる (尽きる) *vi.* (tsu-ki-te [V]) run out; be exhausted.

tsu⌈kisa⌉s·u つきさす (突き刺す) *vt.* (-sash·i-; -sas·a-; -sash·i-te [C]) stick; pierce; stab. (⇨ sasu[2])

tsu⌈kisoi つきそい (付き添い) *n.* attendance; attendant; escort. (⇨ tsukisou)

tsu⌈kiso·u つきそう (付き添う) *vt.* (-so·i-; -sow·a-; -sot-te [C]) accompany; attend; escort:
Haha-oya wa byooki no kodomo ni tsukisotta. (母親は病気の子どもに付き添った) The mother *attended* her sick child. (⇨ tsukisoi)

tsu⌈kitoba⌉s·u つきとばす (突き飛ばす) *vt.* (-tobash·i-; -tobas·a-; -tobash·i-te [C]) thrust away; send flying:
Kare wa watashi o tsukitobashita. (彼は私を突き飛ばした) He *pushed* me *away*.

tsu⌈kitome⌉·ru つきとめる (突き止める) *vt.* (-tome-te [V]) trace; locate; ascertain:
uwasa no dedokoro o tsukitomeru (うわさの出所を突き止める) *trace* the source of the rumor.

tsu⌈kitsuke⌉·ru つきつける (突き付ける) *vt.* (-tsuke-te [V]) point (a weapon); confront with (evidence).

tsu⌈kko⌉m·u つっこむ (突っ込む) *vi.* (-kom·i-; -kom·a-; -koñ-de [C]) thrust into; dip into; run into:
poketto ni te o tsukkomu (ポケットに手を突っ込む) *dip* one's hand into one's pocket.

tsu⌉k·u[1] つく (着く) *vi.* (tsuk·i-; tsuk·a-; tsu·i-te [C]) **1** arrive (at); get (to); reach:
Ikkoo wa buji, sañchoo ni tsuita. (一行は無事, 山頂に着いた) The party safely *arrived* at the summit. (⇨ toochaku)
2 touch; reach:
Teñjoo ga hikui no de atama ga tsuki-soo *da.* (天井が低いので頭がつきそうだ) The ceiling is so low that my head almost *touches* it.
3 sit down; take a seat:
seki ni tsuku (席に着く) *take* a seat / *shokutaku ni* tsuku (食卓に着く) *sit down* to a meal.

tsu⌉k·u[2] つく (付く) *vi.* (tsuk·i-; tsuk·a-; tsu·i-te [C]) **1** stick; adhere:
Kore wa nori de wa tsukimaseñ. (これは糊では付きません) We *cannot stick* these with paste.
2 be stained:
Te ni iñku ga tsuite imasu *yo.* (手にインクが付いていますよ) Your hands *are stained* with ink.
3 have; carry; include:
Kono zasshi ni wa furoku ga tsuite imasu. (この雑誌には付録が付いています) This magazine *has* a supplement.
4 take the side of; side with.
5 (of seed, fruit, etc.) bear; yield; take root; bear (interest).

tsu⌉k·u[3] つく (就く) *vi.* (tsuk·i-; tsuk·a-; tsu·i-te [C]) **1** take; hold; be engaged:
too no iiñchoo no chii ni tsuku (党の委員長の地位に就く) *take* the post of party chairperson.
2 take lessons from; study under (a person).

tsu⌉k·u[4] つく (点く) *vi.* (tsuk·i-; tsuk·a-; tsu·i-te [C]) catch fire; be lighted. (⇨ tsukeru[3])

tsu⌈k·u[5] つく (突く) *vt.* (tsuk·i-; tsuk·a-; tsu·i-te [C]) **1** poke; stab; prick; spear:
Kare wa watashi no wakibara o hiji de tsuita. (彼は私の脇腹をひじで突いた) He *poked* me in the ribs with his elbow.
2 toll (a bell); strike; bounce (a ball).

tsu⌉k·u[6] つく (吐く) *vt.* (tsuk·i-; tsuk·a-; tsu·i-te [C]) tell; sigh:
uso o tsuku (うそをつく) *tell* a lie / *tameiki o* tsuku (ため息をつく) *give* a sigh.

tsu⌈kue つくえ (机) *n.* desk.

tsu⌈kuri⌉ つくり (旁) *n.* the right-hand element of a Chinese character. ★ Often the phonetic element of the character. (⇨ bushu; heñ[3])

tsu⌈ku⌉r·u[1] つくる(作る) *vt.* (tsukur·i-; tsukur·a-; tsukut-te Ⓒ)
1 make; form; shape; manufacture: (⇨ tsukuru[2])
ki de inugoya o tsukuru (木で犬小屋を作る) *make* a kennel of wood.
2 write; compose; make:
shi o tsukuru (詩を作る) *write* a poem / *keeyakusho o* tsukuru (契約書を作る) *draw up* a contract.
3 grow; raise:
kome [*yasai*] *o* tsukuru (米[野菜]を作る) *grow* rice [vegetables].
4 form; organize:
retsu o tsukuru (列を作る) *form* a line / *roodoo-kumiai o* tsukuru (労働組合を作る) *organize* a labor union.
5 cook; make:
yuushoku o tsukuru (夕食を作る) *cook* dinner.

tsu⌈ku⌉r·u[2] つくる(造る) *vt.* (tsukur·i-; tsukur·a-; tsukut-te Ⓒ)
1 build; construct:
ie o tsukuru (家を造る) *build* a house / *hashi o* tsukuru (橋を造る) *construct* a bridge. (⇨ tsukuru[1])
2 mint; coin:
kooka o tsukuru (硬貨を造る) *mint* coins / *shihee o* tsukuru (紙幣を造る) *print* paper money.
3 create:
atarashii toshi o tsukuru (新しい都市を造る) *create* a new city / *tee-eñ o* tsukuru (庭園を造る) *create* a garden.
4 brew: *biiru o* tsukuru (ビールを造る) *brew* beer.

tsu⌈ku⌉s·u つくす(尽くす) *vt.* (tsukush·i-; tsukus·a-; tsukush·i-te Ⓒ) **1** exhaust (energy); use up; consume:
Kare wa zeñryoku o tsukushita. (彼は全力を尽くした) He *has done* his best.
2 devote oneself; serve:
Kanojo wa byooki no otto no tame ni tsukushita. (彼女は病気の夫のために尽くした) She *did all she could* for her sick husband.

tsu⌈kuzu⌉ku つくづく *adv.* (~ to)
1 (of dislike) utterly; really:
Kono wabishii seekatsu ga tsukuzuku *iya ni natta.* (このわびしい生活がつくづくいやになった) I am *utterly* disgusted at this lonely life.
2 carefully; intently:
Watashi wa kore made no jiñsee o tsukuzuku (*to*) *furikaette mita.* (私はこれまでの人生をつくづく(と)振り返ってみた) I *carefully* looked back on my life so far.

tsu⌉ma つま(妻) *n.* wife.
★ '*Tsuma*' refers to one's own wife, or is used as a generic term for wife. '*Kanai*' is used only in the first sense. (↔ otto)

tsu⌈mami[1] つまみ(摘まみ) *n.*
1 knob: tsumami *o mawasu* (つまみを回す) turn a *knob.*
2 pinch:
hito-tsumami *no shio* (一つまみの塩) a *pinch* of salt. (⇨ tsumamu)

tsu⌈mami[2] つまみ *n.* light snacks; hors d'oeuvre.

tsu⌈mamigui つまみぐい(つまみ食い) *n.* eating with the fingers; sneaking a bite of food.
tsumamigui suru (~する) *vt.* eat secretly.

tsu⌈mam·u つまむ(摘まむ) *vt.* (tsumam·i-; tsumam·a-; tsumañ-de Ⓒ) pick up; pinch:
Kamikuzu o tsumañde *kuzukago ni ireta.* (紙くずをつまんでくずかごに入れた) I *picked up* the scraps of paper and put them into the litter bin.

tsu⌈mara⌉na·i つまらない(詰まらない) *a.* (-ku) **1** uninteresting; boring:
Sono shiai wa tsumaranakatta. (その試合はつまらなかった) The match was *not exciting.* (↔ omoshiroi)
2 trifling; foolish; worthless:
Tsumaranai *mono desu ga doozo.* (つまらないものですがどうぞ) This is *nothing special*, but I hope you

will accept it. ⟪⇨ kudaranai⟫

tsuˈmari つまり(詰まり) *conj.* that is; in short; in a word; after all: Tsumari *sore ga kimi no iitai koto desu ne.* (つまりそれが君の言いたいことですね) *In short*, that is what you want to say, isn't it? ⟪⇨ kekkyoku; yoo-suru ni⟫

tsuˈmaˈr·u つまる(詰まる) *vi.* (tsumar·i-; tsumar·a-; tsumat-te Ⓒ) **1** be stopped; be choked up; clog: *Kaze o hiite, hana ga* tsumatta. (かぜをひいて, 鼻が詰まった) I have a cold so my nose *is stuffed up.* **2** be full; be filled up; be packed: *Kabañ no naka wa shorui ga ippai* tsumatte ita. (かばんの中は書類がいっぱい詰まっていた) The briefcase *was packed* full of papers. ⟪⇨ tsumeru⟫

tsuˈmasaki つまさき(爪先) *n.* tiptoe; tip.

tsuˈmazuk·u つまずく(躓く) *vi.* (-zuk·i-; -zuk·a-; -zu·i-te Ⓒ) **1** stumble; trip. **2** (of a project, plan, etc.) fail; go wrong: *Watashi-tachi no keekaku wa saisho kara* tsumazuita. (私たちの計画は最初からつまずいた) Our plan *went wrong* from the beginning.

tsuˈme つめ(爪) *n.* nail; claw.

tsuˈmekake·ru つめかける(詰めかける) *vt.* (-kake-te Ⓥ) besiege; throng; crowd. ⟪⇨ atsumaru⟫

tsuˈmeˈ·ru つめる(詰める) *vt.* (tsume-te Ⓥ) **1** pack; stuff; fill; plug; stop: *Dañbooru-bako ni hoñ o* tsumeta. (段ボール箱に本を詰めた) I *packed* the books in the cardboard boxes. ⟪⇨ tsumaru⟫ **2** move over; stand [sit] closer: *Moo sukoshi oku e* tsumete *kudasai.* (もう少し奥へ詰めてください) Will you *move back* a little more, please? **3** shorten (time); cut (hair).

tsuˈmeta·i つめたい(冷たい) *a.* (-ku) **1** (of temperature) cold; cool; chilly: tsumetai *nomimono* (冷たい飲み物) a *cold* drink / tsumetai *kaze* (冷たい風) a *chill* wind. ⟪↔ atsui[1]⟫ **2** (of a person's attitude) cold; cool: tsumetai *kotoba* (冷たい言葉) *cold* words / tsumetai *hito* (冷たい人) a *coldhearted* person. ⟪↔ atatakai⟫

tsuˈmi つみ(罪) *n.* sin; crime; offense: tsumi *o okasu* (罪を犯す) commit a *sin* [*crime*].

tsuˈmori つもり(積もり) *n.* **1** intention; purpose; idea: *Sono koto wa kare ni iwanai* tsumori *desu.* (そのことは彼に言わないつもりです) I do not *plan* to tell him about that. **2** thought; expectation; conviction: *Kare ni kite moraeru* tsumori de ita. (彼に来てもらえるつもりでいた) I *expected* that he would come. **3** attitude; frame of mind: *Koñdo shippai shitara, kubi da kara sono* tsumori *de.* (今度失敗したら, 首だからそのつもりで) If you fail again, you will be fired, so *be prepared* for that.

tsuˈmor·u つもる(積もる) *vi.* (tsumor·i-; tsumor·a-; tsumot-te Ⓒ) accumulate; be piled up: *Yuki ga takusañ* tsumotta. (雪がたくさん積もった) The snow *lies* very deep.

tsuˈm·u[1] つむ(積む) *vt.* (tsum·i-; tsum·a-; tsuñ-de Ⓒ) **1** pile (up); heap (up); stack. ⟪⇨ kasaneru⟫ **2** load: *torakku ni zaimoku o* tsumu (トラックに材木を積む) *load* a truck with lumber. **3** accumulate (experience, exercise, etc.).

tsuˈm·u[2] つむ(摘む) *vt.* (tsum·i-; tsum·a-; tsuñ-de Ⓒ) pick; gather; pluck; nip: *nohara de hana o* tsumu (野原で花

t

をつむ) *gather* flowers in the field.

tsuˈnaˈ つな(綱) *n.* rope; cord.

tsuˈnagari つながり(繋り) *n.* connection; relation. ((⇨ tsunagaru))

tsuˈnagar·u つながる(繋がる) *vi.* (tsunagar·i-; tsunagar·a-; tsunagat-te [C]) **1** connect; link: *Atarashii hashi de Hoñshuu to Shikoku ga* tsunagatta. (新しい橋で本州と四国がつながった) Honshu and Shikoku *were linked* by new bridges. ((⇨ tsunagu))
2 be related; be linked: *Watashi wa kare to chi ga* tsunagatte imasu. (私は彼と血がつながっています) I *am related* to him by blood. ((⇨ tsunagari))

tsuˈnage·ru つなげる(繋げる) *vt.* (tsunage-te [V]) = tsunagu.

tsuˈnag·u つなぐ(繋ぐ) *vt.* (tsunag·i-; tsunag·a-; tsuna·i-de [C]) **1** tie; fasten; chain: *inu o ki ni* tsunagu (犬を木につなぐ) *tie* a dog to a tree. ((⇨ tsunagaru))
2 connect; join: *hoosu o shookaseñ ni* tsunagu (ホースを消火栓につなぐ) *connect* a hose to a fire hydrant.

tsuˈnami つなみ(津波) *n.* tidal wave; tsunami.

tsuˈne ni つねに(常に) *adv.* (*slightly formal*) always; habitually. ((⇨ itsu-mo))

tsuˈneˈr·u つねる(抓る) *vt.* (tsuner·i-; tsuner·a-; tsunet-te [C]) pinch; nip: *Kanojo wa watashi no ude o* tsunetta. (彼女は私の腕をつねった) She *pinched* me on the arm.

tsuˈnoˈ つの(角) *n.* horn; antler.

tsuˈra·i つらい(辛い) *a.* (-ku) hard; tough; painful; bitter: tsurai *shigoto* (つらい仕事) *hard* work / tsurai *omoi o suru* (つらい思いをする) have a *bitter* experience.

tsuˈranuˈk·u つらぬく(貫く) *vt.* (-nuk·i-; -nuk·a-; -nu·i-te [C]) **1** pierce; run through; penetrate: *Tama wa kabe o* tsuranuita. (弾は壁を貫いた) The bullet *went through* the wall.
2 carry through; accomplish: *Kare wa jibuñ no shiññeñ o* tsuranuita. (彼は自分の信念を貫いた) He *maintained* his convictions *to the end.*

tsuˈre つれ(連れ) *n.* companion.

tsuˈre·ru つれる(連れる) *vt.* (tsure-te [V]) take (a person); bring (a person); be accompanied: *Watashi wa kodomo o doobutsueñ e* tsurete itta. (私は子どもを動物園へ連れて行った) I *took* the children to the zoo.

tsuˈrete つれて *conj.* accordingly; consequently.
... ni tsurete (...に～) as...: *Toshi o toru* ni tsurete *tairyoku ga yowaru.* (年を取るにつれて体力が弱る) *As* one grows older, one's strength decreases. ((⇨ shitagatte[1]))

tsuˈri[1] つり(釣り) *n.* fishing; angling. ((⇨ tsuru[1]))

tsuˈri[2] つり(釣り) *n.* change.
★ Often with '*o-*.' ((⇨ o-tsuri; tsuriseñ))

tsuˈriai つりあい(釣り合い) *n.* balance; proportion; harmony. ((⇨ tsuriau))

tsuˈriaˈ·u つりあう(釣り合う) *vi.* (-a·i-; -aw·a-; -at-te [C]) balance; be in proportion; be in harmony; match. ((⇨ tsuriai))

tsuˈribashi つりばし(吊り橋) *n.* rope bridge; suspension bridge.

tsuˈriseñ つりせん(釣り銭) *n.* small change: Tsuriseñ no nai yoo ni *o-negai shimasu.* (つり銭のないようにお願いします) Please have the *exact amount* ready. ((⇨ o-tsuri))

tsuˈr·u[1] つる(釣る) *vt.* (tsur·i-; tsur·a-; tsut-te [C]) fish; angle; catch. ((⇨ tsuri[1]))

tsuˈr·u[2] つる(吊る) *vt.* (tsur·i-; tsur·a-; tsut-te [C]) hang; suspend: *kaateñ o* tsuru (カーテンをつる) *hang* curtains / *kubi o* tsuru (首をつる) *hang* oneself. 《⇨ tsurusu》

tsuˈru[3] つる (鶴) *n.* crane. 《⇨ kame; señbazuru》

tsuˈrus·u つるす (吊す) *vt.* (tsurush·i-; tsurus·a-; tsurush·i-te Ⓒ) hang; suspend:
señtakumono o tsurusu (洗濯物をつるす) *hang out* the washing. 《⇨ tsuru[2]》

tsuˈtae·ru つたえる (伝える) *vt.* (tsutae-te Ⓥ) **1** tell; inform; notify; communicate.
2 hand down (a tale, custom, religion, etc.); introduce. 《⇨ tsutawaru》

tsuˈta·u つたう (伝う) *vt.* (tsuta·i-; tsutaw·a-; tsutat-te Ⓒ) go along:
yane o tsutatte *nigeru* (屋根を伝って逃げる) flee from roof *to* roof.

tsuˈtawar·u つたわる (伝わる) *vi.* (tsutawar·i-; tsutawar·a-; tsutawat-te Ⓒ) **1** (of information, rumor, etc.) spread; travel; circulate. 《⇨ tsutaeru》
2 (of a tale, tradition, etc.) come down; be handed down. 《⇨ tsutaeru》
3 be transmitted; be introduced:
Bukkyoo ga Nihoñ ni tsutawatta *no wa roku-seeki nakaba desu.* (仏教が日本に伝わったのは6世紀半ばです) It is in the mid-sixth century that Buddhism *was introduced* into Japan. 《⇨ tsutaeru》

tsuˈtomaˈr·u つとまる (勤まる) *vi.* (-mar·i-; -mar·a-; -mat-te Ⓒ) be fit; be equal:
Sono shigoto ga watashi ni tsutomaru *ka doo ka shiñpai desu.* (その仕事が私に勤まるかどうか心配です) I am worried whether I *am equal* to the job.

tsuˈtome[1] つとめ (勤め) *n.* work; job. 《⇨ tsutomeru[1]》

tsuˈtome[2] つとめ (務め) *n.* duty; task:
Kare wa tsutome *o rippa ni hatashita.* (彼は務めを立派に果たした) He discharged his *duties* splendidly. 《⇨ tsutomeru[2]》

tsuˈtomeˈ·ru[1] つとめる (勤める) *vt.* (-me-te Ⓥ) work for; serve:
Kanojo wa shoojigaisha ni tsutomete *imasu.* (彼女は商事会社に勤めています) She *works for* a trading company. 《⇨ kiñmu; tsutome[1]》

tsuˈtomeˈ·ru[2] つとめる (務める) *vt.* (-me-te Ⓥ) act as:
Kare wa kaigi de gichoo o tsutometa. (彼は会議で議長を務めた) He *acted* as chairman at the conference. 《⇨ tsutome[2]》

tsuˈtomeˈ·ru[3] つとめる (努める) *vt.* (-me-te Ⓥ) try; make efforts; endeavor. 《⇨ doryoku》

tsuˈtomesaki つとめさき (勤め先) *n.* one's place of employment. 《⇨ kaisha》

tsuˈtsu つつ (筒) *n.* pipe; tube; cylinder.

tsuˈtsuˈk·u つつく (突つく) *vt.* (tsutsuk·i-; tsutsuk·a-; tsutsu·i-te Ⓒ) poke; peck; nudge.

tsuˈtsuˈm·u つつむ (包む) *vt.* (tsutsum·i-; tsutsum·a-; tsutsuñ-de Ⓒ) **1** wrap; pack:
mono o kami ni tsutsumu (物を紙に包む) *wrap* a thing *up* in paper.
2 cover; veil:
Yama zeñtai ga moya ni tsutsumarete ita. (山全体がもやに包まれていた) The whole mountain *was covered* in mist.

tsuˈtsushimiˈ つつしみ (慎み) *n.* modesty; prudence; discretion; self-control. 《⇨ tsutsushimu》

tsuˈtsushiˈm·u つつしむ (慎む) *vt.* (-shim·i-; -shim·a-; -shiñ-de Ⓒ)
1 be careful; be discreet; be prudent; be cautious:
koodoo o tsutsushimu (行動を慎む) *be prudent* in one's conduct.
2 refrain from; be moderate:
sake o tsutsushimu (酒を慎しむ) *cut down on* one's drinking.

tsuˈu つう (通) *n.* authority; expert:

Ano hito wa kabuki no tsuu *desu.* (あの人は歌舞伎の通です) He is an *authority* on kabuki.

tsuʳuchi つうち (通知) *n.* notice; notification; information.
tsuuchi suru (〜する) *vt.* notify; inform.

tsuʳugaku つうがく (通学) *n.* traveling to school; attending school. ⟪⇨ zaigaku⟫
tsuugaku suru (〜する) *vi.* go to school. ⟪⇨ tsuukiñ⟫

tsuʳuji つうじ (通じ) *n.* bowel movement; evacuation; stool.

tsuʳuji·ru つうじる (通じる) *vi.* (tsuuji-te Ⓥ) **1** lead; run:
Kono michi wa eki e tsuujite imasu. (この道は駅へ通じています) This road *leads* to the station.
2 (of a telephone) get through:
Kanojo no uchi ni deñwa o shita ga tsuujinakatta. (彼女の家に電話をしたが通じなかった) I telephoned her house but I *could not get through.*
3 be understood; make oneself understood:
Watashi no iu koto ga aite ni tsuujinakatta. (私の言うことが相手に通じなかった) I *could not make myself understood* to the other party.
4 be well-informed; be familiar:
Kare wa sono kaisha no naibu-jijoo ni tsuujite iru. (彼はその会社の内部事情に通じている) He *is well-informed* on the internal affairs of the company.

tsuʳujoo つうじょう (通常) *n., adv.* usually; generally:
Neñmatsu mo tsuujoo-doori *ee-gyoo itashimasu.* (年末も通常どおり営業いたします) We will be conducting business *as usual* at the end of the year. ⟪⇨ futsuu[1]⟫

tsuʳuka つうか (通過) *n.* passage.
tsuuka suru (〜する) *vi.* pass:
Kyuukoo wa kono eki o tsuuka shimasu. (急行はこの駅を通過します) The express *does not stop* at this station.

tsuʳuki つうき (通気) *n.* ventilation; air permeabilty.

tsuʳukiñ つうきん (通勤) *n.* commutation; going to work.
tsuukiñ suru (〜する) *vi.* commute; go to work.

tsuʳukoo つうこう (通行) *n.* passing; passage; traffic:
ippoo-tsuukoo (一方通行) a *one-way* street.
tsuukoo suru (〜する) *vi.* pass; go along. ⟪⇨ tooru⟫

tsuʳu-piˀisu ツーピース *n.* two-piece woman's suit.

tsuˀuro つうろ (通路) *n.* passage; way; aisle.

tsuʳushiñ つうしん (通信) *n.* correspondence; communication.
tsuushiñ suru (〜する) *vi.* correspond; communicate.

tsuˀuyaku つうやく (通訳) *n.* interpretation; interpreter:
tsuuyaku *o tooshite hanasu* (通訳を通して話す) speak through an *interpreter.*
tsuuyaku suru (〜する) *vt.* interpret. ⟪⇨ dooji-tsuuyaku⟫

tsuʳuyoo つうよう (通用) *n.* popular use; circulation; currency.
tsuuyoo suru (〜する) *vi.* be used; be accepted; be valid.

tsuʳya つや (艶) *n.* gloss; luster; polish.

tsuʳyoˀ·i つよい (強い) *a.* (-ku)
1 strong; powerful; intense. ⟪↔ yowai⟫ ⟪⇨ tsuyosa⟫
2 (... ni) be good at:
Kare wa suuji ni tsuyoi. (彼は数字に強い) He is *good* at figures. ⟪↔ yowai⟫
3 (... ni) be able to resist; withstand:
Watashi wa samusa ni tsuyoi. (私は寒さに強い) I can *easily stand* the cold. ⟪↔ yowai⟫ ⟪⇨ tsuyosa⟫

tsuʳyoki つよき (強気) *a.n.* (〜 na, ni) bold; aggressive; optimistic:
Kare wa itsu-mo tsuyoki *da.* (彼はいつも強気だ) He is always *firm and resolute.* ⟪↔ yowaki⟫

t

tsuˈyomaˈr·u つよまる (強まる) *vi.* (-mar·i-; -mar·a-; -mat-te [C]) become strong; increase in power [strength]. ⟪⇨ tsuyomeru⟫

tsuˈyomeˈ·ru つよめる (強める) *vt.* (-me-te [V]) strengthen; intensify; emphasize:
ryookoku no musubitsuki o tsuyomeru (両国の結びつきを強める) *strengthen* the ties between two countries. ⟪↔ yowameru⟫ ⟪⇨ tsuyomaru⟫

tsuˈyosa つよさ (強さ) *n.* strength; power, force:
kaze no tsuyosa *o hakaru* (風の強さを測る) measure the *force* of the wind. ⟪⇨ tsuyoi⟫

tsuˈyu[1] つゆ (露) *n.* dew; dewdrop.

tsuˈyu[2] つゆ (梅雨) *n.* the rainy season. ★ The period from June to July, when there are many rainy days. ⟪⇨ baiu; uki[1]⟫

tsuˈyu[3] つゆ (汁) *n.* soup; sauce; juice. ★ Often called '*o-tsuyu*.' ⟪⇨ shiru[2]⟫

tsuˈzuke·ru つづける (続ける) *vt.* (tsuzuke-te [V]) continue; go on; keep up:
Doozo hanashi o tsuzukete *kudasai.* (どうぞ話を続けてください) *Go on* with your story, please. ⟪⇨ tsuzuku⟫

tsuˈzuki つづき (続き) *n.* continuance; continuation; sequel:
Sono hanashi no tsuzuki *ga kikitai.* (その話の続きが聞きたい) I want to hear the *rest* of the story. ⟪⇨ tsuzuku⟫

tsuˈzuk·u つづく (続く) *vi.* (tsuzuk·i-; tsuzuk·a-; tsuzu·i-te [C])
1 continue; go on; last:
Seeteñ ga is-shuukañ tsuzuita. (晴天が一週間続いた) The fine weather *continued* for a week. ⟪⇨ tsuzukeru; tsuzuki⟫
2 follow:
Watashi-tachi wa kare ni tsuzuite *sono heya ni haitta.* (私たちは彼に続いてその部屋に入った) We went into the room, *following* him. ⟪⇨ shitagatte[1]⟫
3 lead; extend:
Kono namikimichi wa ichi-kiro hodo tsuzukimasu. (この並木道は1キロほど続きます) This avenue of trees *extends* for about one kilometer.

tsuˈzumiˈ つづみ (鼓) *n.* Japanese hand drum. ★ Beaten with the fingertips.

ttaˈra[1] ったら *p.* (used to mark the topic of a sentence): ★ Follows a noun or the dictionary form of a verb. An informal form mainly used by women.
Uchi no ko ttara, *asoñde bakari ite, sukoshi mo beñkyoo shinai.* (うちの子ったら, 遊んでばかりいて, 少しも勉強しない) *That child of ours!* He plays around all the time, and does not study one bit.
... ttara nai (...～ない) (used for emphasis or exaggeration):
Kono tokoro mainichi isogashii ttara nai. (このところ毎日忙しいったらない) These days I *am rushed off my feet* every day!

(t)tara[2] (っ)たら *p.* = (t)teba.

(t)teba (っ)てば *p.* (used when emphasizing one's thoughts or opinions to someone who appears not to understand):
★ Sometimes used as a retort or contradiction. Use '*teba*' after '*ñ*,' otherwise '*tteba*.'
"Hayaku ikoo yo." "Wakatte iru tteba." (「早く行こうよ」「わかっているってば」) "Let's hurry up and get along." "Okay, okay, *I understand.*"

U

-u う *infl. end.* = -oo.

u⌈ba⌉·u うばう (奪う) *vt.* (uba·i-; ubaw·a-; ubat-te Ⓒ) take by force; snatch; rob; deprive.

u⌈chi⌉[1] うち (家) *n.* **1** house; home; family. 《⇨ ie[1]》
2 (~ no) my; our:
uchi no *chichi* (うちの父) *my* father / uchi no *gakkoo* [*kaisha*] (うちの学校[会社]) *our* school [company].

u⌈chi[2] うち (内) *n.* **1** inside:
Kono doa wa uchi *kara hiraku.* (このドアは内から開く) This door opens from the *inside.* 《↔ soto》 《⇨ naka[1]》
2 (~ ni) in; within; before:
Kuraku naranai uchi *ni kaerimashoo.* (暗くならないうちに帰りましょう) Let's go back *before* it gets dark.
3 (~ kara) of; out of:
Kono itsutsu no uchi *kara hitotsu tori nasai.* (この五つのうちから一つ取りなさい) Take one *out of* these five.

u⌈chiake·ru うちあける (打ち明ける) *vt.* (-ake-te Ⓥ) confide; confess; unburden.

u⌈chiawase うちあわせ (打ち合わせ) *n.* previous arrangement. 《⇨ uchiawaseru》

u⌈chiawase·ru うちあわせる (打ち合わせる) *vt.* (-awase-te Ⓥ) arrange; make arrangements beforehand. 《⇨ uchiawase》

u⌈chigawa うちがわ (内側) *n.* the inside; interior:
hako no uchigawa (箱の内側) the *inside* of a box. 《↔ sotogawa》

u⌈chikeshi うちけし (打ち消し) *n.* denial; negation. 《⇨ uchikesu》

u⌈chikes·u うちけす (打ち消す) *vt.* (-kesh·i-; -kes·a-; -kesh·i-te Ⓒ) deny (the rumor); negate. 《⇨ uchikeshi》

u⌈chikir·u うちきる (打ち切る) *vt.* (-kir·i-; -kir·a-; -kit-te Ⓒ) discontinue; break off (negotiations).

u⌈chikom·u うちこむ (打ち込む) *vt.* (-kom·i-; -kom·a-; -koñ-de Ⓒ)
1 drive; shoot; smash:
jimeñ ni kui o uchikomu (地面にくいを打ち込む) *drive* a stake into the ground.
2 devote oneself to.

u⌈chiwa[1] うちわ (内輪) *n.* **1** private; family:
uchiwa *dake no atsumari* (内輪だけの集まり) a *private* meeting / uchiwa *no kekkoñ-shiki* (内輪の結婚式) a *family* wedding.
2 conservative; moderate:
Hiyoo wa uchiwa *ni mitsumotte, gojuumañ-eñ kakarimasu.* (費用は内輪に見積もって, 50 万円かかります) *Conservatively* estimated, the cost is half a million yen.

u⌈chi⌉wa[2] うちわ (団扇) *n.* round fan made of paper and bamboo.

u⌈chiwake うちわけ (内訳) *n.* breakdown (of expenditures); item; detail.

u⌉chuu うちゅう (宇宙) *n.* the universe; the cosmos; space.

u⌈de⌉ うで (腕) *n.* **1** arm; forearm.
2 ability; skill:
Kare wa saikiñ gorufu no ude *ga agatta.* (彼は最近ゴルフの腕が上がった) He has recently improved his *skill* in golf. 《⇨ udemae》

u⌈dedo⌉kee うでどけい (腕時計) *n.* wristwatch. 《⇨ tokee》

u⌈degumi⌉ うでぐみ (腕組み) *n.* folding one's arms:
udegumi *o shite kañgaeru* (腕組みをして考える) think with one's *arms folded.*

u⌈demae うでまえ (腕前) *n.* skill; ability. 《⇨ ude》

u⌈doñ うどん *n.* noodles.

u⌈e[1] うえ (上) *n.* **1** on:

u

Kanojo wa yuka no ue *ni juutañ o shiita.* (彼女は床の上にじゅうたんを敷いた) She laid a carpet *on* the floor. ((↔ shita[1]))
2 over; above:
Hikooki wa yama no ue *o toñde ita.* (飛行機は山の上を飛んでいた) The plane was flying *over* the mountain. ((↔ shita[1]))
3 up; upstairs:
Kanojo wa esukareetaa de ue *ni ikimashita.* (彼女はエスカレーターで上に行きました) She went *up* in the escalator. ((↔ shita[1]))
4 top:
Sono hoñ wa ichibañ ue *no tana ni arimasu.* (その本はいちばん上の棚にあります) The book is on the *top* shelf. ((↔ shita[1]))
5 senior; older:
Shujiñ wa watashi yori go-sai ue *desu.* (主人は私より5歳上です) My husband is five years *older* than me. ((↔ shita[1]))
6 superior:
Kono koocha no hoo ga sore yori shitsu ga ue *desu.* (この紅茶の方がそれより質が上です) This tea is *superior* in quality to that one. ((⇨ otoru))
7 after:
Sono koto wa ryooshiñ to soodañ no ue *kimemasu.* (そのことは両親と相談の上決めます) I will decide that matter *after* discussing it with my parents.

u⌈e⌉[2] うえ (飢え) *n.* hunger; starvation. ((⇨ ueru[2]))

u⌈eki うえき (植木) *n.* garden tree [plant]; potted plant.

u⌈e·ru[1] うえる (植える) *vt.* (ue-te [V]) plant (a tree); sow; grow.

u⌈e⌉·ru[2] うえる (飢える) *vi.* (ue-te [V]) be [go] hungry; starve. ((⇨ ue[2]))

u⌈e⌉-shita うえした (上下) *n.* up and down. ((↔ sayuu)) ((⇨ jooge))

u⌈gai うがい (含嗽) *n.* gargling.
ugai suru (〜する) gargle.

u⌈goka⌉s·u うごかす (動かす) *vt.* (ugokash·i-; ugokas·a-; ugokash·i-te [C]) **1** move (a table).
2 operate (a machine, vehicle, etc.); run; start. ((⇨ ugoku))
3 (of feelings, emotions) touch; move; influence:
Sono tegami wa kanojo no kokoro o ugokashita. (その手紙は彼女の心を動かした) That letter *touched* her heart. ((⇨ ugoku))

u⌈goki⌉ うごき (動き) *n.* **1** movement; motion. ((⇨ ugoku))
2 activity; action.
booryokudañ no ugoki *o shiraberu* (暴力団の動きを調べる) investigate the *activities* of criminal gangs.
3 trend; development:
yo no naka no ugoki (世の中の動き) social *trends.* ((⇨ ugoku))

u⌈go⌉k·u うごく (動く) *vi.* (ugok·i-; ugok·a-; ugo·i-te [C]) **1** move; budge; stir:
Kare wa kega o shite, ugokemaseñ. (彼はけがをして, 動けません) He has hurt himself and *cannot move.* ((⇨ ugokasu; ugoki))
2 (of a machine, vehicle, etc.) work; run:
Kono kuruma wa deñki de ugoku. (この車は電気で動く) This car *runs* on electricity. ((⇨ ugokasu))
3 act; get about:
Ima ugoku *no wa keñmee de wa arimaseñ.* (今動くのは賢明ではありません) It is not wise to *act* now.
4 (of feelings, emotions) be influenced; be moved; be touched.

u⌈kabe·ru うかべる (浮かべる) *vt.* (ukabe-te [V]) **1** float; set afloat. ((⇨ ukabu))
2 show (one's feeling); express:
namida o ukaberu (涙を浮かべる) *have* tears in one's eyes. ((⇨ ukabu))

u⌈kab·u うかぶ (浮かぶ) *vt.* (ukab·i-; ukab·a-; ukañ-de [C])
1 float (on the water). ((⇨ ukaberu))
2 (of an idea) come into; occur.
3 (of tears, countenance) appear:

Kanojo no me ni namida ga ukañda. (彼女の目に涙が浮かんだ) Tears *appeared* in her eyes. ⟪⇨ ukaberu⟫

u⌜kaga·u うかがう (伺う) *vt.* (ukaga·i-; ukagaw·a-; ukagat-te Ⓒ) **1** (*humble*) visit; call on [at]: *Asu o-taku ni* ukagatte *mo yoroshii desu ka?* (あすお宅にうかがってもよろしいですか) Is it all right if I *call on* you at home tomorrow?
2 (*humble*) ask: Ukagaitai *koto ga aru ñ desu ga.* (うかがいたいことがあるんですが) There are some questions I'*d like to ask* you.
3 (*humble*) hear; be told: *Anata wa teñkiñ sareta to* ukagatte *orimasu ga.* (あなたは転勤されたとうかがっておりますが) I *hear* that you have been transferred.

u⌜keire·ru うけいれる (受け入れる) *vt.* (-ire-te Ⓥ) accept (a demand, request, proposal, etc.); grant.

u⌜kemi⌝ うけみ (受け身) *n.* passive; passive sentence. ⟪⇨ -rareru; -reru⟫

u⌜kemochi うけもち (受け持ち) *n.* charge; responsibility. ⟪⇨ ukemotsu⟫

u⌜kemots·u うけもつ (受け持つ) *vt.* (-moch·i-; -mot·a-; -mot-te Ⓒ) take charge of; be in charge of: *Dare ga kono kurasu o* ukemotte imasu *ka?* (だれがこのクラスを受け持っていますか) Who *is in charge of* this class? ⟪⇨ ukemochi⟫

u⌜ke⌝·ru うける (受ける) *vt.* (uke-te Ⓥ) **1** catch (a ball).
2 receive (an invitation); get; obtain (permission).
3 suffer: *ooki-na higai o* ukeru (大きな被害を受ける) *suffer* heavy damage.
4 take (an examination); sit for.
5 *vi.* be popular: *Sono sakka no shoosetsu wa josee no aida de* ukete iru. (その作家の小説は女性の間で受けている) That author's novels *are popular* among women. ⟪⇨ niñki⟫

u⌜ketome·ru うけとめる (受け止める) *vt.* (-tome-te Ⓥ) **1** catch (a ball); stop; take.
2 take (a situation); deal with: *jitai o reesee ni* uketomeru (事態を冷静に受け止める) *take* the situation calmly.

u⌜ketori うけとり (受取) *n.* accepting; receipt. ⟪⇨ ryooshuusho; uketoru⟫

u⌜ketor·u うけとる (受け取る) *vt.* (-tor·i-; -tor·a-; -tot-te Ⓒ) **1** receive; get; take; accept: *tegami o* uketoru (手紙を受け取る) *receive* a letter. ⟪⇨ uketori⟫
2 interpret; take: *Ima no wa joodañ to shite* uketotte *kudasai.* (今のは冗談として受け取ってください) Please *take* what I have just said as a joke.

u⌜ketsug·u うけつぐ (受け継ぐ) *vt.* (-tsug·i-; -tsug·a-; -tsu·i-de Ⓒ) succeed to; inherit: *Otto ga shiñda ato, tsuma ga jigyoo o* uketsuida. (夫が死んだ後, 妻が事業を受け継いだ) The wife *succeeded to* the business after her husband's death.

u⌜ketsuke うけつけ (受付) *n.* **1** receptionist; reception desk.
2 acceptance. ⟪⇨ uketsukeru; ukeireru⟫

u⌜ketsuke·ru うけつける (受け付ける) *vt.* (-tsuke-te Ⓥ) accept; receive: *Gañsho wa koñgetsu-matsu made* uketsukemasu. (願書は今月末まで受け付けます) We *accept* applications until the end of this month. ⟪⇨ uketsuke⟫

u⌝ki[1] うき (雨季) *n.* the rainy season. ⟪↔ kañki[2]⟫ ⟪⇨ baiu; tsuyu[2]⟫

u⌜ki[2] うき (浮き) *n.* float (on a fishing line).

u⌜kka⌝ri うっかり *adv.* (~ to; ~ suru) carelessly; inadvertently.

u⌜k·u うく (浮く) *vi.* (uk·i-; uk·a-; u·i-te Ⓒ) **1** float; rise to the surface. ⟪⇨ ukabu⟫

u

2 (of cost, expense) be saved:
Kare no kuruma ni nosete moratta no de takushii-dai ga uita. (彼の車に乗せてもらったのでタクシー代が浮いた) I got a lift in his car, so the taxi fare *was saved*.

u⌈ma⌉ うま (馬) *n*. horse.

u⌈ma⌉·i うまい (旨い) *a*. (-ku)
1 skillful; good:
Kare wa uñteñ ga umai. (彼は運転がうまい) He is *good* at driving.
(⇨ joozu)
2 (of an idea, a project, etc.) great; good: umai *kañgae* (うまい考え) a *great* idea.
3 (of food) delicious; good.
★ Used mainly by men.
(⇨ oishii)
4 successful; profitable; lucky:
Subete umaku *ikimashita*. (すべてうまくいきました) Everything worked out *well*.

u⌈mare うまれ (生まれ) *n*. birth; descent:
Watashi wa umare *mo sodachi mo Tookyoo desu*. (私は生まれも育ちも東京です) I *was born* and brought up in Tokyo. (⇨ umareru)

u⌈mare·ru うまれる (生まれる) *vi*. (umare-te [V]) be born; come into existence. (⇨ tañjoo; umare; umu[1])

u⌈maretsuki うまれつき (生まれ付き) *n*., *adv*. by nature:
Kanojo no koe ga ii no wa umaretsuki *desu*. (彼女の声がいいのは生まれつきです) Her fine voice is something she *was born with*.

u⌈mar·u うまる (埋まる) *vt*. (umar·i-; umar·a-; umat-te [C]) be buried; be filled up:
Kaijoo wa hito de umatta. (会場は人で埋まった) The hall *was filled* with people. (⇨ umeru)

u⌈me うめ (梅) *n*. ume; Japanese apricot; *Prunus mume*.

u⌈meboshi うめぼし (梅干し) *n*. pickled Japanese apricot.

u⌈mekigo⌉e うめきごえ (呻き声) *n*. groan; moan.

u⌈me⌉k·u うめく (呻く) *vi*. (umek·i-; umek·a-; ume·i-te [C]) groan; moan.

u⌈me·ru うめる (埋める) *vt*. (umete [V]) **1** bury; fill in:
Kanojo wa gomi o atsumete, niwa ni umeta. (彼女はごみを集めて, 庭に埋めた) She gathered up the trash and *buried* it in the garden.
(⇨ uzumeru)
2 make up for (a loss, deficit).
(⇨ umaru)

u⌈metate うめたて (埋め立て) *n*. land reclamation. (⇨ umetateru)

u⌈metate⌉·ru うめたてる (埋め立てる) *vt*. (-tate-te [V]) reclaim; fill up; recover. (⇨ umetate)

u⌈mi[1] うみ (海) *n*. sea; ocean.
(↔ riku)

u⌈mi[2] うみ (膿) *n*. pus; discharge.
(⇨ umu[2])

u⌈m·u[1] うむ (生む) *vt*. (um·i-; um·a-; uñ-de [C]) **1** give birth to; breed; lay (an egg). (⇨ umareru)
2 produce; give rise to; yield.

u⌈m·u[2] うむ (膿む) *vi*. (um·i-; um·a-; uñ-de [C]) suppurate; fester; form pus. (⇨ umi[2])

u⌈mu[3] うむ (有無) *n*. existence; presence:
Keekeñ no umu *wa toimaseñ*. (経験の有無は問いません) We do not mind *whether you have* experience *or not*.
umu o iwasezu (～を言わせず) willy-nilly; forcibly.

u⌈ñ[1] うん (運) *n*. luck; fortune; chance:
Kare wa uñ ga ii [warui]. (彼は運がいい[悪い]) He is *lucky* [*unlucky*].
(⇨ uñmee)

u⌈ñ[2] うん *int*. (*informal*) all right:
*"Kore tetsudatte kureru kai." "*Uñ, *ii yo."* (「これ手伝ってくれるかい」「うん, いいよ」) "Can you help me with this?" "*Okay*, fine."
uñ to iu (～と言う) say yes.

u⌈nagi うなぎ (鰻) *n*. eel:
unagi *no kabayaki* (うなぎのかば焼き) broiled *eel*. (⇨ kabayaki)

u

u⌈na⌉r·u うなる (唸る) *vi.* (unar·i-; unar·a-; unat-te Ⓒ) **1** groan; moan; growl.
2 (of a motor, engine, etc.) howl; roar.

u⌈nazuk·u うなずく (頷く) *vi.* (unazuk·i-; unazuk·a-; unazu·i-te Ⓒ) nod (in agreement); approve.

u⌈ñchiñ うんちん (運賃) *n.* fare; charge; freight. 《⇨ ryookiñ》

u⌈ñdoo うんどう (運動) *n.* **1** exercise; sport.
2 movement; campaign:
koogai hañtai no uñdoo (公害反対の運動) anti-pollution *campaigns*.
uñdoo (o) suru (～(を)する) *vi.* take exercise; campaign (for a cause).

u⌈ñdoojoo うんどうじょう (運動場) *n.* playground; playing field.

u⌈ñdo⌉okai うんどうかい (運動会) *n.* sports day; athletic meet.

u⌈ñee うんえい (運営) *n.* management; operation; administration.
uñee (o) suru (～(を)する) *vt.* manage; operate; administer: *jigyoo o* uñee suru (事業を運営する) *manage* a business.

u⌈ñga うんが (運河) *n.* canal.

u⌈ñmee うんめい (運命) *n.* fate; destiny. 《⇨ uñ[1]》

u⌈ñpañ うんぱん (運搬) *n.* carriage; conveyance; transport.
uñpañ suru (～する) *vt.* carry; convey; transport.

u⌈ñteñ うんてん (運転) *n.* driving; operation.
uñteñ (o) suru (～(を)する) *vi., vt.* drive; run; operate.

u⌈ñte⌉ñshu うんてんしゅ (運転手) *n.* driver; chauffeur; motorman.

u⌈ñto うんと *adv.* (*informal*) hard; severely; much:
uñto *beñkyoo suru* (うんと勉強する) study *hard*.

u⌈nubore うぬぼれ (自惚れ) *n.* conceit; self-conceit; vanity. 《⇨ unuboreru》

u⌈nubore·ru うぬぼれる (自惚れる) *vi.* (unubore-te Ⓥ) flatter oneself; be conceited. 《⇨ unubore》

u⌈ñyu うんゆ (運輸) *n.* transport: uñyu-*gaisha* (運輸会社) a *transport* company.

u⌈o うお (魚) *n.* fish. 《⇨ sakana[1]》

u⌈oi⌉chiba うおいちば (魚市場) *n.* fish market.

u⌈ra うら (裏) *n.* **1** the back; the wrong side; the reverse. 《↔ omote》
2 back door:
ura *e mawaru* (裏へ回る) go round to the *back door*. 《↔ omote》
3 back; rear:
ie no ura *no niwa* (家の裏の庭) the garden in the *rear* of the house. 《↔ mae》
4 (of baseball) the second half. 《↔ omote》
5 hidden part; shady side:
ura *no imi* (裏の意味) a *hidden* meaning.

u⌈raga⌉eshi うらがえし (裏返し) *n.* inside out; turning over. 《⇨ uragaesu》

u⌈raga⌉es·u うらがえす (裏返す) *vt.* (-gaesh·i-; -gaes·a-; -gaesh·i-te Ⓒ) turn over; turn inside out:
suteeki o uragaesu (ステーキを裏返す) *turn* a steak *over*. 《⇨ uragaeshi》

u⌈ragi⌉r·u うらぎる (裏切る) *vt.* (-gir·i-; -gir·a-; -git-te Ⓒ) betray; disappoint (someone's hopes).

u⌈raguchi うらぐち (裏口) *n.* back door [entrance].

ur⌈aguchi-nyu⌉ugaku うらぐちにゅうがく (裏口入学) *n.* backdoor admission to a university.

u⌈rami⌉ うらみ (恨み) *n.* grudge; spite; ill-feeling. 《⇨ uramu》

u⌈ramoñ うらもん (裏門) *n.* back [rear] gate. 《↔ omotemoñ》

u⌈ra⌉m·u うらむ (恨む) *vt.* (uram·i-; uram·a-; urañ-de Ⓒ) bear a grudge; think ill of. 《⇨ urami》

u⌈ra-omote うらおもて (裏表) *n.* the top side and the bottom side; both sides.

u

ura-omote ga aru (〜がある) two-faced.

u⌈rayamashi⌉·i うらやましい (羨ましい) *a.* (-ku) envious; jealous. 《⇨ urayamu》

u⌈raya⌉m·u うらやむ (羨む) *vt.* (ura-yam·i-; urayam·a-; urayañ-de Ⓒ) envy; be envious. 《⇨ uraya-mashii》

u⌈re·ru[1] うれる (売れる) *vi.* (ure-te Ⓥ) **1** sell; be sold. 《⇨ deru (16)》
2 (of an entertainer, etc.) be popular; be famous:
Sono kashu no na wa sekeñ ni yo-ku urete imasu. (その歌手の名は世間によく売れています) The name of the singer *is well known* to every-body.

u⌈re⌉·ru[2] うれる (熟れる) *vi.* (ure-te Ⓥ) ripen:
Kono suika wa mada urete inai. (このすいかはまだ熟れていない) This watermelon *is not ripe* yet.

u⌈reshi⌉·i うれしい (嬉しい) *a.* (-ku) glad; happy; pleased. 《⇨ yoro-kobu》《↔ kanashii》

u⌉ri うり (瓜) *n.* type of melon; vegetable such as a gourd, squash, cucumber, etc.
uri-futatsu (うり二つ) double(s); look-alike(s).

u⌈riage うりあげ (売り上げ) *n.* sales; proceeds; turnover:
uriage *o nobasu* (売り上げを伸ばす) increase the *sales*.

u⌈riba うりば (売り場) *n.* counter; department; office:
omocha uriba (おもちゃ売り場) the toy *department*.

u⌈ridashi うりだし (売り出し) *n.* opening sale; bargain [special] sale. 《⇨ uridasu》
uridashi-chuu no (〜中の) up-and-coming: uridashi-chuu no *kashu* (売り出し中の歌手) a singer *coming into popularity*. 《⇨ niñki》

u⌈rida⌉s·u うりだす (売り出す) *vt.* (-dash·i-; -das·a-; -dash·i-te Ⓒ) **1** put on sale; offer for sale. 《⇨ uridashi; uru[1]》
2 win a reputation; become pop-ular. 《⇨ uridashi》

u⌈rikire うりきれ (売り切れ) *n.* sell-out; being out of stock. 《⇨ uri-kireru》

u⌈rikire⌉·ru うりきれる (売り切れる) *vi.* (-kire-te Ⓥ) be sold out; be out of stock. 《⇨ urikire》

u⌈rimono うりもの (売り物) *n.* article for sale; selling point.

u⌈roko うろこ (鱗) *n.* (of fish) scale.

u⌉rouro うろうろ *adv.* (〜 to; 〜 suru) (an aimless or uneasy way of walking):
Heñ na otoko ga urouro (*to*) aruki-mawatte iru. (変な男がうろうろ(と)歩き回っている) There is a strange fel-low *hanging around*.

u⌈r·u[1] うる (売る) *vt.* (ur·i-; ur·a-; ut-te Ⓒ) **1** sell. 《↔ kau[1]》
2 betray (one's country, organi-zation, friend, etc.); sell out.

u⌉·ru[2] うる (得る) *vt.* (e-te Ⓥ) (*literary*) gain. 《⇨ eru》

u⌈rusa⌉·i うるさい (煩い) *a.* (-ku)
1 noisy. 《⇨ yakamashii》
2 (of a demand, request, etc.) annoying; nagging:
Kodomo ga omocha o katte kure to urusai. (子どもがおもちゃを買ってくれとうるさい) My child is *pestering* me to buy him a toy.
3 strict:
Watashi-tachi no señsee wa urusai. (私たちの先生はうるさい) Our teacher is *strict*.
4 particular:
Chichi wa koohii no aji ni urusai. (父はコーヒーの味にうるさい) My fa-ther is *particular* about the taste of his coffee.

u⌈rushi うるし (漆) *n.* Japanese lacquer; japan. 《⇨ shikki[1]》

u⌈ryoo うりょう (雨量) *n.* rainfall; precipitation.

u⌈sagi うさぎ (兎) *n.* rabbit; hare.

u⌈shi うし (牛) *n.* cattle; bull; cow; ox.

u⌈shina·u うしなう(失う) *vt.* (ushina·i-; ushinaw·a-; ushinat-te Ⓒ)
1 lose; be deprived of:
shoku o ushinau (職を失う) *lose* one's job.
2 miss (an opportunity).

u⌈shiro うしろ(後ろ) *n.* **1** back; rear: *kuruma no* ushiro *no seki* (車の後ろの席) the *back* seat of a car. ⟪↔ mae⟫
2 behind:
Ushiro *kara osanai de kudasai.* (後ろから押さないでください) Stop pushing from *behind.* ⟪↔ mae⟫

u⌈shiro⌉ashi うしろあし(後ろ足) *n.* hind leg. ⟪↔ maeashi⟫

u⌉so うそ(嘘) *n.* **1** lie; fib:
Kare wa heeki de uso *o tsuku.* (彼は平気でうそをつく) He makes no bones about telling *lies.*
2 falseness:
Sono uwasa wa uso *da to wakatta.* (そのうわさはうそだとわかった) I found out that the rumor was *false.*

u⌈sugi うすぎ(薄着) *n.* being lightly dressed. ⟪↔ atsugi⟫
usugi (o) suru (~(を)する) *vi.* be lightly dressed; wear light clothes.

u⌈sugura·i うすぐらい(薄暗い) *a.* (-ku) dim; dusky. ⟪⇨ kurai[1]⟫

u⌈su·i うすい(薄い) *a.* (-ku)
1 thin:
usui *kami* [*hoñ*] (薄い紙[本]) a *thin* sheet of paper [book]. ⟪↔ atsui[3]⟫
2 (of taste) weak; thin; lightly-seasoned. ⟪↔ koi[1]⟫
3 (of color) light. ⟪↔ koi[1]⟫
4 (of hair) thin; sparse:
kami ga usuku naru (髪が薄くなる) *lose* one's hair.
5 (of possibility) few; little.

u⌈sume·ru うすめる(薄める) *vt.* (usume-te Ⓥ) dilute; water down.

u⌈ta⌉ うた(歌) *n.* **1** song. ⟪⇨ utau⟫
2 'tanka' poem:
uta *o yomu* (歌を詠む) compose a '*tanka*' *poem.* ⟪⇨ tañka[3]; waka⟫

u⌈tagai うたがい(疑い) *n.*
1 doubt. ⟪⇨ gimoñ; utagau⟫
2 suspicion:
utagai *o idaku* (疑いを抱く) have a *suspicion.* ⟪⇨ utagau⟫

u⌈taga·u うたがう(疑う) *vt.* (utaga·i-; utagaw·a-; utagat-te Ⓒ) doubt; suspect. ⟪⇨ utagai⟫

u⌈tago⌉e うたごえ(歌声) *n.* singing voice.

u⌈ta·u うたう(歌う) *vt.* (uta·i-; utaw·a-; utat-te Ⓒ) sing (a song). ⟪⇨ uta⟫

u⌉teñ うてん(雨天) *n.* rainy weather; rain. ⟪↔ seeteñ⟫

u⌉ts·u[1] うつ(打つ) *vt.* (uch·i-; ut·a-; ut-te Ⓒ) **1** hit; strike; knock:
kanazuchi de kugi o utsu (金づちでくぎを打つ) *strike* a nail with a hammer. ⟪⇨ tataku⟫
2 (of a clock) strike.

u⌉ts·u[2] うつ(撃つ) *vt.* (uch·i-; ut·a-; ut-te Ⓒ) shoot (a rifle); fire.

u⌈tsukushi⌉·i うつくしい(美しい) *a.* (-ku) (*slightly literary*) beautiful; pretty; handsome:
utsukushii *josee* (美しい女性) a *beautiful* woman / utsukushii *koe* (美しい声) a *sweet* voice. ⟪⇨ kiree⟫

u⌈tsumuk·u うつむく(俯く) *vi.* (-muk·i-; -muk·a-; -mu·i-te Ⓒ) look down; hang one's head.

u⌈tsurikawari うつりかわり(移り変わり) *n.* change; transition:
kisetsu no utsurikawari (季節の移り変わり) the *changes* of the seasons.

u⌈tsu⌉r·u[1] うつる(移る) *vi.* (utsur·i-; utsur·a-; utsut-te Ⓒ)
1 move (to a place); shift. ⟪⇨ utsusu[1]⟫
2 move on to (a new topic, subject, etc.). ⟪⇨ utsusu[1]⟫
3 be infected; catch:
Kaze wa utsuri-yasui. (かぜはうつりやすい) Colds *are catching.* ⟪⇨ utsusu[1]⟫

u⌈tsu⌉r·u[2] うつる(写る) *vi.* (utsur·i-; utsur·a-; utsut-te Ⓒ) (of a photograph) be taken; come out. 《⇨ utsusu[2]》

u⌈tsu⌉r·u[3] うつる(映る) *vi.* (utsur·i-; utsur·a-; utsut-te Ⓒ) be reflected; be mirrored. 《⇨ utsusu[3]》

u⌈tsu⌉s·u[1] うつす(移す) *vt.* (utsush·i-; utsus·a-; utsush·i-te Ⓒ)
1 move; remove; transfer. 《⇨ utsuru[1]》
2 give; infect:
Watashi wa anata ni kaze o utsusareta. (私はあなたにかぜをうつされた) I *got* a cold from you. 《⇨ utsuru[1]》

u⌈tsu⌉s·u[2] うつす(写す) *vt.* (utsush·i-; utsus·a-; utsush·i-te Ⓒ)
1 take (a photo). 《⇨ utsuru[2]》
2 copy; trace:
kokubañ ni kaite aru koto o nooto ni utsusu (黒板に書いてあることをノートに写す) *copy* what is written on the blackboard into one's notebook.

u⌈tsu⌉s·u[3] うつす(映す) *vt.* (utsush·i-; utsus·a-; utsush·i-te Ⓒ)
reflect; mirror; project:
suraido o sukuriiñ ni utsusu (スライドをスクリーンに映す) *project* slides onto the screen. 《⇨ utsuru[3]》

u⌈tsuwa うつわ(器) *n.* **1** container; vessel.
2 ability; caliber:
utsuwa *no ookii* [*chiisai*] *hito* (器の大きい[小さい]人) a man of high [poor] *caliber.*

u⌈ttae うったえ(訴え) *n.* **1** lawsuit; legal action.
2 appeal; complaint. 《⇨ uttaeru》

u⌈ttae⌉·ru うったえる(訴える) *vt.* (uttae-te Ⓥ) **1** bring an action; file a suit. 《⇨ uttae》
2 complain (illness, etc.):
zutsuu o uttaeru (頭痛を訴える) *complain* of headaches.
3 appeal; protest (one's innocence).
4 resort (to violence).

u⌈ttooshi⌉·i うっとうしい(鬱陶しい) *a.* (-ku) gloomy; depressing; annoying.

u⌈wagi うわぎ(上着) *n.* coat; jacket.

u⌈waki うわき(浮気) *n.* being fickle; being unfaithful.
uwaki (o) suru (~(を)する) *vi.* have an affair; be unfaithful.
— *a.n.* (~ na) fickle; unfaithful: uwaki *na hito* (浮気な人) a person of *easy virtue.*

u⌈wasa うわさ(噂) *n.* rumor; gossip; hearsay.
uwasa (o) suru (~(を)する) *vi.* talk about; gossip about.

u⌈yama⌉·u うやまう(敬う) *vt.* (-ma·i-; -maw·a-; -mat-te Ⓒ)
respect; worship:
ryooshiñ o uyamau (両親を敬う) *respect* one's parents.

u⌈zu⌉maki うずまき(渦巻) *n.* whirlpool; eddy.

u⌈zumar·u うずまる(埋まる) *vi.* (-mar·i-; -mar·a-; -mat-te Ⓒ)
1 be buried. 《⇨ uzumeru》
2 be filled; overflow:
Hiroba wa oozee no guñshuu de uzumatta. (広場は大勢の群衆でうずまった) The plaza *was overflowing* with people. 《⇨ umeru; uzumeru》

u⌈zume·ru うずめる(埋める) *vt.* (-me-te Ⓥ) bury. 《⇨ umeru; uzumaru》

u

W

w

wa[1 1] わ(輪) *n.* circle; ring; loop.

wa[1 2] わ(和) *n.* **1** unity; harmony: hito no wa (人の和) *good teamwork.*
2 sum; total: wa *o motomeru* (和を求める) work out the *sum.*

wa[3] は *p.* **1** (used to mark the topic of a sentence): ★ Used

when the speaker wants to add something new about the topic. Kore wa *watashi no jisho desu.* (これは私の辞書です) *This* is my dictionary. ⟪⇨ ga[1]⟫
2 (used in making contrasts and comparisons):
Ame wa *futte imasu ga* kaze wa *arimaseñ.* (雨は降っていますが風はありません) *Raining it is*, but there is no *wind*.
3 (used with a negative in a contrastive sense):
Watasha wa tabako wa suimaseñ. (私はたばこは吸いません) I *don't smoke* (but I do drink).
4 (used to indicate a limit):
Koko kara eki made jup-puñ wa *kakarimaseñ.* (ここから駅まで 10 分はかかりません) It does not take *as much as* ten minutes from here to the station. ⟪⇨ mo[2]⟫

wa[4] わ *p.* **1** (used to indicate emotions, such as admiration):
★ Used mainly by women.
Watashi mo gaikoku e ikitai wa. (私も外国へ行きたいわ) I too *want* to go abroad.
2 (used for slight emphasis):
★ Used mainly by women.
Watashi ga iku wa. (私が行くわ) I *am going*.
3 (used to emphasize emotions or feelings of surprise):
Deñsha de ashi o fumareru wa, *saifu o* nusumareru wa, *kyoo wa hidoi hi datta.* (電車で足を踏まれるわ, 財布を盗まれるわ, きょうはひどい日だった) My foot *got stepped on* in the train and my purse *was stolen*. What an awful day it has been today!

-wa わ (羽) *suf.* counter for birds and rabbits. ⟪⇨ APP. 4⟫

wa¹a わあ *int.* hurray; hurrah; gee; wow.

wa⌈apuro ワープロ *n.* word processor.

wa⌈bi わび (詫び) *n.* apology.
★ Often '*o-wabi*.' ⟪⇨ wabiru⟫

wa⌈bi·ru わびる (詫びる) *vt.* (wabite [V]) apologize; make an apology. ⟪⇨ wabi⟫

wa⌈bishi¹·i わびしい (侘びしい) *a.* (-ku) lonely; miserable; dreary. ⟪⇨ mijime; sabishii⟫

wa⌈buñ わぶん (和文) *n.* Japanese; Japanese writing.

wa⌈dai わだい (話題) *n.* topic; subject of conversation.

wa⌈dakamari わだかまり (蟠り) *n.* bad feeling; grudge.

wa⌈ee-ji¹teñ わえいじてん (和英辞典) *n.* Japanese-English dictionary for Japanese people. ⟪⇨ eenichi-jiteñ; eewa-jiteñ; nichiee-jiteñ⟫

wa⌈fuku わふく (和服) *n.* kimono; traditional Japanese costume.
★ More formal than 'kimono.'
⟪↔ yoofuku⟫ ⟪⇨ kimono⟫

wa⌈fuu わふう (和風) *n.* Japanese style: wafuu *no ie* (和風の家) a *Japanese-style* house. ⟪↔ yoofuu⟫

wa¹ga わが (我が) *attrib.* my; our: waga-*sha* (わが社) *our* company / waga-*ya* (わが家) *our* house.

wa⌈gamama¹ わがまま (我儘) *n.* selfishness; willfulness:
wagamama o toosu (わがままを通す) *get one's way*. ⟪⇨ katte[2]⟫
— *a.n.* (~ na, ni) selfish; willful; egoistic.

wa⌈ga¹shi わがし (和菓子) *n.* Japanese confectionery. ⟪↔ yoogashi⟫

wa⌈gomu わゴム (輪ゴム) *n.* rubber band.

wa⌈ishatsu ワイシャツ *n.* shirt; dress shirt. ★ Refers to a shirt with which a tie can be worn.

wa¹iwai わいわい *adv.* (~ to) noisily; boisterously:
waiwai (*to*) *sawagu* (わいわい(と)騒ぐ) make *a lot of noise*.

wa¹ka わか (和歌) *n.* = tañka[3].

wa⌈ka¹·i わかい (若い) *a.* (-ku)
1 young; youthful.
2 immature; inexperienced; green:

W

Soñna koto o iu nañte kimi mo mada wakai. (そんなことを言うなんてきみもまだ若い) You are still *green* to say that sort of thing.

3 (of numbers) low.

wa⌈ka⌉me わかめ (若布) *n.* wakame seaweed. ★ Often served in miso soup.

wa⌈kamono わかもの (若者) *n.* young people; youth. ⟪↔ roojiñ; toshiyori⟫

wa⌈kare⌉ わかれ (別れ) *n.* parting; separation; farewell:

Moo o-wakare shinakereba narimaseñ. (もうお別れしなければなりません) Now, I *have to say good-bye.* ⟪⇨ wakareru[2]⟫

wa⌈kare⌉·ru[1] わかれる (分かれる) *vi.* (wakare-te [V]) branch off; divide; fork; split. ⟪⇨ wakeru⟫

wa⌈kare⌉·ru[2] わかれる (別れる) *vi.* (wakare-te [V]) part; say good-bye; separate; divorce. ⟪⇨ wakare⟫

wa⌈ka⌉r·u わかる (分かる・判る・解る) *vi.* (wakar·i-; wakar·a-; wakat-te [C]) **1** understand:

Watashi no itte iru koto ga wakarimasu *ka?* (私の言っていることがわかりますか) *Do* you *understand* what I am saying? ⟪⇨ rikai⟫

2 know:

Ashita no koto wa wakarimaseñ. (あしたのことはわかりません) *Nobody knows* what will happen tomorrow.

3 turn out; prove:

Kekkyoku kare wa mujitsu to wakatta. (結局彼は無実とわかった) He *turned out* to be innocent after all.

wa⌈kas·u わかす (沸かす) *vt.* (wakash·i-; wakas·a-; wakash·i-te [C]) **1** boil; heat:

furo o wakasu (ふろを沸かす) *get* a bath *ready.* ⟪⇨ waku[2]⟫

2 excite:

Kare no subarashii puree wa kañshuu o wakashita. (彼のすばらしいプレーは観衆を沸かした) His fine play *excited* the spectators. ⟪⇨ waku[2]⟫

wa⌉ke わけ (訳) *n.* **1** reason; cause; grounds:

Futari no rikoñ no wake *o shiritai.* (二人の離婚の訳を知りたい) I'd like to know the *reason* for their divorce.

2 case; circumstances:

Soo-iu wake *nara, dekiru dake no koto wa shimasu.* (そういう訳なら, できるだけのことはします) If that is the *case,* I will do what I can. ⟪⇨ jijoo⟫

3 meaning:

Kono buñ wa nani o itte iru no ka wake *ga wakaranai.* (この文は何を言っているのか訳がわからない) I cannot make out the *meaning* of this sentence.

4 sense:

Shachoo wa wake no wakaru *hito desu.* (社長は訳のわかる人です) Our president is a *sensible* man.

wa⌈ke⌉·ru わける (分ける) *vt.* (wake-te [V]) **1** divide; distribute; share:

rieki o miñna de wakeru (利益をみんなで分ける) *divide* the profits among everyone. ⟪⇨ wakareru[1]⟫

2 classify:

Zoosho o bumoñ-betsu ni waketa. (蔵書を部門別に分けた) I *classified* the book collection according to the different categories. ⟪⇨ buñrui⟫

wa⌉ke wa nai わけはない (訳はない) (*polite*=*wake wa arimaseñ*)

1 there is no reason for...; it cannot be...:

Kare ga soñna ni isogashii wake wa nai. (彼がそんなに忙しいわけはない) It *cannot be* that he is so busy.

2 easy; simple:

Jiteñsha ni noru no nañ ka wake wa nai. (自転車に乗るのなんかわけはない) It is *quite easy* to ride a bicycle.

wa⌈ki⌉ わき (脇) *n.* **1** under one's arm:

Kanojo wa waki *ni hoñ o kakaete*

ita. (彼女はわきに本を抱えていた) She was carrying some books *under her arm.*
2 side:
Chuushajoo wa sono mise no waki *ni arimasu.* (駐車場はその店のわきにあります) The parking lot is at the *side* of the shop.

wa⌈kibara わきばら (わき腹) *n.* one's side:
Kare wa watashi no wakibara *o tsutsuite chuui shita.* (彼は私のわき腹をつついて注意した) He cautioned me by poking me in *the ribs.*

wa⌈kimi⌉ わきみ (脇見) *n.* looking away; glancing aside:
wakimi-*unten* (わき見運転) driving a car *without keeping one's eyes on the road.*
wakimi (o) suru (～(を)する) *vi.* look away.

wa⌈ki-no⌉-shita わきのした (脇の下) *n.* armpit.

wa⌈ku⌉[1] わく (枠) *n.* **1** frame:
mado no waku (窓の枠) a window *frame.*
2 limit: waku *o koeru* (枠を越える) go beyond the *limit.*

wa⌈k·u[2] わく (沸く) *vi.* (wak·i-; wak·a-; wa·i-te [C]) **1** (of water) boil; be heated. (⇨ wakasu)
2 be excited. (⇨ wakasu)

wa⌉kuwaku わくわく *adv.*
wakuwaku suru (～する) get nervous; be exited; be thrilled.

wa⌉ñ[1] わん (椀) *n.* bowl. ★ Often '*o-wañ.*' (⇨ moribachi)

wa⌉ñ[2] わん (湾) *n.* bay; gulf:
Tookyoo wañ (東京湾) Tokyo *Bay.*

wa⌉na わな (罠) *n.* trap; snare:
wana *ni kakaru* (わなにかかる) be caught in a *trap.*

wa⌉ni わに (鰐) *n.* crocodile; alligator.

wa⌈ñpi⌉isu ワンピース *n.* dress; female one-piece garment.

wa⌉ñwañ わんわん **1** bow-wow.
2 (young children's word) doggie.

wa⌉ra わら (藁) *n.* straw.

wa⌈rai わらい (笑い) *n.* laugh; laughter:
warai *o koraeru* (笑いをこらえる) suppress one's *laughter.* (⇨ warau)

wa⌈raigo⌉e わらいごえ (笑い声) *n.* laughing voice; laughter.
(↔ nakigoe[1])

wa⌈ra·u わらう (笑う) *vi.* (wara·i-; waraw·a-; warat-te [C])
1 laugh; grin; smile. (⇨ warai)
2 laugh at; ridicule; make fun of.

wa⌈re-na⌉gara われながら (我ながら) *adv.* if I do say so myself:
Ware-nagara *yoku yatta to omoimasu.* (われながらよくやったと思います) I think I did rather well, *if I may say.*

wa⌈re·ru われる (割れる) *vi.* (ware-te [V]) **1** break; smash:
Sara o otoshita ga warenakatta. (皿を落としたが割れなかった) I dropped the plate, but it *didn't break.* (⇨ kowareru; waru)
2 (of opinions, organization, group, etc.) be divided; split.
(⇨ wakareru[1])

wa⌈reware われわれ (我々) *n.* (*formal*) = watashi-tachi.
we. ★ 'wareware no' = our; 'wareware o' = us. Used mainly by men.

wa⌈ri わり (割) *n.* **1** rate; ratio:
sañsee to hañtai no wari (賛成と反対の割) the *ratio* of supporters and opponents. (⇨ wariai)
2 (unit of ratio) ten percent.
(⇨ bu[2])
wari ni awanai (～に合わない) do not pay; be unprofitable. (⇨ au[2])

wa⌈riai わりあい (割合) *n.* rate; ratio; percentage. (⇨ wari)
— *adv.* (～ ni) comparatively; relatively:
Kyoo wa wariai (ni) *suzushii.* (きょうは割合(に)涼しい) It is *fairly* cool today.

wa⌈riate わりあて (割り当て) *n.* assignment; allotment; quota.
(⇨ wariateru)

wa⌈riate⌉·ru わりあてる (割り当てる) *vt.* (-ate-te V) assign (a task); allot; allocate. ⟪⇨ wariate⟫

wa⌈riba⌉shi わりばし (割り箸) *n.* disposable wooden chopsticks. ⟪⇨ hashi[2]⟫

wa⌈ribiki わりびき (割引) *n.* discount; reduction. ⟪⇨ waribiku⟫

wa⌈ribi⌉k·u わりびく (割り引く) *vt.* (-bik·i-; bik·a-; -bi·i-te C) discount; reduce: ⟪⇨ waribiki⟫
Geñkiñ nara waribikimasu. (現金なら割り引きます) We will *make a discount* if you pay in cash.
waribiite kiku (割り引いて聞く) don't take a person's story at face value.

wa⌈rikañ わりかん (割り勘) *n.* each paying his [her] own way:
Kañjoo wa warikañ ni shimashoo. (勘定は割り勘にしましょう) *Let's split* the bill.

wa⌈riko⌉m·u わりこむ (割り込む) *vi.* (-kom·i-; -kom·a-; -koñ-de C)
1 squeeze oneself:
mañiñ deñsha ni warikomu (満員電車に割り込む) *squeeze oneself* into a crowded train.
2 jump a line; cut in.
3 break into (a conversation).

wa⌈ri ni わりに (割に) *adv.*
1 comparatively; rather; fairly:
Kare wa wari ni *kimuzukashii.* (彼は割に気むずかしい) He is *rather* hard to please.
2 in proportion to; for:
Kare wa toshi no wari ni *fukete mieru.* (彼は年の割に老けて見える) He looks old *for* his age.

wa⌈ri⌉zañ わりざん (割り算) *n.* (of arithmetic) division. ⟪⇨ waru⟫ ⟪↔ kakezañ⟫

wa⌈r·u わる (割る) *vt.* (war·i-; war·a-; wat-te C) **1** break; smash:
tamago o waru (卵を割る) *break* an egg. ⟪⇨ wareru⟫
2 split; chop:
maki o waru (まきを割る) *chop* logs.
3 divide:
Juu-ni waru *yoñ wa sañ desu.* (12割る4は3です) Twelve *divided* by four is three. ⟪⇨ warizañ⟫
4 dilute:
uisukii o mizu de waru (ウイスキーを水で割る) *dilute* the whisky with water. ⟪⇨ mizuwari⟫

wa⌈rugi⌉ わるぎ (悪気) *n.* evil intention; ill will; malice. ⟪⇨ akui⟫

wa⌈ru⌉·i わるい (悪い) *a.* (-ku)
1 bad; evil; wrong:
Uso o tsuku no wa warui *koto desu.* (うそをつくのは悪いことです) It is *wrong* to tell a lie. ⟪↔ yoi[1]⟫
2 (of quality, weather, harvest) bad; poor; inferior. ⟪↔ yoi[1]⟫
3 (of a situation, state, etc.) bad; sick; ill-timed:
Kyoo wa buchoo no kigeñ ga warui. (きょうは部長の機嫌が悪い) The general manager is in a *bad* mood today. ⟪↔ yoi[1]⟫
4 (of luck) bad; unlucky:
Kare wa uñ ga warukatta *dake da.* (彼は運が悪かっただけだ) He was just *unlucky.* ⟪↔ yoi[1]⟫
5 troublesome; harmful:
Tabako wa keñkoo ni warui. (たばこは健康に悪い) Cigarettes are bad for the health.

wa⌈ru⌉kuchi わるくち (悪口) *n.* slander; (verbal) abuse:
hito no warukuchi o iu (人の悪口を言う) *speak ill of* others.

wa⌈sai わさい (和裁) *n.* Japanese dressmaking; kimono making. ⟪↔ yoosai⟫

wa⌈shitsu わしつ (和室) *n.* Japanese-style room. ⟪↔ yooshitsu⟫

wa⌉sho わしょ (和書) *n.* book published in the Japanese language; Japanese book. ⟪↔ yoosho⟫

wa⌈shoku わしょく (和食) *n.* Japanese food. ⟪↔ yooshoku[2]⟫

wa⌈suremono わすれもの (忘れ物) *n.* something left behind:
wasuremono-*toriatsukaijo* (忘れ物取り扱い所) a *lost-and-found* office. ⟪⇨ okiwasureru; wasureru⟫

W

wa⌈sure·ru わすれる(忘れる) *vt.* (wasure-te [V]) **1** forget:
Yuube wa akari o kesu no o wasurete shimatta. (ゆうべは明りを消すのを忘れてしまった) I *forgot* to turn out the lights last night.
2 leave behind:
Deñsha no naka ni kasa o wasurete shimatta. (電車の中に傘を忘れてしまった) I *have left* my umbrella on the train. ⟪⇨ wasuremono⟫

wa⌈ta⌉ わた(綿) *n.* cotton.

wa⌈takushi わたくし(私) *n.* = watashi.

wa⌈takushi-do⌉mo わたくしども(私共) *n.* (*humble*) we; our company [office; store]. ★ Used by service personnel.

wa⌈takushi⌉ritsu わたくしりつ(私立) *n.* = shiritsu[1].

wa⌈tar·u わたる(渡る) *vi.* (watar·i-; watar·a-; watat-te [C])
1 cross; go across; go over:
Kare wa dooro o hashitte watatta. (彼は道路を走って渡った) He ran *across* the street.
2 (of a bird) migrate; (of religion, custom, etc.) be introduced.

wa⌈tashi わたし(私) *n.* (*polite*= watakushi) I: ★ 'watashi no' = my; 'watashi o' = me. Words indicating personal reference are less commonly used in Japanese than in English.
(Watashi *wa*) *kinoo Yamada-sañ ni aimashita.* ((私は)きのう山田さんに会いました) *I* met Mr. Yamada yesterday.
The following are situations in which the use of '*watashi*' is natural:
1 (when contrasting oneself with someone else):
Watashi ni *mo misete kudasai.* (私にも見せてください) Please let *me* have a look at it, too.
2 (when mentioning oneself for the first time): ★ When the topic is already about oneself, '*watashi*' is normally not used.
Watashi *wa Suzuki to iimasu.* (私は鈴木と言います) *My name* is Suzuki.

wa⌈tashibu⌉ne わたしぶね(渡し船) *n.* ferry. ★ A small boat used to carry passengers across a river. ⟪⇨ fune⟫

wa⌈tashi⌉-tachi わたしたち(私達) *n.* we. ★ 'watashi-tachi no'= our; 'watashi-tachi o' = us. ⟪⇨ wareware⟫

wa⌈tas·u わたす(渡す) *vt.* (watash·i-; watas·a-; watash·i-te [C])
1 give; hand over:
Kono tegami o kanojo ni watashite *kudasai.* (この手紙を彼女に渡してください) Please *give* her this letter.
2 lay (a board); stretch (a rope, bridge, etc., between).

wa⌉za-to わざと(態と) *adv.* on purpose; intentionally; deliberately. ⟪⇨ koi[3]⟫
waza-to-rashii (～らしい) put-on; unnatural.

wa⌉zawaza わざわざ(態々) *adv.* specially; expressly:
O-isogashii tokoro o wazawaza *oide itadaki, arigatoo gozaimasu.* (お忙しいところをわざわざお出でいただき, ありがとうございます) Thank you very much for *taking the trouble* to come here when you are so busy.

wa⌉zuka わずか(僅か) *a.n.* (～ na, ni) few; little; slight:
Hoñno wazuka *na hito ga sono kai ni shusseki shita.* (ほんのわずかな人がその会に出席した) Only *a few* people attended the party.
— *adv.* only:
Kyooto ni wa wazuka *mikka ita dake deshita.* (京都にはわずか三日いただけでした) I was in Kyoto for *only* three days. ⟪⇨ hoñno⟫

W

Y

ya[1] や *p.* and: ★ Used to link nouns which are representative of their class.
Sono o-kane de hoñ ya *jisho o kai-mashita.* (そのお金で本や辞書を買いました) I bought books, dictionaries, *and the like*, with that money. 《⇨ dano; to[2]; to ka; yara》

ya[2] や *p.* as soon as: ★ Follows the dictionary form of a verb. Also '*ya ina ya.*' 《⇨ ina》
Kare wa uchi ni kaeru ya (ina ya) *kabañ o oite, mata tobidashite itta.* (彼は家に帰るや(いなや)かばんを置いて、また飛び出して行った) *No sooner* had he come home *than* he put down his bag and rushed out again. 《⇨ sugu》

ya[13] や(矢) *n.* arrow: ya *o iru* (矢を射る) shoot an *arrow.* 《↔ yumi》

ya' やっ *int.* **1** aha: ★ An exclamation of satisfaction or surprise. Ya', *mitsuketa.* (やっ, 見つけた) *Aha!* I have found it.
2 hi; ya:
Ya', *hisashiburi da ne.* (やっ, 久しぶりだね) *Hi!* It has been a long time, hasn't it?

-ya や(屋) *suf.* store; shop; person: yao-ya (八百屋) a *greengrocery* / *sakana*-ya (魚屋) a fish *shop.*

ya˥a やあ *int.* (*informal*) hi; hello.

ya┌bañ やばん(野蛮) *a.n.* (~ na, ni) savage; barbarous:
yabañ *na kooi* (野蛮な行為) a *barbarous* act.

ya┌bure˥·ru[1] やぶれる(破れる) *vi.* (yabure-te Ⓥ) **1** tear; be torn; rip; be ripped:
Kono kami wa sugu yabureru. (この紙はすぐ破れる) This paper *tears* easily. 《⇨ yaburu[1]》
2 (of relationship, balance, etc.) break down; come to nothing:
Kanojo no kekkoñ seekatsu wa sañ-neñ de yabureta. (彼女の結婚生活は3年で破れた) Her married life *came to an end* after three years. 《⇨ yaburu[1]》

ya┌bure˥·ru[2] やぶれる(敗れる・破れる) *vi.* (yabure-te Ⓥ) (of a competitor) lose; be beaten. 《⇨ yaburu[2]》

ya┌bu˥r·u[1] やぶる(破る) *vt.* (yabur·i-; yabur·a-; yabut-te Ⓒ)
1 tear; rip; break:
Kare wa sono tegami o yabutte *suteta.* (彼はその手紙を破って捨てた) He *ripped up* the letter and threw it away. 《⇨ yabureru[1]》
2 break (a promise, agreement, record, etc.).

ya┌bu˥r·u[2] やぶる(敗る・破る) *vt.* (yabur·i-; yabur·a-; yabut-te Ⓒ) beat; defeat. 《⇨ yabureru[2]》

ya˥chiñ やちん(家賃) *n.* (of an apartment, house, etc.) rent.

ya˥do やど(宿) *n.* **1** inn; hotel. 《⇨ ryokañ; yadoya》
2 lodging:
Watashi wa kare ni hito-bañ yado *o kashite yatta.* (私は彼に一晩宿を貸してやった) I gave him a night's *lodging.*

ya┌doya やどや(宿屋) *n.* Japanese-style hotel; Japanese inn. 《⇨ ryokañ; yado》

ya┌gate やがて *adv.* by and by; before long; in the course of time.

ya˥gu やぐ(夜具) *n.* bedding; bedclothes.

ya┌ha˥ri やはり *adv.* (*intensive* = *yappari*) **1** as expected:
Yahari *anata ga yosoo shita toori ni narimashita.* (やはりあなたが予想したとおりになりました) Things turned out *just as you had expected.*
2 still; nonetheless; after all:
Kare wa ima mo yahari *Kama-*

kura ni suñde imasu. (彼は今もやはり鎌倉に住んでいます) He *still* lives in Kamakura.

3 too; also: ★ In the pattern '*... mo yahari.*'

Kare no musuko mo yahari *señsee desu.* (彼の息子もやはり先生です) His son is *also* a teacher.

ya⌉i やい *int.* (*rude*) hey.

ya⌉ji やじ (野次) *n.* jeering; hoot. ⟪⇨ yajiru⟫

ya⌈ji⌉r·u やじる (野次る) *vt.* (yaji-r·i-; yajir·a-; yajit-te [C]) jeer; hoot; jeer; hoot; boo. ⟪⇨ yaji⟫

ya⌈ji⌉rushi やじるし (矢印) *n.* arrow sign.

ya⌈jiuma やじうま (野次馬) *n.* curious onlooker; rubberneck: yajiuma-koñjoo (やじ馬根性) *curiosity.* ⟪⇨ kookishiñ⟫

ya⌈kamashi⌉·i やかましい (喧しい) *a.* (-ku) **1** noisy; loud. ⟪↔ shizuka⟫ ⟪⇨ urusai⟫

2 (of a rule, regulation, etc.) strict.

3 (of a person) particular: *tabemono ni* yakamashii (食べ物にやかましい) be *particular* about food. ⟪⇨ urusai⟫

ya⌉kañ[1] やかん (夜間) *n.* night; nighttime. ⟪↔ hiruma; nitchuu⟫

ya⌈kañ[2] やかん (薬缶) *n.* teakettle; kettle.

ya⌈kedo やけど (火傷) *n.* burn; scald.

yakedo suru (〜する) *vi.* get burned; get scalded.

ya⌈ke·ru やける (焼ける) *vi.* (yake-te [V]) **1** burn; be burned: *Sono mise wa sakuya no kaji de* yaketa. (その店は昨夜の火事で焼けた) That shop *burned down* in last night's fire. ⟪⇨ yaku[1]⟫

2 be broiled; be grilled; be roasted; be baked; be toasted. ⟪⇨ yaku[1]⟫

3 be tanned; get sunburned. ⟪⇨ yaku[1]⟫

4 be discolored: *Kono kiji wa iro ga* yake-yasui. (この生地は色が焼けやすい) This cloth *quickly becomes discolored.*

ya⌈kimashi やきまし (焼き増し) *n.* additional print of a photo.

yakimashi suru (〜する) *vt.* make an additional print [copy].

ya⌈kimo⌉chi やきもち (焼き餅) *n.* toasted rice cake. ⟪⇨ mochi⟫

yakimochi o yaku (〜を焼く) get jealous. ⟪⇨ shitto⟫

ya⌈kitori やきとり (焼き鳥) *n.* chunks of chicken barbecued on a bamboo skewer: yakitori-ya (焼き鳥屋) a *yakitori restaurant.*

ya⌉kkai やっかい (厄介) *n.* burden; trouble:

hoka no hito ni yakkai *o kakeru* (ほかの人にやっかいをかける) cause other people a lot of *trouble.*

— *a.n.* (~ na, ni) troublesome; burdensome.

yakkai ni naru (やっかいになる) depend on; stay.

ya⌉kki やっき (躍起) *a.n.* (~ ni) eager; excited; heated; vehement:

Kare wa yakki ni natte, *sono uwasa o hitee shita.* (彼は躍起になって, そのうわさを否定した) He *vehemently* denied the rumor.

ya⌉kkyoku やっきょく (薬局) *n.* pharmacy; drugstore.

ya⌈k·u[1] やく (焼く) *vt.* (yak·i-; yak·a-; ya·i-te [C]) **1** burn: *kimitsu-shorui o* yaku (機密書類を焼く) *burn* classified documents.

2 tan; get a tan. ⟪⇨ yakeru⟫

3 broil; grill; roast; bake; toast; barbecue. ⟪⇨ yakeru⟫

ya⌉ku[2] やく (役) *n.* **1** role; part. ⟪⇨ yakuwari⟫

2 position; post:

buchoo no yaku (部長の役) the *post* of manager.

yaku ni tatsu (〜に立つ) be useful; be helpful. ⟪⇨ yakudatsu⟫

ya⌉ku[3] やく (約) *adv.* about; some; nearly. ⟪⇨ oyoso⟫

ya⌉ku[4] やく (訳) *n.* translation. ⟪⇨ hoñyaku; tsuuyaku; yakusu⟫

-yaku やく(薬) *suf.* medicine; drug; pill:
suimiñ-yaku (睡眠薬) a sleeping *pill* / doku-yaku (毒薬) *poison.*

ya⌈kuda⌉ts·u やくだつ(役立つ) *vi.* (-dach·i-; -dat·a-; -dat·te Ⓒ) be of use; be useful; be helpful.

ya⌈kugo やくご(訳語) *n.* word; term; equivalent translation.

ya⌈kuhiñ やくひん(薬品) *n.* medicine; drug; chemical. ⟨⇨ kusuri⟩

ya⌈kume⌉ やくめ(役目) *n.* duty; role. ⟨⇨ yaku[2]; yakuwari⟩

ya⌈kuniñ やくにん(役人) *n.* government official; public servant.

ya⌈kusha やくしゃ(役者) *n.* actor; actress. ⟨⇨ haiyuu⟩

ya⌈kusho⌉ やくしょ(役所) *n.* government office:
shi-yakusho (市役所) a city *hall* / *ku*-yakusho (区役所) a ward *office.*

ya⌈kusoku やくそく(約束) *n.* promise; engagement; appointment.
yakusoku ga chigau (～が違う) differ from what was promised.
yakusoku suru (～する) *vt.* promise; make an appointment.

ya⌈ku⌉s·u やくす(訳す) *vt.* (yakush·i-; yakus·a-; yakush·i-te Ⓒ) translate; put...into.... ⟨⇨ yaku[4]⟩

ya⌈kuwari⌉ やくわり(役割) *n.* part; role: *juuyoo na* yakuwari *o hatasu* (重要な役割を果たす) play an important *role.* ⟨⇨ yaku[2]⟩

ya⌈kyuu やきゅう(野球) *n.* baseball.

ya⌈ma⌉ やま(山) *n.* **1** mountain; hill. ★ A hill with a gentle slope and lower than '*yama*' is called '*oka.*' ⟨⇨ oka⟩
2 heap; pile:
gomi no yama (ごみの山) a trash *heap* / *hoñ no* yama (本の山) a *pile* of books.
3 climax; juncture:
Sono jikeñ wa yama *o mukaeta.* (その事件は山を迎えた) The affair has reached a critical *juncture.*
4 guess:
Yama *ga atatta* [*hazureta*]. (やまが当たった[はずれた]) My *guess* hit [missed] the mark.

-yama やま(山) *suf.* Mount; Mt.:
Mihara-yama (三原山) *Mount* Mihara. ⟨⇨ -sañ[2]⟩

ya⌈maimo やまいも(山芋) *n.* yam.

ya⌈maku⌉zure やまくずれ(山崩れ) *n.* landslide.

ya⌈manote やまのて(山の手) *n.*
1 the hilly section of a city.
2 the residential section of a city; uptown. ⟨↔ shitamachi⟩

ya⌈mawake⌉ やまわけ(山分け) *n.* equal division; going halves. ⟨⇨ buñpai⟩
yamawake (ni) suru (～(に)する) *vt.* divide equally; go shares.

ya⌈me·ru[1] やめる(止める) *vt.* (yame-te Ⓥ) **1** stop; discontinue. ⟨⇨ yamu[1]; yosu⟩
2 give up; abandon:
tabako o yameru (たばこをやめる) *give up* smoking. ⟨⇨ akirameru⟩

ya⌈me·ru[2] やめる(辞める) *vt.* (yame-te Ⓥ) resign (one's post); quit.

ya⌈mi⌉ やみ(闇) *n.* **1** darkness.
2 black-marketing; illegal trade.

ya⌈m·u[1] やむ(止む) *vi.* (yam·i-; yam·a-; yañ-de Ⓒ) (of rain) stop; (of wind) die down. ⟨⇨ yameru[1]⟩

ya⌉m·u[2] やむ(病む) *vt., vi.* (yam·i-; yam·a-; yañ-de Ⓒ) be taken sick; suffer from:
zeñsoku o yamu (ぜんそくを病む) *suffer from* asthma. ⟨⇨ byooki⟩

ya⌈mu⌉naku やむなく *adv.* = yamu o ezu.

ya⌈mu o e⌉nai やむをえない(やむを得ない) unavoidable; inevitable.

ya⌈mu o e⌉zu やむをえず(やむを得ず) *adv.* reluctantly; unwillingly.

ya⌉ne やね(屋根) *n.* roof.

ya⌉nushi やぬし(家主) *n.* landlord; landlady.

ya⌈oya やおや(八百屋) *n.* vegetable store; greengrocery; greengrocer.

ya⌈ppa⌉ri やっぱり *adv.* (*intensive*) = yahari.

yara やら *p.* what with...: ★ Used in the pattern '*... yara ... yara*' to link nouns or verbs.
Beñkyoo yara, *arubaito* yara *de, isogashii.* (勉強やら, アルバイトやらで, 忙しい) *What with* my studies *and* my part-time job, I am busy. ⟪⇨ ya[1]⟫

ya⌉reyare やれやれ *int.* well: ★ Used to express a sigh of relief.
Yareyare, *yatto shigoto ga owatta.* (やれやれ, やっと仕事が終わった) *Well, well*, the job is at last finished. ⟪⇨ hotto⟫

ya⌈rikata やりかた (やり方) *n.* way; method:
Sono yarikata *o oshiete kudasai.* (そのやり方を教えてください) Please show me *how to do* it. ⟪⇨ hoo[1]; hoohoo⟫

ya⌈rikome·ru やりこめる (遣り込める) *vt.* (-kome-te [C]) argue a person down; talk down.

ya⌈rinaoshi やりなおし (やり直し) *n.* redoing; doing over again. ⟪⇨ yarinaosu⟫

ya⌈rinao⌉s·u やりなおす (やり直す) *vt.* (-naosh·i-; -naos·a-; -naosh·i-te [C]) do over again; make a fresh start. ⟪⇨ yarinaoshi⟫

ya⌈ri⌉tori やりとり (やり取り) *n.* exchange; giving and taking:
okurimono no yaritori (贈り物のやり取り) an *exchange* of presents.

ya⌈r·u[1] やる (遣る) *vt.* (yar·i-; yar·a-; yat-te [C]) **1** do; play: ★ More informal than '*suru*[1].'
tenisu o yaru (テニスをやる) *play* tennis.
2 keep; run:
Chichi wa hoñya o yatte imasu. (父は本屋をやっています) My father *runs* a bookstore.
3 eat; drink; have; smoke:
Kare wa tabako wa yaranai *ga, sake wa* yaru. (彼はたばこはやらないが, 酒はやる) He *does not* smoke, but *drinks.*

ya⌈r·u[2] やる (遣る) *vt.* (yar·i-; yar·a-; yat-te [C]) **1** give: ★ Never used toward one's superiors.
kodomo ni o-kashi o yaru (子どもにお菓子をやる) *give* candy to a child / *hana ni* mizu o yaru (花に水をやる) *water* the flowers. ⟪⇨ ageru[1]⟫
2 send (a letter).

ya⌈sai やさい (野菜) *n.* vegetable; greens.

ya⌈sashi·i[1] やさしい (易しい) *a.* (-ku) easy; simple; plain.

ya⌈sashi·i[2] やさしい (優しい) *a.* (-ku) gentle; tender; kind:
kimochi no yasashii *hito* (気持ちの優しい人) a *kindhearted* person.

ya⌈se·ru やせる (痩せる) *vi.* (yase-te [V]) lose weight; become thin.

ya⌈shiki⌉ やしき (屋敷) *n.* mansion; residence; premises.

ya⌉shiñ やしん (野心) *n.* ambition: yashiñ-*ka* (野心家) an *ambitious* person.

ya⌈shina·u やしなう (養う) *vt.* (yashina·i-; yashinaw·a-; yashinat-te [C]) **1** support; sustain; feed:
ikka o yashinau (一家を養う) *support* one's family.
2 cultivate; develop; build up:
jitsuryoku o yashinau (実力を養う) *cultivate* one's proficiency.

ya⌈su⌉·i やすい (安い) *a.* (-ku) cheap; low; inexpensive; reasonable. ⟪↔ kooka[2]; takai⟫

-yasu⌉·i やすい (易い) *suf.* (*a.*) (-ku) easy; apt: ★ Added to the continuative base of a verb.
Kare no buñshoo wa yomi-yasui. (彼の文章は読みやすい) His prose is *easy* to read. ⟪↔ -gatai; -nikui; -zurai⟫

ya⌈sume⌉·ru やすめる (休める) *vt.* (yasume-te [V]) rest; relax:
karada o yasumeru (体を休める) *rest* one's body. ⟪⇨ yasumu⟫

ya⌈sumi⌉ やすみ (休み) *n.* **1** rest; break; respite:
hito-yasumi *suru* (ひと休みする) take a *rest.* ⟪⇨ yasumu⟫

2 absence:
Kare wa kyoo wa yasumi desu. (彼はきょうは休みです) He *is off* today. 《⇨ yasumu》
3 being closed:
Kono depaato wa suiyoobi ga yasumi desu. (このデパートは水曜日が休みです) This department store *is closed* on Wednesdays. 《⇨ yasumu》
4 holiday; vacation. 《⇨ kyuuka》

ya⌈sumono やすもの (安物) *n.* cheap article.

ya⌈su⌉m·u やすむ (休む) *vi.* (yasum·i-; yasum·a-; yasuñ-de [C])
1 take a rest; relax. 《⇨ yasumeru; yasumi》
2 be absent; stay away; take a holiday. 《⇨ yasumi》
3 go to bed; sleep. 《⇨ neru[1]; oyasumi nasai》

ya⌈suppo⌉·i やすっぽい (安っぽい) *a.* (-ku) cheap; tawdry:
yasuppoi *kabañ* (安っぽいかばん) a *cheap-looking* bag.

ya⌈tara ni やたらに (矢鱈に) *adv.* freely; haphazardly; thoughtlessly; at random.

ya⌉too やとう (野党) *n.* the opposition party; the opposition. 《↔ yotoo》

ya⌈to⌉·u やとう (雇う) *vt.* (yato·i-; yatow·a-; yatot-te [C]) employ (a person); hire.

ya⌉tsu やつ (奴) *n.* (sometimes *derog.*) fellow; guy; chap.

ya⌈tte k·u⌉ru やってくる (やって来る) *vi.* (k·i-; k·o-; k·i-te [I]) 1 come along; appear; turn up. 《⇨ kuru》
2 continue to do:
Moo juu-neñ kono shigoto o yatte kimashita. (もう10年この仕事をやって来ました) I *have* already *been doing* this job for ten years.

ya⌈tto やっと *adv.* 1 at last; at length; finally.
2 just; barely:
yatto *maniau* (やっと間に合う) be *barely* in time. 《⇨ yooyaku》

ya⌈ttsu⌉ やっつ (八つ) *n.* eight.
★ Used when counting.
《⇨ hachi[1]; APP. 3》

ya⌈ttsuke⌉·ru やっつける *vt.* (yattsuke-te [V]) beat; criticize.

ya⌈wara⌉ka やわらか (柔らか) *a.n.* (~ na, ni) 1 soft; tender:
yawaraka *na kusshoñ* (柔らかなクッション) a *soft* cushion. 《↔ katai》
2 gentle; mild:
yawaraka *na hizashi* (柔らかな日ざし) *mild* sunshine.
3 flexible; supple:
yawaraka *na karada* (柔らかな体) a *supple* body. 《⇨ yawarakai》

ya⌈waraka⌉·i やわらかい (柔かい・軟かい) *a.* (-ku) 1 soft; tender:
yawarakai *niku* (柔らかい肉) *tender* meat. 《↔ katai》
2 gentle; mild: yawarakai *koe* (柔らかい声) a *gentle* voice.
3 (of a way of thinking, etc.) flexible; supple. 《↔ katai》 《⇨ yawaraka》

ya⌉ya やや (稍) *adv.* a little; somewhat:
Keeki wa yaya *yoku natte imasu.* (景気はややよくなっています) Business conditions are improving *slightly*. 《⇨ sukoshi》

ya⌈yakoshi⌉·i ややこしい *a.* (-ku) (*colloq.*) complicated; intricate; complex.

yo⌉[1] よ (世) *n.* 1 world:
kono [*ano*] yo (この[あの]世) this [the other] *world*.
2 times; age.
yo ni deru (~に出る) make one's debut.
yo o saru (~を去る) pass away. 《⇨ shinu》

yo⌉[2] よ (夜) *n.* night. 《⇨ yoru[1]》

yo[3] よ *p.* 1 (used when emphasizing one's thoughts, feeling or opinions, or when reminding someone of something):
Hayaku shinai to okuremasu yo. (早くしないと遅れますよ) *Look*, you will be late unless you hurry up.
2 (used to indicate an invitation or order):

Issho ni ikimashoo yo. (いっしょに行きましょうよ) *Come on*, let's go together.
3 (used to indicate disapproval of someone's thoughts or actions):
Soko de nani o shite iru ñ da yo. (*by men*) (そこで何をしているんだよ) What are you up to there?
4 (*formal*) (used as a form of address):
Waga ko yo. (我が子よ) Oh, my child! / *Kami* yo. (神よ) Oh, God!

-yo よ (余) *suf.* over; more than: *nijuu-yo-neñ* (20 余年) *more than* twenty years.

yoʻake˥ よあけ (夜明け) *n.* dawn; daybreak.

yo˥bi よび (予備) *n.* spare; extra: yobi *no taiya* [*kagi*] (予備のタイヤ[鍵]) a *spare* tire [key]. (⇨ yooi[1])

yoʻbidashi よびだし (呼び出し) *n.*
1 summons:
yobidashi *o ukeru* (呼び出しを受ける) get a *summons*. (⇨ yobidasu)
2 paging. ★ Usually '*o-yobidashi*.' (⇨ yobidasu)
3 (of sumo wrestling) match announcer.

yoʻbida˥s·u よびだす (呼び出す) *vt.* (-dash·i-; -das·a-; -dash·i-te Ⓒ)
1 call; page. (⇨ yobidashi)
2 call [ring] up:
Taroo o deñwa-guchi ni yobidashite *kudasai*. (太郎を電話口に呼び出してください) Please *call* Taro to the phone. (⇨ yobidashi)
3 summon:
Kare wa saibañsho ni yobidasareta. (彼は裁判所に呼び出された) He *was summoned* to court. (⇨ yobidashi)

yoʻbikake よびかけ (呼び掛け) *n.* appeal; plea:
kaku-jikkeñ hañtai no yobikake (核実験反対の呼びかけ) an *appeal* against a nuclear test. (⇨ yobikakeru)

yoʻbikake˥·ru よびかける (呼び掛ける) *vt.* (-kake-te Ⓥ) **1** call (out); address (a person).
2 appeal to (the public). (⇨ yobikake)

yoʻbikoo よびこう (予備校) *n.* cramming school. ★ A school for students who need extra help to pass the university entrance exam.

yoʻbisute よびすて (呼び捨て) *n.* calling a person's name without any title of courtesy.

yoʻboo よぼう (予防) *n.* prevention; precaution; protection.
yoboo suru (～する) *vt.* prevent; protect: *mushiba o* yoboo suru (虫歯を予防する) *prevent* tooth decay.

yoʻboo-chu˥usha よぼうちゅうしゃ (予防注射) *n.* preventive shot [injection].

yoʻb·u よぶ (呼ぶ) *vt.* (yob·i-; yob·a-; yoñ-de Ⓒ) **1** call; call [cry] out: *takushii o* yobu (タクシーを呼ぶ) *call* a taxi.
2 invite:
Paatii ni wa kare o yobitai. (パーティーには彼を呼びたい) I *would like to invite* him to the party.
3 give a name; call.

yoʻbuñ よぶん (余分) *a.n.* (～ na, ni) extra; spare; additional. (⇨ yokee)

yo˥chi よち (余地) *n.* room (for improvement); space.

yoʻfu˥kashi よふかし (夜更かし) *n.* staying up late at night.
yofukashi suru (～する) *vi.* stay up late at night; keep late hours. (↔ asa-neboo)

yoʻfuke˥ よふけ (夜更け) *n.* late hours of the night; midnight. (⇨ yonaka)

yoʻgore よごれ (汚れ) *n.* dirt; stain; soil. (⇨ yogoreru; yogosu)

yoʻgore·ru よごれる (汚れる) *vi.* (yogore-te Ⓥ) become dirty; be soiled; be stained; be polluted. (⇨ yogosu; yogore)

yoʻgos·u よごす (汚す) *vt.* (yogosh·i-; yogos·a-; yogosh·i-te Ⓒ)

make dirty; soil; stain; pollute. 《⇨ yogoreru》

yo⌈hodo よほど(余程) *adv.*
1 very; much; greatly:
Kare wa yohodo *noñda rashii.* (彼はよほど飲んだらしい) He seemed to have drunk *a lot.*
2 nearly; almost:
Yohodo *tsutome o yameyoo ka to omoimashita.* (よほど勤めを辞めようかと思いました) I *almost* decided to quit my job.

yo⌈hoo よほう(予報) *n.* forecast: *teñki* yohoo (天気予報) a weather *forecast.*
yohoo suru (〜する) *vt.* forecast.

yo⌉·i[1] よい(良い・善い) *a.* (-ku) good; fine; excellent:
★ More formal than '*ii.*'
yoi *kañgae* (良い考え) a *good* idea / yoi *shirase* (良い知らせ) *good* news / yoi *teñki* (良い天気) *fine* weather. 《↔ warui》《⇨ ryookoo》
... hoo ga yoi (…ほうが〜) = hoo ga ii.
-te mo yoi (ても〜) can; may:
Kono arubamu o mite mo yoi *desu ka?* (このアルバムを見てもよいですか) *Can* I *have a look* at this photo album?

yo⌉i[2] よい(酔い) *n.* drunkenness; intoxication: yoi ga sameru (酔いがさめる) *sober up.* 《⇨ you》

yo⌉isho よいしょ *int.* heave ho; here we go.

yo⌈jinobor·u よじのぼる(よじ登る) *vi.* (-nobor·i-; -nobor·a-; -nobotte Ⓒ) climb (up); clamber (up). 《⇨ noboru[3]》

yo⌉ka よか(余暇) *n.* leisure; free [spare] time. 《⇨ hima》

yo⌈kee よけい(余計) *a.n.* (〜 na) unnecessary; needless:
Yokee *na o-sewa desu.* (よけいなお世話です) It's *none* of your business.
— *adv.* (〜 ni) (the) more; extra; too many [much]. 《⇨ yobuñ》

yo⌈ke⌉·ru よける(避ける) *vt.* (yoke-te Ⓥ) avoid; dodge:
kaze o yokeru (風をよける) *avoid* the wind / *ame o* yokeru (雨をよける) *seek shelter* from the rain.

yo⌉ki よき(予期) *n.* anticipation; expectation. 《⇨ yosoo》
yoki suru (〜する) *vt.* expect; anticipate.

yo⌈kiñ よきん(預金) *n.* deposit; money on deposit; savings.
★ A deposit in a bank is generally called '*yokiñ,*' and savings put in the post office are called '*chokiñ.*'
yokiñ suru (〜する) *vi., vt.* make a deposit.

yo⌈kka よっか(四日) *n.* four days; the fourth day of the month. 《⇨ APP. 5》

yo⌈ko よこ(横) *n.* **1** width.
★ The horizontal distance from side to side. 《↔ tate》《⇨ haba》
2 side:
Kanojo wa watashi no yoko *ni suwatta.* (彼女は私の横に座った) She sat at my *side.*
3 (〜 ni) sideways; crossways:
Kani wa yoko *ni aruku.* (かには横に歩く) Crabs walk *sideways.*

yo⌈kogaki よこがき(横書き) *n.* horizontal writing. 《↔ tategaki》

yo⌈kogao よこがお(横顔) *n.* (of a face) profile.

yo⌈kogi⌉r·u よこぎる(横切る) *vt.* (-gir·i-; -gir·a-; -git-te Ⓒ) cross; go across: *dooro o* yokogiru (道路を横切る) *cross* a road.

yo⌈ko⌉s·u よこす(寄越す) *vt.* (yokosh·i-; yokos·a-; yokosh·i-te Ⓒ) **1** send; hand over: ★ The recipient is the speaker.
Musuko wa metta ni tegami o yokosanai. (息子はめったに手紙をよこさない) My son *rarely sends* me letters.
2 make a person come to the speaker or writer:
O-ko-sañ o itsu de mo uchi e asobi ni yokoshite *kudasai.* (お子さんをいつでもうちへ遊びによこしてください) Please *send* your child to play at our house anytime.

yo⌈ku[1] よく(欲) *n.* greed; avarice; desire:
Kare wa yoku *ga fukai.* (彼は欲が深い) He *is greedy.*

yo⌉ku[2] よく(良く) *adv.* **1** well; fully; thoroughly:
Osshharu koto wa yoku *wakarimashita.* (おっしゃることはよくわかりました) I understand *perfectly* what you say.
2 kindly; favorably:
Kare wa itsu-mo watashi ni yoku *shite kuremasu.* (彼はいつも私によくしてくれます) He always treats me *kindly.*
3 (used to express wonder, or disapproval):
Yoku *kega o shimaseñ deshita ne.* (よくけがをしませんでしたね) It's *a miracle* that you were not injured, isn't it?

yo⌉ku[3] よく *adv.* frequently; often: *Kare wa* yoku *kaze o hiku.* (彼はよくかぜをひく) He *often* catches colds.

yo⌈ku- よく(翌) *pref.* next; following:
yoku-*go-gatsu tooka* (翌5月10日) the *following* day, that is, May 10.

-yoku よく(欲) *suf.* desire; lust:
chishiki-yoku (知識欲) *thirst* for knowledge / *kiñseñ*-yoku (金銭欲) *desire* for money.

yo⌈kuasa よくあさ(翌朝) *n.* the next [following] morning.
⟪↔ kesa⟫ ⟪⇨ yokuchoo⟫

yo⌈kubari⌉ よくばり(欲張り) *a.n.* (～ na, ni) greedy; avaricious:
yokubari *na hito* (欲張りな人) an *avaricious* person. ⟪↔ muyoku⟫ ⟪⇨ yokubaru⟫

yo⌈kuba⌉r·u よくばる(欲張る) *vi.* (-bar·i-; -bar·a-; -bat-te Ⓒ) be greedy; be avaricious. ⟪⇨ yokubari⟫

yo⌈kuboo よくぼう(欲望) *n.* desire; appetite; craving:
yokuboo *o mitasu* [*osaeru*] (欲望を満たす[抑える]) satisfy [overcome] one's *cravings.*

yo⌈kuchoo よくちょう(翌朝) *n.* (*formal*) the next [following] morning. ⟪⇨ yokuasa⟫

yo⌈kugetsu よくげつ(翌月) *n.* the next [following] month.
⟪⇨ koñgetsu; raigetsu; señgetsu⟫

yo⌈kujitsu よくじつ(翌日) *n.* the next [following] day. ⟪⇨ zeñjitsu⟫

yo⌈kuneñ よくねん(翌年) *n.* the next [following] year. ⟪⇨ kotoshi; kyoneñ⟫

yo⌈kushitsu よくしつ(浴室) *n.* bathroom; bath. ★ In Japanese houses, the bath and toilet are in separate rooms.

yo⌈kushuu よくしゅう(翌週) *n.* the next [following] week.
⟪⇨ raishuu⟫

yo⌈me よめ(嫁) *n.* **1** bride:
yome ni iku (嫁に行く) *marry into a family.* ⟪↔ muko⟫ ⟪⇨ o-yome-sañ⟫
2 daughter-in-law. ⟪↔ muko⟫

yo⌈mi⌉ よみ(読み) *n.* **1** reading.
⟪⇨ yomu⟫
2 judgment; calculation; insight:
Kare wa yomi *ga fukai* [*asai*]. (彼は読みが深い[浅い]) He is a man of deep [shallow] *insight.* ⟪⇨ yomu⟫

yo⌈miga⌉er·u よみがえる(蘇る) *vi.* (-gaer·i-; -gaer·a-; -gaet-te Ⓒ) come back to life; come to oneself; (of memory, impression, etc.) revive; be refreshed.

yo⌉mi-kaki よみかき(読み書き) *n.* reading and writing.

yo⌈mikata よみかた(読み方) *n.* reading; pronunciation; interpretation.

yo⌉m·u よむ(読む) *vt.* (yom·i-; yom·a-; yoñ-de Ⓒ) **1** read:
hoñ o yomu (本を読む) *read* a book / *koe o dashite* yomu (声を出して読む) *read* aloud.
2 read (a person's intention, mind, etc.); fathom. ⟪⇨ yomi⟫

yo⌉ñ よん(四) *n.* four. ⟪⇨ shi[4]; yottsu; APP. 3⟫

yo⌈naka⌉ よなか(夜中) *n.* midnight; the middle of the night.

yo-ˈnoˈ-naka よのなか（世の中） *n.* the world; times; society:
Kare wa yo-no-naka *no koto o yoku shitte iru.*（彼は世の中のことをよく知っている）He has seen much of *the world.* ⟪⇨ yo[1]⟫

yoˈo[1] よう（用） *n.* something to do; business:
Koñbañ wa yoo *ga arimasu.*（今晩は用があります）I have *something to do* this evening. ⟪⇨ yooji[1]⟫
yoo ga nai（〜がない）be no longer useful.
yoo o tasu（〜を足す）do one's business; (*euphemism*) go to the toilet.

yoo[2] よう（様） *a.n.* (〜 na, ni)
1 seem; look: ★ Used to indicate a judgment based on sight, sound, or smell.
Kare wa sono koto o zeñzeñ oboete inai yoo da.（彼はそのことを全然覚えていないようだ）He *does not seem* to remember that at all.
2 like; similar to; of the kind:
Watashi mo kare no yoo na *kashu ni naritai.*（私も彼のような歌手になりたい）I wish to be a singer *like* him.
3 to the effect that:
Yamada-sañ ga kaisha o yameru yoo na *hanashi o kikimashita.*（山田さんが会社を辞めるような話を聞きました）I heard something *to the effect* that Miss Yamada was leaving the company.
4 such; sort: ★ Usually in a negative expression, often with '*kesshite.*'
Watashi wa kesshite uso o tsuku yoo na *niñgeñ de wa arimaseñ.*（私は決してうそをつくような人間ではありません）I am certainly not the *sort of* person who tells lies.
yoo ni（〜に）**1** as; like: *Watashi wa itsu-mo no* yoo ni *roku-ji ni okita.*（私はいつものように6時に起きた）I got up at six *as* usual.
2 so that; so as to: *Miñna ni kikoeru* yoo ni *ooki-na koe de hanashite kudasai.*（みんなに聞こえるように大きな声で話してください）Please speak in a loud voice *so that* everyone can hear you.
yoo ni iu [tanomu]（〜に言う[頼む]）tell [ask]: *Kodomo ni rusubañ suru* yoo ni itta.（子どもに留守番するように言った）I *told* the child to look after the house during my absence.
yoo ni naru（〜になる）reach the point where: *Nihoñgo ga hanaseru* yoo ni narimashita.（日本語が話せるようになりました）I *have reached the stage* at which I can speak Japanese.
yoo ni shite iru（〜にしている）make it a rule to: *Shokuji no ato wa ha o migaku* yoo ni shite imasu.（食事の後は歯を磨くようにしています）I *make it a rule* to brush my teeth after meals.

-yoo よう *infl. end.* [attached to the continuative base of a vowel-stem verb. Irregular verbs are '*shiyoo*' (*suru*) and '*koyoo*' (*kuru*)] ⟪⇨ -oo⟫
1 intend; want:
Ashita wa hayaku okiyoo.（あしたは早く起きよう）I *will get up* early tomorrow.
2 let's:
Issho-ni terebi o miyoo.（一緒にテレビを見よう）*Let's watch* TV together.
-yoo to suru（〜とする）be about to; try: *Uchi o* deyoo to shita *toki, deñwa ga natta.*（家を出ようとしたとき，電話が鳴った）When I *was about to* leave home, the telephone rang.

yoˈobi ようび（曜日） *n.* day of the week. ⟪⇨ APP. 5⟫

yoˈoboo ようぼう（要望） *n.* request; requirement:
yooboo *ni oojiru* [*kotaeru*]（要望に応じる[応える]）meet a person's *requirements*
yooboo suru（〜する）*vt.* ask for; request.

yo⌉obuñ ようぶん(養分) *n.* nourishment; nutriment.

yo⌈ochi ようち(幼稚) *a.n.* (～ na, ni) childish; immature:
yoochi *na kañgae* (幼稚な考え) a *childish* way of thinking.

yo⌈ochi⌉eñ ようちえん(幼稚園) *n.* kindergarten. ⟪⇨ gakkoo⟫

yo⌈oda⌉i ようだい(容体) *n.* condition of a patient.

yo⌈odate⌉·ru ようだてる(用立てる) *n.* (-date-te [V]) lend (money).

yo⌈ofuku ようふく(洋服) *n.* Western clothes; suit; dress. ⟪⇨ fuku[2]⟫ ⟪↔ kimono; wafuku⟫

yo⌈ofuu ようふう(洋風) *n.* Western style:
yoofuu *no ie* (洋風の家) a *Western-style* house. ⟪↔ wafuu⟫

yo⌈oga ようが(洋画) *n.* Western [European] painting; oil painting; foreign film.

yo⌈oga⌉shi ようがし(洋菓子) *n.* cake; Western-style confectionery. ⟪↔ wagashi⟫

yo⌉ogi ようぎ(容疑) *n.* suspicion:
yoogi o ukeru (容疑を受ける) *be suspected* / yoogi *o harasu* (容疑を晴らす) dispel *suspicion*.

yo⌈ogo[1] ようご(用語) *n.* term; word; terminology.

yo⌉ogo[2] ようご(擁護) *n.* support; protection.
yoogo suru (～する) *vt.* support; protect: *keñpoo o* yoogo suru (憲法を擁護する) *support* the constitution.

yo⌉ogu ようぐ(用具) *n.* tool; instrument.

yo⌉oi[1] ようい(用意) *n.* preparation; arrangement; readiness.
yooi (o) suru (～(を)する) *vt.* prepare; arrange; get ready.
⟪⇨ juñbi; shitaku⟫

yo⌈oi[2] ようい(容易) *a.n.* (～ na, ni) easy; simple:
Kono kawa o oyoide wataru no wa yooi *de nai.* (この川を泳いで渡るのは容易でない) It is not *easy* to swim across this river. ⟪⇨ kañtañ⟫

yo⌈oji[1] ようじ(用事) *n.* business; things to do; engagement:
yooji *o sumasu* (用事を済ます) finish one's *job*. ⟪⇨ yoo[1]⟫

yo⌉oji[2] ようじ(幼児) *n.* infant; very young child.

yo⌉ojiñ ようじん(用心) *n.* care; caution; precaution: yoojiñ-boo (用心棒) a *bodyguard*; a *bouncer*.
yoojiñ suru (～する) *vi.* take care; be careful. ⟪↔ buyoojiñ⟫

yo⌈ojiñbuka⌉·i ようじんぶかい(用心深い) *a.* (-ku) cautious; watchful; careful. ⟪↔ keesotsu⟫ ⟪⇨ chuuibukai; shiñchoo[2]⟫

yo⌈oka ようか(八日) *n.* eight days; the eighth day of the month. ⟪⇨ APP. 5⟫

yo⌈oke⌉ñ ようけん(用件) *n.* business. ⟪⇨ yooji[1]⟫

yo⌉oki[1] ようき(容器) *n.* container.

yo⌈oki[2] ようき(陽気) *a.n.* (～ na, ni) cheerful; lively; merry.

yo⌈oki[3] ようき(陽気) *n.* weather:
Ii yooki *desu ne.* (いい陽気ですね) Pleasant *weather*, isn't it?

yo⌈okyuu ようきゅう(要求) *n.* demand; requirement; claim.
yookyuu suru (～する) *vt.* demand; require; claim.
⟪⇨ motomeru⟫

yo⌈omoo ようもう(羊毛) *n.* wool.

yo⌉o-oñ ようおん(拗音) *n.* palatalized consonant. ★ The palatalized sound is represented by a smaller や, ゆ and よ (ャ, ュ, ョ) after the *i*-row *kana* letter of the appropriate consonant: *kya* (きゃ), *kyu* (きゅ), *kyo* (きょ). ⟪⇨ inside front cover; APP. 1⟫

yo⌈oryo⌉o[1] ようりょう(要領) *n.*
1 point; essentials:
Kare no setsumee wa yooryoo *o ete iru.* (彼の説明は要領を得ている) His explanation is to the *point*.
2 knack:
Yatto kuruma no uñteñ no yooryoo *ga wakatta.* (やっと車の運転の要領がわかった) At last I got the *knack* of driving a car.

yooryoo ga ii [warui] (〜がいい[悪い]) clever [clumsy]: *Kare wa* yooryoo ga ii [warui]. (彼は要領がいい[悪い]) He is *quick and smart* [*slow and dull*].

yo⌈oryo⌉o[2] ようりょう (容量) *n.* capacity; volume; bulk. ⟪⇨ taiseki⟫

yo⌈osai ようさい (洋裁) *n.* dressmaking. ⟪↔ wasai⟫

yo⌈osee ようせい (養成) *n.* training; education.

yoosee suru (〜する) *vt.* train; educate; foster.

yo⌉oshi[1] ようし (要旨) *n.* outline; summary; the gist.

yo⌈oshi[2] ようし (養子) *n.* adopted [foster] child.

yo⌈oshitsu ようしつ (洋室) *n.* Western-style room. ⟪↔ washitsu⟫

yo⌈osho ようしょ (洋書) *n.* book published in a European language. ⟪↔ washo⟫

yo⌈oshoku[1] ようしょく (養殖) *n.* culture; farming:

yooshoku-*shiñju* (養殖真珠) a *cultured* pearl.

yooshoku suru (〜する) *vt.* raise; farm: *masu o* yooshoku suru (ますを養殖する) *raise* trout.

yo⌈oshoku[2] ようしょく (洋食) *n.* Western food; Western dishes. ⟪↔ washoku⟫

yo⌉oso ようそ (要素) *n.* element; factor; constituent.

yo⌈osu ようす (様子) *n.* **1** condition; the state of affairs:

yoosu *o ukagau* (様子をうかがう) see *how things stand.*

2 appearance; looks:

machi no yoosu (町の様子) the *look* of the town. ⟪⇨ moyoo⟫

yo⌈o-su⌉ru ni ようするに (要するに) *adv.* in short; in a word; after all.

yo⌈ote⌉ñ ようてん (要点) *n.* point; essence; the gist:

O-hanashi no yooteñ *wa tsukamemashita.* (お話の要点はつかめました) I got the *point* of your talk.

yo⌉oto ようと (用途) *n.* use:

Purasuchikku wa yooto *ga hiroi.* (プラスチックは用途が広い) Plastics have many *uses.*

yo⌈oyaku ようやく (漸く) *adv.*

1 at last; finally. ⟪⇨ tsui ni⟫

2 barely; with difficulty:

Saishuu-deñsha ni yooyaku *maniaimashita.* (最終電車にようやく間に合いました) I was *barely* in time for the last train. ⟪⇨ yatto⟫

yo⌈pparai よっぱらい (酔っぱらい) *n.* drunken person; drunk:

yopparai-*uñteñ* (酔っぱらい運転) *drunken* driving.

yo⌈re⌉ba よれば (依れば) according to: ★ Indicates the source or authority of information received.

Teñki-yohoo ni yoreba, *ashita wa ame ni naru rashii.* (天気予報によれば，あしたは雨になるらしい) *According to* the weather forecast, it will evidently rain.

yo⌉ri より *p.* **1** ...than: ★ Used to make comparisons.

Watashi wa koohii yori *koocha no hoo ga suki desu.* (私はコーヒーより紅茶のほうが好きです) I like tea rather *than* coffee.

2 (*formal*) at; from; than: ★ Indicates a point of origin in time or space. ⟪⇨ kara[3]⟫

Kyoo no kaigi wa sañ-ji yori *hajimemasu.* (きょうの会議は3時より始めます) We will start today's meeting *at* three.

yo⌈rikaka⌉r·u よりかかる (寄り掛かる) *vi.* (-kakar·i-; -kakar·a-; -kakat-te Ⓒ) **1** lean on; recline against: *kabe ni* yorikakaru (壁に寄り掛かる) *lean against* a wall.

2 rely on:

Kare wa mada oya ni yorikakatte iru. (彼はまだ親に寄り掛かっている) He still *relies on* his parents.

yo⌈rimichi よりみち (寄り道) *n.* dropping in; stopover:

yorimichi o suru (寄り道をする) *stop on the way.*

yo⌈riwake⌉·ru よりわける (選り分ける) *vt.* (-wake-te Ⓥ) sort out; classify.

yo⌈roi よろい (鎧) *n.* armor.

yo⌈roke⌉·ru よろける *vi.* (-ke-te Ⓥ) stagger; totter; stumble.

yo⌈rokobi よろこび (喜び) *n.* joy; pleasure; delight; rapture. ⟨⟨↔ kanashimi⟩⟩ ⟨⟨⇨ yorokobu⟩⟩

yo⌈roko⌉b·u よろこぶ (喜ぶ) *vi.* (-kob·i-; -kob·a-; -koñ-de Ⓒ) be glad; be pleased; be delighted. ⟨⟨↔ kanashimu⟩⟩ ⟨⟨⇨ yorokobi⟩⟩
yorokoñde ... suru (喜んで…する) be glad to do: Yorokoñde *o-tetsudai* shimasu. (喜んでお手伝いします) I will *be glad to* help you.

yo⌉roñ よろん (世論) *n.* public opinion:
yoroñ-*choosa* (世論調査) a *public opinion* poll. ⟨⟨⇨ seroñ⟩⟩

yo⌈roshi·i よろしい (宜しい) *a.* (-ku)
★ Formal alternative of '*ii*.'
1 all right; fine; good:
Juñbi wa yoroshii *deshoo ka?* (準備はよろしいでしょうか) You are *ready*, I assume?
2 had better; should:
Kare no iu toori ni shita hoo ga yoroshii *desu yo.* (彼の言うとおりにしたほうがよろしいですよ) You *had better* do as he tells you.
3 can; may:
Kono deñwa o tsukatte mo yoroshii *desu ka?* (この電話を使ってもよろしいですか) *May* I use this telephone? ⟨⟨⇨ yoi[1]⟩⟩

yo⌈roshiku よろしく (宜しく) *adv.*
1 (used to express one's hopes for friendship or favor):
Hajimemashite. Doozo yoroshiku *o-negai shimasu.* (始めまして. どうぞよろしくお願いします) How do you do? *It is a pleasure to meet you.*
★ Greeting used when first meeting someone. / *Kono shigoto o* yoroshiku tanomimasu. (この仕事をよろしく頼みます) *I would be grateful for your help* with this job.
2 (used to express one's regards or best wishes):
O-toosañ ni yoroshiku *o-tsutae kudasai.* (お父さんによろしくお伝えください) Please give my *regards* to your father.

yo⌉royoro よろよろ *adv.* (~ to; ~ suru) staggeringly; totteringly; falteringly. ⟨⟨⇨ hyorohyoro[1]⟩⟩

yo⌉ru[1] よる (夜) *n.* night. ⟨⟨↔ asa[1]⟩⟩ ⟨⟨⇨ bañ[1]; yo[2]⟩⟩

yo⌈r·u[2] よる (寄る) *vi.* (yor·i-; yor·a-; yot-te Ⓒ) **1** draw near; come [go] close.
2 drop in (at a person's house).

yo⌈r·u[3] よる (因る・依る) *vi.* (yor·i-; yor·a-; yot-te Ⓒ) **1** depend:
Shuukaku wa teñkoo ni yorimasu. (収穫は天候によります) The crop *depends* on the weather. ⟨⟨⇨ shidai⟩⟩
2 be based; according to:
Kono monogatari wa jijitsu ni yotte *kakaremashita.* (この物語は事実によって書かれました) This story was written, *based* on fact.
3 be caused; owing to:
Kaji wa tabako no fushimatsu ni yoru *mono datta.* (火事はたばこの不始末によるものだった) The fire was one *caused by* not extinguishing a cigarette. ⟨⟨⇨ yotte⟩⟩

yo⌈sañ よさん (予算) *n.* budget:
yosañ *o tateru* (予算を立てる) make a *budget*.

yo⌈seatsume よせあつめ (寄せ集め) *n.* medley; odds and ends:
yoseatsume *no chiimu* (寄せ集めのチーム) a *scratch* team. ⟨⟨⇨ yoseatsumeru⟩⟩

yo⌈seatsume⌉·ru よせあつめる (寄せ集める) *vt.* (-atsume-te Ⓥ) collect; gather up; bring together. ⟨⟨⇨ yoseatsume⟩⟩

yo⌈se·ru よせる (寄せる) *vt.* (yose-te Ⓥ) **1** bring [draw] up:
Akari o motto hoñ no soba e yose nasai. (あかりをもっと本のそばへ寄せなさい) *Bring* the light *closer* to the book.
2 put [push] aside:

Tsukue o mado no waki ni yoseta. (机を窓のわきに寄せた) I *put* the desk *next to* the window.

yo⌉shi よし (良し・好し) *int.* well; good; all right; OK:
Yoshi, *soo shiyoo.* (よし, そうしよう) *Well*, let's do so.

yo⌈shi⌉ashi よしあし (善し悪し) *n.* good or bad; right or wrong.
yoshiashi da (〜だ) have good and bad points: *Hima ga aru no mo* yoshiashi da. (暇があるのもよしあしだ) *It is not always good* to have ample leisure time.

yo⌉shiyoshi よしよし *int.* (used when consoling someone):
Yoshiyoshi. *Moo nakanai de.* (よしよし. もう泣かないで) *Come come.* You must stop crying now.

yo⌈shuu よしゅう (予習) *n.* preparation (of one's lessons). ⟪↔ fukushuu⟫

yo⌈so⌉ よそ (他所) *n.* **1** (〜 no) another (place); some other (place). ⟪⇨ hoka⟫
2 another person:
kodomo o yoso *ni azukeru* (子どもをよそに預ける) leave one's child in the care of *another*.

yo⌈soo よそう (予想) *n.* expectation; anticipation; guess:
Yosoo *ga atarimashita* [*hazuremashita*]. (予想が当たりました[外れました]) My *guess* proved right [wrong].
yosoo suru (〜する) *vt.* expect; anticipate; guess; predict.

yo⌉s·u よす (止す) *vt.* (yosh·i-; yos·a-; yosh·i-te Ⓒ) stop; give up; quit:
tabako o yosu (たばこをよす) *give up* smoking / *gakkoo o* yosu (学校をよす) *quit* school. ⟪⇨ yameru[1]⟫

yo⌈tee よてい (予定) *n.* plan; schedule; program:
yotee *o tateru* (予定を立てる) make a *plan* / yotee *o heñkoo suru* (予定を変更する) change a *schedule*.
yotee suru (〜する) *vt.* plan; schedule; expect.

yo⌉too よとう (与党) *n.* the ruling [government] party. ⟪↔ yatoo⟫

yo⌈tsukado よつかど (四つ角) *n.* crossroads; intersection.

yo⌈tte よって (依って) ★ Used in the pattern '*... ni yotte.*'
1 by: ★ Used with a passive verb and indicates the agent of a passive sentence.
Kono zoo wa yuumee na chookokuka ni yotte *tsukurareta mono desu.* (この像は有名な彫刻家によって作られたものです) This statue is one that was made *by* a famous sculptor. ⟪⇨ yoru[3]⟫
2 because of; due to: ★ Indicates cause or reason.
Señsoo ni yotte *ooku no hito ga nikushiñ o ushinaimashita.* (戦争によって多くの人が肉親を失いました) Many people lost their families *because of* the war. ⟪⇨ de[1]⟫
3 with; by; through; of: ★ Indicates means, method or material.
Miñna no kyooryoku ni yotte *sono shigoto wa hayaku owatta.* (みんなの協力によってその仕事は早く終わった) The work was finished early *with* the cooperation of everyone.
4 (differ) from...to...: ★ Used in expressions indicating variety or disparity.
Fuuzoku shuukañ wa kuni ni yotte *chigaimasu.* (風俗習慣は国によって違います) Manners and customs vary *from* country *to* country.

yo⌈ttsu⌉ よっつ (四つ) *n.* four. ★ Used when counting. ⟪⇨ shi[4]; yoñ; APP. 3⟫

yo⌉·u よう (酔う) *vi.* (yo·i-; yo·w·a-; yot-te Ⓒ) **1** get tipsy; become drunk. ⟪⇨ yoi[2]; yowaseru⟫
2 get sick:
fune [kuruma] ni you (船[車]に酔う) *get seasick* [*carsick*].
3 be intoxicated; be elated:
Señshu-tachi wa shoori ni yotte ita. (選手たちは勝利に酔っていた) The players *were elated* at the victory.

yoʳwaˡ·i よわい(弱い) *a.* (-ku)
1 weak:
Haha wa karada ga yowai. (母は体が弱い) My mother is physically *weak*. ⟪↔ tsuyoi⟫
2 dim; low:
yowai *hikari* (弱い光) a *dim* light / *Gasu no hi o* yowaku shi nasai. (ガスの火を弱くしなさい) *Turn down* the gas. ⟪↔ tsuyoi⟫
3 (... ni) (of knowledge, etc.) be poor at; weak:
Watashi wa kañji ni yowai. (私は漢字に弱い) I *am poor* at Chinese characters.
4 (... ni) be affected easily:
Chichi wa sake ni yowai. (父は酒に弱い) My father *cannot hold* his liquor very well. ⟪↔ tsuyoi⟫

yoʳwaki よわき(弱気) *a.n.*
(~ na, ni) weak-minded; timid; pessimistic. ⟪↔ tsuyoki⟫

yoʳwameˡ·ru よわめる(弱める) *vt.*
(yowame-te Ⓥ) weaken; turn down (the gas). ⟪↔ tsuyomeru⟫ ⟪⇨ yowaru⟫

yoʳwaˡr·u よわる(弱る) *vi.* (yowar·i-; yowar·a-; yowat-te Ⓒ)
1 become weak; weaken. ⟪⇨ yowameru⟫
2 be perplexed; be in a fix:
Kodomo ni nakarete, yowatta. (子どもに泣かれて, 弱った) I *was at a loss* when the child was crying.

yoʳwaseˡ·ru よわせる(酔わせる) *vt.*
(yowase-te Ⓥ) **1** make a person drunk. ⟪⇨ you⟫
2 charm; enchant:
Kare no eñsoo wa chooshuu o yowaseta. (彼の演奏は聴衆を酔わせた) His performance *enchanted* the audience. ⟪⇨ you⟫

yoʳyaku よやく(予約) *n.* **1** reservation; booking:
yoyaku *o toru* [*torikesu*] (予約をとる[取り消す]) make [cancel] a *reservation.*
2 subscription (to a magazine).
3 appointment (with a dentist).
yoyaku suru (~する) *vt.* reserve; book; subscribe; make an appointment.

yoʳyuu よゆう(余裕) *n.* margin; room; leeway.

yuˡ ゆ(湯) *n.* **1** hot water. ★ Often '*o-yu.*'
2 (hot) bath.

-yu ゆ(油) *suf.* oil:
seki-yu (石油) *petroleum* / too-yu (灯油) *kerosene.*

yuʳbiˡ ゆび(指) *n.* finger; thumb; toe.

yuʳbisaˡs·u ゆびさす(指さす) *vt.* (-sash·i-; -sas·a-; -sash·i-te Ⓒ) point to [at]:
kabe no e o yubisasu (壁の絵を指さす) *point to* a picture on the wall.

yuʳbiwa ゆびわ(指輪) *n.* ring:
yubiwa *o hameru* (指輪をはめる) put on a *ring.*

yuʳdañ ゆだん(油断) *n.* carelessness; inattention; negligence.
yudañ suru (~する) *vi.* be careless; be inattentive; be negligent. ⟪⇨ yoojiñ⟫

yuʳdeˡ·ru ゆでる(茹でる) *vt.* (yude-te Ⓥ) boil: *tamago o* yuderu (卵をゆでる) *boil* an egg.

yuʳde-taˡmago ゆでたまご(茹で卵) *n.* boiled egg. ⟪⇨ hañjuku; tamago⟫

yuʳe ni ゆえに(故に) *conj.* (*formal*) therefore; consequently; hence.

yuʳgame·ru ゆがめる(歪める) *vt.* (yugame-te Ⓥ) distort; twist:
kao o yugameru (顔をゆがめる) *screw up* one's face. ⟪⇨ yugamu⟫

yuʳgam·u ゆがむ(歪む) *vi.* (yugam·i-; yugam·a-; yugañ-de Ⓒ) be twisted; be distorted; be warped; lean. ⟪⇨ yugameru⟫

yuˡge ゆげ(湯気) *n.* steam.

yuˡi-itsu ゆいいつ(唯一) *n.* one and only:
Kare no yui-itsu *no tanoshimi wa tsuri desu.* (彼の唯一の楽しみは釣りです) His *only* pastime is fishing.

yuʳka ゆか(床) *n.* floor: *itabari no* yuka (板張りの床) a boarded *floor.*

yuˈkai ゆかい (愉快) *a.n.* (~ na, ni) pleasant; enjoyable; jolly; amusing. ⟪↔ fuyukai⟫

yuˈkata ゆかた (浴衣) *n.* informal summer kimono.

yuˈketsu ゆけつ (輸血) *n.* blood transfusion.
yuketsu suru (~する) *vi.* transfuse: *kañja ni* yuketsu suru (患者に輸血する) *give* a patient a *blood transfusion.*

yuˈki[1] ゆき (雪) *n.* snow:
Yuki ga futte kita. (雪が降ってきた) It *has begun to snow.*

yuˈki[2] ゆき (行き) *n.* (=iki[2]) going (to a destination):
Deñsha wa yuki *wa koñde ita ga, kaeri wa suite ita.* (電車は行きはこんでいたが, 帰りはすいていた) The train was crowded *on the way there,* but not crowded on the way back. ⟪↔ kaeri⟫ ⟪⇨ iku; yuku⟫

-yuki ゆき (行き) *suf.* bound for:
*Oosaka-*yuki *no ressha* (大阪行きの列車) a train *bound for* Osaka.

yuˈkichigai ゆきちがい (行き違い) *n.*
1 crossing each other:
Tegami ga yukichigai ni natte shimatta. (手紙が行き違いになってしまった) Our letters *have crossed each other.*
2 misunderstanding.

yuˈkidomari ゆきどまり (行き止まり) *n.* dead end. ⟪⇨ ikidomari⟫

yuˈkisaki ゆきさき (行き先) *n.* = yukusaki.

yuˈkkuˈri ゆっくり *adv.* (~ to)
1 slowly; without hurry; leisurely.
2 good; plenty of:
Deñsha ni wa yukkuri *maniaimasu.* (電車にはゆっくり間に合います) We are in *plenty* of time for the train.
yukkuri suru (~する) *vi.* take one's time; stay long.

yuˈk·u ゆく (行く) *vi.* (yuk·i-; yuk·a-; it-te Ⓒ) = iku.

yuˈkue ゆくえ (行方) *n.* whereabouts.

yuˈkue-fuˈmee ゆくえふめい (行方不明) *n.* missing:
Yama de go-niñ ga yukue-fumee ni natta. (山で5人が行方不明になった) Five people *have gone missing* in the mountains.

yuˈkusaki ゆくさき (行く先) *n.* destination; whereabouts. ⟪⇨ ikusaki; yukue⟫

yuˈkusue ゆくすえ (行く末) *n.* future. ⟪⇨ shoorai⟫

yuˈmeˈ ゆめ (夢) *n.* dream; ambition:
Isha ni naru no ga kare no yume desu. (医者になるのが彼の夢です) It is his *dream* to become a doctor.

yuˈmiˈ ゆみ (弓) *n.* bow:
yumi o iru (弓を射る) *shoot an arrow.* ⟪↔ ya[3]⟫

yuˈnomiˈ ゆのみ (湯呑) *n.* cup; teacup. ⟪⇨ chawañ⟫

yuˈnyuu ゆにゅう (輸入) *n.* import; importation.
yunyuu suru (~する) *vt.* import. ⟪↔ yushutsu⟫

yuˈre·ru ゆれる (揺れる) *vi.* (yure-te Ⓥ) **1** shake; tremble; sway.
2 waver:
Sono moñdai de kanojo no kokoro wa yurete iru. (その問題で彼女の心は揺れている) Her heart *is wavering* over that problem.

yuˈruˈ·i ゆるい (緩い) *a.* (-ku)
1 loose; lax:
Kono kutsu wa sukoshi yurui. (この靴は少しゆるい) These shoes are a little *too big* for me. ⟪↔ kitsui⟫ ⟪⇨ yurumeru; yurumu⟫
2 (of a curve, slope, etc.) gentle. ⟪↔ kyuu[1]⟫ ⟪⇨ yuruyaka⟫
3 slow:
yurui *tama o nageru* (ゆるい球を投げる) pitch a *slow* ball. ⟪↔ hayai[2]⟫

yuˈrumeˈ·ru ゆるめる (緩める) *vt.* (yurume-te Ⓥ) **1** loosen; unfasten; relax:
beruto o yurumeru (ベルトをゆるめる) *loosen* one's belt. ⟪⇨ yurumu; yurui⟫
2 make less strict; relax:
Tookyoku wa keekai o yurumeta.

(当局は警戒をゆるめた) The authorities *relaxed* their vigilance. ⟪⇨ yurumu⟫
3 slow down:
Kuruma wa sakamichi de supiido o yurumeta. (車は坂道でスピードをゆるめた) The car *slowed down* on the slope.

yu⌈ru⌉m·u ゆるむ (緩む) *vi.* (yurum·i-; yurum·a-; yuruñ-de Ⓥ)
1 become loose; loosen. ⟪⇨ yurui; yurumeru⟫
2 soften; abate:
Samusa ga yuruñde kita. (寒さがゆるんできた) It *has become less* cold.

yu⌈rushi ゆるし (許し) *n.* permission; pardon. ⟪⇨ kyoka; yurusu⟫

yu⌈ru⌉s·u ゆるす (許す) *vt.* (yurush·i-; yurus·a-; yurush·i-te Ⓒ) permit; allow; forgive:
Go-busata o o-yurushi *kudasai.* (ごぶさたをお許しください) *Forgive* me for not contacting you for so long. ⟪⇨ kañbeñ; kyoka; yurushi⟫

yu⌈ru⌉yaka ゆるやか (緩やか) *a.n.* (~ na, ni) gentle; slow:
yuruyaka *na saka* (ゆるやかな坂) a *gentle* slope. ⟪↔ kitsui⟫

yu⌈shutsu ゆしゅつ (輸出) *n.* export; exportation.
yushutsu suru (~する) *vt.* export. ⟪↔ yunyuu⟫

yu⌈soo ゆそう (輸送) *n.* transport; transportation.
yusoo suru (~する) *vt.* transport; carry.

yu⌈sug·u ゆすぐ (濯ぐ) *vt.* (yusug·i-; yusug·a-; yusu·i-de Ⓒ) rinse out; wash out:
señtakumono o yusugu (洗濯物をゆすぐ) *rinse* one's laundry.

yu⌈sur·u[1] ゆする (揺する) *vt.* (yusur·i-; yusur·a-; yusut-te Ⓒ) shake; rock; swing; roll.

yu⌈sur·u[2] ゆする (強請る) *vt.* (yusur·i-; yusur·a-; yusut-te Ⓒ) extort; blackmail.

y

yu⌉taka ゆたか (豊か) *a.n.* (~ na, ni) abundant; ample; rich; affluent:
yutaka *na shigeñ* (豊かな資源) *abundant* resources. ⟪↔ mazushii; toboshii⟫

yu⌈tta⌉ri ゆったり *adv.* (~ to; ~ suru) at ease; comfortably; loosely:
guriiñsha no zaseki ni yuttari *to suwaru* (グリーン車の座席にゆったりと座る) sit *comfortably* in a first class train seat.

yu·⌈u[1] ゆう (言う) *vi.* (i·i-; yuw·a-; yut-te Ⓒ) = iu.

yu⌉u[2] ゆう (優) *n.* (of a grade, rating) being excellent; A (in schoolwork). ⟪⇨ fuka; ka[2]; ryoo[3]⟫

yu⌈ube[1] ゆうべ (夕べ) *n.* yesterday evening; last night. ⟪⇨ sakuya⟫

yu⌈ube[2] ゆうべ (夕べ) *n.* (*literary*) evening: *oñgaku no* yuube (音楽の夕べ) a musical *evening.*

yu⌈ubiñ ゆうびん (郵便) *n.* **1** mail [postal] service; mail: yuubiñ-*bañgoo* (郵便番号) *zip* [*postal*] code / yuubiñ-*chokiñ* (郵便貯金) *postal* savings.
2 postal matter; mail.

yu⌈ubi⌉ñbutsu ゆうびんぶつ (郵便物) *n.* = yuubiñ (2).

yu⌈ubi⌉ñkyoku ゆうびんきょく (郵便局) *n.* post office. ★ 〒 is the emblem of '*yuubiñkyoku.*'

yu⌈uboku ゆうぼく (遊牧) *n.* nomadism: yuuboku-*miñzoku* (遊牧民族) a *nomadic* tribe.

yu⌈uboo ゆうぼう (有望) *a.n.* (~ na, ni) promising; hopeful.

yu⌈udachi ゆうだち (夕立) *n.* sudden, heavy shower on a summer afternoon.

yu⌈udoku ゆうどく (有毒) *a.n.* (~ na, ni) poisonous.

yu⌈ueki ゆうえき (有益) *a.n.* (~ na, ni) useful; helpful; instructive. ⟪↔ mueki⟫

yu⌈ugai ゆうがい (有害) *a.n.* (~ na, ni) harmful; injurious; bad. ⟪↔ mugai⟫

yu⌈ugata ゆうがた (夕方) *n.* evening. ⟪⇨ asa[1]; bañ[1]; yuube[1]⟫

yu⌈ugure ゆうぐれ (夕暮れ) *n.*

evening. ⟪⇨ yuugata; ban[1]⟫

yu⌈uhañ ゆうはん（夕飯）*n.* supper; dinner. ⟪⇨ yuushoku⟫

yu⌈uhi ゆうひ（夕日）*n.* the evening [setting] sun. ⟪↔ asahi⟫

yu⌈ujiñ ゆうじん（友人）*n.* friend. ⟪⇨ tomo[3]; tomodachi⟫

yu⌈ujoo ゆうじょう（友情）*n.* friendship.

yu⌈ukai ゆうかい（誘拐）*n.* kidnapping; abduction.
yuukai suru（～する）*vt.* kidnap; abduct.

yu⌈ukañ[1] ゆうかん（勇敢）*a.n.* (～ na, ni) brave; courageous:
yuukañ *ni tatakau*（勇敢に闘う）fight *courageously*.

yu⌈ukañ[2] ゆうかん（夕刊）*n.* evening paper; the evening edition of a newspaper. ⟪↔ chookañ[1]⟫ ⟪⇨ shiñbuñ⟫

yu⌉uki ゆうき（勇気）*n.* courage; bravery.

yu⌈ukoo[1] ゆうこう（友好）*n.* friendly relationship; friendship:
yuukoo *o fukameru*（友好を深める）promote *friendship*.

yu⌈ukoo[2] ゆうこう（有効）*a.n.* (～ na, ni) effective; valid. ⟪↔ mukoo[2]⟫

yu⌈umee ゆうめい（有名）*a.n.* (～ na, ni) famous; well-known; notorious. ⟪↔ mumee⟫

yu⌈umeshi ゆうめし（夕飯）*n.* (*informal*) supper; dinner. ⟪⇨ yuushoku⟫

yu⌉umoa ユーモア *n.* humor; joke.

yu⌈unoo ゆうのう（有能）*a.n.* (～ na) able; capable; competent. ⟪↔ munoo⟫

yu⌉uri ゆうり（有利）*a.n.* (～ na, ni) advantageous; favorable. ⟪↔ furi[1]⟫

yu⌈uryoku ゆうりょく（有力）*a.n.* (～ na, ni) influential; strong; leading. ⟪↔ muryoku⟫

yu⌈uryoo ゆうりょう（有料）*n.* charge:
Kono teñrañkai wa yuuryoo *desu.*（この展覧会は有料です）There is a *charge* for this exhibition. ⟪↔ muryoo⟫

yu⌈usee ゆうせい（優勢）*n.* superiority; lead:
yuusee *o tamotsu*（優勢を保つ）retain one's *superiority*.
— *a.n.* (～ na, ni) superior; leading. ⟪↔ ressee⟫

yu⌈useñ ゆうせん（優先）*n.* priority; precedence; preference:
yuuseñ-*juñi*（優先順位）the order of *priority*.
yuuseñ suru（～する）*vi.* have priority; take precedence.

yu⌈useñ-ho⌉osoo ゆうせんほうそう（有線放送）*n.* closed-circuit [cable] broadcasting.

yu⌈ushoku ゆうしょく（夕食）*n.* supper; dinner. ⟪⇨ yuuhañ; bañsañ⟫

yu⌈ushoo ゆうしょう（優勝）*n.* victory; championship.
yuushoo suru（～する）*vi.* win the victory [championship].

yu⌈ushuu ゆうしゅう（優秀）*a.n.* (～ na) excellent; superior; outstanding.

yu⌈usoo ゆうそう（郵送）*n.* sending by mail; post:
yuusoo-ryoo（郵送料）*postage*.
yuusoo suru（～する）*vt.* mail; post; send by mail [post].

yu⌈utoo ゆうとう（優等）*n.* academic honors:
yuutoo *de daigaku o sotsugyoo suru*（優等で大学を卒業する）graduate from college with *honors*.

yu⌈u-utsu ゆううつ（憂鬱）*a.n.* (～ na, ni) depressing; gloomy; melancholy.

yu⌈uwaku ゆうわく（誘惑）*n.* temptation; lure; seduction.
yuuwaku suru（～する）*vt.* tempt; lure; seduce (a woman).

yu⌈uyake ゆうやけ（夕焼け）*n.* glow of the sunset. ⟪↔ asayake⟫

yu⌈uyu⌉u ゆうゆう（悠々）*adv.* (～ to) **1** easily; without difficulty:

yuuyuu *to katsu* (ゆうゆうと勝つ) win an *easy* victory.
2 calmly; sedately; leisurely: *Kare wa sono ba kara* yuuyuu *to tachisatta.* (彼はその場からゆうゆうと立ち去った) He *calmly* went away from the spot.

yu⌈uzuu ゆうずう (融通) *n.*
1 adaptability; flexibility: *Ano hito wa* yuuzuu ga kiku [kikanai]. (あの人は融通がきく[きかない]) He *is flexible and versatile* [*rigid and literal-minded*].
2 loan (of money); financing.
yuuzuu suru (～する) *vt.* accommodate; lend.

yu⌈zur·u ゆずる (譲る) *vt.* (yuzur·i-; yuzur·a-; yuzut-te Ⓒ)
1 hand over; transfer: *kooshiñ ni michi o* yuzuru (後進に道を譲る) *make way* for the younger generation.
2 give; offer; sell: *Shooneñ wa basu de roojiñ ni seki o* yuzutta. (少年はバスで老人に席を譲った) The boy *gave up* his seat to an elderly person on the bus.
3 concede; make a concession.

Z

za⌉azaa ざあざあ *adv.* (～ to) hard: ★ The sound of heavy rainfall.
Ame ga zaazaa (to) futte kita. (雨がざあざあ(と)降ってきた) The rain *began to pour down.*

za⌈buñ ざぶん *adv.* (～ to) with a splash: ★ The sound of a heavy object falling into water.
Kare wa zabuñ to *kawa ni ochita.* (彼はざぶんと川に落ちた) He fell into the river *with a splash.*

za⌈bu⌉toñ ざぶとん (座布団) *n.* cushion for sitting on.

za⌈da⌉ñkai ざだんかい (座談会) *n.* discussion meeting; round-table talk.

-zai ざい (剤) *suf.* medicine; drug; dose: yaku-zai (薬剤) a *medicine* / ge-zai (下剤) a *laxative.*

za⌈igaku ざいがく (在学) *n.* being in school [college].
zaigaku suru (～する) *vi.* attend a school; be in school.
《⇨ tsuugaku》

za⌈iko ざいこ (在庫) *n.* stock: *Sono hoñ wa* zaiko *ga kirete imasu.* (その本は在庫が切れています) The book is out of *stock.*

za⌈imoku ざいもく (材木) *n.* wood; lumber; timber.

za⌈iryo⌉o ざいりょう (材料) *n.* material; stuff; ingredient.

za⌉isañ ざいさん (財産) *n.* property; fortune.

za⌈isee ざいせい (財政) *n.* finance: zaisee *ga kurushii* (財政が苦しい) be in *financial* difficulties.

za⌈iseki[1] ざいせき (在籍) *n.* registration; enrollment: zaiseki-*sha* (在籍者) a *registered* person.
zaiseki suru (～する) *vi.* be registered; be enrolled.

za⌈iseki[2] ざいせき (在席) *n.* being at one's own seat [desk].
zaiseki suru (～する) *vi.* be at one's desk.

za⌈itaku ざいたく (在宅) *n.* being at home: ★ Often with '*go-*.'
Yukari-sañ wa go-zaitaku *desu ka?* (ゆかりさんはご在宅ですか) Is Yukari *at home*?
zaitaku suru (～する) *vi.* be at home.

za⌈kka ざっか (雑貨) *n.* sundries; miscellaneous goods.

za⌉kkubarañ ざっくばらん *a.n.* (～ na, ni) (*informal*) frank; candid; outspoken. 《⇨ sotchoku》

za⌈ñdaka ざんだか (残高) *n.* balance; the remainder (in an account, etc.).

za⌈ñgyoo ざんぎょう(残業) *n.* overtime (work): zañgyoo-*teate* (残業手当) *overtime* pay.
zañgyoo (o) suru (～(を)する) *vi.* work overtime.

za⌈ñkoku ざんこく(残酷) *a.n.* (～ na, ni) cruel; atrocious; brutal.

za⌈ñne⌉ñ ざんねん(残念) *a.n.* (～ na, ni) sorry; regrettable; repentant:
Anata ga paatii ni derarenai no wa zañneñ *desu.* (あなたがパーティーに出られないのは残念です) I am *sorry* that you cannot come to the party.
zañneñ-nagara (～ながら) regrettably; unfortunately.

za⌈ppi ざっぴ(雑費) *n.* miscellaneous [sundry] expenses; incidental expenses.

za⌈seki ざせき(座席) *n.* seat: zaseki *o yoyaku suru* (座席を予約する) reserve a *seat.* ⟪⇨ seki[1]⟫

za⌈setsu ざせつ(挫折) *n.* setback; collapse.
zasetsu suru (～する) *vi.* miscarry; collapse; be discouraged.

za⌈shiki⌉ ざしき(座敷) *n.* tatami-matted reception room with a 'tokonoma.'

za⌈shoo ざしょう(座礁) *n.* stranding; going aground.
zashoo suru (～する) *vi.* go [run] aground.

za⌈sshi ざっし(雑誌) *n.* magazine; periodical. ⟪⇨ hoñ⟫

za⌈ssoo ざっそう(雑草) *n.* weed: *niwa no* zassoo *o toru* (庭の雑草をとる) *weed* the garden. ⟪⇨ kusa⟫

za⌈taku ざたく(座卓) *n.* a low table placed in a Japanese-style room.

za⌈tsu ざつ(雑) *a.n.* (～ na, ni) careless; sloppy; slipshod; rough:
Kare wa shigoto ga zatsu *da.* (彼は仕事が雑だ) He is *careless* in his work.

za⌈tsudañ ざつだん(雑談) *n.* chat; light conversation.

za⌈tsuoñ ざつおん(雑音) *n.* noise; static.

za⌈tto ざっと *adv.* **1** briefly; roughly:
shorui ni zatto *me o toosu* (書類にざっと目を通す) *briefly* look through the papers. ⟪⇨ hitotoori⟫
2 about; approximately.

za⌈ttoo ざっとう(雑踏) *n.* crowd; throng; congestion.
zattoo suru (～する) *vi.* be crowded; be thronged.

za⌉wazawa ざわざわ *adv.* (～ to) **1** (the murmur heard when many people are together):
Kaijoo-nai wa zawazawa *(to) shite ita.* (会場内はざわざわ(と)していた) There was a *stirring* in the hall. ⟪⇨ gayagaya⟫
2 (the sound of leaves rustling in the wind):
Tsuyoi kaze ni ki no ha ga zawazawa (to) yurete iru. (強い風に木の葉がざわざわ(と)揺れている) The leaves *are rustling* in the strong wind.

za⌈yaku ざやく(座薬) *n.* suppository.

ze ぜ *p.* (*colloq.*) (used to emphasize one's opinions or wishes):
★ Used by men.
Sorosoro dekakeyoo ze. (そろそろ出かけようぜ) *Well,* let's be going now.

ze⌉e ぜい(税) *n.* tax; taxation. ⟪⇨ zeekiñ⟫

ze⌈ekañ ぜいかん(税関) *n.* customs; customhouse:
zeekañ-*shiñkokusho* (税関申告書) a *customs* declaration.

ze⌈ekiñ ぜいきん(税金) *n.* tax; duty: zeekiñ *o osameru* (税金を納める) pay a *tax.*

ze⌈emu⌉sho ぜいむしょ(税務署) *n.* tax office.

ze⌈etaku⌉ ぜいたく(贅沢) *n.* luxury; extravagance.
— *a.n.* (～ na, ni) luxurious; extravagant; lavish.

ze⌉hi[1] ぜひ(是非) *adv.* surely; by all means; at any cost:
Kai ni wa zehi *shusseki shite ku-*

dasai. (会にはぜひ出席してください) *Be sure* to attend the party. ⟪⇨ zehi-tomo⟫

zeˈhi[2] ぜひ (是非) ***n.*** right and/or wrong.

zeˈhi-tomo ぜひとも (是非共) ***adv.*** an emphatic form of '*zehi*[1].'

zeˈkkoo[1] ぜっこう (絶好) ***n.*** (~ no) ideal; perfect:
zekkoo *no kikai o nogasu* (絶好の機会を逃す) let a *golden* opportunity slip by.

zeˈkkoo[2] ぜっこう (絶交) ***n.*** breach; breaking off relations.
zekkoo suru (~する) ***vi.*** break off one's friendship.

zeˈkkyoo ぜっきょう (絶叫) ***n.*** shout; scream; exclamation.

zeˈñ[1] ぜん (善) ***n.*** good; right:
zeñ *to aku* (善と悪) *right* and wrong. ⟪↔ aku[3]⟫ ⟪⇨ zeñaku⟫

zeˈñ[2] ぜん (禅) ***n.*** Zen.

zeˈñ-[1] ぜん (全) ***pref.*** all; whole:
zeñ-*sekai* (全世界) the *whole* world / zeñ-*zaisañ* (全財産) one's *whole* fortune.

zeˈñ-[2] ぜん (前) ***pref.*** the former; ex-:
zeñ-*Soori-daijiñ* (前総理大臣) the *former* prime minister. ★ 'Moto (*no*) *Soori-daijiñ*' is *a previous* prime minister. ⟪⇨ moto[2]⟫

-zeñ ぜん (前) ***suf.*** before:
señ-zeñ (戦前) *before* the war / *shoku*-zeñ (食前) *before* a meal.

zeˈñaku ぜんあく (善悪) ***n.*** right and wrong; good and evil. ⟪⇨ zeñ[1]; aku[3]⟫

zeˈñbu ぜんぶ (全部) ***n.*** all; everything; total.

zeˈñgo ぜんご (前後) ***n.*** before and after; in front and in the rear; back and forth.
zeñgo o wasureru (~を忘れる) forget oneself.
zeñgo suru (~する) ***vi.*** be reversed.

-zeˈñgo ぜんご (前後) ***suf.*** about; around: *yoñjus-sai*-zeñgo (40歳前後) *about* forty years old.

zeˈñhañ ぜんはん (前半) ***n.*** the first half: *nijus-seeki* zeñhañ (20世紀前半) *the first half* of the twentieth century. ⟪↔ koohañ⟫

zeˈñiñ ぜんいん (全員) ***n.*** all the members.

zeˈñjitsu ぜんじつ (前日) ***n.*** the day before; the previous day. ⟪⇨ yokujitsu⟫

zeˈñkai ぜんかい (全快) ***n.*** complete recovery.
zeñkai suru (~する) ***vi.*** recover completely.

zeˈñki ぜんき (前期) ***n.*** the first half year; the first term [semester]. ⟪↔ kooki⟫

zeˈñkoku ぜんこく (全国) ***n.*** the whole country; all parts of the country.

zeˈñkoku-teki ぜんこくてき (全国的) ***a.n.*** (~ na, ni) nationwide; all over the country.

zeˈñmetsu ぜんめつ (全滅) ***n.*** annihilation; total destruction.
zeñmetsu suru (~する) ***vi.*** be annihilated; be totally destroyed.

zeˈñpañ ぜんぱん (全般) ***n.*** the whole:
Nihoñ buñka zeñpañ *no chishiki* (日本文化全般の知識) a *general* knowledge of Japanese culture.

zeˈñpañ-teki ぜんぱんてき (全般的) ***a.n.*** (~ na, ni) on the whole; all in all.

zeˈñryaku ぜんりゃく (前略) ***n.*** Dear Mr. [Mrs., Miss, Ms.]...; Dear Sir [Sirs, Madam].
★ Used in the salutation of an informal letter. The corresponding complimentary close is '*soosoo.*' ⟪⇨ haikee[1]; soosoo[2]⟫

zeˈñryoku ぜんりょく (全力) ***n.*** all one's strength:
zeñryoku *o tsukusu* (全力を尽くす) *do one's best.*

zeˈñsha ぜんしゃ (前者) ***n.*** the former. ⟪↔ koosha[2]⟫

zeˈñshiñ[1] ぜんしん (前進) ***n.*** advance; progress.
zeñshiñ suru (~する) ***vi.*** go

ahead; advance; progress.

ze⌈ñshiñ[2] ぜんしん(全身) *n.* the whole body:
Sono ko wa zeñshiñ *doro-darake datta.* (その子は全身泥だらけだった) The child was covered with mud *all over.*

ze⌈ñsoku ぜんそく(喘息) *n.* asthma.

ze⌈ñsoku⌉ryoku ぜんそくりょく(全速力) *n.* full speed.

ze⌈ñtai ぜんたい(全体) *n.* the whole; all: *machi* zeñtai (町全体) *the whole* town.

ze⌈ñtee ぜんてい(前提) *n.* premise; assumption.

ze⌉ñto ぜんと(前途) *n.* future; one's way:
zeñto yuuboo *na wakamono* (前途有望な若者) a *promising* young man.

ze⌉ñzeñ ぜんぜん(全然) *adv.*
1 (with a negative) not at all; never:
Kare ni tsuite wa zeñzeñ *shirimaseñ.* (彼については全然知りません) I know nothing *at all* about him.
2 completely; entirely; altogether. ((⇨ mattaku))

ze⌉ro ゼロ *n.* zero; nothing. ((⇨ ree[4]))
zero kara yarinaosu (～からやり直す) start from scratch once more.

ze⌈tsuboo ぜつぼう(絶望) *n.* despair; hopelessness.
zetsuboo suru (～する) *vi.* despair; give up hope.

ze⌈tsuboo-teki ぜつぼうてき(絶望的) *a.n.* (～ na, ni) desperate; hopeless.

ze⌈tsueñ ぜつえん(絶縁) *n.*
1 breaking off relations.
2 insulation: zetsueñ-*teepu* (絶縁テープ) *insulating* tape.
zetsueñ suru (～する) *vi.* sever relations.

ze⌈ttai ぜったい(絶対) *n., adv.* absoluteness; absolutely:
Koko de wa kañtoku no meeree wa zettai *desu.* (ここでは監督の命令は絶対です) Around here the team manager's orders are *final.*

ze⌈ttai ni ぜったいに(絶対に) *adv.*
1 absolutely; surely:
Koko nara zettai ni *añzeñ desu.* (ここなら絶対に安全です) Provided you are here, you will be *absolutely* safe.
2 (with a negative) never; by no means:
Kono himitsu wa zettai ni *hito ni iimaseñ.* (この秘密は絶対に人に言いません) *Under no circumstances,* will I tell this secret to anybody.

zo ぞ *p.* (*colloq.*) **1** (used rhetorically to oneself in confirming an opinion): ★ Used by men.
Nañ da ka heñ da zo. (何だか変だぞ) *I am sure* something or other is wrong.
2 (used to emphasize one's opinions or wishes): ★ A potentially rude form. Used to close friends and those of lower status. ((⇨ ze))
Sorosoro dekakeru zo. (そろそろ出かけるぞ) *Well,* let's be off now.

-zoi ぞい(沿い) *suf.* along:
*yama-*zoi *no michi* (山沿いの道) a road *along* the foot of a mountain. ((⇨ sou[1]))

zo⌈kugo ぞくご(俗語) *n.* slang; slang word.

zo⌈ku⌉s·u ぞくす(属す) *vi.* (-sh·i-; -s·a-; -sh·i-te Ⓒ) belong to; come under.

zo⌈kuzoku[1] ぞくぞく(続々) *adv.* (～ to) in succession; one after another.

zo⌉kuzoku[2] ぞくぞく *adv.* (～ suru) (the state of feeling chilliness or being excited):
Netsu ga aru no ka, karada ga zokuzoku suru. (熱があるのか, 体がぞくぞくする) I must have a fever because I *have the shivers.*

zo⌈ñji⌉·ru ぞんじる(存じる) *vi.* (zoñji-te Ⓥ) ★ Used in the forms '*zoñjimasu*' and '*zonjite.*' The plain form '*zonjiru*' is never used. The honorific equivalent is '*gozoñji desu.*' ((⇨ gozoñji))

1 (*humble*) know:
Yamada-sañ no koto wa yoku zoñjite orimasu. (山田さんのことはよく存じております) I *know* Mr. Yamada very well. ⟪⇨ shiru[1]⟫
2 (*humble*) hope; feel; think:
Kooee ni zoñjimasu. (光栄に存じます) I *feel* honored.

zo⌈ñza⌉i ぞんざい *a.n.* (~ na, ni) rude; rough; careless; impolite.

zo⌉o ぞう (象) *n.* elephant.

zo⌈odai ぞうだい (増大) *n.* increase; enlargement.
zoodai suru (~する) *vi., vt.* increase. ⟪↔ geñshoo[1]⟫ ⟪⇨ zooka⟫

zo⌈ogeñ ぞうげん (増減) *n.* increase and/or decrease; fluctuation; variation.
zoogeñ suru (~する) *vi., vt.* increase and/or decrease; fluctuate; vary.

zo⌈oka ぞうか (増加) *n.* increase:
jiñkoo no zooka (人口の増加) an *increase* in population.
zooka suru (~する) *vi., vt.* increase. ⟪↔ geñshoo[1]⟫ ⟪⇨ zoodai⟫

zo⌈okiñ ぞうきん (雑巾) *n.* duster; dust cloth; floor cloth.

zo⌈okyoo ぞうきょう (増強) *n.* reinforcement; increase; buildup.
zookyoo suru (~する) *vt.* reinforce; strengthen: *yusooryoku o* zookyoo suru (輸送力を増強する) *augment* the transport capacity.

zo⌈oni ぞうに (雑煮) *n.* soup with rice cakes, chicken and vegetables, served during New Year celebrations. ⟪⇨ shoogatsu⟫

zo⌈ori ぞうり (草履) *n.* zori; Japanese flat sandals.

zo⌈oseñ ぞうせん (造船) *n.* shipbuilding:
zooseñ-jo (造船所) a *shipyard*.

zo⌈osho ぞうしょ (蔵書) *n.* a collection of books; one's personal library.

zo⌈oshuu ぞうしゅう (増収) *n.* increase of income [revenue]. ⟪↔ geñshuu⟫

zo⌉rozoro ぞろぞろ *adv.* (~ to) in a stream; one after another.

zu ず (図) *n.* drawing; figure; diagram; illustration.

zu⌈bo⌉ñ ズボン *n.* trousers; slacks; pants.

zu⌉ibuñ ずいぶん (随分) *adv.* very (much); really; a lot; quite:
Kono heñ wa mukashi to zuibuñ *kawarimashita.* (この辺は昔とずいぶん変わりました) This area has changed *a lot* from the old days.

zu⌈ihitsu ずいひつ (随筆) *n.* essay:
zuihitsu *o kaku* (随筆を書く) write an *essay*.

-zu ni ずに = -nai[1]+-de.

zu⌉ñzuñ ずんずん *adv.* (~ to) quickly; rapidly; on and on.

-zura⌉·i づらい (辛い) *suf.* (*a.*) (-ku) hard; difficult: ★ Added to the continuative base of a verb.
Kono hoñ wa ji ga chiisakute yomi-zurai. (この本は字が小さくて読みづらい) This book has small print and is thus *difficult* to read. ⟪↔ -yasui⟫ ⟪⇨ -gatai; -nikui⟫

zu⌈rari⌉ ずらり *adv.* (~ to) in a line [row]:
Butai ni odoriko ga zurari *to narañda.* (舞台に踊り子がずらりと並んだ) The dancers formed a *straight line* on the stage.

zu⌈ra⌉s·u ずらす *vt.* (zurash·i-; zuras·a-; zurash·i-te Ⓒ) **1** shift; move a little. ⟪⇨ zureru⟫
2 put off; postpone:
nittee o zurasu (日程をずらす) *move back* the schedule. ⟪⇨ zureru⟫

zu⌈re⌉ ずれ *n.* difference; gap:
kañgaekata no zure (考え方のずれ) a *difference* of views. ⟪⇨ zureru⟫

zu⌈re⌉·ru ずれる *vi.* (zure-te Ⓥ)
1 be shifted; be not in the right place. ⟪⇨ zurasu⟫
2 be put off:
Shigoto ga haitte, yotee ga isshuukañ zuremashita. (仕事が入って，予定が1週間ずれました) Because some work has come in, my schedule *is* a week *off*. ⟪⇨ zurasu⟫
3 deviate:

Kare no ikeñ wa teema to sukoshi zurete iru. (彼の意見はテーマと少しずれている) His opinion *is* a bit *off* the topic. 《⇨ zure》

zu⌈ru⌉·i ずるい *a.* (-ku) cunning; tricky; unfair.

zu⌉ruzuru ずるずる *adv.* (~ to) trailingly; draggingly:
Kare wa zuruzuru (*to*) *heñji o nobashita.* (彼はずるずる(と)返事を延ばした) He *kept on* putting off his reply.

zu⌈sañ ずさん (杜撰) *a.n.* (~ na) careless; slipshod; faulty.

-zu⌉tai づたい (伝い) *suf.* along:
*señro-*zutai *no michi* (線路づたいの道) a road *running beside* the railway lines.

zu⌈tazuta ni ずたずたに *adv.* to pieces; to shreds.

-zu⌉tsu ずつ (宛) *suf.* **1** of each; for each; to each: ★ Indicates distribution.
Kono kami o hitori-zutsu *ichi-mai tori nasai.* (この紙を一人ずつ1枚取りなさい) *Each of you* take a sheet of this paper.
2 at a time: ★ Indicates repetition.
Sukoshi-zutsu *arukeru yoo ni narimashita.* (少しずつ歩けるようになりました) *Little by little* I have reached the stage where I am able to walk.

zu⌈tsuu ずつう (頭痛) *n.* headache.
zutsuu no tane (~の種) a source of worry.

zu⌈tto ずっと *adv.* **1** (with a comparative) much; far:
Kare wa watashi yori zutto *wakai.* (彼は私よりずっと若い) He is *much* younger than I. 《⇨ haruka ni》
2 (of time) long:
Zutto *ato ni natte, sono koto ni ki ga tsukimashita.* (ずっと後になって, そのことに気がつきました) I noticed that a *long* time afterward.
3 all the time; all the way.

zu⌈uzuushi⌉·i ずうずうしい (図々しい) *a.* (-ku) impudent; pushy; shameless. 《⇨ atsukamashii》

APPENDIX 1

Guide to Japanese Pronunciation

1. Standard pronunciation of the Japanese language

The variety of Japanese of greatest practical importance for foreign learners is that called **Standard Japanese**. This is understood throughout Japan. The pronunciation of Standard Japanese is based on that of educated people who were born and brought up in Tokyo, or its vicinity.

2. Vowels

2.1 Short and Long Vowels

The vowel system of Japanese (hereafter abbreviated to J) is much simpler than that of English (abbreviated to E). It consists of five short vowels **i**, **e**, **a**, **o**, **u**, and the corresponding long vowels. Long vowels may also be interpreted as double vowels, and in this dictionary they are written **ii**, **ee**, **aa**, **oo**, **uu**. It should be noted that the distinction between short and long vowels is significant in Japanese in that it affects the meanings of words. For example, *i* (stomach) vs. *ii* (good), *tesee* (handmade) vs. *teesee* (correction), *kado* (corner) vs. *kaado* (card), *toru* (take) vs. *tooru* (pass), *kuki* (stem) vs. *kuuki* (air).

In pronouncing a long vowel, foreign learners should nearly double the length of the corresponding short vowel. E speakers are especially advised not to lengthen J short vowels, but to cut them short.

2.2 i and ii (い, イ and いー, イー)

J **i** is phonetically [i] and [i:]. It is close to the French vowel in *qui*, *ici*, etc. E short *i*-vowel in words like *sit*, *miss* is halfway between J **i** and **e**, and, if used, sometimes sounds like **e** to Japanese listeners. It would be better for E-speaking learners to make their *i*-vowel more like long *e*, though they must cut it short. On the other hand, E long *e*-vowel in *be*, *seat*, etc. can safely be used for J **ii**.

2.3 e and ee (え, エ and えー, エー)

J **e** is phonetically halfway between [e] and [ɛ], and is close to the short *e*-vowel in *get*, *less*, etc. The *a*-vowel in *day*, *late*, etc. can safely be used for J **ee**, though the latter is less diphthongal than the former.

2.4 a and aa (あ, ア and あー, アー)
Phonetically between [a] and [ɑ], J **a** has rather a wide range. The nearest vowel to this is British (abbreviated to B hereafter) E short *u*-vowel in *cut*, *fun*, etc. J **a** is halfway between American (abbreviated to A) E short *u*-vowel (*hut*, *luck*, etc.) and short *o*-vowel (*not*, *lock*, etc.) The initial part of the long *i*-vowel in *ice*, *fine*, etc. will also do for J **a**.

Learners are warned against using E short *a*-vowel in *back*, *man*, etc., since this sometimes sounds a little like **e** to Japanese listeners. E *a*-vowel in words like *father*, *Chicago* can be used for J **aa**.

2.5 o and oo (お, オ and おー, オー)
J **o** is phonetically halfway between [o] and [ɔ]. The nearest approach to this vowel is the initial part of A E long *o*-vowel in *go*, *most*, etc., or the B E *au*-vowel in *cause*, *law*, etc., but these should be cut short. B E short *o*-vowel in *hot*, *lock*, etc. is too open for J **o**, and A E short *o*-vowel in *hot*, *lock*, etc. is more like J **a** than J **o**. The nearest vowel to J **oo** is B E *au*-vowel, A E *au*-vowel being too open. It is also like A E long *o*-vowel in *go*, *road*, etc., though less diphthongal. British learners (especially those from southern England) should never use their long *o*-vowel in *go*, *road*, etc., because it sometimes sounds like **au** to Japanese listeners.

2.6 u and uu (う, ウ and うー, ウー)
J **u** is phonetically [ɯ], that is, it lacks the lip-rounding which accompanies the *u*-vowel of most European languages. Therefore learners are advised not to round the corners of their mouths, but to draw them back when making this vowel. This also holds true in the pronunciation of long **uu**.

2.7 Devoicing of vowels
J vowels, especially **i** and **u** are often devoiced (i.e. become voiceless) when they do not carry the accent nucleus (see 5.) and occur between voiceless consonants, or occur at the end of a word or an utterance, preceded by a voiceless consonant. The devoicing is represented by a small circle under the phonetic symbols thus [i̥] and [ɯ̥]. For example, *chikara* [tʃi̥kara] (strength), *pittari* [pi̥ttari] (closely), *ashi* [aʃi̥] (reed); *suppai* [sɯ̥ppai] (sour), *futoi* [ɸɯ̥toi] (thick), *karasu* [karasɯ̥], etc. In the final **su** in *...masu*. or *...desu*., **u** is very often devoiced or dropped completely, and the preceding **s** is compensatorily lengthened. However, failure to devoice these **i**'s and **u**'s does not impair intelligibility.

3. Consonants

3.1 k (**ka** か, カ, **ki** き, キ, **ku** く, ク, **ke** け, ケ, **ko** こ, コ; **kya** きゃ, キャ, **kyu** きゅ, キュ, **kyo** きょ, キョ)
Phoetically [k]. It is like E *k* in *keep*, *cold*, etc., but the aspiration, or *h*-like sound, after J **k** is weaker than in E.

3.2 g (**ga** が, ガ, **gi** ぎ, ギ, **gu** ぐ, グ, **ge** げ, ゲ, **go** ご, ゴ; **gya** ぎゃ, ギャ, **gyu** ぎゅ, ギュ, **gyo** ぎょ, ギョ)
Phonetically [g]. It is like E *g* in *get*, *good*, etc. In the middle of words like *kago* (basket), *agaru* (rise) and in the particle *ga* (が), **g** is often pronounced [ŋ] (as in E *sing*) in traditional standard J, but [ŋ] is currently being replaced by [g]. Foreign learners can safely use [g] in these positions.

3.3 s (**sa** さ, サ, **su** す, ス, **se** せ, セ, **so** そ, ソ)
Phonetically [s], the sound in E *set*, *soon*, etc.

3.4 sh (**shi** し, シ, **sha** しゃ, シャ, **shu** しゅ, シュ, **sho** しょ, ショ)
Phonetically [ʃ]. It is like E *sh* in *shine*, *short*, etc., but lacks the lip-protrusion which often accompanies E *sh*.

3.5 z (**za** ざ, ザ, **zu** ず, ズ, **ze** ぜ, ゼ, **zo** ぞ, ゾ)
At the beginning of words, J **z** is phonetically [dz], like E *ds* in *cards*, *leads*, etc. In the middle of words it is usually [z], like E *z* in *zone*, *lazy*, etc. However, *z* is always intelligible in all positions.

3.6 j (**ji** じ, ジ; **ja** じゃ, ジャ, **ju** じゅ, ジュ, **jo** じょ, ジョ)
Phonetically [dʒ], the sound in E *judge*, *George*, etc.

3.7 t (**ta** た, タ, **te** て, テ, **to** と, ト)
Phonetically dental [t] with the tip of the tongue against the front upper teeth, rather than against the teethridge as in the E *t* in *time*, *talk*, etc., which, however, can safely be used. The aspiration after J **t** is weaker than in E. American learners are warned against using their *t* before a weak vowel as in words like *city*, *matter*, because it sometimes sounds like **r** to Japanese listeners.

3.8 d (**da** だ, ダ, **de** で, デ, **do** ど, ド)
Phonetically [d] pronounced in the same way as J **t** but with voice. However, the E *d* as in in *dark*, *date*, etc., can safely be used for J **d**. Again, Americans should avoid using their *d* before a weak vowel as in *ladder*, *pudding*, etc., since it sometimes sounds like **r** to Japanese listeners.

3.9 ch (**chi** ち, チ; **cha** ちゃ, チャ, **chu** ちゅ, チュ, **cho** ちょ, チョ)
Phonetically [tʃ], the sound in E *church*, *nature*, etc.

3.10 ts (tsu つ, ツ)
Phonetically [ts], the sound in E *cats*, *roots*, etc. English speakers often find it difficult to say [ts] initially as in *tsuzuku* (continue), *tsuru* (crane). You can practice this sound by saying it in words like *cat's-eye* and then omitting the first part of that word (*ca*).

3.11 n (na な, ナ, ni に, ニ, nu ぬ, ヌ, ne ね, ネ, no の, ノ; nya にゃ, ニャ, nyu にゅ, ニュ, nyo にょ, ニョ)
Phonetically dental [n], not alveolar as the E *n* in *night*, *none*, etc., but this causes no practical problems. It is more important that foreign learners should distinguish this sound from **ñ** treated in 3.20.

3.12 h (ha は, ハ, hi ひ, ヒ, he へ, ヘ, ho ほ, ホ; hya ひゃ, ヒャ, hyu ひゅ, ヒュ, hyo ひょ, ヒョ)
Phonetically [h], the sound in E *house*, *hold*, etc. To be more exact, the **h** before **i** and **y** is phonetically [ç], the sound heard in German *ich*. [ç] is accompanied by more friction in the mouth than E *h*.

3.13 f (fu ふ, フ)
Phonetically [ɸ]. Though spelled with **f**, it is slightly different from the *f* in European languages. While European *f* is formed with the lower lip against the upper teeth, the J **f** is produced with the upper and the lower lips close together. The friction sound of J **f** is weaker than European *f*.

3.14 b (ba ば, バ, bi び, ビ, bu ぶ, ブ, be べ, ベ, bo ぼ, ボ; bya びゃ, ビャ, byu びゅ, ビュ, byo びょ, ビョ)
Phonetically [b]. Like E *b* in *be*, *ball*, etc.

3.15 p (pa ぱ, パ, pi ぴ, ピ, pu ぷ, プ, pe ぺ, ペ, po ぽ, ポ; pya ぴゃ, ピャ, pyu ぴゅ, ピュ, pyo ぴょ, ピョ)
Phonetically [p]. It is like E *p* in *pay*, *post*, etc., but the aspiration after J **p** is weaker than in E.

3.16 m (ma ま, マ, mi み, ミ, mu む, ム, me め, メ, mo も, モ; mya みゃ, ミャ, myu みゅ, ミュ, myo みょ, ミョ)
Phonetically [m], the sound in E *meet*, *most*, etc.

3.17 y (ya や, ヤ, yu ゆ, ユ, yo よ, ヨ)
Phonetically [j], the semivowel corresponding to the vowel **i** [i]. It is like the sound in E *yes*, *you*, etc. **ya**, **yu**, **yo** can follow consonants such as **p**, **b**, **k**, **g**, **h**, **m**, **n** and form one syllable. In that case the resulting combinations are called **yoo-oñ**.

3.18 r (ra ら, ラ, ri り, リ, ru る, ル, re れ, レ, ro ろ, ロ; rya りゃ, リャ, ryu りゅ, リュ, ryo りょ, リョ)
Phonetically, J **r** is often a retroflex stop [ɖ] initially and flap [ɾ]

between vowels. Unlike E and other European *r*, it is made with a single tap of the tip of the tongue against the front upper teeth. It sometimes sounds like *d* to a European ear.

3.19 w (wa わ, ワ)

Phonetically [ɰ], the semivowel corresponding to the vowel **u** [ɯ]. Like J **u**, it lacks lip-rounding which usually accompanies European *w*-sound.

3.20 ñ (ん, ン)

ñ is peculiar to J. Learners should never confuse this sound with **n** treated in 3.11. Though usually spelled with the same letter **n** in the Roman alphabet, **n** and **ñ** are quite different in J. While **n** is a pure consonant and is always followed by a vowel or **y**, **ñ** appears word-finally, before a consonant, a vowel, and **y**, but never at the beginning of a word. **ñ** is called **hatsuoñ**. It is always long enough to make a syllable by itself (see 4). Besides, **ñ** has the following varieties according to the position in which it appears. The phonetic property common to all the following variants is that they are syllabic nasals. Thus,

(1) in word-final position: Phonetically syllabic [ɴ], a rather difficult sound for foreign learners. It is made further back than E *ng* [ŋ] (between the backmost part of the tongue and uvula). Examples *eñ* (yen), *hoñ* (book).

(2) before **z**, **j**, **t**, **d**, **ch**, **ts**, **n**, and **r**: Phonetically syllabic [n], nearly the same as E *n*, but longer. Examples *bañzai* (hurrah), *heñji* (answer), *kañtoku* (manager), *koñdo* (this time), *deñchi* (cell), *kañtsuu* (penetration), *oñna* (woman), *señro* (rail).

(3) before **f**, **b**, **p**, and **m**: Phonetically syllabic [m], the same as E *m*, but longer. Examples *iñfure* (inflation), *biñboo* (poverty), *kiñpatsu* (blonde), *koñmori* (thickly).

(4) before **k** and **g**: Phonetically syllabic [ŋ], the same as E *ng*, but longer. Examples *keñka* (quarrel), *sañgo* (coral).

(5) before **s** and **sh**: To be phonetically exact, a nasalized vowel [ĩ], but learners may use [ɴ] in this position. Examples *keñsa* (inspection), *deñsha* (electric train). English-speaking people are advised not to use their *n* here, because they often insert a *t*-sound between *n* and the following *s* or *sh*. The result is *nts* or *nch*, which may sometimes be unintelligible to a Japanese listener.

(6) before **h**, **y**, **w**, and a vowel: Phonetically nasalized vowels like [ĩ], [ẽ], [ɯ̃], etc. Learners, however, may use [ɴ] in these positions. Examples *hañhañ* (fifty-fifty), *pañya* (bakery), *deñwa* (telephone), *heñi* (variation), *dañatsu* (oppression). They should

never use *n* in these positions, since the resulting pronunciation would often be unintelligible. Note the following distinctions: *hiñi* (dignity) vs. *hi ni* (by a day), *kiñeñ* (no smoking) vs. *kineñ* (commemoration), *fuñeñ* (smoke of a volcano) vs. *funeñ* (non-flammable).

3. 21 Double consonants (っ, ッ)

In J, double consonants appear in the combination of **kk**, **ss**, **ssh** (**s**+**sh**), **tt**, **tch** (**t**+**ch**), **tts** (**t**+**ts**), and **pp** as in *sekkeñ* (soap), *bessoo* (villa), *issho* (together), *kitto* (certainly), *itchi* (agreement), *mittsu* (three), *suppai* (sour). English-speaking learners are warned against regarding them as single consonants as in *lesson*, *butter*, *catcher*, etc. They should pronounce them twice as the *c*'s in *thick cloud*, *sh*'s in *reddish shoes*, *t*'s in *hot tea*, *tch* in *hit children*, *p*'s in *hope peace*, etc. To Japanese ears, the first part of a double consonant is considered an independent sound and is counted as consituting another syllable (see 4.). For example, while the second **t** in *kitto* (certainly) is the "normal" **t**, the first **t** is regarded as an independent sound referred to as **sokuoñ** and is written with a smaller *kana* letter っ, ッ (the Roman letter **q** is used by some linguists to represent it, as in *kiqto*), and the word is counted as making three syllables (not two). Likewise, *sekkeñ* (i.e. *seqkeñ*) constitutes four syllables. Note the following distinctions between single and double consonants: *sekeñ* (world) vs. *sekkeñ* (soap), *sasoo to* (in order to stab) vs. *sassoo to* (smartly), *hato* (pigeon) vs. *hatto* (surprisedly), *ichi* (location) vs. *itchi* (agreement), *mitsu* (honey) vs. *mittsu* (three), *supai* (spy) vs. *suppai* (sour).

4. Syllables

J syllables (to be more exact, beats, or technically, morae) are normally composed of a consonant and a vowel in that order, the exceptions being **ñ** ん, ン (see 3.20) and **q** っ, ッ (see 3.21). See the table of the J syllabary on the front endpaper. J syllables tend to be of nearly equal length, though **ñ** and **q** are usually pronounced slightly shorter. Thus, *teashi* (limbs) (three syllables) is said nearly three times longer than *te* (hand) (one syllable).

5. Accent

J does not have an accent system of strong and weak stress like E, and each syllable is said with nearly equal strength. Instead, J has a pitch accent system. The degrees of the pitch of voice depend on the rate of vibration of the vocal cords. When the vibration is fast the pitch is high, and when the rate is slow the pitch is low. The accent patterns of standard J are most clearly explained in terms of two significant levels of pitch: **high** and **low**, and the **accent nucleus**. Words are divided into two classes: words with and without an accent nucleus. In all words which have an accent nucleus, the syllable where the nucleus falls and the preceding syllables (except the first one which is automatically low) are pronounced high, and every syllable that follows the nucleus is said low. In this dictionary accent nucleus is marked with ˥, and the automatic rise on the second syllable is marked with ˹. Thus,

(1) Words with an accent nucleus on the first syllable are: *hi˥* (fire), *ne˥ko* (cat), *i˥nochi* (life), *so˥rosoro* (slowly).

(2) Words with a nucleus on the second syllable are: *i˹nu˥* (dog), *ko˹ko˥ro* (mind), *i˹ke˥bana* (flower arrangement).

(3) Words with a nucleus on the third syllable are: *o˹toko˥* (man), *a˹maga˥sa* (umbrella), *ka˹rai˥bari* (bravado).

(4) Words with a nucleus on the fourth syllable are: *o˹tooto˥* (younger brother), *wa˹tashibu˥ne* (ferry boat), *shi˹dareya˥nagi* (weeping willow).

(5) Words without an accent nucleus are automatically pronounced with the first syllable low and all the succeeding syllables are kept high (though actually with a slight gradual descent). They are: *hi* (day), *u˹shi* (cattle), *ka˹tachi* (shape), *to˹modachi* (friend). Compare the following pair of phrases: *hi˥ ga* (the fire is...) and *hi ˹ga* (the day is...), the former *hi* having a nucleus on it, the latter *hi* without a nucleus.

A word may lose its original accent pattern when it becomes a part of a compound word which then has its own accent pattern as a single word. Thus, *ga˹ikoku* (foreign country) and *yu˹ubiñ* (mail) but *ga˹ikoku-yu˥ubiñ* (foreign mail), *o˥ñgaku* (music) and *ga˹kkoo* (school), but *o˹ñgaku-ga˥kkoo* (music school), and so on. In this dictionary, only those compounds given as main entries are marked with accent.

APPENDIX 2

Outline of Japanese Grammar

1 Noun

Japanese nouns have no gender or case. There is no distinction between singular and plural: *hoñ* (本) means 'a book' or 'books.' But some suffixes are used to indicate the plural: *kare-ra* (they), *kodomo-tachi* (children). Some nouns are capable of forming plurals by reduplication, sometimes with sound changes: *yama-yama* (mountains), and *hito-bito* (people).

1.1 There is a large class of nouns whose function is chiefly grammatical. They are used in making phrases in which these nouns are preceded by a modifier. For example, *kita toki* (when I came), *mita koto* (what I saw), *nani-ka taberu mono* (something to eat), etc. Other examples of such nouns are *aida, tame, tokoro, wake,* etc.

2 Verb

Verbs are classified into the following three groups: consonant-stem verbs, vowel-stem verbs and irregular verbs.

2.1 Consonant-stem verb (*u*-verbs)

The verbs in this group have a consonant preceding final '*u*' in the dictionary form. Note that all verbs ending in vowel plus '*u*' in their dictionary form are also consonant stem verbs; the original '*w*' in these verbs has simply been lost in the modern language: *kawu* > *kau*, *hirowu* > *hirou*, etc.

Consonant-stem verbs are marked [C] in this dictionary.

2.2 Vowel-stem verb (*ru*-verbs)

The verbs in this group end with a final '*-ru*' preceded by '*i*' or '*e*' in the dictionary form. However, not all verbs that end thus are vowel-stem verbs, since there are some consonant-stem verbs which end with '*-iru*' or '*-eru*.'

> *hairu* (enter), *hashiru* (run), *iru* (need), *kiru* (cut), *shiru* (know), *kaeru* (return).

Vowel-stem verbs are marked [V] in this dictionary.

2.3 Irregular verb

There are only two irregular verbs, *suru* (do) (and those verbs formed with *suru*: *meñsuru*, *tassuru*, etc.) and *kuru* (come), which are irregular only in their stems.

Irregular verbs are marked [I] in this dictionary.

3 Conjugations of Verbs

Basic Verb Forms

	Ending	Consonant-stem verbs		Vowel-stem verb	Irregular verb	Irregular verb
Dictionary form	-u	kak·u (write)	yob·u (call)	tabe·ru (eat)	s·uru (do)	k·uru (come)
masu-form	-masu	kaki-masu	yobi-masu	tabe-masu	shi-masu	ki-masu
Negative	-nai	kaka-nai	yoba-nai	tabe-nai	shi-nai	ko-nai
te-form	-t[d]e	kai-te	yoñ-de	tabe-te	shi-te	ki-te
ta-form	-t[d]a	kai-ta	yoñ-da	tabe-ta	shi-ta	ki-ta
tara-form	-t[d]ara	kai-tara	yoñ-dara	tabe-tara	shi-tara	ki-tara
tari-form	-t[d]ari	kai-tari	yoñ-dari	tabe-tari	shi-tari	ki-tari
Desiderative	-tai	kaki-tai	yobi-tai	tabe-tai	shi-tai	ki-tai
Provisional	-ba	kake-ba	yobe-ba	tabere-ba	sure-ba	kure-ba
Tentative	-oo -yoo	kak-oo	yob-oo	tabe-yoo	shi-yoo	ko-yoo
Imperative	-e -ro	kak-e	yob-e	tabe-ro	shi-ro	ko-i
Potential	-eru -rareru	kak-eru	yob-eru	tabe-rareru	(dekiru)	ko-rareru
Passive	-reru -rareru	kaka-reru	yoba-reru	tabe-rareru	sa-reru	ko-rareru
Causative	-seru -saseru	kaka-seru	yoba-seru	tabe-saseru	sa-seru	ko-saseru
Causative-passive	-serareru -saserareru	kaka-serareru	yoba-serareru	tabe-saserareru	saserareru	ko-saserareru

3.1 Dictionary form

This is the form by which verbs are listed in the dictionary. The dictionary form of all Japanese verbs ends in '*u*.' This form is in fact the non-past tense of a verb.

Watashi wa iku. (I go/will go.)

3.2 Continuative form (*masu*-form)

The continuative base of a consonant-stem verb is made by replacing the final '*u*' with '*i*': *kaku* (write) > *kaki-masu*. In the case of a vowel-stem verb, it is made by dropping the final '*ru*': *taberu* (eat) > *tabe-masu*. Irregular verbs are: *suru* (do) > *shi-masu*, *kuru* (come) > *ki-masu*. The following five formal, polite verbs are slightly irregular in dropping '*r*' in their continuative forms.

gozaru (be) — *gozari-masu* > *gozai-masu*
irassharu (go, come) — *irasshari-masu* > *irasshai-masu*
kudasaru (give) — *kudasari-masu* > *kudasai-masu*
nasaru (do) — *nasari-masu* > *nasai-masu*
ossharu (say) — *osshari-masu* > *osshai-masu*

'*-masu*' is used to make the tone of speech polite, and has no concrete meaning in itself.

The conjugation of '*-masu*'

Negative	-maseñ
te-form	-mashi-te
ta-form	-mashi-ta
ba-form	-masure-ba
Tentative	-mashoo

3.3 Negative form (*nai*-form)

The negative base of a consonant-stem verb is made by replacing the final '*u*' with '*a*': *kaku* (write) > *kaka-nai*. In modern Japanese '*w*' is retained only before '*a*,' so those verbs which end in vowel plus '*u*' in the dictionary form in the modern language, but which had an original '*w*' (see 2.1), retain this in the negative form: *ka(w)u* > *kawa-nai*, *hiro(w)u* > *hirowa-nai*. In the case of a vowel-stem verb, the negative base is made by dropping the final '*ru*': *taberu* (eat) > *tabe-nai*. Irregular verbs are: *suru* (do) > *shi-nai*, *kuru* (come) > *ko-nai*.

The conjugation of '*nai*'

te-form	-naku-te
ta-form	-nakat-ta
ba-form	-nakere-ba

3.4 Gerund (*te*-form)

In the case of a vowel-stem verb, the gerund is made by adding '*te*' to the stem.

In the consonant-stem conjugation, however, the verbs undergo sound changes according to the final consonant of the stem.

ka-	ku	ka-	i	-te	write
oyo-	gu	oyo-	i	-de	swim
to-	bu	to-	ñ	-de	jump
no-	mu	no-	ñ	-de	drink
shi-	nu	shi-	ñ	-de	die
hana-	su	hana-	shi	-te	speak
ka-	u	ka-	t	-te	buy
no-	ru	no-	t	-te	ride
ma-	tsu	ma-	t	-te	wait

For the uses of the *te*-form, see under the main entry for '*-te*.' The past tense (*ta*-form) is simply made be replacing the '*-te*' with '*-ta*.'

3.5 Provisional form (*ba*-form)

The provisional form of a verb is made by replacing the final '*-u*' with '*e*' and adding '*-ba*.' This is equivalent to stating that the *ba*-form of a verb is made by dropping the final '*-u*' and adding '*-eba*': *kaku* (write) > *kake-ba*, *taberu* (eat) > *tabere-ba*. Irregular verbs are *suru* (do) > *sure-ba* and *kuru* (come) > *kure-ba*.

This form is also called the conditional form. It indicates the circumstances under which the situation or action in the main clause will be possible.

3.6 Tentative form

The tentative form of a consonant-stem verb is made by changing the final '*u*' to '*oo*': *kaku* (write) > *kak-oo*. In the case of a vowel-stem verb, it is made by changing the final '*-ru*' to '*-yoo*': *taberu* (eat) > *tabe-yoo*. Irregular verbs are *suru* (do) > *shi-yoo*, *kuru* (come) > *ko-yoo*. This form conveys the probable mood and indicates possibility, probability, belief, doubt, etc.

3.7 Imperative form

The imperative form of a consonant-stem verb is made by replacing the final '*u*' with '*e*': *kaku* (write) > *kak-e*. In the case of a vowel-stem verb, it is made by replacing the final '*ru*' with '*ro*': *taberu* (eat) > *tabe-ro*. The irregular verbs are *suru* (do) > *shi-ro* and *kuru* (come) > *ko-i*. This form constitutes a brusque imperative.

The imperative forms of the formal, polite verbs are as follows:

gozaru (be) no form
irassharu (go, come) > *irasshai*
kudasaru (give) > *kudasai*
nasaru (do) > *nasai*
ossharu (say) > *osshai*

3.8 Other verb forms

Forms not dealt with in this 'Outline' can be referred to under the relevant 'ending' in the body of the dictionary.

4 Intransitive and transitive verbs

4.1 Intransitive verb (*vi.*)

An intransitive verb is a verb which is used without a direct object: *aku* (open), *tomaru* (stop), *iku* (go), *kuru* (come), etc.

4.2 Transitive verb (*vt.*)

A transitive verb is a verb which is used with a direct object. The object is usually followed by the particle '*o*.' However, it does not necessarily follow that every noun followed by '*o*' is a direct object, since '*o*' can also denote a location: *kado o magaru* (turn a corner).

Many transitive verbs have intransitive verb partners: *okosu* (wake) / *okiru* (get up), *miru* (look at) / *mieru* (be visible).

Pairs of transitive and intransitive verbs

vt.	*vi.*	Examples
-eru	-aru	ageru (raise) / agaru (rise)
-eru	-u	tsukeru (attach) / tsuku (stick)
-u	-eru	toru (take) / toreru (be taken)
-asu	-u	chirasu (scatter) / chiru (be scattered)
-su	-ru	kaesu (return) / kaeru (come back)

In the case of a small number of verbs, the transitive and intransitive forms are the same: *owaru* (end), *hiraku* (open), etc.

Among the large class of verbs formed by noun plus *suru*, some are transitive, some are intransitive, and some are both transitive and intransitive.

sakusee suru (*vt.*) (I) make (something).
shippai suru (*vi.*) (I) fail.
teñkai suru (*vt.*) (I) develop (something).
(*vi.*) (Something) develops.

5 Copula

The informal form is *da* and the polite form is *desu*.

The conjugation of the copula

	informal	polite
Sentence final form	da	desu
Negative	de nai (ja nai)	de wa arimaseñ (ja arimaseñ)
te-form	de	deshite
ta-form	datta	deshita
ba-form	nara (ba)	deshitara (ba)

6 Adjective

The dictionary form of adjectives ends with '*i*.' Adjectives occur in attributive position: *Kore wa furui kuruma desu.* (This is an old car.), or in predicative position: *Kono kuruma wa furui.* (This car is old.) An adjective can stand by itself as a complete sentence. For example, *Furui* means '(Something) is old.'

Basic adjective forms

Dict. form	samu·i (cold)
ku-form	samu-ku
Negative	samu-kunai
te-form	samu-kute
ta-form	samu-katta
ba-form	samu-kereba

7 Adjectival noun

Adjectival nouns have some functions that ordinary nouns have, and other functions which are similar to adjectives. This class of words is sometimes simply called '*na* word,' since the word '*na*' is used to link an adjectival noun to the following noun or adjectival noun which it modifies. An adjectival noun followed by '*ni*' is an adverb. In this dictionary, '*na*' is treated as a variant of the copula and '*ni*' is a particle indicating manner, and they are written separately: *shizuka na umi* (calm sea), *shizuka ni aruku* (walk quietly).

8 Adverb

Adverbs modify verbs, adjectives and other adverbs. There are true adverbs and derived adverbs. True adverbs include *sugu* (immediately), *mattaku* (very much), *hakkiri* (clearly), etc.
Derived adverbs:

1 Adjectival nouns with the particle '*ni*.'
shizuka ni (quietly)
2 The *ku*-form of adjectives.
hayaku (early), *osoku* (slowly), etc.
3 The *te*-form of verbs.
aratamete (again), *konoñde* (willingly), etc.

9 Interrogative words

When interrogative words are followed by the particles '*ka*' or '*mo*,' or the gerund of the copula plus '*mo*' (i.e. *de mo*), the resulting combinations take on a variety of meanings.

	with 'ka'	with 'mo'		with 'de mo'
		(affirm. verb)	(neg. verb)	
dare (who)	someone	everyone	no one	anyone
dore (which of three or more)	some (one)	every one	none	any one
dochira (which of two)	either	both	neither	either
doo (how)	somehow	every way	no way	any way
doko (where)	somewhere	everywhere	nowhere	anywhere
itsu (when)	sometime	always	never	any time
nani (what)	something	(not used)	nothing	anything

10 Attributive

Attributive refers to a class of words which do not change their form. Some of these correspond to English pronominal adjectives: *kono* (this), *sono* (that), *ano* (that over there), *dono* (which), *koñna* (this kind of), *soñna* (that kind of), *añna* (that kind of), *doñna* (what kind of). *Ooki-na* (large), *chiisa-na* (small), *okashi-na* (funny), etc. are also considered attributives. They cannot be classified as adjectival nouns, even though they are followed by '*na*,' because *ooki*, *chiisa* and *okashi* without '*na*' can neither be used as nouns nor be followed by the copula *da* (*desu*).

ko- here (near the speaker)	so- there (far from the speaker and near the listener)	a- over there (far from both speaker and listener)	do- question
kore this (one)	sore that (one)	are that (one)	dore? which (one)?
kono this	sono that	ano that (over there)	dono? which?
koko here	soko there	asoko over there	doko? where?
kochira this side	sochira that side	achira that side	dochira? which side?
koñna this kind of	soñna that kind of	añna that kind of	doñna? what kind of?
koo like this	soo like that	aa like that	doo? how?

11 Conjunction

A conjunction is a word or phrase which is used to link words, phrases, clauses, or sentences. Many Japanese conjunctions are a combination of two or more words: *sore de* (therefore), *soo suru to* (then).

12 Inflected ending

Inflected endings are attached to a base of a verb, the stem of a verb or adjective, or the copula in order to give a wide range of additional meanings to that verb, adjective or copula: '*-ba*' in *ikeba*, '*-nai*' in *oishikunai*, '*-ta*' in *deshita*, etc.

13 Particle

Particles (*wa*, *ga*, *mo*, *o*, etc.) are unchanging in form and used to indicate the topic, subject, object, etc. of a Japanese sentence as well as functioning in a way similar to prepositions in English: *kara* (away from), *ni* (toward), etc. They are placed after a noun, clause, or sentence, and are sometimes called 'postpositions.'

14 Interjection

An interjection is a word which expresses a strong feeling such as surprise, pain, horror and so on.

aa (oh), *iya* (no), *hora* (look), etc.

15 Prefix

A prefix is a meaning element or a group of meaning elements added to the beginning of a word to form a new word. The new word is written as one word, or sometimes a hyphen is used.

dai- (big), *doo-* (the same), *sai-* (again), etc.

16 Suffix

A suffix is a meaning element or a group of meaning elements added to the end of another word to form a new word; suf. (*a.*) and suf (*a.n.*) indicate that the derived forms are an adjective or adjectival noun respectively.

-dañ (group), *-juu* (through), *-ryuu* (style), etc.

APPENDIX 3

Numbers

Native Japanese counting system

1	hi⌈to⌉tsu	6	mu⌈ttsu⌉
2	fu⌈tatsu⌉	7	na⌈na⌉tsu
3	mi⌈ttsu⌉	8	ya⌈ttsu⌉
4	yo⌈ttsu⌉	9	ko⌈ko⌉notsu
5	i⌈tsu⌉tsu	10	to⌉o
		?	i⌉kutsu

Chinese-derived system

1	i⌈chi⌉ (一)	100	hya⌈ku⌉ (百)
2	ni⌉ (二)	200	ni-⌈hyaku
3	sa⌈ñ (三)	300	sañ⌉-byaku
4	shi⌉, yo⌉ñ (四)	400	yoñ⌉-hyaku
5	go⌉ (五)	500	go-⌈hyaku
6	ro⌈ku⌉ (六)	600	rop-⌈pyaku
7	na⌉na, shi⌈chi⌉ (七)	700	na⌈na⌉-hyaku
8	ha⌈chi⌉ (八)	800	hap-⌈pyaku
9	ku⌉, kyu⌉u (九)	900	kyu⌉u-hyaku
10	ju⌉u (十)	1,000	se⌉ñ (千)
11	ju⌈u-ichi⌉	2,000	ni-⌈se⌉ñ
12	ju⌈u-ni⌉	3,000	sa⌈ñ-ze⌉ñ
13	ju⌉u-sañ	4,000	yo⌈ñ-se⌉ñ
14	ju⌈u-shi⌉, ju⌈u-yoñ⌉	5,000	go-⌈se⌉ñ
15	ju⌉u-go	6,000	ro⌈ku-se⌉ñ
16	ju⌈u-roku⌉	7,000	na⌈na-se⌉ñ
17	ju⌈u-shichi⌉, ju⌈u-na⌉na	8,000	ha⌈s-se⌉ñ
18	ju⌈u-hachi⌉	9,000	kyu⌈u-se⌉ñ
19	ju⌉u-ku, ju⌈u-kyu⌉u	10,000	i⌈chi-ma⌉ñ (1万)
20	ni⌉-juu	100,000	ju⌈u-ma⌉ñ
30	sa⌉ñ-juu	1,000,000	hya⌈ku-ma⌉ñ
40	yo⌉ñ-juu	10,000,000	se⌈ñ-ma⌉ñ
50	go-⌈ju⌉u	100,000,000	i⌈chi⌉-oku (1億)
60	ro⌈ku-ju⌉u	1,000,000,000	ju⌉u-oku
70	shi⌈chi-ju⌉u, na⌈na⌉-juu	10,000,000,000	hya⌈ku⌉-oku
80	ha⌈chi-ju⌉u	100,000,000,000	se⌉ñ-oku
90	kyu⌉u-juu	1,000,000,000,000	i⌉t-choo (1兆)

APPENDIX 4 Counters

	-fuñ (分) minutes	-hai (杯) cups	-haku (泊) stays	-hatsu (発) shots	-heñ (遍) times	-hiki (匹) fish	-ho (歩) steps	-hoñ (本) bottles	-kai (階) floors	-keñ (軒) houses	-soku (足) shoes	-wa (羽) birds
1	i⌉p-puñ	i⌉p-pai	i⌈p-paku	i⌈p-patsu⌉	i⌈p-pe⌉ñ	i⌈p-piki⌉	i⌉p-po	i⌉p-poñ	i⌈k-kai	i⌉k-keñ	i⌈s-soku⌉	i⌈chi⌉-wa
2	ni⌉-fuñ	ni⌉-hai	ni⌉-haku	ni⌉-hatsu	ni-⌈he⌉ñ	ni⌉-hiki	ni⌉-ho	ni⌉-hoñ	ni-⌈kai	ni⌉-keñ	ni⌉-soku	ni⌉-wa
3	sa⌉ñ-puñ	sa⌉ñ-bai	sa⌉ñ-paku	sa⌉ñ-patsu	sa⌉ñ-be⌉ñ	sa⌉ñ-biki	sa⌉ñ-po	sa⌉ñ-boñ	sa⌈ñ-gai	sa⌉ñ-geñ	sa⌉ñ-zoku	sāñ⌉-ba
4	yo⌉ñ-puñ	yo⌉ñ-hai	yo⌉ñ-haku	yo⌉ñ-hatsu	yo⌉ñ-heñ	yo⌉ñ-hiki	yo⌉ñ-ho	yo⌉n-hoñ	yo⌉ñ-kai	yo⌉ñ-keñ	yo⌉ñ-soku	yo⌉ñ-wa
5	go⌉-fuñ	go⌉-hai	go⌉-haku	go⌉-hatsu	go-⌈he⌉ñ	go⌉-hiki	go⌉-ho	go-⌈hoñ	go-⌈kai	go⌉-keñ	go⌉-soku	go⌉-wa
6	ro⌉p-puñ	ro⌉p-pai	ro⌈p-paku	ro⌈p-patsu⌉	ro⌈p-pe⌉ñ	ro⌈p-piki⌉	ro⌉p-po	ro⌉p-poñ	ro⌈k-kai	ro⌉k-keñ	ro⌈ku-soku⌉	ro⌈ku⌉-wa
7	na⌈na⌉-fuñ	na⌈na⌉-hai	na⌈na⌉-haku	na⌈na⌉-hatsu	na⌈na⌉-heñ	na⌈na⌉-hiki	na⌈na⌉-ho	na⌈na⌉-hoñ	na⌈na-kai	na⌈na⌉-keñ	na⌈na⌉-soku	na⌈na⌉-wa
8	ha⌉p-puñ	ha⌉p-pai	ha⌈p-paku	ha⌈p-patsu⌉	ha⌈p-pe⌉ñ	ha⌈p-piki⌉	ha⌉p-po	ha⌉p-poñ	ha⌈k-kai	ha⌉k-keñ	ha⌈s-soku⌉	ha⌈chi⌉-wa
9	kyu⌉u-fuñ	kyu⌉u-hai	kyu⌉u-haku	kyu⌉u-hatsu	kyu⌉u-heñ	kyu⌉u-hiki	kyu⌉u-ho	kyu⌉u-hoñ	kyu⌉u-kai	kyu⌉u-keñ	kyu⌉u-soku	kyu⌉u-wa
10	ji⌉p-puñ	ji⌉p-pai	ji⌈p-paku	ji⌈p-patsu⌉	ji⌈p-pe⌉ñ	ji⌈p-piki⌉	ji⌉p-po	ji⌉p-poñ	ji⌈k-kai	ji⌉k-keñ	ji⌈s-soku⌉	ji⌉p-pa
	ju⌉p-puñ	ju⌉p-pai	ju⌈p-paku	ju⌈p-patsu⌉	ju⌈p-pe⌉ñ	ju⌈p-piki⌉	ju⌉p-po	ju⌉p-poñ	ju⌈k-kai	ju⌉k-keñ	ju⌈s-soku⌉	ju⌉p-pa
How many	na⌉n-puñ	na⌉ñ-bai	na⌉ñ-paku	na⌉ñ-patsu	na⌉ñ-beñ	na⌉ñ-biki	na⌉ñ-po	na⌉ñ-boñ	na⌈ñ-gai	na⌉ñ-geñ	na⌉ñ-zoku	na⌉ñ-ba

APPENDIX 5

Days

1st	tsu⌈itachi⌉	11th	ju⌈u-ichi-nichi⌉	21st	ni⌉juu-ichi-nichi
2nd	fu⌈tsuka	12th	ju⌈u-ni-nichi⌉	22nd	ni⌉juu-ni-nichi
3rd	mi⌈kka	13th	ju⌈u-sa⌉ñ-nichi	23rd	ni⌉juu-sañ-nichi
4th	yo⌈kka	14th	ju⌉u-yokka	24th	ni⌉juu-yokka
5th	i⌈tsuka	15th	ju⌉u-go-nichi	25th	ni⌉juu-go-nichi
6th	mu⌈ika	16th	ju⌈u-roku-nichi⌉	26th	ni⌉juu-roku-nichi
7th	na⌈nu[o]ka	17th	ju⌈u-shichi-nichi⌉	27th	ni⌉juu-shichi-nichi
8th	yo⌈oka	18th	ju⌈u-hachi-nichi⌉	28th	ni⌉juu-hachi-nichi
9th	ko⌈konoka⌉	19th	ju⌉u-ku-nichi	29th	ni⌉juu-ku-nichi
10th	to⌈oka	20th	ha⌈tsuka	30th	sa⌈ñju⌉u-nichi
				31st	sa⌉ñjuu-ichi-nichi

ni⌈chiyo⌉o(bi)	日曜(日)	Sunday
ge⌈tsuyo⌉o(bi)	月曜(日)	Monday
ka⌈yo⌉o(bi)	火曜(日)	Tuesday
su⌈iyo⌉o(bi)	水曜(日)	Wednesday
mo⌈kuyo⌉o(bi)	木曜(日)	Thursday
ki⌈ñyo⌉o(bi)	金曜(日)	Friday
do⌈yo⌉o(bi)	土曜(日)	Saturday

APPENDIX 6

Months

January	i⌈chi-gatsu⌉
February	ni-⌈gatsu⌉
March	sa⌉ñ-gatsu
April	shi-⌈gatsu⌉
May	go⌉-gatsu
June	ro⌈ku-gatsu⌉
July	shi⌈chi-gatsu⌉
August	ha⌈chi-gatsu⌉
September	ku⌉-gatsu
October	ju⌈u-gatsu⌉
November	ju⌈u-ichi-gatsu⌉
December	ju⌈u-ni-gatsu⌉

APPENDIX 7

Japanese Government Ministries and Agencies

Gaimu-shoo (外務省)	Ministry of Foreign Affairs
Hoomu-shoo (法務省)	Ministry of Justice
Kañkyoo-shoo (環境省)	Ministry of the Environment
Keizai-sañgyoo-shoo (経済産業省)	Ministry of Economy, Trade and Industry
Kokudo-kootsuu-shoo (国土交通省)	Ministry of Land, Infrastructure and Transport
Koosee-roodoo-shoo (厚生労働省)	Ministry of Health, Labor and Welfare
Moñbu-kagaku-shoo (文部科学省)	Ministry of Education, Culture, Sports, Science and Technology
Nooriñ-suisañ-shoo (農林水産省)	Ministry of Agriculture, Forestry and Fisheries
Soomu-shoo (総務省)	Ministry of Public Management, Home Affairs, Posts and Telecommunications
Zaimu-shoo (財務省)	Ministry of Finance

Booee-choo (防衛庁) Defense Agency
Booeeshisetsu-choo (防衛施設庁) Defense Facilities Administration Agency
Buñka-choo (文化庁) Agency for Cultural Affairs
Chuushoo-kigyoo-choo (中小企業庁) Small and Medium Enterprise Agency
Kaijoohoañ-choo (海上保安庁) Japan Coast Guard
Kainañshiñpañ-choo (海難審判庁) Marine Accidents Inquiry Agency
Keesatsu-choo (警察庁) National Police Agency
Keñsatsu-choo (検察庁) Public Prosecutors Office
Kiñyuu-choo (金融庁) Financial Service Agency
Kishoo-choo (気象庁) Meteorological Agency
Kokuzee-choo (国税庁) National Tax Agency
Kooañchoosa-choo (公安調査庁) Public Security Investigation Agency
Kunai-choo (宮内庁) Imperial Household Agency
Riñya-choo (林野庁) Forestry Agency
Shakaihokeñ-choo (社会保険庁) Social Insurance Agency
Shigeñ-enerugii-choo (資源ｴﾈﾙｷﾞｰ庁) Agency of Natural Resources and Energy
Shokuryoo-choo (食糧庁) Food Agency
Shooboo-choo (消防庁) Fire and Disaster Management Agency
Suisañ-choo (水産庁) Fisheries Agency
Tokkyo-choo (特許庁) Japan Patent Office

APPENDIX 8

Japanese Political Parties

Jiyuu Miñshutoo	(自由民主党)	Liberal Democratic Party
Shakai Miñshutoo	(社会民主党)	Social Democratic Party
Jiyuutoo	(自由党)	Liberal Party
Koomeitoo	(公明党)	New Komeito
Nihoñ Kyoosañtoo	(日本共産党)	Japanese Communist Party
Miñshutoo	(民主党)	Democratic Party

APPENDIX 9

Japanese Historical Periods and Eras

Joomoñ-jidai	縄 文 時 代	10000 – 300 B.C.
Yayoi-jidai	弥 生 時 代	300 B.C. – A.D. 300
Kofuñ-jidai	古 墳 時 代	A.D. 300 – 710
Nara-jidai	奈 良 時 代	710 – 794
Heeañ-jidai	平 安 時 代	794 – 1192
Kamakura-jidai	鎌 倉 時 代	1192 – 1333
Muromachi-jidai	室 町 時 代	1336 – 1573
Señgoku-jidai	戦 国 時 代	ca. 1480 – ca. 1570
Azuchi-Momoyama-jidai	安土・桃山時代	1573 – 1603
Edo-jidai	江 戸 時 代	1603 – 1867
Meeji-jidai	明 治 時 代	1868 – 1912
Taishoo-jidai	大 正 時 代	1912 – 1926
Shoowa-jidai	昭 和 時 代	1926 – 1989
Heesee-jidai	平 成 時 代	1989 –

After 1868, 'jidai' refers to emperors' names.

APPENDIX 10

Chronological Table of Eras

1868	Meeji	1	1911		44	1954		29
1869	明治	2	1912	Meeji	45	1955		30
1870		3	1913	Taishoo	2	1956		31
1871		4	1914	大正	3	1957		32
1872		5	1915		4	1958		33
1873		6	1916		5	1959		34
1874		7	1917		6	1960		35
1875		8	1918		7	1961		36
1876		9	1919		8	1962		37
1877		10	1920		9	1963		38
1878		11	1921		10	1964		39
1879		12	1922		11	1965		40
1880		13	1923		12	1966		41
1881		14	1924		13	1967		42
1882		15	1925		14	1968		43
1883		16	1926	Taishoo	15	1969		44
1884		17	1927	Shoowa	2	1970		45
1885		18	1928	昭和	3	1971		46
1886		19	1929		4	1972		47
1887		20	1930		5	1973		48
1888		21	1931		6	1974		49
1889		22	1932		7	1975		50
1890		23	1933		8	1976		51
1891		24	1934		9	1977		52
1892		25	1935		10	1978		53
1893		26	1936		11	1979		54
1894		27	1937		12	1980		55
1895		28	1938		13	1981		56
1896		29	1939		14	1982		57
1897		30	1940		15	1983		58
1898		31	1941		16	1984		59
1899		32	1942		17	1985		60
1900		33	1943		18	1986		61
1901		34	1944		19	1987		62
1902		35	1945		20	1988		63
1903		36	1946		21	1989	Shoowa	64
1904		37	1947		22	1990	Heesee	2
1905		38	1948		23	1991	平成	3
1906		39	1949		24	1992		4
1907		40	1950		25	1993		5
1908		41	1951		26	1994		6
1909		42	1952		27	1995		7
1910		43	1953		28	1996		8

A

a *indef. art.* ★ In Japanese, there are no words corresponding to the English articles, and 'a' is not translated: read a book (*hoñ o yomu*) 本を読む.
1 (one) hi⌈to⌉tsu 一つ; i⌈chi⌉ 1: an apple (*riñgo hitotsu*) りんご一つ / a sheet of paper (*ichi-mai no kami*) 1 枚の紙 / an hour (*ichi-jikañ*) 1 時間.
2 (a certain) a⌉ru ある: in a sense (*aru imi de*) ある意味で.
3 (any) ... to i⌈u mono⌉ …というもの: A dog is a faithful animal. (*Inu* (*to iu mono*) *wa chuujitsu na doobutsu desu.*) 犬(というもの)は忠実な動物です.
4 (per) ... ni (tsu⌉ki) …に(つき): I work seven hours a day. (*Watashi wa ichi-nichi ni* (*tsuki*) *nana-jikañ hataraku.*) 私は 1 日に(つき) 7 時間働く.

abandon *vt.* **1** (give up) ... o ya⌈meru …をやめる ⓥ; su⌈teru 捨てる ⓥ: abandon a plan (*keekaku o yameru*) 計画をやめる / abandon hope (*kiboo o suteru*) 希望を捨てる.
2 (leave) ... o mi⌈suteru …を見捨てる ⓥ: He abandoned his wife and children. (*Kare wa tsuma to kodomo o misuteta.*) 彼は妻と子どもを見捨てた.

abbreviate *vt.* ... o sho⌈oryaku suru …を省略する Ⓘ; rya⌈ku⌉su 略す Ⓒ: 'January' is abbreviated to 'Jan.' ('*January*' *wa* '*Jan.*' *to ryakusareru.*) January は Jan. と略される.

abbreviation *n.* sho⌈oryaku 省略; rya⌈kugo 略語: 'TV' is an abbreviation for 'television.' ('*TV*' *wa* '*television*' *no ryakugo desu.*) TV は television の略語です.

ability *n.* **1** (competence) no⌉oryoku 能力: He has the ability to pay. (*Kare wa shiharau nooryoku ga aru.*) 彼は支払う能力がある.
2 (talent) sa⌈inoo 才能: He is a man of great ability. (*Kare wa sainoo no aru hito desu.*) 彼は才能のある人です.

able *adj.* **1** (capable) ... ko⌈to⌉ ga de⌈ki⌉ru …ことができる: She is able to play the piano. (*Kanojo wa piano o hiku koto ga dekiru.*) 彼女はピアノを弾くことができる.
2 (skillful) yu⌈unoo na 有能な: an able manager (*yuunoo na keeeesha*) 有能な経営者.

aboard *prep.* ... ni no⌈tte …に乗って: He is now aboard a ship. (*Kare wa ima fune ni notte imasu.*) 彼は今船に乗っています.
— *adv.* ... ni no⌈tte …に乗って: go aboard (*norikomu*) 乗り込む.

abolish *vt.* ... o ha⌈ishi suru …を廃止する Ⓘ: abolish capital punishment (*shikee o haishi suru*) 死刑を廃止する.

about *prep., adv.* **1** (nearly) ya⌉ku 約; o⌈yoso およそ: We walked about five kilometers. (*Watashi-tachi wa yaku go-kiro aruita.*) 私たちは約 5 キロ歩いた.
2 (concerning) ... ni tsu⌉ite …について: This is a book about dogs. (*Kore wa inu ni tsuite no hoñ desu.*) これは犬についての本です.
3 (around) a⌈chi⌉-kochi あちこち: The children ran about the park. (*Kodomo-tachi wa kooeñ o achikochi kakemawatta.*) 子どもたちは公園をあちこち駆け回った.
be about to do ⟨verb⟩-(y)oo to suru …(よ)うとする Ⓘ: He was about to leave the room. (*Kare wa heya o deyoo to shita.*) 彼は部屋を出ようとした.

above *prep.* **1** (over) ... no u⌈e⌉ ni …の上に: The moon rose above the hill. (*Tsuki ga oka no ue ni nobotta.*) 月が丘の上に昇った.

2 (more than) i˥joo 以上: The height of the tree is above five meters. (*Sono ki no takasa wa go-meetoru ijoo aru.*) その木の高さは5メートル以上ある.

abroad *adv.* ga⌈ikoku e [ni] 外国へ[に]: I would like to go abroad. (*Watashi wa gaikoku e ikitai.*) 私は外国へ行きたい. / She is living abroad. (*Kanojo wa gaikoku ni suñde iru.*) 彼女は外国に住んでいる.

absence *n.* (from school) ke⌈sseki 欠席; (from work) ke⌈kkiñ 欠勤; (lack) ke⌈tsuboo 欠乏: absence of vitamin C (*bitamiñ C no ketsuboo*) ビタミンCの欠乏.

absent *adj.* ya⌈su˥ñde (iru) 休んで(いる); fu⌈zai no 不在の; ke⌈sseki shite 欠席して: He has been absent from school for the past two days. (*Kare wa kono futsuka-kañ gakkoo o yasuñde iru.*) 彼はこの二日間学校を休んでいる.

absolute *adj.* **1** ze⌈ttai no 絶対の: I have absolute trust in him. (*Watashi wa kare ni zettai no shiñrai o oite imasu.*) 私は彼に絶対の信頼をおいています.

2 ma⌈ttaku˥ no まったくの: You are an absolute fool. (*Kimi wa mattaku no baka da.*) 君はまったくのばかだ.

absolutely *adv.* ma⌈ttaku まったく: It's absolutely impossible to do so. (*Soo suru koto wa mattaku fukanoo da.*) そうすることはまったく不可能だ.

absorb *vt.* ... o kyu⌈ushuu suru ...を吸収する Ⓘ; su⌈iko˥mu 吸い込む Ⓒ: This cloth absorbs water well. (*Kono nuno wa mizu o yoku kyuushuu suru.*) この布は水をよく吸収する.

abstain *vi.* (... o) ya⌈meru (...を)やめる Ⓥ; tsu⌈tsushi˥mu 慎む Ⓒ: abstain from smoking (*tabako o yameru*) たばこをやめる.

abstract *adj.* chu⌈ushoo-teki na 抽象的な: an abstract idea (*chuushoo-teki na kañgae*) 抽象的な考え / an abstract painting (*chuushoo-ga*) 抽象画.

absurd *adj.* fu⌈go˥ori na 不合理な; ba⌈ka˥geta ばかげた: make an absurd mistake (*bakageta machigai o suru*) ばかげた間違いをする.

abundant *adj.* ho⌈ofu na 豊富な; yu˥taka na 豊かな: The country is abundant in natural resources. (*Sono kuni wa teñneñ shigeñ ga hoofu da.*) その国は天然資源が豊富だ.

abuse *vt.* (use wrongly) ... o ra⌈ñyoo suru ...を乱用する Ⓘ; a⌈kuyoo suru 悪用する Ⓘ: abuse one's authority (*shokkeñ o rañyoo suru*) 職権を乱用する.

— *n.* (wrong use) ra⌈ñyoo 乱用; (cruel treatment) gya⌈kutai 虐待: child abuse (*jidoo gyakutai*) 児童虐待.

academy *n.* se⌈ñmoñ-ga˥kkoo 専門学校: an academy of music (*oñgaku-gakkoo*) 音楽学校.

accent *n.* **1** na⌈mari˥ なまり: a Northeastern accent (*toohoku namari*) 東北なまり.

2 (pitch accent) a˥kuseñto アクセント: the accent in a word (*tañgo no akuseñto*) 単語のアクセント.

accept *vt.* **1** (take) ... o u⌈ketoru ...を受け取る Ⓒ: He accepted her gift. (*Kare wa kanojo no okurimono o uketotta.*) 彼は彼女の贈り物を受け取った.

2 (agree to) ... o mi⌈tomeru ...を認める Ⓥ: I don't accept what he says. (*Watashi wa kare no iu koto wa mitomemaseñ.*) 私は彼のいうことは認めません.

3 (undertake) ... o to˥ru ...をとる Ⓒ; hi⌈kiuke˥ru 引き受ける Ⓥ: I'll accept responsibility for the accident. (*Watashi ga sono jiko no sekiniñ o torimasu.*) 私がその事故の責任をとります.

acceptable *adj.* **1** (satisfactory) ma˥ñzoku na 満足な; u⌈keirerareru 受け入れられる: Such an offer is not acceptable to me. (*Soñna mooshide wa ukeireraremaseñ.*) そんな申し出は受け入れられません.

2 (pleasing) yo⌈rokobare˥ru 喜ばれる: an acceptable gift (*yoroko-*

bareru okurimono) 喜ばれる贈り物.

acceptance *n.* (accepting) u⌈ke-ire 受け入れ; (approval) sho⌈odaku 承諾: find general acceptance (*ippañ ni ukeirerareru*) 一般に受け入れられる.

accident *n.* ji⌉ko 事故: cause an accident (*jiko o okosu*) 事故を起こす / meet with an accident (*jiko ni au*) 事故にあう / prevent an accident (*jiko o fusegu*) 事故を防ぐ / a traffic accident (*kootsuu jiko*) 交通事故.

by accident *adv.* gu⌈uzeñ 偶然: I met her by accident. (*Watashi wa guuzeñ kanojo ni atta.*) 私は偶然彼女に会った.

accidental *adj.* gu⌈uzeñ no 偶然の; o⌈moigakena⌉i 思いがけない: an accidental meeting (*guuzeñ no deai*) 偶然の出会い.

accommodate *vt.* **1** (of a vehicle) ... o no⌈seru …を乗せる V; (hold) shu⌈uyoo suru 収容する I: This car can accommodate four passengers. (*Kono kuruma wa yoniñ noseru koto ga dekimasu.*) この車は4人乗せることができます. / This hall can accommodate three hundred people. (*Kono hooru wa sañbyaku-niñ o shuuyoo dekimasu.*) このホールは300人を収容できます.

2 (adjust) ... ni na⌈re⌉ru …に慣れる V: He soon accommodated himself to his new circumstances. (*Kare wa atarashii kañkyoo ni sugu nareta.*) 彼は新しい環境にすぐ慣れた.

3 (help) ... ni (... o) ka⌈su …に(…を)貸す C: I accommodated him with some money. (*Watashi wa kare ni o-kane o kashite yatta.*) 私は彼にお金を貸してやった.

accommodation *n.* shu⌈kuhaku-shi⌉setsu 宿泊施設: We need accommodations for five. (*Go-niñ buñ no shukuhaku-shisetsu ga hoshii.*) 5人分の宿泊施設が欲しい.

accompany *vt.* **1** (go with) ... ni tsu⌉ite iku …について行く C: I accompanied him on his walk. (*Watashi wa kare no sañpo ni tsuite itta.*) 私は彼の散歩について行った.

2 (play) ... no ba⌈ñsoo o suru …の伴奏をする I: accompany a song on the piano (*piano de uta no bañsoo o suru*) ピアノで歌の伴奏をする.

3 ... o to⌈mona⌉u …を伴う C: A cold is often accompanied by fever. (*Kaze wa shibashiba netsu o tomonau.*) かぜはしばしば熱を伴う.

accomplish *vt.* ... o tas⌈see suru …を達成する I; ka⌈ñsee suru 完成する I: He accomplished the task in a week. (*Kare wa sono shigoto o isshuu-kañ de kañsee shita.*) 彼はその仕事を1週間で完成した.

accord *n.* i⌈tchi 一致: We came to an accord with them regarding that matter. (*Watashi-tachi wa sono moñdai ni tsuite kare-ra to ikeñ ga itchi shita.*) 私たちはその問題について彼らと意見が一致した.

accordingly *adv.* **1** so⌈re ni ooji⌉te それに応じて; shi⌈tagatte 従って: He understood the danger and acted accordingly. (*Kare wa kikeñ o shitte ite sore ni oojite koodoo shita.*) 彼は危険を知っていてそれに応じて行動した.

2 da⌉ kara だから; so⌈re de それで: She had fever; accordingly we sent her home. (*Kanojo wa netsu ga atta. Da kara uchi made okutta.*) 彼女は熱があった. だから家まで送った.

according to *prep.* ... ni yo⌈re⌉ba …によれば; ... ni shi⌈tagatte …に従って: According to this book, what you say is wrong. (*Kono hoñ ni yoreba, anata no iu koto wa machigatte imasu.*) この本によれば, あなたの言うことは間違っています.

account *n.* **1** (explanation) se⌈tsumee 説明: demand an account (*setsumee o motomeru*) 説明を求める / give an account (*setsumee suru*) 説明する.

2 (of a bank) ko⌈oza 口座: open [close] a bank account (*kooza o hiraku* [*tojiru*]) 口座を開く[閉じる].

3 (of money) ka⌈ñjo⌉o 勘定: We

paid our account of 5,000 yen. (*Goseñ-eñ no kañjoo o haratta.*) 5千円の勘定を払った.

account for *vt.* ...no se⌈tsumee ga tsu⌉ku ...の説明がつく [C]: That accounts for his conduct. (*Sore de kare no koodoo no setsumee ga tsuku.*) それで彼の行動の説明がつく.

accuracy *n.* se⌈ekakusa 正確さ: He took the measurement with accuracy. (*Kare wa suñpoo o seekaku ni hakatta.*) 彼は寸法を正確に測った.

accurate *adj.* se⌈ekaku na 正確な; me⌈ñmitsu na 綿密な: an accurate calculation (*seekaku na keesañ*) 正確な計算 / He is accurate in his work. (*Kare wa shigoto ga meñmitsu da.*) 彼は仕事が綿密だ.

accuse *vt.* ...o ut⌈tae⌉ru ...を訴える [V]; hi⌉nañ suru 非難する [I]: She accused him of stealing her money. (*Kanojo wa kare ga kanojo no o-kane o nusuñda to itte kare o uttaeta.*) 彼女は彼が彼女のお金を盗んだと言って彼を訴えた.

accustom *vt.* ...o na⌈ra⌉su ...を慣らす [C]: accustom a dog to the cold (*inu o samusa ni narasu*) 犬を寒さに慣らす.

be accustomed to ... *vt.* ...ni na⌉rete iru ...に慣れている [V]: I am accustomed to getting up early. (*Watashi wa hayaku okiru koto ni narete iru.*) 私は早く起きることに慣れている.

ache *vi.* ...ga i⌈ta⌉i ...が痛い; u⌈zu⌉ku うずく [C]: My tooth aches. (*Ha ga itai.*) 歯が痛い.

— *n.* i⌈tami⌉ 痛み: The ache in my leg has gone. (*Ashi no itami ga kieta.*) 足の痛みが消えた.

achieve *vt.* ...o ta⌈ssee suru 達成する [I]; na⌈shitoge⌉ru 成し遂げる [V]: achieve one's purpose (*mokuteki o tassee suru*) 目的を達成する.

achievement *n.* **1** ta⌈ssee 達成: the achievement of one's aims (*mokuteki no tassee*) 目的の達成.

2 gyo⌈oseki 業績: His achievements as a scientist are outstanding. (*Kare no kagakusha to shite no gyooseki wa subarashii.*) 彼の科学者としての業績はすばらしい.

acid *adj.* su⌈ppa⌉i 酸っぱい; sa⌈ñsee no 酸性の: sour fruit (*suppai kudamono*) 酸っぱい果物 / acid rain (*sañseeu*) 酸性雨.

— *n.* sa⌉ñ 酸.

acknowledge *vt.* **1** (admit) ... o mi⌈tomeru ...を認める [V]: He acknowledged his mistakes. (*Kare wa jibuñ no machigai o mitometa.*) 彼は自分の間違いを認めた.

2 (express thanks) ... no re⌈e o iu ...の礼を言う [C]: I forgot to acknowledge the gift. (*Okurimono no ree o iu no o wasureta.*) 贈り物の礼を言うのを忘れた.

acknowledgment *n.* **1** (legal admission) ji⌈niñ 自認: acknowledgment of guilt (*yuuzai no jiniñ*) 有罪の自認.

2 (confirmation of receipt) u⌈ketori no tsuuchi 受取の通知; u⌈ketori-shoo 受取証: an acknowledgment of a letter (*tegami o uketotta to iu tsuuchi*) 手紙を受け取ったという通知.

3 (thanks) ka⌉ñsha 感謝.

acquaint *vt.* (let know) ... ni (... o) shi⌈raseru ...に(...を)知らせる [V]: I acquainted him with the fact. (*Watashi wa kare ni sono jijitsu o shiraseta.*) 私は彼にその事実を知らせた.

be acquainted with ... *vt.* ... to shi⌈riai da ...と知り合いだ: He and I have been acquainted for ten years. (*Kare to wa juu-neñ-rai no shiriai desu.*) 彼とは10年来の知り合いです.

acquaintance *n.* chi⌈jiñ 知人; shi⌈riai 知り合い: He's not a friend, only an acquaintance. (*Kare wa yuujiñ de wa naku, tañ-naru shiriai desu.*) 彼は友人ではなく, 単なる知り合いです.

acquire *vt.* **1** (gain) ... o e⌉ru ...を得る [V]; te⌉ ni i⌈reru 手に入れる [V]: acquire land (*tochi o te ni ireru*) 土地を手に入れる.

2 (of a skill, habit) ... o mi ˹ni tsuke˺ru …を身に付ける V; o˹boe˺ru 覚える V: acquire a bad habit (*warui kuse o oboeru*) 悪い癖を覚える.

acre *n.* e˺ekaa エーカー. ★ 1 acre = about 4,050 square meters.

across *prep.* ★ 'Across' does not have exact equivalents, but can often be translated with the particle 'o' and an appropriate verb.

1 (from one side to the other side) ... o yo˹kogi˺tte …を横切って: run across the road (*michi o hashitte yokogiru*) 道を走って横切る / John swam across the river. (*Joñ wa kawa o oyoide watatta.*) ジョンは川を泳いで渡った.

2 (the other side) ... no mu˹koo-gawa ni …の向こう側に: He lives across the street. (*Kare wa michi no mukoogawa ni suñde imasu.*) 彼は道の向こう側に住んでいます.

— *adv.* **1** (width) ha˹ba ga ... 幅が…: This river is 50 meters across. (*Kono kawa wa haba ga gojuu-meetoru aru.*) この川は幅が 50 メートルある.

2 (the other side) mu˹koo e [ni] 向こうへ[に]: go across (*mukoo e iku*) 向こうへ行く.

act *vi.* **1** (do, behave) ko˹odoo suru 行動する I; fu˹ruma˺u 振る舞う C: She acted like a queen. (*Kanojo wa jo-oo no yoo ni furumatta.*) 彼女は女王のように振る舞った.

2 (perform on the stage) (... ni) shu˹tsueñ suru (…に)出演する I: act in a play (*geki ni shutsueñ suru*) 劇に出演する.

3 (have an effect) ki˹ku 効く C: This drug acts quickly. (*Kono kusuri wa sugu kiku.*) この薬はすぐ効く.

— *vt.* **1** (do a play) ... o e˹ñjiru …を演じる V: He acted the part of Hamlet. (*Kare wa Hamuretto no yaku o eñjita.*) 彼はハムレットの役を演じた.

2 (behave) ... ko˹to˺ o suru …ことをする I: act the fool (*baka na koto o suru*) ばかなことをする.

— *n.* **1** (deed) o˹konai 行い; ko˺oi 行為: do an act of kindness (*shiñsetsu na okonai o suru*) 親切な行いをする.

2 (law) ho˹oree 法令; jo˹oree 条令.

3 (division of a play) ma˹ku˺ 幕: a comedy in three acts (*sañ maku no kigeki*) 3 幕の喜劇.

action *n.* **1** (doing something) ka˹tsudoo 活動; ji˹kkoo 実行: I put my plan into action. (*Watashi wa jibuñ no keekaku o jikkoo ni utsushita.*) 私は自分の計画を実行に移した.

2 (behavior) ko˺oi 行為; ko˹odoo 行動: a kind action (*shiñsetsu na kooi*) 親切な行為.

3 (effect) sa˺yoo 作用; ha˹taraki 働き: the action of the heart (*shiñzoo no hataraki*) 心臓の働き.

active *adj.* **1** (lively) ka˹ppatsu na 活発な; ka˹tsudoo-teki na 活動的な: He is not as active as he used to be. (*Kare wa izeñ hodo kappatsu de wa nai.*) 彼は以前ほど活発ではない.

2 (working) ka˹tsudoo shite iru 活動している: an active volcano (*kakkazañ*) 活火山.

activity *n.* **1** (doings) ka˹tsudoo 活動; ka˹tsuyaku 活躍: artistic activities (*geejutsu katsudoo*) 芸術活動.

2 (being active) ka˹ppatsu 活発; ka˹kki 活気: The street was bustling with activity. (*Toori wa kakki ni afurete ita.*) 通りは活気にあふれていた.

actor *n.* ha˹iyuu 俳優; da˹ñyuu 男優: a film actor (*eega haiyuu*) 映画俳優.

actress *n.* jo˹yuu 女優: a stage actress (*butai joyuu*) 舞台女優.

actual *adj.* **1** (real) ji˹ssai no 実際の; ge˹ñjitsu no 現実の: an actual incident (*jissai no jikeñ*) 実際の事件.

2 (present) ge˺ñzai no 現在の: the actual state of affairs (*geñjoo*) 現状.

actually *adv.* **1** (really) ji˹ssai ni 実際に; ho˹ñtoo ni 本当に: Did he

actually do it? (*Kare wa jissai ni soo shita ñ desu ka?*) 彼は実際にそうしたんですか.
2 (as a matter of fact) ji⌈tsu⌉ wa 実は; ho⌈ñtoo wa 本当は: Actually, I failed in the exam. (*Jitsu wa, watashi wa shikeñ ni shippai shita ñ desu.*) 実は, 私は試験に失敗したんです.

acute *adj.* **1** (keen) su⌈rudo⌉i 鋭い; e⌈ebiñ na 鋭敏な: an acute sense of smell (*surudoi shuukaku*) 鋭い臭覚.
2 (of pains and diseases) ha⌈geshi⌉i 激しい; kyu⌈usee no 急性の: an acute pain in the stomach (*i no hageshii itami*) 胃の激しい痛み / acute pneumonia (*kyuusee haieñ*) 急性肺炎.
3 (of a situation) shi⌈ñkoku na 深刻な; ju⌈udai na 重大な: an acute shortage of food (*shiñkoku na shokuryoo-busoku*) 深刻な食料不足.

adapt *vt.* **1** (make suitable) ... ni ka⌈izoo suru ...に改造する [I]; ka⌈isaku suru 改作する [I]: adapt a book for children (*hoñ o kodomo muki ni kakikaeru*) 本を子ども向きに書きかえる.
2 (adjust) ... o (... ni) a⌈wase⌉ru ...を(...に)合わせる [V]; te⌈kigoo saseru 適合させる [V]: adapt a plan to a new situation (*keekaku o atarashii jitai ni awaseru*) 計画を新しい事態に合わせる.

add *vt.* **1** (join) ... o ku⌈waeru ...を加える [V]; ta⌈su 足す [C]: add cream to tea (*koocha ni kuriimu o kuwaeru*) 紅茶にクリームを加える / add five and six (*go to roku o tasu*) 5と6を足す.
2 (say in addition) ... to tsu⌈kekuwaete iu ...とつけ加えて言う [C]: "I wish you good luck," he added. (*"Kouñ o inorimasu" to kare wa tsukekuwaeta.*) 「幸運を祈ります」と彼はつけ加えた.

add to ... *vt.* ... o ma⌈su ...を増す [C]; ... ga fu⌈e⌉ru ...が増える [V]: I am adding to my weight. (*Watashi wa taijuu ga fuete iru.*) 私は体重が増えている.

add up *vt.* ... o go⌈okee suru ...を合計する [I]: add up the figures (*suuji o gookee suru*) 数字を合計する.

addition *n.* **1** (adding) tsu⌈ika 追加.
2 (calculating) ta⌈shi⌉zañ 足し算: be quick at addition (*tashizañ ga hayai*) 足し算が速い.
3 (of a house) ta⌈temashi 建て増し: an addition to a house (*ie no tatemashi*) 家の建て増し.

additional *adj.* tsu⌈ika no 追加の: an additional charge (*tsuika ryookiñ*) 追加料金.

address *n.* **1** (place) ju⌉usho 住所; a⌈tena あて名: Give me your address, please. (*Anata no juusho o oshiete kudasai.*) あなたの住所を教えてください.
2 (speech) e⌈ñzetsu 演説: make an address (*eñzetsu o suru*) 演説をする.
— *vt.* **1** (write) ... ni a⌈tena o ka⌉ku ...にあて名を書く [C]: I addressed the envelopes for the invitation. (*Watashi wa shootaijoo no fuutoo ni atena o kaita.*) 私は招待状の封筒に宛名を書いた.
2 (speak) ... ni ha⌈nashikake⌉ru ...に話しかける [V]; ha⌈nashi⌉ o suru 話をする [I]: I was addressed by a girl. (*Watashi wa oñna-no-ko ni hanashikakerareta.*) 私は女の子に話しかけられた. / address an audience (*chooshuu ni hanashi o suru*) 聴衆に話をする.

adequate *adj.* **1** (enough) ju⌈ubu⌉ñ na 十分な: My salary is not adequate. (*Watashi no kyuuryoo wa juubuñ de wa nai.*) 私の給料は十分ではない.
2 (suitable) (... ni) te⌈ki⌉shita (...に)適した; fu⌈sawashi⌉i ふさわしい: an adequate person for the job (*sono shigoto ni tekishita hito*) その仕事に適した人.

adjective *n.* ke⌈eyo⌉oshi 形容詞.

adjoin *vt.* ... ni ri⌈ñsetsu suru ...に隣接する [I]: My house adjoins the park. (*Watashi no ie wa kooeñ ni* *riñsetsu shite imasu.*) 私の家は公園に隣接しています.

adjust *vt.* **1** (fit) ... o (... ni) cho⌈o-setsu suru …を(…に)調節する ①; a⌈wase⌉ru 合わせる Ⓥ: adjust the stool to the height of the piano (*isu o piano no takasa ni awasete choo-setsu suru*) いすをピアノの高さに合わせて調節する.

2 (settle) ... o se⌈esañ suru …を清算する ①: adjust one's fare (*uñchiñ o seesañ suru*) 運賃を清算する.

— *vi.* (... ni) ju⌈ñnoo suru (…に)順応する ①: adjust to one's new surroundings (*atarashii kañkyoo ni juñnoo suru*) 新しい環境に順応する.

adjustment *n.* cho⌈osee 調整; cho⌈otee 調停; se⌈esañ 清算: make some adjustments to the plan (*keekaku o ikura-ka choosee suru*) 計画をいくらか調整する / fare adjustment (*uñchiñ no seesañ*) 運賃の清算.

administer *vt.* **1** (manage) ... o ka⌉ñri suru …を管理する ①; o⌈same⌉ru 治める ①: administer a company (*kaisha o kañri suru*) 会社を管理する.

2 (give) ... o a⌈taeru …を与える Ⓥ: administer punishment (*batsu o ataeru*) 罰を与える.

administration *n.* **1** (government) se⌉efu 政府; gyo⌈osee 行政.

2 (management) ka⌉ñri 管理; u⌈ñee 運営: the administration of a library (*toshokañ no uñee*) 図書館の運営.

administrator *n.* ka⌈ñri⌉sha 管理者.

admiration *n.* **1** (admiring) ka⌈ñ-tañ 感嘆; sho⌈osañ 称賛: He let out a cry of admiration when he saw the car. (*Kare wa sono kuruma o mite kañtañ no koe o ageta.*) 彼はその車を見て感嘆の声を上げた.

2 (an object admired) a⌈kogare no mato あこがれの的: She is the subject of admiration of young people. (*Kanojo wa wakai hito-tachi no akogare no mato da.*) 彼女は若い人たちのあこがれの的だ.

admire *vt.* **1** (feel admitation for) ... ni ka⌈ñshiñ suru …に感心する ①.

2 (praise) ... o ho⌈me⌉ru …をほめる Ⓥ: He admired her painting. (*Kare wa kanojo no e o hometa.*) 彼は彼女の絵をほめた.

admission *n.* **1** (of a society) nyu⌈ukai 入会; (of a school) nyu⌈u-gaku 入学: gain admission into a club (*kurabu e no nyuukai o yurusareru*) クラブへの入会を許される.

2 (price) nyu⌈ujo⌉o-ryoo 入場料: Admission to the museum is 800 yen. (*Bijutsukañ no nyuujoo-ryoo wa happyaku-eñ desu.*) 美術館の入場料は800円です.

3 (acknowledging) mi⌈tomeru koto⌉ 認めること; sho⌈oniñ 承認: He made an admission that he had told a lie. (*Kare wa uso o tsuita koto o mitometa.*) 彼はうそをついたことを認めた.

admit *vt.* **1** (acknowledge) ... o mi⌈tomeru …を認める Ⓥ: admit one's mistakes (*jibuñ no ayamari o mitomeru*) 自分の誤りを認める.

2 (allow entrance) ... ni ha⌉iru koto o yu⌈ru⌉su …に入ることを許す Ⓒ; ... o to⌉osu …を通す Ⓒ: He was admitted to the school. (*Kare wa sono gakkoo ni hairu koto o yurusareta.*) 彼はその学校に入ることを許された.

admittance *n.* nyu⌈ujoo 入場: No admittance. (*Tachiiri kiñshi.*) 立ち入り禁止.

adopt *vt.* **1** (of a person) ... o yo⌈o-shi ni suru …を養子にする ①: He adopted the child. (*Kare wa sono ko o yooshi ni shita.*) 彼はその子を養子にした.

2 (of a plan) ... o sa⌉iyoo suru …を採用する ①: I decided to adopt your idea. (*Anata no aidea o sai-yoo suru koto ni shimashita.*) あなたのアイデアを採用することにしました.

adore *vt.* **1** (worship) ... o a⌈game⌉ru …をあがめる Ⓥ: adore God (*kami o agameru*) 神をあがめる.

2 (love greatly) ... ni a⌈kogareru ...

a

にあこがれる [V]: adore one's teacher (*señsee ni akogareru*) 先生にあこがれる.
3 (like very much) ... ga da¹isuki da ...が大好きだ: I adore listening to music. (*Watashi wa oñgaku o kiku no ga daisuki desu.*) 私は音楽を聞くのが大好きです.

adult *adj.* (fully grown) se⌈ejiñ no 成人の: an adult man (*seejiñ dañshi*) 成人男子.
— *n.* se⌈ejiñ 成人; o¹tona 大人.

advance *vt.* **1** (bring forward) ... o su⌈sumeru ...を進める [V]; ha⌈yame¹ru 早める [V]: advance a plan (*keekaku o susumeru*) 計画を進める / advance the date of departure (*shuppatsu no hi o hayameru*) 出発の日を早める.
2 (pay, loan) ... o ma⌈eba¹rai suru ...を前払いする [I]; ma⌈egashi suru 前貸しする [I]: advance wages to workers (*roodoosha ni chiñgiñ o maebarai suru*) 労働者に賃金を前払いする.
— *vi.* **1** (move forward) su⌈sumu 進む [C]; ze⌈ñshiñ suru 前進する [I]: advance against the enemy (*teki ni mukatte zeñshiñ suru*) 敵に向かって前進する.
2 (of prices) a⌈garu 上がる [C]: Prices are advancing. (*Bukka wa agatte imasu.*) 物価は上がっています.
— *n.* **1** (progress) shi¹ñpo 進歩: an advance in civilization (*buñmee no shiñpo*) 文明の進歩.
2 (payment) ma⌈eba¹rai 前払い: an advance payment (*maebarai*) 前払い.

in advance *adv.* ma⌈emo¹tte 前もって; a⌈rakajime 予め: I'll let you know in advance. (*Maemotte o-shirase shimasu.*) 前もってお知らせします.

advantage *n.* yu¹uri 有利; ko⌈o-tsu¹goo 好都合; to⌈ku 得: It is a great advantage to live near the station. (*Eki no soba ni sumu no wa totemo beñri desu.*) 駅のそばに住むのはとても便利です.

take advantage of ... *vt.* ... o ri⌈yoo suru ...を利用する [I]: He took advantage of the opportunity. (*Kare wa sono kikai o riyoo shita.*) 彼はその機会を利用した.

adventure *n.* bo⌈okeñ 冒険; a⌈bunai keekeñ 危ない経験: have a lot of adventures (*iroiro abunai kee-keñ o suru*) いろいろ危ない経験をする.

adverb *n.* fu⌈kushi 副詞.

advertise *vt.* ... o ko⌈okoku suru ...を広告する [I]; se⌈ñdeñ suru 宣伝する [I]: advertise a house for sale (*uriya no kookoku o suru*) 売り家の広告をする.
— *vi.* ko⌈okoku o da¹su 広告を出す [C]: That store advertised in a newspaper. (*Sono mise wa shiñbuñ ni kookoku o dashita.*) その店は新聞に広告を出した.

advertisement *n.* ko⌈okoku 広告; se⌈ñdeñ 宣伝: put an advertisement in a magazine (*zasshi ni koo-koku o dasu*) 雑誌に広告を出す.

advice *n.* chu⌈ukoku 忠告; jo⌈geñ 助言; a⌈doba¹isu アドバイス: give advice (*adobaisu o ataeru*) アドバイスを与える / I followed his advice. (*Watashi wa kare no chuukoku ni shitagatta.*) 私は彼の忠告に従った.

advise *vt.* ... ni chu⌈ukoku suru ...に忠告する [I]; jo⌈geñ suru 助言する [I]; ... o su⌈sumeru ...を勧める [I]: No one advised me. (*Dare mo watashi ni chuukoku shite kurena-katta.*) だれも私に忠告してくれなかった. / The doctor advised a change of air. (*Isha wa teñchi o susumeta.*) 医者は転地を勧めた.

aeroplane *n.* ⇨ airplane.

affair *n.* **1** (event) ji¹keñ 事件; de⌈ki¹goto でき事: a strange affair (*fu-shigi na dekigoto*) 不思議なでき事 / current affairs (*geñzai no jookyoo*) 現在の状況.
2 (business) ji¹mu 事務; yo⌈oji 用事: private affairs (*shiji*) 私事.
3 (love affair) jo¹oji 情事.

affect[1] *vt.* **1** (produce an effect) ... ni e⌈ekyoo o ataeru ...に影響を与え

る Ⓥ: The weather greatly affects the growth of crops. (*Teñkoo wa noosakubutsu no seeiku ni ookina eekyoo o ataeru.*) 天候は農作物の生育に大きな影響を与える.
2 (touch) ... o ka⌈ñdoo saseru ...を感動させる Ⓥ: We were deeply affected by his story. (*Watashi-tachi wa kare no hanashi ni fukaku kañdoo shita.*) 私たちは彼の話に深く感動した.

affect[2] *vt.* fu⌈ri⌉ o suru ふりをする Ⓘ: He affected ignorance. (*Kare wa shiranai furi o shita.*) 彼は知らないふりをした.

affected *adj.* ki⌈dotta 気取った; ki⌉za na きざな: an affected way of talking (*kidotta hanashikata*) 気取った話し方.

affection *n.* a⌈ijoo 愛情: feel affection for a person (*hito ni aijoo o idaku*) 人に愛情を抱く.

affectionate *adj.* a⌈ijoo no komo⌉tta [komo⌉tte iru] 愛情のこもった[こもっている]; ya⌈sashii 優しい: He's affectionate to his wife. (*Kare wa tsuma ni yasashii.*) 彼は妻に優しい.

affirm *vt.* ... to da⌈ñge⌉ñ suru ...と断言する Ⓘ; i⌈iki⌉ru 言い切る Ⓒ: He affirmed that she was innocent. (*Kare wa kanojo wa mujitsu da to dañgeñ shita.*) 彼は彼女は無実だと断言した.

affirmation *n.* da⌈ñge⌉ñ 断言; ko⌈otee 肯定.

afford *vt.* 〈verb〉 yo⌈yuu ga a⌉ru ... 余裕がある Ⓒ: I can't afford a new car. (*Shiñsha o kau yoyuu wa nai.*) 新車を買う余裕はない.

afloat *adj., adv.* (floating) u⌈kañde (iru) 浮かんで(いる); (at sea) ka⌈ijoo ni 海上に: get a boat afloat (*booto o ukabaseru*) ボートを浮かばせる.

afraid *adj.* **1** (frightened) o⌈so⌉rete (iru) 恐れて(いる); ... ga ko⌈wa⌉i ...が怖い: I am afraid of going up to high places. (*Watashi wa takai tokoro e agaru no ga kowai.*) 私は高い所へ上がるのが怖い.
2 (fear) shi⌈ñpai shite (iru) 心配して(いる): She is afraid her child might become ill. (*Kanojo wa kodomo ga byooki ni naru ka mo shirenai to shiñpai shite iru.*) 彼女は子どもが病気になるかもしれないと心配している.
I'm afraid ... de wa na⌉i ka to o⌈mo⌉u ...ではないかと思う Ⓒ; ... ka⌉ mo shi⌈renai ...かもしれない: I'm afraid you are wrong. (*Anata wa machigatte iru ka mo shirenai.*) あなたは間違っているかもしれない.

after *prep.* **1** (of time) ... no a⌉to de ...の後で; ... -go⌉ ni ...後に: After that, I'll have coffee. (*Sono ato de koohii o moraimasu.*) その後でコーヒーをもらいます. / He went out after dinner. (*Kare wa yuushoku-go ni gaishutsu shimashita.*) 彼は夕食後に外出しました.
2 (of place, order) ... no u⌈shiro ni ...の後ろに; ... no a⌉to ...の後: I entered the room after him. (*Watashi wa kare no ushiro ni tsuite heya ni haitta.*) 私は彼の後ろについて部屋に入った.
3 (pursuit) ... o o⌈tte ...を追って; ... o mo⌈to⌉mete ...を求めて: The police are after the thief. (*Keesatsu wa sono doroboo o otte iru.*) 警察はそのどろぼうを追っている.
4 (of a clock) su⌈gi⌉ 過ぎ: fifteen minutes after two (*ni-ji juugo-fuñ sugi*) 2時15分過ぎ.
— *conj.* 〈verb〉 a⌉to ni ...後に: He arrived after you left. (*Kare wa anata ga deta ato ni tsukimashita.*) 彼はあなたが出た後に着きました.
— *adv.* a⌉to ni [de] 後に[で]: She returned home soon after. (*Kanojo wa sugu ato ni kitaku shimashita.*) 彼女はすぐ後に帰宅しました.
after all *adv.* ke⌈kkyoku 結局: He didn't come after all. (*Kare wa kekkyoku konakatta.*) 彼は結局来なかった.
After you. (*O-saki ni doozo.*) お先にどうぞ.

afternoon *n.* go⌉go 午後; hi⌈ru sugi⌉ 昼過ぎ: I'll visit you on Monday afternoon. (*Getsuyoobi no *gogo o-tazune shimasu.*) 月曜日の午後お訪ねします. / Is there an afternoon tour? (*Gogo no koosu wa arimasu ka?*) 午後のコースはありますか.

afterward *adv.* a⁊to de 後で; no⸢chi⁊ ni 後に: He told me afterward that he had refused the offer. (*Kare wa sono mooshide o kotowatta to ato de itta.*) 彼はその申し出を断わったと後で言った.

again *adv.* (once more) fu⸢tatabi 再び; ma⸢ta また; mo⸢o ichido もう一度: Come again tomorrow. (*Ashita mata kite kudasai.*) あしたまた来てください. / I'll phone again later. (*Ato de mata deñwa shimasu.*) あとでまた電話します. / Please come again. (*Mata doozo.*) またどうぞ.

against *prep.* **1** (opposition) ... ni ha⸢ñtai shite …に反対して: I am against war. (*Watashi wa señsoo ni hañtai desu.*) 私は戦争に反対です.
2 (contact) ... ni (bu⸢tsukete) …に(ぶつけて): He hit his head against a pillar. (*Kare wa hashira ni atama o butsuketa.*) 彼は柱に頭をぶつけた.
3 (contrast) ... o ha⸢ikee ni …を背景に: The castle looked beautiful against the blue sky. (*Sono shiro wa aozora o haikee ni utsukushiku mieta.*) その城は青空を背景に美しく見えた.

age *n.* **1** (time of life) ne⸢ñree 年齢; to⸢shi⁊ 年; -sai 歳: Write your name and age here, please. (*Koko ni anata no namae to neñree o kaite kudasai.*) ここにあなたの名前と年齢を書いてください. / She got married at the age of 22. (*Kanojo wa nijuu-ni-sai no toki kekkoñ shita.*) 彼女は22歳のとき結婚した.
2 (period) ji⸢dai 時代: the golden age (*oogoñ jidai*) 黄金時代.

agency *n.* da⸢iri⁊teñ 代理店: an advertising agency (*kookoku dairiteñ*) 広告代理店.

agent *n.* da⸢iriniñ 代理人; gyo⁊osha 業者; e⁊ejeñto エージェント: a real estate agent (*fudoosañ gyoosha*) 不動産業者.

aggressive *adj.* **1** (energetic) se⸢kkyoku-teki na 積極的な; ka⸢ppatsu na 活発な: You must be aggressive to succeed in business. (*Jigyoo ni seekoo suru ni wa sekkyoku-teki de nakereba naranai.*) 事業に成功するには積極的でなけらばならない.
2 (ready to attack) ko⸢ogeki-teki na 攻撃的な; shi⸢ñryaku-teki na 侵略的な: an aggressive war (*shiñryaku-señsoo*) 侵略戦争.

ago *adv.* ... ma⁊e ni [no] …前に[の]: He went out five minutes ago. (*Kare wa go-fuñ mae ni gaishutsu shimashita.*) 彼は5分前に外出しました. / I saw her three days ago. (*Watashi wa mikka mae ni kanojo ni aimashita.*) 私は三日前に彼女に会いました.
long ago *adv.* zu⸢tto ma⁊e ni ずっと前に; mu⸢kashi 昔.

agree *vi., vt.* **1** (consent) (... ni) do⸢oi suru (…に)同意する [I]; sa⸢ñsee suru 賛成する [I]: I agree to your proposal. (*Anata no teeañ ni sañsee shimasu.*) あなたの提案に賛成します.
2 (match) (... to) i⸢tchi suru (…と)一致する [I]: What you say does not agree with the facts. (*Kimi ga itte iru koto wa jijitsu to itchi shinai.*) 君が言っていることは事実と一致しない.

agreeable *adj.* **1** (pleasant) ko⸢kochi yo⁊i 心地よい; ka⸢ñji no yo⁊i 感じのよい: an agreeable voice (*kañji no yoi koe*) 感じのよい声.
2 (willing) ... ni sa⸢ñsee shite (iru) …に賛成して(いる): I am quite agreeable to the plan. (*Watashi wa sono añ ni mattaku sañsee desu.*) 私はその案にまったく賛成です.

agreement *n.* **1** (contract) kyo⸢otee 協定; ke⸢eyaku 契約: make an agreement (*kyootee o musubu*) 協定を結ぶ.
2 (agreeing) i⸢tchi 一致; do⸢oi 同意: We are in agreement with their proposal. (*Watashi-tachi wa karera no teeañ ni dooi shite iru.*) 私たちは彼らの提案に同意している.

agriculture *n.* no⌉ogyoo 農業.

ahead *adv.* **1** (in front) ze⌉ñpoo ni 前方に; sa⌈ki ni 先に: We saw a light ahead of us. (*Zeñpoo ni akari ga mieta.*) 前方に明かりが見えた. / He walked ahead of us. (*Kare wa watashi-tachi no saki ni tatte aruita.*) 彼は私たちの先に立って歩いた.
2 (forward) sa⌈ki 先: Our wedding is two weeks ahead. (*Watashi-tachi no kekkoñshiki wa ni-shuukañ saki desu.*) 私たちの結婚式は2週間先です.
go ahead *vi.* sa⌈ki e su⌈sumu 先へ進む [C]: Go ahead. (*Doozo o-saki ni.*) どうぞお先に.

aid *n.* e⌉ñjo 援助; kyu⌈ueñ 救援: ask a person for aid (*hito ni eñjo o motomeru*) 人に援助を求める.
— *vt.* ... o ta⌈suke⌉ru ...を助ける [V]; te⌈tsuda⌉u 手伝う [C]; e⌉ñjo suru 援助する [I]: He aided me in my work. (*Kare wa watashi no shigoto o tetsudatte kureta.*) 彼は私の仕事を手伝ってくれた.

aim *vi.* (... o) me⌈za⌉su (...を)目指す [C]; ne⌈rau ねらう [C]: He is aiming to be a lawyer. (*Kare wa beñgoshi o mezashite iru.*) 彼は弁護士を目指している. / aim at a target (*mato o nerau*) 的をねらう.
— *vt.* ... o (... ni) mu⌈keru ...を(...に)向ける [V]: He aimed a gun at me. (*Kare wa juu o watashi ni muketa.*) 彼は銃を私に向けた.
— *n.* mo⌈kuteki 目的; ne⌈rai ねらい: achieve one's aim (*mokuteki o tassee suru*) 目的を達成する.

air *n.* **1** (gas) ku⌉uki 空気: breathe air (*kuuki o suu*) 空気を吸う.
2 (space) ku⌈uchuu 空中; so⌉ra 空: a balloon floating in the air (*kuuchuu ni tadayou fuuseñ*) 空中に漂う風船.
3 (appearance) ga⌈ikeñ 外見; ta⌉ido 態度: assume an air of indifference (*mukañshiñ na taido o toru*) 無関心な態度をとる.
be on the air *vi.* ho⌈osoo sareru 放送される [V].

air conditioner *n.* e⌈akoñ エアコン; ku⌉uraa クーラー.

aircraft *n.* ko⌈oku⌉uki 航空機.

airfield *n.* hi⌈koojoo 飛行場.

air force *n.* ku⌈uguñ 空軍.

airline *n.* ko⌈okuu⌉uro 航空路; ko⌈okuuga⌉isha 航空会社: Please check other airlines' flights. (*Hoka no kookuugaisha no biñ o shirabete kudasai.*) ほかの航空会社の便を調べてください.

airmail *n.* ko⌈okuu yu⌉ubiñ 航空郵便; ko⌈okuubiñ 航空便: What is the airmail postage for America? (*Amerika made no kookuubiñ wa ikura desu ka?*) アメリカまでの航空便はいくらですか.

airplane *n.* hi⌈ko⌉oki 飛行機: get on [off] an airplane (*hikooki ni noru* [*o oriru*]) 飛行機に乗る[を降りる].

airport *n.* ku⌈ukoo 空港: transportation to the airport (*kuukoo made no kootsuukikañ*) 空港までの交通機関 / domestic airport (*kokunai-kuukoo*) 国内空港 / international airport (*kokusai-kuukoo*) 国際空港.

aisle *n.* tsu⌉uro 通路: Aisle seat, please. (*Tsuuro gawa no seki ni shite kudasai.*) 通路側の席にしてください.

alarm clock *n.* me⌈zamashi-do⌉kee 目覚まし時計.

album *n.* **1** (book) a⌈rubamu アルバム; (holder) -choo 帳: a photo album (*shashiñ-choo*) 写真帳.
2 (record) a⌈rubamu アルバム.

alcohol *n.* a⌈rukooru アルコール; (drinks) a⌈rukooru-i⌉ñryoo アルコール飲料.

alike *adj.* do⌈oyoo na 同様な; yo⌉ku ni⌈te (iru) よく似て(いる): The two of them look alike. (*Futari wa yoku nite iru.*) 二人はよく似ている.
— *adv.* o⌈naji yo⌉o ni 同じように: treat all pupils alike (*seeto o miñna onaji yoo ni atsukau*) 生徒をみんな同じように扱う.

alive *adj.* **1** i⌉kite i⌈ru 生きている: This fish is still alive. (*Kono sa-*

kana wa mada ikite iru.) この魚はまだ生きている.
2 ni⌈giwa⌉tte (iru) にぎわって(いる): The department store was alive with shoppers. (*Depaato wa kai-mono-kyaku de nigiwatte ita.*) デパートは買い物客でにぎわっていた.

all *adj*. ze⌉ñbu (no) 全部(の); su⌉bete (no) すべての; mi⌈ñna みんな: I'd like coins of all types, please. (*Zeñbu no shurui no koiñ ga hoshii.*) 全部の種類のコインが欲しい. / These are all my personal effects. (*Kore wa zeñbu watashi no minomawari-hiñ desu.*) これは全部私の身の回り品です.
— *pron*. su⌉bete no mo⌈no⌉ [hi⌈to⌉] すべてのもの[人]: I'll give you all you want. (*Hoshii mono wa subete age-masu.*) 欲しいものはすべてあげます. / All is over. (*Subete wa owatta.*) すべては終わった.
all together *adv*. ze⌉ñbu de 全部で: How much is it all together? (*Zeñbu de ikura desu ka?*) 全部でいくらですか.

allergic *adj*. a⌈re⌉rugii no アレルギーの: I am allergic to antibiotics. (*Watashi wa kooseebusshitsu no arerugii ga arimasu.*) 私は抗生物質のアレルギーがあります.

allergy *n*. a⌈re⌉rugii アレルギー: I have allergies. (*Watashi wa areru-gii-taishitsu desu.*) 私はアレルギー体質です.

alliance *n*. do⌈omee 同盟; do⌈o-me⌉e-koku 同盟国.

alligator *n*. wa⌉ni わに(鰐): alligator skin [leather] (*wani-gawa*) わに皮.

allot *vt*. ... o wa⌈riate⌉ru ...を割り当てる [V]: I was alloted the difficult work. (*Watashi wa sono muzuka-shii shigoto o wariaterareta.*) 私はその難しい仕事を割り当てられた.

allow *vt*. **1** (permit) ... o yu⌈ru⌉su ...を許す [C]; kyo⌉ka suru 許可する [I]: We were allowed into the room. (*Watashi-tachi wa heya e hairu koto o yurusareta.*) 私たちは部屋へ入ることを許された. / You are not allowed to take pictures here. (*Ko-ko de shashiñ o totte wa ikemaseñ.*) ここで写真を撮ってはいけません.
2 (give) ... ni shi⌈kyuu suru ...に支給する [I]; a⌈taeru 与える [V]: He allows his son ten thousand yen a month. (*Kare wa musuko ni tsuki ichimañ-eñ ataete iru.*) 彼は息子に月 1 万円与えている.

allowance *n*. te⌉ate 手当; ko⌉zu-kai こづかい; ne⌈biki 値引き: a weekly allowance (*is-shuukañ no kozu-kai*) 1 週間の小遣い / make an allowance of 10 per cent (*jup-paaseñto no nebiki o suru*) 10 パーセントの値引きをする.
make allowance(s) for ... *vt*. ... o ko⌉oryo ni i⌈reru ...を考慮に入れる [V]: We have to make allowances for his age. (*Kare no toshi no koto o kooryo ni irenakereba ikenai.*) 彼の年のことを考慮に入れなければいけない.

all right *adj*. **1** (satisfactory) ke⌉kkoo na 結構な; i⌉i いい: That's quite all right. (*Kekkoo desu.*) 結構です. / Is this all right? (*Kore de ii desu ka?*) これでいいですか.
2 (safe) bu⌈ji na 無事な; da⌈ijo⌉obu na 大丈夫な: Are you all right? (*Daijoobu desu ka?*) 大丈夫ですか.
— *adv*. **1** (yes) yo⌈roshii よろしい; i⌉i いい: "Please shut the window." "All right." ("*Mado o shimete kudasai.*" "*Ii desu yo.*") 「窓を閉めてください」「いいですよ」
2 (certainly) ta⌉shika ni 確かに; ma⌈chigai na⌉ku 間違いなく: I paid him all right. (*Watashi wa tashika ni kare ni haraimashita.*) 私は確かに彼に払いました.

ally *vt*. (... to) do⌈omee suru (...と)同盟する [I]: Japan allied itself with the United States. (*Nihoñ wa Bee-koku to doomee shita.*) 日本は米国と同盟した.
— *n*. do⌈ome⌉ekoku 同盟国.

almost *adv*. **1** (for the most part) ho⌈to⌉ñdo ほとんど; ta⌈itee たいてい: I almost always go to bed at eleven. (*Watashi wa hotoñdo itsu-mo juuichi-ji ni nemasu.*) 私はほとんどいつも 11 時に寝ます.

2 (nearly) mo⌈o suko⌉shi de ... ⟨verb⟩ tokoro da もう少しで…ところだ: The cat was almost run over by a car. (*Sono neko wa moo sukoshi de kuruma ni hikareru tokoro datta.*) その猫はもう少しで車にひかれるところだった.

alone *adj.* ta⌉da hi⌈to⌉ri no ただひとりの; ta⌈ñdoku no 単独の: He stayed alone at home. (*Kare wa tada hitori de ie ni ita.*) 彼はただひとりで家にいた.

— *adv.* hi⌈to⌉ri de ひとりで; ta⌈ñdoku de 単独で: She came alone. (*Kanojo wa hitori de kita.*) 彼女はひとりで来た.

along *prep.* ... o to⌉otte …を通って; ... ni so⌉tte …に沿って: walk along the river (*kawa ni sotte aruku*) 川に沿って歩く.

— *adv.* (onward) ma⌉e e 前へ; zu⌈tto ずっと: Move along, please! (*Mae e susuñde kudasai.*) 前へ進んでください.

aloud *adv.* ko⌉e o dashite 声を出して: read aloud (*koe o dashite yomu*) 声を出して読む.

already *adv.* su⌉de ni すでに; mo⌉o もう: I've already paid. (*Daikiñ wa moo haraimashita.*) 代金はもう払いました.

also *adv.* ... mo …も; do⌈oyoo ni 同様に: Also give me an entertainment guide, please. (*Moyooshimono no aññai mo kudasai.*) 催し物の案内もください.

altar *n.* sa⌈idañ 祭壇.

alter *vt.* ... o he⌈ñkoo suru …を変更する [I]; na⌈o⌉su 直す [C]: He altered his plans. (*Kare wa keekaku o heñkoo shita.*) 彼は計画を変更した.

alternate *vi.* ko⌈otai de ⟨verb⟩ 交替で…: My sister and I alternate in doing the dishes. (*Imooto to watashi wa kootai de sara o araimasu.*) 妹と私は交替で皿を洗います.

— *vt.* ... o ko⌉ogo ni ⟨verb⟩ …を交互に…: alternate work and play (*beñkyoo to asobi o koogo ni suru*) 勉強と遊びを交互にする.

— *adj.* ko⌉ogo no 交互の; hi⌈totsu oki⌉ no 一つおきの: I go to the hospital on alternate days. (*Watashi wa ichi-nichi oki ni byooiñ e ikimasu.*) 私は 1 日おきに病院へ行きます.

alternative *adj.* ka⌈wari no 代[替]わりの; do⌉chira ka hi⌈to⌉tsu no どちらか一つの: an alternative plan (*daiañ*) 代案.

— *n.* fu⌈tatsu⌉ ni hi⌈to⌉tsu 二つに一つ: the alternative of going or staying (*iku ka todomaru ka futatsu ni hitotsu*) 行くかとどまるか二つに一つ.

although *conj.* ... ga …が; ... ke⌉redo mo …けれども: Although it was raining, we went out. (*Ame ga futte ita keredo mo watashi-tachi wa dekaketa.*) 雨が降っていたけれども私たちは出かけた.

altitude *n.* ta⌉kasa 高さ; ko⌉odo 高度: fly at an altitude of 10,000 meters (*koodo ichimañ meetoru de tobu*) 高度 1 万メートルで飛ぶ.

altogether *adv.* **1** (entirely) ma⌈ttaku まったく; ka⌈ñzeñ ni 完全に: He gave it up altogether. (*Kare wa sore o kañzeñ ni akirameta.*) 彼はそれを完全にあきらめた.

2 (on the whole) ze⌉ñbu de 全部で; go⌈okee de 合計で: That comes to 5,000 yen altogether. (*Zeñbu de goseñ-eñ ni narimasu.*) 全部で 5 千円になります.

always *adv.* i⌉tsu-mo いつも; tsu⌉ne ni 常に: He always comes late. (*Kare wa itsu-mo okurete kuru.*) 彼はいつも遅れて来る. / I got up at six as always. (*Watashi wa itsu-mo no yoo ni roku-ji ni okita.*) 私はいつものように 6 時に起きた.

not always *adv.* ka⌈narazu⌉shimo ... to wa ka⌈gira⌉nai 必ずしも…とは限らない: The rich are not always happy. (*Kanemochi ga kanarazu shimo shiawase da to wa kagiranai.*) 金持ちが必ずしも幸せだとは限らな

い.

a.m. goˈzeñ 午前; aˈsa 朝: I'm leaving at 8 a.m. tomorrow. (*Watashi wa asu no asa hachi-ji ni tachimasu.*) 私は明日の朝 8 時に発ちます.

amateur *n.* aˈmachua アマチュア; shiˈrooto しろうと.

amaze *vt.* ... o biˈkkuˈri saseru ...をびっくりさせる [V]: I was amazed to learn that he won the prize. (*Kare ga sono shoo o totta koto o shitte, bikkuri shita.*) 彼がその賞を取ったことを知って, びっくりした.

amazement *n.* oˈdorokiˈ 驚き; kyoˈotañ 驚嘆: in amazement (*bikkuri shite*) びっくりして / to one's amazement (*odoroita koto ni wa*) 驚いたことには.

ambassador *n.* taˈishi 大使: an ambassador to Japan (*chuunichi taishi*) 駐日大使.

ambition *n.* taˈimoo 大望; yaˈshiñ 野心: I have no ambition to be a politician. (*Watashi ni wa seejika ni naru yashiñ wa arimaseñ.*) 私には政治家になる野心はありません.

ambitious *adj.* taˈimoo [yaˈshiñ] ga aru 大望[野心]がある; yaˈshiñteki na 野心的な: He is ambitious for fame. (*Kare ni wa yuumee ni naritai to iu yashiñ ga aru.*) 彼には有名になりたいという野心がある.

ambulance *n.* kyuˈukyuˈusha 救急車: call for an ambulance (*kyuukyuusha o yobu*) 救急車を呼ぶ.

amend *vt.* ... o kaˈisee [shuˈusee] suru ...を改正[修正]する [T]: amend the constitution (*keñpoo o kaisee suru*) 憲法を改正する.

America *n.* Aˈmerika アメリカ; Beˈekoku 米国: the United States of America (*Amerika gasshuukoku*) アメリカ合衆国.

American *n.* Aˈmerikaˈjin アメリカ人; Beˈekoˈkumiñ 米国民.
— *adj.* Aˈmerika no アメリカの; Beˈekoku no 米国の: the American language (*beego*) 米語.

among *prep.* **1** (surrounded by) ... ni kaˈkomarete (iru) ...に囲まれて(いる): a village among the mountains (*yama ni kakomareta mura*) 山に囲まれた村.
2 (in the group of) ... no naˈka [aˈida] de ...の中[間]で: Among all the flowers, I like the rose best. (*Hana no naka de watashi wa bara ga ichibañ suki desu.*) 花の中で私はバラがいちばん好きです.

amount *n.* **1** (of money) gaˈku 額; (quantity) ryoˈo 量: spend a large amount of money (*tagaku no okane o tsukau*) 多額のお金を使う / a small amount of butter (*shooryoo no bataa*) 少量のバター.
2 (total) soˈogaku 総額; soˈosuˈu 総数: The amount of the bill comes to 5,000 yen. (*Kañjoo no soogaku wa go-señ-eñ ni narimasu.*) 勘定の総額は 5 千円になります.
— *vi.* (... ni) taˈssuru (...に)達する [T]; naˈru なる [C]: His debts amount to a million yen. (*Kare no shakkiñ wa hyaku-mañ-eñ ni tassuru.*) 彼の借金は 100 万円に達する.

ample *adj.* juˈubuˈñ na 十分な; hoˈofu na 豊富な: ample food (*juubuñ na shokuryoo*) 十分な食料.

amuse *vt.* ... o taˈnoshimaseˈru ...を楽しませる [V]; oˈmoshirogaraseˈru おもしろがらせる [V]: His story amused everyone. (*Kare no hanashi wa miñna o tanoshimaseta.*) 彼の話はみんなを楽しませた.

amusement *n.* taˈnoshiˈmi 楽しみ; goˈraku 娯楽: I play the piano for amusement. (*Watashi wa tanoshimi ni piano o hikimasu.*) 私は楽しみにピアノを弾きます. / There are plenty of amusements in this town. (*Kono machi ni wa goraku ga takusañ aru.*) この町には娯楽がたくさんある.

amusement park *n.* yuˈueˈñchi 遊園地.

amusing *adj.* oˈmoshiroˈi おもしろい; oˈkashiˈi おかしい: an amusing story (*omoshiroi hanashi*) おもしろい話.

analogy *n.* ruˈiji 類似: He drew an

analogy between the two events. (*Kare wa futatsu no jikeñ no ruiji o shiteki shita.*) 彼は二つの事件の類似を指摘した.

analysis *n.* bu⌈ñseki 分析: make an analysis of the situation (*joosee no buñseki o suru*) 情勢の分析をする.

analyze *vt.* ... o bu⌈ñseki suru ...を分析する [I]; ke⌈ñtoo suru 検討する [I]: He analyzed the sales figures. (*Kare wa uriage no suuji o buñseki shita.*) 彼は売り上げの数字を分析した.

ancestor *n.* se⌉ñzo 先祖; so⌉señ 祖先.

anchor *n.* i⌈kari いかり: cast anchor (*ikari o orosu*) いかりを下ろす.

ancient *adj.* ko⌉dai no 古代の; mu⌈kashi no 昔の: ancient civilization (*kodai-buñmee*) 古代文明.

and *conj.* **1** (*n.* and *n.*) to と: a chair and table (*isu to teeburu*) いすとテーブル / 3 and 2 makes 5. (*Sañ to ni de go ni naru.*) 3と2で5になる.

2 (*v.* and *v.*) ⟨verb⟩-tari ⟨verb⟩-tari ...たり...たり: We sang and danced. (*Watashi-tachi wa utattari odottari shita.*) 私たちは歌ったり踊ったりした.

3 (phrase and phrase) so⌈shite そして; ⟨verb⟩-te[de] ...て[で]: She played the piano and I sang. (*Kanojo ga piano o hiite watashi ga utatta.*) 彼女がピアノを弾いて私が歌った. / I opened the door and went inside. (*Watashi wa doa o akete naka e haitta.*) 私はドアを開けて中へ入った.

4 (as a result) (verb)-ba ...ば: Work hard and you will succeed. (*Isshoo-keñmee yareba seekoo shimasu.*) 一生懸命やれば成功します.

anecdote *n.* i⌈tsuwa 逸話.

angel *n.* te⌉ñshi 天使.

anger *n.* i⌈kari 怒り: hold back one's anger (*ikari o osaeru*) 怒りを抑える.

in anger *adv., adj.* o⌈ko⌉tte 怒って: She tore up the letter in anger. (*Kanojo wa okotte sono tegami o yabuita.*) 彼女は怒ってその手紙を破いた.

angle *n.* ka⌉ku 角; ka⌉kudo 角度: a right angle (*chokkaku*) 直角 / consider from various angles (*iroiro na kakudo kara kañgaeru*) いろいろな角度から考える.

angry *adj.* o⌈ko⌉tte (iru) 怒って(いる); ha⌈ra⌉ o ta⌉tete (iru) 腹を立てて(いる): He soon gets angry. (*Kare wa sugu okoru.*) 彼はすぐ怒る. / She looked angry. (*Kanojo wa okotta kao o shita.*) 彼女は怒った顔をした.

animal *n.* do⌈obutsu 動物.

ankle *n.* a⌈shi⌉kubi 足首; ku⌈ru⌉bushi くるぶし: I think I sprained my ankle. (*Ashikubi o kujiita rashii.*) 足首をくじいたらしい.

annex *n.* be⌈kkañ 別館.

anniversary *n.* ki⌈ne⌉ñbi 記念日: a wedding anniversary (*kekkoñ kineñbi*) 結婚記念日.

announce *vt.* ... o ha⌈ppyoo suru ...を発表する [I]; shi⌈raseru 知らせる [V]: They announced their engagement. (*Futari wa koñyaku o happyoo shita.*) 二人は婚約を発表した.

announcement *n.* ha⌈ppyoo 発表; tsu⌈uchi 通知: I read the announcement in a newspaper. (*Sono happyoo o shiñbuñ de yomimashita.*) その発表を新聞で読みました.

announcer *n.* a⌈nau⌉ñsaa アナウンサー.

annoy *vt.* ... o ko⌈marase⌉ru 困らせる [V]; na⌈yama⌉su 悩ます [C]: The crying baby annoyed her. (*Naite iru akañbo ga kanojo o komaraseta.*) 泣いている赤ん坊が彼女を困らせた.

annual *adj.* ma⌈itoshi no 毎年の; i⌈chi-neñ⌉kañ no 1年間の: an annual income (*neñshuu*) 年収.

annul *vt.* ... o to⌈rikesu ...を取り消す [C]; mu⌈koo ni suru 無効にする [I]: annul a contract (*keeyaku o mukoo ni suru*) 契約を無効にする.

anonymous *adj.* to⌈kumee no 匿名の; (of a book) sa⌉kusha fu⌈mee no 作者不明の: an anonymous letter (*tokumee no tegami*) 匿名の手紙.

another *adj.* **1** (one more) mo⌐o hito¬tsu [hito¬ri] no もう一つ[一人]の: How about another cup of tea? (*Ocha o moo ip-pai ikaga desu ka?*) お茶をもう1杯いかがですか.
2 (different) be⌐tsu no 別の; ho⌐ka no ほかの: Can you recommend another hotel? (*Hoka no hoteru o shookai shite kuremaseñ ka?*) ほかのホテルを紹介してくれませんか. / Show me another one, please. (*Hoka no o misete kudasai.*) ほかのを見せてください.

answer *n.* ko⌐ta¬e 答え; he⌐ñji¬ 返事: This answer is wrong. (*Kono kotae wa machigatte iru.*) この答えは間違っている. / Please give me your answer soon. (*Go-heñji o sugu ni kudasai.*) ご返事をすぐに下さい.
— *vt.* ... ni ko⌐tae¬ru 答える Ⓥ; he⌐ñji¬ o suru 返事をする Ⓘ: Nobody answered the question. (*Dare mo sono shitsumoñ ni kotaenakatta.*) だれもその質問に答えなかった. / I will answer you later. (*Ato de heñji o shimasu.*) あとで返事をします.
— *vi.* ko⌐tae¬ru 答える Ⓥ; he⌐ñji¬ o suru 返事をする Ⓘ: Please answer in English. (*Eego de kotaete kudasai.*) 英語で答えてください.

ant *n.* a⌐ri あり.

Antarctic *adj.* na⌐ñkyoku no 南極の: an Antarctic expedition (*nañkyoku tañkeñ*) 南極探検.
— *n.* na⌐ñkyoku 南極.

anticipate *vt.* **1** (expect) ... to yo⌐soo suru …と予想する Ⓘ: I'm anticipating a large attendance today. (*Kyoo wa shussekisha ga ooi to yosoo shite imasu.*) きょうは出席者が多いと予想しています.
2 (act in advance) ... ni se⌐ñte o u¬tsu …に先手を打つ Ⓒ: I anticipated his questions. (*Watashi wa kare no shitsumoñ ni señte o utta.*) 私は彼の質問に先手を打った.

antique *n.* ko⌐ttoohiñ 骨董品; a⌐ñti¬iku アンティーク: Is there an antiques dealer near here? (*Kono chikaku ni kottoo-ya wa arimasu ka?*) この近くに骨董屋はありますか.

anxiety *n.* shi⌐ñpai 心配; fu⌐añ 不安: cause a person anxiety (*hito ni shiñpai o kakeru*) 人に心配をかける.

anxious *adj.* **1** (feeling uneasy) shi⌐ñpai shite (iru) 心配して(いる): I am anxious about his health. (*Kare no keñkoo no koto ga shiñpai desu.*) 彼の健康のことが心配です.
2 (eager) se⌐tsuboo shite (iru) 切望して(いる); ⟨verb⟩-taga¬tte iru …たがっている: She is anxious to meet you. (*Kanojo wa anata ni aitagatte iru.*) 彼女はあなたに会いたがっている.

any *adj.* **1** (some) i⌐kura¬ka no いくらかの. ★ Not translated in Japanese: Do you have any children? (*O-ko-sañ wa o-ari desu ka?*) お子さんはおありですか. / Are there any letters for me? (*Watashi ate no tegami ga todoite imasu ka?*) 私あての手紙が届いていますか.
2 (every) do¬no [do¬ñna] ... de mo どの[どんな]…でも: Any dictionary will do. (*Dono jisho de mo kekkoo desu.*) どの辞書でも結構です.

anybody *pron.* **1** [in negative] da⌐re mo だれも; [interrogative] da¬re-ka だれか: I have't seen anybody. (*Watashi wa dare mo mimaseñ deshita.*) 私はだれも見ませんでした. / Is there anybody who can help me? (*Dare-ka tetsudatte kureru hito wa imaseñ ka?*) だれか手伝ってくれる人はいませんか.
2 [in affirmative] da¬re de mo だれでも: Anybody can do a thing like that. (*Soñna koto wa dare de mo dekimasu.*) そんなことはだれでもできます.

anyhow *adv.* to¬nikaku とにかく; i⌐zure ni shite¬ mo いずれにしても: Anyhow, let's begin. (*Tonikaku hajimeyoo.*) とにかく始めよう.

anything *pron.* **1** (something) na¬ni-ka 何か; na⌐ni mo 何も: I don't know anything about it. (*Sore ni tsuite watashi wa nani mo shirimaseñ.*) それについて私は何も

知りません.
2 (thing) mo⌈no⌉ 物: Is there anything cheaper? (*Motto yasui mono wa arimasu ka?*) もっと安い物はありますか.

anyway *adv.* to⌉nikaku とにかく; i⌈zure ni se⌉yo いずれにせよ: Anyway, let's get to work. (*Tonikaku shigoto o hajimeyoo.*) とにかく仕事を始めよう.

anywhere *adv.* **1** [in negative] do⌉ko e mo どこへも; [interrogative] do⌉ko-ka ni [de] どこかに[で]: Did you see my glasses anywhere? (*Doko-ka de watashi no megane o mimashita ka?*) どこかで私の眼鏡をみましたか. / I didn't go anywhere yesterday. (*Kinoo wa doko e mo ikanakatta.*) きのうはどこへも行かなかった.
2 [in affirmative] do⌉ko e de mo どこへでも: You can go anywhere you like. (*Doko e de mo suki na tokoro e itte ii desu yo.*) どこへでも好きな所へ行っていいですよ.

apart *adv.* ha⌈na⌉rete 離れて; ba⌈rabara ni ばらばらに: They live apart. (*Kare-ra wa hanarete kurashite iru.*) 彼らは離れて暮らしている.

apartment *n.* a⌈pa⌉ato アパート; ma⌉ñshoñ マンション. ★ In Japan '*apaato*' usually refers to an apartment house. '*Apaato*' customarily refers to one- or two-storied wooden structures and is less prestigious than '*mañshoñ*,' which often refers to a condominium.

apologize *vi.* a⌈yama⌉ru 謝る Ⓒ; wa⌈biru わびる Ⓥ: He apologized to her for being late. (*Kare wa okureta koto o kanojo ni ayamatta.*) 彼は遅れたことを彼女に謝った.

apology *n.* wa⌈bi わび; sha⌈zai 謝罪: make an apology (*wabi o iu*) わびを言う.

apparatus *n.* ki⌉gu 器具; so⌉ochi 装置: a heating apparatus (*dañboo soochi*) 暖房装置.

apparent *adj.* a⌈ki⌉raka na 明らかな; ha⌈kki⌉ri shite iru はっきりしている: This fact is apparent to everybody. (*Kono jijitsu wa dare no me ni mo akiraka desu.*) この事実はだれの目にも明らかです.

apparently *adv.* mi⌉ta tokoro ... ra⌈shi⌉i 見たところ…らしい: She was apparently happy. (*Kanojo wa mita tokoro shiawase rashikatta.*) 彼女は見たところ幸せらしかった.

appeal *n.* **1** (request) o-⌈negai お願い; u⌈ttae 訴え: an appeal for help (*eñjo no o-negai*) 援助のお願い.
2 (of a law) ko⌉oso 控訴.
— *vi.* **1** (ask for) (... ni) (... o) ta⌈no⌉mu (…に)(…を)頼む Ⓒ: We appealed to him for support. (*Watashi-tachi wa kare ni shiji o tanoñda.*) 私たちは彼に支持を頼んだ.
2 (attract) (... ni) u⌈ke⌉ru (…に)受ける Ⓥ: The novel appealed to young people. (*Sono shoosetsu wa wakai hito-tachi ni uketa.*) その小説は若い人たちに受けた.
3 (against a legal judgment) ko⌉oso suru 控訴する Ⓘ.

appear *vi.* **1** (become visible) a⌈raware⌉ru 現れる Ⓥ: The moon appeared from behind the mountain. (*Tsuki ga yama no kage kara arawareta.*) 月が山の影から現れた.
2 (present oneself) ... ni de⌉ru …に出る; shu⌈tsueñ suru 出演する: appear on television (*terebi ni deru*) テレビに出る.
3 (seem likely) ... ra⌉shiku mi⌈e⌉ru …らしく見える Ⓥ; ... yo⌉o da …ようだ: He appears to have caught a cold. (*Kare wa kaze o hiite iru yoo da.*) 彼はかぜをひいているようだ.

appearance *n.* **1** (act of appearing) shu⌈sseki 出席; shu⌈tsujoo 出場: make an appearance at a party (*paatii ni shusseki suru*) パーティーに出席する.
2 (outward form) ga⌈ikañ 外観; mi⌈kake 見かけ: You should not judge by appearances. (*Mikake de hañdañ shite wa ikenai.*) 見かけで判断してはいけない.

appendicitis *n.* [technically] chu⌈usu⌉ieñ 虫垂炎; [popularly] mo⌈ocho⌉oen 盲腸炎: have appendicitis (*moochoo ni naru*) 盲腸になる.

appendix *n.* **1** (of a book) fu⌈roku 付録.
2 (bodily organ) chu⌈usui 虫垂; [popularly] mo⌉ochoo 盲腸.

appetite *n.* sho⌈kuyoku 食欲: I have a good [poor] appetite. (*Watashi wa shokuyoku ga aru* [*nai*].) 私は食欲がある[ない].

applaud *vt.* ... ni ha⌉kushu o o⌈kuru ...に拍手を送る [C]: The audience applauded the actor. (*Kañkyaku wa sono haiyuu ni hakushu o okutta.*) 観客はその俳優に拍手を送った.
— *vi.* ha⌉kushu suru 拍手する [I]; ho⌈me⌉ru ほめる [V].

applause *n.* ha⌉kushu 拍手: win the applause of the audience (*kañshuu no hakushu o abiru*) 観衆の拍手を浴びる.

apple *n.* ri⌈ñgo りんご: peel an apple (*riñgo no kawa o muku*) りんごの皮をむく.

applicant *n.* o⌈obo⌉sha 応募者; mo⌈oshikomi⌉sha 申込者: an applicant for a job (*kyuushokusha*) 求職者.

application *n.* **1** (formal request) mo⌈oshikomi 申し込み; shi⌈ñsee 申請: make an application for a job (*shigoto no mooshikomi o suru*) 仕事の申し込みをする.
2 (use) te⌈kiyoo 適用; o⌈oyoo 応用: the application of law (*hoo no tekiyoo*) 法の適用.

apply *vi.* **1** (formally request) (... ni) (... o) mo⌈oshikomu (...に)(...を)申し込む [C]; shi⌈ñsee suru 申請する [I]: I applied for a visa. (*Watashi wa biza no shiñsee o shita.*) 私はビザの申請をした.
2 (fit) (... ni) a⌈tehama⌉ru ...に当てはまる [C]; te⌈kigoo suru 適合する [I]: The rule does not apply to this case. (*Sono kisoku wa kono baai atehamaranai.*) その規則はこの場合当てはまらない.
— *vt.* **1** (make use of) ... o (... ni) o⌈oyoo suru ...を(...に)応用する [I]; te⌈kiyoo suru 適用する [I]: apply new technology to industry (*atarashii gijutsu o sañgyoo ni ooyoo suru*) 新しい技術を産業に応用する.
2 (put) ... o a⌈teru ...を当てる [V]; ha⌈ru はる [C]: apply plaster to a wound (*kizuguchi ni kooyaku o haru*) 傷口にこう薬をはる.

appoint *vt.* **1** (assign) ... o (... ni) ni⌈ñmee suru ...を(...に)任命する [I]; shi⌈mee suru 指名する [I]: They appointed Mr. Yamada chairman. (*Kare-ra wa Yamada-sañ o gichoo ni shimee shita.*) 彼らは山田さんを議長に指名した. / He was appointed professor. (*Kare wa kyooju ni niñmee sareta.*) 彼は教授に任命された.
2 (fix) ... o shi⌈tee suru ...を指定する [I]: appoint the date and place for a meeting (*kaigi no nichiji to basho o shitee suru*) 会議の日時と場所を指定する.

appointment *n.* ya⌈kusoku 約束; yo⌈yaku 予約; a⌈po⌉iñtomeñto アポイントメント: I'd like an appointment for 3 p.m. today. (*Kyoo no sañ-ji ni yoyaku o onegai shitai ñ desu ga.*) きょうの3時に予約をお願いしたいんですが. / make an appointment (*apoiñtomeñto o toru*) アポイントメントをとる.

appreciate *vt.* **1** (be grateful) ... ni ka⌉ñsha suru ...に感謝する [I]; ... o a⌈rigata⌉ku o⌈mo⌉u ...をありがたく思う [C]: I do appreciate your kindness. (*Anata no go-shiñsetsu ni kañsha shimasu.*) あなたのご親切に感謝します.
2 (enjoy) ... o ka⌈ñshoo suru ...を鑑賞する [I]: appreciate good music (*yoi oñgaku o kañshoo suru*) よい音楽を鑑賞する.

appreciation *n.* **1** (grateful recognition) ka⌉ñsha 感謝: I'd like to express my appreciation for your help. (*Go-eñjo ni taishite kañsha mooshiagemasu.*) ご援助にたいして感謝申し上げます.
2 (sensitive awareness) ka⌈ñshoo

鑑賞: appreciation of music (*oñgaku no kañshoo*) 音楽の鑑賞.

approach *vt.* ... ni chi⌈kazu⌉ku ... に近づく [C]; se⌈kkiñ suru 接近する [I]: A typhoon is approaching Kyushu. (*Taifuu ga Kyuushuu ni sekkiñ shite iru.*) 台風が九州に接近している.
— *vi.* chi⌈kazu⌉ku 近づく [C]: Christmas is approaching. (*Kurisumasu ga chikazuite iru.*) クリスマスが近づいている.

appropriate *adj.* te⌈kitoo na 適当な; te⌈kisetsu na 適切な: take appropriate measures (*tekisetsu na shochi o toru*) 適切な処置をとる.
— *vt.* ... o (... ni) a⌈teru ...を(...に)充てる [V]: appropriate the money for repaying a loan (*sono o-kane o rooñ heñsai ni ateru*) そのお金をローン返済に充てる.

approval *n.* sa⌈ñsee 賛成; do⌈oi 同意: receive a person's approval (*hito no sañsee o eru*) 人の賛成を得る.

approve *vt.* ... ni sa⌈ñsee suru ... に賛成する [I]; ... o sho⌈oniñ suru ... を承認する [I]: The committee approved the budget. (*Iiñkai wa yosañañ o shooniñ shita.*) 委員会は予算案を承認した.

April *n.* shi-⌈gatsu⌉ 四月.

apron *n.* e⌉puroñ エプロン: put on an apron (*epuroñ o kakeru*) エプロンをかける.

apt *adj.* 〈verb〉-⌈gachi da ...がちだ; yo⌉ku 〈verb〉 よく...: We are apt to waste time. (*Watashi-tachi wa jikañ o muda ni shi-gachi da.*) 私たちは時間を無駄にしがちだ. / I am apt to forget people's names. (*Watashi wa yoku hito no namae o wasureru.*) 私はよく人の名前を忘れる.

aquarium *n.* su⌈izoku⌉kañ 水族館.

arbitrary *adj.* ni⌉ñi no 任意の; ka⌈tte na 勝手な: an arbitrary choice (*katte na señtaku*) 勝手な選択.

arcade *n.* a⌈ake⌉edo アーケード.

arch *n.* a⌉achi アーチ.

architect *n.* ke⌈ñchikuka 建築家.

architecture *n.* (art) ke⌈ñchiku⌉gaku 建築学; ke⌈ñchiku-gi⌉jutsu 建築技術; (style) ke⌈ñchiku-yo⌉oshiki 建築様式: a church of ancient architecture (*kodai keñchiku-yooshiki no kyookai*) 古代建築様式の教会.

Arctic *adj.* ho⌈kkyoku no 北極の: an Arctic expedition (*hokkyoku tañkeñ*) 北極探検.
— *n.* ho⌈kkyoku 北極; ho⌈kkyoku chi⌉hoo 北極地方.

ardent *adj.* ne⌉sshiñ na 熱心な; ne⌈tsuretsu na 熱烈な: an ardent supporter of the ruling party (*yotoo no netsuretsu na shijisha*) 与党の熱烈な支持者.

area *n.* **1** (space) me⌉ñseki 面積: The area of this floor is 30 square meters. (*Kono yuka no meñseki wa sañjuu heehoo meetoru desu.*) この床の面積は30平方メートルです.
2 (region) chi⌉iki 地域; chi⌉hoo 地方: What type of cooking is this area known for? (*Kono chihoo no meebutsu ryoori wa nañ desu ka?*) この地方の名物料理は何ですか.

argue *vi.* (quarrel) ko⌉oroñ suru 口論する [I]; (discuss) gi⌉roñ suru 議論する [I]: I argued with him about the novel. (*Watashi wa sono shoosetsu ni tsuite kare to giroñ shita.*) 私はその小説について彼と議論した.
— *vt.* ... o ro⌈ñjiru ...を論じる [V]; se⌈ttoku suru 説得する [I]: We argued politics. (*Watashi-tachi wa seeji o roñjita.*) 私たちは政治を論じた.

argument *n.* (quarrel) ko⌉oroñ 口論; (discussion) gi⌉roñ 議論: They had an argument about the plan. (*Kare-ra wa sono keekaku ni tsuite giroñ shita.*) 彼らはその計画について議論した.

arise *vi.* o⌈ko⌉ru 起こる [C]; sho⌈ojiru 生じる [V]: A difficult problem has arisen. (*Muzukashii moñdai ga okotta.*) むずかしい問題が起こった.

arithmetic *n.* sa⌈ñsu⌉u 算数.

arm[1] *n.* u⌈de⌉ 腕: The couple were walking arm in arm. (*Futari wa *ude o kuñde aruite ita.*) 二人は腕を組んで歩いていた.

arm[2] *vt.* ... de bu⌈soo suru ...で武装する [I]: arm oneself with a gun (*juu de busoo suru*) 銃で武装する.

arms *n.* he⌉eki 兵器; bu⌉ki 武器: bear arms (*buki o motsu*) 武器を持つ.

army *n.* ri⌈ku⌉guñ 陸軍; gu⌉ñtai 軍隊.

around *prep.* **1** (circuit) ... no ma⌈wari o [ni] ...の周りを[に]; ... o ka⌈koñde ...を囲んで: run around a tree (*ki no mawari o hashiru*) 木の周りを走る / sit around a fire (*hi o kakoñde suwaru*) 火を囲んで座る.
2 (here and there) a⌈chi-ko⌉chi あちこち: travel around the country (*kuni-juu achi-kochi tabi o suru*) 国中あちこち旅をする.
3 (near) ... no a⌉tari ni ...の辺りに: Her house is around here. (*Kanojo no uchi wa kono atari desu.*) 彼女の家はこの辺りです.
— *adv.* ma⌈wari ni 周りに; a⌉tari ni 辺りに; gu⌈ru⌉ri to ぐるりと: the scenery around (*mawari no keshiki*) 周りの景色 / look around (*atari o mimawasu*) 辺りを見回す/ go around (*mawarimichi o suru*) 回り道をする / hand the papers around (*shorui o mawasu*) 書類を回す.

arouse *vt.* ... o hi⌈kioko⌉su ...を引き起こす [C]; ma⌈ne⌉ku 招く [C]: arouse a person's anger (*hito no ikari o maneku*) 人の怒りを招く.

arrange *vt.* **1** (put into order) ... o ki⌈chi⌉ñto na⌈raberu ...をきちんと並べる [V]: arrange the chairs (*isu o kichiñto naraberu*) 椅子をきちんと並べる / arrange flowers (*hana o ikeru*) 花を生ける.
2 (plan) ... o ki⌈meru ...を決める [V]; te⌉hai suru 手配する [I]: We will arrange the details later. (*Komakai koto wa ato de kimemasu.*) 細かいことは後で決めます. / arrange a car (*kuruma o tehai suru*) 車を手配する.

arrangement *n.* kyo⌈otee 協定; ju⌉ñbi 準備; ha⌈iretsu 配列: come to an arrangement (*kyootee ga seeritsu suru*) 協定が成立する / make the arrangements for one's trip (*ryokoo no juñbi o suru*) 旅行の準備をする.

arrest *vt.* ... o ta⌉iho suru ...を逮捕する [I]: arrest a thief (*doroboo o taiho suru*) 泥棒を逮捕する.
— *n.* ta⌉iho 逮捕.

arrival *n.* to⌈ochaku 到着: arrival time (*toochaku jikañ*) 到着時間.

arrive *vi.* **1** (get to) (... ni) tsu⌉ku (...に)着く [C]; to⌈ochaku suru 到着する [I]: This train arrives at Kyoto at three. (*Kono ressha wa sañ-ji ni Kyooto ni tsukimasu.*) この列車は3時に京都に着きます. / When did the letter arrive? (*Sono tegami wa itsu tsukimashita ka?*) その手紙はいつ着きましたか.
2 (reach) (... ni) ta⌈ssuru (...に)達する [I]: arrive at a conclusion (*ketsuroñ ni tassuru*) 結論に達する.

art *n.* ge⌈ejutsu 芸術; bi⌉jutsu 美術: an art museum (*bijutsu-kañ*) 美術館.

article *n.* **1** (account) ki⌉ji 記事; ro⌈ñbuñ 論文: an article in a magazine (*zasshi no kiji*) 雑誌の記事.
2 (thing) shi⌈namono 品物; -hiñ 品: prohibited articles (*mochikomi kiñshi-hiñ*) 持込み禁止品.
3 (clause) jo⌈okoo 条項: the articles of an agreement (*kyootee no jookoo*) 協定の条項.
4 (of grammar) ka⌈ñshi 冠詞: a definite [an indefinite] article (*tee [futee]-kañshi*) 定[不定]冠詞.

artificial *adj.* ji⌈ñkoo no 人工の; ji⌈ñzoo no 人造の: artificial respiration (*jiñkoo kokyuu*) 人工呼吸 / an artificial flower (*zooka*) 造花.

artist *n.* **1** ge⌈ejutsuka 芸術家.
2 (painter) ga⌈ka 画家; e⌈kaki⌉ 絵かき.

artistic *adj.* ge⌈ejutsu-teki na 芸術的な: artistic beauty (*geejutsu-teki na utsukushisa*) 芸術的な美しさ.

as *conj.* **1** (in the way) ... no yo⌉o ni ...のように; to⌉ori ni とおりに: Do as

you are told. (*Iwareta toori ni shi nasai.*) 言われたとおりにしなさい.
2 (when) ⟨verb⟩ to'ki (ni) …とき(に); (verb) ni tsu'rete …につれて: Just as I was going to bed, there was an earthquake. (*Choodo neyoo to shita toki jishiñ ga atta.*) ちょうど寝ようとしたとき地震があった. / As we grow older, we become forgetful. (*Toshi o toru ni tsurete wasurep-poku naru.*) 年をとるにつれて忘れっぽくなる.
3 (because) … no de …ので; … kara …から: As it rained, I didn't go. (*Ame ga futta no de, watashi wa ikanakatta.*) 雨が降ったので私は行かなかった.
— *prep.* (role) … to shi'te …として: He attended the meeting as an observer. (*Kare wa sono kaigi ni obuzaabaa to shite shusseki shita.*) 彼はその会議にオブザーバーとして出席した.
— *pron.* … no yo'o na …のような: Give me the same thing as this. (*Kore to onaji yoo na mono o kuda-sai.*) これと同じようなものを下さい.
as … as … to o'naji ku'rai …と同じくらい: He is as tall as I am. (*Kare no se no takasa wa watashi to onaji kurai desu.*) 彼の背の高さは私と同じくらいです.

ascertain *vt.* … o ta'shikame'ru …を確かめる V: I ascertained the facts. (*Watashi wa sono jijitsu o tashikameta.*) 私はその事実を確かめた.

ash *n.* ha'i 灰: cigarette ash (*tabako no hai*) たばこの灰.

ashamed *adj.* ha'zukashi'i 恥ずかしい: I am ashamed of myself for having done such a thing. (*Wata-shi wa soñna koto o shite hazuka-shiku omou.*) 私はそんなことをして恥ずかしく思う.

ashtray *n.* ha'izara 灰皿.

aside *adv.* wa'ki' ni わきに: pull a curtain aside (*kaateñ o waki ni hiku*) カーテンをわきに引く / lay a book aside (*hoñ o waki ni oku*) 本をわきに置く.

ask *vt.* **1** (inquire) … ni ki'ku …に聞く C; ta'zune'ru 尋ねる V: Let's ask him about it. (*Sono koto ni tsuite kare ni kiite mimashoo.*) そのことについて彼に聞いてみましょう. / I asked her her address. (*Watashi wa kanojo ni juusho o tazuneta.*) 私は彼女に住所を尋ねた.
2 (request) … ni (… o) ta'no'mu …に(…を)頼む C: I asked him to re-serve a room at a hotel. (*Watashi wa kare ni hoteru no heya no yoyaku o tanoñda.*) 私は彼にホテルの部屋の予約を頼んだ.
ask for … *vt.* … o mo'tome'ru …を求める V: ask for his advice (*kare no jogeñ o motomeru*) 彼の助言を求める.

asleep *adj.* **1** (sleep) ne'mutte (iru) 眠って(いる): The baby is fast asleep. (*Akañboo wa gussuri ne-mutte iru.*) 赤ん坊はぐっすり眠っている.
2 (of a limb) shi'bi're te (iru) しびれて(いる): My left foot is asleep. (*Hidari ashi ga shibireta.*) 左足がしびれた.

aspire *vi.* (… o) ne'tsuboo suru (…を)熱望する I; no'zomu 望む C: He aspired to the position. (*Kare wa sono chii o nozoñde ita.*) 彼はその地位を望んでいた.

aspirin *n.* a'supiriñ アスピリン: take two aspirins (*asupiriñ o ni-joo nomu*) アスピリンを2錠飲む.

assault *vt.* … o shu'ugeki suru …を襲撃する I; o'so'u 襲う C: The robber assaulted the guard. (*Goo-too ga keebiiñ o osotta.*) 強盗が警備員を襲った.
— *n.* shu'ugeki 襲撃; (rape) bo'o-koo 暴行.

assemble *vt.* **1** (gather) … o a'tsume'ru …を集める V: assemble the students in a hall (*seeto o hoo-ru ni atsumeru*) 生徒をホールに集める.
2 (put together) … o ku'mitate'ru …を組み立てる V: assemble a bicy-cle (*jiteñsha o kumitateru*) 自転車を組み立てる.
— *vi.* a'tsuma'ru 集まる C.

assembly *n.* **1** (of people) shu⌈u-kai 集会; ka⌈igoo 会合: The assembly will be held tomorrow. (*Shuukai wa ashita hirakaremasu.*) 集会はあした開かれます.
2 (legislative body) gi⌉kai 議会: the city assembly (*shi-gikai*) 市議会.
3 (of parts) ku⌈mitate 組立: assembly plant (*kumitate-koojoo*) 組立工場.

assert *vt.* **1** (insisit) ... o shu⌈choo suru ...を主張する [I]: assert one's rights (*jibuñ no keñri o shuchoo suru*) 自分の権利を主張する.
2 (declare) ... to da⌈ñge⌉ñ suru ...と断言する [I]; ha⌈kki⌉ri i⌈u はっきり言う [C]: He asserted that he had seen it. (*Kare wa sore o mita to dañgeñ shita.*) 彼はそれを見たと断言した.

assign *vt.* **1** (allot) ... o wa⌈riate⌉ru ...を割り当てる [V]: I assigned the room to them. (*Watashi wa sono heya o kare-ra ni wariateta.*) 私はその部屋を彼らに割り当てた.
2 (fix) ... o shi⌈tee suru ...を指定する [I]; ki⌈meru 決める [V]: assign a day for the meeting (*kaigi no hi o kimeru*) 会議の日を決める.

assignment *n.* shu⌈kudai 宿題; wa⌈riate 割り当て: a summer assignment (*natsuyasumi no shukudai*) 夏休みの宿題.

assist *vt.* ... o te⌈tsuda⌉u ...を手伝う [C]; e⌉ñjo suru 援助する [I]: I assisted him with his work. (*Watashi wa kare no shigoto o tetsudatta.*) 私は彼の仕事を手伝った.
— *vi.* jo⌈ryoku suru 助力する [I].

assistance *n.* e⌉ñjo 援助; jo⌈ryoku 助力: give economic assistance (*keezai eñjo o suru*) 経済援助をする.

assistant *n.* jo⌈shu 助手.

assistant professor *n.* jo⌈kyo⌉oju 助教授.

associate *vi.* ko⌈osai suru 交際する [I]: associate with many people (*ooku no hito to koosai suru*) 多くの人と交際する.
— *vt.* ... o re⌉ñsoo suru ... を連想する [I]: We associate Mt. Fuji with Japan. (*Fuji-sañ to ieba Nihoñ o reñsoo suru.*) 富士山といえば日本を連想する.

associate professor *n.* ju⌈ñkyo⌉oju 準教授.

association *n.* **1** (society) kyo⌈okai 協会; ku⌈miai 組合.
2 (companionship) ko⌈osai 交際.

assume *vt.* **1** (suppose) to⌈ozeñ ... to o⌈mo⌉u 当然...と思う [C]: I assumed that he would come. (*Kare wa toozeñ kuru mono to omotte ita.*) 彼は当然来るものと思っていた.
2 (undertake) ... o hi⌈kiuke⌉ru ...を引き受ける [V]; to⌉ru とる [C]: Who will assume the responsibility? (*Dare ga sono sekiniñ o toru no desu ka?*) だれがその責任をとるのですか.

assumption *n.* ka⌈tee 仮定: It is a mere assumption. (*Sore wa tañnaru katee desu.*) それは単なる仮定です.

assurance *n.* (guarantee) ho⌈shoo 保証; ka⌈kuyaku 確約; (confidence) ka⌈kushiñ 確信: receive assurance (*hoshoo [kakuyaku] o eru*) 保証[確約]を得る.

assure *vt.* (promise) ... ni (... o) ka⌈kuyaku suru ...に(...を)確約する [I]; ho⌈shoo suru 保証する [I]: I assured her of my assistance. (*Watashi wa kanojo ni eñjo o kakuyaku shita.*) 私は彼女に援助を確約した.

assured *adj.* (... o) ka⌈kushiñ shite (iru) (...を)確信して(いる): I am assured of his innocence. (*Watashi wa kare no mujitsu o kakushiñ shite iru.*) 私は彼の無実を確信している.

asthma *n.* ze⌈ñsoku ぜんそく: suffer from asthma (*zeñsoku ni kakaru*) ぜんそくにかかる.

astonish *vt.* ... o o⌈doroka⌉su ...を驚かす [C]; bi⌈kku⌉ri saseru びっくりさせる [V]: I was astonished to hear the news. (*Watashi wa sono shirase o kiite bikkuri shita.*) 私はその知らせを聞いてびっくりした.

astonishment *n.* o⌈doroki⌉ 驚き; bi⌈kku⌉ri びっくり: She looked at me in astonishment. (*Kanojo wa odoroite watashi o mita.*) 彼女は驚いて私を見た.

astound *vt.* ... o bi⌈kku⌉ri gyooteñ sa⌈seru …をびっくり仰天させる Ⓥ: I was astounded by the news. (*Watashi wa sono shirase ni bikkuri gyooteñ shita.*) 私はその知らせにびっくり仰天した.

astronomy *n.* te⌈ñmo⌉ñgaku 天文学.

at *prep.* **1** (position) ... de [ni] …で[に]: I bought this at that store. (*Watashi wa kore o ano mise de kaimashita.*) 私はこれをあの店で買いました. / At that traffic signal turn left. (*Ano shiñgoo de hidari ni magari nasai.*) あの信号で左に曲がりなさい.

2 (time) ... ni [de] …に[で]: Please wake me up at six tomorrow morning. (*Ashita no asa roku-ji ni okoshite kudasai.*) あしたの朝 6 時に起こしてください. / She got married at the age of twenty. (*Kanojo wa hatachi de kekkoñ shita.*) 彼女は 20 歳で結婚した.

3 (direction) ... o …を: The boy stared at me. (*Sono otoko-no-ko wa watashi o jirojiro to mita.*) その男の子は私をじろじろと見た.

4 (cost) ... de …で: I bought this bag at 5,000 yen. (*Watashi wa kono kabañ o goseñ-eñ de katta.*) 私はこのかばんを 5 千円で買った.

athlete *n.* u⌈ñdoo se⌉ñshu 運動選手; su⌈pootsu se⌉ñshu スポーツ選手.

athletics *n.* u⌈ñdoo kyo⌉ogi 運動競技.

Atlantic Ocean *n.* Ta⌈ise⌉eyoo 大西洋.

atlas *n.* chi⌈zuchoo 地図帳.

atmosphere *n.* **1** (feeling) fu⌈ñi⌉ki 雰囲気; ki⌉buñ 気分; mu⌉udo ムード: This restaurant has a nice atmosphere. (*Kono resutorañ wa muudo ga ii.*) このレストランはムードがいい. ★ In this sense, Japanese people often use '*muudo*' (mood).

2 (air) ta⌉iki 大気; ku⌉uki 空気: The atmosphere in the city is polluted. (*Toshi no kuuki wa yogorete iru.*) 都市の空気は汚れている.

atom *n.* ge⌉ñshi 原子.

attach *vt.* **1** (fasten) ... o to⌈ritsukeru …を取り付ける Ⓥ: attach a rope to a boat (*booto ni roopu o toritsukeru*) ボートにロープを取り付ける.

2 (affix) ... o so⌈eru …を添える Ⓥ; tsu⌈kekuwaeru つけ加える Ⓥ: I attached my comments to the document. (*Watashi no ikeñ o sono shorui ni soeta.*) 私の意見をその書類に添えた.

attack *vt.* **1** (use force) ... o ko⌈ogeki suru …を攻撃する Ⓘ; se⌈me⌉ru 攻める Ⓥ: attack the enemy (*teki o koogeki suru*) 敵を攻撃する.

2 (speak or write against) ... o ko⌈ogeki suru …を攻撃する Ⓘ; hi⌉nañ suru 非難する Ⓘ: attack the government (*seefu o koogeki suru*) 政府を攻撃する.

— *n.* ko⌈ogeki 攻撃; hi⌉nañ 非難: a personal attack (*kojiñ-koogeki*) 個人攻撃.

attain *vt.* **1** (achieve) ... o ta⌈ssee suru …を達成する Ⓘ: attain one's hopes (*nozomi o tassee suru*) 望みを達成する.

2 (reach) ... ni ta⌈ssuru …に達する Ⓘ: attain the top of a mountain (*yama no choojoo ni tassuru*) 山の頂上に達する.

attempt *vt.* ⟨verb⟩-(y)oo to suru …(よ)うとする Ⓘ; ku⌈wadate⌉ru 企てる Ⓥ: He attempted to climb the mountain. (*Kare wa sono yama ni noboroo to shita.*) 彼はその山に登ろうとした. / He attempted to stop smoking. (*Kare wa tabako o yameyoo to shita.*) 彼はたばこをやめようとした.

— *n.* ko⌈koromi⌉ 試み; ku⌈wadate⌉ 企て: His attempt failed. (*Kare no kuwadate wa shippai shita.*) 彼の企ては失敗した.

attend *vt.* **1** (be present) ... ni shu⌈sseki suru …に出席する Ⓘ: I attended the party. (*Watashi wa sono kai ni shusseki shita.*) 私はそ

の会に出席した.
2 (nurse) ... o ka⌝ñgo suru ...を看護する [I]; ... ni tsu⌜kiso⌝u ...に付き添う [C]: Who is attending your mother? (*Dare ga o-kaasañ o kañgo shite iru ñ desu ka?*) だれがお母さんを看護しているんですか.
— *vi*. (apply oneself to) ... ni se⌝e o dasu ...に精を出す [C]; se⌜ññeñ suru 専念する [I]: attend to one's business (*shigoto ni see o dasu*) 仕事に精を出す.

attendance *n*. **1** (attending) shu⌜sseki 出席: attendance at a meeting (*kai e no shusseki*) 会への出席.
2 (number present) shu⌜sseki⌝sha 出席者; sa⌜ñka⌝sha 参加者: There was a large attendance at the party. (*Paatii ni wa shussekisha ga oozee ita.*) パーティーには出席者が大勢いた.

attendant *adj*. tsu⌜kisoi no 付き添いの: an attendant nurse (*tsukisoi no kañgofu*) 付き添いの看護婦.
— *n*. tsu⌜kisoi 付き添い; ka⌝kari 係: a parking lot attendant (*chuushajoo no kakari*) 駐車場の係.

attention *n*. **1** (notice) chu⌝ui 注意; chu⌜umoku 注目: attract attention (*chuui o hiku*) 注意を引く / Nobody paid attention to what he said. (*Dare mo kare ga itta koto ni chuui o harawanakatta.*) だれも彼が言ったことに注意を払わなかった.
2 (care) se⌜wa 世話; (consideration) ko⌜koroku⌝bari 心配り.

attic *n*. ya⌜neura(beya) 屋根裏(部屋).

attitude *n*. **1** (behavior) ta⌝ido 態度: He took a defiant attitude. (*Kare wa hañkoo-teki na taido o totta.*) 彼は反抗的な態度を取った.
2 (thinking) ka⌜ñga⌝e 考え: What is your attitude to this problem? (*Kono moñdai ni taisuru anata no kañgae wa doo desu ka?*) この問題に対するあなたの考えはどうですか.

attorney *n*. be⌜ñgo⌝shi 弁護士: consult one's attorney (*beñgoshi ni soodañ suru*) 弁護士に相談する.

attract *vt*. ... o hi⌜kitsuke⌝ru ...を引き付ける [V]; hi⌜ku 引く [C]: A magnet attracts iron. (*Jishaku wa tetsu o hikitsukeru.*) 磁石は鉄を引き付ける. / He tried to attract her attention. (*Kare wa kanojo no chuui o hikoo to shita.*) 彼は彼女の注意を引こうとした.

attraction *n*. mi⌜ryoku 魅力: This painting has no attraction for me. (*Kono e wa watashi ni wa miryoku ga nai.*) この絵は私には魅力がない.

attractive *adj*. mi⌜ryoku-teki na 魅力的な; hi⌜to⌝ o hi⌜kitsuke⌝ru 人を引き付ける: an attractive woman (*miryoku-teki na josee*) 魅力的な女性.

attribute *vt*. ... o (... no) se⌝e ni suru ...を(...の)せいにする [I]: He attributed his failure to illness. (*Kare wa shippai o byooki no see ni shita.*) 彼は失敗を病気のせいにした.

audience *n*. (of a concert) cho⌜oshuu 聴衆; (of a performance) ka⌜ñkyaku 観客; (of a radio) cho⌜oshu⌝sha 聴取者; (of a TV) shi⌜cho⌝osha 視聴者; (of a book) do⌝kusha 読者.

August *n*. ha⌜chi-gatsu⌝ 八月.

aunt *n*. (one's own) o⌜ba おば; (another's) o⌜ba-sañ おばさん. ★ Often sounds derogatory.

Australia *n*. O⌜osutora⌝ria オーストラリア.

Australian *n*. (person) O⌜osutoraria⌝jiñ オーストラリア人.
— *adj*. O⌜osutora⌝ria no オーストラリアの: the Australian flag (*Oosutoraria no kokki*) オーストラリアの国旗.

author *n*. cho⌝sha 著者; sa⌝kusha 作者; (novelist) sa⌝kka 作家.

authority *n*. **1** (right) ke⌜ñge⌝ñ 権限; ke⌝ñryoku 権力: I have no authority to do this. (*Watashi ni wa kono koto o suru keñgeñ wa arimaseñ.*) 私にはこのことをする権限はありません.
2 [*pl*.] to⌝okyoku 当局: the govern-

ment authorities (*seefu tookyoku*) 政府当局.

3 (expert) ta¹ika 大家; ke¹ñi 権威: He is an authority on Japanese history. (*Kare wa Nihoñshi no keñi desu.*) 彼は日本史の権威です.

authorize *vt.* **1** (give right) ... ni ke⌈ñge¹ñ o a⌈taeru ...に権限を与える Ⓥ: The committee authorized him to negotiate. (*Iīñkai wa kare ni kooshoo suru keñgeñ o ataeta.*) 委員会は彼に交渉する権限を与えた.

2 (give permission) ... o ni¹ñka suru 認可する Ⓘ; ko⌈oniñ suru 公認する Ⓘ: an authorized money changer (*kooniñ ryoogaeshoo*) 公認両替商.

automatic *adj.* ji⌈doo-teki na 自動的な: This washing machine is automatic. (*Kono señtakuki wa jidoo desu.*) この洗濯機は自動です.

automobile *n.* ji⌈doosha 自動車; ku⌈ruma 車: drive an automobile (*jidoosha o uñteñ suru*) 自動車を運転する.

autumn *n.* a¹ki 秋.

avenue *n.* (wide street) o⌈odo¹ori 大通り; (with trees on both sides) na⌈miki¹-michi 並木道.

average *n.* he⌈ekiñ 平均: work out an average (*heekiñ o dasu*) 平均を出す.

— *adj.* he⌈ekiñ no 平均の; na⌈mi no 並の: the average temperature (*heekiñ kioñ*) 平均気温 / an average mark (*heekiñ teñ*) 平均点.

avoid *vt.* ... o sa⌈ke¹ru ...を避ける Ⓥ: He seems to be avoiding me. (*Kare wa watashi o sakete iru mitai da.*) 彼は私を避けているみたいだ.

await *vt.* ... o ma¹tsu ...を待つ Ⓒ: I am awaiting your reply. (*Anata no heñji o matte imasu.*) あなたの返事を待っています.

awake *vt.* me¹ o sa⌈ma¹su 目を覚ます Ⓒ: The noise awoke me. (*Sono monooto de me ga sameta.*) その物音で目が覚めた.

— *vi.* ... ni me⌈zame¹ru ...に目覚める Ⓥ; ... o ji⌈kaku suru ...を自覚する Ⓘ: He awoke to his responsibilities. (*Kare wa jibuñ no sekiniñ o jikaku shita.*) 彼は自分の責任を自覚した.

— *adj.* (not asleep) ne⌈murana¹i de (iru) 眠らないで(いる); o¹kite iru 起きている: He is still awake. (*Kare wa mada okite imasu.*) 彼はまだ起きています.

awaken *vt.* ... o yo⌈bioko¹su ...を呼び起こす Ⓒ: awaken a person's interest (*hito no kyoomi o yobiokosu*) 人の興味を呼び起こす.

award *n.* sho¹o 賞; (thing) sho⌈ohiñ 賞品: grant an award (*shoo o ataeru*) 賞を与える / receive an award (*shoo o morau*) 賞をもらう.

— *vt.* ... o a⌈taeru ...を与える Ⓥ: A gold medal was awarded to her. (*Kiñ medaru ga kanojo ni ataerareta.*) 金メダルが彼女に与えられた.

aware *adj.* ... ni ki⌈gatsu¹ite (iru) ...に気がついて(いる); ... o ka⌈ñzu¹ite (iru) ...を感づいて(いる): I was aware of the danger. (*Watashi wa sono kikeñ ni ki ga tsuite ita.*) 私はその危険に気がついていた.

away *adj.* (absent) fu⌈zai de [da] 不在で[だ]; (at a distance) ha⌈na¹rete (iru) 離れて(いる): He is away on a trip. (*Kare wa ryokoo de fuzai desu.*) 彼は旅行で不在です. / How far away is Kobe from Kyoto? (*Koobe wa Kyooto kara dono kurai hanarete imasu ka?*) 神戸は京都からどのくらい離れていますか.

— *adv.* a⌈chira e あちらへ; sa¹tte 去って: drive away (*oiharau*) 追い払う / fly away (*tobi-saru*) 飛び去る / melt away (*toke-saru*) 解け去る / take away (*mochi-saru*) 持ち去る.

awful *adj.* hi⌈do¹i ひどい; ta⌈iheñ na 大変な; su⌈go¹i すごい: an awful pain (*hidoi itami*) ひどい痛み / It was awful yesterday. (*Kinoo wa taiheñ deshita.*) きのうは大変でした.

awfully *adv.* to⌈temo とても; hi¹doku ひどく: It is awfully cold. (*Totemo samui.*) とても寒い.

awkward *adj.* **1** (clumsy) bu⌈ki¹-

a
b

yoo na 不器用な; gi⌈kochina⌉i ぎこちない: an awkward person (*bukiyoo na hito*) 不器用な人.
2 (difficult to deal with) ya⌉kkai na やっかいな; a⌈tsukainiku⌉i 扱いにくい: an awkward problem (*yakkai na moñdai*) やっかいな問題.
3 (embarassing) ba⌈tsu no waru⌉i ばつの悪い; ki⌈mazui 気まずい: I felt awkward. (*Watashi wa kimazui omoi o shita.*) 私は気まずい思いをした.

B

baby *n.* **1** a⌈kañboo 赤ん坊; [pet word] a⌉kachañ 赤ちゃん: a baby boy [girl] (*otoko* [*oñna*] *no akañboo*) 男[女]の赤ん坊 / have a baby (*akañboo o umu*) 赤ん坊を生む.
2 ko⌈domo 子ども: a baby elephant (*zoo no kodomo*) 象の子ども.

baby-sitter *n.* ko⌈mo⌉ri 子守; be⌈bii-shi⌉ttaa ベビーシッター.

bachelor *n.* do⌈kushi⌉ñsha 独身者; hi⌈torimono ひとり者: a bachelor girl (*dokushiñ no josee*) 独身の女性.

back *n.* **1** (of the body) se⌈naka 背中: scratch one's back (*senaka o kaku*) 背中をかく.
2 (the rear) u⌈shiro 後ろ; o⌉ku 奥: the back seat (*ushiro no zaseki*) 後ろの座席 / the back of a room (*heya no oku*) 部屋の奥.
3 (reverse side) u⌈ra 裏: back and front (*ura to omote*) 裏と表.
— *vt.* **1** (support) ... o ko⌈oeñ suru ...を後援する [I]; shi⌉ji suru 支持する [I]: back his plan (*kare no keekaku o shiji suru*) 彼の計画を支持する.
2 (cause to go backward) ... o ko⌈otai saseru ...を後退させる [V].
— *vi.* u⌈shiro e saga⌉ru 後ろへ下がる [C]: The car backed up slowly. (*Kuruma wa yukkuri ushiro e sagatta.*) 車はゆっくり後ろへ下がった.
— *adv.* u⌈shiro ni [e] 後ろに[へ]; mo⌉to no to⌈koro⌉ ni [e] 元の所に[へ]: Put my books back where you got them. (*Watashi no hoñ o moto atta tokoro e modoshi nasai.*) 私の本を元あった所へ戻しなさい. / go back home (*uchi e kaeru*) 家へ帰る.

background *n.* **1** (of scenery) ha⌈ikee 背景: high mountains in the background (*haikee no takai yama*) 背景の高い山.
2 (of conditions) ha⌈ikee 背景; jo⌈okyoo 状況: the economic and social background (*keezai-teki, shakai-teki haikee*) 経済的, 社会的背景.
3 (of a pattern) ji 地: blue spots on a white background (*shiro-ji ni aoi teñ no moyoo*) 白地に青い点の模様.

backward *adj.* **1** u⌈shiro e⌉ no 後ろへの; ko⌈ohoo e⌉ no 後方への: a gentle backward and forward movement (*zeñpoo to koohoo e no yukkuri shita ugoki*) 前方と後方へのゆっくりした動き.
2 o⌈kureta 遅れた; o⌈kurete iru 遅れている: a backward region of a rich country (*yutaka na kuni no okureta chiiki*) 豊かな国の遅れた地域.
— *adv.* u⌈shiro ni [e] 後ろに[へ]; gya⌈ku ni 逆に: The policeman slowly moved backward. (*Keekañ wa yukkuri ushiro e sagatta.*) 警官はゆっくり後ろへ下がった. / I can say the alphabet backward. (*Watashi wa arufabetto o gyaku ni iemasu.*) 私はアルファベットを逆に言えます.

bacon *n.* be⌉ekoñ ベーコン.

bacteria *n.* ba⌈kuteria バクテリア.

bad *adj.* **1** wa⌈ru⌉i 悪い; yo⌉ku nai よくない: bad news (*warui shirase*) 悪い知らせ / bad weather (*warui teñki*) 悪い天気 / My luck was bad. (*Watashi wa uñ ga warukatta.*) 私は運が悪かった.

2 hi⌈do⌉i ひどい: a bad headache (*hidoi zutsuu*) ひどい頭痛.
3 he⌈ta⌉ na 下手な; ma⌈zu⌉i まずい: I wish I weren't so bad at sports. (*Supootsu ga koñna ni heta de nakereba ii ñ da kedo.*) スポーツがこんなに下手でなければいいんだけど.
4 ... ni wa mu⌈kanai ...には向かない: Yesterday was a bad day for the marathon. (*Kinoo wa marasoñ ni wa mukanai hi datta.*) きのうはマラソンには向かない日だった.

badge *n.* ba⌉jji バッジ; ki⌈shoo 記章: wear a badge (*bajji o tsukeru*) バッジをつける.

badly *adv.* ma⌉zuku まずく; hi⌉doku ひどく; to⌈temo とても: He did his work badly. (*Kare no shigoto wa mazukatta.*) 彼の仕事はまずかった. / I was badly hurt. (*Watashi wa hidoi kega o shita.*) 私はひどいけがをした. / I want this badly. (*Watashi wa kore ga totemo hoshii.*) 私はこれがとても欲しい.

bag *n.* 1 fu⌈kuro⌉ 袋: a paper bag (*kami no fukuro*) 紙の袋.
2 (handbag) ha⌈ñdoba⌉ggu ハンドバッグ.

baggage *n.* te⌈ni⌉motsu 手荷物: check in one's baggage (*tenimotsu o chekku-iñ suru*) 手荷物をチェックインする.

bake *vt.* ... o ya⌈ku ...を焼く Ⓒ: bake bread in the oven (*oobuñ de pañ o yaku*) オーブンでパンを焼く.

bakery *n.* pa⌉ñya パン屋; se⌈epañjo 製パン所.

balance *n.* 1 (scales) ha⌈kari はかり; te⌈ñbiñba⌉kari てんびんばかり: weigh something on a balance (*hakari ni kakeru*) はかりにかける.
2 (equilibrium) tsu⌈riai つり合い; ki⌈ñkoo 均衡; he⌈ekoo 平衡; ba⌈rañsu バランス: preserve the balance of power (*chikara no kiñkoo o tamotsu*) 力の均衡を保つ / lose one's balance and fall over (*barañsu o ushinatte taoreru*) バランスを失って倒れる.
3 (remainder) za⌈ñgaku 残額: a bank balance (*giñkoo no zañgaku*) 銀行の残額.
— *vt.* (match) ... o hi⌈kaku suru ...を比較する Ⓘ; ku⌈raberu 比べる Ⓥ: balance the advantages against the disadvantages (*yuuri na teñ to furi na teñ o hikaku suru*) 有利な点と不利な点を比較する.
—*vi.* (keep steady) tsu⌈riai o to⌉ru 釣り合いを取る Ⓒ: balance on one's toes (*tsumasaki de tsuriai o toru*) つま先で釣り合いをとる.

balcony *n.* ba⌈ruko⌉nii バルコニー.

bald *adj.* ha⌉geta はげた; ha⌉gete iru はげている; ke ⌈no na⌉i 毛のない: Mr. Yamaguchi is bald. (*Yamaguchi-sañ wa atama ga hagete iru.*) 山口さんは頭がはげている.

ball *n.* bo⌈oru ボール; ta⌈ma 球; kyu⌉u 球: throw a ball (*booru o nageru*) ボールを投げる / a ball of wool (*keito no tama*) 毛糸の球.

ballet *n.* ba⌉ree バレエ.

balloon *n.* ki⌈kyuu 気球; fu⌈useñ 風船: a hot-air balloon (*netsuki-kyuu*) 熱気球 / blow up a balloon (*fuuseñ o fukuramasu*) 風船をふくらます.

ballpoint (pen) *n.* bo⌈orupeñ ボールペン.

bamboo *n.* ta⌈ke 竹: bamboo shoots and rice (*take-no-ko gohañ*) たけの子ご飯 / a bamboo thicket (*take-yabu*) 竹やぶ.

ban *n.* ki⌈ñshi 禁止: a ban on parking (*chuusha kiñshi*) 駐車禁止.
— *vt.* ... o ki⌈ñshi suru ...を禁止する Ⓘ: ban a protest march (*koogi-demo o kiñshi suru*) 抗議デモを禁止する.

banana *n.* ba⌉nana バナナ.

band[1] *n.* 1 ga⌈kudañ 楽団; ba⌈ñdo バンド: a jazz band (*jazu bañdo*) ジャズバンド.
2 i⌈chi-dañ 一団: a band of robbers (*toozoku no ichi-dañ*) 盗賊の一団.

band[2] *n.* hi⌉mo ひも; ta⌈ga たが; ba⌈ñdo バンド; ri⌉boñ リボン: a band made of iron (*tetsu no taga*) 鉄のたが / a hat with a blue silk band (*aoi *kinu no riboñ o tsuketa booshi*) 青い絹のリボンをつけた帽子.

b

bandage *n.* ho⌈otai 包帯: a clean bandage (*kiree na hootai*) きれいな包帯.
— *vt.* ... ni ho⌈otai o suru ...に包帯をする [I]: bandage up a wound (*kizu ni hootai o suru*) 傷に包帯をする.

banister *n.* te⌈suri 手すり.

bank[1] *n.* gi⌈ñkoo 銀行; ba⌉ñku バンク: a bank account (*giñkoo kooza*) 銀行口座 / withdraw money from a bank (*giñkoo kara o-kane o orosu*) 銀行からお金を下ろす / I deposited a million yen in the bank. (*Watashi wa giñkoo ni hyakumañ-eñ azuketa.*) 私は銀行に 100 万円預けた.

bank[2] *n.* do⌈te 土手; tsu⌈tsumi 堤: the north bank of a river (*kawa no kita-gawa no dote*) 川の北側の土手.

banker *n.* gi⌈ñkooka 銀行家.

bank note *n.* sa⌈tsu 札; shi⌉hee 紙幣.

bankrupt *adj.* ha⌈sañ shita [shite iru] 破産した[している]: go bankrupt (*hasañ suru*) 破産する.

bankruptcy *n.* ha⌈sañ 破産; to⌈osañ 倒産: His company is on the brink of bankruptcy. (*Kare no kaisha wa toosañ shi-soo da.*) 彼の会社は倒産しそうだ.

banquet *n.* e⌈ñkai 宴会: give a banquet (*eñkai o hiraku*) 宴会を開く.

bar[1] *n.* ba⌉a バー; sa⌈kaba 酒場.

bar[2] *n.* bo⌈o 棒; no⌈beboo 延べ棒: a bar of gold (*kiñ no nobeboo*) 金の延べ棒 / an iron bar (*tetsuboo*) 鉄棒 / a bar of chocolate (*ita-choko*) 板チョコ.

bar[3] *vt.* **1** (fasten) ... ni ka⌈ñnu⌉ki o ka⌈ke⌉ru ...にかんぬきを掛ける [V]: bar a door (*doa ni kañnuki o kakeru*) ドアにかんぬきを掛ける.
2 (prevent) ... o sa⌈matage⌉ru ...を妨げる [V]; bo⌈ogai suru 妨害する [I]: bar someone's progress (*hoka no hito ga zeñshiñ suru no o samatageru*) ほかの人が前進するのを妨げる.

barber *n.* to⌈koya 床屋: go to the barber (*tokoya e iku*) 床屋へ行く.

barbershop *n.* to⌈koya 床屋.

bare *adj.* **1** (naked, uncovered) mu⌈kidashi no むき出しの; ha⌈daka no 裸の: bare feet (*hadashi*) はだし / a bare head (*muboo*) 無帽 / The trees are already bare. (*Ko no ha wa moo chitte shimatta.*) 木の葉はもう散ってしまった.
2 (empty) ka⌈ra no からの: a bare cupboard (*karappo no todana*) からっぽの戸棚.
3 (minimum) gi⌈rigiri no ぎりぎりの: a bare majority (*girigiri no kahañsuu*) ぎりぎりの過半数.
4 (unadorned) a⌈rinomama⌉ no (ありのままの): the bare facts (*arinomama no jijitsu*) ありのままの事実.

barefoot *adj.* ha⌈dashi no はだしの: barefoot children (*hadashi no kodomo-tachi*) はだしの子どもたち.
— *adv.* ha⌈dashi de はだしで: walk barefoot (*hadashi de aruku*) はだしで歩く.

barely *adv.* ya⌈tto やっと; ka⌈ro⌉ojite かろうじて: We barely got to Narita in time. (*Watashi-tachi wa karoojite jikañ made ni Narita ni tsuita.*) 私たちはかろうじて時間までに成田に着いた.

bargain *n.* **1** (cheap goods, good buy) ya⌈su⌉i ka⌈imono 安い買い物; (o-)ka⌈idokuhiñ (お)買い得品: make a good bargain (*toku na kaimono o suru*) 得な買い物をする.
2 (agreement) ba⌈ibai-ke⌉eyaku 売買契約; to⌈ri⌉hiki 取り引き; ya⌈kusoku 約束: make a bargain (*keeyaku o musubu*) 契約を結ぶ / drive a hard bargain (*yuuri na jookeñ de torihiki suru*) 有利な条件で取り引きする.
— *vi.* ne⌈biki no kooshoo o suru 値引きの交渉をする [I]; ne⌈gi⌉ru 値切る [C]: I bargained with the shopkeeper over the price. (*Watashi wa mise no shujiñ to nebiki no kooshoo o shita.*) 私は店の主人と値引きの交渉をした.
— *vt.* ... o to⌈rikimeru ...を取り決め

る V; ko⌈oshoo suru 交渉する I: We bargained that we would have no work on Sundays. (*Nichiyoo wa kiñmu shinakute mo yoi yoo ni kooshoo shita.*) 日曜は勤務しなくてもよいように交渉した.

bark *vi.* ho⌈e⌉ru ほえる V: The dog was barking. (*Sono inu wa hoete ita.*) その犬はほえていた.

barn *n.* na⌉ya 納屋; ka⌈chikugoya 家畜小屋.

barrel *n.* ta⌈ru たる: a wooden barrel (*ki no taru*) 木のたる / a barrel of beer (*hito taru no biiru*) 一たるのビール.

barren *adj.* **1** (of land) fu⌈moo no 不毛の; sa⌈ku⌉motsu no de⌈ki⌉nai 作物のできない: a barren land (*fumoo no tochi*) 不毛の土地.

2 (of animals) fu⌈niñ no 不妊の; ko o u⌈manai 子を生まない.

barrier *n.* sa⌈ku さく; sho⌈oheki 障壁; sho⌈ogai 障害: a natural barrier formed by mountains (*yama de tsukurareta shizeñ no kabe*) 山でつくられた自然の壁 / a language barrier (*kotoba no shooheki*) 言葉の障壁.

base *n.* **1** (bottom) so⌈ko 底; do⌈dai 土台: the base of a mountain (*yama no fumoto*) 山のふもと / the base of a pillar (*hashira no dai*) 柱の台.

2 (foundation) ki⌉so 基礎; ki⌈bañ 基盤: a country with a strong economic base (*keezai-teki kibañ ga shikkari shita kuni*) 経済的基盤がしっかりした国.

3 (starting-place) ki⌉chi 基地: a military [naval] base (*rikuguñ [kaiguñ] kichi*) 陸軍[海軍]基地.

4 (of baseball) ru⌉i 塁; be⌉esu ベース: third base (*sañ rui*) 三塁 / home base (*hoomu beesu*) ホームベース.

— *vt.* (... ni) ki⌉so o oku (…に)基礎を置く C; ... ni mo⌈tozu⌉ku …に基づく C: an argument based on sound facts (*shikkari shita jijitsu ni motozuku giroñ*) しっかりした事実に基づく議論.

baseball *n.* ya⌈kyuu 野球; be⌈esubo⌉oru ベースボール: play baseball (*yakyuu o suru*) 野球をする.

basin *n.* **1** (container) se⌈ñme⌉ñki 洗面器; ha⌈chi⌉ 鉢.

2 (area) bo⌈ñchi 盆地.

basis *n.* ki⌉so 基礎; ki⌈juñ 基準: a basis for negotiations (*kooshoo no kiso*) 交渉の基礎 / We work on a five-day week basis. (*Watashi-tachi wa shuu itsuka-see desu.*) 私たちは週5日制です.

basket *n.* ka⌈go かご; za⌈ru ざる: fill [empty] a basket (*kago o ippai [kara] ni suru*) かごをいっぱい[から]にする / a shopping basket (*kaimono kago*) 買い物かご / a wastebasket (*kuzu-kago*) くずかご.

bath *n.* fu⌈ro ふろ; nyu⌈uyoku 入浴: take a bath (*furo ni hairu*) ふろに入る / This bath is too hot. (*Kono furo wa atsu-sugiru.*) このふろは熱すぎる.

bathe *vt.* ... o fu⌈ro⌉ ni i⌈reru …をふろに入れる V; a⌈rau 洗う C: How often do you bathe yourself a week? (*Shuu ni nañ-kai gurai o-furo ni hairimasu ka?*) 週に何回ぐらいおふろに入りますか. / You should bathe that cut in hot water. (*Sono kizu wa o-yu de aratta hoo ga yoi.*) その傷はお湯で洗ったほうがよい.

bathroom *n.* yo⌈kushitsu 浴室; fu⌈roba ふろ場. ★ Japanese bathrooms are not equipped with toilets, and the word ‘bathroom’ is never used to mean ‘toilet.’

battery *n.* de⌉ñchi 電池: This battery is dead. (*Kono deñchi wa kirete iru.*) この電池は切れている. ★ A car battery is called ‘*batterii*’ バッテリー.

battle *n.* **1** (war) ta⌈takai 戦い; se⌈ñsoo 戦争: win [lose] a battle (*tatakai ni katsu [makeru]*) 戦いに勝つ[負ける] / He was wounded in battle. (*Kare wa señsoo de fushoo shita.*) 彼は戦争で負傷した.

2 (struggle) to⌈osoo 闘争; ta⌈takai 戦い; kyo⌈osoo 競争: a battle against corruption (*oshoku to no tatakai*) 汚職との戦い / the battle for existence (*seezoñ kyoosoo*) 生存競争.

bay *n.* wa⌉ñ 湾; i⌈rie 入り江: Tokyo Bay (*Tookyoo wañ*) 東京湾.

be[1] *vi.* **1** [expressing relation] da だ; [polite] desu です: Today is Monday. (*Kyoo wa getsuyoo da.*) 今日は月曜だ. / Miss Yamakawa is a teacher. (*Yamakawa-sañ wa señsee desu.*) 山川さんは先生です.
2 [expressing quality, state, etc.] da だ; [polite] desu です: The room was very quiet. (*Heya wa hijoo ni shizuka datta.*) 部屋は非常に静かだった. / Junko is very happy. (*Juñko-sañ wa totemo shiawase desu.*) 淳子さんはとても幸せです. / I am busy today. (*Watashi wa kyoo isogashii.*) 私はきょう忙しい. ★ An adjective can stand by itself as a complete sentence. The addition of '*desu*' does not change the meaning, but merely makes the sentence more polite.
3 [expressing existence or location of people, animals, and sometimes vehicles] i⌈ru いる V: I was in the garden all afternoon. (*Watashi wa gogo wa zutto niwa ni imashita.*) 私は午後はずっと庭にいました. / There is a cat under the desk. (*Tsukue no shita ni neko ga iru.*) 机の下に猫がいる.
4 [expressing existence or location of inanimate objects] a⌉ru ある C: The pen is in the top drawer. (*Peñ wa ichibañ ue no hikidashi no naka ni arimasu.*) ペンはいちばん上の引き出しの中にあります. / In this country there aren't any high mountains. (*Kono kuni ni wa takai yama wa arimaseñ.*) この国には高い山はありません.
5 [result] ⟨verb⟩-te[de] i⌈ru …て[で]いる V: The light is on. (*Deñki ga tsuite iru.*) 電気がついている. / The window is open. (*Mado ga aite iru.*) 窓が開いている.

be[2] *aux.* **1** [in a progressive tense] ⟨verb⟩-te[de] i⌈ru …て[で]いる V: He is studying very hard. (*Kare wa isshookeñmee beñkyoo shite imasu.*) 彼は一生懸命勉強しています. / What were you doing while I was sleeping? (*Watashi ga nete iru aida anata wa nani o shite imashita ka?*) 私が寝ている間あなたは何をしていましたか.
2 [in the passive] ⟨verb⟩-(ra[sa]) reru …(ら[さ])れる V: My husband and I were invited to her wedding. (*Shujiñ to watashi wa kanojo no kekkoñ-shiki ni shootai sareta.*) 主人と私は彼女の結婚式に招待された. / The boy was scolded by his teacher. (*Sono otoko-no-ko wa señsee ni shikarareta.*) その男の子は先生にしかられた.

beach *n.* ha⌈mabe 浜辺; ka⌈isui-yo⌉kujoo 海水浴場: a sandy beach (*suna-hama*) 砂浜.

beam *n.* **1** (ray of light) ko⌈oseñ 光線; hi⌈kari⌉ 光: The flashlight beam was clearly visible. (*Kaichuu-deñtoo no hikari ga hakkiri mieta.*) 懐中電灯の光がはっきり見えた.
2 (timber) ha⌈ri⌉ はり; ke⌈ta けた: This beam cannot hold up the ceiling. (*Kono hari wa teñjoo o sasaeru koto ga dekinai.*) このはりは天井を支えることができない.

bean *n.* ma⌈me 豆: soya beans (*daizu*) 大豆 / kidney beans (*iñgeñ mame*) いんげん豆 / string beans (*saya eñdoo*) さやえんどう / coffee beans (*koohii mame*) コーヒー豆.

bear[1] ku⌈ma⌉ 熊: a polar bear (*shiro-kuma*) 白熊.

bear[2] *vt.* **1** (support) ... o sa⌈saeru …を支える V: The ice is thick enough to bear your weight. (*Sono koori wa kimi no taijuu o sasaerareru dake no atsumi ga aru.*) その氷はきみの体重を支えられるだけの厚みがある.
2 (give birth to) ko o u⌈mu 子を産む C; (produce) mi ⌈o musubu 実を結ぶ C: My sister bore twins. (*Watashi no ane wa futago o uñda.*) 私の

姉は双子を産んだ. / I was born in 1950. (*Watashi wa señ-kyuu-hyaku-gojuu-neñ ni umaremashita.*) 私は 1950 年に生まれました. / Do you think this tree will bear fruit this year? (*Kono ki wa kotoshi mi ga naru to omoimasu ka?*) この木はことし実がなると思いますか.

3 (endure) ... o ga⌉mañ suru …を我慢する [I]; ... ni ta⌈e⌉ru …に耐える [V]: I couldn't bear to listen to his complaints. (*Watashi wa kare no fuhee o kiku no o gamañ suru koto ga dekinakatta.*) 私は彼の不平を聞くのを我慢することができなかった. / I calmly bore their insults. (*Watashi wa kare-ra no bujoku ni jitto taeta.*) 私は彼らの侮辱にじっと耐えた.

beard *n.* a⌈go⌉hige あごひげ: grow a beard (*agohige o hayasu*) あごひげを生やす.

beat *vt.* **1** (hit) ... o ta⌈ta⌉ku …をたたく [C]; u⌉tsu 打つ [C]: He beat me on the head. (*Kare wa watashi no atama o tataita.*) 彼は私の頭をたたいた. / beat a drum (*taiko o utsu*) たいこを打つ.

2 (defeat) ... o ma⌈kasu …を負かす [C]: We stand no chance of defeating them. (*Kare-ra o makasu mikomi wa nai.*) 彼らを負かす見込みはない.

3 (mix vigorously) ... o ka⌈kimaze⌉ru …をかき混ぜる [V]: beat the milk and eggs together (*gyuunyuu to tamago o issho ni kakimazeru*) 牛乳と卵をいっしょにかき混ぜる.

— *vi.* **1** (hit) (... o) do⌉ñdoñ (to) ta⌈ta⌉ku (…を)どんどん(と)たたく [C]: I beat on the door. (*Watashi wa to o doñdoñ tataita.*) 私は戸をどんどんたたいた.

2 (of a heart) do⌉kidoki na⌈ru どきどき鳴る [C]: Her heart beat with excitement. (*Koofuñ de kanojo no shiñzoo wa dokidoki natta.*) 興奮で彼女の心臓はどきどき鳴った.

— *n.* u⌉tsu o⌈to⌉ 打つ音; (of a heart) do⌈oki どうき(動悸): the beat of a drum (*taiko o utsu oto*) たいこを打つ音 / the beat of a heart (*shiñzoo no dooki*) 心臓のどうき.

beautiful *adj.* **1** (of looks, etc.) ki⌉ree na きれいな; u⌈tsukushi⌉i 美しい: a beautiful woman (*kiree na oñna no hito*) きれいな女の人 / a beautiful voice (*utsukushii koe*) 美しい声 / What a beautiful flower! (*Nañte kiree na hana daroo!*) 何てきれいな花だろう.

2 (splendid) su⌈barashi⌉i すばらしい; su⌈teki na すてきな: It's a beautiful day today. (*Kyoo wa subarashii hi da.*) きょうはすばらしい日だ.

beauty *n.* u⌈tsuku⌉shisa 美しさ; bi⌉ 美; su⌈bara⌉shisa すばらしさ: the beauty of nature (*shizeñ no bi*) 自然の美.

beauty parlor *n.* bi⌈yo⌉oiñ 美容院.

because *conj.* **1** (reason) ... kara …から; ... no de …ので: "Why are you late?" "Because the train was late." (*"Doo shite okureta no?" "Deñsha ga okureta kara desu."*) 「どうして遅れたの」「電車が遅れたからです」/ I took my umbrella because it was raining. (*Ame ga futte ita kara kasa o motte itta.*) 雨が降っていたから傘を持って行った.

2 (just because) ... da⌉ kara to i⌈tte (... nai) …だからといって(…ない): It isn't because you are my cousin that I promoted you. (*Itoko da kara to itte shooshiñ saseta no de wa nai.*) いとこだからといって昇進させたのではない.

because of ... *prep.* ... no ta⌈me⌉ ni …のために; ... ga ge⌈ñiñ de …が原因で: He failed the interview because of his casual attitude. (*Kare wa iikageñ na taido ga geñiñ de meñsetsu ni shippai shita.*) 彼はいいかげんな態度が原因で面接に失敗した.

become *vi.* ⟨noun⟩ ni na⌉ru …になる [C]; ⟨adjective⟩-ku naru …くなる [C]: Our daughter became a nurse. (*Uchi no musume wa kañgofu ni natta.*) うちの娘は看護婦になった. / It will become hot today. (*Kyoo wa atsuku naru deshoo.*) きょうは暑くな

るでしょう. / What has become of Yamamoto? (*Yamamoto wa doo natta deshoo ka?*) 山本はどうなったでしょうか.

becoming *adj.* ni⌈a⌉u 似合う; fu⌈sawashi⌉i ふさわしい: The necklace is very becoming on you. (*Sono nekkuresu wa anata ni yoku niau.*) そのネックレスはあなたによく似合う.

bed *n.* **1** be⌉ddo ベッド; ne⌈doko 寝床: get into bed (*beddo ni hairu*) ベッドに入る / You should not smoke in bed. (*Nedoko de tabako o sutte wa ikemaseñ.*) 寝床でたばこを吸ってはいけません.
2 to⌈ko 床; so⌈ko 底: the bed of a river (*kawadoko*) 川床 / the bed of a lake (*kotee*) 湖底.
go to bed *vi.* ne⌈ru 寝る 🅅; to⌈ko ni tsu⌉ku 床につく 🄲: It's time you went to bed. (*Moo neru jikañ desu.*) もう寝る時間です.

bedroom *n.* shi⌈ñshitsu 寝室.

bee *n.* ha⌈chi はち; mi⌈tsu⌉bachi みつばち: be stung by a bee (*hachi ni sasareru*) はちに刺される.

beef *n.* gyu⌈uniku 牛肉.

beer *n.* bi⌉iru ビール: a bottle of beer (*biiru ip-poñ*) ビール 1 本 / canned beer (*kañ biiru*) 缶ビール / draft beer (*nama biiru*) 生ビール.

beet *n.* bi⌉ito ビート; sa⌈too-da⌉ikoñ 砂糖大根.

before *prep.* **1** (earlier than; prior to) ... no ma⌉e (ni) …の前(に): Can you come before five o'clock? (*Go-ji mae ni koraremasu ka?*) 5 時前に来られますか.
2 (in front of) ... no ma⌉e ni [de] …の前に[で]: the plaza before the station (*eki no mae no hiroba*) 駅の前の広場 / He walked before me. (*Kare wa watashi no mae o aruita.*) 彼は私の前を歩いた.
— *adv.* (earlier) ma⌉e ni 前に; i⌉zeñ (ni) 以前(に): I think I met him before. (*Kare ni wa mae ni atta yoo ni omoimasu.*) 彼には前に会ったように思います.
— *conj.* (earlier than) ‹verb› ma⌉e ni …前に; ‹verb›-nai u⌈chi ni …ないうちに: You must think carefully before you decide. (*Kimeru mae ni shiñchoo ni kañgae nasai.*) 決める前に慎重に考えなさい. / Let's leave before it starts raining. (*Ame ga furi-dasanai uchi ni dekakemashoo.*) 雨が降り出さないうちに出かけましょう.

beg *vt., vi.* **1** (ask for) (... o) (ku⌈re to) ta⌈no⌉mu (…を)(くれと)頼む 🄲: beg for something to eat (*nani-ka tabemono o kure to tanomu*) 何か食べ物をくれと頼む / I beg you to keep silent. (*Tanomu kara damatte ite kudasai.*) 頼むから黙っていてください.
2 (implore) (... o) ko⌉u (…を)請う 🄲: beg for forgiveness (*yurushi o kou*) 許しを請う.
I beg your pardon. (*Shitsuree shimashita.*) 失礼しました; [repeat] (*Moo ichido osshatte kudasai.*) もう一度おっしゃってください.

beggar *n.* ko⌈jiki⌉ 乞食.

begin *vi.* ha⌈jimaru 始まる 🄲; ‹verb›-da⌉su …だす 🄲: School begins at eight and ends at four. (*Gakkoo wa hachi-ji ni hajimari yo-ji ni owaru.*) 学校は 8 時に始まり 4 時に終わる. / It began to rain on the way home. (*Uchi e kaeru tochuu de ame ga furi-dashita.*) 家へ帰る途中で雨が降り出した.
— *vt.* ... o ha⌈jimeru …を始める 🅅; ‹verb›-ha⌈jimeru …始める 🅅: When did you begin work this morning? (*Kesa wa shigoto o nañ-ji ni hajimemashita ka?*) けさは仕事を何時に始めましたか. / I hear that Bob has begun learning Japanese. (*Bobu wa Nihoñgo o narai-hajimeta rashii.*) ボブは日本語を習い始めたらしい.

beginner *n.* sho⌈shi⌉ñsha 初心者; sho⌈ga⌉kusha 初学者: a beginners' Japanese class (*Nihoñgo shokyuu kurasu*) 日本語初級クラス.

beginning *n.* ha⌈jime 初め; sa⌈isho 最初: the beginning of the month (*tsuki no hajime*) 月の初め / I read the book from beginning to end. (*Watashi wa sono hoñ o sai-

sho kara saigo made yomimashita.) 私はその本を最初から最後まで読みました.

behave *vi.* **1** (conduct oneself) fu⌈ruma⌉u ふるまう C: He behaved like a gentleman. (*Kare wa shiñshi-rashiku furumatta.*) 彼は紳士らしくふるまった.

2 (act politely) gyo⌈ogi yo⌉ku suru 行儀よくする I: The children behaved well at the party. (*Kodomo-tachi wa paatii de gyoogi ga yokatta.*) 子どもたちはパーティーで行儀がよかった.

behavior *n.* **1** (way of acting) fu⌈rumai ふるまい; ta⌉ido 態度: selfish behavior (*jibuñ katte na furumai*) 自分勝手なふるまい / arrogant behavior (*oohee na taido*) おうへいな態度.

2 (manners) gyo⌈ogi 行儀: Junko's behavior at the party was good. (*Paatii de Juñko-sañ wa gyoogi ga yokatta.*) パーティーで純子さんは行儀が良かった.

behind *prep.* **1** (at or toward the rear of) ... no u⌈shiro ni [e; de] …の後ろに[へ; で]: The boy was hiding behind a curtain. (*Sono otoko-no-ko wa kaateñ no ushiro ni kakurete ita.*) その男の子はカーテンの後ろに隠れていた.

2 (later than) ... ni o⌈kurete …に遅れて: The Shinkansen trains are behind schedule. (*Shiñkañseñ wa teekoku yori okurete iru.*) 新幹線は定刻より遅れている.

— *adv.* (at or to the back) u⌈shiro ni [e, de] 後ろに[へ, で]; a⌉to ni [e] あとに[へ]: an apartment building with a park behind (*ushiro ni kooeñ no aru apaato*) 後ろに公園のあるアパート / I stayed behind. (*Watashi wa ato ni nokotta.*) 私はあとに残った.

belief *n.* **1** (faith) shi⌈ñkoo 信仰; shi⌈ñji⌉ñ 信心: belief in Christianity (*Kirisuto-kyoo no shiñkoo*) キリスト教の信仰.

2 (opinion) shi⌉ñneñ 信念; ka⌈ñga⌉e 考え; i⌉keñ 意見: To the best of my belief there is no danger. (*Watashi no kañgae de wa kikeñ wa nai to omoimasu.*) 私の考えでは危険はないと思います.

3 (trust) shi⌈ñyoo 信用; shi⌈ñrai 信頼: I have no belief in his ability. (*Watashi wa kare no nooryoku ni shiñrai o oite imaseñ.*) 私は彼の能力に信頼を置いていません.

believe *vt.* **1** (consider to be true) ... o shi⌈ñjiru …を信じる V: We believed her story. (*Wareware wa kanojo no hanashi o shiñjita.*) われわれは彼女の話を信じた.

2 (think) ... to ka⌈ñgae⌉ru …と考える V; o⌈mo⌉u 思う C: I believe that he is honest. (*Kare wa shoojiki da to omoimasu.*) 彼は正直だと思います.

believe in ... *vt.* ... no so⌈ñzai o shiñji⌉ru …の存在を信じる V; ... o shi⌈ñrai suru …を信頼する I: believe in God (*kami no soñzai o shiñjiru*) 神の存在を信じる / I believe in you. (*Watashi wa anata o shiñrai shimasu.*) 私はあなたを信頼します.

bell *n.* **1** (of a church) ka⌈ne 鐘: I hear the ringing of a temple bell. (*O-tera no kane ga naru no ga kikoeru.*) お寺の鐘が鳴るのが聞こえる.

2 (doorbell) be⌉ru ベル: ring a bell (*beru o narasu*) ベルを鳴らす / answer a bell (*beru ni kotaeru*) ベルにこたえる.

3 (sound of a bell) be⌉ru no o⌈to⌉ ベルの音: I thought I heard the bell. (*Beru no oto o kiita yoo ni omou.*) ベルの音を聞いたように思う.

belong *vi.* **1** (be the property of) (... no) mo⌈no⌉ da (…の)ものだ: Who does this umbrella belong to? (*Kono kasa wa dare no mono desu ka?*) この傘はだれのものですか.

2 (be a member of) (... ni) zo⌈kusu⌉ru (…に)属する I; ha⌉itte iru 入っている V: Did you belong to any college societies? (*Nani-ka daigaku no kurabu ni haitte imashita ka?*) 何か大学のクラブに入っていましたか.

below *prep.* **1** (in a lower place, level, etc.) ... no shi⌈ta ni …の下に: Write your name below the line,

b

please. (*Señ no shita ni o-namae o kaite kudasai.*) 線の下にお名前を書いてください.
2 (downstream) ... no ka⌈ryuu ni ... の下流に: The bridge is a kilometer below the waterfall. (*Hashi wa taki no ichi-kiro karyuu ni arimasu.*) 橋は滝の1キロ下流にあります.
3 (less than) mi⌉mañ 未満: Anyone here below 16 must leave. (*Juuroku-sai mimañ no hito wa koko kara dete ikanakereba narimaseñ.*) 16歳未満の人はここから出ていかなければなりません.
— *adv.* (beneath; in lower place) shi⌈ta no [ni] 下の[に]: Miss Ishii lives in the room below. (*Ishii-sañ wa shita no heya ni suñde imasu.*) 石井さんは下の部屋に住んでいます.

belt *n.* **1** (band) be⌈ruto ベルト: a leather belt (*kawa no beruto*) 革のベルト / a safety belt (*añzeñ beruto*) 安全ベルト / wear [loosen] one's belt (*beruto o shimeru* [*yurumeru*]) ベルトを締める[緩める].
2 (area) chi⌉tai 地帯: an earthquake belt (*jishiñ-tai*) 地震帯.

bench *n.* be⌉ñchi ベンチ: sit down on a bench (*beñchi ni suwaru*) ベンチに座る.

bend *vt.* (curve) ... o ma⌈geru ...を曲げる Ⓥ: bend one's back (*senaka o mageru*) 背中を曲げる / It is impossible to bend this iron bar. (*Kono tetsuboo o mageru no wa fukanoo da.*) この鉄棒を曲げるのは不可能だ.
— *vi.* ma⌈garu 曲がる Ⓒ; o⌈re⌉ru 折れる Ⓥ: Just up ahead the road bends sharp left. (*Chotto saki de michi wa kyuu ni hidari ni magarimasu.*) ちょっと先で道は急に左に曲がります.

beneath *prep.* **1** (under) ... no shi⌉ta ni [de] ...の下に[で]: A dog is sleeping beneath the tree. (*Inu ga ki no shita de nete iru.*) 犬が木の下で寝ている.
2 (not worthy of) ... ni fu⌈sawashi⌉ku nai ...にふさわしくない; a⌈tai shinai 値しない: A job like that is clearly beneath a man like him. (*Sono yoo na shigoto wa akiraka ni kare no yoo na otoko ni fusawashiku nai.*) そのような仕事は明らかに彼のような男にふさわしくない.

benefit *n.* **1** (advantage; profit) ri⌉eki 利益; o⌈ñkee 恩恵: a public benefit (*kooeki*) 公益 / The benefits of nuclear energy are great. (*Geñshiryoku enerugii no oñkee wa ookii.*) 原子力エネルギーの恩恵は大きい.
2 (allowance) te⌉ate 手当; kyu⌉ufu 給付: unemployment benefit (*shitsugyoo teate*) 失業手当 / a medical benefit (*iryoo kyuufu*) 医療給付.
be of benefit to ... *vt.* ... no ta⌈me⌉ ni na⌉ru ...のためになる Ⓒ: This book was of great benefit to me. (*Kono hoñ wa totemo tame ni natta.*) この本はとてもためになった.
— *vi.* ri⌉eki o eru 利益を得る Ⓥ; ya⌈ku⌉ ni tatsu 役に立つ Ⓒ: I benefited from the experience. (*Sono keekeñ ga yaku ni tatta.*) その経験が役に立った.
— *vt.* ... no ta⌈me⌉ ni naru ...のためになる Ⓒ; ... ni yo⌉i ...によい: That investment will benefit the company. (*Sono tooshi wa kaisha no tame ni naru deshoo.*) その投資は会社のためになるでしょう.

beside *prep.* **1** (close to) ... no so⌉ba ni ...のそばに; chi⌉kaku ni 近くに: There is a park beside the house. (*Uchi no soba ni kooeñ ga aru.*) 家のそばに公園がある.
2 (compared to) ... to ku⌈raberu to ...と比べると: Beside the artist's earlier work, this picture is rather inferior. (*Sono gaka no shoki no sakuhiñ to kuraberu to kono e wa yaya otoru.*) その画家の初期の作品と比べるとこの絵はやや劣る.

besides *prep.* **1** (in addition to) ... no ho⌈ka ni ...のほかに; ... ni ku⌈waete ...に加えて: Besides John, who else did you invite? (*Joñ no hoka ni dare o yobimashita ka?*)

ジョンのほかにだれを呼びましたか. / You should try to do something besides watching television. (*Terebi o miru hoka ni nani-ka shitara doo desu ka.*) テレビを見るほかに何かしたらどうですか.

2 (apart from) ... iˡgai ni …以外に: I can trust no one besides you. (*Anata igai ni dare mo shiñyoo dekimaseñ.*) あなた以外にだれも信用できません.

— *adv.* (in addition) soˡno ue そのうえ; saˡra ni さらに; hoˡka ni ほかに: This is my favorite picture but I have two more besides. (*Kore wa watashi ga ki ni itte iru e desu ga watashi wa hoka ni ato ni sakuhiñ motte imasu.*) これは私が気に入っている絵ですが私はほかにあと2作品持っています.

best *adj.* moˡttoˡmo yoˡi 最もよい; saˡiryoo no 最良の; iˡchiˡbañ no いちばんの: my best friend (*watashi no ichibañ no shiñyuu*) 私のいちばんの親友 / It is the best book I have ever read. (*Sono hoñ wa watashi ga ima made ni yoñda naka de ichibañ yoi hoñ desu.*) その本は私が今までに読んだ中でいちばんよい本です.

— *adv.* iˡchibañ いちばん: What Japanese food do you like best? (*Ichibañ suki na Nihoñ ryoori wa nañ desu ka?*) いちばん好きな日本料理は何ですか. / Tell me which day will suit you best. (*Ichibañ tsugoo no yoi hi o oshiete kudasai.*) いちばん都合のよい日を教えてください.

— *n.* iˡchibañ yoˡi mono いちばんよいもの: I did it all for the best. (*Sore ga ichibañ yoi to omotte yarimashita.*) それがいちばんよいと思ってやりました.

do one's best *vi.* zeˡñryoku oˡ tsuˡkuˡsu 全力を尽くす Ⓒ: I did my best to rebuild my business. (*Watashi wa kee-ee no tatenaoshi ni zeñryoku o tsukushita.*) 私は経営の建て直しに全力を尽くした.

make the best of ... *vt.* ... o deˡkiru dakeˡ riˡyoo suru …をできるだけ利用する Ⓘ: I made the best of the time left. (*Watashi wa nokosareta jikañ o dekiru dake katsuyoo shita.*) 私は残された時間をできるだけ活用した.

bet *vt.* ... ni kaˡkeˡru …に賭ける Ⓥ: I'll bet you ¥1,000 that I am right. (*Watashi ga tadashii hoo ni señ-eñ kakeru yo.*) 私が正しい方に千円賭けるよ.

— *vi.* (... ni) kaˡkeˡru (…に)賭ける Ⓥ: bet on horses (*uma ni kakeru*) 馬に賭ける.

— *n.* kaˡkeˡ 賭け: make a bet (*kake o suru*) 賭けをする / win [lose] a bet (*kake ni katsu* [*makeru*]) 賭けに勝つ[負ける].

betray *vt.* **1** (be disloyal) ... o uˡragiˡru …を裏切る Ⓒ; uˡru 売る Ⓒ: You have betrayed me. (*Anata wa watashi o uragitta.*) あなたは私を裏切った. / The man betrayed his country to the enemy. (*Sono otoko wa jibuñ no kuni o teki ni utta.*) その男は自分の国を敵に売った.

2 (reveal) ... o moˡraˡsu …を漏らす Ⓒ: He betrayed our secrets to her. (*Kare wa wareware no himitsu o kanojo ni morashita.*) 彼はわれわれの秘密を彼女に漏らした.

better *adj.* **1** (more good) yori [moˡtto; saˡra ni] yoˡi より[もっと; さらに]よい: Your school grades are better than before. (*Kimi no seeseki wa mae yori mo yoi.*) 君の成績は前よりもよい.

2 (of health, etc.) yoˡku natte (iru) よくなって(いる); geˡñki na 元気な: I feel a little better. (*Kibuñ wa sukoshi yoku narimashita.*) 気分は少しよくなりました. / You are looking much better now. (*Kaoiro ga zutto yoku narimashita ne.*) 顔色がずっとよくなりましたね.

— *adv.* moˡtto umaku もっとうまく; yoˡri yoˡku よりよく: I speak Japanese better than I used to. (*Watashi wa Nihoñgo ga mae yori mo umaku hanaseru yoo ni natta.*) 私は日本語が前よりもうまく話せるようになっ

た. / Which do you like better, sushi or tempura? (*Sushi to teñpura de wa dochira ga suki desu ka?*) すしとてんぷらではどちらが好きですか.
had better ⇨ had better.

between *prep.* **1** (space or time) ... no a⌈ida ni [de] …の間に[で]: an old house standing between two skyscrapers (*futatsu no koosoobiru no aida ni hasamareta furui ie*) 二つの高層ビルの間に挟まれた古い家 / Please come between five and six in the evening. (*Yuugata go-ji to roku-ji no aida ni kite kudasai.*) 夕方5時と6時の間に来てください.
2 (range) ... no chu⌈ukañ …の中間; ... no a⌈ida …の間: The price is between ¥10,000 and ¥15,000. (*Nedañ wa ichimañ-eñ to ichimañ-goseñ-eñ no aida desu.*) 値段は1万円と1万5千円の間です.
3 (connection) -⌉kañ no 間の: a Shinkansen journey between Tokyo and Osaka (*Tookyoo Oosaka-kañ no Shiñkañseñ no tabi*) 東京大阪間の新幹線の旅.
4 (dividing) ... no u⌈chi kara hito⌉tsu …のうちから一つ: I don't know how to choose between these neckties. (*Kono nekutai no uchi dore o erañdara yoi ka wakaranai.*) このネクタイのうちどれを選んだらよいかわからない.
— *adv.* a⌈ima ni 合間に: I had two classes and there was no time to go to the toilet between. (*Jugyoo ga futatsu atta ga aima ni toire e iku hima mo nakatta.*) 授業が二つあったが合間にトイレへ行く暇もなかった.

beverage *n.* no⌈mi⌉mono 飲み物; i⌈ñryo⌉o 飲料.

beware *vi.* (... ni) chu⌉ui suru (…に)注意する [I]; ki ⌈o tsuke⌉ru 気をつける [V]: Beware of the dog. (*Inu ni ki o tsuke nasai.*) 犬に気をつけなさい.

beyond *prep.* **1** (position) ... no mu⌈koo ni …の向こうに: The village was visible beyond the lake. (*Mizuumi no mukoo ni mura ga mieta.*) 湖の向こうに村が見えた.
2 (time) ... o su⌉gite …を過ぎて: We can't wait beyond 10:30. (*Juuji-hañ o sugite wa matemaseñ.*) 10時半を過ぎては待てません.
3 (ability; level) ... o ko⌈ete …を越えて; ... i⌉joo ni …以上に: It's beyond me. (*Watashi ni wa wakaranai.*) 私にはわからない.
— *adv.* mu⌈koo ni 向こうに: The explorer crossed the ocean and discovered the continent beyond. (*Tañkeñka wa taiyoo o watari sono mukoo ni tairiku o hakkeñ shita.*) 探検家は大洋を渡りその向こうに大陸を発見した.

bicycle *n.* ji⌈te⌉ñsha 自転車: ride [get on] a bicycle (*jiteñsha ni noru*) 自転車に乗る / get off a bicycle (*jiteñsha kara oriru*) 自転車から下りる / bicycles for rent (*kashi jiteñsha*) 貸し自転車.

bid *n.* nyu⌈usatsu 入札; tsu⌈ke⌉ne 付け値: enter a bid for old books (*kosho no nyuusatsu o suru*) 古書の入札をする.

big *adj.* **1** (of great size) o⌈oki⌉i 大きい; o⌉oki-na 大きな: Do you have a bigger desk? (*Motto ookii tsukue wa arimasu ka?*) もっと大きい机はありますか. / This sweater is too big. (*Kono seetaa wa ooki-sugiru.*) このセーターは大きすぎる. / a big baby (*ooki-na akañboo*) 大きな赤ん坊.
2 (elder) to⌈shiue no 年上の: a big brother (*ani*) 兄 / a big sister (*ane*) 姉.
3 (important; great) ju⌈uyoo na 重要な; ta⌈iheñ na 大変な; o⌈o- 大; da⌈i- 大: a big decision (*juuyoo na kettee*) 重要な決定 / a big mistake (*oo-machigai*) 大間違い / a big incident (*dai-jikeñ*) 大事件.

bike *n.* (bicycle) ji⌈te⌉ñsha 自転車; (motorbike) o⌈oto⌉bai オートバイ.
★ Japanese '*baiku*' refers to a motorbike, not to a bicycle.

bill *n.* **1** (payment) se⌈ekyuusho 請求書; ka⌈ñjo⌉o 勘定: the electricity bill (*deñki-ryoo no seekyuusho*) 電気料の請求書 / It's my treat. I'll pay

the bill. (*Watashi no ogori desu. Kañjoo wa watashi ga haraimasu.*) 私のおごりです. 勘定は私が払います.
2 (paper money) shiˈhee 紙幣; saˈtsu 札: a thousand-yen bill (*señ-eñ satsu*) 千円札.

billion *n.* (one thousand million) juˈu-oku 10億.

bind *vt.* **1** (tie up; bandage) ... o shiˈbaˈru ...を縛る Ⓒ; maˈku 巻く Ⓒ: bind a package with a ribbon (*tsutsumi o riboñ de shibaru*) 包みをリボンで縛る / The doctor bound my wound with a bandage. (*Isha wa watashi no kizuguchi o hootai de maita.*) 医者は私の傷口を包帯で巻いた.
2 (of friendship) ... o muˈsubu ...を結ぶ Ⓒ: Tom and I are bound together by our friendship. (*Tomu to watashi wa yuujoo de musubarete iru.*) トムと私は友情で結ばれている.
3 (of a book) ... o seˈehoñ suru ...を製本する Ⓘ: bind a book (*hoñ o seehoñ suru*) 本を製本する.

bird *n.* toˈri 鳥: a small bird (*kotori*) 小鳥.

birth *n.* taˈñjoo 誕生; uˈmare 生まれ; shuˈsshoo 出生: the birth of a new nation (*atarashii kuni no tañjoo*) 新しい国の誕生 / Breeding is more important than birth. (*Umare yori mo sodachi no hoo ga taisetsu da.*) 生まれよりも育ちのほうが大切だ. / the date of one's birth (*seeneñ gappi*) 生年月日 / a birth certificate (*shusshoo shoomee*) 出生証明.

birthday *n.* taˈñjoˈobi 誕生日: Happy birthday! (*(O-)tañjoobi omedetoo.*) (お)誕生日おめでとう.

biscuit *n.* (U.S.) paˈñ パン; (U.K.) biˈsukeˈtto ビスケット; kuˈraˈkkaa クラッカー.

bishop *n.* (Church of England) shuˈkyoˈo 主教; (Catholic) shiˈkyoo 司教.

bit *n.* **1** (fragment) shoˈoheñ 小片; kaˈkera かけら: bits of glass (*garasu no haheñ*) ガラスの破片 / tear to bits (*biribiri ni saku*) びりびりに裂く.
2 (small amount) suˈkoˈshi 少し; choˈtto ちょっと: I'd like a bit of that ham. (*Sono hamu o sukoshi kudasai.*) そのハムを少し下さい. / Can you just wait a bit? (*Chotto matte moraemasu ka?*) ちょっと待ってもらえますか.
3 (degree) suˈkoˈshi 少し; choˈtto ちょっと: I'm a bit tired. (*Sukoshi tsukaremashita.*) 少し疲れました. / Please turn the volume down a bit. (*Chotto boryuumu o sagete kudasai.*) ちょっとボリュームを下げてください.

bite *vt.* **1** (with teeth) ... o kaˈmu ...をかむ Ⓒ; ... ni kaˈmitsuku ...にかみつく Ⓒ: bite one's nails (*tsume o kamu*) つめをかむ / The big dog bit the girl. (*Ooki-na inu ga oñna-noko ni kamitsuita.*) 大きな犬が女の子にかみついた.
2 (of an insect) ... o saˈsu ...を刺す Ⓒ; kuˈu 食う Ⓒ: I was badly bitten by mosquitoes. (*Watashi wa hidoku ka ni kuwareta.*) 私はひどく蚊に食われた.
— *vi.* kaˈmu かむ Ⓒ; kaˈmitsuku かみつく Ⓒ: This dog doesn't bite. (*Kono inu wa kamitsukimaseñ.*) この犬はかみつきません.
— *n.* hiˈtoˈkajiri ひとかじり; hiˈtoˈkuchi ひと口; saˈshiˈkizu 刺し傷: take a bite from an apple (*riñgo o hitokajiri suru*) りんごをひとかじりする / a bite of bread (*hitokuchi no pañ*) ひと口のパン / an insect bite (*mushi no sashikizu*) 虫の刺し傷.

bitter *adj.* **1** (taste) niˈgaˈi 苦い: bitter coffee (*nigai koohii*) 苦いコーヒー.
2 (emotions; experience) tsuˈrai 辛い; kuˈrushiˈi 苦しい: a bitter memory (*tsurai omoide*) 辛い思い出 / suffer a bitter experience (*kurushii taikeñ o suru*) 苦しい体験をする.
3 (very cold) mi ˈo kiˈru yoo na 身を切るような: a bitter wind (*mi o kiru yoo na kaze*) 身を切るような風.

bitterness *n.* **1** (taste) niˈgami 苦み: chocolate with a touch of bitterness (*chotto nigami no aru cho-*

koreeto) ちょっと苦みのあるチョコレート.
2 (emotions; experience) ku⌈ru-shimi 苦しみ: a man with bitterness in his heart (*kokoro ni kurushimi o idaku hito*) 心に苦しみを抱く人.

black *adj.* **1** (color) ku⌈ro⌉i 黒い: black shoes (*kuroi kutsu*) 黒い靴 / black clouds (*kuroi kumo*) 黒い雲.
2 (race) ko⌈kujiñ no 黒人の: black people (*kokujiñ*) 黒人.
3 (of coffee) bu⌈ra⌉kku no ブラックの: drink one's coffee black (*koohii o burakku de nomu*) コーヒーをブラックで飲む.
4 (bad; threatening) ku⌈rai 暗い: The situation is black. (*Jookyoo wa kurai.*) 状況は暗い.
— *n.* **1** (color) ku⌉ro 黒: Mr. Yamauchi likes dressing in black. (*Yamauchi-sañ wa kuro no fukusoo ga konomi da.*) 山内さんは黒の服装が好みだ.
2 (race) ko⌈kujiñ 黒人: The blacks demanded freedom in South Africa. (*Minami Afurika de kokujiñ-tachi wa jiyuu o yookyuu shita.*) 南アフリカで黒人たちは自由を要求した.
be in the black *vi.* ku⌈roji da 黒字だ.

black-and-white *adj.* ku⌉ro to ⌈shi⌉ro no 黒と白の; shi⌈ro-kuro no 白黒の: a black-and-white roll of film (*shiro-kuro no firumu*) 白黒のフィルム / a black-and-white TV (*shiro-kuro no terebi*) 白黒のテレビ.
★ Note that English and Japanese word orders are opposite.

blade *n.* ha⌉ 刃: the blade of a knife (*naifu no ha*) ナイフの刃 / a razor blade (*kamisori no ha*) かみそりの刃.

blame *vt.* ... no se⌉e ni suru ...のせいにする Ⅰ; ... o se⌈me⌉ru ...を責める Ⅴ: He blamed me for the failure. (*Kare wa sono shippai o watashi no see ni shita.*) 彼はその失敗を私のせいにした. / I don't blame you. (*Kimi o semetari shinai yo.*) きみを責めたりしないよ.

blank *adj.* **1** (not written or printed) na⌈ni mo ka⌉ite nai 何も書いてない; ha⌈kushi no 白紙の: a blank page (*nani mo kaite nai peeji*) 何も書いてないページ / a blank tape (*nani mo rokuoñ sarete inai teepu*) 何も録音されていないテープ.
2 (expressionless) bo⌈ñya⌉ri shita [shite iru] ぼんやりした[している]; hyo⌈o-jo⌉o no na⌉i 表情のない: He looked blank. (*Kare wa hyoojoo no nai kao o shite ita.*) 彼は表情のない顔をしていた.
— *n.* ku⌈usho 空所; ku⌈rañ 空欄; yo⌈haku 余白: Fill in the blanks with a suitable word. (*Kuusho ni tekitoo na go o ire nasai.*) 空所に適当な語を入れなさい.

blanket *n.* mo⌉ofu 毛布: wrap a baby up in a blanket (*akañboo o moofu de kurumu*) 赤ん坊を毛布でくるむ.

blast *n.* **1** (wind) i⌈chijiñ no kaze 一陣の風; to⌈ppuu 突風: a blast of wind (*ichijiñ no kyoofuu*) 一陣の強風.
2 (explosion) ba⌈kuhatsu 爆発; ba⌈kufuu 爆風: the blast of a bomb (*bakudañ no bakuhatsu*) 爆弾の爆発.
— *vt.* (blow up) ... o ba⌈kuha suru ...を爆破する Ⅰ: The door was blasted by someone. (*Doa ga dare-ka ni bakuha sareta.*) ドアがだれかに爆破された.

bleed *vi.* chi ⌈ga de⌉ru 血が出る Ⅴ; shu⌈kketsu suru 出血する Ⅰ: His cut was bleeding. (*Kare no kizuguchi kara chi ga dete ita.*) 彼の傷口から血が出ていた.

blend *vt.* ... o ma⌈ze⌉ru ...を混ぜる Ⅴ; ko⌈ñgoo suru 混合する Ⅰ: blend milk and eggs (*gyuunyuu to tamago o mazeru*) 牛乳と卵を混ぜる.
— *vi.* ma⌈za⌉ru 混ざる Ⓒ: Oil does not blend with water. (*Abura wa mizu to mazaranai.*) 油は水と混ざらない.
— *n.* ko⌈ñgo⌉obutsu 混合物; bu⌈reñdo ブレンド.

bless *vt.* ... o shu⌈kufuku suru ...を

祝福する Ⓘ: The priest blessed the people. (*Shisai wa hitobito o shukufuku shita.*) 司祭は人々を祝福した.
be blessed with … *vt.* … ni me⌈gumareru …に恵まれる Ⓥ: We were blessed with good fortune [weather]. (*Watashi-tachi wa koouñ* [*kooteñ*] *ni megumareta.*) 私たちは好運[好天]に恵まれた.

blessing *n.* ka⌉mi no me⌈gumi 神の恵み; shu⌈kufuku 祝福; i⌈nori 祈り: ask a blessing before [after] a meal (*shokuzeñ* [*shokugo*] *no inori o suru*) 食前[食後]の祈りをする.

blind *adj.* **1** (unable to see) me⌉ no fu⌈ji⌉yuu na 目の不自由な; mo⌈omoku no 盲目の: a blind man (*me no mienai hito*) 目の見えない人.
2 (unable to understand) ... ni ki ⌈ga tsuka⌉nai …に気がつかない; wa⌈kara⌉nai わからない: He was blind to the dangers. (*Kare wa kikeñ ni ki ga tsukanakatta.*) 彼は危険に気がつかなかった.
— *n.* bu⌈raiñdo ブラインド; hi⌈yoke 日よけ: draw up [pull down] the blinds (*buraiñdo o ageru* [*orosu*]) ブラインドを上げる[下ろす].

blindness *n.* mo⌈omoku 盲目: color blindness (*shikimoo*) 色盲.

block *n.* **1** (material) ka⌈tamari 塊: a block of ice (*koori no katamari*) 氷の塊 / a block of wood (*mokuzai*) 木材.
2 (between streets) bu⌈ro⌉kku ブロック; ku⌈kaku 区画.
3 (large building) mu⌈ne 棟: an apartment block (*apaato no mune*) アパートの棟.
— *vt.* ... o fu⌈sagu …をふさぐ Ⓒ; bo⌈ogai suru 妨害する Ⓘ: They blocked the entrance with barricades. (*Kare-ra wa iriguchi o barikeedo de fusaida.*) 彼らは入り口をバリケードでふさいだ.

blood *n.* chi 血; [technical] ke⌈tsu⌉eki 血液: My blood type is B. (*Watashi no ketsueki-gata wa bii desu.*) 私の血液型は B です. / blood pressure (*ketsuatsu*) 血圧.

bloom *n.* ha⌈na⌉ 花: a bloom of a rose (*bara no hana*) バラの花.
be in bloom *vi.* sa⌈ite iru 咲いている Ⓥ: The cherry blossoms are now in full bloom. (*Sakura wa ima ga mañkai desu.*) 桜は今が満開です.
— *vi.* ha⌈na⌉ ga sa⌈ku 花が咲く Ⓒ: Our roses will be blooming in June. (*Uchi no bara wa roku-gatsu ni wa saku deshoo.*) うちのバラは 6 月には咲くでしょう.

blossom *n.* ha⌈na⌉ 花: apple blossoms (*riñgo no hana*) りんごの花.
— *vi.* ha⌈na⌉ ga sa⌈ku 花が咲く Ⓒ: This tree will blossom next week. (*Kono ki wa raishuu saku deshoo.*) この木は来週咲くでしょう.

blotter *n.* su⌈itori⌉gami 吸い取り紙.

blouse *n.* bu⌈ra⌉usu ブラウス: wear a blouse (*burausu o kiru*) ブラウスを着る.

blow[1] *vi.* (wind) fu⌉ku 吹く Ⓒ: The wind is blowing hard. (*Kaze ga hidoku fuite iru.*) 風がひどく吹いている.
— *vt.* (instrument) ... o fu⌉ku …を吹く Ⓒ; (horn) na⌈rasu 鳴らす Ⓒ: blow a trumpet (*torañpetto o fuku*) トランペットを吹く / blow a car horn (*keeteki o narasu*) 警笛を鳴らす.
blow one's nose *vi.* ha⌈na o kamu 鼻をかむ Ⓒ.

blow[2] *n.* **1** (hard stroke) kyo⌉oda 強打; i⌈chigeki 一撃: I received a blow on the head. (*Watashi wa atama ni ichigeki o kuratta.*) 私は頭に一撃をくらった.
2 (shock) da⌈geki 打撃: My father's death was a great blow to me. (*Chichi no shi wa watashi ni totte ooki-na dageki datta.*) 父の死は私にとって大きな打撃だった.

blue *adj.* a⌈o⌉i 青い: the blue sky (*aoi sora*) 青い空 / The lake was blue. (*Mizuumi wa aokatta.*) 湖は青かった.
— *n.* a⌉o 青: dark [light] blue (*koi* [*akarui*] *ao*) 濃い[明るい]青.

blunt *adj.* **1** (of a knife) ni⌈bu⌉i 鈍い; ki⌈re⌉nai 切れない: a blunt knife

b

(*kirenai naifu*) 切れないナイフ.
2 (of people) buꜜkkiraꜜboo na ぶっきらぼうな; soꜜkkenaꜜi そっけない: a blunt manner (*sokkenai taido*) そっけない態度.

blush *vi.* kaꜜo o akarameru 顔を赤らめる Ⓥ; aꜜkaku naꜜru 赤くなる Ⓒ; seꜜkimeñ suru 赤面する Ⓘ: The boy blushed for shame. (*Sono otoko-no-ko wa hazukashisa de akaku natta.*) その男の子は恥ずかしさで赤くなった.
— *n.* seꜜkimeñ 赤面; haꜜjirai no iro 恥じらいの色: hide one's blushes (*hajirai no iro o kakusu*) 恥じらいの色を隠す.

board *n.* **1** (timber) iꜜta 板: a cutting board (*manaita*) まな板.
2 (a official group) iꜜiꜜñkai 委員会: a board of education (*kyooiku iiñkai*) 教育委員会.
— *vt.* **1** (get on) ... ni noꜜru …に乗る Ⓒ: We boarded a plane at Narita. (*Watashi-tachi wa Narita de hikooki ni notta.*) 私たちは成田で飛行機に乗った. / Where can I board the ship to Oshima? (*Ooshima e no fune wa doko de noru ñ desu ka?*) 大島への船はどこで乗るんですか.
2 (cover with boards) ... ni iꜜta o haꜜru …に板を張る Ⓒ: board up a broken window (*kowareta mado ni ita o haru*) 壊れた窓に板を張る.
on board *adv.* (plane) kiꜜnai de 機内で; (ship) seꜜñnai de 船内で: Do they sell tax-free goods on board? (*Kinai de meñzeehiñ no hañbai o shite imasu ka?*) 機内で免税品の販売をしていますか.

boardinghouse *n.* geꜜshukuya 下宿屋.

boast *vi.* jiꜜmañ suru 自慢する Ⓘ: He boasted about his new house. (*Kare wa shiñchiku no ie o jimañ shita.*) 彼は新築の家を自慢した.
— *vt.* ... to jiꜜmañ suru …と自慢する Ⓘ: She boasted that she could read Chinese characters. (*Kanojo wa kañji ga yomeru to jimañ shita.*) 彼女は漢字が読めると自慢した.
— *n.* jiꜜmañ no taꜜne 自慢の種; hoꜜkori 誇り.
make a boast of ... *vt.* ... o jiꜜmañ suru …を自慢する Ⓘ.

boat *n.* **1** (small vessel) boꜜoto ボート: row a boat (*booto o kogu*) ボートをこぐ.
2 (ship) fuꜜne 船: get on a boat (*fune ni noru*) 船に乗る / get off a boat (*fune kara oriru*) 船から降りる / a fishing boat (*gyoseñ*) 漁船 / a sightseeing boat (*yuurañseñ*) 遊覧船. ★ 'Ship' is also called *'fune'*.

body *n.* **1** (including head and limbs) kaꜜrada 体; shiꜜñtai 身体: a strong body (*joobu na karada*) じょうぶな体 / I have aches all over my body. (*Karada-juu ga itai.*) 体中が痛い.
2 (excluding head and limbs) doꜜotai) 胴(体); boꜜdii ボディー: He was hit twice in the body. (*Kare wa bodii o ni-do utareta.*) 彼はボディーを2度打たれた.
3 (corpse) shiꜜtai 死体; iꜜtai 遺体: an unidentified body (*mimoto fumee no itai*) 身元不明の遺体.
4 (main part) shuꜜyoꜜobu 主要部; -tai 体: a car body (*shatai*) 車体 / the body of an airplane (*kitai*) 機体 / the body of a letter (*tegami no hoñbuñ*) 手紙の本文.
5 (group) daꜜñtai 団体; aꜜtsumaꜜri 集まり: a diplomatic body (*gaikoodañ*) 外交団.

boil *vi.* waꜜku 沸く Ⓒ; fuꜜttoo suru 沸騰する Ⓘ: Water boils at 100°C. (*Mizu wa sesshi hyaku-do de futtoo suru.*) 水は摂氏 100 度で沸騰する.
— *vt.* ... o waꜜkasu …を沸かす Ⓒ; niꜜru 煮る Ⓥ; taꜜku 炊く Ⓒ; yuꜜdeꜜru ゆでる Ⓥ: boil water (*o-yu o wakasu*) お湯を沸かす / boil vegetables (*yasai o niru*) 野菜を煮る / boil rice (*gohañ o taku*) ご飯を炊く / Please boil the eggs soft. (*Tamago o hañjuku ni shite kudasai.*) 卵を半熟にしてください. / a boiled egg (*yude tamago*) ゆで卵.

boiler *n.* boꜜiraa ボイラー.

bold *adj.* da⌈ita⌉ñ na 大胆な: a bold plan (*daitañ na keekaku*) 大胆な計画.

bomb *n.* ba⌈kudañ 爆弾: drop a bomb (*bakudañ o otosu*) 爆弾を落とす.
— *vt.* ... o ba⌈kugeki suru ...を爆撃する [I]: bomb a city (*toshi o bakugeki suru*) 都市を爆撃する.

bond *n.* **1** (ties) mu⌈subitsuki 結びつき; ki⌉zuna きずな: a bond of friendship (*yuujoo no kizuna*) 友情のきずな.
2 (restriction) so⌈kubaku 束縛: break one's bonds (*sokubaku o tachikiru*) 束縛を断ち切る.
3 (written promise) sho⌈osho 証書; sho⌈omoñ 証文: He signed the bond. (*Kare wa shoomoñ ni shomee shita.*) 彼は証文に署名した.
4 (interest-bearing certificate) sa⌈ikeñ 債券: a public bond (*koosai*) 公債.

bone *n.* ho⌈ne⌉ 骨: break a bone in one's arm (*ude no hone o oru*) 腕の骨を折る / A fish bone got stuck in my throat. (*Sakana no hone ga nodo ni sasatta.*) 魚の骨がのどに刺さった.

book[1] *n.* ho⌉ñ 本: read [write] a book (*hoñ o yomu* [*kaku*]) 本を読む[書く] / I bought three books. (*Watashi wa hoñ o sañ-satsu katta.*) 私は本を3冊買った. / an instruction book (*shiyoo setsumeesho*) 使用説明書 / a phone book (*deñwachoo*) 電話帳.

book[2] *vt.* ... o yo⌈yaku suru ...を予約する [I]: book a room at a hotel (*hoteru no heya o yoyaku suru*) ホテルの部屋を予約する.

bookseller *n.* ho⌉ñya 本屋.

bookstore *n.* ho⌉ñya 本屋; sho⌈teñ 書店: a second-hand bookstore (*furuhoñya*) 古本屋.

boots *n.* na⌈gagutsu 長靴; bu⌉utsu ブーツ: rubber boots (*gomunaga*) ゴム長.

border *n.* **1** (boundary) ko⌈kkyoo 国境; kyo⌈okai 境界: cross the border (*kokkyoo o koeru*) 国境を越える.
2 (edge) he⌈ri⌉ へり; ha⌈shi 端; fu⌈chi⌉ 縁: a tablecloth with a lace border (*reesu no heri ga aru teeburu-kurosu*) レースのへりがあるテーブルクロス / There was a border of flowers around the lawn. (*Shibafu no mawari wa hana de fuchidorarete ita.*) 芝生の周りは花で縁どられていた.
— *vt.* ... to sa⌈ka⌉i o se⌈ssuru ...と境を接する [I]: Japan borders no other countries. (*Nihoñ wa ta no kuni to sakai o sesshite inai.*) 日本は他の国と境を接していない.

bore[1] *vt.* (make a hole) ... ni a⌈na⌉ o a⌈keru ...に穴をあける [V]: bore a hole in a board (*ita ni ana o akeru*) 板に穴をあける.

bore[2] *vt.* (weary) ... o u⌈ñza⌉ri saseru ...をうんざりさせる [V]; ta⌈ikutsu saseru 退屈させる [V]: Prof. Yamazaki's lecture bored us. (*Yamazaki kyooju no koogi wa taikutsu datta.*) 山崎教授の講義は退屈だった.

boring *adj.* ta⌈ikutsu na 退屈な; tsu⌈mara⌉nai つまらない: a boring job (*taikutsu na shigoto*) 退屈な仕事 / The week-end was really boring. (*Shuumatsu wa hoñtoo ni tsumaranakatta.*) 週末はほんとうにつまらなかった.

born *adj.* **1** u⌈mareta 生まれた: I was born on May 5, 1965. (*Watashi wa señ-kyuuhyaku-rokujuugo-neñ no go-gatsu itsuka ni umaremashita.*) 私は1965年の5月5日に生まれました.
2 u⌈marenagara no 生まれながらの: a born painter (*umarenagara no gaka*) 生まれながらの画家.

borrow *vt.* ... o ka⌈riru ...を借りる [V]: Is it okay if I borrow your notebook? (*Kimi no nooto o karite mo ii desu ka?*) きみのノートを借りてもいいですか. / Mr. Ito borrowed two million yen from the bank. (*Itoo-sañ wa giñkoo kara nihyakumañ-eñ karita.*) 伊藤さんは銀行から200万円

借りた.

both *adj.* ryo⌈ohoo no 両方の; fu⌈tari tomo 二人とも: I don't need both maps. Just give me one. (*Ryoohoo no chizu wa irimaseñ. Ichi-mai dake kudasai.*) 両方の地図はいりません. 1 枚だけ下さい. / Both my parents are getting along very well. (*Ryooshiñ wa futari tomo geñki ni kurashite imasu.*) 両親は二人とも元気に暮らしています.
— *pron.* ryo⌈ohoo 両方; fu⌈tari 二人: There's chocolate and cake. Take both if you want to. (*Chokoreeto to keeki ga arimasu. Yokattara ryoohoo doozo.*) チョコレートとケーキがあります. よかったら両方どうぞ. / Both of us went to the same university. (*Watashi-tachi wa futari tomo onaji daigaku ni kayoimashita.*) 私たちは二人とも同じ大学に通いました.
— *conj.* (both ... and ...) ... mo ... mo ...も...も: He speaks both Chinese and Japanese. (*Kare wa Chuugokugo mo Nihoñgo mo hanashimasu.*) 彼は中国語も日本語も話します.

bother *vt.* ... o na⌈yama⌉su ...を悩ます [C]; u⌈rusagarase⌉ru うるさがらせる [V]; ... ni me⌉ewaku o ka⌈ke⌉ru ...に迷惑をかける [V]: The noise of the passing trains really bothers me. (*Ressha ga tsuuka suru oto wa hoñtoo ni urusai.*) 列車が通過する音はほんとうにうるさい. / I am sorry to bother you at this time of night, but I need some information. (*Yabuñ go-meewaku o kakemasu ga chotto oshiete kudasai.*) 夜分ご迷惑をかけますがちょっと教えてください.
— *vi.* o⌈moinaya⌉mu 思い悩む [C]; ku⌉ ni suru 苦にする [I]: Don't bother about such a trifling matter. (*Soñna tsumaranai koto de omoinayamu no wa yoshi nasai.*) そんなつまらないことで思い悩むのはよしなさい.
— *n.* me⌈ñdo⌉o 面倒; ya⌉kkai やっかい: cause a person bother (*hito ni meñdoo o kakeru*) 人に面倒をかける.

bottle *n.* **1** (container) bi⌉ñ びん: fill [empty] a bottle (*biñ o ippai [kara] ni suru*) びんをいっぱい[から]にする / a bottle full of water (*mizu ga ippai haitta biñ*) 水がいっぱい入ったびん / a milk bottle (*gyuunyuu-biñ*) 牛乳びん.
2 (amount) -hoñ [-boñ; -poñ] 本 (⇨ appendix): I have 2 bottles of whisky. (*Uisukii o ni-hoñ motte imasu.*) ウイスキーを 2 本持っています.

bottle opener *n.* se⌈ñnuki 栓抜き.

bottom *n.* **1** (lowest part) so⌈ko 底: the bottom of a glass (*koppu no soko*) コップの底 / I found my address book at the bottom of my suitcase. (*Juushoroku ga suutsukeesu no soko ni atta.*) 住所録がスーツケースの底にあった.
2 (of a mountain) fu⌈moto⌉ ふもと; (base) shi⌈ta 下: a house at the bottom of the mountain (*yama no fumoto no ie*) 山のふもとの家 / Your mistake is on the third line from the bottom. (*Kimi no machigai wa shita kara sañ-gyoome ni aru.*) 君のまちがいは下から 3 行目にある.
3 (lowest) sa⌈itee no 最低の; (last) sa⌉igo no 最後の; bi⌉ri no びりの: the bottom price (*saitee nedañ*) 最低値段 / He was at the bottom of the class. (*Kare wa kurasu no biri datta.*) 彼はクラスのびりだった.
4 (buttocks) shi⌈ri⌉ 尻: She wiped her baby's dirty bottom. (*Kanojo wa akañboo no yogoreta o-shiri o fuita.*) 彼女は赤ん坊の汚れたお尻を拭いた.

bounce *vi.* ha⌈zumu 弾む [C]; ba⌈uñdo suru バウンドする [I]: This ball bounces well. (*Kono booru wa yoku hazumu.*) このボールはよく弾む.
— *vt.* ... o ha⌈zumaseru ...を弾ませる [V]; ba⌈uñdo saseru バウンドさせる [V]: bounce a ball (*booru o bauñdo saseru*) ボールをバウンドさせる.

bowl *n.* **1** (container) wa⌈ñ わん; cha⌈wañ 茶わん; ha⌈chi⌉ 鉢; bo⌈oru ボール: a rice bowl (*gohañ no cha-*

wañ) ご飯の茶わん / a goldfish bowl (*kiñgyo-bachi*) 金魚鉢 / a salad bowl (*sarada booru*) サラダボール.
2 (amount) -hai [-bai; -pai] 杯 《⇨ appendix》: two bowls of rice (*gohañ ni-hai*) ご飯2杯.

box *n.* **1** (container) ha⌈ko 箱: a wooden box (*ki no hako*) 木の箱 / a lunch box (*beñtoobako*) 弁当箱 / a match box (*matchibako*) マッチ箱.
2 (amount) -hako [-bako; -pako] 箱 《⇨ appendix》: two boxes of tangerines (*mikañ futa-hako*) みかん2箱 / How much do these peaches cost per box? (*Kono momo wa hito-hako ikura desu ka?*) この桃は1箱いくらですか.

boy *n.* o⌈toko⌉-no-ko 男の子; sho⌈o-neñ 少年: Will the boys please line up here? (*Otoko-no-ko-tachi wa koko ni narañde choodai.*) 男の子たちはここに並んでちょうだい. / boys and girls (*shooneñ shoojo*) 少年少女.

bra *n.* bu⌈ra⌉jaa ブラジャー: put on a bra (*burajaa o tsukeru*) ブラジャーをつける.

braid *vt.* ... o a⌉mu ...を編む Ⓒ: braid hair (*kami o amu*) 髪を編む.
— *n.* (hair) o⌈sage⌉gami おさげ髪; (band) ku⌈mi⌉himo 組みひも; mo⌉oru モール: wear one's hair in braids (*kami o osage ni suru*) 髪をおさげにする / gold braid (*kiñ mooru*) 金モール.

brain *n.* **1** (organ) no⌉o 脳; no⌉ozui 脳髄.
2 (intelligence) zu⌉noo 頭脳; a⌈tama 頭; chi⌉ryoku 知力: have good [no] brains (*atama ga yoi [warui]*) 頭がよい[悪い] / use one's brains (*atama o tsukau*) 頭を使う.
3 (intelligent person) chi⌈teki shido⌉osha 知的指導者; bu⌈re⌉eñ ブレーン; (clever person) a⌈tama no i⌉i hito 頭のいい人: He is the brains of the company. (*Kare wa kaisha no bureeñ da.*) 彼は会社のブレーンだ.

brake *n.* bu⌈re⌉eki ブレーキ: put on [take off] the brakes (*bureeki o kakeru [yurumeru]*) ブレーキをかける[緩める].
— *vt.* ... ni bu⌈re⌉eki o ka⌈ke⌉ru ... にブレーキをかける Ⓥ: He braked the car. (*Kare wa kuruma ni bureeki o kaketa.*) 彼は車にブレーキをかけた.
— *vi.* bu⌈re⌉eki o ka⌈ke⌉ru ブレーキをかける Ⓥ: The bus braked suddenly. (*Basu ga kyuu-bureeki o kaketa.*) バスが急ブレーキをかけた.

branch *n.* **1** (tree) e⌈da 枝: break a branch (*eda o oru*) 枝を折る.
2 (office) shi⌈teñ 支店; shi⌉bu 支部: the Iidabashi branch of the Sakura Bank (*Sakura giñkoo no Iidabashi shiteñ*) さくら銀行の飯田橋支店.
3 (part) bu⌉moñ 部門; bu⌉ñka 分科: Geometry is a branch of mathematics. (*Kika wa suugaku no ichi-bumoñ desu.*) 幾何は数学の一部門です.
— *vi.* wa⌈kare⌉ru 分かれる Ⓥ; bu⌉ñ-ki suru 分岐する Ⓘ: This road branches up ahead. (*Kono michi wa saki e itte wakaremasu.*) この道は先へ行って分かれます.

branch line *n.* shi⌈señ 支線.

brassiere *n.* bu⌈ra⌉jaa ブラジャー.

brave *adj.* yu⌉ukañ na 勇敢な; yu⌉uki no [ga] aru 勇気の[が]ある: a brave policeman (*yuukañ na keesatsukañ*) 勇敢な警察官 / It was brave of him to jump into the river to save the child. (*Kodomo o sukuu tame ni kawa ni tobikomu to wa kare mo yuukañ datta.*) 子どもを救うために川に飛び込むとは彼も勇敢だった.

bread *n.* pa⌉ñ パン: a loaf [slice] of bread (*pañ hito katamari [hito kire]*) パンひと塊[ひと切れ] / cut [toast] bread (*pañ o kiru [yaku]*) パンを切る[焼く] / butter bread (*pañ ni bataa o nuru*) パンにバターを塗る.

break[1] *vt.* **1** (destroy) ... o ko⌈wa⌉su ...を壊す Ⓒ: Who broke the toy? (*Omocha o kowashita no wa dare desu ka?*) おもちゃを壊したのはだれですか.
2 (divide) ... o wa⌈ru ...を割る Ⓒ: break an egg (*tamago o waru*) 卵を

b

割る / She broke the glass into pieces. (*Kanojo wa koppu o konagona ni watte shimatta.*) 彼女はコップを粉々に割ってしまった.
3 (snap) ... o o˥ru ...を折る Ⓒ: break a branch from a tree (*ki no eda o oru*) 木の枝を折る / Taro broke his leg. (*Taroo wa ashi o otta.*) 太郎は脚を折った.
4 (smash) ... o ku˹da˥ku ...を砕く Ⓒ: break a rock with a hammer (*hañmaa de iwa o kudaku*) ハンマーで岩を砕く.
5 (violate) ... o ya˹bu˥ru ...を破る Ⓒ: break the law (*hooritsu o yaburu*) 法律を破る / He never breaks a promise. (*Kare wa kesshite yakusoku o yaburanai.*) 彼は決して約束を破らない.
6 (better) ... o ya˹bu˥ru ...を破る Ⓒ: break the world record (*sekai kiroku o yaburu*) 世界記録を破る.
— *vi.* ko˹ware˥ru 壊れる Ⓥ; wa˹reru 割れる Ⓥ; o˹re˥ru 折れる Ⓥ; ku˹dake˥ru 砕ける Ⓥ; ya˹bure˥ru 破れる Ⓥ: This camera has broken. (*Kono kamera wa kowarete shimatta.*) このカメラは壊れてしまった. / My precious vase broke. (*Watashi no daiji na kabiñ ga wareta.*) 私の大事な花びんが割れた.

break[2] *n.* ya˹sumi˥ 休み; kyu˹ukee 休憩: a coffee [tea] break (*nakayasumi*) 中休み / Let's take a quick break. (*Chotto kyuukee shimashoo.*) ちょっと休憩しましょう.

breakfast *n.* cho˹oshoku 朝食; a˹sa-go˥hañ 朝ご飯: have an early breakfast (*hayai chooshoku o toru*) 早い朝食をとる.

breast *n.* **1** (female) chi˥busa 乳房; chi˥chi 乳: suck the breast (*chichi [oppai] o shaburu*) 乳[おっぱい]をしゃぶる.
2 (chest) mu˹ne˥ 胸: have a pain in one's breast (*mune ga itamu*) 胸が痛む.

breath *n.* i˥ki 息; ko˹kyuu 呼吸: take in [give out] breath (*iki o suu [haku]*) 息を吸う[吐く] / have bad breath (*iki ga kusai*) 息が臭い / hold one's breath (*iki o korasu*) 息をこらす / take a deep breath (*shiñkokyuu o suru*) 深呼吸をする.

breathe *vi.* i˥ki o suru 息をする Ⓘ; ko˹kyuu suru 呼吸する Ⓘ: Please breathe in, and then breathe out slowly. (*Iki o sutte sore kara yukkuri haite kudasai.*) 息を吸ってそれからゆっくり吐いてください.
— *vt.* ... o su˹iko˥mu ...を吸い込む Ⓒ: breathe fresh air (*shiñseñ na kuuki o suikomu*) 新鮮な空気を吸い込む.

breeze *n.* so˹yo˥kaze そよ風; bi˹fuu 微風: a cool breeze (*suzushii kaze*) 涼しい風 / a pleasant spring breeze (*kimochi no yoi haru no kaze*) 気持ちのよい春の風.

bribe *n.* wa˥iro わいろ: offer [accept] a bribe (*wairo o sashidasu [uketoru]*) わいろを差し出す[受け取る].
— *vt.* (hito) ni wa˥iro o tsu˹kau (人)にわいろを使う Ⓒ; ... o ba˹ishuu suru ...を買収する Ⓘ: attempt to bribe a mayor (*shichoo o baishuu shiyoo to suru*) 市長を買収しようとする.

brick *n.* re˥ñga れんが: a house built of red bricks (*akai reñga de dekita uchi*) 赤いれんがでできた家.

bride *n.* ha˹na˥yome 花嫁; shi˥ñpu 新婦.

bridegroom *n.* ha˹namu˥ko 花婿; shi˹ñroo 新郎.

bridge *n.* ha˹shi˥ 橋: build a bridge (*hashi o kakeru*) 橋をかける / cross a bridge (*hashi o wataru*) 橋を渡る / a railway bridge (*tekkyoo*) 鉄橋 / a suspension bridge (*tsuribashi*) つり橋.
— *vt.* ... ni ha˹shi˥ o ka˹ke˥ru ...に橋を架ける Ⓥ: We bridged the stream. (*Watashi-tachi wa sono ogawa ni hashi o kaketa.*) 私たちはその小川に橋を架けた.

brief *adj.* mi˹jika˥i 短い; wa˥zuka no わずかの; ta˹ñji˥kañ no 短時間の: a brief speech (*mijikai eñzetsu*) 短い演説 / take a brief rest (*tanjikañ* *no kyuusoku o toru*) 短時間の休息を取る.

— *n.* te[kiyoo 摘要; ga[iyoo 概要.

in brief *adv.* yo[o-su]ru ni 要するに: In brief, he has failed. (*Yoosuru ni kare wa shippai shita.*) 要するに彼は失敗した.

briefcase *n.* bu[riifu-ke]esu ブリーフケース; ka[bañ かばん: I left my briefcase on the train. (*Deñsha no naka ni kabañ o wasuremashita.*) 電車の中にかばんを忘れました.

bright *adj.* **1** (light) a[karui 明るい; ka[gaya]ite (iru) 輝いて(いる): a bright morning (*akaruku hareta asa*) 明るく晴れた朝 / The sun is bright. (*Taiyoo ga akaruku kagayaite iru.*) 太陽が明るく輝いている.

2 (color) a[za]yaka na 鮮やかな: The roses were bright red. (*Bara wa azayaka na akadatta.*) バラは鮮やかな赤だった.

3 (cheerful) ha[re]yaka na 晴れやかな; ka[gaya]ite (iru) 輝いて(いる): a bright, smiling face (*hareyaka na egao*) 晴れやかな笑顔 / His eyes were bright with excitement. (*Kare no me wa koofuñ de kagayaite ita.*) 彼の目は興奮で輝いていた.

4 (clever) ri[koo na 利口な; a[tama] ga i]i 頭がいい: a bright boy (*atama ga ii otoko-no-ko*) 頭がいい男の子.

brighten *vt.* ... o a[karuku suru ...を明るくする Ⅰ; ka[gayakase]ru 輝かせる Ⅴ: A vase of flowers will brighten the room. (*Kabiñ ni hana ga areba heya ga akaruku naru daroo.*) 花びんに花があれば部屋が明るくなるだろう.

— *vi.* a[karuku na]ru 明るくなる Ⓒ: The sky brightened. (*Sora ga akaruku natta.*) 空が明るくなった.

brilliant *adj.* **1** (very bright) hi[kari-kagaya]ku 光り輝く: a brilliant diamond (*hikari-kagayaku daiyamoñdo*) 光り輝くダイヤモンド.

2 (clever) su[gu]rete iru 優れている; su[barashi]i すばらしい: a brilliant student (*sugurete iru gakusee*) 優れている学生 / a brilliant idea (*subarashii kañgae*) すばらしい考え.

bring *vt.* **1** (a thing) ... o mo[tte ku]ru ...を持ってくる Ⅰ: Please bring me some ice and water. (*Koori to mizu o motte kite kudasai.*) 氷と水を持ってきてください.

2 (a person) ... o tsu[rete ku]ru ...を連れてくる Ⅰ: I will bring my brother along with me. (*Otooto o issho ni tsurete kimasu.*) 弟をいっしょに連れてきます.

3 (cause) ... o mo[tara]su ...をもたらす Ⓒ; ma[ne]ku 招く Ⓒ: Our action brought protests from the neighbors. (*Watashi-tachi no koodoo wa kiñjo kara koogi o maneita.*) 私たちの行動は近所から抗議を招いた.

bring up *vt.* ... o so[date]ru ... を育てる Ⅴ: I was brought up in the country. (*Watashi wa inaka de sodatta.*) 私はいなかで育った.

Britain *n.* I[girisu イギリス; E[ekoku 英国.

British *adj.* I[girisu no イギリスの; E[ekoku no 英国の: the British (*Igirisujiñ*) イギリス人; (*Eekokujiñ*) 英国人.

broad *adj.* **1** (wide) ha[ba no hiro]i 幅の広い; (extensive) hi[robi]ro to shita [shite iru] 広々とした[している]: a broad river (*haba no hiroi kawa*) 幅の広い川 / a broad ocean (*hirobiro to shita umi*) 広々とした海 / broad shoulders (*hiroi katahaba*) 広い肩幅.

2 (general) hi[ro]i 広い; o[oza]ppa na おおざっぱな: a broad knowledge of world events (*sekai no dekigoto ni tsuite no hiroi chishiki*) 世界の出来事についての広い知識 / Just give me the broad outline of the plan. (*Sono keekaku no oozappa na gaiyoo o oshiete kudasai.*) その計画のおおざっぱな概要を教えてください.

broadcast *n.* ho[osoo 放送: a broadcast program (*hoosoo bañgumi*) 放送番組 / a live broadcast (*nama-hoosoo*) 生放送 / a satellite broadcast (*eesee hoosoo*) 衛星放送.

— *vt.* ... o ho[osoo suru ...を放送

する [I]: The game will be broadcast on television tonight. (*Sono shiai wa koñya terebi de hoosoo saremasu.*) その試合は今夜テレビで放送されます.

brochure *n.* pa'ñfuretto パンフレット; sho'osa'sshi 小冊子: I'd like a sightseeing brochure for this town. (*Kono machi no kañkoo pañfuretto o itadakitai ñ desu ga.*) この町の観光パンフレットをいただきたいんですが.

broil *vt.* ... o ya'ku ...を焼く [C]; a'bu'ru あぶる [C]: broil chicken legs (*tori no ashi o yaku*) 鶏の脚を焼く.

broken *adj.* **1** (thing) ko'wa'reta 壊れた: a broken cup (*kowareta chawañ*) 壊れた茶碗.
2 (bone) o'reta 折れた; (body part) ke'ga' o shita けがをした: a broken leg (*kossetsu shita ashi*) 骨折した脚.
3 (agreement) ya'bura'reta 破られた; o'kasa'reta 犯された: a broken promise (*yaburareta yakusoku*) 破られた約束 / a broken law (*okasareta hooritsu*) 犯された法律.

brooch *n.* bu'ro'ochi ブローチ.

brook *n.* o'gawa 小川.

broom *n.* ho'oki ほうき: sweep a room with a broom (*hooki de heya o haku*) ほうきで部屋を掃く.

brother *n.* (older) a'ni 兄; (someone else's older brother) (o-)ni'i-sañ (お)兄さん; (younger) o'tooto 弟; (someone else's younger brother) o'tooto-sañ 弟さん: brothers (*kyoodai*) 兄弟. ★ There is no direct Japanese equivalent to 'brother'.

brother-in-law *n.* (older) gi'ri no a'ni [gi'kee] 義理の兄[義兄]; (younger) gi'ri no otooto [gi'tee] 義理の弟[義弟].

brow *n.* (eyebrow) ma'yu まゆ; ma'yuge まゆ毛; (forehead) hi'tai 額: He has strong brows. (*Kare wa futoi mayu o shite iru.*) 彼は太いまゆをしている.

brown *adj.* cha'iro no 茶色の; ka'sshoku no 褐色の: Hiroko has brown eyes [hair]. (*Hiroko-sañ wa chairo no me* [*kami no ke*] *o shite iru.*) 広子さんは茶色の目[髪の毛]をしている. / I painted the chairs and tables brown. (*Watashi wa isu to teeburu o chairo ni nutta.*) 私はいすとテーブルを茶色に塗った.
— *n.* cha'iro 茶色; ka'sshoku 褐色: light brown (*usuchairo*) 薄茶色 / dark brown (*kogechairo*) 焦げ茶色.

bruise *vt.* ... ni a'za' o tsu'ke'ru ...にあざをつける [V]; da'boku'shoo o a'taeru 打撲傷を与える [V]; ki'zu o tsuke'ru 傷をつける [V]: Your blow bruised my cheek. (*Kimi no pañchi de watashi no hoo ni aza ga dekita.*) 君のパンチで私のほおにあざができた. / bruised fruit (*kizu no tsuita kudamono*) 傷のついた果物.
— *vi.* a'za' ni na'ru あざになる [C]; ki'zuato ga tsu'ku 傷あとがつく [C]: I bruise easily. (*Watashi wa sugu aza ni naru.*) 私はすぐあざになる.
— *n.* a'za あざ; ki'zu 傷; da'boku'shoo 打撲傷: She was covered with bruises. (*Kanojo wa aza darake datta.*) 彼女はあざだらけだった.

brush *n.* bu'rashi ブラシ; ha'ke' はけ; fu'de 筆: Use this brush to clean the tiles. (*Tairu o sooji suru no ni kono burashi o tsukai nasai.*) タイルを掃除するのにこのブラシを使いなさい. / I wrote Chinese characters with a brush. (*Fude de kañji o kaita.*) 筆で漢字を書いた.
— *vt.* ... ni bu'rashi o ka'ke'ru ...にブラシをかける [V]; ... o bu'rashi de mi'gaku ...をブラシで磨く [C]: Will you please brush this coat? (*Kono kooto ni burashi o kakete kuremasu ka?*) このコートにブラシをかけてくれますか. / I brush my teeth before going to bed. (*Watashi wa neru mae ni ha o migakimasu.*) 私は寝る前に歯を磨きます.

bubble *n.* a'wa' 泡; a'buku' あぶく: blow (soap) bubbles (*shabonđama o fuku*) シャボン玉を吹く.

bucket *n.* ba'ketsu バケツ; te'oke 手おけ: carry water in a bucket (*baketsu de mizu o hakobu*) バケツで水を運ぶ.

buckle *n.* ba⌝kkuru バックル; shi⌜megane 締め金: fasten [unfasten] one's belt buckle (*beruto no bakkuru o shimeru* [*hazusu*]) ベルトのバックルを締める[はずす].

— *vt.* ... o ba⌜kkuru de shime⌝ru ...をバックルで締める Ⓥ: buckle a belt (*beruto o bakkuru de shimeru*) ベルトをバックルで締める.

bud *n.* me⌝ 芽; tsu⌜bomi⌝ つぼみ: a leaf bud (*ha no me*) 葉の芽 / a flower bud (*hana no tsubomi*) 花のつぼみ / The trees are in bud. (*Ki ga me o dashi-hajimeta.*) 木が芽を出し始めた.

— *vi.* me⌝ o dasu 芽を出す Ⓒ; tsu⌜bomi⌝ o tsu⌜ke⌝ru つぼみをつける Ⓥ: The cherry trees are budding early this year. (*Kotoshi wa sakura ga hayaku tsubomi o tsuke-hajimeta.*) ことしは桜が早くつぼみをつけ始めた.

Buddha *n.* ho⌜toke⌝ 仏; Bu⌝dda ブッダ.

Buddhism *n.* bu⌝kkyoo 仏教: believe in Buddhism (*bukkyoo o shiñkoo suru*) 仏教を信仰する.

budget *n.* yo⌜sañ 予算: make a monthly budget (*maitsuki no yosañ o tateru*) 毎月の予算を立てる / carry out a project within the budget (*yosañ-nai de keekaku o jikkoo suru*) 予算内で計画を実行する.

— *vi.* yo⌜sañ o ta⌜te⌝ru 予算を立てる Ⓥ: We budgeted for the coming year. (*Yokuneñ no yosañ o tateta.*) 翌年の予算を立てた.

build *vt.* **1** (construct) ... o ta⌜te⌝ru ...を建てる Ⓥ; ke⌜ñchiku suru 建築する Ⓘ; ke⌜ñsetsu suru 建設する Ⓘ: The Satos built a new house. (*Satoo-sañ no uchi de wa atarashii uchi o tateta.*) 佐藤さんの家では新しい家を建てた. / Another skyscraper has been built in Shinjuku. (*Moo hitotsu no koosoobiru ga Shiñjuku ni keñsetsu sareta.*) もう一つの高層ビルが新宿に建設された.

2 (develop) ... o ki⌜zu⌝ku ...を築く Ⓒ; tsu⌜ku⌝ru 作る Ⓒ: build a business relationship (*torihiki kañkee o kizuku*) 取り引き関係を築く / I would like to build up my stamina. (*Watashi wa sutamina o tsuketai.*) 私はスタミナをつけたい.

— *n.* ta⌜ikaku 体格: a man with a fine build (*rippa na taikaku o shita otoko no hito*) 立派な体格をした男の人.

builder *n.* ke⌜ñchiku gyo⌝osha 建築業者.

building *n.* ta⌜temo⌝no 建物; bi⌝ru ビル: a ten-year old building (*tatete juu-neñ ni naru biru*) 建てて10年になるビル.

bullet *n.* da⌜ñgañ 弾丸; ta⌜ma⌝ 弾: The bullet hit the wall. (*Tama wa kabe ni atatta.*) 弾は壁に当たった.

bulletin *n.* **1** (official statement) ko⌜ohoo 公報; ko⌜kuji 告示: issue a bulletin (*koohoo o dasu*) 公報を出す.

2 (printed sheet) ka⌜ihoo 会報.

bulletin board *n.* ke⌜ejibañ 掲示板.

bundle *n.* ta⌝ba 束; tsu⌜tsumi⌝ 包み: a bundle of firewood (*maki no taba*) まきの束 / a bundle of clothes (*irui no tsutsumi*) 衣類の包み.

— *vt.* ... o ta⌜bane⌝ru 束ねる Ⓥ; tsu⌜tsumi⌝ ni suru 包みにする Ⓘ: She bundled all her possessions up. (*Kanojo wa mochimono o zeñbu hitomatome ni shita.*) 彼女は持ち物を全部ひとまとめにした.

burden *n.* **1** (load) ni⌝motsu 荷物: She was carrying a heavy burden. (*Kanojo wa omoi nimotsu o hakoñde ita.*) 彼女は重い荷物を運んでいた.

2 (encumbrance) o⌜moni 重荷: The sick child was a burden to her. (*Byooki no kodomo ga kanojo no omoni datta.*) 病気の子どもが彼女の重荷だった.

burn *vt.* **1** (of wood, coal) ... o mo⌜yasu ...を燃やす Ⓒ; ya⌜ku 焼く Ⓒ: Please burn those old papers. (*Kono furui shorui wa moyashite kudasai.*) この古い書類は燃やしてください.

2 (char; damage) ... o ko⌜ga⌝su ...を

焦がす C; ya⌈kedo saseru やけどさせる V: You've gone and burned the bread. (*Pañ o kogashite shimaimashita yo.*) パンを焦がしてしまいましたよ. / I burned my hand lighting the fire. (*Watashi wa hi o tsukete ite te ni yakedo shita.*) 私は火をつけていて手にやけどした.
— *vi.* mo⌈eru 燃える V; ko⌈ge⌉ru 焦げる V: Paper burns easily. (*Kami wa sugu moeru.*) 紙はすぐ燃える. / The cake is burning. (*Keeki ga kogete iru.*) ケーキが焦げている.

burst *vi.* **1** (explode; break open) ha⌈retsu suru 破裂する I; wa⌈reru 割れる V: The bomb burst. (*Bakudañ ga haretsu shita.*) 爆弾が破裂した. / The balloon burst. (*Fuuseñ ga wareta.*) 風船が割れた.
2 (of a bank, dam) ke⌈kkai suru 決壊する I: The water level rose and the dam burst. (*Suii ga agari damu wa kekkai shita.*) 水位が上がりダムは決壊した.
— *vt.* ... o ha⌈retsu saseru ...を破裂させる V; wa⌈ru 割る C: The child burst the soap bubble with a pencil. (*Kodomo wa shaboñdama o eñpitsu de watta.*) 子どもはシャボン玉を鉛筆で割った.
burst into ... *vt.* to⌈tsuzeñ <verb> 突然...: She burst into tears. (*Kanojo wa totsuzeñ naki-dashita.*) 彼女は突然泣き出した.

bus *n.* ba⌉su バス: get on a bus (*basu ni noru*) バスに乗る / get off a bus (*basu o oriru*) バスを降りる / Does this bus go to the airport? (*Kono basu wa kuukoo e ikimasu ka?*) このバスは空港へ行きますか. / a sightseeing bus (*kañkoo basu*) 観光バス.

bush *n.* hi⌈ku⌉i ki 低い木; ka⌈ñboku 灌木; ya⌈bu やぶ: a rose bush (*bara no ki*) ばらの木.

business *n.* **1** (occupation) sho⌈ku⌉gyoo 職業: What business are you in? (*Go-shokugyoo wa nañ desu ka?*) ご職業は何ですか.
2 (trade) sho⌉obai 商売; to⌈ri⌉hiki 取り引き: Business is doing well. (*Shoobai wa umaku itte imasu.*) 商売はうまくいっています.
3 (work) shi⌈goto 仕事; yo⌈oji 用事: Are you here on business or pleasure? (*Koko ni kita no wa shigoto desu ka asobi desu ka?*) ここに来たのは仕事ですか遊びですか. / He went to Osaka on business. (*Kare wa yooji ga atte Oosaka e ikimashita.*) 彼は用事があって大阪へ行きました.
4 (activity) gyo⌉omu 業務; ji⌉mu 事務: Business as usual. (*Gyoomu wa heejoo-doori.*) 業務は平常どおり.
5 (shop) mi⌈se⌉ 店; (firm) ka⌈isha 会社: My father owns five businesses. (*Chichi wa mise o itsutsu motte iru.*) 父は店を五つ持っている.
6 (concern) ko⌈togara 事柄: It's none of your business. (*Sore wa anata ni wa kañkee no nai koto desu.*) それはあなたには関係のないことです.

businessman *n.* ji⌈tsugyooka 実業家; ji⌈tsumuka 実務家. ★ A male office worker is usually called '*bijinesumañ*' (businessman) in Japan.

businesswoman *n.* jo⌈see no jitsugyooka 女性の実業家; jo⌈see no jitsumuka 女性の実務家.

bus stop *n.* ba⌉su no te⌈eryuujo バスの停留所. ★ Often abbreviated to '*basu-tee*' バス停: Where is the bus stop for Shibuya? (*Shibuya-yuki no basu no teeryuujo wa doko desu ka?*) 渋谷行きのバスの停留所はどこですか.

busy *adj.* **1** (actively engaged) i⌈sogashi⌉i 忙しい: a busy person (*isogashii hito*) 忙しい人 / I am afraid the manager is too busy to see you. (*Mooshiwake arimaseñ ga buchoo wa isogashikute o-ai suru koto ga dekimaseñ.*) 申し訳ありませんが部長は忙しくてお会いすることができません.
2 (full of activity; crowded) ni⌈gi⌉yaka na にぎやかな; ko⌉ñzatsu shite iru 混雑している: a busy street (*nigiyaka na toori*) にぎやかな通り / Shin-

juku is the busiest station in Tokyo. (*Shiñjuku wa Tookyoo de ichibañ koñzatsu shite iru eki desu.*) 新宿は東京でいちばん混雑している駅です.
The line is busy. (*O-hanashichuu desu.*) お話中です.

but *conj.* (yet, however) shiˈkaˈshi しかし; deˈ mo でも; daˈ ga だが; keˈredomo けれども: Our family are poor, but happy. (*Watashi-tachi ikka wa mazushii. De mo shiawase desu.*) 私たち一家は貧しい. でも幸せです. / This dress is cheap but well made. (*Kono doresu wa yasui ga yoku dekite iru.*) このドレスは安いがよくできている. / I would like to watch the movie, but I am now busy. (*Eega o mitai keredomo ima wa isogashii.*) 映画を見たいけれども今は忙しい.
not ... but ... ... de wa naˈku(te) mushiro ... ...ではなく(て)むしろ...: The real job of a policeman is not to catch criminals, but to prevent crime. (*Keesatsukañ no hoñrai no shigoto wa hañzaisha o tsukamaeru koto de wa naku mushiro hañzai o fusegu koto desu.*) 警察官の本来の仕事は犯罪者を捕まえることではなくむしろ犯罪を防ぐことです.
— *prep.* ... o noˈzoite ...を除いて; ... no hoˈka ni ...のほかに: Any day but Friday is okay. (*Kiñyoo o nozoite itsu de mo kekkoo desu.*) 金曜を除いていつでも結構です. / There was no one there but me. (*Soko ni wa watashi no hoka dare mo inakatta.*) そこには私のほかだれもいなかった.

butcher *n.* niˈkuˈya 肉屋: buy meat at the butcher's (*nikuya de niku o kau*) 肉屋で肉を買う / a butcher shop (*nikuya*) 肉屋.

butter *n.* baˈtaa バター: I spread the butter on my bread. (*Pañ ni bataa o nutta.*) パンにバターを塗った.

butterfly *n.* choˈo ちょう; choˈochoo ちょうちょう.

button *n.* **1** (clothing) boˈtañ ボタン: sew on a button (*botañ o tsukeru*) ボタンをつける / A button has come off. (*Botañ ga toreta.*) ボタンがとれた.
2 (machine) boˈtañ ボタン; oˈshiboˈtañ 押しボタン: Push the button for the third floor, please. (*Sañ-gai no botañ o oshite kudasai.*) 3 階のボタンを押してください.
— *vt.* boˈtañ o kakeˈru ボタンを掛ける Ⓥ: button up a shirt (*shatsu no botañ o kakeru*) シャツのボタンをかける.

buy *vt.* **1** (purchase) ... o kaˈu ...を買う Ⓒ; koˈonyuu suru 購入する Ⓘ: I want to buy a new television. (*Atarashii terebi o kaitai.*) 新しいテレビを買いたい. / I bought this shirt for five thousand yen. (*Watashi wa kono shatsu o go-señ-eñ de katta.*) 私はこのシャツを 5 千円で買った.
2 (treat) ... o oˈgoru ...をおごる Ⓒ: Bill said he would buy me lunch. (*Biru wa watashi ni o-hiru o ogotte kureru to itta.*) ビルは私にお昼をおごってくれると言った.
— *vi.* kaˈu 買う Ⓒ; koˈonyuu suru 購入する Ⓘ: buying and selling (*baibai*) 売買.

buyer *n.* kaˈite 買い手; shiˈiregaˈkari 仕入れ係; baˈiyaa バイヤー.

by *prep.* **1** (passive) ... ni yoˈtte ...によって: This book was written by a famous author. (*Kono hoñ wa yuumee na sakka ni yotte kakaremashita.*) この本は有名な作家によって書かれました.
2 (means) ... de ...で; ... ni yoˈtte ...によって: How long does it take to go to the airport by taxi? (*Kuukoo made takushii de dono kurai kakarimasu ka?*) 空港までタクシーでどのくらいかかりますか. / Please send this letter by airmail. (*Kono tegami o kookuubiñ de okutte kudasai.*) この手紙を航空便で送ってください. / This machine works by electricity. (*Kono kikai wa deñki de ugoku.*) この機械は電気で動く.
3 (next to) ... no soˈba ni [no; o] ...のそばに[の;を]: a house by the railroad tracks (*señro no soba no uchi*)

線路のそばの家 / She sat by me. (*Kanojo wa watashi no soba ni suwatta.*) 彼女は私のそばに座った.
4 (not later than) ... ma⌉de ni ...までに: Make sure you are here by 8 o'clock tomorrow morning. (*Asu no asa hachi-ji made ni kanarazu koko ni kite kudasai.*) 明日の朝 8 時までに必ずここに来てください.
5 (in accordance with) ... ni shi⌈tagatte ...に従って; ... ni yo⌈tte ...によって: play by the rules (*ruuru ni shitagatte puree suru*) ルールに従ってプレーする / The next song is by request. (*Tsugi no uta wa go-yooboo ni yorimasu.*) 次の歌はご要望によります.
6 (degree; amount) ... dake ...だけ: Land prices have fallen by 10%. (*Tochi no kakaku ga jup-paaseñto dake sagatta.*) 土地の価格が 10%だけ下がった.
7 (to show the part) ... o ... を: He pulled me by the hair. (*Kare wa watashi no kami no ke o hippatta.*) 彼は私の髪の毛を引っ張った. / The mother held the child by the arm. (*Hahaoya wa kodomo no ude o totta.*) 母親は子どもの腕を取った.
8 (measurements) ta⌉te ... yo⌈ko ... 縦...横...: a room 5 meters by 10 meters (*tate go-meetoru yoko juu-meetoru no heya*) 縦 5 メートル横 10 メートルの部屋.
9 (rate; size of units) ... de ...で: ... ta⌉ñi de ...単位で: buy eggs by the dozen (*tamago o ichi-daasu tañi de kau*) 卵を 1 ダース単位で買う. / How much is it by the hour? (*Ichi-jikañ ikura desu ka?*) 1 時間いくらですか.

C

cab *n.* **1** (taxi) ta⌉kushii タクシー.
2 (of a truck) u⌈ñteñdai 運転台: The driver climbed into the cab. (*Uñteñshu wa uñteñdai ni agatta.*) 運転手は運転台に上がった.

cabaret *n.* kya⌉baree キャバレー.

cabbage *n.* kya⌉betsu キャベツ: a Chinese cabbage (*hakusai*) 白菜.

cabin *n.* **1** (small house) ko⌈ya 小屋: a log cabin (*maruta-goya*) 丸太小屋.
2 (mountain lodge) ya⌈magoya 山小屋.
3 (on a ship) se⌈ñshitsu 船室; (on an airplane) jo⌈omui⌉ñshitsu 乗務員室.

cabin crew *n.* (on an airplane) jo⌈omu⌉iñ 乗務員.

cabinet *n.* **1** (furniture) to⌈dana 戸棚; kya⌈bine⌉tto キャビネット: filing cabinet (*fairiñgu kyabinetto*) ファイリング・キャビネット.
2 (of a government) na⌉ikaku 内閣: form [reshuffle] a cabinet (*naikaku o soshiki [kaizoo] suru*) 内閣を組織[改造]する / a cabinet member (*kakuryoo*) 閣僚.

cable *n.* **1** (thick wire) fu⌈to⌉i ke⌉eburu 太いケーブル; (thick rope) fu⌈to⌉i tsu⌈na⌉ 太い綱: an undersea cable (*kaitee keeburu*) 海底ケーブル.
2 (telegram) de⌈ñpoo 電報.

cable car *n.* ke⌈eburu⌉-kaa ケーブルカー: The cable car went up the mountainside. (*Keeburu-kaa wa yama no shameñ o nobotta.*) ケーブルカーは山の斜面を登った.

cable television *n.* yu⌈useñ te⌉rebi 有線テレビ.

cactus *n.* (plant) sa⌈boteñ サボテン.

caddie *n.* (of golf) kya⌉dii キャディー.
— *vi.* (... no) kya⌉dii o suru (...の)キャディーをする [I]: caddie for a person (*hito no kyadii o suru*) 人のキャディーをする.

café *n.* ki⌈ssa⌉teñ 喫茶店. ★ A '*kissateñ*' serves coffee, black tea and may have light meals. For a place where regular meals are served, use '*resutorañ*' レストラン (usually Western food) or '*taishuu shokudoo*' 大衆食堂 (cheap Japanese family-type meals).

cafeteria *n.* ka⌈fete⌉ria カフェテリア. ★ A cafeteria in a school or institution may be called '*shokudoo*' 食堂.

caffeine *n.* ka⌈fe⌉iñ カフェイン: caffeine-free coffee (*kafeiñ nuki no koohii*) カフェイン抜きのコーヒー.

cage *n.* **1** (small one for birds, rodents) ka⌈go かご: a birdcage (*torikago*) 鳥かご.
2 (large one for bigger animals) o⌈ri⌉ 檻.

cake *n.* **1** (as a whole) ke⌉eki ケーキ; (fancy) de⌈koreeshoñ-ke⌉eki デコレーションケーキ; (when sold as individual pieces) yo⌈oga⌉shi 洋菓子: a birthday cake (*baasudee keeki*) バースデーケーキ / bake a cake (*keeki o yaku*) ケーキを焼く.
2 (when counting items) -ko 個: a cake of soap (*sekkeñ ik-ko*) せっけん1個.

calamity *n.* (disaster) sa⌈igai 災害; (unforseen occurrence) sa⌈ina⌉ñ 災難.

calcium *n.* ka⌈rushi⌉umu カルシウム.

calculate *vt.* **1** (figure) ... o ke⌈esañ suru …を計算する Ⓘ: The accounting department calculated the profit for the fiscal year. (*Keeribu wa sono neñdo no rieki o keesañ shita.*) 経理部はその年度の利益を計算した.
2 (estimate) ... o su⌈isoku suru …を推測する Ⓘ; yo⌈soku suru 予測する Ⓘ: calculate the results of an election (*señkyo no kekka o yosoku suru*) 選挙の結果を予測する.

calculating *adj.* da⌈sañ-teki na 打算的な; nu⌈keme no na⌉i 抜け目のない: a calculating politician (*dasañ-teki na seejika*) 打算的な政治家.

calculation *n.* **1** (act of figuring) ke⌈esañ 計算: make a calculation (*keesañ o suru*) 計算をする.
2 (planning) da⌈sañ 打算; ke⌈ekaku 計画.

calculator *n.* ke⌈esa⌉ñki 計算機: a pocket calculator (*deñtaku*) 電卓.

calendar *n.* ka⌈re⌉ñdaa カレンダー. hang a calendar on the wall (*kabe ni kareñdaa o kakeru*) 壁にカレンダーをかける.

calf *n.* **1** (young cow) ko⌈ushi 子牛. ★ The calves of other animals are indicated by the name of the animal to which is added '*... no ko*' …の子: a whale calf (*kujira no ko*) 鯨の子.
2 (part of the leg) fu⌈kurahagi ふくらはぎ.

caliber *n.* **1** (bore) ko⌈okee 口径: a 22-caliber rifle (*nijuu-ni kookee raifuru-juu*) 22口径ライフル銃.
2 (ability) ri⌈kiryoo 力量; shu⌉wañ 手腕: a man of excellent caliber (*shuwañka*) 手腕家.

call *vt.* **1** (telephone) ... ni [e] de⌈ñwa suru …に[へ]電話する Ⓘ; de⌈ñwa o kake⌉ru 電話をかける Ⓥ: I want to call Hawaii. (*Hawai e deñwa shitai ñ desu ga.*) ハワイへ電話したいんですが. / Please tell me how to call this number. (*Kono bañgoo ni deñwa suru hoohoo o oshiete kudasai.*) この番号に電話する方法を教えてください.
2 (ask to come) ... o yo⌈bu …を呼ぶ Ⓒ; ma⌈ne⌉ku 招く Ⓒ: Call a doctor, please. (*Isha o yoñde kudasai.*) 医者を呼んでください. / Please call a taxi for me. (*Takushii o yoñde kudasai.*) タクシーを呼んでください.
3 (utter loudly) ... o yo⌈bu …を呼ぶ Ⓒ: He called Masao's name in a loud voice. (*Kare wa Masao no namae o oogoe de yoñda.*) 彼は正雄の名前を大声で呼んだ.
4 (name) ... to yo⌈bu …と呼ぶ Ⓒ; i⌈u いう Ⓒ: What is this place called? (*Koko wa nañ to iimasu ka?*) ここは何といいますか.
5 (summon) ... o yo⌈bida⌉su …を呼び出す Ⓒ: He was called to the police station. (*Kare wa keesatsusho ni yobidasareta.*) 彼は警察

署に呼び出された.
— *vi.* 1 (shout) yo⌈bu 呼ぶ [C]; sa⌈ke⌉bu 叫ぶ [C]: Someone is calling from upstairs. (*Dare-ka ga ni-kai kara yoñde imasu.*) だれかが2階から呼んでいます.
2 (telephone) de⌈ñwa suru 電話する [I]: I'll call again later. (*Mata ato de deñwa shimasu.*) また後で電話します.
call by *vi.* ta⌈chiyoru 立ち寄る [C]: Call by if you happen to be in the neighborhood. (*Kiñjo ni oide no toki wa tachiyotte kudasai.*) 近所においでの時は立ち寄ってください.
call on *vt.* (visit) ... o ho⌈omoñ suru ...を訪問する [I]; ta⌈zune⌉ru 訪ねる [V]: call on a person (*hito o tazuneru*) 人を訪ねる.
— *n.* 1 (telephone) de⌈ñwa 電話; tsu⌈uwa 通話: I'd like to make a long-distance call. (*Chookyori deñwa o o-negai shimasu.*) 長距離電話をお願いします. / a local call (*shinai deñwa*) 市内電話.
2 (paging) yo⌈bidashi 呼び出し.

calligraphy *n.* (art) sho⌉doo 書道; shu⌈uji 習字; ; (handwriting) hi⌈s-seki 筆跡.

calm *adj.* **1** (not rough) o⌈da⌉yaka na 穏やかな: a calm sea (*odayaka na umi*) 穏やかな海.
2 (not nervous) o⌈chitsuita 落ち着いた; o⌈chitsuite iru 落ち着いている: Be calm. (*Ochitsuki nasai.*) 落ち着きなさい.
— *n.* shi⌈zuke⌉sa 静けさ: the calm before the storm (*arashi no mae no shizukesa*) あらしの前の静けさ.
— *vt.* ... o shi⌈zume⌉ru ...を静める [V]: The teacher calmed her pupils. (*Señsee wa seeto-tachi o shizuka ni saseta.*) 先生は生徒たちを静かにさせた.

calmly *adv.* **1** (quietly) shi⌉zuka ni 静かに: walk calmly (*shizuka ni aruku*) 静かに歩く.
2 (mentally composed) re⌈esee ni 冷静に: Make your decisions calmly. (*Hañdañ wa reesee ni shi nasai.*) 判断は冷静にしなさい.

calorie *n.* ka⌉rorii カロリー: This food is high [low] in calories. (*Kono shokuhiñ wa karorii ga takai [hikui].*) この食品はカロリーが高い[低い].

camel *n.* ra⌈kuda らくだ.

camellia *n.* tsu⌉baki 椿.

camera *n.* ka⌉mera カメラ: load a camera (*kamera ni firumu o ireru*) カメラにフィルムを入れる / a camera shop (*kamera-teñ*) カメラ店.

camp *n.* **1** (hobby) kya⌉ñpu キャンプ: a base camp (*beesu kyañpu*) ベースキャンプ.
2 (military) ya⌈ee 野営: soldiers in a camp (*yaee shite iru heeshi-tachi*) 野営している兵士たち.
3 (for prisoners, refugees) shu⌈u-yoojo 収容所; kya⌉ñpu キャンプ: a refugee camp (*nañmiñ kyañpu*) 難民キャンプ.
— *vi.* 1 (recreation) kya⌉ñpu suru キャンプする [I]; kya⌈ñpu-se⌉ekatsu o suru キャンプ生活をする [I].
2 (military) ya⌈ee suru 野営する [I].

campaign *n.* **1** (for a certain purpose) u⌈ñdoo 運動; ka⌈tsudoo 活動; kya⌈ñpe⌉eñ キャンペーン: launch an election campaign (*señkyo-uñdoo o hajimeru*) 選挙運動を始める / an advertising campaign (*señdeñ-katsudoo*) 宣伝活動.
2 (military) se⌈ñtoo 戦闘; se⌈ñeki 戦役.
— *vi.* 1 (for a certain purpose) u⌈ñdoo o oko⌉su [okonau] 運動を起こす [C] [行う [C]]: The labor union campaigned against the law. (*Roo-doo-kumiai wa sono hooritsu ni hañtai suru uñdoo o okonatta.*) 労働組合はその法律に反対する運動を行った.
2 (military) ju⌈uguñ suru 従軍する [I]; shu⌈ssee suru 出征する [I].

campus *n.* **1** (school site) ko⌉onai 構内; ga⌈ku⌉nai 学内; kya⌉ñpasu キャンパス: a college campus (*dai-gaku no koonai*) 大学の構内 / campus activities (*gakusee-katsudoo*)

学生活動.
2 (branch of a school) bu⌈ñkoo 分校; -koo 校. ★ '*Buñkoo*' is used generically and '*koo*' is used in compounds with proper nouns.

can[1] *aux.* **1** (be able to) de⌈ki⌉ru できる V; ‹consonant-stem verb›-e⌉ru …える; ‹vowel-stem verb›-rare⌉ru …られる; ‹verb› ko⌈to⌉ ga de⌈ki⌉ru …ことができる V: I can write Chinese characters. (*Watashi wa kañji ga kakemasu.*) 私は漢字が書けます. / Can we eat this? (*Kore wa taberaremasu ka?*) これは食べられますか / I can read Chinese. (*Watashi wa Chuugokugo o yomu koto ga dekimasu.*) 私は中国語を読むことができます. / I cannot drive a car. (*Watashi wa jidoosha o uñteñ suru koto ga dekimaseñ.*) 私は自動車を運転することができません.
2 [asking or giving permission] ‹verb›-te[de] mo yo⌉i [i⌉i] …て[で]もよい[いい]; ‹verb›-te[de] mo ka⌈ma-wa⌉nai …て[で]もかまわない: Can one take photographs here? (*Koko de shashiñ o totte mo ii desu ka?*) ここで写真を撮ってもいいですか. / You can do your homework later. (*Shukudai wa ato de shite mo kamaimaseñ.*) 宿題は後でしてもかまいません.
3 [commands] ‹verb› na⌈sa⌉i …なさい: If you don't behave, you can leave. (*Otonashiku shinai nara, dete iki nasai.*) おとなしくしないなら, 出て行きなさい.
4 [negative commands] ‹verb›-te [de] wa i⌈kenai …て[で]はいけない: You can't smoke here. (*Koko de tabako o sutte wa ikenai.*) ここでたばこを吸ってはいけない.
5 [habit or custom] ‹verb› ko⌈to⌉ ga a⌉ru …ことがある C: Mr. Tanaka can be very unpleasant sometimes. (*Tanaka-sañ wa toki ni hidoku iya na taido o toru koto ga aru.*) 田中さんはときにひどくいやな態度をとることがある.
6 [literary form showing possibility] ‹verb›-u⌉ru …得る V: Accidents can happen. (*Jiko wa okoriuru.*) 事故は起こり得る.
7 [negative possibility] ... no ha⌈zu ga na⌉i …のはずがない: His story can't be false. (*Kare no hanashi wa uso no hazu ga arimaseñ.*) 彼の話はうそのはずがありません.
as ... as ... can de⌈kiru dake できるだけ: Try to be as polite as you can in front of the principal. (*Koochoo señsee no mae de wa dekiru dake reegi tadashiku suru yoo ni shi nasai.*) 校長先生の前ではできるだけ礼儀正しくするようにしなさい.
Can you ...? ‹verb›-te[de] ku⌈remase⌉ñ ka? …て[で]くれませんか: Can you hold a minute, please? (*Chotto matte kuremaseñ ka?*) ちょっと待ってくれませんか.

can[2] *n.* **1** (container) ka⌉ñ 缶: three cans of beer (*kañ biiru sañ-ko*) 缶ビール3個 / a trash [garbage] can (*gomibako*) ごみ箱.
2 (canned goods) ka⌈ñzume 缶詰め: a can of pineapples (*paiñ no kañzume*) パインの缶詰め.

Canada *n.* Ka⌉nada カナダ.

Canadian *adj.* Ka⌉nada no カナダの.
— *n.* (inhabitant) Ka⌈nada⌉jiñ カナダ人.

canal *n.* u⌉ñga 運河: the Suez Canal (*Suezu uñga*) スエズ運河 / an irrigation canal (*yoosuiro*) 用水路.

cancel *vt.* **1** (revoke) ... o to⌈ri-kesu …を取り消す C; kya⌉ñseru suru キャンセルする I: Cancel this reservation, please. (*Kono yoyaku o torikeshite kudasai.*) この予約を取り消してください.
2 (cross out) ... o ke⌈su …を消す C: cross out the mistakes (*machigai o kesu*) 間違いを消す.
3 (annul) ... o mu⌈koo ni suru …を無効にする I: The regulations were canceled. (*Sono kisoku wa mukoo ni natta.*) その規則は無効になった.

cancer *n.* **1** (disease) ga⌉ñ 癌: stomach cancer (*igañ*) 胃癌.
2 (zodiacal sign) ka⌈niza かに座.

C

candidate *n.* ko[o]ho]sha 候補者: a candidate for mayor (*shichoo señkyo no koohosha*) 市長選挙の候補者.

candle *n.* ro[o]soku] ろうそく: light [put out] a candle (*roosoku o tsukeru* [*kesu*]) ろうそくをつける[消す].

candy *n.* **1** (Western-style sweets) kya]ñdee キャンデー.
2 (Japanese-style hard sweets) a[me] 飴. ★ Another word for candy, '*kashi*' 菓子, can also include baked goods such as cookies, crackers, and pastries.

cane *n.* **1** (of a plant) ku[ki] 茎.
2 (for walking) su[te]kki ステッキ; tsu]e つえ: walk with a cane (*tsue o tsuite aruku*) つえをついて歩く.

cannon *n.* ta[ihoo 大砲: fire a cannon (*taihoo o utsu*) 大砲を撃つ.

canoe *n.* ka]nuu カヌー: get into [out of] a canoe (*kanuu ni noru* [*kara oriru*]) カヌーに乗る[から降りる].

can opener *n.* ka[ñki]ri 缶切り.

canvas *n.* **1** (cloth) zu]kku ズック.
2 (painting) ka]ñbasu カンバス: paint a picture on canvas (*kañbasu ni e o egaku*) カンバスに絵を描く.

cap *n.* **1** (for the head) bo[oshi 帽子: put on [take off] a cap (*booshi o kaburu* [*nugu*]) 帽子をかぶる[脱ぐ]) / She wore a navy blue cap. (*Kanojo wa koñ no booshi o kabutte ita.*) 彼女は紺の帽子をかぶっていた. ★ 'Hat' is also called '*booshi*'.
2 (for a bottle, etc.) kya]ppu キャップ; fu[ta ふた: a bottle cap (*biñ no futa*) びんのふた.

capable *adj.* **1** (of people) yu[u-noo na 有能な: a capable secretary (*yuunoo na hisho*) 有能な秘書.
2 (of things) ... ga de[ki]ru ...ができる; ka[noo na 可能な: This elevator is capable of carrying 30 persons at a time. (*Kono erebeetaa wa ichido ni sañ-juu-ñiñ o hakobu koto ga dekimasu.*) このエレベーターは一度に30人を運ぶことができます.

capacity *n.* **1** (ability to do something) sa[inoo 才能; no]oryoku 能力: a man of great capacity (*sainoo yutaka na hito*) 才能豊かな人 / This factory doesn't have the capacity to do such a job. (*Kono koojoo ni wa soñna shigoto o konasu nooryoku wa nai.*) この工場にはそんな仕事をこなす能力はない.
2 (maximum amount that can be contained) yo]oseki 容積; shu[u-yo]oryoku 収容力: a barrel with a capacity of 20 liters (*yooseki nijuurittoru no taru*) 容積20リットルのたる / a room with a seating capacity of 50 (*gojuu-niñ buñ no zaseki no aru heya*) 50人分の座席のある部屋.
3 (position) ta[chiba] 立場; shi[kaku 資格: in one's individual capacity (*kojiñ no shikaku de*) 個人の資格で.

cape *n.* **1** (land) mi[saki 岬.
2 (garment) ke]epu ケープ.

capital *n.* **1** (of a nation) shu]to 首都; shu]fu 首府: Tokyo is the capital of Japan. (*Tookyoo wa Nihoñ no shuto desu.*) 東京は日本の首都です.
2 (letter) o[omoji 大文字.
3 (financial resources) shi[ki]ñ 資金: We are short of capital. (*Shikiñ ga tarinai.*) 資金が足りない.
4 (assets) shi[hoñ 資本; ga]ñkiñ 元金: capital and interest (*gañkiñ to rishi*) 元金と利子.

capitalism *n.* shi[hoñshu]gi 資本主義.

capital punishment *n.* shi[ke]e 死刑: The sentence of capital punishment was handed down. (*Shikee no hañketsu ga iiwatasareta.*) 死刑の判決が言い渡された.

capricious *adj.* (spoiled) ki[magurena 気まぐれな; (changeable) ka[wariyasu]i 変わりやすい; (unstable) fu[a]ñtee na 不安定な: capricious weather (*kimagure na teñki*) 気まぐれな天気.

captain *n.* **1** (of a ship) señ]choo 船長; (of an airplane) ki]choo 機長.
2 (of a sports team) kya]puteñ キャプテン.

3 (army rank) ri⌈kuguñ ta⌉ii 陸軍大尉; (navy rank) ka⌉iguñ ta⌈isa 海軍大佐.

captive *n.* ho⌉ryo 捕虜: take a person captive (*hito o horyo ni suru*) 人を捕虜にする.

capture *vt.* (people) ... o to⌈rae⌉ru ...を捕える V; tsu⌈kamaeru 捕まえる V: The police captured the thief. (*Keesatsu wa sono doroboo o tsukamaeta.*) 警察はその泥棒を捕まえた.

car *n.* **1** (automobile) ku⌈ruma 車; ji⌈do⌉osha 自動車; jo⌈oyo⌉osha 乗用車. ★ '*Kuruma*' can conceivably be anything on wheels; a '*jooyoosha*' is an automobile, especially one for passengers: I'd like to rent a car. (*Kuruma o ichi-dai karitai no desu ga.*) 車を1台借りたいのですが. / My car has broken down. (*Kuruma ga koshoo shita.*) 車が故障した. / a hired car (*haiyaa*) ハイヤー.
2 (private car) ma⌈ika⌉a マイカー.
3 (of a train) sha⌈ryoo 車両; -sha 車: Is there a dining car? (*Shokudoosha wa tsuite imasu ka?*) 食堂車はついていますか. / a non-smoking car (*kiñeñsha*) 禁煙車.

caravan *n.* **1** (mobile home) i⌈doo-ju⌉utaku 移動住宅.
2 (of camels) kya⌉rabañ キャラバン.

carbon *n.* ta⌉ñso 炭素.

carbon paper *n.* ka⌈abo⌉ñshi カーボン紙.

carburetor *n.* kya⌈bure⌉taa キャブレター.

card *n.* **1** ka⌉ado カード; (tag) fu⌈da 札; (ticket) ke⌉ñ 券: a credit [charge] card (*kurejitto kaado*) クレジットカード / a bank [cash] card (*kyasshu kaado*) キャッシュカード / a disembarkation [embarkation] card (*nyuukoku* [*shukkoku*] *kaado*) 入国[出国]カード / an identification card (*mibuñ-shoomeesho*) 身分証明書 / a business card (*meeshi*) 名刺.
2 (postcard) ha⌈gaki 葉書: a picture postcard (*ehagaki*) 絵葉書.
3 (playing) to⌈ra⌉ñpu トランプ: a deck of cards (*torañpu hito-kumi*) トランプ1組 / play cards (*torañpu o suru* [*yaru*]) トランプをする[やる].

cardboard *n.* bo⌈orugami ボール紙; a⌈tsugami 厚紙: a corrugated cardboard (*dañ-booru*) 段ボール / a cardboard box (*dañboorubako*) 段ボール箱.

cardinal *adj.* ki⌈hoñ-teki na 基本的な: a cardinal principle (*kihoñ-geñsoku*) 基本原則.

care *n.* **1** (mental distress) shi⌈ñpai 心配; na⌈yami 悩み; ku⌉roo 苦労: a life free from care (*kuroo no nai seekatsu*) 苦労のない生活.
2 (object of attention) yo⌉ojiñ 用心; chu⌉ui 注意: This needs special care. (*Kore wa tokubetsu no chuui ga hitsuyoo desu.*) これは特別の注意が必要です.
3 (help) se⌈wa⌉ 世話: The care of elderly people was discussed at the meeting. (*Roojiñ no sewa ni tsuite kaigoo de hanashiawareta.*) 老人の世話について会合で話し合われた.
in care of (c/o) ... *prep.* ki⌈zuke 気付: c/o Mr. Kazuo Nakamura (*Nakamura Kazuo-sama kizuke*) 中村和夫様気付.
take care *vi.* ki ⌈o tsuke⌉ru 気をつける V: Take care not to fall. (*Korobanai yoo ni ki o tsuke nasai.*) 転ばないように気をつけなさい.
take care of ... *vt.* ... no se⌈wa⌉ o suru ...の世話をする I: I'll take care of the birds. (*Watashi ga tori no sewa o shimashoo.*) 私が鳥の世話をしましょう.
take care of yourself *vi.* da⌈iji⌉ ni suru 大事にする I: Please take good care of yourself. (*Kuregure mo o-karada o odaiji ni.*) くれぐれもお体をお大事に.

career *n.* **1** (occupation) sho⌈ku⌉gyoo 職業: careers open to women (*josee ni kaihoo sarete iru shokugyoo*) 女性に開放されている職業. ★ '*Kyaria*' キャリア is sometimes used for this sense but not in the sense of 'present occupation.'

2 (life) ke[e]reki 経歴: an academic career (*gakureki*) 学歴 / one's professional career (*shokureki*) 職歴.
— *adj.* ho[ñ]shoku no 本職の; ha[e]nuki no 生え抜きの: a career diplomat (*haenuki no gaikookañ*) 生え抜きの外交官 / a career woman (*kyaria uumañ*) キャリアウーマン.

C

careful *adj.* 1 (cautious) chu[ui]bukai 注意深い; shi[ñ]choo na 慎重な: He is very careful with his work. (*Kare wa shigoto ni kañshite hijoo ni chuuibukai.*) 彼は仕事に関して非常に注意深い. / a careful driver (*shiñchoo na uñteñshu*) 慎重な運転手.
2 (thorough) ne[ñ]iri na 念入りな; me[ñ]mitsu na 綿密な: a careful study of Japanese history (*Nihoñshi no meñmitsu na keñkyuu*) 日本史の綿密な研究.
be careful *vi.* ki [o] tsukeru 気をつける [V]: Be careful not to make any noise. (*Oto o tatenai yoo ni ki o tsuke nasai.*) 音を立てないように気をつけなさい.

carefully *adv.* chu[ui]bukaku 注意深く; shi[ñ]choo ni 慎重に: Handle it carefully. (*Shiñchoo ni toriatsukatte kudasai.*) 慎重に取り扱ってください.

careless *adj.* 1 (lack of thought) fu[chu]ui na 不注意な: a careless mistake (*kearesu misu*) ケアレスミス.
2 (inattentive) mu[to]ñchaku na むとんちゃくな: He is careless about how he dresses. (*Kare wa fukusoo ni mutoñchaku da.*) 彼は服装にむとんちゃくだ.
3 (free from cares) no[ñ]ki na のんきな: a careless life (*noñki na kurashi*) のんきな暮らし.

caress *n.* a[i]bu 愛撫; ho[o]yoo 抱擁.
— *vt.* ... o a[i]bu suru ...を愛撫する [I]; na[de]ru なでる [V]: caress a horse's neck (*uma no kubi o naderu*) 馬の首をなでる.

cargo *n.* (freight in general) tsu[mi]ni 積み荷; (specific load) ni[motsu] 荷物: a ship loaded with cargo (*nimotsu o tsuñda fune*) 荷物を積んだ船.

caries *n.* mu[shiba] 虫歯.

carnation *n.* (plant) ka[ane]eshoñ カーネーション; (flower) ka[ane]eshoñ no ha[na] カーネーションの花.

carnival *n.* (festive occasion) ka[a]nibaru カーニバル; (religious occasion) sha[niku]sai 謝肉祭.

carol *n.* (for Christmas) Ku[risu]masu kya[roru] クリスマスキャロル.

carousel *n.* 1 (merry-go-round) ka[iteñ-mo]kuba 回転木馬; me[rii]goora[uñdo] メリーゴーラウンド.
2 (airport luggage pickup) ta[añ]te[eburu] ターンテーブル; ka[iteñdai] 回転台.

carp *n.* (fish) ko[i] こい(鯉): a carp streamer (*koinobori*) 鯉のぼり.

carpenter *n.* da[iku] 大工: carpenter's tools (*daiku-doogu*) 大工道具.

carpet *n.* ju[utañ] じゅうたん; ka[a]petto カーペット: The floor is covered with a thick carpet. (*Yuka ni wa atsui juutañ ga shiite aru.*) 床には厚いじゅうたんが敷いてある.

carrier *n.* 1 (transport company) u[ñ]soo gyo[osha] 運送業者.
2 (mail) yu[ubiñ] haitatsuniñ 郵便配達人.
3 (HIV, etc.) ka[ñse]ñsha 感染者: an HIV carrier (*eichi-ai-bui no kañseñsha*) HIV の感染者.
4 (naval) ku[ubo] 空母: a nuclear aircraft carrier (*geñshiryoku kuubo*) 原子力空母.

carrot *n.* ni[ñ]jiñ にんじん(人参): the carrot and the stick (*ame to muchi*) あめとむち.

carry *vt.* 1 (hold and walk) ... o mo[chiaru]ku ...を持ち歩く [C]; ke[e]tai suru 携帯する [I]: He always carries a camera with him. (*Kare wa itsu-mo kamera o mochiaruite iru.*) 彼はいつもカメラを持ち歩いている. / carry a baby on one's back (*akañboo o oñbu suru*) 赤ん坊をおんぶする.
2 (from one place to another) ... o ha[kobu] ...を運ぶ [C]; mo[tte] iku 持って行く [C]: I'll carry this one.

(*Kore wa watashi ga mochimasu.*) これは私が持ちます.
3 (reach) ... o tsu⌈taeru ...を伝える Ⓥ; to⌉osu 通す Ⓒ: Copper wires carry electricity. (*Doosen̄ wa den̄ki o tooshimasu.*) 銅線は電気を通します.
carry on *vi.* ... o tsu⌈zukeru ...を続ける Ⓥ: Carry on, please. (*Doozo tsuzukete kudasai.*) どうぞ続けてください.
carry out *vt.* ... o ji⌈kkoo suru ...を実行する Ⓘ: carry out a plan (*keekaku o jikkoo suru*) 計画を実行する.

carry-on *n.* ki⌉nai mo⌈chikomi te-ni⌉motsu 機内持ち込み手荷物.

carsick *adj.* ku⌈ruma ni yo⌉tta [yo⌉tte iru] 車に酔った[酔っている]: Michiko gets carsick easily. (*Michiko-san̄ wa sugu kuruma ni yotte shimau.*) 美智子さんはすぐ車に酔ってしまう.

cart *n.* te⌈oshigu⌉ruma 手押し車: a shopping cart (*shoppin̄gu kaato*) ショッピングカート / a golf cart (*gorufu kaato*) ゴルフカート.

cartel *n.* ka⌉ruteru カルテル: form a cartel (*karuteru o tsukuru*) カルテルを作る.

cartoon *n.* **1** (comic book) ma⌈n̄-ga 漫画; (comic strip) re⌈n̄zoku-ma⌉n̄ga 連続漫画.
2 (animated features) a⌈nime アニメ; do⌈oga 動画.

carve *vt.* **1** (inscribe) ... o ki⌈zamu ...を刻む Ⓒ: carve a name on a tree (*namae o ki ni kizamu*) 名前を木に刻む.
2 (form) ... o ho⌉ru 彫る Ⓒ; cho⌈o-koku suru 彫刻する Ⓘ: carve a Buddhist image out of wood (*ki de butsuzoo o horu*) 木で仏像を彫る.
3 (meat, etc.) ... o ki⌉ru ...を切る Ⓒ; ki⌈riwake⌉ru 切り分ける Ⓥ: I carved the turkey for the guests. (*Watashi wa shichimen̄choo o o-kyaku no tame ni kiriwaketa.*) 私は七面鳥をお客のために切り分けた.

carving *n.* cho⌈okoku 彫刻; ho⌈ri-mo⌉no 彫り物.

case[1] *n.* **1** (instance) ba⌈ai 場合: Please give me somewhere to call in case of trouble. (*Jiko no baai no ren̄rakusaki o oshiete kudasai.*) 事故の場合の連絡先を教えてください.
2 (example) ji⌈tsuree 実例; mo⌈n̄-dai 問題: a case of life and death (*shikatsu mon̄dai*) 死活問題.
3 (legal) ji⌉ken̄ 事件: an unsolved case (*meekyuuiri no jiken̄*) 迷宮入りの事件 / a civil [criminal] case (*min̄ji [keeji] jiken̄*) 民事[刑事]事件.
4 (medical) ka⌈n̄ja 患者: There has been another case of cholera in the neighborhood. (*Kin̄jo de moo hitori korera kan̄ja ga deta.*) 近所でもう一人コレラ患者が出た.
in case *adv.* ma⌉n̄ichi ni so⌈na⌉-ete 万一に備えて: I don't think it will rain, but I'll take an umbrella in case. (*Ame wa furanai to omou ga, man̄ichi ni sonaete kasa o motte ikoo.*) 雨は降らないと思うが, 万一に備えて傘を持って行こう.
— *conj.* ‹verb› to i⌈kena⌉i kara ... といけないから: Take an umbrella with you in case it rains. (*Ame ga furu to ikenai kara kasa o motte iki nasai.*) 雨が降るといけないから傘を持って行きなさい.

case[2] *n.* **1** (container) i⌈remono 入れ物; ke⌉esu ケース: a pencil case (*fudebako*) 筆箱 / an attaché case (*tesage kaban̄*) 手さげかばん.
2 (box) ha⌈ko 箱: a case of wine (*budooshu hito-hako*) ぶどう酒一箱.

cash *n.* **1** (currency) ge⌈n̄ki⌉n̄ 現金: pay in cash (*gen̄kin̄ de harau*) 現金で払う.
2 (money) o-⌈kane お金: I'm out of cash now. (*Ima o-kane ga arimasen̄.*) いまお金がありません.
— *vt.* ... o ge⌈n̄ki⌉n̄ ni suru ...を現金にする Ⓘ: I'd like to have this cashed, please. (*Kore o gen̄kin̄ ni shitai no desu ga.*) これを現金にしたいのですが.

cashier *n.* **1** (restaurant, etc.) ka⌈i-kee-ga⌉kari 会計係; re⌈ji-ga⌉kari レジ係; re⌉ji レジ.
2 (bank, commercial establish-

ment, etc.) su'itoo-ga'kari 出納係.

cash register *n.* re'jisutaa レジスター; ki'ñseñ-tooroku'ki 金銭登録器. ★ Or, more commonly, simply '*reji*' レジ.

C

cassette *n.* ka'se'tto カセット: put a cassette into a tape recorder (*kasetto o teepurekoodaa ni ireru*) カセットをテープレコーダーに入れる / play a cassette (*kasetto o kakeru*) カセットをかける / take out a cassette (*kasetto o toridasu*) カセットを取り出す.

cast *vt.* **1** (vote) ... ni to'ohyoo suru …に投票する [I]: I cast a vote for him. (*Watashi wa kare ni toohyoo shita.*) 私は彼に投票した.
2 (direct) ... o mu'keru …を向ける [V]; na'gekake'ru 投げかける [V]: cast suspicion on a person (*hito ni utagai o kakeru*) 人に疑いをかける.
3 (assign) ya'ku' o wa'riate'ru 役を割り当てる [V]: cast Takeshi in the role of Benkee (*Takeshi ni Beñkee no yaku o wariateru*) 健に弁慶の役を割り当てる.
4 (throw) ... o na'ge'ru …を投げる [V]: cast a stone at a dog (*inu ni ishi o nageru*) 犬に石を投げる.
— *n.* **1** (performers) kya'suto キャスト; ha'iyuu 俳優: the whole cast of a film (*eega no kyasuto zeñiñ*) 映画のキャスト全員.
2 (dressing) gi'pusu ギプス: Tony's arm was in a (plaster) cast. (*Tonii wa ude ni gipusu o shite ita.*) トニーは腕にギプスをしていた.

castle *n.* shi'ro 城. ★ In compounds with proper nouns, the Chinese reading, '*joo*' is often used: Himeji Castle (*Himeji-joo*) 姫路城.

casual *adj.* **1** (by chance) na'nigena'i 何気ない: Tom asked a casual question. (*Tomu wa nanigenai shitsumoñ o shita.*) トムは何気ない質問をした.
2 (clothes) fu'da'ñgi no 普段着の; ka'juaru na カジュアルな: casual clothes (*fudañgi*) 普段着 / a casual dress (*kajuaru na doresu*) カジュアルなドレス / shoes for casual wear (*fudañbaki no kutsu*) 普段ばきの靴.
3 (occasional) cho'tto shita ちょっとした: a casual acquaintance (*chotto shita shiriai*) ちょっとした知り合い.

casualty *n.* **1** (injured) fu'sho'osha 負傷者; (dead) shi'sha 死者: casualities (*shishoosha*) 死傷者.
2 (dead from war) se'ñshi'sha 戦死者.

cat *n.* ne'ko 猫: She has a cat. (*Kanojo wa neko o katte iru.*) 彼女は猫を飼っている.

catalog *n.* **1** (of sales) ka'tarogu カタログ: Please give us copies of your catalog. (*O-taku no katarogu o kudasai.*) お宅のカタログを下さい.
2 (of a library, museum, etc.) mo'kuroku 目録: compile a catalog (*mokuroku o sakusee suru*) 目録を作成する / include in a catalog (*mokuroku ni noseru*) 目録に載せる.
3 (of a university, etc.) da'igaku no yooran 大学の要覧; nyu'ugakua'ñnai 入学案内.

cataract *n.* **1** (waterfall) o'oki-na ta'ki 大きな滝.
2 (of the eye) ha'kuna'ishoo 白内障.

catarrh *n.* (medical) ka'taru カタル; [popular term] ha'nakaze 鼻かぜ.

catastrophe *n.* da'isa'igai 大災害: suffer a catastrophe (*daisaigai o koomuru*) 大災害を被る.

catch *vt.* **1** (grasp) ... o tsu'kamaeru …を捕まえる [V]; to'ru とる [C]: Catch that man! (*Ano hito o tsukamaete.*) あの人を捕まえて. / Catch the ball with both hands. (*Booru wa ryoote de tore.*) ボールは両手でとれ.
2 (see) ... o mi'tsukeru …を見つける [V]: The teacher found Yamamoto cheating on a test. (*Señsee wa Yamamoto ga shikeñ de kañniñgu shite iru no o mitsuketa.*) 先生は山本が試験でカンニングしているのを見つけた.
3 (be on time) ... ni ma'nia'u …に間に合う [C]; re'ñraku suru 連絡する [I]: I caught the 10 o'clock train. (*Juu-ji no deñsha ni maniatta.*) 10

時の電車に間に合った. / Where can I catch a taxi? (*Doko de takushii ni noremasu ka?*) どこでタクシーに乗れますか.
4 (contract) ... ni ka⌈ka⌉ru ...にかかる Ⓒ: Hanako caught pneumonia. (*Hanako-sañ wa haieñ ni kakatta.*) 花子さんは肺炎にかかった. / catch a cold (*kaze o hiku*) かぜをひく.
catch up with [to] ... *vt.* ... ni o⌈itsu⌉ku ... に追いつく Ⓒ: He caught up with us later. (*Kare wa ato de watashi-tachi ni oitsuita.*) 彼は後で私達に追いついた.

catcher *n.* kya⌉tchaa キャッチャー; ho⌉shu 捕手: play (the position of) catcher (*kyatchaa o suru*) キャッチャーをする.

category *n.* **1** (division) bu⌉moñ 部門: The materials are classified into two categories. (*Shiryoo wa futatsu no bumoñ ni buñrui sarete iru.*) 資料は二つの部門に分類されている.
2 (philosophy, theory, etc.) ha⌈ñchuu 範疇; ka⌈te⌉gorii カテゴリー: a grammatical category (*buñpoo-hañchuu*) 文法範疇.

caterpillar *n.* **1** (insect) ke⌈mushi 毛虫.
2 (tractor) kya⌈ta⌉piraa キャタピラー.

catfish *n.* na⌈mazu なまず(鯰).

cathedral *n.* da⌈ise⌉edoo 大聖堂; da⌈iji⌉iñ 大寺院.

Catholic *n.* (believer) (Ro⌈oma) Ka⌈torikku-kyo⌉oto (ローマ)カトリック教徒.
— *adj.* (of the Roman Catholic Church) (Ro⌈oma) Katori⌉kku (kyookai) no (ローマ)カトリック(教会)の; kyu⌉ukyoo no 旧教の.

catsup *n.* ke⌈cha⌉ppu ケチャップ.

cattle *n.* **1** (livestock) ka⌈chiku 家畜.
2 (cow) u⌈shi 牛: raise cattle (*ushi o kau*) 牛を飼う / beef cattle (*niku-gyuu*) 肉牛 / dairy cattle (*nyuu-gyuu*) 乳牛.

cauliflower *n.* ka⌈rifura⌉waa カリフラワー.

cause *n.* **1** (responsible for action) ge⌈ñiñ 原因: cause and effect (*geñiñ to kekka*) 原因と結果 / The police are trying to find the cause of the fire. (*Keesatsu wa sono kaji no geñiñ o tsukitomeyoo to shite iru.*) 警察はその火事の原因を突き止めようとしている.
2 (reason) ri⌈yuu 理由: You cannot be absent from the meeting without good reason. (*Seetoo na riyuu naku kaigi o kesseki suru koto wa dekimaseñ.*) 正当な理由なく会議を欠席することはできません.
3 (principle) mo⌈kuhyoo 目標; shu⌈choo 主張.
— *vt.* (bring about) ... no ge⌈ñiñ to na⌉ru ...の原因となる Ⓒ; ... o hi⌈kioko⌉su ...を引き起こす Ⓒ: Careless driving causes accidents. (*Fuchuui na uñteñ wa jiko o hikiokosu.*) 不注意な運転は事故を引き起こす.

caution *n.* **1** (care) chu⌉ui 注意; yo⌉ojiñ 用心: Exercise extreme caution when crossing this street. (*Kono toori o wataru toki ni wa juubuñ ni chuui suru koto.*) この通りを渡る時には十分に注意すること.
2 (warning) ke⌈ekoku 警告: give a person a caution (*hito ni keekoku o ataeru*) 人に警告を与える.
with caution *adv.* yo⌉ojiñ shite 用心して; shiñchoo ni 慎重に.
— *vt.* ... ni ke⌈ekoku suru ...に警告する Ⓘ; chu⌉ui suru 注意する Ⓘ: He cautioned me not to be late. (*Kare wa watashi ni okurenai yoo ni chuui shita.*) 彼は私に遅れないように注意した.

cautious *adj.* shi⌈ñchoo na 慎重な; chu⌉ui shite iru 注意している: Mr. Yamada is a cautious driver. (*Yamada-sañ wa shiñchoo na doraibaa da.*) 山田さんは慎重なドライバーだ. / I was cautious not to overeat. (*Watashi wa tabe-suginai yoo ni chuui shita.*) 私は食べすぎないように注意した.

cave *n.* ho⌈ra-ana ほら穴; do⌈okutsu 洞くつ.

cave-in *n.* (land) ka⌈ñbotsu 陥没;

(mining) ra⌈kubañ 落盤.

cavity *n.* **1** (of a tooth) mu⌈shiba (no a⌈na⌉) 虫歯(の穴).
2 (hole) ku⌈udoo 空洞; a⌈na⌉ 穴.

C

CD *n.* (compact disc) shi⌈idi⌉i シーディー: play a CD (*shiidii o kakeru*) CDをかける.

cease *vt.* ... o ya⌈meru ...をやめる Ⓥ; o⌈eru 終える Ⓥ: cease work [talking] (*shigoto* [*shaberu no*] *o yameru*) 仕事[しゃべるの]をやめる.
— *vi.* ya⌈mu やむ Ⓒ; o⌈waru 終わる Ⓒ: The cheering ceased suddenly. (*See-eñ ga pitari to yañda.*) 声援がぴたりとやんだ.
without ceasing *adv.* ta⌈ema na⌉ku 絶え間なく.

cease-fire *n.* te⌈eseñ 停戦: a cease-fire order (*teeseñ-meeree*) 停戦命令.

cedar *n.* su⌈gi 杉. ★ Strictly speaking '*sugi*' is cryptomeria, the Japanese cedar. '*Seeyoosugi*' 西洋杉 may be used to explain any kind of cedar that is not Japanese.

ceiling *n.* te⌈ñjoo 天井: There are a lot of flies on the ceiling. (*Teñjoo ni takusañ no hae ga tomatte iru.*) 天井にたくさんのはえが止まっている.

celebrate *vt.* ... o i⌈wa⌉u ...を祝う Ⓒ: celebrate his 60th birthday (*kare no kañreki o iwau*) 彼の還暦を祝う.

celebration *n.* i⌈wai 祝い; shu⌈kuteñ 祝典: a birthday celebration (*tañjoobi no o-iwai*) 誕生日のお祝い.

celebrity *n.* yu⌈ume⌉ejiñ 有名人.

celery *n.* se⌉rori セロリ.

cell *n.* **1** (battery) de⌉ñchi 電池.
2 (biology) sa⌈iboo 細胞: brain cells (*noosaiboo*) 脳細胞.
3 (prison) do⌈kuboo 独房; (small room) ko⌈beya 小部屋.

cellar *n.* chi⌈ka⌉shitsu 地下室; chi⌈ka-chozo⌉oko 地下貯蔵庫: wine cellar (*budooshu no chozooko*) ぶどう酒の貯蔵庫.

cello *n.* che⌉ro チェロ: play the cello (*chero o hiku*) チェロを弾く.

cellular phone *n.* i⌈doo-de⌉ñwa 移動電話; ke⌈etai-de⌉ñwa 携帯電話. ★ The latter term is more common.

Celsius *adj.* se⌉sshi no 摂氏の: twenty degrees Celsius (*sesshi nijuu-do*) 摂氏20度. ★ In Japan the Celsius system is used instead of the Fahrenheit system.

cement *n.* se⌈meñto セメント: a bag of cement (*semeñto hito fukuro*) セメント一袋.
— *vt.* **1** (cover) ... ni se⌈meñto o nuru ...にセメントを塗る Ⓒ: cement a floor (*yuka ni semeñto o nuru*) 床にセメントを塗る.
2 (bring together) ... o se⌈meñto de kuttsuke⌉ru ...をセメントでくっつける Ⓥ: cement bricks (*reñga o semeñto de kuttsukeru*) れんがをセメントでくっつける.
3 (of a friendship, etc.) ... o ka⌈tameru ...を固める Ⓥ: cement a friendship (*yuujoo o katameru*) 友情を固める.

cemetery *n.* bo⌉chi 墓地: bury in a cemetery (*bochi ni hoomuru*) 墓地に葬る.

censor *n.* (government official) ke⌈ñetsu⌉kañ 検閲官.
— *vt.* ... o ke⌈ñetsu suru ...を検閲する Ⓘ: Japan censors imported magazines. (*Nihoñ wa yunyuu zasshi o keñetsu suru.*) 日本は輸入雑誌を検閲する.

censorship *n.* ke⌈ñetsu 検閲.

censure *n.* hi⌉nañ 非難.
— *vt.* ... o hi⌉nañ suru ...を非難する Ⓘ: The prime minister was censured in parliament. (*Shushoo wa kokkai de hinañ sareta.*) 首相は国会で非難された.

census *n.* (of a country) ko⌈kusee cho⌉osa 国勢調査: take a census (*jiñkoo choosa o suru*) 人口調査をする.

cent *n.* se⌉ñto セント: 15¢ (*juugo-señto*) 15セント.

center *n.* **1** (middle) chu⌈ushiñ 中心; chu⌈uo⌉o 中央: the center of a circle (*eñ no chuushiñ*) 円の中心 /

the center of a room (*heya no chuuoo*) 部屋の中央 / the center of gravity (*juushiñ*) 重心.
2 (place) chu⌐ushi⌐ñchi 中心地: the center of American theatrical activity (*Amerika no eñgeki katsudoo no chuushiñchi*) アメリカの演劇活動の中心地.
3 (of interest, etc.) chu⌐ushiñ 中心; chu⌐ushiñ ji⌐ñbutsu 中心人物: the center of attention (*chuumoku no mato*) 注目の的 / He is the center of the project. (*Kare wa sono keekaku no chuushiñ jiñbutsu da.*) 彼はその計画の中心人物だ.
4 (facility) -sho[jo] 所; se⌐ñtaa センター: a community center (*chiiki shakai señtaa*) 地域社会センター / a day-care center (*hoikusho*) 保育所 / a shopping center (*shoppiñgu señtaa*) ショッピングセンター / a space center (*uchuukichi*) 宇宙基地.
5 (baseball) se⌐ñtaa センター; chu⌐uken 中堅: play center field (*señtaa o mamoru*) センターを守る / a center fielder (*chuukeñshu*) 中堅手.
— *vt.* 1 (place) ... o chu⌐uo⌐o ni o⌐ku ...を中央に置く Ⓒ: center a table in the room (*teeburu o heya no chuuoo ni oku*) テーブルを部屋の中央に置く.
2 (concentrate) ... ni shu⌐uchuu saseru ...に集中させる Ⓥ: All eyes were centered on him. (*Miñna no me ga kare ni shuuchuu shita.*) みんなの目が彼に集中した.
— *vi.* (... ni) shu⌐uchuu suru (...に) 集中する Ⓘ; a⌐tsuma⌐ru 集まる Ⓒ: The debate centered on the gasoline tax. (*Tooroñ wa gasoriñ no zeekiñ ni shuuchuu shita.*) 討論はガソリンの税金に集中した.

centigrade *adj.* se⌐sshi no 摂氏の: 50° centigrade [Celsius] (*sesshi gojuu-do*) 摂氏 50 度.

centimeter *n.* se⌐ñchi-me⌐etoru センチメートル. ★ Usually abbreviated in speech and writing to '*señchi*': 15 cm (*juugo-señchi*) 15 センチ.

central *adj.* chu⌐ushiñ no 中心の; chu⌐uo⌐o no 中央の: the central part of Australia (*Oosutoraria no chuushiñbu*) オーストラリアの中心部 / Central Post Office (*chuuoo yuubiñkyoku*) 中央郵便局 / central heating (*señtoraru hiitiñgu*) セントラルヒーティング.

century *n.* se⌐eki 世紀: Japan became a modern nation at the end of the 19th century. (*Nihoñ wa juukyuu-seeki matsu ni kiñdai kokka to natta.*) 日本は 19 世紀末に近代国家となった.

ceramics *n.* (art) to⌐ogee 陶芸; (articles) to⌐ojiki⌐rui 陶磁器類.

cereal *n.* **1** (commodity) ko⌐ku⌐motsu 穀物; (grain) ko⌐ku⌐rui 穀類; (plant) ko⌐kusoo 穀草.
2 (breakfast food) shi⌐riaru シリアル.

ceremony *n.* gi⌐shiki 儀式; -⌐shiki 式: an opening [a closing] ceremony (*kaikai[heekai]-shiki*) 開[閉]会式 / a graduation ceremony (*sotsugyoo-shiki*) 卒業式 / a tea ceremony (*cha no yu*) 茶の湯.

certain *adj.* **1** (limited) a⌐ru teedo no ある程度の; i⌐ttee no 一定の: a certain rate (*ittee no hiritsu*) 一定の比率.
2 (not specified but known) a⌐ru ある: Imai didn't come for a certain reason. (*Imai wa aru riyuu de konakatta.*) 今井はある理由で来なかった.
3 (definite) ka⌐kujitsu na 確実な; ma⌐chigai na⌐i 間違いない: He is certain to win. (*Kare ga katsu no wa machigai nai.*) 彼が勝つのは間違いない.
4 (sure) ka⌐kushiñ shite (iru) 確信して(いる); shi⌐ñjite (iru) 信じて(いる): I'm certain of his success. (*Watashi wa kare no seekoo o kakushiñ shite imasu.*) 私は彼の成功を確信しています.
5 (indisputable) ka⌐kujitsu na 確実な; ta⌐shika na 確かな: certain evidence (*tashika na shooko*) 確かな証拠 / a certain cure (*kakujitsu na chiryoohoo*) 確実な治療法.

certainly *adv.* **1** [affirmative reply for permission to ask a question] e⌉e, do⌉ozo ええ, どうぞ: "May I ask you a question?" "Certainly." (*"Shitsumoñ shite mo yoroshii desu ka?" "Ee, doozo."*)「質問してもよろしいですか」「ええ, どうぞ」
2 (without doubt) ta⌉shika ni 確かに; ki⌈tto きっと: John will certainly come. (*Joñ wa kitto kuru yo.*) ジョンはきっと来るよ.

certainty *n.* ka⌈kujitsu na mono⌉ [koto⌉] 確実なもの[こと]: It's a certainty that an earthquake will hit Tokyo someday. (*Tookyoo ni itsuka jishiñ ga kuru no wa kakujitsu da.*) 東京にいつか地震が来るのは確実だ.

certificate *n.* (of attainment) sho⌈omeesho 証明書; (license) me⌈ñkyo⌉joo 免許状: a birth certificate (*shussee shoomeesho*) 出生証明書 / a death certificate (*shiboo shiñdañsho*) 死亡診断書.

certified check *n.* shi⌈harai-hoshoo-kogi⌉tte 支払保証小切手.

certified public accountant *n.* ko⌈oniñ-kaike⌉eshi 公認会計士.

certify *vt.* ... o sho⌈omee suru …を証明する [I]; ho⌈shoo suru 保証する [I]: I hereby certify that the documents are correct. (*Shorui ni machigai no nai koto o koko ni shoomee shimasu.*) 書類に間違いのないことをここに証明します.

chain *n.* ku⌈sari 鎖; che⌉eñ チェーン: a bicycle chain (*jiteñsha no cheeñ*) 自転車のチェーン / put chains on the tires of a car (*kuruma no taiya ni cheeñ o tsukeru*) 車のタイヤにチェーンをつける.
— *vt.* ... o ku⌈sari de tsunagu …を鎖でつなぐ [C]: Keep your dog chained. (*Inu o kusari de tsunaide oki nasai.*) 犬を鎖でつないでおきなさい.

chain store *n.* che⌈eñ-suto⌉a チェーンストア; ka⌈me⌉eteñ 加盟店.

chair *n.* **1** (furniture) i⌈su いす; ko⌈shika⌉ke 腰掛け: sit in a chair (*isu ni suwaru*) いすに座る / rise from a chair (*isu kara tachiagaru*) いすから立ち上がる.
2 (position) gi⌈cho⌉oseki 議長席: take the chair (*gichooseki ni tsuku*) 議長席に着く.
— *vt.* gi⌈choo o tsu⌈tome⌉ru 議長を務める [V]: He chaired the committee. (*Kare wa sono iiñkai no gichoo o tsutometa.*) 彼はその委員会の議長を務めた.

chairman *n.* ⇨ chairperson.

chairperson *n.* **1** (of a business meeting) gi⌈choo 議長; (of a committee) i⌈i⌉ñchoo 委員長.
2 (of a social event) shi⌈ka⌉isha 司会者.

chairwoman *n.* jo⌈see no gi⌉choo [ii⌉ñchoo] 女性の議長[委員長].

chalk *n.* cho⌉oku チョーク; ha⌈kuboku 白墨: write with a piece of chalk (*chooku de kaku*) チョークで書く.

challenge *vt.* **1** (call to contest) ... ni cho⌈oseñ suru …に挑戦する [I]; i⌈do⌉mu 挑む [C]: I challenged him to a game of tennis. (*Watashi wa kare ni tenisu no shiai o idoñda.*) 私は彼にテニスの試合を挑んだ.
2 (stimulate) ... ni (... o) hi⌈tsuyoo to suru …に(…を)必要とする [I]; yo⌈osu⌉ru 要する [I]: This task challenges us to further effort. (*Kono shigoto wa wareware no issoo no doryoku o yoosuru.*) この仕事はわれわれの一層の努力を要する.
3 (object) ... ni i⌉gi o to⌈nae⌉ru …に異議を唱える [V]: I challenged his statement. (*Watashi wa kare ga nobeta koto ni igi o tonaeta.*) 私は彼が述べたことに異議を唱えた.
— *n.* **1** (call to contest) cho⌈oseñ 挑戦: a challenge to violence (*booryoku e no chooseñ*) 暴力への挑戦 / accept a challenge to run a race (*kyoosoo shiyoo to iu chooseñ ni oojiru*) 競走しようという挑戦に応じる.
2 (that which requires ability) ya⌈rigai やりがい; ha⌈riai 張り合い: a job with challenge (*hariai no aru shigoto*) 張り合いのある仕事.
3 (objection) i⌉gi 異議.

chamber *n.* **1** (conference room)

ka⌈igi⌉shitsu 会議室.
2 (judge's) ha⌈ñji⌉shitsu 判事室.
chamber of commerce sho⌈o-koo-kaigisho 商工会議所.
chambermaid *n.* me⌈edo メイド.
chamber music *n.* shi⌈tsuna⌉i-gaku 室内楽.
champagne *n.* sha⌈ñpe⌉ñ シャンペン.
champion *n.* **1** (sports) yu⌈usho⌉o-sha 優勝者; cha⌉ñpioñ チャンピオン: the new world champion (*atarashii sekai chañpioñ*) 新しい世界チャンピオン.
2 (of a cause, etc.) yo⌈ogo⌉sha 擁護者; shi⌈ji⌉sha 支持者: a champion of liberty (*jiyuu no yoogosha*) 自由の擁護者.
3 [adjectivally] yu⌈ushoo- 優勝: a champion team (*yuushoo-chiimu*) 優勝チーム / a champion horse (*yuu-shoo-ba*) 優勝馬.
championship *n.* **1** (position) se⌈ñshu⌉keñ 選手権; cha⌈ñpioñ-shi⌉ppu チャンピオンシップ: win 3 championships (*mittsu no señshu-keñ o kakutoku suru*) 三つの選手権を獲得する.
2 (competition) se⌈ñshukeñ-ji⌉ai [tai⌉kai] 選手権試合[大会]; ke⌈s-sho⌉oseñ 決勝戦.
chance *n.* **1** (coincidence) gu⌈uzeñ 偶然: It was a mere chance that I met him. (*Kare ni atta no wa guu-zeñ no koto datta.*) 彼に会ったのは偶然のことだった.
2 (opportunity) ki⌈ka⌉i 機会; cha⌉ñ-su チャンス: I finally got a chance to go skiing. (*Yooyaku sukii ni iku chañsu ni megumareta.*) ようやくスキーに行くチャンスに恵まれた.
3 (probability) mi⌈komi 見込み: We have a good chance of winning. (*Wareware ni wa kateru mikomi ga juubuñ ni aru.*) われわれには勝てる見込みが十分にある.
by any chance *adv.* hyo⌈tto shita⌉ra ひょっとしたら: Are you Mr. Yamada, by any chance? (*Hyotto shitara, Yamada-sañ de wa arima-señ ka?*) ひょっとしたら, 山田さんではありませんか.
take a chance *vi.* i⌈chi⌉ ka ba⌈chi⌉ ka ya⌈tte mi⌉ru 一か八かやってみる V.
change *n.* **1** (unintentional) he⌉ñ-ka 変化: a change in temperature (*kioñ no heñka*) 気温の変化 / change in the town (*machi no heñka*) 町の変化.
2 (intentional) he⌈ñkoo 変更: the change of schedule (*yotee [kee-kaku] no heñkoo*) 予定[計画]の変更.
3 (return of excess payment) o-⌈tsuri お釣り; tsu⌈riseñ つり銭: Keep the change. (*O-tsuri wa totte oite kudasai.*) お釣りはとっておいてください.
4 (small coins) ko⌈zeni 小銭; ko-⌈maka⌉i o-⌈kane 細かいお金: I'd like to be paid the balance in change. (*Nokori wa kozeni de itadaki ma-shoo.*) 残りは小銭でいただきましょう.
5 (of clothes) ki⌈gae 着替え: Take a change of clothes with you. (*Kigae o motte iki nasai.*) 着替えを持って行きなさい.
6 (transfer transportation) no⌈ri-kae 乗り換え: Make a change at Tokyo for Sendai. (*Señdai e wa Tookyoo de norikae nasai.*) 仙台へは東京で乗り換えなさい.
— *vt.* **1** (make different) ... o ka-⌈eru ...を変える V; he⌈ñkoo suru 変更する I: change one's mind (*kañ-gae o kaeru*) 考えを変える / I want to change my reservation. (*Yoyaku o heñkoo shitai no desu ga.*) 予約を変更したいのですが.
2 (replace) ... o ko⌈okañ suru ...を交換する I; to⌈rikaeru 取り替える V: I changed my car for a bigger one. (*Watashi wa kuruma o ookii no to torikaeta.*) 私は車を大きいのと取り替えた.
3 (transfer) ... ni no⌈rikae⌉ru ...に乗り換える V: change trains for Na-rita at Ueno (*Ueno de Narita-yuki ni norikaeru*) 上野で成田行きに乗り換える.

C

4 (money) ... o ryo⌈ogae suru …を両替する [I]; ku⌈zu⌉su くずす [C]: I'd like to change 100 dollars. (*Hyaku-doru o ryoogae shite kudasai.*) 100ドルを両替してください. / change a ¥1,000 bill (*señ-eñ satsu o kuzusu*) 千円札をくずす.

— *vi.* **1** (become different) (... ni) ka⌈waru (…に)変わる [C]; he⌉ñka suru 変化する [I]: The traffic light changed from red to green. (*Shiñgoo ga aka kara ao ni kawatta.*) 信号が赤から青に変わった.

2 (clothes) (... ni) ki⌈gae⌉ru (…に)着替える [V]: change into a new dress (*atarashii doresu ni kigaeru*) 新しいドレスに着替える.

3 (transportation) (... ni) no⌈rikae⌉ru (…に)乗り換える [V]: change to a bus (*basu ni norikaeru*) バスに乗り換える.

channel *n.* **1** (waterway) su⌉iro 水路 : The Canberra followed the channel into port. (*Kyañbera-goo wa sono suiro o tootte nyuukoo shita.*) キャンベラ号はその水路を通って入港した.

2 (official routes of communication) ke⌉ero 経路; shu⌉dañ 手段: diplomatic channels (*gaikoo ruuto*) 外交ルート.

3 (of a TV, radio, etc.) cha⌈ñneru チャンネル: watch the game on Channel 4 (*yoñ chañneru de shiai o miru*) 4チャンネルで試合を見る.

4 (strait) ka⌈ikyoo 海峡: The English Channel (*Igirisu Kaikyoo*) イギリス海峡.

chaos *n.* (confusion) da⌈iko⌉ñrañ 大混乱: The two-car collision left the street in chaos. (*Ni-dai no kuruma no shoototsu de toori wa daikoñrañ datta.*) 2台の車の衝突で通りは大混乱だった.

chapel *n.* re⌈ehaidoo 礼拝堂; cha⌉peru チャペル.

chapter *n.* **1** (of a book) sho⌉o 章: chapter 10 (*dai jus-shoo*) 第10章.

2 (period) i⌈chiji⌉ki 一時期: open a new chapter in the theater's history (*gekijoo no rekishi ni atarashii ichijiki o kakusu*) 劇場の歴史に新しい一時期を画す.

3 (of an association) shi⌉bu 支部.

character *n.* **1** (moral structure) se⌈ekaku 性格; ji⌉ñkaku 人格; hi⌈togara 人柄; hi⌉ñsee 品性: He has a weak character. (*Kare wa seekaku ga yowai.*) 彼は性格が弱い. / improve one's character (*hiñsee o migaku*) 品性を磨く.

2 (distinguishing feature) to⌈kushitsu 特質: Each town has a character of its own. (*Dono machi ni mo sorezore no tokushitsu ga aru.*) どの町にもそれぞれの特質がある.

3 (of a play, history, etc.) to⌈ojoo ji⌉ñbutsu 登場人物: a main character in the play (*shibai no shuyoo na toojoo jiñbutsu*) 芝居の主要な登場人物.

4 (writing) mo⌉ji 文字: Chinese characters (*kañji*) 漢字.

characteristic *n.* to⌈kuchoo 特徴: Nara even now preserves its old characteristics. (*Nara wa mukashi nagara no tokuchoo o ima mo nokoshite iru.*) 奈良は昔ながらの特徴を今も残している.

— *adj.* do⌈kutoku no 独特の; ... -rashi⌉i …らしい: It's characteristic of Yamada to behave like that. (*Añna furumai o suru to wa ika ni mo Yamada-rashii.*) あんな振る舞いをするとはいかにも山田らしい.

charcoal *n.* su⌈mi⌉ 炭; mo⌈kuta⌉ñ 木炭.

charge *n.* **1** (payment) ryo⌉okiñ 料金; (commission) te⌈su⌉uryoo 手数料: How much is the excess charge? (*Chooka ryookiñ wa ikura desu ka?*) 超過料金はいくらですか. / There is no charge. (*Muryoo desu.*) 無料です. / a rental charge (*shakuyoo-ryoo*) 借用料.

2 (public accusation) hi⌉nañ 非難: deny the charge (*hinañ o hitee suru*) 非難を否定する.

3 (legal accusation) ko⌉kuso 告訴.

4 (management) ka⌉ñri 管理; se⌈ki-

niñ 責任: a person in charge ((*kañri*) *sekiniñsha*) (管理) 責任者.
5 (electricity) de|ñka 電荷: a positive [negative] charge (*see* [*fu*] *deñka*) 正[負]電荷.
6 (attack) ko|ogeki 攻撃: The dog made a charge at the bear. (*Inu wa kuma ni tobikakatta.*) 犬は熊に飛びかかった.
in charge of ... *prep.* ... o ta|ñtoo shite iru ...を担当している V: the teacher in charge of our class (*watashi-tachi no kurasu tañtoo no señsee*) 私たちのクラス担当の先生.
— *vt.* **1** (demand payment) ... o se|ekyuu suru ...を請求する I: charge 20,000 yen for a room (*heya-dai to shite ni-mañ-eñ o seekyuu suru*) 部屋代として2万円を請求する.
2 (record as a debt) ... o ku|rejitto ka|ado de ha|ra|u ...をクレジットカードで払う C; ... o (... no) tsu|ke| ni suru ...を(...の)つけにする I: Please charge it to my account. (*Sore o watashi no kañjoo no tsuke ni shite kudasai.*) それを私の勘定のつけにしてください.
3 (accuse publicly) ... o hi|nañ suru ...を非難する I: He charged that Kimura had let out the secret. (*Kare wa Kimura ga himitsu o morashita to itte hinañ shita.*) 彼は木村が秘密を漏らしたといって非難した.
4 (accuse legally) ... o ko|kuso suru ...を告訴する I: He was charged with theft. (*Kare wa settoozai de kokuso sareta.*) 彼は窃盗罪で告訴された.
5 (with a task, etc.) ... ni (... o) me|ezuru ...に(...を)命ずる I; ma|kase|ru 任せる V: The president charged her secretary with an important task. (*Shachoo wa hisho ni taisetsu na shigoto o makaseta.*) 社長は秘書に大切な仕事を任せた.
6 (energize a battery, etc.) ... o ju|udeñ suru ...を充電する: charge a battery (*deñchi o juudeñ suru*) 電池を充電する.

charitable *adj.* ka|ñdai na 寛大な; ji|hibuka|i 慈悲深い: She was charitable toward him. (*Kanojo wa kare ni kañdai datta.*) 彼女は彼に寛大だった.

charity *n.* **1** (benevolence) o|moiyari 思いやり: charity toward one's neighbors (*kiñjo no hito e no omoiyari*) 近所の人への思いやり.
2 (organization) ji|zeñ-da|ñtai 慈善団体.

charm *n.* **1** (attraction) mi|ryoku 魅力: the charm of her smile (*kanojo no egao no miryoku*) 彼女の笑顔の魅力.
2 (magical formula) ma|jinai まじない; ju|moñ 呪文: lay a charm on a person (*hito ni majinai o kakeru*) 人にまじないをかける.
3 (talisman) o|mamori お守り: He always wears a charm. (*Kare wa itsu-mo omamori o motte iru.*) 彼はいつもお守りを持っている.

charming *adj.* (attractive) mi|ryoku-teki na 魅力的な; cha|amiñgu na チャーミングな: a charming woman (*miryoku-teki* [*chaamiñgu*] *na josee*) 魅力的[チャーミング]な女性.

chart *n.* **1** (sheet of information) zu|hyoo 図表; zu 図; gu|rafu グラフ: a weather chart (*teñkizu*) 天気図 / a bar chart (*boo-gurafu*) 棒グラフ / a pie chart (*eñ-gurafu*) 円グラフ.
2 (nautical) ka|izu 海図: make a chart of the bay (*wañ no kaizu o tsukuru*) 湾の海図を作る.
3 (medical) ka|rute カルテ.

charter *n.* **1** [adjectivally] ka|rikiri no 借り切りの; cha|ataa no チャーターの: a charter flight (*chaataa-biñ*) チャーター便.
2 (of an organization) ke|ñshoo 憲章: the United Nations Charter (*Kokusairеñgoo Keñshoo*) 国際連合憲章.
— *vt.* **1** (hire) ... o cha|ataa suru ...をチャーターする I; ka|riki|ru 借り切る C: charter a bus (*basu o chaataa suru*) バスをチャーターする.
2 (approve) ... ni to|kkyo|joo o

a⌈taeru ...に特許状を与える V.

chartered accountant *n.* ko⌈oniñ-kaike⌉eshi 公認会計士.

chase *vt.* **1** (pursue) ... o o⌈ikake⌉ru ...を追いかける V; tsu⌈iseki suru 追跡する I: The policeman chased the pickpocket. (*Keekañ wa suri o oikaketa.*) 警官はすりを追いかけた.
2 (drive away) ... o o⌈ihara⌉u を追い払う C: The farmer chased the cattle from his field. (*Noofu wa hatake kara ushi o oiharatta.*) 農夫は畑から牛を追い払った.
— *vi.* (... o) o⌈ikake⌉ru (...を)追いかける V: The girls chased after the singer. (*Oñna-no-ko-tachi wa sono kashu no ato o oikaketa.*) 女の子たちはその歌手の後を追いかけた.
— *n.* tsu⌈iseki 追跡; tsu⌈ikyuu 追求: a car chase (*kuruma de no tsuiseki*) 車での追跡.

chassis *n.* (of a car) sha⌈dai 車台; sha⌉shii シャシー.

chat *n.* (light talk) o⌈sha⌉beri おしゃべり; (about various topics) za⌈tsudañ 雑談: Ellen likes to have a chat with me after dinner. (*Ereñ wa shokugo ni watashi to sekeñbanashi o suru no ga suki da.*) エレンは食後に私と世間話をするのが好きだ.
— *vi.* o⌈sha⌉beri suru おしゃべりする I; sha⌈be⌉ru しゃべる C; za⌈tsudañ o suru 雑談をする I: The pupils were chatting about their school trip. (*Seeto-tachi wa shuugaku ryokoo no koto o shabette ita.*) 生徒たちは修学旅行のことをしゃべっていた.

chatter *vi.* **1** (of people) pe⌉chakucha sha⌈be⌉ru ぺちゃくちゃしゃべる C: The old ladies chattered away without regard to the people around. (*Obaasañ-tachi wa mawari no hito o ki ni shinaide pecha-kucha shabette ita.*) おばあさんたちは周りの人を気にしないでぺちゃくちゃしゃべっていた.
2 (of animals) kya⌉kkya to na⌈ku きゃっきゃと鳴く C: The monkeys chattered in the trees. (*Saru ga ki no ue de kyakkya to naita.*) 猿が木の上できゃっきゃと鳴いた.
3 (of objects) ga⌉tagata i⌈u がたがたいう C: Jim's teeth were chattering with fear. (*Jimu no ha wa kyoofu de gatagata itta.*) ジムの歯は恐怖でがたがたいった.
— *n.* **1** (of people) sha⌈berigo⌉e しゃべり声: The chatter of the pupils drowned out the voice of the teacher. (*Seeto no shaberigoe ga señsee no hanashi o keshita.*) 生徒のしゃべり声が先生の話を消した.
2 (of animals) kya⌉kkya to iu na⌈kigo⌉e きゃっきゃという鳴き声.
3 (of objects) ga⌉tagata suru o⌈to⌉ がたがたする音: the chatter of machines (*kikai no gatagata suru oto*) 機械のがたがたする音.

cheap *adj.* **1** (inexpensive) ya⌈su⌉i 安い: a cheap book (*yasui hoñ*) 安い本 / Do you have something a little cheaper? (*Moo sukoshi yasui no wa arimasu ka?*) もう少し安いのはありますか.
2 (inferior) ya⌈suppo⌉i 安っぽい; ya⌈sumono no 安物の: a cheap hat (*yasumono no booshi*) 安物の帽子.
3 (mean) ge⌈hi⌉ñ na 下品な: His cheap jokes make me sick. (*Kare no gehiñ na joodañ ni wa mukamuka suru.*) 彼の下品な冗談にはむかむかする.

cheat *vt.* ... o da⌈ma⌉su ...をだます C: He cheated me out of my money. (*Kare wa watashi o damashite o-kane o totta.*) 彼は私をだましてお金をとった.
— *vi.* (... o) go⌈maka⌉su (...を)ごまかす C; (on examinations) ka⌈ñniñgu o suru カンニングをする I: cheat on taxes (*zeekiñ o gomakasu*) 税金をごまかす / He cheated on the examination. (*Kare wa sono shikeñ de kañniñgu o shita.*) 彼はその試験でカンニングをした.

check *n.* **1** (inspection) sho⌈ogoo 照合; te⌈ñkeñ 点検; che⌉kku チェック: a check of a student's grades (*gakusee no seeseki no shoogoo*) 学生の成績の照合 / a safety check

(*añzeñ no teñkeñ*) 安全の点検.
2 (financial instrument) ko⌈gi⌉tte 小切手: pay a bill by check (*see-kyuusho o kogitte de harau*) 請求書を小切手で払う / a traveler's check (*toraberaazu chekku*) トラベラーズチェック.
3 (bill) ka⌈ñjo⌉o 勘定; (on a piece of paper) ka⌈ñjoogaki 勘定書; de⌈ñ-pyoo 伝票: The bill, please. (*Kañ-joo o onegai shimasu.*) 勘定をお願いします.
4 (mark) che⌉kku no shi⌈rushi チェックの印.
5 (control) yo⌈kusee 抑制; (stop) bo⌈oshi 防止: a check on labor union activity (*roodoo-kumiai-katsudoo no yokusee*) 労働組合活動の抑制.
6 (pattern) che⌈kku[i⌈chimatsu]-mo⌉yoo チェック[市松]模様: a check shirt (*chekku no waishatsu*) チェックのワイシャツ.
— *vt.* **1** (inspect) ... o shi⌈rabe⌉ru ...を調べる Ⓥ; te⌈ñkeñ suru 点検する Ⓘ; ke⌉ñsa suru 検査する Ⓘ: Passports are checked here. (*Pasupooto wa koko de keñsa saremasu.*) パスポートはここで検査されます. / check a car's engine (*kuruma no eñjiñ o teñkeñ suru*) 車のエンジンを点検する.
2 (mark) ... o che⌉kku suru ...をチェックする Ⓘ; ... ni che⌉kku no shi-⌈rushi o tsuke⌉ru ...にチェックの印を付ける Ⓥ.
3 (stop) ... o bo⌈oshi suru ...を防止する Ⓘ; ku⌈itome⌉ru 食い止める Ⓥ: check the spread of cholera (*korera no deñseñ o kuitomeru*) コレラの伝染を食い止める.
check in *vi.* che⌈kku⌉iñ suru チェックインする Ⓘ: The couple checked in to the hotel at four. (*Futari wa yo-ji ni hoteru ni chekkuiñ shita.*) 二人は4時にホテルにチェックインした.
check out *vi.* che⌈kkua⌉uto suru チェックアウトする Ⓘ: I'd like to check out at nine tomorrow morning. (*Asu no asa ku-ji ni chek-kuauto shitai to omoimasu.*) あすの朝9時にチェックアウトしたいと思います.
checkbook *n.* ko⌈gittechoo 小切手帳.
checkers *n.* (draughts) che⌉kkaa チェッカー: play checkers (*chekkaa o suru*) チェッカーをする.
check-in *n.* che⌈kku⌉iñ チェックイン.
checking account *n.* to⌈oza-yo⌉kiñ 当座預金: open a checking account (*tooza-yokiñ no kooza o hiraku*) 当座預金の口座を開く.
checkout *n.* che⌈kkua⌉uto チェックアウト.
checkup *n.* **1** (of health) ke⌈ñkoo-shi⌉ñdañ 健康診断: have a checkup (*keñkooshiñdañ o ukeru*) 健康診断を受ける.
2 (of a car, etc.) ke⌉ñsa 検査.
cheek *n.* ho⌉o ほお: kiss a person on the cheek (*hoo ni kisu suru*) ほおにキスする.
cheer *n.* **1** (applause) ka⌈ssai かっさい: receive cheers from the audience (*chooshuu no kassai o ukeru*) 聴衆のかっさいを受ける.
2 (encouragement) ha⌈gemashi 励まし: words of cheer (*hagemashi no kotoba*) 励ましのことば.
give three cheers *vi.* ba⌈ñza⌉i o sa⌈ñshoo suru 万歳を三唱する.
— *vt.* **1** (encourage) ... o ge⌈ñki-zuke⌉ru ...を元気づける Ⓥ; ha⌈ge-ma⌉su 励ます Ⓒ: Her word cheered him. (*Kanojo no kotoba wa kare o geñkizuketa.*) 彼女の言葉は彼を元気づけた.
2 (shout) ... o se⌈e-eñ suru ...を声援する Ⓘ: cheer the weaker team (*yowai hoo no chiimu o see-eñ suru*) 弱い方のチームを声援する.
cheerful *adj.* **1** (of a person) ge⌉ñ-ki no [ga] ii 元気の[が]いい; ka⌈ika-tsu na 快活な: a cheerful old man (*geñki no ii roojiñ*) 元気のいい老人.
2 (happy) ta⌈noshi⌉i 楽しい; a⌈karui 明るい: cheerful news (*tanoshii shirase*) 楽しい知らせ.
cheese *n.* chi⌉izu チーズ.
chef *n.* ko⌈kku⌉choo コック長; she⌉fu シェフ: Chef's Special (*Hoñjitsu no*

o-susumehiñ) 本日のお勧め品.

chemical *adj.* ka˥gaku no 化学の; ka˹gaku-teki na 化学的な: chemical change (*kagaku heñka*) 化学変化 / a chemical formula (*kagakushiki*) 化学式 / chemical weapons (*kagaku heeki*) 化学兵器.

chemicals *n.* (industrial) ka˹gaku-se˥ehiñ 化学製品; (medicinal) ka˹gaku-ya˥kuhiñ 化学薬品.

chemist *n.* **1** (scientist) ka˹ga˥kusha 化学者.
2 (druggist) ya˹kuza˥ishi 薬剤師.

chemistry *n.* ka˥gaku 化学: organic [inorganic] chemistry (*yuu-[mu]ki kagaku*) 有[無]機化学.
★ When speaking of '*kagaku*,' (chemistry) Japanese speakers will often add parenthically, '*bakegaku*,' (from '*bakeru*' 化ける) to distinguish it from '*kagaku*' 科学 (science).

cheque *n.* ⇨ check *n.* (Sense 2)

cherish *vt.* **1** (protect) ... o ta˹isetsu ni suru ...を大切にする [I]: The mother cherished her baby. (*Hahaoya wa akañboo o taisetsu ni shita.*) 母親は赤ん坊を大切にした.
2 (hold dear) ... o mu˹ne˥ ni hi˹me˥ru ...を胸に秘める [V]: For many years Sally cherished the hope that her son would return. (*Sarii wa naganeñ musuko ga modotte kuru kiboo o mune ni himete ita.*) サリーは長年息子が戻ってくる希望を胸に秘めていた.

cherry *n.* **1** (tree) sa˹kura no ki 桜の木.
2 (fruit) sa˹kurañbo さくらんぼ.
3 (blossom) sa˹kura no hana 桜の花. ★ The cherry blossom is Japan's national flower. Japanese often get together for picnics around cherry trees in blossom, and enjoy merrymaking.

chess *n.* **1** (Western) che˥su チェス: play chess (*chesu o suru*) チェスをする.
2 (Japanese) sho˹ogi 将棋: play Japanese-style chess (*shoogi o sasu*) 将棋を指す.

chest *n.* **1** (breast) mu˹ne˥ 胸: I have a pain in my chest. (*Mune ga itai.*) 胸が痛い.
2 (box) ha˹ko 箱: a chest of drawers (*tañsu*) たんす.

chestnut *n.* **1** (nut) ku˹ri˥ no mi 栗の実; (tree) ku˹ri no˥ ki 栗の木.
2 (color) ku˹ri-iro 栗色.

chew *vt.* ka˥mu 噛む [C]: Chew your food well. (*Tabemono wa yoku kami nasai.*) 食べ物はよくかみなさい.

chicken *n.* **1** (adult bird) ni˹watori 鶏: keep chickens (*niwatori o kau*) 鶏を飼う.
2 (meat) to˹riniku 鶏肉: cook some chicken (*toriniku o ryoori suru*) 鶏肉を料理する / fried chicken (*furaido chikiñ*) フライドチキン.
3 (coward) o˹kubyoomono おくびょう者; yo˹wa˥mushi 弱虫.

chief *n.* (of an organization) *-choo* 長: chief of police (*keesatsu-sho-choo*) 警察署長.
— *adj.* (principle) o˥mo-na 主な; shu˹yoo na 主要な: the chief rivers of Japan (*Nihoñ no omo-na kawa*) 日本の主な川 / the chief aim of the society (*kyookai no shuyoo na mokuteki*) 協会の主要な目的.

chiefly *adv.* shu˥ to shite 主として: The guests were chiefly women. (*O-kyaku wa shu to shite josee datta.*) お客は主として女性だった.

child *n.* **1** (opposite of an adult) ko˹domo 子ども: children (*kodomotachi*) 子どもたち / This book is interesting for both children and adults. (*Kono hoñ wa kodomo ni mo otona ni mo omoshiroi.*) この本は子どもにもおとなにもおもしろい.
2 (son or daughter) ko 子; ko˹domo 子ども: How many children do you have? (*O-kosañ wa nañ-niñ imasu ka?*) お子さんは何人いますか.

childbirth *n.* shu˹ssañ 出産; [technical] bu˹ñbeñ 分娩.

childhood *n.* ko˹domo no to˥ki [ko˥ro] 子供のとき[ころ]: In my childhood, my family lived in Sydney. (*Kodomo no koro, kazoku wa Shidonii ni suñde imashita.*) 子どものころ, 家族はシドニーに住んでいました.

childish *adj.* **1** (like a child) ko⌈domo-rashi⌉i 子どもらしい; ko⌈domo no 子どもの: childish games (*kodomo no asobi*) 子どもの遊び.
2 (silly) ko⌈domoppo⌉i 子供っぽい; yo⌈ochi na 幼稚な: make childish errors (*yoochi na machigai o suru*) 幼稚な間違いをする.

chill *vt.* ... o hi⌈ya⌉su ...を冷やす Ⓒ: chill wine (*waiñ o hiyasu*) ワインを冷やす.
— *n.* 1 (outside temperature) hi⌈e⌉ 冷え; re⌉eki 冷気: autumn chill (*aki no reeki*) 秋の冷気.
2 (body temperature) sa⌈muke⌉ 寒気: I have a slight chill. (*Watashi wa sukoshi samuke ga suru.*) 私は少し寒気がする.

chilly *adj.* **1** (of weather) sa⌈mu⌉i 寒い; ha⌈dasamu⌉i 肌寒い: a chilly room (*samui heya*) 寒い部屋.
2 (of a response) tsu⌈metai 冷たい: a chilly attitude (*tsumetai taido*) 冷たい態度.

chimney *n.* e⌈ñtotsu 煙突: clean a chimney (*eñtotsu o sooji suru*) 煙突を掃除する.

chin *n.* a⌈go⌉ あご: beard on the chin (*ago no hige*) あごのひげ.

china *n.* ji⌉ki 磁器; se⌈tomono 瀬戸物: a china cup (*setomono no chawañ*) 瀬戸物の茶わん.

China *n.* Chu⌉ugoku 中国: People's Republic of China (*Chuukajiñmiñ kyoowakoku*) 中華人民共和国 / Republic of China (*Chuukamiñkoku*) 中華民国.

Chinese *n.* (people) Chu⌈ugoku⌉jiñ 中国人; (language) Chu⌈ugokugo 中国語.
— *adj.* Chu⌉ugoku no 中国の; Chu⌈ugoku⌉jiñ no 中国人の; Chu⌈ugokugo no 中国語の: Chinese cooking (*Chuugoku ryoori*) 中国料理.

chip *n.* **1** (of wood, glass, china, etc.) ka⌈kera かけら: a wood chip (*koppa*) こっぱ.
2 (potato chips, crisps) po⌈teto chi⌉ppusu ポテトチップス.
— *vt.* 1 (break) ... o ka⌈ku ...を欠く Ⓒ: chip a teacup (*chawañ o kaku*) 茶わんを欠く.
2 (carve) ... o ke⌈zuru ...を削る Ⓒ; ke⌈zurito⌉ru 削り取る Ⓒ: chip the ice off the sidewalk (*hodoo kara koori o kezuritoru*) 歩道から氷を削り取る.

chirp *vi.* (of a bird, insect) na⌈ku 鳴く Ⓒ: The crickets are chirping in the garden. (*Koorogi ga niwa de naite iru.*) こおろぎが庭で鳴いている.
— *n.* na⌈kigo⌉e 鳴き声.

chisel *n.* (for wood and stone) no⌉mi のみ; (for metal) ta⌈gane たがね.

chocolate *n.* **1** (sweet) cho⌈kore⌉eto チョコレート: a box of chocolates (*chokoreeto hito hako*) チョコレート一箱.
2 (drink) ko⌉koa ココア: a cup of chocolate (*kokoa ip-pai*) ココア 1 杯.

choice *n.* **1** (act of choosing) e⌈ra⌉bu ko⌈to⌉ 選ぶこと; se⌈ñtaku 選択: make a careful choice of occupations (*shokugyoo o shiñchoo ni erabu*) 職業を慎重に選ぶ.
2 (person) e⌈ra⌉ñda hi⌈to⌉ 選んだ人; (thing) e⌈ra⌉ñda mo⌈no⌉ 選んだ物: Which is your choice? (*Erañda no wa dore desu ka?*) 選んだのはどれですか.
3 (collection to choose from) se⌈ñtaku no shu⌉rui 選択の種類: a great choice of roses (*iroiro na shurui no bara*) いろいろな種類のばら.
— *adj.* (of food, drink) go⌈kujoo no 極上の: choice grapes (*gokujoo no budō*) 極上のぶどう.

choke *vt.* **1** (smother) ... o chi⌈ssoku saseru ...を窒息させる Ⓥ: The baby swallowed a coin and was almost choked. (*Akañboo wa kooka o nomikoñde, moo sukoshi de chissoku suru tokoro datta.*) 赤ん坊は硬貨を飲み込んで, もう少しで窒息するところだった.
2 (block up) ... o fu⌈sagu ...をふさぐ

[C]: The road was choked with cars. (*Dooro wa kuruma de fusagarete ita.*) 道路は車でふさがれていた.
— *vi.* i⌉ki ga tsu⌈ma⌉ru 息が詰まる [C]: We almost choked in the dust. (*Hokori de iki ga tsumari-soo datta.*) ほこりで息が詰まりそうだった.

cholera *n.* ko⌉rera コレラ: contract cholera (*korera ni kakaru*) コレラにかかる.

choose *vt.* (select) ... o e⌈ra⌉bu 選ぶ [C]; se⌈ñtaku suru 選択する [I]: Choose the cake you like best. (*Ichibañ suki na keeki o erabi nasai.*) いちばん好きなケーキを選びなさい. / He was chosen chairman. (*Kare wa gichoo ni erabareta.*) 彼は議長に選ばれた.
— *vi.* e⌈ra⌉bu 選ぶ [C]; se⌈ñtaku suru 選択する [I]: choose between the two (*futatsu no naka kara erabu*) 二つの中から選ぶ.

chop *vt.* **1** (with an ax) ... o ta⌈takiki⌉ru ...をたたき切る [C]; wa⌈ru 割る [C]: chop wood (*maki o waru*) まきを割る.
2 (of vegetables) ... o ki⌈zamu ...を刻む [C]: I chopped up the green onions. (*Watashi wa negi o kizañda.*) 私はねぎを刻んだ.
— *vi.* (... o) ta⌈takiki⌉ru (...を)たたき切る [C]: He chopped at the tree. (*Kare wa sono ki o tatakikitta.*) 彼はその木をたたき切った.
— *n.* a⌈tsugiri no niku⌉ 厚切りの肉; cho⌉ppu チョップ: a pork chop (*butaniku no atsugiri*) 豚肉の厚切り.

chopsticks *n.* ha⌉shi 箸: eat with chopsticks (*hashi de taberu*) 箸で食べる / throwaway chopsticks (*waribashi*) 割りばし.

chore *n.* **1** (duty) za⌈tsuyoo 雑用: daily chores (*mainichi no zatsuyoo*) 毎日の雑用.
2 (burdensome task) me⌈ñdo⌉o na shi⌈goto めんどうな仕事.

chorus *n.* **1** (singing together) ga⌈sshoo 合唱; ko⌉orasu コーラス.
2 (group) ga⌈ssho⌉odañ 合唱団: join a chorus (*gasshoodañ ni hairu*) 合唱団に入る.
3 (composition) ga⌈ssho⌉okyoku 合唱曲.

Christ *n.* Ki⌈risuto キリスト: Jesus Christ (*Iesu Kirisuto*) イエスキリスト / Before Christ (B.C.) (*kigeñ-zeñ*) 紀元前.

Christian *n.* Ki⌈risuto-kyo⌉oto キリスト教徒; Ku⌈ri⌉suchañ クリスチャン.
— *adj.* Ki⌈risuto-kyoo no キリスト教の; Ku⌈ri⌉suchañ no クリスチャンの: the Christian church (*Kirisutokyookai*) キリスト教会.

Christmas *n.* Ku⌈risu⌉masu クリスマス; Ki⌈risuto-koota⌉ñsai キリスト降誕祭: celebrate Christmas (*Kurisumasu o iwau*) クリスマスを祝う / Christmas Eve (*Kurisumasu ibu*) クリスマスイブ.

chronic *adj.* (of disease) ma⌈ñsee no 慢性の: a chronic disease (*mañseebyoo*) 慢性病.
2 (long time) na⌈gabi⌉ku 長引く: a chronic recession (*nagabiku fukyoo*) 長引く不況.

chrysanthemum *n.* ki⌈ku⌉ 菊.

chuckle *vi.* ku⌉sukusu wa⌈rau くすくす笑う [C]: He chuckled over a comic strip. (*Kare wa mañga o mite kusukusu waratta.*) 彼は漫画を見てくすくす笑った.

church *n.* **1** (the body of Christians) kyo⌈okai 教会: members of the church (*kyookai no shiñto*) 教会の信徒.
2 (building) kyo⌈okai 教会; kyo⌈okaidoo 教会堂.
3 (service) re⌈ehai 礼拝: Church begins at 10:00. (*Reehai wa juu-ji ni hajimarimasu.*) 礼拝は10時に始まります.

cider *n.* **1** (alcoholic) ri⌈ñgo⌉shu りんご酒.
2 (non-alcoholic) ri⌈ñgo ju⌉usu りんごジュース. ★ Be careful not to confuse either of these with the generic name for fruit-flavored carbonated drinks in Japan, *'saidaa'* サイダー.

cigar *n.* ha⌈maki 葉巻き.

cigarette *n.* ta⌈bako たばこ; ka⌈mi-maki-ta⌉bako 紙巻きたばこ: smoke a cigarette (*tabako o suu*) たばこを吸う. ★ In Japanese, cigarettes, cigar and tobacco are all called '*tabako*.'

cinema *n.* (theater) e⌈ega⌉-kañ 映画館; (films) e⌉ega 映画: go to the cinema (*eega o mi ni iku*) 映画を見に行く.

circle *n.* **1** (figure) e⌉ñ 円; ma⌈ru まる; wa⌉ 輪: draw a circle (*eñ o egaku*) 円を描く.
2 (company) na⌈kama⌉ 仲間; -sha⌉-kai 社会; -kai 界: the upper circles (*jooryuu-shakai*) 上流社会 / business circles (*jitsugyoo-kai*) 実業界.
3 (cycle) ju⌈ñkañ 循環; shu⌉uki 周期: the circle of seasons (*shiki no juñkañ*) 四季の循環.
— *vi.* ma⌈waru 回る Ⓒ; se⌈ñkai suru 旋回する Ⓘ: The airplane circled over the airfield. (*Hikooki wa hikoojoo no ue o señkai shita.*) 飛行機は飛行場の上を旋回した.
— *vt.* (draw a circle) ... o ma⌈ru de kakomu ...を丸で囲む Ⓒ: circle the correct answers (*tadashii kotae o maru de kakomu*) 正しい答を丸で囲む.

circuit *n.* **1** (motion) i⌈s-shuu 一周; ju⌈ñkai 巡回: The earth makes the circuit of the sun in one year. (*Chikyuu wa ichi-neñ de taiyoo o is-shuu suru.*) 地球は一年で太陽を一周する.
2 (round) ju⌈ñkai chi⌉iki 巡回地域: a postman's circuit (*yuubiñ no haitatsu chiiki*) 郵便の配達地域.
3 (race-track) sa⌉akitto サーキット; shu⌈ukai ko⌉osu 周回コース.
4 (of electricity) ka⌉iro 回路; ka⌈i-señ 回線: a short circuit (*shooto*) ショート.

circular *adj.* **1** (round) ma⌈rui 丸い; e⌉ñ no 円の: a circular movement (*eñ uñdoo*) 円運動.
2 (of a ticket) shu⌈uyuu no 周遊の: a circular ticket (*shuuyuukeñ*) 周遊券.
— *n.* (notice) a⌈ñnaijoo 案内状; chi⌈rashi ちらし.

circulate *vi.* **1** (go round) ju⌈ñkañ suru 循環する Ⓘ: Blood circulates through the body. (*Chi wa karada-juu o juñkañ suru.*) 血は体中を循環する.
2 (spread) hi⌈roma⌉ru 広まる Ⓒ; tsu⌈tawaru 伝わる Ⓒ: The rumor circulated quickly. (*Sono uwasa wa sugu ni hiromatta.*) そのうわさはすぐに広まった.
3 (move from place to place) u⌈gokimawa⌉ru 動き回る Ⓒ: circulate among the guests at a party (*paatii de o-kyaku no aida o ugokimawaru*) パーティーでお客の間を動き回る.
— *vt.* (cause to circulate) ... o ju⌈ñkañ saseru ...を循環させる Ⓥ; ka⌈irañ suru 回覧する Ⓘ: circulate a magazine (*zasshi o kairañ suru*) 雑誌を回覧する.

circulation *n.* **1** (of blood) ju⌈ñkañ 循環; ke⌈kkoo 血行: have a good [bad] circulation (*kekkoo ga yoi [warui]*) 血行がよい[悪い].
2 (of money) ryu⌈utsuu 流通: the circulation of money (*kahee no ryuutsuu*) 貨幣の流通.
3 (number of copies) ha⌈kkoo-busu⌉u 発行部数: have a large [small] circulation (*hakkoo-busuu ga ooi [sukunai]*) 発行部数が多い[少ない].

circumstance *n.* ji⌈joo 事情; jo⌈okyoo 状況: It depends on circumstances. (*Sore wa jijoo ni yorimasu.*) それは事情によります. / Under the present circumstances I can do nothing. (*Geñzai no jookyoo de wa watashi wa nani mo suru koto ga dekimaseñ.*) 現在の状況では私は何もすることができません.

circus *n.* sa⌉akasu サーカス.

cite *vt.* ... o i⌈ñyoo suru ...を引用する Ⓘ; a⌈geru 挙げる Ⓥ: cite an example (*ree o ageru*) 例を挙げる.

citizen *n.* (of a city) shi⌉miñ 市民; (of a state) ko⌈kumiñ 国民: the citizens of Kobe (*Koobe no shimiñ*) 神戸の市民.

city *n.* to⌉shi 都市; to⌈kai 都会; shi⌉

市: Nara is an ancient city. (*Nara wa furui toshi desu.*) 奈良は古い都市です. / I'd like to reserve a hotel room in the city. (*Shinai no hoteru o yoyaku shitai no desu ga.*) 市内のホテルを予約したいのですが.

city hall *n.* shiˈyaˈkusho 市役所.

civil *adj.* **1** (of citizens) shiˈmiñ no 市民の: civil duties (*shimiñ no gimu*) 市民の義務.

2 (not of the armed forces) miˈñkañ no 民間の: civil aviation (*miñkañ-kookuu*) 民間航空.

3 (polite) reˈegi tadashiˈi 礼儀正しい; teˈenee na 丁寧な: make a civil reply (*teenee na heñji o suru*) 丁寧な返事をする.

civilization *n.* buˈñmee 文明: Western civilization (*seeyoo buñmee*) 西洋文明.

civilize *vt.* ... o buˈñmeeka suru ...を文明化する [I]; kyoˈoka suru 教化する [I]: Europe was civilized by the Roman Empire. (*Yooroppa wa Rooma teekoku ni yotte buñmeeka sareta.*) ヨーロッパはローマ帝国によって文明化された.

civilized *adj.* buˈñmeeka shita 文明化した; kyoˈoka sareta 教化された: civilized society (*buñmee shakai*) 文明社会.

claim *vt.* **1** (maintain) ... to shuˈchoo suru ...と主張する [I]; iˈihaˈru 言い張る [C]: He claimed that he is the owner of the land. (*Kare wa sono tochi no shoyuusha da to shuchoo shita.*) 彼はその土地の所有者だと主張した.

2 (demand) ... o yoˈokyuu suru ...を要求する [I]; seˈekyuu suru 請求する [I]: I claimed traveling expenses. (*Watashi wa kootsuuhi o seekyuu shita.*) 私は交通費を請求した.

— *n.* **1** (statement) shuˈchoo 主張: His claim is groundless. (*Kare no shuchoo wa koñkyo ga nai.*) 彼の主張は根拠がない.

2 (demand) yoˈokyuu 要求; seˈekyuu 請求: make a claim for damages (*soñgai-baishoo o seekyuu suru*) 損害賠償を請求する.

3 (right) yoˈokyuu suru keˈñri 要求する権利: He has a claim to the money. (*Kare wa sono o-kane o yookyuu suru keñri ga aru.*) 彼はそのお金を要求する権利がある.

clamor *n.* saˈkebiˈ 叫び; koˈe 声: a clamor against war (*señsoo hañtai no koe*) 戦争反対の声.

— *vi.* saˈwagitateˈru 騒ぎ立てる [V]; yoˈokyuu suru 要求する [I]: They clamored for higher wages. (*Kare-ra wa chiñage o yookyuu shita.*) 彼らは賃上げを要求した.

clap *vt.* ... o taˈtaˈku ...をたたく [C]; poˈñ to taˈtaˈku ぽんとたたく [C]: clap one's hands (*te o tataku*) 手をたたく / He clapped me on the back. (*Kare wa watashi no senaka o poñ to tataita.*) 彼は私の背中をぽんとたたいた.

— *vi.* haˈkushu suru 拍手する [I]: When he appeared on the stage, the audience clapped. (*Kare ga butai ni arawareru to chooshuu wa hakushu shita.*) 彼が舞台に現れると聴衆は拍手した.

— *n.* (clapping) haˈkushu 拍手; (noise) baˈribari [paˈchipachi] to iu oˈtoˈ ばりばり[ぱちぱち]という音: a clap of thunder (*raimee*) 雷鳴.

clash *vi.* **1** (fight) shoˈototsu suru 衝突する [I]: The students and the riot police clashed. (*Gakusee to kidootai ga shoototsu shita.*) 学生と機動隊が衝突した.

2 (conflict) kuˈichigau 食い違う [C]: Their opinions always clash. (*Kare-ra no ikeñ wa itsu-mo kuichigau.*) 彼らの意見はいつも食い違う.

— *n.* shoˈototsu 衝突; fuˈiˈtchi 不一致: a clash of interests (*rigai no shoototsu*) 利害の衝突.

clasp *n.* toˈmegane 留め金: fasten the clasp of a necklace (*nekkuresu no tomegane o tomeru*) ネックレスの留め金を留める.

— *vt.* (with the hand) ... o niˈgirishimeˈru ...を握りしめる [V]; (in the arms) ... o daˈkishimeˈru ...を抱きしめる [V]: The mother clasped her baby to her breast. (*Hahaoya wa akañboo o mune ni dakishimeta.*) 母親は赤ん坊を胸に抱きしめた.

class *n.* **1** (group of students) kuˡrasu クラス; gaˡkkyuu 学級: He and I are in the same class. (*Kare to watashi wa onaji kurasu desu.*) 彼と私は同じクラスです. ★ Japanese '*kurasu*' usually means a specific homeroom.
2 (lesson) juˡgyoo 授業: How many classes do you have today? (*Kyoo wa nañ-jikañ jugyoo ga arimasu ka?*) きょうは何時間授業がありますか.
3 (social group) kaˡikyuu 階級; kaˡisoo 階層: the upper class (*jooryuu-kaikyuu*) 上流階級.
4 (division) buˡrui 部類; shuˡrui 種類: These two things belong to the same class. (*Kore-ra futatsu no mono wa onaji burui ni zokushimasu.*) これら二つの物は同じ部類に属します.
5 (grade) toˡokyuu 等級; kuˡrasu クラス: goods of the highest class (*saikookyuu no shina*) 最高級の品 / first class (*faasuto kurasu*) ファーストクラス.

classic *adj.* **1** (traditional) deˡñtoo-teki na 伝統的な; koˡteñ-teki na 古典的な: a classic event (*deñtoo-teki na gyooji*) 伝統的な行事.
2 (first-rate) iˡchi-ryuu no 一流の: a classic author (*ichi-ryuu no sakka*) 一流の作家.
3 (of literature, art, etc.) koˡteñ no 古典の: classic culture (*koteñ buñka*) 古典文化.
— *n.* (of literature) koˡteñ 古典: the Japanese classics (*Nihoñ no koteñ*) 日本の古典.

classical *adj.* **1** (of music) koˡteñ-shuˡgi no 古典主義の; kuˡrashiˡkku no クラシックの: classical music (*kurashikku oñgaku*) クラシック音楽.
2 (of literature) koˡteñ buˡñgaku no 古典文学の: the classical languages (*koteñgo*) 古典語.

classification *n.* buˡñrui 分類; buˡñruihoo 分類法: the classification of animals.(*doobutsu no buñrui*) 動物の分類.

classify *vt.* ... o buˡñrui suru …を分類する [I]; toˡokyuu ni wakeˡru 等級に分ける [V]: I classified the books by subject. (*Watashi wa hoñ o teema-betsu ni buñrui shita.*) 私は本をテーマ別に分類した.

classmate *n.* doˡokyuˡusee 同級生; doˡokiˡsee 同期生; kuˡrasumeˡeto クラスメート: He is a classmate from high school. (*Kare wa watashi no kookoo kara no dookyuusee desu.*) 彼は私の高校からの同級生です.

classroom *n.* kyoˡoshitsu 教室.

clause *n.* **1** (of grammar) seˡtsu 節.
2 (of a legal document) joˡokoo 条項; kaˡjoo 箇条: amend the third clause of the contract (*keeyaku no dai-sañ-joo o teesee suru*) 契約の第3条を訂正する.

claw *n.* (hooked nail) tsuˡme つめ; kaˡgiˡtsume かぎつめ; (of a crab) haˡsamiˡ はさみ.

clay *n.* neˡñdo 粘土.

clean *adj.* **1** (free from dirt) seˡeketsu na 清潔な; kiˡree na きれいな; yoˡgorete inai 汚れていない: keep one's room clean (*heya o seeketsu ni shite oku*) 部屋を清潔にしておく / clean water (*kiree na mizu*) きれいな水.
2 (unused) naˡni mo kaˡite nai 何も書いてない; miˡshiˡyoo no 未使用の: Please give me a clean sheet of paper. (*Nani mo kaite nai kami o ichi-mai kudasai.*) 何も書いてない紙を1枚下さい.
3 (free from offense) keˡppaku na 潔白な; kiˡree na きれいな: a clean record (*kiree na rireki*) きれいな履歴.
— *adv.* (completely) suˡkkaˡri すっかり; maˡttaku まったく: I clean forgot about it. (*Sono koto wa sukkari wasurete ita.*) そのことはすっかり忘れていた.
— *vt.* ... o seˡeketsu ni suru …を清

C

C

潔にする Ⅰ; mi⌈gaku 磨く Ⓒ; so⌈oji suru 掃除する Ⅰ; se⌈ñtaku suru 洗濯する Ⅰ: clean one's teeth (*ha o migaku*) 歯を磨く / Please clean the room. (*Heya o sooji shite kudasai.*) 部屋を掃除してください. / This is to be cleaned. (*Kore wa señtaku suru mono desu.*) これは洗濯するものです.

cleaner *n.* **1** (person) so⌈oji o suru hito⌉ 掃除をする人; ku⌈riiniñgu-ya クリーニング屋: take one's coat to the cleaner's (*kooto o kuriiniñgu-ya e motte iku*) コートをクリーニング屋へ持っていく.
2 (machine) so⌈oji⌉ki 掃除機.

cleaning *n.* (of a room) so⌈oji 掃除; (of clothes) se⌈ñtaku 洗濯: do the cleaning (*sooji [señtaku] o suru*) 掃除[洗濯]をする.

clear *adj.* **1** (distinct) ha⌈kki⌉ri shita [shite iru] はっきりした[している]; se⌈ñmee na 鮮明な: write in clear letters (*hakkiri shita ji de kaku*) はっきりした字で書く / a clear photograph (*señmee na shashiñ*) 鮮明な写真.
2 (obvious) a⌈ki⌉raka na 明かな; me⌈ehaku na 明白な: It is clear that you are wrong. (*Kimi ga machigatte iru no wa meehaku desu.*) 君が間違っているのは明白です.
3 (bright) a⌈karui 明るい; ha⌉reta 晴れた; ha⌉rete iru 晴れている: clear sunshine (*akarui nikkoo*) 明るい日光 / clear weather (*hareta teñki*) 晴れた天気.
4 (transparent) su⌉ñda 澄んだ; su⌉ñde iru 澄んでいる; to⌈omee na 透明な: clear water (*suñda mizu*) 澄んだ水.
5 (free from obstacles) ja⌈ma ga na⌉i じゃまがない; a⌈ita 空いた; a⌈iteiru 空いている: a clear space (*akichi*) 空き地 / a clear passage (*jiyuu ni tooreru michi*) 自由に通れる道.
— *vt.* **1** (make clear) ... o ki⌉ree ni suru …をきれいにする Ⅰ: clear a mirror (*kagami o kiree ni suru*) 鏡をきれいにする.
2 (remove) ... o to⌈rinozoku …を取り除く Ⓒ: clear the snow from the road (*michi kara yuki o torinozoku*) 道から雪を取り除く.
3 (free from blame) ... o ha⌈ra⌉su …を晴らす Ⓒ: clear a suspect of a crime (*hañzai no utagai o harasu*) 犯罪の疑いを晴らす.
— *vi.* (of the weather) ha⌈re⌉ru 晴れる Ⓥ: The sky is clearing. (*Sora ga harete kita.*) 空が晴れてきた.

clearly *adv.* ha⌈kki⌉ri (to) はっきり(と): I can't hear you clearly. (*Hakkiri kikoemaseñ.*) はっきり聞こえません.

clergyman *n.* bo⌉kushi 牧師; se⌈eshoku⌉sha 聖職者.

clerk *n.* **1** (of an office) ji⌈mu⌉iñ 事務員; sho⌈ku⌉iñ 職員; -in 員: a bank clerk (*giñkooiñ*) 銀行員 / a front desk clerk (*furoñtogakari*) フロント係 / a government clerk (*koomuiñ*) 公務員.
2 (of a shop) te⌈ñiñ 店員: a grocery clerk (*shokuryoohiñteñ no teñiñ*) 食料品店の店員.

clever *adj.* **1** (showing ability) u⌈ma⌉i うまい; ta⌈kumi na 巧みな: a clever idea (*umai kañgae*) うまい考え.
2 (skillful) ki⌉yoo na 器用な: He is clever with his hands. (*Kare wa tesaki ga kiyoo da.*) 彼は手先が器用だ.
3 (intelligent) a⌈tama⌉ ga i⌉i 頭がいい; ri⌈koo na 利口な; ka⌈shiko⌉i 賢い: a clever child (*rikoo na kodomo*) 利口な子ども.

client *n.* i⌈raininñ 依頼人; (of a shop) o-⌈kyaku お客.

cliff *n.* ga⌈ke がけ; ze⌈ppeki 絶壁.

climate *n.* **1** (weather conditions) ki⌈koo 気候: The climate of Japan agrees with me. (*Nihoñ no kikoo wa watashi ni atte imasu.*) 日本の気候は私に合っています.
2 (area) chi⌉hoo 地方; fu⌉udo 風土: live in a warmer climate (*atatakai chihoo de kurasu*) 暖かい地方で暮らす.

climb *vt.* ... ni no⌈boru …に登る Ⓒ:

climb a tree (*ki ni noboru*) 木に登る / Have you ever climbed that mountain? (*Ano yama ni nobotta koto wa arimasu ka?*) あの山に登ったことはありますか.
— *vi.* **1** (go up) (... o) no⌈boru (...を)登る [C]: climb up a ladder (*hashigo o noboru*) はしごを登る.
2 (rise) no⌈boru 昇る [C]; a⌈garu 上がる [C]: The moon climbed above the horizon. (*Tsuki ga chiheeseñ no ue ni nobotta.*) 月が地平線の上に昇った. / Prices are climbing. (*Bukka wa agatte iru.*) 物価は上がっている.
— *n.* no⌈boru koto⌉ 登ること; jo⌈o-shoo 上昇; (of a mountain) to⌈zañ 登山: make a climb (*noboru*) 登る.

cling *vi.* (grip) (... ni) shi⌈gamitsu⌉ku (...に)しがみつく [C]; (stick) ku⌈t-tsu⌉ku くっつく [C]: The mud clung to my shoes. (*Doro ga kutsu ni kuttsuita.*) 泥が靴にくっついた.

clinic *n.* shi⌈ñryoojo 診療所; ku⌈ri⌉nikku クリニック.

clinical thermometer *n.* ta⌈i-o⌉ñkee 体温計.

clip[1] *n.* ku⌈ri⌉ppu クリップ; ka⌈miba⌉sami 紙ばさみ: fasten papers with a clip (*shorui o kurippu de tomeru*) 書類をクリップで留める.
— *vt.* ... o to⌈meru ...を留める [V]: clip a brooch to the lapel (*buroochi o eri ni tomeru*) ブローチをえりに留める.

clip[2] *vt.* (cut) ... o ha⌈sami⌉ de kiru ...をはさみで切る [C]; (trim) ka⌈riko⌉mu 刈り込む [C]: clip an article out of a newspaper (*kiji o shiñbuñ kara kirinuku*) 記事を新聞から切り抜く / She clipped her hair close. (*Kanojo wa kami o mijikaku kari-koñda.*) 彼女は髪を短く刈り込んだ.
— *n.* ka⌈rikomi 刈り込み; (clip-ping) ki⌈rinuki 切り抜き.

cloakroom *n.* ku⌈ro⌉oku(ruumu) クローク(ルーム); ke⌈etaihiñ-azukarijo 携帯品預かり所.

clock *n.* to⌈kee 時計: This clock is five minutes fast [slow]. (*Kono tokee wa go-fuñ susuñde [okurete] iru.*) この時計は5分進んで[遅れて]いる. ★ 'Watch' is also called '*tokee.*'

close[1] *vt.* **1** (shut) ... o to⌈ji⌉ru ...を閉じる [V]; shi⌈me⌉ru 閉める [V]: close one's eyes (*me o tojiru*) 目を閉じる / close a window (*mado o shimeru*) 窓を閉める.
2 (stop up) ... o tsu⌈ukoodome ni suru ...を通行止めにする [I]: The bridge is closed to traffic. (*Hashi wa tsuukoodome ni natte imasu.*) 橋は通行止めになっています.
3 (bring to an end) ... o o⌈eru ...を終える [V]; shu⌈uryoo suru 終了する [I]: close a discussion (*tooroñ o oeru*) 討論を終える.
— *vi.* o⌈waru 終わる [C]; shi⌈ma⌉ru 閉まる [C]: What time does the bank close? (*Giñkoo wa nañ-ji ni shimarimasu ka?*) 銀行は何時に閉まりますか.

close[2] *adj.* **1** (near) se⌈kkiñ shita [shite iru] 接近した[している]; su⌉gu soba (ni) すぐそば(に): His house is close to the station. (*Kare no uchi wa eki no sugu soba desu.*) 彼の家は駅のすぐそばです.
2 (dear) shi⌈tashi⌉i 親しい; shi⌈ñmitsu na 親密な: a close friend (*shiñyuu*) 親友.
3 (careful) sa⌈ishiñ no 細心の: pay close attention (*saishiñ no chuui o harau*) 細心の注意を払う.
— *adv.* su⌉gu so⌉ba ni すぐそばに; chi⌉kaku ni 近くに: Come closer to me. (*Motto chikaku ni ki nasai.*) もっと近くに来なさい.

closed *adj.* shi⌈mera⌉reta 閉められた; shi⌈ma⌉tte iru 閉まっている; kyu⌈u-gyoo no 休業の: Closed today. (*Hoñjitsu kyuugyoo.*) 本日休業.

closely *adv.* **1** (tightly) pi⌈tta⌉ri (to) ぴったり(と); gi⌈sshi⌉ri (to) ぎっしり(と): Her coat fits closely. (*Kanojo no kooto wa pittari atte iru.*) 彼女のコートはぴったり合っている.
2 (carefully) chu⌉ui shite 注意して; me⌈ñmitsu ni 綿密に: listen closely

(*chuui shite kiku*) 注意して聞く.

closet *n.* o'shiire 押し入れ; to'dana 戸棚; ku'ro'zetto クロゼット.

cloth *n.* nu'no 布; ki'ji 生地; ku'rosu クロス: cloth for a dress (*fuku no kiji*) 服の生地 / a tablecloth (*teeburu kurosu*) テーブルクロス.

clothe *vt.* ... ni fu'ku' o ki'seru …に服を着せる Ⓥ: He was clothed in wool. (*Kare wa uuru no fuku o kite ita.*) 彼はウールの服を着ていた.

clothes *n.* fu'ku' 服; i'fuku 衣服; ki'mono 着物: put on [take off] one's clothes (*fuku o kiru [nugu]*) 服を着る[脱ぐ].

clothing *n.* i'rui 衣類; fu'ku' 服; i'ryoohiñ 衣料品: children's clothing (*kodomo-fuku*) 子供服 / food, clothing, and shelter (*ishokujuu*) 衣食住.

cloud *n.* ku'mo 雲: The sun was hidden by a cloud. (*Taiyoo ga kumo ni kakureta.*) 太陽が雲に隠れた.

cloudy *adj.* ku'mo'tta 曇った; ku'mo'tte iru 曇っている; ku'mori' no 曇りの: a cloudy day (*kumori no hi*) 曇りの日 / a cloudy sky (*kumori-zora*) 曇り空 / It is cloudy today. (*Kyoo wa kumotte iru.*) きょうは曇っている.

clover *n.* ku'ro'obaa クローバー: four-leaf clover (*yotsuba no kuroobaa*) 四つ葉のクローバー.

club *n.* **1** (group of people) ku'rabu クラブ; do'oko'okai 同好会: join a golf club (*gorufu kurabu ni hairu*) ゴルフクラブに入る.
2 (stick) ko'ñboo こん棒.

clue *n.* te'ga'kari 手がかり; i'to'guchi 糸口: find [miss] an important clue (*juuyoo na tegakari o mitsukeru [miotosu]*) 重要な手がかりを見つける[見落とす].

clumsy *adj.* bu'ki'yoo na 不器用な; gi'kochina'i ぎこちない: He is clumsy with his hands. (*Kare wa tesaki ga bukiyoo da.*) 彼は手先が不器用だ.

cluster *n.* **1** (bunch) fu'sa' 房: a cluster of grapes (*hito-fusa no budoo*) 1房のぶどう.
2 (group) mu're' 群れ; shu'udañ 集団: a cluster of onlookers (*keñbutsuniñ no mure*) 見物人の群れ.

clutch *vt.* ... o shi'kka'ri to ni'giru …をしっかりと握る Ⓒ; gu'i to tsu'ka'mu ぐいとつかむ Ⓒ: He clutched my arm firmly. (*Kare wa watashi no ude o shikkari to tsukañda.*) 彼は私の腕をしっかりとつかんだ.
— *n.* **1** (grasp) tsu'ka'mu ko'to' つかむこと: The pickpocket made a clutch at her bag. (*Suri wa kanojo no baggu o tsukamoo to shita.*) すりは彼女のバッグをつかもうとした.
2 (control) shi'hai 支配; shu'chuu 手中: fall into the clutches of the enemy (*teki no shuchuu ni ochiiru*) 敵の手中に陥る.

coach *n.* **1** (person) ko'ochi コーチ; shi'do'oiñ 指導員: a baseball coach (*yakyuu no koochi*) 野球のコーチ.
2 (railroad car) kya'kusha 客車; (bus) o'ogata ba'su 大型バス.
3 (carriage) yo'ñriñ oogata ba'sha 四輪大型馬車.
— *vt.* ... o shi'doo suru …を指導する Ⓘ; ko'ochi suru コーチする Ⓘ: I coached her in Japanese. (*Watashi wa kanojo ni Nihoñgo o shidoo shita.*) 私は彼女に日本語を指導した.

coal *n.* se'kita'ñ 石炭: burn coal (*sekitañ o taku*) 石炭をたく.

coarse *adj.* **1** (not fine) tsu'bu no [ga] o'oki'i 粒の[が]大きい: coarse sand (*tsubu no ookii suna*) 粒の大きい砂.
2 (rough) ki'me' no [ga] a'rai きめの[が]粗い: coarse cloth (*kime no arai nuno*) きめの粗い布.
3 (not refined) so'ya na 粗野な; (vulgar) ge'hi'ñ na 下品な: coarse taste (*gehiñ na shumi*) 下品な趣味.

coast *n.* ka'igañ 海岸; e'ñgañ 沿岸: His house is on the coast. (*Kare no ie wa kaigañ ni aru.*) 彼の家は海岸にある.

coat *n.* **1** (outer garment) ko'oto コート; (jacket) u'wagi 上着.
2 (of an animal) ke'gawa 毛皮.
3 (of paint) nu'ri 塗り; to'soo 塗装.

— *vt.* (cover) ... o o⌈ou …を覆う Ⓒ: The furniture was coated with dust. (*Kagu wa hokori de oowarete ita.*) 家具はほこりで覆われていた.

cock *n.* **1** (rooster) o⌉ñdori おんどり. **2** (tap) se⌉ñ 栓; ko⌉kku コック: turn on [off] a cock (*señ o akeru* [*shimeru*]) 栓を開ける[閉める].

cocktail *n.* ka⌉kuteru カクテル.

cocoa *n.* ko⌉koa ココア.

code *n.* **1** (secret words) a⌈ñgoo 暗号; (symbols) fu⌈goo 符号: zip code (*yuubiñ bañgoo*) 郵便番号. **2** (set of laws) ho⌈oteñ 法典: the civil code (*miñpoo*) 民法 / the criminal code (*keehoo*) 刑法. **3** (set of rules) o⌈kite おきて; ki⌉soku 規則: the code of a school (*koosoku*) 校則.

coffee *n.* **1** (drink) ko⌈ohi⌉i コーヒー: make coffee (*koohii o ireru*) コーヒーをいれる / weak [strong] coffee (*usui* [*koi*] *koohii*) 薄い[濃い]コーヒー / a coffee cup (*koohii-jawañ* [*-kappu*]) コーヒー茶碗[カップ] / a coffee pot (*koohii potto*) コーヒーポット. **2** (shrub) ko⌈ohi⌉i no ki⌉ コーヒーの木; (beans) ko⌈ohi⌉i ma⌈me⌉ コーヒー豆.

coffee shop *n.* ko⌈ohii sho⌉ppu コーヒーショップ; ki⌈ssa⌉teñ 喫茶店. ★ A '*kissateñ*' serves only coffee, black tea, and other refreshments.

coffin *n.* hi⌈tsugi ひつぎ; ka⌈ño⌉ke 棺おけ.

cognac *n.* ko⌈nya⌉kku コニャック.

coil *vt.* ... o gu⌉ruguru ma⌈ku …をぐるぐる巻く Ⓒ: coil a rope (*roopu o guruguru maku*) ロープをぐるぐる巻く.
— *vi.* (... ni) ma⌈kitsu⌉ku (…に)巻きつく Ⓒ; (of a snake) to⌈guro⌉ o ma⌈ku とぐろを巻く Ⓒ: The vine coiled around the tree. (*Tsuru ga ki ni makitsuita.*) つるが木に巻きついた.
— *n.* **1** (something coiled) ma⌈ita mono⌉ 巻いたもの; wa⌉ 輪: a coil of wire (*hito-maki no harigane*) 一巻きの針金. **2** (for an electric current) ko⌉iru コイル.

coin *n.* ko⌉oka 硬貨; ko⌉iñ コイン.

coincide *vi.* **1** (happen) do⌉oji ni o⌈ko⌉ru 同時に起こる Ⓒ: The fire coincided with the earthquake. (*Jishiñ to dooji ni kaji ga okotta.*) 地震と同時に火事が起こった. **2** (agree) i⌈tchi suru 一致する Ⓘ: Their tastes in music coincide. (*Kare-ra no oñgaku no shumi wa itchi shite iru.*) 彼らの音楽の趣味は一致している.

Coke *n.* ko⌉ora コーラ.

cold *adj.* **1** (of a thing) tsu⌈metai 冷たい; (of weather) sa⌈mu⌉i 寒い: cold milk (*tsumetai gyuunyuu*) 冷たい牛乳 / It is cold today. (*Kyoo wa samui.*) きょうは寒い. **2** (unkind) re⌈eta⌉ñ na 冷淡な; tsu⌈metai 冷たい: a cold answer (*reetañ na heñji*) 冷淡な返事.
— *n.* **1** (illness) ka⌈ze かぜ: catch a cold (*kaze o hiku*) かぜをひく / I have a cold. (*Watashi wa kaze o hiite imasu.*) 私はかぜをひいています. **2** (low temperature) sa⌉musa 寒さ: shiver with cold (*samusa de furueru*) 寒さで震える.

coldness *n.* (of weather) sa⌉musa 寒さ; (of a thing) tsu⌈meta⌉sa 冷たさ.

collaborate *vi.* kyo⌈odoo de suru 共同でする Ⓘ; kyo⌈oryoku suru 協力する Ⓘ: I collaborated with him on writing the book. (*Watashi wa kare to kyoodoo shite sono hoñ o kaita.*) 私は彼と共同してその本を書いた.

collapse *vi.* **1** (break down) ku⌈zure⌉ru 崩れる Ⓥ; ho⌈okai suru 崩壊する Ⓘ: The bridge collapsed suddenly. (*Sono hashi wa totsuzeñ kuzureta.*) その橋は突然崩れた. **2** (fall down) ta⌈ore⌉ru 倒れる Ⓥ: He collapsed on the job. (*Kare wa shigoto-chuu taoreta.*) 彼は仕事中倒れた. **3** (fail) tsu⌈bureru つぶれる Ⓥ: The project collapsed for lack of funds. (*Sono keekaku wa shikiñ-busoku de tsubureta.*) その計画は資金不足でつぶれた.
— *vt.* (fold together) ... o or⌈ita-

tamu …を折り畳む [C]: collapse an umbrella (*kasa o oritatamu*) 傘を折り畳む.

collar *n.* **1** (of a shirt) ka⌉raa カラー; (of a jacket) e⌈ri⌉ 襟.
2 (of a dog) ku⌈biwa 首輪.

colleague *n.* do⌈oryoo 同僚; na⌈kama⌉ 仲間: He is one of my colleagues. (*Kare wa watashi no dooryoo no hitori desu.*) 彼は私の同僚の一人です.

collect *vt.* ... o a⌈tsume⌉ru …を集める [V]; shu⌈ushuu suru 収集する [I]: collect garbage (*gomi o atsumeru*) ごみを集める / collect stamps (*kitte o shuushuu suru*) 切手を収集する.
— *vi.* a⌈tsuma⌉ru 集まる [C]: Crowds of people collected in front of the building. (*Oozee no hito ga biru no mae ni atsumatta.*) 大勢の人がビルの前に集まった.

collect call *n.* ko⌈rekuto ko⌉oru コレクトコール; ryo⌉okiñ ju⌈shiñniñbarai tsu⌉uwa 料金受信人払い通話: Make this a collect call. (*Kono deñwa wa korekuto kooru ni shite kudasai.*) この電話はコレクトコールにしてください.

collection *n.* **1** (collecting) shu⌈ushuu 収集; ka⌈ishuu 回収; cho⌈oshuu 徴収: garbage collection (*gomi no kaishuu*) ごみの回収 / tax collection (*zeekiñ no chooshuu*) 税金の徴収.
2 (something collected) ko⌈re⌉kushoñ コレクション; shu⌈ushuu⌉butsu 収集物.

college *n.* da⌈igaku 大学; ta⌈ñkada⌉igaku 単科大学: go to college (*daigaku ni kayou*) 大学に通う.
★ 'University' is also called '*daigaku*.'

collide *vi.* **1** (hit) sho⌈ototsu suru 衝突する [I]; bu⌈tsukaru ぶつかる [C]: The bus collided with a truck. (*Sono basu wa torakku to shoototsu shita.*) そのバスはトラックと衝突した.
2 (disagree) i⌈tchi shinai 一致しない; ku⌈ichigau 食い違う [C]: Their views collided over the matter. (*Kare-ra no ikeñ wa sono moñdai de itchi shinakatta.*) 彼らの意見はその問題で一致しなかった.

collision *n.* **1** (crash) sho⌈ototsu 衝突: an automobile collision (*jidoosha no shoototsu*) 自動車の衝突
2 (disagreement) fu⌈i⌉tchi 不一致: a collision of interests (*rigai no fuitchi*) 利害の不一致.

colloquial *adj.* ko⌈ogo no 口語の; ha⌈nashiko⌉toba no 話しことばの: colloquial language (*koogo*) 口語.

colonial *adj.* sho⌈kumi⌉ñchi no 植民地の: a colonial policy (*shokumiñchi seesaku*) 植民地政策.
— *n.* sho⌈kumi⌉ñchi no ju⌈uniñ 植民地の住人.

colony *n.* sho⌈kumi⌉ñchi 植民地; ka⌈itaku⌉chi 開拓地: establish a colony (*shokumiñchi o keñsetsu suru*) 植民地を建設する.

color *n.* i⌈ro⌉ 色; ka⌉raa カラー: Do you have this in another color? (*Kore no irochigai no mono wa arimasu ka?*) これの色違いの物はありますか. / 35 mm color film (*sañjuugo-miri no karaa firumu*) 35 mm のカラーフィルム.
— *vt.* ... ni i⌈ro⌉ o tsu⌈ke⌉ru …に色をつける [V]; i⌈ro⌉ o nu⌈ru 色を塗る [C]: The girl colored the sky blue. (*Sono oñna-no-ko wa sora o aoku nutta.*) その女の子は空を青く塗った.

colorful *adj.* shi⌈kisai ni to⌉ñda 色彩に富んだ; ha⌈na⌉yaka na 華やかな; ka⌉rafuru na カラフルな: colorful folk costumes (*hanayaka na miñzoku ishoo*) 華やかな民族衣装.

column *n.* **1** (of a newspaper) da⌉ñ 段; ko⌉ramu コラム; ra⌉ñ 欄: an advertisement column (*kookokurañ*) 広告欄.
2 (vertical row) ta⌉te no retsu 縦の列: add up the column of figures (*suuji no tate no retsu o gookee suru*) 数字の縦の列を合計する.
3 (pillar) e⌈ñchuu 円柱; ha⌈shira 柱.

comb *n.* ku⌈shi⌉ くし.
— *vt.* ... o ku⌈shi⌉ de to⌈ka⌉su …をくしでとかす [C]: comb one's hair

(*kami o kushi de tokasu*) 髪をくしでとかす.

combat *n.* se⌈ñtoo 戦闘; ka⌈kutoo 格闘.

— *vt.* ... to ta⌈takau …と戦う Ⓒ: combat the enemy (*teki to tatakau*) 敵と戦う.

combination *n.* ke⌈tsugoo 結合; ku⌈miawase 組み合わせ: a good combination of Japanese and Western styles (*Nihoñ-fuu to Seeyoo-fuu no umai kumiawase*) 日本風と西洋風のうまい組み合わせ.

combine *vt.* **1** (join) ... o ke⌈tsugoo suru …を結合する Ⓘ; ga⌈ppee suru 合併する Ⓘ: combine two businesses (*futatsu no jigyoo o gappee suru*) 二つの事業を合併する.

2 (mix) ... o ma⌈ze⌉ru …を混ぜる Ⓥ; (of chemistry) ka⌈goo saseru 化合させる Ⓥ: combine oxygen and hydrogen (*sañso to suiso o kagoo saseru*) 酸素と水素を化合させる.

— *vi.* **1** (unite) ke⌈tsugoo suru 結合する Ⓘ; ga⌈ppee suru 合併する Ⓘ: Our company combined with our competitor. (*Watashi-tachi no kaisha wa kyoosoo-aite to gappee shita.*) 私たちの会社は競争相手と合併した.

2 (of chemistry) ka⌈goo suru 化合する Ⓘ.

come *vi.* **1** (move toward the speaker) ku⌉ru 来る Ⓘ; ya⌈tte ku⌉ru やって来る Ⓘ: When you come to Tokyo, please telephone. (*Tookyoo ni kuru toki wa deñwa o kudasai.*) 東京に来るときは電話をください. / Please come to the hotel tomorrow. (*Ashita hoteru ni kite kudasai.*) あしたホテルに来てください. / He came to see me. (*Kare wa watashi ni ai ni yatte kita.*) 彼は私に会いにやって来た.

2 (move toward the person whom the speaker addresses) i⌈ku [yu⌈ku] 行く Ⓒ ★ '*Yuku*' is somewhat formal and old-fashioned; [polite] u⌈kagau 伺う Ⓒ: I'm coming now. (*Ima ikimasu.*) いま行きます. / I'll come to your hotel tomorrow afternoon. (*Asu no gogo hoteru ni o-ukagai shimasu.*) あすの午後ホテルにお伺いします.

3 (arrive) tsu⌉ku 着く Ⓒ; to⌈ochaku suru 到着する Ⓘ: At last they came to the town. (*Yatto kare-ra wa sono machi ni tsuita.*) やっと彼らはその町に着いた.

4 (reach) (... ni) na⌉ru (…に)なる Ⓒ; ta⌈ssuru 達する Ⓘ: The total comes to 5,000 yen. (*Gookee wa goseñ-eñ ni narimasu.*) 合計は5千円になります.

come back *vi.* mo⌈do⌉ru 戻る Ⓒ: I'll come back right away. (*Sugu modorimasu.*) すぐ戻ります.

come from ... *vt.* ... no shu⌈sshiñ da …の出身だ: He comes from Kyushu. (*Kare wa Kyuushuu shusshiñ desu.*) 彼は九州出身です.

come in *vi.* ha⌉iru 入る Ⓒ: Please come in. (*Doozo o-hairi kudasai.*) どうぞお入りください.

come into ... *vt.* ... e [ni] ha⌉itte kuru …へ[に]入って来る Ⓘ: He came into my room. (*Kare wa watashi no heya e haitte kita.*) 彼は私の部屋へ入って来た.

comedy *n.* ki⌉geki 喜劇.

comet *n.* su⌈isee 彗星; ho⌈oki⌉boshi ほうき星.

comfort *n.* **1** (consolation) na⌈gusame 慰め: His letter gave me great comfort. (*Kare no tegami wa watashi ni ooki-na nagusame to natta.*) 彼の手紙は私に大きな慰めとなった.

2 (freedom from worries) ka⌈iteki 快適; a⌉ñraku 安楽: live in comfort (*añraku ni kurasu*) 安楽に暮らす.

— *vt.* ... o na⌈gusame⌉ru …を慰める Ⓥ: I comforted the crying girl. (*Watashi wa naite iru oñna-no-ko o nagusameta.*) 私は泣いている女の子を慰めた.

comfortable *adj.* **1** (giving comfort) ka⌈iteki na 快適な; ko⌈kochi yo⌉i 心地よい: I had a comfortable journey. (*Watashi wa kaiteki na tabi o shita.*) 私は快適な旅をした.

2 (at ease) ki⌈raku na 気楽な; ku-

C

ˈtsuroˈida くつろいだ: Please make yourself comfortable. (*Doozo o-raku ni.*) どうぞお楽に.

comic *adj.* kiˈgeki no 喜劇の: a comic picture (*kigeki-eega*) 喜劇映画.

— *n.* **1** (comedian) kiˈgeki-haˈi-yuu 喜劇俳優.

2 (in a newspaper) maˈñgaˈrañ 漫画欄.

coming *n.* kuˈru koˈtoˈ 来ること; toˈorai 到来: wait for the coming of spring (*haru ga kuru no o ma-tsu*) 春が来るのを待つ.

— *adj.* tsuˈgiˈ no 次の; koˈñdo no 今度の: the coming generation (*tsugi no sedai*) 次の世代 / the coming summer (*koñdo no natsu*) 今度の夏.

command *vt.* **1** (give an order) ... ni (... to) meˈejiru …に(…と)命じる Ⓥ: He commanded us to halt. (*Kare wa watashi-tachi ni tomare to meejita.*) 彼は私たちに止まれと命じた.

2 (have authority over) ... o shiˈkiˈ suru …を指揮する Ⓘ; shiˈhai suru 支配する Ⓘ: The captain commands his ship. (*Señchoo wa fune o shiki suru.*) 船長は船を指揮する.

— *n.* **1** (order) meˈeree 命令; saˈshizu 指図: give a command (*meeree o kudasu*) 命令を下す / obey a command (*meeree ni shita-gau*) 命令に従う.

2 (ability to control) jiˈyuˈu ni tsu-ˈkaeru chikara 自由に使える力: She has a good command of French. (*Kanojo wa Furañsugo o jiyuu ni tsukaeru.*) 彼女はフランス語を自由に使える.

commander *n.* shiˈkiˈsha 指揮者; shiˈreˈekañ 司令官.

commemoration *n.* kiˈneñ 記念; shuˈkuga 祝賀.

commemorative *adj.* kiˈneñ no 記念の: a commemorative stamp (*kineñ-kitte*) 記念切手.

commence *vt.* ... o kaˈishi suru …を開始する Ⓘ; haˈjimeru 始める Ⓥ: commence an investigation (*choo-sa o kaishi suru*) 調査を開始する.

comment *n.* **1** (remark) roˈñpyoo 論評; iˈkeñ 意見; hiˈhyoo 批評: He gave favorable comments on the book. (*Kare wa sono hoñ ni tsuite kooi-teki na hihyoo o shita.*) 彼はその本について好意的な批評をした.

2 (explanation) kaˈisetsu 解説; se-ˈtsumee 説明.

— *vi.* roˈñpyoo suru 論評する Ⓘ; hiˈhyoo suru 批評する Ⓘ: comment on a new novel (*shiñkañ no shoose-tsu o hihyoo suru*) 新刊の小説を批評する.

commerce *n.* shoˈogyoo 商業; (trade) boˈoeki 貿易: foreign commerce (*gaikoku-booeki*) 外国貿易.

commercial *adj.* **1** (of commerce) shoˈogyoo no 商業の; boˈo-eki no 貿易の: a commercial firm (*shoosha*) 商社.

2 (profit-making) eˈeri no 営利の; shoˈogyoo-teki na 商業的な: a commercial enterprise (*eeri jigyoo*) 営利事業.

— *n.* koˈmaˈasharu コマーシャル; koˈokoku-hoˈosoo 広告放送.

commission *n.* **1** (money) te-ˈsuˈuryoo 手数料; buˈai 歩合: receive a commission of 10 % on sales (*uriage no jup-paaseñto no tesuuryoo o morau*) 売上の 10 パーセントの手数料をもらう.

2 (group of persons) iˈiˈñkai 委員会: a commission of inquiry (*choosa iiñkai*) 調査委員会.

3 (giving authority) iˈniñ 委任; iˈtaku 委託: commission of powers (*keñgeñ no iniñ*) 権限の委任.

commit *vt.* **1** (perform) ... o oˈkaˈsu …を犯す Ⓒ; oˈkonau 行う Ⓒ: commit a crime (*hañzai o okasu*) 犯罪を犯す.

2 (hand over) ... o hiˈkiwataˈsu …を引き渡す Ⓒ; iˈtaku suru 委託する Ⓘ: commit a girl to her uncle (*shoojo o oji ni azukeru*) 少女をおじに預ける.

commitment *n.* (promise) yaˈkusoku 約束; ko⌐oyaku 公約: I made a commitment to help him. (*Watashi wa kare o eñjo suru to yakusoku shita.*) 私は彼を援助すると約束した.

committee *n.* i⌐i⌐ñkai 委員会: a member of a committee (*iiñkai no iiñ*) 委員会の委員.

common *adj.* **1** (usual) fu⌐tsuu no 普通の; yo⌐ku aru よくある: a common mistake (*yoku aru machigai*) よくある間違い.

2 (belonging equally to) kyo⌐otsuu no 共通の; kyo⌐odoo no 共同の: common interests (*kyootsuu no rigai*) 共通の利害.

3 (public) ko⌐okyoo no 公共の; ko⌐oshuu no 公衆の: common land (*kookyoo no tochi*) 公共の土地.

commonly *adv.* i⌐ppañ ni 一般に; fu⌐tsuu wa 普通は: Children commonly like video games. (*Kodomotachi wa ippañ ni terebi geemu ga suki da.*) 子どもたちは一般にテレビゲームが好きだ.

commonplace *adj.* a⌐rifu⌐reta ありふれた; a⌐rifu⌐rete iru ありふれている; he⌐eboñ na 平凡な: a commonplace novel (*heeboñ na shoosetsu*) 平凡な小説.

common sense *n.* jo⌐oshiki 常識; ryo⌐oshiki 良識: He has no common sense. (*Kare wa jooshiki ga nai.*) 彼は常識がない.

communicate *vt.* ... o tsu⌐taeru ...を伝える [V]; shi⌐raseru 知らせる [V]: I will communicate the answer to you. (*Henji wa anata ni tsutaemasu.*) 返事はあなたに伝えます.

— *vi.* re⌐ñraku suru 連絡する [I]: communicate by telephone (*deñwa de reñraku suru*) 電話で連絡する.

communication *n.* **1** (conveying information) de⌐ñtatsu 伝達; i⌐shi no so⌐tsuu 意思の疎通; ko⌐myunike⌐eshoñ コミュニケーション: mass communication (*taishuu deñtatsu*) 大衆伝達, (*masukomi*) マスコミ.

2 (means of communicating) tsu⌐ushiñ (shu⌐dañ) 通信(手段); ko⌐otsuu ki⌐kañ 交通機関: All communication was broken by the storm. (*Arashi no tame subete no tsuushiñ wa todaeta.*) 嵐のためすべての通信は途絶えた.

communist *n.* kyo⌐osañ-shugi⌐sha 共産主義者.

community *n.* **1** (group of people) kyo⌐odoo-sha⌐kai 共同社会; chi⌐iki-sha⌐kai 地域社会: the artists' community (*geejutsuka no shakai*) 芸術家の社会.

2 (the public in general) i⌐ppañ sha⌐kai 一般社会; ko⌐oshuu 公衆: the welfare of the community (*shakai fukushi*) 社会福祉.

commute *vi.* tsu⌐ukiñ suru 通勤する [I]: I commute between Yokohama and Tokyo. (*Watashi wa Yokohama-Tookyoo kañ o tsuukiñ shite imasu.*) 私は横浜—東京間を通勤しています.

compact *adj.* **1** (packed tightly) gi⌐sshi⌐ri tsu⌐ma⌐tta ぎっしり詰まった; mi⌐tsu na 密な: a compact head of cabbage (*gisshiri maita kyabetsu no tama*) ぎっしり巻いたキャベツの玉.

2 (fitted neatly) ko⌐jiñma⌐ri shita [shite iru] こじんまりした[している]; ko⌐ñpakuto na コンパクトな: a compact camera (*koñpakuto kamera*) コンパクトカメラ.

3 (brief) ka⌐ñketsu na 簡潔な: write in a compact style (*kañketsu ni kaku*) 簡潔に書く.

companion *n.* na⌐kama⌐ 仲間; to⌐modachi 友達: He is one of my companions on the journey. (*Kare wa watashi no tabi no nakama no hitori desu.*) 彼は私の旅の仲間の一人です.

company *n.* **1** (business organization) ka⌐isha 会社: What does your company manufacture? (*Anata no kaisha wa nani o tsukutte imasu ka?*) あなたの会社は何を作っていますか. / a trading company (*shooji-gaisha*) 商事会社 / a company employee (*kaishaiñ*) 会社員.

2 (companionship) ko⌈osai 交際; do⌈oseki 同席; do⌈okoo 同行: I was glad to have her company. (*Kanojo to dooseki dekite ureshikatta.*) 彼女と同席できてうれしかった.
3 (friends) na⌈kama⌉ 仲間; to⌈modachi 友達: keep good company (*yoi nakama to tsukiau*) 良い仲間とつき合う.
4 (guests) ra⌈ikyaku 来客: I'm expecting company this evening. (*Koñbañ o-kyaku ga kuru koto ni natte imasu.*) 今晩お客が来ることになっています.
5 (group of people) da⌈ñtai 団体; i⌈kkoo 一行: a theatrical company (*gekidañ*) 劇団.

comparative *adj.* **1** (making a comparison) hi⌈kaku no 比較の: a comparative study of Japanese and American culture (*Nihoñ to Amerika no buñka no hikaku-keñkyuu*) 日本とアメリカの文化の比較研究.
2 (relative) hi⌈kaku-teki 比較的; ka⌉nari no かなりの: The experiment was a comparative success. (*Jikkeñ wa kanari umaku itta.*) 実験はかなりうまくいった.

comparatively *adv.* hi⌈kaku-teki 比較的; ka⌉nari かなり; wa⌈riai (ni) 割合(に): I found the task comparatively easy. (*Sono shigoto wa wariai ni yasashikatta.*) その仕事は割合にやさしかった.

compare *vt.* **1** (examine) ... o hi⌈kaku suru …を比較する [I]; ku⌈raberu 比べる [V]: compare the two pictures (*futatsu no e o hikaku suru*) 二つの絵を比較する.
2 (describe as being the same) ... o (... ni) ta⌈toe⌉ru …を(…に)たとえる [V]: Life is often compared to a voyage. (*Jiñsee wa yoku kookai ni tatoerareru.*) 人生はよく航海にたとえられる.

comparison *n.* hi⌈kaku 比較; ta⌈ishoo 対照: make a comparison between the original and the translation (*geñbuñ to hoñyaku o hikaku shite miru*) 原文と翻訳を比較してみる.

compartment *n.* **1** (separate division) shi⌈kiri 仕切り; ku⌈kaku 区画: The drawer is divided into compartments. (*Hikidashi wa shikiri de kugirarete imasu.*) 引き出しは仕切りで区切られています.
2 (of a train) ko⌈shitsu 個室; ko⌈ñpa⌉atomeñto コンパートメント.

compass *n.* **1** (instrument for showing direction) ji⌉shaku 磁石; ko⌉ñpasu コンパス.
2 (instrument for drawing circles) ko⌉ñpasu コンパス: draw a circle with compasses (*koñpasu de eñ o egaku*) コンパスで円を描く.

compel *vt.* mu⌉ri ni ⟨verb⟩-(sa)seru 無理に…(さ)せる [V]: I was compelled to confess. (*Watashi wa muri ni hakujoo saserareta.*) 私は無理に白状させられた.

compensate *vt.* ... ni ho⌈shoo o suru …に補償をする [I]: The company compensated him for his injury. (*Kaisha wa kare ni shoogai hoshoo o shita.*) 会社は彼に傷害補償をした.

compensation *n.* ho⌈shoo 補償; ba⌈ishoo 賠償: They made compensation for the damage. (*Kare-ra wa sono soñgai no hoshoo o shita.*) 彼らはその損害の補償をした.

compete *vi.* kyo⌈osoo suru 競争する [I]; ki⌈so⌉u 競う [C]: We competed with each other for the prize. (*Watashi-tachi wa shoo o mezashite tagai ni kyoosoo shita.*) 私たちは賞をめざして互いに競争した.

competence *n.* no⌉oryoku 能力; te⌈kisee 適性: I doubt his competence for the task. (*Sono shigoto ni taisuru kare no nooryoku wa gimoñ da.*) その仕事に対する彼の能力は疑問だ.

competent *adj.* no⌉oryoku no [ga] a⌉ru 能力の[が]ある; yu⌈unoo na 有能な: She is competent as a teacher. (*Kanojo wa kyooshi to shite yuunoo da.*) 彼女は教師として有能だ.

competition *n.* **1** (rivalry) kyo⌈o-

soo 競争: They are in competition with each other. (*Kare-ra wa o-tagai ni kyoosoo shite iru.*) 彼らはお互いに競争している.
2 (contest) shi⌈ai 試合; kyo⌉ogi 競技; ko⌉ñtesuto コンテスト.

competitive *adj.* kyo⌈osoo no 競争の; kyo⌈osoo ni taerare⌉ru 競争に耐えられる: a competitive society (*kyoosoo shakai*) 競争社会 / a competitive price (*kyoosoo ni taerare-ru kakaku*) 競争に耐えられる価格.

competitor *n.* kyo⌈oso⌉osha 競争者; kyo⌈osoo-a⌉ite 競争相手: business competitors (*shoobai no kyoo-soo-aite*) 商売の競争相手.

complain *vi.* **1** (state one's displeasure) fu⌈hee [mo⌉ñku] o i⌈u 不平[文句]を言う Ⓒ; bu⌉tsubutsu i⌈u ぶつぶつ言う Ⓒ: He is always complaining. (*Kare wa itsu-mo fuhee o itte iru.*) 彼はいつも不平を言っている.
2 (make a report) (... ni)(... o) u⌈t-ta⌉eru (…に)(…を)訴える Ⓥ: complain to the police about the noise (*keesatsu ni soo-oñ no koto o uttaeru*) 警察に騒音のことを訴える.
— *vt.* ... to fu⌈hee o iu …と不平を言う Ⓒ; ko⌈bo⌉su こぼす Ⓒ: He complains that he has a small income. (*Kare wa shuunyuu ga sukunai to koboshite iru.*) 彼は収入が少ないとこぼしている.

complaint *n.* fu⌈hee 不平; fu⌈mañ 不満; ku⌈joo 苦情: He made a complaint about the poor service at the hotel. (*Kare wa sono hoteru no saabisu ga warui koto ni tsuite kujoo o itta.*) 彼はそのホテルのサービスが悪いことについて苦情を言った.

complete *adj.* **1** (whole) ka⌉ñbi shita [shite iru] 完備した[している]; ze⌉ñbu no 全部の: This room is complete with furniture. (*Kono heya wa kagu ga kañbi shite iru.*) この部屋は家具が完備している.
2 (perfect) ka⌈ñzeñ na 完全な: a complete victory (*kañzeñ na shoori*) 完全な勝利.
3 (finished) ka⌈ñsee shita [shite iru] 完成した[している]: My picture will soon be complete. (*Watashi no e wa moo sugu kañsee shimasu.*) 私の絵はもうすぐ完成します.
— *vt.* ... o ka⌈ñsee suru [saseru] …を完成する Ⓘ [させる Ⓥ]: The bridge is now completed. (*Hashi wa moo kañsee shimashita.*) 橋はもう完成しました.

completely *adv.* ka⌈ñzeñ ni 完全に; ma⌈ttaku まったく; su⌈kka⌉ri すっかり: I completely forgot to thank him. (*Kare ni o-ree o iu no o sukkari wasurete shimatta.*) 彼にお礼を言うのをすっかり忘れてしまった.

completion *n.* ka⌈ñsee 完成; ka⌈ñ-ryoo 完了: I will pay you on completion of the work. (*Shigoto ga kañryoo shitara o-shiharai shimasu.*) 仕事が完了したらお支払いします.

complex *adj.* fu⌈kuzatsu na 複雑な: a complex problem (*fukuzatsu na moñdai*) 複雑な問題.
— *n.* (abnormal mental state) ko⌈ñpure⌉kkusu コンプレックス: an inferiority complex (*rettookañ*) 劣等感.

complicate *vt.* ... o fu⌈kuzatsu ni suru …を複雑にする Ⓘ; me⌈ñdo⌉o ni suru 面倒にする Ⓘ: That complicates matters. (*Soo naru to koto ga meñdoo ni naru.*) そうなると事が面倒になる.

complicated *adj.* fu⌈kuzatsu na 複雑な; ko⌈miitta 込み入った: a complicated machine (*fukuzatsu na kikai*) 複雑な機械.

compliment *n.* **1** (praise) ho⌈me-ko⌉toba ほめことば; sa⌉ñji 賛辞: His achievement deserves a compliment. (*Kare no gyooseki wa sañji ni atai suru.*) 彼の業績は賛辞に値する.
2 (flattery) o⌈seji お世辞: He is always paying her compliments. (*Kare wa itsu-mo kanojo ni oseji o itte iru.*) 彼はいつも彼女にお世辞を言っている.

comply *vi.* (... ni) o⌈ojiru (…に)応じる Ⓥ; shi⌈tagau 従う Ⓒ: We complied with her request. (*Watashi-*

tachi wa kanojo no yookyuu ni oojita.) 私たちは彼女の要求に応じた.

component *n.* ko⌈osee-bu⌉buñ 構成部分; bu⌈hiñ 部品: the components of a camera (*kamera no buhiñ*) カメラの部品.

compose *vt.* **1** (write) ... o tsu⌈ku⌉ru 作る Ⓒ; (of music) sa⌈kkyoku suru 作曲する Ⓘ: compose a poem (*shi o tsukuru*) 詩を作る / compose a song (*uta o sakkyoku suru*) 歌を作曲する.
2 (make up) ... o ko⌈osee suru ...を構成する Ⓘ; ku⌈mitate⌉ru 組み立てる Ⓥ: Six members compose the committee. (*Roku-niñ ga sono iiñkai o koosee shite imasu.*) 6人がその委員会を構成しています.
3 (calm) ... o shi⌈zume⌉ru ...を静める Ⓥ: compose one's mind (*kokoro o shizumeru*) 心を静める.

composer *n.* (of music) sa⌈kkyokuka 作曲家.

composition *n.* **1** (writing) sa⌈kubuñ 作文; (music) sa⌈kkyoku 作曲: I wrote a short composition in Japanese. (*Watashi wa Nihoñgo de mijikai sakubuñ o kaita.*) 私は日本語で短い作文を書いた.
2 (arrangement) ko⌈osee 構成; ko⌈ozoo 構造: the composition of a committee (*iiñkai no koosee*) 委員会の構成.

compound *n.* **1** (mixture) go⌈ose⌉ebutsu 合成物; ko⌈ñgo⌉obutsu 混合物; (word) fu⌈kugoogo 複合語.
2 (chemical substance) ka⌈go⌉obutsu 化合物: a compound of carbon and oxygen (*tañso to sañso no kagoobutsu*) 炭素と酸素の化合物.

compress *vt.* ... o a⌈sshuku suru ...を圧縮する Ⓘ: compress air (*kuuki o asshuku suru*) 空気を圧縮する.

comprise *vt.* (consist of) ... kara na⌉ru ...から成る Ⓒ: The team comprises nine members. (*Sono chiimu wa kyuu-niñ kara naru.*) そのチームは9人から成る.

compromise *n.* da⌈kyoo 妥協; a⌈yumiyori 歩み寄り: arrive at a compromise (*dakyoo ni tassuru*) 妥協に達する.
— *vi.* da⌈kyoo suru 妥協する Ⓘ; a⌈yumiyoru 歩み寄る Ⓒ: I compromised with him on the matter. (*Watashi wa sono keñ de kare to dakyoo shita.*) 私はその件で彼と妥協した.

compulsory *adj.* kyo⌈osee-teki na 強制的な; gi⌈mu-teki na 義務的な: compulsory education (*gimukyooiku*) 義務教育.

computer *n.* ko⌈ñpyu⌉utaa コンピューター; de⌈ñshi-keesa⌉ñki 電子計算機.

comrade *n.* na⌈kama⌉ 仲間; do⌈oryoo 同僚: They are my comrades at school. (*Kare-ra wa watashi no gakkoo no nakama desu.*) 彼らは私の学校の仲間です.

conceal *vt.* ... o ka⌈ku⌉su ...を隠す Ⓒ: He concealed the truth from me. (*Kare wa sono shiñsoo o watashi ni kakushite ita.*) 彼はその真相を私に隠していた.

concede *vt.* **1** (admit) ... o mi⌈tomeru ...を認める Ⓥ: I concede that I am wrong. (*Watashi wa jibuñ ga machigatte iru koto o mitomemasu.*) 私は自分が間違っていることを認めます.
2 (yield) ... o yu⌈zuru ...を譲る Ⓒ: I cannot concede my position in the matter. (*Sono koto ni tsuite wa watashi wa watashi no tachiba o yuzuremaseñ.*) そのことについては私は私の立場を譲れません.

conceit *n.* u⌈nubore うぬぼれ; ji⌈fu⌉shiñ 自負心: He is full of conceit. (*Kare wa unubore ga tsuyoi.*) 彼はうぬぼれが強い.

conceive *vt.* **1** (of feelings) ... o i⌈da⌉ku ...を抱く Ⓒ: He conceived a hatred for them. (*Kare wa kare-ra ni nikushimi o idaita.*) 彼は彼らに憎しみを抱いた.
2 (of a plan) ... o o⌈moitsu⌉ku ...を思いつく Ⓒ: He conceived a good idea. (*Kare wa ii kañgae o omoitsuita.*) 彼はいい考えを思いついた.

concentrate *vt.* **1** (of attention) (... ni) ... o shu⌈uchuu suru (…に)…を集中する [I]: You must concentrate your attention on your work. (*Shigoto ni chuui o shuuchuu shinakereba ikemaseñ.*) 仕事に注意を集中しなければいけません.
2 (of people) (... ni) ... o a⌈tsume⌉ru (…に)…を集める [V]: concentrate troops at one place (*guñtai o ikkasho ni atsumeru*) 軍隊を一か所に集める.
— *vi.* 1 (come together) (... ni) shu⌈uchuu suru …に集中する [I]: People concentrate in large cities. (*Jiñkoo wa dai-toshi ni shuuchuu suru.*) 人口は大都市に集中する.
2 (pay attention) (... ni) shu⌈uchuu suru (…に)集中する [I]: It was quiet, so I could concentrate on my studies. (*Shizuka datta no de watashi wa beñkyoo ni shuuchuu dekita.*) 静かだったので私は勉強に集中できた.

concentration *n.* **1** (of attention) shu⌈uchu⌉uryoku 集中力: Calligraphy requires a great deal of concentration. (*Shodoo wa hijoo ni shuuchuu-ryoku o hitsuyoo to suru.*) 書道は非常に集中力を必要とする.
2 (of things, people) shu⌈uchuu 集中: The concentration of businesses in Tokyo has become a problem. (*Kigyoo no Tookyoo e no shuuchuu ga moñdai ni natte iru.*) 企業の東京への集中が問題になっている.

concept *n.* ga⌉ineñ 概念; ka⌉ñneñ 観念.

conception *n.* ga⌉ineñ 概念; ni⌈ñshiki 認識: He has no conception of the problem. (*Kare wa sono moñdai ni tsuite niñshiki ga nai.*) 彼はその問題について認識がない.

concern *vt.* **1** (have to do with) ... ni ka⌈ñkee suru …に関係する [I]: The matter does not concern me. (*Sono koto wa watashi ni wa kañkee arimaseñ.*) そのことは私には関係ありません.
2 (worry) ... o shi⌈ñpai saseru …を心配させる [V].
To whom it may concern *adv.* ka⌈ñkee ka⌉kui dono 関係各位殿.
— *n.* 1 (anxiety) shi⌈ñpai 心配; ke⌈neñ 懸念: I thank you for your concern. (*Go-shiñpai arigatoo gozaimasu.*) ご心配ありがとうございます.
2 (business) ka⌈ñshi⌉ñji 関心事; ko⌈to⌉ こと: It's no concern of mine. (*Sore wa watashi no shitta koto de wa nai.*) それは私の知ったことではない.
3 (involvement) ka⌈ñkee 関係; ka⌈kawari かかわり: I have no concern in this matter. (*Watashi wa kono koto ni kañkee ga arimaseñ.*) 私はこのことに関係がありません.

concerned *adj.* **1** (worried) shi⌈ñpai shite (iru) 心配して(いる): I'm concerned about my son's future. (*Watashi wa musuko no shoorai ga shiñpai desu.*) 私は息子の将来が心配です.
2 (involved) ka⌈ñkee shite (iru) 関係して(いる): the parties concerned (*kañkeesha*) 関係者.
as far as ... be concerned *adv.* ... ni ka⌈ñsu⌉ru ka⌉giri …に関する限り: As far as I'm concerned, I am against the proposal. (*Watashi ni kañsuru kagiri sono teeañ ni wa hañtai desu.*) 私に関する限りその提案には反対です.

concerning *prep.* ... ni ka⌉ñshite …に関して: If you have any information concerning this matter, please contact us. (*Kono keñ ni kañshite joohoo o o-mochi deshitara go-reñraku kudasai.*) この件に関して情報をお持ちでしたらご連絡ください.

concert *n.* ko⌉ñsaato コンサート; o⌈ñga⌉kukai 音楽会: give a concert (*oñgakukai o hiraku*) 音楽会を開く.

conclude *vt.* **1** (decide) ... to ke⌈tsuroñ o kudasu …と結論を下す [C]; da⌈ñtee suru 断定する [I]: They concluded that his plan was best. (*Kare-ra wa kare no añ ga ichibañ*

yoi to ketsuroñ o kudashita.) 彼らは彼の案がいちばんよいと結論を下した.
2 (finish) ... o o⌈eru を終える Ⓥ: He concluded his speech by thanking his host. (*Kare wa hosuto ni o-ree o nobete supiichi o oeta.*) 彼はホストにお礼を述べてスピーチを終えた.
3 (arrange) ... o mu⌈subu ...を結ぶ Ⓒ: The two countries concluded a peace treaty. (*Ryookoku wa hee-wa-jooyaku o musuñda.*) 両国は平和条約を結んだ.
— *vi.* o⌈waru 終わる Ⓒ: The graduation ceremony concluded with the school song. (*Sotsugyoo-shiki wa kooka de owatta.*) 卒業式は校歌で終わった.

conclusion *n.* **1** (decision) ke⌈tsuroñ 結論: come to a conclusion (*ketsuroñ ni tassuru*) 結論に達する.
2 (end) o⌈wari 終わり: the conclusion of a speech (*eñzetsu no owari*) 演説の終わり.
3 (arrangement) te⌈eketsu 締結: the conclusion of a treaty (*jooyaku no teeketsu*) 条約の締結.

concrete[1] *n.* (building material) ko⌈ñkuri⌉ito コンクリート: The building is built of concrete. (*Sono biru wa koñkuriito de dekite iru.*) そのビルはコンクリートでできている.
— *adj.* ko⌈ñkuri⌉ito no コンクリートの: a concrete building (*koñkuriito no biru*) コンクリートのビル.

concrete[2] *adj.* gu⌈tai-teki na 具体的な: a concrete example (*gutai-teki na jitsuree*) 具体的な実例.

condemn *vt.* **1** (blame) ... o hi⌉-nañ suru ...を非難する Ⓘ; se⌈me⌉ru 責める Ⓥ: Everyone condemns child abuse. (*Dare mo ga kodomo no gyakutai o hinañ suru.*) だれもが子どもの虐待を非難する.
2 (sentence) ... o se⌈ñkoku suru ...を宣告する Ⓘ: He was condemned to life in prison. (*Kare wa shuu-shiñkee o señkoku sareta.*) 彼は終身刑を宣告された.

condense *vt.* **1** (of liquid) ... o ko⌉ku suru ...を濃くする Ⓘ; no⌈o-shuku suru 濃縮する Ⓘ: condense orange juice (*oreñji juusu o noo-shuku suru*) オレンジジュースを濃縮する.
2 (of writing) ... o yo⌈oyaku suru ...を要約する Ⓘ: condense a book for children (*kodomo no tame ni hoñ o yooyaku suru*) 子どものために本を要約する.
— *vi.* gyo⌈oshuku suru 凝縮する Ⓘ: Steam condenses into water when it cools. (*Suijooki wa hieru to gyooshuku shite mizu ni naru.*) 水蒸気は冷えると凝縮して水になる.

condition *n.* **1** (circumstances) jo⌈okyoo 状況; ji⌈joo 事情: housing conditions in Kobe (*Koobe no juu-taku jijoo*) 神戸の住宅事情.
2 (state) jo⌈otai 状態; ko⌈ñdi⌉shoñ コンディション: He's in no condition to travel. (*Kare wa ryokoo dekiru jootai de wa nai.*) 彼は旅行できる状態ではない. / My car is in good condition. (*Watashi no kuruma wa koñdishoñ ga ii.*) 私の車はコンディションがいい.
3 (requirement) jo⌈oke⌉ñ 条件: the conditions of employment (*koyoo jookeñ*) 雇用条件.
— *vt.* ... o sa⌉yuu suru ...を左右する Ⓘ; ke⌈ttee suru 決定する Ⓘ: Our success is conditioned by health. (*Seekoo wa keñkoo ni sayuu sa-reru.*) 成功は健康に左右される.

conditional *adj.* jo⌈okeñ tsuki no 条件付きの; za⌈ñtee-teki na 暫定的な: conditional agreements (*jookeñ tsuki no kyootee*) 条件付きの協定.

conduct *vt.* **1** (carry out) ... o o⌈konau ...を行う Ⓒ; sho⌉ri suru 処理する Ⓘ: conduct negotiations (*kooshoo o suru*) 交渉をする / conduct business affairs (*gyoomu o shori suru*) 業務を処理する.
2 (direct) ... o shi⌈ki⌉ suru ...を指揮する Ⓘ: conduct an orchestra (*ooke-sutora o shiki suru*) オーケストラを指揮する.
3 (guide) ... o a⌈ñna⌉i suru ...を案内する Ⓘ; mi⌈chibi⌉ku 導く Ⓒ: She

conducted the passenger to his seat. (*Kanojo wa jookyaku o seki ni añnai shita.*) 彼女は乗客を席に案内した.
— *n.* **1** (behavior) o⌐konai 行い; ko⌝oi 行為: The teacher praised the child's conduct. (*Señsee wa sono kodomo no okonai o hometa.*) 先生はその子どもの行いをほめた.
2 (management) u⌐ñee 運営; ka⌝ñri 管理: the conduct of a business (*jigyoo no uñee*) 事業の運営.

conductor *n.* **1** (of an orchestra) shi⌐ki⌝sha 指揮者.
2 (of a bus, train) sha⌐shoo 車掌.
3 (guide) a⌐ñnainiñ 案内人: a tour conductor (*teñjooiñ*) 添乗員.

cone *n.* (ice-cream cone) a⌐isu-kuriimu-ko⌝oñ アイスクリームコーン; so⌐futo-kuri⌝imu ソフトクリーム.

confer *vi.* so⌐odañ suru 相談する Ⓘ; u⌐chiawaseru 打ち合わせる Ⓥ: confer with a lawyer (*beñgoshi to soodañ suru*) 弁護士と相談する.

conference *n.* (meeting) ka⌝igi 会議: hold a conference (*kaigi o hiraku*) 会議を開く / Mr. Yamada is in conference now. (*Yamada-sañ wa ima kaigi-chuu desu.*) 山田さんは今会議中です.

confess *vt.* ... o ji⌐haku suru …を自白する Ⓘ; ko⌐kuhaku suru 告白する Ⓘ: He confessed his guilt. (*Kare wa jibuñ no tsumi o kokuhaku shita.*) 彼は自分の罪を告白した.
— *vi.* ji⌐haku suru 自白する Ⓘ; ha⌝kujoo suru 白状する Ⓘ: He refused to confess. (*Kare wa hakujoo shiyoo to shinakatta.*) 彼は白状しようとしなかった.

confession *n.* ji⌐haku 自白; ko⌐kuhaku 告白: make a confession (*jihaku suru*) 自白する.

confide *vt.* ... o u⌐chiakeru …を打ち明ける Ⓥ: He confided his secret to his friend. (*Kare wa tomodachi ni himitsu o uchiaketa.*) 彼は友達に秘密を打ち明けた.
— *vi.* hi⌐mitsu o u⌐chiakeru 秘密を打ち明ける Ⓥ: Teenagers confide in friends rather than in parents. (*Tiiñeejaa wa ryooshiñ yori mo tomodachi ni himitsu o uchiakeru.*) ティーンエージャーは両親よりも友達に秘密を打ち明ける.

confidence *n.* **1** (self-assurance) ji⌐shiñ 自信: I have confidence in myself. (*Watashi wa jibuñ ni jishiñ ga aru.*) 私は自分に自信がある.
2 (belief) ka⌐kushiñ 確信: I have confidence that he will succeed. (*Watashi wa kare ga seekoo suru to iu kakushiñ o motte iru.*) 私は彼が成功するという確信を持っている.
3 (trust) shi⌐ñrai 信頼; shi⌐ñniñ 信任: He betrayed my confidence in him. (*Kare wa watashi no shiñrai o uragitta.*) 彼は私の信頼を裏切った.

confident *adj.* **1** (sure) ka⌐kushiñ shite (iru) 確信して(いる): He is confident that he will pass the examination. (*Kare wa shikeñ ni ukaru to kakushiñ shite iru.*) 彼は試験に受かると確信している.
2 (self-assured) ji⌐shiñ o mo⌝tta [mo⌝tte iru] 自信を持った[持っている]: Be confident in yourself. (*Jibuñ ni jishiñ o mochi nasai.*) 自分に自信を持ちなさい.

confidential *adj.* hi⌐mitsu no 秘密の; na⌐inai no 内々の: This information is confidential. (*Kono joohoo wa himitsu desu.*) この情報は秘密です.

confine *vt.* **1** (restrict) ... o ka⌐gi⌝ru …を限る Ⓒ; to⌐dome⌝ru とどめる Ⓥ: confine a talk to five minutes (*hanashi o go-fuñ ni todomeru*) 話を5分にとどめる.
2 (shut up) ... o to⌐jikome⌝ru …を閉じ込める Ⓥ; ka⌐ñkiñ suru 監禁する Ⓘ: We were confined to the cottage by snow. (*Watashi-tachi wa yuki de yamagoya ni tojikomerareta.*) 私たちは雪で山小屋に閉じ込められた.

confirm *vt.* **1** (verify) ... o ta⌐shikame⌝ru …を確かめる Ⓥ; (make sure) ka⌐kuniñ suru 確認する Ⓘ: confirm a rumor (*uwasa o tashikameru*) うわさを確かめる / The reservation was confirmed at Narita. (*Yoyaku wa Narita de kakuniñ shite arimasu.*) 予約は成田で確認してあります.

2 (strengthen) ... o tsuʳyomeˡru ... を強める V; kaʳtameru 固める V: confirm one's determination (*ketsui o katameru*) 決意を固める.

confirmation *n.* kaʳkuniñ 確認; kaʳkushoo 確証: the confirmation of news (*nyuusu no kakuniñ*) ニュースの確認.

conflict *n.* **1** (disagreement) shoʳototsu 衝突; fuʳiˡtchi 不一致: a conflict of opinions (*ikeñ no shoototsu*) 意見の衝突.

2 (fight) aʳrasoi 争い; taʳtakai 戦い: a conflict between two nations (*ni-koku-kañ no arasoi*) 2国間の争い.

— *vi.* iʳtchi shinai 一致しない; muʳjuñ suru 矛盾する I: Their interests conflicted with each other. (*Kare-ra no rigai wa o-tagai ni itchi shinakatta.*) 彼らの利害はお互いに一致しなかった.

conform *vi.* (... ni) shiʳtagau (…に)従う C: We must conform to rules. (*Wareware wa kisoku ni shitagawanakereba naranai.*) われわれは規則に従わなければならない.

confront *vt.* ... o (... ni) choʳkumeñ saseru …を(…に)直面させる V: They are confronted with difficulties. (*Kare-ra wa koñnañ ni chokumeñ shite iru.*) 彼らは困難に直面している.

confuse *vt.* **1** (bewilder) ... o toʳowaku saseru …を当惑させる V; maʳgotsukaseru まごつかせる V: The unexpected questions confused me. (*Yoki shinai shitsumoñ de magotsuite shimatta.*) 予期しない質問でまごついてしまった.

2 (mistake) ... o koʳñdoo suru …を混同する I; toʳrichigaeru 取り違える V: I confused their names. (*Watashi wa kare-ra no namae o torichigaeta.*) 私は彼らの名前を取り違えた.

confused *adj.* **1** (bewildered) toʳowaku shita [shite iru] 当惑した[している]: He looked confused. (*Kare wa toowaku shita kao o shite ita.*) 彼は当惑した顔をしていた.

2 (mixed up) koʳñrañ shita [shite iru] 混乱した[している]: confused ideas (*koñrañ shita kañgae*) 混乱した考え.

confusing *adj.* toʳowaku saseru 当惑させる; maʳgirawashiˡi 紛らわしい: confusing names (*magirawashii namae*) 紛らわしい名前.

confusion *n.* **1** (confusing) koʳñdoo 混同; koʳñrañ 混乱: Everything was in confusion. (*Subete ga koñrañ shite ita.*) すべてが混乱していた.

2 (bewilderment) toʳowaku 当惑; roʳobai ろうばい: He ran away in confusion. (*Kare wa roobai shite nigete itta.*) 彼はろうばいして逃げて行った.

congratulate *vt.* ... ni (... o) iʳwaˡu …に(…を)祝う C: He congratulated me on my success. (*Kare wa watashi no seekoo o iwatte kureta.*) 彼は私の成功を祝ってくれた.

congratulation *n.* iʳwai 祝い; shuʳkuˡga 祝賀; (words) iʳwai no koʳtobaˡ 祝いのことば: give a speech of congratulation (*shukuji o noberu*) 祝辞を述べる.

Congratulations! Oʳmedetoo. おめでとう: Congratulations on your promotion! (*Go-shooshiñ omedetoo gozaimasu.*) ご昇進おめでとうございます.

congress *n.* koʳkkai 国会; giˡkai 議会.

conjunction *n.* (of grammar) seʳtsuzokuˡshi 接続詞.

connect *vt.* **1** (join) ... o tsuʳnagu …をつなぐ C; seʳtsuzoku suru 接続する I: connect two wires (*harigane o ni-hoñ tsunagu*) 針金を2本つなぐ.

2 (of a telephone) (... ni)... o tsuʳnagu (…に)…をつなぐ C: Please connect me to extension 234. (*Naiseñ*

nii-sañ-yoñ ni tsunaide kudasai.) 内線 234 につないでください.
3 (associate) ... o reˈñsoo suru ...を連想する [I]: People often connect Japan with Mt. Fuji. (*Hito wa yoku Nihoñ to iu to Fujisañ o reñsoo suru.*) 人はよく日本というと富士山を連想する.
— *vi.* tsuˈnagaru つながる [C]; seˈtsuzoku suru 接続する [I]: This train connects with another at Nagoya. (*Kono ressha wa Nagoya de betsu no ressha ni setsuzoku shite imasu.*) この列車は名古屋で別の列車に接続しています.

connection *n.* **1** (relationship) kaˈñkee 関係; kaˈñreñ 関連: the connection between smoking and cancer (*tabako to gañ no kañkee*) たばことがんの関係.
2 (useful person) koˈne コネ: use one's connections (*kone o riyoo suru*) コネを利用する.
3 (train, bus, etc.) reˈñraku 連絡; seˈtsuzoku 接続; noˈritsugi 乗り継ぎ: Is there a connection with this train at Osaka? (*Oosaka de kono ressha wa setsuzoku ga arimasu ka?*) 大阪でこの列車は接続がありますか.
4 (of a telephone) seˈtsuzoku 接続: We have a bad connection. (*Deñwa no setsuzoku ga warui.*) 電話の接続が悪い.

conquer *vt.* **1** (take by force) ... o seˈefuku suru ...を征服する [I]: conquer a country (*kuni o seefuku suru*) 国を征服する.
2 (overcome) ... ni uˈchikaˈtsu ...に打ち勝つ [C]; ... o koˈkufuku suru ...を克服する [I]: conquer obstacles (*shoogai o kokufuku suru*) 障害を克服する.

conqueror *n.* seˈefukuˈsha 征服者; shoˈoriˈsha 勝利者.

conquest *n.* seˈefuku 征服: the Norman conquest (*Norumañjiñ no seefuku*) ノルマン人の征服.

conscience *n.* ryoˈoshiñ 良心: I acted according to my conscience. (*Watashi wa ryooshiñ ni shitagatte koodoo shita.*) 私は良心に従って行動した.

conscious *adj.* **1** (awake) iˈshiki ga aru 意識がある: The patient is still conscious. (*Kañja wa mada ishiki ga aru.*) 患者はまだ意識がある.
2 (aware) kiˈzuˈite (iru) 気づいて(いる): I was conscious of being followed. (*Watashi wa ato o tsukerarete iru no ni kizuite ita.*) 私は後をつけられているのに気づいていた.

consciousness *n.* iˈshiki 意識: lose consciousness (*ishiki o ushinau*) 意識を失う.

consecutive *adj.* reˈñzoku shita [shite iru] 連続した[している]: It rained three consecutive days. (*Mikka reñzoku shite ame ga futta.*) 三日連続して雨が降った. / consecutive holidays (*reñkyuu*) 連休.

consent *vi.* (... ni) doˈoi suru (...に)同意する [I]; shoˈodaku suru 承諾する [I]: I consented to his plan. (*Watashi wa kare no keekaku ni dooi shita.*) 私は彼の計画に同意した.
— *n.* doˈoi 同意; shoˈodaku 承諾: Her parents gave their consent to her marriage. (*Kanojo no ryooshiñ wa kanojo no kekkoñ ni shoodaku o ataeta.*) 彼女の両親は彼女の結婚に承諾を与えた.

consequence *n.* **1** (result) keˈkka 結果; naˈriyuki 成り行き: The accident was a consequence of carelessness. (*Sono jiko wa fuchuui no kekka datta.*) その事故は不注意の結果だった.
2 (importance) juˈuyoosa 重要さ: It is a matter of great consequence to me. (*Sore wa watashi ni totte hijoo ni jyuuyoo na koto desu.*) それは私にとって非常に重要なことです.

consequently *adv.* soˈno kekka その結果; shiˈtagatte 従って: The rain continued for a week, and consequently the road was flooded. (*Ame ga is-shuukañ tsuzuki, sono kekka michi ni mizu ga afureta.*) 雨が1週間続き, その結果道に水があふれた.

C

conservative *adj.* **1** (dislike changing) ho⌈shu-teki na 保守的な: He is conservative in views about education. (*Kare wa kyooiku ni tsuite no kañgaekata ga hoshu-teki da.*) 彼は教育についての考え方が保守的だ.
2 (not extreme) ji⌈mi⌉ na 地味な; hi⌈kaeme na 控えめな: She is conservative in her dress. (*Kanojo wa kiru mono ga jimi da.*) 彼女は着るものが地味だ.

consider *vt.* **1** (regard) ... o (... to) o⌈mo⌉u …を(…と)思う [C]; mi⌈nasu 見なす [C]: I think him unfit for the job. (*Watashi wa kare wa sono shigoto ni tekishite inai to omou.*) 私は彼はその仕事に適していないと思う.
2 (think carefully) ... o yo⌉ku ka⌈ñga⌉eru …をよく考える [V]; ko⌉oryo suru 考慮する [I]: I am considering what to do next. (*Tsugi ni nani o suru ka o kooryo-chuu desu.*) 次に何をするかを考慮中です.
3 (take into account) ... o ko⌉oryo ni i⌈reru …を考慮に入れる [V]: You must consider other people's feelings. (*Hoka no hito no kimochi o kooryo ni irenakereba ikenai.*) ほかの人の気持ちを考慮に入れなければいけない.

considerable *adj.* ka⌉nari no かなりの; so⌈otoo na 相当な: a considerable number of people (*kanari no kazu no hito-tachi*) かなりの数の人たち.

considerably *adv.* ka⌉nari かなり; so⌈otoo ni 相当に: He's considerably older than you. (*Kare wa anata yori mo kanari toshiue desu.*) 彼はあなたよりもかなり年上です.

considerate *adj.* o⌈moiyari no [ga] a⌈ru 思いやりの[が]ある: She is considerate toward old people. (*Kanojo wa o-toshiyori ni omoiyari ga aru.*) 彼女はお年寄りに思いやりがある.

consideration *n.* **1** (fact to be considered) ko⌉oryo su beki ko⌈to⌉ 考慮すべきこと; mo⌈ñda⌉iteñ 問題点: The cost was our main consideration. (*Kosuto ga ooki-na moñdai-teñ datta.*) コストが大きな問題点だった.
2 (careful thought) yo⌉ku ka⌈ñga⌉eru ko⌈to⌉ よく考えること; ko⌉oryo 考慮: We gave our careful consideration to the problem. (*Watashi-tachi wa sono moñdai ni juubuñ na kooryo o haratta.*) 私たちはその問題に十分な考慮を払った.
3 (kindness) o⌈moiyari 思いやり: He has no consideration for other people. (*Kare wa hoka no hito ni taishite omoiyari ga nai.*) 彼はほかの人に対して思いやりがない.

considering *prep.* ... o ka⌈ñga⌉eru to …を考えると; ... no wa⌈ri ni …の割に: She looks young considering her age. (*Kanojo wa toshi no wari ni wakaku mieru.*) 彼女は年の割に若く見える.
— *conj.* ... o ka⌈ñga⌉eru to …を考えると; ... o o⌈mo⌉eba …を思えば: He's done well, considering he has no experience. (*Keekeñ ga nai koto o omoeba kare wa yoku yatta.*) 経験がないことを思えば彼はよくやった.

consist *vi.* **1** (be made up) (... kara) na⌉ru (…から)成る [C]: The committee consists of ten members. (*Iiñkai wa juu-niñ no meñbaa kara natte iru.*) 委員会は 10 人のメンバーから成っている.
2 (be contained) (... ni) a⌉ru (…に)ある [C]: Happiness consists in being contented. (*Koofuku wa mañzoku suru koto ni aru.*) 幸福は満足することにある.

consistency *n.* ik⌈kañsee 一貫性: His opinions lack consistency. (*Kare no ikeñ wa ikkañsee ni kakeru.*) 彼の意見は一貫性に欠ける.

consistent *adj.* **1** (regular) ik⌈kañ shita [shite iru] 一貫した[している]; mu⌈juñ ga na⌉i 矛盾がない: He is consistent in his argument. (*Kare no roñpoo wa ikkañ shite iru.*) 彼の論法は一貫している.
2 (in agreement) i⌈tchi shite (iru) 一致して(いる): His words are not

consistent with his acts. (*Kare wa iu koto to suru koto ga itchi shinai.*) 彼は言うこととすることが一致しない.

console *vt.* ... o na⌜gusame⌝ru ...を慰める [V]: She consoled the crying child. (*Kanojo wa sono naite iru kodomo o nagusameta.*) 彼女はその泣いている子どもを慰めた.

consonant *n.* shi⌜iñ 子音.

conspicuous *adj.* me⌜da⌝tsu 目立つ; hi⌜tome o hiku 人目を引く: Her dress was conspicuous at the party. (*Kanojo no doresu wa paatii de hitome o hiita.*) 彼女のドレスはパーティーで人目を引いた.

constant *adj.* **1** (ceaseless) ta⌜ema (no) na⌝i 絶え間(の)ない; hi⌜kkiri na⌝shi no ひっきりなしの: The constant noise irritated me. (*Taema (no) nai soo-oñ ga watashi o iraira saseta.*) 絶え間(の)ない騒音が私をいらいらさせた.
2 (unchanging) fu⌜heñ no 不変の; i⌜ttee no 一定の: keep the room at a constant temperature (*heya o ittee no oñdo ni tamotsu*) 部屋を一定の温度に保つ.

constantly *adv.* ta⌝ezu 絶えず; i⌝tsu-mo いつも: The issue is constantly on my mind. (*Sono moñdai wa itsu-mo ki ni kakatte iru.*) その問題はいつも気にかかっている.

constitute *vt.* **1** (make up) ... o ko⌜osee suru ...を構成する [I]: Seven members constitute the committee. (*Shichi-niñ no meñbaa ga sono iiñkai o koosee shite iru.*) 7人のメンバーがその委員会を構成している.
2 (set up) ... o se⌜etee suru ...を制定する [I]; (establish) se⌜tsuritsu suru 設立する [I]: constitute a school (*gakkoo o setsuritsu suru*) 学校を設立する.

constitution *n.* **1** (supreme laws) ke⌝ñpoo 憲法: the Constitution of Japan (*Nihoñkoku keñpoo*) 日本国憲法.
2 (structure) ko⌜osee 構成; ko⌜ozoo 構造: the constitution of society (*shakai no koozoo*) 社会の構造.
3 (physical characteristics) ta⌜ishitsu 体質: He has a strong constitution. (*Kare wa joobu na taishitsu da.*) 彼は丈夫な体質だ.

constitutional *adj.* **1** (legal) ke⌝ñpoo no 憲法の; ri⌜kkeñ no 立憲の: constitutional monarchy (*rikkeñ kuñshusee*) 立憲君主制.
2 (of a person) ta⌜ikaku no 体格の; u⌜maretsuki no 生まれつきの: a constitutional weakness (*umaretsuki no byoojaku*) 生まれつきの病弱.

construct *vt.* **1** (build) ... o ku⌜mitate⌝ru ...を組み立てる [V]; ke⌜ñsetsu suru 建設する [I]: construct a bridge (*hashi o keñsetsu suru*) 橋を建設する.
2 (put together) ... o ko⌜osee suru ...を構成する [I]; ku⌜mitate⌝ru 組み立てる [V]: construct a theory (*riroñ o kumitateru*) 理論を組み立てる.

construction *n.* **1** (constructing) ke⌜ñzoo 建造; ke⌜ñsetsu 建設: a building under construction (*keñsetsu-chuu no biru*) 建設中のビル.
2 (something built) ke⌜ñzo⌝obutsu 建造物; ta⌜te⌝mono 建物.

consul *n.* ryo⌝oji 領事.

consulate *n.* ryo⌜oji⌝kañ 領事館.

consult *vt.* **1** (seek advice) ... ni so⌜odañ suru ...に相談する [I]; (of a doctor) mi⌝te morau 診てもらう [C]: consult one's lawyer (*beñgoshi ni soodañ suru*) 弁護士に相談する / consult a doctor (*isha ni mite morau*) 医者に診てもらう.
2 (seek information) ... o shi⌜rabe⌝ru ...を調べる [V]; (of a dictionary) hi⌜ku 引く [C]: consult a dictionary (*jisho o hiku*) 辞書を引く.
— *vi.* so⌜odañ suru 相談する [I]: I consulted with him about the issue. (*Watashi wa sono moñdai ni tsuite kare to soodañ shita.*) 私はその問題について彼と相談した.

consultant *n.* ko⌝moñ 顧問; ko⌜ñsa⌝rutañto コンサルタント: a legal consultant (*hooritsu komoñ*) 法律顧問

/ a management consultant (*kee-ee koñsarutañto*) 経営コンサルタント.

consultation *n.* **1** (meeting) ka⌉igi 会議: They held a consultation on a new project. (*Kare-ra wa atarashii kikaku ni tsuite kaigi o hiraita.*) 彼らは新しい企画について会議を開いた.
2 (consulting) so⌈odañ 相談; kyo⌉ogi 協議: I decided in consultation with him. (*Watashi wa kare to soodañ shite kimeta.*) 私は彼と相談して決めた.

consume *vt.* **1** (use up) ... o sho⌈ohi suru ...を消費する Ⅰ; sho⌈omoo suru 消耗する Ⅰ: How much electricity do you consume a month? (*Ik-kagetsu ni dono kurai deñki o shoohi shimasu ka?*) 1か月にどのくらい電気を消費しますか.
2 (eat) ... o ta⌈be⌉ru ...を食べる Ⅴ; (drink) no⌉mu 飲む Ⓒ: He consumed a bottle of whisky. (*Kare wa uisukii o ip-poñ noñde shimatta.*) 彼はウイスキーを1本飲んでしまった.

consumer *n.* sho⌈ohi⌉sha 消費者.

consumption *n.* sho⌈ohi 消費; (amount consumed) sho⌈ohi⌉ryoo 消費量: consumption tax (*shoohizee*) 消費税.

contact *n.* **1** (touching) fu⌈reai 触れ合い; se⌈sshoku 接触: This disease is passed on by contact. (*Kono byooki wa sesshoku ni yotte deñseñ suru.*) この病気は接触によって伝染する.
2 (communication) re⌈ñraku 連絡; ko⌈oshoo 交渉: I keep in contact with him. (*Watashi wa kare to reñraku o totte imasu.*) 私は彼と連絡をとっています.
3 (business connection) e⌉ñko 縁故; ko⌉ne コネ: I have made good contacts in China. (*Watashi wa Chuugoku de yoi kone o eta.*) 私は中国でよいコネを得た.
— *vt.* ... ni [to] re⌈ñraku suru ...に[と]連絡する Ⅰ; se⌈sshoku suru 接触する Ⅰ: I contacted him on the telephone. (*Watashi wa kare ni deñwa de reñraku shita.*) 私は彼に電話で連絡した.

contagious *adj.* de⌈ñseñsee no 伝染性の: a contagious disease (*deñseñbyoo*) 伝染病.

contain *vt.* **1** (have inside) ... o fu⌈ku⌉mu ...を含む Ⓒ; ... ga ha⌉itte iru ...が入っている Ⅴ: This book contains many illustrations. (*Kono hoñ ni wa sashie ga takusañ haitte iru.*) この本には挿し絵がたくさん入っている.
2 (hold) ha⌉iru 入る Ⓒ: How much does this bottle contain? (*Kono biñ wa dono kurai hairimasu ka?*) このびんはどのくらい入りますか.
3 (be equal to) ... ni hi⌈toshi⌉i ...に等しい: A meter contains 100 centimeters. (*Ichi-meetoru wa hyaku-señchi ni hitoshii.*) 1メートルは100センチに等しい.

container *n.* **1** i⌈remono 入れ物; yo⌉oki 容器: put into a container (*yooki ni ireru*) 容器に入れる.
2 (metal box) ko⌉ñtena コンテナ.

contemplate *vt.* **1** (think seriously) ... o ji⌈kku⌉ri ka⌈ñgae⌉ru ...をじっくり考える Ⅴ; ju⌈kkoo suru 熟考する Ⅰ: I contemplated my future. (*Watashi wa shoorai no koto o jikkuri kañgaeta.*) 私は将来のことをじっくり考えた.
2 (look at) ... o ji⌈tto mitsume⌉ru ...をじっと見つめる Ⅴ; ju⌉kushi suru 熟視する Ⅰ: She contemplated herself in the mirror. (*Kanojo wa kagami no naka no jibuñ o jitto mitsumeta.*) 彼女は鏡の中の自分をじっと見つめた.

contemporary *adj.* **1** (modern) ge⌉ñdai no 現代の: contemporary music (*geñdai oñgaku*) 現代音楽.
2 (living at the same time) so⌈no too⌉ji no その当時の; do⌈o ji⌉dai no 同時代の: He was contemporary with Shakespeare. (*Kare wa Sheekusupia to doo jidai no hito datta.*) 彼はシェークスピアと同時代の人だった.

contempt *n.* ke⌈ebetsu 軽蔑; bu⌈joku 侮辱: I feel contempt for those who are cruel to animals.

(*Watashi wa doobutsu o gyakutai suru hito o keebetsu suru.*) 私は動物を虐待する人を軽蔑する.

contend *vi.* **1** (be in rivalry) (... to) kyo⌈osoo suru (…と)競争する Ⓘ; a⌈raso⌉u 争う Ⓒ: I contended with him for the prize. (*Watashi wa sono shookiñ o neratte kare to arasotta.*) 私はその賞金をねらって彼と争った.
2 (struggle) (... to) ta⌈takau (…と)闘う Ⓒ: contend with difficulties (*koñnañ to tatakau*) 困難と闘う.
— *vt.* (maintain) ... o shu⌈choo suru …を主張する Ⓘ: He contended that I was wrong. (*Kare wa watashi ga machigatte iru to shuchoo shita.*) 彼は私が間違っていると主張した.

content[1] *n.* **1** (subject matter) shu⌉i 趣意; yo⌉oshi 要旨: the content of a speech (*eñzetsu no shui*) 演説の趣意.
2 (substance) na⌈iyoo 内容: a speech with little content (*naiyoo no toboshii eñzetsu*) 内容の乏しい演説.

content[2] *adj.* ma⌉ñzoku shite (iru) 満足して(いる): I am content with my present salary. (*Watashi wa ima no kyuuryoo de mañzoku shite imasu.*) 私は今の給料で満足しています.
— *n.* ma⌉ñzoku 満足: She smiled with content. (*Kanojo wa mañzoku shite hohoeñda.*) 彼女は満足してほほ笑んだ.
— *vt.* ... o ma⌉ñzoku saseru …を満足させる Ⓥ: Nothing can content him. (*Nanigoto mo kare o mañzoku saseru koto wa dekinai.*) 何事も彼を満足させることはできない.

contented *adj.* ma⌉ñzoku shita [shite iru] 満足した[している]: He looked contented. (*Kare wa mañzoku shita yoo ni mieta.*) 彼は満足したように見えた.

contents *n.* **1** (that which is contained) na⌈ka⌉mi 中身; na⌈iyoo 内容: the contents of one's purse (*saifu no nakami*) 財布の中身.
2 (of a book) mo⌈kuji 目次: table of contents (*mokuji*) 目次.

contest *n.* kyo⌈osoo 競争; ko⌉ñtesuto コンテスト: win a speech contest (*beñroñ taikai de yuushoo suru*) 弁論大会で優勝する.
— *vt.* ... o a⌈raso⌉u …を争う Ⓒ: contest a prize (*shoo o arasou*) 賞を争う.

context *n.* bu⌈ñmyaku 文脈; ko⌉ñtekusuto コンテクスト; ze⌈ñgo-ka⌉ñkee 前後関係: guess the meaning of a word from the context (*buñmyaku kara tañgo no imi o suisoku suru*) 文脈から単語の意味を推測する.

continent *n.* ta⌈iriku 大陸: the African Continent (*Afurika-tairiku*) アフリカ大陸.

continental *adj.* ta⌈iriku no 大陸の; ta⌈irikusee no 大陸性の: a continental climate (*tairikusee kikoo*) 大陸性気候.

continual *adj.* re⌈ñzoku-teki na 連続的な; ta⌈ema no na⌉i 絶え間のない: There's continual trouble on the border. (*Kokkyoo de taema no nai fuñsoo ga okite iru.*) 国境で絶え間のない紛争が起きている.

continually *adv.* ta⌈ema na⌉ku 絶え間なく; sho⌉tchuu しょっちゅう: That child is continually crying. (*Ano ko wa shotchuu naite iru.*) あの子はしょっちゅう泣いている.

continue *vt.* ... o tsu⌈zukeru …を続ける Ⓥ; ⟨verb⟩-tsu⌈zukeru 続ける Ⓥ: We continued our journey. (*Watashi-tachi wa ryokoo o tsuzuketa.*) 私たちは旅行を続けた. / He continued to run. (*Kare wa hashiri-tsuzuketa.*) 彼は走り続けた.
— *vi.* tsu⌈zuku 続く Ⓒ; ⟨verb⟩-tsu⌈zuku 続く Ⓒ: His speech continued for two hours. (*Kare no eñzetsu wa ni-jikañ tsuzuita.*) 彼の演説は2時間続いた. / The rain continued all day. (*Ame wa ichinichi-juu furi-tsuzuita.*) 雨は一日中降り続いた.

continuity *n.* re⌈ñzoku 連続;

i⌉kkañsee 一貫性: a continuity of rainy days (*amefuri no reñzoku*) 雨降りの連続 / continuity in government policy (*seesaku no ikkañsee*) 政策の一貫性.

continuous *adj.* ki⌈reme no na⌉i 切れ目のない; re⌈ñzoku-teki na 連続的な: a continuous procession of cars (*kireme no nai kuruma no retsu*) 切れ目のない車の列.

continuously *adv.* ta⌈emana⌉ku 絶え間なく; re⌈ñzoku-teki ni 連続的に: It rained continuously all day. (*Ichinichi-juu taemanaku ame ga futta.*) 一日中絶え間なく雨が降った.

contour *n.* ri⌉ñkaku 輪郭; ga⌈ikee 外形: the contours of a mountain (*yama no riñkaku*) 山の輪郭.

contract[1] *n.* **1** (agreement) ke⌈e-yaku 契約: make a contract (*keeyaku o musubu*) 契約を結ぶ.
2 (written agreement) ke⌈eyaku-sho 契約書: sign a contract (*keeyakusho ni shomee suru*) 契約書に署名する.
— *vt.* **1** (agree by contract) ke⌈e-yaku o suru 契約をする [I]: I contracted to pay cash for the car. (*Watashi wa kuruma no daikiñ o geñkiñ de harau keeyaku o shita.*) 私は車の代金を現金で払う契約をした.
2 (of disease) ... ni ka⌈ka⌉ru ...にかかる [C]: contract pneumonia (*haieñ ni kakaru*) 肺炎にかかる.

contract[2] *vi.* (become smaller) chi⌈jimaru 縮まる [C]: Metals contract when cooled. (*Kiñzoku wa hieru to chijimaru.*) 金属は冷えると縮まる.

contractor *n.* ke⌈eyaku⌉sha 契約者; u⌈keoiniñ 請負人.

contradict *vt.* **1** (deny) ... o hi⌈tee suru ...を否定する [I]: He contradicted the fact. (*Kare wa sono jijitsu o hitee shita.*) 彼はその事実を否定した.
2 (go against) ... to mu⌈juñ suru ...と矛盾する [I]: His account contradicts yours. (*Kare no setsumee wa kimi no to mujuñ suru.*) 彼の説明は君のと矛盾する.

contradiction *n.* **1** (contradicting) ha⌈ñroñ 反論; hi⌈tee 否定: He said nothing in contradiction. (*Kare wa nani mo hañroñ shinakatta.*) 彼は何も反論しなかった.
2 (absence of agreement) mu⌈juñ 矛盾.

contradictory *adj.* mu⌈juñ shita [shite iru] 矛盾した[している]: a rumor contradictory to fact (*jijitsu to mujuñ shita uwasa*) 事実と矛盾したうわさ.

contrary *adj.* **1** (opposite) ha⌈ñtai no 反対の; gya⌈ku no 逆の: They hold contrary opinions. (*Kare-ra wa hañtai no ikeñ o motte iru.*) 彼らは反対の意見を持っている.
2 (opposed) ... ni ha⌈ñsu⌉ru ...に反する: an act contrary to the law (*hooritsu ni hañsuru kooi*) 法律に反する行為.
— *n.* se⌈eha⌉ñtai 正反対.
contrary to ... *prep.* ... ni ha⌉ñshite ...に反して: contrary to one's expectation (*yosoo ni hañshite*) 予想に反して.

contrast *n.* **1** (comparison) ta⌈ishoo 対照; ta⌈ihi 対比; ko⌈ñtora⌉suto コントラスト: the contrast between light and shade (*hikari to kage no taishoo*) 光と陰の対照.
2 (difference) sa⌉i 差異; chi⌈gai 違い: The contrast between winter and summer is great. (*Fuyu to natsu no chigai wa ookii.*) 冬と夏の違いは大きい.
— *vt.* ... o ta⌈ishoo saseru ...を対照させる [V]; ku⌈raberu 比べる [V]: contrast a recent painting with an older one (*saikiñ no e o mukashi no to kuraberu*) 最近の絵を昔のと比べる.
— *vi.* ta⌈ishoo-teki da 対照的だ: Black and white contrasts sharply. (*Kuro to shiro wa kiwamete taishoo-teki da.*) 黒と白はきわめて対照的だ.

contribute *vt.* **1** (give) (... ni) ... o ki⌉fu suru (...に)...を寄付する [I]:

She contributed money to the school. (*Kanojo wa gakkoo ni o-kane o kifu shita.*) 彼女は学校にお金を寄付した.
2 (write) ... o (... ni) ki⌈koo suru …を(…に)寄稿する [I]: He contributed a story to the magazine. (*Kare wa monogatari o sono zasshi ni kikoo shita.*) 彼は物語をその雑誌に寄稿した.
— *vi.* **1** (give) (... ni) ki⌉fu suru (…に)寄付する [I]: contribute to a community chest (*kyoodoo-bokiñ ni kifu suru*) 共同募金に寄付する.
2 (write) (... ni) ki⌈koo suru (…に)寄稿する [I]: contribute to a newspaper (*shiñbuñ ni kikoo suru*) 新聞に寄稿する.
3 (help) (... ni) ya⌈ku⌉ ni tatsu (…に)役に立つ [C]; ko⌈okeñ suru 貢献する [I]: His discovery contributed to the development of science. (*Kare no hakkeñ wa kagaku no hatteñ ni kookeñ shita.*) 彼の発見は科学の発展に貢献した.

contribution *n.* ki⌉fu 寄付; ki⌈zoo 寄贈: make a contribution to a hospital (*byooiñ ni kifu suru*) 病院に寄付する.

control *n.* **1** (directing) shi⌉hai 支配; to⌈osee 統制; (managing) ka⌉ñri 管理: price control (*bukka toosee*) 物価統制 / quality control (*hiñshitsu kañri*) 品質管理.
2 (holding back) yo⌈kusee 抑制; se⌈ege⌉ñ 制限: arms control (*guñbi-seegeñ*) 軍備制限 / birth control (*sañji-seegeñ*) 産児制限.
— *vt.* **1** (direct) ... o to⌈osee suru …を統制する [I]; (manage) ka⌉ñri suru 管理する [I]: control a business (*gyoomu o kañri suru*) 業務を管理する.
2 (hold back) ... o o⌈sae⌉ru …を抑える [V]: control one's anger (*ikari o osaeru*) 怒りを抑える.

controversy *n.* ro⌈ñsoo 論争; gi⌉roñ 議論: The problem is beyond controversy. (*Sono moñdai wa giroñ no yochi ga nai.*) その問題は議論の余地がない.

convenience *n.* **1** (suitableness) ko⌈otsu⌉goo 好都合; be⌉ñri 便利: I bought my present house for its convenience. (*Watashi wa beñri ga ii no de ima no ie o kaimashita.*) 私は便利がいいので今の家を買いました.
2 (apparatus) be⌉ñri na mo⌈no⌉ 便利な物; (facilities) be⌉ñri na setsubi 便利な設備: a hotel with modern conveniences (*kiñdai setsubi no totonotta hoteru*) 近代設備の整ったホテル.

convenient *adj.* **1** (suitable) tsu⌈goo no yo⌉i 都合のよい; (useful) be⌉ñri na 便利な: Is Monday convenient for you? (*Getsuyoo wa go-tsugoo yoroshii desu ka?*) 月曜はご都合よろしいですか. / a convenient kitchen (*beñri na daidokoro*) 便利な台所.
2 (near) chi⌈ka⌉kute beñri ga yoi 近くて便利がよい: His house is convenient for the station. (*Kare no ie wa eki ni chikakute beñri da.*) 彼の家は駅に近くて便利だ.

conveniently *adv.* tsu⌈goo yo⌉ku 都合よく; be⌉ñri ni 便利に: Conveniently, I live near my school. (*Tsugoo yoku watashi wa gakkoo no soba ni suñde imasu.*) 都合よく私は学校のそばに住んでいます.

convention *n.* **1** (meeting) ta⌈ikai 大会: the national convention of a political party (*too no zeñkoku taikai*) 党の全国大会.
2 (custom) shi⌈kitari しきたり; ka⌈ñshuu 慣習: He did not care about convention. (*Kare wa shikitari o ki ni kakenakatta.*) 彼はしきたりを気にかけなかった.

conventional *adj.* ka⌈ta⌉ ni ha⌈matta [ha⌈matte iru] 型にはまった[はまっている]; i⌈ñshuu-teki na 因習的な: conventional ideas (*kata ni hamatta kañgae*) 型にはまった考え.

conversation *n.* ka⌈iwa 会話; da⌈ñwa 談話: Japanese conversation (*Nihoñgo-kaiwa*) 日本語会話 / have a conversation with a person (*hito to hanashi o suru*) 人と話をする.

conversion *n.* he⌈ñkañ 変換; ka⌈ñsañ 換算: a conversion table (*kañsañhyoo*) 換算表.

converse *vi.* ha⌈nashia⌉u 話し合う Ⓒ; ka⌈iwa suru 会話する Ⓘ: We conversed on the matter. (*Watashi-tachi wa sono koto ni tsuite hanashiatta.*) 私たちはそのことについて話し合った.

convert *vt.* **1** (change) ... o (... ni) ka⌈eru ...を(...に)換える Ⓥ; te⌈ñkañ suru 転換する Ⓘ: convert coal to gas (*sekitañ o gasu ni kaeru*) 石炭をガスに変える.
2 (of money) ... o (... ni) ka⌈eru ...を(...に)換える Ⓥ: Can I convert dollars into yen here? (*Koko de doru o eñ ni kaeraremasu ka?*) ここでドルを円に換えられますか.
3 (of religion) ... o (... ni) ka⌈ishuu saseru ...を(...に)改宗させる Ⓥ: He tried to convert me to Christianity. (*Kare wa watashi o kirisutokyoo ni kaishuu saseyoo to shita.*) 彼は私をキリスト教に改宗させようとした.
— *vi.* **1** (change) (... ni) ka⌈waru (...に)変わる Ⓒ: This sofa converts into a bed. (*Kono sofaa wa beddo ni kawarimasu.*) このソファーはベッドに変わります.
2 (of religion) (... ni) ka⌈ishuu suru (...に)改宗する Ⓘ: She converted to Christianity. (*Kanojo wa kirisutokyoo ni kaishuu shita.*) 彼女はキリスト教に改宗した.

convey *vt.* **1** (carry) ... o ha⌈kobu ...を運ぶ Ⓒ; u⌈ñpañ suru 運搬する Ⓘ: convey goods by truck (*shinamono o torakku de hakobu*) 品物をトラックで運ぶ.
2 (make known) (... ni) ... o tsu⌈taeru (...に)...を伝える Ⓥ; de⌈ñtatsu suru 伝達する Ⓘ: Did you convey my message to him? (*Kare ni watashi no messeeji o tsutaemashita ka?*) 彼に私のメッセージを伝えましたか.

convict *vt.* ... o yu⌈uzai to se⌈ñkoku suru ...を有罪と宣告する Ⓘ: He was convicted of theft. (*Kare wa settoo no tsumi de yuuzai to señkoku sareta.*) 彼は窃盗の罪で有罪と宣告された.
— *n.* shu⌈ujiñ 囚人; za⌈iniñ 罪人.

conviction *n.* **1** (strong belief) ka⌈kushiñ 確信; shi⌉ñneñ 信念: I have a strong conviction that I am right. (*Watashi wa tadashii to iu tsuyoi kakushiñ o motte iru.*) 私は正しいという強い確信を持っている.
2 (being convicted) yu⌈uzai no hañketsu 有罪の判決: a previous conviction (*zeñka*) 前科.

convince *vt.* ... o ka⌈kushiñ saseru ...を確信させる Ⓥ; ... o (... ni) na⌈ttoku saseru ...を(...に)納得させる Ⓥ: I am convinced that he told the truth. (*Kare wa hoñtoo no koto o hanashita to kakushiñ shite imasu.*) 彼は本当の事を話したと確信しています. / I convinced him of my innocence. (*Watashi wa jibuñ no muzai o kare ni nattoku saseta.*) 私は自分の無罪を彼に納得させた.

cook *vt.* ... o ryo⌉ori suru ...を料理する Ⓘ; ni⌈ru 煮る Ⓥ: She cooked some chicken. (*Kanojo wa toriniku o ryoori shita.*) 彼女はとり肉を料理した.
— *vi.* ryo⌉ori suru 料理する Ⓘ; ni⌈eru 煮える Ⓥ: These vegetables cook quickly. (*Kore-ra no yasai wa hayaku niemasu.*) これらの野菜は早く煮えます.
— *n.* ryo⌈oriniñ 料理人; ko⌉kku コック: She is a good cook. (*Kanojo wa ryoori ga joozu da.*) 彼女は料理がじょうずだ.

cookie *n.* ku⌉kkii クッキー.

cooking *n.* ryo⌉ori 料理: do the cooking (*ryoori o suru*) 料理をする.
— *adj.* ryo⌈oriyoo no 料理用の: a cooking apple (*ryooriyoo no riñgo*) 料理用のりんご / cooking utensils (*choori kigu*) 調理器具.

cool *adj.* **1** (slightly cold) su⌈zushi⌉i 涼しい; (of a thing) tsu⌈metai 冷たい: a cool breeze (*suzushii kaze*) 涼しい風 / a cool drink (*tsumetai no-

mimono) 冷たい飲物.
2 (calm) re⌈esee na 冷静な; o⌈chitsuita 落ち着いた; o⌈chitsuite iru 落ち着いている: He was cool in the face of danger. (*Kare wa kikeñ ni chokumeñ shite mo reesee datta.*) 彼は危険に直面しても冷静だった.
3 (indifferent) re⌈eta⌉ñ na 冷淡な; ha⌈kujoo na 薄情な: She was cool toward me. (*Kanojo wa watashi ni taishite reetañ datta.*) 彼女は私に対して冷淡だった.
— *vt.* **1** (make cool) ... o hi⌈ya⌉su ...を冷やす; (of temperature) su⌈zu⌉shiku suru 涼しくする [I]: cool a beer in the refrigerator (*biiru o reezooko de hiyasu*) ビールを冷蔵庫で冷やす / I opened the windows to cool the room. (*Watashi wa heya o suzushiku suru tame ni mado o aketa.*) 私は部屋を涼しくするために窓を開けた.
2 (make calm) ... o re⌈esee ni suru ...を冷静にする [I]; shi⌈zume⌉ru 静める [V]: cool one's anger (*ikari o shizumeru*) 怒りを静める.
— *vi.* **1** (become cool) hi⌈e⌉ru 冷える [V]; su⌈zu⌉shiku naru 涼しくなる [C].
2 (become calm) re⌈esee ni na⌉ru 冷静になる [C]; o⌈chitsuku 落ち着く [C].

co-op *n.* se⌈ekyoo 生協; se⌈ekatsu kyoodoo-ku⌉miai 生活協同組合.

cooperate *vi.* kyo⌈oryoku suru 協力する [I]; kyo⌈odoo suru 協同する [I]: If we cooperate, we can finish the work quickly. (*Moshi mo watashi-tachi ga kyooryoku sureba shigoto o hayaku oeru koto ga dekimasu.*) もしも私たちが協力すれば仕事を早く終えることができます.

cooperation *n.* kyo⌈oryoku 協力; kyo⌈odoo 協同: We would be grateful for your cooperation. (*Go-kyooryoku itadakereba arigatai to omoimasu.*) ご協力いただければありがたいと思います.

cooperative *adj.* kyo⌈oryokuteki na 協力的な; kyo⌈odoo no 協同の: They were very cooperative. (*Kare-ra wa hijoo ni kyooryokuteki datta.*) 彼らは非常に協力的だった.

coordinate *vt.* ... o cho⌈owa saseru ...を調和させる [V]; cho⌈osee suru 調整する [I]: We have to coordinate the two plans. (*Sono futatsu no keekaku o choosee shinakereba naranai.*) その二つの計画を調整しなければならない.

cope *vi.* u⌉maku taisho suru うまく対処する [I]; ki⌈rinuke⌉ru 切り抜ける [V]: cope with difficulties (*nañkyoku ni taisho suru*) 難局に対処する.

copper *n.* do⌉o 銅.

copy *n.* **1** (of a book) bu 部; sa⌈tsu 冊: I bought a copy of his book. (*Watashi wa kare no hoñ o issatsu katta.*) 私は彼の本を1冊買った.
2 (imitation) u⌈tsushi⌉ 写し; (reproduction) fu⌈kusee 複製: a copy of a contract (*keeyakusho no utsushi*) 契約書の写し / a copy of a famous painting (*yuumee na e no fukusee*) 有名な絵の複製.
3 (photocopy) ko⌉pii コピー; fu⌈kusha 複写: make two copies of a letter (*tegami o ni-bu kopii suru*) 手紙を2部コピーする.
4 (written material) ko⌉pii コピー; ge⌈ñkoo 原稿; (of an advertisement) ko⌈okoku-bu⌉ñañ 広告文案.
— *vt.* **1** (imitate) ... o u⌈tsu⌉su ...を写す [C]; (reproduce) fu⌈kusee suru 複製する [I]: copy a passage into a notebook (*buñshoo o nooto ni utsusu*) 文章をノートに写す.
2 (make a copy) ... o ko⌉pii suru ...をコピーする [I]; fu⌈kusha suru 複写する [I]: copy a letter (*tegami o kopii suru*) 手紙をコピーする.

cord *n.* **1** (string) hi⌈mo ひも; (rope) tsu⌈na⌉ 綱; na⌈wa⌉ 縄: tie with a cord (*himo de shibaru*) ひもで縛る.
2 (electric cable) ko⌉odo コード.

core *n.* shi⌉ñ 芯: remove a core from an apple (*riñgo no shiñ o toru*) りんごのしんを取る.

cork *n.* ko⌉ruku コルク: pull out a cork (*koruku no señ o nuku*) コルクの栓を抜く.

C

corn *n.* **1** (maize) to⌈omo⌉rokoshi とうもろこし: grow corn (*toomorokoshi o tsukuru*) とうもろこしを作る.
2 (wheat) ko⌈mu⌉gi 小麦.
3 (grain) ko⌈ku⌉motsu 穀物.

corner *n.* **1** (angle) ka⌉do 角; ma⌈garikado 曲がり角: I went to a store on the corner. (*Watashi wa kado no mise e itta.*) 私は角の店へ行った.
2 (hidden place) su⌉mi 隅; ka⌈tasumi 片隅: the corner of a room (*heya no sumi*) 部屋の隅.

corporation *n.* ho⌈ojiñ 法人; ka⌈isha 会社: a trading corporation (*shooji-gaisha*) 商事会社.

correct *adj.* **1** (right) ta⌈dashi⌉i 正しい; se⌈ekaku na 正確な: Can you give me the correct time? (*Tadashii jikañ wa nañ-ji deshoo ka?*) 正しい時間は何時でしょうか.
2 (proper) te⌈kisetsu na 適切な; re⌈egi⌉ ni ka⌈na⌉tta [ka⌈na⌉tte iru] 礼儀にかなった[かなっている]: correct behavior (*reegi ni kanatta furumai*) 礼儀にかなった振る舞い.
— *vt.* **1** (make right) ... o te⌈esee suru …を訂正する Ⅰ; na⌈o⌉su 直す Ⓒ: Please correct me if I'm wrong. (*Watashi ga machigatte itara teesee shite kudasai.*) 私が間違っていたら訂正してください.
2 (punish) ... o shi⌈karu …をしかる Ⓒ; ko⌈rashime⌉ru こらしめる Ⓥ: correct a child for disobedience (*iukoto o kikanai kodomo o shikaru*) 言うことをきかない子どもをしかる.

correction *n.* te⌈esee 訂正; shu⌈usee 修正: make corrections in an estimate (*mitsumori o teesee suru*) 見積もりを訂正する.

correspond *vi.* **1** (agree) (... to) i⌈tchi suru (…と)一致する Ⅰ; cho⌈owa suru 調和する Ⅰ: This does not correspond to the sample. (*Kore wa mihoñ to itchi shinai.*) これは見本と一致しない.
2 (be similar) (... ni) so⌈otoo suru (…に)相当する Ⅰ; ga⌈itoo suru 該当する Ⅰ: The Japanese Diet corresponds to the American Congress. (*Nihoñ no kokkai wa Amerika no gikai ni sootoo shimasu.*) 日本の国会はアメリカの議会に相当します.
3 (exchange letters) bu⌈ñtsuu suru 文通する Ⅰ: We are corresponding with each other. (*Watashi-tachi wa o-tagai ni buñtsuu shite imasu.*) 私たちはお互いに文通しています.

correspondence *n.* **1** (exchanging letters) bu⌈ñtsuu 文通; tsu⌈ushiñ 通信: a correspondence course (*tsuushiñ kyooiku*) 通信教育.
2 (letters) te⌈gami 手紙; sho⌈kañ 書簡: a pile of correspondence (*tegami no yama*) 手紙の山.
3 (agreement) i⌈tchi 一致; cho⌈owa 調和.

correspondent *n.* **1** (of a newspaper) tsu⌈ushi⌉ñiñ 通信員; to⌈kuha⌉iñ 特派員: a foreign correspondent (*kaigai tokuhaiñ*) 海外特派員.
2 (of a letter) bu⌈ntsu⌉usha 文通者.

corresponding *adj.* (... ni) ta⌈ioo suru (…に)対応する; so⌈otoo suru 相当する: duties corresponding to rights (*keñri ni taioo suru gimu*) 権利に対応する義務.

corridor *n.* (indoor) ro⌈oka 廊下; tsu⌉uro 通路: walk along a corridor (*rooka o aruku*) 廊下を歩く.

corrupt *vt.* **1** (debase) ... o da⌈raku saseru …を堕落させる Ⓥ: He was corrupted by evil friends. (*Kare wa warui tomodachi ni yotte daraku saserareta.*) 彼は悪い友だちによって堕落させられた.
2 (bribe) ... o ba⌈ishuu suru …を買収する Ⅰ: corrupt a politician (*seejika o baishuu suru*) 政治家を買収する.
— *adj.* **1** (rotten) da⌈raku shita [shite iru] 堕落した[している]; fu⌈hai shita [shite iru] 腐敗した[している]: The government is corrupt. (*Seefu wa fuhai shite iru.*) 政府は腐敗している.
2 (impure) yo⌈goreta 汚れた; yo⌈gorete iru 汚れている; o⌈señ sareta [sarete iru] 汚染された[されている]:

corrupt air (*yogoreta kuuki*) 汚れた空気.

corruption *n.* (corrupting) da⌈raku 堕落; (bribery) o⌈shoku 汚職; (decay) fu⌈hai 腐敗.

cost *n.* **1** (price) da⌉ika 代価; ka⌈kaku 価格; hi⌉yoo 費用: sell below cost (*geñka o watte uru*) 原価を割って売る / cost of living (*seekatsuhi*) 生活費.

2 (sacrifice) gi⌈see 犠牲; (loss) so⌈ñshitsu 損失: The cost of war is great. (*Señsoo no soñshitsu wa ookii.*) 戦争の損失は大きい.

— *vt.* **1** (of money) (... ga) ka⌈ka⌉ru (...が)かかる Ⓒ; ... suru ...する Ⓘ: About how much will it cost? (*Sore wa ikura-gurai kakarimasu ka?*) それはいくらぐらいかかりますか. / This book cost 3,000 yen. (*Kono hoñ wa sañzeñ-eñ shimashita.*) この本は3千円しました.

2 (of hour, labor) ... ga ka⌈ka⌉ru ... がかかる Ⓒ; ... o yo⌈osu⌉ru ...を要する Ⓘ: This work cost much time and patience. (*Kono shigoto wa ooku no jikañ to koñki o yooshita.*) この仕事は多くの時間と根気を要した.

costly *adj.* **1** (expensive) ko⌉oka na 高価な; ne⌈dañ ga taka⌉i 値段が高い: costly jewels (*kooka na hooseki*) 高価な宝石.

2 (gained at a great loss) gi⌈see [so⌈ñshitsu] no [ga] ooki⌉i 犠牲[損失]の[が]大きい: a costly victory (*gisee no ookii shoori*) 犠牲の大きい勝利.

costume *n.* i⌉shoo 衣装; fu⌈kusoo 服装: Japanese costume (*wasoo*) 和装.

cottage *n.* i⌈nakaya いなか家; sho⌈oju⌉utaku 小住宅.

cotton *n.* (plant) wa⌈ta⌉ 綿; (fibers) mo⌈meñ 木綿; me⌉ñ 綿; (thread) me⌉ñshi 綿糸: a cotton shirt (*momeñ no shatsu*) 木綿のシャツ / cotton goods (*meñ-seehiñ*) 綿製品 / absorbent cotton (*dasshimeñ*) 脱脂綿.

couch *n.* ne⌈isu 寝いす; na⌈gaisu 長いす; ka⌉uchi カウチ: lie on a couch (*nagaisu ni neru*) 長いすに寝る.

cough *vi.* se⌈ki⌉ o suru せきをする: He coughed badly. (*Kare wa hidoku seki o shita.*) 彼はひどくせきをした.

— *n.* se⌈ki⌉ せき; se⌈kiba⌉rai せき払い: I have a cough. (*Seki ga demasu.*) せきが出ます. / give a cough (*sekibarai o suru*) せき払いをする / cough drops (*seki-dome*) せき止め.

could *aux.* **1** [past tense of can] de⌉kita できた: When I was a child, we could swim in this pond. (*Watashi ga kodomo no koro, kono ike de oyogu koto ga dekimashita.*) 私が子どものころ, この池で泳ぐことができました.

2 [in a subordinate clause] de⌈ki⌉ru できる: He asked me if I could drive a car. (*Kare wa watashi ni kuruma no uñteñ ga dekiru ka kiita.*) 彼は私に車の運転ができるか聞いた.

3 [express a possibility] de⌈ki⌉ru daroo できるだろう: I could come tomorrow. (*Ashita kuru koto ga dekiru [korareru] deshoo.*) あした来ることができる[来られる]でしょう.

Could I ...? ⟨verb⟩-te[de] mo i⌉i desu ka? ...て[で]もいいですか: Could I smoke here? (*Koko de tabako o sutte mo ii desu ka?*) ここでたばこを吸ってもいいですか.

Could you ...? ⟨verb⟩-te[de] ku⌈dasaimase⌉ñ [i⌈tadakemase⌉ñ] ka? ...て[で]くださいません[いただけません]か: Could you tell me the way to the station? (*Eki e iku michi o oshiete kudasaimaseñ ka?*) 駅へ行く道を教えてくださいませんか.

council *n.* shi⌈ñgi⌉kai 審議会; kyo⌈ogi⌉kai 協議会.

counselor *n.* **1** (adviser) ka⌉uñseraa カウンセラー; jo⌈ge⌉ñsha 助言者.

2 (lawyer) be⌈ñgo⌉shi 弁護士.

count *vt.* **1** (calculate) ... o ka⌈zoe⌉ru ...を数える Ⓥ; ka⌈ñjo⌉o suru 勘定する Ⓘ: I counted the number of people present. (*Watashi wa shussekisha no kazu o kazoeta.*) 私は出席者の数を数えた.

C

2 (include) ... o ka⌈ñjo⌉o ni i⌈reru …を勘定に入れる Ⓥ: There were six people, counting him. (*Kare o kañjoo ni irete roku-niñ ita.*) 彼を勘定に入れて6人いた.

3 (consider) ... o (... to) o⌈mo⌉u …を(…と)思う Ⓒ: I count myself lucky. (*Watashi wa koouñ da to omou.*) 私は幸運だと思う.

— *vi.* 1 (say numbers) ka⌉zu o ka⌈zoe⌉ru 数を数える Ⓥ: count from 1 to 100 (*ichi kara hyaku made kazoeru*) 1から100まで数える.

2 (be important) ju⌈uyoo da 重要だ: What he says doesn't count. (*Kare ga iu koto wa juuyoo de wa nai.*) 彼が言うことは重要ではない.

count on ... *vt.* ... o a⌈te ni suru …を当てにする Ⓘ: I counted on him. (*Watashi wa kare o ate ni shite ita.*) 私は彼を当てにしていた.

— *n.* 1 (counting) ke⌈esañ 計算; ka⌈ñjo⌉o 勘定: I made three counts. (*Watashi wa sañ-kai keesañ shita.*) 私は3回計算した.

2 (the sum total) so⌈osu⌉u 総数: the death count (*shisha soosuu*) 死者総数.

counter *n.* (long table) ka⌈uñtaa カウンター; u⌈ridai 売り台: Take this baggage to the JAL counter, please. (*Kono nimotsu o Nihoñ kookuu no kauñtaa e hakoñde kudasai.*) この荷物を日本航空のカウンターへ運んでください.

countless *adj.* ka⌈zoekire⌉nai 数えきれない; mu⌈su⌉u no 無数の: the countless stars (*musuu no hoshi*) 無数の星.

country *n.* 1 (nation) ku⌈ni 国; ko⌉kka 国家; -koku 国: Which country are you from? (*Dochira no kuni kara oide desu ka?*) どちらの国からおいでですか. / an agricultural country (*noogyoo-koku*) 農業国 / a developing country (*hatteñ-tojoo-koku*) 発展途上国.

2 (one's native land) so⌉koku 祖国: I love my country. (*Watashi wa sokoku o aisuru.*) 私は祖国を愛する.

3 (land outside town) i⌈naka 田舎; de⌈ñeñ 田園: I want to live in the country. (*Watashi wa inaka ni sumitai.*) 私はいなかに住みたい.

4 (land with special character) chi⌉iki 地域; chi⌉hoo 地方: wooded country (*shiñriñ chihoo*) 森林地方.

county *n.* (in the U.S.) gu⌉ñ 郡; (in England and Wales) shu⌉u 州.

couple *n.* 1 (of things) fu⌈tatsu 二つ; (of people) fu⌈tari 二人: I gave him a couple of apples. (*Watashi wa kare ni riñgo o futatsu ageta.*) 私は彼にりんごを二つあげた.

2 (a man and a woman) ka⌉ppuru カップル; (a man and wife) fu⌉ufu 夫婦: They will make a good couple. (*Kare-ra wa niai no fuufu ni naru daroo.*) 彼らは似合いの夫婦になるだろう.

a couple of ... *adj.* ni- 2: a couple of weeks (*ni-shuukañ*) 2週間 / a couple of shirts (*shatsu ni-mai*) シャツ2枚.

coupon *n.* 1 (of a discount) ku⌈upo⌉ñ-keñ クーポン券.

2 (of a ticket) ka⌈isu⌉ukeñ 回数券.

3 (of a bond) ri⌉fuda 利札.

courage *n.* yu⌉uki 勇気; do⌉kyoo 度胸: a person of courage (*yuuki no aru hito*) 勇気のある人 / take courage (*yuuki o dasu*) 勇気を出す.

courageous *adj.* yu⌉uki no [ga] aru 勇気の[が]ある; yu⌈ukañ na 勇敢な: a courageous person (*yuuki no aru hito*) 勇気のある人.

course *n.* 1 (direction) ho⌈okoo 方向; shi⌉ñro 進路: The ship changed its course. (*Fune wa shiñro o kaeta.*) 船は進路を変えた.

2 (series of studies) ka⌈tee 課程; ka⌈moku 科目: What course are you taking at the college? (*Daigaku de wa doñna kamoku o totte imasu ka?*) 大学ではどんな科目を取っていますか.

3 (of a meal) ko⌉osu コース; ryo⌉ori 料理: a dinner of five courses (*go-shina no ryoori*) 5品の料理.

4 (racecourse) ko⌉osu コース; so⌉oro 走路.

of course *adv.* mo⌈chi⌉roñ もちろん: Of course I'll come. (*Mochiroñ watashi wa ukagaimasu.*) もちろん私は伺います.

court *n.* **1** (of a law trial) ho⌈otee 法廷; sa⌈ibañsho 裁判所: the Supreme Court (*saikoo saibañsho*) 最高裁判所.
2 (of a game) ko⌉oto コート: a tennis court (*tenisu kooto*) テニスコート.
3 (courtyard) na⌈kaniwa 中庭.

courteous *adj.* re⌈egi tadashi⌉i 礼儀正しい; te⌈echoo na 丁重な: courteous greetings (*teechoo na aisatsu*) 丁重なあいさつ.

courtesy *n.* re⌈egi (tada⌉shisa) 礼儀(正しさ); te⌈echoosa 丁重さ: a courtesy visit (*hyookee hoomoñ*) 表敬訪問.

courtyard *n.* na⌈kaniwa 中庭.

cousin *n.* i⌈to⌉ko いとこ: a second cousin (*mata itoko*) またいとこ.

cover *vt.* **1** (spread over) ... o o⌈ou ...を覆う Ⓒ; ka⌈ke⌉ru かける Ⓥ: She covered the table with a tablecloth. (*Kanojo wa teeburu ni teeburukurosu o kaketa.*) 彼女はテーブルにテーブルクロスをかけた.
2 (of wallpaper) ... o ha⌈ru ...を張る Ⓒ; (of paint) nu⌈ru 塗る Ⓒ: I covered the wall with white paint. (*Watashi wa kabe o shiroi peñki de nutta.*) 私は壁を白いペンキで塗った.
3 (hide) ... o ka⌈ku⌉su ...を隠す Ⓒ: She covered her face with her hands. (*Kanojo wa te de kao o kakushita.*) 彼女は手で顔を隠した.
4 (extend over) ... ni wa⌈taru ...にわたる Ⓒ; o⌈yobu 及ぶ Ⓒ: His land covers five square kilometers. (*Kare no tochi wa go-heehoo-kiromeetoru ni oyobu.*) 彼の土地は5平方キロメートルに及ぶ.
5 (travel) ... o i⌈ku ...を行く Ⓒ; tsu⌈uka suru 通過する Ⓘ: You can cover the distance in an hour. (*Sono kyori nara ichi-jikañ de ikemasu.*) その距離なら1時間で行けます.
6 (of insurance) ... o ka⌈ke⌉ru ...をかける Ⓥ: This car is covered by insurance. (*Kono kuruma ni wa hokeñ ga kakete arimasu.*) この車には保険がかけてあります.
7 (report) ... o ho⌈odoo suru ...を報道する Ⓘ; shu⌈zai suru 取材する Ⓘ: The reporter covered the trial. (*Sono kisha wa saibañ o shuzai shita.*) その記者は裁判を取材した.
— *n.* **1** (something which covers) o⌈oi 覆い; ka⌉baa カバー: put a cover on a chair (*isu ni kabaa o kakeru*) いすにカバーをかける.
2 (of a book) hyo⌈oshi 表紙. ★ In Japan, a dust jacket is usually called '*kabaa*' カバー (cover).
3 (shelter) hi⌈nañbasho 避難場所; ka⌈kurebasho 隠れ場所: cover from a storm (*arashi kara no hinañbasho*) あらしからの避難場所.

cow *n.* me⌈ushi 雌牛; nyu⌈ugyuu 乳牛.

coward *n.* o⌈kubyoomono おくびょう者; hi⌈kyoomono ひきょう者.

crab *n.* ka⌈ni かに(蟹): the Crab (*kaniza*) かに座.

crack *vi.* **1** (break) hi⌈bi⌉ ga ha⌉iru ひびが入る Ⓒ: The glass cracked when I poured hot water into it. (*Atsui o-yu o iretara koppu ni hibi ga haitta.*) 熱いお湯を入れたらコップにひびが入った.
2 (make a sharp sound) pa⌉añ [ga⌉ragara, ga⌈cha⌉ñ] to na⌈ru パーン[ガラガラ, ガチャン]と鳴る Ⓒ: The fireworks cracked overhead. (*Hanabi ga zujoo de paañ to natta.*) 花火が頭上でパーンと鳴った.
— *vt.* **1** (cause to break) ... ni hi⌈bi⌉ o i⌈reru ...にひびを入れる Ⓥ; ... o wa⌈ru ...を割る Ⓒ: crack a walnut (*kurumi o waru*) くるみを割る.
2 (cause to make a sharp sound) ... o pa⌈chi⌉tto [pi⌈shi⌉tto] na⌈rasu ...をパチッと[ピシッと]鳴らす Ⓒ: crack a whip (*muchi o pishitto narasu*) むちをピシッと鳴らす.
— *n.* **1** (split) wa⌈reme 割れ目; hi⌈bi⌉ ひび: a crack in a plate (*sara no hibi*) 皿のひび.
2 (sound) ga⌉ragara [ga⌈cha⌉ñ] to

iu o'to ガラガラ[ガチャン]という音: a crack of thunder (*kaminari no bari-bari to iu oto*) 雷のバリバリという音.

cracker *n.* ku'ra'kkaa クラッカー: a rice cracker (*señbee*) せんべい.

cradle *n.* yu'rikago 揺りかご: from the cradle to the grave (*yurikago kara hakaba made*) 揺りかごから墓場まで.

— *vt.* ... o da'ite aya'su ...を抱いてあやす Ⓒ: cradle a baby in one's arms (*akañboo o ude ni daite ayasu*) 赤ん坊を腕に抱いてあやす.

craft *n.* (skill) gi'jutsu 技術; gi'noo 技能: the craft of a wood block printing (*mokuhañga no gijutsu*) 木版画の技術 / arts and crafts (*biju-tsu koogee*) 美術工芸.

crane *n.* **1** (machine) ki'ju'uki 起重機; ku're'eñ クレーン: operate a crane (*kureeñ o ugokasu*) クレーンを動かす.

2 (bird) tsu'ru つる(鶴).

crank *n.* ku'ra'ñku クランク.

crash *vi.* **1** (of a car) sho'ototsu suru 衝突する Ⓘ; (of aircraft) tsu-'iraku suru 墜落する Ⓘ: The car and the bus crashed. (*Kuruma to basu ga shoototsu shita.*) 車とバスが衝突した. / The plane crashed into the sea. (*Sono hikooki wa umi ni tsuiraku shita.*) その飛行機は海に墜落した.

2 (make a noise) ga'cha'ñ [ga'ra-gara] to o'oki-na o'to' o ta'te'ru ガチャン[ガラガラ]と大きな音を立てる Ⓥ: The plate crashed to the floor. (*Sara ga gachañ to yuka ni ochita.*) 皿がガチャンと床に落ちた.

— *vt.* (of a car) ... o sho'ototsu saseru ...を衝突させる Ⓥ; (of an air-craft) tsu'iraku saseru 墜落させる Ⓥ: He crashed his car into the wall. (*Kare wa kuruma o kabe ni shoototsu saseta.*) 彼は車を壁に衝突させた.

— *n.* **1** (of a car) sho'ototsu 衝突; (of an aircraft) tsu'iraku 墜落: Five people were killed in the plane crash. (*Hikooki no tsuiraku jiko de go-niñ ga shiñda.*) 飛行機の墜落事故で5人が死んだ.

2 (noise) ga'cha'ñ ガチャン; ga'ra-gara ガラガラ; do'shi'ñ ドシン: fall with a crash (*doshiñ to taoreru*) ドシンと倒れる.

crawl *vi.* **1** (drag one's body) ha'u はう Ⓒ; ha'tte su'sumu はって進む Ⓒ: He crawled out of the hole. (*Kare wa ana kara hatte deta.*) 彼は穴からはって出た.

2 (move slowly) no'ronoro su'su-mu のろのろ進む Ⓒ: The truck crawled up the steep hill. (*Torakku wa kyuuzaka o noronoro to susuñ-da.*) トラックは急坂をのろのろと進んだ.

crazy *adj.* **1** (sick in mind) ki 'ga kuru'tta [kuru'tte iru] 気が狂った[狂っている]: He must be crazy to do that. (*Soñna koto o suru nañte kare wa ki ga kurutta ni chigai nai.*) そんなことをするなんて彼は気が狂ったにちがいない.

2 (very eager) ne'kkyoo shita [shite iru] 熱狂した[している]; mu-'chuu no 夢中の: He is crazy about video games. (*Kare wa terebi geemu ni muchuu da.*) 彼はテレビゲームに夢中だ.

cream *n.* **1** (of a cosmetic) ku'ri'i-mu クリーム: shaving cream (*hige-sori-yoo kuriimu*) ひげそり用クリーム.

2 (of milk) ku'ri'imu クリーム: ice cream (*aisu kuriimu*) アイスクリーム.

create *vt.* **1** (cause to exist) ... o so'ozoo suru ...を創造する Ⓘ; tsu-'kuridasu 作り出す Ⓒ: create a peaceful world (*heewa na sekai o tsukuridasu*) 平和な世界を作り出す.

2 (produce) ... o hi'kioko'su ...を引き起こす Ⓒ; ma'kioko'su 巻き起こす Ⓒ: create a sensation (*señseeshoñ o makiokosu*) センセーションを巻き起こす.

creation *n.* **1** (creating) so'ozoo 創造; so'osetsu 創設: the creation of a new city (*atarashii toshi no soosetsu*) 新しい都市の創設.

2 (something created) so'osaku 創作; sa'kuhiñ 作品: This is his latest creation. (*Kore wa kare no sai-shiñ-saku desu.*) これは彼の最新作です.

creative *adj.* so⌈ozoo-teki na 創造的な; do⌈kusoo-teki na 独創的な: a creative design (*dokusoo-teki na dezaiñ*) 独創的なデザイン.

creator *n.* so⌈ozo⌉osha 創造者; so⌈osa⌉kusha 創作者.

creature *n.* (living being) i⌈ki⌉mo-no 生き物; (animal) do⌈obutsu 動物; (human being) ni⌈ñgeñ 人間.

credit *n.* **1** (of payment) ku⌈re⌉jitto クレジット; tsu⌈ke⌉ 付け: buy a thing on credit (*mono o kurejitto de kau*) 物をクレジットで買う.
2 (account at a bank) yo⌈kiñ(za⌉ñ-daka) 預金(残高): I have credit at this bank. (*Watashi wa kono giñ-koo ni yokiñ ga arimasu.*) 私はこの銀行に預金があります.
3 (money loaned) ka⌈shitsukekiñ 貸付金; yu⌉ushi 融資.
4 (trust) shi⌈ñrai 信頼; shi⌈ñyoo 信用: I cannot give credit to his story. (*Kare no hanashi wa shiñyoo de-kinai.*) 彼の話は信用できない.
5 (praise) me⌈esee 名声; hyo⌈obañ 評判: a person of credit (*hyoobañ no yoi hito*) 評判のよい人.
— *vt.* (believe) ... o shi⌈ñji⌉ru …を信じる Ⓥ; (trust) shi⌈ñyoo suru 信用する Ⓘ: I cannot credit a rumor like that. (*Soñna uwasa wa shiñ-yoo dekinai.*) そんなうわさは信用できない.

credit card *n.* ku⌈rejitto ka⌉ado クレジットカード: May I use this credit card? (*Kono kurejitto kaado wa tsukaemasu ka?*) このクレジットカードは使えますか.

creditor *n.* sa⌈ike⌉ñsha 債権者; ka⌈shi⌉nushi 貸し主.

creep *vi.* **1** (move quietly) ko⌈s-so⌉ri [yu⌈kku⌉ri] su⌈sumu こっそり[ゆっくり]進む Ⓒ: He crept out of the room. (*Kare wa heya kara kossori dete itta.*) 彼は部屋からこっそり出て行った.
2 (move on hands and knees) ha⌉u はう Ⓒ: The baby crept toward the chair. (*Akañboo wa isu no hoo e hatte itta.*) 赤ん坊はいすのほうへはって行った.

crew *n.* (of a ship) se⌈ñiñ 船員; no-⌈rikumi⌉iñ 乗組員; (of an aircraft) jo⌈omu⌉iñ 乗務員.

crime *n.* tsu⌉mi 罪; ha⌈ñzai 犯罪: commit a crime (*tsumi o okasu*) 罪を犯す / prevent crime (*hañzai o booshi suru*) 犯罪を防止する.

criminal *adj.* ha⌈ñzai no 犯罪の: a criminal act (*hañzai kooi*) 犯罪行為 / He has a criminal record. (*Kare wa zenka ga aru.*) 彼は前科がある.
— *n.* ha⌈ñza⌉isha 犯罪者; ha⌉ñniñ 犯人: arrest a criminal (*hañniñ o taiho suru*) 犯人を逮捕する.

crisis *n.* **1** (time of difficulty) ki⌉ki 危機; na⌈ñkyoku 難局: an oil crisis (*sekiyu kiki*) 石油危機 / an eco-nomic crisis (*keezai kiki*) 経済危機.
2 (turning-point) wa⌈kareme 分かれ目; to⌈oge⌉ 峠: He was seriously ill, but he passed the crisis. (*Kare wa juubyoo datta ga tooge wa ko-shita.*) 彼は重病だったが峠は越した.

crisp *adj.* **1** (of food) pa⌈ripari [ka⌈rikari] no パリパリ[カリカリ]の: crisp lettuce (*paripari no retasu*) パリパリのレタス / crisp toast (*karikari ni yaita toosuto*) カリカリに焼いたトースト.
2 (of manner) te⌉kipaki shita [shite iru] てきぱきした[している]; ha-⌈gire no yo⌉i 歯切れのよい: a crisp way of speaking (*hagire no yoi hanashikata*) 歯切れのよい話し方.
3 (bracing) sa⌈wa⌉yaka na さわやかな; su⌈gasugashi⌉i すがすがしい: a crisp morning (*sugasugashii asa*) すがすがしい朝.

critic *n.* hi⌈hyooka 批評家; hyo⌈o-roñka 評論家: an art critic (*bijutsu hyooroñka*) 美術評論家.

critical[1] *adj.* **1** (fault-finding) hi-⌈hañ-teki na 批判的な; a⌈rasa⌉gashi o suru あら探しをする: He is too criti-cal of others. (*Kare wa hoka no hito no arasagashi bakari suru.*) 彼

はほかの人のあら探しばかりする.
2 (of work) hi꜔hyoo no 批評の; hyo꜔oroñ no 評論の: a critical essay (*hyooroñ*) 評論.

critical[2] *adj.* (dangerous) kiꜜki no 危機の; ki꜔toku no 危篤の; a꜔bunai 危ない: He is in critical condition. (*Kare wa kitoku jootai da.*) 彼は危篤状態だ.

criticism *n.* **1** (disapproval) hi꜔hañ 批判; hiꜜnañ 非難: His conduct drew a lot of criticism. (*Kare no okonai wa ooku-no hinañ o maneita.*) 彼の行いは多くの非難を招いた.
2 (judgment) hi꜔hyoo 批評; hyo꜔oroñ 評論: literary criticism (*buñgee-hyooroñ*) 文芸評論.

criticize *vt.* **1** (find fault with) ... o hi꜔hañ suru ...を批判する Ⓘ; hiꜜnañ suru 非難する Ⓘ: He criticizes everything I do. (*Kare wa watashi ga suru koto o nañ de mo hinañ suru.*) 彼は私がすることを何でも非難する.
2 (judge) ... o hi꜔hyoo suru ...を批評する Ⓘ; hyo꜔oroñ suru 評論する Ⓘ: His new book was criticized in newspapers and magazines. (*Kare no shiñkañ wa shiñbuñ ya zasshi de hihyoo sareta.*) 彼の新刊は新聞や雑誌で批評された.

crocodile *n.* waꜜni わに(鰐).

crooked *adj.* **1** (not straight) ma꜔gatta 曲がった; ma꜔gatte iru 曲がっている: a crooked road (*magatta michi*) 曲がった道.
2 (dishonest) fu꜔see na 不正な: a crooked business deal (*fusee na shootorihiki*) 不正な商取り引き.

crop *n.* **1** (farm product) no꜔osakuꜜbutsu 農作物; sa꜔kuꜜmotsu 作物: gather in a crop (*sakumotsu o toriireru*) 作物を取り入れる.
2 (harvest) shu꜔ukaku 収穫; sa꜔kugara 作柄: The potato crop was large this year. (*Kotoshi wa jagaimo no shuukaku ga ookatta.*) ことしはじゃがいもの収穫が多かった.
— *vt.* (cut short) ... o mi꜔jikaꜜku kiru ...を短く切る Ⓒ; ka꜔rikoꜜmu 刈り込む Ⓒ: crop one's hair (*kami o mijikaku karikomu*) 髪を短く刈り込む.

cross *vt.* **1** (go across) ... o yo꜔kogiꜜru ...を横切る Ⓒ; wa꜔taru 渡る Ⓒ: cross a street (*michi o yokogiru*) 道を横切る / cross a bridge (*hashi o wataru*) 橋を渡る.
2 (place crosswise) ... o ko꜔osa saseru ...を交差させる Ⓥ: cross a knife and fork (*naifu to fooku o koosa saseru*) ナイフとフォークを交差させる.
3 (meet and pass) ... to yu꜔kichigaꜜu ...と行き違う Ⓒ: Your letter crossed mine. (*Kimi no tegami wa watashi no to yukichigai ni natta.*) 君の手紙は私のと行き違いになった.
— *vi.* **1** (go across) yo꜔kogiꜜru 横切る Ⓒ; o꜔odañ suru 横断する Ⓘ: He crossed while the signal was red. (*Kare wa shiñgoo ga aka na no ni oodañ shita.*) 彼は信号が赤なのに横断した.
2 (extend across) ko꜔osa suru 交差する Ⓘ; ma꜔jiwaꜜru 交わる Ⓒ: The roads cross in the center of town. (*Dooro wa machi no chuushiñ de koosa shite imasu.*) 道路は町の中心で交差しています.
3 (pass each other) yu꜔kichigai ni naꜜru 行き違いになる Ⓒ.
— *n.* **1** (two lines placed across) ju꜔ujikee 十字形; ba꜔tsu-jiꜜrushi ×印: mark a place with a cross (*basho ni batsu-jirushi o tsukeru*) 場所に×印をつける.
2 (symbol of crucifixion) ju꜔ujika 十字架.
— *adj.* (having a bad temper) fu꜔kiꜜgeñ na 不機嫌な; (angry) o꜔koꜜtte (iru) 怒って(いる): Since I was late he was cross. (*Watashi ga okureta no de kare wa fukigeñ datta.*) 私が遅れたので彼は不機嫌だった.

crossing *n.* (of roads) ko꜔osateñ 交差点; (of a railway) fu꜔mikiri 踏切.

crouch *vi.* ka꜔gamu かがむ Ⓒ; sha꜔gamu しゃがむ Ⓒ: He crouched and hid behind the curtain. (*Kare wa shagañde kaateñ no kage ni kakureta.*) 彼はしゃがんでカーテンの陰に隠れた.

crow *n.* kaˈrasu からす(鳥).

crowd *n.* **1** (a large group of people) guˈñshuu 群衆; hiˈtogomi 人込み: He disappeared into the crowd. (*Kare wa hitogomi no naka ni sugata o keshita.*) 彼は人込みの中に姿を消した.

2 (the masses) taˈishuu 大衆; miñˈshuu 民衆: appeal to the crowd (*taishuu ni uttaeru*) 大衆に訴える.

a crowd of ... *adj.* oˈozee no 大勢の: There was a crowd of people in the park. (*Kooeñ ni wa oozee no hito ga ita.*) 公園には大勢の人がいた.

— *vt.* **1** (gather) ... ni muˈragaˈru ...に群がる Ⓒ; oˈshikakeˈru 押しかける Ⓥ: Girls crowded the theater. (*Oñna-no-ko-tachi ga gekijoo ni oshikaketa.*) 女の子たちが劇場に押しかけた.

2 (fill) ... o iˈppai ni suru ...をいっぱいにする Ⓘ; (... ni) ... o oˈshikoˈmu (...に)...を押し込む Ⓒ: crowd people into a room (*heya ni hito o oshikomu*) 部屋に人を押し込む.

— *vi.* (come together) (... ni) muˈragaˈru (...に)群がる Ⓒ; aˈtsumaˈru 集まる Ⓒ: The children crowded around the player. (*Kodomo-tachi wa sono señshu no mawari ni atsumatta.*) 子どもたちはその選手の周りに集まった.

crowded *adj.* koˈmiatta 込み合った; koˈmiatte iru 込み合っている; koˈñzatsu shita [shite iru] 混雑した[している]: a crowded bus (*komiatta basu*) 込み合ったバス.

crown *n.* **1** (headdress) kaˈñmuri 冠; oˈokañ 王冠: wear a crown (*kañmuri o kaburu*) 冠をかぶる.

2 (royal position) oˈoi 王位: succeed to the crown (*ooi o tsugu*) 王位を継ぐ.

3 (head) aˈtama 頭; noˈoteˈñ 脳天; (of a mountain) choˈojoˈo 頂上.

— *vt.* **1** (make a king or queen) oˈoi ni tsuˈkaseˈru 王位につかせる Ⓥ: She was crowned in 1558. (*Kanojo wa señ-gohyaku-gojuu-hachi-neñ ni ooi ni tsuita.*) 彼女は1558年に王位についた.

2 (cover) ... no uˈe o ooˈu ...の上を覆う Ⓒ: Snow crowned the mountain. (*Yuki ga yama no ue o ootte ita.*) 雪が山の上を覆っていた.

crucial *adj.* juˈudai na 重大な; keˈttee-teki na 決定的な: a crucial problem (*juudai na moñdai*) 重大な問題.

crude *adj.* **1** (unrefined) teˈñneñ no mamaˈ no 天然のままの; kaˈkoo shite inai 加工していない: crude oil (*geñyu*) 原油.

2 (rough) soˈya na 粗野な; geˈhiˈñ na 下品な: crude behavior (*soya na furumai*) 粗野なふるまい.

cruel *adj.* **1** (merciless) zaˈñkoku na 残酷な; zaˈñgyaku na 残虐な: It is cruel to beat a dog. (*Inu o butsu no wa zañkoku da.*) 犬をぶつのは残酷だ.

2 (painful) hiˈsañ na 悲惨な; muˈzañ na 無惨な: meet with a cruel death (*hisañ na saigo o togeru*) 悲惨な最期を遂げる.

cruelty *n.* zaˈñkoku 残酷; zaˈñgyaku 残虐: treat animals with cruelty (*doobutsu o zañkoku ni atsukau*) 動物を残酷に扱う.

crumb *n.* paˈñ kuˈzu パンくず; paˈñkoˈ パン粉.

crumble *vi.* (boˈroboro ni) kuˈzureˈru (ぼろぼろに)崩れる Ⓥ; kuˈdakeˈru 砕ける Ⓥ: The old wall crumbled down. (*Furui hee ga kuzure-ochita.*) 古い塀が崩れ落ちた.

crush *vt.* **1** (press) ... o oˈshitsubuˈsu ...を押しつぶす Ⓒ: crush an empty beer can (*biiru no akikañ o oshitsubusu*) ビールの空き缶を押しつぶす.

2 (grind) ... o kuˈdaˈku ...を砕く Ⓒ: crush ice (*koori o kudaku*) 氷を砕く.

3 (defeat) ... o kaˈimetsu saseru ...を壊滅させる Ⓥ: crush one's enemies (*teki o kaimetsu saseru*) 敵を

壊滅させる.

— *vi.* (become wrinkled) shiʳwa ni naˡru しわになる Ⓒ: This material crushes easily. (*Kono kiji wa sugu ni shiwa ni naru.*) この生地はすぐにしわになる.

— *n.* **1** (crushing) oʳshitsubuˡsu koʳtoˡ 押しつぶすこと; fuʳñsai 粉砕.
2 (crowded people) zaʳttoo 雑踏; guʳñshuu 群衆: a crush in the subway (*chikatetsu no zattoo*) 地下鉄の雑踏.

crust *n.* paˡñ no kaʳwaˡ パンの皮.

cry *vi.* **1** (weep) naʳku 泣く Ⓒ: She cried when she heard the sad news. (*Sono kanashii shirase o kiite kanojo wa naita.*) その悲しい知らせを聞いて彼女は泣いた.
2 (shout) koˡe o aʳgeru 声を上げる Ⓥ; saʳkeˡbu 叫ぶ Ⓒ: She cried for help. (*Kanojo wa koe o agete tasuke o motometa.*) 彼女は声を上げて助けを求めた.

— *vt.* ... to saʳkeˡbu ...と叫ぶ Ⓒ: "Fire!" he cried. (*"Kaji da" to kare wa sakeñda.*) 「火事だ」と彼は叫んだ.

— *n.* **1** (shout) saʳkebi(goˡe) 叫び(声); oʳgoˡe 大声: give a cry of pain (*kutsuu no sakebigoe o ageru*) 苦痛の叫び声をあげる.
2 (of a bird) naʳkigoˡe 鳴き声; (of a beast) hoʳeˡru koe ほえる声: the cries of wolves (*ookami no hoeru koe*) おおかみのほえる声.

cube *n.* **1** (solid body) riʳppootai 立方体: a cube of sugar (*kakuzatoo*) 角砂糖.
2 (of multiplying) saʳñjoo 3乗.

— *vt.* ... o saʳñjoo suru ...を3乗する Ⓘ: If you cube 2, you will get the answer 8. (*Ni o sañjoo suru to kotae wa hachi desu.*) 2を3乗すると答は8です.

cuff links *n.* kaʳfusu boˡtañ カフスボタン.

cultivate *vt.* **1** (till) ... o taʳgayaˡsu ...を耕す Ⓒ; koʳosaku suru 耕作する Ⓘ: cultivate a field (*hatake o tagayasu*) 畑を耕す.
2 (grow) ... o saʳibai suru ...を栽培する Ⓘ: cultivate mushrooms (*kinoko o saibai suru*) きのこを栽培する.
3 (train) ... o yaʳshinaˡu ...を養う Ⓒ; miʳgaku 磨く Ⓒ: cultivate one's mind (*seeshiñ o yashinau*) 精神を養う.

cultural *adj.* buˡñka no 文化の; kyoʳoyoo no 教養の: cultural exchange (*buñka no kooryuu*) 文化の交流.

culture *n.* **1** (civilization) buˡñka 文化: Japanese culture (*Nihoñ buñka*) 日本文化.
2 (refinement) kyoʳoyoo 教養: a person of culture (*kyooyoo no aru hito*) 教養のある人.
3 (of plants) saʳibai 栽培; (of fish, etc.) yoʳoshoku 養殖: the culture of roses (*bara no saibai*) ばらの栽培 / the culture of pearls (*shiñju no yooshoku*) 真珠の養殖.

cunning *adj.* zuʳruˡi ずるい; waʳrugashikoˡi 悪賢い: I was fooled by his cunning tricks. (*Watashi wa kare no zurui yarikata ni damasareta.*) 私は彼のずるいやりかたにだまされた.

cup *n.* **1** (of Japanese tea) chaʳwañ 茶わん; (of coffee) kaˡppu カップ.
2 (cupful) chaʳwañ [kaˡppu] iˡppai 茶わん[カップ]1杯; -hai 杯: two cups of tea (*koocha ni-hai*) 紅茶2杯. ⟪⇨ appendix⟫
3 (ornamental vessel) yuʳushoˡohai 優勝杯; kaˡppu カップ: win the cup (*yuushoo suru*) 優勝する.

cupboard *n.* (cabinet) shoʳkkiˡdana 食器棚; (closet) toʳdana 戸棚.

curb *n.* (of a street) eˡñseki 縁石.

cure *vt.* **1** (heal) ... o chiʳryoo suru ...を治療する Ⓘ; naʳoˡsu 治す Ⓒ: The doctor cured him of his illness. (*Isha wa kare no byooki o naoshita.*) 医者は彼の病気を治した.
2 (make better) ... o naʳoˡsu ... を直す Ⓒ: cure bad habits (*warui kuse o naosu*) 悪い癖を直す.

— *n.* **1** (remedy) chiʳryoo 治療; ryoʳoyoo 療養: undergo a cure (*chiryoo o ukeru*) 治療を受ける.

2 (method) chi⌈ryoohoo 治療法; (medicine) chi⌈ryo⌉oyaku 治療薬: a cure for cancer (*gañ no chiryoo-yaku*) がんの治療薬.

curiosity *n.* ko⌈oki⌉shiñ 好奇心: satisfy one's curiosity (*kookishiñ o mañzoku saseru*) 好奇心を満足させる.

curious *adj.* **1** (eager) shi⌈ritaga⌉ru 知りたがる; ko⌈oki⌉shiñ no [ga] tsu⌈yo⌉i 好奇心の[が]強い: She is curious to know everything. (*Kanojo wa nañ de mo shiritagaru.*) 彼女は何でも知りたがる.
2 (strange) ki⌉myoo na 奇妙な; me⌈zurashi⌉i 珍しい: It is curious that you have heard nothing from him. (*Kimi ga kare kara nani mo kiite inai no wa kimyoo da.*) 君が彼から何も聞いていないのは奇妙だ.

curiously *adv.* me⌈zurashi-so⌉o ni 珍しそうに: He looked curiously at the insect. (*Kare wa mezurashi-soo ni sono mushi o mita.*) 彼は珍しそうにその虫を見た.

curl *vt.* ... o ka⌉aru saseru …をカールさせる [V]; ma⌈kiage⌉ru 巻き上げる [V]: curl one's hair (*kami o kaaru saseru*) 髪をカールさせる.
— *vi.* ka⌉aru suru カールする [I]; u⌉zu o ma⌈ku 渦を巻く [C]: The smoke curled into the air. (*Kemuri wa uzu o maite kuuchuu ni nobotta.*) 煙は渦を巻いて空中に昇った.
— *n.* ka⌉aru カール; ma⌈kige 巻き毛.

currency *n.* **1** (money) tsu⌉uka 通貨; ka⌉hee 貨幣: paper currency (*shihee*) 紙幣 / foreign currency (*gaika*) 外貨.
2 (being in common) tsu⌈uyoo 通用; ru⌉fu 流布: The rumor soon gained currency. (*Sono uwasa wa sugu ni rufu shita.*) そのうわさはすぐに流布した.

current *n.* **1** (stream) na⌈gare⌉ 流れ; (of the sea) ka⌈iryuu 海流: the current of a river (*kawa no nagare*) 川の流れ / the Japan Current (*Nihoñ-kairyuu*) 日本海流.
2 (of electricity) de⌈ñryuu 電流: alternating current (*kooryuu*) 交流 / direct current (*chokuryuu*) 直流.
3 (of the times) ji⌈ryuu 時流; to⌈ki no nagare⌉ 時の流れ: swim with the current (*jiryuu ni shitagau*) 時流に従う.
— *adj.* **1** (generally accepted) ge⌉ñzai tsu⌈kawarete iru 現在使われている: That word is no longer current. (*Sono kotoba wa geñzai wa tsukawarete inai.*) そのことばは現在は使われていない. / current fashions (*geñzai no ryuukoo*) 現在の流行
2 (of the present time) ge⌉ñzai no 現在の; i⌉ma no 今の: the current month (*koñgetsu*) 今月 / the current year (*kotoshi*) ことし / the current number one CD (*ima ichibañ urete iru shii dii*) 今いちばん売れている CD.

curse *vt.* ... o no⌈noshi⌉ru …をののしる [C]: curse a barking dog (*hoete iru inu o nonoshiru*) ほえている犬をののしる.
— *vi.* (... o) no⌈ro⌉u (…を)のろう [C]: He cursed at his ill luck. (*Kare wa jibuñ no fuuñ o norotta.*) 彼は自分の不運をのろった.
— *n.* no⌈roi のろい; ak⌈uta⌉i 悪態: shout curses at a person (*hito ni akutai o tsuku*) 人に悪態をつく.

curtain *n.* **1** (at a window) ka⌉a-teñ カーテン: draw a curtain (*kaateñ o hiku*) カーテンを引く.
2 (in a theater) ma⌈ku 幕: The curtain rises [falls] at eight. (*Maku wa hachi-ji ni aku [oriru].*) 幕は8時に開く[下りる].

curve *n.* ka⌉abu カーブ; (line) kyo⌈kuseñ 曲線: a curve in the road (*dooro no kaabu*) 道路のカーブ / draw a curve (*kyokuseñ o egaku*) 曲線を描く.
— *vi.* ka⌉abu suru カーブする [I]; ma⌈garu 曲がる [C]; kyo⌈kuseñ o ega⌉ku 曲線を描く [C]: The road curves to the right. (*Michi wa migi ni kaabu shite iru.*) 道は右にカーブしている.

cushion *n.* ku⌉sshoñ クッション; za-

ˈbuˈtoñ 座ぶとん: sit on a cushion (*zabutoñ no ue ni suwaru*) 座ぶとんの上に座る.

custom *n.* **1** (tradition) kaˈñshuu 慣習; fuˈushuu 風習: follow an old custom (*furuku kara no kañshuu ni shitagau*) 古くからの慣習に従う.
2 (habit) shuˈukañ 習慣: It is my custom to get up early. (*Hayaoki wa watashi no shuukañ desu.*) 早起きは私の習慣です.

customary *adj.* shuˈukañ-teki na 習慣的な; kaˈñree no 慣例の: It is customary for me to take a walk. (*Sañpo o suru no wa watashi no shuukañ desu.*) 散歩するのは私の習慣です. / customary law (*kañshuuhoo*) 慣習法.

customer *n.* (of a shop) o-ˈkyaku お客; koˈkyaku 顧客; (of business) toˈrihikisaki 取引先.

customs *n.* **1** (department) zeˈe-kañ 税関: get through customs (*zeekañ o tsuuka suru*) 税関を通過する / a customs declaration form (*zeekañ shiñkokusho*) 税関申告書.
2 (taxes) kaˈñzee 関税: pay customs (*kañzee o harau*) 関税を払う.

cut *vt.* **1** (sever) ... o kiˈru ...を切る Ⓒ; kiˈritoˈru 切り取る Ⓒ: cut a cake into six (*keeki o muttsu ni kiru*) ケーキを六つに切る / cut a branch from a tree (*ki kara eda o kiritoru*) 木から枝を切りとる.
2 (with a sharp edge) ... o kiˈru ...を切る Ⓒ: I cut my finger with a knife. (*Watashi wa naifu de yubi o kitta.*) 私はナイフで指を切った.
3 (delete) ... o saˈkujo suru ...を削除する Ⓘ; keˈzuru 削る Ⓒ; kaˈtto suru カットする Ⓘ: The editor cut the article. (*Heñshuusha wa sono kiji o sakujo shita.*) 編集者はその記事を削除した.
4 (reduce) ... o saˈkugeñ suru ...を削減する Ⓘ; kiˈritsumeˈru 切り詰める Ⓥ: cut one's traveling expenses (*ryohi o kiritsumeru*) 旅費を切り詰める.
5 (shorten) ... o kiˈru ...を切る Ⓒ; (of hair) kaˈru 刈る Ⓒ; kaˈtto suru カットする Ⓘ: cut one's nails (*tsume o kiru*) つめを切る / Cut my hair short, please. (*Kami o mijikaku katte [kitte] kudasai.*) 髪を短く刈って[切って]ください.
— *vi.* **1** (of a knife, etc.) kiˈreˈru 切れる Ⓥ: This razor cuts well. (*Kono kamisori wa yoku kireru.*) このかみそりはよく切れる.
2 (of a road) (... o) tsuˈkkiˈtte suˈsumu (...を)突っ切って進む Ⓒ; yoˈkogiˈru 横切る Ⓒ: I cut through the woods. (*Watashi wa mori o tsukkitte itta.*) 私は森を突っ切って行った.
— *n.* **1** (wound) kiˈriˈkizu 切り傷: I got a cut on my hand. (*Watashi wa te ni kirikizu o koshiraeta.*) 私は手に切り傷をこしらえた.
2 (deletion) saˈkujo 削除; kaˈtto カット: make several cuts in a film (*firumu o suu-kasho katto suru*) フィルムを数か所カットする.
3 (reduction) saˈkugeñ 削減: a tax cut (*geñzee*) 減税.
4 (style) kaˈtaˈ 型: change the cut of one's hair (*kamigata o kaeru*) 髪型を変える.
5 (of meat) kiˈrimiˈ 切り身; hiˈtoˈ-kire ひと切れ: a tender cut of beef (*gyuuniku no yawarakai kirimi*) 牛肉の柔らかい切り身.

cute *adj.* kaˈwaiˈi かわいい; kiˈree na きれいな: a cute baby (*kawaii akañboo*) かわいい赤ん坊.

cycle *n.* **1** (period of time) shuˈuki 周期; juˈñkañ 循環; uˈtsurikawari 移り変わり: the cycle of the seasons (*kisetsu no utsurikawari*) 季節の移り変わり.
2 (bicycle) jiˈteˈñsha 自転車: get on a cycle (*jiteñsha ni noru*) 自転車に乗る / get off a cycle (*jiteñsha kara oriru*) 自転車から降りる.

cycling *n.* saˈikuriñgu サイクリング.

cylinder *n.* eˈñtoo 円筒; eˈñchuu 円柱; shiˈriˈñdaa シリンダー.

D

dagger *n.* ta[ñto]o 短刀; ta[ñkeñ 短剣.

daily *adj.* ma]inichi no 毎日の: one's daily work (*mainichi no shigoto*) 毎日の仕事.

— *adv.* ma]inichi 毎日: Traffic accidents happen daily. (*Kootsuu jiko wa mainichi okoru.*) 交通事故は毎日起こる.

dairy *n.* **1** (farm) ra[kunoojoo 酪農場.

2 (store) nyu[use]ehiñ ha[ñba]iteñ 乳製品販売店.

dairy cattle *n.* nyu[ugyuu 乳牛.

dam *n.* da]mu ダム: build a dam (*damu o tsukuru*) ダムを造る.

damage *n.* so[ñgai 損害; hi]gai 被害: The fire caused a lot of damage. (*Sono kaji wa ooki-na soñgai o ataeta.*) その火事は大きな損害を与えた.

— *vt.* ... ni so[ñgai o a[taeru ...に損害を与える V; ... o ki[zutsuke]ru ...を傷つける V: damage a person's reputation (*hito no meesee o kizutsukeru*) 人の名声を傷つける.

damp *adj.* shi[kke no a]ru 湿気のある; ji]mejime shita [shite iru] じめじめした[している]; nu[reta ぬれた; nu[rete iru ぬれている: damp weather (*jimejime shita teñki*) じめじめした天気 / a damp towel (*nureta taoru*) ぬれたタオル.

— *n.* shi[kke 湿気.

dampen *vt.* ... o shi[meraseru ...を湿らせる V: dampen the clothes before ironing (*airoñ o kakeru mae ni fuku o shimeraseru*) アイロンをかける前に服を湿らせる.

dance *n.* da]ñsu ダンス; o[dori 踊り; da[ñsu pa]atii ダンスパーティー: give a dance (*dañsu paatii o moyoosu*) ダンスパーティーを催す.

— *vi.* o[doru 踊る C: I danced with his daughter. (*Watashi wa kare no musume-sañ to odotta.*) 私は彼の娘さんと踊った.

dandruff *n.* fu[ke ふけ: I have dandruff. (*Watashi wa fukeshoo desu.*) 私はふけ症です.

danger *n.* ki[keñ 危険; ki]ki 危機: This bridge is in danger. (*Kono hashi wa kikeñ da.*) この橋は危険だ. / He is out of danger now. (*Kare wa ima wa kiki o dasshita.*) 彼は今は危機を脱した.

dangerous *adj.* ki[keñ na 危険な; a[bunai 危ない: This river is dangerous to cross. (*Kono kawa o wataru no wa kikeñ da.*) この川を渡るのは危険だ. / It is dangerous to play here. (*Koko de asobu no wa abunai.*) ここで遊ぶのは危ない.

dare *vt., aux.* (be brave enough to do) o[moiki]tte <verb> 思い切って...; a]ete <verb> あえて...: He dared to call on his teacher. (*Kare wa omoikitte señsee o tazuneta.*) 彼は思い切って先生を訪ねた. / I dared not tell her the sad news. (*Watashi wa sono kanashii shirase o totemo kanojo ni ienakatta.*) 私はその悲しい知らせをとても彼女に言えなかった.

dark *adj.* **1** (without light) ku[rai 暗い: a dark night (*kurai yoru*) 暗い夜.

2 (of color) ko]i 濃い; (of hair) ku[ro]i 黒い: dark brown (*koi chairo*) 濃い茶色 / He has dark hair. (*Kare wa kuroi kami o shite iru.*) 彼は黒い髪をしている.

darkness *n.* ku[rayami 暗やみ: The room was in darkness. (*Heya wa kurayami datta.*) 部屋は暗やみだった.

dash *vi.* (rush) to[sshiñ suru 突進する I; i[so]ide i[ku 急いで行く C: He dashed for the bus. (*Kare wa basu ni noroo to isoida.*) 彼はバスに乗ろうと急いだ.

— *n.* ta[ñkyori-kyo]osoo 短距離競

走: a 100 meter dash (*hyaku-mee-toru kyoosoo*) 100 メートル競走.

data *n.* shi⌉ryoo 資料; de⌉eta データ: collect data (*deeta o atsumeru*) データを集める / analyze data (*deeta o buñseki suru*) データを分析する.

date *n.* **1** (day) hi⌈zuke 日付; ki⌉-jitsu 期日: This letter has no date. (*Kono tegami wa hizuke ga nai.*) この手紙は日付がない. / set the date for departure (*shuppatsu no kiji-tsu o kimeru*) 出発の期日を決める.
2 (appointment) de⌉eto デート: have a date with a girlfriend (*gaaru-fureñdo to deeto suru*) ガールフレンドとデートする.
date of birth *n.* se⌈eneñ ga⌉ppi 生年月日.

daughter *n.* mu⌈sume⌉ 娘; (someone else's) o⌈jo⌉o-sañ お嬢さん: one's only daughter (*hitori musume*) 一人娘.

daughter-in-law *n.* (your own) yo⌈me 嫁; (someone else's) o-⌈yo-me-sañ お嫁さん.

dawn *n.* yo⌈ake⌉ 夜明け; a⌈kegata 明け方: They departed at dawn. (*Kare-ra wa akegata ni shuppatsu shita.*) 彼らは明け方に出発した.
— *vi.* yo⌉ ga a⌈keru 夜が明ける Ⓥ: The day dawned. (*Yo ga aketa.*) 夜が明けた.

day *n.* **1** (24 hours) hi 日; i⌈chi-nichi⌉ 一日: What is the fee per day? (*Ichi-nichi no ryookiñ wa ikura desu ka?*) 一日の料金はいくらですか. / What day will it be ready? (*Sore wa nañ nichi ni dekimasu ka?*) それは何日にできますか. / I am staying here three days. (*Koko ni mikka taizai shimasu.*) ここに三日滞在します.
2 (daytime) hi⌈ruma⌉ 昼間; ni⌈tchuu 日中: It was very warm during the day. (*Hiruma wa totemo atataka datta.*) 昼間はとても暖かだった.
the day after tomorrow *n.* a⌈sa⌉tte あさって.
the day before yesterday *n.* o⌈totoi おととい; is⌈saku⌉jitsu 一昨日.

daytime *n.* hi⌈ruma⌉ 昼間; hi⌈ru⌉ 昼; ni⌈tchuu 日中.

dazzle *vt.* ... no me⌉ o ku⌈ramase⌉ru …の目をくらませる Ⓥ: I was dazzled by the car's headlights. (*Watashi wa sono kuruma no heddoraito de me ga kurañda.*) 私はその車のヘッドライトで目がくらんだ.

dead *adj.* **1** (of an animal) shi⌈ñda 死んだ; shi⌈ñde iru 死んでいる: The rat is dead. (*Nezumi wa shiñde iru.*) ねずみは死んでいる.
2 (of a plant) ka⌈reta 枯れた; ka-⌈rete iru 枯れている: dead leaves (*kareha*) 枯れ葉.
3 (of a telephone line) tsu⌈ujinai 通じない: The telephone line went dead after the earthquake. (*Jishiñ no ato de deñwa ga tsuujinaku natta.*) 地震の後で電話が通じなくなった.
4 (of a battery) ki⌉reta 切れた; ki⌉-rete iru 切れている: The battery is dead. (*Deñchi ga kirete iru.*) 電池が切れている.
5 (no longer used) su⌈tareta 廃れた; su⌈tarete iru 廃れている: a dead custom (*sutareta shuukañ*) 廃れた習慣.

dead end *n.* (of a road) yu⌈kido-mari 行き止まり; (of work) yu⌈kizu-mari 行き詰まり: come to a dead end (*yukizumaru*) 行き詰まる.

deadline *n.* shi⌈mekiri 締め切り: meet the deadline (*shimekiri ni maniau*) 締め切りに間に合う.

deaf *adj.* mi⌈mi⌉ ga fu⌈ji⌉yuu na 耳が不自由な; mi⌈mi⌉ ga to⌈oi 耳が遠い: My grandfather is rather deaf. (*Watashi no ojii-sañ wa mimi ga tooi.*) 私のおじいさんは耳が遠い.

deal *vt.* **1** (distribute) ... o ku⌈ba⌉ru …を配る Ⓒ: deal the cards (*kaado o kubaru*) カードを配る.
2 (give) ... o ku⌈waeru …を加える Ⓥ: deal a blow to a person (*hito ni dageki o kuwaeru*) 人に打撃を加える.
— *vi.* **1** (treat) (... o) a⌈tsukau (…を)扱う Ⓒ; sho⌉ri suru 処理する Ⓘ: deal with pupils fairly (*seeto o koo-hee ni atsukau*) 生徒を公平に扱う /

deal with a difficult problem (*muzukashii moñdai o shori suru*) 難しい問題を処理する.
2 (do business) (... o) a[kina]u (...を)商う Ⓒ; (... no) sho]obai o suru (...の)商売をする Ⓘ: He deals in furniture. (*Kare wa kagu no shoobai o shite iru.*) 彼は家具の商売をしている.
— *n.* to[ri]hiki 取り引き; ke[eyaku 契約: make a deal with a company (*kaisha to keeyaku o musubu*) 会社と契約を結ぶ.

dealer *n.* sho]oniñ 商人; ha[ñbai gyo]osha 販売業者: a car dealer (*jidoosha hañbai gyoosha*) 自動車販売業者.

dear *adj.* (much loved) shi[ñai na 親愛な: one's dearest friend (*shiñyuu*) 親友. ★ The greeting in a formal Japanese letter is '*haikee*' 拝啓. However, '*haikee*' requires the use of many other formal expressions at the same time. For an easy-to-use equivalent of the English 'Dear ...,' use '*zeñryaku*' 前略.

death *n.* shi] 死; shi[boo 死亡: Carelessness caused his death. (*Fuchuui ga kare no shi o maneita.*) 不注意が彼の死を招いた. / death penalty (*shikee*) 死刑.

debate *vt.* ... o to]oroñ suru ...を討論する Ⓘ; to]ogi suru 討議する Ⓘ: debate a problem (*moñdai o tooroñ suru*) 問題を討論する.
— *vi.* to]oroñ suru 討論する Ⓘ; to]ogi suru 討議する Ⓘ: They debated all night. (*Kare-ra wa hitobañ-juu tooroñ shita.*) 彼らは一晩中討論した.
— *n.* to]oroñ 討論; to]ogi 討議.

debt *n.* (financial) sha[kki]ñ 借金; fu[sai 負債; (moral) o]ñgi 恩義: pay back a debt (*shakkiñ o kaesu*) 借金を返す / I am in debt to him. (*Watashi wa kare ni kari ga aru.*) 私は彼に借りがある. ★ '*Kari*' means both financial and moral debt.

debtor *n.* ka[ri]nushi 借り主; sa[imu]sha 債務者.

decade *n.* ju[une]ñ-kañ 十年間: the past decade (*koko juuneñ-kañ*) ここ10年間.

decay *vi.* **1** (rot) ku[sa]ru 腐る Ⓒ: This tree began to decay inside. (*Kono ki wa naka ga kusari-hajimeta.*) この木は中が腐り始めた.
2 (decline) o[toroe]ru 衰える Ⓥ: The state's power decayed. (*Kokuryoku ga otoroeta.*) 国力が衰えた.
— *n.* fu[shoku 腐食; o[toroe 衰え: tooth decay (*mushiba*) 虫歯.

deceased *adj.* shi]kyo shita 死去した; bo]o- 亡: his deceased father (*kare no boofu*) 彼の亡父 / the will of the deceased (*kojiñ no isho*) 故人の遺書.

deceit *n.* da[ma]su ko[to] だますこと; sa]gi 詐欺; kyo]gi 虚偽: practice deceit on a person (*hito o damasu*) 人をだます.

deceive *vt.* ... o da[ma]su ...をだます Ⓒ; a[zamu]ku 欺く Ⓒ: The advertisement deceived us. (*Sono kookoku wa watashi-tachi o damashita.*) その広告は私たちをだました.

December *n.* ju[uni-gatsu] 12月.

decent *adj.* **1** (suitable) mi[gurushi]ku nai 見苦しくない; ki[chi]ñto shita [shite iru] きちんとした[している]: He appeared in decent clothes. (*Kare wa kichiñto shita fukusoo de arawareta.*) 彼はきちんとした服装で現われた.
2 (good enough) wa[ru]ku nai 悪くない; ka]nari yoi かなりよい: He makes a decent living. (*Kare wa kanari yoi seekatsu o shite iru.*) 彼はかなりよい生活をしている.

decide *vt.* **1** (resolve) ... to ke]sshiñ suru ...と決心する Ⓘ: He decided to be a lawyer. (*Kare wa beñgoshi ni naroo to kesshiñ shita.*) 彼は弁護士になろうと決心した.
2 (settle) ... ni ki[meru ...に決める Ⓥ: I decided to postpone my departure. (*Watashi wa shuppatsu o nobasu koto ni kimeta.*) 私は出発を延ばすことに決めた.
— *vi.* (... o) ke[ttee suru (...を)決定する Ⓘ: We have to decide on our next plan. (*Tsugi no keekaku o ket-*

tee shinakereba naranai.) 次の計画を決定しなければならない.

decision *n.* ke'ttee 決定; ke'tsuroñ 結論: decision by majority (*tasuuketsu*) 多数決 / come to a decision (*ketsuroñ ni tassuru*) 結論に達する.

d

decisive *adj.* ke'ttee-teki na 決定的な; ki'ppa'ri shita [shite iru] きっぱりした[している]: decisive evidence (*kettee-teki na shooko*) 決定的な証拠 / a decisive answer (*kippari shita kotae*) きっぱりした答え.

deck *n.* **1** (of a ship) de'kki デッキ; ka'ñpañ 甲板.
2 (of a tape) de'kki デッキ: a cassette deck (*kasetto dekki*) カセットデッキ.
3 (of playing cards) hi'to'-kumi 一組: a deck of cards (*torañpu hitokumi*) トランプ一組.

declaration *n.* **1** (announcement) se'ñge'ñ 宣言; fu'koku 布告: the Declaration of Independence (*dokuritsu señgeñ*) 独立宣言 / a declaration of war (*señseñ fukoku*) 宣戦布告.
2 (formal statement) shi'ñkoku 申告: a customs declaration form (*zeekañ shiñkokusho*) 税関申告書.

declare *vt.* **1** (affirm) ... to ge'ñmee suru ...と言明する Ⓘ; da'ñge'ñ suru 断言する Ⓘ: He declared that he was innocent. (*Kare wa jibuñ wa keppaku da to geñmee shita.*) 彼は自分は潔白だと言明した.
2 (say openly) ... o se'ñge'ñ suru ...を宣言する Ⓘ: declare independence (*dokuritsu o señgeñ suru*) 独立を宣言する.
3 (make a statement) ... o shi'ñkoku suru ...を申告する Ⓘ: I have nothing to declare. (*Shiñkoku suru mono wa nani mo arimaseñ.*) 申告するものは何もありません.

decline *vt.* ... o ko'towa'ru ...を断る Ⓒ: She declined my invitation. (*Kanojo wa watashi no shootai o kotowatta.*) 彼女は私の招待を断った.
— *vi.* o'toroe'ru 衰える Ⓥ; sa'ga'ru 下がる Ⓒ: His health is gradually declining. (*Kare no keñkoo wa jojo ni otoroete iru.*) 彼の健康は徐徐に衰えている. / Prices have declined a little. (*Bukka ga sukoshi sagatta.*) 物価が少し下がった.

decorate *vt.* ... o ka'zaru ...を飾る Ⓒ: She decorated her room with flowers. (*Kanojo wa heya o hana de kazatta.*) 彼女は部屋を花で飾った.

decoration *n.* so'oshoku 装飾; ka'zari 飾り: interior decoration (*shitsunai sooshoku*) 室内装飾 / Christmas tree decorations (*Kurisumasu-tsurii no kazari*) クリスマスツリーの飾り.

decrease *vi.* he'ru 減る Ⓒ; su'kuna'ku naru 少なくなる Ⓒ: The population of Tokyo is decreasing. (*Tookyoo no jiñkoo wa hette iru.*) 東京の人口は減っている.
— *vt.* ... o he'rasu ...を減らす Ⓒ: decrease the number of accidents (*jiko no kazu o herasu*) 事故の数を減らす.
— *n.* ge'ñshoo 減少; shu'kushoo 縮小.

decree *n.* (law) ho'oree 法令; se'eree 制令; (ruling) ha'ñketsu 判決: issue a decree (*hooree o happu suru*) 法令を発布する.

dedicate *vt.* (... ni) ... o sa'sageru (...に)...をささげる Ⓥ: He dedicated his life to his work. (*Kare wa shigoto no tame ni isshoo o sasageta.*) 彼は仕事のために一生をささげた.

deed *n.* o'konai 行い; ko'oi 行為: a good deed (*rippa na kooi*) 立派な行為.

deep *adj.* **1** fu'ka'i 深い; fu'kasa ga ... a'ru 深さが...ある: a deep river (*fukai kawa*) 深い川 / This well is 10 meters deep. (*Kono ido wa fukasa ga juu-meetoru aru.*) この井戸は深さが10メートルある. / a deep breath (*shiñ-kokyuu*) 深呼吸.
2 (color) ko'i 濃い; (voice) fu'to'i 太い: a deep red (*koi aka*) 濃い赤 / have a deep voice (*futoi koe o shite iru*) 太い声をしている.

3 (absorbed) mu⌈chuu ni na⌉tte (iru) 夢中になって(いる): He was deep in thought. (*Kare wa kañgaegoto ni muchuu ni natte ita.*) 彼は考え事に夢中になっていた.

deepen *vi.* fu⌈ka⌉ku naru 深くなる Ⓒ; fu⌈kama⌉ru 深まる Ⓒ: The autumn colors have deepened. (*Aki no iro ga fukamatta.*) 秋の色が深まった.

deeply *adv.* fu⌉kaku 深く; ko⌈ko⌉ro kara 心から: breathe deeply (*iki o fukaku suu*) 息を深く吸う / I am deeply grateful to you. (*Watashi wa kokoro kara anata ni kañsha shite orimasu.*) 私は心からあなたに感謝しております.

deer *n.* shi⌈ka しか(鹿): deerskin (*shikagawa*) 鹿皮.

defeat *vt.* ... o ma⌈kasu ...を負かす Ⓒ; ya⌈bu⌉ru 破る Ⓒ: We defeated our opponent by three to one. (*Wareware wa aite o sañ-tai ichi de makashita.*) われわれは相手を3対1で負かした. / be defeated (*makeru*) 負ける.

— *n.* (failure) ma⌈ke 負け; shi⌈ppai 失敗; (in war) ha⌈iboku 敗北: four victories and two defeats (*yoñ shoo ni hai*) 4勝2敗.

defect *n.* (flaw) ke⌈kkañ 欠陥; (fault) ke⌈tte⌉ñ 欠点: a defect in a car (*kuruma no kekkañ*) 車の欠陥.

defend *vt.* 1 (guard) ... o ma⌈mo⌉ru ...を守る Ⓒ; fu⌈se⌉gu 防ぐ Ⓒ: defend oneself from dangers (*kikeñ kara mi o mamoru*) 危険から身を守る.

2 (legal) ... o be⌉ñgo suru ...を弁護する Ⓘ; yo⌉ogo suru 擁護する Ⓘ: I defended his opinions. (*Watashi wa kare no ikeñ o beñgo shita.*) 私は彼の意見を弁護した.

defendant *n.* (person accused) hi⌈koku (niñ) 被告(人).

defense *n.* 1 (protection) bo⌉ogyo 防御; bo⌈oee 防衛: fight in defense of one's country (*kuni no booee no tame ni tatakau*) 国の防衛のために戦う.

2 (argument) be⌉ñgo 弁護; be⌈ñmee 弁明: He made no defense for his behavior. (*Kare wa jibuñ no kooi ni tsuite nani mo beñmee shinakatta.*) 彼は自分の行為について何も弁明しなかった.

deference *n.* ke⌉ei 敬意; so⌈ñkee 尊敬: pay deference to a person (*hito ni keei o harau*) 人に敬意を払う.

deficiency *n.* (shortage) fu⌈soku 不足; ke⌈tsuboo 欠乏: a deficiency of vitamin C (*bitamiñ shii no fusoku*) ビタミンCの不足.

deficit *n.* (loss) ke⌉ssoñ 欠損; (of accounting) a⌈kaji 赤字: a trade deficit (*booeki-akaji*) 貿易赤字.

define *vt.* 1 (explain) ... o te⌉egi suru ...を定義する Ⓘ: define a word (*kotoba o teegi suru*) 言葉を定義する.

2 (fix the limits) ... o ge⌈ñtee suru ...を限定する Ⓘ; sa⌈dame⌉ru 定める Ⓥ: define a boundary (*kyookai o sadameru*) 境界を定める.

definite *adj.* 1 (fixed) i⌈ttee no 一定の: a definite period of time (*ittee kikañ*) 一定期間.

2 (clear) me⌈ekaku na 明確な; ka⌈kujitsu na 確実な: a definite answer (*kakutoo*) 確答.

definitely *adv.* ta⌉shika ni 確かに; me⌈ekaku ni 明確に: He is definitely the best player in the team. (*Kare wa tashika ni chiimu de ichibañ sugureta señshu desu.*) 彼は確かにチームでいちばん優れた選手です.

definition *n.* te⌉egi 定義.

defrost *vt.* 1 (unfreeze) shi⌈mo⌉ [ko⌈ori] o to⌉ru 霜[氷]をとる Ⓒ: defrost a refrigerator (*reezoko no shimo o toru*) 冷蔵庫の霜をとる.

2 (of frozen food) ... o ka⌈itoo suru ...を解凍する Ⓘ: defrost the meat (*niku o kaitoo suru*) 肉を解凍する.

defy *vt.* 1 (challenge) ... ni i⌈do⌉mu ...に挑む Ⓒ: I defied him to solve the problem. (*Watashi wa sono moñdai o toite miro to kare ni idoñda.*) 私はその問題を解いてみろと彼

に挑んだ.
2 (resist) ... **ni ha⌈ñkoo suru** ...に反抗する ⓘ; ... **o mu⌉shi suru** ...を無視する ⓘ: defy public opinion (*yoroñ o mushi suru*) 世論を無視する.

degree *n.* **1** (unit of measure) **do** 度: 10 degrees below zero (*reeka juu do*) 零下 10 度. ★ The Celsius scale is used in Japan.
2 (extent) **te⌉edo** 程度; **da⌈ñkai** 段階: It is a matter of degree. (*Sore wa teedo no moñdai desu.*) それは程度の問題です.
3 (title) **ga⌉kui** 学位: get a master's degree (*shuushi no gakui o toru*) 修士の学位をとる.

delay *vt.* **1** (put off) ... **o no⌈ba⌉su** ...を延ばす Ⓒ; **e⌈ñki suru** 延期する ⓘ: delay one's departure (*shuppatsu o nobasu*) 出発を延ばす.
2 (make late) ... **o o⌈kuraseru** ...を遅らせる Ⓥ: How long will it be delayed? (*Dono kurai okuremasu ka?*) どのくらい遅れますか.

delegate *n.* **da⌈ihyoo** 代表: send a delegate to a convention (*taikai e daihyoo o okuru*) 大会へ代表を送る.
— *vt.* ... **o da⌈ihyoo to shite o⌈kuru** ...を代表として送る Ⓒ; **ha⌈keñ suru** 派遣する ⓘ: The union delegated me to attend the meeting. (*Kumiai wa daihyoo to shite watashi o sono kaigi ni hakeñ shita.*) 組合は代表として私をその会議に派遣した.

delegation *n.* **da⌈ihyo⌉odañ** 代表団.

delete *vt.* ... **o sa⌉kujo suru** ...を削除する ⓘ: delete two lines (*ni-gyoo sakujo suru*) 2 行削除する.

deliberate *adj.* **1** (intentional) **ko⌉i no** 故意の; **ke⌈ekaku-teki na** 計画的な: a deliberate lie (*koi no uso*) 故意のうそ.
2 (careful) **shi⌈ñchoo na** 慎重な: We took deliberate action. (*Watashi-tachi wa shiñchoo na koodoo o totta.*) 私たちは慎重な行動をとった.

deliberately *adv.* **1** (on purpose) **wa⌉zato** わざと; **ko⌉i ni** 故意に: I deliberately told a lie. (*Watashi wa wazato uso o itta.*) 私はわざとうそを言った.
2 (carefully) **shi⌈ñchoo ni** 慎重に: He climbed the stairs deliberately. (*Kare wa shiñchoo ni kaidañ o nobotta.*) 彼は慎重に階段を上った.

delicate *adj.* **1** (fine and beautiful) **se⌈ñsai na** 繊細な; **yu⌉ubi na** 優美な: a delicate piece of silk (*señsai na kinu no orimono*) 繊細な絹の織物.
2 (fragile) **kya⌈sha na** きゃしゃな; **ko⌈ware-yasu⌉i** 壊れやすい: a delicate little girl (*kyasha na oñna-no-ko*) きゃしゃな女の子 / a delicate vase (*koware-yasui kabiñ*) 壊れやすい花びん.
3 (needing careful handling) **bi⌈myoo na** 微妙な; **a⌈tsukai-niku⌉i** 扱いにくい: a very delicate question (*hijoo ni bimyoo na moñdai*) 非常に微妙な問題.

delicious *adj.* **o⌈ishii** おいしい: It's delicious! (*Oishii desu ne.*) おいしいですね.

delight *n.* **o⌈oyo⌉rokobi** 大喜び; **u⌈re⌉shisa** うれしさ: She received the present with delight. (*Kanojo wa ooyorokobi de sono okurimono o uketotta.*) 彼女は大喜びでその贈り物を受け取った.

delightful *adj.* **ta⌈noshi⌉i** 楽しい; **yu⌉kai na** 愉快な: a delightful summer vacation (*tanoshii natsuyasumi*) 楽しい夏休み.

deliver *vt.* **1** (distribute) ... **o ha⌈itatsu suru** ...を配達する ⓘ; **to⌈doke⌉ru** 届ける Ⓥ: Newspapers are delivered twice a day. (*Shiñbuñ wa ichinichi ni ni-do haitatsu sareru.*) 新聞は 1 日に 2 度配達される. / Please deliver this package to him. (*Kono tsutsumi o kare ni todokete kudasai.*) この包みを彼に届けてください.
2 (hand over) ... **o hi⌈kiwata⌉su** ...を引き渡す Ⓒ: deliver a thief to the police (*doroboo o keesatsu ni hikiwatasu*) どろぼうを警察に引き渡す.
3 (speak) ... **o ha⌈na⌉su** 話す Ⓒ; **no-**

ˈbeˈru 述べる V: He delivered a long speech. (*Kare wa nagai eñzetsu o shita.*) 彼は長い演説をした.

delivery *n.* **1** (distribution) haˈitatsu 配達: delivery of goods (*shinamono no haitatsu*) 品物の配達 / express [special] delivery (*sokutatsu*) 速達.
2 (birth of a child) shuˈssañ 出産: an easy [a difficult] delivery (*añ-[nañ]zañ*) 安[難]産.

delusion *n.* moˈosoo 妄想; saˈkkaku 錯覚: suffer from delusions (*moosoo ni nayamu*) 妄想に悩む.

deluxe *adj.* goˈoka na 豪華な; zeˈetaˈku na ぜいたくな: a deluxe hotel (*gooka na hoteru*) 豪華なホテル / a deluxe edition (*gookabañ*) 豪華版.

demand *vt.* **1** (request) ... o yoˈokyuu suru …を要求する I; moˈtomeˈru 求める V: The union demanded higher wages. (*Kumiai wa chiñage o yookyuu shita.*) 組合は賃上げを要求した.
2 (need) ... o yoˈosuˈru …を要する I: This problem demands careful attention. (*Kono mondai wa saishiñ no chuui o yoosuru.*) この問題は細心の注意を要する.
— *n.* **1** (request) yoˈokyuu 要求: He turned down our demands. (*Kare wa wareware no yookyuu o shirizoketa.*) 彼はわれわれの要求を退けた.
2 (desire) juˈyoo 需要: demand and supply (*juyoo to kyookyuu*) 需要と供給.

democracy *n.* (system) miˈñshushuˈgi 民主主義; miˈñshuseˈeji 民主政治; (nation) miˈñshushugiˈkoku 民主主義国.

democratic *adj.* miˈñshushuˈgi no 民主主義の; miˈñshu-teki na 民主的な: His way of doing things is democratic. (*Kare no yarikata wa miñshu-teki da.*) 彼のやり方は民主的だ.

demonstrate *vt.* **1** (show) ... o jiˈssai ni yatte miseˈru …を実際にやって見せる V: He demonstrated how to operate the machine. (*Kare wa sono kikai no ugokashikata o jissai ni yatte miseta.*) 彼はその機械の動かし方を実際にやって見せた.
2 (prove) ... o shoˈomee suru …を証明する I: I demonstrated the correctness of the theory. (*Watashi wa sono riroñ ga tadashii koto o shoomee shita.*) 私はその理論が正しいことを証明した.
— *vi.* (parade) deˈmo o suru デモをする I: They demonstrated against the new taxes. (*Kare-ra wa atarashii zee ni hañtai shite demo o shita.*) 彼らは新しい税に反対してデモをした.

demonstration *n.* **1** (advertising) jiˈtsubutsu-seˈñdeñ 実物宣伝.
2 (teaching) jiˈtsubutsu-kyoˈoiku 実物教育: a demonstration of a new computer (*atarashii koñpyuutaa no jitsubutsu-kyooiku*) 新しいコンピューターの実物教育.
3 (parade) deˈmo デモ: We took part in the demonstrations. (*Watashi-tachi wa sono demo ni sañka shita.*) 私たちはそのデモに参加した.

denial *n.* hiˈtee 否定; hiˈniñ 否認: He made a denial of his connection with the matter. (*Kare wa sono keñ to no kakawari o hitee shita.*) 彼はその件とのかかわりを否定した.

denounce *vt.* ... o hiˈnañ suru …を非難する I: She denounced me as a liar. (*Kanojo wa watashi o usotsuki da to hinañ shita.*) 彼女は私をうそつきだと非難した.

dense *adj.* misˈshuu shita [shite iru] 密集した[している]; koˈi 濃い: a dense forest (*mitsuriñ*) 密林 / a dense fog (*noomu*) 濃霧.

density *n.* miˈtsudo 密度: the density of population (*jiñkoo mitsudo*) 人口密度.

dent *n.* heˈkomi へこみ: I put a dent in my car. (*Watashi wa kuruma ni hekomi o tsukutte shimatta.*) 私は車にへこみをつくってしまった.
— *vt.* ... o heˈkomaseru …をへこま

せる Ⓥ: He dented my car. (*Kare wa watashi no kuruma o hekomaseta.*) 彼は私の車をへこませた.

dentist *n.* ha¹isha 歯医者; shi⌈ka¹i 歯科医: consult a dentist (*haisha ni mite morau*) 歯医者に診てもらう.

deny *vt.* **1** (declare to be untrue) ... o hi⌈tee suru ...を否定する Ⓘ; u⌈chikesu 打ち消す Ⓒ: He denied the rumor. (*Kare wa sono uwasa o hitee shita.*) 彼はそのうわさを否定した.
2 (refuse) ... o ko⌈ba¹mu ...を拒む Ⓒ; ko⌈towa¹ru 断る Ⓒ: The company denied the employees' requests. (*Kaisha wa juugyooiñ no yookyuu o kobañ da.*) 会社は従業員の要求を拒んだ.

depart *vi.* **1** (leave) shu⌈ppatsu suru 出発する Ⓘ; de¹ru 出る Ⓥ: They departed early in the morning. (*Kare-ra wa asa hayaku shuppatsu shita.*) 彼らは朝早く出発した. / The train departs at 8:15. (*Ressha wa hachi-ji juugo-fuñ ni demasu.*) 列車は8時15分に出ます.
2 (change) (... kara) ha⌈zureru (...から)外れる Ⓥ; so⌈re¹ru それる Ⓥ: depart from an original plan (*moto no keekaku kara soreru*) もとの計画からそれる.

department *n.* **1** (office) bu¹moñ 部門; -bu 部: the sales department (*hañbaibu*) 販売部.
2 (store) u⌈riba 売場: the toy department (*omocha-uriba*) おもちゃ売場.
3 (university) ga⌈kka 学科: the department of English (*eebuñka*) 英文科.
4 (government) -shoo 省: the Department of Agriculture (*Noomushoo*) 農務省.

department store *n.* de⌈pa¹ato デパート: go shopping at a department store (*depaato e kaimono ni iku*) デパートへ買い物に行く.

departure *n.* (general) shu⌈ppatsu 出発; (of a train, etc.) ha⌈ssha 発車: What is the departure time of the next flight? (*Tsugi no biñ no shuppatsu jikoku wa nañ-ji desu ka?*) 次の便の出発時刻は何時ですか.

depend *vi.* **1** (rely on) (... o) ta¹yori ni suru (...を)頼りにする Ⓘ; a⌈te ni suru 当てにする Ⓘ: We depend on you. (*Watashi-tachi wa anata o tayori ni shite imasu.*) 私たちはあなたを頼りにしています.
2 (be controlled by) (... ni) yo⌈ru (...に)よる Ⓒ; ... shi¹dai da ...次第だ: Our departure depends on the weather. (*Wareware no shuppatsu wa teñki shidai desu.*) われわれの出発は天気次第です. / It depends. (*Baai ni yorimasu.*) 場合によります.

dependent *adj.* **1** (relying) ... ni ta⌈yo¹tte iru ...に頼っている: He is still dependent on his parents. (*Kare wa mada oya ni tayotte iru.*) 彼はまだ親に頼っている.
2 (being controlled) ... shi¹dai no ...次第の: Your success is dependent on your efforts. (*Anata no seekoo wa doryoku shidai desu.*) あなたの成功は努力次第です.
— *n.* (family member) fu⌈yoo ka¹zoku 扶養家族.

deplore *vt.* **1** (lament) ... o na⌈ge¹ku ...を嘆く Ⓒ; na⌈gekikanashi¹mu 嘆き悲しむ Ⓒ: deplore the death of a close friend (*shiñyuu no shi o nageku*) 親友の死を嘆く.
2 (express regret) ... o za⌈ñne¹ñ [i⌈kañ] ni o⌈mo¹u ...を残念[遺憾]に思う Ⓒ: I deplore the use of violence. (*Watashi wa booryoku no kooshi o zañneñ ni omou.*) 私は暴力の行使を残念に思う.

deport *vt.* ... o tsu⌈ihoo suru ...を追放する Ⓘ; kyo⌈osee-so¹okañ suru 強制送還する Ⓘ: He was deported for having entered the country illegally. (*Kare wa fuhoo nyuukoku no tame ni kyoosee sookañ sareta.*) 彼は不法入国のために強制送還された.

deposit *vt.* ... o yo⌈kiñ suru ...を預金する Ⓘ; a⌈zuke¹ru 預ける Ⓥ: deposit money in a bank (*giñkoo ni o-kane o azukeru*) 銀行にお金を預ける.

— *n.* (of bank) yo⌈kiñ 預金; (of housing) shi⌈ki⌉kiñ 敷金; (part payment) te⌈tsukekiñ 手付け金; a⌈tamakiñ 頭金: pay a deposit (*tetsukekiñ o harau*) 手付け金を払う.

depress *vt.* ... o ki⌈ochi saseru ... を気落ちさせる [V]; ga⌈kka⌉ri saseru がっかりさせる [V]: The news depressed us. (*Sono shirase wa watashi-tachi o gakkari saseta.*) その知らせは私たちをがっかりさせた.

depression *n.* **1** (slump) fu⌈kyoo 不況; fu⌈ke⌉eki 不景気: The industry is now in a depression. (*Sañgyoo-kai wa ima fukyoo desu.*) 産業界は今不況です.
2 (sadness) yu⌈u-utsu ゆううつ; ra⌈kutañ 落胆: mental depression (*ikishoochiñ*) 意気消沈.

deprive *vt.* ... o u⌈ba⌉u ...を奪う [C]: They were deprived of their lands. (*Kare-ra wa tochi o ubawareta.*) 彼らは土地を奪われた.

depth *n.* **1** (deepness) fu⌈ka⌉sa 深さ: measure the depth of a river (*kawa no fukasa o hakaru*) 川の深さを測る.
2 (from front to back) o⌈kuyuki 奥行き: the depth of a building (*tatemono no okuyuki*) 建物の奥行き.

deputy *n.* da⌈iri 代理; da⌈iriniñ 代理人: I acted as his deputy. (*Watashi wa kare no dairi o tsutometa.*) 私は彼の代理を務めた.

derive *vt.* **1** (obtain) ... o e⌉ru ...を得る [V]: derive pleasure from music (*oñgaku kara tanoshimi o eru*) 音楽から楽しみを得る.
2 (originate) ... ni yu⌈rai suru ...に由来する [I]; (... kara) ki⌉te iru (...から)来ている [V]: This word is derived from Latin. (*Kono tañgo wa Rateñgo kara kite iru.*) この単語はラテン語から来ている.

descend *vi.* **1** (go down) ku⌈daru 下る [C]; o⌈ri⌉ru 降りる [V]: We descended from the hilltop. (*Watashi-tachi wa oka no choojoo kara kudatta.*) 私たちは丘の頂上から下った. / The hot-air balloon descended in a field. (*Sono netsukikyuu wa hatake ni orita.*) その熱気球は畑に降りた.
2 (be handed down) tsu⌈tawaru 伝わる [C]: The business descended from father to son. (*Sono shoobai wa chichioya kara musuko e to tsutawatta.*) その商売は父親から息子へと伝わった.
— *vt.* ... o o⌈ri⌉ru ...を下りる [V]: descend the steps (*kaidañ o oriru*) 階段を下りる.

descendant *n.* shi⌉soñ 子孫: a descendant of a famous writer (*yuumee na sakka no shisoñ*) 有名な作家の子孫.

describe *vt.* **1** (give an account) ... o no⌈be⌉ru ...を述べる [V]; i⌈i arawa⌉su 言い表す [C]: He described his experiences. (*Kare wa jibuñ no taikeñ o nobeta.*) 彼は自分の体験を述べた.
2 (tell) ... to i⌈u ...と言う [C]: They described my plan as a failure. (*Kare-ra wa watashi no keekaku wa shippai da to itta.*) 彼らは私の計画は失敗だと言った.

description *n.* ki⌈jutsu 記述; byo⌈osha 描写; (of a person) ni⌉ñsoo 人相: give a full description (*kuwashiku setsumee suru*) 詳しく説明する.

desert[1] *n.* sa⌈baku 砂漠.

desert[2] *vt.* **1** (abandon) ... o mi⌈suteru ...を見捨てる [V]: desert one's wife and children (*saishi o misuteru*) 妻子を見捨てる.
2 (leave) ... o su⌈teru ...を捨てる [V]; da⌈ssoo suru 脱走する [I]: desert a ship (*fune o suteru*) 船を捨てる / The soldiers deserted their posts. (*Heetai-tachi wa mochiba kara dassoo shita.*) 兵隊たちは持ち場から脱走した.

deserve *vt.* ... ni a⌈tai suru ...に値する [I]: His conduct deserves praise. (*Kare no kooi wa shoosañ ni atai suru.*) 彼の行為は称賛に値する.

design *vt.* **1** (draw up a plan) ... o de⌈za⌉iñ suru ...をデザインする [I]; se⌈k-

kee suru 設計する [I]: design a new dress (*atarashii doresu o dezaiñ suru*) 新しいドレスをデザインする / Who designed this house? (*Dare ga kono uchi o sekkee shimashita ka?*) だれがこの家を設計しましたか.
2 (purpose) ... ni yo⌈tee suru ...に予定する [I]: This plot is designed as a parking lot. (*Kono tochi wa chuushajoo ni suru yotee desu.*) この土地は駐車場にする予定です.
— *n.* **1** (pattern) mo⌈yoo 模様: a curtain with a design of roses (*bara no moyoo no kaateñ*) ばらの模様のカーテン.
2 (sketch) de⌈za⌉iñ デザイン; zu⌈añ 図案: a design for an advertisement (*kookoku no zuañ*) 広告の図案.
3 (plan) se⌈kkee 設計: a building under design (*sekkee-chuu no tatemono*) 設計中の建物.

designer *n.* de⌈za⌉inaa デザイナー; se⌈kke⌉esha 設計者: a fashion designer (*fasshoñ dezainaa*) ファッションデザイナー.

desirable *adj.* no⌈zomashi⌉i 望ましい; ko⌈nomashi⌉i 好ましい: desirable surroundings (*nozomashii kañkyoo*) 望ましい環境.

desire *vt.* ... o no⌈zomu 望む [C]: ne⌈ga⌉u 願う [C]: I desire your presence. (*Anata no shusseki o nozomimasu.*) あなたの出席を望みます. / I desire that you answer my letter as soon as possible. (*Dekiru dake hayaku watashi no tegami ni heñji o kudasaru koto o negatte imasu.*) できるだけ早く私の手紙に返事を下さることを願っています.
— *n.* no⌈zomi 望み; ne⌈ga⌉i 願い; yo⌈kuboo 欲望: My desire is to visit your country. (*Watashi no nozomi wa anata no kuni o tazuneru koto desu.*) 私の望みはあなたの国を訪ねることです.

desk *n.* **1** (furniture) tsu⌈kue 机: The letters are all on your desk. (*Tegami wa zeñbu tsukue no ue ni arimasu.*) 手紙は全部机の上にあります.
2 (of a hotel, etc.) u⌈ketsuke 受付.

despair *n.* ze⌈tsuboo 絶望; shi⌈tsuboo 失望: She tried to kill herself out of despair. (*Kanojo wa zetsuboo no amari jisatsu shiyoo to shita.*) 彼女は絶望のあまり自殺しようとした.
— *vi.* ze⌈tsuboo suru 絶望する [I]; a⌈kirame⌉ru あきらめる [V]: We despaired of success. (*Seekoo wa akirameta.*) 成功はあきらめた.

desperate *adj.* **1** (reckless) hi⌈sshi no 必死の: He was desperate to escape. (*Kare wa nigeyoo to hisshi datta.*) 彼は逃げようと必死だった.
2 (hopeless) ze⌈tsuboo-teki na 絶望的な: The situation is desperate. (*Jookyoo wa zetsuboo-teki desu.*) 状況は絶望的です.

despise *vt.* ... o ke⌈ebetsu suru ...を軽蔑する [I]: Don't despise the poor. (*Mazushii hito-tachi o keebetsu shite wa ikenai.*) 貧しい人たちを軽蔑してはいけない.

despite *prep.* ... ni mo ka⌈kawa⌉razu ...にもかかわらず: I attended the meeting despite my illness. (*Watashi wa byooki ni mo kakawarazu sono kai ni shusseki shita.*) 私は病気にもかかわらずその会に出席した.

dessert *n.* de⌈za⌉ato デザート: I'd like some fruit for dessert. (*Dezaato ni kudamono o kudasai.*) デザートに果物を下さい.

destination *n.* mo⌈kuteki⌉chi 目的地; yu⌈kisaki 行き先: We arrived at our destination at five. (*Watashitachi wa mokutekichi ni go-ji ni tsuita.*) 私たちは目的地に5時に着いた.

destiny *n.* u⌉ñmee 運命: It was his destiny to die on the mountain. (*Yama de shinu no ga kare no uñmee datta.*) 山で死ぬのが彼の運命だった.

destroy *vt.* **1** (damage) ... o ha⌈kai suru ...を破壊する [I]; ko⌈wa⌉su 壊す [C]: Three houses were destroyed by a landslide. (*Jisuberi de sañ-geñ no uchi ga hakai sa-*

reta.) 地滑りで3軒の家が破壊された.
2 (ruin) ... o u⌈chikuda⌉ku ...を打ち砕く Ⓒ: His dreams were destroyed by the failure in the examination. (*Shikeñ ni shippai shite kare no yume wa uchikudakareta.*) 試験に失敗して彼の夢は打ち砕かれた.

destruction *n.* ha⌈kai 破壊: environmental destruction (*kañkyoo hakai*) 環境破壊.

detach *vt.* (... kara) ... o to⌈rihazusu (...から)...を取り外す Ⓒ: detach a key from its chain (*kusari kara kagi o torihazusu*) 鎖から鍵を取り外す.

detail *n.* (small item) ko⌈maka⌉i te⌈ñ⌉ 細かい点; sa⌉ibu 細部; sho⌈osai 詳細: I will tell you the details of my plan later. (*Watashi no keekaku no shoosai wa nochi-hodo o-shirase shimasu.*) 私の計画の詳細は後ほどお知らせします.

detain *vt.* **1** (hold back) ... o hi⌈kitome⌉ru ...を引き止める Ⓥ: I won't detain you. (*O-hikitome wa itashimaseñ.*) お引き止めはいたしません.
2 (of the police) ... o ryu⌉uchi [ko⌉ochi] suru ...を留置[拘置]する Ⓘ: He was detained at the police station. (*Kare wa keesatsu ni ryuuchi sareta.*) 彼は警察に留置された.

detect *vt.* ... o mi⌈tsukeru ...を見つける Ⓥ; ha⌈kkeñ suru 発見する Ⓘ: I detected a slight flaw in the lens. (*Reñzu ni kasuka na kizu o mitsuketa.*) レンズにかすかな傷を見つけた.

detective *n.* (police) ke⌉eji 刑事; (civilian) ta⌈ñtee 探偵: a private detective (*shiritsu tañtee*) 私立探偵.

detergent *n.* se⌉ñzai 洗剤: wash with detergent (*señzai de arau*) 洗剤で洗う.

determination *n.* **1** (resolution) ke⌉sshiñ 決心; ke⌈tsuda⌉ñryoku 決断力: a person of determination (*ketsudañryoku no aru hito*) 決断力のある人.
2 (decision) ke⌈ttee 決定: the determination of the date (*hidori no kettee*) 日取りの決定.

determine *vt.* **1** (resolve) ⟨verb⟩ ke⌉sshiñ o suru ...決心をする Ⓘ; ke⌈tsui o suru 決意をする Ⓘ: I determined to go to Japan. (*Watashi wa Nihoñ e iku kesshiñ o shita.*) 私は日本へ行く決心をした.
2 (decide) ... o ki⌈meru ...を決める Ⓥ; ke⌈ttee suru 決定する Ⓘ: We have to determine the date for the next meeting. (*Tsugi no kaigi no hi o kimenakereba naranai.*) 次の会議の日を決めなければならない.

determined *adj.* ka⌈taku ke⌉sshiñ shita [shite iru] 堅く決心した[している]; da⌉ñko to shita [shite iru] 断固とした[している]: He was firmly determined to become a painter. (*Kare wa gaka ni naroo to kataku kesshiñ shite ita.*) 彼は画家になろうと堅く決心していた.

detest *vt.* ... o hi⌉doku ki⌈rau ...をひどく嫌う Ⓒ; ... ga ki⌈rai da ...が嫌いだ: I detest speaking in public. (*Watashi wa hito-mae de hanasu no ga kirai da.*) 私は人前で話すのが嫌いだ.

detour *n.* ma⌈wari⌉michi 回り道: make a detour (*mawarimichi o suru*) 回り道をする.

develop *vt.* **1** ... o ha⌈ttatsu saseru ...を発達させる Ⓥ; ha⌈tteñ saseru 発展させる Ⓥ: He developed the little shop into a large supermarket. (*Kare wa sono chiisa-na mise o hatteñ sasete ooki-na suupaa ni shita.*) 彼はその小さな店を発展させて大きなスーパーにした.
2 (of photograph) ... o ge⌈ñzoo suru ...を現像する Ⓘ: Please develop this film. (*Kono firumu o geñzoo shite kudasai.*) このフィルムを現像してください.

development *n.* **1** (growth) ha⌈ttatsu 発達; ha⌈tteñ 発展: industrial development (*sañgyoo no hattatsu*) 産業の発達 / I was surprised at the unexpected development in the case. (*Jikeñ no igai na hatteñ ni watashi wa odoroita.*) 事件の意外な発展に私は驚いた.

2 (of photograph) ge⌈ñzoo 現像.

device *n.* so⌉ochi 装置; shi⌈kake 仕掛け: a safety device (*añzeñ soochi*) 安全装置.

devil *n.* (evil) a⌉kuma 悪魔; (ogre) o⌈ni 鬼: speaking of the devil ... (*uwasa o sureba ...*) うわさをすれば….

devise *vt.* ... o ko⌈oañ suru …を考案する Ⓘ; ka⌈ñgaeda⌉su 考え出す Ⓒ: He devised a new system of classification. (*Kare wa atarashii buñrui hoohoo o kañgaedashita.*) 彼は新しい分類方法を考え出した.

devoid *adj.* ... ga na⌉i …がない; ka⌈kete iru 欠けている: He is devoid of common sense. (*Kare wa jooshiki ga nai.*) 彼は常識がない.

devote *vt.* ... ni se⌈ññeñ suru …に専念する Ⓘ; ... o (... ni) sa⌈sageru …を(…に)ささげる Ⓥ: He devoted his fortune to the study of cancer. (*Kare wa jibuñ no zaisañ o gañ no keñkyuu ni sasageta.*) 彼は自分の財産をがんの研究にささげた.

dew *n.* tsu⌉yu 露: The grass was wet with dew. (*Kusa no ue ni tsuyu ga orite ita.*) 草の上に露が降りていた.

diabetes *n.* to⌈onyoobyoo 糖尿病.

diagnose *vt.* ... o shi⌈ñdañ suru …を診断する Ⓘ: The doctor diagnosed my illness as pneumonia. (*Isha wa watashi no byooki o haieñ to shiñdañ shita.*) 医者は私の病気を肺炎と診断した.

diagnosis *n.* shi⌈ñdañ 診断: What diagnosis did the doctor make? (*Isha wa doñna shiñdañ o shimashita ka?*) 医者はどんな診断をしましたか.

diagram *n.* zu 図; zu⌈kee 図形: draw a diagram (*zu o kaku*) 図をかく.

dial *n.* (telephone) da⌈iyaru ダイヤル; (watch) mo⌈jibañ 文字盤: turn a dial (*daiyaru o mawasu*) ダイヤルを回す.

— *vt.* ... ni de⌈ñwa o ka⌈ke⌉ru …に電話をかける Ⓥ: dial the police (*keesatsu ni deñwa o kakeru*) 警察に電話をかける.

dialect *n.* ho⌈oge⌉ñ 方言: speak in a dialect (*hoogeñ de hanasu*) 方言で話す.

dialogue *n.* ta⌈iwa 対話: a dialogue between the mayor and citizens (*shichoo to shimiñ to no taiwa*) 市長と市民との対話.

diameter *n.* cho⌈kkee 直径: This circle is one meter in diameter. (*Kono eñ wa chokkee ga ichimeetoru aru.*) この円は直径が1メートルある.

diamond *n.* da⌈iyamo⌉ñdo ダイヤモンド. ★ Often shortened to '*daiya*.': a diamond ring (*daiya no yubiwa*) ダイヤの指輪.

diarrhea *n.* ge⌈ri 下痢: I have diarrhea. (*Watashi wa geri o shite imasu.*) 私は下痢をしています.

diary *n.* ni⌈kki 日記: keep a diary (*nikki o tsukete iru*) 日記をつけている.

dictate *vt.* **1** (secretarial) ... o ka⌈kitoraseru …を書き取らせる Ⓥ; ko⌈ojutsu suru 口述する Ⓘ: dictate a letter to one's secretary (*hisho ni tegami o koojutsu suru*) 秘書に手紙を口述する.

2 (order) ... o o⌈shitsuke⌉ru …を押しつける Ⓥ: dictate the terms of a treaty (*jooyaku no jookeñ o oshitsukeru*) 条約の条件を押しつける.

dictation *n.* ka⌈kitori 書き取り; ko⌈ojutsu 口述: take a dictation (*koojutsu o kakitoru*) 口述を書き取る.

dictator *n.* do⌈kusa⌉isha 独裁者.

dictionary *n.* ji⌉sho 辞書; ji⌈teñ 辞典: consult a dictionary (*jisho o hiku*) 辞書を引く. ★ English-Japanese dictionaries for Japanese are called '*ee-wa jiteñ*' 英和辞典, and for foreigners '*ee-nichi jiteñ*' 英日辞典; Japanese-English dictionaries for Japanese are called '*wa-ee jiteñ*' 和英辞典, and for foreigners '*nichi-ee jiteñ*' 日英辞典.

die *vi.* (animal) shi⌈nu 死ぬ Ⓒ;

(plant) ka^rreru 枯れる Ⓥ: He died from overwork. (*Kare wa karoo de shiñda.*) 彼は過労で死んだ. / This pine tree has died. (*Kono matsu no ki wa karete shimatta.*) この松の木は枯れてしまった.

diet *n.* **1** (regular food) ni⌈chijoo no tabemo⌉no 日常の食べ物; sho⌈kuji 食事; sho⌈ku-se⌉ekatsu 食生活: a well-balanced diet (*barañsu no toreta shokuji*) バランスのとれた食事.
2 (restricted food) da⌉ietto ダイエット; sho⌈kujiryo⌉ohoo 食事療法; ge⌈ñshoku 減食: I am on a diet. (*Watashi wa daietto o shite imasu.*) 私はダイエットをしています.

Diet *n.* ko⌈kkai 国会; gi⌉kai 議会: The Diet is in session. (*Kokkai wa kaikai-chuu desu.*) 国会は開会中です.

differ *vi.* **1** (be unlike) chi⌈gau 違う Ⓒ; ko⌈tona⌉ru 異なる Ⓒ: His brothers differ in character. (*Kare no kyoodai wa seekaku ga chigau.*) 彼の兄弟は性格が違う.
2 (disagree) i⌉keñ ga a⌈wa⌉nai 意見が合わない: I differed with him on the matter. (*Watashi wa sono keñ de kare to ikeñ ga awanakatta.*) 私はその件で彼と意見が合わなかった.

difference *n.* **1** (being different) chi⌈gai 違い; sa 差: I cannot see any difference in these sentences. (*Kono futatsu no buñ no chigai ga wakarimaseñ.*) この二つの文の違いがわかりません. / the difference in temperature (*kioñ no sa*) 気温の差.
2 (disagreement) so⌈oi 相違: differences of opinion (*ikeñ no sooi*) 意見の相違.

different *adj.* **1** (unlike) chi⌈gatta 違った; chi⌈gatte iru 違っている; ko⌈tona⌉tta 異なった; ko⌈tona⌉tte iru 異なっている: The article was different from the sample. (*Shinamono wa mihoñ to chigatte ita.*) 品物は見本と違っていた.
2 (separate) be⌈tsu no 別の: I consulted a different doctor. (*Watashi wa betsu no isha ni mite moratta.*) 私は別の医者に診てもらった.

difficult *adj.* mu⌈zukashi⌉i 難しい; ko⌉ñnañ na 困難な: Japanese grammar is difficult for me. (*Nihoñgo no buñpoo wa watashi ni wa muzukashii.*) 日本語の文法は私には難しい. / It is difficult to go across this mountain. (*Kono yama o koeru no wa koñnañ desu.*) この山を越えるのは困難です.

difficulty *n.* mu⌈zuka⌉shisa 難しさ; ko⌉ñnañ 困難: I understood the difficulty of this job. (*Kono shigoto no muzukashisa ga wakarimashita.*) この仕事の難しさがわかりました.

dig *vt.* ... o ho⌉ru …を掘る Ⓒ; ho⌈rida⌉su 掘り出す Ⓒ: dig a well (*ido o horu*) 井戸を掘る / dig potatoes (*imo o horidasu*) いもを掘り出す.

digest *vt.* ... o sho⌈oka suru …を消化する Ⓘ: Food is digested in the stomach. (*Tabemono wa i de shooka sareru.*) 食べ物は胃で消化される.
— *vi.* sho⌈oka suru 消化する Ⓘ: He had food that was easy to digest. (*Kare wa shooka no yoi mono o tabeta.*) 彼は消化のよいものを食べた.

digestion *n.* sho⌈oka 消化; I have a good [poor] digestion. (*Watashi wa i ga joobu da [yowai].*) 私は胃がじょうぶだ[弱い].

digit *n.* **1** (number) su⌈uji 数字.
2 (place) ke⌈ta 桁: a five-digit number (*go-keta no suu*) 5 桁の数 / the 4th digit (*yoñ-bañme no keta*) 4 番目の桁.

dignity *n.* ki⌈hiñ 気品; i⌈geñ 威厳: a person of dignity (*kihiñ no aru hito*) 気品のある人 / maintain one's dignity (*igeñ o tamotsu*) 威厳を保つ.

dilemma *n.* ji⌈re⌉ñma ジレンマ; i⌈ta-ba⌉sami 板ばさみ: be in a dilemma (*jireñma ni ochiiru*) ジレンマに陥る.

diligent *adj.* ki⌈ñbeñ na 勤勉な; ne⌉sshiñ na 熱心な: a diligent student (*kiñbeñ na gakusee*) 勤勉な学

生 / He is diligent in work. (*Kare wa shigoto nesshiñ desu.*) 彼は仕事熱心です.

dim *adj.* **1** (not bright) u⌈sugurai 薄暗い: a dim room (*usugurai heya*) 薄暗い部屋.
2 (unclear) bo⌈ñya⌉ri shita [shite iru] ぼんやりした[している]; ha⌈kki⌉ri shi⌈nai はっきりしない: I have only a dim memory of the event. (*Sono koto wa boñyari to shika oboete inai.*) そのことはぼんやりとしか覚えていない.

dimension *n.* **1** (size) su⌈ñpoo 寸法: measure the dimensions of a box (*hako no suñpoo o hakaru*) 箱の寸法を測る.
2 (aspect) kyo⌈kumeñ 局面: a new dimension to politics (*seeji no atarashii kyokumeñ*) 政治の新しい局面.
3 (physics) ji⌉geñ 次元: the third dimension (*dai-sañ jigeñ*) 第3次元.

diminish *vi.* he⌈ru 減る Ⓒ; ge⌈ñshoo suru 減少する Ⓘ: The water in the dam is diminishing. (*Damu no mizu ga hette iru.*) ダムの水が減っている.
— *vt.* ... o he⌈rasu ...を減らす Ⓒ; ge⌈ñshoo saseru 減少させる Ⓥ: diminish the risk of war (*señsoo no kikeñ o herasu*) 戦争の危険を減らす.

dine *vi.* sho⌈kuji o suru 食事をする Ⓘ: What time can I dine? (*Shokuji no jikañ wa nañ-ji desu ka?*) 食事の時間は何時ですか.

dining room *n.* sho⌈kudoo 食堂: What time does the dining room open? (*Shokudoo wa nañ-ji ni hirakimasu ka?*) 食堂は何時に開きますか.

dinner *n.* yu⌈ushoku 夕食; sho⌈kuji 食事: Dinner is ready. (*Yuushoku no yooi ga dekimashita.*) 夕食の用意ができました. / I'd like a drink before dinner. (*Shokuji no mae ni nomimono o kudasai.*) 食事の前に飲物を下さい.

dip *vt.* **1** (put in) ... o cho⌉tto hi⌈tasu ...をちょっと浸す Ⓒ: dip a brush into paint (*hake o peñki ni chotto hitasu*) はけをペンキにちょっと浸す
2 (take out) ... o su⌈kuida⌉su ...をすくい出す Ⓒ; ku⌈mida⌉su くみ出す Ⓒ: dip water from a bucket (*baketsu kara mizu o kumidasu*) バケツから水をくみ出す.

diploma *n.* me⌈ñjoo 免状; (of graduation) so⌈tsugyoo sho⌉osho 卒業証書.

diplomacy *n.* ga⌈ikoo 外交.

diplomat *n.* ga⌈iko⌉okañ 外交官.

direct *adj.* **1** (straight) ma⌈ssu⌉gu na 真っすぐな; i⌈tcho⌉kuseñ no 一直線の: a direct road to the station (*eki e tsuujiru massugu na michi*) 駅へ通じる真っすぐな道 / a direct flight from Tokyo to New York (*Tookyoo kara Nyuu Yooku e no chokkoo-biñ*) 東京からニューヨークへの直行便.
2 (immediate) cho⌈kusetsu no 直接の; ji⌉ka no じかの: a direct influence (*chokusetsu no eekyoo*) 直接の影響.
— *adv.* ma⌈ssu⌉gu ni 真っすぐに; cho⌈kusetsu ni 直接に; cho⌈kkoo shite 直行して: This plane flies direct to London. (*Kono hikooki wa Rondoñ e chokkoo shimasu.*) この飛行機はロンドンへ直行します.
— *vt.* **1** (guide) ... ni mi⌈chi o o⌈shieru ...に道を教える Ⓥ: Can you direct me to the station? (*Eki made no michi o oshiete itadakemasu ka?*) 駅までの道を教えていただけますか.
2 (order) ... ni sa⌉shizu suru ...に指図する Ⓘ; me⌈ejiru 命じる Ⓥ: The policeman directed the driver to proceed slowly. (*Keekañ wa uñteñsha ni yukkuri susumu yoo meejita.*) 警官は運転者にゆっくり進むよう命じた.
3 (conduct) ... o shi⌈ki⌉ suru ...を指揮する Ⓘ; e⌈ñshutsu suru 演出する Ⓘ: direct a choir (*gasshoo o shiki suru*) 合唱を指揮する / direct a play (*geki o eñshutsu suru*) 劇を演出する.

direction *n.* **1** (course) ho⌈okoo

方向; ho⌈ogaku 方角: He went in the opposite direction. (*Kare wa hañtai no hookoo e ikimashita.*) 彼は反対の方向へ行きました.
2 (order) shi⌉ji 指示; sa⌉shizu 指図: We obeyed the teacher's directions. (*Watashi-tachi wa señsee no shiji ni shitagatta.*) 私たちは先生の指示に従った.

directly *adv.* **1** (straight) ma⌈ssu⌉gu ni 真っすぐに: I went directly to the hall. (*Watashi wa massugu ni sono kaijoo e itta.*) 私は真っすぐにその会場へ行った.
2 (immediately) cho⌈kusetsu (ni) 直接(に): I bought the goods directly from the wholesaler. (*Watashi wa sono shina o toñya kara chokusetsu katta.*) 私はその品を問屋から直接買った.

director *n.* (company) ju⌈uyaku 重役; to⌈rishimari⌉yaku 取締役; (screen) ka⌈ñtoku 監督; (institution) sho⌈choo 所長; (project) se⌈kini⌉ñsha 責任者: a board of directors (*juuyaku-kai*) 重役会.

directory *n.* (name list) ji⌈ñme⌉ebo 人名簿: a telephone directory (*deñwachoo*) 電話帳.

dirt *n.* (soil) tsu⌈chi⌉ 土; (mud) do⌈ro⌉ 泥; (dust) ho⌈kori ほこり: remove dirt from trousers (*zuboñ no doro o otosu*) ズボンの泥を落とす.

dirty *adj.* (morally and physically) ki⌈tana⌉i 汚い; (physically) yo⌈goreta 汚れた; yo⌈gorete iru 汚れている; (covered with mud) do⌈roda⌉rake no 泥だらけの: a dirty hand (*kitanai te*) 汚い手 / He wore a dirty shirt. (*Kare wa yogoreta shatsu o kite ita.*) 彼は汚れたシャツを着ていた.

disability *n.* (physical) shi⌈ñtai-sho⌉ogai 身体障害: mental disability (*seeshiñ-shoogai*) 精神障害.

disabled *adj.* shi⌈ñtai-sho⌉ogai no aru 身体障害のある: the disabled (*shiñtai shoogaisha*) 身体障害者.

disadvantage *n.* fu⌉ri na ta⌈chiba⌉ 不利な立場; fu⌉ri na ko⌈to⌉ 不利なこと: have the disadvantage of being in a bad location (*ritchi jookeñ ga yokunai to iu furi na teñ ga aru*) 立地条件がよくないという不利な点がある.

disagree *vi.* i⌉keñ ga a⌈wa⌉nai 意見が合わない; i⌈tchi shinai 一致しない: I disagreed with her. (*Watashi wa kanojo to ikeñ ga awanakatta.*) 私は彼女と意見が合わなかった. / What you say disagrees with the facts. (*Kimi ga itte iru koto wa jijitsu to itchi shinai.*) 君が言っていることは事実と一致しない.

disagreeable *adj.* fu⌈yu⌉kai na 不愉快な; i⌈ya⌉ na いやな: a disagreeable smell (*iya na nioi*) いやなにおい.

disagreement *n.* fu⌈i⌉tchi 不一致; i⌉keñ no so⌈oi 意見の相違: There was disagreement between the two reports. (*Futatsu no hookoku no aida ni wa ikeñ no sooi ga atta.*) 二つの報告の間には意見の相違があった.

disappear *vi.* **1** (from sight) mi⌈e⌉naku naru 見えなくなる Ⓒ; su⌉gata o ke⌈su 姿を消す Ⓒ: The moon disappeared behind a cloud. (*Tsuki wa kumo ni kakurete mienaku natta.*) 月は雲に隠れて見えなくなった.
2 (existence) ki⌈ete nakunaru 消えてなくなる Ⓒ: The snow soon disappeared. (*Yuki wa sugu ni kiete nakunatta.*) 雪はすぐに消えてなくなった.

disappoint *vt.* ... o ga⌈kka⌉ri sa⌈seru ...をがっかりさせる Ⓥ; shi⌈tsuboo saseru 失望させる Ⓥ: His remarks disappointed me. (*Kare no hatsugeñ wa watashi o gakkari saseta.*) 彼の発言は私をがっかりさせた.

disappointed *adj.* ga⌈kka⌉ri shita [shite iru] がっかりした[している]; shi⌈tsuboo shita [shite iru] 失望した[している]: I am disappointed with the result. (*Watashi wa sono kekka ni shitsuboo shite imasu.*) 私はその結果に失望しています.

disappointment *n.* shi⌈tsuboo 失望; ki⌈tai-ha⌉zure 期待外れ: The team was a disappointment to us.

(*Sono chiimu wa kitai-hazure datta.*) そのチームは期待外れだった.

disapproval *n.* (non-agreement) fu⌈sho⌉ochi 不承知; fu⌈sa⌉ñsee 不賛成: express one's disapproval (*fusañsee no i o shimesu*) 不賛成の意を示す.

d

disapprove *vi.* sa⌈ñsee shinai 賛成しない; na⌈ñshoku o shime⌉su 難色を示す Ⓒ: My father disapproved of my going abroad. (*Chichi wa watashi ga gaikoku e iku koto ni sañsee shinakatta.*) 父は私が外国へ行くことに賛成しなかった.

disarmament *n.* gu⌉ñbi shu⌈ku-shoo 軍備縮小: nuclear disarmament (*kaku guñshuku*) 核軍縮.

disaster *n.* (literal) sa⌈igai 災害: a disaster area (*hisaichi*) 被災地 / A lot of people died in the disaster. (*Sono saigai de ooku no hito ga nakunatta.*) その災害で多くの人が亡くなった.

disastrous *adj.* da⌈i-sa⌉igai no 大災害の; hi⌈sañ na 悲惨な: a disastrous war (*hisañ na señsoo*) 悲惨な戦争.

discharge *vt.* **1** (release) ... o ka⌈ihoo suru ...を解放する Ⓘ; sha⌈kuhoo suru 釈放する Ⓘ: discharge a prisoner (*shuujiñ o shakuhoo suru*) 囚人を釈放する.
2 (dismiss) ... o ka⌉iko suru ...を解雇する Ⓘ: He discharged his secretary. (*Kare wa hisho o kaiko shita.*) 彼は秘書を解雇した.

discipline *n.* **1** (training) ku⌉ñreñ 訓練; shi⌈tsuke しつけ: Home discipline is important. (*Katee no shitsuke ga daiji desu.*) 家庭のしつけが大事です.
2 (order) ki⌈ritsu 規律; to⌈osee 統制: keep [break] discipline (*kiritsu o mamoru* [*yaburu*]) 規律を守る[破る].

disclose *vt.* ... o a⌈ki⌉raka ni suru ...を明らかにする Ⓘ; ha⌈ppyoo suru 発表する Ⓘ: disclose a secret (*himitsu o akiraka ni suru*) 秘密を明らかにする.

disco *n.* di⌉suko ディスコ.

discomfort *n.* fu⌈kai 不快; fu⌈añ 不安.

disconnect *vt.* (pipe, etc.) ... o ha⌈zusu ...を外す Ⓒ; (telephone, etc.) ... o ki⌉ru ...を切る Ⓒ: disconnect a plug (*puragu o nuku*) プラグを抜く / I've been disconnected. (*Deñwa ga kirete shimatta.*) 電話が切れてしまった.

discontent *n.* fu⌈hee 不平; fu⌈mañ 不満.

discord *n.* **1** (disagreement) fu⌈i⌉tchi 不一致: discord among committee members (*iiñ no aida no ikeñ no fuitchi*) 委員の間の意見の不一致.
2 (argument) fu⌉wa 不和: marital discord (*fuufu kañ no fuwa*) 夫婦間の不和.

discount *n.* wa⌈ribiki 割引: Can you give me a discount on this? (*Kore wa waribiki shite moraemasu ka?*) これは割引してもらえますか.
— *vt.* **1** ... o wa⌈ribi⌉ku ...を割り引く Ⓒ: discount the price 5 percent (*nedañ o go-paaseñto waribiku*) 値段を5%割り引く.
2 (ignore) ... o mu⌉shi suru ...を無視する Ⓘ: You should discount his story. (*Kare no hanashi wa mushi shita hoo ga ii.*) 彼の話は無視したほうがいい.

discourage *vt.* ... o ga⌈kka⌉ri sa⌈seru ...をがっかりさせる Ⓥ; ra⌈kutañ saseru 落胆させる Ⓥ: The failure discouraged him. (*Sono shippai wa kare o gakkari saseta.*) その失敗は彼をがっかりさせた.

discover *vt.* ... o ha⌈kkeñ suru ...を発見する Ⓘ; mi⌈tsukeru 見つける Ⓥ: He discovered a new species of a plant. (*Kare wa shokubutsu no shiñshu o hakkeñ shita.*) 彼は植物の新種を発見した. / I discovered my name on the list. (*Watashi wa meebo ni watashi no namae o mitsuketa.*) 私は名簿に私の名前を見つけた.

discovery *n.* ha⌈kkeñ 発見: He

made some important discoveries. (*Kare wa ikutsu-ka no juuyoo na hakkeñ o shita.*) 彼はいくつかの重要な発見をした.

discreet *adj.* shi¹ryo no aru 思慮のある; fu¹ñbetsu no aru 分別のある; shi⌈ñchoo na 慎重な: He's discreet in his behavior. (*Kare wa koodoo ga shiñchoo da.*) 彼は行動が慎重だ.

discriminate *vt.* (distinguish) ... o ku¹betsu suru …を区別する Ⓘ: discriminate synonyms (*dooigo o kubetsu suru*) 同意語を区別する.
— *vi.* (against) sa¹betsu suru 差別する Ⓘ: discriminate between men and women (*dañsee to josee o sabetsu suru*) 男性と女性を差別する.

discrimination *n.* (prejudice) sa¹betsu 差別: racial discrimination (*jiñshu sabetsu*) 人種差別.

discuss *vt.* ... o ha⌈nashia¹u …を話し合う Ⓒ; to¹ogi suru 討議する Ⓘ: I discussed the problem with him. (*Watashi wa sono moñdai o kare to hanashiatta.*) 私はその問題を彼と話し合った.

discussion *n.* to¹ogi 討議; gi¹roñ 議論; ha⌈nashiai 話し合い: hold a discussion about future plans (*shoorai no keekaku ni tsuite toogi suru*) 将来の計画について討議する.

disease *n.* byo⌈oki 病気: catch [suffer from] a disease (*byooki ni kakaru*) 病気にかかる / prevent [cure] a disease (*byooki o fusegu* [*naosu*]) 病気を防ぐ[治す] / a heart disease (*shiñzoo-byoo*) 心臓病.

disembark *vi.* (from a boat) jo⌈oriku suru 上陸する Ⓘ; (from an airplane) o⌈ri¹ru 降りる Ⓒ.

disgrace *n.* (dishonor) fu⌈me¹eyo 不名誉; (shame) ha⌈ji¹ 恥: Poverty is no disgrace. (*Mazushii koto wa kesshite haji de wa nai.*) 貧しいことは決して恥ではない.

disguise *vt.* ... o he⌈ñsoo saseru …を変装させる Ⓥ: He disguised himself as a policeman. (*Kare wa keekañ ni heñsoo shita.*) 彼は警官に変装した.
— *n.* he⌈ñsoo 変装; ka⌈soo 仮装.

disgust *vt.* ... o mu¹kamuka sa⌈seru …をむかむかさせる Ⓥ; u⌈ñza¹ri sa⌈seru うんざりさせる Ⓥ: I was disgusted at his behavior. (*Kare no taido ni mukamuka shita.*) 彼の態度にむかむかした.
— *n.* ke¹ño 嫌悪; i⌈yake 嫌気: I left the room in disgust. (*Watashi wa iyake ga sashite heya o deta.*) 私は嫌気がさして部屋を出た.

disgusting *adj.* i⌈ya¹ na いやな: a disgusting smell (*iya na nioi*) いやなにおい.

dish *n.* **1** (plate) sa⌈ra 皿: serve fruit in a dish (*kudamono o sara ni irete dasu*) 果物を皿に入れて出す.
2 (food) ryo¹ori 料理; ta⌈bemo¹no 食べ物: This is my favorite French dish. (*Kore wa watashi no ichibañ suki na Furañsu ryoori desu.*) これは私のいちばん好きなフランス料理です.

dishonest *adj.* fu⌈sho¹ojiki na 不正直な; fu⌈see na 不正な: a dishonest transaction (*fusee na torihiki*) 不正な取り引き.

dishonor *n.* fu⌈me¹eyo 不名誉; ku⌈tsujoku 屈辱; ha⌈ji¹ 恥: live in dishonor (*kutsujoku no seekatsu o okuru*) 屈辱の生活を送る / a dishonor to one's family (*ie no haji*) 家の恥.

dishwasher *n.* sho⌈kki-arai¹ki 食器洗い機.

disinfect *vt.* ... o sho⌈odoku suru …を消毒する Ⓘ: disinfect a room (*heya o shoodoku suru*) 部屋を消毒する.

disinfectant *n.* sho⌈odoku¹zai 消毒剤.

disk *n.* e⌈ñbañ 円盤: disk drive (*disuku doraibu*) ディスクドライブ / a hard disk (*haado disuku*) ハードディスク.

dislike *vt.* ... o ki⌈rau …を嫌う Ⓒ; i⌈yaga¹ru いやがる Ⓒ: He seems to dislike me. (*Kare wa watashi o kiratte iru mitai da.*) 彼は私を嫌っているみたいだ. / I dislike living in a large city. (*Dai-toshi ni sumu no *wa iya da.*) 大都市に住むのはいやだ.

disloyal *adj.* chu⌈ujitsu de na⌉i 忠実でない; fu⌈jitsu na 不実な.

dismiss *vt.* **1** (discharge) ... o ku⌈bi ni suru ...を首にする Ⓘ; ka⌉iko suru 解雇する Ⓘ: He dismissed his lazy secretary. (*Kare wa namakemono no hisho o kubi ni shita.*) 彼は怠け者の秘書を首にした.
2 (send away) ... o ka⌈isañ suru ...を解散する Ⓘ: The class was dismissed early today. (*Kyoo wa jugyoo ga hayaku owatta.*) きょうは授業が早く終わった.

disobey *vt.* ... ni shi⌈tagawa⌉nai ...に従わない; so⌈mu⌉ku 背く Ⓒ: disobey a superior (*jooshi ni somuku*) 上司に背く.

disorder *n.* **1** (confusion) ko⌈ñrañ 混乱; ra⌈ñzatsu 乱雑: The room is in disorder. (*Heya ga chirakatte iru.*) 部屋が散らかっている.
2 (disturbance) so⌉odoo 騒動; bo⌈odoo 暴動.

dispatch *vt.* (a person) ... o ha⌈keñ suru ...を派遣する Ⓘ: He was dispatched to China. (*Kare wa Chuugoku e hakeñ sareta.*) 彼は中国へ派遣された.

display *vt.* ... o te⌈ñji suru ...を展示する Ⓘ; chi⌈ñretsu suru 陳列する Ⓘ: display goods for sale (*shoohiñ o chiñretsu suru*) 商品を陳列する.
— *n.* te⌈ñji 展示; chi⌈ñretsu 陳列: His works are now on display. (*Kare no sakuhiñ ga ima chiñretsu sarete iru.*) 彼の作品が今陳列されている.

displease *vt.* ... o o⌈korase⌉ru ...を怒らせる Ⓥ; fu⌈ki⌉geñ ni suru 不機嫌にする Ⓘ: His remarks displeased her. (*Kare no hatsugeñ wa kanojo o okoraseta.*) 彼の発言は彼女を怒らせた.

disposable *adj.* tsu⌈kaisute no 使い捨ての: a disposable lighter (*tsukaisute no raitaa*) 使い捨てのライター.

disposal *n.* sho⌉buñ 処分; sho⌉ri 処理: the disposal of garbage (*gomi no shori*) ごみの処理.

be at one's disposal *vi.* ji⌈yu⌉u ni tsu⌈kaeru 自由に使える Ⓥ: This car is at your disposal. (*Kono kuruma o jiyuu ni o-tsukai kudasai.*) この車を自由にお使いください.

dispose *vi.* (... o) sho⌉buñ suru (...を)処分する Ⓘ; ka⌈tazuke⌉ru 片づける Ⓥ: dispose of garbage [old newspapers] (*gomi [furu-shiñbuñ] o shobuñ suru*) ごみ[古新聞]を処分する.

disposition *n.* se⌈eshitsu 性質; ki⌈shitsu 気質: a man with a cheerful disposition (*yooki na kihitsu no hito*) 陽気な気質の人.

dispute *vi.* ro⌈ñsoo suru 論争する Ⓘ; gi⌉roñ suru 議論する Ⓘ: dispute over a problem (*moñdai ni tsuite roñsoo suru*) 問題について論争する.
— *n.* ro⌈ñsoo 論争; fu⌈ñsoo 紛争: a labor dispute (*roodoo soogi*) 労働争議 / a territorial dispute (*ryoodo fuñsoo*) 領土紛争.

disqualify *vt.* ... no shi⌈kaku o to⌈riageru ...の資格を取り上げる Ⓥ: He was disqualified from taking part in the contest. (*Kare wa sono kyoogi no shutsujoo shikaku o toriagerareta.*) 彼はその競技の出場資格を取り上げられた.

disrupt *vt.* (break up) ... o bu⌈ñretsu saseru ...を分裂させる Ⓥ; (throw into disorder) ko⌈ñrañ saseru 混乱させる Ⓥ: Train service was disrupted by an accident. (*Ressha no unkoo ga jiko no tame ni koñrañ shita.*) 列車の運行が事故のために混乱した.

dissatisfaction *n.* fu⌈mañ 不満; fu⌈hee 不平: express one's dissatisfaction (*fumañ o noberu*) 不満を述べる.

dissatisfied *adj.* fu⌈mañ na 不満な; fu⌈hee na 不平な: He seemed dissatisfied with the terms. (*Kare wa sono jookeñ ni fumañ no yoo datta.*) 彼はその条件に不満のようだった.

dissent *vi.* do⌈oi shinai 同意しない; ha⌈ñtai suru 反対する Ⓘ: Two members dissented from our conclusion. (*Futari ga watashi-tachi no ketsu-

roñ ni hañtai shita.) 二人が私たちの結論に反対した.

dissident *adj*. (opinion) i˥keñ ga chi˥gau 意見が違う; (anti-regime) ha˥ñta˥isee no 反体制の.
— *n*. i˥keñ no chi˥gau hito˥ 意見の違う人; ha˥ñta˥isee no hi˥to˥ 反体制の人.

dissolve *vt*. **1** (make liquid) ... o to˥ka˥su ...を溶かす Ⓒ: dissolve salt in water (*shio o mizu ni tokasu*) 塩を水に溶かす.
2 (break up) ... o ka˥isañ suru ...を解散する Ⓘ: dissolve a parliament (*gikai o kaisañ suru*) 議会を解散する.
— *vi*. to˥ke˥ru 溶ける Ⓥ; ka˥isañ suru 解散する Ⓘ.

distance *n*. kyo˥ri 距離: The distance from here to the station is two kilometers. (*Koko kara eki made no kyori wa ni-kiro desu.*) ここから駅までの距離は2キロです.

distant *adj*. to˥oi 遠い; ha˥na˥reta 離れた; ha˥na˥rete iru 離れている: a distant country (*tooi kuni*) 遠い国 / The town is distant from Tokyo. (*Sono machi wa Tookyoo kara hanarete iru.*) その町は東京から離れている.

distinct *adj*. **1** (different) be˥tsu no 別の; chi˥gatta 違った; chi˥gatte iru 違っている: His method is quite distinct from ours. (*Kare no yarikata wa wareware no to mattaku chigatte iru.*) 彼のやり方はわれわれのとまったく違っている.
2 (clear) ha˥kki˥ri shita [shite iru] はっきりした[している]; me˥eryoo na 明瞭な: She gave me a distinct refusal. (*Kanojo wa hakkiri to watashi ni kotowatta.*) 彼女ははっきりと私に断った.

distinction *n*. ku˥betsu 区別; chi˥gai 違い; to˥kuchoo 特徴: It is important to draw a distinction between official and personal affairs. (*Kooshi no kubetsu o tsukeru koto ga taisetsu desu.*) 公私の区別をつけることが大切です. / I can see no distinction between these plants. (*Kore-ra no shokubutsu no chigai ga wakaranai.*) これらの植物の違いがわからない.

distinguish *vt*. ... o ku˥betsu suru ...を区別する Ⓘ; mi˥wakeru 見分ける Ⓥ: The uniforms are so alike that it is diffiuclt to distinguish the two teams. (*Yunifoomu ga amari nite iru no de ryoo chiimu no kubetsu ga muzukashii.*) ユニフォームがあまり似ているので両チームの区別が難しい.

distinguished *adj*. **1** (of a person) yu˥umee na 有名な; cho˥mee na 著名な: a distinguished writer (*chomee na sakka*) 著名な作家.
2 (of quality) su˥gu˥reta 優れた; su˥gu˥rete iru 優れている: a distinguished performance (*sugureta eñgi*) 優れた演技.

distort *vt*. **1** (twist) ... o yu˥gameru ...をゆがめる Ⓥ; ne˥ji˥ru ねじる Ⓒ: His face was distorted with pain. (*Kare no kao wa kutsuu de yugañda.*) 彼の顔は苦痛でゆがんだ.
2 (of truth, etc.) ... o ma˥geru ...を曲げる Ⓥ: distort the truth (*shiñjitsu o mageru*) 真実を曲げる.

distract *vt*. ... o so˥ra˥su ...をそらす Ⓒ; ma˥gira˥su 紛らす Ⓒ: The noise distracted his attention. (*Sono soooñ ga kare no chuui o sorashita.*) その騒音が彼の注意をそらした.

distress *n*. (worry) na˥yami˥ 悩み; ku˥rushimi 苦しみ; (sorrow) ka˥nashimi 悲しみ.
— *vt*. ... o na˥yama˥su ...を悩ます Ⓒ; ku˥rushime˥ru 苦しめる Ⓥ; ka˥nashimase˥ru 悲しませる Ⓥ: I was distressed at the bad news. (*Watashi wa sono warui shirase ni kokoro o itameta.*) 私はその悪い知らせに心を痛めた.

distribute *vt*. ... o ku˥ba˥ru ...を配る Ⓒ; bu˥ñpai suru 分配する Ⓘ: The teacher distributed handouts to the students. (*Señsee wa seeto ni puriñto o kubatta.*) 先生は生徒にプリントを配った.

distribution *n*. bu˥ñpai 分配;

ha⌈ifu 配布: distribution of profit (*rieki no buñpai*) 利益の分配.

district *n.* **1** (region of a country) chi⌈ho⌉o 地方: the Kantoo district (*Kañtoo chihoo*) 関東地方.
2 (area of a city) chi⌉ku 地区: the business district of a city (*shi no shoogyoo chiku*) 市の商業地区 / an electoral district (*señkyoku*) 選挙区 / a shopping district (*shooteñ-gai*) 商店街.

distrust *vt.* ... o shi⌈ñyoo shinai ...を信用しない; u⌈tagau 疑う Ⓒ: distrust one's own eyes (*jibuñ no me o utagau*) 自分の目を疑う.
— *n.* fu⌈shiñ 不信; gi⌈waku 疑惑: I have a distrust of what he says. (*Kare ga iu koto wa shiñyoo shimaseñ.*) 彼が言うことは信用しません.

disturb *vt.* **1** (interrupt) ... o ja⌈ma suru ...をじゃまする Ⓘ; sa⌈matage⌉ru 妨げる Ⓥ: Don't disturb me while I'm working. (*Shigoto o shite iru toki jama o shinaide kudasai.*) 仕事をしているときじゃまをしないでください.
2 (worry) ... o shi⌈ñpai saseru ...を心配させる Ⓥ; fu⌈añ ni suru 不安にする Ⓘ: The news of the accident disturbed her. (*Sono jiko no shirase wa kanojo o fuañ ni shita.*) その事故の知らせは彼女を不安にした.
3 (stir up) ... o ka⌈kimida⌉su ...をかき乱す Ⓒ: The wind disturbed the papers on the desk. (*Kaze ga tsukue no ue no shorui o kakimidashita.*) 風が机の上の書類をかき乱した.

ditch *n.* mi⌈zo 溝; do⌈bu どぶ; ha⌈isu⌉ikoo 排水溝: an irrigation ditch (*yoosuiro*) 用水路.

dive *vi.* **1** (plunge) (... ni) to⌈biko⌉mu (...に)飛び込む Ⓒ: He dived into the river. (*Kare wa kawa ni tobikoñda.*) 彼は川に飛び込んだ.
2 (go under) (... ni) mo⌈gu⌉ru (...に)潜る Ⓒ: dive for pearls (*shiñju o toru tame ni mizu ni moguru*) 真珠を採るために水に潜る.

diverse *adj.* sa⌈ma⌉zama na さまざまな; i⌈roiro na いろいろな: He has diverse interests. (*Kare wa samazama na shumi o motte iru.*) 彼はさまざまな趣味をもっている.

diversity *n.* ta⌈yoosee 多様性; sa⌈ma⌉zama na ko⌈to⌉ さまざまなこと; so⌈oi 相違: a diversity of opinions (*samazama na ikeñ*) さまざまな意見.

divide *vt.* **1** (separate) ... o wa⌈ke⌉ru ...を分ける Ⓥ; bu⌈ñkatsu suru 分割する Ⓘ: divide a large room into four (*ooki-na heya o yottsu ni wakeru*) 大きな部屋を四つに分ける.
2 (distribute) ... o wa⌈ke⌉ru ...を分ける Ⓥ; bu⌈ñpai suru 分配する Ⓘ: They divided the money among themselves. (*Kare-ra wa sono okane o jibuñ-tachi de waketa.*) 彼らはそのお金を自分たちで分けた.
3 (of mathematics) ... o wa⌈ru ...を割る Ⓒ: divide 8 by 2 (*hachi o ni de waru*) 8を2で割る.
— *vi.* wa⌈kare⌉ru 分かれる Ⓥ; wa⌈reru 割れる Ⓥ: The road divides into two here. (*Michi wa koko de futatsu ni wakaremasu.*) 道はここで二つに分かれます.

dividend *n.* ha⌈itookiñ 配当金.

divine *adj.* (absolute) ka⌉mi no 神の; (holy) shi⌈ñsee na 神聖な: divine grace (*kami no megumi*) 神の恵み.

diving *n.* to⌈bikomi 飛び込み; da⌉ibiñgu ダイビング: scuba diving (*sukyuuba daibiñgu*) スキューバダイビング.

diving board *n.* to⌈bi-ita 飛び板; to⌈bikomidai 飛び込み台.

division *n.* **1** (separation) bu⌈ñkatsu 分割; (distribution) bu⌈ñpai 分配: a division of profits (*rieki no buñpai*) 利益の分配.
2 (section) kyo⌉ku 局; bu 部; ka 課: the sales division (*hañbai-bu*) 販売部.
3 (mathematics) wa⌈ri⌉zañ 割り算: problems in division (*warizañ no moñdai*) 割り算の問題.

divorce *n.* ri⌈koñ 離婚: get a divorce from one's husband (*otto to rikoñ suru*) 夫と離婚する.

— *vt.* ... to ri⌈koñ suru …と離婚する [I]: We got divorced two years ago. (*Watashi-tachi wa ni-neñ mae ni rikoñ shimashita.*) 私たちは2年前に離婚しました.

dizzy *adj.* me⌈ma⌉i ga suru めまいがする: I feel dizzy. (*Watashi wa me-mai ga shimasu.*) 私は目まいがします.

do *vt.* ... o su⌈ru …をする [I]; o⌈konau 行う [C]: do the shopping [cooking] (*kaimono* [*ryoori*] *o suru*) 買い物[料理]をする / What are you doing now? (*Anata wa ima nani o shite imasu ka?*) あなたは今何をしていますか. / What should I do? (*Doo sureba ii deshoo ka?*) どうすればいいでしょうか.
— *vi.* su⌈ru する [I]; ya⌈ru やる [C]: You have done well. (*Yoku yarima-shita.*) よくやりました.

dock *n.* do⌉kku ドック: a floating dock (*uki dokku*) 浮きドック.

doctor *n.* **1** (physician) i⌈sha 医者: see a doctor (*isha ni mite morau*) 医者に診てもらう / Can you get a doctor? (*Isha o yoñde moraemasu ka?*) 医者を呼んでもらえますか.
2 (a person with a degree) ha⌉kase [ha⌉kushi] 博士: a Doctor of Science (*rigaku hakase*) 理学博士.

doctrine *n.* (politics) shu⌉gi 主義; (religion) kyo⌉ogi 教義: preach a doctrine (*kyoogi o toku*) 教義を説く.

document *n.* bu⌉ñsho 文書; sho⌈rui 書類: draw up a document (*shorui o sakusee suru*) 書類を作成する / an official document (*koobuñ-sho*) 公文書.

documentary *n.* (film) ki⌈roku-e⌉ega 記録映画.

dodge *vt.* ... o yo⌈ke⌉ru …をよける [V]; sa⌈ke⌉ru 避ける [V]: dodge a ball (*booru o yokeru*) ボールをよける.

dog *n.* i⌈nu⌉ 犬: He keeps two dogs. (*Kare wa inu o ni-hiki katte iru.*) 彼は犬を2匹飼っている. / I was bitten by a dog. (*Watashi wa inu ni kamareta.*) 私は犬にかまれた.

doghouse *n.* i⌈nugoya 犬小屋.

doings *n.* o⌈konai 行い; ko⌈odoo 行動; ko⌉oi 行為.

doll *n.* ni⌈ñgyoo 人形: play with a doll (*niñgyoo de asobu*) 人形で遊ぶ.

dollar *n.* do⌉ru ドル: Can I change dollars here? (*Koko de doru o kaeraremasu ka?*) ここでドルを換えられますか. / What is the dollar rate? (*Doru wa ikura desu ka?*) ドルはいくらですか.

dolphin *n.* i⌈ruka いるか.

dome *n.* ma⌈ruyane 丸屋根; ma⌈rute⌉ñjoo 丸天井; do⌉omu ドーム.

domestic *adj.* **1** (of the home) ka⌈tee no 家庭の; ka⌈tee-teki na 家庭的な: domestic chores (*kaji*) 家事.
2 (not foreign) ko⌈ku⌉nai no 国内の; ji⌈koku no 自国の: domestic news (*kokunai nyuusu*) 国内ニュース / a domestic flight (*kokunai-biñ*) 国内便 / a domestic animal (*kachiku*) 家畜.

dominant *adj.* shi⌈hai-teki na 支配的な; yu⌈usee na 優勢な: dominant opinion against the tax increase (*zoozee ni hañtai suru shi-hai-teki na ikeñ*) 増税に反対する支配的な意見.

dominate *vt.* ... o shi⌉hai suru …を支配する [I]: The stronger person dominates the weaker. (*Tsuyoi mono ga yowai mono o shihai suru.*) 強い者が弱い者を支配する.

donate *vt.* **1** (money, etc.) ... o ki⌉fu suru …を寄付する [I]; ki⌈zoo suru 寄贈する [I]: I donated some money to the fund. (*Watashi wa o-kane o ikura-ka sono kikiñ ni kifu shita.*) 私はお金をいくらかその基金に寄付した.
2 (organs) ... o te⌈ekyoo suru …を提供する [I]; (blood) keñketsu suru 献血する [I].

donation *n.* ki⌉fu 寄付; (especially money) ki⌈fu⌉kiñ 寄付金: blood donation (*keñketsu*) 献血.

donkey *n.* ro⌉ba ろば.

donor *n.* ki⌈zo⌉osha 寄贈者; te⌈e-kyo⌉osha 提供者: a heart donor (*shiñzoo teekyoosha*) 心臓提供者 / a blood donor (*keñketsusha*) 献血者.

donut *n.* doˈonatsu ドーナツ.
door *n.* dˈoa ドア; to 戸; toˈbira 扉: open [close] a door (*doa o akeru* [*shimeru*]) ドアを開ける[閉める] / Did you lock the door? (*Doa ni kagi o kakemashita ka?*) ドアに鍵をかけましたか. / a front door (*geñkañ*) 玄関 / a back door (*katteguchi*) 勝手口.
dormitory *n.* ryoˈo 寮.
dose *n.* (of medicine) iˈppuku 1 服; (quantity) fuˈkuyoˈoryoo 服用量: Take three doses a day. (*Ichi-nichi sañ-kai fukuyoo no koto.*) 1 日 3 回服用のこと.
dot *n.* teˈñ 点: put a dot over the letter i (*ai no ji no ue ni teñ o utsu*) I の字の上に点を打つ.
on the dot *adv.* kiˈkkaˈri ni きっかりに.
double *adj.* **1** (twice) ni-ˈbai no 2 倍の: His pay is double my pay. (*Kare no kyuuryoo wa watashi no ni-bai da.*) 彼の給料は私の 2 倍だ.
2 (layers) ni-ˈjuu no 二重の: double-glazed windows (*ni-juu mado*) 二重窓.
— *adv.* ni-ˈbai 2 倍: I'll pay double. (*Watashi wa ni-bai haraimasu.*) 私は 2 倍払います.
— *vt.* ... o ni-ˈbai ni suru …を 2 倍にする [I]; ni-ˈjuu ni suru 二重にする [I]: double the sales (*uriage o ni-bai ni suru*) 売り上げを 2 倍にする.
— *vi.* ni-ˈbai ni naˈru 2 倍になる [C]: The population of this town has doubled. (*Kono machi no jiñkoo wa ni-bai ni natta.*) この町の人口は 2 倍になった.
doubt *vt.* ... o uˈtagau …を疑う [C]: giˈmoñ ni omoˈu 疑問に思う [C]: I doubt his innocence. (*Watashi wa kare no mujitsu o utagau.*) 私は彼の無実を疑う. / I doubt if she will come. (*Kanojo ga kuru ka doo ka gimoñ ni omou.*) 彼女が来るかどうか疑問に思う.
— *n.* uˈtagai 疑い; giˈmoñ 疑問: There is some doubt whether he will succeed. (*Kare ga seekoo suru ka doo ka gimoñ da.*) 彼が成功するかどうか疑問だ.
no doubt *adv.* oˈsoˈraku 恐らく; kiˈtto きっと: No doubt he will win. (*Osoraku kare wa katsu deshoo.*) 恐らく彼は勝つでしょう.
doubtful *adj.* uˈtagawashiˈi 疑わしい; kaˈkushiñ ga naˈi 確信がない: I am doubtful whether he will agree to our suggestions. (*Kare ga wareware no teeañ ni sañsee suru ka doo ka utagawashii.*) 彼がわれわれの提案に賛成するかどうか疑わしい.
doubtless *adv.* taˈbuñ たぶん; taˈshika ni 確かに: He will doubtless come later. (*Kare wa tabuñ ato kara kuru deshoo.*) 彼はたぶん後から来るでしょう.
dove *n.* haˈto はと. ★ 'Pigeon' is also called '*hato*.'
down *adv.* shiˈta e 下へ; hiˈkuˈi hoo e 低い方へ: jump down from a tree (*ki kara tobioriru*) 木から跳び下りる / pull the blinds down (*buraiñdo o orosu*) ブラインドを下ろす.
— *prep.* ... no shiˈta e …の下へ; ... no kaˈhoo ni …の下方に: go down a hill (*oka o kudaru*) 丘を下る / The bridge is about two kilometers down the stream. (*Sono hashi wa nagare no yaku ni-kiro karyuu ni aru.*) その橋は流れの約 2 キロ下流にある.
— *adj.* kaˈhoo e no 下方への; kuˈdari no 下りの: a down elevator (*kudari no erebeetaa*) 下りのエレベーター / a down train (*kudari ressha*) 下り列車.
downstairs *adv.* kaˈika e 階下へ: go downstairs (*kaika e oriru*) 階下へ降りる.
— *adj.* kaˈika no 階下の: a downstairs room (*kaika no heya*) 階下の部屋.
downtown *n.* (commercial center) haˈñkaˈgai 繁華街; (city center) toˈshiˈñbu 都心部: go downtown shopping (*hañkagai e kaimono ni iku*) 繁華街へ買い物に行く.
downward *adv.* shiˈta no hoˈo e 下の方へ; shiˈtamuki ni 下向きに: The elevator went downward. (*Ere-

beetaa wa shita e ikimashita.) エレベーターは下へ行きました.

— *adj.* ka⌈hoo e no 下方への; shi⌈tamuki no 下向きの: a downward slope (*kudarizaka*) 下り坂.

doze *vi.* i⌈nemu⌉ri suru 居眠りする Ⓘ; u⌉touto suru うとうとする Ⓘ: I dozed off during the lecture. (*Watashi wa koogi no aida utouto shite shimatta.*) 私は講義の間うとうとしてしまった.

dozen *n.* da⌉asu ダース: one [two] dozen (*ichi* [*ni*] *daasu*) 1 [2]ダース.

draft *n.* **1** (rough copy) shi⌈tagaki 下書き; so⌈oañ 草案: make a draft of a report (*repooto no shitagaki o suru*) レポートの下書きをする.

2 (current of air) su⌈kima⌉kaze すきま風; tsu⌈ufuu 通風: keep out drafts (*sukimakaze o fusegu*) すきま風を防ぐ.

3 (order for payment) ka⌈wase-te⌉gata 為替手形: draw a draft on a bank (*giñkoo ate ni tegata o furidasu*) 銀行宛に手形を振り出す.

drag *vt.* **1** (physically) ... o hi⌈ppa⌉ru ...を引っぱる Ⓒ; hi⌈kizuru 引きずる Ⓒ: We dragged the heavy table across the floor. (*Watashi-tachi wa sono omoi teeburu o hikizutte yuka no ue o ugokashita.*) 私たちはその重いテーブルを引きずって床の上を動かした.

2 (figuratively) ... ni hi⌈kiko⌉mu ...に引き込む Ⓒ: He was dragged into a fight. (*Kare wa keñka ni hikikomareta.*) 彼はけんかに引き込まれた.

drain *vt.* **1** (make flow away) ... no ha⌈isui o suru ...の排水をする Ⓘ: drain the water away from the playground (*uñdoojoo no haisui o suru*) 運動場の排水をする.

2 (remove water) ... no mi⌈zu o ki⌉ru ...の水を切る Ⓒ: She washed the spinach and drained it. (*Kanojo wa hooreñsoo o aratte mizu o kitta.*) 彼女はほうれんそうを洗って水を切った.

drama *n.* (play) ge⌉ki 劇; shi⌈bai 芝居; do⌉rama ドラマ; (study) e⌈ñgeki 演劇: act a drama (*shibai o jooeñ suru*) 芝居を上演する.

dramatic *adj.* **1** (of a play) e⌈ñgeki no 演劇の: dramatic works (*eñgeki sakuhiñ*) 演劇作品.

2 (exciting) ge⌈kiteki na 劇的な: a dramatic incident (*gekiteki na jikeñ*) 劇的な事件.

drastic *adj.* o⌈mo⌉ikitta 思い切った; te⌈ttee-teki na 徹底的な: adopt drastic measures (*omoikitta shudañ o toru*) 思い切った手段をとる.

draw *vt.* **1** (sketch) ... o e⌈ga⌉ku ...を描く Ⓒ; ka⌉ku かく Ⓒ; (of a line) hi⌈ku 引く Ⓒ: Please draw a map here. (*Koko ni chizu o kaite kudasai.*) ここに地図をかいてください / draw a straight line (*chokuseñ o hiku*) 直線を引く.

2 (pull) ... o hi⌈ku ...を引く Ⓒ; hi⌈ppa⌉ru 引っぱる Ⓒ: draw a curtain (*kaateñ o hiku*) カーテンを引く.

3 (attract) ... o hi⌈kitsuke⌉ru ...を引きつける Ⓥ; hi⌈ku 引く Ⓒ: He tried to draw her attention. (*Kare wa kanojo no chuuui o hikoo to shita.*) 彼は彼女の注意を引こうとした.

4 (get) ... o hi⌈kida⌉su ...を引き出す Ⓒ; o⌈ro⌉su おろす Ⓒ: I have to draw some money from the bank. (*Watashi wa giñkoo kara ikura-ka okane o orosanakereba naranai.*) 私は銀行からいくらかお金を下ろさなければならない.

5 (breathe) ... o su⌈u ...を吸う Ⓒ: draw a deep breath (*iki o fukaku suu*) 息を深く吸う.

drawer *n.* hi⌈kidashi 引き出し: open [shut] a drawer (*hikidashi o akeru* [*shimeru*]) 引き出しを開ける[閉める].

drawing *n.* e⌉ 絵; zu 図: She made a drawing of vegetables. (*Kanojo wa yasai no e o kaita.*) 彼女は野菜の絵をかいた.

dread *vt.* ... o o⌈sore⌉ru ...を恐れる Ⓥ; ko⌈waga⌉ru 怖がる Ⓒ: The boy dreaded visiting the dentist. (*Sono otoko-no-ko wa haisha e iku no o kowagatta.*) その男の子は歯医者へ行

くのを怖がった.
— *n.* kyo⌉ofu 恐怖; fu⌈añ 不安.
dreadful *adj.* o⌈soroshi⌉i 恐ろしい; ko⌈wa⌉i 怖い: a dreadful accident (*osoroshii jiko*) 恐ろしい事故.
dream *n.* yu⌈me⌉ 夢: I had a curious dream last night. (*Yuube wa omoshiroi yume o mita.*) ゆうべはおもしろい夢を見た. / It is my dream to live in the country. (*Inaka de kurasu no ga watashi no yume desu.*) 田舎で暮らすのが私の夢です.
— *vi.* yu⌈me⌉ o miru 夢を見る Ⓥ: I seldom dream. (*Watashi wa metta ni yume o minai.*) 私はめったに夢を見ない.
dreamer *n.* yu⌈memi⌉ru hi⌈to⌉ 夢見る人; ku⌈usooka 空想家.
dress *n.* **1** (women's garment) fu⌈ji⌉ñfuku 婦人服; do⌈resu ドレス; wa⌈ñpi⌉isu ワンピース: She wore a pretty dress. (*Kanojo wa kiree na wañpiisu o kite ita.*) 彼女はきれいなワンピースを着ていた.
2 (clothes) fu⌈kusoo 服装; i⌉fuku 衣服: full [formal] dress (*seesoo*) 正装 / casual dress (*fudañgi*) 普段着.
— *vt.* ... ni fu⌈ku⌉ o ki⌈seru ...に服を着せる Ⓥ: dress a doll (*niñgyoo ni fuku o kiseru*) 人形に服を着せる.
— *vi.* fu⌈ku⌉ o ki⌈ru 服を着る Ⓥ: I dressed in my best suit. (*Watashi wa ichibañ ii sebiro o kita.*) 私はいちばんいい背広を着た.
dressing *n.* **1** (bandage) ho⌈otai 包帯.
2 (salad dressing) do⌈re⌉sshiñgu ドレッシング.
dressmaker *n.* do⌈resu me⌉ekaa ドレスメーカー; yo⌈osa⌉ishi 洋裁師.
drift *vi.* **1** (being driven) hyo⌈oryuu suru 漂流する Ⓘ; ta⌈dayo⌉u 漂う Ⓒ: The boat was drifting on the sea. (*Sono booto wa umi no ue o hyooryuu shite ita.*) そのボートは海の上を漂流していた.
2 (without purpose) ma⌈ñzeñ to sugo⌉su 漫然と過ごす Ⓒ: drift through life (*jiñsee o mañzeñ to sugosu*) 人生を漫然と過ごす.
— *vt.* (snow) ... o fu⌈kitsumoraseru ...を吹き積もらせる Ⓥ: The wind drifted the snow. (*Kaze ga yuki o fukitsumoraseta.*) 風が雪を吹き積もらせた.
drill *n.* **1** (tool) ki⌉ri きり; do⌈riru ドリル: use a drill to make a hole (*ana o akeru no ni kiri o tsukau*) 穴を開けるのにきりを使う.
2 (exercise) re⌈ñshuu 練習; ku⌉ñreñ 訓練: drills in Japanese pronunciation (*Nihoñgo no hatsuoñ reñshuu*) 日本語の発音練習.
— *vt.* **1** (make a hole) ... ni a⌈na⌉ o a⌈keru ...に穴を開ける Ⓥ: drill a hole in the wall (*kabe ni ana o akeru*) 壁に穴を開ける.
2 (train) ... o re⌈ñshuu saseru ...を練習させる Ⓥ; o⌈shieko⌉mu 教え込む Ⓒ: The teacher drilled the class in sentence patterns. (*Señsee wa kurasu ni buñkee o oshiekoñda.*) 先生はクラスに文型を教え込んだ.
drink *vt.* ... o no⌉mu ...を飲む Ⓒ: Can I drink this water? (*Kono mizu wa nomemasu ka?*) この水は飲めますか. / I want something to drink. (*Nani-ka nomimono ga hoshii.*) 何か飲み物が欲しい.
— *vi.* no⌉mu 飲む Ⓒ; sa⌈ke o no⌉mu 酒を飲む Ⓒ: I drank too much. (*Nomi-sugimashita.*) 飲み過ぎました.
— *n.* no⌈mi⌉mono 飲み物; sa⌈ke 酒: I'd like a drink before dinner. (*Shokuzeñshu o kudasai.*) 食前酒を下さい.
drip *vi.* po⌉tapota o⌈chi⌉ru ぽたぽた落ちる Ⓥ: The faucet is dripping. (*Jaguchi kara mizu ga potapota ochite iru.*) 蛇口から水がぽたぽた落ちている.
— *n.* shi⌈tatari したたり; shi⌈zuku⌉ しずく: drips of sweat (*ase no shizuku*) 汗のしずく.
drive *vt.* **1** (control) ... o u⌈ñteñ suru ...を運転する Ⓘ: I can drive a bus. (*Watashi wa basu o uñteñ dekiru.*) 私はバスを運転できる.
2 (urge) ... o o⌈itate⌉ru 追い立てる Ⓥ; ka⌈ritate⌉ru 駆り立てる Ⓥ: drive

the cattle to the fields (*ushi o nohara e oiyaru*) 牛を野原へ追いやる.
— *vi.* (car) ku⌈ruma o uñteñ suru 車を運転する [I]; do⌈ra⌉ibu suru ドライブする [I]: We drove around the city. (*Watashi-tachi wa shinai o doraibu shita.*) 私たちは市内をドライブした.

driver *n.* u⌈ñte⌉ñshu 運転手: a taxi driver (*takushii no uñteñshu*) タクシーの運転手.

driveway *n.* sha⌈doo 車道. ★ Japanese does not have a word for 'driveway' especially in its North American sense. A road on private property leading for a public street '*koodoo*' 公道 is a '*shidoo*' 私道 but this can refer to a road on a farm as well. '*Shadoo*' can refer to any public or private street.

droop *vi.* (person) u⌈nadareru うなだれる [V]; (plant) shi⌈oreru しおれる [V]: Her head drooped sadly. (*Kanojo wa kanashi-soo ni unadareta.*) 彼女は悲しそうにうなだれた. / The flowers drooped because they had no water. (*Mizu ga nai no de hana ga shiorete shimatta.*) 水がないので花がしおれてしまった.

drop *vi.* (thing) o⌈chi⌉ru 落ちる [V]; (price, temperature) sa⌈ga⌉ru 下がる [C]: The boy dropped from a tree. (*Sono otoko-no-ko wa ki kara ochita.*) その男の子は木から落ちた. / Stock prices dropped sharply. (*Kabuka ga kyuugeki ni sagatta.*) 株価が急激に下がった.
— *vt.* ... o o⌈to⌉su ...を落とす [C]: You dropped your notebook. (*Techoo o otoshimashita yo.*) 手帳を落としましたよ.
drop out *vi.* (of school) chu⌈uto ta⌉igaku suru 中途退学する [I].
— *n.* (water) shi⌈zuku⌉ しずく; i⌈t-teki 一滴; (price) ge⌈raku 下落; (temperature) ka⌈koo 下降: drops of rain (*ame no shizuku*) 雨のしずく / There was not a drop of water. (*Mizu wa it-teki mo nakatta.*) 水は一滴もなかった. / a sudden drop of temperature (*oñdo no totsuzeñ no kakoo*) 温度の突然の下降.

drown *vi.* o⌈boreshi⌉nu おぼれ死ぬ [C]; su⌈ishi suru 水死する [I]: He almost drowned in the river. (*Kare wa kawa de oboreshinu tokoro datta.*) 彼は川でおぼれ死ぬところだった.

drug *n.* (narcotic) ma⌈yaku 麻薬; (medicine) ku⌈suri 薬: a drug addict (*mayaku jooshuusha*) 麻薬常習者 / take drugs (*mayaku o utsu*) 麻薬を打つ.

drugstore *n.* do⌈raggusuto⌉a ドラッグストア. ★ In Japan, there are pharmacies, but no stores equivalent to drugstores.

drum *n.* **1** (musical instrument) ta⌈iko 太鼓: beat a drum (*taiko o tataku*) 太鼓をたたく.
2 (for oil, etc.) do⌈ramukañ ドラム缶.

drunk *adj.* yo⌉tta 酔った; yo⌉tte iru 酔っている; yo⌈ppa-ratta 酔っぱらった; yo⌈pparatte iru 酔っぱらっている: drunk driving (*yopparai uñteñ*) 酔っぱらい運転 / I got drunk on whisky. (*Watashi wa uisukii de yopparatta.*) 私はウイスキーで酔っぱらった.

dry *adj.* **1** (not wet) ka⌈wa⌉ita 乾いた; ka⌈wa⌉itte iru 乾いている; ka⌈ñsoo shita [shite iru] 乾燥した[している]: dry air (*kawaita kuuki*) 乾いた空気 / The clothes are dry now. (*Fuku wa moo kawaite imasu.*) 服はもう乾いています.
2 (wine) ka⌈rakuchi no 辛口の: I like dry white wine. (*Watashi wa karakuchi no shiro-waiñ ga suki desu.*) 私は辛口の白ワインが好きです.
— *vt.* ... o ka⌈waka⌉su ...を乾かす [C]; ho⌉su 干す [C]: He dried his wet trousers in front of the fire. (*Kare wa nureta zuboñ o hi no mae de kawakashita.*) 彼はぬれたズボンを火の前で乾かした.

dry cleaner *n.* do⌈rai-kuriiniñguya ドライクリーニング屋. ★ In everyday conversation, the dry cleaner's will often be called '*señtakuya*' 洗濯屋.

duck *n.* (domestic) a⌈hiru あひる(家

鴨); (wild) ka˺mo かも(鴨).

due *adj.* **1** (payable) shi˹harawa-na˺kereba na˹ra˺nai 支払わなければならない; shi˹harai kijitsu ga ki˺te iru 支払期日がきている: The bill is due today. (*Sono seekyuusho wa kyoo shiharawanakereba narimaseñ.*) その請求書はきょう支払わなければなりません.
2 (proper) to˹ozeñ no 当然の; se˹e-too na 正当な: I drove with due care. (*Watashi wa toozeñ no chuui o haratte uñteñ shita.*) 私は当然の注意を払って運転した.
3 (expected) ... koto ni na˺tte iru …ことになっている; ... ha˹zu da …はずだ: He is due to come at seven. (*Kare wa shichi-ji ni kuru hazu ni natte iru.*) 彼は7時に来るはずになっている.
due to ... *prep.* ... no ta˹me˺ ni ... のために: Due to the snow the train was delayed. (*Yuki no tame ni ressha ga okureta.*) 雪のために列車が遅れた.

dull *adj.* **1** (uninteresting) tsu˹mara˺nai つまらない; o˹moshi˺roku nai おもしろくない: a dull book (*tsumaranai hoñ*) つまらない本.
2 (weak) ni˹bu˺i 鈍い: a dull pain (*nibui itami*) 鈍い痛み.
3 (blunt) ki˹re˺aji no wa˹ru˺i 切れ味の悪い; na˹makura na なまくらな: a dull knife (*kireaji no warui naifu*) 切れ味の悪いナイフ.
4 (stupid) a˹tama no nibu˺i 頭の鈍い: a dull pupil (*atama no nibui seeto*) 頭の鈍い生徒.
5 (not clear) ha˹kki˺ri shinai はっきりしない: dull weather (*hakkiri shinai teñki*) はっきりしない天気.

dumb *adj.* **1** (mute) ku˹chi no [ga] kikenai 口の[が]きけない; mo˹no˺ o i˹enai 物を言えない: The child was born dumb. (*Sono ko wa umare nagara kuchi ga kikenakatta.*) その子は生まれながら口がきけなかった.
2 (silent) da˹ma˺tte iru 黙っている: He remained dumb about his activities. (*Kare wa jibuñ no koodoo ni tsuite damatte ita.*) 彼は自分の行動について黙っていた.

dump *vt.* ... o na˹gesuteru …を投げ捨てる Ⓥ: Don't dump rubbish into the river. (*Gomi o kawa e nagesutete wa ikemaseñ.*) ごみを川へ投げ捨ててはいけません.
— *n.* go˹misuteba ごみ捨て場.

duplicate *n.* (document) u˹tsushi˺ 写し; (key) a˹ikagi 合い鍵.

durable *adj.* na˹gamochi˺ suru 長持ちする; jo˹obu na じょうぶな: These trousers are made of durable material. (*Kono zuboñ wa joobu na kiji de dekite iru.*) このズボンはじょうぶな生地でできている.

during *prep.* **1** (throughout) ... no a˹ida zutto …の間ずっと; ... chuu …中: I was in Hokkaido during the whole summer. (*Watashi wa natsu no aida zutto Hokkaidoo ni imashita.*) 私は夏の間ずっと北海道にいました.
2 (in the course of) ... no a˹ida ni …の間に: During the night the rain changed to snow. (*Yoru no aida ni ame ga yuki ni kawatta.*) 夜の間に雨が雪に変わった.

dust *n.* ho˹kori ほこり; chi˹ri ちり: The desk is covered with dust. (*Tsukue ni hokori ga tamatte iru.*) 机にほこりがたまっている.
— *vt.* ... no ho˹kori [chi˹ri] o hara˺u …のほこり[ちり]を払う Ⓒ: dust the furniture (*kagu no hokori o harau*) 家具のほこりを払う.

dusty *adj.* ho˹korippo˺i ほこりっぽい; ho˹korida˺rake no ほこりだらけの: a dusty room (*hokoridarake no heya*) ほこりだらけの部屋.

Dutch *adj.* Ora˹ñda no オランダの; (language) Ora˹ñdago no オランダ語の; (people) Ora˹ñda˺jiñ no オランダ人の.
— *n.* (language) Ora˹ñdago オランダ語; (people) Ora˹ñda˺jiñ オランダ人.

duty *n.* **1** (what one ought to do) gi˺mu 義務: carry out [shirk] one's duty (*jibuñ no gimu o hatasu [nogareru]*) 自分の義務を果たす[逃れ

る].

2 (job) ni⌉ñmu 任務; sho⌉kumu 職務: the duties of a policeman (*keekañ no niñmu*) 警官の任務.

3 (tax) ze⌉e 税; ka⌈ñzee 関税: a duty on foreign goods (*gaikoku shoohiñ ni taisuru kañzee*) 外国商品に対する関税.

duty-free shop *n.* me⌈ñze⌉eteñ 免税店.

dwarf *n.* ko⌈bito 小人: a dwarf tree (*boñsai*) 盆栽.

dwell *vi.* su⌉mu 住む Ⓒ; kyo⌈juu suru 居住する Ⓘ: dwell in the country (*inaka ni sumu*) 田舎に住む.

dye *n.* se⌈ñryo⌉o 染料: synthetic dyes (*goosee señryoo*) 合成染料.

— *vt.* ... o so⌈meru ...を染める Ⓥ: He dyed his hair brown. (*Kare wa kami no ke o chairo ni someta.*) 彼は髪の毛を茶色に染めた.

dynamic *adj.* (energetic) ka⌈tsudoo-teki na 活動的な; (great) da⌈inami⌉kku na ダイナミックな: a dynamic person (*katsudoo-teki na hito*) 活動的な人.

dynamite *n.* da⌈inama⌉ito ダイナマイト: explode the dynamite (*dainamaito o bakuha suru*) ダイナマイトを爆破する.

E

each *adj.* so⌈re⌉zore no それぞれの; me⌈eme⌉e no めいめいの: Each student stood up and gave a speech. (*Sorezore no gakusee ga tachiagatte supiichi o shita.*) それぞれの学生が立ち上がってスピーチをした.

— *pron.* so⌈re⌉zore それぞれ; me⌈eme⌉e めいめい: I gave a small tip to each. (*Watashi wa meemee ni chippu o sukoshi yatta.*) 私はめいめいにチップを少しやった.

— *adv.* so⌈re⌉zore それぞれ; me⌈eme⌉e めいめい: I gave the children a slice of cake each. (*Watashi wa kodomo-tachi ni meemee keeki o hito-kire zutsu ageta.*) 私は子どもたちにめいめいケーキを一切れずつあげた.

each other *pron.* ta⌈gai ni 互いに: We looked at each other. (*Watashi-tachi wa o-tagai ni kao o miawaseta.*) 私たちはお互いに顔を見合わせた.

eager *adj.* shi⌈kiri ni ⟨verb⟩-taga⌉tte iru しきりに…たがっている; ne⌈tsuboo shite iru 熱望している; ne⌉sshiñ na 熱心な: He is eager to climb the mountain. (*Kare wa shikiri ni sono yama ni noboritagatte iru.*) 彼はしきりにその山に登りたがっている. / She is eager in her study of Japanese. (*Kanojo wa Nihoñgo no beñkyoo ga nesshiñ da.*) 彼女は日本語の勉強が熱心だ.

eagle *n.* wa⌈shi わし.

ear *n.* **1** (body part) mi⌈mi⌉ 耳: My ears are ringing. (*Watashi wa miminari ga suru.*) 私は耳鳴りがする.

2 (hearing) cho⌉oryoku 聴力; cho⌉okaku 聴覚: have keen ears (*chookaku ga surudoi*) 聴覚が鋭い / I have no ear for music. (*Watashi wa oñgaku ga wakaranai.*) 私は音楽がわからない.

earache *n.* mi⌈mi no itami⌉ 耳の痛み: have an earache (*mimi ga itai*) 耳が痛い.

ear doctor *n.* ji⌈bika⌉-i 耳鼻科医.

eardrum *n.* ko⌈maku 鼓膜.

early *adj.* **1** (before the usual time) ha⌈ya⌉i 早い: I had an early lunch. (*Watashi wa hayai chuushoku o totta.*) 私は早い昼食をとった.

2 (beginning of) ha⌈ya⌉i 早い; ha⌈jime no 初めの: early spring (*sooshuñ*) 早春 / early summer (*shoka*) 初夏 / She got married in her early twenties. (*Kanojo wa nijuu-dai no hajime ni kekkoñ shita.*) 彼女は20代の初めに結婚した.

— *adv.* ha⌉yaku 早く; ha⌈yame ni

早めに: Get up early. (*Hayaku oki nasai.*) 早く起きなさい.

earn *vt.* **1** (money) ... o ka[se]gu ...を稼ぐ Ⓒ: He earns more than ten million yen a year. (*Kare wa ichi-neñ ni is-señ-mañ-eñ ijoo kasegu.*) 彼は1年に1千万円以上稼ぐ.
2 (gain) ... o e]ru ...を得る Ⓥ; to]ru 取る Ⓒ: earn a reputation for honesty (*shoojiki no hyoobañ o toru*) 正直の評判を取る.

earnest *adj.* (serious) ma[jime na まじめな; (eager) ne]sshiñ na 熱心な: an earnest student (*majime na gakusee*) まじめな学生 / He refused her earnest request. (*Kare wa kanojo no nesshiñ na tanomi o kotowatta.*) 彼は彼女の熱心な頼みを断わった.

earth *n.* **1** (globe) chi[kyuu 地球: The spaceship left the earth. (*Uchuuseñ wa chikyuu o hanareta.*) 宇宙船は地球を離れた.
2 (ground) ji]meñ 地面; da]ichi 大地: Snow covered the earth. (*Yuki ga daichi o ootte ita.*) 雪が大地を覆っていた.
3 (soil) tsu[chi] 土; do[joo 土壌: There is not enough earth here to grow a tree. (*Koko wa ki o sodateru no ni juubuñ na dojoo ga nai.*) ここは木を育てるのに十分な土壌がない.

earthquake *n.* ji[shiñ 地震: A strong earthquake hit the island. (*Tsuyoi jishiñ ga shima o osotta.*) 強い地震が島を襲った.

ease *vt.* **1** (relieve) ... o ya[waragel]ru ...を和らげる Ⓥ; ka[ruku suru 軽くする Ⓘ: This medicine should ease your pain. (*Kono kusuri wa itami o yawarageru hazu desu.*) この薬は痛みを和らげるはずです.
2 (loosen) ... o yu[rume]ru ...を緩める Ⓥ: Ease your belt a little. (*Beruto o sukoshi yurume nasai.*) ベルトを少し緩めなさい.
3 (carefully move) ... o so[tto ugoka]su ...をそっと動かす Ⓒ: He eased the car to a stop. (*Kare wa kuruma o sotto tometa.*) 彼は車をそっと止めた.
— *vi.* (lighten) ka[ruku na]ru 軽くなる Ⓒ; ra[ku] ni naru 楽になる Ⓒ: The pain eased. (*Itami wa karuku natta.*) 痛みは軽くなった.
— *n.* (comfort) ki[raku 気楽; a[ñraku 安楽: a life of ease (*kiraku na seekatsu*) 気楽な生活 / The whole family lives in ease. (*Ikka wa añraku ni kurashite imasu.*) 一家は安楽に暮らしています.
with ease *adv.* ya[suya]su to やすやすと: He did the task with ease. (*Kare wa sono shigoto o yasuyasu to yatta.*) 彼はその仕事をやすやすとやった.

easily *adv.* **1** (without difficulty) yo[oi ni 容易に; ta[ya]suku たやすく: He easily solved the problem. (*Kare wa sono mondai o tayasuku toita.*) 彼はその問題をたやすく解いた.
2 (without doubt) u[tagai na]ku 疑いなく; ta]shika ni 確かに: Buy this one. It's easily the best. (*Kore o kai nasai. Sore wa tashika ni ichibañ ii mono desu.*) これを買いなさい. それは確かにいちばんいい物です.

east *n.* **1** (direction) hi[gashi 東: Chiba is to the east of Tokyo. (*Chiba wa Tookyoo no higashi no hoo ni aru.*) 千葉は東京の東の方にある. / North, South, East, West (*too-zai-nañ-boku*) 東西南北.
★ The Japanese order is east, west, south, north.
2 (Orient) To]oyoo 東洋: the Far East (*Kyoku-too*) 極東 / the Middle East (*Chuu-too*) 中東.
— *adj.* hi[gashi no 東の: an east wind (*higashi kaze*) 東風.
— *adv.* hi[gashi e [ni] 東へ[に]: Our balcony faces east. (*Watashitachi no barukonii wa higashi ni muite iru.*) 私たちのバルコニーは東に向いている.

Easter *n.* fu[kkatsu]sai 復活祭.

eastern *adj.* **1** (direction) hi[gashi no 東の: the eastern sky (*higashi no sora*) 東の空.
2 (Oriental) To]oyoo no 東洋の:

Eastern culture (*Tooyoo no buñka*) 東洋の文化.

easy *adj.* **1** (not difficult) ya⸢sashii やさしい; yo⸢oi na 容易な: The problem was easy to solve. (*Sono moñdai wa toku no ga yasashikatta.*) その問題は解くのがやさしかった.
2 (comfortable) ki⸢raku na 気楽な; a⸢ñraku na 安楽な: a person with an easy manner (*kiraku na taido no hito*) 気楽な態度の人 / She leads an easy life. (*Kanojo wa kiraku na seekatsu o okutte iru.*) 彼女は気楽な生活を送っている.

eat *vt.* **1** (consume) ... o ta⸢be⸣ru …を食べる Ⓥ; [honorific] me⸢shiagaru 召し上がる Ⓒ; [humble] i⸢tadaku いただく Ⓒ; [rude] ku⸣u 食う Ⓒ: eat an apple (*riñgo o taberu*) りんごを食べる / What did you eat for breakfast? (*Chooshoku ni nani o tabemashita ka?*) 朝食に何を食べましたか. / What do you eat? (*Nani o meshiagarimasu ka?*) 何を召し上がりますか.
2 (corrode) ... o fu⸢shoku suru …を腐食する Ⓘ: The iron bar was eaten away. (*Sono tetsuboo wa fushoku shite shimatta.*) その鉄棒は腐食してしまった.
— *vi.* ta⸢be⸣ru 食べる Ⓥ: Shall we eat out? (*Soto de tabemasu ka?*) 外で食べますか.

echo *n.* (sound) ha⸢ñkyoo 反響; ko⸢dama こだま: I heard the echo of my voice in the cave. (*Hora-ana no naka de jibuñ no koe no hañkyoo o kiita.*) 洞穴の中で自分の声の反響を聞いた.
— *vi.* ha⸢ñkyoo suru 反響する Ⓘ: The music echoed in the hall. (*Oñgaku ga hooru ni hañkyoo shita.*) 音楽がホールに反響した.

ecology *n.* (study) se⸢eta⸣igaku 生態学; (environment) shi⸢zeñ kañ⸣kyoo 自然環境.

economic *adj.* ke⸢ezaijoo no 経済上の: economic assistance (*keezai eñjo*) 経済援助 / the economic policy of the government (*seefu no keezai-seesaku*) 政府の経済政策.

economical *adj.* ke⸢ezai-teki na 経済的な; se⸢tsuyaku ni na⸣ru 節約になる: an economical car (*keezai-teki na kuruma*) 経済的な車 / He is economical with money. (*Kare wa o-kane o setsuyaku shite iru.*) 彼はお金を節約している.

economics *n.* ke⸢eza⸣igaku 経済学: I study economics at Waseda University. (*Watashi wa Waseda-daigaku de keezaigaku o beñkyoo shite imasu.*) 私は早稲田大学で経済学を勉強しています.

economize *vi.* (... o) se⸢tsuyaku suru (…を)節約する Ⓘ; mu⸢da na⸣ku tsu⸢kau むだなく使う Ⓒ: economize on water (*mizu o setsuyaku suru*) 水を節約する / Make every effort to economize. (*Muda o nakusu yoo ni arayuru doryoku o shi nasai.*) むだをなくすようにあらゆる努力をしなさい.

economy *n.* **1** (saving) se⸢tsuyaku 節約; ke⸢ñyaku 倹約: make economies (*setsuyaku o suru*) 節約をする / try to practice economy (*keñyaku o kokorogakeru*) 倹約を心がける.
2 (system) ke⸣ezai 経済: domestic economy (*katee keezai*) 家庭経済 / the world economy (*sekai keezai*) 世界経済.
— *adj.* ke⸢ezai-teki na 経済的な; ya⸢su⸣i 安い; e⸢ko⸣nomii no エコノミーの: economy passengers (*ekonomii-kurasu no jookyaku*) エコノミークラスの乗客.

edge *n.* **1** (border) ha⸢shi 端; fu⸢chi⸣ 縁; he⸢ri⸣ へり: the edge of a table (*teeburu no hashi*) テーブルの端 / the edge of a cup (*chawañ no fuchi*) 茶わんの縁 / the edge of a tatami (*tatami no heri*) 畳のへり.
2 (of a blade) ha⸣ 刃; ha⸢saki⸣ 刃先: the edge of a razor (*kamisori no ha*) かみそりの刃 / a knife with a sharp edge (*surudoi hasaki o motta naifu*) 鋭い刃先を持ったナイフ.

edit *vt.* ... o he⸢ñshuu suru …を編集する Ⓘ: edit a magazine (*zasshi o heñshuu suru*) 雑誌を編集する.

edition *n.* ha¹ñ 版: the first edition (*sho-hañ*) 初版 / a revised edition (*kaitee-bañ*) 改訂版.

editor *n.* he⌈ñshu¹usha 編集者: the editor in chief (*heñshuu shukañ*) 編集主幹.

editorial *n.* sha⌈setsu 社説; ro⌈ñsetsu 論説: Did you read yesterday's editorial in the Asahi? (*Kinoo no Asahi-shiñbuñ no shasetsu o yomimashita ka?*) きのうの朝日新聞の社説を読みましたか.

educate *vt.* **1** (teach) ... o kyo⌈oiku suru ...を教育する [I]: It costs a lot to educate children. (*Kodomo o kyooiku suru no ni wa o-kane ga kakaru.*) 子どもを教育するのにはお金がかかる.
2 (train) ... o ya⌈shinau ...を養う [C]; ku¹ñreñ suru 訓練する [I]: educate one's ear to appreciate good music (*yoi oñgaku o kañshoo suru mimi o yashinau*) よい音楽を鑑賞する耳を養う.

education *n.* kyo⌈oiku 教育: compulsory education (*gimu-kyooiku*) 義務教育 / receive a good education (*yoi kyooiku o ukeru*) よい教育を受ける.

effect *n.* **1** (result produced) ko¹oka 効果; e⌈ekyoo 影響; sa¹yoo 作用: The PR campaign has had no effect. (*Pii aaru kyañpeeñ wa kooka ga nakatta.*) PR キャンペーンは効果がなかった. / a side effect (*fukusayoo*) 副作用.
2 (result) ke⌈kka 結果: cause and effect (*geñiñ to kekka*) 原因と結果.
3 (meaning) i¹mi 意味; shu¹shi 趣旨: I received a letter to the effect that he would resign his post. (*Kare kara jishoku suru to iu imi no tegami o uketotta.*) 彼から辞職するという意味の手紙を受け取った.
come into effect *vi.* ha⌈kkoo suru 発効する [I]: The law comes into effect next month. (*Sono hooritsu wa raigetsu hakkoo shimasu.*) その法律は来月発効します.
personal effects *n.* mi ⌈no mawarihiñ 身の回り品.
take effect *vi.* ki⌈ku 効く [C]: This medicine soon takes effect. (*Kono kusuri wa sugu kikimasu.*) この薬はすぐ効きます.

effective *adj.* **1** (producing a result) ko¹oka no aru 効果のある; ko⌈oka-teki na 効果的な: His speech was very effective. (*Kare no eñzetsu wa hijoo ni kooka ga atta.*) 彼の演説は非常に効果があった. / make effective use of light and shade (*hikari to kage o kooka-teki ni tsukau*) 光と陰を効果的に使う.
2 (actual) ji⌈ssai no 実際の; ji⌈jitsujoo no 事実上の: He is the effective leader of the group. (*Kare wa sono guruupu no jijitsujoo no shidoosha desu.*) 彼はそのグループの事実上の指導者です.

efficiency *n.* no⌈oritsu 能率: raise [lower] efficiency (*nooritsu o ageru [sageru]*) 能率を上げる[下げる].

efficient *adj.* **1** (of people) yu⌈unoo na 有能な; no¹oryoku no aru 能力のある: an efficient secretary (*yuunoo na hisho*) 有能な秘書 / The teacher was very efficient. (*Sono señsee wa totemo yuunoo datta.*) その先生はとても有能だった.
2 (of methods) ko⌈oka-teki na 効果的な; (of machines) no⌈oritsu-teki na 能率的な: The machines in this factory are very efficient. (*Kono koojoo no kikai wa totemo nooritsu-teki da.*) この工場の機械はとても能率的だ.

effort *n.* **1** (endeavor) do¹ryoku 努力; ho⌈neori¹ 骨折り: We made every effort to find the child. (*Watashi-tachi wa sono ko o sagasu tame ni arayuru doryoku o shita.*) 私たちはその子を捜すためにあらゆる努力をした.
2 (achievement) se¹eka 成果; (work) ro⌈osaku 労作: It is a pretty good effort. (*Sore wa nakanaka yoku dekite iru.*) それはなかなかよくできている.

egg *n.* ta⌈ma¹go 卵: a raw egg (*na-*

ma-tamago) 生卵 / a boiled egg (*yude-tamago*) ゆで卵 / a fried egg (*tamagoyaki*) 卵焼き / scrambled eggs (*iri-tamago*) いり卵 / break an egg (*tamago o waru*) 卵を割る / This egg is soft-boiled [hard-boiled]. (*Kono tamago wa hañjuku* [*kata-yude*] *da.*) この卵は半熟[固ゆで]だ.

egoism *n.* ri⌈koshu⌉gi 利己主義.

eight *pron.* ya⌈ttsu⌉ 八つ; (people) ha⌈chi⌉-niñ 8 人; (things) ha⌈chi⌉-ko [ha⌉k-ko] 8 個: I bought eight apples. (*Riñgo o yattsu* [*hachi-ko*] *katta.*) りんごを八つ[8 個]買った.
— *n.* (figure) ha⌈chi⌉ 8; (hour) ha⌈chi⌉-ji 8 時; (minute) ha⌈chi⌉-fuñ 8 分; (age) ha⌉s-sai 8 歳.
— *adj.* ha⌈chi⌉ no 8 の; ya⌈ttsu⌉ no 八つの; (people) ha⌈chi⌉-niñ no 8 人の; (things) ha⌉k-ko no 8 個の; (age) ha⌉s-sai no 8 歳の.

eighteen *pron.* ju⌈u-hachi⌉ 18; (people) ju⌈uhachi⌉-niñ 18 人; (things) ju⌈uhachi⌉-ko [ju⌈u-ha⌉k-ko] 18 個; (age) ju⌈u-has⌉sai 18 歳.
— *n.* (figure) ju⌈uhachi⌉ 18; (hour) ju⌈uhachi⌉-ji 18 時; (minute) ju⌈u-ha⌉p-puñ 18 分; (age) ju⌈uha⌉ssai 18 歳.
— *adj.* ju⌈u-hachi⌉ no 18 の; (people) ju⌈uhachi⌉-niñ no 18 人の; (things) ju⌈uhachi⌉-ko [ju⌈u-ha⌉k-ko] no 18 個の; (age) ju⌈uha⌉s-sai no 18 歳の.

eighteenth *adj.* ju⌈uhachi-bañme⌉ no 18 番目の; da⌉i-ju⌈uhachi⌉ no 第 18 の.
— *n.* **1** (people) ju⌈uhachi-bañme⌉ no hi⌈to⌉ 18 番目の人; (things) ju⌈u-hachi-bañme⌉ no mo⌈no⌉ 18 番目のもの.
2 (day) ju⌈uhachi-nichi⌉ 18 日.
3 (fraction) ju⌈uhachi-buñ no ichi⌉ 18 分の 1.

eighth *adj.* ha⌈chi-bañme⌉ no 8 番目の; da⌉i-ha⌈chi⌉ no 第 8 の.
— *n.* **1** (people) ha⌈chi-bañme⌉ no hi⌈to⌉ 8 番目の人; (things) ha⌈chi-bañme⌉ no mo⌈no⌉ 8 番目のもの.
2 (day) yo⌈oka 8 日.
3 (fraction) ha⌈chi-buñ no ichi⌉ 8 分の 1.

eightieth *adj.* ha⌈chijuu-bañme⌉ no 80 番目の; da⌉i-ha⌈chiju⌉u no 第 80 の.
— *n.* **1** (people) ha⌈chijuu-bañme⌉ no hi⌈to⌉ 80 番目の人; (things) ha⌈chijuu-bañme⌉ no mo⌈no⌉ 80 番目のもの.
2 (fraction) ha⌈chijuu-buñ no ichi⌉ 80 分の 1.

eighty *pron.* ha⌈chiju⌉u 80; (people) ha⌈chiju⌉u-niñ 80 人; (things) ha⌈chiju⌉k-ko 80 個.
— *n.* (figure) ha⌈chiju⌉u 80; (age) ha⌈chiju⌉s-sai 80 歳.
— *adj.* ha⌈chiju⌉u no 80 の; (people) ha⌈chiju⌉u-niñ no 80 人の; (things) ha⌈chiju⌉k-ko no 80 個の; (age) ha⌈chiju⌉s-sai no 80 歳の.

either *adj.* **1** (one or the other) do⌉chira ka hi⌈to⌉tsu no どちらか一つの; [in the negative] do⌉chira no ... mo (... de na⌉i) どちらの…も(…でない): Please take either slice of cake. (*Keeki o dochira ka hitotsu tori nasai.*) ケーキをどちらか一つとりなさい. / I don't like either Tokyo or Osaka. (*Tookyoo mo Oosaka mo dochira mo suki ja arimaseñ.*) 東京も大阪もどちらも好きじゃありません.
2 (one and the other) do⌉chira no どちらの: There were candles at either end of the table. (*Teeburu no dochira no hashi ni mo roosoku ga atta.*) テーブルのどちらの端にもろうそくがあった.
— *pron.* (one or the other) do⌉chira de mo どちらでも; [in the negative] do⌈chira mo (... de nai) どちらも(…でない): You can choose either of them. (*Sono uchi no dochira de mo erabu koto ga dekimasu.*) そのうちのどちらでも選ぶことができます. / She didn't want either. (*Kanojo wa dochira mo nozomanakatta.*) 彼女はどちらも望まなかった.
— *adv.* [in the negative] ... mo ma⌈ta (... nai) …もまた(…ない): I

don't like sushi, and I don't like tempura either. (*Watashi wa sushi wa suki ja arimaseñ shi, teñpura mo mata suki ja arimaseñ.*) 私はすしは好きじゃありませんし，てんぷらもまた好きじゃありません. / "I can't speak Chinese." "I can't either." (*"Watashi wa Chuugokugo o hanasemaseñ." "Watashi mo hanasemaseñ."*) 「私は中国語を話せません」「私も話せません」

— *conj.* ... ka ma⌈ta⌉ wa ... ka …かまたは…か; [in the negative] ... mo ... mo (... nai) …も…も(…ない): You can have either coffee or tea. (*Koohii ka mata wa koocha ga arimasu.*) コーヒーかまたは紅茶があります. / I cannot write either hiragana or katakana. (*Watashi wa hiragana mo katakana mo kakemaseñ.*) 私はひらがなもカタカナも書けません.

elastic *adj.* da⌈ñryoku no a⌉ru 弾力のある: an elastic band (*wagomu*) 輪ゴム.

— *n.* go⌈mu⌉himo ゴムひも: a piece of elastic (*gomuhimo ip-poñ*) ゴムひも1本.

elbow *n.* hi⌈ji⌉ ひじ: lean forward on one's elbows (*hiji ni yorikakaru*) ひじに寄り掛かる.

— *vt.* ... o hi⌈ji⌉ de o⌈su …をひじで押す 🄲: He elbowed me out of the way. (*Kare wa watashi o oshinoketa.*) 彼は私を押しのけた.

elder *adj.* to⌈shiue no 年上の: my elder brother [sister] (*watashi no ani* [*ane*]) 私の兄[姉].

— *n.* ne⌈ñcho⌉osha 年長者; to⌈shiue no hito⌉ 年上の人: Be polite to your elders. (*Toshiue no hito ni wa reegi tadashiku shi nasai.*) 年上の人には礼儀正しくしなさい.

elderly *adj.* ne⌉ñpai no 年配の; o⌈toshiyori no お年寄りの: an elderly gentleman [lady] (*neñpai no shiñshi* [*josee*]) 年配の紳士[女性].

eldest *adj.* i⌈chibañ toshiue no いちばん年上の; sa⌈ine⌉ñchoo no 最年長の: my eldest brother [sister] (*watashi no ichibañ toshiue no ani* [*ane*]) 私のいちばん年上の兄[姉].

elect *vt.* ... o se⌉ñkyo suru …を選挙する 🄸; e⌈ra⌉bu 選ぶ 🄲: We have to elect a chairman. (*Gichoo o señkyo shinakereba naranai.*) 議長を選挙しなければならない. / The voters elected Mrs. Yasukawa mayor. (*Toohyoosha wa Yasukawa-sañ o shichoo ni erañda.*) 投票者は安川さんを市長に選んだ.

election *n.* se⌉ñkyo 選挙: a general election (*soo-señkyo*) 総選挙 / an election campaign (*señkyo-uñdoo*) 選挙運動 / Our candidate won [lost] the election. (*Wareware no koohosha wa señkyo ni katta* [*maketa*].) われわれの候補者は選挙に勝った[負けた].

electric *adj.* de⌉ñki de u⌈go⌉ku 電気で動く; de⌉ñki no 電気の: an electric clock (*deñki-dokee*) 電気時計 / an electric shaver (*deñki-kamisori*) 電気かみそり / electric current (*deñryuu*) 電流.

electrical *adj.* de⌉ñki no 電気の: an electrical engineer (*deñki gishi*) 電気技師.

electrician *n.* de⌈ñki gi⌉shi 電気技師; de⌈ñki⌉koo 電気工.

electricity *n.* de⌉ñki 電気; (current) de⌈ñryuu 電流: turn on [off] the electricity (*deñki o ireru* [*kiru*]) 電気を入れる[切る] / install electricity (*deñki o hiku*) 電気を引く.

electronic *adj.* de⌉ñshi no 電子の; de⌈ñshi-koo⌉gaku no 電子工学の; e⌈rekutoroni⌉kusu no エレクトロニクスの: an electronic computer (*deñshi keesañki*) 電子計算機 / electronic industries (*erekutoronikusu-sañgyoo*) エレクトロニクス産業.

electronics *n.* de⌈ñshi-ko⌉ogaku 電子工学.

elegant *adj.* jo⌈ohi⌉ñ na 上品な; hi⌈ñ no yo⌉i 品のよい: an elegant lady (*joohiñ na fujiñ*) 上品な婦人 / She was wearing elegant clothes. (*Kanojo wa hiñ no yoi fuku o kite ita.*) 彼女は品のよい服を着ていた.

element *n.* **1** (essential part) yo⌉o-

so 要素; se'ebuñ 成分: An essential element of success is hard work. (*Seekoo ni nakute wa naranai yooso wa kiñbeñ desu.*) 成功になくてはならない要素は勤勉です.
2 (of chemistry) ge'ñso 元素.

elementary *adj.* sho'ho no 初歩の; ki'hoñ no 基本の: the elementary Japanese course (*shokyuu Nihoñgo koosu*) 初級日本語コース.

elementary school *n.* sho'o-ga'kkoo 小学校: enter [leave] an elementary school (*shoogakkoo ni nyuugaku [o sotsugyoo] suru*) 小学校に入学[を卒業]する.

elephant *n.* zo'o 象.

elevator *n.* e'rebe'etaa エレベーター: get on [off] an elevator (*erebeetaa ni noru [kara oriru]*) エレベーターに乗る[から降りる] / take the elevator to the fifth floor (*erebeetaa ni go-kai made noru*) エレベーターに5階まで乗る.

eleven *pron.* ju'uichi' 11; (people) ju'uichi'-niñ 11人; (things) ju'ui'k-ko 11個.
— *n.* (figure) ju'uichi' 11; (hour) ju'u-ichi'-ji 11時; (minute) ju'ui'p-puñ 11分; (age) ju'ui's-sai 11歳.
— *adj.* ju'uichi' no 11の; (people) ju'uichi'-niñ no 11人の; (things) ju'ui'k-ko no 11個の; (age) ju'ui's-sai no 11歳の.

eleventh *adj.* ju'uichi-bañme' no 11番目の; da'i-ju'uichi' no 第11の.
— *n.* **1** (people) ju'uichi-bañme' no h'ito' 11番目の人; (things) ju'u-ichi-bañme' no mo'no' 11番目のもの.
2 (date) ju'uichi-nichi' 11日.
3 (fraction) ju'uichi-buñ no ichi' 11分の1.

eliminate *vt.* ... o no'zoku ...を除く Ⓒ; sa'kujo suru 削除する Ⓘ: It is not easy to eliminate hunger. (*Ue o nozoku no wa yooi de nai.*) 飢えを除くのは容易でない. / eliminate useless words from sentences (*fuyoo na go o buñshoo kara sakujo suru*) 不要な語を文章から削除する.

eloquence *n.* yu'ubeñ 雄弁: a person of eloquence (*yuubeñka*) 雄弁家.

eloquent *adj.* yu'ubeñ na 雄弁な: an eloquent speaker (*yuubeñka*) 雄弁家.

else *adj.* so'no' hoka no そのほかの; ta' no 他の; be'tsu no 別の: No one else came yesterday. (*Kinoo wa sono hoka no hito wa dare mo kimaseñ deshita.*) きのうはそのほかの人はだれも来ませんでした. / I have nothing else to say. (*Hoka ni nani mo iu koto wa arimaseñ.*) ほかに何も言うことはありません.
— *adv.* so'no' hoka ni そのほかに; ta' ni 他に; be'tsu ni 別に: It cannot be bought anywhere else. (*Sore wa hoka no basho de wa kaemaseñ.*) それはほかの場所では買えません.
or else *conj.* so'o shinai to そうしないと: Do as we say, or else! (*Iu toori ni shi nasai. Soo shinai to.*) 言うとおりにしなさい. そうしないと.

elsewhere *adv.* ho'ka no basho de ほかの場所で: They are sold out. Let's buy it elsewhere. (*Sore wa urikire desu. Hoka de kaimashoo.*) それは売り切れです. ほかで買いましょう.

elude *vt.* ... o sa'ke'ru ...を避ける Ⓥ; no'gare'ru 逃れる Ⓥ: elude one's pursuers (*otte o nogareru*) 追っ手を逃れる.

embankment *n.* te'eboo 堤防; do'te 土手.

embark *vi.* (airplane) to'ojoo suru 搭乗する Ⓘ; (ship) jo'oseñ suru 乗船する Ⓘ: We embark for Okinawa next week. (*Watashi-tachi wa raishuu jooseñ shite Okinawa ni mukaimasu.*) 私たちは来週乗船して沖縄に向かいます.

embarkation *n.* (airplane) to'o-joo 搭乗; (ship) jo'oseñ 乗船: an embarkation card (*shukkoku kaado*) 出国カード / an embarkation procedure (*shukkoku tetsuzuki*) 出国手続き / the port of embarkation (*toojoochi*) 搭乗地.

embarrass *vt.* ... o toʳowaku saseru …を当惑させる [V]; ... ni kiʳmazui omoˡi o saʳseru …に気まずい思いをさせる [V]: He embarrassed me with unexpected questions. (*Kare wa igai na shitsumoñ de watashi o toowaku saseta.*) 彼は意外な質問で私を当惑させた.

embarrassed *adj.* kiʳmari waruˡi oʳmoˡi o shita [shite iru] きまり悪い思いをした[している]; toʳowaku shita [shite iru] 当惑した[している]: I was embarrassed when I made the mistake. (*Sono machigai o shita toki kimari warui omoi o shita.*) その間違いをしたときまり悪い思いをした.

embarrassing *adj.* kiʳmazui omoˡi o saʳseru 気まずい思いをさせる; yaˡkkai na 厄介な: an embarrassing question (*yakkai na shitsumoñ*) 厄介な質問.

embarrassment *n.* kiʳmazusa 気まずさ; koʳñwaku 困惑: He tried to hide his embarrassment. (*Kare wa kimazusa o kakusoo to shita.*) 彼は気まずさを隠そうとした.

embassy *n.* taʳishiˡkañ 大使館: the French embassy in Japan (*Nihoñ no Furañsu taishikañ*) 日本のフランス大使館.

embody *vt.* ... o guʳtai-teki ni nobeˡru …を具体的に述べる [V]; guʳtai-ka suru 具体化する [I]: He embodied his ideas in his speech. (*Kare wa eñzetsu no naka de jibuñ no kañgae o gutai-teki ni nobeta.*) 彼は演説の中で自分の考えを具体的に述べた.

embrace *vt.* ... o daʳkishimeˡru …を抱き締める [V]: The mother embraced her child. (*Hahaoya wa kodomo o dakishimeta.*) 母親は子どもを抱き締めた.

— *vi.* daʳkiaˡu 抱き合う [C]: The two lovers embraced. (*Futari no koibito wa dakiatta.*) 二人の恋人は抱き合った.

— *n.* hoʳoyoo 抱擁: a close embrace (*katai hooyoo*) 固い抱擁.

embroider *vt.* ... o shiʳshuu suru …をししゅうする [I]; nuʳikoˡmu 縫い込む [C]: embroider initials on a handkerchief (*hañkachi ni inisharu o nuikomu*) ハンカチにイニシャルを縫い込む.

embroidery *n.* shiʳshuu ししゅう; nuʳitori 縫い取り.

emerald *n.* eʳmeraˡrudo エメラルド.

emerge *vi.* **1** (appear) aʳrawareˡru 現われる [V]; (come out) deˡte kuru 出てくる [I]: The fireman emerged from the burning building. (*Shooboshi ga moete iru biru kara arawareta.*) 消防士が燃えているビルから現われた.

2 (become known) aʳkiˡraka ni naru 明かになる [C]; haʳñmee suru 判明する [I]: The true facts are unlikely to ever emerge. (*Shiñsoo wa doomo akiraka ni narisoo mo nai.*) 真相はどうも明らかになりそうもない.

emergency *n.* kiʳñkyuu jiˡtai 緊急事態; hiʳjoo jiˡtai 非常事態: In an emergency, push this button. (*Hijoo no baai wa kono botañ o oshite kudasai.*) 非常の場合はこのボタンを押してください. / Where is the emergency exit? (*Hijooguchi wa doko ni arimasu ka?*) 非常口はどこにありますか.

eminent *adj.* choʳmee na 著名な; koʳomee na 高名な: an eminent writer (*chomee na sakka*) 著名な作家.

emotion *n.* **1** (feelings) kaʳñjoo 感情: Love and hate are perhaps the strongest emotions. (*Ai to nikushimi wa osoraku mottomo tsuyoi kañjoo de aru.*) 愛と憎しみはおそらくもっとも強い感情である.

2 (excited state) kaʳñdoo 感動; koʳofuñ 興奮: His voice was shaking with emotion. (*Kare no koe wa koofuñ de furuete ita.*) 彼の声は興奮で震えていた.

emperor *n.* (of Japan) teʳñnoˡo 天皇; (of other empires) koʳotee 皇帝: His Majesty the Emperor (*teñnoo heeka*) 天皇陛下 / the present Emperor (*kiñjoo teñnoo*) 今上天皇

/ the Emperor Showa (*Shoowa teñnoo*) 昭和天皇.

emphasis *n.* kyo⌈ochoo 強調; ju⌈ute⌉ñ o o⌈ku koto⌉ 重点を置くこと: speak with emphasis (*kyoochoo shite hanasu*) 強調して話す / put emphasis on oral practice (*kootoo kuñreñ ni juuteñ o oku*) 口頭訓練に重点を置く.

emphasize *vt.* ... o kyo⌈ochoo suru ...を強調する [I]; ri⌈kisetsu suru 力説する [I]: emphasize one's point of view (*jibuñ no ikeñ o kyoochoo suru*) 自分の意見を強調する.

emphatic *adj.* **1** (forceful) kyo⌈o-choo shita [shite iru] 強調した[している]; ki⌈ppa⌉ri to shita [shite iru] きっぱりとした[している]: an emphatic denial (*kippari to shita hiniñ*) きっぱりとした否認.

2 (clear) ha⌈kki⌉ri to shita [shite iru] はっきりとした[している]; a⌈ki⌉raka na 明らかな: an emphatic defeat (*akiraka na haiboku*) 明らかな敗北.

empire *n.* te⌈ekoku 帝国: the Roman Empire (*Rooma teekoku*) ローマ帝国.

employ *vi.* **1** (hire) ... o ya⌈to⌉u ... を雇う [C]: Our family employs three gardeners. (*Uchi de wa niwashi o sañ-niñ yatotte iru.*) うちでは庭師を 3 人雇っている. / Miss Nomura is employed in a bank. (*Nomura-sañ wa giñkoo ni tsutomete iru.*) 野村さんは銀行に勤めている.

2 (use) ... o tsu⌈kau ...を使う [C]; mo⌈chii⌉ru 用いる [V]: Petroleum is employed for many purposes. (*Sekiyu wa iroiro na mokuteki ni tsukawarete iru.*) 石油はいろいろな目的に使われている.

employee *n.* ya⌈towa⌉rete iru hi⌈to⌉ 雇われている人; ju⌈ugyo⌉oiñ 従業員: The employees went on strike. (*Juugyooiñ wa sutoraiki ni haitta.*) 従業員はストライキに入った. / government employees (*koomuiñ*) 公務員 / a company employee (*kaishaiñ*) 会社員.

employer *n.* ya⌈toi⌉nushi 雇い主; ko⌈yo⌉osha 雇用者: Mr. Hayashi was fired by his employer. (*Hayashi-sañ wa yatoinushi ni kubi ni sareta.*) 林さんは雇い主に首にされた.

employment *n.* **1** (being employed) ko⌈yoo 雇用: full employment (*kañzeñ-koyoo*) 完全雇用 / the system of lifetime employment (*shuushiñ koyoo seedo*) 終身雇用制度.

2 (paid work) sho⌈ku 職; shi⌈goto 仕事: Luckily all our graduates found employment. (*Uñ yoku uchi no sotsugyoosee wa zeñiñ shoku ga mitsukatta.*) 運よくうちの卒業生は全員職が見つかった. / look for employment (*shigoto o sagasu*) 仕事を探す.

empress *n.* (of Japan) ko⌈ogo⌉o 皇后; (of other empires) jo⌈tee 女帝: Her Majesty the Empress (*koogoo heeka*) 皇后陛下.

empty *adj.* **1** (containing nothing) ka⌈ra⌉ no 空の: an empty glass (*kara no koppu*) 空のコップ / an empty house (*akiya*) 空き家 / an empty stomach (*kuufuku*) 空腹 / I opened the box, but it was empty. (*Hako o aketa ga kara datta.*) 箱を開けたが空だった.

2 (meaningless) mu⌈i⌉mi na 無意味な; mu⌈nashi⌉i むなしい: an empty promise (*kara-yakusoku*) 空約束 / feel emotionally empty (*munashiku kañjiru*) むなしく感じる.

— *vt.* ... o ka⌈ra⌉ ni suru ...を空にする [I]; a⌈keru 空ける [V]: empty a glass (*koppu o kara ni suru*) コップを空にする / She emptied the water into the bucket. (*Kanojo wa mizu o baketsu ni aketa.*) 彼女は水をバケツに空けた.

enable *vt.* ... no o⌈kage de ... de⌈ki⌉ru ...のおかげで...できる [V]; ... o ka⌈noo ni suru ...を可能にする [I]: The scholarship enabled him to go to college. (*Shoogakukiñ no okage de kare wa daigaku e iku koto ga dekita.*) 奨学金のおかげで彼は大学へ行くことができた. / Proper qualifications will enable you to get a good job. (*Tekitoo na shikaku ga areba yoi shoku ni tsuku koto ga kanoo deshoo.*) 適当な資格があればよい職に就くことが可能でしょう.

enamel *n.* e⌈nameru エナメル; ho⌈o-roo ほうろう: an enamel bowl (*hooroo no booru*) ほうろうのボール.

e

enclose *vt.* **1** (surround) ... o ka⌈kou ...を囲う Ⓒ: The landlord enclosed the vacant lot with a fence. (*Jinushi wa akichi o saku de kakotta.*) 地主は空き地をさくで囲った.
2 (put inside an envelope) ... o do⌈ofuu suru ...を同封する Ⓘ; fu⌈u-nyuu suru 封入する Ⓘ: I am enclosing some family photos with this letter. (*Kazoku no shashiñ o nañ-mai ka kono tegami ni doofuu shimasu.*) 家族の写真を何枚かこの手紙に同封します.

enclosure *n.* **1** (enclosed materials) do⌈ofu⌉ubutsu 同封物.
2 (fence) ka⌈koi 囲い.

encourage *vt.* **1** (give courage, support) ... o ha⌈gema⌉su ...を励ます Ⓒ; ge⌈ñkizuke⌉ru 元気づける Ⓥ: Our teacher always encourages us to study harder. (*Watashi-tachi no señsee wa motto isshookeñmee beñkyoo suru yoo ni watashi-tachi o itsu-mo hagemashite kureru.*) 私たちの先生はもっと一生懸命勉強するように私たちをいつも励ましてくれる. / We were encouraged by our team's success. (*Chiimu no seekoo de watashi-tachi wa geñkizuita.*) チームの成功で私たちは元気づいた.
2 (foster) ... o so⌈kushiñ suru ...を促進する Ⓘ; jo⌈choo suru 助長する Ⓘ: The warm summer encouraged the growth of rice plants. (*Atsui natsu ga ine no seechoo o sokushiñ shita.*) 暑い夏が稲の生長を促進した.

encouragement *n.* ge⌈kiree 激励; sho⌈oree 奨励: give a person encouragement (*hito o gekiree suru*) 人を激励する.

end *n.* **1** (of a period of time; of a story) o⌈wari 終わり; -matsu 末; sa⌉igo 最後: the end of the week (*shuu no owari*) 週の終わり / the end of the month (*getsu-matsu*) 月末.
2 (end point; tip) sa⌈ki 先; se⌈ñtañ 先端; ha⌈shi 端: the end of a stick (*boo no saki*) 棒の先 / the end of a rope (*roopu no señtañ*) ロープの先端 / sit at the end of a bench (*beñchi no hashi ni suwaru*) ベンチの端に座る.
3 (limit) ge⌉ñdo 限度: I am at the end of my patience. (*Watashi wa gamañ no geñdo ni kita.*) 私は我慢の限度にきた.
4 (aim) mo⌈kuteki 目的: He achieved his ends. (*Kare wa mokuteki o tasshita.*) 彼は目的を達した.
— *vi.* (come to an end) o⌈waru 終わる Ⓒ: The exhibition ends next week. (*Teñrañkai wa raishuu owarimasu.*) 展覧会は来週終わります.
— *vt.* (bring to an end) ... o o⌈eru ...を終える Ⓥ; ya⌈meru やめる Ⓥ: The two of you must end your quarrel. (*Futari tomo keñka o yamenakereba ikenai.*) 二人ともけんかをやめなければいけない.

endeavor *vi.* do⌉ryoku suru 努力する Ⓘ: We will endeavor to meet your request. (*Go-yooboo ni sou yoo ni doryoku itashimasu.*) ご要望に添うように努力いたします.
— *n.* do⌉ryoku 努力: make every endeavor (*arayuru doryoku o suru*) あらゆる努力をする.

ending *n.* o⌈wari 終わり; ke⌈tsumatsu 結末: the ending of a movie (*eega no ketsumatsu*) 映画の結末.

endless *adj.* o⌈wari no na⌉i 終わりのない; ha⌈teshina⌉i 果てしない: an endless desert (*hateshinai sabaku*) 果てしない砂漠.

endorse *vt.* ... ni u⌈ragaki suru ...に裏書きする Ⓘ: endorse a check (*kogitte ni uragaki suru*) 小切手に裏書きする.

endurance *n.* ni⌉ñtai 忍耐; ga⌉mañ 我慢: I came to the end of my endurance. (*Watashi wa gamañ no* *geñdo ni kita.*) 私は我慢の限度にきた. / be beyond endurance (*gamañ shi-kirenai*) 我慢しきれない.

endure *vt.* **1** (bear) ... o ga˥mañ suru …を我慢する Ⓘ: endure pain (*kutsuu o gamañ suru*) 苦痛を我慢する.
2 (suffer) ... o ta˥eshino˥bu …を耐え忍ぶ Ⓒ: The explorers endured the harsh winter. (*Tañkeñka-tachi wa kibishii fuyu o taeshinoñda.*) 探検家たちは厳しい冬を耐え忍んだ.

enemy *n.* **1** (person one hates) te˥ki 敵; ka˥taki˥ かたき: A politician always has enemies. (*Seejika wa itsu-mo teki o motte iru.*) 政治家はいつも敵を持っている.
2 (enemy forces) te˥kiguñ 敵軍: The enemy army advanced on us. (*Tekiguñ wa wareware ni mukatte zeñshiñ shite kita.*) 敵軍はわれわれに向かって前進して来た.

energetic *adj.* se˥eryoku-teki na 精力的な; ka˥tsudoo-teki na 活動的な: an energetic businessman (*seeryoku-teki na bijinesumañ*) 精力的なビジネスマン.

energy *n.* **1** (vigor) se˥eryoku 精力; ge˥ñki 元気: work with energy (*seeryoku-teki ni hataraku*) 精力的に働く / He seems to have no energy these days. (*Kare wa saikiñ geñki ga nai yoo da.*) 彼は最近元気がないようだ.
2 (effort) ka˥tsudo˥oryoku 活動力; se˥ekoñ 精魂: I devoted all my energy to the task. (*Watashi wa shigoto ni zeñ seekoñ o katamuketa.*) 私は仕事に全精魂を傾けた.
3 (power) e˥ne˥rugii エネルギー: solar [atomic] energy (*taiyoo [geñshiryoku] enerugii*) 太陽[原子力]エネルギー / We must stop wasting energy. (*Enerugii no mudazukai o yamenakereba naranai.*) エネルギーのむだづかいをやめなければならない.

enforce *vt.* ... o ji˥sshi suru …を実施する Ⓘ; shi˥koo suru 施行する Ⓘ: The law was enforced immediately. (*Sono hooritsu wa tadachi ni jisshi sareta.*) その法律は直ちに実施された.

engage *vt.* **1** (hire; employ) ... o ya˥to˥u …を雇う Ⓒ: We wish to engage an interpreter. (*Tsuuyaku o hitori yatoitai.*) 通訳を一人雇いたい.
2 (reserve) ... o yo˥yaku suru …を予約する Ⓘ: engage seats (*zaseki o yoyaku suru*) 座席を予約する.
3 (attract; occupy) ... o hi˥ku …を引く Ⓒ; ... ni hi˥kiko˥mu …に引き込む Ⓒ: engage a person's attention (*hito no chuui o hiku*) 人の注意を引く.

engaged *adj.* **1** (betrothed) ko˥ñyaku shite (iru) 婚約して(いる): Miss Suzuki is engaged to Mr. Miyashita. (*Suzuki-sañ wa Miyashita-shi to koñyaku shite iru.*) 鈴木さんは宮下氏と婚約している.
2 (be occupied in) ju˥uji shite (iru) 従事して(いる); hi˥ma ga na˥i 暇がない: She is engaged in social work. (*Kanojo wa shakai jigyoo ni juuji shite iru.*) 彼女は社会事業に従事している.
3 (of a telephone) o-ha˥nashi-chuu de お話し中で: The number is engaged. (*Ima o-hanashi-chuu desu.*) 今お話し中です.

engagement *n.* **1** (for marriage) ko˥ñyaku 婚約: break off an engagement (*koñyaku o haki suru*) 婚約を破棄する.
2 (appointment) ya˥kusoku 約束: I have a previous engagement. (*Señyaku ga arimasu.*) 先約があります.

engine *n.* e˥ñjiñ エンジン: start the engine of a car (*jidoosha no eñjiñ o shidoo saseru*) 自動車のエンジンを始動させる.

engineer *n.* gi˥shi 技師: an electrical engineer (*deñki gishi*) 電気技師.

England *n.* I˥ñgurañdo イングランド; (the U.K.) I˥girisu イギリス; E˥ekoku 英国.

English *n.* **1** (language) E˥ego 英語: Do you speak English? (*Anata wa Eego o hanashimasu ka?*) あなたは英語を話しますか.

2 (people) I⌈girisu⌉jiñ イギリス人; E⌈ekoku⌉jiñ 英国人.
— *adj.* 1 (language) E⌈ego no 英語の: Is there an English menu? (*Eego no menyuu wa arimasu ka?*) 英語のメニューはありますか.
2 I⌉ñguranđo no イングランドの: English folk songs (*Iñguranđo no miñyoo*) イングランドの民謡.
3 (British) I⌈girisu no イギリスの; E⌈ekoku no 英国の: English history (*Eekoku no rekishi*) 英国の歴史.
4 (people) I⌈girisu⌉jiñ no イギリス人の; E⌈ekoku⌉jiñ no 英国人の: My grandmother was English. (*Watashi no obaa-sañ wa Igirisujiñ deshita.*) 私のおばあさんはイギリス人でした.

Englishman *n.* I⌈ñguranđo⌉jiñ イングランド人; (born in Britain) I⌈girisu⌉jiñ イギリス人; E⌈ekoku⌉jiñ 英国人.

Englishwoman *n.* I⌉ñguranđo no jo⌈see イングランドの女性; (born in Britain) I⌈girisu [E⌈ekoku] no josee イギリス[英国]の女性.

engrave *vt.* ... o ho⌉ru ...を彫る Ⓒ: engrave letters on stone (*ishi ni moji o horu*) 石に文字を彫る.

enjoy *vt.* 1 (get pleasure) ... o ta⌈noshi⌉mu ...を楽しむ Ⓒ; ... wa ta⌈noshi⌉i ...は楽しい: We really enjoyed our holiday. (*Kyuuka wa hoñtoo ni tanoshikatta.*) 休暇は本当に楽しかった.
2 (experience) ... o mo⌉tte iru ... を持っている Ⓥ; ... ni me⌈gumarete iru ...に恵まれている Ⓥ: Fortunately I enjoy good health. (*Saiwai na koto ni watashi wa keñkoo ni megumarete iru.*) 幸いなことに私は健康に恵まれている.

enjoyable *adj.* ta⌈noshi⌉i 楽しい; yu⌉kai na 愉快な: The play was very enjoyable. (*Shibai wa totemo tanoshikatta.*) 芝居はとても楽しかった.

enjoyment *n.* ta⌈noshi⌉mi 楽しみ; yu⌉kai 愉快; yo⌈rokobi 喜び: Reading is a great enjoyment to me. (*Dokusho wa watashi ni totte ooki-na tanoshimi desu.*) 読書は私にとって大きな楽しみです.

enlarge *vt.* 1 (make larger) ... o o⌉okiku suru ...を大きくする Ⓘ; ka⌈kuchoo suru 拡張する Ⓘ: Our neighbors are planning to enlarge their garden. (*Uchi no tonari no hito wa niwa o kakuchoo suru koto o keekaku shite iru.*) うちの隣の人は庭を拡張することを計画している.
2 (of a photograph) ... o hi⌈kinoba⌉su ...を引き伸ばす Ⓒ: enlarge a photograph (*shashiñ o hikinobasu*) 写真を引き伸ばす.

enlargement *n.* (sha⌈shiñ no) hi⌈kinobashi (写真の)引き伸ばし: I'd like to have an enlargement made. (*Hikinobashi o shite moraitai no desu ga.*) 引き伸ばしをしてもらいたいのですが.

enlist *vi.* (... ni) nyu⌈utai suru (...に)入隊する Ⓘ: enlist in the army (*rikuguñ ni nyuutai suru*) 陸軍に入隊する.

enormous *adj.* kyo⌈dai na 巨大な; ba⌈kudai na 莫大な: an enormous building (*kyodai na tatemono*) 巨大な建物 / an enormous amount of money (*bakudai na kiñgaku*) 莫大な金額.

enough *adj.* ju⌈ubu⌉ñ na 十分な: We don't have enough players to make two teams. (*Chiimu o futatsu tsukuru hodo juubuñ na señshu ga inai.*) チームを二つ作るほど十分な選手がいない.
— *adv.* 1 (to the required degree) ju⌈ubu⌉ñ ni 十分に: This apartment is large enough for our family. (*Kono apaato wa watashi-tachi kazoku ni wa juubuñ hiroi.*) このアパートは私たち家族には十分広い.
2 (to a certain degree) ka⌉nari かなり: The situation is serious enough, but it will get worse. (*Jookyoo wa kanari kibishii ga sara ni waruku naru deshoo.*) 状況はかなり厳しいがさらに悪くなるでしょう.
— *pron.* ju⌈ubu⌉ñ 十分: I can't eat anymore. I've had enough. (*Kore ijoo wa taberaremaseñ. Moo juu-*

buñ itadakimashita.) これ以上は食べられません. もう十分いただきました.

enquire *v.* =inquire.

enroll *vi.* ka⌈iiñ ni na⌉ru 会員になる Ⓒ; (... ni) ha⌉iru (...に) 入る Ⓒ: enroll in the advanced Japanese course (*Nihoñgo jookyuu koosu ni hairu*) 日本語上級コースに入る.

enter *vt.* **1** (go into; come into) ... ni ha⌉iru ...に入る Ⓒ: Can I enter the room now? (*Ima sugu heya ni hairemasu ka?*) 今すぐ部屋に入れますか.

2 (join; take part in) ... ni nyu⌈u-gaku suru ...に入学する Ⓘ; sa⌈ñka suru 参加する Ⓘ: enter a university (*daigaku ni nyuugaku suru*) 大学に入学する / enter a competition (*koñ-tesuto ni sañka suru*) コンテストに参加する.

3 (cause to take part) ... o (... ni) nyu⌈ugaku saseru ...を(...に)入学させる Ⓥ; sa⌈ñka saseru 参加させる Ⓥ: enter a child in a school (*kodomo o gakkoo ni nyuugaku saseru*) 子どもを学校に入学させる / I entered my horse in the race. (*Watashi wa watashi no uma o reesu ni sañka saseta.*) 私は私の馬をレースに参加させた.

4 (write down; insert) ... o ki⌈nyuu suru ...を記入する Ⓘ; i⌈reru 入れる Ⓥ: Please enter your name here. (*Koko ni o-namae o kinyuu shite kudasai.*) ここにお名前を記入してください. / enter data into a computer (*deeta o koñpyuutaa ni ireru*) データをコンピューターに入れる.

enterprise *n.* (commercial) ki⌉-gyoo 企業; (company) ka⌈isha 会社: private enterprises (*miñkañ ki-gyoo*) 民間企業.

entertain *vt.* **1** (amuse) ... o ta-⌈noshimase⌉ru ...を楽しませる Ⓥ: Her jokes entertained us all. (*Kanojo no jooku wa watashi-tachi miñna o tanoshimaseta.*) 彼女のジョークは私たちみんなを楽しませた.

2 (provide hospitality) ... o mo⌈te-na⌉su ...をもてなす Ⓒ; sho⌉otai suru 招待する Ⓘ: I entertained the guests with refreshments. (*Watashi wa chaka de kyaku o motenashita.*) 私は茶菓で客をもてなした. / entertain friends to dinner (*tomodachi o yuushoku ni shootai suru*) 友だちを夕食に招待する.

entertainment *n.* **1** (providing hospitality) se⌉ttai 接待; mo⌈tena-shi もてなし: the entertainment of guests (*o-kyaku no motenashi*) お客のもてなし.

2 (amusement) go⌈raku 娯楽; ta-⌈noshimi 楽しみ: watch television for entertainment (*goraku ni terebi o miru*) 娯楽にテレビを見る.

3 (public events) mo⌈yooshimono 催し物; yo⌈kyoo 余興: this week's entertainments (*koñshuu no moyooshimono*) 今週の催し物.

enthusiasm *n.* ne⌈tchuu 熱中; ne⌉kkyoo 熱狂; -netsu 熱: In Japan, young people's enthusiasm for soccer has recently increased. (*Nihoñ de wa saikiñ wakai hito no sakkaa-netsu ga takamatte iru.*) 日本では最近若い人のサッカー熱が高まっている.

enthusiastic *adj.* ne⌈tsuretsu na 熱烈な; ne⌉sshiñ na 熱心な: an enthusiastic fan (*netsuretsu na fañ*) 熱烈なファン / an enthusiastic supporter (*nesshiñ na shijisha*) 熱心な支持者.

entire *adj.* **1** (whole) ze⌈ñtai no 全体の; ma⌈ruma⌉ru no まるまるの: She stayed in bed the entire day. (*Kanojo wa maru ichi-nichi beddo ni ita.*) 彼女はまる1日ベッドにいた.

2 (complete) ma⌈ttaku⌉ no まったくの: We were in entire ignorance of the events. (*Watashi-tachi wa sono dekigoto o mattaku shiranakatta.*) 私たちはその出来事をまったく知らなかった.

3 (not missing) ka⌈ñzeñ na 完全な: an entire set of the author's works (*sono chosha no sakuhiñ no kañzeñ na setto*) その著者の作品の完全なセット.

entirely *adv.* ma⌈ttaku まったく; su⌈kka⌉ri すっかり: I entirely agree with you. (*Watashi wa anata to mattaku onaji ikeñ desu.*) 私はあなたとまったく同じ意見です.

entitle *vt.* **1** (give a right) ... ni ke⌉ñri o ataeru …に権利を与える Ⓥ; shi⌈kaku o ataeru 資格を与える Ⓥ: He is entitled to a pension. (*Kare wa neñkiñ o ukeru shikaku ga aru.*) 彼は年金を受ける資格がある.

2 (give a title) ... ni da⌉i o tsu⌈ke⌉ru …に題をつける Ⓥ: a book entitled 'A Guide to Japan' (*'Nihoñ Añnai' to dai o tsukerareta hoñ*) 「日本案内」と題をつけれられた本.

entrance *n.* **1** (entry) i⌈riguchi 入り口: I couldn't find the entrance to the car park. (*Chuushajoo no iriguchi ga mitsukaranakatta.*) 駐車場の入り口が見つからなかった.

2 (act of entering) ha⌉iru ko⌈to⌉ 入ること; (of an actor) to⌈ojoo 登場: The security man refused us entrance. (*Gaadomañ wa watashitachi ga hairu koto o kotawatta.*) ガードマンは私たちが入ることを断った.

3 (admission) nyu⌈ugaku 入学: entrance into college (*daigaku nyuugaku*) 大学入学.

entrance examination *n.* (for a school) nyu⌈ugaku shi⌉keñ 入学試験 ★ Often abbreviated to '*nyuushi*' 入試; (for a company) nyu⌈usha shi⌉keñ 入社試験: the entrance examination for Kyoto University (*Kyooto daigaku no nyuugaku shikeñ*) 京都大学の入学試験.

entrust *vt.* ... o (... ni)ma⌈kase⌉ru …を(…に)任せる Ⓥ; a⌈zuke⌉ru 預ける Ⓥ: I entrusted the work to him. (*Watashi wa sono shigoto o kare ni makaseta.*) 私はその仕事を彼に任せた. / She entrusted her savings to her best friend. (*Kanojo wa chokiñ o ichibañ naka no yoi tomodachi ni azuketa.*) 彼女は貯金をいちばん仲のよい友達に預けた.

entry *n.* **1** (act of entering) ha⌉iru ko⌈to⌉ 入ること; ka⌈nyuu 加入: the entry of a country into the United Nations (*kuni no kokureñ e no kanyuu*) 国の国連への加入 / No Entry. (*Tachiiri kiñshi.*) 立ち入り禁止.

2 (written information) ki⌈nyuu 記入; ki⌈sai 記載: She made an entry in her notebook. (*Kanojo wa nooto ni kinyuu shita.*) 彼女はノートに記入した.

3 (a person in a competition) sa⌈ñka⌉sha 参加者.

envelope *n.* fu⌈utoo 封筒: address an envelope (*fuutoo ni atena o kaku*) 封筒に宛名を書く.

envious *adj.* u⌈rayamashi-ga⌉ru うらやましがる; u⌈rayamashi-so⌉o na うらやましそうな: an envious look (*urayamashi-soo na kaotsuki*) うらやましそうな顔つき / Everyone was envious of her success. (*Miñna ga kanojo no seekoo o urayamashi-gatta.*) みんなが彼女の成功をうらやましがった.

environment *n.* ka⌈ñkyoo 環境: protect the environment (*kañkyoo o hogo suru*) 環境を保護する.

envy *vt.* ... o u⌈raya⌉mu …をうらやむ Ⓒ: Many people envy him his good fortune. (*Ooku no hito ga kare no koouñ o urayañde iru.*) 多くの人が彼の好運をうらやんでいる.

— *n.* ne⌈tami⌉ ねたみ; shi⌈tto しっと; u⌈rayami⌉ うらやみ: I feel envy at his success. (*Watashi wa kare no seekoo ga urayamashii.*) 私は彼の成功がうらやましい.

episode *n.* **1** (event) e⌉pisoodo エピソード; de⌈ki⌉goto 出来事: an interesting episode in history (*rekishi-joo no kyoomibukai episoodo*) 歴史上の興味深いエピソード.

2 (of a novel) so⌈owa 挿話.

equal *adj.* **1** (same) o⌈naji 同じ; hi⌈toshi⌉i 等しい: The girls are of equal height. (*Oñna-no-ko-tachi wa onaji se no takasa da.*) 女の子たちは同じ背の高さだ. / He cut the cake into three equal pieces. (*Kare wa keeki o mittsu no hitoshii ookisa ni kitta.*) 彼はケーキを三つの等しい大き

さに切った.

2 (fair) byo[o]doo na 平等な; ta[i]too na 対等な: Every person is born equal. (*Dare de mo umareta toki wa byoodoo desu.*) だれでも生まれたときは平等です.

3 (up to) ta[e]ru 耐える; shi[kaku ga a]ru 資格がある: I am not equal to such a task. (*Watashi ni wa sono yoo na shigoto wa taerarenai.*) 私にはそのような仕事は耐えられない.

— *n.* (people) do[otoo no hito] 同等の人: one's social equals (*shakai-teki ni dootoo no hito-tachi*) 社会的に同等の人たち.

— *vt.* **1** (be the same as) ... ni hi[toshi]i …に等しい: Five plus eight equals thirteen. (*Go tasu hachi wa juusañ desu.*) 5 足す 8 は 13 です.

2 (reach the same standard) ... ni hi[tteki suru …に匹敵する [I]; o[tora]nai 劣らない: Nobody can equal him in mathematics. (*Suugaku de kare ni hitteki suru mono wa inai.*) 数学で彼に匹敵する者はいない.

equality *n.* byo[odoo 平等; ki[ñtoo 均等: equality of the sexes (*dañjo byoodoo*) 男女平等 / equality of opportunity (*kikai kiñtoo*) 機会均等.

equator *n.* se[kidoo 赤道: cross the equator (*sekidoo o koeru*) 赤道を越える.

equilibrium *n.* he[ekoo 平衡; ki[ñkoo 均衡: maintain an equilibrium (*kiñkoo o tamotsu*) 均衡を保つ.

equip *vt.* **1** (fit out) ... o so[nae]ru …を備える [V]; so]obi suru 装備する [I]: The clinic is equipped with an X-ray machine. (*Shiñryoojo wa reñtogeñ shashiñ satsueeki o sonaete iru.*) 診療所はレントゲン写真撮影機を備えている.

2 (prepare) ... o u[kesase]ru …を受けさせる [V]: Parents should equip their children with a good education. (*Oya wa kodomo ni yoi kyooiku o ukesasenakereba naranai.*) 親は子どもによい教育を受けさせなければならない.

equipment *n.* se]tsubi 設備; yo]ogu 用具; so]ochi 装置: equipment costs (*setsubi-hi*) 設備費 / camping equipment (*kyañpu yoogu*) キャンプ用具 / video equipment (*bideo soochi*) ビデオ装置.

equivalent *adj.* do[otoo no 同等の; hi[toshi]i 等しい; so[otoo no 相当の: These two words are equivalent in meaning. (*Kono futatsu no go wa imi ga hitoshii.*) この二つの語は意味が等しい. / What is one dollar equivalent to in Japanese yen? (*Ichi doru wa Nihoñ eñ de ikura ni sootoo shimasu ka?*) 1ドルは日本円でいくらに相当しますか.

— *n.* do[oto]obutsu 同等物; (words) so[otoo-go 相当語: The English equivalent of Japanese 'inu' is 'dog.' (*Nihoñgo no 'inu' ni sootoo suru Eego wa 'dog' desu.*) 日本語の「犬」に相当する英語は 'dog' です.

era *n.* ji[dai 時代; ki]geñ 紀元: the Showa [Meiji] era (*Shoowa [Meeji] jidai*) 昭和[明治]時代 / the Christian era (*Kirisuto kigeñ*) キリスト紀元.

erase *vt.* **1** (of writing) ... o ke[su …を消す [C]; sa]kujo suru 削除する [I]: erase the writing on a blackboard (*kokubañ no ji o kesu*) 黒板の字を消す / Please erase all your mistakes. (*Machigai o zeñbu sakujo shite kudasai.*) 間違いを全部削除してください.

2 (of recording) ... o ke[su … を消す [C]; sho]okyo suru 消去する [I]: erase everything on the tape (*teepu no mono o subete kesu*) テープのものをすべて消す.

eraser *n.* ke[shigomu 消しゴム; ko[kuba]ñ-fuki 黒板ふき: a pencil with an eraser (*keshigomu-tsuki no eñpitsu*) 消しゴムつきの鉛筆 / a blackboard eraser (*kokubañ-fuki*) 黒板ふき.

erect *adj.* cho[kuritsu no 直立の; ma[ssu]gu no 真っすぐの: an erect posture (*chokuritsu no shisee*) 直

立の姿勢 / hold a flag erect (*hata o massugu ni tateru*) 旗を真っすぐに立てる.
— *vt.* ... o ta⌈te⌉ru ...を建てる [V]; ke⌈ñsetsu suru 建設する [I]: erect a monument (*kineñhi o tateru*) 記念碑を建てる / erect a church (*kyookai o keñsetsu suru*) 教会を建設する.

erotic *adj.* se⌈eai no 性愛の; er⌈o-chi⌉kku na エロチックな: a vulgarly erotic film (*poruno eega*) ポルノ映画.

err *vi.* (... o) a⌈yama⌉ru (...を)誤る [C]; ma⌈chiga⌉i o suru 間違いをする [I]: err in one's judgment (*hañdañ o ayamaru*) 判断を誤る.

errand *n.* tsu⌈kai 使い: go on an errand (*tsukai ni iku*) 使いに行く / send a person on an errand (*hito o tsukai ni dasu*) 人を使いに出す.

error *n.* a⌈yamari⌉ 誤り; ma⌈chiga⌉i 間違い: make a serious error (*hidoi machigai o suru*) ひどい間違いをする / I made an error of judgment. (*Watashi wa hañdañ o ayamatta.*) 私は判断を誤った.

erupt *vi.* fu⌈ñka suru 噴火する [I]; ba⌈kuhatsu suru 爆発する [I]: The volcano erupted. (*Kazañ ga fuñka shita.*) 火山が噴火した.

eruption *n.* fu⌈ñka 噴火; ba⌈kuhatsu 爆発: a volcanic eruption (*kazañ no fuñka*) 火山の噴火.

escalator *n.* e⌈sukare⌉etaa エスカレーター: go up [down] an escalator (*esukareetaa de agaru* [*sagaru*]) エスカレーターで上がる[下がる].

escape *vi.* **1** (get free) ni⌈ge⌉ru 逃げる [V]: The prisoners escaped from jail. (*Shuujiñ-tachi wa keemusho kara nigeta.*) 囚人たちは刑務所から逃げた.
2 (leak) mo⌈re⌉ru 漏れる [V]: The gas escaped from the pipe and caused an explosion. (*Gasu ga paipu kara morete bakuhatsu shita.*) ガスがパイプから漏れて爆発した.
— *vt.* (avoid) ... o no⌈gare⌉ru ...を逃れる [V]; ma⌈nugare⌉ru 免れる [V]: escape punishment (*batsu o nogareru*) 罰を逃れる / No one can escape death. (*Dare de mo shi o manugareru koto wa dekinai.*) だれでも死を免れることはできない.
— *n.* **1** (breakout) to⌈oboo 逃亡; da⌈ssoo 脱走: an escape from jail (*keemusho kara no dassoo*) 刑務所からの脱走.
2 (avoiding) ma⌈nugare⌉ru ko⌈to⌉ 免れること: an escape from disaster (*saigai o manugareru koto*) 災害を免れること.
3 (leakage) mo⌈re⌉ 漏れ: an escape of gas (*gasu-more*) ガス漏れ.

escort *n.* **1** (accompaniment) go⌈ee 護衛: A large escort accompanied the premier. (*Oozee no goee ga shushoo ni zuikoo shita.*) 大勢の護衛が首相に随行した.
2 (social companion) tsu⌈kisoi 付き添い; do⌈oha⌉ñsha 同伴者: Who is your escort to tonight's dance? (*Koñya no dañsu paatii no doohañsha wa donata desu ka?*) 今夜のダンスパーティーの同伴者はどなたですか.
— *vt.* **1** (protectively accompany) ... o go⌈ee suru ...を護衛する [I]: Those security men always escort the President. (*Sore-ra no keego no hito-tachi wa itsu-mo daitooryoo o goee shite iru.*) それらの警護の人たちはいつも大統領を護衛している.
2 (socially accompany) ... ni tsu⌈kiso⌉u ...に付き添う [C]; ... o o⌈kuritodoke⌉ru ...を送り届ける [V]: Please allow me to escort you home. (*Otaku made okurasete kudasai.*) お宅まで送らせてください.

especially *adv.* to⌉ku ni 特に; to⌈kubetsu ni 特別に: I am especially interested in music. (*Watashi wa toku ni oñgaku ni kyoomi o motte imasu.*) 私は特に音楽に興味を持っています.

essay *n.* zu⌈ihitsu 随筆; hyo⌈oroñ 評論; sa⌈kubuñ 作文: He wrote an essay about the novel. (*Kare wa sono shoosetsu ni tsuite hyooroñ o kaita.*) 彼はその小説について評論を書いた. / I have to finish this essay by tomorrow. (*Watashi wa kono saku-*

buñ o ashita made ni kakanakereba naranai.) 私はこの作文をあしたまでに書かなければならない.

essential *adj.* **1** (vital) fu⌈ka⌉ketsu na 不可欠な; ze⌉hi hi⌈tsuyoo na ぜひ必要な: A balanced diet is essential for health. (*Barañsu no toreta shokuji wa keñkoo ni fukaketsu desu.*) バランスのとれた食事は健康に不可欠です.
2 (basic) ho⌈ñshitsu-teki na 本質的な; ko⌈ñpoñ-teki na 根本的な: an essential difference (*hoñshitsu-teki na chigai*) 本質的な違い.
— *n.* yo⌈ote⌉ñ 要点: the essentials of Japanese grammar (*Nihoñgo-buñpoo no yooteñ*) 日本語文法の要点.

establish *vt.* **1** (found) ... o se⌈tsuritsu suru ...を設立する Ⓘ; (create) tsu⌈ku⌉ru 作る Ⓒ: establish a school (*gakkoo o setsuritsu suru*) 学校を設立する / establish a new system (*atarashii soshiki o tsukuru*) 新しい組織を作る.
2 (firmly settle) ... ni o⌈chitsukaseru ...に落ち着かせる Ⓥ: They are established in their new house. (*Kare-ra wa shiñkyo ni ochitsuita.*) 彼らは新居に落ち着いた.
3 (of custom, reputation) ... o ka⌈kuritsu suru ...を確立する Ⓘ: That custom is one that was established many years ago. (*Sono shuukañ wa nañ-neñ mo mae ni kakuritsu shita mono desu.*) その習慣は何年も前に確立したものです.
4 (ascertain) ... o sho⌈omee suru ...を証明する Ⓘ: establish one's alibi (*jibuñ no aribai o shoomee suru*) 自分のアリバイを証明する.

establishment *n.* se⌈tsuritsu 設立; se⌈etee 制定: the establishment of a new hospital (*atarashii byooiñ no setsuritsu*) 新しい病院の設立 / the establishment of the constitution (*keñpoo no seetee*) 憲法の制定.

estate *n.* **1** (land) ji⌉sho 地所: We have a small estate in the country. (*Watashi-tachi wa inaka ni chiisana jisho o motte imasu.*) 私たちは田舎に小さな地所を持っています.
2 (property) za⌉isañ 財産: real estate (*fudoosañ*) 不動産.

esteem *n.* (of people) so⌈ñkee 尊敬; (of things) so⌈ñchoo 尊重: hold a person in esteem (*hito o soñkee suru*) 人を尊敬する.
— *vt.* (of people) ... o so⌈ñkee suru ...を尊敬する Ⓘ; (of things) soñchoo suru 尊重する Ⓘ: He is esteemed by everyone. (*Kare wa miñna ni soñkee sarete iru.*) 彼はみんなに尊敬されている. / I esteem your advice highly. (*Watashi wa anata no chuukoku o ooi ni soñchoo itashimasu.*) 私はあなたの忠告を大いに尊重いたします.

estimate *vt.* ... o mi⌈tsumoru ...を見積もる Ⓒ; ha⌉ñdañ suru 判断する Ⓘ: I estimated the cost at a million yen. (*Watashi wa sono hiyoo o hyakumañ-eñ to mitsumotta.*) 私はその費用を100万円と見積もった.
— *vi.* mi⌈tsumori o suru 見積もりをする Ⓘ: estimate for repairs (*shuuri no mitsumori o suru*) 修理の見積もりをする.
— *n.* mi⌈tsumori 見積もり; mi⌈komi 見込み: The carpenter has given us his estimate. (*Daiku wa watashi-tachi ni mitsumori o kureta.*) 大工は私たちに見積もりをくれた.

eternal *adj.* e⌈e-eñ no 永遠の; e⌈ekyuu no 永久の: eternal life (*ee-eñ no seemee*) 永遠の生命 / They pledged their eternal love. (*Kare-ra wa ee-eñ no ai o chikatta.*) 彼らは永遠の愛を誓った.

ethical *adj.* do⌈otokujoo no 道徳上の; ri⌈ñri-teki na 倫理的な: ethical problems (*dootokujoo no moñdai*) 道徳上の問題.

etiquette *n.* re⌈egi-sa⌉hoo 礼儀作法; e⌉chiketto エチケット.

Europe *n.* Yo⌈oro⌉ppa ヨーロッパ; O⌉oshuu 欧州.

European *adj.* Yo⌈oro⌉ppa no ヨーロッパの; O⌉oshuu no 欧州の: European countries (*Yooroppa no kuni-*

guni) ヨーロッパの国々.
— *n.* Yo⌈roppa⌉jiñ ヨーロッパ人.

evade *vt.* **1** (avoid) ... o sa⌈ke⌉ru …を避ける [V]; no⌈gare⌉ru 逃れる [V]: evade the issue (*moñdai o sakeru*) 問題を避ける / evade taxes (*datsuzee suru*) 脱税する.
2 (escape) ... o ma⌈nugare⌉ru …を免れる [V]: evade capture (*taiho o manugareru*) 逮捕を免れる.

eve *n.* **1** (day or night before) ze⌉ñya 前夜; ze⌈ñjitsu 前日; i⌉bu イブ: Christmas Eve (*Kurisumasu ibu*) クリスマスイブ / New Year's Eve (*oomisoka*) 大みそか.
2 (time just before) cho⌈kuzeñ 直前: the eve of an election (*señkyo no chokuzeñ*) 選挙の直前.

even[1] *adv.* **1** [emphasizing a surprising statement] ... de sa⌉e …でさえ; ... de su⌉ra …ですら: He gets up at six even on Sundays. (*Kare wa nichiyoo de sae roku-ji ni okiru.*) 彼は日曜でさえ6時に起きる. / Even a child can answer that. (*Kodomo de sura soñna koto wa kotaerareru.*) 子どもですらそんなことは答えられる.
2 (still; yet) sa⌉ra ni さらに; i⌈ssoo いっそう: This painting is even better than that. (*Kono e wa sono e yori mo sara ni yoi.*) この絵はその絵よりもさらによい. / He made an even worse mistake. (*Kare wa issoo hidoi machigai o shita.*) 彼はいっそうひどい間違いをした.
3 (indeed) so⌈re do⌉koro ka それどころか: I like Sachiko very much, even love her. (*Watashi wa Sachiko-sañ ga suki desu. Sore dokoro ka aishite imasu.*) 私は幸子さんが好きです. それどころか愛しています.
even if ... *conj.* ta⌈toe ⟨verb⟩-te [de] mo たとえ…て[で]も: Even if we fail, it will be a good experience. (*Tatoe shippai shite mo ii keekeñ to naru deshoo.*) たとえ失敗してもいい経験となるでしょう.

even[2] *adj.* **1** (flat) ta⌈ira na 平らな: an even surface (*taira na hyoomeñ*) 平らな表面 / I made the ground even. (*Watashi wa jimeñ o taira ni shita.*) 私は地面を平らにした.
2 (equal) o⌈naji no 同じの; ta⌈itoo no 対等の: an even score (*dooteñ*) 同点 / an even bargain (*taitoo no torihiki*) 対等の取り引き.
3 (of a number) gu⌈usu⌉u no 偶数の: even numbers and odd numbers (*guusuu to kisuu*) 偶数と奇数.
4 (of a level) o⌈naji ta⌉kasa no 同じ高さの: The water was even with my knees. (*Mizu wa watashi no hiza to onaji takasa datta.*) 水は私のひざと同じ高さだった.

evening *n.* ba⌈ñ 晩; yu⌈ugata 夕方: I met him on Saturday evening. (*Watashi wa doyoobi no bañ ni kare ni atta.*) 私は土曜日の晩に彼に会った. / He came back late in the evening. (*Kare wa yuugata osoku kaette kita.*) 彼は夕方遅く帰って来た.

event *n.* **1** (important occurrence) de⌈ki⌉goto 出来事; ji⌉keñ 事件; gyo⌉oji 行事: the major events of that year (*sono toshi no omo na dekigoto*) その年の主な出来事 / a special event (*tokubetsu-gyooji*) 特別行事.
2 (competition) shu⌈moku 種目; kyo⌉ogi 競技: field [track] events (*fiirudo [torakku] shumoku*) フィールド[トラック]種目 / today's main event (*kyoo no shuyoo kyoogi*) きょうの主要競技.
in the event of ... *prep.* ... no ba⌈ai wa …の場合は: in the event of bad weather (*teñki no warui baai wa*) 天気の悪い場合は.

ever *adv.* **1** [in questions] (up to now) i⌈ma ma⌉de ni 今までに; ka⌉tsute かつて: "Have you ever been to Sapporo?" "Yes, I have." (*"Ima made ni Sapporo e itta koto ga arimasu ka?" "Hai, arimasu."*) 「今までに札幌へ行ったことがありますか」「はい, あります」
2 [with negatives] (up to now) ko⌈re ma⌉de (... nai) これまで(…ない): None of us have ever seen it. (*Wareware wa kore made dare

mo sore o mita koto ga arimaseñ.) われわれはこれまでだれもそれを見たことがありません.

3 [with superlative] (up to now) i⌈ma ma⌉de 今まで; ka⌉tsute かつて: This is the most beautiful orchid I have ever seen. (*Kore wa watashi ga ima made mita uchi de ichibañ utsukushii rañ da.*) これは私が今まで見たうちでいちばん美しいらんだ.

4 [used with if] (sometime) i⌉tsu-ka いつか: If you ever come to Kobe, please look us up. (*Itsu-ka Koobe e kita toki wa yotte kuda-sai.*) いつか神戸へ来たときは寄ってください.

every *adj.* **1** (each; all) do⌉no ... mo どの…も; su⌉bete no すべての: Every student wants to win the prize. (*Dono gakusee mo shoo o toritagatte iru.*) どの学生も賞を取りたがっている. / I learned every word in the list. (*Watashi wa risuto ni aru tañgo o subete oboemashita.*) 私はリストにある単語をすべて覚えました.

2 (once in each) ma⌉i- 毎; ... go⌉to ni …ごとに: every day [week, month, year] (*mainichi* [*maishuu, maitsu-ki, maitoshi*]) 毎日[毎週, 毎月, 毎年] / I have the car serviced every six months. (*Watashi wa rok-kagetsu goto ni kuruma o teñkeñ shite moraimasu.*) 私は6か月ごとに車を点検してもらいます.

3 (sufficient; great) ju⌈ubu⌉ñ na 十分な; ka⌈noo na ka⌉giri no 可能な限りの: take every possible measure (*kanoo na kagiri no shochi o toru*) 可能な限りの処置をとる.

every other *adj.* hi⌈totsu oki no 一つおきの: every other day (*ichi-nichi oki*) 1日おき.

everybody *pron.* ⇨ everyone.

everyday *adj.* **1** (daily) ma⌉inichi no 毎日の; ni⌈chijoo no 日常の: ev-eryday life (*mainichi no seekatsu*) 毎日の生活 / everyday conversation (*nichijoo-kaiwa*) 日常会話. ★ Ad-verb 'every day' is '*mainichi*' 毎日.

2 (usual) fu⌉dañ no ふだんの: We all attended the party in everyday clothes. (*Watashi-tachi wa miñna fudañgi de paatii ni shusseki shita.*) 私たちはみんなふだん着でパーティーに出席した.

everyone *pron.* mi⌈ñna⌉ みんな; da⌉re de mo mi⌈na⌉ だれでもみな: Everyone has left. (*Miñna dete iki-mashita.*) みんな出て行きました. / Ev-eryone praises the boy. (*Dare de mo mina sono shooneñ o home-masu.*) だれでもみなその少年をほめます.

everything *pron.* **1** (all things) na⌉ñ de mo mi⌈na⌉ 何でもみな; mi⌈ñ-na⌉ みんな; su⌉bete すべて: I've tried everything, but it's no use. (*Nañ de mo mina yatte mita ga dame datta.*) 何でもみなやってみたがだめだった. / She told the police everything she knew. (*Kanojo wa shitte iru koto wa subete keesatsu ni hana-shita.*) 彼女は知っていることはすべて警察に話した. / Thank you for every-thing. (*Iroiro doomo arigatoo gozaimashita.*) いろいろどうもありがとうございました.

2 (the most important thing) mo⌈t-to⌉mo ta⌈isetsu na mono⌉ 最も大切なもの; su⌉bete すべて: Money isn't everything. (*O-kane ga subete de wa nai.*) お金がすべてではない.

everywhere *adv.* do⌉ko de mo どこでも; i⌈ta⌉ru to⌈koro⌉ ni 至る所に; do⌉ko mo kashiko mo どこもかしこも: Is rice grown everywhere in Ja-pan? (*Nihoñ de wa doko de mo kome ga dekimasu ka?*) 日本ではどこでも米ができますか. / There is mold everywhere. (*Itaru tokoro ni kabi ga haete iru.*) 至る所にかびが生えている.

evidence *n.* **1** (proof) sho⌈oko 証拠: I will believe you if you show me the evidence. (*Sono shooko o misete kurereba anata o shiñji-masu.*) その証拠を見せてくれればあなたを信じます.

2 (testimony) sho⌈ogeñ 証言: The witness stood up and gave her evi-dence. (*Shooniñ wa tachiagatte* *shoogeñ o nobeta.*) 証人は立ち上がって証言を述べた.

evident *adj.* me⌈ehaku na 明白な; a⌈ki⌉raka na 明らかな: an evident mistake (*akiraka na machigai*) 明らかな間違い / It is evident that he lied to us. (*Kare ga uso o tsuita no wa akiraka da.*) 彼がうそをついたのは明らかだ.

evil *adj.* wa⌈ru⌉i 悪い; a⌉kui no 悪意の: an evil custom (*akushuu*) 悪習 / an evil tongue (*dokuzetsu*) 毒舌. — *n.* a⌉ku 悪; a⌉kuji 悪事: good and evil (*zeñ aku*) 善悪 / do evil (*akuji o hataraku*) 悪事を働く.

evoke *vt.* ... o yo⌈bioko⌉su ...を呼び起こす [C]: evoke a memory (*kioku o yobiokosu*) 記憶を呼び起こす.

evolution *n.* ha⌈ttatsu 発達; ha⌈tteñ 発展; shi⌉ñka 進化: the evolution of democracy (*miñshushugi no hattatsu*) 民主主義の発達 / the theory of evolution (*shiñkaroñ*) 進化論.

evolve *vt.* ... o ha⌈ttatsu saseru ...を発達させる [V]; ha⌈tteñ saseru 発展させる [V]: The Japanese have evolved a very interesting culture. (*Nihoñjiñ wa hijoo ni kyoomibukai buñka o hattatsu saseta.*) 日本人は非常に興味深い文化を発達させた. — *vi.* ha⌈tteñ suru 発展する [I]; shi⌉ñka suru 進化する [I]: Man evolved from the apelike creatures. (*Niñgeñ wa ruijiñeñ kara shiñka shita.*) 人間は類人猿から進化した.

exact *adj.* **1** (precise) se⌈ekaku na 正確な: the exact time (*seekaku na jikañ*) 正確な時間 / I didn't understand the exact meaning of the sentence. (*Watashi wa sono buñ no seekaku na imi ga wakaranakatta.*) 私はその文の正確な意味がわからなかった.
2 (accurate; careful) ge⌈ñmitsu na 厳密な; se⌈emitsu na 精密な: The accounts have to be exact. (*Kaikee wa geñmitsu de nakereba ikenai.*) 会計は厳密でなければいけない. / the exact sciences (*seemitsu kagaku*) 精密科学.

exactly *adv.* **1** (precisely) se⌈ekaku ni 正確に; (just) cho⌈odo ちょうど: Explain everything exactly as it happened. (*Okotta mama ni seekaku ni setsumee shi nasai.*) 起こったままに正確に説明しなさい. / I will come at exactly nine o'clock. (*Choodo ku-ji ni kimasu.*) ちょうど9時に来ます.
2 [emphatic use] (quite) so⌈no to⌉ori ni そのとおりに; ma⌈ttaku まったく: Taro did exactly what I told him to. (*Taroo wa watashi ga itta koto o sono toori ni yatta.*) 太郎は私が言ったことをそのとおりにやった.

exaggerate *vt.* ... o o⌈ogesa ni i⌈u ...を大げさに言う [C]; ko⌈choo suru 誇張する [I]: You are exaggerating the danger. (*Anata wa kikeñ o oogesa ni itte iru.*) あなたは危険を大げさに言っている. — *vi.* o⌈ogesa ni iu 大げさに言う [C]: Suzuki tends to exaggerate. (*Suzuki wa oogesa ni iu keekoo ga aru.*) 鈴木は大げさに言う傾向がある.

exaggeration *n.* ko⌈choo 誇張; o⌈ogesa 大げさ: What you say is an exaggeration. (*Kimi ga itte iru koto wa oogesa da.*) 君が言っていることは大げさだ.

examination *n.* **1** (academic) shi⌈ke⌉ñ 試験: take an examination (*shikeñ o ukeru*) 試験を受ける / pass [fail] an examination (*shikeñ ni ukaru* [*ochiru*]) 試験に受かる[落ちる] / an entrance examination of a school (*nyuugaku shikeñ*) 入学試験. ★ Japanese '*shikeñ*' also refers to 'test' and 'quiz.'
2 (medical) shi⌈ñsatsu 診察; shi⌈ñdañ 診断: undergo a physical examination (*keñkoo shiñdañ o ukeru*) 健康診断を受ける.
3 (investigation) ke⌉ñsa 検査; cho⌉osa 調査: carry out an examination of water quality (*suishitsu keñsa o suru*) 水質検査をする.
4 (legal) ji⌈ñmoñ 尋問; shi⌉ñri 審理: the examination of a witness (*shooniñ no jiñmoñ*) 証人の尋問.

examination paper *n.* shi⌈keñ-mo⌉ñdai 試験問題; shi⌈keñ no to⌉o-añ 試験の答案.

examine *vt.* **1** (scrutinize) ... o shi⌈rabe⌉ru ...を調べる [V]; ke⌉ñsa suru 検査する [I]: The customs officer examined my bags. (*Zeekañ no kakarikañ wa watashi no kabañ o shirabeta.*) 税関の係官は私のかばんを調べた.
2 (medically check) ... o shi⌈ñsatsu suru ...を診察する [I]: The doctor carefully examined the patient. (*Isha wa kañja o teenee ni shiñsatsu shita.*) 医者は患者をていねいに診察した.
3 (test) ... ni shi⌈ke⌉ñ o suru ...に試験をする [I]: examine the students in history (*gakusee ni rekishi no shikeñ o suru*) 学生に歴史の試験をする.
4 (question) ... o ji⌈ñmoñ suru ...を尋問する [I]: examine a witness (*shooniñ o jiñmoñ suru*) 証人を尋問する.

example *n.* **1** (illustration) re⌉e 例; ji⌈tsuree 実例: an example of a terrible traffic accident (*hisañ na kootsuu jiko no ree*) 悲惨な交通事故の例.
2 (model) te⌈ho⌉ñ 手本; mo⌈hañ 模範: give a good example to a person (*hito ni yoi tehoñ o shimesu*) 人によい手本を示す.
for example *adv.* ta⌈to⌉eba 例えば.

exceed *vt.* ... o ko⌈su ...を越す [C]; ko⌈eru 越える [V]; cho⌈oka suru 超過する [I]: This year his income will exceed six million yen. (*Kotoshi kare no shuunyuu wa roppyaku-mañ-eñ o koeru daroo.*) 今年彼の収入は 600 万円を越えるだろう. / exceed the speed limit (*seegeñ sokudo o chooka suru*) 制限速度を超過する.

excel *vt.* ... yo⌉ri su⌈gu⌉rete iru ...より優れている [V]; ... ni ma⌈sa⌉ru ...に勝る [C]: Peter excelled the other students in Japanese. (*Piitaa wa Nihoñgo de wa hoka no gakusee yori mo sugurete ita.*) ピーターは日本語ではほかの学生よりも優れていた.
— *vi.* su⌈gu⌉rete iru 優れている [V]; nu⌈kiñde⌉ru 抜きん出る [V]: Mary excels as an interpreter. (*Mearii wa tsuuyaku to shite sugurete iru.*) メアリーは通訳として優れている. / excel at sports (*supootsu de nukiñdete iru*) スポーツで抜きん出ている.

excellent *adj.* su⌈gu⌉reta 優れた; su⌈gu⌉rete iru 優れている; yu⌈ushuu na 優秀な; su⌈barashi⌉i すばらしい: an excellent painting (*sugureta e*) 優れた絵 / an excellent meal (*subarashii shokuji*) すばらしい食事.

except *prep.* ... i⌉gai wa ...以外は; ... o no⌈zoite⌉ wa ...を除いては: everyone except me (*watashi igai wa miñna*) 私以外はみんな / any day except Friday (*kiñyoobi igai wa itsu de mo*) 金曜日以外はいつでも / except the last one (*saigo no mono o nozoite*) 最後のものを除いて / I have nothing to declare except this perfume. (*Kono koosui igai ni wa shiñkoku suru mono wa nani mo arimaseñ.*) この香水以外には申告するものは何もありません.
except for ... *prep.* ... o no⌈zoke⌉ba ...を除けば: Except for a few kanji mistakes, your composition was excellent. (*Jakkañ no kañji no machigai o nozokeba, kimi no sakubuñ wa yoku dekite imashita.*) 若干の漢字の間違いを除けば, 君の作文はよくできていました.

exception *n.* re⌈egai 例外: an exception to a rule (*kisoku no reegai*) 規則の例外 / In this case we can make no exception. (*Kono baai wa reegai to shimaseñ.*) この場合は例外としません.

exceptional *adj.* **1** (unusual) re⌈egai-teki na 例外的な: an exceptional case (*reegai-teki na baai*) 例外的な場合.
2 (remarkable) su⌈gu⌉reta 優れた; su⌈gu⌉rete iru 優れている: an exceptional gift for music (*oñgaku ni taisuru sugureta sainoo*) 音楽に対する

優れた才能.

excess[1] *n.* cho⌈oka 超過; ka⌉do 過度: Any excess in payment will be returned. (*Shiharai no chooka-buñ wa heñkyaku shimasu.*) 支払の超過分は返却します. / go to excess (*do o sugosu*) 度を過ごす.

excess[2] *adj.* cho⌈oka no 超過の; yo⌈buñ no 余分の: excess baggage (*chooka tenimotsu*) 超過手荷物 / pay the excess fare (*yobuñ no ryookiñ o harau*) 余分の料金を払う.

excessive *adj.* ka⌉do no 過度の; ho⌉ogai na 法外な: show an excessive interest (*kado no kyoomi o shimesu*) 過度の興味を示す / These prices are certainly excessive. (*Kono nedañ wa tashika ni hoogai da.*) この値段はたしかに法外だ.

exchange *n.* **1** (of money) ka⌈wase 為替; ryo⌈ogae 両替: foreign exchange (*gaikoku kawase*) 外国為替 / the exchange rate (*kawase reeto*) 為替レート / a bill of exchange (*kawase-tegata*) 為替手形.
2 (giving and taking) ko⌈okañ 交換; ya⌈ri⌉tori やり取り: an exchange student (*kookañ-gakusee*) 交換学生 / an exchange of opinions (*ikeñ no yaritori*) 意見のやり取り.
— *vt.* **1** (give and take) ... o ko⌈okañ suru ...を交換する [I]; ... to to⌈rikaeru ...と取り替える [V]: exchange presents (*okurimono o kookañ suru*) 贈り物を交換する / Excuse me, but could you exchange seats with me? (*Shitsuree desu ga watashi to seki o torikaete itadakemasu ka?*) 失礼ですが私と席を取り替えていただけますか.
2 (of money) ... o ryo⌈ogae suru ...を両替する [I]: Can I exchange dollars for yen here? (*Koko de doru o eñ ni ryoogae dekimasu ka?*) ここでドルを円に両替できますか.

excite *vt.* **1** (stir up) ... o ko⌈ofuñ saseru ...を興奮させる [V]; wa⌉kuwaku sa⌈seru わくわくさせる [V]: The news excited us all. (*Sono shirase wa watashi-tachi miñna o wakuwaku saseta.*) その知らせは私たちみんなをわくわくさせた.
2 (stimulate) ... o so⌈so⌉ru ...をそそる [C]; o⌈kosase⌉ru 起こさせる [V]: The story excited my curiosity. (*Sono hanashi wa watashi no kyoomi o sosotta.*) その話は私の興味をそそった.

excited *adj.* ko⌈ofuñ shita [shite iru] 興奮した[している]; wa⌉kuwaku shita [shite iru] わくわくした[している]: an excited voice (*koofuñ shita koe*) 興奮した声 / We got excited when we saw the movie star. (*Sono eega sutaa o mite watashi-tachi wa wakuwaku shita.*) その映画スターを見て私たちはわくわくした.

excitement *n.* ko⌈ofuñ 興奮: I jumped up in excitement. (*Watashi wa koofuñ shite tobiagatta.*) 私は興奮して跳び上がった.

exciting *adj.* ko⌈ofuñ saseru 興奮させる; wa⌉kuwaku sa⌈seru yo⌉o na わくわくさせるような: an exciting story (*wakuwaku saseru yoo na hanashi*) わくわくさせるような話 / an exciting game (*sugoku omoshiroi shiai*) すごくおもしろい試合.

exclaim *vi.* sa⌈ke⌉bu 叫ぶ [C]; ko⌉e o a⌈geru 声をあげる [V]: The girl exclaimed in joy. (*Sono oñna-no-ko wa yorokoñde koe o ageta.*) その女の子は喜んで声をあげた.
— *vt.* ... to sa⌈ke⌉bu ...と叫ぶ [C]: "I've made a mistake!" he exclaimed. (*"Machigaeta" to kare wa sakeñda.*) 「間違えた」と彼は叫んだ.

exclamation *n.* sa⌈kebigo⌉e 叫び声: give an exclamation of surprise (*odoroki no sakebigoe o ageru*) 驚きの叫び声をあげる.

exclamation mark [point] *n.* ka⌈ñta⌉ñfu 感嘆符.

exclude *vt.* ... o shi⌈medasu ...を締め出す [C]; jo⌈gai suru 除外する [I]: We decided to exclude him from the group. (*Kare o nakama kara shimedasu koto ni kimeta.*) 彼を仲間から締め出すことに決めた.

excluding *prep.* ... o noʳzoite ...を除いて: There were ten members present excluding him. (*Kare o nozoite juu-niñ no kaiiñ ga shusseki shita.*) 彼を除いて 10 人の会員が出席した.

exclusive *adj.* **1** (high class) koʳo-kyuu na 高級な; iʳchiryuu no 一流の: an exclusive hotel (*kookyuu hoteru*) 高級ホテル.

2 (not shared) seʳñyoo no 専用の; doʳkuseñ-teki na 独占的な: This car is for the president's exclusive use. (*Kono kuruma wa shachoo señyoo no kuruma desu.*) この車は社長専用の車です. / an exclusive interview (*dokuseñ-kaikeñ*) 独占会見.

exclusive of ... *prep.* ... o noʳzo-ite ...を除いて: The book costs ¥5,000, exclusive of postage. (*Sono hoñ wa sooryoo o nozoite go-señ-eñ da.*) その本は送料を除いて 5 千円だ.

excursion *n.* eʳñsoku 遠足; kaʳñ-koo-ryoˡkoo 観光旅行: a school excursion (*gakkoo no eñsoku*) 学校の遠足 / go on an excursion to Nikko (*Nikkoo e kañkoo-ryokoo ni iku*) 日光へ観光旅行に行く.

excuse *vt.* **1** (forgive) ... o yuʳruˡ-su ...を許す [C]: Please excuse me for my rudeness. (*Shitsuree o o-yurushi kudasai.*) 失礼をお許しください.

2 (from obligation) ... o meˡñjo suru ...を免除する [I]: The teacher excused me from attending. (*Señ-see wa watashi no shusseki o meñjo shite kureta.*) 先生は私の出席を免除してくれた.

3 (justify) ... no iʳiwake o suru ...の言い訳をする [I]: He excused himself for being late. (*Kare wa okureta koto no iiwake o shita.*) 彼は遅れたことの言い訳をした.

Excuse me. [disturbing someone] (*Chotto shitsuree.*) ちょっと失礼. / [apologizing] (*Gomeñ nasai.*) ごめんなさい.

Excuse me? [asking for repetition] (*Sumimaseñ ga moo ichido o-negai shimasu.*) すみませんがもう一度お願いします.

Excuse me, but .... [addressing or interrupting] (*Shitsuree desu ga ....*) 失礼ですが....

---

execute *vt.* **1** (put to death) ... o shoʳkee suru ...を処刑する [I]: The murderer was executed. (*Sono satsujiñhañ wa shokee sareta.*) その殺人犯は処刑された.

2 (carry out) ... o jiʳkkoo suru ...を実行する [I]: execute an order [a plan] (*meeree [keekaku] o jikkoo suru*) 命令[計画]を実行する.

execution *n.* **1** (lawful killing) shoʳkee 処刑: the execution of a murderer (*satsujiñhañ no shokee*) 殺人犯の処刑.

2 (carrying out) suʳikoo 遂行: the proper execution of one's duties (*jibuñ no shokumu no tadashii sui-koo*) 自分の職務の正しい遂行.

executive *n.* yaʳkuˡiñ 役員; juʳu-yaku 重役; keʳe-eˡesha 経営者.

— *adj.* kaˡñri no 管理の; gyoʳosee-joo no 行政上の: an executive committee (*shikkoo iiñkai*) 執行委員会.

exempt *vt.* ... o meˡñjo suru ...を免除する [I]: be exempted from a tax (*zeekiñ o meñjo sareru*) 税金を免除される.

exercise *n.* **1** (physical) uʳñdoo 運動; taʳisoo 体操: I make sure I get regular exercise. (*Watashi wa itsu-mo kimatta uñdoo o suru yoo ni shite imasu.*) 私はいつも決まった運動をするようにしています.

2 (academic) reʳñshuu 練習; reʳñ-shuu-moˡñdai 練習問題: The grammar exercises are after each lesson. (*Buñpoo no reñshuu-moñdai wa kaku ka no owari ni tsuite imasu.*) 文法の練習問題は各課の終わりについています.

— *vt.* **1** (train) ... o uʳñdoo saseru ...を運動させる [V]: exercise a dog (*inu o uñdoo saseru*) 犬を運動させる.

2 (use) ... o mo⌈chii⌉ru …を用いる 🅅: exercise care (*chuui suru*) 注意する.

exhaust *vt.* **1** (tire out) ... o tsu⌈karehate sase⌉ru …を疲れ果てさせる 🅅: The walk from the station has exhausted me. (*Eki kara aruitara tsukarehateta.*) 駅から歩いたら疲れ果てた.

2 (use up) ... o tsu⌈kaihata⌉su …を使い果たす 🄲: exhaust one's money [strength] (*o-kane* [*tairyoku*] *o tsukaihatasu*) お金[体力]を使い果たす.

exhausted *adj.* tsu⌈kareki⌉tta 疲れきった; tsu⌈kareki⌉tte iru 疲れきっている; he⌈toheto ni na⌉tta [na⌉tte iru] へとへとになった[なっている]: We were all absolutely exhausted. (*Watashitachi wa miñna sukkari tsukarekitte ita.*) 私たちはみんなすっかり疲れきっていた.

exhaust gas *n.* ha⌈ikiga⌉su 排気ガス.

exhausting *adj.* hi⌉doku tsu⌈kare⌉ru ひどく疲れる: an exhausting job (*hidoku tsukareru shigoto*) ひどく疲れる仕事 / The climb to the summit was exhausting. (*Choojoo made no yamanobori wa hidoku tsukareta.*) 頂上までの山登りはひどく疲れた.

exhaustion *n.* **1** (tiredness) hi⌈do⌉i tsu⌈kare⌉ ひどい疲れ: mental [physical] exhaustion (*atama* [*karada*] *no hidoi tsukare*) 頭[体]のひどい疲れ.

2 (using up) tsu⌈kaitsuku⌉su ko⌈to⌉ 使い尽くすこと: the exhaustion of natural resources (*teñneñ shigeñ o tsukaitsukusu koto*) 天然資源を使い尽くすこと.

exhibit *vt.* **1** (put on a show) ... o te⌈ñji suru …を展示する 🄸: She is exhibiting some of her photographs next week. (*Kanojo wa raishuu jibuñ no shashiñ o ikutsu-ka teñji shimasu.*) 彼女は来週自分の写真をいくつか展示します.

2 (show) ... o shi⌈me⌉su …を示す 🄲: She exhibited no interest. (*Kanojo wa nañ no kyoomi mo shimesanakatta.*) 彼女は何の興味も示さなかった.

— *n.* te⌈ñjihiñ 展示品; shu⌈ppi⌉ñbutsu 出品物: exhibits in a museum (*hakubutsukañ no teñjihiñ*) 博物館の展示品.

exhibition *n.* **1** (show) te⌈ñra⌉ñkai 展覧会; te⌈ñji⌉kai 展示会: put on an art exhibition (*bijutsuteñ o hiraku*) 美術展を開く.

2 (act of exhibiting) shi⌈me⌉su ko⌈to⌉ 示すこと; mi⌈se⌉ru ko⌈to⌉ 見せること: a good opportunity for the exhibition of one's talents (*sainoo o shimesu yoi kikai*) 才能を示すよい機会.

exile *n.* **1** (forced absence) tsu⌈ihoo 追放; bo⌈omee 亡命: He was sent into exile. (*Kare wa kokugai ni tsuihoo sareta.*) 彼は国外に追放された. / live in exile (*boomee-seekatsu o okuru*) 亡命生活を送る.

2 (exiled person) tsu⌈ihoo sareta hito⌉ 追放された人; bo⌈ome⌉esha 亡命者: a political exile (*seeji boomeesha*) 政治亡命者.

— *vt.* ... o ko⌈ku⌉gai ni tsu⌈ihoo suru …を国外に追放する 🄸: be exiled from home (*kokoku kara tsuihoo sareru*) 故国から追放される.

exist *vi.* **1** (be) i⌈ru いる 🅅; so⌈ñzai suru 存在する 🄸: No life exists on the moon. (*Tsuki ni wa seebutsu wa inai.*) 月には生物はいない.

2 (stay alive) se⌈ezoñ suru 生存する 🄸; i⌉kite iru 生きている 🅅: The survivors existed only on water. (*Seezoñsha wa mizu dake de ikite ita.*) 生存者は水だけで生きていた.

existence *n.* **1** (existing) so⌈ñzai 存在; ji⌈tsuzai 実在: I believe in the existence of God. (*Watashi wa kami no soñzai o shiñjimasu.*) 私は神の存在を信じます.

2 (survival) se⌈ezoñ 生存; i⌉kite iru ko⌈to⌉ 生きていること: the struggle for existence (*seezoñ-kyoosoo*) 生存競争 / Oxygen is necessary for our existence. (*Sañso wa watashitachi ga ikite iku tame ni hitsu-*

yoo desu.) 酸素は私たちが生きていくために必要です.
3 (way of life) se⌈ekatsu 生活; ku⌈rashi 暮らし: lead a happy existence (*shiawase na kurashi o okuru*) 幸せな暮らしを送る.

exit *n.* de⌉guchi 出口: an emergency exit (*hijooguchi*) 非常口 / The exit is the same as the entrance. (*Deguchi wa iriguchi to onaji desu.*) 出口は入り口と同じです.
— *vi.* ta⌈ijoo suru 退場する Ⅰ.

expand *vi.* **1** (grow large) o⌉okiku naru 大きくなる Ⓒ; (swell) bo⌈ochoo suru 膨張する Ⅰ: This city has expanded rapidly in the last few years. (*Kono toshi wa koko suuneñ de kyuusoku ni ookiku natta.*) この都市はここ数年で急速に大きくなった. / Metals expand when heated. (*Kiñzoku wa nessuru to boochoo suru.*) 金属は熱すると膨張する.
2 (develop) ka⌈kuchoo suru 拡張する Ⅰ; ha⌈tteñ suru 発展する Ⅰ: The store expanded into a large supermarket. (*Sono mise wa kakuchoo shite ooki-na suupaa ni natta.*) その店は拡張して大きなスーパーになった.
3 (explain in detail) ku⌈wa⌉shiku no⌈be⌉ru 詳しく述べる Ⅴ: Could you please expand on the last point? (*Saigo no tokoro o kuwashiku nobete itadakemasu ka?*) 最後の所を詳しく述べていただけますか.
— *vt.* **1** (enlarge) ... o o⌉okiku suru ...を大きくする Ⅰ: The wrestler expanded his chest. (*Resuraa wa mune o ookiku shita.*) レスラーは胸を大きくした.
2 (develop) ... o ka⌈kuchoo suru ...を拡張する Ⅰ; ha⌈tteñ saseru 発展させる Ⅴ: expand one's business (*shoobai o kakuchoo suru*) 商売を拡張する / expand an idea into a theory (*aidea o hatteñ sasete riroñ ni matomeru*) アイデアを発展させて理論にまとめる.

expansion *n.* **1** (in size) ka⌈kuchoo 拡張; ka⌈kudai 拡大: the expansion of territory (*ryoodo no kakuchoo*) 領土の拡張.
2 (in volume) bo⌈ochoo 膨張: the expansion of gases (*kitai no boochoo*) 気体の膨張.
3 (development) ha⌈tteñ 発展: the expansion of trade (*booeki no hatteñ*) 貿易の発展.

expect *vt.* **1** (think) ... daroo to o⌈mo⌉u ...だろうと思う Ⓒ; (anticipate) yo⌉ki suru 予期する Ⅰ: I expect Mr. Miyamoto to come. (*Miyamoto-sañ wa kuru daroo to omou.*) 宮本さんは来るだろうと思う.
2 (wait for) ... o ma⌉tsu ...を待つ Ⓒ: The boss is expecting you. (*Kachoo ga anata o matte imasu yo.*) 課長があなたを待っていますよ.
3 (consider reasonable) ... o ki⌈tai suru ...を期待する Ⅰ: He expects good pay for the work. (*Kare wa sono shigoto ni taishite yoi kyuuryoo o kitai shite iru.*) 彼はその仕事に対して良い給料を期待している.
be expecting (a baby) *vi.* shu⌈s-sañ yo⌉tee da 出産予定だ: I hear that Mary is expecting next month. (*Mearii wa raigetsu shussañ no yotee da soo desu.*) メアリーは来月出産の予定だそうです.

expectation *n.* yo⌈soo 予想; mi⌈komi 見込み; (hopes) ki⌈tai 期待: The outcome was contrary to expectations. (*Kekka wa yosoo ni hañshite ita.*) 結果は予想に反していた. / Our expectations were finally realized. (*Watashi-tachi no kitai wa tsui ni jitsugeñ sareta.*) 私たちの期待はついに実現された.

expedition *n.* (journey) ta⌈ñkeñ 探検; (group) ta⌈ñkeñtai 探検隊: go on an expedition (*tañkeñ ni iku*) 探検に行く.

expel *vt.* ... o o⌈ida⌉su ...を追い出す Ⓒ; tsu⌈ihoo suru 追放する Ⅰ: The illegal immigrants were expelled from Japan. (*Fuhoo ijuusha wa Nihoñ kara tsuihoo sareta.*) 不法移住者は日本から追放された. / be expelled from school (*taigaku ni naru*) 退学になる.

e

expense *n.* **1** (cost) hi˥yoo 費用; shi˥shutsu 支出: They built the church at great expense. (*Kare-ra wa tagaku no hiyoo o kakete sono kyookai o tateta.*) 彼らは多額の費用をかけてその教会を建てた.
2 (necessary costs) ke˥ehi 経費: school expenses (*gakuhi*) 学費 / traveling expenses (*ryohi*) 旅費 / My expenses were paid by the company. (*Watashi no keehi wa kaisha ga haratte kureta.*) 私の経費は会社が払ってくれた.

expense account *n.* hi˥tsuyoo ke˥ehi 必要経費; se˥tta˥ihi 接待費.

expensive *adj.* ko˥oka na 高価な; ta˥ka˥i 高い: That ring looks very expensive. (*Sono yubiwa wa takasoo ni mieru.*) その指輪は高そうに見える. / Do you have a less expensive watch? (*Motto yasui tokee wa arimasu ka?*) もっと安い時計はありますか.

experience *n.* **1** (knowledge or skill) ke˥ekeñ 経験; ta˥ikeñ 体験: I have experience in teaching English. (*Watashi wa Eego no kyooiku ni keekeñ ga arimasu.*) 私は英語の教育に経験があります.
2 (event) ke˥ekeñ [ta˥ikeñ] shita koto˥ 経験[体験]したこと: I had a lot of strange experiences when living abroad. (*Gaikoku ni suñde iru toki fushigi na keekeñ o takusañ shimashita.*) 外国に住んでいるとき不思議な経験をたくさんしました.
— *vt.* ... o ke˥ekeñ suru …を経験する Ⅰ; ta˥ikeñ suru 体験する Ⅰ: I have never before experienced a hardship like this. (*Kono yoo na koñnañ o taikeñ shita koto wa ima made ni arimaseñ.*) このような困難を体験をしたことは今までにありません.

experienced *adj.* ke˥ekeñ no a˥ru 経験のある; be˥terañ no ベテランの: an experienced nurse (*beterañ no kañgofu*) ベテランの看護婦.

experiment *n.* ji˥kkeñ 実験: conduct a chemical experiment (*kagaku no jikkeñ o suru*) 科学の実験をする.
— *vi.* ji˥kkeñ suru 実験する Ⅰ: experiment on animals (*doobutsu jikkeñ o suru*) 動物実験をする.

expert *n.* se˥ñmoñka 専門家; ju˥kure˥ñsha 熟練者; be˥terañ ベテラン: an expert on the Japanese economy (*Nihoñ keezai no señmoñka*) 日本経済の専門家 / She is an expert at teaching Japanese. (*Kanojo wa Nihoñgo kyooiku no beterañ da.*) 彼女は日本語教育のベテランだ.
— *adj.* ju˥kureñ shita [shite iru] 熟練した[している]; ju˥kutatsu shita [shite iru] 熟達した[している]: an expert driver (*jukureñ shita doraibaa*) 熟練したドライバー.

expiration *n.* ma˥ñki 満期; ki˥geñgire 期限切れ: the expiration of one's alien registration certificate (*gaikokujiñ toorokusho no kigeñgire*) 外国人登録書の期限切れ.

expire *vi.* ma˥ñki ni naru 満期になる Ⓒ; ki˥geñ ga ki˥re˥ru 期限が切れる Ⓥ: The validity of my passport has expired. (*Pasupooto no kigeñ ga kireta.*) パスポートの期限が切れた.

explain *vt.* **1** (make clear) ... o se˥tsumee suru …を説明する Ⅰ: explain the structure of a building (*tatemono no koozoo o setsumee suru*) 建物の構造を説明する.
2 (account for) ... o be˥ñmee suru …を弁明する Ⅰ; sha˥kumee suru 釈明する Ⅰ: explain one's absence (*kesseki shita koto o beñmee suru*) 欠席したことを弁明する.

explanation *n.* se˥tsumee 説明; ka˥isetsu 解説; be˥ñmee 弁明: We demand a satisfactory explanation from you. (*Nattoku no yuku setsumee o anata ni yookyuu shimasu.*) 納得のゆく説明をあなたに要求します.

explode *vi.* **1** (of bombs) ba˥kuhatsu suru 爆発する Ⅰ; ha˥retsu suru 破裂する Ⅰ: A bomb exploded. (*Bakudañ ga bakuhatsu shita.*) 爆弾が爆発した.
2 (of emotions) ka˥tto na˥ru かっとなる Ⓒ: He exploded in anger. (*Kare

wa okotte katto natta.) 彼は怒ってかっとなった.

— *vt.* ... o ba⌈kuhatsu saseru …を爆発させる [V]; ha⌈retsu saseru 破裂させる [V]: explode a bomb (*bakudañ o haretsu saseru*) 爆弾を破裂させる.

exploit *vt.* **1** (develop) ... o ka⌈ihatsu suru …を開発する [I]: exploit the natural resources of a country (*kuni no teñneñ shigeñ o kaihatsu suru*) 国の天然資源を開発する.

2 (take advantage of) ... o ri⌈yoo suru …を利用する [I]; sa⌉kushu suru 搾取する [I]; ku⌈imo⌉no ni suru 食い物にする [I]: That company exploits its employees. (*Ano kaisha wa juugyooiñ o kuimono ni shite iru.*) あの会社は従業員を食い物にしている.

explore *vt.* **1** (travel) ... o ta⌈ñkeñ suru …を探検する [I]: explore unknown regions (*michi no chiiki o tañkeñ suru*) 未知の地域を探検する.

2 (examine) ... o cho⌉osa suru …を調査する [I]: explore all aspects of a problem (*moñdai no arayuru meñ o choosa suru*) 問題のあらゆる面を調査する.

explosion *n.* **1** (of a bomb) ba⌈kuhatsu 爆発: a nuclear explosion (*kaku-bakuhatsu*) 核爆発.

2 (of emotions) ba⌈kuhatsu 爆発: an explosion of anger (*ikari no bakuhatsu*) 怒りの爆発 / an explosion of laughter (*bakushoo*) 爆笑.

3 (sudden increase) ba⌈kuhatsuteki na zooka 爆発的な増加: the population explosion (*jiñkoo no bakuhatsu-teki na zooka*) 人口の爆発的な増加.

export *vt.* ... o yu⌈shutsu suru … を輸出する [I]: import raw materials and export finished goods (*geñryoo o yunyuu shite kañseehiñ o yushutsu suru*) 原料を輸入して完成品を輸出する.

— *n.* (exporting) yu⌈shutsu 輸出; (goods) yu⌈shutsuhiñ 輸出品: Exports exceed imports this year. (*Kotoshi wa yushutsu ga yunyuu o uwamawatte iru.*) ことしは輸出が輸入を上回っている.

expose *vt.* **1** (leave unprotected) ... o sa⌈rasu …をさらす [C]: expose one's skin to the sun (*hada o taiyoo ni sarasu*) 肌を太陽にさらす / be exposed to danger and hardship (*kikeñ to koñnañ ni sarasareru*) 危険と困難にさらされる.

2 (disclose) ... o ba⌉kuro suru …を暴露する [I]; a⌈ba⌉ku 暴く [C]: expose the real facts to the public (*shiñsoo o kooshuu ni bakuro suru*) 真相を公衆に暴露する.

exposure *n.* **1** (revelation) ba⌉kuro 暴露; te⌈kihatsu 摘発: the exposure of corruption (*oshoku no bakuro*) 汚職の暴露.

2 (exposing) sa⌈rasu kato⌉ さらすこと: exposure to the sun (*hi ni sarasu koto*) 日にさらすこと.

3 (photography) fi⌉rumu no hito⌉koma フィルムのひとこま: a 36-exposure roll of film (*sañjuu-roku-mai-dori no firumu*) 36 枚どりのフィルム.

express *vt.* **1** (state) ... o hyo⌈oge⌉ñ suru …を表現する [I]; i⌈iarawa⌉su 言い表わす [C]: express one's feelings freely (*kañjite iru koto o jiyuu ni hyoogeñ suru*) 感じていることを自由に表現する / I don't know how to express my gratitude. (*Watashi no kañsha no kimochi o doo iiarawashite yoi ka wakarimaseñ.*) 私の感謝の気持ちをどう言い表わしてよいかわかりません.

2 (show) ... o a⌈rawa⌉su …を表わす [C]; shi⌈me⌉su 示す [C]: Tomoko's tears expressed how sad she was. (*Tomoko-sañ no namida wa kanojo ga doñna ni kanashiñde iru ka o shimeshite ita.*) 友子さんの涙は彼女がどんなに悲しんでいるかを示していた.

3 (send by fast delivery) so⌈kutatsu de okuru 速達で送る [C]: I'd like to have this letter expressed. (*Kono tegami o sokutatsu ni shite itadakitai no desu ga.*) この手紙を速達に

していただきたいのですが.
— *adj.* **1** (especially fast) kyu⌈ukoo no 急行の; so⌈kutatsu no 速達の: an express bus (*kyuukoo basu*) 急行バス / an express letter (*sokutatsu no tegami*) 速達の手紙.
2 (definite) me⌈ekaku na 明確な; ha⌈kki⌉ri shita [shite iru] はっきりした[している]: my father's express wish (*chichi no meekaku na kiboo*) 父の明確な希望.
— *n.* (train) kyu⌈ukoo-re⌉ssha 急行列車: the 8:45 express from Ueno (*Ueno hatsu hachi-ji yoñ-juugo-fuñ no kyuukoo*) 上野発 8:45 の急行.

expression *n.* **1** (showing of opinions, etc.) hyo⌈oge⌉ñ 表現: the expression of ideas (*shisoo no hyoogeñ*) 思想の表現 / give expression to one's feelings (*kañjoo o arawasu*) 感情を表わす.
2 (look) hyo⌈ojo⌉o 表情; ka⌈otsuki 顔つき: a serious expression (*shiñkeñ na hyoojoo*) 真剣な表情 / When I saw her expression, I realized she was angry. (*Kanojo no kaotsuki o mite kanojo ga okotte iru no ga wakatta.*) 彼女の顔つきを見て彼女が怒っているのがわかった.
3 (of words) go⌉ku 語句; i⌈imawashi 言い回し: a set expression (*kimari moñku*) 決まり文句 / There are lots of special polite expressions in Japanese. (*Nihoñgo ni wa tokubetsu teenee na iimawashi ga takusañ aru.*) 日本語には特別丁寧な言い回しがたくさんある.

expressive *adj.* hyo⌈ojo⌉o ni to⌉mu 表情に富む; a⌈rawa⌉shite (iru) 表わして(いる): an expressive look (*hyoojoo ni tomu kaotsuki*) 表情に富む顔つき / be expressive regarding one's gratitude (*kañsha o arawasu*) 感謝を表わす.

express train *n.* kyu⌈ukoo-re⌉ssha 急行列車: a semi-express train (*juñkyuu-ressha*) 準急列車 / a super-express train (*tokkyuu-ressha*) 特急列車.

expressway *n.* ko⌈osoku-jidoosha⌉doo 高速自動車道: the Tomei Expressway between Tokyo and Nagoya (*Tookyoo-Nagoya kañ no Toomee Koosoku*) 東京一名古屋間の東名高速.

exquisite *adj.* **1** (beautiful) hi⌈joo ni utsukushi⌉i 非常に美しい; hi⌈joo ni subarashi⌉i 非常にすばらしい: an exquisite fragrance (*hijoo ni yoi kaori*) 非常によい香り / an exquisite design (*hijoo ni subarashii dezaiñ*) 非常にすばらしいデザイン.
2 (refined) yu⌉uga na 優雅な: a person of exquisite taste (*yuuga na shumi no hito*) 優雅な趣味の人.

extend *vt.* **1** (of time, a line) ... o e⌈ñchoo suru ...を延長する [I]; no⌈ba⌉su 延ばす [C]: I decided to extend my stay in Japan for another year. (*Watashi wa Nihoñ de no taizai o ato ichi-neñ nobasu koto ni kimeta.*) 私は日本での滞在をあと1年延ばすことに決めた. / extend the road to the next town (*tsugi no machi made dooro o eñchoo suru*) 次の町まで道路を延長する.
2 (of an area, activity) ... o ka⌈kuchoo suru ...を拡張する [I]; hi⌈rogeru 広げる [V]: This sidewalk is going to be extended. (*Kono hodoo wa hirogerareru koto ni natte imasu.*) この歩道は広げられることになっています. / extend one's business into a new field (*shigoto o atarashii buñya e kakuchoo suru*) 仕事を新しい分野へ拡張する.
3 (of limbs) ... o no⌈ba⌉su ...を伸ばす [C]: extend an arm (*ude o nobasu*) 腕を伸ばす.
4 (of friendship, credit) ... o a⌈taeru 与える [V]; ho⌈doko⌉su 施す [C]: extend a warm welcome (*atatakaku kañgee suru*) 温かく歓迎する.
— *vi.* **1** (of an area) hi⌈rogaru 広がる [C]; no⌈bi⌉ru 延びる [V]: The paddy field extends as far as the eye can see. (*Miwatasu kagiri suideñ ga hirogatte iru.*) 見渡すかぎり水田が広がっている.

2 (continue to) ke⌜ezoku suru 継続する Ⓘ; zu⌜rekomu ずれ込む Ⓒ: The conference will extend into next week. (*Kaigi wa raishuu made zurekomu deshoo.*) 会議は来週までずれ込むでしょう.

extension *n.* **1** (of a line, space, time) e⌜ñchoo 延長; (of a building) ta⌜temashi 建て増し; zo⌜ochiku 増築: the extension of a railroad (*tetsudoo no eñchoo*) 鉄道の延長 / build an extension to a hospital (*byooiñ no tatemashi o suru*) 病院の建て増しをする.
2 (further development) ka⌜kuchoo 拡張; ka⌜kudai 拡大: the extension of foreign trade (*gaikoku-booeki no kakudai*) 外国貿易の拡大.
3 (of a telephone line) na⌜iseñ 内線: Please give me extension 476. (*Naiseñ yoñ-nana-roku o o-negai shimasu.*) 内線 476 をお願いします.

extensive *adj.* ko⌜oha⌝ñi ni wa⌜taru 広範囲にわたる; ha⌝ñi ga hi⌜ro⌝i 範囲が広い: extensive damage (*koohañi ni wataru higai*) 広範囲にわたる被害.

extent *n.* **1** (expanse) hi⌜rogari 広がり; o⌜okisa 大きさ: a vast extent of land (*tochi no koodai na hirogari*) 土地の広大な広がり.
2 (degree) te⌝edo 程度; ha⌝ñi 範囲: To some extent I agree with you. (*Aru teedo made wa anata ni dooi shimasu.*) ある程度まではあなたに同意します.

exterior *adj.* ga⌝ibu no 外部の; so⌜togawa no 外側の: the exterior walls of a building (*biru no sotogawa no kabe*) ビルの外側の壁.
— *n.* ga⌝ibu 外部; so⌜togawa 外側: a house with a marble exterior (*sotogawa ga dairiseki no ie*) 外側が大理石の家.

external *adj.* **1** (outer) ga⌝ibu no 外部の; so⌝to no 外の: the external appearance of a house (*ie no gaikañ*) 家の外観 / external wounds (*gaishoo*) 外傷.
2 (foreign) ga⌜ikoku no 外国の; ta⌜igai-teki na 対外的な: external affairs (*gaikoku jijoo*) 外国事情 / external trade (*taigai-booeki*) 対外貿易.
3 (superficial) u⌜wabe dake⌝ no うわべだけの: external politeness (*uwabe dake no reegi*) うわべだけの礼儀.

extinct *adj.* ki⌜eta 消えた; ki⌜ete iru 消えている; ze⌜tsumetsu shita [shite iru] 絶滅した[している]: an extinct volcano (*shikazañ*) 死火山 / an extinct animal (*zetsumetsu shita doobutsu*) 絶滅した動物.

extinction *n.* ze⌜tsumetsu 絶滅; sho⌜ometsu 消滅: the complete extinction of a species of bird (*tori no shu no kañzeñ na zetsumetsu*) 鳥の種の完全な絶滅.

extinguish *vt.* ... o chi⌜ñka suru ...を鎮火する Ⓘ; ke⌜su 消す Ⓒ: extinguish a forest fire (*yamakaji o chiñka suru*) 山火事を鎮火する.

extra *adj.* yo⌜buñ na 余分な; ri⌜ñji no 臨時の: I saved some extra money. (*Yobuñ na o-kane wa chokiñ shita.*) 余分なお金は貯金した. / an extra charge (*tokubetsu ryookiñ*) 特別料金 / Wine is not included; it's extra. (*Waiñ wa fukumarete orimaseñ. Sore wa betsu desu.*) ワインは含まれておりません. それは別です.
— *adv.* yo⌜buñ ni 余分に; to⌜kubetsu ni 特別に: an extra good meal (*tokubetsu jootoo no shokuji*) 特別上等の食事 / I gave the bellhop an extra large tip. (*Booi ni tokubetsu ni takusañ chippu o yatta.*) ボーイに特別にたくさんチップをやった.
— *n.* wa⌜rimashi ryo⌝okiñ 割り増し料金; tsu⌜ika ryo⌝okiñ 追加料金: Breakfast is an extra here. (*Koko de wa chooshoku wa betsu-ryookiñ desu.*) ここでは朝食は別料金です.

extract *vt.* **1** (pull out) ... o nu⌜ku ...を抜く Ⓒ; nu⌜kito⌝ru 抜き取る Ⓒ: have a tooth extracted (*ha o nuite morau*) 歯を抜いてもらう / extract a cork from a bottle (*koruku o biñ kara nuku*) コルクをびんから抜く.

2 (squeeze out) ... o shi⌈borida⌉su …を搾り出す Ⓒ; chu⌈ushutsu suru 抽出する Ⓘ: extract juice from an orange (*orenji kara juusu o shiboridasu*) オレンジからジュースを搾り出す.
3 (of information) ... o hi⌈kida⌉su …を引き出す Ⓒ: extract a secret from a person (*hito kara himitsu o hikidasu*) 人から秘密を引き出す.
— *n.* ba⌈ssui 抜粋; i⌈ñyo⌉oku 引用句: an extract from a work of fiction (*shoosetsu kara no iñyoo*) 小説からの引用.

extraordinary *adj.* 1 (unusual) i⌈joo na 異常な; na⌈mihazu⌉reta 並外れた; na⌈mihazu⌉rete iru 並み外れている: an extraordinary event (*ijoo na dekigoto*) 異常な出来事 / a man of extraordinary genius (*namihazureta teñsai no hito*) 並外れた天才の人.
2 (unscheduled) to⌈kubetsu no 特別の; ri⌈ñji no 臨時の: an extraordinary general meeting (*riñji-sookai*) 臨時総会.

extravagance *n.* ze⌈eta⌉ku ぜいたく; ro⌈ohi 浪費: a needless extravagance (*fuhitsuyoo na roohi*) 不必要な浪費.

extravagant *adj.* ze⌈eta⌉ku na ぜいたくな; ro⌈ohi suru 浪費する: an extravagant meal (*zeetaku na shokuji*) ぜいたくな食事.

extreme *adj.* 1 (very great) kyo⌉kudo no 極度の; hi⌈joo-na 非常な: extreme poverty (*kyokudo no hiñkoñ*) 極度の貧困 / live to an extreme old age (*hijoo-na kooree made ikiru*) 非常な高齢まで生きる.
2 (most remote) i⌈chibañ hashi no いちばん端の; se⌈ñtañ no 先端の: We live on the extreme edge of Tokyo. (*Watashi-tachi wa Tookyoo no ichibañ hashi ni suñde imasu.*) 私たちは東京のいちばん端に住んでいます.
3 (drastic) kyo⌈kuta⌉ñ na 極端な: hold extreme views (*kyokutañ na kañgae o motsu*) 極端な考えを持つ.
— *n.* kyo⌈kuta⌉ñ 極端: experience the extremes of heat and cold (*kañsho no ryoo kyokutañ o keekeñ suru*) 寒暑の両極端を経験する.

extremely *adv.* kyo⌈kuta⌉ñ ni 極端に; kyo⌉kudo ni 極度に; ki⌈wa⌉mete きわめて; to⌈temo とても: an extremely difficult problem (*kiwamete muzukashii moñdai*) きわめて難しい問題 / He is extremely angry. (*Kare wa sugoku okotte iru.*) 彼はすごく怒っている.

eye *n.* 1 (organ) me⌉ 目[眼]: have blue [brown, dark] eyes (*aoi [chairoi, kuroi] me o shite iru*) 青い[茶色い, 黒い]目をしている / shut [open] one's eyes (*me o tojiru [akeru]*) 目を閉じる[開ける].
2 (sight) shi⌈ryoku 視力: I have weak eyes. (*Watashi wa shiryoku ga yowai.*) 私は視力が弱い.
3 (discernment) ka⌈ñsatsu⌉ryoku 観察力; me⌉ 目: Mary has an eye for pictures. (*Mearii wa e o miru me o motte iru.*) メアリーは絵を見る眼を持っている.
4 (something like an eye) the eye of a needle (*hari no me*) 針の目 / the eye of a typhoon (*taifuu no me*) 台風の目.

eyeball *n.* ga⌈ñkyuu 眼球.

eyebrow *n.* ma⌉yu 眉; ma⌉yuge 眉毛: knit one's eyebrows (*mayu o shikameru*) 眉をしかめる.

eye doctor *n.* ga⌈ñka⌉-i 眼科医; me⌉isha 目医者.

eyeglasses *n.* me⌉gane 眼鏡.

eyelash *n.* ma⌉tsuge まつげ.

eyelid *n.* ma⌉buta まぶた: the upper [lower] eyelid (*uwa [shita] mabuta*) 上[下]まぶた.

eyesight *n.* shi⌉ryoku 視力: a person with good [poor] sight (*shiryoku no yoi [warui] hito*) 視力のよい[悪い]人 / have one's eyesight tested (*shiryoku o shirabete morau*) 視力を調べてもらう.

F

fable *n.* gu⌈uwa 寓話; de⌈ñsetsu 伝説.

fabric *n.* **1** (cloth) o⌈rimono 織物; ki⌉ji 生地: woolen fabrics (*keorimono*) 毛織物 / weave a fabric (*orimono o oru*) 織物を織る.
2 (structure) ko⌈ozoo 構造; so⌉shiki 組織: the fabric of society (*shakai no koozoo*) 社会の構造.

face *n.* **1** (the front part of the head) ka⌈o 顔: wash one's face (*kao o arau*) 顔を洗う.
2 (look) ka⌈otsuki 顔つき; ka⌈o 顔: put on a sad face (*kanashii kao o suru*) 悲しい顔をする.
3 (surface) hyo⌈ome⌉ñ 表面; (front) o⌈mote⌉ 表: the face of the earth (*chihyoo*) 地表 / the face of a playing card (*torañpu no omote*) トランプの表.
— *vt.* **1** (look toward) ... ni me⌉ñshite iru …に面している [V]: My room faces the south. (*Watashi no heya wa minami ni meñshite imasu.*) 私の部屋は南に面しています.
2 (meet defiantly) ... ni ta⌈chimukau …に立ち向かう [C]: face dangers (*kikeñ ni tachimukau*) 危険に立ち向かう.
3 (present itself to) ... ni sho⌈ojiru …に生じる [V]: A new problem faced us. (*Atarashii moñdai ga wareware ni shoojita.*) 新しい問題がわれわれに生じた.

facilitate *vt.* ... o yo⌈oi ni suru …を容易にする [I]; ra⌈ku⌉ ni suru 楽にする [I]: This computer will facilitate your task. (*Kono koñpyuutaa wa anata no shigoto o raku ni suru deshoo.*) このコンピューターはあなたの仕事を楽にするでしょう.

facility *n.* **1** (means) se⌉tsubi 設備; shi⌉setsu 施設: public facilities (*kookyoo shisetsu*) 公共施設.
2 (conveniences) be⌉ñ 便: transportation facilities (*kootsuu no beñ*) 交通の便.
3 (skill) no⌉oryoku 能力; sa⌈inoo 才能: a facility for language (*gogaku no sainoo*) 語学の才能.

fact *n.* **1** (something that has happened) ji⌉jitsu 事実: I told him the facts. (*Watashi wa kare ni jijitsu o hanashita.*) 私は彼に事実を話した.
2 (reality) ge⌈ñjitsu no hanashi⌉ 現実の話; ji⌉jitsu 事実: a novel based on fact (*jijitsu ni motozuita shoosetsu*) 事実に基づいた小説.

factor *n.* yo⌈oiñ 要因; yo⌉oso 要素: Effort was a factor in his success. (*Doryoku ga kare no seekoo no ichi yooiñ datta.*) 努力が彼の成功の一要因だった.

factory *n.* ko⌈ojo⌉o 工場: He works in this factory. (*Kare wa kono koojoo de hataraite imasu.*) 彼はこの工場で働いています.

faculty *n.* **1** (ability) no⌉oryoku 能力; sa⌈inoo 才能: She has a faculty for music. (*Kanojo wa oñgaku no sainoo ga aru.*) 彼女は音楽の才能がある.
2 (department) ga⌈kubu 学部: the faculty of law (*hoogaku-bu*) 法学部.

fade *vi.* **1** (of a flower) shi⌈bomu しぼむ [C]; shi⌈oreru しおれる [V]: The roses have faded. (*Bara ga shiorete shimatta.*) ばらがしおれてしまった.
2 (of color) a⌈se⌉ru あせる [C]; sa⌈me⌉ru さめる [V]: The shirt faded when it was washed. (*Shatsu o arattara iro ga sameta.*) シャツを洗ったら色がさめた.
3 (disappear) ki⌈esa⌉ru 消え去る [C]: My hopes faded. (*Watashi no nozomi wa kiesatta.*) 私の望みは消え去った.
— *vt.* **1** (of a flower) ... o shi⌈oresasu …をしおれさす [C].
2 (of color) ... o a⌈sesase⌉ru …をあ

せさせる V: Sunlight fades curtains. (*Nikkoo wa kaateñ no iro o asesaseru.*) 日光はカーテンの色をあせさせる.

Fahrenheit *adj.* ka¹shi no 華氏の: eighty degrees Fahrenheit (*kashi hachijuu-do*) 華氏 80 度. ★ In Japan the Celsius system is used instead of the Fahrenheit system.

fail *vi.* **1** (be unsuccessful) shi⌈ppai suru 失敗する I; shi⌈kuji¹ru しくじる C: All his attempts failed. (*Kare no kokoromi wa subete shippai shita.*) 彼の試みはすべて失敗した. / fail in the examination (*shikeñ ni ochiru*) 試験に落ちる.

2 (neglect) (... o) o⌈kota¹ru (...を)怠る C; ⟨verb⟩-na¹i ...ない: He often fails to keep his word. (*Kare wa yakusoku o mamoranai koto ga yoku aru.*) 彼は約束を守らないことがよくある.

3 (break down) ko⌈shoo suru 故障する I; ki⌈kanai 利かない: The brakes failed. (*Bureeki ga kikanakatta.*) ブレーキが利かなかった.

4 (be not enough) fu⌈soku suru 不足する I; fu⌈saku ni na¹ru 不作になる C: The crops failed this year. (*Kotoshi wa fusaku datta.*) ことしは不作だった.

5 (become weak) o⌈toroe¹ru 衰える V; yo⌈wa¹ru 弱る C: My sight has failed. (*Watashi wa shiryoku ga otoroeta.*) 私は視力が衰えた.

— *vt.* **1** (disappoint) ... o shi⌈tsuboo saseru ...を失望させる V; (forsake) mi⌈suteru 見捨てる V: When I wanted his help he failed me. (*Kare no tasuke ga hoshii toki kare wa watashi o misuteta.*) 彼の助けが欲しいとき彼は私を見捨てた.

2 (of a teacher) ... o ra⌈kudai saseru ...を落第させる V; (of a student) ... ni o⌈chi¹ru ...に落ちる C: The teacher failed five students. (*Señsee wa go-niñ o rakudai saseta.*) 先生は 5 人を落第させた. / He failed his exam. (*Kare wa shikeñ ni ochita.*) 彼は試験に落ちた.

failure *n.* **1** (act of failing) shi⌈ppai 失敗: His plan ended in failure. (*Kare no keekaku wa shippai ni owatta.*) 彼の計画は失敗に終わった.

2 (unsuccessful person) shi⌈ppa¹isha 失敗者; ra⌈kuda¹isha 落第者: He is a failure as a politician. (*Kare wa seejika to shite wa rakudai da.*) 彼は政治家としては落第だ.

3 (cessation) te⌈eshi 停止; ko⌈shoo 故障: a power failure (*teedeñ*) 停電 / a heart failure (*shiñzoo mahi*) 心臓まひ.

faint *adj.* **1** (indistinct) ka¹suka na かすかな; ho¹noka na ほのかな: a faint smell (*kasuka na nioi*) かすかなにおい.

2 (vague) ka¹suka na かすかな; wa¹zuka na わずかな: There is still a faint hope. (*Mada kasuka na nozomi ga arimasu.*) まだかすかな望みがあります.

3 (dizzy) me⌈ma¹i ga suru めまいがする: feel faint (*memai ga suru*) めまいがする.

— *vi.* (lose consciousness) shi⌈sshiñ suru 失神する I: She fainted from the heat. (*Kanojo wa atsusa no tame shisshiñ shita.*) 彼女は暑さのため失神した.

— *n.* shi⌈sshiñ 失神; ki⌈zetsu 気絶: fall in a faint (*kizetsu shite taoreru*) 気絶して倒れる.

fair[1] *adj.* **1** (just) ko⌈osee na 公正な; ko⌈ohee na 公平な: a fair judgment (*koosee na hañdañ*) 公正な判断.

2 (considerable) ka¹nari no かなりの; so⌈otoo no 相当の: There were a fair number of people in the room. (*Heya ni wa kanari no kazu no hito ga imashita.*) 部屋にはかなりの数の人がいました.

3 (fine) ha¹reta 晴れた; ha¹rete iru 晴れている: a fair sky (*hareta sora*) 晴れた空.

4 (of hair) ki⌈ñpatsu no 金髪の: She has fair hair. (*Kanojo wa kiñpatsu desu.*) 彼女は金髪です.

5 (of skin) shi⌈ro¹i 白い: She has a fair skin. (*Kanojo wa hada ga shiroi.*) 彼女は肌が白い.

6 (of baseball) fe⌉a na フェアな: a fair ball (*fea booru*) フェアボール.
— *adv.* se⌈ese⌉e do⌈odo⌉o to 正々堂々と; ko⌈omee seedai ni 公明正大に: fight fair (*seesee doodoo to tatakau*) 正々堂々と戦う.

fair[2] *n.* **1** (of farm products) hi⌈ñ-pyo⌉okai 品評会; kyo⌈oshi⌉ñkai 共進会.
2 (exhibition) ha⌈kura⌉ñkai 博覧会; mi⌈ho⌉ñichi 見本市; -fe⌉a フェア: an international trade fair (*kokusai mihoñichi*) 国際見本市.

fairly *adv.* **1** (justly) ko⌈osee ni 公正に; ko⌈ohee ni 公平に: treat pupils fairly (*seeto o koohee ni atsukau*) 生徒を公平に扱う.
2 (quite) ka⌉nari かなり; so⌈otoo (ni) 相当(に): He speaks Japanese fairly well. (*Kare wa Nihoñgo o kanari joozu ni hanashimasu.*) 彼は日本語をかなりじょうずに話します.

fairy tale *n.* o⌈togiba⌉nashi おとぎ話; do⌈owa 童話.

faith *n.* **1** (belief) shi⌈ñkoo 信仰; shi⌉ñneñ 信念: a person of strong faith (*shiñkoo no atsui hito*) 信仰のあつい人.
2 (trust) shi⌈ñrai 信頼; shi⌈ñyoo 信用: I haven't much faith in his ability. (*Watashi wa kare no nooryoku o taishite shiñyoo shite imaseñ.*) 私は彼の能力をたいして信用していません.
3 (loyalty) shi⌉ñgi 信義; se⌈ejitsu 誠実: keep faith with a person (*hito to no shiñgi o mamoru*) 人との信義を守る.

faithful *adj.* **1** (loyal) chu⌈ujitsu na 忠実な; (sincere) se⌈ejitsu na 誠実な: He was faithful to his promise. (*Kare wa yakusoku ni chuujitsu datta.*) 彼は約束に忠実だった.
2 (exact) se⌈ekaku na 正確な; chu⌈ujitsu na 忠実な: a faithful copy (*seekaku na utsushi*) 正確な写し / a translation faithful to the original (*geñbuñ ni chuujitsu na yaku*) 原文に忠実な訳.

fall[1] *n.* (autumn) a⌉ki 秋.

fall[2] *vi.* **1** (go down) o⌈chi⌉ru 落ちる Ⓥ: He fell off a ladder. (*Kare wa hashigo kara ochita.*) 彼ははしごから落ちた.
2 (of rain, etc.) fu⌉ru 降る Ⓒ: The rain began to fall. (*Ame ga furihajimeta.*) 雨が降り始めた.
3 (collapse) ta⌈ore⌉ru 倒れる Ⓥ: I slipped and fell to the ground. (*Watashi wa subette jimeñ ni taoreta.*) 私は滑って地面に倒れた.
4 (become lower) sa⌈ga⌉ru 下がる Ⓒ; hi⌉kuku naru 低くなる Ⓒ: The temperature has fallen five degrees. (*Oñdo ga go-do sagatta.*) 温度が5度下がった.
5 (become) ... ni na⌉ru ...になる Ⓒ: fall ill (*byooki ni naru*) 病気になる / The room fell silent. (*Heya ga shizuka ni natta.*) 部屋が静かになった.
6 (hang down) ta⌈re⌉ru 垂れる Ⓥ: Her hair fell over her shoulders. (*Kanojo no kami no ke wa kata no ue ni tarete ita.*) 彼女の髪の毛は肩の上に垂れていた.

fall down *vi.* ko⌈robu 転ぶ Ⓒ: He fell down on the ice. (*Kare wa koori no ue de koroñda.*) 彼は氷の上で転んだ.
— *n.* **1** (becoming lower) te⌈eka 低下; ge⌈raku 下落: a fall in temperature (*oñdo no teeka*) 温度の低下 / a fall in prices (*bukka no geraku*) 物価の下落.
2 (going down to the ground) te⌈ñtoo 転倒: break one's leg in a fall (*teñtoo shite ashi o oru*) 転倒して脚を折る.
3 (dropping) o⌈chi⌉ru ko⌈to⌉ 落ちること; ra⌈kka 落下: a fall from a horse (*rakuba*) 落馬.
4 (rainfall) ko⌉ou 降雨; (snowfall) ko⌈osetsu 降雪: a heavy fall of snow (*ooyuki*) 大雪.
5 (downfall) bo⌈tsuraku 没落; me⌈tsuboo 滅亡: the fall of the Heike family (*Heeko no metsuboo*) 平家の滅亡.
6 (waterfall) ta⌈ki 滝.

false *adj.* **1** (mistaken) ma⌈chiga⌉tta 間違った; ma⌈chiga⌉tte iru 間

f

違っている: a false account (*machigatta keesañ*) 間違った計算.
2 (not true) u⌈so no うその; i⌈tsuwari no 偽りの: make a false statement (*uso no chiñjutsu o suru*) うその陳述をする.
3 (not genuine) ho⌈ñmono de na⌉i 本物でない; ni⌈se no 偽の: false teeth (*ireba*) 入れ歯.
4 (not loyal) fu⌈se⌉ejitsu na 不誠実な; fu⌈jitsu na 不実な: a false friend (*fujitsu na tomo*) 不実な友.

fame *n.* **1** (being well-known) me⌈esee 名声: come into fame (*yuumee ni naru*) 有名になる.
2 (reputation) hyo⌈obañ 評判: good fame (*yoi hyoobañ*) よい評判.

familiar *adj.* **1** (well-known) yo⌉ku shi⌈rarete iru よく知られている; o-⌈najimi no おなじみの: a familiar song (*o-najimi no uta*) おなじみの歌.
2 (knowing about) shi⌈tte iru 知っている: I am not very familiar with Japanese history. (*Nihoñ no rekishi wa amari yoku shirimaseñ.*) 日本の歴史はあまりよく知りません.
3 (too friendly) u⌈chitoketa 打ち解けた; u⌈chitokete iru 打ち解けている; ku⌈da⌉keta くだけた; ku⌈da⌉kete iru くだけている: a familiar greeting (*uchitoketa aisatsu*) 打ち解けたあいさつ.

familiarity *n.* **1** (close friendship) shi⌈tashimi 親しみ; shi⌈ñkoo 親交: treat one's friend with familiarity (*tomodachi o shitashimi o komete atsukau*) 友だちを親しみをこめて扱う.
2 (being familiar) yo⌉ku shi⌈tte iru koto⌉ よく知っていること; se⌈etsuu 精通: I admire his familiarity with many languages. (*Kare ga ooku no kotoba o shitte iru no ni kañshiñ suru.*) 彼が多くの言葉を知っているのに感心する.

family *n.* **1** (parents and children) ka⌉zoku 家族; se⌈ta⌉i 世帯: We are a family of five in all. (*Watashi no kazoku wa zeñbu de go-niñ desu.*) 私の家族は全部で 5 人です. / Six families live in this apartment house. (*Kono appaato ni wa roku-setai ga suñde imasu.*) このアパートには 6 世帯が住んでいます.
2 (children) ko⌈domo⌉-tachi 子どもたち: He has a large family. (*Kare wa kodomo ga takusañ iru.*) 彼は子どもがたくさんいる.
3 (lineage) i⌈egara 家柄: a person of respectable family (*rippa na iegara no hito*) 立派な家柄の人.
— *adj.* ka⌉zoku no 家族の; ka⌈tee no 家庭の: a family hotel (*kazoku muki no hoteru*) 家族向きのホテル / family life (*katee-seekatsu*) 家庭生活.

family name *n.* se⌉e 姓; myo⌉oji 名字.

famine *n.* ki⌉kiñ ききん: Many people are suffering from famine. (*Oozee no hito ga kikiñ de kurushiñde iru.*) 大勢の人がききんで苦しんでいる.

famous *adj.* yu⌈umee na 有名な: Kyoto is famous for its old temples and shrines. (*Kyooto wa furui tera ya jiñja de yuumee desu.*) 京都は古い寺や神社で有名です. / famous spots (*meesho*) 名所.

fan[1] *n.* (waved in the hand) u⌈chi⌉wa うちわ; (folding fan) se⌈ñsu 扇子; (electric fan) se⌈ñpu⌉uki 扇風機.
— *vt.* ... o a⌈o⌉gu ...をあおぐ Ⓒ: He fanned his face with a hat. (*Kare wa booshi de kao o aoida.*) 彼は帽子で顔をあおいだ.

fan[2] *n.* fa⌉ñ ファン: a baseball fan (*yakyuu fañ*) 野球ファン.

fancy *adj.* **1** (decorated) so⌈oshoku-teki na 装飾的な; ha⌈de⌉ na 派手な: This dress is too fancy for me. (*Kono doresu wa watashi ni wa hade-sugimasu.*) このドレスは私には派手すぎます. / fancy cakes (*dekoreeshoñ keeki*) デコレーションケーキ.
2 (superior) go⌈kujoo no 極上の; to⌈kuseñ no 特選の: fancy fruits (*gokujoo no kudamono*) 極上の果物.
— *n.* **1** (fondness) ko⌈nomi⌉ 好み; a⌈ikoo 愛好: This tie suits my fancy. (*Kono nekutai wa watashi

no konomi ni atte imasu.) このネクタイは私の好みに合っています.
2 (imagination) ku⌈usoo 空想; ge⌈ñ-soo 幻想: a story based on fancy (*kuusoo ni motozuita hanashi*) 空想に基づいた話.
— *vt.* **1** (imagine) ... o so⌈ozoo suru ...を想像する [I]; ku⌈usoo suru 空想する [I]: I cannot fancy her doing such a thing. (*Kanojo ga soñna koto o suru nañte soozoo dekinai.*) 彼女がそんなことをするなんて想像できない.
2 (think) ... to o⌈mo⌉u ...と思う [C]: I fancy she is about thirty. (*Kanojo wa sañjuu gurai da to omoimasu.*) 彼女は30ぐらいだと思います.

fantastic *adj.* **1** (marvelous) su⌈barashi⌉i すばらしい; su⌈teki na すてきな: a fantastic view (*subarashii nagame*) すばらしい眺め.
2 (extravagant) to⌈hoo mo na⌉i 途方もない; to⌈tetsu mo na⌉i とてつもない: a fantastic price (*tohoo mo nai nedañ*) 途方もない値段.
3 (wild) fu⌈uga⌉wari na 風変わりな: a fantastic house (*fuugawari na ie*) 風変わりな家.

fantasy *n.* ku⌈usoo 空想; ge⌈ñsoo 幻想: a world of fantasy (*geñsoo no sekai*) 幻想の世界.

far *adv.* **1** (of a place, distance, etc.) to⌈oku⌉ ni [e] 遠くに[へ]: He hasn't gone so far. (*Kare wa soñna ni tooku e wa itte imaseñ.*) 彼はそんなに遠くへは行っていません. / How far is it to the station? (*Eki made dono kurai arimasu ka?*) 駅までどのくらいありますか.
2 (of time, degree, etc.) ha⌉ruka ni はるかに; zu⌈tto ずっと: His car is far better than mine. (*Kare no kuruma wa watashi no yori haruka ni yoi.*) 彼の車は私のよりはるかによい.
as far as ... *prep.* ... ma⌉de ...まで: I drove as far as Nagoya on Sunday. (*Watashi wa nichiyoo ni Nagoya made kuruma de itta.*) 私は日曜に名古屋まで車で行った.
so far *adv.* i⌈ma ma⌉de 今まで: So far everything has gone off well. (*Ima made no tokoro subete umaku ikimashita.*) 今までのところすべてうまくいきました.
— *adj.* to⌈oi 遠い: Is the hotel far from here? (*Sono hoteru wa koko kara tooi desu ka?*) そのホテルはここから遠いですか.

fare *n.* u⌉ñchiñ 運賃; ryo⌉okiñ 料金: a taxi fare (*takushii ryookiñ*) タクシー料金 / How much is the fare? (*Ryookiñ wa ikura desu ka?*) 料金はいくらですか.

farewell *n.* wa⌈kare⌉ 別れ: a farewell speech (*wakare no aisatsu*) 別れのあいさつ / a farewell party (*soobetsukai*) 送別会.

farm *n.* **1** (area) no⌈ojoo 農場; no⌈oeñ 農園: work on a farm (*noojoo de hataraku*) 農場で働く.
2 (place where animals are bred) shi⌈ikujoo 飼育場: a chicken farm (*yookeejoo*) 養鶏場.
— *vt.* ... o ko⌈osaku suru ...を耕作する [I]: He farms 50 ares. (*Kare wa gojuu-aaru no tochi o koosaku shite imasu.*) 彼は50アールの土地を耕作しています.
— *vi.* no⌉ogyoo o i⌈tona⌉mu 農業を営む [C].

farmer *n.* no⌈ojo⌉onushi 農場主; no⌈ojoo-kee-e⌉esha 農場経営者.

farming *n.* no⌉ogyoo 農業.

farther *adv.* sa⌉ra ni to⌈oku⌉ ni さらに遠くに; mo⌉tto sa⌈ki ni もっと先に: I can walk no farther. (*Moo kore ijoo arukemaseñ.*) もうこれ以上歩けません.
— *adj.* sa⌉ra ni to⌈oku⌉ no さらに遠くの; mo⌉tto sa⌈ki no もっと先の: The station was farther than we had thought. (*Eki wa omotta yori mo sara ni tookatta.*) 駅は思ったよりもさらに遠かった.

farthest *adv.* mo⌈tto⌉mo to⌈oku⌉ ni もっとも遠くに: He was able to throw the ball farthest. (*Kare ga ichibañ tooku made booru o nagerareta.*) 彼がいちばん遠くまでボールを投げられた.
— *adj.* mo⌈tto⌉mo to⌈oi もっとも遠

い: the farthest planet (*mottomo tooi wakusee*) もっとも遠い惑星.

fascinate *vt*. ... o mi⌈ryoo suru ... を魅了する Ⓘ; ... no ko⌈ko⌉ro o u⌈ba⌉u ...の心を奪う Ⓒ: He was fascinated with her beauty. (*Kare wa kanojo no utsukushisa ni kokoro o ubawareta.*) 彼は彼女の美しさに心を奪われた.

fascinating *adj*. mi⌈waku-teki na 魅惑的な; su⌈go⌉ku o⌈moshiro⌉i すごくおもしろい: I found his story fascinating. (*Kare no hanashi wa sugoku omoshirokatta.*) 彼の話はすごくおもしろかった.

fashion *n*. **1** (style) ryu⌈ukoo 流行; fa⌉sshoñ ファッション: She was dressed in the latest fashion. (*Kanojo wa saishiñ ryuukoo no fuku o kite ita.*) 彼女は最新流行の服を着ていた.

2 (manner) ya⌈rikata やり方; shi⌈kata 仕方: He has a strange fashion of speaking. (*Kare wa myoo na hanashikata o suru.*) 彼は妙な話し方をする.

fashionable *adj*. ryu⌈ukoo no 流行の; ha⌈ikara na ハイカラな: a fashionable hairdo (*ryuukoo no heasutairu*) 流行のヘアスタイル.

fast *adj*. **1** (quick) ha⌈ya⌉i 速[早]い; su⌈baya⌉i すばやい: a fast horse (*hayai uma*) 速い馬 / a fast worker (*shigoto no hayai hito*) 仕事の早い人. ★ The kanji '速' is used in reference to 'velocity.'

2 (of a clock) su⌈suñde iru 進んでいる: This clock is five minutes fast. (*Kono tokee wa go-fuñ susuñde iru.*) この時計は5分進んでいる.

3 (firmly fixed) ko⌈tee shita [shite iru] 固定した[している]; (secure) shi⌈kka⌉ri shita [shite iru] しっかりした[している]: make a door fast (*doa o shikkari shimeru*) ドアをしっかり閉める.

4 (of colors) he⌈ñshoku shinai 変色しない; a⌈se⌉nai あせない: a fast color (*asenai iro*) あせない色.

— *adv*. **1** (quickly) ha⌉yaku 速く: He ran as quickly as possible. (*Kare wa dekiru dake hayaku hashitta.*) 彼はできるだけ速く走った.

2 (securely) ka⌈taku 堅く; shi⌈kka⌉ri to しっかりと: bind a rope fast (*tsuna o shikkari shibaru*) 綱をしっかり縛る.

fasten *vt*. **1** (fix firmly) ... o shi⌈kka⌉ri to⌈meru ...をしっかり留める Ⓥ; shi⌈me⌉ru 締める Ⓥ: Please fasten your seat belt. (*Shiito-beruto o shimete kudasai.*) シートベルトを締めてください.

2 (close firmly) ... o shi⌈kka⌉ri shi⌈me⌉ru ...をしっかり閉める Ⓥ: Have you fastened all the windows? (*Mado wa zeñbu shikkari shimemashita ka?*) 窓は全部しっかり閉めましたか.

3 (direct one's looks) ... o ji⌈tto mi⌉ru ...をじっと見る Ⓥ: The child fastened his eyes on me. (*Sono ko wa watashi o jitto mita.*) その子は私をじっと見た.

— *vi*. shi⌈ma⌉ru 閉まる Ⓒ: This door will not fasten. (*Kono to wa doo shite mo shimaranai.*) この戸はどうしても閉まらない.

fat *adj*. **1** (plump) fu⌈to⌉tta 太った; fu⌈to⌉tte iru 太っている: a fat man (*futotta otoko no hito*) 太った男の人 / grow fat (*futoru*) 太る.

2 (greasy) shi⌈boo no [ga] o⌉oi 脂肪の[が]多い; a⌈burakko⌉i 脂っこい: fat meat (*shiboo no ooi niku*) 脂肪の多い肉.

3 (thick) fu⌈kureta ふくれた; fu⌈kurete iru ふくれている; bu⌈atsui 分厚い: a fat wallet (*o-kane de fukureta saifu*) お金でふくれた財布.

— *n*. **1** (used for cooking) a⌈bura 油: fry potatoes in deep fat (*jagaimo o abura de ageru*) じゃがいもを油で揚げる.

2 (formed on the body) shi⌈boo 脂肪: put on fat (*shiboo ga tsuku*) 脂肪がつく.

fatal *adj*. **1** (causing death) chi⌈mee-teki na 致命的な: a fatal wound (*chimee-shoo*) 致命傷.

2 (decisive) u⌉ñmee no 運命の: the

fatal day (*uñmee o kessuru hi*) 運命を決する日.

3 (disastrous) ju⌈udai na 重大な; to⌈rikaeshi no [ga] tsuka⌉nai 取り返しの[が]つかない: make a fatal mistake (*torikaeshi no tsukanai machigai o suru*) 取り返しのつかない間違いをする.

fate *n.* **1** (destiny) u⌉ñmee 運命; shu⌈kumee 宿命: He abandoned himself to his fate. (*Kare wa uñmee ni mi o makaseta.*) 彼は運命に身を任せた.

2 (future) yu⌈kusue 行く末; sho⌉orai 将来: Nobody knows what fate has in store. (*Shoorai doo naru ka dare ni mo wakaranai.*) 将来どうなるかだれにもわからない.

3 (death) shi⌉ 死; sa⌉igo 最期: meet one's fate (*saigo o togeru*) 最期を遂げる.

father *n.* **1** (male parent) chi⌉chi 父; chi⌈chioya 父親; (someone else's) o-⌈to⌉osañ お父さん: My father is a policeman. (*Watashi no chichi wa keesatsukañ desu.*) 私の父は警察官です. / He takes after his father. (*Kare wa o-toosañ ni nite iru.*) 彼はお父さんに似ている.

2 (founder) so⌈oshi⌉sha 創始者; chi⌉chi 父: the Father of Medicine (*igaku no chichi*) 医学の父.

3 (priest) shi⌉ñpu 神父.

fatigue *n.* tsu⌈kare⌉ 疲れ; hi⌈roo 疲労: He became ill with fatigue. (*Kare wa hiroo de byooki ni natta.*) 彼は疲労で病気になった.

faucet *n.* ja⌈guchi 蛇口; se⌉ñ 栓: turn on [off] a faucet (*jaguchi o hinette akeru* [*shimeru*]) 蛇口をひねって開ける[閉める].

fault *n.* **1** (responsibility) (ka⌈shitsu no) se⌈kiniñ (過失の)責任: The fault lies with me. (*Sono sekiniñ wa watashi ni arimasu.*) その責任は私にあります.

2 (imperfection) ke⌈tte⌉ñ 欠点; ke⌈kkañ 欠陥: Everyone has their faults. (*Dare ni mo ketteñ wa aru.*) だれにも欠点はある.

3 (error) a⌈yamari⌉ 誤り; ka⌈shitsu 過失: a fault in grammar (*buñpoojoo no ayamari*) 文法上の誤り.

favor *n.* **1** (kindness) ko⌉oi 好意; shi⌉ñsetsu 親切: I have to return his favor. (*Kare no kooi ni mukuinakereba naranai.*) 彼の好意に報いなければならない.

2 (support) shi⌉ji 支持; sa⌈ñsee 賛成: I am in favor of your plan. (*Watashi wa anata no keekaku ni sañsee desu.*) 私はあなたの計画に賛成です.

3 (unfair partiality) e⌈kohi⌉iki えこひいき: show favor to a person (*hito o ekohiiki suru*) 人をえこひいきする.

ask a favor of ... *vt.* ... ni o-⌈negai suru ...にお願いする Ⓘ: I have a favor to ask of you. (*O-negai ga aru no desu ga.*) お願いがあるのですが.

— *vt.* **1** (show favor to) ... ni ko⌉oi o shi⌈me⌉su ...に好意を示す Ⓒ; sa⌈ñsee suru 賛成する Ⓘ: favor a proposal (*teeañ ni sañsee suru*) 提案に賛成する.

2 (show unfair partiality to) ... o e⌈kohi⌉iki suru ...をえこひいきする Ⓘ; ka⌈waiga⌉ru かわいがる Ⓒ: favor the youngest child (*ichibañ shita no ko o kawaigaru*) いちばん下の子をかわいがる.

favorable *adj.* **1** (showing approval) ko⌈oi-teki na 好意的な; sa⌈ñsee suru 賛成する: I got a favorable answer from him. (*Watashi wa kare kara kooi-teki na heñji o moratta.*) 私は彼から好意的な返事をもらった.

2 (helpful) ko⌈otsu⌉goo na 好都合な; (promising) yu⌈uboo na 有望な: The weather was favorable for hiking. (*Teñkoo wa haikiñgu ni kootsugoo datta.*) 天候はハイキングに好都合だった.

favorite *adj.* o-⌈kiniiri no お気に入りの; i⌈chibañ suki⌉ na いちばん好きな: Who is your favorite singer? (*Anata no ichibañ suki na kashu wa dare desu ka?*) あなたのいちばん好きな歌手はだれですか.

— *n.* o⌈kiniiri お気に入り; (person) ni⌈ñkimono 人気者; (thing) ko⌉obutsu 好物: Sashimi is a favorite of mine. (*Sashimi wa watashi no koobutsu desu.*) 刺し身は私の好物です.

fear *n.* **1** (dread) o⌈sore⌉ 恐れ; kyo⌉ofu 恐怖: I trembled in fear. (*Watashi wa kyoofu de furueta.*) 私は恐怖で震えた.
2 (anxiety) fu⌈añ 不安; shi⌈ñpai 心配: There is no fear of rain today. (*Kyoo wa ame no shiñpai wa nai.*) きょうは雨の心配はない.
— *vt.* **1** (be uneasy) ... o ki⌈zuka⌉u …を気づかう [C]; shi⌈ñpai suru 心配する [I]: He feared that he would fail. (*Kare wa shippai shinai ka to shiñpai datta.*) 彼は失敗しないかと心配だった.
2 (be afraid of) ... o o⌈sore⌉ru …を恐れる [V]; ko⌈waga⌉ru 怖がる [C]: Animals fear fire. (*Doobutsu wa hi o kowagaru.*) 動物は火を怖がる.

fearful *adj.* **1** (terrible) o⌈soroshi⌉i 恐ろしい; mo⌈nosugo⌉i ものすごい: a fearful accident (*osoroshii jiko*) 恐ろしい事故.
2 (afraid) (... o) o⌈so⌉rete (iru) (…を)恐れて(いる); ko⌈waga⌉tte (iru) 怖がって(いる): She was fearful of walking in the dark. (*Kanojo wa kurayami no naka o aruku no o kowagatta.*) 彼女は暗闇の中を歩くのを怖がった.
3 (very bad) hi⌈do⌉i ひどい; ta⌈iheñ na 大変な: make a fearful mistake (*hidoi machigai o suru*) ひどい間違いをする.

fearless *adj.* o⌈sore⌉nai 恐れない; da⌈ita⌉ñ na 大胆な: He was fearless of danger. (*Kare wa kikeñ o osorenakatta.*) 彼は危険を恐れなかった.

feast *n.* **1** (banquet) shu⌈kueñ 祝宴; e⌈ñkai 宴会: give a gorgeous wedding feast (*gooka na kekkoñ no shukueñ o moyoosu*) 豪華な結婚の祝宴を催す.
2 (splendid meal) go⌈chisoo ごちそう: She prepared a feast for us. (*Kanojo wa watashi-tachi ni gochisoo o tsukutte kureta.*) 彼女は私たちにごちそうを作ってくれた.
3 (religious festival) shu⌈kujitsu 祝日; sa⌈ijitsu 祭日.
— *vt.* **1** (give a feast) ... ni go⌈chisoo o suru …にごちそうをする [I]; ... o mo⌈tena⌉su …をもてなす [C]: feast one's guests (*o-kyaku o motenasu*) お客をもてなす.
2 (give pleasure) ... o ta⌈noshimase⌉ru …を楽しませる [V]: feast one's eyes on a painting (*e o mite tanoshimu*) 絵を見て楽しむ.

feather *n.* ha⌈ne 羽; u⌈moo 羽毛.

feature *n.* **1** (characteristic) to⌈kuchoo 特徴; to⌈kushoku 特色: geographical features (*chiri-teki tokuchoo*) 地理的特徴.
2 (special article) to⌈kushuu ki⌉ji 特集記事: a feature in a magazine (*zasshi no tokushuu kiji*) 雑誌の特集記事.
3 (of a movie, TV, etc.) yo⌈bimono 呼び物: a main feature on the program (*puroguramu no yobimono*) プログラムの呼び物.
4 (the face as a whole) ka⌈odachi 顔立ち; yo⌉oboo 容貌: a man of regular features (*kaodachi no totonotta otoko no hito*) 顔立ちの整った男の人.
— *vt.* **1** (of an article) ... o to⌈kushuu suru …を特集する [I]: a magazine featuring overseas travel (*kaigai-ryokoo o tokushuu shita zasshi*) 海外旅行を特集した雑誌.
2 (of a movie, TV, etc.) ... o shu⌈eñ saseru …を主演させる [V]: The movie featured a new actress. (*Sono eega wa shiñjiñ-joyuu o shueñ saseta.*) その映画は新人女優を主演させた.

February *n.* ni-⌈gatsu⌉ 2月.

federal *adj.* re⌈ñgoo no 連合の; re⌈ñpoo no 連邦の: a federal government (*reñpoo seefu*) 連邦政府.

federation *n.* re⌈ñpoo 連邦; re⌈ñmee 連盟.

fee *n.* **1** (payment for a professional service) sha⌈ree 謝礼; ho⌈o-

shuu 報酬; -ryoo 料: a lawyer's fee (*beñgo-ryoo*) 弁護料.
2 (fixed charge) ryoˡokiñ 料金; -ryoo 料: What is the fee per day? (*Ichi-nichi no ryookiñ wa ikura desu ka?*) 1日の料金はいくらですか. / an admission fee (*nyuujoo-ryoo*) 入場料.

feeble *adj.* **1** (weak) yoˊwaˡi 弱い; yoˊwayowashiˡi 弱々しい: a feeble old man (*yowayowashii roojiñ*) 弱弱しい老人.
2 (faint) kaˡsuka na かすかな: I heard a feeble cry. (*Watashi wa kasuka na sakebigoe o kiita.*) 私はかすかな叫び声を聞いた.

feed *vt.* **1** (give food to) ... ni taˊbe-moˡno o aˊtaeru …に食べ物を与える Ⓥ; (of animals) ... ni eˊsaˡ o yaˊru …にえさをやる Ⓒ: She fed her baby with a spoon. (*Kanojo wa akañboo ni saji de tabesaseta.*) 彼女は赤ん坊にさじで食べさせた. / Do not feed the animals. (*Doobutsu ni esa o yara-naide kudasai.*) 動物にえさをやらないでください.
2 (supply) ... o kyoˊokyuu suru …を供給する Ⓘ; iˊreru 入れる Ⓥ: feed data into a computer (*koñpyuutaa ni deeta o ireru*) コンピューターにデータを入れる.
— *vi.* (eat) moˊnoˡ o taˊbeˡru ものを食べる Ⓥ: The cows are feeding in the pasture. (*Ushi ga bokujoo de kusa o tabete iru.*) 牛が牧場で草を食べている.
— *n.* eˊsaˡ えさ; shiˊryoo 飼料.

feel *vi.* **1** (be aware of) kaˊñjiru 感じる Ⓥ: I feel very cold. (*Watashi wa totemo samui.*) 私はとても寒い.
2 (be in a state) kiˡbuñ ga ... da 気分が…だ: How do you feel today? (*Kyoo wa kibuñ wa ikaga desu ka?*) きょうは気分はいかがですか. / I don't feel well. (*Kibuñ ga yoku ari-maseñ.*) 気分がよくありません.
3 (think) (... to) oˊmoˡu (…と)思う Ⓒ: I feel sure of his success. (*Kare wa kitto seekoo suru to omoimasu.*) 彼はきっと成功すると思います.
4 (search) (... o) saˊgasu (…を)探す Ⓒ: I felt in my pocket for the key. (*Watashi wa poketto no naka no kii o sagashita.*) 私はポケットの中のキーを捜した.
— *vt.* **1** (touch) ... ni saˊwatte miˡru …に触ってみる Ⓒ: feel a pulse (*myaku ni sawatte miru*) 脈に触ってみる.
2 (perceive) ... o kaˊñjiru …を感じる Ⓥ: I felt the house shake. (*Watashi wa ie ga yureru no o kañjita.*) 私は家が揺れるのを感じた.
3 (consider) ... to oˊmoˡu …と思う Ⓒ; ... yoˡo na ki ga suru …ような気がする Ⓘ: I feel that he will come. (*Watashi wa kare ga kuru yoo na ki ga suru.*) 私は彼が来るような気がする.
feel like ... *vt.* ⟨verb⟩-tai ki ga suru …たい気がする Ⓘ: I don't feel like eating a meal. (*Shokuji wa tabetaku arimaseñ.*) 食事は食べたくありません.

feeling *n.* **1** (state of mind) kaˊñji 感じ; kiˊmochi 気持ち: a feeling of gratitude (*kañsha no kimochi*) 感謝の気持ち.
2 (emotions) kaˊñjoo 感情; kiˡbuñ 気分: hurt a person's feelings (*hito no kañjoo o gaisuru*) 人の感情を害する.
3 (impression) kaˊñji 感じ; iˊñshoo 印象: I have a feeling that he is working too hard. (*Kare wa hatara-kisugi no yoo na kañji ga suru.*) 彼は働き過ぎのような感じがする.
4 (power to feel) kaˊñkaku 感覚: I lost all feeling in my fingers. (*Wa-tashi wa yubi no kañkaku ga suk-kari nakunatta.*) 私は指の感覚がすっかりなくなった.

fellow *n.* **1** (man) oˊtokoˡ 男; yaˡtsu やつ: He is a pleasant fellow. (*Kare wa yukai na otoko da.*) 彼は愉快な男だ. / a stupid fellow (*baka na yatsu*) ばかなやつ.
2 (comrade) naˊkamaˡ 仲間; doˊo-ryoo 同僚: a fellow student (*ga-kuyuu*) 学友 / a fellow worker (*shi-*

f

goto nakama) 仕事仲間.

fellowship *n.* **1** (friendly association) shi⌈ñkoo 親交; shi⌈ñboku 親睦: enjoy fellowship with people (*hito to shiñkoo o musubu*) 人と親交を結ぶ.
2 (group) da⌈ñtai 団体; ku⌈miai 組合.
3 (money) sho⌈ogakukiñ 奨学金: receive a fellowship (*shoogakukiñ o morau*) 奨学金をもらう.

f

female *adj.* (of people) jo⌈see no 女性の; (of animals) me⌈su⌉ no 雌の: a female child (*oñna-no-ko*) 女の子 / a female dog (*mesu-inu*) 雌犬.
— *n.* (of a person) jo⌈see 女性; (of an animal) me⌈su⌉ 雌.

feminine *adj.* jo⌈see no 女性の; o⌈ñna-rashi⌉i 女らしい: feminine beauty (*joseebi*) 女性美 / a feminine gesture (*oñna-rashii shigusa*) 女らしいしぐさ.

fence *n.* ka⌈koi 囲い; sa⌈ku⌉ さく; ka⌈ki⌉ 垣; fe⌉ñsu フェンス: put up a fence around a garden (*niwa no mawari ni saku o tateru*) 庭の回りにさくを立てる.
— *vt.* ... ni ka⌈koi o suru ...に囲いをする [I]; sa⌈ku⌉ o me⌈gurasu さくを巡らす [C]: I fenced my field. (*Watashi wa hatake ni kakoi o shita.*) 私は畑に囲いをした.

fencing *n.* (with a sword) fe⌉ñshiñgu フェンシング; ke⌈ñjutsu 剣術: Japanese fencing (*keñdoo*) 剣道.

ferocious *adj.* do⌈omoo na どうもうな; kyo⌈oboo na 凶暴な: a ferocious animal (*doomoo na doobutsu*) どうもうな動物.

ferry *n.* fe⌉rii フェリー; re⌈ñrakuseñ 連絡船; wa⌈tashibu⌉ne 渡し船: take a ferry (*ferii de iku*) フェリーで行く.
— *vt.* ... o fu⌉ne de wa⌈tasu ...を船で渡す [C]; ha⌈kobu 運ぶ [C]: ferry people across a river (*hito o fune de kawa o watasu*) 人を船で川を渡す.

fertile *adj.* **1** (of land) ko⌉eta 肥えた; ko⌉ete iru 肥えている; hi⌈yoku na 肥沃な: fertile land (*hiyoku na tochi*) 肥沃な土地.
2 (of mind) yu⌉taka na 豊かな: a fertile imagination (*yutaka na soozooryoku*) 豊かな想像力.

festival *n.* **1** (day) shu⌈kujitsu 祝日; sa⌈ijitsu 祭日.
2 (performances) mo⌈yooshi 催し; ma⌈tsuri 祭り; fe⌉sutibaru フェスティバル; -sai 祭: a music festival (*oñgaku-sai*) 音楽祭.

fetch *vt.* (of a thing) ... o to⌉tte kuru ...を取って来る [I]; (of a person) ... o tsu⌈rete kuru ...を連れて来る [I]: Please fetch me my glasses. (*Megane o totte kite kudasai.*) 眼鏡を取って来てください. / If you would like to meet her, I will fetch her. (*Moshi kanojo ni aitai nara tsurete kimasu yo.*) もし彼女に会いたいなら連れて来ますよ.

fever *n.* **1** (high body temperature) ne⌈tsu⌉ 熱: I have a fever. (*Watashi wa netsu ga aru.*) 私は熱がある.
2 (excitement) ko⌈ofuñ 興奮; ne⌈kkyoo 熱狂: The spectators were in a fever of excitement. (*Kañkyaku wa nekkyoo shite ita.*) 観客は熱狂していた.

few *adj.* **1** (not many) su⌈ko⌉shi shika na⌉i 少ししかない; ho⌈to⌉ñdo na⌉i ほとんどない: I have few friends. (*Watashi ni wa yuujiñ ga hotoñdo imaseñ.*) 私には友人がほとんどいません.
2 (a small number of) sho⌈osu⌉u no 少数の; wa⌉zuka no わずかの: A few people were in the room. (*Wazuka no hito ga sono heya ni imashita.*) わずかの人がその部屋にいました.
— *pron.* sho⌈osu⌉u 少数: Few understood his theories. (*Hoñ no shoosuu no hito shika kare no riroñ o rikai dekinakatta.*) ほんの少数の人しか彼の理論を理解できなかった.

fiancé(e) *n.* ko⌈ñya⌉kusha 婚約者.

fiber *n.* se⌉ñi 繊維: fibers of cotton (*momeñ no señi*) 木綿の繊維.

fiction *n.* **1** (novel) sho⌈osetsu 小説: a writer of fiction (*shoosetsuka*) 小説家.
2 (invented story) tsu⌈kuri-ba⌉na-

shi 作り話: What he says is a fiction. (*Kare ga itte iru koto wa tsukuri-banashi da.*) 彼が言っていることは作り話だ.

field *n.* **1** (for growing crops) ha⌈take 畑; ta⌉ 田: a wheat field (*komugi-batake*) 小麦畑 / a rice field (*tañbo*) たんぼ.

2 (wide area) no⌉ 野; ha⌉ra 原; no⌉hara 野原: field flowers (*no no hana*) 野の花 / pick flowers in a field (*nohara de hana o tsumu*) 野原で花を摘む.

3 (area for sports) kyo⌈ogijoo 競技場; fi⌈irudo フィールド: a playing field (*uñdoojoo*) 運動場.

4 (area of study) bu⌉ñya 分野; ryo⌈oiki 領域: Many people are working in this field. (*Ooku no hito ga kono buñya de hataraite imasu.*) 多くの人がこの分野で働いています.

5 (area of battle) se⌈ñjoo 戦場.

fierce *adj.* **1** (violent) kyo⌈oboo na 凶暴な; o⌈soroshi⌉i 恐ろしい: have a fierce look (*osoroshii kao o suru*) 恐ろしい顔をする.

2 (intense) mo⌈oretsu na 猛烈な; ha⌈geshi⌉i 激しい: a fierce storm (*mooretsu na arashi*) 猛烈な嵐.

fifteen *pron.* ju⌉ugo 15; (people) ju⌉ugo-niñ 15 人; (things) ju⌉ugo-ko 15 個.

— *n.* (figure) ju⌉ugo 15; (hour) ju⌉ugo-ji 15 時; (minute) ju⌉ugo-fuñ 15 分; (age) ju⌉ugo-sai 15 歳.

— *adj.* ju⌉ugo no 15 の; (people) ju⌉ugo-niñ no 15 人の; (things) ju⌉ugo-ko no 15 個の; (age) ju⌉ugo-sai no 15 歳の.

fifteenth *adj.* ju⌈ugo-bañme⌉ no 15 番目の; da⌉i-juugo no 第 15 の.

— *n.* **1** (people) ju⌈ugo-bañme⌉ no hi⌈to⌉ 15 番目の人; (things) ju⌈ugo-bañme⌉ no mo⌈no⌉ 15 番目のもの.

2 (day) ju⌉ugo-nichi 15 日.

3 (fraction) ju⌈ugo-buñ no ichi⌉ 15 分の 1.

fifth *adj.* go-⌈bañme⌉ no 5 番目の; da⌉i-go no 第 5 の.

— *n.* **1** (people) go-⌈bañme⌉ no hi⌈to⌉ 5 番目の人; (things) go-⌈bañme no mono⌉ 5 番目のもの.

2 (day) i⌈tsuka 5 日.

3 (fraction) go-⌈buñ no ichi⌉ 5 分の 1.

fiftieth *adj.* go⌈juu-bañme⌉ no 50 番目の; da⌉i-go⌈ju⌉u no 第 50 の.

— *n.* **1** (people) go⌈juu-bañme⌉ no hi⌈to⌉ 50 番目の人; (things) go⌈juu-bañme⌉ no mo⌈no⌉ 50 番目のもの.

2 (fraction) go⌈juu-buñ no ichi⌉ 50 分の 1.

fifty *pron.* go⌈ju⌉u 50; (people) go⌈ju⌉u-niñ 50 人; (things) go⌈ju⌉k-ko 50 個.

— *n.* (figure) go⌈ju⌉u 50; (minute) go⌈ju⌉p-puñ 50 分; (age) go⌈ju⌉s-sai 50 歳.

— *adj.* go⌈ju⌉u no 50 の; (people) go⌈ju⌉u-niñ no 50 人の; (things) go⌈ju⌉k-ko no 50 個の; (age) go⌈ju⌉s-sai no 50 歳の.

fig *n.* (fruit) i⌈chi⌉jiku いちじく; (tree) i⌈chi⌉jiku no ki いちじくの木.

fight *vi.* **1** (combat) ta⌈takau 戦う [C]: fight against an enemy (*teki to tatakau*) 敵と戦う.

2 (box) na⌈guria⌉u 殴り合う [C]; ke⌈ñka suru けんかする [I]: Two men were fighting on the street. (*Futari no otoko ga toori de keñka shite ita.*) 2 人の男が通りでけんかしていた.

3 (quarrel) ko⌉roñ suru 口論する [I]; i⌈iaraso⌉u 言い争う [C]: They are always fighting. (*Kare-ra wa itsumo iiarasotte iru.*) 彼らはいつも言い争っている.

— *vt.* (struggle) ... to ta⌈takau ...と戦う [C]; ... o a⌈raso⌉u ...を争う [C]: fight inflation (*iñfure to tatakau*) インフレと戦う / fight a losing battle (*makeikusa o tatakau*) 負け戦を戦う.

— *n.* **1** (battle) ta⌈takai 戦い: win [lose] a fight (*tatakai ni katsu* [*makeru*]) 戦いに勝つ[負ける].

2 (struggle) ta⌈takai 闘い; to⌈osoo 闘争: a fight for higher pay (*chiñage-toosoo*) 賃上げ闘争.

fighter *n.* (person who fights) se⌉ñshi 戦士; (boxer) se⌉ñshu 選手; (plane) se⌈ñto⌉oki 戦闘機.

figure *n.* **1** (shape of a person) su⌉gata 姿; hi⌈tokage 人影; ka⌈kkoo 格好: a slender figure (***hossori shita sugata***) ほっそりした姿 / I saw a figure in the dark. (***Watashi wa kurayami no naka ni hitokage o mita.***) 私は暗闇の中に人影を見た.
2 (symbol for a number) su⌈uji 数字: Arabic figures (***Arabia-suuji***) アラビア数字 / double [three] figures (***futaketa*** [***miketa***] ***no suuji***) 2けた[3けた]の数字.
3 (diagram) zu 図; zu⌈kee 図形: The details are shown in figure 2. (***Shoosai wa zu ni ni shimesarete imasu.***) 詳細は図2に示されています.
4 (person) ji⌉ñbutsu 人物: a key figure (***chuushiñ jiñbutsu***) 中心人物.
5 (arithmetic) ke⌈esañ 計算; sa⌈ñsu⌉u 算数: He is good at figures. (***Kare wa keesañ ga tokui da.***) 彼は計算が得意だ.
— *vt.* **1** (think) ... to o⌈mo⌉u ...と思う [C]; ka⌈ñga⌉eru 考える [V]: I figured that he would be late. (***Kare wa okureru to omotte imashita.***) 彼は遅れると思っていました.
2 (calculate) ... o ke⌈esañ suru ...を計算する [I]: figure up a total (***keesañ shite gookee o dasu***) 計算して合計を出す.

file[1] *n.* (folder) to⌈jikomi とじ込み; fa⌉iru ファイル: a file of newspapers (***shiñbuñ no tojikomi***) 新聞のとじ込み.
— *vt.* ... o to⌈jikomu ...をとじ込む [C]; fa⌉iru suru ファイルする [I]: file away papers (***shorui o fairu suru***) 書類をファイルする.

file[2] *n.* (metal tool) ya⌈suri やすり.
— *vt.* ... ni ya⌈suri o kake⌉ru ...にやすりをかける [V]: file one's fingernails (***tsume ni yasuri o kakeru***) つめにやすりをかける.

fill *vt.* **1** (make full) ... o i⌈ppai ni suru ...をいっぱいにする [I]; mi⌈ta⌉su 満たす [C]: fill a bottle with water (***biñ ni mizu o ippai ni ireru***) びんに水をいっぱいに入れる / Sorrow filled my heart. (***Watashi no mune wa kanashimi de ippai datta.***) 私の胸は悲しみでいっぱいだった.
2 (stop up) ... o fu⌈sagu ...をふさぐ [C]; u⌈zumeru うずめる [V]: fill a crack with cement (***sakeme o semeñto de fusagu***) 裂け目をセメントでふさぐ.
— *vi.* i⌈ppai ni na⌉ru いっぱいになる [C]: The hall soon filled. (***Hooru wa sugu ni ippai ni natta.***) ホールはすぐにいっぱいになった.

fill in *vt.* (... ni) ... o ki⌈nyuu suru (...に)...を記入する [I]: Fill in your name on this form, please. (***Kono shorui ni namae o kinyuu shite kudasai.***) この書類に名前を記入してください.

film *n.* **1** (of a photo) fi⌉rumu フィルム: put a film into a camera (***kamera ni firumu o ireru***) カメラにフィルムを入れる / develop a film (***firumu o geñzoo suru***) フィルムを現像する / a 36-exposure roll of film (***sañjuu-roku-mai-dori no firumu***) 36枚撮りのフィルム / a film for color prints [slides] (***karaa-puriñto*** [***suraido***]-***yoo firumu***) カラープリント[スライド]用フィルム.
2 (motion picture) e⌉ega 映画: go to see a film (***eega o mi ni iku***) 映画を見に行く.
3 (thin covering) u⌈sumaku 薄膜; u⌈sukawa 薄皮: a film of oil (***abura no usui maku***) 油の薄い膜.
— *vt.* (make a motion picture) ... o sa⌈tsuee suru ...を撮影する [I]; e⌈ega-ka suru 映画化する [I]: film a novel (***shoosetsu o eega-ka suru***) 小説を映画化する.

filter *n.* (machine) ro⌈ka⌉ki ろ過器; (paper) fi⌉rutaa フィルター: clean water with a filter (***mizu o rokaki de jooka suru***) 水をろ過器で浄化する.
— *vt.* ... o ro⌉ka suru ...をろ過する [I]; ko⌈su こす [C]: filter oil (***abura o kosu***) 油をこす.
— *vi.* (of liquid) shi⌈mide⌉ru しみ出る [V]; (of light) sa⌈shiko⌉mu 差し込

む C: Sunlight filtered through the curtains. (*Hi no hikari ga kaateñ o tooshite sashikoñda.*) 日の光がカーテンを通して差し込んだ.

filthy *adj.* **1** (unclean) fu⌈ketsu na 不潔な; yo⌈goreta 汚れた; yo⌈gorete iru 汚れている: a filthy towel (*yogoreta taoru*) 汚れたタオル.
2 (obscene) mi⌉dara na みだらな; ge⌈hi⌉ñ na 下品な: a filthy story (*gehiñ na hanashi*) 下品な話.

final *adj.* sa⌉igo no 最後の; sa⌈ishuu-teki na 最終的な: the final chapter of a book (*hoñ no saigo no shoo*) 本の最後の章 / a final decision (*saishuu-kettee*) 最終決定.
— *n.* (of a game) ke⌈sshooseñ 決勝戦; (of an exam) sa⌈ishuu shike⌉ñ 最終試験.

finally *adv.* **1** (at last) tsu⌉i ni ついに; yo⌈oyaku ようやく: The engine finally started. (*Eñjiñ ga yooyaku kakatta.*) エンジンがようやくかかった.
2 (lastly) sa⌉igo ni 最後に: Finally, I'd like to say a few words. (*Saigo ni hitokoto mooshiagemasu.*) 最後に一言申し上げます.

finance *n.* (management) za⌈isee 財政; (money) za⌈igeñ 財源: an expert in finance (*zaisee no señmoñka*) 財政の専門家 / the Finance Minister (*ookura daijiñ*) 大蔵大臣.
— *vt.* ... ni shi⌉kiñ o dasu ...に資金を出す C: The company financed his trip. (*Kaisha ga kare no ryohi o dashite kureta.*) 会社が彼の旅費を出してくれた.

financial *adj.* za⌈isee(joo) no 財政(上)の; ki⌈ñyuu no 金融の: the financial condition of a company (*kaisha no zaisee jootai*) 会社の財政状態.

find *vt.* **1** (look for and get) ... o mi⌈tsukeru ...を見つける V; sa⌈gashida⌉su 捜し出す C: I found the key I lost. (*Watashi wa nakushita kii o mitsuketa.*) 私はなくしたキーを見つけた. / I can't find my baggage. (*Watashi no nimotsu ga mitsukarimaseñ.*) 私の荷物が見つかりません.
2 (come up by chance) ... o mi⌈tsukeru ...を見つける V: I found a 100 yen coin on the floor. (*Watashi wa yuka ni hyaku-eñ-dama o mitsuketa.*) 私は床に100円玉を見つけた.
3 (discover) ... o ha⌈kkeñ suru ...を発見する I: find a solution to a problem (*moñdai no kaiketsuhoo o hakkeñ suru*) 問題の解決法を発見する.
4 (learn) ... o shi⌈ru ...を知る C; ... ga wa⌈ka⌉ru ...がわかる C: I found it difficult to climb the mountain. (*Sono yama ni noboru no wa muzukashii koto ga wakatta.*) その山に登るのは難しいことがわかった.
5 (obtain) ... o te⌉ ni i⌈reru ...を手に入れる V; ... ga a⌉ru ...がある C: I cannot find the time to read a book. (*Hoñ o yomu jikañ ga nai.*) 本を読む時間がない.

fine[1] *adj.* **1** (very good) su⌈barashi⌉i すばらしい; mi⌉goto na 見事な; ri⌈ppa na 立派な: The view from here is fine. (*Koko kara no nagame wa subarashii.*) ここからの眺めはすばらしい.
2 (of weather) ha⌉reta 晴れた; ha⌉rete iru 晴れている; yo⌉i teñki no よい天気の: It is fine today. (*Kyoo wa yoi teñki da.*) きょうはよい天気だ.
3 (in good health) ge⌉ñki na 元気な: "How are you?" "Fine, thank you." (*"Genki desu ka?" "Okagesama de (geñki desu)."*)「元気ですか」「おかげさまで(元気です)」
4 (satisfactory) mo⌈oshibuñ na⌉i 申し分ない; ke⌉kkoo na 結構な: "Is this all right?" "That's fine." (*"Kore de yoroshii desu ka?" "Kekkoo desu."*)「これでよろしいですか」「結構です」
5 (thin) ho⌈so⌉i 細い: a fine thread (*hosoi ito*) 細い糸.
— *adv.* u⌉maku うまく; ri⌈ppa ni 立派に: He is doing fine. (*Kare wa umaku yatte imasu.*) 彼はうまくやっています.

fine[2] *n.* ba⌈kkiñ 罰金; ka⌈ryoo 科料: pay a fine (*bakkiñ o shiharau*) 罰金を支払う.

finger *n.* yu⌈bi⌉ 指: the index finger (*hitosashi-yubi*) 人差し指 / the middle finger (*naka-yubi*) 中指 / the ring finger (*kusuri-yubi*) 薬指 / the little finger (*ko-yubi*) 小指.
★ thumb (*oya-yubi*) 親指.

finish *vt.* **1** (bring to an end) ... o o⌈eru ...を終える [V]; su⌈ma⌉su 済ます [C]: I have finished my work. (*Shigoto wa oemashita.*) 仕事は終えました.
2 (consume) ... o ta⌈irage⌉ru ...を平らげる [V]: finish a cake (*keeki o tairageru*) ケーキを平らげる.
3 (make complete) ... no shi⌈age o suru ...の仕上げをする [I]: This painting is beautifully finished. (*Kono e wa utsukushiku shiagatte iru.*) この絵は美しく仕上がっている.
— *vi.* (come to an end) o⌈waru 終わる [C]; su⌉mu 済む [C]: The play finishes at eight. (*Shibai wa hachi-ji ni owarimasu.*) 芝居は8時に終わります.

fire *n.* **1** (flame) hi⌉ 火; ho⌉noo 炎: Fire burns. (*Hi wa moeru.*) 火は燃える.
2 (destructive burning) ka⌉ji 火事: A fire broke out in my neighborhood. (*Watashi no kiñjo de kaji ga atta.*) 私の近所で火事があった.
3 (burning fuel) hi⌉ 火: build a fire (*hi o okosu*) 火をおこす / put out a fire (*hi o kesu*) 火を消す.
— *vt.* **1** (shoot) ... o ha⌈ssha suru ...を発射する [I]; ha⌈ppoo suru 発砲する [I]: fire a gun (*juu o hassha suru*) 銃を発射する.
2 (dismiss) ... o ku⌈bi ni suru ...を首にする [I]; ka⌉iko suru 解雇する [I]: He got fired from his job. (*Kare wa shigoto o kubi ni natta.*) 彼は仕事を首になった.
3 (set fire) ... ni hi⌉ o tsu⌈ke⌉ru ...に火をつける [V]: fire a heap of dead leaves (*kareha no yama ni hi o tsukeru*) 枯れ葉の山に火をつける.

fire engine *n.* sho⌈obo⌉osha 消防車; sho⌈oboo-jido⌉osha 消防自動車.

fireman *n.* sho⌈obo⌉oshi 消防士.

fireplace *n.* da⌉ñro 暖炉.

fire station *n.* sho⌈oboosho 消防署.

fireworks *n.* ha⌉nabi 花火: set off fireworks (*hanabi o ageru*) 花火を上げる.

firm[1] *adj.* **1** (hard) ka⌈tai 堅い; (strong) ga⌈ñjoo na がんじょうな: firm ground (*katai jimeñ*) 堅い地面 / a firm chair (*gañjoo na isu*) がんじょうないす.
2 (steady) shi⌈kka⌉ri shita [shite iru] しっかりした[している]; ke⌈ñjitsu na 堅実な: walk with firm steps (*shikkari shita ashidori de aruku*) しっかりした足どりで歩く.
3 (decided) ki⌈ppa⌉ri shita [shite iru] きっぱりした[している]; da⌉ñko to shita [shite iru] 断固とした[している]: I gave a firm refusal. (*Watashi wa kippari kotowatta.*) 私はきっぱり断わった.

firm[2] *n.* sho⌉okai 商会; sho⌉osha 商社; ka⌈isha 会社: I work for this firm. (*Watashi wa kono kaisha ni tsutomete imasu.*) 私はこの会社に勤めています.

firmly *adv.* ka⌈taku 堅く; shi⌈kka⌉ri (to) しっかり(と): close a door firmly (*doa o shikkari shimeru*) ドアをしっかり閉める.

first *adj.* **1** (of time and place) i⌈chi-bañme⌉ no 1番目の; dai⌉-ichi no 第1の: the first lesson (*dai-ik-ka*) 第1課 / the first floor (*ik-kai*) 1階.
★ BrE = ni-kai 2階.
2 (of order) sa⌈isho no 最初の; se⌈ñtoo no 先頭の; ha⌈jime no 初めの: This is her first novel. (*Kore wa kanojo no saisho no shoosetsu desu.*) これは彼女の最初の小説です. / He was first in line. (*Kare wa retsu no señtoo datta.*) 彼は列の先頭だった.
— *n.* **1** (people) sa⌈isho no hito⌉ 最初の人; (things) sa⌈isho no mono⌉ 最初のもの: He was the first to come. (*Kare ga saisho ni kita hito datta.*) 彼が最初に来た人だった.
2 (date) tsu⌈itachi⌉ 1日.

— *adv.* dai⌉-ichi ni 第 1 に; sa⌈isho ni 最初に; ha⌈ji⌉mete 初めて: He stood first. (*Kare ga dai-ichi-i o shimeta.*) 彼が第 1 位を占めた. / It was ten years ago when I saw him first. (*Kare ni hajimete atta no wa juu-neñ mae desu.*) 彼に初めて会ったのは 10 年前です.

first class *n.* fa⌈asuto ku⌉rasu ファーストクラス; i⌈t-to⌉o 一等.

first-class *adj.* i⌈chiryuu no 一流の; sa⌈iko⌉okyuu no 最高級の: a first-class hotel (*ichiryuu no hoteru*) 一流のホテル.

fiscal *adj.* za⌈iseejoo no 財政上の; ka⌈ikee no 会計の: a fiscal year (*kaikee neñdo*) 会計年度.

fish *n.* sa⌈kana 魚; (flesh) gyo⌈niku 魚肉: catch a fish (*sakana o toru*) 魚をとる.

— *vi.* sa⌈kana o to⌉ru 魚をとる [C]; tsu⌈ri o suru 釣りをする [I]: go fishing (*tsuri ni iku*) 釣りに行く.

— *vt.* ... o tsu⌈ru ...を釣る [C]: fish trout (*masu o tsuru*) マスを釣る.

fisherman *n.* ryo⌉oshi 漁師.

fishery *n.* gyo⌉gyoo 漁業; su⌈isa⌉ñgyoo 水産業.

fishing *n.* tsu⌈ri 釣り; sa⌈kana⌉tori 魚捕り: a fishing boat (*tsuri-bune*) 釣り船 / a fishing line (*tsuri-ito*) 釣り糸 / a fishing rod (*tsuri-zao*) 釣りざお.

fist *n.* ni⌈giri ko⌉bushi 握りこぶし; ge⌈ñkotsu げんこつ: clench one's fist (*kobushi o nigirishimeru*) こぶしを握りしめる / He struck me with his fist. (*Kare wa watashi o geñkotsu de nagutta.*) 彼は私をげんこつで殴った.

fit[1] *vt.* **1** (be the right size) ... ni (pi⌈tta⌉ri) a⌉u ...に(ぴったり)合う [C]: These shoes fit me very well. (*Kono kutsu wa watashi ni pittari da.*) この靴は私にぴったりだ.

2 (make suitable) ... ni a⌈wase⌉ru ...に合わせる [V]: I will fit my schedule to yours. (*Watashi no yotee o anata no ni awasemashoo.*) 私の予定をあなたのに合わせましょう.

3 (put in position) ... ni pi⌈ta⌉ri to ha⌈meru ...にぴたりとはめる [V]; sa⌈shikomu 差し込む [C]: fit a key in the lock (*kagi o joo ni sashikomu*) 鍵を錠に差し込む.

4 (equip with) ... o to⌈ritsukeru ...を取り付ける [V]: I fitted new tires to my car. (*Watashi wa kuruma ni atarashii taiya o toritsuketa.*) 私は車に新しいタイヤを取り付けた.

— *vi.* a⌉u 合う [C]; pi⌈tta⌉ri suru ぴったりする [I]: This door does not fit. (*Kono to wa umaku awanai.*) この戸はうまく合わない.

— *adj.* **1** (suitable) te⌈ki⌉shita 適した; te⌈ki⌉shite iru 適している; fu⌈sawashi⌉i ふさわしい: This water is not fit to drink. (*Kono mizu wa nomu no ni tekishite imaseñ.*) この水は飲むのに適していません.

2 (proper) to⌉o o eta [ete iru] 当を得た[得ている]; o⌈ñtoo na 穏当な: It is not fit for you to say so. (*Anata ga soo iu no wa oñtoo de wa nai.*) あなたがそう言うのは穏当ではない.

3 (in good health) ke⌈ñkoo na 健康な; ge⌉ñki na 元気な: I am feeling very fit. (*Watashi wa totemo geñki desu.*) 私はとても元気です.

fit[2] *n.* (sudden attack of illness) ho⌈ssa 発作: fall down in a fit (*hossa de taoreru*) 発作で倒れる.

five *pron.* i⌈tsu⌉tsu 五つ; (people) go⌈ni⌉ñ 5 人; (things) go⌉-ko 5 個: I want five of these. (*Kore o itsutsu kudasai.*) これを五つ下さい.

— *n.* (figure) go⌉ 5; (hour) go⌉-ji 5 時; (minute) go⌉-fuñ 5 分; (age) go⌉-sai 5 歳.

— *adj.* i⌈tsu⌉tsu no 五つの; (people) go-⌈ni⌉ñ no 5 人の; (things) go⌉-ko no 5 個の; (age) go⌉-sai no 5 歳の.

fix *vt.* **1** (mend) ... o shu⌉uri suru ...を修理する [I]; na⌈o⌉su 直す [C]: I got the camera fixed. (*Watashi wa kamera o shuuri shite moratta.*) 私はカメラを修理してもらった.

2 (prepare) ... o yo⌉oi suru ...を用意する [I]; shi⌈taku suru したくする [I]: She fixed a meal for us. (*Kanojo wa watashi-tachi ni shokuji o yooi*

shite kureta.) 彼女は私たちに食事を用意してくれた.
3 (decide on) ... o ke⌈ttee suru ...を決定する Ⓘ; ki⌈meru 決める Ⓥ: We fixed the time and place for the meeting. (*Watashi-tachi wa kaigi no jikañ to basho o kimeta.*) 私たちは会議の時間と場所を決めた.
4 (make firm) (... ni) ... o ko⌈tee saseru (…に)…を固定させる Ⓥ; to⌈ri-tsuke⌉ru 取り付ける Ⓥ: fix a shelf to the wall (*kabe ni tana o toritsukeru*) 壁に棚を取り付ける.

flag *n.* ha⌈ta⌉ 旗: run up a flag (*hata o kakageru*) 旗を掲げる.

flake *n.* u⌈sui kakera 薄いかけら; ha⌈kuheñ 薄片: flakes of snow (*seppeñ*) 雪片.

flame *n.* ho⌉noo 炎; ka⌈eñ 火炎: burst in flames (*patto moeagaru*) ぱっと燃え上がる.
— *vi.* **1** (burn with flames) ho⌉noo o dasu 炎を出す Ⓒ; mo⌈eaga⌉ru 燃え上がる Ⓒ: The fire flamed brightly. (*Hi wa aka-aka to moeagatta.*) 火は赤々と燃え上がった.
2 (become red) a⌈kaku na⌉ru 赤くなる Ⓒ: Her cheeks flamed. (*Kanojo no hoo ga akaku natta.*) 彼女のほおが赤くなった.

flap *vt.* **1** (move) ... o pa⌉ta pata u⌈goka⌉su …をぱたぱた動かす Ⓒ; (of wings) ha⌈batakase⌉ru 羽ばたかせる Ⓥ: The bird flapped its wings. (*Tori wa hane o habatakaseta.*) 鳥は羽を羽ばたかせた.
2 (give a light blow) ... o ta⌈ta⌉ku …をたたく Ⓒ: flap flies away (*hae o tataite oiharau*) はえをたたいて追い払う.
— *vi.* **1** (of a flag) ha⌈tame⌉ku はためく Ⓒ: The flag was flapping in the wind. (*Hata ga kaze ni hatameite ita.*) 旗が風にはためいていた.
2 (of a bird) ha⌈bata⌉ku 羽ばたく Ⓒ: The bird flapped away. (*Tori ga habataite tobisatta.*) 鳥が羽ばたいて飛び去った.

flash *vi.* **1** (shine quickly) pi⌈ka⌉tto hi⌈ka⌉ru ぴかっと光る Ⓒ; hi⌈rame⌉ku ひらめく Ⓒ: Lightning flashed. (*Inazuma ga pikatto hikatta.*) 稲妻がぴかっと光った.
2 (come suddenly) pa⌉tto u⌈kabu ぱっと浮かぶ Ⓒ: A good idea flashed into my mind. (*Yoi kañgae ga patto atama ni ukañda.*) よい考えがぱっと頭に浮かんだ.
— *vt.* **1** (give out light) ... o pa⌉tto te⌈ra⌉su …をぱっと照らす Ⓒ: flash a light (*akari o patto terasu*) 明かりをぱっと照らす.
2 (show) ... o chi⌈ra⌉ri to mi⌈se⌉ru …をちらりと見せる Ⓥ: flash a badge (*bajji o chirari to miseru*) バッジをちらりと見せる.
— *n.* **1** (bright light) se⌈ñkoo 閃光; hi⌈rameki ひらめき.
2 (for taking photographs) fu⌈ra⌉sshu フラッシュ: Can I use a flash? (*Furasshu o taite mo ii desu ka?*) フラッシュをたいてもいいですか.

flashlight *n.* **1** (torch) ka⌈ichuude⌉ñtoo 懐中電灯: switch on [off] a flashlight (*kaichuudeñtoo o tsukeru [kesu]*) 懐中電灯をつける[消す].
2 (for taking photographs) fu⌈ra⌉sshu フラッシュ.

flat[1] *adj.* **1** (level) ta⌈ira na 平らな; hi⌈ratai 平たい: a flat floor (*taira na yuka*) 平らな床.
2 (spread out) ba⌈tta⌉ri ta⌈o⌉rete (iru) ばったり倒れて(いる): She fell flat on her face. (*Kanojo wa utsubuse ni battari taoreta.*) 彼女はうつ伏せにばったり倒れた.
3 (of a tire) pa⌈ñku shita [shite iru] パンクした[している]: I have a flat tire. (*Taiya ga pañku shimashita.*) タイヤがパンクしました.
4 (absolute) ki⌈ppa⌉ri shita [shite iru] きっぱりした[している]: give a flat refusal (*kippari to kotowaru*) きっぱりと断わる.
— *n.* (surface) he⌈eme⌉ñ 平面; (land) he⌈echi 平地.
— *adv.* **1** (in a flat manner) ta⌈ira ni 平に.
2 (absolutely) ki⌈ppa⌉ri to きっぱりと; ha⌈kki⌉ri はっきり: I told him flat.

(*Watashi wa kare ni hakkiri itte oita.*) 私は彼にはっきり言っておいた.
3 (exactly) ki⌈kka⌉ri きっかり; fu⌈ra⌉t-to フラット: run a course in 10 seconds flat (*koosu o juu-byoo furatto de hashiru*) コースを 10 秒フラットで走る.

flat[2] *n.* (apartment) a⌈pa⌉ato アパート; ma⌉ñshoñ マンション.

flatter *vt.* **1** (praise insincerely) ... ni o⌈seji o iu …にお世辞を言う [C]: She flattered me about my singing. (*Kanojo wa watashi ni uta ga umai to oseji o itta.*) 彼女は私に歌がうまいとお世辞を言った.
2 (give a feeling of pleasure) ... o u⌈reshigarase⌉ru …をうれしがらせる [V]: I am flattered by your invitation. (*Go-shootai o ureshiku omoimasu.*) ご招待をうれしく思います.

flattery *n.* o⌈seji お世辞; o⌈be⌉kka おべっか.

flavor *n.* **1** (taste) a⌈ji 味; (taste and smell) fu⌉umi 風味: This soup has a flavor of garlic. (*Kono suupu wa niñniku no aji ga suru.*) このスープはにんにくの味がする.
2 (atmosphere) o⌈momuki 趣; a⌈ji-wai 味わい: a castle with the flavor of the Middle Ages (*chuusee no omomuki no aru shiro*) 中世の趣のある城.
— *vt.* ... ni fu⌉umi o tsu⌈ke⌉ru …に風味をつける [V]: flavor the tea with lemon (*koocha ni remoñ no fuumi o tsukeru*) 紅茶にレモンの風味をつける.

flaw *n.* ki⌈zu きず: a flaw in a jewel (*hooseki no kizu*) 宝石のきず.

flee *vi.* ni⌈ge⌉ru 逃げる [V]; no⌈gare⌉ru 逃れる [V]: flee from the enemy (*teki kara nogareru*) 敵から逃れる.

fleet *n.* ka⌉ñtai 艦隊; se⌉ñdañ 船団.

flesh *n.* **1** (of an animal) ni⌈ku⌉ 肉; (of a fruit) ka⌉niku 果肉: a flesh eating animal (*nikushoku-doobutsu*) 肉食動物.
2 (body) ni⌉kutai 肉体.

flexible *adj.* **1** (easily bent) ma⌈ge-yasu⌉i 曲げやすい; ji⌈yu⌉u ni ma⌈garu 自由に曲がる: a flexible cord (*jiyuu ni magaru koodo*) 自由に曲がるコード.
2 (adaptable) ju⌉unañ na 柔軟な; yu⌉uzuu no [ga] kiku 融通の[が]きく; fu⌈re⌉kishiburu na フレキシブルな: a flexible plan (*yuuzuu no kiku kee-kaku*) 融通の利く計画.

flight *n.* **1** (journey) so⌉ra no ta⌈bi⌉ 空の旅; fu⌈raito フライト: How was your flight? (*Sora no tabi wa ika-ga deshita ka?*) 空の旅はいかがでしたか.
2 (of a plane) bi⌉ñ 便: Will this flight leave on time? (*Kono biñ wa yotee doori demasu ka?*) この便は予定どおり出ますか. / an extra flight (*riñji-biñ*) 臨時便 /a regular flight (*teeki-biñ*) 定期便.
3 (stairs) ka⌈idañ 階段.

flight attendant *n.* kya⌈kushitsu joomu⌉iñ 客室乗務員.

fling *vt.* (throw) ... o na⌈ge⌉ru …を投げる [V]; ho⌈orida⌉su ほうり出す [C]: He flung his clothes on the floor. (*Kare wa fuku o yuka ni hoorida-shita.*) 彼は服を床にほうり出した.

flint *n.* (for a lighter) ra⌉itaa no i⌈shi⌉ ライターの石.

flip *vt.* ... o ha⌈ji⌉ku …をはじく [C]; po⌉i to na⌈ge⌉ru ぽいと投げる [V]: flip a coin on the counter (*kooka o kauñ-taa no ue ni poi to nageru*) 硬貨をカウンターの上にぽいと投げる.

float *vi.* **1** (stay on the surface) u⌈ku 浮く [C]: Wood floats on water. (*Ki wa mizu ni uku.*) 木は水に浮く.
2 (drift) ta⌈dayo⌉u 漂う [C]: A balloon floated in the air. (*Fuuseñ ga kuuchuu ni tadayotte ita.*) 風船が空中に漂っていた.
— *vt.* ... o u⌈kaberu …を浮かべる [V]; u⌈kaseru 浮かせる [V]: float a raft on the river (*ikada o kawa ni uka-beru*) いかだを川に浮かべる.
— *n.* **1** (on a fishing line) u⌈ki 浮き: The float is moving. (*Uki ga ugoite imasu.*) 浮きが動いています.
2 (vehicle in a procession) da⌈shi⌉ 山車.

flock *n.* mu⌈re⌉ 群れ: a flock of sheep (*hitsuji no mure*) 羊の群れ.

flood *n.* **1** (overflow of water) ko⌈o-zui 洪水; o⌈omi⌉zu 大水: The typhoon caused a bad flood. (*Tai-fuu ga hidoi koozui o hikiokoshita.*) 台風がひどい洪水を引き起こした.
2 (outpouring) a⌈fure⌉ru ko⌈to⌉ あふれること: a flood of tears (*afureru na-mida*) あふれる涙.
— *vt.* **1** (of a place) ... o mi⌈zubita-shi⌉ ni suru ...を水浸しにする [I]; (of a river) ha⌈ñrañ saseru はんらんさせる [V]: The river flooded the village. (*Kawa wa mura o mizubitashi ni shita.*) 川は村を水浸しにした.
2 (fill to overflowing) ... ni sa⌈ttoo suru ...に殺到する [I]: Applicants flooded the office. (*Oobosha ga jimusho ni sattoo shita.*) 応募者が事務所に殺到した.
— *vi.* ha⌈ñrañ suru はんらんする [I]; sa⌈ttoo suru 殺到する [I].

floor *n.* **1** (surface in a room) yu⌈ka 床: sit on the floor (*yuka ni suwa-ru*) 床に座る.
2 (of a building) ka⌉i 階; fu⌈ro⌉a フロア: the second floor (*ni-kai*) 2階. ★ BrE = sañ-gai 3階 / I'd like a room on a higher [lower] floor. (*Motto ue [shita] no kai no heya ni shite kudasai.*) もっと上[下]の階の部屋にしてください.
— *vt.* ... ni yu⌈ka o haru ...に床を張る [C]: floor a room with plastic tiles (*heya ni purasuchikku tairu no yuka o haru*) 部屋にプラスチックタイルの床を張る.

flour *n.* ko⌈mugiko 小麦粉.

flourish *vi.* **1** (grow well) yo⌉ku so⌈da⌉tsu よく育つ [C]; ha⌉ñmo suru 繁茂する [I]: Roses in my garden are flourishing. (*Uchi no niwa no bara wa yoku sodatte imasu.*) うちの庭のばらはよく育っています.
2 (be successful) ha⌉ñjoo suru 繁盛する [I]: His business is flourishing. (*Kare no shoobai wa hañjoo shite iru.*) 彼の商売は繁盛している.
— *vt.* (wave) ... o fu⌈rimawa⌉su ...を振り回す [C]: flourish a sword (*ka-tana o furimawasu*) 刀を振り回す.

flow *vi.* **1** (move along) na⌈gare⌉ru 流れる [V]: The Sumida River flows through Tokyo. (*Sumida-gawa wa Tookyoo o nagarete imasu.*) 墨田川は東京を流れています.
2 (of the tide) sa⌉su 差す [C]; mi-⌈chi⌉ru 満ちる [V]: The tide began to flow. (*Shio ga michite kita.*) 潮が満ちてきた.
— *n.* na⌈gare⌉ 流れ: stop the flow of blood (*chi no nagare o tomeru*) 血の流れを止める.

flower *n.* ha⌈na⌉ 花; ku⌈sa⌉bana 草花: arrange flowers (*hana o ikeru*) 花を生ける / plant flowers (*kusabana o ueru*)) 草花を植える / a flower shop (*hana-ya*) 花屋 / flower ar-rangement (*ikebana*) 生け花.
— *vi.* ha⌈na⌉ ga sa⌈ku⌉ 花が咲く [C]: Tulips flower in spring. (*Chuu-rippu wa haru ni saku.*) チューリップは春に咲く.

flu *n.* i⌈ñfurue⌉ñza インフルエンザ; ryu⌈u-kañ 流感: He has the flu. (*Kare wa ryuukañ ni kakatte iru.*) 彼は流感にかかっている.

fluent *adj.* ryu⌉uchoo na 流ちょうな; na⌈me⌉raka na 滑らかな: He is fluent in Japanese. (*Kare wa Ni-hoñgo ga ryuuchoo desu.*) 彼は日本語が流ちょうです.

fluid *n.* ryu⌈utai 流体; ryu⌈udootai 流動体.
— *adj.* ryu⌈udoosee no 流動性の; ryu⌈udoo-teki na 流動的な: The situation is still fluid. (*Joosee wa mada ryuudoo-teki desu.*) 情勢はまだ流動的です.

flush *vi.* **1** (of water) do⌈tto naga-re⌉ru どっと流れる [V]; ho⌈tobashi⌉ru ほとばしる [C]: The water flushed out from the pipe. (*Mizu ga sono kañ kara hotobashiri-deta.*) 水がその管からほとばしり出た.
2 (blush) pa⌉tto a⌈kaku na⌉ru ぱっと赤くなる [C]; ko⌈ochoo suru 紅潮する [I]: His face flushed with excite-ment. (*Kare no kao wa koofuñ de akaku natta.*) 彼の顔は興奮で赤くなった.

— *vt.* **1** (of water) ... o do˥tto naga˥su …をどっと流す Ⓒ: flush the toilet (*toire no mizu o nagasu*) トイレの水を流す.
2 (blush) ... o a˥karame˥ru …を赤らめる Ⓥ; ko˥ochoo saseru 紅潮させる Ⓥ: She was flushed with fever. (*Kanojo wa netsu de akaku natte ita.*) 彼女は熱で赤くなっていた.
— *n.* ko˥ochoo 紅潮; se˥kimeñ 赤面.

flutter *vi.* **1** (of a bird) ha˥ba˥taki suru 羽ばたきする Ⓘ; (of a butterfly) hi˥rahira to˥bu ひらひら飛ぶ Ⓒ: A butterfly is fluttering about. (*Choo ga ip-piki hirahira toñde iru.*) ちょうが 1 匹ひらひら飛んでいる.
2 (of a flag, etc.) ha˥tame˥ku はためく Ⓒ; hi˥rahira suru ひらひらする Ⓘ: The curtains are fluttering in the breeze. (*Kaateñ ga kaze ni hirahira shite iru.*) カーテンが風にひらひらしている.
— *vt.* ... o ba˥tabata saseru …をばたばたさせる Ⓥ; hi˥rahira saseru ひらひらさせる Ⓥ: The bird fluttered its wings. (*Sono tori wa hane o batabata saseta.*) その鳥は羽をばたばたさせた.
— *n.* ha˥ba˥taki 羽ばたき; ha˥tameki˥ はためき.

fly[1] *vi.* **1** (travel through the air) to˥bu 飛ぶ Ⓒ: These birds fly south in winter. (*Kore-ra no tori wa fuyu ni minami e toñde ikimasu.*) これらの鳥は冬に南へ飛んで行きます.
2 (travel by aircraft) hi˥ko˥oki de i˥ku 飛行機で行く Ⓒ: We flew from Tokyo to Seoul. (*Watashi-tachi wa Tookyoo kara Souru made hikooki de itta.*) 私たちは東京からソウルまで飛行機で行った.
3 (pass quickly) to˥bu yo˥o ni su˥gisaru 飛ぶように過ぎ去る Ⓒ: Time flies. (*Toki wa tobu yoo ni sugisaru.*) 時は飛ぶように過ぎ去る.
4 (wave) hi˥ruga˥eru 翻る Ⓒ: A flag was flying on the mast. (*Masuto ni hata ga hirugaette ita.*) マストに旗が翻っていた.
— *vt.* (in an aircraft) ... o hi˥ko˥oki de to˥bu …を飛行機で飛ぶ Ⓒ: fly the Pacific (*Taiheeyoo o hikooki de tobu*) 太平洋を飛行機で飛ぶ.

fly[2] *n.* **1** (insect) ha˥e はえ: catch a fly (*hae o tsukamaeru*) はえを捕まえる.
2 (fish-hook) ka˥bari 蚊針; ke˥bari 毛針.

foam *n.* a˥wa˥ 泡: the foam of beer (*biiru no awa*) ビールの泡.
— *vi.* a˥wada˥tsu 泡立つ Ⓒ: The beer foamed over the top of the glass. (*Biiru ga awadatte koppu kara afureta.*) ビールが泡立ってコップからあふれた.

focus *n.* **1** (meeting point) sho˥oteñ 焦点; pi˥ñto ピント: the focus of a lens (*reñzu no shooteñ*) レンズの焦点.
2 (center) chu˥ushiñ 中心: the focus of interest (*kyoomi no chuushiñ*) 興味の中心.
— *vt.* **1** (adjust) ... ni sho˥oteñ [pi˥ñto] o a˥wase˥ru …に焦点[ピント]を合わせる Ⓥ: I focused my camera on the flower. (*Watashi wa sono hana ni piñto o awaseta.*) 私はその花にピントを合わせた.
2 (concentrate) ... ni shu˥uchuu saseru …に集中させる Ⓥ: We focused our efforts on the problem. (*Watashi-tachi wa sono moñdai ni doryoku o shuuchuu saseta.*) 私たちはその問題に努力を集中させた.

fog *n.* ki˥ri 霧; mo˥ya もや: a mountain covered with fog (*kiri ni tsutsumareta yama*) 霧に包まれた山.
★ 'Mist' is also called '*kiri*.'
— *vt.* ... o ki˥ri [mo˥ya] de o˥o˥u …を霧[もや]で覆う Ⓒ; ku˥morase˥ru 曇らせる Ⓥ: My glasses were fogged up with steam. (*Megane ga yuge de kumotta.*) 眼鏡が湯気で曇った.

foil *n.* a˥rumi˥-haku はく; ho˥iru ホイル: bake potatoes in aluminum foil (*jagaimo o arumi-haku ni tsutsuñde yaku*) じゃがいもをアルミはくに包んで焼く.

fold *vt.* **1** (double over) ... o o˥ri-

tatamu …を折り畳む [C]: fold a piece of paper in half (*kami o hañbuñ ni oritatamu*) 紙を半分に折り畳む.
2 (bring in close to the body) ... o da⌈kishime⌉ru …を抱き締める [V]: She folded her arms around her child. (*Kanojo wa kodomo o ryooude de dakishimeta.*) 彼女は子どもを両腕で抱き締めた.
3 (enclose) ... o tsu⌈tsu⌉mu …を包む [C]; ku⌈ru⌉mu くるむ [C]: fold a present in paper (*okurimono o kami de tsutsumu*) 贈物を紙で包む.
— *vi.* o⌈ritatameru 折り畳める [V]: This chair folds easily. (*Kono isu wa kañtañ ni oritatamemasu.*) このいすは簡単に折り畳めます.
— *n.* o⌈rime⌉ 折り目; hi⌉da ひだ: the folds of a skirt (*sukaato no hida*) スカートのひだ.

foliage *n.* ha 葉.

folk *n.* **1** (people) hi⌈to⌉bito 人々; hi⌈to⌉-tachi 人たち: country [town] folk (*inaka* [*machi*] *no hito-tachi*) いなか[町]の人たち.
2 (family) ka⌉zoku 家族; (relatives) shi⌉ñzoku 親族: How are your folks? (*O-taku no minasañ wa ikaga desu ka?*) お宅のみなさんはいかがですか.
— *adj.* mi⌈ñkañ no 民間の; mi⌉ñzoku no 民族の: a folk dance (*miñzoku buyoo*) 民族舞踊 / a folk music (*miñzoku oñgaku*) 民族音楽.

folk song *n.* fo⌈oku-so⌉ñgu フォークソング; mi⌈ñyoo 民謡.

follow *vt.* **1** (go after) ... no a⌉to ni tsuite i⌈ku …の後について行く [C]: You go first and I will follow you. (*Anata ga saki ni ikeba ato ni tsuite ikimasu.*) あなたが先に行けば後について行きます.
2 (come after) a⌉to ni kuru 後に来る [I]: Summer follows spring. (*Haru no ato ni natsu ga kuru.*) 春の後に夏が来る.
3 (go along) ... o ta⌈do⌉ru …をたどる [C]; i⌈ku 行く [C]: Follow this road until you get to the station. (*Eki ni tsuku made kono michi o iki nasai.*) 駅に着くまでこの道を行きなさい.
4 (obey) ... ni shi⌈tagau …に従う [C]; ... o ma⌈mo⌉ru …を守る [C]: He didn't follow my instructions. (*Kare wa watashi no shiji ni shitagawanakatta.*) 彼は私の指示に従わなかった.
5 (pursue) ... o o⌈u …を追う [C]; tsu⌈iseki suru 追跡する [I]: We followed the car. (*Watashi-tachi wa sono kuruma o otta.*) 私たちはその車を追った.
6 (understand) ... o ri⌉kai suru …を理解する [I]: I was unable to follow his explanation. (*Watashi wa kare no setsumee ga rikai dekinakatta.*) 私は彼の説明が理解できなかった.
— *vi.* **1** (go [come] after) (... ni) tsu⌉ite iku [kuru] (…に)ついて行く [C] [来る [I]]: The dog followed behind me. (*Sono inu wa watashi ni tsuite kita.*) その犬は私についてきた.
2 (happen) tsu⌈gi⌉ ni o⌈ko⌉ru 次に起こる [C]: No one knows what will follow. (*Tsugi ni nani ga okoru ka dare ni mo wakaranai.*) 次に何が起こるかだれにもわからない.
3 (come as a result) to⌈ozeñ ... to na⌉ru 当然…となる [C]: It follows from this fact that he knows the truth. (*Kono jijitsu kara kare wa toozeñ sono shiñsoo o shitte iru koto ni naru.*) この事実から彼は当然その真相を知っていることになる. / It does not follow that poor people are unhappy. (*Mazushii hito ga fukoo da to wa kagiranai.*) 貧しい人が不幸だとは限らない.

follower *n.* ju⌉usha 従者; shi⌈ñpo⌉osha 信奉者.

following *adj.* tsu⌈gi⌉ no 次の; i⌉ka no 以下の: read the following chapter (*tsugi no shoo o yomu*) 次の章を読む.
— *n.* tsu⌈gi⌉ no ko⌈to⌉ 次のこと; i⌉ka 以下: The following is his answer. (*Ika ga kare no heñji desu.*) 以下が彼の返事です.

fond *adj.* **1** (like) su⌈ki⌉ da 好きだ: She is fond of music. (*Kanojo wa

oñgaku ga suki da.) 彼女は音楽が好きだ.
2 (loving) a⌈ijoo no fuka⌉i 愛情の深い; a⌈mai 甘い: a fond mother (*kodomo ni amai hahaoya*) 子どもに甘い母親.

food *n.* **1** (what is eaten) ta⌈bemo⌉no 食べ物; sho⌈ku⌉motsu 食物: The food is delicious. (*Tabemono ga oishii.*) 食べ物がおいしい. / food and drink (*iñshokubutsu*) 飲食物.
2 (particular kind of food) sho⌈kuhiñ 食品: frozen food (*reetoo-shokuhiñ*) 冷凍食品 / natural foods (*shizeñ-shokuhiñ*) 自然食品.
3 (cooked food) ryo⌉ori 料理: Japanese [Chinese] food (*Nihoñ* [*Chuuka*] *ryoori*) 日本[中華]料理 / local food (*kyoodo ryoori*) 郷土料理.

fool *n.* ba⌈kamono ばか者; o⌈rokamono 愚か者: I was a fool to believe him. (*Kare o shiñjiru nañte watashi mo baka datta.*) 彼を信じるなんて私もばかだった.
— *vt.* ... o da⌈ma⌉su ...をだます Ⓒ: He fooled her out of her money. (*Kare wa kanojo o damashite o-kane o makiageta.*) 彼は彼女をだましてお金を巻き上げた.

foolish *adj.* ba⌉ka na ばかな; o⌉roka na 愚かな: It is foolish of you to do a thing like that. (*Soñna koto o suru nañte kimi mo baka da.*) そんなことをするなんて君もばかだ.

foot *n.* **1** (the part of a leg) a⌈shi⌉ 足: My feet are sore from walking. (*Aruita no de ashi ga itai.*) 歩いたので足が痛い.
2 (bottom) shi⌈ta no bu⌉buñ 下の部分; ne⌈moto⌉ 根元; (of a mountain) fu⌈moto⌉ ふもと: the foot of a page (*peeji no shita no bubuñ*) ページの下の部分 / the foot of a mountain (*yama no fumoto*) 山のふもと.
3 (measure of length) fi⌉ito フィート: He is six feet tall. (*Kare wa shiñchoo ga roku-fiito aru.*) 彼は身長が6フィートある. ★ Japanese use the metric system and 'foot' is not used.

football *n.* **1** (American football) fu⌈ttobo⌉oru フットボール; (association football) sa⌉kkaa サッカー.
2 (ball) fu⌈ttobooru-yoo no booru フットボール用のボール.

footstep *n.* (sound) a⌈shio⌉to 足音: I heard somebody's footsteps. (*Watashi wa dare-ka no ashioto o kiita.*) 私はだれかの足音を聞いた.

for *prep.* **1** (in order to) ... no ta⌈me⌉ ni ...のために: We held a party for him. (*Watashi-tachi wa kare no tame ni paatii o hiraita.*) 私たちは彼のためにパーティーを開いた. / He went out for a walk. (*Kare wa sañpo ni ikimashita.*) 彼は散歩に行きました.
2 (sent to) ... a⌈te no ...あての: Are there any letters for me? (*Watashi ate no tegami wa todoite imasu ka?*) 私あての手紙は届いていますか.
3 (during) ... no a⌈ida ...の間; -kañ 間: I stayed in Kyoto for three days. (*Watashi wa Kyooto ni mikka-kañ taizai shimashita.*) 私は京都に3日間滞在しました. / I'd like to rent this car for 24 hours. (*Kono kuruma o nijuu-yo-jikañ karitai no desu ga.*) この車を24時間借りたいのですが.
4 (as far as) ... no ai⌈da ...の間: I walked for four kilometers. (*Watashi wa yoñ-kiro aruita.*) 私は4キロ歩いた.
5 (suiting) ... muki no ...向きの; ... ni te⌈ki⌉shita ...に適した: This is a car for young people. (*Kore wa wakamono muki no kuruma desu.*) これは若者向きの車です.
6 (in return) ... to hi⌈kikae ni ...と引き換えに; ... ni ta⌉ishite ...に対して: I paid five thousand yen for the tie. (*Watashi wa sono nekutai ni go-señ-eñ haratta.*) 私はそのネクタイに5千円払った.
7 (toward) ... ni mu⌈katte ...に向かって; ... e i⌈ku tame⌉ ni ...へ行くために: He left Tokyo for London. (*Kare wa Roñdoñ ni mukatte Too-

kyoo o tatta.) 彼はロンドンに向かって東京を立った.

8 (in favor of) ... ni sa⌈ñsee no ... に賛成の: Are you for the proposal? (*Anata wa teeañ ni sañsee desu ka?*) あなたは提案に賛成ですか.

9 (on behalf of) ... no ka⌈wari ni ...の代わりに; ... o da⌈ihyoo shite ... を代表して: He spoke for his classmates. (*Kare wa kurasu o daihyoo shite shabetta.*) 彼はクラスを代表してしゃべった.

10 (with regard to) ... ni ta⌉ishite ...に対して: I felt no regret for what I have done. (*Watashi wa jibuñ no shita koto ni taishite kookai shinakatta.*) 私は自分のしたことに対して後悔しなかった.

11 (because of) ... no ri⌈yuu de ...の理由で; ... de ...で: This place is famous for its cherry blossoms. (*Koko wa sakura de yuumee desu.*) ここは桜で有名です.

12 (as) ... to shi⌈te ...として: You mustn't give him up for dead. (*Kare o shiñda mono to shite akiramete wa ikenai.*) 彼を死んだものとしてあきらめてはいけない.

13 (considering) ... no wa⌈ri ni ... の割に: He looks young for his age. (*Kare wa toshi no wari ni wakaku mieru.*) 彼は年の割に若く見える.

forbid *vt.* ... o ki⌈ñjiru ...を禁じる [V]; ki⌈ñshi suru 禁止する [I]: Smoking is forbidden here. (*Kitsueñ wa koko de wa kiñjirarete imasu.*) 喫煙はここでは禁じられています.

force *n.* **1** (violence) bo⌉oryoku 暴力: resort to force (*booryoku ni uttaeru*) 暴力に訴える.

2 (power) chi⌈kara 力: the force of the wind (*kaze no chikara*) 風の力.

3 (organized body) ta⌉i 隊: the armed forces (*guñtai*) 軍隊 / an exploration force (*tañkeñtai*) 探検隊.

4 (influence) e⌈ekyo⌉oryoku 影響力; chi⌈kara⌉ 力: the force of public opinion (*yoroñ no chikara*) 世論の力.

— *vt.* **1** (compel) ... ni [o] mu⌈riyari ⟨verb⟩-(sa)seru ...に[を]無理やり...(さ)せる [V]: They forced him to accept the offer. (*Kare-ra wa kare ni muriyari sono mooshide o uke-saseta.*) 彼らは彼に無理やりその申し出を受けさせた.

2 (do by force) ... o mu⌉ri ni ⟨verb⟩ ...を無理に...: He forced the door open. (*Kare wa muri ni sono doa o aketa.*) 彼は無理にそのドアを開けた.

forecast *vt.* ... o yo⌈hoo suru ...を予報する [I]; yo⌈soo suru 予想する [I]: forecast the weather (*teñki o yohoo suru*) 天気を予報する.

— *n.* yo⌈hoo 予報: weather forecast (*teñki-yohoo*) 天気予報.

forefinger *n.* hi⌈tosashi⌉-yubi 人差し指.

forehead *n.* hi⌈tai 額: a high [low] forehead (*hiroi* [*semai*] *hitai*) 広い[狭い]額.

foreign *adj.* ga⌈ikoku no 外国の; (of people) ga⌈ikoku⌉jiñ no 外国人の: a foreign language (*gaikokugo*) 外国語 / foreign trade (*gaikoku-booeki*) 外国貿易.

foreigner *n.* ga⌈ikoku⌉jiñ 外国人; ga⌈ijiñ 外人.

foresee *vt.* ... o mi⌈toosu ...を見通す [C]; yo⌉chi suru 予知する [I]: Nobody can foresee what will happen. (*Nani ga okoru ka dare ni mo yochi dekinai.*) 何が起こるかだれにも予知できない.

forest *n.* mo⌈ri 森; shi⌈ñriñ 森林.

★ A wood is often called '*hayashi*' 林.

forever *adv.* i⌉tsu made mo いつまでも; e⌈ekyuu ni 永久に: I will remember you forever. (*Anata no koto wa itsu made mo wasuremaseñ.*) あなたのことはいつまでも忘れません.

forget *vt.* **1** (fail to remember) ... o wa⌈sureru ...を忘れる [V]; o⌈moidasenai 思い出せない: I've forgotten her name. (*Kanojo no namae o wasurete shimatta.*) 彼女の名前を忘れてしまった.

2 (leave behind) ... o o⌈kiwasure⌉ru ...を置き忘れる [V]: I often forget my

f

umbrella. (*Watashi wa yoku kasa o okiwasureru.*) 私はよく傘を置き忘れる.

— *vi.* wa⌈sureru 忘れる [V]: Don't forget! (*Wasurenaide.*) 忘れないで.

forgetful *adj.* wa⌈sure-yasu⌉i 忘れやすい; wa⌈sureppo⌉i 忘れっぽい: a forgetful person (*wasureppoi hito*) 忘れっぽい人.

forgive *vt.* **1** (pardon) ... o yu⌈ru⌉su ...を許す [C]; ka⌉ñbeñ suru 勘弁する [I]: I forgave him for his negligence. (*Watashi wa kare no taimañ o yurushite yatta.*) 私は彼の怠慢を許してやった.

2 (let go without payment) ... o me⌉ñjo suru ...を免除する [I]: forgive a debt (*shakkiñ o meñjo suru*) 借金を免除する.

fork *n.* **1** (for food) fo⌉oku フォーク.

2 (gardening tool) ku⌈made⌉ くま手.

3 (place of division) bu⌈ñki⌉teñ 分岐点: a fork in the road (*michi no buñkiteñ*) 道の分岐点.

— *vi.* (divide) bu⌉ñki suru 分岐する [I]; wa⌈kare⌉ru 分かれる [V]: The river forks here. (*Kawa wa koko de futatsu ni wakaremasu.*) 川はここで二つに分かれます.

form *n.* **1** (shape) ka⌈tachi 形; (appearance) ga⌈ikañ 外観: That rock has the form of an animal. (*Ano iwa wa doobutsu no katachi o shite iru.*) あの岩は動物の形をしている.

2 (type) ke⌈etai 形態; (kind) shu⌉rui 種類: There are various forms of government. (*Seeji ni wa iroiro na keetai ga arimasu.*) 政治にはいろいろな形態があります.

3 (printed paper) yo⌈oshi 用紙; (document) sho⌈rui 書類; sho⌈shiki 書式: an application form (*mooshikomi yooshi*) 申し込み用紙.

4 (condition) cho⌈oshi 調子: He is in good form. (*Kare wa chooshi ga ii.*) 彼は調子がいい.

— *vt.* **1** (give shape) ... o ka⌈tachizuku⌉ru ...を形作る [C]; (produce) ... o tsu⌈ku⌉ru ...を作る [C]: form a doll out of clay (*neñdo de niñgyoo o tsukuru*) 粘土で人形を作る.

2 (organize) ... o so⌉shiki suru ...を組織する [I]; ko⌈osee suru 構成する [I]: form a committee (*iiñkai o soshiki suru*) 委員会を組織する.

3 (conceive) ... o ma⌈tomeru ...をまとめる [V]: form ideas (*kañgae o matomeru*) 考えをまとめる.

— *vi.* **1** (take shape) ka⌈tachi o na⌉su 形を成す [C]; de⌈ki⌉ru できる [V]: Icicles formed on the eaves. (*Noki ni tsurara ga dekita.*) 軒につららができた.

2 (come into existence) u⌈mareru 生まれる [V]; u⌈kabu 浮かぶ [C]: A good idea formed in my mind. (*Atama ni ii kañgae ga ukañda.*) 頭にいい考えが浮かんだ.

formal *adj.* **1** (correct for the occasion) ko⌈oshiki no 公式の; se⌈eshiki no 正式の: a formal visit (*kooshiki no hoomoñ*) 公式の訪問 / a formal contract (*seeshiki no keeyaku*) 正式の契約.

2 (not relaxed) ka⌈kushikiba⌉tta 格式ばった; ka⌈kushikiba⌉tte iru 格式ばっている; a⌈ratama⌉tta 改まった: formal behavior (*aratamatta taido*) 改まった態度.

formally *adv.* se⌈eshiki ni 正式に; ko⌈oshiki ni 公式に: I was formally invited to the party. (*Watashi wa seeshiki ni sono paatii ni shootai sareta.*) 私は正式にそのパーティーに招待された.

formation *n.* **1** (shaping) ko⌈osee 構成; ke⌈esee 形成: the formation of character (*jiñkaku no keesee*) 人格の形成.

2 (of troops) ta⌈ikee 隊形.

former *adj.* **1** (of an earlier time) i⌉zeñ no 以前の; ma⌉e no 前の: He is the former president of our company. (*Kare wa watashi-tachi no kaisha no mae no shachoo desu.*) 彼は私たちの会社の前の社長です.

2 (first-mentioned) ze⌉ñsha no 前者の: I prefer the former painting to the latter. (*Watashi wa zeñsha* *no e no hoo ga koosha yori mo suki da.*) 私は前者の絵のほうが後者よりも好きだ.

formerly *adv.* i⌉zeñ wa 以前は; mu⌈kashi wa 昔は: Formerly there was a lake here. (*Izeñ wa koko ni mizuumi ga arimashita.*) 以前はここに湖がありました.

formula *n.* ko⌈oshiki 公式; shi⌈ki⌉ 式: the chemical formula for water (*mizu no kagaku-shiki*) 水の化学式.

f

forsake *vt.* (abandon) ... o mi⌈suteru ...を見捨てる Ⓥ: forsake a friend (*yuujiñ o misuteru*) 友人を見捨てる.

fort *n.* to⌈ride とりで; yo⌈osai 要塞: attack a fort (*toride o koogeki suru*) とりでを攻撃する.

fortieth *adj.* yo⌈ñjuu-bañme⌉ no 40 番目の; da⌉i-yoñjuu no 第 40 の.
— *n.* **1** (things) yo⌈ñjuu-bañme⌉ no mo⌈no⌉ 40 番目のもの; (people) yo⌈ñjuu-bañme⌉ no hi⌈to⌉ 40 番目の人.
2 (fraction) yo⌈ñjuu-buñ no ichi⌉ 40 分の 1.

fortunate *adj.* ko⌈ouñ na 幸運な; u⌉ñ no yoi 運のよい: I was fortunate to survive the accident. (*Watashi wa uñ yoku sono jiko de tasukatta.*) 私は運よくその事故で助かった.

fortunately *adv.* ko⌈ouñ ni⌉ mo 幸運にも; u⌉ñ yoku 運よく: Fortunately nobody was injured in the accident. (*Koouñ ni mo sono jiko de dare mo kega o shinakatta.*) 幸運にもその事故でだれもけがをしなかった.

fortune *n.* **1** (great sum of money) to⌉mi 富; za⌉isañ 財産: inherit a large fortune (*bakudai na zaisañ o soozoku suru*) 莫大な財産を相続する.
2 (luck) u⌉ñ 運; ko⌈ouñ 幸運: try one's fortune (*uñ o kakeru*) 運をかける / He had the good fortune to succeed. (*Koouñ ni mo kare wa seekoo shita.*) 幸運にも彼は成功した.
3 (fate) u⌉ñmee 運命; u⌉ñsee 運勢: tell a persons's fortune (*hito no uñsee o uranau*) 人の運勢を占う.

forty *pron.* yo⌉ñjuu 40; (things) yo⌈ñju⌉k-ko 40 個; (people) yo⌈ñju⌉u-niñ 40 人.
— *n.* (figure) yo⌉ñjuu 40; (minute) yo⌈ñju⌉p-puñ 40 分; (age) yo⌈ñju⌉s-sai 40 歳.
— *adj.* yo⌉ñjuu no 40 の; (things) yo⌈ñju⌉k-ko no 40 個の; (people) yo⌈ñju⌉u-niñ no 40 人の; (age) yo⌈ñju⌉s-sai no 40 歳の.

forward *adv.* **1** (toward the front) ma⌉e e [ni] 前へ[に]; ze⌈ñpoo e [ni] 前方へ[に]: go forward (*zeñshiñ suru*) 前進する / step forward (*mae e susumideru*) 前へ進み出る.
2 (toward the future) sa⌈ki e 先へ; sho⌉orai ni mu⌈katte 将来に向かって: look forward (*shoorai o kañgaeru*) 将来を考える.
— *adj.* **1** (toward the front) ze⌈ñpoo e⌉ no 前方への; ma⌉e no hoo no 前のほうの: The seat is too far forward. (*Seki ga mae no hoo sugiru.*) 席が前のほう過ぎる.
2 (well advanced) ha⌈ya⌉i 早い; so⌈ojuku na 早熟な; shi⌈ñpo-teki na 進歩的な: a forward child (*soojuku na kodomo*) 早熟な子ども / forward opinions (*shiñpo-teki na ikeñ*) 進歩的な意見.
— *vt.* ... o te⌈ñsoo suru ...を転送する Ⓘ: Please forward my mail to this address. (*Yuubiñ wa kono juusho ni teñsoo shite kudasai.*) 郵便はこの住所に転送してください.

foster *vt.* **1** (bring up) ... o yo⌈oiku suru ...を養育する Ⓘ; so⌈date⌉ru 育てる Ⓥ: She fostered the orphan. (*Kanojo wa sono koji o sodateta.*) 彼女はその孤児を育てた.
2 (encourage) ... o so⌈kushiñ suru ...を促進する Ⓘ; jo⌈choo suru 助長する Ⓘ: foster exports (*yushutsu o sokushiñ suru*) 輸出を促進する.
3 (cherish) ... o ko⌈ko⌉ro ni i⌈da⌉ku ...を心に抱く Ⓒ: foster an ambition (*taimoo o idaku*) 大望を抱く.
— *adj.* yo⌈oiku ni yoru 養育による; yo⌉o- 養; sa⌈to- 里: a foster mother (*yoobo*) 養母 / a foster child (*sa-*

togo) 里子.

foul *adj.* **1** (causing disgust) i⌈ya⌉ na いやな; fu⌈kai na 不快な: a foul smell (*iya na nioi*) いやな臭い.
2 (dirty) ki⌈tana⌉i 汚い; yo⌈goreta 汚れた; yo⌈gorete iru 汚れている: a foul room (*kitanai heya*) 汚い部屋.
— *vt.* (make foul) ... o ki⌈tana⌉ku suru ...を汚くする [I]; yo⌈gosu 汚す [C]: This water has been fouled by oil. (*Kono mizu wa abura de yogorete iru.*) この水は油で汚れている.

found *vt.* **1** (establish) ... o se⌈tsuritsu suru ...を設立する [I]; so⌈oritsu suru 創立する [I]: found a school (*gakkoo o sooritsu suru*) 学校を創立する.
2 (base on) ... o ko⌉ñkyo to suru ...を根拠とする [I]; ... ni mo⌈tozu⌉ku ...に基づく [C]: This story is founded upon fact. (*Kono hanashi wa jijitsu ni motozuite iru.*) この話は事実に基づいている.

foundation *n.* **1** (founding) se⌈tsuritsu 設立; so⌈oritsu 創立: foundation of a hospital (*byooiñ no setsuritsu*) 病院の設立.
2 (base) ki⌉so 基礎; do⌈dai 土台: lay the foundations of a house (*ie no kiso o sueru*) 家の基礎を据える.
3 (institution) shi⌉setsu 施設; da⌈ñtai 団体; za⌈idañ 財団.

founder *n.* so⌈oritsu⌉sha 創立者; se⌈tsuritsu⌉sha 設立者.

fountain *n.* **1** (spring of water) fu⌈ñsui 噴水.
2 (source) ge⌈ñseñ 源泉; mi⌈namoto 源: the fountain of knowledge (*chishiki no minamoto*) 知識の源.

fountain pen *n.* ma⌈ñne⌉ñhitsu 万年筆.

four *pron.* yo⌈ttsu 四つ; (things) yo⌉ñ-ko 4個; (people) yo-⌈ni⌉ñ 4人.
— *n.* (figure) yo⌉ñ 4; (hour) yo⌉-ji 4時; (minute) yo⌉ñ-puñ 4分; (age) yo⌉ñ-sai 4歳.
— *adj.* yo⌈ttsu⌉ no 四つの; (things) yo⌉ñ-ko no 4個の; (people) yo-⌈ni⌉ñ no 4人の; (age) yo⌉ñ-sai no 4歳の.

fourteen *pron.* ju⌈uyo⌉ñ 14; (things) ju⌈uyo⌉ñ-ko 14個; (people) ju⌉uyo-niñ 14人.
— *n.* (figure) ju⌈uyo⌉ñ 14; (hour) ju⌈uyo⌉-ji 14時; (minute) ju⌈uyo⌉ñ-puñ 14分; (age) ju⌈uyo⌉ñ-sai 14歳.
— *adj.* ju⌈uyo⌉ñ no 14の; (things) ju⌈uyo⌉ñ-ko no 14個の; (people) ju⌉uyo-niñ no 14人の; (age) ju⌈uyo⌉ñ-sai no 14歳の.

fourteenth *adj.* ju⌈uyoñ-bañme⌉ no 14番目の; da⌉i-ju⌈uyo⌉ñ no 第14の.
— *n.* **1** (things) ju⌈uyoñ-bañme⌉ no mo⌈no⌉ 14番目のもの; (people) ju⌈uyoñ-bañme⌉ no hi⌈to⌉ 14番目の人.
2 (date) ju⌉uyok-ka 14日.
3 (fraction) ju⌈uyon-buñ no ichi⌉ 14分の1.

fourth *adj.* yo⌈ñ-bañme⌉ no 4番目の; da⌉i-yoñ no 第4の.
— *n.* **1** (things) yo⌈ñ-bañme⌉ no mo⌈no⌉ 4番目のもの; (people) yo⌈ñ-bañme⌉ no hi⌈to⌉ 4番目の人.
2 (date) yo⌈k-ka 4日.
3 (fraction) yo⌈ñbuñ no ichi⌉ 4分の1.

fowl *n.* **1** (rooster or hen) ni⌈watori 鶏; (domestic bird) ka⌈kiñ 家禽.
2 (any bird) to⌈ri 鳥: a waterfowl (*mizudori*) 水鳥.

fox *n.* ki⌈tsune きつね(狐).

fragile *adj.* **1** (of a thing) ko⌈wareyasu⌉i 壊れやすい; mo⌈ro⌉i もろい: a fragile vase (*koware-yasui kabiñ*) 壊れやすい花びん.
2 (of a person) kyo⌈jaku na 虚弱な; hi⌈yowa na ひ弱な: a fragile child (*hiyowa na kodomo*) ひ弱な子ども.

fragment *n.* ha⌈heñ 破片; ka⌈kera かけら: The glass broke into fragments. (*Koppu ga konagona ni natta.*) コップが粉々になった.

fragrance *n.* ka⌈ori 香り; ho⌈okoo 芳香; ni⌈o⌉i におい: Roses have a pleasant fragrance. (*Bara wa ii kaori ga suru.*) ばらはいい香りがする.

fragrant *adj.* ka⌈ori no [ga] yo⌉i 香りの[が]よい: fragrant flowers (*kaori* *no yoi hana*) 香りのよい花.

frail *adj.* (weak) ka⌈yowa⌉i か弱い; (fragile) ko⌈ware-yasu⌉i 壊れやすい: a frail child (*kayowai ko*) か弱い子.

frame *n.* **1** (border) wa⌈ku⌉ 枠; fu⌈chi⌉ 縁; fu⌈reemu フレーム: a window frame (*mado-waku*) 窓枠 / a picture frame (*gaku-buchi*) 額縁.
2 (skeleton) ho⌈negumi 骨組み; (of a person) ta⌈ikaku 体格: the frame of a house (*ie no honegumi*) 家の骨組み / a person of large frame (*taikaku no ookii hito*) 体格の大きい人.
3 (structure) ko⌈ozoo 構造; ko⌈osee 構成: the frame of society (*shakai no koozoo*) 社会の構造.
— *vt.* **1** (enclose) ... o wa⌈ku⌉ ni ha⌈meru ...を枠にはめる Ⓥ: frame a picture (*e o gakubuchi ni ireru*) 絵を額縁に入れる.
2 (put together) ... o ku⌈mitate⌉ru ...を組み立てる Ⓥ: frame a house (*ie o kumitateru*) 家を組み立てる / frame a plan (*keekaku o tateru*) 計画を立てる.

framework *n.* ho⌈negumi 骨組み; ko⌈osee 構成; ki⌈koo 機構: the framework of a bridge (*hashi no honegumi*) 橋の骨組み / the framework of a government (*seefu no kikoo*) 政府の機構.

France *n.* Fu⌈rañsu フランス.

frank *adj.* so⌈tchoku na 率直な; za⌉kkubarañ na ざっくばらんな: I'd like to hear your frank opinion. (*Anata no sotchoku na ikeñ o o-kiki shitai.*) あなたの率直な意見をお聞きしたい.

frankly *adv.* so⌈tchoku ni 率直に; za⌉kkubarañ ni ざっくばらんに: He admitted his mistake frankly. (*Kare wa jibuñ no machigai o sotchoku ni mitometa.*) 彼は自分の間違いを率直に認めた. / Frankly, I think you are wrong. (*Sotchoku ni itte kimi wa machigatte iru to omoimasu.*) 率直に言って君は間違っていると思います.

free *adj.* **1** (not bound, controlled) ji⌈yu⌉u na 自由な; so⌈kubaku no [ga] na⌉i 束縛の[が]ない: free speech (*jiyuu na geñroñ*) 自由な言論 / They were glad to be free. (*Karera wa jiyuu ni natte yorokoñda.*) 彼らは自由になって喜んだ.
2 (costing nothing) mu⌈ryoo no 無料の; ta⌉da no ただの; (of tax) mu⌉zee no 無税の: Is there a free city map? (*Muryoo no shigai chizu wa arimasu ka?*) 無料の市街地図はありますか.
3 (not busy) hi⌈ma na 暇な: Are you free tonight? (*Koñbañ o-hima desu ka?*) 今晩お暇ですか.
4 (not occupied) a⌈ite iru 空いている: Do you have any rooms free? (*Aite iru heya wa arimasu ka?*) 空いている部屋はありますか.
5 (without) ... no [ga] na⌉i ...の[が]ない: Her life is quite free from care. (*Kanojo no seekatsu wa mattaku kuroo ga nai.*) 彼女の生活は全く苦労がない.
6 (generous) ki⌈mae no [ga] i⌉i 気前の[が]いい: He is free with his money. (*Kare wa kimae yoku o-kane o tsukau.*) 彼は気前よくお金を使う.
— *vt.* **1** (make free) ... o (... kara) ji⌈yu⌉u ni suru ...を(...から)自由にする Ⓘ; ka⌈ihoo suru 解放する Ⓘ: free a bird from a cage (*tori o kago kara jiyuu ni shite yaru*) 鳥をかごから自由にしてやる.
2 (relieve) ... kara (... o) to⌈rino-zoku ...から(...を)取り除く Ⓒ: free the road of snow (*dooro kara yuki o torinozoku*) 道路から雪を取り除く.

freedom *n.* ji⌈yu⌉u 自由: freedom of speech (*geñroñ no jiyuu*) 言論の自由 / I have freedom to do what I like. (*Watashi wa yaritai'koto ga dekiru jiyuu ga aru.*) 私はやりたいことができる自由がある.

freely *adv.* ji⌈yu⌉u ni 自由に; ka⌉tte ni 勝手に: Everybody can enter this room freely. (*Dare de mo kono heya ni jiyuu ni hairemasu.*) だれでもこの部屋に自由に入れます.

freeze *vi.* **1** (become ice) ko⌈oru

凍る Ⓒ; ko⌈ori ga haru 氷が張る Ⓒ: The lake froze over. (*Mizuumi ichimeñ ni koori ga hatta.*) 湖一面に氷が張った.

2 (be very cold) ko⌈goeru hodo sa⌈mu⌉i 凍えるほど寒い: I am freezing. (*Samukute kogoe-soo da.*) 寒くて凍えそうだ.

3 (become motionless) u⌈goka⌉naku naru 動かなくなる Ⓒ; mi ga su⌈kumu 身がすくむ Ⓒ: I froze at the sight of the snake. (*Watashi wa hebi o mite mi ga sukuñda.*) 私はへびを見て身がすくんだ.

— *vt.* **1** (make ice) ... o ko⌈oraseru ...を凍らせる Ⓥ: The pond was frozen. (*Ike ga kootta.*) 池が凍った.

2 (of food) ... o re⌈etoo suru ...を冷凍する Ⓘ: freeze meat (*niku o reetoo suru*) 肉を冷凍する.

freezer *n.* re⌈eto⌉oko 冷凍庫; fu⌈ri⌉izaa フリーザー; re⌈eto⌉oki 冷凍器: keep food in a freezer (*shokuhiñ o reetooko ni hozoñ suru*) 食品を冷凍庫に保存する.

freight *n.* **1** (carrying) ka⌉motsu u⌈ñsoo 貨物運送: send by air freight (*kookuu kamotsu de okuru*) 航空貨物で送る.

2 (goods) ka⌉motsu 貨物; tsu⌈mini 積み荷.

3 (charge) u⌉ñchiñ 運賃: freight free (*uñchiñ muryoo*) 運賃無料.

French *adj.* Fu⌈rañsu no フランスの; (of people) Fu⌈rañsu⌉jiñ no フランス人の; (of language) Fu⌈rañsugo no フランス語の.

— *n.* (language) Fu⌈rañsugo フランス語; (people) Fu⌈rañsu⌉jiñ フランス人.

frequency *n.* **1** (occurrence) shi⌉bashiba o⌈ko⌉ru ko⌈to⌉ しばしば起こること; hi⌈ñ-patsu 頻発: the frequency of earthquakes in Japan (*Nihoñ ni okeru jishiñ no hiñpatsu*) 日本における地震の頻発.

2 (rate) ka⌈isu⌉u 回数; hi⌉ñdo 頻度: the frequency of crime (*hañzai no hassee-ritsu*) 犯罪の発生率.

frequent *adj.* ta⌈bitabi no たびたびの; shi⌉bashiba no しばしばの: He makes frequent trips to China. (*Kare wa Chuugoku e tabitabi ryokoo shimasu.*) 彼は中国へたびたび旅行します.

frequently *adv.* ta⌈bitabi たびたび; shi⌉bashiba しばしば: He frequently arrives late. (*Kare wa tabitabi chikoku suru.*) 彼はたびたび遅刻する.

fresh *adj.* **1** (newly made) shi⌈ñseñ na 新鮮な: fresh vegetables (*shiñseñ na yasai*) 新鮮な野菜.

2 (new) a⌈tarashi⌉i 新しい: Is there any fresh news? (*Nani-ka atarashii nyuusu wa arimasu ka?*) 何か新しいニュースはありますか.

3 (refreshing) sa⌈wa⌉yaka na さわやかな: I felt fresh after a walk. (*Sañpo no ato sawayaka na kibuñ datta.*) 散歩の後さわやかな気分だった.

4 (bright) a⌈za⌉yaka na 鮮やかな: fresh colors (*azayaka na iro*) 鮮やかな色.

5 (without salt) shi⌈oke no na⌉i 塩気のない; ta⌈ñsui no 淡水の: fresh water (*tañsui*) 淡水.

freshman *n.* shi⌈ñnyu⌉usee 新入生; i⌈chi-ne⌉ñsee 1 年生.

friction *n.* (rubbing) ma⌈satsu 摩擦; (conflict) fu⌉wa 不和: trade friction (*booeki masatsu*) 貿易摩擦.

Friday *n.* ki⌈ñyo⌉o(bi) 金曜(日).

fridge *n.* re⌈ezo⌉oko 冷蔵庫.

fried *adj.* (pan-fried) a⌈bura de i⌈ta⌉meta 油でいためた; (deep-fried) a⌈bura de ageta 油で揚げた; fu⌈rai ni shita フライにした: fried chicken (*furaido chikiñ*) フライドチキン / a fried egg (*medamayaki*) 目玉焼き.

friend *n.* **1** (close companion) to⌈modachi 友だち; yu⌈ujiñ 友人: This is a souvenir for a friend. (*Kore wa yuujiñ e no o-miyage desu.*) これは友人へのおみやげです.

2 (helper) mi⌈kata 味方: a friend of the poor (*mazushii hito-tachi no mikata*) 貧しい人たちの味方.

friendly *adj.* **1** (like a friend) shi⌈tashi⌉i 親しい; yu⌈ukoo-teki na 友好的な: I am on a friendly terms with him. (*Watashi wa kare to wa*

f

shitashii aidagara desu.) 私は彼とは親しい間柄です. / a friendly nation (*yuukookoku*) 友好国.
2 (kind) shi˥ñsetsu na 親切な; ko⌈oi-teki na 好意的な: She is friendly to everybody. (*Kanojo wa dare ni taishite mo shiñsetsu desu.*) 彼女はだれに対しても親切です.

friendship *n.* yu⌈ujoo 友情; yu⌈u-koo-ka˥ñkee 友好関係: The friendship between them lasted long. (*Kare-ra no yuujoo wa nagaku tsuzuita.*) 彼らの友情は永く続いた.

fright *n.* kyo˥ofu 恐怖; ha⌈geshi˥i o⌈doroki˥ 激しい驚き: have a fright (*kyoofu ni osowareru*) 恐怖に襲われる.

frighten *vt.* **1** (make afraid) ... o ko⌈wagarase˥ru ...を怖がらせる Ⓥ; gyo⌈tto saseru ぎょっとさせる Ⓥ: I was frightened by a snake. (*Watashi wa hebi o mite gyotto shita.*) 私は蛇を見てぎょっとした.
2 (scare) ... o o⌈dosu ...を脅す Ⓒ: They frightened him into obedience. (*Kare-ra wa kare o odoshite fukujuu saseta.*) 彼らは彼を脅して服従させた.

frightened *adj.* o⌈bieta おびえた; o⌈biete iru おびえている; gyo⌈tto shita ぎょっとした: I was frightened at the sound. (*Watashi wa sono oto ni gyotto shita.*) 私はその音にぎょっとした.

frightful *adj.* o⌈soroshi˥i 恐ろしい; mo⌈nosugo˥i ものすごい: a frightful sight (*osoroshii kookee*) 恐ろしい光景.

fringe *n.* **1** (ornamental border) fu⌈saka˥zari 房飾り: the fringe of a rug (*juutañ no fusakazari*) じゅうたんの房飾り.
2 (edge) fu⌈chi˥ 縁; he⌈ri˥ へり; ma⌈wari 周り: a park with a fringe of trees (*mawari ni ki no aru kooeñ*) 周りに木のある公園.

frivolous *adj.* (not important) tsu⌈mara˥nai つまらない; to˥ru ni ta⌈ranai 取るに足らない: frivolous matters (*toru ni taranai kotogara*) 取るに足らない事柄.

frog *n.* ka⌈eru かえる(蛙).

from *prep.* **1** (starting point) ... kara ...から: How far is it from here to the station? (*Koko kara eki made dono kurai arimasu ka?*) ここから駅までどのくらいありますか. / rise from a chair (*isu kara tachiagaru*) いすから立ち上がる.
2 (beginning) ... kara ...から: I know her from her childhood. (*Watashi wa kanojo o kodomo no koro kara shitte imasu.*) 私は彼女を子どものころから知っています. / read a book from cover to cover (*hoñ o hajime kara owari made yomu*) 本を初めから終わりまで読む.
3 (distance) ... kara (ha⌈na˥rete) ...から(離れて): The town is four kilometers away from here. (*Sono machi wa koko kara yoñ-kiro hanareta tokoro ni arimasu.*) その町はここから4キロ離れた所にあります / His house is not far from the station. (*Kare no ie wa eki kara tooku nai.*) 彼の家は駅から遠くない.
4 (origin) ... kara ki˥ta ...から来た; ... shu⌈sshiñ no ...出身の: Where are you from? (*Dochira no go-shusshiñ desu ka?*) どちらのご出身ですか. / I come from Hokkaido. (*Watashi wa Hokkaidoo shusshiñ desu.*) 私は北海道出身です.
5 (source) ... kara ...から: A strange sound was heard from within. (*Naka kara heñ na mono-oto ga kikoeta.*) 中から変な物音が聞こえた. / quotations from the Bible (*seesho kara no iñyoo*) 聖書からの引用.
6 (material) ... kara ...から: Wine is made from grapes. (*Budooshu wa budoo kara tsukurimasu.*) ぶどう酒はぶどうから造ります.
7 (cause) ... de ...で; ... ga ge⌈ñiñ de ...が原因で: I was tired from overwork. (*Watashi wa shigoto no shi-sugi de tsukareta.*) 私は仕事のし過ぎで疲れた / He died from a wound. (*Kare wa kizu ga geñiñ de shiñda.*) 彼は傷が原因で死んだ.

front *n.* **1** (part) ma˥e 前; ze˥ñbu 前部: The front of his car was dented. (*Kare no kuruma no zeñbu wa hekoñde ita.*) 彼の車の前部はへこんでいた. / I sat in the front of the car. (*Watashi wa kuruma no mae no seki ni suwatta.*) 私は車の前の席に座った. ★ Japanese '*... no mae*' is used in two senses, 'in front of' and 'at the front of.'
2 (of a building) sho˥ome˥ñ 正面: the front of a house (*ie no shoomeñ*) 家の正面.
3 (in war) ze˥ñseñ 前線; se˥ñseñ 戦線: go to the front (*señseñ ni deru*) 戦線に出る.
in front of ... *prep.* ... no ma˥e ni ...の前に: There is a big tree in front of his house. (*Kare no ie no mae ni wa ooki-na ki ga arimasu.*) 彼の家の前には大きな木があります.
— *adj.* ze˥ñbu ni aru 前部にある; sho˥ome˥ñ no 正面の: the front garden (*zeñtee*) 前庭.

front desk *n.* fu˥roñto フロント; u˥ketsuke 受付: a front desk clerk (*furoñto-gakari*) フロント係.

frontier *n.* **1** (boundary) ko˥kkyoo 国境: cross the frontier by car (*kuruma de kokkyoo o koeru*) 車で国境を越える.
2 (the farthest area of land) fu˥ro˥ñtia フロンティア; he˥ñkyoo 辺境.

frost *n.* **1** (frozen dew) shi˥mo˥ 霜: Frost formed on the ground. (*Jimeñ ni shimo ga orita.*) 地面に霜が降りた.
2 (coldness) ka˥ñki 寒気; hi˥ekomi 冷え込み.
— *vt.* ... o shi˥mo˥ de o˥o˥u ...を霜で覆う [C]: frosted window panes (*shimo de oowareta madogarasu*) 霜で覆われた窓ガラス.

frown *vi.* ma˥yu o hi˥some˥ru まゆをひそめる [V]; shi˥kamettsura o suru しかめっ面をする [I]; i˥ya˥ na ka˥o o suru いやな顔をする [I]: She frowns on my smoking. (*Kanojo wa watashi ga tabako o suu to iya na kao o suru.*) 彼女は私がたばこを吸うといやな顔をする.
— *n.* shi˥kamettsura しかめっ面; shi˥bu˥i kao 渋い顔: He looked at me with a frown. (*Kare wa shibui kao de watashi o mita.*) 彼は渋い顔で私を見た.

frozen *adj.* ko˥otta 凍った; ko˥otte iru 凍っている; re˥etoo shita [shite a˥ru] 冷凍した[してある]: frozen food (*reetoo-shokuhiñ*) 冷凍食品.

fruit *n.* ku˥da˥mono 果物; ka˥jitsu 果実: I'd like some fruit for dessert. (*Dezaato ni kudamono o kudasai.*) デザートに果物を下さい.

fruitful *adj.* mi˥nori no [ga] o˥oi 実りの[が]多い; yu˥ueki na 有益な: a fruitful meeting (*yuueki na kaigoo*) 有益な会合.

frustration *n.* yo˥kkyuu-fu˥mañ 欲求不満; fu˥rasutore˥eshoñ フラストレーション: Her frustration with her job gradually increased. (*Shigoto ni taisuru kanojo no yokkyuu-fumañ wa shidai ni zoodai shita.*) 仕事に対する彼女の欲求不満は次第に増大した.

fry *vt.* (pan-fry) ... o (a˥bura de) i˥tame˥ru ...を(油で)いためる [V]; (deep-fry) (a˥bura de) a˥geru (油で)揚げる [V]; (of an egg) ya˥ku 焼く [C]: Fry me an egg. (*Tamago o yaite kudasai.*) 卵を焼いてください.
— *n.* i˥tamemono いため物; a˥gemono 揚げ物; fu˥rai ryo˥ori フライ料理.

frying pan *n.* fu˥raipañ フライパン.

fuel *n.* ne˥ñryo˥o 燃料: We have enough fuel for this winter. (*Kotoshi no fuyu wa neñryoo ga juubuñ arimasu.*) ことしの冬は燃料が十分あります.

fugitive *n.* (runaway) to˥obo˥osha 逃亡者; (political refugee) bo˥ome˥esha 亡命者.

fulfill *vt.* **1** (perform) ... o ha˥ta˥su ...を果たす [C]: I fulfilled my duty. (*Watashi wa jibuñ no gimu o hatashita.*) 私は自分の義務を果たした.
2 (satisfy) ... o ji˥tsugeñ suru ...を実現する [I]; ka˥nae˥ru かなえる [V]:

He fulfilled his parents' hopes. (*Kare wa ryooshiñ no kiboo o kanaeta.*) 彼は両親の希望をかなえた.

fulfillment *n.* ri⌈koo 履行; ji⌈tsugeñ 実現: fulfillment of a promise (*yakusoku no rikoo*) 約束の履行.

full *adj.* **1** (filled) ... de i⌈ppai na [no] ...でいっぱいな[の]; mi⌉chita 満ちた; mi⌉chite iru 満ちている: The room was full of people. (*Heya wa hito de ippai datta.*) 部屋は人でいっぱいだった. / a glass full of wine (*waiñ ga ippai haitta gurasu*) ワインがいっぱい入ったグラス.

2 (complete) ka⌈ñzeñ na 完全な; ma⌈ñ- 満: The flowers are in full bloom. (*Hana wa mañkai desu.*) 花は満開です. / get full marks (*mañteñ o toru*) 満点をとる. / Full tank, please. (*Mañtañ ni shite kudasai.*) 満タンにしてください.

3 (of food) o-⌈naka ippai no お腹いっぱいの: I am full. (*O-naka ga ippai desu.*) お腹がいっぱいです.

4 (of time) ma⌈ru まる: I waited for a full hour. (*Watashi wa maru ichi-jikañ matta.*) 私はまる1時間待った. / a full five years (*maru go-neñ-kañ*) まる5年間.

full stop *n.* pi⌉riodo ピリオド; shu⌈ushi⌉fu 終止符.

fully *adv.* **1** (completely) ju⌈ubu⌉ñ ni 十分に; ka⌈ñzeñ ni 完全に: I am fully satisfied. (*Watashi wa juubuñ ni mañzoku shite imasu.*) 私は十分に満足しています.

2 (at least) su⌈ku⌉naku tomo 少なくとも; ta⌈ppu⌉ri たっぷり: We walked fully five kilometers. (*Watashi-tachi wa tappuri go-kiro arukimashita.*) 私たちはたっぷり5キロ歩きました.

fun *n.* ta⌈no⌉shisa 楽しさ; o⌈moshi⌉rosa おもしろさ: We had a lot of fun at the party. (*Paatii wa totemo tanoshikatta.*) パーティーはとても楽しかった. / It was fun riding a horse. (*Uma ni noru no wa omoshirokatta.*) 馬に乗るのはおもしろかった.

function *n.* **1** (special job) ha⌈taraki 働き; ki⌉noo 機能: the function of the heart (*shiñzoo no hataraki [kinoo]*) 心臓の働き[機能].

2 (ceremony) gi⌉shiki 儀式; gyo⌉oji 行事; (party) e⌈ñkai 宴会.

— *vi.* u⌈go⌉ku 動く Ⓒ; ki⌉noo suru 機能する Ⓘ: The elevator is not functioning now. (*Erebeetaa wa ima ugoite imaseñ.*) エレベーターは今動いていません.

functional *adj.* ki⌈noo-teki na 機能的な; ji⌈tsuyoo-teki na 実用的な: functional furniture (*kinoo-teki na kagu*) 機能的な家具.

fund *n.* **1** (money) ki⌉kiñ 基金; shi⌉kiñ 資金: a relief fund (*kyuusai shikiñ*) 救済資金.

2 (store) ta⌈kuwae 蓄え; chi⌈kuseki 蓄積: a fund of information (*joohoo no chikuseki*) 情報の蓄積.

fundamental *adj.* **1** (basic) ki⌉so no 基礎の; ki⌈hoñ-teki na 基本的な: fundamental human rights (*kihoñ-teki jiñkeñ*) 基本的人権.

2 (essential) hi⌈ssu no 必須の; ju⌈uyoo na 重要な: Moderate exercise is fundamental to good health. (*Tekido na uñdoo wa keñkoo ni hissu desu.*) 適度な運動は健康に必須です.

funeral *n.* so⌈oshiki 葬式; so⌉ogi 葬儀: attend a funeral (*soogi ni sañretsu suru*) 葬儀に参列する.

funny *adj.* **1** (amusing) o⌈moshiro⌉i おもしろい; ko⌈kkee na こっけいな: a funny story (*omoshiroi hanashi*) おもしろい話.

2 (strange) ki⌉myoo na 奇妙な; he⌉ñ na 変な: This fish has a funny smell. (*Kono sakana wa heñ na nioi ga suru.*) この魚は変なにおいがする.

fur *n.* **1** (skin) ke⌈gawa 毛皮: a fur coat (*kegawa no oobaa*) 毛皮のオーバー.

2 (something made of fur) ke⌈gawa-se⌉ehiñ 毛皮製品: wear expensive furs (*kooka na kegawa o kiru*) 高価な毛皮を着る.

furious *adj.* **1** (very angry) su⌈go⌉ku o⌈kot⌉ta [o⌈kot⌉te iru] すごく怒った[怒っている]; ge⌉kido shita [shite

iru] 激怒した[している]: She is furious with you for sexual discrimination. (*Kanojo wa see sabetsu no koto de kimi no koto o sugoku okotte iru.*) 彼女は性差別のことで君のことをすごく怒っている.
2 (violent) mo⌈oretsu na 猛烈な; mo⌈nosugo⌉i ものすごい: a furious storm (*mooretsu na arashi*) 猛烈なあらし.

furnace *n.* ro 炉; ka⌈mado かまど.

furnish *vt.* **1** (equip) ... ni ka⌉gu o so⌈naetsukeru ...に家具を備え付ける [V]; to⌈ritsukeru 取り付ける [V]: His room is luxuriously furnished. (*Kare no heya ni wa zeetaku na kagu ga okarete iru.*) 彼の部屋にはぜいたくな家具が置かれている.
2 (supply) ... ni (... o) kyo⌈okyuu suru ...に(...を)供給する [I]: The river furnishes this town with water. (*Sono kawa wa kono machi ni mizu o kyookyuu shite imasu.*) その川はこの町に水を供給しています.

furniture *n.* ka⌉gu 家具; bi⌈hiñ 備品: a furniture store (*kaguya*) 家具屋.

furrow *n.* **1** (long cut in the ground) mi⌈zo 溝; (rut) wa⌈dachi わだち.
2 (wrinkle) shi⌈wa しわ.
— *vt.* (wrinkle) ... ni shi⌈wa o yoseru ...にしわを寄せる [V]: furrow one's brow (*hitai ni shiwa o yoseru*) 額にしわを寄せる.

further *adv.* **1** (more) sa⌉ra ni さらに; na⌉o so⌈no ue⌉ ni なおそのうえに: He spoke further on the issue. (*Kare wa sono mondai ni tsuite sara ni hanashita.*) 彼はその問題についてさらに話した.
2 (farther) sa⌉ra ni to⌈oku さらに遠く; mo⌉tto sa⌈ki ni もっと先に: go further away (*motto saki ni iku*) もっと先に行く.
— *adj.* so⌈re i⌉joo no それ以上の: We need further information. (*Sore ijoo no joohoo ga hitsuyoo da.*) それ以上の情報が必要だ.
— *vt.* ... o so⌈kushiñ suru ...を促進する [I]: further public welfare (*kookyoo no fukushi o sokushiñ suru*) 公共の福祉を促進する.

furthermore *adv.* na⌉o なお; so⌈no ue そのうえ.

fury *n.* ha⌈geshi⌉i i⌈kari 激しい怒り; ge⌉kido 激怒: He flew into a fury. (*Kare wa gekido shita.*) 彼は激怒した.

fuss *n.* o⌈osa⌉wagi 大騒ぎ: make a fuss about trifles (*tsumaranai koto ni oosawagi suru*) つまらないことに大騒ぎする.

future *n.* **1** (the time to come) mi⌉rai 未来; sho⌉orai 将来; ko⌉ñgo 今後: No one can tell what will happen in the future. (*Shoorai nani ga okoru ka dare ni mo wakaranai.*) 将来何が起こるかだれにもわからない. / You must be careful in future. (*Kore kara wa motto ki o tsuke nasai.*) これからはもっと気をつけなさい.
2 (prospect) ze⌉ñto 前途; sho⌈orai-see 将来性: a young man with a bright future (*zeñto no akarui seeneñ*) 前途の明るい青年.

G

gain *vt.* **1** (obtain) ... o e⌉ru ...を得る [V]; ka⌈kutoku suru 獲得する [I]: I have gained a lot from it. (*Watashi wa sore kara ooku no mono o eta.*) 私はそれから多くのものを得た.
2 (add) ... o ma⌈su ...を増す [C]: The car gained speed. (*Kuruma wa sokudo o mashita.*) 車は速度を増した.
3 (run fast) su⌈sumu 進む [C]: This watch gains 10 seconds a week. (*Kono tokee wa is-shuukañ ni juu-byoo susumu.*) この時計は1週間に10秒進む.

— *vi.* ri⌉eki o eru 利益を得る V; to ⌈ku o suru 得をする I: How much did you gain in that deal? (*Sono torihiki de ikura mookemashita ka?*) その取り引きでいくらもうけましたか.

— *n.* (profit) ri⌉eki 利益; (increase) zo⌈oka 増加: My losses were greater than my gains. (*Rieki yori mo soñshitsu no hoo ga ookikatta.*) 利益よりも損失のほうが大きかった. / a gain in weight (*taijuu no zooka*) 体重の増加.

g

gallbladder *n.* ta⌈ñnoo 胆のう.

gallant *adj.* i⌈samashi⌉i 勇ましい; yu⌈ukañ na 勇敢な: a gallant leader (*yuukañ na shidoosha*) 勇敢な指導者.

gallery *n.* (for selling art) ga⌈roo 画廊; gya⌉rarii ギャラリー; (for exhibiting art) bi⌈jutsu⌉kañ 美術館.

gallon *n.* ga⌉roñ ガロン: 30 miles per gallon (*ichi-garoñ ni tsuki sañjuu mairu*) 1ガロンにつき30マイル.

★ The gallon is not used in Japan; in the example above, the Japanese would use the liter. There are 4.5 liters in a U.S. gallon.

gallstone *n.* ta⌉ñseki 胆石.

gamble *vi.* ka⌈ke⌉ o suru 賭けをする I; ba⌈kuchi o u⌉tsu ばくちを打つ C: gamble on horses (*keeba ni kane o kakeru*) 競馬に金を賭ける.

— *n.* ka⌈ke⌉ 賭け; ba⌈kuchi ばくち.

game *n.* **1** (sport) shi⌈ai 試合; kyo⌉ogi 競技: win [lose] a game (*shiai ni katsu [makeru]*) 試合に勝つ[負ける].

2 (play) a⌈sobi 遊び; yu⌉ugi 遊戯; ge⌉emu ゲーム: What games do the children play? (*Kodomo-tachi wa doñna asobi o shimasu ka?*) 子どもたちはどんな遊びをしますか.

gang *n.* **1** (criminals) bo⌈oryoku⌉dañ 暴力団; gya⌉ñgu ギャング.

2 (group) i⌈chidañ 一団; (comrade) na⌈kama 仲間: a gang of workers (*roodoosha no ichidañ*) 労働者の一団.

gap *n.* **1** (opening) sa⌈keme 裂け目; su⌈kima すき間: a gap in the wall (*kabe no sakeme*) 壁の裂け目 / fill a gap (*sukima o fusagu*) すき間をふさぐ.

2 (difference) so⌈oi 相違; zu⌈re ずれ; gya⌉ppu ギャップ: There is a big gap between their points of view. (*Kare-ra no kañgae ni wa ooki-na gyappu ga aru.*) 彼らの考えには大きなギャップがある.

garage *n.* sha⌉ko 車庫; ga⌈re⌉eji ガレージ: put a car into the garage (*kuruma o gareeji ni ireru*) 車をガレージに入れる. ★ Japanese '*gareeji*' is not used in the sense of a place where motor vehicles are repaird.

garbage *n.* go⌈mi⌉ ごみ; ku⌉zu くず: take out the garbage (*gomi o dasu*) ごみを出す.

garden *n.* ni⌉wa 庭; (formal) te⌈eeñ 庭園: play in the garden (*niwa de asobu*) 庭で遊ぶ / a kitchen garden (*katee saieñ*) 家庭菜園.

★ 'Yard' and 'court' are also called '*niwa*.'

gardener *n.* u⌈ekiya 植木屋; ni⌈wa⌉shi 庭師.

gargle *vi.* u⌈gai o suru うがいをする I.

— *n.* u⌈gai うがい.

garlic *n.* ni⌈ñniku にんにく; ga⌉arikku ガーリック.

garment *n.* (clothes in general) i⌉rui 衣類; i⌉fuku 衣服: ladies' garments (*fujiñ-yoo no irui*) 婦人用の衣類.

gas *n.* **1** (fuel) ga⌉su ガス: turn on [off] the gas (*gasu o tsukeru [kesu]*) ガスをつける[消す].

2 (air) ki⌈tai 気体; ga⌉su ガス: Hydrogen is a gas at normal temperatures. (*Suiso wa joo-oñ de kitai desu.*) 水素は常温で気体です.

3 (gasoline) ga⌈soriñ ガソリン.

gasoline *n.* ga⌈soriñ ガソリン.

gasp *vi.* a⌈e⌉gu あえぐ C; i⌉ki o ki⌈ra⌉su 息を切らす C: He went up the stairs gasping for breath. (*Kare wa iki o kirashi-nagara kaidañ o nobotta.*) 彼は息を切らしながら階段を上った.

— *n.* aegi あえぎ; i⌈kigire 息切れ: give a gasp of surprise (*odoroite iki o nomu*) 驚いて息をのむ.

gas station *n.* ga⌈sorin̄-suta⌉n̄do ガソリンスタンド; su⌈tan̄do スタンド; kyu⌈uyujo 給油所.

gas tank *n.* (storage facility) ga⌈suta⌉n̄ku ガスタンク; (autos, planes, etc.) ga⌈sorin̄ ta⌉n̄ku ガソリンタンク.

gate *n.* (traditional) mo⌉n̄ 門; (opening in fence, wall) ge⌉eto ゲート: open [close] a gate (*mon̄ o akeru* [*shimeru*]) 門を開ける[閉める].

gather *vt.* **1** (bring together) ... o a⌈tsume⌉ru …を集める Ⓥ: I gathered fallen leaves and burned them. (*Watashi wa ochiba o atsumete moyashita.*) 私は落ち葉を集めて燃やした.
2 (pick; harvest) ... o tsu⌈mu …を摘む Ⓒ; to⌈riireru 取り入れる Ⓥ: gather flowers (*hana o tsumu*) 花を摘む / gather the crops (*sakumotsu o toriireru*) 作物を穫り入れる.
3 (increase) ... o ma⌈su …を増す Ⓒ: The car gathered speed. (*Kuruma wa supiido o mashita.*) 車はスピードを増した.
4 (infer) ... to su⌈isoku suru …と推測する Ⓘ: I gathered that he did not know that fact. (*Kare wa sono jijitsu o shiranai no da to suisoku shita.*) 彼はその事実を知らないのだと推測した.
— *vi.* (assemble) a⌈tsuma⌉ru 集まる Ⓒ: A crowd gathered in the park. (*Kooen̄ ni gun̄shuu ga atsumatta.*) 公園に群集が集まった.

gathering *n.* a⌈tsumari⌉ 集まり; shu⌈ukai 集会.

gauge *n.* ke⌉eki 計器; ge⌉eji ゲージ: a fuel gauge (*nen̄ryookee*) 燃料計 / a pressure gauge (*atsuryokukee*) 圧力計.

gay *adj.* (homosexual) do⌈ose⌉eai no 同性愛の: a gay bar (*geebaa*) ゲイバー.
— *n.* do⌈oseea⌉isha 同性愛者.
★ '*Dooseeaisha*' usually connotes a male in Japan. For females use '*resubian̄*' レスビアン.

gaze *vi.* (... o) ji⌈tto mi⌈tsumeru (…を)じっと見つめる Ⓥ: He gazed into my face. (*Kare wa watashi no kao o jitto mitsumeta.*) 彼は私の顔をじっと見つめた.

gear *n.* **1** (wheels with teeth) gi⌈ya ギヤ; ha⌈gu⌉ruma 歯車: a car with four gears (*yon̄dan̄ giya no kuruma*) 4段ギヤの車.
2 (equipment) yo⌉ogu 用具; yo⌉ohin̄ 用品: fishing gear (*tsuriyoogu*) 釣り用具 / sports gear (*supootsu yoohin̄*) スポーツ用品.
3 (clothing) fu⌈kusoo 服装: hunting gear (*shuryoofuku*) 狩猟服.

gear shift *n.* (on an auto) shi⌉futo シフト.

gem *n.* ho⌈oseki 宝石.

gender *n.* (in grammar) se⌉e 性; (distinction of sex) se⌈ebetsu 性別.

gene *n.* i⌈de⌉n̄shi 遺伝子.

general *adj.* **1** (not specific) i⌈ppan̄ no 一般の; i⌈ppan̄-teki na 一般的な; so⌈ogoo-teki na 総合的な: This book is intended for the general reader. (*Kono hon̄ wa ippan̄ no dokusha o taishoo ni shite iru.*) この本は一般の読者を対象にしている. / the general public (*ippan̄ taishuu*) 一般大衆.
2 (not detailed) ga⌈iryaku no 概略の; da⌈itai no だいたいの: a general plan (*daitai no keekaku*) だいたいの計画.
in general *adv.* i⌈ppan̄ ni 一般に.

generalize *vi.* i⌈ppa⌉n̄ron̄ o no⌈be⌉ru 一般論を述べる Ⓥ: generalize from data (*deeta kara ippan̄ron̄ o noberu*) データから一般論を述べる.

generally *adv.* **1** (usually) i⌈ppan̄ ni 一般に; fu⌈tsuu (wa) 普通(は): I generally get up at six. (*Watashi wa futsuu (wa) roku-ji ni okimasu.*) 私は普通(は)6時に起きます.
2 (widely) hi⌉roku 広く: The fact is generally known. (*Sono jijitsu wa hiroku shirarete iru.*) その事実は広く知られている.

general manager *n.* (of a

bureau) kyoʳkuchoo 局長; (of a department) buʳchoo 部長; (of a store) shiʳteˡñchoo 支店長.

generate *vt.* ... o haʳssee suru ...を発生する ⓘ; oʳkoˡsu 起こす Ⓒ: Friction generates heat. (*Masatsu wa netsu o hassee suru.*) 摩擦は熱を発生する.

generation *n.* daˡi 代; seˡdai 世代: Three generations live in her house. (*Kanojo no ie ni wa sañ-sedai ga suñde iru.*) 彼女の家には3世代が住んでいる. / We are of the same generation. (*Watashi-tachi wa doo sedai da.*) 私たちは同世代だ.

generation gap *n.* seʳdaiˡ kañ no daʳñzetsu 世代間の断絶.

generosity *n.* kiʳmae no yoˡsa 気前のよさ; kaʳñdai 寛大: He showed generosity with his money. (*Kare wa o-kane ni kimae no yoi tokoro o miseta.*) 彼はお金に気前のよいところを見せた.

generous *adj.* **1** (free in giving) kʳimae no yoˡi 気前のよい; moʳno-oˡshimi shinai 物惜しみしない: He made a generous donation. (*Kare wa kimae no yoi kifu o shita.*) 彼は気前のよい寄付をした.
2 (forgiving) kaʳñdai na 寛大な: He was generous regarding my mistake. (*Kare wa watashi no machigai ni taishite kañdai datta.*) 彼は私の間違いに対して寛大だった.

genetics *n.* iʳdeˡñgaku 遺伝学.

genius *n.* **1** (person) teʳñsai 天才: He is a genius in mathematics. (*Kare wa suugaku no teñsai da.*) 彼は数学の天才だ.
2 (ability) saʳinoo 才能: She has a genius for music. (*Kanojo wa oñ-gaku no sainoo ga aru.*) 彼女は音楽の才能がある.

gentle *adj.* **1** (tender) yaʳsashii 優しい; oʳtonashiˡi おとなしい: He is gentle with children. (*Kare wa kodomo ni yasashii.*) 彼は子どもに優しい.
2 (mild) oʳdaˡyaka na 穏やかな; (gradual) yuʳruˡyaka na 緩やかな: a gentle wind (*odayaka na kaze*) 穏やかな風 / a gentle slope (*yuruyaka na saka*) 緩やかな坂.

gentleman *n.* (well-bred man) shiˡñshi 紳士; (male) daʳñsee 男性: behave like a gentleman (*shiñshi-rashiku furumau*) 紳士らしく振る舞う.

gently *adv.* **1** (tenderly) yaʳsa-shiku 優しく; oʳdaˡyaka ni 穏やかに: speak gently (*yasashiku hanasu*) 優しく話す.
2 (gradually) yuʳruˡyaka ni 緩やかに: This road curves gently to the right. (*Kono michi wa yuruyaka ni migi e magatte iru.*) この道は緩やかに右へ曲がっている.

genuine *adj.* **1** (real) hoʳñmono no 本物の; shoʳoshiñ shoomee no 正真正銘の: a genuine diamond (*hoñmono no daiyamoñdo*) 本物のダイヤモンド.
2 (sincere) seʳejitsu na 誠実な; ko-ʳkoˡro kara no 心からの: genuine sympathy (*kokoro kara no doojoo*) 心からの同情.

geography *n.* **1** (study) chiʳriˡga-ku 地理学: physical geography (*shi-zeñ chirigaku*) 自然地理学.
2 (natural features) chiˡri 地理; chiʳsee 地勢: the geography of Japan (*Nihoñ no chiri*) 日本の地理.

geology *n.* chiʳshitsuˡgaku 地質学.

geometry *n.* kiʳkaˡgaku 幾何学.

geranium *n.* zeʳranyuˡumu ゼラニューム.

germ *n.* baʳikiñ ばい菌; saʳikiñ 細菌; byoʳogeñkiñ 病原菌.

gesture *n.* **1** (movement) miˡburi 身ぶり; teˡmane 手まね: I communicated with him with gestures. (*Watashi wa kare to temane de hanashita.*) 私は彼と手まねで話した.
2 (attitude) soˡburi そぶり; jeˡsu-chaa ジェスチャー: His offer of help was a mere gesture. (*Kare no eñjo no mooshide wa tañnaru jesuchaa ni suginakatta.*) 彼の援助の申し出は単なるジェスチャーにすぎなかった.
— *vi.* miˡburi [teˡburi] o suru 身ぶ

り[手ぶり]をする Ⅰ: He gestured to me to keep quiet. (*Kare wa watashi ni damatte iru yoo ni miburi de aizu shita.*) 彼は私に黙っているように身ぶりで合図した.

get *vt.* **1** (receive) ... o u⌈ke⌉ru ...を受ける Ⅴ; u⌈ketoru 受け取る Ⓒ: Who is it that got the phone call? (*Sono deñwa o uketa no wa dare desu ka?*) その電話を受けたのはだれですか. / I got the letter this morning. (*Watashi wa sono tegami o kesa uketorimashita.*) 私はその手紙をけさ受け取りました.
2 (buy) ... o ka⌈u ...を買う Ⓒ: Where did you get that hat? (*Sono booshi o doko de kaimashita ka?*) その帽子をどこで買いましたか.
3 (obtain) ... o e⌉ru ...を得る Ⅴ; to⌉ru 取る Ⓒ; te⌉ ni i⌈reru 手に入れる Ⅴ: He got first prize in the contest. (*Kare wa koñtesuto de it-too-shoo o totta.*) 彼はコンテストで1等賞を取った.
4 (bring) ... o to⌈tte ku⌉ru ...を取ってくる Ⅰ; mo⌈tte ku⌉ru 持ってくる Ⅰ: Get me a chair. (*Isu o motte kite kudasai.*) いすを持ってきてください.
5 (become) ... ni na⌉ru ...になる Ⓒ: He got sick while traveling. (*Kare wa ryokoo saki de byooki ni natta.*) 彼は旅行先で病気になった.
6 (catch) ... o tsu⌈kamaeru ...を捕まえる Ⅴ: The police failed to get the thief. (*Keesatsu wa doroboo o tsukamaeru koto ga dekinakatta.*) 警察はどろぼうを捕まえることができなかった.
7 (understand) ... ga wa⌈ka⌉ru ...がわかる Ⓒ: I get you. (*Wakarimashita.*) わかりました.
— *vi.* **1** (become) na⌉ru なる Ⓒ: It's getting warmer. (*Dañdañ atatakaku natte kite iru.*) だんだん暖かくなってきている.
2 (arrive) (... ni) tsu⌉ku (...に)着く Ⓒ: I'll get there by 5 o'clock. (*Go-ji made ni wa soko ni tsukimasu.*) 5時までにはそこに着きます.
3 (passive) ‹verb›-(ra)reru ...(ら)れる Ⅴ: He got scolded by his teacher. (*Kare wa señsee ni shikarareta.*) 彼は先生にしかられた.

get along *vi.* (live) ku⌈rashite iku 暮らしていく Ⓒ: How are you getting along? (*Ikaga o-kurashi desu ka?*) いかがお暮らしですか.

get away *vi.* ni⌈gedasu 逃げ出す Ⓒ: I could not get away from the meeting. (*Kaigi kara nigedasu koto ga dekinakatta.*) 会議から逃げ出すことができなかった.

get back *vi.* (return) mo⌈do⌉ru 戻る Ⓒ: He'll soon get back. (*Kare wa sugu modoru deshoo.*) 彼はすぐ戻るでしょう.

get down *vi.* o⌈ri⌉ru 降りる Ⅴ; *vt.* o⌈ro⌉su 下(降)ろす Ⓒ: Please get the book down from the shelf. (*Tana kara sono hoñ o oroshite kudasai.*) 棚からその本を下ろしてください.

get in *vi.* na⌉ka ni hairu 中に入る Ⓒ; *vt.* ... ni no⌈ru ...に乗る Ⓒ: I got in a taxi. (*Watashi wa takushii ni notta.*) 私はタクシーに乗った.

get off *vi.* o⌈ri⌉ru 降りる Ⅴ: I'll get off at the next stop. (*Tsugi no teeryuujo de orimasu.*) 次の停留所で降ります.

get on *vt.* ... ni no⌈ru ...に乗る Ⓒ: Where can I get on the bus? (*Sono basu ni wa doko de noru ñ desu ka?*) そのバスにはどこで乗るんですか.

get out of ... *vt.* ... kara de⌉ru ...から出る Ⅴ: Get out of bed. (*Beddo kara de nasai.*) ベッドから出なさい.

get up *vi.* o⌈ki⌉ru 起きる Ⅴ: I have to get up early tomorrow morning. (*Ashita no asa wa hayaku okinakereba naranai.*) あしたの朝は早く起きなければならない.

ghetto *n.* (where a specific minority lives) kyo⌈ju⌉uku 居住区; (slum) hi⌈ñmi⌉ñgai 貧民街.

ghost *n.* yu⌉uree 幽霊: People say a ghost appears at this house. (*Kono uchi ni yuuree ga deru soo da.*) この家に幽霊が出るそうだ.

giant *n.* (person) kyo⌉jiñ 巨人; (figuratively) o⌈omono 大物: an economic giant (*keezai taikoku*) 経済

大国.

— *adj*. kyo⌈dai na 巨大な: a giant Christmas tree (*kyodai na Kurisumasu tsurii*) 巨大なクリスマスツリー.

gift *n*. **1** (present) o⌈kurimono 贈り物; pu⌈re⌉zeñto プレゼント: I sent her a birthday gift. (*Watashi wa kanojo ni tañjoobi no okurimono o okutta.*) 私は彼女に誕生日の贈り物を送った.

2 (talent) sa⌈inoo 才能: She has a gift for painting. (*Kanojo wa e no sainoo ga aru.*) 彼女は絵の才能がある.

g

gift certificate *n*. sho⌈ohi⌉ñkeñ 商品券.

gifted *adj*. sa⌈inoo no [ga] a⌈ru 才能の[が]ある: a gifted painter (*sainoo no aru gaka*) 才能のある画家.

giggle *vi*. ku⌉sukusu wa⌈rau くすくす笑う Ⓒ: The girl started giggling. (*Sono oñna-no-ko wa kusukusu warai-dashita.*) その女の子はくすくす笑い出した.

ginger *n*. (plant) sho⌈oga しょうが(生姜).

ginkgo *n*. (tree) i⌈choo いちょう(銀杏).

ginseng *n*. cho⌈oseñ-ni⌉ñjiñ 朝鮮人参.

giraffe *n*. ki⌈riñ きりん; ji⌉rafu ジラフ.

girl *n*. o⌈ñna⌉-no-ko 女の子; sho⌉ojo 少女: The girls are playing with dolls. (*Oñna-no-ko-tachi wa niñgyoo de asoñde iru.*) 女の子たちは人形で遊んでいる.

girlfriend *n*. (friend who is a girl) o⌈ñna-to⌉modachi 女友達; (in a relationship) ga⌈arufure⌉ñdo ガールフレンド; (lover) ko⌈ibito 恋人.

give *vt*. **1** (to a person) ... o a⌈geru …をあげる Ⓥ; (to an inferior recipient) ya⌈ru やる Ⓒ; (to a superior recipient) sa⌈shiageru 差し上げる Ⓥ: I'll give you this book. (*Anata ni kono hoñ o agemashoo.*) あなたにこの本をあげましょう. / I gave apples to children. (*Watashi wa kodomotachi ni riñgo o yatta.*) 私は子どもたちにりんごをやった. / She gave water to the flowers. (*Kanojo wa hana ni mizu o yatta.*) 彼女は花に水をやった.

2 (to me) ... o ku⌈reru …をくれる Ⓥ; [honorific] ku⌈dasa⌉ru 下さる Ⓒ: My father gave me a fountain pen. (*Chichi wa watashi ni mañneñhitsu o kureta.*) 父は私に万年筆をくれた. / My teacher gave me a notebook. (*Señsee wa watashi ni nooto o kudasatta.*) 先生は私にノートを下さった.

3 (ask for) [imperative] ... o ku⌈dasa⌉i …を下さい: Please give me something to drink. (*Nani-ka nomimono o kudasai.*) 何か飲み物を下さい.

4 (provide) ... o a⌈taeru …を与える Ⓥ: The results will give you satisfaction. (*Sono kekka wa anata ni mañzoku o ataeru deshoo.*) その結果はあなたに満足を与えるでしょう.

5 (hand over) ... o wa⌈tasu …を渡す Ⓒ: I gave my baggage to a porter. (*Watashi wa nimotsu o pootaa ni watashita.*) 私は荷物をポーターに渡した.

6 (show) ... o shi⌈me⌉su …を示す Ⓒ; (state) no⌈be⌉ru 述べる Ⓥ: He gave us a better example. (*Kare wa motto yoi ree o shimeshita.*) 彼はもっとよい例を示した. / I gave a farewell speech. (*Watashi wa wakare no kotoba o nobeta.*) 私は別れの言葉を述べた.

give up *vt*. ... o a⌈kirame⌉ru …をあきらめる Ⓥ: We gave up the plan. (*Watashi-tachi wa sono keekaku o akirameta.*) 私たちはその計画をあきらめた.

given name *n*. na 名. ★ Japanese 'surname' is followed by 'given name.'

glad *adj*. u⌈reshi⌉i うれしい: I'm very glad to see you. (*Anata ni o-me ni kakarete taiheñ ureshii desu.*) あなたにお目にかかれて大変うれしいです.

be glad to do yo⌈roko⌉ñde ⟨verb⟩ 喜んで…: I'd be glad to help you. (*Yorokoñ de o-tetsudai itashimasu.*) 喜んでお手伝いいたします.

gladly *adv*. yo⌈roko⌉ñde 喜んで; ko⌈koroyo⌉ku 快く: I will come gladly. (*Yorokoñde o-ukagai shimasu.*) 喜

んでお伺いします.

glamour *n.* mi⌈ryoku 魅力: the glamour of a beautiful woman (*utsukushii josee no miryoku*) 美しい女性の魅力.

glance *vi.* (... o) chi⌈ratto mi⌉ru (...を)ちらっと見る Ⓥ: She glanced at me. (*Kanojo wa chiratto watashi o mita.*) 彼女はちらっと私を見た.
— *n.* hi⌈to⌉me ひと目: I recognized him at a glance. (*Watashi wa hitome de kare to wakatta.*) 私はひと目で彼とわかった.

gland *n.* se⌉ñ 腺: lymph glands (*riñpaseñ*) リンパ腺.

glare *vi.* **1** (shine) gi⌈ragira ka⌈gaya⌉ku ぎらぎら輝く Ⓒ: The sun glared down on us. (*Taiyoo wa giragira to teritsuketa.*) 太陽はぎらぎらと照りつけた.
2 (stare) (... o) ni⌈ramitsuke⌉ru (...を)にらみつける Ⓥ: He glared at me. (*Kare wa watashi o niramitsuketa.*) 彼は私をにらみつけた.
— *n.* (light) ma⌈bushi⌉i hi⌈kari⌉ まぶしい光; (stare) ni⌈rami⌉ にらみ.

glass *n.* **1** (clear material) ga⌈rasu ガラス: a glass door (*garasu-do*) ガラス戸.
2 (vessel) ko⌈ppu コップ: a glass of water (*koppu ip-pai no mizu*) コップ1杯の水.

glasses *n.* me⌉gane 眼鏡: I put on glasses when I read. (*Watashi wa hoñ o yomu toki megane o kakemasu.*) 私は本を読むとき眼鏡をかけます.

gleam *n.* ka⌉suka na hi⌈kari⌉ かすかな光; bi⌈koo 微光: the gleam of distant fishing boats (*tooku no gyoseñ no hikari*) 遠くの漁船の光.

glide *vi.* su⌈be⌉ru 滑る Ⓒ: They glided down the slope. (*Kare-ra wa shameñ o subette orita.*) 彼らは斜面を滑って下りた.

glimpse *vt.* ... o chi⌈ra⌉ri to mi⌉ru ...をちらりと見る Ⓥ: I glimpsed him in the crowd. (*Watashi wa hitogomi no naka de kare o chirari to mita.*) 私は人込みの中で彼をちらりと見た.
— *n.* hi⌈to⌉me ひと目: I only caught a glimpse of the red car. (*Watashi wa sono akai kuruma o hitome mita dake desu.*) 私はその赤い車をひと目見ただけです.

glitter *vi.* pi⌉kapika hi⌈ka⌉ru ぴかぴか光る Ⓒ; ki⌉rakira ka⌈gaya⌉ku きらきら輝く Ⓒ: Stars are glittering in the sky. (*Sora ni hoshi ga kirakira kagayaite iru.*) 空に星がきらきら輝いている.

global *adj.* **1** (of the earth) chi⌈kyuu (zeñtai) no 地球(全体)の; (of the world) se⌈kai-teki na 世界的な: a global depression (*sekai-teki na fukyoo*) 世界的な不況.
2 (complete) ze⌈ñtai-teki na 全体的な: a global view (*zeñtai o miru kañgae-kata*) 全体を見る考え方.

globe *n.* (of the earth) chi⌈kyu⌉ugi 地球儀.

gloomy *adj.* **1** (dark) u⌈sugurai 薄暗い: a gloomy room (*usugurai heya*) 薄暗い部屋.
2 (low spirited) yu⌈u-utsu na 憂うつな; fu⌈sagiko⌉ñda ふさぎ込んだ: He looked gloomy. (*Kare wa yuu-utsu-soo ni mieta.*) 彼は憂うつそうに見えた.

glorious *adj.* **1** (praiseworthy) e⌈ekoo a⌉ru 栄光ある; me⌉eyo no 名誉の: a glorious victory (*eekoo no shoori*) 栄光の勝利.
2 (wonderful) su⌈barashi⌉i すばらしい; su⌈teki na すてきな: have a glorious holiday (*suteki na kyuujitsu o sugosu*) すてきな休日を過ごす.

glory *n.* **1** (honor) e⌈ekoo 栄光; me⌉eyo 名誉: win glory in battle (*tatakai de meeyo o ukeru*) 戦いで名誉を受ける.
2 (splendor) u⌈tsuku⌉shisa 美しさ; so⌈okañ 壮観: the glory of the setting sun (*yuuhi no utsukushisa*) 夕日の美しさ.

glossary *n.* yo⌈ogo⌉shuu 用語集.

glove *n.* **1** (for hands) te⌈bu⌉kuro 手袋: put on [take off] gloves (*tebukuro o hameru [nugu]*) 手袋をはめる[脱ぐ].

2 (for sports) gu⌈rabu グラブ.

glove compartment *n.* (of a car) ko⌈mono⌉ire 小物入れ.

glow *vi.* **1** (give bright light) a⌈kaku kagaya⌉ku 赤く輝く Ⓒ: The hot iron glowed. (*Nesshita tetsu wa akaku kagayaita.*) 熱した鉄は赤く輝いた.

2 (show rosy color) ko⌈ochoo suru 紅潮する Ⓘ: She glowed with pleasure. (*Kanojo wa yorokobi de koochoo shita.*) 彼女は喜びで紅潮した.

— *n.* (brightness) ka⌈gayaki 輝き; (redness) a⌈karami 赤らみ: The glow of the fire lighted the room. (*Hi no kagayaki ga heya o terashita.*) 火の輝きが部屋を照らした.

glue *n.* (especially for paper) no⌈ri⌉ のり; (bonding agent) se⌈tchaku⌉zai 接着剤: stick paper together with glue (*kami o nori de tsukeru*) 紙をのりでつける.

— *vt.* ... o no⌈rizuke ni suru …をのりづけにする Ⓘ; se⌈tchaku⌉zai de tsu⌈ke⌉ru 接着剤でつける Ⓥ: glue a broken cup together (*wareta chawañ o setchakuzai de tsukeru*) 割れた茶碗を接着剤でつける.

go *vi.* **1** (move) (... e) i⌈ku …へ行く Ⓒ: go to school [church] (*gakkoo [kyookai] e iku*) 学校[教会]へ行く.

2 (travel) (... e) i⌈ku …へ行く Ⓒ: We went to Nikko by bus. (*Watashi-tachi wa Nikkoo e basu de itta.*) 私たちは日光へバスで行った.

3 (leave) i⌈ku 行く Ⓒ; sa⌉ru 去る Ⓒ: I must be going now. (*Moo ikanakereba narimaseñ.*) もう行かなければなりません.

4 (proceed) i⌈ku 行く Ⓒ; shi⌈ñkoo suru 進行する Ⓘ: Everything is going well. (*Subete wa umaku itte imasu.*) すべてはうまくいっています.

5 (attend) ka⌈you 通う Ⓒ: She goes to work on the subway. (*Kanojo wa chikatetsu de shigoto ni kayotte imasu.*) 彼女は地下鉄で仕事に通っています.

6 (disappear) na⌈kunaru なくなる Ⓒ; ki⌈eru 消える Ⓥ: My pain has gone. (*Itami ga nakunatta.*) 痛みがなくなった.

7 (sound) na⌈ru 鳴る Ⓒ: There goes the bell. (*Beru ga natte iru.*) ベルが鳴っている.

go away *vi.* ta⌈chisaru 立ち去る Ⓒ: He went away without a word. (*Kare wa nani mo iwazu ni tachisatta.*) 彼は何も言わずに立ち去った.

go down *vi.* sa⌈ga⌉ru 下がる Ⓒ: Land prices went down. (*Tochi no nedañ ga sagatta.*) 土地の値段が下がった.

going to do ⟨verb⟩ to⌈koro⌉ da ... ところだ: I was just going to phone you. (*Ima choodo deñwa suru tokoro deshita.*) 今ちょうど電話するところでした.

go into ... *vt.* ... ni ha⌉iru …に入る Ⓒ: I went into the room. (*Watashi wa sono heya ni haitta.*) 私はその部屋に入った.

go on doing *vt.* ⟨verb⟩-tsuzukeru ... 続ける Ⓥ: I want to go on working. (*Watashi wa hataraki-tsuzuketai.*) 私は働き続けたい.

go out *vi.* de⌉te iku 出て行く Ⓒ: She went out of the house. (*Kanojo wa uchi kara dete ikimashita.*) 彼女は家から出て行きました.

go up *vi.* a⌈garu 上がる Ⓒ: The temperature suddenly went up. (*Kioñ ga kyuu ni agatta.*) 気温が急に上がった.

goal *n.* **1** (of a game) go⌉oru ゴール; to⌈kuteñ 得点: get a goal (*gooru o kimeru*) ゴールを決める.

2 (aim) mo⌈kuhyoo 目標: reach one's goal (*mokuhyoo o tassee suru*) 目標を達成する. ★ In Japanese, the finish line in a race is usually called '*gooru*' (goal).

goalkeeper *n.* go⌈oru ki⌉ipaa ゴールキーパー.

goalpost *n.* go⌈oru po⌉suto ゴールポスト.

goat *n.* ya⌉gi やぎ(山羊).

go-between *n.* **1** (in a negotiation) chu⌈uka⌉isha 仲介者; a⌈sseñniñ 斡旋人.

2 (matchmaker) na⌈ko⌉odo 仲人; ba⌈ishakuniñ 媒酌人. ★ In Japan marriage is often arranged by a '*nakoodo*.'

god [**God**] *n.* ka⌉mi 神: pray to a god [to God] (*kami ni inoru*) 神に祈る. ★ Christianity in Japan also uses '*kami*' to refer to its deity.

goddess *n.* me⌉gami 女神: the goddess of love (*ai no megami*) 愛の女神.

gold *n.* ki⌉ñ 金; o⌈ogoñ 黄金: This ring is made of gold. (*Kono yubiwa wa kiñ de dekite iru.*) この指輪は金でできている.
— *adj.* ki⌉ñ no 金の: a gold coin (*kiñka*) 金貨.

golden *adj.* **1** (color) ki⌈ñiro no 金色の: golden hair (*kiñpatsu*) 金髪.
2 (made of gold) ki⌈ñsee no 金製の: a golden cup (*kiñsee no kappu*) 金製のカップ.
3 (favorable) ze⌈kkoo no 絶好の: a golden opportunity (*zekkoo no kikai*) 絶好の機会.

golden age *n.* o⌈ogoñ-ji⌉dai 黄金時代; sa⌈ise⌉eki 最盛期.

goldfish *n.* ki⌉ñgyo 金魚.

golf *n.* go⌉rufu ゴルフ: play golf (*gorufu o suru*) ゴルフをする.

golfer *n.* go⌉rufaa ゴルファー: a professional golfer (*puro gorufaa*) プロゴルファー.

good *adj.* **1** (not bad) yo⌉i よい: good news (*yoi shirase*) よい知らせ / good weather (*yoi teñki*) よい天気.
2 (suitable) te⌈ki⌉shite iru 適している: This water is good to drink. (*Kono mizu wa nomu no ni tekishite iru.*) この水は飲むのに適している.
3 (skillful) jo⌈ozu na 上手な; u⌈ma⌉i うまい: You speak good English. (*Anata wa Eego ga o-joozu desu ne.*) あなたは英語がお上手ですね. / He is good at golf. (*Kare wa gorufu ga umai.*) 彼はゴルフがうまい.
4 (kind) shi⌉ñsetsu na 親切な: She was very good to me. (*Kanojo wa watashi ni totemo shiñsetsu deshita.*) 彼女は私にとても親切でした.
5 (beneficial) ta⌈me⌉ ni naru ためになる; yo⌉i よい: Early rising is good for the health. (*Hayaoki wa keñkoo ni yoi.*) 早起きは健康によい.
— *n.* **1** (benefit) ri⌉eki 利益; ta⌈me⌉ ため: I am saying so for your good. (*Anata no tame ni soo itte iru no desu.*) あなたのためにそう言っているのです.
2 (merit) yo⌉i te⌈ñ よい点; to⌈rie⌉ とりえ: I can find no good in him. (*Kare ni wa nani mo torie ga nai.*) 彼には何もとりえがない.

good afternoon *int.* ko⌈ñnichiwa こんにちわ; (when parting) sa⌈yoonara さようなら.

good-bye *int.* sa⌈yoonara さようなら.
— *n.* wa⌈kare no a⌉isatsu 別れのあいさつ: I had no time to say good-bye. (*Wakare no aisatsu o suru hima mo nakatta.*) 別れのあいさつをする暇もなかった.

good evening *int.* ko⌈ñbañwa こんばんは; (when parting) sa⌈yoonara さようなら.

good-looking *adj.* ka⌈odachi no yo⌉i 顔立ちのよい: a good-looking woman (*kaodachi no yoi josee*) 顔立ちのよい女性.

good luck *n.* ko⌈ouñ 幸運: I wish you good luck! (*Koouñ o o-inori shimasu.*) 幸運をお祈りします.

good morning *int.* o⌈hayoo お早う; [polite] o⌈hayoo-gozaimasu お早うございます; (late morning) ko⌈ñnichiwa こんにちは; (when parting) sa⌈yoonara さようなら.

good-natured *adj.* (of young people and women) ki⌈date no yo⌉i 気だてのよい.

good night *int.* o⌈yasumi nasai おやすみなさい; (when parting) sa⌈yoonara さようなら.

goods *n.* sho⌉ohiñ 商品; shi⌈namono 品物: There are a variety of goods in that supermarket. (*Ano suupaa ni wa iroiro na shinamono ga aru.*) あのスーパーにはいろいろな品物がある.

g

goodwill *n.* ko˥oi 好意: show goodwill to a person (*hito ni kooi o shimesu*) 人に好意を示す.

goose *n.* ga⌈choo がちょう.

gorge *n.* kyo⌈okoku 峡谷.

gorgeous *adj.* su⌈barashi˥i すばらしい; ka⌈ree na 華麗な: The bride appeared in a gorgeous dress. (*Hanayome wa karee na ishoo de arawareta.*) 花嫁は華麗な衣装で現れた.

gorilla *n.* go˥rira ゴリラ.

gospel *n.* (of Jesus Christ) fu⌈kuiñ 福音; (book) fu⌈kuiñsho 福音書.

gossip *n.* u⌈wasaba˥nashi うわさ話; go⌈shi˥ppu ゴシップ: The gossip spread at once. (*Sono uwasabanashi wa sugu ni hiromatta.*) そのうわさ話はすぐに広まった.

govern *vt.* **1** (rule) ... o o⌈same˥ru …を治める [V]; shi˥hai suru 支配する [I]: govern a country (*kuni o osameru*) 国を治める.
2 (control) ... o ka˥ñri suru …を管理する [I]: This university is governed by a board of trustees. (*Kono daigaku wa rijikai ni yotte kañri sarete iru.*) この大学は理事会によって管理されている.
3 (influence) ... o sa˥yuu suru …を左右する [I]: Newspapers are often governed by public opinion. (*Shiñbun wa shibashiba yoroñ ni sayuu sareru.*) 新聞はしばしば世論に左右される.

government *n.* **1** (body) se˥efu 政府: The government decided to increase taxes. (*Seefu wa zoozee o kimeta.*) 政府は増税を決めた.
2 (act) se⌈eji 政治: democratic government (*miñshu seeji*) 民主政治.

governor *n.* **1** (elected person) chi˥ji 知事: the governor of a prefecture (*keñchiji*) 県知事.
2 (appointed person) cho⌈okañ 長官; so⌈osai 総裁; ri˥ji 理事.

grab *vt.* ... o hi⌈ttsuka˥mu …をひっつかむ [C]; hi⌈ttaku˥ru ひったくる [C]: The man grabbed the money and ran away. (*Sono otoko wa o-kane o hittakutte nigeta.*) その男はお金をひったくって逃げた.

grace *n.* **1** (beauty) yu˥uga 優雅; jo⌈ohi˥ñ 上品: She danced with grace. (*Kanojo wa yuuga ni odotta.*) 彼女は優雅に踊った.
2 (prayer) sho⌈kuzeñ no ka˥ñsha no i⌈nori 食前の感謝の祈り: say grace (*shokuzeñ no kañsha no inori o suru*) 食前の感謝の祈りをする.

graceful *adj.* yu˥uga na 優雅な; shi⌈to˥yaka na しとやかな: She is graceful in manner. (*Kanojo wa furumai ga shitoyaka da.*) 彼女は振る舞いがしとやかだ.

gracious *adj.* **1** (kind) ya⌈sashii 優しい; shi˥ñsetsu na 親切な: She is gracious to everyone. (*Kanojo wa dare ni mo yasashii.*) 彼女はだれにも優しい.
2 (elegant) yu˥uga na 優雅な: gracious living (*yuuga na seekatsu*) 優雅な生活.

grade *n.* **1** (mark) se⌈eseki 成績; hyo⌈oteñ 評点: I got a good grade in mathematics. (*Watashi wa suugaku de yoi seeseki o totta.*) 私は数学でよい成績をとった.
2 (division of a school) ga⌈kuneñ 学年: The child is in the fifth grade of primary school. (*Sono ko wa shoogakkoo go-neñ-see desu.*) その子は小学校5年生です.
3 (rate) to⌈okyuu 等級; te˥edo 程度: the best grade of meat (*saikookyuu no niku*) 最高級の肉.
— *vt.* ... ni to⌈okyuu o tsu⌈ke˥ru …に等級をつける [V]: grade eggs by size (*ookisa de tamago ni tookyuu o tsukeru*) 大きさで卵に等級をつける.

gradual *adj.* jo˥jo no 徐々の; da⌈ñdañ no だんだんの: a gradual but steady improvement (*jojo de wa aru ga kakujitsu na kaizeñ*) 徐々ではあるが確実な改善.

gradually *adv.* da˥ñdañ to だんだんと; shi⌈dai ni 次第に: His health improved gradually. (*Kare no keñkoo wa jojo ni kaifuku shita.*) 彼の健康は徐々に回復した.

graduate *vi.* (... o) soˈtsugyoo suru (…を)卒業する [I]: He graduated from college with honors. (*Kare wa daigaku o yuutoo de sotsugyoo shita.*) 彼は大学を優等で卒業した.
— *n.* soˈtsugyoˈosee 卒業生.

graduation *n.* soˈtsugyoo 卒業; (ceremony) soˈtsugyoˈo-shiki 卒業式: He went to college after graduation from high school. (*Kare wa kookoo o sotsugyoo shite kara daigaku e shiñgaku shita.*) 彼は高校を卒業してから大学へ進学した.

grain *n.* **1** (a tiny piece) tsuˈbu 粒: a grain of sand (*hito-tsubu no suna*) ひと粒の砂 / grains of wheat (*komugi-tsubu*) 小麦粒.
2 (cereal) koˈkuˈmotsu 穀物: harvest the grain (*kokumotsu o shuukaku suru*) 穀物を収穫する.
3 (a tiny bit) shoˈoryoˈo 少量: He hasn't a grain of sense. (*Kare wa sukoshi no fuñbetsu mo nai.*) 彼は少しの分別もない.

gram *n.* guˈramu グラム: This parcel weighs 500 grams. (*Kono tsutsumi wa gohyaku-guramu aru.*) この包みは500グラムある.

grammar *n.* buˈñpoo 文法: Japanese grammar (*Nihoñgo no buñpoo*) 日本語の文法.

grand *adj.* **1** (magnificent) soˈodai na 壮大な; yuˈudai na 雄大な: The view from the mountain was grand. (*Yama kara no nagame wa yuudai datta.*) 山からの眺めは雄大だった.
2 (dignified) riˈppa na 立派な; iˈdai na 偉大な: a grand gentleman (*rippa na shiñshi*) 立派な紳士.
3 (enjoyable) suˈteki na すてきな: We had a grand time at the party. (*Watashi-tachi wa paatii de suteki na toki o sugoshita.*) 私たちはパーティーですてきな時を過ごした.

grandchild *n.* maˈgoˈ 孫; (someone else's) o-ˈmago-sañ お孫さん.

granddaughter *n.* maˈgomuˈsume 孫娘; (someone else's) oˈñna no o-ˈmago-sañ 女のお孫さん.

grandfather *n.* soˈfu 祖父; (someone else's) o-ˈjiˈi-sañ おじいさん.

grandmother *n.* soˈbo 祖母; (someone else's) o-ˈbaˈa-sañ おばあさん.

grandson *n.* maˈgomuˈsuko 孫息子; (someone else's) oˈtoko no o-ˈmago-sañ 男のお孫さん.

grant *vt.* **1** (consent) ... o kiˈki-ireˈru …を聞き入れる [V]; (agree) shoˈodaku suru 承諾する [I]: He granted us our request. (*Kare wa watashi-tachi no negai o kiki-irete kureta.*) 彼は私たちの願いを聞き入れてくれた.
2 (give) ... ni (... o) aˈtaeru …に(…を)与える [V]: He didn't grant us permission to use the hall. (*Kare wa sono hooru o tsukau kyoka o watashi-tachi ni ataete kurenakatta.*) 彼はそのホールを使う許可を私たちに与えてくれなかった.
3 (admit) ... o miˈtomeru …を認める [V]: I grant that I was wrong. (*Watashi ga machigatte ita koto o mitomemasu.*) 私が間違っていたことを認めます.

grape *n.* buˈdoo ぶどう: a bunch of grapes (*budoo hito-fusa*) ぶどう一房.

grapefruit *n.* guˈreepu-furuˈutsu グレープフルーツ.

graph *n.* guˈrafu グラフ; zuˈhyoo 図表: draw a graph (*gurafu o egaku*) グラフを描く.

grasp *vt.* **1** (hold) ... o shiˈkkaˈri tsuˈkaˈmu …をしっかりつかむ [C]; niˈgirishimeˈru 握りしめる [V]: I grasped his hand and pulled him up. (*Watashi wa te o shikkari tsukañde kare o hippari-ageta.*) 私は手をしっかりつかんで彼を引っ張り上げた.
2 (understand) ... o tsuˈkaˈmu …をつかむ [C]; waˈkaˈru わかる [C]: I cannot grasp the meaning of the word. (*Watashi ni wa sono go no imi ga wakaranai.*) 私にはその語の意味がわからない.
— *vi.* (... ni) tsuˈkamaru (…に)つかまる [C].
— *n.* **1** (holding) shiˈkkaˈri tsu-

⌈ka⌉mu ko⌈to⌉ しっかりつかむこと: have [get] a firm grasp on a rope (*roopu o shikkari tsukamu*) ロープをしっかりつかむ.
2 (understanding) ri⌉kai 理解; ha⌈aku 把握: have a good grasp of the problem (*mondai o yoku haaku suru*) 問題をよく把握する.

grass *n.* (plant) ku⌈sa⌉ 草; (lawn) shi⌈bafu 芝生: Keep off the grass. (*Shibafu ni haitte wa ikenai.*) 芝生に入ってはいけない.

g

grasshopper *n.* ba⌈tta ばった; i⌈nago いなご.

grass roots *n.* (ordinary people) i⌈ppañ taishuu 一般大衆; ku⌈sa no ne 草の根.

grateful *adj.* ka⌉ñsha shite (iru) 感謝して(いる); a⌈riga⌉taku o⌈mo⌉tte (iru) ありがたく思って(いる): I am grateful for your advice. (*Anata no jogeñ o kañsha shite imasu.*) あなたの助言を感謝しています. / I'd be grateful if you would help me. (*Tasukete itadakereba arigataku omoimasu.*) 助けていただければありがたく思います.

gratitude *n.* ka⌉ñsha no ki⌈mochi 感謝の気持ち; ka⌉ñsha 感謝: I showed my gratitude by sending her flowers. (*Watashi wa kanojo ni hana o okutte kañsha no kimochi o arawashita.*) 私は彼女に花を送って感謝の気持ちを表した.

grave[1] *n.* ha⌈ka⌉ 墓; bo⌉chi 墓地: visit a grave (*hakamairi o suru*) 墓参りをする.

grave[2] *adj.* **1** (serious) ju⌈udai na 重大な: He made a grave mistake. (*Kare wa juudai na machigai o shita.*) 彼は重大な間違いをした.
2 (dignified) i⌈geñ no a⌉ru 威厳のある; (solemn) ma⌈jime na まじめな: His face was grave. (*Kare no kao wa majime datta.*) 彼の顔はまじめだった.

gravel *n.* ja⌈ri 砂利: The road was covered with gravel. (*Dooro ni wa jari ga shiite atta.*) 道路には砂利が敷いてあった.

gravity *n.* ju⌉uryoku 重力; i⌉ñryoku 引力: the center of gravity (*juushiñ*) 重心.

gray *adj.* **1** (of a color) ha⌈iiro no 灰色の; gu⌈re⌉e no グレーの; ne⌈zumi iro no ねずみ色の: gray eyes (*haiiro no me*) 灰色の目 / a gray coat (*guree [nezumi iro] no kooto*) グレー[ねずみ色]のコート.
2 (of hair) shi⌈raga(ma⌉jiri) no 白髪(混じり)の: His hair is turning gray. (*Kare no kami no ke wa shiraga ni natte kita.*) 彼の髪の毛は白髪になってきた.
— *n.* ha⌈iiro 灰色; ne⌈zumi iro ねずみ色.

grease *n.* (lubricant) gu⌈ri⌉isu グリース; (animal fat) ju⌉ushi 獣脂; a⌈bura 脂.

great *adj.* **1** (important) i⌈dai na 偉大な; ri⌈ppa na りっぱな: He became a great writer. (*Kare wa idai na sakka ni natta.*) 彼は偉大な作家になった.
2 (nice) su⌈barashi⌉i すばらしい; su⌈teki na すてきな: It is a great idea. (*Sore wa subarashii kañgae da.*) それはすばらしい考えだ.
3 (large in degree) o⌉oki-na 大きな: great joy (*ooki-na yorokobi*) 大きな喜び.
4 (a lot of) ta⌈su⌉u no 多数の; ta⌈kusa⌉ñ no たくさんの: A great number of people attended the opening ceremony. (*Oozee no hito ga sono kaikai-shiki ni shusseki shita.*) 大勢の人がその開会式に出席した.

greatness *n.* i⌈daisa 偉大さ; e⌉rasa 偉さ: his greatness as a statesman (*kare no seejika to shite no idaisa*) 彼の政治家としての偉大さ.

greedy *adj.* **1** (avaricious) yo⌈kuba⌉ri no 欲ばりの: He is too greedy. (*Kare wa yokubari-sugi da.*) 彼は欲張り過ぎだ.
2 (for food) ga⌉tsugatsu shita [shite iru] がつがつした[している]; ku⌈ishi⌉ñboo na 食いしんぼうな: a greedy boy (*kuishiñboo na otoko-no-ko*) 食いしんぼうな男の子.

green *adj.* **1** (color) mi⌈doriiro no 緑色の; gu⌈ri⌉iñ no グリーンの: a green dress (*midori iro no doresu*) 緑色のドレス.
2 (not ripe) u⌈rete nai 熟れてない; ma⌉da a⌈o⌉i まだ青い: green fruit (*urete nai kudamono*) 熟れてない果物.
— *n.* (color) mi⌉dori 緑.

greenhouse *n.* o⌈ñshitsu 温室: the greenhouse effect (*oñshitsu kooka*) 温室効果.

green light *n.* (traffic signal) mi⌉dori no shi⌈ñgoo 緑の信号.

greet *vt.* ... ni a⌉isatsu suru ...にあいさつする Ⓘ: She greeted me with a smile. (*Kanojo wa nikoniko shite watashi ni aisatsu shita.*) 彼女はにこにこして私にあいさつした.

greeting *n.* a⌉isatsu あいさつ: exchange greetings (*aisatsu o kawasu*) あいさつを交わす.

greeting card *n.* gu⌈riitiñgu ka⌉ado グリーティングカード; a⌈isatsu⌉joo あいさつ状. ★ In Japan many people send greetings in the form of a postcard: '*neñgajoo*' 年賀状 at the New Year and some people send '*shochuu mimai*' 暑中見舞い during summer.

grief *n.* fu⌈ka⌉i ka⌈nashimi 深い悲しみ: be filled with grief (*fukai kanashimi ni shizumu*) 深い悲しみに沈む.

grieve *vi.* (... o) fu⌉kaku ka⌈nashi⌉mu (...を)深く悲しむ Ⓒ: He grieved over the death of his friend. (*Kare wa yuujiñ no shi o fukaku kanashiñda.*) 彼は友人の死を深く悲しんだ.

grim *adj.* **1** (stern) i⌈kameshi⌉i いかめしい: a grim face (*ikameshii kao*) いかめしい顔.
2 (unpleasant) i⌈ya⌉ na いやな; fu⌈yu⌉kai na 不愉快な: a grim task (*iya na shigoto*) いやな仕事.
3 (cruel) za⌈ñniñ na 残忍な: War is grim. (*Señsoo wa zañniñ da.*) 戦争は残忍だ.

grin *vi.* ni⌈kko⌉ri wa⌈rau にっこり笑う Ⓒ: He grinned when he saw me. (*Kare wa watashi o mite nikkori waratta.*) 彼は私を見てにっこり笑った.

grind *vt.* **1** (crush) ... o hi⌈ku ...をひく Ⓒ: grind coffee beans (*koohii mame o hiku*) コーヒー豆をひく.
2 (sharpen) ... o to⌉gu ...を研ぐ Ⓒ; (polish) mi⌈gaku 磨く Ⓒ: grind a knife (*naifu o togu*) ナイフを研ぐ / grind a lens (*reñzu o migaku*) レンズを磨く.
3 (rub together) ... o gi⌉shigishi ko⌈su⌉ru ...をぎしぎしこする Ⓒ: grind one's teeth (*hagishiri o suru*) 歯ぎしりをする.

grip *vt.* ... o shi⌈kka⌉ri tsu⌈ka⌉mu ...をしっかりつかむ Ⓒ; ni⌈giru 握る Ⓒ: He gripped me by the arm. (*Kare wa watashi no ude o shikkari tsukañda.*) 彼は私の腕をしっかりつかんだ.
— *n.* **1** (gripping) tsu⌈ka⌉mu ko⌈to⌉ つかむこと.
2 (handle) ni⌈giri にぎり; e 柄: a tool with a wooden grip (*ki no nigiri no doogu*) 木のにぎりの道具.

groan *n.* u⌈mekigo⌉e うめき声; u⌈narigo⌉e うなり声: give a groan (*umekigoe o ageru*) うめき声をあげる.
— *vi.* u⌈me⌉ku うめく Ⓒ: The patient was groaning. (*Sono byooniñ wa umeite ita.*) その病人はうめいていた.

grocery store *n.* sho⌈kuryoohi⌉ñteñ 食料品店: I bought salt and sugar at the grocery store. (*Shokuryoohiñteñ de shio to satoo o katta.*) 食料品店で塩と砂糖を買った. ★ '*Shokuryoohiñteñ*' deals in only food and does not sell household supplies.

grope *vi.* (... o) te⌈sa⌉guri suru (...を)手探りする Ⓘ; te⌈sa⌉guri de sa⌈gasu 手探りで捜す Ⓒ: grope for one's shoes in the dark (*kurayami de kutsu o tesaguri de sagasu*) 暗闇で靴を手探りで捜す.

gross *adj.* **1** (total) so⌈otai no 総体の: the gross amount (*soogaku*) 総額 / a gross profit (*soorieki*) 総利益.
2 (very bad) hi⌈do⌉i ひどい: a gross mistake (*hidoi machigai*) ひどい間違い.

ground *n.* **1** (surface) ji⌉meñ 地面:

The ground is frozen. (*Jimeñ ga kootte iru.*) 地面が凍っている.
2 (soil) to⌈chi 土地; do⌈joo 土壌: rich [poor] ground (*koeta* [*yaseta*] *tochi*) 肥えた[やせた]土地.
3 (for facilities) shi⌈kichi 敷地; ko⌉onai 構内: palace grounds (*kyuudeñ no shikichi*) 宮殿の敷地 / school grounds (*gakkoo no koonai*) 学校の構内.
4 (field) ba⌈sho 場所; u⌈ñdoojoo 運動場; gu⌈rañdo グランド: a baseball ground (*yakyuujoo*) 野球場.
5 (reason) ko⌉ñkyo 根拠; ri⌈yuu 理由: There are no grounds for fear. (*Osoreru riyuu wa nai.*) 恐れる理由はない.
6 (of coffee) ka⌉su かす: coffee grounds (*koohii no kasu*) コーヒーのかす.

ground floor *n.* i⌈k-kai 1 階.

group *n.* mu⌈re⌉ 群れ; shu⌈udañ 集団; gu⌈ru⌉upu グループ: A group of birds flew away. (*Tori no mure ga tobisatta.*) 鳥の群れが飛び去った.
— *vt.* ... o a⌈tsume⌉ru ...を集める Ⓥ: The teacher grouped the children for a photograph. (*Señsee wa shashiñ o toru tame ni kodomotachi o atsumeta.*) 先生は写真を撮るために子どもたちを集めた.

grow *vi.* **1** (of a plant) se⌈echoo suru 生長する Ⓘ; so⌈da⌉tsu 育つ Ⓒ: Oranges grow in warm regions. (*Oreñji wa atatakai chihoo de sodatsu.*) オレンジは暖かい地方で育つ.
2 (of people) se⌈echoo suru 成長する Ⓘ; o⌉okiku naru 大きくなる Ⓒ: Children grow rapidly. (*Kodomo wa ookiku naru no ga hayai.*) 子どもは大きくなるのが早い.
3 (develop) ha⌈tteñ suru 発展する Ⓘ; no⌈bi⌉ru 伸びる Ⓥ: Our company is growing every year. (*Watashi-tashi no kaisha wa maitoshi nobite iru.*) 私たちの会社は毎年伸びている.
4 (become) (... ni) na⌉ru (...に)なる Ⓒ: It is growing dark. (*Dañdañ kuraku natte kita.*) だんだん暗くなってきた.
— *vt.* **1** (cultivate) ... o sa⌈ibai suru ...を栽培する Ⓘ; so⌈date⌉ru 育てる Ⓥ: He grows roses in a greenhouse. (*Kare wa oñshitsu de bara o saibai shite iru.*) 彼は温室でばらを栽培している.
2 (of hair) no⌈ba⌉su 伸ばす Ⓒ; (of a beard) ha⌈ya⌉su 生やす Ⓒ: He grew his hair long. (*Kare wa kami no ke o nagaku nobashita.*) 彼は髪の毛を長く伸ばした.
grow up *vi.* o⌈tona ni na⌉ru おとなになる Ⓒ.

growth *n.* **1** (increase) zo⌈oka 増加: a rapid growth of population (*jiñkoo no kyuusoku na zooka*) 人口の急速な増加.
2 (development) ha⌈tteñ 発展; ha⌈ttatsu 発達: industrial growth (*sañgyoo no hattatsu*) 産業の発達.

grudge *n.* u⌈rami⌉ 恨み; ni⌈kushimi 憎しみ: bear a grudge (*urami o motsu*) 恨みを持つ.

grumble *vi.* fu⌈hee o iu 不平を言う Ⓒ; ku⌈joo o nobe⌉ru 苦情を述べる Ⓥ: Stop grumbling about the food. (*Tabemono no koto de fuhee o iu no wa yoshi nasai.*) 食べ物のことで不平を言うのはよしなさい.
— *n.* fu⌈hee 不平; ku⌈joo 苦情.

guarantee *vt.* ... o ho⌈shoo suru ...を保証する Ⓘ: He guaranteed that the diamond was genuine. (*Kare wa sono daiyamoñdo ga hoñmono de aru koto o hoshoo shita.*) 彼はそのダイヤモンドが本物であることを保証した.
— *n.* ho⌈shoo 保証: This camera has a year guarantee. (*Kono kamera wa ichi-neñ no hoshoo ga tsuite imasu.*) このカメラは 1 年の保証がついています.

guard *vt.* **1** (defend) ... o ma⌈mo⌉ru ...を守る Ⓒ: A big dog was guarding the house. (*Ooki-na inu ga uchi o mamotte ita.*) 大きな犬が家を守っていた.
2 (watch) ... o mi⌈haru ...を見張る Ⓒ: guard a prisoner (*horyo o mi-*

haru) 捕虜を見張る.

— *n.* mi⌈hari 見張り; ga⌉adomañ ガードマン: post a guard at the gate (*moñ ni mihari o tateru*) 門に見張りを立てる / a security guard (*keebiiñ*) 警備員.

guardian *n.* ho⌈go⌉sha 保護者; ko⌈okeññiñ 後見人.

guerilla *n.* ge⌉rira ゲリラ: guerilla warfare (*gerirasen̄*) ゲリラ戦.

guess *vt.* **1** (judge) ... o i⌈iate⌉ru ...を言い当てる Ⓥ; ke⌈ñto⌉o o tsu⌈ke⌉ru 見当をつける Ⓥ: He guessed the right answer. (*Kare wa tadashii kotae o iiateta.*) 彼は正しい答えを言い当てた. / I cannot guess how old she is. (*Kanojo ga nañ-sai ka keñtoo ga tsukanai.*) 彼女が何歳か見当がつかない.

2 (think) ... to o⌈mo⌉u ...と思う Ⓒ: I guess he is wrong. (*Kare wa machigatte iru to omou.*) 彼は間違っていると思う.

— *n.* su⌈isoku 推測; su⌈iryoo 推量.

guest *n.* kya⌈ku 客; [polite] o⌈kyaku(-sañ) お客(さん): We are having guests for dinner today. (*Kyoo wa o-kyaku o yuuhañ ni maneite imasu.*) 今日はお客を夕飯に招いています.

guidance *n.* shi⌈doo 指導: Under Mr. Tanaka's guidance, I learned how to ski. (*Watashi wa Tanaka-sañ no shidoo de sukii o naraimashita.*) 私は田中さんの指導でスキーを習いました.

guide *n.* **1** (person) a⌈ññainiñ 案内人; ga⌉ido ガイド: The guide took us around Kyoto. (*Gaido ga Kyooto o aññai shite kureta.*) ガイドが京都を案内してくれた.

2 (book) ga⌈idobu⌉kku ガイドブック: a guide to Kamakura (*Kamakura no gaidobukku*) 鎌倉のガイドブック.

— *vt.* **1** (direct) ... o a⌈ñna⌉i suru 案内する Ⓘ; mi⌈chibi⌉ku 導く Ⓒ: He guided me around the city. (*Kare ga machi o aññai shite kureta.*) 彼が町を案内してくれた.

2 (control) ... o shi⌉hai suru ...を支配する Ⓘ; mi⌈chibi⌉ku 導く Ⓒ: I was guided by my conscience. (*Watashi wa ryooshiñ ni shitagatta.*) 私は良心に従った.

guide dog *n.* mo⌈odookeñ 盲導犬.

guilt *n.* **1** (of crime) yu⌈uzai 有罪: His guilt was proved by the evidence. (*Kare no yuuzai wa shooko ni yotte risshoo sareta.*) 彼の有罪は証拠によって立証された.

2 (of sense) za⌈iaku⌉kañ 罪悪感; tsu⌉mi no ishiki 罪の意識.

guilty *adj.* yu⌈uzai no 有罪の: He was declared guilty. (*Kare wa yuuzai to señkoku sareta.*) 彼は有罪と宣告された.

guinea pig *n.* (animal) mo⌈rumo⌉tto モルモット; (person) ji⌈kkeñdai 実験台.

guitar *n.* gi⌉taa ギター: play the guitar (*gitaa o hiku*) ギターを弾く.

gulf *n.* wa⌉ñ 湾: the Gulf of Mexico (*Mekishiko wañ*) メキシコ湾.

gum *n.* **1** (chewing gum) chu⌈uiñga⌉mu チューインガム: chew gum (*gamu o kamu*) ガムをかむ.

2 (part of mouth) ha⌉guki 歯ぐき.

gun *n.* (hand-carried weapon) ju⌉u 銃; (hand weapon) ke⌈ñjuu けん銃; pi⌈sutoru ピストル: fire a gun (*juu o hassha suru*) 銃を発射する.

gunshot *n.* ha⌈ppoo 発砲; ju⌈ugeki 銃撃.

gush *vi.* ho⌈tobashiride⌉ru ほとばしり出る Ⓥ; fu⌈ñshutsu suru 噴出する Ⓘ: Water gushed out of the pipe. (*Mizu ga kañ kara fuñshutsu shita.*) 水が管から噴出した.

gym *n.* ta⌈iiku⌉kañ 体育館; ji⌉mu ジム.

gymnastics *n.* ta⌈isoo 体操: rhythmic gymnastics (*shiñtaisoo*) 新体操.

gynecologist *n.* fu⌈jiñka⌉-i 婦人科医.

gynecology *n.* fu⌈jiñ-ka⌉gaku 婦人科学.

H

habit *n.* **1** (behavior) ku⌈se⌉ 癖: That child has the habit of biting his fingernails. (*Sono ko wa yubi no tsume o kamu kuse ga aru.*) その子は指のつめをかむ癖がある.
2 (custom) shu⌈ukañ 習慣: It is his habit to walk his dog every morning. (*Maiasa inu o sañpo saseru no ga kare no shuukañ da.*) 毎朝犬を散歩させるのが彼の習慣だ.

habitual *adj.* shu⌈ukañ-teki na 習慣的な; i⌉tsu-mo no いつもの: one's habitual breakfast (*itsu-mo no chooshoku*) いつもの朝食.

had better <verb> nasa⌉i …なさい; <verb>-ta hoo ga yo⌉i …たほうがよい: You had better do as you are told. (*Iwareta toori ni shi nasai.*) 言われたとおりにしなさい. / You had better not open that door. (*Sono doa wa akenaide oita hoo ga yoi.*) そのドアは開けないでおいたほうがよい.

hail[1] *n.* a⌈rare あられ; hyo⌉o ひょう: A lot of hail fell. (*Hyoo ga takusañ futta.*) ひょうがたくさん降った.

hail[2] *vt.* ... o yo⌈bitome⌉ru …を呼び止める [V]: hail a taxi (*takushii o yobi-tomeru*) タクシーを呼び止める.

hair *n.* **1** (of the head) ka⌈mi no⌉ ke 髪の毛; ka⌈mi⌉ 髪; ke 毛: There is a hair in the soup. (*Suupu ni kami no ke ga ip-poñ haitte iru.*) スープに髪の毛が1本入っている. / I'd like to have my hair cut [set]. (*Kami o katto [setto] shite kudasai.*) 髪をカット[セット]してください.
2 (of the body) ke 毛: a dog hair (*inu no ke*) 犬の毛.

hairbrush *n.* he⌈abu⌉rashi ヘアブラシ.

haircut *n.* sa⌈ñpatsu 散髪: I'd like to have a haircut. (*Sañpatsu o shite moraitai no desu ga.*) 散髪をしてもらいたいのですが.

hairdo *n.* ka⌈migata 髪型; he⌈a-suta⌉iru ヘアスタイル: the latest hairdo (*saishiñ no kamigata*) 最新の髪型.

hairdresser *n.* bi⌈yo⌉oshi 美容師; ri⌈hatsu⌉shi 理髪師: go to the hairdresser's (*biyooiñ e iku*) 美容院へ行く.

hairdryer *n.* do⌈raiyaa ドライヤー.

hairy *adj.* ke⌈buka⌉i 毛深い: a hairy person (*kebukai hito*) 毛深い人.

half *n.* **1** (equal part) ha⌈ñbu⌉ñ 半分; ni-⌈buñ no ichi⌉ 2分の1: Cut the apple in half, please. (*Riñgo o hañbuñ ni kitte kudasai.*) りんごを半分に切ってください. / Half of 32 is 16. (*Sañjuu-ni no ni-buñ no ichi wa juuroku desu.*) 32の2分の1は16です.
2 (of games) ze⌈ñ-[ko⌈o-]hañ 前[後]半: I saw both the first half and the second half of the match. (*Watashi wa shiai no zeñ-hañ to koo-hañ no ryoohoo o mita.*) 私は試合の前半と後半の両方を見た.

half past *prep.* ... ji-ha⌉ñ …時半: I got up at half past six. (*Watashi wa roku-ji-hañ ni okimashita.*) 私は6時半に起きました.

— *adj.* ha⌈ñbu⌉ñ no 半分の; ni-⌈buñ no ichi⌉ no 2分の1の: Half the accidents are due to careless driving. (*Jiko no hañbuñ wa fu-chuui na uñteñ ni yoru.*) 事故の半分は不注意な運転による. / Please give me one and a half kilograms of that meat. (*Sono niku o ichi-kiro hañ kudasai.*) その肉を1キロ半下さい.

— *adv.* **1** (partly) ha⌈ñbu⌉ñ (dake) 半分(だけ); na⌈ka⌉ba 半ば: This job is half done. (*Kono shigoto wa nakaba owarimashita.*) この仕事は半ば終わりました.
2 (not completely) fu⌈ju⌉ubuñ ni 不十分に; fu⌈ka⌉ñzeñ ni 不完全に: These potatoes are only half cooked. (*Kono jagaimo wa juubuñ

ni niete inai.) このじゃがいもは十分に煮えていない.

hall *n.* **1** (hallway) ge⌉ñkañ 玄関: an entrance hall (*omote geñkañ*) 表玄関.
2 (large room) ka⌈ikañ 会館; ho⌉o-ru ホール: a concert hall (*koñsaato hooru*) コンサートホール / a lecture hall (*koodoo*) 講堂 / a city hall (*shi-yakusho*) 市役所.

ham *n.* ha⌉mu ハム: a slice of ham (*hamu hito-kire*) ハム一切れ.

hammer *n.* ka⌈nazu⌉chi 金づち; ha⌉ñmaa ハンマー.
— *vt.* ... o ka⌈nazu⌉chi de u⌈chi-komu ...を金づちで打ち込む Ⓒ: hammer nails into a board (*kanazuchi de ita ni kugi o uchikomu*) 金づちで板にくぎを打ち込む.

hand *n.* **1** (body part) te⌉ 手: What are you holding in your hands? (*Te ni nani o motte iru no desu ka?*) 手に何を持っているのですか. / Raise your hand if you have a question. (*Shitsumoñ ga areba te o age nasai.*) 質問があれば手を挙げなさい.
2 (pointer) ha⌉ri 針: the hour [minute, second] hand (*ji*[*fuñ, byoo*]*-shiñ*) 時[分, 秒]針 / The hands of the clock pointed to 6:30. (*Tokee no hari wa roku-ji hañ o sashite ita.*) 時計の針は6時半を指していた.
3 (assistance) te⌉ 手; te⌈da⌉suke 手助け: Give me a hand with the homework. (*Shukudai ni te o ka-shite kudasai.*) 宿題に手を貸してください.
on the other hand *adv.* ta⌈ho⌉o de wa 他方では.
— *vt.* ... o wa⌈tasu ...を渡す Ⓒ: I handed the money to the taxi driver. (*Watashi wa takushii no uñteñshu ni o-kane o watashita.*) 私はタクシーの運転手にお金を渡した.
hand in *vt.* ... o te⌈eshutsu suru ...を提出する Ⓘ.
hand out *vt.* ... o ku⌈ba⌉ru ...を配る Ⓒ.

handbag *n.* ha⌈ñdoba⌉ggu ハンドバッグ: a leather handbag (*kawa no hañ-dobaggu*) 革のハンドバッグ.

hand baggage *n.* te⌈ni⌉motsu 手荷物.

handful *n.* **1** (amount in the hand) hi⌈to⌉-tsukami ひとつかみ; hi-⌈to⌉-nigiri ひと握り: a handful of flour (*hito-tsukami no komugiko*) ひとつかみの小麦粉.
2 (small number) sho⌈osu⌉u 少数: a handful of spectators (*shoosuu no kañkyaku*) 少数の観客.

handkerchief *n.* ha⌈ñkachi ハンカチ: blow one's nose into one's handkerchief (*hañkachi de hana o ka-mu*) ハンカチではなをかむ.

handle *n.* to⌈tte 取っ手; e 柄; ha⌈ñ-doru ハンドル: a door handle (*doa no totte*) ドアの取っ手 / the handle of a knife (*naifu no e*) ナイフの柄. ★ Japanese '*hañdoru*' is also used in the sense of 'steering wheel.'
— *vt.* **1** (hold) ... o te⌉ de a⌈tsu-kau ...を手で扱う Ⓒ; tsu⌈kau 使う Ⓒ: He handles his chopsticks very well. (*Kare wa hashi o totemo joozu ni tsukau.*) 彼は箸をとてもじょうずに使う.
2 (deal with) ... o to⌈riatsukau ...を取り扱う Ⓒ; sho⌉ri suru 処理する Ⓘ: handle a customer politely (*o-kya-ku o teenee ni atsukau*) お客を丁寧に扱う / handle a problem (*moñdai o shori suru*) 問題を処理する.
3 (deal in) ... o to⌈riatsukau ...を取り扱う Ⓒ; a⌈kina⌉u 商う Ⓒ: handle electrical goods (*deñki-seehiñ o toriatsukau*) 電気製品を取り扱う.

handsome *adj.* **1** (good looking) ka⌈odachi no yo⌉i 顔立ちのよい; ha⌉-ñsamu na ハンサムな: a handsome man (*bidañshi*) 美男子.
2 (large) ka⌉nari no かなりの; so⌈o-too na 相当な: a handsome sum of money (*kanari no kiñgaku*) かなりの金額.
3 (generous) ki⌈mae no yo⌉i 気前のよい: a handsome tip (*kimae no yoi chippu*) 気前のよいチップ.

handwriting *n.* hi⌈sseki 筆跡;

shoʳtai 書体; jiˡ 字: neat handwriting (*kiree na ji*) きれいな字.

handy *adj.* **1** (easy to use) beˡñri na 便利な; teʳgoro na 手ごろな: a handy camera (*tegoro na kamera*) 手ごろなカメラ.
2 (skillful) kiˡyoo na 器用な; joʳozuˡ na じょうずな: He is handy with tools. (*Kare wa doogu o atsukau no ga kiyoo da.*) 彼は道具を扱うのが器用だ.
3 (nearby) teʳjika na 手近な: Keep this dictionary handy. (*Kono jisho o tejika ni oite oki nasai.*) この辞書を手近に置いておきなさい.

h

hang *vt.* **1** (support from above) ... o kaʳkeˡru ...を掛ける V; tsuʳrusu つるす C: Where shall I hang this calendar? (*Kono kareñdaa wa doko ni kakemasu ka?*) このカレンダーはどこに掛けますか. / hang curtains over a window (*mado ni kaateñ o tsurusu*) 窓にカーテンをつるす.
2 (fasten to a wall) ... o kaʳkeˡru ... を掛ける V; kaʳzaru 飾る C: I hung the picture at eye level. (*Watashi wa sono e o me no takasa ni kaketa.*) 私はその絵を目の高さに掛けた.
3 (execute) ... o koʳoshuˡkee ni suru ...を絞首刑にする I; kuʳbi o tsuru 首をつる C: be hanged for murder (*satsujiñzai de kooshukee ni naru*) 殺人罪で絞首刑になる / She committed suicide by hanging herself. (*Kanojo wa kubi o tsutte jisatsu shita.*) 彼女は首をつって自殺した.
— *vi.* kaʳkaˡru 掛かる C; buʳrasagatte iru ぶら下がっている V: The painting hung on the wall. (*Sono e wa kabe ni kakatte ita.*) その絵は壁に掛かっていた. / A long rope was hanging from the ceiling. (*Nagai roopu ga teñjoo kara burasagatte ita.*) 長いロープが天井からぶら下がっていた.
hang up *vi.* deʳñwa o kiˡru 電話を切る C: Hang up and wait, please. (*Ittañ kitte o-machi kudasai.*) いったん切ってお待ちください.

happen *vi.* **1** (occur) oʳkoˡru 起こる C; shoʳojiru 生じる V: Please tell us how the accident happened. (*Doo shite sono jiko ga okita no ka hanashite kudasai.*) どうしてその事故が起きたのか話してください. / What happened? (*Doo shita ñ desu ka?*) どうしたんですか.
2 (chance) guʳuzeñ [taʳmatama] ‹verb› 偶然[たまたま]...: Luckily, I happened to have enough money on me. (*Watashi wa uñ yoku guuzeñ o-kane o juubuñ ni mochiawasete ita.*) 私は運よく偶然お金を十分に持ち合わせていた. / The customer was a woman I happened to know. (*Sono o-kyaku wa tamatama watashi ga shitte iru josee datta.*) そのお客はたまたま私が知っている女性だった.

happening *n.* deʳkiˡgoto 出来事; jiˡkeñ 事件: an unfortunate happening (*fukoo na dekigoto*) 不幸な出来事.

happily *adv.* koʳofuku ni 幸福に; taʳnoshi-soˡo ni 楽しそうに; yuˡkai ni 愉快に: laugh happily (*tanoshisoo ni warau*) 楽しそうに笑う.

happiness *n.* koʳofuku 幸福; (good luck) koʳouñ 幸運; yuˡkai 愉快: I wish you every happiness. (*Anata no go-takoo o o-inori shimasu.*) あなたのご多幸をお祈りします.

happy *adj.* **1** (pleasurable; contented) koʳofuku na 幸福な; shiʳawase na 幸せな; uʳreshiˡi うれしい: a happy life (*koofuku na seekatsu*) 幸福な生活 / a happy marriage (*shiawase na kekkoñ*) 幸せな結婚 / a happy event (*ureshii dekigoto*) うれしい出来事 / I am most happy to meet you. (*O-me ni kakarete ureshii desu.*) お目にかかれてうれしいです. / Happy birthday! (*O-tañjoobi omedetoo.*) お誕生日おめでとう. / Happy New Year! (*Akemashite omedetoo.*) 明けましておめでとう.
2 (satisfied) maˡñzoku na 満足な; naʳttoku shita [shite iru] 納得した[している]: I am happy in my present job. (*Watashi wa ima no shigoto ni mañzoku shite imasu.*) 私は今の

仕事に満足しています.

3 (lucky) ko⌈ouñ na 幸運な; u⌉ñ no yo⌉i 運のよい: I met him by a happy chance. (*Watashi wa uñ yoku kare ni atta.*) 私は運よく彼に会った.

harbor *n.* mi⌈nato 港: arrive in harbor (*minato ni hairu*) 港に入る.

★ Japanese '*minato*' also refers to 'port.'

hard *adj.* **1** (not soft) ka⌈tai 硬い; (solid) ka⌈tai 堅い; (not easy to break) ka⌈tai 固い: hard ground (*katai jimeñ*) 硬い地面 / hard wood (*katai zaimoku*) 堅い材木 / a hard knot (*katai musubime*) 固い結び目 / She boiled the eggs hard. (*Kanojo wa tamago o kataku yudeta.*) 彼女は卵を固くゆでた.

2 (difficult) mu⌈zukashii 難しい; ko⌉ñnañ na 困難な: a hard question (*muzukashii shitsumoñ*) 難しい質問 / It was hard to understand her explanation. (*Kanojo no setsumee o rikai suru no wa koñnañ datta.*) 彼女の説明を理解するのは困難だった.

3 (severe) ki⌈bishi⌉i 厳しい; ge⌈ñkaku na 厳格な: hard training (*kibishii kuñreñ*) 厳しい訓練 / a hard winter (*kibishii fuyu*) 厳しい冬 / The boss is hard on us all. (*Buchoo wa wareware miñna ni tsuraku ataru.*) 部長はわれわれみんなにつらく当たる.

4 (eager) ne⌉sshiñ na 熱心な; ki⌉ñbeñ na 勤勉な: a hard worker (*kiñbeñka*) 勤勉家.

— *adv.* **1** (with effort) ne⌉sshiñ ni 熱心に; i⌈sshooke⌉ñmee (ni) 一生懸命(に): He worked hard. (*Kare wa isshookeñmee (ni) hataraita.*) 彼は一生懸命(に)働いた.

2 (strongly) hi⌉doku ひどく; ha⌈ge⌉shiku 激しく: The wind is blowing hard. (*Kaze ga hageshiku fuite iru.*) 風が激しく吹いている.

harden *vt.* **1** (cause to become hard) ... o ka⌈taku suru ...を堅くする [I]; ka⌈tameru 固める [V]: Heat hardens clay. (*Netsu wa neñdo o kataku suru.*) 熱は粘土を固くする.

2 [figurative use] ... o hi⌈joo ni suru ...を非情にする [I]: harden one's heart (*kokoro o hijoo ni suru*) 心を非情にする.

— *vi.* ka⌈taku na⌉ru 堅くなる [C]; ka⌈tamaru 固まる [C]: The mud hardened. (*Doro ga katamatta.*) 泥が固まった. / Her face hardened with anger. (*Kare no kao wa ikari de kowabatta.*) 彼の顔を怒りでこわばった.

hardly *adv.* **1** (scarcely) ho⌈to⌉ñdo ... na⌉i ほとんど…ない: The old man could hardly walk. (*Sono roojiñ wa hotoñdo aruku koto ga dekinakatta.*) その老人はほとんど歩くことができなかった. / There is hardly any beer left. (*Biiru wa hotoñdo nokotte inai.*) ビールはほとんど残っていない.

2 (not really) to⌈temo ... de⌈ki⌉nai とても…できない: I can hardly demand money from him. (*Totemo kare ni o-kane o yookyuu dekinai.*) とても彼にお金を要求できない.

3 (unlikely) o⌈so⌉raku ... ⟨verb⟩-soo mo na⌉i 恐らく…そうもない: A typhoon is hardly likely to hit us. (*Taifuu wa osoraku ki-soo mo nai.*) 台風は恐らく来そうもない.

hardly ... when ... ⟨verb⟩ ga ha⌈ya⌉i ka ...が早いか: He had hardly seen the policeman when he started running. (*Kare wa keekañ o miru ga hayai ka nigedashita.*) 彼は警官を見るが早いか逃げ出した.

hardship *n.* ku⌉nañ 苦難; ku⌈rushimi⌉ 苦しみ: endure hardship (*kunañ ni taeru*) 苦難に耐える.

hardware *n.* **1** (metal goods) ka⌈namono⌉rui 金物類: a hardware store (*kanomono-teñ*) 金物店.

2 (machinery) ha⌈adoue⌉a ハードウエア.

hardy *adj.* ku⌈kkyoo na 屈強な; ga⌈ñkeñ na 頑健な: a hardy young man (*kukkyoo na wakamono*) 屈強な若者.

hare *n.* no⌈u⌉sagi 野うさぎ.

harm *n.* (damage) ga⌉i 害; (wrong) wa⌈ru⌉i ko⌈to⌉ 悪いこと: do more

harm than good (*eki yori mo gai ni naru*) 益よりも害になる / I meant no harm by what I said. (*Warugi ga atte itta no de wa arimaseñ.*) 悪気があって言ったのではありません.
— *vt.* ... o ga⌈isu⌉ru ...を害する [I]; ki⌈zutsuke⌉ru 傷つける [V]: harm a person's reputation (*hito no meeyo o kizutsukeru*) 人の名誉を傷つける.

harmful *adj.* yu⌈ugai na 有害な; ga⌉i ni naru 害になる: a harmful insect (*yuugai na mushi*) 有害な虫 / Too much alcohol is harmful to the health. (*Arukooru no nomisugi wa keñkoo ni gai ni narimasu.*) アルコールの飲み過ぎは健康に害になります.

harmless *adj.* mu⌉gai na 無害な; a⌉kui no nai 悪意のない: a harmless snake (*mugai na hebi*) 無害なへび / a harmless joke (*akui no nai joodañ*) 悪意のない冗談.

harmonious *adj.* **1** (friendly) na⌉ka no yoi 仲の良い: a harmonious married couple (*naka no yoi fuufu*) 仲の良い夫婦.
2 (tasteful) cho⌈owa shita [shite iru] 調和した[している]: a harmonious combination of colors (*choowa shita iro no kumiawase*) 調和した色の組み合わせ.
3 (tuneful) u⌈tsukushi⌉i 美しい: a harmonious melody (*utsukushii merodii*) 美しいメロディー.

harmony *n.* **1** (pleasing combination) cho⌈owa 調和: The colors in this picture are in harmony. (*Kono e no iro wa choowa ga torete iru.*) この絵の色は調和がとれている.
2 (agreement) i⌈tchi 一致: Your ideas are in harmony with mine. (*Anata no kañgae wa watashi no to itchi shite iru.*) あなたの考えは私のと一致している.
3 (of music) ha⌉amonii ハーモニー; wa⌉see 和声; wa⌉oñ 和音.

harsh *adj.* **1** (rough) a⌈rai 粗い; te⌈za⌉wari ga wa⌈ru⌉i 手触りが悪い: This cloth is harsh to the touch. (*Kono kire wa tezawari ga warui.*) このきれは手触りが悪い.
2 (unpleasant to ears) mi⌈miza⌉wari na 耳障りな; (to eyes) do⌈gitsui どぎつい: a harsh voice (*mimizawari na koe*) 耳障りな声 / harsh colors (*dogitsui iro*) どぎつい色.
3 (severe) ki⌈bishi⌉i 厳しい: a harsh winter (*kibishii fuyu*) 厳しい冬 / a harsh punishment (*geñbatsu*) 厳罰.

harvest *n.* **1** (gathering) shu⌈ukaku 収穫: a rice harvest (*kome no shuukaku*) 米の収穫.
2 (time) shu⌈ukaku⌉ki 収穫期; to⌈ri-ire ji⌉ki 取り入れ時期: The villagers are busy during the harvest. (*Nooson no hito-tachi wa toriire jiki wa isogashii.*) 農村の人たちは取り入れ時期は忙しい.
3 (amount) shu⌈ukaku⌉daka 収穫高: The harvest was worse than anticipated. (*Shuukakudaka wa yosoo yori mo warukatta.*) 収穫高は予想よりも悪かった. / a good [bad] harvest (*hoosaku* [*kyoosaku*]) 豊作[凶作].
4 (consequences) se⌉eka 成果: reap the harvest of one's labors (*doryoku no seeka o te ni suru*) 努力の成果を手にする.
— *vt.* ... o shu⌈ukaku suru ...を収穫する [I]; ka⌈ri-ire⌉ru 刈り入れる [V]: harvest crops (*sakumotsu o kari-ireru*) 作物を刈り入れる.

haste *n.* i⌈sogi⌉ 急ぎ; a⌈wateru koto⌉ 慌てること: a matter requiring haste (*kyuu o yoosuru koto*) 急を要すること / There is no need for all this haste. (*Koñna ni awateru hitsuyoo wa nai.*) こんなに慌てる必要はない.

hasten *vt.* ... o i⌈soga⌉su ...を急がす [C]; ha⌈yame⌉ru 速める [V]: hasten one's pace (*ashi o hayameru*) 足を速める.
— *vi.* i⌈so⌉gu 急ぐ [C]: He hastened home. (*Kare wa isoide uchi e kaetta.*) 彼は急いで家へ帰った.

hat *n.* bo⌈oshi 帽子: put on [take off] a hat (*booshi o kaburu* [*nugu*]) 帽子をかぶる[脱ぐ] / wear a hat (*booshi o kabutte iru*) 帽子をかぶっている.

★ 'Cap' is also called '*booshi*'.

hatch[1] *n.* sho'oko'oguchi 昇降口: an escape hatch (*hijooyoo dasshutsuguchi*) 非常用脱出口.

hatch[2] *vt.* (ta'ma'go o) ka'esu (卵を)かえす Ⓒ; fu'ka suru ふ化する Ⓘ: The hen hatched the eggs. (*Niwatori ga tamago o kaeshita.*) にわとりが卵をかえした.
— *vi.* (ta'ma'go ga) ka'eru (卵が)かえる Ⓒ.

hate *vt.* **1** (detest) ... o (hi'doku) ki'rau ...を(ひどく)嫌う Ⓒ; ni'ku'mu 憎む Ⓒ: The child hates carrots. (*Sono ko wa niñjiñ ga daikirai da.*) その子はにんじんが大嫌いだ. / I hate violence. (*Watashi wa booryoku o nikumu.*) 私は暴力を憎む.
2 (dislike) ... o i'yaga'ru ...をいやがる Ⓒ; ‹verb›-taku nai ...たくない: She hates people interrupting her when she is talking. (*Kanojo wa hanashite iru toki hito ga jama suru no o iyagaru.*) 彼女は話しているとき人がじゃまするのをいやがる. / I hate to bother you. (*Anata o jama shitaku arimaseñ*). あなたをじゃましたくありません.
— *n.* ni'kushimi 憎しみ; zo'o-o 憎悪: love and hate (*ai to nikushimi*) 愛と憎しみ.

hateful *adj.* ni'kumu be'ki 憎むべき; i'ya' na いやな: a hateful crime (*nikumu beki hañzai*) 憎むべき犯罪.

hatred *n.* ni'kushimi 憎しみ; zo'o-o 憎悪: I feel hatred for people who tell lies. (*Watashi wa uso o tsuku hito o nikumu.*) 私はうそをつく人を憎む. / He looked at me with hatred. (*Kare wa zoo-o no me de watashi o mita.*) 彼は憎悪の目で私を見た.

haughty *adj.* ko'omañ na 高慢な; o'ohee na 横柄な: He looks haughty. (*Kare wa koomañ na kao o shite iru.*) 彼は高慢な顔をしている.

have[1] *vt.* **1** (possess) ... o mo'tte iru ...を持っている Ⓥ; (of things) ... ga a'ru ...がある Ⓒ; (of people) ... ga i'ru ...がいる Ⓥ: I have a map. (*Watashi wa chizu o motte imasu.*) 私は地図を持っています. / We have a factory in Kobe. (*Koobe ni koojoo ga arimasu.*) 神戸に工場があります. / Do you have a smaller one? (*Motto chiisai no wa arimasu ka?*) もっと小さいのはありますか. / I have three children. (*Watashi wa kodomo ga sañ-niñ imasu.*) 私は子どもが3人います.
2 (take) ... o to'ru ...をとる Ⓒ; (eat) ta'be'ru 食べる Ⓥ; (drink) no'mu 飲む Ⓒ: have a meal (*shokuji o toru*) 食事をとる / have a drink (*nomimono o nomu*) 飲物を飲む / Can I have breakfast in my room? (*Chooshoku wa heya de toremasu ka?*) 朝食は部屋でとれますか. / What did you have for lunch? (*Chuushoku ni nani o tabemashita ka?*) 昼食に何を食べましたか.
3 (obtain; receive) ... o mo'rau ...をもらう Ⓒ; u'ke'ru 受ける Ⓥ: She had a letter from her mother. (*Kanojo wa haha-oya kara tegami o moratta.*) 彼女は母親から手紙をもらった. / I'll have that red sweater. (*Sono akai seetaa o moraimasu.*) その赤いセーターをもらいます. / May I have a receipt? (*Reshiito o kudasai.*) レシートを下さい.
4 (hold) ... o hi'ra'ku ...を開く Ⓒ; ... ga a'ru ...がある Ⓒ: have a party (*paatii o hiraku*) パーティーを開く / I have a meeting this afternoon. (*Gogo ni kaigi ga arimasu.*) 午後に会議があります.
5 (suffer) ... ni ka'ka'tte i'ru ...にかかっている Ⓥ. ★ The Japanese verb used varies according to the kind of disease, pain, etc: have a headache [toothache] (*atama* [*ha*] *ga itai*) 頭[歯]が痛い / I have a pain here. (*Koko ga itai.*) ここが痛い. / have a cold (*kaze o hiite iru*) かぜをひいている / have a cough (*seki ga deru*) 咳がでる / have a fever (*netsu ga aru*) 熱がある / have chills (*samuke ga suru*) 寒気がする.
6 (think; feel) ... o mo'tte iru ...を持っている Ⓥ: I have some doubts

h

about this project. (*Watashi wa kono keekaku ni ikura-ka gimoñ o motte iru.*) 私はこの計画にいくらか疑問を持っている.

7 (experience) ... o ke⌈ekeñ suru ...を経験する [I]; ta⌈noshi⌉mu 楽しむ [C]: I hope you have a nice holiday. (*Yoi kyuuka o tanoshimu koto o inorimasu.*) よい休暇を楽しむことを祈ります.

8 (give birth) ... o u⌈mu ...を生む [C]: She had a child when she was 35. (*Kanojo wa sañjuu-go-sai no toki akañboo o uñda.*) 彼女は 35 歳のとき赤ん坊を生んだ.

9 [causative use] ‹verb›-(sa)seru ...(さ)せる [V]; ‹verb›-te[de] mo⌈rau ...て[で]もらう [C]: I'll have him come tomorrow. (*Ashita kare o kosase-mashoo.*) あした彼を来させましょう. / I'd like to have these shirts ironed. (*Kono shatsu ni airoñ o kakete moraitai no desu ga.*) このシャツにアイロンをかけてもらいたいのですが.

10 [passive use] ‹verb›-[ra]reru ...[ら]れる [V]: Mrs. Tanaka had all her money stolen. (*Tanaka-sañ wa o-kane o zeñbu nusumareta.*) 田中さんはお金を全部盗まれた. / He had his left leg broken in the accident. (*Kare wa sono jiko de hidari ashi o otta.*) 彼はその事故で左足を折った.

have[2] *aux.* **1** [recent past] ‹verb›-te[de] shi⌈matta ...て[で]しまった: I have already read that book. (*Watashi wa moo sono hoñ o yoñde shi-maimashita.*) 私はもうその本を読んでしまいました.

2 [past experience] ‹verb›-ta ko⌈to⌉ ga aru ...たことがある: I have never been to Kyoto. (*Watashi wa Kyooto e itta koto ga arimaseñ.*) 私は京都へ行ったことがありません.

3 [continuing state] ‹verb›-te[de] i⌈ru ...て[で]いる: We have lived in this house for ten years. (*Watashi-tachi wa kono uchi ni juu-neñ suñde imasu.*) 私たちはこの家に 10 年住んでいます.

haven *n.* (harbor) mi⌈nato 港; (shelter) hi⌈nañjo 避難所.

have to **1** [obligation] ‹verb›-na⌉-kereba na⌈ra⌉nai ...なければならない: Excuse me, but I have to leave now. (*Shitsuree desu ga moo ika-nakereba narimaseñ.*) 失礼ですがもう行かなければなりません. / You have to do as you are told. (*Kimi wa iwa-reta toori ni shinakereba naranai.*) 君は言われたとおりにしなければならない.

2 [negative use] hi⌈tsuyoo wa na⌉i 必要はない: You don't have to go if you don't want to. (*Ikitaku nake-reba iku hitsuyoo wa arimaseñ.*) 行きたくなければ行く必要はありません.

3 [certain inference] ... ni chi⌈gai na⌉i ...にちがいない: You have to be mistaken. (*Anata wa machigaeta ni chigai arimaseñ.*) あなたは間違えたにちがいありません.

hay *n.* ho⌈shikusa 干し草.

hazard *n.* ki⌈keñ 危険: the hazards of mountain-climbing (*tozañ no kikeñ*) 登山の危険.

he *pron.* **1** (male) ka⌉re 彼; a⌈no⌉ hito あの人; [polite] a⌈no kata⌉ あの方: He is a businessman. (*Kare wa jitsugyooka desu.*) 彼は実業家です. / "Who is he?" "He is Mr. Tanaka." (*"Ano hito wa dare desu ka?" "(Ano hito wa) Tanaka-sañ desu."*) 「あの人はだれですか」「(あの人は)田中さんです」 ★ When referring to a person, the occupation or position is used instead of 'he': "Is Mr. Yoshida, the department head, in now?" "He's out on business." (*"Yoshida buchoo wa ima oide desu ka?" "Buchoo wa shigoto de gaishutsu shite orimasu.)* 「吉田部長はいまおいでですか」「部長は仕事で外出しております」

2 (general) ★ Not translated in Japanese: Everybody should do his best. (*Dare mo ga zeñryoku o tsukusu beki da.*) だれもが全力を尽くすべきだ.

head *n.* **1** (body part) a⌈tama⌉ 頭: He hit me on the head. (*Kare wa *watashi no atama o nagutta.*) 彼は私の頭を殴った. / Mind your head. (*Zujoo chuui.*) 頭上注意. ★ English 'head' often corresponds to Japanese '*kao*' (face) and '*kubi*' (neck): / Don't put your head out of the window. (*Mado kara kao* [*kubi*] *o dashite wa ikemaseñ.*) 窓から顔[首]を出してはいけません.

2 (intellect; imagination) a'tama' 頭; zu'noo 頭脳: Come on! Use your head. (*Saa, atama o tsukae.*) さあ, 頭を使え. / A brilliant idea came into my head. (*Umai kañgae ga atama ni ukañda.*) うまい考えが頭に浮かんだ.

3 (top) i'chibañ ue いちばん上; se'ñ-tañ 先端: Your name is at the head of the list. (*Anata no namae wa hyoo no ichibañ ue ni arimasu.*) あなたの名前は表のいちばん上にあります.

4 (chief) -choo 長; ka'shira' 頭: the head of a school (*koochoo*) 校長 / a department head (*buchoo*) 部長.

5 (individual) ni'ñzuu 人数; a'ta-maka'zu 頭数: count heads (*niñzuu o kazoeru*) 人数を数える / twenty head of cattle (*ushi nijut-too*) 牛 20 頭.

6 (of a coin) o'mote' 表: Heads or tails? (*Omote ka ura ka?*) 表か裏か.

— *vt.* **1** (be foremost) ... no se'ñ-too ni ta'tsu ...の先頭に立つ Ⓒ: head a procession (*gyooretsu no señtoo ni tatsu*) 行列の先頭に立つ.

2 (lead) ... o hi'kii'ru ...を率いる Ⓥ: head the association (*kai o hikiiru*) 会を率いる.

3 (direct) ... no ho'o e mu'keru ...の方へ向ける Ⓥ: head a boat for the shore (*booto o kishi no hoo e mukeru*) ボートを岸の方へ向ける.

— *vi.* (... ni mu'katte) su'sumu (...に向かって)進む Ⓒ: head south (*minami ni mukatte susumu*) 南に向かって進む.

headache *n.* zu'tsuu 頭痛: I have a headache. (*Watashi wa zutsuu ga suru.*) 私は頭痛がする.

headline *n.* mi'dashi 見出し: quickly scan the headlines (*midashi o isoide satto miru*) 見出しを急いでさっと見る.

head office *n.* ho'ñsha 本社; ho'ñ-teñ 本店.

headquarters *n.* ho'ñsha 本社; ho'ñbu 本部: the headquarters of a company (*kaisha no hoñsha*) 会社の本社.

heal *vt.* ... o na'o'su ...を治す Ⓒ: It took a long time to heal the broken bone. (*Kossetsu o naosu no ni nagai jikañ ga kakatta.*) 骨折を治すのに長い時間がかかった.

— *vi.* na'o'ru 治る Ⓒ: The wound has finally healed. (*Kizu ga yatto naotta.*) 傷がやっと治った.

health *n.* **1** (being well) ke'ñkoo 健康: Too much alcohol is bad for the health. (*Kado no arukooru wa keñkoo ni warui.*) 過度のアルコールは健康に悪い.

2 (physical condition) ke'ñkoo-jo'otai 健康状態; ka'rada no guai 体の具合: I'm in good [poor] health these days. (*Watashi wa saikiñ karada no guai ga yoi* [*yoku nai*].) 私は最近体の具合がよい[よくない].

health insurance *n.* ke'ñkoo-ho'keñ 健康保険: join a health insurance scheme (*keñkoo-hokeñ ni kanyuu suru*) 健康保険に加入する.

healthy *n.* **1** (having good health) ke'ñkoo na 健康な; ke'ñzeñ na 健全な: a healthy child (*keñkoo na kodomo*) 健康な子ども / I feel very healthy these days. (*Watashi wa saikiñ totemo keñkoo desu.*) 私は最近とても健康です.

2 (producing good health) ke'ñ-koo-teki na 健康的な; ke'ñkoo ni yo'i 健康によい: a healthy lifestyle (*keñkoo-teki na seekatsu-yoo-shiki*) 健康的な生活様式 / The climate here is not very healthy. (*Koko no kikoo wa keñkoo ni amari yoku nai.*) ここの気候は健康にあまりよくない.

heap *n.* tsu'mikasane 積み重ね;

(... no) ya⌈ma⌉ (…の)山: a heap of rubbish (*gomi no yama*) ごみの山 / The magazines and books lay in a heap on the floor. (*Zasshi ya hoñ ga yuka ni tsumikasanete atta.*) 雑誌や本が床に積み重ねてあった.

— *vt.* ... o tsu⌈miage⌉ru …を積み上げる [V]; ya⌈mamori ni suru 山盛りにする [I]: heap up leaves (*ki no ha o tsumiageru*) 木の葉を積み上げる / heap strawberries on a plate (*ichigo o sara ni yamamori ni suru*) いちごを皿に山盛りにする.

hear *vt.* **1** (perceive sounds) ... ga ki⌈koeru …が聞こえる [V]; ... o ki⌈ku …を聞く [C]: Can you hear me? (*Kikoemasu ka?*) 聞こえますか. / I heard the door shut. (*Watashi wa doa ga shimaru oto o kiita.*) 私はドアが閉まる音を聞いた.

2 (be told) ... o ki⌈ku …を聞く [C]; mi⌈mi⌉ ni suru 耳にする [I]: Have you heard the news? (*Sono nyuusu o kikimashita ka?*) そのニュースを聞きましたか. / I heard a strange rumor last night. (*Watashi wa sakuya heñ na uwasa o mimi ni shita.*) 私は昨夜変なうわさを耳にした.

3 (listen to) ... o ki⌈ku …を聞く [C]; ... ni mi⌈mi⌉ o ka⌈tamuke⌉ru …に耳を傾ける [V]: We should hear Miss Watanabe's explanation. (*Wareware wa Watanabe-sañ no setsumee ni mimi o katamukeru beki da.*) われわれは渡辺さんの説明に耳を傾けるべきだ.

— *vi.* mi⌈mi⌉ ga ki⌈koeru 耳が聞こえる [V]: My grandmother cannot hear very well. (*Watashi no sobo wa amari yoku mimi ga kikoenai.*) 私の祖母はあまりよく耳が聞こえない.

hear from … *vt.* ... kara te⌈gami [de⌈ñwa] o mo⌈rau …から手紙[電話]をもらう [C].

hear of … *vt.* ... no u⌈wasa o ki⌈ku …のうわさを聞く [C].

hearing *n.* **1** (sense) cho⌉oryoku 聴力; cho⌉okaku 聴覚: lose one's hearing (*mimi ga kikoenaku naru*) 耳が聞こえなくなる / be hard of hearing (*mimi ga tooi*) 耳が遠い.

2 (enquiry) cho⌈omo⌉ñkai 聴聞会: a public hearing (*koochookai*) 公聴会.

heart *n.* **1** (organ) shi⌈ñzoo 心臓: My heart is beating fast. (*Shiñzoo ga dokidoki shite iru.*) 心臓がどきどきしている.

2 (emotion) ko⌈ko⌉ro 心; ka⌈ñjoo 感情: She has a kind heart. (*Kanojo wa yasashii kokoro o motte iru.*) 彼女は優しい心を持っている.

3 (compassion) a⌈ijoo 愛情; o⌈moiyari 思いやり: He has no heart. (*Kare wa omoiyari ga nai.*) 彼は思いやりがない.

4 (the center) chu⌈ushiñ 中心; ka⌈kushiñ 核心: the heart of the city (*shi no chuushiñbu*) 市の中心部 / the heart of a problem (*jikeñ no kakushiñ*) 事件の核心.

5 (of cards) ha⌈ato ハート: the king of hearts (*haato no kiñgu*) ハートのキング.

heart attack *n.* shi⌈ñzoo-ho⌉ssa 心臓発作; shi⌈ñzoo ma⌉hi 心臓まひ.

heartburn *n.* mu⌈neyake 胸焼け: have heartburn (*muneyake ga suru*) 胸焼けがする.

heart disease *n.* shi⌈ñzoobyoo 心臓病.

hearty *adj.* **1** (very friendly) ko⌈ko⌉ro kara no 心からの: receive a hearty welcome (*kokoro kara no kañgee o ukeru*) 心からの歓迎を受ける.

2 (very cheerful) ge⌉ñki na 元気な; o⌈osee na 旺盛な: have a hearty appetite (*shokuyoku ga oosee da*) 食欲が旺盛だ.

heat *n.* **1** (high temperature) ne⌈tsu⌉ 熱; a⌉tsusa 暑さ: the heat of the sun (*taiyoo netsu*) 太陽熱 / Don't excercise in the heat of the day. (*Nitchuu no atsusa no naka de uñdoo suru no wa yoshi nasai.*) 日中の暑さの中で運動するのはよしなさい.

2 (excitement) ko⌈ofuñ 興奮; ne⌈sshi⌉ñsa 熱心さ: take the heat off (*koofuñ o samasu*) 興奮をさます.

3 (preliminary competition) se¹ñ 選; se¹ñ 戦: trial heats (*yoseñ*) 予選.

— *vt.* ... o ne⌈ssuru ...を熱する Ⓒ; a⌈tatame¹ru 暖[温]める Ⓥ: heat a room (*heya o atatameru*) 部屋を暖める / heat up soup (*suupu o atatameru*) スープを温める / heat water (*oyu o wakasu*) お湯を沸かす.

— *vi.* a¹tsuku naru 熱くなる Ⓒ; a⌈tatama¹ru 暖[温]まる Ⓒ.

heater *n.* da⌈ñbooki¹gu 暖房器具; hi¹itaa ヒーター; su⌈to¹obu ストーブ: an electric [oil] heater (*deñki* [*sekiyu*] *sutoobu*) 電気[石油]ストーブ.

heave *vt.* ... o mo⌈chiageru ...を持ち上げる Ⓥ: heave a heavy suitcase (*omoi suutsukeesu o mochiageru*) 重いスーツケースを持ち上げる.

heaven *n.* 1 (of religion) te¹ñgoku 天国: God is in heaven. (*Kami wa teñgoku ni iru.*) 神は天国にいる.

2 (state of bliss) go⌈kuraku 極楽; ra⌈kueñ 楽園: A hot bath would be sheer heaven. (*Atatakai o-furo wa masa ni gokuraku da.*) 温かいおふろはまさに極楽だ.

heavily *adv.* 1 (excessively) ta⌈iryoo ni 大量に; ta⌈kusa¹ñ たくさん; hi¹doku ひどく: rain heavily (*tairyoo ni ame ga furu*) 大量に雨が降る / smoke heavily (*hidoku tabako o suu*) ひどくたばこを吸う.

2 (densely) mi¹tsu ni 密に: a heavily populated area (*jiñkoo no mitsu na chiiki*) 人口の密な地域.

3 (with weight) o⌈mosoo ni 重そうに; o⌈moku 重く: The fruit hung heavily from the branches. (*Kudamono ga omosoo ni eda ni natte ita.*) 果物が重そうに枝になっていた.

heavy *adj.* 1 (of great weight) o⌈moi 重い: This sofa is too heavy for me to move. (*Kono sofaa wa omokute watashi ni wa ugokasenai.*) このソファーは重くて私には動かせない.

2 (of degree of weight) o⌈mosa ga ... a¹ru 重さが...ある Ⓒ: "How heavy is the suitcase?" "It's twenty kilograms." (*"Kono suutsukeesu wa omosa ga dono kurai arimasu ka?" "Nijuk-kiro arimasu."*) 「このスーツケースは重さがどのくらいありますか」「20キロあります」

3 (of great force, amount, degree) ha⌈geshi¹i 激しい; ta⌈iryoo no 大量の: a heavy blow (*tsuuda*) 痛打 / a heavy drinker (*oozakenomi*) 大酒飲み / a heavy rain (*goou*) 豪雨.

4 (hard) ho⌈ne no ore¹ru 骨の折れる; tsu⌈rai つらい: heavy work (*hone no oreru shigoto*) 骨の折れる仕事 / I had a heavy day yesterday. (*Kinoo wa tsurai ichinichi datta.*) きのうはつらい1日だった.

5 (difficult to digest) shi⌈tsuko¹i しつこい: heavy food (*shitsukoi tabemono*) しつこい食べ物.

6 (sad) shi⌈zuñda 沈んだ; ka⌈nashii 悲しい: a heavy heart (*shizuñda kokoro*) 沈んだ心 / heavy news (*kanashii shirase*) 悲しい知らせ.

heavy industry *n.* ju⌈uko¹ogyoo 重工業.

hedge *n.* 1 (bushes) i⌈kegaki 生け垣: plant a hedge (*ikegaki o megurasu*) 生け垣を巡らす.

2 (protection) bo⌈oe¹esaku 防衛策: a hedge against inflation (*iñfure booeesaku*) インフレ防衛策.

heed *vt.* ... o ko⌈ko¹ro ni to⌈meru ...を心に留める Ⓥ: heed advice [a warning] (*chuukoku* [*chuui*] *o kokoro ni tomeru*) 忠告[注意]を心に留める.

heel *n.* 1 (of a foot) ka⌈kato かかと: have a blister on one's heel (*kakato ni mame ga dekite iru*) かかとにまめができている.

2 (of a shoe) ka⌈kato かかと: shoes with high heels (*kakato no takai kutsu*) かかとの高い靴.

height *n.* 1 (being high) ta¹kasa 高さ; ko¹odo 高度: What is the height of Tokyo Tower? (*Tookyoo Tawaa no takasa wa dono kurai arimasu ka?*) 東京タワーの高さはどのくらいありますか. / We are now flying at a height of 10,000 meters. (*Watashi-tachi wa ima koodo ichimañmeetoru de toñde imasu.*) 私たちは

今高度1万メートルで飛んでいます.
2 (high place) ta⌈ka⌉i to⌈koro⌉ 高い所; ta⌈kadai 高台; cho⌈ojo⌉o 頂上: I am afraid of heights. (*Watashi wa takai tokoro ga kowai.*) 私は高い所が怖い.
3 (extreme degree) ma⌈ssa⌉kari 真っ盛り; ze⌈tchoo 絶頂: We arrived in Rome at the height of the tourist season. (*Watashi-tachi wa kañkoo shiizuñ no massakari ni Rooma ni tsuita.*) 私たちは観光シーズンの真っ盛りにローマに着いた.

heir *n.* so⌈ozokuniñ 相続人: a legal heir (*hootee soozokuniñ*) 法定相続人.

heiress *n.* jo⌈see no soozokuniñ 女性の相続人.

helicopter *n.* he⌈riko⌉putaa ヘリコプター: They hurried to the crash site by helicopter. (*Kare-ra wa herikoputaa de tsuiraku geñba e kyuukoo shita.*) 彼らはヘリコプターで墜落現場へ急行した.

hell *n.* ji⌈goku⌉ 地獄.

hello *int.* **1** (greeting) ya⌉a やあ; (morning) o⌈hayoo お早う; (afternoon) ko⌈ññichi wa こんにちは; (evening) ko⌈ñbañ wa こんばんは.
2 (over the telephone) mo⌉shimoshi もしもし: Hello. Is this Mr. Yamada? (*Moshimoshi. Yamada-sañ desu ka?*) もしもし. 山田さんですか.

helmet *n.* he⌈rume⌉tto ヘルメット: put on [take off] a helmet (*herumetto o kaburu [nugu]*) ヘルメットをかぶる[脱ぐ].

help *vt.* **1** (assist) ... o te⌈tsuda⌉u ...を手伝う Ⓒ: Can you please help me carry this baggage? (*Kono nimotsu o hakobu no o tetsudatte moraemasu ka?*) この荷物を運ぶのを手伝ってもらえますか.
2 (save) ... o ta⌈suke⌉ru ...を助ける Ⓥ: We helped the climbers on the mountain. (*Watashi-tachi wa tozañsha o tasuketa.*) 私たちは登山者を助けた.
3 (be useful) ... ni ya⌈kuda⌉tsu ...に役立つ Ⓒ: Your advice helped us complete the project. (*Anata no jogeñ wa keekaku no kañsee ni yakudachimashita.*) あなたの助言は計画の完成に役立ちました.
4 (relieve) ... o ra⌈ku⌉ ni suru ...を楽にする Ⓘ: This medicine will help your cough. (*Kono kusuri o nomeba seki ga raku ni narimasu yo.*) この薬を飲めば咳が楽になりますよ.
5 (serve food) ... o ji⌈yu⌉u ni to⌉tte ta⌈be⌉ru ...を自由に取って食べる Ⓥ: Help yourself to whatever you want. (*Tabetai mono wa nañ de mo go-jiyuu ni totte o-tabe kudasai.*) 食べたいものは何でもご自由に取ってお食べください.
— *vi.* te⌈tsuda⌉u 手伝う Ⓒ: We can finish quickly if you will help. (*Anata ga tetsudatte kurereba sugu ni owarimasu.*) あなたが手伝ってくれればすぐに終わります.
Can I help you? (in a shop) (*Nani o sashiagemashoo ka?*) 何を差し上げましょうか.
cannot help doing <verb>-zu ni wa i⌈rarenai ...ずにはいられない: I cannot help laughing at him. (*Kare o warawazu ni wa irarenai.*) 彼を笑わずにはいられない.
— *n.* **1** (assistance) ta⌈suke⌉ 助け: We need your help. (*Watashi-tachi wa anata no tasuke ga hitsuyoo desu.*) 私たちはあなたの助けが必要です.
2 (referring to a person) ta⌈suke⌉ ni naru hi⌈to⌉ 助けになる人: You have been a great help. (*Totemo tasukarimashita.*) とても助かりました.
Help Wanted. (*Kyuujiñ.*) 求人.

helper *n.* ta⌈suke⌉ru hi⌈to⌉ 助ける人; te⌈tsuda⌉i 手伝い; he⌉rupaa ヘルパー.

helpful *adj.* yu⌈ueki na 有益な; ya⌈kuda⌉tsu 役立つ: helpful advice (*yuueki na chuukoku*) 有益な忠告 / The computer manual was very helpful. (*Koñpyuutaa no manyuaru wa taiheñ yakudatta.*) コンピューターのマニュアルは大変役だった.

helpless *adj.* **1** (unable to act) do⌉o suru ko⌈to⌉ mo de⌈ki⌉nai どうす

ることもできない: a helpless invalid (*jibuñ de doo suru koto mo dekinai byooniñ*) 自分でどうすることもできない病人.
2 (lacking help) ta⌈suke no na⌉i 助けのない; ta⌈yo⌉ru mo⌈no no na⌉i 頼る者のない: a helpless orphan (*tayoru mono no nai koji*) 頼る者のない孤児.

hem *n.* he⌈ri⌉ へり; fu⌈chi⌉ 縁: the hem of a shirt (*waishatsu no heri*) ワイシャツのへり.

hen *n.* me⌈ñdori めん鳥.

her *pron.* **1** [possessive form] ka⌉-nojo no 彼女の; so⌈no oñna no hito no その女の人の: I think this is her pen. (*Kore wa kanojo no peñ da to omoimasu.*) これは彼女のペンだと思います.
2 [direct object] ka⌉nojo o 彼女を: Do you know her? (*Anata wa kanojo o shitte imasu ka?*) あなたは彼女を知っていますか.
3 [indirect object] ka⌉nojo ni 彼女に: I gave her flowers. (*Watashi wa kanojo ni hana o ageta.*) 私は彼女に花をあげた.
4 [with a preposition] ka⌉nojo 彼女: I just can't live without her. (*Watashi wa kanojo nashi ni wa ikite ikenai.*) 私は彼女なしには生きていけない.

herb *n.* ha⌉abu ハーブ; ko⌈oryoo-shoku⌉butsu 香料植物: medicinal herbs (*yakusoo*) 薬草.

herd *n.* mu⌈re⌉ 群れ: a herd of cows (*ushi no mure*) 牛の群れ.

here *adv.* **1** (at, in, to this place) ko⌈ko ni [de, e] ここに[で, へ]: Mr. Yamada is here. (*Yamada-sañ wa koko ni imasu.*) 山田さんはここにいます. / Wait here a moment, please. (*Koko de chotto matte ite kudasai.*) ここでちょっと待っていてください. / Come here. (*Koko e irasshai.*) ここへいらっしゃい. ★ The meaning is conveyed by the particle: *koko ni* = existence here, movement to here; *koko de* = action here; *koko ni/e* = movement to here; *koko kara* = movement from here.
2 [specifying] ko⌈ko ここ; ko⌈chira こちら: Here's your bag. (*Anata no kabañ wa koko ni arimasu.*) あなたのかばんはここにあります. / Here's the person you were looking for. (*Kochira ga anata ga sagashite ita kata desu.*) こちらがあなたが捜していた方です.
3 [emphasizing] ko⌈ko ここ: This corner here is where the accident happened. (*Kono koko no kado ga jiko no okita tokoro desu.*) このここの角が事故の起きた所です.
4 (hereabouts) ko⌈no この: Is there a post office near here? (*Kono chikaku ni yuubiñkyoku wa arimasu ka?*) この近くに郵便局はありますか.
5 (at this time) i⌉ma 今; ko⌈ko de ここで: Here the story ends. (*Koko de hanashi wa owarimasu.*) ここで話は終わります.
here and there *adv.* a⌈chi ko⌉chi あちこち.

heritage *n.* i⌈sañ 遺産; de⌈ñtoo 伝統.

hero *n.* **1** (brave person) e⌈eyuu 英雄; yu⌉ushi 勇士: a national hero (*kokumiñ-teki eeyuu*) 国民的英雄.
2 (main character) shu⌈ji⌉ñkoo 主人公: the hero of a play (*geki no shujiñkoo*) 劇の主人公.

heroic *adj.* e⌈eyuu-teki na 英雄的な: heroic acts (*eeyuu-teki na kooi*) 英雄的な行為.

heroin *n.* he⌈ro⌉iñ ヘロイン.

heroine *n.* **1** (brave woman) jo⌈see no eeyuu 女性の英雄; jo⌈ketsu 女傑.
2 (main character) o⌈ñna shuji⌉ñ-koo 女主人公; hi⌈ro⌉iñ ヒロイン: the heroine of the novel (*shoosetsu no hiroiñ*) 小説のヒロイン.

herring *n.* ni⌉shiñ にしん: a can of herrings (*nishiñ no kañzume*) にしんの缶詰.

hers *pron.* ka⌉nojo no mo⌈no⌉ 彼女のもの: This magazine is hers. (*Kono zasshi wa kanojo no mono da.*) この雑誌は彼女のものだ.

herself *pron.* **1** [reflexive use] ji⌈buñ ji⌉shiñ o [ni] 自分自身を[に].

h

★ Usually not translated: She cut herself with a knife. (*Kanojo wa naifu de kega o shita.*) 彼女はナイフでけがをした.

2 [emphatic use] ji[bun de 自分で; ka[nojo ji]shin de 彼女自身で: Did Mrs. Yamazaki herself tell you that? (*Yamazaki-sañ jishiñ ga soo itta no desu ka?*) 山崎さん自身がそう言ったのですか.

hesitate *vi.* ta[mera]u ためらう Ⓒ; chu]ucho suru ちゅうちょする Ⓘ; ma[yo]u 迷う Ⓒ: He hesitated about what to do. (*Kare wa nani o shitara yoi ka mayotta.*) 彼は何をしたらよいか迷った.

hiccup *n.* sha]kkuri しゃっくり: have hiccups (*shakkuri o suru*) しゃっくりをする.

hide *vt.* ... o ka[ku]su …を隠す Ⓒ: I hid the money under the tatami. (*Watashi wa sono o-kane o tatami no shita ni kakushita.*) 私はそのお金を畳の下に隠した.

— *vi.* ka[kure]ru 隠れる Ⓥ: The police know where the criminal is hiding. (*Keesatsu wa hañniñ ga doko ni kakurete iru ka shitte iru.*) 警察は犯人がどこに隠れているか知っている.

hideous *adj.* zo[tto suru ぞっとする; o[soroshi]i 恐ろしい: a hideous sight (*zotto suru kookee*) ぞっとする光景 / a hideous crime (*osoroshii hañzai*) 恐ろしい犯罪.

high *adj.* **1** (distance above the ground) ta[ka]i 高い: a high mountain (*takai yama*) 高い山 / The sun was already high. (*Hi wa sude ni takakatta.*) 日はすでに高かった.

2 (in measuring) ta]kasa ga ... a]ru 高さが…ある: The pole is five meters high. (*Sono boo wa takasa ga go-meetoru aru.*) その棒は高さが5メートルある. / How high is Mt. Fuji? (*Fuji-sañ no takasa wa dono kurai desu ka?*) 富士山の高さはどのくらいですか.

3 (of degree, amount, etc.) ta[ka]i 高い: a high temperature (*takai oñdo*) 高い温度 / He drove at high speed. (*Kare wa koosoku de kuruma o uñteñ shita.*) 彼は高速で車を運転した. / The price is too high for me. (*Sono nedañ wa watashi ni wa taka-sugiru.*) その値段は私には高すぎる.

4 (of a voice) ta[ka]i 高い: speak in a high voice (*takai koe de hanasu*) 高い声で話す / sing in a high tone (*takai chooshi de utau*) 高い調子で歌う.

5 (important) ta[ka]i 高い: a high status (*takai chii*) 高い地位 / a high official in the government (*seefu no kookañ*) 政府の高官.

— *adv.* ta]kaku 高く: The birds are flying high in the sky. (*Tori ga sora takaku toñde iru.*) 鳥が空高く飛んでいる. / aim high (*mokuhyoo o takaku motsu*) 目標を高く持つ / rise high in the world (*shusse suru*) 出世する.

higher *adj.* **1** (far above) yo]ri ta[ka]i より高い: mountains higher than Mt. Fuji (*Fuji-sañ yori (mo) takai yama*) 富士山より(も)高い山.

2 (of a degree) ko[otoo na 高等な: higher animals (*kootoo-doobutsu*) 高等動物.

high school *n.* ko[otoo-ga]kkoo 高等学校; chu[u-ga]kkoo 中学校: a junior high school (*chuu-gakkoo*) 中学校 / a senior high school (*kootoo-gakkoo*) 高等学校.

highway *n.* ka[ñseñ do]oro 幹線道路; ko[odoo 公道: a highway linking two cities (*futatsu no toshi o musubu kañseñ dooro*) 2つの都市を結ぶ幹線道路.

hijack *vt.* ... o ha[ija]kku suru …をハイジャックする Ⓘ: hijack an aircraft (*hikooki o haijakku suru*) 飛行機をハイジャックする.

hike *vi.* ha]ikiñgu o suru ハイキングをする Ⓘ; to[horyo]koo o suru 徒歩旅行をする Ⓘ: go hiking (*haikiñgu ni iku*) ハイキングに行く.

— *n.* ha]ikiñgu ハイキング; to[horyo]koo 徒歩旅行: go on a hike

(*haikiñgu ni iku*) ハイキングに行く.

hill *n.* **1** (high ground) o⌈ka 丘; ko⌈yama 小山: go up a hill (*oka ni noboru*) 丘に登る / go down a hill (*oka o oriru*) 丘を下りる.
2 (slope) sa⌈ka⌉ 坂; sa⌈ka⌉michi 坂道: go up [down] a steep hill (*kyuu na sakamichi o agaru* [*kudaru*]) 急な坂道を上がる[下る].

him *pron.* **1** [direct object] ka⌉re o 彼を: I don't know him. (*Watashi wa kare o shirimaseñ.*) 私は彼を知りません.
2 [indirect object] ka⌉re ni 彼に: I gave him a dictionary. (*Watashi wa kare ni jisho o ageta.*) 私は彼に辞書をあげた.
3 [with a preposition] ka⌉re 彼: I went with him. (*Watashi wa kare to issho ni itta.*) 私は彼のといっしょに行った.

himself *pron.* **1** [reflexive use] ji⌈buñ ji⌉shiñ o [ni] 自分自身を[に].
★ Usually not translated: He cut himself while shaving. (*Kare wa hige o sotte ite kitte shimatta.*) 彼はひげをそっていて切ってしまった.
2 [emphatic use] ji⌈buñ de 自分で; ka⌈re ji⌉shiñ de 彼自身で: Mr. Hoshino said so himself. (*Hoshino-shi wa jibuñ de soo iimashita.*) 星野氏は自分でそう言いました.

hind *adj.* u⌈shiro no 後ろの; ko⌉obu no 後部の: the hind legs of a horse (*uma no ushiro ashi*) 馬の後脚.

hinder *vt.* ... o ja⌈ma suru …をじゃまする Ⓘ; o⌈kuraseru 遅らせる Ⓥ: Don't hinder me in my work. (*Watashi no shigoto o jama shinaide kure.*) 私の仕事をじゃましないでくれ. / Construction was hindered by the bad weather. (*Teñki ga warui no de keñsetsu ga okurete shimatta.*) 天気が悪いので建設が遅れてしまった.

hinge *n.* cho⌈otsu⌉gai ちょうつがい: the hinge of a door (*doa no chootsugai*) ドアのちょうつがい.

hint *n.* **1** (suggestion) hi⌉ñto ヒント; a⌈ñji 暗示: drop a hint (*hiñto o ataeru*) ヒントを与える / take a hint (*sore to kañzuku*) それと感づく.
2 (guidance) jo⌈geñ 助言: hints for newly married couples (*shiñkoñ fuufu e no jogeñ*) 新婚夫婦への助言.
3 (sign) ki⌈zashi 兆し: a hint of spring (*haru no kizashi*) 春の兆し.
— *vt.* ... to so⌈re to na⌉ku i⌈u …とそれとなく言う Ⓒ: He hinted to her that he loved her. (*Kare wa kanojo ni aishite iru to sore to naku itta.*) 彼は彼女に愛しているとそれとなく言った.
— *vi.* (... o) ho⌈nomeka⌉su (…を)ほのめかす Ⓒ: The boss hinted at my dismissal. (*Buchoo wa watashi ni kaiko o honomekashita.*) 部長は私に解雇をほのめかした.

hip *n.* ko⌈shi 腰; hi⌉ppu ヒップ.
★ Japanese '*hippu*' usually refers to the buttocks: with one's hands on one's hips (*ryoote o koshi ni atete*) 両手を腰に当てて.

hire *vt.* **1** (employ) ... o ya⌈to⌉u …を雇う Ⓒ: hire a gardener (*niwashi o yatou*) 庭師を雇う / Some workers were hired by the factory. (*Nañniñ ka no roodoosha ga sono koojoo de yatowareta.*) 何人かの労働者がその工場で雇われた.
2 (rent) ... o ka⌈riru …を借りる Ⓥ: hire a car (*kuruma o kariru*) 車を借りる / Our society hired a hall for the party. (*Watashi-tachi no kai de wa paatii no tame ni hooru o karita.*) 私たちの会ではパーティーのためにホールを借りた.
— *n.* chi⌈ñgari 賃借り; chi⌈ñgashi 賃貸し.

his[1] *pron.* ka⌉re no 彼の; so⌈no otoko no hito no その男の人の: His wife is a film star. (*Kare no okusañ wa eega sutaa desu.*) 彼の奥さんは映画スターです. / I know him, but I can't remember his name. (*Watashi wa kare o shitte iru ga namae o omoidasenai.*) 私は彼を知っているが名前を思い出せない. ★ Often omitted in Japanese.

his[2] *pron.* ka⌉re no mo⌈no⌉ 彼のもの; so⌈no otoko no hito no mono⌉ その

男の人のもの: Is this car really his? (*Kono kuruma wa hoñtoo ni kare no mono desu ka?*) この車は本当に彼のものですか. / My shoes are old but his are new. (*Watashi no kutsu wa furui ga kare no wa atarashii.*) 私の靴は古いが彼のは新しい.

historian *n.* re⌈kishika 歴史家.

historic *adj.* re⌈kishi-teki na 歴史的な; re⌈kishi-teki ni yuumee na 歴史的に有名な: a historic event (*rekishi-teki na dekigoto*) 歴史的な出来事 / a historic town (*rekishi-teki ni yuumee na machi*) 歴史的に有名な町.

h

historical *adj.* re⌈kishi-joo no 歴史上の: a historical person (*rekishi-joo no jiñbutsu*) 歴史上の人物 / a historical novel (*rekishi-shoosetsu*) 歴史小説 / places of historical interest (*kyuuseki*) 旧跡.

history *n.* **1** (past events; academic subject) re⌈kishi 歴史: study history (*rekishi o beñkyoo suru*) 歴史を勉強する.

2 (written account) re⌈kishi no ho⌉ñ 歴史の本: a history of Japan (*Nihoñ no rekishi no hoñ*) 日本の歴史の本.

3 (record) ke⌈ereki 経歴; ra⌈ireki 来歴: He related his life history. (*Kare wa jibuñ no keereki o katatta.*) 彼は自分の経歴を語った. / a personal history (*rirekisho*) 履歴書.

hit *vt.* **1** (strike) ... o u⌉tsu ...を打つ [C]; na⌈gu⌉ru 殴る [C]: hit a ball with a bat (*booru o batto de utsu*) ボールをバットで打つ / hit a boy on the head (*kodomo no atama o naguru*) 子どもの頭を殴る.

2 (strike home) ... ni me⌈echuu suru ...に命中する [I]: The stone hit the window. (*Ishi wa mado ni meechuu shita.*) 石は窓に命中した.

3 (contact forcefully; collide with) ... o bu⌈tsukeru ...をぶつける [V]; ... ni butsukaru ...にぶつかる [C]: I hit my knee on the table. (*Watashi wa hiza o teeburu ni butsuketa.*) 私はひざをテーブルにぶつけた. / The car hit the wall. (*Kuruma wa hee ni butsukatta.*) 車は塀にぶつかった.

4 (of misfortune, disaster, etc.) ... o o⌈so⌉u ...を襲う [C]: The typhoon is likely to hit us. (*Taifuu ga wareware o osoi-soo da.*) 台風がわれわれを襲いそうだ.

5 (in baseball) ... o u⌉tsu ...を打つ [C]: hit a homerun (*hoomurañ o utsu*) ホームランを打つ.

— *vi.* **1** (strike) (... ni) na⌈guri-kaka⌉ru (...に)殴りかかる [C]: He hit at me. (*Kare wa watashi ni nagurikakatta.*) 彼は私に殴りかかった.

2 (contact forcefully) (... ni) bu⌈tsukaru (...に)ぶつかる [C]: hit against the wall (*hee ni butsukaru*) 塀にぶつかる.

— *n.* **1** (blow) da⌈geki 打撃: a hard hit (*kyooretsu na dageki*) 強烈な打撃.

2 (successful attempt) a⌈tari 当たり; me⌈echuu 命中: two hits and three misses (*futatsu atari mittsu hazure*) 二つ当たり三つ外れ.

3 (success) se⌈ekoo 成功; hi⌉tto ヒット: a hit song (*hitto soñgu*) ヒットソング / a big hit (*dai-seekoo*) 大成功.

hives *n.* ji⌈ñma⌉shiñ じんましん.

hoarse *adj.* shi⌈wagareta しわがれた; shi⌈wagarete iru しわがれている; ka⌈reta かれた; ka⌈rete iru かれている: a hoarse voice (*shiwagare-goe*) しわがれ声.

hobby *n.* shu⌉mi 趣味; do⌈oraku⌉ 道楽: Stamp collecting is my hobby. (*Kitte shuushuu ga watashi no shumi desu.*) 切手収集が私の趣味です.

hoe *n.* ku⌉wa くわ(鍬).

hog *n.* bu⌈ta 豚.

hold *vt.* **1** (in the hand) te⌉ ni motsu 手に持つ [C]; ka⌈kaeru 抱える [V]; tsu⌈ka⌉mu つかむ [C]: Hold this bag, please. (*Kono kabañ o motte kudasai.*) このかばんを持ってください. / hold a parcel with both hands (*tsutsumi o ryoote de kakaeru*) 包みを両手で抱える / hold a strap tightly while

in a train (*deñsha no naka de tsuri-kawa o shikkari tsukamu*) 電車の中でつり革をしっかりつかむ.
2 (support) ... o sa⌈saeru ...を支える Ⓥ: The chair couldn't hold my weight. (*Isu wa watashi no taijuu o sasaeru koto ga dekinakatta.*) いすは私の体重を支えることができなかった.
3 (keep in a position) ... o ta⌈mo⌉-tsu ...を保つ Ⓒ; ma⌈ma⌉ ni shite oku ままにしておく Ⓒ: Hold the door open, please. (*Doa o aketa mama ni shite oite kudasai.*) ドアを開けたままにしておいてください. / Please hold the line. (*Sono mama kirazu ni o-machi kudasai.*) そのまま切らずにお待ちください.
4 (contain) ... o shu⌈uyoo suru ...を収容する Ⓘ; i⌈reru koto ga deki⌉ru 入れることができる Ⓥ: This hall can hold 2,000 people. (*Kono hooru wa niseñ-niñ shuuyoo dekimasu.*) このホールは2千人収容できます. / How many liters does this bottle hold? (*Kono biñ wa nañ rittoru gurai ireru koto ga dekimasu ka?*) このびんは何リットルぐらい入れることができますか.
5 (make; take place) ... o hi⌈ra⌉ku ...を開く Ⓒ; mo⌈yoo⌉su 催す Ⓒ: hold a meeting (*kaigoo o hiraku*) 会合を開く.
6 (keep; restrain) ... o o⌈sae⌉ru ...を押さえる Ⓥ: Hold him! Don't let him escape! (*Kare o osaero! Niga-su na!*) 彼を押さえろ. 逃がすな.
7 (defend) ... o ma⌈mo⌉ru ...を守る Ⓒ: hold a town against the enemy (*teki kara machi o mamoru*) 敵から町を守る.
8 (think) ... to ka⌈ñgae⌉ru ...と考える: They held that he was guilty. (*Kare-ra wa kare wa yuuzai da to kañgaeta.*) 彼らは彼は有罪だと考えた.
— *vi.* **1** (not break) mo⌈chikota-e⌉ru 持ちこたえる Ⓥ: The rope held. (*Roopu wa mochikotaeta.*) ロープは持ちこたえた.
2 (continue) tsu⌈zuku 続く Ⓒ: The fine weather held. (*Seeteñ ga tsu-zuita.*) 晴天が続いた.
3 (apply) a⌈tehama⌉ru 当てはまる Ⓒ: In this case, that rule does not hold. (*Kono baai, sono kisoku wa atehamaranai.*) この場合その規則は当てはまらない.
— *n.* **1** (grip) tsu⌈ka⌉mu koto つかむこと: release one's hold (*tsukañde iru te o hanasu*) つかんでいる手を離す.
2 (something to hold onto) tsu⌈ka-maru tokoro⌉ つかまる所: There were no holds for my hands. (*Te de tsukamaru tokoro ga nani mo nakatta.*) 手でつかまる所が何もなかった.

hole *n.* **1** (cavity; depression) a⌈na⌉ 穴; ku⌈bomi くぼみ: dig a hole (*ana o horu*) 穴を掘る / a hole in a wall (*kabe no ana*) 壁の穴 / a road full of holes (*ana-darake no dooro*) 穴だらけの道路.
2 (home of an animal) a⌈na⌉ 穴; su⌉ 巣: the hole of a mouse (*nezumi no ana*) ねずみの穴.
— *vt.* ... ni a⌈na⌉ o a⌈keru ...に穴を開ける Ⓥ: The iceberg holed the ship. (*Hyoozañ ga fune ni ana o aketa.*) 氷山が船に穴を開けた.

holiday *n.* **1** (official) shu⌈kujitsu 祝日; sa⌈ijitsu 祭日: a national holiday (*kokumiñ no shukujitsu*) 国民の祝日.
2 (vacation; day off) kyu⌈ujitsu 休日; kyu⌈uka 休暇: the summer holidays (*natsu-yasumi*) 夏休み / I did't take a holiday last month. (*Señgetsu wa kyuuka o toranakatta.*) 先月は休暇をとらなかった.

hollow *adj.* **1** (empty inside) u⌈tsuro no うつろの; ku⌈udoo no 空洞の: a hollow pipe (*naka ga kuudoo no paipu*) 中が空洞のパイプ.
2 (sunken) ku⌈boñda くぼんだ: a person with hollow cheeks (*hoo no ku-boñda hito*) ほおのくぼんだ人.
3 (of sounds) u⌈tsuro na うつろな: a hollow voice (*utsuro na koe*) うつろな声.
— *n.* ku⌈bomi くぼみ; a⌈na⌉ 穴: a hollow in the ground (*jimeñ no kubomi*) 地面のくぼみ.

h

— *vt.* ... o ku⌈rinu⌉ku ...をくりぬく Ⓒ: hollow out a log (*maruta o kurinuku*) 丸太をくりぬく.

holy *adj.* **1** (sacred) shi⌈ñsee na 神聖な: holy ground (*seechi*) 聖地.
2 (devout) shi⌈ñjiñbuka⌉i 信心深い: live a holy life (*shiñkoo-seekatsu o okuru*) 信仰生活を送る.

homage *n.* ke⌉ei 敬意; so⌈ñkee 尊敬: pay homage to a person (*hito ni keei o hyoo suru*) 人に敬意を表する.

home *n.* **1** (abode) ka⌈tee 家庭; ji⌈taku 自宅: a happy home (*tanoshii katee*) 楽しい家庭 / I help out at home. (*Watashi wa jitaku de tetsudai o shite imasu.*) 私は自宅で手伝いをしています.
2 (birthplace; country) ko⌉kyoo 故郷; kyo⌉ori 郷里; ko⌉koku 故国: Where is your home? (*Kyoori wa dochira desu ka?*) 郷里はどちらですか. / My home is in Canada. (*Watashi no kokoku wa Kanada desu.*) 私の故国はカナダです.
3 (property) i⌈e⌉ 家; ju⌈utaku 住宅: He bought a home in the suburbs. (*Kare wa koogai ni ie o katta.*) 彼は郊外に家を買った.
4 (special facility) shi⌉setsu 施設; ho⌉omu ホーム: a home for old people (*roojiñ hoomu*) 老人ホーム.
5 (place of origin) ge⌈ñsa⌉ñchi 原産地; ho⌈ñba 本場: Scotland is the home of whisky. (*Sukottorañdo wa uisukii no hoñba desu.*) スコットランドはウイスキーの本場です.
make oneself at home *vi.* ku⌈tsuro⌉gu くつろぐ Ⓒ.
— *adj.* ka⌈tee no 家庭の; ji⌈taku no 自宅の; ko⌈ku⌉nai no 国内の: home life (*katee-seekatsu*) 家庭生活 / one's home address (*jitaku no juusho*) 自宅の住所 / home and foreign news (*kokunai narabi ni kokugai no nyuusu*) 国内ならびに国外のニュース.
— *adv.* i⌈e⌉ e [ni] 家へ[に]; ko⌉kyoo e 故郷へ; ko⌉koku e 故国へ: write home (*kokyoo e tegami o kaku*) 故郷へ手紙を書く.

homemade *adj.* ji⌈kasee no 自家製の: a homemade cake (*jikasee no keeki*) 自家製のケーキ.

hometown *n.* u⌈mareko⌉kyoo no ma⌈chi⌉ 生まれ故郷の町; ko⌉kyoo 故郷: return to one's hometown (*umarekokyoo e kaeru*) 生まれ故郷へ帰る.

homework *n.* shu⌈kudai 宿題: do [finish] one's homework (*shukudai o suru [sumaseru]*) 宿題をする[済ませる].

homosexual *adj.* do⌈ose⌉eai no 同性愛の.
— *n.* do⌈ose⌉eai no hi⌈to⌉ 同性愛の人.

honest *adj.* **1** (trustworthy) sho⌈oji⌉ki na 正直な; se⌈ejitsu na 誠実な: an honest young man (*shoojiki na wakamono*) 正直な若者 / He is honest in business. (*Kare wa shigoto ni seejitsu da.*) 彼は仕事に誠実だ.
2 (direct; frank) a⌈rinomama⌉ no ありのままの; so⌈tchoku na 率直な: give an honest opinion (*arinomama no ikeñ o noberu*) ありのままの意見を述べる.

honesty *n.* sho⌈oji⌉ki 正直; se⌈ejitsu 誠実: Honesty is the best policy. (*Shoojiki wa saijoo no saku.*) 正直は最上の策.

honey *n.* ha⌈chimitsu はちみつ(蜂蜜).

honor *n.* **1** (high reputation) me⌉eyo 名誉: gain [lose] honor (*meeyo o eru [ushinau]*) 名誉を得る[失う].
2 (high principle) shi⌉ñgi 信義: He is a man of honor. (*Kare wa shiñgi o omoñjiru hito da.*) 彼は信義を重んじる人だ.
3 (respect) ke⌉ei 敬意; so⌈ñkee 尊敬: The citizens showed honor to their hero. (*Shimiñ wa kare-ra no eeyuu ni keei o hyooshita.*) 市民は彼らの英雄に敬意を表した.
4 (degree) yu⌈utoo 優等: graduate from college with honors (*yuutoo de daigaku o sotsugyoo suru*) 優等で大学を卒業する.

— *vt.* ... o so⌈ñkee suru …を尊敬する [I]; u⌈yama⌉u 敬う [C]: honor one's parents (*oya o uyamau*) 親を敬う.

honorable *adj.* **1** (worthy of respect) so⌈ñkee su be⌉ki 尊敬すべき; ri⌈ppa na 立派な: honorable conduct (*rippa na kooi*) 立派な行為.

2 (deserving honor) me⌉eyo aru 名誉ある; ko⌈oee na 光栄な: an honorable position (*meeyo aru chii*) 名誉ある地位.

honorific *adj.* so⌈ñkee no 尊敬の; ke⌈ego no 敬語の: There are many honorific verbs in Japanese. (*Nihoñgo ni wa keego no dooshi ga takusañ arimasu.*) 日本語には敬語の動詞がたくさんあります.

— *n.* ke⌈ego 敬語; ke⌈eshoo 敬称.

hood *n.* **1** (head covering) fu⌉udo フード; zu⌉kiñ ずきん: wear a hood (*fuudo o kaburu*) フードをかぶる.

2 (of a car) bo⌈ñne⌉tto ボンネット.

hoof *n.* hi⌈zume ひずめ.

hook *n.* **1** (for hanging things) ka⌈gi⌉ かぎ; to⌈megane 留め金: hang one's hat on a hook (*booshi o kagi ni kakeru*) 帽子をかぎにかける.

2 (fishhook) tsu⌈ribari 釣り針.

3 (fastener) ho⌉kku ホック: the hooks on a dress (*doresu no hokku*) ドレスのホック.

— *vt.* ... o ka⌈gi⌉ [ho⌉kku] de to⌈meru …をかぎ[ホック]で留める [V]: Please hook this dress at the back for me. (*Kono doresu no ushiro o hokku de tomete kudasai.*) このドレスの後ろをホックで留めてください.

— *vi.* ka⌈gi⌉ [ho⌉kku] de to⌈maru かぎ[ホック]で留まる [C]: This dress hooks at the neck. (*Kono doresu wa kubi no tokoro ga hokku de tomarimasu.*) このドレスは首の所がホックで留まります.

hop *vi.* **1** (on one leg) ka⌈ta-ashi de tobu 片足で跳ぶ [C]: hop along on one's left foot (*hidariashi de toñde aruku*) 左足で跳んで歩く.

2 (jump) hyo⌉i to to⌈bu ひょいと跳ぶ [C]: hop onto a bicycle (*jiteñsha ni hyoi to noru*) 自転車にひょいと乗る / hop across a stream (*ogawa o hyoi to tobikosu*) 小川をひょいと跳び越す.

hope *vt.* ... o no⌈zomu …を望む [C]; ki⌈tai suru 期待する [I]; ⟨verb⟩-tai to o⌈mo⌉u …たいと思う [C]: She's hoping to get into Waseda University. (*Kanojo wa Waseda daigaku e hairu koto o nozoñde imasu.*) 彼女は早稲田大学へ入ることを望んでいます. / I hope to see you next week. (*Raishuu o-ai shitai to omoimasu.*) 来週お会いしたいと思います.

— *vi.* ki⌈boo o mo⌉tsu 希望を持つ [C]; ki⌈tai suru 期待する [I]: We are still hoping. (*Wareware wa mada kiboo o motte imasu.*) われわれはまだ希望を持っています.

— *n.* **1** (expectation) ki⌈boo 希望; no⌈zomi 望み; mi⌈komi 見込み: I lost all hope. (*Watashi wa subete no kiboo o ushinatta.*) 私はすべての希望を失った. / There is little hope that there are any survivors. (*Seezoñsha ga iru mikomi wa hotoñdo arimaseñ.*) 生存者がいる見込みはほとんどありません.

2 (person or thing) ki⌈boo o ataeru mono⌉ 希望を与えるもの; ho⌉opu ホープ: He is our last hope. (*Kare wa wareware no saigo no tanomi no tsuna da.*) 彼はわれわれの最後の頼みの綱だ.

hopeful *adj.* **1** (having hope) ki⌈boo o mo⌉tta [mo⌉tte iru] 希望を持った[持っている]: I feel hopeful about the future. (*Watashi wa shoorai ni kiboo o motte iru.*) 私は将来に希望を持っている.

2 (promising) yu⌈uboo na 有望な; mi⌈komi no a⌉ru 見込みのある: a hopeful young man (*yuuboo na seeneñ*) 有望な青年.

hopeless *adj.* **1** (full of despair) ki⌈boo o ushinatta [ushinatte iru] 希望を失った[失っている]; ze⌈tsuboo shita [shite iru] 絶望した[している]: feel hopeless (*zetsuboo shite iru*) 絶望している.

2 (unpromising) mi⌈komi no na⌉i

見込みのない; ze⌈tsuboo-teki na 絶望的な: a hopeless situation (*zetsu-boo-teki na jitai*) 絶望的な事態.

horizon *n.* **1** (on land) chi⌈heeseñ 地平線: The moon rose above the horizon. (*Tsuki ga chiheeseñ no ue ni nobotta.*) 月が地平線の上に昇った.
2 (at sea) su⌈iheeseñ 水平線.
3 (outlook) ha⌉ñi 範囲; shi⌉ya 視野: broaden one's horizons (*shiya o hiromeru*) 視野を広める.

horizontal *adj.* su⌈ihee na 水平な; yo⌈ko no 横の: a horizontal line (*yokoseñ*) 横線.

h

horn *n.* **1** (of an animal) tsu⌈no⌉ 角: a bull's horns (*ushi no tsuno*) 牛の角.
2 (substance) tsu⌈no-se⌉ehiñ 角製品: These spoons are made of horn. (*Kono supuuñ wa tsuno-see desu.*) このスプーンは角製です.
3 (of a car) ke⌈eteki 警笛: blow a horn (*keeteki o narasu*) 警笛を鳴らす.
4 (musical instrument) ho⌉ruñ ホルン: blow a horn (*horuñ o fuku*) ホルンを吹く.

horoscope *n.* (diagram) te⌈ñkyu⌉u-zu 天宮図; (forecast) se⌈ñse⌉ejutsu 占星術.

horrible *adj.* **1** (causing horror) o⌈soroshi⌉i 恐ろしい: commit a horrible crime (*osoroshii hañzai o okasu*) 恐ろしい犯罪を犯す.
2 (unpleasant) fu⌈yu⌉kai na 不愉快な; (terrible) hi⌈do⌉i ひどい: horrible weather (*fuyukai na teñki*) 不愉快な天気 / a horrible mistake (*hidoi machigai*) ひどい間違い.

horror *n.* **1** (fear) kyo⌉ofu 恐怖; o⌈sore⌉ 恐れ: scream in horror (*kyoofu de himee o ageru*) 恐怖で悲鳴を上げる.
2 (dislike) ke⌉ño 嫌悪: I have a great horror of snakes. (*Watashi wa hebi ga dai-kirai desu.*) 私は蛇が大嫌いです.

hors d'oeuvre *n.* o⌉odoburu オードブル.

horse *n.* u⌈ma⌉ 馬: I like to ride horses. (*Watashi wa uma ni noru no ga suki da.*) 私は馬に乗るのが好きだ. / horse racing (*keeba*) 競馬.

horseback *n.* u⌈ma no se 馬の背: go on horseback (*uma ni notte iku*) 馬に乗って行く.

hose *n.* ho⌉osu ホース: use a hose to water the plants (*shokubutsu ni mizu o yaru no ni hoosu o tsukau*) 植物に水をやるのにホースを使う.

hospitable *adj.* mo⌈tenashi no yo⌉i もてなしのよい; ka⌈ñtai suru 歓待する: He was hospitable to me. (*Kare wa watashi o kañtai shite kureta.*) 彼は私を歓待してくれた.

hospital *n.* byo⌈oiñ 病院: an emergency hospital (*kyuukyuu-byooiñ*) 救急病院 / a maternity hospital (*sañka-byooiñ*) 産科病院 / enter the hospital (*nyuuiñ suru*) 入院する / leave the hospital (*taiiñ suru*) 退院する / Please take me to the hospital. (*Byooiñ e tsurete itte kudasai.*) 病院へ連れて行ってください.

host *n.* **1** (person) shu⌉jiñ 主人; ho⌉suto ホスト: act as host at a party (*paatii de hosuto o tsutomeru*) パーティーでホストを務める.
2 (holder of an event) shu⌈sa⌉isha 主催者: the host city for the Olympic Games (*Oriñpikku no shusai toshi*) オリンピックの主催都市.
3 (on TV) shi⌈ka⌉isha 司会者.
— *vt.* ... o shu⌈sai suru ...を主催する [I]: Kyoto will host the coming conference. (*Kyooto ga koñdo no kaigi o shusai shimasu.*) 京都が今度の会議を主催します.

hostage *n.* hi⌈tojichi 人質: They kept the passengers as hostages. (*Kare-ra wa jookyaku o hitojichi ni shita.*) 彼らは乗客を人質にした.

hostess *n.* **1** (woman who receives guests) o⌈ñna shu⌉jiñ 女主人: act as hostess at a party (*paatii de shujiñyaku o tsutomeru*) パーティーで主人役を務める.
2 (of a night-club) ho⌉sutesu ホステス.

hostile *adj.* **1** (unfriendly) te⌈ki no 敵の; te⌉ki-i no aru 敵意のある: a hostile country (*tekikoku*) 敵国 / a hostile look (*teki-i o motta kao-tsuki*) 敵意を持った顔つき.
2 (disapproving of) ha⌈ñtai no 反対の: He was hostile to the idea. (*Kare wa sono kañgae ni hañtai datta.*) 彼はその考えに反対だった.

hostility *n.* te⌉ki-i 敵意: feel hostility toward a person (*hito ni teki-i o idaku*) 人に敵意を抱く.

hot *adj.* **1** (temperature) a⌈tsu⌉i 暑い; (of heat) a⌈tsu⌉i 熱い: It's hot, isn't it? (*Atsui desu ne.*) 暑いですね. / I like coffee hot. (*Watashi wa atsui koohii ga suki desu.*) 私は熱いコーヒーが好きです.
2 (of taste) pi⌈ri⌉tto ka⌈ra⌉i ぴりっと辛い: hot pepper (*piritto karai koshoo*) ぴりっと辛いこしょう / This curry is too hot for me. (*Kono karee wa kara-sugiru.*) このカレーは辛すぎる.
3 (excitable; angry) ha⌈geshi⌉i 激しい; o⌈ko⌉tta 怒った: a hot debate (*hageshii tooroñ*) 激しい討論 / a person with a hot temper (*tañki na hito*) 短気な人.
4 (fresh) sa⌈ishiñ no 最新の: hot news (*saishiñ nyuusu*) 最新ニュース.

hotel *n.* ho⌉teru ホテル: I'll stay at Yamanaka Hotel. (*Watashi wa Yamanaka hoteru ni tomarimasu.*) 私は山中ホテルに泊まります. / I'd like to reserve a hotel room in the city. (*Shinai no hoteru o yoyaku shite kudasai.*) 市内のホテルを予約してください.

hot spring *n.* o⌈ñseñ 温泉.

hot water *n.* o-⌈yu お湯; yu⌉ 湯.

hour *n.* **1** (60 minutes) ji⌈kañ 時間: I waited for him for two hours. (*Watashi wa kare o ni-jikañ matta.*) 私は彼を2時間待った. / The station is an hour from here. (*Eki wa koko kara ichi-jikañ desu.*) 駅はここから1時間です.
2 (time of an activity) ji⌈kañ 時間: office hours (*kiñmu-jikañ*) 勤務時間 / Our lunch hour is only forty minutes. (*Watashi-tachi no chuushoku-jikañ wa tatta yoñjuugo-fuñ desu.*) 私たちの昼食時間はたった45分です.
3 (time) ji⌉koku 時刻: arrive at the appointed hour (*yakusoku no jikoku ni tsuku*) 約束の時刻に着く.
4 (start of a new hour) sho⌉oji 正時: The bus leaves every hour on the hour. (*Basu wa mai-shooji ni demasu.*) バスは毎正時に出ます.
5 (period) to⌈ki⌉ 時; ji⌉ki 時期: the happiest hours of one's life (*jiñsee de ichibañ tanoshii jiki*) 人生でいちばん楽しい時期.

house *n.* **1** (dwelling) i⌈e⌉ 家; ka⌉oku 家屋: build a house (*ie o tateru*) 家を建てる / He lives in a large house. (*Kare wa ooki-na ie ni suñde iru.*) 彼は大きな家に住んでいる. / a house for rent (*kashiya*) 貸家.
2 (people in a house) i⌈e no mono⌉ 家の者; ka⌉zoku 家族: The whole house felt the earthquake. (*Kazoku miñna no mono ga jishiñ o kañjita.*) 家族みんなの者が地震を感じた.
3 (legislature) gi⌉iñ 議院; gi⌈jidoo 議事堂: the House of Councilors (*Sañgiiñ*) 参議院 / the Houses of Parliament (*kokkai gijidoo*) 国会議事堂.

household *n.* ka⌉zoku 家族: a large household (*dai-kazoku*) 大家族.
— *adj.* ka⌉zoku no 家族の: household affairs (*kaji*) 家事.

housekeeper *n.* ka⌈se⌉efu 家政婦.

housekeeping *n.* ka⌈see 家政; ka⌉ji 家事: housekeeping money (*kakeehi*) 家計費.

housewife *n.* shu⌉fu 主婦.

how *adv.* **1** (in what way) do⌉o yatte どうやって; do⌉ñna fuu ni どんな風に: How can I get to Hiroshima? (*Hiroshima e wa doo yatte ikimasu ka?*) 広島へはどうやって行きますか. / Please tell me how to call this number. (*Kono bañgoo ni deñwa suru hoohoo o oshiete kudasai.*) こ

h

の番号に電話する方法を教えてください. / Please show me how to fill in this form. (*Kono shorui no kaki-kata o oshiete kudasai.*) この書類の書き方を教えてください.
2 (to or by what amount or degree) do⌈no kurai どのくらい; do⌈no te⌉edo どの程度: How long will it take to get to Kobe? (*Koobe made iku no ni dono kurai kakarimasu ka?*) 神戸まで行くのにどのくらいかかりますか. / How much is it? (*Sore wa ikura desu ka?*) それはいくらですか. / How old is your younger sister? (*Imooto-sañ wa nañ-sai desu ka?*) 妹さんは何歳ですか.
3 (in what condition) i⌈ka⌉ga いかが; do⌉ñna guai どんな具合: How is everyone in your family? (*Go-kazoku no minasañ wa ikaga desu ka?*) ご家族のみなさんはいかがですか. / "How do you feel today?" "Not so well." (*"Kyoo wa doñna guai desu ka?" "Amari yoku arimaseñ."*) 「きょうはどんな具合ですか」「あまりよくありません」
4 [for emphasis] na⌉ñ to 何と; na⌉ñte 何て; do⌉ñna ni どんなに: How pretty this flower is! (*Kono hana wa nañte kiree nañ daroo.*) この花はなんてきれいなんだろう. / How I wish I could speak Japanese perfectly! (*Nihoñgo ga kañzeñ ni hanasetara doñna ni ii daroo.*) 日本語が完全に話せたらどんなにいいだろう.
5 [in surprised question] do⌉o shite どうして: How could I have made such a stupid mistake? (*Doo shite añna baka na machigai o shita no daroo?*) どうしてあんなばかな間違いをしたのだろう.
How about ...? ... wa i⌈ka⌉ga desu ka? …はいかがですか: How about a cup of tea? (*O-cha o ip-pai ikaga desu ka?*) お茶を1杯いかがですか.
How about doing? ⟨verb⟩-⌈mase⌉ñ ka? …ませんか: How about playing tennis? (*Tenisu o shimaseñ ka?*) テニスをしませんか.
How are you? 1 (when meeting someone) O-⌈ge⌉ñki desu ka? お元気ですか.
2 (when meeting for the first time) Ha⌈jimema⌉shite. はじめまして.
How do you do? (*Hajimemashite.*) はじめまして.
— *conj.* ... ko⌈to no shidai …ことの次第: I told him how it happened. (*Watashi wa sore ga okotta koto no shidai o kare ni hanashita.*) 私はそれが起こったことの次第を彼に話した.

however *adv.* **1** (to whatever degree) do⌉ñna ni ⟨verb⟩-te[de] mo どんなに…て[で]も: However hard I try, I still can't do it. (*Doñna ni isshookeñmee yatte mo, watashi ni wa mada dekinai.*) どんなに一生懸命にやっても, 私にはまだできない.
2 (in whatever way) do⌉no yoo ni ⟨verb⟩-te[de] mo どのように…て[で]も: However you do it, you are likely to fail. (*Dono yoo ni shite mo kimi wa shippai shi-soo da.*) どのようにしても君は失敗しそうだ.
— *conj.* shi⌈ka⌉shi しかし: However, I will do it in my own way. (*Shikashi watashi wa watashi no yarikata de yarimasu.*) しかし私は私のやり方でやります.

howl *vi.* ho⌈e⌉ru 吠える [V]: A dog is howling in the distance. (*Inu ga tooku de hoete iru.*) 犬が遠くで吠えている.

hug *vt.* ... o da⌈kishime⌉ru …を抱き締める [V]: hug a child (*kodomo o dakishimeru*) 子どもを抱き締める.

huge *adj.* kyo⌈dai na 巨大な; ba⌈kudai na 莫大な: a huge airplane (*kyodai na hikooki*) 巨大な飛行機 / a huge amount of money (*bakudai na kiñgaku*) 莫大な金額.

human *adj.* **1** (of mankind) ni⌈ñgeñ no 人間の; ji⌉ñrui no 人類の: human nature (*niñgeñsee*) 人間性 / the human race (*jiñrui*) 人類.
2 (typical of ordinary people) ni⌈ñgeñ-teki na 人間的な; ni⌈ñgeñrashi⌉i 人間らしい: human interest (*niñgeñ-teki kyoomi*) 人間的興味 /

human feelings (*niñgeñ-rashii kañjoo*) 人間らしい感情.
— *n.* = human being.

human being *n.* niᶠñgeñ 人間; hiᶠto˥ 人.

humane *adj.* ni˥ñjoo no aru 人情のある; jiᶠhibuka˥i 慈悲深い: a man of humane character (*niñjoomi no aru hito*) 人情味のある人.

humanism *n.* jiᶠñbuñshu˥gi 人文主義. ★ In Japanese 'humanitarianism' is called '*hyuumanizumu*' ヒューマニズム.

humanity *n.* **1** (mankind) ji˥ñrui 人類: crimes against humanity (*jiñrui ni taisuru hañzai*) 人類に対する犯罪.
2 (kindness; human feelings) oᶠmoiyari 思いやり; ni˥ñjoo 人情: be lacking in humanity (*niñjoo ni kakeru*) 人情に欠ける.

human relations *n.* niᶠñgeñ-ka˥ñkee 人間関係.

humble *adj.* **1** (modest) hiᶠkaeme na 控えめな; keᶠñsoñ shita [shite iru] 謙そんした[している]: a humble request (*hikaeme na yookyuu*) 控えめな要求 / a humble attitude (*keñsoñ shita taido*) 謙そんした態度.
2 (low) hiᶠku˥i 低い; iᶠyashii 卑しい: a person of humble social standing (*shakai-teki ni mibuñ no hikui hito*) 社会的に身分の低い人.
3 (poor) shi˥sso na 質素な; so˥matsu na 粗末な: a humble house (*shisso na ie*) 質素な家.

humid *adj.* shiᶠmeppo˥i しめっぽい; shiᶠkke no o˥oi 湿気の多い: It's humid this evening. (*Koñya wa shimeppoi.*) 今夜はしめっぽい. / a humid climate (*shikke no ooi kikoo*) 湿気の多い気候.

humidity *n.* shiᶠkke 湿気; shiᶠtsu˥do 湿度: high [low] humidity (*takai* [*hikui*] *shitsudo*) 高い[低い]湿度.

humiliate *vt.* ... ni haᶠji˥ o kaᶠkase˥ru …に恥をかかせる Ⓥ; ... no jiᶠso˥ñshiñ o kiᶠzutsuke˥ru …の自尊心を傷つける Ⓥ: I was humiliated by my blunder. (*Watashi wa hema o yatte haji o kaita.*) 私はへまをやって恥をかいた.

humility *n.* keᶠñsoñ けんそん; hi˥ge 卑下: speak with humility (*keñsoñ shite hanasu*) けんそんして話す.

humor *n.* **1** (being amusing) yu˥umoa ユーモア: a story full of humor (*yuumoa ni tonda hanashi*) ユーモアに富んだ話 / He has no sense of humor. (*Kare wa yuumoa no señsu ga nai.*) 彼はユーモアのセンスがない.
2 (mood) ki˥buñ 気分; kiᶠgeñ きげん: I am in no humor for driving now. (*Ima wa kuruma o uñteñ suru kibuñ ja nai.*) いまは車を運転する気分じゃない. / He was in a good humor. (*Kare wa joo-kigeñ datta.*) 彼は上きげんだった.

humorous *adj.* koᶠkkee na こっけいな; yu˥umoa no aru ユーモアのある: a humorous story (*kokkee na hanashi*) こっけいな話 / a humorous writer (*yuumoa sakka*) ユーモア作家.

hundred *n.* hyaᶠku˥ 100, 百; (people) hyaᶠku˥-niñ 100 人; (things) hya˥k-ko 100 個; (age) hyaᶠku˥-sai 100 歳.
— *adj.* hyaᶠku˥ no 100 の; (people) hyaᶠku˥-niñ no 100 人の; (things) hya˥k-ko no 100 個の.

hundredth *adj.* hyaᶠku-bañme˥ no 100 番目の.
— *n.* **1** (people) hyaᶠku-bañme˥ no hiᶠto˥ 100 番目の人; (things) hyaᶠku-bañme˥ no moᶠno˥ 100 番目のもの.
2 (fraction) hyaᶠku-buñ no ichi˥ 100 分の 1.

hunger *n.* **1** (being hungry) kuᶠufuku 空腹: satisfy one's hunger (*kuufuku o mitasu*) 空腹を満たす.
2 (starvation) uᶠe˥ 飢え: suffer from hunger (*ue ni kurushimu*) 飢えに苦しむ.
3 (strong desire) -yoku 欲; neᶠtsuboo 熱望: a hunger for knowledge (*chishiki-yoku*) 知識欲.

hungry *adj.* **1** (feeling hunger)

u'eta 飢えた; u'ete iru 飢えている; o-ˈnaka ga suita [suite iru] おなかがすいた[すいている]: I am hungry now. (*Watashi wa ima onaka ga suite iru.*) 私は今おなかがすいている.
2 (eager for) neˈtsuboo shite (iru) 熱望して(いる); tsuˈyoku hoˈshigaˈtte (iru) 強く欲しがって(いる): He is hungry for power. (*Kare wa keñryoku o hoshigatte iru.*) 彼は権力を欲しがっている.

hunt *vt.* **1** (chase) ... o kaˈru ...を狩る [C]: We hunted bears in the mountains. (*Watashi-tachi wa yama de kuma-gari o shita.*) 私たちは山で熊狩りをした.
2 (search) ... o saˈgasu ...を探[捜]す [C]; tsuˈiseki suru 追跡する [I]: hunt a better job (*motto yoi shigoto o sagasu*) もっとよい仕事を探す / The bank robber is being hunted by the police. (*Sono giñkoo gootoo wa keesatsu ni tsuiseki sarete iru.*) その銀行強盗は警察に追跡されている.
— *vi.* **1** (chase) kaˈri o suru 狩りをする [I]: go hunting (*kari ni dekakeru*) 狩りに出かける.
2 (search) (... o) saˈgasu (...を)探[捜]す [C]: hunt for a house to rent (*kashiya o sagasu*) 貸家を探す.

hunter *n.* kaˈri o suru hiˈtoˈ 狩りをする人; ryoˈoshi 猟師; haˈñtaa ハンター.

hurry *vi.* (be quick) iˈsoˈgu 急ぐ [C]; aˈwateru 慌てる [V]: hurry to the station (*eki e isogu*) 駅へ急ぐ / Where are you hurrying? (*Awatete doko e iku no desu ka?*) 慌ててどこへ行くのですか.
— *vt.* **1** (cause to be quick) ... o iˈsogaseˈru 急がせる [V]; seˈkitateru せきたてる [V]: You hurried me into making that mistake. (*Kimi ga isogaseta kara añna machigai o shita no da.*) 君が急がせたからあんな間違いをしたのだ.
2 (do quickly) ... o iˈsoˈide <verb> ...を急いで...; aˈwatete <verb> 慌てて...: We have to hurry our work. (*Shigoto o isoide shinakereba naranai.*) 仕事を急いでしなければならない.
— *n.* **1** (quick activity) oˈoiˈsogi 大急ぎ; oˈoaˈwate 大慌て: I'm in a hurry. (*Isoide imasu.*) 急いでいます.
2 (need for quickness) iˈsoˈgu hiˈtsuyoo 急ぐ必要: We can take our time. There is no hurry. (*Yukkuri yareba ii. Isogu hitsuyoo wa arimaseñ.*) ゆっくりやればいい. 急ぐ必要はありません.

hurt *vt.* **1** (injure) ... ni keˈgaˈ o saˈseru ...にけがをさせる [V]; ... o iˈtameˈru ...を痛める [V]: He hurt his knee when he fell. (*Kare wa koroñda toki hiza ni kega o shita.*) 彼は転んだときひざにけがをした.
2 (cause emotional pain) ... o gaˈisuˈru ...を害する [I]; kiˈzu tsukeˈru 傷つける [V]: His remarks hurt her pride deeply. (*Kare no kotoba wa kanojo no puraido o fukaku kizutsuketa.*) 彼の言葉は彼女のプライドを深く傷つけた.
3 (do harm) ... ni gaˈi o aˈtaeru ...に害を与える [V]: The frost hurt the fruit. (*Shimo wa kudamono ni gai o ataeta.*) 霜は果物に害を与えた.
— *vi.* iˈtaˈmu 痛む [C]: My tooth hurts. (*Ha ga itamu.*) 歯が痛む. / Where does it hurt most? (*Doko ga ichibañ itamimasu ka?*) どこがいちばん痛みますか.

husband *n.* oˈtto 夫; shuˈjiñ 主人. ★ The wife refers to her own husband as '*shujiñ*' or '*otto*' and someone else's husband '*go-shujiñ.*': This is a gift for my husband. (*Kore wa shujiñ e no o-miyage desu.*) これは主人へのおみやげです / an ideal husband (*risoo-teki na otto*) 理想的な夫 / husband and wife (*fuufu*) 夫婦.

hush *vt.* ... o shiˈzuka ni saˈseru ...を静かにさせる [V]; daˈmaraseˈru 黙らせる [V]: hush a crying child (*naite iru kodomo o damaraseru*) 泣いている子どもを黙らせる.
— *vi.* shiˈzuka ni naru 静かになる [C]; daˈmaˈru 黙る [C].

hut *n.* koˈya 小屋: a mountain hut (*yama-goya*) 山小屋.

hyphen *n.* ha|ifuñ ハイフン.
hypocrisy *n.* gi⌈zeñ 偽善; ne⌈ko-ka|buri 猫かぶり.
hypocrite *n.* gi⌈ze|ñsha 偽善者: play the hypocrite (*neko o kaburu*) 猫をかぶる.
hypothesis *n.* ka⌈setsu 仮説; ka-⌈tee 仮定: put forward a hypothesis (*kasetsu o tateru*) 仮説を立てる.

I

I *pron.* wa⌈tashi wa [ga] 私は[が]; bo|ku wa [ga] 僕は[が]. ★ '*Boku*' is usually used by boys and young men. Also used by adult men on informal occasions: I'm a tourist. (*Watashi wa kañkookyaku desu.*) 私は観光客です. / I like dogs. (*Boku wa inu ga suki da.*) 僕は犬が好きだ.
ice *n.* ko⌈ori 氷: Please bring me some ice and water. (*Koori to mizu o motte kite kudasai.*) 氷と水を持ってきてください.
ice cream *n.* a⌈isu kuri|imu アイスクリーム.
icicle *n.* tsu⌈rara. つらら.
icy *adj.* **1** (covered with ice) ko⌈ori de oowa|reta [oowa|rete iru] 氷でおおわれた[おおわれている]; hyo⌈oketsu shita [shite iru] 氷結した[している]: an icy road (*hyooketsu shita dooro*) 氷結した道路.
2 (very cold) ko⌈ori no yo|o na 氷のような: Her hands were icy cold. (*Kanojo no te wa koori no yoo ni tsumetakatta.*) 彼女の手は氷のように冷たかった.
3 (unfriendly) re⌈eta|ñ na 冷淡な: an icy manner (*reetañ na taido*) 冷淡な態度.
idea *n.* **1** (thought) ka⌈ñga|e 考え; a⌈ide|a アイデア: That's a good idea. (*Sore wa yoi kañgae da.*) それはよい考えだ. / I hit on a good idea. (*Watashi wa ii aidea o omoitsuita.*) 私はいいアイデアを思いついた.
2 (opinion) i|keñ 意見: We exchanged ideas with each other. (*Watashi-tachi wa o-tagai ni ikeñ o kookañ shita.*) 私たちはお互いに意見を交換した.
3 (imagination) so⌈ozoo 想像; ke⌈ñto|o 見当: I have no idea where he went. (*Kare ga doko e itta no ka keñtoo ga tsukimaseñ.*) 彼がどこへ行ったのか見当がつきません.
ideal *adj.* ri⌈soo-teki na 理想的な: an ideal marriage (*risoo-teki na kekkoñ*) 理想的な結婚.
— *n.* ri⌈soo 理想: He has high ideals. (*Kare wa takai risoo o motte iru.*) 彼は高い理想を持っている.
idealism *n.* ri⌈soo-shu|gi 理想主義; ka⌈ñne|ñroñ 観念論.
idealist *n.* ri⌈sooka 理想家; ri⌈soo-shugi|sha 理想主義者.
identical *adj.* **1** (exactly alike) o⌈naji 同じ; hi⌈toshi|i 等しい: Her dress is identical with mine. (*Kanojo no doresu wa watashi no to onaji da.*) 彼女のドレスは私のと同じだ.
2 (the very same) do⌈oitsu no 同一の: This car is identical to the one that was stolen. (*Kono kuruma wa nusumareta no to dooitsu da.*) この車は盗まれたのと同一だ.
identification *n.* mi⌈buñ sho|o-mee 身分証明: Do you have any identification? (*Nani-ka mibuñ shoomee o o-mochi desu ka?*) 何か身分証明をお持ちですか.
identify *vt.* **1** (recognize) ... o ka-⌈kuniñ suru ...を確認する [I]; mi⌈wa-keru 見分ける [V]: The body has not been identified. (*Sono itai wa mimoto ga kakuniñ sarete imaseñ.*) その遺体は身元が確認されていません.
2 (regard as the same) ... o do⌈o-itsu|shi suru ...を同一視する [I]: identify democracy with liberty (*miñshushugi o jiyuu to dooitsu-*

shi suru) 民主主義を自由と同一視する.

identity *n.* (who or what a person is) mi⌈moto 身元; sho⌉otai 正体: conceal one's identity (*mimoto o kakusu*) 身元を隠す.

idiom *n.* ka⌈ñyoo go⌉ku 慣用語句; se⌈eku 成句.

idiot *n.* ba⌉ka ばか; ma⌈nuke まぬけ.

idle *adj.* **1** (doing nothing) na⌈ni mo shinai 何もしない; a⌈soñde iru 遊んでいる: I spent an idle hour watching TV. (*Watashi wa terebi o minagara nani mo shinai de jikañ o sugoshita.*) 私はテレビを見ながら何もしないで時間を過ごした.
2 (lazy) na⌈ma⌉kete iru 怠けている: an idle fellow (*namakemono*) 怠け者.

idol *n.* (carved image) gu⌈uzoo 偶像; (someone admired) a⌉idoru アイドル.

if *conj.* **1** (supposing that) (mo⌉shi mo) ⟨verb⟩ na⌉ra(ba) (もしも)…なら(ば): If you go, I will go, too. (*Anata ga iku nara(ba) watashi mo ikimasu.*) あなたが行くなら(ば)私も行きます.
2 (provided) ka⌈ri ni ... to ⟨verb⟩-ba 仮に…と…ば: If I were you, I would not do such a thing. (*Kari ni watashi ga anata to sureba soñna koto wa shinai deshoo.*) 仮に私があなたとすればそんなことはしないでしょう.
3 (whether) ... ka do⌉o ka …かどうか: Do you know if he is at home? (*Kare ga uchi ni iru ka doo ka shitte imasu ka?*) 彼が家にいるかどうか知っていますか.
4 (even though) ta⌈toe ... -te [de] mo たとえ…て[で]も: We are happy, if poor. (*Tatoe mazushikute mo watashi-tachi wa shiawase desu.*) たとえ貧しくても私たちは幸せです.

ignorance *n.* mu⌉chi 無知; shi⌈ranai koto⌉ 知らないこと: Ignorance of the law is no excuse. (*Hooritsu o shiranai to iu koto wa iiwake ni naranai.*) 法律を知らないということは言い訳にならない.

ignorant *adj.* **1** (knowing very little) mu⌉chi no 無知の; shi⌈ranai 知らない: I am ignorant about computers. (*Watashi wa koñpyuutaa no koto wa shirimaseñ.*) 私はコンピューターのことは知りません.
2 (uneducated) mu⌉gaku na 無学な: an ignorant person (*mugaku na hito*) 無学な人.
3 (unaware) ki⌈zuka⌉nai 気づかない: I was ignorant of the errors. (*Watashi wa sono machigai ni kizukanakatta.*) 私はその間違いに気づかなかった.

ignore *vt.* ... o mu⌉shi suru …を無視する [I]: He ignored my advice. (*Kare wa watashi no chuukoku o mushi shita.*) 彼は私の忠告を無視した.

ill *adj.* **1** (sick) byo⌈oki de 病気で: He is ill in bed. (*Kare wa byooki de nete imasu.*) 彼は病気で寝ています.
2 (bad) wa⌈ru⌉i 悪い; (harmful) ga⌉i no aru 害のある: ill news (*warui shirase*) 悪い知らせ.
3 (unlucky) fu⌈kitsu na 不吉な: an ill omen (*fukitsu na zeñchoo*) 不吉な前兆.
— *adv.* (badly) wa⌉ruku 悪く: take things ill (*monogoto o waruku toru*) 物事を悪く取る.

illegal *adj.* fu⌈hoo na 不法な; hi⌈go⌉ohoo no 非合法の: an illegal trade (*higoohoo no torihiki*) 非合法の取り引き.

illness *n.* byo⌈oki 病気: He is suffering from a serious illness. (*Kare wa omoi byooki ni kakatte imasu.*) 彼は重い病気にかかっています.

illuminate *vt.* ... o te⌈ra⌉su …を照らす [C]; a⌈karuku suru 明るくする [I]: Candles illuminated the room. (*Roosoku ga heya o akaruku terashita.*) ろうそくが部屋を明るく照らした.

illusion *n.* **1** (false idea) ge⌈ñsoo 幻想; ge⌈ñee 幻影: have illusions about one's future (*jibuñ no mirai ni taishite geñsoo o idaku*) 自分の未来に対して幻想を抱く.
2 (appearance which is not real) sa⌈kkaku 錯覚: an optical illusion

(*me no sakkaku*) 目の錯覚.

illustrate *vt.* **1** (put drawings) ... ni sa⌈shie o ireru ...に挿し絵を入れる Ⓥ; ... o zu⌈kai suru ...を図解する Ⓘ: an illustrated book (*sashie no haitta hoñ*) 挿し絵の入った本.
2 (explain by example) ... o se⌈tsumee suru ...を説明する Ⓘ; re⌈eji suru 例示する Ⓘ: I illustrated my point with examples. (*Watashi wa yooteñ o ree o agete setsumee shita.*) 私は要点を例を挙げて説明した.

illustration *n.* **1** (drawing) sa⌈shie 挿絵; zu 図; i⌈rasuto イラスト.
2 (example) re⌉e 例; ji⌈tsuree 実例.
3 (illustrating) re⌉e ni yoru se⌈tsumee 例による説明; zu⌈kai 図解: Illustration is very useful in teaching. (*Ree ni yoru setsumee wa oshieru no ni taiheñ yakudatsu.*) 例による説明は教えるのに大変役だつ.

image *n.* **1** (mental picture) o⌈mokage 面影; su⌉gata 姿: The image of her is still fresh in my mind. (*Kanojo no omokage ga mada hakkiri to kokoro ni nokotte iru.*) 彼女の面影がまだはっきりと心に残っている.
2 (general opinion) hyo⌈obañ 評判; i⌈me⌉eji イメージ: improve the image of a company (*kaisha o imeeji-appu suru*) 会社をイメージアップする.
3 (close likeness) i⌈kiutsushi 生き写し: She is the image of her mother. (*Kanojo wa o-kaasañ ni ikiutsushi da.*) 彼女はお母さんに生き写しだ.
4 (reflection) e⌈ezoo 映像; su⌉gata 姿: look at one's image in the mirror (*kagami ni utsutta jibuñ no sugata o miru*) 鏡に映った自分の姿を見る.
5 (statue) zo⌉o 像; sho⌈ozoo 肖像: worship images (*guuzoo o suuhai suru*) 偶像を崇拝する.

imaginary *adj.* so⌈ozoo-joo no 想像上の; ka⌈kuu no 架空の: an imaginary animal (*kakuu no doobutsu*) 架空の動物.

imagination *n.* **1** (ability to imagine) so⌈ozo⌉oryoku 想像力: exercise one's imagination (*soozooryoku o hatarakasu*) 想像力を働かす.
2 (ideas in the mind) so⌈ozoo 想像; ki no ma⌈yo⌉i 気の迷い: It's just your imagination. (*Sore wa kimi no ki no mayoi ni suginai.*) それは君の気の迷いにすぎない.

imagine *vt.* **1** (form a mental picture) ... o so⌈ozoo suru ...を想像する Ⓘ; ko⌈ko⌉ro ni e⌈ga⌉ku 心に描く Ⓒ: She imagined life abroad. (*Kanojo wa gaikoku de no seekatsu o soozoo shita.*) 彼女は外国での生活を想像した.
2 (suppose) ... to su⌈isatsu suru ...と推察する Ⓘ; o⌈mo⌉u 思う Ⓒ: I imagine that he will come. (*Kare wa kuru to omoimasu.*) 彼は来ると思います.

imitate *vt.* **1** (copy) ... o ma⌈neru ...をまねる Ⓥ; mo⌈hoo suru 模倣する Ⓘ: imitate the song of a bird (*tori no nakigoe o maneru*) 鳥の鳴き声をまねる.
2 (resemble) ... ni ni⌈seru ...に似せる Ⓥ: This floor is painted to imitate marble. (*Kono yuka wa dairiseki ni nisete nurarete iru.*) この床は大理石に似せて塗られている.

imitation *n.* **1** (imitating) ma⌈ne まね; mo⌈hoo 模倣: He did an imitation of a monkey. (*Kare wa saru no mane o shita.*) 彼は猿のまねをした.
2 (copy) ni⌈semono 偽物; mo⌈zoohiñ 模造品: imitation pearls (*mozoo shiñju*) 模造真珠.

immediate *adj.* **1** (instant) su⌉gu no すぐの; so⌉kuza no 即座の: He gave me an immediate answer. (*Kare wa sugu ni heñji o kureta.*) 彼はすぐに返事をくれた.
2 (direct) cho⌈kusetsu no 直接の: the immediate cause of death (*chokusetsu no shi-iñ*) 直接の死因.
3 (very near) su⌉gu to⌈nari no すぐ隣の: an immediate neighbor (*sugu tonari no hito*) すぐ隣の人.

immediately *adv.* (at once) su⌉gu ni すぐに; ta⌉dachi ni 直ちに: The policeman came immediately. (*Keekañ wa sugu ni kita.*) 警官はすぐに来た.

immense *adj.* (very large) ko⌈odai na 広大な; (very huge) kyo⌈dai na 巨大な: an immense area of desert (*koodai na sabaku chitai*) 広大な砂漠地帯 / an immense statue (*kyodai na zoo*) 巨大な像.

immigrant *n.* i⌈ju⌉usha 移住者; im⌈iñ 移民. ★ Japanese '*imiñ*' means both immigrant and emigrant.

immigration *n.* i⌈juu 移住; i⌈miñ 移民; nyu⌈ukoku 入国: immigration control (*nyuukoku kañri*) 入国管理.

imminent *adj.* sa⌈shisema⌉tta 差し迫った; sa⌈shisema⌉tte iru 差し迫っている; se⌈ppaku shita [shite iru] 切迫した[している]: imminent danger (*sashisematta kikeñ*) 差し迫った危険.

immoral *adj.* fu⌈do⌉otoku na 不道徳な; fu⌈hi⌉ñkoo na 不品行な: immoral conduct (*fudootoku na kooi*) 不道徳な行為.

immorality *n.* fu⌈do⌉otoku 不道徳; fu⌈hi⌉ñkoo 不品行.

immortal *adj.* (never dying) fu⌉shi no 不死の; (eternal) fu⌈kyuu no 不朽の; fu⌈metsu no 不滅の: immortal fame (*fukyuu no meesee*) 不朽の名声.

immortality *n.* fu⌉shi 不死; fu⌈metsu 不滅.

impact *n.* **1** (collision) sho⌈ototsu 衝突; sho⌈ogeki 衝撃: the impact of two cars (*ni-dai no kuruma no shoototsu*) 2台の車の衝突.
2 (effect) e⌈ekyoo 影響: His death had an impact on them. (*Kare no shi wa kare-ra ni eekyoo o ataeta.*) 彼の死は彼らに影響を与えた.

impartial *adj.* ka⌈tayora⌉nai 偏らない; ko⌈ohee na 公平な: an impartial judge (*koohee na saibañkañ*) 公平な裁判官.

impatience *n.* ta⌉ñki 短気; se⌉kkachi せっかち; i⌉raira いらいら: He waited for her with impatience. (*Kare wa iraira shi-nagara kanojo o matta.*) 彼はいらいらしながら彼女を待った.

impatient *adj.* **1** (not patient) ki⌈mijika na 気短な; i⌉raira shite iru いらいらしている: We were impatient at his delay in coming. (*Watashi-tachi wa kare no kuru no ga osoi no de iraira shita.*) 私たちは彼の来るのが遅いのでいらいらした.
2 (eager to do) shi⌈kiri ni ⟨verb⟩-tagaru しきりに…たがる: The children are impatient to go. (*Kodomo-tachi wa shikiri ni ikitagatte iru.*) 子どもたちはしきりに行きたがっている.

imperfect *adj.* fu⌈ka⌉ñzeñ na 不完全な; fu⌈ju⌉ubuñ na 不十分な: Their preparations are imperfect. (*Karera no juñbi wa fukañzeñ da.*) 彼らの準備は不完全だ.

imperial *adj.* (of an empire) te⌈ekoku no 帝国の; (of an emperor) ko⌈otee no 皇帝の: the Imperial Family (*kooshitsu*) 皇室 / the Imperial Palace (in Tokyo) (*Kookyo*) 皇居.

impersonal *adj.* ko⌈jiñ-teki de nai 個人的でない; hi-ko⌈jiñ-teki na 非個人的な: an impersonal letter (*kojiñ ate de nai tegami*) 個人あてでない手紙.

implicit *adj.* a⌉ñ ni shi⌈mesa⌉reta 暗に示された; a⌈ñmoku no 暗黙の: implicit consent (*añmoku no shoodaku*) 暗黙の承諾.

implore *vt.* ... ni ne⌉sshiñ ni ta⌈no⌉mu …に熱心に頼む [C]; ... o ta⌈ñgañ suru …を嘆願する [I]: She implored her husband to give up smoking. (*Kanojo wa otto ni tabako o yameru yoo nesshiñ ni tanoñda.*) 彼女は夫にたばこをやめるよう熱心に頼んだ.

imply *vt.* ... o ho⌈nomeka⌉su …をほのめかす [C]; i⌉mi suru 意味する [I]: Silence often implies resistance. (*Mugoñ wa shibashiba hañkoo o imi suru.*) 無言はしばしば反抗を意味する.

impolite *adj.* bu⌈sa⌉hoo na 無作法な; shi⌈tsu⌉ree na 失礼な: It is impolite of you not to answer him. (*Kare ni heñji o shinai no wa shitsuree da.*) 彼に返事をしないのは失礼だ.

import *vt.* ... o yu⌈nyuu suru …を輸入する Ⅰ: His company imports wine. (*Kare no kaisha wa waiñ o yunyuu shite iru.*) 彼の会社はワインを輸入している.

— *n.* (importing) yu⌈nyuu 輸入; (goods) yu⌈nyuuhiñ 輸入品: Imports this year were greater than exports. (*Kotoshi wa yunyuu no hoo ga yushutsu yori mo ookatta.*) ことしは輸入のほうが輸出よりも多かった.

importance *n.* ju⌈uyoosee 重要性; ju⌈udaisa 重大さ: a matter of great importance (*kiwamete juuyoo na kotogara*) きわめて重要な事柄 / a person of importance (*juuyoo jiñbutsu*) 重要人物.

important *adj.* **1** (of a matter) ju⌈uyoo na 重要な; ta⌈isetsu na 大切な; ju⌈udai na 重大な: It is important to read good books. (*Yoi hoñ o yomu koto wa juuyoo na koto desu.*) よい本を読むことは重要なことです. / Sleeping is important for our health. (*Suimiñ wa keñkoo ni taisetsu desu.*) 睡眠は健康に大切です.

2 (of a person) yu⌈uryoku na 有力な; ju⌈uyoo na 重要な: a very important person (*yoojiñ*) 要人.

impose *vt.* **1** (place) ... o (... ni) ka⌉su …を(…に)課す Ⓒ; o⌈waseru 負わせる Ⓥ: impose a tax on imports (*zeekiñ o yunyuuhiñ ni kasu*) 税金を輸入品に課す.

2 (force) ... o (... ni) o⌈shitsuke⌉ru …を(…に)押しつける Ⓥ: He tried to impose his opinion on me. (*Kare wa kare no ikeñ o watashi ni oshitsukeyoo to shita.*) 彼は彼の意見を私に押しつけようとした.

impossible *adj.* **1** (that cannot be done) fu⌈ka⌉noo na 不可能な: It is impossible to move this stone. (*Kono ishi o ugokasu no wa fukanoo da.*) この石を動かすのは不可能だ.

2 (that cannot happen) a⌈ri e⌉nai あり得ない; shi⌈ñjirare⌉nai 信じられない: It is impossible that he would break his word. (*Kare ga yakusoku o yaburu nañte ari enai.*) 彼が約束を破るなんてあり得ない.

impractical *adj.* hi-ji⌈ssai-teki na 非実際的な; hi-ge⌈ñjitsu-teki na 非現実的な: an impractical plan (*hi-jissai-teki na keekaku*) 非実際的な計画.

impress *vt.* **1** (move deeply) ... ni ka⌈ñmee o ataeru …に感銘を与える Ⓥ: I was deeply impressed by his speech. (*Watashi wa kare no eñzetsu ni fukai kañmee o uketa.*) 私は彼の演説に深い感銘を受けた.

2 (press upon the mind) ... ni i⌈ñshoo o ataeru …に印象を与える Ⓥ: His manner impressed her favorably. (*Kare no taido wa kanojo ni yoi iñshoo o ataeta.*) 彼の態度は彼女によい印象を与えた.

impression *n.* i⌈ñshoo 印象; ka⌈ñmee 感銘: What are your first impressions of Tokyo? (*Tookyoo no dai-ichi iñshoo wa ikaga desu ka?*) 東京の第一印象はいかがですか.

impressive *adj.* tsu⌈yo⌉i i⌈ñshoo o ataeru 強い印象を与える; i⌈ñshoo-teki na 印象的な; ka⌈ñmee o ataeru 感銘を与える: an impressive speech (*hito ni kañmee o ataeru eñzetsu*) 人に感銘を与える演説.

imprison *vt.* ... o ke⌈emu⌉sho ni i⌈reru …を刑務所に入れる Ⓥ; to⌈ogoku suru 投獄する Ⅰ: He was imprisoned for the crime. (*Kare wa sono hañzai no tame ni toogoku sareta.*) 彼はその犯罪のために投獄された.

improper *adj.* **1** (not proper) fu⌈te⌉kitoo na 不適当な; fu⌈sawa⌉shiku na⌉i ふさわしくない: wear dress improper to the occasion (*sono ba ni fusawashiku nai fukusoo o suru*) その場にふさわしくない服装をする.

2 (wrong) ta⌈da⌉shiku na⌉i 正しくない; a⌈yama⌉tta 誤った; a⌈yama⌉tte iru 誤っている: an improper conclusion (*ayamatta ketsuroñ*) 誤った結論.

improve *vt.* ... o ka⌈izeñ suru …を改善する Ⅰ; ka⌈iryoo suru 改良する Ⅰ; jo⌈otatsu saseru 上達させる Ⅴ: improve a product (*seehiñ o kairyoo suru*) 製品を改良する / He improved his Japanese. (*Kare wa Nihoñgo ga jootatsu shita.*) 彼は日本語が上達した.
— *vi.* yo⌉ku naru よくなる Ⓒ; shi⌉ñpo suru 進歩する Ⅰ: His health is improving. (*Kare no keñkoo wa yoku natte imasu.*) 彼の健康はよくなっています.

improvement *n.* ka⌈izeñ 改善; ka⌈iryoo 改良; shi⌉ñpo 進歩: There's room for improvement. (*Kairyoo no yochi ga aru.*) 改良の余地がある.

improvise *vi.* (compose) so⌈kuseki ni tsuku⌉ru 即席に作る Ⓒ; (perform) so⌈kkyoo de eñsoo suru 即興で演奏する Ⅰ: improvise on the piano (*piano o sokkyoo de eñsoo suru*) ピアノを即興で演奏する.

imprudence *n.* ke⌈esotsu 軽率; mu⌈fu⌉ñbetsu 無分別.

imprudent *adj.* ke⌈esotsu na 軽率な; mu⌈fu⌉ñbetsu na 無分別な: What he did was imprudent. (*Kare no shita koto wa keesotsu datta.*) 彼のしたことは軽率だった.

impulse *n.* **1** (sudden desire) sho⌈odoo 衝動; de⌈kigo⌉koro でき心: act on impulse (*shoodoo ni kararete koodoo suru*) 衝動に駆られて行動する / impulse buying (*shoodoogai*) 衝動買い.
2 (sudden force) sho⌈ogeki 衝撃: the impulse of a wave (*nami no shoogeki*) 波の衝撃.

impulsive *adj.* sho⌈odoo-teki na 衝動的な: an impulsive action (*shoodoo-teki na koodoo*) 衝動的な行動.

impure *adj.* (not pure) ju⌈ñsui de na⌉i 純粋でない; (dirty) yo⌈goreta 汚れた; yo⌈gorete iru 汚れている; fu⌈ketsu na 不潔な: The air in this room is impure. (*Kono heya no kuuki wa yogorete iru.*) この部屋の空気は汚れている.

in *prep.* **1** (position) ... ni [de] …に[で]: I live in Tokyo. (*Watashi wa Tookyoo ni suñde imasu.*) 私は東京に住んでいます. / Let's swim in the lake. (*Mizuumi de oyogoo.*) 湖で泳ごう.
2 (time) ... ni [de] …に[で]: Cherry blossoms bloom in April. (*Sakura wa shi-gatsu ni sakimasu.*) 桜は4月に咲きます. / I can finish it in one day. (*Watashi wa ichi-nichi de sore o oeru koto ga dekimasu.*) 私は1日でそれを終えることができます.
3 (motion) ... ni …に: He put his hand in his pocket. (*Kare wa te o poketto ni ireta.*) 彼は手をポケットに入れた.
4 (state) ... no na⌉ka o …の中を: He went out in the rain. (*Kare wa ame no naka o dete itta.*) 彼は雨の中を出て行った.
5 (be means of) ... de …で: write in ink (*iñku de kaku*) インクで書く / Please speak in Japanese. (*Nihoñgo de hanashite kudasai.*) 日本語で話してください.
6 (limitation) ... ni oite …において; ... ga …が: one meter in length (*nagasa ga ichi-meetoru*) 長さが1メートル / We were five in number. (*Wareware wa niñzuu ga go-niñ datta.*) われわれは人数が5人だった.
7 (wearing) ... o ki⌈te …を着て: a woman in white (*shiroi fuku o kita fujiñ*) 白い服を着た婦人.
— *adv.* ... no na⌉ka ni [e] …の中に[へ]: Please come in. (*Doozo naka e o-hairi kudasai.*) どうぞ中へお入りください.
— *adj.* za⌈itaku shite (iru) 在宅して(いる): Is Mr.Tanaka in? (*Tanaka-sañ wa go-zaitaku desu ka?*) 田中さんはご在宅ですか.

inadequate *adj.* fu⌈ju⌉ubuñ na 不十分な; fu⌈te⌉kitoo na 不適当な: an inadequate income (*fujuubuñ na shuunyuu*) 不十分な収入.

inaugurate *vt.* **1** (install) ... o shu⌈uniñ saseru …を就任させる Ⓥ: inaugurate a president (*daitooryoo o shuuniñ saseru*) 大統領を就任させる.
2 (make a start) ... o ka⌈ishi suru …を開始する Ⓘ; ho⌈ssoku saseru 発足させる Ⓥ: inaugurate a long-term plan (*chooki keekaku o hossoku saseru*) 長期計画を発足させる.

incapable *adj.* **1** (not able) de⌈ki⌉nai できない: He's incapable of telling a lie. (*Kare wa uso o tsuku koto ga dekinai.*) 彼はうそをつくことができない.
2 (lacking ability) mu⌈noo na 無能な; mu⌉ryoku na 無力な: an incapable person (*munoo na hito*) 無能な人.

inch *n.* i⌉ñchi インチ: 6 feet 3 inches (*roku-fiito sañ-iñchi*) 6 フィート 3 インチ. ★ Japanese use the metric system and 'inch' is not used.

incident *n.* de⌈ki⌉goto 出来事; ji⌉keñ 事件: He told us about a recent incident. (*Kare wa watashitachi ni saikiñ no dekigoto ni tsuite hanashite kureta.*) 彼は私たちに最近の出来事について話してくれた.

incidentally *adv.* to⌈koro⌉ de ところで; so⌈re wa so⌉o to それはそうと: Incidentally, what time is it now? (*Tokoro de ima nañ-ji desu ka?*) ところで今何時ですか.

inclination *n.* **1** (liking; wish) ko⌉nomi 好み; i⌈koo 意向: I have no inclination to listen to jazz. (*Watashi wa jazu o kiku no wa konomanai.*) 私はジャズを聞くのは好まない.
2 (tendency) ke⌈ekoo 傾向; ku⌈se⌉ 癖: The boy has an inclination to tell lies. (*Sono otoko-no-ko wa uso o tsuku kuse ga aru.*) その男の子はうそをつく癖がある.
3 (sloping) ka⌈tamuki 傾き; ke⌈esha 傾斜; ko⌈obai 勾配: the inclination of a roof (*yane no koobai*) 屋根の勾配.

incline *vt.* (bend) ... o ka⌈tamuke⌉ru …を傾ける Ⓥ; ma⌈geru 曲げる Ⓥ: He inclined his head to hear her words. (*Kare wa kanojo no kotoba o kiku tame ni atama o katamuketa.*) 彼は彼女の言葉を聞くために頭を傾けた.
— *vi.* **1** (lean) ka⌈tamu⌉ku 傾く Ⓒ: The tree inclines toward the left. (*Sono ki wa hidari ni katamuite iru.*) その木は左に傾いている.
2 (tend) ⟨verb⟩-gachi da …がちだ: He inclines to carelessness. (*Kare wa fuchuui ni narigachi da.*) 彼は不注意になりがちだ.
be inclined to do *vi.* **1** (have a willingness) ... ki ni na⌉tte iru …気になっている Ⓥ: He is inclined to go. (*Kare wa iku ki ni natte imasu.*) 彼は行く気になっています.
2 (have a tendency) ke⌈ekoo ga a⌉ru 傾向がある Ⓒ: I am inclined to put on weight. (*Watashi wa futoru keekoo ga aru.*) 私は太る傾向がある.

include *vt.* ... o fu⌈ku⌉mu …を含む Ⓒ; fu⌈kume⌉ru 含める Ⓥ: Is the tax included in this? (*Kore ni zeekiñ wa fukumarete imasu ka?*) これに税金は含まれていますか. / two meals included (*ni-shoku-tsuki*) 2 食付き.

including *prep.* ... o fu⌈ku⌉mete …を含めて; i⌈rete 入れて: All of us, including me, will attend the meeting. (*Watashi mo fukumete zeñiñ ga kai ni shusseki shimasu.*) 私も含めて全員が会に出席します.

income *n.* shu⌈unyuu 収入; sho⌈toku 所得: He has a high income. (*Kare wa koo-shuunyuu o ete iru.*) 彼は高収入を得ている. / income tax (*shotokuzee*) 所得税.

incomparable *adj.* hi⌈kaku deki⌉nai 比較できない; hi⌈rui no na⌉i 比類のない; mu⌉hi no 無比の: incomparable beauty (*hirui no nai utsukushisa*) 比類のない美しさ.

incompatible *adj.* a⌉i-irenai 相容れない; ryo⌈oritsu shinai 両立しない; mu⌈juñ shita [shite iru] 矛盾した[している]: a theory incompatible with the facts (*jijitsu to mujuñ* *shita riroñ*) 事実と矛盾した理論.

incompetent *adj.* mu⌈noo na 無能な; ya⌈ku⌉ ni ta⌈ta⌉nai 役に立たない: He's incompetent as manager. (*Kare wa kañtoku to shite munoo da.*) 彼は監督として無能だ.

incomplete *adj.* fu⌈ka⌉ñzeñ na 不完全な; mi⌈ka⌉ñsee no 未完成の: The bridge is still incomplete. (*Sono hashi wa mada mikañsee desu.*) その橋はまだ未完成です.

inconvenience *n.* fu⌉beñ 不便; fu⌈tsu⌉goo 不都合; me⌉ewaku 迷惑: I hope this will not cause you any inconvenience. (*Kono koto ga go-meewaku ni naranai koto o nozomimasu.*) このことがご迷惑にならないことを望みます.

inconvenient *adj.* fu⌉beñ na 不便な; tsu⌈goo no waru⌉i 都合の悪い: It is inconvenient not to have a car. (*Kuruma ga nai to fubeñ da.*) 車がないと不便だ. / If it is inconvenient for you, I will put off my visit. (*Moshi mo go-tsugoo ga warukereba hoomoñ o nobashimasu.*) もしもご都合が悪ければ訪問を延ばします.

incorporate *vt.* ... o ga⌈ppee saseru ...を合併させる Ⓥ; ku⌈miire⌉ru 組み入れる Ⓥ: incorporate a firm with another (*shoosha o ta no shoosha to gappee saseru*) 商社を他の商社と合併させる.

incorrect *adj.* fu⌈se⌉ekaku na 不正確な; ma⌈chiga⌉tta 間違った; ma⌈chiga⌉tte iru 間違っている: an incorrect answer (*machigatta kotae*) 間違った答え / His information is incorrect. (*Kare no joohoo wa fuseekaku da.*) 彼の情報は不正確だ.

increase *vi.* fu⌈e⌉ru 増える Ⓥ; zo⌈oka suru 増加する Ⓘ: Traffic accidents show a tendency to increase. (*Kootsuu jiko wa zooka suru keekoo ni aru.*) 交通事故は増加する傾向にある.

— *vt.* ... o fu⌈ya⌉su ...を増やす Ⓒ; zo⌈oka saseru 増加させる Ⓥ: The school increased the number of students. (*Sono gakkoo wa seeto no kazu o fuyashita.*) その学校は生徒の数を増やした.

— *n.* zo⌈oka 増加; zo⌈odai 増大: an increase in income (*shuunyuu no zooka*) 収入の増加.

increasingly *adv.* ma⌈su⌉masu ますます; shi⌈dai ni 次第に: It has become increasingly difficult to build a house. (*Ie o tateru no ga masumasu muzukashiku natta.*) 家を建てるのがますます難しくなった.

incredible *adj.* shi⌈ñjirare⌉nai 信じられない; su⌈go⌉i すごい: an incredible story (*shiñjirarenai hanashi*) 信じられない話 / His appetite is incredible. (*Kare no shokuyoku wa sugoi.*) 彼の食欲はすごい.

incur *vt.* ... o ma⌈ne⌉ku ...を招く Ⓒ: incur a person's wrath (*hito no ikari o maneku*) 人の怒りを招く.

indebted *adj.* o⌉ñ o ukete (iru) 恩を受けて(いる); ka⌉ñsha shite (iru) 感謝して(いる): I'm greatly indebted to you for your help. (*Go-joryoku ni taiheñ kañsha shite orimasu.*) ご助力に大変感謝しております.

indeed *adv.* ma⌈ttaku まったく; ho⌈ñtoo ni 本当に; ji⌈tsu⌉ ni 実に: I was indeed very tired. (*Watashi wa mattaku tsukarekitte ita.*) 私はまったく疲れきっていた. / Thank you very much indeed. (*Hoñtoo ni arigatoo gozaimashita.*) 本当にありがとうございました.

independence *n.* do⌈kuritsu 独立; ji⌈ritsu 自立: live a life of independence (*jiritsu shita seekatsu o suru*) 自立した生活をする.

independent *adj.* **1** (not ruled) do⌈kuritsu no 独立の; ji⌉shu no 自主の: an independent country (*dokuritsukoku*) 独立国.

2 (not relying on) ta⌈yora⌉nai 頼らない; ji⌈katsu shita [shite iru] 自活した[している]: My daughter is leading an independent life. (*Musume wa jikatsu shite imasu.*) 娘は自活しています.

3 (separate) be⌈tsubetsu no 別々の; (not connected) mu⌈ka⌉ñkee no 無

関係の: These two problems are independent of each other. (*Kono futatsu no mondai wa o-tagai ni mukañkee desu.*) この二つの問題はお互いに無関係です.

index *n.* **1** (list) sa⌈kuiñ 索引: an index to a book (*hoñ no sakuiñ*) 本の索引.
2 (figure) shi⌈su⌉u 指数: a price index (*bukka shisuu*) 物価指数.

index finger *n.* hi⌈tosashi⌉-yubi 人さし指.

India *n.* I⌉ñdo インド.

indicate *vt.* **1** (point out) ... o sa⌈shishime⌉su ...を指し示す Ⓒ; sa⌉su 指す Ⓒ: He indicated where Matsue was on the map. (*Kare wa Matsue ga doko ni aru ka o chizu de sashi shimeshita.*) 彼は松江がどこにあるかを地図で指し示した.
2 (be a sign of) ... o shi⌈me⌉su ...を示す Ⓒ; a⌈rawa⌉su 表す Ⓒ: The arrow indicates the exit. (*Yajirushi wa deguchi o shimeshite imasu.*) 矢印は出口を示しています.

indication *n.* cho⌈okoo 徴候; ki⌈zashi 兆し: There are indications that business will recover. (*Keeki ga yoku naru kizashi ga aru.*) 景気がよくなる兆しがある.

indifference *n.* mu⌈ka⌉ñshiñ 無関心; re⌈eta⌉ñ 冷淡: an indifference toward politics (*seeji ni taisuru mukañshiñ*) 政治に対する無関心.

indifferent *adj.* mu⌈ka⌉ñshiñ na 無関心な; re⌈eta⌉ñ na 冷淡な: He is indifferent to other people's troubles. (*Kare wa hoka no hito no shiñpaigoto ni wa mukañshiñ da.*) 彼はほかの人の心配事には無関心だ.

indigestion *n.* sho⌈okafu⌉ryoo 消化不良.

indignant *adj.* fu⌈ñgai shita [shite iru] 憤慨した[している]; o⌈ko⌉tta 怒った; o⌈ko⌉tte iru 怒っている: He was indignant at the unfair judgment. (*Kare wa sono fukoohee na hañtee ni fuñgai shita.*) 彼はその不公平な判定に憤慨した.

indignation *n.* i⌈kidoori 憤り; fu⌈ñgai 憤慨: feel indignation about an injustice (*fusee ni taishite ikidoori o kañjiru*) 不正に対して憤りを感じる.

indirect *adj.* **1** (not direct) ma⌈ssu⌉gu de nai 真っすぐでない; ma⌈warimichi no 回り道の: take an indirect route (*mawarimichi o suru*) 回り道をする.
2 (not straightforward) to⌈omawa⌉shi no 遠回しの; so⌈tchoku de na⌉i 率直でない: give an indirect answer (*toomawashi no heñji o suru*) 遠回しの返事をする.
3 (not connected directly) ka⌈ñsetsu no 間接の; ka⌈ñsetsu-teki na 間接的な: an indirect cause (*kañsetsu-teki na geñiñ*) 間接的な原因.

indiscreet *adj.* fu⌈ñbetsu no na⌉i 分別のない; ke⌈esotsu na 軽率な: an indiscreet remark (*keesotsu na hatsugeñ*) 軽率な発言.

indispensable *adj.* ka⌈ku koto no deki⌉nai 欠くことのできない; fu⌈ka⌉ketsu na 不可欠な; ze⌈ttai ni hitsuyoo na 絶対に必要な: Water is indispensable to life. (*Mizu wa seemee ni fukaketsu desu.*) 水は生命に不可欠です.

individual *adj.* **1** (separate) ko⌉ko no 個々の; so⌈re⌉zore no それぞれの: I checked each individual bag. (*Watashi wa sorezore no kabañ o shirabeta.*) 私はそれぞれのかばんを調べた.
2 (of a single person) ko⌉jiñ no 個人の; ko⌈jiñ-teki na 個人的な: an individual matter (*kojiñ-teki na moñdai*) 個人的な問題.
3 (characteristic) ko⌈see-teki na 個性的な; do⌈kutoku no 独特の: an individual style of speaking (*dokutoku no hanashikata*) 独特の話し方.
— *n.* ko⌉jiñ 個人: the rights of the individual (*kojiñ no keñri*) 個人の権利.

indoor *adj.* o⌈ku⌉nai no 屋内の: indoor games (*okunai kyoogi*) 屋内競技.

indoors *adv.* o⌈ku⌉nai de [e] 屋内で

[ㅅ]; u[chi no na]ka de [e] 家の中で [ㅅ]: It began to rain, so I went indoors. (*Ame ga furi-dashita no de watashi wa uchi no naka e haitta.*) 雨が降りだしたので私は家の中へ入った.

induce *vt.* **1** (lead into doing) ... o ‹verb›-(sa)seru …を…(さ)せる [V]: Nothing can induce him to change his mind. (*Nanigoto mo kare no kokoro o kaesaseru koto wa dekinai.*) なにごとも彼の心を変えさせることはできない.
2 (cause) ... o hi[kioko]su …を引き起こす [C]: His illness was induced by overwork. (*Kare no byooki wa karoo ni yotte hikiokosareta.*) 彼の病気は過労によって引き起こされた.

i

indulge *vt.* **1** (spoil) ... o a[maya-ka]su …を甘やかす [C]; ki[mama ni saseru 気ままにさせる [V]: He indulges his children too much. (*Kare wa kodomo o amayakashi-sugiru.*) 彼は子どもを甘やかし過ぎる.
2 (satisfy) ... o ma[ñzoku saseru …を満足させる [V]: indulge one's desires (*yokuboo o mañzoku sa-seru*) 欲望を満足させる.

industrial *adj.* sa[ñgyoo no 産業の; ko]ogyoo no 工業の: an industrial town (*koogyoo toshi*) 工業都市.

industrious *adj.* ki[ñbeñ na 勤勉な; yo]ku ha[taraku よく働く: an industrious student (*kiñbeñ na gaku-see*) 勤勉な学生.

industry *n.* **1** (business) sa[ñgyoo 産業; ko]ogyoo 工業: the automobile industry (*jidoosha-sañgyoo*) 自動車産業.
2 (hard work) ki[ñbeñ 勤勉: He worked with industry. (*Kare wa kiñbeñ ni hataraita.*) 彼は勤勉に働いた.

inevitable *adj.* sa[kerare]nai 避けられない; to[ozeñ no 当然の: Death is inevitable. (*Shi wa sakerarenai.*) 死は避けられない.

inexpensive *adj.* hi]yoo no ka[kara]nai 費用のかからない; ya[su]i 安い: an inexpensive restaurant (*ne-dañ no yasui resutorañ*) 値段の安いレストラン.

infant *n.* yo]oji 幼児.
— *adj.* yo]oji no 幼児の; yo[ojiyoo no 幼児用の: infant food (*yooji-shoku*) 幼児食.

infect *vt.* (give a disease) ... ni ka[ñseñ saseru …に感染させる [V]; byo[oki o utsu]su 病気をうつす [C]: His cold infected his child. (*Kare no kaze ga kodomo ni utsutta.*) 彼のかぜが子どもにうつった.

infection *n.* ka[ñseñ 感染; de[ñ-señ 伝染: prevent infection (*kañ-señ o fusegu*) 感染を防ぐ.

infectious *adj.* ka[ñseñ suru 感染する; ka[ñseñsee no 感染性の: Cancer is not infectious. (*Gañ wa kañ-señ shinai.*) がんは感染しない.

infer *vt.* ... to su[iroñ suru …と推論する [I]; su[isoku suru 推測する [I]: I inferred from his expression that he was angry. (*Kare no hyoojoo kara kare wa okotte iru no da to suisoku shita.*) 彼の表情から彼は怒っているのだと推測した.

inferior *adj.* **1** (poor in quality) o[to]tta 劣った; o[to]tte iru 劣っている; so[aku na 粗悪な: This wine is inferior to that in quality. (*Kono waiñ wa sore yori mo shitsu ga ototte iru.*) このワインはそれよりも質が劣っている.
2 (lower in rank) ka[kyuu no 下級の; ka]i no 下位の: an inferior court (*kakyuu saibañsho*) 下級裁判所.

inferiority *n.* o[to]tte iru ko[to] 劣っていること; re[ttoo 劣等; so[aku 粗悪: an inferiority complex (*ret-tookañ*) 劣等感.

infinite *adj.* ka[giri] no na]i 限りのない; mu[geñ no 無限の: The universe is infinite. (*Uchuu wa mugeñ desu.*) 宇宙は無限です.

inflation *n.* i[ñfure インフレ; i[ñfu-re]eshoñ インフレーション.

inflict *vt.* ... o a[taeru …を与える [V]; o[waseru 負わせる [V]: inflict damage (*soñgai o ataeru*) 損害を与える /

inflict a wound (*kizu o owaseru*) 傷を負わせる.

influence *n.* **1** (effect) e^ekyoo 影響; ka^ñka 感化: the influence of television on children (*kodomotachi ni taisuru terebi no eekyoo*) 子どもたちに対するテレビの影響.
2 (power) se^eryoku 勢力; ke^ñryoku 権力: a person of influence (*yuuryokusha*) 有力者.
3 (person) e^ekyo^oryoku no aru hi^to^ 影響力のある人: a powerful influence in politics (*seekai no oomono jitsuryokusha*) 政界の大物実力者.
— *vt.* ... ni e^ekyoo o ataeru ...に影響を与える Ⓥ: The weather influences the crop. (*Teñkoo wa sakumotsu ni eekyoo o ataeru.*) 天候は作物に影響を与える.

influential *adj.* e^ekyo^oryoku no aru 影響力のある; yu^uryoku na 有力な: an influential politician (*yuuryoku na seejika*) 有力な政治家.

inform *vt.* ... ni (... o) tsu^uchi suru ...に(...を)通知する Ⓘ; shi^raseru 知らせる Ⓥ: I informed my parents of my safe arrival. (*Watashi wa ryooshiñ ni buji ni tsuita koto o shiraseta.*) 私は両親に無事に着いたことを知らせた.

informal *adj.* **1** (not formal) hi^ko^oshiki no 非公式の; rya^kushiki no 略式の: informal clothes (*ryakushiki no fuku*) 略式の服.
2 (colloquial) ku^da^keta くだけた; ku^da^kete iru くだけている; ko^ogo no 口語の: informal expressions (*kudaketa hyoogeñ*) くだけた表現.

information *n.* **1** (news) jo^ohoo 情報: We got a valuable piece of information. (*Watashi-tachi wa kichoo na joohoo o eta.*) 私たちは貴重な情報を得た.
2 (knowledge) chi^shiki 知識: This book gives information about animals. (*Kono hoñ wa doobutsu ni tsuite no chishiki o ataete kureru.*) この本は動物についての知識を与えてくれる.
3 (place) a^ñnaijo 案内所: Where is the tourist information office? (*Kañkoo añnaijo wa doko desu ka?*) 観光案内所はどこですか.

ingenious *adj.* do^kusoo-teki na 独創的な; ri^koo na 利口な: an ingenious theory (*dokusoo-teki na riroñ*) 独創的な理論.

ingredient *n.* za^iryo^o 材料: a list of the ingredients for making cake (*keeki o tsukuru no ni hitsuyoo na zairyoo no risuto*) ケーキを作るのに必要な材料のリスト.

inhabit *vt.* ... ni su^mu ... に住む Ⓒ; kyo^juu suru 居住する Ⓘ: This area is inhabited by rich people. (*Kono chiiki ni wa kanemochi ga suñde iru.*) この地域には金持ちが住んでいる.

inhabitant *n.* ju^umiñ 住民: the inhabitants of a village (*mura no juumiñ*) 村の住民.

inherit *vt.* **1** (receive) ... o so^ozoku suru ...を相続する Ⓘ; u^ketsu^gu 受け継ぐ Ⓒ: She inherited considerable property from her father. (*Kanojo wa chichi-oya kara kanari no zaisañ o soozoku shita.*) 彼女は父親からかなりの財産を相続した.
2 (get from one's parents) ... o u^ketsu^gu ...を受け継ぐ Ⓒ: a characteristic inherited from one's parents (*ryooshiñ kara uketsuida tokushitsu*) 両親から受け継いだ特質.

inheritance *n.* (act) so^ozoku 相続; (money) i^sañ 遺産: He came into a large inheritance from his uncle. (*Kare wa oji kara tagaku no isañ o moratta.*) 彼はおじから多額の遺産をもらった.

initial *adj.* ha^jime no 初めの; sa^isho no 最初の: the initial stage of a disease (*byooki no hajime no dañkai*) 病気の初めの段階.
— *n.* (the first letter) ka^shiramo^ji 頭文字.
— *vt.* ... ni ka^shiramo^ji de sho^mee suru ...に頭文字で署名する Ⓘ: initial a letter (*tegami ni kashiramoji de shomee suru*) 手紙に頭文字で署名する.

initiate *vt.* (start) ... o ka¹ishi suru …を開始する [I]; ... ni cha¹kushu suru …に着手する [I]: initiate reforms (*kaikaku ni chakushu suru*) 改革に着手する.

initiative *n.* shu¹do¹okeñ 主導権; i¹nishia¹chibu イニシアチブ: take the initiative (*inishiachibu o toru*) イニシアチブを取る.

injection *n.* chu¹usha 注射: I had an injection to stop the pain. (*Watashi wa itamidome no chuusha o shite moratta.*) 私は痛み止めの注射をしてもらった.

injure *vt.* ... ni ke¹ga¹ o sa¹seru …にけがをさせる [V]; ... o ki¹zutsuke¹ru …を傷つける [V]: He was slightly injured in the accident. (*Kare wa sono jiko de karui kega o shita.*) 彼はその事故で軽いけがをした. / injure a person's feelings (*hito no kañjoo o kizutsukeru*) 人の感情を傷つける.

injurious *adj.* yu¹ugai na 有害な: Smoking is injurious to the lungs. (*Kitsueñ wa hai ni yuugai desu.*) 喫煙は肺に有害です.

injury *n.* **1** (hurt) fu¹shoo 負傷; ke¹ga¹ けが: suffer injuries to one's head (*atama ni kega o suru*) 頭にけがをする.
2 (harm) ki¹zutsuke¹ru ko¹to¹ 傷つけること; bu¹ree 無礼; bu¹joku 侮辱: an injury to a person's reputation (*meeyo kisoñ*) 名誉毀損.

injustice *n.* fu¹ko¹osee 不公正; fu¹ko¹ohee 不公平: do a person an injustice (*hito o futoo ni atsukau*) 人を不当に扱う.

ink *n.* i¹ñku インク: He signed his name in ink. (*Kare wa namae o iñku de saiñ shita.*) 彼は名前をインクでサインした.

inn *n.* ya¹doya 宿屋: stay at an inn (*yadoya ni tomaru*) 宿屋に泊まる / a Japanese inn (*ryokañ*) 旅館.

inner *adj.* u¹chigawa no 内側の; na¹ibu no 内部の: an inner court (*nakaniwa*) 中庭.

innocence *n.* **1** (freedom from guilt) mu¹zai 無罪: He proved his innocence. (*Kare wa jibuñ no muzai o shoomee shita.*) 彼は自分の無罪を証明した.
2 (purity) mu¹jaki 無邪気; ju¹ñshiñ 純真: childlike innocence (*kodomo no yoo na mujakisa*) 子どものような無邪気さ.

innocent *adj.* **1** (not guilty) mu¹zai no 無罪の; ke¹ppaku na 潔白な: I am innocent. (*Watashi wa keppaku desu.*) 私は潔白です.
2 (knowing no evil) mu¹jaki na 無邪気な; a¹dokena¹i あどけない: an innocent child (*adokenai kodomo*) あどけない子ども.
3 (harmless) mu¹gai na 無害な; a¹kui no nai 悪意のない: innocent jokes (*akui no nai joodañ*) 悪意のない冗談.

innumerable *adj.* ka¹zoekire¹nai 数え切れない; mu¹su¹u no 無数の: innumerable stars (*musuu no hoshi*) 無数の星.

inquire *vt.* ... o ta¹zune¹ru …を尋ねる [V]; to¹iawase¹ru 問い合わせる [V]: He inquired the way to the museum. (*Kare wa bijutsukañ e iku michi o tazuneta.*) 彼は美術館へ行く道を尋ねた.
— *vi.* shi¹tsumoñ suru 質問する [I]; ta¹zune¹ru 尋ねる [V]: inquire at the information desk (*añnaijo de tazuneru*) 案内所で尋ねる.
inquire into ... *vt.* ... o shi¹rabe¹ru …を調べる [V]: inquire into the cause of an accident (*jiko no geñiñ o shiraberu*) 事故の原因を調べる.

inquiry *n.* **1** (asking) to¹iawase 問い合わせ; sho¹okai 照会: a letter of inquiry (*toiawase no tegami*) 問い合わせの手紙.
2 (investigation) cho¹osa 調査; to¹rishirabe 取り調べ: They made inquiries into the matter. (*Kare-ra wa sono moñdai o choosa shita.*) 彼らはその問題を調査した.

insane *adj.* (mad) sho¹oki de na¹i 正気でない; kyo¹oki no 狂気の; (foolish) hi¹jo¹oshiki na 非常識な: an insane scheme (*hijooshiki na* *keekaku*) 非常識な計画.

insect *n.* ko⌈ñchuu 昆虫; mu⌈shi 虫. ★ 'Worm' is also called '*mushi*' in Japanese.

insecure *adj.* **1** (lacking confidence) ji⌈shiñ ga na⌉i 自信がない; fu⌈añ na 不安な: I am insecure about my new job. (*Watashi wa atarashii shigoto ni jishiñ ga nai.*) 私は新しい仕事に自信がない.
2 (not safe) a⌈ñzeñ de na⌉i 安全でない; fu⌈a⌉ñtee na 不安定な: an insecure footing (*fuañtee na ashiba*) 不安定な足場.

insensitive *adj.* do⌈ñkañ na 鈍感な; ka⌈ñji nai 感じない: He is insensitive to other people's feelings. (*Kare wa taniñ no kimochi ni doñkañ da.*) 彼は他人の気持ちに鈍感だ.

insert *vt.* ... o (... ni) sa⌈shiko⌉mu ...を(...に)差し込む Ⓒ; so⌈onyuu suru 挿入する Ⓘ; i⌈reru 入れる Ⓥ: insert a key in a lock (*kagi o joo ni sashikomu*) 鍵を錠に差し込む / insert a coin into a vending machine (*kooka o jidoo hañbaiki ni ireru*) 硬貨を自動販売機に入れる.

inside *adv.* na⌉ka ni [de, e, wa] 中に[で, へ, は]: She went inside. (*Kanojo wa naka ni haitta*) 彼女は中に入った.
— *adj.* na⌉ibu no 内部の; u⌈chigawa no 内側の: inside walls (*uchigawa no kabe*) 内側の壁 / an inside pocket (*uchi poketto*) 内ポケット.
— *n.* na⌉ibu 内部; u⌈chigawa 内側: the inside of a pocket (*poketto no uchigawa*) ポケットの内側 / This door opens from the inside. (*Kono doa wa uchigawa kara hirakimasu.*) このドアは内側から開きます.

insight *n.* do⌈osatsu⌉ryoku 洞察力; ga⌈ñshiki 眼識: a person of insight (*doosatsuryoku no aru hito*) 洞察力のある人.

insincere *adj.* se⌉ei no nai 誠意のない; fu⌈ma⌉jime na ふまじめな: insincere promises (*seei no nai yakusoku*) 誠意のない約束.

insist *vt.* **1** (state) ... to tsu⌉yoku shu⌈choo suru ...と強く主張する Ⓘ; i⌈iha⌉ru 言い張る Ⓒ: He insisted that he was right. (*Kare wa jibuñ ga tadashii to iihatta.*) 彼は自分が正しいと言い張った.
2 (demand) ... to tsu⌉yoku yo⌈okyuu suru ...と強く要求する Ⓘ; kyo⌈oyoo suru 強要する Ⓘ: He insisted that I go. (*Kare wa watashi ni iku yoo ni kyooyoo shita.*) 彼は私に行くように強要した.
— *vi.* (... to) tsu⌉yoku shu⌈choo suru (...と)強く主張する Ⓘ; i⌈iha⌉ru 言い張る Ⓒ: He insisted on his innocence. (*Kare wa muzai da to iihatta.*) 彼は無罪だと言い張った.
if you insist *adv.* ze⌉hi tomo to i⌈u na⌉ra ぜひともというなら: I'll attend if you insist. (*Zehi tomo to iu nara shusseki shimasu.*) ぜひともというなら出席します.

inspect *vt.* **1** (examine) ... o ke⌉ñsa suru ...を検査する Ⓘ; shi⌈rabe⌉ru 調べる Ⓥ: I inspected the house before I bought it. (*Watashi wa sono ie o kau mae ni shirabeta.*) 私はその家を買う前に調べた.
2 (view officially) ... o shi⌈satsu suru ...を視察する Ⓘ: inspect a factory (*koojoo o shisatsu suru*) 工場を視察する.

inspection *n.* ke⌉ñsa 検査; te⌈ñkeñ 点検; shi⌈satsu 視察: an inspection of plants (*shokubutsu no keñsa*) 植物の検査 / a tour of inspection (*shisatsu ryokoo*) 視察旅行.

inspiration *n.* **1** (stimulus) re⌈ekañ 霊感; i⌈ñsupire⌉eshoñ インスピレーション: draw one's inspiration from nature (*shizeñ kara reekañ o ukeru*) 自然から霊感を受ける.
2 (bright idea) myo⌈oañ 妙案; me⌈eañ 名案: I had a sudden inspiration. (*Totsuzeñ meeañ ga hirameita.*) 突然名案がひらめいた.

inspire *vt.* **1** (encourage) ... o fu⌈ruitatase⌉ru ...を奮い立たせる Ⓥ; ko⌉bu suru 鼓舞する Ⓘ: His courage inspired us. (*Kare no yuuki wa watashi-tachi o furuitataseta.*) 彼の

勇気は私たちを奮い立たせた.
2 (produce a feeling) ... o fu⌈kiko⌉mu …を吹き込む Ⓒ; yo⌈bioko⌉su 呼び起こす Ⓒ: The news inspired us with hope. (*Sono shirase wa watashi-tachi ni kiboo o yobiokoshita.*) その知らせは私たちに希望を呼び起こした.

install *vt.* **1** (fix) ... o to⌈ritsukeru …を取り付ける Ⓥ; se⌉tchi suru 設置する Ⓘ: I installed a new air conditioner. (*Watashi wa atarashii kuuraa o toritsuketa.*) 私は新しいクーラーを取り付けた.
2 (place in a position) ... o shu⌈uniñ saseru …を就任させる Ⓥ; ni⌈ñmee suru 任命する Ⓘ: He was installed as chairman. (*Kare wa gichoo ni niñmee sareta.*) 彼は議長に任命された.

installment *n.* **1** (of payments) bu⌈nkatsu-ba⌉rai 分割払い: buy a car on the installment plan (*buñkatsu-barai de kuruma o kau*) 分割払いで車を買う.
2 (of a story, drama) i⌈k-ka⌉i buñ 1回分.

instance *n.* re⌉e 例; ji⌈tsuree 実例: He gave many instances. (*Kare wa takusañ no jitsuree o shimeshita.*) 彼はたくさんの実例を示した.
for instance *adv.* ta⌈to⌉eba 例えば.

instant *adj.* **1** (immediate) so⌉kuza no 即座の; so⌉kuji no 即時の: an instant reply (*sokutoo*) 即答.
2 (of food) i⌈ñsuta⌉ñto no インスタントの: instant coffee (*iñsutañto koohii*) インスタントコーヒー.
— *n.* shu⌈ñkañ 瞬間; so⌉kuji 即時: He was back in an instant. (*Kare wa sugu ni modotte kita.*) 彼はすぐに戻ってきた.

instantaneous *adj.* shu⌈ñkañ no 瞬間の; so⌉kuza no 即座の: instantaneous death (*sokushi*) 即死.

instantly *adv.* so⌉kuza ni 即座に; ta⌉dachi ni 直ちに: be killed instantly (*sokushi suru*) 即死する.

instead *adv.* so⌈no kawari ni その代わりに; ka⌈wari to shite 代わりとして: Give me this instead. (*Sono kawari ni kore o kudasai.*) その代わりにこれを下さい.
instead of ... *prep.* ... no ka⌈wari ni …の代わりに: I went by train instead of by car. (*Watashi wa kuruma no kawari ni deñsha de itta.*) 私は車の代わりに電車で行った.

instinct *n.* ho⌉ñnoo 本能: As winter approaches, swallows fly south by instinct. (*Fuyu ga chikazuku to tsubame wa hoñnoo ni yotte minami e toñde iku.*) 冬が近づくとつばめは本能によって南へ飛んで行く.

institute *n.* (society) ga⌈kkai 学会; (building) ke⌈ñkyuujo 研究所.
— *vt.* ... o mo⌈oke⌉ru …を設ける Ⓥ; se⌈etee suru 制定する: institute new rules (*atarashii kisoku o seetee suru*) 新しい規則を制定する.

institution *n.* **1** (instituting) se⌈tsuritsu 設立; se⌉tchi 設置: the institution of a committee (*iiñkai no setchi*) 委員会の設置.
2 (building) shi⌉setsu 施設; (organization) ki⌉kañ 機関: an institution for the aged (*roojiñ shisetsu*) 老人施設 / a public institution (*kookyoo kikañ*) 公共機関.
3 (established law) ka⌈ñree 慣例; se⌉edo 制度.

instruct *vt.* **1** (teach) ... ni (... o) o⌈shieru …に(…を)教える Ⓥ: Mr. Yagi instructed us in Japanese. (*Yagi señsee ga watashi-tachi ni Nihoñgo o oshiete kureta.*) 八木先生が私たちに日本語を教えてくれた.
2 (order) ... ni (... o) sa⌉shizu suru …に(…を)指図する Ⓘ; shi⌉ji suru 指示する Ⓘ: I instructed him how to do the work. (*Watashi wa kare ni sono shigoto no yarikata o shiji shita.*) 私は彼にその仕事のやり方を指示した.

instruction *n.* **1** (teaching) o⌈shie 教え; kyo⌈oiku 教育: give [receive] instruction in Japanese (*Nihoñgo no kyooiku o suru [ukeru]*) 日本語の教育をする[受ける].
2 (directions) shi⌈yoo setsumee(-

sho) 使用説明(書): the instructions for a watch (*tokee no setsumee-sho*) 時計の説明書.
3 (order) saˡshizu 指図; me⌈eree 命令: We followed our teacher's instructions. (*Watashi-tachi wa señsee no shiji ni shitagatta.*) 私たちは先生の指示に従った.

instructive *adj.* kyo⌈oiku-teki na 教育的な; ta⌈meˡ ni naru ためになる: an instructive book (*tame ni naru hoñ*) ためになる本.

instructor *n.* o⌈shieru hitoˡ 教える人; shi⌈doˡosha 指導者; (of a college) se⌈ñniñ koˡoshi 専任講師.

instrument *n.* **1** (of music) ga⌈k-ki 楽器: He can play several instruments. (*Kare wa ikutsu-ka no gakki o hikeru.*) 彼はいくつかの楽器を弾ける.
2 (tool) kiˡgu 器具; yoˡogu 用具; ki⌈kaˡi 器械: medical instruments (*iryoo kigu*) 医療器具.

insufficient *adj.* fu⌈juˡubuñ na 不十分な; fu⌈soku shite iru 不足している: There are insufficient nurses. (*Kañgofu ga fusoku shite iru.*) 看護婦が不足している.

insult *vt.* ... o bu⌈joku suru ...を侮辱する [I]: insult a person (*hito o bujoku suru*) 人を侮辱する.
— *n.* bu⌈joku 侮辱; buˡree 無礼: What you say is an insult. (*Kimi no iu koto wa bujoku da.*) 君の言うことは侮辱だ.

insurance *n.* **1** (contract) ho⌈keñ 保険; ho⌈keñ-keˡeyaku 保険契約: take out insurance on one's car (*kuruma ni hokeñ o kakeru*) 車に保険をかける / fire insurance (*kasai-hokeñ*) 火災保険 / health insurance (*keñkoo-hokeñ*) 健康保険.
2 (premium) ho⌈keˡñryoo 保険料; ho⌈keñkiñ 保険金: pay one's insurance (*hokeñryoo o shiharau*) 保険料を支払う.

insure *vt.* ... ni ho⌈keñ o kakeˡru ...に保険をかける [V]: He insured his house against fire. (*Kare wa ie ni kasai-hokeñ o kaketa.*) 彼は家に火災保険をかけた.

intake *n.* se⌈sshuˡryoo 摂取量; to⌈ri-ire 取り入れ: a daily intake of calcium (*karushuumu no ichinichi no sesshuryoo*) カルシウムの1日の摂取量.

integrate *vt.* ... o to⌈ogoo suru ...を統合する [I]; to⌈oitsu suru 統一する [I]: Some subjects were integrated into one course. (*Ikutsu-ka no kamoku ga hitotsu no koosu ni toogoo sareta.*) いくつかの課目が一つのコースに統合された.

intellect *n.* chiˡsee 知性; chiˡryoku 知力: a person of intellect (*chisee no aru hito*) 知性のある人.

intellectual *adj.* chi⌈teki na 知的な; chiˡsee no 知性の: Chess is an intellectual game. (*Chesu wa chiteki na geemu desu.*) チェスは知的なゲームです.
— *n.* chi⌈shikiˡjiñ 知識人; i⌈ñteri インテリ.

intelligence *n.* **1** (ability to understand) chiˡnoo 知能; ri⌈kaˡiryoku 理解力: an intelligence quotient (*chinoo shisuu*) 知能指数 / an intelligence test (*chinoo keñsa*) 知能検査.
2 (information) jo⌈ohoo 情報: collect intelligence (*joohoo o atsumeru*) 情報を集める.

intelligent *adj.* **1** (of an animal) chiˡnoo no ta⌈kaˡi 知能の高い; ri⌈koo na 利口な: an intelligent animal (*rikoo na doobutsu*) 利口な動物.
2 (of a building) jo⌈ohooka sareta 情報化された; i⌈ñteˡrijeñto na インテリジェントな: an intelligent building (*iñterijeñto biru*) インテリジェントビル.

intend *vt.* **1** (plan) ... tsu⌈mori da ...つもりだ: I intend to buy a new car. (*Watashi wa shiñsha o kau tsumori desu.*) 私は新車を買うつもりです.
2 (mean) ... tsu⌈mori da ...つもりだ; ... mu⌈ke da ...向けだ: That was intended as a joke. (*Are wa joodañ no tsumori deshita.*) あれは冗談のつ

もりでした. / This book is intended for beginners. (*Kono hoñ wa shoshiñsha muke desu.*) この本は初心者向けです.

intense *adj.* kyo⌈oretsu na 強烈な; mo⌈oretsu na 猛烈な; ha⌈geshi⌉i 激しい: intense heat (*mooretsu na atsusa*) 猛烈な暑さ / a person of intense feelings (*kañjoo no hageshii hito*) 感情の激しい人.

intensity *n.* kyo⌈oretsusa 強烈さ; ha⌈ge⌉shisa 激しさ: the intensity of feeling (*kañjoo no hageshisa*) 感情の激しさ.

intensive *adj.* shu⌈uchuu-teki na 集中的な; te⌈ttee-teki na 徹底的な: an intensive investigation (*tetteeteki na choosa*) 徹底的な調査 / intensive reading (*seedoku*) 精読.

intent *adj.* ne⌉sshiñ na 熱心な; mu⌈chuu na 夢中な: He is intent on the video game. (*Kare wa terebi geemu ni muchuu da.*) 彼はテレビゲームに夢中だ.

intention *n.* i⌉to 意図; i⌈koo 意向; tsu⌈mori つもり: I had no intention of telling a lie. (*Watashi wa uso o tsuku tsumori wa arimaseñ deshita.*) 私はうそをつくつもりはありませんでした.

intentional *adj.* ko⌉i no 故意の; i⌈to-teki na 意図的な: His mistake was intentional. (*Kare no machigai wa ito-teki datta.*) 彼の間違いは意図的だった.

interest *n.* **1** (curiosity) kyo⌉omi 興味: I have an interest in sports. (*Watashi wa supootsu ni kyoomi o motte imasu.*) 私はスポーツに興味を持っています.
2 (matter concerned) ka⌈ñshi⌉ñji 関心事: One of my greatest interests is gardening. (*Watashi no ichibañ no kañshiñji no hitotsu wa eñgee desu.*) 私のいちばんの関心事の一つは園芸です.
3 (benefit) ri⌉eki 利益: He is looking after only his own interests. (*Kare wa jibuñ no rieki dake o motomete iru.*) 彼は自分の利益だけを求めている.
4 (money) ri⌈soku 利息; ri⌉shi 利子: pay interest of 5 percent (*gopaaseñto no risoku o harau*) 5 パーセントの利息を払う.

interested *adj.* kyo⌈omi o mo⌉tte iru 興味を持っている; ka⌈ñshiñ ga a⌉ru 関心がある: We are interested in your products. (*Watashi-domo wa anata no seehiñ ni kyoomi o motte imasu.*) 私どもはあなたの製品に興味を持っています.

interesting *adj.* kyo⌈omi no a⌉ru 興味のある; o⌈moshiro⌉i おもしろい: His story was very interesting. (*Kare no hanashi wa totemo omoshirokatta.*) 彼の話はとてもおもしろかった.

interfere *vi.* **1** (meddle in) (... ni) ka⌈ñshoo suru (…に)干渉する [I]; ku⌈chidashi suru 口出しする [I]: Don't interfere in other people's affairs. (*Hoka no hito no koto ni kuchidashi shite wa ikemaseñ.*) ほかの人のことに口出ししてはいけません.
2 (prevent) (... o) ja⌈ma suru (…を)じゃまする [I]; bo⌈ogai suru 妨害する [I]: He interfered with my plan. (*Kare wa watashi no keekaku o jama shita.*) 彼は私の計画をじゃました.

interference *n.* ka⌈ñshoo 干渉; bo⌈ogai 妨害: I don't like your interference in my work. (*Watashi no shigoto ni kañshoo shite moraitaku nai.*) 私の仕事に干渉してもらいたくない.

interior *adj.* **1** (inside) na⌉ibu no 内部の; u⌈chigawa no 内側の: an inside wall (*uchikabe*) 内壁.
2 (inland) na⌈iriku no 内陸の; ko⌈ku⌉nai no 国内の: interior regions (*nairiku chiiki*) 内陸地域.
— *n.* na⌉ibu 内部; u⌈chigawa 内側: the interior of a house (*ie no naibu*) 家の内部.

intermediate *adj.* chu⌈ukañ no 中間の; chu⌈ukyuu no 中級の: an intermediate course (*chuukyuu koosu*) 中級コース.

internal *adj.* **1** (of the inside)

na⌉ibu no 内部の: internal organs (*naizoo*) 内臓.
2 (domestic) ko⌈ku⌉nai no 国内の; na⌈isee no 内政の: internal affairs (*kokunai jijoo*) 国内事情.

international *adj.* ko⌈kusai no 国際の; ko⌈kusai-teki na 国際的な: an international phone call (*kokusai-deñwa*) 国際電話 / an international airport (*kokusai kuukoo*) 国際空港.

interpret *vt.* **1** (understand) ... o ka⌉ishaku suru …を解釈する ①; (explain) se⌈tsumee suru 説明する ①: How do you interpret this poem? (*Kono shi o doo kaishaku shimasu ka?*) この詩をどう解釈しますか.
2 (translate) ... o tsu⌉uyaku suru …を通訳する ①: She interpreted his speech into Japanese. (*Kanojo wa kare no eñzetsu o Nihoñgo ni tsuuyaku shita.*) 彼女は彼の演説を日本語に通訳した.
— *vi.* tsu⌉uyaku suru 通訳する ①: She interpreted for me. (*Kanojo ga watashi no tsuuyaku o shite kureta.*) 彼女が私の通訳をしてくれた.

interpretation *n.* **1** (understanding) ka⌉ishaku 解釈; (explanation) se⌈tsumee 説明: the interpretation of dreams (*yume no kaishaku*) 夢の解釈.
2 (translation) tsu⌉uyaku 通訳: simultaneous interpretation (*dooji tsuuyaku*) 同時通訳.

interpreter *n.* tsu⌉uyaku 通訳; tsu⌈uyaku⌉sha 通訳者: He acted as interpreter. (*Kare ga tsuuyaku o shita.*) 彼が通訳をした.

interrupt *vt.* **1** (break into) ... o ja⌈ma suru …をじゃまする ①; bo⌈ogai suru 妨害する ①: He interrupted me while I was studying. (*Watashi ga beñkyoo shite iru toki kare wa watashi o jama shita.*) 私が勉強しているとき彼は私をじゃました.
2 (stop) ... o chu⌈udañ suru …を中断する ①; chu⌈ushi suru 中止する ①: He interrupted his work to eat his lunch. (*Kare wa chuushoku o taberu tame ni shigoto o chuudañ shita.*) 彼は昼食を食べるために仕事を中断した.
— *vi.* ja⌈ma suru じゃまする ①: Excuse me for interrupting. (*O-jama shite sumimaseñ.*) おじゃましてすみません.

interruption *n.* (interrupting) bo⌈ogai 妨害; (break) chu⌈udañ 中断: work without interruption (*yasumi naku hataraku*) 休みなく働く.

intersection *n.* (crossroads) ko⌈osa⌉teñ 交差点.

interval *n.* **1** (of time) ka⌈ñkaku 間隔; a⌈ima 合間: Buses leave at fifteen-minute intervals. (*Basu wa juugo-fuñ-kañkaku de dete imasu.*) バスは15分間隔で出ています.
2 (of space) ka⌈ñkaku 間隔; su⌈kima すき間: There is an interval of 2 meters between the houses. (*Ie to ie no aida ni wa ni-meetoru no sukima ga arimasu.*) 家と家の間には2メートルのすき間があります.

intervention *n.* (coming between) chu⌈usai 仲裁; (interference) ka⌈inyuu 介入: military intervention (*guñji-kainyuu*) 軍事介入.

interview *n.* **1** (meeting) me⌈ñsetsu 面接; me⌈ñdañ 面談: a job interview (*shuushoku no meñsetsu*) 就職の面接.
2 (of a reporter) i⌉ñtabyuu インタビュー.
— *vt.* ... to me⌈ñsetsu suru …と面接する ①; ... ni i⌉ñtabyuu suru …にインタビューする ①: The delegation was interviewed by reporters. (*Daihyoodañ wa kisha no iñtabyuu o uketa.*) 代表団は記者のインタビューを受けた.

intimacy *n.* shi⌈ñmitsu 親密; shi⌈tashi⌉i a⌈idagara 親しい間柄: I am on terms of intimacy with him. (*Watashi wa kare to shitashii aidagara desu.*) 私は彼と親しい間柄です.

intimate *adj.* **1** (familiar) shi⌈ñmitsu na 親密な; shi⌈tashi⌉i 親しい: an intimate friend (*shitashii yuujiñ*)

i

親しい友人.
2 (private) ko⌈jiñ-teki na 個人的な; shi⌈teki na 私的な: one's intimate affairs (*shiji*) 私事.
3 (deep and thorough) ku⌈washi⌉i 詳しい; yo⌉ku shi⌈tte iru よく知っている: He has an intimate knowledge of the problem. (*Kare wa sono moñdai o yoku shitte iru.*) 彼はその問題をよく知っている.

into *prep.* **1** (to the inside of) ... no na⌉ka e [ni] …の中へ[に]: go into the house (*ie no naka e hairu*) 家の中へ入る / look into the house (*ie no naka o nozoku*) 家の中をのぞく.
2 (to the condition of) ... ni …に: The rain turned into snow. (*Ame ga yuki ni natta.*) 雨が雪になった. / put a sentence into Japanese (*buñ o Nihoñgo ni yakusu*) 文を日本語に訳す.
3 (against) ... ni …に: His car ran into a tree. (*Kare no kuruma wa ki ni butsukatta.*) 彼の車は木にぶつかった.

intolerable *adj.* ta⌈erare⌉nai 耐えられない; ga⌉mañ de⌈ki⌉nai 我慢できない: intolerable working conditions (*gamañ dekinai roodoo-jookeñ*) 我慢できない労働条件.

intonation *n.* i⌈ñtone⌉eshoñ イントネーション; ko⌉e no yo⌈kuyoo 声の抑揚.

intricate *adj.* ko⌈mi-itta 込み入った; ko⌈mi-itte iru 込み入っている; fu⌈kuzatsu na 複雑な: an intricate story (*komi-itta hanashi*) 込み入った話.

introduce *vt.* **1** (acquaint) ... o sho⌈okai suru …を紹介する Ⓘ: May I introduce Mr. Yamada to you? (*Yamada-sañ o go-shookai itashimasu.*) 山田さんをご紹介いたします.
2 (bring in) ... o to⌈riireru …を取り入れる Ⓥ; tsu⌈taeru 伝える Ⓥ: Tea was introduced into Japan from China. (*O-cha wa Chuugoku kara Nihoñ ni tsutaerareta.*) お茶は中国から日本に伝えられた.
3 (make familiar) ... ni te⌈ho⌉doki suru …に手ほどきする Ⓘ: He introduced me to chess. (*Kare wa watashi ni chesu o tehodoki shite kureta.*) 彼は私にチェスを手ほどきしてくれた.

introduction *n.* **1** (of a person) sho⌈okai 紹介; hi⌈kiawase 引き合わせ: a letter of introduction (*shookaijoo*) 紹介状.
2 (of a book) jo⌈roñ 序論; jo⌈buñ 序文; (of music) jo⌈soo 序奏: write the introduction of a book (*hoñ no joroñ o kaku*) 本の序論を書く.
3 (elementary book) nyu⌈umoñsho 入門書.

intrude *vi.* ... ni ta⌈chiiru ... に立ち入る Ⓒ; ... o ja⌈ma suru …をじゃまする Ⓘ: I don't want to intrude in his private affairs. (*Watashi wa kare no shiteki na koto ni tachiiritaku nai.*) 私は彼の私的なことに立ち入りたくない. / I hope I am not intruding. (*O-jama de nakereba yoi no desu ga.*) おじゃまでなければよいのですが.
— *vt.* ... o (... ni) o⌈shitsuke⌉ru …を(…に)押しつける Ⓥ: intrude one's ideas on others (*jibuñ no kañgae o hoka no hito ni oshitsukeru*) 自分の考えをほかの人に押しつける.

intuition *n.* cho⌈kkañ 直感; cho⌈kkaku 直覚: woman's intuition (*josee no chokkañ*) 女性の直感.

invade *vt.* **1** (enter) ... o shi⌈ñryaku suru …を侵略する Ⓘ; ... ni shi⌈ñnyuu suru …に侵入する Ⓘ: invade other countries (*takoku o shiñryaku suru*) 他国を侵略する.
2 (violate) ... o shi⌈ñgai suru …を侵害する Ⓘ: invade the privacy of others (*tanin no puraibashii o shiñgai suru*) 他人のプライバシーを侵害する.
3 (rush into) ... ni o⌈shiyose⌉ru … に押し寄せる Ⓥ: In summer, crowds of people invade this beach. (*Natsu ni wa oozee no hito ga kono kaigañ ni oshiyosemasu.*) 夏には大勢の人がこの海岸に押し寄せます.

invalid *n.* byo⌈oniñ 病人; byo⌈ojaku⌉sha 病弱者: a permanent invalid (*fuji no byooniñ*) 不治の病人.
— *adj.* byo⌈ojaku na 病弱な; byo⌈oniñ no 病人の: an invalid diet

(*byooniñshoku*) 病人食.

invasion *n.* **1** (entering) shiˈñryaku 侵略; shiˈññyuu 侵入: repel invasion from another country (*takoku no shiñryaku o hanenokeru*) 他国の侵略をはねのける.
2 (violation) shiˈñgai 侵害: invasion of privacy (*puraibashii no shiñgai*) プライバシーの侵害.

invent *vt.* **1** (produce) ... o haˈtsumee suru …を発明する [I]: Who invented the telephone? (*Deñwa o hatsumee shita no wa dare desu ka?*) 電話を発明したのはだれですか.
2 (make up) ... o deˈtchiageˈru …をでっちあげる [V]; koˈshiraeru こしらえる [V]: He invented the story. (*Kare wa sono hanashi o detchiageta.*) 彼はその話をでっちあげた.

invention *n.* **1** (inventing) haˈtsumee 発明; soˈoañ 創案: the invention of television (*terebi no hatsumee*) テレビの発明.
2 (something invented) haˈtsumeehiñ 発明品: The computer is a marvelous invention. (*Koñpyuutaa wa subarashii hatsumeehiñ da.*) コンピューターはすばらしい発明品だ.
3 (false story) tsuˈkurigotoˈ 作り事.

inventor *n.* haˈtsumeˈesha 発明者; koˈoaˈñsha 考案者.

invert *vt.* ... o gyaˈku ni suru …を逆にする [I]; haˈñtai ni suru 反対にする [I]: invert the order (*juñjo o gyaku ni suru*) 順序を逆にする.

invest *vt.* **1** (put money into business) ... o (... ni) toˈoshi suru …を(…に)投資する [I]: He invested all his money in stocks. (*Kare wa okane o zeñbu kabu ni tooshi shita.*) 彼はお金を全部株に投資した.
2 (spend) ... o (... ni) tsuˈiyaˈsu …を(…に)費やす [C]; tsuˈgikoˈmu つぎ込む [C]: He invested a lot of time in his study. (*Kare wa ooku no jikañ o keñkyuu ni tsuiyashita.*) 彼は多くの時間を研究に費やした.

investigate *vt.* ... o choˈosa suru …を調査する [I]; shiˈrabeˈru 調べる [V]: The police are investigating the cause of the accident. (*Keesatsu wa sono jiko no geñiñ o shirabete imasu.*) 警察はその事故の原因を調べています.

investigation *n.* choˈosa 調査; keˈñkyuu 研究: It is under investigation. (*Sore wa choosa-chuu desu.*) それは調査中です.

investigator *n.* choˈosaˈsha 調査者; keˈñkyuˈusha 研究者.

investment *n.* **1** (investing) toˈoshi 投資; shuˈsshi 出資: make an investment in land (*tochi ni tooshi suru*) 土地に投資する.
2 (the amount invested) toˈoshiˈgaku 投資額; shuˈsshiˈgaku 出資額.

invisible *adj.* meˈ ni miˈeˈnai 目に見えない: Germs are invisible to the naked eye. (*Saikiñ wa nikugañ de wa mienai.*) 細菌は肉眼では見えない.

invitation *n.* **1** (inviting) shoˈotai 招待; aˈñnaˈi 案内: accept [decline] an invitation to a party (*paatii e no shootai o ukeru [kotowaru]*) パーティーへの招待を受ける[断る].
2 (letter) shoˈotaˈijoo 招待状: send out invitations to a party (*paatii no shootaijoo o dasu*) パーティーの招待状を出す.

invite *vt.* **1** (ask to come) ... o shoˈotai suru …を招待する [I]; maˈneˈku 招く [C]: I invited her to dinner. (*Watashi wa kanojo o yuushoku ni shootai shita.*) 私は彼女を夕食に招待した.
2 (ask for) ... o moˈtomeˈru …を求める [V]; saˈsou 誘う [C]: Nobody invited his opinion. (*Dare mo kare no ikeñ o motomenakatta.*) だれも彼の意見を求めなかった.
3 (attract) ... o maˈneˈku …を招く [C]; moˈtaraˈsu もたらす [C]: He invited danger by being careless. (*Kare wa fuchuui ni yori kikeñ o maneita.*) 彼は不注意により危険を招いた.

invoice *n.* iˈñboˈisu インボイス; seˈekyuusho 請求書; oˈkurijoo 送り状.

involve *vt.* **1** (mix up) ... o maˈki-

ko⌉mu ...を巻き込む Ⓒ; ka⌈kariai ni suru 掛かり合いにする Ⓘ: I don't want to get involved with the police. (*Watashi wa keesatsu to kakariai ni naritaku nai.*) 私は警察と掛かり合いになりたくない.
2 (require) ... o hi⌈tsuyoo to suru ...を必要とする Ⓘ; to⌈mona⌉u 伴う Ⓒ: This operation involves no risk. (*Kono shujutsu wa kikeñ o tomonawanai.*) この手術は危険を伴わない.
3 (absorb) ... ni mu⌈chuu ni saseru ...に夢中にさせる Ⓥ: He is involved in his book. (*Kare wa hoñ ni muchuu ni natte iru.*) 彼は本に夢中になっている.

inward *adj.* **1** (of the mind) ko⌈koro no na⌉ka no 心の中の; se⌈eshiñ-teki na 精神的な: inward peace (*kokoro no heewa*) 心の平和.
2 (directed toward the inside) u⌈chigawa e⌉ no 内側への: an inward curve (*uchigawa e no kaabu*)内側へのカーブ.
— *adv.* na⌉ka e 中へ; u⌈chigawa e 内側へ: This door opens inward. (*Kono doa wa uchigawa e hirakimasu.*) このドアは内側へ開きます.

iron *n.* **1** (metal) te⌈tsu 鉄.
2 (for clothes) a⌈iroñ アイロン.
— *vt.* ... ni a⌈iroñ o kake⌉ru ...にアイロンをかける Ⓥ: Won't you iron this shirt for me? (*Kono shatsu ni airoñ o kakete kuremaseñ ka?*) このシャツにアイロンをかけてくれませんか.

irony *n.* hi⌈niku 皮肉: the irony of fate (*uñmee no hiniku*) 運命の皮肉.

irregular *adj.* **1** (not regular) fu⌈ki⌉soku na 不規則な; he⌈ñsoku-teki na 変則的な: an irregular diet (*fukisoku na shokuji*) 不規則な食事.
2 (not straight) fu⌈zo⌉roi no ふぞろいの; de⌉koboko shita [shite iru] でこぼこした[している]: an irregular shape (*fuzoroi no katachi*) ふぞろいの形.

irrelevant *adj.* mu⌈ka⌉ñkee no 無関係の; fu⌈te⌉kisetsu na 不適切な: remarks irrelevant to the issues (*moñdai to mukañkee no ikeñ*) 問題と無関係の意見.

irresistible *adj.* te⌈ekoo deki⌉nai 抵抗できない; o⌈saerare⌉nai 抑えられない: irresistible forces (*fukakooryoku*) 不可抗力.

irrespective *adj.* ka⌈ñkee no na⌉i 関係のない.
irrespective of ... *perp.* ... ni ka⌈ñkee na⌉ku ...に関係なく: Anyone can join the club, irrespective of sex. (*Seebetsu ni kañkee naku dare de mo sono kurabu ni hairemasu.*) 性別に関係なくだれでもそのクラブに入れます.

irresponsible *adj.* mu⌈se⌉kiniñ na 無責任な; i⌈ikageñ na いいかげんな: an irresponsible mother (*musekiniñ na hahaoya*) 無責任な母親.

irritate *vt.* ... o i⌉raira saseru ...をいらいらさせる Ⓥ: He was irritated by the noise. (*Kare wa sono soooñ ni iraira shite ita.*) 彼はその騒音にいらいらしていた.

irritation *n.* i⌈radachi いらだち; sho⌈osoo 焦燥.

island *n.* shi⌈ma⌉ 島: What is that island called? (*Ano shima wa nañ to iimasu ka?*) あの島は何と言いますか.

isolate *vt.* **1** ... o ko⌈ritsu saseru ...を孤立させる Ⓥ: The town was isolated because of the heavy snow. (*Sono machi wa ooyuki no tame ni koritsu shita.*) その町は大雪のために孤立した.
2 (of a patient) ... o ka⌈kuri suru ...を隔離する Ⓘ: A patient with an infectious disease must be isolated. (*Deñseñbyoo o motte iru kañja wa kakuri shinakereba naranai.*) 伝染病を持っている患者は隔離しなければならない.

isolation *n.* ko⌈ritsu 孤立; (of a patient) ka⌈kuri 隔離: an isolation ward (*kakuri-byootoo*) 隔離病棟.

issue *n.* **1** (problem) mo⌈ñdai 問題; ro⌈ñte⌉ñ 論点: debate an issue (*moñdai o roñjiru*) 問題を論じる.
2 (printed material) ha⌈kko⌉obutsu 発行物; ka⌈ñko⌉obutsu 刊行物; -goo 号: the March issue of a magazine (*zasshi no sañgatsu-goo*) 雑

誌の3月号.
3 (publication) ha⌈kkoo 発行; ka⌈ñkoo 刊行: the issue of a newspaper (*shiñbuñ no hakkoo*) 新聞の発行.
— *vt.* 1 (publish) ... o ha⌈kkoo suru ...を発行する [I]: issue a passport [magazine] (*ryokeñ* [*zasshi*] *o hakkoo suru*) 旅券[雑誌]を発行する.
2 (give out) ... o da⌉su ...を出す [C]; ko⌈ofu suru 公布する [I]: issue an order (*meeree o dasu*) 命令を出す.
— *vi.* de⌉ru 出る [V]; na⌈garede⌉ru 流れ出る [V]: Blood issued from the wound. (*Chi ga kizuguchi kara nagaredeta.*) 血が傷口から流れ出た.

it *pron.* **1** (the thing that is understood) so⌈re それ: How much is it? (*Sore wa ikura desu ka?*) それはいくらですか.
2 (the thing that is spoken of) so⌈re それ: If you find my umbrella, please return it to me. (*Moshi watashi no kasa o mitsuketara,* (*sore o*) *kaeshite kudasai.*) もし私の傘を見つけたら(それを)返してください. ★ When self-explanatory, '*sore*' is usually omitted.
3 (reference to a general condition) ★ No Japanese equivalent word: It's cold, isn't it? (*Samui desu ne.*) 寒いですね. / It is one o'clock now. (*Ima ichi-ji desu.*) 今1時です. / It is Monday today. (*Kyoo wa getsuyoobi desu.*) きょうは月曜日です. / How far is it from here to the station? (*Koko kara eki made dono kurai arimasu ka?*) ここから駅までどのくらいありますか.

Italian *n.* (people) I⌈taria⌉jiñ イタリア人; (language) I⌈tariago イタリア語.

Italy *n.* I⌈taria イタリア.

itch *vi.* **1** (have a tickling feeling) ka⌈yu⌉i かゆい: I itch all over. (*Karada-juu ga kayui.*) 体じゅうがかゆい.
2 (have a restless desire) mu⌉zumuzu suru むずむずする [I]: He is itching to ask questions. (*Kare wa shitsumoñ o shitakute muzumuzu shite iru.*) 彼は質問をしたくてむずむずしている.

item *n.* **1** (separate article) ko⌈omoku 項目; hi⌈ñmoku 品目: Please check each item on this list. (*Kono risuto no kaku koomoku o shirabete kudasai.*) このリストの各項目を調べてください.
2 (a piece of news) ki⌉ji 記事: I saw the item about the accident in the newspaper. (*Watashi wa sono jiko no kiji o shiñbuñ de mimashita.*) 私はその事故の記事を新聞で見ました.

its *pron.* so⌈re no それの; so⌈no その: I dropped the cup and broke its handle. (*Watashi wa kappu o otoshite* (*sono*) *totte o kowashite shimatta.*) 私はカップを落として(その)取っ手を壊してしまった. ★ When self-explanatory, '*sono*' is usually omitted.

itself *pron.* **1** [reflexive use] so⌈re ji⌉shiñ o [ni] それ自身を[に]: The dog scratched itself. (*Inu wa jibuñ no karada o kaita.*) 犬は自分の体をかいた.
2 [emphatic use] so⌈re ji⌉shiñ ga それ自身が; so⌈no mono ji⌉tai ga そのもの自体が: He is kindness itself. (*Kare wa shiñsetsu sono mono da.*) 彼は親切そのものだ.

ivory *n.* zo⌈oge 象牙.

ivy *n.* tsu⌈ta⌉ つた.

J

jacket *n.* **1** (coat) u⌈wagi 上着; ja⌉ketto ジャケット: put on [take off] a jacket (*uwagi o kiru* [*nugu*]) 上着を着る[脱ぐ].
2 (of a book) ka⌉baa カバー; (of a record) ja⌉ketto ジャケット.

jail *n.* (prison) ke⌈emu⌉sho 刑務所; (detention house) ko⌈ochisho 拘置所; ryu⌈uchijoo 留置場.

jam[1] *n.* ja⌉mu ジャム: spread jam on bread (*pañ ni jamu o nuru*) パンにジャムを塗る.

jam[2] *vt.* **1** (squeeze) ... o (... ni) tsu⌈meko⌉mu …を(…に)詰め込む Ⓒ: jam clothes into a suitcase (*irui o suutsukeesu ni tsumekomu*) 衣類をスーツケースに詰め込む.
2 (push) ... o tsu⌉yoku o⌈su …を強く押す Ⓒ: jam one's foot on the brakes (*bureeki o ashi de fumu*) ブレーキを足で踏む.
3 (block) ... o fu⌈sagu …をふさぐ Ⓒ: The road is jammed with cars. (*Dooro wa kuruma de fusagatte iru.*) 道路は車でふさがっている.
— *vi.* gi⌈sshi⌉ri i⌈ppai ni na⌉ru ぎっしりいっぱいになる Ⓒ: We jammed into the elevator. (*Watashi-tachi wa erebeetaa ni gisshiri ippai notta.*) 私たちはエレベーターにぎっしりいっぱい乗った.

January *n.* i⌈chi-gatsu⌉ 1月.

Japan *n.* Ni⌈ho⌉ñ 日本: Japan is an island country. (*Nihoñ wa shima-guni desu.*) 日本は島国です.

Japanese *n.* (people) Ni⌈hoñji⌉ñ 日本人; (language) Ni⌈hoñgo 日本語: I cannot speak Japanese. (*Watashi wa Nihoñgo o hanasemaseñ.*) 私は日本語を話せません.
— *adj.* Ni⌈ho⌉ñ no 日本の; Ni⌈hoñ-ji⌉ñ no 日本人の; Ni⌈hoñgo no 日本語の: a Japanese doll (*Nihoñ-niñ-gyoo*) 日本人形 / Japanese grammar (*Nihoñgo no buñpoo*) 日本語の文法 / Japanese paper (*washi*) 和紙.

jar *n.* bi⌉ñ びん; tsu⌈bo つぼ: put jam into a jar (*jamu o biñ ni ireru*) ジャムをびんに入れる.

jaw *n.* a⌈go⌉ あご: the lower jaw (*shita-ago*) 下あご / the upper jaw (*uwa-ago*) 上あご.

jealous *adj.* shi⌈ttobuka⌉i しっと深い; ne⌈ta⌉ñde (iru) ねたんで(いる): a jealous husband (*shittobukai otto*) しっと深い夫 / He is jealous of my success. (*Kare wa watashi no see-koo o netañde iru.*) 彼は私の成功をねたんでいる.

jealousy *n.* shi⌈tto しっと; ne⌈tami⌉ ねたみ: burn with jealousy (*shitto ni moeru*) しっとに燃える.

jeans *n.* ji⌉iñzu ジーンズ: He was in jeans. (*Kare wa jiiñzu o haite ita.*) 彼はジーンズをはいていた.

jelly *n.* ze⌉rii ゼリー: apple jelly (*riñ-go no zerii jamu*) りんごのゼリージャム.

jerk *n.* gu⌉i to hi⌈ku koto⌉ ぐいと引くこと: give a rope a jerk (*roopu o gui to hiku*) ロープをぐいと引く.
— *vt.* ... o gu⌉i to hi⌈ku …をぐいと引く Ⓒ: He jerked the window open. (*Kare wa mado o gui to hiraita.*) 彼は窓をぐいと開いた.

jet *n.* **1** (airplane) je⌈tto⌉ki ジェット機: get on board a jet (*jettoki ni noru*) ジェット機に乗る.
2 (strong flow) fu⌈ñshutsu 噴出: a jet of water (*mizu no fuñshutsu*) 水の噴出.

jet lag *n.* ji⌈sa-boke 時差ぼけ.

Jew *n.* Yu⌈daya⌉jiñ ユダヤ人.

jewel *n.* ho⌈oseki 宝石: put on jewels (*hooseki o mi ni tsukeru*) 宝石を身につける.

jewelry *n.* ho⌈oseki⌉rui 宝石類; ho⌈oseki sooshi⌉ñgu 宝石装身具.

Jewish *adj.* Yu⌈daya⌉jiñ no ユダヤ人の: the Jewish people (*Yudaya miñ-zoku*) ユダヤ民族.

job *n.* **1** (employment) tsu⌈tome⌉-guchi 勤め口; sho⌈ku 職: I am looking for a job. (*Watashi wa tsutomeguchi o sagashite imasu.*) 私は勤め口を探しています. / He lost his job. (*Kare wa shoku o ushinatta.*) 彼は職を失った.
2 (work) shi⌈goto 仕事; (duty) tsu⌈tome⌉ 務め: Now let's get on with the job. (*Saa shigoto ni torikakaroo.*) さあ仕事に取りかかろう.

jog *vi.* yu⌈kku⌉ri kake⌉ru ゆっくり駆ける [V]: jo⌈giñgu suru ジョギングする [I]: I jog every morning. (*Watashi wa maiasa jogiñgu o shimasu.*) 私は毎朝ジョギングをします.
— *vt.* ... o cho⌉tto tsu⌈ku ...をちょっと突く [C]: He jogged my elbow. (*Kare wa watashi no hiji o chotto tsuita.*) 彼は私のひじをちょっと突いた.

join *vt.* **1** (become a member) ... ni ku⌈wawa⌉ru ...に加わる [C]; sa⌈ñka suru 参加する [I]: She didn't join us in the game. (*Kanojo wa watashitachi no geemu ni sañka shinakatta.*) 彼女は私たちのゲームに参加しなかった.
2 (put together) ... o tsu⌈nagu ...をつなぐ [C]; ke⌈tsugoo suru 結合する [I]: join two wires (*ni-hoñ no harigane o tsunagu*) 2本の針金をつなぐ.
— *vi.* **1** (meet) a⌈wasa⌉ru 合わさる [C]; ma⌈jiwa⌉ru 交わる [C]: Where do those two roads join? (*Kono futatsu no michi wa doko de majiwarimasu ka?*) この二つの道はどこで交わりますか.
2 (participate) i⌈ssho ni na⌉ru いっしょになる [C]; sa⌈ñka suru 参加する [I]: I joined in the campaign. (*Watashi wa sono uñdoo ni sañka shita.*) 私はその運動に参加した.

joint *n.* **1** (of bones) ka⌈ñsetsu 関節: the joint of the arm (*ude no kañsetsu*) 腕の関節.
2 (of a thing) tsu⌈gime 継ぎ目: a joint in a water pipe (*suidookañ no tsugime*) 水道管の継ぎ目.
— *adj.* kyo⌈odoo no 共同の: a joint statement (*kyoodoo seemee*) 共同声明.

joke *n.* jo⌈oda⌉ñ 冗談; sha⌈re しゃれ; jo⌉oku ジョーク: He often cracks jokes. (*Kare wa yoku joodañ o tobasu.*) 彼はよく冗談を飛ばす.

jolly *adj.* ka⌈ikatsu na 快活な; yo⌈oki na 陽気な: a jolly old man (*yooki na roojiñ*) 陽気な老人.

journal *n.* **1** (magazine) za⌈sshi 雑誌; (newspaper) ni⌈kkañ-shi⌉ñbuñ 日刊新聞: a monthly journal (*gekkañ-zasshi*) 月刊雑誌 / a business journal (*shoogyoo-shiñbuñ*) 商業新聞.
2 (diary) ni⌈sshi 日誌; ni⌈kki 日記: keep a diary (*nikki o tsukeru*) 日記をつける.

journalism *n.* ja⌈anari⌉zumu ジャーナリズム.

journalist *n.* ja⌈anari⌉suto ジャーナリスト; (of a newspaper) shi⌈ñbuñ ki⌉sha 新聞記者; (of a magazine) za⌈sshi ki⌉sha 雑誌記者.

journey *n.* **1** (trip) ryo⌈koo 旅行; ta⌈bi⌉ 旅: He made a journey to China. (*Kare wa Chuugoku e ryokoo shita.*) 彼は中国へ旅行した.
★ 'Trip' and 'travel' are also called '*ryokoo.*'
2 (distance) ryo⌈tee 旅程; ko⌈otee 行程: a day's journey from here (*koko kara ichi-nichi no kootee*) ここから1日の行程.

joy *n.* **1** (feeling) yo⌈rokobi 喜び; u⌈re⌉shisa うれしさ: She was filled with joy at the news. (*Kanojo wa sono shirase ni yorokoñda.*) 彼女はその知らせに喜んだ.
2 (source) yo⌈rokobi no ta⌉ne 喜びの種; u⌈reshi⌉i ko⌈to⌉ うれしいこと: He has tasted the joys and sorrows of life. (*Kare wa jiñsee no yorokobi ya kanashimi o ajiwatte kita.*) 彼は人生の喜びや悲しみを味わってきた.

joyful *adj.* yo⌈rokobashi⌉i 喜ばしい; u⌈reshi⌉i うれしい: joyful news (*ureshii shirase*) うれしい知らせ.

judge *n.* **1** (of a court) sa⌈iba⌉ñkañ 裁判官: The judge sentenced the man to two years in prison. (*Sai-

bañkañ wa sono otoko ni kiñko ni-neñ no kee o iiwatashita.) 裁判官はその男に禁固2年の刑を言い渡した.
2 (umpire) shiˈñpaˈñiñ 審判員: act as judge in a speech contest (*beñ-roñ-taikai no shiñpañiñ o tsu-tomeru*) 弁論大会の審判員を務める.
★ 'Referee' and 'umpire' are also called '*shiñpañ(iñ)*.'
— *vt.* **1** (decide) ... to haˈñdañ suru ...と判断する Ⓘ: I cannot judge which is better. (*Watashi wa dochira ga yoi ka hañdañ dekinai.*) 私はどちらがよいか判断できない.
2 (try) ... o saˈbaˈku ...を裁く Ⓒ; ... ni haˈñketsu o kudasu ...に判決を下す Ⓒ: The court judged him not guilty. (*Hootee wa kare ni muzai no hañketsu o kudashita.*) 法廷は彼に無罪の判決を下した.

judgment *n.* **1** (decision) haˈñdañ 判断; hyoˈoka 評価: make a fair judgment (*koosee na hañdañ o suru*) 公正な判断をする.
2 (ability) haˈñdaˈñryoku 判断力; fuˈñbetsu 分別: a person of judg-ment (*fuñbetsu no aru hito*) 分別のある人.
3 (opinion) iˈkeñ 意見; kaˈñgaˈe 考え: In my judgment, she will make a good president of our company. (*Watashi no kañgae de wa kanojo wa waga-sha no ii shachoo ni naru daroo.*) 私の考えでは彼女は我が社のいい社長になるだろう.
4 (sentence) haˈñketsu 判決: pass judgment on a person (*hito ni hañ-ketsu o kudasu*) 人に判決を下す.

judicial *adj.* shiˈhoo no 司法の; saˈibañ no 裁判の: a judicial deci-sion (*saibañ no hañketsu*) 裁判の判決.

juice *n.* juˈusu ジュース; shiˈru 汁: fruit juice (*kajuu*) 果汁. ★ Japa-nese '*juusu*' usually refers to soft drinks.

July *n.* shiˈchi-gatsuˈ 7月.

jump *vi.* **1** (spring) toˈbu 跳ぶ Ⓒ; toˈbiagaˈru 跳び上がる Ⓒ: He jumped up to catch the ball. (*Kare wa booru o toru tame ni tobi-agatta.*) 彼はボールをとるために跳び上がった.
2 (start) biˈkuˈtto suru びくっとする Ⓘ: When the door banged shut, I jumped. (*Doa ga batañ to shi-matta toki watashi wa bikkutto shita.*) ドアがばたんと閉まったとき私はびくっとした.
3 (rise) kyuˈu ni agaru 急に上がる Ⓒ: Prices have jumped. (*Bukka ga kyuu ni agatta.*) 物価が急に上がった.
— *vt.* ... o toˈbikoeˈru ...を跳び越える Ⓥ: The boy jumped the puddle easily. (*Sono otoko-no-ko wa mizu-tamari o yasuyasu to tobikoeta.*) その男の子は水たまりをやすやすと跳び越えた.
— *n.* choˈoyaku 跳躍; jaˈñpu ジャンプ: the broad [long] jump (*haba-tobi*) 幅跳び / the high jump (*ha-shiri takatobi*) 走り高跳び.

June *n.* roˈku-gatsuˈ 6月.

junior *adj.* **1** (younger) toˈshishita no 年下の: She is three years ju-nior to me. (*Kanojo wa watashi yori sañ-sai toshishita desu.*) 彼女は私より3歳年下です.
2 (lower) shiˈta no 下の; koˈohai no 後輩の: He is junior to me at the office. (*Kare wa kaisha de watashi no koohai desu.*) 彼は会社で私の後輩です.
— *n.* toˈshishita no monoˈ 年下の者; koˈohai 後輩: He is my junior by two years. (*Kare wa watashi yori ni-sai toshishita desu.*) 彼は私より2歳年下です.

jury *n.* baˈishiñ 陪審. ★ In Japan, there is no jury system.

just[1] *adv.* **1** (exactly) choˈodo ちょうど: It's just one o'clock. (*Choodo ichi-ji desu.*) ちょうど1時です.
2 (very recently) taˈtta iˈma たった今: She has just come back. (*Ka-nojo wa tatta ima modotta tokoro desu.*) 彼女はたった今戻ったところです.
3 (only) choˈtto ちょっと; hoˈñ no ほ

んの: Wait just a moment. (*Chotto o-machi kudasai.*) ちょっとお待ちください.

4 (barely) yoʳoyaku ようやく; yaʳtto やっと: He was just in time. (*Kare wa yooyaku maniatta.*) 彼はようやく間に合った.

just[2] *adj.* **1** (fair) koʳosee na 公正な; koʳohee na 公平な: The teacher was just to everyone. (*Señsee wa dare ni mo koohee datta.*) 先生はだれにも公平だった.

2 (reasonable) seʳetoo na 正当な; toʳozeñ na 当然な: a just reward (*seetoo na hooshuu*) 正当な報酬.

justice *n.* **1** (fairness) koʳosee 公正; seˡegi 正義: treat a person with justice (*hito o koosee ni atsukau*) 人を公正に扱う.

2 (judge) saˡibañ 裁判: a court of justice (*saibañsho*) 裁判所.

justification *n.* seʳetooka 正当化; beʳñmee 弁明.

justify *vt.* ... o seʳetooka suru …を正当化する [I]; beʳñmee suru 弁明する [I]: He justified his action. (*Kare wa jibuñ no koodoo o beñmee shita.*) 彼は自分の行動を弁明した.

K

keen *adj.* **1** (of the mind, senses) suʳrudoˡi 鋭い: have a keen intelligence (*surudoi atama o motte iru*) 鋭い頭を持っている / keen eyes 鋭い目.

2 (severe) kiʳbishiˡi 厳しい; haʳgeshiˡi 激しい: a keen, cold winter (*samusa no kibishii fuyu*) 寒さの厳しい冬 / keen competition (*hageshii kyoosoo*) 激しい競争.

3 (sharp) suʳrudoˡi 鋭い: a keen edge (*surudoi ha*) 鋭い刃.

4 (eager) neˡsshiñ na 熱心な: a keen golfer (*nesshiñ na gorufaa*) 熱心なゴルファー / Bill is keen on studying Japanese. (*Biru wa Nihoñgo no beñkyoo ni nesshiñ da.*) ビルは日本語の勉強に熱心だ.

keep *vt.* **1** (have; reserve) ... o moˡtte iru …を持っている [V]; toˡtte oku 取っておく [C]; aʳzukaˡru 預かる [C]: You can keep that book till next week. (*Sono hoñ wa raishuu made motte ite mo ii desu yo.*) その本は来週まで持っていてもいいですよ. / Please keep the change. (*Otsuri wa totte oite kudasai.*) おつりは取っておいてください. / Please keep this baggage until tomorrow. (*Kono nimotsu o ashita made azukatte kudasai.*) この荷物をあしたまで預かってください.

2 (cause to remain) zuʳtto ⟨verb⟩-te [de] oʳku ずっと…て[で]おく [C]: I kept the air-conditioner on all day. (*Kuuraa o ichi-nichi-juu zutto tsukete oita.*) クーラーを1日中ずっとつけておいた. / You mustn't keep your visitor waiting. (*O-kyaku o matasete oite wa ikemaseñ.*) お客を待たせておいてはいけません.

3 (fulfill; guard) ... o maʳmoˡru …を守る [C]: keep a promise [secret] (*yakusoku [himitsu] o mamoru*) 約束[秘密]を守る.

4 (own) ... o moˡtte iru …を持っている [V]; (of an animal) kaˡtte iru 飼っている [V]: He keeps three cars. (*Kare wa kuruma o sañdai motte iru.*) 彼は車を3台持っている. / I keep chickens. (*Watashi wa hiyoko o katte iru.*) 私はひよこを飼っている.

5 (delay) ... o hiʳkitoˡmete oku …を引き止めておく [C]: I won't keep you long. (*Nagaku wa o-hikitome shimaseñ.*) 長くはお引き止めしません.

6 (write) ... o tsuʳkeˡru …をつける [V]: keep a diary (*nikki o tsukeru*) 日記をつける / keep a record of the meeting (*kaigi no kiroku o tsukeru*) 会議の記録をつける.

— vi. **1** (remain) ... maʳmaˡ de iru …ままでいる [V]: He kept awake.

(*Kare wa me o samashita mama de ita.*) 彼は目を覚ましたままでいた. / keep indoors all day (*ichi-nichi-juu ie ni tojikomotta mama de iru*) 1日中家に閉じこもったままでいる.
2 (continue) ⟨verb⟩-tsu[zukeru …続ける [V]: keep crying (*naki-tsuzukeru*) 泣き続ける / It kept raining all day. (*Ichi-nichi-juu ame ga furi-tsuzuita.*) 1日中雨が降り続いた.
3 (last) mo]tsu もつ [C]: The weather will keep till Sunday. (*Kono teñki wa nichiyoobi made motsu deshoo.*) この天気は日曜日までもつでしょう.

kerosene *n.* to[oyu 灯油.

kettle *n.* ya[kañ やかん; yu[wa]kashi 湯沸かし: boil water in a kettle (*yakañ de o-yu o wakasu*) やかんでお湯を沸かす.

key *n.* **1** (to a lock) ka[gi] 鍵: put a key in the lock (*kagi o joo ni sashikomu*) 鍵を錠に差し込む. ★ 'Lock' is also called '*kagi*.'
2 (vital ingredient) ka[gi] 鍵; te[ga]kari 手がかり: This is the key to the problem. (*Kore ga sono moñdai o toku kagi da.*) これがその問題を解く鍵だ.
3 (of a piano, etc.) ki]i キー: the keys of a typewriter (*taipuraitaa no kii*) タイプライターのキー.
— *adj.* (essential) ki[hoñ-teki na 基本的な; ju[uyoo na 重要な: a key color (*kihoñ-shoku*) 基本色 / a key issue (*juuyoo na moñdai*) 重要な問題.

kick *vt.* **1** (with a foot) ... o ke]ru …をける [C]: kick a ball (*booru o keru*) ボールをける.
2 (in sports) bo[oru o ke]tte i[reru ボールをけって入れる [V]: kick a goal (*booru o kette gooru ni ireru*) ボールをけってゴールに入れる.
— *vi.* (... o) ke]ru (…を)ける [C]: The horse kicked at me. (*Sono uma wa watashi o ketta.*) その馬は私をけった.
— *n.* ke]ru ko[to] けること: give a kick at a door (*doa o keru*) ドアをける.

kid *n.* **1** (child) ko[domo 子ども; (young person) wa[kamono 若者.
2 (young goat) ko[ya]gi 子やぎ.
— *vt.* (tease) ... o ka[raka]u …をからかう [C]: He kidded me about my hat. (*Kare wa booshi no koto de watashi o karakatta.*) 彼は帽子のことで私をからかった.
— *vi.* jo[oda]ñ o i[u 冗談を言う [C]: No kidding. (*Joodañ deshoo.*) 冗談でしょう.

kidnap *vt.* ... o yu[ukai suru …を誘拐する [I]: kidnap a child (*kodomo o yuukai suru*) 子どもを誘拐する.

kidnapper *n.* yu[uka]ihañ 誘拐犯.

kill *vt.* **1** (of an animal) ... o ko[rosu …を殺す [C]; (of a plant) ka[rasu 枯らす [C]: Don't kill animals. (*Doobutsu o korosu na.*) 動物を殺すな. / The sudden frost killed the flowers. (*Totsuzeñ no shimo ga hana o karashita.*) 突然の霜が花を枯らした.
2 (in an accident, etc.) ... o shi[boo saseru …を死亡させる [V]: Many passengers were killed in the train crash. (*Ressha no shoototsu de oozee no jookyaku ga shiboo shita.*) 列車の衝突で大勢の乗客が死亡した.
3 (destroy) ... o da[me ni suru …をだめにする [I]; tsu[busu つぶす [C]: His home run killed our hopes of victory. (*Kare no hoomurañ ga wareware no yuushoo no nozomi o tsubushita.*) 彼のホームランがわれわれの優勝の望みをつぶした.
kill time *vi.* ji[kañ o tsubusu 時間をつぶす [C].

killer *n.* sa[tsuji]ñsha 殺人者; ko[roshiya 殺し屋.

kilogram *n.* ki[rogu]ramu キログラム ★ Often shortened to '*kiro*': 250 kilograms of meat (*nihyaku gojuk-kiro no niku*) 250 キロの肉.

kilometer *n.* ki[rome]etoru キロメートル ★ Often shortened to '*kiro*': walk two and a half kilometers (*ni-kiro hañ aruku*) 2 キロ半歩く.

kind[1] *n.* shu]rui 種類; bu]rui 部類:

different kinds of apples (*chigatta shurui no riñgo*) 違った種類のりんご / What kind of tree is this? (*Kore wa nañ to iu shurui no ki desu ka?*) これは何という種類の木ですか.

kind[2] *adj.* shiˈñsetsu na 親切な; yaˈsashii 優しい: Japanese policemen are generally very kind. (*Nihoñ no keesatsukañ wa ippañ ni hijoo ni shiñsetsu desu.*) 日本の警察官は一般に非常に親切です.

be kind enough to do shiˈñsetsu ni mo 〈verb〉 親切にも…: He was kind enough to lend me the money. (*Kare wa shiñsetsu ni mo watashi ni o-kane o kashite kureta.*) 彼は親切にも私にお金を貸してくれた.

kindergarten *n.* yoˈochiˈeñ 幼稚園.

kindly *adv.* **1** (in a kind manner) shiˈñsetsu ni (mo) 親切に(も); yaˈsashiku 優しく: He kindly helped me. (*Kare wa shiñsetsu ni mo watashi o tasukete kureta.*) 彼は親切にも私を助けてくれた.

2 (please) doˈozo どうぞ; doˈo ka どうか: Would you kindly shut the window? (*Doo ka mado o shimete itadakemaseñ ka?*) どうか窓を閉めていただけませんか.

— *adj.* yaˈsashii 優しい; shiˈñsetsu na 親切な: a kindly heart (*yasashii kokoro*) 優しい心.

kindness *n.* **1** (being kind) shiˈñsetsu 親切; yaˈsaˈshisa 優しさ: show kindness to animals (*doobutsu ni yasashiku suru*) 動物に優しくする.

2 (kind action) shiˈñsetsu na koˈoi 親切な行為: I'll never forget your kindness. (*Anata no go-shiñsetsu wa wasuremaseñ.*) あなたのご親切は忘れません.

king *n.* **1** (ruler) oˈo 王; koˈkuoˈo 国王: the King of Sweden (*Suweedeñ kokuoo*) スウェーデン国王.

2 (most important one) ... oˈo ...王: the king of beasts (*hyakujuu no oo*) 百獣の王 / an oil king (*sekiyu-oo*) 石油王.

3 (of cards) kiˈñgu キング: the king of spades (*supeedo no kiñgu*) スペードのキング.

kingdom *n.* **1** (country) oˈokoku 王国: the kingdom of Sweden (*Suweedeñ ookoku*) スウェーデン王国.

2 (of nature) ... ˈkai ...界: the animal [plant] kingdom (*doobutsu-kai* [*shokubutsu-kai*]) 動物界[植物界].

kiss *vt.* ... ni kiˈsu suru ...にキスする ⅠⅠ; seˈppuñ suru 接吻する ⅠⅠ: I kissed my mother on the cheek. (*Watashi wa haha no hoo ni kisu shita.*) 私は母のほおにキスした.

— *n.* kiˈsu キス; kuˈchizuke 口づけ; seˈppuñ 接吻: She gave me a kiss. (*Kanojo wa watashi ni kisu shita.*) 彼女は私にキスした.

kit *n.* yoˈogu hiˈtoˈsoroi 用具ひとそろい; yoˈogubaˈko 用具箱: a first-aid kit (*kyuukyuubako*) 救急箱.

kitchen *n.* daˈidokoro 台所; kiˈtchiñ キッチン: cook in the kitchen (*daidokoro de ryoori suru*) 台所で料理する.

kite *n.* taˈko たこ(凧): fly a kite (*tako o ageru*) たこを揚げる.

knee *n.* hiˈza ひざ: My knees hurt. (*Hiza ga itai.*) ひざが痛い. / She got down on her knees. (*Kanojo wa hizamazuita.*) 彼女はひざまずいた.

kneel *vi.* hiˈzamazuˈku ひざまずく Ⓒ: kneel in prayer (*hizamazuite inoru*) ひざまずいて祈る / I knelt down to pull out a weed. (*Watashi wa zassoo o nuku tame ni hizamazuita.*) 私は雑草を抜くためにひざまずいた.

knife *n.* naˈifu ナイフ; koˈgataˈna 小刀: a kitchen knife (*hoochoo*) 包丁 / He cut the toast with his knife. (*Kare wa toosuto o naifu de kitta.*) 彼はトーストをナイフで切った.

knit *vt.* ... o aˈmu ...を編む Ⓒ: knit a sweater (*seetaa o amu*) セーターを編む.

knob *n.* toˈtte 取っ手; tsuˈmami つまみ: turn the knob of a door (*doa no totte o mawasu*) ドアの取っ手を回す.

knock *vi.* **1** (tap) (... o) taˈtaˈku (...を)たたく Ⓒ; noˈkku suru ノックする

[I]: The teacher knocked on her desk. (*Sensee wa tsukue no ue o tataita.*) 先生は机の上をたたいた. / You must knock before entering the room. (*Heya ni hairu mae ni wa nokku o shinakereba narimaseñ.*) 部屋に入る前にはノックをしなければなりません.

2 (collide) (... ni) tsu⌈kiata⌉ru (...に) 突き当たる [C]; bu⌈tsukaru ぶつかる [C]: Someone knocked into me. (*Dareka ga watashi ni butsukatta.*) だれかが私にぶつかった.

— *vt.* 1 (hit hard) ... o ta⌈ta⌉ku ... をたたく [C]; u⌉tsu 打つ [C]; na⌈gu⌉ru 殴る [C]: knock nails into a board (*ita ni kugi o uchikomu*) 板にくぎを打ち込む / He knocked me on the head. (*Kare wa watashi no atama o nagutta.*) 彼は私の頭を殴った.

2 (hit accidentally) ... ni a⌈taru ...に当たる [C]: He knocked the vase and it fell off the table. (*Kare ga atatte kabiñ ga teeburu kara ochita.*) 彼が当たって花瓶がテーブルから落ちた.

3 (hit intentionally) ... ni bu⌈tsukeru ...にぶつける [V]: The child knocked his head against wall. (*Sono ko wa kabe ni atama o butsuketa.*) その子は壁に頭をぶつけた.

— *n.* ta⌈ta⌉ku ko⌈to⌉ たたくこと; u⌉tsu ko⌈to⌉ 打つこと; no⌉kku ノック: There was a knock on the door. (*Doa o nokku suru oto ga shita.*) ドアをノックする音がした.

knot ***n.* 1** (fastening) mu⌈subime 結び目: make a knot (*musubime o tsukuru*) 結び目を作る.

2 (group) mu⌈re⌉ 群れ; a⌈tsumari 集まり: There were knots of people here and there. (*Achi kochi ni hito no mure ga dekite ita.*) あちこちに人の群れができていた.

3 (in a tree) ko⌈bu⌉ こぶ; fu⌈shi⌉ 節.

4 (measure of speed) no⌉tto ノット: a ship going 30 knots (*sañjuu-notto no fune*) 30ノットの船.

— *vt.* ... o mu⌈subu ...を結ぶ [C]: knot one's tie (*nekutai o musubu*) ネクタイを結ぶ.

know ***vt.* 1** (have knowledge of) ... o shi⌈tte iru ...を知っている [V]: I know that he is honest. (*Kare ga shoojiki na koto wa shitte imasu.*) 彼が正直なことは知っています. / Do you know his name? (*Kare no namae o shitte imasu ka?*) 彼の名前を知っていますか.

2 (recognize) ... to wa⌈ka⌉ru ...とわかる [C]: I knew him at once. (*Sugu kare da to wakatta.*) すぐ彼だとわかった. / You will know my house by the red roof. (*Watashi no uchi wa yane ga akai no de wakarimasu.*) 私の家は屋根が赤いのでわかります.

3 (be acquainted with) ... to shi⌈riai da ...と知り合いだ: I have known him since he was a child. (*Kare to wa kodomo no toki kara no shiriai desu.*) 彼とは子どもの時からの知り合いです.

4 (experience) ... o ke⌈ekeñ suru ...を経験する [I]: He has known both poverty and wealth. (*Kare wa biñboo mo kanemochi mo keekeñ shita.*) 彼は貧乏も金持ちも経験した.

— *vi.* shi⌈tte iru 知っている [V]; wa⌈ka⌉tte iru わかっている [V]: Most people know about the accident. (*Taitee no hito wa sono jiko no koto o shitte imasu.*) たいていの人はその事故のことを知っています.

let ... know *vt.* ... ni o⌈shieru ...に教える [V]: Please let me know when we reach the station. (*Sono eki ni tsuitara oshiete kudasai.*) その駅に着いたら教えてください.

knowledge ***n.* 1** (of facts, information, etc.) chi⌉shiki 知識; shi⌈tte iru koto⌉ 知っていること: My knowledge of Japanese grammar is poor. (*Watashi no Nihoñgo no buñpoo no chishiki wa hiñjaku desu.*) 私の日本語の文法の知識は貧弱です.

2 (learning) ga⌈ku⌉moñ 学問: all branches of knowledge (*gakumoñ no arayuru buñya*) 学問のあらゆる分野.

known *adj.* shi⌈rarete iru 知られている: the oldest known church (*shi-*

rarete iru saiko no kyookai) 知られている最古の教会 / He is known to the public. (*Kare wa sekeñ ni na o shirarete iru.*) 彼は世間に名を知られている.

Korea *n.* Kaˡñkoku 韓国; (historical name) Choˢoseˡñ 朝鮮: the Republic of Korea [South Korea] (*Daikañmiñkoku*) 大韓民国 / the Democratic People's Republic of Korea [North Korea] (*Chooseñ Miñshushugi Jiñmiñ Kyoowakoku*) 朝鮮民主主義人民共和国.

Korean *adj.* Kaˡñkoku no 韓国の; Choˢoseˡñ no 朝鮮の: Korean songs (*Kañkoku [Chooseñ] no uta*) 韓国[朝鮮]の歌.
— *n.* (people) Kaˢñkokuˡjiñ 韓国人; Choˢoseñjiˡn 朝鮮人; (language) Choˢoseñgo 朝鮮語; Kaˢñkokugo 韓国語.

L

label *n.* haˢrigami はり紙; raˡberu ラベル: put a label on one's baggage (*nimotsu ni raberu o tsukeru*) 荷物にラベルをつける.
— *vt.* ... ni haˢrigami o suru ...にはり紙をする [I]; raˡberu o haˢru ラベルをはる [C]: label a box (*hako ni raberu o haru*) 箱にラベルをはる.

labor *n.* **1** (work) roˢodoo 労働; shiˢgoto 仕事; hoˢneori 骨折り: manual labor (*nikutai-roodoo*) 肉体労働 / a labor of love (*suki de suru shigoto*) 好きでする仕事.
2 (workers) roˢodoˡosha 労働者; roˢodookaˡikyuu 労働階級: labor and management (*roodoosha to kee-eesha*) 労働者と経営者.
3 (giving birth) buˢñbeñ 分娩; shuˢssañ 出産: go into labor (*jiñtsuu ga hajimaru*) 陣痛が始まる.
— *vi.* haˢtaraku 働く [C]; hoˢneoˡru 骨折る [C]; doˡryoku suru 努力する [I]: He labored from dawn to dusk. (*Kare wa yoake kara kuraku naru made hataraita.*) 彼は夜明けから暗くなるまで働いた.

laboratory *n.* jiˢkkeˡñshitsu 実験室; keˢñkyuujo 研究所: a chemical laboratory (*kagaku jikkeñshitsu*) 化学実験室.

lace *n.* hiˡmo ひも; reˡesu レース: shoe laces (*kutsu himo*) 靴ひも / a lace curtain (*reesu no kaateñ*) レースのカーテン.
— *vt.* ... no hiˢmo o shimeˡru ...のひもを締める [V]: lace up one's shoes (*kutsu no himo o shimeru*) 靴のひもを締める.

lack *n.* keˢtsuboo 欠乏; fuˢsoku 不足 ★ In a compound '*fusoku*' becomes '*-busoku*': lack of sleep (*suimiñ-busoku*) 睡眠不足 / The plants died for lack of water. (*Mizu-busoku de shokubutsu ga karete shimatta.*) 水不足で植物が枯れてしまった.
— *vt.* ... o kaˢku ...を欠く [C]; ... ga fuˢsoku suru ...が不足する [I]: He lacks courage. (*Kare wa yuuki o kaite iru.*) 彼は勇気を欠いている.

lacking *adj.* fuˢsoku shite iru 不足している; kaˢkete iru 欠けている: Money is lacking for the trip. (*Ryokoo suru ni wa o-kane ga fusoku shite iru.*) 旅行するにはお金が不足している.

lacquer *n.* raˡkkaa ラッカー; uˢrushi 漆: lacquer ware (*shikki*) 漆器.

ladder *n.* haˢshigo はしご: climb up a ladder (*hashigo o noboru*) はしごを上る / set up a ladder against a tree (*ki ni hashigo o kakeru*) 木にはしごをかける.

lady *n.* **1** (woman of high social standing) kiˢfuˡjiñ 貴婦人.
2 (any woman) joˢsee 女性; fuˡjiñ 婦人: I want to buy something for a lady. (*Fujiñ no mono o kaitai no*

desu ga.) 婦人の物を買いたいのですが. / ladies' shoes (*fujiñgutsu*) 婦人靴.

lake *n.* mi⌈zuu⌉mi 湖: row a boat on the lake (*mizuumi de booto o kogu*) 湖でボートをこぐ / Lake Towada (*Towada-ko*) 十和田湖.

lamb *n.* (animal) ko⌈hi⌉tsuji 子羊; (meat) ko⌈hi⌉tsuji no ni⌈ku⌉ 子羊の肉.

lamp *n.* **1** (light) a⌈kari 明かり; de⌈ñki-suta⌉ñdo 電気スタンド: turn on [off] a lamp (*akari o tsukeru* [*kesu*]) 明かりをつける[消す] / a desk lamp (*takujoo sutañdo*) 卓上スタンド.
2 (glass-covered light) ra⌉ñpu ランプ: an oil lamp (*sekiyu rañpu*) 石油ランプ.

land *n.* **1** (ground) to⌈chi 土地; ji⌉meñ 地面: rich land (*koeta tochi*) 肥えた土地.
2 (earth's surface) ri⌈ku 陸; ri⌈kuchi 陸地: We traveled over land and sea. (*Watashi-tachi wa riku ya umi o tabi shita.*) 私たちは陸や海を旅した.
3 (country) ku⌈ni 国; ko⌉kudo 国土: I visited many lands. (*Watashi wa ooku no kuni o tazuneta.*) 私は多くの国を訪ねた.
— *vi.* **1** (from the sea) (... ni) jo⌈oriku suru (…に)上陸する Ⅰ: The party landed at Yokohama. (*Ikkoo wa Yokohama ni jooriku shita.*) 一行は横浜に上陸した.
2 (of an airplane) (... ni) cha⌈kuriku suru (…に)着陸する Ⅰ: The plane landed at Haneda. (*Hikooki wa Haneda ni chakuriku shita.*) 飛行機は羽田に着陸した.
— *vt.* **1** (of people) ... o jo⌈oriku saseru …を上陸させる Ⅴ.
2 (of an airplane) ... o cha⌈kuriku saseru …を着陸させる Ⅴ.

landing *n.* **1** (from the sea) jo⌈oriku 上陸; (of an airplane) cha⌈kuriku 着陸: landing procedures (*jooriku tetsuzuki*) 上陸手続 / a forced landing (*fujichaku*) 不時着.
2 (of stairs) o⌈doriba 踊り場.

landmark *n.* me⌈ji⌉rushi 目印: What landmarks are on the way? (*Tochuu ni doñna mejirushi ga arimasu ka?*) 途中にどんな目印がありますか.

landscape *n.* **1** (scenery) ke⌉shiki 景色; fu⌉ukee 風景: survey the landscape (*keshiki o miwatasu*) 景色を見渡す.
2 (painting) fu⌈ukeega 風景画.

lane *n.* **1** (narrow road) ko⌈michi 小道; ro⌉ji 路地: a blind lane (*fukurokooji*) 袋小路.
2 (division of a road) sha⌈señ 車線; re⌉eñ レーン: change lanes (*shaseñ o heñkoo suru*) 車線を変更する.
3 (regular course) ko⌉oro 航路: an air lane (*kookuuro*) 航空路 / a sea lane (*kooro*) 航路.

language *n.* **1** (speech) ge⌉ñgo 言語; ko⌈toba⌉ 言葉: spoken language (*hanashi-kotoba*) 話し言葉 / written language (*kaki-kotoba*) 書き言葉.
2 (tongue) ko⌈kugo 国語; -go 語: the Japanese language (*Nihoñgo*) 日本語 / a foreign language (*gaikokugo*) 外国語.

lantern *n.* te⌈sage ra⌉ñpu 手提げランプ: a Japanese lantern (*choochiñ*) ちょうちん.

lap *n.* hi⌈za ひざ: The child sat on his mother's lap. (*Sono ko wa hahaoya no hiza no ue ni suwatta.*) その子は母親のひざの上に座った.

large *adj.* **1** (big) o⌈oki⌉i 大きい; o⌉oki-na 大きな: a large dog (*ookii inu*) 大きい犬 / He lives in a large house. (*Kare wa ooki-na ie ni suñde iru.*) 彼は大きな家に住んでいる.
2 (of quantity) ta⌈ryoo no 多量の; (of numbers) ta⌈su⌉u no 多数の: a large income (*tagaku no shuunyuu*) 多額の収入 / a large population (*tasuu no jiñkoo*) 多数の人口.

last[1] *adj.* **1** (final) sa⌉igo no 最後の: the last Sunday of June (*roku-gatsu saigo no nichiyoobi*) 6月最後の日曜日 / This is his last painting. (*Kore wa kare no saigo no e desu.*) これは彼の最後の絵です.
2 (most recent) ko⌈no ma⌉e no この前の; señ- 先; saku- 昨: I met him

on Monday last. (*Kare to wa kono mae no getsuyoobi ni aimashita.*) 彼とはこの前の月曜日に会いました. / last week (*señshuu*) 先週 / last month (*señgetsu*) 先月 / last year (*sakuneñ*) 昨年 / last night (*sakuya*) 昨夜.

— *adv.* sa⌉igo ni 最後に: He spoke last at the meeting. (*Kare wa sono kai de saigo ni hatsugeñ shita.*) 彼はその会で最後に発言した.

— *n.* (people) sa⌉igo no hi⌈to⌉ 最後の人; (thing) sa⌉igo no mo⌈no⌉ 最後のもの: I ate the last of the cake. (*Keeki no saigo wa watashi ga tabemashita.*) ケーキの最後は私が食べました.

last[2] *vi.* **1** (continue) tsu⌈zuku 続く [C]: The rain lasted for a week. (*Ame wa is-shuukañ tsuzuita.*) 雨は1週間続いた.

2 (remain) na⌈gamo⌉chi suru 長持ちする [I]; mo⌉tsu もつ [C]: Cheap shoes won't last long. (*Yasumono no kutsu wa nagaku motanai.*) 安物の靴は長くもたない.

lasting *adj.* e⌈ezoku suru 永続する; e⌈ekyuu no 永久の: a lasting peace (*eekyuu no heewa*) 永久の平和.

latch *n.* ka⌈kegane 掛け金: set the latch (*kakegane o kakeru*) 掛け金をかける.

late *adj.* **1** (after the proper time) o⌈kureta 遅れた; o⌈kurete iru 遅れている: He was late for school. (*Kare wa gakkoo ni okureta.*) 彼は学校に遅れた. / I'm sorry I'm late. (*Okurete sumimaseñ.*) 遅れてすみません.

2 (not early) o⌈soi 遅い: It was late when I went to bed. (*Neta no wa osokatta.*) 寝たのは遅かった.

3 (toward the end) ma⌉kki no 末期の; ko⌉oki no 後期の: It happened in the late sixteenth century. (*Sore wa juuroku seeki no kooki ni okotta.*) それは16世紀の後期に起こった.

4 (recently dead) sa⌈ikiñ nakunatta 最近亡くなった; ko ... 故…: I knew his late father. (*Watashi wa kare no saikiñ nakunatta chichioya o shitte imashita.*) 私は彼の最近亡くなった父親を知っていました. / the late Mr. Yamada (*ko Yamada-shi*) 故山田氏.

— *adv.* **1** (not in time) o⌈kurete 遅れて: The train arrived one hour late. (*Ressha wa ichi-jikañ okurete toochaku shita.*) 列車は1時間遅れて到着した.

2 (not early) o⌈soku 遅く: stay in bed late (*osoku made beddo ni iru*) 遅くまでベッドにいる.

lately *adv.* sa⌈ikiñ 最近; chi⌈ka⌉goro 近ごろ: I haven't seen him lately. (*Watashi wa saikiñ kare ni atte inai.*) 私は最近彼に会っていない. / What books have you read lately? (*Chikagoro doñna hoñ o yomimashita ka?*) 近ごろどんな本を読みましたか.

later *adv.* a⌉to de 後で: I'll call again later. (*Mata ato de deñwa shimasu.*) また後で電話します. / See you later! (*De wa mata.*) ではまた.

— *adj.* mo⌉tto o⌈soi もっと遅い; mo⌉tto ato no もっと後の: I'll take a later train. (*Motto ato no ressha ni norimasu.*) もっと後の列車に乗ります.

latest *adj.* sa⌈ishiñ no 最新の; sa⌈ikiñ no 最近の: Have you heard the latest news? (*Saishiñ no nyuusu o kikimashita ka?*) 最新のニュースを聞きましたか.

latter *adj.* **1** (nearer the end) a⌉to no hoo no 後のほうの; ko⌈ohañ no 後半の: the latter half of the year (*ichi-neñ no koohañ*) 1年の後半.

2 (the second of two) ko⌉osha no 後者の: I prefer the latter picture to the former. (*Watashi wa zeñsha no e yori koosha no hoo ga suki da.*) 私は前者の絵より後者のほうが好きだ.

laugh *vi.* **1** (express amusement) wa⌈rau 笑う [C]: Everyone laughed at his joke. (*Miñna wa kare no jooku ni waratta.*) みんなは彼のジョークに笑った.

2 (scorn) (... o) wa⌈rau (…を)笑う

Ⓒ: He laughed at my mistake. (*Kare wa watashi no machigai o waratta.*) 彼は私の間違いを笑った.
— *n.* wa⌈rai 笑い: He answered with a laugh. (*Kare wa warai-nagara kotaeta.*) 彼は笑いながら答えた.

laughter *n.* wa⌈rai 笑い; wa⌈rai-go⌉e 笑い声: burst into laughter (*fukidasu*) 吹き出す.

launch *vt.* **1** (send off) ... o ha⌈s-sha suru ...を発射する Ⓘ: launch a rocket (*roketto o hassha suru*) ロケットを発射する.
2 (set afloat) ... o shi⌈ñsui saseru ...を進水させる Ⓥ: A new ship was launched. (*Atarashii fune ga shiñ-sui shita.*) 新しい船が進水した.
3 (begin) ... o ha⌈jimeru ...を始める Ⓥ: launch an election campaign (*señkyo-uñdoo o hajimeru*) 選挙運動を始める.

laundry *n.* **1** (clothes, etc.) se⌈ñta-kumono 洗濯物: hang the laundry out to dry (*señtakumono o soto ni hosu*) 洗濯物を外に干す.
2 (place) se⌈ñtakuya 洗濯屋; ku-⌈riiniñgu⌉teñ クリーニング店: send a shirt to the laundry (*waishatsu o kuriiniñguteñ ni dasu*) ワイシャツをクリーニング店に出す.

lavatory *n.* se⌈ñmeñjo 洗面所; to⌉-ire トイレ: I'd like to use the lavatory. (*Toire o o-kari shitai no desu ga.*) トイレをお借りしたいのですが.

lavish *adj.* mo⌈no-o⌉shimi shinai 物惜しみしない; ki⌈mae no yo⌉i 気前のよい: a lavish uncle (*kimae no yoi oji*) 気前のよいおじ.

law *n.* ho⌈o 法; ho⌈oritsu 法律: keep [break] the law (*hoo o mamoru* [*okasu*]) 法を守る[犯す] / It is against the law. (*Sore wa hooritsu ihañ desu.*) それは法律違反です.

lawful *adj.* go⌈ohoo-teki na 合法的な; se⌈etoo na 正当な: a lawful transaction (*goohoo-teki na tori-hiki*) 合法的な取り引き.

lawn *n.* shi⌈bafu 芝生; shi⌈ba 芝: mow the lawn (*shiba o karu*) 芝を刈る.

lawyer *n.* be⌈ñgo⌉shi 弁護士: consult a lawyer (*beñgoshi ni soodañ suru*) 弁護士に相談する.

lay *vt.* **1** (put down) ... o o⌈ku ...を置く Ⓒ: He laid his coat on the chair. (*Kare wa kooto o isu no ue ni oita.*) 彼はコートをいすの上に置いた.
2 (place in a lying position) ... o yo⌈ko ni suru ...を横にする Ⓘ; ne⌈ka-seru 寝かせる Ⓥ: She laid her baby on the bed. (*Kanojo wa akañboo o beddo ni nekaseta.*) 彼女は赤ん坊をベッドに寝かせた.
3 (set in place) ... o shi⌈ku ...を敷く Ⓒ: lay a carpet in the room (*heya ni juutañ o shiku*) 部屋にじゅうたんを敷く.
4 (prepare) ... o yo⌉oi suru ...を用意する Ⓘ: lay the table for dinner (*yuuhañ no shokutaku o yooi suru*) 夕飯の食卓を用意する.
5 (produce) ... o u⌈mu ...を産む Ⓒ: This hen lays an egg every day. (*Kono tori wa mainichi tamago o umu.*) この鶏は毎日卵を産む.

layer *n.* so⌉o 層: a layer of clay (*neñdo no soo*) 粘土の層.

lazy *adj.* ta⌉ida na 怠惰な; na⌈ma⌉-kete iru 怠けている: a lazy student (*taida na gakusee*) 怠惰な学生 / He is lazy. (*Kare wa namakemono da.*) 彼は怠け者だ.

lead[1] *vt.* **1** (guide) ... o mi⌈chibi⌉ku ...を導く Ⓒ; a⌈ñna⌉i suru 案内する Ⓘ: He led us to the hotel. (*Kare wa watashi-tachi o hoteru made añnai shite kureta.*) 彼は私たちをホテルまで案内してくれた.
2 (be first) ... no se⌈ñtoo ni ta⌉tsu ...の先頭に立つ Ⓒ: A band led the parade. (*Gakutai ga kooshiñ no señtoo ni tatta.*) 楽隊が行進の先頭に立った.
3 (direct) ... o shi⌈ki⌉ suru ...を指揮する Ⓘ; hi⌈kii⌉ru 率いる Ⓥ: lead a party (*too o hikiiru*) 党を率いる.
— *vi.* **1** (act as a guide) a⌈ñna⌉i suru 案内する Ⓘ: I'll lead. Please follow me. (*Watashi ga añnai shi-masu. Tsuite kite kudasai.*) 私が案

内します. ついて来てください.

2 (be ahead) se⌈ñtoo ni ta⌉tsu 先頭に立つ Ⓒ: My horse is leading. (*Watashi no uma ga señtoo o hashitte iru.*) 私の馬が先頭を走っている.

3 (of a road) (... ni) tsu⌈ujite iru (...に)通じている Ⓥ: This street leads to the station. (*Kono michi wa eki ni tsuujite imasu.*) この道は駅に通じています.

4 (direct) (... o) shi⌈doo suru (...を)指導する Ⓘ: He led in the campaign. (*Kare ga sono uñdoo o shidoo shita.*) 彼がその運動を指導した.

— *n.* **1** (front position) se⌈ñtoo 先頭; shu⌉i 首位: He is in the lead. (*Kare wa shui ni iru.*) 彼は首位にいる.

2 (advance distance) yu⌉ui 優位; ri⌉ido リード: Our team has a lead of five points. (*Wareware no chiimu wa go-teñ riido shite iru.*) われわれのチームは5点リードしている.

3 (of a play) shu⌈yaku 主役: play the lead in the play (*sono geki de shuyaku o eñjiru*) その劇で主役を演じる.

lead[2] *n.* (metal) na⌈mari 鉛.

leader *n.* **1** (guiding head) shi⌈do⌉osha 指導者; ri⌉idaa リーダー: He acted as our leader. (*Kare wa watashi-tachi no riidaa o tsutometa.*) 彼は私たちのリーダーを務めた.

2 (in a race, competition, etc.) se⌈ñtoo ni ta⌉tsu hi⌈to⌉ 先頭に立つ人; shu⌉i no mo⌈no⌉ 首位の者.

3 (concertmaster) shi⌈ki⌉sha 指揮者.

leadership *n.* shi⌈do⌉okeñ 指導権; shi⌈do⌉oryoku 指導力: seize the leadership (*shidookeñ o nigiru*) 指導権を握る / exercise leadership (*shidooryoku o hakki suru*) 指導力を発揮する.

leading *adj.* **1** (chief) o⌉mo-na 主な; shu⌈yoo na 主要な; i⌈chiryuu no 一流の: the leading countries of Europe (*Yooroppa no ichiryuu-koku*) ヨーロッパの一流国.

2 (important) shu⌈yoo na 主要な: play the leading role (*shuyoo na yakuwari o hatasu*) 主要な役割を果たす.

leaf *n.* **1** (of a plant) ha 葉: sweep up dead leaves (*kareha o hakiatsumeru*) 枯れ葉を掃き集める.

2 (of a book) i⌈chi⌉-mai 1枚; i⌈chi⌉-yoo 1葉: tear a leaf out of a notebook (*nooto kara ichi-mai yabuku*) ノートから1枚破く.

leaflet *n.* chi⌈rashi ちらし; ri⌈ifure⌉tto リーフレット: hand out leaflets (*chirashi o kubaru*) ちらしを配る.

league *n.* do⌈omee 同盟; re⌈ñmee 連盟; ri⌉igu リーグ: join a league (*reñmee ni kanyuu suru*) 連盟に加入する / a league match (*riiguseñ*) リーグ戦.

leak *n.* **1** (hole) mo⌈re⌉guchi 漏れ口; mo⌈reana 漏れ穴: stop a leak (*moreguchi o fusagu*) 漏れ口をふさぐ.

2 (leakage) mo⌈re⌉ 漏れ: a gas leak (*gasu-more*) ガス漏れ.

— *vi.* mo⌉ru 漏る Ⓒ; mo⌈re⌉ru 漏れる Ⓥ: This bucket leaks. (*Kono baketsu wa moru.*) このバケツは漏る. / Gas is leaking from this pipe. (*Kono kañ kara gasu ga morete iru.*) この管からガスが漏れている.

— *vt.* ... o mo⌈ra⌉su ...を漏らす Ⓒ: This boiler leaks water. (*Kono boiraa wa mizu ga moreru.*) このボイラーは水が漏れる. / leak a secret (*himitsu o morasu*) 秘密を漏らす.

lean[1] *vi.* **1** (bend) ka⌈tamu⌉ku 傾く Ⓒ; mi o no⌈rida⌉su 身を乗り出す Ⓒ: The fence leans so much it might fall over. (*Hee ga katamuite taore-soo da.*) 塀が傾いて倒れそうだ. / lean out of the window (*mado kara mi o noridasu*) 窓から身を乗り出す.

2 (rest) (... ni) yo⌈rikaka⌉ru (...に)寄りかかる Ⓒ: lean against a tree (*ki ni yorikakaru*) 木に寄りかかる.

— *vt.* **1** (bend) ... o ka⌈tamuke⌉ru ...を傾ける Ⓥ: lean one's head forward (*kubi o mae ni katamukeru*) 首を前に傾ける.

2 (rest) ... o (... ni) ta⌈tekakeru ...を(...に)立てかける Ⓥ: I leaned my

l

umbrella against the wall. (*Watashi wa kasa o kabe ni tatekaketa.*) 私は傘を壁に立てかけた.

lean[2] *adj.* **1** (thin) ya⌈seta やせた; ya⌈sete iru やせている: a lean horse (*yaseta uma*) やせた馬.

2 (without fat) shi⌈boo no na⌉i 脂肪のない; a⌈kami no 赤身の: lean meat (*akami no niku*) 赤身の肉.

leap *vi.* ha⌈ne⌉ru 跳ねる [V]; to⌈bu 跳ぶ [C]: leap up (*tobiagaru*) 跳び上がる / leap down (*tobioriru*) 跳び降りる / The dog leaped over the fence. (*Sono inu wa hee o tobikoeta.*) その犬は塀を跳び越えた.

learn *vt.* **1** (gain knowledge) ... o ma⌈nabu …を学ぶ [C]; shu⌈utoku suru 習得する [I]: She is learning flower arrangement. (*Kanojo wa ikebana o naratte imasu.*) 彼女は生け花を習っています.

2 (get to know) ... o shi⌈ru …を知る [C]; ki⌈ku 聞く [C]: I've just learned that he is sick. (*Kare ga byooki da to tatta ima shitta.*) 彼が病気だとたった今知った.

3 (memorize) ... o o⌈boe⌉ru …を覚える [V]: learn thirty words a day (*ichi-nichi ni sañjuu-go zutsu oboeru*) 1日に30語ずつ覚える.

— *vi.* ma⌈nabu 学ぶ [C]; na⌈ra⌉u 習う [C]; o⌈boe⌉ru 覚える [V]: Children learn quickly. (*Kodomo wa oboeru no ga hayai.*) 子どもは覚えるのが早い.

learned *adj.* ga⌈ku⌉moñ no aru 学問のある: a learned person (*gakusha*) 学者.

learner *n.* ga⌈kushu⌉usha 学習者; sho⌈shi⌉ñsha 初心者: a learner's dictionary (*gakushuu-jiteñ*) 学習辞典.

learning *n.* **1** (getting knowledge) ma⌈nabu koto⌉ 学ぶこと; ga⌈kushuu 学習: the learning of the Japanese language (*Nihoñgo no gakushuu*) 日本語の学習.

2 (knowledge) ga⌈ku⌉moñ 学問; ga⌈kushiki 学識: a person of learning (*gakumoñ no aru hito*) 学問のある人.

least *adj.* mo⌈tto⌉mo su⌈kuna⌉i もっとも少ない: the least amount (*saishooryoo*) 最少量.

not the least *adv.* su⌈koshi mo ... nai 少しも…ない: I haven't the least interest in the matter. (*Sono keñ ni tsuite wa sukoshi mo kañshiñ ga arimaseñ.*) その件については少しも関心がありません.

— *adv.* mo⌈tto⌉mo su⌈ku⌉naku もっとも少なく: the least expensive method (*mottomo hiyoo no kakaranai hoohoo*) もっとも費用のかからない方法.

leather *n.* ka⌈wa⌉ 革: leather gloves (*kawa no tebukuro*) 革の手袋.

leave[1] *vt.* **1** (go away) ... o sa⌉ru …を去る [C]; de⌉ru 出る [V]: He leaves the house at seven. (*Kare wa shichi-ji ni ie o demasu.*) 彼は7時に家を出ます.

2 (stop being in) ... o ya⌈meru …をやめる [V]: leave the tennis club (*tenisu kurabu o yameru*) テニスクラブをやめる.

3 (go without taking) ... o o⌈kiwasure⌉ru …を置き忘れる [V]: I left my umbrella in a taxi. (*Watashi wa kasa o takushii ni okiwasureta.*) 私は傘をタクシーに置き忘れた.

4 (trust) ... o (... ni) ma⌈kase⌉ru …を(…に)任せる [V]: I'll leave the decision with you. (*Kettee wa anata ni makasemasu.*) 決定はあなたに任せます.

— *vi.* ta⌉tsu 発つ [C]; de⌉ru 出る [V]: I am leaving tomorrow morning. (*Watashi wa ashita no asa tachimasu.*) 私はあしたの朝発ちます. / Will this flight leave on time? (*Kono biñ wa yotee doori demasu ka?*) この便は予定どおり出ますか.

leave[2] *n.* **1** (permission) kyo⌉ka 許可: May I have your leave to go? (*Itte mo yoroshii desu ka?*) 行ってもよろしいですか.

2 (holiday) kyu⌈uka 休暇: take a month's leave (*ik-kagetsu no kyuuka o toru*) 1か月の休暇を取る.

lecture *n.* ko⌉ogi 講義; ko⌈oeñ 講

演: give a lecture on literature (*buñgaku no koogi o suru*) 文学の講義をする.

— *vi.* ko˥ogi [ko˥oeñ] suru 講義[講演]する ①: He lectured on Japanese arts. (*Kare wa Nihoñ no bijutsu ni tsuite kooeñ shita.*) 彼は日本の美術について講演した.

left *adj.* hi˥dari no 左の: He writes with his left hand. (*Kare wa hidarite de kaku.*) 彼は左手で書く.

— *adv.* hi˥dari ni 左に: Turn left at the corner. (*Kado de hidari ni magari nasai.*) 角で左に曲がりなさい.

— *n.* **1** (left side) hi˥dari 左; hi˥darigawa 左側: He sat on her left. (*Kare wa kanojo no hidari ni suwatta.*) 彼は彼女の左に座った.

2 (political party) sa˥yoku 左翼; sa˥ha 左派.

left-handed *adj.* hi˥dari˥kiki no 左利きの: left-handed scissors (*hidarikiki-yoo no hasami*) 左利き用のはさみ.

leftist *n.* sa˥yoku [sa˥ha] no hi˥to˥ 左翼[左派]の人; kyu˥ushiñha no hito˥ 急進派の人.

— *adj.* sa˥yoku [sa˥ha] no 左翼[左派]の; kyu˥ushiñ-teki na 急進的な.

leg *n.* **1** (of an animal) a˥shi˥ 脚 [足]: She has nice legs. (*Kanojo wa kiree na ashi o shite iru.*) 彼女はきれいな脚をしている. ★ In Japanese, both 'leg' and 'foot' are called '*ashi*' あし, but written in different kanji: 'leg' 脚, and 'foot' 足.

2 (of a chair, etc.) a˥shi˥ 脚: One of the legs of the chair is broken. (*Isu no ashi ga ip-poñ orete iru.*) いすの脚が1本折れている.

legal *adj.* **1** (allowed by law) go˥ohoo-teki na 合法的な: a legal act (*goohoo-teki na kooi*) 合法的な行為.

2 (based on law) ho˥otee no 法定の: the legal interest (*hootee rishi*) 法定利子.

legend *n.* de˥ñsetsu 伝説: The story is based on a Japanese legend. (*Sono hanashi wa Nihoñ no deñsetsu ni motozuite imasu.*) その話は日本の伝説に基づいています.

legislation *n.* **1** (law) ho˥oritsu 法律; ho˥oree 法令.

2 (act) ho˥oritsu seetee 法律制定; ri˥ppoo 立法: the power of legislation (*rippookeñ*) 立法権.

legislative *adj.* ri˥ppoo no 立法の: legislative procedure (*rippoo tetsuzuki*) 立法手続き.

legislature *n.* ri˥ppo˥ofu 立法府; ri˥ppoo ki˥kañ 立法機関.

legitimate *adj.* go˥ohoo no 合法の; se˥etoo na 正当な: a legitimate claim (*seetoo na yookyuu*) 正当な要求.

leisure *n.* hi˥ma 暇; yo˥ka 余暇; re˥jaa レジャー: I have no leisure for reading. (*Watashi wa yukkuri hoñ o yomu hima ga nai.*) 私はゆっくり本を読む暇がない. ★ In Japanese, '*rejaa*' is usually associated with 'recreation.'

lemon *n.* re˥moñ レモン: squeeze a lemon (*remoñ o shiboru*) レモンを搾る / tea with lemon (*remoñ tii*) レモンティー.

lend *vt.* ... o ka˥su ...を貸す Ⓒ: Will you lend me your umbrella? (*Anata no kasa o kashite moraemasu ka?*) あなたの傘を貸してもらえますか. / I asked him to lend me some money. (*Watashi wa kare ni o-kane o sukoshi kashite kureru yoo ni tanoñda.*) 私は彼にお金を少し貸してくれるように頼んだ.

length *n.* **1** (of a thing) na˥gasa 長さ: measure the length of curtains (*kaateñ no nagasa o hakaru*) カーテンの長さを測る.

2 (of time) na˥gasa 長さ; ki˥ka˥ñ 期間: the length of a vacation (*kyuuka no nagasa*) 休暇の長さ / the intended length of stay (*yotee taizai kikañ*) 予定滞在期間.

lengthen *vt.* ... o na˥gaku suru ...を長くする ①: lengthen a dress (*doresu no take o nagaku suru*) ドレスの丈を長くする.

— *vi.* na˥gaku naru 長くなる Ⓒ: The days lengthen in spring.

(*Haru ni naru to hi ga nagaku naru.*) 春になると日が長くなる.

lens *n.* re⌉ñzu レンズ: a contact lens (*koñtakuto reñzu*) コンタクトレンズ.

leopard *n.* hyo⌉o ひょう(豹).

less *adj.* yori su⌈kuna⌉i より少ない: I made less money this year than last year. (*Kotoshi wa kyoneñ yori kasegi ga sukunakatta.*) ことしは去年よりかせぎが少なかった. / Please show me something less expensive. (*Moo sukoshi yasui no o misete kudasai.*) もう少し安いのを見せてください.

— *adv.* su⌈ku⌉naku 少なく: The less said the better. (*Kuchikazu wa sukunai hodo yoi.*) 口数は少ないほどよい.

— *pron.* su⌈kuna⌉i ryoo 少ない量: You should eat less. (*Motto taberu ryoo o herasu beki da.*) もっと食べる量を減らすべきだ.

lessen *vi.* su⌈ku⌉naku naru 少なくなる Ⓒ; he⌈ru 減る Ⓒ: The pain has lessened a little. (*Itami ga sukoshi herimashita.*) 痛みが少し減りました.

— *vt.* ... o su⌈ku⌉naku suru …を少なくする Ⓘ; he⌈rasu 減らす Ⓒ: lessen working hours (*roodoo-jikañ o herasu*) 労働時間を減らす.

lesson *n.* **1** (course of study) ga⌈kka 学課; be⌈ñkyoo 勉強: neglect one's lessons (*beñkyoo o okotaru*) 勉強を怠る.

2 (period of teaching) ju⌉gyoo 授業: a lesson in history (*rekishi no jugyoo*) 歴史の授業.

3 (of a textbook) ka 課: the Second Lesson (*dai ni-ka*) 第2課.

4 (wisdom) kyo⌈okuñ 教訓: I learned my lesson from it. (*Ii kyookuñ ni narimashita.*) いい教訓になりました.

lest *conj.* ⟨verb⟩-nai yo⌉o ni …ないように: We spoke quietly lest we disturb others. (*Watashi-tachi wa hoka no hito ni meewaku o kakenai yoo ni hikui koe de hanashita.*) 私たちはほかの人に迷惑をかけないように低い声で話した.

let *vt.* ⟨verb⟩-(sa)seru …(さ)せる Ⓥ; ya⌈raseru やらせる Ⓥ: She let her children play in the park. (*Kanojo wa kodomo-tachi o kooeñ de asobaseta.*) 彼女は子どもたちを公園で遊ばせた. / Please let me do it again. (*Watashi ni moo ichi-do sore o yarasete kudasai.*) 私にもう一度それをやらせてください.

let ... know *vt.* ... ni shi⌈raseru …に知らせる Ⓥ: Please let me know by telephone. (*Deñwa de watashi ni shirasete kudasai.*) 電話で私に知らせてください.

let's do ⟨verb⟩-(y)oo …(よ)う; ⟨verb⟩-mashoo …ましょう: Let's go together. (*Issho ni ikoo.*) いっしょに行こう. / Let's meet again. (*Mata o-ai shimashoo.*) またお会いしましょう.

letter *n.* **1** (written message) te⌈gami 手紙: I wrote a letter to my mother. (*Watashi wa haha ni tegami o kaita.*) 私は母に手紙を書いた. / Please send this letter by airmail. (*Kono tegami o kookuubiñ de dashite kudasai.*) この手紙を航空便で出しください. / letter paper (*biñseñ*) 便せん.

2 (sign in writing) mo⌉ji 文字: small letters (*komoji*) 小文字 / capital letters (*oomoji*) 大文字.

lettuce *n.* re⌉tasu レタス: two heads of lettuce (*retasu ni-ko*) レタス2個.

level *adj.* **1** (flat and even) ta⌈ira na 平らな; su⌈ihee na 水平な: This floor is not level. (*Kono yuka wa suihee ja nai.*) この床は水平じゃない.

2 (of the same height) o⌈naji ta⌉kasa no 同じ高さの: The water was level with my knees. (*Mizu wa watashi no hiza to onaji takasa made atta.*) 水は私のひざと同じ高さまであった.

3 (even) go⌈kaku no 互角の: a level race (*gokaku no kyoosoo*) 互角の競走.

— *n.* **1** (even line or surface) su⌈ihee 水平: bring the shelf to a level (*tana o suihee ni suru*) 棚を水平にする.

2 (height) ta¹kasa 高さ: hang a picture at the level of one's eyes (*e o me no takasa ni kakeru*) 絵を目の高さに掛ける.

— *vt.* 1 (make flat) ... o ta⌈ira ni suru ...を平らにする Ⓘ; na⌈ra¹su ならす Ⓒ: level ground with a bulldozer (*jimeñ o burudoozaa de narasu*) 地面をブルドーザーでならす.

2 (aim) (... ni) ... no ne⌈rai o tsu⌈ke¹ru (...に)...のねらいをつける Ⓥ: level one's gun at a target (*mato ni juu no nerai o tsukeru*) 的に銃のねらいをつける.

liable *adj.* 1 (likely) ⟨verb⟩-gachi¹ na ...がちな; ⟨verb⟩-yasu¹i ...やすい: Difficulties are liable to occur. (*Meñdoo na koto wa okori-gachi da.*) 面倒なことは起こりがちだ. / I am liable to catch colds. (*Watashi wa kaze o hiki-yasui.*) 私はかぜをひきやすい.

2 (responsible) se⌈kiniñ ga a¹ru 責任がある: We are liable for the damage. (*Wareware wa sono soñgai ni taishite sekiniñ ga aru.*) われわれはその損害に対して責任がある.

liar *n.* u⌈so¹tsuki うそつき.

liberal *adj.* 1 (generous) ki⌈mae no yo¹i 気前のよい; ka⌈ñdai na 寛大な: He gave the bellhop a liberal tip. (*Kare wa booi ni kimae no yoi chippu o ageta.*) 彼はボーイに気前のよいチップをあげた.

2 (in politics) ji⌈yuushu¹gi no 自由主義の; sh⌈iñpo-teki na 進歩的な: liberal democracy (*jiyuu miñshu-shugi*) 自由民主主義.

— *n.* ji⌈yuushugi¹sha 自由主義者; ri⌈berari¹suto リベラリスト. ★ Japanese '*riberarisuto*' comes from English 'liberalist'.

liberate *vt.* ... o ji⌈yu¹u ni suru ...を自由にする Ⓘ; ka⌈ihoo suru 解放する Ⓘ: liberate hostages (*hitojichi o kaihoo suru*) 人質を解放する.

liberty *n.* 1 (freedom) ji⌈yu¹u 自由: liberty of speech (*geñroñ no jiyuu*) 言論の自由.

2 (being free from control) ka⌈ihoo 解放.

library *n.* 1 (place) to⌈sho¹kañ 図書館: a public library (*kookyoo toshokañ*) 公共図書館.

2 (collection of books) zo⌈osho 蔵書.

license *n.* 1 (permission) me¹ñkyo 免許; ni¹ñka 認可: get a license to hunt (*shuryoo no meñkyo o morau*) 狩猟の免許をもらう.

2 (written permission) me⌈ñkyo¹shoo 免許証; kyo⌈ka¹shoo 許可証: a driver's license (*uñteñ meñkyo-shoo*) 運転免許証.

— *vt.* ... ni me¹ñkyo [ni¹ñka] o a⌈taeru ...に免許[認可]を与える Ⓥ: His shop is licensed to sell alcohol. (*Kare no mise wa arukooru iñryoo hañbai no niñka o ukete iru.*) 彼の店はアルコール飲料販売の認可を受けている.

lick *vt.* ... o na⌈me¹ru ...をなめる Ⓥ: The dog licked my hand. (*Sono inu wa watashi no te o nameta.*) その犬は私の手をなめた.

lid *n.* fu⌈ta ふた: take off a lid (*futa o akeru*) ふたを開ける.

lie[1] *vi.* 1 (take a flat position) yo⌈ko ni na¹ru 横になる Ⓒ; yo⌈kotawa¹ru 横たわる Ⓒ: I lay on the bench. (*Watashi wa beñchi no ue ni yoko ni natta.*) 私はベンチの上に横になった.

2 (rest) a¹ru ある Ⓒ; o⌈ite a¹ru 置いてある Ⓒ: The book is lying on the desk. (*Hoñ wa tsukue no ue ni oite arimasu.*) 本は机の上に置いてあります.

3 (be situated) ... ni i¹chi suru ...に位置する Ⓘ: The island lies to the south of Tokyo. (*Sono shima wa Tookyoo no minami ni ichi shite iru.*) その島は東京の南に位置している.

4 (exist) a¹ru ある Ⓒ; so⌈ñzai suru 存在する Ⓘ: Happiness lies in health. (*Koofuku wa keñkoo ni aru.*) 幸福は健康にある.

lie[2] *n.* u¹so うそ; i⌈tsuwari 偽り: tell a lie (*uso o tsuku*) うそをつく.

— *vi.* u¹so o tsuku うそをつく Ⓒ; i⌈tsuwa¹ru 偽る Ⓒ: He lied to me about it. (*Kare wa sono koto ni tsuite watashi ni uso o tsuita.*) 彼はそのことについて私にうそをついた.

life *n.* **1** (being alive) se¹emee 生命; i¹nochi 命: He saved the child's life. (*Kare wa sono ko no inochi o sukutta.*) 彼はその子の命を救った.

2 (living thing) i⌜ki¹mono 生き物; se¹ebutsu 生物: There is no life on the moon. (*Tsuki ni wa seebutsu wa inai.*) 月には生物はいない.

3 (the period between birth and death) i⌜sshoo 一生; sho¹ogai 生涯: He remained single throughout his life. (*Kare wa isshoo dokushiñ de tooshita.*) 彼は一生独身で通した.

4 (manner of living) se⌜ekatsu 生活; ku⌜rashi 暮らし: She led a happy life. (*Kanojo wa shiawase na seekatsu o okutta.*) 彼女は幸せな生活を送った.

lift *vt.* (raise) ... o mo⌜chiageru …を持ち上げる [V]: I helped her lift the box up. (*Watashi wa kanojo ga sono hako o mochiageru no o tetsudatta.*) 私は彼女がその箱を持ち上げるのを手伝った.

— *vi.* **1** (go up) a⌜garu 上がる [C]: This lid won't lift. (*Kono futa wa agaranai.*) このふたは上がらない.

2 (disappear) ha⌜re¹ru 晴れる [V]: The fog will soon lift. (*Kiri wa sugu ni hareru deshoo.*) 霧はすぐに晴れるでしょう.

— *n.* **1** (elevator) e⌜rebe¹etaa エレベーター.

2 (ride) ku⌜ruma ni noseru koto¹ 車に乗せること: I gave him a lift to the station. (*Watashi wa kare o eki made kuruma ni nosete yatta.*) 私は彼を駅まで車に乗せてやった.

light[1] *n.* **1** (brightness) hi⌜kari¹ 光; a⌜karusa 明るさ: the light of a candle (*roosoku no hikari*) ろうそくの光 / The light in this room is bad. (*Kono heya no akarusa wa fujuubuñ da.*) この部屋の明るさは不十分だ.

2 (of a lamp) a⌜kari 明かり; (electric light) de⌜ñtoo 電灯: turn on [off] a light (*akari o tsukeru* [*kesu*]) 明かりをつける[消す].

3 (traffic light) ko⌜otsuushi¹ñgoo 交通信号: The lights changed to green [red]. (*Shiñgoo ga ao* [*aka*] *ni kawatta.*) 信号が青[赤]に変わった.

4 (flame) hi¹ 火: strike a light (*hi o tsukeru*) 火をつける.

— *adj.* **1** (bright) a⌜karui 明るい: a light room (*akarui heya*) 明るい部屋.

2 (pale in color) u⌜sui 薄い: light green (*usumidori*) 薄緑.

— *vt.* **1** (set fire to) ... ni hi¹ o tsu⌜ke¹ru …に火をつける [V]: strike a match and light a cigarette (*matchi o sutte tabako ni hi o tsukeru*) マッチをすってたばこに火をつける.

2 (give light to) ... o te⌜ra¹su …を照らす [C]: light the way with a flashlight (*kaichuudeñtoo de michi o terasu*) 懐中電灯で道を照らす.

light[2] *adj.* **1** (of little weight) ka⌜rui 軽い: a light suitcase (*karui suutsukeesu*) 軽いスーツケース.

2 (not much) su⌜kuna¹i 少ない: Traffic is light today. (*Kyoo wa kootsuuryoo ga sukunai.*) きょうは交通量が少ない. / light rain (*kosame*) 小雨.

3 (easy) yo⌜oi na 容易な; ra⌜ku¹ na 楽な: light work (*raku na shigoto*) 楽な仕事.

4 (not serious) ka⌜rui 軽い: light reading (*karui yomimono*) 軽い読み物.

lighten[1] *vt.* (make bright) ... o a⌜karuku suru …を明るくする [I]; te⌜ra¹su 照らす [C]: The white wall lightened the room. (*Shiroi kabe ga heya o akaruku shita.*) 白い壁が部屋を明るくした.

— *vi.* (become bright) a⌜karuku na¹ru 明るくなる [C]: The sky lightened. (*Sora ga akaruku natta.*) 空が明るくなった.

lighten[2] *vt.* (make less heavy) ... o ka⌜ruku suru …を軽くする [I]: I took out some books to lighten my suitcase. (*Watashi wa suutsukeesu o karuku suru tame ni nañ-satsu ka

hoñ o dashita.) 私はスーツケースを軽くするために何冊か本を出した.
— *vi.* (become less heavy) ka⌈ruku na⌉ru 軽くなる Ⓒ: My heart lightened at the news. (*Sono shirase o kiite kokoro ga karuku natta.*) その知らせを聞いて心が軽くなった.

lighter *n.* ra⌉itaa ライター.

lighthouse *n.* to⌈odai 灯台.

lighting *n.* sho⌈omee 照明: direct [indirect] lighting (*chokusetsu* [*kañsetsu*] *shoomee*) 直接[間接]照明.

lightly *adv.* **1** (gently) ka⌈ruku 軽く; so⌈tto そっと: press a bell lightly (*beru o sotto osu*) ベルをそっと押す.
2 (nimbly) ke⌈ekai ni 軽快に: skip lightly along (*keekai ni tobihaneru*) 軽快に跳びはねる.
3 (cheerfully) yo⌈oki ni 陽気に: dance lightly (*yooki ni odoru*) 陽気に踊る.

lightning *n.* i⌈nabi⌉kari 稲光; ka⌈mina⌉ri 雷: be struck by lightning (*kaminari ni utareru*) 雷に打たれる.

like[1] *vt.* **1** (be fond of) ... ga su⌈ki⌉ da ...が好きだ; ... ga ki ⌈ni iru ...が気に入る Ⓒ: I don't like this color. (*Watashi wa kono iro wa suki de wa arimaseñ.*) 私はこの色は好きではありません. / I like this very much. (*Kore ga taiheñ ki ni irimashita.*) これが大変気に入りました.
2 (wish) ⟨verb⟩-ta⌉i no desu ga ...たいのですが: I'd like to change my room. (*Heya o kaetai no desu ga.*) 部屋を替えたいのですが. / I'd like to reserve a hotel room in the city. (*Shinai no hoteru o yoyaku shitai no desu ga.*) 市内のホテルを予約したいのですが.
3 (want to have) ... ga ho⌈shi⌉i ...が欲しい: I'd like a sightseeing brochure for this town. (*Kono machi no kañkoo pañfuretto ga hoshii no desu ga.*) この町の観光パンフレットが欲しいのですが.
Would you like ... ? ... wa i⌈ka⌉ga desu ka? ...はいかがですか: Would you like more coffee? (*Koohii o motto ikaga desu ka?*) コーヒーをもっといかがですか.

like[2] *adj.* (similar) ni⌈te iru 似ている: He is very like his older brother. (*Kare wa niisañ to yoku nite iru.*) 彼は兄さんとよく似ている.
— *prep.* **1** (the same as) ... no yo⌉o na ...のような: a house like a castle (*shiro no yoo na ie*) 城のような家 / What is she like? (*Kanojo wa dono yoo na hito desu ka?*) 彼女はどのような人ですか.
2 (in the same way as) ... no yo⌉o ni ...のように: He climbed the tree like a monkey. (*Kare wa saru no yoo ni sono ki ni nobotta.*) 彼は猿のようにその木に登った.

likely *adj.* **1** (about to happen) ⟨verb⟩-so⌉o na ...そうな: It's likely to be fine this afternoon. (*Gogo wa hare-soo da.*) 午後は晴れそうだ.
2 (probable) a⌈ri-so⌉o na ありそうな; mo⌈ttomo-rashi⌉i もっともらしい: a likely story (*ari-soo na hanashi*) ありそうな話 / a likely explanation (*mottomo-rashii setsumee*) もっともらしい説明.

likewise *adv.* o⌈naji yo⌉o ni 同じように: He took off his shoes and I did likewise. (*Kare wa kutsu o nuida ga watashi mo onaji yoo ni shita.*) 彼は靴を脱いだが私も同じようにした.

liking *n.* ko⌈nomi 好み; shu⌉mi 趣味: He has a particular liking for wine. (*Kare wa toku ni waiñ ga suki da.*) 彼は特にワインが好きだ.

lily *n.* (plant) yu⌈ri ゆり; (flower) yu⌈ri no hana⌉ ゆりの花.

limb *n.* te⌉ashi 手足: He rested his tired limbs. (*Kare wa tsukareta teashi o yasumaseta.*) 彼は疲れた手足を休ませた.

limit *n.* **1** (boundary) ge⌈ñkai 限界; ge⌉ñdo 限度: There is a limit to everything. (*Nanigoto ni mo geñdo ga aru.*) 何事にも限度がある.
2 (restriction) se⌈ege⌉ñ 制限: exceed the weight limit (*juuryoo seegeñ o koeru*) 重量制限を越える.
— *vt.* ... o se⌈ege⌉ñ suru ...を制限す

る [I]: You had better limit the number of cigarettes you smoke. (*Kimi wa suu tabako no hoñsuu o seegeñ shita hoo ga yoi.*) 君は吸うたばこの本数を制限したほうがよい.

limitation *n.* se[egeʼñ 制限; ge[ñ-kai 限界: limitations on imports (*yunyuu seegeñ*) 輸入制限 / know one's limitations (*jibuñ no geñkai o shiru*) 自分の限界を知る.

limited *adj.* **1** (restricted) ka[giraʼ-reta 限られた; ka[giraʼrete iru 限られている: My experience is limited. (*Watashi no keekeñ wa kagirarete imasu.*) 私の経験は限られています.
2 (of a train or bus) to[kkyuu no 特急の: a limited express (*tokkyuu ressha*) 特急列車.

limp *vi.* a[shiʼ o hi[kizuru 足を引きずる [C]: He hurt his ankle and limped back home. (*Kare wa ashi-kubi o itame ashi o hikizutte ie e kaetta.*) 彼は足首を痛め足を引きずって家へ帰った.

line *n.* **1** (long, thin mark) seʼñ 線: draw a straight line (*chokuseñ o hiku*) 直線を引く.
2 (cord) hi[mo ひも; tsu[naʼ 綱: hang the washing on a line (*señta-kumono o himo ni kakeru*) 洗濯物をひもにかける.
3 (row of people) reʼtsu 列: stand in a line (*retsu ni narabu*) 列に並ぶ.
4 (row of words) gyoʼo 行: the fifth line from the top (*ue kara go-gyoo-me*) 上から5行目.
5 (of a telephone) de[ñwaseñ 電話線: The line is busy. (*O-hanashi-chuu desu.*) お話し中です. / Please hold the line. (*Sono mama kirazu ni o-machi kudasai.*) そのまま切らずにお待ちください.
6 (business) shoʼobai 商売; sho-[kuʼgyoo 職業: What is your line? (*Anata no go-shoobai wa nañ desu ka?*) あなたのご商売は何ですか.

linen *n.* a[saʼ 麻.

liner *n.* (ship) te[ekiseñ 定期船; (air-plane) te[eki ryokaʼkki 定期旅客機.

linger *vi.* guʼzuguzu suru ぐずぐずする [I]: Don't linger on your way home. (*Uchi e kaeru tochuu guzu-guzu shinai yoo ni.*) 家へ帰る途中ぐずぐずしないように.

link *vt.* ... o tsu[nagu ...をつなぐ [C]; mu[subu 結ぶ [C]: We linked arms. (*Watashi-tachi wa te o tsunaida.*) 私たちは手をつないだ. / a road linking the two towns (*futatsu no machi o musubu dooro*) 二つの町を結ぶ道路.
— *n.* **1** (ring) waʼ 輪: a link in a chain (*kusari no wa*) 鎖の輪.
2 (anything connecting two things) ka[ñreñ 関連; tsu[nagari つながり: He has links with the political world. (*Kare wa seekai to tsu-nagari ga aru.*) 彼は政界とつながりがある.

lion *n.* ra[ioñ ライオン; shiʼshi 獅子.

lip *n.* ku[chibiru 唇: the lower lip (*shita-kuchibiru*) 下唇 / the upper lip (*uwa-kuchibiru*) 上唇 / bite one's lips (*kuchibiru o kamu*) 唇をかむ. ★ Japanese '*kuchibiru*' refers only to either of the two edges of the mouth, and does not include the skin around them.

lipstick *n.* ku[chibeni 口紅: wear lipstick (*kuchibeni o tsukeru*) 口紅をつける.

liquid *n.* e[kitai 液体.
— *adj.* e[kitai no 液体の; e[kijoo no 液状の: liquid fuel (*ekitai neñ-ryoo*) 液体燃料 / liquid food (*ryuu-dooshoku*) 流動食.

liquor *n.* a[rukooru-iʼñryoo アルコール飲料: a liquor store (*sakaya*) 酒屋.

list *n.* hyo[o 表; i[chirañhyoo 一覧表; riʼsuto リスト; me[ebo 名簿: draw up a list (*ichirañhyoo o tsu-kuru*) 一覧表を作る / Show me a list of your rates, please. (*Ryookiñhyoo o misete kudasai.*) 料金表を見せてください.
— *vt.* ... o hyo[o ni suru ...を表にする [I]; hyo[o ni noseru 表に載せる [V]: I listed the things I had to do. (*Watashi wa suru koto o hyoo ni shita.*) 私はすることを表にした.

listen *vi.* **1** (try to hear) (... o) ki-

ʳku (…を)聞く Ⓒ: listen to the radio (*rajio o kiku*) ラジオを聞く.
2 (follow the advice of) (… ni) miʳmiˡ o kaʳsu (…に)耳を貸す Ⓒ; shiʳtagau 従う Ⓒ: He didn't listen to my advice. (*Kare wa watashi no chuukoku ni mimi o kasanakatta.*) 彼は私の忠告に耳を貸さなかった.

listener *n.* kiʳku hitoˡ 聴く人; kiʳkite 聞き手.

liter *n.* riʳttoru リットル; (of gasoline) riʳttaa リッター: a liter of wine (*ichi-rittoru no waiñ*) 1 リットルのワイン / How much is gasoline per liter? (*Gasoriñ wa rittaa atari ikura desu ka?*) ガソリンはリッターあたりいくらですか. ★ Japanese use the metric system and 'quart' and 'pint' are not used.

literally *adv.* **1** (in the literal sense) moʳjidoˡori ni 文字どおりに: I took what he said literally. (*Watashi wa kare ga itta koto o moji-doori ni uketotta.*) 私は彼が言ったことを文字どおりに受けとった.
2 [intensifier] moʳjidoˡori 文字どおり; hoʳñtoo ni 本当に: He was literally penniless. (*Kare wa moji-doori ichi-moñ nashi datta.*) 彼は文字どおり一文なしだった.

literary *adj.* **1** (of literature) buˡñ-gaku no 文学の: literary works (*buñgaku-sakuhiñ*) 文学作品.
2 (of a written style) buʳñgo no 文語の: literary style (*buñgotai*) 文語体.

literature *n.* **1** (written works) buˡñgaku 文学; buʳñgee 文芸: Japanese literature (*Nihoñ buñ-gaku*) 日本文学.
2 (printed material) buʳñkeñ 文献: I am collecting the literature on Japan. (*Watashi wa Nihoñ ni kañ-suru buñkeñ o atsumete imasu.*) 私は日本に関する文献を集めています.

litter *n.* goʳmiˡ ごみ; kuˡzu くず: No litter, please. (*Gomi o sutenaide kudasai.*) ごみを捨てないでください.
— *vt.* … o chiʳrakasu …を散らかす Ⓒ: The children littered the room with toys. (*Kodomo-tachi wa omo-cha de heya o chirakashita.*) 子どもたちはおもちゃで部屋を散らかした.

little[1] *adj.* **1** (small) chiˡisa-na 小さな; chiʳisaˡi 小さい: a little village (*chiisa-na mura*) 小さな村 / The boy is too little to ride a bicycle. (*Sono ko wa chiisakute jiteñsha ni norenai.*) その子は小さくて自転車に乗れない.
2 (young) neʳñshoo no 年少の; to-ʳshishita no 年下の: a little brother (*otooto*) 弟 / a little sister (*imooto*) 妹.

little[2] *adj.* **1** (small amount) suʳkoˡ-shi no 少しの; waˡzuka na わずかな: There is a little milk in the bottle. (*Biñ ni gyuunyuu ga sukoshi ari-masu.*) びんに牛乳が少しあります.
2 (not much) suʳkoˡshi shika nai 少ししかない; hoʳtoˡñdo nai ほとんどない: I have little money with me. (*O-kane wa sukoshi shika motte imaseñ.*) お金は少ししか持っていません. / There is little hope of his recovery. (*Kare ga kaifuku suru mi-komi wa hotoñdo arimaseñ.*) 彼が回復する見込みはほとんどありません.
— *adv.* **1** (not much) suʳkoˡshi 少し: I feel a little better. (*Kibuñ wa sukoshi yoku narimashita.*) 気分は少し良くなりました. / I speak a little Japanese. (*Nihoñgo o sukoshi ha-nashimasu.*) 日本語を少し話します.
2 (not at all) suʳkoshi mo <verb>-nai 少しも…ない: I little knew that he was ill. (*Kare ga byooki to wa sukoshi mo shiranakatta.*) 彼が病気とは少しも知らなかった.
— *pron.* suʳkoˡshi 少し; shoʳryoo 少量: I'll give you a little of this cake. (*Kono keeki o sukoshi age-mashoo.*) このケーキを少しあげましょう.

live[1] *vi.* **1** (dwell) (… ni) suˡmu (…に)住む Ⓒ: He lives in Kanazawa. (*Kare wa Kanazawa ni suñde imasu.*) 彼は金沢に住んでいます.
2 (be alive) iʳkiˡru 生きる Ⓥ: She lived to the age of eighty. (*Kanojo wa hachijus-sai made ikita.*) 彼女

は80歳まで生きた.
— *vt.* ... no se[r]ekatsu o suru ...の生活をする [I]: live a simple life (*kañso na seekatsu o suru*) 簡素な生活をする.

live[2] *adj.* **1** (living) i[l]kite iru 生きている: a live fish (*ikite iru sakana*) 生きている魚.
2 (of broadcasting) na[l]ma no 生の; ji[r]kkyoo no 実況の: a live TV broadcast (*terebi no nama-hoosoo*) テレビの生放送.
3 (still burning) mo[r]ete iru 燃えている: live coals (*moete iru sekitañ*) 燃えている石炭.
4 (carrying electricity) de[r]ñryuu ga tsuujite iru 電流が通じている: a live battery (*mada tsukaeru deñchi*) まだ使える電池.

livelihood *n.* ku[r]rashi 暮らし; se[r]e-kee 生計: earn one's livelihood (*seekee o tateru*) 生計を立てる.

lively *adj.* **1** (full of life) ge[l]ñki no yoi 元気のよい; ka[r]ppatsu na 活発な: a lively boy (*geñki no yoi shoo-neñ*) 元気のよい少年.
2 (cheerful) yo[r]oki na 陽気な; ni-[r]gi[l]yaka na にぎやかな: The street was lively with shoppers. (*Sono toori wa kaimonokyaku de nigi-yaka datta.*) その通りは買い物客でにぎやかだった.

liver *n.* (organ) ka[r]ñzoo 肝臓; (food) re[l]baa レバー.

living *adj.* **1** (alive) i[l]kite iru 生きている: This fish is still living. (*Kono sakana wa mada ikite iru.*) この魚はまだ生きている.
2 (existing in use) ge[r]ñzoñ no 現存の; ge[l]ñdai no 現代の: living language (*geñdaigo*) 現代語.
— *n.* se[r]ekatsu 生活; ku[r]rashi 暮らし: the standard of living (*seeka-tsu-suijuñ*) 生活水準 / make a living (*seekee o tateru*) 生計を立てる.

living room *n.* i[r]ma[l] 居間.

load *n.* **1** (something which is carried) tsu[r]mini 積み荷; ni[l] 荷: He carried the heavy load on his back. (*Kare wa omoi ni o seotte hakoñ-da.*) 彼は重い荷を背負って運んだ.
2 (something which weighs on the mind) fu[r]tañ 負担; o[r]moni 重荷: It took a load off my mind. (*Sore de watashi no kokoro no omoni ga toreta.*) それで私の心の重荷が取れた.
— *vt.* **1** (put a load on) ... ni (... o) tsu[r]mu ...に(...を)積む [C]: We loaded the truck with vegetables. (*Watashi-tachi wa torakku ni yasai o tsuñda.*) 私たちはトラックに野菜を積んだ.
2 (fill) ... o (... ni) i[r]reru ...を(...に)入れる [V]: load film into a camera (*firumu o kamera ni ireru*) フィルムをカメラに入れる / This gun is not loaded. (*Kono juu ni wa tama ga haitte imaseñ.*) この銃には弾が入っていません.

loaf *n.* hi[r]toka[l]tamari ひと塊: a loaf of bread (*pañ hitokatamari*) パンひと塊.

loan *n.* **1** (lending) ka[r]shitsuke 貸し付け; ka[r]su koto[l] 貸すこと: ask for the loan of money (*o-kane no ka-shitsuke o tanomu*) お金の貸し付けを頼む / Thanks for the loan of your book. (*Hoñ o kashite kurete ariga-too.*) 本を貸してくれてありがとう.
2 (money) ka[r]shitsukekiñ 貸付金; ro[l]oñ ローン: I got a loan from the bank. (*Watashi wa giñkoo kara rooñ o karita.*) 私は銀行からローンを借りた.
— *vt.* ... ni (... o) ka[r]su ...に(...を)貸す [C]; ka[r]shitsuke[l]ru 貸し付ける [V]: I loaned him my car. (*Watashi wa kare ni kuruma o kashite yatta.*) 私は彼に車を貸してやった.

lobby *n.* ro[l]bii ロビー; hi[l]roma 広間: a hotel lobby (*hoteru no robii*) ホテルのロビー.

lobster *n.* ro[l]busutaa ロブスター; i[r]se[l]-ebi 伊勢えび. ★ In Japanese 'prawn' and 'shrimp' are also called '*ebi*.'

local *adj.* **1** (of a certain place) to-[r]chi no 土地の; chi[r]ho[l]o no 地方の: I'd like some local sake. (*Kono* *tochi no sake o nomitai.*) この土地の酒を飲みたい. / a local newspaper (*Chihoo-shiñbuñ*) 地方新聞. ★ Japanese often use '*rookaru*' ローカル (from English 'local') in the sense of 'rural.'

2 (not limited) ka[kueki te]esha no 各駅停車の; fu[tsuu no 普通の: a local train (*futsuu-ressha*) 普通列車.

3 (of a particular part) kyo[kubuteki na 局部的な: a local pain (*kyokubu-teki na itami*) 局部的な痛み.

local call *n.* shi[nai tsu]uwa 市内通話.

local time *n.* ge[ñchi-ji]kañ 現地時間.

locate *vt.* **1** (find the place) ... no ba[sho o sagashi ate]ru …の場所を捜し当てる Ⓥ; sho[zai o tsukitome]ru 所在を突き止める Ⓥ: The police located the missing girl. (*Keesatsu wa yukue fumee no shoojo no shozai o tsukitometa.*) 警察は行方不明の少女の所在を突き止めた.

2 (situate) ... ni a]ru …にある Ⓒ: Where is your hotel located? (*Anata no hoteru wa doko ni arimasu ka?*) あなたのホテルはどこにありますか.

3 (settle) ... o (... ni) o[ku …を(…に)置く Ⓒ: They located their office in Yokohama. (*Kare-ra wa jimusho o Yokohama ni oita.*) 彼らは事務所を横浜に置いた.

location *n.* ba[sho 場所; i]chi 位置; sho[za]ichi 所在地: The new school has a good location. (*Atarashii gakkoo wa ii basho ni aru.*) 新しい学校はいい場所にある.

lock *vt.* **1** (fasten with a lock) ... ni ka[gi] o ka[ke]ru …に鍵をかける Ⓥ; jo[o o oro]su 錠を下ろす Ⓒ: Did you lock the gate? (*Moñ ni kagi o kakemashita ka?*) 門に鍵をかけましたか.

2 (shut in) ... o (... ni) to[jikome]ru …を(…に)閉じ込める Ⓥ; shi[maiko]mu しまい込む Ⓒ: She locked her jewels in the box. (*Kanojo wa hooseki o hako ni shimaikoñda.*) 彼女は宝石を箱にしまい込んだ.

— *vi.* ka[gi] [jo[o] ga ka[ka]ru 鍵[錠]がかかる Ⓒ: This door doesn't lock. (*Kono to wa kagi ga kakaranai.*) この戸は鍵がかからない.

— *n.* jo[o 錠; jo[omae 錠前: open a lock with a key (*kagi de joo o akeru*) 鍵で錠を開ける.

locomotive *n.* ki[ka]ñsha 機関車.

lodge *n.* sa[ñsoo 山荘; ya[magoya 山小屋.

— *vt.* ... o to[meru …を泊める Ⓥ: Can you lodge me overnight? (*Hito-bañ tomete moraemasu ka?*) 一晩泊めてもらえますか.

— *vi.* (... ni) to[maru (…に)泊まる Ⓒ: She lodged at her friend's house. (*Kanojo wa tomodachi no ie ni tomatta.*) 彼女は友だちの家に泊まった.

lodger *n.* ge[shukuniñ 下宿人.

lodging *n.* ka[shima 貸間; ge[shukuya 下宿屋: live in lodgings (*magari suru*) 間借りする.

log *n.* ma[ruta 丸太: a log cabin (*marutagoya*) 丸太小屋.

logic *n.* **1** (way of reasoning) ro]ñri 論理; ro[ñpoo 論法: I cannot follow your logic. (*Kimi no roñri ni wa tsuite ikenai.*) 君の論理にはついていけない.

2 (science) ro[ñri]gaku 論理学.

logical *adj.* ro[ñri-teki na 論理的な; su]ji no tootta [tootte iru] 筋の通った[通っている]: What you say is logical. (*Anata no iu koto wa suji ga tootte iru.*) あなたの言うことは筋が通っている.

loneliness *n.* ko[doku 孤独; sa[bi]shisa 寂しさ: endure loneliness (*kodoku ni taeru*) 孤独に耐える.

lonely *adj.* **1** (alone) ko[doku na 孤独な; hi[toribo]tchi no 独りぼっちの: lead a lonely life (*kodoku na seekatsu o okuru*) 孤独な生活を送る.

2 (unhappy) sa[bishi]i 寂しい: She felt lonely. (*Kanojo wa sabishikatta.*) 彼女は寂しかった.

3 (away from other people) hi[to no sukuna]i 人の少ない; hi[tozato hanaˡreta 人里離れた: a lonely street (*hitodoori no sukunai toori*) 人通りの少ない通り.

long[1] *adj.* **1** (of length, distance, time, etc.) naˡgaˡi 長い: long hair (*nagai kami*) 長い髪 / a long night (*nagai yoru*) 長い夜 / a long vacation (*nagai kyuuka*) 長い休暇.
2 (measuring) naˡgasa no 長さの: a rope five meters long (*go-meetoru no nagasa no roopu*) 5メートルの長さのロープ.
— *adv.* **1** (for a long time) naˡgaku 長く; naˡgaˡi aida 長い間: Have you been waiting long? (*Nagaku machi mashita ka?*) 長く待ちましたか.
2 (at a far distant time) zuˡtto ずっと: He died long ago. (*Kare wa zutto mukashi ni nakunarimashita.*) 彼はずっと昔に亡くなりました.
how long *adv.* doˡno kurai どのくらい: How long are you staying here? (*Dono kurai koko ni taizai shimasu ka?*) どのくらいここに滞在しますか.
So long. (*De wa mata.*) ではまた.

long[2] *vi.* seˡtsuboo suru 切望する [I]; ⟨verb⟩-tai …たい: I'm longing to go home. (*Watashi wa kokyoo e kaeritai.*) 私は故郷へ帰りたい.

long-distance *n.* choˡokyori-deˡñwa 長距離電話.

longing *n.* seˡtsuboo 切望; aˡkogare あこがれ: a longing for fame (*meesee e no akogare*) 名声へのあこがれ.

look *vi.* **1** (try to see) miˡru 見る [V]: I'm just looking. (*Chotto mite iru dake desu.*) ちょっと見ているだけです.
2 (seem to be) ... yoo ni miˡeˡru …ように見える [V]: He looked tired. (*Kare wa tsukareta yoo ni mieta.*) 彼は疲れたように見えた.
— *vt.* **1** (give a look) ... o jiˡtto miˡru …をじっと見る [V]: She looked me in the face. (*Kanojo wa watashi no kao o jitto mita.*) 彼女は私の顔をじっと見た.
2 (notice carefully) ... o taˡshikameˡru …を確かめる [V]: Look to see if he has come yet. (*Kare ga kita ka doo ka tashikame nasai.*) 彼が来たかどうか確かめなさい.
— *n.* **1** (act) miˡru koˡtoˡ 見ること: Please let me have a look at it. (*Sore o misete kudasai.*) それを見せてください.
2 (expression) meˡtsuki 目つき; kaˡotsuki 顔つき: an angry look (*okotta metsuki*) 怒った目つき.
3 (appearance) gaˡikañ 外観; yoˡosu 様子: I don't like the look of the weather. (*Teñki no yoosu ga ki ni iranai.*) 天気の様子が気に入らない.
4 (features) kiˡryoo 器量: She has good looks. (*Kanojo wa kiryoo ga yoi.*) 彼女は器量がよい.
look after … *vt.* ... ni ki ˡo tsukeˡru …に気をつける [V]: look after one's health (*keñkoo ni ki o tsukeru*) 健康に気をつける.
look at … *vt.* ... o yoˡku miru …をよく見る [V]: She looked at herself in the mirror. (*Kanojo wa kagami no naka no jibuñ no sugata o mita.*) 彼女は鏡の中の自分の姿を見た.
look down on … *vt.* ... o miˡkudasu …を見下す [C]: look down on a person (*hito o mikudasu*) 人を見下す.
look for … *vt.* ... o saˡgasu …を捜す [C]: He is looking for his glasses. (*Kare wa megane o sagashite iru.*) 彼は眼鏡を捜している.
look forward to … *vt.* ... o taˡnoshiˡmi ni maˡtsu …を楽しみに待つ [C]: I am looking forward to meeting you. (*O-ai suru no o tanoshimi ni shite imasu.*) お会いするのを楽しみにしています.
look like … *vt.* ... ni niˡte iru …に似ている [V]: He looks like his father. (*Kare wa o-toosañ ni nite iru.*) 彼はお父さんに似ている.
look over … *vt.* ... o shiˡrabeˡru …を調べる [V]: look over the papers (*shorui o shiraberu*) 書類を調べる.
look up *vi.*, *vt.* ... o miˡageˡru …を見上げる [V]; shiˡrabeˡru 調べる [V]: look up into the sky (*sora o mia-*

geru) 空を見上げる / look up a word in a dictionary (*jisho de tañgo o shiraberu*) 辞書で単語を調べる.

lookout *n.* mi[hari 見張り; ke[ekai 警戒: keep a careful lookout (*yudañ naku miharu*) 油断なく見張る.

loop *n.* wa] 輪: make a loop (*wa o tsukuru*) 輪を作る.
— *vt.* ... o wa] ni suru ...を輪にする: loop up a curtain (*kaateñ o wa de tomeru*) カーテンを輪で留める.

loose *adj.* **1** (not tight) yu[ru]i 緩い: a loose knot (*yurui musubime*) 緩い結び目.
2 (not tied) shi[ba]tte nai 縛ってない; (free) ji[yu]u na 自由な: let a dog run loose (*inu o jiyuu ni shite yaru*) 犬を自由にしてやる.
3 (not put up) ta[ba]nete nai 束ねてない; ba]ra no ばらの: buy cakes of soap loose (*sekkeñ o bara de kau*) せっけんをばらで買う.
4 (not careful) fu[se]ekaku na 不正確な; zo[ñza]i na ぞんざいな: a loose translation (*zoñzai na hoñyaku*) ぞんざいな翻訳.
5 (not moral) fu[shi]dara na ふしだらな: a loose life (*fushidara na seekatsu*) ふしだらな生活.

loosen *vt.* ... o yu[rume]ru ...を緩める [V]; to]ku 解く [C]: loosen one's tie (*nekutai o yurumeru*) ネクタイを緩める.
— *vi.* yu[ru]mu 緩む [C]; ta[rumu たるむ [C].

lord *n.* **1** (God) ka]mi 神; (Christ) Ki[risuto キリスト.
2 (peer) ki]zoku 貴族.
3 (ruler) shi[ha]isha 支配者; ku]ñshu 君主.

lose *vt.* **1** (fail to find) ... o na[kusu ...をなくす [C]; o[kiwasure]ru 置き忘れる [V]: I lost my passport. (*Pasupooto o nakushimashita.*) パスポートをなくしました. / He lost his glasses somewhere. (*Kare wa megane o doko-ka ni okiwasureta.*) 彼は眼鏡をどこかに置き忘れた.
2 (have no longer) ... o u[shinau ...を失う [C]: She lost her son in an accident. (*Kanojo wa jiko de musuko o ushinatta.*) 彼女は事故で息子を失った.
3 (fail to win) ... ni ma[keru ...に負ける [V]: lose the baseball game (*yakyuu no shiai ni makeru*) 野球の試合に負ける.
4 (fail to keep) ... o ta[mote]nai ...を保てない; u[shinau 失う [C]: I have lost interest in politics. (*Watashi wa seeji ni kyoomi o ushinatta.*) 私は政治に興味を失った.
5 (fail to see) ... o mi[ushinau ...を見失う [C]; ... ni ma[yo]u ...に迷う [C]: I lost him in the crowd. (*Watashi wa hitogomi de kare o miushinatta.*) 私は人込みで彼を見失った. / I'm lost. (*Michi ni mayotte shimaimashita.*) 道に迷ってしまいました.
6 (waste) ... o mu[da ni suru ...を無駄にする [I]; ro[ohi suru 浪費する [I]: Don't lose any time. (*Jikañ o muda ni shite wa ikenai.*) 時間を無駄にしてはいけない.
7 (of a clock) o[kureru 遅れる: This clock loses a minute a day. (*Kono tokee wa ichi-nichi ni ip-puñ okureru.*) この時計は1日に1分遅れる.
— *vi.* **1** (be defeated) ma[keru 負ける [V]: They lost in the match. (*Kare-ra wa sono shiai de maketa.*) 彼らはその試合で負けた.
2 (suffer loss) so]ñ o suru 損をする [I]: He lost on the bet. (*Kare wa sono kake de soñ o shita.*) 彼はその賭で損をした.

loser *n.* ha]isha 敗者: a bad loser (*makeoshimi o iu hito*) 負け惜しみを言う人.

loss *n.* **1** (losing) na[kusu koto] なくすこと; so[oshitsu 喪失: loss of memory (*kioku sooshitsu*) 記憶喪失.
2 (the amount lost) so[ñgai 損害; so[ñshitsu 損失: His losses were greater than his gains. (*Kare no soñshitsu wa rieki yori mo ookikatta.*) 彼の損失は利益よりも大きかった.
3 (failure to win) ma[ke 負け; ha[iboku 敗北: three wins and two

losses (*sañ-shoo ni-hai*) 3 勝 2 敗.

lost *adj.* **1** (missing) uˈshinatta 失った; fuˈñshitsu shita 紛失した: I looked for my lost watch. (*Watashi wa nakushita tokee o sagashita.*) 私はなくした時計を捜した. / lost articles (*fuñshitsubutsu*) 紛失物.
2 (wasted) muˈda ni naˈtta 無駄になった: make up lost time (*muda ni natta jikañ o umeawaseru*) 無駄になった時間を埋め合わせる.
3 (not won) maˈketa 負けた: a lost game (*maketa shiai*) 負けた試合.
4 (having lost one's way) miˈchi ni mayoˈtta 道に迷った: a lost child (*maigo*) 迷子.

lost-and-found (office) *n.* iˈshitsuˈbutsu toˈriatsukaijoˈ 遺失物取扱所: Where is the lost-and-found? (*Ishitsubutsu toriatsukaijo wa doko desu ka?*) 遺失物取扱所はどこですか.

lot[1] *n.* (great amount) taˈkusañ たくさん: I want a lot more. (*Motto takusañ hoshii.*) もっとたくさん欲しい. / He has a lot of friends. (*Kare wa takusañ tomodachi ga iru.*) 彼はたくさん友だちがいる.

lot[2] *n.* **1** (objects used to decide something) kuˈji くじ: draw lots (*kuji o hiku*) くじを引く.
2 (section of land) jiˈsho 地所; shiˈkichi 敷地: an empty lot (*akichi*) 空き地 / a parking lot (*chuushajoo*) 駐車場.
3 (fate) uˈñmee 運命.

lotion *n.* keˈshoˈosui 化粧水; roˈoshoñ ローション.

lottery *n.* kuˈjibiki くじ引き; taˈkaraˈkuji 宝くじ.

loud *adj.* **1** (strong sound) oˈogoˈe no 大声の; koˈe ga taˈkaˈi 声が高い: We sang in loud voices. (*Watashi-tachi wa oogoe de utatta.*) 私たちは大声で歌った.
2 (noisy) yaˈkamashiˈi やかましい; soˈozooshiˈi 騒々しい: a loud party (*soozooshii paatii*) 騒々しいパーティー.
3 (showy) haˈdeˈ na 派手な; keˈbakebashiˈi けばけばしい: This dress is too loud. (*Kono doresu wa hade sugiru.*) このドレスは派手すぎる.

loudly *adv.* oˈogoˈe de 大声で; yaˈkamaˈshiku やかましく: talk loudly (*oogoe de shaberu*) 大声でしゃべる.

loudspeaker *n.* kaˈkuseˈeki 拡声器; suˈpiˈikaa スピーカー.

lounge *n.* **1** (room) kyuˈukeˈeshitsu 休憩室; raˈuñji ラウンジ; (of an airport) maˈchiaˈishitsu 待合室; roˈbii ロビー.
2 (sofa) neˈisu 寝いす; aˈñrakuˈisu 安楽いす.
— *vi.* buˈrabura suru ぶらぶらする [I]: We lounged on the beach all day. (*Watashi-tachi wa kaigañ de ichi-nichi-juu burabura sugoshita.*) 私たちは海岸で一日中ぶらぶら過ごした.

love *vt.* **1** (feel love) ... o aˈisuˈru ...を愛する [I]: I love you. (*Watashi wa anata o aishite imasu.*) 私はあなたを愛しています. / She is loved by everybody. (*Kanojo wa miñna ni aisarete iru.*) 彼女はみんなに愛されている.
2 (be fond of) ... o koˈnoˈmu ...を好む [C]; ... ga daˈisuki da ...が大好きだ: She loves to travel. (*Kanojo wa ryokoo ga daisuki da.*) 彼女は旅行が大好きだ.
— *n.* **1** (affection) aˈi 愛; aˈijoo 愛情: show a deep love for one's child (*kodomo ni fukai aijoo o shimesu*) 子どもに深い愛情を示す.
2 (sexual feeling) reˈñai 恋愛; koˈi 恋: one's first love (*hatsukoi*) 初恋.
3 (fondness) koˈnomiˈ 好み; shuˈmi 趣味: He has a love of books. (*Kare wa hoñ ga suki da.*) 彼は本が好きだ.

lovely *adj.* **1** (beautiful) uˈtsukushiˈi 美しい; kaˈwaiˈi かわいい: a lovely dress (*utsukushii doresu*) 美しいドレス / a lovely girl (*kawaii shoojo*) かわいい少女.
2 (very pleasant) suˈbarashiˈi すばらしい; suˈteki na すてきな: lovely weather (*subarashii teñki*) すばらしい天気.

lover *n.* **1** (sweetheart) aʳijiñ 愛人; koʳibito 恋人.
2 (person who likes something) aʳikoˡosha 愛好者: a music lover (*oñgaku no aikoosha*) 音楽の愛好者.

loving *adj.* aʳisuˡru 愛する; aʳijoo no komoˡtta [komoˡtte iru] 愛情のこもった[こもっている]: a loving look (*aijoo no komotta manazashi*) 愛情のこもったまなざし.

low *adj.* **1** (not high) hiʳkuˡi 低い: a low building (*hikui tatemono*) 低い建物 / a low temperature (*hikui oñdo*) 低い温度 / a low voice (*hikui koe*) 低い声.
2 (not expensive) yaʳsuˡi 安い: a low price (*yasui nedañ*) 安い値段.
3 (not strong) yoʳwaˡi 弱い: The fire is low. (*Hi ga yowai.*) 火が弱い.
4 (gloomy) geˡñki no [ga] nai 元気の[が]ない: He is in very low spirits today. (*Kare wa kyoo wa geñki ga nai.*) 彼はきょうは元気がない.
— *adv.* hiˡkuku 低く; yaˡsuku 安く: The plane flew low. (*Hikooki wa hikuku toñda.*) 飛行機は低く飛んだ. / buy low and sell high (*yasuku katte takaku uru*) 安く買って高く売る.

lower *adj.* **1** (below another) shiʳta no 下の: I'd like a room on a lower floor. (*Motto shita no kai no heya ni shitai.*) もっと下の階の部屋にしたい.
2 (of low rank) kaʳkyuu no 下級の; kaʳtoo no 下等の: a lower court of law (*kakyuu saibañsho*) 下級裁判所.
— *vt.* **1** (bring down) ... o oʳroˡsu …を下ろす: lower a blind (*buraiñdo o orosu*) ブラインドを下ろす.
2 (reduce) ... o saʳgeˡru …を下げる Ⓥ; oʳtoˡsu 落とす Ⓒ: lower the price (*nedañ o sageru*) 値段を下げる / lower one's voice (*koe o otosu*) 声を落とす.

loyal *adj.* chuʳujitsu na 忠実な; seʳejitsu na 誠実な: a loyal friend (*seejitsu na yuujiñ*) 誠実な友人.

loyalty *n.* chuʳusee 忠誠; chuʳujitsu 忠実; seʳejitsu 誠実: swear one's loyalty (*chuusee o chikau*) 忠誠を誓う.

luck *n.* **1** (chance) uˡñ 運: Luck was with [against] me. (*Uñ ga yokatta [warukatta].*) 運がよかった[悪かった].
2 (fortune) koʳouñ 幸運: I had the luck to win the prize. (*Watashi wa koouñ ni mo shoo o moratta.*) 私は幸運にも賞をもらった.
Good luck! (*Koouñ o inorimasu.*) 幸運を祈ります. ★ For encouragement, Japanese often say '*Gañbatte ne*' 頑張ってね.

luckily *adv.* uˡñ yoku 運よく; koʳouñ niˡ mo 幸運にも: Luckily I caught the train. (*Uñ yoku ressha ni maniatta.*) 運よく列車に間に合った.

lucky *adj.* uˡñ no yoi 運のよい; koʳouñ na 幸運な: It was lucky that we met here. (*Wareware ga koko de aeta no wa koouñ datta.*) われわれがここで会えたのは幸運だった.

luggage *n.* teʳniˡmotsu 手荷物: I'll carry my luggage myself. (*Tenimotsu wa jibuñ de hakobimasu.*) 手荷物は自分で運びます.

lumber *n.* zaʳimoku 材木.

lump *n.* **1** (sugar) kaʳkuzaˡtoo 角砂糖: I take one lump of sugar in my coffee. (*Watashi wa koohii ni kakuzatoo o ik-ko ireru.*) 私はコーヒーに角砂糖を1個入れる.
2 (solid mass) kaʳtamari 塊: a lump of clay (*neñdo no katamari*) 粘土の塊.
3 (swelling) koʳbuˡ こぶ: a lump on the head (*atama no kobu*) 頭のこぶ.
— *vt.* ... o hiʳtoˡmatome ni suru …をひとまとめにする Ⓘ: lump items together (*koomoku o hitomatome ni suru*) 項目をひとまとめにする.

lunch *n.* chuʳushoku 昼食; hiʳrugoˡhañ 昼ご飯; beʳñtoˡo 弁当; raˡñchi ランチ: What did you have for lunch? (*Chuushoku ni nani o tabemashita ka?*) 昼食に何を食べましたか. / take lunch with one (*beñtoo o motte iku*) 弁当を持って行く.

luncheon *n.* chu⌈ushoku⌉kai 昼食会.

lung *n.* ha⌈i 肺: lung cancer (*haigañ*) 肺癌.

luxurious *adj.* ze⌈eta⌉ku na ぜいたくな; go⌉oka na 豪華な: a luxurious hotel (*gooka na hoteru*) 豪華なホテル.

luxury *n.* **1** (great comfort) ze⌈eta⌉ku ぜいたく: live in luxury (*zeetaku ni kurasu*) ぜいたくに暮らす.
2 (thing) ze⌈etakuhiñ ぜいたく品: Jewels are luxuries. (*Hooseki wa zeetakuhiñ da.*) 宝石はぜいたく品だ.

M

machine *n.* ki⌈ka⌉i 機械: Do you know how to operate this machine? (*Kono kikai wa doo yatte ugokasu no ka shitte imasu ka?*) この機械はどうやって動かすのか知っていますか.

machinery *n.* ki⌈ka⌉irui 機械類; ki⌈ka⌉i 機械: This factory has a great deal of machinery. (*Kono koojoo ni wa takusañ no kikai ga aru.*) この工場にはたくさんの機械がある.

mad *adj.* **1** (insane) ki ⌈ga kuru⌉tta [kuru⌉tte iru] 気が狂った[狂っている]: He must be mad to do such a thing. (*Soñna koto o suru nañte kare wa ki ga kurutta ni chigainai.*) そんなことをするなんて彼は気が狂ったに違いない.
2 (foolish) ba⌈ka⌉geta ばかげた; ba⌈ka⌉gete iru ばかげている; mu⌈boo na 無謀な: a mad plan (*muboo na keekaku*) 無謀な計画.
3 (angry) ha⌈ra o ta⌉teta [ta⌉tete iru] 腹を立てた[立てている]: He was mad at me for coming late. (*Kare wa watashi ga okureta no de hara o tateta.*) 彼は私が遅れたので腹を立てた.
4 (enthusiastic) mu⌈chuu ni na⌉tte (iru) 夢中になって(いる): He is mad about horse racing. (*Kare wa keeba ni muchuu ni natte iru.*) 彼は競馬に夢中になっている.

madam *n.* (older woman) o⌉kusama 奥様.

madness *n.* (being insane) kyo⌉oki 狂気; (being enthusiastic) ne⌈kkyoo 熱狂.

magazine *n.* za⌈sshi 雑誌: read a magazine (*zasshi o yomu*) 雑誌を読む / take a magazine (*zasshi o koodoku suru*) 雑誌を購読する / a weekly magazine (*shuukañshi*) 週刊誌 / a monthly magazine (*gekkañshi*) 月刊誌.

magic *n.* **1** (strange powers) ma⌈hoo 魔法: believe in magic (*mahoo o shiñjiru*) 魔法を信じる.
2 (tricks) te⌉jina 手品; ki⌉jutsu 奇術: perform magic (*tejina o suru*) 手品をする.

magnet *n.* ji⌉shaku 磁石: A magnet attracts iron. (*Jishaku wa tetsu o hikitsukeru.*) 磁石は鉄を引きつける.

magnificent *adj.* so⌈odai na 壮大な; su⌈barashi⌉i すばらしい: The views from the mountain were magnificent. (*Yama kara no nagame wa subarashikatta.*) 山からの眺めはすばらしかった.

magnify *vt.* ... o ka⌈kudai suru ...を拡大する [I]: magnify a thing with a lens (*reñzu de mono o kakudai suru*) レンズで物を拡大する.

maid *n.* o-⌈te⌉tsudai お手伝い.

mail *n.* yu⌈ubiñ 郵便: send by mail (*yuubiñ de okuru*) 郵便で送る / deliver the mail (*yuubiñ o haitatsu suru*) 郵便を配達する / Is there any mail for me? (*Watashi ni yuubiñ ga kite imasu ka?*) 私に郵便が来ていますか. / air mail (*kookuubiñ*) 航空便 / sea mail (*funabiñ*) 船便.
— *vt.* ... o yu⌈ubiñ de da⌉su ...を郵便で出す [C]; yu⌈usoo suru 郵送する

Ⓘ: I'd like to mail this letter to China. (*Kono tegami o Chuugoku e okuritai ñ desu ga.*) この手紙を中国へ送りたいんですが.

mailbox *n.* **1** (on a street) po⌉suto ポスト: put a letter into the mailbox (*tegami o posuto ni ireru*) 手紙をポストに入れる.
2 (at a home) yu⌈ubi⌉ñuke 郵便受け: take a letter out of the mailbox (*yuubiñuke kara tegami o toridasu*) 郵便受けから手紙を取り出す.

mailman *n.* yu⌈ubiñ-shuuhaininñ 郵便集配人; yu⌈ubiñya 郵便屋.

main *adj.* o⌉mo-na 主な; shu⌈yoo na 主要な: the main characters in a play (*geki no omo-na toojoo jiñbutsu*) 劇の主な登場人物 / a main road (*shuyoo dooro*) 主要道路 / the main office (*hoñsha*) 本社.
— *n.* ho⌈ñkañ 本管: a gas main (*gasu hoñkañ*) ガス本管.

mainland *n.* ho⌉ñdo 本土: the Chinese mainland (*Chuugoku hoñdo*) 中国本土.

mainly *adv.* o⌉mo ni 主に; shu⌉ to shite 主として: I mainly drink coffee in the morning. (*Asa wa omo ni koohii o nomimasu.*) 朝は主にコーヒーを飲みます.

maintain *vt.* **1** (keep) ... o i⌉ji suru ...を維持する Ⓘ; ta⌈mo⌉tsu 保つ Ⓒ: Food is necessary to maintain life. (*Tabemono wa seemee o iji suru no ni hitsuyoo da.*) 食べ物は生命を維持するのに必要だ. / I tried to maintain a steady speed. (*Watashi wa ittee no sokudo o tamotsu yoo ni shita.*) 私は一定の速度を保つようにした.
2 (support) ... o ya⌈shinau ...を養う Ⓒ: He maintains a large family on his income. (*Kare wa jibuñ no shuunyuu de dai-kazoku o yashinatte iru.*) 彼は自分の収入で大家族を養っている.
3 (declare) ... o shu⌈choo suru ...を主張する Ⓘ: He maintained that he was innocent. (*Kare wa mujitsu da to shuchoo shita.*) 彼は無実だと主張した.

maintenance *n.* i⌉ji 維持; se⌉ebi 整備; ka⌉ñri 管理: the maintenance of peace (*heewa no iji*) 平和の維持 / car maintenance (*kuruma no seebi*) 車の整備 / the maintenance of a building (*biru no kañri*) ビルの管理.

majesty *n.* i⌈geñ 威厳: the majesty of the king (*kokuoo no igeñ*) 国王の威厳 / His Imperial Majesty (*teñnoo heeka*) 天皇陛下 / Her Imperial Majesty (*koogoo heeka*) 皇后陛下.

major *adj.* (greater) o⌈oki⌉i hoo no 大きいほうの; (great) o⌉oki-na 大きな; shu⌈yoo na 主要な: The major part of my data was lost. (*Watashi no deeta no daibubuñ ga kiete shimatta.*) 私のデータの大部分が消えてしまった. / I visited the major cities of Japan. (*Nihoñ no shuyoo na toshi wa tazunemashita.*) 日本の主要な都市は訪ねました.
— *n.* se⌈ñkoo-ka⌉moku 専攻科目: My major is Japanese literature. (*Watashi no señkoo wa Nihoñ buñgaku desu.*) 私の専攻は日本文学です.
major in ... *vt.* ... o se⌈ñkoo suru ...を専攻する Ⓘ: major in mathematics (*suugaku o señkoo suru*) 数学を専攻する.

majority *n.* **1** (most) da⌈ita⌉suu 大多数; da⌈ibu⌉buñ 大部分: The majority of people agree with the plan. (*Daitasuu no hito wa sono añ ni sañsee desu.*) 大多数の人はその案に賛成です.
2 (party) ta⌈suutoo 多数党; ta⌈suuha 多数派.

make *vt.* **1** (create) ... o tsu⌈ku⌉ru ...を作る Ⓒ; se⌈esaku suru 製作する Ⓘ: She made a new dress. (*Kanojo wa atarashii doresu o tsukutta.*) 彼女は新しいドレスを作った. / This box is made of wood. (*Kono hako wa ki de dekite iru.*) この箱は木でできている.
2 (prepare) ... o yo⌉oi suru ...を用意する Ⓘ; to⌈tonoe⌉ru 整える Ⓥ: make a bed (*beddo o yooi suru*) ベッドを用意する / make coffee (*koohii o*

m

ireru) コーヒーを入れる.

3 (do) ... o su⌈ru ...をする [I]; o⌈konau 行う [C]: make a trip (*ryokoo o suru*) 旅行をする / make preparations (*juñbi o suru*) 準備をする.

4 (compel; cause) ... o ⟨verb⟩-(sa)-⌈seru ...を...(さ)せる [V]: I made him go. (*Watashi wa kare o ikaseta.*) 私は彼を行かせた. / He made us laugh. (*Kare wa watashi-tachi o warawaseta.*) 彼は私たちを笑わせた. / The news made everyone glad. (*Sono shirase wa miñna o yorokobaseta.*) その知らせはみんなを喜ばせた.

make out *vt.* ... ga wa⌈ka⌉ru ...がわかる [C]: I cannot make out what you say. (*Anata no ossharu koto ga wakarimaseñ.*) あなたのおっしゃることがわかりません.

make up for ... *vt.* ... o to⌈rikaesu ...を取り返す [C]: I have to make up for lost time. (*Okureta buñ no jikañ o torikaesanakereba naranai.*) 遅れた分の時間を取り返さなければならない.

m

maker *n.* se⌈ezoomoto 製造元; me⌉ekaa メーカー: automakers (*jidoosha meekaa*) 自動車メーカー.

male *adj.* (of people) da⌈ñsee no 男性の; (of animals) o⌈su⌉ no 雄の: a male choir (*dañsee gasshoodañ*) 男性合唱団 / a male dog (*osu no inu*) 雄の犬.

— *n.* (of a person) da⌈ñsee 男性; (of an animal) o⌈su⌉ 雄.

malice *n.* a⌉kui 悪意; te⌉ki-i 敵意: u⌈rami⌉ 恨み: I bear him no malice. (*Watashi wa kare ni nañ no urami mo arimaseñ.*) 私は彼に何の恨みもありません.

man *n.* **1** (male person) o⌈toko 男; da⌈ñsee 男性: men and women (*otoko to oñna*) 男と女.

2 (human beings) ni⌈ñgeñ 人間; hi⌈to 人: Man is mortal. (*Hito wa shinu.*) 人は死ぬ.

3 (manly person) o⌈tokorashi⌉i o⌈toko 男らしい男: He acted like a man. (*Kare wa otokorashiku furumatta.*) 彼は男らしく振る舞った.

manage *vt.* **1** (direct) ... o ke⌈e-ee suru ...を経営する [I]; ka⌉ñri suru 管理する [I]: Who manages this store? (*Dare ga kono mise o kee-ee shite imasu ka?*) だれがこの店を経営していますか.

2 (do with difficulty) do⌉o ni ka ⟨verb⟩ どうにか...: I managed to be in time for the train. (*Doo ni ka ressha ni maniatta.*) どうにか列車に間に合った.

3 (handle) ... o u⌉maku a⌈tsukau ...をうまく扱う [C]: He could not manage the horse well. (*Kare wa sono uma o umaku atsukaenakatta.*) 彼はその馬をうまく扱えなかった.

— *vi.* na⌉ñ toka ya⌈tte iku なんとかやっていく [C]: I can manage alone. (*Hitori de nañ to ka yatte ikemasu.*) 一人でなんとかやっていけます.

management *n.* **1** (managing) ke⌈e-ee 経営; ka⌉ñri 管理: Bad management caused the failure of the business. (*Kee-ee ga mazui tame ni jigyoo ga shippai shita.*) 経営がまずいために事業が失敗した.

2 (persons) ke⌈e-eesha-gawa 経営者側: The management refused to come to terms. (*Kee-eesha-gawa wa dakyoo o kyozetsu shita.*) 経営者側は妥協を拒絶した.

manager *n.* ke⌈e-e⌉esha 経営者; shi⌈ha⌉iniñ 支配人: the manager of a shop (*mise no kee-eesha*) 店の経営者 / the manager of a hotel (*hoteru no shihainiñ*) ホテルの支配人.

managing director *n.* se⌉ñmu to⌈rishimari⌉yaku 専務取締役; (president) sha⌈choo 社長.

manhood *n.* se⌈ejiñ 成人; se⌈ene⌉ñki 成年期: come to manhood 成人する.

manifest *adj.* me⌈ehaku na 明白な; ha⌈kki⌉ri shita [shite iru] はっきりした[している]: His innocence is manifest. (*Kare no mujitsu wa meehaku da.*) 彼の無実は明白だ.

— *vt.* (show) ... o ka⌈o ni da⌉su ...を顔に出す [C]: He manifested displeasure. (*Kare wa fukai o kao ni *dashita.*) 彼は不快を顔に出した.

mankind *n.* ji⌉ñrui 人類; ni⌈ñgeñ 人間: the history of mankind (*jiñrui no rekishi*) 人類の歴史.

manly *adj.* o⌈tokorashi⌉i 男らしい; da⌈ñsee-teki na 男性的な: a manly bearing (*otokorashii taido*) 男らしい態度 / a manly sport (*dañsee-teki na supootsu*) 男性的なスポーツ.

manner *n.* **1** (way) ho⌈ohoo 方法; ya⌈rikata やり方: He did it in his own manner. (*Kare wa jibuñ no yarikata de soo shita.*) 彼は自分のやり方でそうした.
2 (behavior) ta⌉ido 態度: I don't like his arrogant manner. (*Kare no oohee na taido ga ki ni iranai.*) 彼の横柄な態度が気に入らない.
3 (manners) gyo⌈ogi 行儀; sa⌉hoo 作法: He has no manners. (*Kare wa gyoogi ga warui.*) 彼は行儀が悪い.
4 (habits) fu⌈ushuu 風習; fu⌉uzoku 風俗: manners and customs (*fuuzoku shuukañ*) 風俗習慣.

manual *adj.* **1** (of the hand) te⌉ de o⌈konau 手で行う; shu⌈doo no 手動の: manual labor (*te-shigoto*) 手仕事.
2 (of working) ki⌉ñniku no 筋肉の; ni⌈kutai no 肉体の: a manual worker (*nikutai roodoosha*) 肉体労働者.
— *n.* (handbook) sho⌈osa⌉sshi 小冊子; be⌈ñrañ 便覧: an instruction manual (*setsumeesho*) 説明書.

manufacture *vt.* ... o se⌈ezoo suru ...を製造する [I]; se⌈esaku suru 製作する [I]: This factory manufactures automobiles. (*Kono koojoo wa jidoosha o seezoo shite iru.*) この工場は自動車を製造している.
— *n.* se⌈ezoo 製造; se⌈esaku 製作: the date of manufacture (*seezoo neñgappi*) 製造年月日.

manufacturer *n.* se⌈ezoo-gyo⌉o-sha 製造業者: an automobile manufacturer (*jidoosha seezoo-gyoosha*) 自動車製造業者.

manuscript *n.* ge⌈ñkoo 原稿: proofread a manuscript (*geñkoo o koosee suru*) 原稿を校正する.

many *adj.* o⌉oku no 多くの; ta⌈su⌉u no 多数の; ta⌈kusa⌉ñ no たくさんの: Many people think so. (*Ooku no hito ga soo kañgaete imasu.*) 多くの人がそう考えています. / How many eggs are there in this box? (*Kono hako ni tamago wa ikutsu arimasu ka?*) この箱に卵はいくつありますか.
— *pron.* (of people) o⌉oku no hi⌈to⌉ 多く人; (of things) o⌉oku no mo⌈no⌉ (多くの物); ta⌈su⌉u 多数: Many of them were tired. (*Kare-ra no ooku wa tsukarete ita.*) 彼らの多くは疲れていた. / How many came to the party? (*Kai ni wa nañ-niñ kimashita ka?*) 会には何人来ましたか.

map *n.* chi⌉zu 地図: Will you please draw me a map to the station? (*Eki made no chizu o kaite itadakemasu ka?*) 駅までの地図を書いていただけますか.

maple *n.* ka⌈ede かえで; mo⌉miji もみじ.

marble *n.* da⌈iri⌉seki 大理石.

march *vi.* ko⌈oshiñ suru 行進する [I]: We marched around the playground. (*Watashi-tachi wa uñdoojoo no mawari o kooshiñ shita.*) 私たちは運動場の周りを行進した.
— *vt.* ... o ko⌈oshiñ saseru ...を行進させる [V]: The teacher marched the children. (*Señsee wa kodomo-tachi o kooshiñ saseta.*) 先生は子どもたちを行進させた.
— *n.* **1** (walk) ko⌈oshiñ 行進: a march of five kilometers (*go-kiro no kooshiñ*) 5キロの行進.
2 (music) ko⌈oshi⌉ñkyoku 行進曲; ma⌉achi マーチ: play a march (*kooshiñkyoku o eñsoo suru*) 行進曲を演奏する.

March *n.* sa⌉ñ-gatsu 3月.

margin *n.* **1** (space) yo⌈haku 余白; ra⌈ñgai 欄外; ma⌉ajiñ マージン: write down in the margin (*rañgai ni kakikomu*) 欄外に書き込む.
2 (edge) fu⌈chi⌉ 縁; he⌈ri⌉ へり: the

margin of the swimming pool (*puuru no fuchi*) プールの縁.
3 (profit) ri⌈zaya 利ざや; ma⌉ajiñ マージン: a large margin (*ooki-na rizaya*) 大きな利ざや.

marine *adj*. u⌉mi no 海の; ka⌈ijoo no 海上の: marine products (*kaisañbutsu*) 海産物 / marine insurance (*kaijoo-hokeñ*) 海上保険.

mark *n*. **1** (spot) yo⌈gore 汚れ; shi⌈mi 染み; ki⌈zu きず: What are those dirty marks on your trousers? (*Kono zuboñ no kitanai yogore wa nañ desu ka?*) このズボンの汚い汚れは何ですか.
2 (sign) shi⌈rushi 印; ki⌈goo 記号: put a mark on paper (*kami ni shirushi o tsukeru*) 紙に印をつける.
3 (target) mo⌈kuhyoo 目標; ma⌈to 的: aim at the mark (*mato o nerau*) 的をねらう.
4 (grade) te⌈ñsu⌉u 点数: I got 80 marks in mathematics. (*Watashi wa suugaku de hachijut-teñ o totta.*) 私は数学で 80 点を取った.
— *vt*. **1** (put a sign) ... ni shi⌈rushi o tsuke⌉ru ...に印をつける Ⓥ: I marked his house on the map. (*Chizu ni kare no uchi no shirushi o tsuketa.*) 地図に彼の家の印をつけた.
2 (spoil) ... o yo⌈gosu ...を汚す Ⓒ: His shoes marked the floor. (*Kare wa kutsu de yuka o yogoshita.*) 彼は靴で床を汚した.
3 (give marks) ... o sa⌈iteñ suru ...を採点する Ⓘ: mark exam-papers (*shikeñ no tooañ o saiteñ suru*) 試験の答案を採点する.

market *n*. **1** (shops) i⌉chiba 市場: a vegetable market (*aomono ichiba*) 青物市場 / a fish market (*uo ichiba*) 魚市場.
2 (trade) shi⌈joo 市場. ★ '市場' is pronounced '*ichiba*' in meaning 1, and '*shijoo*' in 2: market research (*shijoo choosa*) 市場調査 / put a new product on the market (*shiñseehiñ o shijoo ni dasu*) 新製品を市場に出す.
3 (demand) ju⌈yoo 需要: There is a good market for these kinds of goods. (*Kono shu no shoohiñ wa juyoo ga ookii.*) この種の商品は需要が大きい.
— *vt*. ... o shi⌈joo ni da⌉su ...を市場に出す Ⓒ: They market cars all over the world. (*Kare-ra wa kuruma o sekai-juu no shijoo ni dashite iru.*) 彼らは車を世界中の市場に出している.

marriage *n*. **1** (act) ke⌈kkoñ 結婚: a marriage partner (*kekkoñ aite*) 結婚相手 / an arranged marriage (*miai kekkoñ*) 見合い結婚.
2 (state) ke⌈kkoñ-se⌉ekatsu 結婚生活: Their marriage was not a happy one. (*Kare-ra no kekkoñ-seekatsu wa shiawase de nakatta.*) 彼らの結婚生活は幸せでなかった.
3 (ceremony) ke⌈kko⌉ñshiki 結婚式: perform a marriage (*kekkoñ-shiki o ageru*) 結婚式を挙げる.

marry *vt*. ... to ke⌈kkoñ suru ...と結婚する Ⓘ: He married my sister. (*Kare wa watashi no imooto to kekkoñ shita.*) 彼は私の妹と結婚した. / Will you marry me? (*Watashi to kekkoñ shite kudasai.*) 私と結婚してください.
— *vi*. ke⌈kkoñ suru 結婚する Ⓘ: She married very young. (*Kanojo wa zuibuñ wakai toki ni kekkoñ shita.*) 彼女はずいぶん若いときに結婚した.

marvel *n*. kyo⌉oi 驚異; fu⌈shigi 不思議: the marvels of nature (*shizeñ no kyooi*) 自然の驚異.
— *vi*. (... ni) kyo⌈otañ suru (...に)驚嘆する Ⓘ; o⌈doro⌉ku 驚く Ⓒ: We marveled at his skill. (*Watashi-tachi wa kare no udemae ni kyootañ shita.*) 私たちは彼の腕前に驚嘆した.

marvelous *adj*. su⌈barashi⌉i すばらしい; su⌈teki na すてきな: He made a marvelous invention. (*Kare wa subarashii hatsumee o shita.*) 彼はすばらしい発明をした.

masculine *adj*. o⌈toko no 男の; da⌈nsee no 男性の; (mannish) da⌈ñsee-teki na 男性的な: a masculine woman (*dañsee-teki na josee*) 男性的な女性.

mask *n.* ma˥suku マスク; m˥eñ 面; ka˹meñ 仮面: a gas mask (*boodoku masuku*) 防毒マスク / wear a face mask (*masuku o suru*) マスクをする / put on a mask (*kameñ o kaburu*) 仮面をかぶる.

mass *n.* **1** (lump) o˥oki-na ka˹tamari 大きな塊: a mass of clouds (*kumo no ooki-na katamari*) 雲の大きな塊.
2 (a large number) ta˹su˥u 多数: A mass of people gathered in the park. (*Tasuu no hito ga kooeñ ni atsumatta.*) 多数の人が公園に集まった.
3 (people) ta˹ishuu 大衆; sho˥miñ 庶民: protect the interests of the masses (*shomiñ no rieki o mamoru*) 庶民の利益を守る.

mass communication *n.* ma˹sukomi マスコミ; ta˹ishuu-de˥ñtatsu 大衆伝達. ★ Japanese '*masukomi*' usually refers to 'mass media.'

massive *adj.* do˹sshi˥ri shita [shite iru] どっしりした[している]; ju˹uryo˥okañ no aru 重量感のある: massive furniture (*dosshiri shita kagu*) どっしりした家具 / a massive building (*juuryookañ no aru tatemono*) 重量感のある建物.

mast *n.* ma˥suto マスト; ho˹ba˥shira 帆柱.

master *n.* **1** (head) shu˥jiñ 主人; (employer) ya˹toi˥nushi 雇い主; (of an animal) ka˥inushi 飼い主: He is the master of this house. (*Kare ga kono ie no shujiñ desu.*) 彼がこの家の主人です. / A dog knows his own master. (*Inu wa kainushi o shitte iru.*) 犬は飼い主を知っている.
2 (expert) me˹eji˥ñ 名人; ta˥ika 大家: a great master in painting (*e no taika*) 絵の大家.
3 (a person with an academic degree) shu˥ushi 修士: a Master of Arts (*buñgaku shuushi*) 文学修士.
— *vt.* ... o shu˹utoku suru ...を修得する [I]; ma˥sutaa suru マスターする [I]: She mastered Japanese in a short period. (*Kanojo wa tañkikañ de Nihoñgo o shuutoku shita.*) 彼女は短期間で日本語を修得した.

masterpiece *n.* ke˹ssaku 傑作; me˹esaku 名作: This book is a masterpiece. (*Kono hoñ wa kessaku da.*) この本は傑作だ.

mat *n.* ma˥tto マット; (of straw) mu˹shiro˥ むしろ; go˹za˥ ござ: place a mat (*matto o shiku*) マットを敷く.

match[1] *n.* **1** (game) shi˹ai 試合; kyo˥ogi 競技: have a football match (*futtobooru no shiai o suru*) フットボールの試合をする.
2 (counterpart) kyo˹osoo-a˥ite 競争相手; ko˹ote˥kishu 好敵手: meet one's match (*kootekishu o eru*) 好敵手を得る.
3 (marriage) ke˹kkoñ 結婚: arrange a match (*kekkoñ o matomeru*) 結婚をまとめる.
— *vt.* **1** (suit) ... ni a˥u ...に合う [C]; ... to cho˹owa suru ...と調和する [I]: A red tie will match your suit. (*Akai nekutai ga kimi no fuku ni au deshoo.*) 赤いネクタイが君の服に合うでしょう.
2 (be equal) ... to do˹otoo da ...と同等だ; ... ni ka˹na˥u ...にかなう [C]: Nobody can match him in golf. (*Gorufu de kare ni kanau mono wa inai.*) ゴルフで彼にかなう者はいない.

match[2] *n.* ma˥tchi マッチ: strike a match (*matchi o tsukeru*) マッチをつける.

mate *n.* (companion) na˹kama˥ 仲間; a˹ite˥ 相手: a teammate (*chiimu no nakama*) チームの仲間.

material *n.* **1** (substance) ge˹ñryo˥o 原料; za˹iryo˥o 材料: What are the raw materials for making beer? (*Biiru no geñryoo wa nañ desu ka?*) ビールの原料は何ですか.
2 (data) shi˥ryoo 資料; da˹izai 題材: collect material for a novel (*shoosetsu no shiryoo o atsumeru*) 小説の資料を集める.
— *adj.* **1** (of matter) bu˹sshitsu no 物質の: material civilization

m

(*busshitsu buñmee*) 物質文明.
2 (important) juʼuyoo na 重要な; taʼisetsu na 大切な: material evidence (*juuyoo na shooko*) 重要な証拠.

maternal *adj.* ha'ha no 母の; haʼha-rashi'i 母らしい: maternal love (*boseeai*) 母性愛.

math *n.* suʼugaku 数学.

mathematics *n.* suʼugaku 数学: I am not good at mathematics. (*Suugaku wa nigate da.*) 数学は苦手だ.

matter *n.* **1** (trouble) koʼma'tta koʼto' 困ったこと: What's the matter? (*Doo shita no desu ka?*) どうしたのですか. / Nothing is the matter. (*Nañ de mo arimaseñ.*) 何でもありません.
2 (affair) koʼtogara 事柄; moʼñdai 問題: I don't like to talk about private matters. (*Kojiñ-teki na moñdai ni tsuite wa hanashitaku arimaseñ.*) 個人的な問題については話したくありません.
3 (substance) buʼsshitsu 物質; buʼttai 物体: solid matter (*kotai*) 固体.
— *vi.* moʼñdai to na'ru 問題となる Ⓒ; juʼuyoo da 重要だ: It matters much to me. (*Sore wa watashi ni totte juuyoo na koto desu.*) それは私にとって重要なことです. / It doesn't matter if you come late. (*Osoku kite mo kamaimaseñ.*) 遅く来てもかまいません.

mattress *n.* ma'ttoresu マットレス.

mature *adj.* **1** (ripe) juʼku'shita 熟した; juʼkushite iru 熟している: mature fruit (*jukushita kudamono*) 熟した果物.
2 (fully grown) seʼejuku shita [shite iru] 成熟した[している]: mature girls (*seejuku shita musume-tachi*) 成熟した娘たち.
— *vi.* **1** (grow fully) juʼkusu'ru 熟する Ⓘ: Wine and wisdom mature with age. (*Sake to fuñbetsu wa toshi to tomo ni jukusuru.*) 酒と分別は年とともに熟する.
2 (become due) maʼñki ni na'ru 満期になる Ⓒ: When does this insurance policy mature? (*Kono hokeñ wa itsu mañki ni narimasu ka?*) この保険はいつ満期になりますか.

maximum *adj.* saʼidai no 最大の; saʼikoo no 最高の: the maximum speed [temperature] (*saikoo sokudo* [*kioñ*]) 最高速度[気温].
— *n.* saʼida'igeñ 最大限; saʼiko'oteñ 最高点: This luggage weighs more than the maximum. (*Kono nimotsu no omosa wa saidaigeñdo o koete imasu.*) この荷物の重さは最大限度を越えています.

may *aux.* **1** [possibility] ... ka mo shiʼrenai …かもしれない; oʼso'raku ... daroo おそらく…だろう: It may rain tomorrow. (*Ashita wa ame ga furu ka mo shirenai.*) あしたは雨が降るかもしれない. / It may be true. (*Sore wa osoraku hoñtoo daroo.*) それはおそらく本当だろう.
2 [permission] ⟨verb⟩-te[de] mo i'i …て[で]もいい: You may go if you want to. (*Ikitakereba itte mo ii desu yo.*) 行きたければ行ってもいいですよ. / May I use this phone? (*Kono deñwa o tsukatte mo ii desu ka?*) この電話を使ってもいいですか.
3 [wish] ⟨verb⟩ yo'o ni …ように: May you have a safe journey. (*Ryokoo ga buji de arimasu yoo ni.*) 旅行が無事でありますように.

May *n.* go'-gatsu 5月.

maybe *adv.* mo'shi ka shitara もしかしたら; koʼto ni yoru to ことによると; ta'buñ たぶん: Maybe it will rain tomorrow. (*Moshi ka shitara ashita wa ame ka mo shirenai.*) もしかしたらあしたは雨かもしれない.

mayor *n.* (of a city) shi'choo 市長; (of a town) cho'ochoo 町長: Mr. Tanaka was elected mayor. (*Tanaka-sañ ga shichoo ni erabareta.*) 田中さんが市長に選ばれた.

me *pron.* **1** [direct object] waʼtashi o 私を; [indirect object] waʼtashi ni 私に: He helped me. (*Kare wa watashi o tetsudatte kureta.*) 彼は私を手伝ってくれた. / She gave me

the book. (*Kanojo wa watashi ni sono hoñ o kureta.*) 彼女は私にその本をくれた.
2 (I) wa⌈tashi 私: "Who is there?" "It's me." (*"Soko ni iru no wa dare desu ka?" "Watashi desu."*) 「そこにいるのはだれですか」「私です」

meadow *n.* bo⌈kuso⌉ochi 牧草地.

meal *n.* sho⌈kuji 食事: have three meals a day (*ichi-nichi sañ-kai shokuji o suru*) 1日3回食事をする.

mean[1] *vt.* **1** (indicate) ... o i⌉mi suru ...を意味する Ⅰ: What does the Japanese word '*hana*' mean? (*Nihoñgo no 'hana' to iu go wa doo iu imi desu ka?*) 日本語の「はな」という語はどういう意味ですか.
2 (intend) ... tsu⌈mori da ...つもりだ: I meant it as a joke. (*Joodañ no tsumori de itta no desu.*) 冗談のつもりで言ったのです. / I didn't mean to surprise you. (*Anata o odorokasu tsumori wa arimaseñ deshita.*) あなたを驚かすつもりはありませんでした.

mean[2] *adj.* **1** (base) hi⌈retsu na 卑劣な: mean behavior (*hiretsu na furumai*) 卑劣な振る舞い.
2 (vicious) i⌈ji no waru⌉i 意地の悪い: a mean fellow (*iji no warui hito*) 意地の悪い人.
3 (stingy) ke⌉chi na けちな; ki⌈tana⌉i 汚い: He is mean about money. (*Kare wa o-kane ni kitanai.*) 彼はお金に汚い.

mean[3] *adj.* (middle) chu⌈ukañ no 中間の; (average) he⌈ekiñ no 平均の: the mean annual rainfall (*neñ-kañ no heekiñ koouryoo*) 年間の平均降雨量.
— *n.* chu⌈ukañ 中間; he⌈ekiñ 平均.

meaning *n.* i⌉mi 意味: look up the meaning of the word in a dictionary (*sono go no imi o jisho de sagasu*) その語の意味を辞書で探す.

means *n.* **1** (method) shu⌉dañ 手段; ho⌈ohoo 方法: a means to an end (*mokuteki no tame no shudañ*) 目的のための手段 / a means of transportation (*kootsuu kikañ*) 交通機関.
2 (property) zai⌉sañ 財産; shu⌈unyuu 収入: live within one's means (*jibuñ no shuunyuu no hañi nai de kurasu*) 自分の収入の範囲内で暮らす.

meantime *n.* a⌈ima 合間: in the meantime (*sono kañ ni*) その間に.

meanwhile *adv.* sono ka⌉ñ ni その間に: He went shopping. Meanwhile she prepared the meal. (*Kare wa kaimono ni itta. Sono kañ ni kanojo wa shokuji no shitaku o shita.*) 彼は買い物に行った. その間に彼女は食事の支度をした.

measure *vt.* ... o ha⌈ka⌉ru ...を測る Ⓒ; so⌈kutee suru 測定する Ⅰ: She measured her waist. (*Kanojo wa jibuñ no uesuto o hakatta.*) 彼女は自分のウエストを測った.
— *vi.* ha⌈ka⌉ru 測る Ⓒ; a⌉ru ある Ⓒ: The width of this street measures 5 meters. (*Kono dooro no haba wa go-meetoru aru.*) この道路の幅は5メートルある.
— *n.* **1** (size) su⌈ñpoo 寸法.
2 (instrument) ke⌈eryo⌉oki 計量器; mo⌈nosa⌉shi 物差し: a tape measure (*makijaku*) 巻尺.
3 (unit) ta⌉ñi 単位: The meter is a measure of length. (*Meetoru wa nagasa no tañi desu.*) メートルは長さの単位です.
4 (action) ta⌈isaku 対策; sho⌉chi 処置: We should take strong measures against drunken driving. (*Yopparai uñteñ ni wa kyookoo na taisaku o toru beki da.*) 酔っぱらい運転には強硬な対策をとるべきだ.

measurement *n.* **1** (size) o⌈okisa 大きさ; su⌈ñpoo 寸法: take the measurements for a suit (*yoofuku no suñpoo o toru*) 洋服の寸法を取る / What are the measurements of this room? (*Kono heya no ookisa wa dono kurai desu ka?*) この部屋の大きさはどのくらいですか.
2 (act of measuring) so⌈kutee 測定; so⌈kuryoo 測量: the measurement of time (*jikañ no sokutee*) 時間の測定.

meat *n.* ni⌈ku⌉ 肉: cook meat (*niku o ryoori suru*) 肉を料理する.

mechanic *n.* ki⌈kai⌉koo 機械工; shu⌈uri⌉koo 修理工.

mechanical *adj.* ki⌈ka⌉i no 機械の; ki⌈ka⌉i de u⌈go⌉ku 機械で動く: a mechanical toy (*kikai de ugoku omocha*) 機械で動くおもちゃ.

mechanical pencil *n.* sha⌈apu-pe⌉ñshiru シャープペンシル.

mechanism *n.* ki⌈kaiso⌉ochi 機械装置: The recording mechanism seems to be broken. (*Rokuoñ no kikaisoochi ga kowareta yoo da.*) 録音の機械装置が壊れたようだ.

medal *n.* me⌈daru メダル; ki⌈shoo 記章: win a gold medal (*kiñ-medaru o kakutoku suru*) 金メダルを獲得する.

meddle *vi.* (... ni) ka⌈ñshoo suru (...に)干渉する [I]: Don't meddle in other people's affairs. (*Hoka no hito no koto ni kañshoo suru no wa yame nasai.*) ほかの人のことに干渉するのはやめなさい.

m

media *n.* ma⌈sume⌉dia マスメディア; ma⌈sukomi マスコミ. ⇨ mass communication

mediate *vi.* (... o) cho⌈otee suru (...を)調停する [I]; chu⌈usai suru 仲裁する [I]: mediate between employers and their workers (*koyoosha to juugyooiñ no aida o chootee suru*) 雇用者と従業員の間を調停する.

medical *adj.* i⌉gaku no 医学の; i⌉ryoo no 医療の: a medical college (*ika-daigaku*) 医科大学 / a medical checkup (*keñkoo-shiñdañ*) 健康診断.

medicine *n.* **1** (substance) ku⌈suri 薬: take the medicine for a cold (*kaze no kusuri o nomu*) かぜの薬を飲む / The medicine proved very effective. (*Sono kusuri wa totemo yoku kiita.*) その薬はとてもよく効いた.
2 (science) i⌉gaku 医学; i⌉ryoo 医療: He is studying medicine. (*Kare wa igaku o beñkyoo shite iru.*) 彼は医学を勉強している.

medieval *adj.* chu⌉usee no 中世の: medieval architecture (*chuusee no keñchiku*) 中世の建築.

meditate *vi.* fu⌈ka⌉ku ka⌈ñga⌉eru 深く考える [V]; me⌈esoo suru 瞑想する [I]: meditate on the meaning of life (*jiñsee no igi ni tsuite fukaku kañgaeru*) 人生の意義について深く考える.

meditation *n.* me⌈esoo 瞑想; ju⌈k-koo 熟考: He was deep in meditation. (*Kare wa meesoo ni fukette ita.*) 彼は瞑想にふけっていた.

medium *adj.* chu⌈ukurai no 中くらいの: a man of medium height (*chuukurai no se no dañsee*) 中くらいの背の男性.
— *n.* ba⌈itai 媒体; ki⌉kañ 機関: an advertising medium (*kookoku-baitai*) 広告媒体 / news media (*hoodoo kikañ*) 報道機関.

meet *vt.* **1** (see) ... ni a⌉u ...に会う [C]: I met her in the library. (*Watashi wa toshokañ de kanojo ni atta.*) 私は図書館で彼女に会った.
2 (welcome) ... o de⌈mukaeru ...を出迎える [V]: He went to the station to meet her. (*Kare wa kanojo o demukaeru tame ni eki e itta.*) 彼は彼女を出迎えるために駅へ行った.
3 (join) ... to ma⌈jiwa⌉ru ...と交わる [C]; go⌈oryuu suru 合流する [I]: Where does this street meet the highway? (*Kono dooro wa doko de kañseñ dooro to gooryuu shimasu ka?*) この道路はどこで幹線道路と合流しますか.
4 (satisfy) ... ni o⌈ojiru ...に応じる [V]; ko⌈tae⌉ru こたえる [V]: I'll do what I can to meet your wishes. (*Anata no kiboo ni kotaeru tame ni dekiru dake no koto wa shimasu.*) あなたの希望にこたえるためにできるだけのことはします.
— *vi.* **1** (see) a⌉u 会う [C]: We met quite by chance. (*Watashi-tachi wa mattaku guuzeñ ni atta.*) 私たちはまったく偶然に会った.
2 (come together) a⌈tsuma⌉ru 集まる [C]; ka⌈igoo suru 会合する [I]: We meet together once a week. (*Watashi-tachi wa shuu ni ichi-do atsu-

marimasu.) 私たちは週に一度集まります.

meet with ... *vt.* ... ni a'u ...に遭う: meet with an accident (*jiko ni au*) 事故に遭う.

meeting *n.* ka'i 会; ka'igi 会議; shu'ukai 集会: hold a meeting (*kai o hiraku*) 会を開く / He was absent from the meeting. (*Kare wa kaigi o kesseki shita.*) 彼は会議を欠席した.

melody *n.* se'ñritsu 旋律; me'rodii メロディー: She played a beautiful melody on the piano. (*Kanojo wa utsukushii merodii o piano de hiita.*) 彼女は美しいメロディーをピアノで弾いた.

melt *vi.* to'ke'ru 溶ける V: All the ice has melted. (*Koori ga zeñbu tokete shimatta.*) 氷が全部溶けてしまった.

— *vt.* ... o to'ka'su ...を溶かす C: melt sugar in water (*satoo o mizu ni tokasu*) 砂糖を水に溶かす.

member *n.* ka'iiñ 会員; me'ñbaa メンバー: I am a member of this club. (*Watashi wa kono kurabu no kaiiñ desu.*) 私はこのクラブの会員です.

membership *n.* ka'iiñ no shikaku 会員の資格: He lost his membership. (*Kare wa kaiiñ no shikaku o ushinatta.*) 彼は会員の資格を失った.

memorial *n.* ki'ne'ñbutsu 記念物; ki'ne'ñhi 記念碑.

— *adj.* ki'neñ no 記念の: a memorial festival (*kineñsai*) 記念祭.

memorize *vt.* ... o ki'oku suru ...を記憶する I; a'ñki suru 暗記する I: memorize a poem (*shi o añki suru*) 詩を暗記する.

memory *n.* **1** (power of remembering) ki'oku'ryoku 記憶力: He has a good memory. (*Kare wa kiokuryoku ga ii.*) 彼は記憶力がいい.

2 (something remembered) ki'oku 記憶; o'moide 思い出: I have no memory of my mother. (*Watashi wa haha no kioku ga nai.*) 私は母の記憶がない. / memories of one's childhood (*kodomo no koro no omoide*) 子どもの頃の思い出.

mend *vt.* **1** (repair) ... o na'o'su ...を直す C; shu'uzeñ suru 修繕する I: mend a broken chair (*kowareta isu o naosu*) 壊れたいすを直す.

2 (correct) ... o a'ratame'ru ...を改める V: mend one's ways (*okonai o aratameru*) 行いを改める.

— *vi.* yo'ku naru よくなる C: The child will soon mend. (*Kodomo wa sugu yoku naru deshoo.*) 子どもはすぐよくなるでしょう.

mental *adj.* se'eshiñ no 精神の; chi'noo no 知能の: mental disorders (*seeshiñ shoogai*) 精神障害 / a mental test (*chinoo keñsa*) 知能検査.

mention *vt.* ... o ha'na'su ...を話す C; ... to i'u ...と言う C: He mentioned the plan, but gave no details. (*Kare wa sono keekaku no koto o hanashita ga kuwashii koto wa iwanakatta.*) 彼はその計画のことを話したが詳しいことは言わなかった.

Don't mention it. (*Doo itashimashite.*) どういたしまして.

menu *n.* ko'ñdatehyoo 献立表; me'nyuu メニュー: Can I see the menu? (*Menyuu o misete kudasai.*) メニューを見せてください.

merchandise *n.* sho'ohiñ 商品: general merchandise (*zakka*) 雑貨.

merchant *n.* sho'oniñ 商人: a timber merchant (*zaimokushoo*) 材木商.

merciful *adj.* ji'hibuka'i 慈悲深い; na'sakebuka'i 情け深い: a merciful judge (*jihibukai saibañkañ*) 慈悲深い裁判官.

merciless *adj.* mu'ji'hi na 無慈悲な; na'sake yo'osha no nai 情け容赦のない: merciless criticism (*nasake yoosha no nai hihyoo*) 情け容赦のない批評.

mercury *n.* su'igiñ 水銀.

mercy *n.* **1** (compassion) ji'hi 慈悲; a'waremi' 哀れみ; na'sake 情け: show mercy toward one's enemy (*teki ni nasake o kakeru*) 敵に情けをかける.

2 (blessing) ko'ouñ 幸運: It was a

mercy that it did not rain. (*Ame ga furanakatta no wa koouñ datta.*) 雨が降らなかったのは幸運だった.

mere *adj.* ho⌈ñ no ほんの; ta⌉da no ただの: He is still a mere child. (*Kare wa mada hoñ no kodomo da.*) 彼はまだほんの子どもだ.

merely *adv.* ta⌉ñ ni ... dake 単に…だけ; ta⌉da ... dake ただ…だけ: I said so merely as a joke. (*Tañ ni joodañ to shite itta dake desu.*) 単に冗談として言っただけです.

merge *vi.* **1** (combine) ga⌈ppee suru 合併する [I]; i⌈ssho ni na⌉ru いっしょになる [C]: The roads merge two kilometers ahead. (*Sono michi wa ni-kiro saki de issho ni narimasu.*) その道は2キロ先でいっしょになります.
2 (blend gradually) shi⌈dai ni ... ni na⌉ru 次第に…になる [C]: Twilight slowly merged into darkness. (*Tasogare ga shidai ni kurayami to natta.*) たそがれが次第に暗やみとなった.
— *vt.* ... o ga⌈ppee suru …を合併する [I]; he⌈egoo suru 併合する [I]: The two companies were merged. (*Sono futatsu no kaisha wa gappee shita.*) その二つの会社は合併した.

merit *n.* **1** (worth) ka⌉chi 価値: This work has great merit. (*Kono shigoto wa hijoo ni kachi ga aru.*) この仕事は非常に価値がある.
2 (good quality) cho⌉osho 長所; to⌈rie⌉ とりえ: What are the merits of this plan? (*Kono keekaku no choosho wa nañ desu ka?*) この計画の長所は何ですか.
— *vt.* ... ni a⌈tai suru …に値する [I]: He merits the prize. (*Kare wa sono shoo ni atai suru.*) 彼はその賞に値する.

merry *adj.* yo⌈oki na 陽気な; yu⌉kai na 愉快な: a merry laugh (*yooki na warai*) 陽気な笑い / We had a merry time at the party. (*Watashi-tachi wa paatii de yukai na toki o sugoshita.*) 私たちはパーティーで愉快な時を過ごした.

mess *n.* (untidy condition) chi⌈rakatte iru koto⌉ 散らかっていること; sa⌈ñrañ 散乱; me⌈chakucha めちゃくちゃ: The room was in a mess. (*Heya wa chirakatte ita.*) 部屋は散らかっていた.

message *n.* ko⌈tozuke⌉ 言づけ; de⌈ñgoñ 伝言: I left a message with him. (*Watashi wa kare ni deñgoñ o tanoñda.*) 私は彼に伝言を頼んだ.

messenger *n.* tsu⌈kai no mono⌉ 使いの者; shi⌉sha 使者: dispatch a messenger (*shisha o okuru*) 使者を送る.

metal *n.* ki⌉ñzoku 金属: precious metals (*kikiñzoku*) 貴金属.

meter[1] *n.* me⌈etoru メートル: One meter is equal to about 40 inches. (*Ichi-meetoru wa yaku yoñjuu-iñchi ni hitoshii.*) 1メートルは約40インチに等しい. ★ In Japan the metric system is used.

meter[2] *n.* ke⌈eryo⌉oki 計量器; me⌈etaa メーター: a gas meter (*gasu no meetaa*) ガスのメーター.

method *n.* ho⌈ohoo 方法; ho⌈oshiki 方式: the best method of learning Japanese (*Nihoñgo o manabu saizeñ no hoohoo*) 日本語を学ぶ最善の方法.

metropolis *n.* shu⌉to 首都; shu⌈yoo to⌉shi 主要都市.

metropolitan *adj.* shu⌉to no 首都の; da⌈ito⌉shi no 大都市の: the metropolitan area (*shutokeñ*) 首都圏.

microphone *n.* ma⌈ikuro⌉hoñ マイクロホン; ma⌉iku マイク: speak into a microphone (*maiku de hanasu*) マイクで話す.

microscope *n.* ke⌈ñbikyoo 顕微鏡: examine germs under a microscope (*keñbikyoo de saikiñ o shiraberu*) 顕微鏡で細菌を調べる.

midday *n.* sho⌉ogo 正午; ma⌈hiru 真昼.

middle *n.* **1** (of a place) ma⌈ñnaka 真ん中; chu⌈uo⌉o 中央: There is an island in the middle of the lake. (*Mizuumi no mañnaka ni shima ga aru.*) 湖の真ん中に島がある.
2 (of time) na⌈kagoro 中ごろ; na⌈ka⌉ba 半ば: The cherry blossoms

m

bloom in the middle of April. (*Sakura wa shi-gatsu nakaba ni sakimasu.*) 桜は4月半ばに咲きます.
— *adj.* ma⌈ñnaka no 真ん中の; chu⌈uo⌉o no 中央の: the middle seat in a row (*retsu no mañnaka no seki*) 列の真ん中の席.

middle age *n.* chu⌈uneñ 中年; sho⌈roo 初老: middle age spread (*chuuneñ-butori*) 中年太り.

midnight *n.* ma⌈yo⌉naka 真夜中; yo⌉ru no ju⌈uni⌉-ji 夜の12時: He returned home at midnight. (*Kare wa yoru no juuni-ji ni ie ni kaetta.*) 彼は夜の12時に家に帰った.

might *aux.* **1** [possibility] ... ka mo shi⌈renai ...かもしれない: He might be able to help you. (*Kare wa anata o tasukeru koto ga dekiru ka mo shirenai.*) 彼はあなたを助けることができるかもしれない. / It might rain tomorrow. (*Ashita wa ame ka mo shirenai.*) あしたは雨かもしれない.
2 [permission] ... ⟨verb⟩-te[de] mo yo⌉i ...て[で]もよい: I asked her if I might use the phone. (*Kanojo ni deñwa o tsukatte mo yoi ka to kiita.*) 彼女に電話を使ってもよいかと聞いた.

mighty *adj.* chi⌈karazuyo⌉i 力強い; kyo⌈oryoku na 強力な: a mighty blow (*kyooryoku na ichigeki*) 強力な一撃.

mild *adj.* **1** (of a person) o⌈ñkoo na 温厚な; o⌈ñwa na 穏和な; ya⌈sashii 優しい: He is mild of manner. (*Kare wa taido ga oñkoo da.*) 彼は態度が温厚だ.
2 (of weather) o⌈ñdañ na 温暖な; o⌈da⌉yaka na 穏やかな: We enjoyed a mild winter this year. (*Kotoshi no fuyu wa oñdañ datta.*) ことしの冬は温暖だった.
3 (of taste) tsu⌉yoku nai 強くない; ka⌉raku nai 辛くない: This curry is mild. (*Kono karee wa karaku nai.*) このカレーは辛くない.

mile *n.* ma⌉iru マイル: One mile equals about 1.6 kilometers. (*Ichi-mairu wa yaku it-teñ rok-kiro ni ataru.*) 1マイルは約1.6キロにあたる.
★ In Japan the metric system is used.

military *adj.* gu⌉ñ no 軍の: military forces (*guñtai*) 軍隊 / a military base (*guñji kichi*) 軍事基地.
— *n.* gu⌉ñtai 軍隊.

milk *n.* gyu⌈unyuu 牛乳; mi⌉ruku ミルク: have a glass of milk (*koppu ip-pai no gyuunyuu o nomu*) コップ1杯の牛乳を飲む.
— *vt.* chi⌉chi o shi⌈bo⌉ru 乳を搾る: milk a cow (*ushi no chichi o shiboru*) 牛の乳を搾る.

mill *n.* **1** (machine) se⌈efu⌉ñki 製粉機: a coffee mill (*koohii-hiki*) コーヒーひき.
2 (factory) se⌈efuñjo 製粉所: a water mill (*suishagoya*) 水車小屋.
— *vt.* ... o se⌈efuñ suru ...を製粉する ①: mill grain (*kokurui o seefuñ suru*) 穀類を製粉する.

million *n.* hya⌈ku-ma⌉ñ 100万: ten million (*is-señ-mañ*) 1千万.

millionaire *n.* hya⌈kumañ-cho⌉oja 百万長者; o⌈ogane⌉mochi 大金持ち.

mind *n.* **1** (part of a person) ko⌈ko⌉ro 心; se⌉eshiñ 精神: She is pure in mind. (*Kanojo wa kokoro ga kiree da.*) 彼女は心がきれいだ.
2 (intellect) chi⌉see 知性: improve one's mind (*chisee o migaku*) 知性を磨く.
3 (memory) ki⌈oku 記憶: keep a person's name in mind (*hito no namae o kioku ni todomeru*) 人の名前を記憶にとどめる.
4 (opinion) i⌉keñ 意見; ka⌈ñga⌉e 考え: change one's mind (*kañgae o kaeru*) 考えを変える.
— *vt.* **1** (take care) ... ni chu⌉ui suru ...に注意する ①: Mind your step. (*Ashimoto ni chuui shi nasai.*) 足もとに注意しなさい.
2 [in the negative] ... o i⌈yaga⌉ru ...をいやがる: I don't mind hard work. (*Tsurai shigoto de mo kamaimaseñ.*) つらい仕事でもかまいません.
do you mind if ... ⟨verb⟩-te[de] mo i⌉i desu ka? ...て[で]もいいですか:

m

Do you mind if I smoke here? (*Koko de tabako o sutte mo ii desu ka?*) ここでたばこを吸ってもいいですか.
make up one's mind *vt.* ... to ke|sshiñ suru …と決心する [I]: He made up his mind to be a doctor. (*Kare wa isha ni naroo to kesshiñ shita.*) 彼は医者になろうと決心した.

mine[1] *pron.* wa⌈tashi no mono| 私のもの: This umbrella is mine. (*Kono kasa wa watashi no mono da.*) この傘は私のものだ. / Your shirt is white and mine is blue. (*Kimi no shatsu wa shiro de watashi no wa ao da.*) 君のシャツは白で私のは青だ.

mine[2] *n.* ko|ozañ 鉱山: a diamond mine (*daiyamoñdo koozañ*) ダイヤモンド鉱山 / a coal mine (*tañkoo*) 炭鉱.
— *vt.* ... o ho⌈rida|su …を掘り出す [C]; sa⌈ikutsu suru 採掘する [I]: mine gold (*kiñ o horidasu*) 金を掘り出す.

miner *n.* ko⌈oiñ 坑員; ta⌈ñkoo roodo|osha 炭坑労働者.

mineral *n.* ko|obutsu 鉱物.

mingle *vt.* ... o ma⌈ze|ru …を混ぜる [V]: mingle two colors (*futatsu no iro o mazeru*) 二つの色を混ぜる.
— *vi.* (... to) i⌈rimaji|ru (…と)入り交じる [C]; ma⌈jiwa|ru 交わる [C]: She is too shy to mingle with others. (*Kanojo wa totemo uchiki de hoka no hito to majiwaranai.*) 彼女はとても内気でほかの人と交わらない.

minimum *adj.* sa⌈ishoo no 最小の; sa⌈itee no 最低の: the minimum temperature (*saitee oñdo*) 最低温度 / minimum wages (*saitee chiñgiñ*) 最低賃金.
— *n.* sa⌈isho|ogeñ 最小限; sa⌈ite|egeñ 最低限: have a minimum of eight hours of sleep (*saitee hachi-jikañ no suimiñ o toru*) 最低8時間の睡眠をとる.

minister *n.* da|ijiñ 大臣; ko|oshi 公使: the Prime Minister (*Soori daijiñ*) 総理大臣 / the United States Minister to Japan (*chuunichi Beekoku kooshi*) 駐日米国公使.

ministry *n.* sho|o 省: the Ministry of Finance [Education] (*ookura* [*moñbu*] *shoo*) 大蔵[文部]省.

mink *n.* mi|ñku ミンク.

minor *adj.* **1** (smaller) chi⌈isa|i hoo no 小さいほうの; chi|isa-na 小さな: make a minor alteration to the plan (*sekkee ni chiisa-na heñkoo o kuwaeru*) 設計に小さな変更を加える.
2 (unimportant) ju⌈uyoo de na|i 重要でない; ta|ishita ko⌈to no na|i たいしたことのない: a minor accident (*taishita koto no nai jiko*) たいしたことのない事故.
— *n.* **1** (person) mi⌈seene|ñsha 未成年者: No Minors. (*Miseeneñsha okotowari.*) 未成年者お断り.
2 (music) ta|ñchoo 短調; ta⌈ño|ñkai 短音階.

minority *n.* sho⌈osu|u 少数; sho⌈osuuha 少数派: They were in the minority. (*Kare-ra wa shoosuuha datta.*) 彼らは少数派だった.

minus *adj.* **1** (negative) ma⌈inasu no マイナスの; fu| no 負の: a minus quantity (*fusuu*) 負数.
2 (less than zero) hyo⌈ote|ñka ... 氷点下…; re|eka ... 零下…: The temperature is minus ten degrees. (*Kioñ wa reeka juu-do desu.*) 気温は零下10度です.
— *prep.* (subtract) ... o hi⌈ita …を引いた: Seven minus three is four. (*Nana hiku sañ wa yoñ desu.*) 7引く3は4です.
— *n.* (sign) ma⌈inasu-ki|goo マイナス記号; fu⌈su|u 負数.

minute *n.* **1** (of time) fu|ñ 分: It's five minutes to five. (*Go-ji go-fuñ mae desu.*) 5時5分前です. 《⇨ appendix》
2 (moment) shu⌈ñkañ 瞬間.
in a minute *adv.* su|gu (ni) すぐ(に): I'll do it in a minute. (*Sugu yarimasu.*) すぐやります.
Just a minute. (*Chotto matte kudasai.*) ちょっと待ってください.

miracle *n.* **1** (supernatural event) ki⌈seki 奇跡: perform a miracle (*kiseki o okonau*) 奇跡を行う.

m

2 (wonder) kyo˥oi 驚異; fu⌈shigi na koto˥ 不思議なこと: a miracle of science (*kagaku no kyooi*) 科学の驚異.

mirror *n.* ka⌈gami˥ 鏡: look in a mirror (*kagami o nozoku*) 鏡をのぞく.

miscellaneous *adj.* i⌈roiro na いろいろな; za⌈tta na 雑多な: miscellaneous goods (*zakka*) 雑貨.

mischief *n.* i⌈tazura いたずら: get into mischief (*itazura o hajimeru*) いたずらを始める.

mischievous *adj.* i⌈tazurazuki na いたずら好きな; wa⌈ñpaku na わんぱくな: a mischievous child (*itazurakko*) いたずらっ子.

miser *n.* ke˥chiñboo けちんぼう.

miserable *adj.* **1** (unhappy) mi˥jime na 惨めな; fu⌈ko˥o na 不幸な: I was miserable when I failed in the exam. (*Shikeñ ni shippai shita toki wa mijime datta.*) 試験に失敗したときは惨めだった.

2 (poor) so˥matsu na 粗末な; mi⌈suborashi˥i みすぼらしい: a miserable house (*misuborashii ie*) みすぼらしい家.

3 (unpleasant) fu⌈yu˥kai na 不愉快な; i⌈ya˥ na いやな: miserable weather (*iya na teñki*) いやな天気.

misery *n.* mi˥jime˥sa 惨めさ; kyu⌈uboo 窮乏; ku˥nañ 苦難: live in misery (*mijime na seekatsu o suru*) 惨めな生活をする.

misfortune *n.* fu˥uñ 不運; fu⌈ko˥o 不幸: He had the misfortune to have his wallet stolen. (*Kare wa fukoo ni mo saifu o nusumareta.*) 彼は不幸にも財布を盗まれた.

mishap *n.* fu⌈ko˥o na de⌈ki˥goto 不幸な出来事; ji˥ko 事故.

mislead *vt.* ... o ma⌈yowase˥ru ...を迷わせる Ⓥ; da⌈ma˥su だます Ⓒ: I was misled by his appearance. (*Watashi wa kare no mikake ni damasareta.*) 私は彼の見かけにだまされた.

misleading *adj.* hi⌈to o ayamarase˥ru 人を誤らせる; go⌈kai o mane˥ku 誤解を招く: a misleading explanation (*gokai o maneku setsumee*) 誤解を招く説明.

misprint *n.* mi⌈supuri˥ñto ミスプリント; go⌈shoku 誤植.

miss *vt.* **1** (fail to catch) ... o ⟨verb⟩-sokona˥u ...を...そこなう Ⓒ: miss a catch (*booru o tori-sokonau*) ボールを捕りそこなう / I missed the last train. (*Watashi wa saishuu ressha ni nori-sokonatta.*) 私は最終列車に乗りそこなった.

2 (fail to obtain) ... o no⌈ga˥su ...を逃す Ⓒ: miss a good chance (*yoi kikai o nogasu*) よい機会を逃す.

3 (fail to keep) ... o nu⌈kasu ...を抜かす Ⓒ: Don't miss my name off the list. (*Watashi no namae o meebo kara nukasanaide kudasai.*) 私の名前を名簿から抜かさないでください.

4 (feel sad) sa⌈bi˥shiku o⌈mo˥u 寂しく思う Ⓒ: I will miss you when you move out. (*Anata ga hikkoshi suru to sabishiku narimasu.*) あなたが引っ越しすると寂しくなります.

Miss *n.* -sañ さん: Miss Brown (*Burauñ-sañ*) ブラウンさん.

missing *adj.* yu⌈kuefu˥mee no 行方不明の; mi⌈ataranai 見当たらない: a missing child (*yukuefumee no kodomo*) 行方不明の子ども / My glasses are missing. (*Megane ga miataranai.*) 眼鏡が見当たらない.

mission *n.* shi˥setsu 使節; shi⌈setsu˥dañ 使節団: a trade mission (*booeki shisetsudañ*) 貿易使節団.

mist *n.* ki⌈ri 霧; ka⌈sumi かすみ: The mist has cleared. (*Kiri ga hareta.*) 霧が晴れた.

mistake *n.* ma⌈chiga˥i 間違い; a⌈yamari˥ 誤り. ★ Japanese often say '*misu*' for English 'mistake': Everyone makes mistakes. (*Dare de mo machigai wa suru.*) だれでも間違いはする. / Someone took my umbrella by mistake. (*Dare-ka ga watashi no kasa o machigaete motte itta.*) だれかが私の傘を間違えて持って行った. / It was my mistake. (*Sore wa watashi no misu deshita.*) それは私のミス

m

でした.

— *vt.* ... o ma⌈chigae⌉ru ...を間違える Ⓥ; a⌈yama⌉ru 誤る Ⓒ: I mistook the way. (*Watashi wa michi o machigaeta.*) 私は道を間違えた. / She is often mistaken for her sister. (*Kanojo wa yoku imooto to machigaerareru.*) 彼女はよく妹と間違えられる.

mistaken *adj.* ma⌈chiga⌉eta 間違えた; ma⌈chiga⌉ete iru 間違えている: He was mistaken about the date of the meeting. (*Kare wa kaigi no hi o machigaete ita.*) 彼は会議の日を間違えていた.

mistress *n.* **1** (head of a household) o⌈ñnashu⌉jiñ 女主人; shu⌉fu 主婦.

2 (teacher) o⌈ñna no señse⌉e 女の先生.

mistrust *vt.* ... o shi⌈ñyoo shinai ...を信用しない; shi⌈ñrai shinai 信頼しない: I mistrust what he says. (*Watashi wa kare ga iu koto o shiñyoo shimaseñ.*) 私は彼が言うことを信用しません.

— *n.* fu⌈shiñ 不信; gi⌈waku 疑惑.

misunderstand *vt.* ... o go⌈kai suru ...を誤解する Ⓘ: I misunderstood his meaning. (*Watashi wa kare no imi o gokai shite ita.*) 私は彼の意味を誤解していた.

— *vi.* go⌈kai suru 誤解する Ⓘ: He often misunderstands. (*Kare wa yoku gokai suru.*) 彼はよく誤解する.

misunderstanding *n.* go⌈kai 誤解; i⌉keñ no chi⌈gai 意見の違い: clear up a misunderstanding (*gokai o toku*) 誤解を解く.

misuse *vt.* ... o go⌈yoo suru ...を誤用する Ⓘ; a⌈kuyoo suru 悪用する Ⓘ: misuse a tool (*doogu o goyoo suru*) 道具を誤用する.

— *n.* go⌈yoo 誤用; a⌈kuyoo 悪用.

mix *vt.* **1** (blend) ... o ma⌈ze⌉ru ...を混ぜる Ⓥ: mix cement and sand (*semeñto to suna o mazeru*) セメントと砂を混ぜる.

2 (prepare) ... o ma⌉zete tsu⌈ku⌉ru ...を混ぜて作る Ⓒ: She is mixing a cake. (*Kanojo wa keeki o tsukutte iru tokoro desu.*) 彼女はケーキを作っているところです.

— *vi.* **1** (blend) ma⌈za⌉ru 混ざる Ⓒ; ko⌈ñgoo suru 混合する Ⓘ: Oil and water will not mix. (*Abura to mizu wa mazaranai.*) 油と水は混ざらない.

2 (go together) (... to) ma⌈jiwa⌉ru (...と)交わる Ⓒ: I don't like to mix with people. (*Watashi wa hito to majiwaru no wa suki de wa nai.*) 私は人と交わるのは好きではない.

mixture *n.* **1** (act of mixing) ko⌈ñgoo 混合: mixture of eggs and milk (*tamago to gyuunyuu no koñgoo*) 卵と牛乳の混合.

2 (things mixed) ko⌈ñgo⌉obutsu 混合物: Air is a mixture of gases. (*Kuuki wa kitai no koñgoobutsu desu.*) 空気は気体の混合物です.

mob *n.* bo⌉oto 暴徒; ya⌈jiuma やじ馬.

mock *vt.* **1** (imitate) ... no ma⌈ne o suru ...のまねをする Ⓘ: He mocked his teacher. (*Kare wa señsee no mane o shita.*) 彼は先生のまねをした.

2 (scorn) ... o a⌈zake⌉ru ...をあざける Ⓥ: He mocked my ideas. (*Kare wa watashi no kañgae o azaketta.*) 彼は私の考えをあざけった.

mode *n.* **1** (manner) ho⌈ohoo 方法; yo⌈oshiki 様式: a mode of life (*seekatsu yooshiki*) 生活様式.

2 (fashion) ryu⌈ukoo 流行; mo⌉odo モード: She was dressed in the latest mode. (*Kanojo wa saishiñ ryuukoo no fuku o kite ita.*) 彼女は最新流行の服を着ていた.

model *n.* **1** (small copy) mo⌈kee 模型: a model of a ship (*fune no mokee*) 船の模型.

2 (version) ka⌈ta⌉ 型; de⌈za⌉iñ デザイン: My car is the latest model. (*Watashi no kuruma wa saishiñgata desu.*) 私の車は最新型です.

3 (example) mo⌈hañ 模範; te⌈ho⌉ñ 手本: a model student (*mohañsee*) 模範生 / He made his father his model. (*Kare wa chichioya o tehoñ to shita.*) 彼は父親を手本とした.

4 (person) mo⌉deru モデル: an artist's model (*gaka no moderu*) 画家のモデル.

— *vt.* **1** (shape) ... o tsukuru ...を作る [C]: The children are modeling animals in clay. (*Kodomo-tachi wa neñdo de doobutsu o tsukutte iru.*) 子どもたちは粘土で動物を作っている.

2 (pose as a model) ... no moderu o suru ...のモデルをする [I]: She modeled swimming suits. (*Kanojo wa mizugi no moderu o shita.*) 彼女は水着のモデルをした.

moderate *adj.* **1** (not extreme) tekido no 適度の: moderate exercise (*tekido no uñdoo*) 適度の運動.

2 (temperate) oñkeñ na 穏健な: He is moderate in his opinions. (*Kare wa ikeñ ga oñkeñ da.*) 彼は意見が穏健だ.

3 (reasonable) tegoro na 手ごろな: The prices are moderate. (*Nedañ wa tegoro desu.*) 値段は手ごろです.

modern *adj.* **1** (contemporary) geñdai no 現代の; kiñdai no 近代の: modern times (*geñdai*) 現代 / modern literature (*kiñdai buñgaku*) 近代文学.

2 (new) geñdai-teki na 現代的な; modañ na モダンな: a modern hotel (*geñdaifuu no hoteru*) 現代風のホテル.

modest *adj.* **1** (humble) hikaeme na 控えめな; keñsoñ shita けんそんした: a modest attitude (*hikaeme na taido*) 控えめな態度.

2 (simple) sasayaka na ささやかな; shisso na 質素な: He lives in a modest house. (*Kare wa shisso na ie ni suñde iru.*) 彼は質素な家に住んでいる.

modesty *n.* keñsoñ けんそん; keñkyo 謙虚; (of a woman) shitoyakasa しとやかさ.

modification *n.* heñkoo 変更; shuusee 修正: The plan needs slight modification. (*Keekaku wa sukoshi shuusee ga hitsuyoo da.*) 計画は少し修正が必要だ.

modify *vt.* **1** (change) ... o heñkoo suru ...を変更する [I]: We modified our plans. (*Watashi-tachi wa keekaku o heñkoo shita.*) 私たちは計画を変更した.

2 (revise) ... o shuusee suru ...を修正する [I]: We slightly modified the wording. (*Hyoogeñ o tashoo shuusee shita.*) 表現を多少修正した.

3 (moderate) ... o yurumeru ...を緩める [V]; kageñ suru 加減する [I]: modify one's demand (*yookyuu o yurumeru*) 要求を緩める.

4 (qualify) ... o shuushoku suru ...を修飾する [I]: Adverbs modify verbs. (*Fukushi wa dooshi o shuushoku suru.*) 副詞は動詞を修飾する.

moist *adj.* shimetta 湿った; shimette iru 湿っている; nureta ぬれた; nurete iru ぬれている: moist air (*shimetta kuuki*) 湿った空気.

moisten *vt.* ... o shimerasu ...を湿らす [C]; nurasu ぬらす [C]: moisten one's lips (*kuchibiru o shimerasu*) 唇を湿らす.

— *vi.* shimeru 湿る [C]; nureru ぬれる [V].

moisture *n.* shikke 湿気; suibuñ 水分.

mold[1] *n.* kata 型; nagashigata 流し型: a jelly mold (*zerii no nagashigata*) ゼリーの流し型.

— *vt.* ... o kata ni irete tsukuru ...を型に入れて作る [C]; ... de tsukuru ...で作る [C]: mold a vase out of clay (*neñdo de kabiñ o tsukuru*) 粘土で花びんを作る.

mold[2] *n.* kabi かび: This bread has mold on it. (*Kono pañ wa kabi ga haete iru.*) このパンはかびが生えている.

mole[1] *n.* (animal) mogura もぐら.

mole[2] *n.* (small spot on the skin) hokuro ほくろ.

molecule *n.* buñshi 分子.

moment *n.* **1** (a short period of time) shuñkañ 瞬間; chotto no aida ちょっとの間: Wait a moment, please. (*Chotto matte kudasai.*) ちょっと待ってください. / He went out a moment ago. (*Kare wa chotto mae ni gaishutsu shimashita.*) 彼はちょっと前に外出しました.

m

2 (a particular time) to⌈ki⌉ 時; ba⌈ai 場合: Now is the moment to decide. (*Ima ga ketsudañ suru toki da.*) 今が決断する時だ. / He is not here at the moment. (*Kare wa ima koko ni imaseñ.*) 彼は今ここにいません.

monarch *n.* ku⌉ñshu 君主.

monarchy *n.* ku⌈ñshu-se⌉eji 君主政治; ku⌈ñshu-se⌉etai 君主政体.

monastery *n.* shu⌈udo⌉oiñ 修道院.

Monday *n.* ge⌈tsuyo⌉o(bi) 月曜(日).

money *n.* ka⌈ne 金; o-⌈kane お金; (coin) ko⌉oka 硬貨; (paper note) sa⌈tsu 札; o-⌈satsu お札; shi⌉hee 紙幣: I've spent all my money. (*O-kane wa zeñbu tsukatte shimaimashita.*) お金は全部使ってしまいました. / She is saving money to buy a TV. (*Kanojo wa terebi o kau tame ni o-kane o tamete iru.*) 彼女はテレビを買うためにお金を貯めている.

monkey *n.* sa⌉ru 猿.

monologue *n.* do⌈kuhaku 独白.

monopolize *vt.* ... no do⌈kuseñ-keñ o e⌉ru ...の独占権を得る V; ... o do⌈kuseñ suru ...を独占する I: This company monopolizes the silk market. (*Kono kaisha wa ki-ito shijoo o dokuseñ shite iru.*) この会社は生糸市場を独占している.

monopoly *n.* do⌈kuseñ 独占; se⌈ñbai 専売: a government monopoly (*seefu no señbai*) 政府の専売.

monotonous *adj.* ta⌈ñchoo na 単調な; ta⌈ikutsu na 退屈な: My job was very monotonous. (*Watashi no shigoto wa hijoo ni taikutsu datta.*) 私の仕事は非常に退屈だった.

monotony *n.* ta⌈ñchoo 単調; ta⌈ikutsu 退屈.

monster *n.* ka⌈ibutsu 怪物; ba⌈ke-mono⌉ 化け物.

monstrous *adj.* **1** (huge) kyo⌈dai na 巨大な; ka⌈ibutsu no 怪物の: a monstrous elephant (*kyozoo*) 巨象.
2 (horrible) o⌈soru be⌉ki 恐るべき; to⌈ñdemona⌉i とんでもない: a monstrous lie (*toñdemonai uso*) とんでもないうそ.

month *n.* tsu⌈ki⌉ 月.

monthly *adj.* ma⌈itsuki no 毎月の; tsu⌈ki⌉ i⌈k-ka⌉i no 月1回の: a monthly magazine (*gekkañ zasshi*) 月刊雑誌 / a monthly income (*gesshuu*) 月収.

monument *n.* **1** (structure) ki⌈ne⌉ñhi 記念碑: put up a monument (*kineñhi o tateru*) 記念碑を建てる.
2 (remains) i⌈seki 遺跡: an ancient monument (*kodai no iseki*) 古代の遺跡.

monumental *adj.* **1** (of memory) ki⌈neñ no 記念の: a monumental statue (*kineñzoo*) 記念像.
2 (great) kyo⌈dai na 巨大な; ta⌈i-heñ na 大変な: monumental efforts (*taiheñ na doryoku*) 大変な努力.

mood *n.* ki⌉buñ 気分; ki⌈geñ 機嫌: I'm in no mood for work. (*Shigoto o suru kibuñ de wa nai.*) 仕事をする気分ではない. / She was in a bad mood. (*Kanojo wa kigeñ ga warukatta.*) 彼女は機嫌が悪かった.
⇨ atmosphere.

moon *n.* tsu⌈ki⌉ 月: a full moon (*mañgetsu*) 満月 / a new moon (*shiñgetsu*) 新月.

moonlight *n.* ge⌈kkoo 月光; tsu⌈kia⌉kari 月明かり: walk in the moonlight (*tsukiakari no naka o aruku*) 月明かりの中を歩く.

mop *n.* mo⌉ppu モップ: clean a floor with a mop (*moppu de yuka o fuku*) モップで床をふく.

moral *adj.* do⌈otoku no 道徳の; do⌈otoku-teki na 道徳的な: the moral sense (*dootoku kañneñ*) 道徳観念 / moral education (*dootoku-kyooiku*) 道徳教育.
— *n.* **1** (lesson) kyo⌈okuñ 教訓: There's a moral to this story. (*Kono hanashi ni wa kyookuñ ga aru.*) この話には教訓がある.
2 (principles) do⌈otoku 道徳; mo⌉raru モラル: public morals (*fuuki*) 風紀.

morale *n.* shi⌈ki⌉ 士気: lift morale (*shiki o takameru*) 士気を高める /

Morale is high [low]. (*Shiki ga takai* [*hikui*].) 士気が高い[低い].

morality *n.* **1** (moral quality) do⌈otoku 道徳; do⌉ogi 道義: It is against public morality. (*Sore wa kooshuu dootoku ni hañsuru.*) それは公衆道徳に反する.

2 (virtue) hi⌈ñkoo 品行; to⌈kusee 徳性.

more *adj.* **1** (greater) mo⌉tto ooi もっと多い; mo⌉tto ta⌈kusa⌉ñ no もっとたくさんの: He has more money than me. (*Kare wa watashi yori mo takusañ o-kane o motte iru.*) 彼は私よりもたくさんお金を持っている.

2 (further) so⌈re i⌉joo no それ以上の; mo⌈o もう: One more word. (*Moo hito-koto.*) もう一言. / Please give me two more apples. (*Riñgo o moo futatsu kudasai.*) りんごをもう二つ下さい.

— *pron.* mo⌉tto ooku no hi⌈to⌉ [mo⌈no⌉; ko⌈to⌉] もっと多くの人[物; 事]; ... i⌉joo no hi⌈to⌉ [mo⌈no⌉; ko⌈to⌉] ... 以上の人[物; 事]: I want to know more. (*Motto ooku no koto o shiritai.*) もっと多くの事を知りたい. / More than thirty people were present. (*Sañjuu-niñ ijoo no hito ga shusseki shita.*) 30 人以上の人が出席した.

— *adv.* mo⌉tto もっと; sa⌉ra ni さらに: Be more careful. (*Motto chuui shi nasai.*) もっと注意しなさい. / Let's walk more slowly. (*Motto yukkuri arukimashoo.*) もっとゆっくり歩きましょう.

moreover *adv.* so⌈no ue そのうえ; sa⌉ra ni さらに: The price is too high, and moreover, the product is inferior in quality. (*Nedañ ga takasugi, sono ue hiñshitsu ga otorimasu.*) 値段が高すぎ, そのうえ品質が劣ります.

morning *n.* a⌉sa 朝; go⌉zeñ 午前. ★ '*Asa*' suggests early morning hours and '*gozeñ*' the forenoon: He worked from morning till night. (*Kare wa asa kara bañ made hataraita.*) 彼は朝から晩まで働いた. / I will be free in the morning. (*Gozeñ-chuu wa hima desu.*) 午前中は暇です. / I got up at six this morning. (*Watashi wa kesa roku-ji ni okimashita.*) 私は今朝 6 時に起きました.

mortal *adj.* **1** (certain to die) shi⌈nu koto ni na⌉tte iru 死ぬことになっている: Man is mortal. (*Hito wa dare de mo shinu uñmee ni aru.*) 人はだれでも死ぬ運命にある.

2 (causing death) chi⌈mee-teki na 致命的な: a mortal wound (*chimeeshoo*) 致命傷.

mortgage *n.* te⌈etoo 抵当; ta⌉ñpo 担保: lend money on mortgage (*teetoo o totte kane o kasu*) 抵当を取って金を貸す / He took out a mortgage on his house. (*Kare wa jibuñ no ie o teetoo ni ireta.*) 彼は自分の家を抵当に入れた.

mosquito *n.* ka 蚊: be bitten by a mosquito (*ka ni kuwareru*) 蚊に食われる.

most *adj.* **1** (greatest) mo⌈tto⌉mo ooi もっとも多い: He made the most mistakes. (*Kare ga mottomo ooku no machigai o shita.*) 彼がもっとも多くの間違いをした.

2 (almost all) ta⌈itee no たいていの: Most people think so. (*Taitee no hito wa soo omotte imasu.*) たいていの人はそう思っています.

— *pron.* sa⌈ida⌉igeñ 最大限; da⌈ibu⌉buñ 大部分: This is the most I can do. (*Kore ga watashi no dekiru saidaigeñ desu.*) これが私のできる最大限です. / I did most of the work. (*Sono shigoto no daibubuñ wa watashi ga yarimashita.*) その仕事の大部分は私がやりました.

— *adv.* mo⌈tto⌉mo もっとも; i⌈chibañ いちばん: the most beautiful flower (*mottomo utsukushii hana*) もっとも美しい花 / We can trust him most. (*Kare ga ichiban shiñyoo dekiru.*) 彼がいちばん信用できる.

mostly *adv.* da⌈ibu⌉buñ wa 大部分は; ta⌈itee たいてい: I am out mostly on Sundays. (*Nichiyoo wa taitee* *gaishutsu shite imasu.*) 日曜はたいてい外出しています.

motel *n.* mo¹oteru モーテル: stay overnight at a motel (*hito-bañ mooteru ni tomaru*) ひと晩モーテルに泊まる.

moth *n.* ga が(蛾).

mother *n.* ha¹ha 母; ha⌈haoya 母親; (someone else's) o-⌈ka¹asañ お母さん: My mother is a teacher. (*Haha wa señsee desu.*) 母は先生です. / How old is your mother? (*O-kaasañ wa o-ikutsu desu ka?*) お母さんはおいくつですか.

motion *n.* **1** (movement) u⌈ñdoo 運動; u⌈goki¹ 動き: observe the motion of the stars (*hoshi no ugoki o kañsatsu suru*) 星の動きを観察する.
2 (manner) do¹osa 動作; mi¹buri 身ぶり: The policeman made a motion to me to stop. (*Keekañ wa watashi ni tomaru yoo ni miburi de aizu shita.*) 警官は私に止まるように身ぶりで合図した.
— *vt.* ... ni mi¹buri de shi⌈me¹su ...に身ぶりで示す [C]; a¹izu suru 合図する [I]: He motioned the child away. (*Kare wa sono ko ni mukoo e ike to miburi de shimeshita.*) 彼はその子に向こうへ行けと身ぶりで示した.

motion picture *n.* e¹ega 映画.

motive *n.* do⌈oki 動機: What was your motive for taking an interest in the Japanese language? (*Nihoñgo ni kyoomi o motsu yoo ni natta dooki wa nañ desu ka?*) 日本語に興味を持つようになった動機は何ですか.

motor *n.* mo¹otaa モーター; ha⌈tsudo¹oki 発動機: an electric motor (*deñdooki*) 電動機 / start [cut off] a motor (*mootaa o ugokasu* [*tomeru*]) モーターを動かす[止める].
— *adj.* ji⌈do¹osha no 自動車の: a motor vehicle (*jidoosha*) 自動車 / a motor trip (*jidoosha ryokoo*) 自動車旅行.

motorcycle *n.* o⌈oto¹bai オートバイ; ta⌈ñsha 単車.

motto *n.* hyo⌈ogo 標語; mo¹ttoo モットー.

mound *n.* **1** (bank) tsu⌈ka¹ 塚; tsu⌈tsumi¹ 堤.
2 (of baseball) ma⌈uñdo マウンド: take the mound (*mauñdo ni agaru*) マウンドに上がる.

mount *vt.* **1** (get up on) ... ni no⌈ru ...に乗る [C]: mount a bicycle [horse] (*jiteñsha* [*uma*] *ni noru*) 自転車[馬]に乗る.
2 (go up) ... ni no⌈boru ...に登る [C]; ... o a⌈garu ...を上がる [V]: mount a hill (*koyama ni noboru*) 小山に登る / mount stairs (*kaidañ o agaru*) 階段を上がる.
3 (put in position) ... ni su⌈eru ...に据える [V]; ha⌈ru はる [C]: mount a photograph on cardboard (*daishi ni shashiñ o haru*) 台紙に写真をはる.
— *vi.* **1** (go up) (... ni) no⌈ru (...に)乗る [C]; no⌈boru 上る [C]: mount to the top of a ladder (*hashigo no ue made noboru*) はしごの上まで上る.
2 (increase) zo⌈odai suru 増大する [I]: The number of traffic accidents is mounting. (*Kootsuu jiko no kazu ga zoodai shite iru.*) 交通事故の数が増大している.

mountain *n.* ya⌈ma¹ 山: go up a mountain (*yama ni noboru*) 山に登る / go down a mountain (*yama o kudaru*) 山を下る. ⇨ Mt.

mourn *vt.* ... o na⌈geki-kanashi¹mu ...を嘆き悲しむ [C]: She mourned the death of her father. (*Kanojo wa chichioya no shi o nageki-kanashiñda.*) 彼女は父親の死を嘆き悲しんだ.

mourning *n.* **1** (grief) hi⌈tañ 悲嘆; a⌈itoo 哀悼.
2 (period) mo 喪: go into mourning (*mo ni fukusu*) 喪に服す.

mouse *n.* ne⌈zumi ねずみ; ha⌈tsuka ne¹zumi はつかねずみ. ★ Those that live in Japanese houses are rats.

mouth *n.* **1** (on the face) ku⌈chi 口: open [close] one's mouth (*kuchi o hiraku* [*tojiru*]) 口を開く[閉じる].
2 (opening) ku⌈chi 口: the mouth of a bottle (*biñ no kuchi*) びんの口.

move *vt*. **1** (change the position) ... o u⌈goka⌉su ...を動かす 🄲; i⌈doo suru 移動する 🄸: Please move your car. (*Kuruma o idoo shite kudasai.*) 車を移動してください.
2 (touch the heart) ... o ka⌈ñdoo saseru ...を感動させる 🅅: I was moved by his speech. (*Watashi wa kare no eñzetsu ni kañdoo shita.*) 私は彼の演説に感動した.
3 (propose) ... o te⌈eañ suru ...を提案する 🄸: I move that we close the meeting. (*Watashi wa heekai o teeañ shimasu.*) 私は閉会を提案します.
— *vi*. **1** (be in motion) u⌈go⌉ku 動く 🄲: Don't move while I take your picture. (*Shashiñ o toru aida ugokanaide.*) 写真を撮る間動かないで.
2 (to a new house) i⌈teñ suru 移転する 🄸; hi⌈kko⌉su 引っ越す 🄲: He moved from Tokyo to Osaka. (*Kare wa Tookyoo kara Oosaka e hikkoshita.*) 彼は東京から大阪へ引っ越した.

movement *n*. **1** (moving) u⌈ñdoo 運動; u⌈goki⌉ 動き: observe the movement of stars (*hoshi no ugoki o kañsatsu suru*) 星の動きを観察する.
2 (behavior) do⌉osa 動作; mi⌉buri 身ぶり: Her movements are elegant. (*Kanojo no doosa wa joohiñ da.*) 彼女の動作は上品だ.
3 (activity) u⌈ñdoo 運動: a political movement (*seeji uñdoo*) 政治運動.

movie *n*. e⌉ega 映画: I want to see a movie. (*Nani-ka eega ga [o] mitai.*) 何か映画が[を]見たい. / a movie theater (*eegakañ*) 映画館.

Mr. *n*. -sañ さん; -shi 氏: There's a call for you, Mr. Yamada. (*Yamada-sañ, o-deñwa desu.*) 山田さん, お電話です. / Mr. Murakami was elected mayor. (*Murakami-shi ga shichoo ni erabareta.*) 村上氏が市長に選ばれた.

Mrs. *n*. -sañ さん; -fu⌈jiñ 夫人: May I introduce Mrs. Yamamoto to you? (*Yamamoto-sañ o go-shookai itashimasu.*) 山本さんをご紹介いたします. / This is Mrs. Ishikawa's picture. (*Kore wa Ishikawa-fujiñ no e desu.*) これは石川夫人の絵です.

Ms. *n*. -sañ さん; (teacher) se⌈ñse⌉e 先生: Ms. Kimura (*Kimura-sañ*) 木村さん / Ms. White (*Howaito señsee*) ホワイト先生.

Mt. -sañ 山; -yama 山: Mt. Fuji (Fuji-sañ) 富士山 / Mt. Asama (Asama-yama) 浅間山. ★ '山' is pronounced either '*sañ*' or '*yama*.'

much *adj*. o⌉oku no 多くの; ta⌈kusa⌉ñ no たくさんの: I don't have much time. (*Jikañ wa taishite arimaseñ.*) 時間はたいしてありません. / How much money do you need? (*O-kane wa ikura hitsuyoo desu ka?*) お金はいくら必要ですか.
— *pron*. ta⌈ryoo 多量; ta⌈kusañ たくさん: I don't eat much for lunch. (*Chuushoku wa amari tabemaseñ.*) 昼食はあまり食べません. / I have too much to do. (*Suru koto ga takusañ ari-sugiru.*) することがたくさんありすぎる.
— *adv*. ta⌈iheñ (ni) 大変(に); o⌉oi ni 大いに; hi⌈joo ni 非常に: Thank you very much. (*Taiheñ arigatoo gozaimashita.*) 大変ありがとうございました. / She is much like her mother. (*Kanojo wa hahaoya ni hijoo ni yoku nite iru.*) 彼女は母親に非常によく似ている.

mud *n*. do⌈ro⌉ 泥; nu⌈karumi ぬかるみ: The car splashed me with mud. (*Sono kuruma wa watashi ni doro o haneta.*) その車は私に泥をはねた.

muddy *adj*. do⌈ro-da⌉rake no 泥だらけの; nu⌈karumi no ぬかるみの: get muddy (*doro-darake ni naru*) 泥だらけになる / a muddy road (*nukarumi no michi*) ぬかるみの道.

multiple *adj*. ta⌈yoo na 多様な; fu⌈kugoo no 複合の: multiple vitamin pills (*soogoo bitamiñzai*) 総合ビタミン剤.
— *n*. (of mathematics) ba⌈isu⌉u 倍数.

multiplication *n*. ka⌈ke⌉zañ 掛け算.

multiply *vt.* ... o ka⌈ke⌉ru …を掛ける [V]: Multiply 5 by 3, and you get 15. (*Go ni sañ o kakeru to juugo ni naru.*) 5 に 3 を掛けると 15 になる.

multitude *n.* (number) ta⌈su⌉u 多数; (people) o⌈oze⌉e 大勢: a multitude of flowers (*tasuu no hana*) 多数の花 / a multitude of people (*oozee no hito*) 大勢の人.

mumble *vt.* mo⌉gumogu [bu⌉tsubutsu] (to) i⌈u もぐもぐ[ぶつぶつ](と)言う [C]: He mumbled something. (*Kare wa nani-ka butsubutsu itta.*) 彼は何かぶつぶつ言った.

municipal *adj.* to⌉shi no 都市の; shi⌉ [ma⌈chi⌉] no 市[町]の: a municipal office (*shiyakusho* [*machiyakuba*]) 市役所[町役場] / a municipal government (*chihoo jichitai*) 地方自治体.

murder *n.* sa⌈tsujiñ 殺人; sa⌈tsujiñ ji⌉keñ 殺人事件: commit murder (*satsujiñ o okasu*) 殺人を犯す / There were two murders in this town. (*Kono machi ni satsujiñ jikeñ ga ni-keñ atta.*) この町に殺人事件が 2 件あった.

murderer *n.* sa⌈tsuji⌉ñsha 殺人者; sa⌈tsuji⌉ñhañ 殺人犯.

murmur *n.* **1** (sound) ka⌉suka na o⌈to⌉ かすかな音: I heard the murmur of conversation from the next room. (*Tonari no heya kara hisohiso hanasu koe ga kikoeta.*) 隣の部屋からひそひそ話す声が聞こえた. / the murmur of a stream (*ogawa no sarasara nagareru oto*) 小川のさらさら流れる音.

2 (complaint) fu⌈hee no ko⌉e 不平の声: pay tax without a murmur (*fuhee o iwazu ni zeekiñ o harau*) 不平を言わずに税金を払う.

— *vi.* ka⌉suka na o⌈to⌉ o ta⌈te⌉ru かすかな音を立てる: a murmuring brook (*sarasara nagareru ogawa*) さらさら流れる小川.

muscle *n.* ki⌉ñniku 筋肉: I strained a muscle in my leg. (*Watashi wa ashi no kiñniku o itameta.*) 私は足の筋肉を痛めた.

museum *n.* ha⌈kubutsu⌉kañ 博物館; bi⌈jutsu⌉kañ 美術館: a science museum (*kagaku hakubutsukañ*) 科学博物館 / a museum of modern art (*kiñdai bijutsukañ*) 近代美術館.

mushroom *n.* ki⌉noko きのこ.

music *n.* **1** (art) o⌉ñgaku 音楽; kyo⌉ku 曲: compose music (*sakkyoku suru*) 作曲する.

2 (score) ga⌈kufu 楽譜: play without music (*gakufu nashi de eñsoo suru*) 楽譜なしで演奏する.

musical *adj.* o⌉ñgaku no 音楽の: a musical performance (*eñsoo*) 演奏.

— *n.* myu⌉ujikaru ミュージカル.

musician *n.* o⌈ñgakuka 音楽家; myu⌈uji⌉shañ ミュージシャン.

must *aux.* **1** [obligation] ⟨verb⟩-na⌉kereba na⌈ra⌉nai …なければならない: I must go at once. (*Watashi wa sugu ni ikanakereba naranai.*) 私はすぐに行かなければならない.

2 [in the negative] ⟨verb⟩-te[de] wa i⌈kenai …て[で]はいけない: You must not smoke in this room. (*Kono heya de tabako o sutte wa ikenai.*) この部屋でたばこを吸ってはいけない.

3 [certainty] ... ni chi⌈gaina⌉i …に違いない: If he says so, it must be true. (*Kare ga soo iu nara sore wa hoñtoo ni chigainai.*) 彼がそういうならそれは本当に違いない.

mustache *n.* ku⌈chihige 口ひげ.

mustard *n.* ka⌈rashi からし; ma⌈suta⌉ado マスタード.

mute *adj.* da⌈ma⌉tte iru 黙っている; mu⌈goñ no 無言の: He remained mute. (*Kare wa damatte ita.*) 彼は黙っていた.

mutter *vi.* tsu⌈buya⌉ku つぶやく [C]; bu⌉tsubutsu i⌈u ぶつぶつ言う [C]: I heard him muttering. (*Kare ga butsubutsu itte iru no o kiita.*) 彼がぶつぶつ言っているのを聞いた.

— *vt.* ... o tsu⌈buya⌉ku …をつぶやく [C]; bu⌉tsubutsu i⌈u ぶつぶつ言う [C]: He muttered a reply. (*Kare wa butsubutsu to heñji o shita.*) 彼はぶつぶつと返事をした.

mutton *n.* hi⌈tsuji no ni⌈ku⌉ 羊の肉; yo⌈oniku 羊肉; ma⌉toñ マトン.

mutual *adj.* o⌈tagai no お互いの; so⌉ogo no 相互の: mutual understanding (*soogo rikai*) 相互理解.

my *pron.* wa⌈tashi no 私の: This is my umbrella. (*Kore wa watashi no kasa desu.*) これは私の傘です.

myself *pron.* **1** [reflexive use] wa⌈tashi ji⌉shiñ o [ni] 私自身を[に]; ji⌈buñ o [ni] 自分を[に]: I poured myself a cup of tea. (*Watashi wa jibuñ de o-cha o ireta.*) 私は自分でお茶を入れた.
2 [emphatic use] ji⌈buñ de 自分で; wa⌈tashi ji⌉shiñ de 私自身で: I did it myself. (*Watashi ga jibuñ de sore o yarimashita.*) 私が自分でそれをやりました.

mysterious *adj.* na⌈zo no yo⌉o na 謎のような; fu⌈shigi na 不思議な: a mysterious event (*fushigi na jikeñ*) 不思議な事件.

mystery *n.* fu⌈ka⌉kai na ko⌈to⌉ 不可解なこと; shi⌉ñpi 神秘; na⌈zo 謎: The affair is still shrouded in mystery. (*Sono jikeñ wa ima mo nazo ni tsutsumarete iru.*) その事件は今も謎に包まれている.

myth *n.* shi⌈ñwa 神話: Greek myths (*Girisha-shiñwa*) ギリシャ神話.

N

nail *n.* **1** (fastener) ku⌈gi くぎ: drive a nail into a board (*ita ni kugi o utsu*) 板にくぎを打つ.
2 (of a finger or toe) tsu⌈me つめ: cut one's nails (*tsume o kiru*) つめを切る.

naive *adj.* ta⌈ñjuñ na 単純な; u⌉bu na うぶな: It is naive of you to believe that. (*Soñna koto o shiñjiru nañte kimi mo tañjuñ da.*) そんなことを信じるなんて君も単純だ.

naked *adj.* ha⌈daka no 裸の: a naked body (*ratai*) 裸体.

name *n.* na⌈mae 名前: May I have your name? (*O-namae wa?*) お名前は. / Do you know the name of this flower? (*Kono hana no namae o shitte imasu ka?*) この花の名前を知っていますか. ★ Japanese 'surname' is followed by 'given name.'
— *vt.* ... o (... to) na⌈zuke⌉ru ...を(...と)名付ける Ⓥ: The parents named their child Akemi. (*Ryooshiñ wa kodomo o Akemi to nazuketa.*) 両親は子どもを明美と名付けた.

namely *adv.* su⌈na⌉wachi すなわち; tsu⌉mari つまり: Only one person was absent, namely, Mr. Tanaka. (*Hitori dake kesseki shimashita. Tsumari, Tanaka-sañ desu.*) 一人だけ欠席しました. つまり, 田中さんです.

nap *n.* hi⌈rune 昼寝: take a nap (*hirune o suru*) 昼寝をする.
— *vi.* u⌈tatane suru うたた寝する Ⓘ; hi⌈rune suru 昼寝する Ⓘ.

napkin *n.* na⌉pukiñ ナプキン.

narrow *adj.* se⌈ma⌉i 狭い: a narrow road (*semai michi*) 狭い道.
★ Japanese '*semai*' also means 'small in area.'
— *vi.* se⌉maku naru 狭くなる Ⓒ: The road narrows ahead. (*Kono michi wa saki de semaku natte iru.*) この道は先で狭くなっている.

nasty *adj.* **1** (unkind) i⌈ji⌉waru na 意地悪な: a nasty trick (*ijiwaru na itazura*) 意地悪ないたずら.
2 (unpleasant) i⌈ya⌉ na 嫌な: a nasty smell (*iya na nioi*) 嫌なにおい / nasty weather (*iya na teñki*) 嫌な天気.

nation *n.* **1** (people) ko⌈kumiñ 国民: the voice of the nation (*kokumiñ no koe*) 国民の声.
2 (state) ko⌉kka 国家: a democratic nation (*miñshu kokka*) 民主国家.

national *adj.* **1** (of the people) ko⌈kumiñ no 国民の: national senti-

ment (*kokumiñ kañjoo*) 国民感情.
2 (of the state) ko¹kka no 国家の: the national flower (*kokka*) 国花.
3 (run by the state) ko⌈kuritsu no 国立の: a national theater (*kokuritsu-gekijoo*) 国立劇場.

nationalism *n.* ko⌈kka-shu¹gi 国家主義; mi⌈ñzoku-shu¹gi 民族主義.

nationality *n.* ko⌈kuseki 国籍: acquire Japanese nationality (*Nihoñ kokuseki o toru*) 日本国籍を取る.

nationalization *n.* ko⌈kuyuuka 国有化; ko⌈kuee 国営.

nationalize *vt.* ko⌈kuyuu ni suru 国有にする [I]; ko⌈kuee ni suru 国営にする [I]: nationalize the railroads (*tetsudoo o kokuee ni suru*) 鉄道を国営にする.

native *adj.* **1** (of one's homeland) u⌈mare-ko¹kyoo no 生まれ故郷の: a native place (*umare kokyoo*) 生まれ故郷 / one's native country (*bokoku*) 母国 / native language (*bogo*) 母語.
2 (of that land) do⌈chaku no 土着の: native plants (*dochaku no shokubutsu*) 土着の植物 / native craftwork (*miñgeehiñ*) 民芸品.
3 (innate) u⌈maretsuki no 生まれつきの: native talent (*umaretsuki no sainoo*) 生まれつきの才能.
— *n.* ... u¹mare no hi⌈to¹ …生まれの人: a native of Tokyo (*Tookyoo umare no hito*) 東京生まれの人.

natural *adj.* **1** (of nature) shi⌈zeñ no 自然の; te⌈ñneñ no 天然の: a natural disaster (*shizeñ saigai*) 自然災害 / natural resources (*teñneñ shigeñ*) 天然資源.
2 (to be expected) to⌈ozeñ no 当然の: It is natural that he should get angry. (*Kare ga okoru no wa toozeñ da.*) 彼が怒るのは当然だ.

naturally *adv.* **1** (not forced) shi⌈zeñ ni 自然に: He can speak Japanese naturally. (*Kare wa Nihoñgo o shizeñ ni hanaseru.*) 彼は日本語を自然に話せる.
2 (of course) to⌈ozeñ 当然; mo⌈chi¹roñ もちろん: Naturally, he got angry. (*Toozeñ kare wa okotta.*) 当然彼は怒った.

nature *n.* **1** (environment) shi⌈zeñ 自然: the beauty of nature (*shizeñ no bi*) 自然の美 / protect nature (*shizeñ o mamoru*) 自然を守る.
2 (characteristic) se⌈eshitsu 性質: a cheerful nature (*akarui seeshitsu*) 明るい性質.
by nature *adv.* u⌈maretsuki 生まれつき: He is smart by nature. (*Kare wa umaretsuki atama ga yoi.*) 彼は生まれつき頭が良い.

naughty *adj.* i⌈tazura na いたずらな; i⌈u koto¹ o ki⌈kanai 言うことを聞かない: a naughty child (*itazura na kodomo*) いたずらな子ども.

naval *adj.* ka¹iguñ no 海軍の: a naval base (*kaiguñ kichi*) 海軍基地.

navigation *n.* **1** (on sea) ko¹okai 航海; (in air) ko⌈okuu 航空.
2 (science) ko⌈oka¹ijutsu 航海術; ko⌈oku¹ujutsu 航空術.

navy *n.* ka¹iguñ 海軍: join the navy (*kaiguñ ni hairu*) 海軍に入る.

near *prep.* **1** (position) ... no chi¹kaku ni [e] …の近くに[へ]: He lives near the station. (*Kare wa eki no chikaku ni suñde iru.*) 彼は駅の近くに住んでいる.
2 (time) ... ni chi⌈ka¹i …に近い: It was near noon. (*Shoogo ni chikakatta.*) 正午に近かった.
— *adj.* chi⌈ka¹i 近い: Where is the nearest post office? (*Ichibañ chikai yuubiñkyoku wa doko desu ka?*) いちばん近い郵便局はどこですか. / I will move to Hokkaido in the near future. (*Watashi wa chikai shoorai Hokkaidoo e hikkoshimasu.*) 私は近い将来北海道へ引っ越します.
— *adv.* chi¹kaku ni [e] 近くに[へ]: Do you live near? (*Kono chikaku ni o-sumai desu ka?*) この近くにお住まいですか.

nearly *adv.* **1** (almost) ho⌈to¹ñdo ほとんど; ho¹bo ほぼ; mo⌈o suko¹shi de もう少しで: It is nearly nine o'clock. (*Moo sugu ku-ji da.*) もうす

ぐ9時だ.

2 (closely) mo⌈o suko⌉shi de ... もう少しで…: I was nearly run over by a car. (*Moo sukoshi de kuruma ni hikareru tokoro datta.*) もう少しで車にひかれるところだった.

neat *adj.* ki⌈chi⌉ñto shita [shite iru] きちんとした[している]; ki⌉ree na きれいな: keep one's room neat (*heya o kichiñto shite oku*) 部屋をきちんとしておく / neat handwriting (*kiree na ji*) きれいな字.

neatly *adv.* ki⌈chi⌉ñto きちんと: be neatly dressed (*kichiñto shita minari o shite iru*) きちんとした身なりをしている.

necessarily *adv.* **1** ka⌈narazu 必ず: Important decisions are necessarily slow. (*Juuyoo na kettee wa kanarazu okureru.*) 重要な決定は必ず遅れる.

2 [with a negative] ... to wa ka⌈gira⌉nai …とは限らない: Cheap goods are not necessarily poorly made. (*Yasui mono ga kanarazu shimo osomatsu da to wa kagiranai.*) 安い物が必ずしもお粗末だとは限らない.

necessary *adj.* hi⌈tsuyoo na 必要な: Vitamins are necessary for health. (*Bitamiñ wa keñkoo ni hitsuyoo da.*) ビタミンは健康に必要だ.

necessity *n.* **1** (condition) hi⌈tsuyoo 必要: There is no necessity for you to stay here. (*Anata ga koko ni nokotte iru hitsuyoo wa arimaseñ.*) あなたがここに残っている必要はありません.

2 (thing) hi⌈tsujuhiñ 必需品: Cars are necessities in this town. (*Kuruma wa kono machi de wa hitsujuhiñ desu.*) 車はこの町では必需品です.

neck *n.* **1** (of a body) ku⌈bi 首: I have a stiff neck. (*Kubi ga itakute mawaranai.*) 首が痛くて回らない.

2 (of a garment) e⌈ri⌉ 襟: the neck of a blouse (*burausu no eri*) ブラウスの襟.

3 (anything like a neck) ku⌈bi 首: the neck of a bottle (*biñ no kubi*) びんの首.

necklace *n.* ne⌉kkuresu ネックレス; ku⌈bika⌉zari 首飾り.

necktie *n.* ne⌉kutai ネクタイ.

need[1] *vt.* **1** (want) ... o hi⌈tsuyoo to suru …を必要とする [I]: I need your help. (*Watashi wa anata no eñjo o hitsuyoo to shite imasu.*) 私はあなたの援助を必要としています.

2 (have to do) ⟨verb⟩ hi⌈tsuyoo ga a⌉ru …必要がある; ⟨verb⟩-na⌉kereba na⌈ra⌉nai …なければならない: You need to do this at once. (*Anata wa sugu ni kore o shinakereba naranai.*) あなたはすぐにこれをしなければならない. / You don't need to come. (*Anata wa kuru hitsuyoo ga arimaseñ.*) あなたは来る必要がありません.

— *n.* hi⌈tsuyoo 必要: There is no need for haste. (*Isogu hitsuyoo wa arimaseñ.*) 急ぐ必要はありません. / This car is in need of repairs. (*Kono kuruma wa shuuri ga hitsuyoo da.*) この車は修理が必要だ.

need[2] *aux.* ⟨verb⟩ hi⌈tsuyoo ga a⌉ru …必要がある: "Need I go at once?" "No, you need not." (*"Sugu iku hitsuyoo ga arimasu ka?" "Iie, sono hitsuyoo wa arimaseñ."*) 「すぐ行く必要がありますか」「いいえ, その必要はありません」

needle *n.* ha⌉ri 針; a⌈mi⌉boo 編み棒: sew with a needle (*hari de nuu*) 針で縫う / knit with needles (*amiboo de amu*) 編み棒で編む.

needless *adj.* fu⌈hi⌉tsuyoo na 不必要な; mu⌈da na むだな: one's needless worry (*muda na shiñpai*) むだな心配.

negative *adj.* **1** (refusing) hi⌈tee no 否定の: He gave me a negative answer. (*Kare wa hitee no heñji o yokoshita.*) 彼は否定の返事をよこした.

2 (not positive) sho⌈okyoku-teki na 消極的な; hi⌈kaeme⌉ na 控えめな: take a negative attitude (*shookyoku-teki na taido o toru*) 消極的な態度をとる.

3 (of a disease) i⌈ñsee no 陰性の: The results of the test were nega-

n

tive. (*Keñsa no kekka wa iñsee datta.*) 検査の結果は陰性だった.
— *n.* (photography) ne|ga ネガ; i|ñga 陰画; (math) fu|su|u 負数.

neglect *vt.* ... o o|kota|ru ...を怠る Ⓒ; o|ro|soka ni suru おろそかにする Ⓘ: neglect one's work (*shigoto o orosoka ni suru*) 仕事をおろそかにする.
— *n.* ta|imañ 怠慢; o|kotaru koto| 怠ること: neglect of duty (*shokumu taimañ*) 職務怠慢.

negotiate *vi.* (... to) ko|oshoo suru (...と)交渉する Ⓘ: I have to negotiate with the landlord about the rent. (*Watashi wa yanushi to yachiñ ni tsuite kooshoo shinakereba naranai.*) 私は家主と家賃について交渉しなければならない.
— *vt.* ... o to|rikimeru ...を取り決める Ⓥ: The two countries negotiated a treaty. (*Ryookoku wa jooyaku o torikimeta.*) 両国は条約を取り決めた.

negotiation *n.* ko|oshoo 交渉: enter into negotiations (*kooshoo o hajimeru*) 交渉を始める / The negotiations are now under way. (*Sono kooshoo wa ima shiñkoochuu desu.*) その交渉は今進行中です.

neighbor *n.* ki|ñjo no hi|to| 近所の人.

neighborhood *n.* ki|ñjo 近所: There are many temples in my neighborhood. (*Uchi no kiñjo ni wa o-tera ga takusañ arimasu.*) うちの近所にはお寺がたくさんあります.

neither *adj.* do|chira no ... mo ... na|i どちらの…も…ない: I like neither flower. (*Watashi wa dochira no hana mo suki de wa nai.*) 私はどちらの花も好きではない.
— *pron.* do|chira mo ... na|i どちらも…ない: Neither of them was content. (*Kare-ra wa dochira mo mañzoku shinakatta.*) 彼らはどちらも満足しなかった.
— *adv.* ... mo ma|ta ... na|i …もまた…ない: "I don't want to go." "Neither do I." (*"Watashi wa ikitaku arimaseñ." "Watashi mo ikitaku arimaseñ."*) 「私は行きたくありません」「私も行きたくありません」
neither ... nor ... *adv.* ... mo ... mo ... nai …も…も…ない: Neither he nor I can swim. (*Kare mo watashi mo oyogenai.*) 彼も私も泳げない.

nephew *n.* (one's own) o|i おい; (someone else's) o|igo-sañ おいごさん.

nerve *n.* shi|ñkee 神経: That noise gets on my nerves. (*Ano soo-oñ wa shiñkee ni sawaru.*) あの騒音は神経に障る.

nervous *adj.* shi|ñke|eshitsu na 神経質な; i|raira shita [shite iru] いらいらした[している]; a|gatta あがった; a|gatte iru あがっている: nervous girl. (*shiñkeeshitsu na oñna-no-ko.*) 神経質な女の子. / I was nervous at the interview. (*Watashi wa meñsetsu no toki agatte ita.*) 私は面接のときあがっていた.

nest *n.* su| 巣: Birds have built a nest in our garden. (*Tori ga uchi no niwa ni su o tsukutta.*) 鳥がうちの庭に巣を作った.

net[1] *n.* a|mi| 網; ne|tto ネット: cast a net (*ami o utsu*) 網を打つ / set a net (*ami o haru*) 網を張る.

net[2] *adj.* sho|omi no 正味の; ka|ke|ne no nai 掛け値のない: net weight (*shoomi no omosa*) 正味の重さ / a net profit (*juñeki*) 純益.

network *n.* ho|oso|omoo 放送網; ne|ttowa|aku ネットワーク: a TV network (*terebi hoosoomoo*) テレビ放送網.

neutral *adj.* chu|uritsu no 中立の: a neutral nation (*chuuritsu-koku*) 中立国 / a neutral zone (*chuuritsu chitai*) 中立地帯.

never *adv.* **1** (past experience) ... ko|to| ga nai …ことがない: I have never been abroad. (*Watashi wa gaikoku ni itta koto ga arimaseñ.*) 私は外国に行ったことがありません.
2 (strong negation) ke|sshite ... na|i 決して…ない: I'll never forget you. (*Kesshite anata no koto o wasuremaseñ.*) 決してあなたのことを忘れません.

n

nevertheless *adv.* so⌈re de⌉ mo それでも: He was very tired; nevertheless, he carried on walking. (*Kare wa totemo tsukarete ita ga sore de mo aruki-tsuzuketa.*) 彼はとても疲れていたが, それでも歩き続けた.

new *adj.* **1** (not old) a⌈tarashi⌉i 新しい: a new desk (*atarashii tsukue*) 新しい机 / a new car (*shiñsha*) 新車.
2 (recent) shi⌈ñgata no 新型の: a new model of a word processor (*shiñgata no waapuro*) 新型のワープロ.
3 (just arrived) shi⌈ñniñ no 新任の: a new teacher (*shiñniñ no señsee*) 新任の先生.
4 (unfamiliar) ha⌈ji⌉mete no 初めての: I'm new here. (*Koko wa hajimete desu.*) ここは初めてです.

news *n.* **1** (report) nyu⌉usu ニュース: I heard the news on the radio this morning. (*Sono nyuusu wa kesa rajio de kikimashita.*) そのニュースは今朝ラジオで聞きました.
2 (recent events) ka⌈watta koto⌉ 変わったこと: Is there any news? (*Nani ka kawatta koto wa arimasu ka?*) 何か変わったことはありますか.

newspaper *n.* shi⌈ñbuñ 新聞: take a newspaper (*shiñbuñ o toru*) 新聞をとる / I read the news in the newspaper. (*Sono kiji wa shiñbuñ de yomimashita.*) その記事は新聞で読みました.

new year *n.* shi⌉ññeñ 新年: A Happy New Year (*Shiññeñ omedetoo gozaimasu.*) 新年おめでとうございます. ★ At the New Year many Japanese send greeting cards, '*neñgajoo*' 年賀状.

New Year's Day *n.* ga⌈ñjitsu 元日; ga⌈ñtañ 元旦.

next *adj.* **1** (of place, order) tsu⌈gi⌉ no 次の: I get off at the next stop. (*Tsugi no teeryuujo de orimasu.*) 次の停留所で降ります.
2 (of time) tsu⌈gi⌉ no 次の; yo⌈ku- 翌; rai- 来: next Monday (*tsugi no getsuyoobi*) 次の月曜日 / next day (*yokujitsu*) 翌日 / next week (*raishuu*) 来週 / next month (*raigetsu*) 来月 / next year (*raineñ*) 来年.
— *adv.* tsu⌈gi⌉ ni 次に: What shall I do next? (*Tsugi ni nani o shimashoo ka?*) 次に何をしましょうか.

next to *adj.* ... no to⌈nari ni [no] ... の隣に[の]: the seat next to mine (*watashi no tonari no seki*) 私の隣の席.
— *adv.* (almost) ho⌈to⌉ñdo ほとんど: It is next to impossible to win first prize. (*It-too o toru nañte hotoñdo fukanoo da.*) 一等をとるなんてほとんど不可能だ.

nice *adj.* **1** (good) su⌈teki na すてきな; su⌈barashi⌉i すばらしい: a nice present (*suteki na purezeñto*) すてきなプレゼント / It's nice weather, isn't it? (*Ii o-teñki desu ne.*) いいお天気ですね. / It's nice to meet you. (*Hajimemashite.*) はじめまして.
2 (kind) shi⌉ñsetsu na 親切な: He was nice to me. (*Kare wa watashi ni shiñsetsu ni shite kureta.*) 彼は私に親切にしてくれた.

nickname *n.* a⌈dana あだな; ni⌈kkune⌉emu ニックネーム: give a nickname to a person (*hito ni adana o tsukeru*) 人にあだ名をつける.

niece *n.* (one's own) me⌈e めい; (someone else's) me⌈ego-sañ めいごさん.

night *n.* yo⌉ru 夜; ba⌈ñ 晩: I studied till late at night. (*Watashi wa yoru osoku made beñkyoo shita.*) 私は夜遅くまで勉強した. / I'll stay three nights. (*Koñbañ kara sañpaku shimasu.*) 今晩から3泊します./ a night train (*yakoo ressha*) 夜行列車 / every night (*maibañ*) 毎晩 / last night (*sakuya*) 昨夜.

nightclub *n.* na⌈itoku⌉rabu ナイトクラブ.

nightmare *n.* a⌉kumu 悪夢: have a nightmare (*akumu o miru*) 悪夢を見る.

nine *pron.* ko⌈ko⌉notsu 九つ; (people) kyu⌉u-niñ 9人; (things) kyu⌉u-ko 9個.

— *n.* (figure) ku[1] [kyu[1]u] 九; (hour) ku[1]-ji 9時; (minute) kyu[1]u-fuñ 9分; (age) kyu[1]u-sai 9歳.
— *adj.* ko[r]ko[1]notsu no 九つの; (people) kyu[1]u-niñ no 9人の; (things) kyu[1]u-ko no 9個の; (age) kyu[1]u-sai no 9歳の.

nineteen *pron.* ju[1]uku 19; (people) ju[r]ukyu[1]u-niñ 19人; (things) ju[r]ukyu[1]u-ko 19個.
— *n.* (figure) ju[1]uku 19; (hour) ju[1]uku-ji 19時; (minute) ju[r]ukyu[1]u-fuñ 19分; (age) ju[r]ukyu[1]u-sai 19歳.
— *adj.* ju[1]uku no 19の; (people) ju[r]ukyu[1]u-niñ no 19人の; (things) ju[r]ukyu[1]u-ko no 19個の; (age) ju[r]ukyu[1]u-sai no 19歳の.

nineteenth *adj.* ju[r]ukyuu-bañme[1] no 19番目の; da[1]i-juuku no 第19の.
— *n.* **1** (people) ju[r]ukyuu-bañme[1] no hi[r]to[1] 19番目の人; (things) ju[r]ukyuu-bañme[1] no mo[r]no[1] 19番目のもの.
2 (day) ju[1]uku-nichi 19日.
3 (fraction) ju[r]ukyuu-buñ no ichi[1] 19分の1.

n

ninetieth *adj.* kyu[r]ujuu-bañme[1] no 90番目の; da[1]i-kyuujuu no 第90の.
— *n.* **1** (people) kyu[r]ujuu-bañme[1] no hi[r]to[1] 90番目の人; (things) kyu[r]ujuu-bañme[1] no mo[r]no[1] 90番目のもの.
2 (fraction) kyu[r]ujuu-buñ no ichi[1] 90分の1.

ninety *pron.* kyu[1]ujuu 90; (people) kyu[r]uju[1]u-niñ 90人; (things) kyu[r]uju[1]k-ko 90個.
— *n.* (figure) kyu[1]ujuu 90; (age) kyu[r]uju[1]s-sai 90歳.
— *adj.* kyu[1]ujuu no 90の; (people) kyu[r]uju[1]u-niñ no 90人の; (things) kyu[r]uju[1]k-ko no 90個の; (age) kyu[r]uju[1]s-sai no 90歳の.

ninth *adj.* kyu[r]u-bañme[1] no 9番目の; da[1]i-kyuu [da[1]i-ku] no 第9の.
— *n.* **1** (people) kyu[r]u-bañme[1] no hi[r]to[1] 9番目の人; (things) kyu[r]u-bañme[1] no mo[r]no[1] 9番目のもの.
2 (day) ko[r]konoka 9日.
3 (fraction) kyu[r]u-buñ no ichi[1] 9分の1.

nip *vt.* ... o tsu[r]ne[1]ru …をつねる Ⓒ; ha[r]sa[1]mu はさむ Ⓒ: get one's finger nipped in the door (*doa ni yubi o hasamareru*) ドアに指をはさまれる.

no *adv.* **1** (not so) i[r]ie いいえ; ha[1]i はい. ★ '*Iie*' means 'What you have said is wrong.' and '*hai*' means 'What you have said is right.': "Will you go?" "No, I won't." (*"Anata wa ikimasu ka?" "Iie, ikimaseñ."*)「あなたは行きますか」「いいえ, 行きません」/ "Won't you go?" "No, I won't." (*"Anata wa ikimaseñ ne?" "Hai, ikimaseñ."*)「あなたは行きませんね」「はい, 行きません」/ No, thank you. (*Moo kekkoo desu.*) もう結構です.
2 [before an adjective] ke[r]sshite ... de na[1]i 決して…でない: The job was no easy one. (*Sono shigoto wa kesshite yasashii mono de nakatta.*) その仕事は決してやさしいものでなかった.
— *adj.* (of people) i[r]nai いない; i[r]mase[1]ñ いません; (of things) na[1]i ない; a[r]rimase[1]ñ ありません: He has no children. (*Kare wa kodomo ga imaseñ.*) 彼は子どもがいません. / There is no swimming pool in this hotel. (*Kono hoteru ni wa puuru ga nai.*) このホテルにはプールがない. / No Smoking. (*Kiñeñ.*) 禁煙. / No Admittance. (*Tachiiri kiñshi.*) 立ち入り禁止. / No parking. (*Chuusha kiñshi.*) 駐車禁止.

No. da[1]i ... bañ 第…番; da[1]i ... goo 第…号: No. 5 (*dai-go-bañ*) 第5番 / Room No. 10 (*juu-goo-shitsu*) 10号室.

nobility *n.* **1** (quality) ke[r]daka[1]sa 気高さ; su[r]ukoo 崇高: a person of nobility (*jiñkaku no kedakai hito*) 人格の気高い人.
2 (people) ki[1]zoku 貴族; ki[r]zokuka[1]ikyuu 貴族階級.

noble *adj.* **1** (honorable) ke[r]daka[1]i 気高い; ko[r]oketsu na 高潔な: a noble deed (*kedakai kooi*) 気高い行為.
2 (of high birth) ko[1]oki na 高貴な: a noble family (*kooki na iegara*) 高貴な家柄.

nobody *pron.* da⌈re mo ... na⌉i だれも…ない: Nobody was in the room. (*Heya ni wa dare mo inakatta.*) 部屋にはだれもいなかった.

nod *vi.* **1** (show agreement) u⌈nazu⌉ku うなずく [C]: nod in agreement (*dooi shite unazuku*) 同意してうなずく.
2 (in greeting) e⌉shaku suru 会釈する [I]: I nodded to him. (*Watashi wa kare ni eshaku shita.*) 私は彼に会釈した.
3 (doze) u⌉touto suru うとうとする [I].
— *vt.* **1** (move the head up and down) ... o u⌈nazukase⌉ru …をうなずかせる [V]: She nodded her head. (*Kanojo wa unazuita.*) 彼女はうなずいた.
2 (show agreement) u⌈nazu⌉ite ... o shi⌈me⌉su うなずいて…を示す [C]: She nodded her consent. (*Kanojo wa unazuite shoodaku o shimeshita.*) 彼女はうなずいて承諾を示した.
— *n.* (nodding) u⌈nazuki うなずき; (dozing) i⌈nemu⌉ri 居眠り.

noise *n.* o⌈to⌉ 音; so⌈o-oñ 騒音: Don't make any noise. (*Oto o tatete wa ikemaseñ.*) 音を立ててはいけません.

noisy *adj.* u⌈rusa⌉i うるさい; ya⌈kamashi⌉i やかましい: This room is noisy. (*Kono heya wa urusai.*) この部屋はうるさい.

nominate *vt.* ... o shi⌈mee suru 指名する [I]; ni⌈ñmee suru 任命する [I]: The committee nominated Mr. Yamada for chairman. (*Iiñkai wa Yamada-sañ o gichoo ni shimee shita.*) 委員会は山田さんを議長に指名した.

nomination *n.* shi⌈mee 指名; ni⌈ñmee 任命.

non- *pref.* hi- 非; fu- 不; mu- 無: non-residents (*hi-kyojuusha*) 非居住者 / Non-smoking section, please. (*Kiñeñseki o onegai shimasu.*) 禁煙席をお願いします.

none *pron.* **1** (no things) do⌉re mo ... na⌉i どれも…ない: None of the stories is true. (*Sono hanashi wa dore mo hoñtoo de wa nai.*) その話はどれも本当ではない.
2 (no persons) da⌈re mo ... na⌉i だれも…ない: None have arrived. (*Dare mo kite imaseñ.*) だれも来ていません.
3 (not any) su⌈koshi mo ... na⌉i 少しも…ない; ze⌈ñzeñ ... na⌉i 全然…ない: "How much milk do we have left?" "None." (*"Gyuunyuu wa dore kurai nokotte imasu ka?" "Zeñzeñ arimaseñ."*) 「牛乳はどれくらい残っていますか」「全然ありません」

nonsense *n.* mu⌈i⌉mi 無意味; ba⌈ka⌉geta ko⌈toba⌉ ばかげた言葉; na⌉ñseñsu ナンセンス: talk nonsense (*baka na koto o iu*) ばかなことを言う.
— *int.* Ba⌉ka na. ばかな.

noodle *n.* nu⌉udoru ヌードル: buckwheat noodles (*soba*) そば / wheat noodles (*udoñ*) うどん / Chinese noodles (*raameñ*) ラーメン.

noon *n.* sho⌉ogo 正午; ma⌈hiru 真昼: The bell rings at noon. (*Beru wa shoogo ni narimasu.*) ベルは正午に鳴ります.

no one *pron.* da⌈re mo ... na⌉i だれも…ない. ⇨ nobody

nor *conj.* ... mo ma⌈ta ... ⌉nai …もまた…ない: I can't read French, nor can I speak it. (*Watashi wa Furañsugo ga yomenai shi, hanasu koto mo dekinai.*) 私はフランス語が読めないし, 話すこともできない.

normal *adj.* **1** (standard) hyo⌈ojuñ-teki na 標準的な; fu⌈tsuu no 普通の: normal height (*hyoojuñ-teki na shiñchoo*) 標準的な身長.
2 (usual) se⌈ejoo na 正常な: normal intelligence (*seejoo na chinoo*) 正常な知能.
— *n.* hyo⌈ojuñ 標準; fu⌈tsuu 普通; se⌈ejoo 正常.

normally *adv.* **1** (as usual) se⌈ejoo ni 正常に; i⌈tsu-mo do⌉ori ni いつも通りに: There was an accident an hour ago, but the Shinkansen is running normally. (*Ichi-jikañ mae ni jiko ga atta ga, Shiñkañseñ wa seejoo ni uñkoo shite imasu.*) 1時間前に事故があったが, 新幹線は正常に

運行しています.

2 (ordinarily) fu'tsuu 普通; fu'dañ 普段: I normally get up at six. (*Watashi wa fudañ shichi-ji ni okimasu.*) 私は普段7時に起きます.

north *n.* ki'ta 北: Which way is north? (*Kita wa dochira desu ka?*) 北はどちらですか.

— *adj.* ki'ta no 北の: a north wind (*kita-kaze*) 北風.

— *adv.* ki'ta ni [e] 北に[へ]: My room faces north. (*Watashi no heya wa kitamuki desu.*) 私の部屋は北向きです.

northeast *n.* ho'kutoo 北東.

northern *adj.* ki'ta no 北の: northern countries (*kitaguni*) 北国.

North Pole *n.* Ho'kkyoku 北極.

northward *adv.* ki'ta ni mukatte 北に向かって; ho'ppoo e 北方へ: a northward journey (*hoppoo e no tabi*) 北方への旅.

northwest *n.* ho'kusee 北西.

nose *n.* ha'na 鼻: a long [short] nose (*takai* [*hikui*] *hana*) 高い[低い]鼻 / blow one's nose (*hana o kamu*) 鼻をかむ.

nosebleed *n.* ha'naji 鼻血.

nostril *n.* ha'na no ana' 鼻の穴; bi'koo 鼻孔.

not *adv.* ...(de wa [ja]) na'i ...(では[じゃ])ない; <verb>-nai ...ない: This is not my umbrella. (*Kore wa watashi no kasa de wa arimaseñ.*) これは私の傘ではありません. / He will not succeed. (*Kare wa seekoo shinai deshoo.*) 彼は成功しないでしょう. / This window will not open. (*Kono mado wa dooshite mo akanai.*) この窓はどうしても開かない.

not at all *adv.* **1** ze'ñzeñ ... na'i 全然…ない: I'm not at all tired. (*Watashi wa zeñzeñ tsukarete imaseñ.*) 私は全然疲れていません.

2 (answer to thanks) do'o i'tashima'shite どういたしまして.

notable *adj.* chu'umoku ni atai suru 注目に値する: notable achievements (*chuumoku ni atai suru gyooseki*) 注目に値する業績.

note *n.* **1** (reminder) me'mo メモ: take notes (*memo o toru*) メモを取る.

2 (short letter) mi'jika'i te'gami 短い手紙.

3 (explanation) chu'u 注: notes to a text (*tekisuto no chuu*) テキストの注.

4 (sound) o'to' 音; ne'iro 音色.

— *vt.* ... ni chu'ui suru …に注意する [I]: Note the underlined part. (*Kaseñbu ni chuui shi nasai.*) 下線部に注意しなさい.

notebook *n.* no'oto ノート.

noted *adj.* yu'umee na 有名な; cho'mee na 著名な: a noted writer (*yuumee na sakka*) 有名な作家.

nothing *pron.* na'ni mo ... na'i 何も…ない: I have nothing to declare. (*Shiñkoku suru mono wa nani mo arimaseñ.*) 申告するものは何もありません. / Nothing at all. (*Nañ de mo arimaseñ.*) 何でもありません.

for nothing *adv.* ta'da de ただで: I got it for nothing. (*Watashi wa tada de sore o te ni ireta.*) 私はただでそれを手に入れた.

nothing but ... *adv.* ta'da ... shika ただ…しか: He thinks of nothing but money. (*Kare wa tada kane no koto shika kañgaenai.*) 彼はただ金のことしか考えない.

— *n.* mu' 無: Nothing comes from nothing. (*Mu kara yuu wa shoojinai.*) 無から有は生じない. / come to nothing (*mu ni kisuru*) 無に帰する.

notice *n.* **1** (notification) tsu'uchi 通知; shi'rase 知らせ: give a notice of marriage (*kekkoñ no shirase o dasu*) 結婚の知らせを出す.

2 (bill) ke'eji 掲示: put up a notice of the game (*shiai no keeji o dasu*) 試合の掲示を出す.

3 (attention) chu'ui 注意: Her sudden laughter drew everyone's notice. (*Kanojo no totsuzeñ no warai wa miñna no chuui o hiita.*) 彼女の突然の笑いはみんなの注意を引いた.

4 (warning) yo'koku 予告: He quit his job without giving notice. (*Kare wa yokoku nashi ni shigoto o yameta.*) 彼は予告なしに仕事を辞めた.

— *vt.* (perceive) ... ni ki ˹ga tsu˺ku ...に気が付く Ⓒ; ki˹zu˺ku 気付く Ⓒ: She notices details. (*Kanojo wa komakai koto ni ki ga tsuku.*) 彼女は細かいことに気がつく.

take notice of ... *vt.* ... ni chu˺ui o ha˹ra˺u ...に注意を払う Ⓒ: He took no notice of what I said. (*Kare wa watashi ga itta koto ni chuui o harawanakatta.*) 彼は私が言ったことに注意を払わなかった.

notify *vt.* ... ni tsu˹uchi suru ...に通知する Ⓘ; tsu˹uhoo suru 通報する Ⓘ: notify the police (*keesatsu ni tsuuhoo suru*) 警察に通報する.

notion *n.* **1** (idea) ka˹ñga˺e 考え; (concept) ga˺ineñ 概念: He has odd notions. (*Kare wa okashi-na kañgae o motte iru.*) 彼はおかしな考えを持っている.

2 (intention) i˺to 意図; tsu˹mori つもり: I had no notion of telling the truth. (*Watashi wa hoñtoo no koto o iu tsumori wa nakatta.*) 私は本当のことを言うつもりはなかった.

noun *n.* me˹eshi 名詞.

nourish *vt.* ... o ya˹shina˺u ...を養う Ⓒ; so˹date˺ru 育てる Ⓥ: Milk nourishes a baby. (*Akañboo wa miruku de sodatsu.*) 赤ん坊はミルクで育つ.

nourishment *n.* e˹eyoo 栄養; (food) sho˹ku˺motsu 食物: take nourishment (*eeyoo o toru*) 栄養をとる.

novel[1] *n.* sho˹osetsu 小説: write [read] a novel (*shoosetsu o kaku* [*yomu*]) 小説を書く[読む].

novel[2] *adj.* me˹atarashi˺i 目新しい; za˹ñshiñ na 斬新な: a dress of novel design (*zañshiñ na dezaiñ no doresu*) 斬新なデザインのドレス.

November *n.* ju˹u-ichi-gatsu˺ 11月.

now *adv.* **1** (at this moment) i˺ma 今; mo˺o もう: What time is it now? (*Ima nañ-ji desu ka?*) 今何時ですか. / Where are we flying over now? (*Ima dono heñ o toñde imasu ka?*) 今どの辺を飛んでいますか.

2 (at once) i˺ma sugu 今すぐ: Can I enter the room now? (*Ima sugu heya ni hairemasu ka?*) 今すぐ部屋に入れますか.

3 [as an interjection] sa˺te さて; sa˺a さあ: Now, let's begin. (*Saa, hajimeyoo.*) さあ, 始めよう. / Now it's finished. (*Saa owarimashita.*) さあ終わりました.

4 (at that time) i˺ma ya 今や; so˹no to˺ki そのとき: He was now a national hero. (*Kare wa ima ya kokumiñ no eeyuu datta.*) 彼は今や国民の英雄だった.

just now *adv.* **1** (at the moment) i˺ma wa 今は: I'm busy just now. (*Ima wa isogashii desu.*) 今は忙しいです.

2 (a moment ago) tsu˺i sakki ついさっき: She was here just now. (*Kanojo wa tsui sakki koko ni imashita.*) 彼女はついさっきここにいました.

— *conj.* ... da˺ kara ...だから: Now that you've grown up, you must be responsible for your own actions. (*Anata wa moo otona da kara, jibuñ no koodoo ni sekiniñ o motaneba naranai.*) あなたはもう大人だから, 自分の行動に責任を持たねばならない.

— *n.* i˺ma 今: Now is the time to do what we promised. (*Ima koso yakusoku o hatasu toki da.*) 今こそ約束を果たすときだ.

by now *adv.* i˹ma goro wa mo˺o 今ごろはもう: She will be in Tokyo by now. (*Kanojo wa ima goro wa moo Tookyoo ni tsuite iru daroo.*) 彼女は今ごろはもう東京に着いているだろう.

for now *adv.* i˹ma no tokoro˺ (wa) 今のところ(は): I am free for now. (*Ima no tokoro wa hima desu.*) 今のところは暇です.

nowadays *adv.* ko˹no-goro wa このごろは; sa˹ikiñ wa 最近は: Everything is expensive nowadays. (*Kono-goro wa nañ de mo takai.*) このごろは何でも高い.

nowhere *adv.* do˹ko ni mo ... na˺i どこにも…ない: He was nowhere to be seen. (*Kare wa doko ni mo ina-*

n

katta.) 彼はどこにもいなかった.

nuclear *adj.* ge[ñshi]ryoku no 原子力の; ka]ku no 核の: nuclear energy (*geñshiryoku*) 原子力 / a nuclear weapon (*kakuheeki*) 核兵器.

nude *adj.* ha[daka no 裸の; nu]udo no ヌードの: a nude photo (*nuudo shashiñ*) ヌード写真.

— *n.* ra[tai 裸体.

nuisance *n.* u[rusa]i mo[no] うるさいもの; ya]kkai na mo[no] 厄介なもの: What a nuisance that child is! (*Ano ko wa nañte urusai ñ daroo.*) あの子は何てうるさいんだろう.

numb *adj.* ka[ñkaku no na]i 感覚のない: My feet are numb with cold. (*Samusa de ashi no kañkaku ga nakunatta.*) 寒さで足の感覚がなくなった.

number *n.* **1** (figure) ka]zu 数: a high [low] number (*ookii* [*chiisai*] *kazu*) 大きい[小さい]数 / cardinal [ordinal] numbers (*ki* [*guu*] *suu*) 奇[偶]数.

2 (No.) ba[ñgo]o 番号: Please tell me how to call this number. (*Kono bañgoo ni deñwa suru hoohoo o oshiete kudasai.*) この番号に電話する方法を教えてください. / a telephone number (*deñwa bañgoo*) 電話番号 / a passport number (*ryokeñ bañgoo*) 旅券番号 / a seat number (*zaseki bañgoo*) 座席番号.

a great number of ... *adj.* ta[kusa]ñ no たくさんの: There are a great number of parks in this town. (*Kono machi ni wa takusañ no kooeñ ga aru.*) この町にはたくさんの公園がある.

— *vt.* **1** (assign a number to) ... ni ba[ñgo]o o tsu[ke]ru ...に番号をつける [V]: number the pages (*peeji ni bañgoo o tsukeru*) ページに番号をつける.

2 (reach) ... ni ta[ssuru ...に達する [I]: Those who attended numbered thirty. (*Shussekisha wa sañjuuniñ ni tasshita.*) 出席者は30人に達した.

numeral *n.* su[uji 数字: Roman numerals (*rooma suuji*) ローマ数字.

numerous *adj.* (of things) ta[su]u no 多数の; (of people) o[oze]e no 大勢の: There are numerous people waiting in the room. (*Heya de matte iru hito ga oozee imasu.*) 部屋で待っている人が大勢います.

nun *n.* shu[udo]ojo 修道女; ni[soo 尼僧.

nurse *n.* **1** (female) ka[ñgo]fu 看護婦; (male) ka[ñgo]shi 看護士.

2 (nanny) u]ba 乳母.

— *vt.* **1** (take care of) ... o ka]ñbyoo suru ...を看病する [I]: She nursed her sick mother. (*Kanojo wa byooki no hahaoya o kañbyoo shita.*) 彼女は病気の母親を看病した.

2 (give milk) ... ni chi]chi o no[mase]ru ...に乳を飲ませる [V]: She is nursing her baby. (*Kanojo wa akañboo ni chichi o nomasete iru.*) 彼女は赤ん坊に乳を飲ませている.

nursery *n.* (for children) ho[iku]eñ 保育園; ta[kujisho 託児所.

nut *n.* **1** (edible seed) ko] no mi 木の実; na]ttsu ナッツ.

2 (for fastening) na]tto ナット.

nylon *n.* na]iroñ ナイロン.

O

oak *n.* (tree) o]oku オーク; (material) o[oku]zai オーク材.

oar *n.* ka]i かい; o[oru オール: pull on the oars (*ooru o kogu*) オールをこぐ.

oath *n.* chi[kai 誓い; se[eyaku 誓約: break [keep] one's oath (*chikai o yaburu* [*mamoru*]) 誓いを破る[守る].

oatmeal *n.* o[otomi]iru オートミール.

obedience *n.* fu[kujuu 服従; ju[ujuñ 従順: obedience to an order (*meeree no fukujuu*) 命令の服従.

obedient *adj.* ju[ujuñ na 従順な;

su⌉nao na 素直な: an obedient child (*sunao na kodomo*) 素直な子ども.

obey *vt.* ... ni shi⌈tagau …に従う [C]; shi⌈tagatte koodoo suru 従って行動する [I]: We should obey the law. (*Watashi-tachi wa hooritsu ni shitagawanakereba naranai.*) 私たちは法律に従わなければならない.

object[1] *n.* **1** (material thing) mo⌈no⌉ 物; bu⌈ttai 物体: I saw a strange object in the dark. (*Watashi wa kurayami no naka de heñ na mono o mita.*) 私は暗闇の中で変な物を見た.
2 (thing or person to which thought is directed) ta⌈ishoo 対象; ta⌈isho⌉obutsu 対象物: an object of interest (*kyoomi no taishoo*) 興味の対象.
3 (aim) mo⌈kuteki 目的; me⌉ate 目当て: realize one's object (*mokuteki o tassee suru*) 目的を達成する.
4 (of grammar) mo⌈kutekigo 目的語: the direct [indirect] object (*chokusetsu* [*kañsetsu*] *mokutekigo*) 直接[間接]目的語.

object[2] *vi.* (... ni) ha⌈ñtai suru (…に)反対する [I]: He objected to my plan. (*Kare wa watashi no keekaku ni hañtai shita.*) 彼は私の計画に反対した. / I object to smoking in the room. (*Watashi wa heya de tabako o suu no ni wa hañtai desu.*) 私は部屋でたばこを吸うのには反対です.

objection *n.* ha⌈ñtai 反対; i⌉gi 異議: He made no objection to my suggestion. (*Kare wa watashi no teeañ ni nani mo igi o tonaenakatta.*) 彼は私の提案に何も異議を唱えなかった.

objective *n.* mo⌈kuteki 目的: achieve one's objective (*mokuteki o tassee suru*) 目的を達成する.
— *adj.* kya⌈kkañ-teki na 客観的な: objective data (*kyakkañ-teki na deeta*) 客観的なデータ.

obligation *n.* **1** (duty) gi⌉mu 義務; se⌈kiniñ 責任: I have an obligation to support my family. (*Watashi wa kazoku o yashinau gimu ga aru.*) 私は家族を養う義務がある.
2 (debt) o⌉ñgi 恩義; o⌉ñ 恩: repay an obligation (*oñ ni mukuiru*) 恩に報いる.

obligatory *adj.* gi⌈muzukera⌉rete iru 義務づけられている; gi⌈mu-teki na 義務的な: Attendance at the meeting is obligatory. (*Sono kai e no shusseki wa gimuzukerarete imasu.*) その会への出席は義務づけられています.

oblige *vt.* **1** (compel) ya⌈mu o e⌉zu ⟨verb⟩ やむを得ず…; kyo⌈osee suru 強制する [I]: He was obliged to sell his house to pay his debts. (*Kare wa shakkiñ heñsai no tame ni yamu o ezu ie o utta.*) 彼は借金返済のためにやむを得ず家を売った.
2 (do a favor) ... ni o⌈ñkee o ho⌈doko⌉su …に恩恵を施す [C]: Will you oblige me with some money? (*Watashi ni o-kane o sukoshi kashite itadakemaseñ ka?*) 私にお金を少し貸していただけませんか.
be obliged *vi.* a⌈rigata⌉ku o⌈mo⌉u ありがたく思う [C]: I am much obliged to you for your kindness. (*Go-shiñsetsu hoñtoo ni arigatoo gozaimasu.*) ご親切本当にありがとうございます.

oblique *adj.* (slanting) na⌈na⌉me no 斜めの; ha⌈su no はすの: an oblique line (*shaseñ*) 斜線.

obscure *adj.* **1** (not clear) ha⌈kki⌉ri shinai はっきりしない; ai⌈mai na あいまいな: He gave an obscure explanation. (*Kare wa aimai na setsumee o shita.*) 彼はあいまいな説明をした.
2 (not well known) mu⌈mee no 無名の: an obscure writer (*mumee no sakka*) 無名の作家.
— *vt.* ... o mi⌈e⌉naku suru …を見えなくする [I]; o⌈oikaku⌉su 覆い隠す [C]: The moon was obscured by clouds. (*Tsuki ga kumo ni kakureta.*) 月が雲に隠れた.

obscurity *n.* ha⌈kki⌉ri shinai koto⌉ はっきりしないこと; fu⌈me⌉eryoo 不明瞭: His essay is full of obscurities. (*Kare no roñbun wa fumee-ryoo na teñ ga ooi.*) 彼の論文は不明瞭な点が多い.

observation *n.* **1** (watching) ka⌈ñsatsu 観察; ka⌈ñsoku 観測: the observation of the stars (*hoshi no kañsoku*) 星の観測.
2 (comment) i⌉keñ 意見; ka⌈ñga⌉e 考え: He made some observations on the subject. (*Kare wa sono moñdai ni tsuite ikutsu-ka kañgae o nobeta.*) 彼はその問題についていくつか考えを述べた.

observatory *n.* ka⌈ñsokujo⌉ 観測所; (astronomical) te⌈ñmoñdai 天文台; (meteorological) ki⌈shoodai 気象台.

observe *vt.* **1** (watch) ... o ka⌈ñsatsu suru ...を観察する Ⓘ; ka⌈ñsoku suru 観測する Ⓘ: observe the behavior of birds (*tori no koodoo o kañsatsu suru*) 鳥の行動を観察する.
2 (notice) ... ni ki ⌈ga tsu⌉ku ...に気がつく Ⓒ: I observed a letter on the desk. (*Watashi wa tsukue no ue no tegami ni ki ga tsuita.*) 私は机の上の手紙に気がついた.
3 (obey) ... o ma⌈mo⌉ru ...を守る Ⓒ; ju⌉ñshu suru 遵守する Ⓘ: observe the traffic regulations (*kootsuu hooki o mamoru*) 交通法規を守る.
4 (celebrate) ... o i⌈wa⌉u ...を祝う Ⓒ: observe someone's birthday (*tañjoobi o iwau*) 誕生日を祝う.
5 (remark) ... to no⌈be⌉ru ...と述べる Ⓥ; i⌈u 言う Ⓒ: "It's a lovely day," he observed. (*"Ii (o-)teñki desu ne." to kare wa itta.*) 「いい(お)天気ですね」と彼は言った.
— *vi.* **1** (watch) ka⌈ñsatsu [ka⌈ñsoku] suru 観察[観測]する Ⓘ.
2 (remark) i⌉keñ [ka⌈ñga⌉e] o no⌈be⌉ru 意見[考え]を述べる Ⓥ.

observer *n.* **1** (watcher) ka⌈ñsatsu⌉sha 観察者; ka⌈ñsoku⌉sha 観測者.
2 (of a meeting) o⌈buza⌉abaa オブザーバー; ta⌈chiainiñ 立ち会い人.

obstacle *n.* sho⌈oga⌉i 障害; ja⌈ma (mono) じゃま(物): clear an obstacle from the road (*dooro kara shoogai-butsu o torinozoku*) 道路から障害物を取り除く.

obstinate *adj.* ga⌉ñko na 頑固な; go⌈ojoo na 強情な: an obstinate child (*goojoo na kodomo*) 強情な子ども.

obstruct *vt.* ... o ja⌈ma suru ...をじゃまする Ⓘ; sa⌈matage⌉ru 妨げる Ⓥ; bo⌈ogai suru 妨害する Ⓘ: Trees obstructed the view. (*Ki ga shikai o samatagete ita.*) 木が視界を妨げていた.

obtain *vt.* (get) ... o ⌈te⌉ ni i⌈reru ...を手に入れる Ⓥ; e⌈ru 得る Ⓥ: Where did you obtain the perfume? (*Sono koosui wa doko de te ni iremashita ka?*) その香水はどこで手に入れましたか.

obvious *adj.* a⌈ki⌉raka na 明らかな; me⌈ehaku na 明白な: It was obvious that the driver had been drinking. (*Uñteñsha ga sake o noñde ita no wa akiraka datta.*) 運転者が酒を飲んでいたのは明らかだった.

obviously *adv.* a⌈ki⌉raka ni 明らかに; me⌈ehaku ni 明白に: Obviously, he needs some help. (*Akiraka ni kare wa tasuke o hitsuyoo to shite iru.*) 明らかに彼は助けを必要としている.

occasion *n.* **1** (particular time) ba⌈ai 場合; to⌈ki⌉ とき: I met her on the occasion of my first visit there. (*Watashi wa saisho ni soko o tazuneta toki kanojo to aimashita.*) 私は最初にそこを訪ねたとき彼女と会いました.
2 (special event) gyo⌉oji 行事: The party was a great occasion. (*Paatii wa seekai deshita.*) パーティーは盛会でした.
3 (opportunity) ki⌈ka⌉i 機会; o⌈ri⌉ 折: I want to change my job if the occasion arises. (*Kikai ga areba shoku o kaetai.*) 機会があれば職を替えたい.
— *vt.* ... o hi⌈kioko⌉su ...を引き起こす Ⓒ: His remarks occasioned the quarrel. (*Kare no kotoba ga kooroñ o hikiokoshita.*) 彼の言葉が口論

を引き起こした.

occasional *adj.* to⌈kiori no 時折の; to⌈kidoki no 時々の: Tokyo will be cloudy with occasional rain. (*Tookyoo wa kumori de tokidoki ame deshoo.*) 東京は曇りで時々雨でしょう.

occasionally *adv.* to⌈kiori 時折; to⌈kidoki 時々: My son occasionally writes to me. (*Musuko wa tokidoki tegami o yokoshimasu.*) 息子は時々手紙をよこします.

occupation *n.* **1** (job) sho⌈ku⌉gyoo 職業; shi⌈goto 仕事: What is his occupation? (*Kare no shokugyoo wa nañ desu ka?*) 彼の職業は何ですか. / He is a writer by occupation. (*Kare no shokugyoo wa sakka desu.*) 彼の職業は作家です.
2 (holding possession of) se⌈ñryoo 占領; se⌈ñyuu 占有: an occupation army (*señryooguñ*) 占領軍.

occupy *vt.* **1** (hold) ... o shi⌈me⌉ru ...を占める V: He occupies an important position in this firm. (*Kare wa kono kaisha de juuyoo na chii o shimete imasu.*) 彼はこの会社で重要な地位を占めています.
2 (fill) ... o fu⌈sagu ...をふさぐ C: Is this seat occupied? (*Kono seki wa fusagatte imasu ka?*) この席はふさがっていますか. / The toilet is occupied. (*Toire wa shiyoo-chuu desu.*) トイレは使用中です.
3 (take possession of) ... o se⌈ñryoo suru ...を占領する I: They occupied the enemy's capital. (*Kare-ra wa teki no shuto o señryoo shita.*) 彼らは敵の首都を占領した.

occur *vi.* **1** (happen) o⌈ko⌉ru 起こる C; sho⌈ojiru 生じる V: That accident occurred here. (*Sono jiko wa koko de okorimashita.*) その事故はここで起こりました.
2 (come to mind) o⌈moitsu⌉ku 思いつく C; a⌈tama⌉ ni u⌈kabu 頭に浮かぶ C: A good idea occurred to me. (*Ii kañgae ga atama ni ukañda.*) いい考えが頭に浮かんだ.

occurrence *n.* **1** (event) de⌈ki⌉goto 出来事: an unfortunate occurrence (*fukoo na dekigoto*) 不幸な出来事.
2 (happening) ha⌈ssee 発生: the occurrence of a fire (*kaji no hassee*) 火事の発生.

ocean *n.* ta⌈iyoo 大洋; (sea) u⌉mi 海: the Pacific Ocean (*Taiheeyoo*) 太平洋 / the Atlantic Ocean (*Taiseeyoo*) 大西洋 / go swimming in the ocean (*umi e oyogi ni iku*) 海へ泳ぎに行く.

o'clock *adv.* -ji 時: I get up at six o'clock. (*Watashi wa roku-ji ni okimasu.*) 私は6時に起きます. / He came at exactly nine o'clock. (*Kare wa choodo ku-ji ni kimashita.*) 彼はちょうど9時に来ました.

October *n.* ju⌈u-gatsu⌉ 10月.

oculist *n.* ga⌈ñka⌉-i 眼科医.

odd *adj.* **1** (of a number) ki⌈su⌉u no 奇数の: an odd number (*kisuu*) 奇数.
2 (strange) he⌉ñ na 変な; myo⌉o na 妙な: His behavior is odd. (*Kare no taido wa heñ da.*) 彼の態度は変だ. / I smell an odd odor. (*Myoo na nioi ga suru.*) 妙なにおいがする.
3 (occasional) ri⌈ñji no 臨時の: odd jobs (*riñji no shigoto*) 臨時の仕事.
4 (separated) ka⌈ta⌉hoo dake no 片方だけの: an odd glove (*katahoo dake no tebukuro*) 片方だけの手袋.

odds *n.* ka⌈chime⌉ 勝ち目; mi⌈komi 見込み: The odds are fifty-fifty. (*Kachime wa gobugobu desu.*) 勝ち目は五分五分です.

odor *n.* ni⌈o⌉i におい; ka⌈ori 香り: the odor of medicine (*kusuri no nioi*) 薬のにおい / the sweet odor of roses (*bara no yoi kaori*) バラのよい香り.

of *prep.* **1** (belonging) ... no ...の: the leg of a table (*teeburu no ashi*) テーブルの脚 / the teacher of our school (*watashi-tachi no gakkoo no señsee*) 私たちの学校の先生.
2 (containing) ... no ...の; ... no ryo⌉o no ...の量の: a cup of coffee (*ip-pai no koohii*) 1杯のコーヒー / a box of chocolates (*hito-hako no*

chokoreeto) 1 箱のチョコレート.
3 (forming) ... no ...の; ... no u⌈chi de ...のうちで: He is one of my friends. (*Kare wa watashi no tomodachi no hitori desu.*) 彼は私の友だちの一人です. / Summer is the warmest season of the year. (*Natsu wa ichi-neñ no uchi de ichibañ atsui kisetsu desu.*) 夏は一年のうちでいちばん暑い季節です.
4 (made from) ... de de⌉kite iru ... でできている: a plate of silver (*giñ de dekite iru sara*) 銀でできている皿.
5 (consisting) ... kara na⌉ru ...から成る: a committee of ten members (*juu-niñ kara naru iiñkai*) 10 人から成る委員会.
6 (origin) ... no ...の; ... kara ...から: the works of Shakespeare (*Sheekusupia no sakuhiñ*) シェークスピアの作品.

off *prep.* **1** (away from) ... kara (ha⌈na⌉rete) ...から(離れて): He fell off a ladder. (*Kare wa hashigo kara ochita.*) 彼ははしごから落ちた. / I took the book off the shelf. (*Watashi wa sono hoñ o tana kara totta.*) 私はその本を棚から取った.
2 (out of) ... kara ...から; ... o ...を: I got off the bus. (*Watashi wa basu o orita.*) 私はバスを降りた.
3 (not occupied) ... o ha⌈na⌉rete ... を離れて; ma⌈nuga⌉rete 免れて: He is off duty. (*Kare wa hibañ desu.*) 彼は非番です.
— *adv.* 1 (away) ha⌈na⌉rete 離れて: The plane takes off at two. (*Hikooki wa ni-ji ni ririku shimasu.*) 飛行機は 2 時に離陸します.
2 (not being worn) nu⌉ide 脱いで: take off one's shoes (*kutsu o nugu*) 靴を脱ぐ.
3 (reduced) wa⌈ribiki shite 割引して: take ten percent off (*ichi-wari waribiku*) 1 割割り引く.
4 (free from work) ya⌈su⌉ñde 休んで: He had a few days off. (*Kare wa ni-, sañ-nichi yasuñda.*) 彼は 2, 3 日休んだ.
— *adj.* 1 (far) ha⌈na⌉rete (iru) 離れて(いる): The station is two kilometers off. (*Eki wa ni-kiro saki desu.*) 駅は 2 キロ先です.
2 (not connected) ki⌉rete (iru) 切れて(いる): The switch is off. (*Suitchi wa kirete imasu.*) スイッチは切れています.
3 (gone away) sa⌉tte (iru) 去って(いる): I must be off now. (*Moo oitoma shinakereba narimaseñ.*) もうおいとましなければなりません.

offend *vt.* **1** (make angry) ... o o⌈korase⌉ru ...を怒らせる [V]: She was offended by his remarks. (*Kanojo wa kare no kotoba ni okotta.*) 彼女は彼の言葉に怒った.
2 (displease) ... ni fu⌈ka⌉ikañ o a⌈taeru ...に不快感を与える [V]: That tall building offends the eye. (*Ano takai biru wa mezawari da.*) あの高いビルは目障りだ.
— *vi.* tsu⌉mi o o⌈ka⌉su 罪を犯す [C]; ... ni ha⌈ñsu⌉ru ...に反する [I]: offend agaist custom (*shuukañ ni hañsuru*) 習慣に反する.

offense *n.* **1** (crime) tsu⌉mi 罪; i⌈hañ 違反: a traffic offense (*kootsuu-ihañ*) 交通違反.
2 (displeasure) ki ⌈o wa⌉ruku suru ko⌈to⌉ 気を悪くすること: She is quick to take offense. (*Kanojo wa sugu ki o waruku suru.*) 彼女はすぐ気を悪くする.
3 (attack) ko⌈ogeki 攻撃: Offense is the best defense. (*Koogeki wa sairyoo no boogyo da.*) 攻撃は最良の防御だ.

offensive *adj.* **1** (unpleasant) i⌈ya na いやな; fu⌈kai na 不快な: a noise offensive to the ear (*mimizawari na oto*) 耳障りな音.
2 (insulting) ki ⌈ni sawaru 気に障る; bu⌈ree na 無礼な: offensive language (*hito no ki ni sawaru kotoba*) 人の気に障る言葉.
3 (used to attack) ko⌈ogeki-yoo no 攻撃用の: offensive weapons (*koogeki-yoo no buki*) 攻撃用の武器.

offer *vt.* **1** (put forward) ... o te⌈ekyoo suru ...を提供する [I]; mo⌈oshideru 申し出る Ⓥ: I was offered a good post. (*Watashi wa yoi chii o teekyoo sareta.*) 私はよい地位を提供された.

2 (present for sale) ... o u⌈ri ni da⌉su ...を売りに出す Ⓒ: He offered his car for a million yen. (*Kare wa jibuñ no kuruma o hyakumañ-eñ de uri ni dashita.*) 彼は自分の車を100万円で売りに出した.

— *n.* te⌈ekyoo 提供; mo⌈oshide 申し出: accept [decline] an offer (*mooshide o ukeireru* [*jitai suru*]) 申し出を受け入れる[辞退する].

office *n.* **1** (room) ji⌈mu⌉sho 事務所; ji⌈mu⌉shitsu 事務室: an information office (*añnaijo*) 案内所 / a doctor's office (*shiñryoo-shitsu*) 診療室.

2 (building) ka⌈isha 会社; ya⌈kusho 役所: He works in an office. (*Kare wa kaisha ni tsutomete imasu.*) 彼は会社に勤めています. / a post office (*yuubiñkyoku*) 郵便局.

3 (department) cho⌉o 庁: the Patent Office (*Tokkyochoo*) 特許庁.

4 (position) ka⌈ñshoku 官職; sho⌈ku 職: stay in office (*zaishoku suru*) 在職する / take office (*shuuniñ suru*) 就任する.

officer *n.* **1** (of armed forces) shi⌉kañ 士官: an army officer (*rikuguñ shikañ*) 陸軍士官.

2 (policeman) ke⌈esatsu⌉kañ 警察官; ke⌈ekañ 警官. ★ Often called '*omawari-sañ*' お巡りさん.

official *n.* ko⌈omu⌉iñ 公務員; ya⌈kuniñ 役人: a government official (*kokka koomuiñ*) 国家公務員.

— *adj.* **1** (of a position) ko⌈omujoo no 公務上の; o⌈oyake no 公の: official documents (*koobuñsho*) 公文書.

2 (authorized) ko⌈oniñ no 公認の; ko⌈oshiki no 公式の: an official record (*kooniñ-kiroku*) 公認記録.

officially *adv.* ko⌈oshiki ni 公式に; se⌈eshiki ni 正式に: The hall was officially opened yesterday. (*Sono hooru wa kinoo seeshiki ni kaikañ shita.*) そのホールはきのう正式に開館した.

often *adv.* yo⌉ku よく; ta⌈bitabi たびたび; shi⌉bashiba しばしば: He is often absent. (*Kare wa shibashiba kesseki suru.*) 彼はしばしば欠席する.

how often *adv.* na⌉ñ kai 何回: How often do I take the medicine? (*Kusuri wa nañ-kai nomu no desu ka?*) 薬は何回飲むのですか.

oh *int.* o⌉o おお; a⌉a ああ; o⌉ya おや: Oh! I'v forgotten again. (*Aa, mata wasurete shimatta.*) ああ, また忘れてしまった.

oil *n.* **1** (liquid) a⌈bura 油; o⌉iru オイル: machine oil (*kikai-abura*) 機械油 / salad oil (*sarada-yu*) サラダ油.

2 (petroleum) se⌈kiyu 石油: heavy oil (*juuyu*) 重油.

3 (paints) e⌈nogu 絵の具: paint in oils (*aburae o kaku*) 油絵をかく.

— *vt.* (put on) ... ni a⌈bura o nuru ...に油を塗る Ⓒ; (put into) a⌈bura o sa⌉su 油を差す Ⓒ: oil a bicycle (*jiteñsha ni abura o sasu*) 自転車に油を差す.

OK *adv.* o⌉okee オーケー; yo⌈roshi⌉i よろしい: OK, I'll do it. (*Yoroshii, watashi ga yarimashoo.*) よろしい, 私がやりましょう.

— *adj.* o⌉okee オーケー; yo⌈roshi⌉i よろしい; ke⌉kkoo da 結構だ: Everything is OK. (*Subete ookee desu.*) すべてオーケーです.

— *vt.* ... o sho⌈oniñ suru ...を承認する Ⓘ: My boss OK'd my plan. (*Buchoo wa watashi no keekaku o shooniñ shita.*) 部長は私の計画を承認した.

old *adj.* **1** (advanced in age) to⌈shi to⌉tta [to⌉tte iru] 年取った[取っている]; ro⌈ojiñ no 老人の: He's far too old for the job. (*Kare wa sono shigoto ni wa toshi o torisugite iru.*) 彼はその仕事には年を取りすぎている. / a hospital for old people (*roojiñ no tame no byooiñ*) 老人のための病院.

2 (of age) -sai no 歳の; (of a building) -neñ[tsuki] ni na⌉ru 年[月]になる: He is sixty years old. (*Kare wa*

rokujus-sai desu.) 彼は60歳です. / How old is your son? (*Musuko-sañ wa nañ-sai desu ka?*) 息子さんは何歳ですか. / This building is fifty years old. (*Kono biru wa tatte kara gojuu-neñ ni naru.*) このビルは建ってから50年になる.
3 (elder) to⌈shiue no 年上の: She is three years older than me. (*Kanojo wa watashi yori mo mittsu toshi-ue desu.*) 彼女は私よりも三つ年上です. / my oldest brother [sister] (*watashi no ichibañ ue no ani* [*ane*]) 私のいちばん上の兄[姉].
4 (not new) fu⌈ru⌉i 古い; fu⌉ruku kara no 古くからの: an old building (*furui tatemono*) 古い建物 / an old friend (*furuku kara no tomodachi*) 古くからの友だち.

olive *n.* (tree) o⌈ri⌉ibu no ki⌉ オリーブの木; (fruit) o⌈ri⌉ibu no mi オリーブの実.

omelet *n.* o⌈muretsu オムレツ.

omen *n.* ze⌈ñchoo 前兆; ki⌈zashi きざし: a good omen (*kitchoo*) 吉兆 / a bad omen (*kyoochoo*) 凶兆.

omission *n.* sho⌈oryaku 省略; da⌈tsuraku 脱落: I noticed several omissions in the list of names. (*Watashi wa meebo ni namae ga ikutsu-ka datsuraku shite iru no ni ki ga tsuita.*) 私は名簿に名前がいくつか脱落しているのに気がついた.

omit *vt.* **1** (leave out) ... o nu⌈kasu ...を抜かす Ⓒ; ha⌈bu⌉ku 省く Ⓒ; sho⌈oryaku suru 省略する Ⓘ: Let's omit this chapter. (*Kono shoo wa shooryaku shimashoo.*) この章は省略しましょう.
2 (fail to do) ... o wa⌈sureru ...を忘れる Ⓥ: I omitted to sign the letter. (*Tegami ni saiñ suru no o wasurete shimatta.*) 手紙にサインするのを忘れてしまった.

on *prep.* **1** (touching) ... no u⌈e ni [o] ...の上に[を]; ... ni se⌈sshite ...に接して: The book is on the desk. (*Sono hoñ wa tsukue no ue ni arimasu.*) その本は机の上にあります. / I hung her picture on the wall. (*Watashi wa kanojo no e o kabe ni kaketa.*) 私は彼女の絵を壁にかけた. / Please sit on this chair. (*Kono isu ni o-suwari kudasai.*) このいすにお座りください.
2 (wearing) ... o mi ⌈ni tsu⌉kete ... を身につけて: put a hat on one's head (*booshi o kaburu*) 帽子をかぶる.
3 (of a day) ... ni ...に: She often goes to church on Sundays. (*Kanojo wa nichiyoo ni yoku kyookai e ikimasu.*) 彼女は日曜によく教会へ行きます.
4 (towards) ... ni mu⌈katte ...に向かって; ... no ho⌉o ni ...の方に: She turned her back on me. (*Kanojo wa watashi no hoo ni se o muketa.*) 彼女は私の方に背を向けた.
5 (concerning) ... ni tsu⌉ite ...について; ... ni ka⌈ñsu⌉ru ...に関する: He lectured on democracy. (*Kare wa miñshushugi ni tsuite kooeñ shita.*) 彼は民主主義について講演した.
6 (by means of) ... de ...で: I talked with him on the phone. (*Watashi wa kare to deñwa de hanashita.*) 私は彼と電話で話した.
7 (supported by) ... o mo⌈to⌉ ni ... を基に: His story is based on experience. (*Kare no hanashi wa keekeñ o moto ni shite iru.*) 彼の話は経験を基にしている.
8 (as soon as) <verb> to su⌉gu ...とすぐ: On leaving school, she went to France. (*Sotsugyoo suru to sugu kanojo wa Furañsu e itta.*) 卒業するとすぐ彼女はフランスへ行った.
— *adv.* **1** (forward) ma⌉e e 前へ; sa⌈ki e 先へ: go on (*susumu*) 進む / further on (*sara ni saki no hoo e*) さらに先の方へ.
2 (continuing) tsu⌈zuite 続いて: It went on raining. (*Ame ga furi-tsuzuita.*) 雨が降り続いた.
3 (worn) ... o mi ⌈ni tsu⌉kete ...を身につけて: I had nothing on. (*Watashi wa nani mo mi ni tsukete inakatta.*) 私は何も身につけていなかった.

once *adv.* **1** (single time) i⌈chi-do 一度; i⌈k-kai 1回: I go to the bookstore once a week. (*Watashi wa shuu ni ichi-do sono hoñya e iki-masu.*) 私は週に一度その本屋へ行きます.

2 (formerly) ka¹tsute かつて; i¹zeñ 以前: I once lived in Nagasaki. (*Watashi wa katsute Nagasaki ni suñde imashita.*) 私はかつて長崎に住んでいました.

— *conj.* i⌈ttañ ⟨verb⟩ to いったん…と: Once he begins, he never gives up. (*Ittañ hajimeru to kare wa akiramenai.*) いったん始めると彼はあきらめない.

at once *adv.* su¹gu ni すぐに: He came at once. (*Kare wa sugu ni kimashita.*) 彼はすぐに来ました.

once in a while *adv.* to⌈kidoki 時々: I go to the movies once in a while. (*Watashi wa tokidoki eega ni ikimasu.*) 私は時々映画に行きます.

once more *adv.* mo⌈o ichi-do もう一度: Let me try once more. (*Moo ichi-do yarasete kudasai.*) もう一度やらせてください.

once upon a time *adv.* mu⌈ka-shi mukashi 昔々.

one[1] *pron.* hi⌈to¹tsu 一つ; (people) hi⌈to¹ri 一人; (thing) i¹k-ko 1個: He is one of my friends. (*Kare wa watashi no tomodachi no hitori desu.*) 彼は私の友だちの一人です.

— *n.* (figure) i⌈chi¹ 1; (hour) i⌈chi¹-ji 1時; (minute) i¹p-puñ 1分; (age) i¹s-sai 1歳.

— *adj.* **1** (single) hi⌈to¹tsu no 一つの; (people) hi⌈to¹ri no 一人の; (thing) i¹k-ko no 1個の; (age) i¹s-sai no 1歳の.

2 (certain) a¹ru ある: one fine day (*aru hareta hi*) ある晴れた日 / one night (*aru bañ*) ある晩.

one[2] *pron.* **1** (thing) mo⌈no¹ もの: I want a cheaper one. (*Motto yasui mono ga hoshii.*) もっと安いものが欲しい. / Show me another one, please. (*Hoka no mono o misete kudasai.*) ほかものを見せてください.

2 (person) hi⌈to 人: One must do one's best. (*Hito wa saizeñ o tsu-kusu beki da.*) 人は最善を尽くすべきだ.

oneself *pron.* ji⌈buñ ji¹shiñ 自分自身.

onion *n.* ta⌈mane¹gi たまねぎ.

only *adj.* **1** (of people) ta¹da hi⌈to¹ri no ただ一人の; (of a thing) ta¹da hi⌈to¹tsu no ただ一つの; ta¹da ... dake no ただ…だけの: He is the only friend that I have. (*Kare wa wata-shi no tada hitori no yuujiñ desu.*) 彼は私のただ一人の友人です. / They are the only people who know the truth. (*Sono shiñsoo o shitte iru no wa kare-ra dake da.*) その真相を知っているのは彼らだけだ.

2 (best) sa⌈iryoo no 最良の; sa⌈i-teki no 最適の: He is the only man for the job. (*Kare wa sono shigoto ni saiteki no hito da.*) 彼はその仕事に最適の人だ.

— *adv.* **1** (merely) ta⌈tta ... shika たった…しか: I had only two hun-dred yen. (*Watashi wa tatta ni-hyaku-eñ shika motte inakatta.*) 私はたった200円しか持っていなかった.

2 (solely) ta¹da ... dake ただ…だけ: Only he could solve the problem. (*Kare dake ga sono moñdai o toketa.*) 彼だけがその問題を解けた.

onto *prep.* ... no u⌈e¹ e [ni] …の上へ[に]: He jumped onto the stage. (*Kare wa butai no ue ni tobiagatta.*) 彼は舞台の上に飛び上がった.

opal *n.* o⌈pa¹aru オパール.

open *vt.* **1** (move) ... o a⌈keru …を開ける Ⓥ; (unfold) hi⌈ra¹ku 開く Ⓒ: May I open the window? (*Mado o akete mo ii desu ka?*) 窓を開けてもいいですか. / Open your books to page five. (*Hoñ no go-peeji o hi-raki nasai.*) 本の5ページを開きなさい.

2 (start) ... o ha⌈jimeru …を始める Ⓥ; hi⌈ra¹ku 開く Ⓒ: open a busi-ness (*jigyoo o hajimeru*) 事業を始める.

3 (make public) ... o ko⌈okai suru …を公開する Ⓘ; hi⌈ra¹ku 開く Ⓒ: open the gallery to the public (*biju-tsukañ o ippañ ni kookai suru*) 美

O

術館を一般に公開する.
— *vi.* **1** (become open) hi⌈ra⌉ku 開く Ⓒ: This door won't open. (*Kono to wa doo shite mo hirakanai.*) この戸はどうしても開かない.
2 (begin) ha⌈jimaru 始まる Ⓒ: In Japan school opens in April. (*Nihoñ de wa gakkoo wa shi-gatsu ni hajimarimasu.*) 日本では学校は 4 月に始まります.
— *adj.* **1** (not closed) a⌈ite iru 開いている: The doors are open. (*To wa aite imasu.*) 戸は開いています.
2 (operating) a⌈ite iru 開いている: Is the bank still open? (*Giñkoo wa mada aite imasu ka?*) 銀行はまだ開いていますか.
3 (free to all) da⌉re de mo sa⌈ñka deki⌉ru だれでも参加できる: an open competition (*dare de mo sañka dekiru koñtesuto*) だれでも参加できるコンテスト.
4 (not hidden) ka⌈kushidate no na⌉i 隠しだてのない; ko⌈ozeñ no 公然の: an open secret (*koozeñ no himitsu*) 公然の秘密.

opener *n.* a⌈keru mono⌉ 開けるもの: a bottle opener (*señnuki*) 栓抜き / a can opener (*kañkiri*) 缶切り.

opening *n.* **1** (hole) a⌈na⌉ 穴; su⌈kima すき間: an opening in a wall (*kabe no ana*) 壁の穴.
2 (beginning) ka⌈ishi 開始; o⌉opuniñgu オープニング: the opening of a new theater (*atarashii gekijoo no oopuniñgu*) 新しい劇場のオープニング.
3 (opportunity for work) shu⌈ushoku⌉guchi 就職口; a⌈ki 空き: Is there an opening in this firm? (*Kono kaisha ni shoku no aki wa arimasu ka?*) この会社に職の空きはありますか.

openly *adv.* ko⌈ozeñ to 公然と; (frankly) so⌈tchoku ni 率直に: criticize openly (*koozeñ to hinañ suru*) 公然と非難する / speak openly (*sotchoku ni hanasu*) 率直に話す.

opera *n.* o⌉pera オペラ: stage an opera (*opera o jooeñ suru*) オペラを上演する.

operate *vt.* ... o u⌈ñteñ suru ...を運転する Ⓘ; u⌈goka⌉su 動かす Ⓒ: operate a truck (*torakku o uñteñ suru*) トラックを運転する.
— *vi.* **1** (perform an operation) (... ni) shu⌉jutsu suru (...に)手術する Ⓘ: The surgeon operated on him for an appendicitis. (*Geka-i wa kare ni moochoo no shujutsu o shita.*) 外科医は彼に盲腸の手術をした.
2 (work) sa⌈doo suru 作動する Ⓘ; u⌈go⌉ku 動く Ⓒ: The machine is operating properly. (*Kikai wa chooshi yoku ugoite imasu.*) 機械は調子よく動いています.

operation *n.* **1** (of surgery) shu⌉jutsu 手術: He had an operation on his eye. (*Kare wa me no shujutsu o uketa.*) 彼は目の手術を受けた.
2 (action) sa⌉gyoo 作業; ka⌈tsudoo 活動: a rescue operation (*kyuujo katsudoo*) 救助活動.
3 (working) u⌈ñteñ 運転; so⌉osa 操作: The operation of this machine is simple. (*Kono kikai no soosa wa kañtañ desu.*) この機械の操作は簡単です.

operator *n.* **1** (of a machine) u⌈ñte⌉ñsha 運転者: an elevator operator (*erebeetaa uñteñgakari*) エレベーター運転係.
2 (of a telephone switchboard) ko⌈oka⌉ñshu 交換手.

opinion *n.* **1** (view) i⌉keñ 意見; ka⌈ñga⌉e 考え: express one's opinion (*jibuñ no ikeñ o noberu*) 自分の意見を述べる / public opinion (*yoroñ*) 世論.
2 (judgment) hyo⌉oka 評価; ha⌉ñdañ 判断: He has a good opinion of the method. (*Kare wa sono hoohoo o takaku hyooka shite iru.*) 彼はその方法を高く評価している.

opponent *n.* a⌈ite⌉ 相手; te⌈ki 敵: defeat one's opponent (*aite o yaburu*) 相手を破る.

opportune *adj.* tsu⌈goo no i⌉i 都合のいい; te⌈kisetsu na 適切な: He appeared at an opportune moment. (*Kare wa tsugoo no ii toki ni arawareta.*) 彼は都合のいいときに現れた.

opportunity *n.* ki⌉kai 機会; ko⌉o-ki 好機; cha⌉ñsu チャンス: I have little opportunity for speaking Japanese. (*Watashi wa Nihoñgo o hanasu kikai ga hotoñdo arimaseñ.*) 私は日本語を話す機会がほとんどありません.

oppose *vt.* ... ni ha⌈ñtai suru ...に反対する [I]: We opposed his plan. (*Watashi-tachi wa kare no keekaku ni hañtai shita.*) 私たちは彼の計画に反対した.

opposite *adj.* **1** (contrary) ha⌈ñtai no 反対の; gya⌈ku no 逆の: go in the opposite direction (*hañtai no hookoo ni iku*) 反対の方向に行く / the opposite sex (*isee*) 異性.

2 (on the other side) ha⌈ñtaigawa no 反対側の; mu⌈koogawa no 向こう側の: The post office is on the opposite side of the street. (*Yuubiñkyoku wa toori no mukoogawa ni arimasu.*) 郵便局は通りの向こう側にあります.

— *n.* gya⌈ku no koto⌉ 逆のこと; se⌈eha⌉ñtai no mo⌈no⌉ 正反対のもの: I thought quite the opposite. (*Watashi wa mattaku gyaku no koto o kañgaeta.*) 私はまったく逆のことを考えた.

— *prep.* ... no mu⌈kaigawa ni [no] ...の向かい側に[の]: the house opposite mine (*watashi no ie no mukai no ie*) 私の家の向かいの家 / We sat opposite each other. (*Watashi-tachi wa mukaiatte suwatta.*) 私たちは向かい合って座った.

opposition *n.* ha⌈ñtai 反対: My plan met with opposition. (*Watashi no keekaku wa hañtai ni atta.*) 私の計画は反対にあった. / the opposition party (*yatoo*) 野党.

oppress *vt.* **1** (govern cruelly) ... o a⌈ppaku suru ...を圧迫する [I]; shi⌈itage⌉ru 虐げる [V]: oppress the people (*kokumiñ o shiitageru*) 国民を虐げる.

2 (depress) ... o yu⌈u-utsu ni suru ...を憂うつにする [I]; me⌈irase⌉ru めいらせる [V]: I felt oppressed by the heat. (*Atsusa de meitte shimatta.*) 暑さでめいってしまった.

oppression *n.* a⌈ppaku 圧迫; a⌈ssee 圧制: suffer under oppression (*assee no moto ni kurushimu*) 圧制の下に苦しむ.

optimism *n.* ra⌈kkañ 楽観; ra⌈kuteñ-shu⌉gi 楽天主義.

optimistic *adj.* ra⌈kuteñ-teki na 楽天的な; ra⌈kkañ-teki na 楽観的な: I am optimistic about the future. (*Watashi wa shoorai ni tsuite rakkañ-teki desu.*) 私は将来について楽観的です.

option *n.* se⌈ñtaku⌉keñ 選択権; o⌉pushoñ オプション: I have no option in the matter. (*Watashi wa sono keñ de wa señtakukeñ ga arimaseñ.*) 私はその件では選択権がありません.

or *conj.* **1** [show an alternative] ... ka so⌈re to⌉mo ... ka ...かそれとも...か; ... ka ... ka ...か...か: Which would you like, tea or coffee? (*Koocha ni shimasu ka, sore tomo koohii ni shimasu ka?*) 紅茶にしますか, それともコーヒーにしますか. / Are your shoes brown or black? (*Anata no kutsu wa chairo desu ka kuro desu ka?*) あなたの靴は茶色ですか黒ですか. / Are you coming or not? (*Anata wa kuru no desu ka konai no desu ka?*) あなたは来るのですか来ないのですか.

2 (otherwise) sa⌉mo nai to さもないと: Hurry up or you'll be late. (*Isogi nasai. Samo nai to okuremasu yo.*) 急ぎなさい. さもないと遅れますよ.

oral *adj.* ko⌈otoo no 口頭の; (spoken) ko⌈ojutsu no 口述の: an oral examination (*koojutsu shikeñ*) 口述試験.

orange *n.* o⌈re⌉ñji オレンジ: orange juice (*oreñji juusu*) オレンジジュース.

— *adj.* o⌈reñji iro no オレンジ色の: an orange dress (*oreñji iro no doresu*) オレンジ色のドレス.

orator *n.* e⌈ñzetsu⌉sha 演説者; (eloquent) yu⌈ubeñka 雄弁家.

orbit *n.* ki⌈doo 軌道: put a satellite in orbit (*eesee o kidoo ni noseru*) 衛星を軌道に乗せる.

orchard *n.* ka⌈ju⌉eñ 果樹園: an apple orchard (*riñgoeñ*) りんご園.

orchestra *n.* o⌈oke⌉sutora オーケストラ; ka⌈ñgeñga⌉kudañ 管弦楽団: a symphony orchestra (*kookyoogakudañ*) 交響楽団.

order *n.* **1** (arrangement) ju⌈ñ 順; ju⌉ñjo 順序; ju⌈ñbañ 順番: put names in alphabetical order (*namae o arufabetto-juñ ni naraberu*) 名前をアルファベット順に並べる.

2 (command) me⌈eree 命令; sa⌉shizu 指図: I obeyed the doctor's orders. (*Watashi wa isha no sashizu ni shitagatta.*) 私は医者の指図に従った.

3 (request) chu⌈umoñ 注文: give out [cancel] an order (*chuumoñ o dasu* [*torikesu*]) 注文を出す[取り消す] / My order hasn't come yet. (*Chuumoñ shita mono ga mada kimaseñ.*) 注文したものがまだ来ません.

4 (condition properly arranged) se⌈etoñ 整頓; se⌉eri 整理: set a room in order (*heya o seetoñ suru*) 部屋を整頓する.

5 (peaceful condition) chi⌉tsujo 秩序: keep order (*chitsujo o tamotsu*) 秩序を保つ.

out of order *adj.* ko⌈shoo shite (iru) 故障して(いる): The elevator is out of order. (*Erebeetaa wa koshoo desu.*) エレベーターは故障です.

— *vt.* **1** (give a command) ⟨verb⟩ yo⌉o ni me⌈ejiru …ように命じる Ⓥ; shi⌉ji suru 指示する Ⓘ: He was ordered not to smoke. (*Kare wa tabako o suwanai yoo ni meejirareta.*) 彼はたばこを吸わないように命じられた.

2 (request) ... o chu⌈umoñ suru …を注文する Ⓘ: I ordered the book from the publisher. (*Watashi wa sono hoñ o shuppañsha ni chuumoñ shita.*) 私はその本を出版社に注文した.

orderly *adj.* se⌈etoñ sareta [sarete iru] 整頓された[されている]; ki⌈chi⌉ñto shita [shite iru] きちんとした[している]: keep one's room orderly (*heya o kichiñto shite oku*) 部屋をきちんとしておく.

ordinary *adj.* **1** (usual) fu⌈tsuu no 普通の; tsu⌈ujoo no 通常の: ordinary clothes (*futsuu no fuku*) 普通の服 / an ordinary meeting (*reekai*) 例会.

2 (common) he⌈eboñ na 平凡な; (average) na⌈mi no 並の: an ordinary person (*heeboñ na hito*) 平凡な人.

organ *n.* **1** (of a body) ki⌉kañ 器官; zo⌉oki 臓器: the digestive organs (*shooka kikañ*) 消化器官 / an organ transplant (*zooki-ishoku*) 臓器移植.

2 (means) ki⌉kañ 機関; so⌉shiki 組織: organs of government (*seeji kikañ*) 政治機関.

3 (musical instrument) o⌈rugañ オルガン: play the organ (*orugañ o hiku*) オルガンを弾く.

organic *adj.* **1** (of a chemical compound) yu⌈uki⌉butsu no 有機物の: organic fertilizer (*yuuki hiryoo*) 有機肥料.

2 (of a bodily organ) ki⌉kañ no 器官の; zo⌉oki no 臓器の: organic disease (*naizoo no byooki*) 内臓の病気.

organization *n.* **1** (organized group) so⌉shiki 組織; da⌈ñtai 団体: a religious organization (*shuukyoo-dañtai*) 宗教団体.

2 (organizing) so⌈shiki-ka 組織化; he⌈ñsee 編成: the organization of working people (*hataraku hitotachi no soshiki-ka*) 働く人たちの組織化.

organize *vt.* **1** (form into a group) ... o so⌉shiki suru …を組織する Ⓘ; he⌈ñsee suru 編成する Ⓘ: organize a political party (*seetoo o soshiki suru*) 政党を組織する / organize a baseball team (*yakyuu no chiimu o heñsee suru*) 野球のチームを編成する.

2 (arrange) ... o ju⌉ñbi suru …を準

O

備する [I]: organize a conference (*kaigi o juñbi suru*) 会議を準備する.
3 (put into working order) ke^r^etoodate^l^ru 系統だてる [V]; ma^r^tomeru まとめる [V]: organize one's thoughts (*kañgae o matomeru*) 考えをまとめる.

Orient *n.* to^l^oyoo 東洋.

oriental *adj.* to^l^oyoo no 東洋の: oriental art (*tooyoo bijutsu*) 東洋美術.

origin *n.* **1** (beginning) ki^l^geñ 起源; ha^r^jimari 始まり: the origins of civilization (*buñmee no kigeñ*) 文明の起源.
2 (birth) u^r^mare 生まれ; su^r^joo 素性: an American of Japanese origin (*nikkee Amerikajiñ*) 日系アメリカ人.

original *adj.* **1** (first) sa^r^isho no 最初の; mo^l^to no 元の: the original plan (*saisho no keekaku*) 最初の計画.
2 (creative) do^r^kusoo-teki na 独創的な: an original design (*dokusoo-teki na dezaiñ*) 独創的なデザイン.
3 (new) ki^r^batsu na 奇抜な: an original idea (*kibatsu na aidea*) 奇抜なアイデア.
— *n.* (of art) ge^r^ñga 原画; (of literature) ge^r^ñsho 原書: read a book in the original (*hoñ o geñsho de yomu*) 本を原書で読む.

originality *n.* do^r^kuso^l^oryoku 独創力; do^r^kusoosee 独創性.

originally *adv.* mo^l^to wa 元は; ha^r^jime wa 初めは: Originally the firm was a small factory. (*Sono kaisha wa moto wa chiisa-na koojoo dat-ta.*) その会社は元は小さな工場だった.

originate *vi.* (come into being) ha^r^ssee suru 発生する [I]; o^r^ko^l^ru 起こる [C]: The accident originated from carelessness. (*Sono jiko wa fuchuui kara okotta.*) その事故は不注意から起こった.
— *vt.* (bring into being) ... o o^r^ko^l^su ...を起こす [C]; ha^r^jimeru 始める [V]: originate a new movement (*atarashii uñdoo o okosu*) 新しい運動を起こす.

ornament *n.* so^r^oshokuhiñ 装飾品; ka^r^zari 飾り: ornaments for a Christmas tree (*Kurisumasu tsurii no kazari*) クリスマスツリーの飾り.
— *vt.* ... o ka^r^zaru ...を飾る [C]: ornament a room with flowers (*heya o hana de kazaru*) 部屋を花で飾る.

orphan *n.* ko^l^ji 孤児; mi^r^nashi^l^go みなしご.

orthodox *adj.* se^r^etoo-teki na 正統的な; o^r^osodo^l^kkusu na オーソドックスな: the orthodox way of singing (*seetoo-teki na utaikata*) 正統的な歌い方.

ostrich *n.* da^r^choo だちょう.

other *adj.* **1** (different) ho^r^ka no ほかの; ta^l^ no 他の; be^r^tsu no 別の: Please check other airlines' flights. (*Hoka no kookuugaisha no biñ o shirabete kudasai.*) ほかの航空会社の便を調べてください.
2 (being the one left of two) mo^r^o ippo^l^o no もう一方の; ta^r^ho^l^o no 他方の: Show me your other hand. (*Moo ippoo no te o mise nasai.*) もう一方の手を見せなさい.
3 (being the ones left of several) no^r^kori no 残りの: The other children returned home. (*Nokori no kodomo-tachi wa ie ni kaerima-shita.*) 残りの子どもたちは家に帰りました.
4 (opposite) mu^r^koogawa no 向こう側の: the other side of the road (*dooro no mukoogawa*) 道路の向こう側.
5 (recently past) ko^r^no aida no この間の: the other night (*kono aida no yoru*) この間の夜 / the other day (*señjitsu*) 先日.
— *pron.* **1** (different thing) ho^r^ka no mono^l^ ほかの物; (different people) ho^r^ka no hito^l^ ほかの人: Show me some others. (*Hoka no mono o misete kudasai.*) ほかの物を見せてください. / She is always kind to others. (*Kanojo wa itsu-mo hoka no hito-tachi ni yasashii.*) 彼女はいつもほかの人たちに優しい.
2 (the remaining ones) mo^r^o ippo^l^o no mo^r^no^l^ [hi^r^to^l^] もう一方の物[人];

O

so⌈no⌉ hoka no mo⌈no⌉ [hi⌈to⌉] そのほかの物[人]: Two of them went out and the others stayed behind. (*Futari ga dekake sono hoka no hito wa ato ni nokorimashita.*) 二人が出かけそのほかの人は後に残りました.

otherwise *adv.* **1** (in different way) be⌈tsu no hoohoo de 別の方法で: He seems to think otherwise. (*Kare wa betsu no kañgaekata no yoo da.*) 彼は別の考え方のようだ.
2 (in other respects) so⌈no⌉ ta no te⌈ñ de⌉ wa その他の点では: The rent is high, but is otherwise satisfactory. (*Yachiñ ga takai ga sono ta no teñ de wa mooshibuñ arimaseñ.*) 家賃が高いがその他の点では申し分ありません.
— *conj.* sa⌉mo nai to さもないと: Start at once, otherwise you will be late. (*Sugu shuppatsu shi nasai. Samo nai to okuremasu yo.*) すぐ出発しなさい. さもないと遅れますよ.

ouch *int.* i⌈ta⌉i 痛い: Ouch! Stop that! (*Itai. Yamete.*) 痛い. やめて.

ought *aux. v.* **1** [obligation] ⟨verb⟩ be⌉ki de aru …べきである; ⟨verb⟩-na⌉kereba i⌈kenai …なければいけない: We ought to follow rules. (*Wareware wa kisoku ni shitagau beki de aru.*) われわれは規則に従うべきである. / You ought to be more careful. (*Motto ki o tsukenakereba ikenai.*) もっと気をつけなければいけない.
2 [indicates what is advisable] ⟨verb⟩-ta ho⌉o ga i⌉i …たほうがいい: You ought to see a doctor. (*Isha ni mite moratta hoo ga ii yo.*) 医者に診てもらったほうがいいよ.
3 [likelihood] ... ha⌈zu da …はずだ: The weather ought to be fine tomorrow. (*Ashita wa teñki ni naru hazu da.*) あしたは天気になるはずだ.

ounce *n.* o⌉ñsu オンス: This parcel weighs 20 ounces. (*Kono tsutsumi wa omosa ga nijuu-oñsu aru.*) この包みは重さが20オンスある. ★ In Japan the metric system is used.

our *pron.* wa⌈tashi⌉-tachi no 私たちの; [formal] wa⌈reware no われわれの: This is our house. (*Kore ga watashi-tachi no ie desu.*) これが私たちの家です.

ours *pron.* wa⌈tashi⌉-tachi no (mo⌈no⌉) 私たちの(もの); [formal] wa⌈reware no mono⌉ われわれの(もの): This car is ours. (*Kono kuruma wa watashi-tachi no (mono) desu.*) この車は私たちの(もの)です.

ourselves *pron.* **1** [reflexive use] ji⌈bun ji⌉shiñ o [ni] 自分自身を[に]. ★ Usually not translated: We were careful not to hurt ourselves. (*Watashitachi wa kega o shinai-yoo ni ki o tsuketa.*) 私たちはけがをしないように気をつけた.
2 [emphatic use] ji⌈bu⌉ñ-tachi de 自分たちで; wa⌈tashi-tachi ji⌉shiñ de わたしたち自身で: We went to see him ourselves. (*Watashi-tachi wa watashi-tachi jishiñ de kare ni ai ni itta.*) 私たちは私たち自身で彼に会いに行った.

out *adv.* **1** (away from inside) so⌉to e [ni] 外へ[に]: He has gone out to lunch. (*Kare wa chuushoku ni soto e ikimashita.*) 彼は昼食に外へ行きました.
2 (from inside) ⟨verb⟩-dasu …出す: take out a pen (*peñ o toridasu*) ペンを取り出す.
3 (far away) to⌈oku no 遠くの: He lives out in the country. (*Kare wa tooku no inaka ni suñde imasu.*) 彼は遠くの田舎に住んでいます.
4 (completely) su⌈kka⌉ri すっかり: I am tired out. (*Watashi wa sukkari tsukarete shimatta.*) 私はすっかり疲れてしまった.
5 (clearly) ha⌈kki⌉ri to はっきりと: speak out (*hakkiri to noberu*) はっきりと述べる.
— *adj.* **1** (absent) fu⌈zai de 不在で; ga⌈ishutsu shite (iru) 外出して(いる): My father is out. (*Chichi wa gaishutsu-chuu desu.*) 父は外出中です.
2 (being outside) so⌉to ni dete

(iru) 外に出て(いる): He is out in the garden. (*Kare wa niwa ni dete imasu.*) 彼は庭に出ています.

3 (in the open) de⌉te (iru) 出て(いる): The stars are out. (*Hoshi ga dete iru.*) 星が出ている.

out of ... *prep.* **1** (from inside of) ... kara ...から: He went out of the room. (*Kare wa heya kara dete itta.*) 彼は部屋から出て行った.

2 (from) ... kara ...から: drink out of a cup (*kappu kara nomu*) カップから飲む.

3 (without) ... ga ki⌉rete ...が切れて: My car is out of gas. (*Watashi no kuruma wa gasoriñ ga kireta.*) 私の車はガソリンが切れた.

outbreak *n.* ha⌈ssee 発生; bo⌈ppatsu 勃発: an outbreak of dysentery (*sekiri no hassee*) 赤痢の発生 / an outbreak of war (*señsoo no boppatsu*) 戦争の勃発.

outcome *n.* ke⌈kka 結果; se⌉eka 成果: the outcome of an election (*señkyo no kekka*) 選挙の結果.

outdoor *adj.* ko⌉gai no 戸外の; o⌈ku⌉gai no 屋外の / an outdoor swimming pool (*okugai puuru*) 屋外プール.

outdoors *adv.* ko⌉gai de [e] 戸外で[へ]; o⌈ku⌉gai de [e] 屋外で[へ]; u⌈chi no so⌉to de [e] 家の外で[へ]: It is cold outdoors. (*Soto wa samui.*) 外は寒い.

— *n.* ko⌉gai 戸外; o⌈ku⌉gai 屋外.

outer *adj.* so⌉togawa no 外側の; ga⌉ibu no 外部の: the outer walls (*soto-kabe*) 外壁 / the outer world (*gaikai*) 外界.

outfit *n.* so⌉obi i⌈sshiki 装備一式: a traveling outfit (*ryokoo yoogu isshiki*) 旅行用具一式.

outlet *n.* **1** (passage) de⌉guchi 出口; ha⌈ke⌉guchi はけ口: an outlet for water (*mizu no hakeguchi*) 水のはけ口.

2 (means of releasing) ha⌈ke⌉guchi はけ口: an outlet for emotion (*kañjoo no hakeguchi*) 感情のはけ口.

3 (wall socket) ko⌉ñseñto コンセント: put a plug in the outlet (*puragu o koñseñto ni sashikomu*) プラグをコンセントに差し込む.

outline *n.* **1** (line) ri⌈ñkaku 輪郭; ga⌈ikee 外形: draw an outline (*riñkaku o egaku*) 輪郭を描く.

2 (summary) ga⌈iryaku 概略; ta⌈iyoo 大要; a⌈ramashi あらまし: give an outline of a story (*hanashi no taiyoo o noberu*) 話の大要を述べる.

— *vt.* **1** (draw) ... no ri⌈ñkaku o ega⌉ku ...の輪郭を描く Ⓒ; rya⌈kuzu o ka⌉ku 略図を書く Ⓒ: He outlined the map of his town. (*Kare wa machi no ryakuzu o kaita.*) 彼は町の略図を書いた.

2 (give the main features of) ... no a⌈ramashi [ga⌈iryaku] o nobe⌉ru ...のあらまし[概略]を述べる Ⓥ: I outlined my plans to my friends. (*Watashi wa keekaku no gairyaku o tomodachi ni hanashita.*) 私は計画の概略を友だちに話した.

outlook *n.* **1** (view) na⌈game⌉ 眺め; mi⌈harashi 見晴らし: His house has a splendid outlook. (*Kare no uchi wa nagame ga subarashii.*) 彼の家は眺めがすばらしい.

2 (prospect) mi⌈tooshi 見通し; mi⌈komi 見込み: The business outlook for this year is bright. (*Kotoshi no keeki no mitooshi wa akarui.*) ことしの景気の見通しは明るい.

output *n.* **1** (quantity) se⌈esa⌉ñdaka 生産高: The output of this factory is increasing. (*Kono koojoo no seesañdaka wa fuete imasu.*) この工場の生産高は増えています.

2 (of a computer) a⌈utopu⌉tto アウトプット.

3 (power) shu⌈tsu⌉ryoku 出力.

outrage *n.* ra⌈ñboo 乱暴; bo⌈okoo 暴行: acts of outrage (*booryoku kooi*) 暴力行為.

— *vt.* ... o fu⌈ñgai saseru ...を憤慨させる Ⓥ: I was outraged by his behavior. (*Watashi wa kare no taido ni fuñgai shita.*) 私は彼の態度に憤慨した.

outrageous *adj.* bu⌈sa⌉hoo na 無

作法な; ho⌉ogai na 法外な: outrageous behavior (*busahoo na furumai*) 無作法な振る舞い / an outrageous price (*hoogai na nedañ*) 法外な値段.

outside *adv.* so⌉to ni [de, e, wa] 外に[で, へ, は]: play outside (*soto de asobu*) 外で遊ぶ / take one's dog outside (*inu o soto e tsuredasu*) 犬を外へ連れ出す.

— *adj.* so⌈togawa no 外側の; ga⌉ibu no 外部の: the outside door (*sotogawa no to*) 外側の戸 / outside interference (*gaibu kara no kañshoo*) 外部からの干渉.

— *n.* so⌈togawa 外側; ga⌉ibu 外部: I painted the outside of the house white. (*Watashi wa ie no sotogawa o peñki de shiroku nutta.*) 私は家の外側をペンキで白く塗った.

outsider *n.* bu⌈ga⌉isha 部外者; yo⌈somono よそ者: They did not welcome outsiders. (*Kare-ra wa yosomono o kañgee shinakatta.*) 彼らはよそ者を歓迎しなかった.

outskirts *n.* ko⌉ogai 郊外: He lives on the outskirts of Tokyo. (*Kare wa Tookyoo no koogai ni suñde imasu.*) 彼は東京の郊外に住んでいます.

outstanding *adj.* **1** (prominent) me⌈da⌉tsu 目立つ; ke⌈sshutsu shita [shite iru] 傑出した[している]: He is outstanding as a statesman. (*Kare wa seejika to shite kesshutsu shite iru.*) 彼は政治家として傑出している.

2 (unpaid) mi⌈ha⌉rai no 未払いの; (unsettled) mi⌈ka⌉iketsu no 未解決の: That problem is still outstanding. (*Sono moñdai wa mada mikaiketsu da.*) その問題はまだ未解決だ.

outward *adj.* **1** (of the outside) ga⌈imeñ-teki na 外面的な; u⌈wabe no うわべの: You should not judge by the outward appearance of things. (*Monogoto no gaikeñ dake de hañdañ shite wa ikenai.*) 物事の外見だけで判断してはいけない.

2 (going out) so⌉to e mu⌈kau 外へ向かう: an outward voyage (*yuki no kooro*) 行きの航路.

— *adv.* **1** (toward the outside) so⌉to e [ni] 外へ[に]: This door opens outward. (*Kono to wa soto ni hirakimasu.*) この戸は外に開きます.

2 (away from home) ko⌈ku⌉gai e [ni] 国外へ[に]: a ship bound outward (*gaikoku yuki no fune*) 外国行きの船.

oven *n.* o⌉obuñ オーブン; te⌉ñpi 天火: a microwave oven (*deñshi-reñji*) 電子レンジ.

over *prep.* **1** (above) ... no u⌈e ni [o] …の上に[を]: Our plane flew over the mountains. (*Watashi-tachi no hikooki wa yama no ue o toñda.*) 私たちの飛行機は山の上を飛んだ.

2 (covering) ... o o⌈otte …をおおって: She put her hands over her face. (*Kanojo wa ryoote de kao o ootta.*) 彼女は両手で顔をおおった.

3 (across) ... o ko⌈ete …を越えて: My house is over the hill. (*Watashi no ie wa ano oka o koeta tokoro ni arimasu.*) 私の家はあの丘を越えた所にあります.

4 (more than) ... i⌉joo no …以上の; ... o ko⌈ete …を越えて: He is over eighty. (*Kare wa hachijuu o koete imasu.*) 彼は 80 を越えています.

5 (while doing) ⟨verb⟩-nagara …ながら: We talked over a glass of beer. (*Watashi-tachi wa biiru o nominagara hanashita.*) 私たちはビールを飲みながら話した.

6 (during) ... ni wa⌈tatte …にわたって; ... no a⌈ida …の間: I read the book over the weekend. (*Watashi wa shuumatsu no aida-juu sono hoñ o yoñda.*) 私は週末の間じゅうその本を読んだ.

7 (concerning) ... no ko⌈to⌉ de …のことで: They quarreled over money. (*Kare-ra wa o-kane no koto de iiarasotta.*) 彼らはお金のことで言い争った.

— *adv.* **1** (above) jo⌈ohoo ni 上方に; zu⌈joo ni 頭上に: A helicopter

flew over. (*Herikoputaa ga zujoo o tonde itta.*) ヘリコプターが頭上を飛んで行った.
2 (to another side) mu⌈koo e 向こうへ; so⌈chira [ko⌈chira] e そちら[こちら]へ: go over to France (*Furañsu e wataru*) フランスへ渡る / I'll be right over. (*Sugu ni sochira e ikimasu.*) すぐにそちらへ行きます.
3 (again) mo⌈o ichido もう一度: I had to do it over. (*Watashi wa sore o moo ichido yaranakereba naranakatta.*) 私はそれをもう一度やらなければならなかった.
over there *adv.* a⌈soko ni [de] あそこに[で]: The ticket machine is over there. (*Keñbaiki wa asoko desu.*) 券売機はあそこです.
— *adj.* (finished) o⌈watte (iru) 終わって(いる): The rainy season is over. (*Tsuyu ga owatta.*) 梅雨が終わった.

over- *pref.* **1** ka⌉do ni 過度に; a⌈mari ni o⌉oku あまりに多く: overestimate (*kadai-hyooka suru*) 過大評価する / overproduction (*seesañ-kajoo*) 生産過剰.
2 u⌈e ni [kara] 上に[から]: overhang (*... no ue ni sashikakaru*) …の上にさしかかる.

overall *adj.* ze⌈ñtai no 全体の; ze⌉ñbu no 全部の: the overall length of a bridge (*hashi no zeñchoo*) 橋の全長.
— *adv.* ze⌉ñbu de 全部で: How much will it cost overall? (*Zeñbu de ikura kakarimasu ka?*) 全部でいくらかかりますか.

overcoat *n.* o⌉obaa オーバー; ga⌈i-too 外套: put on [take off] an overcoat (*oobaa o kiru [nugu]*) オーバーを着る[脱ぐ].

overcome *vt.* **1** (defeat) ... ni u⌈chikatsu …に打ち勝つ Ⓒ; ... o ma⌈kasu …を負かす Ⓒ: ovecome all difficulties (*arayuru koñnañ ni uchi-katsu*) あらゆる困難に打ち勝つ / overcome the enemy (*teki o makasu*) 敵を負かす.
2 (exhaust) ... o ma⌈irase⌉ru …を参らせる Ⓥ: I was overcome by the heat. (*Atsusa de maitta.*) 暑さで参った.

overdo *vt.* **1** (carry too far) ... o ya⌈ri-sugi⌉ru …をやりすぎる Ⓥ; do ⌈o kosu 度を越す Ⓒ: Don't overdo exercise. (*Uñdoo o yari-suginai yoo ni.*) 運動をやりすぎないように.
2 (cook too long) ... o ni-⌈sugi⌉ru …を煮すぎる Ⓥ; ya⌈ki-sugi⌉ru 焼きすぎる Ⓥ: overdo a piece of meat (*niku o yaki-sugiru*) 肉を焼きすぎる.

overflow *vi.* **1** (flow over the edge) a⌈fure⌉ru あふれる Ⓥ; (of a river) ha⌈ñrañ suru はんらんする Ⓘ: This river overflows every year. (*Kono kawa wa maitoshi hañrañ suru.*) この川は毎年はんらんする.
2 (be filled) i⌈ppai de a⌉ru いっぱいである Ⓒ; a⌈riama⌉ru あり余る Ⓒ: My heart is overflowing with joy. (*Watashi no kokoro wa yorokobi de ippai desu.*) 私の心は喜びでいっぱいです.
— *vt.* ... kara a⌈furede⌉ru …からあふれ出る Ⓥ: The crowd overflowed the hall into the street. (*Guñshuu wa hooru kara toori ni afuredeta.*) 群衆はホールから通りにあふれ出た.

overhead *adv.* zu⌈joo ni 頭上に; ta⌉kaku 高く: The moon was shining overhead. (*Tsuki ga zujoo ni kagayaite ita.*) 月が頭上に輝いていた.

overlap *vi.* ka⌈sanaru 重なる Ⓒ: overlapping tiles (*kasanatte iru tairu*) 重なっているタイル / His vacation overlapped with mine. (*Kare no kyuuka ga watashi no kyuuka to kasanatta.*) 彼の休暇が私の休暇と重なった.

overlook *vt.* **1** (look down on) ... o mi⌈orosu …を見下ろす Ⓒ; mi⌈watasu 見渡す Ⓒ: We overlook the lake from the room. (*Heya kara mizuumi ga miwatasemasu.*) 部屋から湖が見渡せます.
2 (fail to see) ... o mi⌈otosu …を見落とす Ⓒ: overlook a typographical error (*goshoku o miotosu*) 誤植を見落とす.

3 (ignore) ... o o⌐ome ni mi⌝ru …を大目に見る Ⓥ; mi⌐nogasu 見逃す Ⓒ: overlook bad conduct (*warui okonai o oome ni miru*) 悪い行いを大目に見る.

overnight *adv.* **1** (during the night) yo⌐dooshi 夜通し; hi⌐tobañjuu 一晩中: stay overnight (*hitobañ tomaru*) ひと晩泊まる.

2 (suddenly) i⌐chi⌝ya ni shite 一夜にして; to⌐tsuzeñ 突然: become rich overnight (*ichiya ni shite kanemochi ni naru*) 一夜にして金持ちになる.

— *adj.* i⌐ppaku no 一泊の: an overnight trip (*ippaku-ryokoo*) 一泊旅行.

overseas *adv.* ka⌝igai e 海外へ; ga⌐ikoku e 外国へ: go overseas (*gaikoku e iku*) 外国へ行く.

— *adj.* ka⌝igai no 海外の; ka⌐igaimuke no 海外向けの: make an overseas trip (*kaigai-ryokoo o suru*) 海外旅行をする / an overseas broadcast (*kaigaimuke no hoosoo*) 海外向けの放送.

overtake *vt.* **1** (catch up with) ... ni o⌐itsu⌝ku …に追いつく Ⓒ: I overtook him at the entrance. (*Watashi wa iriguchi no tokoro de kare ni oitsuita.*) 私は入り口の所で彼に追いついた.

2 (pass) ... o o⌐iko⌝su …を追い越す Ⓒ: He overtook several cars. (*Kare wa nañ-dai mo kuruma o oikoshita.*) 彼は何台も車を追い越した.

overthrow *vt.* **1** (overturn) ... o hi⌐kkurika⌝esu …をひっくり返す Ⓒ; ta⌐o⌝su 倒す Ⓒ: The tree was overthrown by the storm. (*Sono ki wa arashi de taosareta.*) その木は嵐で倒された.

2 (defeat) ... o ta⌐o⌝su …を倒す: overthrow the government (*seefu o taosu*) 政府を倒す.

— *n.* da⌐too 打倒; te⌐ñpuku 転覆.

overtime *n.* cho⌐oka ki⌝ñmu 超過勤務; za⌐ñgyoo 残業: do overtime (*zañgyoo o suru*) 残業をする.

— *adj.* ji⌐ka⌝ñgai no 時間外の; cho⌐oka ki⌝ñmu no 超過勤務の: overtime pay (*chooka kiñmu teate*) 超過勤務手当.

— *adv.* ji⌐ka⌝ñgai de 時間外で; cho⌐oka ki⌝ñmu de 超過勤務で: work overtime (*jikañgai kiñmu o suru*) 時間外勤務をする.

overturn *vi.* hi⌐kkurika⌝eru ひっくり返る Ⓒ; te⌐ñpuku suru 転覆する Ⓘ: The boat was hit by a wave and it overturned. (*Booto wa oonami o ukete teñpuku shita.*) ボートは大波を受けて転覆した.

— *vt.* ... o hi⌐kkurika⌝esu …をひっくり返す Ⓒ; ta⌐o⌝su 倒す Ⓒ: The rebels overturned the government. (*Hañrañguñ ga seefu o taoshita.*) 反乱軍が政府を倒した.

overwhelm *vt.* **1** (defeat) ... o a⌐ttoo suru …を圧倒する Ⓘ: be overwhelmed by the enemy (*teki ni attoo sareru*) 敵に圧倒される.

2 (overcome) ... o ma⌐irase⌝ru …を参らせる Ⓥ; u⌐chihishi⌝gu 打ちひしぐ Ⓒ: She was overwhelmed with grief. (*Kanojo wa kanashimi ni uchihishigareta.*) 彼女は悲しみに打ちひしがれた.

overwhelming *adj.* a⌐ttoo-teki na 圧倒的な: an overwhelming majority (*attoo-teki na tasuu*) 圧倒的な多数.

overwork *vt.* ... o ha⌐tarakase-sugi⌝ru …を働かせすぎる Ⓥ; ko⌝kushi suru 酷使する Ⓘ: overwork a horse (*uma o kokushi suru*) 馬を酷使する.

— *vi.* ha⌐taraki-sugi⌝ru 働きすぎる Ⓥ: He always overworks. (*Kare wa itsu-mo hataraki-sugiru.*) 彼はいつも働きすぎる.

— *n.* ka⌐roo 過労; ha⌐taraki-sugi 働きすぎ: fall ill from overwork (*karoo de byooki ni naru*) 過労で病気になる.

owe *vt.* **1** (be in debt) ... ni ka⌐ri ga a⌝ru …に借りがある Ⓒ: I owe her five thousand yen. (*Watashi wa kanojo ni go-señ-eñ kari ga aru.*) 私は彼女に5千円借りがある.

2 (be obliged) ... no o⌐kage da …のおかげだ: I owe my success to you.

(*Watashi no seekoo wa anata no okage desu.*) 私の成功はあなたのおかげです.
3 (be under an obligation) ... no gi¹mu ga aru ...の義務がある Ⓒ; ⟨verb⟩-ba na⁽ra¹nai ...ばならない: I owe him my thanks. (*Kare ni o-ree o iwanakereba naranai.*) 彼にお礼を言わなければならない.
— *vi.* sha⁽kki¹ñ shite iru 借金している Ⓥ.

owl *n.* fu⁽kuro¹o ふくろう; mi⁽mi¹zuku みみずく.

own *adj.* ji⁽buñ ji¹shiñ no 自分自身の: I saw it with my own eyes. (*Watashi wa sore o jibuñ jishiñ no me de mimashita.*) 私はそれを自分自身の目で見ました.
— *pron.* ji⁽buñ ji¹shiñ no mo⁽no¹ 自分自身のもの: This house is my own. (*Kono ie wa watashi jishiñ no mono desu.*) この家は私自身のものです.
— *vt.* (possess) ... o mo¹tte iru ...を持っている Ⓒ; sho⁽yuu suru 所有する Ⓘ: I own a car. (*Watashi wa kuruma o motte imasu.*) 私は車を持っています.

owner *n.* mo⁽chi¹nushi 持ち主; sho⁽yu¹usha 所有者: Who is the owner of this land? (*Kono tochi no shoyuusha wa dare desu ka?*) この土地の所有者はだれですか. / a store owner (*shooteñ kee-eesha*) 商店経営者.

ox *n.* o⁽ushi 雄牛. ★ '*Ushi*' is the generic term for ox, bull, cow, etc.

oxygen *n.* sa¹ñso 酸素: an oxygen mask (*sañso masuku*) 酸素マスク.

oyster *n.* ka¹ki かき(牡蠣).

P

pace *n.* **1** (step) ho⁽choo 歩調: walk at a slow pace (*yukkuri shita hochoo de aruku*) ゆっくりした歩調で歩く.
2 (stride) i¹p-po 1 歩; ho⁽haba 歩幅: step backward two steps (*ni-ho ushiro e sagaru*) 2 歩後へ下がる.
3 (rate of speed) ha¹yasa 速さ; pe¹esu ペース: He worked at his own pace. (*Kare wa jibuñ no peesu de hataraita.*) 彼は自分のペースで働いた.
— *vi.* yu⁽kku¹ri a⁽ru¹ku ゆっくり歩く Ⓒ: pace up and down (*ittari kitari suru*) 行ったり来たりする.
— *vt.* ... o a⁽rukima¹waru ...を歩き回る Ⓒ: pace the floor (*yuka no ue o arukimawaru*) 床の上を歩き回る.

Pacific *adj.* Ta⁽ihe¹eyoo no 太平洋の: the Pacific Ocean (*Taiheeyoo*) 太平洋.
— *n.* Ta⁽ihe¹eyoo 太平洋.

pack *vt.* **1** (wrap together) ... o ni⁽zu¹kuri suru ...を荷造りする Ⓘ; ko⁽ñpoo suru 梱包する Ⓘ: pack goods (*shinamono o koñpoo suru*) 品物を梱包する.
2 (put together) ... o tsu⁽me¹ru ...を詰める Ⓥ: pack one's clothes into a suitcase (*irui o suutsukeesu ni tsumeru*) 衣類をスーツケースに詰める.
3 (fill) ... o tsu⁽mekomu ...を詰め込む Ⓒ: pack passengers into a bus (*jookyaku o basu ni tsumekomu*) 乗客をバスに詰め込む.
— *vi.* ni⁽zu¹kuri o suru 荷造りをする Ⓘ: Please help me pack. (*Nizukuri o suru no o tetsudatte kudasai.*) 荷造りをするのを手伝ってください.
— *n.* **1** (bundle) tsu⁽tsumi¹ 包み; ni¹motsu 荷物: carry a pack on one's back (*nimotsu o seotte hakobu*) 荷物を背負って運ぶ.
2 (packet) hi⁽to¹-hako ひと箱: I smoke two packs of cigarettes a day. (*Watashi wa ichi-nichi ni tabako o futa-hako suimasu.*) 私は1日にたばこを二箱吸います.

package *n.* tsu⁽tsumi¹ 包み; ko⁽zu¹tsumi 小包: open a package (*kozu-

tsumi o akeru) 小包を開ける.
— *vt.* ... o ni⌈zu⌉kuri suru ...を荷造りする ⎕I⎕: package books (*hoñ o nizukuri suru*) 本を荷造りする.

packet *n.* chi⌉isa-na tsu⌈tsumi⌉ 小さな包み; ta⌉ba 束: a packet of letters (*tegami no taba*) 手紙の束.

pad *n.* **1** (cushion) tsu⌈me⌉mono 詰め物; a⌈temono 当て物; pa⌉ddo パッド.
2 (sheets of paper) tsu⌈zuri つづり: a writing pad (*biñseñ no tsuzuri*) 便箋のつづり.
— *vt.* ... ni tsu⌈me⌉mono o suru ...に詰め物をする ⎕I⎕: pad a cushion with cotton (*kusshoñ ni wata o tsumeru*) クッションに綿を詰める.

page *n.* pe⌈eji ページ: turn pages (*peeji o mekuru*) ページをめくる.

pail *n.* ba⌈ketsu バケツ; te⌈oke 手おけ: carry water in a pail (*mizu o teoke de hakobu*) 水を手おけで運ぶ.

pain *n.* **1** (hurting) i⌈tami⌉ 痛み: I have a dull pain in my back. (*Watashi wa senaka ni nibui itami ga aru.*) 私は背中に鈍い痛みがある.
2 (suffering) ku⌈tsuu 苦痛; ku⌉noo 苦悩: She is in pain. (*Kanojo wa kunoo shite iru.*) 彼女は苦悩している.
take pains *vi.* ho⌈ne⌉ o o⌈ru 骨を折る ⎕C⎕: He took pains to complete the work. (*Kare wa sono shigoto o kañsee suru no ni hone o otta.*) 彼はその仕事を完成するのに骨を折った.

painful *adj.* **1** (sore) i⌈ta⌉i 痛い: a painful wound (*itai kizu*) 痛い傷.
2 (unpleasant) tsu⌈rai つらい; ku⌈rushi⌉i 苦しい: That job was painful to me. (*Sono shigoto wa watashi ni wa tsurakatta.*) その仕事は私にはつらかった.

painkiller *n.* chi⌈ñtsu⌉uzai 鎮痛剤; i⌈tamidome 痛み止め.

paint *vt.* **1** (decorate) ... o pe⌈ñki de nuru ...をペンキで塗る ⎕C⎕: I painted the chair white. (*Watashi wa isu o peñki de shiroku nutta.*) 私はいすをペンキで白く塗った.
2 (make a picture) e⌉ o kaku 絵をかく ⎕C⎕: She painted flowers. (*Kanojo wa hana no e o kaita.*) 彼女は花の絵をかいた.
— *vi.* e⌉ o kaku 絵をかく ⎕C⎕: paint in oils (*aburae o kaku*) 油絵をかく.
— *n.* **1** (of decoration) pe⌈ñki ペンキ; to⌈ryoo 塗料: put bright paint on the walls (*kabe ni akarui peñki o nuru*) 壁に明るいペンキを塗る / Wet [Fresh] Paint. (*Peñki nuritate.*) ペンキ塗り立て.
2 (of a picture) e⌈nogu 絵の具: water paints (*suisai enogu*) 水彩絵の具.

painter *n.* **1** (artist) e⌈kaki⌉ 絵かき; ga⌈ka 画家: a painter in the Japanese style (*Nihoñ gaka*) 日本画家.
2 (person whose work is painting) pe⌈ñkiya ペンキ屋.

painting *n.* **1** (picture) e⌉ 絵: make a painting (*e o kaku*) 絵をかく.
2 (work) e⌉ o kaku ko⌈to⌉ 絵をかくこと: I like painting. (*Watashi wa e o kaku koto ga suki desu.*) 私は絵をかくことが好きです.

pair *n.* **1** (two things) hi⌈to⌉-kumi ひと組; i⌈t-tsui 一対: a pair of gloves (*tebukuro hito-kumi*) 手袋ひと組 / a pair of shoes (*kutsu is-soku*) 靴1足.
2 (single thing) i⌉k-ko 1個; i⌈t-chaku 1着: a pair of glasses (*megane ik-ko*) 眼鏡1個 / a pair of trousers (*zuboñ it-chaku*) ズボン1着 / a pair of scissors (*hasami it-choo*) はさみ1丁.
3 (man and woman) hi⌈to⌉-kumi no dañjo 1組の男女; ka⌉ppuru カップル: a nice pair (*niai no kappuru*) 似合いのカップル.
4 (male and female animals) tsu⌈gai つがい: two pairs of doves (*hato futa-tsugai*) はと二つがい.
— *vt.* ... o ku⌈miawase⌉ru ...を組み合わせる ⎕V⎕; tsu⌈i ni suru 対にする ⎕I⎕: The two of them were paired at the party. (*Sono futari ga paatii de tsui ni natta.*) その二人がパーティーで対になった.

pajamas *n.* pa⌉jama パジャマ; ne⌈maki 寝巻き: a pair of pajamas (*pajama it-chaku*) パジャマ1着.

pal *n.* to⌜modachi 友だち; na⌜kama⌝ 仲間; na⌜ka⌝yoshi 仲良し: a drinking pal (*nomi tomodachi*) 飲み友だち.

palace *n.* (royal residence) kyu⌜u-deñ 宮殿; (large house) da⌜i-te⌝e-taku 大邸宅.

pale *adj.* **1** (wan) ka⌜oiro ga waru⌝i 顔色が悪い; a⌜ojiro⌝i 青白い: You look pale. (*Kaoiro ga warui desu ne.*) 顔色が悪いですね.
2 (faint) u⌜sui 薄い; a⌜wa⌝i 淡い: pale blue (*usui aoiro*) 薄い青色.
— *vi.* **1** (turn pale) a⌜ozame⌝ru 青ざめる Ⓥ: She paled at the news. (*Kanojo wa sono shirase o kiite aozameta.*) 彼女はその知らせを聞いて青ざめた.
2 (seem less important) i⌜roa⌝sete mi⌜e⌝ru 色あせて見える Ⓥ: My work pales beside yours. (*Watashi no sakuhiñ wa kimi no to narabu to iroasete mieru.*) 私の作品は君のと並ぶと色あせて見える.

palm *n.* te-⌜no⌝-hira 手のひら: read a person's palm (*hito no tesoo o miru*) 人の手相を見る.

pamphlet *n.* pa⌝ñfuretto パンフレット; sho⌜osa⌝sshi 小冊子.

pan *n.* hi⌜ranabe 平なべ: a frying-pan (*furaipañ*) フライパン.

pancake *n.* pa⌜ñke⌝eki パンケーキ.

panel *n.* **1** (flat piece of wood) pa⌝neru パネル.
2 (group of people) -da⌝ñ 団; i⌝iñ 委員: a panel of judges (*shiñsaiñ-dañ*) 審査員団 / a panel of experts (*señmoñka no iiñ-tachi*) 専門家の委員たち.
3 (section containing dials) ke⌜eki-bañ 計器盤.

panic *n.* kyo⌜okoo 恐慌; pa⌝nikku パニック: They were in a panic. (*Kare-ra wa kyookoo jootai ni atta.*) 彼らは恐慌状態にあった.

panorama *n.* pa⌜norama パノラマ; ze⌜ñkee 全景.

pant *vi.* a⌜e⌝gu あえぐ Ⓒ; ha⌝a haa i⌜u はあはあ言う Ⓒ: He panted as he ran. (*Kare wa hashiri-nagara haa haa itta.*) 彼は走りながらはあはあ言った.
— *vt.* ... o a⌜egi-na⌝gara i⌜u ...をあえぎながら言う Ⓒ: He panted out the news. (*Kare wa aegi-nagara sono shirase o tsutaeta.*) 彼はあえぎながらその知らせを伝えた.

panties *n.* pa⌝ñtii パンティー.

pants *n.* (trousers) zu⌜bo⌝ñ ズボン; (short undergarment) pa⌝ñtsu パンツ.

paper *n.* **1** (thin sheet) ka⌜mi⌝ 紙: two sheets of paper (*ni-mai no kami*) 2枚の紙 / a paper bag (*kami-bukuro*) 紙袋 / a paper cup (*kami-koppu*) 紙コップ.
2 (newspaper) shi⌜ñbuñ 新聞: subscribe to a paper (*shiñbuñ o koo-doku suru*) 新聞を購読する.
3 (exam paper) to⌜oañ(yo⌝oshi) 答案(用紙): mark papers (*tooañ o sai-teñ suru*) 答案を採点する.
4 (document) sho⌜rui 書類; bu⌝ñ-sho 文書: look through papers (*shorui ni me o toosu*) 書類に目を通す.
5 (report) ro⌜ñbuñ 論文; re⌜po⌝oto レポート: a paper on the population problem (*jiñkoo-moñdai ni kañ-suru roñbuñ*) 人口問題に関する論文.
— *vt.* ... ni ka⌜mi⌝ o ha⌜ru ...に紙をはる Ⓒ: paper a wall green (*kabe ni guriiñ no kabegami o haru*) 壁にグリーンの壁紙をはる.

parachute *n.* pa⌜rashu⌝uto パラシュート; ra⌜kka⌝sañ 落下傘.

parade *n.* ko⌜oshiñ 行進; gyo⌜ore-tsu 行列; pa⌜re⌝edo パレード.
— *vi.* ko⌜oshiñ suru 行進する Ⓘ: They paraded through the streets. (*Kare-ra wa gairo o kooshiñ shita.*) 彼らは街路を行進した.

paradise *n.* te⌝ñgoku 天国; ra⌜ku-eñ 楽園: This amusement park is a paradise for children. (*Kono yuueñ-chi wa kodomo no teñgoku da.*) この遊園地は子どもの天国だ.

paradox *n.* gya⌜kusetsu 逆説; pa⌜rado⌝kkusu パラドックス.

paragraph *n.* da⌝ñraku 段落; pa⌝ragurafu パラグラフ.

parallel *adj.* **1** (running side by side) heʳekoo no 平行の; heʳekoo shita [shite iru] 平行した[している]: parallel lines (*heekooseñ*) 平行線 / The highway runs parallel to the railroad. (*Kañseñdooro wa señro to heekoo shite hashitte iru.*) 幹線道路は線路と平行して走っている.
2 (similar) niʳte iru 似ている; ruʳiji shita [shite iru] 類似した[している]: Our case is parallel to yours. (*Wareware no jijoo wa anata no baai to nite iru.*) われわれの事情はあなたの場合と似ている.
— *n.* 1 (line) heʳekooseñ 平行線: draw a parallel (*heekooseñ o hiku*) 平行線を引く.
2 (likeness) ruʳiji (suru mono˥) 類似(するもの); hiʳtteki (suru mono˥) 匹敵(するもの): There is no parallel to it. (*Sore ni hitteki suru mono wa nai.*) それに匹敵するものはない.
3 (of latitude) iʳdoseñ 緯度線.
— *vt.* ... to heʳekoo shite iru ...と平行している [V]: The road parallels the river. (*Dooro wa kawa to heekoo shite iru.*) 道路は川と平行している.

paralysis *n.* ma˥hi まひ: infantile paralysis (*shooni mahi*) 小児まひ.

paralyze *vt.* ... o ma˥hi saseru ...をまひさせる [V]; fuʳzui ni suru 不随にする [I]: My right arm was paralyzed. (*Migi ude ga mahi shita.*) 右腕がまひした.

parcel *n.* tsuʳtsumi˥ 包み; koʳzu˥tsumi 小包: wrap up a parcel (*kozutsumi o hoosoo suru*) 小包を包装する.

pardon *n.* yuʳrushi˥ 許し: ask for a person's pardon (*hito no yurushi o kou*) 人の許しを乞う.
— *vt.* yuʳru˥su 許す [C]: Please pardon me my rudeness. (*Busahoo o o-yurushi kudasai.*) 無作法をお許しください. / Pardon me for interrupting. (*Ojama shite sumimaseñ.*) おじゃましてすみません.

I beg your pardon. [apologizing] (*Gomen nasai.*) ごめんなさい. / [disturbing someone] (*Shitsuree shimasu.*) 失礼します. / I beg your pardon for being late. (*Okurete sumimaseñ.*) 遅れてすみません. / I beg your pardon? [asking for repetition] (*Osoreirimasu ga moo ichido osshatte kudasai.*) 恐れ入りますがもう一度おっしゃってください.

---

parent *n.* oʳya˥ 親: one's parents (*ryooshiñ*) 両親 / a parent bird (*oya-dori*) 親鳥.

parenthesis *n.* (maʳru)ka˥kko (丸)かっこ; pa˥areñ パーレン.

park *n.* **1** (public piece of ground) koʳoeñ 公園: play in the park (*kooeñ de asobu*) 公園で遊ぶ.
2 (car park) chuʳushajoo 駐車場.
— *vt.* ... o chuʳusha suru ...を駐車する [I]: Can I park my car on this street? (*Kono dooro ni kuruma o chuusha shite mo ii desu ka?*) この道路に車を駐車してもいいですか.

parking *n.* chuʳusha 駐車: No Parking. (*Chuusha kiñshi.*) 駐車禁止.

parliament *n.* (of the United Kingdom) gi˥kai 議会; koʳkkai 国会. ★ In Japan, 'the Diet' is called '*kokkai*,' and in the United States 'the Congress' is called '*gikai*.'

part *n.* **1** (section) bu˥buñ 部分: parts of the body (*karada no bubuñ*) 体の部分.
2 (piece) buʳhiñ 部品: automobile parts (*jidoosha no buhiñ*) 自動車の部品.
3 (region) chiʳho˥o 地方; chi˥iki 地域: What part of Japan are you from? (*Nihoñ no dono chihoo no shusshiñ desu ka?*) 日本のどの地方の出身ですか.
4 (of a book) -bu 部; he˥ñ 編: a novel in three parts (*sañ-bu-saku no shoosetsu*) 3部作の小説.
5 (duty) yaʳkuwa˥ri 役割; yaʳkume˥ 役目: play a part (*yakume o hatasu*) 役目を果たす.
take part *vi.* ... ni saʳñka suru ...に参加する [I]: I took part in the

demonstration. (*Watashi wa sono demo ni sañka shita.*) 私はそのデモに参加した.

— *vt.* **1** (divide) ... o wa⌈ke⌉ru ... 分ける Ⓥ; bu⌈ñkatsu suru 分割する Ⓘ: part an apple in two (*riñgo o futatsu ni wakeru*) りんごを二つに分ける.

2 (separate) ... o hi⌈kihana⌉su ...を引き離す Ⓒ: part the fighting children (*keñka shite iru kodomotachi o hikihanasu*) けんかしている子どもたちを引き離す.

— *vi.* wa⌈kare⌉ru 別れる Ⓥ: We parted at the station. (*Watashitachi wa eki de wakareta.*) 私たちは駅で別れた.

partial *adj.* **1** (of a part) i⌈chibu⌉-buñ no 一部分の; bu⌈buñ-teki na 部分的な: partial damage (*bubuñ-teki na soñgai*) 部分的な損害.

2 (biased) fu⌈ko⌉ohee na 不公平な: A referee should not be partial. (*Shiñpañ wa fukoohee de atte wa naranai.*) 審判は不公平であってはならない.

partially *adv.* bu⌈buñ-teki ni 部分的に: The bridge is partially completed. (*Hashi wa bubuñ-teki ni kañsee shite iru.*) 橋は部分的に完成している.

participate *vt.* ... ni sa⌈ñka suru ...に参加する Ⓘ; ka⌈nyuu suru 加入する Ⓘ: I participated in the discussion. (*Watashi wa sono tooroñ ni sañka shita.*) 私はその討論に参加した.

participation *n.* sa⌈ñka 参加; ka⌈nyuu 加入: participation in a demonstration (*demo ni sañka suru koto*) デモに参加すること.

particle *n.* **1** chi⌉isa-na tsubu 小さな粒: A particle of dirt was in my eye. (*Gomi no tsubu ga me ni haitta.*) ごみの粒が目に入った.

2 (of grammar) fu⌈heñka⌉shi 不変化詞.

particular *adj.* **1** (specific) to⌈kutee no 特定の: Do you have a particular color in mind? (*Tokutee no iro o o-kañgae desu ka?*) 特定の色をお考えですか.

2 (special) to⌈kubetsu no 特別の: pay particular attention (*tokubetsu no chuui o harau*) 特別の注意を払う / I have nothing particular to do today. (*Kyoo wa toku ni suru koto wa arimaseñ.*) きょうは特にすることはありません.

3 (hard to please) ya⌈kamashi⌉i やかましい; ki⌈muzukashi⌉i 気難しい: He is particular about his food. (*Kare wa taberu mono ni yakamashii.*) 彼は食べるものにやかましい.

— *n.* (details) sho⌈osai 詳細: go into particulars (*shoosai ni wataru*) 詳細にわたる.

particularly *adv.* to⌉ku ni 特に; to⌈riwake とりわけ: I am particularly interested in Japanese history. (*Watashi wa toku ni Nihoñ no rekishi ni kyoomi o motte imasu.*) 私は特に日本の歴史に興味を持っています.

partly *adv.* **1** (not wholly) i⌈chibu⌉buñ wa 一部分は; bu⌈buñ-teki ni 部分的に: The bridge was partly damaged. (*Hashi wa ichibu ga kowareta.*) 橋は一部が壊れた.

2 (to some extent) a⌈ru te⌉edo ある程度: His success is due partly to luck. (*Kare no seekoo wa aru teedo uñ ni yoru.*) 彼の成功はある程度運による.

partner *n.* **1** (one of two people) a⌈ite⌉ 相手; pa⌉atonaa パートナー: a tennis partner (*tenisu no paatonaa*) テニスのパートナー / a dancing partner (*dañsu no aite*) ダンスの相手.

2 (person who shares in the same activity) na⌈kama⌉ 仲間; kyo⌈oryoku⌉sha 協力者: a partner in business (*jigyoo no nakama*) 事業の仲間.

partnership *n.* kyo⌈oryoku 協力; te⌈ekee 提携: I entered into partnership with him. (*Watashi wa kare to teekee shita.*) 私は彼と提携した.

part-time *adj.* pa⌈ato-ta⌉imu no パートタイムの; a⌈ruba⌉ito no アルバイト

p

の; hi⌈jo⌉okiñ no 非常勤の: a part-time job (*paato-taimu no shigoto*) パートタイムの仕事 / a part-time teacher (*hijookiñ kooshi*) 非常勤講師.

party *n.* **1** (gathering) a⌈tsumari⌉ 集まり; pa⌉atii パーティー; ka⌉i 会: give a party (*paatii o hiraku*) パーティーを開く / a welcome party (*kañgeekai*) 歓迎会.
2 (political group) se⌈etoo 政党; to⌉o 党: the Liberal Democratic Party (*Jimiñ-too*) 自民党.
3 (group of people) i⌈chidañ 一団; i⌈kkoo 一行: The party left for London. (*Ikkoo wa Roñdoñ e mukatte tachimashita.*) 一行はロンドンへ向かって立ちました. / a party of tourists (*kañkoodañ*) 観光団.

pass *vi.* **1** (of time) ta⌉tsu たつ Ⓒ; ke⌈eka suru 経過する Ⓘ: Two weeks have passed since I came to Tokyo. (*Tookyoo e kite kara ni-shuukañ tachimashita.*) 東京へ来てから2週間たちました.
2 (go) to⌉oru 通る Ⓒ; su⌈sumu 進む Ⓒ: Where are we passing now? (*Ima doko o tootte iru no desu ka?*) 今どこを通っているのですか.
3 (go away) ki⌈esa⌉ru 消え去る Ⓒ; na⌈kunaru なくなる Ⓒ: The pain has passed. (*Itami ga nakunarimashita.*) 痛みがなくなりました.
4 (of a test) (... ni) u⌈ka⌉ru (…に)受かる Ⓒ; go⌈okaku suru 合格する Ⓘ: pass in an examination (*shikeñ ni gookaku suru*) 試験に合格する.
— *vt.* **1** (go through) ... o to⌉oru …を通る Ⓒ: No one is allowed to pass this gate. (*Dare mo kono moñ o tooru koto wa dekimaseñ.*) だれもこの門を通ることはできません.
2 (overtake) ... o o⌈iko⌉su …を追い越す Ⓒ: He passed my car on the road. (*Kare wa michi de watashi no kuruma o oikoshita.*) 彼は道で私の車を追い越した.
3 (hand) ... o wa⌈tasu …を渡す Ⓒ: ma⌈wasu 回す Ⓒ: Please pass this note to him. (*Kono memo o kare ni watashite kudasai.*) このメモを彼に渡してください.
4 (of a test) ... ni u⌈ka⌉ru 受かる Ⓒ; go⌈okaku suru 合格する Ⓘ: She passed her driving test. (*Kanojo wa uñteñmeñkyo shikeñ ni ukatta.*) 彼女は運転免許試験に受かった.
5 (enact) ... o ka⌈ketsu suru …を可決する Ⓘ: The Diet passed the bill. (*Kokkai wa sono giañ o kaketsu shita.*) 国会はその議案を可決した.
6 (give a judgment) ... o ku⌈dasu …を下す Ⓒ; no⌈be⌉ru 述べる Ⓥ: The judge passed sentence on him. (*Saibañkañ wa kare ni hañketsu o kudashita.*) 裁判官は彼に判決を下した.
7 (spend) ... o su⌈go⌉su …を過ごす Ⓒ: I passed the summer in the country. (*Watashi wa inaka de natsu o sugoshita.*) 私は田舎で夏を過ごした.
8 (of a ball) ... o pa⌉su suru …をパスする Ⓘ: pass a ball to a person (*hito ni booru o pasu suru*) 人にボールをパスする.
— *n.* **1** (free ticket) mu⌈ryoo-nyuujo⌉okeñ 無料入場券: a boarding pass (*toojoo-keñ*) 搭乗券.
2 (narrow path) to⌈oge⌉ 峠; ya⌈ma⌉-michi 山道: cross a pass (*tooge o kosu*) 峠を越す.
3 (successful result in an examination) go⌈okaku 合格; kyu⌈udai 及第.

passage *n.* **1** (way) tsu⌉uro 通路: Don't leave your bicycle in the passage. (*Tsuuro ni jiteñsha o oite wa ikemaseñ.*) 通路に自転車を置いてはいけません.
2 (act of passing) tsu⌈ukoo 通行; tsu⌈uka 通過: block a person's passage (*hito no tsuukoo o jama suru*) 人の通行をじゃまする.
3 (journey) ryo⌈koo 旅行; (by sea) fu⌉ne no ta⌈bi⌉ 船の旅; (by air) so⌉ra no ta⌈bi⌉ 空の旅.
4 (of time) na⌈gare⌉ 流れ; ke⌈eka 経過: the passage of time (*toki no nagare*) 時の流れ.
5 (part of writing) i⌈ssetsu 一節: a passage from the Bible (*seesho*

kara no issetsu) 聖書からの一節.

passenger *n.* jo⌈okyaku 乗客; ryo⌈kaku 旅客: passengers on a bus (*basu no jyookyaku*) バスの乗客 / a passenger ship (*kyakuseñ*) 客船.

passing *adj.* **1** (going by) tsu⌈uka suru 通過する; to⌈origakari no 通りがかりの: catch a passing taxi (*toorigakari no takushii o tsukamaeru*) 通りがかりのタクシーを捕まえる.
2 (lasting only a short time) i⌈chi⌉ji no 一時の; tsu⌈kanoma no つかの間の: passing joys (*tsukanoma no yorokobi*) つかの間の喜び.
— *n.* tsu⌈uka 通過; tsu⌈ukoo 通行: No passing. (*Oikoshi kiñshi.*) 追い越し禁止.

passion *n.* **1** (strong feeling) ge⌈kijoo 激情; jo⌈onetsu 情熱: a person of passion (*joonetsu-teki na hito*) 情熱的な人.
2 (strong liking) ne⌈tchuu 熱中; ne⌈tsuai 熱愛: He has a passion for golf. (*Kare wa gorufu ni netchuu shite iru.*) 彼はゴルフに熱中している.
3 (strong anger) ge⌉kido 激怒: fly into a passion (*katto natte okoru*) かっとなって怒る.

passionate *adj.* jo⌈onetsu-teki na 情熱的な; ne⌈tsuretsu na 熱烈な: a passionate woman (*joonetsu-teki na josee*) 情熱的な女性 / a passionate speech (*netsuretsu na eñzetsu*) 熱烈な演説.

passive *adj.* **1** (not active) ju⌈dooteki na 受動的な; sho⌈okyoku-teki na 消極的な: He is passive in everything. (*Kare wa nani o suru ni mo shookyoku-teki da.*) 彼は何をするにも消極的だ.
2 (of grammar) u⌈kemi no 受身の; ju⌈dootai no 受動態の: a passive sentence (*judoo buñ*) 受動文.
— *n.* (passive voice) ju⌈dootai 受動態.

passport *n.* pa⌈supo⌉oto パスポート; ryo⌈keñ 旅券: I lost my passport. (*Pasupooto o nakushimashita.*) パスポートをなくしました. / a passport number (*ryokeñ-bañgoo*) 旅券番号.

past *adj.* **1** (gone by) su⌈gisatta 過ぎ去った; ka⌉ko no 過去の: The danger is past now. (*Kikeñ wa moo sugisatta.*) 危険はもう過ぎ去った. / He spoke about his past life. (*Kare wa jibuñ no kako no seekatsu ni tsuite katatta.*) 彼は自分の過去の生活について語った.
2 (recent) ko⌈no この; señ- 先: She has been ill for the past three days. (*Kono mikka-kañ kanojo wa byooki deshita.*) この三日間彼女は病気でした. / the past week (*señshuu*) 先週.
3 (former) mo⌉to no 元の: the past president (*moto no shachoo*) 元の社長.
4 (of grammar) ka⌉ko no 過去の: the past form of a verb (*dooshi no kakokee*) 動詞の過去形.
— *n.* **1** (the time gone by) ka⌉ko 過去; su⌈gisatta koto⌉ 過ぎ去ったこと: Let's forget the past. (*Kako no koto wa wasuremashoo.*) 過去のことは忘れましょう.
2 (one's earlier life) ka⌉ko no re⌈kishi 過去の歴史: Nobody knows his past. (*Kare no kako wa dare mo shiranai.*) 彼の過去はだれも知らない.
— *prep.* **1** (beyond) ... o to⌈orisu⌉gite …を通り過ぎて: A taxi went past me. (*Takushii ga watashi no yoko o toorisugite itta.*) タクシーが私の横を通り過ぎて行った. / I rode past my stop. (*Norikoshite shimaimashita.*) 乗り越してしまいました.
2 (after) ... o su⌉gite …を過ぎて: It's a quarter past eight. (*Hachi-ji juugo-fuñ sugi desu.*) 8時15分過ぎです. / I got up at half past six. (*Watashi wa roku-ji hañ ni okimashita.*) 私は6時半に起きました.
— *adv.* to⌈orisu⌉gite 通り過ぎて: He ran past. (*Kare wa hashitte toorisugita.*) 彼は走って通り過ぎた.

paste *n.* **1** (mixture of flour and water) no⌈ri⌉ のり: seal an envelope with paste (*fuutoo o nori de haru*) 封筒をのりではる.
2 (any mixture) ne⌈ri⌉mono 練り物;

pe⌉esuto ペースト: tooth paste (*neri hamigaki*) 練り歯磨き.
— *vt.* ... o no⌈ri⌉ de ha⌈ru ...をのりではる Ⓒ: paste pictures in an album (*shashiñ o arubamu ni haru*) 写真をアルバムにはる.

pasture *n.* bo⌈kujoo 牧場.

pat *vt.* ... o ka⌈ruku tata⌉ku ...を軽くたたく Ⓒ: He patted me on the shoulder. (*Kare wa watashi no kata o karuku tataita.*) 彼は私の肩を軽くたたいた.
— *n.* ka⌈ruku tata⌉ku ko⌈to⌉ 軽くたたくこと.

patch *n.* **1** (piece of material) tsu⌈gikire 継ぎきれ; a⌈tenuno 当て布: a jacket with patches on the elbows (*hiji ni atenuno o shita uwagi*) ひじに当て布をした上着.
2 (bandage put on an eye) ga⌈ñtai 眼帯.
3 (small section of land) ha⌈take 畑: a patch of cabbages (*kyabetsu-batake*) キャベツ畑.
— *vt.* ... ni tsu⌈gi o ateru ...に継ぎを当てる Ⓥ: patch trousers (*zuboñ ni tsugi o ateru*) ズボンに継ぎを当てる.

patent *n.* to⌉kkyo 特許; to⌉kkyo⌉keñ 特許権: take out a patent on an invention (*hatsumee no tokkyo o toru*) 発明の特許を取る.
— *adj.* to⌉kkyo no aru 特許のある: a patent lock (*tokkyo no aru joo*) 特許のある錠.
— *vt.* ... no to⌉kkyo o toru ...の特許を取る Ⓒ.

path *n.* **1** (narrow way) ko⌈michi 小道; ho⌈so⌉michi 細道: a mountain path (*yama no komichi*) 山の小道.
2 (course) to⌈ori⌉michi 通り道; ki⌈doo 軌道: the path of a satellite (*eesee no kidoo*) 衛星の軌道.

pathetic *adj.* (causing pity) a⌉ware na 哀れな; i⌈tamashi⌉i 痛ましい: a pathetic sight (*itamashii kookee*) 痛ましい光景.

patience *n.* ni⌉ñtai 忍耐; shi⌉ñboo 辛抱: She waited for the delayed bus with patience. (*Kanojo wa okureta basu o shiñboo-zuyoku matta.*) 彼女は遅れたバスを辛抱強く待った.

patient *n.* ka⌈ñja 患者; byo⌈onin 病人: The doctor examined the patient carefully. (*Isha wa kañja o teenee ni shiñsatsu shita.*) 医者は患者を丁寧に診察した.
— *adj.* ga⌈mañ-zuyo⌉i 我慢強い; shi⌈ñboo-zuyo⌉i 辛抱強い: He is a very patient man. (*Kare wa totemo gamañ-zuyoi otoko da.*) 彼はとても我慢強い男だ.

patriot *n.* a⌈iko⌉kusha 愛国者.

patriotism *n.* a⌈iko⌉kushiñ 愛国心.

patrol *vt.* ... o ju⌈ñkai suru ...を巡回する Ⓘ; pa⌈toro⌉oru suru パトロールする Ⓘ: Policemen patrol this street. (*Keekañ ga kono toori o patorooru shite imasu.*) 警官がこの通りをパトロールしています.
— *n.* ju⌈ñkai 巡回; pa⌈toro⌉oru パトロール: a patrol car (*patokaa*) パトカー.

patron *n.* (supporter) ko⌈oe⌉ñsha 後援者; (customer) o⌈tokui お得意; hi⌈iki⌉kyaku ひいき客.

pattern *n.* **1** (design) mo⌈yoo 模様; ga⌈ra 柄: What does this pattern represent? (*Kono moyoo wa nani o arawashimasu ka?*) この模様は何を表しますか.
2 (model) ge⌈ñkee 原型; ka⌈tagami 型紙: make a dress from a pattern (*katagami ni shitagatte doresu o tsukuru*) 型紙に従ってドレスを作る.
3 (way of acting) ka⌈ta⌉ 型; yo⌈oshiki 様式; pa⌈ta⌉an パターン: new patterns of life (*atarashii seekatsu yooshiki*) 新しい生活様式.
— *vt.* (copy) ... o ma⌈neru ...をまねる Ⓥ; te⌈ho⌉ñ to suru 手本とする Ⓘ: He patterned himself after his father. (*Kare wa chichioya o tehoñ to shita.*) 彼は父親を手本とした.

pause *n.* sho⌈okyu⌉ushi 小休止; chu⌈udañ 中断: a pause in the conversation (*kaiwa no chuudañ*) 会話の中断.
— *vi.* **1** (make a brief stop) cho⌉t-

to ya⌈su⌉mu ちょっと休む Ⓒ; to⌈gire⌉ru 途切れる Ⓥ: He paused to light a cigarette. (*Kare wa chotto te o yasumete tabako ni hi o tsuketa.*) 彼はちょっと手を休めてたばこに火をつけた.
2 (hesitate) ta⌈mera⌉u ためらう Ⓒ: pause to find the right word (*tekitoo na kotoba o motomete tamerau*) 適当な言葉を求めてためらう.

pave *vt.* ... o ho⌈soo suru …を舗装する Ⓘ: pave a road with asphalt (*dooro o asufaruto de hosoo suru*) 道路をアスファルトで舗装する.

pavement *n.* **1** (surface) ho⌈soo 舗装: a crack in the pavement (*hosoo no hibiware*) 舗装のひび割れ.
2 (sidewalk) ho⌈doo 歩道: walk on the pavement (*hodoo o aruku*) 歩道を歩く.

paw *n.* a⌈shi⌉ 足: a dog's paw (*inu no ashi*) 犬の足.
— *vt.* ... o a⌈shi⌉ de kaku …を足でかく Ⓒ: The bull pawed the ground. (*Ushi wa ashi de jimeñ o kaita.*) 牛は足で地面をかいた.

pay *vt.* **1** (give money) ... o ha⌈ra⌉u …を払う Ⓒ; shi⌈hara⌉u 支払う Ⓒ: I paid two thousand yen for the book. (*Watashi wa sono hoñ ni niseñ-eñ haratta.*) 私はその本に2千円払った.
2 (settle) ... o shi⌈hara⌉u …を支払う Ⓥ: I haven't paid taxes yet. (*Zeekiñ o mada shiharatte imaseñ.*) 税金をまだ支払っていません.
3 (give) ... o ha⌈ra⌉u …を払う Ⓒ: pay attention to the matter (*sono mondai ni chuui o harau*) その問題に注意を払う.
4 (make) su⌈ru する Ⓘ: pay a call on a person (*hito o hoomoñ suru*) 人を訪問する.
— *vi.* **1** (give money) shi⌈harai o suru 支払いをする Ⓘ; da⌉ikiñ o ha⌈ra⌉u 代金を払う Ⓒ: Can I pay with a traveler's check? (*Ryokoo kogitte de shiharai dekimasu ka?*) 旅行小切手で支払いできますか.
2 (be profitable) hi⌈kia⌉u 引き合う Ⓒ; mo⌈oka⌉ru もうかる Ⓒ: This business doesn't pay. (*Kono shoobai wa hikiawanai.*) この商売は引き合わない.
— *n.* kyu⌉uryoo 給料; ho⌈oshuu 報酬: We get our pay at the end of the month. (*Watashi-tachi wa kyuuryoo o getsumatsu ni moraimasu.*) 私たちは給料を月末にもらいます.

payment *n.* **1** (paying) shi⌈harai 支払い: What are the terms of payment? (*Shiharai jookeñ wa doo natte imasu ka?*) 支払い条件はどうなっていますか.
2 (amount) shi⌈haraikiñ 支払い金.

pea *n.* e⌈ñdo⌉omame えんどう豆.

peace *n.* **1** (freedom from war) he⌈ewa 平和: The country is now at peace. (*Sono kuni wa ima heewa desu.*) その国はいま平和です.
2 (freedom from disturbance) chi⌈añ 治安; chi⌉tsujo 秩序: keep the peace (*chiañ o mamoru*) 治安を守る.
3 (freedom from anxiety) he⌈eoñ 平穏; ya⌈suragi 安らぎ: peace of mind (*kokoro no yasuragi*) 心のやすらぎ.

peaceful *adj.* **1** (be fond of peace) he⌈ewa o kono⌉mu 平和を好む; he⌈ewa-teki na 平和的な: solve a dispute by peaceful means (*fuñsoo o heewa-teki na shudañ de kaiketsu suru*) 紛争を平和的な手段で解決する.
2 (quiet) shi⌉zuka na 静かな; he⌈ewa na 平和な: spend a peaceful day (*shizuka na ichi-nichi o sugosu*) 静かな一日を過ごす.

peach *n.* mo⌈mo 桃; (fruit) mo⌈mo no mi 桃の実; (tree) mo⌈mo no ki⌉ 桃の木. ★ Japanese peaches are larger than those of Europe and North America.

peak *n.* **1** (top of a mountain) sa⌈ñchoo 山頂; mi⌈ne⌉ 峰: The mountain peak was covered with snow. (*Yama no mine wa yuki ni oowarete ita.*) 山の峰は雪におおわれていた.
2 (highest point) sa⌈iko⌉oteñ 最高点; ze⌈tchoo 絶頂: She was at the peak of her popularity. (*Kanojo wa*

p

niñki no zetchoo ni atta.) 彼女は人気の絶頂にあった.

— *vi.* cho'oteñ [pi'iku] ni ta'ssuru 頂点[ピーク]に達する Ⓘ: The sales peaked in June. (*Uriage wa roku-gatsu ni piiku ni tasshita.*) 売り上げは6月にピークに達した.

peanut *n.* pi'inattsu ピーナッツ; ra'k-ka'see 落花生.

pear *n.* se'eyo'o-nashi 西洋なし.

★ Japanese pears (simply '*nashi*') are round.

pearl *n.* shi'ñju 真珠: an imitation pearl (*jiñzoo shiñju*) 人造真珠.

— *adj.* shi'ñju no 真珠の; shi'ñju-iro no 真珠色の: pearl earrings (*shiñju no mimikazari*) 真珠の耳飾り.

peasant *n.* no'ofu 農夫; no'omiñ 農民.

pebble *n.* ko'ishi 小石.

peck *vi.* (of a bird) ku'chibashi de tsutsu'ku くちばしでつつく Ⓒ: The bird pecked at my finger. (*Sono tori wa watashi no yubi o kuchiba-shi de tsutsuita.*) その鳥は私の指をくちばしでつついた.

— *vt.* ... o tsu'tsu'ku ...をつつく Ⓒ; tsu'iba'mu ついばむ Ⓒ: The birds pecked the corn. (*Tori-tachi wa toomorokoshi o tsuibañda.*) 鳥たちはとうもろこしをついばんだ.

peculiar *adj.* **1** (strange) myo'o na 妙な; he'ñ na 変な: This meat has a peculiar taste. (*Kono niku wa heñ na aji ga suru.*) この肉は変な味がする.

2 (special) to'kubetsu no 特別の; to'kushu no 特殊の: a matter of peculiar interest (*toku ni kyoomi-bukai moñdai*) 特に興味深い問題.

3 (distinctive) to'kuyuu no 特有の; do'kutoku no 独特の: a custom peculiar to Japan (*Nihoñ tokuyuu no shuukañ*) 日本特有の習慣.

pedal *n.* pe'daru ペダル.

— *vt.* pe'daru o fuñde hashira-se'ru ペダルを踏んで走らせる Ⓥ: pedal a bicycle (*jiteñsha o hashiraseru*) 自転車を走らせる.

pedestrian *n.* ho'ko'osha 歩行者.

— *adj.* to'ho no 徒歩の; ho'ko'o-sha no 歩行者の: a pedestrian crossing (*oodañhodoo*) 横断歩道.

pediatrician *n.* sho'onika'-i 小児科医.

peel *vt.* **1** (of fruit and vegetables) ... no ka'wa' o mu'ku ...の皮をむく Ⓒ: peel a banana (*banana no kawa o muku*) バナナの皮をむく.

2 (of a tree) ... no ka'wa' o hagu ...の皮をはぐ Ⓒ: peel the bark off a tree (*ki no kawa o hagu*) 木の皮をはぐ.

— *n.* ka'wa' 皮: the peel of an apple (*riñgo no kawa*) りんごの皮.

peep *vi.* no'zokimi suru のぞき見する Ⓘ: He peeped through the keyhole. (*Kare wa kagiana kara nozokimi shita.*) 彼は鍵穴からのぞき見した.

— *n.* no'zokimi のぞき見; chi'ra'ri to miru ko'to' ちらりと見ること: She took a peep at him. (*Kanojo wa kare o chirari to mita.*) 彼女は彼をちらりと見た.

peer *n.* **1** (nobleman) ki'zoku 貴族.

2 (equal in rank) do'otoo no mono' 同等の者; do'oryoo 同僚; na'kama' 仲間: He asked for the opinion of his peers. (*Kare wa dooryoo no ikeñ o motometa.*) 彼は同僚の意見を求めた.

peg *n.* to'mekugi 止めくぎ; ka'ke-kugi 掛けくぎ: hang one's coat on a peg (*uwagi o kakekugi ni kakeru*) 上着を掛けくぎにかける / a hat peg (*booshikake*) 帽子掛け.

— *vt.* ... o ku'gi de tomeru ...をくぎで留める Ⓥ: peg a notice to the wall (*keeji o kugi de kabe ni tomeru*) 掲示をくぎで壁に留める.

pen[1] *n.* (instrument for writing) pe'ñ ペン: write with a pen (*peñ de kaku*) ペンで書く / a ballpoint pen (*boorupeñ*) ボールペン / a fountain pen (*mañneñhitsu*) 万年筆.

pen[2] *n.* (small enclosure) ka'koi 囲い; o'ri' おり.

— *vt.* ... o ka'koi [o'ri'] ni i'reru ...を囲い[おり]に入れる Ⓥ.

p

penalty *n.* **1** (punishment) ke¹ebatsu 刑罰; ba¹tsu 罰: The penalty for drunken driving is heavy. (*Yopparai uñteñ no batsu wa omoi.*) 酔っぱらい運転の罰は重い.
2 (fine) ba⌈kkiñ 罰金: pay a penalty for violating the rules (*kisoku ihañ no bakkiñ o harau*) 規則違反の罰金を払う.

pencil *n.* e⌈ñpitsu 鉛筆: sharpen a pencil (*eñpitsu o kezuru*) 鉛筆を削る / the lead of a pencil (*eñpitsu no shiñ*) 鉛筆のしん / a mechanical pencil (*shaapu peñshiru*) シャープペンシル.

pendant *n.* pe¹ñdañto ペンダント.

penetrate *vt.* **1** (enter) ... o tsu⌈ranu¹ku ...を貫く Ⓒ; ka⌈ñtsuu suru 貫通する Ⓘ: The bullet penetrated the wall. (*Dañgañ wa kabe o kañtsuu shita.*) 弾丸は壁を貫通した.
2 (spread) ... ni hi⌈rogaru ...に広がる Ⓒ: The smell penetrated the room. (*Sono nioi ga heya ni hirogatta.*) そのにおいが部屋に広がった.
— *vi.* tsu⌈ranu¹ku 貫く Ⓒ; shi⌈mito¹oru しみ通る Ⓒ: The rain penetrated through my coat. (*Ame ga uwagi ni shimitootta.*) 雨が上着にしみ通った.

peninsula *n.* ha⌈ñtoo 半島.

pension *n.* ne⌈ñkiñ 年金; o⌈ñkyuu 恩給: He lives on a pension. (*Kare wa neñkiñ de kurashite iru.*) 彼は年金で暮らしている.

people *n.* **1** (persons) hi⌈to¹bito 人人; hi⌈to 人: The street was crowded with people. (*Toori wa hito de koñzatsu shite ita.*) 通りは人で混雑していた. / There were thirty people present at the meeting. (*Kai ni wa sañjuu-niñ ga shusseki shita.*) 会には30人が出席した.
2 (nation) ko⌈kumiñ 国民: the Japanese people (*Nihoñ kokumiñ*) 日本国民.
3 (race) mi¹ñzoku 民族: There are many English-speaking peoples. (*Eego o hanasu miñzoku wa ooi.*) 英語を話す民族は多い.

pepper *n.* ko⌈sho¹o こしょう: put pepper on meat (*niku ni koshoo o furikakeru*) 肉にこしょうを振りかける.
— *vt.* ... ni ko⌈sho¹o o fu⌈rikake¹ru ...にこしょうを振りかける Ⓥ.

per *prep.* ... ni tsu¹ki ...につき: What is the fee per day? (*Ryookiñ wa ichi-nichi ni tsuki ikura desu ka?*) 料金は一日につきいくらですか. / 60 kilometers per hour (*jisoku rokujuk-kiro*) 時速60キロ.

perceive *vt.* **1** (become aware of) ... ni ki⌈zu¹ku ...に気づく Ⓒ: I perceived the difference between them. (*Watashi wa ryoosha no chigai ni kizuita.*) 私は両者の違いに気づいた.
2 (understand) ... ga wa⌈ka¹ru ...がわかる Ⓒ: I quickly perceived his joke. (*Watashi wa kare no jooku ga sugu ni wakatta.*) 私は彼のジョークがすぐにわかった.

percent *n.* pa⌈ase¹ñto パーセント: Ten percent equals one '*wari*'. (*Jup-paaseñto wa ichi-wari desu.*) 10パーセントは1割です. / an interest of three percent (*sañ-paaseñto no risoku*) 3パーセントの利息.

percentage *n.* **1** (rate) hya⌈kubu¹ñritsu 百分率; bu⌈ai 歩合: on a percentage basis (*buaisee de*) 歩合制で.
2 (part) wa⌈riai 割合; bu¹buñ 部分: The greater percentage of students go to university. (*Seeto no daibubuñ wa daigaku e ikimasu.*) 生徒の大部分は大学へ行きます.

perception *n.* chi⌈kaku 知覚: a person of keen perception (*chikaku no surudoi hito*) 知覚の鋭い人.

perfect *adj.* **1** (complete) ka⌈ñzeñ na 完全な; ka⌈ñpeki na 完ぺきな: a perfect crime (*kañzeñ-hañzai*) 完全犯罪 / Nobody is perfect. (*Kañpeki na hito wa inai.*) 完ぺきな人はいない.
2 (exact) se⌈ekaku na 正確な: draw a perfect circle (*seekaku na eñ o egaku*) 正確な円を描く.
3 (excellent) sa⌈iteki no 最適の: mo⌈oshibuñ no na¹i 申し分のない: He is perfect for this job. (*Kare*

wa kono shigoto ni saiteki da.) 彼はこの仕事に最適だ.
4 (thorough) ma⌈ttaku⌉ no まったくの: He is a perfect stranger. (*Ano hito wa mattaku shiranai hito desu.*) あの人はまったく知らない人です.
— *vt.* ... o ka⌈ñsee suru …を完成する [I]: perfect one's theory (*jibuñ no riroñ o kañsee suru*) 自分の理論を完成する.

perfection *n.* ka⌈ñzeñ 完全; ka⌈ñpeki 完ぺき; ka⌈ñsee 完成: Perfection is difficult to achieve. (*Kañpeki o kisuru no wa muzukashii.*) 完ぺきを期するのは難しい.

perfectly *adv.* ka⌈ñzeñ ni 完全に; ka⌈ñpeki ni 完ぺきに: He speaks Japanese perfectly. (*Kare wa Nihoñgo o kañpeki ni hanashimasu.*) 彼は日本語を完ぺきに話します.

perform *vt.* **1** (carry out) ... o ji⌈kkoo suru …を実行する [I]; ha⌈ta⌉su 果たす [C]: I performed the task faithfully. (*Watashi wa sono shigoto o chuujitsu ni hatashita.*) 私はその仕事を忠実に果たした.
2 (of a play) ... o jo⌈oeñ suru …を上演する [I]; (of music) e⌈ñsoo suru 演奏する [I]: perform a musical (*myuujikaru o jooeñ suru*) ミュージカルを上演する.
— *vi.* (of a play) (... o) e⌈ñjiru (…を)演じる [V]; (of music) e⌈ñsoo suru 演奏する [I]: perform on the violin (*baioriñ o eñsoo suru*) バイオリンを演奏する.

performance *n.* **1** (of a play) ko⌈oeñ 公演; jo⌈oeñ 上演; (of music) e⌈ñsoo 演奏: What time does the performance begin? (*Kaieñ wa nañ-ji desu ka?*) 開演は何時ですか.
2 (doing) ji⌈kkoo 実行; su⌈ikoo 遂行: the performance of one's duty (*shokumu no jikkoo*) 職務の実行.
3 (ability) se⌈enoo 性能; no⌉oryoku 能力: engine performance (*eñjiñ no seenoo*) エンジンの性能.

performer *n.* (of a play) e⌈ñgi⌉sha 演技者; (of music) e⌈ñso⌉osha 演奏者.

perfume *n.* **1** (liquid) ko⌈osui 香水: put on perfume (*koosui o tsukeru*) 香水をつける.
2 (smell) ka⌈ori 香り; ni⌈o⌉i におい: the perfume of roses (*bara no kaori*) ばらの香り.

perhaps *adv.* ko⌈to ni yoru to ことによると; ta⌉buñ 多分; o⌈so⌉raku 恐らく: Perhaps he will come. (*Tabuñ kare wa kuru deshoo.*) 多分彼は来るでしょう.

peril *n.* ki⌈keñ 危険: He faced many perils. (*Kare wa ooku no kikeñ ni chokumeñ shita.*) 彼は多くの危険に直面した.

period *n.* **1** (length of time) ki⌉kañ 期間; ji⌉ki 時期: He stayed here for a short period of time. (*Kare wa tañkikañ koko ni taizai shita.*) 彼は短期間ここに滞在した.
2 (punctuation mark) pi⌉riodo ピリオド; shu⌈ushi⌉fu 終止符: put a period at the end of a sentence (*buñ no saigo ni shuushifu o utsu*) 文の最後に終止符を打つ.
3 (division of a school day) ji⌈geñ 時限; ji⌈kañ 時間: the third period (*dai sañ-jigeñ*) 第3時限 / a study period (*jishuu-jikañ*) 自習時間.
4 (era) ji⌈dai 時代: the Kamakura period (*Kamakura jidai*) 鎌倉時代.
5 (menstrual period) se⌉eri 生理; ge⌈kkee 月経.

periodical *n.* te⌈eki kañko⌉obutsu 定期刊行物; za⌈sshi 雑誌.

perish *vi.* (die) shi⌈nu 死ぬ [C]; (be destroyed) ho⌈robi⌉ru 滅びる [V]: Hundreds of people perished in the earthquake. (*Nañ-byaku-niñ mo no hito ga sono jishiñ de shiñda.*) 何百人もの人がその地震で死んだ.

permanent *adj.* e⌈ekyuu no 永久の; fu⌈heñ no 不変の: permanent peace (*eekyuu no heewa*) 永久の平和 / a permanent domicile (*hoñseki*) 本籍.
— *n.* (permanent wave) pa⌈amane⌉ñto パーマネント; pa⌉ama パーマ: A soft [tight] permanent, please. (*Karuku* [*Kitsuku*] *paama shitekuda-*

sai.) 軽く[きつく]パーマしてください.

permission *n.* kyo⌉ka 許可; yu⌈rushi⌉ 許し; ni⌉ñka 認可: The teacher gave me permission to leave early. (*Señsee wa watashi ni sootai no kyoka o kureta.*) 先生は私に早退の許可をくれた.

permit *vt.* ... o kyo⌉ka suru ...を許可する [I]; yu⌈ru⌉su 許す [C]: My father permitted me to go abroad. (*Chichi wa watashi ga gaikoku e iku no o yurushite kureta.*) 父は私が外国へ行くのを許してくれた. / Smoking is not permitted here. (*Koko wa kiñeñ desu.*) ここは禁煙です.

— *vi.* yu⌈ru⌉su 許す [C]: We will depart tomorrow if the weather permits. (*Teñkoo ga yuruseba asu shuppatsu shimasu.*) 天候が許せば明日出発します.

— *n.* kyo⌈ka⌉shoo 許可証; me⌈ñ-kyo⌉shoo 免許証: an International Driving Permit (*Kokusai uñteñ meñkyoshoo*) 国際運転免許証.

perpetual *adj.* **1** (continuing) ta⌈ema no na⌉i 絶え間のない: perpetual noise (*taema no nai soo-oñ*) 絶え間のない騒音.

2 (lasting) e⌈ekyuu no 永久の; fu⌈kyuu no 不朽の: perpetual fame (*fukyuu no meesee*) 不朽の名声.

perplex *vt.* ... o na⌈yamase⌉ru ...を悩ませる [V]; to⌈owaku saseru 当惑させる [V]: The problem perplexed me. (*Sono moñdai wa watashi o nayamaseta.*) その問題は私を悩ませた.

persecute *vt.* ... o ha⌈kugai suru ...を迫害する [I]: They were persecuted for their religion. (*Kare-ra wa shiñkoo no tame ni hakugai sareta.*) 彼らは信仰のために迫害された.

persevere *vi.* (... o) shi⌉ñboo suru (...を)辛抱する [I]; ga⌈ñba⌉ru がんばる [C]: He persevered in his work. (*Kare wa shigoto o gañbatta.*) 彼は仕事をがんばった.

persist *vt.* **1** (continue firmly) ko⌈shitsu suru 固執する [I]; a⌈ku⌉made to⌉osu あくまで通す [C]: persist in one's opinion (*jibuñ no ikeñ o akumade mo toosu*) 自分の意見をあくまでも通す.

2 (last) tsu⌈zuku 続く [C]: The rain persisted for three days. (*Ame wa mikka tsuzuita.*) 雨は三日続いた.

persistent *adj.* **1** (continuing) ko⌈shitsu suru 固執する; shi⌈tsuko⌉i しつこい: a persistent salesman (*shitsukoi seerusumañ*) しつこいセールスマン.

2 (lasting) na⌉gaku tsu⌈zuku 長く続く: a persistent rain (*nagaku tsuzuku ame*) 長く続く雨.

person *n.* hi⌈to 人; (human being) ni⌈ñgeñ 人間: He is a very nice person. (*Kare wa totemo yoi hito desu.*) 彼はとてもよい人です. / How many persons are there in the room? (*Heya ni wa nañ-niñ imasu ka?*) 部屋には何人いますか.

personal *adj.* **1** (private) ko⌉jiñ no 個人の; ko⌈jiñ-teki na 個人的な: This is my personal affair. (*Kore wa watashi no kojiñ-teki na moñdai desu.*) これは私の個人的な問題です.

2 (one's own) ji⌈buñ no 自分の: This camera is for my personal use. (*Kono kamera wa watashi ga jibuñ de tsukatte iru mono desu.*) このカメラは私が自分で使っているものです.

3 (done by oneself) ho⌉ñniñ no 本人の; ji⌉shiñ no 自身の: The mayor made a personal visit to him. (*Shichoo jishiñ ga kare o hoomoñ shita.*) 市長自身が彼を訪問した.

personal effects *n.* mi-⌈no-mawari-hiñ 身の回り品.

personality *n.* **1** (character) ji⌈ñ-kaku 人格; ko⌉see 個性: He has a very strong personality. (*Kare wa kosee ga tsuyoi.*) 彼は個性が強い.

2 (well-known person) yu⌈ume⌉ejiñ 有名人; ta⌉reñto タレント: a TV personality (*terebi tareñto*) テレビタレント.

personally *adv.* **1** (in person) cho⌈kusetsu jibuñ de 直接自分で: He wrote the answer personally. (*Kare wa chokusetsu jibuñ de sono heñji o kaita.*) 彼は直接自分で

p

その返事を書いた.

2 (as a person) ni⌈ñgeñ [ko⌉jiñ] to shite⌉ (wa) 人間[個人]として(は): I don't like him personally, but I respect his talent. (*Kojiñ-teki ni wa suki de wa nai ga, kare no sainoo wa soñkee shite imasu.*) 個人的には好きではないが, 彼の才能は尊敬しています.

3 (as far as oneself is concerned) ji⌈buñ to shite⌉ wa 自分としては: Personally, I am against the plan. (*Watashi to shite wa sono keekaku ni hañtai desu.*) 私としてはその計画に反対です.

personnel *n.* ji⌈ñiñ 人員; sho⌈ku⌉iñ 職員: a personnel department (*jiñji-ka*) 人事課.

perspective *n.* **1** (the way of drawing) e⌈ñkiñ-ga⌉hoo 遠近画法.

2 (view) mi⌈tooshi 見通し: get a clear perspective on a problem (*moñdai ni tsuite hakkiri shita mitooshi o motsu*) 問題についてはっきりした見通しを持つ.

persuade *vt.* **1** (make someone do by talking) ... o to⌈kifuse⌉ru ...を説き伏せる [V]; se⌈ttoku shite <verb>-(sa)seru 説得して...(さ)せる [V]: I persuaded him to go. (*Watashi wa kare o tokifusete ikaseta.*) 私は彼を説き伏せて行かせた.

2 (convince) ... o na⌈ttoku saseru ...を納得させる [V]; ka⌈kushiñ saseru 確信させる [V]: I persuaded him that I was right. (*Watashi wa kare ni watashi ga tadashii koto o nattoku saseta.*) 私は彼に私が正しいことを納得させた.

persuasion *n.* **1** (persuading) se⌈ttoku 説得: I gave in to his persuasion. (*Watashi wa kare no settoku ni shitagatta.*) 私は彼の説得に従った.

2 (belief) ka⌈kushiñ 確信: I have a strong persuasion that this is true. (*Watashi wa kore wa tadashii to tsuyoi kakushiñ o motte iru.*) 私はこれは正しいと強い確信を持っている.

pertinent *adj.* (relevant) ka⌈ñkee ga a⌉ru 関係がある; te⌈kisetsu na 適切な: His remarks are not pertinent to this issue. (*Kare ga nobeta koto wa kono moñdai to kañkee ga nai.*) 彼が述べたことはこの問題と関係がない.

pet *n.* pe⌉tto ペット; a⌈igañ-do⌉obutsu 愛玩動物: I have a rabbit as a pet. (*Watashi wa usagi o petto ni katte imasu.*) 私はうさぎをペットに飼っています.

— *adj.* **1** (kept as a pet) pe⌉tto no ペットの: a pet turtle (*petto no kame*) ペットのかめ.

2 (favorite) o-⌈ki ni iri no お気に入りの; to⌈kui no 得意の: It is his pet theme. (*Sore wa kare no tokui no teema da.*) それは彼の得意のテーマだ.

petrol *n.* ga⌈soriñ ガソリン.

petty *adj.* to⌉ru ni ta⌈ranai 取るに足らない; sa⌉sai na ささいな: petty faults (*sasai na ketteñ*) ささいな欠点.

pharmacist *n.* ya⌈kuza⌉ishi 薬剤師.

pharmacy *n.* ya⌈kkyoku 薬局; ku⌈suriya 薬屋.

phase *n.* **1** (aspect) me⌉ñ 面; so⌈kumeñ 側面: a problem with many phases (*ooku no sokumeñ o motsu moñdai*) 多くの側面を持つ問題.

2 (stage) da⌈ñkai 段階: We entered a new phase in the negotiations. (*Wareware wa kooshoo no atarashii dañkai ni haitta.*) われわれは交渉の新しい段階に入った.

phenomenon *n.* ge⌈ñshoo 現象: a natural phenomenon (*shizeñ-geñshoo*) 自然現象.

philosopher *n.* te⌈tsugaku⌉sha 哲学者.

philosophy *n.* te⌈tsu⌉gaku 哲学.

phone *n.* de⌈ñwa 電話: talk on the phone (*deñwa de hanasu*) 電話で話す / make a phone call (*deñwa o kakeru*) 電話をかける / May I use your phone? (*Deñwa o o-kari dekimasu ka?*) 電話をお借りできますか. / a phone book (*deñwachoo*) 電話帳 / a phone booth (*deñwa bokkusu*) 電話ボックス / a phone number (*deñwa-bañgoo*) 電話番号.

p

photo *n.* sha⌈shiñ 写真.

photograph *n.* sha⌈shiñ 写真: Can I take photographs here? (*Koko de shashiñ o totte mo ii desu ka?*) ここで写真を撮ってもいいですか. / No Photographs. (*Satsuee kiñshi.*) 撮影禁止.

photographer *n.* ka⌈mera⌉mañ カメラマン; sha⌈shiñ-ka 写真家: a press photographer (*shiñbuñsha no kameramañ*) 新聞社のカメラマン.
★ In Japan, professional photographers are called '*kameramañ*' (cameraman).

photography *n.* sha⌈shi⌉ñjutsu 写真術; sha⌈shiñ-sa⌉tsuee 写真撮影.

phrase *n.* **1** (group of words) ku⌉ 句; fu⌈re⌉ezu フレーズ: a noun phrase (*meeshi-ku*) 名詞句 / a set phrase (*seeku*) 成句.
2 (expression) ko⌈tobazu⌉kai 言葉遣い; i⌈imawashi 言い回し: a happy turn of phrase (*umai iimawashi*) うまい言い回し.

physical *adj.* **1** (of the body) shi⌉ñtai no 身体の; ni⌈kutai no 肉体の: a physical examination (*shiñtai keñsa*) 身体検査.
2 (material) bu⌈sshitsu no 物質の; shi⌈ze⌉ñ no 自然の: the physical world (*shizeñkai*) 自然界.
3 (of the natural science) bu⌈tsuri-teki na 物理的な: a physical change (*butsuri-teki heñka*) 物理的変化.

physician *n.* na⌈ika⌉-i 内科医; (doctor) i⌉shi 医師; i⌈sha 医者: You'd better see a physician. (*Isha e itta hoo ga ii desu yo.*) 医者へ行ったほうがいいですよ.

physics *n.* bu⌈tsuri⌉gaku 物理学: nuclear physics (*geñshi butsuri-gaku*) 原子物理学.

pianist *n.* pi⌈ani⌉suto ピアニスト; pi⌈ano eñsooka ピアノ演奏家.

piano *n.* pi⌈ano ピアノ: She played Chopin on the piano. (*Kanojo wa piano de Shopañ o hiita.*) 彼女はピアノでショパンを弾いた.

pick *vt.* **1** (select) ... o e⌈ra⌉bu ...を選ぶ Ⓒ: He picked a nice tie. (*Kare wa suteki na nekutai o erañda.*) 彼はすてきなネクタイを選んだ.
2 (of a flower) ... o tsu⌈mu ...を摘む Ⓒ; (of a fruit) ... o mo⌉gu ...をもぐ Ⓒ: pick flowers (*hana o tsumu*) 花を摘む / pick apples (*riñgo o mogu*) りんごをもぐ.
3 (take off) ... o ho⌈ji⌉ru ...をほじる Ⓒ: pick one's nose (*hana o hojiru*) 鼻をほじる.
4 (dig into) ... o tsu⌈tsu⌉ku ...をつつく Ⓒ: pick a little hole (*tsutsuite chiisa-na ana o akeru*) つついて小さな穴を開ける.
pick up *vt.* ... o te⌉ ni toru ...を手に取る Ⓒ: May I pick it up? (*Te ni totte mo ii desu ka?*) 手に取ってもいいですか.

pickle *n.* pi⌉kurusu ピクルス; tsu⌈ke-mono 漬物.

picnic *n.* (pleasure trip) pi⌈kuni⌉kku ピクニック: go on a picnic to the lake (*mizuumi e pikunikku ni iku*) 湖へピクニックに行く.

picture *n.* **1** (painting) e⌉ 絵: draw a picture (*e o kaku*) 絵をかく / a picture frame (*gakubuchi*) 額縁.
2 (photograph) sha⌈shiñ 写真: May I take your picture? (*Anata no shashiñ o totte mo yoroshii desu ka?*) あなたの写真を撮ってもよろしいですか.
3 (movie) e⌉ega 映画: go to the pictures (*eega o mi ni iku*) 映画を見に行く.
— *vt.* (imagine) ... o ko⌈ko⌉ro ni e⌈ga⌉ku ...を心に描く Ⓒ: I pictured the scene. (*Watashi wa sono bameñ o kokoro ni egaita.*) 私はその場面を心に描いた.

picture postcard *n.* e⌈ha⌉gaki 絵はがき.

picturesque *adj.* e⌉ no yoo ni u⌈tsukushi⌉i 絵のように美しい: a picturesque view (*e no yoo ni utsukushii nagame*) 絵のように美しい眺め.

pie *n.* pa⌉i パイ: bake a pie (*pai o yaku*) パイを焼く.

piece *n.* **1** (single thing) hi⌈to⌉tsu 一つ; i⌉k-ko 1 個: I have 3 pieces of

p

baggage in all. (*Nimotsu wa zeñbu de sañ-ko desu.*) 荷物は全部で3個です. ★ Japanese use different counters, depending on the type of thing being counted: a piece of paper (*kami ichi-mai*) 紙1枚 / a piece of chalk (*chooku ip-poñ*) チョーク1本 / a piece of furniture (*kagu it-teñ*) 家具1点 / a piece of information (*joohoo hitotsu*) 情報一つ.
2 (part) bu⌉buñ 部分; ku⌈kaku 区画: cut a pie into six equal pieces (*pai o roku-toobuñ suru*) パイを6等分する.
3 (work) sa⌈kuhiñ 作品: write a piece for the piano (*piano no tame no sakuhiñ o kaku*) ピアノのための作品を書く.

pier *n.* sa⌈ñbashi 桟橋; fu⌈too 埠頭.

pierce *vt.* **1** (pass through) ... o tsu⌈kisa⌉su …を突き刺す Ⓒ; tsu⌈ra-nu⌉ku 貫く Ⓒ: A nail pierced the tire. (*Kugi ga taiya o tsukisashita.*) くぎがタイヤを突き刺した.
2 (make a hole) ... ni a⌈na⌉ o a⌈keru …に穴を開ける Ⓥ: pierce a hole in the wall (*kabe ni ana o akeru*) 壁に穴を開ける.

pig *n.* bu⌈ta 豚.

pigeon *n.* ha⌉to はと(鳩).

pile *n.* tsu⌈mikasane 積み重ね; ya⌈ma⌉ 山: a pile of newspapers (*shiñbuñ no yama*) 新聞の山.
— *vt.* ... o tsu⌈mikasane⌉ru …を積み重ねる Ⓥ: I piled old newspapers in the corner. (*Watashi wa furu-shiñbuñ o sumi ni tsumikasaneta.*) 私は古新聞を隅に積み重ねた.

pill *n.* ga⌈ñyaku 丸薬; jo⌈ozai 錠剤; ku⌈suri 薬: take a pill (*gañyaku [joozai] o nomu*) 丸薬[錠剤]を飲む / a sleeping pill (*suimiñyaku*) 睡眠薬.

pillar *n.* ha⌈shira 柱; shi⌈chuu 支柱: set up a pillar (*hashira o tateru*) 柱を立てる.

pillow *n.* ma⌉kura 枕: pillowcase (*makura kabaa*) 枕カバー.

pilot *n.* **1** (of an airplane) so⌈oju⌉u-shi 操縦士; pa⌈iro⌉tto パイロット: a jet pilot (*jettoki no pairotto*) ジェット機のパイロット.
2 (of a ship) mi⌈zusaki añnainiñ 水先案内人.
— *adj.* (experimental) shi⌈ke⌉ñ no 試験の; ji⌈kkeñ no 実験の: a pilot farm (*shikeñ-noojoo*) 試験農場.
— *vt.* **1** (act as a pilot) ... o so⌈o-juu suru …を操縦する Ⓘ: pilot a plane (*hikooki o soojuu suru*) 飛行機を操縦する.
2 (guide) ... o a⌈ñna⌉i suru …を案内する Ⓘ: He piloted me through Tokyo. (*Kare ga Tookyoo o añnai shite kureta.*) 彼が東京を案内してくれた.

pin *n.* pi⌉ñ ピン; to⌈meba⌉ri 留め針.
— *vt.* ... o pi⌉ñ de to⌈meru …をピンで留める Ⓥ: pin a flower to a coat (*hana o piñ de uwagi ni tomeru*) 花をピンで上着に留める.

pinch *vt.* **1** (squeeze) ... o tsu⌈ne⌉ru …をつねる Ⓒ: She pinched my arm. (*Kanojo wa watashi no ude o tsunetta.*) 彼女は私の腕をつねった.
2 (press tightly) ... o ha⌈sa⌉mu …を挟む Ⓒ: I pinched my finger in the door. (*Watashi wa yubi o doa ni hasañda.*) 私は指をドアに挟んだ.
— *n.* tsu⌈ne⌉ru ko⌈to⌉ つねること; ha⌈sa⌉mu ko⌈to⌉ 挟むこと: give a child a pinch on the cheek (*kodomo no hoo o tsuneru*) 子どもの頬をつねる.

pine *n.* ma⌉tsu 松; (tree) ma⌉tsu no ki 松の木.

pink *adj.* mo⌈moiro no 桃色の; pi⌉ñ-ku no ピンクの: a pink rose (*momo-iro no bara*) 桃色のばら.
— *n.* mo⌈moiro 桃色; pi⌉ñku ピンク.

pint *n.* pa⌉iñto パイント. ★ In Japan the metric system is used.

pioneer *n.* **1** (early settler) ka⌈i-ta⌉kusha 開拓者.
2 (person who is the first) se⌈ñku⌉-sha 先駆者; so⌈oshi⌉sha 創始者: He is a pioneer in this field. (*Kare wa kono buñya no señkusha da.*) 彼はこの分野の先駆者だ.

pious *adj.* ke⌈ekeñ na 敬虔な; shi⌈ñ-jiñbuka⌉i 信心深い: a pious Christian (*keekeñ na kurisuchañ*) 敬虔な

p

クリスチャン.

pipe *n.* **1** (tube) ka¹ñ 管; pa⌈ipu パイプ: a gas pipe (*gasu-kañ*) ガス管.
2 (of tobacco) pa⌈ipu パイプ: smoke a pipe (*paipu de ippuku suu*) パイプで一服吸う.
— *vt.* ... o ka¹ñ [pa⌈ipu] de o⌈kuru …を管[パイプ]で送る Ⓒ: The oil is piped into the tank. (*Sekiyu wa paipu de tañku ni okuraremasu.*) 石油はパイプでタンクに送られます.

pit *n.* **1** (hole) a⌈na¹ 穴: dig a pit for rubbish (*gomi o ireru ana o horu*) ごみを入れる穴を掘る.
2 (coal-mine) ta⌈ñkoo 炭坑.

pitch *n.* **1** (of a sound) ta¹kasa 高さ; cho⌈oshi 調子: the pitch of a voice (*koe no takasa*) 声の高さ.
2 (throwing) to⌈okyuu 投球: a wild pitch (*bootoo*) 暴投.
3 (slope) ko⌈obai 勾配: the pitch of a roof (*yane no koobai*) 屋根の勾配.
— *vt.* **1** (throw) ... o na⌈ge¹ru …を投げる Ⓥ: pitch a fast ball (*sokkyuu o nageru*) 速球を投げる.
2 (set up) ... o ha⌈ru …を張る Ⓒ; ta⌈te¹ru 立てる Ⓥ: pitch a tent (*teñto o haru*) テントを張る.
— *vi.* (rise and fall) jo¹oge ni yu⌈reru 上下に揺れる Ⓥ: The ship pitched violently in the storm. (*Fune wa arashi de jooge ni hageshiku yureta.*) 船は嵐で上下に激しく揺れた.

pitcher[1] *n.* (container) mi⌈zusashi¹ 水差し: pour water into a pitcher (*mizusashi ni mizu o sosogu*) 水差しに水を注ぐ.

pitcher[2] *n.* (baseball player) to¹oshu 投手; pi¹tchaa ピッチャー.

pitiful *adj.* ka⌈waiso¹o na かわいそうな; a¹ware na 哀れな: a pitiful sight (*aware na kookee*) 哀れな光景.

pity *n.* **1** (feeling of sorrow) a⌈waremi 哀れみ; do⌈ojoo 同情: I feel pity for him. (*Kare o ki no doku ni omou.*) 彼を気の毒に思う.
2 (regret) za⌈ñne¹ñ na ko⌈to¹ 残念なこと: It's a pity that he cannot come. (*Kare ga korarenai no wa zañneñ da.*) 彼が来られないのは残念だ.
— *vt.* ... o ki ⌈no doku¹ ni o⌈mo¹u …を気の毒に思う Ⓒ: I pity the sick old man. (*Watashi wa sono byooki no roojiñ o ki no doku ni omou.*) 私はその病気の老人を気の毒に思う.

place *n.* **1** (location) ba⌈sho 場所; to⌈koro¹ 所: Is there a place to change money near here? (*Kono chikaku ni ryoogae o suru tokoro wa arimasu ka?*) この近くに両替をする所はありますか.
2 (spot) ka¹sho 箇所; to⌈koro¹ 所: He rubbed the sore place on his arm. (*Kare wa ude no itamu kasho o sasutta.*) 彼は腕の痛む箇所をさすった.
3 (house) ju⌈utaku 住宅; i⌈e¹ 家: He has a nice place in the suburbs. (*Kare wa koogai ni ii ie ga aru.*) 彼は郊外にいい家がある.
4 (position) ju¹ñi 順位: I took second place in the race. (*Watashi wa kyoosoo de ni-i datta.*) 私は競走で2位だった.
5 (job) sho⌈ku 職; shi⌈goto 仕事: He found a new place in the firm. (*Kare wa sono kaisha de atarashii shoku o mitsuketa.*) 彼はその会社で新しい職を見つけた.
— *vt.* **1** (put) ... o o⌈ku …を置く Ⓒ: She placed a vase on the table. (*Kanojo wa kabiñ o teeburu no ue ni oita.*) 彼女は花びんをテーブルの上に置いた.
2 (of an order) ... o da¹su …を出す Ⓒ; su⌈ru する Ⓘ: I placed an order for the book with the bookstore. (*Watashi wa sono hoñ o shoteñ ni chuumoñ shita.*) 私はその本を書店に注文した.
3 (entrust) ... o o⌈ku …を置く Ⓒ: I place my confidence in him. (*Watashi wa kare ni shiñrai o oite imasu.*) 私は彼に信頼を置いています.

plain *adj.* **1** (not decorated) mu¹ji no 無地の: a plain blouse (*muji no burausu*) 無地のブラウス.
2 (clear) me⌈ehaku na 明白な; ha⌈k-

p

ki⌉ri shita [shite iru] はっきりした[している]: It is quite plain that he wants to quit his job. (*Kare ga shigoto o yametagatte iru no wa hakkiri shite iru.*) 彼が仕事を辞めたがっているのははっきりしている.

3 (easy to understand) wa⌈kari-yasu⌉i わかりやすい: explain in plain language (*wakariyasui kotoba de setsumee suru*) わかりやすい言葉で説明する.

4 (simple) ka⌉ñso na 簡素な; shi⌉s-so na 質素な: a plain way of life (*shisso na kurashikata*) 質素な暮らし方.

5 (not pretty) na⌈mi no 並の; bu-⌈ki⌉ryoo na 不器量な.

— *adv.* ha⌈kki⌉ri to はっきりと: speak plain (*hakkiri to hanasu*) はっきりと話す.

— *n.* he⌈echi 平地; he⌈eya 平野.

plainly *adv.* **1** (clearly) wa⌈kari-ya⌉suku わかりやすく; ha⌈kki⌉ri to はっきりと: explain one's ideas plainly (*jibuñ no kañgae o hakkiri to se-tsumee suru*) 自分の考えをはっきりと説明する.

2 (obviously) a⌈ki⌉raka ni 明らかに; me⌈ehaku ni 明白に: Plainly, he is wrong. (*Akiraka ni kare wa machi-gatte iru.*) 明らかに彼は間違っている.

3 (simply) ka⌉ñso ni 簡素に; shi⌉s-so ni 質素に: She was dressed plainly. (*Kanojo wa shisso na fuku-soo o shite ita.*) 彼女は質素な服装をしていた.

plan *n.* **1** (idea) ke⌈ekaku 計画; a⌉ñ 案; pu⌉rañ プラン: carry out a plan (*keekaku o jikkoo suru*) 計画を実行する.

2 (line drawing) zu⌈meñ 図面: plans for a new library (*atarashii toshokañ no zumeñ*) 新しい図書館の図面.

— *vt.* **1** (think out) ... o ke⌈ekaku suru ...を計画する [I]; yo⌈tee suru 予定する [I]: He is planning a tour of Hokkaido this summer. (*Kare wa kono natsu Hokkaidoo-ryokoo o keekaku shite iru.*) 彼はこの夏北海道旅行を計画している.

2 (make a drawing) ... o se⌈kkee suru ...を設計する [I]; ... no zu⌈meñ o ka⌉ku ...の図面をかく [C]: plan a garden (*niwa o sekkee suru*) 庭を設計する.

plane[1] *n.* hi⌈ko⌉oki 飛行機: get on a plane (*hikooki ni noru*) 飛行機に乗る / get off a plane (*hikooki kara oriru*) 飛行機から降りる / take a plane to Hawaii (*hikooki de Ha-wai e iku*) 飛行機でハワイへ行く.

plane[2] *n.* he⌈emeñ 平面; me⌉ñ 面: a horizontal plane (*suiheemeñ*) 水平面.

— *adj.* ta⌈ira na 平らな: a plane surface (*taira na hyoomeñ*) 平らな表面.

— *vt.* ... ni ka⌈ñna⌉ o ka⌈ke⌉ru ...にかんなをかける [V]: plane a board smooth (*ita ni kañna o kakete na-meraka ni suru*) 板にかんなをかけて滑らかにする.

planet *n.* wa⌈kusee 惑星.

plant *n.* **1** (living thing) sho⌈ku⌉bu-tsu 植物; (grass) ku⌈sa⌉ 草: grow a plant (*shokubutsu o saibai suru*) 植物を栽培する.

2 (factory) ko⌈ojo⌉o 工場: a chemi-cal plant (*kagaku-koojoo*) 化学工場.

— *vt.* **1** (put into the ground) ... o u⌈eru ...を植える [V]: plant roses in a garden (*niwa ni bara o ueru*) 庭にばらを植える.

2 (instill) ... o u⌈etsuke⌉ru ...を植え付ける [V]; fu⌈kiko⌉mu 吹き込む [C]: plant an idea (*kañgae o fukikomu*) 考えを吹き込む.

plaster *n.* shi⌈kkui しっくい.

— *vt.* ... ni shi⌈kkui o nuru ...にしっくいを塗る [C]: plaster walls (*kabe ni shikkui o nuru*) 壁にしっくいを塗る.

plastic *adj.* pu⌈rasuchikkusee no プラスチック製の; go⌈oseeju⌉shi no 合成樹脂の; bi⌈niirusee no ビニール製の: a plastic dish (*purasuchikku no sara*) プラスチックの皿 / a plastic bag (*biniiru-bukuro*) ビニール袋. ★ Japa-nese '*purasuchikku*' refers only to a hard material.

— *n.* pu[rasuchi]kku プラスチック; go[oseeju]shi 合成樹脂; bi[ni]iru ビニール.

plate *n.* **1** (flat dish) sa[ra 皿; hi[razara 平皿: a soup plate (*suupuzara*) スープ皿.
2 (plateful) hi[tosara]buñ 一皿分: a plate of vegetables (*yasai hitosara*) 野菜一皿.
3 (sheet of metal) ki[ñzokubañ 金属板; i[tagane 板金: a steel plate (*koobañ*) 鋼板.
4 (license plate) na[ñbaa-pure]eto ナンバープレート.

platform *n.* **1** (of a station) pu[rattoho]omu プラットホーム; ho]omu ホーム: Which platform does the train leave from? (*Sono ressha wa dono hoomu kara demasu ka?*) その列車はどのホームから出ますか.
2 (raised part) da]ñ 壇; e[ñdañ 演壇: stand on a platform (*eñdañ ni tatsu*) 演壇に立つ.

platinum *n.* pu[rachina プラチナ; ha[kkiñ 白金.

platter *n.* o[ozara 大皿.

play *vi.* **1** (have fun) a[sobu 遊ぶ Ⓒ: The children are playing with their toys. (*Kodomo-tachi wa omocha de asoñde imasu.*) 子どもたちはおもちゃで遊んでいます.
2 (take part in a game) kyo]ogi ni sa[ñka suru 競技に参加する Ⓘ; shi[ai o suru 試合をする Ⓘ: We played against their team. (*Watashi-tachi wa kare-ra to shiai o shita.*) 私たちは彼らと試合をした.
3 (perform music) e[ñsoo suru 演奏する Ⓘ: play in an orchestra (*ookesutora de eñsoo suru*) オーケストラで演奏する.
4 (act in a play) shu[tsueñ suru 出演する Ⓘ: She played in the movie. (*Kanojo wa sono eega ni shutsueñ shita.*) 彼女はその映画に出演した.
— *vt.* **1** (take part in) ... o su[ru …をする Ⓘ: play baseball (*yakyuu o suru*) 野球をする / play a game (*shiai o suru*) 試合をする / play chess (*chesu o suru*) チェスをする.
2 (of a musical instrument) ... o hi[ku …を弾く Ⓒ; e[ñsoo suru 演奏する Ⓘ: play the piano (*piano o hiku*) ピアノを弾く.
3 (of a drama) ... o e[ñjiru …を演じる Ⓥ: play the part of Hamlet (*Hamuretto no yaku o eñjiru*) ハムレットの役を演じる.
4 (perform) ... o ha[ta]su …を果たす Ⓒ: play an important role (*juuyoo na yakuwari o hatasu*) 重要な役割を果たす.
— *n.* **1** (recreation) a[sobi 遊び; ki[barashi 気晴らし.
2 (drama) ge]ki 劇; e[ñgeki 演劇; shi[bai 芝居: go to a play (*shibai o mi ni iku*) 芝居を見に行く.
3 (playing of the game) shi[aiburi 試合ぶり; pu[re]e プレー: fair play (*fea-puree*) フェアプレー.

player *n.* **1** (of a game) kyo[ogi]sha 競技者; se]ñshu 選手: a tennis player (*tenisu no señshu*) テニスの選手.
2 (of a musical instrument) e[ñso]osha 演奏者.
3 (of a drama) ya[kusha 役者; ha[iyuu 俳優.
4 (record player) pu[re]eyaa プレーヤー; e[ñsoo so]ochi 演奏装置.

playground *n.* (of a school) u[ñdoojoo 運動場; (of a park) a[sobiba 遊び場.

plea *n.* ta[ñgañ 嘆願: make a plea for help (*eñjo o tañgañ suru*) 援助を嘆願する.

plead *vi.* **1** (ask earnestly) (... ni) ta[ñgañ suru (…に)嘆願する Ⓘ: She pleaded with him not to go. (*Kanojo wa kare ni ikanai yoo ni tañgañ shita.*) 彼女は彼に行かないように嘆願した.
2 (speak in support of) (... o) be]ñgo suru (…を)弁護する Ⓘ: plead for the defendant (*hikoku no beñgo o suru*) 被告の弁護をする.
— *vt.* (give as an excuse) ... o be[ñkai suru …を弁解する Ⓘ; i[iwake o suru 言い訳をする Ⓘ: He pleaded ignorance of the rule. (*Kare wa*

sono kisoku wa shiranakatta to beñkai shita.) 彼はその規則は知らなかったと弁解した.

pleasant *adj.* **1** (enjoyable) ta⌈no-shi⌉i 楽しい; ka⌈iteki na 快適な: We had a pleasant time. (*Watashi-tachi wa tanoshii toki o sugoshita.*) 私たちは楽しい時を過ごした.
2 (nice) i⌉i いい; ki⌈mochi ga yo⌉i 気持ちがよい: It is pleasant this morning. (*Kesa wa kimochi ga yoi.*) けさは気持ちがよい.
3 (agreeable) ka⌈ñji no i⌉i 感じのいい: a pleasant person (*kañji no ii hito*) 感じのいい人.

please[1] *adv.* **1** [asking politely] do⌉ozo どうぞ; <verb>-te[de] ku⌈da-sa⌉i ... て[で]ください; o-⌈negai shima-su お願いします: Please sit down. (*Doozo o-kake kudasai.*) どうぞお掛けください. / Let me off here, please. (*Koko de oroshite kudasai.*) ここで降ろしてください. / Speak slowly, please. (*Yukkuri hanashite kuda-sai.*) ゆっくり話してください. / The check, please. (*O-kañjoo o o-negai shimasu.*) お勘定をお願いします.
2 [calling attention] su⌈mimase⌉ñ ga すみませんが; do⌉oka どうか: Will you pass the salt, please? (*Sumima-señ ga shio o totte itadakemasu ka?*) すみませんが塩を取っていただけますか. / Will you please come with me? (*Dooka watashi to issho ni kite kudasai.*) どうか私といっしょに来てください.

please[2] *vt.* **1** (give pleasure) ... o yo⌈rokobase⌉ru ...を喜ばせる Ⓥ; (satisfy) ma⌉ñzoku saseru 満足させる Ⓥ: You cannot please every-body. (*Subete no hito o mañzoku saseru koto wa dekinai.*) すべての人を満足させることはできない.
2 (like) ... o ko⌈no⌉mu ...を好む Ⓒ: Do what you please. (*Suki na yoo ni shi nasai.*) 好きなようにしなさい.

pleased *adj.* yo⌈roko⌉ñde 喜んで; ma⌉ñzoku shite (iru) 満足して(いる); ki ⌈ni itte (iru) 気に入って(いる): She is pleased with her new dress. (*Kanojo wa atarashii doresu ga ki ni itte imasu.*) 彼女は新しいドレスが気に入っています.
be pleased to do yo⌈roko⌉ñde <verb> 喜んで...: I am pleased to help you. (*Yorokoñde o-tetsudai shimasu.*) 喜んでお手伝いします.

pleasure *n.* **1** (feeling of happi-ness) ta⌈noshi⌉mi 楽しみ; yo⌈rokobi 喜び: I find pleasure in listening to music. (*Watashi wa oñgaku o kiku no ga tanoshimi desu.*) 私は音楽を聴くのが楽しみです.
2 (cause of happiness) ta⌈noshi⌉i ko⌈to⌉ 楽しいこと; (satisfaction) ka⌉i-raku 快楽: It is a pleasure to watch TV. (*Terebi o miru no wa tano-shii koto desu.*) テレビを見るのは楽しいことです.

pledge *n.* chi⌈kai 誓い; se⌈eyaku 誓約: He gave me a ring as a pledge of his love. (*Kare wa ai no chikai to shite yubiwa o watashi ni ku-reta.*) 彼は愛の誓いとして指輪を私にくれた.
— *vt.* ... o chi⌈ka⌉u ...を誓う Ⓒ; ya⌈kusoku suru 約束する Ⓘ: He pledged to do his best. (*Kare wa saizeñ o tsukusu koto o chikatta.*) 彼は最善を尽くすことを誓った.

plentiful *adj.* ta⌈kusañ a⌉ru たくさんある; ju⌈ubu⌉ñ na 十分な; ho⌈ofu na 豊富な: Fish are plentiful in this lake. (*Kono mizuumi ni wa sakana ga takusañ imasu.*) この湖には魚がたくさんいます.

plenty *n.* ta⌈ppu⌉ri たっぷり; ju⌈ubu⌉ñ 十分; ho⌈ofu 豊富: We have plenty of time to go there. (*Soko e iku jikañ wa tappuri arimasu.*) そこへ行く時間はたっぷりあります. / I have plenty of money for my trip. (*Ryo-koo no o-kane wa juubuñ arimasu.*) 旅行のお金は十分あります.

plot *n.* **1** (secret plan) i⌈ñboo 陰謀; ta⌈kurami たくらみ: hatch a plot to overthrow the government (*seefu o taosu iñboo o kuwadateru*) 政府を倒す陰謀を企てる.
2 (of a novel, play) su⌉ji 筋; ko⌈o-

soo 構想: The novel has a complicated plot. (*Sono shoosetsu wa suji ga komiitte iru.*) その小説は筋が込み入っている.
3 (small piece of land) to'chi 土地; ji'sho 地所: a vegetable plot (*saieñ*) 菜園.
— *vt.* **1** (plan) ... o ta'kura'mu ... をたくらむ C; ke'ekaku suru 計画する I: They plotted to kidnap the girl. (*Kare-ra wa sono shoojo o yuukai suru koto o takurañda.*) 彼らはその少女を誘拐することをたくらんだ.
2 (outline) ... o chi'zu ni ki'nyuu suru ...を地図に記入する I: plot a ship's course (*fune no koosu o chizu ni kinyuu suru*) 船のコースを地図に記入する.
— *vi.* i'ñboo o ta'kura'mu 陰謀をたくらむ C.

plow *n.* su'ki すき: turn over the earth with a plow (*suki de tochi o tagayasu*) すきで土地を耕す.
— *vt.* ... o ta'gaya'su ...を耕す C: plow a field (*hatake o tagayasu*) 畑を耕す.

pluck *vt.* **1** (pull) ... o hi'ppa'ru ... を引っ張る C: pluck a person's sleeve (*hito no sode o hipparu*) 人のそでを引っ張る.
2 (pull out feathers) ... o mu'shiru ...をむしる C: pluck feathers from a chicken (*niwatori no hane o mushiru*) 鶏の羽をむしる.
3 (pick) ... o mo'gu ...をもぐ C; to'ru 取る C: pluck an apple from a tree (*riñgo o ki kara mogu*) りんごを木からもぐ.

plug *n.* **1** (object used to block a hole) se'ñ 栓: pull out a plug (*señ o nuku*) 栓を抜く.
2 (of electricity) sa'shikomi 差し込み; pu'ragu プラグ: insert a plug in an outlet (*puragu o koñseñto ni sashikomu*) プラグをコンセントに差し込む.
— *vt.* ... ni se'ñ o tsu'me'ru ...に栓を詰める V: plug up a hole (*ana ni señ o tsumeru*) 穴に栓を詰める.

plum *n.* pu'ramu プラム; su'momo すもも.

plunder *vt.* ... o rya'kudatsu suru ...を略奪する I; go'odatsu suru 強奪する I: plunder a village (*mura o ryakudatsu suru*) 村を略奪する.

plunge *vt.* (thrust) ... o tsu'kko'mu ...を突っ込む C: plunge one's hand into the water (*te o mizu ni tsukkomu*) 手を水に突っ込む.
— *vi.* (throw oneself) (... ni) to'biko'mu (...に)飛び込む C: plunge into the river (*kawa ni tobikomu*) 川に飛び込む.
— *n.* to'biko'mu ko'to' 飛び込むこと: take a plunge into a pool (*puuru ni tobikomu*) プールに飛び込む.

plural *adj.* fu'kusu'u no 複数の; fu'tatsu i'joo no 二つ以上の: a plural noun (*fukusuu-meeshi*) 複数名詞.
— *n.* fu'kusuukee 複数形.

plus *adj.* **1** (above zero) pu'rasu no プラスの; se'e no 正の: a plus quantity (*seesuu*) 正数.
2 (more than) ... i'joo ...以上: It will cost ¥10,000 plus. (*Sore wa ichi-mañ-eñ ijoo kakaru deshoo.*) それは1万円以上かかるでしょう.
— *prep.* ... o ku'waete ...を加えて; ta'shite 足して: Three plus four equals seven. (*Sañ tasu yoñ wa nana desu.*) 3足す4は7です.
— *n.* (sign) pu'rasu-ki'goo プラス記号; se'esu'u 正数.

p.m. *adv., adj.* go'go 午後: 11 p.m. (*gogo juuichi-ji*) 午後11時 / I'd like to make an appointment for 5 p.m. today. (*Kyoo no gogo go-ji ni o-ai shitai no desu ga.*) きょうの午後5時にお会いしたいのですが.

pneumonia *n.* ha'ieñ 肺炎.

pocket *n.* po'ke'tto ポケット: He put the money in his pocket. (*Kare wa sono o-kane o poketto ni ireta.*) 彼はそのお金をポケットに入れた. / a pocket calculator (*deñtaku*) 電卓.

poem *n.* shi 詩: write a poem (*shi o kaku*) 詩を書く. ★ 'Poetry' is also called '*shi*.'

poet *n.* shi'jiñ 詩人.

poetic *adj.* shi no 詩の; shi-'teki

na 詩的な: a poetic drama (*shigeki*) 詩劇.

poetry *n.* shi 詩; shi'ika 詩歌: a collection of poetry (*shishuu*) 詩集. ★ 'Poem' is also called '*shi*.'

point *n.* **1** (sharp tip) sa'ki 先; se'ñtañ 先端: the point of a needle (*hari no saki*) 針の先.
2 (exact spot) te'ñ 点; chi'teñ 地点: a starting point (*shuppatsu-teñ*) 出発点.
3 (dot) te'ñ 点: a decimal point (*shoosuu-teñ*) 小数点.
4 (special quality) to'kuchoo 特徴; to'kushitsu 特質: a strong point (*choosho*) 長所 / a weak point (*tañsho*) 短所.
5 (mark in scoring) te'ñsu'u 点数; to'kuteñ 得点: win by three points (*sañ-teñ-sa de katsu*) 3点差で勝つ.
6 (important part) yo'ote'ñ 要点; po'iñto ポイント: the point of one's speech (*eñzetsu no yooteñ*) 演説の要点.
7 (place on a scale) te'ñ 点; do 度: the boiling point of water (*mizu no futteñ*) 水の沸点.
— *vi.* (hold out a finger) (... o) yu'bisa'su (…を)指さす Ⓒ: He pointed to the picture. (*Kare wa sono e o yubisashita.*) 彼はその絵を指さした.
— *vt.* (direct) ... o mu'keru …を向ける Ⓥ: point a gun toward a bird (*juu o tori ni mukeru*) 銃を鳥に向ける.
point out *vt.* ... o shi'teki suru …を指摘する Ⓘ: Please point out where I am on this map. (*Kono chizu de geñzai iru tokoro o sashite kudasai.*) この地図で現在いる所を指してください.

pointed *adj.* to'ga'tta とがった; to'ga'tte iru とがっている; su'rudo'i 鋭い: a pointed tower (*togatta too*) とがった塔 / a pointed beak (*surudoi kuchibashi*) 鋭いくちばし.

poison *n.* do'ku' 毒; do'kuyaku 毒薬: She tried to kill herself by taking poison. (*Kanojo wa doku o noñde jisatsu shiyoo to shita.*) 彼女は毒を飲んで自殺しようとした.
— *vt.* ... o do'kusatsu suru …を毒殺する Ⓘ; do'ku' de ko'rosu 毒で殺す Ⓒ: poison rats (*nezumi o doku de korosu*) ねずみを毒で殺す.

poisoning *n.* chu'udoku 中毒: food poisoning (*shoku-chuudoku*) 食中毒.

poisonous *adj.* yu'udoku na 有毒な; yu'ugai na 有害な: a poisonous snake (*dokuhebi*) 毒へび.

poke *vt.* **1** (prod) ... o tsu'ku …を突く Ⓒ; tsu'tsu'ku つつく Ⓒ: He poked me in the ribs. (*Kare wa watashi no wakibara o tsuita.*) 彼は私のわき腹を突いた.
2 (protrude) ... o tsu'kida'su …を突き出す Ⓒ: poke one's head out of the window (*mado kara atama o tsukidasu*) 窓から頭を突き出す.
— *vi.* (... o) tsu'tsu'ku (…を)つつく Ⓒ: poke at a frog with a stick (*boo de kaeru o tsutsuku*) 棒でかえるをつつく.

pole[1] *n.* bo'o 棒; sa'o' さお: support with a pole (*boo de sasaeru*) 棒で支える.

pole[2] *n.* kyo'ku 極: the North Pole (*hokkyoku*) 北極 / the South Pole (*nañkyoku*) 南極.

police *n.* **1** (department) ke'esatsu 警察: Get me the police. (*Keesatsu ni tsunaide kudasai.*) 警察につないでください. / a police box (*koobañ*) 交番.
2 (members) ke'esatsu'kañ 警察官; ke'esatsu 警察: The police are looking for the criminal. (*Keesatsu wa sono hañniñ o sagashite iru.*) 警察はその犯人を捜している.

policeman *n.* ke'ekañ 警官; o'ma'wari-sañ お巡りさん: ask a policeman the way to the station (*keekañ ni eki e iku michi o kiku*) 警官に駅へ行く道を聞く / Call a policeman. (*Keekañ o yoñde kudasai.*) 警官を呼んでください.

policewoman *n.* fu'jiñ-ke'ekañ 婦人警官; fu'kee 婦警.

policy *n.* **1** (of a government) se-

p

ˈesaku 政策; (of a company) hoˈoshiñ 方針: a foreign policy (*gaikoo-seesaku*) 外交政策.
2 (method) hoˈosaku 方策; shuˈdañ 手段: A strike is not the best policy. (*Sutoraiki wa saizeñ no shudañ de wa nai.*) ストライキは最善の手段ではない.

polish *vt.* **1** (make shiny) ... o miˈgaku ...を磨く Ⓒ; ... no tsuˈya o daˈsu ...のつやを出す Ⓒ: polish one's shoes (*kutsu o migaku*) 靴を磨く.
2 (improve) ... ni miˈgaki o kakeˈru ...に磨きをかける Ⓥ: polish one's performance (*eñgi ni migaki o kakeru*) 演技に磨きをかける.

polite *adj.* **1** (courteous) reˈegi tadashiˈi 礼儀正しい; teˈenee na 丁寧な: He has a polite way of speaking. (*Kare wa kotobazukai ga teenee da.*) 彼は言葉遣いが丁寧だ.
2 (cultured) seˈñreñ sareta 洗練された; joˈoryuu no 上流の: polite society (*jooryuu shakai*) 上流社会.

politeness *n.* reˈegi tadaˈshisa 礼儀正しさ; teˈenee 丁寧.

political *adj.* seˈeji(joo) no 政治(上)の; seˈeji-teki na 政治的な: a political party (*seetoo*) 政党 / a political problem (*seeji-teki na moñdai*) 政治的な問題.

politician *n.* seˈejika 政治家.

politics *n.* **1** (management of political affairs) seˈeji 政治: I have no interest in politics. (*Watashi wa seeji ni wa kyoomi ga arimaseñ.*) 私は政治には興味がありません.
2 (science) seˈejiˈgaku 政治学: major in politics (*seejigaku o señkoo suru*) 政治学を専攻する.
3 (political principles) seˈesaku 政策; (political opinions) seˈekeñ 政見.

poll *n.* **1** (voting) toˈohyoo 投票: The poll will be held tomorrow. (*Toohyoo wa ashita okonawaremasu.*) 投票はあした行われます.
2 (the number of votes) toˈohyoˈosuu 投票数; toˈohyoo-keˈkka 投票結果: declare the poll (*toohyoo-kekka o happyoo suru*) 投票結果を発表する.
3 (opinion poll) yoˈroñ-choˈosa 世論調査.

pollute *vt.* ... o yoˈgosu ...を汚す Ⓒ; osˈeñ suru 汚染する Ⓘ: Smoke from factories is polluting the air. (*Koojoo kara no kemuri ga taiki o yogoshite iru.*) 工場からの煙が大気を汚している.

pollution *n.* yoˈgosu kotoˈ 汚すこと; osˈeñ 汚染: air pollution (*taiki-oseñ*) 大気汚染.

polo shirt *n.* poˈroshatsu ポロシャツ.

polyester *n.* poˈrieˈsuteru ポリエステル.

pond *n.* iˈkeˈ 池: row a boat on a pond (*ike de booto o kogu*) 池でボートをこぐ.

pool *n.* **1** (swimming pool) puˈuru プール: He went swimming in the pool. (*Kare wa puuru e oyogi ni itta.*) 彼はプールへ泳ぎに行った.
2 (small area of still water) miˈzutamari 水たまり: The rain left pools on the road. (*Ame de dooro ni mizutamari ga dekita.*) 雨で道路に水たまりができた.

poor *adj.* **1** (having little money) maˈzushiˈi 貧しい; biˈñboo na 貧乏な: She was too poor to buy a coat. (*Kanojo wa mazushikute kooto ga kaenakatta.*) 彼女は貧しくてコートが買えなかった.
2 (of bad quality) shiˈtsu no waruˈi 質の悪い; soˈmatsu na 粗末な: goods of poor quality (*shitsu no warui shinamono*) 質の悪い品物.
3 (not good) heˈtaˈ na へたな; oˈtoˈtta 劣った; oˈtoˈtte iru 劣っている: I am poor at Japanese. (*Watashi wa Nihoñgo ga heta desu.*) 私は日本語がへたです.
4 (deserving pity) aˈware na 哀れな; kaˈwaisoˈo na かわいそうな: The poor bird had broken its wing. (*Kawaisoo na tori wa hane o otte ita.*) かわいそうな鳥は羽を折っていた.

pop[1] *adj.* taˈishuu muki no 大衆向きの; poˈpyuraa na ポピュラーな: pop music (*popyuraa oñgaku*) ポピュラー音楽.

pop² *vi.* **1** (make a short sound) po¹ñ to o¹to¹ o ta¹te¹ru ポンと音を立てる Ⓥ: The balloon popped. (*Fuuseñ ga poñ to wareta.*) 風船がポンと割れた.

2 (move in a sudden way) kyu¹u ni ugo¹ku 急に動く Ⓒ: pop out of bed (*beddo kara kyuu ni okidasu*) ベッドから急に起き出す.

— *vt.* ... o po¹ñ to nu¹ku ...をポンと抜く Ⓒ: pop a cork (*koruku no señ o poñ to nuku*) コルクの栓をポンと抜く.

— *n.* po¹ñ to iu o¹to¹ ポンという音.

popular *adj.* **1** (well-liked) ni¹ñki no a¹ru 人気のある; ha¹ya¹tte iru はやっている: The circus is popular with children. (*Saakasu wa kodomotachi ni niñki ga aru.*) サーカスは子どもたちに人気がある. / What is popular now? (*Ima nani ga hayatte imasu ka?*) 今何がはやっていますか.

2 (favored among the public) ta¹ishuumuki no 大衆向きの; po¹pyuraa na ポピュラーな: a popular magazine (*taishuu-zasshi*) 大衆雑誌 / a popular song (*ryuukooka*) 流行歌.

popularity *n.* ni¹ñki 人気; ryu¹ukoo 流行: win popularity (*niñki o hakusu*) 人気を博す.

population *n.* ji¹ñkoo 人口: What is the population of this country? (*Kono kuni no jiñkoo wa dono kurai desu ka?*) この国の人口はどのくらいですか.

porch *n.* **1** (roofed entrance) ge¹ñkañ 玄関; po¹ochi ポーチ.

2 (veranda) be¹rañda ベランダ.

pork *n.* bu¹taniku 豚肉; po¹oku ポーク: roast some pork (*butaniku o yaku*) 豚肉を焼く.

port *n.* (harbor) mi¹nato 港; (city) mi¹nato¹machi 港町: clear port (*shukkoo suru*) 出港する / come into port (*nyuukoo suru*) 入港する.

portable *adj.* mo¹chihakobi deki¹ru 持ち運びできる; ke¹etaiyoo no 携帯用の; po¹otaburu no ポータブルの: a portable radio (*pootaburu rajio*) ポータブルラジオ.

— *n.* ke¹etaiyoo ki¹gu 携帯用器具; po¹otaburu ポータブル.

porter *n.* po¹otaa ポーター; a¹kaboo 赤帽: Please get me a porter. (*Pootaa o yoñde kudasai.*) ポーターを呼んでください.

portion *n.* **1** (part) bu¹buñ 部分; i¹chi¹bu 一部: He sold a portion of his land. (*Kare wa tochi no ichibu o utta.*) 彼は土地の一部を売った.

2 (share) wa¹kema¹e 分け前: He asked for his portion of the money. (*Kare wa o-kane no wakemae o yookyuu shita.*) 彼はお金の分け前を要求した.

3 (one serving of food) i¹chi-niñ mae 一人前: order three portions of steak (*suteeki o sañ-niñ mae chuumoñ suru*) ステーキを3人前注文する.

portrait *n.* sho¹ozooga 肖像画; ji¹ñbutsuga 人物画.

pose *n.* **1** (position) shi¹see 姿勢; po¹ozu ポーズ: assume a relaxed pose (*kutsuroida shisee o toru*) くつろいだ姿勢をとる.

2 (false manner) mi¹sekake 見せかけ; ki¹dori 気取り: What he says is a mere pose. (*Kare ga iu koto wa tañnaru misekake da.*) 彼が言うことは単なる見せかけだ.

— *vi.* **1** (hold a position) po¹ozu o toru ポーズをとる Ⓒ: She posed for her portrait. (*Kanojo wa shoozooga o kaite morau tame ni poozu o totta.*) 彼女は肖像画をかいてもらうためにポーズをとった.

2 (pretend to be) ... no fu¹ri¹ o suru ...のふりをする Ⓘ: He posed as a doctor. (*Kare wa isha no furi o shita.*) 彼は医者のふりをした.

position *n.* **1** (location) i¹chi 位置; ba¹sho 場所: I found the position of the village on the map. (*Watashi wa sono mura no basho o chizu de mitsuketa.*) 私はその村の場所を地図で見つけた.

2 (the way of holding the body) shi¹see 姿勢: sit in a comfortable

p

position (*raku na shisee de suwaru*) 楽な姿勢で座る.
3 (job) tsu⌈tome⌉guchi 勤め口; sho⌈ku 職: He got a position as a lecturer. (*Kare wa kooshi no tsutomeguchi o mitsuketa.*) 彼は講師の勤め口を見つけた.
4 (stand) ta⌈chiba⌉ 立場; kyo⌈oguu 境遇: Put yourself in my position. (*Watashi no tachiba ni mo natte mite kudasai.*) 私の立場にもなってみてください.
5 (rank) chi⌉i 地位; mi⌉buñ 身分: a high position in society (*takai shakai-teki chii*) 高い社会的地位.

positive *adj.* **1** (not negative) se⌈kkyoku-teki na 積極的な: take a positive attitude (*sekkyoku-teki na taido o toru*) 積極的な態度をとる.
2 (certain) ka⌈kushiñ shita [shite iru] 確信した[している]: I am positive of his innocence. (*Watashi wa kare no muzai o kakushiñ shite imasu.*) 私は彼の無罪を確信しています.
3 (of a disease) yo⌈osee no 陽性の: The results of the test were positive. (*Keñsa no kekka wa yoosee datta.*) 検査の結果は陽性だった.
4 (affirmative) ko⌈otee-teki na 肯定的な: a positive answer (*kooteeteki na heñji*) 肯定的な返事.
— *n.* (photography) po⌉ji ポジ; yo⌈oga 陽画; (math) se⌈esu⌉u 正数.

possess *vt.* **1** (own) ... o sho⌈yuu suru …を所有する [I]; mo⌉tte iru 持っている [V]: He possesses a villa in the country. (*Kare wa inaka ni bessoo o motte iru.*) 彼は田舎に別荘を持っている.
2 (have) ... ga a⌈ru …がある [C]: He possesses the ability to do it. (*Kare ni wa sore o suru nooryoku ga aru.*) 彼にはそれをする能力がある.

possession *n.* **1** (ownership) sho⌈yuu 所有; mo⌉tte iru ko⌈to⌉ 持っていること: the possession of land (*tochi no shoyuu*) 土地の所有.
2 (thing possessed) sho⌈yu⌉ubutsu 所有物; za⌉isañ 財産: He lost all his possessions in the fire. (*Kare wa kaji de zeñ zaisañ o ushinatta.*) 彼は火事で全財産を失った.

possibility *n.* **1** (state of being possible) ka⌈noosee 可能性: There is no possibility of war. (*Señsoo no kanoosee wa nai.*) 戦争の可能性はない.
2 (likelihood) o⌈koriu⌉ru ko⌈to⌉ 起こりうること; a⌈riu⌉ru ko⌈to⌉ ありうること: Failure is a possibility. (*Shippai wa ariuru koto da.*) 失敗はありうることだ.

possible *adj.* **1** (able to be done) ka⌈noo na 可能な; ⟨verb⟩ ko⌈to⌉ ga de⌈ki⌉ru …ことができる: It is possible to prevent disease. (*Byooki no yoboo wa kanoo desu.*) 病気の予防は可能です. / Is it possible to look around your factory? (*Anata no koojoo o keñgaku suru koto wa dekimasu ka?*) あなたの工場を見学することはできますか.
2 (likely to happen) o⌈koriu⌉ru 起こりうる; ⟨verb⟩-soo na …そうな: Rain is possible tomorrow. (*Ashita wa ame ga furi-soo da.*) あしたは雨が降りそうだ.
if possible *adv.* de⌈ki⌉reba できれば: If possible, I'll come tomorrow. (*Dekireba ashita ikimasu.*) できればあした行きます.

possibly *adv.* **1** (perhaps) ko⌈to ni yoru to ことによると; mo⌉shi ka suru to もしかすると: Possibly it will be true. (*Moshi ka suru to sore wa hoñtoo ka mo shirenai.*) もしかするとそれは本当かもしれない.
2 (in any possible way) na⌉ñ to ka shite 何とかして; de⌈kiru ka⌉giri できる限り: I will do everything I possibly can. (*Dekiru kagiri no koto wa yarimasu.*) できる限りのことはやります.

post[1] *n.* **1** (mail) yu⌈ubiñ 郵便: send a book by post (*hoñ o yuubiñ de okuru*) 本を郵便で送る.
2 (letters, parcels, etc.) yu⌈ubi⌉ñbutsu 郵便物.
— *vt.* ... o yu⌈ubiñ de da⌉su …を郵便で出す [C]; yu⌈usoo suru 郵送する [I]: I posted the letter yesterday.

(*Sono tegami wa kinoo dashimashita.*) その手紙はきのう出しました.

post[2] *n.* (upright pole) ha⌈shira 柱; ku⌉i くい: set fence posts (*saku no hashira o tateru*) 柵の柱を立てる.
— *vt.* ... o ha⌈ru ... をはる [C]; ke⌈eji suru 掲示する [I]: post a notice on a door (*doa no ue ni keeji o haru*) ドアの上に掲示をはる.

post[3] *n.* **1** (position) chi⌉i 地位; sho⌈ku 職: get a post as professor (*kyooju no chii ni tsuku*) 教授の地位に就く.
2 (place of duty) mo⌈chiba 持ち場; bu⌉sho 部署: leave one's post (*mochiba o hanareru*) 持ち場を離れる.

postage *n.* yu⌈ubiñ-ryo⌉okiñ 郵便料金: How much did the postage cost? (*Yuubiñ-ryookiñ wa ikura kakarimashita ka?*) 郵便料金はいくらかかりましたか.

postage stamp *n.* yu⌈ubiñ-ki⌉tte 郵便切手; ki⌈tte 切手.

postcard *n.* yu⌈ubiñ-ha⌉gaki 郵便はがき; ha⌈gaki はがき: I'd like to send this postcard by air mail. (*Kono hagaki o kookuubiñ de onegai shimasu.*) このはがきを航空便でお願いします. / a picture postcard (*e-hagaki*) 絵はがき.

poster *n.* po⌉sutaa ポスター: put up a poster (*posutaa o haru*) ポスターをはる.

postman *n.* yu⌈ubiñ shuuhainiñ 郵便集配人.

post office *n.* yu⌈ubi⌉ñkyoku 郵便局: Where is the post office? (*Yuubiñkyoku wa doko desu ka?*) 郵便局はどこですか.

postpone *vt.* ... o e⌈ñki suru ...を延期する [I]; o⌈kuraseru 遅らせる [V]: I postponed my trip because of illness. (*Watashi wa byooki no tame ni ryokoo o eñki shita.*) 私は病気のために旅行を延期した.

postponement *n.* e⌈ñki 延期; a⌈toma⌉washi 後回し.

postposition *n.* ko⌈ochi⌉shi 後置詞.

pot *n.* **1** (used for cooking) na⌉be なべ; fu⌈kanabe 深なべ: I cooked the soup in a pot. (*Watashi wa nabe de suupu o tsukutta.*) 私はなべでスープを作った.
2 (round container) tsu⌈bo つぼ; ha⌈chi⌉ 鉢; bi⌉ñ びん; po⌉tto ポット.
— *vt.* ... o ha⌈chi⌉ ni u⌈eru ...を鉢に植える: pot a plant (*kusabana o hachi ni ueru*) 草花を鉢に植える.

potage *n.* po⌈ta⌉aju ポタージュ.

potato *n.* ja⌈gaimo じゃがいも: boil [bake] potatoes (*jagaimo o yuderu [yaku]*) じゃがいもをゆでる[焼く].

potential *adj.* ka⌈noosee no a⌉ru 可能性のある; se⌈ñzai suru 潜在する: potential ability (*señzai nooryoku*) 潜在能力.
— *n.* ka⌈noosee 可能性; se⌈ñza⌉iryoku 潜在力.

pound[1] *n.* **1** (unit of weight) po⌉ñdo ポンド. ★ In Japan the metric system is used.
2 (unit of money) po⌉ñdo ポンド.

pound[2] *vt.* **1** (hit) ... o do⌉ñdoñ ta⌈ta⌉ku ...をどんどんたたく [C]; re⌉ñda suru 連打する [I]: pound a door (*doa o doñdoñ tataku*) ドアをどんどんたたく.
2 (crush) ... o u⌈chikuda⌉ku ...を打ち砕く [C]; tsu⌉ite ko⌈na⌉ ni suru ついて粉にする [I]: pound corn into meal (*toomorokoshi o tsuite kona ni suru*) とうもろこしをついて粉にする.
— *vi.* do⌉ñdoñ ta⌈ta⌉ku どんどんたたく [C]; tsu⌉yoku utsu 強く打つ [C]: I feel my heart pound. (*Shiñzoo ga dokidoki suru no ga wakaru.*) 心臓がどきどきするのがわかる.

pour *vt.* ... o so⌈sogu ...を注ぐ [C]; tsu⌈gu つぐ [C]: She poured wine into my glass. (*Kanojo wa waiñ o watashi no gurasu ni sosoida.*) 彼女はワインを私のグラスに注いだ.
— *vi.* **1** (flow) na⌈garede⌉ru 流れ出る [V]: Water is pouring from the pipe. (*Mizu ga paipu kara nagaredete iru.*) 水がパイプから流れ出ている.
2 (of people) do⌉tto de⌉ru どっと出る [V]: The crowd poured out of the stadium. (*Guñshuu ga kyoogijoo

kara dotto dete kita.) 群衆が競技場からどっと出てきた.

3 (of rain) ha⌈ge⌉shiku fu⌈ru 激しく降る Ⓒ: The rain poured down last night. (*Yuube wa ame ga hageshiku futta.*) ゆうべは雨が激しく降った.

poverty *n.* bi⌉ñboo 貧乏; hi⌈ñkoñ 貧困: live in poverty (*mazushii kurashi o suru*) 貧しい暮らしをする.

powder *n.* ko⌈na⌉ 粉; fu⌈ñmatsu 粉末: grind into powder (*hiite kona ni suru*) ひいて粉にする.

— *vt.* (apply powder) ... ni o⌈shiroi o tsu⌈ke⌉ru …におしろいをつける Ⓥ: She powdered her face. (*Kanojo wa kao ni oshiroi o tsuketa.*) 彼女は顔におしろいをつけた.

power *n.* **1** (ability) no⌉oryoku 能力; chi⌈kara 力: He has the power to tell the future. (*Kare ni wa mirai o yogeñ suru nooryoku ga aru.*) 彼には未来を予言する能力がある. / I will do all in my power. (*Dekiru kagiri no koto wa yarimasu.*) できる限りのことはやります.

2 (force) chi⌈kara 力; do⌉oryoku 動力; (electric power) de⌈ñryoku 電力: atomic power (*geñshi-ryoku*) 原子力 / The power went out in the hotel. (*Hoteru ga teedeñ ni natta.*) ホテルが停電になった.

3 (authority) ke⌉ñryoku 権力; chi⌈kara 力: the power of the law (*hooritsu no chikara*) 法律の力.

4 (right) ke⌈ñge⌉ñ 権限: The police have the power of arrest. (*Keesatsu wa taiho no keñgeñ o motte iru.*) 警察は逮捕の権限を持っている.

5 (strong country) kyo⌈okoku 強国; ta⌈ikoku 大国: an economic power (*keezai taikoku*) 経済大国.

powerful *adj.* **1** (strong) kyo⌈oryoku na 強力な; tsu⌈yo⌉i 強い: a powerful engine (*kyooryoku na eñjiñ*) 強力なエンジン.

2 (influential) se⌉eryoku no aru 勢力のある; yu⌈uryoku na 有力な: a powerful politician (*yuuryoku na seejika*) 有力な政治家.

practical *adj.* **1** (learned through practice) ji⌈ssai no 実際の; ji⌈tchi no 実地の: practical experience (*jissai no keekeñ*) 実際の経験.

2 (useful) ji⌈tsuyoo-teki na 実用的な; ya⌈ku⌉ ni tatsu 役に立つ: Your invention is practical. (*Kimi no hatsumee wa jitsuyoo-teki da.*) 君の発明は実用的だ.

3 (concerned with actual conditions) ge⌈ñjitsu-teki na 現実的な; ji⌈ssai-teki na 実際的な: His ideas are hardly practical. (*Kare no kañgae wa jissai-teki to wa ienai.*) 彼の考えは実際的とは言えない.

practically *adv.* **1** (almost) ho⌈to⌉ñdo ... mo do⌈ozeñ de ほとんど…も同然で: The work is practically finished. (*Shigoto wa hotoñdo owatta mo doozeñ da.*) 仕事はほとんど終わったも同然だ.

2 (in a practical way) ji⌈ssai-joo wa 実際上は; ji⌈sshitsu-teki ni⌉ wa 実質的には: Practically, the plan didn't work well. (*Jissai ni wa sono keekaku wa umaku ikanakatta.*) 実際にはその計画はうまくいかなかった.

practice *n.* **1** (repeated exercise) re⌈ñshuu 練習; ke⌉eko けいこ: You need more practice to play the piano. (*Kimi wa piano o hiku no ni motto reñshuu ga hitsuyoo da.*) 君はピアノを弾くのにもっと練習が必要だ.

2 (habit) shu⌈ukañ 習慣; ka⌈ñree 慣例: It is my practice to get up early. (*Hayaoki ga watashi no shuukañ desu.*) 早起きが私の習慣です.

3 (actual doing) ji⌈kkoo 実行; ji⌈sshi 実施: He put his plan into practice. (*Kare wa jibuñ no keekaku o jikkoo ni utsushita.*) 彼は自分の計画を実行に移した.

4 (work) gyo⌉omu 業務: He has a practice in Tokyo. (*Kare wa Tookyoo de kaigyoo shite iru.*) 彼は東京で開業している.

— *vt.* **1** (do exercises) ... o re⌈ñshuu [ke⌉eko] suru …を練習[けいこ]する Ⓘ: practice speaking Japanese (*Nihoñgo o hanasu reñshuu o*

suru) 日本語を話す練習をする.
2 (follow) ... o kaᶠigyoo suru …を開業する Ⓘ: Ten years have passed since he started practicing medicine. (*Kare wa isha o kaigyoo shite kara juu-neñ ni naru.*) 彼は医者を開業してから 10 年になる.
3 (carry out) ... o reᶠekoo suru …を励行する Ⓘ: practice economy (*keñyaku o reekoo suru*) 倹約を励行する.
— *vi.* **1** (do exercises) (... o) reᶠñshuu suru (…を)練習する Ⓘ: practice on the violin (*baioriñ o reñshuu suru*) バイオリンを練習する.
2 (follow) (... o) kaᶠigyoo suru (…を)開業する Ⓘ: practice as a lawyer (*beñgoshi o kaigyoo suru*) 弁護士を開業する.

praise *vt.* ... o hoᶠme˥ru …をほめる Ⓥ; shoᶠosañ suru 賞賛する Ⓘ: Everybody praised his courage. (*Dare mo ga kare no yuuki o hometa.*) だれもが彼の勇気をほめた.
— *n.* hoᶠme˥ru koᶠto˥ ほめること; shoᶠosañ 賞賛: His deeds are worthy of praise. (*Kare no kooi wa shoosañ ni atai suru.*) 彼の行為は賞賛に値する.

prawn *n.* kuᶠruma˥ebi 車海老. ★ In Japanese, 'lobster,' 'prawn,' and 'shrimp' are all called '*ebi*.'

pray *vi.* iᶠno˥ru 祈る Ⓒ; ki˥gañ suru 祈願する Ⓘ: She knelt down and prayed. (*Kanojo wa hizamazuite inotta.*) 彼女はひざまづいて祈った.
— *vt.* ... ni iᶠno˥ru …に祈る Ⓒ: pray God (*kami ni inoru*) 神に祈る.

prayer *n.* **1** (act of praying) iᶠnori˥ 祈り; ki˥gañ 祈願: a prayer for peace (*heewa no inori*) 平和の祈り.
2 (words) iᶠnori no kotoba˥ 祈りの言葉: say one's prayers (*o-inori o iu*) お祈りを言う.

preach *vt.* (give a sermon) ... o seᶠkkyo˥o suru …を説教する Ⓘ; to˥ku 説く Ⓒ: preach the Gospel (*fukuiñ o toku*) 福音を説く.
— *vi.* (advise) (... ni) seᶠkkyo˥o suru (…に)説教する Ⓘ: He preached to his son. (*Kare wa musuko ni sekkyoo shita.*) 彼は息子に説教した.

precaution *n.* yo˥ojiñ 用心; keᶠekai 警戒: take an umbrella as a precaution (*yoojiñ no tame ni kasa o motte iku*) 用心のために傘を持って行く.

precede *vt.* (come before) ... yo˥ri mo saᶠki ni ku˥ru …よりも先に来る Ⓘ; (go before) ... yo˥ri mo saᶠki ni iku …よりも先に行く Ⓒ: She preceded me into the room. (*Kanojo wa watashi yori mo saki ni heya ni haitta.*) 彼女は私よりも先に部屋に入った.

preceding *adj.* ma˥e no 前の; saᶠki no 先の: the preceding page (*mae no peeji*) 前のページ.

precious *adj.* kiᶠchoo na 貴重な; ko˥oka na 高価な; taᶠisetsu na 大切な: waste one's precious time (*kichoo na jikañ o muda ni suru*) 貴重な時間を無駄にする / precious metals (*kikiñzoku*) 貴金属.

precise *adj.* (exact) seᶠekaku na 正確な; teᶠkikaku na 的確な: a precise translation (*seekaku na hoñyaku*) 正確な翻訳 / a precise explanation (*tekikaku na setsumee*) 的確な説明.

precisely *adv.* seᶠekaku ni 正確に; choᶠodo ちょうど: The plane took off at twelve precisely. (*Hikooki wa juuni-ji choodo ni ririku shita.*) 飛行機は 12 時ちょうどに離陸した.

precision *n.* seᶠekaku 正確; seᶠemitsu 精密: speak with precision (*seekaku ni hanasu*) 正確に話す / precision instruments (*seemitsu kikai*) 精密機械.

predecessor *n.* zeᶠñni˥ñsha 前任者; seᶠñpai 先輩.

predict *vt.* ... to yoᶠgeñ suru …と予言する Ⓘ; yoᶠsoku suru 予測する Ⓘ: Scientists predicted that there would be an earthquake. (*Kagakusha-tachi wa jishiñ ga okoru daroo to yogeñ shita.*) 科学者たちは地震が起こるだろうと予言した.

preface *n.* joᶠbuñ 序文.

prefecture *n.* ke˥ñ 県; fu˥ 府: Chiba Prefecture (*Chiba-keñ*) 千葉

県 / Osaka-fu (*Oosaka-fu*) 大阪府.
★ '*Fu*' is only used with reference to Osaka and Kyoto.

prefer *vt.* ... no ho⌉o ga su⌈ki⌉ da …のほうが好きだ; ... no ho⌉o ga ii …のほうがいい: Which do you prefer, tea or coffee? (*Koocha to koohii to dochira ga o-suki desu ka?*) 紅茶とコーヒーとどちらがお好きですか. / I prefer going by train to flying. (*Watashi wa hikooki yori mo ressha de iku hoo ga ii.*) 私は飛行機よりも列車で行くほうがいい.

preferable *adj.* ko⌈nomashi⌉i 好ましい; no⌈zomashi⌉i 望ましい: It is preferable that you have knowledge of Japanese. (*Nihoñgo no chishiki o motte iru koto ga nozomashii.*) 日本語の知識を持っていることが望ましい.

preference *n.* ko⌈nomi 好み: Her preference in reading is mysteries. (*Kanojo no dokusho no konomi wa misuterii desu.*) 彼女の読書の好みはミステリーです.

pregnant *adj.* ni⌈ñshiñ shite iru 妊娠している: She is six months pregnant. (*Kanojo wa niñshiñ rok-kagetsu desu.*) 彼女は妊娠 6 か月です.

prejudice *n.* he⌈ñkeñ 偏見; se⌈ñnyu⌉ukañ 先入観: He has a prejudice against modern art. (*Kare wa geñdai geejutsu ni heñkeñ o motte iru.*) 彼は現代芸術に偏見を持っている.
— *vt.* ... ni he⌈ñkeñ o mo⌈tase⌉ru …に偏見を持たせる [V]; ha⌈ñkañ o motase⌉ru 反感を持たせる [V]: He is prejudiced against the police. (*Kare wa keesatsu ni taishite hañkañ o motte iru.*) 彼は警察に対して反感を持っている.

preliminary *adj.* yo⌉bi no 予備の; ju⌉ñbi no 準備の: a preliminary examination (*yobi shikeñ*) 予備試験.

preparation *n.* ju⌉ñbi 準備: The meal is in preparation. (*Shokuji wa juñbi-chuu desu.*) 食事は準備中です.

prepare *vt.* **1** (make ready) ... no ju⌉ñbi o suru …の準備をする [I]; yo⌉oi o suru 用意をする [I]: He is preparing his speech for tomorrow. (*Kare wa ashita no kooeñ no juñbi o shite imasu.*) 彼はあしたの講演の準備をしています.
2 (put together) ... no shi⌈taku o suru …のしたくをする [I]: I'll prepare the table. (*Watashi ga shokuji no shitaku o shimasu.*) 私が食事のしたくをします.
— *vi.* ju⌉ñbi suru 準備する [I]; yo⌉oi suru 用意する [I]: prepare for an examination (*shikeñ no juñbi o suru*) 試験の準備をする.

preposition *n.* ze⌈ñchi⌉shi 前置詞.

prescribe *vt.* **1** (of a medicine) ... o sho⌈hoo suru …を処方する [I]: The doctor prescribed a medicine for my stomach pains. (*Isha wa watashi no fukutsuu ni kusuri o shohoo shite kureta.*) 医者は私の腹痛に薬を処方してくれた.
2 (state) ... o ki⌈tee suru …を規定する [I]; shi⌉ji suru 指示する [I]: The rules prescribe what we should do. (*Kisoku wa wareware ga nani o nasu beki ka kitee shite iru.*) 規則はわれわれが何をなすべきか規定している.

prescription *n.* sho⌈hoo 処方; sho⌈hooseñ 処方せん: Please fill this prescription. (*Kono shohooseñ de kusuri o kudasai.*) この処方せんで薬を下さい.

presence *n.* **1** (attendance) shu⌈sseki 出席: Your presence is requested. (*Go-shusseki o o-negai itashimasu.*) ご出席をお願いいたします.
2 (the fact of being present) so⌈ñzai 存在; i⌈ru koto⌉ いること: No one noticed his presence. (*Kare ga iru koto ni dare mo kizukanakatta.*) 彼がいることにだれも気づかなかった.

present[1] *adj.* **1** (being at the place) shu⌈sseki shite iru 出席している: Were you present at the party? (*Anata wa sono kai ni shusseki shimashita ka?*) あなたはその会に出席しましたか.
2 (existing now) ge⌉ñzai no 現在の: the present government (*geñzai no seefu*) 現在の政府.

3 (of grammar) ge^ñzai no 現在の: the present form of a verb (*dooshi no geñzai-kee*) 動詞の現在形.

— *n.* ge^ñzai 現在; i^ma 今: He is not here at present. (*Kare wa ima koko ni imaseñ.*) 彼は今ここにいません.

present[2] *n.* (gift) o^kurimono 贈り物; pu^re^zeñto プレゼント: This is a present for you. (*Kore wa anata e no okurimono desu.*) これはあなたへの贈り物です.

present[3] *vt.* **1** (give) ... o o^kuru …を贈る Ⓒ; zo^otee suru 贈呈する Ⓘ: I presented a book to her. (*Watashi wa hoñ o kanojo ni okutta.*) 私は本を彼女に贈った.

2 (offer) ... o te^eshutsu suru …を提出する Ⓘ: He presented his plan at the meeting. (*Kare wa kaigi ni jibuñ no keekaku o teeshutsu shita.*) 彼は会議に自分の計画を提出した.

3 (introduce) ... o sho^okai suru …を紹介する Ⓘ: May I present Mr. Ogawa to you? (*Ogawa-shi o go-shookai itashimasu.*) 小川氏をご紹介いたします.

4 (of a play) ... o jo^oeñ suru …を上演する Ⓘ: present a drama (*geki o jooeñ suru*) 劇を上演する.

presently *adv.* **1** (soon) ma-^mo^naku まもなく; ya^gate やがて: He will be here presently. (*Kare wa ma-mo-naku koko e yatte kuru deshoo.*) 彼はまもなくここへやって来るでしょう.

2 (now) ge^ñzai wa 現在は; mo^kka 目下: She is presently abroad. (*Kanojo wa geñzai gaikoku ni imasu.*) 彼女は現在外国にいます.

preservation *n.* **1** (keeping) ho^zoñ 保存; cho^zoo 貯蔵: preservation of food (*shokuryoo no hozoñ*) 食糧の保存.

2 (protection) ho^go 保護: preservation of nature (*shizeñ hogo*) 自然保護.

preserve *vt.* **1** (keep) ... o ho^zoñ suru …を保存する Ⓘ; ho^kañ suru 保管する Ⓘ: preserve old documents (*furui shorui o hozoñ suru*) 古い書類を保存する.

2 (protect) ... o ho^go suru …を保護する Ⓘ: preserve the environment (*kañkyoo o hogo suru*) 環境を保護する.

3 (maintain) ... o ta^mo^tsu …を保つ Ⓒ; i^ji suru 維持する Ⓘ: preserve one's health (*keñkoo o tamotsu*) 健康を保つ.

4 (of food) ... o ho^zoñ suru …を保存する Ⓘ; tsu^keru 漬ける Ⓥ: preserve fruit in sugar (*kudamono o satoo-zuke ni suru*) 果物を砂糖漬けにする.

preside *vi.* (act as chairman) gi^choo o suru 議長をする Ⓘ; (of a meeting) shi^kai o suru 司会をする Ⓘ: preside over a meeting (*kaigi no shikai o suru*) 会議の司会をする.

president *n.* (of a republic) da^ito^oryoo 大統領; (of a company) sha^choo 社長; (of a university) ga^kuchoo 学長.

press *vt.* **1** (push) ... o o^su …を押す Ⓒ: press a doorbell (*doa no beru o osu*) ドアのベルを押す.

2 (squeeze out) ... o shi^bo^ru …を搾る Ⓒ: press the juice out of grapes (*budoo kara juusu o shiboru*) ぶどうからジュースを搾る.

3 (iron) a^iroñ o kake^ru アイロンをかける Ⓥ: This is to be pressed. (*Kore wa airoñ o kakeru mono desu.*) これはアイロンをかけるものです.

4 (hold close) ... o ni^girishime^ru …を握り締める Ⓥ; da^kishime^ru 抱き締める Ⓥ: He pressed my hand firmly. (*Kare wa watashi no te o shikkari to nigirishimeta.*) 彼は私の手をしっかりと握り締めた.

5 (urge) ... o se^kitateru …をせきたてる Ⓥ; se^ma^ru 迫る Ⓒ: He pressed me for an answer. (*Kare wa watashi ni kaitoo o sematta.*) 彼は私に回答を迫った.

— *vi.* **1** (weigh down) (... o) o^shitsuke^ru (…を)押しつける Ⓥ; (with a foot) (... o) fu^mitsuke^ru (…を)踏みつける Ⓥ: He pressed down on the brake pedal. (*Kare wa bureeki o

fuñda.) 彼はブレーキを踏んだ.
2 (crowd) (... ni) o⌈shiyose⌉ru (…に)押し寄せる [V]: They pressed around her. (*Kare-ra wa kanojo no mawari ni oshiyoseta.*) 彼らは彼女の周りに押し寄せた.
3 (urge) (... o) se⌈ga⌉mu (…を)せがむ [C]; sa⌉isoku suru 催促する [I]: He pressed for payment. (*Kare wa shiharai o saisoku shita.*) 彼は支払いを催促した.
— *n.* 1 (newspapers) shi⌈ñbuñ 新聞; (magazines) za⌈sshi 雑誌; (publishing) shu⌈ppañ 出版: freedom of the press (*shuppañ no jiyuu*) 出版の自由.
2 (people) ho⌈odo⌉ojiñ 報道陣; ki⌈sha⌉dañ 記者団: The Premier meets the press on Monday. (*Shushoo wa getsuyoo ni kishadañ to au.*) 首相は月曜に記者団と会う.
3 (printing press) i⌈ñsatsu⌉ki 印刷機.

pressing *adj.* kyu⌈u o yoosu⌉ru 急を要する; ki⌈ñkyuu no 緊急の: pressing business (*kyuu o yoosuru shigoto*) 急を要する仕事.

pressure *n.* **1** (force) a⌈tsu⌉ryoku 圧力: the air pressure in a tire (*taiya no kuuki no atsuryoku*) タイヤの空気の圧力 / blood pressure (*ketsuatsu*) 血圧.
2 (strain) a⌈ppaku 圧迫; ju⌈uatsu 重圧: mental pressure (*seeshiñ-teki na juuatsu*) 精神的な重圧.

prestige *n.* me⌈esee 名声; i⌈shiñ 威信: The doctor enjoys great prestige. (*Sono isha wa meesee ga takai.*) その医者は名声が高い.

presume *vt.* (suppose) ... to su⌈itee suru …と推定する [I]; ... da to o⌈mo⌉u …だと思う [C]: I presume him innocence. (*Watashi wa kare wa muzai da to omou.*) 私は彼は無罪だと思う.

pretend *vt.* **1** (give a false appearance) ... no fu⌈ri⌉ o suru …のふりをする [I]: She pretended not to know me. (*Kanojo wa watashi o shiranai furi o shita.*) 彼女は私を知らないふりをした.
2 (imagine) ... go⌉kko o suru …ごっこをする [I]: Let's pretend that we are pirates. (*Kaizoku-gokko o shiyoo.*) 海賊ごっこをしよう.

pretext *n.* ko⌈ojitsu 口実; be⌈ñkai 弁解: He was absent on the pretext of illness. (*Kare wa byooki o koojitsu ni yasuñda.*) 彼は病気を口実に休んだ.

pretty *adv.* ka⌉nari かなり; so⌈otoo 相当: I'm pretty tired. (*Watashi wa kanari tsukaremashita.*) 私はかなり疲れました.
— *adj.* 1 (of a child) ka⌈wairashi⌉i かわいらしい; ki⌉ree na きれいな: a pretty girl (*kawairashii oñna-noko*) かわいらしい女の子.
2 (of a thing) ki⌉ree na きれいな: a pretty garden (*kiree na niwa*) きれいな庭.

prevail *vi.* **1** (be widespread) fu⌈kyuu shite iru 普及している [V]; ryu⌈ukoo suru 流行する [I]: This style will prevail this summer. (*Kono sutairu ga kono natsu ryuukoo suru deshoo.*) このスタイルがこの夏流行するでしょう.
2 (win out) (... ni) u⌈chika⌉tsu (…に)打ち勝つ [C]: prevail over an enemy (*teki ni uchikatsu*) 敵に打ち勝つ.

prevalent *adj.* ryu⌈ukoo shite iru 流行している; ha⌈ya⌉tte iru はやっている: Colds are prevalent now. (*Kaze ga ima hayatte iru.*) かぜが今はやっている.

prevent *vt.* **1** (stop) ... o fu⌈se⌉gu …を防ぐ [C]; bo⌈oshi suru 防止する [I]: prevent accidents (*jiko o fusegu*) 事故を防ぐ.
2 (hinder) ... o sa⌈matage⌉ru …を妨げる [V]; ja⌈ma suru じゃまする [I]: He prevented us from getting married. (*Kare wa watashi-tachi no kekkoñ o jama shita.*) 彼は私たちの結婚をじゃました.

prevention *n.* bo⌈oshi 防止; yo⌈boo 予防: Prevention is better than cure. (*Yoboo wa chiryoo ni masaru.*) 予防は治療に勝る.

preventive *adj.* yo⌈boo no 予防の:

P

preventive measures (*yoboosaku*) 予防策.
— *n.* yo⌈bo⌉oyaku 予防薬.

previous *adj.* sa⌈ki no 先の; ma⌉e no 前の: The figure is on the previous page. (*Zu wa mae no peeji ni arimasu.*) 図は前のページにあります. / I have a previous engagement. (*Watashi wa señyaku ga arimasu.*) 私は先約があります.

previously *adv.* i⌉zeñ ni 以前に; ma⌉e ni 前に: He had arrived three days previously. (*Kare wa mikka mae ni tsuite ita.*) 彼は三日前に着いていた.

prey *n.* e⌉jiki えじき: The lion leaped upon its prey. (*Raioñ wa ejiki ni tobikakatta.*) ライオンはえじきに飛びかかった.
— *vi.* (... o) e⌉jiki ni suru (…を)えじきにする [I]: Large animals prey upon smaller ones. (*Ookii doobutsu wa chiisai doobutsu o ejiki ni suru.*) 大きい動物は小さい動物をえじきにする.

price *n.* **1** (amount of money) ne⌈dañ 値段; ka⌈kaku 価格: What is the price of this bag? (*Kono kabañ no nedañ wa ikura desu ka?*) このかばんの値段はいくらですか. / a fixed price (*teeka*) 定価.
2 (what one must suffer) da⌈ishoo 代償; gi⌈see 犠牲: He succeeded at the price of his health. (*Kare wa keñkoo o gisee ni shite seekoo shita.*) 彼は健康を犠牲にして成功した.
— *vt.* ... ni ne⌈dañ o tsu⌈ke⌉ru …に値段をつける [V]: The watch was priced at 10,000 yen. (*Sono tokee wa ichi-mañ-eñ no nedañ ga tsuite ita.*) その時計は1万円の値段がついていた.

prick *vt.* ... o chi⌈ku⌉ri to sa⌉su …をちくりと刺す [C]: I pricked my finger with a pin. (*Watashi wa piñ de yubi o chikuri to sashita.*) 私はピンで指をちくりと刺した.

pride *n.* **1** (pleasant feeling of satisfaction) ji⌈mañ 自慢; to⌈kui 得意: He takes pride in his son. (*Kare wa jibuñ no musuko o jimañ shite iru.*) 彼は自分の息子を自慢している.
2 (self-respect) ji⌈so⌉ñshiñ 自尊心; ho⌈kori 誇り: His pride was hurt by her words. (*Kanojo no kotoba de kare no jisoñshiñ wa kizutsukerareta.*) 彼女の言葉で彼の自尊心は傷つけられた.
3 (conceit) u⌈nubore うぬぼれ.

priest *n.* shi⌉sai 司祭: a Buddhist priest (*boosañ*) 坊さん.

primarily *adv.* o⌉mo ni 主に; shu⌉ to shite 主として: This idea is primarily his. (*Kono aidea wa omo ni kare no mono desu.*) このアイデアは主に彼のものです.

primary *adj.* **1** (first in order) sho⌈kyuu no 初級の; sho⌈too no 初等の: primary education (*shotoo kyooiku*) 初等教育.
2 (first) da⌉i-ichi no 第一の; (most important) mo⌈tto⌉mo ju⌈uyoo na 最も重要な: The primary cause of the accident is his carelessness. (*Sono jiko no dai-ichi no geñiñ wa kare no fuchuui desu.*) その事故の第一の原因は彼の不注意です.
3 (chief) shu⌈yoo na 主要な; o⌉mona 主な: a primary road (*shuyoo dooro*) 主要道路.

primary school *n.* sho⌈oga⌉kkoo 小学校.

prime *adj.* **1** (most important) mo⌈tto⌉mo ju⌈uyoo na 最も重要な: Safety is a matter of prime importance. (*Añzeñ ga mottomo juuyoo na kotogara desu.*) 安全が最も重要な事柄です.
2 (best) sa⌈iryoo no 最良の; go⌈kujoo no 極上の: prime beef (*gokujoo no gyuuniku*) 極上の牛肉.
— *n.* ze⌈ñsee 全盛; sa⌈kari 盛り: He is already past his prime. (*Kare wa sude ni sakari o sugita.*) 彼はすでに盛りを過ぎた.

prime minister *n.* so⌈ori-da⌉ijiñ 総理大臣; shu⌈shoo 首相.

primitive *adj.* **1** (of the earliest times) ge⌉ñshi no 原始の: primitive man (*geñshijiñ*) 原始人.

p

2 (simple) ge⌈ñshi-teki na 原始的な: primitive weapons (*geñshi-teki na buki*) 原始的な武器.

prince *n.* **1** (son of a king or queen) o⌉oji 王子: a crown prince (*kootaishi*) 皇太子.
2 (ruler) ku⌉ñshu 君主.

princess *n.* **1** (daughter of a king or queen) o⌉ojo 王女.
2 (wife of a prince) hi⌉ 妃: a crown princess (*kootaishi-hi*) 皇太子妃.

principal *adj.* (most important) mo⌈tto⌉mo ju⌈uyoo na 最も重要な; (chief) o⌉mo na 主な: the principal cities of Japan (*Nihoñ no omo na toshi*) 日本の主な都市.
— *n.* **1** (head of a school) ko⌈o-choo 校長.
2 (amount of money) ga⌉ñkiñ 元金.

principally *adv.* shu⌉ to shite 主として; o⌉mo ni 主に: Accidents occur principally on rainy days. (*Jiko wa omo ni ame no hi ni okorimasu.*) 事故は主に雨の日に起こります.

principle *n.* **1** (general truth) ge⌉ñri 原理; (rule) ge⌈ñsoku 原則: the principles of economics (*keezai-gaku no geñri*) 経済学の原理.
2 (guide to behavior) shu⌉gi 主義; shi⌈ñjoo 信条: That is against my principles. (*Sore wa watashi no shiñjoo ni hañsuru.*) それは私の信条に反する.
3 (scientific law) ge⌉ñri 原理: the principle of the lever (*teko no geñri*) てこの原理.
in principle *adv.* geñsoku to shite 原則として.
on principle *adv.* shu⌉gi to shite 主義として.

print *vt.* **1** (on paper) ... o i⌈ñsatsu suru ...を印刷する Ⓘ; su⌈ru 刷る Ⓒ: The publisher printed 7,000 copies of his book. (*Shuppañsha wa kare no hoñ o nana-señ-bu iñsatsu shita.*) 出版社は彼の本を7千部印刷した.
2 (write) ... o ka⌈tsujitai de ka⌉ku ...を活字体で書く Ⓒ: Please print your name. (*Namae o katsujitai de kaite kudasai.*) 名前を活字体で書いてください.
3 (of a photograph) ... o ya⌈kitsu-ke⌉ru ...を焼き付ける Ⓥ: print out a negative (*nega o yakitsukeru*) ネガを焼き付ける.
— *n.* **1** (act of printing) i⌈ñsatsu 印刷.
2 (printed lettering) i⌈ñsatsu shita mo⌉ji 印刷した文字; ka⌈tsuji 活字: a book in large print (*ooki-na katsuji no hoñ*) 大きな活字の本.
3 (printed reproduction) ha⌈ñga 版画: a woodblock print (*mokuhañ-ga*) 木版画.
4 (photography) i⌈ñga 印画; pu⌈riñ-to プリント: a film for color prints (*karaa puriñto-yoo firumu*) カラープリント用フィルム.
5 (mark) a⌉to 跡: the print of a foot (*ashiato*) 足跡.

printed matter *n.* i⌈ñsatsu⌉butsu 印刷物.

printer *n.* **1** (people) i⌈ñsatsu⌉koo 印刷工; i⌈ñsatsu gyo⌉osha 印刷業者.
2 (machine) i⌈ñsatsu⌉ki 印刷機; pu⌈riñtaa プリンター.

printing *n.* **1** (work of printer) i⌈ñsatsu 印刷; i⌈ñsatsu⌉gyoo 印刷業.
2 (printed copies) i⌈ñsatsu busu⌉u 印刷部数; ha⌉ñ 版; su⌈ri⌉ 刷り: a first printing of 5,000 copies (*shohañ go-señ-bu*) 初版5千部.

prior *adj.* ma⌉e no 前の; sa⌈ki no 先の: I have a prior engagement. (*Watashi wa señyaku ga arimasu.*) 私は先約があります.

priority *n.* yu⌈useñ 優先; (right) yu⌈use⌉ñkeñ 優先権: This plan has priority over others. (*Kono keekaku wa ta ni yuuseñ shimasu.*) この計画は他に優先します. / give priority to elderly people (*o-toshiyori o yuuseñ suru*) お年寄りを優先する.

prison *n.* ke⌈emu⌉sho 刑務所; ko⌈o-chisho 拘置所: He is in prison. (*Kare wa keemusho ni haitte iru.*) 彼は刑務所に入っている.

prisoner *n.* shu⌈ujiñ 囚人: release a prisoner (*shuujiñ o shakuhoo suru*) 囚人を釈放する / a prisoner of war (*horyo*) 捕虜.

privacy *n.* pu⌈ra⌉ibashii プライバシー; shi⌉ji 私事: an invasion of privacy (*puraibashii no shiñgai*) プライバシーの侵害.

private *adj.* **1** (personal) ko⌉jiñ no 個人の; ko⌈jiñ-teki na 個人的な: These are my private affairs. (*Kore wa watashi no kojiñ-teki na moñdai desu.*) これは私の個人的な問題です. **2** (secret) na⌈imitsu no 内密の; hi⌈mitsu no 秘密の: Please keep this private. (*Kore wa naimitsu ni shite oite kudasai.*) これは内密にしておいてください. **3** (not public) shi⌉ritsu no 私立の: a private university (*shiritsu-daigaku*) 私立大学.

privately *adv.* na⌈isho⌉ de ないしょで; ko⌉jiñ-teki ni 個人的に: I'd like to speak to you privately. (*Naisho de o-hanashi o shitai no desu ga.*) ないしょでお話をしたいのですが.

privilege *n.* (special advantage) to⌈kuteñ 特典; (right) to⌈kkeñ 特権: They were given the privilege of using the room. (*Kare-ra wa sono heya o tsukau tokkeñ o ataerareta.*) 彼らはその部屋を使う特権を与えられた.

prize *n.* sho⌉o 賞; sho⌈ohiñ 賞品: She received a prize for her painting. (*Kanojo wa e de shoo o totta.*) 彼女は絵で賞を取った. / win first prize (*it-too-shoo o toru*) 1 等賞を取る.

probability *n.* **1** (likelihood) mi⌈komi 見込み; ko⌈osañ 公算: Is there any probability that he will win? (*Kare wa katsu mikomi wa arimasu ka?*) 彼は勝つ見込みはありますか. **2** (something that is probable) o⌈kori-so⌉o na ko⌈to⌉ 起こりそうなこと: It is a probability. (*Sore wa okori-soo na koto da.*) それは起こりそうなことだ.

probable *adj.* a⌈ri-so⌉o na ありそうな; ta⌉buñ ... daroo たぶん…だろう: It is probable that he will succeed. (*Kare wa tabuñ seekoo suru daroo.*) 彼はたぶん成功するだろう.

probably *adv.* ta⌉buñ たぶん; o⌈so⌉raku 恐らく: I'll probably be a little late. (*Tabuñ sukoshi okureru deshoo.*) たぶん少し遅れるでしょう.

problem *n.* **1** (question) mo⌈ñdai 問題: the problem of housing (*juutaku-moñdai*) 住宅問題 / solve a problem in mathematics (*suugaku no moñdai o toku*) 数学の問題を解く. **2** (difficulty) ya⌉kkai na ko⌈to⌉ やっかいなこと; mo⌈ñdai 問題: There is little problem about it. (*Sore wa taishita moñdai de wa nai.*) それはたいした問題ではない. / a problem child (*moñdaiji*) 問題児.

No problem. (*Ii desu tomo.*) いいですとも; (*Doo itashimashite.*) どういたしまして.

procedure *n.* te⌈tsu⌉zuki 手続き; te⌉juñ 手順: an embarkation procedure (*shukkoku tetsuzuki*) 出国手続き / a landing procedure (*jooriku tetsuzuki*) 上陸手続き.

proceed *vi.* **1** (go on) (... ni) su⌈sumu (…に)進む Ⓒ: After lunch we proceeded to the next destination. (*Chuushoku-go watashi-tachi wa tsugi no mokutekichi ni susuñda.*) 昼食後私たちは次の目的地に進んだ. **2** (continue) (... o) tsu⌈zukeru (…を)続ける Ⓥ: Please proceed with your story. (*Doozo o-hanashi o tsuzukete kudasai.*) どうぞお話を続けてください.

process *n.* **1** (series of changes) ka⌉tee 課程: the process of learning (*gakushuu no katee*) 学習の課程. **2** (method) se⌈ehoo 製法; ko⌈otee 工程: make glass by a new process (*atarashii seehoo de garasu o tsukuru*) 新しい製法でガラスを作る.
— *vt.* (of a material) ... o ka⌈koo suru …を加工する Ⓘ; (of information) ... o sho⌉ri suru …を処理する Ⓘ: process the data by computer (*deeta o koñpyuutaa de shori suru*) データをコンピューターで処理する.

procession *n.* gyo⌈oretsu 行列: a funeral procession (*soogi no* *gyooretsu*) 葬儀の行列.

proclaim *vt*. ... o se[ñge]ñ suru ...を宣言する Ⅰ; ko[ohyoo suru 公表する Ⅰ: The colony proclaimed its independence. (*Sono shokumiñchi wa dokuritsu o señgeñ shita.*) その植民地は独立を宣言した.

proclamation *n*. se[ñge]ñ 宣言; fu[koku 布告: a proclamation of war (*señseñ fukoku*) 宣戦布告.

produce *vt*. **1** (manufacture) ... o tsu[ku]ru ...を作る Ⓒ; se[esañ suru 生産する Ⅰ: This factory produces motorcycles. (*Kono koojoo wa ootobai o tsukutte imasu.*) この工場はオートバイを作っています.

2 (bring forth) ... o u[mu ...を産む Ⓒ; sa[ñshutsu suru 産出する Ⅰ: Hens produce an egg a day. (*Meñdori wa ichi-nichi ni ik-ko tamago o umu.*) めんどりは1日に1個卵を産む.

3 (cause) ... o hi[kioko]su ...を引き起こす Ⓒ; mo[tara]su もたらす Ⓒ: Hard work produces good results. (*Isshookeñmee yareba yoi kekka o motarashimasu.*) 一生懸命やればよい結果をもたらします.

4 (show) ... o da]shite mi[se]ru ...を出して見せる Ⓥ: He produced his driver's license. (*Kare wa uñteñ meñkyoshoo o dashite miseta.*) 彼は運転免許証を出して見せた.

5 (bring to the public) ... o se[esaku suru ...を製作する Ⅰ; (of a play) jo[oeñ suru 上演する Ⅰ: produce a new play (*shiñsaku no shibai o jooeñ suru*) 新作の芝居を上演する.

producer *n*. **1** (of a play, movie, etc.) pu[rodyu]usaa プロデューサー; se[esa]kusha 制作者.

2 (of goods) se[esa]ñsha 生産者.

product *n*. **1** (something produced) sa[ñbutsu 産物; se]ehiñ 製品: a new product (*shiñ-seehiñ*) 新製品.

2 (result) ke[kka 結果; se]eka 成果: products of endeavor (*doryoku no kekka*) 努力の結果.

production *n*. **1** (act of making) se[esañ 生産; se[ezoo 製造: mass production (*tairyoo-seesañ*) 大量生産 / the production of arms (*buki no seezoo*) 武器の製造.

2 (the amount produced) se[esa]ñdaka 生産高: the production of automobiles (*jidoosha no seesañdaka*) 自動車の生産高.

3 (of a play, movie, etc.) se[esaku 制作; e[ñshutsu 演出.

productive *adj*. (producing much) se[esa]ñryoku no aru 生産力のある; (fertile) hi[yoku na 肥沃な; (fruitful) mi[nori no o]oi 実りの多い: The discussion was productive. (*Sono tooroñ wa minori ga ookatta.*) その討論は実りが多かった.

productivity *n*. se[esa]ñryoku 生産力; se[esañsee 生産性: low costs and high productivity (*hikui kosuto to takai seesañsee*) 低いコストと高い生産性.

profess *vt*. (state) ... to ko[ogeñ suru ...と公言する Ⅰ; ha[kki]ri i[u はっきり言う Ⓒ: He professed to know nothing about the matter. (*Kare wa sono koto ni tsuite nani mo shiranai to hakkiri itta.*) 彼はそのことについて何も知らないとはっきり言った.

profession *n*. **1** (occupation) sho[ku]gyoo 職業; se[ñmo]ñshoku 専門職: He is a lawyer by profession. (*Kare no shokugyoo wa beñgoshi desu.*) 彼の職業は弁護士です.

2 (open declaration) ko[ogeñ 公言; ko[kuhaku 告白: professions of faith (*shiñkoo no kokuhaku*) 信仰の告白.

professional *adj*. **1** (of a profession) sho[ku]gyoo no 職業の; se[ñmoñ-teki na 専門的な: professional skill (*señmoñ-teki na gijutsu*) 専門的な技術.

2 (not amateur) ho[ñshoku no 本職の; pu]ro no プロの: a professional golfer (*puro gorufaa*) プロゴルファー.

— *n*. ho[ñshoku no hito] 本職の人; pu]ro プロ.

professor *n*. kyo[oju 教授: a professor of Japanese literature (*Ko-*

kubuñgaku kyooju) 国文学教授.

profile *n.* yo⌈kogao 横顔; pu⌈rofi⌉iru プロフィール.

profit *n.* **1** (money) ri⌉eki 利益; mo⌈oke⌉ もうけ: make a profit (*rieki o ageru*) 利益をあげる / a net profit (*juñeki*) 純益.
2 (benefit) to⌈ku 得; e⌉ki 益: There is no profit in complaining. (*Fuhee o itte mo nañ no toku ni mo naranai.*) 不平を言っても何の得にもならない.
— *vi.* ri⌉eki o e⌉ru 利益を得る [V]: He profited from the sale of his land. (*Kare wa tochi o utte rieki o eta.*) 彼は土地を売って利益を得た.

profitable *adj.* **1** (producing profit) mo⌈oke⌉ ni naru もうけになる; yu⌉uri na 有利な: a profitable business (*yuuri na jigyoo*) 有利な事業.
2 (benefit) ta⌈me⌉ ni naru ためになる; yu⌈ueki na 有益な: profitable advice (*yuueki na jogeñ*) 有益な助言.

profound *adj.* **1** (deep understanding) shi⌈ñeñ na 深遠な; fu⌈ka⌉i 深い: a man of profound learning (*gakushiki no fukai hito*) 学識の深い人.
2 (very deep) ko⌈ko⌉ro no so⌈ko kara⌉ no 心の底からの; fu⌈ka⌉i 深い: profound sorrow (*fukai kanashimi*) 深い悲しみ.

program *n.* **1** (details of events) pu⌈rogu⌉ramu プログラム; (of a TV and radio) ba⌈ñgumi 番組: the program of a concert (*oñgakukai no puroguramu*) 音楽会のプログラム.
2 (plan) ke⌈ekaku 計画: draw up a business program (*jigyoo-keekaku o tateru*) 事業計画を立てる.
3 (of a computer) pu⌈rogu⌉ramu プログラム.

progress *n.* **1** (development) shi⌉ñpo 進歩; ha⌈ttatsu 発達: the progress of civilization (*buñmee no hattatsu*) 文明の発達.
2 (forward movement) ze⌈ñshiñ 前進; shi⌈ñkoo 進行: We made slow progress through the crowd. (*Watashi-tachi wa guñshuu no aida o yukkuri zeñshiñ shita.*) 私たちは群衆の間をゆっくり前進した.
— *vi.* **1** (advance) ze⌈ñshiñ suru 前進する [I]; shi⌈ñkoo suru 進行する [I]: How is the work progressing? (*Shigoto wa ikaga shiñkoo shite imasu ka?*) 仕事はいかが進行していますか.
2 (develop) shi⌉ñpo suru 進歩する [I]; jo⌈otatsu suru 上達する [I]: He progressed in Japanese little by little. (*Kare no Nihoñgo wa sukoshi zutsu jootatsu shita.*) 彼の日本語は少しずつ上達した.

progressive *adj.* **1** (going ahead) ze⌈ñshiñ suru 前進する; shi⌈ñkoo shite iru 進行している: progressive movement (*zeñshiñ-uñdoo*) 前進運動.
2 (using new ideas) shi⌈ñpo-teki na 進歩的な: a progressive policy (*shiñpo-teki na seesaku*) 進歩的な政策.

prohibit *vt.* **1** (forbit) ... o ki⌈ñshi suru ...を禁止する [I]; ki⌈ñjiru 禁じる [V]: Parking is prohibited in this area. (*Kono chiiki wa chuusha ga kiñshi sarete imasu.*) この地域は駐車が禁止されています. / prohibited articles (*mochikomi kiñshihiñ*) 持込み禁止品.
2 (prevent) ... o sa⌈matage⌉ru ...を妨げる [V]; ha⌈ba⌉mu 阻む [C]: The rain prohibited us from going out. (*Ame ga watashi-tachi no gaishutsu o habañda.*) 雨が私たちの外出を阻んだ.

prohibition *n.* ki⌈ñshi 禁止; (order) ki⌈ñshi-me⌉eree 禁止命令: a prohibition against swimming (*yuuee kiñshi*) 遊泳禁止.

project[1] *n.* ke⌈ekaku 計画; ki⌈kaku 企画: carry out one's project (*keekaku o jikkoo suru*) 計画を実行する.

project[2] *vt.* **1** (throw an image) ... o e⌈esha suru ...を映写する [I]; to⌈oee suru 投影する [I]: project a slide on a screen (*suraido o sukuriiñ ni eesha suru*) スライドをスクリーンに映写する.
2 (plan) ... o ke⌈ekaku suru ...を計画する [I]: A new dam is projected

for this area. (*Atarashii damu ga kono chiiki ni keekaku sarete imasu.*) 新しいダムがこの地域に計画されています.

— *vi.* (stick out) tsu⌈kide⌉ru 突き出る: The rock projected from the sea. (*Sono iwa wa umi kara tsukidete ita.*) その岩は海から突き出ていた.

prolong *vt.* ... o e⌈ñchoo suru ...を延長する [I]; hi⌈kinoba⌉su 引き延ばす [C]: He prolonged his visit. (*Kare wa taizai o eñchoo shita.*) 彼は滞在を延長した.

prominent *adj.* **1** (standing out) tsu⌈kide⌉ta 突き出た; tsu⌈kide⌉te iru 突き出ている: His front teeth are prominent. (*Kare no maeba wa tsukidete iru.*) 彼の前歯は突き出ている.
2 (famous) su⌈gu⌉reta 優れた; su⌈gu⌉rete iru 優れている; cho⌈mee na 著名な: a prominent politician (*chomee na seejika*) 著名な政治家.

promise *vt.* **1** (give one's word) ... ni (... to) ya⌈kusoku suru ...に(...と)約束する [I]: He promised me to come at three. (*Kare wa watashi ni sañ-ji ni kuru to yakusoku shita.*) 彼は私に3時に来ると約束した.
2 (give a reason to expect) ... no mi⌈komi ga a⌉ru ...の見込みがある [C]; ... ni na⌈ri-so⌉o da ...になりそうだ: It promises to be fine tomorrow. (*Ashita wa teñki ni nari-soo da.*) あしたは天気になりそうだ.

— *n.* **1** (agreement) ya⌈kusoku 約束: keep [carry out] one's promise (*yakusoku o mamoru* [*jikkoo suru*]) 約束を守る[実行する].
2 (expectation) mi⌈komi 見込み; yu⌈uboo 有望: a young writer of promise (*zeñto yuuboo na wakai sakka*) 前途有望な若い作家.

promising *adj.* mi⌈komi no a⌉ru 見込みのある; ze⌉ñto yu⌈uboo na 前途有望な: She is a promising pianist. (*Kanojo wa zeñto yuuboo na pianisuto desu.*) 彼女は前途有望なピアニストです.

promote *vt.* **1** (advance in rank) ... o sho⌈oshiñ saseru ...を昇進させる [V]; (of a student) ... o shi⌈ñkyuu saseru ...を進級させる [V]: He was promoted to manager. (*Kare wa kachoo ni shooshiñ shita.*) 彼は課長に昇進した.
2 (encourage) ... o so⌈kushiñ suru ...を促進する [I]; zo⌈oshiñ suru 増進する [I]: promote the sale of new products (*shiñ-seehiñ no hañbai o sokushiñ suru*) 新製品の販売を促進する.

promotion *n.* **1** (raising to a higher rank) sho⌈oshiñ 昇進; sho⌈okaku 昇格: He got a promotion last month. (*Kare wa señgetsu shooshiñ shita.*) 彼は先月昇進した.
2 (encouragement) so⌈kushiñ 促進; zo⌈oshiñ 増進: the promotion of world peace (*sekai-heewa no sokushiñ*) 世界平和の促進.

prompt *adj.* bi⌈ñsoku na 敏速な; ha⌈ya⌉i 速い: prompt action (*biñsoku na koodoo*) 敏速な行動 / He is prompt in his payments. (*Kare wa shiharai ga hayai.*) 彼は支払いが速い.

— *vt.* ... o u⌈naga⌉su ...を促す [C]; shi⌈geki suru 刺激する [I]: What prompted this hasty action? (*Nani ga kono yoo na hayamatta koodoo o unagashita no daroo ka?*) 何がこのような早まった行動を促したのだろうか.

promptly *adv.* bi⌈ñsoku ni 敏速に; so⌉kuza ni 即座に: He promptly answered my letter. (*Kare wa sokuza ni heñji o kureta.*) 彼は即座に返事をくれた.

pronoun *n.* da⌈ime⌉eshi 代名詞.

pronounce *vt.* **1** (speak sounds) ... o ha⌈tsuoñ suru ...を発音する [I]: How do you pronounce this word? (*Kono go wa doo hatsuoñ shimasu ka?*) この語はどう発音しますか.
2 (declare officially) ... o se⌈ñge⌉ñ suru ...を宣言する [I]; se⌈ñkoku suru 宣告する [I]; da⌈ñge⌉ñ suru 断言する [I]: pronounce sentence on a prisoner (*hikoku ni hañketsu o kudasu*) 被告に判決を下す / The doctor pronounced the patient cured. (*Isha wa kañja wa naotta to dañ-*

geñ shita.) 医者は患者は治ったと断言した.

pronunciation *n.* ha⌈tsuoñ 発音: Her pronunciation is clear. (*Kanojo no hatsuoñ wa hakkiri shite iru.*) 彼女の発音ははっきりしている.

proof *n.* **1** (evidence) sho⌈oko 証拠; sho⌈omee 証明: We have no proof that he is guilty. (*Kare ga yuuzai da to iu shooko wa nai.*) 彼が有罪だという証拠はない.
2 (trial print) ko⌈oseezuri 校正刷り: correct the proofs of a textbook (*tekisuto no kooseezuri o naosu*) テキストの校正刷りを直す.

proper *adj.* **1** (suitable) te⌈kisetsu na 適切な; te⌈kitoo na 適当な: I am looking for a proper place for the meeting. (*Kaigi ni tekitoo na basho o sagashite iru tokoro desu.*) 会議に適当な場所を探しているところです.
2 (well-mannered) re⌈egi tadashi⌉i 礼儀正しい; sa⌉hoo ni ka⌈na⌉tta [ka⌈na⌉tte iru] 作法にかなった[かなっている]: His behavior is not proper. (*Kare no taido wa sahoo ni kanatte inai.*) 彼の態度は作法にかなっていない.

properly *adv.* **1** (correctly) ta⌈da⌉shiku 正しく: speak Japanese properly (*Nihoñgo o tadashiku hanasu*) 日本語を正しく話す.
2 (suitably) te⌈kitoo ni 適当に; ki⌈chi⌉ñto きちんと: He did his work properly. (*Kare wa shigoto o kichiñto yatta.*) 彼は仕事をきちんとやった.

property *n.* **1** (something owned) za⌉isañ 財産; shi⌉sañ 資産: real property (*fudoosañ*) 不動産.
2 (land) sho⌈yu⌉uchi 所有地; ji⌉sho 地所: He has a large property in Tokyo. (*Kare wa Tookyoo ni ookina tochi o motte iru.*) 彼は東京に大きな土地を持っている.
3 (characteristic) to⌈kusee 特性: the properties of metal (*kiñzoku no tokusee*) 金属の特性.

proportion *n.* **1** (ratio) wa⌈riai 割合; hi⌈ritsu 比率: The proportion of boys to girls in this class is three to two. (*Kono kurasu no dañshi to joshi no hiritsu wa sañ tai ni desu.*) このクラスの男子と女子の比率は 3 対 2 です.
2 (part) bu⌉buñ 部分: The larger proportion of the earth is covered with water. (*Chikyuu no daibubuñ wa mizu de oowarete iru.*) 地球の大部分は水で覆われている.
3 (balance) tsu⌈riai つり合い; ki⌈ñkoo 均衡: The desk and the chair are not in proportion. (*Tsukue to isu ga tsuriatte inai.*) 机といすがつり合っていない.
4 (of mathematics) hi⌈ree 比例: direct proportion (*seehiree*) 正比例 / inverse proportion (*hañpiree*) 反比例.

proposal *n.* **1** (something proposed) te⌈eañ 提案; mo⌈oshikomi 申し込み: My proposal was not accepted. (*Watashi no teeañ wa uke-irerarenakatta.*) 私の提案は受け入れられなかった.
2 (offer of marriage) ke⌈kkoñ no mooshikomi 結婚の申し込み; pu⌈ropo⌉ozu プロポーズ: make a proposal to a woman (*josee ni puropoozu suru*) 女性にプロポーズする.

propose *vt.* **1** (suggest) ... o te⌈eañ suru ...を提案する Ⓘ; mo⌈oshide⌉ru 申し出る Ⓥ: I proposed another meeting. (*Watashi wa moo ichi-do kaigi o hiraku koto o teeañ shita.*) 私はもう一度会議を開くことを提案した.
2 (plan) ... o ke⌈ekaku suru ...を計画する Ⓘ; (intend) tsu⌈mori da つもりだ: He proposed to buy a car. (*Kare wa kuruma o kau tsumori datta.*) 彼は車を買うつもりだった.
— *vi.* (make an offer of marriage) ke⌈kkoñ o mooshiko⌉mu 結婚を申し込む Ⓒ; pu⌈ropo⌉ozu suru プロポーズする Ⓘ: He proposed to her. (*Kare wa kanojo ni kekkoñ o mooshikoñda.*) 彼は彼女に結婚を申し込んだ.

proposition *n.* **1** (proposal) te⌈eañ 提案; ke⌈ekaku 計画: I accepted his proposition to share expenses. (*Watashi wa hiyoo o wakeau to iu*

kare no teeañ o ukeireta.) 私は費用を分け合うという彼の提案を受け入れた.
2 (statement) shuˈchoo 主張; chiˈñ-jutsu 陳述.

prose *n.* saˈñbuñ 散文: write in prose (*sañbuñ de kaku*) 散文で書く.

prosecute *vt.* **1** (put on trial) ... o kiˈso suru ...を起訴する [I]: The man was prosecuted for theft. (*Sono otoko wa nusumi no kado de kiso sareta.*) その男は盗みのかどで起訴された.
2 (carry on) ... o oˈkonau ...を行う [C]; suˈikoo suru 遂行する [I]: prosecute an inquiry (*choosa o okonau*) 調査を行う.

prospect *n.* **1** (outlook) miˈkomi 見込み; kiˈtai 期待: There is little prospect of his success. (*Kare no seekoo no mikomi wa amari nai.*) 彼の成功の見込みはあまりない.
2 (view) naˈgameˈ 眺め; miˈharashi 見晴らし: The hotel commands a fine prospect. (*Sono hoteru wa nagame ga subarashii.*) そのホテルは眺めがすばらしい.

prospectus *n.* aˈñnaisho 案内書; (of books) shiˈñkañ-aˈñnai 新刊案内.

prosper *vi.* haˈñee suru 繁栄する [I]; haˈñjoo suru 繁盛する [I]: His business is prospering. (*Kare no shoobai wa hañjoo shite iru.*) 彼の商売は繁盛している.

prosperity *n.* haˈñee 繁栄; haˈñ-joo 繁盛; seˈekoo 成功: I wish you happiness and prosperity. (*Go-takoo to go-seekoo o o-inori ita-shimasu.*) ご多幸とご成功をお祈りいたします.

prosperous *adj.* haˈñee shite iru 繁栄している; haˈñjoo shite iru 繁盛している: a prosperous business (*hañ-joo shite iru shoobai*) 繁盛している商売.

protect *vt.* ... o hoˈgo suru ...を保護する [I]; maˈmoˈru 守る [C]: protect wild animals (*yasee no doobutsu o hogo suru*) 野生の動物を保護する / protect children from danger (*ko-domo-tachi o kikeñ kara mamoru*) 子どもたちを危険から守る.

protection *n.* **1** (act of protecting) hoˈgo 保護: I asked for police protection. (*Watashi wa keesatsu no hogo o motometa.*) 私は警察の保護を求めた.
2 (something that protects) hoˈgo suru moˈnoˈ 保護する物: a protection from the sun (*hiyoke*) 日よけ.

protectionism *n.* hoˈgobooeki-shuˈgi 保護貿易主義; hoˈgoseˈe-saku 保護政策.

protective *adj.* hoˈgo suru 保護する: protective trade (*hogo booeki*) 保護貿易.

protest *vi.* (... ni) koˈogi suru (...に) 抗議する [I]; iˈgi o moˈoshitateru 異議を申し立てる [V]: We protested against the new tax. (*Watashi-tachi wa atarashii zee ni koogi shita.*) 私たちは新しい税に抗議した.
— *vt.* **1** (object) ... ni koˈogi suru ...に抗議する [I]: He protested the umpire's decision. (*Kare wa shiñ-pañ no hañtee ni koogi shita.*) 彼は審判の判定に抗議した.
2 (insist) ... o shuˈchoo suru ...を主張する [I]: I protested my innocence. (*Watashi wa keppaku o shuchoo shita.*) 私は潔白を主張した.
— *n.* koˈogi 抗議; iˈgi no moˈoshi-tate 異議の申し立て: a protest march (*koogi-demo*) 抗議デモ.

Protestant *n.* shiˈñkyoˈoto 新教徒; puˈroteˈsutañto プロテスタント.
— *adj.* shiˈñkyoo no 新教の.

proud *adj.* **1** (feeling satisfaction) hoˈkori ni omoˈu 誇りに思う; toˈkuˈi na 得意な: I am proud of my profession. (*Watashi wa jibuñ no shigoto o hokori ni omotte iru.*) 私は自分の仕事を誇りに思っている.
2 (conceited) uˈnuboreta うぬぼれた; uˈnuborete iru うぬぼれている; koˈo-mañ na 高慢な: I don't like his proud manner. (*Kare no koomañ na taido ga ki ni iranai.*) 彼の高慢な態度が気に入らない.
3 (having self-respect) jiˈsoˈñshiñ no aru 自尊心のある; hoˈkori no ta-

P

ˈkaˈi 誇りの高い: He was too proud to accept the money. (*Kare wa jisoñshiñ ga aru kara sono o-kane o uketoranakatta.*) 彼は自尊心があるからそのお金を受け取らなかった.

proudly *adv.* hoˈkorashiˈge ni 誇らしげに; jiˈmañ shite 自慢して: He talked about his experience proudly. (*Kare wa jibuñ no keekeñ o hokorashige ni katatta.*) 彼は自分の経験を誇らしげに語った.

prove *vt.* **1** (show to be true) ... o shoˈomee suru ...を証明する [I]; riˈsshoo suru 立証する [I]: I proved him to be innocent. (*Watashi wa kare ga keppaku de aru koto o shoomee shita.*) 私は彼が潔白であることを証明した.
2 (test) ... o taˈmeˈsu ...を試す [C]: prove a new engine (*atarashii eñjiñ o tamesu*) 新しいエンジンを試す.
— *vi.* (turn out) ... de aˈru koto ga waˈkaˈru ...であることがわかる [C]: The rumor proved to be false. (*Sono uwasa wa uso de aru koto ga wakatta.*) そのうわさはうそであることがわかった.

proverb *n.* koˈtowaza ことわざ; kaˈkugeñ 格言.

provide *vt.* **1** (supply) ... o kyoˈokyuu suru ...を供給する [I]; aˈtaeru 与える [V]; yoˈoi suru 用意する [I]: We provided the victims with food. (*Watashi-tachi wa hisaisha ni tabemono o ataeta.*) 私たちは被災者に食べ物を与えた.
2 (set forth) ... to kiˈtee suru ...と規定する [I]: It is provided that the rent should be paid monthly. (*Yachiñ wa tsuki goto ni shiharau yoo ni kitee sarete iru.*) 家賃は月ごとに支払うように規定されている.
— *vi.* **1** (prepare) (... ni) soˈnaeˈru (...に)備える [V]; juˈñbi suru 準備する [I]: provide against typhoon (*taifuu ni sonaeru*) 台風に備える.
2 (support) (... o) yaˈshinaˈu (...を)養う [C]: provide for one's family (*kazoku o yashinau*) 家族を養う.

provided *conj.* moˈshi <verb>-ba もし...ば: I can buy it provided I have enough money. (*Moshi o-kane ga juubuñ ni areba sore o kau koto ga dekimasu.*) もしお金が十分にあればそれを買うことができます.

province *n.* **1** (region) chiˈhoo 地方; iˈnaka いなか: He is from the provinces. (*Kare wa chihoo shusshiñ desu.*) 彼は地方出身です.
2 (field of knowledge) buˈñya 分野; haˈñi 範囲: It does not come within my province. (*Sore wa watashi no buñya de wa arimaseñ.*) それは私の分野ではありません.
3 (division of a country) shuˈu 州.

provision *n.* **1** (preparation) yoˈoi 用意; juˈñbi 準備: I have to make provision for old age. (*Roogo no juñbi o shinakereba narimaseñ.*) 老後の準備をしなければなりません.
2 (food) shoˈkuˈryoo 食糧: Provisions have run out. (*Shokuryoo ga nakunatta.*) 食糧がなくなった.
3 (rule) kiˈtee 規定; joˈokoo 条項.

provoke *vt.* **1** (make angry) ... o oˈkoraseˈru ...を怒らせる [V]: Don't provoke the animals. (*Doobutsu o okorasete wa ikemaseñ.*) 動物を怒らせてはいけません.
2 (rouse) ... o hiˈkiokoˈsu ...を引き起こす [C]: His words provoked laughter. (*Kare no kotoba wa warai o hikiokoshita.*) 彼の言葉は笑いを引き起こした.

prudent *adj.* shiˈñchoo na 慎重な; fuˈñbetsu no aˈru 分別のある: a prudent attitude (*shiñchoo na taido*) 慎重な態度.

prune[1] *n.* puˈruˈuñ プルーン; hoˈshisuˈmomo 干しすもも.

prune[2] *vt.* ... o kaˈrikoˈmu ...を刈り込む [C]; kiˈritoru 切り取る [C]: prune hedges (*ikegaki o karikomu*) 生け垣を刈り込む / prune off dead branches (*kare-eda o kiritoru*) 枯れ枝を切り取る.

psychological *adj.* shiˈñri-teki na 心理的な: a psychological effect (*shiñri-teki kooka*) 心理的効果.

psychology *n.* shiˈñriˈgaku 心理

p

学: child psychology (*jidoo shiñri-gaku*) 児童心理学.

public *adj.* **1** (of the people as a whole) ko⌈okyoo no 公共の: a public library (*kookyoo toshokañ*) 公共図書館.
2 (for the use of everyone) ko⌈o-shuu no 公衆の: a public telephone (*kooshuu-deñwa*) 公衆電話 / Is there a public restroom near here? (*Kono chikaku ni kooshuu toire wa arimasu ka?*) この近くに公衆トイレはありますか.
3 (acting for the people) ko⌉omu no 公務の: a public official (*koomuiñ*) 公務員.
4 (known by all) shu⌉uchi no 周知の: a matter of public knowledge (*shuuchi no kotogara*) 周知の事柄.
— *n.* (people in general) ji⌈ñmi⌉ñ 人民; ko⌈kumiñ 国民; ko⌈oshuu 公衆: The public has a right to know. (*Kokumiñ wa shiru keñri ga aru.*) 国民は知る権利がある.

publication *n.* **1** (something published) shu⌈ppa⌉ñbutsu 出版物; ka⌈ñ-ko⌉obutsu 刊行物: new publications (*shiñkañsho*) 新刊書.
2 (publishing) shu⌈ppañ 出版; ha⌈k-koo 発行; ka⌈ñkoo 刊行: the date of publication (*hakkoo neñgappi*) 発行年月日.

publicity *n.* **1** (being widely known) yo⌉ku shi⌈rewata⌉ru ko⌈to⌉ よく知れ渡ること; hyo⌈obañ 評判: His novel gained wide publicity. (*Kare no shoosetsu wa hiroku hyoobañ ni natta.*) 彼の小説は広く評判になった.
2 (advertising) ko⌈okoku 広告; se⌈ñdeñ 宣伝: publicity for a movie (*eega no señdeñ*) 映画の宣伝.

publish *vt.* **1** (bring out) ... o shu⌈ppañ suru …を出版する [I]; ha⌈k-koo suru 発行する [I]; ka⌈ñkoo suru 刊行する [I]: His new novel will be published in September. (*Kare no atarashii shoosetsu wa ku-gatsu ni shuppañ saremasu.*) 彼の新しい小説は9月に出版されます.
2 (make known) ... o ha⌈ppyoo suru …を発表する [I]; ko⌈ohyoo suru 公表する [I]: publish a secret (*himitsu o koohyoo suru*) 秘密を公表する.

publisher *n.* shu⌈ppa⌉ñsha 出版社; shu⌈ppañ gyo⌉osha 出版業者.

puff *n.* **1** (small blast) hi⌈to⌉fuki ひと吹き; pu⌉tto fuku ko⌈to⌉ ぷっと吹くこと: blow out a candle in one puff (*roosoku o hito-fuki de kesu*) ろうそくをひと吹きで消す.
2 (soft round object) fu⌈wa⌉tto shita mo⌈no⌉ ふわっとした物: puffs of cloud (*fuwatto shita kumo*) ふわっとした雲 / a cream puff (*shuukuriimu*) シュークリーム.
— *vi.* **1** (blow out) pu⌉tto fu⌈ki-da⌉su ぷっと吹き出す [C]: puff at one's pipe (*paipu o fukasu*) パイプを吹かす.
2 (breathe hard) i⌉ki o ki⌈ra⌉su 息を切らす [C]; a⌈e⌉gu あえぐ [C]: He puffed up the stairs. (*Kare wa aegi-nagara kaidañ o nobotta.*) 彼はあえぎながら階段を上った.
— *vt.* pa⌉ppato haku ぱっぱと吐く [C]: puff cigarette smoke (*tabako no kemuri o haku*) たばこの煙を吐く.

pull *vt.* **1** (draw) ... o hi⌈ppa⌉ru …を引っ張る [C]; hi⌈ku 引く [C]: pull a rope (*tsuna o hipparu*) 綱を引っ張る / He pulled my sleeve. (*Kare wa watashi no sode o hiita.*) 彼は私のそでを引いた.
2 (pluck out) ... o nu⌈ku …を抜く [C]; mu⌈shiru むしる [C]: I need to pull a tooth. (*Ha o ip-poñ nukanakereba naranai.*) 歯を1本抜かなければならない. / pull up weeds in the garden (*niwa no zassoo o mushiru*) 庭の雑草をむしる.
— *vi.* **1** (draw) (... o) hi⌈ppa⌉ru (…を)引っ張る [C]; hi⌈ku 引く [C]: A fish is pulling on the line. (*Sakana ga ito o hiite iru.*) 魚が糸を引いている.
2 (row) ko⌉gu 漕ぐ [C]: He pulled toward the shore. (*Kare wa kishi e mukatte koida.*) 彼は岸へ向かって漕いだ.
3 (steer) (... ni) yo⌈ru (…に)寄る [C]: The car pulled into the side of the road. (*Kuruma wa dooro waki ni*

yotta.) 車は道路わきに寄った.
— *n.* **1** (act of pulling) hi⌈ppa⌉ru ko⌈to⌉ 引っ張ること; hi⌈ku koto⌉ 引くこと: give the handle a pull (*hañdoru o gui to hiku*) ハンドルをぐいと引く.
2 (pulling force) hi⌈ku chikara⌉ 引く力; i⌉ñryoku 引力: the pull of the moon (*tsuki no iñryoku*) 月の引力.

pulse *n.* mya⌈kuhaku 脈拍; mya⌈ku⌉ 脈: feel a person's pulse (*hito no myaku o miru*) 人の脈を診る.

pump *n.* po⌉ñpu ポンプ: a bicycle pump (*kuuki-ire*) 空気入れ.
— *vt.* ... o po⌉ñpu de su⌈ida⌉su ...をポンプで吸い出す Ⓒ; ku⌈mida⌉su くみ出す Ⓒ: pump water from a well (*ido kara mizu o poñpu de kumidasu*) 井戸から水をポンプでくみ出す.

pumpkin *n.* ka⌈bocha かぼちゃ.

punch *vt.* ... o ge⌈ñkotsu de u⌉tsu ...をげんこつで打つ Ⓒ; ... ni pa⌉ñchi o ku⌈rawasu ...にパンチをくらわす Ⓒ: He punched me on the chin. (*Kare wa watashi no ago ni pañchi o kurawaseta.*) 彼は私のあごにパンチをくらわせた.
— *n.* pa⌉ñchi パンチ; ge⌈ñkotsu de u⌉tsu ko⌈to⌉ げんこつで打つこと: give a person a punch in the face (*hito no kao o naguru*) 人の顔を殴る.

punctual *adj.* (on time) ji⌈kañ o mamo⌉ru 時間を守る; (of a date) ki⌉jitsu o ma⌈mo⌉ru 期日を守る: He is always punctual for appointments. (*Kare wa itsu-mo yakusoku no jikañ o mamoru.*) 彼はいつも約束の時間を守る.

punish *vt.* ... o ba⌈ssuru ...を罰する Ⓘ; ko⌈rashime⌉ru 懲らしめる Ⓥ: He was punished for cheating in the exam. (*Kare wa shikeñ de kañniñgu o shite basserareta.*) 彼は試験でカンニングをして罰せられた.

punishment *n.* sho⌉batsu 処罰; ke⌉ebatsu 刑罰: inflict punishment on a person (*hito o shobatsu suru*) 人を処罰する.

pupil[1] *n.* (child) se⌉eto 生徒: This school has 500 pupils. (*Kono gakkoo ni wa seeto ga go-hyaku-niñ iru.*) この学校には生徒が 500 人いる.

pupil[2] *n.* (of the eye) hi⌈tomi ひとみ; do⌈okoo どう孔.

purchase *vt.* ... o k⌈au ...を買う Ⓒ; ko⌈onyuu suru 購入する Ⓘ: He purchased a new car. (*Kare wa shiñsha o katta.*) 彼は新車を買った.
— *n.* **1** (buying) ko⌈onyuu 購入; ka⌈iire 買い入れ: save money for the purchase of a house (*ie o koonyuu suru tame ni o-kane o tameru*) 家を購入するためにお金をためる.
2 (article) ko⌈onyuuhiñ 購入品; ka⌈imono 買い物: make a good purchase (*toku na kaimono o suru*) 得な買い物をする.

pure *adj.* **1** (not mixed) ju⌈ñsui na 純粋な; ma⌈jirike no na⌉i 混じり気のない: pure gold (*juñkiñ*) 純金.
2 (clean) se⌈eketsu na 清潔な; ki⌉ree na きれいな: pure water (*kiree na mizu*) きれいな水.

purity *n.* (being pure) ju⌈ñsui 純粋; (cleanness) se⌈eketsu 清潔.

purple *adj.* mu⌈rasaki iro no 紫色の: a purple flower (*murasaki iro no hana*) 紫色の花.
— *n.* mu⌈rasaki-iro 紫色.

purpose *n.* **1** (aim) mo⌈kuteki 目的; mo⌈kuhyoo 目標: What is the purpose of your trip? (*Anata no ryokoo no mokuteki wa nañ desu ka?*) あなたの旅行の目的は何ですか. / He attained his purpose. (*Kare wa mokuteki o tasshita.*) 彼は目的を達した.
2 (use) yo⌉oto 用途: This tool has various purposes. (*Kono doogu wa iroiro na yooto o motte imasu.*) この道具はいろいろな用途を持っています.

purse *n.* **1** (handbag) ha⌈ñdoba⌉ggu ハンドバッグ.
2 (small bag for carrying money) ko⌈zeni⌉-ire 小銭入れ; ga⌈maguchi がま口.

purser *n.* (of an airplane, ship) pa⌉asaa パーサー.

pursue *vt.* **1** (chase) ... o o⌈ikake⌉ru ...を追いかける Ⓥ; tsu⌈iseki suru 追跡する Ⓘ: He pursued the thief. (*Kare wa doroboo o oikaketa.*) 彼は

どろぼうを追いかけた.

2 (continue) ... o tsuˈzukeru ...を続ける [V]: I want to pursue my research at the university. (*Watashi wa daigaku de keñkyuu o tsuzuketai.*) 私は大学で研究を続けたい.

pursuit *n.* **1** (pursuing) tsuˈiseki 追跡; tsuˈikyuu 追求: the pursuit of happiness (*koofuku no tsuikyuu*) 幸福の追求.

2 (occupation) shiˈgoto 仕事; shoˈkuˈgyoo 職業: daily pursuits (*nichijoo no shigoto*) 日常の仕事.

3 (hobby) shuˈmi 趣味: Fishing is my favorite pursuit. (*Tsuri ga watashi no shumi desu.*) 釣りが私の趣味です.

push *vt.* **1** (press) ... o oˈsu ...を押す [C]: push a button (*botañ o osu*) ボタンを押す / He pushed the door open. (*Kare wa doa o oshite aketa.*) 彼はドアを押して開けた.

2 (urge on) ... ni (... o) kaˈritateˈru ...に(...を)駆り立てる [V]; seˈkitateru せきたてる [V]: He pushed me for payment. (*Kare wa watashi ni shiharai o sekitateta.*) 彼は私に支払いをせきたてた.

3 (promote) ... o oˈshisusumeˈru ...を押し進める [V]; gaˈñbaˈru がんばる [C]: push one's plans (*keekaku o oshisusumeru*) 計画を押し進める.

— vi. **1** (press) oˈsu 押す [C]: You push while I pull. (*Watashi ga hikimasu kara oshite kudasai.*) 私が引きますから押してください.

2 (advance with effort) oˈshisusuˈmu 押し進む [C]: I pushed through the crowd. (*Watashi wa hitogomi no naka o oshisusuñda.*) 私は人込みの中を押し進んだ.

— n. **1** (pushing) oˈsu kotoˈ 押すこと; oˈshi 押し: give a door a hard push (*doa o tsuyoku osu*) ドアを強く押す.

2 (vigorous effort) gaˈñbariˈ がんばり; doˈryoku 努力: make a push (*gañbaru*) がんばる.

put *vt.* **1** (place) ... o oˈku ...を置く [C]; suˈeru 据える [V]: She put the vase by the window. (*Kanojo wa kabiñ o mado no soba ni oita.*) 彼女は花びんを窓のそばに置いた.

2 (cause to be in a condition) ... o ... suˈru ...を...する [I]: I put my room in order. (*Watashi wa heya o seetoñ shita.*) 私は部屋を整頓した.

3 (submit) ... o daˈsu ...を出す [C]; teˈeshutsu suru 提出する [I]: He put several questions to me. (*Kare wa watashi ni ikutsu-ka shitsumoñ o shita.*) 彼は私にいくつか質問をした.

4 (express) ... o iˈiarawaˈsu ...を言い表す [C]: put one's thoughts into words (*kañgae o kotoba ni iiarawasu*) 考えを言葉に言い表す.

5 (attach) ... o tsuˈkeˈru ...を付ける [V]: put a knob on a door (*doa ni totte o tsukeru*) ドアに取っ手を付ける.

6 (write down) ... o kaˈkikomu ...を書き込む [C]; kiˈnyuu suru 記入する [I]: He put something in his notebook. (*Kare wa nooto ni nani-ka o kakikoñda.*) 彼はノートに何かを書き込んだ.

put away *vt.* ... o kaˈtazukeˈru ...を片づける [V]: put toys away (*omocha o katazukeru*) おもちゃを片づける.

put down *vt.* ... o shiˈta ni oku ...を下に置く [C]: put a glass down (*koppu o shita ni oku*) コップを下に置く.

put in *vt.* ... ni iˈreru ...に入れる [V]: Put the garbage in here. (*Gomi wa koko ni ire nasai.*) ごみはここに入れなさい.

put on *vt.* ... o mi ˈni tsukeˈru ...を身につける [V]: put on a coat (*kooto o kiru*) コートを着る / put on shoes (*kutsu o haku*) 靴をはく / put on a hat (*booshi o kaburu*) 帽子をかぶる / put on glasses (*megane o kakeru*) 眼鏡をかける / put on a ring (*yubiwa o hameru*) 指輪をはめる.

put out *vt.* ... o keˈsu ...を消す [C]: put out a light (*akari o kesu*) 明かりを消す.

puzzle *vt.* (perplex) ... o koˈmaraseˈru ...を困らせる [V]; naˈyamaˈsu 悩ます [C]: I am puzzled about what to do. (*Watashi wa doo shite yoi ka*

nayañde iru.) 私はどうしてよいか悩んでいる.
— *vi.* (think hard) a⌈tama⌉ o shi⌈bo⌉ru 頭を絞る Ⓒ: He puzzled over the question. (*Kare wa sono moñdai ni atama o shibotta.*) 彼はその問題に頭を絞った.
— *n.* **1** (problem) na⌈ñmoñ 難問; na⌈zo なぞ: His behavior is a puzzle to us. (*Kare no koodoo wa watashi-tachi ni totte nazo da.*) 彼の行動は私たちにとってなぞだ.
2 (game) pa⌉zuru パズル: a jigsaw puzzle (*jigusoo pazuru*) ジグソーパズル.

Q

quaint *adj.* fu⌈uga⌉wari na 風変わりな: quaint customs (*fuugawari na shuukañ*) 風変わりな習慣.

qualification *n.* **1** (diploma) shi⌈kaku 資格: She has a nurse's qualifications. (*Kanojo wa kañgofu no shikaku o motte imasu.*) 彼女は看護婦の資格を持っています.
2 (restriction) jo⌈oke⌉ñ 条件: The committee accepted my suggestion without any qualification. (*Iiñkai wa nañ no jookeñ mo nashi de watashi no teeañ o mitometa.*) 委員会は何の条件もなしで私の提案を認めた.

qualified *adj.* shi⌈kaku no a⌉ru 資格のある: a qualified architect (*shikaku no aru keñchikushi*) 資格のある建築士.

qualify *vt.* **1** (make fit) ... ni shi⌈kaku o ataeru …に資格を与える Ⓥ: She is qualified to teach Japanese. (*Kanojo wa Nihoñgo o oshieru shikaku ga arimasu.*) 彼女は日本語を教える資格があります.
2 (make less strict) ... o ya⌈warage⌉ru …を和らげる Ⓥ: qualify one's anger (*ikari o yawarageru*) 怒りを和らげる.
3 (modify) ... o shu⌈ushoku suru …を修飾する Ⓘ: Adjectives qualify nouns. (*Keeyooshi wa meeshi o shuushoku suru.*) 形容詞は名詞を修飾する.
— *vi.* shi⌈kaku o e⌉ru 資格を得る Ⓥ: He qualified to receive a scholarship. (*Kare wa shoogakukiñ o morau shikaku o eta.*) 彼は奨学金をもらう資格を得た.

quality *n.* **1** (nature) shi⌈tsu 質; hi⌈ñshitsu 品質: goods of good [poor] quality (*shitsu no yoi [warui] shinamono*) 質のよい[悪い]品物.
2 (characteristic) to⌈kushitsu 特質; to⌈kusee 特性: Hardness is one quality of iron. (*Katai no ga tetsu no hitotsu no tokusee desu.*) 硬いのが鉄の一つの特性です.
3 (excellence) ryo⌈oshitsu 良質; ko⌈okyuu 高級: quality goods (*kookyuuhiñ*) 高級品.

quantity *n.* ryo⌉o 量; su⌈uryo⌉o 数量; bu⌈ñryo⌉o 分量: I prefer quality to quantity. (*Watashi wa ryoo yori mo shitsu o erabimasu.*) 私は量よりも質を選びます. / a large [small] quantity of cement (*tairyoo [shooryoo] no semeñto*) 大量[少量]のセメント.

quarantine *n.* ka⌈kuri 隔離; ke⌈ñeki 検疫: put a person in quarantine (*hito o kakuri suru*) 人を隔離する.
— *vt.* ... o ka⌈kuri suru …を隔離する Ⓘ; ke⌈ñeki suru 検疫する Ⓘ: All the passengers were quarantined. (*Jookyaku wa zeñiñ keñeki o uketa.*) 乗客は全員検疫を受けた.

quarrel *vi.* ko⌉oroñ suru 口論する Ⓘ; ke⌈ñka suru けんかする Ⓘ: He quarreled with his wife over trifles. (*Kare wa tsumaranai koto de okusañ to kooroñ shita.*) 彼はつまらないことで奥さんと口論した. / They are always quarreling with each other.

(*Kare-ra wa o-tagai ni keñka bakari shite iru.*) 彼らはお互いにけんかばかりしている.
— *n.* ko'roñ 口論; ku'chige'ñka 口げんか: He had a quarrel with her. (*Kare wa kanojo to kuchigeñka o shita.*) 彼は彼女と口げんかをした.

quart *n.* ku'o'oto クォート. ★ In Japan the metric system is used.

quarter *n.* **1** (fourth part) yo'ñbuñ no ichi' 4 分の 1: a quarter of a kilometer (*yoñbuñ no ichi-kiro*) 4 分の 1 キロ / three quarters (*yoñbuñ no sañ*) 4 分の 3.
2 (15 minutes) ju'ugo-fuñ 15 分: It's quarter past seven. (*Shichi-ji juugo-fuñ sugi desu.*) 7 時 15 分過ぎです.
3 (three months) shi'ha'ñki 4 半期: the profits for the first quarter (*dai-ichi shihañki no rieki*) 第一 4 半期の利益.
4 (region) chi'iki 地域; chi'ku 地区: the residential quarter (*juukyo chiku*) 住居地区.
— *vt.* ... o yo'ttsu' ni wa'ke'ru ... を 4 つに分ける Ⓥ; yo'ñtoobuñ suru 4 等分する Ⓘ: quarter an apple (*riñgo o yottsu ni kiru*) りんごを 4 つに切る.

queen *n.* **1** (ruler) jo-'o'o 女王: the Queen of England (*Eekoku jo-oo*) 英国女王.
2 (excellent woman) jo-'o'o 女王; ha'nagata 花形: a beauty queen (*bijiñ koñtesuto no jo-oo*) 美人コンテストの女王.

queer *adj.* **1** (strange) ki'myoo na 奇妙な; he'ñ na 変な: It is queer that he didn't show up. (*Kare ga sugata o misenakatta no wa heñ da.*) 彼が姿を見せなかったのは変だ.
2 (causing suspicion) a'yashii 怪しい; u'tagawashii 疑わしい: There was a queer noise in the attic. (*Yaneura de ayashii mono-oto ga shita.*) 屋根裏で怪しい物音がした.
3 (sick) ki'buñ ga wa'ru'i 気分が悪い: I do feel a bit queer. (*Watashi wa sukoshi kibuñ ga warui.*) 私は少し気分が悪い.

quench *vt.* ... o i'ya'su ...をいやす Ⓒ: quench one's thirst (*nodo no kawaki o iyasu*) のどの渇きをいやす.

question *n.* **1** (expression) shi'tsumoñ 質問; to'i 問い: May I ask you a question? (*Shitsumoñ shite mo yoroshii desu ka?*) 質問してもよろしいですか.
2 (problem) mo'ñdai 問題: the housing question (*juutaku-moñdai*) 住宅問題.
3 (doubt) gi'moñ 疑問; u'tagai 疑い: There is no question that he is telling the truth. (*Kare ga hoñtoo no koto o itte iru no wa utagai nai.*) 彼が本当のことを言っているのは疑いない.
— *vt.* **1** (ask a question) ... ni shi'tsumoñ suru ...に質問する Ⓘ: I was questioned by a policeman. (*Watashi wa keekañ ni shitsumoñ sareta.*) 私は警官に質問された.
2 (doubt) ... o u'tagau ...を疑う Ⓒ: I question his honesty. (*Watashi wa kare no shoojikisa o utagau.*) 私は彼の正直さを疑う.

question mark *n.* gi'mo'ñfu 疑問符.

queue *n.* re'tsu 列: form a queue (*retsu o tsukuru*) 列を作る.
— *vi.* re'tsu o tsu'ku'ru 列を作る Ⓒ; na'rañde ma'tsu 並んで待つ Ⓒ: We queued up for a taxi. (*Watashi-tachi wa ichi-retsu ni narañde takushii o matta.*) 私たちは一列に並んでタクシーを待った.

quick *adj.* **1** (fast) ha'ya'i 速[早]い: He is a quick walker. (*Kare wa aruku no ga hayai.*) 彼は歩くのが速い.
2 (alert) bi'ñkañ na 敏感な; ha'ya'i 早い: She is quick at learning Japanese. (*Kanojo wa Nihoñgo o oboeru no ga hayai.*) 彼女は日本語を覚えるのが早い.
3 (easily aroused) o'korippo'i 怒りっぽい: Mr. Tanaka has a quick temper. (*Tanaka-sañ wa okorippoi.*) 田中さんは怒りっぽい.
— *adv.* ha'yaku 速[早]く; i'so'ide 急いで: Can't you run quicker? (*Motto hayaku hashirenai no?*) もっ

q

と速く走れないの. / Come quick. (*Isoide ki nasai.*) 急いで来なさい.

quickly *adv.* ha¹yaku 速く[早]; i⌈so¹-ide 急いで; su¹gu ni すぐに: Quickly, please. (*Hayaku o-negai shimasu.*) 早くお願いします. / He walked quickly. (*Kare wa isoide aruita.*) 彼は急いで歩いた. / The doctor came quickly. (*Isha wa sugu ni kita.*) 医者はすぐに来た.

quiet *adj.* **1** (not noisy) shi¹zuka na 静かな: I'd like a quiet room. (*Shizuka na heya o tanomimasu.*) 静かな部屋を頼みます.
2 (peaceful) he⌈eoñ na 平穏な; he⌈e-wa na 平和な: live a quiet life (*heeoñ na kurashi o suru*) 平穏な暮らしをする.
3 (still) shi¹zuka na 静かな; u⌈goka¹-nai 動かない: The lake is quiet. (*Mizuumi wa shizuka da.*) 湖は静かだ.
4 (gentle) o⌈tonashi¹i おとなしい; shi⌈to¹yaka na しとやかな: a quiet woman (*shitoyaka na josee*) しとやかな女性.
5 (not showy) ji⌈mi¹ na 地味な: a quiet color (*jimi na iro*) 地味な色.
— *n.* **1** (quietness) shi⌈zuke¹sa 静けさ; se⌈ejaku 静寂: the quiet after a storm (*arashi no ato no shizukesa*) 嵐の後の静けさ.
2 (peace) he⌈eoñ 平穏; he⌈ewa 平和.
— *vt.* ... o shi⌈zume¹ru ...を静める Ⓥ; na⌈dame¹ru なだめる Ⓥ: quiet a crying baby (*naite iru akañboo o nadameru*) 泣いている赤ん坊をなだめる.
— *vi.* shi⌈zuma¹ru 静まる Ⓒ: The storm quieted down. (*Arashi wa shizumatta.*) 嵐は静まった.

quietly *adv.* shi¹zuka ni 静かに: walk quietly (*shizuka ni aruku*) 静かに歩く.

quit *vt.* ... o ya⌈meru ...を辞める Ⓥ: He quit his job last month. (*Kare wa señgetsu tsutome o yamemashita.*) 彼は先月勤めを辞めました.

quite *adv.* **1** (completely) ma⌈ttaku まったく; ka⌈ñzeñ ni 完全に: I quite agree with you. (*Watashi mo anata to mattaku onaji ikeñ desu.*) 私もあなたとまったく同じ意見です. / He is not quite well yet. (*Kare wa mada kañzeñ ni yoku natte imaseñ.*) 彼はまだ完全によくなっていません.
2 (rather) na⌈kanaka なかなか; ka¹-nari かなり: It is quite cold this morning. (*Kesa wa kanari samui.*) けさはかなり寒い.

quiz *n.* **1** (short test) sho⌈o-shike¹ñ 小試験; sho⌈o-te¹suto 小テスト.
2 (game) ku¹izu クイズ.

quotation *n.* i⌈ñyoo 引用; i⌈ñyoo-buñ 引用文.

quote *vt.* ... o i⌈ñyoo suru ...を引用する Ⓘ: He quoted the phrase from the Bible. (*Kare wa sono ku o seesho kara iñyoo shita.*) 彼はその句を聖書から引用した.

R

race[1] *n.* **1** (competition in speed) kyo⌈osoo 競走; re¹esu レース: run a race (*kyoosoo suru*) 競走する / the races (*keeba*) 競馬.
2 (contest) kyo⌈osoo 競争: an arms race (*guñbi-kyoosoo*) 軍備競争.
— *vi.* (... to) kyo⌈osoo suru (...と) 競走する Ⓘ: I raced with him. (*Watashi wa kare to kyoosoo shita.*) 私は彼と競走した.
— *vt.* ... to kyo⌈osoo suru ...と競走する Ⓘ: I'll race you to the station. (*Eki made kimi to kyoosoo shiyoo.*) 駅まで君と競走しよう.

race[2] *n.* ji⌈ñshu 人種; mi¹ñzoku 民族: the race problem (*jiñshu-moñdai*) 人種問題.

rack *n.* **1** (shelf) o⌈kidana 置き棚: a baggage rack (*amidana*) 網棚.

2 (framework) -ˈkake 掛け: a hat rack (*booshi-kake*) 帽子掛け / a towel rack (*taoru-kake*) タオル掛け.

racket *n.* raˈkeˈtto ラケット.

radar *n.* reˈedaa レーダー: a radar system (*reedaa soochi*) レーダー装置.

radiate *vt.* ... o hoˈosha suru …を放射する [I]: A fire radiates heat. (*Hi wa netsu o hoosha suru.*) 火は熱を放射する.

— *vi.* hoˈosha suru 放射する [I].

radiation *n.* hoˈosha 放射; hoˈone-tsu 放熱: radiation of heat (*netsu no hoosha*) 熱の放射.

radical *adj.* **1** (extreme) kaˈgeki na 過激な; kyuˈushiñ-teki na 急進的な: radical students (*kageki na gakusee-tachi*) 過激な学生たち / a radical politician (*kyuushiñ-teki na seejika*) 急進的な政治家.

2 (basic) koˈñpoñ-teki na 根本的な; (thorough) teˈttei-teki na 徹底的な: make radical improvements to the tax system (*zeesee o koñ-poñ-teki ni kaizen suru*) 税制を根本的に改善する.

radio *n.* raˈjio ラジオ: turn the radio on [off] (*rajio o tsukeru* [*kesu*]) ラジオをつける[消す] / listen to the radio (*rajio o kiku*) ラジオを聞く.

rag *n.* boˈro ぼろ; boˈroˈkire ぼろきれ.

rage *n.* **1** (great anger) iˈkari 怒り; geˈkido 激怒: fly into a rage (*katto naru*) かっとなる.

2 (violence) haˈgeˈshisa 激しさ; moˈoi 猛威: the rage of the wind (*kaze no mooi*) 風の猛威.

— *vi.* **1** (show great anger) geˈkido suru 激怒する [I]; haˈraˈ o taˈteˈru 腹を立てる [V]: He raged when he heard the news. (*Kare wa sono shirase o kiite gekido shita.*) 彼はその知らせを聞いて激怒した.

2 (be violent) moˈoi o fuˈruu 猛威をふるう [C]; aˈrekuruˈu 荒れ狂う [C]: The storm raged all night. (*Arashi wa hito-bañ-juu arekurutta.*) 嵐は一晩中荒れ狂った.

ragged *adj.* **1** (torn) boˈroboro no ぼろぼろの: a ragged coat (*boroboro no uwagi*) ぼろぼろの上着.

2 (uneven) giˈzagiza no ぎざぎざの: a ragged coastline (*gizagiza no kai-gañseñ*) ぎざぎざの海岸線.

raid *n.* **1** (sudden attack) shuˈugeki 襲撃; kyuˈushuu 急襲: make a raid on the enemy (*teki o kyuushuu suru*) 敵を急襲する.

2 (sudden entry by the police) te-ˈireˈ 手入れ: make a raid on a night-club (*naitokurabu no teire o oko-nau*) ナイトクラブの手入れを行う.

— *vt.* ... o oˈsou …を襲う [C]; te-ˈireˈ o suru 手入れをする [I]: The thieves raided the bank. (*Doroboo ga giñkoo o osotta.*) どろぼうが銀行を襲った.

rail *n.* **1** (track) reˈeru レール; seˈñro 線路: run on rails (*reeru no ue o hashiru*) レールの上を走る.

2 (railroad) teˈtsudoo 鉄道: lay rails (*tetsudoo o shiku*) 鉄道を敷く.

3 (bar of wood or metal) yoˈkoboo 横棒; teˈsuri 手すり: lean on a rail (*tesuri ni yorikakaru*) 手すりに寄り掛かる.

railroad *n.* teˈtsudoo 鉄道: a rail-road crossing (*tetsudoo no fumi-kiri*) 鉄道の踏切 / a railroad bridge (*tekkyoo*) 鉄橋.

— *vt.* ... o teˈtsudoo de yusoo suru …を鉄道で輸送する [I].

railway *n.* = railroad.

rain *n.* aˈme 雨: It looks like rain. (*Ame ni nari-soo da.*) 雨になりそうだ. / The rain stopped suddenly. (*Ame ga kyuu ni yañda.*) 雨が急にやんだ.

— *vi.* aˈme ga furu 雨が降る [C]: It has begun raining. (*Ame ga furi-hajimeta.*) 雨が降り始めた.

rainbow *n.* niˈji にじ: After the rain, a rainbow formed in the sky. (*Ame no ato de sora ni niji ga deta.*) 雨の後で空ににじが出た.

rain check *n.* (ticket) uˈteñ hi-ˈkikaˈekeñ 雨天引換券; (promise) goˈjitsu no shoˈotai 後日の招待: Give me a rain check. (*Mata no kikai ni yoroshiku.*) またの機会によろしく.

raincoat *n.* re⌈eñko⌉oto レーンコート.

rainfall *n.* ko⌈ou⌉ryoo 降雨量: the annual average rainfall (*neñkañ heekiñ koouryoo*) 年間平均降雨量.

rainy *adj.* a⌉me no 雨の; a⌈me⌉furi no 雨降りの: a rainy day (*ame no hi*) 雨の日 / the rainy season (*tsuyu*) 梅雨.

raise *vt.* **1** (lift) ... o a⌈geru ...を上げる [V]: She raised her hand and waved. (*Kanojo wa te o agete futta.*) 彼女は手を上げて振った.
2 (make higher) ... o a⌈geru ...を上げる [V]: raise the rent (*yachiñ o ageru*) 家賃を上げる.
3 (bring up) ... o so⌈date⌉ru ...を育てる [V]: I was born and raised in Tokyo. (*Watashi wa Tookyoo de umare sodatta.*) 私は東京で生まれ育った.
4 (grow) ... o sa⌈ibai suru ...を栽培する [I]: raise vegetables in a field (*hatake de yasai o saibai suru*) 畑で野菜を栽培する.
5 (gather) ... o a⌈tsume⌉ru ...を集める [V]: raise money for charity (*jizeñ no tame ni o-kane o atsumeru*) 慈善のためにお金を集める.
6 (bring forward) ... o te⌉eki suru ...を提起する [I]: raise an important question (*juuyoo na moñdai o teeki suru*) 重要な問題を提起する.
— *n.* (of pay) sho⌈okyuu 昇給; chi⌈ñage 賃上げ: demand a raise (*chiñage o yookyuu suru*) 賃上げを要求する.

raisin *n.* ho⌈shibu⌉doo 干しぶどう.

rake *n.* ku⌈made くま手; re⌉eki レーキ.
— *vt.* ... o ka⌈kiatsume⌉ru ...をかき集める [V]; ka⌈kinara⌉su かきならす [C]: rake fallen leaves (*ochiba o kakiatsumeru*) 落ち葉をかき集める / rake the flower beds (*kadañ o kakinarasu*) 花壇をかきならす.

rally *vi.* **1** (come together) a⌈tsuma⌉ru 集まる [C]: rally around the leader (*shidoosha no moto ni atsumaru*) 指導者のもとに集まる.
2 (recover strength) ka⌈ifuku suru 回復する [I]: As the fever left him, he began to rally. (*Netsu ga tore, kare wa kaifuku shi-hajimeta.*) 熱が取れ, 彼は回復し始めた.
— *vt.* ... o fu⌈tatabi atsume⌉ru ...を再び集める [V]: rally the scattered soldiers (*barabara ni natta heetai-tachi o futatabi atsumeru*) ばらばらになった兵隊たちを再び集める.
— *n.* da⌈i-shu⌉ukai 大集会; ta⌈ikai 大会: a peace rally (*heewa-uñdoo shuukai*) 平和運動集会.

random *adj.* **1** (without method) te⌈atarishi⌉dai no 手当たり次第の; de⌈tarame na でたらめな: a random guess (*detarame na suisoku*) でたらめな推測.
2 (statistics) mu⌈sa⌉kui no 無作為の; ni⌉ñi no 任意の.
at random *adv.* de⌈tarame ni でたらめに: select at random (*detarame ni erabu*) でたらめに選ぶ.

range *n.* **1** (extent) ha⌉ñi 範囲; ha⌈ba 幅: a wide range of knowledge (*hiroi hañi no chishiki*) 広い範囲の知識 / a range of prices (*nedañ no haba*) 値段の幅.
2 (row or line) na⌈rabi 並び; tsu⌈zuki 続き: a mountain range (*sañmyaku*) 山脈.
3 (distance) kyo⌉ri 距離: fire a gun at close range (*shikiñ kyori kara happoo suru*) 至近距離から発砲する.
— *vi.* o⌈yobu 及ぶ [C]: The children's ages range from 5 to 10. (*Kodomo-tachi no neñree wa go-sai kara jus-sai ni oyoñde iru.*) 子どもたちの年齢は5歳から10歳に及んでいる.
— *vt.* ... o na⌈raberu ...を並べる [V]: range the pupils in a line (*seeto o ichi-retsu ni naraberu*) 生徒を一列に並べる.

rank *n.* **1** (grade) ka⌈ikyuu 階級; to⌈okyuu 等級: people of all ranks (*arayuru kaikyuu no hito-tachi*) あらゆる階級の人たち / a painter of the first rank (*ichi-ryuu no gaka*) 一流の画家.
2 (row) re⌉tsu 列: stand in a rank (*retsu ni narabu*) 列に並ぶ.

— *vt.* **1** (arrange) ... o na⌈raberu …を並べる [V]: rank books on a shelf (*tana ni hoñ o naraberu*) 棚に本を並べる.
2 (make much of) ... o hyo⌉oka suru …を評価する [I]: I rank his abilities high. (*Watashi wa kare no sainoo o takaku hyooka shite iru.*) 私は彼の才能を高く評価している.
— *vi.* (hold a position) shi⌈me⌉ru 占める [V]: He ranks first in his class. (*Kare wa kurasu de ichibañ o shimete iru.*) 彼はクラスで一番を占めている.

rank and file *n.* (company workers) i⌈ppañ sha⌉iñ 一般社員; (soldiers) he⌉eshi-tachi 兵士たち.

ransom *n.* mi⌈noshirokiñ 身代金: They held the child for ransom. (*Kare-ra wa sono ko o hitojichi ni shite minoshirokiñ o yookyuu shita.*) 彼らはその子を人質にして身代金を要求した.

rap *vi.* (... o) ko⌉tsukotsu [to⌉ñtoñ] to ta⌈ta⌉ku (…を)こつこつ[とんとん]とたたく [C]: rap at a door (*doa o toñtoñ to tataku*) ドアをとんとんとたたく.
— *n.* ko⌉tsukotsu [to⌉ñtoñ] to ta⌈ta⌉ku o⌈to⌉ こつこつ[とんとん]とたたく音.

rape *vt.* ... o go⌈okañ suru …を強姦する [I]; re⌉epu suru レイプする [I].

rapid *adj.* ha⌈ya⌉i 速い; kyu⌈usoku na 急速な: a rapid river (*nagare no hayai kawa*) 流れの速い川 / make rapid progress (*kyuusoku na shiñpo o togeru*) 急速な進歩を遂げる.

rapidly *adv.* ha⌉yaku 速く; su⌈ba⌉yaku すばやく: Don't speak so rapidly. (*Sonna ni hayaku shaberanaide kudasai.*) そんなに速くしゃべらないでください.

rapture *n.* u⌈cho⌉oteñ 有頂天; kyo⌉oki 狂喜: He was in raptures about the news. (*Kare wa sono shirase ni uchooteñ datta.*) 彼はその知らせに有頂天だった.

rare[1] *adj.* **1** (unusual) ma⌈re⌉ na まれな; me⌈zurashi⌉i 珍しい: It is rare for him to be absent. (*Kare ga yasumu no wa mezurashii.*) 彼が休むのは珍しい.
2 (thin) u⌈sui 薄い; ki⌈haku na 希薄な: The air is rare in the high mountains. (*Takai yama wa kuuki ga kihaku desu.*) 高い山は空気が希薄です.

rare[2] *adj.* (partly cooked) na⌈mayake no 生焼けの; re⌉a no レアの: I like rare beef. (*Watashi wa namayake no gyuuniku ga suki desu.*) 私は生焼けの牛肉が好きです.

rarely *adv.* ma⌈re⌉ ni まれに; me⌉tta ni ⟨verb⟩-nai めったに…ない: I'm rarely ill. (*Watashi wa metta ni byooki o shinai.*) 私はめったに病気をしない.

rash[1] *adj.* ke⌈esotsu na 軽率な; mu⌈fu⌉ñbetsu na 無分別な: It was rash of you to say so. (*Kimi ga soo itta no wa keesotsu datta.*) 君がそう言ったのは軽率だった.

rash[2] *n.* ha⌈sshiñ 発疹; fu⌈kidemono 吹き出物.

rat *n.* ne⌈zumi ねずみ. ★ In Japanese 'mouse' is also called '*nezumi.*'

rate *n.* **1** (amount) ri⌉tsu 率; wa⌈riai 割合: interest rates (*ri-ritsu*) 利率 / an exchange rate (*kookañ-ritsu*) 交換率 / the rate of discount (*waribiki-ritsu*) 割引率.
2 (speed) so⌉kudo 速度; ha⌉yasa 速さ: drive at the rate of 50 kilometers an hour (*jisoku gojuk-kiro no hayasa de kuruma o uñteñ suru*) 時速 50 キロの速さで車を運転する.
3 (price) ryo⌉okiñ 料金; ne⌈dañ 値段: a telephone rate (*deñwa-ryookiñ*) 電話料金 / What's the rate? (*Ryookiñ wa ikura desu ka?*) 料金はいくらですか.
— *vi.* (set a value) ... to mi⌈tsumoru …と見積もる [C]: I rated the diamond at 50,000 yen. (*Watashi wa sono daiyamoñdo o go-mañ-eñ to mitsumotta.*) 私はそのダイヤモンドを5万円と見積もった.

rather *adv.* **1** (more willing) mu⌉shiro むしろ: I would rather stay home than go out. (*Watashi wa dekakeru yori mo mushiro uchi ni*

itai.) 私は出かけるよりもむしろ家にいたい.
2 (somewhat) ka˥nari かなり; da˹ibu だいぶ: I am rather tired. (*Watashi wa kanari tsukareta.*) 私はかなり疲れた. / It's rather hot, isn't it? (*Daibu atsui desu ne.*) だいぶ暑いですね.

ratio *n.* hi˥ 比; hi˹ritsu 比率; wa˹ri-ai 割合: The ratio of boys and girls is two to one. (*Otoko-no-ko to oñna-no-ko no hiritsu wa ni tai ichi desu.*) 男の子と女の子の比率は2対1です.

rational *adj.* **1** (able to reason) ri˥-see no aru 理性のある; ri˹see-teki na 理性的な: Man is a rational animal. (*Niñgeñ wa risee-teki na doobutsu desu.*) 人間は理性的な動物です.
2 (reasonable) go˹ori-teki na 合理的な: a rational explanation (*goori-teki na setsumee*) 合理的な説明.

rattle *vi.* **1** (cause sounds) ga˥ra-gara o˹to˥ ga suru がらがら音がする [I]; ga˥tagata na˹ru がたがた鳴る [C]: The windows rattled in the wind. (*Mado ga kaze de gatagata natta.*) 窓が風でがたがた鳴った.
2 (move with sounds) ga˥tagata to ha˹shi˥ru がたがたと走る [C]: The old car rattled by. (*Furui kuruma ga gatagata to hashitte itta.*) 古い車ががたがたと走って行った.
— *n.* ga˥tagata iu o˹to˥ がたがたいう音.

raw *adj.* **1** (uncooked) na˥ma no 生の: a raw egg (*nama-tamago*) 生卵 / sliced raw fish (*sashimi*) 刺身.
2 (not prepared) ge˹ñryo˥o no ma˹ma no 原料のままの: raw petroleum (*geñyu*) 原油 / raw silk (*ki-ito*) 生糸.
3 (sore) a˹kamuke no 赤むけの; hi˥-rihiri suru ひりひりする: a raw wound (*akamuke no kizu*) 赤むけの傷.
4 (inexperienced) mi˹ke˥ekeñ no 未経験の; mi˥juku na 未熟な: a raw recruit (*shiñpee*) 新兵.

ray *n.* **1** (beam) ko˹oseñ 光線: the sun's rays (*taiyoo-kooseñ*) 太陽光線 / ultraviolet rays (*shigaiseñ*) 紫外線.
2 (tiny amount) wa˥zuka わずか: a ray of hope (*wazuka na nozomi*) わずかな望み.

razor *n.* ka˹miso˥ri かみそり: shave one's face with a razor (*kamisori de kao o soru*) かみそりで顔をそる.

reach *vt.* **1** (arrive at) ... ni tsu˥ku …に着く [C]; to˹ochaku suru 到着する [I]: Telephone me when you reach Narita. (*Narita ni tsuitara deñwa o kudasai.*) 成田に着いたら電話をください. / They reached their destination safely. (*Kare-ra wa buji ni mokutekichi ni toochaku shita.*) 彼らは無事に目的地に到着した.
2 (touch) ... ni te˥ ga to˹do˥ku …に手が届く [C]: Can you reach the top shelf? (*Ichibañ ue no tana ni te ga todokimasu ka?*) いちばん上の棚に手が届きますか.
3 (get to) ... ni to˹do˥ku …に届く [C]; ta˥ssuru 達する [I]: The letter reached me this morning. (*Sono tegami wa kesa todokimashita.*) その手紙は今朝届きました.
— *vi.* (extend a hand) te˥ o no˹ba˥su 手を伸ばす [C]: He reached out for a cigarette. (*Kare wa tabako o toroo to te o nobashita.*) 彼はたばこを取ろうと手を伸ばした.

react *vi.* **1** (act in response) ha˹ñnoo suru 反応する [I]: Our eyes react to light. (*Me wa hikari ni hañnoo suru.*) 目は光に反応する.
2 (act opposing) ha˹ñpatsu suru 反発する [I]: react against despotism (*señsee-seeji ni hañpatsu suru*) 専制政治に反発する.

reaction *n.* **1** (response) ha˹ñnoo 反応: What was his reaction to your proposal? (*Anata no teeañ ni taisuru kare no hañnoo wa doo deshita?*) あなたの提案に対する彼の反応はどうでした.
2 (opposing action) ha˹ñpatsu 反発; ha˹ñkoo 反抗: reaction against the tax increase (*zoozee ni taisuru hañpatsu*) 増税に対する反発.

read *vt.* **1** (get the meaning) ... o yo˥mu …を読む [C]: Have you read this book? (*Kono hoñ wa yomima-*

shita ka?) この本は読みましたか.
2 (speak printed words) ko⌉e o dashite yomu 声を出して読む Ⓒ; ro⌈odoku suru 朗読する Ⓘ: read a textbook aloud (*kyookasho o roodoku suru*) 教科書を朗読する.
— *vi.* do⌉kusho suru 読書する Ⓘ: I want more time to read. (*Motto dokusho suru jikañ ga hoshii.*) もっと読書する時間が欲しい.

reader *n.* **1** (person) do⌉kusha 読者; do⌈kushoka 読書家: I am a slow reader. (*Watashi wa hoñ o yomu no ga osoi.*) 私は本を読むのが遅い.
2 (textbook) kyo⌈oka⌉sho 教科書; to⌈kuhoñ 読本.

readily *adv.* **1** (willingly) ko⌈koroyo⌉ku 快く: He lent me the money readily. (*Kare wa kokoroyoku sono o-kane o kashite kureta.*) 彼は快くそのお金を貸してくれた.
2 (easily) ta⌈ya⌉suku たやすく: I cannot readily answer the question. (*Sono moñdai wa tayasuku heñtoo dekimaseñ.*) その問題はたやすく返答できません.

reading *n.* **1** (act of reading) do⌉kusho 読書: She is fond of reading. (*Kanojo wa dokusho ga suki da.*) 彼女は読書が好きだ.
2 (something to be read) yo⌈mimo⌉no 読み物: suitable reading for children (*kodomo-tachi ni fusawashii yomimono*) 子どもたちにふさわしい読み物.
3 (of a gauge) hyo⌈oji 表示; shi⌉do 示度: the reading on a thermometer (*oñdokee no shido*) 温度計の示度.

ready *adj.* **1** (prepared) yo⌉oi no dekita [dekite iru] 用意のできた[できている]: Dinner is ready. (*Yuuhañ no yooi ga dekimashita.*) 夕飯の用意ができました. / Are you ready to go out? (*Dekakeru yooi wa dekimashita ka?*) 出かける用意はできましたか.
2 (willing) yo⌈roko⌉ñde ⟨verb⟩ 喜んで…: I am always ready to help. (*Itsu de mo yorokoñde o-tetsudai shimasu.*) いつでも喜んでお手伝いします.
3 (about to) i⌉ma ni mo ⟨verb⟩-soo da いまにも…そうだ: She was ready to cry. (*Kanojo wa ima ni mo nakidashi-soo datta.*) 彼女はいまにも泣きだしそうだった.

ready-made *adj.* de⌈kiai no 出来合いの; ki⌈see-hiñ no 既製品の: ready-made clothes (*kisee-fuku*) 既製服.

real *adj.* **1** (actually existing) ji⌈tsuzai no 実在の; ji⌈ssai no 実際の: a real person in history (*rekishi-joo jitsuzai no jiñbutsu*) 歴史上実在の人物 / real events (*jissai no dekigoto*) 実際の出来事.
2 (true) ho⌈ñtoo no 本当の; shi⌉ñ no 真の: What is the real reason for his absence? (*Kare no kesseki no hoñtoo no riyuu wa nañ desu ka?*) 彼の欠席の本当の理由は何ですか.
3 (genuine) ho⌈ñmono no 本物の: a real pearl (*hoñmono no shiñju*) 本物の真珠.

reality *n.* ge⌈ñjitsu 現実: His dream became a reality. (*Kare no yume wa geñjitsu to natta.*) 彼の夢は現実となった.

realization *n.* **1** (understanding) ri⌉kai 理解; ni⌈ñshiki 認識: I have a full realization of the situation. (*Jookyoo wa juubuñ niñshiki shite imasu.*) 状況は十分認識しています.
2 (making real) ji⌈tsugeñ 実現; ta⌈ssee 達成: the realization of one's hopes (*kiboo no jitsugeñ*) 希望の実現.

realize *vt.* **1** (understand) ... o ri⌉kai suru …を理解する Ⓘ; sa⌈toru 悟る Ⓒ: He realized that he was mistaken. (*Kare wa jibuñ ga machigatte iru koto o satotta.*) 彼は自分が間違っていることを悟った.
2 (make real) ... o ji⌈tsugeñ suru …を実現する Ⓘ: She realized her dream of becoming an actress. (*Kanojo wa joyuu ni naru to iu yume o jitsugeñ shita.*) 彼女は女優になるという夢を実現した.

really *adv.* **1** (truly) ho⌈ñtoo ni 本

r

当に; ji⌐ssai ni 実際に: I really don't know. (*Watashi wa hoñtoo ni shirimaseñ.*) 私は本当に知りません.
2 (indeed) ma⌐ttaku まったく: It is really a pity. (*Mattaku zañneñ da.*) まったく残念だ.

realm *n.* **1** (area) ryo¬oiki 領域; ha¬ñi 範囲: the realm of science (*kagaku no ryooiki*) 科学の領域.
2 (kingdom) o⌐okoku 王国; (national territory) ko¬kudo 国土.

reap *vt.* ... o ka⌐ri-ire¬ru …を刈り入れる Ⓥ; shu⌐ukaku suru 収穫する Ⓘ: reap crops (*sakumotsu o kari-ireru*) 作物を刈り入れる.
— *vi.* ka⌐rito¬ru 刈り取る Ⓒ: reap as one has sown (*jibuñ no maita tane o karitoru*) 自分のまいた種を刈り取る.

rear[1] *adj.* u⌐shiro no 後ろの; u⌐ra no 裏の: a rear entrance (*uraguchi*) 裏口.
— *n.* u⌐shiro 後ろ; ko¬obu 後部: the rear of a house (*ie no ushiro*) 家の後ろ.

rear[2] *vt.* **1** (bring up) ... o so⌐date¬ru …を育てる Ⓥ: rear one's children (*kodomo o sodateru*) 子どもを育てる.
2 (lift up) ... o mo⌐chiageru …を持ち上げる Ⓥ: The snake reared its head. (*Hebi wa atama o mochiageta.*) へびは頭を持ち上げた.

reason *n.* **1** (cause) ri⌐yuu 理由; wa¬ke 訳: What is the reason for your absence? (*Anata ga kesseki shita riyuu wa nañ desu ka?*) あなたが欠席した理由は何ですか. / He resigned for some reason. (*Kare wa doo iu wake ka jishoku shita.*) 彼はどういう訳か辞職した.
2 (the power to think) ri¬see 理性; ha⌐ñda¬ñ-ryoku 判断力: Animals have no reason. (*Doobutsu ni wa risee ga nai.*) 動物には理性がない.
3 (good judgment) fu¬ñbetsu 分別; sho⌐oki 正気: lose one's reason (*fuñbetsu o nakusu*) 分別をなくす.
— *vt.* ... o se⌐ttoku shite <verb>-(sa)seru …を説得して…(さ)せる Ⓥ: I reasoned him into giving up the plan. (*Watashi wa kare o settoku shite sono keekaku o akiramesaseta.*) 私は彼を説得してその計画をあきらめさせた.
— *vi.* su¬iri suru 推理する Ⓘ: the ability to reason (*suiriryoku*) 推理力.

reasonable *adj.* **1** (sensible) mo⌐tto¬mo na もっともな; ri⌐kutsu ni a¬tta 理屈に合った: reasonable demands (*mottomo na yookyuu*) もっともな要求.
2 (fair) te⌐goro na 手ごろな; ho⌐do yo¬i ほどよい: a reasonable price (*tegoro na nedañ*) 手ごろな値段.

reasoning *n.* su¬iri 推理; su⌐iroñ 推論: Your reasoning is correct. (*Kimi no suiri wa tadashii.*) 君の推理は正しい.

reassure *vt.* ... o a⌐ñshiñ saseru …を安心させる Ⓥ: The doctor reassured him that he would soon get well. (*Isha wa sugu yoku narimasu to itte kare o añshiñ saseta.*) 医者はすぐよくなりますと言って彼を安心させた.

rebel *vi.* (... ni) ha⌐ñkoo suru (…に)反抗する Ⓘ; so⌐mu¬ku 背く Ⓒ: rebel against a ruler (*shihaisha ni hañkoo suru*) 支配者に反抗する.
— *n.* ha⌐ñgyaku¬sha 反逆者; ha⌐ñko¬osha 反抗者.

rebellion *n.* ha⌐ñrañ 反乱; mu¬hoñ 謀反: rise in rebellion (*hañrañ o okosu*) 反乱を起こす.

rebuild *vt.* ... o ta⌐tenao¬su …を建て直す Ⓒ; ka⌐ichiku suru 改築する Ⓘ: rebuild an old house (*furui ie o tatenaosu*) 古い家を建て直す.

recall *vt.* **1** (remember) ... o o⌐moida¬su …を思い出す Ⓒ: I can't recall his name. (*Watashi wa kare no namae o omoidasenai.*) 私は彼の名前を思い出せない.
2 (call back) ... o yo⌐bimodo¬su …を呼び戻す Ⓒ; sho⌐okañ suru 召還する Ⓘ: He was recalled to the head office. (*Kare wa hoñsha e yobimodosareta.*) 彼は本社へ呼び戻された.
3 (take back) ... o to⌐rimodo¬su …

r

を取り戻す [C]; ka⌈ishuu suru 回収する [I]: recall defective cars (*kekkañ-sha o kaishuu suru*) 欠陥車を回収する.

— *n.* **1** (order to return) sho⌈o-kañ 召還: the recall of an ambassador (*taishi no shookañ*) 大使の召還.
2 (remembrance) ki⌈oku⌉ryoku 記憶力: He has total recall. (*Kare wa subarashii kiokuryoku o motte iru.*) 彼はすばらしい記憶力を持っている.
3 (by a vote) ri⌈ko⌉oru リコール.

receipt *n.* **1** (written statement) ryo⌈oshuusho 領収書; re⌈shi⌉ito レシート: May I have a receipt? (*Re-shiito o kudasai.*) レシートを下さい.
2 (receiving) u⌈ketoru koto⌉ 受け取ること; ju⌈ryoo 受領: On receipt of your payment, we will send you the goods. (*O-shiharai o uketori shidai shinamono o hassoo itashi-masu.*) お支払いを受け取り次第品物を発送いたします.

receive *vt.* **1** (get) ... o u⌈ketoru ...を受け取る [C]; u⌈ke⌉ru 受ける [V]: I received your letter yesterday. (*Ki-noo o-tegami o uketorimashita.*) きのうお手紙を受け取りました. / She received her education abroad. (*Ka-nojo wa gaikoku de kyooiku o uketa.*) 彼女は外国で教育を受けた.
2 (welcome) ... o mu⌈kaeru ...を迎える [V]; mo⌈tena⌉su もてなす [C]: He received his guests warmly. (*Kare wa o-kyaku o atatakaku mukaeta.*) 彼はお客を温かく迎えた.

receiver *n.* **1** (of a telephone) ju-⌈wa⌉ki 受話器; (of a radio) ju⌈shi⌉ñ-ki 受信機: pick up [hang up] the receiver (*juwaki o toru* [*oku*]) 受話器を取る[置く].
2 (person) u⌈ketoriniñ 受け取り人.

recent *adj.* sa⌈ikiñ no 最近の; chi-⌈ka⌉goro no 近ごろの: Have you read his recent work? (*Kare no sai-kiñ saku o yomimashita ka?*) 彼の最近作を読みましたか.

recently *adv.* sa⌈ikiñ 最近; chi-⌈ka⌉goro 近ごろ: I have put on weight recently. (*Watashi wa sai-kiñ futotta.*) 私は最近太った.

reception *n.* **1** (party) ka⌈ñge⌉e-kai 歓迎会; re⌈se⌉pushoñ レセプション: give a reception (*kañgeekai o hiraku*) 歓迎会を開く / a wedding reception (*kekkoñ hirooeñ*) 結婚披露宴.
2 (welcome) ka⌈ñgee 歓迎; se⌉ttai 接待: They got a cordial reception. (*Kare-ra wa kokoro kara no kañ-gee o uketa.*) 彼らは心からの歓迎を受けた.
3 (receiving) ju⌈ryoo 受領; (of a radio) ju⌈shiñ 受信.

recess *n.* **1** (pause) kyu⌈ukee 休憩; ya⌈sumi⌉ 休み: take a ten-minute recess (*jup-puñ-kañ kyuukee suru*) 10分間休憩する.
2 (hidden place) o⌈kuma⌉tta to-⌈koro⌉ 奥まった所.

recipe *n.* cho⌈orihoo 調理法; tsu-⌈kurikata⌉ 作り方: a recipe for stew (*shichuu no tsukurikata*) シチューの作り方.

reciprocal *adj.* so⌉ogo no 相互の; o⌈tagai no お互いの: reciprocal help (*soogo fujo*) 相互扶助.

recite *vt.* **1** (repeat aloud from memory) ... o a⌈ñshoo suru ...を暗唱する [I]: recite a poem (*shi o añ-shoo suru*) 詩を暗唱する.
2 (tell in detail) ku⌈wa⌉shiku no-⌈be⌉ru 詳しく述べる [V]: He recited his adventures. (*Kare wa jibuñ no bookeñdañ o kuwashiku nobeta.*) 彼は自分の冒険談を詳しく述べた.

reckless *adj.* mu⌈ko⌉omizu na 向こう見ずな; mu⌈boo na 無謀な: a reckless boy (*mukoomizu na otoko-no-ko*) 向こう見ずな男の子 / reckless driving (*muboo-uñteñ*) 無謀運転.

recline *vt.* (of a seat) ta⌈o⌉su 倒す [C]; yo⌈kotae⌉ru 横たえる [V]: May I recline my seat? (*Shiito o taoshite mo ii desu ka?*) シートを倒してもいいですか.

— *vi.* mo⌈tare⌉ru もたれる [V]; yo⌈ko ni na⌉ru 横になる [C].

recognition *n.* (recognizing) mi-⌈tomeru koto⌉ 認めること; sho⌈oniñ

r

承認: recognition of defeat (*haiboku o mitomeru koto*) 敗北を認めること / recognition of a new state (*shiñkokka no shooniñ*) 新国家の承認.

recognize *vt.* **1** (know) ... to wa⌈ka⌉ru ...とわかる Ⓒ; (recall) ... o o⌈moida⌉su ...を思い出す Ⓒ: I recognized him as one of my old friends. (*Watashi wa kare ga kyuuyuu no hitori da to wakatta.*) 私は彼が旧友の一人だとわかった.
2 (admit) ... o mi⌈tomeru ...を認める Ⓥ: He did not recognize his mistake. (*Kare wa jibuñ no machigai o mitomenakatta.*) 彼は自分の間違いを認めなかった.
3 (accept) ... o mi⌈tomeru ...を認める Ⓥ; sho⌈oniñ suru 承認する Ⓘ: recognize a new government (*shiñseefu o shooniñ suru*) 新政府を承認する.

recollect *vt.* ... o o⌈moida⌉su ...を思い出す Ⓒ: I cannot recollect his name. (*Watashi wa kare no namae ga omoidasenai.*) 私は彼の名前が思い出せない.

recollection *n.* **1** (memory) ki⌈oku 記憶; o⌈moida⌉su ko⌈to⌉ 思い出すこと: I have no recollection of it. (*Watashi ni wa sono kioku wa nai.*) 私にはその記憶はない.
2 (something in one's memory) o⌈moide 思い出; tsu⌈ioku 追憶: happy recollections (*tanoshii omoide*) 楽しい思い出.

recommend *vt.* **1** (praise) ... o su⌈sumeru ...を勧める Ⓥ; o⌈shieru 教える Ⓥ; su⌈iseñ suru 推薦する Ⓘ: The teacher recommended the dictionary to us. (*Señsee wa sono jisho o watashi-tachi ni susumeta.*) 先生はその辞書を私たちに勧めた. / Can you recommend a good restaurant near here? (*Kono chikaku no yoi resutorañ o oshiete kudasai.*) この近くのよいレストランを教えてください. / I recommended him for the job. (*Watashi wa kare o sono shigoto ni suiseñ shita.*) 私は彼をその仕事に推薦した.
2 (advise) ⟨verb⟩ yo⌉o ni su⌈sumeru ...ように勧める Ⓥ; chu⌈ukoku suru 忠告する Ⓘ: The doctor recommended that he should give up smoking. (*Isha wa kare ni tabako o yameru yoo ni susumeta.*) 医者は彼にたばこをやめるように勧めた.

recommendation *n.* **1** (advice) su⌈iseñ 推薦; su⌈sume 勧め: a letter of recommendation (*suiseñjoo*) 推薦状 / I bought this car on his recommendation. (*Watashi wa kare no susume de kono kuruma o katta.*) 私は彼の勧めでこの車を買った.
2 (written statement) su⌈iseñjoo 推薦状: write a recommendation (*suiseñjoo o kaku*) 推薦状を書く.

reconcile *vt.* **1** (make friendly) na⌈kana⌉ori saseru 仲直りさせる Ⓥ: The couple are completely reconciled. (*Futari wa kañzeñ ni nakanaori shita.*) 二人は完全に仲直りした.
2 (harmonize) ... o cho⌈owa saseru ...を調和させる Ⓥ; i⌈tchi saseru 一致させる Ⓥ: reconcile one's ideal with reality (*risoo to geñjitsu o itchi saseru*) 理想と現実を一致させる.

reconfirm *vt.* ... o sa⌈ika⌉kuniñ suru ...を再確認する Ⓘ: I'd like to reconfirm a reservation. (*Yoyaku o saikakuniñ shitai no desu ga.*) 予約を再確認したいのですが.

reconstruct *vt.* ... o sa⌈ikeñ suru ...を再建する Ⓘ: reconstruct an old temple (*furui tera o saikeñ suru*) 古い寺を再建する.

reconstruction *n.* sa⌈ikeñ 再建: reconstruction of a bridge (*hashi no saikeñ*) 橋の再建 / reconstruction of the economy (*keezai no saikeñ*) 経済の再建.

record *vt.* **1** (write down) ... o ki⌈roku suru ...を記録する Ⓘ; ka⌈kitomeru 書き留める Ⓥ: record an event in a diary (*dekigoto o nikki ni kiroku suru*) 出来事を日記に記録する.
2 (set down on a disk or tape) ... o ro⌈kuoñ suru ...を録音する Ⓘ: I re-

r

corded his speech on tape. (*Watashi wa kare no eñzetsu o teepu ni rokuoñ shita.*) 私は彼の演説をテープに録音した.

— *n.* **1** (written report) ki⌈roku 記録: I kept a record of everything discussed. (*Tooroñ sareta koto wa subete kiroku ni totta.*) 討論されたことはすべて記録に取った.

2 (best performance) ki⌈roku 記録: break the world record (*sekai-kiroku o yaburu*) 世界記録を破る.

3 (collected facts) ke⌈ereki 経歴; se⌈eseki 成績: The child has a good school record. (*Sono ko wa gakkoo no seeseki ga yoi.*) その子は学校の成績がよい.

4 (disk) re⌈ko⌉odo レコード: play a record (*rekoodo o kakeru*) レコードをかける.

recording *n.* (radio) ro⌈kuoñ 録音; (TV) ro⌈kuga 録画: make a recording of music on tape (*oñgaku o teepu ni rokuoñ suru*) 音楽をテープに録音する.

recover *vt.* (get back) ... o to⌈rimodo⌉su …を取り戻す Ⓒ: The police recovered the stolen jewelry. (*Keesatsu wa nusumareta hooseki o torimodoshita.*) 警察は盗まれた宝石を取り戻した.

— *vi.* (return to a normal condition) ka⌈ifuku suru 回復する Ⓘ: The patient recovered quickly. (*Kañja wa sugu ni kaifuku shita.*) 患者はすぐに回復した.

recovery *n.* ka⌈ifuku 回復; ka⌈ishuu 回収: an economic recovery (*keezai no kaifuku*) 経済の回復 / the recovery of stolen jewels (*nusumareta hooseki no kaishuu*) 盗まれた宝石の回収.

recreation *n.* ki⌈barashi 気晴らし; go⌈raku 娯楽; re⌈kurie⌉eshoñ レクリエーション: My favorite recreation is fishing. (*Watashi no ichibañ no kibarashi wa tsuri desu.*) 私のいちばんの気晴らしは釣りです. / a recreation ground (*yuueñchi*) 遊園地

recruit *n.* **1** (new member) shi⌈ñ-ka⌉iiñ 新会員; shi⌈ñjiñ 新人.

2 (soldier) shi⌉ñpee 新兵.

— *vt.* ... o bo⌈shuu suru …を募集する Ⓘ: recruit new employees (*shiñnyuu shaiñ o boshuu suru*) 新入社員を募集する.

rectangle *n.* ku⌈kee 矩形; cho⌈oho⌉okee 長方形.

red *adj.* a⌈kai 赤い; a⌈kairo no 赤色の: a red rose (*akai bara*) 赤いばら / a red traffic light (*akashiñgoo*) 赤信号 / He turned red with anger. (*Kare wa okotte akaku natta.*) 彼は怒って赤くなった.

— *n.* a⌉ka 赤.

be in the red *vi.* a⌈kaji o da⌉shite iru 赤字を出している Ⓥ.

redeem *vt.* ... o to⌈rimodo⌉su …を取り戻す Ⓒ; ka⌈ifuku suru 回復する Ⓘ: redeem a mortgage (*teetoo o torimodosu*) 抵当を取り戻す.

reduce *vt.* ... o he⌈rasu …を減らす Ⓒ; su⌈ku⌉naku suru 少なくする Ⓘ: reduce one's weight (*taijuu o herasu*) 体重を減らす / reduce a price (*nedañ o sageru*) 値段を下げる / reduce speed (*supiido o otosu*) スピードを落とす.

reduction *n.* **1** (making less) ge⌈ñshoo 減少: tax reduction (*geñzee*) 減税.

2 (discount) wa⌈ribiki 割引: I bought this sweater at a reduction of 10 percent. (*Watashi wa kono seetaa o ichi-waribiki de katta.*) 私はこのセーターを1割引きで買った.

refer *vi.* **1** (look for information) (... o) sa⌈ñshoo suru (…を)参照する Ⓘ: refer to a book (*hoñ o sañshoo suru*) 本を参照する.

2 (mention) (... o) ku⌈chi ni da⌉su (…を)口に出す Ⓒ: He often refers to his mother. (*Kare wa yoku hahaoya no koto o kuchi ni dasu.*) 彼はよく母親のことを口に出す.

3 (concern) (... ni) te⌈kiyoo sareru (…に)適用される Ⓥ: This rule refers only to students. (*Kono kisoku wa gakusee dake ni tekiyoo sareru.*) この規則は学生だけに適用される.

— *vt.* **1** (send) ... o i⌈kaseru …を行かせる Ⓥ: I referred him to a doctor. (*Watashi wa kare o isha ni ikaseta.*) 私は彼を医者に行かせた.
2 (assign) ... o ma⌈kase⌉ru …を任せる Ⓥ: They referred the problem to the committee. (*Kare-ra wa sono moñdai o iiñkai ni makaseta.*) 彼らはその問題を委員会に任せた.

referee *n.* re⌉ferii レフェリー; shi⌈ñ-pañ 審判; shi⌈ñpa⌉ñiñ 審判員.
★ 'Judge' and 'umpire' are also called '*shiñpañ*(*iñ*).'

reference *n.* **1** (mentioning) fu⌈reru koto⌉ 触れること: He made no reference to the accident. (*Kare wa sono jiko ni furenakatta.*) 彼はその事故に触れなかった.
2 (consulting) sa⌈ñshoo 参照; sa⌈ñ-koo 参考: He keeps a dictionary on his desk for easy reference. (*Kare wa sugu sañshoo dekiru yoo ni jisho o tsukue no ue ni oite iru.*) 彼はすぐ参照できるように辞書を机の上に置いている.
3 (note about one's character) ji⌉ñ-butsu sho⌈omeesho 人物証明書; su⌈iseñjoo 推薦状: an excellent reference from a former employer (*mae no yatoinushi kara no rippa na suiseñjoo*) 前の雇い主からのりっぱな推薦状.

refine *vt.* **1** (make pure) ... o se⌈e-see suru …を精製する Ⓘ: refine sugar (*satoo o seesee suru*) 砂糖を精製する.
2 (polish) ... o jo⌈ohi⌉ñ ni suru …を上品にする Ⓘ: refine one's language (*kotobazukai o joohiñ ni suru*) 言葉遣いを上品にする.

refined *adj.* **1** (polished) se⌈ñreñ sareta 洗練された; jo⌈ohi⌉ñ na 上品な: refined manners (*joohiñ na monogoshi*) 上品な物腰.
2 (purified) se⌈esee shita 精製した: refined sugar (*seeseetoo*) 精製糖.

refinement *n.* **1** (good manners) jo⌈ohi⌉ñ 上品; se⌈ñreñ 洗練: a lady of refinement (*joohiñ na fujiñ*) 上品な婦人.
2 (refining) se⌈esee 精製: the refinement of oil (*sekiyu no seesee*) 石油の精製.

reflect *vt.* **1** (throw back) ... o ha⌈ñsha suru …を反射する Ⓘ: The white sand reflects heat. (*Shiroi suna wa netsu o hañsha suru.*) 白い砂は熱を反射する.
2 (give back an image) ... o u⌈tsu⌉su …を映す Ⓒ: White clouds are reflected on the lake. (*Shiroi kumo ga mizuumi ni utsutte iru.*) 白い雲が湖に映っている.
3 (express) ... o a⌈rawa⌉su …を表す Ⓒ: His clothes reflect his good taste. (*Kare no fuku wa kare no yoi shumi o arawashite iru.*) 彼の服は彼のよい趣味を表している.
4 (think carefully) ... o ha⌈ñsee suru …を反省する Ⓘ: reflect one's past errors (*kako no ayamachi o hañsee suru*) 過去の過ちを反省する.
— *vi.* **1** (give back) ha⌈ñsha suru 反射する Ⓘ; u⌈tsu⌉su 映す Ⓒ: Light reflected on the roof. (*Hikari ga yane de hañsha shite ita.*) 光が屋根で反射していた.
2 (consider) yo⌉ku ka⌈ñga⌉eru よく考える Ⓥ: reflect on what to do (*nani o suru ka yoku kañgaeru*) 何をするかよく考える.

reflection *n.* **1** (image) e⌈ezoo 映像; u⌈tsu⌉tta sugata 映った姿: look at one's reflection in the mirror (*kagami ni utsutta jibuñ no sugata o miru*) 鏡に映った自分の姿を見る.
2 (reflecting) ha⌈ñsha 反射: the reflection of light (*hikari no hañsha*) 光の反射.
3 (consideration) yo⌉ku ka⌈ñga⌉eru ko⌈to⌉ よく考えること; ha⌈ñsee 反省: He has bought it without much reflection. (*Kare wa yoku kañgaenai de sore o katte shimatta.*) 彼はよく考えないでそれを買ってしまった.

reform *vt.* **1** (improve) ... o ka⌈i-kaku suru …を改革する Ⓘ; ka⌈isee suru 改正する Ⓘ: reform the tax system (*zeesee o kaisee suru*) 税制

を改正する.

2 (make better) ... o ka⌉ishiñ saseru ...を改心させる Ⓥ; kyo⌈osee suru 矯正する Ⓘ: reform a criminal (*hañzaisha o kaishiñ saseru*) 犯罪者を改心させる.

— *vi.* (become better) ka⌉ishiñ suru 改心する Ⓘ.

— *n.* ka⌈ikaku 改革; ka⌈izeñ 改善: social reforms (*shakai-kaikaku*) 社会改革.

refrain *vi.* (... o) tsu⌈tsushi⌉mu (...を)慎む Ⓒ; e⌈ñryo suru 遠慮する Ⓘ: Please refrain from smoking. (*Tabako wa go-eñryo kudasai.*) たばこはご遠慮ください.

refresh *vt.* **1** (give energy) ... o sa⌈wa⌉yaka ni suru ...をさわやかにする Ⓘ; ge⌈ñki-zuke⌉ru 元気づける Ⓥ: I felt refreshed after a short nap. (*Sukoshi netara kibuñ ga sawayaka ni natta.*) 少し寝たら気分がさわやかになった.

2 (make fresh) ... o a⌉rata ni suru ...を新たにする Ⓘ: refresh one's memory (*kioku o arata ni suru*) 記憶を新たにする.

refreshment *n.* **1** (food and drink) ka⌈rui shokuji 軽い食事; cha⌈ga⌉shi 茶菓子: serve refreshments at a party (*paatii de karui shokuji o dasu*) パーティーで軽い食事を出す.

2 (time to recover) kyu⌈uyoo 休養; ge⌉ñki ka⌈ifuku 元気回復: You need some refreshment. (*Anata wa sukoshi kyuuyoo o toru hitsuyoo ga arimasu.*) あなたは少し休養をとる必要があります.

refrigerator *n.* re⌈ezo⌉oko 冷蔵庫: Meat should be kept in the refrigerator. (*Niku wa reezooko ni irete okanakereba narimaseñ.*) 肉は冷蔵庫に入れておかなければなりません.

refugee *n.* na⌈ñmiñ 難民; hi⌈na⌉ñsha 避難者.

refund *vt.* ... o ha⌈raimodo⌉su ...を払い戻す Ⓒ; ka⌉esu 返す Ⓒ: He refunded the money to me. (*Kare wa watashi ni sono o-kane o kaeshite kureta.*) 彼は私にそのお金を返してくれた.

refusal *n.* kyo⌈zetsu 拒絶; kyo⌉hi 拒否: He gave me a flat refusal. (*Kare wa watashi ni kippari to kotowatta.*) 彼は私にきっぱりと断った.

refuse *vt.* ... o ko⌈towa⌉ru ...を断る Ⓒ; kyo⌈zetsu suru 拒絶する Ⓘ; kyo⌉hi suru 拒否する Ⓘ: He refused our offer. (*Kare wa wareware no mooshide o kotowatta.*) 彼はわれわれの申し出を断った. / refuse a request (*yookyuu o kyozetsu suru*) 要求を拒絶する.

— *vi.* ko⌈towa⌉ru 断る Ⓒ.

regard *vt.* **1** (consider) ... to ka⌈ñga⌉eru ...と考える Ⓥ: I regard the situation as serious. (*Watashi wa jitai wa juudai da to kañgaete iru.*) 私は事態は重大だと考えている.

2 (pay attention) ... ni chu⌉ui o ha⌈ra⌉u ...に注意を払う Ⓒ: He did not regard our warning. (*Kare wa watashi-tachi no keekoku ni chuui o harawanakatta.*) 彼は私たちの警告に注意を払わなかった.

3 (respect) ... o so⌈ñchoo suru ...を尊重する Ⓘ: regard the rights of others (*hoka no hito no keñri o sonchoo suru*) ほかの人の権利を尊重する.

— *n.* **1** (attention) chu⌉ui 注意; ka⌈ñshiñ 関心: He pays no regard to his safety. (*Kare wa añzeñ ni chuui o harawanai.*) 彼は安全に注意を払わない.

2 (respect) so⌈ñkee 尊敬; ke⌉ei 敬意: I have high regard for my teacher. (*Watashi wa señsee o taiheñ soñkee shite imasu.*) 私は先生を大変尊敬しています.

regarding *prep.* ... ni ka⌉ñshite (wa) ...に関して(は): Have you any suggestions regarding this problem? (*Kono moñdai ni kañshite nani ka teeañ wa arimasu ka?*) この問題に関して何か提案はありますか.

regime *n.* se⌈ekeñ 政権: a military regime (*guñji-seekeñ*) 軍事政権.

region *n.* **1** (area) chi⌈ho⌉o 地方; (district) chi⌉iki 地域; chi⌉tai 地帯:

r

tropical regions (*nettai chihoo*) 熱帯地方 / an industrial region (*koogyoo chitai*) 工業地帯.
2 (part of the body) bu'i 部位; a'tari あたり: I have a pain in the region of my stomach. (*I no atari ga itai.*) 胃のあたりが痛い.

register *vt.* **1** (enter) ... o to'oroku suru …を登録する [I]; to'doke'ru 届ける [V]: register the names of members (*kaiiñ no namae o tooroku suru*) 会員の名前を登録する / register a birth (*shusshoo* [*shussee*] *o todokeru*) 出生を届ける.
2 (record) ... o ki'roku suru …を記録する [I]; sa'su 指す [C]: The thermometer registered minus 5 degrees. (*Oñdokee wa mainasu godo o sashite ita.*) 温度計はマイナス5度を指していた.
3 (of mail) ... o ka'kitome ni suru …を書留にする [I]: Please register this letter. (*Kono tegami o kakitome ni shite kudasai.*) この手紙を書留にしてください.
— *vi.* (... ni) to'oroku suru (…に)登録する [I]; ki'mee suru 記名する [I]: register at a hotel (*hoteru no shukuhakusha-meebo ni kimee suru*) ホテルの宿泊者名簿に記名する.
— *n.* **1** (list) to'oroku'bo 登録簿; me'ebo 名簿: the register of voters (*señkyoniñ meebo*) 選挙人名簿.
2 (device) ji'doo-kiroku'ki 自動記録器: a cash register (*kiñseñ toorokuki*) 金銭登録器.

registration *n.* to'oroku 登録: a registration number (*tooroku-bañgoo*) 登録番号 / a registration card (*shukuhakusha kaado*) 宿泊者カード.

regret *vt.* **1** (feel sorry) ... o za'ñne'ñ ni o'mo'u …を残念に思う [C]: I regret that you have to resign. (*Anata ga taishoku shinakereba naranai no o zañneñ ni omoimasu.*) あなたが退職しなければならないのを残念に思います.
2 (remember with remorse) ... o ko'okai suru …を後悔する [I]: You will regret what you have done. (*Anata wa shita koto o kookai suru deshoo.*) あなたはしたことを後悔するでしょう.
— *n.* za'ñne'ñ 残念; ko'okai 後悔: a matter for regret (*zañneñ na koto*) 残念なこと / I feel regret for having been unkind to her. (*Kanojo ni taishite fushiñsetsu datta koto o kookai shite imasu.*) 彼女に対して不親切だったことを後悔しています.

regular *adj.* **1** (usual) te'eki-teki na 定期的な: a regular meeting (*teeki-teki na atsumari*) 定期的な集まり / a regular holiday (*teekyuubi*) 定休日 / a regular flight (*teekibiñ*) 定期便.
2 (steady) ki'soku-teki na 規則的な: lead a regular life (*kisoku tadashii seekatsu o suru*) 規則正しい生活をする.
3 (balanced) to'tono'tta 整った: have regular features (*totonotta kao o shite iru*) 整った顔をしている.
4 (formal) se'eshiki no 正式の: a regular player (*see-señshu*) 正選手.
— *n.* se'ekai'iñ 正会員; re'gyuraa レギュラー.

regularly *adv.* te'eki-teki ni 定期的に; ki'soku-teki ni 規則的に: We meet regularly once a month. (*Watashi-tachi wa tsuki ni ichi-do kimatte kaigoo o hirakimasu.*) 私たちは月に一度きまって会合を開きます.

regulate *vt.* **1** (control) ... o ki'see suru …を規制する [I]; to'rishima'ru 取り締まる [C]: regulate air pollution (*taiki oseñ o kisee suru*) 大気汚染を規制する.
2 (adjust) ... o cho'osetsu suru …を調節する [I]: regulate the room temperature (*shitsuoñ o choosetsu suru*) 室温を調節する.

regulation *n.* **1** (rule) ki'soku 規則; ki'tee 規定: traffic regulations (*kootsuu kisoku*) 交通規則.
2 (regulating) ki'see 規制: the regulation of prices (*bukka no kisee*) 物価の規制.
3 (adjustment) cho'osetsu 調節:

the regulation of temperature (*oñdo no choosetsu*) 温度の調節.

rehearsal *n.* ke'eko けいこ; re'ñshuu 練習; ri'ha'asaru リハーサル: hold a rehearsal (*rihaasaru o suru*) リハーサルをする.

reign *n.* chi'see 治世; ku'ñriñ 君臨: The king's reign lasted a long time. (*Sono oo no chisee wa nagaku tsuzuita.*) その王の治世は長く続いた.
— *vi.* ku'ñriñ suru 君臨する [I]; to'ochi suru 統治する [I].

reinforce *vt.* ... o ho'kyoo suru ... を補強する [I]; zo'okyoo suru 増強する [I]: reinforce a bridge (*hashi o hokyoo suru*) 橋を補強する / reinforce staff members (*staffu o zookyoo suru*) スタッフを増強する.

reissue *vt.* ... o sa'iha'kkoo suru ...を再発行する [I]: Can I have the certificate reissued? (*Shoomeesho o saihakkoo shite moraemasu ka?*) 証明書を再発行してもらえますか.
— *n.* sa'iha'kkoo 再発行.

reject *vt.* ... o kyo'zetsu suru ...を拒絶する [I]; ko'towa'ru 断る [C]: He rejected my proposal. (*Kare wa watashi no teeañ o kotowatta.*) 彼は私の提案を断った.

rejoice *vi.* (... o) yo'roko'bu (...を) 喜ぶ [C]; u'reshiga'ru うれしがる [C]: She rejoiced at the news. (*Kanojo wa sono shirase o yorokoñda.*) 彼女はその知らせを喜んだ.

relate *vt.* **1** (tell) ... o ha'na'su ...を話す [C]: We listened as he related his experiences. (*Watashi-tachi wa kare ga taikeñ o hanasu no o kiita.*) 私たちは彼が体験を話すのを聞いた.
2 (connect) ... o ka'ñreñzuke'ru ...を関連づける [V]: relate the two events (*sono futatsu no jikeñ o kañreñzukeru*) その二つの事件を関連づける.
— *vi.* (... ni) ka'ñkee ga a'ru (...に) 関係がある [C]: The letter relates to him. (*Sono tegami wa kare ni kañkee suru mono desu.*) その手紙は彼に関係するものです.

related *adj.* **1** (of the same family) shi'ñrui no 親類の; ke'tsueñ no 血縁の: She is not related to me. (*Kanojo wa watashi no shiñrui de wa arimaseñ.*) 彼女は私の親類ではありません.
2 (connected) ka'ñkee no a'ru 関係のある; ka'ñreñ shita 関連した: a related question (*kañreñ-shitsumoñ*) 関連質問.

relation *n.* **1** (connection) ka'ñkee 関係; ka'ñreñ 関連: Weight has a close relation to health. (*Taijuu wa keñkoo to missetsu na kañkee ga arimasu.*) 体重は健康と密接な関係があります. / business relations (*torihiki-kañkee*) 取引関係.
2 (relative) shi'ñrui 親類; shi'ñseki 親戚: Is he a relation of yours? (*Ano kata wa anata no go-shiñseki desu ka?*) あの方はあなたのご親戚ですか.

relationship *n.* ka'ñkee 関係; ka'ñreñ 関連: We have a good relationship with our neighbors. (*Watashi-tachi wa tonari no hito-tachi to yoi kañkee ni arimasu.*) 私たちは隣の人たちとよい関係にあります.

relative *adj.* hi'kaku-teki 比較的: live in relative luxury (*hikaku-teki zeetaku na seekatsu o suru*) 比較的ぜいたくな生活をする.
— *n.* (relation) ni'kushiñ 肉親; mi'uchi 身内; shi'ñseki 親戚: All his relatives attended the wedding. (*Kare no nikushiñ wa miñna kekkoñshiki ni shusseki shita.*) 彼の肉親はみんな結婚式に出席した. / She is a relative on my father's side. (*Kanojo wa watashi no chichi-kata no shiñseki desu.*) 彼女は私の父方の親戚です.

relatively *adv.* hi'kaku-teki 比較的; wa'riai 割合: It is relatively warm today. (*Kyoo wa wariai atataka desu.*) きょうはわりあい暖かです.

relax *vt.* **1** (make less tight) ... o ku'tsurogase'ru ...をくつろがせる [V]; ri'ra'kkusu saseru リラックスさせる [V]: I felt relaxed after a bath. (*Ofuro ni haittara kutsuroida kibuñ*

r

ni natta.) おふろに入ったらくつろいだ気分になった.
2 (loosen) ... o yu⌈rume⌉ru ...を緩める Ⓥ: I relaxed my grip on the rope. (*Watashi wa roopu o nigiru te o yurumeta.*) 私はロープを握る手を緩めた.
3 (make less strict) ... o ka⌈ñwa suru ...を緩和する Ⓘ: relax import regulations (*yunyuu kisee o kañwa suru*) 輸入規制を緩和する.
— *vi.* **1** (rest from work) ku⌈tsuro⌉gu くつろぐ Ⓒ: relax by going fishing (*sakanatsuri ni itte kutsurogu*) 魚釣りに行ってくつろぐ.
2 (become less severe) yu⌈ru⌉mu 緩む Ⓒ: The cold has been relaxing. (*Samusa ga yuruñde kita.*) 寒さが緩んできた.

relaxation *n.* kyu⌈uyoo 休養; ho⌈neya⌉sume 骨休め.

release *vt.* **1** (set free) ... o ha⌈na⌉su ...を放す Ⓒ; ka⌈ihoo suru 解放する Ⓘ: I released the bird from the cage. (*Watashi wa tori o kago kara hanashite yatta.*) 私は鳥をかごから放してやった.
2 (offer to the public) ... o ko⌈okai suru ...を公開する Ⓘ; (of a movie) fu⌈uki⌉ru 封切る Ⓒ; (of a record) ha⌈tsubai suru 発売する Ⓘ: The new film will be released next week. (*Sono eega wa raishuu fuukiraremasu.*) その映画は来週封切られます.
— *n.* **1** (setting free) sha⌈kuhoo 釈放; ka⌈ihoo 解放: a release from prison (*keemusho kara no shakuhoo*) 刑務所からの釈放.
2 (of news) ha⌈ppyoo 発表; (of a movie) fu⌈ukiri 封切り; (of a record) ha⌈tsubai 発売.

relevant *adj.* (related) ka⌈ñreñ shita [shite iru] 関連した[している]; (pertinent) te⌈kisetsu na 適切な: the relevant data (*kañreñ shita shiryoo*) 関連した資料 / a relevant remark (*tekisetsu na kotoba*) 適切なことば.

reliable *adj.* (dependable) shi⌈ñrai deki⌉ru 信頼できる; ta⌉shika na 確かな: a reliable person (*shiñrai dekiru hito*) 信頼できる人 / reliable information (*tashika na joohoo*) 確かな情報.

reliance *n.* shi⌈ñrai 信頼; shi⌈ñyoo 信用: put reliance on a person (*hito o shiñyoo suru*) 人を信用する.

relic *n.* i⌈butsu 遺物; i⌈seki 遺跡: relics of an ancient civilization (*kodai buñmee no iseki*) 古代文明の遺跡.

relief[1] *n.* **1** (feeling of comfort) ho⌈tto suru koto⌉ ほっとすること; a⌈ñshiñ 安心: It was a great relief to find nothing had been stolen. (*Nani mo nusumarenakatta to wakari hotto shita.*) 何も盗まれなかったとわかりほっとした.
2 (lessening of pain) ke⌈egeñ 軽減; jo⌉kyo 除去: a drug for the relief of pain (*kutsuu o keegeñ suru kusuri*) 苦痛を軽減する薬.
3 (help) kyu⌈usai 救済; kyu⌉ujo 救助: The money was used for the relief of the poor. (*Sono o-kane wa mazushii hito-tachi no kyuusai no tame ni tsukawareta.*) そのお金は貧しい人たちの救済のために使われた.

relief[2] *n.* (sculpture) u⌈kibori 浮き彫り; re⌈ri⌉ifu レリーフ.

relieve *vt.* **1** (lessen) ... o ya⌈warage⌉ru ...を和らげる Ⓥ; ra⌈ku⌉ ni suru 楽にする Ⓘ: This medicine will relieve your pain. (*Kono kusuri wa anata no itami o yawaragemasu.*) この薬はあなたの痛みを和らげます.
2 (free from worry) ... o ho⌈tto saseru ...をほっとさせる Ⓥ; a⌈ñshiñ saseru 安心させる Ⓥ: I was relieved to be back home. (*Uchi ni kaette hotto shita.*) 家に帰ってほっとした.
3 (replace) ... o ko⌈otai saseru ...を交替させる Ⓥ: I will be relieved at five. (*Watashi wa go-ji ni kootai shimasu.*) 私は5時に交替します.

religion *n.* shu⌉ukyoo 宗教; shi⌈ñkoo 信仰: What is your religion? (*Anata no shuukyoo wa nañ desu ka?*) あなたの宗教は何ですか.

r

religious *adj.* shu⌉ukyoo no 宗教の; shi⌈ñkoo no 信仰の: religious freedom (*shiñkoo no jiyuu*) 信仰の自由.

relish *n.* (of food) a⌈jiwai 味わい; (liking) ko⌈nomi 好み: She drank the wine with relish. (*Kanojo wa sono waiñ o oishisoo ni noñda.*) 彼女はそのワインをおいしそうに飲んだ.

reluctance *n.* ki ⌈ga susumanai koto⌉ 気が進まないこと; i⌈yaga⌉ru ko⌈to⌉ 嫌がること: He accepted the offer with reluctance. (*Kare wa iyaiya nagara sono mooshide ni oojita.*) 彼はいやいやながらその申し出に応じた.

reluctant *adj.* ki ⌈ga susumanai 気が進まない; i⌈yaga⌉ru 嫌がる: I am reluctant to ask for his help. (*Kare no eñjo o motomeru no wa ki ga susumanai.*) 彼の援助を求めるのは気が進まない.

rely *vi.* ta⌉nomi ni su⌈ru 頼みにする [I]; shi⌈ñrai suru 信頼する [I]: You can rely on him. (*Kare wa shiñrai dekimasu.*) 彼は信頼できます.

remain *vi.* **1** (stay) to⌈doma⌉ru とどまる [C]: He went out but I remained. (*Kare wa dekaketa ga watashi wa todomatta.*) 彼は出かけたが私はとどまった.
2 (continue to be) ... no ma⌈ma⌉ de i⌈ru ...のままでいる [V]: She remained silent for a long time. (*Kanojo wa nagai aida damatta mama de ita.*) 彼女は長い間黙ったままでいた.
3 (be left) no⌈ko⌉ru 残る [C]: The snow still remains. (*Yuki wa mada nokotte iru.*) 雪はまだ残っている.

remainder *n.* no⌈kori⌉ 残り; no⌈korimono 残り物: give the remainder of the meal to a dog (*shokuji no nokori o inu ni yaru*) 食事の残りを犬にやる.

remark *n.* **1** (comment) i⌉keñ 意見; ka⌈ñsoo 感想: He made some remarks on the work. (*Kare wa sono sakuhiñ ni tsuite ikura ka kañsoo o nobeta.*) 彼はその作品についていくらか感想を述べた.
2 (notice) chu⌈umoku 注目; chu⌉ui 注意: a novel worthy of remark (*chuumoku ni atai suru shoosetsu*) 注目に値する小説.
— *vt.* (say) ... to no⌈be⌉ru ...と述べる [V]; i⌈u 言う [C]: He remarked that she was beautiful. (*Kanojo wa bijiñ da to kare wa itta.*) 彼女は美人だと彼は言った.

remarkable *adj.* chu⌈umoku su be⌉ki 注目すべき; i⌈chijirushi⌉i 著しい: a remarkable event (*chuumoku su beki jikeñ*) 注目すべき事件 / make remarkable progress (*ichijirushii shiñpo o suru*) 著しい進歩をする.

remedy *n.* **1** (cure) chi⌈ryoohoo 治療法; ryo⌈ohoo 療法: Is there any good remedy for colds? (*Kaze ni yoi chiryoohoo wa arimasu ka?*) かぜによい治療法はありますか.
2 (means of correcting) ka⌈ize⌉ñsaku 改善策; kyo⌈oseehoo 矯正法: a remedy for unemployment (*shitsugyoo no kaizeñsaku*) 失業の改善策.
— *vt.* (put to right) ... o kyo⌈osee suru ...を矯正する [I]; ka⌈izeñ suru 改善する [I]: remedy a deficiency (*kekkañ o kyoosee suru*) 欠陥を矯正する.

remember *vt.* **1** (keep in the mind) ... o o⌈bo⌉ete iru ...を覚えている [V]; ki⌈oku shite iru 記憶している [V]: I don't remember his name. (*Watashi wa kare no namae o oboete imaseñ.*) 私は彼の名前を覚えていません.
2 (recall) ... o o⌈moida⌉su ...を思い出す [C]: I cannot remember where I met him. (*Doko de kare ni atta ka omoidasenai.*) どこで彼に会ったか思い出せない.
3 (take care not to forget) wa⌈surena⌉ide <verb> 忘れないで...: I'll remember to mail this letter. (*Kono tegami o wasurenaide dashimasu.*) この手紙を忘れないで出します.
— *vi.* o⌈moida⌉su 思い出す [C]; ki⌈oku suru 記憶する [I]: If I remember rightly, he is a graduate of this

r

school. (*Watashi no kioku ni machigai nakereba, kare wa koko no gakkoo no sotsugyoosee da.*) 私の記憶に間違いなければ，彼はここの学校の卒業生だ.

remembrance *n.* ki⌈oku 記憶; o⌈moide 思い出: I have no remembrance of the accident. (*Sono jiko wa kioku ga nai.*) その事故は記憶がない. / I have many good remembrances of my schooldays. (*Watashi wa gakusee-jidai no yoi omoide ga takusañ aru.*) 私は学生時代のよい思い出がたくさんある.

remind *vt.* **1** (make remember) ... ni (... o) o⌈moidasase⌉ru ...に(...を)思い出させる Ⓥ: This picture reminds me of my home town. (*Kono e wa watashi ni furusato o omoidasaseru.*) この絵は私にふるさとを思い出させる.
2 (make think of) ... ni (... o) ki⌈zukase⌉ru ...に(...を)気づかせる Ⓥ; chu⌉ui suru 注意する Ⓘ: Please remind me to take my medicine. (*Kusuri o nomu yoo ni watashi ni chuui shite kudasai.*) 薬を飲むように私に注意してください.

remorse *n.* ko⌉okai 後悔; ryo⌉oshiñ no ka⌈shaku 良心のかしゃく: I feel remorse for what I have done. (*Watashi wa shita koto o kookai shite iru.*) 私はしたことを後悔している.

remote *adj.* **1** (of a place) to⌈oku hana⌉reta 遠く離れた; he⌉ñpi na へんぴな: a remote village (*heñpi na mura*) へんぴな村.
2 (of time) to⌈oi 遠い: the remote past (*tooi mukashi*) 遠い昔.
3 (not closely related) ka⌈ñkee no usui 関係の薄い; to⌈oi 遠い: remote relatives (*tooi shiñrui*) 遠い親類.
4 (slight) ka⌉suka na かすかな: a remote chance (*kasuka na chañsu*) かすかなチャンス.

removal *n.* **1** (moving) i⌈doo 移動; i⌈teñ 移転: removal to a new office (*atarashii jimusho e no iteñ*) 新しい事務所への移転.
2 (taking away) jo⌉kyo 除去.

remove *vt.* **1** (get rid of) ... o to⌈rinozoku ...を取り除く Ⓒ: remove the snow on a street (*toori no yuki o torinozoku*) 通りの雪を取り除く.
2 (take off) ... o nu⌉gu ...を脱ぐ Ⓒ: remove one's hat and coat (*booshi to kooto o nugu*) 帽子とコートを脱ぐ.
3 (dismiss) ... o me⌈ñshoku suru ...を免職する Ⓘ: He was removed from office. (*Kare wa meñshoku sareta.*) 彼は免職された. / be removed from school (*taigaku saserareru*) 退学させられる.
— *vi.* (move house) hi⌈kko⌉su 引っ越す Ⓒ: remove from Tokyo to Yokohama (*Tookyoo kara Yokohama e hikkosu*) 東京から横浜へ引っ越す.

render *vt.* **1** (give) ... o a⌈taeru ...を与える Ⓥ: Nobody rendered him help. (*Dare mo kare ni eñjo o ataenakatta.*) だれも彼に援助を与えなかった.
2 (make) ... o ... ni su⌈ru ...を...にする Ⓘ: render a contract invalid (*keeyaku o mukoo ni suru*) 契約を無効にする.
3 (perform) ... o e⌈ñjiru ...を演じる Ⓥ: render the part of Hamlet (*Hamuretto no yaku o eñjiru*) ハムレットの役を演じる.

renew *vt.* **1** (begin again) ... o sa⌈ikai suru ...を再開する Ⓘ: renew negotiations (*kooshoo o saikai suru*) 交渉を再開する.
2 (make new) ... o a⌈tarashi⌉ku suru ...を新しくする Ⓘ: I renewed the door by painting it. (*Watashi wa doa ni peñki o nutte atarashiku shita.*) 私はドアにペンキを塗って新しくした.
3 (replace) ... o ko⌈oshiñ suru ...を更新する Ⓘ: renew a driver's license (*uñteñ meñkyoshoo o kooshiñ suru*) 運転免許証を更新する.

rent *n.* chi⌈ñta⌉iryoo 賃貸料; (of a house) ya⌉chiñ 家賃; (of a room) he⌈yadai 部屋代; (of land) chi⌉[ji⌉]dai 地代: How much is the rent for this house? (*Koko no yachiñ* *wa ikura desu ka?*) ここの家賃はいくらですか.

— *vt.* **1** (pay) ... o chi˹ñgari suru ...を賃借りする [I]; ka˹riru 借りる [V]: I'd like to rent a car. (*Kuruma o ichi-dai karitai no desu ga.*) 車を一台借りたいのですが.

2 (receive) ... o chi˹ñgashi suru ...を賃貸しする [I]; ka˹su 貸す [C]: She rents a room to a student. (*Kanojo wa gakusee ni heya o kashite iru.*) 彼女は学生に部屋を貸している.

rent-a-car *n.* re˹ñta˺kaa レンタカー: Can I reserve a rent-a-car here? (*Koko de reñtakaa o yoyaku dekimasu ka?*) ここでレンタカーを予約できますか.

repair *vt.* **1** (mend) ... o shu˺uri suru ...を修理する [I]; (of a part) shu˹uzeñ suru 修繕する [I]: Can you repair this camera? (*Kono kamera o shuuri dekimasu ka?*) このカメラを修理できますか. / I repaired the roof. (*Watashi wa yane o shuuzeñ shita.*) 私は屋根を修繕した.

2 (correct) ... o ta˹da˺su ...を正す [C]: repair a mistake (*ayamari o tadasu*) 誤りを正す.

— *n.* **1** (reparing) shu˺uri 修理; shu˹uzeñ 修繕: The bridge is under repair. (*Hashi wa shuurichuu desu.*) 橋は修理中です. / make repairs on a house (*ie o shuuzeñ suru*) 家を修繕する.

2 (condition) te˹ire˺ no jo˹otai 手入れの状態: The car is in good repair. (*Kuruma wa teire ga yukitodoite iru.*) 車は手入れが行き届いている.

repay *vt.* **1** (pay back) ... o he˹ñsai suru ...を返済する [I]; ka˺esu 返す [C]: I repaid him the money. (*Watashi wa kare ni sono o-kane o kaeshita.*) 私は彼にそのお金を返した.

2 (reward) ... ni mu˹kui˺ru ...に報いる [V]; o˹ñga˺eshi suru 恩返しする [I]: repay a person's kindness (*hito no shiñsetsu ni mukuiru*) 人の親切に報いる / How can I ever repay you? (*Anata ni doo yatte oñgaeshi o shite ii ka wakarimaseñ.*) あなたにどうやって恩返しをしていいかわかりません.

repeat *vt.* **1** (say again) ... o ku˹rika˺eshite i˹u ...を繰り返して言う [C]; mo˹o ichido iu もう一度言う [C]: Could you repeat that? (*Moo ichido itte itadakemaseñ ka?*) もう一度言っていただけませんか.

2 (do again) ... o ku˹rika˺esu ...を繰り返す [C]: Don't repeat the same error. (*Onaji machigai o kurikaeshite wa ikenai.*) 同じ間違いを繰り返してはいけない.

3 (recite) ... o a˹ñshoo suru ...を暗唱する [I]: repeat a poem (*shi o añshoo suru*) 詩を暗唱する.

— *vi.* (say again) ku˹rika˺eshite i˹u 繰り返して言う [C]; ku˹rika˺esu 繰り返す [C]: Please repeat after me. (*Ato ni tsuite kurikaeshite itte kudasai.*) 後について繰り返して言ってください.

repent *vi.* ko˺okai suru 後悔する [I]: He repented and changed his ways. (*Kare wa kookai shite okonai o aratameta.*) 彼は後悔して行いを改めた.

— *vt.* ... o ko˺okai suru ...を後悔する [I]; ku˹ya˺mu 悔やむ [C]: He repented having said no. (*Kare wa kotowatta koto o kookai shita.*) 彼は断ったことを後悔した.

repetition *n.* ku˹rikaeshi 繰り返し; ha˹ñpuku 反復: Repetition is important in learning a language. (*Kotoba o narau ni wa hañpuku ga juuyoo desu.*) 言葉を習うには反復が重要です.

replace *vt.* **1** (put back) mo˺to no to˹koro˺ ni o˹ku 元の所に置く [C]; mo˹do˺su 戻す [C]: replace a book on the shelf (*hoñ o tana ni modosu*) 本を棚に戻す.

2 (change) ... o to˹rikaeru ...を取り替える [V]; ko˹okañ suru 交換する [I]: replace a worn tire (*hetta taiya o torikaeru*) 減ったタイヤを取り替える.

3 (take the place of) ... ni to˺ttekawaru ...に取って代わる [C]; ... no a˺to o tsu˹gu ...の後を継ぐ [C]: Mr. Aoki replaced Mr. Yamada as our company president. (*Aoki-shi ga Ya-*

mada-shi no ato o tsuide wareware no shachoo ni natta.) 青木氏が山田氏の後を継いでわれわれの社長になった.

reply *vi.* (... ni) he⌈ñji⌉ o suru (...に) 返事をする [I]; ko⌈tae⌉ru 答える [V]: I replied to his letter at once. (*Watashi wa kare no tegami ni sugu ni heñji o shita.*) 私は彼の手紙にすぐに返事をした.

— *vt.* ... to ko⌈tae⌉ru ...と答える [V]: He replied that he knew nothing about it. (*Kare wa sore ni tsuite nani mo shiranai to kotaeta.*) 彼はそれについて何も知らないと答えた.

— *n.* he⌈ñji⌉ 返事; ko⌈ta⌉e 答え: I have received no reply from him yet. (*Kare kara mada nani mo heñji o moratte imaseñ.*) 彼からまだ何も返事をもらっていません.

report *n.* **1** (statement) ho⌈okoku 報告; (written form) ho⌈okokusho 報告書; sho⌈omeesho 証明書: a police report on the accident (*keesatsu no jiko hookokusho*) 警察の事故報告書 / Please make out a theft report. (*Toonañ shoomeesho o tsukutte kudasai.*) 盗難証明書を作ってください.

2 (piece of news) ho⌈odoo 報道; ki⌉ji 記事: a newspaper report (*shiñbuñ kiji*) 新聞記事.

3 (school report) se⌈esekihyoo 成績表; tsu⌈uchihyoo 通知表.

4 (of an explosion) ba⌈kuhatsu⌉oñ 爆発音; (of a shot) ju⌈usee 銃声.

— *vt.* **1** (give a statement) ... o ho⌈okoku suru ...を報告する [I]: He reported the results of the election at the meeting. (*Kare wa señkyo no kekka o kai de hookoku shita.*) 彼は選挙の結果を会で報告した.

2 (give an account) ... o ho⌈odoo suru ...を報道する [I]; ho⌈ojiru 報じる [V]: It is reported that a ship is missing. (*Fune ga is-seki yukuefumee da to hoojirarete iru.*) 船が1隻行方不明だと報じられている.

3 (notify) ... o to⌈dokede⌉ru ...を届け出る [V]; shi⌈ñkoku suru 申告する [I]: I reported the accident to the police. (*Watashi wa sono jiko o keesatsu ni todoketa.*) 私はその事故を警察に届けた.

— *vi.* **1** (make a statement) ho⌈okoku suru 報告する [I]: He reported on the conference. (*Kare wa sono kaigi ni tsuite hookoku shita.*) 彼はその会議について報告した.

2 (appear) shu⌈ttoo suru 出頭する [I]: He was told to report to the police. (*Kare wa keesatsu ni shuttoo suru yoo ni iwareta.*) 彼は警察に出頭するように言われた.

reporter *n.* shu⌈zai ki⌉sha 取材記者; (of a newspaper) shi⌈ñbuñ ki⌉sha 新聞記者; re⌈po⌉otaa レポーター.

represent *vt.* **1** (act for) ... o da⌈ihyoo suru ...を代表する [I]: We chose committee members to represent us. (*Watashi-tachi wa watashi-tachi o daihyoo suru iiñ o erañda.*) 私たちは私たちを代表する委員を選んだ.

2 (stand for) ... o a⌈rawa⌉su ...を表す [C]: The blue lines on the map represent rivers. (*Chizu no aoi señ wa kawa o arawashimasu.*) 地図の青い線は川を表します.

3 (show) ... o e⌈ga⌉ku ...を描く [C]: This painting represents a storm at sea. (*Kono e wa umi no arashi o egaite imasu.*) この絵は海の嵐を描いています.

4 (be an example of) ... no te⌈ñkee o shime⌉su ...の典型を示す [C]: He represents the Japanese businessman. (*Kare wa Nihoñjiñ no jitsugyooka no teñkee o shimeshite iru.*) 彼は日本人の実業家の典型を示している.

representation *n.* hyo⌈oge⌉ñ 表現; byo⌈osha 描写: This novel provides a vivid representation of rural life. (*Kono shoosetsu wa inaka no seekatsu o iki-iki to byoosha shite iru.*) この小説は田舎の生活を生き生きと描写している.

representative *n.* **1** (person acting for others) da⌈ihyoo 代表: We sent a representative to the meeting. (*Wareware wa sono*

shuukai ni daihyoo o okutta.) われわれはその集会に代表を送った.
2 (member of the House of Representatives) da⌈igi⌉shi 代議士: a representative from Tokyo (*Tookyoo señshutsu no daigishi*) 東京選出の代議士.
— *adj.* **1** (representing) da⌈ihyoo suru 代表する: a representative body (*daihyoodañ*) 代表団.
2 (typical) da⌈ihyoo-teki na 代表的な; te⌈ñkee-teki na 典型的な: This is one of the buildings representative of modern architecture. (*Kore wa kiñdai keñchiku no daihyoo-teki na tatemono no hitotsu desu.*) これは近代建築の代表的な建物のひとつです.

reprimand *vt.* ... o shi⌈sseki suru ...を叱責する Ⓘ; shi⌈karu しかる Ⓒ: He was reprimanded for his negligence in his job. (*Kare wa shokumu taimañ o shisseki sareta.*) 彼は職務怠慢を叱責された.
— *n.* shi⌈sseki 叱責; cho⌈okai 懲戒.

reproach *vt.* (scold) ... o shi⌈karu ...をしかる Ⓒ; (blame) hi⌉nañ suru 非難する Ⓘ: I reproached him for carelessness. (*Watashi wa kare no fuchuui o shikatta.*) 私は彼の不注意をしかった.
— *n.* (scolding) shi⌈sseki 叱責; (blaming) hi⌉nañ 非難: a look of reproach (*hinañ no kaotsuki*) 非難の顔つき.

reproduce *vt.* **1** (produce again) ... o sa⌈isee suru ...を再生する Ⓘ; sa⌈igeñ suru 再現する Ⓘ: Tape recorders reproduce sound. (*Teepu-rekoodaa wa oto o saisee suru.*) テープレコーダーは音を再生する.
2 (copy) ... o fu⌈kusee suru ...を複製する Ⓘ; fu⌈kusha suru 複写する Ⓘ: This picture was reproduced from the original. (*Kono e wa geñga o fukusee shita mono desu.*) この絵は原画を複製したものです.
— *vi.* (have offspring) ha⌈ñshoku suru 繁殖する Ⓘ: Insects reproduce by laying eggs. (*Koñchuu wa tamago o uñde hañshoku suru.*) 昆虫は卵を生んで繁殖する.

reproduction *n.* **1** (reproducing) sa⌈isee 再生; sa⌈igeñ 再現: the reproduction of sound (*oto no saisee*) 音の再生.
2 (copy) fu⌈kusha 複写; fu⌈kusee 複製: This picture is a reproduction. (*Kono e wa fukusee desu.*) この絵は複製です.

republic *n.* kyo⌈owa⌉koku 共和国: the People's Republic of China (*Chuuka jiñmiñ kyoowakoku*) 中華人民共和国.

republican *adj.* (of a country) kyo⌈owa⌉koku no 共和国の; (of a party) kyo⌈owatoo no 共和党の.
— *n.* kyo⌈owashugi⌉sha 共和主義者; kyo⌈owato⌉oiñ 共和党員.

reputation *n.* **1** (opinion) hyo⌈obañ 評判: He has a good [bad] reputation. (*Kare wa hyoobañ ga ii* [*warui*].) 彼は評判がいい[悪い].
2 (good name) me⌈esee 名声; ko⌈ohyoo 好評: The scandal damaged his reputation. (*Sono sukyañdaru wa kare no meesee o kizu tsuketa.*) そのスキャンダルは彼の名声を傷つけた.

request *n.* **1** (demand) ne⌈ga⌉i 願い; ta⌈nomi⌉ 頼み; yo⌈osee 要請: I have a request to make of you. (*Onegai ga aru no desu ga.*) お願いがあるのですが. / I bought this at her request. (*Kanojo no tanomi de kore o katta.*) 彼女の頼みでこれを買った.
2 (something asked for) ne⌈gaigoto⌉ 願い事; ri⌈kue⌉suto リクエスト: grant a request (*negaigoto o kanaeru*) 願い事をかなえる / play requests from listeners (*chooshusha kara no rikuesuto-kyoku o eñsoo suru*) 聴取者からのリクエスト曲を演奏する.
— *vt.* ... o ta⌈no⌉mu ...を頼む Ⓒ; yo⌈okyuu suru 要求する Ⓘ: I requested his help. (*Watashi wa kare no eñjo o tanoñda.*) 私は彼の援助を頼んだ.

r

require *vt.* **1** (need) ... o hi⌈tsuyoo to suru …を必要とする Ⓘ: Is there anything else you require? (*Hoka ni nani ka hitsuyoo to suru mono wa arimasu ka?*) ほかに何か必要とするものはありますか. / The roof requires repairing. (*Yane wa shuuri ga hitsuyoo da.*) 屋根は修理が必要だ.
2 (demand) ... o yo⌈okyuu suru …を要求する Ⓘ; me⌈ejiru 命じる Ⓥ: We have done all that is required of us. (*Yookyuu sareta koto wa subete yarimashita.*) 要求されたことはすべてやりました.

requirement *n.* hi⌈tsuyoo na mono⌉ 必要な物; hi⌈tsuyoojo⌉oken̄ 必要条件: This store can supply all your requirements. (*Kono mise ni wa anata ga hitsuyoo to suru mono wa subete arimasu.*) この店にはあなたが必要とする物はすべてあります.

rescue *vt.* ... o su⌈kuu …を救う Ⓒ; kyu⌉ujo suru 救助する Ⓘ: He rescued a drowning child. (*Kare wa oborekakete iru kodomo o sukutta.*) 彼はおぼれかけている子どもを救った.
— *n.* kyu⌈ushutsu 救出; kyu⌉ujo 救助: go to the rescue of a person (*hito no kyuujo ni iku*) 人の救助に行く.

research *n.* cho⌉osa 調査; ke⌈n̄kyuu 研究: carry out market research (*shijoo choosa o okonau*) 市場調査を行う / He is engaged in cancer research. (*Kare wa gan̄ no ken̄kyuu ni juuji shite iru.*) 彼はがんの研究に従事している.
— *vi.* (... o) cho⌉osa suru (…を)調査する Ⓘ; ke⌈n̄kyuu suru 研究する Ⓘ: We are researching into the problem. (*Watashi-tachi wa sono mon̄dai no choosa o shite imasu.*) 私たちはその問題の調査をしています.

resemblance *n.* ru⌈iji 類似; ni⌈te iru tokoro⌉ 似ているところ: There is little resemblance between them. (*Kare-ra ni wa nite iru tokoro ga hoton̄do nai.*) 彼らには似ているところがほとんどない.

resemble *vt.* ... ni ni⌈te iru …に似ている Ⓥ: She resembles her mother. (*Kanojo wa hahaoya ni nite iru.*) 彼女は母親に似ている.

resent *vt.* ... ni ha⌈ra⌉ o ta⌈te⌉ru …に腹を立てる Ⓥ; fu⌈n̄gai suru 憤慨する Ⓘ: He resented my remarks. (*Kare wa watashi no kotoba ni hara o tateta.*) 彼は私の言葉に腹を立てた.

resentment *n.* fu⌈n̄gai 憤慨; i⌈kidoori 憤り: I felt resentment at the way I had been treated. (*Watashi wa uketa taiguu ni fun̄gai shita.*) 私は受けた待遇に憤慨した.

reservation *n.* yo⌈yaku 予約: I'd like to make a reservation for 7:00. (*Shichi-ji ni yoyaku shite kudasai.*) 7時に予約してください. / Cancel this reservation, please. (*Kono yoyaku o torikeshite kudasai.*) この予約を取り消してください.

reserve *vt.* **1** (book) ... o yo⌈yaku suru …を予約する Ⓘ: I reserved a table at the restaurant for seven. (*Watashi wa sono resutoran̄ ni shichi-ji ni teeburu o yoyaku shita.*) 私はそのレストランに7時にテーブルを予約した.
2 (set apart) ... o to⌉tte oku …をとっておく Ⓒ: reserve Sunday for fishing (*tsuri ni nichiyoo o totte oku*) 釣りに日曜をとっておく.
— *n.* **1** (store) ta⌈kuwae 蓄え: a reserve of food (*shokuryoo no takuwae*) 食糧の蓄え.
2 (troops) yo⌈bi⌉gun̄ 予備軍.

reservoir *n.* cho⌈su⌉ichi 貯水池.

reside *vi.* su⌉mu 住む Ⓒ; kyo⌈juu suru 居住する Ⓘ: He resides in the suburbs. (*Kare wa koogai ni sun̄de iru.*) 彼は郊外に住んでいる.

residence *n.* ju⌉ukyo 住居; ju⌈utaku 住宅: take up residence in the country (*inaka ni kyo o sadameru*) 田舎に居を定める.

resident *n.* kyo⌈ju⌉usha 居住者: foreign residents (*kyoryuu gaikokujin̄*) 居留外国人.
— *adj.* kyo⌈juu suru 居住する; su⌈mikomi no 住み込みの: a resident

r

tutor (*sumikomi no katee kyooshi*) 住み込みの家庭教師.

resign *vi.* ji⌈shoku suru 辞職する [I]; ya⌈meru 辞める [V]: He decided to resign from his job. (*Kare wa shigoto o yameru koto ni kimeta.*) 彼は仕事を辞めることに決めた.

— *vt.* ... o ji⌈shoku suru …を辞職する [I]; ji⌈niñ suru 辞任する [I]: He resigned his post as headmaster. (*Kare wa koochoo no shoku o jiniñ shita.*) 彼は校長の職を辞任した.

resignation *n.* **1** (the act of resigning) ji⌈shoku 辞職; ji⌈niñ 辞任. **2** (written statement) ji⌈hyoo 辞表: send in one's resignation (*jihyoo o dasu*) 辞表を出す.

resist *vt.* **1** (oppose) ... ni te⌈ekoo suru …に抵抗する [I]: The crowd resisted the police. (*Guñshuu wa keekañtai ni teekoo shita.*) 群衆は警官隊に抵抗した.

2 (withstand) ... ni ta⌈e⌉ru …に耐える [V]; ... o ga⌉mañ suru …を我慢する [I]: resist temptation (*yuuwaku ni taeru*) 誘惑に耐える / I can't resist sweets. (*Watashi wa amai mono o gamañ dekinai.*) 私は甘いものを我慢できない.

resistance *n.* te⌈ekoo 抵抗; ha⌈ñtai 反対: They put up a strong resistance to our plan. (*Kare-ra wa watashi-tachi no keekaku ni tsuyoi hañtai o shimeshita.*) 彼らは私たちの計画に強い反対を示した. / resistance to disease (*byooki ni taisuru teekooryoku*) 病気に対する抵抗力.

resolute *adj.* da⌉ñko to shita 断固とした; ke⌈tsuzeñ to shita 決然とした: I am resolute against war. (*Watashi wa dañko to shite señsoo ni hañtai da.*) 私は断固として戦争に反対だ.

resolution *n.* **1** (formal agreement) ke⌉tsugi 決議: adopt a resolution for building a new city hall (*shiñ-shichoosha keñsetsu no ketsugi o saitaku suru*) 新市庁舎建設の決議を採択する.

2 (firm decision) ke⌉tsui 決意; ke⌉sshiñ 決心: I made a resolution to get up early. (*Watashi wa hayaoki no ketsui o shita.*) 私は早起きの決意をした.

3 (determination) ke⌈tsuda⌉ñ-ryoku 決断力: a man of great resolution (*ketsudañ-ryoku no aru hito*) 決断力のある人.

4 (solution) ka⌈iketsu 解決: the resolution of the problem (*moñdai no kaiketsu*) 問題の解決.

resolve *vt.* **1** (decide) ... to ke⌉sshiñ suru …と決心する [I]: I resolved to quit smoking. (*Watashi wa tabako o yameyoo to kesshiñ shita.*) 私はたばこをやめようと決心した.

2 (pass a resolution) ... o ke⌉tsugi suru …を決議する [I]: It was resolved to raise the membership fee. (*Kaihi o neage suru koto ga ketsugi sareta.*) 会費を値上げすることが決議された.

3 (settle) ... o ka⌈iketsu suru …を解決する [I]: resolve a conflict (*arasoi o kaiketsu suru*) 争いを解決する.

— *vi.* (... o) ke⌉sshiñ suru (…を)決心する [I]; ki⌈meru 決める [V]: She resolved on marrying him. (*Kanojo wa kare to kekkoñ suru koto o kimeta.*) 彼女は彼と結婚することを決めた.

resort *vi.* (turn for help) ta⌈yo⌉ru 頼る [C]; u⌈ttae⌉ru 訴える [V]: resort to violence (*booryoku ni uttaeru*) 暴力に訴える.

— *n.* **1** (vacation place) ko⌈oraku⌉chi 行楽地; ri⌈zo⌉oto リゾート: a summer resort (*natsu no koorakuchi*) 夏の行楽地.

2 (turning for help) ta⌉yori 頼り: You are my only resort. (*Anata dake ga tayori desu.*) あなただけが頼りです.

resource *n.* **1** (reserve) shi⌉geñ 資源; za⌈igeñ 財源: natural resources (*teñneñ shigeñ*) 天然資源 / We have limited financial resources. (*Wareware no zaigeñ wa kagirarete iru.*) われわれの財源は限られている.

r

2 (means) shu⌉dañ 手段; ho⌈ohoo 方法: We had no other resource but to apologize. (*Watashi-tachi wa ayamaru yori hoka ni hoohoo ga nakatta.*) 私たちは謝るよりほかに方法がなかった.

respect *n.* **1** (polite regard) so⌈ñkee 尊敬; ke⌉ei 敬意: I have respect for my teacher. (*Watashi wa señsee o soñkee shite imasu.*) 私は先生を尊敬しています.
2 (concern) so⌈ñchoo 尊重; chu⌉ui 注意: have respect for the law (*hooritsu o soñchoo suru*) 法律を尊重する.
3 (point) te⌈ñ 点: I cannot agree with you in some respects. (*Watashi wa aru teñ de anata ni dooi dekinai.*) 私はある点であなたに同意できない.
4 (regards) yo⌈roshiku よろしく: Give my respects to your mother. (*O-kaasañ ni yoroshiku.*) お母さんによろしく.
— *vt.* **1** (look up to) ... o u⌈yama⌉u …を敬う Ⓒ; so⌈ñkee suru 尊敬する Ⓘ: He is respected by everyone. (*Kare wa miñna ni soñkee sarete iru.*) 彼はみんなに尊敬されている.
2 (show consideration for) ... o so⌈ñchoo suru …を尊重する Ⓘ: respect another's rights (*hoka no hito no keñri o soñchoo suru*) ほかの人の権利を尊重する.

respectable *adj.* **1** (proper) ma⌈tomo na まともな: get a respectable job (*matomo na shoku ni tsuku*) まともな職に就く.
2 (decent) ki⌈chi⌉ñto shita [shite iru] きちんとした[している]: He looked respectable. (*Kare wa kichiñto shita kakkoo o shite ita.*) 彼はきちんとした格好をしていた.
3 (fairly large) ka⌉nari no かなりの: a respectable income (*kanari no shuunyuu*) かなりの収入.

respectful *adj.* ke⌉ei o hyo⌈osu⌉ru 敬意を表する; te⌉enee na 丁寧な: be respectful to one's superiors (*ue no hito ni keei o hyoosuru*) 上の人に敬意を表する / make a respectful bow (*teenee na ojigi o suru*) 丁寧なおじぎをする.

respective *adj.* so⌈re⌉zore no それぞれの; me⌈eme⌉e no めいめいの: They went their respective ways. (*Karera wa meemee no michi o itta.*) 彼らをめいめいの道を行った.

respectively *adv.* so⌈re⌉zore それぞれ; me⌈eme⌉e ni めいめいに: Taro and Jiro were first and second, respectively. (*Taroo to Jiroo wa sorezore ichi-bañ to ni-bañ ni natta.*) 太郎と次郎はそれぞれ一番と二番になった.

respond *vi.* **1** (answer) (... ni) ko⌈tae⌉ru (…に)答える Ⓥ: respond to a question (*shitsumoñ ni kotaeru*) 質問に答える / respond to a letter (*tegami ni heñji o dasu*) 手紙に返事を出す.
2 (react) (... ni) ha⌈ñnoo suru (…に)反応する Ⓘ; o⌈ojiru 応じる Ⓥ: He didn't respond to our demands. (*Kare wa wareware no yookyuu ni oojinakatta.*) 彼はわれわれの要求に応じなかった.

response *n.* **1** (answer) he⌈ñtoo 返答: I made a quick response to his inquiry. (*Kare no toiawase ni sugu ni heñtoo shita.*) 彼の問い合わせにすぐに返答した.
2 (reaction) ha⌈ñnoo 反応: response to a stimulus (*shigeki ni taisuru hañnoo*) 刺激に対する反応.

responsibility *n.* se⌈kiniñ 責任: I will take responsibility for the consequences. (*Kekka ni taishite wa watashi ga sekiniñ o torimasu.*) 結果に対しては私が責任を取ります.

responsible *adj.* **1** (having duty) se⌈kiniñ ga a⌉ru 責任がある: Drivers are responsible for their passengers' safety. (*Uñtenshu wa jookyaku no añzeñ ni sekiniñ ga aru.*) 運転手は乗客の安全に責任がある.
2 (reliable) shi⌈ñrai deki⌉ru 信頼できる: He is a responsible person. (*Kare wa shiñrai dekiru hito desu.*) 彼は信頼できる人です.

3 (being the cause) ge⌈ñiñ no 原因の: What is responsible for the accident? (*Jiko no geñiñ wa nañ desu ka?*) 事故の原因は何ですか.

rest[1] *n.* **1** (taking one's ease) ya⌈sumi⌉ 休み; kyu⌈usoku 休息: We stopped for a rest. (*Watashi-tachi wa yasumu tame ni tomatta.*) 私たちは休むために止まった. / take a rest (*hitoyasumi suru*) ひと休みする.

2 (sleep) su⌈imiñ 睡眠: have a good night's rest (*hito-bañ juubuñ ni suimiñ o toru*) 一晩十分に睡眠をとる.

3 (being still) te⌈eshi 停止: The machine is now at rest. (*Kikai wa ima teeshi shite imasu.*) 機械は今停止しています.

— *vi.* **1** (take one's ease) ya⌈su⌉mu 休む Ⓒ; kyu⌈usoku suru 休息する Ⓘ: You must rest for a time after a meal. (*Shokugo wa shibaraku yasumanakereba ikemaseñ.*) 食後はしばらく休まなければいけません.

2 (be at ease) a⌈ñshiñ shite iru 安心している Ⓥ: He couldn't rest until he found his wallet. (*Kare wa saifu o mitsukeru made añshiñ dekinakatta.*) 彼は財布を見つけるまで安心できなかった.

3 (lie) (... ni) no⌈tte iru (…に)のっている Ⓘ: The statue rested on a pedestal. (*Zoo wa dai no ue ni notte ita.*) 像は台の上にのっていた.

4 (rely) (... ni) ka⌈ka⌉tte iru (…に)かかっている Ⓥ: Our hopes rest on you. (*Watashi-tachi no kiboo wa anata ni kakatte imasu.*) 私たちの希望はあなたにかかっています.

— *vt.* **1** (give rest) ... o ya⌈sumase⌉ru …を休ませる Ⓥ; kyu⌈usoku saseru 休息させる Ⓥ: I stopped reading and rested my eyes. (*Watashi wa dokusho o yamete me o yasumaseta.*) 私は読書をやめて目を休ませた.

2 (set) ... o o⌈ku …を置く Ⓒ; (lean) ta⌈tekake⌉ru 立てかける Ⓥ: rest a pair of skis against the wall (*kabe ni sukii o tatekakeru*) 壁にスキーを立てかける.

rest[2] *n.* **1** (remainder) no⌈kori 残り: I saved the rest of the money. (*Nokori no o-kane wa chokiñ shimashita.*) 残りのお金は貯金しました.

2 (people) no⌈kori no hi⌈to⌉-tachi 残りの人たち: The rest stayed behind. (*Nokori no hito-tachi wa ato ni nokorimashita.*) 残りの人たちは後に残りました.

restaurant *n.* re⌉sutorañ レストラン; ryo⌈ori⌉ya 料理屋; sho⌈kudoo 食堂: Is there a Japanese restaurant near here? (*Kono chikaku ni Nihoñ ryooriya wa arimasu ka?*) この近くに日本料理屋はありますか.

restless *adj.* o⌈chitsukanai 落ち着かない; so⌉wasowa shita [shite iru] そわそわした[している]: a restless child (*ochitsukanai kodomo*) 落ち着かない子ども.

restoration *n.* ka⌈ifuku 回復; shu⌈ufuku 修復: the restoration of order (*chitsujo no kaifuku*) 秩序の回復 / the restoration of a building (*tatemono no shuufuku*) 建物の修復.

restore *vt.* **1** (repair) ... o fu⌈kkyuu suru …を復旧する Ⓘ: restore an old temple (*furui tera o fukkyuu suru*) 古い寺を復旧する.

2 (of health) ... o ka⌈ifuku saseru …を回復させる Ⓥ: He has been restored to health. (*Kare wa keñkoo o kaifuku shita.*) 彼は健康を回復した.

3 (bring back) ... o mo⌉to ni mo⌈do⌉su …を元に戻す Ⓒ; ka⌉esu 返す Ⓒ: I restored the book to its rightful owner. (*Watashi wa sono hoñ o tadashii mochinushi ni kaeshita.*) 私はその本を正しい持ち主に返した.

restrain *vt.* ... o o⌈sae⌉ru …を抑える Ⓥ; se⌈eshi suru 制止する Ⓘ: He could not restrain his anger. (*Kare wa ikari o osaeru koto ga dekinakatta.*) 彼は怒りを抑えることができなかった.

restraint *n.* yo⌈kusee 抑制; ko⌈osoku 拘束: put restraints on prices (*bukka o yokusee suru*) 物価を抑制する / He is kept under restraint.

(*Kare wa koosoku sarete iru.*) 彼は拘束されている.

restrict *vt.* ... o se⌈ege⌉ñ suru ...を制限する Ⓘ; ge⌈ñtee suru 限定する Ⓘ: The speed is restricted to 40 kilometers an hour here. (*Koko de wa sokudo wa jisoku yoñjuk-kiro ni seegeñ sarete imasu.*) ここでは速度は時速 40 キロに制限されています.

restriction *n.* se⌈ege⌉ñ 制限; ge⌈ñtee 限定: place restrictions on the import of oranges (*oreñji no yunyuu ni seegeñ o kuwaeru*) オレンジの輸入に制限を加える.

rest room *n.* te⌈a⌉rai 手洗い; to⌉ire トイレ: Where is the rest room? (*Toire wa doko desu ka?*) トイレはどこですか.

result *n.* **1** (outcome) ke⌈kka 結果: the results of an election (*señkyo no kekka*) 選挙の結果.
2 (final score) ke⌈kka 結果; se⌈eseki 成績: baseball results (*yakyuu no shiai no kekka*) 野球の試合の結果 / the results of an examination (*shikeñ no seeseki*) 試験の成績.
3 (answer) ko⌈ta⌉e 答え: What is the result of the calculation? (*Keesañ no kotae wa ikura desu ka?*) 計算の答えはいくらですか.
— *vi.* (... ni) ki⌈iñ suru (...に)起因する Ⓘ: His illness resulted from overwork. (*Kare no byooki wa karoo ni kiiñ suru.*) 彼の病気は過労に起因する.

r

resume *vt.* ... o fu⌈tatabi hajimeru ...を再び始める Ⓥ; sa⌈ikai suru 再開する Ⓘ: He resumed working after lunch. (*Kare wa chuushoku-go futatabi shigoto o hajimeta.*) 彼は昼食後再び仕事を始めた.
— *vi.* fu⌈tatabi hajimaru 再び始まる Ⓒ; sa⌈ikai suru 再開する Ⓘ: After tea, the meeting resumed. (*O-cha o noñde kara kaigi wa saikai shita.*) お茶を飲んでから会議は再開した.

retail *n.* ko⌈uri 小売り: a retail price (*kouri kakaku*) 小売り価格.
— *vi.* ko⌈uri sareru 小売りされる Ⓥ; u⌈rareru 売られる Ⓥ: This article retails at 100 yen. (*Kono shina wa hyaku-eñ de urarete imasu.*) この品は 100 円で売られています.

retain *vt.* **1** (keep) ... o ta⌈mo⌉tsu ...を保つ Ⓒ: This china dish retains heat well. (*Kono tooki no sara wa netsu o yoku tamochimasu.*) この陶器の皿は熱をよく保ちます.
2 (remember) ... o o⌈bo⌉ete iru ...を覚えている Ⓥ: I cannot retain everything I learned. (*Naratta koto o subete oboete iru koto wa dekimaseñ.*) 習ったことをすべて覚えていることはできません.

retaliate *vi.* shi⌈kaeshi suru 仕返しする Ⓘ; ho⌈ofuku suru 報復する Ⓘ: I will retaliate if kicked. (*Moshi keraretara shikaeshi shite yaru.*) もし蹴られた仕返ししてやる.

retire *vi.* **1** (stop working) ta⌈ishoku suru 退職する Ⓘ: He retired at the age of sixty. (*Kare wa rokujussai de taishoku shimashita.*) 彼は 60 歳で退職しました.
2 (withdraw) hi⌈kisaga⌉ru 引き下がる Ⓒ: He retired to the study after dinner. (*Kare wa yuushoku-go shosai ni hikisagatta.*) 彼は夕食後書斎に引き下がった.
— *vt.* ... o ta⌈ishoku saseru ...を退職させる Ⓥ; i⌈ñtai saseru 引退させる Ⓥ: He was compulsorily retired. (*Kare wa muri ni taishoku saserareta.*) 彼は無理に退職させられた.

retirement *n.* ta⌈ishoku 退職; i⌈ñtai 引退: give written notice of one's retirement (*taishoku negai o dasu*) 退職願いを出す.

retreat *vi.* shi⌈rizo⌉ku 退く Ⓒ; ta⌈ikyaku suru 退却する Ⓘ: The troops retreated from the village. (*Guñtai wa sono mura kara taikyaku shita.*) 軍隊はその村から退却した.
— *n.* ta⌈ikyaku 退却; ko⌈otai 後退.

retrieve *vt.* **1** (get back) ... o to⌈rimodo⌉su ...を取り戻す Ⓒ; ka⌈ishuu suru 回収する Ⓘ: I retrieved my lost bag. (*Watashi wa nakushita kabañ o torimodoshita.*) 私はなくしたかばんを取り戻した.

2 (computing) ... o ke⌈ñsaku suru …を検索する [I]; hi⌈ki⌉dasu 引き出す [C]: retrieve data (*deeta o keñsaku suru*) データを検索する.

return *vi.* ka⌉eru 帰る [C]; mo⌈do⌉ru 戻る [C]: He returned to his hometown. (*Kare wa kokyoo e kaerimashita.*) 彼は故郷へ帰りました. / What time will he return? (*Kare wa nañji ni modorimasu ka?*) 彼は何時に戻りますか.
— *vt.* ... o ka⌉esu …を返す [C]: Please return this umbrella to her. (*Kono kasa o kanojo ni kaeshite kudasai.*) この傘を彼女に返してください.
— *n.* **1** (coming back) ka⌈eri 帰り: I am looking forward to your return from China. (*Anata no Chuugoku kara no o-kaeri o o-machi shite imasu.*) あなたの中国からのお帰りをお待ちしています.
2 (paying back) he⌈ñkyaku 返却: He is demanding the return of the money. (*Kare wa sono o-kane no heñkyaku o yookyuu shite iru.*) 彼はそのお金の返却を要求している.

reunion *n.* **1** (meeting) sa⌈ikai no atsumari⌉ 再会の集まり: a class reunion (*doosookai*) 同窓会.
2 (coming together again) sa⌈ikai 再会: a family reunion (*kazoku no saikai*) 家族の再会.

reveal *vt.* **1** (disclose) ... o a⌈ki⌉raka ni suru …を明らかにする [I]: He did not reveal his identity. (*Kare wa jibuñ no mimoto o akiraka ni shinakatta.*) 彼は自分の身元を明らかにしなかった.
2 (show) ... o shi⌈me⌉su …を示す [C]; mi⌈se⌉ru 見せる [V]: I opened the door and revealed the garden. (*Watashi wa doa o hiraite niwa o miseta.*) 私はドアを開いて庭を見せた.

revenge *vt.* ... ni fu⌈kushuu suru …に復讐する [I]; shi⌈kaeshi o suru 仕返しをする [I]: He revenged himself on his enemies. (*Kare wa teki ni fukushuu shita.*) 彼は敵に復讐した.
— *n.* fu⌈kushuu 復讐; shi⌈kaeshi 仕返し: take revenge on a person (*hito ni shikaeshi o suru*) 人に仕返しをする.

revenue *n.* (of a government) sa⌈inyuu 歳入; (income) shu⌈unyuu 収入.

revenue stamp *n.* shu⌈unyuui⌉ñshi 収入印紙.

reverence *n.* so⌈ñkee 尊敬; ke⌈eai 敬愛: He is held in reverence by many people. (*Kare wa ooku no hito ni keeai sarete imasu.*) 彼は多くの人に敬愛されています.

reverse *n.* **1** (opposite) gya⌈ku 逆; ha⌈ñtai 反対: He did the reverse of what I expected. (*Kare wa watashi no yosoo to hañtai no koto o shita.*) 彼は私の予想と反対のことをした.
2 (back side) u⌈ra⌉ 裏; ri⌉meñ 裏面: the reverse of a painting (*e no ura*) 絵の裏.
3 (misfortune) fu⌉uñ 不運; shi⌈ppai 失敗: suffer a reverse (*fuuñ ni mimawareru*) 不運に見舞われる.
4 (reverse gear) ba⌉kku バック: shift into reverse (*giya o bakku ni ireru*) ギヤをバックに入れる.
— *adj.* **1** (contrary) gya⌈ku no 逆の; a⌈bekobe no あべこべの: read the numbers in reverse order (*suuji o gyaku no juñ ni yomu*) 数字を逆の順に読む.
2 (back) u⌈ra⌉ no 裏の: the reverse side of a dress (*doresu no uragawa*) ドレスの裏側.
— *vt.* **1** (change to the opposite) ... o gya⌈ku ni suru …を逆にする [I]: reverse the order (*juñjo o gyaku ni suru*) 順序を逆にする.
2 (turn backward) ... o ba⌉kku saseru …をバックさせる [V]: reverse one's car (*kuruma o bakku saseru*) 車をバックさせる.
— *vi.* (go backward) gya⌈kushiñ suru 逆進する [I].

review *n.* **1** (criticism) hi⌈hyoo 批評; hyo⌈oroñ 評論: a book review (*shohyoo*) 書評.
2 (studying again) fu⌈kushuu 復習: a review of today's lesson (*kyoo no jugyoo no fukushuu*) きょうの授業の

r

復習.

— *vt.* **1** (criticize) ... o hi⌈hyoo suru ...を批評する Ⅰ: The play was favorably reviewed. (*Sono shibai wa koohyoo datta.*) その芝居は好評だった.

2 (study again) ... o fu⌈kushuu suru ...を復習する Ⅰ: review the main subjects (*omo-na kamoku o fukushuu suru*) 主な科目を復習する.

3 (investigate again) ... o sa⌈icho⌉osa suru ...を再調査する Ⅰ; sa⌈ike⌉ñtoo suru 再検討する Ⅰ: review the cause of an accident (*jiko geñiñ o saichoosa suru*) 事故原因を再調査する.

— *vi.* hi⌈hyoo [hyo⌈oroñ] o ka⌉ku 批評[評論]を書く Ⓒ: He reviews for that magazine. (*Kare wa sono zasshi ni hyooroñ o kaite iru.*) 彼はその雑誌に評論を書いている.

revise *vt.* **1** (bring up-to-date) ... o ka⌈itee suru ...を改訂する Ⅰ: revise a dictionary (*jisho o kaitee suru*) 辞書を改訂する.

2 (amend) ... o shu⌈usee suru ...を修正する Ⅰ: He revised his opinion. (*Kare wa jibuñ no ikeñ o shuusee shita.*) 彼は自分の意見を修正した.

revision *n.* ka⌈itee 改訂; shu⌈usee 修正.

revival *n.* fu⌈kkatsu 復活; fu⌈kkoo 復興: the revival of an old custom (*furui shuukañ no fukkatsu*) 古い習慣の復活 / the Revival of Learning (*Buñgee fukkoo*) 文芸復興.

revive *vi.* **1** (come back to life) i⌈kika⌉eru 生き返る Ⓒ; ka⌈ifuku suru 回復する Ⅰ: The flower will revive if you water it. (*Mizu o yareba sono hana wa ikikaeru deshoo.*) 水をやればその花は生き返るでしょう.

2 (become popular again) fu⌈kkatsu suru 復活する Ⅰ: The old custom is reviving. (*Sono furui shuukañ wa fukkatsu shite kite iru.*) その古い習慣は復活してきている.

— *vt.* **1** (bring to life) ... o i⌈kikarase⌉ru ...を生き返らせる Ⓥ; i⌉shiki o ka⌈ifuku saseru 意識を回復させる Ⓥ: He revived her with cold water. (*Kare wa tsumetai mizu de kanojo no ishiki o kaifuku saseta.*) 彼は冷たい水で彼女の意識を回復させた.

2 (make popular again) ... o fu⌈kkatsu saseru ...を復活させる Ⓥ; sa⌈ijo⌉oeñ suru 再上演する Ⅰ: revive an old play (*furui geki o saijooeñ suru*) 古い劇を再上演する.

revolt *vt.* ha⌈ñrañ o oko⌉su 反乱を起こす Ⓒ; ha⌈ñkoo suru 反抗する Ⅰ: revolt against a ruler (*shihaisha ni taishite hañrañ o okosu*) 支配者に対して反乱を起こす.

— *n.* ha⌈ñrañ 反乱; ha⌈ñkoo 反抗.

revolution *n.* **1** (great social change) ka⌈kumee 革命: the French Revolution (*Furañsu-kakumee*) フランス革命 / the Industrial Revolution (*Sañgyoo-kakumee*) 産業革命.

2 (circular movement) ka⌈iteñ 回転: the revolution of the moon around the earth (*tsuki no chikyuu o meguru kaiteñ*) 月の地球をめぐる回転.

revolutionary *adj.* ka⌈kumee no 革命の; ka⌈kumee-teki na 革命的な: a revolutionary invention (*kakumee-teki na hatsumee*) 革命的な発明.

revolve *vi.* ka⌈iteñ suru 回転する Ⅰ; ma⌈waru 回る Ⓒ: The earth revolves around the sun. (*Chikyuu wa taiyoo no mawari o mawaru.*) 地球は太陽の周りを回る.

revue *n.* re⌉byuu レビュー.

reward *n.* **1** (something given in return) ho⌈oshuu 報酬; ho⌈obi ほうび: He was given a watch as a reward for his services. (*Kare wa kare no jiñryoku no hoobi to shite tokee o moratta.*) 彼は彼の尽力のほうびとして時計をもらった.

2 (money) ho⌈oshookiñ 報奨金; sha⌈reekiñ 謝礼金: A reward of a million yen is offered for useful information. (*Yuueki na joohoo ni hyakumañ-eñ no sharee-kiñ ga teekyoo sarete iru.*) 有益な情報に 100

万円の謝礼金が提供されている.
— *vt*. ... ni mu⌈kui⌉ru ...に報いる [V]; sha⌈ree [ho⌈obi] o ataeru 謝礼[ほうび]を与える [V]: I'll reward the person who brings back the lost dog. (*Inaku natta inu o tsurete kite kureta hito ni sharee o itashimasu.*) いなくなった犬を連れてきてくれた人に謝礼をいたします.

rhythm *n*. ri⌉zumu リズム; ri⌈tsudoo 律動.

rib *n*. **1** (bone) ro⌈kkotsu 肋骨: He broke a rib in his fall. (*Kare wa koroñde rokkotsu o ip-poñ otta.*) 彼は転んで肋骨を1本折った.
2 (of an umbrella) ho⌈ne⌉ 骨: the ribs of an umbrella (*kasa no hone*) 傘の骨.

ribbon *n*. ri⌉boñ リボン: put on a ribbon (*riboñ o tsukeru*) リボンをつける.

rice *n*. ko⌈me 米; go⌉hañ ごはん.
★ Japanese refer to 'rice' in various ways depending on the stage of production: rice plant (*ine*) 稲, rough rice (*momi*) もみ, grains (*kome*) 米, brown rice (*geñmai*) 玄米, polished rice (*hakumai*) 白米, cooked rice (*gohañ, raisu*) ごはん, ライス.

rice cake *n*. mo⌈chi 餅: make [grill] rice cake (*mochi o tsuku* [*yaku*]) 餅をつく[焼く].

rich *adj*. **1** (wealthy) ka⌈nemochi no 金持ちの: He is a rich man. (*Kare wa kanemochi da.*) 彼は金持ちだ.
2 (having much) ho⌈ofu na 豊富な; yu⌉taka na 豊かな: Oranges are rich in vitamin C. (*Oreñji wa bitamiñ shii ga hoofu desu.*) オレンジはビタミンCが豊富です.
3 (producing much) ko⌉eta 肥えた; ko⌉ete iru 肥えている: rich land (*koeta tochi*) 肥えた土地.
4 (full of fats, sugar, etc.) shi⌈tsuko⌉i しつこい: a rich diet (*shitsukoi shokuji*) しつこい食事.

rid *vt*. ... o to⌈rinozoku ...を取り除く [C]; jo⌉kyo suru 除去する [I]: rid a garden of weeds (*niwa kara kusa o torinozoku*) 庭から草を取り除く.

get rid of ... *vt*. ... o no⌈zoku ...を除く [C]; ka⌈tazuke⌉ru 片づける [V]: I have finally got rid of my debt. (*Watashi wa yatto shakkiñ o katazuketa.*) 私はやっと借金を片づけた.

riddle *n*. na⌈zo なぞ; na⌈zonazo なぞなぞ: solve a riddle (*nazo o toku*) なぞを解く.

ride *vi*. (... ni) no⌈ru (...に)乗る [C]: ride in a train (*ressha ni noru*) 列車に乗る / He was riding on a horse. (*Kare wa uma ni notte ita.*) 彼は馬に乗っていた.
— *vt*. ... ni no⌈tte iku ...に乗って行く [C]: I ride my bicycle to school. (*Watashi wa jiteñsha ni notte gakkoo e ikimasu.*) 私は自転車に乗って学校へ行きます.
— *n*. no⌈ru [no⌈seru] koto⌉ 乗る[乗せる]こと: give a person a ride (*hito o nosete yaru*) 人を乗せてやる.

rider *n*. no⌈ru hito⌉ 乗る人; (of a horse) ki⌉shu 騎手.

ridge *n*. o⌉ne 尾根; ya⌈ma no se 山の背: walk along mountain ridges (*one-zutai ni aruku*) 尾根伝いに歩く.

ridiculous *adj*. ba⌈ka⌉geta ばかげた; ba⌈ka⌉gete iru ばかげている; o⌈kashi⌉i おかしい: a ridiculous idea (*bakageta kañgae*) ばかげた考え.

rifle *n*. ra⌈ifuru⌉juu ライフル銃: shoot a rifle (*raifurujuu de utsu*) ライフル銃で撃つ.

right[1] *adj*. **1** (correct) ta⌈dashi⌉i 正しい; se⌈ekaku na 正確な: You are right. (*Anata wa tadashii.*) あなたは正しい. / Will you tell me the right time? (*Seekaku na jikañ o oshiete kudasai.*) 正確な時間を教えてください. / That's right. (*Soo desu.*) そうです.
2 (proper) te⌈kitoo na 適当な; fu⌈sawashi⌉i ふさわしい: the right dress for the occasion (*sono ba ni fusawashii doresu*) その場にふさわしいドレス.
3 (morally good) ta⌈dashi⌉i 正しい; yo⌉i よい: Telling lies is not right. (*Uso o tsuku no wa yoku nai.*) うそをつくのはよくない.
4 (satisfactory) mo⌈oshibuñ no na⌉i

申し分のない: Everything is just right. (*Subete mooshibuñ arimaseñ.*) すべて申し分ありません.
5 (healthy) ke⌈ñkoo na 健康な; cho⌈oshi no yo⌉i 調子のよい: I feel perfectly all right now. (*Ima wa karada no chooshi wa totemo yoi.*) 今は体の調子はとてもよい.
— *adv.* **1** (correctly) ta⌈da⌉shiku 正しく; se⌈ekaku ni 正確に: He answered right. (*Kare wa tadashiku kotaeta.*) 彼は正しく答えた.
2 (directly) ma⌈ssu⌉gu ni 真っすぐに: Go right on to the end of this street. (*Kono michi no tsukiatari made massugu ni iki nasai.*) この道の突き当たりまで真っすぐに行きなさい.
3 (exactly) cho⌈odo ちょうど; ma⌈ttaku まったく: The ball hit me right on the head. (*Booru wa choodo watashi no atama ni atatta.*) ボールはちょうど私の頭に当たった.
right away *adv.* su⌉gu ni すぐに: I'll come back right away. (*Sugu ni modorimasu.*) すぐに戻ります.
— *n.* **1** (lawful claim) ke⌉ñri 権利: rights and duties (*keñri to gimu*) 権利と義務 / stand on one's rights (*jibuñ no keñri o shuchoo suru*) 自分の権利を主張する.
2 (what is right) ta⌈dashi⌉i ko⌈to⌉ 正しいこと: I always did right. (*Watashi wa itsu-mo tadashii koto o shimashita.*) 私はいつも正しいことをしました.

right[2] *adj.* mi⌈gi no 右の: write with one's right hand (*migite de kaku*) 右手で書く.
— *adv.* mi⌈gi ni 右に: turn right (*migi ni magaru*) 右に曲がる.
— *n.* **1** (right side) mi⌈gi 右; mi⌈gigawa 右側: keep to the right (*migigawa o tsuukoo suru*) 右側を通行する.
2 (political party) u⌉yoku 右翼; u⌉ha 右派.

right-handed *adj.* mi⌈gikiki no 右利きの: a right-handed person (*migikiki no hito*) 右利きの人.

rightist *n.* u⌉yoku [u⌉ha] no hi⌈to⌉ 右翼[右派]の人; ho⌈shuha no hito⌉ 保守派の人.

rigid *adj.* **1** (stiff) ka⌈tai 堅い; ko⌈waba⌉tta こわばった; ko⌈waba⌉tte iru こわばっている: a rigid bar (*katai boo*) 堅い棒 / a rigid face (*kowabatta kao*) こわばった顔.
2 (severe) ge⌈ñkaku na 厳格な; ki⌈bishi⌉i 厳しい: The rules are rigid. (*Kisoku ga kibishii.*) 規則が厳しい.

rigor *n.* ki⌈bi⌉shisa 厳しさ; ge⌈ñkaku 厳格: enforce the law with rigor (*hooritsu o geñkaku ni shikoo suru*) 法律を厳格に施行する.

rigorous *adj.* ki⌈bishi⌉i 厳しい; ge⌈ñkaku na 厳格な: a rigorous training (*kibishii kuñreñ*) 厳しい訓練 / a rigorous climate (*kibishii kikoo*) 厳しい気候.

ring[1] *n.* **1** (circle) wa⌉ 輪: We sat in a ring. (*Watashi-tachi wa wa ni natte suwatta.*) 私たちは輪になって座った.
2 (round band) yu⌈biwa 指輪: She wears a diamond ring. (*Kanojo wa daiyamoñdo no yubiwa o shite iru.*) 彼女はダイヤモンドの指輪をしている.

ring[2] *vi.* **1** (sound) na⌈ru 鳴る Ⓒ: The telephone is ringing. (*Deñwa ga natte imasu.*) 電話が鳴っています.
2 (summon) be⌉ru o na⌈rashite yobu ベルを鳴らして呼ぶ Ⓒ: ring for a bellboy (*beru o narashite booi o yobu*) ベルを鳴らしてボーイを呼ぶ.
— *vt.* **1** (cause to sound) ... o na⌈rasu ...を鳴らす Ⓒ: ring the bell (*beru o narasu*) ベルを鳴らす.
2 (summon) ... o na⌈rashite yobu ...を鳴らして呼ぶ Ⓒ: He rang the bell for the nurse. (*Kare wa beru o narashite kañgofu o yoñda.*) 彼はベルを鳴らして看護婦を呼んだ.
ring up *vt.* ... ni de⌈ñwa suru ...に電話する Ⓘ: I'll ring you up tonight. (*Koñya deñwa shimasu.*) 今夜電話します.

rinse *vt.* ... o yu⌈sugu ...をゆすぐ Ⓒ; su⌈sugu すすぐ Ⓒ: rinse one's mouth (*kuchi o yusugu*) 口をゆすぐ / rinse out socks (*kutsushita o *susugu*) 靴下をすすぐ.

riot *n.* bo⌈odoo 暴動: raise [put down] a riot (*boodoo o okosu* [*chiñatsu suru*]) 暴動を起こす[鎮圧する].

ripe *adj.* ju⌈ku⌉shita 熟した; ju⌈ku⌉shite iru 熟している; ta⌈begoro no 食べごろの: Apples are not ripe yet. (*Riñgo wa mada jukushite imaseñ.*) りんごはまだ熟していません. / ripe cheese (*tabegoro no chiizu*) 食べごろのチーズ.

ripen *vi.* ju⌈ku⌉su 熟す Ⓒ; u⌈re⌉ru うれる Ⓥ: The corn has ripened. (*Toomorokoshi ga jukushita.*) とうもろこしが熟した.

rise *vi.* **1** (increase) ma⌈su 増す Ⓒ; a⌈garu 上がる Ⓒ: The river is rising after a heavy rain. (*Ooame no ato de kawa no mizu ga mashite iru.*) 大雨の後で川の水が増している. / Prices will rise again. (*Bukka wa mata agaru deshoo.*) 物価はまた上がるでしょう.

2 (move upward) no⌈boru 昇る Ⓒ: The sun rises in the east. (*Taiyoo wa higashi kara noboru.*) 太陽は東から昇る.

3 (stand up) ta⌈chiagaru 立ち上がる Ⓒ: She rose from her chair. (*Kanojo wa isu kara tachiagatta.*) 彼女はいすから立ち上がった.

4 (get up) o⌈ki⌉ru 起きる Ⓥ: I have to rise early tomorrow morning. (*Ashita no asa wa hayaku okinakereba naranai.*) あしたの朝は早く起きなければならない.

5 (slope upwards) so⌈bie⌉ru そびえる Ⓥ: The mountain rose above the clouds. (*Yama wa kumo no ue ni sobiete ita.*) 山は雲の上にそびえていた.

— *n.* **1** (increase) jo⌈oshoo 上昇: a rise in wages (*chiñgiñ no jooshoo*) 賃金の上昇.

2 (slope) no⌈borizaka 昇り坂; (hill) ta⌈kadai 高台: His villa was built on a rise. (*Kare no bessoo wa takadai ni taterareta.*) 彼の別荘は高台に建てられた.

risk *n.* ki⌈keñ 危険: run a risk (*kikeñ o okasu*) 危険を冒す / There is no risk of your drowning in this stream. (*Kono nagare de wa oboreru kikeñ wa arimaseñ.*) この流れでは溺れる危険はありません.

at one's own risk *adv.* ji⌈buñ no sekiniñ de 自分の責任で: Do it at your own risk. (*Anata no sekiniñ de yari nasai.*) あなたの責任でやりなさい.

— *vt.* ... o ka⌈ke⌉ru ...を賭ける Ⓥ: He risked his life to save the child. (*Kare wa sono ko o sukuu tame ni inochi o kaketa.*) 彼はその子を救うために命を賭けた.

ritual *n.* gi⌉shiki 儀式; sa⌈ishiki 祭式: a religious ritual (*shuukyooteki na gishiki*) 宗教的な儀式.

rival *n.* kyo⌈osoo a⌉ite 競争相手; ra⌉ibaru ライバル: He and I are rivals for the job. (*Kare to watashi wa shigoto-joo no raibaru dooshi da.*) 彼と私は仕事上のライバル同士だ.

— *vt.* ... to kyo⌈osoo suru ...と競争する Ⓘ; ... ni ta⌈ikoo suru ...に対抗する Ⓘ: The two of them rivaled each other for first place. (*Futari wa o-tagai ni taikoo shite ichi-i o arasotta.*) 二人はお互いに対抗して1位を争った.

river *n.* ka⌈wa⌉ 川: fish in the river (*kawa de tsuri o suru*) 川で釣りをする / the Tone river (*Tonegawa*) 利根川.

road *n.* **1** (way) do⌉oro 道路; mi⌈chi 道: Be careful when you cross the road. (*Michi o wataru toki wa ki o tsuke nasai.*) 道を渡るときは気をつけなさい. / Does this road go to Nikko? (*Kono michi wa Nikkoo e ikimasu ka?*) この道は日光へ行きますか.

2 (course) mi⌈chi 道; ho⌈ohoo 方法: the road to success (*seekoo e no michi*) 成功への道.

road map *n.* do⌈oro chi⌉zu 道路地図.

roar *vi.* **1** (of an animal) ho⌈e⌉ru ほえる Ⓥ: The lion roared in anger. (*Raioñ wa okotte hoeta.*) ライオンは

r

怒ってほえた.

2 (make a deep sound) go⌈o-oñ o ta⌈te⌉ru ごう音を立てる [V]: A truck roared down the road. (*Torakku ga goo-oñ o tatete hashiri-satta.*) トラックがごう音を立てて走り去った.

3 (shout) do⌈na⌉ru どなる [C]; (laugh) o⌈owa⌉rai suru 大笑いする [I]: He roared with laughter. (*Kare wa oowarai shita.*) 彼は大笑いした.

— *n.* ho⌈e⌉ru ko⌉e ほえる声; do⌈yo-meki⌉ どよめき: the roars of a tiger (*tora no hoeru koe*) とらのほえる声.

roast *vt.* **1** (of meat) ... o ya⌈ku ... を焼く [C]; a⌈bu⌉ru あぶる [C]: roast meat in an oven (*teñpi de niku o yaku*) 天火で肉を焼く.

2 (of beans) ... o i⌉ru 炒る [C]: roast coffee beans (*koohii mame o iru*) コーヒー豆を炒る.

rob *vt.* ... kara (... o) u⌈ba⌉u ...から(...を)奪う [C]: ... o o⌈so⌉u ...を襲う [C]: The man robbed her of her money. (*Sono otoko wa kanojo kara o-kane o ubatta.*) その男は彼女からお金を奪った. ★ The object of English 'rob' is a person or an office, etc., but the object of the Japanese equivalent is a 'thing.' / The jewelry store was robbed last night. (*Sono hoosekiteñ wa sakuya osowareta.*) その宝石店は昨夜襲われた.

robber *n.* go⌈otoo 強盗; do⌈roboo どろぼう: catch a robber (*doroboo o tsukamaeru*) どろぼうを捕まえる.

robbery *n.* go⌈otoo 強盗; go⌈oda-tsu 強奪: commit a bank robbery (*giñkoo gootoo o hataraku*) 銀行強盗を働く.

robe *n.* re⌈efuku 礼服; ro⌉obu ローブ.

robin *n.* ko⌈ma⌉dori こまどり; ro⌉biñ ロビン.

robot *n.* ro⌈bo⌉tto ロボット: industrial robots (*sañgyooyoo robotto*) 産業用ロボット.

robust *adj.* ta⌈kumashi⌉i たくましい; kyo⌈okeñ na 強健な: a robust young man (*takumashii seeneñ*) たくましい青年.

rock[1] *n.* **1** (mass) i⌈wa⌉ 岩; ga⌉ñ-seki 岩石: a house built on a rock (*iwa no ue ni taterareta ie*) 岩の上に建てられた家.

2 (pieces) i⌈shi 石: They threw rocks at the police. (*Kare-ra wa keekañ ni ishi o nageta.*) 彼らは警官に石を投げた.

rock[2] *vt.* ... o yu⌈riugoka⌉su ...を揺り動かす [C]: rock a cradle (*yurikago o yuriugokasu*) 揺りかごを揺り動かす.

— *vi.* yu⌈reru 揺れる [V]: The boat rocked to and fro. (*Booto wa zeñ-go ni yureta.*) ボートは前後に揺れた.

rocket *n.* ro⌈ke⌉tto ロケット: launch a rocket (*roketto o uchiageru*) ロケットを打ち上げる.

rocky *adj.* i⌈wa no o⌉oi 岩の多い; i⌈wada⌉rake no 岩だらけの: a rocky coastline (*iwadarake no kaigañ*) 岩だらけの海岸.

rod *n.* bo⌈o 棒; sa⌈o⌉ さお: hang curtains on a rod (*kaateñ o boo ni tsurusu*) カーテンを棒につるす / a fishing rod (*tsurizao*) 釣ざお.

roe *n.* sa⌈kana no tama⌉go 魚の卵.

role *n.* **1** (of an actor) ya⌈ku⌉ 役: play the leading role (*shuyaku o eñjiru*) 主役を演じる.

2 (part) ya⌈kuwari 役割; ya⌈kume⌉ 役目: play an important role in the convention (*taikai de juuyoo na yakuwari o hatasu*) 大会で重要な役割を果たす.

roll *vi.* **1** (turn over) ko⌈rogaru 転がる [C]: The ball rolled into the hole. (*Booru wa korogatte ana ni haitta.*) ボールは転がって穴に入った.

2 (move on) su⌈sumu 進む [C]: The car rolled down the street. (*Kuruma wa michi o susuñde itta.*) 車は道を進んで行った.

3 (rock) yo⌈ko ni yureru 横に揺れる [V]: The ship rolled in the storm. (*Fune wa arashi no naka de yoko ni yureta.*) 船は嵐の中で横に揺れた.

4 (move gently) u⌈ne⌉ru うねる [C]: The waves are rolling. (*Nami ga unette iru.*) 波がうねっている.

— *vt.* **1** (cause to turn over) ... o ko⌈rogasu ...を転がす [C]: roll a bar-

r

rel over (*taru o korogasu*) たるを転がす.

2 (wind round) ... o ma⌈rumeru ...を丸める Ⓥ; ma⌈ku 巻く Ⓒ: roll an umbrella (*kasa o maku*) 傘を巻く.

3 (make flat) ... o na⌈ra⌉su ...をならす Ⓒ: roll a road (*michi o narasu*) 道をならす.

— *n.* **1** (anything rolled) ma⌈ita mono⌉ 巻いた物; hi⌈to⌉maki ひと巻き: a roll of toilet paper (*toiretto peepaa hitomaki*) トイレットペーパーひと巻き / a 36-exposure roll of film (*sañjuu-roku-mai-dori no firumu*) 36枚撮りのフィルム.

2 (list) me⌈ebo 名簿: Is my name on the rolls? (*Watashi no namae wa meebo ni notte imasu ka?*) 私の名前は名簿に載っていますか.

3 (bread) ro⌈oru⌉pañ ロールパン.

romance *n.* **1** (love affair) ro⌈ma⌉ñsu ロマンス; re⌈ñai ji⌉keñ 恋愛事件.

2 (story) de⌈ñki sho⌉osetsu 伝奇小説; re⌈ñai sho⌉osetsu 恋愛小説.

romantic *adj.* **1** (fanciful) ku⌈usoo-teki na 空想的な; ro⌈mañchi⌉kku na ロマンチックな: a romantic poem (*romañchikku na shi*) ロマンチックな詩.

2 (of art) ro⌈mañshu⌉gi no ロマン主義の; ro⌈mañha no ロマン派の: the Romantic Movement (*Romañshugi uñdoo*) ロマン主義運動.

romanticism *n.* ro⌈mañshu⌉gi ロマン主義.

roof *n.* ya⌉ne 屋根.

— *vt.* ... ni ya⌉ne o tsu⌈ke⌉ru ...に屋根をつける Ⓥ; ya⌉ne o fu⌈ku 屋根をふく Ⓒ: roof a house with tiles (*kawara de yane o fuku*) かわらで屋根をふく.

room *n.* **1** (of a house) he⌈ya⌉ 部屋; -shitsu 室; -ma 間; -doo 堂: enter a room (*heya ni hairu*) 部屋に入る / leave a room (*heya kara deru*) 部屋から出る / a bathroom (*yokushitsu*) 浴室 / a living room (*ima*) 居間 / a dining room (*shokudoo*) 食堂.

2 (space) ku⌈ukañ 空間; ba⌈sho 場所: A piano takes up room. (*Piano wa basho o toru.*) ピアノは場所を取る. / Make room, please. (*Basho o akete kudasai.*) 場所を空けてください.

3 (chance) yo⌉chi 余地; ki⌈ka⌉i 機会: There is room for improvement. (*Kaizeñ no yochi ga arimasu.*) 改善の余地があります.

root *n.* **1** (of a plant) ne⌉ 根: the root of a tree (*ki no ne*) 木の根.

2 (of a hair, tooth, etc.) tsu⌈kene 付け根: the root of a hair (*mookoñ*) 毛根.

3 (origin) ko⌈ñge⌉ñ 根源; (cause) ge⌈ñiñ 原因: Love of money is the root of all evil. (*Kiñseñyoku ga shoaku no koñgeñ da.*) 金銭欲が諸悪の根源だ. / What is the root of the trouble? (*Momegoto no geñiñ wa nañ desu ka?*) もめごとの原因は何ですか.

rope *n.* na⌈wa⌉ 縄; tsu⌈na⌉ 綱; ro⌉opu ロープ: tie with a rope (*nawa de shibaru*) 縄で縛る.

— *vt.* ... o na⌈wa⌉ [ro⌉opu] de shi⌈ba⌉ru ...を縄[ロープ]で縛る Ⓒ: rope a box to the roof of a car (*hako o kuruma no yane ni roopu de shibaru*) 箱を車の屋根にロープで縛る.

rose *n.* **1** (flower) ba⌈ra ばら: a wild rose (*nobara*) 野ばら.

2 (color) ba⌈rairo ばら色: Her dress was rose colored. (*Kanojo no doresu wa barairo datta.*) 彼女のドレスはばら色だった.

rosy *adj.* **1** (rose-colored) ba⌈rairo no ばら色の; ke⌈sshoku no yo⌉i 血色のよい: rosy cheeks (*kesshoku no yoi hoo*) 血色のよいほお.

2 (bright) a⌈karui 明るい; yu⌈uboo na 有望な: a rosy future (*akarui mirai*) 明るい未来.

rot *vi.* ku⌈sa⌉ru 腐る Ⓒ: The tomatoes are rotting in the basket. (*Tomato ga kago no naka de kusatte iru.*) トマトがかごの中で腐っている.

— *vt.* ... o ku⌈sarase⌉ru ...を腐らせる Ⓥ: Too much water rotted the roots. (*Mizu o yarisugite ne ga kusatte shimatta.*) 水をやりすぎて根が腐ってしまった.

— *n.* fu⌈hai 腐敗.

rotate *vi.* ka⌈iteñ suru 回転する [I]: The earth rotates once in twenty-four hours. (*Chikyuu wa nijuuyo-jikañ de ichi-do kaiteñ suru.*) 地球は24時間で一度回転する.

rotation *n.* ka⌈iteñ 回転: the rotation of an engine (*eñjiñ no kaiteñ*) エンジンの回転.

rough *adj.* **1** (not smooth) a⌈rai 粗い; za⌉razara shita [shite iru] ざらざらした[している]; (uneven) de⌈koboko no でこぼこの: rough paper (*zarazara shita kami*) ざらざらした紙 / a rough road (*dekoboko no michi*) でこぼこの道.

2 (not complete) o⌈omaka na 大まかな; o⌈oza⌉ppa na 大ざっぱな: a rough estimate of repair costs (*shuurihi no oozappa na mitsumori*) 修理費の大ざっぱな見積もり.

3 (not gentle) so⌉ya na 粗野な; bu⌈sa⌉hoo na 無作法な: He is a man with rough manners. (*Kare wa busahoo na otoko da.*) 彼は無作法な男だ.

4 (not finished) mi⌈ka⌉ñsee no 未完成の; fu⌈ka⌉ñzeñ na 不完全な: a rough copy (*shitagaki*) 下書き.

roughly *adv.* **1** (about) o⌈yoso およそ; da⌈itai 大体; ya⌉ku 約: It will cost roughly ten thousand yen. (*Oyoso ichi-mañ-eñ kakarimasu.*) およそ1万円かかります.

2 (in a rough manner) ra⌈ñboo ni 乱暴に; te⌈araku 手荒く: treat a person roughly (*hito o tearaku atsukau*) 人を手荒く扱う.

round[1] *prep.* **1** (in a circle) ... no ma⌈wari o …の周りを: The earth goes round the sun. (*Chikyuu wa taiyoo no mawari o mawaru.*) 地球は太陽の周りを回る.

2 (on all sides of) ... no ma⌈wari ni …の周りに: We sat round the table. (*Watashi-tachi wa teeburu no mawari ni suwatta.*) 私たちはテーブルの周りに座った.

3 (here and there) ... o a⌈chi⌉kochi …をあちこち: He looked round the room. (*Kare wa heya no naka o achikochi mimawashita.*) 彼は部屋の中をあちこち見回した.

— *adv.* **1** (in a circle) gu⌈ru⌉ri to ぐるりと; ka⌈iteñ shite 回転して: turn a chair round (*isu o gururi to mawasu*) いすをぐるりと回す.

2 (in circumference) shu⌉ui ga 周囲が: His waist measures 82 centimeters round. (*Kare wa koshi no shuui ga hachijuu-ni-señchi aru.*) 彼は腰の周囲が82センチある.

3 (from one to another) tsu⌈gi⌉ kara tsu⌈gi⌉ e to 次から次へと: Drinks were passed round. (*Nomimono ga tsugi kara tsugi e to mawasareta.*) 飲物が次から次へと回された.

round[2] *adj.* **1** (shaped like a ball) ma⌈rui 丸い; kyu⌈ukee no 球形の: The earth is round. (*Chikyuu wa marui.*) 地球は丸い.

2 (circular) ma⌈rui 丸い; e⌈ñkee no 円形の: a round plate (*marui sara*) 丸い皿.

3 (plump) ma⌈ruma⌉ru to shita [shite iru] 丸々とした[している]: a round face (*marumaru to shita kao*) 丸々とした顔.

4 (complete) ka⌉ñzeñ na 完全な; ha⌈su⌉u no na⌉i 端数のない: a round number (*hasuu no nai kazu*) 端数のない数.

— *n.* **1** (beat) ju⌈ñkai 巡回: make one's rounds (*juñkai suru*) 巡回する.

2 (one complete game) hi⌈to⌉-shoobu ひと勝負; hi⌈to⌉shiai ひと試合: play a round (*hitoshoobu suru*) ひと勝負する.

— *vt.* ... o ma⌈waru …を回る [C]; ma⌈garu 曲がる [C]: round a corner (*kado o magaru*) 角を曲がる.

round-trip ticket *n.* o⌈ofuku-ki⌉ppu 往復切符.

rouse *vt.* ... no me⌉ o sa⌈masase⌉ru …の目を覚まさせる [V]; ... o o⌈ko⌉su …を起こす [C]: Please rouse me at six. (*Roku-ji ni okoshite kudasai.*) 6時に起こしてください.

route *n.* mi⌈chi 道; ru⌉uto ルート:

That restaurant is on our route. (*Sono resutorañ wa watashi-tachi ga iku michi no tochuu ni arimasu.*) そのレストランは私たちが行く道の途中にあります. / an air route (*kookuuro*) 航空路.

routine *n.* ki⌈mariki⌉tta shi⌈goto 決まりきった仕事: one's daily routine (*mainichi no kimatta shigoto*) 毎日の決まった仕事.

— *adj.* ki⌈mariki⌉tta 決まりきった; te⌈eki-teki na 定期的な: a routine physical exam (*teeki-teki na keñkoo shiñdañ*) 定期的な健康診断.

row[1] *n.* re⌉tsu 列: a row of trees (*namiki*) 並木 / sit in the front row (*ichibañ mae no retsu ni suwaru*) いちばん前の列に座る.

row[2] *vt.* **1** (move) ... o ko⌉gu ...をこぐ Ⓒ: row a boat (*booto o kogu*) ボートをこぐ.

2 (carry) ... o ko⌉ide ha⌈kobu ...をこいで運ぶ Ⓒ: He rowed me across the river. (*Kare wa fune o koide watashi o kawa mukoo made hakoñde kureta.*) 彼は舟をこいで私を川向こうまで運んでくれた.

— *vi.* fu⌉ne o ko⌉gu 舟をこぐ Ⓒ.

row[3] *n.* o⌈oge⌉ñka 大げんか; sa⌉wagi 騒ぎ: He had a row with his wife. (*Kare wa okusañ to oogeñka o shita.*) 彼は奥さんと大げんかをした.

royal *adj.* o⌉o no 王の: a royal family (*oozoku*) 王族 / a royal palace (*ookyuu*) 王宮.

rub *vt.* ... o ko⌈su⌉ru ...をこする Ⓒ; su⌈riko⌉mu すり込む Ⓒ: rub one's eyes (*me o kosuru*) 目をこする / rub oil on one's skin (*hada ni abura o surikomu*) 肌にオイルをすり込む.

— *vi.* su⌈re⌉ru すれる Ⓥ; ko⌈su⌉ru こする Ⓒ: The wheel is rubbing against something. (*Shariñ ga nani-ka kosutte iru.*) 車輪が何かこすっている.

rubber *n.* **1** (elastic substance) go⌉mu ゴム: a rubber band (*wagomu*) 輪ゴム / a rubber stamp (*gomuiñ*) ゴム印.

2 (eraser) ke⌈shigomu 消しゴム.

3 (condom) ko⌈ñdo⌉omu コンドーム.

rubbish *n.* go⌈mi⌉ ごみ; ku⌉zu くず: throw rubbish away (*gomi o suteru*) ごみを捨てる.

ruby *n.* ru⌉bii ルビー.

rude *adj.* **1** (not polite) shi⌈tsu⌉ree na 失礼な; bu⌉ree na 無礼な; bu⌈sa⌉hoo na 無作法な: It is rude of you not to thank him. (*Kare ni o-ree o iwanai no wa shitsuree desu.*) 彼にお礼を言わないのは失礼です. / say rude things (*buree na koto o iu*) 無礼なことを言う.

2 (rough) ra⌈ñboo na 乱暴な: rude treatment (*rañboo na toriatsukai*) 乱暴な取り扱い.

rug *n.* shi⌈kimono 敷物; ju⌉utañ じゅうたん.

rugby *n.* ra⌉gubii ラグビー.

rugged *adj.* **1** (uneven) de⌈koboko no でこぼこの: a rugged road (*dekoboko no michi*) でこぼこの道.

2 (strong-looking) i⌈katsui いかつい: rugged features (*ikatsui kaodachi*) いかつい顔立ち.

3 (not refined) se⌈ñreñ sarete inai 洗練されていない: rugged manners (*señreñ sarete inai furumai*) 洗練されていない振る舞い.

ruin *vt.* ... o ha⌈metsu saseru ...を破滅させる Ⓥ; da⌈inashi ni suru 台なしにする Ⓘ: Drink ruined his career. (*Sake ga kare no isshoo o dainashi ni shita.*) 酒が彼の一生を台なしにした.

— *n.* **1** (destruction) ha⌈metsu 破滅; ko⌈ohai 荒廃: The castle fell into ruin. (*Sono shiro wa koohai shite shimatta.*) その城は荒廃してしまった.

2 (building) ha⌉ikyo 廃虚; i⌈seki 遺跡: ancient Greek ruins (*kodai Girisha no iseki*) 古代ギリシャの遺跡.

rule *n.* **1** (regulation) ki⌉soku 規則; ki⌈tee 規定: obey [break] a rule (*kisoku o mamoru [yaburu]*) 規則を守る[破る] / It's against the rules. (*Kisoku ihañ da.*) 規則違反だ.

2 (reign) shi⌉hai 支配; to⌉ochi 統治: The country was under mili-

r

tary rule. (*Sono kuni wa guñ no shihaika ni atta.*) その国は軍の支配下にあった.
3 (custom) shuˈukañ 習慣; naˈrawashi 習わし: It is my rule to rise early. (*Hayaku okiru no ga watashi no shuukañ desu.*) 早く起きるのが私の習慣です.
— *vt.* **1** (govern) ... o shiˈhai suru ...を支配する [I]; toˈochi suru 統治する [I]: The queen ruled her country for a long period. (*Jo-oo wa kuni o nagai aida toochi shita.*) 女王は国を長い間統治した.
2 (decide) ... o saˈiketsu suru ...を裁決する [I]; haˈñtee suru 判定する [I]: The court ruled him innocent. (*Hootee wa kare o muzai to saiketsu shita.*) 法廷は彼を無罪と裁決した.
3 (draw) seˈñ o hiˈku 線を引く [C]: rule straight lines on paper (*kami ni massugu na señ o hiku*) 紙に真っすぐな線を引く.
— *vi.* **1** (govern) shiˈhai suru 支配する [I].
2 (decide) haˈñketsu suru 判決する [I]; kiˈtee suru 規定する [I].

ruler *n.* **1** (person) shiˈhaˈisha 支配者; toˈochiˈsha 統治者.
2 (material) joˈogi 定規; moˈnosaˈshi 物差し: draw a line with a ruler (*joogi de señ o hiku*) 定規で線を引く.

ruling *n.* **1** (decision) haˈñketsu 判決; saˈitee 裁定: a ruling of the Supreme Court (*Saikoo-saibañsho no hañketsu*) 最高裁判所の判決.
2 (governing) shiˈhai 支配; toˈochi 統治.
— *adj.* shiˈhai shite iru 支配している: the ruling class (*shihai-kaikyuu*) 支配階級 / the ruling party (*yotoo*) 与党.

rumor *n.* uˈwasa うわさ: There is a rumor that they are getting married. (*Kare-ra wa kekkoñ suru to iu uwasa da.*) 彼らは結婚するといううわさだ.

run *vi.* **1** (move rapidly) haˈshiˈru 走る [C]; kaˈkeˈru 駆ける [V]: I ran to the station. (*Watashi wa eki made hashitta.*) 私は駅まで走った.
2 (escape) niˈgeˈru 逃げる [V]: I ran for my life. (*Watashi wa inochi karagara nigeta.*) 私は命からがら逃げた.
3 (take part in a race) kyoˈosoo ni deˈru 競走に出る [V]; riˈkkoˈoho suru 立候補する [I]: He ran in the 100-meter race. (*Kare wa hyaku-meetoru kyoosoo ni deta.*) 彼は100メートル競走に出た. / run for mayor (*shichoo ni rikkooho suru*) 市長に立候補する.
4 (work) uˈgoˈku 動く [C]: This car runs by electricity. (*Kono kuruma wa deñki de ugokimasu.*) この車は電気で動きます.
5 (travel regularly) uˈñkoo suru 運行する [I]; haˈshiˈru 走る [C]: The buses run every fifteen minutes. (*Basu wa juugo-fuñ oki ni hashitte imasu.*) バスは15分おきに走っています.
6 (flow) naˈgareˈru 流れる [V]: Sweat was running from his forehead. (*Ase ga kare no hitai kara nagarete ita.*) 汗が彼の額から流れていた.
7 (extend) toˈotte iru 通っている [V]: The path runs through the woods. (*Sono komichi wa mori no naka o tootte imasu.*) その小道は森の中を通っています.
8 (continue) tsuˈzuku 続く [C]: The play ran for three months. (*Sono shibai wa sañ-kagetsu tsuzuita.*) その芝居は3か月続いた.
— *vt.* **1** (cause to run) ... o haˈshiraseˈru ...を走らせる: run a dog (*inu o hashiraseru*) 犬を走らせる.
2 (cause to work) ... o uˈgokaˈsu ...を動かす [C]: run a machine (*kikai o ugokasu*) 機械を動かす.
3 (manage) ... o keˈe-ee suru ...を経営する [I]: run a hotel (*hoteru o kee-ee suru*) ホテルを経営する.
4 (publish) ... o daˈsu ...を出す [C]: run an advertisement in a newspaper (*shiñbuñ ni kookoku o dasu*)

新聞に広告を出す.

— *n.* **1** (running) ha⌈shi⌉ru ko⌈to⌉ 走ること: I was tired after my run. (*Hashitta no de tsukareta.*) 走ったので疲れた.

2 (series) re⌈ñzoku 連続; tsu⌈zuki 続き: a run of fine weather (*kooteñ tsuzuki*) 好天続き.

3 (score) to⌈kuteñ 得点: score three runs (*sañ-teñ ageru*) 3 点あげる / a home run (*hoomurañ*) ホームラン.

4 (ladder) de⌈ñseñ 伝線: get a run in one's tights (*taitsu ni deñseñ ga dekiru*) タイツに伝線ができる.

runner *n.* ha⌈shi⌉ru hi⌈to⌉ 走る人; so⌉osha 走者; ra⌉ññaa ランナー: a long-distance runner (*chookyori rañnaa*) 長距離ランナー.

rural *adj.* i⌈naka no 田舎の: a rural town (*inaka no machi*) 田舎の町 / rural life (*deñeñ-seekatsu*) 田園生活.

rush *vi.* **1** (hurry) to⌈sshiñ suru 突進する [I]; i⌈so⌉gu 急ぐ [C]: The police rushed to the scene. (*Keekañtai wa geñba e isoida.*) 警官隊は現場へ急いだ.

2 (act in haste) ke⌈esotsu ni koodoo suru 軽率に行動する [I]: She rushed into marriage. (*Kanojo wa keesotsu ni kekkoñ shita.*) 彼女は軽率に結婚した.

— *vt.* (casue to rush) ... o to⌈sshiñ saseru …を突進させる [V]; i⌈sogase⌉ru 急がせる [V]: Don't rush me. (*Isogasenaide kudasai.*) 急がせないでください.

— *n.* to⌈sshiñ 突進; sa⌈ttoo 殺到: make a rush for the door (*doa ni mukatte sattoo suru*) ドアに向かって殺到する.

rust *n.* sa⌈bi⌉ さび: a knife covered with rust (*sabitsuita naifu*) さびついたナイフ.

— *vi.* sa⌈bi⌉ru さびる [V]: This bicycle does not rust. (*Kono jiteñsha wa sabimaseñ.*) この自転車はさびません.

rustic *adj.* i⌈naka no いなかの: rustic life (*deñeñ seekatsu*) 田園生活.

rusty *adj.* sa⌉bita さびた; sa⌉bite iru さびている: a rusty nail (*sabita kugi*) さびた釘.

rye *n.* ra⌈imugi ライ麦; ha⌈dakamu⌉gi 裸麦.

S

sack *n.* o⌈obu⌉kuro 大袋: a potato sack (*jagaimo no fukuro*) じゃがいもの袋 / a sack of coal (*sekitañ hitofukuro*) 石炭ひと袋.

sacred *adj.* shi⌈ñsee na 神聖な: a sacred book (*seeteñ*) 聖典.

sacrifice *n.* gi⌈see 犠牲: I made great sacrifices to educate my children. (*Watashi wa kodomo o kyooiku suru no ni tadai no gisee o haratta.*) 私は子どもを教育するのに多大の犠牲を払った.

— *vt.* **1** (give up) ... o gi⌈see ni suru …を犠牲にする [I]: I cannot sacrifice business for pleasure. (*Watashi wa asobi no tame ni shigoto o gisee ni suru koto wa dekinai.*) 私は遊びのために仕事を犠牲にすることはできない.

2 (offer to a deity) ... o i⌈kenie to shite sasageru …をいけにえとしてささげる [V]: sacrifice sheep to gods (*hitsuji o kami ni ikenie to shite sasageru*) 羊を神にいけにえとしてささげる.

sad *adj.* ka⌈nashii 悲しい; a⌉ware na 哀れな: the sad news (*kanashii shirase*) 悲しい知らせ / We all felt sad about his death. (*Watashi-tachi wa miñna kare no shi o kanashiñda.*) 私たちはみんな彼の死を悲しんだ.

saddle *n.* (of a horse) ku⌈ra⌉ くら; (of a bicycle) sa⌈doru サドル: put a saddle on a horse (*uma ni kura o oku*) 馬にくらを置く.

sadly *adv.* ka⌈nashi⌉ñde 悲しんで; ka⌈nashi-so⌉o ni 悲しそうに: The girl was weeping sadly. (*Sono oñna-no-ko wa kanashi-soo ni naite ita.*) その女の子は悲しそうに泣いていた.

sadness *n.* ka⌈nashimi 悲しみ; hi⌈ai 悲哀.

safe[1] *adj.* **1** (out of danger) a⌈ñzeñ na 安全な: We are safe here. (*Koko ni ireba añzeñ desu.*) ここにいれば安全です.
2 (not injured) bu⌈ji na 無事な: I hope that you have a safe trip. (*Tabi no go-buji o inorimasu.*) 旅のご無事を祈ります.

safe[2] *n.* ki⌉ñko 金庫: put the money in the safe (*kiñko ni o-kane o shimau*) 金庫にお金をしまう.

safely *adv.* a⌈ñzeñ ni 安全に; bu⌈ji ni 無事に: He reached home safely. (*Kare wa buji ni kitaku shimashita.*) 彼は無事に帰宅しました.

safety *n.* a⌈ñzeñ 安全; bu⌈ji 無事: Safety First. (*Añzeñ dai-ichi.*) 安全第一.

sail *n.* ho⌉ 帆: raise [lower] a sail (*ho o ageru* [*orosu*]) 帆を揚げる[下ろす].
— *vi.* ha⌈ñsoo suru 帆走する [I]; ko⌉okai suru 航海する [I]: They sailed across the Pacific. (*Kare-ra wa Taiheeyoo o watatte kookai shita.*) 彼らは太平洋を渡って航海した.

sailor *n.* **1** (crew) se⌈ñiñ 船員; fu⌈na⌉nori 船乗り: a good [poor] sailor (*fune ni tsuyoi* [*yowai*] *hito*) 船に強い[弱い]人.
2 (not officer) su⌉ihee 水兵.

saint *n.* se⌈ejiñ 聖人; se⌉eja 聖者.

sake *n.* (... no) ta⌈me⌉ (…の)ため; mo⌈kuteki 目的: They fought for their country's sake. (*Kare-ra wa sokoku no tame ni tatakatta.*) 彼らは祖国のために戦った.
for the sake of ... *adv.* ... no ta⌈me⌉ ni …のために: He would do anything for the sake of money. (*Kane no tame nara kare wa nañ de mo yaru.*) 金のためなら彼は何でもやる.

salad *n.* sa⌉rada サラダ: make a vegetable salad (*yasai sarada o tsukuru*) 野菜サラダを作る.

salary *n.* kyu⌉uryoo 給料; sa⌉rarii サラリー: a high [low] salary (*takai* [*hikui*] *kyuuryoo*) 高い[低い]給料 / I can't live on my salary now. (*Ima no kyuuryoo de wa seekatsu dekinai.*) 今の給料では生活できない.

sale *n.* **1** (act of selling) ha⌈ñbai 販売: make a sale (*hañbai o suru*) 販売をする.
2 (at lower prices) ya⌈suuri 安売り; to⌈kubai 特売: I bought this coat at a sale. (*Watashi wa kono kooto o tokubai de katta.*) 私はこのコートを特売で買った.
3 (the amount sold) u⌈riage 売り上げ: The sales of cars are up [down] this month. (*Kuruma no uriage ga koñgetsu wa agatta* [*sagatta*].) 車の売り上げが今月は上がった[下がった].

salesman *n.* te⌈ñiñ 店員; se⌈erusu⌉mañ セールスマン: The salesmen in this store are all very kind. (*Koko no mise no teñiñ wa miñna shiñsetsu da.*) ここの店の店員はみんな親切だ. / a car salesman (*kuruma no seerusumañ*) 車のセールスマン.
★ Japanese '*seerusumañ*' refers only to 'commercial traveler.'

saleswoman *n.* jo⌈see-te⌉ñiñ 女性店員.

salmon *n.* sa⌉ke 鮭.

salt *n.* shi⌈o⌉ 塩: This soup needs a little more salt. (*Kono suupu wa moo sukoshi shio o kikaseta hoo ga ii.*) このスープはもう少し塩を利かせたほうがいい. / Please pass the salt. (*Shio o mawashite kudasai.*) 塩を回してください.

salute *vt.* **1** (show respect) ... ni ke⌈eree suru …に敬礼する [I]: salute the flag (*kokki ni keeree suru*) 国旗に敬礼する.
2 (greet) ... ni a⌉isatsu suru …にあいさつする [I]: She saluted me with a smile. (*Kanojo wa egao de watashi ni aisatsu shita.*) 彼女は笑顔で私にあいさつした.

S

salvation *n.* kyu⌈usai 救済; kyu⌉u-jo 救助.

same *adj.* o⌈naji 同じ; do⌈oitsu no 同一の: He and I are the same age. (*Kare to watashi wa onaji toshi desu.*) 彼と私は同じ年です.
— *pron.* o⌈naji mono⌉ [koto⌉] 同じ物[事]: She ordered coffee and I ordered the same. (*Kanojo wa koohii o chuumoñ shita ga watashi mo onaji mono o chuumoñ shita.*) 彼女はコーヒーを注文したが私も同じ物を注文した.

sample *n.* mi⌈hoñ 見本; sa⌉ñpuru サンプル: This is different from the sample. (*Kore wa mihoñ to chigau.*) これは見本と違う.
— *vt.* ... no a⌈ji o mi⌉ru …の味をみる [V]: sample wine (*waiñ no aji o miru*) ワインの味をみる.

sand *n.* su⌈na 砂.

sandal *n.* sa⌈ñdaru サンダル.

sandwich *n.* sa⌈ñdoi⌉tchi サンドイッチ: make a ham sandwich (*hamu sañdoitchi o tsukuru*) ハムサンドイッチを作る.

sandy *adj.* su⌈na no 砂の; su⌈nachi no 砂地の: a sandy beach (*sunahama*) 砂浜.

sane *adj.* sho⌈oki no 正気の; ke⌈ñzeñ na 健全な: He doesn't seem sane at all. (*Kare wa totemo shooki to wa omoenai.*) 彼はとても正気とは思えない. / make a sane decision (*keñzeñ na ketsudañ o suru*) 健全な決断をする.

sanitary *adj.* e⌈esee-teki na 衛生的な; se⌈eketsu na 清潔な: The public lavatory in the park was not sanitary. (*Kooeñ no kooshuu beñjo wa seeketsu de nakatta.*) 公園の公衆便所は清潔でなかった.

sarcasm *n.* hi⌈niku 皮肉; i⌈yami⌉ 嫌み: bitter sarcasm (*tsuuretsu na hiniku*) 痛烈な皮肉.

sarcastic *adj.* hi⌈niku na 皮肉な; i⌈yami⌉ o i⌈u 嫌みをいう: a sarcastic person (*hinikuya*) 皮肉屋.

sardine *n.* i⌈washi いわし; sa⌉radiñ サーディン.

sash *n.* o⌉bi 帯; ka⌈zario⌉bi 飾り帯.

satellite *n.* **1** (natural body) e⌈esee 衛星: The moon is a satellite of the earth. (*Tsuki wa chikyuu no eesee desu.*) 月は地球の衛星です. **2** (man-made body) ji⌈ñkoo-e⌉esee 人工衛星: launch a satellite (*jiñkoo-eesee o uchiageru*) 人工衛星を打ち上げる / satellite broadcasting (*eesee hoosoo*) 衛星放送.

satin *n.* shu⌉su しゅす; sa⌉teñ サテン.

satisfaction *n.* ma⌉ñzoku 満足; na⌈ttoku 納得: The matter was settled to the satisfaction of all. (*Sono koto wa miñna ga mañzoku suru yoo ni kaiketsu shita.*) そのことはみんなが満足するように解決した.

satisfactory *adj.* ma⌉ñzoku no i⌈ku 満足のいく; na⌈ttoku no iku 納得のいく: He gave a satisfactory explanation. (*Kare wa nattoku no iku setsumee o shita.*) 彼は納得のいく説明をした.

satisfied *adj.* ma⌉ñzoku shita [shite iru] 満足した[している]; na⌈ttoku shita [shite iru] 納得した[している]: She was satisfied with her new house. (*Kanojo wa atarashii ie ni mañzoku shite ita.*) 彼女は新しい家に満足していた.

satisfy *vt.* ... o ma⌉ñzoku saseru 満足させる [V]; na⌈ttoku saseru 納得させる [V]: His explanation failed to satisfy her. (*Kare no setsumee wa kanojo o nattoku saseru koto ga dekinakatta.*) 彼の説明は彼女を納得させることができなかった.

saturate *vt.* ... ni shi⌈mikoma⌉su …にしみ込ます [C]; ... o zu⌈bunure ni suru …をずぶぬれにする [I]: a cloth saturated with oil (*abura no shimikoñda kire*) 油のしみ込んだ布.

Saturday *n.* do⌈yo⌉o(bi) 土曜(日).

sauce *n.* so⌉osu ソース. ★ In Japan, it usually refers to a thick brown sauce.

saucer *n.* u⌈ke⌉zara 受け皿: a cup and saucer (*ukezara tsuki no chawañ*) 受け皿付きの茶わん.

sausage *n.* so⌈ose⌉eji ソーセージ:

Vienna sausage (*Uiñna sooseeji*) ウインナソーセージ.

savage *adj.* **1** (cruel) do⌈omoo na どうもうな; za⌈ñkoku na 残酷な: a savage beast (*doomoo na kemono*) どうもうな獣.
2 (uncivilized) ya⌈bañ na 野蛮な: savage customs (*yabañ na fuushuu*) 野蛮な風習.

save *vt.* **1** (rescue) ... o su⌈kuu ...を救う [C]; ta⌈suke⌉ru 助ける [V]: He saved the child's life. (*Kare wa sono ko no inochi o sukutta.*) 彼はその子の命を救った.
2 (store up) ... o ta⌈kuwae⌉ru ...を蓄える [V]; cho⌈kiñ suru 貯金する [I]: I save some money out of my salary every month. (*Watashi wa maitsuki kyuuryoo kara ikura ka chokiñ shite imasu.*) 私は毎月給料からいくらか貯金しています.
3 (avoid wasting) ... o se⌈tsuyaku suru ...を節約する [I]; ha⌈bu⌉ku 省く [C]: He saved his bus fares and walked. (*Kare wa basu-dai o setsuyaku shite aruita.*) 彼はバス代を節約して歩いた.

savings *n.* yo⌈kiñ 預金; cho⌈kiñ 貯金: savings account (*futsuuyokiñ kooza*) 普通預金口座.

savior *n.* kyu⌈usa⌉isha 救済者; su⌈kui⌉nushi 救い主.

saw *n.* no⌈kogi⌉ri のこぎり: cut wood with a saw (*nokogiri de ki o kiru*) のこぎりで木を切る.
— *vt.* ... o no⌈kogi⌉ri de ki⌉ru ...をのこぎりで切る [C]: saw a tree down (*ki o nokogiri de kitte taosu*) 木をのこぎりで切って倒す.

say *vt.* **1** (speak) ... to i⌈u ...と言う [C]; ha⌈na⌉su 話す [C]: They say that you are wrong. (*Miñna wa kimi ga machigatte iru to itte iru.*) みんなは君が間違っていると言っている. / What did he say about the problem? (*Sono moñdai ni tsuite kare wa nañ to itte imashita ka?*) その問題について彼は何と言っていましたか.
2 (state) ... to ka⌉ite aru ...と書いてある [C]: The sign says "Danger." (*Sono hyooshiki ni wa "Kikeñ" to kaite aru.*) その標識には「危険」と書いてある.
3 (indicate) ... o shi⌈me⌉su ...を示す [C]; sa⌉su 指す [C]: My watch says ten o'clock. (*Watashi no tokee wa juu-ji o sashite iru.*) 私の時計は10時を指している.
4 (order) ... to shi⌉ji suru ...と指示する [I]; i⌈u 言う [C]: We must do whatever the teacher says. (*Señsee no iu koto wa nañ de mo shinakereba naranai.*) 先生の言うことは何でもしなければならない.

scale[1] *n.* **1** (of a measure) me⌈mori 目盛り: read the scale on a thermometer (*oñdokee no memori o yomu*) 温度計の目盛りを読む.
2 (of a map) shu⌈kushaku 縮尺: a map with a scale of one centimeter to one kilometer (*ichi-kiro o isseñchi ni shukushaku shita chizu*) 1キロを1センチに縮尺した地図.
3 (size) ki⌉bo 規模: a business on a large scale (*dai-kibo na jigyoo*) 大規模な事業.
4 (of music) o⌈ñkai 音階.

scale[2] *n.* te⌈ñbiñ てんびん; ta⌈ijuukee 体重計: weigh oneself on the bathroom scales (*yokushitsu no taijuukee de taijuu o hakaru*) 浴室の体重計で体重を量る.

scan *vt.* **1** (look at attentively) ... o ji⌈tto mitsumeru ...をじっと見つめる [V]: scan the horizon for a ship (*fune o motomete suiheeseñ o jitto mitsumeru*) 船を求めて水平線をじっと見つめる.
2 (glance) ... ni za⌈tto me⌉ o toosu ...にざっと目を通す [C]: scan a newspaper (*shiñbuñ ni zatto me o toosu*) 新聞にざっと目を通す.

scandal *n.* su⌈kya⌉ñdaru スキャンダル; o⌈shoku ji⌉keñ 汚職事件: cause a scandal (*sukyañdaru o okosu*) スキャンダルを起こす.

scanty *adj.* to⌈boshi⌉i 乏しい; wa⌉zuka na わずかな: scanty information (*toboshii joohoo*) 乏しい情報.

scar *n.* ki⌈zuato 傷跡: He has a scar

S

on his face. (*Kare wa kao ni kizu-ato ga aru.*) 彼は顔に傷跡がある.

scarce *adj.* fu⌈soku shite (iru) 不足して(いる); su⌈kuna⌉i 少ない: Vegetables are scarce and dear. (*Yasai ga fusoku shite nedañ ga takai.*) 野菜が不足して値段が高い.

scarcely *adv.* **1** (hardly) ho⌈to⌉ñdo ... na⌉i ほとんど…ない: He was so tired that he could scarcely walk. (*Kare wa hijoo ni tsukarete ite hotoñdo aruku koto ga dekinakatta.*) 彼は非常に疲れていてほとんど歩くことができなかった.
2 (barely) ya⌈tto やっと; karo⌉ojite かろうじて: Scarcely 10 people were present. (*Yatto juu-niñ ga shusseki shita.*) やっと10人が出席した.

scare *vt.* ... o bi⌈kku⌉ri saseru …をびっくりさせる [V]; o⌈doka⌉su 脅かす [C]: I was scared by the sudden barking. (*Totsuzeñ inu ga hoete bikkuri shita.*) 突然犬がほえてびっくりした.

scarf *n.* su⌈ka⌉afu スカーフ; e⌈ri⌉maki えり巻き: wear a scarf (*sukaafu o kakeru*) スカーフをかける.

scarlet *adj.* hi⌈iro no 緋色の; shi⌈ñkuiro no 深紅色の: He turned scarlet. (*Kare wa kao ga makka ni natta.*) 彼は顔が真っ赤になった.
— *n.* hi⌈iro 緋色; shi⌈ñkuiro 深紅色.

scatter *vt.* **1** (sprinkle) ... o ba⌈rama⌉ku …をばらまく [C]; ma⌈kichirasu まき散らす [C]: scatter seed over the fields (*hatake ni tane o maku*) 畑に種をまく.
2 (drive) ... o o⌈ichira⌉su …を追い散らす [C]: The police scattered the crowd. (*Keekañ-tachi wa guñshuu o oichirashita.*) 警官たちは群集を追い散らした.
— *vi.* chi⌈rijiri ni na⌉ru ちりぢりになる [C]: The children scattered when it began to rain. (*Ame ga furi-dasu to kodomo-tachi wa chirijiri ni natta.*) 雨が降り出すと子どもたちはちりぢりになった.

scene *n.* **1** (the place of occurrence) ge⌈ñba 現場: We rushed to the scene of the accident. (*Watashi-tachi wa jiko no geñba ni isoida.*) 私たちは事故の現場に急いだ.
2 (view) ke⌉shiki 景色; fu⌉ukee 風景: I like to paint rural scenes. (*Watashi wa inaka no fuukee o egaku no ga suki da.*) 私は田舎の風景を描くのが好きだ.
3 (part of a play) ba 場; ba⌉meñ 場面: She appears in Act I, Scene 2. (*Kanojo wa dai ichi-maku dai ni-ba ni toojoo suru.*) 彼女は第1幕第2場に登場する.

scenery *n.* **1** (view) fu⌉ukee 風景; ke⌉shiki 景色: The mountain scenery was beautiful. (*Yama no keshiki wa utsukushikatta.*) 山の景色は美しかった.
2 (of a stage) ha⌈ikee 背景; bu⌈taiso⌉ochi 舞台装置.

scent *n.* ni⌈o⌉i におい; ka⌈ori 香り: the scent of flowers (*hana no kaori*) 花の香り.
— *vt.* ... o ka⌈gitsuke⌉ru …をかぎつける [V]: The dog scented a fox. (*Inu ga kitsune no nioi o kagitsuketa.*) 犬がきつねのにおいをかぎつけた.

schedule *n.* **1** (plan) yo⌈tee 予定; yo⌈teehyoo 予定表; su⌈ke⌉juuru スケジュール: My schedule for tomorrow is very tight. (*Ashita no yotee wa gisshiri tsumatte iru.*) あしたの予定はぎっしり詰まっている.
2 (timetable) ji⌈kokuhyoo 時刻表: a train schedule (*ressha no jikokuhyoo*) 列車の時刻表.
— *vt.* ... o yo⌈tee suru …を予定する [I]: The next meeting is scheduled for Monday. (*Tsugi no kaigi wa getsuyoobi ni yotee sarete iru.*) 次の会議は月曜日に予定されている.

scheme *n.* **1** (plan) ke⌈ekaku 計画: carry out a scheme (*keekaku o jikkoo suru*) 計画を実行する.
2 (plot) i⌈ñboo 陰謀; ta⌈kurami たくらみ: He had a scheme to rob the bank. (*Kare wa giñkoo o osou koto o takurañde ita.*) 彼は銀行を襲うことをたくらんでいた.
— *vt.* ... o ke⌈ekaku suru …を計画

S

する [I]: He schemed to escape from the prison. (*Kare wa datsugoku o keekaku shita.*) 彼は脱獄を計画した.

scholar *n.* ga⌈kusha 学者: a famous scholar of Japanese literature (*Nihoñ buñgaku no yuumee na gakusha*) 日本文学の有名な学者.

scholarship *n.* **1** (financial aid) sho⌈ogakukiñ 奨学金: receive a scholarship to university (*daigaku shiñgaku no shoogakukiñ o ukeru*) 大学進学の奨学金を受ける.
2 (learning) ga⌈ku⌉moñ 学問; ga⌈kushiki 学識: a person of great scholarship (*hijoo-ni gakushiki no aru hito*) 非常に学識のある人.

school *n.* **1** (building) ga⌈kkoo 学校: He goes to school by bus. (*Kare wa basu de gakkoo ni kayotte iru.*) 彼はバスで学校に通っている.
2 (class) ju⌉gyoo 授業: We have no school today. (*Kyoo wa jugyoo wa arimaseñ.*) きょうは授業はありません.
3 (department) ga⌈kubu 学部: medical school (*igakubu*) 医学部.
4 (group) ryu⌉uha 流派: a school of flower arrangement (*ikebana no ryuuha*) いけばなの流派.

schoolboy *n.* da⌈ñshi-se⌉eto 男子生徒.

school building *n.* ko⌉osha 校舎.

schoolchild *n.* ga⌈kudoo 学童.

schoolgirl *n.* jo⌈shi-se⌉eto 女子生徒.

schoolteacher *n.* se⌈ñse⌉e 先生; kyo⌉oshi 教師.

science *n.* ka⌉gaku 科学: natural science (*shizeñ kagaku*) 自然科学.

scientific *adj.* ka⌉gaku no 科学の; ka⌈gaku-teki na 科学的な: His methods are scientific. (*Kare no hoohoo wa kagaku-teki da.*) 彼の方法は科学的だ.

scientist *n.* ka⌈ga⌉kusha 科学者: a social scientist (*shakai kagakusha*) 社会科学者.

scissors *n.* ha⌈sami⌉ はさみ: use scissors (*hasami o tsukau*) はさみを使う.

scold *vt.* ... o shi⌈karu ...をしかる [C]: She scolded her son for being lazy. (*Kanojo wa musuko ga namakete iru no de shikatta.*) 彼女は息子が怠けているのでしかった.

scope *n.* ha⌉ñi 範囲; shi⌉ya 視野: broaden the scope of an investigation (*choosa no hañi o hirogeru*) 調査の範囲を広げる.

score *n.* **1** (points in a game) to⌈kuteñ 得点; (in a test) te⌈ñsu⌉u 点数: win by a score of three to two (*sañ tai ni de katsu*) 3 対 2 で勝つ / I got a score of eighty on the math test. (*Watashi wa suugaku no shikeñ de hachijut-teñ o totta.*) 私は数学の試験で 80 点を取った.
2 (of music) ga⌈kufu 楽譜; su⌈ko⌉a スコア.
— *vt.* ... te⌈ñ o to⌉ru ...点を取る [C]: We scored five points late in the game. (*Wareware wa shiai no koohañ de go-teñ ireta.*) われわれは試合の後半で 5 点入れた.

scorn *n.* ke⌈ebetsu 軽蔑: She looked at me with scorn. (*Kanojo wa watashi o keebetsu shita me de mita.*) 彼女は私を軽蔑した目で見た.
— *vt.* ... o ke⌈ebetsu suru ...を軽蔑する [I]: I scorn people who tell lies. (*Watashi wa uso o tsuku hito o keebetsu suru.*) 私はうそをつく人を軽蔑する.

scornful *adj.* ke⌈ebetsu shita [shite iru] 軽蔑した[している]: a scornful look (*keebetsu shita kaotsuki*) 軽蔑した顔つき / He was scornful of us. (*Kare wa watashi-tachi o keebetsu shite ita.*) 彼は私たちを軽蔑していた.

scout *n.* **1** (soldier) se⌈kkoo 斥候: send out scouts (*sekkoo o dasu*) 斥候を出す.
2 (Boy Scouts) bo⌈oisuka⌉uto ボーイスカウト.
— *vi.* (... o) sa⌈gashimawa⌉ru (...を)探し回る [C]: scout about for a good restaurant (*yoi shokudoo o sagashimawaru*) よい食堂を探し回る.

scramble *vi.* **1** (climb) (... ni) yo-

S

⌐jinobo¬ru (…に)よじ登る Ⓒ: scramble up into a tree (*ki ni yojinoboru*) 木によじ登る.
2 (struggle) (… o) u⌐baia¬u (…を)奪い合う Ⓒ: scramble for good seats (*yoi seki o toriau*) よい席を取り合う.

scrambled eggs *n.* i⌐rita¬mago いり卵.

scrap *n.* **1** (fragment) ki⌐rehashi 切れ端; sho⌐oheñ 小片: a scrap of paper (*kamikire*) 紙切れ.
2 (refuse) su⌐kura¬ppu スクラップ; ha⌐ibutsu 廃物: This old car will soon go for scrap. (*Kono furui kuruma wa moo sugu sukurappu da.*) この古い車はもうすぐスクラップだ.

scrape *vt.* **1** (rub) … o ko⌐surioto¬su …をこすり落とす Ⓒ: scrape the mud off one's shoes (*kutsu no doro o kosuriotosu*) 靴の泥をこすり落とす.
2 (injure) … o su⌐rimu¬ku …をすりむく Ⓒ: I fell and scraped my knee. (*Watashi wa koroñde hiza o surimuita.*) 私は転んでひざをすりむいた.

scratch *vt.* **1** (tear) … o hi⌐kka¬ku …をひっかく Ⓒ: The cat scratched me with its claws. (*Neko ga watashi o tsume de hikkaita.*) 猫が私を爪でひっかいた.
2 (rub) … o ka¬ku …をかく Ⓒ; ko⌐su¬ru こする Ⓒ: scratch one's head (*atama o kaku*) 頭をかく.
— *n.* ka⌐ki¬kizu かき傷: He got a scratch on his hand. (*Kare wa te ni kakikizu o koshiraeta.*) 彼は手にかき傷をこしらえた.

scream *vi.* ka⌐nakirigo¬e o a⌐geru 金切り声を上げる Ⓥ: She screamed for help. (*Kanojo wa sukui o motomete kanakirigoe o ageta.*) 彼女は救いを求めて金切り声を上げた.
— *n.* ka⌐nakirigo¬e 金切り声: give a scream (*kanakirigoe o dasu*) 金切り声を出す.

screen *n.* **1** (partition) tsu⌐itate ついたて; shi⌐kiri しきり: a sliding screen (*shooji*) 障子.
2 (display surface) ga¬meñ 画面; su⌐kuri¬iñ スクリーン: a TV screen (*terebi no gameñ*) テレビの画面.
3 (net) a⌐mi¬do 網戸: put up screens to keep out insects (*mushi ga hairanai yoo ni amido o tsukeru*) 虫が入らないように網戸をつける.
— *vt.* **1** (hide) … o (… kara) sa⌐egi¬ru …を(…から)さえぎる Ⓒ: The tall trees screened us from view. (*Takai ki ga shikai o saegitte ita.*) 高い木が視界をさえぎっていた.
2 (separate) … o shi⌐ki¬ru …を仕切る Ⓒ: Part of the room was screened off. (*Heya no ichibu wa shikirarete ita.*) 部屋の一部は仕切られていた.

screw *n.* **1** (metal nail) ne¬ji ねじ: tighten a screw (*neji o shimeru*) ねじを締める.
2 (propeller) (of a ship) su⌐ku¬ryuu スクリュー; (of a plane) pu⌐ropera プロペラ.
— *vt.* **1** (fasten) … o ne¬ji de shi⌐me¬ru …をねじで締める Ⓥ: screw a box shut (*hako o neji de shimeru*) 箱をねじで締める.
2 (twist) … o hi⌐ne¬ru …をひねる Ⓒ; ne⌐ji¬ru ねじる Ⓒ: screw the lid onto a jar (*biñ no futa o hinette shimeru*) びんのふたをひねって締める.

scribble *vt.* … o zo⌐ñza¬i ni ka¬ku …をぞんざいに書く Ⓒ; ha⌐shirigaki suru 走り書きする Ⓘ: scribble a message (*messeeji o hashirigaki suru*) メッセージを走り書きする.

script *n.* **1** (the text of a play) da⌐ihoñ 台本: read from a script (*daihoñ o yomu*) 台本を読む.
2 (handwriting) te⌐gaki 手書き.

scroll *n.* ma⌐kimono 巻物; ka⌐ke¬jiku 掛け軸.

scrub *vt.* … o go¬shigoshi a⌐rau …をごしごし洗う Ⓒ: scrub the floor with a brush (*burashi de yuka o goshigoshi arau*) ブラシで床をごしごし洗う.

scrutiny *n.* se⌐emitsu na ke¬ñsa 精密な検査; gi¬ñmi 吟味: undergo careful scrutiny (*shiñchoo na keñsa o ukeru*) 慎重な検査を受ける.

sculpture *n.* cho⌐okoku 彫刻.

S

sea *n.* u⌉mi 海: swim in the sea (*umi de oyogu*) 海で泳ぐ / I like traveling by sea. (*Watashi wa funatabi ga suki da.*) 私は船旅が好きだ.

seal[1] *n.* **1** (impression) ha⌉ñ 判; i⌉ñ 印: attach one's seal to a document (*shorui ni iñ o osu*) 書類に印を押す. ★ In Japan the seal has legal force and is used instead of a signature.
2 (enclosure) shi⌉iru シール.
— *vt.* **1** (mark with a seal) ha⌉ñ o o⌈su 判を押す Ⓒ; cho⌈oiñ suru 調印する Ⓘ: sign and seal a treaty (*jooyaku ni shomee chooiñ suru*) 条約に署名調印する.
2 (close) ... ni fu⌉u o suru …に封をする Ⓘ: seal an envelope (*fuutoo ni fuu o suru*) 封筒に封をする.

seal[2] *n.* (animal) a⌈za⌉rashi あざらし; o⌈tto⌉see おっとせい.

seam *n.* nu⌈ime⌉ 縫い目: The sleeve has come apart at the seam. (*Sode no nuime ga hokorobita.*) そでの縫い目がほころびた.

seaman *n.* se⌈ñiñ 船員; fu⌈na⌉nori 船乗り.

search *vt.* **1** (look for) ... o sa⌈gasu …を捜す Ⓒ: I searched the room for the lost pen. (*Watashi wa nakushita peñ o heyajuu sagashita.*) 私はなくしたペンを部屋中捜した.
2 (examine) ... o shi⌈rabe⌉ru …を調べる Ⓥ; ke⌉ñsa suru 検査する Ⓘ: My bag was searched at customs. (*Watashi no kabañ wa zeekañ de shiraberareta.*) 私のかばんは税関で調べられた.
— *n.* so⌈osaku 捜索; tsu⌈ikyuu 追求: He came to Tokyo in his search for work. (*Kare wa shoku o motomete Tookyoo e kita.*) 彼は職を求めて東京へ来た.

seashore *n.* ka⌈igañ 海岸; u⌈mibe 海辺.

seasick *adj.* fu⌉ne ni yotta [yotte iru] 船に酔った[酔っている]: get seasick (*fune ni you*) 船に酔う.

seaside *n.* ka⌈igañ 海岸; u⌈mibe 海辺: a seaside hotel (*umibe no hoteru*) 海辺のホテル.

season *n.* **1** (of the year) ki⌉setsu 季節: Autumn is the best season for traveling. (*Aki wa ryokoo ni ichibañ ii kisetsu desu.*) 秋は旅行にいちばんいい季節です.
2 (period) ji⌉ki 時期; shi⌉izuñ シーズン: the harvest season (*toriire no jiki*) 取り入れの時期 / the rainy season (*uki*) 雨季.
— *vt.* ... ni a⌈ji o tsuke⌉ru …に味をつける Ⓥ; cho⌉omi suru 調味する Ⓘ: season meat with salt and pepper (*niku ni shio to koshoo de aji o tsukeru*) 肉に塩とこしょうで味をつける.

seat *n.* za⌈seki 座席; se⌉ki 席: Is this seat occupied? (*Kono seki wa fusagatte imasu ka?*) この席はふさがっていますか. / Please have a seat. (*Doozo o-kake kudasai.*) どうぞおかけください.
— *vt.* ... o se⌉ki ni tsu⌈kase⌉ru …を席に着かせる Ⓥ: I seated myself beside her. (*Watashi wa kanojo no soba ni suwatta.*) 私は彼女のそばに座った.

second[1] *adj.* **1** (after the first) ni⌈bañme⌉ no 2番目の; dai⌉-ni no 第2の: He was second in the race. (*Kare wa kyoosoo de ni-bañ datta.*) 彼は競争で2番だった. / the Second World War (*dai-niji sekai taiseñ*) 第2次世界大戦.
2 (another) mo⌈o hito⌉tsu no もう一つの: have a second helping (*okawari o suru*) お代わりをする.
— *n.* **1** (people) dai⌉-ni no hi⌈to⌉ 第2の人; (things) dai⌉-ni no mo⌈no⌉ 第2のもの: You are the second to ask that question. (*Kimi wa sono shitsumoñ o suru futari-me da.*) 君はその質問をする二人目だ.
2 (day) fu⌈tsuka 2日.

second[2] *n.* **1** (one sixtieth of a minute) byo⌉o 秒: three minutes and fifty seconds (*sañ-pun gojuu-byoo*) 3分50秒.
2 (moment) cho⌉tto no ma ちょっとの間: Wait a second. (*Chotto matte kudasai.*) ちょっと待ってください.

secondary *adj.* dai⌉-ni no 第2の;

ni-ʳji-teki na 2 次的な: a secondary product (*fukusañbutsu*) 副産物.

secondary school *n.* chuʳutoo-gaˡkkoo 中等学校.

secret *n.* hiʳmitsu 秘密; kiʳmitsu 機密: keep [reveal] a secret (*himitsu o mamoru* [*uchiakeru*]) 秘密を守る[打ち明ける] / The secret has leaked out. (*Sono himitsu wa moreta.*) その秘密は漏れた. / the secret of success (*seekoo no himitsu*) 成功の秘密.

— *adj.* hiʳmitsu no 秘密の: We have to keep this secret from him. (*Kore wa kare ni himitsu ni shite okanakereba naranai.*) これは彼に秘密にしておかなければならない.

secretary *n.* **1** (of an office) hiˡsho 秘書: She is the president's secretary. (*Kanojo wa shachoo no hisho desu.*) 彼女は社長の秘書です.

2 (of an organization) shoʳki 書記: a chief secretary (*shokichoo*) 書記長.

3 (of a government) choʳokañ 長官: the Secretary of State (U. S.) (*Kokumu-chookañ*) 国務長官.

secretly *adv.* hiʳmitsu ni 秘密に; koʳssoˡri to こっそりと: He secretly copied the document. (*Kare wa kossori sono shorui o kopii shita.*) 彼はこっそりその書類をコピーした.

sect *n.* (religion) shuˡuha 宗派; (group) buˡñpa 分派; (party) toˡoha 党派.

section *n.* **1** (part) buˡbuñ 部分: cut a cake into six sections (*o-kashi o muttsu ni kiru*) お菓子を六つに切る.

2 (department) buˡmoñ 部門; kaˡ 課: the personnel section (*jiñjika*) 人事課.

3 (area) chiˡku 地区; kuˡiki 区域: a city's business section (*toshi no shoogyoo chiku*) 都市の商業地区.

4 (division) seˡtsu 節; raˡñ 欄: Section 2 of Chapter 1 (*dai is-shoo dai ni-setsu*) 第1章第2節 / the sports section of a newspaper (*shiñbuñ no supootsu-rañ*) 新聞のスポーツ欄.

secure *adj.* **1** (safe) aʳñzeñ na 安全な: This house is secure in an earthquake. (*Kono uchi wa jishiñ ga kite mo añzeñ desu.*) この家は地震がきても安全です.

2 (firm) shiʳkkaˡri shita [shite iru] しっかりした[している]: Is the door secure? (*Doa wa shikkari shimatte imasu ka?*) ドアはしっかり閉まっていますか.

— *vt.* **1** (obtain) ... o kaˡkuho suru ...を確保する Ⅰ: I secured my seat early. (*Watashi wa seki o hayame ni kakuho shita.*) 私は席を早めに確保した.

2 (fasten tightly) ... o shiʳkkaˡri shiʳmeˡru ...をしっかり閉める Ⅴ: secure a window (*mado o shikkari shimeru*) 窓をしっかり閉める.

3 (make safe) ... o aʳñzeñ ni suru ...を安全にする Ⅰ: secure one's house against robbery (*uchi ni gootoo ga hairanai yoo ni suru*) 家に強盗が入らないようにする.

security *n.* **1** (protection) boʳoee 防衛; hoʳshoo 保障: social security (*shakai-hoshoo*) 社会保障.

2 (safety) aʳñzeñ 安全: peace and security (*heewa to añzeñ*) 平和と安全.

3 (pledge) hoʳshoo 保証: security against loss (*soñgai ni taisuru hoshoo*) 損害に対する保証.

see *vt.* **1** (perceive with eyes) ... ga miʳeˡru ...が見える Ⅴ: Can you see the bird over there? (*Asoko no tori ga miemasu ka?*) あそこの鳥が見えますか. / I saw her enter the room. (*Kanojo ga heya ni hairu no ga mieta.*) 彼女が部屋に入るのが見えた.

2 (look at) ... o miˡru ...を見る Ⅴ: I saw the game on TV. (*Sono shiai wa terebi de mimashita.*) その試合はテレビで見ました. / See page 12. (*Juu-ni-peeji o mi nasai.*) 12ページを見なさい.

3 (understand) ... ga waʳkaˡru ...がわかる Ⓒ: I don't see why he failed. (*Kare ga doo shite shippai shita no ka wakaranai.*) 彼がどうして失敗したのかわからない.

4 (meet) ... ni a⌝u …に会う C: I'm seeing her today. (*Kyoo kanojo ni au koto ni natte iru.*) きょう彼女に会うことになっている. / It's nice to see you. (*O-ai dekite ureshii desu.*) お会いできてうれしいです.

— *vi.* **1** (have the power of sight) mi⌜e⌝ru 見える V: Cats can see in the dark. (*Neko wa kurayami de mo me ga mieru.*) ねこは暗闇でも目が見える.

2 (understand) wa⌜ka⌝ru わかる C: I see. (*Wakarimashita.*) わかりました.

see off *vt.* ... o mi⌜okuru …を見送る C: I saw him off at the station. (*Watashi wa kare o eki de miokutta.*) 私は彼を駅で見送った.

seed *n.* **1** (of a plant) ta⌝ne 種: sow seeds (*tane o maku*) 種をまく.

2 (source) ta⌝ne 種: the seeds of doubt (*utagai no tane*) 疑いの種.

seek *vt.* **1** (look for) ... o sa⌜gasu …を捜す C: seek shelter from the rain (*amayadori no basho o sagasu*) 雨宿りの場所を捜す.

2 (try to obtain) ... o mo⌜tome⌝ru …を求める V: She sought help from a lawyer. (*Kanojo wa beñgoshi ni sukui o motometa.*) 彼女は弁護士に救いを求めた.

seem *vi.* ... no yo⌝o ni mi⌜e⌝ru …のように見える V; ... no yo⌝o da …のようだ: She seems tired. (*Kanojo wa tsukarete iru yoo ni mieru.*) 彼女は疲れているように見える. / It seems that the weather is improving. (*Teñki wa kaifuku suru yoo da.*) 天気は回復するようだ.

seize *vt.* **1** (grasp) ... o tsu⌜ka⌝mu …をつかむ C: He seized me by the arm. (*Kare wa watashi no ude o tsukañda.*) 彼は私の腕をつかんだ.

2 (take possession of) ... o o⌜oshuu suru …を押収する I: The police seized a lot of drugs. (*Keesatsu wa tairyoo no mayaku o ooshuu shita.*) 警察は大量の麻薬を押収した.

— *vi.* (... o) tsu⌜ka⌝mu (…を)つかむ C; to⌜rae⌝ru とらえる V: seize on a chance (*kikai o toraeru*) 機会をとらえる.

seldom *adv.* me⌝tta ni <verb>-nai めったに…ない: My father is seldom ill. (*Chichi wa metta ni byooki o shinai.*) 父はめったに病気をしない. / He is seldom at home. (*Kare wa metta ni uchi ni inai.*) 彼はめったに家にいない.

select *vt.* ... o e⌜ra⌝bu …を選ぶ C; se⌜ñtaku suru 選択する I: I selected the present carefully. (*Watashi wa okurimono o shiñchoo ni erañda.*) 私は贈り物を慎重に選んだ.

selection *n.* se⌜ñtaku 選択; e⌜ra⌝bu ko⌜to⌝ 選ぶこと: His selection of a computer took a long time. (*Kare wa koñpyuutaa o erabu no ni nagai jikañ ga kakatta.*) 彼はコンピューターを選ぶのに長い時間がかかった. / That store has a good selection of wines. (*Sono mise wa yoi waiñ o soroete iru.*) その店はよいワインをそろえている.

self *n.* ji⌜buñ 自分; ji⌜shiñ 自身: reveal one's true self (*hoñshoo o arawasu*) 本性を現わす.

selfish *adj.* ji⌜buñ ho⌝ñi no 自分本位の; wa⌜gama⌝ma na わがままな: That's too selfish. (*Sore wa añmari jibuñ katte sugiru.*) それはあんまり自分勝手すぎる. / a selfish child (*wagamama na kodomo*) わがままな子ども.

sell *vt.* **1** (give something for money) ... o u⌜ru …を売る C: He sold his motorbike for ¥100,000. (*Kare wa baiku o juu-mañ-eñ de utta.*) 彼はバイクを10万円で売った.

2 (deal in) ... o u⌜tte iru …を売っている V: That store sells fruits. (*Ano mise wa kudamono o utte iru.*) あの店は果物を売っている.

— *vi.* u⌜ru 売る C; u⌜reru 売れる V: This book is selling well. (*Kono hoñ wa yoku urete iru.*) この本はよく売れている.

seller *n.* **1** (people) u⌜rite 売り手; ha⌜ñbainiñ 販売人.

2 (things) u⌜reru mono⌝ 売れるもの: a good seller (*yoku ureru mono*) よ

S

く売れるもの.

senate *n.* jo⌈oiñ 上院. ★ The Japanese equivalent is the House of Councilors (*Sañgiiñ*) 参議院) of the Japanese Diet.

senator *n.* jo⌈oiñ gi⌉iñ 上院議員. ★ The Japanese equivalent is a member of the House of Councilors of the Japanese Diet.

send *vt.* **1** (of things) ... o o⌈kuru ...を送る Ⓒ: I sent her a picture postcard. (*Watashi wa kanojo ni ehagaki o okutta.*) 私は彼女に絵はがきを送った.

2 (of people) ... o i⌈kaseru ...を行かせる Ⓥ: He is going to send his son to college. (*Kare wa musuko o daigaku e ikaseru tsumori de iru.*) 彼は息子を大学へ行かせるつもりでいる.

send for ... *vt.* ... o yo⌈bi⌉ ni ya⌈ru ...を呼びにやる Ⓒ: send for a doctor (*isha o yobi ni yaru*) 医者を呼びにやる.

senior *adj.* **1** (older) to⌈shiue no 年上の: He is senior to me by three years. (*Kare wa watashi yori sañsai toshiue da.*) 彼は私より3歳年上だ.

2 (higher in rank) u⌈wayaku no 上役の; (in length of service) se⌈ñpai no 先輩の: Mr. Yamada is senior to me in our firm. (*Yamada-sañ wa kaisha de watashi no señpai desu.*) 山田さんは会社で私の先輩です.

3 (of a student) sa⌈ijo⌉okyuu no 最上級の.

— *n.* ne⌈ñcho⌉osha 年長者; se⌈ñpai 先輩; sa⌈ijookyu⌉usee 最上級生.

sensation *n.* **1** (feeling) ka⌈ñkaku 感覚; ka⌈ñji 感じ: have a sensation of fear (*osoroshii kañji ga suru*) 恐ろしい感じがする.

2 (excitement) da⌈ihyo⌉obañ 大評判; se⌈ñse⌉eshoñ センセーション: His novel caused a sensation. (*Kare no shoosetsu wa daihyoobañ ni natta.*) 彼の小説は大評判になった.

sense *n.* **1** (power to feel) ka⌈ñkaku 感覚: the sense of hearing (*chookaku*) 聴覚.

2 (feeling) ka⌈ñji 感じ: a sense of fatigue (*hirookañ*) 疲労感.

3 (wisdom) shi⌉ryo 思慮; fu⌉ñbetsu 分別; jo⌈oshiki 常識: a person of sense (*fuñbetsu no aru hito*) 分別のある人.

4 (ability to appreciate) ... o ka⌈isu⌉ru ko⌈ko⌉ro ...を解する心; ka⌉ññeñ 観念: a sense of humor (*yuumoa o kaisuru kokoro*) ユーモアを解する心 / a sense of time (*jikañ no kaññeñ*) 時間の観念.

5 (meaning) i⌉mi 意味: the sense of a word (*gogi*) 語義 / This sentence does not make sense. (*Kono buñ wa imi o nasanai.*) この文は意味をなさない. / What he says is right in a sense. (*Kare no itte iru koto wa aru imi de wa tadashii.*) 彼の言っていることはある意味では正しい.

— *vt.* ... o ka⌈ñjiru ...を感じる Ⓥ: sense danger (*kikeñ o kañjiru*) 危険を感じる.

senseless *adj.* **1** (unconcious) ki ⌈o ushinatta [ushinatte iru] 気を失った[失っている]; mu⌈i⌉shiki no 無意識の: He was knocked senseless. (*Kare wa nagurarete ki o ushinatta.*) 彼は殴られて気を失った.

2 (foolish) o⌉roka na 愚かな; mu⌈fu⌉ñbetsu na 無分別な: senseless behavior (*oroka na koodoo*) 愚かな行動.

sensibility *n.* ka⌈ñkaku 感覚; (delicate feeling) ka⌈ñjusee 感受性: the sensibility of the skin to heat and cold (*kañdañ ni taisuru hifu no kañkaku*) 寒暖に対する皮膚の感覚 / a writer of great sensibility (*kañjusee no yutaka na sakka*) 感受性の豊かな作家.

sensible *adj.* fu⌉ñbetsu no a⌉ru 分別のある; ke⌈ñmee na 賢明な: It was sensible of you to follow his advice. (*Kare no chuukoku ni shitagatta no wa keñmee datta.*) 彼の忠告に従ったのは賢明だった.

sensitive *adj.* **1** (easily affected) bi⌈ñkañ na 敏感な: a sensitive ear (*biñkañ na mimi*) 敏感な耳.

S

2 (easily hurt) su⌉gu ki ni suru すぐ気にする: She is sensitive to gossip. (*Kanojo wa uwasa o sugu ki ni suru.*) 彼女はうわさをすぐ気にする.

sentence *n.* **1** (group of words) bu⌉ñ 文; bu⌉ñshoo 文章: write a sentence (*buñ o kaku*) 文を書く.
2 (judgment) ha⌈ñketsu 判決; ke⌉e 刑: a sentence of death (*shikee no hañketsu*) 死刑の判決 / serve one's sentence (*kee ni fukusu*) 刑に服す.

sentiment *n.* **1** (feeling) ka⌈ñjoo 感情: appeal to sentiment (*kañjoo ni uttaeru*) 感情に訴える.
2 (emotion) ka⌈ñshoo 感傷: There is no room for sentiment in competition. (*Shoobu ni kañshoo ga hairu yochi wa nai.*) 勝負に感傷が入る余地はない.
3 (thought) i⌉keñ 意見; ka⌈ñsoo 感想: What are your sentiments about this problem? (*Kono moñdai ni tsuite no anata no kañsoo wa doo desu ka?*) この問題についてのあなたの感想はどうですか.

sentimental *adj.* ka⌈ñshoo-teki na 感傷的な; na⌈midamoro⌉i 涙もろい: a sentimental movie (*kañshoo-teki na eega*) 感傷的な映画 / a sentimental girl (*namidamoroi oñna-no-ko*) 涙もろい女の子.

separate *vt.* **1** (divide) ... o wa⌈ke⌉ru ...分ける [V]; ku⌈gi⌉ru 区切る [C]: The two prefectures are separated by the river. (*Sono futatsu no keñ wa kawa de wakerarete iru.*) その二つの県は川で分けられている.
2 (keep apart) ... o ki⌈rihana⌉su ...を切り離す [C]; bu⌉ñri suru 分離する [I]: separate cream from milk (*kuriimu o gyuunyuu kara buñri suru*) クリームを牛乳から分離する.
— *vi.* wa⌈kare⌉ru 別れる [V]; ha⌈nare⌉ru 離れる [V]: We separated at the station. (*Watashi-tachi wa eki de wakareta.*) 私たちは駅で別れた.
— *adj.* **1** (not together) wa⌈ka⌉reta 分かれた; wa⌈ka⌉rete iru 分かれている: two separate gardens (*futatsu ni wakareta niwa*) 二つに分かれた庭.
2 (different) be⌈tsubetsu no 別々の: sit at separate tables (*betsubetsu no teeburu ni suwaru*) 別々のテーブルに座る.

separately *adv.* wa⌈ka⌉rete 分かれて; be⌈tsubetsu ni 別々に: We paid separately. (*Watashi-tachi wa betsubetsu ni okane o haratta.*) 私たちは別々にお金を払った.

separation *n.* **1** (being apart) bu⌉ñri 分離; be⌉tsuri 別離: I met him after a long separation. (*Kare to wa hisashiburi ni atta.*) 彼とは久しぶりに会った.
2 (living apart) be⌈kkyo 別居.

September *n.* ku⌉-gatsu 9月.

sequence *n.* **1** (order) ju⌉ñjo 順序: arrange the names in alphabetical sequence (*namae o arufabetto juñ ni naraberu*) 名前をアルファベット順に並べる.
2 (series) re⌈ñzoku 連続: a sequence of lectures (*ichireñ no koogi*) 一連の講義.

serene *adj.* no⌉doka na のどかな; (peaceful) he⌈ewa na 平和な: serene weather (*nodoka na teñki*) のどかな天気 / lead a serene life (*heewa na seekatsu o okuru*) 平和な生活を送る.

series *n.* hi⌈to⌉tsuzuki ひと続き; re⌈ñzoku 連続: A series of rainy days followed. (*Amefuri no hi ga tsuzuita.*) 雨降りの日が続いた. / a television series (*reñzoku terebi bañgumi*) 連続テレビ番組.

serious *adj.* **1** (grave) ju⌈udai na 重大な: a serious mistake (*juudai na ayamari*) 重大な誤り.
2 (in earnest) ma⌈jime na まじめな; shi⌈ñkeñ na 真剣な: He looked serious. (*Kare wa shiñkeñ na kao o shite ita.*) 彼は真剣な顔をしていた.

seriously *adv.* o⌈moku 重く; ma⌈jime ni まじめに: He is seriously ill. (*Kare wa juubyoo desu.*) 彼は重病です. / Don't take it seriously. (*Majime ni toranaide kudasai.*) まじめにとらないでください.

sermon *n.* seˡkkyoo 説教: preach a sermon (*sekkyoo suru*) 説教する.

serpent *n.* heˡbi 蛇.

servant *n.* shiˡyooniñ 使用人; meˡshitsuˡkai 召し使い: engage [dismiss] a servant (*shiyooniñ o yatou* [*kaiko suru*]) 使用人を雇う[解雇する].

serve *vt.* **1** (wait at table) ... o daˡsu ...を出す Ⓒ: She served us sushi. (*Kanojo wa watashi-tachi ni sushi o dashite kureta.*) 彼女は私たちにすしを出してくれた. / What time is dinner served? (*Yuushoku wa nañ-ji desu ka?*) 夕食は何時ですか.
2 (work) ... ni tsuˡkaeru ...に仕える Ⓥ; haˡtaraku 働く Ⓒ: Mr. Suzuki served this company for thirty years. (*Suzuki-sañ wa kono kaisha ni sañjuu-neñ-kañ hataraita.*) 鈴木さんはこの会社に30年間働いた.
3 (be useful) ... no yaˡkuˡ ni tatsu ...の役に立つ Ⓒ: I am glad if I can serve you. (*O-yaku ni tateba ureshiku omoimasu.*) お役に立てばうれしく思います.
4 (supply) ... ni kyoˡokyuu suru ...に供給する Ⓘ: serve a town with water (*machi ni mizu o kyookyuu suru*) 町に水を供給する.
— *vi.* **1** (work) tsuˡtomeˡru 勤める Ⓥ: She serves as secretary. (*Kanojo wa hisho to shite tsutomete iru.*) 彼女は秘書として勤めている.
2 (be useful) yaˡkuˡ ni tatsu 役に立つ Ⓒ: This box serves for a seat. (*Kono hako wa isu to shite yaku ni tatsu.*) この箱はいすとして役に立つ.

service *n.* **1** (attention) saˡabisu サービス: The service at this store is poor. (*Kono mise no saabisu wa yoku nai.*) この店のサービスはよくない. / Does this bill include the service charge? (*Kono kañjoo ni saabisu-ryoo wa fukumarete imasu ka?*) この勘定にサービス料は含まれていますか.
★ The Japanese '*saabisu*' is often used in the sense of 'discount' or 'a free gift.'
2 (business) jiˡgyoo 事業; gyoˡomu 業務: the telephone service (*deñwa jigyoo*) 電話事業 / domestic [international] airline service (*kokunaiseñ* [*kokusaiseñ*]) 国内[国際]線.
3 (duty) tsuˡtomeˡ 勤め: public service (*koomu*) 公務.
4 (helpful act) jiˡñryoku 尽力; hoˡneoriˡ 骨折り: do a person a service (*hito no yaku ni tatsu*) 人の役に立つ.

session *n.* **1** (meeting) kaˡigi 会議: go into session (*kaikai suru*) 開会する.
2 (period) kaˡiki 会期: a session of the Diet (*kokkai no kaiki*) 国会の会期.

set *vt.* **1** (put) ... o oˡku ...を置く Ⓒ: set a book on the desk (*tsukue no ue ni hoñ o oku*) 机の上に本を置く.
2 (arrange) ... o toˡtonoeˡru ...を整える Ⓥ; seˡtto suru セットする Ⓘ: I want my hair washed and set. (*Kami o aratte setto shite kudasai.*) 髪を洗ってセットしてください.
3 (fix) ... o kiˡmeru ...を決める Ⓥ: set the date for a meeting (*kaigi no hidori o kimeru*) 会議の日取りを決める.
4 (record) ... o taˡteˡru ...を立てる Ⓥ: set a new record (*shiñ kiroku o tateru*) 新記録を立てる.
— *vi.* **1** (sink) shiˡzumu 沈む Ⓒ: The sun sets in the west. (*Taiyoo wa nishi ni shizumu.*) 太陽は西に沈む.
2 (become solid) kaˡtamaru 固まる Ⓒ: The jelly has set. (*Zerii ga katamatta.*) ゼリーが固まった.
— *n.* **1** (group) hiˡtoˡsoroi ひとそろい; seˡtto セット: a set of tools (*doogu hitosoroi*) 道具ひとそろい / a coffee set (*koohii setto*) コーヒーセット.
2 (apparatus) juˡshiˡñki 受信機; juˡzoˡoki 受像機: a television set (*terebi juzooki*) テレビ受像機.
— *adj.* **1** (fixed) kiˡmerareta 決められた: a set phrase (*kimari moñku*) 決まり文句.
2 (ready) ⟨verb⟩-(y)oo to suru ...(よ)うとする: I was set to leave when he came. (*Dekakeyoo to shita toki*

kare ga kita.) 出かけようとしたとき彼が来た.
set about ... *vt.* ... o ha⌈jimeru ...を始める [V]: set about a job (*shigoto o hajimeru*) 仕事を始める.
set off *vi.* shu⌈ppatsu suru 出発する [I]: set off on a trip (*tabi ni shuppatsu suru*) 旅に出発する.
set up *vt.* ... o su⌈etsuke⌉ru ...を据え付ける [V]: set up a tent (*teñto o haru*) テントを張る.

setting *n.* bu⌈tai so⌉ochi 舞台装置; ha⌈ikee 背景: Kyoto is the setting of this play. (*Kyooto ga kono geki no butai desu.*) 京都がこの劇の舞台です.

settle *vt.* **1** (put in order) ... o ka⌈iketsu suru ...を解決する [I]: The lawyer settled the matter. (*Beñgoshi wa sono moñdai o kaiketsu shita.*) 弁護士はその問題を解決した.
2 (place) ... o o⌈ku ...を置く [C]: She gently settled the vase on the table. (*Kanojo wa sono kabiñ o sotto teeburu no ue ni oita.*) 彼女はその花びんをそっとテーブルの上に置いた.
3 (pay) ... o shi⌈hara⌉u ...を支払う [C]; se⌈esañ suru 清算する [I]: settle a bill (*kañjoo o harau*) 勘定を払う.
— *vi.* **1** (make a home) (... ni) te⌈ejuu suru (...に)定住する [I]; sho⌈kumiñ suru 植民する [I]: They decided to settle in Hokkaido. (*Karera wa Hokkaidoo ni teejuu suru koto ni kimeta.*) 彼らは北海道に定住することに決めた.
2 (be decided) ki⌈maru 決まる [C]: Have you settled on a date for your departure? (*Shuppatsu no hi wa kimarimashita ka?*) 出発の日は決まりましたか.
3 (come to rest) (... ni) to⌈maru (...に)止まる [C]: The birds settled on the branches. (*Tori ga eda ni tomatta.*) 鳥が枝に止まった.

settlement *n.* **1** (agreement) ka⌈iketsu 解決: the settlement of a dispute (*fuñsoo no kaiketsu*) 紛争の解決.
2 (payment) se⌈esañ 清算: the settlement of debts (*shakkiñ no seesañ*) 借金の清算.
3 (colony) sho⌈kumi⌉ñchi 植民地.

seven *pron.* na⌈na⌉tsu 七つ; (things) na⌈na⌉-ko 7 個; (people) shi⌈chi⌉-niñ 7 人.
— *n.* (figure) na⌉na [shi⌈chi⌉] 7; (hour) shi⌈chi⌉-ji 7 時; (minute) shi⌈chi⌉[na⌈na⌉]-fuñ 7 分; (age) na⌈na⌉-sai 7 歳.
— *adj.* na⌈na⌉tsu no 七つの; (people) shi⌈chi⌉-niñ no 7 人の; (things) na⌈na⌉-ko no 7 個の; (age) na⌈na⌉-sai no 7 歳の.

seventeen *pron.* ju⌈ushichi⌉ [ju⌈una⌉na] 17; (people) ju⌈ushichi⌉-niñ 17 人; (things) ju⌈unana⌉-ko 17 個.
— *n.* (figure) ju⌈ushichi⌉ [ju⌈una⌉na] 17; (hour) ju⌈ushichi⌉-ji 17 時; (minute) ju⌈unana⌉-fuñ 17 分; (age) ju⌈unana⌉-sai 17 歳.
— *adj.* ju⌈ushichi⌉ [ju⌈una⌉na] no 17 の; (people) ju⌈ushichi⌉-niñ no 17 人の; (things) ju⌈unana⌉-ko no 17 個の; (age) ju⌈unana⌉-sai no 17 歳の.

seventeeth *adj.* ju⌈unana-bañme⌉ no 17 番目の; da⌉i-ju⌈una⌉na no 第 17 の.
— *n.* **1** (people) ju⌈unana-bañme⌉ no hi⌈to⌉ 17 番目の人; (things) ju⌈unana-bañme⌉ no mo⌈no⌉ 17 番目のもの.
2 (day) ju⌈ushichi-nichi⌉ 17 日.
3 (fraction) ju⌈ushichi-buñ no ichi⌉ 17 分の 1.

seventh *adj.* na⌈na-bañme⌉ no 7 番目の; da⌉i-⌈na⌉na no 第 7 の.
— *n.* **1** (people) na⌈na-bañme⌉ no hi⌈to⌉ 7 番目の人; (things) na⌈na-bañme⌉ no mo⌈no⌉ 7 番目のもの.
2 (day) na⌈noka 7 日.
3 (fraction) na⌈na-buñ no ichi⌉ 7 分の 1.

seventieth *adj.* na⌈najuu-bañme⌉ no 70 番目の; da⌉i-na⌈na⌉juu no 第 70 の.
— *n.* **1** (people) na⌈najuu-bañme⌉ no hi⌈to⌉ 70 番目の人; (things) na⌈na-juu-bañme⌉ no mo⌈no⌉ 70 番目のもの.

seventy *pron.* shi⌈chiju⌉u [na⌈na⌉-juu] 70; (people) shi⌈chiju⌉u-niñ 70 人; (things) shi⌈chiju⌉k-ko [na⌈na-ju⌉k-ko] 70 個.
— *n.* (figure) shi⌈chiju⌉u [na⌈na⌉juu] 70; (age) shi⌈chiju⌉s-sai [na⌈naju⌉s-sai] 70 歳.
— *adj.* shi⌈chiju⌉u no 70 の; (people) shi⌈chiju⌉u-niñ no 70 人の; (things) shi⌈chiju⌉k-ko [na⌈naju⌉k-ko] no 70 個の; (age) shi⌈chiju⌉s-sai [na⌈naju⌉s-sai] 70 歳の.

several *adj.* i⌉kutsu-ka no いくつかの; (people) su⌈u-niñ no 数人の; (things) su⌉u-ko no 数個の: I stayed at the hotel for several days. (*Watashi wa sono hoteru ni suu-jitsu taizai shita.*) 私はそのホテルに数日滞在した.

severe *adj.* **1** (strict, rigorous) ki⌈bishi⌉i 厳しい: a severe teacher (*kibishii señsee*) 厳しい先生 / a severe winter (*kibishii fuyu*) 厳しい冬.
2 (keen) ha⌈geshi⌉i 激しい: severe competition (*hageshii kyoosoo*) 激しい競争.

sew *vt.* ... o nu⌉u ...を縫う Ⓒ: sew a dress (*doresu o nuu*) ドレスを縫う.

sewer *n.* (underground pipe) ge⌈su⌉idoo 下水道; ge⌈suikañ 下水管.

sex *n.* se⌉e 性; se⌈ebetsu 性別; se⌉kkusu セックス: Anybody can apply, regardless of sex. (*Seebetsu ni kañkee naku dare de mo oobo dekimasu.*) 性別に関係なくだれでも応募できます. ★ The Japanese '*sekkusu*' is used only in the sense of 'sexual behavior.'

sexual *adj.* se⌉e no 性の; se⌈e-teki na 性的な: sexual harassment (*seku-hara*) セクハラ / sexual intercourse (*see-kooshoo*) 性交渉.

sexy *adj.* se⌈e-teki miryoku no a⌉ru 性的魅力のある; se⌉kushii na セクシーな: a sexy woman (*sekushii na josee*) セクシーな女性.

shabby *adj.* bo⌈roboro no ぼろぼろの; ki⌈furu⌉shita 着古した: a shabby coat (*boroboro no uwagi*) ぼろぼろの上着.

shade *n.* **1** (shelter) ka⌉ge 陰; hi⌈kage 日陰: Please dry it in the shade. (*Sore wa hikage ni hoshite kudasai.*) それは日陰に干してください.
2 (color) i⌈roai 色合い: a lighter shade of green (*usui iroai no midori*) 薄い色合いの緑.
3 (of a lamp) ka⌉sa かさ; (of a window) hi⌈yoke 日除け; bu⌈raiñdo ブラインド: pull down [up] the shades (*buraiñdo o sageru* [*ageru*]) ブラインドを下げる[上げる].
— *vt.* ... o sa⌈egi⌉ru ...を遮る Ⓒ: I shaded my eyes from the sun with my hand. (*Watashi wa te de hizashi o saegitta.*) 私は手で日差しを遮った.

shadow *n.* **1** (dark image) ka⌉ge 影: a man's shadow on the wall (*kabe ni utsutta hito no kage*) 壁に映った人の影.
2 (darkness) ka⌉ge 陰: The north side of the house is in shadow. (*Ie no kitagawa wa kage ni natte iru.*) 家の北側は陰になっている.

shady *adj.* ka⌉ge no ooi 陰の多い; hi⌈kage no 日陰の: a shady path (*hikage no komichi*) 日陰の小道.

shaft *n.* e 柄; ji⌈ku 軸: the shaft of an ax (*ono no e*) 斧の柄 / the shaft of an arrow (*ya no jiku*) 矢の軸.

shake *vt.* **1** (move quickly) ... o fu⌈ru ...を振る Ⓒ; yu⌈suru 揺する Ⓒ: He shook his head. (*Kare wa kubi o yoko ni futta.*) 彼は首を横に振った. / An earthquake shook the building. (*Jishiñ ga biru o yusutta.*) 地震がビルを揺すった.
2 (disturb) ... o do⌈oyoo saseru ...を動揺させる Ⓥ: We were shaken by the news. (*Watashi-tachi wa sono shirase ni dooyoo shita.*) 私たちはその知らせに動揺した.
— *vi.* fu⌈rueru 震える Ⓥ; yu⌈reru 揺れる Ⓥ: The children were shaking with cold. (*Kodomo-tachi wa samukute furuete ita.*) 子どもたちは寒くて震えていた.
— *n.* shi⌈ñdoo 振動[震動]: give a pole a shake (*sao o yusuru*) さおを揺

S

する.

shall *aux.* **1** [show the future] ... de⌈sho⌉o …でしょう; da⌈ro⌉o だろう: I shall succeed this time. (*Kon̄do wa seekoo suru deshoo.*) 今度は成功するでしょう.

2 [request] ⟨verb⟩-masho⌉o …ましょう: Shall I open the window? (*Mado o akemashoo ka?*) 窓を開けましょうか. / Shall we dance? (*Odorimashoo ka?*) 踊りましょうか.

shallow *adj.* **1** (not deep) a⌈sai 浅い: a shallow lake (*asai mizuumi*) 浅い湖.

2 (not serious) a⌈sa⌉haka na あさはかな: a shallow mind (*asahaka na kokoro*) あさはかな心.

sham *n.* mi⌈sekake 見せかけ; go⌈makashi ごまかし: His bravery is a mere sham. (*Kare no yuuki wa tan̄naru misekake da.*) 彼の勇気は単なる見せかけだ.

— *adj.* ni⌈se no 偽の: a sham pearl (*nise no shin̄ju*) 偽の真珠.

shame *n.* **1** (feeling) ha⌈zukashi⌉i o⌈mo⌉i 恥ずかしい思い: The child blushed with shame. (*Sono ko wa hazukashikute akaku natta.*) その子は恥ずかしくて赤くなった.

2 (disgrace) ha⌈ji⌉ 恥: His behavior brought shame on his school. (*Kare no koodoo wa gakkoo ni haji o kakaseta.*) 彼の行動は学校に恥をかかせた.

3 (pity) za⌈n̄ne⌉n̄ na ko⌈to⌉ 残念なこと: It's a shame that you missed the party. (*Kimi ga paatii ni derarenakatta no wa zan̄nen̄ da.*) 君がパーティーに出られなかったのは残念だ.

— *vt.* ... ni ha⌈ji⌉ o ka⌈kase⌉ru …に恥をかかせる Ⓥ: He has shamed his parents. (*Kare wa oya ni haji o kakaseta.*) 彼は親に恥をかかせた.

shameful *adj.* ha⌈zube⌉ki 恥ずべき: shameful conduct (*hazubeki kooi*) 恥ずべき行為.

shameless *adj.* ha⌈jishi⌉razu no 恥知らずの; zu⌈uzuushi⌉i ずうずうしい: a shameless liar (*hajishirazu no usotsuki*) 恥知らずのうそつき.

shampoo *n.* sha⌉n̄puu シャンプー; se⌈n̄patsu 洗髪.

— *vt.* ka⌈mi⌉ o a⌈rau 髪を洗う Ⓒ: Shampoo and set, please. (*Kami o aratte setto shite kudasai.*) 髪を洗ってセットしてください.

shape *n.* **1** (figure) ka⌈tachi 形; su⌉gata 姿: What shape is it? (*Sore wa don̄na katachi o shite imasu ka?*) それはどんな形をしていますか.

2 (condition) jo⌈otai 状態; cho⌈oshi 調子: He is in good shape. (*Kare wa karada no chooshi ga yoi.*) 彼は体の調子がよい.

— *vt.* ... no ka⌈tachi ni tsuku⌉ru …の形に作る Ⓒ: shape clay into a cup (*nen̄do de chawan̄ o tsukuru*) 粘土で茶碗を作る.

shapeless *adj.* ka⌈tachi ga kuzu⌉reta [kuzu⌉rete iru] 形が崩れた[崩れている]; bu⌈ka⌉kkoo na 不格好な: a shapeless hat (*bukakkoo na booshi*) 不格好な帽子.

share *vt.* ... o wa⌈ke⌉ru …を分ける Ⓥ: We shared the profits equally. (*Watashi-tachi wa rieki o hitoshiku waketa.*) 私たちは利益を等しく分けた.

— *vi.* (... o) bu⌈n̄tan̄ suru (…を)分担する Ⓘ: share in the expense (*hiyoo o bun̄tan̄ suru*) 費用を分担する.

— *n.* **1** (part) wa⌈kema⌉e 分け前: He asked for a share of the property. (*Kare wa zaisan̄ no wakemae o yookyuu shita.*) 彼は財産の分け前を要求した.

2 (stock) ka⌈bu 株: I have shares in that company. (*Watashi wa ano kaisha no kabu o motte imasu.*) 私はあの会社の株を持っています.

shareholder *n.* ka⌈bu⌉nushi 株主.

sharp *adj.* **1** (of an edge) su⌈rudo⌉i 鋭い: a sharp knife (*surudoi naifu*) 鋭いナイフ.

2 (abrupt; steep) kyu⌈u na 急な: make a sharp turn (*kyuu-kaabu o kiru*) 急カーブを切る / a sharp slope (*kyuu na sakamichi*) 急な坂道.

3 (clear) ha⌈kki⌉ri shita [shite iru] はっきりした[している]: a sharp con-

S

trast (*hakkiri shita taishoo*) はっきりした対照.

4 (shrewd) a⌈tama no kire⌉ru 頭の切れる: a sharp businessman (*atama no kireru jitsugyooka*) 頭の切れる実業家.

— *n.* (musical note) sha⌉apu シャープ.

shapen *vt.* ... o to⌈garaseru ...をとがらせる [V]; ke⌈zuru 削る [C]: sharpen a pencil (*eñpitsu o kezuru*) 鉛筆を削る.

shatter *vt.* ... o ko⌈nagona ni kowa⌉su ...を粉々に壊す [C]: The ball shattered the window. (*Sono booru wa mado o konagona ni kowashita.*) そのボールは窓を粉々に壊した.

shave *vi.* hi⌈ge o so⌉ru ひげをそる [C]: I shave every day. (*Watashi wa mainichi hige o soru.*) 私は毎日ひげをそる.

— *vt.* ... o so⌉ru ...をそる [C]: shave one's beard (*hige o soru*) ひげをそる.

— *n.* hi⌈gesori⌉ ひげそり: Haircut and shave, please. (*Sañpatsu to higesori o o-negai shimasu.*) 散髪とひげそりをお願いします.

she *pron.* ka⌉nojo 彼女; a⌈no oñna no hito⌉ あの女の人; [polite] a⌈no kata⌉ あの方: She wanted to know my name. (*Kanojo wa watashi no namae o kikitagatta.*) 彼女は私の名前を聞きたがった. / She is my teacher. (*Ano oñna no hito wa watashi no señsee desu.*) あの女の人は私の先生です. / Who is she? (*Ano kata wa dare desu ka?*) あの方はだれですか.

shed[1] *n.* ko⌈ya 小屋; mo⌈nookigoya 物置小屋.

shed[2] *vt.* **1** (make flow) ... o na⌈ga⌉su ...を流す [C]: shed tears (*namida o nagasu*) 涙を流す.

2 (drop off) ... o o⌈to⌉su ...を落とす [C]: Those trees shed their leaves in autumn. (*Kono ki wa aki ni ha o otoshimasu.*) この木は秋に葉を落とします.

sheep *n.* hi⌈tsuji 羊.

sheer *adj.* **1** (complete) ma⌈ttaku no まったくの: It's sheer nonsense to try that. (*Soñna koto o suru no wa mattaku no nañseñsu da.*) そんなことをするのはまったくのナンセンスだ.

2 (very thin) go⌉ku u⌈sui ごく薄い: sheer stockings (*goku usui sutokkiñgu*) ごく薄いストッキング.

sheet *n.* **1** (cloth) shi⌉itsu シーツ; shi⌈kifu 敷布: put clean sheets on the bed (*kiree na shiitsu o beddo ni shiku*) きれいなシーツをベッドに敷く.

2 (single piece) i⌈chi⌉-mai 1枚: a sheet of paper (*kami ichi-mai*) 紙1枚.

sheet music *n.* ga⌈kufu 楽譜.

shelf *n.* ta⌈na 棚: fix a shelf (*tana o tsukeru*) 棚をつける / put a book on the shelf (*hoñ o tana no ue ni oku*) 本を棚の上に置く.

shell *n.* **1** (seashell) ka⌈igara 貝殻: gather shells (*kaigara o hirou*) 貝殻を拾う.

2 (nutshell) ka⌈ra⌉ 殻: peanut shells (*piinattsu no kara*) ピーナッツの殻.

3 (pod) sa⌉ya さや.

— *vt.* ... o ka⌈ra⌉ kara to⌈rida⌉su ...を殻から取り出す [C]; ... no sa⌉ya o mu⌈ku ...のさやをむく [C]: shell peas (*mame no saya o muku*) 豆のさやをむく.

shellfish *n.* ka⌉i 貝.

shelter *n.* **1** (protection) hi⌉nañ 避難; ho⌉go 保護: take shelter from the rain (*amayadori o suru*) 雨宿りをする.

2 (place) hi⌈nañjo 避難所: a bus shelter (*basu no machiaijo*) バスの待合所.

— *vt.* ... o ho⌉go suru ...を保護する [I]: The trees sheltered the house from a storm. (*Ki ga arashi kara ie o mamotta.*) 木が嵐から家を守った.

— *vi.* hi⌉nañ suru 避難する [I]: shelter under a tree (*ki no shita ni hinañ suru*) 木の下に避難する.

shepherd *n.* hi⌈tsuji⌉kai 羊飼い.

sherbet *n.* sha⌉abetto シャーベット.

shield *n.* (protection against weapons) ta⌉te 楯; (protective cover) ho⌈go⌉butsu 保護物.

— *vt.* ... o ho'go suru …を保護する [I]; ka'ba'u かばう [C]: He shielded me from danger. (*Kare wa kikeñ kara watashi o kabatte kureta.*) 彼は危険から私をかばってくれた.

shift *vt.* (change) ... o ka'eru …を変える [V]; (move) u'tsu'su 移す [C]: I shifted the bed from the room. (*Watashi wa beddo o heya kara utsushita.*) 私はベッドを部屋から移した.
— *vi.* ka'waru 変わる [C]; u'tsu'ru 移る [C]: The wind shifted to the south. (*Kaze ga minami muki ni kawatta.*) 風が南向きに変わった.
— *n.* **1** (change) he'ñka 変化; te'ñkañ 転換: a shift in policy (*seesaku no teñkañ*) 政策の転換.
2 (a period of work) ko'otai 交替: They work in eight-hour shifts. (*Kare-ra wa hachi-jikañ kootai de hataraku.*) 彼らは8時間交替で働く.

shine *vi.* ka'gaya'ku 輝く [C]; hi'ka'ru 光る [C]: The moon is shining brightly. (*Tsuki ga akaruku kagayaite iru.*) 月が明るく輝いている.
— *vt.* **1** (give out light) ... o te'ra'su …を照らす [C]: He shone a flashlight on me. (*Kare wa watashi ni kaichuu-deñtoo o terashita.*) 彼は私に懐中電灯を照らした.
2 (polish) ... o mi'gaku …を磨く [C]: shine one's shoes (*kutsu o migaku*) 靴を磨く.

ship *n.* fu'ne 船: When does the ship sail? (*Fune wa nañ-ji ni demasu ka?*) 船は何時に出ますか. / a passenger ship (*kyakuseñ*) 客船.
★ 'Boat' is also called *'fune.'*
— *vt.* **1** (send) ... o o'kuru …を送る [C]: We will ship the goods to you immediately. (*Shinamono wa sugu ni o-okuri shimasu.*) 品物はすぐにお送りします.
2 (carry by ship) ... o fu'ne de ha'kobu …を船で運ぶ [C]: The cars were shipped to Hokkaido. (*Kuruma wa fune de Hokkaidoo e hakobareta.*) 車は船で北海道へ運ばれた.

shipment *n.* ha'ssoo 発送; (goods) tsu'mini 積み荷: The goods are ready for shipment. (*Shinamono wa hassoo no juñbi ga dekite imasu.*) 品物は発送の準備ができています. / When can we expect the shipment to arrive? (*Tsumini wa itsu tsukimasu ka?*) 積み荷はいつ着きますか.

shirt *n.* **1** (garment) wa'ishatsu ワイシャツ: put on [take off] a shirt (*waishatsu o kiru [nugu]*) ワイシャツを着る[脱ぐ].
2 (undershirt) sha'tsu シャツ.
★ Japanese '*shatsu*' is used only in this sense.

shiver *vi.* fu'rueru 震える [V]: He was shivering with cold. (*Kare wa samukute furuete ita.*) 彼は寒くて震えていた.
— *n.* fu'rue 震え; mi'bu'rui 身震い.

shock *n.* **1** (blow) da'geki 打撃; sho'kku ショック: My father's death was a great shock to me. (*Chichi no shi wa watashi ni totte ooki-na dageki datta.*) 父の死は私にとって大きな打撃だった.
2 (violent shake) sho'ogeki 衝撃; shi'ñdoo 震動: the shock of an explosion (*bakuhatsu no shoogeki*) 爆発の衝撃 / the shock of an earthquake (*jishiñ no shiñdoo*) 地震の震動.
— *vt.* ... ni sho'ogeki [sho'kku] o a'taeru …に衝撃[ショック]を与える [V]: We were shocked by the accident. (*Watashi-tachi ni wa sono jiko wa shokku datta.*) 私たちにはその事故はショックだった.

shoe *n.* ku'tsu 靴: put on [take off] one's shoes (*kutsu o haku [nugu]*) 靴をはく[脱ぐ] / shoe store (*kutsuya*) 靴屋.

shoemaker *n.* ku'tsu'ya 靴屋; ku'tsuna'oshi 靴直し.

shoot *vt.* **1** (fire) ... o u'tsu …を撃つ [C]: shoot a gun (*teppoo o utsu*) 鉄砲を撃つ.
2 (make a film) ... o sa'tsuee suru …を撮影する [I]: The film was shot in New York. (*Sono eega wa Nyuu Yooku de satsuee sareta.*) そ

の映画はニューヨークで撮影された.

— *vi.* **1** (fire) (... o) u˺tsu (...を)撃つ [C]: He shot at the target. (*Kare wa mato o megakete utta.*) 彼は的をめがけて撃った.

2 (move quickly) i˹kioi yo˺ku to˹bida˺su 勢いよく飛び出す [C]: A cat shot out of the room. (*Neko ga heya kara ikioi yoku tobidashita.*) 猫が部屋から勢いよく飛び出した.

— *n.* (bud) shi˹ñme 新芽: a bamboo shoot (*take no ko*) 筍.

shop *n.* mi˹se˺ 店; sho˺oteñ 商店: open [close] a shop (*mise o hiraku* [*shimeru*]) 店を開く[閉める] / an antique shop (*kottoohiñ-teñ*) 骨董品店 / a duty-free shop (*meñzee-teñ*) 免税店.

— *vi.* ka˹imono o suru 買い物をする [I]: I always shop at this supermarket. (*Watashi wa itsu-mo koko no suupaa de kaimono o shimasu.*) 私はいつもここのスーパーで買い物をします.

shopping *n.* ka˹imono 買い物: Can we do some shopping at the airport? (*Kono kuukoo de kaimono wa dekimasu ka?*) この空港で買い物はできますか. / a shopping street (*shooteñgai*) 商店街.

shore *n.* ki˹shi˺ 岸; (seashore) ka˹igañ 海岸.

short *adj.* **1** (not long) mi˹jika˺i 短い: I had my hair cut short. (*Kami o mijikaku katte moratta.*) 髪を短く刈ってもらった. / a short vacation (*mijikai kyuuka*) 短い休暇.

2 (not tall) se˺ no hi˹ku˺i 背の低い: He is shorter than you. (*Kare wa kimi yori se ga hikui.*) 彼は君より背が低い.

3 (not enough) fu˹soku shite iru 不足している: We are short of hands. (*Hitode ga fusoku shite iru.*) 人手が不足している.

shortage *n.* fu˹soku 不足; ke˹tsuboo 欠乏: a shortage of food (*shokuryoo no fusoku*) 食料の不足.

shorten *vt.* ... o mi˹ji˺kaku suru ...を短くする [I]: shorten trousers by three centimeters (*zuboñ o sañseñchi mijikaku suru*) ズボンを3センチ短くする.

shorthand *n.* so˹kki 速記: write in shorthand (*sokki de kaku*) 速記で書く.

shortly *adv.* ma˹mo˺naku まもなく; su˺gu ni すぐに: He will arrive shortly. (*Kare wa mamonaku toochaku suru deshoo.*) 彼はまもなく到着するでしょう.

shorts *n.* sho˹otopa˺ñtsu ショートパンツ; ha˹ñzu˺boñ 半ズボン.

shot *n.* **1** (firing) ha˹ssha 発射; ha˹ppoo 発砲: take a shot at a bird (*tori o neratte utsu*) 鳥をねらって撃つ.

2 (sound) ju˹usee 銃声: I heard two shots. (*Watashi wa juusee o ni-hatsu kiita.*) 私は銃声を2発聞いた.

3 (bullet) ta˹ma˺ 弾: fire a shot (*tama o utsu*) 弾を撃つ.

4 (photograph) sa˹tsuee 撮影; sha˹shiñ 写真: take a shot of a shrine (*jiñja no shashiñ o toru*) 神社の写真を撮る.

5 (golf) sho˺tto ショット.

should *aux.* **1** [obligation] <verb> be˺ki da ...べきだ: You should go as soon as possible. (*Kimi wa dekiru dake hayaku iku beki da.*) 君はできるだけ早く行くべきだ. / What should I do? (*Doo sureba yoi deshoo?*) どうすればよいでしょう.

2 [expectation] ... ha˹zu da ...はずだ: The bus should be coming soon. (*Basu wa sugu kuru haza da.*) バスはすぐ来るはずだ.

3 [concessive conditional] ma˺ñichi <verb>-te[de] mo 万一...て[で]も: If I should fail, I will try again. (*Mañichi shippai shite mo moo ichido yarimasu.*) 万一失敗してももう一度やります.

shoulder *n.* ka˺ta 肩: carry a bag over one's shoulder (*kabañ o kata ni kakeru*) かばんを肩にかける.

shout *vi.* o˹ogo˺e de sa˹ke˺bu 大声で叫ぶ [C]: He shouted for help. (*Kare wa tasuke o motomete oogoe de sakeñda.*) 彼は助けを求めて大

声で叫んだ.

shove *vt.* ... o o⌈shinoke⌉ru …を押しのける Ⓥ: He shoved me aside. (*Kare wa watashi o waki ni oshi-noketa.*) 彼は私を脇に押しのけた.

— *n.* hi⌈to⌉oshi ひと押し; tsu⌈ki 突き: give a shove (*gutto osu* [*tsuku*]) ぐっと押す[突く].

shovel *n.* sha⌉beru シャベル: remove snow with a shovel (*shaberu de yuki o kaku*) シャベルで雪をかく.

— *vt.* ... o sha⌉beru de su⌈kuu …をシャベルですくう Ⓒ: shovel sand into a bucket (*suna o shaberu de su-kutte baketsu in ireru*) 砂をシャベルですくってバケツに入れる.

show *vt.* **1** (let be seen) ... o mi-⌈se⌉ru …を見せる Ⓥ: Please show me some rings. (*Yubiwa o misete kudasai.*) 指輪を見せてください. / Please show me another. (*Hoka no o misete kudasai.*) ほかのを見せてください.

2 (point out) ... o o⌈shieru …を教える Ⓥ: Please show me how to fill in this form. (*Kono shorui no kaki-kata o oshiete kudasai.*) この書類の書き方を教えてください. / Show me the way, please. (*Michi o oshiete kudasai.*) 道を教えてください.

3 (prove) ... o shi⌈me⌉su …を示す Ⓒ: He showed that he was right. (*Kare wa jibuñ ga tadashii koto o shimeshita.*) 彼は自分が正しいことを示した.

4 (guide) ... o a⌈ñna⌉i suru …を案内する Ⓘ: Please show me to my seat. (*Watashi no seki e añnai shite kudasai.*) 私の席へ案内してください.

— *vi.* (appear) a⌈raware⌉ru 現れる Ⓥ; mi⌈e⌉ru 見える Ⓥ: Light was showing under the door. (*Doa no shita kara akari ga miete ita.*) ドアの下から明かりが見えていた.

— *n.* **1** (performance) sho⌉o ショー; mi⌈semono⌉ 見せ物: I would like to see a show while in town. (*Machi ni iru aida ni shoo o mitai.*) 町にいる間にショーを見たい.

2 (exhibition) te⌈ñji⌉kai 展示会; te⌈ñra⌉ñkai 展覧会.

shower *n.* **1** (bath) sha⌉waa シャワー: take a shower (*shawaa o abiru*) シャワーを浴びる / I'd like a room with shower. (*Shawaa tsuki no heya ni shitai.*) シャワーつきの部屋にしたい. ★ Japanese '*shawaa*' is used only in this sense.

2 (rain) ni⌈waka-a⌉me にわか雨: I was caught in a shower. (*Watashi wa niwaka-ame ni atta.*) 私はにわか雨に遭った.

— *vi.* **1** (wash) sha⌉waa o a⌈biru シャワーを浴びる Ⓥ: I shower every morning. (*Watashi wa maiasa sha-waa o abiru.*) 私は毎朝シャワーを浴びる.

2 (rain) ni⌈waka-a⌉me ga furu にわか雨が降る Ⓒ: Suddenly it began to shower. (*Totsuzeñ niwaka-ame ga furi-dashita.*) 突然にわか雨が降り出した.

shriek *vi.* ka⌈nakirigo⌉e o dasu 金切り声を出す Ⓒ; kya⌉tto sa⌈ke⌉bu きゃっと叫ぶ Ⓒ: She shrieked in hor-ror. (*Kanojo wa osoroshikute kyatto sakeñda.*) 彼女は恐ろしくてきゃっと叫んだ.

shrill *adj.* su⌈rudo⌉i 鋭い; ka⌈ñdaka⌉i かん高い: a shrill whistle (*surudoi keeteki*) 鋭い警笛.

— *n.* ka⌈nakirigo⌉e 金切り声; hi-⌈mee 悲鳴.

shrimp *n.* ko⌈ebi 小えび. ★ In Japanese, 'lobster,' 'prawn,' and 'shrimp' are all called '*ebi.*'

shrine *n.* ji⌉ñja 神社: Meiji Shrine (*Meeji jiñguu*) 明治神宮.

shrink *vi.* **1** (become smaller) chi-⌈jimu 縮む Ⓒ: The shirt shrank when it was washed. (*Arattara sha-tsu ga chijiñda.*) 洗ったらシャツが縮んだ.

2 (draw back) hi⌈ru⌉mu ひるむ Ⓒ; shi⌈rigo⌉mi suru しりごみする Ⓘ: He didn't shrink from danger. (*Kare wa kikeñ ni hirumanakatta.*) 彼は危険にひるまなかった.

shrub *n.* te⌈eboku 低木; ka⌈ñboku 灌木.

shun *vt.* ... o sa⌈ke⌉ru …を避ける Ⓥ: shun temptation (*yuuwaku o sakeru*) 誘惑を避ける.

shut *vt.* **1** (close) ... o shi⌈me⌉ru …を閉める Ⓥ: Please shut the window. (*Mado o shimete kudasai.*) 窓を閉めてください.
2 (fold) ... o to⌈ji⌉ru …を閉じる Ⓥ: shut a book (*hoñ o tojiru*) 本を閉じる.
— *vi.* shi⌈ma⌉ru 閉まる Ⓒ: This door won't shut. (*Kono doa wa shimaranai.*) このドアは閉まらない.

shutter *n.* **1** (of a camera) sha⌉ttaa シャッター: press the shutter (*shattaa o osu*) シャッターを押す.
2 (of a house) a⌈ma⌉do 雨戸; sha⌉ttaa シャッター: The shutter doesn't work well. (*Shattaa no guai ga warui.*) シャッターのぐあいが悪い.

shy *adj.* ha⌈zukashigari no 恥ずかしがりの; u⌈chiki na 内気な: She is shy and dislikes parties. (*Kanojo wa hazukashigari de paatii ga kirai da.*) 彼女は恥ずかしがりでパーティーが嫌いだ.

sick *adj.* **1** (ill) byo⌈oki no 病気の: He is sick in bed. (*Kare wa byooki de nete imasu.*) 彼は病気で寝ています.
2 (ready to vomit) ha⌈kike⌉ ga suru 吐き気がする; mu⌉kamuka suru むかむかする: I am going to be sick. (*Haki-soo da.*) 吐きそうだ. / I feel sick. (*Kibuñ ga warui.*) 気分が悪い.
3 (tired of) u⌈ñza⌉ri shite (iru) うんざりして(いる): I am sick of the rain. (*Kono ame ni wa uñzari da.*) この雨にはうんざりだ.

sickness *n.* byo⌈oki 病気: absence due to sickness (*byooki no tame no kesseki*) 病気のための欠席.

side *n.* **1** (edge) ga⌈wa⌉ 側: the right [left] side of a road (*michi no migi[hidari]gawa*) 道の右[左]側.
2 (outside) so⌈kume⌉ñ 側面; yo⌈ko 横: the side of a building (*biru no sokumeñ*) ビルの側面.
3 (surface) me⌉ñ 面: the right [wrong] side of the paper (*kami no omote [ura] meñ*) 紙の表[裏]面.
4 (of a body) wa⌈kibara わき腹: I feel a pain in my side. (*Wakibara ga itai.*) わき腹が痛い.
5 (next to something) so⌉ba そば; wa⌈ki⌉ わき: Come and sit by my side. (*Soba e kite suwari nasai.*) そばへ来て座りなさい.
— *adj.* yo⌈ko no 横の; so⌈kume⌉ñ no 側面の: a side gate (*yoko no moñ*) 横の門.

sideboard *n.* sho⌈kki⌉dana 食器棚: put the dishes in a sideboard (*shokkidana ni sara o ireru*) 食器棚に皿を入れる.

sidewalk *n.* ho⌈doo 歩道: walk on the sidewalk (*hodoo o aruku*) 歩道を歩く.

siege *n.* ho⌈oikoˈogeki 包囲攻撃: break a siege (*hooi o yaburu*) 包囲を破る.

sigh *vi.* ta⌈mei⌉ki o tsuku ため息をつく Ⓒ: He sighed with relief. (*Kare wa hotto shite tameiki o tsuita.*) 彼はほっとしてため息をついた.
— *n.* ta⌈mei⌉ki ため息: breathe a deep sigh (*fukai tameiki o tsuku*) 深いため息をつく.

sight *n.* **1** (power) shi⌉ryoku 視力: have weak sight (*shiryoku ga yowai*) 視力が弱い.
2 (act) mi⌉ru ko⌈to⌉ 見ること: I caught sight of him in the crowd. (*Watashi wa hitogomi no naka de kare o mitsuketa.*) 私は人込みの中で彼を見つけた.
3 (view) ko⌈okee 光景; na⌈game⌉ 眺め: The sight of the lake was wonderful. (*Mizuumi no nagame wa subarashikatta.*) 湖の眺めはすばらしかった.
4 (something worth seeing) me⌈esho⌉ 名所: the sights of Kyoto (*Kyooto no meesho*) 京都の名所.

sightseeing *n.* ka⌈ñkoo 観光: I'd like a sightseeing brochure for this town. (*Kono machi no kañkoo pañfuretto ga hoshii no desu ga.*) この町の観光パンフレットが欲しいのですが. / a sightseeing bus (*kañkoo basu*) 観光バス / a sightseeing boat (*yuurañ-*

S

señ) 遊覧船.

sign *n.* **1** (notice) ke⌈eji 掲示; hyo⌈oshiki 標識: a road sign (*dooro hyooshiki*) 道路標識.
2 (signal) shi⌈ñgoo 信号: a stop sign (*teeshi shiñgoo*) 停止信号.
3 (indication) cho⌈okoo 兆候; ki⌈zashi 兆し: a sign of spring (*haru no kizashi*) 春の兆し.
4 (gesture) a⌉izu 合図: He gave me a sign to go. (*Kare wa ike to watashi ni aizu shita.*) 彼は行けと私に合図した.
— *vt.* ... ni sho⌈mee suru ...に署名する Ⅰ; sa⌉iñ suru サインする Ⅰ: He signed the check. (*Kare wa kogitte ni shomee shita.*) 彼は小切手に署名した. ★ Japanese use '*saiñ*' in the sense of 'signature.'
— *vi.* sho⌈mee suru 署名する Ⅰ; sa⌉iñ suru サインする Ⅰ: Please sign here. (*Koko ni saiñ shite kudasai.*) ここにサインしてください.

signal *n.* shi⌈ñgoo 信号; a⌉izu 合図: a signal of danger (*kikeñ shiñgoo*) 危険信号 / the signal for the start (*sutaato no aizu*) スタートの合図.
— *vt.* ... ni a⌉izu suru ...に合図する Ⅰ: signal a taxi (*takushii ni aizu suru*) タクシーに合図する.
— *vi.* (... ni) a⌉izu suru (...に)合図する Ⅰ: The policeman signaled to me to stop. (*Sono keekañ wa watashi ni tomare to aizu shita.*) その警官は私に止まれと合図した.

signature *n.* sho⌈mee 署名; sa⌉iñ サイン: put one's signature on a document (*shorui ni shomee suru*) 書類に署名する.

significance *n.* **1** (importance) ju⌈uyoosee 重要性; ju⌈udaisa 重大さ: a matter of great significance (*juuyoo na moñdai*) 重要な問題.
2 (meaning) i⌉gi 意義; i⌉mi 意味: the significance of a symbol (*kigoo no imi*) 記号の意味.

significant *adj.* **1** (important) ju⌈uyoo na 重要な: a significant promise (*juuyoo na yakusoku*) 重要な約束.
2 (having a meaning) i⌉miarige na 意味ありげな: a significant gesture (*imiarige na miburi*) 意味ありげな身ぶり.

signify *vt.* **1** (mean) ... o i⌉mi suru ...を意味する Ⅰ: What does this road sign signify? (*Kono dooro hyooshiki wa nani o imi shimasu ka?*) この道路標識は何を意味しますか.
2 (show) ... o shi⌈me⌉su ...を示す Ⓒ; shi⌈raseru 知らせる Ⓥ: He signified his agreement by raising his right hand. (*Kare wa migite o agete sañi o shimeshita.*) 彼は右手を挙げて賛意を示した.

silence *n.* **1** (stillness) shi⌈zuke⌉sa 静けさ: the silence of the night (*yoru no shizukesa*) 夜の静けさ.
2 (no talking) chi⌈ñmoku 沈黙: break [keep] the silence (*chiñmoku o yaburu* [*mamoru*]) 沈黙を破る[守る].

silent *adj.* **1** (quiet) shi⌉zuka na 静かな: a silent forest (*shizuka na mori*) 静かな森.
2 (not speaking) da⌈ma⌉tte iru 黙っている; mu⌈goñ no 無言の: He remained silent. (*Kare wa damatte ita.*) 彼は黙っていた. / a silent protest (*mugoñ no koogi*) 無言の抗議.

silently *adv.* shi⌉zuka ni 静かに; da⌈ma⌉tte 黙って: The child nodded silently. (*Sono ko wa damatte unazuita.*) その子は黙ってうなずいた.

silk *n.* ki⌉nu 絹: raw silk (*ki-ito*) 生糸.

silkworm *n.* ka⌉iko かいこ.

silly *adj.* ba⌉ka na ばかな; ba⌈ka⌉geta ばかげた; ba⌈ka⌉gete iru ばかげている: Stop being silly. (*Baka na koto wa yoshi nasai.*) ばかなことはよしなさい. / a silly question (*bakageta shitsumoñ*) ばかげた質問.

silver *n.* gi⌉ñ 銀: This ring is made of silver. (*Kono yubiwa wa giñ de dekite iru.*) この指輪は銀でできている.
— *adj.* gi⌉ñ no 銀の; gi⌈ñsee no 銀製の: a silver spoon (*giñ no supuuñ*) 銀のスプーン.

similar *adj.* ru⌈iji shita [shite iru]

類似した[している]; ni[te iru 似ている: Our tastes are similar. (*Watashi-tachi no shumi wa nite iru.*) 私たちの趣味は似ている.

similarity *n.* ru[iji 類似; ni[te iru koto] 似ていること: There are some similarities between their opinions. (*Kare-ra no ikeñ ni wa nita tokoro ga aru.*) 彼らの意見には似たところがある.

similarly *adv.* do[oyoo ni 同様に; o[na]jiku 同じく: I am to blame. But similarly, you are wrong. (*Watashi wa warui. Shikashi kimi mo dooyoo ni yoku nai.*) 私は悪い. しかし君も同様によくない.

simple *adj.* **1** (easy) ka[ñtañ na 簡単な; ya[sashii やさしい: a simple task (*kañtañ na shigoto*) 簡単な仕事 / The question was simple. (*Sono moñdai wa yasashikatta.*) その問題はやさしかった.
2 (plain) shi]sso na 質素な: lead a simple life (*shisso na seekatsu o okuru*) 質素な生活を送る.
3 (natural) ju[ñshiñ na 純真な: He is as simple as a child. (*Kare wa kodomo no yoo ni juñshiñ da.*) 彼は子どものように純真だ.

simplicity *n.* **1** (easiness) ka[ñtañ 簡単; yo[oi 容易: The problem is simplicity itself. (*Sono moñdai wa mattaku kañtañ da.*) その問題はまったく簡単だ.
2 (plainness) shi]sso 質素: I like the simplicity of her dress. (*Kanojo no fukusoo no shisso na tokoro ga suki da.*) 彼女の服装の質素なところが好きだ.
3 (naturalness) ju[ñshiñsa 純真さ; mu[jaki]sa 無邪気さ: a look of simplicity (*mujaki na hyoojoo*) 無邪気な表情.

simplify *vt.* ... o ka[ñtañ ni suru …を簡単にする [I]; ka[ñketsu ni suru 簡潔にする [I]: simplify sentences (*buñshoo o kañketsu ni suru*) 文章を簡潔にする.

simply *adv.* **1** (easily) ka[ñtañ ni 簡単に; wa[kariya]suku わかりやすく: explain simply (*wakariyasuku setsumee suru*) わかりやすく説明する.
2 (merely) ta]ñ ni ... dake 単に…だけ; ta]da ただ: He did it simply for the money. (*Kare wa tada o-kane no tame ni dake sore o yatta.*) 彼はただお金のためにだけそれをやった.
3 (really) ma[ttaku まったく; ji[tsu] ni 実に: That's simply ridiculous. (*Sore wa mattaku bakagete iru.*) それはまったくばかげている.

simultaneous *adj.* do[oji no 同時の: simultaneous interpretation (*dooji tsuuyaku*) 同時通訳.

sin *n.* tsu]mi 罪: commit a sin (*tsumi o okasu*) 罪を犯す.

since *prep.* ... i]rai …以来; i]go 以後: I haven't seen her since last year. (*Kyoneñ irai kanojo ni atte imaseñ.*) 去年以来彼女に会っていません.
— *conj.* **1** (after that time) <verb>-te[de] i]rai …て[で]以来; <verb>-te [de] kara …て[で]から: Two years have passed since I came to Japan. (*Nihoñ ni kite kara ni-neñ tachimashita.*) 日本に来てから2年たちました.
2 (because) ... kara …から: Since I have a meeting, I must go. (*Kaigi ga arimasu kara, ikanakereba nari-maseñ.*) 会議がありますから, 行かなければなりません.

sincere *adj.* ko[ko]ro kara no 心からの; se[ejitsu na 誠実な: sincere thanks (*kokoro kara no kañsha*) 心からの感謝 / a sincere politician (*seejitsu na seejika*) 誠実な政治家.

sincerely *adv.* ko[ko]ro kara 心から; ho[ñtoo ni 本当に: I sincerely hope you will get well soon. (*Hayaku yoku narareru koto o kokoro kara o-inori shimasu.*) 早く良くなれることを心からお祈りします.
Sincerely yours, (at the end of a letter) ke]egu 敬具.

sincerity *n.* se[ejitsu 誠実; se]ei 誠意: He spoke with sincerity. (*Kare wa seei o motte hanashita.*) 彼は誠意をもって話した.

sing *vi.* **1** (with the voice) u[ta] o

S

uˈtau 歌を歌う Ⓒ: I like to sing. (*Watashi wa uta o utau no ga suki da.*) 私は歌を歌うのが好きだ.
2 (of birds, etc.) naˈku 鳴く Ⓒ; saˈezuˈru さえずる Ⓒ: The crickets are singing. (*Koorogi ga naite iru.*) こおろぎが鳴いている. / The birds are singing. (*Tori ga saezutte iru.*) 鳥がさえずっている.
— *vt.* ... o uˈtau …を歌う Ⓒ: She sang a sad song. (*Kanojo wa kanashii uta o utatta.*) 彼女は悲しい歌を歌った.

singer *n.* kaˈshu 歌手; uˈtau hitoˈ 歌う人: an opera singer (*opera kashu*) オペラ歌手.

single *adj.* **1** (only one) taˈtta hiˈtoˈtsu no たった一つの: I missed my single chance. (*Watashi wa tatta hitotsu no chañsu o nogashita.*) 私はたった一つのチャンスを逃した.
2 (unmarried) doˈkushiñ no 独身の: He remained single. (*Kare wa dokushiñ de tooshita.*) 彼は独身で通した.
3 (for one person) hiˈtori-yoo no 一人用の: reserve a single room (*hitori-beya o yoyaku suru*) 一人部屋を予約する.
— *n.* **1** (one thing) hiˈtoˈtsu no moˈnoˈ 一つのもの.
2 (ticket) kaˈtamichi-kiˈppu 片道切符.
3 (baseball) taˈñda 単打; shiˈñguru hiˈtto シングルヒット.

singles *n.* (of tennis) shiˈñgurusu シングルス: the men's singles (*dañshi shiñgurusu no shiai*) 男子シングルスの試合.

singular *adj.* **1** (remarkable) naˈmihazureta 並外れた; naˈmihazurete iru 並外れている; maˈre ni miˈru まれに見る: a woman of singular beauty (*mare ni miru bijiñ*) まれに見る美人.
2 (strange) kiˈmyoo na 奇妙な; fuˈugaˈwari na 風変わりな: a person of singular habits (*fuugawari na kuse no hito*) 風変わりな癖の人.
3 (in grammar) taˈñsuˈu no 単数の: a singular form (*tañsuu-kee*) 単数形.

sink *vi.* **1** (go down) shiˈzumu 沈む Ⓒ: The ship hit a rock and sank. (*Sono fune wa iwa ni atatte shizuñda.*) その船は岩に当たって沈んだ.
2 (go lower) saˈgaˈru 下がる Ⓒ: Prices are sinking. (*Bukka ga sagatte iru.*) 物価が下がっている.
— *vt.* ... o shiˈzumeru …を沈める Ⓥ: sink a ship (*fune o shizumeru*) 船を沈める.
— *n.* naˈgashiˈ 流し: wash the dishes in the sink (*nagashi de sara o arau*) 流しで皿を洗う.

sip *vt.* ... o suˈkoshi zutsu noˈmu …を少しずつ飲む Ⓒ; suˈsuru すする Ⓒ: sip hot coffee (*atsui koohii o susuru*) 熱いコーヒーをすする.

sir *n.* [used in polite expressions]: Good morning, sir. (*Ohayoo gozaimasu.*) お早うございます. / May I help you, sir? (*Irasshaimase.*) いらっしゃいませ. ★ There is no direct Japanese equivalent. Various polite expressions are used instead.

sister *n.* (older) aˈne 姉; (someone else's older sister) (o-)ˈneˈesañ (お)姉さん; (younger) iˈmootoˈ 妹; (someone else's younger sister) iˈmooto-sañ 妹さん: sisters (*shimai*) 姉妹. ★ There is no direct Japanese equivalent to 'sister.'

sister-in-law *n.* (older) giˈri no ane 義理の姉; (younger) giˈri no imootoˈ 義理の妹.

sit *vi.* **1** (rest) (... ni) suˈwaru (…に)座る Ⓒ; kaˈkeˈru かける Ⓥ: May I sit here? (*Koko ni suwatte mo ii desu ka?*) ここに座ってもいいですか. / He sat on the stool. (*Kare wa sono maruisu ni kaketa.*) 彼はその丸いすにかけた.
2 (perch) (... ni) toˈmaru (…に)止まる Ⓒ: A strange bird is sitting in the tree. (*Minarenai tori ga ki ni tomatte iru.*) 見慣れない鳥が木に止まっている.

sit down *vi.* suˈwaru 座る Ⓒ: Please sit down. (*Doozo o-suwari* *kudasai*.) どうぞお座りください.

site *n.* **1** (land) yo⌉ochi 用地; shi⌈kichi 敷地: a site for a factory (*koojoo no yoochi*) 工場の用地.
2 (place) ba⌈sho 場所; ge⌈ñba 現場: the site of an accident (*jikogeñba*) 事故現場.

situation *n.* **1** (state of affairs) jo⌈osee 情勢; jo⌈okyoo 状況: The political situation has changed. (*Seeji-joosee ga kawatta.*) 政治情勢が変わった.
2 (position) ta⌈chiba⌉ 立場; kyo⌈oguu 境遇: I am now in an awkward situation. (*Watashi wa ima mazui tachiba ni aru.*) 私はいままずい立場にある.
3 (job) tsu⌈tome⌉guchi 勤め口; sho⌈ku 職: He's looking for a situation. (*Kare wa shoku o sagashite iru.*) 彼は職を探している.

six *pron.* mu⌈ttsu⌉ 六つ; (people) ro⌈ku⌉-niñ 6 人; (things) ro⌉k-ko 6 個.
— *n.* (figure) ro⌈ku 6; (hour) ro⌈ku⌉-ji 6 時; (minute) ro⌉p-puñ 6 分; (age) ro⌈ku⌉-sai 6 歳.
— *adj.* mu⌈ttsu⌉ no 六つの; (people) ro⌈ku⌉-niñ no 6 人の; (things) ro⌉k-ko no 6 個の; (age) ro⌈ku⌉-sai no 6 歳の.

sixteen *pron.* ju⌈uroku⌉ 16; (people) ju⌈uroku⌉-niñ 16 人; (things) ju⌈uro⌉k-ko 16 個.
— *n.* (figure) ju⌈uroku⌉ 16; (hour) ju⌈uroku⌉-ji 16 時; (minute) ju⌈uro⌉p-puñ 16 分; (age) ju⌈uroku⌉-sai 16 歳.
— *adj.* ju⌈uroku⌉ no 16 の; (people) ju⌈uroku⌉-niñ no 16 人の; (things) ju⌈uro⌉k-ko no 16 個の; (age) ju⌈uroku⌉-sai no 16 歳の.

sixteenth *adj.* ju⌈uroku-bañme⌉ no 16 番目の; da⌉i-ju⌈uroku⌉ no 第 16 の.
— *n.* **1** (people) ju⌈uroku-bañme⌉ no hi⌈to⌉ 16 番目の人; (things) ju⌈uroku-bañme⌉ no mo⌈no⌉ 16 番目のもの.
2 (day) ju⌈uroku-nichi⌉ 16 日.
3 (fraction) ju⌈uroku-buñ no ichi⌉ 16 分の 1.

sixth *adj.* ro⌈ku-bañme⌉ no 6 番目の; da⌉i-ro⌈ku⌉ no 第 6 の.
— *n.* **1** (things) ro⌈ku-bañme⌉ no mo⌈no⌉ 6 番目のもの; (people) ro⌈ku-bañme⌉ no hi⌈to⌉ 6 番目の人.
2 (day) mu⌈ika 6 日.
3 (fraction) ro⌈ku-buñ no ichi⌉ 6 分の 1.

sixtieth *adj.* ro⌈kujuu-bañme⌉ no 60 番目の; da⌉i-ro⌈kuju⌉u no 第 60 の.
— *n.* **1** (things) ro⌈kujuu-bañme⌉ no mo⌈no⌉ 60 番目のもの; (people) ro⌈kujuu-bañme⌉ no hi⌈to⌉ 60 番目の人.
2 (fraction) ro⌈kujuu-buñ no ichi⌉ 60 分の 1.

sixty *pron.* ro⌈kuju⌉u 60; (people) ro⌈kuju⌉u-niñ 60 人; (things) ro⌈kuju⌉k-ko 60 個.
— *n.* (figure) ro⌈kuju⌉u 60; (minute) ro⌈kuju⌉p-puñ 60 分; (age) ro⌈kuju⌉s-sai 60 歳.
— *adj.* ro⌈kuju⌉u no 60 の; (people) ro⌈kuju⌉u-niñ no 60 人の; (things) ro⌈kuju⌉k-ko no 60 個の; (age) ro⌈kuju⌉s-sai no 60 歳の.

size *n.* **1** (bigness) o⌈okisa 大きさ: The two rooms are the same size. (*Sono futatsu no heya wa onaji ookisa desu.*) その二つの部屋は同じ大きさです. / Show me something in this size, please. (*Kono ookisa no mono o misete kudasai.*) この大きさの物を見せてください.
2 (measurement) sa⌉izu サイズ; su⌈ñpoo 寸法: What is your shoe size? (*Anata no kutsu no saizu wa dono kurai desu ka?*) あなたの靴のサイズはどのくらいですか.

skate *n.* su⌈keeto⌉-gutsu スケート靴: a pair of skates (*sukeeto-gutsu issoku*) スケート靴 1 足. ★ Japanese '*sukeeto*' is used in the sense of 'skating.'
— *vi.* su⌈keeto o suru スケートをする ①: skate on a pond (*ike de sukeeto o suru*) 池でスケートをする / go skating (*sukeeto ni iku*) スケートに行く.

skeleton *n.* **1** (bones) ko⌈kkaku 骨格; ga⌉ikotsu がい骨.

S

2 (building) ho⌈negumi⌉ 骨組み: the steel skeleton of a building (*biru no tekkotsu no honegumi*) ビルの鉄骨の骨組み.

sketch *n.* **1** (drawing) su⌈ke⌉tchi スケッチ; rya⌈kuzu 略図: make a sketch of a tree (*ki no suketchi o suru*) 木のスケッチをする.
2 (outline) a⌈rasuji あら筋; ga⌈i-ryaku 概略: I gave them a rough sketch of my plan. (*Watashi wa kare-ra ni keekaku no gairyaku o shimeshita.*) 私は彼らに計画の概略を示した.
— *vt.* ... no su⌈ke⌉tchi o kaku ...のスケッチをかく Ⓒ; ... o sha⌈see suru ...を写生する Ⓘ: sketch a cat (*neko o shasee suru*) ねこを写生する.

ski *n.* su⌈ki⌉i スキー: glide on skis (*sukii de suberu*) スキーで滑る.
★ Japanese '*sukii*' is used in the sense of 'skiing.'
— *vi.* su⌈ki⌉i o suru スキーをする Ⓘ: ski down a slope (*shameñ o sukii de suberioriru*) 斜面をスキーで滑り下りる.

skill *n.* **1** (ability) shu⌉wañ 手腕; jo⌈ozu じょうず: play the violin with skill (*baioriñ o joozu ni hiku*) バイオリンをじょうずに弾く.
2 (craft) gi⌉noo 技能; gi⌉jutsu 技術: Reading and writing are different skills. (*Yomu no to kaku no wa chigau ginoo da.*) 読むのと書くのは違う技能だ.

skilled *adj.* u⌈de no i⌉i 腕のいい; ju-⌈kureñ shita [shite iru] 熟練した[している]: a skilled carpenter (*ude no ii daiku*) 腕のいい大工 / skilled hands (*jukureñkoo*) 熟練工.

skillfull *adj.* ju⌈kureñ shita [shite iru] 熟練した[している]; jo⌈ozu⌉ na じょうずな: a skillful surgeon (*jukureñ shita geka-i*) 熟練した外科医 / He is skillful at teaching. (*Kare wa oshieru no ga joozu da.*) 彼は教えるのがじょうずだ.

skim *vt.* **1** (remove) ... o su⌈kuito⌉ru ...をすくい取る Ⓒ: skim the cream off the milk (*gyuunyuu kara kuriimu o sukuitoru*) 牛乳からクリームをすくい取る.
2 (read quickly) ... o za⌈tto yo⌉mu ...をざっと読む Ⓒ: skim the headlines of a newspaper (*shiñbuñ no midashi o zatto yomu*) 新聞の見出しをざっと読む.
3 (move swiftly) ... o su⌈resure ni tobu ...をすれすれに飛ぶ Ⓒ: A bird skimmed the water. (*Tori ga suimeñ o suresure ni toñda.*) 鳥が水面をすれすれに飛んだ.
— *vi.* **1** (look through) za⌈tto me⌉ o toosu ざっと目を通す Ⓒ: skim through a catalog (*katarogu ni zatto me o toosu*) カタログにざっと目を通す.
2 (glide lightly) su⌈be⌉ru yoo ni su-⌈sumu 滑るように進む Ⓒ: The motorboat seemed to skim over the surface of the water. (*Mootaabooto ga suijoo o suberu yoo ni susuñda.*) モーターボートが水上を滑るように進んだ.

skin *n.* **1** (of a human) hi⌉fu 皮膚; ha⌉da 肌: She has fair skin. (*Kanojo wa hada ga shiroi.*) 彼女は肌が白い.
2 (of an animal) ka⌈wa⌉ 皮; ke-⌈gawa 毛皮: a coat made from a fox skin (*kitsune no kegawa no kooto*) きつねの毛皮のコート.
3 (peel) ka⌈wa⌉ 皮: an apple skin (*riñgo no kawa*) りんごの皮.
— *vt.* (hide) ... no ka⌈wa o ha⌉gu ...の皮をはぐ Ⓒ; (peel) ... no ka⌈wa⌉ o mu⌈ku ...の皮をむく Ⓒ: skin a deer (*shika no kawa o hagu*) 鹿の皮をはぐ.

skip *vi.* **1** (hop) to⌈bihane⌉ru 飛び跳ねる Ⓥ; su⌈ki⌉ppu suru スキップする Ⓘ: skip about (*hanemawaru*) 跳ね回る.
2 (pass over) sho⌈oryaku suru 省略する Ⓘ; to⌈bashite yo⌉mu 飛ばして読む Ⓒ: I skipped chapter two of the book. (*Watashi wa sono hoñ no dai-ni-shoo o tobashite yoñda.*) 私はその本の第2章を飛ばして読んだ.
— *vt.* **1** (jump) ... o to⌈biko⌉su ...を飛び越す Ⓒ: skip a stream (*ogawa*

o tobikosu) 小川を飛び越す.
2 (miss out) ... o sho[ryaku suru ...を省略する [I]; nu[ku 抜く [C]: skip breakfast (*chooshoku o nuku*) 朝食を抜く.

skirt *n.* su[ka]ato スカート: put on [wear] a skirt (*sukaato o haku* [*haite iru*]) スカートをはく[はいている].

skull *n.* zu[ga]ikotsu 頭蓋骨; do]-kuro どくろ.

sky *n.* so]ra 空: a blue sky (*aozora*) 青空 / a cloudy sky (*kumorizora*) 曇り空 / There was not a cloud in the sky. (*Sora ni wa kumo hitotsu nakatta.*) 空には雲一つなかった.

slacks *n.* su[ra]kkusu スラックス: put on slacks (*surakkusu o haku*) スラックスをはく. ★ Japanese '*surakkusu*' usually refers to casual trousers.

slam *vt.* **1** (shut violently) ba[ta]ñ to shi[me]ru ばたんと閉める [V]: slam the door shut (*to o batañ to shimeru*) 戸をばたんと閉める.
2 (place violently) do[su]ñ to o[ku どすんと置く [C]: slam a parcel on the floor (*nimotsu o yuka ni dosuñ to oku*) 荷物を床にどすんと置く.

slander *n.* wa[ru]kuchi 悪口; chu[u-shoo 中傷.

slang *n.* zo[kugo 俗語; su[ra]ñgu スラング.

slant *vi.* ka[tamu]ku 傾く [C]: His handwriting slants to the left. (*Kare no ji wa hidari ni katamuite iru.*) 彼の字は左に傾いている.
— *vt.* ... o ka[tamuke]ru ...を傾ける [V]: The picture is a little slanted. (*Sono e wa sukoshi katamuite iru.*) その絵は少し傾いている.
— *n.* ke[esha 傾斜; sha]meñ 斜面: The slant of this roof is steep. (*Kono yane no keesha wa kyuu da.*) この屋根の傾斜は急だ.

slap *vt.* ... o hi[rate de pisha]ri to ta[ta]ku ...を平手でぴしゃりとたたく [C]: slap someone on the face (*hito no kao o pishari to tataku*) 人の顔をぴしゃりとたたく.
— *n.* hi[rateuchi 平手打ち: She gave him a slap on the cheek. (*Kanojo wa kare no hoo ni hirateuchi o kurawashita.*) 彼女は彼のほおに平手打ちをくらわした.

slash *vt.* **1** (cut) ... o ki]ru ...を切る [C]: The knife slipped and I slashed my finger. (*Naifu ga subette yubi o kitte shimatta.*) ナイフが滑って指を切ってしまった.
2 (reduce) ... o ki[risageru ...を切り下げる [V]: slash prices (*nedañ o kirisageru*) 値段を切り下げる.
— *vi.* ta[takitsuke]ru たたきつける [V]: slash the bushes with a stick (*boo de yabu o tatakitsukeru*) 棒でやぶをたたきつける.
— *n.* ki[ri]kizu 切り傷: a slash on one's cheek (*hoo no kirikizu*) ほおの切り傷.

slate *n.* su[reeto スレート; se[kibañ 石板.

slaughter *n.* (people) gya[kusatsu 虐殺; (animals) chi[kusatsu 畜殺.
— *vt.* ... o gya[kusatsu suru ...を虐殺する [I]; chi[kusatsu suru 畜殺する [I]: slaughter hogs for food (*shokuryoo no tame ni buta o chikusatsu suru*) 食料のために豚を畜殺する.

slave *n.* do[ree 奴隷: work like a slave (*doree no yoo ni hataraku*) 奴隷のように働く.

slavery *n.* (condition) do[ree no mi]buñ 奴隷の身分; (system) do[ree se]edo 奴隷制度.

sled *n.* so]ri そり.

sleep *vi.* ne[muru 眠る [C]; ne[mureru 眠れる [V]: The baby is sleeping. (*Akañboo wa nemutte iru.*) 赤ん坊は眠っている. / I slept well last night. (*Sakuya wa yoku nemureta.*) 昨夜はよく眠れた.
— *n.* ne[muri 眠り; su[imiñ 睡眠: get some sleep (*sukoshi suimiñ o toru*) 少し睡眠をとる.

sleeping pill *n.* su[imi]ñyaku 睡眠薬: take a sleeping pill (*suimiñyaku o nomu*) 睡眠薬を飲む.

sleepy *adj.* ne[mui 眠い: I feel sleepy. (*Nemuku natta.*) 眠くなった. / I was sleepy all day today. (*Kyoo wa ichinichi-juu nemukatta.*) きょう

は一日中眠かった.

sleeve *n.* so⌈de そで: a dress with long sleeves (*nagasode no doresu*) 長そでのドレス.

slender *adj.* ho⌈sso⌉ri shita [shite iru] ほっそりした[している]; su⌈ra⌉ri to shita [shite iru] すらりとした[している]: slender fingers (*hossori shita yubi*) ほっそりした指 / a slender girl (*surari to shita shoojo*) すらりとした少女.

slice *n.* hi⌈to⌉-kire 一切れ: a slice of bread (*pañ hito-kire*) パン一切れ.

— *vt.* ... o u⌈suku ki⌉ru ...を薄く切る Ⓒ; ki⌈ritoru 切り取る Ⓒ: slice a cake (*keeki o usuku kiru*) ケーキを薄く切る / slice off a piece of ham (*hamu o hito-kire kiritoru*) ハムを一切れ切り取る.

slide *vi.* su⌈be⌉ru 滑る Ⓒ: Let's slide on the ice. (*Koori no ue o suberoo.*) 氷の上を滑ろう.

— *vt.* ... o su⌈berase⌉ru ...を滑らせる Ⓥ: slide a glass across a table (*koppu o teeburu no ue de suberaseru*) コップをテーブルの上で滑らせる.

— *n.* **1** (sliding) su⌈be⌉ru ko⌈to⌉ 滑ること; ka⌈ssoo 滑走.

2 (apparatus) su⌈beri⌉dai 滑り台: play on a slide (*suberidai de asobu*) 滑り台で遊ぶ.

3 (film) su⌈raido スライド: a film for color slides (*suraido-yoo firumu*) スライド用フィルム.

slight *adj.* wa⌉zuka na わずかな; su⌈ko⌉shi no 少しの: There is a slight difference between the two. (*Sono futatsu ni wa wazuka na chigai ga aru.*) その二つにはわずかな違いがある.

slightly *adv.* wa⌉zuka ni わずかに; su⌈koshi ba⌉kari 少しばかり: It was raining slightly. (*Ame ga sukoshi futte ita.*) 雨が少し降っていた.

slim *adj.* ho⌈sso⌉ri shita [shite iru] ほっそりした[している]; su⌈ra⌉ri to shita [shite iru] すらりとした[している]: She has a slim figure. (*Kanojo wa surari to shita karada o shite iru.*) 彼女はすらりとした体をしている.

— *vi.* ta⌈ijuu o herasu 体重を減らす Ⓒ: I'm slimming down now. (*Watashi wa ima taijuu o herashite imasu.*) 私はいま体重を減らしています.

slip[1] *vi.* **1** (slide) su⌈be⌉ru 滑る Ⓒ: I slipped on the ice and hurt my hand. (*Watashi wa koori de subette te ni kega o shita.*) 私は氷で滑って手にけがをした.

2 (escape) so⌈tto nige⌉ru そっと逃げる Ⓥ: He slipped out of the room. (*Kare wa sotto heya kara dete itta.*) 彼はそっと部屋から出て行った.

3 (move smoothly) su⌈be⌉ru yoo ni u⌈go⌉ku 滑るように動く Ⓒ: The ship slipped through the waves. (*Fune wa nami no aida o suberu yoo ni hashitta.*) 船は波の間を滑るように走った.

— *vt.* ... o su⌈berase⌉ru ...を滑らせる Ⓥ; so⌈tto ⟨verb⟩ そっと...: He slipped his wallet out of his pocket. (*Kare wa poketto kara saifu o sotto dashita.*) 彼はポケットから財布をそっと出した.

— *n.* **1** (slipping) su⌈be⌉ru ko⌈to⌉ 滑ること.

2 (mistake) ma⌈chiga⌉i 間違い: a slip of the pen (*kakichigai*) 書き違い.

3 (undergarment) su⌈ri⌉ppu スリップ; shi⌈mi⌉izu シミーズ.

slip[2] *n.* ho⌈sonaga⌉i ka⌈mikire⌉ 細長い紙切れ; de⌈ñpyoo 伝票: a sales slip (*uriage-deñpyoo*) 売上伝票.

slipper *n.* shi⌈tsunaibaki 室内ばき. ★ In Japan 'mules' or 'scuffs' are called '*surippa*' スリッパ.

slippery *adj.* su⌈beriyasu⌉i 滑りやすい; tsu⌉rutsuru shita [shite iru] つるつるした[している]: a slippery floor (*suberiyasui yuka*) 滑りやすい床.

slogan *n.* su⌈ro⌉ogañ スローガン; hyo⌈ogo 標語.

slope *n.* sa⌈ka⌉ 坂; sa⌈ka⌉michi 坂道: a steep [gentle] slope (*kyuu* [*yuruyaka*] *na saka*) 急[緩やか]な坂.

slot *n.* su⌈ro⌉tto スロット; mi⌈zo 溝.

slow *adj.* **1** (not fast) o⌈soi 遅い; no⌈ro⌉i のろい: a slow worker (*shigoto ga osoi hito*) 仕事が遅い人.

2 (of clocks) o⌈kurete iru 遅れている:

This clock is three minutes slow. (*Kono tokee wa sañ-puñ okurete iru.*) この時計は 3 分遅れている.
3 (dull) o⌈soi 遅い; ni⌈bu⌉i 鈍い: He is slow in his movements. (*Kare wa doosa ga nibui.*) 彼は動作が鈍い.
4 (not busy) fu⌈ke⌉eki na 不景気な: Business is slow now. (*Ima wa fukeeki da.*) いまは不景気だ.
— *adv.* yu⌈kku⌉ri to ゆっくりと; o⌈soku 遅く: Drive slower, please. (*Motto yukkuri uñteñ shite kudasai.*) もっとゆっくり運転してください.
— *vt.* ... o o⌈soku suru ...を遅くする Ⓘ.
slow down *vi.* su⌈piido o oto⌉su スピードを落とす Ⓒ.

slowly *adv.* yu⌈kku⌉ri to ゆっくりと; o⌈soku 遅く: Please speak a little more slowly. (*Moo sukoshi yukkuri hanashite kudasai.*) もう少しゆっくり話してください.

slum *n.* su⌈ramu⌉gai スラム街.

slumber *n.* u⌈tatane うたた寝; ma⌈doromi まどろみ: fall into a slumber (*utatane suru*) うたた寝する.
— *vi.* ne⌈muru 眠る Ⓒ; ma⌈doro⌉mu まどろむ Ⓒ.

sly *adj.* zu⌈ru⌉i ずるい; wa⌈rugashiko⌉i 悪賢い: He is as sly as a fox. (*Kare wa kitsune no yoo ni zurui.*) 彼はきつねのようにずるい.

smack *vt.* **1** (slap) ... o pi⌈sha⌉ri to utsu ...をぴしゃりと打つ Ⓒ: smack a naughty child (*itazura na ko o pishari to utsu*) いたずらな子をぴしゃりと打つ.
2 (kiss) ... ni chu⌉tto kisu o suru ...にちゅっとキスをする Ⓘ: She smacked a kiss on my cheek. (*Kanojo wa watashi no hoo ni chutto kisu o shita.*) 彼女は私のほおにちゅっとキスをした.
— *n.* (sound) pi⌈shatto iu oto⌉ ぴしゃっという音; (blow) hi⌈rateuchi 平手打ち.

small *adj.* **1** (little in size) chi⌈isa⌉i 小さい; chi⌉isa-na 小さな: Do you have a smaller one? (*Motto chiisai no wa arimasu ka?*) もっと小さいのはありますか. / a small car (*chiisa-na kuruma*) 小さな車.
2 (little in amount) su⌈kuna⌉i 少ない: a small number (*shoosuu*) 少数 / a small sum (*shoogaku*) 少額.
3 (not important) tsu⌈mara⌉nai つまらない; ku⌈daranai くだらない: a small problem (*tsumaranai moñdai*) つまらない問題.

smart *adj.* **1** (clever) ri⌈koo na 利口な; a⌈tama no yo⌉i 頭のよい: a smart student (*atama no yoi gakusee*) 頭のよい学生.
2 (stylish) su⌈ma⌉ato na スマートな: a smart uniform (*sumaato na seefuku*) スマートな制服.
3 (painful) ha⌈geshi⌉i 激しい; hi⌉rihiri suru ひりひりする: a smart pain in the side (*wakibara no hageshii itami*) わき腹の激しい痛み.
— *vi.* hi⌉rihiri i⌈ta⌉mu ひりひり痛む Ⓒ: The cut smarts. (*Kirikizu ga itamu.*) 切り傷が痛む.

smash *vt.* **1** (crush) ... o ko⌈na-gona ni waru 粉々に割る Ⓒ: She dropped the plate and smashed it. (*Kanojo wa sara o otoshite kona-gona ni watte shimatta.*) 彼女は皿を落として粉々に割ってしまった.
2 (hit) ... o na⌈gu⌉ru ...を殴る Ⓒ: He smashed me with his fist. (*Kare wa watashi o geñkotsu de nagutta.*) 彼は私をげんこつで殴った.
— *vi.* ge⌈kitotsu suru 激突する Ⓘ: The car smashed into a tree. (*Sono kuruma wa ki ni gekitotsu shita.*) その車は木に激突した.

smear *vt.* **1** (spread) ... ni (... o) nu⌈ru ...に(...を)塗る Ⓒ: smear one's face with cream (*kao ni kuriimu o nuru*) 顔にクリームを塗る.
2 (smudge) ... o yo⌈gosu ...を汚す Ⓒ: The boy smeared the table with jam. (*Sono ko wa jamu de teeburu o yogoshita.*) その子はジャムでテーブルを汚した.
3 (spoil) ... o ki⌈zutsuke⌉ru ...を傷つける Ⓥ: smear a person's reputation (*hito no meesee o kizutsukeru*) 人の名声を傷つける.

smell *n.* **1** (odor) ni'o'i におい; (aroma) ka'ori 香り: There is a smell of something burning. (*Nani-ka ga kogete iru nioi ga suru.*) 何かが焦げているにおいがする. / the smell of coffee (*koohii no kaori*) コーヒーの香り.
2 (sense) shu'ukaku 臭覚: Dogs have a keen sense of smell. (*Inu wa surudoi shuukaku o motte iru.*) 犬は鋭い臭覚を持っている.
— *vi.* ni'o'i ga suru においがする [I]: This flower smells sweet. (*Kono hana wa ii nioi ga suru.*) この花はいいにおいがする.
— *vt.* ... no ni'o'i o ka'gu ...のにおいをかぐ [C]: He smelled the fish. (*Kare wa sono sakana no nioi o kaida.*) 彼はその魚のにおいをかいだ.

smile *vi.* bi'shoo suru 微笑する [I]; ni'kko'ri suru にっこりする [I]; ho'hoe'mu ほほ笑む [C]: She smiled when she saw me. (*Kanojo wa watashi o mite nikkori shita.*) 彼女は私を見てにっこりした.
— *vt.* bi'shoo shite ‹verb› 微笑して...: He smiled his thanks. (*Kare wa bishoo shite kañsha shita.*) 彼は微笑して感謝した.
— *n.* bi'shoo 微笑; ho'hoemi ほほ笑み: a cheerful smile (*tanoshi-soo na bishoo*) 楽しそうな微笑 / with a smile (*nikoniko shite*) にこにこして.

smog *n.* su'mo'ggu スモッグ; e'ñmu 煙霧.

S

smoke *n.* **1** (from burning) ke'muri 煙: I see black smoke coming out of the chimney. (*Eñtotsu kara kuroi kemuri ga dete iru no ga mieru.*) 煙突から黒い煙が出ているのが見える.
2 (smoking) ki'tsueñ 喫煙; i'ppuku 一服: have a smoke (*ippuku suru*) 一服する.
— *vi.* **1** (of a cigarette) ta'bako o suu たばこを吸う [C]: Do you mind if I smoke here? (*Koko de tabako o sutte mo ii desu ka?*) ここでたばこを吸ってもいいですか.
2 (give off smoke) ke'muri o da'su 煙を出す [C]: The volcano is smoking. (*Kazañ ga kemuri o dashite iru.*) 火山が煙を出している.
— *vt.* **1** (inhale) ... o su'u ...を吸う [C]: smoke a cigar (*hamaki o suu*) 葉巻を吸う.
2 (treat) ... o ku'ñsee ni suru ...を薫製にする [I]: smoke salmon (*sake o kuñsee ni suru*) さけを薫製にする.

smoking *n.* ki'tsueñ 喫煙: No smoking. (*Kiñeñ.*) 禁煙 / a smoking car (*kitsueñsha*) 喫煙車.

smooth *adj.* **1** (not rough) na'me'raka na 滑らかな; su'besube no すべすべの: smooth skin (*subesube no hada*) すべすべの肌.
2 (even surface) he'eta'ñ na 平坦な: a smooth road (*heetañ na michi*) 平坦な道.
3 (calm) shi'zuka na 静かな: smooth water on the lake (*mizuumi no shizuka na suimeñ*) 湖の静かな水面.
4 (steady in motion) na'me'raka na 滑らかな; e'ñkatsu na 円滑な: smooth driving (*nameraka na uñteñ*) 滑らかな運転.
— *vt.* ... o na'me'raka ni suru ...を滑らかにする [I]; ta'ira ni suru 平らにする [I]: smooth a board with sandpaper (*kamiyasuri de ita o nameraka ni suru*) 紙やすりで板を滑らかにする.

smoothly *adv.* na'me'raka ni 滑らかに; ju'ñchoo ni 順調に: Everything went smoothly. (*Subete juñchoo ni itta.*) すべて順調にいった.

smuggle *vt.* ... o mi'tsuyu suru ...を密輸する [I]: smuggle in [out] drugs (*mayaku o mitsuyunyuu [mitsuyushutsu] suru*) 麻薬を密輸入[密輸出]する.

snack bar *n.* ke'esho'kudoo 軽食堂; su'na'kku スナック.

snake *n.* he'bi 蛇.

snap *vi.* **1** (break) pu'tsu'ri to ki're'ru ぷつりと切れる [V]; po'ki'ñ to o're'ru ぽきんと折れる [V]: The rope snapped when I pulled it tight. (*Sono tsuna wa gyuutto hippattara*

putsuri to kireta.) その綱はぎゅーっと引っぱったらぷつりと切れた. / The branch snapped off. (*Eda ga pokiñ to oreta.*) 枝がぽきんと折れた.
2 (close) pa⌈chi⌉ñ to shi⌈ma⌉ru ぱちんと閉まる [C]: The lock snapped shut. (*Kagi wa pachiñ to shimatta.*) 鍵はぱちんと閉まった.
3 (try to bite) (... ni) ka⌈mitsuko⌉o to suru (…に)かみつこうとする [I]: The dog snapped at me. (*Sono inu wa watashi ni kamitsukoo to shita.*) その犬は私にかみつこうとした.
4 (speak) (... ni) ga⌉migami i⌈u (…に)がみがみ言う [C]: She snapped at the child. (*Kanojo wa sono ko ni gamigami itta.*) 彼女はその子にがみがみ言った.
— *vt.* ... o pa⌈chi⌉ñ to na⌈rasu …をぱちんと鳴らす [C]: snap a whip (*pachiñ to muchi o narasu*) ぱちんとむちを鳴らす / snap down a lid (*pachiñ to futa o shimeru*) ぱちんとふたを閉める.
— *n.* **1** (sound) pa⌈chi⌉ñ [po⌈ki⌉ri] to i⌈u oto⌉ ぱちん[ぽきり]という音.
2 (fastening device) to⌈megane 留め金; su⌈na⌉ppu スナップ.

snapshot *n.* su⌈nappu-sha⌉shiñ スナップ写真: take a snapshot of a child (*kodomo no sunappu-shashiñ o toru*) 子どものスナップ写真を撮る.

snatch *vt.* ... o hi⌈ttaku⌉ru …をひったくる [C]; u⌈baito⌉ru 奪い取る [C]: The thief snatched the money and ran away. (*Doroboo wa kane o ubaitotte nigeta.*) どろぼうは金を奪い取って逃げた.
— *n.* hi⌈ttakuri ひったくり: make a snatch at a bag (*baggu o hittakuroo to suru*) バッグをひったくろうとする.

sneer *vi.* re⌈eshoo suru 冷笑する [I]; a⌈zawara⌉u あざ笑う [C]: He sneered at my idea. (*Kare wa watashi no aidea o azawaratta.*) 彼は私のアイデアをあざ笑った.

sneeze *vi.* ku⌈sha⌉mi o suru くしゃみをする [I]: She had a cold and was sneezing. (*Kanojo wa kaze o hiite kushami o shite ita.*) 彼女はかぜを引いてくしゃみをしていた.
— *n.* ku⌈sha⌉mi くしゃみ: give a sneeze (*kushami o suru*) くしゃみをする.

snore *vi.* i⌈biki⌉ o kaku いびきをかく [C]: He snores loudly. (*Kare wa ooki-na ibiki o kaku.*) 彼は大きないびきをかく.

snow *n.* yu⌈ki⌉ 雪: Ten centimeters of snow covered the ground. (*Yuki ga jus-señchi tsumotta.*) 雪が10センチ積もった.
— *vi.* yu⌈ki⌉ ga furu 雪が降る [C]: It snowed all night. (*Yuki ga hito-bañ-juu futta.*) 雪がひと晩中降った.

snowman *n.* yu⌈kida⌉ruma 雪だるま: make a snowman (*yukidaruma o tsukuru*) 雪だるまを作る.

snowstorm *n.* fu⌉buki 吹雪.

snowy *adj.* yu⌈ki⌉ ni o⌈owareta [o⌈owarete iru] 雪に覆われた[覆われている]: snowy mountains (*yuki ni oowareta yama*) 雪に覆われた山.

so *adv.* **1** (to such a degree) so⌈re hodo それほど; so⌈ñna ni そんなに: This problem is not so difficult. (*Kono moñdai wa sore hodo muzukashiku nai.*) この問題はそれほど難しくない.
2 (in such a way) so⌉o そう; so⌈no yo⌉o ni そのように: Is that really so? (*Hoñtoo ni soo desu ka?*) 本当にそうですか.
3 (as a result) so⌈ko de そこで; so⌈re de それで: He caught a cold and so he stayed away from school. (*Kare wa kaze o hiita. Sore de gakoo o yasuñda.*) 彼はかぜを引いた. それで学校を休んだ.
4 (very) hi⌈joo ni 非常に; ta⌈iheñ 大変: I was so tired. (*Watashi wa hijoo ni tsukareta.*) 私は非常に疲れた.
5 (also) ... mo ma⌈ta …もまた: He's left-handed and so am I. (*Kare wa hidari-kiki da ga watashi mo mata soo desu.*) 彼は左利きだが私もまたそうです.
So long. Sa⌈yoona⌉ra. さようなら.
so ... that ... hi⌈joo ni ... na no

de 非常に…なので: It was raining so hard that I didn't go out. (*Ame ga hidoku futte ita no de gaishutsu shinakatta.*) 雨がひどく降っていたので外出しなかった.

so that ... can do ... de⌈ki⌉ru yoo ni …できるように: I worked hard so that I could pass the examination. (*Shikeñ ni ukaru yoo ni isshookeñmee ni beñkyoo shita.*) 試験に受かるように一生懸命に勉強した.

soak *vt.* **1** (place in liquid) ... o hi⌈tasu …を浸す Ⓒ: soak beans in water (*mame o mizu ni hitasu*) 豆を水に浸す.

2 (make wet) ... o zu⌈bunure ni suru …をずぶぬれにする Ⓘ: I got soaked in a shower. (*Watashi wa yuudachi de zubunure ni natta.*) 私は夕立でずぶぬれになった.

3 (suck up) ... o su⌈ito⌉ru …を吸い取る Ⓒ: use a sponge to soak up the spilled water (*koboreta mizu o suitoru no ni supoñji o tsukau*) こぼれた水を吸い取るのにスポンジを使う.

— *vi.* **1** (remain in liquid) (... ni) tsu⌈keru (…に)つける Ⓥ: let the clothes soak in water (*fuku o mizu ni tsukeru*) 服を水につける.

2 (penetrate) (... ni) shi⌈mito⌉oru (…に)しみ通る Ⓒ: The rain soaked through my coat. (*Ame ga kooto ni shimitootta.*) 雨がコートにしみ通った.

soap *n.* se⌈kkeñ せっけん: wash with soap and water (*sekkeñ to mizu de arau*) せっけんと水で洗う.

soar *vi.* **1** (fly up) ma⌈iaga⌉ru 舞い上がる Ⓒ; ta⌉kaku a⌈garu 高く上がる Ⓒ: The skylark soared into the sky. (*Hibari wa sora ni maiagatta.*) ひばりは空へ舞い上がった.

2 (rise) ko⌈otoo suru 高騰する Ⓘ: Prices have soared. (*Bukka ga kootoo shita.*) 物価が高騰した.

sob *vi.* su⌈surina⌉ku すすり泣く Ⓒ; shi⌉kushiku na⌈ku しくしく泣く Ⓒ: She sobbed at the news. (*Kanojo wa sono shirase o kiite susurinaita.*) 彼女はその知らせを聞いてすすり泣いた.

sober *adj.* yo⌉tte inai 酔っていない; shi⌉rafu no しらふの: He was the only sober man at the party. (*Sono paatii de yotte inai no wa kare dake datta.*) そのパーティーで酔っていないのは彼だけだった. / become sober (*yoi ga sameru*) 酔いが覚める.

so-called *adj.* i⌈wayu⌉ru いわゆる: so-called high society (*iwayuru jooryuu shakai*) いわゆる上流社会.

soccer *n.* sa⌉kkaa サッカー: play soccer (*sakkaa o suru*) サッカーをする.

sociable *adj.* sha⌈koo-teki na 社交的な; sha⌈koozuki na 社交好きな: He is a sociable man. (*Kare wa shakoo-teki na otoko da.*) 彼は社交的な男だ.

social *adj.* **1** (of human society) sha⌉kai no 社会の: a social problem (*shakai-moñdai*) 社会問題.

2 (of companionship) sha⌈koojoo no 社交上の; sha⌈koo-teki na 社交的な: a social club (*shakoo kurabu*) 社交クラブ / a social gathering (*koñshiñkai*) 懇親会.

society *n.* **1** (community) sha⌉kai 社会: a civilized society (*buñmee shakai*) 文明社会.

2 (organization) kyo⌈okai 協会; ka⌉i 会: set up a society (*kyookai o setsuritsu suru*) 協会を設立する.

3 (upper class) jo⌈oryuu sha⌉kai 上流社会.

sock *n.* ku⌈tsu⌉shita 靴下: a pair of socks (*kutsushita is-soku*) 靴下1足. ★ Japanese '*kutsushita*' refers to 'socks' and 'stockings.'

socket *n.* so⌈ke⌉tto ソケット; sa⌈shikomi 差し込み.

soda *n.* so⌉oda ソーダ; ta⌈ñsa⌉ñsui 炭酸水: a whisky and soda (*haibooru*) ハイボール.

sofa *n.* so⌉faa ソファー: sit on a sofa (*sofaa ni suwaru*) ソファーに座る.

soft *adj.* **1** (not hard) ya⌈waraka⌉i 柔らかい: a soft bed (*yawarakai beddo*) 柔らかいベッド / a soft-boiled egg (*hañjuku-tamago*) 半熟卵.

2 (smooth) na⌈me⌉raka na 滑らかな:

Silk is soft to the touch. (*Kinu wa tezawari ga nameraka da.*) 絹は手触りが滑らかだ.
3 (gentle) ya⌈sashii 優しい: She has a soft heart. (*Kanojo wa yasashii kokoro o motte iru.*) 彼女は優しい心を持っている.
4 (quiet) shi⌉zuka na 静かな: soft music (*shizuka na oñgaku*) 静かな音楽.

soften *vt.* ... o ya⌈wara⌉kaku suru …を柔らかくする [I]: soften leather (*kawa o yawarakaku suru*) 革を柔らかくする
— *vi.* ya⌈wara⌉kaku naru 柔らかくなる [C]: Wax softens when heated. (*Roo wa nessuru to yawarakaku naru.*) ろうは熱すると柔らかくなる.

software *n.* so⌈futoue⌉a ソフトウェア.

soil *n.* tsu⌈chi⌉ 土: cultivate the soil (*tsuchi o tagayasu*) 土を耕す.

solar *adj.* ta⌉iyoo no 太陽の: solar heat (*taiyoo-netsu*) 太陽熱 / a solar battery (*taiyoo deñchi*) 太陽電池.

soldier *n.* he⌉eshi 兵士; he⌈etai 兵隊; ri⌈ku⌉guñ no gu⌈ñjiñ 陸軍の軍人.

sole *adj.* ta⌉da hi⌈to⌉tsu no ただ一つの; yu⌉i-itsu no 唯一の: He is the sole survivor. (*Kare wa yui-itsu no seezoñsha da.*) 彼は唯一の生存者だ.

solemn *adj.* **1** (serious) ma⌈jime na まじめな: a solemn face (*majime na kao*) まじめな顔.
2 (sacred) o⌈go⌉soka na 厳かな: a solemn ceremony (*ogosoka na gishiki*) 厳かな儀式.

solicit *vt.* ... o se⌈ga⌉mu …をせがむ [C]; mo⌈tome⌉ru 求める [V]: He solicited my help. (*Kare wa watashi no eñjo o motometa.*) 彼は私の援助を求めた.

solid *adj.* **1** (hard) ko⌈tai no 固体の; ko⌈kee no 固形の: Water is liquid and ice is solid. (*Mizu wa ekitai de koori wa kotai desu.*) 水は液体で氷は固体です. / solid fuel (*kokee-neñryoo*) 固形燃料.
2 (strong) ga⌈ñjoo na がんじょうな: This desk is solid. (*Kono tsukue wa gañjoo da.*) この机はがんじょうだ.
3 (not hollow) chu⌈ukuu de na⌉i 中空でない: a solid bar of iron (*chuukuu de nai tetsu no boo*) 中空でない鉄の棒.
— *n.* ko⌈tai 固体.

solitary *adj.* ko⌈doku na 孤独な; sa⌈bishi⌉i 寂しい: a solitary traveler (*kodoku na tabibito*) 孤独な旅人.

solitude *n.* ko⌈doku 孤独; hi⌈tori-kiri ひとりきり: enjoy solitude (*kodoku o tanoshimu*) 孤独を楽しむ.

soluble *adj.* to⌈ke⌉ru 溶ける; to⌈keyasu⌉i 溶けやすい: Vitamin B is soluble in water. (*Bitamiñ bii wa mizu ni tokeyasui.*) ビタミンBは水に溶けやすい.

solution *n.* **1** (answer) ko⌈ta⌉e 答え; ka⌈iketsu 解決: I found the solution to the question. (*Sono moñdai no kotae ga wakatta.*) その問題の答えがわかった.
2 (dissolving) yo⌈okai 溶解; yo⌉o-eki 溶液: a solution of salt in water (*shio no yooeki*) 塩の溶液.

solve *vt.* ... o to⌉ku …を解く [C]; ka⌈iketsu suru 解決する [I]: I have solved all the problems. (*Moñdai wa zeñbu toita.*) 問題は全部解いた. / solve a difficult case (*muzukashii jikeñ o kaiketsu suru*) 難しい事件を解決する.

some *adj.* ★ There is no Japanese equivalent to 'some' and it is often not translated: I need some bread and milk. (*Pañ to miruku ga hoshii.*) パンとミルクが欲しい. / Would you like some tea? (*O-cha wa ikaga desu ka?*) お茶はいかがですか.
1 (of a number) i⌉kutsu ka no いくつかの: I bought some apples. (*Watashi wa riñgo o ikutsu ka katta.*) 私はりんごをいくつか買った.
2 (of an amount) i⌉kura ka no いくらかの: I'd like some coins in the change. (*Kozeni mo ikura ka mazete kudasai.*) 小銭もいくらか混ぜてください. / Can we do some shopping in this airport? (*Kono kuukoo de ikura ka kaimono ga dekimasu*

S

ka?) この空港でいくらか買物ができますか.
3 (of people) na¹ñniñ ka no 何人かの: Some people were injured in the accident. (*Sono jiko de nañniñ ka no hito ga kega o shita.*) その事故で何人かの人がけがをした.
4 (certain) a¹ru ... ある…; na¹ni-ka no 何かの: For some reason, the train was delayed. (*Nani-ka no riyuu de ressha ga okureta.*) 何かの理由で列車が遅れた.
— *pron.* **1** (of a number) i¹kutsu ka いくつか: I have read some of these books. (*Kono hoñ no naka no ikutsu ka wa yomimashita.*) この本の中のいくつかは読みました.
2 (of an amount) i¹kura ka いくらか: Some of the milk was spilled on the table. (*Gyuunyuu no ikura ka ga teeburu no ue ni koboreta.*) 牛乳のいくらかがテーブルの上にこぼれた.
3 (of people) a¹ru hi¹to¹-tachi ある人たち: Some agreed with me. (*Aru hito-tachi wa watashi ni sañsee shita.*) ある人たちは私に賛成した.
— *adv.* ya¹ku 約; o¹yoso およそ: It is some five kilometers. (*Yaku go-kiro desu.*) 約5キロです.

somebody *pron.* a¹ru hi¹to¹ ある人; da¹re-ka だれか: There's somebody at the door. (*Geñkañ ni dare-ka kite imasu.*) 玄関にだれか来ています.

someday *adv.* i¹tsu-ka いつか; ya¹gate やがて: Someday you'll understand. (*Itsu-ka kimi mo wakaru daroo.*) いつか君もわかるだろう.

somehow *adv.* na¹ñ to ka 何とか; to¹mokaku (mo) ともかく(も): I'll finish the work somehow. (*Nañ to ka sono shigoto o kañsee shimasu.*) 何とかその仕事を完成します.

someone *pron.* a¹ru hi¹to¹ ある人; da¹re-ka だれか: Can someone here speak English? (*Dare-ka koko de Eego ga hanasemasu ka?*) だれかここで英語が話せますか. / Please send someone for my baggage. (*Nimotsu o tori ni dare-ka o yokoshite kudasai.*) 荷物を取りにだれかをよこしてください.

something *pron.* a¹ru mo¹no¹ あるもの; na¹ni-ka 何か: I want to buy something for a man. (*Otoko mono o kaitai no desu ga.*) 男ものを買いたいのですが. / Can you give me something to read? (*Nani-ka yomu mono o kudasai.*) 何か読むものをください.

sometime *adv.* i¹tsu-ka いつか: I think I can meet him sometime next week. (*Raishuu no itsu-ka kare ni aeru to omoimasu.*) 来週のいつか彼に会えると思います.

sometimes *adv.* to¹kidoki 時々; to¹ki¹ ni wa 時には: I sometimes play tennis with him. (*Watashi wa tokidoki kare to tenisu o shimasu.*) 私は時々彼とテニスをします. / Sometimes I do the washing by myself. (*Toki ni wa jibuñ de señtaku o shimasu.*) 時には自分で洗濯をします.

somewhat *adv.* su¹ko¹shi 少し; i¹kubuñ いくぶん; ya¹ya やや: The train arrived somewhat late. (*Ressha wa sukoshi okurete toochaku shita.*) 列車は少し遅れて到着した. / I am somewhat tired. (*Watashi wa yaya tsukareta.*) 私はやや疲れた.

somewhere *adv.* do¹ko-ka ni どこかに; do¹ko-ka e どこかへ: I left my gloves somewhere. (*Watashi wa tebukuro o doko-ka ni okiwasureta.*) 私は手袋をどこかに置き忘れた. / Let's go somewhere quiet. (*Doko-ka shizuka na tokoro e ikoo.*) どこか静かな所へ行こう.

son *n.* mu¹suko 息子; (someone else's) mu¹suko-sañ 息子さん: I have two sons. (*Watashi ni wa musuko ga futari iru.*) 私には息子が二人いる.

song *n.* **1** (of music) u¹ta¹ 歌: sing a song (*uta o utau*) 歌を歌う / a popular song (*ryuukooka*) 流行歌.
2 (of birds) sa¹ezuri さえずり; (of insects) na¹kigo¹e 鳴き声: the song of birds (*tori no saezuri*) 鳥のさえずり / the song of insects (*mushi no nakigoe*) 虫の鳴き声.

S

soon *adv.* **1** (in a short time) ma⌈mo⌉naku まもなく: The train is leaving soon. (*Ressha wa mamonaku demasu.*) 列車はまもなく出ます.
2 (quickly) ha⌉yaku 早く: Please come as soon as possible. (*Dekiru dake hayaku kite kudasai.*) できるだけ早く来てください.
3 (early) ha⌈yame⌉ ni 早めに: The sooner, the better. (*Hayakereba hayai hodo yoi.*) 早ければ早いほどよい. / Come again soon! (*Mata kite kudasai.*) また来てください.

soot *n.* su⌉su すす; ba⌈ieñ 煤煙.

soothe *vt.* ... o na⌈dame⌉ru …をなだめる [V]; na⌈gusame⌉ru 慰める [V]: soothe an angry person (*okotte iru hito o nadameru*) 怒っている人をなだめる.

sophisticated *adj.* **1** (of taste) se⌉ñreñ sareta [sarete iru] 洗練された[されている]: sophisticated tastes (*señreñ sareta shumi*) 洗練された趣味.
2 (well-developed) se⌈ekoo na 精巧な: a sophisticated machine (*seekoo na kikai*) 精巧な機械.

sore *adj.* i⌈ta⌉i 痛い: I have a sore throat. (*Nodo ga itai.*) のどが痛い.

sorrow *n.* **1** (sadness) ka⌈nashimi 悲しみ: We felt deep sorrow at his death. (*Watashi-tachi wa kare no shi o fukaku kanashiñda.*) 私たちは彼の死を深く悲しんだ.
2 (regret) i⌉kañ 遺憾: He expressed sorrow for what he had done. (*Kare wa jibuñ no shita koto ni taishite ikañ no i o arawashita.*) 彼は自分のしたことに対して遺憾の意を表した.

sorry *adj.* **1** (full of sorrow) ki⌈nodoku⌉ na 気の毒な: I'm sorry that you're sick. (*Go-byooki de kinodoku desu.*) ご病気で気の毒です.
2 (regretful) za⌈ññ⌉eñ na 残念な: I'm sorry I can't come to the party. (*Zaññeñ desu ga paatii ni wa deraremaseñ.*) 残念ですがパーティーには出られません.
Sorry. Go⌈meñ nasa⌉i. ごめんなさい; Su⌈mimase⌉ñ. すみません.

sort *n.* **1** (kind) shu⌉rui 種類: What sort of music do you like best? (*Doo iuu shurui no oñgaku ga ichibañ suki desu ka?*) どういう種類の音楽がいちばん好きですか.
2 (type) ... no hi⌈to⌉ …の人: He is a good sort. (*Kare wa ii hito da.*) 彼はいい人だ.
— *vt.* ... o bu⌈ñrui suru …を分類する [I]: sort business cards (*meeshi o buñrui suru*) 名刺を分類する.

soul *n.* **1** (spirit) ta⌉mashii 魂; re⌉ekoñ 霊魂: Christians believe that at death their soul goes to heaven. (*Kurisuchañ wa shinu to tamashii wa teñgoku e iku to shiñjite iru.*) クリスチャンは死ぬと魂は天国へ行くと信じている.
2 (mind) se⌉eshiñ 精神; ko⌈ko⌉ro 心: body and soul (*nikutai to seeshiñ*) 肉体と精神.
3 (deep feeling) ne⌉tsujoo 熱情; ki⌉haku 気迫: His painting has no soul. (*Kare no e ni wa kihaku ga nai.*) 彼の絵には気迫がない.
4 (person) ni⌈ñgeñ 人間; hi⌈to⌉ 人: Not a soul left the room. (*Dare hitori heya kara dete ikanakatta.*) だれ一人部屋から出て行かなかった.

sound[1] *n.* o⌈to⌉ 音; mo⌈no-oto⌉ 物音: make a sound (*oto o tateru*) 音を立てる / There was no sound. (*Mono-oto hitotsu shinakatta.*) 物音一つしなかった.
— *vi.* **1** (make a sound) na⌉ru 鳴る [C]: The doorbell sounded. (*Doa no beru ga natta.*) ドアのベルが鳴った.
2 (seem) ... no yo⌉o ni o⌈moware⌉ru …のように思われる [V]; ... mi⌉tai da …みたいだ: The plan sounds all right. (*Sono keekaku wa ii yoo ni omowareru.*) その計画はいいように思われる.
— *vt.* ... o na⌈rasu …を鳴らす [C]: sound a horn (*keeteki o narasu*) 警笛を鳴らす.

sound[2] *adj.* **1** (healthy) ke⌈ñzeñ na 健全な: He is sound in mind and body. (*Kare wa shiñshiñ tomo ni*

S

keñzeñ da.) 彼は心身ともに健全だ.
2 (secure) shi⌈kka⌉ri shita [shite iru] しっかりした[している]; ke⌈ñjitsu na 堅実な: a sound investment (*keñjitsu na tooshi*) 堅実な投資.
3 (sensible) ta⌈dashi⌉i 正しい; da⌈too na 妥当な: a sound judgment (*datoo na hañdañ*) 妥当な判断.
4 (complete) ju⌈ubu⌉ñ na 十分な: have a sound sleep (*jukusui suru*) 熟睡する.

soup *n.* su⌉upu スープ: eat soup (*suupu o nomu*) スープを飲む. ★ Don't say '*suupu o taberu*' スープを食べる. / miso soup (*misoshiru*) みそ汁.

sour *adj.* **1** (acid taste) su⌈ppa⌉i 酸っぱい: Those grapes taste sour. (*Kono budoo wa suppai.*) このぶどうは酸っぱい.
2 (unpleasant) fu⌈ki⌉geñ na 不きげんな: He was in a sour mood. (*Kare wa fukigeñ datta.*) 彼は不きげんだった.

source *n.* **1** (origin) mi⌈namoto [ge⌉ñ] 源: a source of income (*shuunyuu-geñ*) 収入源.
2 (the beginning of a river) mi⌈namoto 源; su⌈igeñ 水源: This river has its source in Lake Suwa. (*Kono kawa wa Suwako ni minamoto o hassuru.*) この川は諏訪湖に源を発する.
3 (of information) de⌈do⌉koro 出所; su⌉ji 筋: information from a reliable source (*tashika na suji kara no joohoo*) 確かな筋からの情報.

south *n.* mi⌈nami 南; na⌉ñbu 南部: The birds flew to the south. (*Tori wa minami e toñde itta.*) 鳥は南へ飛んで行った.
— *adj.* mi⌈nami no 南の: a south wind (*minami-kaze*) 南風.
— *adv.* mi⌈nami e [ni] 南へ[に]: go south (*minami e iku*) 南へ行く.

southeast *n.* na⌈ñtoo 南東.

southern *adj.* mi⌈nami no 南の: Southern Europe (*Minami Yooroppa*) 南ヨーロッパ.

southwest *n.* na⌈ñsee 南西.

souvenir *n.* ki⌈neñhiñ 記念品; o⌈miyage おみやげ; mi⌈yage みやげ: I bought a doll as a souvenir. (*Watashi wa o-miyage ni niñgyoo o katta.*) 私はおみやげに人形を買った.
★ Japanese '*miyage*' refers to something that is given to others.

sovereign *n.* ku⌉ñshu 君主; ge⌉ñshu 元首; shu⌈ke⌉ñsha 主権者.
— *adj* **1** (ruling) shu⌈keñ no a⌉ru 主権のある: sovereign authority (*shukeñ*) 主権.
2 (independent) do⌈kuritsu no 独立の: a sovereign state (*dokuritsu-koku*) 独立国.

sow *vt.* ... o ma⌉ku ...をまく Ⓒ: He sowed wheat in the field. (*Kare wa hatake ni mugi o maita.*) 彼は畑に麦をまいた.
— *vi.* ta⌉ne o maku 種をまく Ⓒ: As you sow, so shall you reap. (*Maita tane wa karanakereba naranai.*) まいた種は刈らなければならない.

soybean *n.* da⌈izu 大豆: fermented soybean paste (*miso*) みそ / soybean paste soup (*misoshiru*) みそ汁.

soy sauce *n.* sho⌈oyu しょうゆ.

space *n.* **1** (universe) u⌉chuu 宇宙: travel in space (*uchuu o ryokoo suru*) 宇宙を旅行する. ★ 'Universe' is also called '*uchuu*.'
2 (empty part) ku⌈ukañ 空間: time and space (*jikañ to kuukañ*) 時間と空間.
3 (distance) ka⌈ñkaku 間隔; su⌈kima すきま: Leave a space between the cars. (*Kuruma no aida ni kañkaku o ake nasai.*) 車の間に間隔を空けなさい.
4 (room) ku⌈usho 空所; yo⌉chi 余地; su⌈pe⌉esu スペース: There is no space for another bed. (*Moo hitotsu beddo o ireru yochi wa arimaseñ.*) もう一つベッドを入れる余地はありません.

spacious *adj.* hi⌈robi⌉ro to shita [shite iru] 広々とした[している]; ko⌈odai na 広大な: a spacious living-room (*hirobiro to shita ima*) 広々とした居間.

spade *n.* (tool) su⌈ki すき(鋤).

span *n.* **1** (stretch) na⌉gasa 長さ;

ze⌈ñchoo 全長; ze⌈ñpuku 全幅: the span of one's arms (*ryoo-ude o hirogeta nagasa*) 両腕を広げた長さ / the span of a bridge (*hashi no zeñchoo*) 橋の全長.
2 (space of time) ki⌉kañ 期間: the average span of life (*heekiñ jumyoo*) 平均寿命.
— *vt.* ... ni ka⌈ka⌉ru ...に架かる Ⓒ: The bridge spans the river. (*Hashi wa sono kawa ni kakatte iru.*) 橋はその川に架かっている.

spare *vt.* **1** (afford) ... o sa⌉ku ...を割く Ⓒ: Can you spare me five minutes? (*Jikañ o go-fuñ saite itadakemasu ka?*) 時間を5分割いていただけますか.
2 (keep from using) ... o o⌈shi⌉mu ...を惜しむ Ⓒ: He spared no efforts. (*Kare wa doryoku o oshimanakatta.*) 彼は努力を惜しまなかった.
3 (save) ... o ha⌈bu⌉ku ...を省く Ⓒ: This will save me trouble. (*Kore de tema ga habukeru.*) これで手間が省ける.

spark *n.* hi⌉bana 火花: produce sparks (*hibana o dasu*) 火花を出す.

sparkle *vi.* ka⌈gaya⌉ku 輝く Ⓒ; ki⌈rame⌉ku きらめく Ⓒ: The diamond sparkled in the sunlight. (*Daiyamoñdo ga hi no hikari o ukete kirameita.*) ダイヤモンドが日の光を受けてきらめいた.
— *n.* ka⌈gayaki 輝き; ki⌈rameki きらめき.

sparrow *n.* su⌈zume すずめ.

speak *vi.* **1** (say words) ha⌈na⌉su 話す Ⓒ: May I speak in English? (*Eego de hanashite mo ii desu ka?*) 英語で話してもいいですか. / Please speak more slowly. (*Motto yukkuri hanashite kudasai.*) もっとゆっくり話してください.
2 (give a speech) e⌈ñzetsu suru 演説する Ⓘ: The lecturer spoke for about an hour. (*Kooshi wa yaku ichi-jikañ eñzetsu shita.*) 講師は約1時間演説した.
— *vt.* **1** (say words) ... o ha⌈na⌉su ...を話す Ⓒ; sha⌈be⌉ru しゃべる Ⓒ: I speak only a little Japanese. (*Watashi wa Nihoñgo o sukoshi dake hanashimasu.*) 私は日本語を少しだけ話します.
2 (tell) ... o ka⌈taru ...を語る Ⓒ: speak the truth (*shiñjitsu o kataru*) 真実を語る.

speaker *n.* **1** (person) ha⌈na⌉su hi⌈to⌉ 話す人; e⌈ñzetsu⌉sha 演説者: a native speaker (*bokokugo o hanasu hito*) 母国語を話す人 / a fine speaker (*eñzetsu no umai hito*) 演説のうまい人.
2 (chairperson) gi⌉choo 議長.
3 (loudspeaker) su⌈pi⌉ikaa スピーカー; ka⌈kuse⌉eki 拡声器.

special *adj.* **1** (not ordinary) to⌈kubetsu no 特別の: This is a special present for you. (*Kore wa anata e no tokubetsu no okurimono desu.*) これはあなたへの特別の贈り物です.
2 (particular) to⌈kuyuu no 特有の: a custom special to Japan (*Nihoñ tokuyuu no shuukañ*) 日本特有の習慣.
3 (not general) se⌈ñmon no 専門の; to⌈kushu na 特殊な: What is your special field of study? (*Anata no señmoñ buñya wa nañ desu ka?*) あなたの専門分野は何ですか.
4 (exceptional) ri⌈ñji no 臨時の: a special issue of a magazine (*zasshi no riñji zookañ-goo*) 雑誌の臨時増刊号.

specialist *n.* se⌈ñmoñka 専門家; (doctor) se⌈ñmo⌉ñ-i 専門医: a specialist in heart diseases (*shiñzoobyoo no señmoñ-i*) 心臓病の専門医.

specialize *vi.* (... o) se⌈ñmoñ ni suru (...を)専門にする Ⓘ; se⌈ñkoo suru 専攻する Ⓘ: She specializes in Japanese literature. (*Kanojo wa Nihoñ buñgaku o senkoo shite iru.*) 彼女は日本文学を専攻している.

specially *adv.* to⌈kubetsu ni 特別に; wa⌉zawaza わざわざ: I came here specially to see you. (*Kimi ni wazawaza ai ni kita ñ da.*) 君にわざわざ会いに来たんだ.

specialty *n.* **1** (special study) se⌈ñmoñ 専門; se⌈ñkoo 専攻.
2 (special product) to⌈kuseehiñ 特製品; (food) me⌈ebutsu ryo⌉ori 名物料理.

species *n.* shu⌉ 種: butterflies of many species (*kakushu no choo*) 各種のちょう.

specific *adj.* **1** (definite) me⌈e-kaku na 明確な; gu⌈taiteki na 具体的な: make specific plans for a trip (*ryokoo no gutai-teki na keekaku o suru*) 旅行の具体的な計画をする.
2 (particular) to⌈kushu no 特殊の: a specific remedy (*tokushu ryoohoo*) 特殊療法.

specifically *adv.* to⌉ku ni 特に; to⌈riwake とりわけ: a book written specifically for children (*toku ni kodomo no tame ni kakareta hoñ*) 特に子どものために書かれた本.

specify *vt.* ... o shi⌈tee suru ...を指定する [I]; me⌈egeñ suru 明言する [I]: Please specify the time and place. (*Jikañ to basho o shitee shite kudasai.*) 時間と場所を指定してください.

specimen *n.* mi⌈hoñ 見本; hyo⌈o-hoñ 標本: specimens of a new product (*shiñ-seehiñ no mihoñ*) 新製品の見本 / butterfly specimens (*choo no hyoohoñ*) ちょうの標本.

speck *n.* chi⌈isa⌉i shi⌈mi [ki⌈zu] 小さい染み[きず]: a speck of ink (*iñku no chiisai shimi*) インクの小さい染み.

spectacle *n.* (unusual sight) ko⌉okee 光景; so⌈okañ 壮観: The sunrise was a splendid spectacle. (*Hinode wa subarashii kookee datta.*) 日の出はすばらしい光景だった.

spectacles *n.* me⌉gane 眼鏡.

spectacular *adj.* su⌈barashi⌉i すばらしい; so⌈okañ na 壮観な: a spectacular view of the Alps (*Arupusu no subarashii nagame*) アルプスのすばらしい眺め.

spectator *n.* ka⌈ñkyaku 観客; ke⌈ñbutsuniñ 見物人: spectators at a game (*shiai no kañkyaku*) 試合の観客.

speculate *vi.* **1** (guess) sui⌈soku suru 推測する [I]; a⌈re⌉-kore ka⌈ñ-gae⌉ru あれこれ考える [V]: speculate about one's future life (*shoorai no seekatsu ni tsuite are-kore kañgaeru*) 将来の生活についてあれこれ考える.
2 (engage in risky business) to⌉oki suru 投機する [I]: speculate in land (*tochi ni tooki suru*) 土地に投機する.

speculation *n.* **1** (guess) su⌈i-soku 推測: Your speculations are close to the truth. (*Anata no sui-soku wa shiñjitsu ni chikai.*) あなたの推測は真実に近い.
2 (investment) to⌉oki 投機: speculation in stocks (*kabu no tooki*) 株の投機.

speech *n.* **1** (public talk) e⌈ñzetsu 演説; ko⌈oeñ 講演; sup⌈i⌉ichi スピーチ: He made an impromptu speech. (*Kare wa sokuseki de eñzetsu o shita.*) 彼は即席で演説をした. / an opening [closing] speech (*kaikai [heekai] no ji*) 開会[閉会]の辞.
2 (the act of speaking) ha⌈na⌉su ko⌈to⌉ 話すこと; ge⌈ñroñ 言論: freedom of speech (*geñroñ no jiyuu*) 言論の自由.
3 (the manner of speaking) ha⌈na-shika⌉ta 話し方; ha⌈nashiburi 話しぶり: His speech is not clear. (*Kare no hanashikata wa hakkiri shinai.*) 彼の話し方ははっきりしない.

speed *n.* **1** (swiftness) ha⌉yasa 速さ; so⌈ku⌉ryoku 速力: the speed of light (*hikari no hayasa*) 光の速さ / The train gradually gathered speed. (*Ressha wa jojo ni sokuryoku o mashita.*) 列車は徐々に速力を増した.
2 (velocity) so⌉kudo 速度; su⌈piido スピード: He drove at a speed of 50 kilometers an hour. (*Kare wa ji-soku gojuk-kiro no sokudo de uñteñ shita.*) 彼は時速 50 キロの速度で運転した.

speedy *adj.* bi⌈ñsoku na 敏速な; ha⌈ya⌉i 速い: a speedy worker (*shi-goto no hayai hito*) 仕事の速い人.

spell[1] *vt.* ... o tsu⌈zuru ...をつづる [C]:

How do you spell your name? (*Anata no namae wa doo tsuzuri-masu ka?*) あなたの名前はどうつづりますか.

spell[2] *n.* **1** (period) hi⌈to⌉tsuzuki ひと続き; shi⌈ba⌉raku no aida しばらくの間: a long spell of rainy weather (*nagai uteñ no tsuzuki*) 長い雨天の続き.

2 (work) hi⌈to⌉shigoto ひと仕事; ko⌈otai 交替: take a spell at the oars (*kootai de ooru o kogu*) 交替でオールをこぐ.

spelling *n.* tsu⌈zuri つづり; su⌈pe⌉-riñgu スペリング.

spend *vt.* **1** (pay out) ... o tsu⌈kau ...を使う Ⓒ; tsu⌈iya⌉su 費やす Ⓒ: He spends a lot of money on books. (*Kare wa hoñ ni o-kane o takusañ tsukau.*) 彼は本にお金をたくさん使う.

2 (pass) ... o su⌈go⌉su ...を過ごす Ⓒ: Where do you spend the summer vacation? (*Natsuyasumi wa doko de sugoshimasu ka?*) 夏休みはどこで過ごしますか.

sphere *n.* **1** (round object) kyu⌉u 球; kyu⌈ukee 球形.

2 (range) ha⌉ñi 範囲; ryo⌈oiki 領域: a sphere of activity (*katsudoo hañi*) 活動範囲.

spice *n.* ya⌈kumi 薬味; ko⌈oshi⌉ñ-ryoo 香辛料: use spices in cooking (*ryoori ni kooshiñryoo o tsukau*) 料理に香辛料を使う.

spider *n.* ku⌉mo くも(蜘蛛).

spill *vt.* ... o ko⌈bo⌉su ...をこぼす Ⓒ: Who is it that spilled water on the floor? (*Yuka ni mizu o koboshita no wa dare desu ka?*) 床に水をこぼしたのはだれですか.

— *vi.* ko⌈bore⌉ru こぼれる Ⓥ: Milk spilled from the glass. (*Gyuunyuu ga koppu kara koboreta.*) 牛乳がコップからこぼれた.

spin *vt.* **1** (turn) ... o ma⌈wasu ...を回す Ⓒ: spin a top (*koma o ma-wasu*) こまを回す.

2 (twist) ... o tsu⌈mu⌉gu ...を紡ぐ Ⓒ: spin wool into thread (*yoomoo o tsumuide ito ni suru*) 羊毛を紡いで糸にする.

3 (form a thread) ... o ka⌈ke⌉ru ...をかける Ⓥ: Spiders spin webs. (*Ku-mo wa su o kakeru.*) くもは巣をかける.

— *vi.* ku⌉rukuru ma⌈waru くるくる回る Ⓒ: The wheel began to spin around. (*Shariñ ga mawari-haji-meta.*) 車輪が回り始めた.

— *n.* ka⌈iteñ 回転.

spinach *n.* ho⌈ore⌉ñsoo ほうれん草.

spirit *n.* **1** (mind) ko⌈ko⌉ro 心: the poor in spirit (*kokoro no mazushii hito-tachi*) 心の貧しい人たち.

2 (mood) ki⌉buñ 気分; ki⌈geñ きげん: He is in good spirits. (*Kare wa kigeñ ga ii.*) 彼はきげんがいい.

3 (principle) se⌉eshiñ 精神: fighting spirit (*tooshi*) 闘志.

4 (vigor) ka⌈kki 活気; ge⌉ñki 元気: a team with lots of spirit (*kakki no aru chiimu*) 活気のあるチーム.

5 (soul) re⌉ekoñ 霊魂; yu⌉uree 幽霊: believe in spirits (*yuuree o shiñjiru*) 幽霊を信じる.

6 (alcohol) a⌈rukooru アルコール; tsu⌈yo⌉i sake 強い酒.

spiritual *adj.* se⌈eshiñ-teki na 精神的な: spiritual love (*seeshiñ-teki na ai*) 精神的な愛.

spit *vt.* ... o ha⌈kida⌉su ...を吐き出す Ⓒ: He spat out the grape seeds. (*Kare wa budoo no tane o hakida-shita.*) 彼はぶどうの種を吐き出した.

— *vi.* tsu⌉ba o haku つばを吐く Ⓒ: Don't spit on the road. (*Dooro ni tsuba o haite wa ikemaseñ.*) 道路につばを吐いてはいけません.

spite *n.* a⌉kui 悪意; i⌈ji⌉waru 意地悪: do something out of spite (*akui kara nani-ka o suru*) 悪意から何かをする.

in spite of ... *prep.* ... ni mo ka-⌈kawa⌉razu ...にもかかわらず: In spite of his efforts, he failed. (*Doryoku ni mo kakawarazu kare wa ship-pai shita.*) 努力にもかかわらず彼は失敗した.

splash *vt.* ... o ha⌈neka⌉su ...をはねかす Ⓒ; ha⌈nekake⌉ru はねかける Ⓥ: The car splashed mud on me. (*So-*

S

no kuruma wa watashi ni doro o hanekaketa.) その車は私に泥をはねかけた.

— *vi.* ba¹shabasha ha⌈neka¹su ばしゃばしゃはねかす Ⓒ: We splashed through the river. (*Watashi-tachi wa mizu o bashabasha hanekashite kawa o watatta.*) 私たちは水をばしゃばしゃはねかして川を渡った.

splendid *adj.* **1** (magnificent) so⌈oree na 壮麗な; go¹oka na 豪華な: He lives in a splendid house. (*Kare wa gooka na uchi ni suñde iru.*) 彼は豪華な家に住んでいる.

2 (brilliant) su⌈barashi¹i すばらしい; su⌈teki na すてきな: I hit on a splendid idea. (*Watashi wa subarashii kañgae o omoitsuita.*) 私はすばらしい考えを思いついた.

3 (glorious) ka⌈gayakashi¹i 輝かしい: splendid achievements (*kagayakashii gyooseki*) 輝かしい業績.

splendor *n.* (brightness) ka⌈gayaki¹ 輝き; (magnificence) so⌈oreesa 壮麗さ: the splendor of a palace (*ookyuu no sooreesa*) 王宮の壮麗さ.

split *vt.* **1** (break) ... o wa⌈ru ...を割る Ⓒ: split logs (*maki o waru*) まきを割る.

2 (divide) ... o bu⌈ñkatsu suru ...を分割する Ⓘ; wa⌈ke¹ru 分ける Ⓥ: I split the profits with him. (*Watashi wa rieki o kare to waketa.*) 私は利益を彼と分けた.

— *vi.* **1** (break) wa⌈reru 割れる Ⓥ: The ship split on a rock. (*Fune wa iwa ni atatte futatsu ni wareta.*) 船は岩に当たって二つに割れた.

2 (separate) bu⌈ñretsu suru 分裂する Ⓘ: The party split up into two factions. (*Too wa futa-ha ni buñretsu shita.*) 党は二派に分裂した.

spoil *vt.* **1** (damage) ... o da⌈me¹ ni suru ...をだめにする Ⓘ: She spoiled the soup by putting too much salt in it. (*Kanojo wa suupu ni shio o iresugite dame ni shita.*) 彼女はスープに塩を入れすぎてだめにした.

2 (overindulge) ... o a⌈mayakashite dame¹ ni suru ...を甘やかしてだめにする Ⓘ: spoil a child (*kodomo o amayakashite dame ni suru*) 子どもを甘やかしてだめにする.

— *vi.* da⌈me¹ ni naru だめになる Ⓒ; wa¹ruku naru 悪くなる Ⓒ: Food spoils quickly in summer. (*Natsu wa tabemono ga sugu ni waruku naru.*) 夏は食べ物がすぐに悪くなる.

sponge *n.* su⌈poñji スポンジ; ka⌈imeñ 海綿: wash a car with a sponge (*supoñji de kuruma o arau*) スポンジで車を洗う.

— *vt.* ... o su⌈poñji de nugu¹u ...をスポンジでぬぐう Ⓒ: sponge out a stain (*yogore o supoñji de nugutte toru*) 汚れをスポンジでぬぐって取る.

sponsor *n.* **1** (of advertising) su⌈po¹ñsaa スポンサー.

2 (responsible person) ho⌈shooniñ 保証人: stand sponsor for a person (*hito no hoshooniñ to naru*) 人の保証人となる.

— *vt.* ... no su⌈po¹ñsaa to naru ...のスポンサーとなる Ⓒ: sponsor a TV program (*terebi bañgumi no supoñsaa to naru*) テレビ番組のスポンサーとなる.

spontaneous *adj.* ji⌈hatsu-teki na 自発的な; shi⌈zeñ ni oko¹ru 自然に起こる: a spontaneous action (*jihatsuteki na koodoo*) 自発的な行動 / break into spontaneous song (*shizeñ ni utaidasu*) 自然に歌い出す.

spoon *n.* su⌈pu¹uñ スプーン; sa¹ji さじ: eat soup with a spoon (*supuuñ de suupu o nomu*) スプーンでスープを飲む.

sport *n.* su⌈po¹otsu スポーツ; u⌈ñdoo 運動: play sports (*supootsu o suru*) スポーツをする / sports equipment (*supootsu yoohiñ*) スポーツ用品.

sportsman *n.* su⌈pootsu¹mañ スポーツマン; u⌈ñdoozuki no hito¹ 運動好きの人. ★ Japanese '*spootsumañ*' usually refers to 'athlete.'

spot *n.* **1** (mark) shi⌈mi 染み; yo⌈gore 汚れ: You have a spot on your dress. (*Doresu ni shimi ga tsuite imasu yo.*) ドレスに染みがついていますよ.

2 (place) chi⌉teñ 地点; ba⌈sho 場所: a good fishing spot (*yoi tsuri-ba*) よい釣り場 / famous spots (*mee-sho*) 名所.

— *vt.* **1** (see) ... o mi⌈tsukeru ...を見つける [V]: I spotted his car in the parking lot. (*Watashi wa chuusha-joo de kare no kuruma o mitsu-keta.*) 私は駐車場で彼の車を見つけた.

2 (mark) ... ni shi⌈mi o tsuke⌉ru ...に染みをつける [V]; ... o yo⌈gosu ...を汚す [C]: I spotted my tie with sauce. (*Watashi wa soosu de neku-tai o yogoshita.*) 私はソースでネクタイを汚した.

sprain *vt.* ... o ku⌈ji⌉ku ...をくじく [C]: I think I have sprained my ankle. (*Ashi o kujiita rashii.*) 足をくじいたらしい.

sprawl *vi.* te⌉ashi o no⌈ba⌉su 手足を伸ばす [C]; ne⌈sobe⌉ru 寝そべる [C]: sprawl on the lawn (*shibafu ni ne-soberu*) 芝生に寝そべる.

spray *n.* **1** (mist) shi⌈buki⌉ しぶき: Spray from the waterfall hit our faces. (*Taki no shibuki ga wata-shi-tachi no kao ni kakatta.*) 滝のしぶきが私たちの顔にかかった.

2 (instrument) fu⌈ñmu⌉ki 噴霧器; su⌈pu⌉ree スプレー: use a spray to kill insects (*mushi o korosu no ni su-puree o tsukau*) 虫を殺すのにスプレーを使う.

— *vt.* ... o sa⌉ñpu suru ...を散布する [I]; fu⌈kikake⌉ru 吹きかける [V]: She sprayed perfume on herself. (*Ka-nojo wa jibuñ ni koosui o fukika-keta.*) 彼女は自分に香水を吹きかけた.

spread *vt.* **1** (open out) ... o hi⌈ro-geru ...を広げる [V]: He spread a newspaper on the table. (*Kare wa teeburu no ue ni shiñbuñ o hiro-geta.*) 彼はテーブルの上に新聞を広げた.

2 (cover) ... o nu⌈ru ...を塗る [C]: spread butter on bread (*pañ ni bataa o nuru*) パンにバターを塗る.

3 (scatter) ... o ma⌈kichira⌉su ...をまき散らす [C]: Flies spread disease. (*Hae wa byooki o makichirasu.*) はえは病気をまき散らす.

— *vi.* **1** (be extended) hi⌈rogaru 広がる [C]: The fire spread to the house next door. (*Kaji wa tonari no uchi ni hirogatta.*) 火事は隣の家に広がった.

2 (be scattered) hi⌈roma⌉ru 広まる [C]: The news spread fast. (*Sono shirase wa sugu ni hiromatta.*) その知らせはすぐに広まった.

— *n.* hi⌈rogari 広がり; fu⌈kyuu 普及: the spread of education (*kyooiku no fukyuu*) 教育の普及.

spring[1] *n.* ha⌉ru 春: Plants start to grow in spring. (*Shokubutsu wa haru ni seechoo shi-hajimeru.*) 植物は春に生長し始める.

spring[2] *vi.* **1** (leap) ha⌈ne⌉ru 跳ねる [V]; to⌈biaga⌉ru 跳び上がる [C]: He sprang into the boat. (*Kare wa booto ni tobinotta.*) 彼はボートに跳び乗った.

2 (come into being) a⌈raware⌉ru 現れる [V]; u⌈mareru 生まれる [V]: A new town sprang up at that site. (*Sono basho ni atarashii machi ga uma-reta.*) その場所に新しい町が生まれた.

3 (flow forth) wa⌈kide⌉ru 湧き出る [V]: Hot water sprang out of the earth. (*Jimeñ kara oñseñ ga waki-deta.*) 地面から温泉が湧き出た.

— *n.* **1** (flow of water) i⌈zumi 泉; su⌈igeñ 水源: a hot spring (*oñseñ*) 温泉.

2 (coil) ba⌉ne ばね; su⌈puriñgu スプリング.

3 (jump) cho⌈oyaku 跳躍.

sprinkle *vt.* ... o ma⌉ku ...をまく [C]: sprinkle water on the lawn (*shiba-fu ni mizu o maku*) 芝生に水をまく.

sprout *vi.* me⌉ o dasu 芽を出す [C]: The seeds began to sprout. (*Tane ga me o dashi-hajimeta.*) 種が芽を出し始めた.

— *n.* me⌉ 芽; shi⌈ñme 新芽: bean sprouts (*moyashi*) もやし.

spur *n.* **1** (metal device) ha⌈kusha 拍車: put spurs to a horse (*uma ni hakusha o kakeru*) 馬に拍車をかける.

2 (stimulus) shi⌈geki 刺激: put spurs to a person (*hito ni shigeki o*

ataeru) 人に刺激を与える.
— *vt.* **1** (apply spurs) ... ni ha⌈ku-sha o ateru ...に拍車を当てる [V]: spur a horse on (*uma ni hakusha o atete hashiraseru*) 馬に拍車を当てて走らせる.
2 (urge) ... o ka⌈ritate⌉ru ...を駆り立てる [V]; shi⌈geki suru 刺激する [I]: The prize money spurred him on. (*Shookiñ ga kare o karitateta.*) 賞金が彼を駆り立てた.

spy *n.* su⌉pai スパイ: an industrial spy (*sañgyoo supai*) 産業スパイ.
— *vi.* (... o) su⌉pai suru (...を)スパイする [I]; ko⌈sso⌉ri shi⌈rabe⌉ru こっそり調べる [V]: His job is to spy on the enemy. (*Kare no shigoto wa teki o supai suru koto da.*) 彼の仕事は敵をスパイすることだ.
— *vt.* ... o sa⌈gurida⌉su ...を探り出す [C]: spy out a secret (*himitsu o saguridasu*) 秘密を探り出す.

square *n.* **1** (flat figure) se⌈eho⌉o-kee 正方形; shi⌈ka⌉kukee 四角形.
2 (open area) hi⌉roba 広場: a town square (*machi no hiroba*) 町の広場.
3 (mathematics) he⌈ehoo 平方; ni-⌈joo 2 乗: Nine is the square of three. (*Kyuu wa sañ no heehoo da.*) 9 は 3 の平方だ.
— *adj.* **1** (shape) se⌈eho⌉okee no 正方形の; shi⌈kaku⌉i 四角い: a square table (*shikakui teeburu*) 四角いテーブル.
2 (mathematics) he⌈ehoo no 平方の: A table 2 meters square has an area of 4 square meters. (*Ni-mee-toru heehoo no teeburu no meñ-seki wa yoñ heehoo meetoru aru.*) 2 メートル平方のテーブルの面積は 4 平方メートルある.
— *vt.* ... o he⌈ehoo suru ...を平方する [I]; ni-⌈joo suru 2 乗する [I]: 3 squared is 9. (*Sañ no ni-joo wa kyuu.*) 3 の 2 乗は 9.

squash *n.* (vegetable) ka⌈bocha かぼちゃ.

squeak *vi.* ki⌈shi⌉ru きしる [C]: This door squeaks. (*Kono doa wa ki-shiru.*) このドアはきしる.
— *n.* chu⌉u-chuu na⌈ku ko⌉e ちゅうちゅう鳴く声; ki⌉i-kii to iu o⌈to⌉ きーきーという音: the squeak of a mouse (*nezumi no chuu-chuu naku koe*) ねずみのちゅうちゅう鳴く声.

squeeze *vt.* **1** (press hard) ... o tsu⌉yoku o⌈su ...を強く押す [C]; tsu⌉-yoku ni⌈giru 強く握る [C]: I took his hand and squeezed it. (*Watashi wa kare no te o totte tsuyoku ni-gitta.*) 私は彼の手をとって強く握った.
2 (extract) ... o shi⌈bo⌉ru ...を搾る [C]; shi⌈borida⌉su 搾り出す [C]: squeeze the juice from a lemon (*remoñ kara juusu o shiboridasu*) レモンからジュースを搾り出す. ★ Japanese '*shiboru*' also means 'wring.'
3 (cram) ... o tsu⌈mekomu ...を詰め込む [C]: squeeze things into a suit-case (*suutsukeesu ni mono o tsume-komu*) スーツケースにものを詰め込む.
— *vi.* wa⌈riko⌉mu 割り込む [C]: squeeze between two cars (*ni-dai no kuruma no aida ni warikomu*) 2 台の車の間に割り込む.
— *n.* shi⌈bo⌉ru ko⌈to⌉ 搾ること; da-⌈kishime⌉ru ko⌈to⌉ 抱き締めること.

squirrel *n.* ri⌉su りす.

stab *vt.* ... o tsu⌈kisa⌉su ...を突き刺す [C]: The man stabbed him with a knife. (*Sono otoko wa naifu de kare o sashita.*) その男はナイフで彼を刺した.
— *vi.* (... ni) tsu⌈kikaka⌉ru (...に)突きかかる [C]: He stabbed at me. (*Ka-re wa watashi ni tsukikakatta.*) 彼は私に突きかかった.
— *n.* (thrust) sa⌉su ko⌈to⌉ 刺すこと; (wound) sa⌈shi⌉kizu 刺し傷.

stability *n.* a⌈ñtee 安定; a⌈ñteesee 安定性: political stability (*seeji-teki na añtee*) 政治的な安定.

stable[1] *adj.* **1** (unchanging) a⌈ñtee shita [shite iru] 安定した[している]: Prices are stable now. (*Bukka wa ima añtee shite iru.*) 物価はいま安定している.
2 (firm) shi⌈kka⌉ri shita [shite iru] しっかりした[している]: stable foundations (*shikkari shita kiso*) しっかりし

S

た基礎.

stable[2] *n.* **1** (of a horse) u˹magoya 馬小屋; u˹maya 馬屋.
2 (club) ku˺rabu クラブ: a stable of sumo wrestlers (*sumoo-beya*) 相撲部屋.

stack *n.* **1** (pile) tsu˹mikasane 積み重ね; ya˹ma˺ 山: a stack of old newspapers (*furushiñbuñ no yama*) 古新聞の山.
2 (haystack) ho˹shikusa no yama˺ 干し草の山.
— *vt.* ... o tsu˹mikasane˺ru ...を積み重ねる [V]: He stacked the books on the desk. (*Kare wa tsukue no ue ni hoñ o tsumikasaneta.*) 彼は机の上に本を積み重ねた.

stadium *n.* su˹ta˺jiamu スタジアム; kyo˹ogijoo 競技場.

staff *n.* sho˹ku˺iñ 職員; bu˹iñ 部員; su˹ta˺ffu スタッフ: the teaching staff of a school (*gakkoo no kyooshokuiñ*) 学校の教職員 / the editorial staff (*heñshuu buiñ*) 編集部員.
★ Japanese '*sutaffu*' usually refers to a staff member.

stage *n.* **1** (of a theater) bu˺tai 舞台; su˹te˺eji ステージ: appear on the stage (*butai ni tatsu*) 舞台に立つ.
2 (period) da˹ñkai 段階; ji˺ki 時期: The research is still in the testing stage. (*Keñkyuu wa mada jikkeñ dañkai da.*) 研究はまだ実験段階だ.
— *vt.* ... o jo˹oeñ suru ...を上演する [I]: They staged the play for the first time. (*Kare-ra wa sono geki o hajimete jooeñ shita.*) 彼らはその劇を初めて上演した.

stagger *vi.* **1** (sway) yo˹rome˺ku よろめく [C]; yo˺royoro a˹ru˺ku よろよろ歩く [C]: The drunk man staggered along the road. (*Yopparai wa yoroyoro michi o aruite itta.*) 酔っぱらいはよろよろ道を歩いて行った.
2 (be shocked) gu˹ratsuku ぐらつく [C]; ta˹jiro˺gu たじろぐ [C]: He was staggered by the price. (*Kare wa sono nedañ ni tajiroida.*) 彼はその値段にたじろいだ.
— *vt.* **1** (make stagger) ... o yo˹romeka˺su ...をよろめかす [C]: The blow staggered him. (*Sono ichigeki ga kare o yoromekashita.*) その一撃が彼をよろめかした.
2 (shock) ... o gu˹ratsukaseru ...をぐらつかせる [V]: The news staggered his determination. (*Sono shirase wa kare no kesshiñ o guratsukaseta.*) その知らせは彼の決心をぐらつかせた.

stain *vt.* ... o yo˹gosu ...を汚す [C]: The coffee he spilt stained his trousers. (*Kare wa koohii o koboshite zuboñ o yogoshita.*) 彼はコーヒーをこぼしてズボンを汚した.
— *vi.* yo˹goreru 汚れる [V]: White cloth stains easily. (*Shiroi nuno wa sugu yogoreru.*) 白い布はすぐ汚れる.
— *n.* yo˹gore 汚れ; shi˹mi 染み: remove a stain (*shimi o toru*) 染みをとる.

stair *n.* ka˹idañ 階段: go up [down] the stairs (*kaidañ o agaru [oriru]*) 階段を上がる[下りる].

staircase *n.* ka˹idañ 階段: a spiral staircase (*raseñ-kaidañ*) らせん階段.

stake *n.* ku˺i くい; bo˹o 棒: drive a stake into the ground (*kui o jimeñ ni uchikomu*) くいを地面に打ち込む.

stale *adj.* fu˺ruku natta 古くなった; shi˹ñseñ de na˺i 新鮮でない: stale bread (*furuku natta pañ*) 古くなったパン.

stalk *n.* (stem of a plant) ku˹ki˺ 茎.

stall *n.* ba˹iteñ 売店; ya˺tai 屋台.

stammer *vi.* ku˹chigomo˺ru 口ごもる [C]; do˹mo˺ru どもる [C]: He stammers when he is angry. (*Kare wa okotte iru toki domoru.*) 彼は怒っているときどもる.
— *vt.* ... o ku˹chigomori-na˺gara i˹u ...を口ごもりながら言う [C]; do˹mori-na˺gara i˹u どもりながら言う [C]: He stammered an apology. (*Kare wa domori-nagara ayamatta.*) 彼はどもりながら謝った.

stamp *n.* **1** (of a letter) ki˹tte 切手; (of tax) i˹ñshi 印紙: a postage stamp (*yuubiñ-kitte*) 郵便切手 / a commemorative stamp (*kineñ-*

kitte) 記念切手 / a revenue stamp (*shuunyuu-iñshi*) 収入印紙.
2 (seal) su⌈tañpu スタンプ; ha⌉ñ 判; i⌉ñ 印: a rubber stamp (*gomu-iñ*) ゴム印.
— *vt.* 1 (bring one's foot down) ... o fu⌈mitsuke⌉ru ...を踏みつける Ⓥ; fu⌈minara⌉su 踏み鳴らす Ⓒ: He stamped his foot in anger. (*Kare wa okotte ashi o fuminarashita.*) 彼は怒って足を踏み鳴らした.
2 (print) ... ni ha⌉ñ o o⌈su ...に判を押す Ⓒ: stamp a passport (*pasupooto ni hañ o osu*) パスポートに判を押す.
3 (paste) ... ni ki⌈tte [i⌈ñshi] o haru ...に切手[印紙]をはる Ⓒ: stamp a letter (*tegami ni kitte o haru*) 手紙に切手をはる.
— *vi.* (... o) fu⌈mitsuke⌉ru (...を)踏みつける Ⓥ: He stamped on the insect. (*Kare wa sono mushi o fumitsuketa.*) 彼はその虫を踏みつけた.

stand *vi.* **1** (be in an upright position) ta⌉tte iru 立っている Ⓥ: He was standing by the window. (*Kare wa mado no soba ni tatte ita.*) 彼は窓のそばに立っていた.
2 (rise to one's feet) ta⌈chiagaru 立ち上がる Ⓒ: Everybody stood when the teacher came in. (*Señsee ga haitte kita toki zeñiñ ga tachiagatta.*) 先生が入って来たとき全員が立ち上がった.
3 (be situated) a⌉ru ある Ⓒ: The castle stands on a hill. (*Sono shiro wa oka no ue ni arimasu.*) その城は丘の上にあります.
4 (be stopped) to⌈matte iru 止まっている Ⓥ: A taxi was standing in front of the station. (*Takushii ga eki no mae ni tomatte ita.*) タクシーが駅の前に止まっていた.
— *vt.* 1 (place in an upright position) ... o ta⌈te⌉ru ...を立てる Ⓥ: stand a candle on the table (*roosoku o teeburu no ue ni tateru*) ろうそくをテーブルの上に立てる.
2 (bear) ... o ga⌉mañ suru ...を我慢する Ⓘ: I cannot stand her smoking. (*Watashi wa kanojo ga tabako o suu no o gamañ dekinai.*) 私は彼女がたばこを吸うのを我慢できない.
stand for ... *vt.* ... o a⌈rawa⌉su ...を表す Ⓒ: What does this mark stand for? (*Kono shirushi wa nani o arawashimasu ka?*) この印は何を表しますか.
stand out *vi.* me⌈da⌉tsu 目立つ Ⓒ: The tall man stood out from the rest. (*Sono se no takai hito wa hoka no hito yori mo medatta.*) その背の高い人はほかの人よりも目立った.
— *n.* 1 (position) ta⌈chiba⌉ 立場: He made his stand on the question clear. (*Kare wa sono moñdai ni tsuite no tachiba o akiraka ni shita.*) 彼はその問題についての立場を明らかにした.
2 (for spectators) ka⌈ñkyaku⌉seki 観客席; su⌈tañdo スタンド.

standard *n.* hyo⌈ojuñ 標準; sui⌈juñ 水準: the living standard (*seekatsu-suijuñ*) 生活水準.
— *adj.* hyo⌈ojuñ no 標準の; fu⌈tsuu no 普通の: standard size (*hyoojuñ saizu*) 標準サイズ.

standing *n.* mi⌉buñ 身分; chi⌉i 地位: people of high standing (*mibuñ no takai hito-tachi*) 身分の高い人たち / the social standing of women (*josee no shakai-teki chii*) 女性の社会的地位.

standpoint *n.* ta⌈chiba⌉ 立場; ke⌉ñchi 見地: consider the problem from various standpoints (*iroiro na keñchi kara moñdai o kañgaeru*) いろいろな見地から問題を考える.

star *n.* **1** (heavenly body) ho⌈shi 星; (figure) ho⌈shiji⌉rushi 星印.
2 (famous performer) su⌈ta⌉a スター: a movie star (*eega sutaa*) 映画スター.
— *vi.* shu⌈eñ suru 主演する Ⓘ: She starred in the movie. (*Kanojo wa sono eega de shueñ shita.*) 彼女はその映画で主演した.

stare *vi.* (... o) ji⌈tto mitsumeru (...を)じっと見つめる Ⓥ: She was staring out of the window. (*Kanojo wa*

S

mado kara soto o jitto mitsumete ita.) 彼女は窓から外をじっと見つめていた.
— *vt.* ... o ji⌈tto mitsumeru …をじっと見つめる [V]; ji⌈rojiro na⌈gameˈru じろじろ眺める [V]: She stared me in the face. (*Kanojo wa watashi no kao o jitto mitsumeta.*) 彼女は私の顔をじっと見つめた.

start *vi.* **1** (begin) ha⌈jimaru 始まる [C]: The concert starts at seven. (*Koñsaato wa shichi-ji ni hajimarimasu.*) コンサートは 7 時に始まります.
2 (leave) shu⌈ppatsu suru 出発する [I]; de⌈kakeru 出かける [V]: He started on his trip yesterday. (*Kare wa kinoo ryokoo ni shuppatsu shimashita.*) 彼はきのう旅行に出発しました.
— *vt.* **1** (casue to begin) ... o ha⌈jimeru …を始める [V]: He started working at six in the morning. (*Kare wa asa roku-ji ni shigoto o hajimeta.*) 彼は朝 6 時に仕事を始めた.
2 (set in motion) ... o shi⌈doo saseru …を始動させる [V]: start the engine (*eñjiñ o shidoo saseru*) エンジンを始動させる.
— *n.* **1** (beginning) ka⌈ishi 開始; ha⌈jime 始め: The play was boring at the start. (*Sono geki wa hajime wa tsumaranakatta.*) その劇は始めはつまらなかった.
2 (leaving) shu⌈ppatsu 出発; su⌈taˈato スタート: make an early start (*hayame ni shuppatsu suru*) 早めに出発する.

startle *vt.* ... o bi⌈kkuˈri saseru びっくりさせる [V]; to⌈biagaraseˈru 跳び上がらせる [V]: I was startled to hear the news. (*Watashi wa sono shirase o kiite bikkuri shita.*) 私はその知らせを聞いてびっくりした.

starve *vi.* **1** (suffer from hunger) u⌈eˈru 飢える [V]; gaˈshi suru 餓死する [I]: There was no food and many people starved to death. (*Taberu mono ga nakute ooku no hito ga gashi shita.*) 食べる物がなくて多くの人が餓死した.
2 (be very hungry) o⌈naka ga pekopeko da お腹がぺこぺこだ: I'm starving. (*O-naka ga pekopeko da.*) お腹がぺこぺこだ.
— *vt.* ... o u⌈esaseˈru …を飢えさせる [V]; gaˈshi saseru 餓死させる [V]: starve animals (*doobutsu o gashi saseru*) 動物を餓死させる.

state *n.* **1** (country) koˈkka 国家; (administrative unit) shuˈu 州: an independent state (*dokuritsu kokka*) 独立国家 / There are fifty states in the U.S. (*Gasshuukoku ni wa gojuu no shuu ga aru.*) 合衆国には 50 の州がある.
2 (condition) jo⌈otai 状態: I inquired about her state of health. (*Watashi wa kanojo no keñkoo-jootai ni tsuite tazuneta.*) 私は彼女の健康状態について尋ねた.
— *vt.* ... o no⌈beˈru …を述べる [V]: state one's opinion (*jibuñ no ikeñ o noberu*) 自分の意見を述べる.

stately *adj.* do⌈odoˈo to shita [shite iru] 堂々とした[している]; i⌈geñ no aˈru 威厳のある: a stately building (*doodoo to shita tatemono*) 堂堂とした建物.

statement *n.* **1** (the act of stating) chi⌈ñjutsu 陳述; mo⌈oshitate 申し立て: make a false statement (*uso no chiñjutsu o suru*) うその陳述をする.
2 (formal declaration) se⌈emee 声明; su⌈teˈetomeñto ステートメント: a joint statement (*kyoodoo-seemee*) 共同声明.

statesman *n.* se⌈ejika 政治家.

station *n.* **1** (stopping place) eˈki 駅: I get off at the next station. (*Tsugi no eki de orimasu.*) 次の駅で降ります. / Where is the nearest subway station? (*Ichibañ chikai chikatetsu no eki wa doko desu ka?*) いちばん近い地下鉄の駅はどこですか.
2 (building) shoˈ 署; kyoˈku 局: a police station (*keesatsu-sho*) 警察署 / a fire station (*shooboo-sho*) 消防署 / a broadcasting station (*hoosoo-kyoku*) 放送局.

stationery *n.* (materials for writing) bu⌈ñbo⌉ogu 文房具; (letter paper) bi⌈ñseñ 便せん.

statistics *n.* to⌈okee 統計: Statistics show that the population is increasing. (*Tookee ni yoreba jiñkoo wa fuete iru.*) 統計によれば人口は増えている.

statue *n.* zo⌉o 像; cho⌈ozoo 彫像: a bronze statue (*doozoo*) 銅像 / a wooden statue (*mokuzoo*) 木像.

status *n.* **1** (position) chi⌉i 地位; mi⌉buñ 身分: the social status of women (*josee no shakai-teki chii*) 女性の社会的地位.

2 (condition) jo⌈otai 状態: the current status of the negotiations (*geñzai no kooshoo no jootai*) 現在の交渉の状態.

stay *vi.* **1** (remain) (... ni) to⌈doma⌉ru (…に)とどまる Ⓒ; i⌈ru いる Ⓥ: I stayed in the house all day. (*Watashi wa ichi-nichi-juu ie ni imashita.*) 私は一日中家にいました.

2 (live for a time) (... ni) ta⌈izai suru (…に)滞在する Ⓘ; to⌈maru 泊まる Ⓒ: How long are you staying here? (*Dono kurai koko ni taizai shimasu ka?*) どのくらいここに滞在しますか. / I'll stay at the Tokyo Hotel. (*Watashi wa Tookyoo Hoteru ni tomarimasu.*) 私は東京ホテルに泊まります.

3 (continue to be) ma⌈ma⌉ de i⌈ru ままでいる Ⓥ: Please stay seated. (*Doozo suwatta mama de ite kudasai.*) どうぞ座ったままでいてください.

— *n.* ta⌈izai 滞在: I hope you enjoy your stay in Kyoto. (*Kyooto ni go-taizai-chuu wa tanoshiku o-sugoshi kudasai.*) 京都にご滞在中は楽しくお過ごしください.

steadily *adv.* cha⌈kujitsu ni 着実に; shi⌈kka⌉ri to しっかりと: His Japanese is improving steadily. (*Kare no Nihoñgo wa chakujitsu ni jootatsu shite imasu.*) 彼の日本語は着実に上達しています.

steady *adj.* **1** (not changing) ka⌈wa-ranai 変わらない; i⌈chiyoo na 一様な: walk at a steady pace (*kawaranai hochoo de aruku*) 変わらない歩調で歩く.

2 (firm) shi⌈kka⌉ri shita [shite iru] しっかりした[している]; a⌈ñtee shita [shite iru] 安定した[している]: This table is steady. (*Kono teeburu wa shikkari shite iru.*) このテーブルはしっかりしている.

3 (serious) ke⌈ñjitsu na 堅実な; ma⌈jime na まじめな: a steady young man (*majime na seeneñ*) まじめな青年.

— *vt.* ... o a⌈ñtee saseru …を安定させる Ⓥ; o⌈chitsukaseru 落ち着かせる Ⓥ: These pills will steady your nerves. (*Kono kusuri wa anata no shiñkee o ochitsukaseru deshoo.*) この薬はあなたの神経を落ち着かせるでしょう.

steak *n.* su⌈te⌉eki ステーキ; bi⌈futeki ビフテキ.

steal *vt.* ... o nu⌈su⌉mu …を盗む Ⓒ: Somebody has stolen my bag. (*Dare-ka ga watashi no kabañ o nusuñda.*) だれかが私のかばんを盗んだ. / I had my wallet stolen. (*Watashi wa saifu o nusumareta.*) 私は財布を盗まれた.

— *vi.* nu⌈sumi⌉ o suru 盗みをする Ⓘ: It is wrong to steal. (*Nusumi o suru koto wa warui koto da.*) 盗みをすることは悪いことだ.

steam *n.* su⌈ijo⌉oki 水蒸気; yu⌉ge 湯気: Steam is rising from the kettle. (*Yakañ kara yuge ga agatte iru.*) やかんから湯気が上がっている.

— *vt.* ... o mu⌉su …を蒸す Ⓒ; fu⌈ka⌉su ふかす Ⓒ: steam potatoes (*jagaimo o fukasu*) じゃがいもをふかす.

— *vi.* yu⌉ge o ta⌈te⌉ru 湯気を立てる Ⓥ; ku⌈mo⌉ru 曇る Ⓒ: My glasses steamed up. (*Megane ga kumotta.*) 眼鏡が曇った.

steamer *n.* (steamship) ki⌈señ 汽船; (container) mu⌈shi⌉ki 蒸し器.

steamship *n.* ki⌈señ 汽船.

steel *n.* ko⌈otetsu 鋼鉄; ha⌈gane 鋼: This tool is made of steel. (*Kono doogu wa kootetsu de dekite iru.*) この道具は鋼鉄でできている.

steep *adj.* kyu⌈u na 急な; ke⌈wa-shi⌉i 険しい: a steep slope (*kyuu na saka*) 急な坂 / a steep hill (*kewa-shii oka*) 険しい丘.

steer *vt.* (direct the movement) (... ni) ... o mu⌈keru (…に)…を向ける Ⓥ: The ship steered a course for the island. (*Fune wa shima no hoo ni koosu o muketa.*) 船は島の方にコースを向けた.
— *vi.* (of a car) u⌈ñteñ suru 運転する Ⓘ; (of a ship) ka⌉ji o toru 舵を取る Ⓒ: This car steers easily. (*Kono kuruma wa uñteñ shi-yasui.*) この車は運転しやすい.

steering wheel *n.* (of a car) ha⌈ñdoru ハンドル.

stem *n.* (trunk) mi⌉ki 幹; (stalk) ku⌈ki⌉ 茎.

stenographer *n.* so⌈kki⌉sha 速記者.

stenography *n.* so⌈kki 速記; so⌈kki⌉jutsu 速記術.

step *n.* **1** (one motion of the leg) a⌈yumi⌉ 歩み; i⌉p-po 一歩: He took a step back. (*Kare wa ip-po ushiro e sagatta.*) 彼は一歩後ろへ下がった.
2 (gait) a⌈rukiburi⌉ 歩きぶり; a⌈shi-dori⌉ 足どり: walk with a light step (*karui ashidori de aruku*) 軽い足どりで歩く.
3 (sound) a⌈shioto⌉ 足音: I heard steps outside. (*Soto de ashioto ga kikoeta.*) 外で足音が聞こえた.
4 (of a stair) ka⌈idañ 階段; su⌈te⌉p-pu ステップ.
— *vi.* (walk) a⌈ru⌉ku 歩く Ⓒ; su-⌈sumu 進む Ⓒ: step forward (*mae e susumu*) 前へ進む.

stereo *n.* su⌈tereo ステレオ; su⌈tereo so⌉ochi ステレオ装置: record in stereo (*sutereo de rokuoñ suru*) ステレオで録音する.

sterile *adj.* (of land) fu⌈moo no 不毛の; (of animals) fu⌈niñ no 不妊の; (of germs) mu⌈kiñ no 無菌の.

stern *adj.* ge⌈ñkaku na 厳格な; ki-⌈bishi⌉i 厳しい: a stern teacher (*geñ-kaku na señsee*) 厳格な先生 / He is stern to his pupils. (*Kare wa seeto ni kibishii.*) 彼は生徒に厳しい.

stew *n.* shi⌈chu⌉u シチュー.
— *vt.* ... o to⌈robi de niru ...をとろ火で煮る Ⓥ; shi⌈chu⌉u ni suru シチューにする Ⓘ: stewed beef (*biifu shi-chuu*) ビーフシチュー.

steward *n.* su⌈chuwa⌉ado スチュワード; kyu⌉uji 給仕.

stewardess *n.* su⌈chuwa⌉adesu スチュワーデス.

stick[1] *vt.* **1** (pierce) ... o tsu⌈kisa⌉-su ...を突き刺す Ⓒ: I stuck my hand with a pin. (*Watashi wa piñ de te o tsukisashita.*) 私はピンで手を突き刺した.
2 (thrust) ... ni tsu⌈kko⌉mu ...に突っ込む Ⓒ: He stuck his hands in his pockets. (*Kare wa ryoote o poket-to ni tsukkoñda.*) 彼は両手をポケットに突っ込んだ.
3 (fasten) ... o ku⌈ttsuke⌉ru ...をくっつける Ⓥ; ha⌈ru はる Ⓒ; to⌈meru 留める Ⓥ: stick a stamp on an envelope (*fuutoo ni kitte o haru*) 封筒に切手をはる / stick a notice on the wall with tacks (*bira o kabe ni byoo de tomeru*) ビラを壁にびょうで留める.
— *vi.* **1** (be pierced) sa⌈sa⌉ru 刺さる Ⓒ: A nail stuck in the tire. (*Kugi ga taiya ni sasatta.*) くぎがタイヤに刺さった.
2 (be fastened) ku⌈ttsu⌉ku くっつく Ⓒ: This glue sticks well. (*Kono nori wa yoku kuttsuku.*) こののりはよくくっつく.

stick[2] *n.* **1** (twig) bo⌈okire 棒切れ; ki⌈gire⌉ 木切れ: collect sticks for firewood (*takigi ni suru tame ni kigire o atsumeru*) 薪にするために木切れを集める.
2 (slender piece) bo⌈ojoo no mono⌉ 棒状のもの: a stick of candy (*boojoo no kyañdee*) 棒状のキャンデー.
3 (cane) tsu⌉e つえ; su⌈te⌉kki ステッキ: walk with a stick (*tsue o tsuite aruku*) つえをついて歩く.

sticky *adj.* ne⌉baneba suru ねばねばする; be⌈tobeto na べとべとな: His fingers are sticky with jam. (*Kare no yubi wa jamu de betobeto da.*)

S

彼の指はジャムでべとべとだ.

stiff *adj.* **1** (rigid) ka⌈tai 堅い; ko⌈waba⌉tta こわばった; ko⌈waba⌉tte iru こわばっている: stiff cardboard (*katai boorugami*) 堅いボール紙.
2 (formal) ka⌈takurushi⌉i 堅苦しい; (awkward) gi⌈kochina⌉i ぎこちない: make a stiff bow (*katakurushii ojigi o suru*) 堅苦しいおじぎをする / a stiff style of writing (*gikochinai buñtai*) ぎこちない文体.

stiffen *vt.* ... o ka⌈taku suru ...を硬くする Ⓘ; ko⌈wabarase⌉ru こわばらせる Ⓥ: stiffen a collar with starch (*karaa o nori de kataku suru*) カラーをのりで硬くする.
— *vi.* ka⌈taku na⌉ru 硬くなる Ⓒ: The body stiffens with age. (*Karada wa toshi o toru to kataku naru.*) 体は年をとると硬くなる.

still[1] *adv.* **1** (up to now) ma⌉da まだ; i⌉ma mo 今も: He is still in bed. (*Kare wa mada nete iru.*) 彼はまだ寝ている. / I still don't feel well. (*Mada kibuñ wa yoku arimaseñ.*) まだ気分は良くありません.
2 (nevertheless) so⌈re de⌉ mo nao それでもなお: He failed, but still he wants to try again. (*Kare wa shippai shita ga sore de mo nao moo ichi-do yatte mitai to omotte iru.*) 彼は失敗したがそれでもなおもう一度やってみたいと思っている.
3 (even) na⌉o i⌈ssoo なおいっそう; sa⌉ra ni さらに: It became still colder. (*Nao issoo samuku natta.*) なおいっそう寒くなった.

still[2] *adj.* **1** (quiet) shi⌉zuka na 静かな; shi⌉ñ to shita [shite iru] しんとした[している]: a still night (*shizuka na yoru*) 静かな夜 / The empty house was still. (*Akiya wa shiñ to shite ita.*) 空き家はしんとしていた.
2 (motionless) se⌈eshi shita [shite iru] 静止した[している]; jit⌈to shita [shite iru] じっとした[している]: sit still (*jitto suwatte iru*) じっと座っている.

stimulate *vt.* **1** (excite) ... o shi⌈geki suru ...を刺激する Ⓘ; ko⌈ofuñ saseru 興奮させる Ⓥ: The smells of cooking stimulated his appetite. (*Ryoori no nioi ga kare no shokuyoku o shigeki shita.*) 料理のにおいが彼の食欲を刺激した.
2 (encourage) ... no ha⌈gemi⌉ to na⌉ru ...の励みとなる Ⓒ: Praise stimulated him to further efforts. (*Homerareta koto ga hagemi to natte kare wa issoo doryoku shita.*) ほめられたことが励みとなって彼はいっそう努力した.

stimulus *n.* shi⌈geki 刺激; shi⌈geki⌉butsu 刺激物: a stimulus to industrial development (*sañgyoo no hattatsu o unagasu shigeki*) 産業の発達を促す刺激.

sting *vt.* **1** (prick) ... o sa⌉su ...を刺す Ⓒ: An insect stung me. (*Mushi ga watashi o sashita.*) 虫が私を刺した.
2 (cause pain) ... o hi⌉rihiri saseru ...をひりひりさせる Ⓥ: The salt water made my cut sting. (*Shiomizu de kizuguchi ga hirihiri shita.*) 塩水で傷口がひりひりした.
— *vi.* sa⌉su 刺す Ⓒ: This bee does not sting. (*Kono hachi wa sashimaseñ.*) この蜂は刺しません.

stingy *adj.* ke⌉chi na けちな; ke⌈chikusa⌉i けちくさい: a stingy person (*kechi na hito*) けちな人.

stir *vt.* **1** (mix) ... o ka⌈kimawasu ...をかき回す Ⓒ; ka⌈kimazeru かき混ぜる Ⓥ: stir some sugar into one's coffee (*koohii ni satoo o irete kakimazeru*) コーヒーに砂糖を入れてかき混ぜる.
2 (excite) ... o ka⌈kitateru ...をかき立てる Ⓥ: His story stirred my curiosity. (*Kare no hanashi wa watashi no kookishiñ o kakitateta.*) 彼の話は私の好奇心をかき立てた.
— *vi.* (move) u⌈go⌉ku 動く Ⓒ: Something stirred in the darkness. (*Nani-ka ga kurayami de ugoita.*) 何かが暗やみで動いた.

stitch *n.* hi⌈to⌉-hari ひと針; hi⌈to⌉-nui ひと縫い: take up a stitch (*hito-hari nuu*) ひと針縫う.

stock *n.* **1** (shares) ka⌈bu 株; ka-

ʳbuˡshiki 株式: Stocks are going up. (*Kabu ga agatte iru.*) 株が上がっている.
2 (supply) taʳkuwae 蓄え; choʳzoo 貯蔵: The stock of food is getting low. (*Shokuryoo no takuwae ga geñshoo shite iru.*) 食糧の蓄えが減少している.
3 (store of goods) zaʳiko 在庫: The book is in stock. (*Sono hoñ wa zaiko ga arimasu.*) その本は在庫があります.
4 (livestock) kaʳchiku 家畜.

stocking *n.* kuʳtsuˡshita 靴下; suʳtoˡkkiñgu ストッキング: put on [take off] one's stockings (*kutsushita o haku* [*nugu*]) 靴下をはく[脱ぐ].
★ 'Socks' are also called '*kutsushita.*'

stomach *n.* **1** (organ) i 胃: I have a pain in my stomach. (*Watashi wa i ga itai.*) 私は胃が痛い. / stomach medicine (*i no kusuri*) 胃の薬.
2 (abdomen) haʳraˡ 腹; oʳnaka お腹.

stomachache *n.* iʳtsuu 胃痛; fuʳkutsuu 腹痛: I have a stomachache. (*I* [*Onaka*] *ga itai.*) 胃[お腹]が痛い.

stone *n.* iʳshiˡ 石; koʳishi 小石: a monument built of stone (*ishi de dekite iru kineñhi*) 石でできている記念碑 / The stone hit the window. (*Koishi ga mado ni atatta.*) 小石が窓に当たった.

stool *n.* maʳruisu 丸いす; koʳshikakeˡ 腰掛け.

stoop *vi.* maʳekaˡgami ni naru 前かがみになる Ⓒ; kaʳgamu かがむ Ⓒ: I stooped down and picked up a pencil. (*Watashi wa kagañde eñpitsu o hiroiageta.*) 私はかがんで鉛筆を拾い上げた.

stop *vt.* **1** (halt) ... o toʳmeru …を止める Ⓥ: I stopped my car at the traffic lights. (*Watashi wa shiñgoo de kuruma o tometa.*) 私は信号で車を止めた.
2 (discontinue) ... o chuʳushi suru …を中止する Ⓘ; yaʳmeru やめる Ⓥ: He stopped smoking. (*Kare wa tabako o suu no o yameta.*) 彼はたばこを吸うのをやめた.
— *vi.* **1** (cease moving) toʳmaru 止まる Ⓒ: Does this train stop at Nara? (*Kono ressha wa Nara ni tomarimasu ka?*) この列車は奈良に止まりますか.
2 (come to an end) chuʳudañ suru 中断する Ⓘ; yaʳmu やむ Ⓒ: The rain has stopped. (*Ame ga yañda.*) 雨がやんだ.
3 (stay) (... ni) taʳizai suru (…に)滞在する Ⓘ; toʳmaru 泊まる Ⓒ: I'm going to stop at a hotel. (*Watashi wa hoteru ni tomarimasu.*) 私はホテルに泊まります.
— *n.* **1** (halting) toʳmaru kotoˡ 止まること: come to a stop (*tomaru*) 止まる / This train goes to Ueno without a stop. (*Kono ressha wa Ueno made tomarazu ni ikimasu.*) この列車は上野まで止まらずに行きます.
2 (place where a bus stops) teʳeryuujo 停留所; (of a train) teʳeshaba 停車場: I get off at the next stop. (*Tsugi no teeryuujo de orimasu.*) 次の停留所で降ります.
3 (stay) taʳizai 滞在; shuʳkuhaku 宿泊: I want to make a week's stop in Kyoto. (*Watashi wa Kyooto ni is-shuukañ taizai shitai.*) 私は京都に1週間滞在したい.

store *n.* **1** (shop) miʳseˡ 店; shoˡoteñ 商店: The store opens at ten o'clock. (*Mise wa juu-ji ni hirakimasu.*) 店は10時に開きます.
2 (stock) taʳkuwae 蓄え; choʳzoo 貯蔵: have a good store of food (*tabemono o juubuñ ni takuwaete aru*) 食べ物を十分に蓄えてある.
— *vt.* **1** (put aside) ... o taʳkuwaeˡru …を蓄える Ⓥ: store up fuel for the winter (*fuyu ni sonaete neñryoo o takuwaeru*) 冬に備えて燃料を蓄える.
2 (put in a storehouse) ... o (... ni) hoʳkañ suru …を(…に)保管する Ⓘ: store the furniture in a warehouse (*kagu o sooko ni hokañ suru*) 家具を倉庫に保管する.

stork *n.* koʳonoˡtori こうのとり.

S

storm *n.* a˥rashi 嵐; bo˩ofu˥u-u 暴風雨: The antenna was damaged by the storm. (*Añtena ga arashi de kowareta.*) アンテナが嵐で壊れた.
— *vi.* a˥rashi ga fuku 嵐が吹く Ⓒ: It stormed all night long. (*Arashi ga hito-bañ-juu fuita.*) 嵐が一晩中吹いた.

story[1] *n.* **1** (imaginary account) mo˩noga˥tari 物語; (novel) sho˩osetsu 小説: a love story (*koi monogatari*) 恋物語 / a detective story (*suiri-shoosetsu*) 推理小説.
2 (true account) ha˩nashi˥ 話; (news) ki˥ji 記事: It is the same old story. (*Sore wa yoku aru hanashi da.*) それはよくある話だ.

story[2] *n.* (level of building) ka˥i 階: the upper [lower] story (*ue* [*shita*] *no kai*) 上[下]の階.

stove *n.* (cooking device) re˥ñji レンジ; (heater) su˩to˥obu ストーブ.
★ Japanese '*sutoobu*' is used only for 'heater.'

straight *adj.* **1** (without a bend) ma˩ssu˥gu na 真っすぐな; i˩tcho˥kuseñ no 一直線の: a straight path (*massugu na michi*) 真っすぐな道.
2 (upright) cho˩kuritsu shita [shite iru] 直立した[している]; ma˩ssu˥gu na 真っすぐな: drive a stake straight into the ground (*kui o jimeñ ni massugu ni uchikomu*) くいを地面に真っすぐに打ち込む.
3 (in good order) ki˩chi˥ñto shita [shite iru] きちんとした[している]: keep one's room straight (*heya o kichiñto shite oku*) 部屋をきちんとしておく.
— *adv.* **1** (directly) cho˩kusetsu ni 直接に; ma˩ssu˥gu 真っすぐ: I went straight home. (*Watashi wa massugu uchi e kaerimashita.*) 私は真っすぐ家へ帰りました.
2 (in a straight line) ma˩ssu˥gu ni 真っすぐに; i˩tcho˥kuseñ ni 一直線に: Keep straight on. (*Massugu ni iki nasai.*) 真っすぐに行きなさい.

straighten *vt.* **1** (make straight) ... o ma˩ssu˥gu ni suru ...を真っすぐにする Ⓘ: straighten one's tie (*nekutai o massugu ni naosu*) ネクタイを真っすぐに直す.
2 (put in order) ... o se˩etoñ suru ...を整頓する Ⓘ: straighten one's room (*heya o seetoñ suru*) 部屋を整頓する.

strain *vt.* **1** (hurt) ... o i˩tame˥ru ...を痛める Ⓥ: I strained my eyes by reading too much. (*Hoñ o yomisugite me o itameta.*) 本を読みすぎて目を痛めた.
2 (stretch tight) pi˩ñ to haru ぴんと張る Ⓒ: strain a wire (*harigane o piñ to haru*) 針金をぴんと張る.
3 (separate a liquid) ... o ko˩su ...をこす Ⓒ; mi˩zu o ki˥ru 水を切る Ⓒ: strain the coffee (*koohii o kosu*) コーヒーをこす / strain the vegetables (*yasai no mizu o kiru*) 野菜の水を切る.
— *vi.* **1** (pull) (... o) hi˩ppa˥ru (...を)引っぱる Ⓒ: We strained at the rope. (*Watashi-tachi wa sono roopu o hippatta.*) 私たちはそのロープを引っ張った.
2 (try very hard) ke˩ñmee ni do˥ryoku suru 懸命に努力する Ⓘ: strain for victory (*shoori o mezashite keñmee ni doryoku suru*) 勝利を目指して懸命に努力する.
— *n.* **1** (force exerted) hi˩ppa˥ru chi˩kara˥ 引っ張る力: The rope broke under the strain. (*Hipparu chikara ga tsuyokute tsuna ga kireta.*) 引っ張る力が強くて綱が切れた.
2 (overwork) ka˩roo 過労: The strain made him ill. (*Karoo de kare wa byooki ni natta.*) 過労で彼は病気になった.

strange *adj.* **1** (odd) ki˥myoo na 奇妙な; he˥ñ na 変な: There is something strange about him. (*Kare wa doko-ka heñ da.*) 彼はどこか変だ.
2 (unfamiliar) mi˩shiranu 見知らぬ; shi˩ranai 知らない: visit a strange land (*shiranai kuni o tazuneru*) 知らない国を訪ねる.

stranger *n.* **1** (unknown person) shi˩ranai hito˥ 知らない人: The dog barked at a stranger. (*Inu ga shi-*

S

ranai hito ni hoeta.) 犬が知らない人にほえた.

2 (outsider) ha⌈ji⌉mete no hi⌈to⌉ 初めての人: I am a stranger here. (*Watashi wa koko wa hajimete desu.*) 私はここは初めてです.

strap *n.* (narrow strip) ka⌈wahimo 革ひも; (of a train) tsu⌈rikawa つり革: hold on to a strap (*tsurikawa ni tsukamaru*) つり革につかまる.
— *vt.* ... o ka⌈wahimo de shiba⌉ru ...を革ひもで縛る [C]: strap up a trunk (*torañku o kawahimo de shibaru*) トランクを革ひもで縛る.

strategy *n.* **1** (military operations) se⌈ñryaku 戦略: nuclear strategy (*kaku señryaku*) 核戦略.

2 (skill) se⌈ñryaku 戦略; shu⌉dañ 手段: marketing strategy (*maaketiñgu señryaku*) マーケティング戦略.

straw *n.* **1** (stalk) wa⌉ra わら: a straw hat (*mugiwara-booshi*) 麦わら帽子.

2 (for drinking) su⌈to⌉roo ストロー: drink orange juice through a straw (*oreñji juusu o sutoroo de nomu*) オレンジュースをストローで飲む.

strawberry *n.* i⌉chigo いちご(苺).

streak *n.* su⌉ji 筋; shi⌈ma⌉ しま: He has streaks of gray in his hair. (*Kare wa kami no ke ni shiraga ga majitte iru.*) 彼は髪の毛に白髪が混じっている. / streaks of lightning (*inazuma*) 稲妻.

stream *n.* **1** (brook) o⌈gawa 小川: cross a stream (*ogawa o wataru*) 小川を渡る.

2 (current) na⌈gare⌉ 流れ: go with [against] the stream (*nagare ni shitagau* [*sakarau*]) 流れに従う[逆らう].
— *vi.* na⌈gare⌉ru 流れる [V]: Tears streamed down her cheeks. (*Namida ga kanojo no hoo o nagareochita.*) 涙が彼女のほおを流れ落ちた.

street *n.* to⌈ori⌉ 通り; ga⌉iro 街路: His house is on this street. (*Kare no uchi wa kono toori ni arimasu.*) 彼の家はこの通りにあります. / Follow this street. (*Kono toori o iki nasai.*) この通りを行きなさい. / a street map (*gairo chizu*) 街路地図.

streetcar *n.* ro⌈meñde⌉ñsha 路面電車.

strength *n.* **1** (power) chi⌈kara⌉ 力; ta⌉iryoku 体力: I don't have the strength to lift the box. (*Watashi ni wa sono hako o mochiageru chikara ga nai.*) 私にはその箱を持ち上げる力がない. / He regained his strength. (*Kare wa tairyoku o kaifuku shita.*) 彼は体力を回復した.

2 (mental power) chi⌉ryoku 知力: strength of mind (*seeshiñryoku*) 精神力.

strengthen *vt.* ... o tsu⌉yoku suru ...を強くする [I]; jo⌈obu ni suru 丈夫にする [I]: strengthen one's body (*karada o joobu ni suru*) 体を丈夫にする.

stress *n.* **1** (pressure) a⌈tsu⌉ryoku 圧力: the stress of a roof on a beam (*hari ni kakaru yane no atsuryoku*) はりにかかる屋根の圧力.

2 (worry) su⌈to⌉resu ストレス: diseases caused by stress (*sutoresu de okoru byooki*) ストレスで起こる病気.

3 (emphasis) kyo⌈ochoo 強調; ju⌈ushi 重視: Our school places stress on foreign languages. (*Watashitachi no gakkoo wa gaikokugo o juushi shite iru.*) 私たちの学校は外国語を重視している.
— *vt.* ... o kyo⌈ochoo suru ...を強調する [I]: He stressed the importance of health. (*Kare wa keñkoo no juuyoosa o kyoochoo shita.*) 彼は健康の重要さを強調した.

stretch *vt.* ... o no⌈ba⌉su ...を伸ばす [C]; hi⌈rogeru 広げる [V]: stretch one's arms and yawn (*ude o nobashite akubi o suru*) 腕を伸ばしてあくびをする / I stretched the carpet on the floor. (*Watashi wa sono juutañ o yuka ni hirogeta.*) 私はそのじゅうたんを床に広げた.
— *vi.* no⌈bi⌉ru 伸びる [V]; hi⌈rogaru 広がる [C]: My sweater stretched in the wash. (*Arattara seetaa ga nobite shimatta.*) 洗ったらセーターが伸びてしまった. / The lake stretched

away into the distance. (*Mizuumi wa eñpoo made hirogatte ita.*) 湖は遠方まで広がっていた.

strict *adj.* **1** (rigid) ki⌈bishi⌉i 厳しい; ge⌈ñkaku na 厳格な: a strict teacher (*kibishii señsee*) 厳しい先生.
2 (exact) ge⌈ñmitsu na 厳密な; se⌈ekaku na 正確な: a strict translation (*seekaku na hoñyaku*) 正確な翻訳.

strictly *adv.* ki⌈bi⌉shiku 厳しく; ge⌈ñmitsu ni 厳密に: Strictly speaking, this is illegal. (*Geñmitsu ni iu to kore wa ihoo da.*) 厳密に言うとこれは違法だ.

stride *vi.* o⌈omata ni aru⌉ku 大またに歩く Ⓒ: He strode along the street. (*Kare wa toori o oomata ni aruita.*) 彼は通りを大またに歩いた.
— *n.* o⌈omata no i⌉ppo 大またの一歩; hi⌈to⌉matagi ひとまたぎ: in one stride (*hitomatagi de*) ひとまたぎで.

strife *n.* a⌈raso⌉i 争い; to⌈osoo 闘争: factional strife (*habatsu no arasoi*) 派閥の争い.

strike *vt.* **1** (hit) ... o u⌉tsu …を打つ Ⓒ; ... ni bu⌈tsukaru …にぶつかる Ⓒ: strike a ball (*booru o utsu*) ボールを打つ / The car struck the guardrail. (*Kuruma wa gaadoreeru ni butsukatta.*) 車はガードレールにぶつかった.
2 (give a blow) ... o na⌈gu⌉ru …を殴る Ⓒ: He hit me in the face. (*Kare wa watashi no kao o nagutta.*) 彼は私の顔を殴った.
3 (make a sound) ... o u⌉tsu …を打つ Ⓒ; na⌈rasu 鳴らす Ⓒ: The clock struck seven. (*Tokee ga shichi-ji o utta.*) 時計が7時を打った.
4 (set on fire) ... o su⌉ru … をする Ⓒ; tsu⌈ke⌉ru つける Ⓥ: He struck a match and lit a cigarette. (*Kare wa matchi o sutte tabako ni hi o tsuketa.*) 彼はマッチを擦ってたばこに火をつけた.
5 (enter the mind) ko⌈ko⌉ro ni u⌈kabu 心に浮かぶ Ⓒ: A good idea struck me. (*Yoi kañgae ga atama ni ukañda.*) よい考えが頭に浮かんだ.
— *vi.* **1** (hit) (... ni) na⌈guri-kaka⌉ru (…に)殴りかかる Ⓒ: He struck at the dog with a stick. (*Kare wa boo de inu ni naguri-kakatta.*) 彼は棒で犬に殴りかかった.
2 (quit work) su⌈tora⌉iki o suru ストライキをする Ⓘ: They are striking for higher wages. (*Kare-ra wa chiñage no tame ni sutoraiki o shite iru.*) 彼らは賃上げのためにストライキをしている.
3 (attack) (... o) ko⌈ogeki suru (…を)攻撃する Ⓘ: strike at the enemy (*teki o koogeki suru*) 敵を攻撃する.
— *n.* **1** (the act of hitting) u⌉tsu ko⌈to⌉ 打つこと; ko⌈ogeki 攻撃.
2 (the act of quitting work) su⌈tora⌉iki ストライキ; su⌉to スト: go on strike (*suto ni hairu*) ストに入る.
3 (in baseball) su⌈tora⌉iku ストライク.

striking *adj.* me⌈da⌉tsu 目立つ: a striking dress (*medatsu doresu*) 目立つドレス.

string *n.* **1** (thin cord) hi⌈mo ひも; (thread) i⌉to 糸: tie up a parcel with string (*tsutsumi o himo de shibaru*) 包みをひもで縛る.
2 (connected series) re⌈ñzoku 連続; re⌉tsu 列: a string of cars (*kuruma no retsu*) 車の列.

strip[1] *vt.* **1** (take off) ... o ha⌈ga⌉su …をはがす Ⓒ; mu⌉ku むく Ⓒ: strip the wallpaper off (*kabegami o hagasu*) 壁紙をはがす / strip the bark from a tree (*ki no kawa o muku*) 木の皮をむく.
2 (make bare) ... o ha⌈daka ni suru …を裸にする Ⓘ: strip oneself (*hadaka ni naru*) 裸になる.
3 (remove) ... o to⌈rihara⌉u …を取り払う Ⓒ: strip a room of furniture (*heya kara kagu o toriharau*) 部屋から家具を取り払う.

strip[2] *n.* ho⌈sonaga⌉i ki⌈re⌉ 細長い切れ: a strip of paper (*hosonagai kami kire*) 細長い紙切れ.

stripe *n.* su⌉ji 筋; shi⌈ma⌉ しま: a tie with stripes (*shima no nekutai*) しまのネクタイ.

strive *vi.* do⌉ryoku suru 努力する Ⓘ; tsu⌈tome⌉ru 努める Ⓥ: strive to win (*yuushoo shiyoo to tsutomeru*)

S

優勝しようと努める.

stroke[1] *n.* **1** (blow) i⌈chigeki 一撃; da⌈geki 打撃: fell a tree with one stroke of the ax (*ono no ichigeki de ki o taosu*) おのの一撃で木を倒す.
2 (sudden attack of illness) ho⌈ssa 発作; so⌈tchuu 卒中: have a stroke (*sotchuu ni kakaru*) 卒中にかかる.
3 (mark made in writing) hi⌈to⌉fude 一筆; fu⌈dezu⌉kai 筆づかい: the final stroke (*shiage no hitofude*) 仕上げの一筆.
4 (movement) do⌉osa 動作; su⌈toro⌉oku ストローク: He swam with strong strokes. (*Kare wa chikarazuyoi sutorooku de oyoida.*) 彼は力強いストロークで泳いだ.

stroke[2] *vt.* ... o na⌈de⌉ru ...をなでる [V]; sa⌈suru さする [C]: stroke a cat (*neko o naderu*) 猫をなでる.

stroll *vi.* bu⌉rabura a⌈ru⌉ku ぶらぶら歩く [C]; sa⌈ñpo suru 散歩する [I]: I strolled along the beach. (*Watashi wa umibe o burabura sañpo shita.*) 私は海辺をぶらぶら散歩した.

strong *adj.* **1** (powerful) tsu⌈yo⌉i 強い: a strong man (*tsuyoi otoko*) 強い男 / strong winds (*tsuyoi kaze*) 強い風.
2 (durable) jo⌈obu na 丈夫な: strong cloth (*joobu na kiji*) 丈夫な生地.
3 (of drinks) ko⌉i 濃い: strong black coffee (*koi burakku koohii*) 濃いブラックコーヒー.

strongly *adv.* kyo⌈okoo ni 強硬に; ne⌉sshiñ ni 熱心に: protest strongly (*kyookoo ni koogi suru*) 強硬に抗議する.

structure *n.* **1** (construction) ko⌈ozoo 構造; so⌉shiki 組織: the structure of a machine (*kikai no koozoo*) 機械の構造.
2 (building) ke⌈ñzo⌉obutsu 建造物; ta⌈te⌉mono 建物: a marble structure (*dairiseki no tatemono*) 大理石の建物.

struggle *n.* **1** (great effort) do⌉ryoku 努力; fu⌈ñtoo 奮闘: a desperate struggle (*hisshi no doryoku*) 必死の努力.
2 (fight) kyo⌈osoo 競争; to⌈osoo 闘争: the struggle for existence (*seezoñ-kyoosoo*) 生存競争.
— *vi.* fu⌈ñtoo suru 奮闘する [I]; do⌉ryoku suru 努力する [I]: struggle for a living (*seekatsu no tame ni fuñtoo suru*) 生活のために奮闘する.

stubborn *adj.* ga⌉ñko na がんこな; go⌈ojoo na 強情な: a stubborn child (*goojoo na kodomo*) 強情な子ども.

student *n.* ga⌈kusee 学生; se⌉eto 生徒. ★ Junior and senior high school students are called '*seeto*' and college and university students '*gakusee*': a foreign student (*ryuugakusee*) 留学生.

studio *n.* **1** (of an artist) shi⌈gotoba 仕事場; a⌈torie アトリエ.
2 (of a broadcasting station) ho⌈oso⌉oshitsu 放送室; su⌈tajio スタジオ.

study *vt.* **1** (learn) ... o be⌈ñkyoo suru ...を勉強する [I]; ke⌈ñkyuu suru 研究する [I]: I am studying law. (*Watashi wa hooritsu o beñkyoo shite imasu.*) 私は法律を勉強しています.
2 (examine) ... o shi⌈rabe⌉ru ...を調べる [V]; cho⌉osa suru 調査する [I]: study a timetable (*jikokuhyoo o shiraberu*) 時刻表を調べる.
— *vi.* be⌈ñkyoo suru 勉強する [I]: He is studying to be a lawyer. (*Kare wa beñgoshi ni naru tame ni beñkyoo shite iru.*) 彼は弁護士になるために勉強している.
— *n.* **1** (learning) be⌈ñkyoo 勉強; ga⌈kushuu 学習: I like study better than sports. (*Watashi wa uñdoo yori beñkyoo no hoo ga suki da.*) 私は運動より勉強のほうが好きだ.
2 (research) ke⌈ñkyuu 研究: the study of physics (*butsurigaku no keñkyuu*) 物理学の研究.
3 (room) sho⌈sai 書斎; ke⌈ñkyu⌉ushitsu 研究室.

stuff *n.* **1** (substance) mo⌈no⌉ もの; (material) ge⌈ñryo⌉o 原料: What is this black stuff? (*Kono kuroi mono*

S

wa nañ desu ka?) この黒いものは何ですか.
2 (belongings) mo⌈chi⌉mono 持ち物: empty all the stuff from one's pockets (*poketto no naka no mochimono o zeñbu kara ni suru*) ポケットの中の持ち物を全部空にする.
— *vt.* ... ni (... o) tsu⌈mekomu ...に(...を)詰め込む Ⓒ: I stuffed the bag with old clothes. (*Watashi wa kabañ ni furugi o tsumekoñda.*) 私はかばんに古着を詰め込んだ.

stumble *vi.* **1** (trip) tsu⌈mazuku つまずく Ⓒ; yo⌈rome⌉ku よろめく Ⓒ: She stumbled on a stone and fell. (*Kanojo wa ishi ni tsumazuite koroñda.*) 彼女は石につまずいて転んだ.
2 (hesitate in speaking) tsu⌈kae⌉ru つかえる Ⓥ; do⌈mo⌉ru どもる Ⓒ: stumble over one's words (*kotoba ga tsukaeru*) 言葉がつかえる.

stump *n.* ki⌈ri⌉kabu 切り株: sit on a stump (*kirikabu ni suwaru*) 切り株に座る.

stun *vt.* **1** (make unconcious) ... o ki⌈zetsu saseru ...を気絶させる Ⓥ: The blow stunned him. (*Sono ichi geki de kare wa kizetsu shita.*) その一撃で彼は気絶した.
2 (surprise) ... o gyo⌈oteñ saseru ...を仰天させる Ⓥ: We were stunned by the news. (*Watashi-tachi wa sono shirase ni gyooteñ shita.*) 私たちはその知らせに仰天した.

stunt *n.* myo⌉ogi 妙技; ha⌈nare-waza⌉ 離れ技: perform a stunt (*myoogi o okonau*) 妙技を行う.

stupid *adj.* ba⌉ka na ばかな; o⌈roka na 愚かな: a stupid mistake (*baka na ayamari*) ばかな誤り / It was stupid of me to believe that. (*Sore o shiñjiru to wa watashi mo oroka datta.*) それを信じるとは私も愚かだった.

stupidity *n.* o⌈roka⌉sa 愚かさ; ba⌉ka ばか.

sturdy *adj.* (strong) ta⌈kumashi⌉i たくましい; (firm) ga⌈ñjoo na 頑丈な: He is small but sturdy. (*Kare wa chiisai ga takumashii.*) 彼は小さいがたくましい. / a sturdy chair (*gañjoo na isu*) 頑丈ないす.

stutter *vi.* do⌈mo⌉ru どもる Ⓒ; ku⌈chigomo⌉ru 口ごもる Ⓒ: He stutters a little. (*Kare wa sukoshi domoru.*) 彼は少しどもる.

style *n.* **1** (manner) ya⌈rikata やり方; yo⌈oshiki 様式: change one's style of living (*seekatsu-yooshiki o kaeru*) 生活様式を変える.
2 (fashion) ryu⌈ukoo(gata) 流行(型); su⌈ta⌉iru スタイル: the latest style in shoes (*kutsu no saishiñ ryuukoogata*) 靴の最新流行型.
3 (original way of writing) bu⌈ñtai 文体: write in an easy style (*wakariyasui buñtai de kaku*) わかりやすい文体で書く.

subdue *vt.* ... o se⌈efuku suru ...を征服する Ⓘ; chi⌈ñatsu suru 鎮圧する Ⓘ: subdue a revolt (*boodoo o chiñatsu suru*) 暴動を鎮圧する.

subject[1] *n.* **1** (theme) shu⌈dai 主題; wa⌈dai 話題: change the subject (*wadai o kaeru*) 話題を変える.
2 (course of study) ka⌈moku 科目: What is your favorite subject? (*Anata no suki na kamoku wa nañ desu ka?*) あなたの好きな科目は何ですか.
3 (of grammar) shu⌉bu 主部; (word) shu⌉go 主語.
4 (person) ko⌈kumiñ 国民.
— *adj.* **1** (likely to receive) (... ni) ka⌈kariyasu⌉i (...に)かかりやすい: I am subject to colds. (*Watashi wa kaze o hiki-yasui.*) 私はかぜを引きやすい.
2 (depending on) (... o) u⌈ke⌉ru hi⌈tsuyoo ga a⌉ru (...を)受ける必要がある: The plan is subject to his approval. (*Sono keekaku wa kare no shooniñ o ukeru hitsuyoo ga aru.*) その計画は彼の承認を受ける必要がある.
3 (under the power of) shi⌉hai o u⌈ke⌉ru 支配を受ける: We are subject to the laws. (*Wareware wa hoo no shihai o ukete iru.*) われわれは法の支配を受けている.

subject[2] *vt.* **1** (bring under control) ... o fu⌈kujuu saseru ...を服従させる Ⓥ; ... no shi⌈ha⌉ika ni o⌈ku ...の

支配下に置く [C]: The country was subjected to foreign rule. (*Sono kuni wa gaikoku no shihaika ni okareta.*) その国は外国の支配下に置かれた.
2 (cause to suffer) ... o u⌈ke⌉ru …を受ける [V]: He was subjected to cruel treatment. (*Kare wa zañkoku na atsukai o uketa.*) 彼は残酷な扱いを受けた.

subjective *adj.* shu⌈kañ-teki na 主観的な: a subjective judgment (*shukañ-teki na hañdañ*) 主観的な判断.

submarine *n.* se⌈ñsuikañ 潜水艦: a nuclear submarine (*geñshiryoku señsuikañ*) 原子力潜水艦.

submission *n.* (obedience) fu⌈kujuu 服従; ko⌈ofuku 降伏.

submit *vt.* ... o te⌈eshutsu suru …を提出する [I]: I submitted the application form to the office. (*Watashi wa mooshikomi-yooshi o yakusho ni teeshutsu shita.*) 私は申込用紙を役所に提出した.
— *vi.* (... ni) fu⌈kujuu suru (…に)服従する: They submitted without a fight. (*Kare-ra wa tatakawazu ni fukujuu shita.*) 彼らは戦わずに服従した.

subordinate *adj.* ka⌉i no 下位の; ju⌈uzoku shita 従属した: a subordinate rank (*kai no kurai*) 下位の位.

subscribe *vi.* **1** (of a magazine, etc.) (... o) te⌈eki-ko⌉odoku suru (…を)定期購読する [I]: I subscribe to two newspapers. (*Watashi wa shiñbuñ o ni-shi teeki koodoku shite iru.*) 私は新聞を2紙定期購読している.
2 (contribute) (... ni) ki⌉fu suru (…に)寄付する [I]: subscribe to a relief fund (*eñjo kikiñ ni kifu suru*) 援助基金に寄付する.

subscription *n.* te⌈eki-ko⌉odoku 定期購読: cancel [renew] one's subscription (*teeki-koodoku o yameru* [*kooshiñ suru*]) 定期購読をやめる[更新する].

subside *vi.* (of land) chi⌈ñka suru 沈下する [I]; (of floods) hi⌈ku 引く [C]; (of a storm) o⌈sama⌉ru 収まる [C].

subsidy *n.* jo⌈seekiñ 助成金; ho⌈jokiñ 補助金.

substance *n.* **1** (matter) bu⌈sshitsu 物質; -tai 体: a chemical substance (*kagaku-busshitsu*) 化学物質 / a liquid [gaseous] substance (*eki*[*ki*]*tai*) 液[気]体.
2 (essential part) na⌈ka⌉mi 中身; na⌈iyoo 内容: an argument of little substance (*nakami no nai giroñ*) 中身のない議論.

substantial *adj.* **1** (large) ka⌉nari no かなりの; so⌈otoo na 相当な: a substantial sum of money (*kanari no gaku no kane*) かなりの額の金.
2 (strong) ga⌈ñjoo na がんじょうな: The house doesn't look very substantial. (*Sono uchi wa amari gañjoo ni mienai.*) その家はあまりがんじょうに見えない.
3 (rich) na⌈ka⌉mi no aru 中身のある; ta⌈ppu⌉ri shita [shite iru] たっぷりした[している]: have a substantial meal (*tappuri shita shokuji o toru*) たっぷりした食事をとる.
4 (essential) ho⌈ñshitsu-teki na 本質的な; ji⌈jitsujoo no 事実上の: We are in substantial agreement. (*Wareware wa hoñshitsu-teki ni ikeñ ga itchi shite iru.*) われわれは本質的に意見が一致している.

substitute *vt.* ... o ka⌈wari ni tsukau …を代わりに使う [C]: substitute margarine for butter (*bataa no kawari ni maagariñ o tsukau*) バターの代わりにマーガリンを使う.
— *vi.* (... no) ka⌈wari ni na⌉ru (…の)代わりになる [C]: I'm looking for someone who will substitute for me. (*Watashi wa watashi no kawari ni naru hito o sagashite iru.*) 私は私の代わりになる人を探している.
— *n.* (people) da⌈iriniñ 代理人; (things) da⌈iyoohiñ 代用品.

subtle *adj.* **1** (delicate) bi⌈myoo na 微妙な: There is a subtle difference between them. (*Ryoosha no aida ni wa bimyoo na chigai ga*

S

aru.) 両者の間には微妙な違いがある.
2 (faint) ka⌉suka na かすかな: a subtle perfume (*kasuka na kaori*) かすかな香り.
3 (sensitive) bi⌈ñkañ na 敏感な; su⌈rudo⌉i 鋭い: a subtle observer (*surudoi kañsatsusha*) 鋭い観察者.

subtract *vt.* ... o hi⌈ku …を引く [C]; ge⌈ñjiru 減じる [V]: Subtract 2 from 5 and you get 3. (*Go kara ni o hiku to sañ ni naru.*) 5から2を引くと3になる.

subtraction *n.* hi⌈ki⌉zañ 引き算: do subtraction (*hikizañ o suru*) 引き算をする.

suburb *n.* ko⌉ogai 郊外: He lives in the suburbs. (*Kare wa koogai ni suñde iru.*) 彼は郊外に住んでいる.

subway *n.* chi⌈katetsu 地下鉄: Where is the nearest subway station? (*Ichibañ chikai chikatetsu no eki wa doko desu ka?*) いちばん近い地下鉄の駅はどこですか.

succeed[1] *vi.* (... ni) se⌈ekoo suru (…に)成功する [I]; go⌈okaku suru 合格する [I]: He succeeded in his business. (*Kare wa shoobai ni seekoo shita.*) 彼は商売に成功した. / succeed in an examination (*shikeñ ni gookaku suru*) 試験に合格する.

succeed[2] *vt.* ... no a⌉to o tsu⌈gu …の跡を継ぐ [C]: elect a person who succeeds the mayor (*shichoo no ato o tsugu hito o señkyo suru*) 市長の跡を継ぐ人を選挙する.
— *vi.* (... o) tsu⌈gu (…を)継ぐ [C]: He succeeded to his father's business. (*Kare wa chichioya no shoobai o tsuida.*) 彼は父親の商売を継いだ.

success *n.* se⌈ekoo 成功: She achieved great success as a singer. (*Kanojo wa kashu to shite hijoo na seekoo o osameta.*) 彼女は歌手として非常な成功を収めた. / I wish you success. (*Go-seekoo o inorimasu.*) ご成功を祈ります.

successful *adj.* se⌈ekoo shita [shite iru] 成功した[している]; go⌈okaku shita [shite iru] 合格した[している]: a successful plan (*seekoo shita keekaku*) 成功した計画 / He was successful in the entrance examination. (*Kare wa nyuugaku shikeñ ni gookaku shita.*) 彼は入学試験に合格した.

successfully *adv.* shu⌈bi⌉-yoku 首尾よく; u⌉maku うまく: Everything turned out successfully. (*Subete umaku ikimashita.*) すべてうまくいきました.

succession *n.* **1** (series) re⌈ñzoku 連続; -tsu⌉zuki 続き: a succession of misfortunes (*fukoo no reñzoku*) 不幸の連続 / a succession of fine days (*seeteñ-tsuzuki*) 晴天続き.
2 (the right to succeed) ke⌈eshoo 継承; ke⌈esho⌉okeñ 継承権: the succession to the throne (*ooi keeshoo*) 王位継承.

successive *adj.* tsu⌈zuite⌉ no 続いての; re⌈ñzoku no 連続の: It rained three successive days. (*Mikka-kañ tsuzuite ame ga futta.*) 3日間続いて雨が降った.

successor *n.* ko⌈oke⌉esha 後継者; ko⌈oniñ 後任; ke⌈esho⌉osha 継承者: the president's successor (*shachoo no kooniñ*) 社長の後任 / the successor to the throne (*ooi keeshoosha*) 王位継承者.

such *adj.* so⌈no yo⌉o na そのような; so⌈ñna そんな: Can you recommend such a place? (*Sono yoo na tokoro o hitotsu oshiete moraemasu ka?*) そのような所を一つ教えてもらえますか. / I don't know such a person. (*Soñna hito wa shirimaseñ.*) そんな人は知りません.
such as ... ... no yo⌉o na …のような: I like a painting such as this. (*Watashi wa kono yoo na e ga suki desu.*) 私はこのような絵が好きです.
— *adv.* so⌈ñna ni そんなに: Is he such a good golf player? (*Kare wa soñna ni gorufu no joozu na hito desu ka?*) 彼はそんなにゴルフのじょうずな人ですか.

suck *vt.* **1** (draw in) ... o su⌈u …を吸う [C]; su⌈iko⌉mu 吸い込む [C]: suck

the juice from an orange (*oreñji no shiru o suu*) オレンジの汁を吸う.
2 (lick) ... o sha⌈buru ...をしゃぶる Ⓒ; na⌈me⌉ru なめる Ⓥ: suck a candy (*kyañdee o shaburu*) キャンデーをしゃぶる.

sudden *adj.* to⌈tsuzeñ no 突然の; kyu⌈u na 急な: His sudden death was a shock. (*Kare no totsuzeñ no shi wa shokku datta.*) 彼の突然の死はショックだった. / There was a sudden change in the weather. (*Teñkoo ga kyuu ni kawatta.*) 天候が急に変わった.

suddenly *adv.* to⌈tsuzeñ 突然; fu⌈i ni 不意に: Suddenly the light went out. (*Totsuzeñ akari ga kieta.*) 突然明かりが消えた.

sue *vt.* ... o ko⌉kuso suru ...を告訴する Ⓘ: I sued him for libel. (*Watashi wa meeyo-kisoñ de kare o kokuso shita.*) 私は名誉毀損で彼を告訴した.
— *vi.* so⌈shoo o oko⌉su 訴訟を起こす Ⓒ: sue for damages (*soñgai-baishoo no soshoo o okosu*) 損害賠償の訴訟を起こす.

suffer *vt.* **1** (experience) ... o ko⌈omu⌉ru ...を被る Ⓒ; o⌈u 負う Ⓒ: The company suffered great losses. (*Sono kaisha wa dai-soñgai o koomutta.*) その会社は大損害を被った. / suffer serious wounds (*juushoo o ou*) 重傷を負う.
2 (endure) ... ni ta⌈e⌉ru ...に耐える Ⓥ: I cannot suffer such insults. (*Watashi wa sono yoo na bujoku ni taerarenai.*) 私はそのような侮辱に耐えられない.
— *vi.* **1** (feel pain) (... ni) ku⌈rushi⌉mu (...に)苦しむ Ⓒ: They are suffering from hunger. (*Kare-ra wa ue ni kurushiñde iru.*) 彼らは飢えに苦しんでいる.
2 (of illness) (... o) ya⌉mu (...を)病む Ⓒ; wa⌈zurau 患う Ⓒ: suffer from gout (*tsuufuu o yamu*) 痛風を病む / suffer from rheumatism (*ryuumachi o wazurau*) リューマチを患う.
3 (receive ill treatment) i⌈tade o uke⌉ru 痛手を受ける Ⓥ: It is always the consumers who suffer. (*Itade o ukeru no wa itsu-mo shoohisha da.*) 痛手を受けるのはいつも消費者だ.

suffering *n.* ku⌈rushimi 苦しみ; ku⌉roo 苦労: endure suffering (*kurushimi ni taeru*) 苦しみに耐える.

sufficient *adj.* ju⌈ubu⌉ñ na 十分な; ta⌈riru 足りる: There is sufficient food for us all. (*Shokuryoo wa watashi-tachi miñna ni juubuñ arimasu.*) 食糧は私たちみんなに十分あります. / The pension is not sufficient for living expenses. (*Neñkiñ wa seekatsuhi ni tarinai.*) 年金は生活費に足りない.

sufficiently *adv.* ju⌈ubu⌉ñ ni 十分に; ta⌈riru dake 足りるだけ: The water was sufficiently warm to swim in. (*Mizu wa oyogeru hodo juubuñ ni atatakakatta.*) 水は泳げるほど十分に温かかった.

sugar *n.* sa⌈to⌉o 砂糖: Do you take sugar in your coffee? (*Koohii ni satoo o iremasu ka?*) コーヒーに砂糖を入れますか.

suggest *vt.* **1** (propose) ... o te⌈eañ suru ...を提案する Ⓘ: He suggested a new plan to the committee. (*Kare wa atarashii keekaku o iiñkai ni teeañ shita.*) 彼は新しい計画を委員会に提案した.
2 (hint) ... o a⌉ñ ni shi⌈me⌉su ...を暗に示す Ⓒ: Clouds suggest rain. (*Kumo wa ame ga furu koto o añ ni shimeshite iru.*) 雲は雨が降ることを暗に示している.
3 (bring to mind) ... o o⌈moidasaseru ...を思い出させる Ⓥ: This music suggests the ocean. (*Kono oñgaku wa umi o omoidasaseru.*) この音楽は海を思い出させる.

suggestion *n.* (proposal) te⌈eañ 提案; (hint) shi⌉sa 示唆: make a new suggestion (*atarashii teeañ o suru*) 新しい提案をする / a newspaper article full of suggestions (*shisa ni tomu shiñbuñ kiji*) 示唆に富む新聞記事.

suicide *n.* ji⌈satsu 自殺: commit

suicide (*jisatsu suru*) 自殺する.

suit *n.* **1** (clothes) su⌉utsu スーツ; se⌈biro jo⌉oge 背広上下: put on a suit (*suutsu o kiru*) スーツを着る.
2 (lawsuit) so⌈shoo 訴訟; ko⌉kuso 告訴: a civil [criminal] suit (*miñji* [*keeji*] *soshoo*) 民事[刑事]訴訟.
— *vt.* **1** (be convenient) ... ni tsu⌈goo ga yo⌉i 都合がよい: Would ten o'clock suit you? (*Juu-ji de go-tsugoo wa yoroshii desu ka?*) 10時でご都合はよろしいですか.
2 (satisfy) ... ni te⌈kisuru ...に適する Ⅰ: The climate suits me very well. (*Ima no kikoo wa watashi ni hijoo-ni tekishite iru.*) 今の気候は私に非常に適している.
3 (be becoming) ... ni ni⌈a⌉u ...に似合う Ⓒ: Long hair doesn't suit her. (*Nagai kami wa kanojo ni niawanai.*) 長い髪は彼女に似合わない.

suitable *adj.* te⌈kitoo na 適当な; ... ni mu⌈ita [mu⌈ite iru] ...に向いた[向いている]: I found a suitable present for her. (*Kanojo ni tekitoo na okurimono o mitsuketa.*) 彼女に適当な贈り物を見つけた. / Those shoes are not suitable for mountain climbing. (*Kono kutsu wa yamanobori ni wa muite inai.*) この靴は山登りには向いていない.

suitcase *n.* su⌈utsuke⌉esu スーツケース.

sullen *adj.* fu⌈ki⌉geñ na 不機嫌な; mu⌈ttsu⌉ri shita [shite iru] むっつりした[している]: a sullen look (*fukigeñ na kao*) 不機嫌な顔.

sum *n.* **1** (of money) ga⌉ku 額: a large [small] sum of money (*tagaku* [*shoogaku*] *no o-kane*) 多額[少額]のお金.
2 (total) go⌈okee 合計; so⌈okee 総計; wa⌉ 和: find the sum (*gookee o motomeru*) 合計を求める.
3 (of arithmetic) ke⌈esañ 計算: do sums (*keesañ suru*) 計算する.
— *vt.* ... o ma⌈tomeru ...をまとめる Ⓥ; yo⌈oyaku suru 要約する Ⅰ: sum up the main points of the story (*hanashi no yooteñ o matomeru*) 話の要点をまとめる.

summary *n.* ga⌈iyoo 概要; yo⌈oyaku 要約: a summary of a speech (*eñzetsu no gaiyoo*) 演説の概要.
— *adj.* te⌈mijika na 手短な: a summary account (*temijika na setsumee*) 手短な説明.

summer *n.* na⌈tsu⌉ 夏: summer clothes (*natsu fuku*) 夏服.

summit *n.* **1** (top) cho⌈ojo⌉o 頂上: the summit of a hill (*oka no choojoo*) 丘の頂上.
2 (meeting) shu⌈noo ka⌉idañ 首脳会談.

summon *vt.* ... o yo⌈bida⌉su ...を呼び出す Ⓒ; sho⌈okañ suru 召喚する Ⅰ: He was summoned to appear in court. (*Kare wa saibañsho ni shuttoo suru yoo yobidasareta.*) 彼は裁判所に出頭するよう呼び出された.

summons *n.* sho⌈okañ 召喚; yo⌈bidashi 呼び出し: receive a summons (*yobidashi o ukeru*) 呼び出しを受ける.

sun *n.* **1** (heavenly body) ta⌉iyoo 太陽: The sun rises in the east and sets in the west. (*Taiyoo wa higashi kara nobori nishi ni shizumu.*) 太陽は東から上り西に沈む.
2 (heat and light) ni⌉kkoo 日光; hi 日: My room gets a lot of sun. (*Watashi no heya wa yoku hi ga ataru.*) 私の部屋はよく日が当たる.

sunbeam *n.* ni⌉kkoo 日光; ta⌈iyoo-ko⌉oseñ 太陽光線.

sunburn *n.* hi⌈yake 日焼け: suffer from sunburn (*hiyake suru*) 日焼けする.

Sunday *n.* ni⌈chiyo⌉o(bi) 日曜(日).

sunglasses *n.* sa⌈ñgu⌉rasu サングラス: He was wearing sunglasses. (*Kare wa sañgurasu o kakete ita.*) 彼はサングラスをかけていた.

sunlight *n.* ni⌉kkoo 日光: the right to sunlight (*nisshookeñ*) 日照権.

sunny *adj.* hi⌈atari no yo⌉i 日当たりのよい: a sunny room (*hiatari no yoi heya*) 日当たりのよい部屋.

sunrise *n.* hi-⌈no-de 日の出: get up before sunrise (*hi-no-de mae ni*

S

okiru) 日の出前に起きる.

sunset *n.* hi-ʳno-iri 日の入り; niʳchi-botsu 日没; hiʳgure 日暮れ: go home at sunset (*higure ni ie ni kaeru*) 日暮れに家に帰る.

sunshine *n.* niˡkkoo 日光; hiʳnata ひなた: play in the sunshine (*hinata de asobu*) ひなたで遊ぶ.

superb *adj.* suʳbarashiˡi すばらしい; miˡgoto na 見事な: a superb performance (*migoto na eñgi*) 見事な演技.

superficial *adj.* **1** (of the surface) hyoʳomeˡñ no 表面の; aʳsai 浅い: a superficial wound (*gaishoo*) 外傷.
2 (not thorough) hyoʳomeñ-teki na 表面的な; hiʳsoo-teki na 皮相的な: superficial observation (*hyoomeñ-teki na kañsatsu*) 表面的な観察.

superfluous *adj.* yoʳbuñ no 余分の; yoʳkee na よけいな: a superfluous remark (*yokee na hitokoto*) よけいなひと言.

superintendent *n.* (of work) kaʳñtoku 監督; (of a building) kaʳñriniñ 管理人; (police officer) keʳesatsu-shoˡchoo 警察署長.

superior *adj.* **1** (better) suʳguˡreta 優れた; suʳguˡrete iru 優れている; joʳotoo no 上等の: His computer is superior to this one. (*Kare no koñpyuutaa wa kore yori mo sugurete iru.*) 彼のコンピューターはこれよりも優れている.
2 (higher) joʳokyuu no 上級の; joˡoi no 上位の: a superior court (*jookyuu saibañsho*) 上級裁判所.
— *n.* (person) uʳwayaku 上役; joˡoshi 上司: He is my superior. (*Kare wa watashi no jooshi desu.*) 彼は私の上司です.

superiority *n.* yuʳuetsu 優越; taʳkuetsu 卓越: a sense of superiority (*yuuetsukañ*) 優越感.

supermarket *n.* suʳupaamaˡaketto スーパーマーケット; suˡupaa スーパー: go shopping at a supermarket (*suupaa e kaimono ni iku*) スーパーへ買い物に行く.

superstition *n.* meʳeshiñ 迷信: believe in superstitions (*meeshiñ o shiñjiru*) 迷信を信じる.

supervise *vt.* ... o kaʳñtoku suru ...を監督する [I]; kaˡñri suru 管理する [I]: supervise work (*shigoto o kañtoku suru*) 仕事を監督する.

supervision *n.* kaʳñtoku 監督; kaˡñri 管理: The research was carried out under his supervision. (*Choosa wa kare no kañtoku no moto de okonawareta.*) 調査は彼の監督のもとで行われた.

supervisor *n.* kaʳñtokuˡsha 監督者; kaʳñriniñ 管理人.

supper *n.* yuʳushoku 夕食; yuʳugoˡhañ 夕ご飯: have a steak for supper (*yuushoku ni suteeki o taberu*) 夕食にステーキを食べる.

supplement *n.* fuʳroku 付録; hoʳsoku 補足: a supplement to a magazine (*zasshi no furoku*) 雑誌の付録.

supply *vt.* ... ni (... o) kyoʳokyuu suru ...に(...を)供給する [I]; aʳtaeru 与える [V]: We supplied them with food. (*Watashi-tachi wa kare-ra ni taberu mono o ataeta.*) 私たちは彼らに食べる物を与えた.
— *n.* **1** (the act of supplying) kyoʳokyuu 供給: supply and demand (*kyookyuu to juyoo*) 供給と需要.
2 (store) taʳkuwae 蓄え; soʳnae 備え: We have a good supply of food. (*Tabemono no sonae wa juubuñ ni aru.*) 食べ物の備えは十分にある.
3 (things needed) seʳekatsu hitsujuhiñ 生活必需品.

support *vt.* **1** (hold up) ... o saʳsaeru ...を支える [V]: The walls support the roof. (*Kabe ga yane o sasaete iru.*) 壁が屋根を支えている.
2 (provide for) ... o yaʳshinaˡu ...を養う [C]; fuʳyoo suru 扶養する [I]: He supports a large family. (*Kare wa dai-kazoku o yashinatte iru.*) 彼は大家族を養っている.
3 (help prove) ... o uʳrazukeˡru ...を裏づける [V]: The theory was supported by facts. (*Sono riroñ wa jijitsu ni yotte urazukerareta.*) その

S

理論は事実によって裏づけられた.

— n. 1 (the act of supporting) sa⌈sae 支え; shi⌉ji 支持: The baby stood without support. (*Akañboo wa sasae nashi de tatta.*) 赤ん坊は支えなしで立った. / win public support (*taishuu no shiji o eru*) 大衆の支持を得る.

2 (person) se⌈ekatsu o sasaeru hito⌉ 生活を支える人: He is the sole support of his family. (*Kare wa hitori de ikka o sasaete iru.*) 彼は一人で一家を支えている.

suppose *vt.* **1** (think) ... to o⌈mo⌉u ...と思う Ⓒ: What do you suppose he will do? (*Kare wa doo suru to omoimasu ka?*) 彼はどうすると思いますか.

2 (assume) ... to ka⌈tee suru ...と仮定する Ⓘ: Let's suppose you are right. (*Kimi ga tadashii to katee shite miyoo.*) 君が正しいと仮定してみよう.

be supposed to do ⟨verb⟩ ko⌈to⌉ ni na⌉tte iru ...ことになっている Ⓥ: I am supposed to meet him at five. (*Kare to go-ji ni au koto ni natte iru.*) 彼と5時に会うことになっている.

suppress *vt.* **1** (subdue) ... o yo⌈kuatsu suru ...を抑圧する Ⓘ; chi⌈ñatsu suru 鎮圧する Ⓘ: The rebellion was suppressed. (*Hañrañ wa chiñatsu sareta.*) 反乱は鎮圧された.

2 (keep back) ... o o⌈sae⌉ru ...を抑える Ⓥ: suppress one's anger (*ikari o osaeru*) 怒りを抑える.

3 (hide) ... o ka⌈ku⌉su ...を隠す Ⓒ: suppress the truth (*shiñsoo o kakusu*) 真相を隠す.

supreme *adj.* sa⌈ikoo no 最高の: the supreme commander (*saikoo shireekañ*) 最高司令官 / the Supreme Court (*Saikoo-saibañsho*) 最高裁判所.

sure *adj.* **1** (confident) ka⌈kushiñ shite (iru) 確信して(いる): I am sure of his innocence. (*Watashi wa kare no muzai o kakushiñ shite imasu.*) 私は彼の無罪を確信しています.

2 (unlikely to fail) ki⌈tto ⟨verb⟩ きっと...: He is sure to succeed. (*Kare wa kitto seekoo suru.*) 彼はきっと成功する. / When you visit Tokyo, please be sure to come to see us. (*Tookyoo e kita toki wa kitto yotte kudasai.*) 東京へ来たときはきっと寄ってください.

3 (reliable) shi⌈ñrai de⌈ki⌉ru 信頼できる; ta⌉shika na 確かな: a sure friend (*shiñrai dekiru yuujiñ*) 信頼できる友人 / sure proof (*tashika na shooko*) 確かな証拠.

make sure *vt.* ... o ta⌈shikame⌉ru ...を確かめる Ⓥ: I telephoned to make sure that she was coming. (*Kanojo ga kuru koto o tashikameru tame ni deñwa o shita.*) 彼女が来ることを確かめるために電話をした.

— adv. 1 (certainly) ke⌉kkoo desu けっこうです; do⌉ozo どうぞ: "May I smoke here?" "Sure." (*"Koko de tabako o sutte mo ii desu ka?" "Ee, doozo."*) 「ここでたばこを吸ってもいいですか」「ええ, どうぞ」

2 (surely) ta⌉shika ni 確かに; ma⌈ttaku まったく: It sure is hot. (*Iya mattaku atsui.*) いやまったく暑い.

surely *adv.* **1** (without doubt) ta⌉shika ni 確かに; ki⌈tto きっと: He will surely succeed. (*Kare wa kitto seekoo suru deshoo.*) 彼はきっと成功するでしょう.

2 [with a negative] ma⌉saka まさか: Surely you are not going alone? (*Masaka hitori de iku no de wa nai deshoo ne?*) まさか一人で行くのではないでしょうね.

3 (certainly) i⌉i desu tomo いいですとも; mo⌈chi⌉roñ もちろん: "May I come with you?" "Surely." (*"Issho ni itte mo ii desu ka?" "Ii desu tomo."*) 「いっしょに行ってもいいですか」「いいですとも」

surf *n.* yo⌈seru nami⌉ 寄せる波.

— vi. na⌈minori⌉ o suru 波乗りをする Ⓘ; sa⌉afiñ o suru サーフィンをする Ⓘ: go surfing (*saafiñ ni iku*) サーフィンに行く.

surface *n.* **1** (outer side) hyo⌈o-

S

me˥ñ 表面: the surface of the earth (*chikyuu no hyoomeñ*) 地球の表面 / the surface of water (*suimeñ*) 水面.
2 (outer appearance) u˦wabe うわべ; ga˦ikañ 外観: look only at the surface of things (*monogoto no uwabe dake o miru*) 物事のうわべだけを見る.
— *adj.* hyo˦ome˥ñ no 表面の; u˦wabe dake no うわべだけの: surface friendship (*uwabe dake no yuujoo*) うわべだけの友情.

surface mail *n.* fu˦tsuu-yu˥ubiñ 普通郵便.

surgeon *n.* ge˦ka˥-i 外科医.

surgery *n.* **1** (science) ge˦ka 外科: plastic surgery (*keesee-geka*) 形成外科.
2 (operation) shu˥jutsu 手術.
3 (operating room) shu˦jutsu˥-shitsu 手術室.

surmount *vt.* ... o no˦rikoe˥ru ...を乗り越える [V]; ... ni u˦chika˥tsu ...に打ち勝つ [C]: surmount difficulties (*koñnañ o norikoeru*) 困難を乗り越える.

surname *n.* se˥e 姓; myo˥oji 名字.
★ Japanese 'surname' is followed by 'given name.'

surpass *vt.* ... o u˦wamawa˥ru ...を上回る [C]; ko˦eru 越える [V]: The result surpasses our expectations. (*Kekka wa watashi-tachi no yosoo o uwamawatta.*) 結果は私たちの予想を上回った.

surplus *n.* a˦mari 余り; yo˦joo 余剰: have a surplus of rice (*kome ga amaru*) 米が余る.
— *adj.* yo˦buñ na 余分な; ka˦joo no 過剰の: a surplus population (*kajoo-jiñkoo*) 過剰人口.

surprise *vt.* **1** (cause a feeling of wonder) ... o o˦doroka˥su ...を驚かす [C]; bi˦kku˥ri saseru びっくりさせる [V]: The news surprised us. (*Sono shirase wa watashi-tachi o odorokashita.*) その知らせは私たちを驚かした. / I was surprised to hear the news. (*Watashi wa sono shirase o kiite bikkuri shita.*) 私はその知らせを聞いてびっくりした.
2 (attack unexpectedly) ... o fu˦i-uchi suru ...を不意打ちする [I]; ki˦shuu suru 奇襲する [I]: surprise the enemy (*teki o fuiuchi suru*) 敵を不意打ちする.
— *n.* **1** (astonishment) o˦doroki˥ 驚き: jump with surprise (*odoroite tobiagaru*) 驚いて跳び上がる.
2 (something unexpected) i˦gai na koto˥ 意外なこと: His visit was a surprise. (*Kare no hoomoñ wa igai datta.*) 彼の訪問は意外だった.

surprised *adj.* o˦doro˥ita 驚いた; o˦doro˥ite iru 驚いている; bi˦kku˥ri shita [shite iru] びっくりした[している]: He looked surprised. (*Kare wa bikkuri shita kao o shite ita.*) 彼はびっくりした顔をしていた.

surprising *adj.* o˦doroku be˥ki 驚くべき; i˦gai na 意外な: It is not surprising that he failed. (*Kare ga shippai shita no wa igai de wa nai.*) 彼が失敗したのは意外ではない.

surrender *vi.* (... ni) ko˦ofuku suru (...に)降伏する [I]: surrender to the enemy (*teki ni koofuku suru*) 敵に降伏する.
— *vt.* ... o ho˥oki suru ...を放棄する [I]; su˦teru 捨てる [V]: surrender hope (*kiboo o suteru*) 希望を捨てる.
— *n.* ko˦ofuku 降伏: an unconditional surrender (*mujookeñ koofuku*) 無条件降伏.

surround *vt.* ... o ka˦komu ...を囲む [C]; to˦rimaku 取り巻く [C]: The house is surrounded by trees. (*Sono uchi wa ki ni kakomarete iru.*) その家は木に囲まれている. / The girls surrounded the singer. (*Oñna-no-ko-tachi wa sono kashu o torimaita.*) 女の子たちはその歌手を取り巻いた.

surroundings *n.* ka˦ñkyoo 環境: social surroundings (*shakai-kañkyoo*) 社会環境.

survey *vt.* **1** (measure) ... o so˦ku-ryoo suru ...を測量する [I]: survey the land (*tochi o sokuryoo suru*) 土地を測量する.

2 (look over) ... o mi⌈watasu …を見渡す Ⓒ: He stood on the hill and surveyed the scenery. (*Kare wa oka no ue ni tatte keshiki o miwatashita.*) 彼は丘の上に立って景色を見渡した.
— *n.* **1** (examination) cho⌉osa 調査; so⌈kuryoo 測量: a market survey (*shijoo choosa*) 市場調査.
2 (general study) ga⌈ikañ 概観; ga⌈isetsu 概説: a survey of Japanese history (*Nihoñshi no gaisetsu*) 日本史の概説.

survival *n.* se⌈ezoñ 生存; i⌈kinoko⌉ru ko⌈to⌉ 生き残ること: The climber's survival is doubtful. (*Sono tozañka no seezoñ wa utagawashii.*) その登山家の生存は疑わしい.

survive *vt.* **1** (remain alive) ... yori na⌈gaiki⌉ suru …より長生きする Ⓘ: She suvived her husband by ten years. (*Kanojo wa otto yori juu-neñ nagaiki shita.*) 彼女は夫より10年長生きした.
2 (continue to live) ... o i⌈kinobi⌉ru …を生き延びる Ⓥ: Only one person survived the plane crash. (*Sono hikooki jiko de wa tatta hitori ga seezoñ shite ita.*) その飛行機事故ではたった一人が生存していた.
— *vi.* i⌈kinoko⌉ru 生き残る Ⓒ; za⌈ñzoñ suru 残存する Ⓘ: That custom still survives. (*Sono shuukañ wa mada zañzoñ shite iru.*) その習慣はまだ残存している.

S

susceptible *adj.* (easily influenced) ka⌈ñji-yasu⌉i 感じやすい; (easily affected) ka⌈kari-yasu⌉i かかりやすい: She is susceptible to colds. (*Kanojo wa kaze o hiki-yasui.*) 彼女はかぜをひきやすい.

suspect *vt.* **1** (believe a person to be guilty) ... ni u⌈tagai o ka⌈ke⌉ru …に疑いをかける Ⓥ: The police suspects him of murder. (*Keesatsu wa kare ni satsujiñ no utagai o kakete iru.*) 警察は彼に殺人の疑いをかけている.
2 (believe to be probable) ... de wa nai ka to o⌈mo⌉u …ではないかと思う Ⓒ: I suspect that he is ill. (*Kare wa byooki de wa nai ka to omou.*) 彼は病気ではないかと思う.
3 (have doubts) ... o u⌈tagau …を疑う Ⓒ: I suspect his honesty. (*Watashi wa kare no shoojikisa o utagau.*) 私は彼の正直さを疑う. ★ Japanese '*utagau*' is also used in the sense of 'doubt.'
— *n.* yo⌈ogi⌉sha 容疑者: The police arrested two suspects. (*Keesatsu wa yoogisha o futari taiho shita.*) 警察は容疑者を二人逮捕した.

suspend *vt.* **1** (hang) ... o tsu⌈rusu …をつるす Ⓒ: suspend a lamp from the ceiling (*teñjoo kara rañpu o tsurusu*) 天井からランプをつるす.
2 (stop temporarily) ... o i⌈chi⌉ji chu⌈ushi suru …を一時中止する Ⓘ: The project was suspended. (*Sono keekaku wa ichiji chuushi sareta.*) その計画は一時中止された.
3 (keep out of a job) ... o te⌈eshoku saseru …を停職させる Ⓥ; (of a school) te⌈egaku saseru 停学させる Ⓥ: He was suspended from school. (*Kare wa teegaku ni natta.*) 彼は停学になった.

suspense *n.* **1** (uncertainty) fu⌈añ 不安; ki⌈ga⌉kari 気がかり: wait in suspense for the result (*harahara shite kekka o matsu*) はらはらして結果を待つ.
2 (of a novel) sa⌈supe⌉ñsu サスペンス.

suspicion *n.* u⌈tagai 疑い; gi⌈waku 疑惑: He looked at me with suspicion. (*Kare wa utagai no me de watashi o mita.*) 彼は疑いの目で私を見た. / arouse suspicion (*giwaku o umu*) 疑惑を生む.

suspicious *adj.* u⌈tagawashi⌉i 疑わしい; a⌈yashi⌉i 怪しい: I am suspicious of his story. (*Watashi wa kare no hanashi wa ayashii to omotte iru.*) 私は彼の話は怪しいと思っている.

sustain *vt.* **1** (maintain) ... o i⌉ji suru …を維持する Ⓘ; tsu⌈zukeru 続ける Ⓥ: sustain one's efforts (*doryoku o tsuzukeru*) 努力を続ける.

2 (undergo) ... o u⌈ke⌉ru …を受ける V; o⌈u 負う C: sustain a serious injury (*juushoo o ou*) 重傷を負う.

swallow *vt.* **1** (take into the stomach) ... o no⌈mikomu …を飲み込む C: swallow food without chewing (*tabemono o kamazu ni nomikomu*) 食べ物をかまずに飲み込む.
2 (take in) ... o no⌈mikomu …を飲み込む C: The boat was swallowed by the waves. (*Booto wa nami ni nomikomarete shimatta.*) ボートは波に飲み込まれてしまった.
3 (accept) ... o u⌈nomi⌉ ni suru …をうのみにする I: He swallows everything that he is told. (*Kare wa iwareta koto wa nañ de mo unomi ni suru.*) 彼は言われたことは何でもうのみにする.

swamp *n.* nu⌈machi 沼地; shi⌈tchi 湿地.

swan *n.* ha⌈kuchoo 白鳥.

swarm *n.* mu⌈re⌉ 群れ: a swarm of bees (*hachi no mure*) はちの群れ / swarms of tourists (*kañkookyaku no mure*) 観光客の群れ.
— *vi.* mu⌈raga⌉ru 群がる C; mu⌈re⌉ o nasu 群れをなす C: Shoppers swarmed into the store. (*Kaimonokyaku ga mure o nashite mise ni haitta.*) 買い物客が群れをなして店に入った.

sway *vi.* **1** (move back and forth) yu⌈reru 揺れる V: The flowers are swaying in the breeze. (*Hana ga kaze ni yurete iru.*) 花が風に揺れている.
2 (lean) ka⌈tamu⌉ku 傾く C: The car swayed to the left on the curve. (*Kuruma wa kaabu de hidari ni katamuita.*) 車はカーブで左に傾いた.
— *vt.* **1** (move) ... o yu⌈riugoka⌉su …を揺り動かす C: The wind swayed the branches of the trees. (*Kaze ga ki no eda o yuriugokashita.*) 風が木の枝を揺り動かした.
2 (influence) ... o u⌈goka⌉su …を動かす C: His speech swayed the audience. (*Kare no eñzetsu wa chooshuu no kokoro o ugokashita.*) 彼の演説は聴衆の心を動かした.

swear *vi.* **1** (curse) (... o) no⌈noshi⌉ru (…を)ののしる C: The drunk swore at the policeman. (*Yopparai wa keekañ o nonoshitta.*) 酔っぱらいは警官をののしった.
2 (state with an oath) chi⌈ka⌉u 誓う C; da⌈ñge⌉ñ suru 断言する I: swear on the Bible (*seesho ni te o oite chikau*) 聖書に手を置いて誓う.
— *vt.* ... o chi⌈ka⌉u …を誓う C: swear eternal love (*ee-eñ no ai o chikau*) 永遠の愛を誓う.

sweat *n.* a⌉se 汗: wipe the sweat off one's brow (*hitai no ase o nuguu*) 額の汗をぬぐう.
— *vi.* a⌉se o kaku 汗をかく: Running fast made me sweat. (*Isoide hashittara ase o kaita.*) 急いで走ったら汗をかいた.

sweater *n.* se⌉etaa セーター: put on [take off] a sweater (*seetaa o kiru [nugu]*) セーターを着る[脱ぐ] / She was wearing a red sweater. (*Kanojo wa akai seetaa o kite ita.*) 彼女は赤いセーターを着ていた.

sweep *vt.* **1** (clean) ... o ha⌉ku …を掃く C; so⌈oji suru 掃除する I: sweep a floor (*yuka o haku*) 床を掃く / I swept the room clean. (*Watashi wa heya o kiree ni sooji shita.*) 私は部屋をきれいに掃除した.
2 (push away) ... o o⌈shinaga⌉su …を押し流す C; (blow away) fu⌈kitoba⌉su 吹き飛ばす C: The flood swept away the bridge. (*Koozui ga sono hashi o oshinagashita.*) 洪水がその橋を押し流した.
— *vi.* ha⌉ku 掃く C; so⌈oji suru 掃除する I: She is busy sweeping. (*Kanojo wa sooji ni isogashii.*) 彼女は掃除に忙しい.

sweet *adj.* **1** (having the taste of sugar) a⌈mai 甘い: I like sweet things. (*Watashi wa amai mono ga suki desu.*) 私は甘いものが好きです.
2 (pleasant) ko⌈koroyo⌉i 快い; u⌈tsukushi⌉i 美しい: a sweet sleep (*kokoroyoi nemuri*) 快い眠り / a sweet voice (*utsukushii koe*) 美しい声.

S

— *n.* a⌈mai mono⌉ 甘い物; kya⌉ñ-dee キャンデー.

sweeten *vt.* ... o a⌈maku suru ...を甘くする Ⓘ: sweeten coffee (*koohii o amaku suru*) コーヒーを甘くする.

swell *vi.* **1** (become larger) fu⌈kuramu 膨らむ Ⓒ: The buds are swelling. (*Tsubomi ga fukurañde kite iru.*) つぼみが膨らんできている.
2 (of limbs) ha⌈reru はれる Ⓥ: My injured arm began to swell. (*Kega shita ude ga hare-dashita.*) けがした腕がはれだした.
— *vt.* ... o fu⌈kuramaseru ...を膨らませる Ⓥ: The wind swelled the sails. (*Kaze ga ho o fukuramaseta.*) 風が帆を膨らませた.

swift *adj.* **1** (very fast) ha⌈ya⌉i 速い: a swift horse (*ashi no hayai uma*) 足の速い馬.
2 (prompt) su⌉gu ni ⟨verb⟩ すぐに...: He was swift to act. (*Kare wa sugu ni koodoo shita.*) 彼はすぐに行動した.

swim *vi.* o⌈yo⌉gu 泳ぐ Ⓒ: The children swam in the pond. (*Kodomo-tachi wa ike de oyoida.*) 子どもたちは池で泳いだ.
— *vt.* ... o o⌈yo⌉gu ...を泳ぐ Ⓒ; o⌈yo⌉ide wa⌈taru 泳いで渡る Ⓒ: He swam the river. (*Kare wa sono kawa o oyoide watatta.*) 彼はその川を泳いで渡った.

swimming *n.* o⌈yogi 泳ぎ; su⌈iee 水泳: a swimming pool (*puuru*) プール.

swindler *n.* sa⌈gi⌉shi 詐欺師; pe⌈te⌉ñshi ぺてん師.

swing *vi.* **1** (move back and forth) yu⌈reru 揺れる Ⓥ; bu⌉rabura suru ぶらぶらする Ⓘ: The lamp is swinging in the wind. (*Rañpu ga kaze ni yurete iru.*) ランプが風に揺れている.
2 (turn) gu⌈ru⌉ri to ma⌈waru ぐるりと回る Ⓒ: He swung around and stared at me. (*Kare wa gururi to mawatte watashi o mitsumeta.*) 彼はぐるりと回って私を見つめた.
— *vt.* ... o fu⌈ru ...を振る Ⓒ; gu⌈ru⌉ri to ma⌈wasu ぐるりと回す Ⓒ: swing a bat (*batto o furu*) バットを振る.
— *n.* bu⌉rañko ぶらんこ: get on a swing (*burañko ni noru*) ぶらんこに乗る.

switch *n.* **1** (device) su⌈i⌉tchi スイッチ: turn on [off] a switch (*suitchi o ireru* [*kiru*]) スイッチを入れる[切る].
2 (change) te⌈ñkañ 転換; he⌈ñkoo 変更: a switch of plans (*keekaku no heñkoo*) 計画の変更.
— *vt.* ... o ka⌈eru ...を替える Ⓥ: switch seats (*seki o kaeru*) 席を替える.
— *vi.* su⌈i⌉tchi o hi⌈ne⌉ru スイッチをひねる Ⓒ: switch on [off] the radio (*suitchi o hinette rajio o tsukeru* [*kesu*]) スイッチをひねってラジオをつける[消す].

sword *n.* ka⌈tana⌉ 刀; ke⌉ñ 剣: draw [sheath] a sword (*katana o nuku* [*osameru*]) 刀を抜く[納める].

symbol *n.* **1** (something that stands for) sho⌈ochoo 象徴: The dove is a symbol of peace. (*Hato wa heewa no shoochoo desu.*) はとは平和の象徴です.
2 (sign) ki⌈goo 記号: a chemical symbol (*kagaku-kigoo*) 化学記号.

symbolic *adj.* sho⌈ochoo-teki na 象徴的な: a symbolic meaning (*shoochoo-teki na imi*) 象徴的な意味.

symbolize *vt.* ... o sho⌈ochoo suru ...を象徴する Ⓘ: This picture symbolizes the sun. (*Kono e wa taiyoo o shoochoo shite iru.*) この絵は太陽を象徴している.

symmetry *n.* (sa⌉yuu)ta⌈ishoo (左右)対称; tsu⌈riai つり合い.

sympathetic *adj.* do⌈ojoo-teki na 同情的な; o⌈moiyari no a⌉ru 思いやりのある: a sympathetic person (*omoiyari no aru hito*) 思いやりのある人.

sympathize *vi.* (... ni) do⌈ojoo suru (...に)同情する Ⓘ: He sympathized with me when I was in trouble. (*Kare wa watashi ga komatte iru toki doojoo shite kureta.*) 彼は

私が困っているとき同情してくれた.

sympathy *n.* **1** (feeling for another) do⌈ojoo 同情; o⌈moiyari 思いやり: feel sympathy for the poor (*mazushii hito-tachi ni doojoo suru*) 貧しい人たちに同情する / a letter of sympathy (*o-kuyami no tegami*) お悔やみの手紙.
2 (agreement) do⌈okañ 同感; sa⌈ñsee 賛成: I have no sympathy with their plans. (*Watashi wa kare-ra no keekaku ni sañsee dekinai.*) 私は彼らの計画に賛成できない.

symphony *n.* ko⌈okyo⌉okyoku 交響曲; shi⌉ñfonii シンフォニー.

symptom *n.* cho⌈okoo 徴候; ki⌈zashi 兆し: A cough is a symptom of the common cold. (*Seki wa kaze no chookoo desu.*) せきはかぜの徴候です.

syrup *n.* shi⌉roppu シロップ.

system *n.* **1** (organization) so⌉shiki 組織: a system of government (*seeji soshiki*) 政治組織.
2 (a set of things) ta⌈ikee 体系; ke⌈etoo 系統: the solar system (*taiyoo-kee*) 太陽系 / the nervous system (*shiñkee-keetoo*) 神経系統.
3 (plan) ho⌈oshiki 方式; (method) ho⌈ohoo 方法: a sales system (*hañbai-hoohoo*) 販売方法.

systematic *adj.* so⌈shiki-teki na 組織的な; ke⌈etoo-teki na 系統的な: a systematic method (*keetoo-teki na hoohoo*) 系統的な方法.

T

table *n.* **1** (furniture) te⌈eburu テーブル; sho⌈kutaku 食卓; da⌉i 台: set [clear] the table (*shokutaku o yooi-suru* [*katazukeru*]) 食卓を用意する[片づける] / sit at the negotiating table (*kooshoo no teeburu ni tsuku*) 交渉のテーブルにつく.
2 (list) hyo⌈o 表: a table of contents (in a book) (*mokuji*) 目次 / a multiplication table (*kuku no hyoo*) 九九の表. ★ The Japanese system covers as far as 9×9.

tablecloth *n.* te⌈eburu ku⌉rosu テーブルクロス; te⌈eburu⌉kake テーブル掛け.

table d'hôte *n.* te⌈eshoku 定食: I'll have the table d'hôte. (*Watashi wa teeshoku ni shimasu.*) 私は定食にします.

tablespoon *n.* o⌈osaji 大さじ.

tablet *n.* jo⌈ozai 錠剤: Take two tablets after each meal. (*Mai-shokugo ni ni-joo nomi nasai.*) 毎食後に 2 錠飲みなさい.

tacit *adj.* a⌈ñmoku no 暗黙の; mu⌈goñ no 無言の: tacit consent (*añmoku no shoodaku*) 暗黙の承諾.

taciturn *adj.* mu⌉kuchi na 無口な; ku⌈chikazu no sukuna⌉i 口数の少ない: a taciturn child (*mukuchi na kodomo*) 無口な子ども.

tack *n.* byo⌉o びょう; to⌈megane 留め金.
— *vt.* ... o byo⌉o de to⌈meru ...をびょうで留める Ⓥ: tack down a carpet (*juutañ o byoo de tomeru*) じゅうたんをびょうで留める.

tact *n.* ki⌈teñ 機転; jo⌈saina⌉sa 如才なさ: He has great tact. (*Kare wa hijoo ni kiteñ ga kiku.*) 彼は非常に機転がきく.

tactics *n.* se⌈ñjutsu 戦術; se⌈ñpoo 戦法; ka⌈ke⌉hiki 駆け引き: use clever tactics (*koomyoo na señjutsu o toru*) 巧妙な戦術をとる / surprise [delaying] tactics (*kishuu* [*hikinobashi*] *señpoo*) 奇襲[引き延ばし]戦法.

tag *n.* fu⌈da 札: a name tag (*nafuda*) 名札 / a price tag (*nefuda*) 値札.

tail *n.* **1** (part of an animal's body) o⌉ 尾; shi⌈ppo⌉ しっぽ: wag a tail (*shippo o furu*) しっぽを振る.
2 (end) bi⌉bu 尾部; ko⌉obu 後部; sa⌉igo 最後: I joined the tail of the line. (*Watashi wa retsu no saigo*

s
t

ni tsuita.) 私は列の最後についた.
3 (coin) u⌈ra⌉ 裏: Heads or tails? (*Ura desu ka omote desu ka?*) 裏ですか表ですか.
— *vt.* ... o bi⌈koo suru ...を尾行する Ⓘ: tail a suspect (*yoogisha o bikoo suru*) 容疑者を尾行する.

tailor *n.* yo⌈ofuku-ya 洋服屋; te⌉eraa テーラー: a tailor's shop (*shiñshi-fuku-teñ*) 紳士服店.
— *vt.* ... o shi⌈tate⌉ru ...を仕立てる Ⓥ: His suit is well tailored. (*Kare no fuku wa shitate ga ii.*) 彼の服は仕立てがいい.

tailor-made *adj.* chu⌈umoñ ni yoru 注文による; a⌈tsurae no あつらえの: a tailor-made suit (*atsurae no suutsu*) あつらえのスーツ.

take *vt.* **1** (carry) ... o mo⌈tte iku ...を持って行く Ⓒ; tsu⌈rete iku 連れていく Ⓒ: Please take this baggage to the taxi stand. (*Kono nimotsu o takushii noriba made motte itte kudasai.*) この荷物をタクシー乗り場まで持って行ってください. / Please take me to the hospital. (*Byooiñ e tsurete itte kudasai.*) 病院へ連れて行ってください.
2 (hold) ... o mo⌉tsu ...を持つ Ⓒ; to⌉ru 取る Ⓒ: She took his hand and helped him across the road. (*Kanojo wa kare no te o totte dooro o wataraseta.*) 彼女は彼の手を取って道路を渡らせた.
3 (need) ... o hi⌈tsuyoo to suru ...を必要とする Ⓘ; (of time) ... ga ka⌈ka⌉ru ...がかかる Ⓒ: This task took two hours. (*Kono shigoto wa ni-jikañ kakatta.*) この仕事は2時間かかった. / How long does it take to go to the airport by taxi? (*Kuukoo made takushii de dono kurai kakari-masu ka?*) 空港までタクシーでどのくらいかかりますか.
4 (use) ... o ri⌈yoo suru ...を利用する Ⓘ: I take a bus to school. (*Gakkoo e wa basu o riyoo shite imasu.*) 学校へはバスを利用しています.
5 (do) ... o su⌈ru ...をする Ⓘ: take a bath (*nyuuyoku suru*) 入浴する / take a walk (*sañpo o suru*) 散歩をする / take good care of a pet (*petto no sewa o yoku suru*) ペットの世話をよくする.
6 (record) ... o to⌉ru ...をとる Ⓒ: take notes (*memo o toru*) メモをとる / May I take your picture? (*Anata no shashiñ o totte mo ii desu ka?*) あなたの写真を撮ってもいいですか.
7 (occupy) ... o to⌉ru ...をとる Ⓒ; shi⌈me⌉ru 占める Ⓥ: This desk takes too much space. (*Kono tsukue wa basho o tori-sugiru.*) この机は場所をとりすぎる. / Is this seat taken? (*Kono seki wa fusagatte imasu ka?*) この席はふさがっていますか.
8 (choose; buy) ... o e⌈ra⌉bu ...を選ぶ; ... ni su⌈ru ...にする Ⓘ: OK. I'll take this. (*Wakarimashita. Kore ni shimasu.*) わかりました. これにします.
9 (consume) ... o ta⌈be⌉ru ...を食べる Ⓥ; no⌉mu 飲む Ⓒ: How many times a day should I take this medicine? (*Kono kusuri wa ichi-nichi ni nañ-kai nomu no desu ka?*) この薬は一日に何回飲むのですか. / Do you take sugar in your tea? (*Koocha ni satoo o iremasu ka?*) 紅茶に砂糖を入れますか.
10 (consider) ... o (... to) to⌉ru ...を(...と)とる Ⓒ; u⌈ketomeru 受け止める Ⓥ: Don't take my joke as for an insult. (*Joodañ o waruguchi to toranaide kudasai.*) 冗談を悪口ととらないでください. / He doesn't take what I say seriously. (*Kare wa watashi no iu koto o shiñkeñ ni uketomenai.*) 彼は私の言うことを真剣に受け止めない.
11 (assume) ... o hi⌈kiuke⌉ru ...を引き受ける Ⓥ; to⌉ru とる Ⓒ: take a job of baby-sitting (*komori o hikiukeru*) 子守を引き受ける / take responsibility (*sekiniñ o toru*) 責任をとる.
12 (accept) ... o u⌈keireru ...を受け入れる Ⓥ; o⌈u 負う Ⓒ: take advice (*chuukoku o ukeireru*) 忠告を受け入れる / take the blame (*seme o ou*) 責めを負う.
13 (measure) ... o ha⌈ka⌉ru ...を測る

t

[C]: A nurse took my temperature. (*Kañgofu ga watashi no taioñ o hakatta.*) 看護婦が私の体温を測った.
14 (feel) ... o mo˥tsu ...を持つ [C]; i˥da˥ku 抱く [C]: She takes no interest in my offer. (*Kanojo wa watashi no mooshide ni mattaku kyoomi o motte inai.*) 彼女は私の申し出に全く興味を持っていない.
take off *vt.* **1** (remove) ... o nu˥gu ...を脱ぐ [C]: take off one's shoes (*kutsu o nugu*) 靴を脱ぐ.
2 (have holidays) ya˥sumi˥ o toru 休みをとる [C]: I took yesterday off. (*Kinoo wa yasumi o totta.*) きのうは休みをとった.
— *vi.* (of an aircraft) ri˥riku suru 離陸する [I].
take out *vt.* **1** (go out with) ... o tsu˥reda˥su ...を連れ出す [C]: I took her out for a meal. (*Kanojo o shokuji ni tsurete itta.*) 彼女を食事に連れて行った.
2 (remove) ... o to˥ridasu ...を取り出す [C]: take a book out of a bag (*hoñ o kabañ kara toridasu*) 本をカバンから取り出す.
take up *vt.* (start doing) ... o ha˥jimeru ...を始める [V]: take up golf (*gorufu o hajimeru*) ゴルフを始める.

takeoff *n.* ri˥riku 離陸.

tale *n.* **1** (story) ha˥nashi˥ 話; mo˥noga˥tari 物語: a fairy tale (*otogibanashi*) おとぎ話.
2 (lie) tsu˥kuri-ba˥nashi 作り話.

talent *n.* sa˥inoo 才能: She has a talent for music [drawing]. (*Kanojo ni wa oñgaku* [*e*] *no sainoo ga aru.*) 彼女には音楽[絵]の才能がある. ★ In Japan, a 'TV personality' is called '(*terebi*) *tareñto*' (テレビ)タレント, literally '(TV) talent.'

talk *vi.* ha˥na˥su 話す [C]; ha˥nashi˥ o suru 話をする [I]: He is going to talk about the political reform tonight. (*Koñbañ kare wa seeji-kaikaku ni tsuite hanashimasu.*) 今晩彼は政治改革について話します.
— *vt.* ... no ko˥to˥ o ha˥na˥su ...のことを話す [C]: talk music (*oñgaku no koto o hanasu*) 音楽のことを話す.
— *n.* **1** (conversation) ha˥nashi˥ 話; ha˥nashiai 話し合い: I had a long talk about the matter with him. (*Sono koto ni tsuite kare to nagaku hanashiatta.*) そのことについて彼と長く話し合った.
2 (conference) ka˥idañ 会談; kyo˥ogi 協議: high-level talks (*kookañ ni yoru kyoogi*) 高官による協議.

talkative *adj.* ha˥nashizuki na 話好きな; o˥sha˥beri na おしゃべりな: a talkative person (*oshaberi na hito*) おしゃべりな人.

tall *adj.* **1** (high) ta˥ka˥i 高い; (of a person) se˥ ga ta˥ka˥i 背が高い: a tall building (*takai biru*) 高いビル / a tall man (*se no takai hito*) 背の高い人 / "How tall are you?" "I'm 170 centimeters tall." ("*Shiñchoo wa dono kurai desu ka?*" "*Hyaku nanajus-señchi desu.*") 「身長はどのくらいですか」「170 センチです」
2 (unreasonable) shi˥ñjirare˥nai 信じられない: a tall story (*shiñjirarenai hanashi*) 信じられない話.

tame *adj.* **1** (not wild) ka˥inarasa˥reta 飼いならされた; ka˥inarasa˥rete iru: a tame animal (*kainarasareta doobutsu*) 飼いならされた動物.
2 (unexciting) tsu˥mara˥nai つまらない; ta˥ñchoo na 単調な: a tame job (*tañchoo na shigoto*) 単調な仕事.
— *vt.* (train) ... o ka˥inara˥su ...を飼いならす [C]; (control) o˥moido˥ori ni suru 思い通りにする [I]: tame a bear (*kuma o narasu*) 熊をならす.

tan *n.* hi˥yake 日焼け: get a tan (*hiyake suru*) 日焼けする.
— *vt.* (expose to the sun) ... o hi˥yake saseru ...を日焼けさせる [V]: He is deeply tanned. (*Kare wa hidoku hiyake shite iru.*) 彼はひどく日焼けしている.
— *vi.* hi ˥ni yakeru 日に焼ける [V]: I tan easily. (*Watashi wa sugu hi ni yakeru.*) 私はすぐ日に焼ける.

tangle *vt.* ... o mo˥tsure saseru ...をもつれさせる [V]; ka˥ramase˥ru 絡ませる [V]: Your hair is tangled. (*Kami*

t

no ke ga motsurete imasu yo.) 髪の毛がもつれていますよ.

tank *n.* **1** (container) ta⌉ñku タンク: a water [fish] tank (*suisoo*) 水槽. **2** (military vehicle) se⌉ñsha 戦車.

tanker *n.* (ship) ta⌉ñkaa タンカー; (truck) ta⌈ñku ro⌉orii タンクローリー.

tap *vt.* (hit gently) ... o ka⌈ruku ta-ta⌉ku ...を軽くたたく [C]; (beat repeatedly) ko⌉tsukotsu to ta⌈ta⌉ku こつこつとたたく [C]: He tapped me on the shoulder. (*Kare wa watashi no kata o poñ to tataita.*) 彼は私の肩をポンとたたいた.
— *n.* (water-controlling handle) ja⌈guchi 蛇口; (for gas, etc.) se⌉ñ 栓: turn the tap on [off] (*jaguchi o akeru* [*shimeru*]) 蛇口を開ける[締める].

tape *n.* **1** (strip) te⌉epu テープ; hi⌈mo ひも: bind a parcel with tape (*tsutsumi o teepu de shibaru*) 包みをテープで縛る.
2 (of a cassette) ka⌈setto te⌉epu カセットテープ; (of a video) bi⌈deo te⌉epu ビデオテープ: play a tape (*teepu o kakeru*) テープをかける / rewind [fast-forward] a tape (*teepu o maki-modosu* [*hayaokuri suru*]) テープを巻き戻す[早送りする].
3 (sticky tape) ne⌈ñchaku te⌉epu 粘着テープ: insulating tape (*zetsueñ teepu*) 絶縁テープ.
— *vt.* (record on cassette) ... o ro⌈kuoñ suru ...を録音する [I]; (on video) ro⌈kuga suru 録画する [I]: record TV programs (*terebi-bañgumi o rokuga suru*) テレビ番組を録画する.

tape recorder *n.* te⌈epu reko⌉o-daa テープレコーダー.

tar *n.* ta⌉aru タール.

target *n.* **1** (mark) ma⌈to 的; hyo⌈oteki 標的: The missile hit the target. (*Misairu wa hyooteki ni meechuu shita.*) ミサイルは標的に命中した.
2 (objective) mo⌈kuhyoo 目標; (numerical) mo⌈kuhyo⌉ochi 目標値; (monetary) mo⌈kuhyo⌉ogaku 目標額: set a target (*mokuhyoochi o settee suru*) 目標値を設定する.

task *n.* shi⌈goto 仕事: I was assigned a difficult task. (*Watashi wa yakkai na shigoto o waria-terareta.*) 私は厄介な仕事を割り当てられた.

taste *n.* **1** (flavor) a⌈ji 味: This orange has a sweet taste. (*Kono oreñji wa amai.*) このオレンジは甘い.
2 (sense) mi⌈kaku 味覚: This herb is bitter to the taste. (*Kono haabu wa aji ga nigai.*) このハーブは味が苦い.
3 (appreciation) se⌉ñsu センス: She has excellent taste in clothes. (*Kanojo wa fuku no señsu ga totemo ii.*) 彼女は服のセンスがとてもいい.
4 (liking) ko⌉nomi 好み; shu⌉mi 趣味: It's a matter of taste. (*Sore wa konomi no moñdai desu.*) それは好みの問題です. / This music isn't to my taste. (*Kono oñgaku wa watashi no shumi ni awanai.*) この音楽は私の趣味に合わない.
— *vi.* (have a flavor) ... no a⌈ji ga suru ...の味がする [I]: This soup tastes of garlic. (*Kono suupu wa niñniku no aji ga suru.*) このスープはにんにくの味がする.
— *vt.* **1** (test) ... no a⌈ji o mi⌉ru ...の味を見る [V]: She tasted the soup. (*Kanojo wa sono suupu no aji o mita.*) 彼女はそのスープの味を見た.
2 (experience) ... o a⌈jiwa⌉u ...を味わう [C]: taste the bitterness of defeat (*haiboku no kurushimi o aji-wau*) 敗北の苦しみを味わう.

tax *n.* ze⌉e 税; ze⌈ekiñ 税金: an income tax (*shotoku-zee*) 所得税 / collect taxes (*zeekiñ o chooshuu suru*) 税金を徴収する / Does this include tax and service? (*Kore wa zee to saabisuryoo komi desu ka?*) これは税とサービス料込みですか.
— *vt.* ... ni ze⌈ekiñ o ka⌈ke⌉ru ...に税金をかける [V]; ka⌈zee suru 課税する [I]: Alcohol is heavily taxed. (*Sake ni wa omoi zeekiñ ga kakerarete iru.*) 酒には重い税金がかけられている.

tax-free *adj.* me⌈ñzee no 免税の;

mu˥zee no 無税の: Do they sell tax-free goods on board? (*Meñzee-hiñ wa kinai de hañbai shite imasu ka?*) 免税品は機内で販売していますか.
— *adv.* me⌈ñzee de 免税で: Can I buy it tax-free? (*Sore wa meñzee de kaemasu ka?*) それは免税で買えますか.

taxi *n.* ta˥kushii タクシー: Please call a taxi for me. (*Takushii o yoñde kudasai.*) タクシーを呼んでください. / Where can I catch a taxi? (*Takushii ni wa doko de noremasu ka?*) タクシーにはどこで乗れますか.

taxi stand *n.* ta⌈kushii no˥riba タクシー乗り場: Where is the taxi stand? (*Takushii noriba wa doko ni arimasu ka?*) タクシー乗り場はどこにありますか.

taxpayer *n.* no⌈oze˥esha 納税者.

tea *n.* o-⌈cha お茶; ti˥i ティー: black tea (*koocha*) 紅茶 / green tea (*ryokucha*) 緑茶 / strong [weak] tea (*koi [usui] o-cha*) 濃い[薄い]お茶 / make tea (*o-cha o ireru*) お茶を入れる.

teach *vt.* ... o o⌈shieru ...を教える [V]: He teaches English to junior high school students. (*Kare wa chuugakusee ni Eego o oshiete imasu.*) 彼は中学生に英語を教えています. / She taught me how to swim. (*Kanojo ga watashi ni oyogikata o oshiete kureta.*) 彼女が私に泳ぎ方を教えてくれた.
— *vi.* o⌈shieru 教える [V]: He teaches at senior high school. (*Kare wa kookoo de oshiete imasu.*) 彼は高校で教えています.

teacher *n.* se⌈ñse˥e 先生; [formal] kyo˥oshi 教師: a teacher of mathematics (*suugaku no señsee*) 数学の先生.

teaching *n.* **1** (art or job) o⌈shieru koto˥ 教えること: go into teaching (*kyooshoku ni tsuku*) 教職に就く.
2 (beliefs) o⌈shie 教え: the teachings of Gandhi (*Gañjii no oshie*) ガンジーの教え.

team *n.* **1** (of sports) chi˥imu チーム; -bu 部: What is your favorite professional baseball team? (*Anata no suki na puro yakyuu no chiimu wa doko desu ka?*) あなたの好きなプロ野球のチームはどこですか. / He is on the tennis team. (*Kare wa tenisu-bu no ichiiñ desu.*) 彼はテニス部の一員です.
2 (group) -dañ 団; -hañ 班: a team of medical doctors (*ishi-dañ*) 医師団.

tear[1] *vt.* **1** (pull apart) ... o ya⌈bu˥ru ...を破る [C]: I have torn my shirt on a nail. (*Watashi wa shatsu o kugi ni hikkakete yabuite shimatta.*) 私はシャツをくぎに引っ掛けて破いてしまった.
2 (remove) ... o ha⌈gito˥ru ...をはぎ取る [C]; ya⌈burito˥ru 破り取る [C]: tear a poster off a wall (*kabe kara posutaa o hagitoru*) 壁からポスターをはぎ取る / He tore the page out of the book. (*Kare wa hoñ kara sono peeji o yaburitotta.*) 彼は本からそのページを破り取った.
— *vi.* ya⌈bure˥ru 破れる [V]: This fabric does not tear easily. (*Kono kiji wa kañtañ ni yaburenai.*) この生地は簡単に破れない.
tear down *vt.* ... o to⌈rikowa˥su ...を取り壊す [C]: tear down an old house (*furui ie o torikowasu*) 古い家を取り壊す.
— *n.* ya⌈bureme 破れ目; (of clothes) ka⌈gizaki かぎ裂き: mend a tear (*kagizaki o tsukurou*) かぎ裂きを繕う.

tear[2] *n.* na˥mida 涙: wipe one's tears (*namida o nuguu*) 涙をぬぐう / hold back one's tears (*namida o koraeru*) 涙をこらえる / Tears streamed down his cheeks. (*Namida ga kare no hoo o tsutatta.*) 涙が彼のほおを伝った.

tease *vt.* ... o ka⌈raka˥u ...をからかう [C]: They teased him about his new hairdo. (*Kare-ra wa kare no atarashii kamigata o karakatta.*) 彼らは彼の新しい髪型をからかった.

t

teaspoon *n.* ko⌈saji 小さじ; cha⌈saji 茶さじ.

technical *adj.* **1** (of technique) gi⌈jutsujoo no 技術上の; gi⌈jutsu-teki na 技術的な: technical cooperation (*gijutsu teekee*) 技術提携.
2 (special) se⌈ñmoñ-teki na 専門的な: technical knowledge (*señmoñ chishiki*) 専門知識 / technical terms (*señmoñ yoogo*) 専門用語.

technician *n.* (skilled worker) gi⌈jutsu⌉sha 技術者; gi⌉shi 技師; (specialist) se⌈ñmoñka 専門家: an electrical technician (*deñki gishi*) 電気技師.

technique *n.* **1** (skill) gi⌉jutsu 技術; te⌉kunikku テクニック: improve one's technique (*gijutsu o takameru*) 技術を高める / That pianist has an excellent technique. (*Ano pianisuto wa tekunikku ga subarashii.*) あのピアニストはテクニックがすばらしい.
2 (method) ho⌈ohoo 方法: teaching techniques (*kyoojuhoo*) 教授法.

technological *adj.* ka⌈gakugi⌉jutsu no 科学技術の; gi⌈jutsu-teki na 技術的な: technological advances (*kagakugijutsu no hattatsu*) 科学技術の発達 / a highly technological problem (*kiwamete gijutsu-teki na moñdai*) きわめて技術的な問題.

technology *n.* ka⌈gakugi⌉jutsu 科学技術; te⌈kuno⌉rojii テクノロジー: high technology (*señtañ gijutsu*) 先端技術 / an institute of technology (*kooka [koogyoo] daigaku*) 工科[工業]大学.

t

tedious *adj.* ta⌈ikutsu na 退屈な; tsu⌈mara⌉nai つまらない: a tedious lecture (*taikutsu na koogi*) 退屈な講義.

teenager *n.* ti⌈iñe⌉ejaa ティーンエージャー; ju⌉udai no wa⌈kamono 十代の若者.

teens *n.* ju⌉udai 十代: He is in his early [late] teens. (*Kare wa juudai zeñhañ [koohañ] desu.*) 彼は十代前半[後半]です.

telegram *n.* de⌈ñpoo 電報: Send this telegram, please. (*Kono deñpoo o utte kudasai.*) この電報を打ってください. / an urgent telegram (*shikyuu deñpoo*) 至急電報 / a telegram of congratulations [condolence] (*shukudeñ [choodeñ]*) 祝電[弔電].

telegraph *n.* de⌈ñshiñ 電信; de⌈ñpoo 電報: a telegraph office (*deñpookyoku*) 電報局.
— *vt.* ... ni de⌈ñpoo o u⌉tsu …に電報を打つ Ⓒ: His parents telegraphed him to come home immediately. (*Kare no ryooshiñ wa kare ni sugu kaeru yoo ni deñpoo o utta.*) 彼の両親は彼にすぐ帰るように電報を打った.

telephone *n.* de⌈ñwa 電話; (machine) de⌈ñwa⌉ki 電話機: a public telephone (*kooshuu deñwa*) 公衆電話 / make a telephone call (*deñwa o kakeru*) 電話をかける / answer the telephone (*deñwa ni deru*) 電話に出る / install a telephone (*deñwa o hiku*) 電話を引く / Can I use your telephone? (*Deñwa o karite mo ii desu ka?*) 電話を借りてもいいですか.
— *vt.* ... ni de⌈ñwa o kake⌉ru …に電話をかける Ⓥ: I telephoned her that I couldn't make it. (*Watashi wa kanojo ni ikenaku natta to deñwa shita.*) 私は彼女に行けなくなったと電話した.
— *vi.* de⌈ñwa o kake⌉ru 電話をかける Ⓥ: I telephoned for a taxi. (*Watashi wa deñwa o kakete takushii o yoñda.*) 私は電話をかけてタクシーを呼んだ.

telephone directory *n.* de⌈ñwachoo 電話帳.

telephone number *n.* de⌈ñwaba⌉ñgoo 電話番号: What is your telephone number? (*Deñwa-bañgoo wa nañ-bañ desu ka?*) 電話番号は何番ですか. / Give me your telephone number. (*Deñwa-bañgoo o oshiete kudasai.*) 電話番号を教えてください.

telescope *n.* bo⌈oeñkyoo 望遠鏡:

look at stars through a telescope (*booeñkyoo de hoshi o miru*) 望遠鏡で星を見る / an astronomical telescope (*teñtai-booeñkyoo*) 天体望遠鏡.

television *n.* te⌉rebi テレビ: turn on [off] the television (*terebi o tsukeru* [*kesu*]) テレビをつける[消す] / I watched the game on television. (*Watashi wa sono shiai o terebi de mimashita.*) 私はその試合をテレビで見ました.

tell *vt.* **1** (say) ... o i⌈u ...を言う Ⓒ; (talk) ha⌈na⌉su 話す Ⓒ: tell a lie (*uso o tsuku*) うそをつく / Tell me about your experiences in Africa. (*Afurika de no keekeñ ni tsuite hanashite kudasai.*) アフリカでの経験について話してください.
2 (inform) ... ni (... o) o⌈shieru ...に(...を)教える Ⓥ; tsu⌈taeru 伝える Ⓥ: Please tell me the way to the station. (*Eki e iku michi o oshiete kudasai.*) 駅へ行く道を教えてください. / Please tell him to call me. (*Kare ni deñwa suru yoo tsutaete kudasai.*) 彼に電話するよう伝えてください.
3 (order) ... ni (... to) me⌈ejiru ...に(...と)命じる Ⓥ; i⌈u 言う Ⓒ: I told him not to be late again. (*Kare ni nido to chikoku suru na to itta.*) 彼に二度と遅刻するなと言った.
4 (know) ... ga [wa] wa⌈ka⌉ru ...が[は]わかる Ⓒ: Nobody can tell the truth. (*Dare ni mo sono shiñsoo wa wakaranai.*) だれにもその真相はわからない.
— *vi.* ha⌈na⌉su 話す Ⓒ; i⌈u 言う Ⓒ: He told about his strange experience. (*Kare wa jibuñ no fushigi na taikeñ ni tsuite hanashita.*) 彼は自分の不思議な体験について話した.

temper *n.* **1** (mood) ki⌈geñ 機嫌; (nature) ki⌈shoo 気性: He is in a good [bad] temper. (*Kare wa kigeñ ga ii* [*warui*].) きげんがいい[悪い]. / He has a quick temper. (*Kare wa kishoo ga hageshii.*) 彼は気性が激しい.
2 (rage) ka⌈ñshaku かんしゃく: He is in a temper. (*Kare wa kañshaku o okoshite iru.*) 彼はかんしゃくを起こしている.

temperance *n.* **1** (self-control) se⌈ssee 節制; ji⌈see 自制: temperance in eating and drinking (*iñshoku no sessee*) 飲食の節制.
2 (the taking of no alcohol) ki⌈ñshu 禁酒.

temperate *adj.* **1** (of climate) o⌈ñdañ na 温暖な: a temperate climate (*oñdañ na kikoo*) 温暖な気候.
2 (of a person) o⌈da⌉yaka na 穏やかな: a temperate disposition (*odayaka na seekaku*) 穏やかな性格.

temperature *n.* **1** (of atmosphere) ki⌈oñ 気温: The average temperature of Tokyo is about 15°C. (*Tookyoo no heekiñ kioñ wa sesshi juugo-do gurai desu.*) 東京の平均気温は摂氏 15 度ぐらいです.
2 (of a person) ta⌉ioñ 体温: My temperature went up [came down]. (*Taioñ ga agatta* [*sagatta*].) 体温が上がった[下がった].

tempest *n.* o⌈oa⌉rashi 大嵐; bo⌈ofu⌉u-u 暴風雨.

temple[1] *n.* (of a god) shi⌈ñdeñ 神殿; (in Buddhism) ji⌉iñ 寺院; te⌈ra 寺; -ji 寺. ★ Used at the end of the name of a temple: Horyuji Temple (*Hooryuuji*) 法隆寺.

temple[2] *n.* (parts of a head) ko⌈mekami こめかみ.

temporarily *adv.* i⌈chiji-teki ni 一時的に; ka⌈ri ni 仮に: The shop is temporarily closed. (*Sono mise wa ichiji-teki ni shimatte imasu.*) その店は一時的に閉まっています.

temporary *adj.* i⌈chiji-teki na 一時的な; ka⌈ri no 仮の; ri⌈ñji no 臨時の: a temporary place of refuge (*riñji no hinañjo*) 臨時の避難所 / The economic recovery was only temporary. (*Keezai no kaifuku wa hoñno ichiji-teki na mono datta.*) 経済の回復はほんの一時的なものだった.

tempt *vt.* **1** (try to persuade) ... o yu⌈uwaku shiyo⌉o to suru ...を誘惑しようとする Ⓘ: He tempted me with

money. (*Kare wa watashi o okane de yuuwaku shiyoo to shita.*) 彼は私をお金で誘惑しようとした.
2 (attract) ... o sa⌈sou ...を誘う Ⓒ; su⌈ru ki ni saseru する気にさせる Ⓥ: The beautiful weather tempted me to go out. (*Seeteñ ni sasowarete watashi wa soto ni deta.*) 晴天に誘われて私は外に出た.

temptation *n.* **1** (tempting) yu⌈uwaku 誘惑: resist [succumb to] temptation (*yuuwaku ni makenai* [*kussuru*]) 誘惑に負けない[屈する].
2 (thing that tempts) yu⌈uwaku⌉butsu 誘惑物: Big cities provide many temptations. (*Dai-tokai wa yuuwakubutsu ga ooi.*) 大都会は誘惑物が多い.

ten *pron.* to⌉o [ju⌉u] 十; (people) ju⌉u-niñ 10人; (things) ju⌉k-ko 10個.
— *n.* (figure) ju⌉u 10; (hour) ju⌉u-ji 10時; (minute) ju⌉p-puñ 10分; (age) ju⌉s-sai 10歳.
— *adj.* ju⌉u no 10の; (people) ju⌉u-niñ no 10人の; (things) ju⌉k-ko no 10個の; (age) ju⌉s-sai no 10歳の.

ten thousand *n.* ma⌉ñ 万.

tenacious *adj.* ko⌈shitsu suru 固執する; ne⌈barizuyo⌉i 粘り強い: He was tenacious of his rights. (*Kare wa jibuñ no keñri ni koshitsu shita.*) 彼は自分の権利に固執した.

tenant *n.* (of a house) sha⌈kuyaniñ 借家人; (of land) sha⌈kuchiniñ 借地人; (of a building) te⌈nañto テナント.

tend *vi.* ... ke⌈ekoo ni a⌉ru ...傾向にある Ⓒ; <verb>-gachi da ...がちだ: Prices are tending to go up. (*Bukka wa agaru keekoo ni aru.*) 物価は上がる傾向にある. / He tends to be late. (*Kare wa okure-gachi da.*) 彼は遅れがちだ.

tendency *n.* ke⌈ekoo 傾向: Unemployment is showing a tendency to increase. (*Shitsugyooritsu wa zooka no keekoo o shimeshite iru.*) 失業率は増加の傾向を示している.

tender[1] *adj.* **1** (soft) ya⌈waraka⌉i 柔らかい: a tender steak (*yawarakai suteeki*) 柔らかいステーキ.
2 (kind) ya⌈sashii 優しい; o⌈moiyari no a⌉ru 思いやりのある: He was tender to me. (*Kare wa watashi ni yasashikatta.*) 彼は私に優しかった. / She has a tender heart. (*Kanojo wa omoiyari ga aru.*) 彼女は思いやりがある.
3 (sore) sa⌈waru to ita⌉i 触ると痛い: The bruise is still tender. (*Uchimi wa sawaru to mada itai.*) 打ち身は触るとまだ痛い.

tender[2] *vt.* ... o te⌈eshutsu suru ...を提出する Ⓘ: tender a resignation (*jihyoo o teeshutsu suru*) 辞表を提出する.

tennis *n.* te⌉nisu テニス: play tennis (*tenisu o suru*) テニスをする.

tense *adj.* **1** (tightly stretched) pi⌉ñ to ha⌈tta [ha⌈tte iru] ぴんと張った[張っている]: a tense rope (*piñ to hatta roopu*) ぴんと張ったロープ.
2 (nervous) ki⌈ñchoo shita [shite iru] 緊張した[している]; ha⌈ritsu⌉meta 張りつめた; ha⌈ritsumete iru 張りつめている: a tense situation (*haritsumeta joosee*) 張りつめた情勢.

tension *n.* **1** (being tense) ha⌈ri 張り; ha⌈ritsume⌉ru ko⌈to⌉ 張りつめること: lessen the tension of a net (*netto no hari o yurumeru*) ネットの張りを緩める.
2 (mental strain) ki⌈ñchoo 緊張: She was under extreme tension. (*Kanojo wa kyokudo ni kiñchoo shite ita.*) 彼女は極度に緊張していた.

tent *n.* te⌉ñto テント: put up [take down] a tent (*teñto o haru* [*tatamu*]) テントを張る[畳む].

tentative *adj.* (not definite) ka⌈ri no 仮の; za⌈ñtee-teki na 暫定的な: a tentative agreement (*kari no gooi*) 仮の合意.

tenth *adj.* ju⌈ubañme⌉ no 10番目の; da⌉i-juu no 第10の.
— *n.* **1** (people) ju⌈ubañme⌉ no hi⌈to⌉ 10番目の人; (things) ju⌈ubañme⌉ no mo⌈no⌉ 10番目のもの.
2 (day) to⌈oka 10日.
3 (fraction) ju⌈u-buñ no ichi⌉ 10分

t

の1.

tepid *adj.* na⌈manuru⌉i なまぬるい: tepid water (*nurumayu*) ぬるま湯.

term *n.* **1** (period) ki⌉kañ 期間; (of an office) ni⌉ñki 任期: a prison term (*keeki*) 刑期 / His term expires next year. (*Kare no niñki wa raineñ de kireru.*) 彼の任期は来年で切れる.

2 (of a school) ga⌈kki 学期: the spring term (*haru no gakki*) 春の学期.

3 (words) se⌈ñmoñ yo⌉ogo 専門用語; (wording) ko⌈tobazu⌉kai 言葉づかい: technical [legal] terms (*señmoñ* [*hooritsu*] *yoogo*) 専門[法律]用語.

4 (conditions) jo⌈oke⌉ñ 条件: the terms of employment (*koyoo jookeñ*) 雇用条件 / I sold my apartment on favorable terms. (*Watashi wa yuuri na jookeñ de mañshoñ o utta.*) 私は有利な条件でマンションを売った.

5 (relationship) a⌈idagara 間柄; ka⌈ñkee 関係: I am on good terms with him. (*Watashi to kare wa naka no yoi aidagara desu.*) 私と彼は仲のよい間柄です.

in terms of ... *prep.* ... no te⌈ñ de ...の点で: In terms of rent this room is much better. (*Yachiñ no teñ de wa kono heya no hoo ga zutto ii.*) 家賃の点ではこの部屋の方がずっといい.

terminal *n.* **1** (of a station) shu⌈uteñ 終点; ta⌉aminaru ターミナル(駅); (of an airport) (e⌈a)ta⌉aminaru (エア)ターミナル.

2 (of an electric circuit) de⌈ñkyoku 電極; (of a computer) ta⌈ñmatsu 端末: the positive [negative] terminal (*purasu* [*mainasu*] *kyoku*) プラス[マイナス]極.

— *adj.* **1** (of a station) shu⌈uteñ no 終点の; ta⌉aminaru no ターミナルの.

2 (of disease) ma⌉kki no 末期の: terminal cancer (*makki gañ*) 末期癌.

terminate *vt.* ... o o⌈waraseru ...を終わらせる Ⓥ; ya⌈meru やめる Ⓥ: terminate a discussion (*hanashiai o yameru*) 話し合いをやめる.

— *vi.* o⌈waru 終わる Ⓒ; to⌈maru 止まる Ⓒ: The meeting terminated at three. (*Kaigi wa sañ-ji ni owatta.*) 会議は3時に終わった.

terrace *n.* (of a house) te⌉rasu テラス; (of land) da⌈ñkyuu 段丘.

terrible *adj.* **1** (bad) hi⌈do⌉i ひどい; hi⌉doku he⌈ta⌉ na ひどくへたな: The weather was terrible. (*Hidoi teñki datta.*) ひどい天気だった. / He is a terrible golfer. (*Kare wa gorufu ga heta da.*) 彼はゴルフがへただ.

2 (fearful) o⌈soroshi⌉i 恐ろしい: a terrible disaster (*osoroshii saigai*) 恐ろしい災害.

terribly *adv.* hi⌉doku ひどく; (very) hi⌈joo ni 非常に: I'm terribly busy today. (*Kyoo wa hidoku isogashii.*) 今日はひどく忙しい. / I'm terribly sorry. (*Hoñtoo ni mooshiwake arimaseñ.*) 本当に申し訳ありません.

terrific *adj.* **1** (wonderful) su⌈barashi⌉i すばらしい: terrific weather (*subarashii teñki*) すばらしい天気.

2 (extreme) mo⌈nosugo⌉i ものすごい: a terrific noise (*monosugoi soo-oñ*) ものすごい騒音.

terrify *vt.* ... o ko⌈wagarase⌉ru ...を怖がらせる Ⓥ; zo⌈tto saseru ぞっとさせる Ⓥ: The passengers were terrified by the turbulence. (*Jookyaku wa rañkiryuu ni zotto shita.*) 乗客は乱気流にぞっとした.

territory *n.* **1** (region) chi⌉iki 地域: an uninhabited territory (*hito no suñde inai chiiki*) 人の住んでいない地域.

2 (the land ruled by a government) ryo⌉odo 領土: This island is Japanese territory. (*Kono shima wa Nihoñ no ryoodo desu.*) この島は日本の領土です.

3 (of knowledge) (se⌈ñmoñ)bu⌉ñya (専門)分野: Accounting is outside my territory. (*Kaikeegaku wa watashi no señmoñgai desu.*) 会計学は私の専門外です.

terror *n.* kyo⌉ofu 恐怖: I couldn't even speak because of terror. (*Kyoofu no amari koe mo denakatta.*) 恐怖のあまり声も出なかった.

test *n.* te⌉suto テスト; shi⌈ke⌉ñ 試験; ke⌉ñsa 検査: take [give] a test (*shikeñ o ukeru [suru]*) 試験を受ける[する] / pass [fail] a test (*shikeñ ni ukaru [ochiru]*) 試験に受かる[落ちる] / a blood [vision] test (*ketsueki [shiryoku] keñsa*) 血液[視力]検査.
— *vt.* ... o te⌉suto suru …をテストする [I]; ke⌉ñsa suru 検査する [I]; shi⌈rabe⌉ru 調べる [V]: I had my eyes tested. (*Watashi wa me o keñsa shite moratta.*) 私は目を検査してもらった.

testify *vi.* (in a court) sho⌈ogeñ suru 証言する [I]: The witness testified for the plaintiff. (*Shooniñ wa geñkoku ni yuuri na shoogeñ o shita.*) 証人は原告に有利な証言をした.
— *vt.* (give evidence) ... to sho⌈ogeñ suru …と証言する [I]; ... no sho⌈oko to na⌉ru …の証拠となる [C]: He testified that he had seen nobody. (*Kare wa dare mo minakatta to shoogeñ shita.*) 彼はだれも見なかったと証言した.

testimony *n.* (statement) sho⌈ogeñ 証言; (evidence) sho⌈oko 証拠: She gave testimony against the accused. (*Kanojo wa hikoku ni furi na shoogeñ o shita.*) 彼女は被告に不利な証言をした.

text *n.* **1** (main part) ho⌉ñbuñ 本文: The text of this book exceeds 200 pages. (*Kono hoñ no hoñbuñ wa nihyaku-peeji o koeru.*) この本の本文は 200 ページを超える. ★ Japanese '*tekisuto*' (text) often means 'textbook.'
2 (original) ge⌈ñbuñ 原文: consult the original text (*geñteñ ni ataru*) 原典に当たる.

textbook *n.* kyo⌈oka⌉sho 教科書; te⌉kisuto テキスト: a Japanese textbook (*Nihoñgo no kyookasho*) 日本語の教科書. ★ 'Textbook' is usually called '*tekisuto*' in Japanese.

textile *n.* o⌈rimono 織物.

than *conj.* ... yo⌉ri mo …よりも; ... no ho⌈ka ni …のほかに: It was hotter than I had expected. (*Omotta yori mo atsukatta.*) 思ったよりも暑かった. / Don't you have any other colors than this? (*Kono hoka ni ta no iro wa nai ñ desu ka?*) このほかに他の色はないんですか.
— *prep.* ... yo⌉ri mo …よりも: He is five years older than me. (*Kare wa watashi yori mo go-sai toshiue desu.*) 彼は私よりも 5 歳年上です.

thank *vt.* ... ni o-⌈ree [re⌈e] o iu …にお礼[礼]を言う [C]; ka⌉ñsha suru 感謝する [I]: I thanked him for the present. (*Watashi wa kare ni okurimono no o-ree o itta.*) 私は彼に贈り物のお礼を言った. / She thanked you for your help. (*Kanojo wa anata no eñjo o kañsha shite imashita.*) 彼女はあなたの援助を感謝していました.

thankful *adj.* ka⌉ñsha shite iru 感謝している; a⌈riga⌉taku o⌈mo⌉u ありがたく思う: I am thankful for my good fortune. (*Watashi wa koouñ o kañsha shite imasu.*) 私は好運を感謝しています.

thanks *int.* a⌈ri⌉gatoo ありがとう; do⌉omo どうも: Thanks a lot. (*Doomo arigatoo.*) どうもありがとう. / Many thanks for a wonderful dinner. (*Oishii yuuhañ o arigatoo gozaimashita.*) おいしい夕飯をありがとうございました. / No, thanks. (*Iya, kekkoo desu.*) いや, 結構です.
— *n.* ka⌉ñsha (no ki⌈mochi) 感謝(の気持ち); o-⌈ree [re⌈e] お礼[礼]: I wrote her a letter of thanks. (*Watashi wa kanojo ni o-ree no tegami o kaita.*) 私は彼女にお礼の手紙を書いた.
thanks to ... *prep.* ... no ta⌈me⌉ ni …のために: Thanks to the bad weather, the match was canceled. (*Akuteñkoo no tame ni shiai wa chuushi ni natta.*) 悪天候のために試合は中止になった.

thank you *int.* **1** [expressing gratitude] a⌈ri⌉gatoo ありがとう; ka⌉ñsha shimasu 感謝します: Thank you very much for everything. (*Iroiro doomo arigatoo gozaimashita.*) いろいろどうもありがとうございました. / Thank you very much for your attention. (*Go-seechoo o kañsha shimasu.*) ご清聴を感謝します. / No, thank you. (*Iie, kekkoo desu.*) いいえ, 結構です.

2 [at the conclusion of a speech] ko⌈re de owarima⌉su これで終わります; i⌉joo desu 以上です.

that[1] *pron.* **1** [something located at some distance from both the speaker and the listener] a⌈re あれ: Give me the same thing as that. (*Are to onaji mono o kudasai.*) あれと同じものを下さい. / Who's that? (*Are wa dare desu ka?*) あれはだれですか.

2 [something located away from the speaker and close to the listener] so⌈re それ: Where can I buy that? (*Sore wa doko de kaemasu ka?*) それはどこで買えますか.

3 (substitute) (... no) so⌈re (…の)それ: The climate here is like that of California. (*Koko no kikoo wa Kariforunia no sore to nite iru.*) ここの気候はカリフォルニアのそれと似ている.

— *adj.* a⌈no あの; so⌈no その: That car is mine. (*Ano [Sono] kuruma wa watashi no desu.*) あの[その]車は私のです. / What is that building? (*Ano tatemono wa nañ desu ka?*) あの建物は何ですか.

— *adv.* so⌈ñna ni そんなに; so⌈re hodo それほど: It's not that bad. (*Sore wa soñna ni waruku arimaseñ.*) それはそんなに悪くありません. / Playing tennis is not that easy. (*Tenisu o suru no wa sore hodo kañtañ ja nai.*) テニスをするのはそれほど簡単じゃない.

that[2] *conj.* ... to i⌈u (koto⌉) …という(こと); to と: The problem is that we are short of money. (*Moñdai wa o-kane ga tarinai to iu koto da.*) 問題はお金が足りないということだ. / I think that you are right. (*Watashi wa anata wa tadashii to omou.*) 私はあなたは正しいと思う.

so that *conj.* ... yo⌉o ni …ように: She got up early so that she could catch the first train. (*Kanojo wa shihatsu ni maniau yoo ni hayaku okita.*) 彼女は始発に間に合うように早く起きた.

so … that a⌈mari ... no de あまり…ので: I was so tired that I went to bed early. (*Amari tsukareta no de hayaku nemashita.*) あまり疲れたので早く寝ました.

that[3] *rel. pron.* ... (to⌈koro⌉ no) …(ところの): This is the picture that I painted. (*Kore ga watashi ga kaita (tokoro no) e desu.*) これが私がかいた(ところの)絵です. ★ The insertion of '*tokoro no*' sounds unnatural, so it is usually omitted.

thaw *vi.* (melt) to⌈ke⌉ru 解ける Ⓥ; (of frozen food) ka⌈itoo suru 解凍する Ⓘ: The snow began to thaw. (*Yuki ga toke-hajimeta.*) 雪が解け始めた. / The frozen meat took one hour to thaw. (*Sono reetoo niku wa kaitoo suru no ni ichi-jikañ kakatta.*) その冷凍肉は解凍するのに1時間かかった.

— *vt.* (melt) ... o to⌈ka⌉su …を解かす Ⓒ; (of frozen food) ka⌈itoo suru 解凍する Ⓘ: thaw out frozen food (*reetoo shokuhiñ o kaitoo suru*) 冷凍食品を解凍する.

— *n.* (of snow) yu⌈kidoke 雪解け.

the[1] *def. art.* **1** [before a noun mentioned previously] so⌈no その: Once there lived a queen. The queen had two daughters. (*Mukashi jo-oo ga suñde ita. (Sono) jo-oo ni wa futari no musume ga ita.*) 昔女王が住んでいた. (その)女王には二人の娘がいた.

2 [before a noun understood] re⌉e no 例の; i⌉tsu-mo no いつもの: Come and meet me at the station. ((*Itsu-mo no) eki e mukae ni kite kudasai.*) (いつもの)駅へ迎えに来てください.

3 [before an adjective] (of people) hi⌈to⌉-tachi 人たち; (of a thing) mo-

t

ˈnoˈ もの: the poor (*mazushii hitotachi*) 貧しい人たち / the beautiful (*utsukushii mono*) 美しいもの.
4 [before a unit] ... taˈñi de ... 単位で: It's cheaper to buy by the dozen. (*Daasu tañi de katta hoo ga yasui.*) ダース単位で買った方が安い.

the[2] *adv.* [used in comparisons] soˈre dake それだけ: With one of us away, the task is all the tougher. (*Hitori inai no de sore dake shigoto ga taiheñ da.*) 一人いないのでそれだけ仕事が大変だ.
the ..., the ... ‹adjective› -ba ... hoˈdo ...ば...ほど: The sooner, the better. (*Hayakereba hayai hodo yoi.*) 早ければ早いほどよい.

theater *n.* geˈkijoo 劇場: a movie theater (*eegakañ*) 映画館.

theatrical *adj.* geˈkijoo no 劇場の; eˈñgeki no 演劇の: a theatrical company (*gekidañ*) 劇団.

theft *n.* nuˈsumiˈ 盗み; [formal] seˈttoˈo 窃盗: commit theft (*nusumi o hataraku*) 盗みを働く.

their *pron.* (people) aˈno hitoˈ-tachi no あの人たちの; kaˈre-ra no 彼らの; (females) kaˈnojo-ra no 彼女らの; (things) soˈre(ˈ-ra) no それ(ら)の: They helped their father's business. (*Kare-ra wa chichioya no shigoto o tetsudatta.*) 彼らは父親の仕事を手伝った.

theirs *pron.* (people) aˈno hitoˈ-tachi no moˈnoˈ あの人たちのもの; kaˈre-ra no moˈnoˈ 彼らのもの; (females) kaˈnojo-ra[-tachi] no moˈnoˈ 彼女ら[たち]のもの: These books are theirs. (*Kono hoñ wa kare-ra no mono desu.*) この本は彼らのものです.

them *pron.* **1** [direct object] (people) aˈno hitoˈ-tachi o あの人たちを; kaˈre-ra[-tachi] o 彼らを; (females) kaˈnojo-ra[-tachi] o 彼女[たち]を; (things) soˈre(ˈ-ra) o それ(ら)を: I visited them yesterday. (*Watashi wa kinoo kare-ra o tazuneta.*) 私はきのう彼らを訪ねた. / We ate them with salt. (*Watashi-tachi wa sore o shio de tabeta.*) 私たちはそれを塩で食べた.
2 [indirect object] (people) aˈno hitoˈ-tachi ni あの人たちに; kaˈre-ra ni 彼らに; (females) kaˈnojo-ra ni 彼女らに; (things) soˈre(ˈ-ra) ni それ(ら)に: Give them the rest. (*Nokori wa kare-ra ni age nasai.*) 残りは彼らにあげなさい.

theme *n.* **1** (subject) daˈimoku 題目; teˈema テーマ; (topic) waˈdai 話題: the theme of an essay (*roñbuñ no teema*) 論文のテーマ.
2 (of music) shuˈdai 主題: a theme song (*shudaika*) 主題歌.

themselves *pron.* **1** [reflexive use] jiˈbuˈñ-tachi jiˈshiñ o [ni] 自分たち自身を[に]; soˈreˈ-ra jiˈtai o [ni] それら自体を[に]: They had to take care of themselves. (*Kare-ra wa jibuñ-tachi jishiñ no sewa o shinakereba naranakatta.*) 彼らは自分たち自身の世話しなければならなかった.
2 [emphatic use] kaˈre-ra jiˈshiñ de 彼ら自身で; jiˈbuˈñ-tachi jiˈshiñ de 自分たち自身で: They did the job themselves. (*Kare-ra wa jibuñ-tachi de sono shigoto o shita.*) 彼らは自分たちでその仕事をした.

then *adv.* **1** (at that time) soˈno toˈki その時; toˈoji 当時: I have not seen her since then. (*Kanojo ni wa sono toki irai atte imaseñ.*) 彼女にはその時以来会っていません. / I was still a student then. (*Watashi wa tooji wa mada gakusee deshita.*) 私は当時はまだ学生でした.
2 (after that) soˈre kara それから: I stayed in Kyoto and then went to Nara. (*Watashi wa Kyooto ni tomari sore kara Nara e itta.*) 私は京都に泊まりそれから奈良へ行った.
3 (in that case) soˈre naˈra それなら: "I don't quite agree." "What do you think we should do, then?" (*"Watashi wa sañsee to iu wake de wa arimaseñ." "Sore nara doo sureba ii to omoimasu ka?"*) 「私は賛成というわけではありません」「それならどうすればいいと思いますか」

theoretical *adj.* riˈroñ-teki na 理

論的な; ri'roñjoo no 理論上の: theoretical linguistics (*riroñ geñgogaku*) 理論言語学.

theory *n.* **1** (general principles) ri'roñ 理論: In theory it is possible but in practice I don't know. (*Riroñ-teki ni wa kanoo desu ga, jissai wa wakarimaseñ.*) 理論的には可能ですが, 実際はわかりません.
2 (idea offered) ga'kusetsu 学説; -roñ 論: the theory of relativity (*sootaisee riroñ*) 相対性理論.

there[1] *adv.* **1** (that place) so'ko ni [e, de] そこに[へ, で]; a'soko ni [e, de] あそこに[へ, で]: Sit there. (*Soko ni suwari nasai.*) そこに座りなさい. / The accident took place there. (*Jiko wa asoko de okotta.*) 事故はあそこで起こった. ★ '*Soko*' refers to a place near the listener and slightly distant from the speaker, and '*asoko*' refers to a place which is some distance away from both the speaker and the listener.
2 (in that respect) so'no teñ de その点で: There I cannot agree with you. (*Sono teñ de watashi wa anata ni dooi dekimaseñ.*) その点で私はあなたに同意できません.
— *int.* ho'ra ほら; so're それ: There, I told you so. (*Hora, watashi ga itta toori deshoo.*) ほら, 私が言ったとおりでしょう.

there[2] **is [are]** *vi.* **1** [with an inanimate subject] ... ga a'ru ...がある Ⓒ: Is there a bookstore near here? (*Kono chikaku ni hoñya wa arimasu ka?*) この近くに本屋はありますか.
2 [with an animate subject] ... ga i'ru ...がいる Ⓥ: How many students are there in your school? (*Anata no gakkoo wa gakusee ga nañ-niñ imasu ka?*) あなたの学校は学生が何人いますか.

thereafter *adv.* so'no go その後: Thereafter we got out of touch. (*Sono go watashi-tachi wa reñraku o toriatte imaseñ.*) その後私たちは連絡を取り合っていません.

thereby *adv.* so're ni yotte それによって: I went on a diet and thereby lost five kilos. (*Daietto o yari, sore ni yotte go-kiro yasemashita.*) ダイエットをやり, それによって 5 キロやせました.

therefore *adv.* so're yue' ni それゆえに; so'ko de そこで; shi'tagatte 従って: It was a rainy day; therefore I didn't go out. (*Sono hi wa amefuri deshita. Soko de watashi wa gaishutsu shimaseñ deshita.*) その日は雨降りでした. そこで私は外出しませんでした.

thermometer *n.* o'ñdokee 温度計; ka'ñdañkee 寒暖計; (clinical) ta'ioñkee 体温計: The thermometer stands at 10°C. (*Oñdokee wa sesshi juu-do o sashite iru.*) 温度計は摂氏 10 度を指している. ★ In Japan the Celsius scale is used.

these *pron.* ko're'-ra これら; ko're これ: These are all my books. (*Kore wa miñna watashi no hoñ desu.*) これはみんな私の本です.
— *adj.* ko're'-ra no これらの; ko'no この: These people are all nice. (*Kono hito-tachi wa mina shiñsetsu desu.*) この人たちは皆親切です.

thesis *n.* ro'ñbuñ 論文: a doctoral thesis (*hakase-roñbuñ*) 博士論文.

they *pron.* **1** (people) a'no hito'-tachi あの人たち; ka're-ra 彼ら; (females) ka'nojo-ra[-tachi] 彼女ら[たち]; (things) so're('-ra) それ(ら); a're あれ: They are tourist. (*Kare-ra wa kañkookyaku desu.*) 彼らは観光客です. / What are they? (*Sore wa nañ desu ka?*) それは何ですか.
2 (generic) ★ In Japanese, it is omitted: Do they carry cigarettes at that store? (*Asoko no mise de wa tabako o utte imasu ka?*) あそこの店ではたばこを売っていますか. / They say there will be a wet spell. (*Ame no hi ga tsuzuku to iu koto desu.*) 雨の日が続くということです.

thick *adj.* **1** (not thin) a'tsui 厚い; a'tsusa ga ... a'ru 厚さが...ある: a thick book (*atsui hoñ*) 厚い本 / The ice was two centimeters thick. (*Koori wa atsusa ga ni-señchi atta.*)

氷は厚さが2センチあった.
2 (great in diameter) fu⌈to⌉i 太い: thick neck [tree-trunk] (*futoi kubi* [*miki*]) 太い首[幹].
3 (dense) mi⌉tsu na 密な; (of liquid) ko⌉i 濃い: a thick forest (*mitsuriñ*) 密林 / thick soup [fog] (*koi suupu* [*kiri*]) 濃いスープ[霧].

thicken *vt.* **1** (make thick) ... o a⌈tsuku suru ...を厚くする Ⓘ: thicken a wall (*kabe o atsuku suru*) 壁を厚くする.
2 (of liquid) ... o ko⌉ku suru ...を濃くする Ⓘ: thicken soup (*suupu o koku suru*) スープを濃くする.
— *vi.* a⌈tsuku na⌉ru 厚くなる Ⓒ; ko⌉ku naru 濃くなる Ⓒ: The clouds are thickening. (*Kumo ga atsuku natte kite iru.*) 雲が厚くなってきている. / The fog is thickening. (*Kiri ga koku natte kite iru.*) 霧が濃くなってきている.

thicket *n.* shi⌈gemi⌉ 茂み; ya⌈bu やぶ: hide in a thicket (*shigemi no naka ni kakureru*) 茂みの中に隠れる.

thickness *n.* a⌈tsusa 厚さ; (of a diameter) fu⌉tosa 太さ: a board with a thickness of two centimeters (*atsusa ni-señchi no ita*) 厚さ2センチの板 / The tree is two meters in thickness. (*Sono ki wa futosa ga ni-meetoru aru.*) その木は太さが2メートルある.

thief *n.* do⌈roboo どろぼう: catch a thief (*doroboo o tsukamaeru*) どろぼうを捕まえる.

thigh *n.* fu⌈tomomo 太もも.

thimble *n.* yu⌈binuki 指ぬき.

thin *adj.* **1** (not thick) u⌈sui 薄い: a thin blanket (*usui moofu*) 薄い毛布.
2 (small in diameter) ho⌈so⌉i 細い: a thin wire (*hosoi harigane*) 細い針金.
3 (not fat) ya⌈seta やせた; ya⌈sete iru やせている: She is thin. (*Kanojo wa yasete iru.*) 彼女はやせている.
4 (not dense) ma⌈bara na まばらな: a thin audience (*mabara na chooshuu*) まばらな聴衆.
5 (watery) u⌈sui 薄い; mi⌈zuppo⌉i 水っぽい: thin soup (*mizuppoi suupu*) 水っぽいスープ.
— *vt.* ... o u⌈sumeru ...を薄める Ⓥ: thin soup (*suupu o usumeru*) スープを薄める.
— *vi.* u⌈suku na⌉ru 薄くなる Ⓒ: I'm thinning on top. (*Kami ga usuku natte kite iru.*) 髪が薄くなってきている.

thing *n.* **1** (object) mo⌈no⌉ 物: There are a lot of things on the desk. (*Tsukue no ue ni wa iroiro na mono ga aru.*) 机の上にはいろいろな物がある.
2 (matter) ko⌈to⌉ こと: I have a lot of things to do. (*Shinakereba naranai koto ga takusañ aru.*) しなければならないことがたくさんある.
3 (belongings) mo⌈chi⌉mono 持ち物; sho⌈jihiñ 所持品: pack one's things (*shojihiñ o matomeru*) 所持品をまとめる.
4 (circumstances) jo⌈okyoo 状況; ji⌈joo 事情: Things are getting better. (*Jookyoo wa yoku natte kite imasu.*) 状況はよくなってきています.
5 (event) mo⌈no⌉goto 物事; ko⌈to⌉ 事: A strange thing happened. (*Fushigi na koto ga okotta.*) 不思議な事が起こった.

think *vt.* **1** (form in the mind) ... to o⌈mo⌉u ...と思う Ⓒ: What do you think of Tokyo? (*Tookyoo o doo omoimasu ka?*) 東京をどう思いますか. / I don't think she will come. (*Kanojo ga kuru to wa omoimaseñ.*) 彼女が来るとは思いません.
2 (consider) ... to ka⌈ñga⌉eru ...と考える Ⓥ: I am thinking what to do next. (*Tsugi ni nani o shiyoo ka to kañgaete iru tokoro desu.*) 次に何をしようかと考えているところです.
— *vi.* **1** (have in the mind) ka⌈ñga⌉eru 考える Ⓥ: I'm still thinking. (*Mada kañgae-chuu desu.*) まだ考え中です.
2 (consider) yo⌉ku ka⌈ñga⌉eru よく考える Ⓥ: We have to think hard about the problem. (*Wareware wa sono moñdai ni tsuite yoku kañgaenakereba naranai.*) われわれはその

t

問題についてよく考えなければならない.

think of … *vt.* … o o⌈moitsu⌉ku …を思いつく [C]: I can't think of any good ideas. (*Ii kañgae ga omoi tsukanai.*) いい考えが思いつかない.

third *adj.* sa⌈ñ-bañme⌉ no 3 番目の; da⌉i-sañ no 第 3 の.

— *n.* **1** (people) sa⌈ñ-bañme⌉ no hi⌈to⌉ 3 番目の人; (things) sa⌈ñ-bañme⌉ no mo⌈no⌉ 3 番目のもの.

2 (day) mi⌈kka 三日.

3 (of a fraction) sa⌈ñ-buñ no ichi⌉ 3 分の 1.

— *adv.* sa⌈ñbañme⌉ ni 3 番目に: Nagoya is the third largest city in Japan. (*Nagoya wa Nihoñ de sañbañme ni ooki-na toshi desu.*) 名古屋は日本で 3 番目に大きな都市です.

thirst *n.* **1** (feeling of dryness) no⌉do no ka⌈waki⌉ のどの渇き: quench one's thirst (*nodo no kawaki o iyasu*) のどの渇きをいやす.

2 (desire) ka⌈tsuboo 渇望; yo⌈kuboo 欲望: a thirst for knowledge (*chishikiyoku*) 知識欲.

thirsty *adj.* **1** (suffering from thirst) no⌉do ga ka⌈wa⌉ita [ka⌈wa⌉ite iru] のどが渇いた[渇いている]: I'm thirsty. (*Nodo ga kawaita.*) のどが渇いた.

2 (eager) tsu⌉yoku mo⌈to⌉mete iru 強く求めている: He is thirsty for information. (*Kare wa joohoo o tsuyoku motomete iru.*) 彼は情報を強く求めている.

thirteen *pron.* ju⌉usañ 13; (people) ju⌈usa⌉ñ-niñ 13 人; (things) ju⌈usa⌉ñ-ko 13 個.

— *n.* (figure) ju⌉usañ 13; (hour) ju⌈usa⌉ñ-ji 13 時; (minute) ju⌈usa⌉ñ-puñ 13 分; (age) ju⌈usa⌉ñ-sai 13 歳.

— *adj.* ju⌉usañ no 13 の; (people) ju⌈usa⌉ñ-niñ no 13 人の; (things) ju⌈usa⌉ñ-ko no 13 個の; (age) ju⌈usa⌉ñ-sai no 13 歳の.

thirteenth *adj.* ju⌈usañ-bañme⌉ no 13 番目の; da⌉i-⌈ju⌉usañ no 第 13 の.

— *n.* **1** (people) ju⌈usañ-bañme⌉ no hi⌈to⌉ 13 番目の人; (things) ju⌈usañ-bañme⌉ no mo⌈no⌉ 13 番目のもの.

2 (day) ju⌈usa⌉ñ-nichi 13 日.

3 (fraction) ju⌈usañ-buñ no ichi⌉ 13 分の 1.

thirtieth *adj.* sa⌈ñjuu-bañme⌉ no 30 番目の; da⌉i-⌈sa⌉ñjuu no 第 30 の.

— *n.* **1** (people) sañ⌈juu-bañme⌉ no hi⌈to⌉ 30 番目の人; (things) sa⌈ñjuu-bañme⌉ no mo⌈no⌉ 30 番目のもの.

2 (day) sa⌈ñju⌉u-nichi 30 日.

3 (fraction) sa⌈ñjuu-buñ no ichi⌉ 30 分の 1.

thirty *pron.* sa⌉ñjuu 30; (people) sa⌈ñju⌉u-niñ 30 人; (things) sa⌈ñju⌉k-ko 30 個.

— *n.* (figure) sa⌉ñjuu 30; (minute) sa⌈ñju⌉p-puñ 30 分; (age) sa⌈ñju⌉s-sai 30 歳.

— *adj.* sa⌉ñjuu no 30 の; (people) sa⌈ñju⌉u-niñ no 30 人の; (things) sa⌈ñju⌉k-ko no 30 個の; (age) sa⌈ñjus-sai no 30 歳の.

this *pron.* **1** [something that is closer to the speaker] ko⌈re これ: What's this? (*Kore wa nañ desu ka?*) これは何ですか. / Do you have one like this? (*Kore to onaji mono wa arimasu ka?*) これと同じものはありますか. / I'll take this. (*Kore o kudasai.*) これを下さい.

2 [someone that is closer to the speaker] ko⌈chira こちら: This is my teacher. (*Kochira wa watashi no señsee desu.*) こちらは私の先生です.

3 [something a person is about to describe] ko⌈re これ: This is my first visit to Japan. (*Nihoñ e kita no wa kore ga hajimete desu.*) 日本へ来たのはこれが初めてです.

4 (here) ko⌈ko ここ: This is where I was born. (*Koko ga watashi no umareta tokoro desu.*) ここが私の生まれたところです.

— *adj.* **1** (being the one near) ko⌈no この: This room is 303. (*Kono heya wa sañ maru sañ desu.*) この部屋は 303 です. / This apple is delicious. (*Kono riñgo wa oishii.*) このリンゴはおいしい.

2 (present) ge⌈ñzai no 現在の; ko⌈ñ- 今: this week (*koñ-shuu*) 今週 / (*koñ-getsu*) 今月 / this year (*kotoshi*) ことし / this morning (*kesa*) けさ / this evening (*koñ-bañ*) 今晩.

— *adv.* ko⌈ñna ni こんなに: I didn't expect this many people. (*Koñna ni ooku no hito ga kuru to wa omowanakatta.*) こんなに多くの人が来るとは思わなかった.

thorn *n.* to⌈ge⌉ とげ: get a thorn in one's finger (*yubi ni toge ga sasaru*) 指にとげが刺さる / remove a thorn (*toge o nuku*) とげを抜く.

thorough *adj.* **1** (complete) ka⌈ñzeñ na 完全な; te⌈ttee shita [shite iru] 徹底した[している]: a thorough investigation (*tettee shita choosa*) 徹底した調査.

2 (of a person) ki⌈choome⌉ñ na きちょうめんな: He is thorough in his work. (*Kare wa shigoto ga kichoomeñ da.*) 彼は仕事がきちょうめんだ.

thoroughly *adv.* ka⌈ñzeñ ni 完全に; te⌈tteeteki ni 徹底的に: He searched his room thoroughly for the papers. (*Kare wa sono shorui o motomete heya-juu o tetteeteki ni sagashita.*) 彼はその書類を求めて部屋中を徹底的に捜した.

those *pron.* **1** ko⌈re(⌉-ra) これ(ら); a⌈re(⌉-ra) あれ(ら): Those are all my books. (*Kore wa miñna watashi no hoñ desu.*) これはみんな私の本です. / Those are my children. (*Are wa watashi no kodomo-tachi desu.*) あれは私の子どもたちです.

2 (of people) hi⌈to⌉(-tachi) 人(たち): Those who are interested, raise your hands. (*Kyoomi no aru hito wa te o agete kudasai.*) 興味のある人は手を挙げてください.

— *adj.* so⌈re⌉-ra no それらの; so⌈no その; a⌈re⌉-ra no あれらの; a⌈no あの: Who are those people? (*Ano hito-tachi wa dare desu ka?*) あの人たちはだれですか.

though *conj.* **1** (despite) ke⌉redomo けれども; ... ni mo ka⌈kawa⌉razu にもかかわらず: He went out, though it was raining. (*Ame ga futte ita keredomo kare wa gaishutsu shita.*) 雨が降っていたけれども彼は外出した. / Though she had a high fever, she went to work. (*Kanojo wa koonetsu ga atta ni mo kakawarazu, shigoto ni itta.*) 彼女は高熱があったにもかかわらず, 仕事に行った.

2 (even if) ta⌈toe ... -te[de] mo たとえ…て[で]も: Though you don't feel like it, you have to go. (*Tatoe ki ga susumanakute mo, anata wa ikanakereba narimaseñ.*) たとえ気が進まなくても, あなたは行かなければなりません.

— *adv.* (however) de⌉ mo でも; ya⌈ha⌉ri やはり: The work was hard. I enjoyed it, though. (*Shigoto wa kitsukatta. De mo tanoshikatta.*) 仕事はきつかった. でも楽しかった.

thought *n.* **1** (idea) ka⌈ñga⌉e 考え; (opinion) i⌉keñ 意見: Tell me your thoughts on this matter. (*Kono moñdai ni tsuite anata no ikeñ o kikasete kudasai.*) この問題についてあなたの意見を聞かせてください.

2 (thinking) ka⌈ñgae⌉ru ko⌈to⌉ 考えること; mo⌈noo⌉moi もの思い: I haven't given it enough thought yet. (*Sore ni tsuite wa mada juubuñ ni kañgaete imaseñ.*) それについてはまだ十分に考えていません. / He was deep in thought. (*Kare wa monoomoi ni fukette ita.*) 彼はもの思いにふけっていた.

thoughtful *adj.* **1** (considerate) o⌈moiyari no a⌉ru 思いやりのある; (kind) shi⌉ñsetsu na 親切な: a thoughtful person (*omoiyari no aru hito*) 思いやりのある人 / It is thoughtful of you to do that. (*Soo shite kudasaru no wa go-shiñsetsu na koto desu.*) そうしてくださるのはご親切なことです.

2 (thinking deeply) ka⌈ñgaeko⌉ñde iru 考え込んでいる: She looks thoughtful. (*Kanojo wa kañgae-koñde iru yoo da.*) 彼女は考え込んで

いるようだ.

thoughtless *adj.* ke⌈esotsu na 軽率な; fu⌈chu⌉ui na 不注意な: thoughtless behavior (*keesotsu na furumai*) 軽率な振る舞い.

thousand *n.* se⌉ñ 千: ten thousand (*ichi-mañ*) 1万 / fourteen thousand (*ichi-mañ yoñ-señ*) 1万4千 / a hundred thousand (*juu-mañ*) 10万 / Thousands of people were killed in the earthquake. (*Sono jishiñ de nañ-zeñ to iu hito ga shiñda.*) その地震で何千という人が死んだ.
— *adj.* se⌉ñ no 千の: There are a thousand meters in a kilometer. (*Ichi-kiro wa señ-meetoru desu.*) 1キロは千メートルです.

thread *n.* **1** (string) i⌉to 糸: sew with silk thread (*kinu-ito de nuu*) 絹糸で縫う.
2 (plot) su⌉ji 筋; (course) su⌈ji⌉-michi 筋道: I cannot follow the thread of his story. (*Watashi wa kare no hanashi no suji ni tsuite ikenai.*) 私は彼の話の筋についていけない.
— *vt.* ... ni i⌉to o toosu ...に糸を通す Ⓒ: thread a needle (*hari ni ito o toosu*) 針に糸を通す.

threat *n.* **1** (warning) o⌈doshi 脅し: They carried out their threat to go on strike. (*Kare-ra wa sutoraiki o suru to odoshi o kaketa.*) 彼らはストライキをすると脅しをかけた.
2 (source of danger) kyo⌉oi 脅威: The excessive appreciation of the yen is a threat to the Japanese economy. (*Eñdaka no ikisugi wa Nihoñ keezai ni totte kyooi da.*) 円高の行き過ぎは日本経済にとって脅威だ.

threaten *vt.* **1** (make a threat) ... o o⌈dosu ...を脅す Ⓒ; [formal] kyo⌈ohaku suru 脅迫する Ⓘ: The man threatened me with a knife. (*Sono otoko wa watashi o naifu de odoshita.*) その男は私をナイフで脅した.
2 (give a sign) ⟨verb⟩-so⌉o da ...そうだ: It is threatening to rain. (*Ame ga furi-soo da.*) 雨が降りそうだ.

three *pron.* mi⌈ttsu 三つ; (people) sa⌈ñ-ni⌉ñ 3人; (things) sa⌉ñ-ko 3個.
— *n.* (figure) sa⌈ñ 3; (hour) sa⌉ñ-ji 3時; (minute) sa⌉ñ-puñ 3分; (age) sa⌉ñ-sai 3歳.
— *adj.* mi⌈ttsu⌉ no 三つの; sa⌈ñ no 3の; (people) sa⌈ñ-ni⌉ñ no 3人の; (things); sa⌉ñ-ko no 3個の; (age) sa⌉ñ-sai no 3歳の.

threshold *n.* **1** (of a doorway) shi⌈kii 敷居: cross the threshold (*shikii o matagu*) 敷居をまたぐ.
2 (beginning) ha⌈jime 始め: He is on the threshold of a new career. (*Kare wa atarashii shigoto o hajimeyoo to shite iru.*) 彼は新しい仕事を始めようとしている.

thrifty *adj.* ke⌈ñyaku suru 倹約する; tsu⌈mashi⌉i つましい: a thrifty meal (*tsumashii shokuji*) つましい食事.

thrill *n.* (feeling) zo⌉kuzoku [wa⌉kuwaku] suru ka⌈ñji ぞくぞく[わくわく]する感じ; su⌉riru スリル: It is a real thrill to meet the star in person. (*Ano sutaa ni jika ni aeru nañte wakuwaku suru.*) あのスターにじかに会えるなんてわくわくする.
— *vt.* ... o zo⌉kuzoku [wa⌉kuwaku] saseru ...をぞくぞく[わくわく]させる Ⓥ: She was thrilled by the invitation. (*Kanojo wa sono shootai ni wakuwaku shita.*) 彼女はその招待にわくわくした.

thrive *vi.* **1** (prosper) sa⌈kae⌉ru 栄える Ⓥ; ha⌈ñee suru 繁栄する Ⓘ: His business is thriving. (*Kare no shoobai wa sakaete iru.*) 彼の商売は栄えている.
2 (grow) so⌈da⌉tsu 育つ Ⓒ: This plant thrives in a warm climate. (*Kono shokubutsu wa atatakai tokoro de sodachimasu.*) この植物は暖かい所で育ちます.

throat *n.* no⌉do のど: I have a sore throat. (*Nodo ga itai.*) のどが痛い. / clear one's throat (*sekibarai o suru*) せき払いをする.

throb *vi.* (of a heart) do⌉kidoki suru どきどきする Ⓘ; (of a wound) zu⌉kizuki suru ずきずきする Ⓘ: The cut was throbbing with pain. (*Kirikizu ga itami de zukizuki shite ita.*) 切

り傷が痛みでずきずきしていた.

— *n.* do⌈oki 動悸; ko⌈doo 鼓動: a throb of the heart (*shiñzoo no dooki*) 心臓の動悸.

throne *n.* o⌉oza 王座; o⌉oi 王位: come to the throne (*ooi ni tsuku*) 王位につく.

throng *n.* gu⌈ñshuu 群集; mu⌈re⌉ 群れ: a throng of people (*hito no mure*) 人の群れ.

— *vi.* mu⌈raga⌉ru 群がる Ⓒ; sa⌈ttoo suru 殺到する Ⓘ: The returning spectators thronged toward the exit. (*Kaeri no kañkyaku ga deguchi ni sattoo shita.*) 帰りの観客が出口に殺到した.

— *vt.* ... ni mu⌈raga⌉ru …に群がる Ⓒ; ... de go⌈ttaga⌉esu …でごった返す Ⓒ: The street was thronged with shoppers. (*Sono toori wa kaimonokyaku de gottagaeshite ita.*) その通りは買物客でごった返していた.

through *prep.* **1** (from side to side) ... o to⌉otte …を通って: The river runs through the city. (*Sono kawa wa shichuu o tootte nagarete iru.*) その川は市中を通って流れている.

2 (from beginning to end) sa⌈isho kara sa⌉igo made 最初から最後まで; -juu 中: I read through the book. (*Watashi wa sono hoñ o saigo made yoñda.*) 私はその本を最後まで読んだ. / The rain lasted all through the night. (*Ame wa hitobañ-juu futta.*) 雨は一晩中降った.

3 (up to) ... ma⌉de …まで: I work from Monday through Friday. (*Watashi wa getsuyoo kara kiñyoo made hatarakimasu.*) 私は月曜から金曜まで働きます.

4 (by means of) ... ni yo⌈tte …によって; ... o to⌉oshite …を通して: He reserved a hotel room through a travel agency. (*Kare wa ryokoodairiteñ o tooshite hoteru no heya o yoyaku shita.*) 彼は旅行代理店を通してホテルの部屋を予約した.

— *adv.* **1** to⌉oshite 通して: I have a permit; let me through. (*Kyokashoo ga aru no de tooshite kudasai.*) 許可証があるので通してください.

2 (from beginning to end) sa⌉igo made 最後まで: Please hear me through. (*Doo ka saigo made kiite kudasai.*) どうか最後まで聞いてください.

— *adj.* **1** (finished) o⌈watte 終わって; su⌉ñ de 済んで: Are you through? (*Moo sumimashita ka?*) もう済みましたか.

2 (direct) cho⌈kutsuu no 直通の: a through train (*chokutsuu ressha*) 直通列車.

throughout *prep.* **1** (in every part) ... no su⌉mi kara sumi made …の隅から隅まで; -juu 中: search throughout the house (*ie-juu sagasu*) 家中捜す.

2 (from beginning to end) -juu (zu⌈tto) 中(ずっと): He was asleep throughout the lecture. (*Kare wa koogi no aida-juu zutto nete ita.*) 彼は講義の間じゅうずっと寝ていた.

throw *vt.* **1** (hurl) ... o na⌈ge⌉ru …を投げる Ⓥ: I threw the ball to him. (*Watashi wa sono booru o kare ni nageta.*) 私はそのボールを彼に投げた.

2 (make fall down) ... o na⌈getoba⌉su …を投げ飛ばす Ⓒ: He threw his wrestling opponent. (*Kare wa resuriñgu no aite o nagetobashita.*) 彼はレスリングの相手を投げ飛ばした

3 (put on hastily) ... o sa⌉tto ki⌈ru …をさっと着る Ⓥ; (take off) nu⌉gu 脱ぐ Ⓒ: throw one's jacket on [off] (*uwagi o satto kiru* [*nugu*]) 上着をさっと着る[脱ぐ].

4 (cast) ... o mu⌈keru …を向ける Ⓥ: He threw me a threatening look. (*Kare wa watashi ni odosu yoo na shiseñ o muketa.*) 彼は私に脅すような視線を向けた.

thrust *vt.* **1** (push) ... o tsu⌉yoku o⌈su …を強く押す Ⓒ; tsu⌈kko⌉mu 突っ込む Ⓒ: He thrust me aside. (*Kare wa watashi o waki e tsuyoku oshita.*) 彼は私をわきへ強く押した. / He thrust his wallet into his pocket. (*Kare wa saifu o poketto no naka ni tsukkoñda.*) 彼は財布をポケットの

中に突っ込んだ.
2 (stab) ... o tsu⌈kisa⌉su …を突き刺す [C]: thrust a knife into a person's back (*hito no senaka ni naifu o tsukisasu*) 人の背中にナイフを突き刺す.
— *vi.* (push) o⌈su 押す [C]; (stab) sa⌉su 刺す [C]: thrust through a crowd (*hitogomi o oshiwakete susumu*) 人込みを押し分けて進む.

thumb *n.* o⌈yayubi 親指: raise one's thumb (*oyayubi o tateru*) 親指を立てる.

thunder *n.* ka⌈mina⌉ri 雷; ra⌈imee 雷鳴: the rolling sound of thunder (*kaminari no gorogoro iu oto*) 雷のごろごろいう音.
— *vi.* ka⌈mina⌉ri ga na⌈ru 雷が鳴る [C]; (make a loud noise) go⌈o-oñ o tate⌉ru 轟音を立てる [V]: It's thundering in the distance. (*Tooku de kaminari ga natte iru.*) 遠くで雷が鳴っている.

Thursday *n.* mo⌈kuyo⌉o(bi) 木曜(日).

thus *adv.* **1** (in this way) ko⌈no yo⌉o ni このように: Do it thus. (*Kono yoo ni yari nasai.*) このようにやりなさい.
2 (for this reason) da⌉kara だから; shi⌈tagatte 従って: He is ill and thus absent. (*Kare wa byooki desu. Shitagatte yasuñde imasu.*) 彼は病気です. 従って休んでいます.

ticket *n.* ki⌈ppu 切符; ke⌉ñ 券; chi⌈ke⌉tto チケット: Where can I buy a ticket for a sightseeing bus? (*Kañkoo basu no kippu wa doko de kaemasu ka?*) 観光バスの切符はどこで買えますか. / Can I cancel this ticket? (*Kono kippu wa torikesemasu ka?*) この切符は取り消せますか.

tickle *vt.* ... o ku⌈suguru …をくすぐる [C]: The mother tickled her baby's feet. (*Hahaoya wa akañboo no ashi o kusugutta.*) 母親は赤ん坊の足をくすぐった.

tide *n.* **1** (of the sea) shi⌈o⌉ 潮: The tide is coming in [going out]. (*Shio ga michi-hajimete [hiki-hajimete] iru.*) 潮が満ち始めて[引き始めて]いる.
2 (trend) fu⌈uchoo 風潮; jo⌈osee 情勢; ke⌈esee 形勢: the tide of international affairs (*kokusai-joosee*) 国際情勢 / The tide turned against me. (*Keesee wa watashi ni furi ni natta.*) 形勢は私に不利になった.

tidy *adj.* ki⌈chi⌉ñto shita [shite iru] きちんとした[している]: keep a kitchen tidy (*daidokoro o kichiñto shite oku*) 台所をきちんとしておく / She always looks tidy. (*Kanojo wa itsumo minari ga kichiñto shite iru.*) 彼女はいつも身なりがきちんとしている.

tie *n.* **1** (necktie) ne⌉kutai ネクタイ: put on [take off] a tie (*nekutai o shimeru [hazusu]*) ネクタイを締める[はずす] / a tie pin (*taipiñ*) タイピン.
2 (something that joins) tsu⌈nagari つながり; ki⌉zuna きずな: business ties (*shoobai-joo no tsunagari*) 商売上のつながり / family ties (*kazoku no kizuna*) 家族のきずな.
3 (draw) do⌈oteñ 同点; hi⌈kiwake 引き分け: The game ended in a tie. (*Shiai wa hikiwake ni owatta.*) 試合は引き分けに終わった.
— *vt.* **1** (fasten) ... o mu⌈subu …を結ぶ [C]; shi⌈ba⌉ru 縛る [C]: tie one's shoelaces (*kutsu no himo o musubu*) 靴のひもを結ぶ / tie a parcel with string (*kozutsumi o himo de shibaru*) 小包をひもで縛る.
2 (bind) ... o so⌈kubaku suru …を束縛する [I]; shi⌈baritsuke⌉ru 縛りつける [V]: I work all day tied to my desk. (*Watashi wa ichinichi-juu tsukue ni shibaritsukerarete shigoto o shite iru.*) 私は一日中机に縛りつけられて仕事をしている.
3 (equal) ... to do⌈oteñ ni na⌉ru …と同点になる [C]: The Giants tied the Tigers in the ninth inning. (*Jaiañtsu wa kyuukai ni Taigaasu to dooteñ ni natta.*) ジャイアンツは9回にタイガースと同点になった.

tiger *n.* to⌈ra とら(虎).

tight *adj.* **1** (fitting closely) shi⌈ma⌉tta 締まった; shi⌈ma⌉tte iru 締っている; ki⌈tchi⌉ri shita [shite iru] きっちりした[している]; ki⌈tsui きつい: shut

a door tight (*to o kitchiri shimeru*) 戸をきっちり閉める / My trousers are too tight. (*Watashi no zuboñ wa kitsu-sugiru.*) 私のズボンはきつすぎる.
2 (stretched) pi˹ñ to hatta [hatte iru] ぴんと張った[張っている]: a tight rope (*piñ to hatta roopu*) ぴんと張ったロープ.
3 (strict) yoyu˹u no na˺i 余裕のない; ki˹tsui きつい: a tight schedule (*yoyuu no nai yotee*) 余裕のない予定.

tighten *vt.* ... o shi˹kka˺ri to shi˹me˺ru ...をしっかりと締める V: tighten up a screw (*neji o shikkari to shimeru*) ねじをしっかりと締める.

tightly *adv.* shi˹kka˺ri to しっかりと; ki˹tsuku きつく.

tile *n.* ta˺iru タイル; (of a Japanese roof) ka˺wara かわら.

till *prep.* ... ma˺de ...まで: He worked from nine till five. (*Kare wa kuji kara goji made hataraita.*) 彼は9時から5時まで働いた. / I haven't heard of it till now. (*Watashi wa sore ni tsuite ima made kiita koto ga nakatta.*) 私はそれについて今まで聞いたことがなかった.
— *conj.* ... ma˺de ...まで: I waited there till the rain let up. (*Watashi wa ame ga yamu made soko de matte ita.*) 私は雨がやむまでそこで待っていた.

tilt *vt.* ... o ka˹tamuke˺ru ...を傾ける V: He tilted the chair backward. (*Kare wa isu o ushiro ni katamuketa.*) 彼はいすを後ろに傾けた.
— *vi.* ka˹tamu˺ku 傾く C: The pillar tilted and fell. (*Sono hashira wa katamuite taoreta.*) その柱は傾いて倒れた.

timber *n.* za˹imoku 材木; mo˹ku˺zai 木材.

time *n.* **1** (passing hours) to˹ki˺ 時; ji˹kañ 時間: Time is money. (*Toki wa kane nari.*) 時は金なり. / waste time (*jikañ o muda ni suru*) 時間を無駄にする / kill time (*jikañ o tsubusu*) 時間をつぶす.
2 (the hour of the day) ji˹koku 時刻; ji˹kañ 時間; -ji 時: What time is it? (*Ima nañ-ji desu ka?*) 今何時ですか. / What time does the dining room open? (*Shokudoo wa nañ-ji ni akimasu ka?*) 食堂は何時に開きますか.
3 (particular moment) ji˹kañ 時間: It's time for bed. (*Neru jikañ desu.*) 寝る時間です. / Do you have time? (*O-jikañ wa arimasu ka?*) お時間はありますか.
4 (experience) to˹ki˺ 時: We had a good time this evening. (*Koñya wa tanoshii toki o sugoshita.*) 今夜は楽しい時を過ごした.
5 (period) ki˺kañ 期間; a˹ida 間: for a long time (*nagai aida*) 長い間 / for some time (*shibaraku no aida*) しばらくの間 / for the time being (*toobuñ no aida*) 当分の間.
6 (age) ji˹dai 時代: the good old times (*furuki yoki jidai*) 古きよき時代.
7 (number of times) -ka˺i 回; -do 度: We meet three times a week for practice. (*Watashi-tachi wa reñshuu no tame ni shuu sañ-kai aimasu.*) 私たちは練習のために週3回会います. / How many times have you come to Tokyo? (*Tookyoo ni wa nañ-do koraremashita ka?*) 東京には何度来られましたか.
8 (multiplication) -bai 倍: China is 26 times larger than Japan. (*Chuugoku no hirosa wa Nihoñ no nijuuroku-bai desu.*) 中国の広さは日本の26倍です.

at a time *adv.* i˹chi-do˺ ni 一度に: Can you eat that much at a time? (*Ichi-do ni soñna ni taberaremasu ka?*) 一度にそんなに食べられますか.

in time *adv., adj.* ma˹nia˺tte 間に合って: We arrived just in time for the concert. (*Koñsaato ni nañ to ka maniatta.*) コンサートに何とか間に合った.

on time *adv., adj.* ji˹kañ do˺ori ni 時間どおりに: The train arrived on time. (*Deñsha wa jikañ doori ni toochaku shita.*) 電車は時間どおり

に到着した.

time difference *n.* ji⌉sa 時差: The time difference between Tokyo and New York is 14 hours. (*Tookyoo to Nyuu Yooku no jisa wa juuyo-jikañ desu.*) 東京とニューヨークの時差は 14 時間です.

timetable *n.* (of transportation) ji⌈kokuhyoo 時刻表; (of school) ji⌈kañwari 時間割.

timid *adj.* o⌈kubyo⌉o na 臆病な; u⌈chiki na 内気な: a timid person (*okubyoo na hito*) 臆病な人.

tin *n.* **1** (can) ka⌉ñ 缶; (canned food) ka⌈ñzu⌉me 缶詰.
2 (metal) su⌉zu すず(錫); (tinplate) bu⌈riki ブリキ.
— *vt.* ... o ka⌈ñzu⌉me ni suru ...を缶詰にする [I]: tin fruit (*kudamono o kañzume ni suru*) 果物を缶詰にする.

tiny *adj.* chi⌈tcha⌉ na ちっちゃな: a tiny little boy (*chitcha na otoko-no-ko*) ちっちゃな男の子.

tip[1] *n.* chi⌉ppu チップ: I gave the taxi driver a good tip. (*Watashi wa sono takushii no uñteñshu ni tappuri chippu o hazuñda.*) 私はそのタクシーの運転手にたっぷりチップを弾んだ.
— *vt.* ... ni chi⌉ppu o ya⌈ru ...にチップをやる [C]: I tipped the bellboy. (*Watashi wa booi ni chippu o yatta.*) 私はボーイにチップをやった.

tip[2] *n.* sa⌉ki 先; se⌈ñtañ 先端: the tip of the finger (*yubi no saki*) 指の先.

tire[1] *vt.* **1** (exhaust) ... o tsu⌈kare sase⌉ru ...を疲れさせる [V]: Walking tired the patient. (*Hokoo wa byooniñ o tsukare saseta.*) 歩行は病人を疲れさせた.
2 (make weary) a⌈kia⌉ki saseru あきあきさせる [V]; u⌈ñza⌉ri saseru うんざりさせる [V]: His same old story tired her. (*Kare no onaji hanashi wa kanojo o uñzari saseta.*) 彼の同じ話は彼女をうんざりさせた.

tire[2] *n.* ta⌈iya タイヤ: pump up a tire (*taiya ni kuuki o ireru*) タイヤに空気を入れる / I got a flat tire. (*Taiya ga pañku shita.*) タイヤがパンクした.

tired *adj.* **1** (exhausted) tsu⌈ka⌉reta 疲れた; tsu⌈ka⌉rete iru 疲れている: I'm tired from swimming. (*Watashi wa suiee de tsukareta.*) 私は水泳で疲れた.
2 (wearied) a⌉kita 飽きた; a⌉kite iru 飽きている: I'm tired of your conversation. (*Kimi no hanashi ni wa moo akita.*) 君の話にはもう飽きた.

tireless *adj.* tsu⌈kare⌉ o shi⌈ranai 疲れを知らない; se⌈eryoku-teki na 精力的な: a tireless worker (*tsukare o shiranai hatarakimono*) 疲れを知らない働き者.

tiresome *adj.* ya⌉kkai na やっかいな; ta⌈ikutsu na 退屈な: a tiresome child (*yakkai na kodomo*) やっかいな子ども / a tiresome game (*taikutsu na shiai*) 退屈な試合.

tissue *n.* **1** (of organs) so⌉shiki 組織: nervous tissue (*shiñkee soshiki*) 神経組織.
2 (paper) ti⌉sshu ティッシュ; chi⌈rigami ちり紙: toilet tissue (*toiretto peepaa*) トイレットペーパー. ★ 'Tissue' is often called '*tisshu peepaa*' (tissue paper).

title *n.* **1** (name) da⌈imee 題名: the title of a book (*hoñ no daimee*) 本の題名.
2 (of a rank) ka⌈tagaki 肩書き: a person with a title (*katagaki no aru hito*) 肩書きのある人.
3 (championship) se⌈ñshu⌉keñ 選手権: She holds the world title. (*Kanojo wa sekai chañpioñ da.*) 彼女は世界チャンピオンだ.

to[1] *prep.* **1** (toward) ... e [ni] ...へ[に]: Is this the bus to Shibuya? (*Kore wa Shibuya e iku basu desu ka?*) これは渋谷へ行くバスですか. / I wrote a letter to her. (*Watashi wa kanojo ni tegami o kaita.*) 私は彼女に手紙を書いた.
2 (as far as) ... ma⌉de ...まで: It is two kilometers from my house to the station. (*Watashi no uchi kara eki made ni-kiro desu.*) 私の家から駅まで 2 キロです.

t

3 (till) ... ma⌉de まで: He worked from morning to night. (*Kare wa asa kara bañ made hataraita.*) 彼は朝から晩まで働いた.

4 (concerning) ... ni (to⌉tte) …に(とって): His resignation is a great loss to our company. (*Kare ga yameta no wa kaisha ni totte ooki-na soñshitsu da.*) 彼が辞めたのは会社にとって大きな損失だ.

5 (connection) ... no …の: an assistant to Dr. Kimura (*Kimura hakase no joshu*) 木村博士の助手 / the key to a laboratory (*keñkyuushitsu no kagi*) 研究室の鍵.

6 (comparison) ... ni ta⌉ishite …に対して: We won the game by a score of three to two. (*Watashi-tachi wa sañ tai ni de shiai ni katta.*) 私たちは 3 対 2 で試合に勝った.

7 (agreement) ... ni a⌈wa⌉sete …に合わせて: We danced to the music. (*Watashi-tachi wa sono oñgaku ni awasete odotta.*) 私たちはその音楽に合わせて踊った.

to[2] [marking the infinitive] **1** [noun use] ... ko⌈to⌉ …こと; ... no ga [wa] …のが[は]: I decided to work there. (*Watashi wa soko de hataraku koto ni shita.*) 私はそこで働くことにした. / I like to play tennis. (*Watashi wa tenisu o suru no ga suki desu.*) 私はテニスをするのが好きです. / It's good to keep early hours. (*Hayane hayaoki o suru no wa ii koto desu.*) 早寝早起きをするのはいいことです.

2 [adjective use] ... ta⌈me⌉ no …ための; ... be⌉ki …べき: a house to live in (*sumu tame no ie*) 住むための家 / I want something to eat. (*Nani-ka taberu mono ga hoshii.*) 何か食べる物が欲しい. / I have no friends to talk with. (*Watashi ni wa tomo ni kataru beki tomo wa inai.*) 私には共に語るべき友はいない.

3 [adverb use] ... ta⌈me⌉ ni …ために; 〈verb〉-te[de] …て[で]: We eat to live. (*Watashi-tachi wa ikiru tame ni taberu.*) 私たちは生きるために食べる. / I'm very glad to see you again. (*Anata to mata o-ai dekite ureshii desu.*) あなたとまたお会いできてうれしいです.

toast *n.* to⌉osuto トースト: a slice of toast (*toosuto ichi-mai*) トースト 1 枚 / make toast (*pañ o yaku*) パンを焼く.

tobacco *n.* ki⌈zami-ta⌉bako 刻みたばこ: chewing tobacco (*kami tabako*) かみたばこ.

today *adv.* **1** (this day) kyo⌉o (wa) きょう(は): I'm busy today. (*Kyoo wa isogashii.*) きょうは忙しい.

2 (the present time) ge⌉ñzai de wa 現在では; ko⌉ñnichi de wa 今日では: Studying abroad is not unusual today. (*Ryuugaku wa koñnichi de wa mezurashiku arimaseñ.*) 留学は今日では珍しくありません.

— *n.* kyo⌉o きょう: today's newspaper (*kyoo no shiñbuñ*) きょうの新聞.

toe *n.* (of a foot) a⌈shi no yubi⌉ 足の指; (of a shoe, sock) tsu⌈masaki つま先: the big [little] toe (*ashi no oyayubi [koyubi]*) 足の親指[小指] / a hole in the toe of a sock (*kutsushita no tsumasaki no ana*) 靴下のつま先の穴.

together *adv.* **1** (in company) i⌈ssho ni いっしょに; to⌉mo ni 共に: Let's go together. (*Issho ni ikimashoo.*) いっしょに行きましょう. / How about having dinner together? (*Yuuhañ o go-issho ni ikaga desu ka?*) 夕飯をごいっしょにいかがですか.

2 (joined) a⌈wa⌉sete 合わせて: How much is it all together? (*Awasete zeñbu de ikura desu ka?*) 合わせて全部でいくらですか.

3 (at the same time) do⌉oji ni 同時に: They got a promotion together. (*Kare-ra wa dooji ni shookaku shita.*) 彼らは同時に昇格した.

toil *vi.* (... ni) ho⌈ne⌉ o oru (…に)骨を折る [C]; se⌉e o dasu 精を出す [C]: toil at the task (*shigoto ni see o dasu*) 仕事に精を出す.

— *n.* ho⌈neori⌉ 骨折り; ku⌉roo 苦労.

toilet *n.* se⌈ñmeñjo 洗面所; to⌉ire トイレ; be⌈ñjo⌉ 便所: flush a toilet (*toire no mizu o nagasu*) トイレの水

を流す / a public toilet (*kooshuu-beñjo*) 公衆便所.

token *n.* **1** (sign) shiˈrushi 印: This is just a token of my gratitude. (*Kore wa watashi no hoñ no kañsha no shirushi desu.*) これは私のほんの感謝の印です.
2 (keepsake) kiˈneñ no shina 記念の品: He gave me a necklace as a token of our first date. (*Kare wa saisho no deeto no kineñ ni nekkuresu o kureta.*) 彼は最初のデートの記念にネックレスをくれた.

tolerable *adj.* gaˈmañ deˈkiˈru 我慢できる: This heat is not tolerable. (*Kono atsusa wa gamañ dekinai.*) この暑さは我慢できない.

tolerant *adj.* kaˈñdai na 寛大な; kaˈñyoo na 寛容な: He is tolerant of other's errors. (*Kare wa hoka no hito no machigai ni taishite kañdai da.*) 彼はほかの人の間違いに対して寛大だ.

tolerate *vt.* **1** (allow) ... o yuˈruˈsu …を許す [C]: We should not tolerate any violence. (*Doñna booryoku mo yurusu wake ni wa ikanai.*) どんな暴力も許す訳にはいかない.
2 (endure) ... o gaˈmañ suru …を我慢する [I]: I cannot tolerate this noise. (*Kono soo-oñ wa gamañ dekinai.*) この騒音は我慢できない.

toll *n.* **1** (charge) ryoˈokiñ 料金: pay a toll to cross a bridge (*hashi o wataru no ni ryookiñ o harau*) 橋を渡るのに料金を払う / a toll road (*yuuryoo dooro*) 有料道路.
2 (casualty) shiˈshoˈosha 死傷者; giˈseˈesha 犠牲者; (damage) soˈñgai 損害: the death toll in the accident (*sono jiko no giseesha*) その事故の犠牲者.

tomato *n.* toˈmato トマト: tomato juice (*tomato juusu*) トマトジュース.

tomb *n.* haˈkaˈ 墓: a tombstone (*hakaishi*) 墓石.

tomorrow *adv.* aˈshitaˈ (wa) あした(は); aˈsuˈ (wa) あす(は); [formal] myoˈonichi 明日: It'll be fine tomorrow. (*Ashita wa hareru deshoo.*) あしたは晴れるでしょう.
— *n.* aˈshitaˈ あした; aˈsuˈ あす: Tomorrow is a holiday. (*Ashita wa kyuujitsu desu.*) あしたは休日です. / I am leaving tomorrow morning. (*Watashi wa asu no asa tachimasu.*) 私はあすの朝立ちます. / the day after tomorrow (*asatte [myoogonichi]*) あさって[明後日].

ton *n.* toˈñ トン: One cubic meter of water weighs a ton. (*Ichi-rippoo-meetoru no mizu no omosa wa it-toñ desu.*) 1立方メートルの水の重さは1トンです.

tone *n.* **1** (sound) choˈoshi 調子; neˈiro 音色: the clear tone of a flute (*furuuto no suñda neiro*) フルートの澄んだ音色.
2 (of a voice) kuˈchoo 口調: He spoke in a gentle tone. (*Kare wa yasashii kuchoo de hanashita.*) 彼はやさしい口調で話した.
3 (shade of color) iˈroai 色合い; shiˈkichoo 色調: a picture in warm tones (*atatakai shikichoo no e*) 暖かい色調の絵.

tongs *n.* -baˈsami ばさみ: ice tongs (*koori-basami*) 氷ばさみ / coal tongs (*sekitañ-basami*) 石炭ばさみ.

tongue *n.* **1** (organ) shiˈtaˈ 舌: stick out one's tongue (*shita o dasu*) 舌を出す.
2 (food) taˈñ タン: ox-tongue (*gyuu tañ*) 牛タン.
3 (language) koˈtobaˈ 言葉: Watch your tongue. (*Kotoba ni ki o tsuke nasai.*) 言葉に気をつけなさい.

tonight *adv.* koˈñya (wa) 今夜(は): I'm free tonight. (*Koñya wa hima desu.*) 今夜は暇です.
— *n.* koˈñya 今夜; koˈñbañ 今晩: Can I get a room for tonight? (*Koñbañ tomaremasu ka?*) 今晩泊まれますか.

too[1] *adv.* (also) ... mo …も; maˈta また: I'm tired, too. (*Watashi mo tsukaremashita.*) 私も疲れました. / He can speak Chinese, and Korean, too. (*Kare wa Chuugokugo o hanasemasu shi, mata Kañkokugo mo*

t

hanasemasu.) 彼は中国語を話せますし，また韓国語も話せます.

too[2] *adv.* **1** (to a great extent) -sugi⌉ru すぎる: This room is too small. (*Kono heya wa sema-sugiru.*) この部屋は狭すぎる. / It's too expensive for me. (*Watashi ni wa taka-sugimasu.*) 私には高すぎます. / Don't eat too much. (*Tabe-suginai yoo ni.*) 食べすぎないように.
2 (very) hi⌈joo ni 非常に; [in the negative] a⌈mari ... -na⌉i あまり…ない: I'm not feeling too well. (*Watashi wa amari kibuñ ga yokunai.*) 私はあまり気分がよくない.

tool *n.* do⌈ogu⌉ 道具: the tools of one's trade (*shoobai-doogu*) 商売道具.

tooth *n.* ha⌉ 歯: brush one's teeth (*ha o migaku*) 歯を磨く / pull a tooth (*ha o nuku*) 歯を抜く / a bad tooth (*mushiba*) 虫歯 / a false tooth (*ireba*) 入れ歯.

toothache *n.* ha⌉ no i⌈tami⌉ 歯の痛み; shi⌈tsuu 歯痛: I have a toothache. (*Ha ga itai.*) 歯が痛い.

toothbrush *n.* ha⌈bu⌉rashi 歯ブラシ.

toothpaste *n.* ne⌈rihami⌉gaki 練り歯磨き.

toothpick *n.* tsu⌈mayo⌉oji つまようじ; yo⌈oji ようじ.

top *n.* **1** (upper part) u⌈e 上; jo⌉obu 上部: the fifth line from the top (*ue kara go-gyoo-me*) 上から5行目.
2 (surface) u⌈e 上; hyo⌈ome⌉ñ 表面: clear a table top (*teeburu no ue o katazukeru*) テーブルの上を片付ける.
3 (of a mountain) cho⌈ojo⌉o 頂上: We finally reached the top of the mountain. (*Watashi-tachi wa yatto choojoo ni tsuita.*) 私たちはやっと頂上に着いた.
4 (highest rank) i⌈chi⌉bañ 一番; to⌉ppu トップ: He is at the top of our class. (*Kare wa kurasu de ichi-bañ desu.*) 彼はクラスで一番です.
★ In Japan 'leading runner' is often called '*toppu rañnaa*' (top runner).
5 (covering) fu⌈ta ふた; se⌉ñ 栓: a box top (*hako no futa*) 箱のふた.
— *vt.* **1** (crown) ... no i⌈tadaki o oo⌉u …の頂を覆う [C]: Snow topped the mountain. (*Yuki ga yama no itadaki o ootta.*) 雪が山の頂を覆った.
2 (surpass) ... yori su⌈gure⌉ru …より優れる [V]: He topped all the others at golf. (*Kare wa gorufu de wa hoka no dare yori mo sugurete ita.*) 彼はゴルフではほかのだれよりも優れていた.

topic *n.* wa⌈dai 話題: bring up a topic (*wadai o kiridasu*) 話題を切り出す / the topic for a discussion (*kaigi no gidai*) 会議の議題.

torch *n.* (flaming light) ta⌉imatsu たいまつ; (flashlight) ka⌈ichuude⌉ñtoo 懐中電灯: turn on a torch (*kaichuu-deñtoo o tsukeru*) 懐中電灯をつける.

torment *n.* ku⌈tsuu 苦痛; ku⌉noo 苦悩: He is in torment. (*Kare wa kunoo shite iru.*) 彼は苦悩している.
— *vt.* ... o ku⌈rushime⌉ru …を苦しめる [V]: She is tormented with a headache. (*Kanojo wa zutsuu de kurushiñde iru.*) 彼女は頭痛で苦しんでいる.

torture *n.* **1** (of punishment) go⌈o-moñ 拷問: He was put to torture. (*Kare wa goomoñ ni kakerareta.*) 彼は拷問にかけられた.
2 (suffering) ku⌈tsuu 苦痛: It was torture doing it over again. (*Sore o mata yarinaosu no wa kutsuu datta.*) それをまたやり直すのは苦痛だった.
— *vt.* (punish) ... o go⌈omoñ ni kake⌉ru …を拷問にかける [V]; (make suffer) ku⌈rushime⌉ru 苦しめる [V]: He was tortured into making a confession. (*Kare wa goomoñ ni kakerarete jihaku shita.*) 彼は拷問にかけられて自白した.

toss *vt.* **1** (throw) ... o na⌈ge⌉ru …を投げる [V]: Toss that bag to me. (*Sono kabañ o nagete kudasai.*) そのかばんを投げてください.
2 (in cooking) ... o ka⌈kimazeru …をかき混ぜる [V]: toss a salad (*sarada o kakimazeru*) サラダをかき混ぜる.
— *vi.* **1** (move up and down) yu⌈reru 揺れる [V]: The ship tossed on

the waves. (*Fune wa nami no ue de yurete ita.*) 船は波の上で揺れていた.
2 (flip a coin) to⌉su de ki⌈meru トスで決める Ⓥ: Let's toss up. (*Tosu de kimeyoo.*) トスで決めよう.
— *n.* na⌈geru koto⌉ 投げること: decide by the toss of a coin (*koiñ o nagete kimeru*) コインを投げて決める.

total *n.* so⌈okee 総計; go⌈okee 合計: The total comes to 5,000 yen. (*Sookee wa goseñ-eñ ni narimasu.*) 総計は5千円になります.
— *adj.* **1** (whole) ze⌈ñtai no 全体の; so⌈o- 総: What will be the total amount? (*Soo-gaku wa ikura desu ka?*) 総額はいくらですか.
2 (complete) ma⌈ttaku⌉ no まったくの; ka⌈ñzeñ na 完全な: a total failure (*kañzeñ na shippai*) 完全な失敗.
— *vt.* ... o go⌈okee suru …を合計する Ⓘ: total the expenditures (*hiyoo o gookee suru*) 費用を合計する.

totally *adv.* ma⌈ttaku まったく; ka⌈ñzeñ ni 完全に: I was totally unaware of his illness. (*Watashi wa kare no byooki no koto o mattaku shiranakatta.*) 私は彼の病気のことをまったく知らなかった.

touch *vt.* **1** (contact) ... ni sa⌈waru …に触る Ⓒ; fu⌈reru 触れる Ⓥ: Do not touch the exhibits. (*Teñjihiñ ni sawaranaide kudasai.*) 展示品に触らないでください. / The branch almost touches the electric wire. (*Sono eda wa deñseñ ni fure-soo da.*) その枝は電線に触れそうだ.
2 (move) ... o ka⌈ñdoo saseru …を感動させる Ⓥ: I was touched by his words. (*Watashi wa kare no kotoba ni kañdoo shita.*) 私は彼の言葉に感動した.
3 (eat, drink) ... ni te⌉ o tsu⌈ke⌉ru …に手をつける Ⓥ: She didn't touch the supper. (*Kanojo wa yuushoku ni te o tsukenakatta.*) 彼女は夕食に手をつけなかった.
— *n.* **1** (sensation) ka⌈ñshoku 感触; (of a hand) te⌈za⌉wari 手触り: the soft touch of fur (*kegawa no yawarakai tezawari*) 毛皮の柔らかい手触り.
2 (act of touching) sa⌈waru koto⌉ 触ること; se⌈sshoku 接触: I felt a touch on my arm. (*Watashi wa dare-ka ga ude ni sawaru no o kañjita.*) 私はだれかが腕に触るのを感じた.
3 (communication) re⌈ñraku 連絡: It has been a long time since he went out of touch. (*Kare kara reñraku ga todaete moo kanari tatsu.*) 彼から連絡が途絶えてもうかなりたつ.
4 (bit) su⌈ko⌉shi 少し: This salad needs a touch of salt. (*Kono sarada wa sukoshi shio ga tarinai.*) このサラダは少し塩が足りない.

tough *adj.* **1** (difficult) ko⌉ñnañ na 困難な; mu⌈zukashii 難しい: He is in a tough position now. (*Kare wa ima muzukashii tachiba ni aru.*) 彼は今難しい立場にある.
2 (not tender) ka⌈tai 堅い: This steak is rather tough. (*Kono suteeki wa sukoshi katai.*) このステーキは少し堅い.
3 (strong) tsu⌈yo⌉i 強い; jo⌈obu na 丈夫な; ta⌉fu na タフな: tough shoes (*joobu na kutsu*) 丈夫な靴 / He's tough. (*Kare wa tafu da.*) 彼はタフだ.

tour *n.* **1** (journey) ryo⌈koo 旅行: She went on a tour of China. (*Kanojo wa Chuugoku ryokoo ni itta.*) 彼女は中国旅行に行った.
2 (visit) ke⌈ñbutsu 見物; tsu⌉aa ツアー: Is there an all-day tour? (*Ichinichi no tsuaa wa arimasu ka?*) 一日のツアーはありますか.

tourist *n.* (traveler) ryo⌈ko⌉osha 旅行者; (sightseeing) ka⌈ñko⌉okyaku 観光客: I'm a tourist. (*Watashi wa kañkookyaku desu.*) 私は観光客です. / a tourist information office (*kañkoo annaijo*) 観光案内所.

tournament *n.* to⌉onameñto トーナメント: a tennis tournament (*tenisu no toonameñto*) テニスのトーナメント.

toward *prep.* **1** (in the direction of) ... no ho⌉o e [ni] …の方へ[に]; ...

t

e mu⌐katte …へ向かって: He went toward the door. (*Kare wa doa no hoo e itta.*) 彼はドアの方へ行った. / The plane is flying toward the south. (*Hikooki wa minami e mukatte toñde imasu.*) 飛行機は南へ向かって飛んでいます.

2 (in relation to) ... ni ta⌐ishite …に対して: He was friendly toward me. (*Kare wa watashi ni taishite kooi-teki datta.*) 彼は私に対して好意的だった.

3 (of time) ... ni chi⌐kaku …に近く; ko⌐ro ころ: He returned toward midnight. (*Kare wa mayonaka chi-kaku ni kaette kita.*) 彼は真夜中近くに帰ってきた.

4 (leading to) ... ni mu⌐katte …に向かって: the first step toward peace (*heewa ni mukatte no dai-ip-po*) 平和に向かっての第一歩.

towel *n.* ta⌐oru タオル: a bath towel (*basu taoru*) バスタオル / He dried his hands with a towel. (*Kare wa taoru de te o fuita.*) 彼はタオルで手をふいた.

tower *n.* to⌐o 塔; ta⌐waa タワー: a church tower (*kyookai no too*) 教会の塔.

— *vi.* (rise high) ta⌐kaku so⌐bie-ta⌐tsu 高くそびえ立つ Ⓒ: The building towers over this town. (*Sono biru wa kono machi ni takaku sobietatte iru.*) そのビルはこの街に高くそびえ立っている.

town *n.* ma⌐chi 町; (city) to⌐shi 都市; to⌐kai 都会. ★ Large towns are often called '*shi*' 市: Where is the shopping district in this town? (*Kono machi no shooteñgai wa doko ni arimasu ka?*) この町の商店街はどこにありますか. / an industrial town (*sañgyoo toshi*) 産業都市.

toy *n.* o⌐mo⌐cha おもちゃ: a toy gun (*omocha no pisutoru*) おもちゃのピストル / a toy shop (*omocha-ya*) おもちゃ屋.

— *vi.* ... o mo⌐teasobu …をもてあそぶ Ⓒ: The boy was toying with his food. (*Sono ko wa tabemono o moteasoñde ita.*) その子は食べ物をもてあそんでいた.

trace *n.* **1** (mark) a⌐to 跡; (footprint) a⌐shia⌐to 足跡: The police followed the trace of the man. (*Keesatsu wa sono otoko no ato o otta.*) 警察はその男の跡を追った.

2 (small amount) ho⌐ñno wa⌐zuka ほんのわずか: Traces of poison were found in the food. (*Tabemono ni hoñno wazuka no doku ga mitsu-katta.*) 食べ物にほんのわずかの毒が見つかった.

— *vt.* ... o ta⌐do⌐ru …をたどる Ⓒ: trace the history of a race (*miñ-zoku no rekishi o tadoru*) 民族の歴史をたどる.

track *n.* **1** (trace) to⌐otta ato 通った跡; (footprint) a⌐shia⌐to 足跡: follow tire tracks in the sand (*suna ni tsuita taiya no ato o tadoru*) 砂についたタイヤの跡をたどる.

2 (railroad line) se⌐ñro 線路; -señ 線: The train for Osaka leaves from track 2. (*Oosaka yuki no deñ-sha wa ni-bañ-señ kara hassha shi-masu.*) 大阪行きの電車は2番線から発車します.

3 (path) ko⌐michi 小道: A track runs through the woods. (*Komichi ga mori no naka o tootte iru.*) 小道が森の中を通っている.

4 (racetrack) kyo⌐oso⌐oro 競走路; to⌐ra⌐kku トラック: a cycling track (*jiteñsha kyosooro*) 自転車競走路 / track events (*torakku kyoogi*) トラック競技.

tract *n.* **1** (land) hi⌐rogari 広がり; chi⌐tai 地帯: large tracts of forest (*koodai na shiñriñ chitai*) 広大な森林地帯.

2 (organ) ka⌐ñ 管: the digestive tract (*shooka-kañ*) 消化管.

tractor *n.* to⌐ra⌐kutaa トラクター.

trade *n.* **1** (business transaction) to⌐ri⌐hiki 取り引き; bo⌐oeki 貿易: foreign trade (*gaikoku-booeki*) 外国貿易 / promote trade with Asian nations (*Ajia shokoku to no boo-eki o sokushiñ suru*) アジア諸国との

t

貿易を促進する.
2 (occupation) sho⌈ku⌉gyoo 職業; sho⌉obai 商売: He is a shoemaker by trade. (*Kare no shokugyoo wa kutsu-ya desu.*) 彼の職業は靴屋です.
— *vi.* (buy and sell) (... o) ba⌉ibai suru …を売買する [I]; a⌈tsukau 扱う [C]: His firm trades in groceries. (*Kare no kaisha wa shokuryoohiñ o atsukatte iru.*) 彼の会社は食料品を扱っている.
— *vt.* (exchange) ... o ko⌈okañ suru …を交換する [I]: trade stamps with a friend (*kitte o tomodachi to kookañ suru*) 切手を友達と交換する.

trader *n.* bo⌈oeki gyo⌉osha 貿易業者; sho⌉oniñ 商人.

tradition *n.* **1** (customs) de⌈ñtoo 伝統; ka⌈ñree 慣例: maintain an old tradition (*furuku kara no deñtoo o mamoru*) 古くからの伝統を守る.
2 (story) de⌈ñsetsu 伝説; i⌈itsutae 言い伝え.

traditional *adj.* de⌈ñtoo-teki na 伝統的な: a traditional costume (*deñtoo-teki na ishoo*) 伝統的な衣装.

traditionally *adv.* de⌈ñtoo-teki ni 伝統的に: Traditionally, the students of this school wear a uniform. (*Deñtoo-teki ni kono gakkoo no seeto wa seefuku o kite iru.*) 伝統的にこの学校の生徒は制服を着ている.

traffic *n.* ko⌈otsuu 交通: a traffic accident (*kootsuu jiko*) 交通事故 / Traffic is heavy around here. (*Kono heñ wa kootsuu ga hageshii.*) この辺は交通が激しい.
— *vi.* (... o) ba⌉ibai suru (…を)売買する [I]: traffic in drugs (*mayaku o baibai suru*) 麻薬を売買する.

tragedy *n.* **1** (drama) hi⌉geki 悲劇: Shakespeare's tragedies (*Sheekusupia no higeki*) シェークスピアの悲劇.
2 (unfortunate event) hi⌈sañ na [ka⌈nashii] de⌈ki⌉goto 悲惨な[悲しい]出来事: His death was a great tragedy for his family. (*Kare no shi wa kazoku ni totte hijoo ni kanashii dekigoto datta.*) 彼の死は家族にとって非常に悲しい出来事だった.

tragic *adj.* hi⌉geki no 悲劇の; (disastrous) hi⌈sañ na 悲惨な: a tragic air accident (*hisañ na kookuuki jiko*) 悲惨な航空機事故.

trail *n.* **1** (track) a⌉to 跡: follow the trail of a bear (*kuma no ato o tadoru*) 熊の跡をたどる.
2 (path) ko⌈michi 小道: a mountain trail (*yama no komichi*) 山の小道.
— *vt.* **1** (drag) ... o hi⌈kizuru …を引きずる [C]: She trailed her long skirt along the floor. (*Kanojo wa nagai sukaato o yuka ni hikizutte aruita.*) 彼女は長いスカートを床に引きずって歩いた.
2 (follow) ... no a⌉to ni tsuite i⌈ku …の後について行く [C]; ... o bi⌈koo suru …を尾行する [I]: A detective trailed the suspect. (*Keeji wa yoogisha o bikoo shita.*) 刑事は容疑者を尾行した.

train[1] *n.* **1** (of a railroad) re⌈ssha 列車; de⌉ñsha 電車. ★ '*Ressha*' usually refers to a long-distance train: Does this train stop at Sendai? (*Kono ressha wa Señdai ni tomarimasu ka?*) この列車は仙台に止まりますか. / get on a train (*deñsha ni noru*) 電車に乗る / get off a train (*deñsha o oriru*) 電車を降りる / change trains (*deñsha o norikaeru*) 電車を乗り換える.
2 (line) re⌉tsu 列: a funeral train (*sooshiki no retsu*) 葬式の列.

train[2] *vt.* ... o ku⌉ñreñ suru …を訓練する [I]: train employees for an emergency (*hijoojitai ni sonaete juugyooiñ o kuñreñ suru*) 非常事態に備えて従業員を訓練する / He was trained as an interpreter. (*Kare wa tsuuyaku to shite no kuñreñ o uketa.*) 彼は通訳としての訓練を受けた.

training *n.* ku⌉ñreñ 訓練; (of sports) re⌈ñshuu 練習; to⌈re⌉eniñgu トレーニング: vocational training (*shokugyoo kuñreñ*) 職業訓練 / baseball training (*yakyuu no reñshuu*)

t

野球の練習.

traitor *n.* ha⌈ñgyaku⌉sha 反逆者; u⌈ragirimono 裏切り者.

tram *n.* ro⌈meñ-de⌉ñsha 路面電車.

tramp *vi.* **1** (walk with heavy steps) do⌈shi⌉ñdoshiñ to a⌈ru⌉ku どしんどしんと歩く C: He tramped along the corridor. (*Kare wa rooka o doshiñdoshiñ to aruita.*) 彼は廊下をどしんどしんと歩いた.

2 (walk over) te⌉kuteku a⌈ru⌉ku てくてく歩く C: I tramped five kilometers in the heat. (*Watashi wa atsui naka o go-kiro tekuteku aruita.*) 私は暑い中を5キロてくてく歩いた.

— *n.* **1** (long walk) to⌈horyo⌉koo 徒歩旅行: go for a tramp (*tohoryokoo ni dekakeru*) 徒歩旅行に出かける.

2 (homeless person) fu⌈ro⌉osha 浮浪者.

trample *vt.* ... o fu⌈mitsuke⌉ru ...を踏みつける V: The children trampled the flower bed. (*Kodomotachi wa kadañ o fumitsuketa.*) 子どもたちは花壇を踏みつけた.

— *vi.* (... o) fu⌈miniji⌉ru (...を)踏みにじる C: trample on a person's feelings (*hito no kañjoo o fuminijiru*) 人の感情を踏みにじる.

tranquil *adj.* shi⌉zuka na 静かな; o⌈da⌉yaka na 穏やかな: a tranquil lake (*shizuka na mizuumi*) 静かな湖.

transaction *n.* to⌈ri⌉hiki 取り引き; gyo⌉omu 業務: business transactions (*shootorihiki*) 商取引.

transfer *vt.* ... o u⌈tsu⌉su ...を移す C: transfer a document from the drawer to the shelf (*shorui o hikidashi kara tana e utsusu*) 書類を引き出しから棚へ移す / He was transferred to the personnel department. (*Kare wa jiñjibu ni utsusareta.*) 彼は人事部に移された.

— *vi.* (move) u⌈tsu⌉ru 移る C; (change) no⌈rika⌉eru 乗り換える V: transfer to another school (*teñkoo suru*) 転校する / At what station do I transfer? (*Dono eki de norikaeru no desu ka?*) どの駅で乗り換えるのですか.

— *n.* i⌈doo 移動; (of transportation) no⌈rikae 乗り換え.

transform *vt.* ... o tsu⌈kurika⌉eru ...を造り変える V; su⌈kka⌉ri ka⌈eru すっかり変える V: transform a storehouse to a disco (*sooko o disuko ni tsukurikaeru*) 倉庫をディスコに造り変える.

transistor *n.* to⌈rañji⌉sutaa トランジスター.

transit *n.* **1** (carrying) yu⌈soo 輸送; u⌉ñsoo 運送: My baggage was lost in transit. (*Watashi no nimotsu wa yusoo-chuu ni fuñshitsu shita.*) 私の荷物は輸送中に紛失した.

2 (at an airport) no⌈ritsugi 乗り継ぎ: I'm in transit to Hong Kong. (*Watashi wa Hoñkoñ e iku noritsugi-kyaku desu.*) 私は香港へ行く乗り継ぎ客です.

transition *n.* u⌈tsurikawari 移り変わり; i⌈koo 移行: a transition from communism to liberalism (*kyoosañshugi kara jiyuushugi e no ikoo*) 共産主義から自由主義への移行.

translate *vt.* **1** (put into another language) ... o ya⌈ku⌉su ...を訳す C; ho⌈ñyaku suru 翻訳する I: translate a book from Japanese into English (*hoñ o Nihoñgo kara Eego ni yakusu*) 本を日本語から英語に訳す.

2 (interpret) ... o ka⌉ishaku suru ...を解釈する I: How would you translate his silence? (*Kare no chiñmoku o doo kaishaku shimasu ka?*) 彼の沈黙をどう解釈しますか.

translation *n.* ho⌈ñyaku 翻訳; -yaku 訳: This translation is full of errors. (*Kono hoñyaku wa machigai darake da.*) この翻訳は間違いだらけだ. / literal translation (*chokuyaku*) 直訳 / free translation (*iyaku*) 意訳.

translator *n.* ya⌉kusha 訳者; ho⌈ñyakuka 翻訳家.

transmission *n.* **1** (of a message) de⌈ñtatsu 伝達; (of a disease) de⌈ñseñ 伝染: the transmission of information (*joohoo no deñtatsu*)

情報の伝達 / the transmission of a disease (*byooki no deñseñ*) 病気の伝染.
2 (broadcast) ho^ro^soo 放送: the transmission of a TV program (*terebi-bañgumi no hoosoo*) テレビ番組の放送.

transmit *vt.* **1** (send) ... o o^kuru ...を送る [C]: transmit a message by radio (*tsuushiñ o mudeñ de okuru*) 通信を無電で送る.
2 (pass on) ... o tsu^taeru ...を伝える [V]; (of a disease) de^ñseñ saseru 伝染させる [V]: transmit a tradition to the younger generation (*deñtoo o wakai sedai ni tsutaeru*) 伝統を若い世代に伝える / Rats transmit diseases. (*Nezumi wa byooki o deñseñ saseru.*) ねずみは病気を伝染させる.
3 (of a TV station, etc.) ... o ho^o-soo suru ...を放送する [I]: The accident was transmitted live from the site. (*Sono jiko wa geñba kara nama de hoosoo sareta.*) その事故は現場から生で放送された.

transparent *adj.* to^omee na 透明な; su^kito^otte iru 透き通っている: a transparent plastic case (*toomee na purasuchikku no keesu*) 透明なプラスチックのケース.

transplant *vt.* ... o i^shoku suru ...を移植する [I]: transplant a heart (*shiñzoo o ishoku suru*) 心臓を移植する.
— *n.* i^shoku 移植.

transport *n.* yu^soo 輸送; u^ñsoo 運送: a transport ship (*yusoo-señ*) 輸送船.
— *vt.* ... o yu^soo suru ...を輸送する [I]; u^ñsoo suru 運送する [I]: transport goods by truck (*nimotsu o torakku de yusoo suru*) 荷物をトラックで輸送する.

transportation *n.* yu^soo 輸送; u^ñsoo 運送: a transportation company (*uñsoo-gaisha*) 運送会社.

trap *n.* **1** (device) wa^na わな; o^to-shi^ana 落とし穴: set a trap for a fox (*kitsune ni wana o shikakeru*) きつねにわなをしかける.
2 (trick) ke^eryaku 計略; wa^na わな: fall into a trap (*wana ni hamaru*) わなにはまる.
— *vt.* ... o wa^na de to^rae^ru ...をわなで捕らえる [V]: trap an animal (*doobutsu o wana de toraeru*) 動物をわなで捕らえる.

trash *n.* go^mi^ ごみ; ku^zu くず: sweep up trash (*gomi o haku*) ごみを掃く.

travel *vi.* **1** (journey) ryo^koo suru 旅行する [I]; ta^bi^ o suru 旅をする [I]: He traveled around the world. (*Kare wa sekai-is-shuu-ryokoo o shita.*) 彼は世界一周旅行をした.
2 (move) su^sumu 進む [C]; tsu^tawaru 伝わる [C]: Sound travels through the air. (*Oto wa kuuchuu o tsutawaru.*) 音は空中を伝わる.
3 (go as a salesperson) se^erusu shite ma^waru セールスして回る [C]: She travels selling insurance. (*Kanojo wa hokeñ o seerusu shite mawatte iru.*) 彼女は保険をセールスして回っている.
— *n.* ryo^koo 旅行; ta^bi^ 旅: I've just returned from my travels. (*Watashi wa ryokoo kara kaette kita tokoro desu.*) 私は旅行から帰って来たところです. ★ 'Journey,' 'trip' and 'tour' are also called '*ryokoo.*'

traveler *n.* ryo^ko^osha 旅行者; ta^bibito 旅人: a fellow traveler (*tabi no michizure*) 旅の道連れ.

traveler's check *n.* ryo^koosha kogi^tte 旅行者小切手; to^rabe-raazu che^kku トラベラーズチェック: Can I pay with a traveler's check? (*Ryokoosha kogitte de shiharai dekimasu ka?*) 旅行者小切手で支払いできますか. / I'd like to cash this traveler's check. (*Kono torabe-raazu chekku o geñkiñ ni shite kudasai.*) このトラベラーズチェックを現金にしてください.

tray *n.* bo^ñ 盆: carry glasses on a tray (*gurasu o boñ ni nosete hakobu*) グラスを盆に乗せて運ぶ.

treacherous *adj.* u^ragiri no 裏切りの; fu^jitsu na 不実な: a treacher-

t

ous act (*uragiri kooi*) 裏切り行為.

tread *vi.* (... o) fu⌐mu (…を)踏む Ⓒ; fu⌐mitsuke⌉ru 踏みつける Ⓥ: He trod on my foot. (*Kare wa watashi no ashi o fuñda.*) 彼は私の足を踏んだ.
— *vt.* ... o fu⌐mu …を踏む Ⓒ; fu⌐mitsubu⌉su 踏みつぶす Ⓒ: tread out one's cigarette (*tabako no hi o fuñde kesu*) たばこの火を踏んで消す.

treason *n.* ha⌐ñgyaku 反逆; mu⌉hoñ 謀反: plot treason (*muhoñ o takuramu*) 謀反をたくらむ.

treasure *n.* **1** (gold, jewels, etc.) ta⌐kara(mono⌉) 宝(物); za⌐ihoo 財宝: hidden treasure (*kakusareta takara*) 隠された宝.
2 (valued object) ki⌐choohiñ 貴重品: national treasures (*kokuhoo*) 国宝.
— *vt.* ... o ta⌐isetsu ni suru …を大切にする Ⓘ: I treasure the watch he gave me. (*Watashi wa kare ga kureta tokee o taisetsu ni shite imasu.*) 私は彼がくれた時計を大切にしています.

treasurer *n.* ka⌐ikeega⌉kari 会計係.

treasury *n.* (of a government) ko⌉oko 公庫; (funds) shi⌉kiñ 資金; (of a book) ho⌐oteñ 宝典.

treat *vt.* **1** (behave toward) ... o a⌐tsukau …を扱う Ⓒ: He treated me as one of the family. (*Kare wa watashi o kazoku no ichiiñ no yoo ni atsukatte kureta.*) 彼は私を家族の一員のように扱ってくれた.
2 (consider) ... o (... to) mi⌐na⌉su …を(…と)みなす Ⓒ: They treated the rumor as a fact. (*Kare-ra wa sono uwasa o jijitsu to minashita.*) 彼らはそのうわさを事実とみなした.
3 (give medical care) ... o chi⌐ryoo suru …を治療する Ⓘ; te⌉ate suru 手当てする Ⓘ: treat a patient with a new drug (*atarashii kusuri de kañja o chiryoo suru*) 新しい薬で患者を治療する.
4 (discuss) ... o ro⌐ñjiru …を論じる Ⓥ; no⌐be⌉ru 述べる Ⓥ: treat a subject thoroughly (*moñdai o tetteeteki ni roñjiru*) 問題を徹底的に論じる.
5 (of a meal) ... ni (... o) o⌐goru …に(…を)おごる Ⓒ: I'll treat you. (*Ogotte yaru yo.*) おごってやるよ.

treatment *n.* **1** (treating) to⌐riatsukai 取り扱い; a⌐tsukaikata 扱い方: receive kind treatment (*shiñsetsu na toriatsukai o ukeru*) 親切な取り扱いを受ける.
2 (of a disease) chi⌐ryoo(hoo) 治療(法): She is under treatment in the hospital. (*Kanojo wa byooiñ de chiryoo o ukete imasu.*) 彼女は病院で治療を受けています. / a new treatment for cancer (*gañ no atarashii chiryoohoo*) がんの新しい治療法.

treaty *n.* jo⌐oyaku 条約: conclude a peace treaty (*heewa-jooyaku o musubu*) 平和条約を結ぶ.

tree *n.* ki⌉ 木: cut down a tree (*ki o kiritaosu*) 木を切り倒す.

tremble *vi.* **1** (of a body) fu⌐rueru 震える Ⓥ: His hands were trembling with cold. (*Kare no te wa samusa de furuete ita.*) 彼の手は寒さで震えていた.
2 (of a thing) yu⌐reru 揺れる Ⓥ; shi⌐ñdoo suru 震動する Ⓘ: This bridge trembles as cars cross it. (*Kono hashi wa kuruma ga tooru to yureru.*) この橋は車が通ると揺れる.

tremendous *adj.* **1** (enormous) kyo⌐dai na 巨大な: a tremendous pumpkin (*kyodai na kabocha*) 巨大なかぼちゃ.
2 (extraordinay) mo⌐nosugo⌉i ものすごい; o⌐soroshi⌉i 恐ろしい: a tremendous explosion (*monosugoi bakuhatsu*) ものすごい爆発.

trench *n.* mi⌐zo 溝; ho⌐ri⌉ 堀: dig a trench (*mizo o horu*) 溝を掘る.

trend *n.* ke⌐ekoo 傾向; na⌐riyuki 成り行き: Prices are on an upward trend. (*Bukka wa jooshoo no keekoo ni aru.*) 物価は上昇の傾向にある.

trespass *vi.* (... ni) shi⌐ñnyuu suru (…に)侵入する Ⓘ; (... o) shi⌐ñgai suru (…を)侵害する Ⓘ: trespass on a person's privacy (*hito no puraiba-*

t

shii o shiñgai suru) 人のプライバシーを侵害する / No Trespassing. (*Tachiiri kiñshi.*) 立ち入り禁止.

trial *n.* **1** (legal process) sa^l^ibañ 裁判; shi^l^ñri 審理: a criminal trial (*keeji saibañ*) 刑事裁判 / stand trial (*saibañ o ukeru*) 裁判を受ける.
2 (test) shi^r^ke^l^ñ 試験; ko^r^koromi 試み: put a machine to trial (*kikai o tameshi ni tsukatte miru*) 機械を試しに使ってみる / He succeeded on his second trial. (*Kare wa ni-dome no kokoromi de seekoo shita.*) 彼は2度目の試みで成功した.
3 (trouble) shi^l^reñ 試練; sai^r^na^l^ñ 災難: a time of trial (*shireñ no toki*) 試練の時.

triangle *n.* sa^l^ñkaku 三角; (shape) sa^r^ñka^l^kukee 三角形; (set triangle) sa^r^ñkaku jo^l^ogi (三角定規).

tribe *n.* shu^l^zoku 種族; bu^l^zoku 部族.

tribute *n.* **1** (expression of praise) sa^l^ñji 賛辞; (something given to show respect) o^r^kurimono 贈り物: a floral tribute (*keñka*) 献花.
2 (payment to a ruler) mi^r^tsugimono 貢ぎ物: pay tribute to a ruler (*shihaisha ni mitsugimono o suru*) 支配者に貢ぎ物をする.

trick *n.* **1** (joke) jo^r^oda^l^ñ 冗談; i^r^tazura いたずら: play a trick on a person (*hito ni itazura o suru*) 人にいたずらをする.
2 (artifice) ta^r^kurami たくらみ; sa^r^kuryaku 策略: He got the license by a trick. (*Kare wa sakuryaku o tsukatte sono meñkyo o eta.*) 彼は策略を使ってその免許を得た.
3 (magic) te^l^jina 手品; ki^l^jutsu 奇術: card tricks (*torañpu no tejina*) トランプの手品.
— *vt.* ... o da^r^ma^l^su ...をだます Ⓒ: He tricked the old woman out of her money. (*Kare wa sono rooba o damashite kane o totta.*) 彼はその老婆をだまして金を取った.

trifle *n.* **1** (anything of little value) tsu^r^mara^l^nai mo^r^no^l^ つまらない物; ku^r^daranai mono^l^ くだらない物: quarrel over trifles (*tsumarani koto de keñka o suru*) つまらないことでけんかをする.
2 (small amount of money) wa^l^zuka na o-^r^kane わずかなお金: It cost me just a trifle. (*Hoñno wazuka na o-kane shika kakarimaseñ deshita.*) ほんのわずかなお金しかかかりませんでした.

trifling *adj.* ku^r^daranai くだらない; sa^l^sai na ささいな: a trifling error (*sasai na ayamari*) ささいな誤り.

trim *vt.* **1** (clip) ... o ka^r^riko^l^mu ... を刈り込む Ⓒ; (of hair) a^r^tama^l^ o ka^r^ru 頭を刈る Ⓒ: trim a hedge (*ikegaki o karikomu*) 生け垣を刈り込む / I got my hair trimmed. (*Watashi wa atama o katte moratta.*) 私は頭を刈ってもらった.
2 (decorate) ... o ka^r^zaru ...を飾る Ⓒ: trim a dress with lace (*fuku o reesu de kazaru*) 服をレースで飾る.
— *adj.* ki^r^chi^l^ñto shita [shite iru] きちんとした[している]; te^r^ire no yo^l^i 手入れのよい: a trim garden (*teire no yoi niwa*) 手入れのよい庭.

trip *n.* ryo^r^koo 旅行; ta^r^bi^l^ 旅: go on a trip (*ryokoo ni dekakeru*) 旅行に出かける / make a business trip to China (*shigoto de Chuugoku e ryokoo suru*) 仕事で中国へ旅行する / Have a good trip! (*Yoi go-ryokoo o.*) よいご旅行を. ★ 'Journey,' 'tour' and 'travel' are also called '*ryokoo.*'
— *vi.* (catch one's foot) (... ni) tsu^r^mazuku (...に)つまずく Ⓒ: trip on the root of a tree (*ki no ne ni tsumazuku*) 木の根につまずく.

triple *adj.* sa^l^ñ-juu no 3 重の; sa^l^ñbai no 3 倍の: a triple mirror (*sañmeñkyoo*) 三面鏡.

tripod *n.* sa^r^ñkyaku 三脚.

triumph *n.* sho^l^ori 勝利; da^r^ise^l^ekoo 大成功: win a triumph (*shoori o kachitoru*) 勝利を勝ち取る.

trivial *adj.* (of little importance) sa^l^sai na ささいな; (of a person) ku^r^daranai くだらない: trivial mistakes (*sasai na ayamari*) ささいな誤り / a trivial man (*kudaranai otoko*) くだらない男.

t

troop *n.* **1** (crowd) mu[re] 群れ; i[chiguñ 一群; i[chidañ 一団: a troop of demonstrators (*demotai no ichiguñ*) デモ隊の一群.
2 (of soldiers) gu]ñtai 軍隊.
trophy *n.* to]rofii トロフィー; sho[o-hiñ 賞品: win a trophy (*torofii o kakutoku suru*) トロフィーを獲得する.
tropical *adj.* ne[ttai no 熱帯の; ne[ttai chi]hoo no 熱帯地方の: a tropical fish (*nettaigyo*) 熱帯魚 / a tropical climate (*nettai-see kikoo*) 熱帯性気候.
trot *vi.* (horse) ha[ya]-ashi de ka[ke]ru 速足で駆ける [V]; (people) i[so]ide a[ru]ku 急いで歩く [C]: The horse trotted down the road. (*Uma ga haya-ashi de michi o kakete itta.*) 馬が速足で道を駆けて行った.
— *n.* ha[ya]-ashi 速足; i[sogi]-ashi 急ぎ足.
trouble *n.* **1** (inconvenience) me]ewaku 迷惑; ya]kkai やっかい: I'm sorry I've given you so much trouble. (*Taiheñ go-meewaku o o-kake shite sumimaseñ.*) 大変ご迷惑をおかけしてすみません.
2 (difficulty) ko]ñnañ 困難; ku]roo 苦労; ho[neori] 骨折り: I had a lot of trouble finding the book. (*Sono hoñ o mitsukeru no ni taiheñ ku-roo shita.*) その本を見つけるのに大変苦労した.
3 (worry) shi[ñpai(goto]) 心配(事); na[yami] 悩み: Tell me your troubles if you have any. (*Shiñpaigoto ga areba watashi ni hanashi nasai.*) 心配事があれば私に話しなさい.
4 (illness) byo[oki 病気: heart trouble (*shiñzoobyoo*) 心臓病.
5 (disturbance) go[tagota] ごたごた; fu[ñsoo 紛争: labor troubles (*roo-doo soogi*) 労働争議.
— *vt.* **1** (cause worry) ... o shi[ñ-pai saseru ...を心配させる [V]; na[yama]su 悩ます [C]: He is troubled about family matters. (*Kare wa katee no koto de nayañde iru.*) 彼は家庭のことで悩んでいる.
2 (cause inconvenience) ... ni me]ewaku o ka[ke]ru ...に迷惑をかける [V]; ya]kkai o ka[ke]ru やっかいをかける [V]: I don't like to trouble you about a thing like this. (*Koñna koto de go-meewaku o kaketaku arimaseñ.*) こんなことでご迷惑をかけたくありません.
troublesome *adj.* ya]kkai na やっかいな; me[ñdo]o na 面倒な: a troublesome problem (*meñdoo na moñ-dai*) 面倒な問題.
trousers *n.* zu[bo]ñ ズボン: put on [take off] trousers (*zuboñ o haku* [*nugu*]) ズボンをはく[脱ぐ].
truck *n.* (car) to[ra]kku トラック: transport goods by truck (*shina-mono o torakku de yusoo suru*) 品物をトラックで輸送する.
true *adj.* **1** (of a story) ho[ñtoo no 本当の; ji]jitsu no 事実の: Do you think his story is true? (*Kare no hanashi wa hoñtoo da to omoi-masu ka?*) 彼の話は本当だと思いますか.
2 (genuine) ho[ñmono no 本物の; shi]ñ no 真の: a true friend (*shiñ no tomo*) 真の友.
3 (faithful) se[ejitsu na 誠実な; chu[ujitsu na 忠実な: He was true to his word. (*Kare wa yakusoku ni seejitsu datta.*) 彼は約束に誠実だった.
truly *adj.* **1** (truthfully) shi]ñjitsu ni 真実に; i[tsuwari na]ku 偽りなく: speak truly (*shiñjitsu o kataru*) 真実を語る.
2 (sincerely) se[ejitsu ni 誠実に; ko[ko]ro kara 心から: I feel truly grateful. (*Kokoro kara kañsha shimasu.*) 心から感謝します.
3 (really) ho[ñtoo ni 本当に; ma[t-taku まったく: I am truly happy. (*Watashi wa hoñtoo ni shiawase desu.*) 私は本当に幸せです.
trumpet *n.* to[rañpe]tto トランペット: blow a trumpet (*torañpetto o fuku*) トランペットを吹く.
trunk *n.* **1** (of a tree) mi]ki 幹.
2 (of an elephant) zo]o no ha[na 象の鼻.
3 (box) to[ra]ñku トランク.

4 (body) do˥otai 胴体.

trust *vt.* **1** (have confidence) ... o shi˹ñrai suru ...を信頼する [I]; shi˹ñyoo suru 信用する [I]: We can trust what he says. (*Kare no iu koto wa shiñyoo dekimasu.*) 彼の言うことは信用できます.

2 (entrust) ... o a˹zuke˥ru ...を預ける [V]; ma˹kase˥ru 任せる [V]: I trusted the details to him. (*Komakai koto wa kare ni makasemashita.*) 細かいことは彼に任せました.

3 (expect) ... o ki˹tai suru ...を期待する [I]; ka˹kushiñ suru 確信する [I]: I trust you will have a good journey. (*Yoi tabi o kitai shite imasu.*) よい旅を期待しています.

— *n.* **1** (confidence) shi˹ñrai 信頼; shi˹ñyoo 信用: have trust in a person (*hito o shiñyoo suru*) 人を信用する.

2 (charge) i˹taku 委託; ho˹kañ 保管; (care) ho˥go 保護: I left my valuables in trust with him. (*Watashi wa kichoohiñ o kare ni hokañ shite moratta.*) 私は貴重品を彼に保管してもらった.

3 (responsibility) se˹kiniñ 責任: a position of great trust (*omoi sekiniñ no aru chii*) 重い責任のある地位.

trustworthy *adj.* shi˹ñrai deki˥ru 信頼できる; a˹te ni na˥ru 当てになる: a trustworthy driver (*shiñrai dekiru uñteñshu*) 信頼できる運転手.

truth *n.* **1** (true fact) ho˹ñtoo no koto˥ 本当のこと; ji˥jitsu 事実; shi˹ñsoo 真相: tell the truth (*hoñtoo no koto o hanasu*) 本当のことを話す

2 (trueness) shi˥ñri 真理: seek truth (*shiñri o tañkyuu suru*) 真理を探究する.

truthful *adj.* se˹ejitsu na 誠実な; sho˹oji˥ki na 正直な: a truthful child (*shoojiki na kodomo*) 正直な子ども.

try *vt.* **1** (attempt) ... to tsu˹tome˥ru ...と努める [V]; do˥ryoku suru 努力する [I]: I tried to do my best. (*Watashi wa zeñryoku o tsukusoo to tsutometa.*) 私は全力を尽くそうと努めた.

2 (test) ... o ta˹me˥su ...を試す [C]; ko˹koromi˥ru 試みる [V]: He tried a different method. (*Kare wa chigau hoohoo o tameshite mita.*) 彼は違う方法を試してみた.

3 (conduct the trial) ... o shi˥ñri suru ...を審理する [I]; sa˹ba˥ku 裁く [C]: try the case (*jikeñ o shiñri suru*) 事件を審理する.

— *vi.* ya˹tte mi˥ru やってみる [V]: I tried again and again. (*Watashi wa nañ-do mo yatte mita.*) 私は何度もやってみた.

try on *vt.* ... o ki˹te mi˥ru ...を着てみる [V]: May I try this on? (*Kore o kite mite mo ii desu ka?*) これを着てみてもいいですか.

tub *n.* **1** (container) o˥ke おけ: wash clothes in a tub (*oke de kimono o arau*) おけで着物を洗う.

2 (of a bath) yo˹kusoo 浴槽; yu˥bune 湯ぶね.

tube *n.* **1** (pipe) ka˥ñ 管; tsu˹tsu 筒: a rubber tube (*gomu-kañ*) ゴム管.

2 (container) chu˥ubu チューブ: a tube of paint (*enogu no chuubu*) 絵の具のチューブ.

tuck *vt.* **1** (gather up) ... o ma˹kuriage˥ru ...をまくり上げる [V]: tuck up one's sleeves (*sode o makuriageru*) そでをまくり上げる.

2 (push) ... o o˹shiko˥mu ...を押し込む [C]: tuck a handkerchief in one's pocket (*hañkachi o poketto ni oshikomu*) ハンカチをポケットに押し込む.

3 (fold) ... o ku˹rumiko˥mu ...をくるみ込む [C]: tuck a baby in a bed (*akañboo o beddo ni kurumikoñde nekaseru*) 赤ん坊をベッドにくるみ込んで寝かせる.

Tuesday *n.* ka˹yo˥o(bi) 火曜(日).

tug *vt.* ... o hi˹ku ...を引く [C]; hi˹ppa˥ru 引っ張る [C]: I tugged the door but it wouldn't open. (*Watashi wa doa o hippatta ga akanakatta.*) 私はドアを引っ張ったが開かなかった.

— *n.* tsuˡyoku hiˈku kotoˡ 強く引くこと: He gave me a tug at my hair. (*Kare wa watashi no kami no ke o tsuyoku hippatta.*) 彼は私の髪の毛を強く引っ張った.

tumble *vi.* **1** (fall) taˈoreˡru 倒れる Ⓥ; koˈrobu 転ぶ Ⓒ: I tumbled over the roots of a tree. (*Watashi wa ki no ne ni tsumazuite koroñda.*) 私は木の根につまずいて転んだ.
2 (roll over) koˈrogemawaˡru 転げ回る Ⓒ: The children tumbled about on the grass. (*Kodomo-tachi wa kusa no ue o korogemawatta.*) 子どもたちは草の上を転げ回った.

tune *n.* **1** (musical tones) kyoˡku 曲; (melody) meˡrodii メロディー: play a tune on the piano (*piano de kyoku o hiku*) ピアノで曲を弾く.
2 (correct pitch) choˈoshi 調子: Your violin is out of tune. (*Kimi no baioriñ wa chooshi ga kurutte iru.*) 君のバイオリンは調子が狂っている.
— *vt.* **1** (of a radio, TV) ... o aˈwaseˡru ...を合わせる Ⓥ: tune the television to Channel 1 (*terebi o dai-ichi chañneru ni awaseru*) テレビを第1チャンネルに合わせる.
2 (of an instrument) ... no choˈoshi o awaseˡru ...の調子を合わせる Ⓥ; ... o choˈoritsu suru ...を調律する Ⓘ: tune a piano (*piano o chooritsu suru*) ピアノを調律する.

tunnel *n.* toˈñneru トンネル: build a tunnel (*toñneru o horu*) トンネルを掘る.

turf *n.* shiˈba 芝: artificial turf (*jiñkoo-shiba*) 人口芝.

turkey *n.* shiˈchimeñchoo 七面鳥.

turmoil *n.* saˡwagi 騒ぎ; koˈñrañ 混乱: The town was in a turmoil during the election. (*Señkyo no aida machi wa oosawagi datta.*) 選挙の間町は大騒ぎだった.

turn *vt.* **1** (revolve) ... o maˈwasu ...を回す Ⓒ; kaˈiteñ saseru 回転させる Ⓥ: turn the knob of a door (*doa no totte o mawasu*) ドアの取っ手を回す / turn the wheel to the right (*hañdoru o migi e mawasu*) ハンドルを右へ回す.
2 (move around) ... o hiˈkkurikaˡesu ...をひっくり返す Ⓒ; uˈragaˡesu 裏返す Ⓒ; (of a page) meˈkuru めくる Ⓒ: turn the steak over (*suteeki o uragaesu*) ステーキを裏返す / turn the pages of a book (*hoñ no peeji o mekuru*) 本のページをめくる.
3 (go around) ... o maˈgaru ...を曲がる Ⓒ; maˈwaru 回る Ⓒ: The car turned the corner. (*Sono kuruma wa kado o magatta.*) その車は角を曲がった.
4 (change direction) ... o kaˈeru ...を変える Ⓥ; muˈkeru 向ける Ⓥ: She turned her back to me. (*Kanojo wa senaka o watashi no hoo e muketa.*) 彼女は背中を私の方へ向けた.
5 (change) ... o kaˈeru ...を変える Ⓥ: Heat turns water into vapor. (*Netsu wa mizu o jooki ni kaeru.*) 熱は水を蒸気に変える.
— *vi.* **1** (rotate) maˈwaru 回る Ⓒ; kaˈiteñ suru 回転する Ⓘ: The faucet turned easily. (*Señ wa kañtañ ni mawatta.*) 栓は簡単に回った.
2 (change direction) muˡki o kaˈeru 向きを変える Ⓥ; maˈgaru 曲がる Ⓒ: Turn to the left at the next corner. (*Tsugi no kado o hidari e magari nasai.*) 次の角を左へ曲がりなさい.
3 (change) kaˈwaru 変わる Ⓒ: The traffic light turned from red to green. (*Shiñgoo ga aka kara ao ni kawatta.*) 信号が赤から青に変わった.

turn off *vt.* ... o toˈmeru ...を止める Ⓥ; keˈsu 消す Ⓒ: turn off the gas (*gasu o tomeru*) ガスを止める / turn off the radio (*rajio o kesu*) ラジオを消す.

turn on *vt.* ... o daˡsu ...を出す Ⓒ; tsuˈkeˡru つける Ⓥ: turn on the water (*mizu o dasu*) 水を出す / turn on the television (*terebi o tsukeru*) テレビをつける.

turn out *vt.* ... o keˈsu ...を消す Ⓒ: turn out the light (*akari o kesu*) 明かりを消す.

— *n.* **1** (turning) maˈwasu kotoˡ

回すこと; ma⌈waru koto⌉ 回ること; ka⌈iteñ 回転: I gave the handle a turn to the right. (*Watashi wa hañdoru o migi e mawashita.*) 私はハンドルを右へ回した.
2 (change of direction) ma⌈garu koto⌉ 曲がること; te⌈ñkai 転回: make a turn to the left (*hidari e magaru*) 左へ曲がる.
3 (rightful duty) ju⌈ñbañ 順番; ba⌉ñ 番: Now it's your turn to sing. (*Koñdo wa kimi ga utau bañ da.*) 今度は君が歌う番だ.
4 (change) he⌉ñka 変化; te⌈ñkai 展開: an unexpected turn of events (*yoki shinai koto no teñkai*) 予期しない事の展開.
5 (turning point) ka⌈warime 変わり目: the turn of the century (*seeki no kawarime*) 世紀の変わり目.

turnip *n.* ka⌈bu かぶ(蕪).

turnpike *n.* ko⌈osoku yuuryoo do⌉oro 高速有料道路.

TV *n.* te⌉rebi テレビ: I watched the baseball game on TV. (*Watashi wa sono yakyuu no shiai o terebi de mita.*) 私はその野球の試合をテレビで見た. / a TV set (*terebi juzooki*) テレビ受像機.

twelfth *adj.* ju⌈uni-bañme⌉ no 12 番目の; da⌉i-ju⌈uni⌉ no 第12の.
— *n.* **1** (person) ju⌈uni-bañme⌉ no hi⌈to⌉ 12番目の人; (things) ju⌈uni-bañme⌉ no mo⌈no⌉ 12番目のもの.
2 (day) ju⌈uni-nichi⌉ 12日.
3 (fraction) ju⌈unibuñ no ichi⌉ 12分の1.

twelve *pron.* ju⌈uni⌉ 12; (people) ju⌈uni⌉-niñ 12人; (things) ju⌈uni⌉-ko 12個.
— *n.* (figure) ju⌈uni⌉ 12; (hour) ju⌈uni⌉-ji 12時; (minute) ju⌈uni⌉-fuñ 12分; (age) ju⌈uni⌉-sai 12歳.
— *adj.* ju⌈uni⌉ no 12の; (people) ju⌈uni⌉-niñ no 12人の; (things) ju⌈uni⌉-ko no 12個の; (age) ju⌈uni⌉-sai no 12歳の.

twentieth *adj.* ni⌈juu-bañme⌉ no 20番目の; da⌉i-nijuu no 第20の.
— *n.* **1** (person) ni⌈juu-bañme⌉ no hi⌈to⌉ 20番目の人; (thing) ni⌈juu-bañme⌉ no mo⌈no⌉ 20番目のもの.
2 (day) ha⌈tsuka 20日.
3 (fraction) ni⌈juubuñ no ichi⌉ 20分の1.

twenty *pron.* ni⌉juu 20; (people) ni⌉ju⌉u-niñ 20人; (things) ni⌈ju⌉k-ko 20個.
— *n.* (figure) ni⌉juu 20; (hour) ni⌈ju⌉u-ji 20時; (minute) ni⌈ju⌉p-puñ 20分; (age) ni⌈ju⌉s-sai [ha⌉tachi] 20歳.
— *adj.* ni⌉juu no 20の; (people) ni⌈ju⌉u-niñ no 20人の; (of things) ni⌈ju⌉k-ko no 20個の; (age) ni⌈ju⌉s-sai [ha⌉tachi] no 20歳の.

twice *adv.* **1** (two times) ni-⌈do 2度; ni-⌈ka⌉i 2回: I have visited Kyoto twice. (*Watashi wa Kyooto e ni-kai ikimashita.*) 私は京都へ2回行きました.
2 (two times as much) ni-⌈bai 2倍: I worked twice as hard as you. (*Watashi wa anata no ni-bai hataraita.*) 私はあなたの2倍働いた.

twilight *n.* ta⌈sogare たそがれ; u⌈su-a⌉kari 薄明かり: stroll in the twilight (*tasogare no naka o sañpo suru*) たそがれの中を散歩する.

twin *n.* so⌈ose⌉eji 双生児; fu⌈tago 双子.
— *adj.* fu⌈tago no 双子の: twin brothers (*futago no kyoodai*) 双子の兄弟 / twin sisters (*futago no shimai*) 双子の姉妹.

twin bed *n.* tsu⌈iñ be⌉ddo ツインベッド.

twist *vt.* **1** (turn) ... o ne⌈ji⌉ru ...をねじる Ⓒ; hi⌈ne⌉ru ひねる Ⓒ: twist a knob (*totte o hineru*) 取っ手をひねる.
2 (wind) ... o ma⌈ku ...を巻く Ⓒ: twist a cord around a package (*tsutsumi ni himo o maku*) 包みにひもを巻く.
3 (wind together) ... o yo⌉ru ...をよる Ⓒ; a⌉mu 編む Ⓒ: twist wires to make a rope (*harigane o yotte roopu o tsukuru*) 針金をよってロープを作る.
— *vi.* **1** (of a path) ma⌈garikune⌉-

ru 曲がりくねる Ⓒ: The road twists through the mountains. (*Michi wa yama no aida o magarikunette iru.*) 道は山の間を曲がりくねっている.

2 (of a body) mi o moˈgaˈku 身をもがく Ⓒ: She twisted with pain. (*Kanojo wa kutsuu de mi o mogaita.*) 彼女は苦痛で身をもがいた.

— *n.* **1** (twisting) neˈjiri ねじり; yoˈri より: give a twist to a person's arm (*hito no ude o nejiru*) 人の腕をねじる.

2 (bend) maˈgari 曲がり; kaˈabu カーブ: The road has a lot of twists. (*Sono michi wa kaabu ga ooi.*) その道はカーブが多い.

two *pron.* fuˈtatsuˈ 二つ; (people) fuˈtariˈ 二人; (things) niˈ-ko 2 個.

— *n.* (figure) niˈ 2; (hour) niˈ-ji 2 時; (minute) niˈ-fuñ 2 分; (age) niˈ-sai 2 歳.

— *adj.* fuˈtatsuˈ no 二つの; (people) fuˈtariˈ no 二人の; (things) niˈ-ko no 2 個の; (age) niˈ-sai no 2 歳の.

type *n.* **1** (kind) kaˈtaˈ 型; taˈipu タイプ: cars of the same type (*onaji kata no kuruma*) 同じ型の車 / My blood type is B. (*Watashi no ketsueki-gata wa B desu.*) 私の血液型は B です.

2 (letter used in printing) kaˈtsuji 活字: set up type (*katsuji o kumu*) 活字を組む / italic type (*itarikku-tai*) イタリック体.

— *vt.* ... o taˈipu suru ...をタイプする Ⓘ: type a letter (*tegami o taipu suru*) 手紙をタイプする.

typewriter *n.* taˈipuraˈitaa タイプライター: write a letter on a typewriter (*taipuraitaa de tegami o kaku*) タイプライターで手紙を書く.

typical *adj.* **1** (representative) teˈñkee-teki na 典型的な; daˈihyoo-teki na 代表的な: a typical Japanese dish (*daihyoo-teki na Nihoñ ryoori*) 代表的な日本料理.

2 (characteristic) doˈkutoku na 独特な; toˈkuyuu no 特有の: his typical way of speaking (*kare tokuyuu no hanashikata*) 彼特有の話し方.

typically *adv.* iˈppañ ni 一般に; gaˈishite 概して: Typically, winter in Japan is mild. (*Gaishite Nihoñ no fuyu wa oñdañ desu.*) 概して日本の冬は温暖です.

typist *n.* taˈipiˈsuto タイピスト.

tyranny *n.* seˈñsee-seˈeji 専制政治; aˈssee 圧制.

tyrant *n.* seˈñsee kuˈñshu 専制君主; boˈokuñ 暴君.

U

ugly *adj.* **1** (unpleasing) miˈnikuˈi 醜い; miˈgurushiˈi 見苦しい: an ugly duckling (*minikui ahiru no ko*) 醜いあひるの子.

2 (disgusting) fuˈkai na 不快な; iˈyaˈ na いやな: an ugly rumor (*iya na uwasa*) いやなうわさ.

ulcer *n.* kaˈiyoo 潰瘍: stomach ulcers (*ikaiyoo*) 胃潰瘍.

ultimate *adj.* **1** (final) saˈigo no 最後の; saˈishuu no 最終の: an ultimate decision (*saishuu kettee*) 最終決定.

2 (greatest) saˈikoo no 最高の: the ultimate speed (*saikoo sokudo*) 最高速度.

ultimately *adv.* saˈigo ni 最後に; keˈkkyoku 結局: Ultimately, he decided not to go. (*Kekkyoku kare wa ikanai koto ni kimeta.*) 結局彼は行かないことに決めた.

umbrella *n.* kaˈsa 傘: put up an umbrella (*kasa o sasu*) 傘をさす / open [close] an umbrella (*kasa o hirogeru* [*tatamu*]) 傘を広げる[畳む] / a collapsible umbrella (*oritatami no kasa*) 折り畳みの傘.

umpire *n.* shiˈñpañ 審判; shiˈñpaˈñ-iñ 審判員; aˈñpaˈia アンパイア.

★ 'Judge' and 'referee' are also

called '*shiñpañ(iñ).*'

unable *adj.* ... ga de˹ki˺nai …ができない: I was unable to attend the party. (*Watashi wa sono paatii ni shusseki suru koto ga dekinakatta.*) 私はそのパーティーに出席することができなかった.

unaccompanied *adj.* (of a person) tsu˹re no na˺i 連れのない; (of baggage) be˹ssoo no 別送の: Please send this as unaccompanied baggage. (*Kore o bessoo tenimotsu ni shite okutte kudasai.*) これを別送手荷物にして送ってください.

unanimous *adj.* ma˹ñjoo itchi no 満場一致の: a unanimous decision (*mañjoo itchi no kettee*) 満場一致の決定.

unanimously *adv.* ma˹ñjoo itchi de 満場一致で: He was elected chairperson unanimously. (*Kare wa mañjoo itchi de gichoo ni erabareta.*) 彼は満場一致で議長に選ばれた.

unaware *adj.* ... o shi˹rana˺i de …を知らないで; ... ni ki ˹ga tsuka˺nai de …に気がつかないで: I was unaware that she was there. (*Watashi wa kanojo ga soko ni iru no ni ki ga tsukanakatta.*) 私は彼女がそこにいるのに気がつかなかった.

unbearable *adj.* ta˹erare˺nai 耐えられない; ga˺mañ de˹ki˺nai 我慢できない: This heat is unbearable. (*Kono atsusa wa gamañ dekinai.*) この暑さは我慢できない.

unbelievable *adj.* shi˹ñjirare˺nai 信じられない: His good luck is unbelievable. (*Kare no koouñ wa shiñjirarenai.*) 彼の幸運は信じられない.

unbutton *vt.* ... no bo˺tañ o ha˹zusu …のボタンをはずす Ⓒ: unbutton one's coat (*uwagi no botañ o hazusu*) 上着のボタンをはずす.

uncertain *adj.* **1** (not sure) ka˹kushiñ ga na˺i 確信がない: I am uncertain of success. (*Seekoo no kakushiñ wa arimaseñ.*) 成功の確信はありません.

2 (not definite) fu˹ka˺kujitsu na 不確実な; ha˹kki˺ri shinai はっきりしない: The date of their arrival is uncertain. (*Kare-ra no toochaku suru hi wa hakkiri shimaseñ.*) 彼らの到着する日ははっきりしません.

3 (not steady) fu˹a˺ñtee na 不安定な; ka˹wariyasu˺i 変わりやすい: uncertain weather (*kawariyasui teñki*) 変わりやすい天気.

uncertainty *n.* fu˹ka˺kujitsu 不確実; fu˹a˺ñtee 不安定.

unchangeable *adj.* ka˹waranai 変わらない; fu˹heñ no 不変の: unchangeable facts (*fuheñ no jijitsu*) 不変の事実.

uncle *n.* o˹ji おじ: I stayed at my uncle's. (*Watashi wa oji no ie ni tomatta.*) 私はおじの家に泊まった.

uncomfortable *adj.* **1** (not comfortable) ⟨verb⟩-gokochi no yo˺ku nai …心地のよくない: an uncomfortable chair (*suwari-gokochi no yoku nai isu*) 座り心地のよくないいす / an uncomfortable uniform (*ki-gokochi no yoku nai seefuku*) 着心地のよくない制服.

2 (uneasy) o˹chitsukanai 落ち着かない; fu˹añ na 不安な: I feel uncomfortable with strangers. (*Shiranai hito to iru to ochitsukanai.*) 知らない人といると落ち着かない.

uncommon *adj.* **1** (rare) me˹zurashi˺i 珍しい; ma˹re na まれな: an uncommon bird (*mezurashii tori*) 珍しい鳥.

2 (remarkable) i˹joo na 異常な; hi˹boñ na 非凡な: uncommon ability (*hiboñ na sainoo*) 非凡な才能.

unconscious *adj.* **1** (not conscious) i˺shiki o u˹shinatta [u˹shinatte iru] 意識を失った[失っている]: become unconscious (*ishiki o ushinau*) 意識を失う.

2 (not aware) (... ni) ki˹zuka˺nai (…に)気づかない: He was unconscious of his mistake. (*Kare wa jibuñ no ayamari ni kizukanakatta.*) 彼は自分の誤りに気づかなかった.

3 (not intended) mu˹i˺shiki no 無意識の: an unconscious habit (*mu-*

ishiki ni deru kuse) 無意識に出る癖.

uncover *vt.* **1** (remove) ... no fu⌈ta o to⌉ru …のふたを取る Ⓒ: uncover a box (*hako no futa o toru*) 箱のふたを取る.
2 (make known) ... o ba⌉kuro suru …を暴露する Ⓘ; a⌈ba⌉ku 暴く Ⓒ: uncover a conspiracy (*iñboo o abaku*) 陰謀を暴く.

undecided *adj.* (of a person) ke⌉sshiñ ga tsu⌉ite nai 決心がついてない; (of a matter) ki⌈matte na⌉i 決まってない; mi⌈tee no 未定の: The date of the meeting is still undecided. (*Kaigi no hi wa mada mitee desu.*) 会議の日はまだ未定です.

undeniable *adj.* hi⌈tee deki⌉nai 否定できない; me⌈ehaku na 明白な: undeniable facts (*meehaku na jijitsu*) 明白な事実.

under *prep.* **1** (below) ... no shi⌈ta ni [de] …の下に[で]: The cat is under the table. (*Neko wa teeburu no shita ni imasu.*) 猫はテーブルの下にいます. / We took a rest under a tree. (*Watashi-tachi wa ki no shita de yasuñda.*) 私たちは木の下で休んだ.
2 (less than) ... mi⌉mañ no [de] …未満の[で]: children under 13 years of age (*juusañ-sai mimañ no kodomo-tachi*) 13 歳未満の子どもたち.
3 (directed by) ... no mo⌈to⌉ de …のもとで: I studied law under Professor Tanaka. (*Watashi wa Tanaka kyooju no moto de hooritsu o manañda.*) 私は田中教授のもとで法律を学んだ.
4 (in course of) ... chuu no …中の: a road under repair (*shuuri-chuu no dooro*) 修理中の道路.

undergo *vt.* ... o u⌈ke⌉ru …を受ける Ⓥ; ke⌈ekeñ suru 経験する Ⓘ: undergo an operation (*shujutsu o ukeru*) 手術を受ける / undergo many hardships (*ooku no koñnañ o keekeñ suru*) 多くの困難を経験する.

underground *adj.* **1** (beneath the surface of the earth) chi⌉ka no 地下の: an underground passage (*chika no tsuuro*) 地下の通路.
2 (secret) hi⌈mitsu no 秘密の: an underground organization (*himitsu soshiki*) 秘密組織.
— *n.* (subway) chi⌈katetsu 地下鉄.

underline *vt.* ... no shi⌈ta ni se⌉ñ o hi⌈ku …の下に線を引く Ⓒ: underline a word (*go no shita ni señ o hiku*) 語の下に線を引く.
— *n.* ka⌈señ 下線; u⌈ñdaara⌉iñ アンダーライン.

underneath *prep.* ... no shi⌈ta ni [o] …の下に[を]: I have nothing on beneath my sweater. (*Watashi wa seetaa no shita ni nani mo kite imaseñ.*) 私はセーターの下に何も着ていません. / look beneath a bed (*beddo no shita o miru*) ベッドの下を見る.

undershirt *n.* shi⌈tagi 下着; sha⌉tsu シャツ.

undershorts *n.* pa⌉ñtsu パンツ.

understand *vt.* **1** (get the meaning of) ... o ri⌉kai suru …を理解する Ⓘ; ... ga wa⌈ka⌉ru …がわかる Ⓒ: Do you understand what I say? (*Watashi no iu koto ga wakarimasu ka?*) 私の言うことがわかりますか.
2 (interpret) ... to o⌈mo⌉u …と思う Ⓒ; ka⌉ishaku suru 解釈する Ⓘ: I understood his silence to be a refusal. (*Watashi wa kare ga damatte iru no wa iya na no da to omotta.*) 私は彼が黙っているのはいやなのだと思った.
3 (know the feelings) ... o ri⌉kai suru …を理解する Ⓘ: No one understood her. (*Dare mo kanojo o rikai shinakatta.*) だれも彼女を理解しなかった.
— *vi.* ri⌉kai suru 理解する Ⓘ; wa⌈ka⌉ru わかる Ⓒ: Do you understand? (*Wakarimashita ka?*) わかりましたか.

understanding *n.* ri⌉kai 理解; ri⌈ka⌉iryoku 理解力: I have a full understanding of the situation. (*Jookyoo wa yoku rikai shite imasu.*) 状況はよく理解しています.

undertake *vt.* **1** (accept) ... o hi-

ʳkiukeˡru …を引き受ける Ⓥ: undertake a task (*shigoto o hikiukeru*) 仕事を引き受ける.
2 (enter on) ... ni chaˡkushu suru …に着手する Ⓘ; ... o haʳjimeru …を始める Ⓥ: undertake an enterprise (*jigyoo o hajimeru*) 事業を始める.

undertaking *n.* jiˡgyoo 事業; shiʳgoto 仕事: a social undertaking (*shakai jigyoo*) 社会事業 / a difficult undertaking (*muzukashii shigoto*) 難しい仕事.

undesirable *adj.* noʳzomashiku naˡi 望ましくない; koʳnomashiku naˡi 好ましくない: an undesirable friend (*konomashiku nai tomodachi*) 好ましくない友だち.

undo *vt.* **1** (unfasten) ... o hoʳdoˡku …をほどく Ⓒ; hiʳraˡku 開く Ⓒ; haʳzusu 外す Ⓒ: undo a knot (*musubime o hodoku*) 結び目をほどく / undo a package (*tsutsumi o hiraku*) 包みを開く / undo a button (*botañ o hazusu*) ボタンをはずす.
2 (reverse) ... o moˡto ni moʳdoˡsu …を元に戻す Ⓒ: What is done cannot be undone. (*Shite shimatta koto wa moto ni modoranai.*) してしまったことは元に戻らない.

undress *vt.* ... no fuʳkuˡ o nuʳgaseˡru …の服を脱がせる Ⓥ: undress a child (*kodomo no fuku o nugaseru*) 子どもの服を脱がせる.

uneasiness *n.* fuʳañ 不安; shiʳñpai 心配: give a person uneasiness (*hito o fuañ ni suru*) 人を不安にする.

uneasy *adj.* fuʳañ na 不安な; shiʳñpai na 心配な: I feel uneasy about my son's future. (*Watashi wa musuko no shoorai ga fuañ da.*) 私は息子の将来が不安だ.

unemployed *adj.* shiʳgoto no naˡi 仕事のない; shiʳtsugyoo shita [shite iru] 失業した[している]: He was unemployed for three months. (*Kare wa sañ-kagetsu shigoto ga nakatta.*) 彼は3か月仕事がなかった. / the unemployed (*shitsugyoosha*) 失業者.

unemployment *n.* shiʳtsugyoo 失業: unemployment benefit (*shitsugyoo teate*) 失業手当.

unequal *adj.* hiʳtoˡshiku naˡi 等しくない; doʳotoo de naˡi 同等でない: rooms of unequal size (*ookisa ga hitoshiku nai heya*) 大きさが等しくない部屋.

uneven *adj.* taʳira de naˡi 平らでない; deʳkoboko no でこぼこの: an uneven road (*dekoboko no michi*) でこぼこの道.

unexpected *adj.* yoˡki shiʳnai 予期しない; iʳgai na 意外な: an unexpected accident (*yoki shinai jiko*) 予期しない事故 / That's unexpected. (*Sore wa igai da.*) それは意外だ.

unexpectedly *adv.* oʳmoigakenaˡku 思いがけなく; iʳgai ni 意外に: I unexpectedly met him at the station. (*Watashi wa omoigakenaku kare to eki de deatta.*) 私は思いがけなく彼と駅で出会った.

unfair *adj.* fuʳkoˡohee na 不公平な; fuʳtoo na 不当な: receive unfair treatment (*fukoohee na atsukai o ukeru*) 不公平な扱いを受ける.

unfamiliar *adj.* yoˡku shiʳranai よく知らない; miʳnarenai 見慣れない; naʳjimi no naˡi なじみのない: The subject is unfamiliar to me. (*Sono moñdai wa yoku shirimaseñ.*) その問題はよく知りません.

unfavorable *adj.* tsuʳgoo no waʳruˡi 都合の悪い; fuˡri na 不利な: unfavorable conditions (*furi na jookeñ*) 不利な条件.

unfit *adj.* fuʳteˡkitoo na 不適当な; fuˡmuki no 不向きの: This water is unfit for drinking. (*Kono mizu wa iñyoo ni tekisanai.*) この水は飲用に適さない.

unfold *vt.* ... o hiʳrogeru …を広げる Ⓥ; hiʳraˡku 開く Ⓒ: unfold a map (*chizu o hirogeru*) 地図を広げる.

unforgettable *adj.* waʳsurerarenai 忘れられない: an unforgettable experience (*wasurerarenai keekeñ*) 忘れられない経験.

unfortunate *adj.* fuˡuñ na 不運な; fuʳkoˡo na 不幸な: He was unfor-

u

tunate to meet with the accident. (*Kare ga sono jiko ni atta no wa fuuñ datta.*) 彼がその事故に遭ったのは不運だった.

unfortunately *adv.* u'ñ waruku 運悪く; a'iniku あいにく: Unfortunately it began to rain. (*Uñ waruku ame ga furi-dashita.*) 運悪く雨が降りだした. / Unfortunately I have a previous engagement. (*Ainiku señyaku ga arimasu.*) あいにく先約があります.

ungrateful *adj.* o'ñshi'razu no 恩知らずの: an ungrateful person (*oñshirazu no hito*) 恩知らずの人.

unhappy *adj.* **1** (not happy) fu'ko'o na 不幸な; mi'jime na 惨めな: lead an unhappy life (*fukoo na seekatsu o okuru*) 不幸な生活を送る.
2 (not satisfactory) fu'mañ na 不満な; o'moshiro'ku nai おもしろくない: We were unhappy about the result. (*Watashi-tachi wa sono kekka ni fumañ datta.*) 私たちはその結果に不満だった.

unhealthy *adj.* fu'ke'ñkoo na 不健康な; ke'ñkoo ni waru'i 健康に悪い: unhealthy habits (*keñkoo ni warui shuukañ*) 健康に悪い習慣.

uniform *n.* se'efuku 制服; yu'nifo'omu ユニフォーム.
— *adj.* **1** (not changing) i'chiyoo na 一様な; i'ttee no 一定の: drive at a uniform speed (*ittee no sokudo de kuruma o uñteñ suru*) 一定の速度で車を運転する.
2 (not different) do'oitsu no 同一の; o'naji katachi no 同じ形の: a row of uniform houses (*onaji katachi no ie no narabi*) 同じ形の家の並び.

unify *vt.* ... o to'oitsu suru …を統一する [I]; to'ogoo suru 統合する [I]: unify factions (*tooha o tooitsu suru*) 党派を統一する.

unimportant *adj.* ju'uyoo de na'i 重要でない; sa'sai na ささいな: an unimportant problem (*juuyoo de nai moñdai*) 重要でない問題.

union *n.* **1** (organization) ku'miai 組合: join a union (*kumiai ni kanyuu suru*) 組合に加入する / a labor union (*roodoo-kumiai*) 労働組合.
2 (act of uniting) ke'tsugoo 結合; ga'ppee 合併: the union of two companies (*futatsu no kaisha no gappee*) 二つの会社の合併.
3 (of states) re'ñpoo 連邦; re'ñgoo ko'kka 連合国家.

unique *adj.* ru'i no nai 類のない; do'kutoku no 独特の: a unique building (*rui no nai tatemono*) 類のない建物 / This custom is one that is unique to Japan. (*Kono fuushuu wa Nihoñ dokutoku no mono desu.*) この風習は日本独特のものです.

unit *n.* **1** (single group) ta'ñi 単位: The family is a unit of society. (*Kazoku wa shakai no tañi desu.*) 家族は社会の単位です.
2 (measurement) ta'ñi 単位: A meter is a unit of length. (*Meetoru wa nagasa no tañi desu.*) メートルは長さの単位です.

unite *vt.* **1** (join together) ... o ke'tsugoo suru …を結合する [I]; mu'subitsuke'ru 結びつける [V]: unite theory and practice (*riroñ to jisseñ o musubitsukeru*) 理論と実践を結びつける.
2 (act together) ... o da'ñketsu saseru …を団結させる [V]: We were united in our efforts. (*Wareware wa dañketsu shite doryoku shita.*) われわれは団結して努力した.
— *vi.* **1** (join together) ga'ppee suru 合併する [I]: The two companies united to form a new company. (*Sono futatsu no kaisha wa gappee shite hitotsu no atarashii kaisha ni natta.*) その二つ会社は合併して一つの新しい会社になった.
2 (act together) da'ñketsu suru 団結する [I]: unite in fighting (*dañketsu shite tatakau*) 団結して戦う.

united *adj.* da'ñketsu shita [shite iru] 団結した[している]; i'tchi shita [shite iru] 一致した[している]: make a united effort (*itchi kyooryoku suru*) 一致協力する.

United States of America *n.* A⌈merika (gasshu⌉ukoku) アメリカ(合衆国); Be⌈ekoku 米国.

unity *n.* ta⌈ñitsu 単一; to⌈oitsu 統一: the unity of a race (*miñzoku no tooitsu*) 民族の統一.

universal *adj.* **1** (of the whole world) ze⌈ñ se⌉kai no 全世界の: universal peace (*sekai-heewa*) 世界平和.
2 (general) fu⌈heñ-teki na 普遍的な; i⌈ppañ-teki na 一般的な: a universal rule (*ippañ hoosoku*) 一般法則.

universe *n.* u⌉chuu 宇宙; ze⌈ñ se⌉kai 全世界. ★ 'Space' is also called '*uchuu*.'

university *n.* da⌈igaku 大学; so⌈ogoo-da⌉igaku 総合大学: a university student (*daigakusee*) 大学生 / go to university (*daigaku e iku*) 大学へ行く. ★ 'College' is also called '*daigaku*.'

unjust *adj.* fu⌈ko⌉ohee na 不公平な; fu⌈see na 不正な: an unjust judge (*fukoohee na saibañkañ*) 不公平な裁判官.

unkind *adj.* fu⌈shi⌉ñsetsu na 不親切な; ha⌈kujoo na 薄情な: He was very unkind to me. (*Kare wa watashi ni hijoo ni fushiñsetsu datta.*) 彼は私に非常に不親切だった.

unknown *adj.* shi⌈rarete inai 知られていない; mi⌉chi no 未知の; mu⌈mee no 無名の: an unknown place (*michi no basho*) 未知の場所 / an unknown actress (*mumee no joyuu*) 無名の女優.

unlawful *adj.* fu⌈hoo na 不法な; hi⌈goohoo-teki na 非合法的な: unlawful entry (*fuhoo shiññyuu*) 不法侵入.

unless *conj.* moshi ... (-)na⌉kereba もし…なければ: Don't go unless you want to. (*Ikitaku nakereba iku no wa yoshi nasai.*) 行きたくなければ行くのはよしなさい. / I will go unless it rains. (*Ame ga furanakereba ikimasu.*) 雨が降らなければ行きます.

unlike *adj.* ni⌈te inai 似ていない; o⌈naji de na⌉i 同じでない: The two sisters are quite unlike. (*Futari no shimai wa mattaku nite inai.*) 二人の姉妹はまったく似ていない.
— *prep.* ... ni ni⌈te inai de …に似ていないで; ... to chi⌈gatte …と違って: The picture is quite unlike him. (*Sono shashiñ wa kare ni marude nite inai.*) その写真は彼にまるで似ていない.

unlikely *adj.* ⟨verb⟩-soo mo na⌉i …そうもない: an unlikely story (*ari-soo mo nai hanashi*) ありそうもない話 / He is unlikely to come. (*Kare wa ki-soo mo nai.*) 彼は来そうもない.

unlimited *adj.* ka⌈giri na⌉i 限りない; mu⌈geñ no 無限の: unlimited liability (*mugeñ sekiniñ*) 無限責任.

unload *vt.* (... kara) ni⌉ o o⌈ro⌉su (…から)荷を降ろす Ⓒ: unload the cargo from a ship (*fune kara ni o orosu*) 船から荷を降ろす.

unlock *vt.* ... no jo⌈o [ka⌈gi⌉] o a⌈keru …の錠[鍵]を開ける Ⓥ: unlock a door (*doa no joo o akeru*) ドアの錠を開ける.

unlucky *adj.* u⌉ñ no wa⌈ru⌉i 運の悪い; fu⌈uñ na 不運な: an unlucky person (*uñ no warui hito*) 運の悪い人.

unnatural *adj.* **1** (not natural) fu⌈shi⌉zeñ na 不自然な; i⌈joo na 異常な: an unnatural silence (*fushizeñ na shizukesa*) 不自然な静けさ.
2 (artificial) wa⌈za-to-rashi⌉i わざとらしい: an unnatural smile (*tsukuri warai*) 作り笑い.

unnecessary *adj.* hi⌈tsuyoo ga na⌉i 必要がない; fu⌈hitsu⌉yoo na 不必要な: It is unnecessary for you to go there. (*Anata wa soko e iku hitsuyoo wa arimaseñ.*) あなたはそこへ行く必要はありません.

unoffical *adj.* hi⌈ko⌉oshiki no 非公式の; shi⌈teki na 私的な: an unofficial meeting (*hikooshiki no kaigoo*) 非公式の会合.

unpaid *adj.* mi⌈ha⌉rai no 未払いの: an unpaid bill (*miharai no seekyuusho*) 未払いの請求書.

unpleasant *adj.* fu⌐yu⌝kai na 不愉快な; i⌐ya⌝ na いやな: unpleasant noises (*fuyukai na soo-oñ*) 不愉快な騒音 / have an unpleasant experience (*iya na keekeñ o suru*) いやな経験をする.

unreasonable *adj.* **1** (not sensible) su⌝ji ga to⌐ora⌝nai 筋が通らない; mu⌐fu⌝ñbetsu na 無分別な: What he says is unreasonable. (*Kare no iu koto wa suji ga tooranai.*) 彼の言うことは筋が通らない.
2 (too great) fu⌐too na 不当な; ho⌝ogai na 法外な: unreasonable prices (*hoogai na nedañ*) 法外な値段.

unrest *n.* fu⌐añ 不安; shi⌐ñpai 心配: social unrest (*shakai fuañ*) 社会不安.

unsatisfactory *adj.* fu⌐ma⌝ñzoku na 不満足な; fu⌐ju⌝ubuñ na 不十分な: His answer was unsatisfactory. (*Kare no kotae wa fumañzoku datta.*) 彼の答えは不満足だった.

unspeakable *adj.* ko⌐toba⌝ de a⌐rawase⌝nai 言葉で表せない; i⌐iyoo no na⌝i 言いようのない: unspeakable suffering (*iiyoo no nai kurushimi*) 言いようのない苦しみ.

unsteady *adj.* fu⌐a⌝ñtee na 不安定な; gu⌝ragura suru ぐらぐらする: an unsteady table (*guragura suru teeburu*) ぐらぐらするテーブル.

unthinkable *adj.* ka⌐ñgaerare⌝nai 考えられない; o⌐mo⌝i mo yo⌐ranai 思いもよらない: Cancellation at this stage is unthinkable. (*Kono dañkai de chuushi nañte kañgaerarenai.*) この段階で中止なんて考えられない.

untidy *adj.* da⌐rashi na⌝i だらしない; chi⌐rakatta 散らかった; chi⌐rakatte iru 散らかっている: an untidy appearance (*darashi nai kakkoo*) だらしない格好 / an untidy room (*chirakatta heya*) 散らかった部屋.

untie *vt.* ... o to⌝ku ...を解く Ⓒ; ho⌐do⌝ku ほどく Ⓒ: untie a knot (*musubime o hodoku*) 結び目をほどく.

until *prep.* ... ma⌝de ...まで: I was waiting for you until three o'clock. (*Watashi wa sañ-ji made anata o matte imashita.*) 私は3時まであなたを待っていました. / He will not come home until Monday. (*Kare wa getsuyoo made uchi ni kaette kimaseñ.*) 彼は月曜まで家に帰って来ません.
— *conj.* ... ma⌝de ...まで: Please keep this baggage until I come back. (*Kono nimotsu o watashi ga modoru made azukatte kudasai.*) この荷物を私が戻るまで預かってください.

unusual *adj.* fu⌐tsuu de na⌝i 普通でない; me⌐zurashi⌝i 珍しい: It is unusual for him to be absent. (*Kare ga yasumu no wa mezurashii.*) 彼が休むのは珍しい.

unwilling *adj.* i⌐yaiya-na⌝gara no いやいやながらの; ki ⌐ga susumanai 気が進まない: He was unwilling to go. (*Kare wa iku no wa ki ga susumanakatta.*) 彼は行くのは気が進まなかった.

unworthy *adj.* a⌐taishinai 値しない; ka⌝chi no nai 価値のない: conduct unworthy of praise (*shoosañ ni ataishinai kooi*) 賞賛に値しない行為.

up *adv.* **1** (to or in a higher place) u⌐e e [ni] 上へ[に]; ta⌐ka⌝i to⌐koro⌝ ni [de] 高い所に[で]: pull one's socks up (*kutsushita o ue e hipparu*) 靴下を上へ引っ張る / He lives five floors up. (*Kare wa go-kai ue ni suñde imasu.*) 彼は5階上に住んでいます.
2 (totally) su⌐kka⌝ri すっかり: We ate up the cake. (*Watashi-tachi wa keeki o sukkari tabete shimatta.*) 私たちはケーキをすっかり食べてしまった.
— *prep.* **1** (to a higher place) ... no u⌐e ni ...の上に: We climbed up the hill. (*Watashi-tachi wa oka no ue ni nobotta.*) 私たちは丘の上に登った.
2 (along) ... ni so⌝tte ...に沿って: walk up the street (*michi ni sotte aruku*) 道に沿って歩く.
— *adj.* no⌐bori no 上りの: an up elevator (*nobori no erebeetaa*) 上りのエレベーター / an up train (*nobori-*

u

ressha) 上り列車.

up to ... *prep.* ... ma¹de ...まで: I was up to my knees in water. (*Watashi wa hiza made mizu ni tsukatta.*) 私はひざまで水につかった.

uphold *vt.* ... o shi¹ji suru ...を支持する [I]: He upheld my opinions. (*Kare wa watashi no ikeñ o shiji shite kureta.*) 彼は私の意見を支持してくれた.

upper *adj.* **1** (higher) u^re no 上の: an upper room (*ue no heya*) 上の部屋 / the upper lip (*uwa-kuchibiru*) 上唇.
2 (superior) jo¹oi no 上位の; jo^ro-kyuu no 上級の: the upper class (*jooryuu kaikyuu*) 上流階級.

upright *adj.* **1** (erect) ma^rssu¹gu na 真っすぐな; cho^rkuritsu no 直立の: an upright tree (*massugu na ki*) 真っすぐな木 / an upright posture (*chokuritsu no shisee*) 直立の姿勢.
2 (honest) sho^roji¹ki na 正直な; ko^rosee na 公正な: upright dealings (*koosee na torihiki*) 公正な取り引き.
— *adv.* ma^rssu¹gu ni 真っすぐに: stand upright (*massugu ni tatsu*) 真っすぐに立つ.

uproar *n.* o^rosa¹wagi 大騒ぎ; so¹odoo 騒動.

upset *vt.* **1** (turn over) ... o hi^rk-kurika¹esu ...をひっくり返す [C]: upset a cup (*chawañ o hikkurikaesu*) 茶碗をひっくり返す.
2 (disturb) ... o da^rme¹ ni suru ...をだめにする [I]: The rain upset our plans. (*Ame ga watashi-tachi no keekaku o dame ni shita.*) 雨が私たちの計画をだめにした.
3 (cause to worry) ... o ro^robai saseru ...をろうばいさせる [V]: The bad news upset him. (*Sono warui shirase wa kare o roobai saseta.*) その悪い知らせは彼をろうばいさせた.
— *n.* **1** (upsetting) te^rñpuku 転覆: the upset of a boat (*booto no teñpuku*) ボートの転覆.
2 (confusion) ko¹ñrañ 混乱: an upset of one's plans (*keekaku no koñrañ*) 計画の混乱.
3 (slight illness) fu^rchoo 不調: a stomach upset (*i no fuchoo*) 胃の不調.

upside down *adv.* sa^rkasama ni 逆さまに; hi^rkkurika¹ette ひっくり返って: turn a glass upside down (*koppu o hikkurikaesu*) コップをひっくり返す.

upstairs *adv.* u^re no ka¹i e [ni] 上の階へ[に]: go upstairs (*ue no kai e iku*) 上の階へ行く.
— *adj.* ka^rijoo no 階上の: the upstairs rooms (*kaijoo no heya*) 階上の部屋.

up-to-date *adj.* sa^rishiñ no 最新の: an up-to-date catalog (*saishiñ no katarogu*) 最新のカタログ.

upward *adv.* u^re no ho¹o 上の方: look upward (*ue no hoo o miru*) 上の方を見る.
— *adj.* u^rwamuki no 上向きの: an upward slope (*noborizaka*) 上り坂.

uranium *n.* u¹rañ ウラン; u^rrani¹umu ウラニウム.

urban *adj.* to¹shi no 都市の; to^rkai no 都会の: urban life (*toshi-seekatsu*) 都市生活.

urge *vt.* **1** (force onward) ... o ka^rritate¹ru ...を駆り立てる [V]; se^rkitateru せきたてる [V]: urge a horse on (*uma o karitateru*) 馬を駆り立てる.
2 (ask earnestly) ... ni shi^rkiri ni susumeru ...にしきりに勧める [V]: I urged him to stay overnight. (*Watashi wa kare ni ip-paku suru yoo ni shikiri ni susumeta.*) 私は彼に1泊するようにしきりに勧めた.
3 (press upon) ... o shu^rchoo suru ...を主張する [I]; ri^rkisetsu suru 力説する [I]: He urged restraint. (*Kare wa jisee o shuchoo shita.*) 彼は自制を主張した.

urgent *adj.* ki^rñkyuu no 緊急の: He went to Osaka on urgent business. (*Kare wa kiñkyuu no yooji de Oosaka e ikimashita.*) 彼は緊急の用事で大阪へ行きました. / an urgent telegram (*shikyuu-deñpoo*) 至急電報.

urinate *vi.* sho^robe¹ñ o suru 小便を

する [I]; hoˈonyoo suru 放尿する [I].

us *pron.* **1** [direct object] waˈreware o われわれを; waˈtashiˈ-tachi o 私たちを: She showed us into the room. (*Kanojo wa wareware o heya ni tooshita.*) 彼女はわれわれを部屋に通した.

2 [indirect object] waˈreware ni われわれに; waˈtashiˈ-tachi ni 私たちに: She showed us her picture. (*Kanojo wa watashi-tachi ni kanojo no shashiñ o miseta.*) 彼女は私たちに彼女の写真を見せた.

U.S.A. *n.* Aˈmerika (gasshuˈukoku) アメリカ(合衆国); Beˈekoku 米国.

use[1] *vt.* **1** (employ) ... o tsuˈkau ...を使う [C]; riˈyoo suru 利用する [I]: May I use this telephone? (*Kono deñwa o tsukatte mo ii desu ka?*) この電話を使ってもいいですか. / He used a taxi to go there. (*Kare wa soko e iku no ni takushii o riyoo shita.*) 彼はそこへ行くのにタクシーを利用した.

2 (consume) ... o shoˈohi suru ...を消費する [I]; tsuˈkau 使う [C]: She used up all the soap. (*Kanojo wa sekkeñ o zeñbu tsukatte shimatta.*) 彼女はせっけんを全部使ってしまった.

use[2] *n.* **1** (using) shiˈyoo 使用; riˈyoo 利用: This park is for the use of children. (*Kono kooeñ wa kodomo-tachi no riyoo no tame ni arimasu.*) この公園は子どもたちの利用のためにあります.

2 (purpose) yoˈoto 用途; moˈkuteki 目的: This tool has several uses. (*Kono doogu wa iroiro na yooto ga aru.*) この道具はいろいろな用途がある.

3 (value) koˈoyoo 効用; yaˈkuˈ ni tatsu koˈtoˈ 役に立つこと: These shoes are of no use. (*Kono kutsu wa yaku ni tatanai.*) この靴は役に立たない.

make use of ... *vt.* ... o riˈyoo suru ...を利用する [I].

used *adj.* tsuˈkatta 使った; chuˈuko no 中古の: a used car (*chuukosha*) 中古車 / used nuclear fuel (*shiyoozumi no kakuneñryoo*) 使用済みの核燃料.

used to[1] *vi.* iˈzeñ [muˈkashi] wa ⟨verb⟩-ta 以前[昔]は…た: He used to work hard but does not now. (*Izeñ wa kare wa yoku hataraita ga ima wa soo de nai.*) 以前は彼はよく働いたが今はそうでない.

used to[2] *adj.* ... ni naˈrete iru ...に慣れている: He is used to driving a car. (*Kare wa kuruma no uñteñ ni narete iru.*) 彼は車の運転に慣れている.

useful *adj.* yaˈkuˈ ni taˈtsu 役に立つ; yuˈueki na 有益な: This guidebook was very useful to me. (*Kono añnaisho wa totemo yaku ni tatta.*) この案内書はとても役に立った. / useful information (*yuueki na joohoo*) 有益な情報.

useless *adj.* yaˈkuˈ ni taˈtaˈnai 役に立たない; muˈda na 無駄な: This tool is useless. (*Kono doogu wa yaku ni tatanai.*) この道具は役に立たない. / a useless attempt (*muda na kokoromi*) 無駄な試み.

usher *vt.* ... o aˈñnaˈi suru ...を案内する [I]; seˈñdoo suru 先導する [I]: She ushered me into the room. (*Kanojo wa watashi o heya ni añnai shite kureta.*) 彼女は私を部屋に案内してくれた.

— *n.* aˈñnaigaˈkari 案内係.

usual *adj.* iˈtsu-mo no いつもの; fuˈtsuu no 普通の: He took his usual seat at the table. (*Kare wa teeburu no itsu-mo no seki ni tsuita.*) 彼はテーブルのいつもの席に着いた. / It is usual for him to sit up late at night. (*Kare ga yoru osoku made okite iru no wa futsuu desu.*) 彼が夜遅くまで起きているのは普通です.

as usual *adv.* iˈtsu-mo no toˈori いつものとおり.

usually *adv.* fuˈtsuu wa 普通は; iˈtsu-mo wa いつもは: I usually get up at six. (*Watashi wa futsuu wa roku-ji ni okimasu.*) 私は普通は6時に起きます.

utility *n.* yuˈuyoosee 有用性; koˈoyoo 効用: the utility of cars (*ku-*

ruma no kooyoo) 車の効用.
— *adj.* ji⌈tsuyoo-teki na 実用的な: utility furniture (*jitsuyoo-teki na kagu*) 実用的な家具.

utilize *vt.* ... o ri⌈yoo suru …を利用する [I]; ka⌈tsuyoo suru 活用する [I]: utilize atomic power for peaceful purposes (*geñshiryoku o heewa mokuteki ni riyoo suru*) 原子力を平和目的に利用する.

utmost *adj.* sa⌈idai no 最大の; sa⌈ikoo no 最高の: with one's utmost effort (*saidai no doryoku o shite*) 最大の努力をして.
do one's utmost *vi.* ze⌈ñryoku o tsu⌈ku⌉su 全力を尽くす [C].

utter[1] *adj.* ma⌈ttaku⌉ no まったくの; ka⌈ñzeñ na 完全な: He is an utter stranger to me. (*Kare wa watashi ga mattaku shiranai hito desu.*) 彼は私がまったく知らない人です.

utter[2] *vt.* (of a word) ... o ha⌈ssuru …を発する [I]; (of a cry) a⌈geru 上げる [V]: He did not utter a word. (*Kare wa hitokoto mo hasshinakatta.*) 彼はひと言も発しなかった. / utter a cry (*sakebigoe o ageru*) 叫び声を上げる

utterly *adv.* ma⌈ttaku まったく; su⌈kka⌉ri すっかり: He was utterly exhausted. (*Kare wa sukkari tsukarete ita.*) 彼はすっかり疲れていた.

V

vacant *adj.* **1** (empty) a⌈ite iru 空いている; ka⌈ra⌉ no 空の: a vacant seat (*aite iru seki*) 空いている席 / Are there any vacant rooms in this hotel? (*Kono hoteru ni akishitsu wa arimasu ka?*) このホテルに空室はありますか.
2 (free from work) hi⌈ma na 暇な; yo⌈oji no na⌉i 用事のない: vacant hours (*hima na jikañ*) 暇な時間.

vacation *n.* kyu⌈uka 休暇; kyu⌈ujitsu 休日; ya⌈sumi⌉ 休み: take a vacation of a week (*is-shuukañ no kyuuka o toru*) 1週間の休暇を取る / a summer vacation (*natsu-yasumi*) 夏休み.

vacuum *n.* **1** (space) shi⌈ñkuu 真空: Sound does not travel in a vacuum. (*Oto wa shiñkuu-chuu de wa tsutawaranai.*) 音は真空中では伝わらない.
2 (cleaner) de⌈ñki-sooji⌉ki 電気掃除機.

vacuum bottle *n.* ma⌈ho⌉obiñ 魔法びん.

vacuum cleaner *n.* de⌈ñki-sooji⌉ki 電気掃除機.

vague *adj.* ha⌈kki⌉ri shinai はっきりしない; a⌈imai na あいまいな; ba⌈kuzeñ to shita [shite iru] 漠然とした[している]: give a vague answer (*aimai na heñji o suru*) あいまいな返事をする.

vain *adj.* **1** (useless) mu⌈da na 無駄な; mu⌈eki na 無益な: make a vain effort (*muda na doryoku o suru*) 無駄な努力をする.
2 (too proud) u⌈nubore no tsuyo⌉i うぬぼれの強い; kyo⌈e⌉eshiñ no tsu⌈yo⌉i 虚栄心の強い: She is vain about her beauty. (*Kanojo wa jibuñ no biboo o unuborete iru.*) 彼女は自分の美貌をうぬぼれている.
in vain *adv., adj.* mu⌈da ni 無駄に; mu⌈na⌉shiku むなしく: I tried, but in vain. (*Yatte mita ga muda datta.*) やってみたが無駄だった.

valid *adj.* **1** (reasonable) da⌈too na 妥当な; se⌈etoo na 正当な: He didn't have a valid reason for his absence. (*Kare wa kesseki shita koto no seetoo na riyuu o motte inakatta.*) 彼は欠席したことの正当な理由を持っていなかった.
2 (legally effective) yu⌈ukoo na 有効な; go⌈ohoo-teki na 合法的な: This passport is valid for five years. (*Kono pasupooto wa go-neñkañ yuukoo desu.*) このパスポートは5年間

有効です.

validity *n.* se⌈etoosa 正当さ; da⌈toosee 妥当性; yu⌈ukoo 有効: the term of validity (*yuukoo kikañ*) 有効期間.

valley *n.* ta⌈ni⌉ 谷; ta⌈nima⌉ 谷間: The river flows through the valley. (*Sono kawa wa tanima o nagarete iru.*) その川は谷間を流れている.

valuable *adj.* **1** (worth much) ka⌉chi no aru 価値のある; ki⌈choo na 貴重な: a valuable experience (*kichoo na keekeñ*) 貴重な経験.

2 (costly) ko⌉oka na 高価な: a valuable jewel (*kooka na hooseki*) 高価な宝石.

— *n.* ki⌈choohiñ 貴重品: Please leave your valuables at the reception desk. (*Kichoohiñ wa furoñto ni azukete kudasai.*) 貴重品はフロントに預けてください.

value *n.* **1** (worth) ka⌉chi 価値; ne⌈uchi 値打ち: the value of education (*kyooiku no kachi*) 教育の価値.

2 (price) ka⌈kaku 価格; ne⌈dañ 値段: What is the value of this house? (*Kono ie no kakaku wa ikura desu ka?*) この家の価格はいくらですか.

— *vt.* **1** (place a value) ... o hyo⌉oka suru …を評価する [T]: He valued the land at five million yen. (*Kare wa sono tochi o gohyakumañ-eñ to hyooka shita.*) 彼はその土地を500万円と評価した.

2 (think highly of) ... o so⌈ñchoo suru …を尊重する [T]; ta⌈isetsu ni suru 大切にする [T]: I value his friendship. (*Watashi wa kare no yuujoo o taisetsu ni shite iru.*) 私は彼の友情を大切にしている.

valve *n.* be⌉ñ 弁; ba⌈rubu バルブ: a safety valve (*añzeñ-beñ*) 安全弁.

van *n.* ba⌉ñ バン; yu⌈ugai-tora⌉kku 有蓋トラック.

vanilla *n.* ba⌉nira バニラ: vanilla ice cream (*banira no aisu kuriimu*) バニラのアイスクリーム.

vanish *vi.* **1** (disappear) ki⌈eru 消える [V]; mi⌈e⌉naku naru 見えなくなる [C]: The man vanished in the crowd. (*Sono otoko wa hitogomi no naka de mienakunatta.*) その男は人込みの中で見えなくなった.

2 (cease to exist) sho⌈ometsu suru 消滅する [I]; na⌈kunaru なくなる [C]: Many species of animal have vanished from the earth. (*Ooku no shu no doobutsu ga chijoo kara shoometsu shita.*) 多くの種の動物が地上から消滅した.

vanity *n.* kyo⌈e⌉eshiñ 虚栄心; u⌈nubore うぬぼれ: Miss Takahashi is full of vanity. (*Takahashi-sañ wa kyooeeshiñ ga tsuyoi.*) 高橋さんは虚栄心が強い.

vapor *n.* jo⌉oki 蒸気: water vapor (*suijooki*) 水蒸気.

variable *adj.* **1** (changeable) ka⌈wariyasu⌉i 変わりやすい: variable weather (*kawariyasui teñki*) 変わりやすい天気.

2 (that can be changed) ka⌈erareru 変えられる: The temperature in this room is variable. (*Kono heya no oñdo wa kaeraremasu.*) この部屋の温度は変えられます.

variation *n.* he⌉ñka 変化; he⌈ñdoo 変動: variations in air pressure (*kiatsu no heñka*) 気圧の変化.

varied *adj.* sa⌈ma⌉zama na さまざまな; ta⌈sai na 多彩な: He has had varied careers. (*Kare wa samazama na shoku ni tsuita.*) 彼はさまざまな職に就いた.

variety *n.* **1** (change) he⌉ñka 変化; ta⌈yoosee 多様性: a life full of variety (*heñka ni toñda jiñsee*) 変化に富んだ人生.

2 (kind) shu⌉rui 種類: a new variety of tulip (*chuurippu no shiñshu*) チューリップの新種.

a variety of ... *adj.* i⌈roiro na いろいろな: a variety of magazines (*iroiro na zasshi*) いろいろな雑誌.

various *adj.* **1** (different) i⌈roiro na いろいろな; sa⌈ma⌉zama na さまざまな: I planted various seeds. (*Watashi wa iroiro na tane o maita.*) 私はいろいろな種をまいた.

2 (several) i⌉kutsu ka no いくつかの; o⌉oku no 多くの: Various people asked me about you. (*Ooku no hito ga watashi ni anata no koto o kiita.*) 多くの人が私にあなたのことを聞いた.

varnish *n.* ni⌉su ニス: put varnish on the floor (*yuka ni nisu o nuru*) 床にニスを塗る.

vary *vi.* **1** (change) ka⌈waru 変わる [C]: The weather varies from day to day. (*Teñkoo wa hi goto ni kawaru.*) 天候は日ごとに変わる.
2 (differ) ko⌈tona⌉ru 異なる [C]; chi⌈gau 違う [C]: Customs vary from country to country. (*Shuukañ wa kuni ni yotte kotonaru.*) 習慣は国によって異なる.
— *vt.* ... o ka⌈eru ...を変える [V]: She varied her hair style. (*Kanojo wa kamigata o kaeta.*) 彼女は髪型を変えた.

vase *n.* ka⌈biñ 花びん: put flowers in a vase (*kabiñ ni hana o sasu*) 花びんに花を挿す.

vast *adj.* **1** (very great in extent) ko⌈odai na 広大な: a vast desert (*koodai na sabaku*) 広大な砂漠.
2 (very great in amount) ba⌈kudai na 莫大な: a vast sum of money (*bakudai na kiñgaku no o-kane*) 莫大な金額のお金.

vault *n.* (roof) a⌈achigata no teñjoo アーチ形の天井; (cellar) chi⌈ka⌉shitsu 地下室.

veal *n.* ko⌈ushi no niku⌉ 子牛の肉.

vegetable *n.* ya⌈sai 野菜: grow vegetables (*yasai o saibai suru*) 野菜を栽培する / fresh vegetables (*shiñseñ na yasai*) 新鮮な野菜.

vehement *adj.* ha⌈geshi⌉i 激しい; ge⌈kiretsu na 激烈な: a vehement argument (*gekiroñ*) 激論.

vehicle *n.* no⌈rimono 乗り物; ku⌈ruma 車: The road was crowded with vehicles. (*Dooro wa kuruma de koñde ita.*) 道路は車で込んでいた.

veil *n.* be⌉eru ベール; ka⌈burimono かぶり物: wear a veil (*beeru o kaburu*) ベールをかぶる.

vein *n.* **1** (blood vessel) jo⌈omyaku 静脈.
2 (in a leaf) yo⌈omyaku 葉脈; (in rock) ko⌈omyaku 鉱脈.
3 (mood) ki⌉buñ 気分: in a light-hearted vein (*karui kibuñ de*) 軽い気分で.

velocity *n.* so⌉kudo 速度; ha⌉yasa 速さ.

velvet *n.* bi⌈roodo ビロード.

venerable *adj.* so⌈ñkee sube⌉ki 尊敬すべき; ri⌉ppa na 立派な: a venerable scholar (*rippa na gakusha*) 立派な学者.

vengeance *n.* fu⌈kushuu 復讐: take vengeance on a person (*hito ni fukushuu suru*) 人に復讐する.

ventilation *n.* ka⌈zetooshi 風通し; ka⌈ñki 換気.

venture *n.* bo⌈okeñ 冒険; to⌉oki 投機: a venture business (*tooki-teki jigyoo*) 投機的事業.
— *vt.* o⌈mo⌉ikitte ⟨verb⟩ 思い切って...: We ventured a protest. (*Watashi-tachi wa omoikitte koogi shita.*) 私たちは思い切って抗議した.

verb *n.* do⌈oshi 動詞: a transitive verb (*tadooshi*) 他動詞 / an intransitive verb (*jidooshi*) 自動詞.

verge *n.* fu⌈chi⌉ 縁; kyo⌈okai 境界: the verge of a cliff (*gake no fuchi*) がけの縁.

verify *vt.* ... o ta⌈shikame⌉ru ...を確かめる [V]: verify a fact (*jijitsu o tashikameru*) 事実を確かめる.

verse *n.* i⌈ñbuñ 韻文; shi 詩: a story written in verse (*iñbuñ de kakareta monogatari*) 韻文で書かれた物語 / epic [lyrical] verse (*joji [jojoo]-shi*) 叙事[叙情]詩.

version *n.* **1** (translation) -ya⌉ku 訳: I have the French version of the book. (*Watashi wa sono hoñ no Furañsugo-yaku o motte iru.*) 私はその本のフランス語訳を持っている.
2 (particular form) -bañ 版: an abridged version of a dictionary (*jisho no kañyaku-bañ*) 辞書の簡約版.
3 (description) se⌈tsumee 説明:

He gave a different version of the accident. (*Kare wa sono jiko ni tsuite chigatta setsumee o shita.*) 彼はその事故について違った説明をした.

versus *prep.* ... ta⌉i ...対: Waseda versus Keio (*Waseda tai Keeoo*) 早稲田対慶応.

vertical *adj.* su⌈ichoku no 垂直の; ta⌉te no 縦の: The cliff is almost vertical. (*Gake wa hotoñdo suichoku da.*) がけはほとんど垂直だ. / a vertical line (*tate no señ*) 縦の線.
— *n.* su⌈ichokuseñ 垂直線.

very *adv.* **1** (extremely) hi⌈joo ni 非常に; to⌈temo とても; ta⌈iheñ 大変: I'm very tired. (*Watashi wa hijoo ni tsukaremashita.*) 私は非常に疲れました. / Your story is very interesting. (*Kimi no hanashi wa taiheñ omoshiroi.*) 君の話は大変おもしろい.
2 (really) ma⌈ttaku まったく; ho⌈ñtoo ni 本当に: It was the very first time that I met him. (*Kare ni atta no wa mattaku hajimete deshita.*) 彼に会ったのはまったく初めてでした.
— *adj.* ma⌉sa ni so⌈no まさにその: This is the very book I was looking for. (*Kore wa masa ni watashi ga sagashite ita sono hoñ desu.*) これはまさに私が捜していたその本です.

vessel *n.* **1** (ship) fu⌉ne 船.
2 (container) yo⌉oki 容器; i⌈remono 入れ物.

vest *n.* (waistcoat) cho⌈kki チョッキ: a life vest (*kyumee dooi*) 救命胴衣.

veteran *n.* ro⌈oreñ na hito⌉ 老練な人; be⌈terañ ベテラン. ★ Japanese '*beterañ*' is usually used in the sense of an 'experienced person.'

via *prep.* ... ke⌈eyu de ...経由で; ... o he⌉te ...を経て: I went to Japan via Hawaii. (*Watashi wa Hawai keeyu de Nihoñ e ikimashita.*) 私はハワイ経由で日本へ行きました.

vibrate *vi.* **1** (quiver) shi⌈ñdoo suru 振動する [I]: The house vibrates whenever a heavy truck passes. (*Omoi torakku ga tooru tabi ni ie ga shiñdoo suru.*) 重いトラックが通るたびに家が振動する.
2 (resound) na⌈rihibi⌉ku 鳴り響く [C]: The hall vibrated with cheers. (*Hooru ni hakushu ga narihibiita.*) ホールに拍手が鳴り響いた.
— *vt.* ... o shi⌈ñdoo saseru ...を振動させる [V]; yu⌈riugoka⌉su 揺り動かす [C].

vice *n.* **1** (bad habit) a⌈kushuu 悪習: the vice of smoking (*kitsueñ no akushuu*) 喫煙の悪習.
2 (evil) a⌉ku 悪; a⌈kutoku 悪徳: virtue and vice (*bitoku to akutoku*) 美徳と悪徳.

vice president *n.* fu⌈ku-daito⌉oryoo 副大統領; (of a company) fu⌈ku-sha⌉choo 副社長.

vicinity *n.* ki⌉ñjo 近所; fu⌉kiñ 付近: There is no hospital in my vicinity. (*Kiñjo ni byooiñ wa arimaseñ.*) 近所に病院はありません.

vicious *adj.* a⌉kui no aru 悪意のある; i⌈ji no waru⌉i 意地の悪い: vicious remarks (*akui no aru kotoba*) 悪意のある言葉.

victim *n.* gi⌈se⌉esha 犠牲者; hi⌈ga⌉isha 被害者: victims of war (*señsoo no giseesha*) 戦争の犠牲者 / the victim of an accident (*jiko no higaisha*) 事故の被害者.

victor *n.* sho⌈ori⌉sha 勝利者; (winner) yu⌈usho⌉osha 優勝者.

victory *n.* sho⌉ori 勝利: lead a team to victory (*chiimu o shoori ni michibiku*) チームを勝利に導く / win a victory in an election (*señkyo ni katsu*) 選挙に勝つ.

video *n.* bi⌉deo ビデオ: record a movie on video (*eega o bideo ni rokuga suru*) 映画をビデオに録画する.

vie *vi.* ki⌈soia⌉u 競い合う [C]; ha⌈ria⌉u 張り合う [C]: vie with one another for a prize (*shoo o mezashite otagai ni kisoiau*) 賞を目指してお互いに競い合う.

view *n.* **1** (scene) na⌈game⌉ 眺め; mi⌈harashi 見晴らし: We reserved a room with a good view. (*Watashitachi wa nagame no yoi heya o yoyaku shita.*) 私たちは眺めのよい部

屋を予約した.
2 (act of seeing) mi¹ru ⌈koto¹ 見ること: It was our first view of Mt. Fuji. (*Watashi-tachi wa Fuji-sañ o hajimete mita.*) 私たちは富士山を初めて見た.
3 (opinion) ka⌈ñga¹e 考え; i¹keñ 意見: Tell me your views on the matter. (*Sono moñdai ni tsuite anata no kañgae o kikasete kudasai.*) その問題についてあなたの考えを聞かせてください.
— *vt.* ... o na⌈game¹ru ...を眺める Ⓥ: view a lake from an airplane (*hikooki kara mizuumi o nagameru*) 飛行機から湖を眺める.

viewpoint *n.* ka¹ñteñ 観点; ke¹ñchi 見地: Look at the problem from a different viewpoint. (*Sono moñdai o chigatta kañteñ kara mite gorañ nasai.*) その問題を違った観点から見てご覧なさい.

vigor *n.* ka⌈tsu¹ryoku 活力; ki⌈ryoku 気力: I don't have the vigor to begin a new job. (*Watashi wa atarashii shigoto o hajimeru kiryoku ga nai.*) 私は新しい仕事を始める気力がない.

vigorous *adj.* se¹eryoku o⌈osee na 精力旺盛な; ka⌈kki ni mi¹chita [mi¹chite iru] 活気に満ちた[満ちている]: a vigorous young man (*kakki ni michita wakamono*) 活気に満ちた若者.

vile *adj.* (mean) ge⌈retsu na 下劣な; (disgusting) i⌈ya¹ na いやな: a vile smell (*iya na nioi*) いやなにおい.

village *n.* mu⌈ra¹ 村: live in a village (*mura ni sumu*) 村に住む.

villain *n.* wa⌈rumono 悪者; a⌈kuto¹o 悪党.

vine *n.* **1** (grapevine) bu⌈doo no ki¹ [tsuru¹] ぶどうの木[つる].
2 (climbing plant) tsu⌈ru¹ つる; tsu⌈rukusa つる草: Pumpkins grow on vines. (*Kabocha wa tsuru ni naru.*) かぼちゃはつるになる.

vinegar *n.* su¹ 酢.

violate *vt.* **1** (break) ... o ya⌈bu¹ru ...を破る Ⓒ; o⌈ka¹su 犯す Ⓒ: violate an agreement (*kyootee o yaburu*) 協定を破る / violate the law (*hooritsu o okasu*) 法律を犯す.
2 (disturb) ... o shi⌈ñgai suru ...を侵害する Ⓘ; sa⌈matage¹ru 妨げる Ⓥ: violate a person's privacy (*hito no puraibashii o shiñgai suru*) 人のプライバシーを侵害する.

violation *n.* i⌈hañ 違反; shi⌈ñgai 侵害: violation of the law (*hooritsu-ihañ*) 法律違反 / violation of human rights (*jiñkeñ shiñgai*) 人権侵害.

violence *n.* **1** (conduct) bo¹oryoku 暴力; ra⌈ñboo 乱暴: use violence (*booryoku o mochiiru*) 暴力を用いる.
2 (great strength) ha⌈ge¹shisa 激しさ; mo¹oi 猛威: the violence of a typhoon (*taifuu no mooi*) 台風の猛威.

violent *adj.* **1** (showing great force) ha⌈geshi¹i 激しい; mo⌈oretsu na 猛烈な: a violent earthquake (*hageshii jishiñ*) 激しい地震.
2 (showing strong feelings) ha⌈geshi¹i 激しい: a person of violent temper (*hageshii kishoo no hito*) 激しい気性の人.
3 (wild) ra⌈ñboo na 乱暴な; bo⌈oryoku-teki na 暴力的な: resort to violent means (*booryoku ni uttaeru*) 暴力に訴える.

violently *adv.* ha⌈ge¹shiku 激しく; mo⌈oretsu ni 猛烈に: The wind is blowing violently. (*Kaze ga hageshiku fuite iru.*) 風が激しく吹いている.

violet *n.* (flower) su⌈mire すみれ; (color) su⌈mireiro すみれ色; mu⌈rasaki-iro 紫色.

violin *n.* ba⌈iorin バイオリン: play the violin (*baioriñ o hiku*) バイオリンを弾く.

virgin *n.* sho¹jo 処女.
— *adj.* sho¹jo no 処女の; ju⌈ñketsu na 純潔な: virgin snow (*shojo yuki*) 処女雪.

virtue *n.* **1** (morality) to⌈ku 徳; bi⌈toku 美徳: a person of virtue (*toku no aru hito*) 徳のある人.

V

2 (merit) cho⌝osho 長所; ri⌜ten 利点: This house has the virtue of being easy to clean. (*Kono uchi wa sooji shi-yasui to iu riteñ ga aru.*) この家は掃除しやすいという利点がある.

visa *n.* bi⌝za ビザ; sa⌜shoo 査証: I applied for a visa to China. (*Watashi wa Chuugoku e no biza o shiñsee shita.*) 私は中国へのビザを申請した.
— *vt.* ... ni sa⌜shoo suru ...に査証する [I]; bi⌝za o a⌜taeru ビザを与える [V]: get one's passport visaed (*pasupooto ni biza o morau*) パスポートにビザをもらう.

visible *adj.* 1 (able to be seen) me⌝ ni mi⌜e⌝ru 目に見える: That star is visible to the naked eye. (*Sono hoshi wa nikugañ de miemasu.*) その星は肉眼で見えます.
2 (evident) a⌜ki⌝raka na 明らかな; me⌜ehaku na 明白な: a visible increase in crime (*hañzai no meehaku na zooka*) 犯罪の明白な増加.

vision *n.* 1 (sight) shi⌝ryoku 視力; shi⌜kaku 視覚: I am slowly losing my vision. (*Watashi wa sukoshi zutsu shiryoku ga ochite iru.*) 私は少しずつ視力が落ちている.
2 (imagination) so⌜ozo⌝oryoku 想像力; do⌜osatsu⌝ryoku 洞察力: a statesman of vision (*doosatsuryoku no aru seejika*) 洞察力のある政治家.

visit *vt.* 1 (call on) ... o ta⌜zune⌝ru ...を訪ねる [V]; ho⌜omoñ suru 訪問する [I]: I visited him at his office. (*Watashi wa kare o kaisha ni tazuneta.*) 私は彼を会社に訪ねた.
2 (go to see) ... o o⌜tozure⌝ru 訪れる [V]; ke⌜ñbutsu ni iku 見物に行く [C]: Many people visit Kyoto. (*Oozee no hito ga Kyooto o otozuremasu.*) 大勢の人が京都を訪れます.
3 (stay) ... ni to⌜maru ...に泊まる [C]; ta⌜izai suru 滞在する [I]: They visited us for a week. (*Kare-ra wa watashi-tachi no tokoro ni isshuukañ tomatta.*) 彼らは私たちのところに1週間泊まった.
— *n.* ho⌜omoñ 訪問; ke⌜ñbutsu 見物; ta⌜izai 滞在: This is my second visit. (*Kore ga ni-kaime no hoomoñ desu.*) これが2回目の訪問です. / a visit to Nikko (*Nikkoo keñbutsu*) 日光見物.

visitor *n.* 1 (caller) ho⌜omo⌝ñkyaku 訪問客; ra⌜ikyaku 来客: We had two visitors today. (*Kyoo wa raikyaku ga futari atta.*) きょうは来客が二人あった.
2 (sightseer) ka⌜ñko⌝okyaku 観光客: visitors to Tokyo from Hawaii (*Hawai kara Tookyoo e yatte kuru kañkookyaku*) ハワイから東京へやって来る観光客.

visual *adj.* shi⌜kaku no 視覚の; shi⌝ryoku no 視力の: visual effects (*shikaku kooka*) 視覚効果 / a visual test (*shiryoku keñsa*) 視力検査.

vital *adj.* 1 (important) ki⌜wa⌝mete ju⌜udai na きわめて重大な; (essential) ze⌜ttai ni hitsuyoo na 絶対に必要な: make a vital decision (*kiwamete juudai na kesshiñ o suru*) きわめて重大な決心をする / Your help is vital for our success. (*Wareware ga seekoo suru tame ni wa anata no eñjo ga zettai ni hitsuyoo desu.*) われわれが成功するためにはあなたの援助が絶対に必要です.
2 (of life) se⌝emee no 生命の: vital energy (*katsuryoku*) 活力.

vitality *n.* ka⌜kki 活気; ka⌜tsu⌝ryoku 活力: a person full of vitality (*kakki ni michita hito*) 活気に満ちた人.

vitamin *n.* bi⌜ta⌝miñ ビタミン: vitamin pills (*bitamiñzai*) ビタミン剤.

vivid *adj.* 1 (full of life) i⌜ki-i⌝ki to shita [shite iru] 生き生きとした[している]: a vivid performance (*iki-iki to shita eñgi*) 生き生きとした演技.
2 (bright) a⌜za⌝yaka na 鮮やかな: vivid colors (*azayaka na iro*) 鮮やかな色.

vocabulary *n.* go⌝i 語い: He has a large vocabulary. (*Kare wa goi ga hoofu da.*) 彼は語いが豊富だ.

vocal *adj.* 1 (of the voice) ko⌝e no 声の: vocal sounds (*oñsee*) 音声 /

vocal music (*seegaku*) 声楽.

2 (oral) ko⌈otoo no 口頭の: a vocal communication (*kootoo no deñtatsu*) 口頭の伝達.

vogue *n.* ryu⌈ukoo 流行; ha⌈yari⌉ はやり: Long hair is no longer in vogue. (*Choohatsu wa moo hayari de wa arimaseñ.*) 長髪はもうはやりではありません.

voice *n.* **1** (sound) ko⌉e 声: She spoke in a quiet voice. (*Kanojo wa shizuka na koe de hanashita.*) 彼女は静かな声で話した.

2 (expressed opinion) i⌉keñ 意見; ko⌉e 声: the voice for peace (*heewa o motomeru koe*) 平和を求める声.

volcano *n.* ka⌉zañ 火山: When is it that this volcano last erupted? (*Kono kazañ ga saigo ni fuñka shita no wa itsu desu ka?*) この火山が最後に噴火したのはいつですか.

volleyball *n.* ba⌈reebo⌉oru バレーボール: play volleyball (*bareebooru o suru*) バレーボールをする.

volume *n.* **1** (book) ho⌉ñ 本; -kañ 巻; -satsu 冊: a dictionary in two volumes (*ni-kañ kara naru jisho*) 2巻からなる辞書 / You can borrow three volumes at a time. (*Ichi-do ni sañ-satsu kariraremasu.*) 一度に3冊借りられます.

2 (loudness) o⌈ñryoo 音量; bo⌈ryuumu ボリューム: turn up [down] the volume on the TV (*terebi no oñryoo o ookiku* [*chiisaku*] *suru*) テレビの音量を大きく[小さく]する.

3 (solid content) ta⌉iseki 体積; (the amount of space inside) yo⌉oseki 容積: The volume of this box is 10 cubic centimeters. (*Kono hako no yooseki wa juu-rippoo-señchi-meetoru desu.*) この箱の容積は10立方センチメートルです.

4 (amount) ryo⌉o 量: a large volume of sales (*ooku no hañbairyoo*) 多くの販売量.

voluntary *adj.* ji⌈hatsu-teki na 自発的な; ji⌈yu⌉u na ishi ni yo⌈ru 自由な意志による: a voluntary helper (*jihatsu-teki na eñjosha*) 自発的な援助者.

volunteer *n.* shi⌈ga⌉ñsha 志願者; yu⌉ushi 有志; bo⌈ra⌉ñtia ボランティア.

— *vt.* ... o su⌈suñde mooshide⌉ru ...を進んで申し出る [V]: I volunteered to do the job. (*Watashi wa susuñde sono shigoto o suru koto o mooshideta.*) 私は進んでその仕事をすることを申し出た.

— *vi.* ji⌈hatsu-teki ni mooshide⌉ru 自発的に申し出る [V].

vomit *vt.* ... o ha⌉ku ...を吐く [C]; mo⌈do⌉su もどす [C]: The boy vomited up what he had eaten. (*Sono otoko-no-ko wa tabeta mono o haita.*) その男の子は食べたものを吐いた.

vote *n.* **1** (choice) to⌈ohyoo 投票: We took a vote on the matter. (*Watashi-tachi wa sono moñdai ni tsuite toohyoo o okonatta.*) 私たちはその問題について投票を行った.

2 (ballot) to⌈ohyo⌉osuu 投票数; hyo⌈osu⌉u 票数: count the votes (*hyoosuu o kazoeru*) 票数を数える.

— *vi.* to⌈ohyoo o suru 投票をする [I]: I voted for [against] the project. (*Watashi wa sono keekaku ni sañsee* [*hañtai*] *no toohyoo o shita.*) 私はその計画に賛成[反対]の投票をした.

— *vt.* ... o to⌈ohyoo de kimeru ...を投票で決める [V]: We voted to go on a hike next Sunday. (*Tsugi no nichiyoobi ni haikiñgu ni iku koto o toohyoo de kimeta.*) 次の日曜日にハイキングに行くことを投票で決めた.

voter *n.* to⌈ohyooniñ 投票人; to⌈ohyo⌉osha 投票者.

vow *n.* chi⌈kai 誓い; se⌈eyaku 誓約: make a vow (*chikai o tateru*) 誓いを立てる.

— *vt.* ... o chi⌈ka⌉u ...を誓う [C]: He vowed never to smoke. (*Kare wa kesshite tabako o suwanai to chikatta.*) 彼は決してたばこを吸わないと誓った.

vowel *n.* bo⌈iñ 母音.

voyage *n.* ko⌉okai 航海; fu⌈natabi 船旅: go on a long voyage (*nagai kookai ni deru*) 長い航海に出る.

vulgar *adj.* zo⌈kuaku na 俗悪な; ge-

ˈhiˈn̄ na 下品な: a vulgar TV program (*zokuaku na terebi ban̄gumi*) 俗悪なテレビ番組 / vulgar language (*gehin̄ na kotoba*) 下品な言葉.

vulnerable *adj*. kiˈzutsuki-yasuˈi 傷つきやすい; yoˈwaˈi 弱い: a vulnerable girl (*kizutsuki-yasui shoojo*) 傷つきやすい少女.

W

wade *vi*. aˈruˈite suˈsumu 歩いて進む Ⓒ: wade across a stream (*nagare o aruite wataru*) 流れを歩いて渡る.

waffle *n*. waˈffuru ワッフル.

wage *n*. chiˈn̄gin̄ 賃金; kyuˈuryoo 給料: He works for low wages. (*Kare wa hikui chin̄gin̄ de hataraite iru.*) 彼は低い賃金で働いている.

wagon *n*. **1** (used to carry food) waˈgon̄ ワゴン.
2 (four-wheeled vehicle pulled by horses) niˈbaˈsha 荷馬車.

waist *n*. **1** (of a person) uˈeˈsuto ウエスト; koˈshi 腰: She has a slender waist. (*Kanojo wa hossori shita uesuto o shite iru.*) 彼女はほっそりしたウエストをしている. ★ Japanese '*koshi*' refers to 'waist,' 'hips,' and 'lower back.'
2 (of a garment) uˈeˈsuto ウエスト.

wait *vi*. (... o) maˈtsu (...を)待つ Ⓒ: Wait a moment, please. (*Chotto matte kudasai.*) ちょっと待ってください. / Are you waiting for someone? (*Dare-ka o matte iru no desu ka?*) だれかを待っているのですか.

waiter *n*. uˈeˈetaa ウエーター; boˈoi ボーイ; kyuˈuji 給仕: Waiter, please. (*Booi-san̄.*) ボーイさん.

waiting room *n*. maˈchiaˈishitsu 待合室.

waitress *n*. uˈeˈetoresu ウエートレス.

wake *vi*. meˈ ga saˈmeˈru 目が覚める Ⓥ; oˈkiˈru 起きる Ⓥ: I woke up early this morning. (*Watashi wa kesa hayaku me ga sameta.*) 私はけさ早く目が覚めた.
— *vt*. ... o oˈkoˈsu ...を起こす Ⓒ; ... no meˈ o saˈmaˈsu ...の目を覚ます Ⓒ: Please wake me up at six. (*Roku-ji ni okoshite kudasai.*) 6時に起こしてください.

walk *vi*. **1** aˈruˈku 歩く Ⓒ; aˈruˈite iku 歩いて行く Ⓒ: He walked two kilometers. (*Kare wa ni-kiro aruita.*) 彼は2キロ歩いた. / I walk to school. (*Watashi wa aruite gakkoo e ikimasu.*) 私は歩いて学校へ行きます.
2 (take a walk) saˈn̄po suru 散歩する Ⓘ.
— *vt*. **1** (travel on foot) ... o aˈruˈku ...を歩く Ⓒ; aˈruki-mawaˈru 歩き回る Ⓒ: I walked the beach for hours. (*Watashi wa nan̄-jikan̄ mo umibe o aruita.*) 私は何時間も海辺を歩いた.
2 (accompany) ... o oˈkuru ...を送る Ⓒ: He walked her home. (*Kare wa kanojo o ie made okutta.*) 彼は彼女を家まで送った.
— *n*. **1** (stroll) saˈn̄po 散歩: My grandfather usually goes out for a walk in the afternoon. (*Sofu wa taitee gogo san̄po ni dekakeru.*) 祖父はたいてい午後散歩に出かける.
2 (distance to walk) miˈchinori 道のり: It's a ten-minute walk from here to the station. (*Koko kara eki made wa aruite jup-pun̄ desu.*) ここから駅までは歩いて10分です.
3 (path) hoˈdoo 歩道; saˈn̄poˈmichi 散歩道; yuˈuhoˈdoo 遊歩道.
4 (manner of walking) aˈruki-kaˈta 歩き方; aˈruki-buri 歩き振り: I recognized him by his walk. (*Watashi wa aruki-kata de kare da to wakatta.*) 私は歩き方で彼だとわかった.

wall *n*. **1** (of a room) kaˈbe 壁: hang a calendar on the wall (*kabe ni karen̄daa o kakeru*) 壁にカレンダー

をかける.

2 (outside) heꜛe 塀: The house has a brick wall around it. (*Sono ie wa mawari ni reñga no hee ga aru.*) その家は周りにれんがの塀がある.

— *vt.* (surround) ... o heꜛe de kakomu ...を塀で囲む Ⓒ; ... ni heꜛe o megurasu ...に塀を巡らす Ⓒ: The garden is walled in. (*Sono niwa wa hee de kakomarete iru.*) その庭は塀で囲まれている.

wallet *n.* saꜛifu 財布: My wallet was lifted in the train. (*Saifu o deñsha no naka de surareta.*) 財布を電車の中ですられた.

walnut *n.* (nut) kuꜛrumi くるみ; (tree) kuꜛrumi no kiꜜ くるみの木.

waltz *n.* waꜜrutsu ワルツ: dance a waltz (*warutsu o odoru*) ワルツを踊る.

wander *vi.* **1** (walk aimlessly) aꜛruki-mawaꜜru 歩き回る Ⓒ; buꜛratsuku ぶらつく Ⓒ: She wandered about the town to kill time. (*Kanojo wa jikañ o tsubusu tame ni machi o buratsuita.*) 彼女は時間をつぶすために町をぶらついた.

2 (go astray) haꜛgureꜜru はぐれる Ⓥ: He wandered away from his companions. (*Kare wa nakama kara hagurete shimatta.*) 彼は仲間からはぐれてしまった.

3 (move away) yoꜛkomichi e soreꜜru 横道へそれる Ⓥ: The speaker often wandered from the subject. (*Kooeñsha wa shibashiba wadai kara yokomichi e soreta.*) 講演者はしばしば話題から横道へそれた.

want *vt.* **1** (want something) [with 1st and 2nd persons] ... ga hoꜛshiꜜi ...が欲しい; [with 1st person] ... o kuꜛdasaꜜi ...を下さい; [with 3rd person] ... o hoꜛshigaꜜru ...を欲しがる Ⓒ: I want a better seat. (*Motto yoi seki ga hoshii.*) もっと良い席が欲しい. / Do you want this book? (*Anata wa kono hoñ ga hoshii desu ka?*) あなたはこの本が欲しいですか. / Please, I want five of these. (*Kore o itsutsu kudasai.*) これを五つ下さい. / The girl wants a doll for her birthday. (*Sono oñna-no-ko wa tañjoobi ni niñgyoo o hoshigatte iru.*) その女の子は誕生日に人形を欲しがっている.

2 (want to do) [with 1st and 2nd persons] ‹verb›-tai ...たい; [with 3rd person] ‹verb›-tagaru ...たがる Ⓒ: I want to read a detective story. (*Suiri shoosetsu ga yomitai.*) 推理小説が読みたい. / Where do you want to go? (*Doko e ikitai desu ka?*) どこへ行きたいですか. / These days, many young people want to go abroad. (*Chikagoro wa oozee no wakamono ga gaikoku e ikitagaru.*) 近頃は大勢の若者が外国へ行きたがる.

3 (want someone to do) (... ni) ‹verb›-te[de] hoꜛshiꜜi (...に)...て[で]欲しい, ‹verb›-te[de] moꜛraitai ...て[で]もらいたい: I want you to go shopping for me. (*Kimi ni kawari ni kaimono ni itte moraitai.*) 君に代わりに買い物に行ってもらいたい.

4 (want something done) ‹verb›-te[de] kuꜛdasaꜜi ...て[で]ください: I want my hair washed and set. (*Kami o aratte setto shite kudasai.*) 髪を洗ってセットしてください.

5 (call) ... o yoꜛbu ...を呼ぶ Ⓒ: "Mom, Dad wants you." (*"O-kaasañ, O-toosañ ga yoñde iru yo."*) 「お母さん, お父さんが呼んでいるよ」/ Somebody wants you on the phone. (*Anata ni deñwa desu.*) あなたに電話です.

— *n.* **1** (lack) fuꜛsoku 不足; keꜛtsuboo 欠乏: The tree is dying from want of water. (*Ki wa mizu ga fusoku shite karekakete iru.*) 木は水が不足して枯れかけている.

2 (need) hiꜛtsuyoo 必要; nyuꜛuyoo 入用: I am in want of money. (*Watashi wa o-kane o hitsuyoo to shite imasu.*) 私はお金を必要としています.

wanting *adj.* ... ni taꜛrinai ...に足りない; kaꜛkete iru 欠けている: She is wanting in courtesy. (*Kanojo wa reegi ni kakete iru.*) 彼女は礼儀に欠けている.

war *n.* se[ñsoo 戦争: A war broke out. (*Señsoo ga hajimatta.*) 戦争が始まった. / At that time Japan was at war with China. (*Tooji Nippoñ wa Chuugoku to señsoo chuu datta.*) 当時日本は中国と戦争中だった. / World War II (*dai ni-ji sekai taiseñ*) 第二次世界大戦.

warble *vi.* sa[ezu]ru さえずる Ⓒ: A bird is warbling in a tree. (*Tori ga ki de saezutte iru.*) 鳥が木でさえずっている.

ward *n.* **1** (of a hospital) byo[otoo 病棟: a children's ward (*shooni byootoo*) 小児病棟.
2 (division in an area) ku] 区: Chiyoda Ward (*Chiyoda-ku*) 千代田区.
3 (person) hi-ho[go]sha 被保護者.

wardrobe *n.* **1** (closet) yo[ofuku-da]ñsu 洋服だんす; i[shoo-da]ñsu 衣装だんす.
2 (clothes) fu[ku] 服; i]rui 衣類: She has a large wardrobe. (*Kanojo wa ishoo o takusañ motte iru.*) 彼女は衣装をたくさん持っている.

warehouse *n.* so]oko 倉庫; cho[zoojo 貯蔵所.

warfare *n.* se[ñsoo 戦争: nuclear warfare (*kaku señsoo*) 核戦争 / guerilla warfare (*gerira-señ*) ゲリラ戦.

warm *adj.* **1** (comfortably warm) a[tataka]i 暖かい: It's getting warmer day by day. (*Hi ni hi ni atatakaku natte kite iru.*) 日に日に暖かくなってきている.
2 (uncomfortably warm) a[tsu]i 暑い: This room is too warm. (*Kono heya wa atsui.*) この部屋は暑い.
3 (kind) a[tataka]i 温かい: He has a warm heart. (*Kare wa atatakai kokoro o motte iru.*) 彼は温かい心を持っている. / They gave her a warm welcome. (*Kare-ra wa kanojo o atatakaku mukaeta.*) 彼らは彼女を温かく迎えた.
— *vt.* **1** (of things) ... o a[tatame]ru ...を暖[温]める Ⓥ; a[tata]kaku suru 暖かくする Ⓘ: warm up a room (*heya o atatameru*) 部屋を暖める / I'll warm the soup. (*Watashi ga suupu o atatamemashoo.*) 私がスープを温めましょう.
2 (of heart) ... o a[tatame]ru ...を温める Ⓥ; a[tataka]i ki[mochi ni saseru 温かい気持ちにさせる Ⓥ: It warms my heart to hear her story. (*Kanojo no hanashi o kiku to kokoro ga atatamaru.*) 彼女の話を聞くと心が温まる.
— *vi.* a[tatama]ru 暖[温]まる Ⓒ; a[tataka]ku naru 暖[温]かくなる Ⓒ: The soup on the stove is warming. (*Reñji ni kaketa suupu ga atatamatte kita.*) レンジにかけたスープが温まってきた

warmth *n.* **1** (of things) a[tata]kasa 暖かさ: The warmth of the room felt good. (*Heya no atatakasa ga kokochi yokatta.*) 部屋の暖かさが心地よかった.
2 (of heart) o[moiyari 思いやり; shi]ñsetsu 親切: He has no warmth. (*Kare wa omoiyari ga nai.*) 彼は思いやりがない.

warn *vt.* **1** (caution) ... ni ke[ekoku suru ...に警告する Ⓘ; chu]ui suru 注意する Ⓘ: The police warned reckless drivers. (*Keesatsu wa muboo na uñteñsha ni keekoku shita.*) 警察は無謀な運転者に警告した.
2 (tell in advance) ... ni (... to) yo[koku suru ...に(...と)予告する Ⓘ: The boss warned him that he would be fired in a month. (*Jooshi wa kare ni ikkagetsu-go ni kaiko suru to yokoku shita.*) 上司は彼に1か月後に解雇すると予告した.

warning *n.* ke[ekoku 警告; chu]ui 注意: I gave him a warning not to go there. (*Watashi wa kare ni soko e iku na to keekoku shita.*) 私は彼にそこへ行くなと警告した.

warrior *n.* bu]shi 武士; gu[ñjiñ 軍人.

wash *vt.* **1** (clean) ... o a[rau ...を洗う Ⓒ: I washed my car clean. (*Watashi wa kuruma o kiree ni aratta.*) 私は車をきれいに洗った.
2 (of clothes) ... o se[ñtaku suru ...

W

を洗濯する [I]; a⌈rau 洗う [C]: wash trousers (*zuboñ o señtaku suru*) ズボンを洗濯する.
3 (sweep) ... o o⌈shinaga⌉su ...を押し流す [C]: The bridge was washed away by the flood. (*Hashi ga koozui de oshinagasareta.*) 橋が洪水で押し流された.
4 (flow) ... ni u⌈chiyoseru ...に打ち寄せる [V]: Waves are washing the beach. (*Nami ga kishi ni uchiyosete iru.*) 波が岸に打ち寄せている.
— *vi.* **1** (clean) a⌈rau 洗う [C]: wash before meals (*shokuji no mae ni te o arau.*) 食事の前に手を洗う.
2 (can be washed) se⌈ñtaku ga kiku 洗濯がきく [C]: This curtain washes well. (*Kono kaateñ wa señtaku ga kiku.*) このカーテンは洗濯がきく.
3 (of detergents) yo⌈gore o oto⌉su 汚れを落とす [C]: This detergent doesn't wash well. (*Kono señzai wa amari ochinai.*) この洗剤はあまり落ちない.
4 (do the laundry) se⌈ñtaku suru 洗濯する [I]: Mr. Tanaka washes on Mondays. (*Tanaka-sañ wa getsuyoobi ni señtaku suru.*) 田中さんは月曜日に洗濯する.
— *n.* **1** (act of washing) a⌈rau koto⌉ 洗うこと; (of clothes) se⌈ñtaku 洗濯: I gave my car a good wash. (*Watashi wa kuruma o yoku aratta.*) 私は車をよく洗った.
2 (laundry) se⌈ñtakumono 洗濯物: I have a big wash today. (*Kyoo wa señtakumono ga takusañ aru.*) 今日は洗濯物がたくさんある.

washing machine *n.* se⌈ñtaku⌉ki 洗濯機: wash in a washing machine (*señtakuki de arau*) 洗濯機で洗う.

washroom *n.* se⌈ñmeñjo 洗面所; te⌈a⌉rai 手洗い.

waste *vt.* ... o mu⌈da ni suru ...を無駄にする [I]; ro⌈ohi suru 浪費する [I]: Don't waste money. (*O-kane o muda ni shite wa ikemaseñ.*) お金を無駄にしてはいけません.
— *vi.* **1** (spend carelessly) mu⌈da ni suru 無駄にする [I].
2 (lose strength) su⌈ijaku suru 衰弱する [I]: He wasted away through an illness. (*Kare wa byooki no tame ni suijaku shita.*) 彼は病気のために衰弱した.
— *n.* **1** (meaningless use) mu⌈da 無駄; ro⌈ohi 浪費: It's a waste of time. (*Sore wa jikañ no muda da.*) それは時間の無駄だ.
2 (refuse) ha⌈iki⌉butsu 廃棄物; (liquid) ha⌈ieki 廃液: industrial waste (*sañgyoo haikibutsu*) 産業廃棄物.

wasteful *adj.* mu⌈da na 無駄な; fu⌈ke⌉ezai na 不経済な: This method is wasteful. (*Kono hoohoo wa fukeezai da.*) この方法は不経済だ.

watch[1] *n.* (wristwatch) u⌈dedo⌉kee 腕時計; (pocket watch) ka⌈ichuudo⌉kee 懐中時計: a watch shop (*tokee-teñ*) 時計店. ★ 'Clock' is also called '*tokee*.'

watch[2] *vt.* **1** (look at) ... o mi⌉ru ...を見る [V]: watch TV (*terebi o miru*) テレビを見る.
2 (keep watch) ... o mi⌈haru ...を見張る [C]: Will you watch my bags while I go to make a phone call? (*Deñwa o kakete kuru aida, nimotsu o mihatte ite kuremaseñ ka?*) 電話をかけてくる間, 荷物を見張っていてくれませんか.
— *vi.* **1** (watch carefully) yo⌉ku miru よく見る [V]: Watch while I write this kanji. (*Watashi ga kono kañji o kaku aida yoku mite i nasai.*) 私がこの漢字を書く間よく見ていなさい.
2 (be careful) ki ⌈o tsuke⌉ru 気をつける [V]; chu⌉ui suru 注意する [I]: Watch when you cross the street. (*Michi o wataru toki wa ki o tsuke nasai.*) 道を渡るときは気をつけなさい.
3 (await) (... o) ma⌈chikamae⌉ru (...を)待ち構える [V]: We were watching for an opportunity. (*Watashi-tachi wa chañsu o machikamaete ita.*) 私たちはチャンスを待ち構えていた.

watchful *adj.* yo⌐ojiñbuka˥i 用心深い; yu⌐dañ no [ga] na˥i 油断の[が]ない: watchful eyes (*yoojiñbukai me*) 用心深い目.

water *n.* **1** (cold) mi⌐zu 水; (hot) (o)⌐yu˥ (お)湯: Please give me a glass of water. (*Mizu o ip-pai kudasai.*) 水を1杯下さい. / The water is boiling. (*O-yu ga waite imasu.*) お湯が沸いています.
2 (in water) su⌐ichuu 水中: jump into the water (*suichuu ni tobikomu*) 水中に飛び込む.
3 (sea) u˥mi 海; (lake) mi⌐zu˥umi 湖; (river) ka⌐wa˥ 川.
4 (territorial waters) ryo⌐okai 領海: A ship of unknown nationality violated Japanese waters. (*Kokuseki fumee no fune ga Nihoñ no ryookai o shiñpañ shita.*) 国籍不明の船が日本の領海を侵犯した.
5 [compound words] -sui 水: soda water (*tañsañ-sui*) 炭酸水 / toilet water (*keshoo-sui*) 化粧水.
— *vt.* ... ni mi⌐zu o yaru …に水をやる Ⓒ: water the flowers (*hana ni mizu o yaru*) 花に水をやる.

waterfall *n.* ta⌐ki 滝.

waterproof *adj.* bo⌐osui no 防水の: This watch is waterproof. (*Kono udedokee wa boosui desu.*) この腕時計は防水です.

watt *n.* wa˥tto ワット.

wave *n.* **1** (of water) na⌐mi˥ 波: The waves are high. (*Nami ga takai.*) 波が高い.
2 (of a hand) te˥ o fu⌐ru koto˥ 手を振ること: She gave me a cheerful wave when she recognized me. (*Kanojo wa watashi ni ki ga tsuku to ureshi-soo ni te o futta.*) 彼女は私に気がつくとうれしそうに手を振った.
— *vi.* **1** (move a hand) te˥ o fu⌐ru 手を振る Ⓒ: When she saw me, she waved at me. (*Kanojo wa watashi o mite te o futta.*) 彼女は私を見て手を振った.
2 (move to and fro) yu⌐reru 揺れる Ⓥ; (of cloth) hi⌐ruga˥eru 翻る Ⓒ: The sheet on the washline waved in the wind. (*Monohoshi no shiitsu ga kaze ni hirugaette ita.*) 物干しのシーツが風に翻っていた.
— *vt.* **1** (of hand, flag, etc.) ... o fu⌐ru …を振る Ⓒ: Children waved small flags as the procession went by. (*Kodomo-tachi wa gyooretsu ga toorisugiru toki kobata o futta.*) 子どもたちは行列が通り過ぎるとき小旗を振った.
2 (of greeting) ... ni te˥ o fu⌐ru …に手を振る Ⓒ: He waved her goodbye. (*Kare wa kanojo ni te o futte wakare o tsugeta.*) 彼は彼女に手を振って別れを告げた.

waver *vi.* (be uncertain) ma⌐yo˥u 迷う Ⓒ; ta⌐mera˥u ためらう Ⓒ: He wavered in his judgment. (*Kare wa hañdañ ni mayotta.*) 彼は判断に迷った.

wax *n.* (beeswax) ro˥o ろう; (polish) wa˥kkusu ワックス.

way *n.* **1** (method) ho⌐ohoo 方法; ya⌐rikata やり方: Please tell me the best way to do this. (*Kore o yaru ichibañ yoi hoohoo o oshiete kudasai.*) これをやるいちばんよい方法を教えてください.
2 (direction) ho⌐okoo 方向: This way, please. (*Kochira e doozo.*) こちらへどうぞ. / He didn't know which way to go. (*Kare wa dotchi no hookoo e ikeba ii no ka wakaranakatta.*) 彼はどっちの方向へ行けばいいのかわからなかった.
3 (road) mi⌐chi 道: Will you tell me the way to the station? (*Eki e iku michi o oshiete kudasai.*) 駅へ行く道を教えてください.
4 (distance) mi⌐chinori 道のり; kyo˥ri 距離: We still have quite a way to walk. (*Watashi-tachi wa mada kanari no michinori o arukanakereba naranai.*) 私たちはまだかなりの道のりを歩かなければならない.
5 (respect) te˥ñ 点; me˥ñ 面: His advice was helpful in many ways. (*Kare no adobaisu wa ooku no meñ de yaku ni tatta.*) 彼のアドバイスは多くの面で役に立った.

W

all the way *adv.* (from beginning to end) zu[']tto ずっと: The train was crowded and I stood all the way to Tokyo. (*Ressha ga koñde ite, watashi wa Tookyoo made zutto tatte ita.*) 列車が込んでいて, 私は東京までずっと立っていた.
by the way *adv.* to[']koro[']de ところで.
in the way *adv., adj.* ja[']ma ni na[']tte (iru) じゃまになって(いる): You'll be in the way if you stand there. (*Soko ni tatsu to jama ni narimasu.*) そこに立つとじゃまになります.
on the way *adv., adj.* to[']chuu (de) 途中(で): What landmarks are on the way? (*Tochuu no mejirushi wa nañ desu ka?*) 途中の目印は何ですか.

we *pron.* wa[']tashi[']-tachi 私たち; [formal] wa[']reware われわれ. ★ Used mainly by men. Women use '*watashi-tachi*.'

weak *adj.* **1** (of a body, character, etc.) yo[']wa[']i 弱い: My mother is physically weak. (*Haha wa karada ga yowai.*) 母は体が弱い/ He is weak-willed so he gives up easily. (*Kare wa ishi ga yowai no de sugu akirameru.*) 彼は意志が弱いのですぐあきらめる.
2 (of knowledge, ability, etc.) (... ga) ni[']gate na (…が)苦手な; (... ni) yo[']wa[']i 弱い: He is weak in math. (*Kare wa suugaku ga nigate da.*) 彼は数学が苦手だ. / weak point (*jakuteñ*) 弱点.

weaken *vt.* ... o yo[']wame[']ru …を弱める [V]; yo[']waku suru 弱くする [I]: The illness weakened him. (*Kare wa byooki de yowatta.*) 彼は病気で弱った.
— *vi.* yo[']waku naru 弱くなる [C].

weakness *n.* **1** (frailty) yo[']wasa 弱さ; yo[']wa[']i ko[']to[']弱いこと: His physical weakness was his parents' constant worry. (*Kare no karada ga yowai koto wa ryooshiñ no shiñpai no tane datta.*) 彼の体が弱いことは両親の心配の種だった.
2 (shortcoming) ja[']kute[']ñ 弱点; ta[']ñsho 短所; ke[']tte[']ñ 欠点: Everyone has weaknesses. (*Dare de mo jakuteñ wa aru.*) だれでも弱点はある.

wealth *n.* to[']mi 富; za[']isañ 財産: He aquired great wealth through land speculation. (*Kare wa tochitooki de ooki-na zaisañ o kizuita.*) 彼は土地投機で大きな財産を築いた.

wealthy *adj.* yu[']ufuku na 裕福な; ka[']nemochi no 金持ちの: He comes from a wealthy family. (*Kare wa yuufuku na iegara no de desu.*) 彼は裕福な家柄の出です.

weapon *n.* bu[']ki 武器; he[']eki 兵器: nuclear weapons (*kaku-heeki*) 核兵器 / conventional weapons (*tsuujoo-heeki*) 通常兵器.

wear *vt.* **1** (of clothes) ... o ki[']te iru …を着ている [V]; (of shoes, trousers, skirt) ha[']ite iru はいている [V]; (of a hat) ka[']bu[']tte iru かぶっている [V]; (of glasses) ka[']kete iru かけている [V]; (of a necktie) shi[']mete iru 締めている [V]; (of gloves, ring) ha[']mete iru はめている [V]; (of a scarf, watch) shi[']te iru している [V]; (of a ribbon, perfume) tsu[']kete iru つけている [V]: Miss Yamada was wearing a kimono. (*Yamada-sañ wa kimono o kite ita.*) 山田さんは着物を着ていた.
2 (of a mustache) ... o ha[']ya[']shite iru …を生やしている [V]; (of hair) yu[']tte iru 結っている [V]: Mr. Tanaka wears a mustache. (*Tanaka-sañ wa kuchi hige o hayashite iru.*) 田中さんは口ひげを生やしている. / My wife wears her hair short. (*Kanai wa kami o mijikaku shite iru.*) 家内は髪を短くしている.
3 (of an expression) ... o shi[']te iru …をしている [V]: His face wore a troubled look. (*Kare wa shiñpai-soo na kao o shite ita.*) 彼は心配そうな顔をしていた
4 (make thin) ... o su[']riherasu をすり減らす [C]: The carpet is worn thin. (*Juutañ ga surihette usuku natte iru.*) じゅうたんがすり減って薄くな

W

っている.

— *vi.* **1** (last) mo^ltsu もつ Ⓒ: This cloth will wear for years. (*Kono kiji wa nañ-neñ mo motsu deshoo.*) この生地は何年ももつでしょう.
2 (become worn) su^rriheru すり減る Ⓒ; (of cloth) su^rrikireru すり切れる Ⓥ: The heels of these shoes are worn down. (*Kono kutsu wa kakato ga surihette iru.*) この靴はかかとがすり減っている.

— *n.* **1** (use of clothing) cha^rku-yoo 着用: clothes for everyday wear (*fudañ-gi*) ふだん着.
2 (clothes) i^lrui 衣類; i^lfuku 衣服: men's [ladies'] wear (*shiñshi [fujiñ] fuku*) 紳士[婦人]服.
3 (damage) su^rrikire すり切れ; (clothes) ki^rfurushi 着古し: The coat showed signs of wear. (*Sono kooto wa kifurushita ato ga atta.*) そのコートは着古した跡があった.

weary *adj.* **1** (tired) tsu^rka^lreta 疲れた; tsu^rka^lrete iru 疲れている: I was weary from the long walk. (*Nagai aida aruita no de tsukaremashita.*) 長い間歩いたので疲れました.
2 (bored) a^rkia^lki shite (iru) 飽き飽きして(いる); u^rñza^lri shite (iru) うんざりして(いる): I'm weary of sitting at home. (*Watashi wa ie ni iru no wa uñzari da.*) 私は家にいるのはうんざりだ.

weather *n.* te^lñki 天気; te^rñkoo 天候: How is the weather? (*O-teñki wa doo desu ka?*) お天気はどうですか. / It's nice weather, isn't it? (*Ii o-teñki desu ne.*) いいお天気ですね.

weatherman *n.* te^rñkiyoho^lokañ 天気予報官; ki^rshoo yoho^loshi 気象予報士.

weave *vt.* ... o o^lru ...を織る Ⓒ: She is weaving a rug. (*Kanojo wa juutañ o otte iru.*) 彼女はじゅうたんを織っている.

wedding *n.* ke^rkko^lñshiki 結婚式: I was invited to my cousin's wedding. (*Watashi wa itoko no kekkoñshiki ni shootai sareta.*) 私はいとこの結婚式に招待された.

wedge *n.* ku^rsabi くさび: drive a wedge into a log (*maruta ni kusabi o uchikomu*) 丸太にくさびを打ち込む.

Wednesday *n.* su^riyo^lo(bi) 水曜(日).

weed *n.* za^rssoo 雑草: pull weeds (*zassoo o nuku*) 雑草を抜く.

week *n.* **1** shu^lu 週: last week (*señshuu*) 先週 / this week (*koñshuu*) 今週 / next week (*raishuu*) 来週/ the week after next (*saraishuu*) 再来週 / every week (*maishuu*) 毎週 / How many Japanese lessons do you take a week? (*Shuu ni nañ-do Nihoñgo no ressuñ o ukemasu ka?*) 週に何度日本語のレッスンを受けますか.
2 i^rs-shu^lukañ 1 週間: two weeks (*ni-shuukañ*) 2 週間 / I haven't seen him for weeks. (*Watashi wa nañ-shuukañ mo kare ni atte imaseñ.*) 私は何週間も彼に会っていません.

weekday *n.* he^rejitsu 平日; shu^rujitsu 週日; u^ri^likudee ウイークデー: I am very busy on weekdays. (*Watashi wa heejitsu wa hijoo ni isogashii.*) 私は平日は非常に忙しい.

weekend *n.* shu^rumatsu 週末: We went skiing over the weekend. (*Watashi-tachi wa shuumatsu ni sukii ni ikimashita.*) 私たちは週末にスキーに行きました.

weekly *adj.* (every week) ma^rishuu no 毎週の; (once a week) shu^lu i^rk-ka^li no 週 1 回の; (published once a week) shu^rukañ no 週刊の: weekly wages (*shuukyuu*) 週給 / a weekly magazine (*shuukañshi*) 週刊誌.

— *n.* (magazine) shu^ruka^lñshi 週刊誌; (newspaper) shu^ruka^lñshi 週刊紙.

weep *vi.* na^rku 泣く Ⓒ: She wept at the news. (*Kanojo wa sono shirase o kiite naita.*) 彼女はその知らせを聞いて泣いた.

weigh *vt.* ... no o^rmosa o haka^lru ...の重さを量る Ⓒ: weigh a parcel (*kozutsumi no omosa o hakaru*) 小包の重さを量る / I weighed myself. (*Jibuñ no taijuu o hakatta.*) 自分の

体重を量った.

— *vi.* o⌈mosa ga ... a⌉ru 重さが…ある Ⓒ: "How much do you weigh?" "About 50 kilograms." (*"Taijuu wa dono kurai arimasu ka?" "Go-juk-kiro kurai desu."*) 「体重はどのくらいありますか」「50 キロくらいです」

weight *n.* **1** (things) o⌈mosa 重さ; (people) ta⌈ijuu 体重: gain [lose] weight (*taijuu ga fueru* [*heru*]) 体重が増える[減る].

2 (burden) o⌈moni 重荷; ju⌈uatsu 重圧: That's a real weight off my mind. (*Sore de watashi no kokoro no omoni mo toreta.*) それで私の心の重荷もとれた.

welcome *int.* yo⌉okoso ようこそ: Welcome to Japan! (*Nihoñ e yoo-koso.*) 日本へようこそ.

— *vt.* ... o ka⌈ñgee suru …を歓迎する Ⓘ: They welcomed the guest. (*Kare-ra wa kyaku o kañgee shita.*) 彼らは客を歓迎した.

— *adj.* ka⌈ñgee sareru 歓迎される; yo⌈rokobashi⌉i 喜ばしい: a welcome guest (*kañgee sareru o-kyaku*) 歓迎されるお客 / welcome news (*yoro-kobashii nyuusu*) 喜ばしいニュース.

— *n.* ka⌈ñgee 歓迎: They gave their guest a warm welcome. (*Kare-ra wa o-kyaku o atatakaku mukaeta.*) 彼らはお客を温かく迎えた.

You are welcome. Do⌉o i⌈ta-shima⌉shite. どういたしまして: "Thank you very much." "You're welcome." (*"Arigatoo gozaimasu." "Doo itashimashite."*) 「ありがとうございます」「どういたしまして」

welfare *n.* fu⌈ku⌉shi 福祉: promote welfare (*fukushi o zooshiñ suru*) 福祉を増進する / welfare work (*fu-kushi-jigyoo*) 福祉事業 / social wel-fare (*shakai-fukushi*) 社会福祉.

well[1] *adv.* **1** (skillfully) u⌉maku うまく; jo⌈ozu⌉ ni 上手に: sing a song well (*uta o umaku utau*) 歌をうまく歌う.

2 (satisfactorily) yo⌉ku よく; u⌉ma-ku うまく: Well done! (*Yoku yatta.*) よくやった. / The shutter of my cam-era doesn't work well. (*Kamera no shattaa ga umaku ugokanai.*) カメラのシャッターがうまく動かない.

3 (thoroughly) yo⌉ku よく; ju⌈ubu⌉ñ ni 十分に: I know her well. (*Wata-shi wa kanojo o yoku shitte imasu.*) 私は彼女をよく知っています.

4 (much) ka⌉nari かなり; ju⌈ubu⌉ñ ni 十分に: He is well over sixty. (*Kare wa rokujus-sai o kanari koete iru.*) 彼は 60 歳をかなり越えている.

... **as well** *adv.* so⌈no ue ... mo その上…も: He speaks Japanese, and Chinese as well. (*Kare wa Nihoñ-go o hanasemasu shi, Chuugo-kugo mo hanasemasu.*) 彼は日本語を話せますし, 中国語も話せます.

may as well do ⟨verb⟩-te[de] mo i⌉i daroo …て[で]もいいだろう: You may as well know the truth. (*Shiñjitsu o shitte oite mo ii daroo.*) 真実を知っておいてもいいだろう.

may well do ... no mo mo⌈tto⌉-mo da …のももっともだ: He may well think so. (*Kare ga soo omou no mo mottomo da.*) 彼がそう思うのももっともだ.

— *adj.* **1** (healthy) ke⌈ñkoo na 健康な; ge⌉ñki na 元気な: My family are well. (*Kazoku wa miñna geñki desu.*) 家族はみんな元気です. / I don't feel well. (*Kibuñ ga yoku arima-señ.*) 気分がよくありません.

2 (good) mo⌈oshibuñ na⌉i 申し分ない; u⌉maku i⌈tte iru うまくいっている: All's well. (*Bañji mooshibuñ nai.*) 万事申し分ない.

— *int.* **1** (used in reply) So⌉o desu ne. そうですね.; E⌉e maa. ええまあ.

2 (to change the subject) to⌈koro⌉ de ところで; sa⌉te さて.

well[2] *n.* i⌉do 井戸: draw water from a well (*ido kara mizu o kumu*) 井戸から水をくむ.

well-known *adj.* yu⌈umee na 有名な; yo⌉ku shi⌈rarete iru よく知られている: This restaurant is best-known for its good wine. (*Kono resutorañ wa waiñ ga yoi no de

W

ichibañ yoku shirarete imasu.) このレストランはワインがよいのでいちばんよく知られています.

west *n.* **1** (direction) ni⌈shi 西: The wind is blowing from the west. (*Kaze wa nishi kara fuite imasu.*) 風は西から吹いています.
2 (Occident) se⌉eyoo 西洋.
— *adj.* ni⌈shi no 西の: a west wind (*nishi kaze*) 西風.
— *adv.* ni⌈shi ni [e] 西に[へ]: This room faces west. (*Kono heya wa nishi-muki desu.*) この部屋は西向きです.

western *adj.* ni⌈shi no 西の; (Occidental) se⌉eyoo no 西洋の: the western sky (*nishi no sora*) 西の空 / Western countries (*seeyoo sho-koku*) 西洋諸国.

westward *adv.* ni⌈shi no ho⌉o e 西の方へ: The ship turned westward. (*Fune wa nishi no hoo e mukatta.*) 船は西の方へ向かった.
— *adj.* ni⌈shi ni mukau 西に向かう: a westward voyage (*nishi ni mukau kookai*) 西に向かう航海.

wet *adj.* **1** (covered with liquid) nu⌈reta ぬれた; nu⌈rete iru ぬれている; shi⌈metta 湿った; shi⌈mette iru 湿っている: a wet towel (*nureta taoru*) ぬれたタオル / I got wet in the rain. (*Ame de nureta.*) 雨でぬれた. / Wet Paint. (*Peñki nuritate.*) ペンキ塗り立て.
2 (rainy) a⌈me⌉furi no 雨降りの; a⌉me no [ga] ooi 雨の[が]多い: wet weather (*ame moyoo no teñki*) 雨模様の天気 / the wet season (*uki*) 雨季.
— *vt.* ... o nu⌈rasu …をぬらす Ⓒ; shi⌈meraseru 湿らせる Ⓥ: He wet the towel with water. (*Kare wa taoru o mizu de shimeraseta.*) 彼はタオルを水で湿らせた.

whale *n.* ku⌈jira 鯨.

what[1] *pron.* **1** (inquiry) na⌉ni 何; (things) do⌉ñna mo⌈no⌉ どんなもの; (state) do⌉ñna ko⌈to⌉ どんなこと: What is this? (*Kore wa nañ desu ka?*) これは何ですか. / What is 'goboo'? (*'Goboo' to wa doñna mono desu ka?*) 「ごぼう」とはどんなものですか. / What did he talk about? (*Kare wa doñna koto o hanashimashita ka?*) 彼はどんなことを話しましたか. / What does this mean? (*Kore wa doo iu imi desu ka?*) これはどういう意味ですか.
2 (of money) i⌉kura いくら: What is the fee per day? (*Ichi-nichi no ryoo-kiñ wa ikura desu ka?*) 一日の料金はいくらですか. / What is the dollar rate? (*Doru no reeto wa ikura desu ka?*) ドルのレートはいくらですか.
What about ...? ... wa do⌉o desu ka? …はどうですか: What about a drink? (*Ippai doo desu ka?*) 一杯どうですか. / What about going to a movie? (*Eega ni iku no wa doo desu ka?*) 映画に行くのはどうですか.
— *adj.* **1** [question] na⌉ñ no 何の; na⌉ñ to iu 何という; do⌉ñna どんな; na⌉ni [na⌉ñ]- 何: What time is it? (*Nañ-ji desu ka?*) 何時ですか. / What day of the week is it today? (*Kyoo wa nañ-yoobi desu ka?*) 今日は何曜日ですか. / What flowers do you like? (*Anata wa doñna hana ga suki desu ka?*) あなたはどんな花が好きですか.
2 [exclamation] na⌉ñte 何て; na⌉ñ-to 何と: What a cute baby! (*Nañte kawaii aka-chañ deshoo!*) 何てかわいい赤ちゃんでしょう.
— *adv.* do⌈re hodo どれほど; do⌈no te⌉edo どの程度: What does it matter? (*Sore ga dore hodo moñdai ni naru no ka?*) それがどれほど問題になるのか.
— *int.* **1** [used when a person could not catch what another said] e' えっ; na⌉ni 何.
2 [shows surprise] na⌉ñ datte 何だって; na⌉ni 何.

what[2] *rel. pron.* ... ko⌈to⌉ …こと; ... mo⌈no⌉ …もの: What he said is not true. (*Kare ga itta koto wa hoñtoo de wa arimaseñ.*) 彼が言ったことは本当ではありません. / The girl showed her mother what her grandmother

W

gave her. (*Sono oñna-no-ko wa sobo ga kureta mono o hahaoya ni miseta.*) その女の子は祖母がくれたものを母親に見せた.

whatever *rel. pron.* **1** ... mo⌈no [ko⌈to] wa na⌉ñ de mo ...もの[こと]は何でも: You may do whatever you like. (*Anata wa nañ de mo suki na koto o shite kamaimaseñ.*) あなたは何でも好きなことをしてかまいません.
2 (no matter what) na⌉ni ga ⟨verb⟩-te[de] mo 何が...て[で]も: Whatever happens, don't give up. (*Nani ga atte mo, akiramete wa ikenai.*) 何があってもあきらめてはいけない.
— *rel. adj.* **1** do⌉ñna ... de mo どんな...でも: You may read whatever book you like. (*Kimi ga suki na hoñ nara doñna hoñ de mo yoñde yoi.*) 君が好きな本ならどんな本でも読んでよい.
2 (no matter what) do⌉ñna ⟨verb⟩-(y)oo to mo どんな...(よ)うとも: Whatever results follow, I will go. (*Doñna kekka ni naroo to mo, watashi wa ikimasu.*) どんな結果になろうとも, 私は行きます.

wheat *n.* ko⌈mu⌉gi 小麦: Bread is made from wheat. (*Pañ wa ko-mugi kara tsukurareru.*) パンは小麦から作られる.

wheel *n.* **1** sha⌈riñ 車輪; ku⌈ruma 車: The wheel of my bicycle came off. (*Watashi no jiteñsha no sha-riñ ga hazurete shimatta.*) 私の自転車の車輪がはずれてしまった.
2 (steering wheel) ha⌈ñdoru ハンドル: take the wheel of a car (*kuruma no hañdoru o nigiru*) 車のハンドルを握る.
— *vi.* **1** (turn around) ku⌈ruri to mu⌉ki o ka⌈eru くるりと向きを変える Ⓥ: He wheeled around and looked at me. 彼はくるりと向きを変えて私を見た.
2 (move in circles) se⌈ñkai suru 旋回する Ⓘ: Gulls are wheeling around over the sea. (*Kamome ga umi no ue o señkai shite iru.*) カモメが海の上を旋回している.
— *vt.* (push) ... o o⌈su ...を押す Ⓒ; (pull) hi⌈ku 引く Ⓒ: She wheeled the baby carriage around the park. (*Kanojo wa kooeñ de ubaguruma o oshite aruita.*) 彼女は公園で乳母車を押して歩いた.

when[1] *adv.* i⌉tsu いつ: When did you come to Japan? (*Anata wa itsu Nihoñ e koraremashita ka?*) あなたはいつ日本へ来られましたか. / I don't know when she will get back. (*Kanojo ga itsu kaette kuru ka wakarimaseñ.*) 彼女がいつ帰ってくるかわかりません.
— *pron.* i⌉tsu いつ: Untill when are you going to stay here? (*Itsu made koko ni irasshaimasu ka?*) いつまでここにいらっしゃいますか.

when[2] *conj.* **1** ... to⌉ki ...とき: When it rains, I usually stay at home. (*Ame no toki wa taitee uchi ni imasu.*) 雨のときはたいてい家にいます. / I was reading a book when he came in. (*Kare ga haitte kita toki, watashi wa hoñ o yoñde ita.*) 彼が入ってきたとき, 私は本を読んでいた.
2 (whenever) ... toki wa i⌉tsu-mo ...ときはいつも: He calls on me when he comes to Osaka. (*Kare wa Oo-saka ni kuru toki wa itsu-mo wata-shi o tazunete kimasu.*) 彼は大阪に来るときはいつも私を訪ねて来ます.

when[3] *rel. adv.* ... to⌉ki ...時: Mon-day is when I'm busiest. (*Getsu-yoobi wa watashi ga ichibañ iso-gashii toki desu.*) 月曜日は私がいちばん忙しい時です.

whenever *conj.* **1** ... toki wa i⌉tsu-mo ...ときはいつも: Whenever he goes for a walk he takes his dog with him. (*Kare wa sañpo ni deka-keru toki wa itsu-mo inu o tsurete ikimasu.*) 彼は散歩に出かけるときはいつも犬を連れて行きます.
2 (no matter when) i⌉tsu ⟨verb⟩-te [de] mo いつ...て[で]も: Whenever I phone him, he is out. (*Watashi ga itsu deñwa o shite mo, kare wa dekakete iru.*) 私がいつ電話をしても, 彼は出かけている.

where[1] *adv.* do⌝ko どこ; [polite] do⌝chira どちら: Where is the post office? (*Yuubiñkyoku wa doko desu ka?*) 郵便局はどこですか. / Where do you live? (*Dochira ni o-sumai desu ka?*) どちらにお住まいですか. / Where can I change money? (*O-kane wa doko de kaeraremasu ka?*) お金はどこで換えられますか. / I don't know where she went. (*Watashi wa kanojo ga doko e itta no ka shirimaseñ.*) 私は彼女がどこへ行ったのか知りません.

— *pron.* do⌝ko どこ; [polite] do⌝chira どちら: Where are you from? (*Shusshiñchi wa dochira desu ka?*) 出身地はどちらですか.

where[2] *rel. adv.* ... to⌜koro⌝ ...ところ: This is where we keep towels. (*Koko ga taoru o shimatte oku tokoro desu.*) ここがタオルをしまっておくところです. / This is the town where I was born. (*Koko ga watashi no umareta machi desu.*) ここが私の生まれた町です.

— *conj.* ... to⌜koro⌝ ni [e, o] ...所に[へ, を]: Please stay where you are. (*Ima iru tokoro ni ite kudasai.*) 今いる所にいてください. / I will go where you go. (*Watashi wa anata no iku tokoro e ikimasu.*) 私はあなたの行く所へ行きます.

wherever *conj.* **1** ... to⌜koro wa do⌝ko de mo ...所はどこでも: Please sit wherever you like. (*Doko de mo o-suki na tokoro ni o-suwari kudasai.*) どこでもお好きな所にお座りください.

2 (no matter where) ta⌜toe do⌝ko ni [e] ⟨verb⟩-te[de] mo たとえどこに[へ]...て[で]も: Wherever you go, please write to us. (*Tatoe doko e itte mo, tegami o kudasai.*) たとえどこへ行っても, 手紙を下さい.

whether *conj.* **1** [expressing doubt] ... ka do⌝o ka ...かどうか: I don't know whether that is true or not. (*Watashi wa sore ga hoñtoo ka doo ka shirimaseñ.*) 私はそれが本当かどうか知りません.

2 (no matter) ⟨verb⟩-te[de] mo ...て[で]も: Whether he comes or not, the result will be the same. (*Kare ga kite mo konakute mo, kekka wa onaji deshoo.*) 彼が来ても来なくても, 結果は同じでしょう.

which *pron.* **1** [selection from two things] do⌝chira どちら: Which way shall we go? (*Dochira no michi o ikimasu ka?*) どちらの道を行きますか. / Which do you like better, coffee or tea? (*Koohii to koocha to dochira ga suki desu ka?*) コーヒーと紅茶とどちらが好きですか.

2 [selection of one out of three or more things] do⌝re どれ: Which of these flowers do you like best? (*Kore-ra no hana no uchi dore ga ichibañ suki desu ka?*) これらの花のうちどれがいちばん好きですか.

— *adj.* do⌝chira no どちらの; do⌝no どの: Which umbrella is yours? (*Dono kasa ga anata no desu ka?*) どの傘があなたのですか.

whichever *pron.* **1** (of things) do⌝chira de mo どちらでも; do⌝re de mo どれでも: Take whichever you like. (*Dochira de mo suki na hoo o tori nasai.*) どちらでも好きな方を取りなさい.

2 (of people) da⌝re de mo だれでも: Whichever of you finishes first will receive a prize. (*Dare de mo it-too ni natta hito wa shoohiñ ga moraemasu.*) だれでも 1 等になった人は賞品がもらえます.

3 (no matter which) do⌝chira ga [o, ni] ⟨verb⟩-te[de] mo どちらが[を, に]...て[で]も: Whichever you choose, there won't be much difference. (*Dochira o erañde mo amari chigai wa nai deshoo.*) どちらを選んでもあまり違いはないでしょう.

— *adj.* **1** do⌝chira no ... de mo どちらの...でも; do⌝no ... de mo どの...でも: Take whichever book you like. (*Dochira de mo anata no suki na hoñ o tori nasai.*) どちらでもあなたの好きな本を取りなさい.

2 (no matter which) do⌝chira ga

⟨verb⟩-te[de] mo どちらが…て[で]も: Whichever side wins, I don't care. (*Dochira no gawa ga katte mo, watashi wa kamaimaseñ.*) どちらの側が勝っても私はかまいません.

while *conj.* **1** (during the time) ... a⌈ida ...間: Did anyone call while I was away? (*Watashi ga inai aida ni dare-ka kara deñwa ga arimashita ka?*) 私がいない間にだれかから電話がありましたか.
2 (on the other hand) i⌈ppo⌉o de wa 一方では: The book was scorned by critics, while it was applauded by the public. (*Sono hoñ wa hihyooka ni keebetsu sareta ga, ippoo de wa taishuu ni kañgee sareta.*) その本は批評家に軽蔑されたが, 一方では大衆に歓迎された.
3 (although) ... ga ...が: While I understand what you say, I can't agree with your plan. (*Anata no ossharu koto wa mitomemasu ga, anata no keekaku ni wa sañsee dekimaseñ.*) あなたのおっしゃることは認めますが, あなたの計画には賛成できません.

whim *n.* ki⌈magure 気まぐれ; mu⌈raki むら気: full of whims (*kimagure na*) 気まぐれな.

whip *n.* mu⌉chi むち: beat a person with a whip (*hito o muchi de utsu*) 人をむちで打つ.
— *vt.* ... o mu⌉chi de utsu ...をむちで打つ [C]: He whipped the horse to make it run faster. (*Kare wa uma ga motto hayaku hashiru yoo ni muchi de utta.*) 彼は馬がもっと早く走るようにむちで打った.

whirl *vi.* gu⌉ruguru ma⌈waru ぐるぐる回る [C]; u⌈zuma⌉ku 渦巻く [C]: Scraps of paper whirled in the wind. (*Kamikire ga kaze de guruguru mawatte ita.*) 紙切れが風でぐるぐる回っていた.
— *vt.* ... o gu⌉ruguru ma⌈wasu ...をぐるぐる回す [C]; u⌉zu o ma⌈kaseru 渦を巻かせる [V]: The wind whirled the fallen leaves about. (*Kaze ga ochiba o fuite uzu o makaseta.*) 風が落ち葉を吹いて渦を巻かせた.
— *n.* (spin) ka⌈iteñ 回転, se⌈ñkai 旋回.

whisk(e)y *n.* u⌈i⌉sukii ウイスキー: whiskey and water (*uisukii no mizuwari*) ウイスキーの水割り / whiskey and soda (*haibooru*) ハイボール.

whisper *vi.* sa⌈saya⌉ku ささやく [C]: She whispered in his ear. (*Kanojo wa kare no mimi ni sasayaita.*) 彼女は彼の耳にささやいた.
— *vt.* ... o sa⌈saya⌉ku ...をささやく [C]: She whispered a word or two to me. (*Kanojo wa watashi ni hitokoto futakoto sasayaita.*) 彼女は私に一言二言ささやいた.
— *n.* sa⌈sayaki ささやき; ko⌈goe 小声.

whistle *vi.* **1** (make a sound using the lips) ku⌈chibue o fu⌉ku 口笛を吹く [C]: The boy whistled to his dog. (*Sono otoko-no-ko wa inu ni mukatte kuchibue o fuita.*) その男の子は犬に向かって口笛を吹いた.
2 (blow a whistle) fu⌈e o narasu 笛を鳴らす [C]: The policeman whistled for the car to stop. (*Keekañ wa fue o narashite sono kuruma ni tomare to meejita.*) 警官は笛を鳴らしてその車に止まれと命じた.
— *vt.* ... o ku⌈chibue de fu⌉ku ...を口笛で吹く [C]: He was whistling a march. (*Kare wa kuchibue de maachi o fuite ita.*) 彼は口笛でマーチを吹いていた.
— *n.* **1** (musical instrument) fu⌈e 笛; (used for warning) ke⌈eteki 警笛; (of a steam train, ship, etc.) ki⌈teki 汽笛.
2 (the sound made by the lips) ku⌈chibue 口笛.

white *adj.* **1** (as opposed to black) shi⌈ro⌉i 白い; (of hair) shi⌈raga no 白髪の: white clouds (*shiroi kumo*) 白い雲 / His hair turned white. (*Kare no kami wa shiroku natta.*) 彼の髪は白くなった.
2 (pale) a⌈ojiro⌉i 青白い; (bloodless) chi ⌈no ke no na⌉i 血の気のない: Her face turned white at the news. (*Kanojo wa sono shirase o kiite*

massao ni natta.) 彼女はその知らせを聞いて真っ青になった.

3 (race) ha⌈kujiñ no 白人の; shi⌈ro⌉i 白い.

— *n.* 1 (color) shi⌉ro 白; ha⌈kushoku 白色.

2 (race) ha⌈kujiñ 白人.

whiteness *n.* shi⌉rosa 白さ.

who *pron.* da⌉re だれ; [polite] do⌉nata どなた: Who is it? (*Donata desu ka?*) どなたですか. / Who said so? (*Dare ga soo iimashita ka?*) だれがそう言いましたか. / Who is it you wish to see? (*Dare ni aitai no desu ka?*) だれに会いたいのですか.

whoever *pron.* 1 (anyone who) da⌉re de mo だれでも: Whoever comes will be welcome. (*Dare de mo kuru hito wa kañgee shimasu.*) だれでも来る人は歓迎します.

2 (no matter who) da⌉re ga ⟨verb⟩-te[de] mo だれが…て[で]も: Whoever says so, I won't change my mind. (*Dare ga soo itte mo watashi wa kañgae o kaeru tsumori wa arimaseñ.*) だれがそう言っても私は考えを変えるつもりはありません.

whole *adj.* 1 (entire) ze⌈ñtai no 全体の; (everything) ze⌉ñbu no 全部の; ze⌈ñ- 全: the whole world (*zeñsekai*) 全世界 / the whole class (*kurasu zeñ-iñ*) クラス全員 / He devoted his whole life to education. (*Kare wa isshoo o kyooiku ni sasageta.*) 彼は一生を教育に捧げた.

2 (as much as) ma⌈ru ... 丸…: a whole year (*maru ichi-ñeñ*) 丸 1 年 / three whole days (*maru mikkakañ*) 丸 3 日間.

— *n.* ze⌈ñtai 全体; ze⌉ñbu 全部: the whole of Japan (*Nihoñ zeñtai*) 日本全体.

on the whole *adv.* ze⌈ñtai to shite 全体として: Everything went well on the whole. (*Zeñtai to shite subete umaku itta.*) 全体としてすべてうまくいった.

wholesale *adj.* o⌈roshiuri no 卸し売りの: a wholesale dealer (*oroshiuri gyoosha*) 卸売業者.

— *n.* o⌈roshi⌉uri 卸し売り.

wholesome *adj.* ke⌈ñkoo ni yo⌉i 健康によい: wholesome exercise (*keñkoo ni yoi uñdoo*) 健康によい運動.

wholly *adv.* su⌈kka⌉ri すっかり; ma⌈ttaku まったく; ka⌈ñzeñ ni 完全に: His suggestion was wholly unacceptable. (*Kare no teeañ wa mattaku ukeirerarenai mono datta.*) 彼の提案はまったく受け入れられないものだった.

whom *pron.* da⌉re o [ni] だれを[に]; [polite] do⌉nata o [ni] どなたを[に]: Whom did you choose captain? (*Anata-tachi wa dare o kyaputeñ ni erabimashita ka?*) あなたたちはだれをキャプテンに選びましたか. / Whom did you meet? (*Anata wa dare ni aimashita ka?*) あなたはだれに会いましたか.

whose *pron.* da⌉re no だれの; [polite] do⌉nata no どなたの: Whose bag is this? (*Kore wa dare no kabañ desu ka?*) これはだれのかばんですか. / Whose is this? (*Kore wa dare no desu ka?*) これはだれのですか.

why *adv.* na⌉ze なぜ; do⌉o-shite どうして: Why aren't the subways running? (*Naze chikatetsu wa ugoite inai no desu ka?*) なぜ地下鉄は動いていないのですか. / Tell me why he did such a thing. (*Kare ga doo-shite añna koto o shita no ka oshiete kudasai.*) 彼がどうしてあんなことをしたのか教えてください.

Why don't ...? ⟨verb⟩-maseñ ka? ませんか: Why don't we go for a walk? (*Sañpo ni ikimaseñ ka?*) 散歩に行きませんか. / Why don't you come and see me next Sunday? (*Koñdo no nichiyoobi ni asobi ni kimaseñ ka?*) 今度の日曜日に遊びに来ませんか.

Why not? do⌉o shite ⟨verb⟩-nai no ka? どうして…ないのか: "I am not going to the pary." "Why not?" (*"Watashi wa paatii e ikimaseñ." "Doo shite ikanai no?"*) 「私はパーティーへ行きません」「どうして行かないの」

W

— *rel. adv.* ri⌈yuu 理由; wa⌉ke 訳: This is why he came. (*Kore ga kare ga kita riyuu desu.*) これが彼が来た理由です.

— *int.* o⌉ya おや; ma⌉a まあ.

why ever *adv.* i⌈ttai na⌉ze [do⌉o-shite] いったいなぜ[どうして]: Why ever did she say such a thing? (*Ittai naze kanojo wa soñna koto o itta no desu ka?*) いったいなぜ彼女はそんなことを言ったのですか.

wicked *adj.* wa⌈ru⌉i 悪い; ja⌈aku na 邪悪な: a wicked man (*akuniñ*) 悪人 / a wicked deed (*akuji*) 悪事.

wicket *n.* (of a station) ka⌈isatsu⌉-guchi 改札口; (of a ticket office) ma⌈do⌉guchi 窓口.

wide *adj.* **1** (broad) hi⌈ro⌉i 広い: a wide road (*hiroi michi*) 広い道 / wide knowledge (*hiroi chishiki*) 広い知識. ★ Japanese '*hiroi*' also means 'large in area.'

2 [used with measurements] ha⌈ba ga ... (a⌉ru) 幅が…(ある): "How wide is the doorway?" "It's 70 cm wide." (*"Toguchi no haba wa dono kurai arimasu ka?" "Haba wa nanajus-señchi arimasu."*) 「戸口の幅はどのくらいありますか」「幅は70センチあります」

3 (of eyes, doors, etc.) o⌉okiku hi-⌈ra⌉ita [hi⌈ra⌉ite iru] 大きく開いた[開いている]: The child stared with wide eyes. (*Sono kodomo wa me o maruku shite mitsumeta.*) その子どもは目を丸くして見つめた. / He opened the window wide. (*Kare wa mado o ookiku aketa.*) 彼は窓を大きく開けた.

— *adv.* hi⌉roku 広く; o⌉okiku hi⌈ra⌉ite (iru) 大きく開いて(いる): The door was wide open. (*Doa wa ookiku hiraite ita.*) ドアは大きく開いていた.

widely *adv.* **1** (to a wide extent) hi⌉roku 広く; ko⌈oha⌉ñi ni 広範囲に: He has traveled widely. (*Kare wa hiroku achikochi ryokoo shita.*) 彼は広くあちこち旅行した.

2 (greatly) o⌉okiku 大きく; o⌉oi ni 大いに; hi⌈joo ni 非常に: differ widely (*ooi ni kotonaru*) 大いに異なる.

widen *vt.* ... o hi⌉roku suru 広くする [I]: The city is planning to widen the road. (*Shi wa sono michi o hiroku suru keekaku o shite iru.*) 市はその道を広くする計画をしている.

— *vi.* hi⌉roku naru 広くなる [C]: The river widens up ahead. (*Kawa wa kono saki de hiroku natte imasu.*) 川はこの先で広くなっています.

widespread *adj.* hi⌈roma⌉tta 広まった; hi⌈roma⌉tte iru 広まっている; fu-⌈kyuu shita [shite iru] 普及した[している]: Fear of the disease is widespread among the people. (*Sono byooki ni taisuru kyoofu wa hitobito no aida ni hiromatte iru.*) その病気に対する恐怖は人々の間に広まっている.

widow *n.* mi⌈bo⌉ojiñ 未亡人; ya-⌈mome やもめ.

widower *n.* o⌈tokoya⌉mome 男やもめ.

width *n.* ha⌈ba 幅; hi⌈rosa 広さ: What is the width of this road? (*Kono michi no haba wa dore kurai desu ka?*) この道の幅はどれくらいですか. / The width of the fabric is 90 cm. (*Sono kiji no haba wa kyuujus-señchi arimasu.*) その生地の幅は90センチあります.

wife *n.* (one's own and generic) tsu⌉ma 妻; (one's own) ka⌉nai 家内; (someone else's) o⌉kusañ 奥さん: This is my wife. (*Kore ga kanai desu.*) これが家内です.

wig *n.* ka⌈tsura かつら: wear a wig (*katsura o tsukeru*) かつらをつける.

wild *adj.* **1** (of plants and animals) ya⌈see no 野生の: wild plants (*yasee shokubutsu*) 野生植物 / wild dogs (*yakeñ*) 野犬.

2 (of land) shi⌈zeñ no mama no 自然のままの; a⌈reha⌉teta 荒れ果てた; a⌈reha⌉tete iru 荒れ果てている: a wild land (*arechi*) 荒れ地.

3 (of the weather, sea, etc.) a⌈reta 荒れた; a⌈rete iru 荒れている: a wild sea (*araumi*) 荒海.

4 (violent) ra⌈ñboo na 乱暴な; kyo⌈oboo na 凶暴な: He was wild in his youth. (*Kare wa wakai koro wa rañboo datta.*) 彼は若い頃は乱暴だった.

5 (crazy) kyo⌈oki ji⌉mita [ji⌉mite iru] 狂気じみた[じみている]; (excited) ko⌈ofuñ shita [shite iru] 興奮した[している]: He was wild with anger. (*Kare wa gekido shite ita.*) 彼は激怒していた.

wilderness *n.* a⌈reno 荒れ野; a⌈rechi 荒れ地; mi⌈ka⌉ichi 未開地.

wildly *adv.* (violently) ra⌈ñboo ni 乱暴に; kyo⌈oboo ni 凶暴に; (crazily) ki ⌈ga kuru⌉tta yoo ni 気が狂ったように: They were beating on the door wildly. (*Kare-ra wa ki ga kurutta yoo ni doa o tataite ita.*) 彼らは気が狂ったようにドアをたたいていた.

will *aux.* 1 [future] ‹verb› da⌈ro⌉o …だろう; [polite] ‹verb› de⌈sho⌉o …でしょう: It will be fine tomorrow. (*Ashita wa hareru daroo.*) あしたは晴れるだろう. / He will graduate next year. (*Kare wa raineñ sotsugyoo suru deshoo.*) 彼は来年卒業するでしょう.

2 [probability] ‹verb› da⌈ro⌉o …だろう; [polite] ‹verb› de⌈sho⌉o …でしょう: He will become a good teacher. (*Kare wa yoi señsee ni naru deshoo.*) 彼はよい先生になるでしょう / How long will it take? (*Jikañ wa dono kurai kakaru deshoo ka?*) 時間はどのくらいかかるでしょうか.

3 [intention] ‹verb› tsu⌈mori da …つもりだ; ‹verb›-(y)o⌉o to o⌈mo⌉u …(よ)うと思う: I will ask him for advice. (*Watashi wa kare ni jogeñ o motomeru tsumori da.*) 私は彼に助言を求めるつもりだ.

4 [asking for a favor] ‹verb›-te[de] ku⌈remase⌉ñ ka …て[で]くれませんか: Will you help me move this table? (*Kono teeburu o ugokasu no o tetsudatte kuremaseñ ka?*) このテーブルを動かすのを手伝ってくれませんか.

5 [insist] do⌉oshite mo ‹verb›-(y)o⌉o to suru どうしても…(よ)うとする: He will have his own way. (*Kare wa dooshite mo jibuñ no suki na yoo ni shiyoo to suru.*) 彼はどうしても自分の好きなようにしようとする.

will *n.* 1 (wish) i⌉shi 意志; i⌉to 意図: free will (*jiyuu ishi*) 自由意志 / He has a strong will. (*Kare wa ishi ga tsuyoi.*) 彼は意志が強い.

2 (document) yu⌈igoñ 遺言; yu⌈igoñsho⌉ 遺言書: make a will (*yuigoñsho o tsukuru*) 遺言書を作る.

willful *adj.* wa⌈gama⌉ma na わがままな; go⌈ojoo na 強情な: a willful child (*wagamama na kodomo*) わがままな子ども.

willing *adj.* 1 (don't mind) ‹verb›-te[de] mo ka⌈mawa⌉nai …て[で]もかまわない; ... no o i⌈towa⌉nai …のをいとわない: The old couple was willing to take care of their grandchildren. (*Sono roo-fuufu wa mago no sewa o shite mo kamawanai to omotte ita.*) その老夫婦は孫の世話をしてもかまわないと思っていた.

2 (eager) su⌈suñde suru 進んでする; ko⌈ko⌉ro kara no 心からの: willing help (*kokoro kara no eñjo*) 心からの援助.

willingly *adv.* yo⌈roko⌉ñde 喜んで; ko⌈koroyo⌉ku 快く; su⌈suñde 進んで: He willingly helped me move into this house. (*Kare wa watashi ga kono ie ni hikkosu no o yorokoñde tetsudatte kureta.*) 彼は私がこの家に引っ越すのを喜んで手伝ってくれた.

win *vt.* 1 (of a game, battle, etc.) ... ni ka⌉tsu …に勝つ Ⓒ: Our team won the game 5–3. (*Watashi-tachi no chiimu wa go tai sañ de shiai ni katta.*) 私たちのチームは5対3で試合に勝った. / Who will win the election? (*Dare ga señkyo ni katsu daroo?*) だれが選挙に勝つだろう.

2 (of a victory, prize, etc.) ... o ka⌈chitoru …を勝ち取る Ⓒ; ka⌈kutoku suru 獲得する Ⓘ: He won first prize in the contest. (*Kare wa koñtesuto de it-too-shoo o kachitotta.*) 彼はコンテストで一等賞を勝ち取った.

3 (of a fame, trust, etc.) ... o e⌉ru

…を得る [V]; te͏ˈ ni iˈreru 手に入れる [V]: He won the confidence of those around him. (*Kare wa mawari no hito no shiñrai o eta.*) 彼は周りの人の信頼を得た.

— *vi.* kaˈtsu 勝つ [C].

— *n.* shoˈori 勝利; kaˈchiˈ 勝ち: The team has had three wins and two losses. (*Chiimu wa sañ-shoo ni-hai da.*) チームは3勝2敗だ.

wind[1] *n.* kaˈze 風: a strong wind (*tsuyoi kaze*) 強い風 / The wind is blowing from the north. (*Kaze wa kita kara fuite iru.*) 風は北から吹いている.

wind[2] *vt.* ... o maˈku …を巻く [C]: wind a watch (*tokee no neji o maku*) 時計のねじを巻く / wind thread onto a spool (*ito o itomaki ni maku*) 糸を糸巻きに巻く.

— *vi.* **1** (curve) maˈgarikuneˈru 曲がりくねる [C]: The road winds around the hills. (*Michi wa oka no aida o magarikunette iru.*) 道は丘の間を曲がりくねっている.

2 (wrap around) maˈkitsuˈku 巻きつく [C]; kaˈramitsuˈku 絡みつく [C]: The morning glories wind around the pole. (*Asagao wa sao ni karamitsuku.*) 朝顔はさおに絡みつく.

window *n.* **1** maˈdo 窓: open [close] the window (*mado o akeru [shimeru]*) 窓を開ける[閉める] / look out the window (*mado kara soto o miru*) 窓から外を見る.

2 (windowpane) maˈdo-gaˈrasu 窓ガラス.

3 (of a ticket office) maˈdoˈguchi 窓口: Tickets are sold at window No. 2. (*Kippu wa ni-bañ no madoguchi de utte imasu.*) 切符は2番の窓口で売っています.

windy *adj.* kaˈze no tsuyoˈi 風の強い; kaˈze no [ga] aˈru 風の[が]ある: a windy night (*kaze no tsuyoi yoru*) 風の強い夜.

wine *n.* **1** (from grapes) waˈiñ ワイン; buˈdoˈoshu ぶどう酒: red [white] wine (*aka [shiro] waiñ*) 赤[白]ワイン.

2 (from other fruits) kaˈjitsuˈshu 果実酒: apple wine (*riñgoshu*) りんご酒.

wing *n.* **1** (of birds) tsuˈbasa 翼; (of insects) haˈne 羽.

2 (of planes, etc.) tsuˈbasa 翼.

3 (of buildings) yoˈku 翼; soˈde そで: the south wing of a building (*tatemono no minami no yoku*) 建物の南の翼.

wink *vi.* (... ni) uˈiˈñku suru (…に)ウインクする [I]; meˈkuˈbase suru 目くばせする [I]: She winked at me. (*Kanojo wa watashi ni uiñku shita.*) 彼女は私にウインクした.

— *n.* (intentional) meˈkuˈbase 目くばせ; uˈiˈñku ウインク; (unintentional) maˈbaˈtaki まばたき.

winner *n.* **1** (victor) shoˈosha 勝者: the winner of the race (*reesu no shoosha*) レースの勝者.

2 (person who wins a prize) juˈshoˈosha 受賞者; nyuˈushoˈosha 入賞者: a Nobel prize winner (*Noo-beru-shoo jushoosha*) ノーベル賞受賞者.

winter *n.* fuˈyuˈ 冬: We had a cold winter this year. (*Kotoshi no fuyu wa samukatta.*) 今年の冬は寒かった.

wipe *vt.* ... o fuˈku …をふく [C]; fuˈkitoˈru ふき取る [C]: He wiped the spilled soup off the table. (*Kare wa teeburu ni koboreta suupu o fukitotta.*) 彼はテーブルにこぼれたスープをふき取った.

— *n.* fuˈku kotoˈ ふくこと; nuˈguˈu koˈtoˈ ぬぐうこと; nuˈguitoˈru koˈtoˈ ぬぐい取ること.

wire *n.* **1** haˈrigane 針金; (of electricity) deˈñseñ 電線: telephone wires (*deñwa señ*) 電話線/ barbed wire (*yuushi tesseñ*) 有刺鉄線.

2 (telegram) deˈñpoo 電報: Send him a wire. (*Kare ni deñpoo o utte kudasai.*) 彼に電報を打ってください.

— *vt.* ... ni deˈñpoo o uˈtsu …に電報を打つ [C]: She wired her friend to congratulate her on her marriage. (*Kanojo wa tomodachi ni kekkoñ o iwau deñpoo o utta.*) 彼女は友達に結婚を祝う電報を打った.

— *vi.* de⌈ñpoo o u⌉tsu 電報を打つ 🄲.

wisdom *n.* ka⌈shiko⌉i ko⌈to⌉ 賢いこと; ke⌈ñmee 賢明; chi⌈e⌉ 知恵; fu⌈ñbetsu 分別: He had enough wisdom to refuse the offer. (*Kare ni wa sono mooshide o kotowaru dake no fuñbetsu ga atta.*) 彼にはその申し出を断わるだけの分別があった.

wise *adj.* ka⌈shiko⌉i 賢い; ke⌈ñmee na 賢明な; fu⌈ñbetsu no [ga] a⌉ru 分別の[が]ある: a wise judgment (*keñmee na hañdañ*) 賢明な判断 / You were wise to have withheld any comment. (*Anata ga komeñto o saketa no wa keñmee datta.*) あなたがコメントを避けたのは賢明だった.

wisely *adv.* **1** ke⌈ñmee ni 賢明に; shi⌈ryobu⌉kaku 思慮深く: You have chosen wisely. (*Anata wa keñmee na señtaku o shita.*) あなたは賢明な選択をした.

2 [sentence qualifier] ke⌈ñmee ni⌉ mo 賢明にも: He wisely kept his secret. (*Kare wa keñmee ni mo himitsu o mamotta.*) 彼は賢明にも秘密を守った.

wish *vt.* **1** (have a desire) ⟨verb⟩-ba[tara] yo⌉i [i⌉i] no ni (to o⌈mo⌉u) …ば[たら]よい[いい]のに(と思う 🄲): I wish I could go with you. (*Anata to issho ni iketara ii no ni.*) あなたといっしょに行けたらいいのに. / I wished I hadn't said such a thing. (*Watashi wa añna koto o iwanakereba yokatta to omotta.*) 私はあんなことを言わなければよかったと思った.

2 (want to do) [1st and 2nd persons] ⟨verb⟩-tai (to o⌈mo⌉u) …たい(と思う 🄲); [3rd person] ⟨verb⟩-tagaru …たがる 🄲: I wish to become a doctor. (*Watashi wa isha ni naritai to omotte imasu.*) 私は医者になりたいと思っています. / The boss wishes to see you. (*Jooshi ga kimi ni aitai to itte imasu.*) 上司が君に会いたいと言っています.

3 (hope for) ... o i⌈no⌉ru …を祈る 🄲; ne⌈ga⌉u 願う 🄲: I wish you luck. (*Koouñ o inorimasu.*) 幸運を祈ります. / I wish you a happy new year. (*Yoi shiññeñ o omukae kudasai.*) よい新年をお迎えください.

wish for … *vt.* ... o no⌈zomu … を望む 🄲: We wish for world peace. (*Watashi-tachi wa sekai heewa o nozomimasu.*) 私たちは世界平和を望みます.

— *n.* no⌈zomi 望み; ne⌈ga⌉i 願い; ga⌈ñboo 願望: Her wish to go abroad has finally come true. (*Gaikoku e ikitai to iu kanojo no negai wa tsui ni jitsugeñ shita.*) 外国へ行きたいという彼女の願いはついに実現した.

send one's best wishes to … *vt.* ... ni yo⌈roshiku⌉ to tsu⌈taeru …によろしくと伝える 🅅: Please send my best wishes to your mother. (*Doozo o-kaasañ ni yoroshiku otsutae kudasai.*) どうぞお母さんによろしくお伝えください.

wit *n.* **1** (humor) ki⌉chi 機知; u⌈i⌉tto ウイット: a person of wit (*kichi ni tonda hito*) 機知に富んだ人.

2 (intelligence) ri⌈kai⌉ryoku 理解力, chi⌈e⌉ 知恵: have quick [slow] wits (*rikai ga hayai* [*osoi*]) 理解が早い[遅い].

witch *n.* ma⌉jo 魔女; o⌈ñnamahoo-tsu⌉kai 女魔法使い.

with *prep.* **1** (together) ... to i⌈ssho ni といっしょに; to⌉mo ni ともに: She lives with her aunt. (*Kanojo wa oba to issho ni kurashite imasu.*) 彼女はおばといっしょに暮らしています. / Please come with me. (*Issho ni kite kudasai.*) いっしょに来てください.

2 (having) ... no [ga] a⌉ru …の[が]ある; -tsu⌈ki no つきの: a box with a lid (*futa ga aru hako*) ふたがある箱 / I'd like a room with bath. (*Furo-tsuki no heya ni shitai.*) 風呂つきの部屋にしたい.

3 (carrying) ... o mo⌉tte …を持って: Take an umbrella with you. (*Kasa o motte iki nasai.*) 傘を持って行きなさい.

4 (using) ... de …で; ... o tsu⌈katte …を使って: write with a pen (*peñ de kaku*) ペンで書く.

5 (cause) ... de ...で; ... no se⌉e de ...のせいで: tremble with rage (*ikari de furueru*) 怒りで震える.
6 (concerning) ... ni ka⌉ñshite ...に関して; ... ni に: He was angry with me. (*Kare wa watashi ni hara o tatete ita.*) 彼は私に腹を立てていた.
7 (against) ... to ...と; ... o a⌈ite⌉ ni ...を相手に: I discussed the matter with him. (*Watashi wa sono koto o kare to hanashiatta.*) 私はそのことを彼と話し合った.
8 (at the same time) ... to do⌉oji ni ...と同時に; ... to to⌉mo ni ...とともに: rise with the sun (*taiyoo to tomo ni okiru*) 太陽とともに起きる.
9 (corresponding to) ... ni tsu⌈rete ...につれて; ... to to⌉mo ni ...とともに: His memory faded with time. (*Kare no omoide wa toki to tomo ni usureta.*) 彼の思い出は時とともに薄れた.

withdraw *vt.* **1** (of money) ... o hi⌈kida⌉su ...を引き出す Ⓒ; o⌈ro⌉su 下ろす Ⓒ: I withdrew 30,000 yen from my account. (*Watashi wa kooza kara sañmañ-eñ oro-shita.*) 私は口座から3万円を下ろした.
2 (of troops) ... o te⌈ttai saseru ...を撤退させる Ⓥ; (from school) ta⌈i-gaku saseru 退学させる Ⓥ: The country withdrew its troops. (*Sono kuni wa guñtai o tettai saseta.*) その国は軍隊を撤退させた. / His parents withdrew him from school. (*Ryoo-shiñ wa kare o taigaku saseta.*) 両親は彼を退学させた.
3 (of an offer) ... o te⌈kkai suru ...を撤回する Ⓘ: withdraw an offer (*mooshide o tekkai suru*) 申し出を撤回する.
— *vi.* hi⌈kisaga⌉ru 引き下がる Ⓒ; ta⌈ishutsu suru 退出する Ⓘ: The children withdrew to their own rooms at bedtime. (*Neru jikañ ni naru to kodomo-tachi wa jibuñ no heya ni hikisagatta.*) 寝る時間になると子どもたちは自分の部屋に引き下がった.

wither *vi.* shi⌈oreru しおれる Ⓥ; ka⌈reru 枯れる Ⓥ: The flowers withered because they had no water. (*Mizu ga nai no de hana ga karete shimatta.*) 水がないので花が枯れてしまった.

withhold *vt.* ... o sa⌈shihikae⌉ru 差し控える Ⓥ; ho⌈ryuu suru 保留する Ⓘ: withhold a question (*shitsu-moñ o sashihikaeru*) 質問を差し控える.

within *prep.* ... i⌉nai ni [de] ...以内に[で]; ... no ha⌈ñi⌉nai ni [de] ...の範囲内に[で]: I'll be back within five minutes. (*Go-fuñ inai ni modotte kimasu.*) 5分以内に戻ってきます. / live within one's income (*shuu-nyuu no hañinai de kurasu*) 収入の範囲内で暮らす.

without *prep.* **1** (not having) ... no na⌉i ...のない; ... na⌉shi de ...なしで: a room without a window (*mado no nai heya*) 窓のない部屋 / I usually drink coffee without cream. (*Watashi wa futsuu kuriimu nashi de koohii o nomimasu.*) 私は普通クリームなしでコーヒーを飲みます.
2 (without ~ing) <verb>-nai de ...ないで; <verb>-zu ni ...ずに: He went out without saying good-by. (*Kare wa sayonara o iwanai de dete itta.*) 彼はさよならを言わないで出て行った.
3 (if it wasn't for) ... ga na⌉kattara ...がなかったら: Without water, we couldn't live. (*Mizu ga nakattara watashi-tachi wa ikite ikenai.*) 水がなかったら私たちは生きていけない.

witness *n.* **1** (eyewitness) mo⌈ku-geki⌉sha 目撃者; sho⌈oniñ 証人: a witness of the accident (*jiko no mokugekisha*) 事故の目撃者.
2 (someone who testifies in court) sho⌈oniñ 証人: a witness for the defense (*hikoku-gawa no shooniñ*) 被告側の証人.
3 (evidence) sho⌈oko 証拠; (testimony) sho⌈ogeñ 証言: bear witness (*shoogeñ suru*) 証言する.
— *vt.* ... o mo⌈kugeki suru ...を目撃する Ⓘ: Did you witness the accident? (*Anata wa sono jiko o moku-geki shita no desu ka?*) あなたはその

W

事故を目撃したのですか.

witty *adj.* ki꜔chi ni ton̄da [ton̄de iru] 機知に富んだ[富んでいる]; sa꜔iki no [ga] aru 才気の[が]ある: witty remarks (*kichi ni ton̄da hatsugen̄*) 機知に富んだ発言.

wolf *n.* o꜔okami 狼.

woman *n.* o꜒n̄na-no-hito꜔ 女の人; jo꜒see 女性; fu꜒jin̄ 婦人; o꜒n̄na꜔ 女. ★ '*On̄na*' often has a derogatory connotation, especially when referring to a young woman.

wonder *vt.* **1** (want to know) ... da꜒ro꜔o ...だろう: I wonder where he went. (*Kare wa doko e itta no daroo.*) 彼はどこへ行ったのだろう. / I wonder what happened. (*Nani ga okotta no daroo.*) 何が起こったのだろう.

2 (think) ... to ka꜒n̄ga꜔eru ...と考える Ⓥ: I'm now wondering what to do next Sunday. (*Tsugi no nichiyoo wa nani o shiyoo ka to kan̄gaete iru tokoro desu.*) 次の日曜は何をしようかと考えているところです.

— *vi.* **1** (doubt) u꜒tagau 疑う Ⓒ; i꜒buka꜔ru いぶかる Ⓒ: I wonder about his innocence. (*Watashi wa kare no keppaku o utagau.*) 私は彼の潔白を疑う.

2 (be surprised) fu꜒shigi ni omo꜔u 不思議に思う Ⓒ; o꜒doro꜔ku 驚く Ⓒ: Everybody wondered at the boy's talent. (*Min̄na ga sono shoonen̄ no sainoo ni odoroita.*) みんながその少年の才能に驚いた.

— *n.* o꜒doroki꜔ 驚き: It's a wonder you came back safe. (*Anata ga buji ni kaette kita no wa odoroki da.*) あなたが無事に帰ってきたのは驚きだ.

wonderful *adj.* **1** (good) su꜒barashi꜔i すばらしい; su꜒teki na すてきな: The view from the top of the mountain was wonderful. (*Yama no choojoo kara no nagame wa subarashikatta.*) 山の頂上からの眺めはすばらしかった. / Many thanks for a wonderful dinner. (*Suteki na yuushoku o arigatoo gozaimashita.*) すてきな夕食をありがとうございました.

2 (strange) fu꜒shigi na 不思議な; (surprising) o꜒doroku be꜔ki 驚くべき: a wonderful story (*fushigi na monogatari*) 不思議な物語.

wood *n.* **1** (lumber) mo꜒ku꜔zai 木材; za꜒imoku 材木; (material) ki꜔ 木: This table is made of wood. (*Kono teeburu wa ki de dekite imasu.*) このテーブルは木でできています.

2 (forest) mo꜒ri 森; ha꜒yashi 林. ★ '*Mori*' refers to a large area of land more thickly covered with trees than '*hayashi*.'

wooden *adj.* mo꜒kusee no 木製の; ki꜔ de dekita [dekite iru] 木でできた[できている]: a wooden chair (*mokusee no isu*) 木製のいす / wooden Japanese-style clogs (*geta*) げた.

wool *n.* **1** (hair) yo꜒omoo 羊毛.

2 (yarn) ke꜒ito 毛糸: wind up knitting wool (*keito o maku*) 毛糸を巻く.

3 (fabric) u꜔uru ウール; ke꜒orimono 毛織物: I wear wool in winter. (*Fuyu wa uuru o kimasu.*) 冬はウールを着ます.

woolen *adj.* yo꜒omoo no 羊毛の; ke꜒ori no 毛織りの: a woolen blanket (*yoomoo no moofu*) 羊毛の毛布.

word *n.* **1** (unit of language) ta꜒n̄go 単語; go꜔ 語; ko꜒toba꜔ 言葉: What does this word mean? (*Kono tan̄go wa doo iu imi desu ka?*) この単語はどういう意味ですか.

2 (talk) ha꜒nashi꜔ 話: I'd like to have a word with you. (*O-hanashi ga shitai no desu ga.*) お話がしたいのですが.

3 (news) shi꜒rase 知らせ; ta꜔yori 便り; sho꜒osoku 消息: Word came that it was snowing in Tokyo. (*Tookyoo de wa yuki ga futte iru to iu shirase ga todoita.*) 東京では雪が降っているという知らせが届いた.

4 (promise) ya꜒kusoku 約束: keep one's word (*yakusoku o mamoru*) 約束を守る.

in other words *adv.* i꜒ika꜔ereba 言いかえれば.

work *n.* **1** (task) shi꜒goto 仕事;

W

sa⌉gyoo 作業; ro⌈odoo 労働; (study) be⌈ñkyoo 勉強: hard [easy] work (*tsurai* [*raku na*] *shigoto*) つらい[楽な]仕事 / I have a lot of work to do today. (*Kyoo wa shinakereba naranai shigoto ga takusañ aru.*) 今日はしなければならない仕事がたくさんある.

2 (job) shi⌈goto 仕事; tsu⌈tome⌉guchi 勤め口: He is looking for work. (*Kare wa tsutomeguchi o sagashite iru.*) 彼は勤め口を探している.

3 (workplace) tsu⌈tomesaki 勤め先; sho⌈kuba 職場; ka⌈isha 会社: He goes to work by train. (*Kare wa deñsha de kaisha ni ikimasu.*) 彼は電車で会社に行きます.

4 (handiwork) sa⌈iku⌉ 細工; (of one's making) se⌈esaku 製作: Making this brooch required careful work. (*Kono buroochi o tsukuru ni wa neñiri na saiku ga hitsuyoo datta.*) このブローチを作るには念入りな細工が必要だった.

5 (work of art) sa⌈kuhiñ 作品: This sculpture is Rodin's work. (*Kono chookoku wa Rodañ no sakuhiñ desu.*) この彫刻はロダンの作品です.

6 (factory) ko⌈ojo⌉o 工場.

— *vi.* **1** (do work) ha⌈taraku 働く Ⓒ; shi⌈goto o suru 仕事をする Ⓘ: He works at a bank. (*Kare wa giñkoo de hataraite imasu.*) 彼は銀行で働いています. / I work for a trading company. (*Watashi wa booekigaisha ni tsutomete imasu.*) 私は貿易会社に勤めています.

2 (study) be⌈ñkyoo suru 勉強する Ⓘ: I'm working at my Japanese. (*Watashi wa Nihoñgo o beñkyoo shite imasu.*) 私は日本語を勉強しています.

3 (operate) u⌈go⌉ku 動く Ⓒ: Is the elevator working? (*Erebeetaa wa ugoite imasu ka?*) エレベーターは動いていますか. / This shutter doesn't work well. (*Kono shattaa wa guai ga warui.*) このシャッターは具合が悪い.

4 (of plans) u⌉maku i⌈ku うまくいく Ⓒ; (of medicine, etc.) ki⌈ku 効く Ⓒ: The plan worked well. (*Sono keekaku wa umaku itta.*) その計画はうまくいった. / This medicine works for headaches. (*Kono kusuri wa zutsuu ni kiku.*) この薬は頭痛に効く.

— *vt.* **1** (operate) ... o u⌈goka⌉su …を動かす Ⓒ; u⌈ñteñ suru 運転する Ⓘ: How do you work this machine? (*Kono kikai wa doo yatte ugokasu ñ desu ka?*) この機械はどうやって動かすんですか.

2 (make work) ... o ha⌈tarakaseru …を働かせる Ⓥ; ko⌉kitsukau こき使う Ⓒ: You must not work your employees too hard. (*Juugyooiñ o hatarakase-sugite wa ikenai.*) 従業員を働かせ過ぎてはいけない.

work on ... *vt.* ... ni to⌈rikumu …に取り組む Ⓒ: They are working on a new project. (*Kare-ra wa atarashii purojekuto ni torikuñde iru.*) 彼らは新しいプロジェクトに取り組んでいる.

work out *vt.* (think of) ka⌈ñgaeda⌉su 考え出す Ⓒ: work out a solution to a problem (*moñdai no kaiketsuhoo o kañgaedasu*) 問題の解決法を考え出す.

— *vi.* (turn out) na⌉ru なる Ⓒ: How did your plan work out? (*Anata no keekaku wa doo narimashita ka?*) あなたの計画はどうなりましたか.

worker *n.* ha⌈taraku hito⌉ 働く人; ro⌈odo⌉osha 労働者: factory workers (*koojoo roodoosha*) 工場労働者.

working *adj.* **1** (having a job) ha⌈taraku 働く: working people (*hataraku hitobito*) 働く人々.

2 (useful) ji⌈ssai ni yakuda⌉tsu 実際に役立つ; ji⌈tsuyoo-teki na 実用的な: a working knowledge of Japanese (*Nihoñgo no jitsuyooteki na chishiki*) 日本語の実用的な知識.

workshop *n.* **1** (place) sa⌈gyooba 作業場; shi⌈gotoba 仕事場.

2 (study group) wa⌈akusho⌉ppu ワ

W

ークショップ; ke[ñkyuushu]ukai 研究集会; ke[ñkyuu guru]upu 研究グループ.

world *n.* **1** (the earth) se]kai 世界: travel around the world (*sekai isshuu no tabi o suru*) 世界一周の旅をする / That is the highest building in the world. (*Are ga sekai de ichibañ takai biru desu.*) あれが世界でいちばん高いビルです. / a world record (*sekai kiroku*) 世界記録.
2 (people) se[kaijuu no hito]bito 世界中の人々: The news shocked the world. (*Sono nyuusu wa sekaijuu no hitobito ni shoogeki o ataeta.*) そのニュースは世界中の人々に衝撃を与えた.
3 (society) yo-[no]-naka 世の中; se]keñ 世間: It's a small world. (*Seken wa semai.*) 世間は狭い.

worldwide *adj.* se[kai-teki na 世界的な; se[kai-juu ni shirewata]tta [shirewatta]te iru] 世界中に知れわたった[知れわたっている]: His fame is worldwide. (*Kare no meesee wa sekai-juu ni shirewattatte iru.*) 彼の名声は世界中に知れわたっている.
— *adv.* se[kai-juu ni [de] 世界中に[で]; se[kai-teki ni 世界的に: spread worldwide (*sekai-juu ni hiromaru*) 世界中に広まる.

worm *n.* mu[shi 虫; (earthworm) mi[mizu みみず; (caterpillar) ke[mushi] 毛虫. ★ 'Insects' is also called '*mushi.*'

worn *adj.* **1** (being used) su[rikireta すり切れた; su[rikirete iru すり切れている: worn clothes (*surikireta fuku*) すり切れた服.
2 (being tired) tsu[karekiꜛtta 疲れきった; tsu[karekiꜛtte iru 疲れきっている; ya[tsu]reta やつれた; ya[tsu]rete iru やつれている: a worn face (*yatsureta kao*) やつれた顔.

worried *adj.* shi[ñpai-soo na 心配そうな; shi[ñpai shite iru 心配している: a worried look (*shiñpai-soo na kao*) 心配そうな顔 / I am worried about his health. (*Watashi wa kare no keñkoo o shiñpai shite iru.*) 私は彼の健康を心配している.

worry *vi.* shi[ñpai suru 心配する [I]; na[ya]mu 悩む [C]: You worry too much. (*Anata wa shiñpai shi-sugiru.*) あなたは心配しすぎる. / Don't worry. (*Shiñpai wa irimaseñ.*) 心配はいりません.
— *vt.* **1** (annoy) ... o na[yama]su 悩ます [C]; i]raira sa[seru いらいらさせる [V]: The child worried its mother by asking difficult questions. (*Sono kodomo wa muzukashii shitsumoñ o shite hahaoya o nayamashita.*) その子どもは難しい質問をして母親を悩ました.
2 (make anxious) ... no ki [o momaseru …の気をもませる [V]; ... o shi[ñpai saseru …を心配させる [V]: Her long absence from school worried her classmates. (*Kanojo no chooki kesseki wa kurasumeeto o shiñpai saseta.*) 彼女の長期欠席はクラスメートを心配させた.
— *n.* **1** (anxiety) shi[ñpai 心配; ki[gu]roo 気苦労: Worry kept me awake. (*Shiñpai de watashi wa nemurenakatta.*) 心配で私は眠れなかった.
2 (cause for anxiety) shi[ñpaigoto 心配事; shi[ñpai no ta]ne 心配の種: Life is full of worries. (*Jiñsee ni wa shiñpaigoto ga ooi.*) 人生には心配事が多い.

worse *adj.* mo]tto wa[ru]i もっと悪い; ... yori wa[ru]i …より悪い: The weather is getting worse. (*Teñki ga dañdañ waruku natte kite iru.*) 天気がだんだん悪くなってきている. / The patient is worse than yesterday. (*Byooniñ wa kinoo yori guai ga warui.*) 病人はきのうより具合が悪い.
— *adv.* mo]tto waruku もっと悪く; mo]tto hidoku もっとひどく: It's raining worse than before. (*Mae yori hidoku ame ga futte iru.*) 前よりひどく雨が降っている.

worship *n.* **1** (reverence) su[uhai 崇拝; so[ñkee 尊敬: hero worship (*eeyuu suuhai*) 英雄崇拝.
2 (of a church) re[ehai 礼拝; (of a

shrine, temple) sa⌈ñpai 参拝.

— *vt.* (give worship) ... o su⌈uhai suru 崇拝する [I]; so⌈ñkee suru 尊敬する [I]: He worships his father. (*Kare wa chichioya o soñkee shite iru.*) 彼は父親を尊敬している.

— *vi.* (take part in worship) re⌈ehai suru 礼拝する [I]: I worship at that church. (*Watashi wa ano kyookai de reehai shite imasu.*) 私はあの教会で礼拝しています.

worst *adj.* mo⌈tto⌉mo [i⌈chibañ] wa⌈ru⌉i もっとも[いちばん]悪い; sa⌈iaku no 最悪の: This is the worst time for young people to look for work. (*Ima wa wakai hito ga shoku o sagasu no ni saiaku no toki da.*) 今は若い人が職を探すのに最悪の時だ.

— *adv.* mo⌈tto⌉mo [i⌈chibañ] wa⌉ruku もっとも[いちばん]悪く; mo⌈tto⌉mo [i⌈chibañ] hi⌉doku もっとも[いちばん]ひどく: That child behaves the worst in this class. (*Sono ko wa kono kurasu de ichibañ taido ga warui.*) その子はこのクラスでいちばん態度が悪い.

worth *adj.* **1** (equal in value) ka⌉chi ga aru 価値がある; ne⌈uchi ga a⌉ru 値打ちがある: This old car is worth 200,000 yen. (*Kono chuukosha wa nijuumañ-eñ no neuchi ga aru.*) この中古車は 20 万円の値打ちがある.

2 (good enough) ka⌉chi ga aru 価値がある; ne⌈uchi ga a⌉ru 値打ちがある; ... ni a⌈tai suru …に値する: That is worth trying. (*Sore wa yatte miru kachi ga aru.*) それはやってみる価値がある.

— *n.* (value) ka⌉chi 価値: a painting of great worth (*hijoo ni kachi no aru e*) 非常に価値のある絵.

worthless *adj.* ka⌉chi no [ga] nai 価値の[が]ない; ya⌈ku⌉ ni ta⌈ta⌉nai 役に立たない: a worthless book (*kachi no nai hoñ*) 価値のない本.

worthwhile *adj.* ka⌉chi no [ga] aru 価値の[が]ある; ya⌈rigai no [ga] a⌉ru やりがいの[が]ある: a worthwhile job (*yarigai no aru shigoto*) やりがいのある仕事.

worthy *adj.* ... ni a⌈tai suru …に値する; fu⌈sawashi⌉i ふさわしい: His action is worthy of praise. (*Kare no kooi wa shoosañ ni atai suru.*) 彼の行為は賞賛に値する.

would *aux.* **1** [future] ⟨verb⟩ da⌈ro⌉o …だろう; [polite] ⟨verb⟩ de⌈sho⌉o …でしょう: I thought you would come. (*Watashi wa anata ga kuru daroo to omoimashita.*) 私はあなたが来るだろうと思いました.

2 [intention] ⟨verb⟩ tsu⌈mori da … つもりだ: He said he would go on a trip next month. (*Kare wa raigetsu ryokoo ni iku tsumori da to itta.*) 彼は来月旅行に行くつもりだと言った.

3 [determination] do⌉o shite mo ⟨verb⟩-(y)o⌉o to suru どうしても …(よ)うとする: He would do everything his way. (*Kare wa nañ de mo doo shite mo jibuñ no yarikata de shiyoo to suru.*) 彼は何でもどうしても自分のやり方でしようとする.

4 [possibility] ⟨verb⟩ da⌈ro⌉o …だろう; [polite] ⟨verb⟩ de⌈sho⌉o …でしょう: If I were you, I would accept the offer. (*Moshi watashi ga anata dattara sono mooshide o ukeireta deshoo.*) もし私があなただったらその申し出を受け入れたでしょう.

I would like … ... o ku⌈dasa⌉i …を下さい: I would like a roll of film. (*Firumu o ip-poñ kudasai.*) フィルムを 1 本下さい.

I would like to do ⟨verb⟩-tai …たい: I would like to see the room. (*Watashi wa sono heya o mitai no desu ga.*) 私はその部屋を見たいのですが.

Would you …? ⟨verb⟩-te[de] i⌈tadakemase⌉ñ ka? …て[で]いただけませんか: Would you please open the window? (*Mado o akete itadakemaseñ ka?*) 窓を開けていただけませんか.

wound *vt.* **1** (injure physically) ... o fu⌈shoo saseru …を負傷させる [V]; ... ni ke⌈ga⌉ o sa⌈seru …にけがをさせる [V]: Fifty people were wounded in the railway accident. (*Sono ressha

jiko de gojuu-niñ ga fushoo shita.) その列車事故で 50 人が負傷した.
2 (hurt feelings) ... o ki⌈zutsuke⌉ru …を傷つける Ⓥ: His words wounded her. (*Kare no kotoba wa kanojo o kizutsuketa.*) 彼の言葉は彼女を傷つけた.
— *n.* ke⌈ga⌉ けが; ki⌈zu 傷; fu⌈shoo 負傷: a slight wound (*keeshoo*) 軽傷 / He suffered a fatal wound. (*Kare wa chimeeshoo o otta.*) 彼は致命傷を負った.

wrap *vt.* ... o tsu⌈tsu⌉mu …を包む Ⓒ; ku⌈ru⌉mu くるむ Ⓒ: She wrapped the present in paper. (*Kanojo wa purezeñto o kami ni tsutsuñda.*) 彼女はプレゼントを紙に包んだ.

wrapper *n.* tsu⌈tsumi⌉gami 包み紙; ho⌈oso⌉oshi 包装紙.

wreath *n.* ha⌈nawa 花輪: a funeral wreath (*soogi no hanawa*) 葬儀の花輪.

wreck *n.* **1** (ruin of a ship) na⌈ñpa 難破; so⌈onañ 遭難; (damaged ship) na⌈ñpaseñ 難破船: The storm caused many wrecks. (*Sono arashi de soonañ jiko ga ooku deta.*) その嵐で遭難事故が多く出た.
2 (what is left of anything destroyed) za⌈ñgai 残骸: clear away the wreck of the plane that crashed (*tsuiraku shita hikooki no zañgai o katazukeru*) 墜落した飛行機の残骸を片づける.
— *vt.* (of a ship) ... o na⌈ñpa saseru …を難破させる Ⓥ; (of a vehicle) ... o ko⌈wa⌉su …を壊す Ⓒ; ta⌉iha saseru 大破させる Ⓥ: The ship was wrecked in a storm. (*Sono fune wa arashi de nañpa shita.*) その船は嵐で難破した.

wrestle *vi.* **1** (with a person) to⌈kkumiai o suru 取っ組み合いをする Ⓘ; re⌉suriñgu o suru レスリングをする Ⓘ: The boys are wrestling. (*Sono otoko-no-ko-tachi wa tokkumiai o shite iru.*) その男の子たちは取っ組み合いをしている.
2 (with a difficulty) (... to) to⌈rikumu (…と)取り組む Ⓒ: We must wrestle with the problem. (*Watashi-tachi wa sono moñdai ni torikumanakereba naranai.*) 私たちはその問題に取り組まなければならない.

wrestler *n.* re⌉suriñgu no señshu レスリングの選手: a sumo wrestler (*sumootori*) 相撲取り.

wrestling *n.* re⌉suriñgu レスリング.

wretched *adj.* (miserable) mi⌉jime na 惨めな; a⌉ware na 哀れな: lead a wretched life (*mijime na seekatsu o okuru*) 惨めな生活を送る.

wring *vt.* **1** (squeeze) ... o shi⌈bo⌉ru …を絞る Ⓒ: Wring the towels before you hang them out to dry. (*Hosu mae ni taoru o shibori nasai.*) 干す前にタオルを絞りなさい. ★ Japanese '*shiboru*' also means 'squeeze.'
2 (twist) ... o hi⌈ne⌉ru …をひねる Ⓒ: I'll wring your neck if you say that again! (*Moo ichido ittara kubi o hineru zo!*) もう一度言ったら首をひねるぞ.
3 (clasp) ... o ka⌈taku nigiru …を固く握る Ⓒ: He wrung his friend's hand. (*Kare wa yuujiñ no te o kataku nigitta.*) 彼は友人の手を固く握った.

wrinkle *n.* shi⌈wa しわ: smooth out the wrinkles of one's jacket (*uwagi no shiwa o nobasu*) 上着のしわを伸ばす / She has wrinkles about her mouth. (*Kanojo wa kuchi no mawari ni shiwa ga aru.*) 彼女は口の回りにしわがある
— *vt.* ... ni shi⌈wa o yoseru …にしわを寄せる Ⓥ: He wrinkled his forehead. (*Kare wa hitai ni shiwa o yoseta.*) 彼は額にしわを寄せた.
— *vi.* shi⌈wa ga yoru しわが寄る Ⓒ; shi⌈wa ni na⌉ru しわになる Ⓒ: This cloth wrinkles easily. (*Kono kire wa shiwa ni nari-yasui.*) このきれはしわになりやすい.

wrist *n.* te⌉kubi 手首: He seized me by the wrist. (*Kare wa watashi no tekubi o tsukañda.*) 彼は私の手首をつかんだ.

wristwatch *n.* u⌈dedo⌉kee 腕時計.

write *vt.* ... o ka¹ku ...を書く Ⓒ: Please write your name here. (*Koko ni namae o kaite kudasai.*) ここに名前を書いてください. / He is writing a book. (*Kare wa hoñ o kaite iru.*) 彼は本を書いている.

— *vi.* ka¹ku 書く Ⓒ; (of a letter) te[gami o ka¹ku 手紙を書く Ⓒ: write in pencil (*eñpitsu de kaku*) 鉛筆で書く / I write to my parents every month. (*Watashi wa maitsuki ryooshiñ ni tegami o kakimasu.*) 私は毎月両親に手紙を書きます.

write down *vt.* ... o ka[kitomeru ...を書き留める Ⓥ: write down a phone number (*deñwa bañgoo o kakitomeru*) 電話番号を書き留める.

writer *n.* **1** (one who wrote) ka¹ita hi[to¹ 書いた人; hi¹ssha 筆者; (of fiction) sa¹kusha 作者: the writer of this letter (*kono tegami o kaita hito*) この手紙を書いた人 / the writer of a novel (*shoosetsu no sakusha*) 小説の作者.

2 (author) sa[kka 作家; (reporter) ki¹sha 記者.

writing *n.* **1** (act of writing) ka¹ku ko[to¹ 書くこと; shi[ppitsu 執筆.

2 (handwriting) ji¹ 字; hi¹sseki 筆跡: His writing is neat. (*Kare no ji wa kiree da.*) 彼の字はきれいだ.

3 (something that is written) ka¹ita mo[no¹ 書いたもの; sho[meñ 書面: Please submit complaints in writing. (*Kujoo wa shomeñ de teeshutsu shite kudasai.*) 苦情は書面で提出してください.

4 (work) cho[saku 著作; sa[kuhiñ 作品: the writings of Yukio Mishima (*Mishima Yukio no sakuhiñ*) 三島由紀夫の作品.

writing paper *n.* bi[ñseñ 便せん.

written *adj.* **1** (not oral) ka¹ita 書いた; hi[kki no 筆記の: a written test (*hikki shikeñ*) 筆記試験.

2 (of language) ka[kiko¹toba no 書き言葉の: written language (*kakikotoba*) 書き言葉.

wrong *adj.* **1** (bad) wa[ru¹i 悪い; fu[see na 不正な: It is wrong to tell a lie. (*Uso o tsuku koto wa warui.*) うそをつくことは悪い.

2 (incorrect) ma[chiga¹tta 間違った; ma[chiga¹tte iru 間違っている; a[yama¹tta 誤った; a[yama¹tte iru 誤っている: a wrong answer (*machigatta kotae*) 間違った答え / You got the wrong number. (*Bañgoo ga chigaimasu.*) 番号が違います.

3 (of a condition) gu[ai no [ga] waru¹i 具合の[が]悪い; cho[oshi ga kuru¹tte iru 調子が狂っている: This clock is wrong. (*Kono tokee wa kurutte iru.*) この時計は狂っている. / What's wrong with him? (*Kare wa doo shita no desu ka?*) 彼はどうしたのですか.

4 (inappropriate) fu[te¹kitoo na 不適当な; ma[zu¹i まずい: He came at the wrong time. (*Kare wa mazui toki ni yatte kita.*) 彼はまずい時にやって来た.

— *adv.* **1** (badly) wa¹ruku 悪く; fu[see ni 不正に.

2 (incorrectly) ma[chiga¹tte 間違って; a[yama¹tte 誤って: answer wrong (*machigatta kotae o suru*) 間違った答えをする.

3 (not properly) gu[ai ga wa¹ruku 具合が悪く; cho[oshi ga kuru¹tte 調子が狂って.

go wrong *vi.* shi[ppai suru 失敗する Ⓘ: Our plans went wrong. (*Watashi-tachi no keekaku wa shippai shita.*) 私たちの計画は失敗した.

— *n.* a¹ku 悪; fu[see 不正; wa[ru¹i ko[to¹ 悪いこと: do wrong (*warui koto o suru*) 悪いことをする / know right from wrong (*zeñaku no kubetsu ga tsuku*) 善悪の区別がつく.

be in the wrong *vi.* ma[chiga¹tte iru 間違っている Ⓥ: I admit I was in the wrong. (*Watashi ga machigatte ita koto o mitomemasu.*) 私が間違っていたことを認めます.

W

X

Xerox *n.* [trademark] Ze⌈ro⌉kkusu ゼロックス.

X-rated *adj.* (for adults) se⌈ejiñ-muki no 成人向きの: an X-rated movie (*seejiñ-muki eega*) 成人向き映画.

X-ray *n.* **1** (ray) re⌈ñtogeñ-señ レントゲン線; e⌈kkusu-señ エックス線.
2 (photograph) re⌈ñtogeñ-sha⌉shiñ レントゲン写真.
— *vt.* ... no re⌈ñtogeñ-sha⌉shiñ o toru …のレントゲン写真を撮る Ⓒ: I was X-rayed. (*Watashi wa reñtogeñ-shashiñ o totte moratta.*) 私はレントゲン写真を撮ってもらった.

xylophone *n.* shi⌉rohoñ シロホン; mo⌈kkiñ 木琴: play the xylophone (*mokkiñ o eñsoo suru*) 木琴を演奏する.

Y

yacht *n.* yo⌉tto ヨット; ka⌈isooseñ 快走船. ★ Japanese '*yotto*' usually refers to a dinghy or sailboat.

yard[1] *n.* (ground) ni⌈wa 庭: The children are playing in the yard. (*Kodomo-tachi ga niwa de asoñde iru.*) 子どもたちが庭で遊んでいる.
★ Japanese '*niwa*' also refers to a 'garden.'

yard[2] *n.* (measure) ya⌉ado ヤード; ya⌉aru ヤール: 1 yard (*ichi-yaado*) 1 ヤード (= about 91.4 centimeters).
★ In Japan the metric system is used.

yarn *n.* i⌉to 糸; ke⌈ito 毛糸: spin a yarn (*ito o tsumugu*) 糸を紡ぐ.

yawn *vi.* a⌈kubi o suru あくびをする Ⓘ: He yawned and fell asleep. (*Kare wa akubi o shite nete shimatta.*) 彼はあくびをして寝てしまった.
— *n.* a⌈kubi あくび: give [stifle] a yawn (*akubi o suru* [*koraeru*]) あくびをする[こらえる].

year *n.* **1** (time period) ne⌉ñ 年: I came to Japan three years ago. (*Watashi wa sañ-neñ mae ni Nihoñ e kimashita.*) 私は 3 年前に日本へ来ました. / this year (*kotoshi*) ことし / last year (*kyoneñ* [*sakuneñ*]) 去年[昨年] / next year (*raineñ*) 来年.
2 (age) -sai 歳: My son will be 18 years old next month. (*Watashi no musuko wa raigetsu juuhas-sai ni narimasu.*) 私の息子は来月 18 歳になります.
3 (school year) ga⌈kuneñ 学年: We were in the same year in high school. (*Watashi-tachi wa kookoo de onaji gakuneñ deshita.*) 私たちは高校で同じ学年でした.

yearly *adj.* **1** (every year) ma⌈ito-shi no 毎年の: a yearly event (*mai-toshi no gyooji*) 毎年の行事.
2 (for a year) i⌈chi-ne⌉ñkañ no 1 年間の: a yearly income (*neñshuu*) 年収.

yearn *vi.* (... ni) a⌈kogareru (…に)あこがれる Ⓥ; (... o) ne⌈tsuboo suru (…を)熱望する Ⓘ: yearn for fame (*meesee ni akogareru*) 名声にあこがれる / He yearns to go to Greece. (*Kare wa Girisha e iku koto o netsuboo shite iru.*) 彼はギリシャへ行くことを熱望している.

yeast *n.* ko⌈obokiñ 酵母菌; i⌈isuto イースト.

yell *vi.* o⌈ogo⌉e o a⌈geru 大声を上げる Ⓥ; sa⌈ke⌉bu 叫ぶ Ⓒ: He yelled for help. (*Kare wa oogoe o agete tasuke o motometa.*) 彼は大声を上げて

助けを求めた.
— *n.* sa⌈kebigo⌉e 叫び声: give a yell (*sakebigoe o ageru*) 叫び声を上げる.

yellow *adj.* ki⌈iroi 黄色い: a yellow flower (*kiiroi hana*) 黄色い花.
— *n.* ki⌈iro 黄色: deep [light] yellow (*koi* [*usui*] *kiiro*) 濃い[薄い]黄色.

yen *n.* e⌉ñ 円: The yen has gone up [down]. (*Eñ ga agatta* [*sagatta*].) 円が上がった[下がった]. / What is the current exchange rate of the yen against the dollar? (*Geñzai no doru ni taisuru eñ no kawase-sooba wa ikura desu ka?*) 現在のドルに対する円の為替相場はいくらですか. / I'd like to change some dollars into yen. (*Doru o eñ ni kaetai no desu ga.*) ドルを円に換えたいのですが.

yes *adv.* **1** [in answer to an affirmative question] ha⌉i はい; so⌉o desu そうです: "Is this your car?" "Yes, it is." (*"Kore wa anata no kuruma desu ka?" "Hai, soo desu."*) 「これはあなたの車ですか」「はい, そうです」
★ '*Hai*' literally means 'That's right' and is used to confirm a statement, whether affirmative or negative. Note that this use is different from that of 'yes' and 'no' in English.
2 [in answer to a negative question] i⌈ie いいえ; chi⌈gaima⌉su 違います: "Isn't it raining?" "Yes, it is." (*"Ame wa futte inai no desu ka?" "Iie, futte imasu."*) 「雨は降っていないのですか」「いいえ, 降っています」
3 [in answer to a call] ha⌉i はい: "Mr. Yamada." "Yes." (*"Yamada-kuñ." "Hai."*) 「山田君」「はい」

yesterday *adv.* ki⌈no⌉o (wa) きのう(は); sa⌈ku⌉jitsu (wa) 昨日(は): I was at home yesterday. (*Kinoo wa ie ni imashita.*) きのうは家にいました.
— *n.* ki⌈no⌉o きのう; sa⌈ku⌉jitsu 昨日: Yesterday was my birthday. (*Kinoo wa watashi no tañjoobi deshita.*) きのうは私の誕生日でした. / the day before yesterday (*ototoi*) おととい.

yet *adv.* **1** [with a negative] ma⌉da まだ: My order hasn't come yet. (*Chuumoñ shita mono ga mada kimaseñ.*) 注文したものがまだ来ません.
2 [in questions] mo⌉o もう; su⌉de ni すでに: Has he come yet? (*Kare wa moo kimashita ka?*) 彼はもう来ましたか.
3 [in the affirmative] ma⌉da まだ; i⌉ma nao 今なお: I have yet much to say. (*Watashi wa mada iu koto ga takusañ arimasu.*) 私はまだ言うことがたくさんあります.

yield *vt.* **1** (produce) ... o mo⌈tara⌉su ...をもたらす Ⓒ; u⌈mu 生む Ⓒ: The land yielded a good crop. (*Sono tochi wa yoi shuukaku o motarashita.*) その土地はよい収穫をもたらした. / His business yielded large profits. (*Kare no shoobai wa ooki-na rieki o uñda.*) 彼の商売は大きな利益を生んだ.
2 (give up) ... o yu⌈zuru ...を譲る Ⓒ: He yielded his property to his son. (*Kare wa musuko ni zaisañ o yuzutta.*) 彼は息子に財産を譲った.
— *vi.* (submit) (... ni) ma⌈keru (...に)負ける Ⓥ; ku⌈ssuru 屈する Ⓘ: They never yielded to violence. (*Kare-ra wa kesshite booryoku ni kusshinakatta.*) 彼らは決して暴力に屈しなかった.

yolk *n.* ta⌈ma⌉go no ki⌈mi 卵の黄身; ra⌈ñoo 卵黄.

you *pron.* **1** [the person spoken to] a⌈na⌉ta あなた; ki⌈mi 君; [plural] a⌈nata gata あなたがた; ki⌈mi⌉-tachi 君たち: May I take a picture of you? (*Anata no shashiñ o totte mo ii desu ka?*) あなたの写真を撮ってもいいですか. / You are right. (*Kimi no iu toori da.*) 君の言うとおりだ.
★ '*Anata*' is used toward those of the same or lower status. Those who are higher in status are referred to by their occupation or position. '*Kimi*' is used among males of the same status or toward subordinates..

2 [any person] hi⌈to wa (da⌉re de mo) 人は(だれでも). ★ Often omitted in Japanese: You have to be careful in crossing the street. (*Michi o oodañ suru toki wa ki o tsukenakereba ikemaseñ.*) 道を横断するときは気をつけなければいけません.

young *adj.* **1** (not old) wa⌈ka⌉i 若い: He looks young for his age. (*Kare wa toshi no wari ni wakaku mieru.*) 彼は年の割に若く見える.
2 (of age) to⌈shi shita no 年下の: I am three years younger than Mr. Yamakawa. (*Watashi wa Yamakawa-sañ yori sañ-sai toshi shita desu.*) 私は山川さんより 3 歳年下です.

your *pron.* a⌈na⌉ta no あなたの; ki⌈mi no 君の; [plural] a⌈nata gata no あなたがたの; ki⌈mi⌉-tachi no 君たちの: Where is your company? (*Anata no kaisha wa doko ni arimasu ka?*) あなたの会社はどこにありますか. / Is this your school? (*Kore wa kimi-tachi no gakkoo desu ka?*) これは君たちの学校ですか. ★ Often omitted in Japanese: May I have your name? (*O-namae o kikasete kudasai.*) お名前を聞かせてください. ⇨ you 1 ★

yours *pron.* a⌈na⌉ta no mo⌈no⌉ あなたのもの; ki⌈mi no mono⌉ 君のもの; [plural] a⌈nata-gata no mono⌉ あなたがたのもの; ki⌈mi⌉-tachi no mo⌈no⌉ 君たちのもの: Are these shoes yours? (*Kono kutsu wa anata no mono desu ka?*) この靴はあなたのものですか. / Yours is better than mine. (*Kimi no mono no hoo ga watashi no yori mo yoi.*) 君のものの方が私のよりもよい. ⇨ you 1 ★
Yours sincerely [truly], ke⌉egu 敬具.

yourself *pron.* **1** [reflexive use] ji⌈buñ ji⌉shiñ o [ni] 自分自身を[に]. ★ Usually not translated: How did you hurt yourself?. (*Doo shite kega o shita no desu ka?*) どうしてけがをしたのですか. / Please take good care of yourself. (*O-karada o taisetsu ni.*) お体を大切に.
2 [emphatic use] ji⌈buñ de 自分で; a⌈nata ji⌉shiñ de あなた自身で: Do it yourself. (*Anata ga jibuñ de sore o yari nasai.*) あなたが自分でそれをやりなさい.

yourselves *pron.* **1** [reflexive use] ji⌈buñ ji⌉shiñ o [ni] 自分自身を[に]. ★ Usually not translated: You should be ashamed of yourselves. (*Kimi-tachi wa haji to omou beki da.*) 君たちは恥と思うべきだ.
2 [emphatic use] ji⌈bu⌉ñ-tachi de 自分たちで; a⌈natagata ji⌉shiñ de あなたがた自身で: You said so yourselves. (*Anatagata jishiñ ga soo itta de wa nai ka.*) あなたがた自身がそう言ったではないか.

youth *n.* **1** (period) se⌈eneñ [se⌈eshuñ] ji⌉dai 青年[青春]時代; wa⌈ka⌉i koro 若いころ: the friends of my youth (*watashi no seeshuñ jidai no yuujiñ-tachi*) 私の青春時代の友人たち.
2 (young man) wa⌈kamono 若者; se⌈eneñ 青年: a group of youths (*wakamono no ichidañ*) 若者の一団.
3 (being young) wa⌉kasa 若さ: keep one's youth (*wakasa o tamotsu*) 若さを保つ.

youthful *adj.* wa⌈kawakashi⌉i 若若しい; ge⌉ñki na 元気な: He has a very youthful face. (*Kare wa totemo wakawakashii kao o shite iru.*) 彼はとても若々しい顔をしている.

Z

zeal *n.* ne¹tsui 熱意; ne¹sshiñ 熱心: work with great zeal (*hijoo ni nesshiñ ni hataraku*) 非常に熱心に働く.

zealous *adj.* ne¹sshiñ na 熱心な; ne⌈kkyoo-teki na 熱狂的な: zealous efforts (*nesshiñ na doryoku*) 熱心な努力.

zero *n.* **1** (number) ze¹ro ゼロ; re¹e 零.
2 (on a thermometer) re¹edo 零度; (no score) re⌈ete¹ñ 零点: The temperature dropped to zero. (*Oñdo ga reedo ni sagatta.*) 温度が零度に下がった.

zigzag *n.* ji⌈guzagu ジグザグ.
— *adj.* ji⌈guzagu no ジグザグの: a zigzag path (*jiguzagu no michi*) ジグザグの道.
— *vi.* ji⌈guzagu ni susumu ジグザグに進む Ⓒ.

zip code *n.* yu⌈ubiñ-ba¹ñgoo 郵便番号.

zipper *n.* (fastener) ji¹ppaa ジッパー; fa¹sunaa ファスナー; cha¹kku チャック: do up one's zipper (*jippaa o shimeru*) ジッパーを締める.

zone *n.* **1** (area) chi¹tai 地帯; chi¹iki 地域; chi¹ku 地区: a safety [danger] zone (*añzeñ* [*kikeñ*] *chitai*) 安全[危険]地帯 / a residential zone (*juutaku chiku*) 住宅地区.
2 (earth's surface) -tai 帯: the frigid zone (*kañtai*) 寒帯 / the temperate zone (*oñtai*) 温帯 / the torrid zone (*nettai*) 熱帯.
— *vt.* ... o chi¹ku ni wa⌈ke¹ru …を地区に分ける Ⓥ: This area is zoned for industry. (*Kono chiiki wa sañgyoo chiku ni natte iru.*) この地域は産業地区になっている.

zoo *n.* do⌈obutsu¹eñ 動物園: I took my children to the zoo. (*Watashi wa kodomo-tachi o doobutsueñ ni tsurete itta.*) 私は子どもたちを動物園に連れて行った.

Roomaji	Hiragana Katakana

A Table of Japanese Sounds

a	あ ア	ka	か カ	ga	が ガ	sa	さ サ	za	ざ ザ	ta	た タ	da	だ ダ	na	な ナ
i	い イ	ki	き キ	gi	ぎ ギ	shi *si	し シ	ji *zi	じ ジ	chi *ti	ち チ	ji *zi	ぢ ヂ	ni	に ニ
u	う ウ	ku	く ク	gu	ぐ グ	su	す ス	zu	ず ズ	tsu *tu	つ ツ	zu	づ ヅ	nu	ぬ ヌ
e	え エ	ke	け ケ	ge	げ ゲ	se	せ セ	ze	ぜ ゼ	te	て テ	de	で デ	ne	ね ネ
o	お オ	ko	こ コ	go	ご ゴ	so	そ ソ	zo	ぞ ゾ	to	と ト	do	ど ド	no	の ノ
		kya	きゃ キャ	gya	ぎゃ ギャ	sha *sya	しゃ シャ	ja *zya	じゃ ジャ	cha *tya	ちゃ チャ	ja *zya	ぢゃ ヂャ	nya	にゃ ニャ
		kyu	きゅ キュ	gyu	ぎゅ ギュ	shu *syu	しゅ シュ	ju *zyu	じゅ ジュ	chu *tyu	ちゅ チュ	ju *zyu	ぢゅ ヂュ	nyu	にゅ ニュ
		kyo	きょ キョ	gyo	ぎょ ギョ	sho *syo	しょ ショ	jo *zyo	じょ ジョ	cho *tyo	ちょ チョ	jo *zyo	ぢょ ヂョ	nyo	にょ ニョ

* Alternative romanization according to the Kunrei system

Romanization

The romanization is based on the standard Hepburn system with the following modifications:

- Long vowels are indicated by double vowel letters. (paatii, shuuchuu)
- When the vowel sequence '**ei**' is pronounced as a long vowel, it is indicated as '**ee**.' (seeto, zeekiñ)
- The syllabic '**n**' is transcribed as '**ñ**.' (shiñbuñ)

ha は ハ	ba ば バ	pa ぱ パ	ma ま マ	ya や ヤ	ra ら ラ	wa わ ワ	ñ ん ン
hi ひ ヒ	bi び ビ	pi ぴ ピ	mi み ミ		ri り リ	▲i ゐ ヰ	
fu *hu ふ フ	bu ぶ ブ	pu ぷ プ	mu む ム	yu ゆ ユ	ru る ル		
he へ ヘ	be べ ベ	pe ぺ ペ	me め メ		re れ レ	▲e ゑ ヱ	
ho ほ ホ	bo ぼ ボ	po ぽ ポ	mo も モ	yo よ ヨ	ro ろ ロ	o を ヲ	
hya ひゃ ヒャ	bya びゃ ビャ	pya ぴゃ ピャ	mya みゃ ミャ		rya りゃ リャ		
hyu ひゅ ヒュ	byu びゅ ビュ	pyu ぴゅ ピュ	myu みゅ ミュ		ryu りゅ リュ		
hyo ひょ ヒョ	byo びょ ビョ	pyo ぴょ ピョ	myo みょ ミョ		ryo りょ リョ		

▲ Not used in modern Japanese.

aa	ii	uu	ee	oo
ああ あー	いい いー	うう うー	ええ えい えー	おお おう おー
アア アー	イイ イー	ウウ ウー	エエ エイ エー	オオ オウ オー

Long vowels as described in this dictionary.

fa	fi	fo
ファ	フィ	フォ
di	**dii**	**tii**
ディ	ディー	ティー

Used for words of foreign origin.